MW00449061

Joel Whitburn's

TOP COUNTRY SONGS

1944 to 2005

Billboard®

Chart Data Compiled from *Billboard's* Country Singles Charts, 1944-2005

Cover design by Dean Eggert Design

ISBN 0-89820-165-9

Record Research Inc.
P.O. Box 200
Menomonee Falls, Wisconsin 53052-0200 U.S.A.

Phone: (262) 251-5408
Fax: (262) 251-9452
E-Mail: books@recordresearch.com
Web site: www.recordresearch.com

CONTENTS

Dedicated to...Eddy Arnold

Eddy Arnold has continually ranked as the #1 all-time artist in each edition of *Joel Whitburn's Top Country Singles* book, beginning with my first edition in 1971 through this current sixth edition! Among his remarkable feats is the fact that he is the only artist in history to have a chart hit in seven consecutive decades!

Eddy, your chart stats are amazing — solid evidence that your wonderful recordings and classy style are cherished by music fans the world over.

The author wishes to extend a special note of thanks to his Record Research staff:

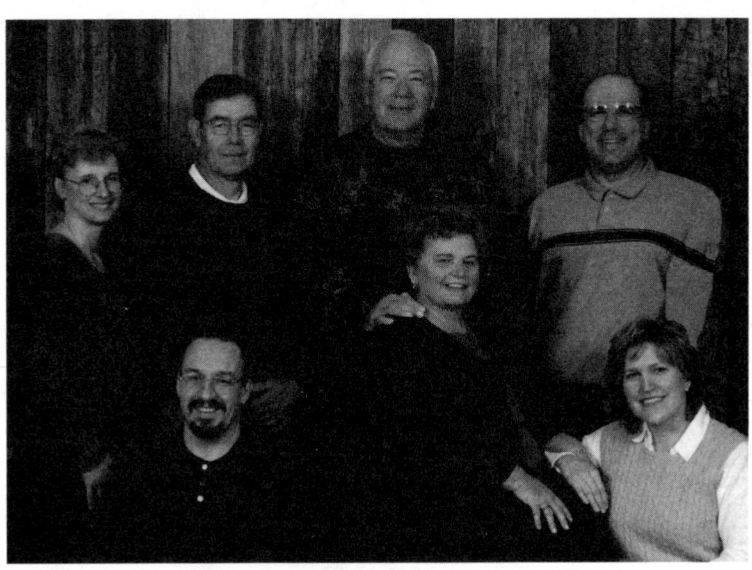

Front: Brent Olynick, Fran Whitburn, Kim Bloxdorf
Back: Jeanne Olynick, Nestor Vidotto, Joel Whitburn, Paul Haney

AUTHOR'S NOTE

Top Country Songs represents more than just an update of my *Top Country Singles* book. For this brand new edition, I wanted to be able to look up an artist and see all of their accomplishments at a glance in a clean and easy-to-read format. To complete this vision, I loaded up the following pages with fresh new features, such as:

- Songwriters are now shown for every hit! Names like Harlan Howard, Cindy Walker and Bob McDill now receive their due credit.
- Many pre-1944 Artists and Songs are included. Influential pioneers such as Vernon Dahlhart, Jimmie Rodgers and The Carter Family are now shown in their proper historical context.
- All Grammy and CMA Award winners are noted. Artist awards are now shown after the bio. Song and Single awards are featured in title trivia.
- Decade and All-Time Artist rankings now appear directly to the right of the artist name.
- Grand Ole Opry and Country Music Hall of Fame Induction years are now highlighted for easy access.
- Artists with 60 or more charted hits have an alphabetical listing of their songs below their chronological listing. For those same artists a double line now separates the songs by decade.
- All bios now contain at least one line about the artist. Previous bios have been updated with loads of new information.
- All vinyl label and number information is provided from 1944-1989. Starting in 1990, record labels started drastically cutting back the number of singles released to the general public. Because of this practice, the title and label and catalog number of the album for a charted song is shown in title trivia from 1990-present.

In addition to all of these new features, you get all the reliable chart stats you've come to expect from Record Research. The entire history of this uniquely American music is now at your fingertips. I hope that you are enriched and entertained by the information in the upcoming pages.

JOEL WHITBURN

ABOUT THE AUTHOR

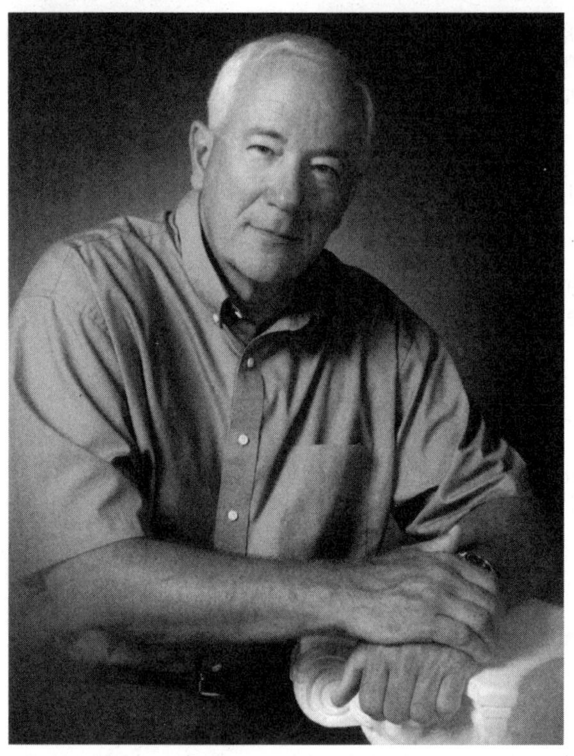

When Joel Whitburn spun his first 78 rpm single back in 1950, little did he know that his part-time passion would spin off into a lifelong career and the uncontested title of "The World's #1 Chart Authority."

From a few chart facts scribbled on 3x5 note cards as a hobby to help organize his personal record collection, to a vast computerized database encompassing over a century of charted music, Joel's research has developed a richness and diversity rivaling that of the music it documents.

Joel published his first book — a slim, 104-page volume on Pop music singles — in 1970. With 105 Record Research volumes published to date, Joel has proven himself to be a prolific compiler of chart research books covering a wide variety of Billboard's singles and albums charts: Country, Pop, R&B, Dance/Disco, Christmas, Adult Contemporary, Album Rock and Modern Rock. His research on the music charts stretches back to 1890, and his book formats run the gamut from yearly record rankings to artist-by-artist compilations of charted record data to reproductions of the original charts themselves.

Joel's own record collection remains unrivaled the world over and includes every charted Hot 100 and pop single (back to 1936), every charted pop album (back to 1945), collections of nearly every charted Country, R&B, Bubbling Under The Hot 100 and Adult Contemporary records, and every video to chart since Billboard began its video charts in 1979. Ever the consummate collector, Joel also owns one of the world's largest picture sleeve collections, many of which he displays in the series of Top 40 Hits books he writes for Billboard's book division.

Joel's ongoing collaborations with Rhino Records have also produced nearly 150 CD volumes featuring his personal picks of Billboard's top Rock 'n' Roll, Pop, Country, R&B, Soul, Dance, Jazz, Gospel, Album Rock, Modern Rock, and Christmas hits.

In person, this walking music encyclopedia stands 6'6" – a definite advantage when he played college and semi-pro basketball. An avid sports fan, Joel participates in a wide variety of water, winter and motor sports. The Wisconsinite and his wife, Fran, a native of Honduras, enjoy spending time in southern Florida and central Wisconsin, and especially love being with their grandchildren Samantha and Nathaniel. Their daughter, Kim Bloxdorf, is vice president of Record Research, and other key employees are Brent Olynick, Paul Haney, Jeanne Olynick and Nestor Vidotto. Joel's lifelong passion for music, old and new, and his penchant for accurate detail continues into the 21st century.

SYNOPSIS OF BILLBOARD'S COUNTRY SINGLES CHARTS 1944-2005

JUKE BOX

Date	Positions	Chart Title
1/8/44	2-8	Most Played Juke Box Folk Records (9/6/47-11/1/47 shown as Most-Played Juke Box Hillbilly Records)
1/31/48	9-15	Most Played Juke Box Folk Records
6/25/49	7-15	Most Played Juke Box (Country & Western) Records
11/4/50	6-10	Most Played Juke Box Folk (Country & Western) Records
11/15/52	8-10	Most Played in Juke Boxes
6/30/56	9-10	Most Played C&W in Juke Boxes
6/17/57		final chart

BEST SELLERS

Date	Positions	Chart Title
5/15/48	10-15	Best Selling Retail Folk Records
6/25/49	5-15	Best Selling Retail Folk (Country & Western) Records
11/15/52	8-10	National Best Sellers
2/20/54	9-15	Best Sellers in Stores
6/30/56	13-20	C&W Best Sellers in Stores
10/13/58		final chart

JOCKEYS

Date	Positions	Chart Title
12/10/49	8-10	Country & Western Records Most Played By Folk Disk Jockeys
11/15/52	9-15	Most Played by Jockeys
6/30/56	12-15	Most Played C&W by Jockeys
10/13/58		final chart

HOT COUNTRY SINGLES

Date	Positions	Chart Title
10/20/58	30	Hot C&W Sides
11/3/62	30	Hot Country Singles
1/11/64	50	Hot Country Singles
10/15/66	75	Hot Country Singles
7/14/73	100	Hot Country Singles
1/20/90*	75	Hot Country Singles
2/17/90	75	Hot Country Singles & Tracks
1/6/01	60	Hot Country Singles & Tracks
4/30/05	60	Hot Country Songs

**Billboard* began compiling chart with information provided by Nielsen Broadcast Data Systems, which electronically monitors actual radio airplay. Songs were ranked by their gross impressions, which multiplied each play by the Arbitron-estimated audience for the station at the time of the play. On December 5, 1992, *Billboard* eliminated the gross impressions method and began compiling the chart strictly on the number of detections or plays registered by each song. On January 15, 2005, *Billboard* returned to the audience impressions method of ranking song popularity.

HOT COUNTRY SINGLES SALES

10/20/84	30	Hot Country Singles Sales
5/31/86	40	Hot Country Singles Sales
8/2/86	30	Hot Country Singles Sales
1/21/89–6/24/95		No chart published
7/1/95*	25	Top Country Singles Sales
7/20/02	10	Top Country Singles Sales
4/30/05	10	Country Singles Sales

**Billboard* began compiling chart from a national sample of retail store and rack sales reports collected, compiled, and provided by Nielsen SoundScan; this data is not a factor in the airplay-only *Hot Country Songs* chart.

HOT COUNTRY SINGLES AIRPLAY

10/20/84	30	Hot Country Singles Airplay
5/31/86	40	Hot Country Singles Airplay
8/2/86	30	Hot Country Singles Airplay
5/16/87		final chart

First "Hot C&W Sides" Chart — 10/20/58

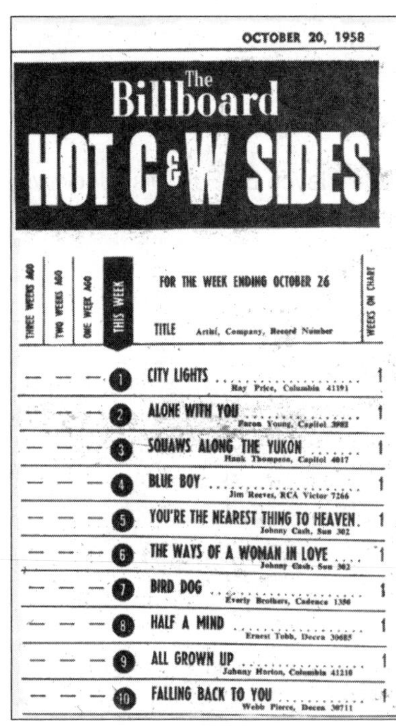

OCTOBER 20, 1958

The Billboard

HOT C&W SIDES

FOR THE WEEK ENDING OCTOBER 26

THREE WEEKS AGO	TWO WEEKS AGO	ONE WEEK AGO	THIS WEEK	TITLE Artist, Company, Record Number	WEEKS ON CHART
—	—	—	1	CITY LIGHTS — Ray Price, Columbia 41191	1
—	—	—	2	ALONE WITH YOU — Faron Young, Capitol 3982	1
—	—	—	3	SQUAWS ALONG THE YUKON — Hank Thompson, Capitol 4017	1
—	—	—	4	BLUE BOY — Jim Reeves, RCA Victor 7266	1
—	—	—	5	YOU'RE THE NEAREST THING TO HEAVEN — Johnny Cash, Sun 302	1
—	—	—	6	THE WAYS OF A WOMAN IN LOVE — Johnny Cash, Sun 302	1
—	—	—	7	BIRD DOG — Everly Brothers, Cadence 1350	1
—	—	—	8	HALF A MIND — Ernest Tubb, Decca 30685	1
—	—	—	9	ALL GROWN UP — Johnny Horton, Columbia 41210	1
—	—	—	10	FALLING BACK TO YOU — Webb Pierce, Decca 30711	1

THREE WEEKS AGO	TWO WEEKS AGO	ONE WEEK AGO	THIS WEEK	TITLE Artist, Company, Record Number	WEEKS ON CHART
—	—	—	11	MY BABY'S GONE — Louvin Brothers, Capitol 4055	1
—	—	—	12	SEND ME THE PILLOW YOU DREAM ON — Hank Locklin, RCA Victor 7127	1
—	—	—	13	TUPELO COUNTY JAIL — Webb Pierce, Decca 30711	1
—	—	—	14	GIVE MYSELF A PARTY — Don Gibson, RCA Victor 7330	1
—	—	—	15	THAT'S THE WAY I FEEL — Faron Young, Capitol 4050	1
—	—	—	16	TALK TO ME LONESOME HEART — James O'Gwynne, D 1006	1
—	—	—	17	PICK ME UP ON YOUR WAY DOWN — Charlie Walker, Columbia 41211	1
—	—	—	18	LONELY ISLAND PEARL — Johnnie and Jack, RCA Victor 7324	1
—	—	—	19	WHAT DO I CARE! — Johnny Cash, Columbia 41251	1
—	—	—	20	TOUCH AND GO HEART — Kitty Wells, Decca 30736	1
—	—	—	21	DEEP PURPLE BLUES — Ernest Tubb, Decca 30685	1
—	—	—	22	HEY, SHERIFF — Rusty and Doug, Hickory 1083	1
—	—	—	23	INVITATION TO THE BLUES — Ray Price, Columbia 41191	1
—	—	—	24	WOULD YOU CARE! — Jim Edward, Maxine and Bonnie Brown, RCA Victor 7311	1
—	—	—	25	LOOK WHO'S BLUE — Don Gibson, RCA Victor 7330	1
—	—	—	26	BLUE, BLUE DAY — Don Gibson, RCA Victor 7010	1
—	—	—	27	GUESS THINGS HAPPEN THAT WAY — Johnny Cash, Sun 295	1
—	—	—	28	HEY, MR. BLUEBIRD — Ernest Tubb and Wilburn Brothers, Decca 30610	1
—	—	—	29	SHE WAS ONLY SEVENTEEN — Marty Robbins, Columbia 41208	1
—	—	—	30	ALL OVER AGAIN — Johnny Cash, Columbia 41251	1

RESEARCHING BILLBOARD'S COUNTRY CHARTS

This book covers the entire history of *Billboard* magazine's Country singles charts from 1944 through June 25, 2005. Over 17,800 charted hits and over 2,300 artists are listed in all.

MULTIPLE COUNTRY SINGLES CHARTS, 1948-1958

Billboard published its first Country singles chart, *Juke Box Folk Records*, on January 8, 1944. All chart data from 1944 through May 8, 1948, refers to the Juke Box chart. On May 15, 1948, *Billboard* introduced another Country singles chart, *Best Selling Retail Folk Records.* A third Country singles chart, *Most Played by Folk Disk Jockeys,* made its debut on December 10, 1949. All of these charts were published on a weekly basis and each focused on specific areas of the music trade. The *Juke Box* chart was discontinued on June 17, 1957. On October 20, 1958, the *Best Seller* and *Disk Jockey* charts were replaced by one all-encompassing Top 30 Country singles chart titled *Hot C&W Sides.* This chart has changed in name and size over time and is known, today, as *Hot Country Singles & Tracks.* For a more detailed history of all of *Billboard's* Country singles charts, see the "Synopsis of *Billboard's* Country Singles Charts" on the previous page.

During the years of multiple charts, 1948-1958, many singles hit more than one chart. In our research, the single's debut date is taken from the chart on which it first appeared. The single's peak position is taken from the chart on which it achieved its highest ranking. Listed to the right of the title (before the listing of the B-side) is an indication of the chart(s) and peak position on which it hit. (See "Peak Position Attained On Various Country Charts" in the USER'S GUIDE for a further explanation.) The single's weeks charted and weeks at positions #1 or #2 are taken from the chart on which it achieved its highest total.

CHART METHODOLOGIES

For decades, *Billboard's* Country singles charts were compiled from playlists reported by radio stations and sales reports reported by stores. These airplay and sales reports established the weekly rankings on *Billboard's* airplay charts (*Jockeys, Hot Country Singles Airplay*) and sales charts (*Best Sellers, Hot Country Singles Sales*), and were combined for the compilation of the *Hot Country Singles* charts.

On January 20, 1990, *Billboard* began basing their chart entirely on airplay with information gathered by Nielsen Broadcast Data Systems; a subsidiary of *Billboard* that electronically monitors actual radio airplay. They have installed monitors throughout the country that track the airplay of songs 24 hours a day, seven days a week. These monitors can identify each song played by an encoded audio "fingerprint." *Billboard* determined weekly rankings according to gross impressions, which multiplied each play by the Arbitron-estimated audience for the station at the time of the play.

On December 5, 1992, *Billboard* began compiling the Country singles chart strictly on the number of detections or plays registered by each song. On January 15, 2005, *Billboard* returned to the previous gross impressions method of ranking song popularity.

COUNTRY SINGLES SALES AND AIRPLAY CHARTS

Billboard began publication of the *Hot Country Singles Sales and Airplay* charts on October 20, 1984. These charts were the two ingredients that made up the *Hot Country Singles* chart. The airplay chart was discontinued in 1987; the *Hot Country Singles* chart essentially became the airplay chart after *Billboard* began compiling that chart with Nielsen Broadcast Data Systems data. The sales chart experienced a six-year hiatus beginning in 1989; however, when it returned in July of 1995, it was not figured into the compilation of the *Hot Country Singles* chart.

ISSUE DATE vs. COLLECTION DATE

All dates within *Top Country Songs* refer to the issue dates of *Billboard* magazine and not the "week ending" dates as shown on the various charts when they were originally published. The issue and week ending dates were different until January 13, 1962, when *Billboard* began using one date system for both the issue and the charts inside. *Billboard's* issue dates were all Saturdays, except from April 29, 1957 to December 25, 1961, when they changed to a Monday issue date. On January 6, 1962, *Billboard* reverted to a permanent Saturday issue date.

The *Hot Country Songs* chart reports on airplay activity from the seven-day period ending 12 days prior. For example, *Billboard* compiled the *Hot Country Songs* chart dated September 24, 2005 (Saturday) on September 12 (Monday). The radio airplay reports for this chart covered a seven-day period beginning at 12:01 a.m. on September 5 (Monday) and ending at midnight on September 11, 2005 (Sunday). Delivery of the September 24 issue began on September 16 (Friday). *Billboard's* timing has changed slightly over the years.

First "Hot Country Singles" Chart — 11/3/62

BILLBOARD MUSIC WEEK

HOT COUNTRY SINGLES

This Week	Last Week	By special survey for week ending 11/3 Title, Artist, Label & No.	Weeks on Chart
1	1	MAMA SANG A SONG Bill Anderson, Decca 31404	15
2	3	I'M GONNA CHANGE EVERYTHING Jim Reeves, RCA Victor 8080	10
3	4	I'VE BEEN EVERYWHERE Hank Snow, RCA Victor 8072	8
4	2	DEVIL WOMAN Marty Robbins, Columbia 42486	14
5	5	DON'T GO NEAR THE INDIANS Rex Allen, Mercury 71997	6
6	7	COW TOWN Webb Pierce, Decca 31421	5
7	9	A GIRL I USED TO KNOW George Jones and the Jones Boys, United Artists 500	5
8	8	HELLO OUT THERE Carl Belew, RCA Victor 8058	6
9	6	PRIDE Ray Price, Columbia 42518	7
10	17	LITTLE BLACK BOOK Jimmy Dean, Columbia 42529	6
11	12	FOOTSTEPS OF A FOOL Judy Lynn, United Artists 472	12
12	11	THE BURNING OF ATLANTA Claude King, Columbia 42581	3
13	15	AFTER LOVING YOU Eddy Arnold, RCA Victor 8048	14
14	18	KICKIN' OUR HEARTS AROUND Buck Owens, Capitol 4826	2
15	28	HE STANDS REAL TALL Del Reeves, Decca 31417	2
16	—	WE MISSED YOU Kitty Wells, Decca 31422	1
17	10	IF YOU DON'T KNOW I AIN'T GONNA TELL YOU George Hamilton IV, RCA Victor 8062	11
18	—	THE VIOLET AND A ROSE "Little" Jimmy Dickens, Columbia 42485	1
19	19	SOONER OR LATER Webb Pierce, Decca 31421	4
20	24	SILVER THREADS AND GOLDEN NEEDLES Springfields, Philips 40038	10
21	25	I CAN'T STOP (MY LOVIN' YOU) Buck Owens, Capitol 4826	2
22	—	THEN A TEAR FELL Earl Scott, Kapp 854	1
23	27	SEND ME THE PILLOW YOU DREAM ON Johnny Tillotson, Cadence 1424	9
24	16	WILLIE THE WEEPER Billy Walker, Columbia 42492	10
25	20	DADDY STOPPED IN Claude Gray, Mercury 72001	3
26	13	BIG FOOL OF THE YEAR George Jones and the Jones Boys, United Artists 500	4
27	23	UNDER COVER OF THE NIGHT Dave Dudley, Jubilee 5436	8
28	22	A LITTLE HEARTACHE Eddy Arnold, RCA Victor 8048	19
29	26	SHAME ON ME Bobby Bare, RCA Victor 8032	8
30	14	EVERYBODY BUT ME Ernest Ashworth, Hickory 1170	19

USER'S GUIDE

The artist section lists each artist's charted hits in chronological order. Each of an artist's song titles is sequentially numbered. All #1 hits are shaded for quick identification.

EXPLANATION OF COLUMNAR HEADINGS

DEBUT: Date first charted

PEAK: Highest charted position (highlighted in bold type). All #1 singles are identified by a special #1 symbol (➊).

WKS: Total weeks charted

Gold: ● Gold single*

▲ Platinum single* (additional million units sold are indicated by a numeral following the symbol)

Country Chart Hit: Song title of chart hit

Songwriter: Name(s) of the song's writer(s).

Label (& Number): Original record label and number of single when charted (1944-1989 only). For songs from 1990-on, only the label is shown and the album from which the track is taken is noted below the title along with its label and number.

*The primary source used to determine gold and platinum singles is the Recording Industry Association of America (RIAA), which began certifying gold singles in 1958 and platinum singles in 1976. From 1958 through 1988, RIAA required sales of one million units for a gold single and two million units for a platinum single; however, as of January 1, 1989, RIAA lowered the certification requirements for gold singles to sales of 500,000 units and for platinum to one million units. Some record labels have never requested RIAA certifications for their hits. In order to fill in the gaps, especially during the period prior to 1958, various other trade publications and reports were used to supplement RIAA's certifications.

LETTER(S) IN BRACKETS AFTER TITLES

C - Comedy
F - Foreign language
I - Instrumental
L - Live
N - Novelty
R - Re-entry, re-recording, or re-release of a previously recorded single by that artist
S - Spoken
X - Christmas

EXPLANATION OF SYMBOLS

3^2 Superior number to the right of the #1, #2 or #3 peak position is the total weeks the song held that position.

+ Indicates song peaked in the year after it first charted.

/ Divides a two-sided hit. Complete chart data (debut date, peak position, etc.) is shown for both sides. If a title never achieved its own peak position, **flip** is shown and weeks charted are the number of weeks it was shown as a "tag along."

↑ Indicates the weeks charted data is subject to change since the song was still charted as of the 9/24/2005 research cut-off date.

PEAK POSITIONS ATTAINED ON VARIOUS POP CHARTS

Prior to publishing the all-encompassing *Hot C&W Sides* chart in 1958, *Billboard* published three weekly Country singles charts: *Best Sellers In Stores*, *Most Played By Jockeys* and *Most Played In Juke Boxes*. The peak position shown in the Peak column for these charts is taken from the chart on which it achieved its highest position. The individual peak positions attained on these three charts is listed to the right of the A-side title. Also, the peak positions attained on the *Hot Country Singles Sales* and *Hot Country Singles Airplay* charts are listed to the right of the chart hit titles. All of the Country singles charts consulted are listed below. The following letter designations precede the peak position attained on these charts:

- **A:** Airplay (*Most Played By Jockeys* and *Hot Country Singles Airplay*)
- **S:** Sales (*Best Sellers In Stores* and *Hot Country Singles Sales*)
- **J:** *Most Played In Juke Boxes*

PICTURES OF THE TOP 200 ARTISTS

A picture of each of the Top 200 artists is shown next to their listing in the artist section.

ARTIST & TITLE NOTES

Below every artist name are brief notes about the artist. Directly under some song titles are notes indicating backing vocalists, guest instrumentalists, the title of the movie in which the song was featured, the name of a famous songwriter or producer, etc. Duets and other important name variations are shown in bold letters next to the title. Names of artists mentioned in the artist and title notes of others, who have their own chart hits elsewhere in this book, are highlighted in bold type; a name is shown bold the first time it appears in an artist's biography. All movie, TV and album titles, and other major works, are shown in italics.

As always, we gladly welcome any corrections/updates to our artist biographies or title trivia notes. Please include solid evidence.

ARTIST'S BIGGEST HIT

The biggest chart hit of any artist with 10 or more hits is underlined. The top hit is a reflection of chart performance only and may or may not relate to an artist's best seller or most popular song over the years. A tie is broken based on total weeks at the peak position, total weeks in the Top 10, total weeks in the Top 40, and finally, total weeks charted.

WHAT'S NEW WITH THIS EDITION

In our continuing efforts to improve each subsequent edition of *Top Country Songs*, we added the following to this sixth edition:

SONGWRITERS

Directly to the right of each chart hit is the name(s) of the song's writer(s). A listing of Top Country Songwriters is shown on page 597. Songwriters that charted infrequently as artists (such as Harlan Howard) have their songwriter ranking to the right of their artist name (shown as: **SW: #rank**).

PRE-1944 ARTISTS AND SONGS

Many influential pioneers and songs have been added to the main artist listings. Pre-1944 hits are shown directly beneath the artist bio.

ARTIST RANKINGS

Decade and All-Time artist rankings are now shown directly to the right of the artist name for easy reference.

TOP COUNTRY SONGS & ARTISTS AWARDS

COUNTRY MUSIC ASSOCIATION AWARDS

Country music industry professionals in Nashville founded the Country Music Association (**CMA**) in 1958. In 1961 the CMA created the Country Music Hall of Fame (**HOF**). The Induction Year for each individual is shown to the right of his or her **artist heading**.

In November 1967, the CMA held its first awards show; one year later the event was televised for the first time and has been every year since. Nominees and winners are determined by a vote of Country music industry professionals. Below each **artist bio**, you will find winners for Entertainer, Male and Female Vocalist, Vocal Group, Vocal Duo, Musician, Instrumental Group, Comedian and Horizon (New Artist) of the Year. In **title trivia**, you will find winners for Single, Song, Vocal Event and Musical Event of the Year.

GRAMMY AWARDS

The National Academy of Recording Arts & Sciences introduced the Grammy Awards in 1958. Each year thousands of music industry professionals vote for winners in several music genres, including Country. The actual awards show is televised each February. In **title trivia**, you will find winners for Single, Song, Male and Female Vocal, Vocal Duo/Group and Vocal Collaboration of the year.

GRAMMY HALL OF FAME

The Recording Academy's Trustees established the Grammy Hall of Fame Award in 1973 to honor **recordings** of lasting qualitative or historical significance that are at least 25 years old. A special committee of eminent and knowledgeable music professionals selects inductees annually each January. The Country songs inducted are noted in **title trivia**.

GRAND OLE OPRY

The *Grand Ole Opry* radio show was first broadcast on Nashville's WSM radio station on Saturday night, November 28, 1925. The show was picked up by NBC radio in October 1939 and was heard throughout the nation. The show has also been televised on various network and cable outlets over the years. Periodically, the current members vote to induct a new member. The induction year is shown directly beneath the **artist bio** (**OPRY**).

NATIONAL RECORDING REGISTRY

In 2000, the U.S. Congress passed a bill to establish the National Recording Registry in the Library of Congress to maintain and preserve sound recordings that are culturally, historically or aesthetically significant. Each April, new inductees are announced. These recordings are noted in title trivia (**NRR**).

ROLLING STONE 500

In 2004, *Rolling Stone* magazine polled 172 music industry professionals (including Joel Whitburn) to vote for their favorite songs of all time. The results were later published and the Country songs that made the list are noted in title trivia (**RS500**).

A-Z SONG LISTING FOR MAJOR ARTISTS

Artists with 60 or more charted hits have an alphabetical listing of their hits below their chronological listing. For those artists, a double line separates the songs by decade.

UPDATED AND EXPANDED BIOS

Every artist bio now contains at least one line about the artist. Previous bios have been updated with new information.

LABEL AND NUMBER INFORMATION

All vinyl label and number information is provided from 1944-1989. From 1990-present, the album title, label and catalog number information is shown in title trivia.

ARTIST SECTION

Lists, alphabetically by artist name, every song in chronological sequence that charted on *Billboard's* Country Singles charts from January 8, 1944 through June 25, 2005.

Billboard DEBUT	PEAK	WKS	GOLD	ARTIST Ranking / Country Chart Hit	Songwriter	Label (& Number)

A

ABBOTT, Jerry

Born on 12/10/1947 in Dallas, Texas. Male singer/songwriter/guitarist.

DEBUT	PEAK	WKS	GOLD	Country Chart Hit	Songwriter	Label (& Number)
4/29/78	**63**	7		1 **I Want A Little Cowboy**	*Jerry Abbott/Patty Jackson*	Churchill 7712
9/9/78	**80**	6		2 **I Owe It All To You**	*Jerry Abbott*	Churchill 7715
1/9/82	**82**	4		3 **One Night Stanley**	*Jerry Abbott/Charles Stewart*	Dallas Star 102581

ABERNATHY, Mack

Born Raleigh Mack Abernathy in Austin, Texas. Male singer/songwriter/guitarist.

DEBUT	PEAK	WKS	GOLD	Country Chart Hit	Songwriter	Label (& Number)
11/12/88	**98**	2		1 **Slippin' Around**	*Floyd Tillman*	CMI 1988-8
2/18/89	**80**	3		2 **Different Situations**	*Mack Abernathy*	CMI 1988-9

ACUFF, Roy — 1940s: #19 / All-Time: #292 // HOF: 1962

Born on 9/15/1903 in Maynardville, Tennessee. Died of heart failure on 11/23/1992 (age 89). Male singer/songwriter/guitarist. The Smoky Mountain Boys consisted of Beecher "Bashful Brother Oswald" Kirby (dobro; died on 10/17/2002, age 90), Howard "Howdy" Forrester (fiddle; died on 8/1/1987, age 65) and Jimmie Riddle (harmonica, piano; died on 12/10/1982, age 64). Formed Acuff-Rose music publishing company in 1942 and the Hickory record label in 1953 with **Fred Rose**. Twice ran for governor of Tennessee. Won Grammy's Lifetime Achievement Award in 1987. Known as "The King Of Country Music." Also see **Heart Of Nashville**.

EARLY HITS: Great Speckle Bird (1938) / Wabash Cannon Ball (1938) // OPRY: 1938

ROY ACUFF and his Smoky Mountain Boys:

DEBUT	PEAK	WKS	GOLD	Country Chart Hit	Songwriter	Label (& Number)
2/12/44	**4**	2		1 **The Prodigal Son**	*Floyd Jenkins*	Okeh 6716
11/4/44	**3^1**	8		2 **I'll Forgive You But I Can't Forget /**	*Jay Frank/Pee Wee King*	
11/11/44	**6**	4		3 **Write Me Sweetheart**	*Roy Acuff*	Okeh 6723
4/19/47	**4**	6		4 (Our Own) **Jole Blon**	*Roy Acuff*	Columbia 37287
2/7/48	**8**	5		5 **The Waltz Of The Wind**	J:8 / S:13 *Fred Rose*	Columbia 38042
6/19/48	**14**	2		6 **Unloved And Unclaimed**	S:14 *Roy Acuff/Vit Pellettieri*	Columbia 38189
8/7/48	**12**	1		7 **This World Can't Stand Long**	S:12 *Roy Acuff*	Columbia 20454
11/6/48	**12**	1		8 **Tennessee Waltz**	J:12 *Pee Wee King/Redd Stewart*	Columbia 20551
12/18/48	**14**	1		9 **A Sinner's Death**	S:14 *Roy Acuff*	Columbia 20475
3/31/58	**8**	7		10 **Once More**	A:8 *Dusty Owens*	Hickory 1073
12/29/58+	**16**	11		11 **So Many Times**	*Don Gibson*	Hickory 1090
6/15/59	**20**	3		12 **Come And Knock** (On The Door Of My Heart)	*Charlie Louvin/Ira Louvin*	Hickory 1097

ROY ACUFF:

DEBUT	PEAK	WKS	GOLD	Country Chart Hit	Songwriter	Label (& Number)
5/15/65	**45**	5		13 **Freight Train Blues**	*Roy Acuff*	Hickory 1291
11/27/71	**56**	6		14 **I Saw The Light** ***[w/ Nitty Gritty Dirt Band]***	*Hank Williams*	United Artists 50849
2/16/74	**51**	11		15 **Back In The Country**	*Eddy Raven*	Hickory/MGM 314
6/22/74	**97**	3		16 **Old Time Sunshine Song**	*Eddy Raven*	Hickory/MGM 319
6/17/89	**87**	2		17 **The Precious Jewel** ***[w/ Charlie Louvin]***	*Roy Acuff*	Hal Kat 63058

ADAMS, Don

Born on 1/4/1941 in Ross County, Ohio. Male singer/songwriter/guitarist.

DEBUT	PEAK	WKS	GOLD	Country Chart Hit	Songwriter	Label (& Number)
4/1/67	**64**	4		1 **Two Of The Usual**	*Fred Carter*	Jack O'Diamonds 1002
7/14/73	**91**	5		2 **I'll Be Satisfied**	*Tyran Carlo/Berry Gordy*	Atlantic 4002
11/24/73+	**34**	12		3 **I've Already Stayed Too Long**	*Ben Peters*	Atlantic 4009
4/27/74	**80**	4		4 **Baby Let Your Long Hair Down** ***[w/ The Greenfield Express]***	*Rory Bourke/Eddie Rabbitt*	Atlantic 4017
8/17/74	**52**	9		5 **That's Love**	*Don Adams/Gary Adams*	Atlantic 4027

ADAMS, Kay, with The Cliffie Stone Group

Born Princetta Kay Adams on 4/9/1941 in Knox City, Texas; raised in Vernon, Texas. Female singer.

DEBUT	PEAK	WKS	GOLD	Country Chart Hit	Songwriter	Label (& Number)
10/15/66	**30**	7		**Little Pink Mack**	*Chris Roberts/Jim Thornton/Scott Turner*	Tower 269

ADAMS, Kaylee

Born on 9/10/1955 in Navarre, Ohio. Female singer.

DEBUT	PEAK	WKS	GOLD	Country Chart Hit	Songwriter	Label (& Number)
10/18/86	**68**	4		**I Can't Help The Way I Don't Feel**	*Michael Garvin/Tom Shapiro/Chris Waters*	Warner 28567

ADAMS, Peggy Jo

Born in Arkansas. Female singer.

DEBUT	PEAK	WKS	GOLD	Country Chart Hit	Songwriter	Label (& Number)
7/8/78	**90**	4		**Hello, This Is Anna** ***[w/ O.B. McClinton]***	*Ron Crick/Nate Herman*	Epic 50563

ADEN, Terry

Born on 8/11/1952 in Poplar Bluff, Missouri. Died on 11/28/2001 (age 49). Male singer.

DEBUT	PEAK	WKS	GOLD	Country Chart Hit	Songwriter	Label (& Number)
10/31/81	**81**	3		1 **What's So Good About Goodbye**	*David Hodges*	B&B 21
4/3/82	**73**	5		2 **She Doesn't Belong To You**	*Chris Hill*	AMI 1303

Billboard			G O L D	ARTIST Ranking	
DEBUT	PEAK	WKS		Country Chart Hit.......... Songwriter	Label (& Number)

ADKINS, Trace — 2000s: #20 / All-Time: #183

Born on 1/13/1962 in Springhill, Louisiana; raised in Sarepta, Louisiana. Male singer/songwriter/guitarist. Sang with the New Commitment gospel group while in high school. Played football for Louisiana Tech. Also see **America The Beautiful**.

OPRY: 2003

DEBUT	PEAK	WKS		Country Chart Hit	Songwriter	Label (& Number)
4/13/96	**20**	20	1	**There's A Girl In Texas**	S:7 *Trace Adkins/Carl Vipperman*	Capitol
8/24/96	**3**[1]	21	2	**Every Light In The House**	S:2 *Kent Robbins*	Capitol
1/25/97	❶[1]	20	3	**(This Ain't) No Thinkin' Thing**	*Tim Nichols/Mark D. Sanders*	Capitol
4/26/97	**2**[2]	20	4	**I Left Something Turned On At Home**	*Billy Lawson/John Schweers*	Capitol
				above 4 from the album *Dreamin' Out Loud* on Capitol 37222		
9/6/97	**4**	22	5	**The Rest Of Mine**	S:6 *Trace Adkins/Kenny Beard*	Capitol
1/17/98	**11**	20	6	**Lonely Won't Leave Me Alone**	S:14 *Mary Danna/Jody Alan Sweet*	Capitol
5/9/98	**27**	20	7	**Big Time**	*Kenny Beard/Larry Boone/Paul Nelson*	Capitol
				above 3 from the album *Big Time* on Capitol 55856		
12/26/98+	**64**	3	8	**The Christmas Song**	*Mel Torme/Robert Wells* **[X]**	Capitol
9/18/99+	**27**	20	9	**Don't Lie**	*Chet Biggers/Frank Rogers*	Capitol
1/29/00	**10**	23	10	**More**	*Del Gray/Thom McHugh*	Capitol
7/29/00	**36**	20	11	**I'm Gonna Love You Anyway**	*Stacy Dean Campbell/Dean Miller*	Capitol
				above 3 from the album *More...* on Capitol 96618		
7/7/01	**6**	32	12	**I'm Tryin'**	*Anthony Smith/Jeffrey Steele/Chris Wallin*	Capitol
3/2/02	**17**	23	13	**Help Me Understand**	*Chris Farren/Wayne Hector/Steve Mac*	Capitol
9/28/02+	**10**	25	14	**Chrome**	*Anthony Smith/Jeffrey Steele*	Capitol
				above 3 from the album *Chrome* on Capitol 30618		
3/15/03	**9**	28	15	**Then They Do**	*Jim Collins/Sunny Russ*	Capitol
				from the album *Greatest Hits Collection, Volume I* on Capitol 81512		
9/27/03+	**5**	28	16	**Hot Mama**	*Casey Beathard/Tom Shapiro*	Capitol
4/17/04	**13**	31	17	**Rough & Ready**	*Blair Mackichan/Brian White/Craig Wiseman*	Capitol
				above 2 from the album *Comin' On Strong* on Capitol 40517		
12/18/04+	**2**[1]	28	18	**Songs About Me**	*Ed Hill/Shayne Smith*	Capitol
4/9/05	**58**	1	19	**Honky Tonk Badonk Adonk**	*Dallas Davidson/Randy Houser/Jamey Johnson*	Capitol
6/11/05	**16**	16↑	20	**Arlington**	*Jeremy Spillman/Dave Turnbull*	Capitol
				above 3 from the album *Songs About Me* on Capitol 64512		

ADKINS, Wendel

Born on 1/15/1947 in Louisville, Kentucky; raised in Fremont, Ohio. Male singer.

DEBUT	PEAK	WKS		Country Chart Hit	Songwriter	Label (& Number)
2/19/77	**80**	4	1	**I Will**	*Oskar Solomon*	Hitsville 6050
4/30/77	**91**	3	2	**Laid Back Country Picker**	*Jim Casey/Vince Matthews*	Hitsville 6055
11/26/77	**98**	2	3	**Julieanne (Where Are You Tonight)?**	*Fred Schoonmaker/Larry Schoonmaker*	MC/Curb 5002

AKEMAN, David "Stringbean"

Born on 6/17/1916 in Annville, Kentucky. Shot to death on 11/10/1973 (age 57). Comic singer/banjo player. Regular on TV's *Hee Haw*. He and his wife were killed by robbers after a performance at the *Grand Ole Opry*.

OPRY: 1945

AKINS, Rhett

Born Thomas Rhett Akins on 10/13/1969 in Valdosta, Georgia. Male singer/songwriter/guitarist.

DEBUT	PEAK	WKS		Country Chart Hit	Songwriter	Label (& Number)
10/1/94	**35**	20	1	**What They're Talkin' About**	*Rhett Akins/Larry Boone/Paul Nelson*	Decca
1/21/95	**36**	14	2	**I Brake For Brunettes**	*Rhett Akins/Sandy Ramos*	Decca
5/13/95	**3**[1]	21	3	**That Ain't My Truck**	S:15 *Rhett Akins/Tom Shapiro/Chris Waters*	Decca
10/21/95+	**17**	22	4	**She Said Yes**	*Rhett Akins/Joe Doyle*	Decca
				above 4 from the album *A Thousand Memories* on Decca 11098		
3/30/96	❶[1]	21	5	**Don't Get Me Started**	*Rhett Akins/Sam Hogin/Mark D. Sanders*	Decca
9/7/96	**38**	13	6	**Love You Back**	*Bob DiPiero/Craig Wiseman*	Decca
12/7/96+	**51**	10	7	**Every Cowboy's Dream**	*Rhett Akins/Randy Boudreaux/Kim Williams*	Decca
3/22/97	**69**	1	8	**Somebody Knew**	*Larry Bastian/Dean Dillon*	Decca
				above 4 from the album *Somebody New* on Decca 11424		
10/4/97	**41**	20	9	**More Than Everything**	S:16 *Marv Green/Aimee Mayo*	Decca
1/24/98	**47**	11	10	**Better Than It Used To Be**	*Mark D. Sanders/Neil Thrasher*	Decca
				above 2 from the album *What Livin's All About* on Decca 70001		
4/18/98	**56**	9	11	**Drivin' My Life Away**	*David Malloy/Eddie Rabbitt/Even Stevens*	Decca
				from the movie *Black Dog* starring Patrick Swayze (soundtrack on Decca 70027)		
6/1/02	**55**	3	12	**Highway Sunrise**	*Ken Lamb/Jeff Stevens*	Audium
5/10/03	**57**	2	13	**In Your Love**	*Marv Green/Ken Lamb/Anthony Little*	Audium
				above 2 from the album *Friday Night In Dixie* on Audium 8153		

Billboard DEBUT	PEAK	WKS	GOLD	ARTIST / Country Chart Hit	Ranking / Songwriter	Label (& Number)

ALABAMA — 1980s: #5 / 1990s: #7 / All-Time: #16 // HOF: 2005

Group formed in Fort Payne, Alabama: Randy Owen (vocals, guitar; born on 12/13/1949), Jeff Cook (keyboards, fiddle; born on 8/27/1949), Teddy Gentry (bass; born on 1/22/1952) and Bennett Vartanian (drums). Owen, Cook and Gentry are cousins. Jackie Owen (another cousin) replaced Vartanian briefly in 1976; Rick Scott then took over as drummer later that same year. Mark Herndon (born on 5/11/1955) replaced Scott as drummer in 1979.

CMA: Vocal Group 1981, 1982 & 1983 / Instrumental Group 1981 & 1982 / Entertainer 1982, 1983 & 1984

DEBUT	PEAK	WKS		Country Chart Hit	Songwriter	Label (& Number)
7/23/77	**78**	8		1 **I Wanna Be With You Tonight**	*Jeff Cook/Teddy Gentry/Randy Owen/Rick Scott*	GRT 129
9/29/79	**33**	12		2 **I Wanna' Come Over**	*Michael Berardi/Richard Berardi*	MDJ 7906
2/2/80	**17**	13		3 **My Home's In Alabama**	*Teddy Gentry/Randy Owen*	MDJ 1002
5/31/80	❶[1]	17		4 **Tennessee River**	*Randy Owen*	RCA 12018
9/20/80	❶[1]	19		5 **Why Lady Why**	*Teddy Gentry/Rick Scott*	RCA 12091
2/14/81	❶[1]	14		6 **Old Flame**	*Donny Lowery/Mac McAnally*	RCA 12169
5/23/81	❶[2]	13		7 **Feels So Right**	*Randy Owen*	RCA 12236
10/24/81	❶[2]	16		8 **Love In The First Degree**	*Tim DuBois/Jim Hurt*	RCA 12288
3/6/82	❶[1]	18		9 **Mountain Music** Grammy: Vocal Group	*Randy Owen*	RCA 13019
5/29/82	❶[1]	17		10 **Take Me Down**	*Mark Gray/J.P. Pennington*	RCA 13210
8/28/82	❶[1]	17		11 **Close Enough To Perfect**	*Carl Chambers*	RCA 13294
12/11/82+	**35**	7		12 **Christmas In Dixie**	*Jeff Cook/Teddy Gentry/Randy Owen* **[X]**	RCA 13358
2/12/83	❶[1]	16		13 **Dixieland Delight**	*Ronnie Rogers*	RCA 13446
5/14/83	❶[1]	17		14 **The Closer You Get** Grammy: Vocal Group	*Mark Gray/J.P. Pennington*	RCA 13524
8/20/83	❶[1]	20		15 **Lady Down On Love**	*Randy Owen*	RCA 13590
1/21/84	❶[1]	17		16 **Roll On (Eighteen Wheeler)**	*Dave Loggins*	RCA 13716
4/21/84	❶[1]	19		17 **When We Make Love**	*Troy Seals/Mentor Williams*	RCA 13763
8/4/84	❶[1]	19		18 **If You're Gonna Play In Texas (You Gotta Have A Fiddle In The Band) /**	S:❶[1] / A:2 *Murry Kellum/Dan Mitchell*	
8/4/84	**flip**	2		19 **I'm Not That Way Anymore**	*Greg Fowler/Teddy Gentry/Mark Herndon/Randy Owen*	RCA 13840
11/10/84+	❶[1]	19		20 **(There's A) Fire In The Night**	A:❶[1] / S:2 *Bob Corbin*	RCA 13926
2/9/85	❶[1]	21		21 **There's No Way**	S:❶[1] / A:❶[1] *John Jarrard/Lisa Palas/Will Robinson*	RCA 13992
5/18/85	❶[1]	19		22 **Forty Hour Week (For A Livin')**	A:❶[1] / S:2 *Dave Loggins/Don Schlitz/Lisa Silver*	RCA 14085
8/24/85	❶[1]	22		23 **Can't Keep A Good Man Down**	S:❶[1] / A:❶[1] *Bob Corbin*	RCA 14165
1/25/86	❶[1]	21		24 **She And I**	A:❶[2] / S:❶[1] *Dave Loggins*	RCA 14281
9/20/86	❶[1]	20		25 **Touch Me When We're Dancing**	S:❶[1] / A:❶[1] *Ken Bell/Terry Skinner/J.L. Wallace*	RCA 5003
12/6/86+	**10**	15		26 **Deep River Woman** *[w/ Lionel Richie]*	S:❶[1] / A:10 *Lionel Richie*	Motown 1873
1/24/87	❶[1]	22		27 **"You've Got" The Touch**	A:❶[1] / S:3 *John Jarrard/Lisa Palas/Will Robinson*	RCA 5081
8/22/87	**7**	17		28 **Tar Top**	S:5 *Randy Owen*	RCA 5222
12/5/87+	❶[1]	22		29 **Face To Face** K.T. Oslin (guest vocal)	S:3 *Randy Owen*	RCA 5328
4/23/88	❶[1]	17		30 **Fallin' Again**	S:3 *Greg Fowler/Teddy Gentry/Randy Owen*	RCA 6902
11/26/88+	❶[1]	19		31 **Song Of The South**	S:10 *Bob McDill*	RCA 8744
3/11/89	❶[1]	19		32 **If I Had You**	*Kerry Chater/Danny Mayo*	RCA 8817
8/12/89	❶[1]	24		33 **High Cotton**	*Scott Anders/Roger Murrah*	RCA 8948
12/9/89+	❶[1]	26		34 **Southern Star**	*Rich Alves/Steve Dean/Roger Murrah*	RCA 9083
4/28/90	**3**[3]	21		35 **Pass It On Down**	*Teddy Gentry/Randy Owen/Will Robinson/Ronnie Rogers*	RCA
7/28/90	❶[4]	20		36 **Jukebox In My Mind**	*Dave Gibson/Ronnie Rogers*	RCA
11/17/90+	❶[1]	20		37 **Forever's As Far As I'll Go**	*Mike Reid*	RCA
3/2/91	❶[3]	20		38 **Down Home**	*Rick Bowles/Josh Leo*	RCA
6/8/91	**2**[1]	20		39 **Here We Are** above 5 from the album *Pass It On Down* on RCA 2108	*Beth Nielsen Chapman/Vince Gill*	RCA
9/28/91	**4**	20		40 **Then Again**	*Rick Bowles/Jeff Silbar*	RCA
1/11/92	**2**[1]	20		41 **Born Country** above 2 from the album *Greatest Hits II* on RCA 61040	*Byron Hill/John Schweers*	RCA
6/6/92	**2**[1]	20		42 **Take A Little Trip**	*Ronnie Rogers/Mark Wright*	RCA
9/26/92	❶[2]	20		43 **I'm In A Hurry (And Don't Know Why)**	*Roger Murrah/Randy Vanwarmer*	RCA
12/26/92+	**3**[2]	20		44 **Once Upon A Lifetime**	*Gary Baker/Frank J. Myers*	RCA
4/10/93	**3**[1]	20		45 **Hometown Honeymoon** above 4 from the album *American Pride* on RCA 66044	*Josh Leo/Jim Photoglo*	RCA
9/11/93	❶[1]	20		46 **Reckless**	*Michael Clark/Jeff Stevens*	RCA
12/18/93+	**7**	20		47 **T.L.C. A.S.A.P.**	*Gary Baker/Frank J. Myers*	RCA
12/25/93+	**51**	6		48 **Angels Among Us**	S:6 *Don Goodman/Becky Hobbs* **[X]**	RCA
4/16/94	**13**	20		49 **The Cheap Seats**	*Marcus Hummon/Randy Sharp*	RCA
9/10/94	**6**	20		50 **We Can't Love Like This Anymore**	*John Jarrard/Wendell Mobley*	RCA
12/31/94+	**28**	14		51 **Angels Among Us** #46-49 & 51: from the album *Cheap Seats* on RCA 66296	*Don Goodman/Becky Hobbs* **[X-R]**	RCA
1/28/95	**75**	1		52 **Sweet Home Alabama** from the various artists album *Skynyrd Frynds* on MCA 11097	*Ed King/Gary Rossington/Ronnie Van Zant*	MCA
2/11/95	**3**[1]	20		53 **Give Me One More Shot** #50 & 53 from the album *Greatest Hits - Vol. III* on RCA 66410	*Teddy Gentry/Randy Owen/Ronnie Rogers*	RCA
7/1/95	**2**[1]	20		54 **She Ain't Your Ordinary Girl**	S:21 *Robert Jason*	RCA
9/30/95	**4**	20		55 **In Pictures**	S:6 *Bobby Boyd/Joe Doyle*	RCA

DEBUT	PEAK	WKS	GOLD	ARTIST / Ranking / Country Chart Hit	Songwriter	Label (& Number)
				ALABAMA — cont'd		
1/13/96	**19**	20		56 **It Works**	S:18 *Mickey Cates/Mark Alan Springer*	RCA
5/18/96	**38**	7		57 **Say I**	*Steve Bogard/Jeff Stevens*	RCA
7/20/96	**4**	20		58 **The Maker Said Take Her**	*Ronnie Rogers/Mark Wright*	RCA
				above 5 from the album *In Pictures* on RCA 66525		
1/4/97	**72**	2		59 **The Blessings**	*Greg Fowler/Teddy Gentry/Randy Owen/Ronnie Rogers* **[X]**	RCA
				from the album *Christmas Volume II* on RCA 66927		
3/1/97	**2**[1]	20		60 **Sad Lookin' Moon**	S:14 *Greg Fowler/Teddy Gentry/Randy Owen*	RCA
6/28/97	**3**[1]	20		61 **Dancin', Shaggin' On The Boulevard**	*Greg Fowler/Teddy Gentry/Randy Owen*	RCA
10/11/97	**22**	20		62 **Of Course I'm Alright**	*Billy Kirsch*	RCA
12/27/97+	**47**	3		63 **Christmas In Dixie**	*Jeff Cook/Teddy Gentry/Randy Owen* **[X-R]**	RCA
2/14/98	**21**	20		64 **She's Got That Look In Her Eyes**	*Teddy Gentry/Randy Owen*	RCA
				#60-62 & 64: from the album *Dancin' On The Boulevard* on RCA 67426		
8/1/98	**2**[1]	21		65 **How Do You Fall In Love**	*Greg Fowler/Teddy Gentry/Randy Owen*	RCA
12/5/98+	**14**	20		66 **Keepin' Up**	*Greg Fowler/Teddy Gentry/Randy Owen/Ronnie Rogers*	RCA
				above 2 from the album *For The Record - 41 Number One Hits* on RCA 67633		
12/19/98+	**40**	4		67 **Christmas In Dixie**	*Jeff Cook/Teddy Gentry/Randy Owen* **[X-R]**	RCA
1/9/99	**71**	1		68 **Santa Claus (I Still Believe In You)**	*Greg Fowler/Linda Gentry/Teddy Gentry/John Jarrard/Randy Owen* **[X]**	RCA
5/1/99	**3**[3]	23		69 **God Must Have Spent A Little More Time On You** ***[w/ *NSYNC]***	S:3 *Evan Rogers/Carl Sturken*	RCA
10/16/99+	**24**	20		70 **Small Stuff**	*Mark Collie/Hillary Kanter/Even Stevens*	RCA
12/11/99+	**37**	5		71 **Christmas In Dixie**	*Jeff Cook/Teddy Gentry/Randy Owen* **[X-R]**	RCA
				#63, 67, 68 & 71: from the album *Christmas* on RCA 7014		
12/25/99+	**64**	3		72 **Rockin' Around The Christmas Tree**	*Johnny Marks* **[X]**	RCA
				from the album *Christmas Volume II* on RCA 66927		
1/15/00	**51**	3		73 **Twentieth Century**	S:8 *Chris Cummings/Don Schlitz*	RCA
1/15/00	**55**	1		74 **New Year's Eve 1999** ***[w/ Gretchen Peters]***	*Gretchen Peters*	RCA
5/20/00	**63**	3		75 **We Made Love**	*Tom Douglas/Billy Kirsch*	RCA
				#69, 70, 73 & 75: from the album *Twentieth Century* on RCA 67793		
11/4/00+	**15**	20		76 **When It All Goes South**	*Janis Carnes/Rick Carnes/John Jarvis*	RCA
5/5/01	**41**	11		77 **Will You Marry Me**	*Al Anderson/Jeffrey Steele*	RCA
				above 2 from the album *When It All Goes South* on RCA 69337		
6/8/02	**48**	9		78 **I'm In The Mood**	*Lewis Anderson/Ronnie Rogers*	RCA
				from the album *In The Mood: Love Songs* on RCA 67052		

Angels Among Us ['94, '95] · Blessings ['97] · Born Country ['92] · Can't Keep A Good Man Down ['85] · Cheap Seats ['94] · Christmas In Dixie ['83, '98, '99, '00] · Close Enough To Perfect ['82] · Closer You Get ['83] · Dancin', Shaggin' On The Boulevard ['97] · Deep River Woman ['87] · Dixieland Delight ['83] · Down Home ['91] · Face To Face ['88] · Fallin' Again ['88] · Feels So Right ['81] · Forever's As Far As I'll Go ['91] · Forty Hour Week (For A Livin') ['85] · Give Me One More Shot ['95] · God Must Have Spent A Little More Time On You ['99] · Here We Are ['91] · High Cotton ['89] · Hometown Honeymoon ['93] · How Do You Fall In Love ['98] · I Wanna Be With You Tonight ['77] · I Wanna' Come Over ['79] · I'm In A Hurry (And Don't Know Why) ['92] · I'm In The Mood ['02] · I'm Not That Way Anymore ['84] · If I Had You ['89] · If You're Gonna Play In Texas (You Gotta Have A Fiddle In The Band) ['84] · In Pictures ['95] · It Works ['96] · Jukebox In My Mind ['90] · Keepin' Up ['99] · Lady Down On Love ['83] · Love In The First Degree ['81] · Maker Said Take Her ['96] · Mountain Music ['82] · My Home's In Alabama ['80] · New Year's Eve 1999 ['00] · Of Course I'm Alright ['97] · Old Flame ['81] · Once Upon A Lifetime ['93] · Pass It On Down ['90] · Reckless ['93] · Rockin' Around The Christmas Tree ['00] · Roll On (Eighteen Wheeler) ['84] · Sad Lookin' Moon ['97] · Santa Claus (I Still Believe In You) ['99] · Say I ['96] · She Ain't Your Ordinary Girl ['95] · She And I ['86] · She's Got That Look In Her Eyes ['98] · Small Stuff ['00] · Song Of The South ['89] · Southern Star ['90] · Sweet Home Alabama ['95] · T.L.C. A.S.A.P. ['94] · Take A Little Trip ['92] · Take Me Down ['82] · Tar Top ['87] · Tennessee River ['80] · Then Again ['91] · (There's A) Fire In The Night ['85] · There's No Way ['85] · Touch Me When We're Dancing ['86] · Twentieth Century ['00] · We Can't Love Like This Anymore ['94] · We Made Love ['00] · When It All Goes South ['01] · When We Make Love ['84] · Why Lady Why ['80] · Will You Marry Me ['01] · "You've Got" The Touch ['87]

ALAN, Buddy — All-Time: #277

Born Alvis Alan Owens on 5/23/1948 in Mesa, Arizona. Singer/songwriter/guitarist. Son of **Buck Owens** and **Bonnie Owens**.

DEBUT	PEAK	WKS	GOLD	Country Chart Hit	Songwriter	Label (& Number)
7/27/68	**7**	15		1 **Let The World Keep On A Turnin'** ***[w/ Buck Owens]***	*Buck Owens*	Capitol 2237
11/23/68	**54**	6		2 **When I Turn Twenty-One**	*Merle Haggard*	Capitol 2305
10/25/69	**23**	10		3 **Lodi**	*John Fogerty*	Capitol 2653
2/7/70	**23**	8		4 **Big Mama's Medicine Show**	*Buddy Alan*	Capitol 2715
5/2/70	**38**	9		5 **Down In New Orleans**	*Buck Owens*	Capitol 2784
8/8/70	**57**	7		6 **Santo Domingo**	*Buck Owens*	Capitol 2852
11/7/70	**19**	12		7 **Cowboy Convention** ***[w/ Don Rich]***	*Peter Barnfather/John Carter*	Capitol 2928
1/16/71	**37**	9		8 **Lookin' Out My Back Door**	*John Fogerty*	Capitol 3010
3/6/71	**54**	5		9 **I'm On The Road To Memphis** ***[w/ Don Rich]***	*Mike Collings/Ron White*	Capitol 3040
6/5/71	**48**	9		10 **Fishin' On The Mississippi**	*Bob Morris*	Capitol 3110
8/21/71	**46**	9		11 **I Will Drink Your Wine**	*Buddy Alan*	Capitol 3146
12/4/71+	**29**	10		12 **Too Old To Cut The Mustard** ***[w/ Buck Owens]***	*Bill Carlisle*	Capitol 3215
3/4/72	**68**	4		13 **White Line Fever**	*Merle Haggard*	Capitol 3266
6/24/72	**47**	10		14 **I'm In Love**	*Freddie Hart*	Capitol 3346
9/23/72	**49**	7		15 **Things**	*Bobby Darin*	Capitol 3427
12/30/72+	**60**	6		16 **Move It On Over**	*Hank Williams*	Capitol 3485
4/7/73	**64**	4		17 **Why, Because I Love You**	*Buddy Alan*	Capitol 3555
5/19/73	**67**	4		18 **Caribbean**	*Mitchell Torok*	Capitol 3598
8/11/73	**68**	6		19 **Summer Afternoons**	*Buddy Alan*	Capitol 3680
11/24/73+	**67**	8		20 **All Around Cowboy Of 1964**	*Buddy Alan/Ray McDonald*	Capitol 3749
5/4/74	**70**	8		21 **I Never Had It So Good**	*Roger Nichols/Paul Williams*	Capitol 3861
2/15/75	**35**	11		22 **Chains**	*Gerry Goffin/Carole King*	Capitol 4019
6/7/75	**88**	5		23 **Another Saturday Night**	*Sam Cooke*	Capitol 4075

ALBERT, Urel

Born on 5/28/1928 in Chicago, Illinois. Died on 4/29/1992 (age 63). Male comedian/impressionist.

DEBUT	PEAK	WKS	GOLD	Country Chart Hit	Songwriter	Label (& Number)
10/13/73	**97**	2		**Country And Pop Music**	*Johnny Elgin* **[N]**	Toast 311
				"live" effects are dubbed-in		

DEBUT	PEAK	WKS	GOLD	ARTIST / Ranking / Country Chart Hit	Songwriter	Label (& Number)
				ALDEAN, Jason		
				Born on 2/28/1977 in Macon, Georgia. Male singer/guitarist.		
4/23/05	**15↑**	23↑		**Hicktown**	*Kenny Alphin/Vicky McGehee/John Rich*	Broken Bow
				from the album *Jason Aldean* on Broken Bow 7657		
				ALEXANDER, Daniele		
				Born on 12/2/1954 in Fort Worth, Texas. Female singer/songwriter.		
7/22/89	**19**	20		1 **She's There**	*Daniele Alexander*	Mercury 874330
11/11/89	**53**	8		2 **Where Did The Moon Go Wrong**	*Daniele Alexander/Paul Nelson*	Mercury 876228
12/1/90+	**56**	9		3 **It Wasn't You, It Wasn't Me** ***[w/ Butch Baker]***	*Daniele Alexander/Austin Gardner*	Mercury
				ALEXANDER, Jessi		
				Born in 1972 in Jackson, Tennessee; raised in Memphis, Tennessee. Female singer/songwriter/guitarist.		
5/8/04	**52**	5		1 **Honeysuckle Sweet**	*Jessi Alexander/Sally Barris*	Columbia
10/2/04	**57**	1		2 **Make Me Stay Or Make Me Go**	*Jessi Alexander/Al Anderson/Gary Nicholson*	Columbia
				above 2 from the album *Honeysuckle Sweet* on Columbia 90849		
				ALEXANDER, Wyvon		
				Born on 7/2/1954 in Weaverville, California. Male singer/songwriter.		
2/14/81	**90**	2		1 **Frustration**	*Wyvon Alexander*	Gervasi 633
4/18/81	**86**	2		2 **Old Familiar Feeling**	*Wyvon Alexander*	Gervasi 644
8/15/81	**74**	4		3 **Women /**	*Kendal Franceschi/Ed Jones/Cindy Walker*	
1/16/82	**83**	3		4 **Don't Lead Me On**	*Wyvon Alexander*	Gervasi 659
8/28/82	**69**	6		5 **Alice In Dallas (Sweet Texas)**	*Merle Haggard/Dave Kirby*	Gervasi 660
11/27/82	**76**	4		6 **Midnight Cabaret**	*Kirk Stirland*	Gervasi 661
12/10/83+	**68**	8		7 **The Look Of A Lovin' Lady**	*Bill Anderson/Blake Mevis*	Gervasi 663
				ALIBI		
				Vocal group from Canada.		
10/3/87	**84**	2		1 **Roller Coaster**	*Bryon O'Donnell*	Comstock 1856
5/21/88	**61**	6		2 **Do You Have Any Doubts**	*Mike Rheault/Colin Weinmaster*	Comstock 1884
				ALLAN, Gary — **2000s: #14 / All-Time: #206**		
				Born Gary Herzberg on 12/5/1967 in Montebello, California; raised in La Mirada, California. Male singer/guitarist.		
8/24/96+	**7**	23		1 **Her Man**	*Kent Robbins*	Decca
1/11/97	**70**	1		2 **Please Come Home For Christmas**	*Charles Brown/Gene Redd* **[X]**	Decca
				from the various artists album *A Country Christmas 1996* on MCA 40019 (available only at Target stores)		
1/18/97	**44**	11		3 **Forever And A Day**	*Frank Dycus/Jim Lauderdale*	Decca
4/12/97	**43**	15		4 **From Where I'm Sitting**	*Garth Brooks/Kent Maxon*	Decca
8/23/97	**43**	12		5 **Living In A House Full Of Love**	*Billy Sherrill/Glenn Sutton*	Decca
				#1 & 3-5: from the album *Used Heart For Sale* on Decca 11482		
2/14/98	**7**	23		6 **It Would Be You**	S:15 *Dana Oglesby/Kent Robbins*	Decca
8/1/98	**43**	11		7 **No Man In His Wrong Heart**	*Trey Bruce/Randy Rogers*	Decca
11/7/98+	**47**	17		8 **I'll Take Today**	*Kent Robbins/Will Robinson*	Decca
				above 3 from the album *It Would Be You* on Decca 70012		
8/14/99+	**12**	29		9 **Smoke Rings In The Dark**	*Houston Robert/Rivers Rutherford*	MCA Nashville
1/22/00	**74**	1		10 **Runaway**	*Max Crook/Del Shannon*	MCA Nashville
4/1/00	**34**	20		11 **Lovin' You Against My Will**	*Jamie O'Hara*	MCA Nashville
4/22/00+	**5**	48		12 **Right Where I Need To Be**	*Casey Beathard/Kendell Marvel*	MCA Nashville
				above 4 from the album *Smoke Rings In The Dark* on MCA Nashville 70101		
7/7/01	**18**	24		13 **Man Of Me**	*Rivers Rutherford/George Teren*	MCA Nashville
1/19/02	**3**^{2}	34		14 **The One**	*Billy Lee/Karen Manno*	MCA Nashville
10/5/02+	**❶**^{1}	31		15 **Man To Man**	*Jamie O'Hara*	MCA Nashville
				above 3 from the album *Alright Guy* on MCA Nashville 70201		
6/28/03	**❶**^{2}	24		16 **Tough Little Boys**	*Harley Allen/Don Sampson*	MCA Nashville
11/22/03+	**12**	24		17 **Songs About Rain**	*Pat McLaughlin/Liz Rose*	MCA Nashville
6/26/04	**❶**^{2}	33		18 **Nothing On But The Radio**	*Odie Blackmon/Byron Hill/Brice Long*	MCA Nashville
				above 3 from the album *See If I Care* on MCA Nashville 000111		
6/11/05	**18↑**	16↑		19 **Best I Ever Had**	*Matt Scannell*	MCA Nashville
				ALLANSON, Susie — **All-Time: #295**		
				Born on 3/17/1952 in Las Vegas, Nevada. Female singer/actress. Performed in the musical *Hair* and both the musical and movie version of *Jesus Christ Superstar*. Formerly married to music executive Ray Ruff.		
7/9/77	**23**	14		1 **Baby, Don't Keep Me Hangin' On**	*Ray Broome/Llloyd Schoonmaker*	Oak 1001
11/5/77+	**20**	14		2 **Baby, Last Night Made My Day**	*Bobby Lee Springfield*	Warner/Curb 8473
3/4/78	**7**	13		3 **Maybe Baby**	*Buddy Holly/Norman Petty*	Warner/Curb 8534
6/24/78	**2**^{2}	13		4 **We Belong Together**	*Carol Chase*	Warner/Curb 8597
10/28/78	**17**	11		5 **Back To The Love**	*Bobby Lee Springfield*	Warner/Curb 8686
2/3/79	**8**	11		6 **Words**	*Barry Gibb/Maurice Gibb/Robin Gibb*	Elektra/Curb 46009
4/28/79	**6**	12		7 **Two Steps Forward And Three Steps Back**	*Jerry Crutchfield/Molly-Ann Leikin*	Elektra/Curb 46036
8/18/79	**79**	4		8 **Without You**	*Tom Evans/Pet Ham*	Elektra/Curb 46503
12/1/79+	**38**	10		9 **I Must Be Crazy**	*Bob McDill*	Elektra/Curb 46565
8/2/80	**31**	12		10 **While I Was Makin' Love To You**	*Michael Dunn/Curly Putman*	United Artists 1365
11/8/80+	**23**	14		11 **Dance The Two Step**	*Lee Holdridge/Molly-Ann Leikin*	Liberty 1383
5/30/81	**53**	7		12 **Run To Her**	*Gerry Goffin/Jack Keller*	Liberty/Curb 1408
9/5/81	**44**	8		13 **Love Is Knockin' At My Door (Here Comes Forever Again)**	*Mark Wright*	Liberty/Curb 1425
12/5/81	**60**	7		14 **Hearts (Our Hearts)**	*Deborah Allen/Ken Beal*	Liberty/Curb 1422

Billboard DEBUT	PEAK	WKS	GOLD	ARTIST / Country Chart Hit	Ranking / Songwriter	Label (& Number)
				ALLANSON, Susie — cont'd		
4/24/82	**62**	6		15 **Wasn't That Love**	*Mitch Johnson/Harry Shannon*	Liberty/Curb 1460
12/27/86+	**67**	7		16 **Where's The Fire**	*Susan Longacre/Sam Lorber*	TNP 75001
6/20/87	**70**	5		17 **She Don't Love You**	*Jerry Butler/Calvin Carter/Curtis Mayfield*	TNP 75005
				ALLEN, Deborah	**All-Time: #293**	
				Born Deborah Lynn Thurmond on 9/30/1953 in Memphis, Tennessee. Female singer/songwriter. Married to songwriter Rafe Van Hoy from 1982-93. Regular on TV's *The **Jim Stafford** Show* in 1975.		
6/23/79	**10**	14		1 **Don't Let Me Cross Over** *[w/ Jim Reeves]*	*Penny Jay*	RCA 11564
11/3/79+	**6**	15		2 **Oh, How I Miss You Tonight** *[w/ Jim Reeves]*	*Joe Burke/Benny Davis/Mark Fisher*	RCA 11737
4/12/80	**10**	16		3 **Take Me In Your Arms And Hold Me** *[w/ Jim Reeves]*	*Cindy Walker*	RCA 11946
11/22/80+	**24**	15		4 **Nobody's Fool**	*Deborah Allen/Don Cook/Rafe Van Hoy*	Capitol 4945
8/15/81	**20**	11		5 **You (Make Me Wonder Why)**	*Deborah Allen/Rafe Van Hoy*	Capitol 5014
1/9/82	**33**	10		6 **You Look Like The One I Love**	*Deborah Allen/Rafe Van Hoy*	Capitol 5080
5/29/82	**82**	3		7 **After Tonight**	*Steve Diamond/Troy Seals/Eddie Setser*	Capitol 5110
8/20/83	**4**	24		8 **Baby I Lied**	*Deborah Allen/Rory Bourke/Rafe Van Hoy*	RCA 13600
1/28/84	**2**[2]	24		9 **I've Been Wrong Before**	*Deborah Allen/Don Cook/Rafe Van Hoy*	RCA 13694
5/26/84	**10**	20		10 **I Hurt For You**	*Deborah Allen/Rafe Van Hoy*	RCA 13776
10/20/84	**23**	17		11 **Heartache And A Half**	A:20 / S:26 *Deborah Allen/Eddie Struzick/Rafe Van Hoy*	RCA 13921
12/5/92+	**29**	20		12 **Rock Me (In The Cradle Of Love)**	*Deborah Allen/Rafe Van Hoy*	Giant
4/17/93	**44**	13		13 **If You're Not Gonna Love Me**	*Deborah Allen/Mark Collie/Rafe Van Hoy*	Giant
				above 2 from the album *Delta Dreamland* on Giant 24485		
5/7/94	**66**	2		14 **Break These Chains**	*Deborah Allen/Kye Fleming/Mary Ann Kennedy*	Giant
				from the album *All That I Am* on Giant 24552		
				ALLEN, Joe		
				Born in Aspen, Colorado. Male singer/songwriter/session musician.		
1/25/75	**83**	5		1 **Should I Come Home (Or Should I Go Crazy)**	*Joe Allen*	Warner 8052
7/5/75	**88**	8		2 **Carolyn At The Broken Wheel Inn**	*Bob McDill*	Warner 8098
				ALLEN, Judy		
				Born in Canada. Female singer.		
1/28/78	**94**	4		**Sweet Little Devil**	*Don Goodman/Mark Sherrill*	Polydor 14440
				ALLEN, Melody		
				Born in 1955 in Moline, Illinois. Female singer.		
2/1/75	**91**	6		1 **Once Again I Go To Sleep With Lovin' On My Mind**	*Kallie Jean*	Mercury 73638
5/10/75	**68**	8		2 **May You Rest In Peace**	*Kallie Jean*	Mercury 73674
				ALLEN, Red		
				Born Harley Allen on 2/12/1930 in Pigeon Roost, Kentucky. Died on 4/3/1993 (age 63). Male singer/guitarist.		
3/24/58	**13**	2		**Once More** *[w/ The Osborne Brothers]*	A:13 *Dusty Owens*	MGM 12583
				ALLEN, Rex		
				Born on 12/31/1920 in Willcox, Arizona. Died after being struck by a car on 12/17/1999 (age 78). Male singer/guitarist/actor. Professional rodeo rider as a teenager. Starred in numerous western movies. Narrator for several Disney nature movies. Played "Bill Baxter" on TV's *Frontier Doctor*. Father of **Rex Allen Jr.**		
9/3/49	**14**	1		1 **Afraid** *[w/ The Arizona Wranglers & Jerry Byrd]*	J:14 *Fred Rose*	Mercury 6192
4/21/51	**10**	1		2 **Sparrow In The Tree Top**	J:10 *Bob Merrill*	Mercury 5597-X45
				Harry Geller (orch.); Jud Conlin Singers (backing vocals)		
8/8/53	**4**	13		3 **Crying In The Chapel**	J:4 / S:4 / A:6 *Artie Glenn*	Decca 28758
8/14/61	**21**	4		4 **Marines, Let's Go**	*Martin Phillips*	Mercury 71844
				title song from the movie starring *Tom Reese*		
9/29/62	**4**	13		5 **Don't Go Near The Indians**	*Lorene Mann*	Mercury 71997
				The Merry Melody Singers (backing vocals)		
1/11/64	**44**	3		6 **Tear After Tear**	*Fred Burch/Marijohn Wilkin*	Mercury 72205
6/22/68	**71**	5		7 **Tiny Bubbles**	*Leon Pober*	Decca 32322

Billboard DEBUT	PEAK	WKS	GOLD	ARTIST / Country Chart Hit	Ranking / Songwriter	Label (& Number)
				ALLEN, Rex Jr.	**All-Time: #163**	
				Born on 8/23/1947 in Chicago, Illinois. Male singer/songwriter/guitarist. Son of **Rex Allen**. Traveled with his father from age six. Formed the groups the Townsmen and Saturday's Children. Served in the U.S. Army from 1967-69. Hosted TNN's *Nashville On The Road* and worked as a regular performer on ***The Statler Brothers** Show*.		
12/29/73+	**63**	10		1 **The Great Mail Robbery**	*Joe Allen*	Warner 7753
4/20/74	**19**	14		2 **Goodbye**	*Larry Butler/Buddy Killen*	Warner 7788
8/24/74	**31**	14		3 **Another Goodbye Song**	*Larry Butler/Martha Sharp*	Warner 8000
12/7/74+	**36**	11		4 **Never Coming Back Again**	*Larry Butler/Jan Crutchfield*	Warner 8046
5/31/75	**70**	7		5 **Lying In My Arms**	*Joe Allen*	Warner 8095
1/24/76	**34**	9		6 **Play Me No Sad Songs**	*Roger Bowling/Larry Butler*	Warner 8171
5/1/76	**17**	12		7 **Can You Hear Those Pioneers**	*Rex Allen Jr./Judy Maude*	Warner 8204
				Rex Allen and **The Sons of The Pioneers** (guest vocals)		
8/7/76	**18**	13		8 **Teardrops In My Heart**	*Vaughn Horton*	Warner 8236

Billboard DEBUT	PEAK	WKS	GOLD	ARTIST / Ranking / Country Chart Hit	Songwriter	Label (& Number)

ALLEN, Rex Jr. — cont'd

DEBUT	PEAK	WKS	Rank	Country Chart Hit	Songwriter	Label (& Number)
12/11/76+	**8**	16	9	**Two Less Lonely People**	*Wayland Holyfield*	Warner 8297
4/9/77	**10**	12	10	**I'm Getting Good At Missing You (Solitaire)**	*Wayland Holyfield*	Warner 8354
8/6/77	**15**	11	11	**Don't Say Goodbye**	*Rex Allen Jr.*	Warner 8418
11/12/77+	**8**	15	12	**Lonely Street**	*Carl Belew/Kenny Sowder/W.S. Stevenson*	Warner 8482
3/25/78	**8**	15	13	**No, No, No (I'd Rather Be Free)**	*Wayland Holyfield/Bob McDill*	Warner 8541
7/29/78	**10**	12	14	**With Love**	*Rex Allen Jr.*	Warner 8608
11/25/78+	**12**	14	15	**It's Time We Talk Things Over** *[w/ The Boys]*	*Rex Allen Jr./Judy Maude*	Warner 8697
4/14/79	**9**	12	16	**Me And My Broken Heart**	*Curtis Allen*	Warner 8786
8/4/79	**18**	12	17	**If I Fell In Love With You**	*Rafe Van Hoy*	Warner 49020
2/16/80	**25**	10	18	**Yippy Cry Yi**	*Joe Allen/Bucky Lindsey*	Warner 49168
5/24/80	**14**	13	19	**It's Over**	*Rex Allen Jr./Danny DeMarco/Joe Holcolmb*	Warner 49128
9/27/80	**25**	12	20	**Drink It Down, Lady**	*Sonny Throckmorton*	Warner 49562
12/20/80+	**12**	14	21	**Cup Of Tea** *[w/ Margo Smith]*	*Harlan White*	Warner 49626
3/14/81	**35**	9	22	**Just A Country Boy**	*Rex Allen Jr.*	Warner 49682
6/13/81	**26**	12	23	**While The Feeling's Good** *[w/ Margo Smith]*	*Roger Bowling/Freddie Hart*	Warner 49738
3/27/82	**43**	10	24	**Last Of The Silver Screen Cowboys** **Rex Allen** and **Roy Rogers** (guest vocals)	*Milton Brown/Steve Dorff/Snuff Garrett*	Warner 50035
7/10/82	**44**	10	25	**Cowboy In A Three Piece Business Suit**	*Dewayne Blackwell*	Warner 29968
11/27/82	**85**	3	26	**Ride Cowboy Ride**	*Curtis Allen/Rex Allen Jr./Danny DeMarco*	Warner 29890
10/22/83	**37**	15	27	**The Air That I Breathe**	*Albert Hammond/Mike Hazlewood*	Moon Shine 3017
3/10/84	**44**	9	28	**Sweet Rosanna**	*Buck Moore/A.L. "Doodle" Owens*	Moon Shine 3022
7/14/84	**18**	16	29	**Dream On Texas Ladies**	*Steve Mills*	Moon Shine 3030
11/10/84+	**24**	19	30	**Running Down Memory Lane** S:17 / A:26	*Eddy Raven*	Moon Shine 3034
4/20/85	**62**	7	31	**When You Held Me In Your Arms**	*Hugh Moffatt*	Moon Shine 3036
11/14/87	**59**	8	32	**We're Staying Together**	*Thom Schuyler*	TNP 75010

ALLEN, Rosalie

Born Julie Marlene Bedra on 6/27/1924 in Old Forge, Pennsylvania. Died of heart failure on 9/23/2003 (age 79). Female singer. Hosted own TV show in New York City from 1949-53. Known as "The Prairie Star" and "Queen of The Yodelers."

DEBUT	PEAK	WKS	Rank	Country Chart Hit	Songwriter	Label (& Number)
8/10/46	**5**	1	1	**I Want To Be A Cowboy's Sweetheart /**	*Patsy Montana*	
8/17/46	**3**[2]	4	2	**Guitar Polka (Old Monterey)**	*Al Dexter*	RCA Victor 20-1924
2/4/50	**7**	4	3	**Beyond The Sunset** *[w/ The Three Suns & Elton Britt]* A:7	*Blanche Brock/Virgil Brock*	RCA Victor 47-3105
2/25/50	**3**[2]	10	4	**Quicksilver** *[w/ Elton Britt]* A:3 / J:6 / S:9	*Edward Pola/Irving Taylor/George Wyle*	RCA Victor 48-0168

ALLEY, Jim

Born in Hemphill, West Virginia. Male singer/songwriter/guitarist.

DEBUT	PEAK	WKS	Rank	Country Chart Hit	Songwriter	Label (& Number)
1/20/68	**73**	2	1	**Only Daddy That'll Walk The Line**	*Jimmy Bryant*	Dot 17051
3/15/75	**96**	2	2	**Her Memory's Gonna Kill Me**	*Jim Alley/Roger Bowling*	Avco 606

ALMOST BROTHERS, The

Duo formed in New York: guitarist/songwriter/producer Mike Ragogna and guitarist/pianist Steve Mosto.

DEBUT	PEAK	WKS	Rank	Country Chart Hit	Songwriter	Label (& Number)
8/17/85	**55**	7	1	**Don't Tell Me Love Is Kind**	*Mike Ragogna*	MTM 72053
2/22/86	**63**	6	2	**Birds Of A Feather**	*Mike Ragogna*	MTM 72062
8/9/86	**72**	6	3	**What's Your Name**	*Claude Johnson*	MTM 72072
11/22/86	**52**	8	4	**I Don't Love Her Anymore**	*Mike Ragogna*	MTM 72079

ALVIN & THE CHIPMUNKS — see CHIPMUNKS, The

AMARILLO — see GRANT, Barry

AMAZING RHYTHM ACES, The

Country-rock group from Memphis, Tennessee: **Russell Smith** (vocals, guitar), Barry "Byrd" Burton (guitar), Billy Earhart III (keyboards), James Hooker (piano), Jeff "Stick" Davis (bass) and Butch McDade (drums). Burton left in 1977; replaced by Duncan Cameron. Earhart joined **The Bama Band** in 1986. Cameron joined **Sawyer Brown** in 1991. McDade died of cancer on 11/29/1998 (age 52).

DEBUT	PEAK	WKS	Rank	Country Chart Hit	Songwriter	Label (& Number)
7/5/75	**11**	14	1	**Third Rate Romance**	*Russell Smith*	ABC 12078
11/29/75+	**9**	14	2	**Amazing Grace (Used To Be Her Favorite Song)**	*Russell Smith*	ABC 12142
8/7/76	**12**	14	3	**The End Is Not In Sight (The Cowboy Tune)** **Grammy: Vocal Group**	*Russell Smith*	ABC 12202
7/15/78	**100**	1	4	**Ashes Of Love**	*Jack Anglin/Jim Anglin/Johnny Wright*	ABC 12369
3/24/79	**88**	4	5	**Lipstick Traces (On A Cigarette)**	*Naomi Neville*	ABC 12454
11/29/80	**77**	6	6	**I Musta Died And Gone To Texas**	*Russell Smith*	Warner 49600

AMERICA THE BEAUTIFUL

All-star group: **Trace Adkins**, **Billy Dean**, **Vince Gill**, **Carolyn Dawn Johnson**, **Toby Keith**, **Brenda Lee**, **Lonestar**, **Martina McBride**, **Jamie O'Neal**, **Kenny Rogers** and **Keith Urban**.

DEBUT	PEAK	WKS	Rank	Country Chart Hit	Songwriter	Label (& Number)
7/21/01	**58**	6		**America The Beautiful**	*Katherine Bates/Samuel Ward*	(no label)

AMES, Durelle

Born Durelle Upchurch on 5/4/1965 in Gaffney, South Carolina. Female singer. Also recorded as **De De Ames**.

DEBUT	PEAK	WKS	Rank	Country Chart Hit	Songwriter	Label (& Number)
8/15/87	**72**	5	1	**Dancin' In The Moonlight**	*Fred Goodman/John Schnall*	Advantage 175
1/16/88	**75**	4	2	**Break Down The Walls** *[De De Ames]*	*Fred Goodman*	Advantage 185

AMY

Born Amy Barrett in Atlanta, Georgia. Female singer.

DEBUT	PEAK	WKS	Rank	Country Chart Hit	Songwriter	Label (& Number)
2/3/79	**76**	4		**Please Be Gentle**	*Mac Davis*	Scorpion 0570

Billboard DEBUT	PEAK	WKS	GOLD		ARTIST / Country Chart Hit	Ranking / Songwriter	Label (& Number)

ANDERSON, Bill 1960s: #8 / 1970s: #18 / All-Time: #30 // HOF: 2001

Born James William Anderson III on 11/1/1937 in Columbia, South Carolina. Male singer/songwriter. Worked as a sportswriter and as a DJ in Georgia. Appeared in such movies as *Las Vegas Hillbillies, Forty Acre Feud* and *Road To Nashville*. Hosted own TV show in 1966. Hosted TV game shows *The Better Sex* and *Fandango*. Hosted TNN's *Opry Backstage*. Known as "Whispering Bill."

OPRY: 1961

DEBUT	PEAK	WKS	GOLD		Country Chart Hit	Songwriter	Label (& Number)
12/29/58+	12	17		1	That's What It's Like To Be Lonesome	Bill Anderson	Decca 30773
7/6/59	13	19		2	Ninety-Nine	Bill Anderson	Decca 30914
12/28/59+	19	8		3	Dead Or Alive	Bill Anderson	Decca 30993
6/20/60	7	18		4	The Tip Of My Fingers	Bill Anderson	Decca 31092
12/26/60+	9	14		5	Walk Out Backwards	Bill Anderson	Decca 31168
7/10/61	9	19		6	Po' Folks	Bill Anderson	Decca 31262
4/21/62	14	10		7	Get A Little Dirt On Your Hands also see #63 below	Bill Anderson	Decca 31358
7/28/62	❶[7]	27		8	Mama Sang A Song	Bill Anderson [S]	Decca 31404
2/23/63	❶[7]	27		9	Still	Bill Anderson	Decca 31458
8/24/63	2[2]	23		10	8 X 10	Bill Anderson/Walter Haynes	Decca 31521
1/25/64	5	18		11	Five Little Fingers /	Bill Anderson	
2/15/64	14	20		12	Easy Come-Easy Go	Bill Anderson	Decca 31577
7/25/64	8	16		13	Me	Alex Zanetis [S]	Decca 31630
11/7/64	38	5		14	In Case You Ever Change Your Mind /	Bill Anderson	
11/14/64+	8	18		15	Three A.M.	Bill Anderson/Jerry Todd	Decca 31681
4/3/65	12	17		16	Certain	Bill Anderson	Decca 31743
9/4/65	11	16		17	Bright Lights And Country Music	Bill Anderson/Jimmy Gateley	Decca 31825
1/22/66	11	13		18	Golden Guitar /	Billy Gray/Curtis Leach [S]	
2/12/66	4	24		19	I Love You Drops	Bill Anderson	Decca 31890
2/19/66	29	8		20	I Know You're Married (But I Love You Still) *[w/ Jan Howard]* /	Mack Magaha/Don Reno	
3/12/66	44	1		21	Time Out *[w/ Jan Howard]*	Harlan Howard/Richard Johnson	Decca 31884
8/27/66	❶[1]	20		22	I Get The Fever	Bill Anderson	Decca 31999
1/14/67	5	19		23	Get While The Gettin's Good	Bill Anderson	Decca 32077
7/1/67	10	19		24	No One's Gonna Hurt You Anymore /	Ted Cooper/Steve Karliski	
7/15/67	64	5		25	Papa	Bill Anderson [S]	Decca 32146
10/28/67	❶[4]	20		26	For Loving You *[w/ Jan Howard]*	Steve Karliski [S]	Decca 32197
11/11/67	42	9		27	Stranger On The Run	Bill Anderson/Kay Scott	Decca 32215
3/16/68	2[1]	18		28	Wild Week-End	Bill Anderson	Decca 32276
8/17/68	2[2]	16		29	Happy State Of Mind	Bill Anderson	Decca 32360
3/1/69	❶[2]	19		30	My Life (Throw It Away If I Want To)	Bill Anderson	Decca 32445
7/12/69	2[3]	15		31	But You Know I Love You	Mike Settle	Decca 32514
11/15/69+	2[1]	15		32	If It's All The Same To You *[w/ Jan Howard]*	Bill Anderson	Decca 32511
3/14/70	5	15		33	Love Is A Sometimes Thing *[w/ The Po' Boys]*	Jan Howard [L]	Decca 32643
6/20/70	4	15		34	Someday We'll Be Together *[w/ Jan Howard]*	Jackey Beavers/Johnny Bristol/Harvey Fuqua	Decca 32689
10/24/70	6	14		35	Where Have All Our Heroes Gone	Bill Anderson/Bob Talbert [S]	Decca 32744
3/13/71	6	15		36	Always Remember	Jerry Bradley/Patsy Lawley	Decca 32793
7/24/71	3[3]	17		37	Quits	Bill Anderson	Decca 32850
10/9/71	4	15		38	Dis-Satisfied *[w/ Jan Howard]*	Bill Anderson/Carter Howard/Jan Howard	Decca 32877
3/18/72	5	15		39	All The Lonely Women In The World	Bill Anderson	Decca 32930
9/9/72	2[2]	16		40	Don't She Look Good	Jerry Chesnut	Decca 33002
2/24/73	2[1]	14		41	If You Can Live With It (I Can Live Without It)	Bill Anderson	MCA 40004
7/7/73	2[3]	15		42	The Corner Of My Life	Bill Anderson	MCA 40070
12/15/73+	❶[1]	14		43	World Of Make Believe	Marion Carpenter/Pee Wee Maddux/Pete McCord	MCA 40164
6/1/74	24	14		44	Can I Come Home To You	Jan Crutchfield/Buddy Killen	MCA 40243
10/5/74	7	13		45	Every Time I Turn The Radio On	Bill Anderson	MCA 40304
2/8/75	14	11		46	I Still Feel The Same About You	Bill Anderson	MCA 40351
5/10/75	36	11		47	Country D.J.	Bill Anderson	MCA 40404
8/23/75	24	11		48	Thanks	Phil Coulter/Bill Martin	MCA 40443
11/29/75+	❶[1]	16		49	Sometimes *[w/ Mary Lou Turner]*	Bill Anderson	MCA 40488
3/27/76	7	12		50	That's What Made Me Love You *[w/ Mary Lou Turner]*	Larry Shoberg	MCA 40533
8/14/76	10	14		51	Peanuts And Diamonds	Bobby Braddock	MCA 40595
12/4/76+	6	14		52	Liars One, Believers Zero	Glenn Martin	MCA 40661
5/7/77	7	13		53	Head To Toe	Bobby Braddock	MCA 40713
7/16/77	18	12		54	Where Are You Going, Billy Boy *[w/ Mary Lou Turner]*	Dave Kirby/Glenn Martin	MCA 40753
10/1/77	11	12		55	Still The One	Johanna Hall/John Hall	MCA 40794
1/28/78	25	10		56	I'm Way Ahead Of You *[w/ Mary Lou Turner]*	Curly Putman/Sonny Throckmorton	MCA 40852
4/29/78	4	14		57	I Can't Wait Any Longer	Bill Anderson/Buddy Killen	MCA 40893
11/11/78	30	9		58	Double S	Bill Anderson/Buddy Killen [S]	MCA 40964
2/17/79	20	13		59	This Is A Love Song	Jim Weatherly	MCA 40992
7/21/79	40	9		60	The Dream Never Dies *[w/ The Po' Folks]*	Richard Cooper	MCA 41060
12/8/79+	51	8		61	More Than A Bedroom Thing	Bill Anderson	MCA 41150

DEBUT	PEAK	WKS	GOLD		ARTIST / Country Chart Hit	Songwriter	Label (& Number)
					ANDERSON, Bill — cont'd		
4/12/80	**35**	9		62	**Make Mine Night Time**	*Mike Kosser/Curly Putman*	MCA 41212
6/21/80	**46**	7		63	**Get A Little Dirt On Your Hands** *[w/ David Allan Coe]* new version of #7 above	*Bill Anderson* [R]	Columbia 11277
8/23/80	**58**	7		64	**Rock 'N' Roll To Rock Of Ages**	*Jane Abbott/Bill Anderson*	MCA 41297
11/22/80	**83**	3		65	**I Want That Feelin' Again**	*Bill Anderson*	MCA 51017
2/21/81	**44**	8		66	**Mister Peepers**	*Mark Charron*	MCA 51052
8/15/81	**74**	4		67	**Homebody**	*Bill Anderson*	MCA 51150
12/26/81+	**76**	4		68	**Whiskey Made Me Stumble (The Devil Made Me Fall)**	*Hugh Moffatt*	MCA 51204
8/21/82	**42**	10		69	**Southern Fried**	*Bill Anderson*	Southern Tracks 1007
12/25/82+	**82**	5		70	**Laid Off**	*Bill Anderson*	Southern Tracks 1011
3/12/83	**70**	6		71	**Thank You Darling**	*Tom Lazaros* [S]	Southern Tracks 1014
7/9/83	**71**	6		72	**Son Of The South /**	*Bill Anderson*	
7/9/83	**flip**	6		73	**20th Century Fox**	*Jane Abbott/Bill Anderson*	Southern Tracks 1021
5/12/84	**76**	7		74	**Your Eyes**	*Terry Carisse*	Southern Tracks 1026
2/9/85	**58**	7		75	**Wino The Clown**	*Ron Hellard/Bucky Jones/Curly Putman*	Swanee 4013
4/27/85	**62**	6		76	**Pity Party**	*Bill Anderson*	Swanee 5015
8/17/85	**75**	5		77	**When You Leave That Way You Can Never Go Back**	*Stephen Clark/Johnny MacRae*	Swanee 5018
12/27/86+	**80**	5		78	**Sheet Music**	*Bill Anderson/Aubrey Cain/D. Mathis Cothran*	Southern Tracks 1067
5/9/87	**78**	5		79	**No Ordinary Memory**	*Michael Clark/Stephen Clark/Johnny MacRae*	Southern Tracks 1077
2/9/91	**60**	6		80	**Deck Of Cards** from the album *Best Of Bill Anderson* on Curb 77436	*"T" Texas Tyler* [S]	Curb

All The Lonely Women In The World ['72]
Always Remember ['71]
Bright Lights And Country Music ['65]
But You Know I Love You ['69]
Can I Come Home To You ['74]
Certain ['65]
Corner Of My Life ['73]
Country D.J. ['75]
Dead Or Alive ['60]
Deck Of Cards ['91]
Dis-Satisfied ['71]
Don't She Look Good ['72]
Double S ['78]
Dream Never Dies ['79]
Easy Come-Easy Go ['64]
8 X 10 ['63]
Every Time I Turn The Radio On ['74]
Five Little Fingers ['64]
For Loving You ['67]
Get A Little Dirt On Your Hands ['62, '80]
Get While The Gettin's Good ['67]
Golden Guitar ['66]
Happy State Of Mind ['68]
Head To Toe ['77]
Homebody ['81]
I Can't Wait Any Longer ['78]
I Get The Fever ['66]
I Know You're Married (But I Love You Still) ['66]
I Love You Drops ['66]
I Still Feel The Same About You ['75]
I Want That Feelin' Again ['80]
I'm Way Ahead Of You ['78]
If It's All The Same To You ['70]
If You Can Live With It (I Can Live Without It) ['73]
In Case You Ever Change Your Mind ['64]
Laid Off ['83]
Liars One, Believers Zero ['77]
Love Is A Sometimes Thing ['70]
Make Mine Night Time ['80]
Mama Sang A Song ['62]
Me ['64]
Mister Peepers ['81]
More Than A Bedroom Thing ['80]
My Life (Throw It Away If I Want To) ['69]
Ninety-Nine ['59]
No One's Gonna Hurt You Anymore ['67]
No Ordinary Memory ['87]
Papa ['67]
Peanuts And Diamonds ['76]
Pity Party ['85]
Po' Folks ['61]
Quits ['71]
Rock 'N' Roll To Rock Of Ages ['80]
Sheet Music ['87]
Someday We'll Be Together ['70]
Sometimes ['76]
Son Of The South ['83]
Southern Fried ['82]
Still ['63]
Still The One ['77]
Stranger On The Run ['67]
Thank You Darling ['83]
Thanks ['75]
That's What It's Like To Be Lonesome ['59]
That's What Made Me Love You ['76]
This Is A Love Song ['79]
Three A.M. ['65]
Time Out ['66]
Tip Of My Fingers ['60]
20th Century Fox ['83]
Walk Out Backwards ['61]
When You Leave That Way You Can Never Go Back ['85]
Where Are You Going, Billy Boy ['77]
Where Have All Our Heroes Gone ['70]
Whiskey Made Me Stumble (The Devil Made Me Fall) ['82]
Wild Week-End ['68]
Wino The Clown ['85]
World Of Make Believe ['74]
Your Eyes ['84]

ANDERSON, Ivie

Born on 7/10/1905 in Gilroy, California. Died of asthma on 12/28/1949 (age 44). Black female singer.

DEBUT	PEAK	WKS	GOLD		Country Chart Hit	Songwriter	Label (& Number)
4/8/44	**4**	2			**Mexico Joe** *[w/ Ceele Burke's Orch.]*	*Johnny Lange/Leon Rene*	Exclusive 3113

ANDERSON, John — 1980s: #30 / 1990s: #41 / All-Time: #63

Born on 12/13/1954 in Orlando, Florida; raised in Apopka, Florida. Male singer/songwriter/guitarist. While a teenager led the groups the Weed Seeds and the Living End. Sang with sister Donna in the early 1970s. Moved to Nashville in 1971. Worked construction on the new Grand Ole Opry building. Worked as a staff writer with Gallico Music.

CMA: Horizon 1983

DEBUT	PEAK	WKS	GOLD		Country Chart Hit	Songwriter	Label (& Number)
12/10/77+	**62**	8		1	**I've Got A Feelin' (Somebody Stealin')**	*John Anderson/Michael Garvin/Ervan James*	Warner 8480
6/24/78	**69**	5		2	**Whine, Whistle, Whine**	*Don Goodman/Mark Sherrill*	Warner 8585
11/25/78	**40**	9		3	**The Girl At The End Of The Bar**	*John Anderson/Lionel Delmore*	Warner 8705
3/24/79	**41**	8		4	**My Pledge Of Love**	*Joe Stafford*	Warner 8770
7/14/79	**31**	11		5	**Low Dog Blues**	*John Anderson/Lionel Delmore*	Warner 8863
10/27/79+	**15**	16		6	**Your Lying Blue Eyes**	*Ken McDuffie*	Warner 49089
3/15/80	**13**	15		7	**She Just Started Liking Cheatin' Songs**	*Kent Robbins*	Warner 49191
7/26/80	**21**	14		8	**If There Were No Memories**	*Ron McCown*	Warner 49275
11/22/80+	**7**	17		9	**1959**	*Gary Gentry*	Warner 49582
3/28/81	**4**	16		10	**I'm Just An Old Chuck Of Coal (But I'm Gonna Be A Diamond Someday)**	*Billy Joe Shaver*	Warner 49699
8/1/81	**8**	15		11	**Chicken Truck /**	*John Anderson/Monroe Fields/Ervan Parker*	
8/1/81	**54**	15		12	**I Love You A Thousand Ways**	*Jim Beck/Lefty Frizzell*	Warner 49772
11/21/81+	**7**	18		13	**I Just Came Home To Count The Memories**	*Glenn Ray*	Warner 49860
4/17/82	**6**	19		14	**Would You Catch A Falling Star**	*Bobby Braddock*	Warner 50043
9/25/82	**❶[2]**	20		15	**Wild And Blue**	*John Sherrill*	Warner 29917
1/15/83	**❶[1]**	22	●	16	**Swingin'** CMA : Single	*John Anderson/Lionel Delmore*	Warner 29788
6/25/83	**5**	17		17	**Goin' Down Hill**	*John Anderson/Aries Lincoln*	Warner 29585
9/24/83	**❶[1]**	21		18	**Black Sheep**	*Robert Altman/Dan Darst*	Warner 29497
1/14/84	**10**	16		19	**Let Somebody Else Drive**	*Merle Kilgore/Mack Vickery*	Warner 29385
5/12/84	**14**	17		20	**I Wish I Could Write You A Song**	*John Anderson/Lionel Delmore*	Warner 29276
8/18/84	**3[1]**	25		21	**She Sure Got Away With My Heart** S:3 / A:3	*Walt Aldridge/Tom Brasfield*	Warner 29207
12/8/84+	**20**	17		22	**Eye Of A Hurricane** S:18 / A:21	*Jerry Fuller*	Warner 29127
5/4/85	**15**	17		23	**It's All Over Now** A:14 / S:15	*Bobby Womack/Shirley Womack*	Warner 29002

DEBUT	PEAK	WKS	GOLD	ARTIST / Country Chart Hit	Ranking / Songwriter	Label (& Number)
				ANDERSON, John — cont'd		
8/24/85	**30**	14		24 **Tokyo, Oklahoma**	A:29 / S:30 *Mack Vickery*	Warner 28916
11/16/85+	**12**	22		25 **Down In Tennessee**	S:11 / A:14 *Wayland Holyfield*	Warner 28855
3/22/86	**31**	11		26 **You Can't Keep A Good Memory Down**	*Bruce Burch/Michael Murrah/Roger Murrah*	Warner 28748
8/16/86	**10**	22		27 **Honky Tonk Crowd**	S:4 / A:11 *Larry Cordle/Lionel Delmore*	Warner 28639
12/6/86+	**44**	12		28 **Countrified**	*Tom Lazaros*	Warner 28502
3/7/87	**55**	8		29 **What's So Different About You**	*John Anderson/Fred Carter*	Warner 28433
9/5/87	**48**	8		30 **When Your Yellow Brick Road Turns Blue**	*Bernie Nelson/Gary Vincent*	MCA 53155
12/5/87+	**23**	15		31 **Somewhere Between Ragged And Right** ***[w/ Waylon Jennings]***	*Waylon Jennings/Roger Murrah*	MCA 53226
4/23/88	**65**	4		32 **It's Hard To Keep This Ship Together**	*John Anderson/Fred Carter*	MCA 53307
7/9/88	**35**	12		33 **If It Ain't Broke Don't Fix It**	*John Anderson/Tony Stampley*	MCA 53366
11/5/88	**68**	4		34 **Down In The Orange Grove**	*John Anderson/Lionel Delmore/Herb McCullough*	MCA 53441
2/11/89	**73**	4		35 **Lower On The Hog**	*Larry Cordle/Lionel Delmore*	MCA 53485
10/14/89	**66**	5		36 **Who's Lovin' My Baby**	*Curtis Wright*	Universal 66020
9/28/91	**67**	3		37 **Who Got Our Love**	*John Anderson/Lionel Delmore*	BNA
12/21/91+	**❶**^{1}	20		38 **Straight Tequila Night**	*Debbie Hupp/Kent Robbins*	BNA
4/18/92	**3**^{1}	20		39 **When It Comes To You**	*Mark Knopfler*	BNA
8/15/92	**2**^{2}	20		40 **Seminole Wind**	*John Anderson*	BNA
11/28/92+	**7**	20		41 **Let Go Of The Stone**	*Max D. Barnes/Max T. Barnes*	BNA
				above 5 from the album *Seminole Wind* on BNA 61029		
5/1/93	**❶**^{1}	20		42 **Money In The Bank**	*Bob DiPiero/John Jarrard/Mark D. Sanders*	BNA
8/28/93	**13**	20		43 **I Fell In The Water**	*Jerry Salley/Jeff Stevens*	BNA
12/11/93+	**3**^{1}	20		44 **I've Got It Made**	*Max D. Barnes*	BNA
4/23/94	**4**	20		45 **I Wish I Could Have Been There**	*John Anderson/Kent Robbins*	BNA
				above 4 from the album *Solid Ground* on BNA 66232		
10/1/94	**35**	10		46 **Country 'Til I Die**	*John Anderson/Troy Seals/Eddie Setser*	BNA
12/10/94+	**3**^{3}	20		47 **Bend It Until It Breaks**	*John Anderson/Lionel Delmore*	BNA
12/31/94+	**57**	2		48 **Christmas Time**	*John Anderson/Lionel Delmore* **[X]**	BNA
				from the album *Christmas Time* on BNA 66411		
4/22/95	**15**	20		49 **Mississippi Moon**	*Tony Joe White/Carson Whitsett*	BNA
				#46, 47 & 49: from the album *Country 'Til I Die* on BNA 66417		
12/9/95+	**26**	20		50 **Paradise**	*Bob McDill/Roger Murrah*	BNA
3/9/96	**51**	10		51 **Long Hard Lesson Learned**	*Donna Anderson/John Anderson/Michael Anderson*	BNA
6/22/96	**67**	4		52 **My Kind Of Crazy**	*John Jarrard/Delbert McClinton/Gary Nicholson*	BNA
				above 3 from the album *Paradise* on BNA 66810		
7/5/97	**22**	20		53 **Somebody Slap Me**	S:11 *Bob McDill/Roger Murrah*	Mercury
9/27/97	**44**	11		54 **Small Town**	*John Anderson/Gary Scruggs*	Mercury
1/17/98	**41**	12		55 **Takin' The Country Back**	*Marty Stuart/Curtis Wright*	Mercury
				above 3 from the album *Takin' The Country Back* on Mercury 536004		
4/29/00	**56**	8		56 **You Ain't Hurt Nothin' Yet**	S:25 *Al Anderson/Billy Lawson*	Columbia
9/30/00	**55**	9		57 **Nobody's Got It All**	S:14 *Layng Martine Jr./Kent Robbins*	Columbia
				above 2 from the album *Nobody's Got It All* on Columbia 63990		
				ANDERSON, Keith		
				Born in 1968 in Miami, Oklahoma. Male singer/songwriter/guitarist.		
12/25/04+	**8**	32		**Pickin' Wildflowers**	*Keith Anderson/John Rich/Kim Williams*	Arista Nashville
				from the album *Three Chord Country And American Rock & Roll* on Arista Nashville 66294		
				ANDERSON, Liz		
				Born Elizabeth Jane Haaby on 3/13/1930 in Roseau, Minnesota; raised in Grand Forks, North Dakota. Female singer/songwriter/guitarist. Mother of **Lynn Anderson**.		
4/2/66	**23**	10		1 **Go Now Pay Later**	*Liz Anderson*	RCA Victor 8778
7/30/66	**45**	4		2 **So Much For Me, So Much For You**	*Liz Anderson*	RCA Victor 8861
10/15/66	**5**	17		3 **The Game Of Triangles** ***[w/ Bobby Bare & Norma Jean]***	*Cy Coben*	RCA Victor 8963
12/3/66+	**22**	12		4 **The Wife Of The Party**	*Liz Anderson*	RCA Victor 8999
4/22/67	**5**	17		5 **Mama Spank**	*Liz Anderson*	RCA Victor 9163
9/2/67	**24**	13		6 **Tiny Tears**	*Liz Anderson*	RCA Victor 9271
12/23/67+	**40**	12		7 **Thanks A Lot For Tryin' Anyway**	*Jim Glaser*	RCA Victor 9378
2/24/68	**21**	12		8 **Mother, May I** ***[w/ Lynn Anderson]***	*Liz Anderson/Lynn Anderson*	RCA Victor 9445
5/11/68	**43**	9		9 **Like A Merry-Go-Round**	*Liz Anderson*	RCA Victor 9508
8/24/68	**65**	7		10 **Me, Me, Me, Me, Me /**	*Liz Anderson*	
8/31/68	**58**	4		11 **Cry, Cry Again**	*Liz Anderson/Dick Land*	RCA Victor 9586
11/23/68	**51**	5		12 **Love Is Ending**	*Bonnie Patterson*	RCA Victor 9650
2/14/70	**26**	8		13 **Husband Hunting**	*Liz Anderson*	RCA Victor 9796
8/15/70	**64**	6		14 **All Day Sucker**	*Casey Anderson/Liz Anderson*	RCA Victor 9876
12/19/70	**75**	2		15 **When I'm Not Lookin'**	*Bonnie Patterson*	RCA Victor 9924
10/23/71	**69**	3		16 **It Don't Do No Good To Be A Good Girl**	*Liz Anderson*	Epic 10782
4/8/72	**56**	7		17 **I'll Never Fall In Love Again**	*Burt Bacharach/Hal David*	Epic 10840
8/12/72	**67**	4		18 **Astrology**	*Liz Anderson*	Epic 10896
3/17/73	**72**	2		19 **Time To Love Again**	*Helen Cornelius*	Epic 10952

Billboard DEBUT	PEAK	WKS	GOLD	ARTIST / Country Chart Hit	Ranking / Songwriter	Label (& Number)

ANDERSON, Lynn — **1970s: #13 / All-Time: #57**

Born on 9/26/1947 in Grand Forks, North Dakota; raised in Sacramento, California. Female singer/songwriter/guitarist/actress. Daughter of **Liz Anderson**. An accomplished equestrian, she was the California Horse Show Queen in 1966. Regular on **Lawrence Welk**'s TV show from 1968. Acted in the movie *Country Gold*. Married to **Glenn Sutton** from 1968-77. Also see **Heart Of Nashville** and **Tomorrow's World**.

CMA: Female Vocalist 1971

DEBUT	PEAK	WKS	GOLD	Country Chart Hit	Songwriter	Label (& Number)
10/29/66+	**36**	17		1 **Ride, Ride, Ride**	*Liz Anderson*	Chart 1375
3/18/67	**5**	19		2 **If I Kiss You (Will You Go Away)**	*Liz Anderson*	Chart 1430
7/1/67	**49**	6		3 **Keeping Up Appearances** ***[w/ Jerry Lane]***	*Liz Anderson*	Chart 1425
8/12/67	**28**	13		4 **Too Much Of You**	*Gene Hood*	Chart 1475
12/2/67+	**4**	18		5 **Promises, Promises**	*Lynn Anderson/Carlisle Hughey/William Smith*	Chart 1010
2/24/68	**21**	12		6 **Mother, May I** ***[w/ Liz Anderson]***	*Liz Anderson/Lynn Anderson*	RCA Victor 9445
3/30/68	**8**	14		7 **No Another Time**	*Jerry "Max" Lane*	Chart 1026
8/3/68	**12**	14		8 **Big Girls Don't Cry**	*Liz Anderson*	Chart 1042
11/30/68+	**11**	14		9 **Flattery Will Get You Everywhere**	*Liz Anderson*	Chart 1059
3/8/69	**18**	12		10 **Our House Is Not A Home (If It's Never Been Loved In)**	*Shirley Mayo/Curly Putman*	Chart 5001
8/2/69	**2^{2}**	15		11 **That's A No No**	*Ben Peters*	Chart 5021
11/22/69+	**15**	12		12 **He'd Still Love Me**	*Hugh X. Lewis/Glenn Sutton*	Chart 5040
2/14/70	**16**	10		13 **I've Been Everywhere**	*Geoff Mack*	Chart 5053
3/21/70	**7**	16		14 **Stay There 'Til I Get There**	*Glenn Sutton*	Columbia 45101
6/6/70	**17**	10		15 **Rocky Top**	*Boudleaux Bryant/Felice Bryant*	Chart 5068
8/1/70	**15**	12		16 **No Love At All /**	*Wayne Carson/Johnny Christopher*	
8/1/70	**flip**	12		17 **I Found You Just In Time**	*Billy Sherrill/Glenn Sutton*	Columbia 45190
10/31/70	**20**	11		18 **I'm Alright**	*Bill Anderson*	Chart 5098
11/7/70	**❶^{5}**	20	●	19 **Rose Garden**	*Joe South*	Columbia 45252
				Grammy: Female Vocal		
2/6/71	**20**	13		20 **It Wasn't God Who Made Honky Tonk Angels**	*Joe Miller*	Chart 5113
5/8/71	**❶^{2}**	15		21 **You're My Man**	*Glenn Sutton*	Columbia 45356
5/15/71	**74**	3		22 **Jim Dandy**	*Lincoln Chase*	Chart 5125
7/24/71	**54**	5		23 **He Even Woke Me Up To Say Goodbye**	*Doug Gilmore/Mickey Newbury*	Chart 5136
8/21/71	**❶^{3}**	16		24 **How Can I Unlove You**	*Joe South*	Columbia 45429
1/29/72	**3^{1}**	16		25 **Cry**	*Churchill Kohlman*	Columbia 45529
6/10/72	**4**	13		26 **Listen To A Country Song**	*Alan Garth/Jim Messina*	Columbia 45615
10/14/72	**4**	14		27 **Fool Me**	*Joe South*	Columbia 45692
1/13/73	**❶^{1}**	16		28 **Keep Me In Mind**	*George Richey/Glenn Sutton*	Columbia 45768
6/2/73	**2^{1}**	15		29 **Top Of The World**	*John Bettis/Richard Carpenter*	Columbia 45857
9/15/73	**3^{2}**	17		30 **Sing About Love**	*Glenn Sutton*	Columbia 45918
3/9/74	**15**	13		31 **Smile For Me**	*Rory Bourke*	Columbia 46009
6/29/74	**7**	14		32 **Talkin' To The Wall**	*Warner Mack*	Columbia 46056
10/26/74	**❶^{1}**	13		33 **What A Man, My Man Is**	*Glenn Sutton*	Columbia 10041
3/8/75	**13**	12		34 **He Turns It Into Love Again**	*Larry Cheshier/Murry Kellum/Glenn Sutton*	Columbia 10100
6/28/75	**14**	14		35 **I've Never Loved Anyone More**	*Linda Hargrove/Michael Nesmith*	Columbia 10160
11/22/75+	**26**	11		36 **Paradise**	*John Prine*	Columbia 10240
2/7/76	**20**	14		37 **All The King's Horses**	*J.C. Cunningham*	Columbia 10280
6/5/76	**44**	9		38 **Rodeo Cowboy /**	*Glenn Sutton*	
6/5/76	**flip**	3		39 **Dixieland, You Will Never Die**	*J.C. Cunningham*	Columbia 10337
9/25/76	**23**	11		40 **Sweet Talkin' Man**	*J.C. Cunningham*	Columbia 10401
1/22/77	**12**	14		41 **Wrap Your Love All Around Your Man**	*J.C. Cunningham*	Columbia 10467
5/28/77	**22**	10		42 **I Love What Love Is Doing To Me**	*J.C. Cunningham*	Columbia 10545
9/3/77	**19**	12		43 **He Ain't You**	*Jeff Barry/Brad Burg/Lisa Hartman/Dene Hofheinz*	Columbia 10597
12/3/77+	**26**	13		44 **We Got Love**	*Roy Culbertson/Harold Forness/Larry Keith/Steve Pippin*	Columbia 10650
4/29/78	**44**	9		45 **Rising Above It All**	*Jerry Foster/Bill Rice*	Columbia 10721
9/2/78	**43**	8		46 **Last Love Of My Life**	*Pat Bunch/Johnny Christopher*	Columbia 10809
3/10/79	**10**	13		47 **Isn't It Always Love**	*Karla Bonoff*	Columbia 10909
6/23/79	**18**	12		48 **I Love How You Love Me**	*Larry Kolber/Barry Mann*	Columbia 11006
10/13/79	**33**	9		49 **Sea Of Heartbreak**	*Hal David/Paul Hampton*	Columbia 11104
7/5/80	**26**	13		50 **Even Cowgirls Get The Blues**	*Rodney Crowell*	Columbia 11296
10/25/80	**27**	13		51 **Blue Baby Blue**	*Michael Clark*	Columbia 11374
4/9/83	**42**	11		52 **You Can't Lose What You Never Had**	*Michael Garvin/Tom Shapiro/Chris Waters*	Permian 82000
7/16/83	**18**	16		53 **What I Learned From Loving You**	*John Hooker/Russell Smith*	Permian 82001
12/17/83+	**9**	23		54 **You're Welcome To Tonight** ***[w/ Gary Morris]***	*Grant Boatwright/Larry Henley/Jim Hurt*	Permian 82003
9/13/86	**49**	9		55 **Fools For Each Other** ***[w/ Ed Bruce]***	S:28 *Guy Clark*	RCA 5005
12/20/86+	**45**	9		56 **Didn't We Shine**	*Don Schlitz/Jesse Winchester*	Mercury 888209
9/19/87	**38**	12		57 **Read Between The Lines**	*Kathie Baillie/Michael Bonagura/Don Schlitz*	Mercury 888839
7/30/88	**24**	17		58 **Under The Boardwalk**	S:24 *Artie Resnick/Kenny Young*	Mercury 870528
12/3/88+	**50**	10		59 **What He Does Best**	*Thom Schuyler*	Mercury 872220
3/11/89	**69**	6		60 **How Many Hearts**	*Bobby Borchers/Nelson Larkin/Pam Wolfe*	Mercury 872602

Billboard DEBUT	PEAK	WKS	GOLD	ARTIST / Country Chart Hit	Ranking / Songwriter	Label (& Number)

ANDERSON, Lynn — cont'd

All The King's Horses ['76]
Big Girls Don't Cry ['68]
Blue Baby Blue ['80]
Cry ['72]
Didn't We Shine ['87]
Dixieland, You Will Never Die ['76]
Even Cowgirls Get The Blues ['80]
Flattery Will Get You Everywhere ['69]
Fool Me ['72]
Fools For Each Other ['86]
He Ain't You ['77]
He Even Woke Me Up To Say Goodbye ['71]
He Turns It Into Love Again ['75]
He'd Still Love Me ['70]
How Can I Unlove You ['71]
How Many Hearts ['89]
I Found You Just In Time ['70]
I Love How You Love Me ['79]
I Love What Love Is Doing To Me ['77]
I'm Alright ['70]
I've Been Everywhere ['70]
I've Never Loved Anyone More ['75]
If I Kiss You (Will You Go Away) ['67]
Isn't It Always Love ['79]
It Wasn't God Who Made Honky Tonk Angels ['71]
Jim Dandy ['71]
Keep Me In Mind ['73]
Keeping Up Appearances ['67]
Last Love Of My Life ['78]
Listen To A Country Song ['72]
Mother, May I ['68]
No Another Time ['68]
No Love At All ['70]
Our House Is Not A Home (If It's Never Been Loved In) ['69]
Paradise ['76]
Promises, Promises ['68]
Read Between The Lines ['87]
Ride, Ride, Ride ['67]
Rising Above It All ['78]
Rocky Top ['70]
Rodeo Cowboy ['76]
Rose Garden ['70]
Sea Of Heartbreak ['79]
Sing About Love ['73]
Smile For Me ['74]
Stay There 'Til I Get There ['70]
Sweet Talkin' Man ['76]
Talkin' To The Wall ['74]
That's A No No ['69]
Too Much Of You ['67]
Top Of The World ['73]
Under The Boardwalk ['88]
We Got Love ['78]
What A Man, My Man Is ['74]
What He Does Best ['89]
What I Learned From Loving You ['83]
Wrap Your Love All Around Your Man ['77]
You Can't Lose What You Never Had ['83]
You're My Man ['71]
You're Welcome To Tonight ['84]

ANDI AND THE BROWN SISTERS

Vocal trio from Albany, Oregon: Andi Brown and her sister Robin Brown, with Darby Huffman.

DEBUT	PEAK	WKS	GOLD	#	Country Chart Hit	Songwriter	Label (& Number)
10/8/88	94	2		1	I'd Do Anything For You, Baby	Tommy Dee/Tom Hamilton	Killer 1013
2/4/89	90	2		2	This Old Feeling	Tommy Dee/Tom Hamilton	Killer 115
					ANDY & THE BROWN SISTERS (above 2)		
5/6/89	79	4		3	Labor Of Love	Karen Mills/Marcia Sandford	Door Knob 323
7/8/89	84	3		4	Gently Hold Me	Mack Jackson	Door Knob 329
9/30/89	90	2		5	Lighter Shade Of Blue	Keith Longbotham/Dave Salyer	Door Knob 331
11/25/89	70	6		6	Shows You What I Know	Kathy Bazinet/Carl Hunt	Door Knob 337

ANDREWS, Jessica — 2000s: #46

Born on 12/29/1983 in Huntingdon, Tennessee. Female singer/songwriter.

DEBUT	PEAK	WKS	GOLD	#	Country Chart Hit	Songwriter	Label (& Number)
2/6/99	28	20		1	I Will Be There For You	S:4 Rick Bowles/Josh Leo/Tom Shapiro	DreamWorks
7/10/99	25	20		2	You Go First (Do You Wanna Kiss)	Kerry Chater/Lynn Chater/Cyril Rawson	DreamWorks
12/11/99+	24	20		3	Unbreakable Heart	S:4 Benmont Tench	DreamWorks
6/24/00	53	8		4	I Do Now	Franne Golde/Tom Snow	DreamWorks
					above 4 from the album *Heart Shaped World* on DreamWorks 450104		
11/4/00+	❶[3]	33		5	Who I Am	Brett James/Troy Verges	DreamWorks
6/9/01	31	19		6	Helplessly, Hopelessly	Brett James/Troy Verges	DreamWorks
1/26/02	47	6		7	Karma	Marv Green/Aimee Mayo	DreamWorks
					above 3 from the album *Who I Am* on DreamWorks 450248		
12/7/02+	17	26		8	There's More To Me Than You	Jessica Andrews/Marcel Chagnon/James Slater	DreamWorks
8/9/03	49	5		9	Good Time	Jessica Andrews/Bekka Bramlett/Annie Roboff	DreamWorks
					above 2 from the album *Now* on DreamWorks 450356		
10/9/04	45	16		10	All I Ever Needed *[w/ Bret Michaels]*	Bret Michaels	Poor Boy

ANDREWS, Sheila

Born in Alabama; raised in Ohio. Female singer.

DEBUT	PEAK	WKS	GOLD	#	Country Chart Hit	Songwriter	Label (& Number)
12/16/78+	88	4		1	Too Fast For Rapid City	Layng Martine Jr.	Ovation 1116
9/22/79	88	3		2	I Gotta Get Back The Feeling	Robert Jones/Mike Kosser	Ovation 1128
1/26/80	48	7		3	What I Had With You *[w/ Joe Sun]*	Curly Putman/Sonny Throckmorton	Ovation 1138
7/26/80	42	10		4	It Don't Get Better Than This	Jack Fisher/Don Harp	Ovation 1146
11/29/80	58	8		5	Where Could You Take Me	Skippy Barrett/Gene Dobbins	Ovation 1160

ANDREWS SISTERS — 1940s: #32

Highly popular vocal trio from Minneapolis, Minnesota: sisters Patty Andrews (born on 2/26/1918), Maxene Andrews (born on 1/3/1916; died on 10/21/1995, age 79) and LaVerne Andrews (born on 7/6/1911; died on 5/8/1967, age 55). The trio appeared in several movies.

DEBUT	PEAK	WKS	GOLD	#	Country Chart Hit	Songwriter	Label (& Number)
1/8/44	❶[5]	11	●	1	Pistol Packin' Mama *[w/ Bing Crosby]*	Al Dexter	Decca 23277
4/9/49	2[1]	16		2	I'm Bitin' My Fingernails And Thinking Of You *[w/ Ernest Tubb]* /	J:2 / S:4 Ernie Benedict/Lenny Sanders/Ernest Tubb/Roy West	
4/16/49	6	5		3	Don't Rob Another Man's Castle *[w/ Ernest Tubb]*	J:6 / S:10 Jenny Lou Carson	Decca 24592

ANGELLE, Lisa

Born on 12/27/1965 in New Orleans, Louisiana. Female singer/songwriter.

DEBUT	PEAK	WKS	GOLD	#	Country Chart Hit	Songwriter	Label (& Number)
4/6/85	78	4		1	Love, It's The Pits	Holly Dunn/Chris Waters	EMI America 8258
11/16/85	96	3		2	Bring Back Love	Ronnie Scott/Steve Wolfe	EMI America 8294
9/25/99+	19[S]	12		3	I Wear Your Love	Lisa Angelle/Andrew Gold	DreamWorks
10/30/99	75	1		4	Kiss This	Lisa Angelle/Andrew Gold	DreamWorks
					above 2 from the album *Twisted* on DreamWorks 50196		
8/5/00	62	2		5	A Woman Gets Lonely	Lisa Angelle	DreamWorks
3/3/01	50	5		6	I Will Love You	Robert Wasserman	DreamWorks
					above 2 from the album *Lisa Angelle* on DreamWorks 50116		

ANTHONY, Rayburn

Born on 5/23/1937 in Humboldt, Tennessee. Male singer/guitarist.

DEBUT	PEAK	WKS	GOLD	#	Country Chart Hit	Songwriter	Label (& Number)
10/9/76	84	5		1	Crazy Again	Bob McDill	Polydor 14346
3/26/77	39	9		2	Lonely Eyes	Bob McDill	Polydor 14380
6/25/77	57	8		3	Hold Me	Jerry Foster/Bill Rice	Polydor 14398
10/15/77	75	5		4	She Keeps Hangin' On	Mitch Johnson/Steve Stone	Polydor 14423
3/25/78	31	9		5	Maybe I Should've Been Listenin'	Buzz Rabin	Polydor 14457
10/21/78	75	5		6	I Thought You Were Easy	Bob McDill	Mercury 55042
2/3/79	28	11		7	Shadows Of Love	Wayland Holyfield	Mercury 55053
6/23/79	79	3		8	It Won't Go Away	Bob McDill	Mercury 55063
10/6/79	60	6		9	The Wild Side Of Life *[w/ Kitty Wells]*	Arlie Carter/William Warren	Mercury 57006

Billboard DEBUT	PEAK	WKS	GOLD	ARTIST Ranking / Country Chart Hit	Songwriter	Label (& Number)

ANTHONY, Vince, with The "Country" Blue Notes

Born Vincent Anthony Guzzetta in Berwick, Louisiana. Male singer/songwriter/guitarist. The "Country" Blue Notes: Chet Guzzetta (Vince's brother), Joe Auenson, Cookie Gaudet and Ronnie Ghirardi.

DEBUT	PEAK	WKS	GOLD	Country Chart Hit	Songwriter	Label (& Number)
3/6/82	**82**	3		Call Me Friend	*Vince Anthony*	Midnight Gold 160

ANTON, Susan

Born on 10/12/1950 in Oak Glen, California. Female actress/model/singer. Appeared in several movies and TV shows. Married actor Jeff Lester on 8/15/1992.

DEBUT	PEAK	WKS	GOLD	Country Chart Hit	Songwriter	Label (& Number)
11/29/80+	**10**	18		Killin' Time *[w/ Fred Knoblock]*	*Jeff Harrington/Jeff Pennig*	Scotti Brothers 609

ARATA, Tony

Born on 10/10/1957 in Savannah, Georgia. Male singer/songwriter/guitarist.

DEBUT	PEAK	WKS	GOLD	Country Chart Hit	Songwriter	Label (& Number)
9/22/84	**76**	4		1 Come On Home	*Tony Arata/David Hodge*	Noble Vision 106
2/9/85	**65**	7		2 Sure Thing	*Tony Arata*	Noble Vision 108

ARCHER PARK

Duo of Randy Archer (born on 2/20/1959 in Swainsboro, Georgia) and Johnny Park (born on 10/30/1957 in Arlington, Texas).

DEBUT	PEAK	WKS	GOLD	Country Chart Hit	Songwriter	Label (& Number)
8/20/94	**29**	14		1 Where There's Smoke	*Bobby Barker/Mark Collie*	Atlantic
12/3/94	**63**	6		2 We Got A Lot In Common	*Randy Archer/Bobby Barker/Johnny Park*	Atlantic
				above 2 from the album *Where There's Smoke* on Atlantic 87211		

ARGO, Judy

Born on 12/8/1947 in Atlanta, Georgia. Female singer.

DEBUT	PEAK	WKS	GOLD	Country Chart Hit	Songwriter	Label (& Number)
4/7/79	**83**	6		1 Night Time Music Man	*Tom Grant*	ASI 1019
8/11/79	**95**	3		2 He's A Good Man	*David Tanner*	MDJ 51379
9/29/79	**55**	7		3 Hide Me (In The Shadow Of Your Love)	*Jess Hudson/Kenny Seratt*	MDJ 4633

ARMAND, Reneé

Born on 10/14/1945 in Los Angeles, California. Female singer.

DEBUT	PEAK	WKS	GOLD	Country Chart Hit	Songwriter	Label (& Number)
8/24/74	**8**	16		Boney Fingers *[w/ Hoyt Axton]*	*Renee Armand/Hoyt Axton*	A&M 1607

ARMSTRONG, Wayne

Born in Tulsa, Oklahoma. Male singer.

DEBUT	PEAK	WKS	GOLD	Country Chart Hit	Songwriter	Label (& Number)
8/9/80	**59**	8		Hot Sunday Morning	*Allen Chapman/Jeff Tweel*	NSD 57

ARNOLD, Eddy — 1940s: #1 / 1950s: #2 / 1960s: #5 / All-Time: #1 // HOF: 1966

Born Richard Edward Arnold on 5/15/1918 in Henderson, Tennessee. Male singer/songwriter/guitarist. Own radio show on WMPS in Memphis, Tennessee (1934-39). Lead singer of **Pee Wee King**'s Golden West Cowboys from 1940-43. Hosted own TV show from 1952-56. Hosted TV's *Out On The Farm* in 1954. Hosted TV's *Today On The Farm* in 1960. Once known as "The Tennessee Plowboy." Also see **Heart Of Nashville** and **Some Of Chet's Friends**.

EARLY HIT: The Cattle Call (1945) // CMA: Entertainer 1967

EDDY ARNOLD and his Tennessee Plowboys:

DEBUT	PEAK	WKS	GOLD	Country Chart Hit	Songwriter	Label (& Number)
6/30/45	**5**	2		1 Each Minute Seems A Million Years	*Cook Watson*	Bluebird 33-0527
7/13/46	**7**	1		2 All Alone In This World Without You	*Owen Bradley/Vic McAlpin/Betty Wade*	RCA Victor 20-1855
10/12/46	**2**[4]	17		3 That's How Much I Love You /	*Eddy Arnold/Wally Fowler/J. Graydon Hall*	
10/12/46	**3**[1]	2		4 Chained To A Memory	*Jenny Lou Carson*	RCA Victor 20-1948
3/1/47	**❶**[1]	22		5 What Is Life Without Love	*Eddy Arnold/Owen Bradley/Vernice McAlpin*	RCA Victor 20-2058
5/31/47	**❶**[5]	38		6 It's A Sin /	*Fred Rose/Zeb Turner*	
6/21/47	**4**	2		7 I Couldn't Believe It Was True	*Eddy Arnold/Wally Fowler*	RCA Victor 20-2241
8/23/47	**❶**[21]	46		8 I'll Hold You In My Heart (Till I Can Hold You In My Arms) J:❶[21] / S:7	*Eddy Arnold/Tommy Dilbeck*	RCA Victor 20-2332
				also see #29 below		
11/8/47	**2**[2]	15		9 To My Sorrow J:2	*Vernice McAlpin*	RCA Victor 20-2481
2/7/48	**10**	2		10 Molly Darling J:10 / S:14	*Will Hays*	RCA Victor 20-2489
3/20/48	**❶**[9]	39	●	11 Anytime / J:❶[9] / S:❶[3]	*Herb Lawson*	
3/27/48	**2**[5]	21		12 What A Fool I Was J:2 / S:7	*Stu Davis*	RCA Victor 20-2700
5/15/48	**❶**[19]	54	●	13 Bouquet Of Roses / S:❶[19] / J:❶[18]	*Bob Hilliard/Steve Nelson*	
5/15/48	**❶**[3]	26		14 Texarkana Baby J:❶[3] / S:❶[1]	*Cottonseed Clark/Fred Rose*	RCA Victor 20-2806

EDDY ARNOLD, The Tennessee Plowboy and his Guitar:

DEBUT	PEAK	WKS	GOLD	Country Chart Hit	Songwriter	Label (& Number)
8/28/48	**❶**[8]	32	●	15 Just A Little Lovin' (Will Go A Long, Long Way) / J:❶[8] / S:❶[4]	*Eddy Arnold/Zeke Clements*	
8/28/48	**5**	19		16 My Daddy Is Only A Picture S:5 / J:6	*Tommy Dilbeck*	RCA Victor 20-3013
11/20/48	**❶**[1]	21		17 A Heart Full Of Love (For A Handful Of Kisses) / S:❶[1] / J:3	*Eddy Arnold/Steve Nelson/Ray Soehnel*	
11/20/48+	**2**[1]	17		18 Then I Turned And Walked Slowly Away J:2 / S:4	*Red Fortner*	RCA Victor 20-3174
2/5/49	**10**	1		19 Many Tears Ago J:10	*Jenny Lou Carson*	RCA Victor 20-1871
2/12/49	**3**[1]	10		20 There's Not A Thing (I Wouldn't Do For You) / J:3 / S:7	*Billy Hughes*	
2/19/49	**❶**[12]	31		21 Don't Rob Another Man's Castle J:❶[12] / S:❶[6]	*Jenny Lou Carson*	RCA Victor 21-0002
5/14/49	**❶**[3]	22		22 One Kiss Too Many J:❶[3] / S:2	*Eddy Arnold/Ed Nelson/Steve Nelson*	RCA Victor 48-0083
5/21/49	**2**[3]	19		23 The Echo Of Your Footsteps S:2 / J:3	*Jenny Lou Carson*	RCA Victor 21-0051
7/2/49	**❶**[4]	22		24 I'm Throwing Rice (At The Girl That I Love) S:❶[4] / J:❶[3]	*Eddy Arnold/Ed Nelson/Steve Nelson*	RCA Victor 48-0080
7/16/49	**7**	4		25 Show Me The Way Back To Your Heart S:7 / J:11	*Eddy Arnold/Steve Nelson/Ray Soehnel*	RCA Victor 21-0083
11/19/49	**7**	8		26 C-H-R-I-S-T-M-A-S / S:7 / A:7 / J:9	*Eddy Arnold/Jenny Lou Carson* [X]	
12/10/49	**5**	4		27 Will Santy Come To Shanty Town A:5 / J:6 / S:8	*Eddy Arnold/Ed Nelson/Steve Nelson* [X]	RCA Victor 48-0127
12/17/49+	**6**	2		28 There's No Wings On My Angel J:6 / S:11	*Eddy Arnold/Cy Coben/Irving Melsher*	RCA Victor 48-0137
				from the movie *Feudin' Rhythm* starring Arnold		

Billboard DEBUT	PEAK	WKS	GOLD	ARTIST / Country Chart Hit	Ranking / Songwriter	Label (& Number)
				ARNOLD, Eddy — cont'd		
12/31/49+	❶^{1}	17		29 Take Me In Your Arms And Hold Me / (answer to #8 above)	J:❶^{1} / A:4 / S:5 *Cindy Walker*	
1/14/50	6	7		30 Mama And Daddy Broke My Heart	S:6 / J:8 *Spade Cooley*	RCA Victor 48-0150
4/15/50	3^{1}	12		31 Little Angel With The Dirty Face /	S:3 / J:7 / A:10 *Dale Parker*	
4/22/50	3^{1}	13		32 Why Should I Cry?	J:3 / A:5 / S:5 *Zeke Clements*	RCA Victor 48-0300
7/1/50	2^{2}	17		33 Cuddle Buggin' Baby /	S:2 / J:3 / A:4 *Red Rowe*	
7/1/50	6	12		34 Enclosed, One Broken Heart	J:6 / A:7 / S:7 *Eddy Arnold/Sadie Sallis*	RCA Victor 48-0342
9/30/50	2^{8}	16		35 The Lovebug Itch /	S:2 / J:2 / A:2 *Roy Botkin/Jenny Lou Carson*	
12/9/50	10	1		36 A Prison Without Walls	J:10 *Steve Nelson/Jack Rollins*	RCA Victor 48-0382
1/13/51	❶^{11}	23		37 There's Been A Change In Me	A:❶^{11} / S:❶^{4} / J:2 *Cy Coben*	RCA Victor 48-0412
2/24/51	8	5		38 May The Good Lord Bless And Keep You	S:8 / A:10 *Meredith Willson*	RCA Victor 48-0425
4/14/51	❶^{3}	17		39 Kentucky Waltz	S:❶^{3} / J:❶^{3} / A:4 *Bill Monroe*	RCA Victor 48-0444
6/23/51	❶^{11}	24		40 I Wanna Play House With You /	J:❶^{11} / S:❶^{6} / A:2 *Cy Coben*	
7/7/51	4	9		41 Something Old, Something New	J:4 / S:7 *Eddy Arnold/Cy Coben/Charles Grean*	RCA Victor 48-0476
10/27/51	2^{1}	16		42 Somebody's Been Beatin' My Time /	J:2 / A:3 / S:5 *Zeke Clements*	
10/27/51	5	12		43 Heart Strings	S:5 / J:8 *Merle Moore*	RCA Victor 47-4273
1/26/52	4	12		44 Bundle Of Southern Sunshine /	J:4 / S:4 / A:5 *Sunny Clapp*	
2/23/52	9	1		45 Call Her Your Sweetheart	A:9 *Leon Payne*	RCA Victor 47-4413
4/5/52	❶^{1}	14		46 Easy On The Eyes	S:❶^{1} / A:4 / J:6 *Eddy Arnold/Cy Coben*	RCA Victor 47-4569
7/19/52	❶^{4}	18		47 A Full Time Job	A:❶^{4} / S:3 / J:3 *Jerry Teifer*	RCA Victor 47-4787
10/25/52	3^{1}	11		48 Older And Bolder /	S:3 / J:4 / A:7 *Cy Coben*	
12/6/52	9	1		49 I'd Trade All Of My Tomorrows (For Just One Yesterday)	J:9 *Jenny Lou Carson*	RCA Victor 47-4954
1/24/53	❶^{3}	13		50 Eddy's Song	S:❶^{3} / J:2 / A:5 *Cy Coben/Charles Grean*	RCA Victor 5108
6/20/53	4	9		51 Free Home Demonstration /	S:4 / A:5 / J:5 *Cy Coben/Charles Grean*	
7/18/53	4	10		52 How's The World Treating You	A:4 / J:7 *Chet Atkins/Boudleaux Bryant*	RCA Victor 5305
10/3/53	4	10		53 Mama, Come Get Your Baby Boy	A:4 / S:9 / J:9 *Alvin Alton/Leon Merritt*	RCA Victor 5415
1/9/54	❶^{1}	37		54 I Really Don't Want To Know	J:❶^{1} / S:2 / A:2 *Howard Barnes/Don Robertson*	RCA Victor 5525
4/10/54	7	9		55 My Everything	A:7 / S:7 *Jerry Lacy*	RCA Victor 5634
8/21/54	7	14		56 Hep Cat Baby /	J:7 / S:9 / A:14 *Cy Coben*	
8/28/54	3^{1}	23		57 This Is The Thanks I Get (For Loving You)	S:3 / A:3 / J:3 *Tommy Dilbeck*	RCA Victor 5805
				EDDY ARNOLD and his Guitar:		
12/18/54+	12	3		58 Christmas Can't Be Far Away	A:12 *Boudleaux Bryant* [X]	RCA Victor 47-5905
1/29/55	2^{4}	25		59 I've Been Thinking /	J:2 / S:3 / A:4 *Boudleaux Bryant*	
2/5/55	12	7		60 Don't Forget	S:12 *Fred Ebb/Norman Leyden*	RCA Victor 6000
4/23/55	6	9		61 In Time /	A:6 / S:7 / J:flip *John Bellah/Barbara Cross*	
4/23/55	9	8		62 Two Kinds Of Love	S:9 / J:9 *Ed Nelson/Steve Nelson/Eddie Thorpe*	RCA Victor 6069
6/25/55	❶^{2}	26		63 The Cattle Call /	S:❶^{2} / J:2 / A:4 *Tex Owens*	
7/9/55	8	7		64 The Kentuckian Song (from the movie *The Kentuckian* starring Burt Lancaster)	J:8 *Irving Gordon*	RCA Victor 6139
8/20/55	❶^{2}	15		65 That Do Make It Nice /	J:❶^{2} / A:4 / S:11 *Eddy Arnold/Fred Ebb/Paul Klein*	
8/20/55	2^{7}	31		66 Just Call Me Lonesome	J:2 / S:2 / A:2 *Rex Griffin*	RCA Victor 6198
11/12/55	10	10		67 The Richest Man (In The World) /	S:10 / A:14 *Boudleaux Bryant*	
11/26/55	6	8		68 I Walked Alone Last Night	S:6 *Robert Arthur/Jack Wolf*	RCA Victor 6290
1/28/56	7	3		69 Trouble In Mind	S:7 *Richard Jones*	RCA Victor 6365
				EDDY ARNOLD:		
8/25/56	15	1		70 Casey Jones (The Brave Engineer)	A:15 *Eddie Newton/T. Lawrence Seibert*	RCA Victor 6601
9/1/56	10	8		71 You Don't Know Me	S:10 / A:15 *Eddy Arnold/Cindy Walker*	RCA Victor 6502
5/27/57	12	3		72 Gonna Find Me A Bluebird	A:12 / S:15 *Marvin Rainwater*	RCA Victor 6905
3/16/59	12	9		73 Chip Off The Old Block	*James Lee*	RCA Victor 7435
6/22/59	5	19		74 Tennessee Stud	*Jimmie Driftwood*	RCA Victor 7542
1/9/61	23	3		75 Before This Day Ends	*Roy Drusky/Vic McAlpin/Marie Wilson*	RCA Victor 7794
5/29/61	27	1		76 (Jim) I Wore A Tie Today	*Cindy Walker*	RCA Victor 7861
10/16/61	17	10		77 One Grain Of Sand	*Rosella LaRue*	RCA Victor 7926
3/17/62	7	10		78 Tears Broke Out On Me	*Hank Cochran*	RCA Victor 7984
6/30/62	3^{1}	19		79 A Little Heartache /	*Wayne Walker*	
8/4/62	7	19		80 After Loving You	*John Lantz/Eddie Miller*	RCA Victor 8048
12/8/62+	5	15		81 Does He Mean That Much To You?	*Don Robertson/Jack Rollins*	RCA Victor 8102
4/27/63	11	10		82 Yesterday's Memories	*Hank Cochran*	RCA Victor 8160
8/10/63	13	12		83 A Million Years Or So	*Charlie Williams*	RCA Victor 8207
12/7/63+	12	12		84 Jealous Hearted Me	*A.P. Carter*	RCA Victor 8253
2/1/64	5	20		85 Molly *[w/ The Needmore Creek Singers]*	*Steve Karliski*	RCA Victor 8296
7/18/64	26	13		86 Sweet Adorable You	*Baker Knight*	RCA Victor 8363
11/7/64+	8	19		87 I Thank My Lucky Stars	*Wayne Walker*	RCA Victor 8445
3/27/65	❶^{2}	25		88 What's He Doing In My World	*Carl Belew/Eddie Bush/Billy Joe Moore*	RCA Victor 8516
9/18/65	15	9		89 I'm Letting You Go	*Billy Grammar*	RCA Victor 8632
10/9/65	❶^{3}	25		90 Make The World Go Away (Grammy: Hall of Fame)	*Hank Cochran*	RCA Victor 8679
2/12/66	❶^{6}	19		91 I Want To Go With You	*Hank Cochran*	RCA Victor 8749
5/14/66	2^{1}	16		92 The Last Word In Lonesome Is Me	*Roger Miller*	RCA Victor 8818
7/23/66	3^{4}	15		93 The Tip Of My Fingers	*Bill Anderson*	RCA Victor 8869
10/15/66	❶^{4}	19		94 Somebody Like Me	*Wayne Carson*	RCA Victor 8965

DEBUT	PEAK	WKS	GOLD		ARTIST / Country Chart Hit	Ranking / Songwriter	Label (& Number)
					ARNOLD, Eddy — cont'd		
12/24/66+	51	8		95	The First Word	*Billy Sherrill/Bob Tubert*	RCA Victor 9027
2/18/67	❶[2]	16		96	Lonely Again	*Jean Chapel*	RCA Victor 9080
5/6/67	3[3]	16		97	Misty Blue	*Bob Montgomery*	RCA Victor 9182
8/26/67	❶[1]	16		98	Turn The World Around	*Ben Peters*	RCA Victor 9265
12/2/67+	2[2]	15		99	Here Comes Heaven	*Joy Byers/Bob Tubert*	RCA Victor 9368
2/17/68	4	14		100	Here Comes The Rain, Baby	*Mickey Newbury*	RCA Victor 9437
6/1/68	4	12		101	It's Over	*Jimmie Rodgers*	RCA Victor 9525
8/31/68	❶[2]	14		102	Then You Can Tell Me Goodbye	*John D. Loudermilk*	RCA Victor 9606
11/23/68+	10	14		103	They Don't Make Love Like They Used To	*Red Lane*	RCA Victor 9667
3/29/69	10	13		104	Please Don't Go	*Alfredo Bracchi/Tony D'Amzi/Carl Sigman*	RCA Victor 0120
6/28/69	19	12		105	But For Love	*Terry Cashman/Gene Pistilli/Tommy West*	RCA Victor 0175
9/27/69	69	2		106	You Fool	*Martha Sharp*	RCA Victor 0226
12/27/69+	73	2		107	Since December	*Hank Cochran/Glenn Martin*	RCA Victor 0282
2/28/70	22	11		108	Soul Deep	*Wayne Carson*	RCA Victor 9801
6/13/70	28	11		109	A Man's Kind Of Woman /	*George Rizzo*	
6/20/70	flip	10		110	Living Under Pressure	*Baker Knight*	RCA Victor 9848
9/12/70	22	9		111	From Heaven To Heartache	*Ben Peters*	RCA Victor 9889
1/2/71	26	12		112	Portrait Of My Woman	*Glen Sherley*	RCA Victor 9935
5/1/71	49	8		113	A Part Of America Died	*Harry Koch* [S]	RCA Victor 9968
7/3/71	34	9		114	Welcome To My World	*John Hathcock/Ray Winkler*	RCA Victor 9993
11/13/71	55	7		115	I Love You Dear	*Jack Moran*	RCA Victor 0559
2/26/72	38	9		116	Lonely People	*Harlan Howard*	RCA Victor 0641
8/5/72	62	4		117	Lucy	*Alex Harvey*	RCA Victor 0747
1/20/73	28	12		118	So Many Ways	*Bobby Stevenson*	MGM 14478
5/19/73	56	9		119	If The Whole World Stopped Lovin'	*Ben Peters*	MGM 14535
8/18/73	29	11		120	Oh, Oh, I'm Falling In Love Again	*Al Hoffman/Dick Manning/Mark Markwell*	MGM 14600
12/8/73+	24	13		121	She's Got Everything I Need	*Wayne Carson*	MGM 14672
3/30/74	56	9		122	Just For Old Times Sake	*Hank Hunter/Jack Keller*	MGM 14711
8/3/74	19	12		123	I Wish That I Had Loved You Better	*Chick Rains*	MGM 14734
12/28/74+	47	9		124	Butterfly	*Ralph Bernet/Mike Curb/Mack David/Danyel Gerard*	MGM 14769
6/7/75	60	12		125	Red Roses For A Blue Lady	*Roy Bennett/Sid Tepper*	MGM 14780
10/11/75	86	6		126	Middle Of A Memory	*Bud Johnston*	MGM 14827
6/19/76	13	13		127	Cowboy	*Ron Fraser/Harry Shannon*	RCA Victor 10701
10/23/76	43	9		128	Put Me Back Into Your World	*Lorene Mann*	RCA 10794
3/5/77	22	13		129	(I Need You) All The Time	*Boudleaux Bryant/Felice Bryant*	RCA 10899
7/23/77	53	7		130	Freedom Ain't The Same As Being Free	*Jackie Johnson*	RCA 11031
11/12/77	83	3		131	Where Lonely People Go	*Floyd Huddleston*	RCA 11133
4/22/78	23	12		132	Country Lovin'	*Alan Bernstein/Richard Ziegler*	RCA 11257
8/5/78	91	2		133	I'm The South	*Alberta Carruth/Fred Foster*	RCA 11319
12/9/78+	13	14		134	If Everyone Had Someone Like You	*Bobby Lee Springfield*	RCA 11422
4/14/79	21	11		135	What In Her World Did I Do	*Bobby Fischer/Don Wayne*	RCA 11537
8/4/79	22	11		136	Goodbye	*Larry Butler/Buddy Killen*	RCA 11668
11/17/79+	28	13		137	If I Ever Had To Say Goodbye To You	*Steve Gibb*	RCA 11752
3/8/80	6	13		138	Let's Get It While The Gettin's Good	*Bobby Lee Springfield*	RCA 11918
6/28/80	10	15		139	That's What I Get For Loving You	*Bobby Lee Springfield*	RCA 12039
12/6/80+	11	16		140	Don't Look Now (But We Just Fell In Love)	*Jeff Silbar/Johnny Slate*	RCA 12136
5/16/81	32	10		141	Bally-Hoo Days /	*Larry Henley/Larry Keith/Steve Pippin/Rafe Van Hoy*	
6/20/81	flip	5		142	Two Hearts Beat Better Than One	*Dan Hoffman/Mary Ann Kennedy/Ricky Page*	RCA 12226
12/12/81+	30	11		143	All I'm Missing Is You	*Wayland Holyfield*	RCA 13000
4/24/82	73	5		144	Don't Give Up On Me	*Ben Peters*	RCA 13094
3/19/83	76	6		145	The Blues Don't Care Who's Got 'Em	*Wayland Holyfield/Dickey Lee*	RCA 13452
12/25/99	18[S]	2		146	Cattle Call *[w/ LeAnn Rimes]*	*Tex Owens* [R]	Curb

After Loving You ['62]
All Alone In This World Without You ['46]
All I'm Missing Is You ['82]
Anytime ['48]
Bally-Hoo Days ['81]
Before This Day Ends ['61]
Blues Don't Care Who's Got 'Em ['83]
Bouquet Of Roses ['48]
Bundle Of Southern Sunshine ['52]
But For Love ['69]
Butterfly ['75]
Call Her Your Sweetheart ['52]
Casey Jones (The Brave Engineer) ['56]
Cattle Call ['55]
Cattle Call ['99]
Chained To A Memory ['46]
Chip Off The Old Block ['59]
C-H-R-I-S-T-M-A-S ['49]
Christmas Can't Be Far Away ['55]
Country Lovin' ['78]
Cowboy ['76]
Cuddle Buggin' Baby ['50]
Does He Mean That Much To You? ['63]
Don't Forget ['55]
Don't Give Up On Me ['82]
Don't Look Now (But We Just Fell In Love) ['81]
Don't Rob Another Man's Castle ['49]
Each Minute Seems A Million Years ['45]
Easy On The Eyes ['52]
Echo Of Your Footsteps ['49]
Eddy's Song ['53]
Enclosed, One Broken Heart ['50]
First Word ['67]
Free Home Demonstration ['53]
Freedom Ain't The Same As Being Free ['77]
From Heaven To Heartache ['70]
Full Time Job ['52]
Gonna Find Me A Bluebird ['57]
Goodbye ['79]
Heart Full Of Love (For A Handful Of Kisses) ['48]
Heart Strings ['51]
Hep Cat Baby ['54]
Here Comes Heaven ['68]
Here Comes The Rain, Baby ['68]
How's The World Treating You ['53]
I Couldn't Believe It Was True ['47]
I Love You Dear ['71]
(I Need You) All The Time ['77]
I Really Don't Want To Know ['54]
I Thank My Lucky Stars ['65]
I Walked Alone Last Night ['55]
I Wanna Play House With You ['51]
I Want To Go With You ['66]
I Wish That I Had Loved You Better ['74]
I'd Trade All Of My Tomorrows (For Just One Yesterday) ['52]
I'll Hold You In My Heart (Till I Can Hold You In My Arms) ['47]
I'm Letting You Go ['65]
I'm The South ['78]
I'm Throwing Rice (At The Girl That I Love) ['49]
I've Been Thinking ['55]
If Everyone Had Someone Like You ['79]
If I Ever Had To Say Goodbye To You ['80]
If The Whole World Stopped Lovin' ['73]
In Time ['55]
It's A Sin ['47]
It's Over ['68]
Jealous Hearted Me ['64]
(Jim) I Wore A Tie Today ['61]
Just A Little Lovin' (Will Go A Long, Long Way) ['48]
Just Call Me Lonesome ['55]
Just For Old Times Sake ['74]
Kentuckian Song ['55]
Kentucky Waltz ['51]
Last Word In Lonesome Is Me ['66]
Let's Get It While The Gettin's Good ['80]
Little Angel With The Dirty Face ['50]
Little Heartache ['62]
Living Under Pressure ['70]
Lonely Again ['67]
Lonely People ['72]
Lovebug Itch ['50]
Lucy ['72]
Make The World Go Away ['65]
Mama And Daddy Broke My Heart ['50]
Mama, Come Get Your Baby Boy ['53]
Man's Kind Of Woman ['70]
Many Tears Ago ['49]
May The Good Lord Bless And Keep You ['51]
Middle Of A Memory ['75]
Million Years Or So ['63]
Misty Blue ['67]
Molly Darling ['48]
Molly ['64]
My Daddy Is Only A Picture ['48]
My Everything ['54]
Oh, Oh, I'm Falling In Love Again ['73]
Older And Bolder ['52]
One Grain Of Sand ['61]
One Kiss Too Many ['49]
Part Of America Died ['71]
Please Don't Go ['69]
Portrait Of My Woman ['71]
Prison Without Walls ['50]
Put Me Back Into Your World ['76]
Red Roses For A Blue Lady ['75]
Richest Man (In The World) ['55]
She's Got Everything I Need ['74]
Show Me The Way Back To Your Heart ['49]
Since December ['70]
So Many Ways ['73]
Somebody Like Me ['66]

ARNOLD, Eddy — cont'd

Somebody's Been Beatin' My Time ['51]
Something Old, Something New ['51]
Soul Deep ['70]
Sweet Adorable You ['64]
Take Me In Your Arms And Hold Me ['50]
Tears Broke Out On Me ['62]
Tennessee Stud ['59]
Texarkana Baby ['48]
That Do Make It Nice ['55]
That's How Much I Love You ['46]
That's What I Get For Loving You ['80]
Then I Turned And Walked Slowly Away ['49]
Then You Can Tell Me Goodbye ['68]
There's Been A Change In Me ['51]
There's No Wings On My Angel ['50]
There's Not A Thing (I Wouldn't Do For You) ['49]
They Don't Make Love Like They Used To ['69]
This Is The Thanks I Get (For Loving You) ['54]
Tip Of My Fingers ['66]
To My Sorrow ['47]
Trouble In Mind ['56]
Turn The World Around ['67]
Two Hearts Beat Better Than One ['81]
Two Kinds Of Love ['55]
Welcome To My World ['71]
What A Fool I Was ['48]
What In Her World Did I Do ['79]
What Is Life Without Love ['47]
What's He Doing In My World ['65]
Where Lonely People Go ['77]
Why Should I Cry? ['50]
Will Santy Come To Shanty Town ['49]
Yesterday's Memories ['63]
You Don't Know Me ['56]
You Fool ['69]

ARNOLD, Rick

Born in Tennessee. Male singer/songwriter/guitarist.

DEBUT	PEAK	WKS	#	Title	Songwriter	Label
9/16/89	89	2		I Must Be Crazy	Rick Arnold	Lynn 51088

ASHLEY, Leon

Born Leon Walton on 5/18/1936 in Newton County, Georgia. Male singer/songwriter/guitarist. Married **Margie Singleton** on 2/20/1965. Formed own Ashley record label in 1967.

DEBUT	PEAK	WKS	#	Title	Songwriter	Label
7/29/67	❶[1]	18	1	Laura (What's He Got That I Ain't Got)	Leon Ashley/Margie Singleton	Ashley 2003
11/11/67	54	7	2	Hangin' On *[w/ Margie Singleton]*	Ira Allen/Buddy Mize	Ashley 2015
12/2/67+	28	12	3	Anna, I'm Taking You Home	Leon Ashley/Margie Singleton	Ashley 2025
3/30/68	14	14	4	Mental Journey	Leon Ashley/Margie Singleton	Ashley 2075
5/11/68	55	6	5	You'll Never Be Lonely Again *[w/ Margie Singleton]*	Leon Ashley/Margie Singleton	Ashley 3000
7/27/68	8	15	6	Flower Of Love	Leon Ashley/Margie Singleton	Ashley 4000
1/11/69	25	9	7	While Your Lover Sleeps	Leon Ashley/Buddy Mize/Margie Singleton	Ashley 7000
4/19/69	23	10	8	Walkin' Back To Birmingham	Leon Ashley/Margie Singleton	Ashley 9000
8/16/69	55	7	9	Ain't Gonna Worry	Leon Ashley/Margie Singleton	Ashley 22

ASHTON, Susan

Born Susan Rae Hill on 7/17/1967 in Irving, Texas. Female singer/songwriter.

DEBUT	PEAK	WKS	#	Title	Songwriter	Label
1/30/99	51	9	1	Faith Of The Heart	S:25 Diane Warren	Capitol
5/29/99	37	20	2	You're Lucky I Love You	Marla Cannon/Neil Thrasher	Capitol
				above 2 from the album *Closer* on Capitol 97745		
9/20/03	56	6	3	She Is	Susan Ashton/Pat Bunch/Tommy Lee James	Capitol

ASHWORTH, Ernest — 1960s: #32 / All-Time: #228

Born on 12/15/1928 in Huntsville, Alabama. Singer/songwriter/guitarist. Appeared in the movie *The Farmer's Other Daughter.*

OPRY: 1964

DEBUT	PEAK	WKS	#	Title	Songwriter	Label
5/30/60	4	16	1	Each Moment ('Spent With You)	Ernest Ashworth/Billy Hogan	Decca 31085
10/24/60	8	20	2	You Can't Pick A Rose In December	Leon Payne	Decca 31156
5/15/61	15	2	3	Forever Gone	Ernest Ashworth/Billy Hogan	Decca 31237
6/30/62	3[1]	20	4	Everybody But Me	LeRoy Harris	Hickory 1170
12/29/62+	7	15	5	I Take The Chance	Charlie Louvin/Ira Louvin	Hickory 1189
6/22/63	❶[1]	36	6	Talk Back Trembling Lips	John D. Loudermilk	Hickory 1214
2/1/64	10	20	7	A Week In The Country	Baker Knight	Hickory 1237
6/20/64	4	23	8	I Love To Dance With Annie	Boudleaux Bryant/Felice Bryant	Hickory 1265
11/7/64+	11	21	9	Pushed In A Corner	Ruby Rivers	Hickory 1281
5/15/65	18	13	10	Because I Cared	Jack Turner	Hickory 1304
8/7/65	8	20	11	The DJ Cried	Joyce Allsup	Hickory 1325
				ERNIE ASHWORTH:		
1/29/66	28	11	12	I Wish	Ernest Ashworth	Hickory 1358
7/16/66	13	17	13	At Ease Heart	Jimmy Jay	Hickory 1400
12/3/66+	31	9	14	Sad Face	Eve Jay/Doug Kershaw	Hickory 1428
4/1/67	63	4	15	Just An Empty Place	Ronald Blackwell	Hickory 1445
8/5/67	48	10	16	My Love For You (Is Like A Mountain Range)	Ernest Ashworth/Tommy Moreland/Harold Watson	Hickory 1466
11/25/67	48	7	17	Tender And True	Ernest Ashworth/Tommy Moreland/Harold Watson	Hickory 1484
5/25/68	39	8	18	A New Heart	Ernest Ashworth/Arless Clark	Hickory 1503
3/29/69	69	4	19	Where Do You Go (When You Don't Go With Me)	Joe Melson/Susie Melson	Hickory 1528
7/12/69	72	3	20	Love, I Finally Found It	Ernest Ashworth/Robert Owens	Hickory 1538
7/18/70	72	3	21	That Look Of Good-Bye	Joe Melson/Susie Melson	Hickory 1570

ASLEEP AT THE WHEEL

Group from Paw Paw, West Virginia: **Ray Benson** (male vocals, guitar), Chris O'Connell (female vocals, guitar) Reuben "Lucky Oceans" Gosfield (steel guitar), Danny Levin (fiddle, mandolin) and Jim "Floyd Domino" Haber (piano). Numerous personnel changes with Benson the only constant. **Jann Browne** was a member from 1981-83. **Rosie Flores** joined in 1997.

DEBUT	PEAK	WKS	#	Title	Songwriter	Label
12/21/74+	69	8	1	Choo Choo Ch'Boogie	Denver Darling/Milt Gabler/Vaughn Horton	Epic 50045
8/9/75	10	18	2	The Letter That Johnny Walker Read	Ray Benson/Chris Frayne/Leroy Preston	Capitol 4115
12/13/75+	31	11	3	Bump Bounce Boogie	Ray Benson/Jim Haber/Leroy Preston	Capitol 4187
4/3/76	35	11	4	Nothin' Takes The Place Of You	Toussaint McCall/Pat Robinson	Capitol 4238
8/28/76	48	8	5	Route 66	Bobby Troup	Capitol 4319
11/20/76+	38	10	6	Miles And Miles Of Texas	Tom Camfield/Diane Johnston	Capitol 4357
3/19/77	42	9	7	The Trouble With Lovin' Today	Kevin Farrell	Capitol 4393
12/2/78	75	6	8	Texas Me & You	Ray Benson	Capitol 4659
2/28/87	39	14	9	Way Down Texas Way	S:27 Billy Joe Shaver	Epic 06671
5/30/87	17	18	10	House Of Blue Lights	S:10 Don Raye/Freddie Slack	Epic 07125
10/17/87	53	7	11	Boogie Back To Texas	Ray Benson	Epic 07610

Billboard DEBUT	PEAK	WKS	GOLD	ARTIST / Country Chart Hit	Ranking / Songwriter	Label (& Number)

ASLEEP AT THE WHEEL — cont'd

DEBUT	PEAK	WKS		Country Chart Hit	Songwriter	Label (& Number)
1/9/88	**59**	9	12	**Blowin' Like A Bandit**	*Guy Clark*	Epic 07659
7/23/88	**55**	6	13	**Walk On By**	*Kendall Hayes*	Epic 07966
10/29/88	**65**	11	14	**Hot Rod Lincoln**	S:29 *Charlie Ryan/W.S. Stevenson*	Epic 08087
9/1/90	**54**	4	15	**Keepin' Me Up Nights**	*J.D. Hicks/Byron Hill*	Arista
12/1/90+	**60**	14	16	**That's The Way Love Is**	*Leroy Preston*	Arista
3/16/91	**71**	2	17	**Dance With Who Brung You**	*Ray Benson*	Arista
				above 3 from the album *Keepin' Me Up Nights* on Arista 8550		
3/19/94	**73**	1	18	**Corine, Corina** ***[w/ Brooks & Dunn]***	*Bo Chapman/Mitchell Parish/J. Mayo Williams*	Liberty
				from Asleep At The Wheel's album *Tribute To The Music Of* **Bob Wills And The Texas Playboys** on Liberty 81470		
3/25/00	**65**	1	19	**Roly Poly** ***[w/ Dixie Chicks]***	*Fred Rose*	DreamWorks
				from the album *Ride With Bob* on DreamWorks 50117		

ATCHER, Bob — 1940s: #40

Born on 5/11/1914 in Hardin County, Kentucky. Died on 10/31/1993 (age 79). Male singer/songwriter/guitarist/fiddler. Joined the WLS *National Barn Dance* in 1948. Mayor of Schaumburg, Illinois (1959-75).

EARLY HIT: Pins And Needles In My Heart [w/ Bonnie Blue Eyes] (1943)

DEBUT	PEAK	WKS		Country Chart Hit	Songwriter	Label (& Number)
7/13/46	**7**	1	1	**I Must Have Been Wrong**	*Bob Atcher*	Columbia 36983
1/31/48	**6**	11	2	**Signed, Sealed And Delivered**	*Cowboy Copas/Lois Mann*	Columbia 37991
5/7/49	**12**	1	3	**Tennessee Border**	J:12 *Jimmy Work*	Columbia 20557
10/8/49	**9**	2	4	**Why Don't You Haul Off And Love Me**	J:9 *Lonnie Glosson*	Columbia 20611

ATKINS, Big Ben

Born on 9/23/1943 in Vernon, Alabama. Male singer.

DEBUT	PEAK	WKS		Country Chart Hit	Songwriter	Label (& Number)
5/13/78	**72**	4		**We Don't Live Here, We Just Love Here**	*Mickey Buckins*	GRT 161

ATKINS, Chet — HOF: 1973

Born on 6/20/1924 in Luttrell, Tennessee. Died of cancer on 6/30/2001 (age 77). Moved to Nashville in 1950 and became a prolific studio guitarist and producer. RCA's A&R manager in Nashville from 1960-68; RCA vice president from 1968-82. Won Grammy's Lifetime Achievement Award in 1993. Recipient of *Billboard's* Century Award in 1997. Inducted into the Rock and Roll Hall of Fame in 2002. Also see **Some Of Chet's Friends**.

CMA: Musician 1967, 1968, 1969, 1981, 1982, 1983, 1984, 1985 & 1988 // OPRY: 1950

DEBUT	PEAK	WKS		Country Chart Hit	Songwriter	Label (& Number)
1/15/55	**13**	2	1	**Mister Sandman**	A:13 / S:15 *Pat Ballard* **[I]**	RCA Victor 5956
4/2/55	**15**	1	2	**Silver Bell** ***[w/ Hank Snow]***	S:15 *Edward Madden/Percy Wenrich* **[I]**	RCA Victor 5995
6/26/65	**4**	19	3	**Yakety Axe**	*Boots Randolph/James Rich* **[I]**	RCA Victor 8590
10/15/66	**30**	10	4	**Prissy**	*Priscilla Hubbard* **[I]**	RCA Victor 8927
12/1/73	**75**	6	5	**Fiddlin' Around**	*Johnny Gimble* **[I]**	RCA Victor 0146
9/20/75	**77**	5	6	**The Night Atlanta Burned**	*John D. Loudermilk* **[I]**	RCA Victor 10346
				THE ATKINS STRING COMPANY		
6/12/76	**40**	12	7	**Frog Kissin'**	*Buddy Kalb* **[L-N]**	RCA Victor 10614
3/1/80	**83**	3	8	**Blind Willie**	*Buddy Kalb* **[L]**	RCA 11892
8/23/80	**83**	4	9	**I Can Hear Kentucky Calling Me**	*Boudleaux Bryant/Felice Bryant*	RCA 12064
12/17/83+	**6**	18	10	**We Didn't See A Thing** ***[w/ Ray Charles & George Jones]***	*Gary Gentry*	Columbia 04297

ATKINS, Rodney

Born on 3/28/1969 in Knoxville, Tennessee. Male singer/songwriter.

DEBUT	PEAK	WKS		Country Chart Hit	Songwriter	Label (& Number)
8/30/97	**74**	1	1	**In A Heartbeat**	*Rodney Atkins/Brian Gowan/Ted Hewitt*	Curb
				from the album *Rodney Atkins* on Curb 77896		
5/18/02	**37**	16	2	**Sing Along**	*Rodney Atkins/Bruce Gaitsch/Ted Hewitt*	Curb
10/5/02	**36**	17	3	**My Old Man**	*Rodney Atkins/Ted Hewitt*	Curb
6/21/03+	**4**	33	4	**Honesty (Write Me A List)**	S:5 *Patsy Clements/David Kent*	Curb
4/10/04	**41**	12	5	**Someone To Share It With**	*Rodney Atkins/Brian Gowan/Ted Hewitt*	Curb
				above 4 from the album *Honesty* on Curb 78745		

ATLANTA

Group from Atlanta: Brad Griffis and Bill Davidson (vocals), Tony Ingram (vocals, fiddle; **Spurzz**), Alan David (guitar), Allen Collay and Bill Packard (keyboards), Jeff Baker (harmonica), Dick Stevens (bass) and John Holder (drums).

DEBUT	PEAK	WKS		Country Chart Hit	Songwriter	Label (& Number)
5/21/83	**9**	17	1	**Atlanta Burned Again Last Night**	*James Dotson/Dwain Rowe/Jeff Stevens*	MDJ 4831
9/10/83	**11**	19	2	**Dixie Dreaming**	*John Gilbert*	MDJ 4832
2/18/84	**5**	23	3	**Sweet Country Music**	*A.P. Carter/James Dotson/Dwain Rowe/Jeff Stevens*	MCA 52336
6/16/84	**35**	12	4	**Pictures**	*Rex Gosdin/Carole Halupke*	MCA 52391
9/15/84	**22**	16	5	**Wishful Drinkin'**	S:17 / A:27 *Blake Mevis/Bill Shore*	MCA 52452
				from the movie *Ellie* starring Shelley Winters		
4/6/85	**57**	10	6	**My Sweet-Eyed Georgia Girl**	*Stewart Harris/John Rosasco*	MCA 52552
6/22/85	**58**	7	7	**Why Not Tonight**	*Bucky Jones/Tom Shapiro/Chris Waters*	MCA 52603
1/31/87	**75**	6	8	**We Always Agree On Love**	*Doug Johnson*	Southern Tracks 1074
1/23/88	**70**	5	9	**Sad Cliches**	*Buddy Buie/Ronnie Hammond*	Southern Tracks 1091

ATLANTA POPS — see COLEMAN, Albert

ATLANTA RHYTHM SECTION

Group from Doraville, Georgia: Ronnie Hammond (vocals), Barry Bailey and J.R. Cobb (guitars), Dean Daughtry (keyboards), Paul Goddard (bass) and Robert Nix (drums; replaced by Roy Yeager in 1980).

DEBUT	PEAK	WKS		Country Chart Hit	Songwriter	Label (& Number)
7/7/79	**92**	3	1	**Do It Or Die**	*Buddy Buie/J.R. Cobb/Ronnie Hammond*	Polydor 14568
12/6/80	**75**	7	2	**Silver Eagle**	*Buddy Buie/J.R. Cobb*	Polydor 2142

Billboard DEBUT	PEAK	WKS	GOLD	ARTIST / Country Chart Hit	Ranking / Songwriter	Label (& Number)

AUSTIN, Bobby

Born on 5/5/1933 in Wenatchee, Washington. Died on 1/6/2002 (age 68). Male singer/songwriter/bassist.

DEBUT	PEAK	WKS		Country Chart Hit	Songwriter	Label (& Number)
10/8/66	21	14	1	**Apartment #9**	*Fern Foley/Fuzzy Owen/Johnny Paycheck*	Tally 500
4/8/67	59	6	2	**Cupid's Last Arrow**	*Bobby Austin/Charles Tanner*	Capitol 5867
12/30/67+	68	5	3	**This Song Is Just For You**	*Cecil Harris/Perk Williams*	Capitol 2039
12/27/69+	65	4	4	**For Your Love**	*Ed Townsend*	Capitol 2681
11/11/72	39	8	5	**Knoxville Station**	*Jerry McBee*	Atlantic 2913

AUSTIN, Bryan

Born on 9/12/1967 in Pass Christian, Mississippi. Male singer/songwriter/guitarist.

DEBUT	PEAK	WKS		Country Chart Hit	Songwriter	Label (& Number)
5/28/94	62	9		**Radio Active**	*Bucky Jones/L. David Lewis/Kim Williams*	Patriot
				from the album *Bryan Austin* on Patriot 27909		

AUSTIN, Chris

Born in Boone, North Carolina. Died in a plane crash on 3/16/1991 (age 27). Male singer/guitarist/fiddler. Member of **Reba McEntire**'s band. Plane crash also killed **Paula Kay Evans**.

DEBUT	PEAK	WKS		Country Chart Hit	Songwriter	Label (& Number)
7/30/88	62	5	1	**Lonesome For You**	*Larry Cordle/Larry Shell*	Warner 27815
12/10/88	89	6	2	**I Know There's A Heart In There Somewhere**	*Bruce Burch/J.D. Hicks*	Warner 27661
4/1/89	54	7	3	**Blues Stay Away From Me**	*Alton Delmore/Rabon Delmore/Henry Glover/Wayne Raney*	Warner 27531

AUSTIN, Darlene

Born in Salina, Kansas. Female singer.

DEBUT	PEAK	WKS		Country Chart Hit	Songwriter	Label (& Number)
6/26/82	68	6	1	**Sunday Go To Cheatin' Clothes**	*David Heavener*	Myrtle 1002
10/9/82	75	5	2	**Take Me Tonight**	*Don Singleton*	Myrtle 1003
3/12/83	79	4	3	**I'm On The Outside Looking In**	*Teddy Randazzo/Bob Weinstein*	Myrtle 1004
7/5/86	81	4	4	**Guilty Eyes**	*Brent Mason/Jim McBride*	CBT 4146
9/12/87	63	6	5	**I Had A Heart**	*Jason Blume/Bryan Cumming*	Magi 4444

AUSTIN, Kay

Born on 2/3/1954 in Long Beach, California. Female singer.

DEBUT	PEAK	WKS		Country Chart Hit	Songwriter	Label (& Number)
5/31/80	86	3	1	**The Rest Of Your Life**	*Robert Duncan*	e.i.o. 1122
9/13/80	75	4	2	**Two Hearts Beat** (Better Than One)	*Dan Hoffman/Mary Ann Kennedy/June Page*	e.i.o. 1127

AUSTIN, Sherrié

Born Sherrié Krenn on 8/28/1970 in Sydney, Australia; raised in Townsville, Australia. Female singer/songwriter/actress. Played "Pippa McKenna" on TV's *The Facts of Life* (1987-88). Former member of pop duo Colourhaus (under her real last name).

DEBUT	PEAK	WKS		Country Chart Hit	Songwriter	Label (& Number)
5/24/97	34	20	1	**Lucky In Love**	S:12 *Sherrié Austin/Blair Daly/Will Rambeaux*	Arista
9/13/97	41	15	2	**One Solitary Tear**	S:19 *Sherrié Austin/Steve Mandile*	Arista
1/31/98	34	16	3	**Put Your Heart Into It**	S:13 *Sherrié Austin/Will Rambeaux*	Arista
7/11/98	74	1	4	**Innocent Man**	*Kent Agee/Will Rambeaux*	Arista
				above 4 from the album *Words* on Arista 18843		
5/22/99	29	20	5	**Never Been Kissed**	S:❶[4] *Sherrié Austin/Greg Barnhill/Will Rambeaux*	Arista
11/6/99	49	8	6	**Little Bird**	S:4 *Sherrié Austin/Jon Davis/Will Rambeaux*	Arista
				above 2 from the album *Love In The Real World* on Arista 18881		
4/14/01	55	3	7	**Jolene**	*Dolly Parton*	WE
				from the album *Followin' A Feelin'* on WE 1161		
6/14/03	18	26	8	**Streets Of Heaven**	*Sherrié Austin/Paul Duncan/Al Kasha*	Broken Bow
3/20/04	50	6	9	**Drivin' Into The Sun**	*Sherrié Austin/Georgia Middleman*	Broken Bow
				above 2 from the album *Streets Of Heaven* on Broken Bow 75872		
5/22/04	46	11	10	**Son Of A Preacher Man**	*John Hurley/Ronnie Wilkins*	Broken Bow

AUTRY, Gene — 1940s: #6 / 1950s: #41 / All-Time: #137 // HOF: 1969

Born Orvon Gene Autry on 9/29/1907 in Tioga, Texas. Died of respiratory failure on 10/2/1998 (age 91). Male singer/songwriter/guitarist/actor. Worked as a cowboy and telegraph operator for the Frisco Railroad. Played saxophone and guitar with the Fields Brothers Marvelous Medicine Show. Sang on KVOO in Tulsa in 1929 as "The Oklahoma Yodeling Cowboy." Joined the WLS *National Barn Dance* in 1930. Hosted own *Melody Ranch* radio series. Acted in several western movies. Starred in own TV western from 1950-56. Later owned several businesses (including the California Angels major league baseball team).

EARLY HITS: The Last Round-Up (1933) / That Silver-Haired Daddy Of Mine [w/ Jimmy Long] (1935) / Tumbling Tumbleweeds (1935) / South Of The Border (1939) / Back In The Saddle Again (1940)

DEBUT	PEAK	WKS		Country Chart Hit	Songwriter	Label (& Number)
1/29/44	3[1]	9	1	**I'm Thinking Tonight Of My Blue Eyes**	*A.P. Carter*	Okeh 6648
4/29/44	4	1	2	**I Hang My Head And Cry**	*Gene Autry/Fred Rose/Ray Whitley*	Okeh 6627
2/10/45	2[1]	8	3	**Gonna Build A Big Fence Around Texas /**	*Cliff Friend/George Olsen/Katherine Phillips*	
2/17/45	4	3	4	**Don't Fence Me In**	*Cole Porter*	Okeh 6728
				from the movie *Hollywood Canteen* starring Bette Davis		
4/28/45	❶[8]	22	5	**At Mail Call Today /**	*Gene Autry/Fred Rose*	
4/28/45	7	2	6	**I'll Be Back**	*Gene Autry*	Okeh 6737
10/27/45	4	2	7	**Don't Hang Around Me Anymore**	*Gene Autry/Denver Darling/Vaughn Horton*	Columbia 36840
12/29/45	4	1	8	**I Want To Be Sure /**	*Gene Autry/Merle Travis*	
12/29/45	4	1	9	**Don't Live A Lie**	*Gene Autry/Johnny Bond*	Columbia 36880
2/23/46	4	5	10	**Silver Spurs** (On The Golden Stairs)	*Gene Autry/Cindy Walker*	Columbia 36904
5/25/46	3[2]	7	11	**I Wish I Had Never Met Sunshine**	*Gene Autry/Dale Evans/Oakley Haldeman*	Columbia 36970
6/15/46	4	8	12	**Wave To Me, My Lady**	*Frank Loesser/Willie Stein*	Columbia 36984
7/6/46	7	1	13	**You Only Want Me When You're Lonely**	*Gene Autry/Steve Nelson*	Columbia 36970
10/19/46	3[2]	12	14	**Have I Told You Lately That I Love You /**	*Scott Wiseman*	
10/26/46	4	3	15	**Someday You'll Want Me To Want You**	*Jimmie Hodges*	Columbia 37079

DEBUT	PEAK	WKS	GOLD	ARTIST / Country Chart Hit	Ranking / Songwriter	Label (& Number)

AUTRY, Gene — cont'd

DEBUT	PEAK	WKS	GOLD	Country Chart Hit	Songwriter	Label (& Number)
3/8/47	3[1]	2		16 You're Not My Darlin' Anymore	Rosalie Allen/Sam Martin/Fred Rose	Columbia 37201
1/3/48	5	1	●	17 Here Comes Santa Claus (Down Santa Claus Lane)	Gene Autry/Oakley Haldeman [X]	Columbia 37942
10/9/48	6	12		18 Buttons And Bows from the movie *The Paleface* starring Bob Hope	S:6 / J:6 Ray Evans/Jay Livingston	Columbia 20469
11/27/48	4	7		19 Here Comes Santa Claus (Down Santa Claus Lane)	S:4 / J:7 Gene Autry/Oakley Haldeman [X-R]	Columbia 20377
12/10/49+	❶[1]	5	●	20 Rudolph, The Red-Nosed Reindeer *[w/ The Pinafores]* Grammy: Hall of Fame	A:❶[1] / S:4 / J:7 Johnny Marks [X]	Columbia 38610
12/10/49+	8	3		21 Here Comes Santa Claus (Down Santa Claus Lane)	A:8 / S:13 Gene Autry/Oakley Haldeman [X-R]	Columbia 20377
4/8/50	3[2]	4		22 Peter Cottontail	S:3 / A:5 / J:7 Steve Nelson/Jack Rollins	Columbia 38750
12/9/50+	4	4	●	23 Frosty The Snow Man *[w/ The Cass County Boys]*	S:4 Steve Nelson/Jack Rollins	Columbia 38907
12/16/50	5	3		24 Rudolph, The Red-Nosed Reindeer *[w/ The Pinafores]*	S:5 / A:5 / J:5 Johnny Marks [X-R]	Columbia 38610
6/9/51	9	1		25 Old Soldiers Never Die	A:9 Gene Autry	Columbia 4-39405
12/26/98+	55	3		26 Rudolph, The Red-Nosed Reindeer	Johnny Marks [X-R]	Columbia
12/18/99+	60	2		27 Rudolph, The Red-Nosed Reindeer	Johnny Marks [X-R]	Columbia

AXTON, Hoyt

Born on 3/25/1938 in Duncan, Oklahoma. Died of a heart attack on 10/26/1999 (age 61). Singer/songwriter/guitarist/actor. Son of songwriter Mae Axton ("Heartbreak Hotel"). Started own Jeremiah label in 1978. Acted in such movies as *The Black Stallion* and *Gremlins.*

DEBUT	PEAK	WKS	GOLD	Country Chart Hit	Songwriter	Label (& Number)
3/30/74	10	15		1 When The Morning Comes *[w/ Linda Ronstadt]*	Hoyt Axton	A&M 1497
8/24/74	8	16		2 Boney Fingers *[w/ Reneé Armand]*	Renee Armand/Hoyt Axton	A&M 1607
2/8/75	61	9		3 Nashville	Hoyt Axton	A&M 1657
5/10/75	57	7		4 Lion In The Winter *[w/ Linda Ronstadt]*	Hoyt Axton	A&M 1683
5/15/76	18	14		5 Flash Of Fire	Hoyt Axton/Catherine Smith	A&M 1811
4/16/77	57	7		6 You're The Hangnail In My Life	Woody Bowles/Mike Montgomery	MCA 40711
6/18/77	65	6		7 Little White Moon	Mark Dawson	MCA 40731
5/12/79	17	15		8 Della And The Dealer	Hoyt Axton	Jeremiah 1000
10/6/79	14	14		9 A Rusty Old Halo	Bob Merrill	Jeremiah 1001
1/12/80	21	12		10 Wild Bull Rider	Hoyt Axton	Jeremiah 1003
4/12/80	37	12		11 Evangelina	Hoyt Axton/Ken Higginbotham	Jeremiah 1005
10/11/80	80	3		12 Where Did The Money Go	Hoyt Axton/Mark Dawson	Jeremiah 1008
5/9/81	78	3		13 Flo's Yellow Rose from the TV series *Flo* starring Polly Holliday	Susie Glickman/Fred Werner	Elektra 47133
7/25/81	86	4		14 The Devil	Hoyt Axton	Jeremiah 1011

AZAR, Steve

Born on 4/11/1964 in Greenville, Mississippi. Male singer/songwriter/guitarist.

DEBUT	PEAK	WKS	GOLD	Country Chart Hit	Songwriter	Label (& Number)
3/16/96	51	10		1 Someday	Steve Azar/A.J. Masters/Bob Regan	River North
7/6/96	50	15		2 I Never Stopped Lovin' You above 2 from the album *Heartbreak Town* on River North 161172	Steve Azar/Jason Blume	River North
10/6/01+	2[1]	44		3 I Don't Have To Be Me ('Til Monday)	Steve Azar/R.C. Bannon/Jason Young	Mercury
8/3/02	28	25		4 Waitin' On Joe above 2 from the album *Waitin' On Joe* on Mercury 170269	Steve Azar	Mercury
6/4/05	47	11		5 Doin' It Right	Steve Azar/Tony Colton/A.J. Masters	Mercury

B

BACKROADS

Group from Tennessee. Led by singer/songwriter Jerry Marcum.

DEBUT	PEAK	WKS	GOLD	Country Chart Hit	Songwriter	Label (& Number)
2/19/83	72	5		So Close	Jerry Marcum	Soundwaves 4698

BACKTRACK Featuring John Hunt

Group from Texas. Led by singer/songwriter John Hunt.

DEBUT	PEAK	WKS	GOLD	Country Chart Hit	Songwriter	Label (& Number)
4/6/85	94	3		Mexico	John Hunt	Goldmine 11

BADALE, Andy

Born Angelo Badalamenti on 3/22/1937 in Brooklyn, New York. Composed several TV and movie scores.

DEBUT	PEAK	WKS	GOLD	Country Chart Hit	Songwriter	Label (& Number)
1/26/80	93	4		Nashville Beer Garden	Andy Badale/Virginia Johnson/Charlie Monk/Frank Stanton [I]	GP 577

BAILES, Eddy

Born on 4/21/1934 in Parkersburg, West Virginia. Died on 6/17/2002 (age 78). Male singer/guitarist.

DEBUT	PEAK	WKS	GOLD	Country Chart Hit	Songwriter	Label (& Number)
2/21/76	93	3		Love Isn't Love (Till You Give It Away)	Bobby Fischer/Ricci Mareno	Cin Kay 101

BAILEY, DeFord **HOF: 2005**

Born on 12/14/1899 in Smith County, Tennessee. Died on 7/2/1982 (age 82). Black singer/harmonica player. The first black superstar in country music.

OPRY: 1925

BAILEY, Glen

Born in 1952 in Thunder Bay, Ontario, Canada. Male singer.

DEBUT	PEAK	WKS	GOLD	Country Chart Hit	Songwriter	Label (& Number)
3/6/82	87	3		1 Stompin' On My Heart	Steve Reed	Yatahey 1221
6/26/82	85	3		2 Designer Jeans	Bob Keith/Ed Michaels	Yatahey 3024

BAILEY, Johnny

Born in Atlanta, Georgia. Male singer/songwriter.

DEBUT	PEAK	WKS	GOLD	Country Chart Hit	Songwriter	Label (& Number)
2/5/83	86	2		1 What's She Doing To My Mind /	Johnny Bailey	
2/5/83	flip	2		2 This Country Music's Driving Me Crazy	Johnny Fox	Soundwaves 4695

DEBUT	PEAK	WKS	GOLD	ARTIST / Country Chart Hit	Ranking / Songwriter	Label (& Number)

BAILEY, Judy

Born on 1/6/1955 in Winchester, Kentucky. Female singer.

DEBUT	PEAK	WKS	#	Country Chart Hit	Songwriter	Label (& Number)
11/29/80+	**10**	14	1	**Following The Feeling** *[w/ Moe Bandy]*	*Charlie Craig*	Columbia 11395
5/9/81	**56**	7	2	**Slow Country Dancin'**	*Len Green/Lorraine Walden*	Columbia 02045
10/3/81	**54**	7	3	**The Best Bedroom In Town**	*Charlie Craig*	Columbia 02505
2/12/83	**72**	4	4	**Tender Lovin' Lies**	*Dennis Adkins/Billy Lindsey*	Warner 29799
2/9/85	**96**	3	5	**There's A Lot Of Good About Goodbye**	*Rory Bourke/Dan Mitchell*	White Gold 22249

BAILEY, Lynn

Born on 4/18/1942 in Indianapolis, Indiana. Female singer.

DEBUT	PEAK	WKS	#	Country Chart Hit	Songwriter	Label (& Number)
4/5/80	**94**	2		**Cheater Fever**	*Ron Hellard/Lamar Morris*	Wartrace 613

BAILEY, Mary

Born in 1945 in Toronto, Ontario, Canada. Female singer/songwriter. Became **Shania Twain**'s first manager in the late 1980s.

DEBUT	PEAK	WKS	#	Country Chart Hit	Songwriter	Label (& Number)
8/15/81	**84**	3		**Too Much, Too Little, Too Late**	*Mary Bailey*	E & R 8101

BAILEY, Razzy — 1980s: #48 / All-Time: #157

Born Rasie Michael Bailey on 2/14/1939 in Five Points, Alabama. Male singer/songwriter/guitarist. First recorded for B&K label in 1949. Worked as a truck driver, insurance salesman and furniture salesman during the early 1960s. Formed the group Daily Bread in 1968. Formed the Aquarians in 1972. Recorded as Razzy for MGM in 1974.

DEBUT	PEAK	WKS	#	Country Chart Hit	Songwriter	Label (& Number)
10/30/76	**99**	2	1	**Keepin' Rosie Proud Of Me**	*Don Goodman/Troy Seals*	Erastus 526
8/12/78	**9**	15	2	**What Time Do You Have To Be Back To Heaven**	*Steve Pippin/Johnny Slate*	RCA 11338
12/23/78+	**6**	14	3	**Tonight She's Gonna Love Me (Like There Was No Tomorrow)**	*Steve Pippin/Johnny Slate*	RCA 11446
4/21/79	**6**	13	4	**If Love Had A Face**	*Steve Jobe/Steve Pippin*	RCA 11536
8/18/79	**10**	14	5	**I Ain't Got No Business Doin' Business Today**	*Danny Morrison/Johnny Slate*	RCA 11682
12/22/79+	**5**	14	6	**I Can't Get Enough Of You**	*Danny Morrison/Johnny Slate*	RCA 11885
4/19/80	**13**	14	7	**Too Old To Play Cowboy**	*Dave Kirby/Danny Morrison*	RCA 11954
8/2/80	**❶[1]**	15	8	**Loving Up A Storm**	*Danny Morrison/Johnny Slate*	RCA 12062
11/22/80+	**❶[1]**	17	9	**I Keep Coming Back /**	*Jim Hurt/Larry Keith/Johnny Slate*	
11/22/80+	**flip**	17	10	**True Life Country Music**	*Sam Lorber/Danny Morrison/Jeff Silbar*	RCA 12120
3/28/81	**❶[1]**	16	11	**Friends /**	*Danny Morrison/Johnny Slate*	
3/28/81	**flip**	16	12	**Anywhere There's A Jukebox**	*Razzy Bailey*	RCA 12199
7/11/81	**❶[1]**	18	13	**Midnight Hauler /**	*Tim DuBois/Wood Newton*	
7/11/81	**8**	18	14	**Scratch My Back (And Whisper In My Ear)**	*Earl Cage/Raymond Moore/Marcell Strong*	RCA 12268
12/19/81+	**❶[1]**	20	15	**She Left Love All Over Me**	*Chester Lester*	RCA 13007
4/10/82	**10**	15	16	**Everytime You Cross My Mind (You Break My Heart)**	*Larry Keith/Danny Morrison/Johnny Slate*	RCA 13084
8/21/82	**8**	17	17	**Love's Gonna Fall Here Tonight**	*Kendal Franceschi*	RCA 13290
12/4/82+	**30**	14	18	**Poor Boy**	*Dobie Gray/Mark Gray/Jerry Michael*	RCA 13383
4/30/83	**19**	13	19	**After The Great Depression**	*Razzy Bailey/Hank Cochran/Royce Porter*	RCA 13512
10/29/83	**62**	10	20	**This Is Just The First Day**	*Razzy Bailey/Hank Cochran/Royce Porter*	RCA 13630
2/25/84	**14**	17	21	**In The Midnight Hour**	*Steve Cropper/Wilson Pickett*	RCA 13718
8/4/84	**29**	14	22	**Knock On Wood**	*Steve Cropper/Eddie Floyd*	MCA 52421
12/8/84+	**43**	13	23	**Touchy Situation**	*Chester Lester*	MCA 52500
3/23/85	**51**	10	24	**Modern Day Marriages**	*Razzy Bailey*	MCA 52547
7/27/85	**78**	4	25	**Fightin' Fire With Fire**	*Bobby Harden*	MCA 52628
12/14/85+	**48**	9	26	**Old Blue Yodeler**	*Razzy Bailey*	MCA 52701
6/28/86	**63**	7	27	**Rockin' In The Parkin' Lot**	*Razzy Bailey/Mentor Williams*	MCA 52851
10/31/87	**69**	5	28	**If Love Ever Made A Fool**	*Clarence Boyd*	SOA 001
1/23/88	**58**	6	29	**Unattended Fire**	*Razzy Bailey/Rusty French*	SOA 002
12/24/88+	**73**	6	30	**Starting All Over Again**	*Phillip Mitchell*	SOA 003
4/29/89	**65**	5	31	**But You Will**	*Razzy Bailey/Con Fullam*	SOA 006

BAILLIE AND THE BOYS

Trio of songwriters/session singers: Kathie Baillie (born on 2/20/1951 in Morristown, New Jersey) and husband Michael Bonagura (born on 3/26/1953 in Newark, New Jersey) with Alan LeBoeuf. Baillie and Bonagura married on 8/29/1981. LeBoeuf starred as **Paul McCartney** in Broadway show *Beatlemania*. Group became a duo when LeBoeuf left in January 1989.

DEBUT	PEAK	WKS	#	Country Chart Hit	Songwriter	Label (& Number)
4/18/87	**9**	21	1	**Oh Heart**	S:18 *Kathie Baillie/Michael Bonagura/Don Schlitz*	RCA 5130
8/8/87	**18**	16	2	**He's Letting Go**	S:29 *Pat Bunch/Mary Ann Kennedy/Pam Rose*	RCA 5227
12/19/87+	**9**	18	3	**Wilder Days**	S:23 *Craig Bickhardt/Michael Bonagura*	RCA 5327
10/1/88+	**5**	27	4	**Long Shot**	S:9 *Don Schlitz/Gary Scruggs*	RCA 8631
2/4/89	**8**	21	5	**She Deserves You**	*Kathie Baillie/Michael Bonagura/Don Schlitz*	RCA 8796
7/1/89	**4**	24	6	**(I Wish I Had A) Heart Of Stone**	*Wayland Holyfield/Richard Leigh*	RCA 8944
11/4/89+	**9**	26	7	**I Can't Turn The Tide**	*Kathie Baillie/Craig Bickhardt/Michael Bonagura*	RCA 9076
4/14/90	**23**	14	8	**Perfect**	*Mark Nevin*	RCA
8/11/90	**5**	21	9	**Fool Such As I**	*William Trader*	RCA
1/5/91	**18**	20	10	**Treat Me Like A Stranger**	*Michael Bonagura/Peter McCann*	RCA

above 3 from the album *The Lights Of Home* on RCA 2114

DEBUT	PEAK	WKS	GOLD	ARTIST / Country Chart Hit	Songwriter	Label (& Number)
				BAKER, Adam		
				Born on 5/26/1964 in Oklahoma City, Oklahoma; raised in Edmond, Oklahoma. Male singer/songwriter.		
3/9/85	**97**	3		1 **I Can See Him In Her Eyes**	*David Chamberlain/Becky Jones*	Signature 22484
2/8/86	**48**	10		2 **In Love With Her**	*Adam Baker*	Avista 8610
10/18/86	**46**	9		3 **Weren't You Listening**	*Michael Garvin/Tom Shapiro/Chris Waters*	Avista 8602
2/7/87	**54**	7		4 **You've Got A Right**	*Bruce Channel/Kieran Kane*	Avista 8703
10/31/87	**63**	4		5 **Standing Invitation**	*Ron Hellard/Bucky Jones/Curly Putman*	Avista 8704
				BAKER, Butch		
				Born on 10/22/1958 in Sweetwater, Tennessee. Male singer/songwriter/guitarist. Also see **Tomorrow's World**.		
8/4/84	**80**	3		1 **Burn Georgia Burn (There's A Fire In Your Soul)**	*Jim Elliott*	Mercury 880020
10/27/84	**56**	7		2 **Thinking 'Bout Leaving**	*Randy Albright/Butch Paulson/Mark D. Sanders*	Mercury 880256
8/9/86	**41**	14		3 **That's What Her Memory Is For**	*J.D. Hicks/Roger Murrah/John Schweers*	Mercury 884857
11/15/86	**53**	9		4 **Your Loving Side**	*Roger Murrah/John Schweers/Carson Whitsett*	Mercury 888133
5/16/87	**51**	10		5 **Don't It Make You Wanta Go Home**	*Joe South*	Mercury 888543
11/28/87	**60**	10		6 **I'll Fall In Love Again**	*Todd Cerney/Austin Roberts*	Mercury 888926
7/2/88	**69**	5		7 **Party People**	*Leo Clyde*	Mercury 870486
9/2/89	**64**	6		8 **Our Little Corner**	*Chuck Leonard/Bill McCorvey*	Mercury 874746
11/18/89	**66**	9		9 **Wonderful Tonight**	*Eric Clapton*	Mercury 876226
12/1/90+	**56**	9		10 **It Wasn't You, It Wasn't Me** ***[w/ Daniele Alexander]***	*Daniele Alexander/Austin Gardner*	Mercury
				BAKER, Carroll		
				Born on 3/4/1949 in Port Medway, Nova Scotia, Canada. Female singer/songwriter. Hosted Canadian TV show *Sounds Good Country*.		
7/4/81	**82**	3		1 **Mama What Does Cheatin' Mean**	*Buddy Pahl*	Excelsior 1013
7/6/85	**95**	1		2 **It Always Hurts Like The First Time**	*Steve Bogard/Rory Bourke*	Tembo 8520
				BAKER, George, Selection		
				Born Johannes Bouwens on 12/9/1944 in the Netherlands. His Selection included Lydia Bont (female vocals), Jan Hop, Jacobus Greuter, George The and Jan Visser.		
1/10/76	**33**	15		**Paloma Blanca**	*George Baker*	Warner 8115
				BAKER, "Two Ton"		
				Born Richard Baker on 5/2/1916 in Chicago, Illinois. Died on 5/4/1975 (age 59). Novelty pianist/bandleader. Disc jockey at WGN radio beginning in 1944; hosted a children's TV program in Chicago in the 1950s.		
2/9/46	**2^{1}**	16		**Sioux City Sue** ***[w/ Hoosier Hot Shots]***	*Ray Freedman/Dick Thomas* **[N]**	Decca 18745
				BAKER & MYERS		
				Songwriting team of Gary Baker and Frank J. Myers. Baker was a member of **The Shooters**.		
9/30/95	**67**	6		1 **These Arms**	*Gary Baker/Frank J. Myers*	Curb
2/10/96	**48**	17		2 **Years From Here**	*Gary Baker/Frank J. Myers/Jerry Williams*	Curb
8/24/96	**71**	1		3 **A Little Bit Of Honey**	*Gary Baker/Frank J. Myers*	Curb
				all of above from the album *Baker & Myers* on Curb 77806		
				BALL, David		
				Born on 7/9/1953 in Rock Hill, South Carolina. Male singer/songwriter/guitarist.		
5/7/88	**46**	10		1 **Steppin' Out**	*David Ball/Mark Wright*	RCA 6899
8/20/88	**55**	7		2 **You Go, You're Gone**	*David Ball/Frank Dycus/Mark Wright*	RCA 8636
9/2/89	**64**	4		3 **Gift Of Love**	*David Ball/Frank Dycus*	RCA 8975
4/16/94	**2^{1}**	20		4 **Thinkin' Problem**	*David Ball/Allen Shamblin/Stuart Ziff*	Warner
9/10/94	**7**	20		5 **When The Thought Of You Catches Up With Me**	*David Ball*	Warner
1/14/95	**11**	20		6 **Look What Followed Me Home**	*David Ball/Tommy Polk*	Warner
5/20/95	**48**	10		7 **What Do You Want With His Love**	*David Ball/William Jefferies*	Warner
9/16/95	**50**	9		8 **Honky Tonk Healin'**	*David Ball/Tommy Polk*	Warner
				above 5 from the album *Thinkin' Problem* on Warner 45562		
5/4/96	**49**	9		9 **Circle Of Friends**	S:18 *David Ball/Billy Spencer*	Warner
8/10/96	**67**	3		10 **Hangin' In And Hangin' On**	*Ray Herndon/Terry McBride/Gary Nicholson/Billy Thomas*	Warner
				above 2 from the album *Starlite Lounge* on Warner 46244		
5/1/99	**47**	10		11 **Watching My Baby Not Coming Back**	*David Ball/Brad Paisley*	Warner
8/7/99	**67**	1		12 **I Want To With You**	*Steve Bogard/Jeff Stevens*	Warner
				above 2 from the album *Play* on Warner 47270		
9/8/01	**2^{1}**	22		13 **Riding With Private Malone**	*Wood Newton/Tom Shepherd*	Dualtone
				from the album *Amigo* on Dualtone 01109		
10/30/04	**60**	1		14 **Louisiana Melody**	*David Ball/Allen Shamblin*	Quarterback
				from the album *Freewheeler* on Quarterback 79200		
				BALL, Marcia		
				Born Marcia Mouton on 3/20/1949 in Orange, Texas; raised in Vinton, Louisiana. Female singer.		
11/18/78	**91**	2		**I'm A Fool To Care**	*Ted Daffan*	Capitol 4633
				BALLARD, Roger		
				Born in Kentwood, Louisiana. Male singer/songwriter.		
9/25/93	**68**	3		**Two Steps In The Right Direction**	*Roger Ballard/Don Goodman/A.J. Masters*	Atlantic
				from the album *Little Piece Of Heaven* on Atlantic 82470		
				BALLEW, Michael		
				Born in Austin, Texas. Male singer/songwriter/guitarist.		
11/7/81	**67**	6		1 **Your Daddy Don't Live In Heaven (He's In Houston)**	*Michael Ballew/Bob Moulds*	Liberty 1437
2/13/82	**71**	5		2 **Pretending Fool**	*Michael Ballew/John English*	Liberty 1447

Billboard DEBUT	PEAK	WKS	GOLD	ARTIST / Ranking / Country Chart Hit	Songwriter	Label (& Number)

BAMA BAND, The

Backing band for **Hank Williams, Jr.**: **Lamar Morris** (vocals, guitar), Wayne "Animal" Turner (guitar), Edward "Cowboy" Long (steel guitar), Paul Eugene "Dixie" Hatfield (keyboards), Jerry McKinney (sax), Vernon Derrick (fiddle), Ray Barrickman (bass) and William Claude Marshall (drums). Billy Earhart (of **Amazing Rhythm Aces**) replaced Hatfield in 1986.

DEBUT	PEAK	WKS	Country Chart Hit	Songwriter	Label (& Number)
12/18/82+	**54**	9	1 **Dallas**	*Bill Boutwell/John Crocker/Jerry Puckett*	Oasis 1
5/7/83	**56**	9	2 **Tijuana Sunrise**	*Dixie Hatfield*	Soundwaves 4707
7/20/85	**60**	8	3 **What Used To Be Crazy**	*Joe Chambers/Larry Jenkins*	Compleat 144
3/29/86	**70**	4	4 **I've Changed My Mind**	*David Steen*	Compleat 152
1/31/87	**64**	7	5 **Suddenly Single**	*Max D. Barnes/Troy Seals*	Compleat 163
8/27/88	**71**	5	6 **Southern Accent**	*Robert Alley/Patti Flores*	Mercury 870603
12/24/88+	**69**	6	7 **Real Old-Fashioned Broken Heart**	*Bob McDill*	Mercury 872150
3/18/89	**87**	3	8 **When We Get Back To The Farm**	*Michael Garvin/Tom Shapiro/Chris Waters*	Mercury 872650

BANDANA

Group formed in Nashville: Lon Wilson (vocals), **Tim Mensy** and Joe Van Dyke (guitars), Jerry Fox (bass) and Jerry Ray Johnston (drums). In 1986 Mensy, Van Dyke and Johnston left, replaced by Michael Black and Billy Kemp (guitars) and Bob Mummert (drums). Disbanded in 1987.

DEBUT	PEAK	WKS	Country Chart Hit	Songwriter	Label (& Number)
1/9/82	**37**	12	1 **Guilty Eyes**	*Kent Blazy/Jim Dowell*	Warner 49872
5/1/82	**61**	7	2 **Cheatin' State Of Mind**	*Jerry Fox/Joe Van Dyke/Lonnie Wilson*	Warner 50045
8/21/82	**17**	18	3 **The Killin' Kind**	*Jim Dowell/Ronnie Friend*	Warner 29936
12/11/82+	**29**	15	4 **I Can't Get Over You (Getting Over Me)**	*Jim Dowell/Ronnie Friend*	Warner 29831
9/3/83	**18**	18	5 **Outside Lookin' In**	*Jerry Fox/Lonnie Wilson*	Warner 29524
4/14/84	**26**	13	6 **Better Our Hearts Should Bend (Than Break)**	*Bill McCarthy*	Warner 29315
8/18/84	**52**	12	7 **All I Wanna Do (Is Make Love To You)**	*Kieran Kane*	Warner 29226
5/4/85	**46**	13	8 **It's Just Another Heartache**	*Steve Bogard/Rick Giles*	Warner 29029
9/14/85	**37**	12	9 **Lovin' Up A Storm**	*Jerry Fox/Lonnie Wilson*	Warner 28939
5/17/86	**54**	9	10 **Touch Me**	*Gary Harrison/Dave Robbins/Lonnie Wilson*	Warner 28721

BANDIT BAND, The

Group from Lexington, Kentucky.

DEBUT	PEAK	WKS	Country Chart Hit	Songwriter	Label (& Number)
4/4/87	**73**	4	**Do You Wanna Fall In Love**	*Ken Bell/Rick Cox*	Pegasus 108

BANDIT BROTHERS

Studio group assembled by producers John Range and Karl Shannon.

DEBUT	PEAK	WKS	Country Chart Hit	Songwriter	Label (& Number)
4/6/91	**57**	5	**Women** (parody of "Men" by **The Forester Sisters**)	*Robert Byrne/Alan Schulman* **[N]**	Curb

BANDY, Charlie

Born in 1954 in Grundy, Virginia. Male singer. No relation to Moe Bandy.

DEBUT	PEAK	WKS	Country Chart Hit	Songwriter	Label (& Number)
7/28/84	**95**	2	**Tenamock Georgia**	*J.C. Cunningham*	RCI 2386

BANDY, Moe — 1980s: #33 / All-Time: #68

Born Marion Bandy on 2/12/1944 in Meridian, Mississippi; raised in San Antonio, Texas. Male singer/guitarist. Played in his father's band, the Mission City Playboys; also worked as a rodeo rider. Regular on the local San Antonio TV show *Country Corner* in 1973. Started his own theater in Branson, Missouri.

CMA: Vocal Duo (w/ Joe Stampley) 1980

DEBUT	PEAK	WKS	Country Chart Hit	Songwriter	Label (& Number)
3/30/74	**17**	15	1 **I Just Started Hatin' Cheatin' Songs Today**	*A.L. "Doodle" Owens/Whitey Shafer*	GRC 2006
8/3/74	**24**	11	2 **Honky Tonk Amnesia**	*A.L. "Doodle" Owens/Whitey Shafer*	GRC 2024
11/23/74+	**7**	14	3 **It Was Always So Easy (To Find An Unhappy Woman)**	*A.L. "Doodle" Owens/Whitey Shafer*	GRC 2036
3/22/75	**13**	11	4 **Don't Anyone Make Love At Home Anymore**	*Dallas Frazier*	GRC 2055
6/28/75	**7**	16	5 **Bandy The Rodeo Clown**	*Lefty Frizzell/Whitey Shafer*	GRC 2070
12/20/75+	**2**[2]	15	6 **Hank Williams, You Wrote My Life**	*Paul Craft*	Columbia 10265
4/17/76	**27**	10	7 **The Biggest Airport In The World**	*Whitey Shafer*	Columbia 10313
7/4/76	**11**	14	8 **Here I Am Drunk Again**	*Clyde Beavers/Autry Inman*	Columbia 10361
10/30/76+	**11**	15	9 **She Took More Than Her Share**	*Whitey Shafer*	Columbia 10428
3/5/77	**9**	14	10 **I'm Sorry For You, My Friend**	*Hank Williams*	Columbia 10487
6/18/77	**13**	12	11 **Cowboys Ain't Supposed To Cry**	*Jack Owen*	Columbia 10558
10/8/77	**11**	14	12 **She Just Loved The Cheatin' Out Of Me**	*A.L. "Doodle" Owens/Whitey Shafer*	Columbia 10619
1/28/78	**13**	14	13 **Soft Lights And Hard Country Music**	*Whitey Shafer*	Columbia 10671
5/20/78	**11**	14	14 **That's What Makes The Juke Box Play**	*Jimmy Work*	Columbia 10735
9/16/78	**7**	13	15 **Two Lonely People**	*Tom Benjamin/Ed Penney*	Columbia 10820
1/27/79	**2**[2]	15	16 **It's A Cheating Situation** (**Janie Fricke** (backing vocal))	*Curly Putman/Sonny Throckmorton*	Columbia 10889
6/16/79	**9**	14	17 **Barstool Mountain**	*Wayne Carson/Donn Tankersley*	Columbia 10974
7/14/79	**❶**[1]	16	18 **Just Good Ol' Boys** *[w/ Joe Stampley]*	*Ansley Fleetwood*	Columbia 11027
10/6/79	**❶**[1]	14	19 **I Cheated Me Right Out Of You**	*Bobby Barker*	Columbia 11090
11/17/79+	**7**	14	20 **Holding The Bag** *[w/ Joe Stampley]*	*Pat Bunch/Buck Moore*	Columbia 11147
2/2/80	**13**	12	21 **One Of A Kind**	*Bobby Fischer/Sonny Throckmorton*	Columbia 11184
4/12/80	**11**	15	22 **Tell Ole I Ain't Here, He Better Get On Home** *[w/ Joe Stampley]*	*Wayne Kemp*	Columbia 11244
4/26/80	**22**	12	23 **The Champ**	*Dave Kirby/Warren Robb*	Columbia 11255
8/2/80	**10**	15	24 **Yesterday Once More**	*Jim Mundy/Peggy White*	Columbia 11305

DEBUT	PEAK	WKS	GOLD	ARTIST / Ranking / Country Chart Hit	Songwriter	Label (& Number)
				BANDY, Moe — cont'd		
11/29/80+	**10**	14		25 **Following The Feeling** *[w/ Judy Bailey]*	*Charlie Craig*	Columbia 11395
3/14/81	**10**	15		26 **Hey Joe** (Hey Moe) *[w/ Joe Stampley]*	*Boudleaux Bryant*	Columbia 60508
4/18/81	**15**	14		27 **My Woman Loves The Devil Out Of Me**	*Bobby Barker*	Columbia 02039
8/1/81	**12**	14		28 **Honky Tonk Queen** *[w/ Joe Stampley]*	*Robby Hicks*	Columbia 02198
10/17/81+	**10**	17		29 **Rodeo Romeo**	*Dan Mitchell*	Columbia 02532
2/27/82	**21**	16		30 **Someday Soon**	*Ian Tyson*	Columbia 02735
6/19/82	**4**	18		31 **She's Not Really Cheatin'** (She's Just Gettin' Even)	*Randy Shaffer*	Columbia 02966
10/23/82+	**12**	19		32 **Only If There Is Another You**	*Dan Mitchell*	Columbia 03309
3/5/83	**19**	15		33 **I Still Love You In The Same Ol' Way**	*Virgil Warner*	Columbia 03625
6/25/83	**10**	18		34 **Let's Get Over Them Together** *[w/ Becky Hobbs]*	*Charlie Craig/Keith Stegall*	Columbia 03970
11/5/83	**34**	16		35 **You're Gonna Lose Her Like That**	*Peggy Forman/Wayne Forman*	Columbia 04204
2/18/84	**31**	13		36 **It Took A Lot Of Drinkin'** (To Get That Woman Over Me)	*Byron Gallimore/Blake Mevis/Bill Shore*	Columbia 04353
6/2/84	**8**	16		37 **Where's The Dress** *[w/ Joe Stampley]*	*George Cummings/Bucky Lindsey/Tony Stampley* [N]	Columbia 04477
8/4/84	**12**	22		38 **Woman Your Love**	A:8 / S:12 *Bill Shore/David Wills*	Columbia 04466
10/13/84	**36**	10		39 **The Boy's Night Out** *[w/ Joe Stampley]*	*David Rosson/Joe Stampley/Tony Stampley*	Columbia 04601
1/26/85	**48**	10		40 **Daddy's Honky Tonk** *[w/ Joe Stampley]*	*Bobby Keel/Buck Moore*	Columbia 04756
4/20/85	**58**	8		41 **Still On A Roll** *[w/ Joe Stampley]*	*John Greenebaum/Becky Hobbs/Blake Mevis*	Columbia 04843
8/10/85	**45**	14		42 **Barroom Roses**	*Byron Gallimore/Blake Mevis/Bill Shore*	Columbia 05438
11/15/86	**42**	14		43 **One Man Band**	*Ken Bell/Bud McGuire*	MCA/Curb 52950
2/28/87	**6**	27		44 **Till I'm Too Old To Die Young**	A:10 / S:11 *Scott Dooley/John Hadley/Kevin Welch*	MCA/Curb 53033
8/1/87	**11**	27		45 **You Haven't Heard The Last Of Me**	S:14 *Eric Kaz/Tom Snow*	MCA/Curb 53132
1/30/88	**8**	21		46 **Americana**	S:11 *Larry Alderman/Richard Fagan/Patti Ryan*	Curb 10504
6/25/88	**47**	10		47 **Ashes In The Wind**	*Hank Cochran/Jeff Tweel*	Curb 10510
9/10/88	**21**	19		48 **I Just Can't Say No To You**	*Steve Gibson/Parker McGee*	Curb 10513
2/25/89	**34**	13		49 **Many Mansions**	*Carol Etheridge/Alice Randall/Mark D. Sanders*	Curb 10524
6/10/89	**53**	8		50 **Brotherly Love**	*Tim Nichols/Jimmy Stewart*	Curb 10537
9/16/89	**49**	10		51 **This Night Won't Last Forever**	*Roy Freeland/Bill LaBounty*	Curb 10555
				BANNON, R.C.		
				Born Daniel Shipley on 5/2/1945 in Dallas, Texas. Male singer/songwriter/guitarist. Married to **Louise Mandrell** from 1979-91.		
7/30/77	**99**	1		1 **Southbound**	*R.C. Bannon/Harlan Sanders*	Columbia 10570
10/1/77	**90**	4		2 **Rainbows And Horseshoes**	*R.C. Bannon*	Columbia 10612
12/24/77+	**33**	12		3 **It Doesn't Matter Anymore**	*Paul Anka*	Columbia 10655
4/22/78	**64**	7		4 (The Truth Is) **We're Livin' A Lie**	*R.C. Bannon/John Bettis*	Columbia 10714
11/11/78	**64**	5		5 **Somebody's Gonna Do It Tonight**	*Ben Peters*	Columbia 10847
3/10/79	**46**	8		6 **I Thought You'd Never Ask** *[w/ Louise Mandrell]*	*Don Cook/Curly Putman*	Epic 50668
6/2/79	**13**	12		7 **Reunited** *[w/ Louise Mandrell]*	*Dino Fekaris/Freddie Perren*	Epic 50717
9/22/79	**26**	11		8 **Winners And Losers**	*Ken Bell/Terry Skinner/J.L. Wallace*	Columbia 11081
11/17/79	**48**	8		9 **We Love Each Other** *[w/ Louise Mandrell]*	*Buddy Killen*	Epic 50789
3/1/80	**65**	5		10 **Lovely Lonely Lady**	*Wayland Holyfield/Mark Wright*	Columbia 11210
5/24/80	**61**	7		11 **If You're Serious About Cheatin'**	*R.C. Bannon/John Schweers*	Columbia 11267
9/13/80	**36**	10		12 **Never Be Anyone Else** *[w/ Louise Mandrell]*	*Baker Knight*	Columbia 11346
11/28/81+	**35**	11		13 **Where There's Smoke There's Fire** *[w/ Louise Mandrell]*	*Kye Fleming/Dennis W. Morgan*	RCA 12359
1/23/82	**46**	11		14 **Til Something Better Comes Along**	*R.C. Bannon/John Bettis*	RCA 13029
6/5/82	**56**	7		15 **Our Wedding Band** *[w/ Louise Mandrell]* /	*Don Pfrimmer/Charles Quillen*	
6/5/82	**flip**	7		16 **Just Married** *[w/ Louise Mandrell]*	*Jack Clement/Carol Hall*	RCA 13095
12/11/82+	**35**	7		17 **Christmas Is Just A Song For Us This Year** *[w/ Louise Mandrell]*	*R.C. Bannon* [X]	RCA 13358
				BARBER, Ava		
				Born on 6/28/1954 in Knoxville, Tennessee. Female singer/pianist. Regular on **Lawrence Welk**'s TV show from 1974-82.		
2/12/77	**70**	8		1 **Waitin' At The End Of Your Run**	*Jerry Foster/Bill Rice*	Ranwood 1071
6/18/77	**92**	2		2 **Your Love Is My Refuge**	*Wayland Holyfield*	Ranwood 1077
8/13/77	**69**	8		3 **Don't Take My Sunshine Away**	*Jerry Foster/Bill Rice*	Ranwood 1080
2/4/78	**14**	14		4 **Bucket To The South**	*Gail Davies*	Ranwood 1083
6/17/78	**44**	7		5 **You're Gonna Love Love**	*Wayland Holyfield*	Ranwood 1085
10/28/78	**75**	6		6 **Healin'**	*Bob McDill*	Ranwood 1087
2/28/81	**70**	5		7 **I Think I Could Love You Better Than She Did**	*Debbie Hupp/Bob Morrison*	Oak 1029
				BARBER, Debra		
				Born on 11/3/1953 in Tupelo, Mississippi. Female singer.		
3/22/75	**98**	1		1 **You Can't Follow Where He's Been** /	*James Gilreath/Danny Walls*	
3/29/75	**97**	1		2 **Help Yourself To Me**	*Bucky Jones/Royce Porter*	RCA Victor 10190
				BARBER, Glenn		
				Born Martin Glenn Barber on 2/2/1935 in Hollis, Oklahoma; raised in Pasadena, Texas. Singer/songwriter/multi-instrumentalist.		
1/25/64	**48**	2		1 **How Can I Forget You**	*Glenn Barber*	Sims 148
8/22/64	**42**	7		2 **If Anyone Can Show Cause** /	*Adrian Roland*	
8/29/64	**27**	9		3 **Stronger Than Dirt**	*Glenn Barber*	Starday 676
11/9/68	**41**	8		4 **Don't Worry 'Bout The Mule** (Just Load The Wagon)	*Glenn Barber*	Hickory 1517
9/20/69	**24**	11		5 **Kissed By The Rain, Warmed By The Sun**	*Gene Thomas*	Hickory 1545
1/10/70	**28**	11		6 **She Cheats On Me**	*Glenn Barber*	Hickory 1557
6/20/70	**72**	2		7 **Poison Red Berries**	*Mickey Newbury*	Hickory 1568
1/16/71	**75**	2		8 **Yes, Dear, There Is A Virginia**	*Doug Kershaw*	Hickory 1585
3/25/72	**28**	12		9 **I'm The Man On Susie's Mind**	*Glenn Barber/Joe Melson*	Hickory 1626

DEBUT	PEAK	WKS	GOLD	ARTIST / Country Chart Hit	Songwriter	Label (& Number)
				BARBER, Glenn — cont'd		
8/5/72	**23**	12		10 **Unexpected Goodbye**	*Glenn Barber/Joe Melson*	Hickory 1645
1/6/73	**67**	4		11 **Yes Ma'm (I Found Her In A Honky Tonk)**	*Glenn Barber*	Hickory 1653
9/8/73	**61**	8		12 **Country Girl (I Love You Still)**	*Eddy Raven*	Hickory/MGM 302
12/29/73+	**45**	11		13 **Daddy Number Two**	*Glenn Barber/Joe Melson*	Hickory/MGM 311
4/13/74	**65**	7		14 **You Only Live Once (In Awhile)**	*Mickey Newbury*	Hickory/MGM 316
11/26/77	**79**	6		15 **(You Better Be) One Hell Of A Woman**	*Glenn Barber*	Groovy 102
1/14/78	**67**	6		16 **Cry, Cry Darling**	*Joe Miller/Jimmy Newman*	Groovy 103
9/30/78	**30**	10		17 **What's The Name Of That Song?**	*Betty Barber/Glenn Barber*	Century 21 100
1/6/79	**27**	10		18 **Love Songs Just For You**	*Marsha Barber/Joe Melson*	Century 21 101
4/14/79	**76**	2		19 **Everybody Wants To Disco**	*Jim Mundy*	MMI 1029
6/23/79	**70**	4		20 **Woman's Touch**	*Ken Bell/Terry Skinner/J.L. Wallace*	MMI 1031
8/16/80	**74**	5		21 **First Love Feelings**	*Betty Ann Barber/Glenn Barber*	Sunbird 7551

BARE, Bobby **1960s: #23 / 1970s: #40 / All-Time: #54**

Born on 4/7/1935 in Ironton, Ohio. Male singer/songwriter/guitarist. Recorded the song "The All American Boy" which hit #2 on the pop charts in 1959, credited to the song's co-writer Bill Parsons. Served in the U.S. Army from 1958-61. Acted in the movie *A Distant Trumpet*. Hosted TNN's *Bobby Bare and Friends*. Father of **Bobby Bare Jr.** His daughter Cari, heard on "Singin' In The Kitchen," died of heart failure in 1976 at age 15. Also see **Heart Of Nashville** and **Some Of Chet's Friends**.

OPRY: 1965

DEBUT	PEAK	WKS	GOLD	Country Chart Hit	Songwriter	Label (& Number)
9/15/62	**18**	8		1 **Shame On Me**	*Bill Enis/Lawton Williams*	RCA Victor 8032
7/6/63	**6**	18		2 **Detroit City** Grammy: Single	*Danny Dill/Mel Tillis*	RCA Victor 8183
10/26/63+	**5**	16		3 **500 Miles Away From Home**	*Bobby Bare/Charlie Williams*	RCA Victor 8238
2/8/64	**4**	17		4 **Miller's Cave**	*Jack Clement*	RCA Victor 8294
6/6/64	**47**	3		5 **Have I Stayed Away Too Long**	*Frank Loesser*	RCA Victor 8358
11/14/64+	**3^{2}**	19		6 **Four Strong Winds**	*Ian Tyson*	RCA Victor 8443
3/13/65	**11**	12		7 **A Dear John Letter** *[w/ Skeeter Davis]*	*Billy Barton/Fuzzy Owen/Lewis Talley*	RCA Victor 8496
3/27/65	**30**	8		8 **Times Are Gettin' Hard**	*Bobby Bare*	RCA Victor 8509
6/5/65	**7**	16		9 **It's Alright**	*Mac Gayden/Jerry Tuttle*	RCA Victor 8571
10/2/65	**31**	6		10 **Just To Satisfy You**	*Don Bowman/Waylon Jennings*	RCA Victor 8654
11/20/65+	**26**	12		11 **Talk Me Some Sense**	*Keith Colley/Nancie Mantz*	RCA Victor 8699
3/12/66	**34**	6		12 **In The Same Old Way**	*Spooner Oldham/Dan Penn*	RCA Victor 8758
6/25/66	**5**	20		13 **The Streets Of Baltimore**	*Tompall Glaser/Harlan Howard*	RCA Victor 8851
10/15/66	**5**	17		14 **The Game Of Triangles** *[w/ Norma Jean & Liz Anderson]*	*Cy Coben*	RCA Victor 8963
11/5/66	**38**	11		15 **Homesick**	*Billy Cole*	RCA Victor 8988
3/4/67	**16**	13		16 **Charleston Railroad Tavern**	*Jerry Smith*	RCA Victor 9098
5/20/67	**14**	16		17 **Come Kiss Me Love**	*Ian Campbell*	RCA Victor 9191
10/7/67	**15**	13		18 **The Piney Wood Hills**	*Buffy Sainte-Marie*	RCA Victor 9314
3/2/68	**15**	11		19 **Find Out What's Happening**	*Jerry Crutchfield*	RCA Victor 9450
7/27/68	**14**	13		20 **A Little Bit Later On Down The Line**	*Chip Taylor*	RCA Victor 9568
10/26/68	**16**	12		21 **The Town That Broke My Heart**	*Tom T. Hall*	RCA Victor 9643
3/15/69	**4**	17		22 **(Margie's At) The Lincoln Park Inn**	*Tom T. Hall*	RCA Victor 0110
8/2/69	**19**	11		23 **Which One Will It Be**	*Hank Cochran/Glenn Martin*	RCA Victor 0202
11/15/69	**16**	12		24 **God Bless America Again**	*Bobby Bare/Boyce Hawkins*	RCA Victor 0264
1/24/70	**22**	7		25 **Your Husband, My Wife** *[w/ Skeeter Davis]*	*Irwin Levine/Toni Wine*	RCA Victor 9789
8/8/70	**3^{2}**	16		26 **How I Got To Memphis**	*Tom T. Hall*	Mercury 73097
12/26/70+	**7**	17		27 **Come Sundown**	*Kris Kristofferson*	Mercury 73148
5/15/71	**8**	15		28 **Please Don't Tell Me How The Story Ends**	*Kris Kristofferson*	Mercury 73203
9/25/71	**57**	9		29 **Short And Sweet**	*Billy Joe Shaver*	Mercury 73236
4/1/72	**13**	14		30 **What Am I Gonna Do**	*Carole King/Toni Stern*	Mercury 73279
8/26/72	**12**	14		31 **Sylvia's Mother**	*Shel Silverstein*	Mercury 73317
1/6/73	**25**	11		32 **I Hate Goodbyes**	*Jerry Foster/Bill Rice*	RCA Victor 0866
4/14/73	**11**	15		33 **Ride Me Down Easy**	*Billy Joe Shaver*	RCA Victor 0918
9/8/73	**30**	13		34 **You Know Who**	*Shel Silverstein*	RCA Victor 0063
12/22/73+	**2^{2}**	16		35 **Daddy What If** *[w/ Bobby Bare Jr.]*	*Shel Silverstein* **[N]**	RCA Victor 0197
5/4/74	**❶^{1}**	18		36 **Marie Laveau**	*Shel Silverstein/Baxter Taylor* **[L]**	RCA Victor 0261
11/16/74+	**29**	13		37 **Singin' In The Kitchen** *[w/ The Family]*	*Shel Silverstein* **[N]**	RCA Victor 10096
3/15/75	**23**	11		38 **Back In Huntsville Again**	*Shel Silverstein*	RCA Victor 10223
7/19/75	**18**	12		39 **Alimony**	*Shel Silverstein*	RCA Victor 10318
10/25/75	**29**	11		40 **Cowboys And Daddys**	*Marty Cooper*	RCA Victor 10409
3/13/76	**13**	14		41 **The Winner**	*Shel Silverstein*	RCA Victor 10556
7/10/76	**23**	11		42 **Put A Little Lovin' On Me**	*Bob McDill*	RCA Victor 10718
10/9/76	**17**	11		43 **Dropkick Me, Jesus**	*Paul Craft*	RCA 10790
1/8/77	**30**	9		44 **Vegas** *[w/ Jeannie Bare]*	*Shel Silverstein*	RCA 10852
3/12/77	**21**	14		45 **Look Who I'm Cheating On Tonight /**	*Bob McDill*	
3/12/77	**flip**	14		46 **If You Think I'm Crazy Now (You Should Have Seen Me When I Was A Kid)**	*Bob McDill*	RCA 10902
7/30/77	**85**	3		47 **Red-Neck Hippie Romance**	*Shel Silverstein*	RCA 11037
4/15/78	**29**	11		48 **Too Many Nights Alone**	*Shel Silverstein/Even Stevens*	Columbia 10690
10/14/78	**11**	12		49 **Sleep Tight, Good Night Man**	*Sam Lorber/Jeff Silbar*	Columbia 10831

DEBUT	PEAK	WKS	GOLD	ARTIST Ranking / Country Chart Hit	Songwriter	Label (& Number)
				BARE, Bobby — cont'd		
1/27/79	**23**	11		50 **Healin'**	*Bob McDill*	Columbia 10891
6/9/79	**42**	8		51 **Till I Gain Control Again**	*Rodney Crowell*	Columbia 10998
9/8/79	**17**	12		52 **No Memories Hangin' Round** ***[w/ Rosanne Cash]***	*Rodney Crowell*	Columbia 11045
1/5/80	**11**	14		53 **Numbers**	*Shel Silverstein* **[L-N]**	Columbia 11170
4/26/80	**31**	12		54 **Tequila Sheila**	*Mac Davis/Shel Silverstein* **[L]**	Columbia 11259
10/4/80	**41**	8		55 **Food Blues**	*Shel Silverstein*	Columbia 11365
12/20/80+	**19**	12		56 **Willie Jones** — **Charlie Daniels** (backing vocal)	*Charlie Daniels*	Columbia 11408
4/25/81	**28**	13		57 **Learning To Live Again**	*Bob McDill*	Columbia 02038
8/8/81	**28**	11		58 **Take Me As I Am (Or Let Me Go)**	*Boudleaux Bryant*	Columbia 02414
11/7/81	**35**	11		59 **Dropping Out Of Sight**	*Tom T. Hall*	Columbia 02577
1/30/82	**18**	16		60 **New Cut Road**	*Guy Clark*	Columbia 02690
5/29/82	**31**	11		61 **If You Ain't Got Nothin' (You Ain't Got Nothin' To Lose)**	*Red Lane/Dan Wilson*	Columbia 02895
8/21/82	**37**	11		62 **(I'm Not) A Candle In The Wind**	*Bill Rice/Mary Sharon Rice*	Columbia 03149
11/20/82	**83**	3		63 **Praise The Lord And Send Me The Money**	*Hugh Moffatt*	Columbia 03334
3/12/83	**30**	14		64 **It's A Dirty Job** ***[w/ Lacy J. Dalton]***	*Don Cook/Rafe Van Hoy*	Columbia 03628
5/28/83	**29**	15		65 **The Jogger**	*Shel Silverstein* **[N]**	Columbia 03809
10/1/83	**69**	7		66 **Diet Song**	*Shel Silverstein*	Columbia 04092
8/10/85	**53**	9		67 **When I Get Home**	*Bill Little/Ed Raetzloff*	EMI America 8279
11/23/85	**76**	4		68 **Reno And Me**	*John Hadley/Kevin Welch*	EMI America 8296
8/2/86	**67**	6		69 **Real Good**	*Troy Seals*	EMI America 8333

Alimony ['75]
Back In Huntsville Again ['75]
Charleston Railroad Tavern ['67]
Come Kiss Me Love ['67]
Come Sundown ['71]
Cowboys And Daddys ['75]
Daddy What If ['74]
Dear John Letter ['65]
Detroit City ['63]
Diet Song ['83]
Dropkick Me, Jesus ['76]
Dropping Out Of Sight ['81]
Find Out What's Happening ['68]
500 Miles Away From Home ['64]
Food Blues ['80]
Four Strong Winds ['65]
Game Of Triangles ['66]
God Bless America Again ['69]
Have I Stayed Away Too Long ['64]
Healin' ['79]
Homesick ['66]
How I Got To Memphis ['70]
I Hate Goodbyes ['73]
(I'm Not) A Candle In The Wind ['82]
If You Ain't Got Nothin' (You Ain't Got Nothin' To Lose) ['82]
If You Think I'm Crazy Now (You Should Have Seen Me When I Was A Kid) ['77]
In The Same Old Way ['66]
It's A Dirty Job ['83]
It's Alright ['65]
Jogger ['83]
Just To Satisfy You ['65]
Learning To Live Again ['81]
Little Bit Later On Down The Line ['68]
Look Who I'm Cheating On Tonight ['77]
(Margie's At) The Lincoln Park Inn ['69]
Marie Laveau ['74]
Miller's Cave ['64]
New Cut Road ['82]
No Memories Hangin' Round ['79]
Numbers ['80]
Piney Wood Hills ['67]
Please Don't Tell Me How The Story Ends ['71]
Praise The Lord And Send Me The Money ['82]
Put A Little Lovin' On Me ['76]
Real Good ['86]
Red-Neck Hippie Romance ['77]
Reno And Me ['85]
Ride Me Down Easy ['73]
Shame On Me ['62]
Short And Sweet ['71]
Singin' In The Kitchen ['75]
Sleep Tight, Good Night Man ['78]
Streets Of Baltimore ['66]
Sylvia's Mother ['72]
Take Me As I Am (Or Let Me Go) ['81]
Talk Me Some Sense ['66]
Tequila Sheila ['80]
Till I Gain Control Again ['79]
Times Are Gettin' Hard ['65]
Too Many Nights Alone ['78]
Town That Broke My Heart ['68]
Vegas ['77]
What Am I Gonna Do ['72]
When I Get Home ['85]
Which One Will It Be ['69]
Willie Jones ['81]
Winner ['76]
You Know Who ['73]
Your Husband, My Wife ['70]

BARE, Bobby Jr.

Born in 1968 in Nashville, Tennessee. Male singer/songwriter/guitarist. Son of **Bobby Bare**.

DEBUT	PEAK	WKS	GOLD	Country Chart Hit	Songwriter	Label (& Number)
12/22/73+	**2^{2}**	16		1 **Daddy What If** ***[w/ Bobby Bare]***	*Shel Silverstein* **[N]**	RCA Victor 0197
9/7/74	**41**	8		2 **Where'd I Come From** ***[w/ Jeannie Bare]***	*Jerry Foster/Bill Rice* **[N]**	RCA Victor 10037

BAREFOOT JERRY

Group of Nashville session musicians led by Wayne Moss and Russ Hicks.

DEBUT	PEAK	WKS	GOLD	Country Chart Hit	Songwriter	Label (& Number)
6/1/74	**22**	13		1 **Boogie Woogie (a/k/a T.D.'s Boogie Woogie)** ***[w/ Charlie McCoy]***	*Clarence "Pine Top" Smith* **[I]**	Monument 8611
2/5/77	**98**	3		2 **Summit Ridge Drive** ***[w/ Charlie McCoy]***	*Artie Shaw* **[I]**	Monument 45210

BARKER, Aaron

Born on 4/23/1968 in San Antonio, Texas. Male singer/songwriter.

DEBUT	PEAK	WKS	GOLD	Country Chart Hit	Songwriter	Label (& Number)
7/18/92	**73**	2		**The Taste Of Freedom** — from the album *The Taste Of Freedom* on Atlantic 82354	*Aaron Barker*	Atlantic

BARLOW, Jack

Born Jack Butcher in 1925 in Muscatine, Iowa. Male singer/guitarist. Also recorded as **Zoot Fenster**.

DEBUT	PEAK	WKS	GOLD	Country Chart Hit	Songwriter	Label (& Number)
10/26/68	**40**	4		1 **Baby, Ain't That Love**	*Jack Moran/Glenn Tubb*	Dot 17139
5/3/69	**55**	6		2 **Birmingham Blues**	*Don Wayne*	Dot 17212
12/13/69+	**68**	5		3 **Nobody Wants To Hear It Like It Is**	*Glenn Tubb*	Dot 17317
1/23/71	**59**	4		4 **Dayton, Ohio**	*Don Wayne*	Dot 17366
11/6/71+	**26**	13		5 **Catch The Wind**	*Jerry Gillespie/Ricci Mareno*	Dot 17396
5/13/72	**58**	7		6 **They Call The Wind Maria** — from the movie *Paint Your Wagon* starring **Clint Eastwood**	*Alan Jay Lerner/Frederick Loewe*	Dot 17414
8/4/73	**55**	9		7 **Oh Woman**	*Milton Blackford*	Dot 17468
11/8/75	**30**	10		8 **The Man On Page 602** ***[Zoot Fenster]***	*Helen Fischer/Gene Strasser/George Winters* **[N]**	Antique 106

BARLOW, Randy — All-Time: #264

Born on 3/29/1943 in Detroit, Michigan. Male singer/songwriter/guitarist.

DEBUT	PEAK	WKS	GOLD	Country Chart Hit	Songwriter	Label (& Number)
7/20/74	**80**	6		1 **Throw Away The Pages**	*Fred Kelly*	Capitol 3883
2/14/76	**74**	6		2 **Johnny Orphan**	*Randy Barlow/Fred Kelly*	Gazelle 153
5/15/76	**53**	9		3 **Goodnight My Love**	*John Marascalco/George Motola*	Gazelle 217
8/21/76	**46**	9		4 **Lonely Eyes**	*Fred Kelly*	Gazelle 280
11/27/76+	**18**	14		5 **Twenty-Four Hours From Tulsa**	*Burt Bacharach/Hal David*	Gazelle 330
3/26/77	**26**	11		6 **Kentucky Woman**	*Neil Diamond*	Gazelle 381
6/25/77	**31**	9		7 **California Lady**	*Randy Barlow/Fred Kelly*	Gazelle 413
10/1/77	**48**	8		8 **Walk Away With Me**	*Fred Kelly*	Gazelle 427
4/1/78	**10**	17		9 **Slow And Easy**	*Fred Kelly/Barbara Muir*	Republic 017
8/12/78	**10**	13		10 **No Sleep Tonight**	*Randy Barlow/Fred Kelly*	Republic 024
12/9/78+	**10**	14		11 **Fall In Love With Me Tonight**	*Randy Barlow/Fred Kelly*	Republic 034
4/7/79	**10**	12		12 **Sweet Melinda**	*Randy Barlow/Fred Kelly*	Republic 039

DEBUT	PEAK	WKS	GOLD	ARTIST / Ranking / Country Chart Hit	Songwriter	Label (& Number)
				BARLOW, Randy — cont'd		
8/11/79	**25**	10		13 **Another Easy Lovin' Night**	*Fred Kelly*	Republic 044
11/3/79+	**13**	14		14 **Lay Back In The Arms Of Someone**	*Mike Chapman/Nicky Chinn*	Republic 049
10/25/80	**46**	8		15 **Willow Run**	*Randy Barlow/Fred Kelly*	Paid 110
1/24/81	**25**	10		16 **Dixie Man**	*Ken Bell/Terry Skinner/J.L. Wallace*	Paid 116
4/18/81	**13**	13		17 **Love Dies Hard**	*Fred Kelly*	Paid 133
9/12/81	**32**	10		18 **Try Me**	*Randy Barlow/Fred Kelly*	Paid 144
12/19/81+	**30**	13		19 **Love Was Born**	*Ron Eden/Fred Kelly*	Jamex 002
10/29/83	**67**	6		20 **Don't Leave Me Lonely Loving You**	*J.R. Dooley/Fred Kelly*	Gazelle 001
				BARMBY, Shane		
				Born on 2/12/1954 in Sacramento, California. Male singer. Also see **Tomorrow's World**.		
5/13/89	**77**	3		1 **Let's Talk About Us**	*Otis Blackwell*	Mercury 874168
11/4/89	**77**	3		2 **A Rainbow Of Our Own**	*Buddy Cannon/Dean Dillon*	Mercury 876020
				BARNES, Benny		
				Born on 1/1/1936 in Beaumont, Texas. Died on 8/27/1987 (age 51). Male singer/songwriter/guitarist.		
9/29/56	**2^1**	17		1 **Poor Man's Riches** J:2 / A:8 / S:15	*Benny Barnes/Dee Marais*	Starday 262
6/12/61	**22**	4		2 **Yearning**	*Eddie Eddings/George Jones*	Mercury 71806
7/30/77	**94**	2		3 **I've Got Some Gettin' Over You To Do**	*Jerry Foster/Bill Rice*	Playboy 5808
				BARNES, Kathy		
				Born on 3/29/1954 in Henderson, Kentucky. Female singer.		
4/26/75	**64**	9		1 **I'm Available (For You To Hold Me Tight)**	*Dave Burgess/Don Earl*	MGM 14797
8/30/75	**94**	3		2 **Shhh**	*Don Earl*	MGM 14822
12/6/75	**92**	5		3 **Be Honest With Me**	*Gene Autry/Fred Rose*	MGM 14836
5/15/76	**73**	6		4 **Sleeping With A Memory**	*Rick Klang/Don Pfrimmer*	Republic 223
9/11/76	**39**	11		5 **Someday Soon**	*Ian Tyson*	Republic 293
1/8/77	**37**	9		6 **Good 'N' Country**	*Rick Klang/Don Pfrimmer*	Republic 338
3/26/77	**92**	3		7 **If We Can't Do It Right** *[w/ Larry Barnes]*	*Ben Peters*	Republic 369
4/2/77	**50**	8		8 **Catch The Wind**	*Donovan Leitch*	Republic 376
7/9/77	**88**	3		9 **Tweedle-O-Twill**	*Gene Autry/Fred Rose*	Republic 389
10/8/77	**62**	7		10 **The Sun In Dixie**	*Rick Klang/Don Pfrimmer*	Republic 005
12/24/77+	**81**	5		11 **Something's Burning**	*Mac Davis*	Republic 012
				BARNES, Max D. **SW: #59**		
				Born Max Duane Barnes on 7/24/1936 in Hardscratch, Iowa. Died of pneumonia on 1/11/2004 (age 67). Male singer/songwriter/guitarist.		
10/22/77	**97**	1		1 **Allegheny Lady**	*Rayburn Anthony/Max D. Barnes*	Polydor 14419
1/5/80	**88**	5		2 **Dear Mr. President**	*Max D. Barnes* **[S]**	Ovation 1139
3/8/80	**79**	4		3 **Mean Woman Blues**	*Max D. Barnes*	Ovation 1142
6/28/80	**68**	6		4 **Cowboys Are Common As Sin**	*Max D. Barnes*	Ovation 1149
11/22/80	**88**	3		5 **Heaven On A Freight Train**	*Max D. Barnes*	Ovation 1158
3/7/81	**84**	2		6 **Don't Ever Leave Me Again**	*Max D. Barnes*	Ovation 1164
				BARNETT, Bobby		
				Born on 2/15/1936 in Cushing, Oklahoma. Male singer.		
10/10/60	**24**	1		1 **This Old Heart**	*Eddie Miller/Bob Morris*	Razorback 306
2/22/64	**47**	2		2 **Worst Of Luck**	*Joe Poovey*	Sims 159
5/20/67	**52**	12		3 **Down, Down, Came The World**	*Bozo Darnell/Waylon Jennings*	K-Ark 741
10/14/67	**74**	2		4 **The Losing Kind**	*Curtis Wayne*	K-Ark 766
8/10/68	**14**	14		5 **Love Me, Love Me**	*George Richey/Glenn Sutton*	Columbia 44589
1/4/69	**44**	10		6 **Your Sweet Love Lifted Me**	*George Richey/Glenn Sutton*	Columbia 44716
6/21/69	**59**	8		7 **Drink Canada Dry**	*Larry Kingston*	Columbia 44861
3/18/78	**97**	3		8 **Burn Atlanta Down**	*Dave Kirby*	Cin Kay 128
				BARNETT, Mandy		
				Born on 9/28/1975 in Crossville, Tennessee. Female singer/actress. Portrayed **Patsy Cline** in the Nashville musical *Always Patsy Cline.*		
1/13/96	**43**	16		1 **Now That's All Right With Me**	*Kostas/Tony Perez*	Asylum
5/18/96	**65**	6		2 **Maybe**	*Rodney Crowell/Jim Lauderdale/John Leventhal*	Asylum
8/31/96	**72**	4		3 **A Simple I Love You**	*Karen Brooks/Randy Sharp*	Asylum
				above 3 from the album *Mandy Barnett* on Asylum 61810		
				BARNHILL, Joe		
				Born on 6/13/1965 in Turkey, Texas; raised in California and Tennessee. Male singer. Son of Joe Bob Barnhill, leader of **Joe Bob's Nashville Sound Company**.		
7/15/89	**56**	7		1 **Your Old Flame's Goin' Out Tonite**	*Wayne Perry*	Universal 66014
12/2/89+	**57**	7		2 **Good As Gone**	*Joe Bob Barnhill/Joe Hunter/Don Miller*	Universal 66032
				BARNHILL, Leslee		
				Born in Shawnee, Oklahoma. Female singer.		
2/25/78	**92**	2		1 **Let's Call It A Day (And Get On With The Night)**	*Dave Burgess/Don Pfrimmer*	Republic 014
5/19/79	**62**	6		2 **Bad Day For A Breakup**	*Randy Barlow/Fred Kelly*	Republic 040
				BASS, Sam D.		
				Born in Oklahoma. Male singer/guitarist/bassist. Joined the backing bands of **Tommy Duncan**, **Tex Ritter**, **T. Texas Tyler** and **Moon Mullican**.		
7/5/80	**92**	2		**How Could I Do This To Me**	*Steve Spurgin*	3J 1003

DEBUT	PEAK	WKS	GOLD	ARTIST / Country Chart Hit	Songwriter	Label (& Number)
				BATES, Jeff		
				Born on 9/19/1963 in Bunker Hill, Mississippi. Male singer/songwriter/guitarist.		
1/4/03	**8**	30		1 **The Love Song**	*Jeff Bates/Kenny Beard/Casey Beathard*	RCA
9/13/03	**47**	6		2 **Rainbow Man**	*Harley Allen/Jeff Bates*	RCA
1/24/04	**23**	24		3 **I Wanna Make You Cry**	*Jeff Bates/Kenny Beard*	RCA
9/25/04+	**17**	38		4 **Long, Slow Kisses**	*Jeff Bates/Gordon Bradberry/Ben Hayslip*	RCA
				above 4 from the album *Rainbow Man* on RCA 67071		
				BAUER, Kathy		
				Born on 8/3/1951 in League City, Texas. Female singer.		
4/23/83	**82**	4		**Hold Me Till The Last Waltz Is Over**	*Bill Nash*	NSD 164
				BAUGH, Phil		
				Born on 12/13/1936 in Marysville, California. Died of heart failure on 11/4/1990 (age 53). Male guitarist/songwriter. Member of the **Nashville Superpickers**. Former owner of the Soundwaves record label.		
6/12/65	**16**	15		1 **Country Guitar** *[w/ Vern Stovall]*	*Phil Baugh/Vern Stovall* **[N]**	Longhorn 559
11/6/65	**27**	7		2 **One Man Band**	*Curtis Leach* **[N]**	Longhorn 563
				BAXTER, BAXTER & BAXTER		
				Trio of brothers from Rockford, Illinois: Rick Baxter, Mark Baxter and Duncan Baxter.		
2/28/81	**76**	4		**Take Me Back To The Country**	*Boomer Castleman*	Sun 1160
				BEACH BOYS, The		
				Surf-rock group from Hawthorne, California. Lineup in 1996: brothers Brian Wilson and Carl Wilson, their cousin Mike Love, Al Jardine and Bruce Johnston. Carl Wilson died of cancer on 2/6/1998 (age 51). Inducted into the Rock and Roll Hall of Fame in 1988. Won Grammy's Lifetime Achievement Award in 2001.		
8/24/96	**69**	1		1 **Little Deuce Coupe** *[w/ James House]*	*Roger Christian/Brian Wilson*	River North
9/7/96	**73**	1		2 **Don't Worry Baby** *[w/ Lorrie Morgan]*	*Roger Christian/Brian Wilson*	River North
10/12/96	**69**	1		3 **Long Tall Texan** *[w/ Doug Supernaw]*	*Henry Strzelecki*	River North
				above 3 from the album *Stars And Stripes Vol. 1* on River North 1205		
				BEAN, Jim		
				Born in Miami, Florida. Male singer.		
9/17/88	**96**	1		**Lay, Lady Lay**	*Bob Dylan*	Hub 47
				BEAR CREEK BAND Featuring Leonda		
				Group from Durand, Wisconsin. Led by Leonda Sundlin (vocals) and Dan Calllan (keyboards).		
10/22/88	**99**	1		**Falling In Love Right & Left**	*Ken Harvey*	Bear Creek 103
				BEARDS, The		
				Duo from Indiana: brothers Randy Beard (guitar, vocals) and Ronnie Beard (drums, vocals).		
5/14/88	**75**	4		1 **Stone Cold Love**	*Randy Beard/Ronnie Beard*	Beardo 001
11/26/88	**71**	6		2 **Fearless Heart**	*Steve Earle*	Beardo 002
				BEATTY, Susi		
				Born on 6/1/1962 in Alexandria, Virginia. Female singer.		
9/30/89	**71**	5		1 **Hard Baby To Rock**	*Mark Collie/David Luttrell/Phil Thomas*	Starway 1205
12/9/89+	**65**	6		2 **Heart From A Stone**	*Beth Nielsen Chapman/Mark Germino*	Starway 1206
				BEAVERS, Clyde		
				Born on 6/8/1932 in Tennega, Georgia. Male singer.		
10/24/60	**13**	15		1 **Here I Am Drunk Again**	*Autry Inman/Jack Kay*	Decca 31173
3/16/63	**27**	2		2 **Still Loving You**	*Bob Montgomery*	Tempwood V 1039
8/3/63	**21**	1		3 **Sukiyaki (I Look Up When I Walk)**	*Rokusuke Ei/Hachidai Nakamura*	Tempwood V 1044
3/12/66	**47**	3		4 **That's You (And What's Left Of Me)**	*Jimmy Jay/Dean Mathis*	Hickory 1346
				BECKHAM, Bob		
				Born on 7/8/1927 in Stratford, Oklahoma. Male singer.		
9/2/67	**73**	2		**Cherokee Strip**	*Glen Spencer/Tim Spencer*	Monument 1018
				BECKHAM, Charlie		
				Born in Houston, Texas. Male singer/songwriter.		
6/18/88	**84**	3		**Think I'll Go Home**	*Charlie Beckham*	Oak 1048
				BEE, Kathy		
				Born in 1955 in Bloomingburg, Ohio. Female singer/songwriter.		
10/8/88	**100**	1		**Let's Go Party**	*Kathy Bee*	Lilac 1213
				BEE, Molly		
				Born Molly Beachboard on 8/18/1939 in Oklahoma City, Oklahoma. Female singer/actress.		
9/21/74	**55**	8		1 **She Kept On Talkin'**	*Gary U.S. Bonds/Charles Whitehead/Jerry Williams*	Granite 509
2/22/75	**83**	7		2 **Right Or Left At Oak Street**	*Joe Nixon/Charlie Williams*	Granite 515
				BEE GEES		
				Trio of brothers from Manchester, England: Barry Gibb, with twins Robin Gibb and Maurice Gibb. Maurice died of heart failure on 1/12/2003 (age 53). Inducted into the Rock and Roll Hall of Fame in 1997.		
11/25/78+	**39**	12		**Rest Your Love On Me**	*Barry Gibb*	RSO 913
				BEESON, Marc		
				Born on 12/20/1954 in Champaign, Illinois. Male singer/songwriter/guitarist. Founding member of **Burnin' Daylight**.		
9/3/94	**70**	2		**A Wing And A Prayer**	*Marc Beeson/Steve Bogard*	BNA

Billboard DEBUT	PEAK	WKS	GOLD	ARTIST / Country Chart Hit	Ranking / Songwriter	Label (& Number)
				BELEW, Carl		
				Born on 4/21/1931 in Salina, Oklahoma. Died of cancer on 10/31/1990 (age 59). Male singer/songwriter/guitarist.		
4/6/59	9	20		1 Am I That Easy To Forget	*Carl Belew/W.S. Stevenson*	Decca 30842
6/13/60	19	15		2 Too Much To Lose	*Tommy Blake/Lester Vanadore*	Decca 31086
9/29/62	8	12		3 Hello Out There	*Wayne Walker/Kent Westberry*	RCA Victor 8058
9/26/64	23	13		4 In The Middle Of A Memory	*Carl Belew/Clyde Pitts*	RCA Victor 8406
8/7/65	12	18		5 Crystal Chandelier	*Ted Harris*	RCA Victor 8633
2/5/66	43	4		6 Boston Jail	*Tony Senn/Tommy Stough*	RCA Victor 8744
11/26/66	64	3		7 Walking Shadow, Talking Memory	*Jean Chapel*	RCA Victor 8996
9/9/67	65	2		8 Girl Crazy	*Carl Belew/Van Givens*	RCA Victor 9272
3/16/68	68	2		9 Mary's Little Lamb	*Carl Belew*	RCA Victor 9446
4/24/71	51	10		10 All I Need Is You *[w/ Betty Jean Robinson]*	*Betty Jean Robinson*	Decca 32802
9/14/74	56	11		11 Welcome Back To My World	*Carl Belew/Joe Johnson/Max Powell*	MCA 40276
				BELL, Delia		
				Born Delia Nowell on 4/16/1938 in Bonham, Texas; raised in Hugo, Oklahoma. Female singer.		
5/7/83	45	11		1 Flame In My Heart	*George Jones/Bernard Spurlock*	Warner 29653
8/13/83	82	3		2 Coyote Song	*Ray Park*	Warner 29550
				BELL, James		
				Born James Mullins in Tulsa, Oklahoma. Male singer/songwriter.		
5/4/68	51	7		He Ain't Country	*James Bell*	Bell 710
				BELL, Tommy		
				Born in 1950 in Lansing, Michigan. Male singer.		
10/2/82	83	3		1 Georgiana	*Bob Morrison*	Gold Sound 8013
9/24/83	97	2		2 Honky Tonk Crazy	*Dean Dillon/Frank Dycus*	Gold Sound 8016
				BELL, Vivian		
				Born in Austin, Texas. Female singer.		
3/19/77	71	7		The Angel In Your Arms	*Tom Brasfield/Herbert Ivey/Terry Woodford*	GRT 118
				BELLAMY BROTHERS	**1980s: #16 / All-Time: #70**	
				Duo from Darby, Florida: brothers Howard Bellamy (born on 2/2/1946) and David Bellamy (born on 9/16/1950). Both graduated from the University of Florida; Howard with a degree in veterinary medicine and David with a degree in psychology. David was a member of the Accidents in 1967. Both were members of Jericho from 1968-71. Moved to Los Angeles in 1975. Started own Bellamy Brothers record label in 1992. Howard married **Sharon Vaughn** on 6/10/2002.		
3/13/76	21	12		1 Let Your Love Flow	*Larry Williams*	Warner/Curb 8169
2/18/78	86	4		2 Bird Dog	*Boudleaux Bryant*	Warner/Curb 8521
4/29/78	19	12		3 Slippin' Away	*Frank Saulino/Jim Valentini*	Warner/Curb 8558
9/16/78	99	2		4 Wild Honey	*Howard Bellamy*	Warner/Curb 8627
11/18/78+	16	14		5 Lovin' On	*Ben Peters*	Warner/Curb 8692
3/24/79	❶^{3}	15		6 If I Said You Have A Beautiful Body Would You Hold It Against Me	*David Bellamy*	Warner/Curb 8790
8/18/79	5	13		7 You Ain't Just Whistlin' Dixie	*David Bellamy*	Warner/Curb 49032
2/2/80	❶^{1}	14		8 Sugar Daddy	*David Bellamy*	Warner/Curb 49160
5/24/80	❶^{1}	17		9 Dancin' Cowboys	*David Bellamy*	Warner/Curb 49241
10/11/80	3^{3}	15		10 Lovers Live Longer	*David Bellamy*	Warner/Curb 49573
1/17/81	❶^{1}	13		11 Do You Love As Good As You Look	*Charlie Black/Rory Bourke/Jerry Gillespie*	Warner/Curb 49639
6/6/81	12	13		12 They Could Put Me In Jail	*Bob McDill*	Warner/Curb 49729
10/10/81	7	17		13 You're My Favorite Star	*David Bellamy*	Warner/Curb 49815
12/19/81+	62	7		14 It's So Close To Christmas (And I'm So Far From Home)	*David Bellamy* [X]	Curb/Warner 49875
3/27/82	❶^{1}	18		15 For All The Wrong Reasons	*David Bellamy*	Elektra/Curb 47431
7/17/82	21	13		16 Get Into Reggae Cowboy	*David Bellamy*	Elektra/Curb 69999
9/25/82	❶^{1}	18		17 Redneck Girl	*David Bellamy*	Warner/Curb 29923
1/15/83	❶^{1}	18		18 When I'm Away From You	*Frankie Miller*	Elektra/Curb 69850
5/21/83	4	17		19 I Love Her Mind	*David Bellamy*	Warner/Curb 29645
9/10/83	15	15		20 Strong Weakness	*David Bellamy*	Warner/Curb 29514
6/2/84	5	18		21 Forget About Me	*Frankie Miller/Troy Seals/Eddie Setser*	Curb/MCA 52380
9/22/84	6	21		22 World's Greatest Lover	A:5 / S:6 *David Bellamy*	Curb/MCA 52446
1/19/85	❶^{1}	20		23 I Need More Of You	S:❶^{1} / A:❶^{1} *David Bellamy*	Curb/MCA 52518
5/4/85	2^{2}	20		24 Old Hippie	S:❶^{1} / A:2 *David Bellamy*	Curb/MCA 52579
9/14/85	2^{1}	22		25 Lie To You For Your Love	S:2 / A:2 *Jeff Barry/David Bellamy/Howard Bellamy/Frankie Miller*	Curb/MCA 52668
2/8/86	2^{1}	20		26 Feelin' The Feelin'	S:2 / A:2 *David Bellamy*	Curb/MCA 52747
9/27/86	❶^{1}	20		27 Too Much Is Not Enough *[w/ The Forester Sisters]*	S:❶^{1} / A:❶^{1} *David Bellamy/Ron Taylor*	Curb/MCA 52917
1/24/87	❶^{1}	22		28 Kids Of The Baby Boom	A:❶^{1} / S:7 *David Bellamy*	Curb/MCA 53018
5/9/87	31	10		29 Country Rap	S:30 *David Bellamy*	Curb/MCA 52834
8/15/87	3^{1}	24		30 Crazy From The Heart	S:9 *David Bellamy/Don Schlitz*	Curb/MCA 53154
1/9/88	5	21		31 Santa Fe	S:8 *David Bellamy/Ron Taylor*	Curb/MCA 53222
5/7/88	6	21		32 I'll Give You All My Love Tonight	S:16 *David Bellamy/Billy Crain/Wally Dentz*	Curb/MCA 53310
9/3/88	9	19		33 Rebels Without A Clue	S:8 *David Bellamy*	Curb/MCA 53399

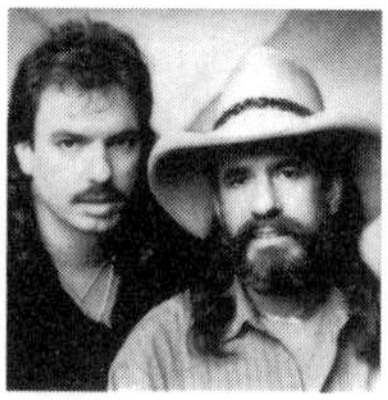

DEBUT	PEAK	WKS	GOLD	ARTIST / Country Chart Hit	Ranking / Songwriter	Label (& Number)
				BELLAMY BROTHERS — cont'd		
1/7/89	**5**	20		34 **Big Love**	*David Bellamy*	Curb/MCA 53478
5/6/89	**51**	7		35 **Hillbilly Hell**	*David Bellamy/Bobby Braddock*	Curb/MCA 53642
7/1/89	**10**	27		36 **You'll Never Be Sorry**	*David Bellamy/Howard Bellamy/Don Schlitz*	Curb/MCA 53672
11/11/89	**37**	12		37 **The Center Of My Universe**	*David Bellamy/Howard Bellamy/Don Schlitz*	Curb/MCA 53719
4/14/90	**63**	7		38 **Drive South** ***[w/ The Forester Sisters]*** from the Forester Sisters' album *Come Hold Me* on Warner/Curb 26141	*John Hiatt*	Warner/Curb
6/30/90	**7**	21		39 **I Could Be Persuaded** from the album *Reality Check* on Curb/MCA 42340	*David Bellamy/Howard Bellamy/Don Schlitz*	Curb/MCA
3/23/91	**46**	18		40 **She Don't Know That She's Perfect**	*David Bellamy/Howard Bellamy/J.L. Williams*	Atlantic
8/17/91	**74**	2		41 **All In The Name Of Love** above 2 from the album *Rollin' Thunder* on Atlantic 82232	*Jerry Lynn Williams*	Atlantic
6/6/92	**23**	20		42 **Cowboy Beat**	*John Beland/David Bellamy*	Bellamy Brothers
10/17/92	**64**	6		43 **Can I Come On Home To You**	*David Bellamy*	Bellamy Brothers
3/13/93	**62**	7		44 **Hard Way To Make An Easy Livin'** above 3 from the album *The Latest And The Greatest* on Bellamy Brothers 9108	*John Beland/David Bellamy/Howard Bellamy*	Bellamy Brothers
8/7/93	**66**	6		45 **Rip Off The Knob**	*David Bellamy*	Bellamy Brothers
1/15/94	**71**	3		46 **Not** above 2 from the album *Rip Off The Knob* on Bellamy Brothers 9109	*David Bellamy*	Bellamy Brothers
				BENEDICT, Ernie, and His Polkateers Born on 6/20/1917 in Green River, Wyoming. Died on 9/3/2000 (age 83). Accordian player/bandleader. Formed his Polkateers group in Cleveland, Ohio. Hosted local *Polka Picnic* TV show.		
10/8/49	**15**	1		**Over Three Hills**	J:15 *Ernie Benedict/Dolly Kendall/Lenny Sanders/Roy Uest*	RCA Victor 20-3389
				BENONI, Arne Born in Napp, Norway. Male singer/guitarist.		
6/24/89	**96**	1		1 **Southern Lady**	*Jeff Garris*	Round Robin 1879
10/7/89	**88**	2		2 **If I Live To Be A Hundred (I'll Die Young)**	*Mae Boren Axton/Ed Hunnicutt/Roger Wade*	Round Robin 1881
				BENSON, Matt Born in Chattanooga, Tennessee. Male singer.		
7/29/89	**63**	5		**When Will The Fires End**	*Roger Ball/Jesse Shofner*	Step One 406
				BENSON, Ray Born Raymond Benson Siefert on 3/16/1951 in Philadelphia, Pennsylvania. Male singer/songwriter/guitarist. Leader of **Asleep At The Wheel**.		
9/21/91	**67**	4		**Four Scores And Seven Beers Ago**	*Danny Morrison/Kerry Kurt Phillips/Andy Spooner*	Arista
				BENTLEY, Dierks Born on 11/20/1975 in Phoenix, Arizona. Male singer/songwriter/guitarist. ***OPRY: 2005***		
4/12/03	**❶** [1]	35		1 **What Was I Thinkin'**	S:2 *Brett Beavers/Dierks Bentley/Deric Ruttan*	Capitol
10/25/03+	**17**	27		2 **My Last Name**	*Harley Allen/Dierks Bentley*	Capitol
5/15/04+	**4**	37		3 **How Am I Doin'** above 3 from the album *Dierks Bentley* on Capitol 39814	*Jim Beavers/Dierks Bentley*	Capitol
2/5/05	**3** [5]	25		4 **Lot Of Leavin' Left To Do** from the album *Modern Day Drifter* on Capitol 66475	*Brett Beavers/Dierks Bentley/Deric Ruttan*	Capitol
				BENTLEY, Stephanie Born on 4/29/1963 in Thomasville, Georgia. Female singer/songwriter. Married Brian Prout of **Diamond Rio** on 12/28/2001.		
10/14/95+	**21**	20		1 **Heart Half Empty** ***[w/ Ty Herndon]*** from Herndon's album *What Mattered Most* on Epic 66397	S:10 *Gary Burr/Desmond Child*	Epic
2/3/96	**32**	20		2 **Who's That Girl**	*Stephanie Bentley/Don Pfrimmer/George Teren*	Epic
7/27/96	**60**	16		3 **Once I Was The Light Of Your Life**	*Hugh Prestwood*	Epic
2/22/97	**47**	11		4 **The Hopechest Song** above 3 from the album *Hopechest* on Epic 66877	*Angela Kaset*	Epic
				BENTON, Barbi Born Barbara Klein on 1/28/1950 in Sacramento, California. Singer/actress/model. Regular on TV's *Hee Haw* and *Sugar Time*.		
3/15/75	**5**	14		1 **Brass Buckles**	*Bobby Borchers/Mack Vickery*	Playboy 6032
8/16/75	**61**	8		2 **Movie Magazine, Stars In Her Eyes**	*Bobby Borchers/Mack Vickery*	Playboy 6043
10/18/75	**32**	9		3 **Roll You Like A Wheel** ***[w/ Mickey Gilley]*** **MICKEY GILLEY & BARBI BENTON**	*Vic McAlpin*	Playboy 6045
12/27/75+	**74**	5		4 **The Reverend Bob**	*Glenn Sutton*	Playboy 6056
				BERG, Matraca Born on 2/3/1964 in Nashville, Tennessee. Female singer/songwriter. Daughter of Nashville session singer/songwriter Icee Berg. Married Jeff Hanna of the **Nitty Gritty Dirt Band** in 1993.		
6/9/90	**36**	10		1 **Baby, Walk On**	*Matraca Berg/Ronnie Samoset*	RCA
9/8/90	**36**	15		2 **The Things You Left Undone**	*Matraca Berg/Ronnie Samoset*	RCA
1/12/91	**43**	16		3 **I Got It Bad**	*Matraca Berg/Jim Photoglo*	RCA
5/25/91	**55**	13		4 **I Must Have Been Crazy** above 4 from the album *Lying To The Moon* on RCA 2066	*Matraca Berg/Ronnie Samoset*	RCA
11/16/91	**66**	5		5 **It's Easy To Tell** from the album *Bittersweet Surrender* on RCA 61050	*Pam Hayes/Stephony Smith*	RCA
9/13/97	**59**	4		6 **That Train Don't Run**	*Matraca Berg/Gary Harrison*	Rising Tide
2/14/98	**51**	11		7 **Back In The Saddle** above 2 from the album *Sunday Morning To Saturday Night* on Rising Tide 53047	*Matraca Berg/Stan Lynch*	Rising Tide

Billboard DEBUT	PEAK	WKS	GOLD	ARTIST / Ranking / Country Chart Hit ... Songwriter	Label (& Number)

BERNARD, Crystal

Born on 9/30/1961 in Garland, Texas. Female singer/songwriter/actress. Played "Helen Chapel" on TV's *Wings*.

DEBUT	PEAK	WKS	GOLD	Country Chart Hit ... Songwriter	Label (& Number)
11/2/96	**57**	15		1 **Have We Forgotten What Love Is** ... S:13 *Crystal Bernard/Billy Dean* **Billy Dean** (backing vocal)	River North
3/15/97	**70**	3		2 **State Of Mind** ... S:14 *Crystal Bernard/David Rhyne*	River North

BERRY, John — 1990s: #46 / All-Time: #244

Born on 9/14/1959 in Aiken, South Carolina; raised in Atlanta, Georgia. Male singer/songwriter/guitarist. Began performing in 1981 in Athens, Georgia. Survived a motorcycle crash in 1981 and brain surgery in 1994. Also see **Hope**.

DEBUT	PEAK	WKS	GOLD	Country Chart Hit ... Songwriter	Label (& Number)
6/5/93	**51**	11		1 **A Mind Of Her Own** ... *John Berry/Charles Jones*	Liberty
9/25/93	**22**	20		2 **Kiss Me In The Car** ... *John Berry/Chris Waters*	Liberty
2/12/94	**❶**[1]	20		3 **Your Love Amazes Me** *Amanda Hunt/Chuck Jones*	Liberty
6/25/94	**5**	20		4 **What's In It For Me** ... *Gary Burr/John Jarrard*	Liberty
10/15/94+	**4**	20		5 **You And Only You** ... *Chuck Jones/J.D. Martin* above 5 from the album *John Berry* on Liberty 80472	Liberty
3/4/95	**2**[1]	20		6 **Standing On The Edge Of Goodbye** ... *John Berry/Stewart Harris*	Patriot
7/8/95	**4**	20		7 **I Think About It All The Time** ... *Billy Livsey/Don Schlitz*	Patriot
10/21/95	**25**	20		8 **If I Had Any Pride Left At All** ... *John Greenebaum/Troy Seals/Eddie Setser*	Patriot
1/6/96	**55**	2		9 **O Holy Night** ... *Adolphe Adam/John Dwight* **[X]** from the album *O Holy Night* on Capitol 32663	Capitol
2/17/96	**34**	11		10 **Every Time My Heart Calls Your Name** ... *Gary Heyde/J.B. Rudd* #6-8 & 10: from the album *Standing On The Edge Of Goodbye* on Patriot 28495	Patriot
7/27/96	**10**	20		11 **Change My Mind** ... S:5 *Jason Blume*	Capitol
12/7/96+	**2**[2]	20		12 **She's Taken A Shine** ... S:10 *Richard Bach/Greg Barnhill*	Capitol
4/19/97	**19**	20		13 **I Will, If You Will** ... *Randy Goodrum/John Jarvis* above 3 from the album *Faces* on Capitol 35464	Capitol
9/20/97	**59**	6		14 **The Stone** ... *Danny Mayo/Bob Regan*	Capitol
1/10/98	**63**	1		15 **O Holy Night** ... *Adolphe Adam/John Dwight* **[X-R]** from the album *O Holy Night* on Capitol 32663	Capitol
4/25/98	**62**	7		16 **Over My Shoulder** ... *Marcus Hummon/Roger Murrah*	Capitol
8/8/98	**75**	1		17 **Better Than A Biscuit** ... *Gene Cook* above 2 from the album *Better Than A Biscuit* on Capitol 59933	Capitol
6/26/99	**53**	10		18 **Love Is For Giving** ... *Robert Ellis Orrall/David Tyson*	Lyric Street
9/4/99	**43**	17		19 **Power Windows** ... *Billy Falcon* above 2 from the album *Wildest Dreams* on Lyric Street 65005	Lyric Street
10/2/99	**70**	1		20 **There He Goes** *[w/ Patsy Cline]* ... *Durwood Haddock/Eddie Miller/William Stevenson* from Cline's album *Duets Volume 1* on Private I 417097	Private I

BEVERLY HILL BILLIES

Pioneering group formed in California: Cyprian "Ezra Longnecker" Paulette (vocals; died on 3/19/1952, age 46), Tom "Pappy" Murray (guitar; died on 12/28/1964, age 65), Leo "**Zeke Manners**" Mannes (accoridian; died on 10/14/2000, age 89) and Harry "Hank Skillet" Blaeholder (fiddle; died on 4/27/1960, age 61).

EARLY HITS: When The Bloom Is On The Sage (1930) / My Pretty Quadroon (1930)

BICKHARDT, Craig

Born on 9/7/1954 in Haverton, Pennsylvania. Male singer/songwriter. Member of **Schuyler, Knobloch & Bickhardt**.

DEBUT	PEAK	WKS	GOLD	Country Chart Hit ... Songwriter	Label (& Number)
5/26/84	**86**	4		**You Are What Love Means To Me** ... *Craig Bickhardt* from the movie *Tender Mercies* starring Robert Duvall	Liberty 1518

BIG & RICH

Duo from Texas: "Big" Kenny Alphin and **John Rich** (former member of **Lonestar**).

DEBUT	PEAK	WKS	GOLD	Country Chart Hit ... Songwriter	Label (& Number)
12/27/03+	**21**	20		1 **Wild West Show** ... S:❶[2] *Kenny Alphin/Blair Daly/John Rich*	Warner
4/24/04	**11**	21		2 **Save A Horse (Ride A Cowboy)** ... *Kenny Alphin/John Rich*	Warner
10/2/04+	**15**	20		3 **Holy Water** ... *Kenny Alphin/Jeff Cohen/Vicky McGehee/John Rich*	Warner
2/19/05	**20**	20		4 **Big Time** ... *Kenny Alphin/Angie Aparo/John Rich* above 4 from the album *Horse Of A Different Color* on Warner 48520	Warner

BIG HOUSE

Group from Bakersfield, California: brothers Monty Byrom (vocals) and Tanner Byrom (drums), with David Neuhauser and Chuck Seaton (guitars), Sonny California (harmonica) and Ron Mitchell (bass).

DEBUT	PEAK	WKS	GOLD	Country Chart Hit ... Songwriter	Label (& Number)
2/8/97	**30**	20		1 **Cold Outside** ... S:21 *Monty Byrom/Dennis Knutson/David Neuhauser/Max Reese*	MCA
5/24/97	**57**	11		2 **You Ain't Lonely Yet** ... *Monty Byrom/David Neuhauser*	MCA
10/11/97	**71**	4		3 **Love Ain't Easy** ... *Monty Byrom/Pride Hutchison/Scott Hutchison/David Neuhauser* above 3 from the album *Big House* on MCA 11446	MCA
5/23/98	**63**	6		4 **Faith** ... *Monty Byrom/Scott Hutchinson* from the album *Travelin' Kind* on MCA 70015	MCA

BILLY HILL

Group formed in Nashville, Tennessee: **Dennis Robbins** (vocals), Bob DiPiero and John Scott Sherrill (guitars), Reno Kling (bass) and Martin Parker (drums). DiPiero was formerly married to **Pam Tillis**. Also see **Tomorrow's World**.

DEBUT	PEAK	WKS	GOLD	Country Chart Hit ... Songwriter	Label (& Number)
7/8/89	**25**	17		1 **Too Much Month At The End Of The Money** ... *Bob DiPiero/Dennis Robbins/John Scott Sherrill*	Reprise 22942
12/9/89+	**58**	6		2 **I Can't Help Myself (Sugar Pie Honey Bunch)** ... *Lamont Dozier/Brian Holland/Eddie Holland*	Reprise 22746

BILLY THE KID

Born in Bakersfield, California. Male singer.

DEBUT	PEAK	WKS	GOLD	Country Chart Hit ... Songwriter	Label (& Number)
6/16/79	**50**	7		**What I Feel Is You** ... *Kelly Bach/Betty Jones*	Cyclone 103

DEBUT	PEAK	WKS	GOLD	ARTIST / Country Chart Hit	Songwriter	Label (& Number)

BIRD, Vicki

Born on 7/9/1955 in Bird's Hollow, West Virginia. Female singer. Regular on TV's *Hee Haw* from 1989-91.

DEBUT	PEAK	WKS	GOLD	Country Chart Hit	Songwriter	Label (& Number)
10/24/87	64	6		1 I've Got Ways Of Making You Talk	*Tom Brasfield/S. Alan Taylor*	16th Avenue 70405
4/23/88	61	6		2 A Little Bit Of Lovin' (Goes A Long Long Way) same song as "Just A Little Bit" by **The Diamonds**	*Roger Cook/Bobby Wood*	16th Avenue 70413
4/8/89	73	4		3 Mem'ries	*Linda Hargrove/Sue Hargrove*	16th Avenue 70421
10/14/89	87	2		4 Moanin' The Blues	*Hank Williams*	16th Avenue 70431

BISHOP, Bob

Born Bishop Sykes on 8/6/1928 in Henry County, Tennessee. Died on 11/7/1994 (age 66). Male singer/songwriter/guitarist.

DEBUT	PEAK	WKS	GOLD	Country Chart Hit	Songwriter	Label (& Number)
11/9/68	42	6		Roses To Reno	*Bob Bishop/Wayne Walker*	ABC 11132

BISHOP, Joni

Born in Tennessee. Female singer.

DEBUT	PEAK	WKS	GOLD	Country Chart Hit	Songwriter	Label (& Number)
8/1/87	71	4		Heart Out Of Control	*Ilze Platais*	Columbia 07225

BISHOP, Terri

Born in Phoenix, Arizona. Female singer.

DEBUT	PEAK	WKS	GOLD	Country Chart Hit	Songwriter	Label (& Number)
7/22/78	97	3		One More Kiss	*Dick St. Nicklaus*	United Artists 1194

BLACK('S), Bill, Combo

Born on 9/17/1926 in Memphis, Tennessee. Died of a brain tumor on 10/21/1965 (age 39). Bass guitarist. Backed **Elvis Presley** on most of his early records. Formed own band in 1959. Gilbert Michael, Larry Rogers and Bob Tucker led group after Black's death.

DEBUT	PEAK	WKS	GOLD	Country Chart Hit	Songwriter	Label (& Number)
4/5/75	29	13		1 Boilin' Cabbage	*Gilbert Michael/Larry Rogers/Bob Tucker* [I]	Hi 2283
9/20/75	84	5		2 Back Up And Push	*Gilbert Michael/Larry Rogers/Bob Tucker* [I]	Hi 2291
1/24/76	57	8		3 Fire On The Bayou	*Gilbert Michael* [I]	Hi 2301
7/24/76	100	2		4 Jump Back Joe Joe	*Gilbert Michael/Larry Rogers/Bob Tucker* [I]	Hi 2311
11/20/76	89	7		5 Redneck Rock	*Larry Rogers/Bob Tucker* [L]	Hi 2317
4/8/78	96	4		6 Cashin' In (A Tribute To Luther Perkins)	*Johnny Cash/Merle Kilgore/Claude King* [I]	Hi 78508

BLACK, Clint — 1990s: #4 / 2000s: #43 / All-Time: #49

Born on 2/4/1962 in Long Branch, New Jersey; raised in Houston, Texas. Male singer/songwriter/guitarist. Began singing professionally in 1981 at the Benton Springs Club in Houston. Married actress Lisa Hartman on 10/20/1991.
Also see **Same Old Train**.

CMA: Horizon 1989 / Male Vocalist 1990 // OPRY: 1991

DEBUT	PEAK	WKS	GOLD	Country Chart Hit	Songwriter	Label (& Number)
2/18/89	❶[1]	24		1 A Better Man	*Clint Black/Hayden Nicholas*	RCA 8781
7/15/89	❶[1]	21		2 Killin' Time	*Clint Black/Hayden Nicholas*	RCA 8945
11/18/89+	❶[3]	26		3 Nobody's Home	*Clint Black*	RCA 9078
3/10/90	❶[2]	25		4 Walkin' Away	*Clint Black/Dick Gay/Hayden Nicholas*	RCA
7/7/90	3[1]	21		5 Nothing's News above 2 from the album *Killin' Time* on RCA 9668	*Clint Black*	RCA
10/27/90	4	20		6 Put Yourself In My Shoes	*Clint Black/Hayden Nicholas/Shake Russell*	RCA
2/2/91	❶[2]	20		7 Loving Blind	*Clint Black*	RCA
4/27/91	7	20		8 One More Payment	*Clint Black/Hayden Nicholas/Shake Russell*	RCA
7/27/91	❶[2]	20		9 Where Are You Now	*Clint Black/Hayden Nicholas*	RCA
11/2/91	42	10		10 Hold On Partner *[w/ Roy Rogers]* from Rogers' album *Roy Rogers Tribute* on RCA 3024	*Bobby Paine/Larsen Paine*	RCA
4/25/92	61	8		11 This Nightlife #6-9 & 11: from the album *Put Yourself In My Shoes* on RCA 2372	*Clint Black/Hayden Nicholas*	RCA
6/20/92	2[2]	20		12 We Tell Ourselves	*Clint Black/Hayden Nicholas*	RCA
9/26/92	4	20		13 Burn One Down	*Clint Black/Frankie Miller/Hayden Nicholas*	RCA
1/16/93	❶[2]	20		14 When My Ship Comes In above 3 from the album *The Hard Way* on RCA 66003	*Clint Black/Hayden Nicholas*	RCA
5/15/93	2[1]	20		15 A Bad Goodbye *[w/ Wynonna]*	*Clint Black*	RCA
8/14/93	3[1]	20		16 No Time To Kill	*Clint Black/Hayden Nicholas*	RCA
10/30/93	54	20		17 Desperado from the various artists album *Common Thread: The Songs Of The* **Eagles** on Giant 24531	*Glenn Frey/Don Henley*	Giant
11/20/93+	2[2]	20		18 State Of Mind	*Clint Black*	RCA
2/5/94	74	1		19 Tuckered Out	*Clint Black/Hayden Nicholas*	RCA
3/5/94	❶[1]	20		20 A Good Run Of Bad Luck	*Clint Black/Hayden Nicholas*	RCA
6/4/94	4	20		21 Half The Man #15, 16 & 18-21: from the album *No Time To Kill* on RCA 66239	*Clint Black/Hayden Nicholas*	RCA
9/24/94	4	20		22 Untanglin' My Mind	*Clint Black/Merle Haggard*	RCA
12/31/94+	3[1]	20		23 Wherever You Go	*Clint Black/Hayden Nicholas*	RCA
4/8/95	❶[3]	20		24 Summer's Comin'	*Clint Black/Hayden Nicholas*	RCA
7/8/95	2[2]	20		25 One Emotion	*Clint Black/Hayden Nicholas*	RCA
10/14/95	4	20		26 Life Gets Away above 5 from the album *One Emotion* on RCA 66419	*Clint Black/Hayden Nicholas/Thom Schuyler*	RCA
12/16/95+	58	4		27 Til' Santa's Gone (Milk And Cookies)	*Clint Black/Hayden Nicholas/Shake Russell* [X]	RCA
1/6/96	71	1		28 The Kid above 2 from the album *Looking For Christmas* on RCA 66593	*Clint Black/Merle Haggard/Hayden Nicholas* [X]	RCA

Billboard DEBUT	PEAK	WKS	GOLD	ARTIST / Country Chart Hit	Ranking / Songwriter	Label (& Number)

BLACK, Clint — cont'd

DEBUT	PEAK	WKS	GOLD	#	Country Chart Hit	Songwriter	Label (& Number)
9/7/96	❶[3]	20		29	Like The Rain	*Clint Black/Hayden Nicholas*	RCA
11/30/96+	6	20		30	Half Way Up above 2 from the album *The Greatest Hits* on RCA 66671	*Clint Black/Hayden Nicholas*	RCA
1/4/97	65	2		31	Til' Santa's Gone (Milk And Cookies) [X-R] from the album *Looking For Christmas* on RCA 66593	*Clint Black/Hayden Nicholas/Shake Russell*	RCA
6/14/97	11	20		32	Still Holding On *[w/ Martina McBride]*	*Matraca Berg/Clint Black/Marty Stuart*	RCA
8/30/97	2[3]	21		33	Something That We Do	S:6 *Clint Black/Skip Ewing*	RCA
10/18/97+	❶[2]	29		34	Nothin' But The Taillights	S:18 *Clint Black/Steve Wariner*	RCA
1/3/98	40	2		35	Til' Santa's Gone (Milk And Cookies) [X-R] from the album *Looking For Christmas* on RCA 66593	*Clint Black/Hayden Nicholas/Shake Russell*	RCA
4/11/98	❶[1]	20		36	The Shoes You're Wearing	S:20 *Clint Black/Hayden Nicholas*	RCA
8/15/98	12	20		37	Loosen Up My Strings	*Clint Black/Hayden Nicholas*	RCA
12/26/98+	38	3		38	Til' Santa's Gone (I Just Can't Wait) [X-R]	*Clint Black/Hayden Nicholas/Shake Russell*	RCA
1/9/99	67	1		39	The Kid [X-R] above 2 from the album *Looking For Christmas* on RCA 66593	*Clint Black/Merle Haggard/Hayden Nicholas*	RCA
1/30/99	29	15		40	You Don't Need Me Now #32-34, 36, 37 & 40: from the album *Nothin' But The Taillights* on RCA 67515	*Clint Black/Shake Russell*	RCA
9/4/99	❶[2]	27		41	When I Said I Do *[w/ Lisa Hartman Black]*	*Clint Black*	RCA
12/11/99+	34	5		42	Til' Santa's Gone (I Just Can't Wait) [X-R]	*Clint Black/Hayden Nicholas/Shake Russell*	RCA
1/8/00	71	1		43	The Kid [X-R] above 2 from the album *Looking For Christmas* on RCA 66593	*Clint Black/Merle Haggard/Hayden Nicholas*	RCA
1/15/00	5	22		44	Been There *[w/ Steve Wariner]*	*Clint Black/Steve Wariner*	RCA
6/24/00	30	20		45	Love She Can't Live Without #41, 44 & 45: from the album *D'lectrified* on RCA 67823	*Clint Black/Skip Ewing*	RCA
9/22/01	27	20		46	Easy For Me To Say *[w/ Lisa Hartman Black]*	*Clint Black/Hayden Nicholas*	RCA
2/16/02	50	6		47	Money Or Love above 2 from the album *Greatest Hits II* on RCA 67005	*Clint Black*	RCA
3/29/03	42	7		48	I Raq And Roll only available as a free download on Black's official website	*Clint Black/Hayden Nicholas*	clintblack.com
11/1/03+	16	22		49	Spend My Time	*Clint Black/Hayden Nicholas*	Equity
5/1/04	51	9		50	The Boogie Man	*Clint Black/Will Jennings*	Equity
5/29/04	8	20		51	Hey Good Lookin' *[w/ Jimmy Buffett/Kenny Chesney/Alan Jackson/ Toby Keith/George Strait]* from Buffett's album *License To Chill* on RCA 62270	*...Hank Williams*	RCA
7/31/04	42	8		52	My Imagination #49, 50 & 52: from the album *Spend My Time* on Equity 3001	*Clint Black/Matt Rollings*	Equity
1/8/05	54	1		53	Christmas With You [X] from the album *Christmas With You* on Equity 3004	*Clint Black/Hayden Nicholas*	Equity

BLACK, Jeanne

Born Gloria Jeanne Black on 10/25/1937 in Pomona, California. Female singer. Regular on **Cliffie Stone**'s TV show.

DEBUT	PEAK	WKS	GOLD	#	Country Chart Hit	Songwriter	Label (& Number)
5/2/60	6	12	●		He'll Have To Stay answer to "He'll Have To Go" by **Jim Reeves**	*Audrey Allison/Joe Allison/Charles Grean*	Capitol 4368

BLACKHAWK — All-Time: #236

Trio of music veterans Henry Paul (member of Southern-rock bands The Outlaws and Henry Paul Band) with the songwriting team of Dave Robbins and Van Stephenson. Stephenson died of cancer on 4/8/2001 (age 47). Touring bassist Randy Threet became the third member in 2002.

DEBUT	PEAK	WKS	GOLD	#	Country Chart Hit	Songwriter	Label (& Number)
11/20/93+	11	20		1	Goodbye Says It All	*Charlie Black/Bobby Fischer/Fred MacRae*	Arista
4/16/94	2[1]	20		2	Every Once In A While	*Henry Paul/Dave Robbins/Van Stephenson*	Arista
8/20/94	9	20		3	I Sure Can Smell The Rain	*Walt Aldridge/John Jarrard*	Arista
12/17/94+	10	20		4	Down In Flames	*Michael Clark/Jeff Stevens*	Arista
4/15/95	7	20		5	That's Just About Right above 5 from the album *BlackHawk* on Arista 18708	*Jeff Black*	Arista
7/29/95	2[2]	20		6	I'm Not Strong Enough To Say No	S:3 *Mutt Lange*	Arista
11/11/95+	3[1]	20		7	Like There Ain't No Yesterday	*Walt Aldridge/Mark Narmore*	Arista
2/24/96	11	20		8	Almost A Memory Now	*Dale Oliver/Dave Robbins/Van Stephenson*	Arista
6/15/96	17	20		9	Big Guitar	S:24 *Henry Gross/Henry Paul*	Arista
10/26/96	49	9		10	King Of The World above 5 from the album *Strong Enough* on Arista 18792	*Jeff Black*	Arista
6/28/97	31	20		11	Hole In My Heart	S:13 *Desmond Child/Dave Robbins/Van Stephenson*	Arista
10/18/97	37	17		12	Postmarked Birmingham above 2 from the album *Love & Gravity* on Arista 18837	*Don Sampson/Phil Vassar*	Arista
1/10/98	75	1		13	We Three Kings (Star Of Wonder) [X] from the various artists album *Country Cares For Kids* on BNA 67518	*John Henry Hopkins*	BNA
8/29/98+	4	28		14	There You Have It	S:11 *Steve Bogard/Rick Giles*	Arista
2/6/99	27	20		15	Your Own Little Corner Of My Heart above 2 from the album *The Sky's The Limit* on Arista 18872	*Walt Aldridge/Brad Crisler*	Arista
3/4/00	40	19		16	I Need You All The Time from the album *Greatest Hits* on Arista 18907	*Pat Bunch/Jimmy Price/Shane Teeters*	Arista
11/3/01+	37	20		17	Days Of America	*Lee Miller/Henry Paul/Dave Robbins*	Columbia
6/8/02	51	5		18	One Night In New Orleans above 2 from the album *Spirit Dancer* on Columbia 85968	*Rick Giles/Gilles Godard/Tim Nichols*	Columbia

BLACKJACK — see GRAYSON, Jack

BLACK TIE

All-star trio: Jimmy Griffin (Bread; **The Remingtons**), Randy Meisner (**Eagles**; **Poco**) and **Billy Swan**.

DEBUT	PEAK	WKS	GOLD	#	Country Chart Hit	Songwriter	Label (& Number)
12/15/90+	59	8			Learning The Game from the album *When The Night Falls* on Bench 101	*Buddy Holly*	Bench

DEBUT	PEAK	WKS	GOLD	ARTIST / Country Chart Hit	Songwriter	Label (& Number)
				BLACKWELL, Karon		
				Born in Ellisville, Mississippi. Female singer. Married comedian Marty Allen in 1984.		
1/22/77	**93**	3		**Blue Skies And Roses**	*Jimmy Dallas*	Blackland 254
				BLACKWOOD, R.W., and The Blackwood Singers		
				Born on 11/27/1946 in Tennessee. Male singer. Member of The Blackwood Brothers gospel group.		
8/7/76	**32**	10		1 **Sunday Afternoon Boatride In The Park On The Lake**	*Ted Brown/Ron Hellard*	Capitol 4302
11/13/76	**91**	4		2 **Memory Go Round**	*Gary S. Paxton*	Capitol 4346
10/28/78	**57**	6		3 **Dolly** *[R.W. Blackwood]* tribute to **Dolly Parton**	*Buzz Cason/Austin Roberts*	Scorpion 0561
				BLAIR, Kenny		
				Born in Austin, Texas. Male singer.		
7/2/88	**84**	2		**Lost In Austin**	*Lane Caudell/Don Goodman*	Awesome 119
				BLAKE & BRIAN		
				Duo of Blake Weldon (born on 9/13/1966 in Lufkin, Texas) and Brian Gowen (born on 1/7/1969 in Temple, Texas).		
7/19/97	**45**	16		1 **Another Perfect Day**	*Phil Barnhart/Brian Tabor/Conley White*	Curb
11/22/97+	**62**	8		2 **The Wish** above 2 from the album *Blake & Brian* on Curb 77900	*Phil Barnhart/Sam Hogin/Conley White*	Curb
4/25/98	**68**	1		3 **Amnesia**	*Larry Boone/Rick Bowles*	Curb
				BLAKER, Clay, and The Texas Honky-Tonk Band		
				Born on 6/27/1950 in Houston, Texas; raised in Almeda, Texas. Male singer/guitarist.		
5/16/87	**91**	2		1 **South Of The Border**	*Michael Carr/James Kennedy*	Texas Musik 6153
2/27/88	**75**	5		2 **A Honky Tonk Heart (And A Hillbilly Soul)**	*Dan McCoy*	Rain Forest 120187
				BLANCH, Arthur		
				Born in 1926 in Wollun, New South Wales, Australia. Male singer/guitarist. Father of **Jewel Blanch**.		
9/16/78	**73**	4		1 **The Little Man's Got The Biggest Smile In Town**	*Porter Jordan/Jerry Styner*	MC/Curb 5015
9/1/79	**82**	7		2 **Maybe I'll Cry Over You**	*Elton Britt*	Ridgetop 00479
				BLANCH, Jewel		
				Born in Australia. Female singer/actress. Daughter of **Arthur Blanch**. Played "Charlotte Sutter" in the 1975 movie *Against A Crooked Sky*.		
9/30/78	**68**	6		1 **So Good**	*Bob Morrison*	RCA 11329
2/10/79	**33**	12		2 **Can I See You Tonight**	*Deborah Allen/Rafe Van Hoy*	RCA 11464
				BLANCHARD, Jack, & Misty Morgan		
				Husband-and-wife duo. Both born in Buffalo, New York. Jack (born on 5/8/1942) plays saxophone and keyboards. Misty (born on 5/23/1945) plays keyboards. Met and married while working in Florida in 1963.		
3/1/69	**59**	4		1 **Big Black Bird (Spirit Of Our Love)**	*Jack Blanchard*	Wayside 1028
2/7/70	**❶[2]**	19		2 **Tennessee Bird Walk**	*Jack Blanchard* **[N]**	Wayside 010
6/20/70	**5**	13		3 **Humphrey The Camel**	*Jack Blanchard* **[N]**	Wayside 013
9/26/70	**27**	11		4 **You've Got Your Troubles (I've Got Mine)**	*Roger Cook/Roger Greenaway*	Wayside 015
7/24/71	**25**	13		5 **There Must Be More To Life (Than Growing Old)** /	*Jack Blanchard*	
7/24/71	**46**	13		6 **Fire Hydrant #79**	*Jack Blanchard*	Mega 0031
11/6/71+	**15**	14		7 **Somewhere In Virginia In The Rain**	*Jack Blanchard*	Mega 0046
3/25/72	**38**	11		8 **The Legendary Chicken Fairy**	*Jack Blanchard* **[N]**	Mega 0063
9/30/72	**60**	7		9 **Second Tuesday In December**	*Jack Blanchard*	Mega 0089
3/10/73	**65**	4		10 **A Handfull Of Dimes**	*Jack Blanchard*	Mega 0101
12/1/73+	**23**	13		11 **Just One More Song**	*Jack Blanchard*	Epic 11058
5/11/74	**53**	10		12 **Something On Your Mind**	*Jack Blanchard*	Epic 11097
9/28/74	**41**	12		13 **Down To The End Of The Wine**	*Jack Blanchard*	Epic 50023
7/26/75	**74**	7		14 **Because We Love**	*Jack Blanchard/Misty Morgan*	Epic 50122
12/27/75+	**68**	6		15 **I'm High On You**	*Jack Blanchard*	Epic 50181
				BLANTON, Loy		
				Born on 7/14/1945 in Victoria, Texas. Male singer.		
6/15/85	**77**	4		1 **California Sleeping**	*Dave Kirby/Curly Putman*	Soundwaves 4750
9/7/85	**63**	11		2 **Sailing Home To Me**	*Dave Kirby/Danny Morrison*	Soundwaves 4760
				BLIXSETH, Tim		
				Born in Oklahoma. Male singer/songwriter. Also recorded as **T.L. Lee**.		
5/4/85	**91**	2		1 **It Can't Be Done** **TIM BLIXSETH (with Kathy Walker)**	*Tim Blixseth/Norman Saleet*	Compleat 141
2/21/87	**78**	4		2 **A Silent Understanding** **T.L. LEE (with Kathy Walker)**	*Edra Blixseth/Tim Blixseth*	Compleat 164
				BLOCK, Doug		
				Born on 8/13/1946 in Brooklyn, New York. Died in January 1986 (age 39). Male singer.		
1/31/81	**82**	3		1 **Have Another Drink** *[Douglas]*	*Ray Davies*	Door Knob 143
12/22/84	**73**	4		2 **Have Another Drink** above 2 are the same version	*Ray Davies* **[R]**	Revolver 005
				BLUE, Bobby		
				Born in Los Angeles, California. Male singer.		
2/1/86	**80**	3		**Once Upon A Time**	*Gary Tanner*	Nite 108

DEBUT	PEAK	WKS	GOLD	#	ARTIST / Country Chart Hit	Songwriter	Label (& Number)

BLUE BOYS Featuring Bud Logan

Backing band for **Jim Reeves**: **Bud Logan** (vocals, bass), Leo Jackson (guitar), Bunky Keels (piano) and Jimmy Orr (drums).

DEBUT	PEAK	WKS	GOLD	#	Country Chart Hit	Songwriter	Label (& Number)
7/15/67	**63**	3		1	**My Cup Runneth Over** — from the musical *I Do! I Do!* starring Mary Martin and Robert Preston	*Tom Jones/Harvey Schmidt*	RCA Victor 9201
2/3/68	**58**	6		2	**I'm Not Ready Yet**	*Tom T. Hall*	RCA Victor 9418

BLUE COUNTY

Vocal duo formed in Nashville, Tennessee: Aaron Benward (from Auburn, Indiana) and Scott Reeves (from Delight, Arkansas). Reeves played "Ryan McNeil" on TV's *The Young And The Restless.*

DEBUT	PEAK	WKS	GOLD	#	Country Chart Hit	Songwriter	Label (& Number)
10/18/03+	**11**	30		1	**Good Little Girls**	*Brett Jones/Troy Seals*	Curb
5/15/04	**24**	22		2	**That's Cool**	*Aaron Benward/Lee Miller/Scott Reeves*	Curb
12/18/04+	**38**	14		3	**Nothin' But Cowboy Boots**	*Aaron Benward/Lee Miller*	Curb
4/23/05	**53**	8		4	**That Summer Song** — above 4 from the album *Blue County* on Curb 78833	*Tanya Leah/Stephanie Lewis/Brian Nash*	Curb

BLUE RIDGE RANGERS — see FOGERTY, John

BLUESTONE

Duo of **Ray Pennington** and **Jerry McBee**.

DEBUT	PEAK	WKS	GOLD	#	Country Chart Hit	Songwriter	Label (& Number)
2/9/80	**84**	3			**Haven't I Loved You Somewhere Before**	*Jerry McBee/Ray Pennington*	Dimension 1002

BOARDO, Liz

Born on 10/22/62 in Dorchester, Massachusetts. Female singer.

DEBUT	PEAK	WKS	GOLD	#	Country Chart Hit	Songwriter	Label (& Number)
2/7/87	**58**	6		1	**There's Still Enough Of Us**	*Ronnie Friend*	Master 02
6/27/87	**65**	5		2	**I Need To Be Loved Again**	*Don Goodman/Pal Rakes*	Master 03

BOGGUSS, Suzy — All-Time: #212

Born Susan Kay Bogguss on 12/30/1956 in Aledo, Illinois. Female singer/songwriter/guitarist. Married to songwriter/engineer Doug Crider. Also see **The Red Hots** and **Tomorrow's World**.

CMA: Horizon 1992

DEBUT	PEAK	WKS	GOLD	#	Country Chart Hit	Songwriter	Label (& Number)
3/14/87	**68**	6		1	**I Don't Want To Set The World On Fire**	*Bennie Benjamin/Eddie Durham/Sol Marcus/Eddie Seiler*	Capitol 5669
8/15/87	**69**	6		2	**Love Will Never Slip Away**	*Stan Munsey*	Capitol 44045
8/13/88	**77**	2		3	**I Want To Be A Cowboy's Sweetheart**	*Patsy Montana*	Capitol 44187
3/11/89	**46**	13		4	**Somewhere Between**	*Merle Haggard*	Capitol 44270
6/3/89	**14**	26		5	**Cross My Broken Heart**	*Rhonda Fleming/Verlon Thompson*	Capitol 44399
10/14/89	**38**	13		6	**My Sweet Love Ain't Around**	*Hank Williams Sr.*	Capitol 44450
9/1/90	**72**	1		7	**Under The Gun**	*Hugh Prestwood*	Capitol
12/15/90	**72**	4		8	**All Things Made New Again** — above 2 from the album *Moment Of Truth* on Capitol 92653	*Dan Seals/Rafe Van Hoy*	Capitol
5/11/91	**12**	20		9	**Hopelessly Yours** ***[w/ Lee Greenwood]*** — from Greenwood's album *A Perfect 10* on Capitol 95541	*Curly Putman/Keith Whitley*	Capitol
9/14/91	**12**	20		10	**Someday Soon**	*Ian Tyson*	Capitol
1/4/92	**9**	20		11	**Outbound Plane**	*Nanci Griffith/Tom Russell*	Capitol
4/4/92	**9**	20		12	**Aces**	*Cheryl Wheeler*	Capitol
8/15/92	**6**	20		13	**Letting Go** — above 4 from the album *Aces* on Capitol 95847	*Doug Crider/Matt Rollings*	Capitol
12/5/92+	**2^1**	20		14	**Drive South**	*John Hiatt*	Liberty
3/27/93	**23**	15		15	**Heartache** — above 2 from the album *Voices In The Wind* on Liberty 98585	*Lowell George/Ivan Ulz*	Liberty
8/7/93	**5**	20		16	**Just Like The Weather**	*Suzy Bogguss/Doug Crider*	Liberty
12/4/93+	**5**	20		17	**Hey Cinderella**	*Matraca Berg/Suzy Bogguss/Gary Harrison*	Liberty
5/7/94	**43**	9		18	**You Wouldn't Say That To A Stranger**	*Pat Bunch/Doug Crider*	Liberty
8/27/94	**65**	3		19	**Souvenirs** — above 4 from the album *Something Up My Sleeve* on Liberty 89261	*Gretchen Peters*	Liberty
6/1/96	**60**	6		20	**Give Me Some Wheels**	*Matraca Berg/Suzy Bogguss/Gary Harrison*	Capitol
9/14/96	**53**	9		21	**No Way Out**	*Marcus Hummon/Darrell Scott*	Capitol
3/22/97	**57**	9		22	**She Said, He Heard** — above 3 from the album *Give Me Some Wheels* on Capitol 36460	*Suzy Bogguss/Don Schlitz*	Capitol
4/11/98	**33**	19		23	**Somebody To Love**	*Matraca Berg/Suzy Bogguss/Doug Crider*	Capitol
9/19/98	**63**	4		24	**Nobody Love, Nobody Gets Hurt**	*Bobbie Cryner*	Capitol
11/28/98+	**67**	3		25	**From Where I Stand** — above 3 from the album *Nobody Love, Nobody Gets Hurt* on Capitol 57310	*Kim Richey/Tia Sillers*	Capitol
8/28/99	**66**	5		26	**Goodnight** — from the album *Suzy Bogguss* on Platinum 9358	*Charlie Black/Dana Hunt*	Platinum
5/12/01	**51**	6		27	**Keep Mom And Dad In Love** ***[w/ Billy Dean]***	*Lisa Brokop/Cyril Rawson/Richard Wold*	Dreamcatcher

BOLT, Al

Born Almos Bolt on 6/23/1938 in Atlanta, Texas. Male singer.

DEBUT	PEAK	WKS	GOLD	#	Country Chart Hit	Songwriter	Label (& Number)
2/28/76	**85**	6		1	**I'm In Love With My Pet Rock** **[N]**	*Bill Pineo*	Cin Kay 102
6/12/76	**92**	3		2	**Family Man**	*Bill Martin*	Cin Kay 103

BONAMY, James

Born on 4/29/1972 in Winter Park, Florida; raised in Daytona Beach, Florida. Male singer/guitarist.

DEBUT	PEAK	WKS	GOLD	#	Country Chart Hit	Songwriter	Label (& Number)
11/11/95	**64**	4		1	**Dog On A Toolbox**	*Monty Holmes/Gerry House*	Epic
12/16/95+	**26**	20		2	**She's Got A Mind Of Her Own**	*Billy Livsey/Don Schlitz*	Epic
5/11/96	**2^1**	21		3	**I Don't Think I Will**	*Doug Johnson*	Epic
10/26/96+	**27**	20		4	**All I Do Is Love Her** — above 4 from the album *What I Live To Do* on Epic 67069	*Skip Ewing/Wayland Patton*	Epic

DEBUT	PEAK	WKS	GOLD	ARTIST / Ranking / Country Chart Hit	Songwriter	Label (& Number)
				BONAMY, James — cont'd		
4/5/97	**31**	20		5 **The Swing**	S:22 *Robert Ellis Orrall/Bob Regan*	Epic
8/16/97	**65**	6		6 **Naked To The Pain**	*Don Pfrimmer/Richard Wold*	Epic
11/22/97	**63**	4		7 **Little Blue Dot**	*Rick Giles/Susan Longacre*	Epic
				above 3 from the album *Roots And Wings* on Epic 67878		
				BOND, Bobby		
				Born in Grand Rapids, Michigan. Male singer.		
9/30/72	**66**	7		**You Don't Mess Around With Jim**	*Jim Croce*	Hickory 1649
				BOND, Johnny		
				Born Cyrus Bond on 6/1/1915 in Enville, Oklahoma. Died of a heart attack on 6/12/1978 (age 63). Male singer/songwriter/guitarist. Regular on radio shows *Melody Ranch*, *Hollywood Barn Dance* and *Town Hall Party*. Acted in several western movies. Wrote book *The **Tex Ritter** Story*.		
2/22/47	**4**	1		1 **Divorce Me C.O.D.**	*Cliffie Stone/Merle Travis*	Columbia 37217
3/8/47	**3**[1]	5		2 **So Round, So Firm, So Fully Packed**	*Eddie Kirk/Cliffie Stone/Merle Travis*	Columbia 37255
8/16/47	**4**	3		3 **The Daughter Of Jole Blon**	*Fred Rose*	Columbia 37566
				JOHNNY BOND and his Red River Valley Boys (above 3)		
6/12/48	**9**	6		4 **Oklahoma Waltz**	J:9 *Jimmy Kenton*	Columbia 38160
4/9/49	**12**	2		5 **Till The End Of The World**	J:12 *Vaughn Horton*	Columbia 20549
7/23/49	**11**	1		6 **Tennessee Saturday Night**	J:11 *Billy Hughes*	Columbia 20545
4/15/50	**8**	2		7 **Love Song In 32 Bars**	J:8 *Roy Brodsky/Sid Tepper*	Columbia 20671
8/4/51	**7**	3		8 **Sick, Sober And Sorry**	J:7 *Tex Atchison/Eddie Hazelwood*	Columbia 4-20808
11/2/63	**30**	1		9 **Three Sheets In The Wind**	*Tex Atchison/Johnny Bond*	Starday 649
2/6/65	**2**[4]	21		10 **10 Little Bottles**	*Johnny Bond* **[L-N-S]**	Starday 704
2/20/71	**59**	6		11 **Here Come The Elephants**	*Jim Owens* **[N]**	Starday 916
				BON JOVI, Jon		
				Born on 3/2/1962 in Perth Amboy, New Jersey. Male singer/songwriter/guitarist/actor. Leader of rock group Bon Jovi. Acted in several movies.		
10/3/98	**68**	5		**Bang A Drum** ***[w/ Chris LeDoux]***	*Jon Bon Jovi*	Capitol
				from LeDoux's album *One Road Man* on Capitol 21942		
				BONNERS, The		
				Black vocal group from Cucamonga, California: Jim and wife Edith Bonner, with children Teresa, Cheryl, Kenny and Jim Jr.		
9/10/88	**99**	1		**Way Beyond The Blue**	*Randy Albright/Mark D. Sanders/Lisa Silver*	OL 126
				BONNIE LOU		
				Born Mary Kath on 10/27/1924 in Towanda, Illinois. Female singer/guitarist. Regular on the WLW *Midwestern Hayride*.		
5/9/53	**7**	5		1 **Seven Lonely Days**	A:7 / S:8 / J:9 *Marshall Brown/Alden Schuman/Earl Schuman*	King 1192
9/19/53	**6**	9		2 **Tennessee Wig Walk**	S:6 / J:6 *Larry Coleman/Johnny Gimble*	King 1237
				BONSALL, "Cat" Joe		
				Born on 5/18/1948 in Philadelphia, Pennsylvania. Male singer. Member of the **Oak Ridge Boys**.		
9/13/86	**11**	18		**Out Goin' Cattin'** ***[w/ Sawyer Brown]***	A:11 / S:12 *Mark Miller/Randy Scruggs*	Capitol/Curb 5629
				BOOKER, Jay		
				Born in Pensacola, Florida. Male singer/songwriter/guitarist.		
5/2/87	**61**	8		**Hot Red Sweater**	*Jay Booker*	EMI America 8379
				BOONE, Debby		
				Born on 9/22/1956 in Leonia, New Jersey. Daughter of **Pat Boone** and granddaughter of **Red Foley**. Worked with the Boone Family from 1969; sang with her sisters in gospel quartet. Went solo in 1977. Won the 1977 Best New Artist Grammy Award. Married Gabriel Ferrer, the son of singer Rosemary Clooney and actor Jose Ferrer, on 9/1/1979.		
10/22/77	**4**	14	▲	1 **You Light Up My Life**	*Joe Brooks*	Warner/Curb 8455
				title song from the movie starring Didi Conn		
4/29/78	**33**	11		2 **Baby, I'm Yours /**	*Van McCoy*	
5/20/78	**22**	8		3 **God Knows**	*Franne Golde/Peter Noone/Allee Willis*	Warner/Curb 8554
11/18/78	**61**	4		4 **In Memory Of Your Love**	*Carol Chase*	Warner/Curb 8700
1/13/79	**11**	13		5 **My Heart Has A Mind Of Its Own**	*Howard Greenfield/Jack Keller*	Warner/Curb 8739
5/26/79	**25**	10		6 **Breakin' In A Brand New Broken Heart**	*Howard Greenfield/Jack Keller*	Warner/Curb 8814
9/1/79	**41**	7		7 **See You In September**	*Sherman Edwards/Sid Wayne*	Warner/Curb 49042
11/10/79	**48**	6		8 **Everybody's Somebody's Fool**	*Howard Greenfield/Jack Keller*	Warner/Curb 49107
2/16/80	❶[1]	15		9 **Are You On The Road To Lovin' Me Again**	*Debbie Hupp/Bob Morrison*	Warner/Curb 49176
7/26/80	**14**	13		10 **Free To Be Lonely Again**	*Diane Pfeifer*	Warner/Curb 49281
11/8/80	**44**	10		11 **Take It Like A Woman**	*Norman Sallitt*	Warner/Curb 49585
2/7/81	**23**	12		12 **Perfect Fool**	*Diane Pfeifer*	Warner/Curb 49652
6/27/81	**46**	7		13 **It'll Be Him**	*Billy Ray Reynolds*	Warner/Curb 49720
				BOONE, Larry		
				Born on 6/7/1956 in Cooper City, Florida. Male singer/songwriter/guitarist.		
7/26/86	**64**	9		1 **Stranger Things Have Happened**	*David Chamberlain*	Mercury 884858
10/25/86	**52**	9		2 **She's The Trip That I've Been On**	*Dallas Frazier/Whitey Shafer*	Mercury 888044
3/21/87	**48**	10		3 **Back In The Swing Of Things Again**	*Bob Moulds/David Wills*	Mercury 888427
6/6/87	**52**	8		4 **I Talked A Lot About Leaving**	*Bobby Keel/Charles Quillen/Tony Stampley*	Mercury 888598
12/19/87+	**44**	19		5 **Roses In December**	*Larry Boone/Paul Nelson*	Mercury 870086
4/9/88	**48**	10		6 **Stop Me (If You've Heard This One Before)**	*Tim Daniels/Gene Dobbins/Tommy Rocco*	Mercury 870267
6/18/88	**10**	19		7 **Don't Give Candy To A Stranger**	S:18 *Larry Boone/Dave Gibson/Jimbeau Hinson*	Mercury 870454
11/19/88+	**16**	21		8 **I Just Called To Say Goodbye Again**	*Bud McGuire/Paul Nelson*	Mercury 872046

Billboard			G O L D	ARTIST Ranking		
DEBUT	PEAK	WKS		Country Chart Hit	Songwriter	Label (& Number)
				BOONE, Larry — cont'd		
3/25/89	**19**	14		9 **Wine Me Up**	*Billy Deaton/Faron Young*	Mercury 872728
7/8/89	**39**	9		10 **Fool's Paradise**	*Gene Nelson/Paul Nelson*	Mercury 874538
3/17/90	**75**	1		11 **Everybody Wants To Be Hank Williams**	*Larry Boone/Paul Nelson*	Mercury
				from the album *Down That River Road* on Mercury 842156		
3/9/91	**57**	8		12 **I Need A Miracle**	*Larry Boone/Danny Mayo/Paul Nelson*	Columbia
5/25/91	**34**	20		13 **To Be With You**	*Gretchen Peters*	Columbia
				above 2 from the album *One Way To Go* on Columbia 47050		
4/24/93	**65**	5		14 **Get In Line**	*Larry Boone/Tom Shapiro/Chris Waters* **[L]**	Columbia
				from the album *Get In Line* on Columbia 48968		
				BOONE, Pat		
				Born Charles Eugene Patrick Boone on 6/1/1934 in Jacksonville, Florida. Male singer. Married **Red Foley**'s daughter, Shirley, on 11/7/1953. Father of **Debby Boone**.		
4/5/75	**72**	7		1 **Indiana Girl**	*Marty Cooper*	Melodyland 6005
9/27/75	**84**	6		2 **I'd Do It With You** *[w/ Shirley Boone]*	*Bobby Lee Springfield*	Melodyland 6018
7/17/76	**34**	10		3 **Texas Woman**	*Robert Duncan/Steve Stone*	Hitsville 6037
10/16/76	**86**	4		4 **Oklahoma Sunshine**	*Mike Settle*	Hitsville 6042
11/15/80	**60**	6		5 **Colorado Country Morning**	*J.C. Cunningham/Robert Duncan*	Warner/Curb 49596
				BOOTH, Larry		
				Born in Tampa, Florida. Male singer/bassist. Brother of **Tony Booth**. Member of **Gene Watson**'s band.		
5/27/78	**99**	2		**I See Love In Your Eyes**	*Ira Allen/Dan Newman*	Cream 7823
				BOOTH, Tony		
				Born on 2/7/1943 in Tampa, Florida. Male singer/guitarist. Brother of **Larry Booth**. Member of **Gene Watson**'s band.		
3/28/70	**67**	3		1 **Irma Jackson**	*Merle Haggard*	MGM 14112
12/4/71+	**45**	12		2 **Cinderella**	*Buddy Mize*	Capitol 3214
3/25/72	**15**	15		3 **The Key's In The Mailbox**	*Harlan Howard*	Capitol 3269
7/8/72	**18**	12		4 **A Whole Lot Of Somethin'**	*Buddy Alan*	Capitol 3356
9/30/72	**16**	13		5 **Lonesome 7-7203**	*Justin Tubb*	Capitol 3441
1/27/73	**32**	10		6 **When A Man Loves A Woman (The Way That I Love You)**	*Buck Owens*	Capitol 3515
4/28/73	**41**	8		7 **Loving You**	*Buck Owens*	Capitol 3582
7/7/73	**49**	6		8 **Old Faithful**	*Buck Owens*	Capitol 3639
10/6/73	**47**	11		9 **Secret Love**	*Sammy Fain/Paul Francis Webster*	Capitol 3723
12/29/73+	**49**	11		10 **Happy Hour**	*Buck Owens*	Capitol 3795
4/20/74	**84**	6		11 **Lonely Street**	*Carl Belew/Kenny Sowder/W.S. Stevenson*	Capitol 3853
8/31/74	**27**	13		12 **Workin' At The Car Wash Blues**	*Jim Croce*	Capitol 3943
12/28/74+	**72**	8		13 **Watch Out For Lucy**	*Lonnie Mack*	Capitol 3994
5/21/77	**95**	2		14 **Letting Go**	*Dave Kirby/Glenn Martin*	United Artists 962
				BORCHERS, Bobby		
				Born on 6/19/1952 in Cincinnati, Ohio; raised in Kentucky. Male singer/songwriter.		
3/6/76	**29**	10		1 **Someone's With Your Wife Tonight, Mister**	*Rory Bourke/Johnny Wilson*	Playboy 6065
8/21/76	**32**	9		2 **They Don't Make 'Em Like That Anymore**	*Rory Bourke*	Playboy 6083
12/4/76+	**12**	15		3 **Whispers**	*Rory Bourke/Gene Dobbins/Johnny Wilson*	Playboy 6092
5/14/77	**7**	14		4 **Cheap Perfume And Candlelight**	*Sterling Whipple*	Playboy 5803
9/3/77	**18**	11		5 **What A Way To Go**	*Bobby David/Jim Rushing*	Playboy 5816
12/10/77+	**18**	13		6 **I Promised Her A Rainbow**	*Rory Bourke*	Playboy 5823
4/8/78	**23**	10		7 **I Like Ladies In Long Black Dresses**	*Rory Bourke*	Playboy 5827
8/12/78	**20**	11		8 **Sweet Fantasy**	*Rory Bourke*	Epic 50585
1/13/79	**32**	8		9 **Wishing I Had Listened To Your Song**	*Jerry Chesnut*	Epic 50650
5/5/79	**43**	8		10 **I Just Wanna Feel The Magic**	*Rory Bourke/Mel McDaniel*	Epic 50687
2/21/87	**80**	3		11 **It Was Love What It Was**	*Whitey Shafer/Sonny Throckmorton*	Longhorn 3002
5/2/87	**86**	2		12 (I Remember When I Thought) **Whiskey Was A River**	*Bobby Borchers*	Longhorn 3003
				BOTTOMS, Dennis		
				Born on 8/28/1954 in Springfield, Illinois. Male singer/banjo player.		
4/27/85	**74**	7		1 **Did I Stay Too Long**	*Larry Keith/John Reid/Johnny Slate*	Warner 29035
8/3/85	**80**	5		2 **Bring On The Sunshine**	*Danny Morrison/John Reid/Johnny Slate*	Warner 28944
				BOUCHER, Jessica		
				Born in New York. Female singer. One-half of **Merrill And Jessica** duo.		
5/5/84	**39**	10		**Memory Lane** *[w/ Joe Stampley]*	*Dave McComb/David Rosson/Tony Stampley*	Epic 04446
				BOWES, Margie		
				Born on 3/18/1941 in Roxboro, North Carolina. Female singer/actress. Acted in the movie *The Gold Guitar*. Once married to Doyle Wilburn of the **Wilburn Brothers**.		
				OPRY: 1959		
3/23/59	**10**	16		1 **Poor Old Heartsick Me**	*Helen Carter*	Hickory 1094
8/31/59	**15**	14		2 **My Love And Little Me**	*Phil Everly*	Hickory 1102
7/24/61	**21**	6		3 **Little Miss Belong To No One**	*Wayne Walker*	Mercury 71845
1/11/64	**33**	4		4 **Our Things**	*Ramona Redd/Mitchell Torok*	Decca 31557
5/23/64	**26**	7		5 **Understand Your Gal**	*Johnny Cash*	Decca 31606
				answer to "Understand Your Man" by **Johnny Cash**		

Billboard			G O L D	ARTIST	Ranking	
DEBUT	PEAK	WKS		Country Chart Hit	Songwriter	Label (& Number)

BOWLING, Roger

Born on 12/3/1944 in Harlan, Kentucky. Committed suicide on 12/26/1982 (age 38). Male singer/songwriter/guitarist.

DEBUT	PEAK	WKS	GOLD	Country Chart Hit	Songwriter	Label (& Number)
6/10/78	**96**	5		1 **Dance With Me Molly**	*Roger Bowling/Steve Tutsie*	Louisiana Hayride 783
9/16/78	**90**	5		2 **A Loser's Just A Learner (On His Way To Better Things)**	*Roger Bowling/Steve Tutsie*	Louisiana Hayride 784
2/23/80	**55**	7		3 **Friday Night Fool**	*Roger Bowling*	NSD 37
5/31/80	**78**	3		4 **The Diplomat**	*Roger Bowling/Billy Edd Wheeler*	NSD 46
8/23/80	**52**	8		5 **Long Arm Of The Law**	*Roger Bowling/Billy Edd Wheeler*	NSD 58
11/29/80+	**30**	15		6 **Yellow Pages**	*Roger Bowling/George Nowak*	NSD 71
4/11/81	**50**	8		7 **A Little Bit Of Heaven**	*Roger Bowling/Paul Richey*	Mercury 57049

BOWMAN, Billy Bob, and The Beaumont Bag & Burlap Company

Born Hiram Abiff Collie on 11/25/1926 in Little Rock, Arkansas; raised in San Antonio, Texas. Died on 2/19/1992 (age 65). Popular DJ under the name Biff Collie. Formerly married to **Shirley Collie**.

DEBUT	PEAK	WKS	GOLD	Country Chart Hit	Songwriter	Label (& Number)
11/4/72	**55**	5		**Miss Pauline**	*Leon Malphrus*	United Artists 50957

BOWMAN, Don

Born on 8/26/1937 in Lubbock, Texas. Male singer/songwriter/guitarist/comedian. Discovered by **Chet Atkins**. Original host of radio's *American Country Countdown*. Also see **Some Of Chet's Friends**.

CMA: Comedian 1967

DEBUT	PEAK	WKS	GOLD	Country Chart Hit	Songwriter	Label (& Number)
7/25/64	**14**	16		1 **Chit Akins, Make Me A Star**	*Don Bowman* **[N]**	RCA Victor 8384
6/18/66	**49**	2		2 **Giddyup Do-Nut** parody of "Giddyup Go" by **Red Sovine**	*Don Bowman/Tommy Hill/Red Sovine* **[N]**	RCA Victor 8811
12/3/66	**73**	2		3 **Surely Not**	*Jerry Reed* **[N]**	RCA Victor 8990
2/24/68	**72**	2		4 **For Loving You** ***[w/ Skeeter Davis]***	*Steve Karliski* **[N]**	RCA Victor 9415
10/5/68	**74**	2		5 **Folsom Prison Blues #2** parody of "Folsom Prison Blues" by **Johnny Cash**	*Don Bowman/Johnny Cash* **[N]**	RCA Victor 9617
5/17/69	**70**	5		6 **Poor Old Ugly Gladys Jones** ***[w/ Friends]*** **Bobby Bare**, **Waylon Jennings** and **Willie Nelson** (guest vocals)	*Don Bowman/Waylon Jennings* **[N]**	RCA Victor 0133

BOWSER, Donnie

Born Donald Bowshier on 4/14/1937 in Madison Mills, Ohio. Died of a heart attack on 2/22/2002 (age 64). Male singer/guitarist.

DEBUT	PEAK	WKS	GOLD	Country Chart Hit	Songwriter	Label (& Number)
9/16/89	**90**	1		**Falling For You**	*Allen Greene*	Ridgewood 3002

BOXCAR WILLIE

Born Lecil Martin on 9/1/1931 in Sterratt, Texas. Died of leukemia on 4/12/1999 (age 67). Male singer/songwriter/guitarist. Adopted his on-stage hobo attire in 1976.

OPRY: 1981

DEBUT	PEAK	WKS	GOLD	Country Chart Hit	Songwriter	Label (& Number)
4/26/80	**95**	3		1 **Train Medley** Fireball Mail/Train of Love/Walking Cane/Wreck of the Old #97/Orange Blossom Special/Wabash Cannonball/Night Train to Memphis; also see #7 below	*Owen Bradley/A.P. Carter/Johnny Cash/Marvin Hughes/Floyd Jenkins/ Lecil Martin/C.W. Noell/Ervin Rouse/Hank Whitter*	Column One 1012
3/13/82	**36**	12		2 **Bad News**	*John D. Loudermilk*	Main Street 951
7/10/82	**77**	5		3 **We Made Memories** ***[w/ Penny DeHaven]***	*Jess Hudson/Kenny Seratt*	Main Street 952
9/11/82	**80**	4		4 **Last Train To Heaven /**	*Jan Shuster/Guy Workman*	
11/13/82	**70**	6		5 **Keep On Rollin' Down The Line**	*Boxcar Willie*	Main Street 953
2/5/83	**76**	6		6 **Country Music Nightmare /**	*Lecil Martin* **[N]**	
4/16/83	**61**	8		7 **Train Medley** same version as #1 above	*Owen Bradley/A.P. Carter/Johnny Cash/Marvin Hughes/Floyd Jenkins/ Lecil Martin/C.W. Noell/Ervin Rouse/Hank Whitter* **[R]**	Main Street 954
12/24/83+	**44**	12		8 **The Man I Used To Be**	*Lathan Hudson/Larry Kingston*	Main Street 93017
5/5/84	**87**	3		9 **Not On The Bottom Yet**	*Bobby Caraway/Martin Llone*	Main Street 93020
7/14/84	**69**	6		10 **Luther**	*Ken Jones/Larry Kingston*	Main Street 93021

BOYD, Bill, and his Cowboy Ramblers

Born on 9/29/1910 in Fannin County, Texas. Died on 12/7/1977 (age 67). Male singer/songwriter/guitarist. Not to be confused with William "Hopalong Cassidy" Boyd. The Cowboy Ramblers included his younger brother Jim Boyd (guitar), Ken Pitts (fiddle), Knocky Parker (piano) and Marvin "Smoky" Montgomery (banjo). Group appeared in several western movies.

DEBUT	PEAK	WKS	GOLD	Country Chart Hit	Songwriter	Label (& Number)
9/8/45	**4**	2		1 **Shame On You**	*Spade Cooley*	Bluebird 33-0530
8/24/46	**5**	1		2 **New Steel Guitar Rag**	*Bill Boyd*	RCA Victor 20-1907

BOYD, Jimmy

Born on 1/9/1939 in McComb, Mississippi. Male singer/actor. Played "Howard Meechim" on TV's *Bachelor Father* (1958-61).

DEBUT	PEAK	WKS	GOLD	Country Chart Hit	Songwriter	Label (& Number)
12/20/52	**7**	3	●	**I Saw Mommy Kissing Santa Claus**	J:7 / A:7 *Tommy Connor* **[X-N]**	Columbia 4-39871

BOYD, Mike

Born in Houston, Texas. Male singer/songwriter.

DEBUT	PEAK	WKS	GOLD	Country Chart Hit	Songwriter	Label (& Number)
5/22/76	**98**	2		1 **The Leaving Was Easy**	*Mike Boyd*	Claridge 417
8/20/77	**93**	6		2 **Stop And Think It Over**	*Jack Graffagnino*	MBI 4816
2/11/78	**80**	5		3 **Love And Hate**	*Vincent Kickerillo/Mike Ruggeri*	Inergi 305

BOYER TWINS, The

Duo of twin brothers Gene Boyer and Dean Boyer.

DEBUT	PEAK	WKS	GOLD	Country Chart Hit	Songwriter	Label (& Number)
2/9/80	**91**	4		**Three Little Words**	*Dave Loggins*	Sabre 4516

BOY HOWDY

Group formed in Los Angeles, California: brothers Cary Park and Larry Park (guitars), **Jeffrey Steele** (vocals, bass) and Hugh Wright (drums). Cary and Larry are the sons of noted bluegrass fiddler Ray Park.

DEBUT	PEAK	WKS	GOLD	Country Chart Hit	Songwriter	Label (& Number)
7/4/92	**43**	16		1 **Our Love Was Meant To Be**	*Chris Farren/Jeffrey Steele*	Curb
6/19/93	**12**	20		2 **A Cowboy's Born With A Broken Heart** above 2 from the album *Welcome To Howdywood* on Curb 77562	*Chris Farren/Jeffrey Steele*	Curb

Billboard			G O L D	ARTIST	Ranking	
DEBUT	PEAK	WKS		Country Chart Hit	Songwriter	Label (& Number)
				BOY HOWDY — cont'd		
11/6/93+	**4**	20		3 **She'd Give Anything**	*Chris Farren/Vince Melamed/Jeffrey Steele*	Curb
4/2/94	**2^{1}**	20		4 **They Don't Make 'Em Like That Anymore**	*Chris Farren/Jeffrey Steele*	Curb
				above 2 from the album *She'd Give Anything* on Curb 77656		
12/10/94+	**23**	20		5 **True To His Word**	*Chris Farren/Gary Harrison/Jeffrey Steele*	Curb
4/8/95	**57**	6		6 **Bigger Fish To Fry**	*Jeffrey Steele*	Curb
7/1/95	**48**	10		7 **She Can't Love You**	*Chris Farren/Randy Sharp/Jeffrey Steele*	Curb
				above 3 from the album *Born That Way* on Curb 77691		
				BRADDOCK, Bobby	**SW: #39**	
				Born on 8/5/1940 in Auburndale, Florida. Male singer/songwriter/pianist.		
7/29/67	**74**	4		1 **I Know How To Do It**	*Bobby Braddock*	MGM 13737
1/11/69	**62**	6		2 **The Girls In Country Music**	*Bobby Braddock*	MGM 14017
6/2/79	**58**	5		3 **Between The Lines**	*Bobby Braddock/Sparky Lawrence*	Elektra 46038
2/9/80	**87**	3		4 **Nag, Nag, Nag**	*Bobby Braddock* **[N]**	Elektra 46585
				BRADFORD, Keith		
				Born Arthur Guilbeault in Burrillville, Rhode Island. Male singer.		
6/17/78	**83**	4		1 **Lonely People**	*Jimmie Crane*	Mu-Sound 421
3/17/79	**86**	2		2 **Lonely Coming Down**	*Porter Wagoner*	Scorpion 0572
				BRADING, Susie		
				Born Susan Storment in Lincoln, Illinois. Female singer.		
2/4/84	**94**	3		**Dream Lover**	*Don Riddle*	Riddle 1010
				BRADLEY, Owen, Quintet	**HOF: 1974**	
				Born on 10/21/1915 in Westmoreland, Tennessee. Died on 1/7/1998 (age 82). Music director at WSM-Nashville from 1940-58. Nashville producer for Decca from 1947. Country A&R director for Decca from 1958-68. Vice president of MCA from 1968.		
12/3/49+	**7**	4		**Blues Stay Away From Me** A:7 / J:8 / S:9	*Alton Delmore/Rabon Delmore/Henry Glover/Wayne Raney*	Coral 60107
				Jack Shook and Dottie Dillard (vocals)		
				BRADSHAW, Carolyn		
				Born on 1/2/1936 in Oklahoma. Died on 2/14/1993 (age 57). Female singer. Regular on the *Louisiana Hayride*.		
8/22/53	**10**	1		**Marriage Of Mexican Joe** J:10	*Mitchell Torok*	Abbott 141
				sequel to "Mexican Joe" by **Jim Reeves**		
				BRADSHAW, Terry		
				Born on 9/2/1948 in Shreveport, Louisiana. Pro football quarterback with the Pittsburgh Steelers from 1970-83. Acted in the movies *Hooper, Smokey and The Bandit II* and *Cannonball Run*. Current TV football analyst (on Fox's *NFL Sunday*).		
1/31/76	**17**	13		1 **I'm So Lonesome I Could Cry**	*Hank Williams*	Mercury 73760
7/10/76	**90**	4		2 **The Last Word In Lonesome Is Me**	*Roger Miller*	Mercury 73808
4/26/80	**73**	5		3 **Until You**	*Claire Cloninger/Jerry Crutchfield*	Benson 2001
				BRANDON, T.C.		
				Born in Fullerton, California. Female singer.		
9/2/89	**93**	1		**You Belong To Me**	*Pee Wee King/Chilton Price/Redd Stewart*	Bear 2006
				BRANDT, Paul		
				Born on 7/21/1972 in Calgary, Alberta, Canada. Male singer/songwriter/guitarist.		
3/9/96	**5**	22		1 **My Heart Has A History** S:10	*Paul Brandt/Mark D. Sanders*	Reprise
6/8/96	**2^{2}**	23		2 **I Do** S:3	*Paul Brandt*	Reprise
11/16/96+	**39**	20		3 **I Meant To Do That**	*Paul Brandt/Kerry Chater/Lynn Chater*	Reprise
3/29/97	**38**	15		4 **Take It From Me**	*Paul Brandt/Roy Hurd*	Reprise
				above 4 from the album *Calm Before The Storm* on Reprise 46180		
10/18/97	**45**	10		5 **A Little In Love**	*Rick Bowles/Josh Leo*	Reprise
1/24/98	**68**	3		6 **What's Come Over You**	*Gene Nelson/Doug Swander*	Reprise
				above 2 from the album *Outside The Frame* on Reprise 46635		
4/17/99	**47**	20		7 **That's The Truth**	*Paul Brandt/Chris Farren*	Reprise
9/18/99+	**38**	20		8 **It's A Beautiful Thing** S:25	*Jeffrey Steele/Craig Wiseman*	Reprise
12/18/99+	**66**	3		9 **Six Tons Of Toys**	*Dave Dudley* **[X]**	Reprise
				from the album *A Paul Brandt Christmas - Shall I Play For You?* on Reprise 47264		
2/5/00	**68**	4		10 **That Hurts**	*Gary Burr/Gerry House*	Reprise
				#7, 8 & 10: from the album *That's The Truth* on Reprise 47319		
				BRANE, Sherry		
				Born in Kansas. Female singer.		
12/9/78+	**56**	7		1 **It's My Party**	*John Gluck/Wally Gold/Herb Wiener*	Oak 1013
5/17/80	**83**	2		2 **Little Girls Need Daddies**	*Dixie Smallwood*	Tejas 1015
10/11/80	**86**	2		3 **Falling In Trouble Again**	*Raleigh Squires*	e.i.o. 1129
				BRANNON, Kippi		
				Born Kippi Brinkley in 1966 in Goodlettsville, Tennessee. Female singer.		
9/26/81	**37**	11		1 **Slowly**	*Tommy Hill/Webb Pierce*	MCA 51166
4/3/82	**55**	7		2 **If I Could See You Tonight**	*Mark Collie*	MCA 52023
9/11/82	**87**	4		3 **He Don't Make Me Cry**	*Sorrells Pickard*	MCA 52096
2/1/97	**42**	20		4 **Daddy's Little Girl** S:6	*Angela Kaset/Kenya Walker/Stan Webb*	Curb/Universal
6/28/97	**53**	8		5 **I'd Be With You**	*Angela Kaset/Kenya Walker/Stan Webb*	Curb/Universal
				above 2 from the album *I'd Be With You* on Curb/Universal 53092		

Billboard DEBUT	PEAK	WKS	GOLD	ARTIST / Country Chart Hit	Ranking / Songwriter	Label (& Number)

BRASFIELD, Rod — HOF: 1987

Born on 8/22/1910 in Smithville, Mississippi. Died of heart failure on 9/12/1958 (age 48). Legendary comedian. Known for his baggy suit, button shoes, beat-up hat, rubbery face and clacking false teeth.

OPRY: 1944

BREAKFAST BARRY — see GRANT, Barry

BRENNAN, Walter

Born on 7/25/1894 in Swampscott, Massachusetts. Died on 9/21/1974 (age 80). Acted in several movies. Played "Grandpa" on TV's *The Real McCoys*.

DEBUT	PEAK	WKS	Country Chart Hit	Songwriter	Label (& Number)
5/5/62	3^{1}	13	**Old Rivers** — The Johnny Mann Singers (backing vocals)	*Cliff Crofford* [S]	Liberty 55436

BRENTWOOD

Vocal trio formed in Nashville, Tennessee: Jay Kencke, Kenny Wrinn and Ron Freeman.

DEBUT	PEAK	WKS	Country Chart Hit	Songwriter	Label (& Number)
10/1/83	96	1	1 **Love The One You're With**	*Stephen Stills*	Hot Schatz 0051
3/17/84	80	3	2 **Anything For Your Love**	*Stewart Harris/Roger Murrah*	Hot Schatz 0052

BRESH, Tom

Born on 2/23/1948 in Hollywood, California. Male singer/songwriter/guitarist/actor. Son of **Merle Travis**. Worked as a stuntman as a child. Member of **Hank Penny**'s band. Appeared in the musicals *Finian's Rainbow*, *Harvey* and *The Music Man*.

DEBUT	PEAK	WKS	Country Chart Hit	Songwriter	Label (& Number)
4/24/76	6	16	1 **Home Made Love**	*Richard Mainegra*	Farr 004
8/14/76	17	11	2 **Sad Country Love Song**	*John Beland*	Farr 009
11/20/76+	33	11	3 **Hey Daisy (Where Have All The Good Times Gone)**	*John Beland*	Farr 012
6/11/77	57	7	4 **Until I Met You**	*Tom Bresh*	ABC/Dot 17703
9/24/77	48	7	5 **That Old Cold Shoulder**	*Sterling Whipple*	ABC/Dot 17720
1/28/78	78	4	6 **Smoke! Smoke! Smoke! (That Cigarette)**	*Merle Travis/Tex Williams*	ABC/Dot 17738
4/29/78	74	6	7 **Ways Of A Woman In Love**	*Don Cook*	ABC 12352
8/12/78	84	4	8 **First Encounter Of A Close Kind**	*Tom Bresh*	ABC 12389
12/11/82	77	5	9 **When It Comes To Love** *[w/ Lane Brody]*	*Thom Schuyler*	Liberty 1487

BR5-49

Group formed in Nashville, Tennessee: Gary Bennett (vocals, guitar), Chuck Mead (guitar), Don Herron (mandolin), Jay McDowell (bass) and Randall Wilson (drums). Group named after the fictional telephone number used by **Junior Samples** on TV's *Hee-Haw*.

DEBUT	PEAK	WKS	Country Chart Hit	Songwriter	Label (& Number)
9/21/96	44	20	1 **Cherokee Boogie**	*Moon Mullican/Chief William Redbird*	Arista Nashville
1/18/97	68	1	2 **Even If It's Wrong**	*Gary Bennett*	Arista Nashville
2/22/97	61	6	3 **Little Ramona (Gone Hillbilly Nuts)** — above 3 from the album *BR5-49* on Arista Nashville 18818	*Chuck Mead*	Arista Nashville
6/23/01	11^{S}	22	4 **Too Lazy To Work, Too Nervous To Steal** — from the album *This Is BR5-49* on Lucky Dog 85456	*Chuck Mead*	Monument

BRICKMAN, Jim

Born on 11/20/1961 in Cleveland, Ohio. New Age pianist/songwriter.

DEBUT	PEAK	WKS	Country Chart Hit	Songwriter	Label (& Number)
2/22/97+	9	20	1 **Valentine** *[w/ Martina McBride]* — from McBride's album *Evolution* on RCA 67516	*Jim Brickman/Jack Kugell*	RCA
10/25/97	51	11	2 **The Gift** *[w/ Collin Raye]* — from Raye's album *Direct Hits* on Epic 67893	*Jim Brickman/Tom Douglas* [X]	Epic
1/22/00	74	2	3 **Your Love** *[w/ Michelle Wright]* — from Brickman's album *Destiny* on Windham Hill 11396	*Jim Brickman/Dane DeVillar/Sean Hosein*	Windham Hill

BRILEY, Jebry Lee

Born in Brooklyn, New York. Female singer.

DEBUT	PEAK	WKS	Country Chart Hit	Songwriter	Label (& Number)
10/13/79	89	3	1 **I Just Wonder Where He Could Be Tonight** *[w/ Hilka]*	*Hilka Cornelius*	IBC 0004
2/13/82	80	4	2 **Let Your Fingers Do The Walkin'**	*Pat Briley*	Paid 141

BRITT, Catherine

Born in 1985 in Newcastle, New South Wales, Australia. Female singer.

DEBUT	PEAK	WKS	Country Chart Hit	Songwriter	Label (& Number)
8/14/04	36	19	**The Upside Of Being Down** — from the album *Too Far Gone* on RCA 57261	*Christi Baker/Shari Baker/Rory Lee Feek*	RCA

BRITT, Elton — 1940s: #13 / All-Time: #284

Born James Elton Baker on 6/27/1913 in Zack, Arkansas. Died of a heart attack on 6/23/1972 (age 58). Male singer/songwriter/guitarist. Appeared in the movies *Laramie*, *The Last Doggie* and *The Prodigal Son*.

EARLY HIT: There's A Star-Spangled Banner Waving Somewhere (1942)

DEBUT	PEAK	WKS	Country Chart Hit	Songwriter	Label (& Number)
1/27/45	7	1	1 **I'm A Convict With Old Glory In My Heart**	*Dave McEnery/Bob Miller*	Bluebird 33-0517
1/26/46	2^{5}	18	2 **Someday**	*Jimmie Hodges*	Bluebird 33-0521
3/16/46	3^{2}	9	3 **Wave To Me, My Lady /**	*Frank Loesser/Willie Stein*	
4/13/46	4	1	4 **Blueberry Lane**	*Lee David/Bob Miller*	Victor 20-1789
5/11/46	5	1	5 **Detour**	*Paul Westmoreland*	RCA Victor 20-1817
7/27/46	6	1	6 **Blue Texas Moonlight** *[w/ The Skytoppers]*	*Layman Cameron/Eddie Smith*	RCA Victor 20-1873
8/24/46	4	1	7 **Gotta Get Together With My Gal**	*Max Rich/Esther Van Sciver*	RCA Victor 20-1927
10/30/48	6	6	8 **Chime Bells** *[w/ The Skytoppers]*	S:6 / J:12 *Elton Britt/Bob Miller*	RCA Victor 20-3090
3/19/49	4	12	9 **Candy Kisses** *[w/ The Skytoppers]*	S:4 / J:12 *George Morgan*	RCA Victor 21-0006
2/4/50	7	4	10 **Beyond The Sunset** *[w/ The Three Suns & Rosalie Allen]*	A:7 *Blanche Brock/Virgil Brock*	RCA Victor 47-3105
2/25/50	3^{2}	10	11 **Quicksilver** *[w/ Rosalie Allen]*	A:3 / J:6 / S:9 *Edward Pola/Irving Taylor/George Wyle*	RCA Victor 48-0168
5/4/68	26	10	12 **The Jimmie Rodgers Blues**	*Elton Britt/Vaughn Horton*	RCA Victor 9503
1/4/69	71	4	13 **The Bitter Taste**	*Vaughn Horton*	RCA Victor 9658

DEBUT	PEAK	WKS	GOLD	#	ARTIST / Country Chart Hit	Songwriter	Label (& Number)
					BROCK, Chad		
					Born on 7/31/1963 in Ocala, Florida. Male singer/songwriter/guitarist.		
8/1/98	**51**	16		1	**Evangeline**	*Carson Chamberlain/Bob McDill*	Warner
11/7/98+	**3**^{3}	29		2	**Ordinary Life**	S:8 *Bonnie Baker/Connie Harrington*	Warner
5/22/99	**19**	26		3	**Lightning Does The Work**	S:5 *Chad Brock/Kelly Garrett/John Hadley*	Warner
					above 3 from the album *Chad Brock* on Warner 47071		
11/20/99+	**30**	13		4	**A Country Boy Can Survive** ***[w/ Hank Williams, Jr. & George Jones]***	S:2 *Hank Williams Jr.*	Warner
2/19/00	❶^{3}	36		5	**Yes!**	S:3 *Chad Brock/Jim Collins/Stephony Smith*	Warner
8/5/00	**21**	20		6	**The Visit**	*Gene Ellsworth/Brad Rodgers/Charley Stefl*	Warner
					above 3 from the album *Yes!* on Warner 47659		
8/18/01	**47**	10		7	**Tell Me How**	*John Bettis/Jason Deere/Larry Stewart*	Warner
					from the album *III* on Warner 48008		
7/20/02	**60**	1		8	**A Man's Gotta Do**	*Chad Brock/Brett Jones*	Broken Bow
3/15/03	**58**	3		9	**That Was Us**	*Tony Lane/Craig Wiseman*	Broken Bow
12/20/03+	**48**	7		10	**You Are**	*Steve Dean/Noah Gordon/Wil Nance*	Broken Bow
					above 3 from the album *Free* on Broken Bow 75372		
10/16/04	**53**	6		11	**That Changed Me**	*Michael Dulaney/Steven Jones/Jason Sellers*	Broken Bow
					BROCK, Joe		
					Born in Lake Placid, Florida. Male singer.		
5/29/76	**98**	3			**Everything You'd Never Want To Be**	*Fred Koller/Charlie Williams*	Ronnie 7601
					BRODY, Lane		
					Born Lynn Voorlas on 9/24/1955 in Oak Park, Illinois; raised in Racine, Wisconsin. Female singer/actress. Also recorded as **Lynn Nilles**.		
2/12/77	**93**	4		1	**You're Gonna Make Love To Me** ***[Lynn Nilles]***	*L. Russell Brown/Irwin Levine*	GRT 100
4/24/82	**60**	6		2	**He's Taken**	*Lane Brody*	Liberty 1457
7/17/82	**61**	7		3	**More Nights**	*Paula Breedlove/Bob Morrison*	Liberty 1470
12/11/82	**77**	5		4	**When It Comes To Love** ***[w/ Tom Bresh]***	*Thom Schuyler*	Liberty 1487
5/21/83	**15**	19		5	**Over You**	*Bobby Hart/Austin Roberts*	Liberty 1498
					from the movie *Tender Mercies* starring Robert Duvall		
11/19/83	**60**	7		6	**It's Another Silent Night**	*Ken Bell/Terry Skinner*	Liberty 1509
2/4/84	❶^{1}	22		7	**The Yellow Rose** ***[w/ Johnny Lee]***	*Lane Brody/Johnny Lee*	Warner 29375
					same melody as "The Yellow Rose Of Texas" with new lyrics; from the TV series starring Cybill Shepherd		
5/12/84	**59**	7		8	**Hanging On**	*Ira Allen/Buddy Mize*	Liberty 1519
8/25/84	**81**	5		9	**Alibis**	*Pat Killough/Rock Killough*	EMI America 8218
5/18/85	**29**	14		10	**He Burns Me Up**	S:29 / A:29 *Bobby Lee Springfield*	EMI America 8266
9/7/85	**51**	10		11	**Baby's Eyes**	*Lane Brody*	EMI America 8283
4/5/86	**50**	8		12	**I Could Get Used To This** ***[w/ Johnny Lee]***	*Jan Buckingham/Bruce Miller*	Warner 28747
					BROKOP, Lisa		
					Born on 6/6/1973 in Surrey, British Columbia, Canada. Female singer/songwriter.		
8/20/94	**52**	10		1	**Give Me A Ring Sometime**	*Sharon Anderson/Kris Bergsnes/Bob Moulds*	Capitol
11/26/94+	**52**	20		2	**Take That**	*Gary Burr/Tom Shapiro*	Capitol
4/15/95	**64**	5		3	**One Of Those Nights**	*Troy Seals/Conway Twitty*	Capitol
7/29/95	**60**	7		4	**Who Needs You**	*Mickey Cates/Skip Ewing*	Capitol
					above 4 from the album *Every Little Girl's Dream* on Capitol 89252		
11/25/95+	**55**	12		5	**She Can't Save Him**	*Liz Hengber/Bob Regan*	Capitol
3/23/96	**63**	7		6	**Before He Kissed Me**	*Liz Hengber/Mark Irwin*	Capitol
					above 2 from the album *Lisa Brokop* on Capitol 33875		
5/23/98	**59**	7		7	**How Do I Let Go**	*Lisa Brokop/Karen Taylor-Good*	Columbia
11/14/98	**64**	3		8	**When You Get To Be You**	*Michael Ehmig/Dennis Robbins/Curtis Wright*	Columbia
2/20/99	**65**	3		9	**Ain't Enough Roses**	*Lisa Brokop/Sam Hogin/Bob Reagan*	Columbia
					above 3 from the album *When You Get To Be You* on Columbia		

BROOKS, Garth — **1990s: #1 / 2000s: #25 / All-Time: #29**

Born Troyal Garth Brooks on 2/7/1962 in Luba, Oklahoma; raised in Yukon, Oklahoma. Male singer/songwriter/guitarist. His mother, Colleen Carroll, recorded with Capitol in 1954 and was a regular on **Red Foley**'s *Ozark Jubilee* TV show. Attended Oklahoma State University on a track scholarship. Played local clubs and worked as a bouncer. Also recorded as alter-ego **Chris Gaines**. Engaged to **Trisha Yearwood** on 5/25/2005. Also see **One Heart At A Time**.

CMA: Horizon 1990 / Entertainer 1991, 1992, 1997 & 1998 // OPRY: 1990

DEBUT	PEAK	WKS	GOLD	#	Country Chart Hit	Songwriter	Label (& Number)
3/25/89	**8**	26		1	**Much Too Young (To Feel This Damn Old)**	*Garth Brooks/Randy Taylor*	Capitol 44342
9/9/89	❶^{1}	26		2	**If Tomorrow Never Comes**	*Kent Blazy/Garth Brooks*	Capitol 44430
1/20/90	**2**^{1}	25		3	**Not Counting You**	*Garth Brooks*	Capitol
5/5/90	❶^{3}	21		4	**The Dance**	*Tony Arata*	Capitol
					above 2 from the album *Garth Brooks* on Capitol 90897		
8/18/90	❶^{4}	20		5	**Friends In Low Places**	*Dewayne Blackwell/Earl Bud Lee*	Capitol
					CMA: Single		
11/3/90+	❶^{2}	20		6	**Unanswered Prayers**	*Pat Alger/Larry Bastian/Garth Brooks*	Capitol
2/9/91	❶^{1}	20		7	**Two Of A Kind, Workin' On A Full House**	*Bobby Boyd/Warren Haynes/Dennis Robbins*	Capitol
5/18/91	❶^{2}	20		8	**The Thunder Rolls**	*Pat Alger/Garth Brooks*	Capitol
					above 4 from the album *No Fences* on Capitol 93866		
8/17/91	**3**^{1}	20		9	**Rodeo**	*Larry Bastian*	Capitol

Billboard DEBUT	PEAK	WKS	GOLD	ARTIST / Ranking / Country Chart Hit	Songwriter	Label (& Number)
				BROOKS, Garth — cont'd		
10/19/91	❶^{2}	20		10 **Shameless**	*Billy Joel*	Capitol
1/4/92	❶^{4}	20		11 **What She's Doing Now**	*Pat Alger/Garth Brooks*	Capitol
2/1/92	3^{1}	20		12 **Papa Loved Mama**	*Garth Brooks/Kim Williams*	Capitol
3/21/92	66	20		13 **Against The Grain**	*Bruce Bouton/Larry Cordle/Carl Jackson*	Capitol
5/2/92	❶^{1}	20		14 **The River**	*Garth Brooks/Victoria Shaw*	Capitol
				#9-14: from the album *Ropin' The Wind* on Capitol 96330		
9/12/92	12	20		15 **We Shall Be Free**	*Garth Brooks/Stephanie Davis*	Liberty
10/17/92+	❶^{1}	20		16 **Somewhere Other Than The Night**	*Kent Blazy/Garth Brooks*	Liberty
12/26/92+	48	4		17 **The Old Man's Back In Town**	*Larry Bastain/Garth Brooks/Randy Taylor* **[X]**	Liberty
				from the album *Beyond The Season* on Liberty 98742		
2/6/93	2^{1}	20		18 **Learning To Live Again**	*Stephanie Davis/Don Schlitz*	Liberty
2/13/93	73	1		19 **Dixie Chicken**	*Lowell George/Martin Kibbee*	Liberty
5/8/93	❶^{1}	20		20 **That Summer**	*Pat Alger/Garth Brooks/Sandy Mahl*	Liberty
				#15, 16 & 18-20: from the album *The Chase* on Liberty 98743		
8/7/93	❶^{2}	20		21 **Ain't Going Down (Til The Sun Comes Up)**	*Kent Blazy/Garth Brooks/Kim Williams*	Liberty
9/11/93	❶^{1}	20		22 **American Honky-Tonk Bar Association**	*Bryan Kennedy/Jim Rushing*	Liberty
9/18/93+	2^{1}	20		23 **Callin' Baton Rouge**	*Dennis Linde*	Liberty
9/18/93+	3^{3}	20		24 **Standing Outside The Fire**	*Garth Brooks/Jenny Yates*	Liberty
9/18/93+	7	20		25 **One Night A Day**	*Gary Burr/Pete Wasner*	Liberty
7/16/94	67	11		26 **Hard Luck Woman**	*Paul Stanley*	Mercury
				from the various artists album *Kiss My Ass: Classic Kiss Regrooved* on Mercury 522123		
11/26/94+	49	20		27 **The Red Strokes**	*Garth Brooks/James Garver/Lisa Sanderson/Jenny Yates*	Liberty
				#21-25 & 27: from the album *In Pieces* on Liberty 80857		
1/7/95	70	1		28 **White Christmas**	*Irving Berlin* **[X]**	Liberty
				from the album *Beyond The Season* on Liberty 98742		
9/9/95	❶^{1}	20		29 **She's Every Woman**	*Garth Brooks/Victoria Shaw*	Capitol
11/25/95	23	14		30 **The Fever**	*Bryan Kennedy/Joe Perry/Dan Roberts/Steven Tyler*	Capitol
12/9/95+	❶^{1}	20		31 **The Beaches Of Cheyenne**	*Garth Brooks/Bryan Kennedy/Dan Roberts*	Capitol
12/9/95+	4	20		32 **That Ol' Wind**	*Garth Brooks/Leigh Reynolds*	Capitol
12/9/95+	5	32		33 **It's Midnight Cinderella**	*Kent Blazy/Garth Brooks/Kim Williams*	Capitol
12/9/95+	19	20		34 **The Change**	*Tony Arata/Wayne Tester*	Capitol
12/9/95	64	4		35 **The Old Stuff**	*Garth Brooks/Bryan Kennedy/Dan Roberts*	Capitol
12/9/95	71	1		36 **Rollin'**	*Harley Allen/Garth Brooks/Leigh Reynolds*	Capitol
				#29-36: from the album *Fresh Horses* on Capitol 32080		
8/23/97	2^{2}	20		37 **In Another's Eyes** ***[w/ Trisha Yearwood]***	*Garth Brooks/John Peppard/Bobby Wood*	MCA
				Grammy: Vocal Collaboration; from Yearwood's album *Songbook - A Collection Of Hits* on MCA 70011		
11/22/97	❶^{3}	20		38 **Longneck Bottle**	*Rick Carnes/Steve Wariner*	Capitol
12/6/97+	❶^{1}	28		39 **Two Piña Coladas**	*Shawn Camp/Benita Hill/Sandy Mason*	Capitol
12/6/97+	2^{1}	20		40 **She's Gonna Make It**	*Kent Blazy/Garth Brooks/Kim Williams*	Capitol
12/6/97+	13	20		41 **Do What You Gotta Do**	*Patrick Flynn*	Capitol
12/6/97+	41	8		42 **Belleau Wood**	*Garth Brooks/Joe Henry* **[X]**	Capitol
12/6/97	52	2		43 **Cowboy Cadillac**	*Garth Brooks/Bryan Kennedy*	Capitol
12/6/97	57	2		44 **Take The Keys To My Heart**	*Bonnie Hill/Tommy Smith/Pam Wolfe*	Capitol
12/6/97	59	2		45 **How You Ever Gonna Know**	*Kent Blazy/Garth Brooks*	Capitol
12/6/97	68	1		46 **A Friend To Me**	*Garth Brooks/Victoria Shaw*	Capitol
12/6/97	70	1		47 **I Don't Have To Wonder**	*Shawn Camp/Taylor Dunn*	Capitol
				#38-47: from the album *Sevens* on Capitol 56599		
1/3/98	56	2		48 **Santa Looked A Lot Like Daddy**	*Buck Owens/Don Rich* **[X]**	Liberty
1/3/98	59	2		49 **The Old Man's Back In Town**	*Larry Bastain/Garth Brooks/Randy Taylor* **[X-R]**	Liberty
				above 2 from the album *Beyond The Season* on Liberty 98742		
5/9/98	26	20		50 **Burnin' The Roadhouse Down** ***[w/ Steve Wariner]***	*Rick Carnes/Steve Wariner*	Capitol
				from Wariner's album *Burnin' The Roadhouse Down* on Capitol 94482		
5/16/98	❶^{1}	20		51 **To Make You Feel My Love**	*Bob Dylan*	Capitol
				from the movie *Hope Floats* starring Sandra Bullock (soundtrack on Capitol 93402)		
5/23/98	65	4		52 **Uptown Down-Home Good Ol' Boy**	*Dewayne Blackwell/Earl Lee*	Capitol
5/23/98	68	1		53 **Something With A Ring To It**	*Mark Collie/Aaron Tippin*	Capitol
				above 2 from the album *The Limited Series* on Capitol 94572		
8/29/98	3^{1}	20		54 **You Move Me**	*Gordon Kennedy/Pierce Pettis*	Capitol
				from the album *Sevens* on Capitol 56599		
9/19/98	18	20		55 **Where Your Road Leads** ***[w/ Trisha Yearwood]***	*Desmond Child/Victoria Shaw*	MCA Nashville
				from Yearwood's album *Where Your Road Leads* on MCA Nashville 70023		
11/14/98	9	20		56 **It's Your Song**	*Benita Hill/Pam Wolfe*	Capitol
12/5/98	63	2		57 **Tearin' It Up (And Burnin' It Down)**	*Kent Blazy/Garth Brooks/Kim Williams*	Capitol
12/5/98	65	1		58 **Wild As The Wind** ***[w/ Trisha Yearwood]***	*Charles Quatro/Pete Wasner*	Capitol
				above 3 from Brooks's album *Double Live* on Capitol 97424		
1/2/99	65	2		59 **Belleau Wood**	*Garth Brooks/Joe Henry* **[X-R]**	Capitol
				from the album *Sevens* on Capitol 56599		
1/9/99	72	1		60 **Go Tell It On The Mountain**	*(traditional)* **[X]**	Liberty
				from the album *Beyond The Season* on Liberty 98742		
8/7/99	62	4		61 **Lost In You**	*Gordon Kennedy/Wayne Kirkpatrick/Tommy Sims*	Capitol
8/28/99	24	15		62 **It Don't Matter To The Sun** S:❶^{10}	*Gordon Kennedy/Wayne Kirkpatrick/Tommy Sims*	Capitol
				GARTH BROOKS AS CHRIS GAINES (above 2)		
				above 2 from the album *Garth Brooks In...The Life Of Chris Gaines* on Capitol 20051		
12/11/99+	65	4		63 **White Christmas**	*Irving Berlin* **[X-R]**	Liberty
12/18/99+	54	4		64 **Sleigh Ride**	*Leroy Anderson/Mitchell Parish* **[X]**	Capitol
12/18/99	62	3		65 **Baby Jesus Is Born**	*Randy Handley/Cam King* **[X]**	Capitol

DEBUT	PEAK	WKS	GOLD	ARTIST / Ranking / Country Chart Hit	Songwriter	Label (& Number)
				BROOKS, Garth — cont'd		
12/25/99+	**56**	3		66 **It's The Most Wonderful Time Of The Year**	*Edward Pola/George Wyle* **[X]**	Capitol
12/25/99+	**63**	3		67 (There's No Place Like) **Home For The Holidays**	*Robert Allen/Al Stillman* **[X]**	Capitol
1/8/00	**69**	1		68 **God Rest Ye Merry Gentlemen**	*(traditional)* **[X]**	Capitol
				#63-68: from the album *Garth Brooks & The Magic Of Christmas* on Capitol 23550		
5/13/00	**21**	20		69 **When You Come Back To Me Again**	*Garth Brooks/Jenny Yates*	Capitol
				from the movie *Frequency* starring Dennis Quaid		
6/17/00	**22**	20		70 **Katie Wants A Fast One** *[w/ Steve Wariner]*	*Rick Carnes/Steve Wariner*	Capitol
				from Wariner's album *Faith In You* on Capitol 23503		
11/25/00+	**7**	20		71 **Wild Horses**	*Bill Shore/David Wills*	Capitol
				from the 1990 album *No Fences* on Capitol 93866		
10/13/01	**24**	20		72 **Beer Run** *[w/ George Jones]*	*Keith Anderson/Kent Blazy/George Ducas/Amanda Williams/Kim Williams*	Bandit
				from Jones's album *The Rock: Stone Cold Country 2001* on Bandit 67029		
10/27/01+	**5**	20		73 **Wrapped Up In You**	*Wayne Kirkpatrick*	Capitol
12/1/01+	**16**	20		74 **Squeeze Me In** *[w/ Trisha Yearwood]*	*Delbert McClinton/Gary Nicholson*	Capitol
12/1/01+	**18**	20		75 **Thicker Than Blood**	*Garth Brooks/Jenny Yates*	Capitol
1/5/02	**55**	2		76 **Call Me Claus** S:4	*Garth Brooks/Lisa Sanderson/Jenny Yates* **[X]**	Capitol
1/5/02	**56**	1		77 **'Zat You, Santa Claus?**	*Jack Fox* **[X]**	Capitol
				above 2 from the album *Garth Brooks & The Magic Of Christmas: Songs From Call Me Claus* on Capitol 35624		
3/8/03	**24**	15		78 **Why Ain't I Running**	*Tony Arata/Kent Blazy/Garth Brooks*	Capitol
				#73-75 & 78: from the album *Scarecrow* on Capitol 31330		

Against The Grain ['92]
Ain't Going Down (Til The Sun Comes Up) ['93]
American Honky-Tonk Bar Association ['93]
Baby Jesus Is Born ['99]
Beaches Of Cheyenne ['96]
Beer Run ['01]
Belleau Wood ['98, '99]
Burnin' The Roadhouse Down ['98]
Call Me Claus ['02]
Callin' Baton Rouge ['94]
Change ['96]
Cowboy Cadillac ['97]
Dance ['90]
Dixie Chicken ['93]
Do What You Gotta Do ['00]
Fever ['95]
Friend To Me ['97]
Friends In Low Places ['90]
Go Tell It On The Mountain ['99]
God Rest Ye Merry Gentlemen ['00]
Hard Luck Woman ['94]
How You Ever Gonna Know ['97]
I Don't Have To Wonder ['97]
If Tomorrow Never Comes ['89]
In Another's Eyes ['97]
It Don't Matter To The Sun ['99]
It's Midnight Cinderella ['96]
It's The Most Wonderful Time Of The Year ['00]
It's Your Song ['98]
Katie Wants A Fast One ['00]
Learning To Live Again ['93]
Longneck Bottle ['97]
Lost In You ['99]
Much Too Young (To Feel This Damn Old) ['89]
Not Counting You ['90]
Old Man's Back In Town ['93, '98]
Old Stuff ['95]
One Night A Day ['94]
Papa Loved Mama ['92]
Red Strokes ['95]
River ['92]
Rodeo ['91]
Rollin' ['95]
Santa Looked A Lot Like Daddy ['98]
Shameless ['91]
She's Every Woman ['95]
She's Gonna Make It ['98]
Sleigh Ride ['00]
Something With A Ring To It ['98]
Somewhere Other Than The Night ['93]
Squeeze Me In ['02]
Standing Outside The Fire ['94]
Take The Keys To My Heart ['97]
Tearin' It Up (And Burnin' It Down) ['98]
That Ol' Wind ['96]
That Summer ['93]
(There's No Place Like) Home For The Holidays ['00]
Thicker Than Blood ['02]
Thunder Rolls ['91]
To Make You Feel My Love ['98]
Two Of A Kind, Workin' On A Full House ['91]
Two Piña Coladas ['98]
Unanswered Prayers ['91]
Uptown Down-Home Good Ol' Boy ['98]
We Shall Be Free ['92]
What She's Doing Now ['92]
When You Come Back To Me Again ['00]
Where Your Road Leads ['98]
White Christmas ['95, '99]
Why Ain't I Running ['03]
Wild As The Wind ['98]
Wild Horses ['01]
Wrapped Up In You ['02]
You Move Me ['98]
'Zat You, Santa Claus? ['02]

BROOKS, Karen

Born on 4/29/1954 in Dallas, Texas. Female singer.

DEBUT	PEAK	WKS	GOLD	Country Chart Hit	Songwriter	Label (& Number)
7/31/82	**17**	19		1 **New Way Out**	*Randy Sharp*	Warner 29958
11/20/82+	❶[1]	20		2 **Faking Love** *[w/ T.G. Sheppard]*	*Matraca Berg/Bobby Braddock*	Warner/Curb 29854
2/5/83	**21**	14		3 **If That's What You're Thinking**	*Randy Sharp*	Warner 29789
6/18/83	**30**	12		4 **Walk On**	*Karen Brooks*	Warner 29644
4/28/84	**40**	11		5 **Born To Love You**	*Charlie Black/Layng Martine Jr.*	Warner 29302
7/21/84	**19**	16		6 **Tonight I'm Here With Someone Else**	*Dave Loggins*	Warner 29225
1/5/85	**63**	8		7 **A Simple I Love You**	*Karen Brooks/Randy Sharp*	Warner 29154
7/13/85	**45**	9		8 **I Will Dance With You** *[w/ Johnny Cash]*	*Jack Routh*	Warner 28979

BROOKS, Kix

Born Leon Brooks III on 5/12/1955 in Shreveport, Louisiana. Male singer/songwriter. Joined with **Ronnie Dunn** in 1991 in duo **Brooks & Dunn**. Also see **Tomorrow's World**.

DEBUT	PEAK	WKS	GOLD	Country Chart Hit	Songwriter	Label (& Number)
9/10/83	**73**	4		1 **Baby, When Your Heart Breaks Down**	*Kix Brooks*	Avion 103
1/28/89	**87**	2		2 **Sacred Ground**	*Kix Brooks/Vern Rust*	Capitol 44275

BROOKS & DUNN — 1990s: #8 / 2000s: #5 / All-Time: #43

Duo of **Kix Brooks** (born on 5/12/1955 in Shreveport, Louisiana) and **Ronnie Dunn** (born on 6/1/1953 in Coleman, Texas). Brooks had written several hits and Dunn had won a national talent competition before teaming up. One of the most successful musical duos of all-time.

CMA: Vocal Duo 1992, 1993, 1994, 1995, 1996, 1997, 1998, 1999, 2001, 2002, 2003 & 2004 / Entertainer 1996

DEBUT	PEAK	WKS	GOLD	Country Chart Hit	Songwriter	Label (& Number)
6/22/91	❶[2]	20		1 **Brand New Man**	*Kix Brooks/Don Cook/Ronnie Dunn*	Arista
10/12/91	❶[2]	20		2 **My Next Broken Heart**	*Kix Brooks/Don Cook/Ronnie Dunn*	Arista
2/1/92	❶[2]	20		3 **Neon Moon**	*Ronnie Dunn*	Arista
5/23/92	❶[4]	20		4 **Boot Scootin' Boogie**	*Ronnie Dunn*	Arista
9/19/92	**6**	20		5 **Lost And Found**	*Kix Brooks/Don Cook*	Arista
				above 5 from the album *Brand New Man* on Arista 18658		
2/6/93	**4**	20		6 **Hard Workin' Man**	*Ronnie Dunn*	Arista
				Grammy: Vocal Duo		
5/15/93	**2**[2]	20		7 **We'll Burn That Bridge**	*Don Cook/Ronnie Dunn*	Arista
9/4/93	❶[1]	20		8 **She Used To Be Mine**	*Ronnie Dunn*	Arista
12/11/93+	**2**[2]	20		9 **Rock My World** (Little Country Girl)	*Bill LaBounty/Steve O'Brien*	Arista
3/5/94	**73**	4		10 **Ride 'em High, Ride 'em Low**	*Ronnie Dunn*	MCA
				from the movie *8 Seconds* starring Luke Perry (soundtrack on MCA 10927)		
3/19/94	**73**	1		11 **Corine, Corina** *[w/ Asleep At The Wheel]*	*Bo Chapman/Mitchell Parish/J. Mayo Williams*	Liberty
				from Asleep At The Wheel's album *Tribute To The Music Of* ***Bob Wills And The Texas Playboys*** on Liberty 81470		
4/9/94	❶[1]	20		12 **That Ain't No Way To Go**	*Kix Brooks/Don Cook/Ronnie Dunn*	Arista
				#6-9 & 12: from the album *Hard Workin' Man* on Arista 18716		
8/27/94	❶[2]	20		13 **She's Not The Cheatin' Kind**	*Ronnie Dunn*	Arista

Billboard DEBUT	PEAK	WKS	GOLD		ARTIST / Country Chart Hit	Ranking	Songwriter	Label (& Number)
					BROOKS & DUNN — cont'd			
11/12/94+	**6**	20		14	**I'll Never Forgive My Heart**		*Dean Dillon/Janine Dunn/Ronnie Dunn*	Arista
2/18/95	**❶**[1]	20		15	**Little Miss Honky Tonk**		*Ronnie Dunn*	Arista
6/10/95	**❶**[2]	20		16	**You're Gonna Miss Me When I'm Gone**		*Kix Brooks/Don Cook/Ronnie Dunn*	Arista
9/23/95	**5**	20		17	**Whiskey Under The Bridge**		*Kix Brooks/Don Cook/Ronnie Dunn*	Arista
					above 5 from the album *Waitin' On Sundown* on Arista 18765			
4/6/96	**❶**[3]	20		18	**My Maria**	S:❶[8]	*Daniel Moore/B.W. Stevenson*	Arista Nashville
					Grammy: Vocal Duo			
4/27/96	**2**[2]	20		19	**I Am That Man**	S:8	*Terry McBride/Monty Powell*	Arista Nashville
9/14/96	**13**	20		20	**Mama Don't Get Dressed Up For Nothing**	S:15	*Kix Brooks/Don Cook/Ronnie Dunn*	Arista Nashville
12/7/96+	**❶**[1]	20		21	**A Man This Lonely**	S:12	*Ronnie Dunn/Tommy Lee James*	Arista Nashville
3/22/97	**8**	20		22	**Why Would I Say Goodbye**		*Kix Brooks/Chris Waters*	Arista Nashville
					above 5 from the album *Borderline* on Arista Nashville 18810			
8/30/97	**3**[1]	20		23	**Honky Tonk Truth**		*Ronnie Dunn/Kim Williams/Lonnie Wilson*	Arista Nashville
10/18/97+	**2**[2]	24		24	**He's Got You**		*Ronnie Dunn/Terry McBride*	Arista Nashville
					above 2 from the album *The Greatest Hits Collection* on Arista Nashville 18852			
5/2/98	**❶**[2]	20		25	**If You See Him/If You See Her** *[w/ Reba]*		*Tommy Lee James/Jennifer Kimball/Terry McBride*	Arista Nashville
7/4/98	**❶**[3]	21		26	**How Long Gone**		*Shawn Camp/John Scott Sherrill*	Arista Nashville
9/26/98	**❶**[1]	20		27	**Husbands And Wives**		*Roger Miller*	Arista Nashville
1/16/99	**5**	20		28	**I Can't Get Over You**		*Ronnie Dunn/Terry McBride*	Arista Nashville
5/1/99	**41**	10		29	**South Of Santa Fe**		*Larry Boone/Kix Brooks/Paul Nelson*	Arista Nashville
					above 5 from the album *If You See Her* on Arista Nashville 18865			
8/7/99	**15**	20		30	**Missing You**		*Mark Leonard/Charles Sandford/John Waite*	Arista Nashville
10/9/99+	**19**	20		31	**Beer Thirty**		*Ronnie Dunn/Terry McBride*	Arista Nashville
11/27/99+	**53**	13		32	**Against The Wind**		*Bob Seger*	Elektra
					from the animated TV series *King Of The Hill* (soundtrack on Elektra 62441)			
1/22/00	**60**	8		33	**Goin' Under Gettin' Over You**		*Ronnie Dunn/Terry McBride*	Arista Nashville
3/18/00	**5**	29		34	**You'll Always Be Loved By Me**		*Ronnie Dunn/Terry McBride*	Arista Nashville
					#30, 31, 33 & 34: from the album *Tight Rope* on Arista Nashville 18895			
2/17/01	**❶**[6]	29		35	**Ain't Nothing 'Bout You**		*Rivers Rutherford/Tom Shapiro*	Arista Nashville
6/23/01	**❶**[1]	33		36	**Only In America**		*Kix Brooks/Don Cook/Randy Rogers*	Arista Nashville
10/27/01+	**❶**[1]	27		37	**The Long Goodbye**		*Kix Brooks/Ronnie Dunn/Mark Wright*	Arista Nashville
4/13/02	**5**	20		38	**My Heart Is Lost To You**		*Brett Beavers/Connie Harrington*	Arista Nashville
9/7/02	**12**	20		39	**Every River**		*Tom Littlefield/Angelo Petraglia/Kim Richey*	Arista Nashville
					above 5 from the album *Steers & Stripes* on Arista Nashville 67003			
12/28/02+	**41**	3		40	**It Won't Be Christmas Without You**		*Steven Busch/Ronnie Dunn/Jerry Williams* **[X]**	Arista Nashville
12/28/02+	**47**	3		41	**Hangin' Round The Mistletoe**		*Kostas* **[X]**	Arista Nashville
1/4/03	**57**	2		42	**Winter Wonderland**		*Felix Bernard/Richard Smith* **[X]**	Arista Nashville
1/11/03	**57**	1		43	**Rockin' Little Christmas**		*Deborah Allen/Bruce Channel* **[X]**	Arista Nashville
					above 4 from the album *It Won't Be Christmas Without You* on Arista Nashville 67053			
4/19/03	**❶**[1]	29		44	**Red Dirt Road**		*Kix Brooks/Ronnie Dunn*	Arista Nashville
9/20/03+	**3**[5]	23		45	**You Can't Take The Honky Tonk Out Of The Girl**		*Bart Allmand/Bob DiPiero*	Arista Nashville
2/14/04	**6**	22		46	**That's What She Gets For Loving Me**		*Ronnie Dunn/Terry McBride*	Arista Nashville
					above 3 from the album *Red Dirt Road* on Arista Nashville 67070			
7/10/04	**2**[1]	23		47	**That's What It's All About**		*Kix Brooks/Ronnie Dunn*	Arista Nashville
12/4/04+	**❶**[1]	26		48	**It's Getting Better All The Time**		*Don Cook/Ronnie Dunn*	Arista Nashville
					above 2 from the album *Greatest Hits II* on Arista Nashville 63271			
6/4/05	**❶**[1]	17↑		49	**Play Something Country**		*Ronnie Dunn/Terry McBride*	Arista Nashville
					from the album *Hillbilly Deluxe* on Arista Nashville 69946			
					BROOKS BROTHERS BAND			
					Group from Dallas, Texas. Led by brothers Bill Brooks and Randy Brooks.			
1/12/85	**81**	6			**Hurry On Home**		*Keith Stegall/Chris Waters*	Buckboard 115
					BROTHER PHELPS			
					Duo of brothers Ricky Lee Phelps (born on 10/8/1953) and Doug Phelps (born on 2/16/1960). Both formerly with **The Kentucky Headhunters**. Doug returned to Kentucky Headhunters in 1996.			
7/3/93	**6**	20		1	**Let Go**		*Dickie Brown*	Asylum
11/13/93+	**28**	18		2	**Were You Really Livin'**		*Doug Phelps/Ricky Lee Phelps*	Asylum
3/26/94	**53**	9		3	**Eagle Over Angel**		*Gerald Guinn/Yvonne Guinn/James H. Peters*	Asylum
9/3/94	**62**	5		4	**Ever-Changing Woman**		*Dave Kirby/Curly Putman*	Asylum
					above 4 from the album *Let Go* on Asylum 61544			
2/18/95	**54**	11		5	**Anyway The Wind Blows**		*J.J. Cale*	Asylum
6/3/95	**65**	6		6	**Not So Different After All**		*Jeff Hughes/Irene Kelley*	Asylum
					above 2 from the album *Anyway The Wind Blows* on Asylum 61724			
					BROWN, Billy			
					Born in 1956 in Port Orange, Florida. Male singer.			
12/15/79	**95**	3			**What It Means To Be An American**		*Ernie Johnson* **[S]**	Bernes 101
					BROWN, Cooter			
					Born in Tampa, Florida. Male singer.			
12/16/95	**71**	1			**Pure Bred Redneck**		*Glenn Ashworth/Buddy Causey/Dana Sigmon* **[N]**	Reprise
					BROWN, Floyd			
					Born in Greenwell Springs, Louisiana. Male singer/songwriter.			
6/18/77	**100**	1		1	**Let's Get Acquainted Again**		*Dan Penn*	ABC/Dot 17702
7/9/83	**79**	6		2	**Kiss Me Just One More Time**		*Floyd Brown*	Magnum 1002

Billboard DEBUT	PEAK	WKS	GOLD	ARTIST / Country Chart Hit	Ranking / Songwriter	Label (& Number)

BROWN, Jim Ed

1970s: #32 / All-Time: #88

Born on 4/1/1934 in Sparkman, Arkansas. Male singer/guitarist. Recorded in duo with older sister **Maxine Brown** in 1953; joined by younger sister Bonnie in 1955 (recorded as **The Browns**). Began solo recording in 1965. Hosted TNN's *You Can Be A Star* and *Going Our Way*. Also see **Some Of Chet's Friends**.

CMA: Vocal Duo (with Helen Cornelius) 1977 // OPRY: 1963

JIM EDWARD BROWN:

DEBUT	PEAK	WKS	GOLD	#	Country Chart Hit	Songwriter	Label (& Number)
7/10/65	**33**	8		1	**I Heard From A Memory Last Night**	*Ralph Freed/Jerry Livingston*	RCA Victor 8566
10/16/65	**37**	5		2	**I'm Just A Country Boy**	*Marshall Baker/Fred Hellerman*	RCA Victor 8644
4/9/66	**41**	4		3	**Regular On My Mind**	*Bill Hjerpe*	RCA Victor 8766
7/30/66	**23**	10		4	**A Taste Of Heaven**	*David Briggs/Jimmy Rule*	RCA Victor 8867
11/19/66	**57**	7		5	**The Last Laugh**	*Bobby Braddock/Jim Ed Brown/Curly Putman*	RCA Victor 8997
2/4/67	**18**	11		6	**You Can Have Her**	*Bill Cook*	RCA Victor 9077

JIM ED BROWN:

DEBUT	PEAK	WKS	GOLD	#	Country Chart Hit	Songwriter	Label (& Number)
5/20/67	**3**^{2}	20		7	**Pop A Top**	*Nat Stuckey*	RCA Victor 9192
10/14/67	**13**	13		8	**Bottle, Bottle**	*Larry Kingston*	RCA Victor 9329
2/10/68	**23**	11		9	**The Cajun Stripper**	*Billy Deaton/Doug Kershaw/Rusty Kershaw*	RCA Victor 9434
5/25/68	**13**	12		10	**The Enemy**	*Jonny Adcock*	RCA Victor 9518
9/28/68	**49**	8		11	**Jack And Jill**	*Lane Caudell/John Major*	RCA Victor 9616
12/14/68+	**35**	12		12	**Longest Beer Of The Night**	*Carson Parks*	RCA Victor 9677
3/22/69	**17**	11		13	**Man And Wife Time**	*Dave Pittman/Buzz Rabin*	RCA Victor 0114
7/19/69	**29**	10		14	**The Three Bells**	*Bert Reisfeld/Jean Villard*	RCA Victor 0190
12/13/69+	**35**	9		15	**Ginger Is Gentle And Waiting For Me /**	*Jill Williams*	
12/27/69+	**flip**	7		16	**Drink Boys, Drink**	*Jack Ripley*	RCA Victor 0274
4/4/70	**71**	4		17	**Lift Ring, Pull Open**	*Joey Cooper/John Galli*	RCA Victor 9810
7/11/70	**31**	9		18	**Baby, I Tried**	*Skip Gibbs*	RCA Victor 9858
10/24/70	**4**	18		19	**Morning**	*Bill Graham*	RCA Victor 9909
3/27/71	**13**	15		20	**Angel's Sunday**	*Hank Mills*	RCA Victor 9965
9/18/71	**37**	13		21	**She's Leavin' (Bonnie, Please Don't Go)**	*Kevin Johnson*	RCA Victor 0509
3/4/72	**55**	7		22	**Evening**	*Don Devaney/Chuck Rogers*	RCA Victor 0642
6/10/72	**57**	8		23	**How I Love Them Old Songs**	*Mickey Newbury*	RCA Victor 0712
9/30/72	**67**	6		24	**All I Had To Do**	*Ron Oates/Ed Penney*	RCA Victor 0785
12/16/72+	**29**	12		25	**Unbelievable Love**	*Ben Peters/Curly Putman*	RCA Victor 0846
4/28/73	**6**	15		26	**Southern Loving**	*Jim Owen*	RCA Victor 0928
9/1/73	**15**	14		27	**Broad-Minded Man**	*Jim Owen*	RCA Victor 0059
12/8/73+	**10**	15		28	**Sometime Sunshine**	*James Coleman/Johnny Wilson*	RCA Victor 0180
5/4/74	**10**	17		29	**It's That Time Of Night**	*Bill Graham*	RCA Victor 0267
9/21/74	**47**	8		30	**Get Up I Think I Love You**	*Larry Gatlin*	RCA Victor 10047
1/11/75	**63**	7		31	**Don Junior**	*Tony Romeo*	RCA Victor 10131
3/29/75	**41**	9		32	**Barroom Pal, Goodtime Gals**	*Bucky Jones/Royce Porter*	RCA Victor 10233
9/20/75	**52**	10		33	**Fine Time To Get The Blues**	*Red Lane/Curly Putman/Sonny Throckmorton*	RCA Victor 10370
1/3/76	**24**	12		34	**Another Morning**	*Bill Graham*	RCA Victor 10531
4/17/76	**69**	6		35	**Let Me Love You Where It Hurts**	*Gary S. Paxton*	RCA Victor 10619

JIM ED BROWN/HELEN CORNELIUS:

DEBUT	PEAK	WKS	GOLD	#	Country Chart Hit	Songwriter	Label (& Number)
7/4/76	❶^{2}	16		36	**I Don't Want To Have To Marry You**	*Fred Imus/Phil Sweet*	RCA Victor 10711
10/16/76	**65**	7		37	**I've Rode With The Best** *[Jim Ed Brown]*	*Bill Graham/Mike Haviland*	RCA 10786
11/20/76+	**2**^{1}	17		38	**Saying Hello, Saying I Love You, Saying Goodbye**	*Jeff Barry/Brad Burg/Dene Hofheinz*	RCA 10822
5/7/77	**12**	12		39	**Born Believer**	*Gary Harju*	RCA 10967
8/20/77	**12**	12		40	**If It Ain't Love By Now**	*Jeff Barry/Doug Haywood*	RCA 11044
11/12/77	**66**	8		41	**When I Touch Her There** *[Jim Ed Brown]*	*Sam Weedman*	RCA 11134
12/24/77+	**91**	3		42	**Fall Softly Snow**	*Jean Surrey* **[X]**	RCA 11162
3/11/78	**11**	13		43	**I'll Never Be Free**	*Bennie Benjamin/George Weiss*	RCA 11220
7/29/78	**6**	15		44	**If The World Ran Out Of Love Tonight**	*Michael Garin/Blake Mevis/Kelly Wilson/Steve Wilson*	RCA 11304
11/25/78+	**10**	14		45	**You Don't Bring Me Flowers**	*Alan Bergman/Marilyn Bergman/Neil Diamond*	RCA 11435
3/31/79	**2**^{2}	13		46	**Lying In Love With You**	*Gary Harrison/Dean Rutherford*	RCA 11532
8/4/79	**3**^{2}	13		47	**Fools**	*Johnny Duncan*	RCA 11672
10/27/79	**38**	11		48	**You're The Part Of Me** *[Jim Ed Brown]*	*Hank Martin/John Schweers*	RCA 11742
3/8/80	**5**	14		49	**Morning Comes Too Early**	*Kye Fleming/Dennis W. Morgan*	RCA 11927
7/19/80	**24**	12		50	**The Bedroom**	*Russ Allison/Ron Muir*	RCA 12037
5/9/81	**13**	14		51	**Don't Bother To Knock**	*Kye Fleming/Dennis W. Morgan*	RCA 12220

BROWN, Josie

Born Linda Brown in 1943 in Corning, New York. Died of heart failure on 8/16/1998 (age 55). Female singer.

DEBUT	PEAK	WKS	GOLD	#	Country Chart Hit	Songwriter	Label (& Number)
9/15/73	**44**	13		1	**Precious Memories Follow Me**	*Frances Rhodes*	RCA Victor 0042
2/2/74	**58**	8		2	**Both Sides Of The Line**	*Marian Frances*	RCA Victor 0209
5/18/74	**83**	7		3	**Satisfy Me And I'll Satisfy You**	*Bill Dees*	RCA Victor 0266

Billboard DEBUT	PEAK	WKS	GOLD	ARTIST / Country Chart Hit	Ranking / Songwriter	Label (& Number)
				BROWN, Junior		
				Born Jamieson Brown on 6/12/1952 in Cottonwood, Arizona. Male singer/songwriter/guitarist.		
8/26/95	**73**	2		1 **Highway Patrol**	*Dennis Payne/Ray Rush/Red Simpson*	MCG/Curb
2/17/96	**68**	4		2 **My Wife Thinks You're Dead**	*Junior Brown*	MCG/Curb
				above 2 from the album *Junior High* on MCG/Curb 77783		
				BROWN, Marti		
				Born in Chattanooga, Tennessee. Female singer.		
7/21/73	**78**	5		**Let My Love Shine**	*Gayle Barnhill/Rory Bourke*	Atlantic 4003
				BROWN, Marty		
				Born Dennis Marty Brown on 7/25/1965 in Maceo, Kentucky. Male singer/songwriter/guitarist.		
5/22/93	**74**	3		**It Must Be The Rain**	*Marty Brown*	MCA
				from the album *Wild Kentucky Skies* on MCA 10672		
				BROWN, Max		
				Born in Louisville, Kentucky. Male singer/songwriter.		
5/19/79	**91**	5		1 **Take Time To Smell The Flowers**	*Max Brown*	Door Knob 095
8/18/79	**73**	8		2 **Take Good Care Of My Love**	*Max Brown*	Door Knob 105
				BROWN, Maxine		
				Born Ella Maxine Brown on 4/27/1931 in Campti, Louisiana. Female singer/songwriter. Eldest member of **The Browns**.		
12/14/68+	**64**	11		**Sugar Cane County**	*Maxine Brown*	Chart 1061
				BROWN, Roy, and his Orchestra		
				Born on 9/10/1925 in New Orleans, Louisiana. Died of a heart attack on 5/25/1981 (age 55). Black singer/pianist. One of the most successful R&B artists from 1948-51.		
12/25/48	**12**	1		**'Fore Day In The Morning**	J:12 *Roy Brown*	DeLuxe 3198
				BROWN, Shannon		
				Born in Spirit Lake, Iowa. Female singer.		
11/7/98	**58**	11		1 **I Won't Lie**	*Bruce Bouton/Hillary Lindsey*	Arista Nashville
9/15/01	**40**	15		2 **Baby I Lied**	*Deborah Allen/Rory Bourke/Rafe Van Hoy*	BNA
2/16/02	**58**	4		3 **Untangle My Heart**	*Shannon Brown/Jim Collins/Melba Montgomery*	BNA
				above 2 from the album *Untangle My Heart* on BNA 67021		
				**BROWN, T. Graham**	**All-Time: #190**	
				Born Anthony Graham Brown on 12/30/1954 in Atlanta, Georgia. Male singer/songwriter/actor. Former jingle singer. Acted in the movies *Greased Lightning*, *The Farm* and *Heartbreak Hotel*. Also see **Tomorrow's World**.		
7/27/85	**39**	10		1 **Drowning In Memories**	*Gary Nicholson/Chick Rains*	Capitol 5499
10/19/85+	**7**	27		2 **I Tell It Like It Used To Be**	S:7 / A:7 *Michael Garvin/Ron Hellard/Bucky Jones*	Capitol 5524
4/26/86	**3**[1]	19		3 **I Wish That I Could Hurt That Way Again**	S:2 / A:5 *Don Cook/Curly Putman/Rafe Van Hoy*	Capitol 5571
9/6/86	**❶**[1]	23		4 **Hell And High Water**	S:❶[1] / A:❶[1] *T. Graham Brown/Alex Harvey*	Capitol 5621
1/31/87	**❶**[1]	21		5 **Don't Go To Strangers**	S:❶[2] / A:❶[1] *J.D. Martin/Russell Smith*	Capitol 5664
5/30/87	**9**	20		6 **Brilliant Conversationalist**	S:3 *John Hadley/Gary Nicholson*	Capitol 44008
9/12/87	**4**	22		7 **She Couldn't Love Me Anymore**	S:5 *Billy Henderson/Billy Maddox/Mike McGuire*	Capitol 44061
1/23/88	**4**	20		8 **The Last Resort**	S:13 *Bruce Bouton/T. Graham Brown/Bruce Burch*	Capitol 44125
7/30/88	**❶**[1]	21		9 **Darlene**	S:5 *Mike Geiger/Woody Mullis/Ricky Rector*	Capitol 44205
12/10/88+	**7**	20		10 **Come As You Were**	*Paul Craft*	Capitol 44273
4/29/89	**30**	13		11 **Never Say Never**	*Walt Aldridge/Tom Brasfield*	Capitol 44349
4/7/90	**6**	21		12 **If You Could Only See Me Now**	*Rick Giles/Susan Longacre*	Capitol
6/23/90	**6**	21		13 **Don't Go Out** ***[w/ Tanya Tucker]***	*Radney Foster/Bill Lloyd*	Capitol
				from Tucker's album *Tennessee Woman* on Capitol 91821		
9/15/90	**18**	20		14 **Moonshadow Road**	*T. Graham Brown/Gary Nicholson/Verlon Thompson*	Capitol
1/12/91	**53**	11		15 **I'm Sending One Up For You**	*T. Graham Brown/Ray Kennedy/Gary Nicholson*	Capitol
				#12, 14 & 15: from the album *Bumper To Bumper* on Capitol 91780		
4/20/91	**31**	12		16 **With This Ring**	*Luther Dixon/Tony Hester/Richard Wylie*	Capitol
				from the album *You Can't Take It With You* on Capitol 93547		
9/19/98+	**44**	20		17 **Wine Into Water**	*T. Graham Brown/Bruce Burch/Ted Hewitt*	Intersound
2/27/99	**68**	6		18 **Happy Ever After**	*Gary Nicholson/Kevin Welch*	Intersound
6/5/99	**63**	3		19 **Never In A Million Tears**	*Daryl Burgess/Ty Tyler*	Intersound
10/23/99	**73**	5		20 **Memphis Women & Chicken**	*Donnie Fritts/Gary Nicholson/Dan Penn*	Intersound
				above 4 from the album *Wine Into Water* on Intersound 9346		
9/2/00	**59**	12		21 **Now That's Awesome!** ***[w/ Bill Engvall/Tracy Byrd/Neal McCoy]***	S:13 *Bill Engvall/Porter Howell* **[N]**	BNA
				from Engvall's album *Now That's Awesome!* on BNA 69311		
12/20/03	**58**	1		22 **Middle Age Crazy**	*Sonny Throckmorton*	Intersound
				from the album *The Next Right Thing* on Intersound 5499		

Billboard DEBUT	PEAK	WKS	GOLD	ARTIST / Country Chart Hit	Ranking / Songwriter	Label (& Number)

BROWNE, Jann

Born on 3/14/1954 in Anderson, Indiana; raised in Shelbyville, Indiana. Female singer/songwriter. Member of **Asleep At The Wheel** from 1981-83. Married songwriter Roger Stebner in 1985.

DEBUT	PEAK	WKS	GOLD	Country Chart Hit	Songwriter	Label (& Number)
7/1/89	**19**	21		1 **You Ain't Down Home**	*Jamie O'Hara*	Curb 10530
11/25/89+	**18**	26		2 **Tell Me Why**	*Gail Davies/Harry Stinson*	Curb 10568
9/15/90	**75**	1		3 **Louisville** from the album *Tell Me Why* on Curb 10630	*Jann Browne/Pat Gallaghor*	Curb

BROWNS, The — 1950s: #25 / All-Time: #217

Brother-and-sister trio from Sparkman, Arkansas: **Jim Ed Brown**, **Maxine Brown** and Bonnie Brown. Maxine and Jim Ed had worked as a duo from the late 1940s and Bonnie joined them in 1955. The trio worked **Red Foley**'s *Arkansas Jamboree* radio shows. Sister Norma subbed for Jim Ed while he was in the service. The trio disbanded in 1967, with Jim Ed and Maxine continuing as solo artists.

OPRY: 1963

DEBUT	PEAK	WKS	GOLD	Country Chart Hit	Songwriter	Label (& Number)
				JIM EDWARD & MAXINE BROWN:		
6/26/54	**8**	15		1 **Looking Back To See** A:8	*Jim Ed Brown/Maxine Brown*	Fabor 107
				JIM EDWARD, MAXINE & BONNIE BROWN:		
11/12/55	**7**	7		2 **Here Today And Gone Tomorrow** A:7	*Jim Ed Brown/Maxine Brown*	Fabor 126
4/28/56	**2**[1]	24		3 **I Take The Chance** A:2 / S:6 / J:9	*Charlie Louvin/Ira Louvin*	RCA Victor 6480
9/22/56	**11**	2		4 **Just As Long As You Love Me** A:11	*Charlie Louvin/Ira Louvin*	RCA Victor 6631
3/23/57	**15**	1		5 **Money** A:15	*Zeb Turner*	RCA Victor 6823
9/2/57	**4**	17		6 **I Heard The Bluebirds Sing** A:4 / S:15	*Hod Pharis*	RCA Victor 6995
				THE BROWNS:		
10/20/58	**13**	2		7 **Would You Care**	*Jim Ed Brown/Preston Temple*	RCA Victor 7311
2/23/59	**11**	12		8 **Beyond The Shadow**	*Tommy Russell*	RCA Victor 7427
8/3/59	**❶**[10]	19	●	9 **The Three Bells**	*Bert Reisfeld/Jean Villard*	RCA Victor 7555
11/9/59+	**7**	16		10 **Scarlet Ribbons (For Her Hair)**	*Evelyn Danzig/Jack Segal*	RCA Victor 7614
				THE BROWNS Featuring Jim Edward Brown:		
4/11/60	**20**	7		11 **The Old Lamplighter**	*Nat Simon/Charles Tobias*	RCA Victor 7700
12/31/60	**23**	3		12 **Send Me The Pillow You Dream On**	*Hank Locklin*	RCA Victor 7804
1/18/64	**42**	1		13 **Oh No!**	*Clint Ballard/Ted Cooper*	RCA Victor 8242
5/16/64	**12**	26		14 **Then I'll Stop Loving You**	*Jim Reeves*	RCA Victor 8348
11/7/64	**40**	6		15 **Everybody's Darlin', Plus Mine**	*Frances Hur*	RCA Victor 8423
2/5/66	**46**	4		16 **Meadowgreen**	*Roger Miller*	RCA Victor 8714
				THE BROWNS:		
7/2/66	**16**	13		17 **I'd Just Be Fool Enough**	*Melvin Endsley*	RCA Victor 8838
10/8/66	**19**	10		18 **Coming Back To You**	*Floyd Robinson*	RCA Victor 8942
5/6/67	**54**	7		19 **I Hear It Now**	*Chip Taylor*	RCA Victor 9153
12/16/67+	**52**	7		20 **Big Daddy** /	*John D. Loudermilk*	
12/30/67+	**64**	4		21 **I Will Bring You Water**	*Keith Colley/Nancie Mantz*	RCA Victor 9364

BRUCE, Ed — All-Time: #149

Born William Edwin Bruce, Jr. on 12/29/1940 in Keiser, Arkansas; raised in Memphis, Tennessee. Male singer/songwriter/guitarist/actor. Recorded for Sun in 1957. Moved to Nashville in 1964 and worked with the Marijohn Wilkins Singers. Did TV commercials as "The Tennessean." Played "Tom Guthrie" on TV's *Bret Maverick*. Hosted TV's *American Sports Cavalcade* and *Truckin' U.S.A.*

DEBUT	PEAK	WKS	GOLD	Country Chart Hit	Songwriter	Label (& Number)
1/14/67	**57**	9		1 **Walker's Woods**	*Kay Arnold*	RCA Victor 9044
4/15/67	**69**	5		2 **Last Train To Clarksville**	*Tommy Boyce/Bobby Hart*	RCA Victor 9155
7/13/68	**52**	5		3 **Painted Girls And Wine**	*Jack Ripley*	RCA Victor 9553
1/4/69	**53**	10		4 **Song For Jenny**	*Ed Bruce*	Monument 1118
5/24/69	**52**	7		5 **Everybody Wants To Get To Heaven**	*Ed Bruce*	Monument 1138
12/15/73+	**77**	8		6 **July, You're A Woman**	*John Stewart*	United Artists 353
11/15/75+	**15**	14		7 **Mammas Don't Let Your Babies Grow Up To Be Cowboys**	*Ed Bruce/Patsy Bruce*	United Artists 732
3/20/76	**32**	10		8 **The Littlest Cowboy Rides Again**	*Glenn Ray*	United Artists 774
6/19/76	**57**	7		9 **Sleep All Mornin'**	*Alex Harvey*	United Artists 811
9/25/76	**36**	10		10 **For Love's Own Sake**	*Julie Didier/Casey Kelly*	United Artists 862
8/13/77	**52**	10		11 **When I Die, Just Let Me Go To Texas**	*Bobby Borchers/Ed Bruce/Patsy Bruce*	Epic 50424
11/19/77	**54**	10		12 **Star-Studded Nights**	*Sonny Throckmorton*	Epic 50475
2/11/78	**57**	7		13 **Love Somebody To Death**	*Red Lane/Glenn Martin*	Epic 50503
5/20/78	**94**	3		14 **Man Made Of Glass**	*Dennis Wilson*	Epic 50544
10/7/78	**70**	6		15 **The Man That Turned My Mama On**	*Ed Bruce*	Epic 50613
12/16/78+	**60**	9		16 **Angeline**	*Ronnie Rogers*	Epic 50645
3/8/80	**21**	15		17 **Diane**	*Ronnie Rogers*	MCA 41201
7/5/80	**12**	15		18 **The Last Cowboy Song** **Willie Nelson** (guest vocal)	*Ed Bruce/Ron Peterson*	MCA 41273
11/8/80+	**14**	16		19 **Girls, Women And Ladies**	*Ed Bruce/Patsy Bruce/Ron Peterson*	MCA 51018
3/28/81	**24**	14		20 **Evil Angel**	*Jesse Winchester*	MCA 51076
7/25/81	**14**	15		21 (When You Fall In Love) **Everything's A Waltz**	*Ed Bruce/Patsy Bruce/Ron Peterson*	MCA 51139

Billboard DEBUT	PEAK	WKS	GOLD	ARTIST Ranking / Country Chart Hit	Songwriter	Label (& Number)

BRUCE, Ed — cont'd

DEBUT	PEAK	WKS	#	Country Chart Hit	Songwriter	Label (& Number)
11/28/81+	❶[1]	21	22	You're The Best Break This Old Heart Ever Had	Randy Hatch/Wayland Holyfield	MCA 51210
4/24/82	13	16	23	Love's Found You And Me	Ed Bruce/Ronnie Rogers	MCA 52036
8/28/82	4	19	24	Ever, Never Lovin' You	Ed Bruce/Patsy Bruce/Glenn Ray	MCA 52109
1/22/83	6	18	25	My First Taste Of Texas	Ed Bruce/Ronnie Rogers	MCA 52156
5/14/83	21	15	26	You're Not Leavin' Here Tonight	Charlie Black/Kerry Chater/Tommy Rocco	MCA 52210
8/6/83	19	17	27	If It Was Easy	Larry Kingston/Harlan Sanders	MCA 52251
11/12/83+	4	21	28	After All	Ed Bruce/Patsy Bruce	MCA 52295
8/18/84	45	12	29	Tell 'Em I've Gone Crazy	Ed Bruce/Patsy Bruce/Ron Peterson	MCA 52433
11/3/84+	3[2]	22	30	You Turn Me On (Like A Radio)	S:3 / A:3 Bob McDill/Jim Weatherly	RCA 13937
3/23/85	17	16	31	When Givin' Up Was Easy	S:13 / A:18 Keith Palmer	RCA 14037
8/3/85	20	16	32	If It Ain't Love	A:18 / S:20 Mark Nesler	RCA 14150
4/12/86	4	19	33	Nights	S:4 / A:4 Byron Hill/Tony Hiller	RCA 14305
9/13/86	49	9	34	Fools For Each Other *[w/ Lynn Anderson]*	S:28 Guy Clark	RCA 5005
12/6/86+	36	14	35	Quietly Crazy	Steve Cropper/Mentor Williams	RCA 5077

BRUNER, Cliff

Born Clifton Bruner on 4/25/1915 in Texas City, Texas. Died of cancer on 8/25/2000 (age 85). Highly influential "texas swing" fiddle player.

EARLY HIT: It Makes No Difference Now (1938)

BRUSH ARBOR

Bluegrass group from San Diego, California: brothers Jim Rice (guitar), Joe Rice (mandolin) and Wayne Rice (banjo), with Ken Munds (vocals, guitar), Dave Rose (bass) and Dale Cooper (drums).

DEBUT	PEAK	WKS	#	Country Chart Hit	Songwriter	Label (& Number)
11/25/72+	56	10	1	Proud Mary	John Fogerty	Capitol 3468
3/10/73	41	7	2	Brush Arbor Meeting	Ken Munds	Capitol 3538
8/4/73	72	4	3	Alone Again (Naturally)	Gilbert O'Sullivan	Capitol 3672
11/17/73	98	2	4	Now That It's Over	Dennis Agajanian/Bonnie Blakey	Capitol 3733
12/8/73+	73	8	5	Trucker And The U.F.O.	Ken Munds	Capitol 3774
7/31/76	90	3	6	Emmylou	Buzz Cason	Monument 8702
11/12/77	56	11	7	Get Down Country Music	Jim Rice	Monument 230

BRYANT, Jimmy — see ORVILLE & IVY

BRYANT, Keith

Born in Lexington, Virginia. Male singer/songwriter/guitarist.

DEBUT	PEAK	WKS	#	Country Chart Hit	Songwriter	Label (& Number)
7/17/04	47	15		Ridin' With The Legend tribute to Dale Earnhardt; from the album *Ridin' With The Legend* on Lofton Creek 9002	John Detterline/Gary Gentry	Lofton Creek

BRYANT, Ronnie

Born in Atlanta, Georgia. Male singer.

DEBUT	PEAK	WKS	#	Country Chart Hit	Songwriter	Label (& Number)
11/4/89	81	2		Neither One Of Us	Jim Weatherly	Evergreen 1102

BRYCE, Sherry

Born in Duncanville, Alabama. Female singer/songwriter. Married to **Mack Sanders**; together they owned the Pilot label.

DEBUT	PEAK	WKS	#	Country Chart Hit	Songwriter	Label (& Number)
6/5/71	8	15	1	Take My Hand *[w/ Mel Tillis]*	Helen Acton/Les Acton/Shirley Price	MGM 14255
10/30/71	9	14	2	Living And Learning *[w/ Mel Tillis]*	Terry Skinner	MGM 14303
4/8/72	38	10	3	Anything's Better Than Nothing *[w/ Mel Tillis]*	Marie Wilson	MGM 14365
8/11/73	64	10	4	Leaving's Heavy On My Mind	Jim Rister/Sonny Rister	MGM 14548
11/17/73+	26	13	5	Let's Go All The Way Tonight *[w/ Mel Tillis]*	Mel Tillis	MGM 14660
2/9/74	45	11	6	Don't Stop Now	Sherry Bryce	MGM 14695
4/13/74	11	14	7	Don't Let Go *[w/ Mel Tillis]*	Jesse Stone	MGM 14714
6/29/74	62	9	8	Treat Me Like A Lady	Sherry Bryce	MGM 14726
10/5/74	70	6	9	Oh, How Happy	Charles Hetsher	MGM 14747
1/4/75	14	13	10	You Are The One *[w/ Mel Tillis]*	Hal Harbour/Kent Westberry	MGM 14776
4/26/75	96	3	11	Love Song	Tom Brasfield/Carolyn Shields	MGM 14793
5/17/75	32	13	12	Mr. Right And Mrs. Wrong *[w/ Mel Tillis]*	Hal Harbour/Kent Westberry	MGM 14803
2/28/76	97	2	13	Hang On Feelin'	Mike Kosser/Richard Mainegra	MGM 14842
11/13/76	93	3	14	Everything's Coming Up Love	Sherry Bryce	MCA 40630
10/1/77	79	5	15	The Lady Ain't For Sale	Sherry Bryce	Pilot 45100

BUCHANAN, Wes

Born in Vallejo, California. Male singer/songwriter/actor. Hosted own *Hollywood Jamboree* TV series in 1967. Appeared in the movie *From Nashville With Love.*

DEBUT	PEAK	WKS	#	Country Chart Hit	Songwriter	Label (& Number)
12/7/68	72	3		Warm Red Wine	Wes Buchanan	Columbia 44686

BUCHANAN BROTHERS

Duo of twin brothers from Canton, Ohio: Lester Buchanan (born on 10/17/1920; died on 8/6/2005, age 84) and Chester Buchanan (born on 10/17/1920; died on 5/15/1999, age 79).

DEBUT	PEAK	WKS	#	Country Chart Hit	Songwriter	Label (& Number)
6/29/46	6	3		Atomic Power	Fred Kirby	RCA Victor 20-1850

BUCK, Gary

Born on 3/21/40 in Thessalon, Ontario, Canada. Died of cancer on 10/14/2003 (age 63). Singer/songwriter/guitarist. Not to be confused with Gary Buck of The Four Guys.

DEBUT	PEAK	WKS	#	Country Chart Hit	Songwriter	Label (& Number)
6/29/63	11	17	1	Happy To Be Unhappy	Bobby Bare	Petal 1011
4/11/64	37	3	2	The Wheel Song	Frances Long/Pat Slatton	Petal 1500
2/13/82	93	2	3	Midnight Magic	Jerry McBee/Ray Pennington	Dimension 1029

DEBUT	PEAK	WKS	GOLD	ARTIST / Country Chart Hit	Ranking / Songwriter	Label (& Number)

BUCKAROOS, The

Backing band for **Buck Owens**: **Don Rich** (vocals, guitar, fiddle), Tom Brumley (steel guitar), **Doyle Holly** (bass) and Jerry Wiggins (drums). Rich was killed in a motorcycle accident on 7/17/1974 (age 32).

CMA: Instrumental Group 1967 & 1968

DEBUT	PEAK	WKS		Country Chart Hit	Songwriter	Label (& Number)
11/25/67	**69**	4		1 **Chicken Pickin'**	*Buck Owens/Don Rich* **[I]**	Capitol 2010
6/8/68	**38**	9		2 **I'm Coming Back Home To Stay**	*Don Rich*	Capitol 2173
9/21/68	**50**	8		3 **I'm Goin' Back Home Where I Belong**	*Don Rich*	Capitol 2264
4/19/69	**63**	2		4 **Anywhere U.S.A.**	*Don Holiman/Don Rich*	Capitol 2420
10/25/69	**43**	6		5 **Nobody But You**	*Don Rich*	Capitol 2629
4/4/70	**71**	3		6 **The Night They Drove Old Dixie Down**	*Robbie Robertson*	Capitol 2750

BUDDE, Rusty

Born in Houston, Texas. Male singer.

DEBUT	PEAK	WKS		Country Chart Hit	Songwriter	Label (& Number)
12/27/86	**77**	4		**Misty Mississippi**	*Don Goodman/Roger Lavoie/Pal Rakes/Mike Sullivan*	BPC 1002

BUFF, Beverly

Born in Washington, Georgia. Female singer.

DEBUT	PEAK	WKS		Country Chart Hit	Songwriter	Label (& Number)
11/24/62+	**22**	3		1 **I'll Sign**	*Kathy Mulkey/Truman Mulkey*	Bethlehem 3027
3/30/63	**23**	5		2 **Forgive Me**	*Arnold Bennett*	Bethlehem 3065

BUFFALO CLUB, The

Trio formed by former **Restless Heart** drummer John Dittrich, with singer Ron Hemby and guitarist Charlie Kelley.

DEBUT	PEAK	WKS		Country Chart Hit	Songwriter	Label (& Number)
1/18/97	**9**	20		1 **If She Don't Love You**	*Marc Beeson/Trey Bruce*	Rising Tide
6/7/97	**26**	20		2 **Nothin' Less Than Love**	*Wayne Tester/Russell Young*	Rising Tide
10/11/97	**53**	8		3 **Heart Hold On**	*Mike Lawler/Vicky McGehee/Henry Paul*	Rising Tide
				above 3 from the album *The Buffalo Club* on Rising Tide 53044		

BUFFETT, Jimmy — All-Time: #287

Born on 12/25/1946 in Pascagoula, Mississippi; raised in Mobile, Alabama. Singer/songwriter/guitarist. Earned a degree in journalism from the University of Southern Mississippi. Nashville correspondent for *Billboard* magazine from 1969-70. Settled in Key West in 1971. Owner of the Margaritaville record label and a line of tropical clothing. Authored the novels *Tales From Margaritaville* and *Where Is Joe Merchant*.

DEBUT	PEAK	WKS		Country Chart Hit	Songwriter	Label (& Number)
5/12/73	**58**	10		1 **The Great Filling Station Holdup**	*Jimmy Buffett*	Dunhill/ABC 4348
6/15/74	**58**	7		2 **Come Monday**	*Jimmy Buffett*	Dunhill/ABC 4385
8/23/75	**88**	5		3 **Door Number Three**	*Jimmy Buffett/Steve Goodman*	ABC 12113
4/30/77	**13**	17		4 **Margaritaville**	*Jimmy Buffett*	ABC 12254
10/1/77	**24**	10		5 **Changes In Latitudes, Changes In Attitudes**	*Jimmy Buffett*	ABC 12305
8/19/78	**91**	3		6 **Livingston Saturday Night**	*Jimmy Buffett*	ABC 12391
9/8/84	**42**	13		7 **When The Wild Life Betrays Me**	*Jimmy Buffett/Will Jennings/Michael Utley*	MCA 52438
12/8/84+	**58**	13		8 **Bigger Than The Both Of Us**	*Rhonda Coullet*	MCA 52499
3/23/85	**37**	15		9 **Who's The Blonde Stranger?**	S:24 *Jimmy Buffett/Will Jennings/Josh Leo/Michael Utley*	MCA 52550
6/29/85	**56**	9		10 **Gypsies In The Palace**	*Jimmy Buffett/Glenn Frey/Will Jennings*	MCA 52607
9/7/85	**16**	19		11 **If The Phone Doesn't Ring, It's Me**	A:11 / S:16 *Jimmy Buffett/Will Jennings/Michael Utley*	MCA 52664
2/8/86	**50**	9		12 **Please Bypass This Heart**	*Jimmy Buffett/Will Jennings/Michael Utley*	MCA 52752
8/28/93	**74**	1		13 **Another Saturday Night**	*Sam Cooke*	MCA
				from the album *Margaritaville Cafe Late Night Menu* on MCA 10824		
11/6/99	**63**	3		14 **Margaritaville** ***[w/ Alan Jackson]***	*Jimmy Buffett* **[R]**	Arista Nashville
				from Jackson's album *Under The Infleunce* on Arista Nashville 18892		
6/21/03	❶[8]	27		15 **It's Five O'Clock Somewhere** ***[w/ Alan Jackson]***	*Jim Brown/Don Rollins*	Arista Nashville
				Grammy: Song / CMA: Vocal Event; from Jackson's album *Greatest Hits Volume II and Some Other Stuff* on Arista Nashville 53097		
5/29/04	**8**	20		16 **Hey Good Lookin'** ***[w/ Clint Black/Kenny Chesney/Alan Jackson/Toby Keith/George Strait]***	*Hank Williams*	RCA
9/4/04	**20**	20		17 **Trip Around The Sun** ***[w/ Martina McBride]***	*Al Anderson/Steve Bruton/Sharon Vaughn*	Mailboat
				above 2 from Buffett's album *License To Chill* on RCA 62270		

BUNZOW, John

Born on 5/2/1951 in Portland, Oregon. Male singer/songwriter.

DEBUT	PEAK	WKS		Country Chart Hit	Songwriter	Label (& Number)
4/8/95	**69**	4		**Easy As One, Two, Three**	*John Bunzow*	Liberty
				from the album *Stories Of The Years* on Liberty 28246		

BURBANK, Gary, with Band McNally

Born in Cincinnati, Ohio. DJ at WHAS in Louisville, Kentucky, at the time of his hit.

DEBUT	PEAK	WKS		Country Chart Hit	Songwriter	Label (& Number)
7/26/80	**91**	2		**Who Shot J.R.?**	*Gary Burbank/Ron Reed/Ed Vanover* **[N]**	Ovation 1150
				inspired by the shooting of "J.R. Ewing" (Larry Hagman) on TV's *Dallas*		

BURBANK STATION

Group from Fargo, North Dakota. Features female singer Bunny Davis.

DEBUT	PEAK	WKS		Country Chart Hit	Songwriter	Label (& Number)
8/6/88	**77**	3		1 **Divided**	*John Jarrard/Jim Rushing*	Prairie Dust 8841
5/27/89	**90**	2		2 **Get Out Of My Way**	*Kent Robbins/Will Robinson*	Prairie Dust 112

BURCH SISTERS, The

Vocal trio from Jacksonville, Florida: sisters Cathy Burch (born on 12/28/1960), Charlene Burch (born on 9/19/1962) and Cindy Burch (born on 8/1/1963). Also see **Tomorrow's World**.

DEBUT	PEAK	WKS		Country Chart Hit	Songwriter	Label (& Number)
5/21/88	**23**	18		1 **Everytime You Go Outside I Hope It Rains**	S:28 *Hal Coleman/Ken Gibbons*	Mercury 870362
10/15/88	**61**	5		2 **What Do Lonely People Do**	*Harlan Howard*	Mercury 870687
12/17/88+	**45**	11		3 **I Don't Want To Mention Any Names**	*Larry Cordle/Lisa Palas*	Mercury 872324
4/1/89	**46**	11		4 **Old Flame, New Fire**	*Paul Harrison/Bob McDill*	Mercury 872730
7/1/89	**59**	8		5 **The Way I Want To Go**	*Chick Rains*	Mercury 874560

DEBUT	PEAK	WKS	GOLD	ARTIST / Country Chart Hit	Songwriter	Label (& Number)

BURDICK, Kathy

Born in Peoria, Illinois. Female singer.

DEBUT	PEAK	WKS	#	Country Chart Hit	Songwriter	Label (& Number)
11/8/80+	30	12		Lost In Love *[w/ Dickey Lee]*	*Graham Russell*	Mercury 57036

BURGESS, Frank

Born in West Virginia. Male singer.

DEBUT	PEAK	WKS	#	Country Chart Hit	Songwriter	Label (& Number)
11/26/88	88	3	1	American Man	*Bobby Braddock/Don Henry*	True 94
5/13/89	81	3	2	What It Boils Down To	*Hank Williams Jr.*	True 96

BURGESS, Wilma

Born on 6/11/1939 in Orlando, Florida. Died of a heart attack on 8/26/2003 (age 64). Female singer.

DEBUT	PEAK	WKS	#	Country Chart Hit	Songwriter	Label (& Number)
12/11/65+	7	18	1	Baby	*Ray Griff*	Decca 31862
5/7/66	12	17	2	Don't Touch Me	*Hank Cochran*	Decca 31941
10/29/66	4	18	3	Misty Blue	*Bob Montgomery*	Decca 32027
3/25/67	24	15	4	Fifteen Days	*Cindy Walker*	Decca 32105
8/26/67	16	15	5	Tear Time	*Jan Crutchfield*	Decca 32178
8/17/68	59	9	6	Look At The Laughter	*Tony Senn/Tommy Stough*	Decca 32359
3/22/69	68	3	7	Parting (Is Such Sweet Sorrow)	*Ray Griff*	Decca 32437
8/9/69	48	10	8	The Woman In Your Life	*Ted Harris*	Decca 32522
12/27/69+	48	9	9	The Sun's Gotta' Shine	*Ted Harris*	Decca 32593
7/11/70	63	6	10	Lonely For You	*Ben Peters*	Decca 32684
9/22/73	61	11	11	I'll Be Your Bridge (Just Lay Me Down)	*Paul Huffman/Royce Porter*	Shannon 813
12/22/73+	14	17	12	Wake Me Into Love *[w/ Bud Logan]*	*Red Lane/Tom McKeon/Royce Porter*	Shannon 816
7/6/74	53	10	13	The Best Day Of The Rest Of Our Love *[w/ Bud Logan]*	*Bucky Jones/Royce Porter*	Shannon 820
9/14/74	46	11	14	Love Is Here /	*Bucky Jones/Royce Porter*	
2/8/75	86	6	15	Sweet Lovin' Baby	*Gerald Nelson/Chuck Taylor*	Shannon 821

BURKE, Fiddlin' Frenchie

Born Leon Bourke in Kaplan, Louisiana. Male singer/songwriter/fiddler.

DEBUT	PEAK	WKS	#	Country Chart Hit	Songwriter	Label (& Number)
11/23/74+	39	15	1	Big Mamou **FIDDLIN' FRENCHIE BOURQUE and THE OUTLAWS**	*Link Davis*	20th Century 2152
4/19/75	30	9	2	Colinda	*Jimmy Williams*	20th Century 2182
10/11/75	73	5	3	The Fiddlin' Of Jacques Pierre Bordeaux **FIDDLIN' FRENCHIE BURKE & THE OUTLAWS** (above 2)	*Dallas Frazier/A.L. "Doodle" Owens*	20th Century 2225
7/1/78	94	5	4	Knock Knock Knock **FRENCHIE BURKE**	*Joel Sonnier*	Cherry 644
3/28/81	93	3	5	(Frenchie Burke's) Fire On The Mountain	*Frenchie Burke* [I]	Delta 11332

BURKHART, Jerry

Born in Waco, Texas. Male singer/songwriter/guitarist. Owns an auto repair shop.

DEBUT	PEAK	WKS	#	Country Chart Hit	Songwriter	Label (& Number)
2/22/03	56	1		Cryin' Steel from the album *Cryin' Country* on Cupit 7774	*Jerry Cupit*	Cupit

BURNETTE, Billy

Born on 5/8/1953 in Memphis, Tennessee. Male singer/songwriter/guitarist. Son of **Dorsey Burnette**, nephew of Johnny Burnette and cousin of Rocky Burnette. Member of Fleetwood Mac from 1987-1993. Acted in the movie *Saturday Night Special.*

DEBUT	PEAK	WKS	#	Country Chart Hit	Songwriter	Label (& Number)
11/3/79	76	5	1	What's A Little Love Between Friends	*Billy Burnette/Larry Henley*	Polydor 2024
8/10/85	51	8	2	Ain't It Just Like Love	*Billy Burnette/Pat Robinson*	Curb/MCA 52626
12/28/85+	68	9	3	Try Me	*Billy Burnette/Steve Cropper*	Curb/MCA 52749
7/12/86	54	7	4	Soldier Of Love	*Richard Brannan/Anthony Crawford/David Malloy*	Curb/MCA 52852
3/7/92	64	6	5	Nothin' To Do (And All Night To Do It)	*Deborah Allen/Billy Burnette/Rafe Van Hoy*	Warner

BURNETTE, Billy Joe

Born in 1945 in Richmond, Virginia. Male singer/songwriter.

DEBUT	PEAK	WKS	#	Country Chart Hit	Songwriter	Label (& Number)
1/6/90	90	1		Three Flags	*Billy Joe Burnette/Dale Royal* [S]	Badger 1004

BURNETTE, Dorsey

Born on 12/28/1932 in Memphis, Tennessee. Died of a heart attack on 8/19/1979 (age 46). Male singer/songwriter/guitarist. Older brother of Johnny Burnette and father of **Billy Burnette**.

DEBUT	PEAK	WKS	#	Country Chart Hit	Songwriter	Label (& Number)
5/13/72	21	12	1	In The Spring (The Roses Always Turn Red)	*Dorsey Burnette*	Capitol 3307
9/2/72	40	8	2	I Just Couldn't Let Her Walk Away	*Charles Bell/Alton Harkins*	Capitol 3404
2/17/73	42	9	3	I Let Another Good One Get Away	*Dorsey Burnette/Steve Stone*	Capitol 3529
5/12/73	53	5	4	Keep Out Of My Dreams	*Dorsey Burnette/Steve Stone*	Capitol 3588
8/11/73	26	14	5	Darlin' (Don't Come Back) *[w/ Sound Company]*	*Dorsey Burnette/Kelly Gordon/Steve Stone*	Capitol 3678
1/12/74	85	7	6	It Happens Every Time *[w/ Sound Company]*	*Milton Brown/Steve Dorff*	Capitol 3796
3/9/74	69	8	7	Bob, All The Playboys And Me *[w/ Sound Company]*	*Charlie Williams*	Capitol 3829
6/15/74	62	8	8	Daddy Loves You Honey	*Tony Hiller*	Capitol 3887
11/23/74	71	5	9	What Ladies Can Do (When They Want To)	*Rory Bourke*	Capitol 3963
5/31/75	28	12	10	Molly (I Ain't Gettin' Any Younger)	*Dennis Linde*	Melodyland 6007
10/18/75	97	3	11	Lyin' In Her Arms Again	*Gary Branson*	Melodyland 6019
4/24/76	74	5	12	Ain't No Heartbreak	*Dorsey Burnette/Steve Stone*	Melodyland 6031
6/11/77	31	15	13	Things I Treasure	*Dorsey Burnette*	Calliope 8004
11/5/77	53	7	14	Soon As I Touched Her	*Nate Helms/Ken Hirsch*	Calliope 8012
9/1/79	77	4	15	Here I Go Again	*Dorsey Burnette/J.C. Cunningham*	Elektra 46513

BURNIN' DAYLIGHT

Trio of **Marc Beeson** (vocals), Sonny Lemaire (bass; **Exile**) and Kurt Howell (keyboards; **Southern Pacific**).

DEBUT	PEAK	WKS	#	Country Chart Hit	Songwriter	Label (& Number)
10/19/96	49	16	1	Love Worth Fighting For	*Marc Beeson/Kurt Howell/Sonny Lemaire*	Curb
2/15/97	37	20	2	Say Yes	*Marc Beeson/Chuck Jones*	Curb
6/21/97	58	6	3	Live To Love Again	*Marc Beeson/Trey Bruce/Kurt Howell/Sonny Lemaire*	Curb

above 3 from the album *Burnin' Daylight* on Curb 77850

BURNS, Brent

Born in Seminole, Oklahoma; raised in Phoenix, Arizona. Male singer/guitarist.

DEBUT	PEAK	WKS	#	Country Chart Hit	Songwriter	Label (& Number)
5/6/78	91	4		I Hear You Coming Back	*Yvonne Smith*	Pantheon Desert 79

BURNS, George

Born Nathan Birnbaum on 1/20/1896 in Brooklyn, New York. Died on 3/9/1996 (age 100). Legendary comedian/actor.

DEBUT	PEAK	WKS	#	Country Chart Hit	Songwriter	Label (& Number)
1/5/80	15	14	1	I Wish I Was Eighteen Again	*Sonny Throckmorton*	Mercury 57011
5/24/80	85	4	2	The Arizona Whiz	*Max D. Barnes/Harlan Sanders*	Mercury 57021
2/14/81	66	5	3	Willie, Won't You Sing A Song With Me	*Glenn Sutton*	Mercury 57045

BURNS, Hughie

Born in Phoenix, Arizona. Male singer.

DEBUT	PEAK	WKS	#	Country Chart Hit	Songwriter	Label (& Number)
3/8/80	95	2		The Family Inn	*Barry Grant/Lee Likes*	C-S-I 002

BURNS, Jackie

Born in Long Beach, California. Female singer.

DEBUT	PEAK	WKS	#	Country Chart Hit	Songwriter	Label (& Number)
10/11/69	60	5	1	Something's Missing (It's You)	*Larry Butler*	Honor Brigade 5
10/21/72	71	2	2	(If Loving You Is Wrong) I Don't Want To Be Right	*Homer Banks/Carl Hampton/Raymond Jackson*	JMI 8

BURRITO BROTHERS

Group formed in 1968 as the **Flying Burrito Brothers** by **Chris Hillman** and Gram Parsons, ex-members of folk-rock band The Byrds. By 1980, consisted of "Sneaky" Pete Kleinow (steel guitar), Floyd "Gib" Guilbeau (fiddle; father of Ronnie Guilbeau of **Palomino Road**), Skip Battin (bass), Greg Harris (guitar) and Ed Ponder (drums). In 1981, relocated to Nashville, dropped "Flying" from band name, Harris and Ponder left and John Beland (guitar) joined. By late 1981, reduced to a duo of Guilbeau and Beland.

DEBUT	PEAK	WKS	#	Country Chart Hit	Songwriter	Label (& Number)
3/1/80	95	2	1	White Line Fever *[Flying Burrito Brothers]*	*Merle Haggard* [L]	Regency 45001
1/24/81	67	5	2	She's A Friend Of A Friend	*John Beland/Gib Guilbeau*	Curb 5402
4/18/81	20	13	3	Does She Wish She Was Single Again	*Milton Blackford/Richard Leigh*	Curb 01011
8/8/81	16	14	4	She Belongs To Everyone But Me	*John Beland/Gib Guilbeau*	Curb 02243
12/26/81+	27	14	5	If Something Should Come Between Us (Let It Be Love)	*John Beland/Gib Guilbeau*	Curb 02641
4/17/82	40	10	6	Closer To You	*John Beland/Gib Guilbeau*	Curb 02835
7/24/82	39	10	7	I'm Drinkin' Canada Dry	*Johnny Cymbal/Austin Roberts*	Curb 03023
11/13/82	48	10	8	Blue And Broken Hearted Me	*Buddy Cannon/Raleigh Squires*	Curb 03314
1/28/84	49	9	9	Almost Saturday Night	*John Fogerty*	Curb 52329
5/26/84	53	8	10	My Kind Of Lady	*Joel Hirschhorn/Al Kasha*	Curb 52379

BUSH, Johnny — All-Time: #272

Born John Bush Shin III on 2/17/1935 in Houston, Texas. Male singer/songwriter/guitarist/drummer. Worked with **Ray Price** and **Willie Nelson** in the 1960s. Known as "The Country Caruso."

DEBUT	PEAK	WKS	#	Country Chart Hit	Songwriter	Label (& Number)
11/25/67	69	3	1	You Oughta Hear Me Cry	*Willie Nelson*	Stop 126
3/16/68	29	13	2	What A Way To Live	*Willie Nelson*	Stop 160
8/3/68	10	16	3	Undo The Right	*Hank Cochran/Willie Nelson*	Stop 193
12/28/68+	16	13	4	Each Time	*Ray Price*	Stop 232
3/22/69	7	15	5	You Gave Me A Mountain	*Marty Robbins*	Stop 257
8/16/69	26	10	6	My Cup Runneth Over	*Tom Jones/Harvey Schmidt*	Stop 310
1/3/70	56	8	7	Jim, Jack, And Rose /	*Larry Kingston*	
1/10/70	flip	5	8	I'll Go To A Stranger	*Dave Kirby/Ray Pennington*	Stop 354
5/16/70	25	11	9	Warmth Of The Wine	*Larry Kingston*	Stop 371
11/7/70	44	11	10	My Joy	*Frank Dycus/Larry Kingston*	Stop 380
4/10/71	53	6	11	City Lights	*Bill Anderson*	Stop 392
4/22/72	17	12	12	I'll Be There	*Rusty Gabbard/Ray Price*	Million 1
7/22/72	14	15	13	Whiskey River	*Johnny Bush/Paul Stroud*	RCA Victor 0745

also see #24 below

DEBUT	PEAK	WKS	#	Country Chart Hit	Songwriter	Label (& Number)
12/30/72+	34	9	14	There Stands The Glass	*Audrey Grisham/Russ Hull/Mary Shurtz*	RCA Victor 0867
5/5/73	38	11	15	Here Comes The World Again	*Steve Karliski/Larry Kolber*	RCA Victor 0931
9/1/73	53	8	16	Green Snakes On The Ceiling	*Jimmie Peters/Elton Williams*	RCA Victor 0041
12/1/73+	37	10	17	We're Back In Love Again	*Glenn Martin/Sonny Throckmorton*	RCA Victor 0164
3/23/74	48	10	18	Toy Telephone /	*Frank Dycus/Larry Kingston*	
5/4/74	flip	4	19	From Tennessee To Texas	*Johnny Bush/Larry Kingston*	RCA Victor 0240
10/15/77	78	7	20	You'll Never Leave Me Completely /	*Chuck Howard/Dave Kirby*	
4/29/78	99	2	21	Put Me Out Of My Memory	*Johnny Bush*	Gusto 165
9/2/78	89	3	22	She Just Made Me Love You More	*James Coleman/Moe Lytle*	Gusto 9006
5/19/79	83	5	23	When My Conscience Hurts The Most	*Vic McAlpin/Lester Vanadore*	Whiskey River 791
2/28/81	92	2	24	Whiskey River	*Johnny Bush* [R]	Delta 10041

new version of #13 above

BUTLER, Bobby "Sofine"

Born in El Paso, Texas. Male singer/songwriter/DJ.

DEBUT	PEAK	WKS	#	Country Chart Hit	Songwriter	Label (& Number)
12/4/76	98	2	1	Teddy Toad	*Brent Burns/Bobby Butler*	Pantheon Desert 77
5/26/79	46	6	2	Cheaper Crude Or No More Food	*Brent Burns* [N]	IBC 0001

Billboard DEBUT	PEAK	WKS	GOLD	ARTIST / Country Chart Hit ... Songwriter	Ranking	Label (& Number)

BUTLER, Carl, and Pearl — All-Time: #296

Husband-and-wife duo from Knoxville, Tennessee. Carl was born on 6/2/1927; died on 9/4/1992 (age 65). Pearl was born Pearl Dee Jones on 9/20/1927; died on 3/1/1989 (age 61). Both appeared in the movie *Second Fiddle To A Steel Guitar.*

OPRY: 1962

DEBUT	PEAK	WKS	#	Country Chart Hit	Songwriter	Label (& Number)
8/7/61	25	2	1	**Honky Tonkitis** *[Carl Butler]*	*Tex Atchison*	Columbia 41997
12/8/62	❶^{11}	24	2	**Don't Let Me Cross Over**	*Penny Jay*	Columbia 42593
7/6/63	14	14	3	**Loving Arms**	*Irene Stanton/Wayne Walker*	Columbia 42778
1/11/64	9	8	4	**Too Late To Try Again /**	*Carl Butler*	
1/11/64	36	1	5	**My Tears Don't Show**	*Carl Butler*	Columbia 42892
6/6/64	14	16	6	**I'm Hanging Up The Phone**	*Wanda Rogers/Weldon Rogers*	Columbia 43030
9/26/64	23	10	7	**Forbidden Street**	*Penny Jay*	Columbia 43102
2/27/65	38	10	8	**We'd Destroy Each Other /**	*Benny Joy/Kent Westberry*	
3/27/65	22	13	9	**Just Thought I'd Let You Know**	*Hugh X. Lewis*	Columbia 43210
12/11/65	42	2	10	**Our Ship Of Love**	*Larry Kingston*	Columbia 43433
8/6/66	31	7	11	**Little Pedro**	*Cecil Null*	Columbia 43685
8/17/68	28	12	12	**Punish Me Tomorrow**	*Harlan Howard*	Columbia 44587
1/4/69	46	8	13	**I Never Got Over You**	*Sudie Callaway/Marie Wilson*	Columbia 44694
7/5/69	63	6	14	**We'll Sweep Out The Ashes In The Morning**	*Joyce Allsup*	Columbia 44862

BUZZI, Ruth

Born on 7/24/1936 in Westerley, Rhode Island. Female comedian/actress. Regular on TV's *Laugh-In.*

DEBUT	PEAK	WKS	#	Country Chart Hit	Songwriter	Label (& Number)
4/2/77	90	4		**You Oughta Hear The Song**	*Roger Bowling/Jodie Emerson*	United Artists 951

BUZZIN' COUSINS

Group that appeared in the movie *Falling From Grace*: **John Cougar Mellencamp** (director/star of the movie), **Dwight Yoakam**, **Joe Ely**, John Prine, and James McMurtry.

DEBUT	PEAK	WKS	#	Country Chart Hit	Songwriter	Label (& Number)
2/15/92	68	5		**Sweet Suzanne** from the movie *Falling From Grace* starring **John Cougar Mellencamp** (soundtrack on Mercury 512004)	*John Mellencamp*	Mercury

BYERS, Brenda

Born in Canterbury, Connecticut. Female singer/banjo player.

DEBUT	PEAK	WKS	#	Country Chart Hit	Songwriter	Label (& Number)
10/26/68	51	9	1	**The Auctioneer**	*Buddy Black/Leroy Van Dyke*	MTA 160
10/11/69	65	6	2	**Thank You For Loving Me**	*Tony Hatch/Jackie Trent*	MTA 176
1/24/70	66	4	3	**Homeward Bound**	*Paul Simon*	MTA 177

BYRAM, Judy

Born in Pelham, Alabama. Female singer.

DEBUT	PEAK	WKS	#	Country Chart Hit	Songwriter	Label (& Number)
12/5/87	71	5	1	**No More One More Time**	*Dave Kirby/Troy Seals*	F&L 554
6/4/88	74	5	2	**One Fire Between Us**	*Charlie Craig*	Regal 001

BYRD, Jerry

Born on 3/9/1920 in Lima, Ohio. Died on 4/11/2005 (age 85). Steel guitarist.

DEBUT	PEAK	WKS	#	Country Chart Hit	Songwriter	Label (& Number)
9/3/49	14	1		**Afraid** *[w/ Rex Allen & The Arizona Wranglers]*	J:14 *Fred Rose*	Mercury 6192

BYRD, Tracy — 1990s: #36 / 2000s: #26 / All-Time: #121

Born on 12/17/1966 in Beaumont, Texas; raised in Vidor, Texas. Male singer/songwriter/guitarist. Studied business at Southwest Texas State. In 1991, became a regular performer at Cutter's Nightclub in Beaumont. Signed to MCA in 1992.

DEBUT	PEAK	WKS	#	Country Chart Hit	Songwriter	Label (& Number)
8/22/92	71	3	1	**That's The Thing About A Memory**	*Lewis Anderson/Tracy Byrd/Keith Stegall*	MCA
2/13/93	42	20	2	**Someone To Give My Love To**	*Jerry Foster/Bill Rice*	MCA
6/19/93	❶^{1}	20	3	**Holdin' Heaven**	*Bill Kenner/Thom McHugh*	MCA
10/30/93	39	15	4	**Why Don't That Telephone Ring** above 4 from the album *Tracy Byrd* on MCA 10649	*Ron Hellard/Charles Quillen*	MCA
4/30/94	4	20	5	**Lifestyles Of The Not So Rich And Famous**	*Byron Hill/Wayne Tester*	MCA
8/13/94	4	20	6	**Watermelon Crawl**	*Buddy Brock/Zack Turner*	MCA
11/19/94+	5	20	7	**The First Step**	*Doug Crider/Verlon Thompson*	MCA
1/21/95	2^{2}	20	8	**The Keeper Of The Stars** above 4 from the album *No Ordinary Man* on MCA 10991	*Dickey Lee/Danny Mayo/Karen Staley*	MCA
6/3/95	15	20	9	**Walking To Jerusalem**	S:3 *Sam Hogin/Mark D. Sanders*	MCA
9/9/95	9	20	10	**Love Lessons**	S:6 *Owen Hewitt/Jerry Kilgore/Sarah Majors/Monty Powell*	MCA
2/3/96	14	20	11	**Heaven In My Woman's Eyes**	*Mark Nesler*	MCA
5/25/96	21	20	12	**4 To 1 In Atlanta** above 4 from the album *Love Lessons* on MCA 11242	*L. Russell Brown/Bill Kenner*	MCA
9/21/96+	3^{2}	20	13	**Big Love**	S:13 *Michael Clark/Jeff Stevens*	MCA
1/25/97	4	20	14	**Don't Take Her She's All I Got**	*Gary U.S. Bonds/Jerry Williams*	MCA
5/17/97	17	20	15	**Don't Love Make A Diamond Shine**	*Mike Dekle/Craig Wiseman*	MCA
9/27/97	47	10	16	**Good Ol' Fashioned Love** above 4 from the album *Big Love* on MCA 11485	*Tony Martin/Mark Nesler*	MCA
2/7/98	3^{2}	28	17	**I'm From The Country**	S:7 *Marty Brown/Stan Webb/Richard Young*	MCA Nashville
6/20/98	9	23	18	**I Wanna Feel That Way Again** above 2 from the album *I'm From The Country* on MCA Nashville 70016	*Steve Bogard/Michelle Leigh/Jeff Stevens*	MCA Nashville

DEBUT	PEAK	WKS	GOLD	ARTIST / Ranking / Country Chart Hit... Songwriter	Label (& Number)
				BYRD, Tracy — cont'd	
12/19/98+	31	20		19 **When Mama Ain't Happy** ... *Rick Giles/Gilles Godard/Tim Nichols*	MCA Nashville
				from the album *Keepers / Greatest Hits* on MCA Nashville 70048	
9/25/99+	11	25		20 **Put Your Hand In Mine** ... *Jimmy Barber/Skip Ewing*	RCA
1/1/00	55	2		21 **Merry Christmas From Texas Y'all** ... *Clint Bullard/Doug Nichols* **[X]**	RCA
4/1/00	44	12		22 **Love, You Ain't Seen The Last Of Me** ... *Kendal Francheski*	RCA
9/2/00	43	8		23 **Take Me With You When You Go** ... *Jennifer Hanson/Mark Nesler*	RCA
				#20, 22 & 23: from the album *It's About Time* on RCA 67881	
9/2/00	59	12		24 **Now That's Awesome!** ***[w/ Bill Engvall/Neal McCoy/T. Graham Brown]***	
				from Engvall's album *Now That's Awesome!* on BNA 69311 ...S:13 *Bill Engvall/Porter Howell* **[N]**	BNA
3/24/01	21	20		25 **A Good Way To Get On My Bad Side** ***[w/ Mark Chesnutt]*** ... *Rivers Rutherford/George Teren*	RCA
8/25/01+	9	28		26 **Just Let Me Be In Love** ... *Tony Martin/Mark Nesler/Tom Shapiro*	RCA
4/6/02	❶[1]	32		27 **Ten Rounds With José Cuervo** *Casey Beathard/Marla Cannon/Mike Heeney*	RCA
				above 3 from the album *Ten Rounds* on RCA 67009	
11/9/02+	38	16		28 **Lately (Been Dreamin' 'Bout Babies)** ... *Ralph Hamm*	RCA
3/15/03	13	21		29 **The Truth About Men** ... *Tim Johnson/Rory Lee/Paul Overstreet* **[N]**	RCA
				Andy Griggs, **Montgomery Gentry** and **Blake Shelton** (guest vocals)	
8/9/03+	7	27		30 **Drinkin' Bone** ... *Casey Beathard/Kerry Kurt Phillips*	RCA
3/27/04	53	6		31 **How'd I Wind Up In Jamaica** ... *Casey Beathard/Mike Heeney*	RCA
				above 3 from the album *The Truth About Men* on RCA 67073	
10/2/04	34	20		32 **Revenge Of A Middle-Aged Woman** ... *Dave Berg/Annie Tate/Sam Tate*	BNA
				from the album *Greatest Hits* on BNA 64861	

C

DEBUT	PEAK	WKS	GOLD	ARTIST / Country Chart Hit... Songwriter	Label (& Number)
				CACTUS CHOIR	
				Group from San Francisco, California: Marty Atkinson (vocals), Gary Hooker (guitar), Dave Ristrim (steel guitar), Tim Hensley (banjo), Shane Hicks (keyboards), Cal Ball (bass) and Eric Nelson (drums).	
1/24/98	62	8		**Step Right Up** ... *Tom Haller*	Curb
				CAGLE, Buddy	
				Born Walter Cagle on 2/8/1936 in Concord, North Carolina; raised in Winston-Salem, North Carolina. Male singer/guitarist.	
5/18/63	29	3		1 **Your Mother's Prayer** ... *Eddie Miller*	Capitol 4923
11/16/63	26	2		2 **Sing A Sad Song** ... *Wynn Stewart*	Capitol 5043
9/25/65	37	8		3 **Honky Tonkin' Again** ... *Bobby George/Curtis Leach/Claude McBride/Vern Stoval*	Mercury 72452
4/23/66	31	10		4 **Tonight I'm Coming Home** ... *Scott Turner/Charlie Williams*	Imperial 66161
1/14/67	57	7		5 **Apologize** ... *Freddie Hart*	Imperial 66218
8/12/67	75	2		6 **Longtime Traveling** ... *Oscar Brand/Paul Nassau*	Imperial 66245
				CAGLE, Chris — **2000s: #36**	
				Born Christian Cagle on 11/10/1968 in Louisiana; raised in Baytown, Texas. Male singer/songwriter/guitarist.	
7/29/00	15	23		1 **My Love Goes On And On** ...S:10 *Chris Cagle/Don Pfrimmer*	Virgin
12/2/00+	8	31		2 **Laredo** ... *Chris Cagle*	Virgin
9/22/01+	❶[1]	36		3 **I Breathe In, I Breathe Out** *Chris Cagle/Jon Robbin*	Capitol
5/4/02	33	20		4 **Country By The Grace Of God** ... *Chris Cagle/Michael Greene/Bryan Wayne*	Capitol
				above 4 from the album *Play It Loud* on Capitol 34170	
11/9/02+	4	32		5 **What A Beautiful Day** ... *Chris Cagle/Monty Powell*	Capitol
6/28/03	5	30		6 **Chicks Dig It** ... *Chris Cagle/Charlie Crowe*	Capitol
1/31/04	39	13		7 **I'd Be Lying** ... *Chris Cagle*	Capitol
				above 3 from the album *Chris Cagle* on Capitol 40516	
6/25/05	28↑	14↑		8 **Miss Me Baby** ... *Chris Cagle/Monty Powell*	Capitol
				CAIN, Hunter	
				Born in Hendersonville, Tennessee. Male singer.	
7/16/88	82	2		1 **Hollywood Heroes /** ... *Mike Reid/Troy Seals/Eddie Setser*	
5/13/89	95	1		2 **She's Too Good To Be Cheated This Way** ... *T. Graham Brown/Bruce Burch*	Discovery 4587
				CALAMITY JANE	
				Female group: **Pam Rose** (vocals), Mary Fielder (guitar), Linda Moore (bass) and Mary Ann Kennedy (drums).	
10/17/81	61	7		1 **Send Me Somebody To Love** ... *Tim Krekel*	Columbia 02503
2/27/82	44	9		2 **I've Just Seen A Face** ... *John Lennon/Paul McCartney*	Columbia 02715
6/19/82	60	7		3 **Walkin' After Midnight** ... *Alan Block/Don Hecht*	Columbia 02958
10/16/82	87	3		4 **Love Wheel** ... *Pat Bunch/Mary Ann Kennedy/Pam Rose*	Columbia 03229
				CALHOUN, Linda	
				Born in Little Rock, Arkansas. Female singer.	
4/28/79	85	4		**I Can Feel Love** ... *Jim Hayner*	Grape 2004
				CAMERON, Bart	
				Born in Louisville, Kentucky. Male singer.	
11/1/86	76	4		1 **Dark Eyed Lady** ... *James Britt/Bob Leroy*	Revolver 013
5/30/87	77	3		2 **Do It For The Love Of It** ... *Rita Grimm/Dani Hayes*	Revolver 015
				CAMP, Colleen	
				Born on 6/7/1953 in San Francisco, California. Female singer/actress.	
1/23/82	72	4		**One Day Since Yesterday** ... *Earl Ball/Peter Bogdanovich*	Moon Pictures 0001

Billboard DEBUT	PEAK	WKS	GOLD	ARTIST / Ranking / Country Chart Hit	Songwriter	Label (& Number)

CAMP, Shawn

Born on 8/29/1966 in Little Rock, Arkansas; raised in Perryville, Arkansas. Male singer/songwriter/guitarist/fiddler.

DEBUT	PEAK	WKS	GOLD	Country Chart Hit	Songwriter	Label (& Number)
7/31/93	39	20		1 **Fallin' Never Felt So Good**	*Shawn Camp/Will Smith*	Reprise
11/20/93+	39	20		2 **Confessin' My Love**	*Shawn Camp/John Scott Sherrill*	Reprise
				above 2 from the album *Shawn Camp* on Reprise 45450		

CAMPBELL, Archie

Born on 11/7/1914 in Bulls Gap, Tennessee. Died of heart failure on 8/29/1987 (age 72). Singer/songwriter/comedian. Chief writer and cast member of the TV series *Hee Haw.* Hosted TNN's *Yesteryear In Nashville.* Also see **Some Of Chet's Friends.**

CMA: Comedian 1969 // OPRY: 1958

DEBUT	PEAK	WKS	GOLD	Country Chart Hit	Songwriter	Label (& Number)
3/14/60	24	4		1 **Trouble In The Amen Corner**	*Archie Campbell* [S]	RCA Victor 7660
1/22/66	16	8		2 **The Men In My Little Girl's Life**	*Mary Candy/Eddie Deane/Gloria Shayne*	RCA Victor 8741
3/11/67	44	10		3 **The Cockfight**	*Fred Blalock/Maxine Kelton* [S]	RCA Victor 9081
1/6/68	24	15		4 **The Dark End Of The Street** ***[w/ Lorene Mann]***	*Chips Moman/Dan Penn*	RCA Victor 9401
6/29/68	31	10		5 **Tell It Like It Is** ***[w/ Lorene Mann]***	*George Davis/Lee Diamond*	RCA Victor 9549
9/28/68	57	8		6 **Warm And Tender Love** ***[w/ Lorene Mann]***	*Bobby Robinson*	RCA Victor 9615
1/4/69	36	9		7 **My Special Prayer** ***[w/ Lorene Mann]***	*Wini Scott*	RCA Victor 9691
12/8/73	87	4		8 **Freedom Ain't The Same As Bein' Free**	*Jackie Johnson*	RCA Victor 0155

CAMPBELL('S), Cecil, Tennessee Ramblers

Born on 3/22/1911 in Danbury, North Carolina. Died on 6/18/1989 (age 78). Singer/songwriter/steel guitarist. Appeared in the movies *My Darling Clementine* and *Swing Your Partner.*

DEBUT	PEAK	WKS	GOLD	Country Chart Hit	Songwriter	Label (& Number)
5/21/49	9	1		**Steel Guitar Ramble**	J:9 *Cecil Campbell*	RCA Victor 21-0014

CAMPBELL, Glen 1960s: #34 / 1970s: #24 / All-Time: #39 // HOF: 2005

Born on 4/22/1936 in Delight, Arkansas. Male singer/songwriter/guitarist/actor. With his uncle Dick Bills's band, 1954-58. To Los Angeles; recorded with The Champs in 1960. Became prolific studio musician; with The Hondells in 1964, **The Beach Boys** in 1965 and Sagittarius in 1967. Own TV show *The Glen Campbell Goodtime Hour,* 1968-72. Acted in the movies *True Grit, Norwood* and *Strange Homecoming;* voice in the animated movie *Rock-A-Doodle.*

CMA: Male Vocalist 1968 / Entertainer 1968

DEBUT	PEAK	WKS	GOLD	Country Chart Hit	Songwriter	Label (& Number)
12/29/62	20	5		1 **Kentucky Means Paradise** ***[w/ The Green River Boys]***	*Merle Travis*	Capitol 4867
12/10/66+	18	13		2 **Burning Bridges**	*Walter Scott*	Capitol 5773
4/29/67	73	2		3 **I Gotta Have My Baby Back**	*Floyd Tillman*	Capitol 5854
7/29/67	30	12		4 **Gentle On My Mind**	*John Hartford*	Capitol 5939
				Grammy: Single, Song & Male Vocal; also see #9 below		
10/28/67+	2[2]	18		5 **By The Time I Get To Phoenix**	*Jimmy Webb*	Capitol 2015
				Grammy: Hall of Fame / RS500		
2/3/68	13	12		6 **Hey Little One**	*Dorsey Burnette/Barry DeVorzon*	Capitol 2076
4/13/68	❶[3]	16		7 **I Wanna Live**	*John D. Loudermilk*	Capitol 2146
7/6/68	3[2]	15		8 **Dreams Of The Everyday Housewife**	*Chris Gantry*	Capitol 2224
10/19/68	44	3		9 **Gentle On My Mind**	*John Hartford/John Hartford* [R]	Capitol 5939
				reissue of #4 above		
11/2/68	❶[2]	19	●	10 **Wichita Lineman**	*Jimmy Webb*	Capitol 2302
				Grammy: Hall of Fame / RS500		
11/23/68	44	7		11 **Less Of Me** ***[w/ Bobbie Gentry]***	*Glen Campbell*	Capitol 2314
2/8/69	14	14		12 **Let It Be Me** ***[w/ Bobbie Gentry]***	*Gilbert Becaud/Mann Curtis*	Capitol 2387
3/15/69	❶[3]	14	●	13 **Galveston**	*Jimmy Webb*	Capitol 2428
5/10/69	28	10		14 **Where's The Playground Susie**	*Jimmy Webb*	Capitol 2494
7/26/69	9	12		15 **True Grit**	*Elmer Bernstein/Don Black*	Capitol 2573
				title song from the movie starring John Wayne and Campbell		
10/25/69	2[1]	13		16 **Try A Little Kindness**	*Bobby Austin/Curt Sapaugh*	Capitol 2659
1/24/70	2[3]	13		17 **Honey Come Back**	*Jimmy Webb*	Capitol 2718
2/21/70	6	13		18 **All I Have To Do Is Dream** ***[w/ Bobbie Gentry]***	*Boudleaux Bryant*	Capitol 2745
4/25/70	25	9		19 **Oh Happy Day**	*Edwin Hawkins*	Capitol 2787
7/18/70	5	12		20 **Everything A Man Could Ever Need**	*Mac Davis*	Capitol 2843
				from the movie *Norwood* starring Campbell		
9/19/70	3[2]	15		21 **It's Only Make Believe**	*Jack Nance/Conway Twitty*	Capitol 2905
3/13/71	7	14		22 **Dream Baby (How Long Must I Dream)**	*Cindy Walker*	Capitol 3062
7/3/71	21	14		23 **The Last Time I Saw Her**	*Gordon Lightfoot*	Capitol 3123
10/30/71	40	8		24 **I Say A Little Prayer/By The Time I Get To Phoenix** ***[w/ Anne Murray]***	*...Burt Bacharach/Hal David/Jimmy Webb*	Capitol 3200
1/8/72	15	12		25 **Oklahoma Sunday Morning**	*Hammond Hazelwood/Tony MacAulay*	Capitol 3254
4/1/72	6	13		26 **Manhattan Kansas**	*Joe Allen*	Capitol 3305
8/26/72	45	10		27 **I Will Never Pass This Way Again**	*Ronnie Gaylord*	Capitol 3411
12/16/72+	33	10		28 **One Last Time**	*Dick Addrisi/Don Addrisi*	Capitol 3483
3/24/73	48	8		29 **I Knew Jesus (Before He Was A Star)**	*Neal Hefti/Stan Styne*	Capitol 3548
7/28/73	49	9		30 **Bring Back My Yesterday**	*Robert Relf/Barry White*	Capitol 3669
10/20/73	20	12		31 **Wherefore And Why**	*Gordon Lightfoot*	Capitol 3735
2/2/74	20	10		32 **Houston (I'm Comin' To See You)**	*David Paich*	Capitol 3808
8/3/74	3[2]	18		33 **Bonaparte's Retreat**	*Pee Wee King*	Capitol 3926
12/14/74+	16	13		34 **It's A Sin When You Love Somebody**	*Jimmy Webb*	Capitol 3988

DEBUT	PEAK	WKS	GOLD	ARTIST / Ranking / Country Chart Hit	Songwriter	Label (& Number)
				CAMPBELL, Glen — cont'd		
6/7/75	❶[3]	21	●	35 **Rhinestone Cowboy**	*Larry Weiss*	Capitol 4095
11/1/75	3[2]	15		36 **Country Boy** (You Got Your Feet In L.A.)	*Dennis Lambert/Brian Potter*	Capitol 4155
4/10/76	4	12		37 **Don't Pull Your Love/Then You Can Tell Me Goodbye**	*...Dennis Lambert/John D. Loudermilk/Brian Potter*	Capitol 4245
7/10/76	18	11		38 **See You On Sunday**	*Dennis Lambert/Brian Potter*	Capitol 4288
1/29/77	❶[2]	17	●	39 **Southern Nights**	*Allen Toussaint*	Capitol 4376
7/2/77	4	15		40 **Sunflower**	*Neil Diamond*	Capitol 4445
12/3/77+	39	10		41 **God Must Have Blessed America**	*Allen Toussaint*	Capitol 4515
6/10/78	21	12		42 **Another Fine Mess** from the movie *The End* starring **Burt Reynolds**	*Paul Williams*	Capitol 4584
9/23/78	16	16		43 **Can You Fool**	*Michael Smotherman*	Capitol 4638
2/17/79	13	11		44 **I'm Gonna Love You**	*Michael Smotherman*	Capitol 4682
5/26/79	45	7		45 **California**	*Michael Smotherman*	Capitol 4715
9/1/79	25	10		46 **Hound Dog Man**	*Tommy Stuart*	Capitol 4769
11/24/79	66	6		47 **My Prayer**	*Michael Smotherman*	Capitol 4799
5/24/80	60	6		48 **Somethin' 'Bout You Baby I Like** ***[w/ Rita Coolidge]***	*Richie Supa*	Capitol 4865
8/30/80	80	4		49 **Hollywood Smiles**	*Larry Weiss*	Capitol 4909
9/27/80	59	6		50 **Dream Lover** ***[w/ Tanya Tucker]***	*Bobby Darin*	MCA 41323
11/22/80+	10	17		51 **Any Which Way You Can** from the movie starring **Clint Eastwood**	*Milton Brown/Steve Dorff/Snuff Garrett*	Warner 49609
2/7/81	54	7		52 **I Don't Want To Know Your Name**	*Michael Smotherman*	Capitol 4959
4/11/81	85	4		53 **Why Don't We Just Sleep On It Tonight** ***[w/ Tanya Tucker]***	*Glenn Riggs/Harry Shannon*	Capitol 4986
8/8/81	15	12		54 **I Love My Truck** from the movie *The Night The Lights Went Out In Georgia* starring Kristy McNichol	*Joe Rainey*	Mirage 3845
10/30/82	44	8		55 **Old Home Town**	*David Pomeranz*	Atlantic Amer. 99967
1/15/83	17	17		56 **I Love How You Love Me**	*Larry Kolber/Barry Mann*	Atlantic Amer. 99930
6/11/83	85	3		57 **On The Wings Of My Victory**	*Bob Corbin*	Atlantic Amer. 99893
6/23/84	10	22		58 **Faithless Love**	*J.D. Souther*	Atlantic Amer. 99768
10/27/84	47	12		59 **Slow Nights** ***[w/ Mel Tillis]***	*Bob Albright*	MCA 52474
12/1/84+	4	20		60 **A Lady Like You**	A:4 / S:5 *Keith Stegall/Jim Weatherly*	Atlantic Amer. 99691
5/18/85	14	21		61 **(Love Always) Letter To Home**	A:11 / S:18 *Carl Jackson*	Atlantic Amer. 99647
11/16/85+	7	21		62 **It's Just A Matter Of Time**	A:7 / S:7 *Brook Benton/Belford Hendricks/Clyde Otis*	Atlantic Amer. 99600
4/26/86	38	11		63 **Cowpoke**	A:37 *Stan Jones*	Atlantic Amer. 99559
7/26/86	52	8		64 **Call Home**	*Mike Reid/Troy Seals*	Atlantic Amer. 99525
5/30/87	6	28		65 **The Hand That Rocks The Cradle** ***[w/ Steve Wariner]***	S:11 *Ted Harris*	MCA 53108
10/3/87+	5	23		66 **Still Within The Sound Of My Voice**	S:20 *Jimmy Webb*	MCA 53172
2/20/88	32	12		67 **I Remember You**	*Johnny Mercer/Victor Schertzinger*	MCA 53245
5/28/88	7	23		68 **I Have You**	S:28 *Gene Nelson/Paul Nelson*	MCA 53218
10/1/88	35	10		69 **Light Years**	*Jimmy Webb*	MCA 53426
1/21/89	47	14		70 **More Than Enough**	*Jimmy Webb*	MCA 53493
9/30/89	6	26		71 **She's Gone, Gone, Gone**	*Harlan Howard*	Universal 66024
3/17/90	61	8		72 **Walkin' In The Sun** from the album *Walkin' In The Sun* on Capitol 93884	*Jeff Barry*	Capitol
1/26/91	27	16		73 **Unconditional Love**	*Tim DuBois/Donny Lowery/Randy Sharp*	Capitol
6/1/91	70	5		74 **Livin' In A House Full Of Love** above 2 from the album *Unconditional Love* on Capitol 90992	*Billy Sherrill/Glenn Sutton*	Capitol
1/23/93	66	9		75 **Somebody Like That** from the album *Somebody Like That* on Liberty 97962	*Larry Bryant/Geoff Thurman*	Liberty

All I Have To Do Is Dream ['70]
Another Fine Mess ['78]
Any Which Way You Can ['81]
Bonaparte's Retreat ['74]
Bring Back My Yesterday ['73]
Burning Bridges ['67]
By The Time I Get To Phoenix ['68]
California ['79]
Call Home ['86]
Can You Fool ['78]
Country Boy (You Got Your Feet In L.A.) ['75]
Cowpoke ['86]
Don't Pull Your Love/Then You Can Tell Me Goodbye ['76]
Dream Baby (How Long Must I Dream) ['71]
Dream Lover ['80]
Dreams Of The Everyday Housewife ['68]
Everything A Man Could Ever Need ['70]
Faithless Love ['84]
Galveston ['69]
Gentle On My Mind ['67, '68]
God Must Have Blessed America ['78]
Hand That Rocks The Cradle ['87]
Hey Little One ['68]
Hollywood Smiles ['80]
Honey Come Back ['70]
Hound Dog Man ['79]
Houston (I'm Comin' To See You) ['74]
I Don't Want To Know Your Name ['81]
I Gotta Have My Baby Back ['67]
I Have You ['88]
I Knew Jesus (Before He Was A Star) ['73]
I Love How You Love Me ['83]
I Love My Truck ['81]
I Remember You ['88]
I Say A Little Prayer/By The Time I Get To Phoenix ['71]
I Wanna Live ['68]
I Will Never Pass This Way Again ['72]
I'm Gonna Love You ['79]
It's A Sin When You Love Somebody ['75]
It's Just A Matter Of Time ['86]
It's Only Make Believe ['70]
Kentucky Means Paradise ['62]
Lady Like You ['85]
Last Time I Saw Her ['71]
Less Of Me ['68]
Let It Be Me ['69]
Light Years ['88]
Livin' In A House Full Of Love ['91]
(Love Always) Letter To Home ['85]
Manhattan Kansas ['72]
More Than Enough ['89]
My Prayer ['79]
Oh Happy Day ['70]
Oklahoma Sunday Morning ['72]
Old Home Town ['82]
On The Wings Of My Victory ['83]
One Last Time ['73]
Rhinestone Cowboy ['75]
See You On Sunday ['76]
She's Gone, Gone, Gone ['89]
Slow Nights ['84]
Somebody Like That ['93]
Somethin' 'Bout You Baby I Like ['80]
Southern Nights ['77]
Still Within The Sound Of My Voice ['88]
Sunflower ['77]
True Grit ['69]
Try A Little Kindness ['69]
Unconditional Love ['91]
Walkin' In The Sun ['90]
Where's The Playground Susie ['69]
Wherefore And Why ['73]
Why Don't We Just Sleep On It Tonight ['81]
Wichita Lineman ['68]

CAMPBELL, Jo Ann

Born on 7/20/1938 in Jacksonville, Florida. Female singer/actress. Appeared in the movies *Johnny Melody*, *Go Johnny Go* and *Hey, Let's Twist.* Married **Troy Seals**; recorded together as Jo Ann & Troy in 1964.

DEBUT	PEAK	WKS	GOLD	Country Chart Hit	Songwriter	Label (& Number)
9/22/62	24	3		**(I'm The Girl On) Wolverton Mountain** answer to "Wolverton Mountain" by **Claude King**	*Merle Kilgore/Claude King*	Cameo 223

CAMPBELL, Mike

Born in Odessa, Texas. Male singer/songwriter/guitarist.

DEBUT	PEAK	WKS	GOLD	Country Chart Hit	Songwriter	Label (& Number)
12/26/81+	65	6		1 **Barroom Games**	*Mike Campbell/Jerry Crutchfield/Gerry House*	Columbia 02622
10/2/82	57	8		2 **No Room To Cry**	*Mike Campbell*	Columbia 03154
5/14/83	76	5		3 **Don't Say You Love Me** (Just Love Me Again)	*Claire Cloninger/Jerry Crutchfield*	Columbia 03838
12/17/83+	57	9		4 **Sweet And Easy To Love**	*Sam Phillips*	Columbia 04225

DEBUT	PEAK	WKS	GOLD	ARTIST / Ranking / Country Chart Hit	Songwriter	Label (& Number)
				CAMPBELL, Mike — cont'd		
3/17/84	**52**	10		5 **One Sided Love Affair**	*Eddie Rabbitt/Even Stevens*	Columbia 04387
7/14/84	**77**	3		6 **You're The Only Star (In My Blue Heaven)**	*Gene Autry*	Columbia 04488
				CAMPBELL, Stacy Dean		
				Born on 7/27/1967 in Carlsbad, New Mexico. Male singer/songwriter.		
7/4/92	**54**	8		1 **Rosalee**	*Craig Bickhardt/Brent Maher/Don Schlitz*	Columbia
10/17/92	**65**	3		2 **Baby Don't You Know**	*Jamie O'Hara*	Columbia
12/26/92+	**55**	11		3 **Poor Man's Rose**	*Stacy Dean Campbell/Bill Owsley/Jody Spence*	Columbia
				above 3 from the album *Lonesome Wins Again* on Columbia 47872		
8/12/95	**61**	6		4 **Honey I Do**	*Al Anderson/Stacy Dean Campbell*	Columbia
				from the album *Hurt City* on Columbia 57214		
				CANADIAN SWEETHEARTS, The		
				Husband-and-wife duo from Canada: Bob Regan and **Lucille Starr**. Regan was born on 3/13/1931; died on 3/5/1990 (age 58). Starr was born Lucille Savoie in St. Boniface, Manitoba, Canada. Divorced in 1977.		
2/1/64	**45**	1		1 **Hootenanny Express**	*Bob Regan*	A&M 727
2/10/68	**51**	5		2 **Let's Wait A Little Longer**	*Curly Putman/Billy Sherrill*	Epic 10258
1/3/70	**50**	9		3 **Dream Baby** ***[Bob Regan & Lucille Starr]***	*Cindy Walker*	Dot 17327
				CANNON, Ace		
				Born Hubert Cannon on 5/4/1934 in Grenada, Mississippi. Male saxophonist. Worked with **Bill Black's Combo**.		
2/19/77	**73**	4		**Blue Eyes Crying In The Rain**	*Fred Rose* **[I]**	Hi 2313
				CANNON, Jimmi		
				Born in Sylacauga, Alabama. Female singer/dancer. Member of **Dean Martin**'s Golddiggers from 1971-73.		
10/24/81	**63**	5		1 **Whole Lot Of Cheatin' Goin' On**	*Jerry Hayes/Ronny Scaife/Don Singleton*	Warner 49806
3/20/82	**78**	5		2 **Even If It's Wrong**	*Jimmy Louis*	Warner 50024
8/28/82	**81**	4		3 **Fool's Gold**	*Steve Berg/Don Stalker*	Warner 29949
				CANNONS, The		
				Family trio from Oklahoma: twins Karla Cannon (piano, trumpet, fiddle) and Darla Cannon (guitar, saxophone), with brother Larry Cannon (guitar, trumpet, banjo).		
12/3/83	**90**	2		1 **One Step Closer**	*Bill Rice/Mary Sharon Rice*	Compleat 116
11/8/86	**72**	7		2 **Do You Mind If I Step Into Your Dreams**	*Shelby Kennedy/Tony Von Dollen*	Mercury 888048
8/1/87	**73**	4		3 **Love'll Come Lookin' For You**	*Sandy Ramos/Jon Vezner*	Mercury 888648
				CANYON		
				Group from Texas: Steve Cooper (vocals, guitar), Johnny Boatright (guitar), Jay Brown (keyboards), Randy Rigney (bass) and Keech Rainwater (drums). Rainwater later joined **Lonestar**.		
2/6/88	**59**	6		1 **Overdue**	*Rick Bowles/Tom Brasfield/Robert Byrne*	16th Avenue 70410
5/28/88	**54**	9		2 **In The Middle Of The Night**	*Mike Geiger/Woody Mullis/Ricky Rector*	16th Avenue 70415
9/10/88	**55**	9		3 **I Guess I Just Missed You**	*Walt Aldridge/Tom Brasfield*	16th Avenue 70419
11/26/88+	**47**	10		4 **Love Is On The Line**	*Steve Cooper*	16th Avenue 70423
5/13/89	**44**	8		5 **Right Track, Wrong Train**	*S. Alan Taylor/Lonnie Wilson*	16th Avenue 70426
8/12/89	**40**	10		6 **Hot Nights**	*Fred Knoblock/Jim Weatherly*	16th Avenue 70433
11/25/89+	**53**	8		7 **Radio Romance**	*Reed Nielsen/Monty Powell/Jack White*	16th Avenue 70437
5/12/90	**74**	1		8 **Carryin' On**	*Bob DiPiero/Gerry House*	16th Avenue
				from the album *Radio Romance* on 16th Avenue 70556		
11/3/90	**71**	4		9 **Dam These Tears**	*Mike Geiger/Woody Mullis*	16th Avenue
				CANYON, George		
				Born Fred George Lays in 1970 in Pictou, Nova Scotia, Canada. Male singer/songwriter/guitarist.		
3/5/05	**44**	11		**My Name**	*George Canyon/Gordie Sampson*	Universal South
				from the album *One Good Friend* on Universal South 003159		
				CAPITALS, The		
				Vocal group from Columbus, Ohio: Arti Portilla, Ronnie Cochran, Terry Kaufman and Jack Crum.		
1/5/80	**91**	4		1 **Me Touchin' You**	*Bobby Bond*	Ridgetop 00779
9/27/80	**29**	11		2 **A Little Ground In Texas**	*Bobby Fischer*	Ridgetop 01080
3/7/81	**45**	8		3 **Bridge Over Broadway**	*Gene Dobbins/Tommy Rocco*	Ridgetop 01281
				CAPPS, Hank		
				Born in Fayetteville, North Carolina. Male singer.		
9/16/72	**33**	13		**Bowling Green**	*Phil Everly/Terry Slater*	Capitol 3416
				CAPTAIN & TENNILLE, The		
				Husband-and-wife duo: Daryl "The Captain" Dragon (born on 8/27/1942 in Los Angeles, California) and Toni Tennille (born on 5/8/1943 in Montgomery, Alabama). Own TV show on ABC from 1976-77. Dragon is the son of noted conductor Carmen Dragon.		
5/6/78	**97**	3		**I'm On My Way**	*Mark Safan*	A&M 2027
				CAPTAIN STUBBY & THE BUCCANEERS		
				Born Thomas Fouts on 11/24/1918 in Carroll County, Indiana. Played novelty instruments, such as a toilet seat with guitar strings ("gitarlet"). Worked on WLW-Cincinnati, own band from 1937. On WLS *National Barn Dance* for 10 years; made appearances on Don McNeil's *Breakfast Club*. Own *Polka-Go-Round* TV series on ABC from 1965-68. Later worked as a DJ on WLS-Chicago. The Buccaneers: Dwight "Tiny" Stokes (vocals, bass), Jerald Richards (tin whistle), Sonny Fleming (guitar) and Peter Kunatz (accordian).		
2/12/49	**13**	1		1 **Lavender Blue (Dilly Dilly)** ***[w/ Burl Ives]***	S:13 *Eliot Daniel/Larry Morey*	Decca 24547
7/16/49	**12**	1		2 **Money, Marbles And Chalk**	J:12 *Pop Eckler*	Decca 46149
				Windy Breeze (vocal)		
7/23/49	**14**	1		3 **Come Wet Your Mustache With Me**	J:14 *Jack Manus/Milton Shaw/Michael Stoner*	Decca 46169
				STUBBY AND THE BUCCANEERS (above 2)		

Billboard DEBUT	PEAK	WKS	GOLD	ARTIST / Country Chart Hit	Ranking / Songwriter	Label (& Number)

CARDWELL, Jack

Born on 11/9/1930 in Chapman, Alabama; raised in Mobile, Alabama. Male singer/songwriter/guitarist.

DEBUT	PEAK	WKS	GOLD	Country Chart Hit	Songwriter	Label (& Number)
2/14/53	3^2	9		1 **The Death Of Hank Williams**	S:3 / A:4 / J:5 *Jack Cardwell*	King 1172
9/26/53	7	2		2 **Dear Joan**	S:7 *Jack Cardwell*	King 1269

answer to "A Dear John Letter" by **Jean Shepard**

CARGILL, Henson

Born on 2/5/1941 in Oklahoma City, Oklahoma. Male singer/guitarist. Studied animal husbandry at Colorado State; worked as a deputy sheriff in Oklahoma County. Appeared on the TV series *Country Hayride* in Cincinnati. Later operated a large cattle ranch in Stillwater, Oklahoma.

DEBUT	PEAK	WKS	GOLD	Country Chart Hit	Songwriter	Label (& Number)
12/9/67+	❶^5	19		1 **Skip A Rope**	*Jack Moran/Glenn Tubb*	Monument 1041
4/27/68	11	12		2 **Row Row Row**	*Dallas Frazier*	Monument 1065
8/10/68	39	8		3 **She Thinks I'm On That Train**	*Dallas Frazier/A.L. "Doodle" Owens*	Monument 1084
1/25/69	8	14		4 **None Of My Business**	*Jack Moran*	Monument 1122
5/31/69	40	8		5 **This Generation Shall Not Pass**	*Dallas Frazier*	Monument 1142
9/20/69	32	9		6 **Then The Baby Came**	*Chuck Rogers*	Monument 1158
5/16/70	18	11		7 **The Most Uncomplicated Goodbye I've Ever Heard**	*Dallas Frazier/Whitey Shafer*	Monument 1198
7/17/71	44	9		8 **Pencil Marks On The Wall**	*Richard Ahlert/Eddie Snyder*	Mega 0030
11/27/71	65	3		9 **Naked And Crying**	*Lionel Delmore*	Mega 0043
3/4/72	64	4		10 **I Can't Face The Bed Alone**	*Patty Burt/Richard Burt*	Mega 0060
10/14/72	62	7		11 **Red Skies Over Georgia**	*Gene Dobbins*	Mega 0090
10/13/73	28	13		12 **Some Old California Memory**	*A.L. "Doodle" Owens/Warren Robb*	Atlantic 4007
3/2/74	78	7		13 **She Still Comes To Me (To Pour The Wine)**	*Dick Feller*	Atlantic 4016
5/25/74	29	13		14 **Stop And Smell The Roses**	*Mac Davis/Doc Severinsen*	Atlantic 4021
12/22/79+	29	13		15 **Silence On The Line**	*Sterling Whipple*	Copper Mountain 201
5/3/80	67	5		16 **Have A Good Day**	*Hal Bynum/Dave Kirby*	Copper Mountain 589

CARLETTE

Born Carlette West in Austin, Texas. Female singer. Married to Oak Records owner Ray Ruff.

DEBUT	PEAK	WKS	GOLD	Country Chart Hit	Songwriter	Label (& Number)
2/9/85	60	5		1 **Any Way That You Want Me**	*Chip Taylor*	Oak 1079
4/6/85	71	5		2 **Showdown**	*Hank Garfield/Chet McCracken*	Luv 106
6/8/85	52	9		3 **You Can't Measure My Love**	*Delaney Bramlett/Billy Burnette*	Luv 107
8/17/85	65	7		4 **Tonight's The Night**	*Larry Fargo/Carlette Ruff*	Luv 109
2/22/86	72	5		5 **Two Steps From The Blues**	*Stephanie Winslow*	Luv 116
4/12/86	61	6		6 **Sugar Shack**	*Keith McCormack/Faye Voss*	Luv 118
10/18/86	52	7		7 **We Belong Together**	*Carol Chase*	Luv 125
5/2/87	63	4		8 **Waltzin' With Daddy**	*David Featherstone*	Luv 137
5/30/87	57	4		9 **You've Lost That Loving Feeling**	*Barry Mann/Phil Spector/Cynthia Weil*	Luv 142

CARLILE, Tom

Born in 1943 in Miami, Florida. Male singer/songwriter.

DEBUT	PEAK	WKS	GOLD	Country Chart Hit	Songwriter	Label (& Number)
6/20/81	93	2		1 **Gold Cadillac**	*Tom Carlile*	Door Knob 157
8/29/81	73	6		2 **Get It While You Can**	*Tom Carlile*	Door Knob 162
10/17/81	49	12		3 **Catch Me If You Can**	*Tom Carlile*	Door Knob 167
1/30/82	84	3		4 **Feel**	*Tom Carlile*	Door Knob 172
2/20/82	70	5		5 **Lover (Right Where I Want You)**	*Tom Carlile*	Door Knob 170
5/8/82	59	9		6 **Hurtin' For Your Love**	*Tom Carlile*	Door Knob 176
7/17/82	39	11		7 **Back In Debbie's Arms**	*Tom Carlile*	Door Knob 180
10/23/82	37	12		8 **Green Eyes**	*Tom Carlile*	Door Knob 187
1/8/83	55	7		9 **Rainin' Down In Nashville**	*Tom Carlile*	Door Knob 191

CARLISLE, Bob

Born on 9/29/1956 in Santa Anna, California. Male singer/songwriter/guitarist.

DEBUT	PEAK	WKS	GOLD	Country Chart Hit	Songwriter	Label (& Number)
5/24/97	45	12		**Butterfly Kisses**	*Bob Carlisle/Randy Thomas*	DMG/Jive

Grammy: Song; from the album *Butterfly Kisses (Shades Of Grace)* on Jive 41613

CARLISLES, The — 1950s: #34

Group formed by **Bill Carlisle** (born on 12/19/1908 in Wakefield, Kentucky; died of a stroke on 3/17/2003, age 94) in 1951. Group also consisted of Tommy Bishop and Betty Amos. From 1930-47, Bill performed with his brother Cliff (born on 5/6/1904 in Mount Eden, Kentucky; died on 4/2/1983, age 78) as the **Carlisle Brothers**.

OPRY: 1953

DEBUT	PEAK	WKS	GOLD	Country Chart Hit	Songwriter	Label (& Number)
10/26/46	5	1		1 **Rainbow At Midnight** ***[Carlisle Brothers]***	*John Miller* **[N]**	King 535
6/19/48	14	2		2 **Tramp On The Street** ***[Bill Carlisle]***	S:14 / J:14 *Grady Cole/Hazel Cole* **[N]**	King 697
12/15/51+	6	8		3 **Too Old To Cut The Mustard**	A:6 *Bill Carlisle*	Mercury 6348
1/10/53	❶^4	24		4 **No Help Wanted**	A:❶^4 / J:❶^4 / S:2 *Bill Carlisle*	Mercury 70028
4/11/53	3^1	13		5 **Knothole**	A:3 / S:8 *Bill Carlisle/Virginia Suber* **[N]**	Mercury 70109
7/25/53	2^1	8		6 **Is Zat You, Myrtle**	A:2 / S:9 *Bill Carlisle/Charlie Louvin/Ira Louvin* **[N]**	Mercury 70174
11/7/53+	5	6		7 **Tain't Nice (To Talk Like That)** ***[w/ Bill Carlisle]***	A:5 / J:6 *Bill Carlisle/Virginia Suber*	Mercury 70232
7/3/54	15	1		8 **Shake-A-Leg**	A:15 *Bill Carlisle/Charlie Louvin/Ira Louvin*	Mercury 70351
10/9/54	12	5		9 **Honey Love**	A:12 *Clyde McPhatter/Jerry Wexler*	Mercury 70435
12/11/65+	4	17		10 **What Kinda Deal Is This** ***[Bill Carlisle]***	*Wayne Gilbreath* **[N]**	Hickory 1348

CARLLILE, Kathy

Born Mary Katherine Carllile in 1963 in Nashville, Tennessee. Female singer. Daughter of Kenneth Ray "Thumbs" Carllile (guitarist with **Jimmy Dickens** and **Roger Miller**).

DEBUT	PEAK	WKS	GOLD	Country Chart Hit	Songwriter	Label (& Number)
4/5/80	61	8		**Stay Until The Rain Stops**	*Wayne Carson/Bonnie Owens/Ronnie Reno*	Frontline 705

CARLSON, Paulette

Born on 10/11/1952 in Northfield, Minnesota. Female singer/songwriter/guitarist. Lead singer of **Highway 101**.

DEBUT	PEAK	WKS	#	Country Chart Hit	Songwriter	Label (& Number)
6/25/83	65	7	1	**You Gotta Get To My Heart (Before You Lay A Hand On Me)**	*Buzz Arledge/Jerry McBee*	RCA 13546
12/3/83	67	8	2	**I'd Say Yes**	*Michael Garvin/Tom Shapiro/Chris Waters*	RCA 13599
3/10/84	72	4	3	**Can You Fool**	*Michael Smotherman*	RCA 13745
12/7/91+	21	20	4	**I'll Start With You**	*Paulette Carlson/Tom Shapiro/Chris Waters*	Capitol
5/30/92	68	1	5	**Not With My Heart You Don't**	*Paulette Carlson/Mike Nobel/Jeff Pennig*	Capitol
				above 2 from the album *Love Goes On* on Capitol 97711		

CARMEN, Eric

Born on 8/11/1949 in Cleveland, Ohio. Male singer/songwriter/pianist. Lead singer of rock group the Raspberries from 1970-74.

DEBUT	PEAK	WKS	#	Country Chart Hit	Songwriter	Label (& Number)
4/9/88	51	9		**As Long As We Got Each Other** ***[w/ Louise Mandrell]***	*John Bettis/Steve Dorff*	RCA 20288
				from the TV series *Growing Pains* starring Alan Thicke and Joanna Kerns		

CARNES, Kim

Born on 7/20/1945 in Los Angeles, California. Female singer/songwriter/pianist. Member of The New Christy Minstrels with husband/co-writer Dave Ellingson and **Kenny Rogers** in the late 1960s. Also see **USA For Africa**.

DEBUT	PEAK	WKS	#	Country Chart Hit	Songwriter	Label (& Number)
7/29/78	99	2	1	**You're A Part Of Me** ***[w/ Gene Cotton]***	*Kim Carnes*	Ariola America 7704
4/5/80	3^{3}	14	2	**Don't Fall In Love With A Dreamer** ***[w/ Kenny Rogers]***	*Kim Carnes/Dave Ellingson*	United Artists 1345
11/10/84	70	10	3	**What About Me?** ***[w/ Kenny Rogers & James Ingram]***	*David Foster/Richard Marx/Kenny Rogers*	RCA 13899
8/20/88	70	7	4	**Speed Of The Sound Of Loneliness**	*John Prine*	MCA 53387
				Lyle Lovett (backing vocal)		
10/29/88	68	5	5	**Crazy In Love**	*Randy McCormick/Even Stevens*	MCA 53433

CARNES, Rick & Janis

Husband-and-wife duo: Rick Carnes (born on 6/30/1950 in Fayetteville, Arkansas) and Janis Carnes (born on 5/21/1947 in Shelbyville, Tennessee). Married in 1973; moved to Nashville in 1978.

DEBUT	PEAK	WKS	#	Country Chart Hit	Songwriter	Label (& Number)
12/18/82+	67	6	1	**Have You Heard**	*Janis Carnes/Rick Carnes/Chip Hardy*	Elektra 69928
7/30/83	51	8	2	**Poor Girl**	*Janis Carnes/Rick Carnes/Chip Hardy*	Warner 29656
11/26/83+	32	16	3	**Does He Ever Mention My Name**	*Janis Carnes/Rick Carnes/Chip Hardy*	Warner 29448
8/18/84	74	4	4	**Long Lost Causes**	*Janis Carnes/Rick Carnes/Chip Hardy*	MCA 52414

CAROLINA RAIN

Male trio formed in Nashville, Tennessee: Rhean Boyer (vocals, guitar), Jeremy Baxter (mandolin) and Marvin Evatt (guitar).

DEBUT	PEAK	WKS	#	Country Chart Hit	Songwriter	Label (& Number)
9/25/04	41	12		**I Ain't Scared**	*Rhean Boyer/Gary Lloyd/Stephony Smith*	Equity

CARPENTER, Kris

Born in Amarillo, Texas. Male singer/guitarist.

DEBUT	PEAK	WKS	#	Country Chart Hit	Songwriter	Label (& Number)
2/21/81	76	4		**My Song Don't Sing The Same**	*John English*	Door Knob 146

CARPENTER, Mary-Chapin — 1990s: #29 / All-Time: #152

Born on 2/21/1958 in Princeton, New Jersey. Female singer/songwriter/guitarist. Father was an executive with *Life* magazine. Graduated from Brown University with a degree in American civilization.

CMA: Female Vocalist 1992 & 1993

DEBUT	PEAK	WKS	#	Country Chart Hit	Songwriter	Label (& Number)
4/15/89	19	22	1	**How Do**	*Mary-Chapin Carpenter*	Columbia 68677
9/2/89	8	26	2	**Never Had It So Good**	*Mary-Chapin Carpenter/John Jennings*	Columbia 69050
1/6/90	7	26	3	**Quittin' Time**	*Roger Linn/Robb Royer*	Columbia
6/16/90	14	21	4	**Something Of A Dreamer**	*Mary-Chapin Carpenter*	Columbia
				above 2 from the album *State Of The Heart* on Columbia 44228		
10/20/90+	16	20	5	**You Win Again**	*Mary-Chapin Carpenter*	Columbia
2/16/91	15	20	6	**Right Now**	*Sylvester Bradford*	Columbia
6/8/91	2^{1}	20	7	**Down At The Twist And Shout**	*Mary-Chapin Carpenter*	Columbia
				Grammy: Female Vocal		
10/26/91+	14	20	8	**Going Out Tonight**	*Mary-Chapin Carpenter/John Jennings*	Columbia
				above 4 from the album *Shooting Straight In The Dark* on Columbia 46077		
5/30/92	4	20	9	**I Feel Lucky**	*Mary-Chapin Carpenter/Don Schlitz*	Columbia
				Grammy: Female Vocal		
9/12/92	15	20	10	**Not Too Much To Ask** ***[w/ Joe Diffie]***	*Mary-Chapin Carpenter/Don Schlitz*	Columbia
12/26/92+	4	20	11	**Passionate Kisses**	*Lucinda Williams*	Columbia
				Grammy: Song & Female Vocal		
2/13/93	27	20	12	**Romeo** ***[w/ Dolly Parton/Billy Ray Cyrus/Kathy Mattea/Pam Tillis/Tanya Tucker]***	*Dolly Parton*	Columbia
				from Parton's album *Slow Dancing With The Moon* on Columbia 53199		
4/17/93	11	20	13	**The Hard Way**	*Mary-Chapin Carpenter*	Columbia
8/21/93	16	20	14	**The Bug**	*Mark Knopfler*	Columbia
12/18/93+	2^{1}	20	15	**He Thinks He'll Keep Her**	*Mary-Chapin Carpenter/Don Schlitz*	Columbia
4/30/94	2^{1}	20	16	**I Take My Chances**	*Mary-Chapin Carpenter/Don Schlitz*	Columbia
				#9-11 & 13-16: from the album *Come On Come On* on Columbia 48881		
9/10/94	❶^{1}	20	17	**Shut Up And Kiss Me**	*Mary-Chapin Carpenter*	Columbia
				Grammy: Female Vocal		
12/10/94+	6	20	18	**Tender When I Want To Be**	*Mary-Chapin Carpenter*	Columbia
3/25/95	21	13	19	**House Of Cards**	*Mary-Chapin Carpenter*	Columbia
7/1/95	45	9	20	**Why Walk When You Can Fly**	*Mary-Chapin Carpenter*	Columbia
				above 4 from the album *Stones In The Road* on Columbia 64327		

DEBUT	PEAK	WKS	GOLD	ARTIST / Country Chart Hit	Ranking / Songwriter	Label (& Number)
				CARPENTER, Mary-Chapin — cont'd		
10/5/96+	**11**	20		21 **Let Me Into Your Heart**	S:18 *Mary-Chapin Carpenter*	Columbia
2/1/97	**35**	12		22 **I Want To Be Your Girlfriend**	*Mary-Chapin Carpenter*	Columbia
4/19/97	**64**	7		23 **The Better To Dream Of You**	*Mary-Chapin Carpenter*	Columbia
7/19/97	**58**	5		24 **Keeping The Faith**	*Mary-Chapin Carpenter*	Columbia
				above 4 from the album *A Place In The World* on Columbia 67501		
12/19/98	**67**	9		25 **It's Only Love** ***[w/ Randy Scruggs]***	*Mary-Chapin Carpenter/Randy Scruggs*	Reprise
				from Scruggs's album *Crown Of Jewels* on Reprise 46930		
4/10/99	**22**	21		26 **Almost Home**	S:11 *Mary-Chapin Carpenter/Beth Nielsen Chapman/Annie Roboff*	Columbia
10/9/99	**55**	7		27 **Wherever You Are**	*Mary-Chapin Carpenter*	Columbia
				above 2 from the album *Party Doll And Other Favorites* on Columbia 68571		
5/5/01	**53**	6		28 **Simple Life**	S:8 *Mary-Chapin Carpenter*	Columbia
				from the album *Time* Sex* Love** on Columbia 85176		
				CARPENTERS		
				Brother-sister duo from New Haven, Connecticut: Richard (born on 10/15/1946) and Karen (born on 3/2/1950) Carpenter. Karen died of heart failure due to anorexia nervosa on 2/4/1983 (age 32). Won the 1970 Best New Artist Grammy Award.		
2/18/78	**8**	14		**Sweet, Sweet Smile**	*Juice Newton/Otha Young*	A&M 2008
				written by **Juice Newton**		
				CARR, Eddie Lee		
				Born in Dallas, Texas. Male singer.		
7/29/89	**98**	1		**Big Bad Mama**	*Murry Kellum/Dan Mitchell*	Evergreen 1092
				CARR, Joe "Fingers"		
				Born Lou Busch on 7/18/1910 in Louisville, Kentucky. Died on 9/19/1979 (age 69). Honky-tonk pianist.		
3/3/51	**8**	2		**Tailor Made Woman** ***[w/ Tennessee Ernie Ford]***	J:8 *Jimmy Bryant/Bill Kemp*	Capitol F1349
				CARR, Kenny		
				Born in New Orleans, Louisiana. Male singer.		
9/10/88	**96**	1		1 **The Writing On The Wall**	*Bobby Fischer/Freddy Weller*	Kottage 0090
5/20/89	**88**	3		2 **Tell Me**	*Neal James*	Kottage 0091
				CARRINGTON, Rodney		
				Born in Longview, Texas. Male comedian. Starred in the 2004 TV sitcom *Rodney.*		
10/7/00	**71**	1		1 **More Of A Man**	*Rodney Carrington/Bob Hoban/Tim Northern* **[N]**	Capitol
				from the album *Morning Wood* on Capitol 24827		
3/15/03	**60**	1		2 **Don't Look Now**	*Rodney Carrington* **[N]**	Capitol
				from the album *Nut Sack* on Capitol 36579		
				CARSON, Fiddlin' John		
				Born on 3/23/1868 in Fannin County, Georgia. Died on 12/11/1949 (age 81). Pioneering fiddle player/recording artist/radio performer. Great-great-grandfather of singer **Brad Wolf**.		
				EARLY HITS: The Little Log Cabin In The Lane (1924) / You Will Never Miss Your Mother Until She Is Gone (1924) / Fare You Well, Old Joe Clark (1924) / Old Dan Tucker (1925)		
				CARSON, Jeff		
				Born Jeff Herndon on 12/16/1964 in Tulsa, Oklahoma; raised in Gravette, Arkansas. Male singer/songwriter/guitarist.		
3/11/95	**69**	4		1 **Yeah Buddy**	*Bob Regan/Mark D. Sanders*	MCG/Curb
6/3/95	**❶**[1]	20		2 **Not On Your Love**	S:5 *Tony Martin/Troy Martin/Reese Wilson*	MCG/Curb
10/7/95	**3**[1]	20		3 **The Car**	S:6 *Gary Heyde/Michael Spriggs*	MCG/Curb
1/6/96	**70**	1		4 **Santa Got Lost In Texas**	*Ken Darby* **[X]**	MCG/Curb
3/2/96	**6**	20		5 **Holdin' Onto Somethin'**	*Thom McHugh/Tom Shapiro*	MCG/Curb
8/10/96	**62**	6		6 **That Last Mile**	*Larry Boone/Will Robinson*	MCG/Curb
				#1-3, 5 & 6: from the album *Jeff Carson* on MCG/Curb 77744		
4/5/97	**55**	10		7 **Do It Again**	*Jess Brown/Brett James*	Curb
6/14/97	**66**	7		8 **Butterfly Kisses**	*Bob Carlisle/Randy Thomas*	Curb
8/16/97	**64**	4		9 **Here's The Deal**	S:6 *Jody Harris/Bobby Taylor*	Curb
1/24/98	**52**	10		10 **Cheatin' On Her Heart**	*Porter Howell/Mark D. Sanders*	Curb
				above 4 from the album *Butterfly Kisses* on Curb 77859		
7/18/98	**49**	13		11 **Shine On**	*Jim Daddario/Tony Marty*	Curb
5/26/01	**14**	28		12 **Real Life (I Never Was The Same Again)**	*James Janosky/Neil Thrasher*	Curb
3/2/02	**46**	10		13 **Until We Fall Back In Love Again**	*Jeff Carson/Philip Douglas/Jim Weatherly*	Curb
				above 3 from the album *Real Life* on Curb 77937		
6/14/03	**50**	10		14 **I Can Only Imagine**	*Bart Millard*	Curb
				from the various artists album *God Bless The USA 2003* on Curb 78810		
				CARSON, Joe		
				Born in 1937 in Brownwood, Texas. Died in a car crash on 2/28/1964 (age 27). Male singer.		
8/3/63	**27**	2		1 **I Gotta Get Drunk (And I Shore Do Dread It)**	*Willie Nelson*	Liberty 55578
11/9/63+	**19**	10		2 **Helpless**	*Bob Morris*	Liberty 55614
3/7/64	**34**	11		3 **Double Life**	*Dave Burgess/Clyde Pitts*	Liberty 55664
				CARSON, Wayne		
				Born Wayne Carson Thompson on 5/5/1942 in Denver, Colorado. Male singer/songwriter.		
9/29/73	**77**	7		1 **You're Gonna Love Yourself In The Morning**	*Donnie Fritts*	Monument 8581
12/25/76+	**82**	5		2 **Barstool Mountain**	*Wayne Carson/Donn Tankersley*	Elektra 45358
6/25/77	**99**	2		3 **Bugle Ann**	*Gary Head/Shorty Thompson*	Elektra 45407
4/2/83	**61**	7		4 **1 Yr 2 Mo 11 Days**	*Wayne Carson/Ronnie Reno*	EMH 0017

DEBUT	PEAK	WKS	GOLD	ARTIST / Country Chart Hit ... Songwriter	Ranking	Label (& Number)

CARTEE, Alan

Born in Nashville, Tennessee. Male singer/songwriter.

DEBUT	PEAK	WKS	GOLD	#	Country Chart Hit	Songwriter	Label (& Number)
10/8/77	98	1			**Let My Fingers Do The Walking (I'm Your Telephone Man)** answer to "Telephone Man" by **Meri Wilson**	*Ava Aldridge/Alan Cartee* [N]	Groovy 101

CARTER, Anita

Born Ina Anita Carter on 3/31/1933 in Maces Springs, Virginia. Died on 7/29/1999 (age 66). Female singer/songwriter. Member of **The Carter Family**. Daughter of Maybelle and Ezra Carter; sister of Helen and **June Carter**.

DEBUT	PEAK	WKS	GOLD	#	Country Chart Hit	Songwriter	Label (& Number)
4/21/51	4	11		1	**Bluebird Island** *[w/ Hank Snow]* / S:4 / J:7	*Hank Snow*	
5/12/51	2^{1}	14		2	**Down The Trail Of Achin' Hearts** *[w/ Hank Snow]* J:2 / S:7 / A:7	*Jimmy Kennedy/Nat Simon*	RCA Victor 48-0441
9/3/66	44	3		3	**I'm Gonna Leave You**	*Anita Carter/Helen Carter*	RCA Victor 8923
10/21/67	61	3		4	**Love Me Now (While I Am Living)**	*Harlan Howard*	RCA Victor 9307
3/30/68	4	15		5	**I Got You** *[w/ Waylon Jennings]*	*Gordon Galbraith/Ricci Mareno*	RCA Victor 9480
11/9/68	65	5		6	**To Be A Child Again**	*Jerry Chesnut*	United Artists 50444
4/12/69	50	7		7	**The Coming Of The Roads** *[w/ Johnny Darrell]*	*Billy Edd Wheeler*	United Artists 50503
1/16/71	41	8		8	**Tulsa County**	*Pamela Polland*	Capitol 2994
10/23/71	61	8		9	**A Whole Lotta Lovin'**	*Ben Peters/George Richey*	Capitol 3194

CARTER, Benny, And His Orchestra

Born Bennett Lester Carter on 8/8/1907 in Harlem, New York. Died of bronchitis on 7/12/2003 (age 95). Black saxophonist/trumpeter/clarinetist/pianist. Won Grammy's Lifetime Achievement Award in 1987.

DEBUT	PEAK	WKS	GOLD	#	Country Chart Hit	Songwriter	Label (& Number)
2/19/44	2^{1}	5			**Hurry, Hurry!** Savannah Churchill (vocal)	*Benny Carter/Richard Larkin*	Capitol 144

CARTER, Brenda

Born in Tennessee. Female singer.

DEBUT	PEAK	WKS	GOLD	#	Country Chart Hit	Songwriter	Label (& Number)
9/28/68	12	12			**Milwaukee, Here I Come** *[w/ George Jones]*	*Lee Fikes*	Musicor 1325

CARTER, Carlene

Born Rebecca Carlene Smith on 9/26/1955 in Madison, Tennessee. Female singer/songwriter/guitarist. Daughter of **June Carter** and **Carl Smith**. Worked with **The Carter Family** from the late 1960s into the early 1970s. Went solo thereafter. Appeared in the London production of **Pump Boys And Dinettes**. Married to singer Nick Lowe from 1979-90.

DEBUT	PEAK	WKS	GOLD	#	Country Chart Hit	Songwriter	Label (& Number)
10/27/79	42	8		1	**Do It In A Heartbeat**	*Carlene Carter/Nick Lowe/John McFee*	Warner 49083
10/25/80	76	5		2	**Baby Ride Easy** *[w/ Dave Edmunds]*	*Richard Dobson*	Warner 49572
12/2/89+	26	18		3	**Time's Up** *[w/ Southern Pacific]*	*Harry Stinson/Wendy Waldman/Kevin Welch*	Warner 22714
7/14/90	3^{1}	21		4	**I Fell In Love**	*Carlene Carter/Howie Epstein/Perry Lamek/Benmont Tench*	Reprise
10/27/90+	3^{1}	20		5	**Come On Back**	*Carlene Carter*	Reprise
3/16/91	25	17		6	**The Sweetest Thing**	*Carlene Carter/Robert Ellis Orrall*	Reprise
8/10/91	33	12		7	**One Love** above 4 from the album *I Fell In Love* on Reprise 26139	*Carlene Carter/Howie Epstein/Perry Lamek*	Reprise
5/29/93	3^{2}	20		8	**Every Little Thing**	*Al Anderson/Carlene Carter*	Giant
10/9/93	51	8		9	**Unbreakable Heart**	*Benmont Tench*	Giant
2/5/94	50	9		10	**I Love You 'Cause I Want To** above 3 from the album *Little Love Letters* on Giant 24499	*Carlene Carter/Radney Foster*	Giant
5/14/94	43	10		11	**Something Already Gone** from the movie *Maverick* starring Mel Gibson and Jodie Foster (soundtrack on Atlantic 82595)	*Al Anderson/Carlene Carter*	Atlantic
1/7/95	66	1		12	**Rockin' Little Christmas**	*Al Anderson/Carlene Carter* [X]	Giant
7/22/95	70	3		13	**Love Like This**	*Pat Bunch/Mary Ann Kennedy/Pam Rose*	Giant
8/26/95	75	1		14	**Hurricane** above 2 from the album *Little Acts Of Treason* on Giant 24581	*Al Anderson/Carlene Carter*	Giant

CARTER, Deana

Born on 1/4/1966 in Nashville, Tennessee. Female singer/songwriter. Daughter of **Fred Carter, Jr.**

DEBUT	PEAK	WKS	GOLD	#	Country Chart Hit	Songwriter	Label (& Number)
8/17/96	❶^{2}	20		1	**Strawberry Wine** S:❶^{3} **CMA: Single**	*Matraca Berg/Gary Harrison*	Capitol
12/14/96+	❶^{2}	20		2	**We Danced Anyway** S:❶^{5}	*Matraca Berg/Randy Scruggs*	Capitol
3/29/97	5	20		3	**Count Me In**	*Deana Carter/Chuck Jones*	Capitol
8/2/97	❶^{1}	20		4	**How Do I Get There**	*Deana Carter/Chris Farren*	Capitol
11/1/97	25	17		5	**Did I Shave My Legs For This?** S:9 above 5 from the album *Did I Shave My Legs For This?* on Capitol 37514	*Deana Carter/Rhonda Hart*	Capitol
9/26/98	16	20		6	**Absence Of The Heart**	*Deana Carter/Chris Farren/Chuck Jones*	Capitol
1/23/99	36	12		7	**You Still Shake Me**	*Tim Ryan/Leslie Satcher*	Capitol
4/3/99	35	16		8	**Angels Working Overtime** above 3 from the album *Everything's Gonna Be Alright* on Capitol 21142	*Michael Dulaney/Michael Lunn*	Capitol
10/26/02+	14	26		9	**There's No Limit**	*Deana Carter/Randy Scruggs*	Arista Nashville
5/24/03	35	12		10	**I'm Just A Girl** above 2 from the album *I'm Just A Girl* on Arista Nashville 67054	*Deana Carter/Bill Mann*	Arista Nashville
4/9/05	55	5		11	**One Day At A Time** from the album *The Story Of My Life* on Vanguard 79765	*Deana Carter*	Vanguard

CARTER, Fred Jr.

Born on 12/31/1933 in Winnsboro, Louisiana. Male singer/guitarist. Father of **Deana Carter**.

DEBUT	PEAK	WKS	GOLD	#	Country Chart Hit	Songwriter	Label (& Number)
10/14/67	70	3			**And You Wonder Why**	*Bill Anderson*	Monument 1022

Billboard DEBUT	PEAK	WKS	GOLD	ARTIST / Country Chart Hit	Ranking / Songwriter	Label (& Number)

CARTER, June

Born Valerie June Carter on 6/23/1929 in Maces Springs, Virginia. Died of heart failure on 5/15/2003 (age 73). Female singer/songwriter. Member of **The Carter Family**. Daughter of Maybelle and Ezra Carter, sister of Helen and **Anita Carter**. Married to **Carl Smith** from 1952-56; their daughter is **Carlene Carter**. Worked with **Elvis Presley**, then joined the **Johnny Cash** road show in 1961. Married Cash in March 1968.

CMA: Vocal Group (with Johnny Cash) 1969

DEBUT	PEAK	WKS	GOLD	Country Chart Hit	Songwriter	Label (& Number)
8/27/49	**9**	1		1 **Baby, It's Cold Outside** *[w/ Homer & Jethro]* ....S:9 from the movie *Neptune's Daughter* starring Esther Williams	*Frank Loesser* **[N]**	RCA Victor 48-0075
				JOHNNY CASH & JUNE CARTER:		
11/7/64+	**4**	22		2 **It Ain't Me, Babe**	*Bob Dylan*	Columbia 43145
3/4/67	**2**[1]	17		3 **Jackson** Grammy: Vocal Duo	*Gaby Rodgers/Billy Edd Wheeler*	Columbia 44011
6/24/67	**6**	17		4 **Long-Legged Guitar Pickin' Man**	*Marshall Grant*	Columbia 44158
1/24/70	**2**[1]	15		5 **If I Were A Carpenter** Grammy: Vocal Duo	*Tim Hardin*	Columbia 45064
4/3/71	**27**	11		6 **A Good Man** *[June Carter Cash]*	*June Carter*	Columbia 45338
9/11/71	**15**	13		7 **No Need To Worry**	*Sarah Jane Cooper/G.P. White*	Columbia 45431
7/15/72	**29**	7		8 **If I Had A Hammer**	*Lee Hays/Pete Seeger*	Columbia 45631
1/20/73	**27**	10		9 **The Loving Gift**	*Kris Kristofferson*	Columbia 45758
9/29/73	**69**	10		10 **Allegheny**	*Chris Gantry*	Columbia 45929
11/20/76+	**26**	11		11 **Old Time Feeling**	*Tom Jans/Will Jennings*	Columbia 10436

CARTER, Wilf "Montana Slim"

Born on 12/18/1904 in Guysboro, Nova Scotia, Canada. Died on 12/5/1996 (age 91). Legendary singer/songwriter/guitarist. Worked as a cowboy and rodeo performer. Known for his "three-in-one yodel" style.

CARTER, Woody, and his Hoedown Boys

Born on 9/4/1915 in Washington DC; raised in Houston, Texas. Died on 9/21/1996 (age 81). Male singer/guitarist.

DEBUT	PEAK	WKS	GOLD	Country Chart Hit	Songwriter	Label (& Number)
9/17/49	**14**	1		**Sittin' On The Doorstep** J:14	*Sam Lewis/Lew Pollack/Joe Young*	Macy's 100

CARTER FAMILY, The — HOF: 1970

Founded by Alvin Pleasant "A.P." Carter (born on 12/15/1891 in Maces Springs, Virginia; died on 11/7/1960, age 68); with wife Sara Dougherty (born on 7/21/1899 in Flatwoods, Virginia; died on 1/8/1979, age 79) and sister-in-law Maybelle Addington (born on 5/10/1909 in Nickelsville, Virginia; died on 10/23/1978, age 69). Joined from 1936-39 by Maybelle's daughters Helen, **Anita Carter**, and **June Carter**, and A.P.'s children Janette and Joe. Helen died on 6/2/1998 (age 70). Anita died on 7/29/1999 (age 66). June died on 5/15/2003 (age 73). This group disbanded in 1943 and was re-formed by Maybelle and her daughters as the Carter Sisters and Mother Maybelle. Joined **Johnny Cash**'s road show in 1961. Known as "The First Family of Country Music." Chart hits below feature Maybelle and her daughters.

EARLY HITS: Bury Me Under The Weeping Willow (1928) / Wildwood Flower (1928) / I'm Thinking Tonight Of My Blue Eyes (1929) / Can The Circle Be Unbroken (1935) // OPRY: 1950

DEBUT	PEAK	WKS	GOLD	Country Chart Hit	Songwriter	Label (& Number)
4/6/63	**13**	3		1 **Busted** *[w/ Johnny Cash]*	*Harlan Howard*	Columbia 42665
9/4/71	**37**	11		2 **A Song To Mama** *[w/ Johnny Cash]*	*Helen Carter/June Carter/Glenn Jones*	Columbia 45428
4/29/72	**42**	7		3 **Travelin' Minstrel Band**	*Jerry Foster/Bill Rice*	Columbia 45581
9/30/72	**35**	8		4 **The World Needs A Melody** *[w/ Johnny Cash]*	*Larry Henley/Red Lane/Johnny Slate*	Columbia 45679
8/4/73	**57**	7		5 **Praise The Lord And Pass The Soup** *[w/ Johnny Cash & The Oak Ridge Boys]*	*Albert Hammond/Mike Hazlewood*	Columbia 45890
11/17/73+	**34**	10		6 **Pick The Wildwood Flower** *[Johnny Cash w/ Mother Maybelle Carter]*	*Joe Allen*	Columbia 45938

CARTWRIGHT, Lionel

Born on 2/10/1960 in Gallipolis, Ohio; raised in Milton, West Virginia. Male singer/songwriter/guitarist.

DEBUT	PEAK	WKS	GOLD	Country Chart Hit	Songwriter	Label (& Number)
11/19/88+	**45**	13		1 **You're Gonna Make Her Mine**	*Lionel Cartwright*	MCA 53444
2/18/89	**14**	25		2 **Like Father Like Son**	*Paul Overstreet/Don Schlitz*	MCA 53498
6/17/89	**3**[1]	24		3 **Give Me His Last Chance**	*Lionel Cartwright*	MCA 53651
10/14/89+	**12**	21		4 **In My Eyes**	*Lionel Cartwright*	MCA 53723
3/24/90	**8**	23		5 **I Watched It All (On My Radio)**	*Lionel Cartwright/Don Schlitz*	MCA
7/28/90	**7**	20		6 **My Heart Is Set On You**	*Lionel Cartwright*	MCA
12/1/90+	**31**	15		7 **Say It's Not True** above 3 from the album *I Watched It On The Radio* on MCA 42336	*Lionel Cartwright*	MCA
7/6/91	**❶**[1]	20		8 **Leap Of Faith**	*Lionel Cartwright*	MCA
11/16/91+	**24**	20		9 **What Kind Of Fool**	*Lionel Cartwright*	MCA
4/4/92	**62**	4		10 **Family Tree** above 3 from the album *Chasin' The Sun* on MCA 10307	*Lionel Cartwright*	MCA
8/15/92	**63**	11		11 **Be My Angel**	*Jennifer Kimball/Bob McDill/Dan Seals*	MCA
10/31/92	**50**	15		12 **Standing On The Promises**	*Lionel Cartwright/Allen Shamblin*	MCA

CARVER, Johnny — All-Time: #229

Born on 11/24/1940 in Jackson, Mississippi. Male singer/songwriter/guitarist. Began singing in the family's Gospel group. Started his own band, the Capital Cowboys, while still a teenager. Moved to Los Angeles in 1965; became leader of the house band at the Palomino Club.

DEBUT	PEAK	WKS	GOLD	Country Chart Hit	Songwriter	Label (& Number)
12/23/67+	**21**	13		1 **Your Lily White Hands**	*Ray Griff*	Imperial 66268
6/1/68	**48**	8		2 **I Still Didn't Have The Sense To Go**	*Patti George*	Imperial 66297
12/7/68+	**32**	11		3 **Hold Me Tight**	*Johnny Nash*	Imperial 66341
4/5/69	**26**	9		4 **Sweet Wine**	*Ray Griff*	Imperial 66361
8/2/69	**41**	10		5 **That's Your Hang Up**	*Johnny Carver/Sonny Throckmorton*	Imperial 66389
12/13/69+	**43**	9		6 **Willie And The Hand Jive**	*Johnny Otis*	Imperial 66423
6/20/70	**68**	4		7 **Harvey Harrington IV**	*Wayne Kemp/Mack Vickery*	Imperial 66442
12/12/70	**73**	2		8 **If You See My Baby**	*Eddie Miller/Bob Morris*	United Artists 50713

Billboard DEBUT	PEAK	WKS	GOLD	ARTIST / Ranking / Country Chart Hit	Songwriter	Label (& Number)
				CARVER, Johnny — cont'd		
8/14/71	**34**	15		9 **If You Think That It's All Right**	*Johnny Carver*	Epic 10760
12/25/71+	**27**	11		10 **I Start Thinking About You**	*Johnny Carver*	Epic 10813
6/24/72	**35**	9		11 **I Want You**	*Johnny Carver*	Epic 10872
4/7/73	**5**	17		12 **Yellow Ribbon**	*L. Russell Brown/Irwin Levine*	ABC 11357
7/28/73	**6**	13		13 **You Really Haven't Changed**	*Johnny Carver/Ron Chancey*	ABC 11374
12/8/73+	**12**	16		14 **Tonight Someone's Falling In Love**	*Bobby Braddock/Jimmy Gilmer*	ABC 11403
4/13/74	**27**	12		15 **Country Lullabye**	*Barry Mann/Cynthia Weil*	ABC 11425
8/24/74	**10**	16		16 **Don't Tell (That Sweet Ole Lady Of Mine)**	*L. Russell Brown/Irwin Levine*	ABC 12017
1/18/75	**39**	11		17 **January Jones**	*Rory Bourke*	ABC 12052
6/7/75	**64**	7		18 **Strings**	*Tupper Saussy/Bill Wills*	ABC 12097
10/4/75	**74**	7		19 **Start All Over Again**	*Bill Dees*	ABC/Dot 17576
3/6/76	**77**	5		20 **Snap, Crackle And Pop**	*Danny Morrison/Rafe Van Hoy*	ABC/Dot 17614
7/4/76	**9**	14		21 **Afternoon Delight**	*Bill Danoff*	ABC/Dot 17640
11/6/76	**47**	9		22 **Love Is Only Love (When Shared By Two)**	*Johnny Carver/Ron Chancey*	ABC/Dot 17661
2/12/77	**48**	6		23 **Sweet City Woman**	*Rich Dodson*	ABC/Dot 17675
3/12/77	**29**	10		24 **Living Next Door To Alice**	*Mike Chapman/Nicky Chinn*	ABC/Dot 17685
6/18/77	**36**	9		25 **Down At The Pool**	*Don Goodman/Bud Reneau*	ABC/Dot 17707
11/26/77	**72**	6		26 **Apartment**	*Bobby Braddock*	ABC/Dot 17729
6/14/80	**90**	3		27 **Fingertips**	*Johnny Carver*	Equity 1902
1/24/81	**73**	5		28 **S.O.S.**	*Stig Anderson/Benny Andersson/Bjorn Ulvaeus*	Tanglewood 1905

CASEY, Karen

Born in Reno, Nevada. Female singer.

DEBUT	PEAK	WKS	GOLD	Country Chart Hit	Songwriter	Label (& Number)
2/23/80	**92**	2		**Leavin' On Your Mind**	*Webb Pierce/Wayne Walker*	Western Pride 112

CASH, Johnny 1950s: #9 / 1960s: #4 / 1970s: #11 / All-Time: #3 // HOF: 1980

Born J.R. Cash on 2/26/1932 in Kingsland, Arkansas; raised in Dyess, Arkansas. Died of diabetes on 9/12/2003 (age 71). Legendary singer/songwriter/guitarist. In U.S. Air Force, 1950-54, where he adopted the name John Ray. Backed by The Tennessee Two: Luther Perkins (guitar) and Marshall Grant (bass). First recorded for Sun in 1955. On *Louisiana Hayride* in 1957. Own TV show for ABC from 1969-71. Worked with **June Carter** from 1961; married her in March 1968. Father of **Rosanne Cash** and stepfather of **Carlene Carter**. Brother of **Tommy Cash**. Acted on numerous TV shows. Known as "The Man In Black." Inducted into the Rock and Roll Hall of Fame in 1992. Won Grammy's Living Legends Award in 1999.

CMA: Vocal Group (with June Carter) 1969 / Male Vocalist 1969 / Entertainer 1969 // OPRY: 1956

DEBUT	PEAK	WKS	GOLD	Country Chart Hit	Songwriter	Label (& Number)
11/26/55	**14**	1		1 **Cry! Cry! Cry!**	S:14 *Johnny Cash*	Sun 221
2/4/56	**4**	23		2 **So Doggone Lonesome /**	J:4 / A:6 / S:6 *Johnny Cash*	
2/11/56	**4**	20		3 **Folsom Prison Blues** — **Grammy: Hall of Fame / RS500**; also see #62 below	A:4 / S:5 / J:5 *Johnny Cash*	Sun 232
6/9/56	**❶[6]**	43		4 **I Walk The Line /** — **Grammy: Hall of Fame / RS500**	J:❶[6] / A:❶[1] / S:2 *Johnny Cash*	
6/9/56	**flip**	9		5 **Get Rhythm** — also see #65 below	S:flip / J:flip *Johnny Cash*	Sun 241
12/22/56+	**❶[5]**	28		6 **There You Go /**	J:❶[5] / S:2 / A:2 *Johnny Cash*	
12/22/56+	**7**	24		7 **Train Of Love**	A:7 / S:13 / J:flip *Johnny Cash*	Sun 258
5/27/57	**9**	15		8 **Next In Line /**	S:9 / A:9 *Johnny Cash*	
6/17/57	**flip**	9		9 **Don't Make Me Go**	S:flip *Johnny Cash*	Sun 266
9/16/57	**3[1]**	23		10 **Home Of The Blues /**	A:3 / S:5 *Johnny Cash/Glenn Douglas/Lillie McAlpin*	
10/7/57	**13**	2		11 **Give My Love To Rose**	A:13 / S:flip *Johnny Cash*	Sun 279
1/20/58	**❶[10]**	23		12 **Ballad Of A Teenage Queen /** — also see #134 below	A:❶[10] / S:❶[8] *Jack Clement*	
2/10/58	**4**	14		13 **Big River** — also see #72 below	A:4 / S:flip *Johnny Cash*	Sun 283
5/26/58	**❶[8]**	24		14 **Guess Things Happen That Way /**	S:❶[8] / A:❶[3] *Jack Clement*	
6/2/58	**6**	13		15 **Come In Stranger**	A:6 / S:flip *Johnny Cash*	Sun 295
8/25/58	**2[4]**	16		16 **The Ways Of A Woman In Love /**	S:2 / A:2 *Bill Justis/Charlie Rich*	
9/1/58	**5**	16		17 **You're The Nearest Thing To Heaven**	A:5 / S:flip *Jim Atkins/Johnny Cash/Hoyt Johnson*	Sun 302
10/13/58	**4**	19		18 **All Over Again /**	A:6 *Johnny Cash*	
10/13/58	**7**	15		19 **What Do I Care**	*Johnny Cash*	Columbia 41251
1/19/59	**❶[6]**	20		20 **Don't Take Your Guns To Town**	*Johnny Cash*	Columbia 41313
1/19/59	**30**	1		21 **It's Just About Time**	*Jack Clement*	Sun 309
3/30/59	**8**	13		22 **Luther Played The Boogie /**	*Johnny Cash*	
3/30/59	**12**	9		23 **Thanks A Lot**	*Charlie Rich*	Sun 316
5/4/59	**9**	11		24 **Frankie's Man, Johnny /**	*(traditional)*	
5/11/59	**13**	11		25 **You Dreamer You**	*Johnny Cash*	Columbia 41371
7/20/59	**11**	11		26 **Katy Too**	*Johnny Cash/Jack Clement*	Sun 321
8/10/59	**4**	20		27 **I Got Stripes /**	*Johnny Cash/Charlie Williams*	
8/24/59	**14**	9		28 **Five Feet High And Rising**	*Johnny Cash*	Columbia 41427
11/9/59	**22**	5		29 **Goodbye Little Darlin'**	*Gene Autry/Johnny Marvin*	Sun 331
1/4/60	**24**	1		30 **The Little Drummer Boy**	*Katherine Davis/Henry Onorati/Harry Simeone* **[X]**	Columbia 41481
2/15/60	**16**	10		31 **Straight A's In Love /**	*Johnny Cash*	
3/7/60	**20**	2		32 **I Love You Because** *[w/ The Gene Lowery Singers]*	*Leon Payne*	Sun 334
4/25/60	**10**	15		33 **Seasons Of My Heart /**	*Darrell Edwards/George Jones*	
5/9/60	**13**	8		34 **Smiling Bill McCall**	*Johnny Cash* **[N]**	Columbia 41618

Billboard DEBUT	PEAK	WKS	GOLD	Ranking	ARTIST / Country Chart Hit	Songwriter	Label (& Number)
					CASH, Johnny — cont'd		
8/22/60	15	7		35	Second Honeymoon	*Autry Inman*	Columbia 41707
12/26/60	30	1		36	Mean Eyed Cat	*Johnny Cash*	Sun 347
					JOHNNY CASH And The Tennessee Two (all of above Sun Records, except #32)		
2/6/61	13	9		37	Oh Lonesome Me *[w/ The Gene Lowery Singers]*	*Don Gibson*	Sun 355
					all Sun records recorded from 1955-58		
6/12/61	24	2		38	The Rebel - Johnny Yuma	*Andrew Fenady/Richard Markowitz*	Columbia 41995
					from the TV series *The Rebel* starring Nick Adams		
12/18/61+	11	14		39	Tennessee Flat-Top Box	*Johnny Cash*	Columbia 42147
3/31/62	24	3		40	The Big Battle	*Johnny Cash*	Columbia 42301
7/14/62	8	10		41	In The Jailhouse Now	*Jimmie Rodgers*	Columbia 42425
4/6/63	13	3		42	Busted *[w/ The Carter Family]*	*Harlan Howard*	Columbia 42665
6/8/63	❶^{7}	26		43	Ring Of Fire	*June Carter/Merle Kilgore*	Columbia 42788
					Grammy: Hall of Fame / RS500		
11/9/63	2^{3}	16		44	The Matador	*June Carter/Johnny Cash*	Columbia 42880
2/22/64	❶^{6}	22		45	Understand Your Man /	*Johnny Cash*	
3/7/64	49	1		46	Dark As A Dungeon	*Merle Travis*	Columbia 42964
7/11/64	3^{3}	20		47	The Ballad Of Ira Hayes /	*Peter LaFarge*	
7/25/64	8	15		48	Bad News	*John D. Loudermilk*	Columbia 43058
11/7/64+	4	22		49	It Ain't Me, Babe *[w/ June Carter]*	*Bob Dylan*	Columbia 43145
2/20/65	3^{3}	16		50	Orange Blossom Special	*Ervin Rouse*	Columbia 43206
7/10/65	15	13		51	Mister Garfield	*Jack Elliott*	Columbia 43313
9/4/65	10	9		52	The Sons Of Katie Elder	*Elmer Bernstein/Ernie Sheldon*	Columbia 43342
					from the movie starring John Wayne		
11/20/65+	9	14		53	Happy To Be With You	*June Carter/Johnny Cash/Merle Kilgore*	Columbia 43420
2/12/66	2^{2}	18		54	The One On The Right Is On The Left	*Jack Clement* [N]	Columbia 43496
7/2/66	17	9		55	Everybody Loves A Nut	*Jack Clement* [N]	Columbia 43673
9/10/66	39	5		56	Boa Constrictor	*Shel Silverstein* [N]	Columbia 43763
12/24/66+	20	13		57	You Beat All I Ever Saw	*Johnny Cash*	Columbia 43921
3/4/67	2^{1}	17		58	Jackson *[w/ June Carter]*	*Gaby Rodgers/Billy Edd Wheeler*	Columbia 44011
					Grammy: Vocal Duo		
6/24/67	6	17		59	Long-Legged Guitar Pickin' Man *[w/ June Carter]*	*Marshall Grant*	Columbia 44158
10/28/67	60	6		60	The Wind Changes	*Johnny Cash*	Columbia 44288
12/23/67+	2^{2}	15		61	Rosanna's Going Wild	*Anita Carter/Helen Carter/June Carter*	Columbia 44373
6/1/68	❶^{4}	18		62	Folsom Prison Blues	*Johnny Cash* [L]	Columbia 44513
					Grammy: Male Vocal		
12/7/68+	❶^{6}	20		63	Daddy Sang Bass	*Carl Perkins*	Columbia 44689
7/26/69	❶^{5}	14	●	64	A Boy Named Sue	*Shel Silverstein* [L-N]	Columbia 44944
					Grammy: Song & Male Vocal / CMA: Single; recorded at San Quentin prison		
10/11/69	23	12		65	Get Rhythm	*Johnny Cash* [R]	Sun 1103
					same version as #5 above with "live" effects dubbed-in		
11/22/69	4	13		66	Blistered /	*Billy Edd Wheeler*	
11/29/69	flip	12		67	See Ruby Fall	*Johnny Cash*	Columbia 45020
1/24/70	2^{1}	15		68	If I Were A Carpenter *[w/ June Carter]*	*Tim Hardin*	Columbia 45064
					Grammy: Vocal Duo		
2/28/70	35	7		69	Rock Island Line	*Johnny Cash*	Sun 1111
4/18/70	3^{2}	14		70	What Is Truth	*Johnny Cash* [S]	Columbia 45134
9/5/70	❶^{2}	15		71	Sunday Morning Coming Down	*Kris Kristofferson* [L]	Columbia 45211
12/5/70	41	8		72	Big River	*Johnny Cash* [R]	Sun 1121
					same version as #13 above		
12/19/70+	❶^{1}	13		73	Flesh And Blood	*Johnny Cash*	Columbia 45269
					from the movie *I Walk The Line* starring Gregory Peck		
3/27/71	3^{2}	13		74	Man In Black	*Johnny Cash*	Columbia 45339
6/26/71	18	10		75	Singing In Viet Nam Talking Blues	*Johnny Cash* [S]	Columbia 45393
9/4/71	37	11		76	A Song To Mama *[w/ The Carter Family]*	*Helen Carter/June Carter/Glenn Jones*	Columbia 45428
9/11/71	15	13		77	No Need To Worry *[w/ June Carter]*	*Sarah Jane Cooper/G.P. White*	Columbia 45431
10/16/71	16	11		78	Papa Was A Good Man *[w/ The Evangel Temple Choir]*	*Hal Bynum*	Columbia 45460
1/29/72	2^{1}	16		79	A Thing Called Love *[w/ The Evangel Temple Choir]*	*Jerry Reed*	Columbia 45534
5/6/72	2^{3}	12		80	Kate	*Marty Robbins*	Columbia 45590
7/15/72	29	7		81	If I Had A Hammer *[w/ June Carter Cash]*	*Lee Hays/Pete Seeger*	Columbia 45631
8/26/72	2^{2}	15		82	Oney	*Jerry Chesnut*	Columbia 45660
9/30/72	35	8		83	The World Needs A Melody *[w/ The Carter Family]*	*Larry Henley/Red Lane/Johnny Slate*	Columbia 45679
12/23/72+	3^{1}	15		84	Any Old Wind That Blows	*Dick Feller*	Columbia 45740
1/20/73	27	10		85	The Loving Gift *[w/ June Carter Cash]*	*Kris Kristofferson*	Columbia 45758
4/21/73	30	9		86	Children	*Joe South*	Columbia 45786
					from the movie *The Gospel Road* starring Cash		
8/4/73	57	7		87	Praise The Lord And Pass The Soup *[w/ The Carter Family & The Oak Ridge Boys]*	*...Albert Hammond/Mike Hazlewood*	Columbia 45890
9/29/73	69	10		88	Allegheny *[w/ June Carter]*	*Chris Gantry*	Columbia 45929
11/17/73+	34	10		89	Pick The Wildwood Flower *[w/ Mother Maybelle Carter]*	*Joe Allen*	Columbia 45938
2/23/74	52	8		90	Orleans Parish Prison	*Dick Feller*	Columbia 45997
4/27/74	31	13		91	Ragged Old Flag	*Johnny Cash*	Columbia 46028
12/14/74+	14	12		92	Lady Came From Baltimore	*Tim Hardin*	Columbia 10066
4/12/75	42	9		93	My Old Kentucky Home (Turpentine And Dandelion Wine)	*Randy Newman*	Columbia 10116
7/26/75	17	12		94	Look At Them Beans	*Joe Tex*	Columbia 10177
11/15/75+	35	12		95	Texas - 1947	*Guy Clark*	Columbia 10237

DEBUT	PEAK	WKS	GOLD	#	ARTIST / Country Chart Hit	Songwriter	Label (& Number)
					CASH, Johnny — cont'd		
2/7/76	**54**	7		96	**Strawberry Cake**	*Johnny Cash*	Columbia 10279
4/10/76	**❶[2]**	15		97	**One Piece At A Time**	*Wayne Kemp* **[N]**	Columbia 10321
7/24/76	**29**	8		98	**Sold Out Of Flagpoles**	*Johnny Cash*	Columbia 10381
10/23/76	**41**	8		99	**It's All Over**	*Johnny Cash*	Columbia 10424
					JOHNNY CASH & The Tennessee Three (above 3)		
11/20/76+	**26**	11		100	**Old Time Feeling** ***[w/ June Carter Cash]***	*Tom Jans/Will Jennings*	Columbia 10436
2/26/77	**38**	9		101	**The Last Gunfighter Ballad**	*Guy Clark*	Columbia 10483
8/6/77	**46**	9		102	**Lady**	*Johnny Cash*	Columbia 10587
10/22/77	**32**	12		103	**After The Ball**	*Johnny Cash*	Columbia 10623
2/11/78	**12**	13		104	**I Would Like To See You Again**	*Larry Atwood/Charlie Craig*	Columbia 10681
5/20/78	**2[2]**	13		105	**There Ain't No Good Chain Gang** ***[w/ Waylon Jennings]***	*Hal Bynum/Dave Kirby*	Columbia 10742
9/9/78	**44**	8		106	**Gone Girl**	*Jack Clement*	Columbia 10817
12/9/78	**89**	2		107	**It'll Be Her**	*Billy Ray Reynolds*	Columbia 10855
1/13/79	**21**	13		108	**I Will Rock And Roll With You**	*Johnny Cash*	Columbia 10888
5/19/79	**2[1]**	16		109	**(Ghost) Riders In The Sky**	*Stan Jones*	Columbia 10961
10/20/79	**42**	7		110	**I'll Say It's True**	*Johnny Cash*	Columbia 11103
					George Jones (guest vocal)		
11/17/79+	**22**	12		111	**I Wish I Was Crazy Again** ***[w/ Waylon Jennings]***	*Bob McDill*	Columbia 10742
4/19/80	**66**	5		112	**Bull Rider**	*Rodney Crowell*	Columbia 11237
6/7/80	**54**	8		113	**Song Of The Patriot**	*Shirl Milete/Marty Robbins*	Columbia 11283
					Marty Robbins (harmony vocal)		
8/23/80	**53**	8		114	**Cold Lonesome Morning**	*Johnny Cash*	Columbia 11340
11/29/80	**85**	4		115	**The Last Time**	*Kris Kristofferson*	Columbia 11399
1/24/81	**78**	5		116	**Without Love**	*Nick Lowe*	Columbia 11424
3/21/81	**10**	15		117	**The Baron**	*Paul Richey/Billy Sherrill/Jerry Taylor*	Columbia 60516
7/25/81	**60**	5		118	**Mobile Bay**	*Dave Kirby/Curly Putman*	Columbia 02189
1/23/82	**71**	5		119	**The Reverend Mr. Black /**	*Jimmy Peters/Billy Edd Wheeler*	
1/23/82	**flip**	5		120	**Chattanooga City Limit Sign**	*Bob Drawdy*	Columbia 02669
4/17/82	**26**	12		121	**The General Lee**	*Tom Bresh/Johnny Cash*	Scotti Brothers 02803
					from the TV series *The Dukes Of Hazzard* starring **John Schneider** and **Tom Wopat**		
8/7/82	**55**	8		122	**Georgia On A Fast Train**	*Billy Joe Shaver*	Columbia 03058
2/26/83	**84**	2		123	**We Must Believe In Magic**	*Bob McDill/Allen Reynolds*	Columbia 03524
9/24/83	**75**	4		124	**I'm Ragged But I'm Right**	*Johnny Cash*	Columbia 04060
5/12/84	**84**	5		125	**That's The Truth**	*Paul Kennerley*	Columbia 04428
7/14/84	**45**	11		126	**The Chicken In Black**	*Gary Gentry* **[N]**	Columbia 04513
5/18/85	**❶[1]**	20		127	**Highwayman** ***[w/ Waylon Jennings/Willie Nelson/Kris Kristofferson]***	S:❶[1] / A:❶[1] *Jimmy Webb*	Columbia 04881
					Grammy: Song		
7/13/85	**45**	9		128	**I Will Dance With You** ***[w/ Karen Brooks]***	*Jack Routh*	Warner 28979
9/14/85	**15**	18		129	**Desperados Waiting For A Train** ***[w/ Waylon Jennings/Willie Nelson/Kris Kristofferson]***	S:15 / A:16 *Guy Clark*	Columbia 05594
5/17/86	**35**	11		130	**Even Cowgirls Get The Blues** ***[w/ Waylon Jennings]***	A:34 *Rodney Crowell*	Columbia 05896
3/28/87	**43**	11		131	**The Night Hank Williams Came To Town**	*Bobby Braddock/Charlie Williams*	Mercury 888459
					Waylon Jennings (guest vocal)		
12/12/87	**72**	5		132	**W. Lee O'Daniel (And The Light Crust Dough Boys)**	*James Talley*	Mercury 870010
9/24/88	**21**	20		133	**That Old Wheel** ***[w/ Hank Williams, Jr.]***	S:17 *Johnny Pierce*	Mercury 870688
2/25/89	**45**	9		134	**Ballad Of A Teenage Queen** ***[w/ Rosanne Cash & The Everly Brothers]***	*Jack Clement* **[R]**	Mercury 872420
					new version of #12 above		
3/3/90	**25**	14		135	**Silver Stallion** ***[w/ Waylon Jennings/Willie Nelson/Kris Kristofferson]***	*Lee Clayton*	Columbia
					from their album *Highwayman 2* on Columbia 45240		
9/22/90	**69**	4		136	**Goin' By The Book**	*Chester Lester*	Mercury
					from the album *The Mystery Of Life* on Mercury 848051		
12/25/93+	**54**	10		137	**The Devil Comes Back To Georgia** ***[w/ Mark O'Connor/Charlie Daniels/Marty Stuart/Travis Tritt]***	*Tom Crain/Charlie Daniels/Joe DiGregorio/Fred Edwards/Charles Hayward/Jim Marshall*	Warner
					from O'Connor's album *Heroes* on Warner 45257		
11/7/98	**61**	6		138	**I Walk The Line Revisited** ***[w/ Rodney Crowell]***	*Johnny Cash/Rodney Crowell*	Sugar Hill
					from Crowell's album *The Houston Kid* on Sugar Hill 1065		
3/8/03	**56**	1		139	**Hurt**	S:❶[14] *Trent Reznor*	American
					CMA: Single; single certified double platinum; from the album *American IV: The Man Comes Around* on American 063339		

After The Ball ['77]
All Over Again ['58]
Allegheny ['73]
Any Old Wind That Blows ['73]
Bad News ['64]
Ballad Of A Teenage Queen ['58, '89]
Ballad Of Ira Hayes ['64]
Baron ['81]
Big Battle ['62]
Big River ['58, '70]
Blistered ['69]
Boa Constrictor ['66]
Boy Named Sue ['69]
Bull Rider ['80]
Busted ['63]
Chattanooga City Limit Sign ['82]
Chicken In Black ['84]
Children ['73]
Cold Lonesome Morning ['80]
Come In Stranger ['58]
Cry! Cry! Cry! ['55]
Daddy Sang Bass ['69]
Dark As A Dungeon ['64]
Desperados Waiting For A Train ['85]
Devil Comes Back To Georgia ['94]
Don't Make Me Go ['57]
Don't Take Your Guns To Town ['59]
Even Cowgirls Get The Blues ['86]
Everybody Loves A Nut ['66]
Five Feet High And Rising ['59]
Flesh And Blood ['71]
Folsom Prison Blues ['56, '68]
Frankie's Man, Johnny ['59]
General Lee ['82]
Georgia On A Fast Train ['82]
Get Rhythm ['56, '69]
(Ghost) Riders In The Sky ['79]
Give My Love To Rose ['57]
Goin' By The Book ['90]
Gone Girl ['78]
Goodbye Little Darlin' ['59]
Guess Things Happen That Way ['58]
Happy To Be With You ['66]
Highwayman ['85]
Home Of The Blues ['57]
Hurt ['03]
I Got Stripes ['59]
I Love You Because ['60]
I Walk The Line ['56]
I Walk The Line Revisited ['98]
I Will Dance With You ['85]
I Will Rock And Roll With You ['79]
I Wish I Was Crazy Again ['80]
I Would Like To See You Again ['78]
I'll Say It's True ['79]
I'm Ragged But I'm Right ['83]
If I Had A Hammer ['72]
If I Were A Carpenter ['70]
In The Jailhouse Now ['62]
It Ain't Me, Babe ['65]
It'll Be Her ['78]
It's All Over ['76]
It's Just About Time ['59]
Jackson ['67]
Kate ['72]
Katy Too ['59]
Lady ['77]
Lady Came From Baltimore ['75]
Last Gunfighter Ballad ['77]
Last Time ['80]
Little Drummer Boy ['60]
Long-Legged Guitar Pickin' Man ['67]
Look At Them Beans ['75]
Loving Gift ['73]
Luther Played The Boogie ['59]
Man In Black ['71]
Matador ['63]
Mean Eyed Cat ['60]
Mister Garfield ['65]
Mobile Bay ['81]
My Old Kentucky Home (Turpentine And Dandelion Wine) ['75]
Next In Line ['57]
Night Hank Williams Came To Town ['87]
No Need To Worry ['71]
Oh Lonesome Me ['61]
Old Time Feeling ['77]
One On The Right Is On The Left ['66]
One Piece At A Time ['76]
Oney ['72]
Orange Blossom Special ['65]
Orleans Parish Prison ['74]
Papa Was A Good Man ['71]
Pick The Wildwood Flower ['74]
Praise The Lord And Pass The Soup ['73]
Ragged Old Flag ['74]
Rebel - Johnny Yuma ['61]
Reverend Mr. Black ['82]
Ring Of Fire ['63]
Rock Island Line ['70]
Rosanna's Going Wild ['68]
Seasons Of My Heart ['60]
Second Honeymoon ['60]
See Ruby Fall ['69]
Silver Stallion ['90]
Singing In Viet Nam Talking Blues ['71]
Smiling Bill McCall ['60]
So Doggone Lonesome ['56]
Sold Out Of Flagpoles ['76]
Song Of The Patriot ['80]
Song To Mama ['71]
Sons Of Katie Elder ['65]
Straight A's In Love ['60]
Strawberry Cake ['76]

Billboard DEBUT	PEAK	WKS	GOLD	ARTIST / Country Chart Hit	Ranking / Songwriter	Label (& Number)

CASH, Johnny — cont'd

Sunday Morning Coming Down ['70]
Tennessee Flat-Top Box ['62]
Texas - 1947 ['76]
Thanks A Lot ['59]
That Old Wheel ['88]
That's The Truth ['84]
There Ain't No Good Chain Gang ['78]
There You Go ['57]
Thing Called Love ['72]
Train Of Love ['57]
Understand Your Man ['64]
W. Lee O'Daniel (And The Light Crust Dough Boys) ['87]
Ways Of A Woman In Love ['58]
We Must Believe In Magic ['83]
What Do I Care ['58]
What Is Truth ['70]
Wind Changes ['67]
Without Love ['81]
World Needs A Melody ['72]
You Beat All I Ever Saw ['67]
You Dreamer You ['59]
You're The Nearest Thing To Heaven ['58]

CASH, Rosanne — 1980s: #37 / All-Time: #132

Born on 5/24/1956 in Memphis, Tennessee. Female singer/songwriter. Daughter of **Johnny Cash** and Vivian Liberto. Raised by her mother in California, then moved to Nashville after high school graduation. Worked in the Johnny Cash Road Show. Married to **Rodney Crowell** from 1979-92. Moved to New York. Married producer John Leventhal in 1995. Released short-story collection *Bodies Of Water* in 1996.

Debut	Peak	Wks	Country Chart Hit	Songwriter	Label (& Number)
9/8/79	17	12	1 No Memories Hangin' Round *[w/ Bobby Bare]*	*Rodney Crowell*	Columbia 11045
2/2/80	15	13	2 Couldn't Do Nothin' Right	*Kix Brooks/Gary Nunn*	Columbia 11188
5/31/80	25	12	3 Take Me, Take Me	*Keith Sykes*	Columbia 11268
2/21/81	❶[1]	19	4 Seven Year Ache	*Rosanne Cash*	Columbia 11426
8/29/81	❶[1]	16	5 My Baby Thinks He's A Train	*Leroy Preston*	Columbia 02463
12/19/81+	❶[1]	18	6 Blue Moon With Heartache	*Rosanne Cash*	Columbia 02659
5/29/82	4	18	7 Ain't No Money	*Rodney Crowell*	Columbia 02937
10/9/82+	8	20	8 I Wonder	*Leroy Preston*	Columbia 03283
3/12/83	14	15	9 It Hasn't Happened Yet	*John Hiatt*	Columbia 03705
6/1/85	❶[1]	24	10 I Don't Know Why You Don't Want Me	S:❶[1] / A:❶[1] *Rosanne Cash/Rodney Crowell*	Columbia 04809
			Grammy: Female Vocal		
10/5/85+	❶[1]	24	11 Never Be You	S:❶[1] / A:❶[1] *Tom Petty/Benmont Tench*	Columbia 05621
2/15/86	5	22	12 Hold On	S:5 / A:5 *Rosanne Cash*	Columbia 05794
7/19/86	5	20	13 Second To No One	A:4 / S:6 *Rosanne Cash*	Columbia 06159
6/27/87	❶[1]	23	14 The Way We Make A Broken Heart	S:❶[1] *John Hiatt*	Columbia 07200
11/14/87+	❶[1]	22	15 Tennessee Flat Top Box	S:❶[3] *Johnny Cash*	Columbia 07624
1/23/88	❶[1]	23	16 It's Such A Small World *[w/ Rodney Crowell]*	S:❶[3] *Rodney Crowell*	Columbia 07693
4/2/88	❶[1]	22	17 If You Change Your Mind	S:❶[2] *Rosanne Cash/Hank DeVito*	Columbia 07746
8/13/88	❶[1]	23	18 Runaway Train	S:❶[1] *John Stewart*	Columbia 07988
2/25/89	45	9	19 Ballad Of A Teenage Queen *[w/ Johnny Cash & The Everly Brothers]*	*Jack Clement*	Mercury 872420
3/25/89	❶[1]	21	20 I Don't Want To Spoil The Party	*John Lennon/Paul McCartney*	Columbia 68599
11/4/89	37	11	21 Black And White	*Paul Smith*	Columbia 73054
3/3/90	63	6	22 One Step Over The Line *[w/ Nitty Gritty Dirt Band & John Hiatt]*	*John Hiatt*	Universal
			from The Nitty Gritty Dirt Band's album *Will The Circle Be Unbroken Volume II* on Universal 12500		
9/29/90	39	11	23 What We Really Want	*Rosanne Cash*	Columbia
2/23/91	69	1	24 On The Surface	*Rosanne Cash/Jimmy Tittle*	Columbia
			above 2 from the album *Interiors* on Columbia 46079		

CASH, Tommy — All-Time: #282

Born on 4/5/1940 in Dyess, Arkansas. Male singer/songwriter/guitarist. Younger brother of **Johnny Cash**.

Debut	Peak	Wks	Country Chart Hit	Songwriter	Label (& Number)
8/31/68	41	9	1 The Sounds Of Goodbye	*Dick Heard/Eddie Rabbitt*	United Artists 50337
6/21/69	43	11	2 Your Lovin' Takes The Leavin' Out Of Me	*Eddie Rabbitt*	Epic 10469
11/22/69+	4	16	3 Six White Horses	*Larry Murray*	Epic 10540
3/28/70	9	14	4 Rise And Shine	*Carl Perkins*	Epic 10590
7/18/70	9	13	5 One Song Away	*Don Reid*	Epic 10630
11/21/70	36	9	6 The Tears On Lincoln's Face	*Hugh X. Lewis/Glenn Sutton*	Epic 10673
3/13/71	20	11	7 So This Is Love	*Lew DeWitt/Don Reid*	Epic 10700
7/10/71	28	10	8 I'm Gonna Write A Song	*Glenn Sutton*	Epic 10756
12/4/71	67	2	9 Roll Truck Roll	*Tommy Collins*	Epic 10795
3/25/72	32	11	10 You're Everything	*Billy Sherrill/Glenn Sutton*	Epic 10838
7/15/72	22	11	11 That Certain One	*Don Reid*	Epic 10885
10/28/72	24	11	12 Listen	*Tommy Cash/Jimmy Peppers*	Epic 10915
3/24/73	37	10	13 Workin' On A Feelin'	*Red Lane/Tom McKeon/Royce Porter*	Epic 10964
7/28/73	16	13	14 I Recall A Gypsy Woman	*Bob McDill/Allen Reynolds*	Epic 11026
11/24/73+	21	13	15 She Met A Stranger, I Met A Train	*Danny Morrison/Johnny Slate*	Epic 11057
3/22/75	58	9	16 The One I Sing My Love Songs To	*Wayland Holyfield*	Elektra 45241
1/10/76	94	4	17 Broken Bones	*Porter Jordan/Jerry Styner*	20th Century 2263
7/16/77	63	6	18 The Cowboy And The Lady	*Peggy Russell*	Monument 45222
2/11/78	98	3	19 Take My Love To Rita	*Tom Mayberry/Mack Vickery*	Monument 45238

CASHMAN & WEST

Duo of singer/songwriters Dennis "Terry Cashman" Minogue and Thomas "Tommy West" Picardo.

Debut	Peak	Wks	Country Chart Hit	Songwriter	Label (& Number)
2/10/73	69	2	Songman	*Terry Cashman/Tommy West*	Dunhill/ABC 4333

CASSADY, Linda

Born on 7/10/1957 in Sacramento, California. Female singer/songwriter.

Debut	Peak	Wks	Country Chart Hit	Songwriter	Label (& Number)
5/22/76	83	8	1 C.B. Widow	*Linda Cassady*	Cin Kay 107
9/11/76	91	4	2 If It's Your Song You Sing It	*Linda Cassady*	Cin Kay 111
1/29/77	79	6	3 Little Things Mean A Lot	*Edith Lindeman/Carl Stutz*	Cin Kay 115
4/9/77	92	4	4 I Don't Hurt Anymore	*Don Robertson/Jack Rollins*	Cin Kay 116

DEBUT	PEAK	WKS	GOLD	ARTIST / Ranking / Country Chart Hit / Songwriter	Label (& Number)
				CASSADY, Linda — cont'd	
2/4/78	91	3		5 **Little Teardrops** (Are Smarter Than You Think) ... *Aaron Allan*	Cin Kay 127
4/29/78	87	4		6 (There's Nothing Like The Love) **Between A Woman And A Man** *[w/ Bobby Spears]* ...*Danny Hice/Ruby Hice*	Cin Kay 129
8/5/78	76	6		7 **Lonely Side Of The Bed** ... *Jimmy Anthony/Linda Cassady*	Cin Kay 047
				CATES SISTERS, The	
				Duo of from Independence, Missouri: sisters Margie Cates and Marcy Cates.	
9/11/76	82	5		1 **Mr. Guitar** ... *Joe Hunter/Roger LeBlanc*	Caprice 2024
1/29/77	50	8		2 **Out Of My Mind** *[The Cates]* ... *Joe Hunter/Roger LeBlanc*	Caprice 2030
5/21/77	74	6		3 **Can't Help It** ... *Joe Hunter/Roger LeBlanc*	Caprice 2032
8/13/77	87	5		4 **Throw Out Your Loveline** ... *Joe Hunter/Roger LeBlanc*	Caprice 2038
10/1/77	30	11		5 **I'll Always Love You** ... *Bobby Lee*	Caprice 2036
12/24/77+	29	11		6 **I've Been Loved** *Barbara Lewis*	Caprice 2041
3/18/78	61	7		7 **Long Gone Blues** ... *Dave Hanner*	Caprice 2047
9/2/78	39	8		8 **Lovin' You Off My Mind** ... *Don Lewis*	Caprice 2051
				THE CATES:	
2/17/79	78	5		9 **Going Down Slow** ... *Bobby Bond*	Ovation 1123
6/30/79	57	8		10 **Make Love To Me** ... *George Brunies/Allan Copeland/Paul Mares/Walt Melrose/ Bill Norvas/Ben Pollack/Leon Roppolo/Mel Stitzel*	Ovation 1126
12/22/79+	68	7		11 **Let's Go Through The Motions** ... *Dave Gillon*	Ovation 1134
5/24/80	72	5		12 **Gonna Get Along Without You Now** ... *Milton Kellem*	Ovation 1144
10/25/80	75	4		13 **Lightnin' Strikin'** ... *Buddy Wayne*	Ovation 1155
				CATO, Connie	
				Born Connie Ann Cato on 3/30/1955 in Carlinville, Illinois. Female singer.	
2/2/74	33	16		1 **Superskirt** ... *Ron Hellard/Gary S. Paxton*	Capitol 3788
7/13/74	73	7		2 **Super Kitten** ... *Gene Crysler*	Capitol 3908
10/19/74	92	6		3 **Lincoln Autry** ... *Bill Anthony/Bob Morrison*	Capitol 3958
3/8/75	14	14		4 **Hurt** *Jimmie Crane/Al Jacobs*	Capitol 4035
7/26/75	83	6		5 **Yes** ... *Terry Woodford/Barbara Wyrick*	Capitol 4113
11/22/75+	53	10		6 **Who Wants A Slightly Used Woman** ... *Thomas Boyce/Mel Powers*	Capitol 4169
4/24/76	91	4		7 **I Love A Beautiful Guy** ... *Jack Lebsock*	Capitol 4243
8/7/76	80	5		8 **Here Comes That Rainy Day Feeling Again** ... *Roger Cook/Roger Greenaway/Tony MacAulay*	Capitol 4303
11/6/76	76	6		9 **I'm Sorry** ... *Dub Allbritten/Ronnie Self*	Capitol 4345
2/19/77	92	3		10 **Don't You Ever Get Tired** (Of Hurting Me) ... *Hank Cochran*	Capitol 4379
8/16/80	49	7		11 **You Better Hurry Home** (Somethin's Burnin') ... *Terry Henry/Glenn Martin*	MCA 41287
				CAUDELL, Lane	
				Born on 4/25/1952 in Asheboro, North Carolina. Male singer/songwriter/actor. Played "Woody King" on TV's *Days Of Our Lives.*	
9/19/87	66	5		1 **Souvenirs** ... *Bruce Burch/Lane Caudell*	16th Avenue 70403
4/16/88	77	5		2 **I Need A Good Woman Bad** ... *Tom Brasfield/Earl Thomas Conley*	16th Avenue 70411
				C COMPANY Featuring TERRY NELSON	
				Group of studio musicians led by DJ/singer Terry Nelson from Russellville, Alabama.	
5/1/71	49	3	●	**Battle Hymn Of Lt. Calley** ... *James Smith/Julian Wilson* [S]	Plantation 73
				CEDAR CREEK	
				Group formed in Nashville, Tennessee: Dave Holcraft, Ken Harden, Don Edmunds and Ron Spearman (vocals), Sam Stricklan (guitar), Garland Craft (keyboards), Tony Perkins (bass) and Chris Golden (drums). Golden is the son of **William Lee Golden** and a member of **The Goldens**.	
11/14/81	80	4		1 **Looks Like A Set-Up To Me** ... *Alan Rhody*	Moon Shine 3001
2/6/82	42	10		2 **Took It Like A Man, Cried Like A Baby** ... *Charlie Black/Rory Bourke/Tommy Rocco*	Moon Shine 3003
1/22/83	83	3		3 **Take A Ride On A Riverboat** ... *Jeff Pollard*	Moon Shine 3008
8/6/83	81	3		4 **Lonely Heart** ... *Paul Overstreet*	Moon Shine 3013
				CERRITO	
				Born William Lanzi in New Jersey. Male singer.	
4/22/89	84	3		1 **Daydream** ... *John Sebastian*	Soundwaves 4818
9/23/89	79	3		2 **Bad Moon Rising** ... *John Fogerty*	Soundwaves 4826
				CHAIN, Michael	
				Born on 7/5/1955 in San Fernando, California. Male singer/songwriter.	
3/18/00	67	1		**Let's Go Chase Some Women** ... *Michael Chain* from the album *Let's Go Chase Some Women* on Hard Ten 1062	Hard Ten
				CHAMBERLAIN, David	
				Born on 12/23/1944 in Fort Worth, Texas. Male singer/songwriter.	
1/30/88	72	4		**I Owe, I Owe** (It's Off To Work I Go) ... *David Chamberlain/Mark Sherrill*	Country Int'l. 214
				CHAMBERS, Carl	
				Born on 12/17/1946 in Lakeland, Florida. Male singer/songwriter/guitarist.	
2/28/81	91	2		**Take Me Home With You** ... *Carl Chambers/Nancy Chambers*	Prairie Dust 8001
				CHANCE	
				Group from Texas: brothers Jeff Barosh (vocals, steel guitar) and Mick Barosh (drums), with John Buckley (guitar), Jon Mulligan (keyboards) and Billy Hafer (bass). Jeff Barosh began solo career in 1988 as **Jeff Chance**.	
4/20/85	35	13		1 **To Be Lovers** ... *Buzz Arledge/Carson Whitsett*	Mercury 880555
7/27/85	45	11		2 **You Could Be The One Woman** ... *Jim Bacon/Ed Tree*	Mercury 880959

DEBUT	PEAK	WKS	GOLD	ARTIST / Ranking Country Chart Hit	Songwriter	Label (& Number)
				CHANCE — cont'd		
10/26/85	**30**	15		3 **She Told Me Yes**	A:26 / S:30 *Rob Crosby*	Mercury 884178
3/29/86	**53**	7		4 **I Need Some Good News Bad**	*Buzz Arledge/Carson Whitsett*	Mercury 884545
8/30/86	**60**	10		5 **What Did You Do With My Heart**	*Jim Calhoun*	Mercury 884918
				CHANCE, Jeff		
				Born Jeff Barosh in El Campo, Texas. Male singer/steel guitarist. Member of **Chance**.		
3/19/88	**64**	7		1 **So Far Not So Good /**	*Edwin Rowell*	
6/18/88	**52**	7		2 **Hopelessly Falling**	*Edwin Rowell*	Curb 10506
11/26/88+	**57**	9		3 **Let It Burn**	*Tony Haselden/Tim Mensy*	Curb 10516
				CHANEY, Hank		
				Born in Florida. Male singer.		
8/16/86	**98**	1		**Be-Bop-A-Lula "86"**	*Tex Davis/Gene Vincent*	CMI 04
				CHANTILLY		
				Female group: Kim Williams (lead vocals), Debbie Pierce and P.J. Allman. Pierce, daughter of **Webb Pierce**, was later replaced by Joci Stevens.		
5/1/82	**81**	4		1 **Whatever Turns You On**	*Jerry Fuller*	Jaroco 31082
6/26/82	**43**	10		2 **Stumblin' In**	*Mike Chapman/Nicky Chinn*	Jaroco 51282
				CHANTILLY (Featuring Kim Williams) (above 2)		
10/9/82	**65**	6		3 **Right Back Loving You Again**	*Lewis Anderson/Casey Kelly*	F&L 519
12/25/82+	**75**	6		4 **Better Off Blue**	*Allan Chapman/Jimmy Prichett*	F&L 520
2/12/83	**60**	7		5 **Storm Of Love**	*Buzz Cason/Todd Cerney*	F&L 523
9/17/83	**60**	7		6 **Have I Got A Heart For You**	*Marvin Morrow/Keith Stegall*	F&L 527
2/11/84	**72**	4		7 **Baby's Walkin'**	*Kye Fleming/Dennis W. Morgan/Charles Quillen*	F&L 534
				CHAPARRAL BROTHERS		
				Duo of brothers John Chaparral and Paul Chaparral.		
5/11/68	**65**	4		1 **Standing In The Rain**	*Don Ducon*	Capitol 2153
2/14/70	**70**	2		2 **Running From A Memory**	*Chris Roberts/Scott Turner*	Capitol 2708
				CHAPARRO, Tammy		
				Born in 1967 in Billings, Montana. Female singer.		
5/7/83	**89**	3		**Stay With Me**	*Donny Cummings/Chuck Deal*	Compass 60
				CHAPMAN, Cee Cee		
				Born Melissa Carol Chapman on 12/13/1958 in Portsmouth, Virginia. Female singer/guitarist. Santa Fe is her backing band.		
11/26/88	**60**	8		1 **Gone But Not Forgotten** *[w/ Santa Fe]*	*Charlie Black/Bobby Fischer/Austin Roberts*	Curb 10518
4/8/89	**51**	10		2 **Frontier Justice**	*Charlie Black/Bobby Fischer/Austin Roberts*	Curb 10529
8/5/89	**49**	7		3 **Twist Of Fate**	*Charlie Black/Bobby Fischer/Austin Roberts*	Curb 10547
11/4/89	**64**	4		4 **Love Is A Liar**	*Charlie Black/Bobby Fischer/Austin Roberts*	Curb 10529
1/2/93	**64**	6		5 **Two Ships That Passed In The Moonlight**	*Hugh Prestwood*	Curb/Capitol
				from the album *Cee Cee Chapman* on Curb/Capitol 94373		
				CHAPMAN, Donovan		
				Born in 1975 in Farmerville, Louisiana (white father; Hawaiian mother). Male singer/songwriter/guitarist. Decorated member of the pararescue team of the U.S. Air Force.		
11/29/03	**58**	1		1 **There Is No War**	*Donovan Chapman*	Curb
3/6/04	**56**	1		2 **Hey Hollywood**	*Franklin Highland/Aaron Sain*	Curb
				CHAPMAN, Gary		
				Born on 8/19/1957 in Waurika, Oklahoma; raised in DeLeon, Texas. Male singer/songwriter. Married to singer Amy Grant from 1982-99. Hosted TNN's *Prime Time Country* from 1996-99.		
1/9/88	**60**	6		1 **When We're Together**	*Gary Chapman/Amy Sky/Mark Wright*	RCA 5285
4/16/88	**76**	4		2 **Everyday Man**	*Gary Chapman/Jerry McPherson*	RCA 7601
				CHAPMAN, Marshall		
				Born on 1/7/1949 in Spartanburg, South Carolina. Male singer/songwriter/guitarist.		
3/5/77	**100**	2		**Somewhere South Of Macon**	*Marshall Chapman/Jim Rushing*	Epic 50307
				CHARLENE		
				Born Charlene D'Angelo on 6/1/1950 in Hollywood, California. Female singer.		
4/10/82	**60**	8		**I've Never Been To Me**	*Ken Hirsch/Ron Miller*	Motown 1611
				CHARLES, Kim		
				Born in Chicago, Illinois. Male singer.		
2/10/79	**35**	9		**Want To Thank You**	*Rory Bourke*	MCA 40987
				CHARLES, Ray		
				Born Ray Charles Robinson on 9/23/1930 in Albany, Georgia; raised in Greenville, Florida. Died of liver disease on 6/10/2004 (age 73). Black singer/pianist. Partially blind at age five, completely blind at seven (glaucoma). Studied classical piano and clarinet at State School for Deaf and Blind Children, St. Augustine, Florida, 1937-45. Formed own band in 1954. Inducted into the Rock and Roll Hall of Fame in 1986. Won Grammy's Lifetime Achievement Award in 1987. Legendary performer, with many TV and movie appearances. Also see **USA For Africa**.		
11/22/80	**55**	10		1 **Beers To You** *[w/ Clint Eastwood]*	*Steve Dorff/John Durrill/Snuff Garrett/Sandy Pinkard*	Warner 49608
				from the movie *Any Which Way You Can* starring Eastwood		
12/18/82+	**20**	18		2 **Born To Love Me**	*Bob Morrison*	Columbia 03429
4/23/83	**37**	11		3 **3/4 Time**	*Tony Joe White*	Columbia 03810
9/24/83	**82**	3		4 **Ain't Your Memory Got No Pride At All**	*Bucky Jones/Red Lane/Royce Porter*	Columbia 04083
12/17/83+	**6**	18		5 **We Didn't See A Thing** *[w/ George Jones & Chet Atkins]*	*Gary Gentry*	Columbia 04297

DEBUT	PEAK	WKS	GOLD	ARTIST / Country Chart Hit	Ranking / Songwriter	Label (& Number)
				CHARLES, Ray — cont'd		
4/14/84	**50**	10		6 **Do I Ever Cross Your Mind**	*Billy Burnette/Michael Smotherman*	Columbia 04420
8/4/84	**14**	18		7 **Rock And Roll Shoes** ***[w/ B.J. Thomas]***	S:14 / A:21 *Paul Kennerley/Graham Lyle*	Columbia 04531
12/15/84+	**❶[1]**	27		8 **Seven Spanish Angels** ***[w/ Willie Nelson]***	S:❶[1] / A:❶[1] *Troy Seals/Eddie Setser*	Columbia 04715
5/4/85	**12**	17		9 **It Ain't Gonna Worry My Mind** ***[w/ Mickey Gilley]***	A:11 / S:12 *Richard Leigh*	Columbia 04860
8/31/85	**14**	17		10 **Two Old Cats Like Us** ***[w/ Hank Williams, Jr.]***	S:13 / A:17 *Troy Seals*	Columbia 05575
7/19/86	**34**	13		11 **The Pages Of My Mind**	*Byron Hill/J. Remington Wilde*	Columbia 06172
11/1/86	**66**	4		12 **Dixie Moon /**	*Troy Seals/Eddie Setser*	
1/31/87	**76**	3		13 **A Little Bit Of Heaven**	*Kent Robbins/Paul Williams*	Columbia 06370
				CHARLESTON EXPRESS with Jesse Wales		
				Group from Charleston, South Carolina: Jesse Wales (vocals, bass), Dennis Tee (guitar), Geoff Conine (guitar), Jim Bryan (steel guitar) and Tommy Smith (drums).		
12/15/84+	**69**	7		1 **Sweet Love, Don't Cry**	*Jimmy Fuller*	Soundwaves 4743
5/18/85	**82**	4		2 **Leaving**	*Jimmy Fuller*	Soundwaves 4749
				CHARNISSA		
				Born Charnissa Moore in Phoenix, Arizona. Female singer.		
5/8/76	**49**	8		**Gone At Last** ***[w/ Johnny Paycheck]***	*Paul Simon*	Epic 50215
				CHASE, Becky		
				Born in Wheaton, Illinois. Female singer.		
1/12/85	**77**	6		**Until The Music Is Gone**	*Mark James*	Spirit Horse 102
				CHASE, Carol		
				Born Carol Schulte in Stanley, North Dakota. Female singer.		
11/10/79+	**32**	13		1 **This Must Be My Ship**	*Scott Anders/Roger Murrah/Tina Murrah*	Casablanca 4501
12/15/79	**92**	4		2 **Can't Love On Lies** ***[w/ Jim West]***	*Jim West*	Macho 003
2/23/80	**48**	7		3 **Sexy Song**	*Milton Brown/Steve Dorff/Snuff Garrett*	Casablanca 4502
10/18/80	**87**	3		4 **Regrets**	*Barbara Wyrick*	Casablanca 2301
				CHASTAIN, Dawn		
				Born in Springfield, Illinois. Female singer. Former fashion model.		
4/15/78	**83**	4		1 **Never Knew (How Much I Loved You 'Til I Lost You)**	*Kelly Bach/Betty Jones*	Prairie Dust 7623
1/6/79	**72**	4		2 **Me Plus You Equals Love**	*Bobby Lee Springfield*	Oak 1018
5/5/79	**91**	2		3 **Love Talks**	*Curly Putman/Rafe Van Hoy*	SCR 164
9/8/79	**74**	4		4 **That's You, That's Me**	*Bobby Lee Springfield/Van Stephenson*	SCR 178
				CHER		
				Born Cherilyn Sarkisian on 5/20/1946 in El Centro, California. Adopted by stepfather at age 15 and last name changed to La Piere. Female singer/actress. Starred in several movies. In 1963 formed successful recording duo Sonny & Cher with Sonny Bono, her husband from 1963-75.		
7/14/79	**87**	2		**It's Too Late To Love Me Now**	*Rory Bourke/Gene Dobbins/Johnny Wilson*	Casablanca 987
				CHERRY, Don		
				Born on 1/11/1924 in Wichita Falls, Texas. Male singer.		
10/5/68	**71**	2		**Take A Message To Mary**	*Boudleaux Bryant/Felice Bryant*	Monument 1088

DEBUT	PEAK	WKS	GOLD	ARTIST / Country Chart Hit	Ranking / Songwriter	Label (& Number)
				CHESNEY, Kenny	**1990s: #44 / 2000s: #3 / All-Time: #66**	
				Born on 3/26/1968 in Knoxville, Tennessee; raised in Luttrell, Tennessee. Male singer/songwriter/guitarist. Attended East Tennessee State University. Moved to Nashville in 1990. Worked as a staff writer at Acuff-Rose prior to his recording contract. Married actress Renee Zellweger on 5/9/2005; marriage annulled on 9/16/2005. Also see **The Grigsby Twins**.		
				CMA: Entertainer 2004		
12/18/93+	**59**	8		1 **Whatever It Takes**	*Buddy Brock/Kenny Chesney/Kim Williams*	Capricorn
5/14/94	**70**	6		2 **The Tin Man**	*Kenny Chesney/David Lowe/Stacey Slate*	Capricorn
				also see #22 below; above 2 from the album *In My Wildest Dreams* on Capricorn 42023		
4/1/95	**6**	20		3 **Fall In Love**	S:14 *Buddy Brock/Kenny Chesney/Kim Williams*	BNA
7/29/95	**8**	20		4 **All I Need To Know**	*Steve Seskin/Mark Alan Springer*	BNA
11/11/95+	**23**	20		5 **Grandpa Told Me So**	*J.D. Hicks/Mark Alan Springer*	BNA
				above 3 from the album *All I Need To Know* on BNA 66562		
4/6/96	**41**	16		6 **Back In My Arms Again**	S:22 *Rory Bourke/Lewis Moore/Lee Roy Parnell*	BNA
7/20/96	**2[1]**	20		7 **Me And You**	S:7 *Skip Ewing/Ray Herndon*	BNA
12/21/96+	**2[2]**	21		8 **When I Close My Eyes**	*Nettie Musick/Mark Alan Springer*	BNA
				above 3 from the album *Me And You* on BNA 66908		
5/31/97	**❶[3]**	20		9 **She's Got It All**	S:8 *Craig Wiseman/Drew Womack*	BNA
10/11/97+	**11**	22		10 **A Chance**	*Dean Dillon/Royce Porter*	BNA
3/7/98	**2[1]**	25		11 **That's Why I'm Here**	S:10 *Shaye Smith/Mark Alan Springer*	BNA
8/15/98	**27**	20		12 **I Will Stand**	S:7 *Casey Beathard/Mark Germino*	BNA
				above 4 from the album *I Will Stand* on BNA 67498		
11/28/98	**64**	6		13 **Touchdown Tennessee**	*Kenny Chesney/Dean Dillon*	BNA
12/12/98+	**❶[6]**	37		14 **How Forever Feels**	S:❶[2] *Wendell Mabley/Tony Mullins*	BNA
2/13/99	**72**	1		15 **Team Of Destiny**	*Kenny Chesney/Dean Dillon*	BNA
4/17/99	**❶[1]**	32		16 **You Had Me From Hello**	*Kenny Chesney/Skip Ewing*	BNA
6/26/99+	**11**	21		17 **She Thinks My Tractor's Sexy**	*Jim Collins/Paul Overstreet*	BNA

DEBUT	PEAK	WKS	GOLD	#	ARTIST / Country Chart Hit	Songwriter	Label (& Number)
					CHESNEY, Kenny — cont'd		
1/8/00	67	1		18	Away In A Manger	*John McFarland/James Murray* [X]	RCA
					from the various artists album *Country Christmas Classics* on RCA 67698		
1/22/00	8	25		19	What I Need To Do	*Tom Damphier/Bill Luther*	BNA
					#14, 16, 17 & 19: from the album *Everywhere We Go* on BNA 67655		
8/19/00	3[1]	25		20	I Lost It	*Jimmy Olander/Neil Thrasher*	BNA
					Pam Tillis (backing vocal)		
1/20/01	❶[1]	30		21	Don't Happen Twice	*Curtis Lance/Thom McHugh*	BNA
7/28/01	19	20		22	The Tin Man	*Kenny Chesney/David Lowe/Stacey Slate* [R]	BNA
					new version of #2 above; above 3 from the album *Greatest Hits* on BNA 67976		
12/29/01+	2[2]	25		23	Young	*Steve McEwan/Naoise Sheridan/Craig Wiseman*	BNA
5/4/02	❶[7]	31		24	The Good Stuff	*Jim Collins/Craig Wiseman*	BNA
5/11/02	60	1		25	Live Those Songs	*Chris Bain/Cole Degges/David Lowe*	BNA
6/29/02+	6	25		26	A Lot Of Things Different	*Bill Anderson/Dean Dillon*	BNA
1/18/03	2[2]	23		27	Big Star	*Stephony Smith*	BNA
5/24/03	2[5]	23		28	No Shoes, No Shirt, No Problems	*Casey Beathard*	BNA
					#23-28: from the album *No Shoes, No Shirt, No Problems* on BNA 67038		
10/25/03	❶[7]	20		29	There Goes My Life	*Wendell Mobley/Neil Thrasher*	BNA
					from the album *When The Sun Goes Down* on BNA 55801		
12/13/03+	30	5		30	All I Want For Christmas Is A Real Good Tan	*Paul Overstreet* [X]	BNA
12/20/03	60	1		31	I'll Be Home For Christmas	*Kim Gannon/Walter Kent/Buck Ram* [X]	BNA
12/27/03+	49	3		32	Jingle Bells	*James Pierpont* [X]	BNA
1/10/04	45	1		33	Pretty Paper *[w/ Willie Nelson]*	*Willie Nelson* [X]	BNA
1/10/04	54	1		34	Silver Bells	*Ray Evans/Jay Livingston* [X]	BNA
1/10/04	57	1		35	Silent Night *[w/ The Grigsby Twins]*	*Franz Gruber/Josef Mohr* [X]	BNA
1/10/04	60	1		36	Thank God For Kids	*Eddy Raven* [X]	BNA
					#30-36: from the album *All I Want For Christmas Is A Real Good Tan* on BNA 51808		
2/7/04	❶[5]	22		37	When The Sun Goes Down *[w/ Uncle Kracker]*	*Brett James*	BNA
5/1/04	2[7]	22		38	I Go Back	*Kenny Chesney*	BNA
5/29/04	8	20		39	Hey Good Lookin' *[w/ Jimmy Buffett/Clint Black/Alan Jackson/Toby Keith/George Strait]*		
					from Buffett's album *License To Chill* on RCA 62270	*Hank Williams*	RCA
9/4/04	2[1]	21		40	The Woman With You	*David Frasier/Craig Wiseman*	BNA
1/1/05	❶[2]	24		41	Anything But Mine	*Scooter Carusoe*	BNA
2/5/05	53	2		42	Guitars And Tiki Bars	*Kenny Chesney/Dean Dillon/Michael Tamburino*	BNA
					from the album *Be As You Are: Songs From An Old Blue Chair* on BNA 61530		
5/7/05	6	20		43	Keg In The Closet	*Kenny Chesney/Brett James*	BNA
					#37, 38, 40, 41 & 43: from the album *When The Sun Goes Down* on BNA 58801		

CHESNUT, Jim

Born on 12/1/1944 in Midland, Texas. Male singer/songwriter/pianist.

DEBUT	PEAK	WKS	GOLD	#	Country Chart Hit	Songwriter	Label (& Number)
7/23/77	99	1		1	Let Me Love You Now	*Jim Chesnut*	ABC/Hickory 54013
12/10/77+	76	8		2	The Wrong Side Of The Rainbow	*Whitey Shafer*	ABC/Hickory 54021
4/15/78	76	6		3	The Ninth Of September	*Steve Collom*	ABC/Hickory 54027
8/5/78	56	9		4	Show Me A Sign	*Jim Chesnut*	ABC/Hickory 54033
11/18/78	57	7		5	Get Back To Loving Me	*Steve Collom*	ABC/Hickory 54038
6/2/79	80	3		6	Just Let Me Make Believe	*Ronald Blackwell*	MCA 41015
9/15/79	27	11		7	Let's Take The Time To Fall In Love Again	*Jim Chesnut*	MCA 41106
9/13/80	46	9		8	Out Run The Sun	*Billy Burnette/Larry Henley*	United Artists 1372
6/6/81	36	10		9	Bedtime Stories	*Chester Lester/Danny Morrison*	Liberty 1405
10/24/81	70	4		10	The Rose Is For Today	*John Schweers*	Liberty 1434

CHESNUTT, Mark — 1990s: #11 / 2000s: #50 / All-Time: #82

Born on 9/6/1963 in Beaumont, Texas. Male singer/songwriter/guitarist. Son of regional Texas star Bob Chesnutt. Played drums in a rock band in the early 1980s. First recorded for the Axbar label in 1984.

CMA: Horizon 1993

DEBUT	PEAK	WKS	GOLD	#	Country Chart Hit	Songwriter	Label (& Number)
8/4/90	3[3]	20		1	Too Cold At Home	*Bobby Harden*	MCA
11/24/90+	❶[2]	20		2	Brother Jukebox	*Paul Craft*	MCA
3/30/91	5	20		3	Blame It On Texas	*Ronnie Rogers/Mark Wright*	MCA
7/13/91	3[2]	20		4	Your Love Is A Miracle	*Bill Kenner/Mark Wright*	MCA
10/26/91+	10	20		5	Broken Promise Land	*Bill Rice/Mary Sharon Rice*	MCA
					above 5 from the album *Too Cold At Home* on MCA 10032		
2/29/92	5	20		6	Old Flames Have New Names	*Bobby Braddock/Rafe Van Hoy*	MCA
6/13/92	❶[1]	20		7	I'll Think Of Something	*Jerry Foster/Bill Rice*	MCA
6/20/92	4	25		8	Bubba Shot The Jukebox	*Dennis Linde*	MCA
1/2/93	4	20		9	Old Country	*Bobby Harden*	MCA
					above 4 from the album *Longnecks & Short Stories* on MCA 10530		
5/22/93	❶[1]	20		10	It Sure Is Monday	*Dennis Linde*	MCA
9/4/93	❶[1]	20		11	Almost Goodbye	*Billy Livsey/Don Schlitz*	MCA
12/11/93+	❶[1]	20		12	I Just Wanted You To Know	*Gary Harrison/Tim Mensy*	MCA

DEBUT	PEAK	WKS	GOLD	#	ARTIST / Country Chart Hit	Ranking / Songwriter	Label (& Number)
					CHESNUTT, Mark — cont'd		
4/2/94	**21**	20		13	**Woman, Sensuous Woman**	*Gary S. Paxton*	MCA
					above 4 from the album *Almost Goodbye* on MCA 10851		
7/23/94	**6**	20		14	**She Dreams**	*Gary Harrison/Tim Mensy*	Decca
10/29/94+	**2**^{2}	20		15	**Goin' Through The Big D**	*Ronnie Rogers/Jon Wright/Mark Wright*	Decca
2/25/95	❶^{1}	20		16	**Gonna Get A Life**	*Frank Dycus/Jim Lauderdale*	Decca
6/17/95	**23**	17		17	**Down In Tennessee**	*Wayland Holyfield*	Decca
					above 4 from the album *What A Way To Live* on Decca 11094		
9/23/95	**18**	20		18	**Trouble**	*Todd Snider*	Decca
12/30/95+	**7**	20		19	**It Wouldn't Hurt To Have Wings**	*Jerry Foster/Roger Lavoie/Johnny Morris*	Decca
5/4/96	**37**	20		20	**Wrong Place, Wrong Time**	*Scott Miller/Jimmy Stewart*	Decca
					above 3 from the album *Wings* on Decca 11261		
10/5/96+	❶^{2}	23		21	**It's A Little Too Late**	*Mark Chesnutt/Slugger Morrissette/Roger Springer*	Decca
1/4/97	**75**	1		22	**What Child Is This**	*(traditional)* **[X]**	MCA
					from the various artists album *A Country Christmas* on MCA 9720		
3/15/97	**8**	20		23	**Let It Rain**	S:16 *Mark Chesnutt/Steve Leslie/Roger Springer*	Decca
					#21 & 23: from the album *Greatest Hits* on Decca 11529		
8/2/97	**2**^{1}	21		24	**Thank God For Believers**	S:16 *Tim Johnson/Mark Alan Springer/Roger Springer*	Decca
12/13/97+	**34**	13		25	**It's Not Over** ***[w/ Vince Gill & Alison Krauss]***	*Larry Kingston/Mark Wright*	Decca
3/14/98	**18**	20		26	**I Might Even Quit Lovin' You**	*Mark Chesnutt/Slugger Morrissette/Roger Springer*	Decca
9/26/98	**45**	9		27	**Wherever You Are**	*Tony Martin/Roger Springer/Reese Wilson*	Decca
					above 4 from the album *Thank God For Believers* on Decca 70006		
11/21/98+	❶^{2}	25		28	**I Don't Want To Miss A Thing**	S:❶^{8} *Diane Warren*	Decca
					from the movie *Armageddon* starring Bruce Willis		
4/24/99	**17**	21		29	**This Heartache Never Sleeps**	*Daryl Burgess/Tim Johnson*	Decca
					above 2 from the album *I Don't Want To Miss A Thing* on Decca 70035		
4/22/00	**52**	10		30	**Fallin' Never Felt So Good**	*Shawn Camp/Will Smith*	MCA Nashville
9/30/00	**59**	8		31	**Lost In The Feeling**	*Lewis Anderson*	MCA Nashville
					above 2 from the album *Lost In The Feeling* on MCA Nashville 170125		
3/24/01	**21**	20		32	**A Good Way To Get On My Bad Side** ***[w/ Tracy Byrd]***	*Rivers Rutherford/George Teren*	RCA
					from Byrd's album *Ten Rounds* on RCA 67009		
2/9/02	**11**	33		33	**She Was**	*Neal Coty/Jimmy Melton*	Columbia
10/26/02	**47**	10		34	**I Want My Baby Back**	*Tony Martin/Mark Nesler/Tom Shapiro*	Columbia
2/15/03	**48**	10		35	**I'm In Love With A Married Woman**	*Marc Beeson/Tim Johnson*	Columbia
					above 3 from the album *Mark Chesnutt* on Columbia 86540		
7/17/04	**36**	14		36	**The Lord Loves The Drinkin' Man**	*Kevin Fowler*	Vivaton!
10/30/04+	**33**	20		37	**I'm A Saint**	*Tony Martin/Jimmy Richey/Jason Sellers*	Vivaton!
5/14/05	**59**	2		38	**A Hard Secret To Keep**	*Jim McBride/Jerry Salley*	Vivaton!
					above 3 from the album *Savin' The Honky Tonk* on Vivaton! 01		
					CHEVALIER, Jay, And Shelley Ford		
					Vocal duo. Jay Chevalier was born on 3/4/1936 in Forest Hill, Louisiana. Shelley Ford was born in New Orleans, Louisiana. Couple later married.		
3/17/79	**90**	2			**Disco Blues**	*Jay Chevalier*	Creole Gold 1114
					CHICK AND HIS HOT RODS — see RENO & SMILEY		
					CHILDRESS, Lisa		
					Born in Boliver, Missouri. Female singer.		
4/26/86	**51**	8		1	**This Time It's You**	*Bobby Reed*	A.M.I. 1941
1/17/87	**55**	6		2	**It's Goodbye And So-Long To You**	*Harold Breau/Raymond Couture*	A.M.I. 1947
5/7/88	**63**	6		3	(I Wanna Hear You) **Say You Love Me Again**	*Bobby Reed*	True 89
8/20/88	**73**	3		4	**You Didn't Have To Jump The Fence**	*Bobby Reed*	True 91
1/21/89	**65**	5		5	(Here Comes) **That Old Familiar Feeling**	*Bobby Reed*	True 95
7/15/89	**83**	3		6	**Maybe There**	*Bobby Reed*	True 97
					CHILDS, Andy		
					Born on 12/7/1962 in Memphis, Tennessee. Male singer/guitarist. Member of **Sixwire**.		
7/3/93	**73**	2		1	**I Wouldn't Know**	*Marc Beeson/Robert Byrne/Mike McGuire*	RCA
10/2/93	**62**	6		2	**Broken**	*Thom Schuyler*	RCA
4/2/94	**61**	5		3	**Simple Life**	*Mac McAnally*	RCA
					above 3 from the album *Andy Childs* on RCA 66253		
					CHINNOCK, Billy		
					Born in New Jersey. Male singer/songwriter/guitarist.		
1/19/85	**91**	3			**The Way She Makes Love**	*Billy Chinnock*	Paradise 630
					CHIPMUNKS, The		
					Characters created by Ross Bagdasarian ("David Seville") who named Alvin, Simon and Theodore after Liberty executives Alvin Bennett, Simon Waronker and Theodore Keep. The Chipmunks starred in own prime-time animated TV show in the early 1960s and a Saturday morning cartoon series in the mid-1980s. Bagdasarian died on 1/16/1972 (age 52). His son, Ross Jr., resurrected the act in 1980.		
10/31/92	**71**	1			**Achy Breaky Heart**	*Don Von Tress* **[N]**	Epic
					Billy Ray Cyrus (guest vocal); from the album *Chipmunks In Low Places* on Epic 53006		
					CHOATES, Harry		
					Born on 12/26/1922 in Rayne, Louisiana; raised in Port Arthur, Texas. Died on 7/17/1951 while in jail (age 28) in Austin, Texas. Male singer/fiddler. Record label misspelled last name as Coates.		
1/4/47	**4**	2			**Jole Blon** ***[Harry Coates]***	*Roy Acuff*	Modern Mountain 511

DEBUT	PEAK	WKS	GOLD	ARTIST / Ranking / Country Chart Hit ... Songwriter	Label (& Number)
				CHRIS & LENNY	
				Female-male vocal duo: Chris Thompson and Lenny Grasso.	
8/5/89	**93**	2		**When Daddy Did The Driving** ... *Chris Thompson*	Happy Man 821
				CHRISTINE, Anne	
				Born Anne Christine Poux on 12/17/1933 in Meadville, Pennsylvania. Female singer/songwriter.	
7/17/71	**69**	5		**Summer Man** ... *Anne Christine*	CME 4634
				CHURCH, Claudia	
				Born in 1962 in Lenoir, North Carolina. Female singer/songwriter. Married **Rodney Crowell** in 1997.	
1/16/99	**41**	20		1 **What's The Matter With You Baby** ... S:19 *Beth Nielsen Chapman/Annie Roboff*	Reprise
6/26/99	**63**	3		2 **Home In My Heart (North Carolina)** ... *Claudia Church/Rodney Crowell*	Reprise
				CLANTON, Darrell	
				Born in Indianapolis, Indiana. Male singer/guitarist/banjo player.	
10/15/83+	**24**	19		1 **Lonesome 7-7203** ... *Justin Tubb*	Audiograph 474
3/31/84	**75**	6		2 **I'll Take As Much Of You As I Can Get** ... *Chuck Howard*	Audiograph 479
1/19/85	**56**	9		3 **I Forgot That I Don't Live Here Anymore** ... *Michael Garvin/Tom Shapiro/Chris Waters*	Warner 29185
				CLAPTON, Eric	
				Born Eric Patrick Clapp on 3/30/1945 in Ripley, England. Male rock singer/songwriter/guitarist. Nicknamed "Slowhand." Inducted into the Rock and Roll Hall of Fame in 2000.	
3/18/78	**26**	9	●	1 **Lay Down Sally** ... *Eric Clapton/Marcy Levy/George Terry*	RSO 886
10/21/78	**82**	7		2 **Promises** ... *Richard Feldman/Roger Linn*	RSO 910
				CLARK, Guy	
				Born on 11/6/1941 in Monahans, Texas; raised in Rockport, Texas. Male singer/songwriter/guitarist.	
1/6/79	**96**	2		1 **Fools For Each Other** ... *Guy Clark*	Warner 8714
7/11/81	**38**	11		2 **The Partner Nobody Chose** ... *Guy Clark/Rodney Crowell*	Warner 49740
7/2/83	**42**	13		3 **Homegrown Tomatoes** ... *Guy Clark*	Warner 29595
				CLARK, Jameson	
				Born in 1972 in Starr, South Carolina. Male singer/songwriter/guitarist.	
9/8/01	**52**	9		1 **Don't Play Any Love Songs** ... *Jameson Clark/Don Poythress/Don Skaggs*	Capitol
9/28/02	**51**	4		2 **You Da Man** ... *Jameson Clark/Craig Wiseman*	Capitol
				from the album *Workin' On A Groove* on Capitol 32301	
				CLARK, Jay	
				Born in 1958 in Missouri; raised in Round Rock, Texas. Male singer/songwriter/guitarist.	
12/21/85	**73**	5		1 **Love Gone Bad** ... *Jay Clark*	Concorde 301
4/12/86	**75**	4		2 **Modern Day Cowboy** ... *Jay Clark*	Concorde 302
				CLARK, Lucky	
				Born in Dallas, Texas. Male singer.	
6/4/77	**99**	1		**Everytime Two Fools Collide** ... *Jan Dyer/Jeff Tweel*	Polydor 14393
				CLARK, Mickey	
				Born Michael Clark on 5/2/1940 in Louisville, Kentucky. Male singer/songwriter/guitarist.	
3/12/83	**74**	6		1 **She's Gone To L.A. Again** ... *Mickey Clark*	Monument 03519
2/14/87	**54**	9		2 **When I'm Over You (What You Gonna Do)** ... *Mark Germino/Chuck Keuning*	Evergreen 1051
9/26/87	**76**	4		3 **You Take The Leavin' Out Of Me** ... *Mickey Clark*	Evergreen 1058
				CLARK, Petula	
				Born on 11/15/1932 in Epsom, Surrey, England. Female pop singer/actress. Appeared in several British movies.	
2/6/82	**20**	14		**Natural Love** ... *Kim Espy/Phil Gernhard/Jeff Harrington/Jeff Pennig*	Scotti Brothers 02676

CLARK, Roy **1970s: #49 / All-Time: #116**

Born on 4/15/1933 in Meherrin, Virginia. Male singer/songwriter/guitarist/banjo player. Acted on TV's *The Beverly Hillbillies* as both "Cousin Roy" and "Big Mama Halsey." Co-hosted the TV series *Hee-Haw.*

CMA: Comedian 1970 / Entertainer 1973 / Instrumental Group (with Buck Trent) 1975 & 1976 / Musician 1977, 1978 & 1980 // OPRY: 1987

DEBUT	PEAK	WKS	GOLD	Country Chart Hit ... Songwriter	Label (& Number)
7/6/63	**10**	16		1 **Tips Of My Fingers** ... *Bill Anderson*	Capitol 4956
2/8/64	**31**	3		2 **Through The Eyes Of A Fool** ... *Bobby Bare/Charlie Williams*	Capitol 5099
3/20/65	**37**	10		3 **When The Wind Blows In Chicago** ... *Audie Murphy/Scott Turner*	Capitol 5350
8/3/68	**53**	8		4 **Do You Believe This Town** ... *Joe Nixon/Charlie Williams*	Dot 17117
1/18/69	**57**	6		5 **Love Is Just A State Of Mind** ... *Joe Allison/Red Lane*	Dot 17187
6/7/69	**9**	16		6 **Yesterday, When I Was Young** ... *Charles Aznavour/Herbert Kretzmer*	Dot 17246
9/27/69	**40**	7		7 **September Song** ... *Maxwell Anderson/Kurt Weill*	Dot 17299
12/6/69+	**21**	9		8 **Right Or Left At Oak Street** ... *Joe Nixon/Charlie Williams*	Dot 17324
1/24/70	**31**	9		9 **Then She's A Lover** ... *Bobby Russell*	Dot 17335
6/6/70	**5**	15		10 **I Never Picked Cotton** ... *Bobby George/Charlie Williams*	Dot 17349
9/26/70	**6**	14		11 **Thank God And Greyhound** ... *Larry Kingston/Ed Nix*	Dot 17355
3/27/71	**74**	2		12 **(Where Do I Begin) Love Story** ... *Francis Lai/Carl Sigman*	Dot 17370
				from the movie starring Ali MacGraw and Ryan O'Neal	
4/24/71	**45**	9		13 **A Simple Thing As Love** ... *John Hartford*	Dot 17368

DEBUT	PEAK	WKS	GOLD	ARTIST / Ranking / Country Chart Hit	Songwriter	Label (& Number)
				CLARK, Roy — cont'd		
8/14/71	**63**	4		14 **She Cried**	*Glenn Martin*	Dot 17386
10/30/71	**39**	9		15 **Magnificent Sanctuary Band**	*Dorsey Burnette*	Dot 17395
8/19/72	**9**	14		16 **The Lawrence Welk - Hee Haw Counter-Revolution Polka**	*Vaughn Horton* **[N]**	Dot 17426
2/17/73	**❶[1]**	16		17 **Come Live With Me**	*Boudleaux Bryant/Felice Bryant*	Dot 17449
7/7/73	**27**	11		18 **Riders In The Sky**	*Stan Jones* **[I]**	Dot 17458
10/27/73+	**2[1]**	16		19 **Somewhere Between Love And Tomorrow**	*Tom Lazaros/Bud Reneau*	Dot 17480
3/16/74	**4**	16		20 **Honeymoon Feelin'**	*Ron Hellard/Gary S. Paxton*	Dot 17498
8/17/74	**12**	17		21 **The Great Divide**	*Ron Hellard/Gary S. Paxton*	Dot 17518
12/21/74+	**64**	6		22 **Dear God**	*Len Chiriacka/Chris Gantry*	ABC/Dot 17530
3/29/75	**35**	10		23 **You're Gonna Love Yourself In The Morning**	*Donnie Fritts*	ABC/Dot 17545
8/9/75	**16**	14		24 **Heart To Heart**	*Dave Gillon*	ABC/Dot 17565
1/24/76	**2[2]**	16		25 **If I Had It To Do All Over Again**	*Bobby Lee Springfield*	ABC/Dot 17605
6/5/76	**21**	11		26 **Think Summer**	*Paul Evans/Paul Parnes*	ABC/Dot 17626
12/25/76+	**26**	11		27 **I Have A Dream, I Have A Dream /**	*Boudleaux Bryant/Felice Bryant*	
4/9/77	**80**	4		28 **Half A Love**	*Roy Clark/Red Lane*	ABC/Dot 17667
8/13/77	**40**	10		29 **We Can't Build A Fire In The Rain**	*Bud Reneau*	ABC/Dot 17712
2/11/78	**60**	6		30 **Must You Throw Dirt In My Face**	*Bill Anderson*	ABC 12328
6/3/78	**65**	6		31 **Where Have You Been All Of My Life**	*Wayland Holyfield*	ABC 12365
9/23/78	**89**	2		32 **The Happy Days /**	*Charles Aznavour/Bradford Craig*	
2/17/79	**34**	10		33 **Shoulder To Shoulder (Arm And Arm)**	*Bob Morrison/Jim Zerface*	ABC 12402
12/15/79+	**21**	13		34 **Chain Gang Of Love**	*Roger Bowling/Billy Edd Wheeler*	MCA 41153
4/12/80	**48**	7		35 **If There Were Only Time For Love**	*Wayne Moss*	MCA 41208
8/16/80	**73**	5		36 **For Love's Own Sake**	*Julie Didier/Casey Kelly*	MCA 41288
12/20/80+	**60**	8		37 **I Ain't Got Nobody**	*Roger Bowling/Larry Butler*	MCA 51031
4/4/81	**86**	2		38 **She Can't Give It Away**	*Curly Putman/Sonny Throckmorton*	MCA 51079
5/23/81	**63**	6		39 **Love Takes Two**	*Red Lane/Danny Morrison*	MCA 51111
9/26/81	**73**	4		40 **The Last Word In Jesus Is Us**	*Bob Morrison/Bill Zerface/Jim Zerface*	Songbird 51167
5/15/82	**54**	9		41 **Paradise Knife And Gun Club**	*Chick Rains*	Churchill 94002
9/11/82	**85**	3		42 **Tennessee Saturday Night**	*Billy Hughes*	Churchill 94007
10/30/82	**65**	7		43 **Here We Go Again**	*Don Lanier/Red Steagall*	Churchill 94011
2/19/83	**74**	5		44 **I'm A Booger /**	*J. Martin Johnson/Bucky Jones/Red Lane*	
2/19/83	**flip**	5		45 **A Way Without Words**	*Bucky Jones/Chris Water*	Churchill 94017
8/27/83	**55**	9		46 **Wildwood Flower**	*A.P. Carter* **[I]**	Churchill 94025
10/27/84	**48**	11		47 **Another Lonely Night With You**	*Casey Anderson/Roy Clark*	Churchill 52469
4/12/86	**56**	7		48 **Tobacco Road**	*John D. Loudermilk*	Silver Dollar 0001
8/30/86	**61**	7		49 **Juke Box Saturday Night /**	*Stewart Harris/John Rosasco*	
8/30/86	**flip**	7		50 **Night Life**	*Walt Breeland/Paul Buskirk/Willie Nelson*	Silver Dollar 0004
3/11/89	**73**	4		51 **What A Wonderful World**	*Bob Thiele/George Weiss*	Hallmark 0001
10/14/89	**68**	5		52 **But, She Loves Me**	*Jerry Fuller*	Hallmark 0004
				CLARK, Sanford		
				Born on 10/24/1935 in Tulsa, Oklahoma. Male singer/songwriter/guitarist.		
10/6/56	**14**	1		**The Fool**	A:14 *Naomi Ford*	Dot 15481
				CLARK, Steve		
				Born in Big Hill, Kentucky. Male singer/songwriter.		
3/10/84	**68**	5		**That It's All Over Feeling (All Over Again)**	*Steve Clark/Johnny MacRae*	Mercury 818058

CLARK, Terri **2000s: #37 / All-Time: #182**

Born Terri Sauson (Clark is her stepfather's last name) on 8/5/1968 in Montreal, Quebec, Canada; raised in Medicine Hat, Alberta, Canada. Female singer/songwriter/guitarist. Discovered while performing at Tootsie's Orchid Lounge in Nashville. Also see **Hope**.

OPRY: 2004

DEBUT	PEAK	WKS	GOLD	Ranking / Country Chart Hit	Songwriter	Label (& Number)
7/15/95	**3[1]**	20		1 **Better Things To Do**	S:11 *Terri Clark/Tom Shapiro/Chris Waters*	Mercury
10/28/95+	**3[2]**	20		2 **When Boy Meets Girl**	S:6 *Terri Clark/Tom Shapiro/Chris Waters*	Mercury
3/9/96	**8**	20		3 **If I Were You**	S:4 *Terri Clark*	Mercury
7/13/96	**34**	12		4 **Suddenly Single**	*Terri Clark/Tom Shapiro/Chris Waters*	Mercury
				above 4 from the album *Terri Clark* on Mercury 526991		
10/12/96	**5**	20		5 **Poor, Poor Pitiful Me**	S:6 *Warren Zevon*	Mercury
1/11/97	**10**	20		6 **Emotional Girl**	S:6 *Rick Bowles/Terri Clark/Chris Waters*	Mercury
5/17/97	**49**	10		7 **Just The Same**	S:23 *Terri Clark/Tom Shapiro/Chris Waters*	Mercury
				above 3 from the album *Just The Same* on Mercury 532879		
4/4/98	**2[2]**	26		8 **Now That I Found You**	S:9 *Paul Begaud/Vanessa Corish/J.D. Martin*	Mercury
8/29/98	**❶[3]**	26		9 **You're Easy On The Eyes**	*Terri Clark/Tom Shapiro/Chris Waters*	Mercury
2/6/99	**12**	20		10 **Everytime I Cry**	*Bob Regan/Karen Staley*	Mercury
5/29/99	**47**	10		11 **Unsung Hero**	*Tina Arena/Dean McTaggart/David Tyson*	Mercury
				above 4 from the album *How I Feel* on Mercury 558211		
7/22/00	**13**	25		12 **A Little Gasoline**	*Dean Miller/Tammy Rogers*	Mercury
2/10/01	**27**	20		13 **No Fear**	*Mary-Chapin Carpenter/Terri Clark*	Mercury

DEBUT	PEAK	WKS	GOLD	ARTIST / Ranking / Country Chart Hit	Songwriter	Label (& Number)
				CLARK, Terri — cont'd		
7/7/01	**41**	11		14 **Getting There**	*Gary Burr/Terri Clark*	Mercury
				above 3 from the album *Fearless* on Mercury 170157		
8/31/02+	**2^{1}**	34		15 **I Just Wanna Be Mad**	S:9 *Kelley Lovelace/Lee Miller*	Mercury
3/22/03	**30**	18		16 **Three Mississippi**	*Hillary Lindsey/Angelo Petraglia/Troy Verges*	Mercury
8/16/03+	**3^{1}**	30		17 **I Wanna Do It All**	*Rick Giles/Gilles Godard/Tim Nichols*	Mercury
				above 3 from the album *Pain To Kill* on Mercury 170325		
4/24/04	**❶[1]**	24		18 **Girls Lie Too**	*Connie Harrington/Kelley Lovelace/Tim Nichols*	Mercury
				from the album *Greatest Hits 1994-2004* on Mercury 001906		
11/20/04+	**26**	19		19 **The World Needs A Drink**	*Casey Beathard/Eric Church*	Mercury
				from the album *Life Goes On* on Mercury 002579		
				CLARK FAMILY EXPERIENCE, The		
				Bluegrass group from Rocky Mount, Virginia: brothers Alan Clark (guitar), Ashley Clark (fiddle), Austin Clark (dobro), Adam Clark (mandolin), Aaron Clark (bass) and Andrew Clark (drums).		
7/29/00	**18**	27		1 **Meanwhile Back At The Ranch**	S:5 *Gordon Kennedy/Wayne Kirkpatrick*	Curb
5/5/01	**34**	16		2 **Standin' Still**	*Robin Lee Bruce/Christine Dannemiller/Camille Harrison*	Curb
10/20/01	**51**	12		3 **To Quote Shakespeare**	*Greg Barnhill/Mary Lamar*	Curb
5/4/02	**44**	12		4 **Going Away**	*Ashley Clark*	Curb
				above 4 from the album *The Clark Family Experience* on Curb 77754		
				CLARKSON, Kelly		
				Born on 4/24/1982 in Burleson, Texas. Female pop singer. Winner of TV's first *American Idol* talent series.		
10/26/02	**58**	1	●	**A Moment Like This**	*Jorgen Elofsson/John Reid*	RCA
				from the various artists album *American Idol: Greatest Moments* on RCA 68141		
				CLAYPOOL, Philip		
				Born on 4/15/1958 in Memphis, Tennessee. Male singer/songwriter/guitarist.		
6/24/95	**71**	5		1 **Swinging On My Baby's Chain**	*Philip Claypool/Tom DeVoursney/David Steen*	Curb
9/2/95	**60**	8		2 **Feel Like Makin' Love**	*Paul Rodgers*	Curb
2/3/96	**73**	2		3 **The Strength Of A Woman**	*Philip Claypool*	Curb
6/15/96	**70**	7		4 **Circus Leaving Town**	*Philip Claypool*	Curb
				above 4 from the album *A Circus Leaving Town* on Curb 77755		
				CLEMENT, Jack — **SW: #88**		
				Born on 4/5/1932 in Memphis, Tennessee. Male singer/guitarist.		
6/24/78	**86**	4		1 **We Must Believe In Magic /**	*Bob McDill/Allen Reynolds*	
6/24/78	**flip**	4		2 **When I Dream**	*Sandy Theoret*	Elektra 45474
9/16/78	**84**	4		3 **All I Want To Do In Life**	*Allen Reynolds/Sandy Theoret*	Elektra 45518
				CLEMENTS, Boots		
				Born in Tiffin, Ohio; raised in San Diego, California. Male singer.		
4/19/86	**96**	1		**Sukiyaki "My First Lonely Night"**	*Buzz Cason/Rohusuke Ei/Tom Leslie/Hachidai Nakamura*	West 719
				#1 Pop hit for Kyu Sakamoto in 1963		
				CLEMENTS, Vassar		
				Born on 4/25/1928 in Kinard, Florida; raised in Kissimmee, Florida. Died of cancer on 8/16/2005 (age 77). Male singer/fiddler. Popular session musician.		
7/12/80	**70**	5		1 **There'll Be No Teardrops Tonight**	*Hank Williams*	Flying Fish 4004
4/9/88	**83**	2		2 **I Hear The South**	*R.C. Bannon/John Bettis*	Shikata 10102
				CLIFFORD, Buzz		
				Born Reese Francis Clifford III on 10/8/1942 in Berwyn, Illinois. Male pop singer.		
3/20/61	**28**	1		**Baby Sittin' Boogie**	*Johnny Parker* **[N]**	Columbia 41876
				CLINE, Patsy — **All-Time: #222 // HOF: 1973**		
				Born Virginia Patterson Hensley on 9/8/1932 in Gore, Virginia. Died in a plane crash on 3/5/1963 (age 30) near Camden, Tennessee (with **Cowboy Copas** and **Hawkshaw Hawkins**). Female singer. Jessica Lange portrayed Cline in the 1985 movie biography *Sweet Dreams.* Won Grammy's Lifetime Achievement Award in 1995.		
				OPRY: 1961		
3/2/57	**2^{2}**	19		1 **Walkin' After Midnight /**	J:2 / S:3 / A:3 *Alan Block/Don Hecht*	
6/10/57	**14**	1		2 **A Poor Man's Roses (Or A Rich Man's Gold)**	A:14 *Milton DeLugg/Bob Hilliard*	Decca 30221
4/3/61	**❶[2]**	39		3 **I Fall To Pieces**	*Hank Cochran/Harlan Howard*	Decca 31205
				Grammy: Hall of Fame / RS500; also see #17 and #19 below		
11/13/61+	**2^{2}**	21		4 **Crazy**	*Willie Nelson*	Decca 31317
				Grammy: Hall of Fame / RS500 / NRR		
3/3/62	**❶[5]**	19		5 **She's Got You**	*Hank Cochran*	Decca 31354
6/2/62	**10**	12		6 **When I Get Thru With You (You'll Love Me Too) /**	*Harlan Howard*	
6/30/62	**21**	3		7 **Imagine That**	*Justin Tubb*	Decca 31377
8/25/62	**14**	10		8 **So Wrong**	*Carl Perkins*	Decca 31406
2/16/63	**8**	17		9 **Leavin' On Your Mind**	*Wayne Walker*	Decca 31455
5/11/63	**5**	16		10 **Sweet Dreams (Of You)**	*Don Gibson*	Decca 31483
9/14/63	**7**	13		11 **Faded Love**	*Bob Wills/Johnnie Lee Wills*	Decca 31522
1/11/64	**47**	3		12 **When You Need A Laugh**	*Hank Cochran*	Decca 31552
10/31/64	**23**	12		13 **He Called Me Baby**	*Harlan Howard*	Decca 31671
1/25/69	**73**	2		14 **Anytime**	*Herb Lawson*	Decca 25744
4/8/78	**98**	1		15 **Life's Railway To Heaven**	*W.S. Stevenson*	4 Star 1033
8/30/80	**18**	12		16 **Always**	*Irving Berlin*	MCA 41303
12/20/80+	**61**	7		17 **I Fall To Pieces**	*Hank Cochran/Harlan Howard* **[R]**	MCA 51038
				newly mixed version of #3 above (with orchestra and chorus added)		

DEBUT	PEAK	WKS	GOLD	ARTIST / Ranking / Country Chart Hit	Songwriter	Label (& Number)
				CLINE, Patsy — cont'd		
11/7/81+	5	17		18 **Have You Ever Been Lonely** (Have You Ever Been Blue) *[w/ Jim Reeves]*	*...George Brown/Peter DeRose*	RCA 12346
				Cline and Reeves never recorded together; their voices were spliced together electronically		
6/5/82	54	8		19 **I Fall To Pieces** *[w/ Jim Reeves]*	*Hank Cochran/Harlan Howard* [R]	MCA 52052
				new version of #3 above		
10/2/99	70	1		20 **There He Goes** *[w/ John Berry]*	*Durwood Haddock/Eddie Miller/William Stevenson*	Private I
				from Cline's album *Duets Volume I* on Private I 417097		
				CLOWER, Jerry		
				Born on 9/28/1926 in Liberty, Mississippi. Died of heart failure on 8/24/1998 (age 71). Legendary comedian/storyteller. Former fertilizer salesman. His routines were based on people he knew growing up in Mississippi.		
				OPRY: 1973		
				COCHRAN, Anita		
				Born on 2/6/1967 in Pontiac, Michigan. Female singer/songwriter/guitarist.		
4/5/97	64	4		1 **I Could Love A Man Like That**	*Anita Cochran*	Warner
8/9/97	69	1		2 **Daddy Can You See Me**	*Anita Cochran*	Warner
11/8/97+	❶[1]	23		3 **What If I Said** *[w/ Steve Wariner]*	S:3 *Anita Cochran*	Warner
4/4/98	69	4		4 **Will You Be Here**	*Anita Cochran*	Warner
				above 4 from the album *Back To You* on Warner 46395		
7/31/99	58	9		5 **For Crying Out Loud**	*Bob McDill/Tommy Rocco*	Warner
5/20/00	50	8		6 **Good Times**	*Anita Cochran/Bob DiPiero*	Warner
8/5/00	61	7		7 **You With Me**	*Anita Cochran*	Warner
				above 3 from the album *Anita* on Warner 47318		
6/26/04	57	6		8 **(I Wanna Hear) A Cheatin' Song** *[w/ Conway Twitty]*	*Anita Cochran*	Warner
				Twitty's vocals created from various snippets of his past recordings; from Cochran's album *God Created Woman* on Warner 48009		
				COCHRAN, Cliff		
				Born in Pascagoula, Mississippi; raised in Greenville, Mississippi. Male singer. Cousin of **Hank Cochran**.		
8/10/74	54	10		1 **The Way I'm Needing You**	*Hank Cochran/Jane Kinsey*	Enterprise 9103
1/11/75	73	7		2 **All The Love You'll Ever Need**	*Jeannie Seely*	Enterprise 9109
5/26/79	24	13		3 **Love Me Like A Stranger**	*John Schweers/David Wills*	RCA 11562
9/22/79	29	9		4 **First Thing Each Morning** (Last Thing At Night)	*Kye Fleming/Dennis W. Morgan*	RCA 11711
				COCHRAN, Hank — **SW: #11**		
				Born Garland Perry Cochran on 8/2/1935 in Greenville, Mississippi. Male singer/songwriter/guitarist. Cousin of **Cliff Cochran**. Formerly married to **Jeannie Seeley**.		
9/1/62	20	5		1 **Sally Was A Good Old Girl**	*Harlan Howard*	Liberty 55461
11/10/62	23	2		2 **I'd Fight The World**	*Joe Allison/Hank Cochran*	Liberty 55498
10/5/63	25	1		3 **A Good Country Song**	*Bob Forshee*	Gaylord 6431
4/15/67	70	2		4 **All Of Me Belongs To You**	*Merle Haggard*	Monument 994
7/8/78	91	4		5 **Willie** *[w/ Merle Haggard]*	*Glenn Martin*	Capitol 4585
10/14/78	77	5		6 **Ain't Life Hell** *[w/ Willie Nelson]*	*Hank Cochran*	Capitol 4635
11/8/80	57	9		7 **A Little Bitty Tear** *[w/ Willie Nelson]*	*Hank Cochran*	Elektra 47062
				COCHRAN, Tammy		
				Born on 1/30/1970 in Austinburg, Ohio. Female singer/songwriter.		
4/8/00	41	17		1 **If You Can**	S:12 *Joy Swinea*	Epic
9/9/00	51	12		2 **So What**	S:15 *Roxie Dean/Jamie O'Neal/Sonny Tillis*	Epic
3/31/01	9	32		3 **Angels In Waiting**	*Tammy Cochran/Stewart Harris/Jim McBride*	Epic
11/17/01+	18	28		4 **I Cry**	*Mark Selby/Tia Sillers*	Epic
				above 4 from the album *Tammy Cochran* on Epic 69736		
6/1/02	20	22		5 **Life Happened**	*P.J. Matthews/Kerry Kurt Phillips*	Epic
12/7/02+	31	20		6 **Love Won't Let Me**	S:5 *Jason Deere/Franne Golde/Kasia Livingston*	Epic
				above 2 from the album *Life Happened* on Epic 86052		
				CODY, Betty		
				Born Rita Coté on 8/17/1921 in Sherbrooke, Quebec, Canada; raised in Auburn, Maine. Female singer.		
12/26/53	10	1		**I Found Out More Than You Ever Knew**	J:10 *Cecil Null*	RCA Victor 5462
				answer to "I Forgot More Than You'll Ever Know" by **The Davis Sisters**		
				COE, David Allan — **All-Time: #233**		
				Born on 9/6/1939 in Akron, Ohio. Male singer/songwriter/guitarist/actor. Billed as "The Mysterious Rhinestone Cowboy" until 1978. Acted in such movies as *Take This Job And Shove It*, *The Last Days Of Frank And Jesse James* and *Stagecoach*.		
11/30/74	80	6		1 **(If I Could Climb) The Walls Of The Bottle**	*Don Goodman/Troy Seals*	Columbia 10024
5/10/75	91	4		2 **Would You Be My Lady**	*David Allan Coe*	Columbia 10093
7/5/75	8	17		3 **You Never Even Called Me By My Name**	*Steve Goodman*	Columbia 10159
12/27/75+	17	11		4 **Longhaired Redneck**	*David Allan Coe*	Columbia 10254
4/24/76	60	6		5 **When She's Got Me** (Where She Wants Me)	*David Allan Coe*	Columbia 10323
9/25/76	25	11		6 **Willie, Waylon And Me**	*David Allan Coe* [N]	Columbia 10395
2/26/77	49	8		7 **Lately I've Been Thinking Too Much Lately**	*David Allan Coe*	Columbia 10475
8/6/77	82	5		8 **Just To Prove My Love For You**	*David Allan Coe*	Columbia 10583
10/29/77	92	3		9 **Face To Face**	*David Allan Coe*	Columbia 10621
3/25/78	86	3		10 **Divers Do It Deeper**	*David Allan Coe*	Columbia 10701
7/22/78	85	4		11 **You Can Count On Me**	*David Allan Coe*	Columbia 10753
9/9/78	45	8		12 **If This Is Just A Game**	*David Allan Coe*	Columbia 10816
3/17/79	72	5		13 **Jack Daniel's, If You Please**	*David Allan Coe*	Columbia 10911
6/21/80	46	7		14 **Get A Little Dirt On Your Hands** *[w/ Bill Anderson]*	*Bill Anderson*	Columbia 11277

DEBUT	PEAK	WKS	GOLD	ARTIST / Country Chart Hit	Ranking / Songwriter	Label (& Number)

COE, David Allan — cont'd

DEBUT	PEAK	WKS	GOLD	Country Chart Hit	Songwriter	Label (& Number)
3/14/81	88	3		15 Stand By Your Man	*Billy Sherrill/Tammy Wynette*	Columbia 60501
7/4/81	77	5		16 Tennessee Whiskey	*Dean Dillon/Linda Hargrove*	Columbia 02118
1/23/82	62	5		17 Now I Lay Me Down To Cheat	*Walt Aldridge/Billy Henderson*	Columbia 02678
4/10/82	58	8		18 Take Time To Know Her	*Steve Davis*	Columbia 02815
3/19/83	4	19		19 The Ride	*John Detterline/Gary Gentry*	Columbia 03778
7/23/83	45	10		20 Cheap Thrills	*Bob McDill*	Columbia 03997
10/22/83	85	5		21 Crazy Old Soldier	*Paul Kennerley/Troy Seals*	Columbia 04136
12/24/83+	48	13		22 Ride 'Em Cowboy	*Paul Davis*	Kat Family 04258
3/17/84	2[1]	22		23 Mona Lisa Lost Her Smile	*J.C. Cunningham*	Columbia 04396
8/25/84	44	11		24 It's Great To Be Single Again	*David Allan Coe*	Columbia 04553
12/8/84+	11	19		25 She Used To Love Me A Lot	S:9 / A:19 *Kye Fleming/Dennis W. Morgan/Charles Quillen*	Columbia 04688
4/13/85	29	12		26 Don't Cry Darlin' George Jones (recitation)	S:27 / A:30 *Dean Dillon*	Columbia 04846
11/2/85	52	8		27 I'm Gonna Hurt Her On The Radio	*Tom Brasfield/Mac McAnally*	Columbia 05631
5/10/86	44	10		28 A Country Boy (Who Rolled The Rock Away)	*Buddy Cannon/Jimmy Darrell/Dean Dillon*	Columbia 05876
8/2/86	56	8		29 I've Already Cheated On You *[w/ Willie Nelson]*	S:29 *David Allan Coe/Willie Nelson*	Columbia 06227
2/14/87	34	16		30 Need A Little Time Off For Bad Behavior	S:22 *David Allan Coe/Bobby Keel/Larry Latimer*	Columbia 06661
6/6/87	62	5		31 Tanya Montana	*David Allan Coe/Billy Sherrill*	Columbia 07129

COFFEY, Kellie

Born on 4/22/1978 in Moore, Oklahoma. Female singer/songwriter.

DEBUT	PEAK	WKS	GOLD	Country Chart Hit	Songwriter	Label (& Number)
12/22/01+	8	33		1 When You Lie Next To Me	*Kellie Coffey/Trina Harmon/J.D. Martin*	BNA
8/3/02+	18	26		2 At The End Of The Day	*Kellie Coffey/Brett James*	BNA
3/1/03	44	10		3 Whatever It Takes above 3 from the album *When You Lie Next To Me* on BNA 67040	*Kellie Coffey/Gordon O'Brien*	BNA
10/11/03+	24	22		4 Texas Plates	*Kellie Coffey/Brett James*	BNA
6/5/04	41	11		5 Dance With My Father above 2 from the album *A Little More Me* on BNA 55846	*Richard Marx/Luther Vandross*	BNA

COHN, Marc

Born on 7/5/1959 in Cleveland, Ohio. Male pop singer/songwriter/keyboardist. Won the 1991 Best New Artist Grammy Award.

DEBUT	PEAK	WKS	GOLD	Country Chart Hit	Songwriter	Label (& Number)
8/3/91	74	1		Walking In Memphis	*Marc Cohn*	Atlantic

COHRON, Phil

Born in Crestview, Florida. Male singer.

DEBUT	PEAK	WKS	GOLD	Country Chart Hit	Songwriter	Label (& Number)
1/6/90	86	2		Across The Room From You	*Donald White*	Air 182

COIN, R.C.

Born Richard Carey Coin on 1/1/1951 San Antonio, Texas. Male singer.

DEBUT	PEAK	WKS	GOLD	Country Chart Hit	Songwriter	Label (& Number)
10/17/87	76	3		Bed Of Roses	*Rex Benson/Steve Gillette*	BGM 82087

COLDER, Ben — see WOOLEY, Sheb

COLE, Brenda

Born in Los Angeles, California. Female singer/songwriter.

DEBUT	PEAK	WKS	GOLD	Country Chart Hit	Songwriter	Label (& Number)
6/27/87	83	3		1 But I Never Do	*Brenda Cole*	Melody Dawn 77701
12/19/87	86	3		2 Gone, Gone, Gone	*Brenda Cole*	Melody Dawn 77702
4/16/88	84	2		3 Boots (These Boots Are Made For Walking)	*Lee Hazlewood*	Melody Dawn 77703

COLE, Nat "King" — **1940s: #36**

Born Nathaniel Adams Coles on 3/17/1919 in Montgomery, Alabama; raised in Chicago, Illinois. Died of cancer on 2/15/1965 (age 45). Black pop singer/songwriter/pianist. Father of singer Natalie Cole. Won Grammy's Lifetime Achievement Award in 1990. Formed **The King Cole Trio** in 1939: Cole (vocals, piano), Oscar Moore (guitar) and Wesley Prince (bass).

DEBUT	PEAK	WKS	GOLD	Country Chart Hit	Songwriter	Label (& Number)
5/13/44	❶[6]	15		1 Straighten Up And Fly Right *[The King Cole Trio]* / **Grammy: Hall of Fame**	*Nat "King" Cole/Irving Mills*	
5/20/44	2[1]	5		2 I Can't See For Lookin' *[The King Cole Trio]*	*Nadine Robinson/Doc Stanford*	Capitol 154

COLE, Patsy

Born in Galesburg, Illinois; raised in Maquon, Illinois. Female singer.

DEBUT	PEAK	WKS	GOLD	Country Chart Hit	Songwriter	Label (& Number)
4/22/89	89	2		1 I Never Had A Chance With You	*Johnny McCollum/Dan Mitchell*	Tra-Star 1225
7/15/89	80	3		2 Death And Taxes (And Me Lovin' You)	*Charlie Black/Bobby Fischer/Austin Roberts*	Tra-Star 1226
11/4/89	91	2		3 You And The Horse (That You Rode In On)	*Chris Blake/Bobby Fischer/Doug Rock*	Tra-Star 1227

COLE, Sami Jo — see SAMI JO

COLEMAN('S), Albert, Atlanta Pops

Born in Paris, France; later based in Atlanta, Georgia. Conductor of the Atlanta Pops.

DEBUT	PEAK	WKS	GOLD	Country Chart Hit	Songwriter	Label (& Number)
5/29/82	42	15		1 Just Hooked On Country (Parts I & II) [I] **Part I medley:** Tennesse Waltz/Turkey In The Straw/Wabash Cannon Ball/Wildwood Flower/I Can't Stop Loving You/Orange Blossom Special/Jambalaya/Games People Play; **Part II medley:** Rose Garden/Rocky Top/Under The Double Eagle/You Are My Sunshine/Green, Green Grass Of Home/Your Cheating Heart/Don't It Make You Want To Go Home/Young Love/Battle Hymn Of The Republic	*Boudleaux Bryant/Felice Bryant/A.P. Carter/Ric Cartey/Jimmie Davis/Don Gibson/Julia Ward Howe/Carole Joyner/Pee Wee King/Charles Mitchell/Curly Putman/Joe South/William Steffe/Redd Stewart/Hank Williams*	Epic 02938
9/25/82	77	4		2 Just Hooked On Country (Part III) [I] medley: Last Date/Steel Guitar Rag/Walking The Floor Over You/I Walk The Line/Cold Cold Heart/Soldier's Joy/Walk A Mile In My Shoes/Oh Lonesome Me	*Johnny Cash/Floyd Cramer/Jimmie Driftwood/Don Gibson/Leon McAuliffe/Joe South/Cliffie Stone/Merle Travis/Ernest Tubb/Hank Williams*	Epic 03215

COLLIE, Biff — see BOWMAN, Billy Bob

COLLIE, Mark — All-Time: #299

Born George Mark Collie on 1/18/1956 in Waynesboro, Tennessee. Male singer/songwriter/guitarist.

DEBUT	PEAK	WKS	#	Country Chart Hit	Songwriter	Label (& Number)
2/10/90	**54**	11	1	**Something With A Ring To It**	*Mark Collie/Aaron Tippin*	MCA
6/9/90	**35**	21	2	**Looks Aren't Everything**	*Mark Collie*	MCA
10/6/90	**59**	5	3	**Hardin County Line**	*Mark Collie/Ronny Scaife*	MCA
2/9/91	**18**	20	4	**Let Her Go**	*Mark Collie*	MCA
				above 4 from the album *Hardin County Line* on MCA 42333		
6/29/91	**31**	18	5	**Calloused Hands**	*Pat Alger/Gene Levine*	MCA
10/26/91+	**28**	20	6	**She's Never Comin' Back**	*Mark Collie/Gerry House*	MCA
3/7/92	**70**	4	7	**It Don't Take A Lot**	*Mark Collie/Larry Shell*	MCA
				above 3 from the album *Born And Raised In Black & White* on MCA 10321		
8/29/92	**5**	20	8	**Even The Man In The Moon Is Crying**	*Mark Collie/Don Cook*	MCA
1/30/93	**6**	20	9	**Born To Love You**	*Mark Collie/Don Cook/Chick Rains*	MCA
6/5/93	**26**	19	10	**Shame Shame Shame Shame**	*Mark Collie/Jackson Leap*	MCA
9/18/93	**24**	20	11	**Something's Gonna Change Her Mind**	*Mark Collie/Don Cook*	MCA
				above 4 from the album *Mark Collie* on MCA 10658		
5/7/94	**53**	8	12	**It Is No Secret**	*Mark Collie/Mike Reid*	MCA
9/10/94+	**13**	20	13	**Hard Lovin' Woman**	*Mark Collie/Don Cook/John Jarvis*	MCA
				above 2 from the album *Unleashed* on MCA 11055		
6/17/95	**25**	20	14	**Three Words, Two Hearts, One Night**	*Mark Collie/Gerry House*	Giant
11/25/95	**65**	2	15	**Steady As She Goes**	*Bob DiPiero/Michael Mugrage/John Scott Sherrill*	Giant
				above 2 from the album *Tennessee Plates* on Giant 24620		
2/24/96	**72**	2	16	**Love To Burn**	*Mary Ann Kennedy/Bill McDermott/Rich Wayland*	Columbia
				from the various artists album *NASCAR: Hotter Than Asphalt* on Columbia 67510		

COLLIE, Shirley

Born Shirley Caddell on 3/16/1931 in Chillicothe, Missouri. Female singer. Formerly married to **Biff Collie** and **Willie Nelson**.

DEBUT	PEAK	WKS	#	Country Chart Hit	Songwriter	Label (& Number)
6/12/61	**25**	5	1	**Dime A Dozen**	*Harlan Howard*	Liberty 55324
9/11/61	**23**	3	2	**Why, Baby, Why** *[w/ Warren Smith]*	*Darrell Edwards/George Jones*	Liberty 55361
3/17/62	**10**	13	3	**Willingly** *[w/ Willie Nelson]*	*Hank Cochran*	Liberty 55403

COLLINS, Brian

Born on 10/19/1950 in Baltimore, Maryland; raised in Texas City, Texas. Male singer/songwriter/guitarist.

DEBUT	PEAK	WKS	#	Country Chart Hit	Songwriter	Label (& Number)
10/16/71	**67**	3	1	**All I Want To Do Is Say I Love You**	*Jerry Foster/Bill Rice*	Mega 0038
2/21/72	**47**	8	2	**There's A Kind Of Hush (All Over The World)**	*Les Reed/Geoff Stephens*	Mega 0058
7/1/72	**61**	6	3	**Spread It Around**	*Jerry Foster/Bill Rice*	Mega 0078
7/14/73	**24**	14	4	**I Wish (You Had Stayed)**	*Rhett Davis*	Dot 17466
12/8/73+	**43**	12	5	**I Don't Plan On Losing You**	*Arthur Kent/Frank Stanton*	Dot 17483
5/18/74	**10**	15	6	**Statue Of A Fool**	*Jan Crutchfield*	Dot 17499
11/9/74+	**23**	14	7	**That's The Way Love Should Be**	*Milton Blackford/Joe Dougherty/Dave Gillon*	ABC/Dot 17527
4/26/75	**84**	5	8	**I'd Still Be In Love With You**	*A.L. "Doodle" Owens/Warren Robb*	ABC/Dot 17546
12/6/75	**83**	5	9	**Queen Of Temptation**	*Jerry House*	ABC/Dot 17593
3/6/76	**65**	8	10	**To Show You That I Love You**	*Marshall Chapman/Jim Rushing*	ABC/Dot 17613
5/7/77	**83**	6	11	**If You Love Me (Let Me Know)**	*John Rostill*	ABC/Dot 17694
6/24/78	**86**	3	12	**Old Flames (Can't Hold A Candle To You)**	*Hugh Moffatt/Pebe Sebert*	RCA 11277
3/10/79	**94**	3	13	**Hello Texas**	*Robby Campbell/Brian Collins*	RCA 11478
4/17/82	**80**	4	14	**Before I Got To Know Her**	*Brian Collins*	Primero 1001
7/2/83	**80**	4	15	**Nickel's Worth Of Heaven**	*Brian Collins/Rick Doss*	Primero 1018

COLLINS, Dugg

Born on 7/2/1943 in Memphis, Texas. Male singer/songwriter/DJ.

DEBUT	PEAK	WKS	#	Country Chart Hit	Songwriter	Label (& Number)
5/21/77	**92**	4	1	**I'm The Man**	*Bernard Spurlock*	SCR 143
9/17/77	**99**	2	2	**How Do You Talk To A Baby**	*Webb Pierce/Wayne Walker*	SCR 147

COLLINS, Gwen & Jerry

Wife-and-husband duo from Miami, Florida.

DEBUT	PEAK	WKS	#	Country Chart Hit	Songwriter	Label (& Number)
1/17/70	**34**	9		**Get Together**	*Chet Powers*	Capitol 2710

COLLINS, Jim

Born in 1959 in Nacogdoches, Texas; raised in Houston, Texas. Male singer/songwriter/guitarist.

DEBUT	PEAK	WKS	#	Country Chart Hit	Songwriter	Label (& Number)
6/8/85	**78**	3	1	**You Can Always Say Good-Bye In The Morning**	*Jim Weatherly*	White Gold 22250
8/24/85	**59**	6	2	**I Wanna Be A Cowboy 'Til I Die**	*David Rosson*	White Gold 22252
12/14/85	**75**	6	3	**What A Memory You'd Make**	*Charlie Black/Rory Bourke/Tommy Rocco*	White Gold 22251
6/21/86	**65**	5	4	**(Because Of You) The Things I've Done To Me**	*Murray Cannon/Jimmy Darrell/Donny Lowery*	TKM 111216
11/1/86	**59**	5	5	**Romance**	*David Rosson*	TKM 111217
11/22/97+	**55**	8	6	**The Next Step**	*Kent Blazy/Sharon Blazy/Marcus Hummon*	Arista Nashville
3/7/98	**73**	4	7	**My First, Last, One And Only**	*Jim Collins/Bob Regan/Chris Waters*	Arista Nashville
				above 2 from the album *The Next Step* on Arista Nashville 18858		

COLLINS, Judy

Born on 5/1/1939 in Seattle, Washington. Female folk singer/songwriter.

DEBUT	PEAK	WKS	#	Country Chart Hit	Songwriter	Label (& Number)
9/29/84	**57**	9		**Home Again** *[w/ T.G. Sheppard]*	*Gerry Goffin/Michael Masser*	Elektra 69697

Billboard DEBUT	PEAK	WKS	GOLD	ARTIST / Country Chart Hit	Ranking / Songwriter	Label (& Number)
				COLLINS, Tommy	**1950s: #39**	
				Born Leonard Raymond Sipes on 9/28/1930 in Bethany, Oklahoma. Died of emphysema on 3/14/2000 (age 69). Male singer/songwriter/guitarist. Regular on the *Town Hall Party* radio series in the early 1950s. Wrote several hits for **Merle Haggard**. The song "Leonard" by Haggard is about Collins.		
2/20/54	2^{7}	21		1 **You Better Not Do That**	A:2 / J:2 / S:2 *Tommy Collins*	Capitol 2701
9/4/54	4	15		2 **Whatcha Gonna Do Now**	A:4 / S:7 *Tommy Collins*	Capitol 2891
2/5/55	10	1		3 **Untied**	J:10 / S:15 *Tommy Collins*	Capitol 3017
4/30/55	5	9		4 **It Tickles**	J:5 / A:9 / S:10 *Tommy Collins/Wanda Collins*	Capitol 3082
10/1/55	13	2		5 **I Guess I'm Crazy /**	S:13 *Werly Fairburn*	
10/1/55	15	2		6 **You Oughta See Pickles Now**	S:15 *Dick Reynolds*	Capitol 3190
1/11/64	47	1		7 **I Can Do That** ***[w/ Wanda Collins]***	*Tommy Collins*	Capitol 5051
2/5/66	7	13		8 **If You Can't Bite, Don't Growl**	*Tommy Collins*	Columbia 43489
7/16/66	47	2		9 **Shindig In The Barn**	*Tommy Collins*	Columbia 43628
2/11/67	62	4		10 **Don't Wipe The Tears That You Cry For Him (On My Good White Shirt) /**	*Bob Morris*	
3/4/67	60	5		11 **Birmingham**	*Tommy Collins*	Columbia 43972
9/23/67	52	6		12 **Big Dummy**	*Tommy Collins*	Columbia 44260
1/13/68	64	6		13 **I Made The Prison Band**	*Earl Ball/Jimmy Bryant/Tommy Collins*	Columbia 44386
				COLTER, Jessi		
				Born Mirriam Johnson on 5/25/1943 in Phoenix, Arizona. Female singer/songwriter/pianist. Mother of **Shooter Jennings**. Married to **Duane Eddy** from 1961-68. Married **Waylon Jennings** on 10/26/1969.		
11/14/70	25	10		1 **Suspicious Minds** ***[w/ Waylon Jennings]*** also see #7 below	*Mark James*	RCA Victor 9920
6/19/71	39	8		2 **Under Your Spell Again** ***[w/ Waylon Jennings]***	*Buck Owens/Dusty Rhodes*	RCA Victor 9992
2/15/75	❶^{1}	18		3 **I'm Not Lisa**	*Jessi Colter*	Capitol 4009
8/23/75	5	17		4 **What's Happened To Blue Eyes**	*Jessi Colter*	Capitol 4087
1/3/76	11	13		5 **It's Morning (And I Still Love You)**	*Jessi Colter*	Capitol 4200
4/17/76	50	7		6 **Without You**	*Jessi Colter*	Capitol 4252
5/1/76	2^{1}	14		7 **Suspicious Minds** ***[w/ Waylon Jennings]*** same version as #1 above	*Mark James* **[R]**	RCA Victor 10653
9/4/76	29	12		8 **I Thought I Heard You Calling My Name**	*Lee Emerson*	Capitol 4325
11/4/78	45	10		9 **Maybe You Should've Been Listening**	*Buzz Rabin*	Capitol 4641
4/14/79	91	4		10 **Love Me Back To Sleep**	*Zack Van Arsdale*	Capitol 4696
2/21/81	17	12		11 **Storms Never Last** ***[w/ Waylon Jennings]***	*Jessi Colter*	RCA 12176
6/6/81	10	13		12 **Wild Side Of Life/It Wasn't God Who Made Honky Tonk Angels** ***[w/ Waylon Jennings]***	*...Arlie Carter/Joe Miller/William Warren*	RCA 12245
2/13/82	70	4		13 **Holdin' On**	*Jessi Colter/Waylon Jennings/Basil McDavid*	Capitol 5073
				COMEAUX, Amie		
				Born on 12/4/1976 in Brusly, Louisiana. Died in a car crash on 12/21/1997 (age 21). Female singer.		
1/14/95	64	4		**Who's She To You** from the album *Moving Out* on Polydor 523710	*Donny Kees/Frank J. Myers*	Polydor
				COMMANDER CODY And His Lost Planet Airmen		
				Born George Frayne on 7/19/1944 in Boise, Idaho; raised in Brooklyn, New York. Male rock singer/keyboardist. His Lost Planet Airmen: John Tichy, Don Bolton and Bill Kirchen (guitars), Andy Stein (fiddle, sax), Bruce Barlow (bass) and Lance Dickerson (drums).		
5/6/72	51	9		1 **Hot Rod Lincoln**	*Charlie Ryan/W.S. Stevenson* **[N]**	Paramount 0146
7/28/73	97	2		2 **Smoke! Smoke! Smoke! (That Cigarette)**	*Merle Travis/Tex Williams* **[N]**	Paramount 0216
				COMO, Perry		
				Born Pierino Como on 5/18/1912 in Canonsburg, Pennsylvania. Died on 5/12/2001 (age 88). Legendary pop singer. Won Grammy's Lifetime Achievement Award in 2002.		
1/17/76	100	1		**Just Out Of Reach**	*Virgil Stewart*	RCA Victor 10402
				COMPTON BROTHERS, The		
				Duo from St. Louis, Missouri: brothers Bill Compton (vocals, guitar) and Harry Compton (vocals, guitar, drums). Won a Columbia Records talent contest in 1965. Operated their own publishing company, Wepedol Music.		
12/31/66+	61	5		1 **Pickin' Up The Mail**	*Ron Kitson*	Dot 16948
3/23/68	64	5		2 **Honey**	*Jan Crutchfield*	Dot 17070
8/3/68	75	2		3 **Two Little Hearts**	*Aileen Mnich*	Dot 17110
11/23/68	62	5		4 **Everybody Needs Somebody**	*Buck Owens*	Dot 17167
9/20/69	11	12		5 **Haunted House** "live" effects dubbed-in	*Robert Geddins*	Dot 17294
1/24/70	16	11		6 **Charlie Brown**	*Jerry Leiber/Mike Stoller*	Dot 17336
8/22/70	61	3		7 **That Ain't No Stuff**	*Dallas Frazier*	Dot 17352
6/12/71	65	6		8 **Pine Grove**	*Harry Compton*	Dot 17378
9/4/71	62	6		9 **May Old Acquaintance Be Forgot (Before I Lose My Mind)**	*Harry Compton*	Dot 17391
2/26/72	49	10		10 **Yellow River**	*Jeff Christie*	Dot 17408
8/26/72	41	9		11 **Claudette**	*Roy Orbison*	Dot 17427
10/6/73	65	12		12 **California Blues (Blue Yodel No. 4)**	*Jimmie Rodgers*	Dot 17477
3/15/75	97	2		13 **Cat's In The Cradle**	*Harry Chapin/Sandy Chapin*	ABC/Dot 17538
				CONCRETE COWBOY BAND		
				Group of Nashville session musicians led by Buddy Skipper. Vocals by **Donna Hazard** and Nancy Walker.		
7/11/81	87	2		**Country Is The Closest Thing To Heaven (You Can Hear)**	*Ed Keeley/Steve Vining*	Excelsior 1011

Billboard DEBUT	PEAK	WKS	GOLD	ARTIST / Country Chart Hit	Ranking / Songwriter	Label (& Number)

CONFEDERATE RAILROAD — All-Time: #269

Country-rock group from Marietta, Georgia: **Danny Shirley** (vocals; born on 8/12/1956), Michael Lamb (guitar), Gates Nichols (steel guitar; born on 5/26/1944), Chris McDaniel (keyboards; born on 2/4/1965), Wayne Secrest (bass; born on 4/29/1950) and Mark DuFresne (drums; born on 8/6/1953). Jimmy Dormire (born on 3/8/1960) replaced Lamb in 1995. Cody McCarver replaced McDaniel in 1999.

DEBUT	PEAK	WKS	GOLD	Country Chart Hit	Songwriter	Label (& Number)
4/4/92	37	19		1 **She Took It Like A Man**	*Danny Mayo/Paul Nelson/Karen Staley*	Atlantic
7/4/92	4	20		2 **Jesus And Mama**	*J.D. Hicks/Danny Mayo*	Atlantic
11/21/92+	2^{1}	20		3 **Queen Of Memphis**	*Dave Gibson/Kathy Louvin*	Atlantic
4/10/93	14	20		4 **When You Leave That Way You Can Never Go Back**	*Stephen Clark/Fred MacRae*	Atlantic
7/24/93	10	20		5 **Trashy Women**	*Christopher Wall*	Atlantic
12/11/93+	27	20		6 **She Never Cried**	*Danny Mayo/Diana Rae/Freddy Weller*	Atlantic
				above 6 from the album *Confederate Railroad* on Atlantic 82335		
3/12/94	9	20		7 **Daddy Never Was The Cadillac Kind**	*Dave Gibson/Bernie Nelson*	Atlantic
7/9/94	20	20		8 **Elvis And Andy**	*Craig Wiseman*	Atlantic
11/5/94	55	7		9 **Summer In Dixie**	*Gene Levine/Jon Robbin*	Atlantic
				above 3 from the album *Notorious* on Atlantic 82505		
5/13/95	24	20		10 **When And Where**	*J.J. Brown/Bill Jones/Jeff Pennig*	Atlantic
9/9/95	54	8		11 **Bill's Laundromat, Bar And Grill**	*Mark Germino/Jimmy Stewart*	Atlantic
11/4/95	66	5		12 **When He Was My Age**	*Kenny Chesney/Billy Lawson/David Lowe*	Atlantic
5/25/96	51	9		13 **See Ya**	*Thom McHugh/Chris Ward*	Atlantic
				above 4 from the album *When And Where* on Atlantic 82774		
11/21/98	66	9		14 **The Big One**	*Jon Ims/Pam Matthews*	Atlantic
4/3/99	70	2		15 **Cowboy Cadillac**	*Danny Wells/Craig Wiseman*	Atlantic
				above 2 from the album *Keep On Rockin'* on Atlantic 83024		
9/2/00	71	1		16 **Toss A Little Bone**	*Steve Bogard/Rick Giles*	Atlantic
				from the album *Rockin' Country Party Pack* on Atlantic 83207		
9/8/01	39	12		17 **That's What Brothers Do**	*Anthony Smith/Chris Wallin*	Audium
4/20/02	59	1		18 **She Treats Her Body Like A Temple**	*Rivers Rutherford/Craig Wiseman*	Audium
				above 2 from the album *Unleashed* on Audium 8137		

CONLEE, John — 1980s: #26 / All-Time: #100

Born on 8/11/1946 in Versailles, Kentucky. Male singer/songwriter/guitarist. Worked as a mortician for six years, then a newsreader in Fort Knox. Moved to WLAC-Nashville in 1971; worked as a DJ and music director.

OPRY: 1981

DEBUT	PEAK	WKS	GOLD	Country Chart Hit	Songwriter	Label (& Number)
5/27/78	5	20		1 **Rose Colored Glasses**	*George Baber/John Conlee*	ABC 12356
11/4/78+	❶^{1}	16		2 **Lady Lay Down**	*Don Cook/Rafe Van Hoy*	ABC 12420
3/3/79	❶^{1}	15		3 **Backside Of Thirty**	*John Conlee*	ABC 12455
8/11/79	2^{2}	15		4 **Before My Time**	*Ben Peters*	MCA 41072
12/15/79+	7	14		5 **Baby, You're Something**	*Don Cook/Curly Putman/Rafe Van Hoy*	MCA 41163
5/3/80	2^{2}	16		6 **Friday Night Blues**	*Sonny Throckmorton/Rafe Van Hoy*	MCA 41233
9/13/80	2^{2}	17		7 **She Can't Say That Anymore**	*Sonny Throckmorton*	MCA 41321
1/24/81	12	14		8 **What I Had With You**	*Curly Putman/Sonny Throckmorton*	MCA 51044
5/30/81	26	12		9 **Could You Love Me (One More Time)**	*Carter Stanley*	MCA 51112
8/29/81	2^{2}	20		10 **Miss Emily's Picture**	*Red Lane*	MCA 51164
2/20/82	6	18		11 **Busted**	*Harlan Howard*	MCA 52008
7/3/82	26	12		12 **Nothing Behind You, Nothing In Sight**	*Harlan Howard/Ron Peterson*	MCA 52070
10/2/82+	10	22		13 **I Don't Remember Loving You**	*Bobby Braddock/Harlan Howard*	MCA 52116
3/5/83	❶^{1}	19		14 **Common Man**	*Sammy Johns*	MCA 52178
6/25/83	❶^{1}	20		15 **I'm Only In It For The Love**	*Deborah Allen/Kix Brooks/Rafe Van Hoy*	MCA 52231
10/15/83+	❶^{1}	23		16 **In My Eyes**	*Barbara Wyrick*	MCA 52282
3/10/84	❶^{1}	19		17 **As Long As I'm Rockin' With You**	*Bruce Channel/Kieran Kane*	MCA 52351
6/23/84	4	19		18 **Way Back**	*Jerry Fuller*	MCA 52403
10/20/84+	2^{2}	21		19 **Years After You**	S:❶^{1} / A:2 *Thom Schuyler*	MCA 52470
3/2/85	7	20		20 **Working Man**	S:7 / A:7 *Jim Hurt/Billy Ray Reynolds*	MCA 52543
7/6/85	15	17		21 **Blue Highway**	A:14 / S:15 *Don Henry/Drew Womack*	MCA 52625
10/26/85+	5	21		22 **Old School**	S:4 / A:5 *Don Schlitz/Russell Smith*	MCA 52695
2/22/86	10	20		23 **Harmony**	S:9 / A:11 *Rich Beresford/Jimbeau Hinson*	Columbia 05778
6/14/86	❶^{1}	22		24 **Got My Heart Set On You**	S:❶^{1} / A:3 *Dobie Gray/Bud Reneau*	Columbia 06104
10/25/86+	6	19		25 **The Carpenter**	S:❶^{1} / A:6 *Guy Clark*	Columbia 06311
2/28/87	4	24		26 **Domestic Life**	S:3 / A:6 *Gary Harrison/J.D. Martin*	Columbia 06707
7/18/87	11	21		27 **Mama's Rockin' Chair**	S:6 *Johnny MacRae/Tim Mensy*	Columbia 07203
11/28/87	55	7		28 **Living Like There's No Tomorrow (Finally Got To Me Tonight)**	*Jim McBride/Roger Murrah*	Columbia 07643
1/21/89	43	10		29 **Hit The Ground Runnin'**	*Bobby Fischer/Rick Giles*	16th Avenue 70424
4/8/89	48	9		30 **Fellow Travelers**	*Wayland Patton/Jim Rushing*	16th Avenue 70427
8/19/89	67	5		31 **Hopelessly Yours**	*Don Cook/Curly Putman/Keith Whitley*	16th Avenue 70432
12/15/90+	61	9		32 **Doghouse**	*Kenny Beard/John Bicknell/Michael Grady*	16th Avenue

CONLEY, Earl Thomas — 1980s: #12 / All-Time: #72

Born on 10/17/1941 in West Portsmouth, Ohio. Male singer/songwriter/guitarist. Served in the U.S. Army from 1960-62. Worked in a steel mill in Huntsville, Alabama, in the early 1970s. Also recorded as **The ETC Band**.

Billboard DEBUT	PEAK	WKS	GOLD	ARTIST / Country Chart Hit	Songwriter	Label (& Number)
				EARL CONLEY:		
7/26/75	87	4		1 **I Have Loved You Girl (But Not Like This Before)** also see #15 below	*Earl Thomas Conley*	GRT 027
11/22/75	87	5		2 **It's The Bible Against The Bottle (In The Battle For Daddy's Soul)**	*Mel Howard/Janis Wolverton*	GRT 032
3/27/76	67	6		3 **High And Wild**	*Earl Thomas Conley*	GRT 041
8/14/76	77	5		4 **Queen Of New Orleans**	*Earl Thomas Conley*	GRT 064
1/6/79	32	12		5 **Dreamin's All I Do**	*Earl Thomas Conley*	Warner 8717
				EARL THOMAS CONLEY:		
6/23/79	41	8		6 **Middle-Age Madness**	*Earl Thomas Conley*	Warner 8798
10/6/79	26	11		7 **Stranded On A Dead End Street** *[The ETC Band]*	*Earl Thomas Conley*	Warner 49072
11/15/80+	7	20		8 **Silent Treatment**	*Earl Thomas Conley*	Sunbird 7556
4/4/81	❶^{1}	19		9 **Fire & Smoke**	*Earl Thomas Conley*	Sunbird 7561
10/17/81+	10	18		10 **Tell Me Why**	*John Acklen/Earl Thomas Conley*	RCA 12344
2/6/82	16	13		11 **After The Love Slips Away /**	*Earl Thomas Conley*	
2/6/82	flip	13		12 **Smokey Mountain Memories**	*Earl Thomas Conley/Richmond Devereux*	RCA 13053
6/12/82	8	18		13 **Heavenly Bodies**	*Elaine Litton/Gloria Nissenson*	RCA 13246
10/2/82	❶^{1}	18		14 **Somewhere Between Right And Wrong**	*Earl Thomas Conley*	RCA 13320
1/15/83	2^{2}	21		15 **I Have Loved You, Girl (But Not Like This Before)** [R] new version of #1 above	*Earl Thomas Conley*	RCA 13414
5/14/83	❶^{1}	19		16 **Your Love's On The Line**	*Earl Thomas Conley/Randy Scruggs*	RCA 13525
9/10/83	❶^{1}	25		17 **Holding Her And Loving You**	*Walt Aldridge/Tom Brasfield*	RCA 13596
1/14/84	❶^{1}	18		18 **Don't Make It Easy For Me**	*Earl Thomas Conley/Randy Scruggs*	RCA 13702
5/5/84	❶^{1}	21		19 **Angel In Disguise**	*Earl Thomas Conley/Randy Scruggs*	RCA 13758
9/8/84	❶^{1}	22		20 **Chance Of Lovin' You** S:❶^{1} / A:❶^{1}	*Earl Thomas Conley/Randy Scruggs*	RCA 13877
11/10/84+	8	21		21 **All Tangled Up In Love** *[w/ Gus Hardin]* S:5 / A:8	*Bob McDill/Jim Weatherly*	RCA 13938
1/5/85	❶^{1}	22		22 **Honor Bound** S:❶^{1} / A:❶^{1}	*Charlie Black/Austin Roberts/Tommy Rocco*	RCA 13960
5/4/85	❶^{1}	19		23 **Love Don't Care (Whose Heart It Breaks)** S:❶^{1} / A:❶^{1}	*Earl Thomas Conley/Randy Scruggs*	RCA 14060
9/14/85	❶^{1}	22		24 **Nobody Falls Like A Fool** S:❶^{1} / A:❶^{1}	*Peter McCann/Mark Wright*	RCA 14172
2/1/86	❶^{1}	22		25 **Once In A Blue Moon** A:❶^{2} / S:❶^{1}	*Tom Brasfield/Robert Byrne*	RCA 14282
8/2/86	2^{1}	20		26 **Too Many Times** *[w/ Anita Pointer]* S:❶^{1} / A:2	*Tony McShear/Scott Page/Micheal Smotherman*	RCA 14380
11/29/86+	❶^{1}	23		27 **I Can't Win For Losin' You** A:❶^{1} / S:5	*Rick Bowles/Robert Byrne*	RCA 5064
4/4/87	❶^{1}	21		28 **That Was A Close One** S:4 / A:18	*Robert Byrne*	RCA 5129
8/1/87	❶^{1}	23		29 **Right From The Start** S:9	*Billy Herzig/Randy Watkins*	RCA 5226
3/12/88	❶^{1}	23		30 **What She Is (Is A Woman In Love)** S:4	*Paul Harrison/Bob McDill*	RCA 6894
7/2/88	❶^{1}	21		31 **We Believe In Happy Endings** *[w/ Emmylou Harris]* S:3	*Bob McDill*	RCA 8632
11/12/88+	❶^{1}	24		32 **What I'd Say** S:13	*Robert Byrne/Will Robinson*	RCA 8717
3/18/89	❶^{1}	21		33 **Love Out Loud**	*Thom Schuyler*	RCA 8824
10/7/89	26	15		34 **You Must Not Be Drinking Enough**	*Danny Kortchmar*	RCA 8973
2/24/90	11	22		35 **Bring Back Your Love To Me**	*John Hiatt*	RCA
7/14/90	61	6		36 **Who's Gonna Tell Her Goodbye** above 2 from the album *Greatest Hits, Volume II* on RCA 2043	*Bill Rice/Mary Sharon Rice*	RCA
6/1/91	8	20		37 **Shadow Of A Doubt**	*Robert Byrne/Tom Wopat*	RCA
9/7/91	2^{1}	20		38 **Brotherly Love** *[w/ Keith Whitley]*	*Tim Nichols/Jimmy Stewart*	RCA
1/11/92	36	13		39 **Hard Days And Honky Tonk Nights**	*Earl Thomas Conley/Randy Scruggs*	RCA
5/23/92	74	3		40 **If Only Your Eyes Could Lie** above 4 from the album *Yours Truly* on RCA 3116	*John Jarrard/Bob McDill*	RCA

CONWAY, Dave

Born in Seattle, Washington. Male singer.

DEBUT	PEAK	WKS	GOLD	Country Chart Hit	Songwriter	Label (& Number)
8/6/77	68	6		**If You're Gonna Love (You Gotta Hurt)**	*DeWayne Orender/Lee Satterfield*	True 105

COOK, Steven Lee

Born in Shelbyville, Kentucky. Male singer.

DEBUT	PEAK	WKS	GOLD	Country Chart Hit	Songwriter	Label (& Number)
12/22/79+	92	5		**Please Play More Kenny Rogers** *[w/ The Jordanaires]* [N]	*Ralph Gabbard/John Ireson*	Grinder's Switch 1709

COOLEY, Spade — 1940s: #18

Born Donnell Clyde Cooley on 12/17/1910 in Grand, Oklahoma. Died of a heart attack on 11/23/1969 (age 58). Male singer/fiddler/actor. Acted in numerous movies. Hosted own TV shows from the late 1940s to 1958. Married Ella Mae Evans in 1945; murdered her on 4/3/1961. Sentenced to life imprisonment at Vacaville, California. Died performing at the Oakland Deputy Sheriff's Show two months before he was to be paroled.

DEBUT	PEAK	WKS	GOLD	Country Chart Hit	Songwriter	Label (& Number)
3/3/45	❶^{9}	31		1 **Shame On You /** **Tex Williams** and Oakie (vocals)	*Spade Cooley*	
4/28/45	8	1		2 **A Pair Of Broken Hearts**	*Jenny Lou Carson/Fred Rose*	Okeh 6731
10/6/45	4	1		3 **I've Taken All I'm Gonna Take From You**	*Jenny Lou Carson/Fred Rose*	Okeh 6746

Billboard DEBUT	PEAK	WKS	GOLD	ARTIST / Country Chart Hit	Ranking / Songwriter	Label (& Number)

COOLEY, Spade — cont'd

DEBUT	PEAK	WKS	GOLD	Country Chart Hit	Songwriter	Label (& Number)
3/16/46	**2**[1]	11		4 **Detour** / Oakie, Arkie and **Tex Williams** (vocals)	*Paul Westmoreland*	
4/20/46	**3**[1]	11		5 **You Can't Break My Heart**	*Spade Cooley/Smokey Rogers*	Columbia 36935
3/8/47	**4**	1		6 **Crazy 'Cause I Love You** **Tex Williams** (vocal: #2, 3, 5 & 6)	*Spade Cooley*	Columbia 37058

COOLIDGE, Rita

Born on 5/1/1944 in Nashville, Tennessee. Female singer/songwriter/pianist. Married to **Kris Kristofferson** from 1973-80. Known as "The Delta Lady." Acted in the 1983 movie *Club Med.*

DEBUT	PEAK	WKS	GOLD	Country Chart Hit	Songwriter	Label (& Number)
12/22/73+	**92**	5		1 **A Song I'd Like To Sing** *[w/ Kris Kristofferson]*	*Kris Kristofferson*	A&M 1475
3/23/74	**98**	2		2 **Loving Arms** *[w/ Kris Kristofferson]*	*Tom Jans*	A&M 1498
8/31/74	**94**	5		3 **Mama Lou**	*Larry Murray*	A&M 1545
12/28/74+	**87**	4		4 **Rain** *[w/ Kris Kristofferson]*	*Larry Gatlin*	Monument 8630
10/15/77	**82**	8	●	5 **We're All Alone**	*Boz Scaggs*	A&M 1965
11/25/78	**63**	9		6 **The Jealous Kind** /	*Robert Guidrey*	
11/25/78	**83**	9		7 **Love Me Again**	*David Lasley/Allee Willis*	A&M 2090
12/22/79+	**32**	10		8 **I'd Rather Leave While I'm In Love**	*Peter Allen/Carole Bayer Sager*	A&M 2199
5/24/80	**60**	6		9 **Somethin' 'Bout You Baby I Like** *[w/ Glen Campbell]*	*Richie Supa*	Capitol 4865
1/31/81	**72**	4		10 **Fool That I Am**	*Bruce Roberts/Carole Bayer Sager*	A&M 2281

COOPER, Jerry

Born in Arlington, Virginia. Male singer.

DEBUT	PEAK	WKS	GOLD	Country Chart Hit	Songwriter	Label (& Number)
10/3/87	**88**	2		1 **I'll Forget You**	*Eddie Burton/Kent Westberry*	Bear 178
1/9/88	**83**	3		2 **As Long As There's Women Like You**	*Eddie Burton/Kent Westberry*	Bear 187

COOPER, Wilma Lee & Stoney, and The Clinch Mountain Clan — 1950s: #50

Wife-and-husband duo: Wilma Leigh Leary (born on 2/7/1921 in Valley Head, West Virginia; vocals, guitar, banjo, piano) and Dale Troy "Stoney" Cooper (born on 10/16/1918 in Harman, West Virginia; died on 3/22/1977, age 58; vocals, fiddle). Own band, The Clinch Mountain Clan. Daughter Carolee Cooper is leader of The Carol Lee Singers.

OPRY: 1957

DEBUT	PEAK	WKS	GOLD	Country Chart Hit	Songwriter	Label (& Number)
9/29/56	**14**	1		1 **Cheated Too**	A:14 *Wilma Lee Cooper*	Hickory 1051
12/15/58+	**4**	26		2 **Come Walk With Me** *[w/ Carolee]*	*Burkett Graves*	Hickory 1085
5/25/59	**4**	23		3 **Big Midnight Special**	*Wilma Lee Cooper*	Hickory 1098
10/19/59	**3**[4]	24		4 **There's A Big Wheel**	*Don Gibson*	Hickory 1107
5/16/60	**17**	8		5 **Johnny, My Love (Grandma's Diary)**	*Boudleaux Bryant/Felice Bryant*	Hickory 1118
9/12/60	**16**	14		6 **This Ole House**	*Stuart Hamblen*	Hickory 1126
6/12/61	**8**	7		7 **Wreck On The Highway**	*Dorsey Dixon*	Hickory 1147

COPAS, Cowboy — 1940s: #17 / All-Time: #239

Born Lloyd Estel Copas on 7/15/1913 in Blue Creek, Ohio. Died in a plane crash on 3/5/1963 (age 49) near Camden, Tennessee (with **Patsy Cline** and **Hawkshaw Hawkins**). Male singer/songwriter/guitarist. Replaced **Eddy Arnold** as lead singer with **Pee Wee King**'s Golden West Cowboys.

OPRY: 1946

DEBUT	PEAK	WKS	GOLD	Country Chart Hit	Songwriter	Label (& Number)
8/31/46	**4**	1		1 **Filipino Baby** *[Cowboy (Pappy) Copas]*	*Billy Cox/Clarke Van Ness*	King 505
1/3/48	**2**[3]	20		2 **Signed Sealed And Delivered** also see #14 below	*Cowboy Copas/Lois Mann*	King 658
5/1/48	**3**[1]	17		3 **Tennessee Waltz**	S:3 / J:4 *Pee Wee King/Redd Stewart*	King 696
7/3/48	**7**	9		4 **Tennessee Moon**	S:7 / J:7 *Gene Branch*	King 714
9/18/48	**12**	1		5 **Breeze**	J:12 *Al Lewis/Tony Sacco/Richard Smith*	King 618
2/12/49	**12**	1		6 **I'm Waltzing With Tears In My Eyes**	S:12 *Cowboy Copas/Syd Nathan*	King 775
2/19/49	**5**	13		7 **Candy Kisses**	J:5 / S:7 *George Morgan*	King 777
11/12/49	**14**	2		8 **Hangman's Boogie** from the movie *Square Dance Jubilee*	S:14 / J:14 *Larry Cassidy*	King 811
4/28/51	**5**	11		9 **The Strange Little Girl**	A:5 / S:7 / J:10 *Richard Adler/Jerry Ross*	King 45-951
1/19/52	**8**	3		10 **'Tis Sweet To Be Remembered**	A:8 *Mac Wiseman*	King 45-1000
7/4/60	**❶**[12]	34		11 **Alabam**	*Cowboy Copas*	Starday 501
4/24/61	**9**	8		12 **Flat Top**	*Cowboy Copas/Tommy Hill*	Starday 542
7/31/61	**12**	10		13 **Sunny Tennessee**	*Cowboy Copas*	Starday 552
9/11/61	**10**	8		14 **Signed Sealed And Delivered** new version of #2 above	*Cowboy Copas/Lois Mann* **[R]**	Starday 559
4/27/63	**12**	14		15 **Goodbye Kisses**	*Cowboy Copas/Lefty Frizzell*	Starday 621

CORBIN, Ray

Born in Lubbock, Texas. Died of a gunshot wound on 10/26/1971 (age 35). Also known as Slim Corbin.

DEBUT	PEAK	WKS	GOLD	Country Chart Hit	Songwriter	Label (& Number)
1/11/69	**67**	2		**Passin' Through**	*Bobby Bare*	Monument 1102

CORBIN/HANNER BAND, The

Duo of Bob Corbin (born on 4/9/1951 in Butler, Pennsylvania) and Dave Hanner (born on 2/22/1949 in Kittanning, Pennsylvania). Band included Al Snyder (keyboards), Kip Paxton (bass) and Dave Freeland (drums).

DEBUT	PEAK	WKS	GOLD	Country Chart Hit	Songwriter	Label (& Number)
1/20/79	**85**	4		1 **America's Sweetheart** *[Corbin & Hanner]*	*Bob Corbin*	Lifesong 1783
5/30/81	**64**	6		2 **Time Has Treated You Well**	*Dave Hanner*	Alfa 7001
8/8/81	**46**	9		3 **Livin' The Good Life**	*Bob Corbin*	Alfa 7007
11/28/81+	**49**	10		4 **Oklahoma Crude**	*Bob Corbin*	Alfa 7010
4/10/82	**46**	9		5 **Everyone Knows I'm Yours**	*Dave Hanner*	Alfa 7022
12/4/82	**75**	7		6 **One Fine Morning**	*Bob Corbin*	Lifesong 45120

DEBUT	PEAK	WKS	GOLD	ARTIST / Country Chart Hit	Ranking / Songwriter	Label (& Number)
				CORBIN/HANNER:		
8/11/90	**55**	8		7 **Work Song**	*Bob Corbin*	Mercury
3/9/91	**59**	4		8 **Concrete Cowboy**	*Bob Corbin*	Mercury
				above 2 from the album *Black And White Photograph* on Mercury 846326		
9/12/92	**73**	2		9 **Just Another Hill**	*Bob Corbin/Dave Hanner*	Mercury
12/12/92+	**49**	14		10 **I Will Stand By You**	*Bob Corbin*	Mercury
4/24/93	**71**	3		11 **Any Road**	*Bob Corbin/Dave Hanner/Kevin Herring*	Mercury
				above 3 from the album *Just Another Hill* on Mercury 512288		
				CORNELIUS, Helen	**All-Time: #256**	
				Born Helen Johnson on 12/6/1941 in Monroe City, Missouri. Female singer/songwriter. Staff writer with Screen Gems in 1970. Teamed with **Jim Ed Brown** and appeared on the *Nashville On The Road* TV series from 1976-80.		
				CMA:Vocal Duo (with Jim Ed Brown) 1977		
				JIM ED BROWN/HELEN CORNELIUS:		
7/4/76	❶^{2}	16		1 **I Don't Want To Have To Marry You**	*Fred Imus/Phil Sweet*	RCA Victor 10711
10/30/76	**91**	3		2 **There's Always A Goodbye** ***[Helen Cornelius]***	*Randy Richards*	RCA 10795
11/20/76+	**2^{1}**	17		3 **Saying Hello, Saying I Love You, Saying Goodbye**	*Jeff Barry/Brad Burg/Dene Hofheinz*	RCA 10822
5/7/77	**12**	12		4 **Born Believer**	*Gary Harju*	RCA 10967
8/20/77	**12**	12		5 **If It Ain't Love By Now**	*Jeff Barry/Doug Haywood*	RCA 11044
12/24/77+	**91**	3		6 **Fall Softly Snow**	*Jean Surrey* **[X]**	RCA 11162
3/11/78	**11**	13		7 **I'll Never Be Free**	*Bennie Benjamin/George Weiss*	RCA 11220
7/29/78	**6**	15		8 **If The World Ran Out Of Love Tonight**	*Michael Garin/Blake Mevis/Kelly Wilson/Steve Wilson*	RCA 11304
9/30/78	**30**	8		9 **What Cha Doin' After Midnight, Baby** ***[Helen Cornelius]***	*Michael Garvin/Blake Mevis*	RCA 11375
11/25/78+	**10**	14		10 **You Don't Bring Me Flowers**	*Alan Bergman/Marilyn Bergman/Neil Diamond*	RCA 11435
3/31/79	**2^{2}**	13		11 **Lying In Love With You**	*Gary Harrison/Dean Rutherford*	RCA 11532
8/4/79	**3^{2}**	13		12 **Fools**	*Johnny Duncan*	RCA 11672
12/1/79	**68**	5		13 **It Started With A Smile** ***[Helen Cornelius]***	*Helen Cornelius/Johnny Koonse*	RCA 11753
3/8/80	**5**	14		14 **Morning Comes Too Early**	*Kye Fleming/Dennis W. Morgan*	RCA 11927
7/19/80	**24**	12		15 **The Bedroom**	*Russ Allison/Ron Muir*	RCA 12037
5/9/81	**13**	14		16 **Don't Bother To Knock**	*Kye Fleming/Dennis W. Morgan*	RCA 12220
12/5/81+	**42**	10		17 **Love Never Comes Easy** ***[Helen Cornelius]***	*Johnny MacRae/Bob Morrison*	Elektra 47237
11/26/83	**70**	6		18 **If Your Heart's A Rollin' Stone** ***[Helen Cornelius]***	*Blake Mevis/Bill Shore/David Wills*	Ameri-Can 1011
				CORNOR, Randy		
				Born on 7/28/1954 in Houston, Texas. Male singer/songwriter/guitarist.		
11/1/75+	**9**	15		1 **Sometimes I Talk In My Sleep**	*Eddy Raven*	ABC/Dot 17592
5/15/76	**33**	11		2 **Heart Don't Fail Me Now**	*Lynn Jones*	ABC/Dot 17625
10/2/76	**72**	6		3 **I Guess You Never Loved Me Anyway**	*Eddy Raven*	ABC/Dot 17655
3/5/77	**86**	3		4 **Love Doesn't Live Here Anymore**	*Ray Griff*	ABC/Dot 17676
7/1/78	**95**	3		5 **Ring Telephone Ring (Damn Telephone)**	*Randy Cornor/Lynn Jones*	Cherry 643
12/23/78	**100**	2		6 **Hurt As Big As Texas**	*Mike Kosser/Curly Putman*	Cherry 783
				COTTER, Brad		
				Born on 9/29/1973 in Opelika, Alabama; raised in Auburn, Alabama. Male singer/songwriter. Winner of TV's second *Nashville Star* talent series.		
5/22/04	**35**	16		1 **I Meant To**	S:❶^{9} *Steve Bogard/Brad Cotter/Rick Giles*	Epic
9/11/04	**59**	2		2 **Can't Tell Me Nothin'**	*Steve Bogard/Rick Giles*	Epic
11/13/04	**59**	2		3 **I Miss Me**	*Steve Bogard/Brad Cotter/Rick Giles*	Epic
				above 3 from the album *Patient Man* on Epic 92559		
				COTTON, Gene		
				Born on 6/30/1944 in Columbus, Ohio. Male singer/songwriter/guitarist.		
12/11/76+	**92**	7		1 **You've Got Me Runnin'**	*Parker McGee*	ABC 12227
7/29/78	**99**	2		2 **You're A Part Of Me** ***[w/ Kim Carnes]***	*Kim Carnes*	Ariola America 7704
5/22/82	**78**	4		3 **If I Could Get You (Into My Life)**	*Gene Cotton*	Knoll 5002
				COTY, Neal		
				Born in Maryland. Male singer/songwriter/guitarist.		
11/11/00+	**49**	14		**Legacy**	S:11 *Neal Coty/Randy Vanwarmer*	Mercury
				from the album *Legacy* on Mercury 170161		
				COUCH, Orville		
				Born on 2/21/1935 in Ferris, Texas. Died of heart failure on 5/26/2002 (age 67). Male singer/songwriter/guitarist.		
11/24/62+	**5**	21		1 **Hello Trouble**	*Orville Couch/Eddie McDuff*	Vee Jay 470
9/28/63	**25**	1		2 **Did I Miss You?**	*Orville Couch/Eddie McDuff*	Vee Jay 528
				COULTERS, The		
				Family trio from Durham, North Carolina.		
2/26/83	**70**	5		**Caroline's Still In Georgia**	*Wayland Holyfield*	Dolphin 45003
				COUNTRY CAVALEERS, The		
				Duo of **James Marvell** and Buddy Good. Both were members of the vocal group Mercy.		
10/20/73	**99**	2		1 **Humming Bird**	*Jack Anglin/Jim Anglin/Johnnie Wright*	MGM 14606
8/28/76	**97**	2		2 **Te' Quiero (I Love You In Many Ways)**	*Buddy Good/James Marvell*	Country Show. 171
				COUNTRY GENTLEMEN, The		
				Bluegrass group: Charlie Waller (vocals, guitar), John Duffey (mandolin; died on 12/10/1996, age 62), Eddie Adcock (banjo) and Ed McGlothlin (string bass). Numerous personnel changes through the years. **Ricky Skaggs** played fiddle in the group in 1972.		
10/30/65	**43**	4		**Bringing Mary Home**	*John Duffey/Larry Kingston/Chaw Mank*	Rebel 250

DEBUT	PEAK	WKS	GOLD	ARTIST / Country Chart Hit	Ranking / Songwriter	Label (& Number)

COWBOY TROY

Born Troy Coleman in Dallas, Texas. Black male singer/songwriter/rapper. Calls his style of music "hick-hop."

DEBUT	PEAK	WKS		Country Chart Hit	Songwriter	Label (& Number)
4/2/05	**48**	4		**I Play Chicken With The Train** from the album *Loco Motive* on Raybaw 49316	*Angie Aparo/Troy Coleman/John Rich*	Raybaw

COX, Don

Born in Texas. Male singer/guitarist.

DEBUT	PEAK	WKS		Country Chart Hit	Songwriter	Label (& Number)
12/1/79	**94**	3		**Smooth Southern Highway**	*Curly Putman/Sonny Throckmorton*	ARC 5902

COX, Don

Born on 1/14/1964 in Belhaven, North Carolina. Male singer. Former member of the **Super Grit Cowboy Band**.

DEBUT	PEAK	WKS		Country Chart Hit	Songwriter	Label (& Number)
4/9/94	**53**	13		**All Over Town** from the album *All Over Town* on Step One 83	*Tommy Barnes/Richard Rankin*	Step One

CRADDOCK, Billy "Crash" — 1970s: #21 / All-Time: #97

Born on 6/13/1939 in Greensboro, North Carolina. Male singer/songwriter/guitarist. With his brother Ronald in rock band the Four Rebels in 1957. First recorded for Colonial in 1957. Semi-retired from recording and worked outside of music in Greensboro from 1960-69. Known as "Mr. Country Rock."

DEBUT	PEAK	WKS		Country Chart Hit	Songwriter	Label (& Number)
2/13/71	**3^{2}**	17	1	**Knock Three Times**	*L. Russell Brown/Irwin Levine*	Cartwheel 193
6/19/71	**5**	14	2	**Dream Lover**	*Bobby Darin*	Cartwheel 196
11/6/71	**10**	14	3	**You Better Move On**	*Arthur Alexander*	Cartwheel 201
3/4/72	**10**	16	4	**Ain't Nothin' Shakin'** (But The Leaves On The Trees)	*Dallas Frazier/A.L. "Doodle" Owens*	Cartwheel 210
7/1/72	**5**	16	5	**I'm Gonna Knock On Your Door**	*Aaron Schroeder/Sid Wayne*	Cartwheel 216
11/18/72+	**22**	12	6	**Afraid I'll Want To Love Her One More Time**	*David Wilkins*	ABC 11342
2/24/73	**33**	9	7	**Don't Be Angry**	*Wade Jackson*	ABC 11349
5/26/73	**14**	11	8	**Slippin' And Slidin'**	*Richard Penniman*	ABC 11364
9/1/73	**8**	15	9	**'Till The Water Stops Runnin'**	*L. Russell Brown/Irwin Levine*	ABC 11379
1/5/74	**3^{2}**	16	10	**Sweet Magnolia Blossom**	*Gayle Barnhill/Rory Bourke*	ABC 11412
6/1/74	**❶^{2}**	16	11	**Rub It In**	*Layng Martine Jr.*	ABC 12013
11/9/74+	**❶^{1}**	14	12	**Ruby, Baby**	*Jerry Leiber/Mike Stoller*	ABC 12036
2/22/75	**4**	14	13	**Still Thinkin' 'Bout You**	*Johnny Christopher/Bobby Wood*	ABC 12068
6/21/75	**10**	14	14	**I Love The Blues And The Boogie Woogie**	*Darrell Statler*	ABC 12104
10/18/75	**2^{3}**	17	15	**Easy As Pie**	*Rory Bourke/Gene Dobbins/Johnny Wilson*	ABC/Dot 17584
4/3/76	**7**	13	16	**Walk Softly**	*Van McCoy*	ABC/Dot 17619
7/4/76	**4**	13	17	**You Rubbed It In All Wrong**	*John Adrian*	ABC/Dot 17635
10/23/76+	**❶^{1}**	16	18	**Broken Down In Tiny Pieces**	*John Adrian*	ABC/Dot 17659
3/12/77	**28**	10	19	**Just A Little Thing**	*Layng Martine Jr.*	ABC/Dot 17682
6/4/77	**7**	15	20	**A Tear Fell**	*Dorian Burton/Eugene Randolph*	ABC/Dot 17701
11/12/77+	**10**	15	21	**The First Time**	*John Adrian*	ABC/Dot 17725
2/4/78	**4**	15	22	**I Cheated On A Good Woman's Love**	*Del Bryant*	Capitol 4545
2/18/78	**92**	2	23	**Another Woman**	*Buzz Cason/Dan Penn*	ABC 12335
5/6/78	**50**	9	24	**Think I'll Go Somewhere** (And Cry Myself To Sleep)	*Bill Anderson*	ABC 12357
5/20/78	**28**	10	25	**I've Been Too Long Lonely Baby**	*John Adrian*	Capitol 4575
7/29/78	**57**	6	26	**Don Juan**	*Layng Martine Jr.*	ABC 12384
9/16/78	**14**	12	27	**Hubba Hubba**	*Layng Martine*	Capitol 4624
1/6/79	**4**	14	28	**If I Could Write A Song As Beautiful As You**	*John Adrian*	Capitol 4672
4/28/79	**28**	10	29	**My Mama Never Heard Me Sing**	*John Adrian*	Capitol 4707
8/4/79	**16**	13	30	**Robinhood**	*Larry Cheshire/Murry Kellum*	Capitol 4753
11/10/79+	**24**	14	31	**Till I Stop Shaking**	*John Adrian*	Capitol 4792
3/15/80	**22**	11	32	**I Just Had You On My Mind**	*Sue Richards*	Capitol 4838
6/14/80	**50**	8	33	**Sea Cruise**	*Huey Smith/John Vincent*	Capitol 4875
10/18/80	**20**	13	34	**A Real Cowboy** (You Say You're)	*David Heavener*	Capitol 4935
2/14/81	**37**	10	35	**It Was You**	*Bob House/Billy Stone*	Capitol 4972
6/20/81	**11**	16	36	**I Just Need You For Tonight**	*Ken Bell/Terry Skinner/J.L. Wallace*	Capitol 5011
10/17/81	**38**	10	37	**Now That The Feeling's Gone**	*Mickey Buckins/Randy McCormick*	Capitol 5051
7/17/82	**28**	12	38	**Love Busted**	*Red Lane/Alan Rhody*	Capitol 5139
11/20/82	**62**	5	39	**The New Will Never Wear Off Of You** *[Crash Craddock]*	*Craig Morris*	Capitol 5170
10/22/83	**86**	2	40	**Tell Me When I'm Hot**	*Debbie Hupp/Lisa Palas*	Cee Cee 5400
8/5/89	**68**	7	41	**Just Another Miserable Day** (Here In Paradise)	*...Charles Browder/Elroy Kahanek/Nelson Larkin/Ewell Rousell/Tom Smith*	Atlantic 88851

CRAFT, Paul

Born on 8/12/1938 in Memphis, Tennessee; raised in Richmond, Virginia. Male singer/songwriter.

DEBUT	PEAK	WKS		Country Chart Hit	Songwriter	Label (& Number)
10/12/74	**55**	10	1	**It's Me Again, Margaret**	*Paul Craft* **[N]**	Truth 3205
6/11/77	**98**	2	2	**We Know Better**	*Paul Craft*	RCA 10971
10/1/77	**55**	7	3	**Lean On Jesus** "Before He Leans On You"	*Mark Germino/Rob Stanley*	RCA 11078
3/4/78	**84**	6	4	**Teardrops In My Tequila**	*Paul Craft*	RCA 11211

Billboard			G O L D	ARTIST	Ranking	
DEBUT	PEAK	WKS		Country Chart Hit	Songwriter	Label (& Number)

CRAMER, Floyd — HOF: 2003

Born on 10/27/1933 in Samti, Louisiana; raised in Huttig, Arkansas. Died of cancer on 12/31/1997 (age 64). Male pianist/songwriter. Popular session musician. Also see **Some Of Chet's Friends**.

DEBUT	PEAK	WKS	GOLD	Country Chart Hit	Songwriter	Label (& Number)
11/7/60+	**11**	18	●	1 **Last Date** **Grammy: Hall of Fame**	*Floyd Cramer* [I]	RCA Victor 7775
6/19/61	**8**	10		2 **San Antonio Rose**	*Bob Wills* [I]	RCA Victor 7893
2/18/67	**53**	7		3 **Stood Up**	*Al Gorgoni/Jerry Teifer* [I]	RCA Victor 9065
4/16/77	**67**	7		4 **Rhythm Of The Rain** ***[w/ The Keyboard Kick Band]*** The Keyboard Kick Band is Floyd Cramer playing eight different keyboards	*John Gummoe* [I]	RCA 10908
3/15/80	**32**	10		5 **Dallas** from the TV series starring Larry Hagman	*Jerrold Immel* [I]	RCA 11916

CRAWFORD, Calvin

Born on 5/25/1931 in Alabama. Died of cancer on 12/23/1999 (age 68). Male singer/bassist.

DEBUT	PEAK	WKS	GOLD	Country Chart Hit	Songwriter	Label (& Number)
9/27/75	**69**	6		**Sweet Molly** ***[w/ David Houston]***	*Anne Young*	Epic 50134

CRAWFORD/WEST

Duo of Rick Crawford (from Texas) and Kenny West (from Arkansas).

DEBUT	PEAK	WKS	GOLD	Country Chart Hit	Songwriter	Label (& Number)
6/14/97	**75**	1		**Summertime Girls**	*Rick Crawford/Kim Tribble/Jim Varsos*	Warner

CREECH, Alice

Born in Panther Branch, North Carolina. Female singer.

DEBUT	PEAK	WKS	GOLD	Country Chart Hit	Songwriter	Label (& Number)
5/29/71	**73**	2		1 **The Hunter**	*Gloria Van Cleve/Bob Wilson*	Target 00313
11/13/71	**33**	11		2 **The Night They Drove Old Dixie Down**	*Robbie Robertson*	Target 0138
2/12/72	**34**	11		3 **We'll Sing In The Sunshine**	*Gale Garnett*	Target 0144

CREEDENCE CLEARWATER REVIVAL

Rock group from El Cerrito, California: **John Fogerty** (vocals, guitar), brother Tom Fogerty (guitar), Stu Cook (keyboards, bass) and Doug Clifford (drums). Group disbanded in 1972. Tom Fogerty died on 9/6/1990 (age 48). Group inducted into the Rock and Roll Hall of Fame in 1993.

DEBUT	PEAK	WKS	GOLD	Country Chart Hit	Songwriter	Label (& Number)
12/5/81+	**50**	8		**Cotton Fields** recorded in 1969	*Huddie Ledbetter*	Fantasy 920

CREWS, Dwayne

Born on 5/7/1956 in Dallas, Texas. Male singer/guitarist.

DEBUT	PEAK	WKS	GOLD	Country Chart Hit	Songwriter	Label (& Number)
1/6/90	**81**	2		**Selfish Man**	*Mike Garman*	Killer 124

CRITTENDEN, Melodie

Born in 1969 in Moore, Oklahoma. Female singer/songwriter.

DEBUT	PEAK	WKS	GOLD	Country Chart Hit	Songwriter	Label (& Number)
1/17/98	**42**	15		1 **Broken Road**	*Bobby Boyd/Jeff Hanna/Marcus Hummon*	Asylum
5/9/98	**72**	3		2 **I Should've Known** above 2 from the album *Melodie Crittenden* on Asylum 62043	*Melodie Crittenden/Eric Silver*	Asylum

CROCE, Jim

Born on 1/10/1943 in Philadelphia, Pennsylvania. Killed in a plane crash on 9/20/1973 (age 30) in Natchitoches, Louisiana. Pop-rock singer/songwriter/guitarist.

DEBUT	PEAK	WKS	GOLD	Country Chart Hit	Songwriter	Label (& Number)
4/13/74	**68**	7		**I'll Have To Say I Love You In A Song**	*Jim Croce*	ABC 11424

CROCKETT, Howard

Born Howard Hausey on 12/25/1925 in Minden, Louisiana. Died on 12/27/1994 (age 69). Male singer/songwriter.

DEBUT	PEAK	WKS	GOLD	Country Chart Hit	Songwriter	Label (& Number)
5/19/73	**52**	10		**Last Will And Testimony (Of A Drinking Man)**	*Howard Crockett*	Dot 17457

CROFT, Sandy

Born in 1969 in Chattanooga, Tennessee. Female singer.

DEBUT	PEAK	WKS	GOLD	Country Chart Hit	Songwriter	Label (& Number)
1/22/83	**61**	8		1 **Easier**	*Jan Buckingham/Pam Tillis*	Angelsong 1821
8/4/84	**91**	2		2 **Easier** above 2 are the same version	*Jan Buckingham/Pam Tillis* [R]	Capitol 5363
6/15/85	**68**	6		3 **Piece Of My Heart**	*Bert Berns*	Capitol 5471

CROSBY, Bing

Born Harry Lillis Crosby on 5/3/1903 in Tacoma, Washington. Died of a heart attack on 10/14/1977 (age 74). Male singer/actor. One of the most popular entertainers of all-time.

DEBUT	PEAK	WKS	GOLD	Country Chart Hit	Songwriter	Label (& Number)
1/8/44	❶[5]	11	●	1 **Pistol Packin' Mama** ***[w/ Andrews Sisters]***	*Al Dexter*	Decca 23277
8/30/52	**10**	1		2 **Till The End Of The World** ***[w/ Grady Martin]***	J:10 *Vaughn Horton*	Decca 9-28265

CROSBY, Eddie

Born in Brooklyn, New York. Male singer.

DEBUT	PEAK	WKS	GOLD	Country Chart Hit	Songwriter	Label (& Number)
12/10/49	**7**	2		**Blues Stay Away From Me**	A:7 / J:10 *Alton Delmore/Rabon Delmore/Henry Glover/Wayne Raney*	Decca 46180

CROSBY, Rob

Born Robert Crosby Hoar on 4/25/1954 in Sumter, South Carolina. Male singer/songwriter/guitarist.

DEBUT	PEAK	WKS	GOLD	Country Chart Hit	Songwriter	Label (& Number)
11/10/90+	**12**	20		1 **Love Will Bring Her Around**	*Rob Crosby/Will Robinson*	Arista
4/20/91	**15**	20		2 **She's A Natural**	*Rick Bowles/Rob Crosby*	Arista
9/28/91	**20**	20		3 **Still Burnin' For You**	*Rob Crosby*	Arista
2/1/92	**28**	14		4 **Working Woman** above 4 from the album *Solid Ground* on Arista 8662	*Rob Crosby/Tim DuBois/Will Robinson*	Arista
7/4/92	**53**	9		5 **She Wrote The Book**	*Steve Bogard/Rick Giles*	Arista
12/26/92+	**48**	12		6 **In The Blood** above 2 from the album *Another Time And Place* on Arista 18710	*Bob DiPiero/John Jarrard/Mark D. Sanders*	Arista
9/30/95	**64**	8		7 **The Trouble With Love**	*Rob Crosby/Sonny Lemaire*	River North
1/20/96	**64**	6		8 **Lady's Man** above 2 from the album *Starting Now* on River North 1162	*Gary Cotton/Rob Crosby*	River North

DEBUT	PEAK	WKS	GOLD	ARTIST Ranking / Country Chart Hit	Songwriter	Label (& Number)

CROSBY, STILLS & NASH

Folk-rock trio: David Crosby (guitar; from The Byrds); Stephen Stills (guitar, bass; from The Buffalo Springfield) and Graham Nash (guitar; from The Hollies). Occasionally joined by **Neil Young** (guitar). Inducted into the Rock and Roll Hall of Fame in 1997. Also see **The Red Hots**.

DEBUT	PEAK	WKS	GOLD	Country Chart Hit	Songwriter	Label (& Number)
8/14/82	**87**	4		1 **Wasted On The Way**	*Graham Nash*	Atlantic 4058
3/11/89	**92**	2		2 **This Old House** **CROSBY, STILLS, NASH & YOUNG**	*Neil Young*	Atlantic 88966

CROSS CANADIAN RAGWEED

Group from Stillwater, Oklahoma: Cody Canada (vocals, guitar), Grady Cross (guitar), Jeremy Plato (bass) and Randy Ragsdale (drums).

DEBUT	PEAK	WKS	GOLD	Country Chart Hit	Songwriter	Label (& Number)
11/2/02	**57**	3		1 **17**	*Jason Boland/Cody Canada*	Universal South
1/17/04	**57**	2		2 **Constantly** above 2 from the album *Cross Canadian Ragweed* on Universal South 064414	*Cody Canada*	Universal South
3/6/04	**46**	13		3 **Sick And Tired**	*Cody Canada*	Universal South
1/15/05	**46**	20		4 **Alabama** above 2 from the album *Soul Gravy* on Universal South 001887	*Cody Canada/Ted Roberson*	Universal South

CROW, Alvin, And The Pleasant Valley Boys

Born on 9/29/1950 in Oklahoma City, Oklahoma. Leader of The Pleasant Valley Boys based in Austin, Texas.

DEBUT	PEAK	WKS	GOLD	Country Chart Hit	Songwriter	Label (& Number)
6/11/77	**83**	4		1 **Yes She Do, No She Don't (I'm Satisfied With My Gal)**	*Peter DeRose/Jackie Trent*	Polydor 14387
9/10/77	**97**	2		2 **Crazy Little Mama (At My Front Door)**	*Ewart Abner/John Moore*	Polydor 14410
12/17/77	**94**	4		3 **Nyquil Blues** *[Alvin Crow]*	*Herb Steiner*	Polydor 14437

CROW, Sheryl

Born on 2/11/1962 in Kennett, Missouri. Adult Alternative rock singer/songwriter/guitarist. Won the 1994 Best New Artist Grammy Award.

DEBUT	PEAK	WKS	GOLD	Country Chart Hit	Songwriter	Label (& Number)
10/12/02+	**21**	33	●	1 **Picture** *[w/ Kid Rock]* S:❶[52] from Kid Rock's album *Cocky* on Lava 83482	*Robert Ritchie*	Lava
11/1/03+	**35**	20		2 **The First Cut Is The Deepest** from the album *The Very Best Of Sheryl Crow* on A&M 152102	*Cat Stevens*	A&M
10/2/04	**55**	1		3 **No Depression In Heaven** from the various artists album *The Unbroken Circle: The Musical Heritage Of* ***The Carter Family*** on Dualtone 1162	*A.P. Carter*	Dualtone

CROWELL, Rodney — All-Time: #188

Born on 8/7/1950 in Houston, Texas. Male singer/songwriter/guitarist. Moved to Nashville in 1972 and worked as staff writer for **Jerry Reed**. Worked with **Emmylou Harris** from 1975-77. Married to **Rosanne Cash** from 1979-92. Married **Claudia Church** in 1997. Cousin of **Larry Willoughby**. Member of **The Notorious Cherry Bombs**.

DEBUT	PEAK	WKS	GOLD	Country Chart Hit	Songwriter	Label (& Number)
9/9/78	**95**	3		1 **Elvira**	*Dallas Frazier*	Warner 8637
5/19/79	**90**	3		2 **(Now And Then, There's) A Fool Such As I**	*William Trader*	Warner 8794
5/31/80	**78**	6		3 **Ashes By Now**	*Rodney Crowell*	Warner 49224
10/10/81	**30**	11		4 **Stars On The Water**	*Rodney Crowell*	Warner 49810
2/13/82	**34**	11		5 **Victim Or A Fool**	*Rodney Crowell*	Warner 50008
11/15/86+	**38**	12		6 **When I'm Free Again** S:29	*Rodney Crowell/Will Jennings*	Columbia 06415
3/21/87	**71**	7		7 **She Loves The Jerk**	*John Hiatt*	Columbia 06584
6/20/87	**59**	8		8 **Looking For You**	*Rosanne Cash/Rodney Crowell*	Columbia 07137
1/23/88	**❶[1]**	23		9 **It's Such A Small World** *[w/ Rosanne Cash]* S:❶[3]	*Rodney Crowell*	Columbia 07693
6/11/88	**❶[1]**	21		10 **I Couldn't Leave You If I Tried** S:❶[4]	*Rodney Crowell*	Columbia 07918
10/15/88+	**❶[1]**	19		11 **She's Crazy For Leavin'** S:❶[2]	*Guy Clark/Rodney Crowell*	Columbia 08080
2/25/89	**❶[1]**	21		12 **After All This Time** **Grammy: Song**	*Rodney Crowell*	Columbia 68585
7/1/89	**❶[1]**	20		13 **Above And Beyond**	*Harlan Howard*	Columbia 68948
10/14/89+	**3[1]**	26		14 **Many A Long & Lonesome Highway**	*Rodney Crowell/Will Jennings*	Columbia 73042
3/3/90	**6**	26		15 **If Looks Could Kill**	*Rodney Crowell*	Columbia
7/14/90	**22**	15		16 **My Past Is Present**	*Rodney Crowell/Stuart Smith*	Columbia
10/20/90+	**17**	20		17 **Now That We're Alone**	*Rodney Crowell*	Columbia
4/27/91	**72**	5		18 **Things I Wish I'd Said** above 4 from the album *Keys To The Highway* on Columbia 45242	*Rodney Crowell*	Columbia
3/7/92	**10**	20		19 **Lovin' All Night**	*Rodney Crowell*	Columbia
6/27/92	**11**	20		20 **What Kind Of Love** above 2 from the album *Life Is Messy* on Columbia 47985	*Rodney Crowell/Will Jennings/Roy Orbison*	Columbia
4/2/94	**60**	7		21 **Let The Picture Paint Itself**	*Rodney Crowell*	MCA
9/17/94	**75**	1		22 **Big Heart** above 2 from the album *Let The Picture Paint Itself* on MCA 11042	*Rodney Crowell*	MCA
4/29/95	**69**	9		23 **Please Remember Me** from the album *Jewel Of The South* on MCA 11223	*Rodney Crowell/Will Jennings*	MCA
11/7/98	**61**	6		24 **I Walk The Line Revisited** *[w/ Johnny Cash]* from Crowell's album *The Houston Kid* on Sugar Hill 1065	*Johnny Cash/Rodney Crowell*	Sugar Hill
11/8/03	**60**	1		25 **Earthbound** from the album *Fate's Right Hand* on DMZ/Epic 89082	*Rodney Crowell*	DMZ/Epic

DEBUT	PEAK	WKS	GOLD	ARTIST / Ranking / Country Chart Hit	Songwriter	Label (& Number)

CROWLEY, J.C.

Born John Crowley on 11/13/1947 in Houston, Texas. Male singer/songwriter/guitarist. Former member of the pop group Player ("Baby Come Back").

DEBUT	PEAK	WKS	GOLD	Country Chart Hit	Songwriter	Label (& Number)
9/3/88	**49**	7		1 **Boxcar 109**	*Josh Leo/Harry Stinson*	RCA 8634
10/29/88+	**13**	19		2 **Paint The Town And Hang The Moon Tonight**	*J.C. Crowley/Jack Routh*	RCA 8747
3/25/89	**21**	15		3 **I Know What I've Got**	*J.C. Crowley/Jeff Silbar*	RCA 8822
7/22/89	**55**	9		4 **Beneath The Texas Moon**	*J.C. Crowley/Jack Routh*	RCA 9012

CRUM, Simon — see HUSKY, Ferlin

CRYNER, Bobbie

Born on 9/13/1961 in Woodland, California. Female singer/songwriter.

DEBUT	PEAK	WKS	GOLD	Country Chart Hit	Songwriter	Label (& Number)
7/3/93	**63**	6		1 **Daddy Laid The Blues On Me**	*Bobbie Cryner*	Epic
11/20/93	**68**	5		2 **He Feels Guilty**	*Tommy Polk/Verlon Thompson*	Epic
5/14/94	**72**	3		3 **You Could Steal Me**	*Bobbie Cryner/Jesse Hunter*	Epic
				above 3 from the album *Bobbie Cryner* on Epic 53238		
10/14/95	**63**	8		4 **I Just Can't Stand To Be Unhappy**	*Hugh Prestwood*	MCA Nashville
3/2/96	**56**	7		5 **You'd Think He'd Know Me Better**	*Bobbie Cryner*	MCA Nashville
				above 2 from the album *Girl Of Your Dreams* on MCA Nashville 11324		

CUMMINGS, Barbara

Born on 3/26/1942 in Greenfield, Ohio. Died on 7/25/2000 (age 58). Female singer/songwriter.

DEBUT	PEAK	WKS	GOLD	Country Chart Hit	Songwriter	Label (& Number)
12/24/66+	**69**	8		**She's The Woman**	*Barbara Cummings/Bob Cummings*	London 104

CUMMINGS, Burton

Born on 12/31/1947 in Winnipeg, Manitoba, Canada. Male singer/songwriter/pianist. Lead singer of rock group The Guess Who.

DEBUT	PEAK	WKS	GOLD	Country Chart Hit	Songwriter	Label (& Number)
3/3/79	**33**	12		**Takes A Fool To Love A Fool**	*Burton Cummings*	Portrait 70024

CUMMINGS, Chris

Born on 8/11/1975 in Norton, New Brunswick, Canada. Male singer/songwriter.

DEBUT	PEAK	WKS	GOLD	Country Chart Hit	Songwriter	Label (& Number)
12/20/97+	**50**	7		**The Kind Of Heart That Breaks**	*Chris Cummings/Phillip Douglas/Kim Tribble*	Warner
				from the album *Chris Cummings* on Warner 46672		

CUNHA, Rick

Born on 7/19/1945 in Los Angeles, California. Male singer/songwriter/guitarist.

DEBUT	PEAK	WKS	GOLD	Country Chart Hit	Songwriter	Label (& Number)
5/18/74	**49**	10		(I'm A) **YoYo Man**	*Martin Cooper/Rick Cunha*	GRC 2016

CUNNINGHAM, J.C.

Born John Collins Cunningham on 11/13/1950 in Brownsville, Texas. Male singer/songwriter.

DEBUT	PEAK	WKS	GOLD	Country Chart Hit	Songwriter	Label (& Number)
7/5/80	**85**	2		1 **The Pyramid Song**	*J.C. Cunningham* **[N]**	Scotti Brothers 601
4/21/84	**70**	6		2 **Light Up**	*J.C. Cunningham*	Viva 29311

CURB, Mike, Congregation

Born on 12/24/1944 in Savannah, Georgia. Pop music mogul and politician. President of MGM Records from 1969-73. Elected lieutenant governor of California in 1978; served as governor of California in 1980. Formed own company, Sidewalk Records, in 1964; became Curb Records in 1974.

DEBUT	PEAK	WKS	GOLD	Country Chart Hit	Songwriter	Label (& Number)
8/1/70	❶^{2}	15		1 **All For The Love Of Sunshine** ***[w/ Hank Williams, Jr.]***	*Mike Curb/Harley Hatcher/Lalo Schifrin*	MGM 14152
				from the movie *Kelly's Heroes* starring **Clint Eastwood**		
12/19/70+	**3**^{2}	15		2 **Rainin' In My Heart** ***[w/ Hank Williams, Jr.]***	*Slim Harpo/Jerry West*	MGM 14194
12/18/71+	**7**	14		3 **Ain't That A Shame** ***[w/ Hank Williams, Jr.]***	*Dave Bartholomew/Fats Domino*	MGM 14317
5/27/72	**24**	11		4 **Gone (Our Endless Love)** ***[w/ Billy Walker]***	*Darrell Glenn/Billy Walker*	MGM 14377

CURLESS, Dick — All-Time: #275

Born on 3/17/1932 in Fort Fairfield, Maine. Died of cancer on 5/25/1995 (age 63). Male singer/songwriter/guitarist. Had own radio show as "The Tumbleweed Kid" in Ware, Massachusetts, in 1948. On Armed Forces Radio Network as "The Rice-Paddy Ranger" from 1951-54.

DEBUT	PEAK	WKS	GOLD	Country Chart Hit	Songwriter	Label (& Number)
3/13/65	**5**	17		1 **A Tombstone Every Mile**	*Dan Fulkerson*	Tower 124
6/19/65	**12**	13		2 **Six Times A Day (The Trains Came Down)**	*Dan Fulkerson*	Tower 135
11/6/65	**42**	3		3 **'Tater Raisin' Man**	*Dan Fulkerson*	Tower 161
1/15/66	**44**	3		4 **Travelin' Man**	*Nancy Chase/Pauline Curless*	Tower 193
10/15/66	**63**	3		5 **The Baron**	*Dick Curless/Manny Hobbs*	Tower 255
2/4/67	**28**	11		6 **All Of Me Belongs To You**	*Merle Haggard*	Tower 306
7/29/67	**72**	1		7 **House Of Memories**	*Merle Haggard*	Tower 335
11/4/67	**70**	2		8 **Big Foot**	*Jack Ripley*	Tower 362
3/23/68	**55**	7		9 **Bury The Bottle With Me**	*Hank Cochran/Darrell McCall*	Tower 399
6/15/68	**34**	9		10 **I Ain't Got Nobody**	*Roger Graham/Dave Tayton/Spencer Williams*	Tower 415
5/2/70	**27**	11		11 **Big Wheel Cannonball**	*Vaughn Horton*	Capitol 2780
				new "trucker" version of "Wabash Cannonball"		
8/8/70	**31**	10		12 **Hard, Hard Traveling Man**	*Bobby Bond*	Capitol 2848
11/21/70	**29**	9		13 **Drag 'Em Off The Interstate, Sock It To 'Em, J.P. Blues**	*Vaughn Horton*	Capitol 2949
2/20/71	**41**	9		14 **Juke Box Man**	*Hank Mills*	Capitol 3034
7/31/71	**36**	9		15 **Loser's Cocktail**	*Jerry Crutchfield/Don Earl/Nick Nixon*	Capitol 3105
10/2/71	**40**	10		16 **Snap Your Fingers**	*Grady Martin/Alex Zanetis*	Capitol 3182
2/26/72	**34**	11		17 **January, April And Me**	*Buddy Mize*	Capitol 3267
7/1/72	**31**	9		18 **Stonin' Around**	*Mel Tillis*	Capitol 3354
11/25/72	**55**	7		19 **She Called Me Baby**	*Harlan Howard*	Capitol 3470
3/24/73	**54**	7		20 **Chick Inspector (That's Where My Money Goes)**	*Vaughn Horton*	Capitol 3541
7/14/73	**80**	3		21 **China Nights (Shina No Yoru)**	*Sylvia Eisenberg*	Capitol 3630
9/15/73	**65**	7		22 **The Last Blues Song**	*Barry Mann/Cynthia Weil*	Capitol 3698

Billboard DEBUT	PEAK	WKS	GOLD		ARTIST / Country Chart Hit	Songwriter	Label (& Number)

CURREY, Diana Sicily

Born in San Antonio, Texas. Female singer.

DEBUT	PEAK	WKS	GOLD		Country Chart Hit	Songwriter	Label (& Number)
10/21/89	91	2			Longneck Lone Star (And Two Step Dancin')	Jerry Taylor	Condor 13

CURRINGTON, Billy

Born on 11/19/1973 in Savannah, Georgia; raised in Rincon, Georgia. Male singer/songwriter/guitarist.

DEBUT	PEAK	WKS	GOLD		Country Chart Hit	Songwriter	Label (& Number)
5/3/03	8	30		1	Walk A Little Straighter	S:3 *Casey Beathard/Carson Chamberlain/Billy Currington*	Mercury
1/17/04	5	33		2	I Got A Feelin'	*Casey Beathard/Carson Chamberlain/Billy Currington*	Mercury
					above 2 from the album *Billy Currington* on Mercury 000164		
9/18/04	7	20		3	Party For Two ***[w/ Shania Twain]***	*Mutt Lange/Shania Twain*	Mercury
					from Twain's album *Greatest Hits* on Mercury 003072		
6/11/05	29↑	16↑		4	Must Be Doin' Somethin' Right	*Marty Dodson/P.J. Matthews*	Mercury
					from the album *Doin' Somethin' Right* on Mercury 003712		

CURTIS, Larry

Born in Van Nuys, California. Male singer.

DEBUT	PEAK	WKS	GOLD		Country Chart Hit	Songwriter	Label (& Number)
6/10/78	88	5			It Feels Like Love For The First Time	*Larry Lynum/Tom Wargo*	ScrimShaw 1315

CURTIS, Mac

Born Wesley Erwin Curtis on 1/16/1939 in Fort Worth, Texas; raised in Olney, Texas. Male singer/songwriter.

DEBUT	PEAK	WKS	GOLD		Country Chart Hit	Songwriter	Label (& Number)
6/15/68	64	5		1	The Quiet Kind	*Harlan Howard*	Epic 10324
10/19/68	54	7		2	The Sunshine Man	*Ray Pennington*	Epic 10385
5/24/69	63	7		3	Happiness Lives In This House	*Dave Kirby/Ray Pennington*	Epic 10468
11/8/69	60	5		4	Don't Make Love	*Ray Griff*	Epic 10530
2/28/70	43	9		5	Honey, Don't	*Carl Perkins*	Epic 10574
10/17/70	35	10		6	Early In The Morning	*Bobby Darin/Woody Harris*	GRT 26

CURTIS, Sonny

Born on 5/9/1937 in Meadow, Texas. Male singer/songwriter/guitarist. Member of Buddy Holly & The Three Tunes.

DEBUT	PEAK	WKS	GOLD		Country Chart Hit	Songwriter	Label (& Number)
10/8/66	49	2		1	My Way Of Life	*Sonny Curtis*	Viva 602
9/23/67	50	11		2	I Wanna Go Bummin' Around	*Sonny Curtis*	Viva 617
2/24/68	36	11		3	Atlanta Georgia Stray	*Chris Cantry*	Viva 626
7/20/68	45	9		4	The Straight Life	*Sonny Curtis*	Viva 630
11/29/75	78	5		5	Lovesick Blues	*Cliff Friend/Irving Mills*	Capitol 4158
9/15/79	77	6		6	The Cowboy Singer	*Sonny Curtis*	Elektra 46526
1/19/80	86	3		7	Do You Remember Roll Over Beethoven	*Sonny Curtis*	Elektra 46568
3/29/80	38	9		8	The Real Buddy Holly Story	*Sonny Curtis*	Elektra 46616
7/19/80	29	10		9	Love Is All Around	*Sonny Curtis*	Elektra 46663
					theme from TV's *The Mary Tyler Moore Show*		
11/8/80	70	3		10	Fifty Ways To Leave Your Lover	*Paul Simon*	Elektra 47048
4/25/81	15	16		11	Good Ol' Girls	*Dan Wilson*	Elektra 47129
8/22/81	33	10		12	Married Women	*Bob McDill*	Elektra 47176
1/25/86	69	5		13	Now I've Got A Heart Of Gold	*Sonny Curtis*	'Steem 110185

CYRUS, Billy Ray — 1990s: #50 / All-Time: #201

Born on 8/25/1961 in Flatwoods, Kentucky. Male singer/songwriter/guitarist/actor. Attended Kentucky's Georgetown University. Moved to Los Angeles in 1984; worked as an exotic dancer and car salesman. Formed backing band, Sly Dog, in 1986. Plays "Dr. Clint Cassidy" on the PAX-TV series *Doc.*

DEBUT	PEAK	WKS	GOLD		Country Chart Hit	Songwriter	Label (& Number)
4/4/92	❶[5]	20	▲	1	Achy Breaky Heart	*Don Von Tress*	Mercury
					CMA: Single		
6/13/92+	52	12		2	Some Gave All	*Billy Ray Cyrus/Cindy Cyrus*	Mercury
7/4/92	2[1]	20		3	Could've Been Me	*Reed Nielsen/Monty Powell*	Mercury
9/5/92+	6	20		4	She's Not Cryin' Anymore	*Buddy Cannon/Billy Ray Cyrus/Terry Shelton*	Mercury
10/17/92	23	20		5	Wher'm I Gonna Live?	*Billy Ray Cyrus/Cindy Cyrus*	Mercury
					above 5 from the album *Some Gave All* on Mercury 510635		
2/13/93	27	20		6	Romeo ***[w/ Dolly Parton/Mary-Chapin Carpenter/Kathy Mattea/Pam Tillis/T. Tucker]***	*Dolly Parton*	Columbia
					from Parton's album *Slow Dancing With The Moon* on Columbia 53199		
7/3/93	3[1]	20		7	In The Heart Of A Woman	*Brett Cartwright/Keith Hinton*	Mercury
10/23/93	9	20		8	Somebody New	*Michael Curtis/Tom Harvey*	Mercury
1/29/94	12	20		9	Words By Heart	*Reed Nielsen/Monty Powell*	Mercury
6/4/94	63	2		10	Talk Some	*Don Von Tress*	Mercury
					above 4 from the album *It Won't Be The Last* on Mercury 514758		
10/22/94	33	18		11	Storm In The Heartland	*Donald Burns/Billy Henderson*	Mercury
2/4/95	66	4		12	Deja Blue	*Donny Lowery/Craig Wiseman*	Mercury
					above 2 from the album *Storm In The Heartland* on Mercury 526081		
8/19/95	75	1		13	The Fastest Horse In A One Horse Town	*Tony Haselden/Don Von Tress*	Columbia
					from the various artists album *NASCAR: Runnin' Wide Open* on Columbia 67020		
8/31/96	69	5		14	Trail Of Tears	*Billy Ray Cyrus*	Mercury
2/8/97	65	6		15	Three Little Words	*Jim Collins/Dave Perkins*	Mercury
					above 2 from the album *Trail Of Tears* on Mercury 532829		
5/31/97	19	20		16	It's All The Same To Me	*Jerry Laseter/Kerry Kurt Phillips*	Mercury
					from the album *The Best Of Billy Ray Cyrus: Cover To Cover* on Mercury 534837		
8/1/98	70	5		17	Time For Letting Go	*Jude Cole*	Mercury
10/31/98+	3[3]	27		18	Busy Man	*Bob Regan/George Teren*	Mercury
4/10/99	41	14		19	Give My Heart To You	*Walt Aldridge/Bob DiPiero*	Mercury
					above 3 from the album *Shot Full Of Love* on Mercury 558347		
7/8/00	17	23		20	You Won't Be Lonely Now	S:5 *John Bettis/Brett James*	Monument
11/4/00	60	2		21	We The People	*Monty Powell/Jimmie Lee Sloas/Anna Wilson*	Monument

DEBUT	PEAK	WKS	GOLD	ARTIST / Country Chart Hit	Ranking / Songwriter	Label (& Number)
				CYRUS, Billy Ray — cont'd		
1/20/01	**43**	10		22 **Burn Down The Trailer Park**	*Pat MacDonald/Billy Maddox/Paul Thorn*	Monument
4/21/01	**58**	1		23 **Crazy 'Bout You Baby**	*Ed Berghoff/Jeffrey Steele*	Monument
6/9/01	**45**	10		24 **Southern Rain**	*Billy Ray Cyrus/Michael Sagraves/Donald Von Tress*	Monument
				above 5 from the album *Southern Rain* on Monument 62105		
7/5/03	**60**	1		25 **Back To Memphis**	*T.W. Hale/Russell Tabor*	Madacy
				from the album *Time Flies* on Madacy 4114		
2/7/04	**54**	1		26 **Face Of God**	*Bob DiPiero/Rivers Rutherford/Tom Shapiro*	Word-Curb
				from the album *The Other Side* on Word-Curb 886274		

D

DEBUT	PEAK	WKS	GOLD	ARTIST / Country Chart Hit	Ranking / Songwriter	Label (& Number)
				DAFFAN('S), Ted, Texans	**1940s: #14**	
				Born Theron Eugene Daffan on 9/21/1912 in Beauregarde Parish, Louisiana; raised in Houston, Texas. Died of cancer on 10/6/1996 (age 84). Male singer/songwriter/guitarist. His Texans: Buddy Buller, Harry Sorensen and Freddy Courtney.		
1/8/44	**2^3**	8		1 **No Letter Today /**	*Frank Brown*	
				Chuck Keeshan and Leon Seago (vocals)		
1/15/44	**3^5**	21		2 **Born To Lose**	*Frank Brown*	Okeh 6706
6/3/44	**4**	2		3 **Look Who's Talkin'**	*Ted Daffan*	Okeh 6719
				Leon Seago (vocal, above 2)		
2/24/45	**6**	2		4 **Time Won't Heal My Broken Heart /**	*Ted Daffan/Billy Martin*	
3/3/45	**5**	3		5 **You're Breaking My Heart**	*Ted Daffan*	Okeh 6729
				Ted Daffan (vocal, above 2)		
8/25/45	**5**	3		6 **Shadow On My Heart /**	*Ted Daffan*	
9/1/45	**2^3**	13		7 **Headin' Down The Wrong Highway**	*Ted Daffan*	Okeh 6744
				"Idaho" (vocal, above 2)		
10/26/46	**5**	3		8 **Shut That Gate**	*Ted Daffan/Dick James*	Columbia 37087
				George Strange (vocal)		
				DAISY, Pat		
				Born Patricia Deasy on 10/10/1944 in Gallatin, Tennessee. Female singer.		
2/19/72	**20**	13		1 **Everybody's Reaching Out For Someone**	*Dickey Lee/Allen Reynolds*	RCA Victor 0637
7/29/72	**48**	7		2 **Beautiful People**	*Kenny O'Dell*	RCA Victor 0743
5/5/73	**49**	7		3 **The Lonesomest Lonesome**	*Mac Davis*	RCA Victor 0932
10/13/73	**53**	9		4 **My Love Is Deep, My Love Is Wide**	*Ben Peters*	RCA Victor 0087
				DALE, Kenny		
				Born Kenneth Dale Eoff on 10/3/1951 in Artesia, New Mexico. Male singer/songwriter/guitarist.		
3/5/77	**11**	17		1 **Bluest Heartache Of The Year**	*W.W. Wimberly*	Capitol 4389
7/30/77	**11**	14		2 **Shame, Shame On Me (I Had Planned To Be Your Man)**	*W.W. Wimberly*	Capitol 4457
1/21/78	**17**	14		3 **Red Hot Memory**	*W.W. Wimberly*	Capitol 4528
5/6/78	**28**	11		4 **The Loser**	*Darrell McCall/Lamar Morris*	Capitol 4570
9/2/78	**18**	13		5 **Two Hearts Tangled In Love**	*W.W. Wimberly*	Capitol 4619
4/21/79	**16**	11		6 **Down To Earth Woman**	*Steve Pippin/Johnny Slate*	Capitol 4704
7/21/79	**7**	15		7 **Only Love Can Break A Heart**	*Burt Bacharach/Hal David*	Capitol 4746
11/3/79	**15**	13		8 **Sharing**	*Steve Pippin/Johnny Slate*	Capitol 4788
2/23/80	**23**	10		9 **Let Me In**	*Larry Keith/Steve Pippin/Johnny Slate*	Capitol 4829
6/28/80	**33**	11		10 **Thank You, Ever-Lovin'**	*Kenny O'Dell*	Capitol 4882
11/22/80+	**31**	13		11 **When It's Just You And Me**	*Kenny O'Dell*	Capitol 4943
3/6/82	**65**	6		12 **Moanin The Blues**	*J.D. Meister/Jennifer Meister/W.W. Wimberly*	Funderburg 5001
1/28/84	**85**	6		13 **Two Will Be One**	*Kenny Dale*	Republic 8301
9/1/84	**86**	3		14 **Take It Slow**	*Michael Ballew/Bob Moulds*	Republic 8403
4/13/85	**83**	3		15 **Look What Love Did To Me**	*Kenny Dale*	Saba 9214
5/31/86	**63**	7		16 **I'm Going Crazy**	*Bobby Pruett*	BGM 30186
				DALE, Terry		
				Born in Florida. Male singer.		
1/9/82	**93**	2		1 **Intimate Strangers**	*Ken Bell/Terry Skinner/J.L. Wallace*	Lanedale 1001
3/27/82	**73**	4		2 **Loving You Is Always On My Mind**	*Fred MacRae/Bob Morrison*	Lanedale 711
				DALHART, Vernon	**HOF: 1981**	
				Born Marion Slaughter on 4/6/1883 in Jefferson, Texas. Died on 9/15/1948 (age 65). Began career as an opera singer; later switched to hugely popular "hillbilly" style. One of the top-selling recording artists of the 1920s.		
				EARLY HITS: The Prisoner's Song (1925) / The Wreck Of The Old 97 (1925) / The Death Of Floyd Collins (1925) / My Blue Ridge Mountain Home (1928)		
				DALICE		
				Born in Texas. Female singer.		
1/6/90	**87**	2		**Crazy Driver**	*Gary Potterton*	Country Pride 0021
				DALLAS, Johnny		
				Born Joseph Poovey on 3/6/1937 in Plano, Texas. Male singer.		
12/24/66+	**62**	7		**Heart Full Of Love**	*Larry Kingston*	Little Darlin' 0013

DEBUT	PEAK	WKS	GOLD	ARTIST / Country Chart Hit	Ranking / Songwriter	Label (& Number)
				DALLEY, Amy		
				Born in Kingsport, Tennessee. Singer/songwriter/guitarist.		
3/8/03	**27**	20		1 **Love's Got An Attitude (It Is What It Is)**	*Bonnie Baker/Amy Dalley/Lee Miller*	Curb
8/23/03	**43**	13		2 **I Think You're Beautiful**	*Amy Dalley/Lee Miller*	Curb
2/14/04	**23**	28		3 **Men Don't Change**	*Amy Dalley/Lee Miller*	Curb
11/13/04+	**29**	20		4 **I Would Cry**	*Bonnie Baker/Amy Dalley*	Curb
				DALTON, Bob		
				Born in Itman, West Virginia. Male singer.		
10/17/70	**73**	3		**Mama, Call Me Home**	*Ann Dougherty/Doyle Marsh/Hope Neathamer*	Mega 0003

DEBUT	PEAK	WKS	GOLD	ARTIST / Country Chart Hit	Ranking / Songwriter	Label (& Number)
				DALTON, Lacy J.	**All-Time: #181**	
				Born Jill Byrem on 10/13/1946 in Bloomsburg, Pennsylvania. Female singer/songwriter/guitarist. Formed the psychedelic rock band Office in 1968. Recorded as Jill Croston in 1978.		
10/6/79	**17**	13		1 **Crazy Blue Eyes**	*Lacy J. Dalton/Mary McFadden*	Columbia 11107
2/2/80	**18**	12		2 **Tennessee Waltz**	*Pee Wee King/Redd Stewart*	Columbia 11190
4/26/80	**14**	14		3 **Losing Kind Of Love**	*Lacy J. Dalton/Mark Sherrill*	Columbia 11253
8/30/80	**7**	14		4 **Hard Times**	*Bobby Braddock*	Columbia 11343
12/13/80+	**8**	15		5 **Hillbilly Girl With The Blues**	*Lacy J. Dalton*	Columbia 11410
4/4/81	**10**	13		6 **Whisper**	*Lacy J. Dalton/Mark Sherrill*	Columbia 01036
7/18/81	**2**[2]	18		7 **Takin' It Easy**	*Lacy J. Dalton/Billy Sherrill/Mark Sherrill*	Columbia 02188
12/5/81+	**5**	17		8 **Everybody Makes Mistakes /**	*Lacy J. Dalton/Billy Sherrill*	
12/5/81+	**flip**	16		9 **Wild Turkey**	*Hugh Moffatt/Pebe Sebert*	Columbia 02637
5/1/82	**13**	15		10 **Slow Down**	*Lacy J. Dalton/Billy Sherrill/Mark Sherrill*	Columbia 02847
9/11/82	**7**	19		11 **16th Avenue**	*Thom Schuyler*	Columbia 03184
3/12/83	**30**	14		12 **It's A Dirty Job** *[w/ Bobby Bare]*	*Don Cook/Rafe Van Hoy*	Columbia 03628
6/11/83	**9**	20		13 **Dream Baby (How Long Must I Dream)**	*Cindy Walker*	Columbia 03926
10/15/83	**54**	8		14 **Windin' Down**	*Lacy J. Dalton/Fred Koller/Mark Sherrill*	Columbia 04133
11/24/84+	**15**	20		15 **If That Ain't Love**	S:12 / A:16 *Jeff Harrington/Jeff Pennig*	Columbia 04696
4/27/85	**19**	18		16 **Size Seven Round (Made Of Gold)** *[w/ George Jones]*	S:17 / A:19 *Monroe Fields/Gary Lumpkin*	Epic 04876
6/8/85	**20**	17		17 **You Can't Run Away From Your Heart**	S:19 / A:20 *Wendy Waldman*	Columbia 04884
10/19/85	**58**	8		18 **The Night Has A Heart Of It's Own**	*Lacy J. Dalton/Paul Worley*	Columbia 05644
1/18/86	**43**	16		19 **Don't Fall In Love With Me**	*Lacy J. Dalton/Mary McFadden*	Columbia 05759
6/14/86	**16**	19		20 **Working Class Man**	S:16 / A:16 *Jonathan Cain*	Columbia 06098
12/6/86+	**33**	14		21 **This Ol' Town**	*Rick Giles/George Green*	Columbia 06360
1/28/89	**13**	16		22 **The Heart**	*Kris Kristofferson*	Universal 53487
5/13/89	**57**	6		23 **I'm A Survivor**	*Mark Erwin/Bill Tinker*	Universal 66007
7/22/89	**38**	10		24 **Hard Luck Ace**	*Aaron Anderson/Lacy J. Dalton*	Universal 66015
3/31/90	**15**	22		25 **Black Coffee**	*Hillary Kanter/Even Stevens*	Capitol
				from the album *Lacy J.* on Capitol 93912		
				DALTON, Larry, and The Dalton Gang		
				Born Lawrence Pursley on 4/24/1946 in Big Stone Gap, Virginia. Male singer/songwriter.		
9/5/81	**82**	3		**Cowboy**	*Larry Dalton*	Soundwaves 4645
				DANDY		
				Trio of studio musicians from Nashville, Tennessee: **Hilka** Cornelius, Jeff Tweel and Jack "Stackatrack" Gromshal. Also recorded as **The Doolittle Band**.		
4/14/79	**57**	6		1 **Stay With Me**	*J.P. Pennington*	Warner/Curb 8771
7/28/79	**67**	5		2 **I Don't Want To Love You Anymore**	*Larry Keith/Mike Snow*	Warner/Curb 8880
12/1/79	**71**	6		3 **I'm Just Your Yesterday**	*James Dugan*	Warner/Curb 49111
10/18/80	**54**	7		4 **Who Were You Thinkin' Of** **THE DOOLITTLE BAND**	*Paul Gauvin/Jim Glaser/Cathy Pelletier*	Columbia 11355
				DANIEL		
				Born Daniel Willis on 11/23/1953 in Washington DC. Male singer.		
6/25/77	**91**	3		1 **But Tonight I'm Gonna Love You**	*David Connors/Steve Monahan*	LS 122
12/3/77	**100**	1		2 **Stolen Moments**	*Ray Griff*	LS 136
7/29/78	**78**	5		3 **I Bow My Head (When They Say Grace)**	*Bobby Barker/Dennis W. Morgan*	LS 166
				DANIEL, Cooter		
				Born on 11/9/1956 in Knoxville, Tennessee. Male singer/songwriter. Owner of the Connection record label.		
3/22/80	**89**	2		**Where Are We Going From Here**	*Cooter Daniel/Harold Dickinson*	Connection 1
				DANIEL, Davis		
				Born Robert Andrykowski on 3/1/1961 in Arlington Heights, Illinois; raised in Nebraska; later based in Denver, Colorado. Male singer/songwriter.		
5/11/91	**28**	20		1 **Picture Me**	*Brian Shaw/Mentor Williams*	Mercury
8/31/91	**13**	20		2 **For Crying Out Loud**	*James Compton/Phil Wood*	Mercury
1/4/92	**27**	20		3 **Fighting Fire With Fire**	*Conley White/Michael White*	Mercury

DEBUT	PEAK	WKS	GOLD	ARTIST / Ranking / Country Chart Hit	Songwriter	Label (& Number)

DANIEL, Davis — cont'd

DEBUT	PEAK	WKS	GOLD	Country Chart Hit	Songwriter	Label (& Number)
5/9/92	**48**	13		4 **Still Got A Crush On You**	*Dean Dillon/Paul Overstreet*	Mercury
				above 4 from the album *Fighting Fire With Fire* on Mercury 848291		
4/30/94	**74**	2		5 **I Miss Her Missing Me**	*Ronnie Samoset/Craig Wiseman*	Polydor
9/3/94	**64**	6		6 **William And Mary**	*George McCorkle/Rick Williamson*	Polydor
1/28/95	**58**	9		7 **Tyler**	*Davis Daniel/Lance Rogge*	Polydor
				above 3 from the album *Davis Daniel* on Polydor 518815		

DANIEL, Pebble

Born on 7/28/1947 in Waco, Texas. Died on 12/4/1995 (age 48). Female singer.

DEBUT	PEAK	WKS	GOLD	Country Chart Hit	Songwriter	Label (& Number)
6/21/80	**86**	3		**Goodbye Eyes**	*Dave Loggins*	Elektra 46643

DANIÉLLE, Tina

Born in Jena, Louisiana. Female singer.

DEBUT	PEAK	WKS	GOLD	Country Chart Hit	Songwriter	Label (& Number)
11/15/86	**75**	4		1 **Standing Too Close To The Moon**	*Leland Domann/Eric Thorson*	Charta 202
2/14/87	**71**	5		2 **Burned Out**	*Don Dozier/Sara Dozier/Jan Rasmussen*	Charta 204
5/9/87	**73**	4		3 **Warmed Over Romance**	*Charles Fields*	Charta 206

DANIELS, Charlie, Band — **All-Time: #194**

Born on 10/28/1936 in Wilmington, North Carolina. Male singer/songwriter/fiddler. His band: Tom Crain (guitar), Joe "Taz" DiGregorio (keyboards), Charles Hayward (bass), Jim Marshall (drums) and Fred Edwards (drums). Marshall and Edwards left in 1986; replaced by Jack Gavin. Group appeared in the movie *Urban Cowboy*.

CMA: Instrumental Group 1979 & 1980 / Musician 1979

DEBUT	PEAK	WKS	GOLD	Country Chart Hit	Songwriter	Label (& Number)
8/4/73	**67**	6		1 **Uneasy Rider** *[Charlie Daniels]*	*Charlie Daniels* [N]	Kama Sutra 576
1/31/76	**36**	11		2 **Texas**	*Charlie Daniels*	Kama Sutra 607
6/26/76	**22**	11		3 **Wichita Jail**	*Charlie Daniels*	Epic 50243
1/22/77	**75**	4		4 **Billy The Kid**	*Charlie Daniels*	Epic 50322
10/22/77	**85**	5		5 **Heaven Can Be Anywhere (Twin Pines Theme)**	*Charlie Daniels*	Epic 50456
6/30/79	**❶**[1]	14	▲	6 **The Devil Went Down To Georgia**	*Tom Crain/Charlie Daniels/Joe DiGregorio/Fred Edwards/ Charles Hayward/Jim Marshall*	Epic 50700
				Grammy: Vocal Group / CMA: Single; also see #29 & #30 below		
10/6/79	**19**	11		7 **Mississippi**	*Charlie Daniels*	Epic 50768
1/12/80	**87**	4		8 **Behind Your Eyes**	*John Boylan*	Epic 50806
2/23/80	**27**	10		9 **Long Haired Country Boy**	*Charlie Daniels*	Epic 50845
6/7/80	**13**	11		10 **In America**	*Tom Crain/Charlie Daniels/Joe DiGregorio/Fred Edwards/Charles Hayward/Jim Marshall*	Epic 50888
9/6/80	**80**	4		11 **The Legend Of Wooley Swamp**	*Tom Crain/Charlie Daniels/Joe DiGregorio/Fred Edwards/ Charles Hayward/Jim Marshall*	Epic 50921
12/27/80+	**44**	10		12 **Carolina (I Remember You)**	*Tom Crain/Charlie Daniels/Joe DiGregorio/Fred Edwards/ Charles Hayward/Jim Marshall*	Epic 50955
7/25/81	**94**	2		13 **Sweet Home Alabama**	*Ed King/Gary Rossington/Ronnie Van Zant* [L]	Epic 02185
7/17/82	**76**	4		14 **Ragin' Cajun**	*Tom Crain/Charlie Daniels/Joe DiGregorio/Fred Edwards/Charles Hayward/Jim Marshall*	Epic 02995
10/16/82	**69**	5		15 **We Had It All One Time**	*Charlie Daniels*	Epic 03251
8/13/83	**65**	6		16 **Stroker's Theme**	*Charlie Daniels*	Epic 03918
				from the movie *Stroker Ace* starring **Burt Reynolds**		
10/5/85	**54**	10		17 **American Farmer**	*Tom Crain/Charlie Daniels/Joe DiGregorio/Fred Edwards/Charles Hayward*	Epic 05638
12/7/85+	**33**	17		18 **Still Hurtin' Me**	S:29 *Brian Cadd*	Epic 05699
3/22/86	**8**	22		19 **Drinkin' My Baby Goodbye**	S:7 / A:7 *Charlie Daniels*	Epic 05835
8/20/88	**10**	17		20 **Boogie Woogie Fiddle Country Blues**	...S:4 *Tom Crain/Charlie Daniels/Joe DiGregorio/Jack Gavin/Charles Hayward*	Epic 08002
1/21/89	**36**	11		21 **Cowboy Hat In Dallas**	*Tom Crain/Charlie Daniels/Joe DiGregorio/Jack Gavin/Charles Hayward*	Epic 68542
4/22/89	**43**	9		22 **Midnight Train**	*Tom Crain/Charlie Daniels/Joe DiGregorio/Jack Gavin/Charles Hayward*	Epic 68738
10/14/89+	**12**	26		23 **Simple Man**	*Charlie Daniels/Joe DiGregorio/Jack Gavin/Charles Hayward*	Epic 73030
2/24/90	**34**	18		24 **Mister DJ**	*Tom Crain/Charlie Daniels/Joe DiGregorio/Fred Edwards/Charles Hayward*	Epic
8/25/90	**56**	5		25 **(What This World Needs Is) A Few More Rednecks**	*Charlie Daniels/Joe DiGregorio/ Jack Gavin/Charles Hayward*	Epic
				above 2 from the album *Simple Man* on Epic 45316		
				CHARLIE DANIELS:		
4/27/91	**65**	7		26 **Honky Tonk Life**	*Charlie Daniels*	Epic
11/2/91	**47**	14		27 **Little Folks**	*Charlie Daniels*	Epic
				above 2 from the album *Renegade* on Epic 46835		
3/20/93	**73**	2		28 **America, I Believe In You**	*Charlie Daniels/Joe DiGregorio/Charles Hayward*	Liberty
				from the album *America, I Believe In You* on Liberty 80477		
12/25/93+	**54**	10		29 **The Devil Comes Back To Georgia** *[w/ Mark O'Connor/Johnny Cash/Marty Stuart/Travis Tritt]*	...*Tom Crain/Charlie Daniels/Joe DiGregorio/Fred Edwards/Charles Hayward/Jim Marshall*	Warner
				from O'Connor's album *Heroes* on Warner 45257; sequel to #6 above		
6/20/98	**60**	7		30 **The Devil Went Down To Georgia**	*Tom Crain/Charlie Daniels/Joe DiGregorio/Fred Edwards/ Charles Hayward/Jim Marshall* [R]	Epic
				same version as #6 above; from the album *Super Hits* on Epic 64182		
9/23/00	**31**	21		31 **All Night Long** *[w/ Montgomery Gentry]*	S:7 *Bruce Brown/Charlie Daniels/Joe DiGregorio/ Jack Gavin/Charles Hayward*	Columbia
				from Montgomery Gentry's album *Tattoos & Scars* on Columbia 69156		
11/10/01	**33**	13		32 **This Ain't No Rag, It's A Flag**	*Charlie Daniels*	Blue Hat
				from the album *The Live Record* on Blue Hat 8133		
1/25/03	**51**	6		33 **Southern Boy** *[w/ Travis Tritt]*	*Charlie Daniels/Travis Tritt*	Blue Hat
				from the album *Redneck Fiddlin' Man* on Blue Hat 8159		
7/19/03	**58**	1		34 **My Beautiful America**	*Charlie Daniels* [S]	Blue Hat
				from the album *Freedom And Justice For All* on Blue Hat 8188		

DEBUT	PEAK	WKS	GOLD		ARTIST / Country Chart Hit	Songwriter	Label (& Number)

DANIELS, Clint

Born on 8/24/1974 in Panama City, Florida. Male singer/songwriter/guitarist.

DEBUT	PEAK	WKS	GOLD	#	Country Chart Hit	Songwriter	Label (& Number)
6/13/98	44	12		1	A Fool's Progress	*Clint Daniels/Tony Martin*	Arista
10/17/98	53	9		2	When I Grow Up	*Tony Martin/Calvin Sweat*	Arista
					above 2 from the album *Clint Daniels* on Arista 18868		
5/17/03	56	1		3	The Letter (Almost Home)	*Lisa Threet/Randy Threet*	Epic

DARIN, Bobby

Born Walden Robert Cassotto on 5/14/1936 in the Bronx, New York. Died of heart failure on 12/20/1973 (age 37). Popular male singer/songwriter/actor. Appeared in several movies and TV shows. Married to actress Sandra Dee from 1960-67. Inducted into the Rock and Roll Hall of Fame in 1990.

DEBUT	PEAK	WKS	GOLD	#	Country Chart Hit	Songwriter	Label (& Number)
8/4/58	14	3	●		Splish Splash	S:14 *Bobby Darin/Jean Murray*	Atco 6117

DARLING, Helen

Born on 5/1/1965 in Baton Rouge, Louisiana; raised in Houston, Texas. Female singer.

DEBUT	PEAK	WKS	GOLD	#	Country Chart Hit	Songwriter	Label (& Number)
8/5/95	69	3			Jenny Come Back	*Tia Sillers/John Tirro*	Decca
					from the album *Helen Darling* on Decca 11259		

DARRELL, Johnny

Born on 7/23/1940 in Hopewell, Alabama. Died of diabetes on 10/7/1997 (age 57). Male singer/guitarist.

DEBUT	PEAK	WKS	GOLD	#	Country Chart Hit	Songwriter	Label (& Number)
12/25/65+	30	7		1	As Long As The Wind Blows	*Curly Putman*	United Artists 943
6/4/66	44	3		2	Johnny Lose It All	*Bill Hughey*	United Artists 50008
11/12/66	72	4		3	She's Mighty Gone	*June Carter/Johnny Cash*	United Artists 50047
4/1/67	9	15		4	Ruby, Don't Take Your Love To Town	*Mel Tillis*	United Artists 50126
7/22/67	73	3		5	My Elusive Dreams	*Curly Putnam/Billy Sherrill*	United Artists 50183
10/7/67	37	10		6	Come See What's Left Of Your Man	*Ronnie Self*	United Artists 50207
12/23/67+	22	14		7	The Son Of Hickory Holler's Tramp	*Dallas Frazier*	United Artists 50235
4/27/68	3^{1}	18		8	With Pen In Hand	*Bobby Goldsboro*	United Artists 50292
9/21/68	27	10		9	I Ain't Buying	*Billy Edd Wheeler*	United Artists 50442
11/30/68+	20	13		10	Woman Without Love	*Jerry Chesnut*	United Artists 50481
4/12/69	50	7		11	The Coming Of The Roads *[w/ Anita Carter]*	*Billy Edd Wheeler*	United Artists 50503
4/26/69	17	13		12	Why You Been Gone So Long	*Mickey Newbury*	United Artists 50518
9/13/69	23	10		13	River Bottom	*Billy Edd Wheeler*	United Artists 50572
2/14/70	68	7		14	Mama Come'n Get Your Baby Boy	*Dewayne Blackwell*	United Artists 50629
7/11/70	75	2		15	Brother River	*Hank Cochran/Red Lane*	United Artists 50675
11/14/70	74	2		16	They'll Never Take Her Love From Me	*Leon Payne*	United Artists 50716
7/28/73	66	10		17	Dakota The Dancing Bear	*Larry Murray*	Monument 8579
10/12/74	63	9		18	Orange Blossom Special	*Ervin Rouse*	Capricorn 0207

DARREN, James

Born James Ercolani on 6/8/1936 in Philadelphia, Pennsylvania. Male pop singer/actor. Appeared in several movies and TV shows.

DEBUT	PEAK	WKS	GOLD	#	Country Chart Hit	Songwriter	Label (& Number)
7/29/78	53	9			Let Me Take You In My Arms Again	*Neil Diamond*	RCA 11316

DAVE & SUGAR — **All-Time: #218**

Trio consisting of **Dave Rowland** (born on 1/26/1942), Vicki Hackeman (born on 8/4/1950) and Jackie Frantz (born on 10/8/1950). Trio worked as backup singers for **Charley Pride**. Frantz was replaced by **Sue Powell** in 1977. Hackeman was replaced by Melissa Dean in 1979. Powell was replaced by Jamie Jaye in 1980. Rowland went solo in 1982.

DEBUT	PEAK	WKS	GOLD	#	Country Chart Hit	Songwriter	Label (& Number)
11/15/75+	25	17		1	Queen Of The Silver Dollar	*Shel Silverstein*	RCA Victor 10425
4/17/76	❶^{1}	19		2	The Door Is Always Open	*Dickey Lee/Bob McDill*	RCA Victor 10625
9/11/76	3^{1}	17		3	I'm Gonna Love You	*Baker Knight*	RCA 10768
2/12/77	5	13		4	Don't Throw It All Away	*Gary Benson/David Mindel*	RCA 10876
7/16/77	7	14		5	That's The Way Love Should Be	*Milton Blackford/Joe Dougherty/Dave Gillon*	RCA 11034
10/29/77	2^{4}	16		6	I'm Knee Deep In Loving You	*Sonny Throckmorton*	RCA 11141
4/8/78	4	14		7	Gotta' Quit Lookin' At You Baby	*Jerry Foster/Bill Rice*	RCA 11251
8/12/78	❶^{1}	16		8	Tear Time	*Jan Crutchfield*	RCA 11322
1/20/79	❶^{3}	14		9	Golden Tears	*John Schweers*	RCA 11427
6/30/79	6	13		10	Stay With Me	*J.P. Pennington*	RCA 11654
10/20/79	4	14		11	My World Begins And Ends With You /	*Larry Keith/Steve Pippin*	
10/20/79	flip	14		12	Why Did You Have To Be So Good	*Jerry Foster/Bill Rice*	RCA 11749
4/5/80	18	12		13	New York Wine And Tennessee Shine	*Wayland Holyfield*	RCA 11947
8/16/80	40	8		14	A Love Song	*Jan Crutchfield*	RCA 12063
2/7/81	32	9		15	It's A Heartache	*Ronnie Scott/Steve Wolfe*	RCA 12168
					DAVE ROWLAND & SUGAR:		
5/9/81	6	15		16	Fool By Your Side	*Bobby Cox*	Elektra 47135
8/29/81	32	8		17	The Pleasure's All Mine	*Kieran Kane/Curly Putman*	Elektra 47177
					DAVE ROWLAND:		
5/15/82	77	5		18	Natalie /	*Dean Dillon/Gary Stewart/Tanya Tucker*	
5/15/82	flip	5		19	Why Didn't I Think Of That	*Jamie O'Hara/John Potts*	Elektra 47442
7/31/82	84	3		20	Lovin' Our Lives Away	*Jerry Foster/Bill Rice*	Elektra 69998

DAVIDSON, Clay

Born on 4/4/1971 in Saltville, Virginia. Male singer/songwriter/guitarist.

DEBUT	PEAK	WKS	GOLD	#	Country Chart Hit	Songwriter	Label (& Number)
1/15/00	3^{1}	31		1	Unconditional	S:7 *Deanna Bryant/Liz Hengber/Rivers Rutherford*	Virgin
7/29/00	26	20		2	I Can't Lie To Me	*Kenny Beard/Casey Beathard/Clay Davidson*	Virgin
1/27/01	21	20		3	Sometimes	*Kenny Beard/Casey Beathard/Clay Davidson*	Virgin
					above 3 from the album *Unconditional* on Virgin 48854		

Billboard DEBUT	PEAK	WKS	GOLD		ARTIST / Country Chart Hit	Ranking / Songwriter	Label (& Number)

DAVIES, Gail — All-Time: #221

Born Patricia Gail Dickerson on 6/5/1948 in Broken Bow, Oklahoma. Female singer/songwriter/guitarist. Did session work in Los Angeles and worked as a staff writer for Vogue Music. Moved to Nashville in the mid-1970s. Lead singer with the **Wild Choir** in 1986.

DEBUT	PEAK	WKS	GOLD	#	Country Chart Hit	Songwriter	Label (& Number)
7/8/78	26	12		1	**No Love Have I**	*Mel Tillis*	Lifesong 1771
10/21/78	27	12		2	**Poison Love**	*Elmer Laird*	Lifesong 1777
2/10/79	11	16		3	**Someone Is Looking For Someone Like You**	*Gail Davies*	Lifesong 1784
11/17/79+	7	16		4	**Blue Heartache**	*Paul Craft*	Warner 49108
3/22/80	21	11		5	**Like Strangers**	*Boudleaux Bryant*	Warner 49199
6/28/80	21	12		6	**Good Lovin' Man**	*Gail Davies*	Warner 49263
11/29/80+	4	16		7	**I'll Be There** (If You Ever Want Me)	*Rusty Gabbard/Ray Price*	Warner 49592
4/4/81	5	18		8	**It's A Lovely, Lovely World**	*Boudleaux Bryant*	Warner 49694
8/15/81	9	15		9	**Grandma's Song**	*Gail Davies*	Warner 49790
2/13/82	9	18		10	**'Round The Clock Lovin'**	*Rory Bourke/K.T. Oslin*	Warner 50004
6/26/82	17	15		11	**You Turn Me On I'm A Radio**	*Joni Mitchell*	Warner 29972
10/30/82+	24	15		12	**Hold On**	*Rick Clark/Mark Marchetti*	Warner 29892
3/26/83	17	15		13	**Singing The Blues**	*Melvin Endsley*	Warner 29726
10/15/83	18	19		14	**You're A Hard Dog** (To Keep Under The Porch)	*Susanna Clark/Harlan Howard*	Warner 29472
2/25/84	19	17		15	**Boys Like You**	*Gail Davies/Walker Igleheart*	Warner 29374
8/4/84	55	12		16	**It's You Alone**	*Ron Davies*	Warner 29219
10/6/84	20	25		17	**Jagged Edge Of A Broken Heart**	A:18 / S:20 *Walker Igleheart/Mike Joyce*	RCA 13912
2/23/85	37	12		18	**Nothing Can Hurt Me Now**	*Paul Kennerley/Bob McDill*	RCA 14017
6/22/85	56	8		19	**Unwed Fathers**	*Bobby Braddock/John Prine*	RCA 14095
9/21/85	15	25		20	**Break Away**	S:12 / A:15 *Wayland Holyfield/Gary Nicholson*	RCA 14184
3/11/89	50	10		21	**Waiting Here For You**	*Gail Davies*	MCA 53505
6/24/89	69	4		22	**Hearts In The Wind**	*Ken Cummings/Gail Davies*	MCA 53442

DAVIS, Carrie

Born in Scottsdale, Arizona. Female singer.

DEBUT	PEAK	WKS	GOLD	#	Country Chart Hit	Songwriter	Label (& Number)
3/4/89	84	3			**Another Heart To Break The Fall**	*Del Gray/David Lee Murphy*	Fountain Hills 130

DAVIS, Danny, & The Nashville Brass

Born George Nowlan on 4/29/1925 in Dorchester, Massachusetts. Trumpet player/bandleader. Played with many swing bands including Gene Krupa, Bob Crosby, Freddy Martin, Blue Barron, and Sammy Kaye. Producer for Joy and MGM Records in the late 1950s. Production assistant to **Chet Atkins** in 1965. Owner of the Wartrace record label. Formed The Nashville Brass in 1968.

CMA: Instrumental Group 1969, 1970, 1971, 1972, 1973 & 1974

DEBUT	PEAK	WKS	GOLD	#	Country Chart Hit	Songwriter	Label (& Number)
1/3/70	68	3		1	**Please Help Me, I'm Falling** ***[w/ Hank Locklin]***	*Blair/Don Robertson*	RCA Victor 0287
2/14/70	63	3		2	**Wabash Cannon Ball**	*A.P. Carter* **[I]**	RCA Victor 9785
6/27/70	56	6		3	**Flying South** ***[w/ Hank Locklin]***	*Cindy Walker*	RCA Victor 9849
7/4/70	70	2		4	**Columbus Stockade Blues**	*Jimmie Davis/Eva Sargent* **[I]**	RCA Victor 9847
10/15/77	91	6		5	**How I Love Them Old Songs**	*Mickey Newbury*	RCA 11073
2/2/80	20	12		6	**Night Life** ***[w/ Willie Nelson]***	*Walt Breeland/Paul Buskirk/Willie Nelson*	RCA 11893
5/17/80	41	8		7	**Funny How Time Slips Away** ***[w/ Willie Nelson]***	*Willie Nelson*	RCA 11999
3/23/85	82	3		8	**I Dropped Your Name** Arlene Baird (vocal)	*Ken Bell/Terry Skinner*	Wartrace 730
10/10/87	62	5		9	**Green Eyes** (Cryin' Those Blue Tears) ***[w/ Dona Mason]***	*Mary Fielder/Kim Morrison*	Jaroco 8742

DAVIS, Dianne

Born in Celina, Tennessee. Female singer.

DEBUT	PEAK	WKS	GOLD	#	Country Chart Hit	Songwriter	Label (& Number)
7/29/89	75	4			**Baby Don't Go**	*Karla Bonoff/Kenny Edwards*	16th Avenue 70430

DAVIS, Gene

Born in Dallas, Texas. Male singer/songwriter.

DEBUT	PEAK	WKS	GOLD	#	Country Chart Hit	Songwriter	Label (& Number)
11/27/76	97	4			**Oh Those Texas Women**	*Gene Davis*	Maverick 301

DAVIS, Jimmie — 1940s: #25 // HOF: 1972

Born on 9/11/1899 in Beech Grove, Louisiana. Died on 11/5/2000 (age 101). Male singer/songwriter/guitarist. Appeared in several movies. Governor of Louisiana from 1944-48 and 1960-64.

EARLY HITS: Nobody's Darling But Mine (1937) / Meet Me Tonight In Dreamland (1938) / You Are My Sunshine (1940)

DEBUT	PEAK	WKS	GOLD	#	Country Chart Hit	Songwriter	Label (& Number)
9/2/44	3[1]	2		1	**Is It Too Late Now /**	*Jimmie Davis*	
9/30/44	4	2		2	**There's A Chill On The Hill Tonight**	*Nelson Cogane/Jimmie Davis/Sammy Mysels/Dick Robertson*	Decca 6100
2/17/45	❶[1]	18		3	**There's A New Moon Over My Shoulder**	*Lee Blastic/Jimmie Davis/Ekko Whelan*	Decca 6105
3/2/46	4	1		4	**Grievin' My Heart Out For You**	*Jimmie Davis/Logan Snodgrass*	Decca 18756
1/18/47	4	2		5	**Bang Bang**	*Jimmie Davis*	Decca 46016
6/16/62	15	9		6	**Where The Old Red River Flows**	*Jimmie Davis*	Decca 31368

DAVIS, Joey

Born in Waynesboro, Virginia. Male singer/songwriter.

DEBUT	PEAK	WKS	GOLD	#	Country Chart Hit	Songwriter	Label (& Number)
8/12/78	99	1		1	**Why Don't You Leave Me Alone**	*Joey Davis*	MRC 1017
12/16/78	94	3		2	**Takin' It Easy**	*Joey Davis*	MRC 1023

DAVIS, Linda

Born on 11/26/1962 in Dodson, Texas. Female singer. One-half of **Skip and Linda** duo. Married to **Lang Scott**.

DEBUT	PEAK	WKS	GOLD	#	Country Chart Hit	Songwriter	Label (& Number)
10/29/88	50	10		1	**All The Good One's Are Taken**	*Max T. Barnes/Randy Hardison*	Epic 08057
2/4/89	51	6		2	**Back In The Swing Again**	*Al DeLory/Lee Johnson/Carson Whitsett*	Epic 68544
6/10/89	67	5		3	**Weak Nights**	*Kix Brooks/Mary Fielder*	Epic 68919

Billboard DEBUT	PEAK	WKS	GOLD	ARTIST Ranking / Country Chart Hit	Songwriter	Label (& Number)
				DAVIS, Linda — cont'd		
1/12/91	**61**	7		4 **In A Different Light**	*Ed Hill/Jonathan Yudkin*	Capitol
5/4/91	**68**	5		5 **Some Kinda Woman**	*Annette Cotter/David Leonard*	Capitol
				above 2 from the album *In A Different Light* on Capitol 94829		
8/28/93	❶[1]	20		6 **Does He Love You** *[w/ Reba McEntire]*	*Sandy Knox/Billy Stritch*	MCA
				Grammy: Vocal Collaboration / CMA: Vocal Event; from McEntire's album *Greatest Hits Volume Two* on MCA 10906		
2/26/94	**43**	13		7 **Company Time**	*Mac McAnally*	Arista
6/18/94	**58**	8		8 **Love Didn't Do It**	*Steven Jones/Bobby Tomberlin*	Arista
				above 2 from the album *Shoot For The Moon* on Arista 18749		
12/2/95+	**13**	20		9 **Some Things Are Meant To Be** S:12	*Michael Garvin/Gordon Payne*	Arista
4/13/96	**33**	19		10 **A Love Story In The Making**	*Al Anderson/Craig Wiseman*	Arista
				above 2 from the album *Some Things Are Meant To Be* on Arista 18804		
5/16/98	**20**	21		11 **I Wanna Remember This**	*Jennifer Kimball/Annie Roboff*	Decca
				from the movie *Black Dog* starring Patrick Swayze (soundtrack on Decca 70027)		
10/31/98+	**38**	19		12 **I'm Yours**	*Phillip Coleman/Carolyn Dawn Johnson*	DreamWorks
4/3/99	**60**	7		13 **From The Inside Out**	*Marc Beeson/Angela Kaset*	DreamWorks
				above 2 from the album *I'm Yours* on DreamWorks 50100		

DAVIS, Mac — **All-Time: #187**

Born Scott Davis on 1/21/1942 in Lubbock, Texas. Male singer/songwriter/guitarist. Worked as a regional rep for Vee-Jay and Liberty Records. Acted in several movies. Host of own musical variety TV series from 1974-76.

DEBUT	PEAK	WKS	GOLD	Country Chart Hit	Songwriter	Label (& Number)
4/25/70	**43**	13		1 **Whoever Finds This, I Love You**	*Mac Davis*	Columbia 45117
8/29/70	**68**	4		2 **I'll Paint You A Song**	*Mac Davis*	Columbia 45192
				from the movie *Norwood* starring **Glen Campbell**		
8/26/72	**26**	11	●	3 **Baby Don't Get Hooked On Me**	*Mac Davis*	Columbia 45618
2/24/73	**47**	8		4 **Dream Me Home**	*Mac Davis*	Columbia 45773
5/12/73	**36**	11		5 **Your Side Of The Bed**	*Mac Davis*	Columbia 45839
9/1/73	**29**	15		6 **Kiss It And Make It Better**	*Mac Davis*	Columbia 45911
9/7/74	**40**	12		7 **Stop And Smell The Roses**	*Mac Davis/Doc Severinsen*	Columbia 10018
1/4/75	**29**	11		8 **Rock N' Roll (I Gave You The Best Years Of My Life)**	*Kevin Johnson*	Columbia 10070
4/12/75	**69**	6		9 **(If You Add) All The Love In The World**	*Ian Page*	Columbia 10111
6/7/75	**31**	12		10 **Burnin' Thing**	*Mac Davis*	Columbia 10148
9/27/75	**81**	5		11 **I Still Love You (You Still Love Me)**	*Mac Davis/Mickey James*	Columbia 10187
3/27/76	**17**	13		12 **Forever Lovers**	*Sterling Whipple*	Columbia 10304
10/9/76	**34**	10		13 **Every Now And Then**	*Mac Davis*	Columbia 10418
5/21/77	**42**	9		14 **Picking Up The Pieces Of My Life**	*Mac Davis*	Columbia 10535
6/10/78	**92**	5		15 **Music In My Life**	*Mac Davis*	Columbia 10745
3/22/80	**10**	12		16 **It's Hard To Be Humble**	*Mac Davis* **[N]**	Casablanca 2244
7/12/80	**10**	15		17 **Let's Keep It That Way**	*Curly Putman/Rafe Van Hoy*	Casablanca 2286
10/11/80	**9**	17		18 **Texas In My Rear View Mirror**	*Mac Davis*	Casablanca 2305
2/21/81	**2[2]**	15		19 **Hooked On Music**	*Mac Davis*	Casablanca 2327
7/18/81	**47**	10		20 **Secrets**	*Sam Lorber/Mike Noble/Jeff Silbar*	Casablanca 2336
10/24/81+	**5**	18		21 **You're My Bestest Friend**	*Mac Davis*	Casablanca 2341
5/29/82	**37**	10		22 **Rodeo Clown**	*Mac Davis*	Casablanca 2350
9/25/82	**58**	8		23 **The Beer Drinkin' Song**	*Mac Davis*	Casablanca 2355
12/18/82+	**62**	7		24 **Lying Here Lying**	*Walt Aldridge/Mac Davis*	Casablanca 2363
2/11/84	**41**	14		25 **Most Of All**	*Mac Davis*	Casablanca 818168
5/19/84	**76**	5		26 **Caroline's Still In Georgia**	*Wayland Holyfield*	Casablanca 818929
5/25/85	**10**	24		27 **I Never Made Love (Till I Made Love With You)** S:9 / A:10	*Bob McDill*	MCA 52573
10/5/85	**34**	16		28 **I Feel The Country Callin' Me**	*Joe Richie*	MCA 52669
2/1/86	**46**	9		29 **Sexy Young Girl**	*Mac Davis/Barbara Wyrick*	MCA 52765
6/7/86	**65**	5		30 **Somewhere In America**	*Steve Davis/Even Stevens*	MCA 52826

DAVIS, Paul

Born in West Virginia. Male singer.

DEBUT	PEAK	WKS	GOLD	Country Chart Hit	Songwriter	Label (& Number)
7/18/60	**28**	5		**One Of Her Fools**	*Dewey Stone*	Doke 107

DAVIS, Paul

Born on 4/21/1948 in Meridian, Mississippi. Male singer/songwriter/producer.

DEBUT	PEAK	WKS	GOLD	Country Chart Hit	Songwriter	Label (& Number)
1/11/75	**47**	8		1 **Ride 'Em Cowboy**	*Paul Davis*	Bang 712
12/16/78+	**85**	4		2 **Sweet Life**	*Susan Collins/Paul Davis*	Bang 738
				also see #5 below		
8/30/86	❶[1]	21		3 **You're Still New To Me** *[w/ Marie Osmond]* S:❶[1] / A:❶[1]	*Paul Davis/Paul Overstreet*	Curb/Capitol 5613
11/21/87+	❶[1]	24		4 **I Won't Take Less Than Your Love** *[w/ Tanya Tucker & Paul Overstreet]* ...S:2	*Paul Overstreet/Don Schlitz*	Capitol 44100
8/20/88	**47**	8		5 **Sweet Life** *[w/ Marie Osmond]*	*Susan Collins/Paul Davis*	Curb/Capitol 44215

Billboard DEBUT	PEAK	WKS	GOLD	ARTIST Ranking / Country Chart Hit	Songwriter	Label (& Number)

DAVIS, Sammy Jr.

Born on 12/8/1925 in Harlem, New York. Died of cancer on 5/16/1990 (age 64). Black singer/dancer/actor. Numerous appearances on TV, Broadway and in movies. Won Grammy's Lifetime Achievement Award in 2001.

DEBUT	PEAK	WKS	GOLD	Country Chart Hit	Songwriter	Label (& Number)
12/11/82	89	2		**Smoke, Smoke, Smoke (That Cigarette)**	*Merle Travis/Tex Williams*	Applause 100

DAVIS, Skeeter — 1960s: #25 / All-Time: #120

Born Mary Penick on 12/30/1931 in Dry Ridge, Kentucky. Died of cancer on 9/19/2004 (age 72). Female singer/songwriter. Worked as **The Davis Sisters** with friend Betty Jack Davis, and later with Georgia Davis. Went solo in 1956. Married to **Ralph Emery** from 1960-64. Married to Joey Spampinato, the bassist of rock band NRBQ, from 1983-96. Also see **Some Of Chet's Friends**.

OPRY: 1959

DEBUT	PEAK	WKS	GOLD	Country Chart Hit	Songwriter	Label (& Number)
2/24/58	15	1		1 **Lost To A Geisha Girl** A:15 answer to "Geisha Girl" by **Hank Locklin**	*Lawton Williams*	RCA Victor 7084
3/30/59	5	17		2 **Set Him Free** also see #24 below	*Skeeter Davis/Helen Moyers/Marie Wilson*	RCA Victor 7471
9/21/59	15	13		3 **Homebreaker**	*Skeeter Davis/Marie Wilson*	RCA Victor 7570
3/7/60	11	12		4 **Am I That Easy To Forget?**	*Carl Belew/W.S. Stevenson*	RCA Victor 7671
8/29/60	2^3	16		5 **(I Can't Help You) I'm Falling Too** answer to "Please Help Me, I'm Falling" by **Hank Locklin**	*Hal Blair/Don Robertson*	RCA Victor 7767
12/31/60+	5	13		6 **My Last Date (With You)** answer to "Last Date" by **Floyd Cramer**	*Boudleaux Bryant/Floyd Cramer/Skeeter Davis*	RCA Victor 7825
4/24/61	11	11		7 **The Hand You're Holding Now**	*Marty Robbins*	RCA Victor 7863
10/16/61	10	11		8 **Optimistic**	*Aubrey Freeman*	RCA Victor 7928
3/10/62	9	9		9 **Where I Ought To Be /**	*Harlan Howard*	
6/2/62	23	3		10 **Something Precious**	*Lorene Mann*	RCA Victor 7979
9/8/62	22	1		11 **The Little Music Box**	*Skeeter Davis/Rudy Thacker*	RCA Victor 8055
12/15/62+	2^3	24		12 **The End Of The World**	*Sylvia Dee/Arthur Kent*	RCA Victor 8098
5/25/63	9	14		13 **I'm Saving My Love**	*Alex Zanetis*	RCA Victor 8176
10/12/63	14	10		14 **I Can't Stay Mad At You**	*Gerry Goffin/Carole King*	RCA Victor 8219
1/25/64	17	15		15 **He Says The Same Things To Me**	*Gary Geld/Peter Udell*	RCA Victor 8288
5/16/64	8	14		16 **Gonna Get Along Without You Now**	*Milton Kellem*	RCA Victor 8347
9/26/64	45	4		17 **Let Me Get Close To You**	*Gerry Goffin/Carole King*	RCA Victor 8397
11/14/64	38	5		18 **What Am I Gonna Do With You**	*Gerry Goffin/Russ Titelman*	RCA Victor 8450
3/13/65	11	12		19 **A Dear John Letter** *[w/ Bobby Bare]*	*Billy Barton/Fuzzy Owen/Lewis Talley*	RCA Victor 8496
9/11/65	30	7		20 **Sun Glasses**	*John D. Loudermilk*	RCA Victor 8642
10/15/66	36	9		21 **Goin' Down The Road (Feelin' Bad)**	*Skeeter Davis*	RCA Victor 8932
1/28/67	11	16		22 **Fuel To The Flame**	*Bill Owens/Dolly Parton*	RCA Victor 9058
7/22/67	5	18		23 **What Does It Take (To Keep A Man Like You Satisfied)**	*Jim Glaser*	RCA Victor 9242
12/16/67+	52	7		24 **Set Him Free** new version of #2 above	*Skeeter Davis/Helen Moyers/Marie Wilson* **[R]**	RCA Victor 9371
2/24/68	72	2		25 **For Loving You** *[w/ Don Bowman]*	*Steve Karliski* **[N]**	RCA Victor 9415
3/23/68	54	7		26 **Instinct For Survival**	*Jim Glaser*	RCA Victor 9459
6/22/68	16	10		27 **There's A Fool Born Every Minute**	*Paul Evans/Paul Parnes*	RCA Victor 9543
1/11/69	66	7		28 **The Closest Thing To Love (I've Ever Seen)**	*Ronny Light*	RCA Victor 9695
12/13/69+	9	15		29 **I'm A Lover (Not A Fighter)**	*Ronny Light*	RCA Victor 0292
1/24/70	22	7		30 **Your Husband, My Wife** *[w/ Bobby Bare]*	*Irwin Levine/Toni Wine*	RCA Victor 9789
5/9/70	65	5		31 **It's Hard To Be A Woman**	*Johnny Christopher/Richard Mainegra/Red West*	RCA Victor 9818
8/8/70	69	3		32 **We Need A Lot More Of Jesus**	*Wayne Raney*	RCA Victor 9871
9/26/70	65	2		33 **Let's Get Together** *[w/ George Hamilton IV]*	*Chet Powers*	RCA Victor 9893
3/6/71	21	13		34 **Bus Fare To Kentucky**	*Ronny Light*	RCA Victor 9961
7/17/71	58	8		35 **Love Takes A Lot Of My Time**	*Ronny Light*	RCA Victor 9997
1/8/72	54	7		36 **One Tin Soldier** from the movie *Billy Jack* starring Tom Laughlin	*Dennis Lambert/Brian Potter*	RCA Victor 0608
5/20/72	46	8		37 **Sad Situation**	*Clyde Pitts*	RCA Victor 0681
6/16/73	12	17		38 **I Can't Believe That It's All Over**	*Ben Peters*	RCA Victor 0968
12/15/73+	44	10		39 **Don't Forget To Remember**	*Barry Gibb/Maurice Gibb*	RCA Victor 0188
5/25/74	65	8		40 **One More Time**	*Ronny Light*	RCA Victor 0277
9/18/76	60	7		41 **I Love Us**	*Jeff Tweel*	Mercury 73818

DAVIS, Stephanie

Born in Montana. Female singer/songwriter.

DEBUT	PEAK	WKS	GOLD	Country Chart Hit	Songwriter	Label (& Number)
8/28/93	72	2		**It's All In The Heart** from the album *Stephanie Davis* on Asylum 61546	*Stephanie Davis*	Asylum

DAVIS SISTERS, The

Vocal duo from Lexington, Kentucky: **Skeeter Davis** and Betty Jack Davis. The two were not related. Betty Jack was killed and Skeeter was seriously injured in a car crash on 8/2/1953. Betty Jack was replaced by her sister Georgia.

DEBUT	PEAK	WKS	GOLD	Country Chart Hit	Songwriter	Label (& Number)
8/15/53	❶^{8}	26		**I Forgot More Than You'll Ever Know** A:❶^{8} / S:❶^{6} / J:❶^{2}	*Cecil Null*	RCA Victor 5345

DAWSON, Peter, Band

Born in 1979 in Dallas, Texas. Male singer/songwriter/guitarist.

DEBUT	PEAK	WKS	GOLD	Country Chart Hit	Songwriter	Label (& Number)
10/21/00	72	1		**Willie Nelson For President** from the album *Do You Do or Do You Don't* on Radio 3200	*Peter Dawson/James Wood* **[N]**	Radio

DEBUT	PEAK	WKS	GOLD	ARTIST / Country Chart Hit ... Songwriter	Ranking	Label (& Number)
				DAY, Jennifer		
				Born on 8/22/1979 in McAlpin, Florida. Female singer.		
12/4/99+	**31**	20		1 **The Fun Of Your Love** ... S:5 *Beth Nielsen Chapman/Jennifer Day/Annie Roboff*		BNA
6/3/00	**67**	3		2 **What If It's Me** ... *Robert Byrne/Angela Kaset*		BNA
				above 2 from the album *The Fun Of Your Love* on BNA 67799		
				DEAL, Don		
				Born in 1939 in Iowa. Male singer/guitarist.		
6/16/79	**90**	2		**Second Best (Is Too Far Down The Line)** ... *Wynn Stewart*		Donjim 1008

DEBUT	PEAK	WKS	GOLD	ARTIST / Country Chart Hit ... Songwriter	Ranking	Label (& Number)
				DEAN, Billy	**1990s: #45 / All-Time: #169**	
				Born on 4/1/1962 in Quincy, Florida. Male singer/songwriter/guitarist. Atteneded college in Decatur, Mississippi, on a basketball scholarship. Also see **America The Beautiful** and **One Heart At A Time**.		
12/22/90+	**3**[1]	22		1 **Only Here For A Little While** ... *Wayland Holyfield/Richard Leigh*		Capitol
5/4/91	**3**[2]	20		2 **Somewhere In My Broken Heart** ... *Billy Dean/Richard Leigh*		Capitol
				above 2 from the album *Young Man* on Capitol 94302		
9/14/91	**4**	20		3 **You Don't Count The Cost** ... *Bucky Jones/Tom Shapiro/Chris Waters*		Capitol
1/4/92	**4**	20		4 **Only The Wind** ... *Chuck Jones/Tom Shapiro*		Capitol
5/23/92	**4**	20		5 **Billy The Kid** ... *Billy Dean/Paul Nelson*		Capitol
8/29/92	**3**[2]	20		6 **If There Hadn't Been You** ... *Ron Hellard/Tom Shapiro*		Capitol
				above 4 from the album *Billy Dean* on Capitol 96728		
12/12/92+	**6**	20		7 **Tryin' To Hide A Fire In The Dark** ... *Billy Dean/Tim Nichols*		Liberty
4/10/93	**22**	20		8 **I Wanna Take Care Of You** ... *Billy Dean/Judy Jones*		Liberty
8/21/93	**34**	13		9 **I'm Not Built That Way** ... *Don Pfrimmer/George Teren*		Liberty
11/13/93+	**9**	20		10 **We Just Disagree** ... *Jim Krueger*		Liberty
				above 4 from the album *Fire In The Dark* on Liberty 98947		
3/5/94	**53**	8		11 **Once In A While** ... *John Bettis/Steve Dorff*		MCA
				from the movie *8 Seconds* starring Luke Perry (soundtrack on MCA 10927)		
6/4/94	**24**	20		12 **Cowboy Band** ... *Jule Medders/Monty Powell*		Liberty
10/8/94	**60**	6		13 **Men Will Be Boys** ... *Guy Clark/Verlon Thompson*		Liberty
				above 2 from the album *Men'll Be Boys* on Liberty 27760		
2/3/96	**5**	20		14 **It's What I Do** ... S:17 *Chuck Jones/Tom Shapiro*		Capitol
6/15/96	**4**	20		15 **That Girl's Been Spyin' On Me** ... S:13 *Max T. Barnes/Tom Shapiro*		Capitol
11/2/96	**45**	14		16 **I Wouldn't Be A Man** ... *Rory Bourke/Mike Reid*		Capitol
				above 3 from the album *It's What I Do* on Capitol 30525		
7/4/98	**33**	18		17 **Real Man** ... *Billy Dean*		Capitol
11/21/98	**68**	3		18 **Innocent Bystander** ... *Billy Dean/David Gates*		Capitol
				above 2 from the album *Real Man* on Capitol 55406		
10/30/99+	**❶**[1]	37		19 **Buy Me A Rose** ***[w/ Kenny Rogers & Alison Krauss]*** *Jim Funk/Erik Hickenlooper*		Dreamcatcher
				from Rogers' album *She Rides Wild Horses* on Dreamcatcher 004		
5/12/01	**51**	6		20 **Keep Mom And Dad In Love** ***[w/ Suzy Bogguss]*** ... *Lisa Brokop/Cyril Rawson/Richard Wold*		Dreamcatcher
9/27/03	**52**	16		21 **I'm In Love With You** ... *Chuck Cannon/Billy Dean*		Curb
3/6/04	**27**	20		22 **Thank God I'm A Country Boy** ... *John Martin Sommers*		Curb
9/11/04+	**8**	31		23 **Let Them Be Little** ... *Billy Dean/Richie McDonald*		Curb
6/18/05	**52**	2		24 **This Is The Life** ... *Chuck Cannon/Billy Dean*		Curb
				above 4 from the album *Let Them Be Little* on Curb 78862		
				DEAN, Eddie		
				Born Edgar Dean Glosup on 7/9/1907 in Posey, Texas. Died of emphysema on 3/4/1999 (age 91). Male singer/songwriter/guitarist. Regular on the WLS *National Barn Dance* and Judy Canova's radio show. Acted in several movies from 1937-48.		
9/25/48	**11**	1		1 **One Has My Name (The Other Has My Heart)** ... S:11 *Hal Blair/Dearest Dean/Eddie Dean*		Crystal 132
1/22/55	**10**	3		2 **I Dreamed Of A Hill-Billy Heaven** ... J:10 / A:10 / S:15 *Eddie Dean/Hal Southern*		Sage and Sand 180
				The Frontiersmen (instrumental backing, above 2)		

DEBUT	PEAK	WKS	GOLD	ARTIST / Country Chart Hit ... Songwriter	Ranking	Label (& Number)
				DEAN, Jimmy	**1960s: #40 / All-Time: #197**	
				Born on 8/10/1928 in Plainview, Texas. Male singer/songwriter/guitarist. Hosted own CBS-TV series from 1957-58; ABC-TV series from 1963-66. Business interests include a line of pork sausage. Married **Donna Meade** on 10/27/1991. Also see **Some Of Chet's Friends**.		
3/7/53	**5**	7		1 **Bumming Around** ***[Jimmie Dean]*** ... A:5 / S:9 / J:10 *Pete Graves*		4 Star 1613
10/16/61	**❶**[2]	22	●	2 **Big Bad John** *Jimmy Dean* **[S]**		Columbia 42175
				Grammy: Single		
2/3/62	**9**	10		3 **Dear Ivan** ... *Jimmy Dean* **[S]**		Columbia 42259
2/10/62	**16**	10		4 **The Cajun Queen /** ... *Wayne Walker* **[S]**		
3/10/62	**15**	6		5 **To A Sleeping Beauty** ... *Jackie Gleason/Gus Kahn/Larry Markes/Egbert Van Alstyne* **[S]**		Columbia 42282
				also see #24 below		

DEBUT	PEAK	WKS	GOLD	ARTIST / Country Chart Hit	Songwriter	Label (& Number)
				DEAN, Jimmy — cont'd		
4/21/62	3^{1}	13		6 **P.T. 109** based on the sinking of John F. Kennedy's torpedo boat in 1943	*Fred Burch/Marijohn Wilkin*	Columbia 42338
9/29/62	**10**	11		7 **Little Black Book**	*Jimmy Dean*	Columbia 42529
2/1/64	**35**	6		8 **Mind Your Own Business**	*Hank Williams*	Columbia 42934
6/5/65	❶^{2}	17		9 **The First Thing Ev'ry Morning (And The Last Thing Ev'ry Night)**	*Jimmy Dean/Ruth Roberts*	Columbia 43263
10/30/65	**35**	6		10 **Harvest Of Sunshine**	*Jimmy Dean/Bill Katz/Ruth Roberts*	Columbia 43382
10/22/66	**10**	18		11 **Stand Beside Me**	*Tompall Glaser*	RCA Victor 8971
2/18/67	**16**	14		12 **Sweet Misery**	*Jan Crutchfield/Wayne Walker*	RCA Victor 9091
7/22/67	**41**	9		13 **Ninety Days**	*Jan Crutchfield/Jimmy Rule*	RCA Victor 9241
11/18/67+	**30**	10		14 **I'm A Swinger**	*Larry Lee*	RCA Victor 9350
3/9/68	**21**	14		15 **A Thing Called Love**	*Jerry Reed*	RCA Victor 9454
8/10/68	**52**	8		16 **Born To Be By Your Side**	*Jerry Reed*	RCA Victor 9567
11/9/68	**22**	11		17 **A Hammer And Nails**	*Ben Peters*	RCA Victor 9652
4/5/69	**52**	7		18 **A Rose Is A Rose Is A Rose**	*Gordon Galbraith/Ricci Mareno*	RCA Victor 0122
1/30/71	**29**	11		19 **Slowly** *[w/ Dottie West]*	*Tommy Hill/Webb Pierce*	RCA Victor 9947
4/17/71	**54**	7		20 **Everybody Knows**	*Charlie Rich*	RCA Victor 9966
1/1/72	**38**	12		21 **The One You Say Good Mornin' To**	*Ted Harris*	RCA Victor 0600
10/6/73	**90**	6		22 **Your Sweet Love (Keeps Me Homeward Bound)**	*Jan Crutchfield*	Columbia 45922
5/15/76	**9**	6	●	23 **I.O.U.** also see #25 & #26 below	*Jimmy Dean/Larry Markes* **[S]**	Casino 052
9/25/76	**85**	3		24 **To A Sleeping Beauty** new version of #5 above	*Jackie Gleason/Gus Kahn/Larry Markes/Egbert Van Alstyne* **[S-R]**	Casino 074
5/14/77	**90**	2		25 **I.O.U.** same version as #23 above	*Jimmy Dean/Larry Markes* **[S-R]**	Casino 052
5/14/83	**77**	4		26 **I.O.U.** new version of #23 above	*Jimmy Dean/Larry Markes* **[S-R]**	Churchill 94024
				DEAN, Larry Born in Perrytown, Texas. Male singer/songwriter/guitarist. Married actress Philece Sampler on 7/10/1999.		
10/7/89	**91**	2		**Outside Chance**	*Wayne Carson/Larry Dean*	USA 620
				DEAN, Roxie Born on 3/23/1974 in Baton Rouge, Louisiana. Female singer/songwriter.		
11/22/03	**60**	1		1 **Everyday Girl**	S:2 *Bonnie Baker/Robin Lee Bruce/Roxie Dean*	DreamWorks
2/12/05	8^{S}	4		2 **A Soldier's Wife** from the album *Ms. America* on Valhalla 123	*Roxie Dean*	Valhalla
				DEBONAIRES Male vocal group from Tyler, Texas.		
4/13/85	**79**	6		**I'm On Fire**	*Bruce Springsteen*	MTM 72051
				DEE, Duane Born Duane DeRosia on 1/16/1940 in Hartford, Wisconsin. Male singer.		
11/11/67+	**44**	12		1 **Before The Next Teardrop Falls**	*Vivian Keith/Ben Peters*	Capitol 5986
12/21/68+	**58**	7		2 **True Love Travels On A Gravel Road**	*Dallas Frazier/A.L. "Doodle" Owens*	Capitol 2332
2/6/71	**71**	2		3 **I've Got To Sing**	*Milton Blackford/Dan Wilson*	Cartwheel 192
10/16/71	**36**	13		4 **How Can You Mend A Broken Heart**	*Barry Gibb/Robin Gibb*	Cartwheel 200
3/4/72	**64**	6		5 **Sweet Apple Wine**	*Sharon Dobbins/Jim Powell*	Cartwheel 207
4/20/74	**88**	3		6 **Morning Girl**	*Tupper Saussy*	ABC 11417
				DEE, Gordon Born Gordon Dillingham in New Bridge, North Carolina. Male singer/guitarist.		
12/15/84	**87**	5		**(Nothing Left Between Us) But Alabama**	*Red Lane/Larry Latimer*	Southern Tracks 1029
				DEE, Kathy Born Kathleen Dearth on 4/7/1933 in Moundsville, West Virginia. Died on 11/3/1968 (age 35). Female singer.		
9/21/63	**18**	3		1 **Unkind Words**	*Allan Sippola/Jimmy Walker*	United Artists 627
2/15/64	**44**	4		2 **Don't Leave Me Lonely Too Long**	*Roy Drusky*	United Artists 687
				DEER, John — see JOHN DEER		
				DeHAVEN, Penny Born Charlotte DeHaven on 5/17/1948 in Winchester, Virginia. Female singer/actress. Acted in the movies *Valley Of Blood*, *Traveling Light* and *Country Music Story*. Also recorded as **Penny Starr**.		
1/7/67	**69**	3		1 **A Grain Of Salt** *[Penny Starr]*	*Jerry Fuller*	Band Box 372
8/9/69	**34**	11		2 **Mama Lou**	*Larry Murray*	Imperial 66388
11/15/69	**37**	10		3 **Down In The Boondocks**	*Joe South*	Imperial 66421
3/21/70	**59**	5		4 **I Feel Fine**	*John Lennon/Paul McCartney*	Imperial 66437
5/30/70	**20**	12		5 **Land Mark Tavern** *[w/ Del Reeves]*	*Jerry Chesnut*	United Artists 50669
9/19/70	**69**	2		6 **Awful Lotta Lovin'**	*Jerry Chesnut*	United Artists 50703
1/30/71	**46**	9		7 **The First Love**	*Laurel Hanson/Scott Turner*	United Artists 50742
6/19/71	**42**	9		8 **Don't Change On Me**	*Jimmy Holiday/Eddie Reeves*	United Artists 50787
12/25/71+	**61**	9		9 **Another Day Of Loving**	*Penny DeHaven/Scott Turner*	United Artists 50854
6/24/72	**54**	6		10 **Crying In The Rain** *[w/ Del Reeves]*	*Howard Greenfield/Carole King*	United Artists 50829
7/14/73	**96**	2		11 **The Lovin' Of Your Life**	*Dallas Frazier/Whitey Shafer*	Mercury 73384
12/1/73+	**67**	8		12 **I'll Be Doggone**	*Warren Moore/Smokey Robinson/Marvin Tarplin*	Mercury 73434
5/4/74	**93**	5		13 **Play With Me**	*Jerry Foster/Bill Rice*	Mercury 73468
8/7/76	**83**	4		14 **(The Great American) Classic Cowboy**	*Bobby Fischer/Scott Turner*	Starcrest 066

DEBUT	PEAK	WKS	GOLD		ARTIST / Ranking / Country Chart Hit	Songwriter	Label (& Number)
					DeHAVEN, Penny — cont'd		
7/10/82	**77**	5		15	**We Made Memories** *[w/ Boxcar Willie]*	*Jess Hudson/Kenny Seratt*	Main Street 952
11/5/83	**74**	5		16	**Only The Names Have Been Changed**	*Kent Robbins*	Main Street 93015
4/14/84	**78**	4		17	**Friendly Game Of Hearts**	*Don Cook/Ron Hellard/Curly Putman*	Main Street 93019
					DEKLE, Mike		
					Born in Panama City, Florida; raised in Athens, Georgia. Male singer/songwriter.		
6/30/84	**93**	2		1	**Hanky Panky**	*Mike Dekle*	NSD 188
11/3/84	**79**	4		2	**The Minstrel**	*Mike Dekle*	NSD 195
					DELICATO, Paul		
					Born in St. Louis, Missouri. Male singer/bassist.		
9/13/75	**91**	5			**Lean On Me**	*Bill Withers*	Artists Of America 101
					DELMORE BROTHERS — **HOF: 2001**		
					Duo from Elkmont, Alabama: brothers Alton Delmore (born on 12/25/1908; died on 6/8/1964, age 55) and Rabon Delmore (born on 12/3/1916; died on 12/4/1952, age 36). Both were singers/songwriters/guitarists/fiddle players.		
					OPRY: 1933		
12/14/46	**2**^{1}	4		1	**Freight Train Boogie**	*Bob Nobar/Jim Scott*	King 570
9/17/49+	**❶**^{1}	23		2	**Blues Stay Away From Me** J:❶^1 / S:2 / A:3	*Alton Delmore/Rabon Delmore/Henry Glover/Wayne Raney*	King 803
2/18/50	**7**	1		3	**Pan American Boogie** J:7	*Alton Delmore/Rabon Delmore*	King 826
					DELRAY, Martin		
					Born Michael Ray Martin on 9/26/1949 in Texarkana, Arkansas. Male singer/songwriter. Also recorded as **Mike Martin**.		
3/23/85	**76**	3		1	**Temptation** *[Mike Martin]*	*Mitch Johnson/Mike Martin*	Compleat 139
2/23/91	**27**	20		2	**Get Rhythm** — **Johnny Cash** (guest vocal)	*Johnny Cash*	Atlantic
7/20/91	**58**	9		3	**Lillies White Lies**	*Wood Newton/Billy Ray Reynolds*	Atlantic
2/1/92	**51**	12		4	**Who, What, Where, When, Why, How** — above 3 from the album *Get Rhythm* on Atlantic 82176	*Jeff Crossan*	Atlantic
12/19/92+	**61**	9		5	**What Kind Of Man** — from the album *What Kind Of Man* on Atlantic 82439	*Kenny Beard/J. Francis Keus*	Atlantic
					DENNEY, Kevin		
					Born in Monticello, Kentucky. Male singer/songwriter/guitarist.		
12/8/01+	**16**	24		1	**That's Just Jessie** S:2	*Kevin Denney/P.J. Matthews/Kerry Kurt Phillips*	Lyric Street
6/15/02	**30**	20		2	**Cadillac Tears**	*Leslie Satcher/Wynn Varble*	Lyric Street
11/9/02+	**43**	15		3	**It'll Go Away** — above 3 from the album *Kevin Denney* on Lyric Street 65020	*Kevin Denney/Don Sampson*	Lyric Street
10/11/03	**44**	16		4	**A Year At A Time**	*Jay DeMarcus/Lonnie Wilson*	Lyric Street
					DENNIS, Wesley		
					Born on 4/22/1963 in Clanton, Alabama; raised in Montgomery, Alabama. Male singer/songwriter.		
2/25/95	**46**	11		1	**I Don't Know (But I've Been Told)**	*Wesley Dennis*	Mercury
6/3/95	**51**	10		2	**Don't Make Me Feel At Home**	*L. David Lewis/Kim Williams*	Mercury
9/2/95	**58**	8		3	**Who's Counting** — all of above from the album *Wesley Dennis* on Mercury 526582	*Tony Martin/Roger Springer/Reese Wilson*	Mercury
					DENNY, Burch		
					Born in Louisville, Kentucky. Male singer.		
3/4/89	**86**	2			**Yesterday Is Too Far Away**	*Val Stecklein*	Oak 1068
					DENTON, Jack		
					Born in Toronto, Ontario, Canada. Male singer.		
10/7/89	**95**	1			**Anna ("Go With Him")**	*Arthur Alexander*	M.V.P. 10001

DEBUT	PEAK	WKS	GOLD		ARTIST / Ranking / Country Chart Hit	Songwriter	Label (& Number)
					DENVER, John — **All-Time: #200**		
					Born Henry John Deutschendorf on 12/31/1943 in Roswell, New Mexico. Died on 10/12/1997 (age 53) at the controls of a light plane that crashed off the California coast. Male singer/songwriter/guitarist. With the Chad Mitchell Trio from 1965-68. Starred in the 1977 movie *Oh, God.*		
					CMA: Entertainer 1975		
6/26/71	**50**	12	●	1	**Take Me Home, Country Roads** — **Grammy: Hall of Fame**; Fat City (Bill Danoff & Taffy Nivert of **Starland Vocal Band**; backing vocals)	*Bill Danoff/John Denver/Taffy Nivert*	RCA Victor 0445
12/15/73+	**69**	7		2	**Please, Daddy**	*Bill Danoff/Taffy Nivert* [X]	RCA Victor 0182
2/16/74	**42**	12	●	3	**Sunshine On My Shoulders**	*John Denver/Richard Kniss/Mike Taylor*	RCA Victor 0213
6/8/74	**9**	14	●	4	**Annie's Song** — written for his wife Annie Martell (married 1967-83)	*John Denver*	RCA Victor 0295
9/28/74	**❶**^{1}	14	●	5	**Back Home Again**	*John Denver*	RCA Victor 10065
1/4/75	**7**	12		6	**Sweet Surrender**	*John Denver* [L]	RCA Victor 10148
3/29/75	**❶**^{1}	14	●	7	**Thank God I'm A Country Boy**	*John Martin Sommers* [L]	RCA Victor 10239
8/16/75	**❶**^{1}	18	●	8	**I'm Sorry**	*John Denver*	RCA Victor 10353
12/13/75+	**12**	11		9	**Fly Away** — **Olivia Newton-John** (backing vocal)	*John Denver*	RCA Victor 10517
3/13/76	**30**	10		10	**Looking For Space**	*John Denver*	RCA Victor 10586

Billboard DEBUT	PEAK	WKS	GOLD	ARTIST / Ranking / Country Chart Hit	Songwriter	Label (& Number)
				DENVER, John — cont'd		
5/29/76	**70**	5		11 **It Makes Me Giggle**	*John Denver*	RCA Victor 10687
9/18/76	**34**	9		12 **Like A Sad Song**	*John Denver*	RCA 10774
12/18/76+	**22**	11		13 **Baby, You Look Good To Me Tonight**	*Bill Danoff*	RCA 10854
3/12/77	**62**	7		14 **My Sweet Lady**	*John Denver*	RCA 10911
11/26/77+	**22**	13		15 **How Can I Leave You Again**	*John Denver*	RCA 11036
2/25/78	**72**	6		16 **It Amazes Me**	*John Denver*	RCA 11214
2/17/79	**64**	5		17 **Downhill Stuff**	*John Denver*	RCA 11479
4/7/79	**47**	7		18 **What's On Your Mind /**	*John Denver*	
4/7/79	**flip**	7		19 **Sweet Melinda**	*Steve Gillette/David MacKechnie*	RCA 11535
3/1/80	**84**	5		20 **Autograph**	*John Denver*	RCA 11915
6/13/81	**10**	18		21 **Some Days Are Diamonds (Some Days Are Stone)**	*Dick Feller*	RCA 12246
11/14/81	**50**	9		22 **The Cowboy And The Lady**	*Bobby Goldsboro*	RCA 12345
7/9/83	**14**	19		23 **Wild Montana Skies** ***[w/ Emmylou Harris]***	*John Denver*	RCA 13562
12/14/85+	**9**	21		24 **Dreamland Express**	A:7 / S:10 *John Denver*	RCA 14227
8/30/86	**57**	9		25 **Along For The Ride ('56 T-Bird)**	*Bill Braun/Danny O'Keefe*	RCA 14406
10/29/88	**96**	2		26 **Country Girl In Paris**	*John Denver*	Windstar 75720
5/27/89	**14**	23		27 **And So It Goes** ***[w/ Nitty Gritty Dirt Band]***	*Paul Overstreet/Don Schlitz*	Universal 66008
				DERAILERS, The		
				Group from Austin, Texas: Tony Villanueva (vocals, guitar), Brian Hofeldt (guitar), Ed Adkins (bass) and Mark Horn (drums).		
12/4/99	**71**	1		**The Right Place** — from the album *Full Western Dress* on Sire 31062	*Bill Carter/Ruth Ellsworth/Tony Villanueva*	Sire
				DERN, Daisy		
				Born in 1967 in San Francisco, California. Female singer/songwriter. Distant cousin of actors Bruce Dern and Laura Dern.		
11/3/01+	**43**	15		**Gettin' Back To You**	*Brad Davis/Daisy Dern/Dave Gibson*	Mercury
				DESERT ROSE BAND, The — **All-Time: #253**		
				Group from California. Core members: **Chris Hillman** (born on 12/4/1944), John Jorgenson (born on 7/6/1956) and **Herb Pedersen** (born on 4/27/1944). Hillman was a founding member of The Byrds and the **Flying Burrito Brothers**. Jorgenson left in 1992. Disbanded in early 1994.		
3/21/87	**26**	18		1 **Ashes Of Love**	*Jack Anglin/Jim Anglin/Johnny Wright*	Curb/MCA 53048
7/11/87	**6**	21		2 **Love Reunited**	S:19 *Steve Hill/Chris Hillman*	Curb/MCA 53142
10/31/87+	**2**[1]	25		3 **One Step Forward**	S:6 *Chris Hillman/Bill Wildes*	Curb/MCA 53201
3/26/88	❶[1]	19		4 **He's Back And I'm Blue**	S:7 *Robert Anderson/Mike Woody*	Curb/MCA 53274
7/30/88	**2**[1]	20		5 **Summer Wind**	S:8 *Steve Hill/Chris Hillman*	Curb/MCA 53354
11/26/88+	❶[1]	20		6 **I Still Believe In You**	*Steve Hill/Chris Hillman*	Curb/MCA 53454
3/18/89	**3**[2]	20		7 **She Don't Love Nobody**	*John Hiatt*	Curb/MCA 53616
7/8/89	**11**	22		8 **Hello Trouble**	*Orville Couch/Eddie McDuff*	Curb/MCA 53671
11/4/89+	**6**	26		9 **Start All Over Again**	*Steve Hill/Chris Hillman*	Curb/MCA 53746
3/24/90	**13**	23		10 **In Another Lifetime**	*Steve Hill/Chris Hillman*	Curb/MCA
7/21/90	**10**	20		11 **Story Of Love** — above 2 from the album *Pages Of Life* on Curb/MCA 42332	*Steve Hill/Chris Hillman*	Curb/MCA
2/9/91	**37**	12		12 **Will This Be The Day**	*Steve Hill/Chris Hillman*	Curb/MCA
5/25/91	**65**	6		13 **Come A Little Closer** — above 2 from the album *A Dozen Roses - Greatest Hits* on Curb/MCA 77571	*Steve Hill/Chris Hillman*	Curb/MCA
10/5/91	**53**	11		14 **You Can Go Home**	*Chris Hillman/Jack Tempchin*	Curb/MCA
1/25/92	**67**	3		15 **Twilight Is Gone** — above 2 from the album *True Love* on Curb/MCA 77572	*Steve Hill/Chris Hillman*	Curb/MCA
9/4/93	**71**	1		16 **What About Love** — from the album *Life Goes On* on Curb 77627	*Steve Hill/Chris Hillman*	Curb
				DESERT WIND BAND, The — see SHAW, Ron		
				DeVAL, Buddy — see LORRIE, Myrna		
				DeWITT, Lew		
				Born on 3/12/1938 in Roanoke, Virginia. Died on 8/15/1990 (age 52). Male singer. Member of **The Statler Brothers** from 1955-82.		
11/30/85	**77**	7		**You'll Never Know**	*Mack Gordon/Harry Warren*	Compleat 147

DEBUT	PEAK	WKS	GOLD	ARTIST / Ranking / Country Chart Hit	Songwriter	Label (& Number)
				DEXTER, Al, and his Troopers — **1940s: #4 / All-Time: #147**		
				Born Clarence Albert Poindexter on 5/4/1905 in Troup, Texas. Died on 1/28/1984 (age 78). Male singer/songwriter/guitarist. Owned his own Round-Up club in Longview, Texas. His Troopers included Aubrey Gass, Paul Sells and Holly Hollinger.		
1/8/44	❶[3]	10	●	1 **Pistol Packin' Mama /** — **Grammy: Hall of Fame**	*Al Dexter*	
1/8/44	❶[1]	25		2 **Rosalita**	*Al Dexter*	Okeh 6708
3/11/44	❶[13]	30		3 **So Long Pal /**	*Al Dexter*	
3/11/44	❶[2]	30		4 **Too Late To Worry**	*Al Dexter*	Okeh 6718
1/20/45	❶[7]	21		5 **I'm Losing My Mind Over You /**	*Al Dexter/James Paris*	
1/27/45	**2**[1]	10		6 **I'll Wait For You Dear**	*Al Dexter*	Okeh 6727

DEBUT	PEAK	WKS	GOLD		ARTIST / Country Chart Hit	Songwriter	Label (& Number)
					DEXTER, Al, and his Troopers — cont'd		
7/7/45	2^{5}	11		7	Triflin' Gal /	Cindy Walker	
8/25/45	5	3		8	I'm Lost Without You	Al Dexter/Frankie Marvin	Okeh 6740
2/2/46	❶^{16}	29		9	Guitar Polka /	Al Dexter [I]	
2/9/46	2^{1}	8		10	Honey Do You Think It's Wrong	Al Dexter/Frankie Marvin	Columbia 36898
8/31/46	❶^{5}	13		11	Wine, Women And Song /	Al Dexter	
9/14/46	3^{1}	5		12	It's Up To You	Al Dexter/James Paris	Columbia 37062
1/25/47	4	1		13	Kokomo Island	Al Dexter/Cindy Walker	Columbia 37200
5/10/47	4	7		14	Down At The Roadside Inn	Al Dexter	Columbia 37303
7/3/48	14	1		15	Rock And Rye Rag	J:14 Al Dexter [I]	Columbia 20422
9/18/48	11	2		16	Calico Rag	J:11 Al Dexter/James Paris	Columbia 20438

DIAMOND, Neil

Born on 1/24/1941 in Brooklyn, New York. Pop singer/songwriter/guitarist.

DEBUT	PEAK	WKS	GOLD		Country Chart Hit	Songwriter	Label (& Number)
11/25/78	70	8	▲	1	You Don't Bring Me Flowers *[w/ Barbra Streisand]*	Alan Bergman/Marilyn Bergman/Neil Diamond	Columbia 10840
2/17/79	73	7		2	Forever In Blue Jeans	Richard Bennett/Neil Diamond	Columbia 10897

DIAMOND RIO — 1990s: #20 / 2000s: #28 / All-Time: #92

Group formed in Nashville, Tennessee: Marty Roe (vocals; born on 12/28/1960), Jimmy Olander (guitar; born on 8/26/1961), Gene Johnson (mandolin; born on 8/10/1949), Dan Truman (piano; born on 8/29/1956), Dana Williams (bass; born on 5/22/1961) and Brian Prout (drums; born on 12/4/1955). Prout was formerly married to Nancy Given of **Wild Rose**; married **Stephanie Bentley** on 12/28/2001. Also see **Jed Zeppelin**.

CMA: Vocal Group 1992, 1993, 1994 & 1997 // OPRY: 1998

DEBUT	PEAK	WKS	GOLD		Country Chart Hit	Songwriter	Label (& Number)
3/23/91	❶^{2}	20		1	Meet In The Middle	James Foster/Chapin Hartford/Don Pfrimmer	Arista
7/20/91	3^{1}	20		2	Mirror Mirror	Bob DiPiero/John Jarrard/Mark D. Sanders	Arista
11/16/91+	9	20		3	Mama Don't Forget To Pray For Me	Larry Cordle/Larry Shell	Arista
3/28/92	2^{2}	20		4	Norma Jean Riley	Robert Honey/Monty Powell/Dan Truman	Arista
7/11/92	7	20		5	Nowhere Bound	Jule Medders/Monty Powell	Arista
					above 5 from the album *Diamond Rio* on Arista 8673		
11/21/92+	2^{2}	20		6	In A Week Or Two	Gary Burr/James House	Arista
4/3/93	5	20		7	Oh Me, Oh My, Sweet Baby	Michael Garvin/Tom Shapiro	Arista
7/24/93	13	20		8	This Romeo Ain't Got Julie Yet	Jimmy Olander/Eric Silver	Arista
11/27/93+	21	20		9	Sawmill Road	Sam Hogin/Jim McBride/Dan Truman	Arista
					above 4 from the album *Close To The Edge* on Arista 18656		
5/28/94	2^{2}	20		10	Love A Little Stronger	Billy Ray Crittenden/Chuck Jones/Gregory Swint	Arista
10/22/94+	9	20		11	Night Is Fallin' In My Heart	Dennis Linde	Arista
2/4/95	16	20		12	Bubba Hyde	S:11 Craig Wiseman	Arista
5/20/95	19	20		13	Finish What We Started	Mike Noble/Monty Powell	Arista
					above 4 from the album *Love A Little Stronger* on Arista 18745		
12/16/95+	2^{1}	20		14	Walkin' Away	S:20 Annie Roboff/Craig Wiseman	Arista
5/4/96	4	20		15	That's What I Get For Lovin' You	Kent Blazy/Joe Thrasher	Arista
8/24/96	15	20		16	It's All In Your Head	Tony Martin/Van Stephenson/Reese Wilson	Arista
12/14/96+	4	20		17	Holdin'	Kelly Garrett/Craig Wiseman	Arista
					above 4 from the album *IV* on Arista 18812		
6/7/97	❶^{3}	22		18	How Your Love Makes Me Feel	Max T. Barnes/Trey Bruce	Arista Nashville
11/1/97+	4	21		19	Imagine That	Derek George/John Tirro/Bryan White	Arista Nashville
					above 2 from the album *Greatest Hits* on Arista Nashville 18844		
5/30/98	4	23		20	You're Gone	Jon Vezner/Paul Williams	Arista Nashville
10/31/98+	2^{2}	29		21	Unbelievable	Al Anderson/Jeffrey Steele	Arista Nashville
3/27/99	33	20		22	I Know How The River Feels	Steven Jones/Amy Powers	Arista Nashville
					above 3 from the album *Unbelievable* on Arista Nashville 18866		
5/20/00	36	17		23	Stuff	Kelly Garrett/Tim Owens	Arista Nashville
11/4/00+	❶^{2}	33		24	One More Day	Steven Jones/Bobby Tomberlin	Arista Nashville
5/12/01	18	20		25	Sweet Summer	Michael Dulaney/Neil Thrasher	Arista Nashville
10/20/01	42	10		26	That's Just That	Kelly Garrett/Tim Owens	Arista Nashville
					above 4 from the album *One More Day* on Arista Nashville 67999		
4/13/02	❶^{2}	45		27	Beautiful Mess	Sonny Lemaire/Clay Mills/Shane Minor	Arista Nashville
11/23/02+	❶^{2}	34		28	I Believe	Skip Ewing/Donny Kees	Arista Nashville
8/2/03	16	22		29	Wrinkles	Ronny Scaife/Neil Thrasher	Arista Nashville
1/31/04	45	8		30	We All Fall Down	Arlis Albritton/Steve Jones	Arista Nashville
					above 4 from the album *Completely* on Arista Nashville 67046		
8/14/04	43	5		31	Can't You Tell	Joleen Belle/Eric Silver	Arista Nashville
3/12/05	45	9		32	One Believer	Marc Beeson/Don Pfrimmer/Mike Reid	Arista Nashville

DIAMONDS, The

Vocal group from Canada: Bob Duncan, Gary Cech, Gary Owens and Steve Smith. The original group consisting of Dave Somerville, Ted Kowalski, Phil Levitt and Bill Reed charted 16 pop hits from 1956-61. Duncan joined in 1978 and recruited the other three members in 1982.

DEBUT	PEAK	WKS	GOLD		Country Chart Hit	Songwriter	Label (& Number)
2/14/87	63	8		1	Just A Little Bit	Roger Cook/Bobby Wood	Churchill 94101
7/11/87	83	3		2	Two Kinds Of Woman	Craig Bickhardt	Churchill 94102

Billboard DEBUT	PEAK	WKS	GOLD	ARTIST Ranking / Country Chart Hit.......Songwriter	Label (& Number)

DIANA

Born Diana Murrell on 5/26/1955 in Cincinnati, Ohio. Female singer.

DEBUT	PEAK	WKS	GOLD	Country Chart Hit / Songwriter	Label (& Number)
6/23/79	40	8		1 Just When I Needed You Most ... *Randy Vanwarmer*	Elektra 46061
10/6/79	41	9		2 Lonely Together ... *Bobby Lee Springfield*	Elektra 46539
8/1/81	29	12		3 He's The Fire ... *Chester Lester/Danny Morrison*	Sunbird 7564
12/18/82	88	3		4 Who's Been Sleeping In My Bed ... *Jim Jensing/Quentin Powers*	Adamas 103

DICKENS, "Little" Jimmy — 1940s: #39 / All-Time: #263 // HOF: 1983

Born on 12/19/1920 in Bolt, West Virginia. Male singer/songwriter/guitarist. Stands just 4'11". Hosted own local radio shows throughout the midwest during the 1940s. Nicknamed "Tater."

OPRY: 1948

DEBUT	PEAK	WKS	GOLD	Country Chart Hit / Songwriter	Label (& Number)
4/16/49	7	7		1 Take An Old Cold 'Tater (And Wait) *[Jimmie Dickens]* ... S:7 / J:11 *Eugene Bartlett* [N]	Columbia 20548
6/25/49	7	10		2 Country Boy ... S:7 / J:8 *Boudleaux Bryant/Felice Bryant*	Columbia 20585
9/3/49	12	1		3 Pennies For Papa *[Jimmie Dickens]* ... S:12 *Connie Taylor*	Columbia 20548
9/24/49	10	1		4 My Heart's Bouquet ... J:10 *Jimmy Dickens*	Columbia 20598
1/14/50	6	3		5 A-Sleeping At The Foot Of The Bed ... S:6 / A:7 *Luther Patrick/Gene Wilson*	Columbia 20644
4/22/50	3^{2}	10		6 Hillbilly Fever ... A:3 / S:5 / J:9 *George Vaughn*	Columbia 20677
8/7/54	9	7		7 Out Behind The Barn ... A:9 *Boudleaux Bryant*	Columbia 21247
11/3/62	10	8		8 The Violet And A Rose ... *Bud Auge/John Reinfield/Mel Tillis*	Columbia 42485
12/14/63	28	2		9 Another Bridge To Burn ... *Harlan Howard*	Columbia 42845
4/10/65	21	18		10 He Stands Real Tall ... *Cal Veale*	Columbia 43243
10/9/65	❶^{2}	19		11 **May The Bird Of Paradise Fly Up Your Nose** *Neal Merritt* [N]	Columbia 43388
2/26/66	27	8		12 When The Ship Hit The Sand ... *Larry Kingston* [N]	Columbia 43514
7/9/66	41	5		13 Who Licked The Red Off Your Candy ... *Larry Kingston* [N]	Columbia 43701
3/11/67	23	14		14 Country Music Lover ... *Bobby Braddock* [N]	Columbia 44025
				JIMMY DICKENS:	
7/6/68	69	5		15 How To Catch An African Skeeter Alive ... *Dallas Frazier* [N]	Decca 32326
1/25/69	55	8		16 When You're Seventeen ... *Leon Payne*	Decca 32426
5/9/70	75	2		17 (You've Been Quite A Doll) Raggedy Ann ... *Red Lane*	Decca 32644
2/13/71	70	3		18 Everyday Family Man ... *L.E. White*	United Artists 50730
4/15/72	61	6		19 Try It, You'll Like It ... *Gary S. Paxton*	United Artists 50889

DICKEY, Dan

Born on 6/22/1949 in Houston, Texas. Male singer/songwriter/guitarist.

DEBUT	PEAK	WKS	GOLD	Country Chart Hit / Songwriter	Label (& Number)
6/9/79	96	2		1 Hot Mama ... *Dan Dickey*	Chartwheel 123
10/6/79	96	2		2 Bye, Bye, Baby ... *Dan Dickey*	Chartwheel 126

DIFFIE, Joe — 1990s: #13 / All-Time: #91

Born on 12/28/1958 in Tulsa, Oklahoma; raised in Duncan, Oklahoma. Male singer/songwriter/guitarist. Worked in a foundry while playing local nightclubs in Oklahoma. Moved to Nashville in 1986 to work for Gibson Guitars. Signed to Epic in early 1990. Also see **Same Old Train**.

OPRY: 1993

DEBUT	PEAK	WKS	GOLD	Country Chart Hit / Songwriter	Label (& Number)
8/25/90	❶^{1}	20		1 **Home** *William Lehner/Andy Spooner*	Epic
12/15/90+	2^{2}	20		2 If You Want Me To ... *Joe Diffie/Lonnie Wilson*	Epic
4/6/91	❶^{1}	20		3 **If The Devil Danced (In Empty Pockets)** *Ken Spooner/Kim Williams*	Epic
8/3/91	2^{2}	20		4 New Way (To Light Up An Old Flame) ... *Joe Diffie/Lonnie Wilson* above 4 from the album *A Thousand Winding Roads* on Epic 46047	Epic
12/7/91+	5	20		5 Is It Cold In Here ... *Joe Diffie/Danny Morrison/Kerry Kurt Phillips*	Epic
4/18/92	5	20		6 Ships That Don't Come In ... *Dave Gibson/Paul Nelson*	Epic
8/15/92	16	20		7 Next Thing Smokin' ... *Joe Diffie/Danny Morrison/Johnny Slate*	Epic
9/12/92	15	20		8 Not Too Much To Ask *[w/ Mary-Chapin Carpenter]* ... *Mary-Chapin Carpenter/Don Schlitz* from Carpenter's album *Come On Come On* on Columbia 48881	Columbia
12/19/92+	41	13		9 Startin' Over Blues ... *Whitey Shafer/Lonnie Williams* #5-7 & 9: from the album *Regular Joe* on Epic 47477	Epic
3/20/93	5	20		10 Honky Tonk Attitude ... *Lee Bogan/Joe Diffie*	Epic
7/24/93	3^{1}	20		11 Prop Me Up Beside The Jukebox (If I Die) ... *Rick Blaylock/Howard Perdew/Kerry Kurt Phillips*	Epic
11/13/93+	5	20		12 John Deere Green ... *Dennis Linde*	Epic
3/12/94	19	20		13 In My Own Backyard ... *Joe Diffie/Kerry Kurt Phillips/Andy Spooner* above 4 from the album *Honky Tonk Attitude* on Epic 53002	Epic
7/16/94	❶^{2}	20		14 **Third Rock From The Sun** *John Greenebaum/Tony Martin/Sterling Whipple*	Epic
10/22/94	❶^{4}	20		15 **Pickup Man** *Howard Perdew/Kerry Kurt Phillips*	Epic
2/4/95	2^{2}	20		16 So Help Me Girl ... S:8 *Howard Perdew/Andy Spooner*	Epic
5/27/95	21	12		17 I'm In Love With A Capital "U" ... S:22 *Paul Nelson/Craig Wiseman*	Epic
8/12/95	40	11		18 That Road Not Taken ... *Deborah Beasley/Casey Kelly* above 5 from the album *Third Rock From The Sun* on Epic 64357	Epic
12/2/95+	❶^{2}	20		19 **Bigger Than The Beatles** S:11 *Jeb Stuart Anderson/Steve Dukes*	Epic
12/16/95+	33	5		20 Leroy The Redneck Reindeer ... *Joe Diffie/Steve Pippin/Stacey Slate* [X-N] from the album *Mr. Christmas* on Epic 67045	Epic
3/2/96	23	20		21 C-O-U-N-T-R-Y ... *Dusty Drake/Ron Harbin/Ed Hill*	Epic

Billboard DEBUT	PEAK	WKS	GOLD	ARTIST / Ranking / Country Chart Hit	Songwriter	Label (& Number)

DIFFIE, Joe — cont'd

DEBUT	PEAK	WKS	GOLD	Country Chart Hit	Songwriter	Label (& Number)
6/22/96	**23**	20		22 **Whole Lotta Gone**	*Bryan Burns/Mark Oliverius*	Epic
				#19, 21 & 22: from the album *Life's So Funny* on Epic 67405		
12/21/96+	**46**	4		23 **Leroy The Redneck Reindeer**	*Joe Diffie/Steve Pippin/Stacey Slate* [X-N-R]	Epic
				from the album *Mr. Christmas* on Epic 67045		
3/8/97	**25**	17		24 **This Is Your Brain**	S:23 *Kelly Garrett/Craig Wiseman*	Epic
7/5/97	**40**	11		25 **Somethin' Like This**	*Michael Higgins/Ron Williams*	Epic
10/25/97	**61**	4		26 **The Promised Land**	*William Lehner/Andy Spooner*	Epic
				above 3 from the album *Twice Upon A Time* on Epic 67693		
12/20/97+	**54**	4		27 **Leroy The Redneck Reindeer**	*Joe Diffie/Steve Pippin/Stacey Slate* [X-N-R]	Epic
				from the album *Mr. Christmas* on Epic 67045		
4/4/98	**4**	25		28 **Texas Size Heartache**	*Zack Turner/Lonnie Wilson*	Epic
9/12/98	**43**	10		29 **Poor Me**	*Al Anderson/Bob DiPiero*	Epic
				above 2 from the album *Greatest Hits* on Epic 69137		
11/28/98	**64**	10		30 **Behind Closed Doors**	*Kenny O'Dell*	Epic
				from the various artists album *Tribute To Tradition* on Columbia 68073		
3/13/99	**6**	29		31 **A Night To Remember**	S:4 *Max T. Barnes/Terry Welborn*	Epic
9/4/99+	**21**	23		32 **The Quittin' Kind**	S:7 *Phil Barnhart/Sam Hogin/Mark D. Sanders*	Epic
2/12/00	**5**	37		33 **It's Always Somethin'**	*Marv Green/Aimee Mayo*	Epic
				above 3 from the album *A Night To Remember* on Epic 69815		
7/28/01+	**10**	34		34 **In Another World**	*Tom Shapiro/Wally Wilson/Jimmy Yeary*	Monument
4/6/02	**49**	6		35 **This Pretender**	*Gary LeVox/Zack Turner/Lonnie Wilson*	Monument
				above 2 from the album *In Another World* on Monument 85373		
1/24/04	**19**	28		36 **Tougher Than Nails**	*Max T. Barnes/Kendell Marvell/Phil O'Donnell*	Broken Bow
8/21/04	**50**	8		37 **If I Could Only Bring You Back**	*Charles Davis/Frank J. Myers*	Broken Bow
				above 2 from the album *Tougher Than Nails* on Broken Bow 75082		

DILLINGHAM, Craig

Born on 2/11/1958 in Brownwood, Texas. Male singer/songwriter/guitarist.

DEBUT	PEAK	WKS	GOLD	Country Chart Hit	Songwriter	Label (& Number)
12/3/83+	**32**	14		1 **Have You Loved Your Woman Today**	*Kent Robbins/David Wills*	MCA/Curb 52301
3/31/84	**47**	9		2 **Honky Tonk Women Make Honky Tonk Men**	*Bobby Braddock/Sonny Throckmorton*	MCA/Curb 52352
7/21/84	**58**	6		3 **1984**	*Craig Dillingham/Bill Graham*	MCA/Curb 52406
8/31/85	**78**	5		4 **Next To You**	*Jerry Fuller*	MCA/Curb 52647
6/14/86	**80**	3		5 **I'll Pull You Through** *[w/ Tish Hinojosa]*	*Joe Lubinsky/Howard Pfeifer*	MCA/Curb 52823

DILLON, Dean — **SW: #32**

Born on 3/26/1955 in Lake City, Tennessee. Male singer/songwriter/guitarist.

DEBUT	PEAK	WKS	GOLD	Country Chart Hit	Songwriter	Label (& Number)
12/15/79+	**30**	12		1 **I'm Into The Bottle (To Get You Out Of My Mind)**	*Steve Abbott/Dean Rutherford*	RCA 11881
5/31/80	**28**	12		2 **What Good Is A Heart**	*Dean Dillon*	RCA 12003
11/1/80+	**25**	15		3 **Nobody In His Right Mind (Would've Left Her)**	*Dean Dillon*	RCA 12109
5/30/81	**57**	6		4 **They'll Never Take Me Alive**	*Dean Dillon/Frank Dycus*	RCA 12234
10/17/81	**77**	5		5 **Jesus Let Me Slide**	*Dean Dillon/Frank Dycus/Albert Gore*	RCA 12319
4/10/82	**41**	11		6 **Brotherly Love** *[w/ Gary Stewart]*	*Dean Dillon/Gary Stewart*	RCA 13049
6/19/82	**74**	4		7 **Play This Old Working Day Away**	*Red Lane*	RCA 13208
9/18/82	**65**	6		8 **You To Come Home To**	*Clyde Phillips*	RCA 13295
1/8/83	**47**	12		9 **Those Were The Days** *[w/ Gary Stewart]*	*Dean Dillon/Rex Huston/Gary Stewart*	RCA 13401
4/16/83	**71**	4		10 **Smokin' In The Rockies** *[w/ Gary Stewart]*	*Buddy Cannon/Dean Dillon/Frank Dycus/Gary Stewart*	RCA 13472
11/12/83	**67**	6		11 **Famous Last Words Of A Fool**	*Dean Dillon/Rex Huston*	RCA 13628
7/2/88	**51**	9		12 **The New Never Wore Off My Sweet Baby**	*Dean Dillon/Frank Dycus/Blake Mevis*	Capitol 44179
9/17/88	**39**	12		13 **I Go To Pieces**	*Del Shannon*	Capitol 44239
12/24/88+	**58**	9		14 **Hey Heart**	*Dean Dillon*	Capitol 44294
8/26/89	**61**	6		15 **It's Love That Makes You Sexy**	*Dean Dillon/Frank Dycus*	Capitol 44400
11/18/89	**66**	5		16 **Back In The Swing Of Things**	*Buddy Cannon/Dean Dillon/Vern Gosdin*	Capitol
				from the album *I've Learned To Live* on Capitol 92079		
2/23/91	**69**	6		17 **Holed Up In Some Honky Tonk**	*Dean Dillon/Frank Dycus/Blake Mevis*	Atlantic
6/22/91	**39**	12		18 **Friday Night's Woman**	*Buddy Cannon/Dean Dillon/Hodges Rippy*	Atlantic
9/21/91	**62**	12		19 **Don't You Even (Think About Leavin')**	*Dean Dillon/Randy Scruggs*	Atlantic
				above 3 from the album *Out Of Your Ever-Lovin' Mind* on Atlantic 82163		
5/22/93	**62**	5		20 **Hot, Country And Single**	*Dean Dillon/John Northrup*	Atlantic
				from the album *Hot, Country And Single* on Atlantic 82438		

DILLON, Lola Jean — see WHITE, L.E.

DIMICHELE, Mickey

Born in Los Angeles, California. Male singer/songwriter/bassist.

DEBUT	PEAK	WKS	GOLD	Country Chart Hit	Songwriter	Label (& Number)
2/28/04	**57**	1		**Jolene**	*Mickey Dimichele*	BroadBand

DIRKSEN, Senator Everett McKinley

Born on 1/4/1896 in Pekin, Illinois. Died on 9/7/1969 (age 73). Served as a United States senator from 1950-69.

DEBUT	PEAK	WKS	GOLD	Country Chart Hit	Songwriter	Label (& Number)
1/7/67	**58**	7		**Gallant Men**	*John Cacavas/Charles Osgood* [S]	Capitol 5805

DIXIANA

Group from Greenville, South Carolina: Cindy Murphy (vocals), brothers Phil Lister (guitar) and Mark Lister (bass), Randall Griffith (keyboards) and Colonel Shuford (drums).

DEBUT	PEAK	WKS	GOLD	Country Chart Hit	Songwriter	Label (& Number)
2/22/92	**39**	20		1 **Waitin' For The Deal To Go Down**	*Charlie Black/Bobby Fischer/Austin Roberts*	Epic
6/27/92	**40**	13		2 **That's What I'm Working On Tonight**	*Mary Francis/Lonzo Williams/Nancy Williams*	Epic
4/24/93	**66**	3		3 **Now You're Talkin'**	*Joe Collins/Mike Heeney*	Epic
				above 3 from the album *Dixiana* on Epic 48620		

DEBUT	PEAK	WKS	GOLD	ARTIST / Country Chart Hit	Ranking / Songwriter	Label (& Number)

DIXIE CHICKS

2000s: #12 / All-Time: #142

Female trio: Natalie Maines (lead vocals), with sisters Martha "Martie" Erwin (fiddle, mandolin) and Emily Erwin (guitar, banjo). Natalie was born on 10/14/1974 in Lubbock, Texas. Daughter of Lloyd Maines (of **The Maines Brothers Band**). Married to Michael Tarabay from 1997-99; married actor Adrian Pasdar on 6/24/2000. Martie was born on 10/12/1969 in York, Pennsylvania. Married to Ted Seidel from 1995-99; married Gareth Maguire (took his last name) on 8/10/2001. Emily was born on 8/16/1972 in Pittsfield, Massachusetts. Married **Charlie Robison** (took his last name) on 5/1/1999. Several radio stations banned their songs after Maines made a controversial statement about President Bush in March 2003. Group named after the Little Feat song "Dixie Chicken."

CMA: Vocal Group 1999, 2000 & 2002 / Entertainer 2000

DEBUT	PEAK	WKS	GOLD	Country Chart Hit	Songwriter	Label (& Number)
10/25/97+	7	26		1 **I Can Love You Better**	S:5 *Pamela Brown/Kostas*	Monument
4/11/98	❶[2]	29		2 **There's Your Trouble** — Grammy: Vocal Group	S:3 *Mark Selby/Tia Sillers*	Monument
8/22/98	❶[4]	27		3 **Wide Open Spaces** — CMA: Single	S:5 *Susan Gibson*	Monument
12/12/98+	❶[2]	25		4 **You Were Mine**	*Martie Maguire/Emily Robison*	Monument
4/3/99	6	20		5 **Tonight The Heartache's On Me**	*Mary Francis/Johnny MacRae/Bob Morrison*	Monument
6/5/99	64	13		6 **Let 'Er Rip** — above 6 from the album *Wide Open Spaces* on Monument 68195	*Billy Crain/Sandy Ramos*	Monument
7/10/99	2[1]	20		7 **Ready To Run** — Grammy: Vocal Group	*Marcus Hummon/Martie Maguire*	Monument
8/14/99	60	11		8 **You Can't Hurry Love** — above 2 from the movie *Runaway Bride* starring Julia Roberts (soundtrack on Columbia 69923)	*Lamont Dozier/Brian Holland/Eddie Holland*	Columbia
9/11/99+	❶[3]	41		9 **Cowboy Take Me Away**	*Marcus Hummon/Martie Maguire*	Monument
9/11/99+	❶[1]	32		10 **Without You**	*Natalie Maines/Eric Silver*	Monument
9/11/99+	13	32	●	11 **Goodbye Earl**	S:2 *Dennis Linde*	Monument
9/11/99+	52	20		12 **Sin Wagon**	*Natalie Maines/Emily Robison/Stephony Smith*	Monument
9/18/99+	3[1]	21		13 **If I Fall You're Going Down With Me**	*Matraca Berg/Annie Roboff*	Monument
3/25/00	65	1		14 **Roly Poly** ***[w/ Asleep At The Wheel]*** — from Asleep At The Wheel's album *Ride With Bob* on DreamWorks 50117	*Fred Rose*	DreamWorks
5/20/00	10	20		15 **Cold Day In July**	*Richard Leigh*	Monument
6/30/01	23	16		16 **Heartbreak Town**	*Darrell Scott*	Monument
9/29/01+	7	27		17 **Some Days You Gotta Dance** — #9-13 & 15-17: from the album *Fly* on Monument 69678	*Troy Johnson/Marshall Morgan*	Monument
1/26/02+	❶[1]	25		18 **Travelin' Soldier**	*Bruce Robison*	Monument
6/8/02	2[2]	20		19 **Long Time Gone** — Grammy: Vocal Group	S:❶[12] *Darrell Scott*	Monument
9/7/02	2[2]	22		20 **Landslide**	S:2 *Stevie Nicks*	Monument
9/14/02	56	1		21 **White Trash Wedding**	*Martie Maguire/Natalie Maines/Emily Robison*	Monument
9/14/02	58	1		22 **Tortured, Tangled Hearts**	*Martie Maguire/Natalie Maines/Marty Stuart*	Monument
6/7/03	48	9		23 **Godspeed (Sweet Dreams)** — above 6 from the album *Home* on Monument 86840	*Radney Foster*	Monument

DR. HOOK

Pop-rock group formed in New Jersey: **Ray Sawyer** (vocals), Dennis Locorriere (vocals, guitar), Rik Elswit (guitar), Bob Henke (guitar), Billy Francis (keyboards), Jance Garfat (bass) and John Wolters (drums). Wolters was a member of **Tennessee Pulleybone**; died of cancer on 6/16/1997 (age 52).

DEBUT	PEAK	WKS	GOLD	Country Chart Hit	Songwriter	Label (& Number)
3/6/76	55	8	●	1 **Only Sixteen**	*Sam Cooke*	Capitol 4171
6/19/76	51	12		2 **A Couple More Years**	*Dennis Locorriere/Shel Silverstein*	Capitol 4280
12/4/76+	26	13		3 **If Not You**	*Dennis Locorriere*	Capitol 4364
6/25/77	92	3		4 **Walk Right In**	*Gus Cannon/Hosie Woods*	Capitol 4423
10/7/78	50	11	●	5 **Sharing The Night Together**	*Ava Aldridge/Eddie Struzick*	Capitol 4621
2/10/79	82	4		6 **All The Time In The World**	*Shel Silverstein/Even Stevens*	Capitol 4677
5/19/79	68	9	●	7 **When You're In Love With A Beautiful Woman**	*Even Stevens*	Capitol 4705
11/3/79	91	4		8 **Better Love Next Time**	*Larry Keith/Steve Pippin/Johnny Slate*	Capitol 4785

DODD, Deryl

Born on 4/12/1964 in Comanche, Texas; raised in Dallas, Texas. Male singer/songwriter/guitarist.

DEBUT	PEAK	WKS	GOLD	Country Chart Hit	Songwriter	Label (& Number)
10/5/96	68	3		1 **Friends Don't Drive Friends...**	*Deryl Dodd/Harry Stinson*	Columbia
11/9/96+	36	20		2 **That's How I Got To Memphis**	*Tom T. Hall*	Columbia
5/17/97	61	8		3 **Movin' Out To The Country** — above 3 from the album *One Ride In Vegas* on Columbia 67544	*Deryl Dodd*	Columbia
4/18/98	62	6		4 **Time On My Hands**	*Caren Day/Shane Decker/Deryl Dodd*	Columbia
9/12/98+	26	23		5 **A Bitter End**	S:13 *Kenny Beard/Deryl Dodd*	Columbia
2/27/99	59	20		6 **Sundown**	*Gordon Lightfoot*	Columbia
3/27/99	65	3		7 **Good Idea Tomorrow**	*Deryl Dodd*	Columbia
5/29/99	64	3		8 **John Roland Wood** — #5, 7 & 8: from the album *Deryl Dodd* on Columbia 68793	*Troy Jones*	Columbia
10/16/99	71	3		9 **On Earth As It Is In Texas** — #6 & 9: from the album *Pearl Snaps* on Columbia 85754	*Brett Beavers/Deryl Dodd*	Columbia
12/18/04	59	1		10 **Let Me Be** — from the album *Stronger Proof* on Dualtone 1191	*Brett Beavers/Deryl Dodd*	Dualtone

DODSON, Darrell

Born in Murfreesboro, Tennessee. Male singer.

DEBUT	PEAK	WKS	GOLD	Country Chart Hit	Songwriter	Label (& Number)
4/16/77	99	2		**Love Song Sing Along**	*Bob Millsap*	SCR 139

DEBUT	PEAK	WKS	GOLD	ARTIST / Country Chart Hit	Ranking / Songwriter	Label (& Number)
				DOLAN, Madonna		
				Born in McLeansboro, Illinois. Female singer/multi-instrumentalist.		
9/24/88	**82**	3		**The Home Team**	*Nancy Whipple/Sterling Whipple*	True 92
				DOLAN, Ramblin' Jimmie		
				Born on 10/29/1916 in Gardena, California. Died on 7/31/1994 (age 77). Male singer/guitarist. Known as "America's Country Troubador."		
2/3/51	**7**	4		**Hot Rod Race**	S:7 *George Wilson* **[N]**	Capitol F1322
				DOLLAR, Johnny		
				Born on 3/8/1933 in Kilgore, Texas. Died on 4/13/1986 (age 53). Male singer/songwriter/guitarist.		
2/12/66	**49**	2		1 **Tear-Talk**	*Alex Zanetis*	Columbia 43343
3/19/66	**15**	15		2 **Stop The Start (Of Tears In My Heart)**	*Fred Carr/Johnny Dollar/Ken Milburn/Danny Ross*	Columbia 43537
2/25/67	**65**	5		3 **Your Hands**	*Johnny Dollar/Ken Milburn/Danny Ross*	Dot 16990
9/16/67	**47**	12		4 **The Wheels Fell Off The Wagon Again**	*Ray Buzzeo*	Date 1566
1/13/68	**42**	12		5 **Everybody's Got To Be Somewhere**	*Charlene Yates*	Date 1585
11/16/68	**48**	7		6 **Big Rig Rollin' Man**	*Charles Fields/Don Riis*	Chart 1057
3/15/69	**65**	4		7 **Big Wheels Sing For Me**	*Johnny Dollar/Bill Morrow*	Chart 1070
2/14/70	**71**	3		8 **Truck Driver's Lament**	*Joe Gibson*	Chart 5049
				DOMINO, Fats		
				Born Antoine Domino on 2/26/1928 in New Orleans, Louisiana. Black male singer/pianist. Inducted into the Rock and Roll Hall of Fame in 1986. Won Grammy's Hall of Fame and Lifetime Achievement Awards in 1987.		
12/20/80+	**51**	9		**Whiskey Heaven**	*Cliff Crofford/John Durrill/Snuff Garrett*	Warner 49610
				from the movie *Any Which Way You Can* starring **Clint Eastwood**		
				DONALDSON, Craig		
				Born in Charleston, West Virginia. Male singer.		
9/25/76	**99**	2		**I Believe He's Gonna Drive That Rig To Glory**	*Tim Schumacher*	Great American 281
				DON JUAN		
				Vocal trio from Rock Island, Illinois: Stu Stuart, Ed Allen and Toby Strause.		
3/12/88	**75**	4		1 **We're Gonna Love Tonight**	*Val Pratt/Eddie Rager*	Maxx 821
8/20/88	**78**	2		2 **Let It Go**	*Karon Penning*	Maxx 827
				DOOLITTLE BAND, The — see DANDY		
				DOTSON, Amber		
				Born in Garland, Texas. Female singer/songwriter.		
4/2/05	**59**	1		**I'll Try Anything**	*Amber Dotson/Phil O'Donnell*	Capitol
				DOTTSY		
				Born Dottsy Brodt on 4/6/1954 in Seguin, Texas. Female singer.		
5/31/75	**17**	17		1 **Storms Never Last**	*Jessi Colter*	RCA Victor 10280
11/22/75+	**12**	14		2 **I'll Be Your San Antone Rose**	*Susanna Clark*	RCA Victor 10423
5/29/76	**86**	4		3 **The Sweetest Thing (I've Ever Known)**	*Otha Young*	RCA Victor 10666
9/25/76	**68**	6		4 **Love Is A Two-Way Street**	*Sterling Whipple*	RCA 10766
6/4/77	**10**	16		5 **(After Sweet Memories) Play Born To Lose Again**	*Kent Robbins*	RCA 10982
10/29/77	**22**	13		6 **It Should Have Been Easy**	*Bob McDill*	RCA 11138
2/11/78	**20**	12		7 **Here In Love**	*Kent Robbins*	RCA 11203
7/8/78	**21**	11		8 **I Just Had You On My Mind**	*Sue Richards*	RCA 11293
1/20/79	**12**	14		9 **Tryin' To Satisfy You**	*Waylon Jennings*	RCA 11448
				Waylon Jennings (backing vocal)		
6/16/79	**22**	10		10 **Slip Away**	*William Armstrong/Marcus Daniel/Wilbur Terrell*	RCA 11610
11/10/79	**34**	10		11 **When I'm Gone**	*Bonnie Murray*	RCA 11743
6/27/81	**32**	12		12 **Somebody's Darling, Somebody's Wife**	*Linda Young*	Tanglewood 1908
9/19/81	**58**	8		13 **Let The Little Bird Fly**	*Bobby Fischer/Don Wayne*	Tanglewood 1910
				DOUGLAS — see BLOCK, Doug		
				DOUGLAS, Joe		
				Born in New Orleans, Louisiana. Male singer/songwriter.		
1/20/79	**84**	5		1 **You're Still On My Mind**	*Luke McDaniel*	D 1315
1/26/80	**88**	2		2 **Back Street Affair**	*Billy Wallace*	Foxy Cajun 1001
6/20/81	**75**	4		3 **Leavin You Is Easier (Than Wishing You Were Gone) /**	*Joe Douglas/Merrill Lane*	
6/20/81	**flip**	4		4 **Louisiana Joe**	*Doug Badon*	Foxy Cajun 1005
				DOUGLAS, Steve		
				Born on 2/17/1951 in Greenville, Mississippi. Male singer.		
6/7/80	**67**	7		1 **This Is True**	*Melvin McGill*	Demon 1954
8/5/89	**91**	2		2 **To A San Antone Rose**	*J.D. Lawrence*	Dorman 98915
1/13/90	**80**	1		3 **Funny Ways Of Loving Me**	*J.D. Lawrence*	Dorman 98111
				DOUGLAS, Tony		
				Born on 4/12/1929 in Martins Mill, Texas. Male singer/songwriter.		
3/30/63	**23**	1		1 **His And Hers**	*Orville Couch/Tony Douglas/Chuck Jennings*	Vee Jay 481
				also see #5 below		
12/30/72+	**35**	15		2 **Thank You For Touching My Life**	*Tommy Williamson*	Dot 17443
6/30/73	**37**	9		3 **My Last Day**	*Tommy Williamson*	Dot 17464

DEBUT	PEAK	WKS	GOLD	Ranking	ARTIST / Country Chart Hit	Songwriter	Label (& Number)
					DOUGLAS, Tony — cont'd		
12/13/75+	**72**	7		4	**If I Can Make It** (Through The Mornin')	*David Cash/Tony Douglas*	20th Century 2257
2/20/82	**87**	3		5	**His 'N Hers**	*Orville Couch/Tony Douglas/Chuck Jennings* **[R]**	Cochise 118
					new version of #1 above		
					DOVE, Ronnie		
					Born on 9/7/1935 in Herndon, Virginia; raised in Baltimore, Maryland. Male singer.		
1/29/72	**61**	8		1	**Kiss The Hurt Away**	*Finley Duncan/Chuck Reed*	Decca 32919
2/3/73	**69**	5		2	**Lilacs In Winter**	*J.D. Brock*	Decca 33038
4/12/75	**75**	7		3	**Please Come To Nashville**	*Bobby David/Niki Shrode*	Melodyland 6004
6/14/75	**25**	12		4	**Things**	*Bobby Darin*	Melodyland 6011
4/25/87	**77**	4		5	**Heart**	*Jimmy Elledge*	Diamond 378
11/7/87	**73**	7		6	**Rise And Shine**	*Paul Overstreet/Thom Schuyler*	Diamond 379
					DOWNEY, Sean Morton		
					Born on 12/9/1933 in Los Angeles, California. Died of cancer on 3/12/2001 (age 67). TV talk show host better known as Morton Downey, Jr.		
3/14/81	**95**	2			**Green Eyed Girl**	*Jerry Fuller*	ESO 932
					DOWNING, Big Al		
					Born on 1/9/1940 in Centralia, Oklahoma; raised in Lenapah, Oklahoma. Died of leukemia on 7/4/2005 (age 65). Black singer/songwriter/pianist.		
12/2/78+	**20**	13		1	**Mr. Jones**	*Al Downing*	Warner 8716
4/21/79	**18**	13		2	**Touch Me** (I'll Be Your Fool Once More)	*Al Downing*	Warner 8787
9/8/79	**59**	5		3	**Midnight Lace**	*Al Downing*	Warner 49034
11/17/79	**73**	4		4	**I Ain't No Fool**	*Al Downing*	Warner 49141
2/9/80	**33**	8		5	**The Story Behind The Story**	*Al Downing*	Warner 49161
7/12/80	**20**	11		6	**Bring It On Home**	*Wallace Burdette/Al Downing/Joe Martin*	Warner 49270
7/3/82	**48**	9		7	**I'll Be Loving You**	*Al Downing/Lance Quinn*	Team 1001
10/23/82	**67**	7		8	**Darlene**	*Al Downing/Lance Quinn*	Team 1002
2/12/83	**38**	11		9	**It Takes Love**	*Al Downing/Lance Quinn*	Team 1004
10/1/83	**64**	5		10	**Let's Sing About Love**	*Al Downing*	Team 1003
1/7/84	**45**	11		11	**The Best Of Families**	*Woody Bomar/John Jarrard*	Team 1007
4/28/84	**76**	4		12	**There'll Never Be A Better Night For Bein' Wrong**	*Larry Cheshier/Murry Kellum/Dan Mitchell*	Team 1008
1/17/87	**69**	5		13	**How Beautiful You Are** (To Me)	*Al Downing*	Vine St. 103
9/12/87	**67**	5		14	**Just One Night Won't Do**	*Mac Gayden/Dave Gillon/Sam Hogin*	Vine St. 105
8/5/89	**82**	3		15	**I Guess By Now**	*Al Downing*	Door Knob 328
					DOWNS, Laverne		
					Born in Dallas, Texas. Female singer.		
7/4/60	**16**	7			**But You Use To**	*Tommy Downs/Martha Kinslow*	Peach 735
					DRAKE, Dusty		
					Born on 2/23/1964 in Monaca, Pennsylvania. Male singer/songwriter/guitarist.		
8/10/02	**57**	3		1	**And Then**	S:7 *Bob Feldman/Ray Vega/Robert Vega*	Warner
3/22/03	**26**	20		2	**One Last Time**	*P.J. Matthews/Kerry Kurt Phillips*	Warner
8/9/03	**50**	6		3	**Smaller Pieces**	*Dusty Drake/Ron Harbin/Kerry Kurt Phillips*	Warner
					above 3 from the album *Dusty Drake* on Warner 48051		
9/25/04	**43**	9		4	**I Am The Working Man**	*Gary Harrison/Shane Teeters*	Warner
					DRAKE, Guy		
					Born on 7/24/1904 in Weir, Kentucky. Died on 6/17/1984 (age 79). Male singer/songwriter/comedian.		
1/10/70	**6**	14			**Welfare Cadilac**	*Guy Drake* **[N-S]**	Royal American 1
					DRAPER, Rusty		
					Born Farrell Draper on 1/25/1923 in Kirksville, Missouri. Died of pneumonia on 3/28/2003 (age 80). Male singer/guitarist. Known as "Ol' Redhead."		
8/29/53	**6**	5	●	1	**Gambler's Guitar**	S:6 / J:6 *Jim Lowe*	Mercury 70167
7/8/67	**70**	3		2	**My Elusive Dreams**	*Curly Putman/Billy Sherrill*	Monument 1019
3/2/68	**70**	4		3	**California Sunshine**	*Harlan Howard*	Monument 1044
8/3/68	**58**	3		4	**Buffalo Nickel**	*John Jarboe*	Monument 1074
4/25/70	**73**	2		5	**Two Little Boys**	*Bob Braden*	Monument 1188
1/19/80	**87**	3		6	**Harbor Lights**	*Jimmy Kennedy/Hugh Williams*	KL 001
					DRESSER, Lee		
					Born on 5/22/1941 in Washington DC; raised in Moberly, Missouri. Male singer/songwriter/guitarist.		
2/11/78	**78**	5		1	**You're All The Woman I'll Ever Need**	*Lee Dresser*	Capitol 4529
12/2/78	**86**	5		2	**A Beautiful Song** (For A Beautiful Lady)	*Lee Dresser*	Capitol 4613
4/2/83	**77**	4		3	**The Hero**	*Lee Dresser*	Air Int'l. 10021
9/3/83	**96**	1		4	**Feelings Feelin Right**	*Lee Dresser*	Air Int'l. 10022
					DRIFTING COWBOYS, The		
					Former backing band for **Hank Williams**. The 1978 lineup consisted of original members Bob McNett (guitar; born on 10/16/1925), Don Helms (steel guitar; born on 2/28/1927) and Jerry Rivers (fiddle; born on 8/25/1928; died of cancer on 10/4/1996, age 68), with new members Bobby Andrews (bass) and Jimmy Heap, Jr. (drums; son of **Jimmy Heap**). Rivers was also a member of **The Homesteaders**.		
1/28/78	**97**	2		1	**Lovesick Blues** *[w/ Jim Owen]*	*Cliff Friend/Irving Mills*	Epic 50498
5/6/78	**90**	4		2	**Rag Mop**	*Deacon Anderson/Johnnie Lee Wills*	Epic 50543

Billboard DEBUT	PEAK	WKS	GOLD	ARTIST / Country Chart Hit	Ranking / Songwriter	Label (& Number)

DRIFTWOOD, Jimmie

Born James Corbett Morris on 6/20/1907 in Mountain View, Arkansas. Died of heart failure on 7/12/1998 (age 91). Male singer/songwriter/guitarist.

OPRY: 1960

DEBUT	PEAK	WKS	GOLD	Country Chart Hit	Songwriter	Label (& Number)
6/8/59	**24**	3		**The Battle Of New Orleans**	*Jimmie Driftwood*	RCA Victor 7534

DRUMM, Don

Born in Springfield, Massachusetts. Male singer/guitarist/pianist.

DEBUT	PEAK	WKS	GOLD	Country Chart Hit	Songwriter	Label (& Number)
11/30/74+	**86**	7		1 **In At Eight And Out At Ten**	*Skippy Barrett/Ricci Mareno*	Chart 5223
1/7/78	**18**	14		2 **Bedroom Eyes**	*Ray Hillburn*	Churchill 7704
5/27/78	**35**	8		3 **Just Another Rhinestone**	*Ray Hillburn*	Churchill 7710
10/7/78	**81**	3		4 **Something To Believe In**	*Bob Millsap*	Churchill 7717

DRUSKY, Roy — 1960s: #16 / All-Time: #106

Born on 6/22/1930 in Atlanta, Georgia. Died of emphysema on 9/23/2004 (age 74). Male singer/songwriter/guitarist. Studied veterinary medicine at Emory University. Hosted own radio show on WEAS in Decatur, Georgia. Acted in the movies *The Golden Guitar* and *Forty-Acre Feud.*

OPRY: 1959

DEBUT	PEAK	WKS	GOLD	Country Chart Hit	Songwriter	Label (& Number)
1/18/60	**2^{3}**	24		1 **Another**	*Roy Drusky/Vic McAlpin*	Decca 31024
7/11/60	**3^{3}**	20		2 **Anymore**	*Roy Drusky/Vic McAlpin/Marie Wilson*	Decca 31109
12/19/60	**26**	3		3 **I Can't Tell My Heart That** *[w/ Kitty Wells]*	*Jack Anglin/Jim Anglin/Johnnie Wright*	Decca 31164
2/20/61	**10**	12		4 **I'd Rather Loan You Out /**	*Roy Drusky/Vic McAlpin/Lester Vanadore*	
3/13/61	**2^{4}**	27		5 **Three Hearts In A Tangle**	*Ray Starr/Sonny Thompson*	Decca 31193
9/11/61	**9**	20		6 **I Went Out Of My Way** (To Make You Happy)	*Roy Drusky/Jean Elrod/Vic McAlpin*	Decca 31297
4/21/62	**17**	2		7 **There's Always One** (Who Loves A Lot)	*Floyd Biggs/Mary Biggs/Hargus "Pig" Robbins*	Decca 31366
12/22/62+	**3^{4}**	21		8 **Second Hand Rose**	*Harlan Howard*	Decca 31443
12/7/63+	**8**	19		9 **Peel Me A Nanner**	*Bill Anderson*	Mercury 72204
5/9/64	**13**	16		10 **Pick Of The Week**	*Liz Anderson*	Mercury 72265
12/26/64+	**41**	3		11 **Summer, Winter, Spring And Fall**	*Roy Drusky/Vic McAlpin*	Decca 31717
1/16/65	**6**	21		12 (From Now On All My Friends Are Gonna Be) **Strangers**	*Liz Anderson*	Mercury 72376
5/29/65	**❶^{2}**	23		13 **Yes, Mr. Peters** *[w/ Priscilla Mitchell]*	*Steve Karliski/Larry Kolber*	Mercury 72416
10/23/65	**21**	15		14 **White Lightnin' Express**	*Hal Mills*	Mercury 72471
12/4/65	**45**	2		15 **Slippin' Around** *[w/ Priscilla Mitchell]*	*Floyd Tillman*	Mercury 72497
2/26/66	**20**	14		16 **Rainbows And Roses**	*Ted Harris*	Mercury 72532
6/25/66	**10**	16		17 **The World Is Round**	*Tony Senn/Tommy Stough*	Mercury 72586
11/19/66+	**12**	14		18 **If The Whole World Stopped Lovin'**	*Ben Peters*	Mercury 72627
3/25/67	**61**	5		19 **I'll Never Tell On You** *[w/ Priscilla Mitchell]*	*Steve Karliski/Larry Kolber*	Mercury 72650
6/24/67	**25**	11		20 **New Lips**	*Johnny Carver*	Mercury 72689
11/11/67+	**18**	16		21 **Weakness In A Man**	*Jerry Chesnut*	Mercury 72742
3/30/68	**28**	10		22 **You Better Sit Down Kids**	*Sonny Bono*	Mercury 72784
7/20/68	**24**	11		23 **Jody And The Kid**	*Kris Kristofferson*	Mercury 72823
1/25/69	**10**	15		24 **Where The Blue And Lonely Go**	*Bill Silva/Jerry Warren*	Mercury 72886
6/7/69	**14**	11		25 **My Grass Is Green**	*Roy Drusky*	Mercury 72928
10/4/69	**7**	11		26 **Such A Fool**	*Roy Drusky/Marvin Moore/Lester Vanadore*	Mercury 72964
1/17/70	**11**	11		27 **I'll Make Amends**	*Bud Moore*	Mercury 73007
5/9/70	**5**	16		28 **Long Long Texas Road**	*Dennis Linde*	Mercury 73056
9/19/70	**9**	12		29 **All My Hard Times**	*Joe South*	Mercury 73111
3/6/71	**15**	12		30 **I Love The Way That You've Been Lovin' Me**	*Gordon Galbraith/Ricci Mareno*	Mercury 73178
7/3/71	**37**	10		31 **I Can't Go On Loving You**	*Hank Mills*	Mercury 73212
12/11/71+	**17**	13		32 **Red Red Wine**	*Neil Diamond*	Mercury 73252
5/20/72	**58**	9		33 **Sunshine And Rainbows /**	*Curly Putman*	
5/20/72	**flip**	2		34 **The Night's Not Over Yet**	*Jerry Foster/Bill Rice*	Mercury 73293
8/12/72	**25**	12		35 **The Last Time I Called Somebody Darlin'**	*Dallas Frazier/A.L. "Doodle" Owens*	Mercury 73314
1/13/73	**32**	10		36 **I Must Be Doin' Something Right**	*Ben Peters*	Mercury 73356
5/12/73	**50**	7		37 **That Rain Makin' Baby Of Mine**	*Dallas Frazier/Warren Robb*	Mercury 73376
8/4/73	**25**	11		38 **Satisfied Mind**	*Joe Hayes/Jack Rhodes*	Mercury 73405
4/20/74	**81**	6		39 **Close To Home**	*Alex Harvey*	Capitol 3859
9/21/74	**45**	11		40 **Dixie Lily**	*Elton John/Bernie Taupin*	Capitol 3942
1/15/77	**81**	5		41 **Night Flying**	*Sterling Whipple*	Scorpion 0521
8/13/77	**91**	4		42 **Betty's Song**	*Warren Ortiz/David Reeves*	Scorpion 0540

DUCAS, George

Born on 8/1/1966 in Texas City, Texas; raised in San Diego, California; later based in Houston, Texas. Male singer/songwriter/guitarist.

DEBUT	PEAK	WKS	GOLD	Country Chart Hit	Songwriter	Label (& Number)
9/10/94	**38**	12		1 **Teardrops**	*George Ducas/Terry McBride*	Liberty
12/10/94+	**9**	20		2 **Lipstick Promises**	*George Ducas/Tia Sillers*	Liberty
5/13/95	**52**	10		3 **Hello Cruel World**	*George Ducas/Angelo Petraglia/Ty Tyler*	Liberty
9/23/95	**72**	3		4 **Kisses Don't Lie**	*George Ducas/Mike Heeney*	Liberty

above 4 from the album *George Ducas* on Liberty 28329

Billboard DEBUT	PEAK	WKS	GOLD	ARTIST / Country Chart Hit	Ranking / Songwriter	Label (& Number)

DUCAS, George — cont'd

DEBUT	PEAK	WKS	#	Country Chart Hit	Songwriter	Label (& Number)
6/8/96	**57**	12	5	**Every Time She Passes By**	S:22 *George Ducas/Mike Heeney*	Capitol
2/8/97	**55**	9	6	**Long Trail Of Tears**	*George Ducas/Mike Heeney*	Capitol

above 2 from the album *Where I Stand* on Capitol 35463

DUDLEY, Dave — **1960s: #27 / All-Time: #107**

Born David Pedruska on 5/3/1928 in Spencer, Wisconsin; raised in Stevens Point, Wisconsin. Died of a heart attack on 12/22/2003 (age 75). Male singer/songwriter/guitarist. Worked as a DJ at radio stations WTWT in Wausua, Wisconsin, KBOK in Waterloo, Iowa, KCHA in Charles City, Idaho and KEVE in Minneapolis. Known as the pioneer of "truck driving" songs.

DEBUT	PEAK	WKS	#	Country Chart Hit	Songwriter	Label (& Number)
10/16/61	**28**	2	1	**Maybe I Do**	*Noah Gordon/Tracy Hagans*	Vee 7003
9/15/62	**18**	9	2	**Under Cover Of The Night**	*Dave Dudley*	Jubilee 5436
6/1/63	$\mathbf{2}^{2}$	21	3	**Six Days On The Road**	*Earl Green/Carl Montgomery*	Golden Wing 3020
10/5/63	$\mathbf{3}^{2}$	20	4	**Cowboy Boots**	*Baker Knight*	Golden Ring 3030
12/14/63+	**7**	16	5	**Last Day In The Mines**	*Jimmy Key*	Mercury 72212
10/10/64	**6**	17	6	**Mad**	*Tom T. Hall*	Mercury 72308
3/13/65	**15**	17	7	**Two Six Packs Away**	*Ronnie Self*	Mercury 72384
7/10/65	$\mathbf{3}^{3}$	21	8	**Truck Drivin' Son-Of-A-Gun**	*Dixie Dean/Ray King*	Mercury 72442
11/20/65+	**4**	16	9	**What We're Fighting For**	*Tom T. Hall*	Mercury 72500
3/12/66	**12**	12	10	**Viet Nam Blues**	*Kris Kristofferson* [S]	Mercury 72550
7/2/66	**13**	14	11	**Lonelyville**	*Dave Burgess*	Mercury 72585
10/8/66	**15**	12	12	**Long Time Gone**	*Dave Dudley/Dick Marrison*	Mercury 72618
2/25/67	**12**	15	13	**My Kind Of Love**	*Jerry Reed*	Mercury 72655
7/15/67	**23**	14	14	**Trucker's Prayer**	*Jim Thornton/Scott Turner*	Mercury 72697
11/4/67+	**12**	16	15	**Anything Leaving Town Today**	*Dave Dudley/Tom T. Hall*	Mercury 72741
3/2/68	**10**	13	16	**There Ain't No Easy Run**	*Dave Dudley/Tom T. Hall*	Mercury 72779
7/13/68	**14**	11	17	**I Keep Coming Back For More**	*Dave Dudley*	Mercury 72818
11/16/68+	**10**	16	18	**Please Let Me Prove (My Love For You)**	*Jimmy Key*	Mercury 72856
3/29/69	**12**	15	19	**One More Mile**	*Tom T. Hall*	Mercury 72902
8/30/69	**10**	13	20	**George (And The North Woods)**	*Tom T. Hall*	Mercury 72952
3/14/70	❶^{1}	16	21	**The Pool Shark**	*Tom T. Hall*	Mercury 73029
8/1/70	**20**	12	22	**This Night (Ain't Fit For Nothing But Drinking)**	*Tom T. Hall*	Mercury 73089
11/14/70	**23**	13	23	**Day Drinkin'** *[w/ Tom T. Hall]*	*Tom T. Hall*	Mercury 73139
12/26/70+	**15**	13	24	**Listen Betty (I'm Singing Your Song)**	*Tom T. Hall*	Mercury 73138
4/17/71	**8**	14	25	**Comin' Down**	*Dave Dudley*	Mercury 73193
8/21/71	**8**	15	26	**Fly Away Again**	*Dave Dudley*	Mercury 73225
3/18/72	**14**	14	27	**If It Feels Good Do It**	*Jerry Chesnut*	Mercury 73274
7/22/72	**12**	16	28	**You've Gotta Cry Girl**	*Rich Barish/Dave Dudley*	Mercury 73309
12/9/72+	**40**	10	29	**We Know It's Over** *[w/ Karen O'Donnal]*	*Randy Rogers*	Mercury 73345
3/3/73	**19**	12	30	**Keep On Truckin'**	*Randy Rogers*	Mercury 73367
8/4/73	**37**	9	31	**It Takes Time**	*Dave Dudley/John Huhta*	Mercury 73404
11/3/73	**47**	12	32	**Rollin' Rig**	*Roy Baham*	Rice 5064
4/6/74	**67**	7	33	**Have It Your Way**	*Dave Dudley*	Rice 5067
8/31/74	**61**	9	34	**Counterfeit Cowboy**	*Ronnie Rogers*	Rice 5069
2/8/75	**74**	10	35	**How Come It Took So Long (To Say Goodbye)**	*Dave Dudley/Jack Key/Randy Rogers*	United Artists 585
5/3/75	**21**	12	36	**Fireball Rolled A Seven**	*Roy Baham*	United Artists 630
10/25/75+	**12**	15	37	**Me And Ole C.B.**	*Dave Dudley/Randy Rogers*	United Artists 722
2/28/76	**47**	8	38	**Sentimental Journey**	*Les Brown/Bud Green/Ben Homer*	United Artists 766
8/21/76	**83**	5	39	**38 And Lonely**	*Randy Rogers*	United Artists 836
3/4/78	**95**	3	40	**One A.M. Alone**	*Dave Dudley/Ronnie Rogers*	Rice 5077
9/6/80	**77**	5	41	**Rolaids, Doan's Pills And Preparation H**	*Marie Dudley/Max Harter*	Sun 1154

DUFF, Arlie

Born Arleigh Duff on 3/28/1924 in Jack's Branch, Texas. Died on 7/4/1996 (age 72). Male singer/songwriter.

DEBUT	PEAK	WKS	#	Country Chart Hit	Songwriter	Label (& Number)
12/5/53+	**7**	10		**You All Come**	S:7 / A:7 / J:8 *Arlie Duff*	Starday 104

DUGAN, Jeff

Born in Broussard, Louisiana. Male singer/songwriter/guitarist.

DEBUT	PEAK	WKS	#	Country Chart Hit	Songwriter	Label (& Number)
8/15/87	**68**	12	1	**Once A Fool, Always A Fool**	*Dean Dillon/Bob Melton/Royce Porter*	Warner 28376
5/28/88	**52**	8	2	**I Wish It Was That Easy Going Home**	*Hank Cochran/Red Lane*	Warner 27995

DUKE OF PADUCAH — see FORD, Whitey

Billboard DEBUT	PEAK	WKS	GOLD	ARTIST Ranking / Country Chart Hit.......... Songwriter		Label (& Number)

DUNCAN, Johnny — 1970s: #46 / All-Time: #125

Born on 10/5/1938 in Dublin, Texas. Male singer/songwriter/guitarist. Attended Texas Christian University. Lived in Clovis, New Mexico (1959-64). Moved tro Nashville in 1964 and worked as a DJ on WAGG in Franklin, Tennessee. Related to **Brady Seals**, **Dan Seals** and **Troy Seals**.

DEBUT	PEAK	WKS	GOLD	Country Chart Hit	Songwriter	Label (& Number)
8/12/67	54	7		1 **Hard Luck Joe**	*Bobby Goldsboro*	Columbia 44196
1/13/68	67	3		2 **Baby Me Baby**	*Harlan Howard*	Columbia 44383
8/17/68	47	9		3 **To My Sorrow**	*Vic McAlpin*	Columbia 44580
10/19/68	21	8		4 **Jackson Ain't A Very Big Town** *[w/ June Stearns]*	*Vic McAlpin*	Columbia 44656
2/8/69	70	4		5 **I Live To Love You**	*Glenn Sutton*	Columbia 44693
3/15/69	74	3		6 **Back To Back** (We're Strangers) *[w/ June Stearns]*	*Marian Francis*	Columbia 44752
6/21/69	30	12		7 **When She Touches Me**	*Carolyn Varga*	Columbia 44864
12/13/69+	65	6		8 **Window Number Five**	*Charlie Craig*	Columbia 45006
5/9/70	39	10		9 **You're Gonna Need A Man**	*Bobby Goldsboro*	Columbia 45124
9/19/70	68	3		10 **My Woman's Love**	*Larry Butler*	Columbia 45201
10/31/70	27	13		11 **Let Me Go** (Set Me Free)	*Johnny Duncan*	Columbia 45227
3/13/71	19	13		12 **There's Something About A Lady**	*Johnny Duncan*	Columbia 45319
7/24/71	39	9		13 **One Night Of Love**	*Johnny Duncan*	Columbia 45418
11/27/71+	12	13		14 **Baby's Smile, Woman's Kiss**	*Billy Edd Wheeler*	Columbia 45479
3/18/72	19	12		15 **Fools**	*Johnny Duncan*	Columbia 45556
9/30/72	66	5		16 **Here We Go Again**	*Don Lanier/Red Steagall*	Columbia 45674
3/31/73	6	16		17 **Sweet Country Woman**	*Sandy St. John/Charles Tharp*	Columbia 45818
9/8/73	18	14		18 **Talkin' With My Lady**	*Don Goodman/Troy Seals*	Columbia 45917
4/6/74	47	9		19 **The Pillow**	*Johnny Duncan*	Columbia 46018
9/21/74	66	9		20 **Scarlet Water**	*Spooner Oldham/Freddy Weller*	Columbia 10007
3/8/75	57	8		21 **Charley Is My Name**	*Johnny Duncan*	Columbia 10085
8/23/75	26	14		22 **Jo And The Cowboy**	*Johnny Duncan*	Columbia 10182
12/20/75+	86	7		23 **Gentle Fire**	*Johnny Duncan*	Columbia 10262
3/27/76	4	20		24 **Stranger**	*Kris Kristofferson*	Columbia 10302
10/2/76	❶[2]	17		25 **Thinkin' Of A Rendezvous**	*Bobby Braddock/Sonny Throckmorton*	Columbia 10417
2/5/77	❶[1]	15		26 **It Couldn't Have Been Any Better**	*Ray Griff*	Columbia 10474
6/4/77	5	16		27 **A Song In The Night**	*Bobby Lee Springfield*	Columbia 10554
10/29/77+	4	16		28 **Come A Little Bit Closer** *[w/ Janie Fricke]*	*Tommy Boyce/Wes Farrell/Bobby Hart*	Columbia 10634
3/11/78	❶[1]	18		29 **She Can Put Her Shoes Under My Bed** (Anytime)	*Robert Halley/Aaron Schroeder*	Columbia 10694
7/15/78	4	14		30 **Hello Mexico** (And Adios Baby To You)	*Steve Davis/Billy Sherrill/Glenn Sutton*	Columbia 10783
2/24/79	6	14		31 **Slow Dancing**	*Jack Tempchin*	Columbia 10915
9/29/79	9	12		32 **The Lady In The Blue Mercedes**	*Dan Darst/Gary Gentry*	Columbia 11097
1/5/80	17	14		33 **Play Another Slow Song**	*Kieran Kane/Richard Kane*	Columbia 11185
6/7/80	17	14		34 **I'm Gonna Love You Tonight** (In My Dreams)	*Wayland Holyfield*	Columbia 11280
7/12/80	17	14		35 **He's Out Of My Life** *[w/ Janie Fricke]*	*Tom Bahler*	Columbia 11312
11/8/80+	16	14		36 **Acapulco**	*Larry Collins/Mike Leath*	Columbia 11385
11/7/81	40	10		37 **All Night Long**	*Dennis Cavalier*	Columbia 02570
4/12/86	69	6		38 **The Look Of A Lady In Love**	*Lewis Anderson/Brent Mason*	Pharoah 2502
8/16/86	81	2		39 **Texas Moon**	*Stewart Harris/Mark Robbins*	Pharoah 2503

DUNCAN, Tommy, And His Western All Stars

Born on 1/11/1911 in Hillsboro, Texas. Died of a heart attack on 7/25/1967 (age 56). Featured vocalist with **Bob Wills**.

DEBUT	PEAK	WKS	GOLD	Country Chart Hit	Songwriter	Label (& Number)
8/13/49	8	3		**Gamblin' Polka Dot Blues**	S:8 / J:8 *Ray Hall/Jimmie Rodgers*	Capitol 40178

DUNCAN, Whitney

Born in Knoxville, Tennessee. Female singer.

DEBUT	PEAK	WKS	GOLD	Country Chart Hit	Songwriter	Label (& Number)
7/31/04	60	1		**My World Is Over** *[w/ Kenny Rogers]* from Rogers' album *42 Ultimate Hits* on Capitol 98794	*Whitney Duncan/Brian Nash/Mike Post*	Capitol

DUNN, Holly — All-Time: #209

Born on 8/22/1957 in San Antonio, Texas. Female singer/songwriter/guitarist. Sister of **Chris Waters**. Former staff writer at CBS and MTM Records. Worked as a DJ at WWWW in Detroit. Also see **Tomorrow's World**.

CMA: Horizon 1987 // OPRY: 1989

DEBUT	PEAK	WKS	GOLD	Country Chart Hit	Songwriter	Label (& Number)
6/8/85	62	6		1 **Playing For Keeps**	*Holly Dunn/Tom Shapiro/Chris Waters*	MTM 72052
10/5/85	64	8		2 **My Heart Holds On**	*Hugh Prestwood*	MTM 72057
5/17/86	39	12		3 **Two Too Many**	S:39 / A:39 *Holly Dunn*	MTM 72064
8/23/86	7	25		4 **Daddy's Hands**	S:4 / A:7 *Holly Dunn*	MTM 72075
2/7/87	4	21		5 **A Face In The Crowd** *[w/ Michael Martin Murphey]*	A:4 / S:15 *Gary Harrison/Karen Staley*	Warner 28471
5/2/87	2[2]	25		6 **Love Someone Like Me**	S:❶[1] *Holly Dunn/Radney Foster*	MTM 72082
8/29/87	4	25		7 **Only When I Love**	S:❶[1] *Holly Dunn/Tom Shapiro/Chris Waters*	MTM 72091
1/16/88	7	24		8 **Strangers Again**	S:2 *Holly Dunn/Chris Waters*	MTM 72093
6/25/88	5	20		9 **That's What Your Love Does To Me**	S:3 *Bill Caswell/Chick Rains*	MTM 72108
11/5/88+	11	19		10 (It's Always Gonna Be) **Someday**	*Holly Dunn/Tom Shapiro/Chris Waters*	MTM 72116
5/27/89	❶[1]	23		11 **Are You Ever Gonna Love Me**	*Holly Dunn/Tom Shapiro/Chris Waters*	Warner 22957
9/23/89	4	26		12 **There Goes My Heart Again**	*Joe Diffie/Wayne Perry/Lonnie Wilson*	Warner 22796

DEBUT	PEAK	WKS	GOLD	ARTIST / Ranking / Country Chart Hit	Songwriter	Label (& Number)
				DUNN, Holly — cont'd		
2/17/90	**25**	13		13 **Maybe** ***[w/ Kenny Rogers]***	*Bill Rice/Mary Sharon Rice*	Reprise
				from Rogers' album *Something Inside So Strong* on Reprise 25792		
6/2/90	**63**	4		14 **My Anniversary For Being A Fool**	*Holly Dunn*	Warner
9/1/90	**❶** [1]	20		15 **You Really Had Me Going**	*Holly Dunn/Tom Shapiro/Chris Waters*	Warner
1/5/91	**19**	20		16 **Heart Full Of Love**	*Kostas*	Warner
				above 3 from the album *Heart Full Of Love* on Warner 26173		
7/13/91	**48**	9		17 **Maybe I Mean Yes**	*Holly Dunn/Tom Shapiro/Chris Waters*	Warner
				from the album *Milestones - Greatest Hits* on Warner 26630		
4/25/92	**67**	4		18 **No Love Have I**	*Mel Tillis*	Warner
8/1/92	**68**	7		19 **As Long As You Belong To Me**	*Holly Dunn/Tom Shapiro/Chris Waters*	Warner
12/26/92+	**51**	10		20 **Golden Years**	*Sam Hogin/Gretchen Peters*	Warner
				above 3 from the album *Getting It Dunn* on Warner 26949		
4/8/95	**56**	11		21 **I Am Who I Am**	*Holly Dunn/Tom Shapiro/Chris Waters*	River North
				from the album *Life And Love And All The Stages* on River North 161140		
				DUNN, Ronnie		
				Born on 6/1/1953 in Coleman, Texas. Male singer/songwriter. One-half of **Brooks & Dunn** duo.		
3/5/83	**59**	7		1 **It's Written All Over Your Face**	*Tom Brasfield/Robert Byrne*	Churchill 94018
6/23/84	**59**	8		2 **She Put The Sad In All His Songs**	*Robert Byrne/Mac McAnally*	Churchill 52383
				DURHAM, Bobby		
				Born in Bakersfield, California. Male singer/songwriter/guitarist.		
5/21/88	**92**	2		**Let's Start A Rumor Today**	*Bobby Durham/Wayne Durham/Theresa Spanke*	Hightone 502
				DURRENCE, Sam		
				Born in Orlando, Florida. Male singer.		
9/15/73	**98**	3		**Last Days Of Childhood**	*John Wilkins*	River 3875
				DYCKE, Jerry		
				Born in Topeka, Kansas. Male singer/songwriter/guitarist.		
5/3/80	**93**	3		1 **Daddy Played Harmonica**	*Jerry Dycke*	Churchill 7757
2/28/81	**94**	2		2 **Beethoven Was Before My Time**	*Jerry Dycke*	Churchill 7766

E

DEBUT	PEAK	WKS	GOLD	ARTIST / Ranking / Country Chart Hit	Songwriter	Label (& Number)
				EAGLES		
				Rock-country group formed in Los Angeles, California: **Don Henley** (vocals, drums), Glenn Frey (vocals, guitar), Randy Meisner (bass) and Bernie Leadon (guitar). Meisner founded **Poco**. Leadon had been in the **Flying Burrito Brothers**. Frey and Henley were with **Linda Ronstadt**. Don Felder (guitar) added in 1975. Leadon replaced by Joe Walsh in 1975. Meisner replaced by Timothy B. Schmit in 1977. Disbanded in 1982. Henley, Frey, Felder, Walsh and Schmit reunited in 1994. Group inducted into the Rock and Roll Hall of Fame in 1998.		
10/11/75	**8**	13		1 **Lyin' Eyes**	*Glenn Frey/Don Henley*	Asylum 45279
1/8/77	**43**	12	•	2 **New Kid In Town**	*Glenn Frey/Don Henley/J.D. Souther*	Asylum 45373
1/24/81	**55**	7		3 **Seven Bridges Road**	*Steve Young* **[L]**	Asylum 47100
11/12/94	**58**	6		4 **The Girl From Yesterday**	*Glenn Frey/Jack Tempchin*	Geffen
				from the album *Hell Freezes Over* on Geffen 24725		
				EAKES, Bobbie		
				Born on 7/25/1961 in Warner Robins, Georgia. Female singer/actress. Regular on the TV soap operas *The Bold And The Beautiful* and *All My Children.* Married actor David Steen on 7/4/1992.		
6/24/00	**50**	17		**Tired Of Loving This Way** ***[w/ Collin Raye]***	*Gene Lesage/Allison Mellon*	Epic
				from Raye's album *Tracks* on Epic 69995		
				EARLE, Kenny		
				Born in Moblie, Alabama. Male singer/songwriter. Member of **The Wolfpack**.		
5/9/81	**84**	3		1 **We Have To Start Meeting Like This**	*Ken Bell/Terry Skinner/J.L. Wallace*	Kik 904
9/19/81	**73**	4		2 **Wasn't It Supposed To Be Me**	*Ken Bell/Terry Skinner/J.L. Wallace*	Kari 124
				EARLE, Steve		
				Born on 1/17/1955 in Fort Monroe, Virginia; raised in Schertz, Texas. Male singer/songwriter/guitarist.		
10/1/83	**70**	4		1 **Nothin' But You** ***[w/ The Dukes]***	*Steve Earle*	Epic 04070
12/8/84	**76**	6		2 **What'll You Do About Me?**	*Dennis Linde*	Epic 04666
3/22/86	**37**	13		3 **Hillbilly Highway**	*Steve Earle/Jimbeau Hinson*	MCA 52785
6/21/86	**7**	22		4 **Guitar Town**	S:6 / A:8 *Steve Earle*	MCA 52856
10/25/86	**28**	15		5 **Someday**	A:28 / S:30 *Steve Earle*	MCA 52920
2/14/87	**8**	19		6 **Goodbyes All We've Got Left**	A:8 / S:15 *Steve Earle*	MCA 53011
6/13/87	**20**	16		7 **Nowhere Road**	*Steve Earle/Reno Kling*	MCA 53103
10/17/87	**37**	13		8 **Sweet Little '66** ***[w/ The Dukes]***	*Steve Earle*	MCA 53182
1/9/88	**29**	13		9 **Six Days On The Road** ***[w/ The Dukes]***	*Earl Green/Carl Montgomery*	Hughes/MCA 53249
				from the movie *Planes, Trains & Automobiles* starring Steve Martin and John Candy		
				EARWOOD, Mundo — **All-Time: #290**		
				Born Raymond Earwood on 10/13/1952 in Del Rio, Texas. Male singer/songwriter/guitarist.		
10/21/72	**57**	10		1 **Behind Blue Eyes**	*Mundo Earwood*	Royal American 65
				also see #7 below		
6/29/74	**59**	10		2 **Let's Hear It For Loneliness**	*Ronald Dickson/Mundo Earwood*	GRT 003
10/25/75	**91**	4		3 **She Brings Her Lovin' Home To Me** ***[Mundo Ray]***	*Mundo Earwood*	Epic 50141

DEBUT	PEAK	WKS	GOLD	ARTIST / Ranking / Country Chart Hit	Songwriter	Label (& Number)
				EARWOOD, Mundo — cont'd		
2/7/76	**86**	7		4 **I Can't Quit Cheatin' On You**	*John Barnes/Henry Strzelecki*	Epic 50185
6/26/76	**70**	7		5 **Lonesome Is A Cowboy**	*Cliff Downs/Roger Hallmark/Gaston Nichols*	Epic 50232
3/19/77	**86**	4		6 **I Can Give You Love**	*Mundo Earwood*	True 101
7/9/77	**32**	11		7 **Behind Blue Eyes** same version as #1 above	*Mundo Earwood* **[R]**	True 104
12/17/77+	**69**	8		8 **Angelene**	*Mundo Earwood/Dick Heard*	True 111
5/20/78	**36**	11		9 **When I Get You Alone**	*Milton Blackford/Richard Leigh*	GMC 102
9/2/78	**18**	13		10 **Things I'd Do For You**	*Mundo Earwood*	GMC 104
12/2/78+	**25**	13		11 **Fooled Around And Fell In Love**	*Mundo Earwood*	GMC 105
4/28/79	**38**	10		12 **My Heart Is Not My Own**	*Mundo Earwood*	GMC 106
8/4/79	**34**	9		13 **We Got Love**	*Mundo Earwood*	GMC 107
10/13/79	**73**	3		14 **Philodendron /**	*Mundo Earwood*	
11/24/79	**67**	6		15 **Sometimes Love**	*Mundo Earwood*	GMC 108
4/5/80	**27**	13		16 **You're In Love With The Wrong Man** **Mel Tillis** (harmony vocal)	*Mundo Earwood*	GMC 109
9/27/80	**26**	12		17 **Can't Keep My Mind Off Of Her**	*Raleigh Squires*	GMC 111
2/14/81	**40**	9		18 **Blue Collar Blues**	*Mundo Earwood*	Excelsior 1005
5/16/81	**32**	12		19 **Angela**	*Mundo Earwood*	Excelsior 1010
10/17/81	**45**	8		20 **I'll Still Be Loving You**	*Mundo Earwood*	Excelsior 1019
4/17/82	**58**	8		21 **All My Lovin**	*John Lennon/Paul McCartney*	Primero 1002
9/4/82	**68**	5		22 **Pyramid Of Cans**	*Buddy Cannon/Bob Corbin/Jimmy Darrell*	Primero 1009
4/15/89	**80**	3		23 **A Woman's Way**	*Mundo Earwood*	Pegasus 110
				EAST, Lyndel Born in Oklahoma City, Oklahoma. Female singer.		
7/29/78	**97**	2		**Why Do You Come Around**	*Lyndel East*	NSD 2
				EASTON, Sheena Born Sheena Orr on 4/27/1959 in Bellshill, Scotland. Pop singer/actress. Won the 1981 Best New Artist Grammy Award.		
1/29/83	**❶**[1]	17		1 **We've Got Tonight** ***[w/ Kenny Rogers]***	*Bob Seger*	Liberty 1492
3/24/84	**86**	7		2 **Almost Over You**	*Jennifer Kimball/Cindy Richardson*	EMI America 8186
				EASTWOOD, Clint Born on 5/31/1930 in San Francisco, California. Legendary movie actor/director/producer. Served as mayor of Carmel, California (1986-88).		
5/17/80	**❶**[1]	16		1 **Bar Room Buddies** ***[w/ Merle Haggard]***	*Milton Brown/Cliff Crofford/Steve Dorff/Snuff Garrett*	Elektra 46634
11/22/80	**55**	10		2 **Beers To You** ***[w/ Ray Charles]***	*Steve Dorff/John Durrill/Snuff Garrett/Sandy Pinkard*	Warner 49608
				EATON, Connie Born on 3/1/1950 in Nashville, Tennessee. Female singer.		
2/7/70	**34**	7		1 **Angel Of The Morning**	*Chip Taylor*	Chart 5048
5/23/70	**44**	9		2 **Hit The Road Jack** ***[w/ Dave Peel]***	*Percy Mayfield*	Chart 5066
11/7/70	**56**	7		3 **It Takes Two** ***[w/ Dave Peel]***	*Sylvia Moy/William Stevenson*	Chart 5099
2/6/71	**74**	2		4 **Sing A Happy Song**	*Bill Graham/Charlie Williams*	Chart 5110
9/11/71	**56**	10		5 **Don't Hang No Halos On Me**	*Wayne Carson*	Chart 5138
1/25/75	**23**	13		6 **Lonely Men, Lonely Women**	*Bill Dees*	Dunhill/ABC 15022
6/14/75	**93**	4		7 **If I Knew Enough To Come Out Of The Rain**	*L. Russell Brown/Irwin Levine*	ABC 12098
				EATON, Skip — see SKIP & LINDA		
				EBERLY, Bob, with The Sunshine Serenaders Born Robert Eberle on 7/24/1916 in Mechanicsville, New York. Died of a heart attack on 11/17/1981 (age 65). Vocalist with Jimmy Dorsey from 1935-43.		
1/1/49	**8**	1		**One Has My Name The Other Has My Heart** J:8 / S:15	*Hal Blair/Dearest Dean/Eddie Dean*	Decca 24492
				EDDY, Duane Born on 4/26/1938 in Corning, New York. Originator of the "twangy" guitar sound. Married to **Jessi Colter** from 1961-68. Inducted into the Rock and Roll Hall of Fame in 1994.		
8/4/58	**17**	5		1 **Rebel-'Rouser** S:17 The Sharps (later known as The Rivingtons, rebel yells)	*Duane Eddy/Lee Hazlewood* **[I]**	Jamie 1104
5/7/77	**69**	6		2 **You Are My Sunshine** ***[w/ Waylon Jennings/Willie Nelson/Kin Vassy/Deed Eddy]*** instrumental version recorded by Eddy on his 1960 album *The Twangs The Thang*	*Jimmie Davis/Charles Mitchell*	Elektra 45359
				EDGE, Kathy Born in Huntsville, Alabama; raised in Memphis, Tennessee. Female singer.		
3/21/87	**89**	5		**I Take The Chance**	*Charlie Louvin/Ira Louvin*	NSD 228
				EDMUNDS, Dave Born on 4/15/1944 in Cardiff, Wales. Rock singer/songwriter/guitarist/producer.		
10/25/80	**76**	5		**Baby Ride Easy** ***[w/ Carlene Carter]***	*Richard Dobson*	Warner 49572
				EDWARDS, Bobby Born Robert Moncrief on 1/18/1926 in Anniston, Alabama. Male singer/songwriter.		
9/4/61	**4**	24		1 **You're The Reason** The Four Young Men (backing vocals)	*Bobby Edwards/Terry Fell/Fred Henley/Mildred Imes*	Crest 1075
9/14/63	**23**	2		2 **Don't Pretend**	*Robert Moncrief/Jerry Russell/Rose Russell*	Capitol 5006

DEBUT	PEAK	WKS	GOLD	ARTIST / Country Chart Hit	Ranking / Songwriter	Label (& Number)
				EDWARDS, Jimmy		
				Born James Bullington on 2/9/1933 in Senath, Missouri. Male singer/songwriter.		
11/11/57+	12	6		Love Bug Crawl	A:12 *Jimmy Edwards/Jack Foshee*	Mercury 71209
				EDWARDS, Jonathan		
				Born on 7/28/1946 in Aitkin, Minnesota; raised in Virginia. Male singer/guitarist.		
9/17/88	64	6		1 We Need To Be Locked Away	*Tony Haselden/Stan Munsey*	MCA/Curb 53390
12/10/88+	56	14		2 Look What We Made (When We Made Love)	*Mike Chapman/Dave Loggins/Russell Smith*	MCA/Curb 53467
3/18/89	59	7		3 It's A Natural Thing	*Tom Brasfield/Mac McAnally*	MCA/Curb 53613
				EDWARDS, Meredith		
				Born on 3/15/1984 in Clinton, Mississippi. Female singer.		
2/3/01	37	13		1 A Rose Is A Rose	S:8 *Dave Berg/Deanna Bryant/Sunny Russ*	Mercury
5/26/01	47	9		2 The Bird Song	*Buzz Cason/Neil Thrasher*	Mercury
				above 2 from the album *Reach* on Mercury 170188		
				EDWARDS, Stoney		
				Born Frenchy Edwards on 12/24/1929 in Seminole, Oklahoma. Died on 4/5/1997 (age 67). Black singer/songwriter/guitarist.		
1/23/71	68	3		1 A Two Dollar Toy	*Stoney Edwards*	Capitol 3005
4/3/71	61	7		2 Poor Folks Stick Together	*John Schweers*	Capitol 3061
8/28/71	73	2		3 The Cute Little Waitress	*Stoney Edwards*	Capitol 3131
11/11/72+	20	14		4 She's My Rock	*Sharon Dobbins*	Capitol 3462
3/17/73	54	6		5 You're A Believer	*Sharon Dobbins*	Capitol 3550
8/11/73	39	10		6 Hank And Lefty Raised My Country Soul	*Dallas Frazier/A.L. "Doodle" Owens*	Capitol 3671
12/22/73+	85	7		7 Daddy Bluegrass	*Boudleaux Bryant/Felice Bryant*	Capitol 3766
2/8/75	77	8		8 Clean Your Own Tables	*Chip Taylor*	Capitol 4015
4/19/75	20	12		9 Mississippi You're On My Mind	*Jesse Winchester*	Capitol 4051
11/29/75+	41	11		10 Blackbird (Hold Your Head High)	*Chip Taylor*	Capitol 4188
4/10/76	51	8		11 Love Still Makes The World Go 'Round	*Aaron Allen*	Capitol 4246
10/23/76	90	4		12 Don't Give Up On Me	*Merle Haggard*	Capitol 4337
11/4/78	60	7		13 If I Had It To Do All Over Again	*Danny Wolfe*	JMI 47
5/24/80	53	10		14 No Way To Drown A Memory	*Curtis Wayne*	Music America 107
9/20/80	85	3		15 One Bar At A Time	*Jim Busby*	Music America 109
				ELAM, Katrina		
				Born in 1981 in Bray, Oklahoma. Female singer/songwriter.		
7/31/04	29	21		1 No End In Sight	*Robin Lee Bruce/Christine Dannemiller/Katrina Elam*	Universal South
3/19/05	59	3		2 I Want A Cowboy	*Katrina Elam/Wayne Kirkpatrick/Jimmie Lee Sloas*	Universal South
				above 2 from the album *Katrina Elam* on Universal South 002610		
				ELLEDGE, Jimmy		
				Born on 1/8/1943 in Nashville, Tennessee. Male singer/pianist.		
5/17/75	95	4		One By One	*Kelly Bach/Jean Lane*	4 Star 1003
				ELLIOTT, Alecia		
				Born on 12/25/1982 in Muscle Shoals, Alabama. Female singer/songwriter.		
10/2/99+	50	20		1 I'm Diggin' It	S:3 *Daryl Burgess/Michele McCord*	MCA Nashville
5/13/00	70	10		2 You Wanna What?	*Andy Bohatiuk/Alecia Elliott/Bill Terry*	MCA Nashville
				above 2 from the album *I'm Diggin' It* on MCA Nashville 170087		
				ELLIS, Darryl & Don		
				Duo of brothers Darryl Ellis Gatlin (born on 12/1/1964) and Don Ellis Gatlin (born on 7/2/1967). Both born in Norfolk, Virginia; raised in Beaver Falls, Pennsylvania.		
6/27/92	70	2		1 Goodbye Highway	*Bob DiPiero/Jim Photoglo*	Epic
9/5/92	58	8		2 No Sir	*Steve Dean/Don Ellis/Billy Montana*	Epic
11/21/92	73	4		3 Something Moving In Me	*Rory Bourke/Mike Reid*	Epic
				ELLIS, Mike		
				Born in San Antonio, Texas. Male singer/guitarist.		
7/29/78	89	3		I Never Meant To Harm You	*Jimmy Anthony/Donnie Sanders*	Cin Kay 130
				ELLWANGER, Sandy		
				Born on 9/10/1963 in Fremont, California. Female singer/songwriter/pianist.		
7/29/89	96	2		1 I Just Came In Here (To Let A Little Hurt Out)	*McKay Phillips/Doug Zepp*	Door Knob 326
11/11/89	79	2		2 What Kind Of Girl Do You Think I Am	*Sandy Ellwanger/Ralph Porter*	Door Knob 334
				ELMO & PATSY		
				Husband-and-wife team of Elmo Shropshire and Patsy Trigg. Divorced in 1985.		
1/7/84	92	2		1 Grandma Got Run Over By A Reindeer *[Elmo 'N Patsy]*	*Randy Brooks* **[X-N]**	Soundwaves 4658
1/3/98	64	2		2 Grandma Got Run Over By A Reindeer	*Randy Brooks* **[X-N-R]**	Epic
				above 2 are different versions		
12/25/99+	48	3		3 Grandma Got Run Over By A Reindeer	*Randy Brooks* **[X-N-R]**	Epic
				above 2 are the same version; from the album *Grandma Got Run Over By A Reindeer* on Epic 39931		
				ELY, Joe		
				Born on 2/9/1947 in Amarillo, Texas; raised in Lubbock, Texas. Male singer/songwriter/guitarist. Member of the **Buzzin' Cousins**.		
2/12/77	89	3		All My Love	*Joe Ely*	MCA 40666

DEBUT	PEAK	WKS	GOLD	ARTIST / Country Chart Hit	Songwriter	Label (& Number)
				EME		
				Vocal group from Texas.		
2/21/81	**86**	2		**Every Breath I Take**	*Gerry Goffin/Carole King*	EPI 1541
				EMERICK, Scotty		
				Born on 6/16/1975 in Vero Beach, Florida. Male singer/songwriter/guitarist.		
7/26/03	**24**	23		1 **I Can't Take You Anywhere** ***[w/ Toby Keith]***	S:2 *Scotty Emerick/Toby Keith*	DreamWorks
2/14/04	**47**	10		2 **The Coast Is Clear**	*Scotty Emerick/Red Lane*	DreamWorks
				above 2 from the album *The Coast Is Clear* on DreamWorks 450434		
6/12/04	**49**	7		3 **The Watch**	*Dean Dillon/Scotty Emerick/Leslie Satcher*	DreamWorks
				EMERSON DRIVE		
				Group from Grande Prairie, Alberta, Canada: Brad Mates (vocals; born on 7/21/1978), Danick Dupelle (guitar; born on 9/29/1973), Chris Hartman (keyboards; born on 1/2/1978), Pat Allingham (fiddle; born on 7/9/1978), Jeff Loberg (bass) and Mike Melancon (drums; born on 8/13/1978).		
11/10/01+	**4**	35		1 **I Should Be Sleeping**	S:2 *Lisa Drew/Shaye Smith*	DreamWorks
6/29/02+	**3^{3}**	36		2 **Fall Into Me**	*Danny Orton/Jeremy Stover*	DreamWorks
4/5/03	**23**	24		3 **Only God (Could Stop Me Loving You)**	*Mutt Lange*	DreamWorks
				above 3 from the album *Emerson Drive* on DreamWorks 450272		
1/24/04	**21**	22		4 **Last One Standing**	S:5 *Richard Marx/Fee Waybill*	DreamWorks
8/28/04	**41**	9		5 **November**	*Brett James/Angelo Petraglia*	DreamWorks
				above 2 from the album *What If?* on DreamWorks 000071		
				EMERY, Ralph		
				Born Walter Ralph Emery on 3/10/1933 in McEwen, Tennessee. Popular radio DJ/TV personality. Former host of TNN's *Nashville Now.* Married to **Skeeter Davis** from 1960-64.		
8/28/61	**4**	15		**Hello Fool**	*James Coleman/Willie Nelson* **[S]**	Liberty 55352
				answer to "Hello Walls" by **Faron Young**		
				EMILIO		
				Born Emilio Navaira on 8/23/1962 in San Antonio, Texas. Male singer.		
8/19/95	**27**	20		1 **It's Not The End Of The World**	S:20 *Larry Boone/Earl Clark/Paul Nelson*	Capitol
1/20/96	**41**	15		2 **Even If I Tried**	S:10 *Chris Faulk/Nettie Musick/Bob Regan*	Capitol
5/11/96	**56**	7		3 **I Think We're On To Something**	*Jeff Pennig/Bob Regan*	Capitol
10/12/96	**62**	1		4 **Have I Told You Lately**	*Van Morrison*	Capitol
				above 4 from the album *Life Is Good* on Capitol 32392		
2/15/97	**56**	9		5 **I'd Love You To Love Me**	S:22 *Marv Green/Thom McHugh*	Capitol
6/7/97	**64**	3		6 **She Gives**	*Steve Bogard/Jeff Stevens*	Capitol
				above 2 from the album *It's On The House* on Capitol 52180		
				ENGLAND, Ty		
				Born on 12/5/1963 in Oklahoma City, Oklahoma. Male singer/guitarist.		
6/10/95	**3^{1}**	20		1 **Should've Asked Her Faster**	S:11 *Al Anderson/Bob DiPiero/Joe Klemick*	RCA
10/28/95+	**44**	16		2 **Smoke In Her Eyes**	S:25 *Hugh Prestwood*	RCA
2/24/96	**55**	7		3 **Redneck Son**	*Bob Carlisle/Randy Thomas*	RCA
				above 3 from the album *Ty England* on RCA 66522		
8/10/96	**22**	20		4 **Irresistible You**	S:17 *Billy Lawson*	RCA
12/28/96+	**46**	9		5 **All Of The Above**	*Jon Robbin/Chris Waters*	RCA
				above 2 from the album *Two Ways To Fall* on RCA 66930		
2/3/01	**53**	9		6 **I Drove Her To Dallas** ***[Tyler England]***	*Tony Martin/Mark Narmore*	Capitol
				from the album *Highways & Dance Halls* on Capitol 521657		
				ENGLISH, Robin		
				Born in 1971 in Texas. Female singer/songwriter.		
12/1/01+	**10^{S}**	33		**Girl In Love**	*Robin English/Marcus Hummon*	Columbia
				ENGVALL, Bill		
				Born on 7/27/1957 in Galveston, Texas. Stand-up comedian/actor. Played "Bill Pelton" on TV's *The **Jeff Foxworthy** Show.*		
1/25/97	**29**	20	●	1 **Here's Your Sign (Get The Picture)** ***[w/ Travis Tritt]***	S:❶^{8} *Bill Engvall/Scott Rouse/Ronny Scaife* **[C]**	Warner
				from Engvall's album *Here's Your Sign* on Warner 46263		
8/16/97	**56**	5		2 **Warning Signs** ***[w/ John Michael Montgomery]***	S:21 *Bill Engvall/Scott Rouse/Ronny Scaife* **[C]**	Warner
				from the album *Warning Signs* on Warner 43934		
2/14/98	**72**	1		3 **It's Hard To Be A Parent**	*Bill Engvall/Jim Hollihan* **[N]**	Warner
10/17/98	**60**	8		4 **I'm A Cowboy**	*Aaron Barker/Bill Engvall* **[N]**	Warner
12/12/98+	**39**	5		5 **Here's Your Sign Christmas**	S:❶^{9} *Bill Engvall/Doug Grau* **[X-C]**	Warner
4/24/99	**72**	1		6 **Hollywood Indian Guides**	*Bill Engvall/Doug Grau/Porter Howell* **[N]**	Warner
12/11/99+	**46**	5		7 **Here's Your Sign Christmas**	*Bill Engvall/Doug Grau* **[X-C-R]**	Warner
				above 4 from the album *Dorkfish* on Warner 47090		
4/15/00	**63**	6		8 **The Blue Collar Dollar Song** ***[w/ Jeff Foxworthy & Marty Stuart]*** from Foxworthy's album *Big Funny* on DreamWorks 50200	*Bill Engvall/Jeff Foxworthy/ Doug Grau/Porter Howell* **[N]**	DreamWorks
9/2/00	**59**	12		9 **Now That's Awesome!** ***[w/ Tracy Byrd/Neal McCoy/T. Graham Brown]***	S:13 *Bill Engvall/Porter Howell* **[N]**	BNA
12/9/00	**71**	2		10 **Shoulda Shut Up**	*Bill Engvall/Porter Howell* **[C]**	BNA
				above 2 from the album *Now That's Awesome!* on BNA 69311		
				ERIKA JO		
				Born Erika Jo Heriges on 11/2/1986 in Angelton, Texas; raised in Nashville, Tennessee. Female singer. Winner of the second season of TV's *Nashville Star* talent contest.		
5/14/05	**53**	1		**I Break Things**	*Monty Criswell/Wade Kirby*	Universal South
				from the album *Erika Jo* on Universal South 004522		

Billboard DEBUT	PEAK	WKS	GOLD	ARTIST / Country Chart Hit	Songwriter	Label (& Number)

ESMERELDY And Her Novelty Band

Born Verna Sherrill on 6/1/1920 in Middleton, Tennessee. Female novelty singer. Known as "The Streamlined Hillbilly." Mother of pop singer Amy Holland.

DEBUT	PEAK	WKS	#	Country Chart Hit	Songwriter	Label (& Number)
3/20/48	**10**	1		**Slap Her Down Again Paw**	*Polly Arnold/Eddie Asherman/Alice Cornett* **[N]**	Musicraft 524

ETC BAND, The — see CONLEY, Earl Thomas

ETHEL & THE SHAMELESS HUSSIES

Female trio from Huntsville, Alabama: "Ethel Beaverton" (**Gayle Zeiler**), "Blanche Hickey" (Valerie Hunt) and "Bunny O'Hare" (Beki Fogle). Name taken from a line in "The Streak" by **Ray Stevens**.

DEBUT	PEAK	WKS	#	Country Chart Hit	Songwriter	Label (& Number)
5/21/88	**71**	5	1	**One Nite Stan**	*Jon Iger/Kacey Jones* **[N]**	MCA 53323
1/21/89	**86**	2	2	**It's Just The Whiskey Talkin'**	*Justin Ezzi*	MCA 53472

EVANGELINE

Female group from Louisiana: Kathleen Stieffel (vocals, guitar), Rhonda Lohmeyer (guitar), Sharon Leger (bass) and Beth McKee (keyboards).

DEBUT	PEAK	WKS	#	Country Chart Hit	Songwriter	Label (& Number)
1/22/94	**70**	4		**Let's Go Spend Your Money Honey**	*Kostas/Kelly Willis*	MCA

EVANS, Ashley

Born in Kentucky. Female singer.

DEBUT	PEAK	WKS	#	Country Chart Hit	Songwriter	Label (& Number)
1/6/90	**76**	2		**I'm So Afraid Of Losing You Again**	*Dallas Frazier/A.L. "Doodle" Owens*	Door Knob 338

EVANS, Paul

Born on 3/5/1938 in Brooklyn, New York. Male singer/songwriter.

DEBUT	PEAK	WKS	#	Country Chart Hit	Songwriter	Label (& Number)
5/20/78	**57**	10	1	**Hello, This Is Joannie (The Telephone Answering Machine Song)**	*Paul Evans/Fred Tobias*	Spring 183
5/5/79	**81**	4	2	**Disneyland Daddy**	*Paul Evans/Paul Parnes*	Spring 193
8/16/80	**80**	4	3	**One Night Led To Two**	*Bob Alan/Paul Evans*	Cinnamon 604

EVANS, Paula Kay

Born on 11/10/1957 in Garland, Texas. Died in a plane crash on 3/16/1991 (age 33). Backing singer for **Reba McEntire**. Plane crash also killed **Chris Austin**.

DEBUT	PEAK	WKS	#	Country Chart Hit	Songwriter	Label (& Number)
4/23/77	**100**	2		**Runnin' Out Again**	*Milton Blackford/Richard Mainegra*	Autumn 368

EVANS, Sara — 2000s: #16 / All-Time: #225

Born on 2/5/1971 in Boonville, Missouri; raised in Boonesboro, Missouri. Female singer/songwriter.

DEBUT	PEAK	WKS	#	Country Chart Hit	Songwriter	Label (& Number)
3/29/97	**59**	6	1	**True Lies**	*Al Anderson/Sara Evans/Mary Sharon Rice*	RCA
7/12/97	**44**	11	2	**Three Chords And The Truth**	*Sara Evans/Ron Harbin/Aimee Mayo*	RCA
12/27/97+	**48**	8	3	**Shame About That**	*Sara Evans/Jamie O'Hara*	RCA
				above 3 from the album *Three Chords And The Truth* on RCA 66995		
6/13/98	**56**	10	4	**Cryin' Game**	*Jamie O'Hara*	RCA
10/3/98+	❶^{1}	30	5	**No Place That Far**	S:3 *Sara Evans/Tony Martin/Tom Shapiro*	RCA
4/3/99	**32**	20	6	**Fool, I'm A Woman**	*Matraca Berg/Sara Evans*	RCA
				above 3 from the album *No Place That Far* on RCA 67653		
3/25/00	**22**	28	7	**That's The Beat Of A Heart** ***[w/ The Warren Brothers]***	*Tena Clark/Tim Heintz*	BNA
				from the movie *Where The Heart Is* starring Natalie Portman (soundtrack on RCA 67963)		
7/1/00+	❶^{1}	35	8	**Born To Fly**	*Sara Evans/Marcus Hummon/Darrell Scott*	RCA
2/17/01	2^{3}	26	9	**I Could Not Ask For More**	*Diane Warren*	RCA
9/15/01+	**16**	22	10	**Saints & Angels**	*Victoria Banks*	RCA
3/16/02	**5**	32	11	**I Keep Looking**	*Sara Evans/Tony Martin/Tom Shapiro*	RCA
				above 4 from the album *Born To Fly* on RCA 67964		
3/1/03	**16**	26	12	**Backseat Of A Greyhound Bus**	*Chris Lindsey/Hillary Lindsey/Aimee Mayo/Troy Verges*	RCA
9/20/03+	2^{1}	33	13	**Perfect**	*Sara Evans/Tony Martin/Tom Shapiro*	RCA
5/8/04	❶^{1}	31	14	**Suds In The Bucket**	*Billy Montana/Tammy Wagoner*	RCA
12/4/04+	**41**	14	15	**Tonight**	*Bonnie Baker/Tim Johnson*	RCA
				above 4 from the album *Restless* on RCA 67074		
5/7/05	❶^{2}	22↑	16	**A Real Fine Place To Start**	*George Ducas/Radney Foster*	RCA
				from the album *Real Fine Place* on RCA 69486		

EVERETTE, Leon — All-Time: #215

Born Leon Everette Baughman on 6/21/1948 in Aiken, South Carolina; raised in New York. Male singer/songwriter/guitarist.

DEBUT	PEAK	WKS	#	Country Chart Hit	Songwriter	Label (& Number)
12/3/77	**84**	5	1	**I Love That Woman (Like The Devil Loves Sin)**	*Paul Huffman/Bucky Jones/Joane Keller*	True 110
				also see #6 below		
1/20/79	**89**	3	2	**We Let Love Fade Away**	*Jim McBride/Roger Murrah*	Orlando 100
4/7/79	**81**	4	3	**Giving Up Easy**	*Jerry Foster/Bill Rice*	Orlando 102
				also see #9 below		
6/9/79	**33**	10	4	**Don't Feel Like The Lone Ranger**	*Roger Murrah*	Orlando 103
9/15/79	**42**	7	5	**The Sun Went Down In My World Tonight**	*Scott Anders/Roger Murrah*	Orlando 104
12/8/79+	**28**	12	6	**I Love That Woman (Like The Devil Loves Sin)**	*Paul Huffman/Bucky Jones/Joane Keller* **[R]**	Orlando 105
				new version of #1 above		
3/1/80	**30**	12	7	**I Don't Want To Lose**	*Tim Lewis/Roger Murrah*	Orlando 106
5/31/80	**10**	17	8	**Over**	*Jerry Foster/Bill Rice*	Orlando 107
10/25/80+	**5**	18	9	**Giving Up Easy**	*Jerry Foster/Bill Rice* **[R]**	RCA 12111
				same version as #3 above		
3/7/81	**11**	13	10	**If I Keep On Going Crazy**	*Jim McBride/Roger Murrah*	RCA 12177
7/18/81	**4**	16	11	**Hurricane**	*Stewart Harris/Thom Schuyler/Keith Stegall*	RCA 12270
11/14/81+	**9**	17	12	**Midnight Rodeo**	*DeWayne Orender/Rodger Ware*	RCA 12355
3/27/82	**7**	18	13	**Just Give Me What You Think Is Fair**	*Rex Gosdin/V.L. Haywood/Jeff Tweel*	RCA 13079
8/7/82	**10**	17	14	**Soul Searchin'**	*Bill Rice/Mary Sharon Rice*	RCA 13282
11/27/82+	**15**	18	15	**Shadows Of My Mind**	*E.E. Collins*	RCA 13391

DEBUT	PEAK	WKS	GOLD	#	ARTIST / Country Chart Hit	Ranking / Songwriter	Label (& Number)
					EVERETTE, Leon — cont'd		
3/19/83	**9**	18		16	**My Lady Loves Me (Just As I Am)**	*Keith Stegall/Chris Waters*	RCA 13466
8/13/83	**31**	13		17	**The Lady, She's Right** **Rex Gosdin** (harmony vocal)	*V.L. Haywood/Chris Ryder*	RCA 13584
2/4/84	**6**	20		18	**I Could'a Had You**	*Bill Rice/Mary Sharon Rice*	RCA 13717
7/7/84	**30**	14		19	**Shot In The Dark**	*Ronnie Rogers*	RCA 13834
3/30/85	**47**	10		20	**Too Good To Say No To**	*Bill Rice/Mary Sharon Rice*	Mercury 880611
6/15/85	**53**	9		21	**A Good Love Died Tonight**	*Roger Murrah*	Mercury 880829
10/5/85	**44**	9		22	**'Til A Tear Becomes A Rose**	*Bill Rice/Mary Sharon Rice*	Mercury 884040
5/24/86	**46**	9		23	**Danger List (Give Me Someone I Can Love)**	*Larry Crane/John Mellencamp*	Orlando 112
8/2/86	**59**	5		24	**Sad State Of Affairs**	*Pam Belford/Kent Blazy/Jim Dowell*	Orlando 114
11/15/86	**56**	6		25	**Still In The Picture**	*Phil Barnhart/Kent Blazy/Jim Dowell*	Orlando 115
					EVERLY, Don Born Isaac Donald Everly on 2/1/1937 in Brownie, Kentucky. Male singer/songwriter. One-half of **The Everly Brothers**.		
4/10/76	**50**	8		1	**Yesterday Just Passed My Way Again**	*Darlene Shafer/Whitey Shafer*	Hickory/MGM 368
2/5/77	**84**	4		2	**Since You Broke My Heart**	*Don Everly*	ABC/Hickory 54005
5/7/77	**96**	4		3	**Brother Juke-Box**	*Paul Craft*	ABC/Hickory 54012
					EVERLY, Phil Born on 1/19/1939 in Chicago, Illinois. Male singer/songwriter. One-half of **The Everly Brothers**.		
12/27/80+	**63**	7		1	**Dare To Dream Again**	*Phil Everly*	Curb 5401
6/13/81	**52**	8		2	**Sweet Southern Love**	*Phil Everly/Joe Sauseris*	Curb 02116
2/19/83	**37**	12		3	**Who's Gonna Keep Me Warm**	*Kevin McKnelly/Don Stirling*	Capitol 5197
					EVERLY BROTHERS, The Duo of vocalists/guitarists/songwriters: brothers **Don Everly** (born on 2/1/1937) and **Phil Everly** (born on 1/19/1939). Duo split up in July 1973 and reunited in September 1983. Inducted into the Rock and Roll Hall of Fame in 1986. Won Grammy's Lifetime Achievement Award in 1997. ***OPRY: 1957***	**1950s: #19 / All-Time: #214 // HOF: 2001**	
5/13/57	**❶**^{7}	26	●	1	**Bye Bye Love** **Grammy: Hall of Fame / RS500**	S:❶^{7} / A:❶^{7} *Boudleaux Bryant/Felice Bryant*	Cadence 1315
9/30/57	**❶**^{8}	22	●	2	**Wake Up Little Susie**	A:❶^{8} / S:❶^{7} *Boudleaux Bryant/Felice Bryant*	Cadence 1337
2/10/58	**4**	13		3	**This Little Girl Of Mine /**	S:4 / A:5 *Ray Charles*	
3/24/58	**10**	1		4	**Should We Tell Him**	A:10 / S:flip *Don Everly/Phil Everly*	Cadence 1342
4/28/58	**❶**^{3}	20	●	5	**All I Have To Do Is Dream /** **Grammy: Hall of Fame / RS500**	S:❶^{3} / A:❶^{1} *Boudleaux Bryant*	
6/16/58	**15**	1		6	**Claudette**	A:15 *Roy Orbison*	Cadence 1348
8/18/58	**❶**^{6}	13	●	7	**Bird Dog /**	S:❶^{6} / A:3 *Boudleaux Bryant*	
9/1/58	**7**	5		8	**Devoted To You**	A:7 *Boudleaux Bryant*	Cadence 1350
12/1/58+	**17**	7		9	**Problems**	*Boudleaux Bryant/Felice Bryant*	Cadence 1355
8/31/59	**8**	12		10	**('Til) I Kissed You**	*Don Everly*	Cadence 1369
3/6/61	**25**	3		11	**Ebony Eyes**	*John D. Loudermilk*	Warner 5199
9/29/84	**49**	12		12	**On The Wings Of A Nightingale**	*Paul McCartney*	Mercury 880213
1/5/85	**44**	11		13	**The First In Line**	*Paul Kennerley*	Mercury 880423
3/1/86	**17**	18		14	**Born Yesterday**	S:12 / A:18 *Don Everly*	Mercury 884428
7/5/86	**56**	6		15	**I Know Love /**	*Brian Neary/Jim Photoglo*	
9/13/86	**57**	8		16	**These Shoes**	*John Goin/Larry Lee*	Mercury 884694
2/25/89	**45**	9		17	**Ballad Of A Teenage Queen** *[w/ Johnny Cash & Rosanne Cash]*	*Jack Clement*	Mercury 872420
					E.W.B. Vocal trio from Dallas, Texas: Jerrel Elliott, Richard Wesley, Gerald Bennett.		
9/12/81	**96**	2			**We Could Go On Forever**	*Jerrel Elliott*	Paid 142
					EWING, Skip Born Donald Ralph Ewing on 3/6/1964 in Redlands, California. Male singer/songwriter/guitarist.		
3/5/88	**17**	18		1	**Your Memory Wins Again**	*Skip Ewing/Mike Geiger/Woody Mullis*	MCA 53271
6/25/88	**8**	24		2	**I Don't Have Far To Fall**	S:17 *Skip Ewing/Don Sampson*	MCA 53353
10/29/88+	**3**^{1}	22		3	**Burnin' A Hole In My Heart**	S:21 *Skip Ewing/Mike Geiger/Woody Mullis*	MCA 53435
3/4/89	**10**	20		4	**The Gospel According To Luke**	*Skip Ewing/Don Sampson*	MCA 53481
6/24/89	**15**	24		5	**The Coast Of Colorado**	*Max D. Barnes/Skip Ewing*	MCA 53663
10/7/89+	**5**	26		6	**It's You Again**	*Skip Ewing/Mike Geiger/Woody Mullis*	MCA 53732
3/3/90	**70**	5		7	**If A Man Could Live On Love Alone** from the album *The Will To Love* on MCA 42301	*Skip Ewing/Red Lane*	MCA
8/18/90	**69**	4		8	**I'm Your Man** from the album *Healin' Fire* on MCA 42344	*Rick Bowles/Skip Ewing*	MCA
5/25/91	**73**	1		9	**I Get The Picture**	*Skip Ewing/Red Lane*	Capitol
3/28/92	**71**	1		10	**Naturally** above 2 from the album *Naturally* on Capitol 96097	*Rick Bowles/Skip Ewing*	Capitol
1/6/96	**68**	1		11	**Christmas Carol** from the album *Following Yonder Star* on MCA 10068	*Skip Ewing/Don Sampson* **[X]**	MCA
4/19/97	**58**	12		12	**Mary Go Round**	*Skip Ewing/Phil Vassar*	Word
8/23/97	**66**	7		13	**Answer To My Prayer** above 2 from the album *Until I Found You* on Word 471202	*Skip Ewing/Victoria Shaw*	Word
12/27/97+	**60**	3		14	**Christmas Carol**	*Skip Ewing/Don Sampson* **[X-R]**	MCA
12/25/99+	**44**	3		15	**Christmas Carol** above 2 from the album *Following Yonder Star* on MCA 10068	*Skip Ewing/Don Sampson* **[X-R]**	MCA

Billboard DEBUT	PEAK	WKS	GOLD	ARTIST Ranking / Country Chart Hit	Songwriter	Label (& Number)

EXILE — 1980s: #50 / All-Time: #153

Group from Richmond, Kentucky: **J.P. Pennington** (vocals, guitar; born on 1/22/1949), **Les Taylor** (guitar; born on 12/27/1948), Marlon Hargis (keyboards; born on 5/13/1949), Sonny Lemaire (bass; born on 9/16/1946) and Steve Goetzman (drums; born on 9/1/1950). **Mark Gray** (born on 10/24/1953) was a member from 1979-82. Member Bernie Faulkner formed **Hazard**. Hargis was replaced by Lee Carroll (born on 1/27/1953) in 1985. Pennington was replaced by Paul Martin (born on 12/22/1962) in 1989. Taylor was replaced by Mark Jones (born on 7/18/1954) in 1989.

DEBUT	PEAK	WKS	#	Country Chart Hit		Songwriter	Label (& Number)
8/20/83	27	16	1	High Cost Of Leaving		Mark Gray/Sonny Lemaire/J.P. Pennington	Epic 04041
12/3/83+	❶[1]	22	2	Woke Up In Love		J.P. Pennington	Epic 04247
4/7/84	❶[1]	24	3	I Don't Want To Be A Memory		Sonny Lemaire/J.P. Pennington	Epic 04421
8/11/84	❶[1]	26	4	Give Me One More Chance	A:❶[2] / S:❶[1]	Sonny Lemaire/J.P. Pennington	Epic 04567
12/8/84+	❶[1]	23	5	Crazy For Your Love	S:❶[1] / A:❶[1]	Sonny Lemaire/J.P. Pennington	Epic 04722
3/30/85	86	4	6	Stay With Me recorded in 1978		J.P. Pennington	Curb/MCA 52551
4/6/85	❶[1]	22	7	She's A Miracle	S:❶[1] / A:❶[1]	Sonny Lemaire/J.P. Pennington	Epic 04864
8/17/85	❶[1]	24	8	Hang On To Your Heart	S:❶[1] / A:❶[1]	Sonny Lemaire/J.P. Pennington	Epic 05580
12/7/85+	❶[1]	22	9	I Could Get Used To You	S:❶[1] / A:❶[1]	Sonny Lemaire/J.P. Pennington	Epic 05723
4/5/86	14	16	10	Super Love	A:13 / S:14	Sonny Lemaire/J.P. Pennington	Epic 05860
7/26/86	❶[1]	22	11	It'll Be Me	A:❶[1] / S:3	Sonny Lemaire/J.P. Pennington	Epic 06229
6/6/87	❶[1]	23	12	She's Too Good To Be True	S:2	Sonny Lemaire/J.P. Pennington	Epic 07135
10/10/87+	❶[1]	22	13	I Can't Get Close Enough	S:❶[2]	Sonny Lemaire/J.P. Pennington	Epic 07597
2/20/88	60	4	14	Feel Like Foolin' Around		Sonny Lemaire/J.P. Pennington/Les Taylor	Epic 07710
4/23/88	9	18	15	Just One Kiss	S:5	Sonny Lemaire/J.P. Pennington	Epic 07775
9/3/88	21	18	16	It's You Again	S:23	Sonny Lemaire/J.P. Pennington	Epic 08020
12/16/89+	17	25	17	Keep It In The Middle Of The Road		Sonny Lemaire/J.P. Pennington	Arista 9911
4/14/90	2[1]	21	18	Nobody's Talking		Sonny Lemaire/Randy Sharp	Arista
9/1/90	7	20	19	Yet		Sonny Lemaire/Randy Sharp	Arista
12/15/90+	32	20	20	There You Go above 3 from the album *Still Standing* on Arista 8624		Donny Lowery/Randy Sharp	Arista
6/22/91	16	20	21	Even Now from the album *Justice* on Arista 8675		Marc Beeson/Randy Sharp	Arista

F

FAIRCHILD, Barbara — All-Time: #223

Born on 11/12/1950 in Knobel, Arkansas; raised in St. Louis, Missouri. Female singer/songwriter/guitarist. First appeared on local St. Louis TV shows in 1963; made her first recording in 1965. Began recoding gospel music in 1990.

DEBUT	PEAK	WKS	#	Country Chart Hit	Songwriter	Label (& Number)
5/31/69	69	5	1	Love Is A Gentle Thing	Ann Burns/Barbara Fairchild/Ruby Van Noy	Columbia 44797
8/9/69	66	6	2	A Woman's Hand	Jan Crutchfield	Columbia 44925
2/14/70	26	11	3	A Girl Who'll Satisfy Her Man	Jerry Crutchfield	Columbia 45063
8/1/70	52	6	4	Find Out What's Happenin'	Jerry Crutchfield	Columbia 45173
1/2/71	33	10	5	(Loving You Is) Sunshine	Jerry Crutchfield	Columbia 45272
4/10/71	62	8	6	What Do You Do	Linda Cassady	Columbia 45344
8/7/71	28	11	7	Love's Old Song	Jerry Crutchfield	Columbia 45422
1/15/72	38	8	8	Color My World	Tony Hatch/Jackie Trent	Columbia 45522
5/27/72	29	10	9	Thanks For The Mem'ries	Jerry Crutchfield	Columbia 45589
10/14/72	53	9	10	A Sweeter Love (I'll Never Know)	Jerry Crutchfield	Columbia 45690
12/30/72+	❶[2]	19	11	Teddy Bear Song	Don Earl/Nick Nixon	Columbia 45743
7/28/73	2[2]	16	12	Kid Stuff	Jerry Crutchfield/Don Earl	Columbia 45903
1/26/74	6	14	13	Baby Doll	Jerry Crutchfield/Don Earl	Columbia 45988
6/29/74	17	13	14	Standing In Your Line	Barbara Fairchild	Columbia 46053
11/2/74	31	10	15	Little Girl Feeling	Helen Cornelius/Jerry Crutchfield	Columbia 10047
5/10/75	52	10	16	Let's Love While We Can	Ronny Scaife	Columbia 10128
9/6/75	41	11	17	You've Lost That Lovin' Feelin'	Barry Mann/Phil Spector/Cynthia Weil	Columbia 10195
12/20/75+	63	8	18	I Just Love Being A Woman	Barbara Fairchild/Penni Lane	Columbia 10261
4/10/76	65	7	19	Under Your Spell Again	Buck Owens/Dusty Rhodes	Columbia 10314
7/24/76	31	11	20	Mississippi	Werner Theunissen	Columbia 10378
10/30/76	15	13	21	Cheatin' Is	Rafe Van Hoy	Columbia 10423
3/12/77	22	14	22	Let Me Love You Once Before You Go	Steve Dorff/Molly-Ann Leikin	Columbia 10485
10/1/77	49	8	23	For All The Right Reasons	Susan Barrett/Billy Ray Reynolds	Columbia 10607
3/4/78	96	3	24	She Can't Give It Away	Curly Putman/Sonny Throckmorton	Columbia 10686
5/27/78	72	6	25	The Other Side Of The Morning	Steve O'Brian/Pam Tillis	Columbia 10607
10/14/78	91	5	26	It's Sad To Go To The Funeral (Of A Good Love That Has Died)	Barbara Fairchild/Randy Reinhard	Columbia 10825
7/12/80	74	5	27	Let Me Be The One *[w/ Billy Walker]*	Jimbeau Henson	Paid 102
10/11/80	79	3	28	Love's Slipping Through Our Fingers (Leaving Time On Our Hands) *[w/ Billy Walker]* /	John Riggs/Billy Walker	
12/20/80+	70	7	29	Bye Bye Love *[w/ Billy Walker]*	Boudleaux Bryant/Felice Bryant	Paid 107
5/17/86	84	4	30	Just Out Riding Around	Tim Goodman/Dave Lehman	Capitol 5582

Billboard DEBUT	PEAK	WKS	GOLD	ARTIST / Country Chart Hit	Ranking / Songwriter	Label (& Number)
				FAIRCHILD, Shelly		
				Born on 8/23/1977 in Clinton, Mississippi. Female singer/songwriter.		
10/16/04+	**35**	17		**You Don't Lie Here Anymore** S:4	*Shelly Fairchild/Sonny Lemaire/Clay Mills*	Columbia
				from the album *Ride* on Columbia 90355		
				FAIRGROUND ATTRACTION		
				Pop group from England: Eddi Reader (female vocals), Mark Nevin (guitar), Simon Edwards (bass) and Roy Dodds (drums).		
1/28/89	**85**	2		**Perfect**	*Mark Nevin*	RCA 8789
				FALLS, Ruby		
				Born Bertha Dorsey on 1/16/1946 in Jackson, Tennessee; raised in Milwaukee, Wisconsin. Died of a brain hemorrhage on 6/15/1986 (age 40). Black singer/songwriter.		
3/15/75	**86**	7		1 **Sweet Country Music**	*Charles Fields/Don Riis*	50 States 31
7/12/75	**77**	8		2 **He Loves Me All To Pieces**	*Charles Fields/Don Riis*	50 States 33
2/7/76	**81**	9		3 **Show Me Where**	*Ray Griff*	50 States 39
7/17/76	**81**	7		4 **Beware Of The Woman (Before She Gets To Your Man)**	*Vera Lakey*	50 States 43
3/12/77	**88**	4		5 **Do The Buck Dance**	*Charles Fields/Don Riis*	50 States 50
9/24/77	**40**	8		6 **You've Got To Mend This Heartache**	*Ruby Falls/Charles Fields/Don Riis*	50 States 56
4/15/78	**81**	5		7 **Three Nights A Week**	*Fats Domino*	50 States 60
9/30/78	**86**	3		8 **If That's Not Loving You (You Can't Say I Didn't Try)**	*Ruby Falls/Bill Rainsford/Don Riis*	50 States 63
6/9/79	**56**	7		9 **I'm Gettin' Into Your Love**	*Jim McBride/Roger Murrah*	50 States 70
				FAMILY BROWN		
				Family group from Ottawa, Ontario, Canada: father Joe Brown (died on 10/30/1986, age 60), with children Barry Brown, Lawanda Brown and Tracey Brown.		
7/18/81	**57**	8		1 **It's Really Love This Time**	*Robert Jones/Mike Kosser*	Ovation 1174
1/23/82	**30**	11		2 **But It's Cheating**	*Barry Brown*	RCA 13015
8/21/82	**61**	7		3 **Some Never Stand A Chance**	*Barry Brown*	RCA 13285
10/22/83	**67**	5		4 **We Really Got A Hold On Love**	*Tony Brown/Michael Foster*	RCA 13565
3/3/84	**56**	10		5 **Repeat After Me**	*Barry Brown*	RCA 13734
11/30/85	**66**	7		6 **Feel The Fire**	*Danny Hogan/Don Singleton/Rick Yancey*	RCA 50837
4/5/86	**80**	3		7 **What If It's Right**	*Barry Brown*	RCA 50851

FARGO, Donna — **1970s: #27 / All-Time: #115**

Born Yvonne Vaughan on 11/10/1945 in Mount Airy, North Carolina. Female singer/songwriter. Graduated from High Point College in North Carolina; taught English at a high school in Covina, California. Married record producer Stan Silver in 1969. Hosted own syndicated TV show (1978-79). Diagnosed with multiple sclerosis in 1979.

DEBUT	PEAK	WKS	GOLD	Country Chart Hit	Songwriter	Label (& Number)
3/25/72	❶[3]	23	●	1 **The Happiest Girl In The Whole U.S.A.**	*Donna Fargo*	Dot 17409
				Grammy: Female Vocal / CMA: Single		
9/2/72	❶[3]	16	●	2 **Funny Face**	*Donna Fargo*	Dot 17429
2/17/73	❶[1]	14		3 **Superman**	*Donna Fargo*	Dot 17444
5/26/73	❶[1]	14		4 **You Were Always There**	*Donna Fargo*	Dot 17460
9/29/73	**2**[1]	14		5 **Little Girl Gone**	*Donna Fargo*	Dot 17476
2/23/74	**6**	12		6 **I'll Try A Little Bit Harder**	*Donna Fargo*	Dot 17491
6/8/74	❶[1]	15		7 **You Can't Be A Beacon (If Your Light Don't Shine)**	*Martin Cooper*	Dot 17506
10/12/74+	**9**	15		8 **U.S. Of A**	*Donna Fargo*	ABC/Dot 17523
2/15/75	**7**	11		9 **It Do Feel Good**	*Donna Fargo*	ABC/Dot 17541
6/7/75	**14**	14		10 **Hello Little Bluebird**	*Donna Fargo*	ABC/Dot 17557
10/4/75	**38**	11		11 **Whatever I Say**	*Donna Fargo*	ABC/Dot 17579
12/20/75+	**58**	7		12 **What Will The New Year Bring?**	*Donna Fargo*	ABC/Dot 17586
2/28/76	**60**	6		13 **You're Not Charlie Brown (And I'm Not Raggedy Ann)**	*Donna Fargo*	ABC/Dot 17609
4/3/76	**20**	10		14 **Mr. Doodles**	*Donna Fargo*	Warner 8186
7/17/76	**15**	13		15 **I've Loved You All Of The Way**	*Donna Fargo*	Warner 8227
10/23/76+	**3**[1]	19		16 **Don't Be Angry**	*Wade Jackson*	ABC/Dot 17660
2/12/77	**9**	13		17 **Mockingbird Hill**	*Vaughn Horton*	Warner 8305
4/30/77	❶[1]	14		18 **That Was Yesterday**	*Donna Fargo*	Warner 8375
9/10/77	**8**	15		19 **Shame On Me**	*Bill Enis/Lawton Williams*	Warner 8431
1/7/78	**2**[2]	15		20 **Do I Love You (Yes In Every Way)**	*Paul Anka/Yves Dessca/Alain LeGovic/Michel Pelay/Maxime Piolat*	Warner 8509
5/27/78	**19**	11		21 **Ragamuffin Man**	*Stewart Harris*	Warner 8578
8/26/78	**10**	13		22 **Another Goodbye**	*Scott English/Barry Mann/Cynthia Weil*	Warner 8643
1/13/79	**6**	15		23 **Somebody Special**	*Donna Fargo*	Warner 8722
7/21/79	**14**	13		24 **Daddy**	*Donna Fargo*	Warner 8867
11/17/79	**45**	7		25 **Preacher Berry**	*Donna Fargo*	Warner 49093
3/8/80	**43**	7		26 **Walk On By**	*Kendall Hayes*	Warner 49183
8/9/80	**63**	7		27 **Land Of Cotton**	*David Chamberlain/Jim Vest*	Warner 49514
11/1/80	**55**	6		28 **Seeing Is Believing**	*Glenn Martin*	Warner 49575
8/1/81	**73**	6		29 **Lonestar Cowboy**	*Donna Fargo*	Warner 49757
11/21/81	**72**	4		30 **Jacamo**	*Dan Foliart/Tom Shapiro*	Warner 49852
7/10/82	**40**	9		31 **It's Hard To Be The Dreamer (When I Used To Be The Dream)**	*Joe Chambers/Larry Jenkins/Conway Twitty*	RCA 13264

Billboard DEBUT	PEAK	WKS	GOLD	ARTIST / Country Chart Hit	Ranking / Songwriter	Label (& Number)

FARGO, Donna — cont'd

DEBUT	PEAK	WKS	#	Country Chart Hit	Songwriter	Label (& Number)
10/9/82	80	3	32	Did We Have To Go This Far (To Say Goodbye)	*Dallas Frazier/A.L. "Doodle" Owens*	RCA 13329
10/1/83	72	4	33	The Sign Of The Times	*Donna Fargo*	Columbia 04097
7/7/84	80	4	34	My Heart Will Always Belong To You	*Kent Blazy*	Cleveland Int'l 1
7/19/86	58	8	35	Woman Of The 80's	S:33 *Donna Fargo*	Mercury 884712
11/8/86+	29	17	36	Me And You	S:20 *Donna Fargo*	Mercury 888093
6/27/87	23	15	37	Members Only *[w/ Billy Joe Royal]*	S:21 *Larry Addison*	Mercury 888680
2/16/91	71	2	38	Soldier Boy	*Luther Dixon/Florence Green*	Cleveland Int'l

FAUCETT, Dawnett

Born in Abilene, Texas. Female singer.

DEBUT	PEAK	WKS	Country Chart Hit	Songwriter	Label (& Number)
9/30/89	74	3	Money Don't Make A Man A Lover	*John Jarrard*	Step One 407

FAUTHEREE, Jimmy Lee — see JIMMY & JOHNNY

FELICIANO, José

Born on 9/8/1945 in Lares, Puerto Rico; raised in the Bronx, New York. Blind since birth. Male singer/songwriter/guitarist. Won the 1968 Best New Artist Grammy Award.

DEBUT	PEAK	WKS	Country Chart Hit	Songwriter	Label (& Number)
9/3/83	64	7	Let's Find Each Other Tonight	*Jose Feliciano*	Motown 1674

FELL, Terry, & The Fellers

Born on 5/13/1921 in Dora, Alabama. Male singer/songwriter/guitarist.

DEBUT	PEAK	WKS	Country Chart Hit	Songwriter	Label (& Number)
8/7/54	4	11	Don't Drop It	J:4 / S:11 / A:12 *Terry Fell*	"X" 0010

FELLER, Dick

Born on 1/2/1943 in Bronaugh, Missouri. Male singer/songwriter/guitarist.

DEBUT	PEAK	WKS	#	Country Chart Hit	Songwriter	Label (& Number)
11/17/73+	22	11	1	Biff, The Friendly Purple Bear	*Dick Feller* [S]	United Artists 316
6/8/74	11	14	2	Makin' The Best Of A Bad Situation	*Dick Feller* [N]	Asylum 11037
9/21/74	10	15	3	The Credit Card Song	*Dick Feller* [N]	United Artists 535
12/6/75+	49	9	4	Uncle Hiram And The Homemade Beer	*Dick Feller* [N]	Asylum 45290

FELTS, Narvel

All-Time: #154

Born Albert Narvel Felts on 11/11/1938 near Keiser, Arkansas; raised near Bernie, Missouri. Male singer/songwriter/guitarist. Known as "Narvel The Marvel." Hosted own radio show on KDEX in Dexter, Missouri. Member of **The Wolfpack**.

DEBUT	PEAK	WKS	#	Country Chart Hit	Songwriter	Label (& Number)
6/16/73	8	16	1	Drift Away	*Mentor Williams*	Cinnamon 763
10/13/73	13	13	2	All In The Name Of Love	*Jerry Foster/Bill Rice*	Cinnamon 771
1/19/74	14	14	3	When Your Good Love Was Mine	*Jerry Foster/Bill Rice*	Cinnamon 779
4/27/74	39	11	4	Until The End Of Time *[w/ Sharon Vaughn]*	*Jerry Foster/Bill Rice*	Cinnamon 793
5/11/74	26	13	5	I Want To Stay	*Jerry Foster/Bill Rice*	Cinnamon 798
9/14/74	33	13	6	Raindrops	*Dee Clark*	Cinnamon 809
4/5/75	2[1]	21	7	Reconsider Me	*Margaret Lewis/Myra Smith*	ABC/Dot 17549
8/23/75	12	15	8	Funny How Time Slips Away	*Willie Nelson*	ABC/Dot 17569
12/6/75+	10	16	9	Somebody Hold Me (Until She Passes By)	*Ava Aldridge/Roy Aldridge/Sue Richards*	ABC/Dot 17598
4/3/76	5	16	10	Lonely Teardrops	*Tyran Carlo/Berry Gordy*	ABC/Dot 17620
8/7/76	14	11	11	My Prayer	*Georges Boulanger/Jimmy Kennedy*	ABC/Dot 17643
11/13/76+	20	12	12	My Good Thing's Gone	*Johnny Elgin/Ted Fuller*	ABC/Dot 17664
2/26/77	19	11	13	The Feeling's Right	*Jerry Foster/Bill Rice*	ABC/Dot 17680
5/28/77	37	10	14	I Don't Hurt Anymore	*Don Robertson/Jack Rollins*	ABC/Dot 17700
8/20/77	22	11	15	To Love Somebody	*Barry Gibb/Robin Gibb*	ABC/Dot 17715
12/3/77+	34	11	16	Please /	*Ken Bell/Terry Skinner*	
1/7/78	flip	6	17	Blue Darlin'	*Lessie Lyle*	ABC/Dot 17731
3/18/78	30	10	18	Runaway	*Max Crook/Del Shannon*	ABC 12338
7/1/78	31	9	19	Just Keep It Up	*Otis Blackwell*	ABC 12374
10/21/78	26	10	20	One Run For The Roses	*Jerry Chesnut*	ABC 12414
1/6/79	14	11	21	Everlasting Love	*Buzz Cason/Mac Gayden*	ABC 12441
4/21/79	43	8	22	Moment By Moment	*Terry Skinner/J.L. Wallace*	MCA 41011
7/7/79	33	9	23	Tower Of Strength	*Burt Bacharach/Bob Hilliard*	MCA 41055
10/20/79	73	4	24	Because Of Losing You	*Jerry Foster/Bill Rice*	Collage 101
8/22/81	67	5	25	Louisiana Lonely	*Don Earl/Scott Phelps*	GMC 114
12/12/81	84	4	26	Fire In The Night	*Don Earl*	GMC 115
2/13/82	58	8	27	I'd Love You To Want Me **Lobo** (backing vocal)	*Lobo*	Lobo 3
6/5/82	84	3	28	Sweet Southern Moonlight	*Joe Stanley*	Lobo 8
7/17/82	64	6	29	Roll Over Beethoven	*Chuck Berry*	Lobo 11
11/13/82	84	3	30	Smoke Gets In Your Eyes /	*Otto Harbach/Jerome Kern*	
12/11/82	82	4	31	You're The Reason	*Bobby Edwards/Terry Fell/Fred Henley/Mildred Imes*	Compleat 101
4/2/83	52	9	32	Cry Baby	*Jerry Foster/Roger Lavoie/Johnny Morris*	Compleat 104
9/17/83	79	4	33	Anytime You're Ready	*Jerry Foster/Johnny Morris/Mark Severs*	Evergreen 1011
12/10/83+	52	10	34	Fool	*Terry Skinner*	Evergreen 1014
3/10/84	70	6	35	You Lay So Easy On My Mind	*Charles Fields/Bobby G. Rice/Don Riis*	Evergreen 1017

DEBUT	PEAK	WKS	GOLD		ARTIST / Country Chart Hit	Songwriter	Label (& Number)
					FELTS, Narvel — cont'd		
6/30/84	**53**	8		36	**Let's Live This Dream Together**	*Steve Nathan/Terry Skinner/J.L. Wallace*	Evergreen 1022
10/6/84	**63**	5		37	**I'm Glad You Couldn't Sleep Last Night**	*Steve Nathan/Terry Skinner/J.L. Wallace*	Evergreen 1025
1/5/85	**51**	10		38	**Hey Lady**	*Eddie Burton/Jacquelyn Sharp/Timothy Sharp*	Evergreen 1027
6/1/85	**68**	4		39	**If It Was Any Better (I Couldn't Stand It)**	*Eddie Burton/Tom Grant/Melanie Morris*	Evergreen 1030
9/7/85	**71**	5		40	**Out Of Sight Out Of Mind**	*Ivory Joe Hunter/Clyde Otis*	Evergreen 1034
6/7/86	**70**	5		41	**Rockin' My Angel**	*Charlie Black/Austin Roberts/Tommy Rocco*	Evergreen 1041
5/16/87	**60**	7		42	**When A Man Loves A Woman**	*Calvin Lewis/Andrew Wright*	Evergreen 1054
					FENDER, Freddy — **All-Time: #213**		
					Born Baldemar Huerta on 6/4/1937 in San Benito, Texas. Male singer/songwriter/guitarist. Acted in the movie *The Milagro Beanfield War*. Joined the Texas Tornados in 1990. Underwent a kidney transplant (donated by his daughter Marla) on 1/24/2002.		
1/11/75	❶^{2}	17	●	1	**Before The Next Teardrop Falls** CMA: Single	*Vivian Keith/Ben Peters*	ABC/Dot 17540
6/21/75	❶^{2}	16	●	2	**Wasted Days And Wasted Nights**	*Wayne Duncan/Freddy Fender*	ABC/Dot 17558
10/4/75	**10**	14		3	**Since I Met You Baby**	*Ivory Joe Hunter*	GRT 031
10/11/75	❶^{1}	16		4	**Secret Love**	*Sammy Fain/Paul Francis Webster*	ABC/Dot 17585
1/10/76	**13**	12		5	**Wild Side Of Life**	*Arlie Carter/William Warren*	GRT 039
2/7/76	❶^{1}	15		6	**You'll Lose A Good Thing**	*Barbara Lynn*	ABC/Dot 17607
5/22/76	**7**	13		7	**Vaya Con Dios**	*Inez James/Buddy Pepper/Larry Russell*	ABC/Dot 17627
9/18/76	**2**^{2}	14		8	**Living It Down**	*Ben Peters*	ABC/Dot 17652
3/19/77	**4**	15		9	**The Rains Came /**	*Huey Meaux*	
3/19/77	**flip**	15		10	**Sugar Coated Love**	*Jay Miller*	ABC/Dot 17686
7/30/77	**11**	12		11	**If You Don't Love Me (Why Don't You Just Leave Me Alone)**	*Tommy McLain*	ABC/Dot 17713
11/26/77+	**18**	11		12	**Think About Me**	*Gaylan Latimar*	ABC/Dot 17730
3/11/78	**34**	9		13	**If You're Looking For A Fool**	*Bob McRee/Clifton Thomas/Edward Thomas*	ABC 12339
6/17/78	**13**	12		14	**Talk To Me**	*Joe Seneca*	ABC 12370
10/14/78	**26**	9		15	**I'm Leaving It All Up To You**	*Don Harris/Dewey Terry*	ABC 12415
2/17/79	**22**	12		16	**Walking Piece Of Heaven**	*Marty Robbins*	ABC 12453
6/23/79	**22**	11		17	**Yours**	*Albert Gamse/Gonzalo Roig/Jack Sherr*	Starflite 4900
10/13/79	**61**	5		18	**Squeeze Box**	*Pete Townshend*	Starflite 4904
1/12/80	**83**	3		19	**My Special Prayer**	*Wini Scott*	Starflite 4906
4/5/80	**82**	3		20	**Please Talk To My Heart**	*Jimmy Fautheree/Johnny Mathis*	Starflite 4908
2/19/83	**87**	3		21	**Chokin' Kind**	*Harlan Howard*	Warner 29794
					FENDERMEN, The		
					Duo of Jim Sundquist (from Niagara, Wisconsin) and Phil Humphrey (from Stoughton, Wisconsin). Both guitarists were born on 11/26/1937.		
7/11/60	**16**	8			**Mule Skinner Blues**	*Jimmie Rodgers/George Vaughn*	Soma 1137
					FENSTER, Zoot — see BARLOW, Jack		
					FERRARI, CW		
					CW Ferrari is actually pianist/songwriter Bill Ferreira.		
3/19/88	**76**	4			**Country Highways**	*Bill Ferreira* **[I]**	Southern Sound 1001
					FINNEY, Maury		
					Born in Humboldt, Minnesota. Male saxophonist/songwriter.		
1/3/76	**84**	9		1	**Maiden's Prayer /** vocals by a female chorus	*Maury Finney* **[F]**	
1/3/76	**flip**	9		2	**San Antonio Stroll**	*Peter Noah* **[I]**	Soundwaves 4525
4/24/76	**76**	7		3	**Rollin' In My Sweet Baby's Arms /**	*Jay Frank* **[I]**	
4/24/76	**78**	7		4	**Wild Side Of Life**	*Arlie Carter/William Warren* **[I]**	Soundwaves 4531
9/4/76	**81**	7		5	**Waltz Across Texas /**	*Billy Tubb* **[I]**	
9/4/76	**flip**	7		6	**Off And Running**	*Maury Finney* **[I]**	Soundwaves 4536
1/29/77	**85**	6		7	**Everybody's Had The Blues**	*Merle Haggard* **[I]**	Soundwaves 4541
6/25/77	**72**	10		8	**Coconut Grove** vocals by a female chorus	*John Sebastian/Zal Yanovsky*	Soundwaves 4548
11/19/77	**85**	5		9	**Poor People Of Paris /**	*Marguerite Monnot* **[I]**	
11/19/77	**flip**	5		10	**Almost Persuaded**	*Billy Sherrill/Glenn Sutton* **[I]**	Soundwaves 4557
4/15/78	**88**	6		11	**I Don't Wanna Cry**	*Larry Gatlin* **[I]**	Soundwaves 4566
8/12/78	**84**	7		12	**Whispering**	*Richard Coburn/Vincent Rose/John Schonberger* **[I]**	Soundwaves 4572
2/3/79	**92**	2		13	**Happy Sax**	*Maury Finney* **[I]**	Soundwaves 4578
6/16/79	**93**	2		14	**Your Love Takes Me So High /**	*Maury Finney/Steve Finney* **[I]**	
6/16/79	**flip**	2		15	**I Want To Play My Horn On The Grand Ole' Opry** vocals by Finney and a female chorus	*Faith Finney/Maury Finney*	Soundwaves 4585
9/20/80	**75**	5		16	**Lonely Wine**	*Robert Wells* **[I]**	Soundwaves 4613
					FIRST EDITION, The — see ROGERS, Kenny		
					FISCHOFF, George		
					Born on 8/3/1938 in South Bend, Indiana. Prolific pianist/songwriter.		
3/31/79	**74**	7			**The Piano Picker**	*George Fischoff* **[I]**	Drive 6273
					FITZGERALD, Ella		
					Born on 4/25/1918 in Newport News, Virginia. Died of diabetes on 6/15/1996 (age 78). Legendary jazz singer. Won Grammy's Lifetime Achievement Award in 1967.		
3/18/44	**2**^{1}	1			**When My Sugar Walks Down The Street**	*Gene Austin/Jimmy McHugh/Irving Mills*	Decca 18587

5 RED CAPS

R&B vocal group from Los Angeles, California: Steve Gibson, Emmett Matthews, Dave Patillo, Jimmy Springs and Romaine Brown. Patillo died in September 1967 (age 53). Springs died on 10/4/1987 (age 75). Brown died in January 1988 (age 73). Gibson died on 3/14/1996 (age 81).

DEBUT	PEAK	WKS		Country Chart Hit	Songwriter	Label (& Number)
4/29/44	2^1	8		**I Learned A Lesson, I'll Never Forget**	*Joe Davis*	Beacon 7120

FLATT & SCRUGGS — 1960s: #44 / All-Time: #252 // HOF: 1985

Bluegrass duo of Lester Flatt (guitar) and **Earl Scruggs** (banjo). Flatt was born on 6/14/1914 in Overton County, Tennessee. Died on 5/11/1979 (age 64). Scruggs was born on 1/6/1924 in Flintville, North Carolina. Both were members of **Bill Monroe**'s band from 1944-48. Left Monroe to form the Foggy Mountain Boys.

OPRY: 1955

LESTER FLATT, EARL SCRUGGS & The Foggy Mountain Boys:

DEBUT	PEAK	WKS		Country Chart Hit	Songwriter	Label (& Number)
2/2/52	9	1	1	**'Tis Sweet To Be Remembered**	A:9 *Mac Wiseman*	Columbia 4-20886
6/8/59	9	30	2	**Cabin In The Hills**	*Lester Flatt/Earl Scruggs*	Columbia 41389
2/1/60	21	6	3	**Crying My Heart Out Over You**	*Carl Butler/Louise Certain/George Sherry/Gladys Stacey*	Columbia 41518
12/5/60+	12	14	4	**Polka On A Banjo**	*Leon Luallen/Rich Tillman/George Williams*	Columbia 41786
10/9/61	10	16	5	**Go Home**	*Onie Wheeler*	Columbia 42141
4/7/62	16	8	6	**Just Ain't**	*Ginger Willis/Hal Willis*	Columbia 42280
6/23/62	27	1	7	**The Legend Of The Johnson Boys**	*Lester Flatt/Earl Scruggs*	Columbia 42413
12/8/62+	❶^3	20	8	**The Ballad Of Jed Clampett**	*Paul Henning*	Columbia 42606
				theme from the TV series *The Beverly Hillbillies* starring Buddy Ebsen (as "Jed Clampett")		
5/11/63	8	11	9	**Pearl Pearl Pearl**	*Paul Henning* **[N]**	Columbia 42755
				"Cousin Pearl" (Bea Benaderet) was a featured character on TV's *The Beverly Hillbillies*		
9/28/63	26	3	10	**New York Town**	*Woody Guthrie*	Columbia 42840
2/15/64	12	18	11	**You Are My Flower /**	*A.P. Carter*	
2/22/64	40	2	12	**My Saro Jane**	*Lester Flatt/Earl Scruggs*	Columbia 42954

LESTER FLATT & EARL SCRUGGS:

DEBUT	PEAK	WKS		Country Chart Hit	Songwriter	Label (& Number)
3/14/64	14	11	13	**Petticoat Junction**	*Paul Henning/Cliff Massey*	Columbia 42982
				theme from the TV series starring Edgar Buchanan		
8/15/64	21	15	14	**Workin' It Out**	*Walter Raim/Shel Silverstein*	Columbia 43080
3/13/65	43	10	15	**I Still Miss Someone**	*Johnny Cash/Roy Cash*	Columbia 43204
4/15/67	54	5	16	**Nashville Cats**	*John Sebastian*	Columbia 44040
7/29/67	20	14	17	**California Up Tight Band**	*Tom T. Hall*	Columbia 44194

FLATT & SCRUGGS:

DEBUT	PEAK	WKS		Country Chart Hit	Songwriter	Label (& Number)
1/13/68	45	8	18	**Down In The Flood /**	*Bob Dylan*	
4/6/68	58	6	19	**Foggy Mountain Breakdown**	*Earl Scruggs* **[I]**	Columbia 44380
				Grammy: Instrumental Duo & Hall Of Fame / NRR; from the movie *Bonnie & Clyde* starring Warren Beatty and Faye Dunaway; also charted on Mercury 72739 as "Theme From Bonnie & Clyde (Foggy Mountain Breakdown)"		
9/14/68	58	8	20	**Like A Rolling Stone**	*Bob Dylan*	Columbia 44623

FLETCHER, Vicky

Born in San Antonio, Texas. Female singer.

DEBUT	PEAK	WKS		Country Chart Hit	Songwriter	Label (& Number)
7/20/74	92	3	1	**Touching Me, Touching You**	*George Richey/Billy Sherrill/Carmol Taylor*	Columbia 46043
6/12/76	97	2	2	**Ain't It Good To Be In Love Again**	*DeWayne Orender*	Music Row 213

FLORES, Rosie

Born on 9/10/1956 in San Antonio, Texas; raised in San Diego, California. Female singer. Joined **Asleep At The Wheel** in 1997.

DEBUT	PEAK	WKS		Country Chart Hit	Songwriter	Label (& Number)
9/12/87	51	10	1	**Crying Over You**	*James Intveld*	Reprise 28250
12/26/87+	67	6	2	**Somebody Loses, Somebody Wins**	*Ron Coleman/Bill Graham/Alan Laney*	Reprise 28134
7/9/88	74	3	3	**He Cares**	*Paul Overstreet/Don Schlitz*	Reprise 27980

FLOYD, Charlie

Born in Aynor, South Carolina. Male singer/songwriter/guitarist.

DEBUT	PEAK	WKS		Country Chart Hit	Songwriter	Label (& Number)
10/23/93	75	1	1	**I've Fallen In Love (And I Can't Get Up)**	*Ronnie Samoset/Craig Wiseman*	Liberty
1/1/94	58	7	2	**Good Girls Go To Heaven**	*Richard Fagan/Kim Williams*	Liberty
				above 2 from the album *Charlie's Nite Life* on Liberty 80475		

FLYING BURRITO BROTHERS — see BURRITO BROTHERS

FOGELBERG, Dan

Born on 8/13/1951 in Peoria, Illinois. Male singer/songwriter/guitarist.

DEBUT	PEAK	WKS		Country Chart Hit	Songwriter	Label (& Number)
2/16/80	85	8	1	**Longer**	*Dan Fogelberg*	Full Moon 50824
4/20/85	56	16	2	**Go Down Easy**	*Jay Bolotin*	Full Moon 04835
8/24/85	33	13	3	**Down The Road Mountain Pass**	*Lester Flatt/Dan Fogelberg/Earl Scruggs*	Full Moon 05446

FOGERTY, John

Born on 5/28/1945 in Berkeley, California. Male singer/songwriter/guitarist. Leader of **Creedence Clearwater Revival**. Also recorded solo as **The Blue Ridge Rangers**.

DEBUT	PEAK	WKS		Country Chart Hit	Songwriter	Label (& Number)
2/10/73	66	6	1	**Jambalaya (On The Bayou)** *[The Blue Ridge Rangers]*	*Hank Williams*	Fantasy 689
2/2/85	38	11	2	**Big Train (From Memphis)**	*John Fogerty*	Warner 29100
8/16/97	67	2	3	**Southern Streamline**	*John Fogerty*	Warner
				from the album *Blue Moon Swamp* on Warner 45426		

FOLEY, Betty

Born on 2/3/1933 in Chicago, Illinois; raised in Berea, Kentucky. Died on 6/27/1990 (age 57). Female singer. Daughter of **Red Foley**.

DEBUT	PEAK	WKS		Country Chart Hit	Songwriter	Label (& Number)
3/6/54	8	10	1	**As Far As I'm Concerned** *[w/ Red Foley]*	J:8 / A:8 / S:11 *Dale Parker*	Decca 29000
6/25/55	3^1	23	2	**Satisfied Mind** *[w/ Red Foley]*	J:3 / S:4 / A:6 *Joe Hays/Jack Rhodes*	Decca 29526
8/31/59	7	12	3	**Old Moon**	*Waco Austin/O'Brein Fisher*	Bandera 1304

Billboard DEBUT	PEAK	WKS	GOLD	ARTIST / Country Chart Hit	Ranking / Songwriter	Label (& Number)

FOLEY, Red

1940s: #5 / 1950s: #5 / All-Time: #33 // HOF: 1967

Born Clyde Foley on 6/17/1910 in Blue Lick, Kentucky. Died of a heart attack on 9/19/1968 (age 58). Male singer/songwriter. Father of **Betty Foley**. On the WLS *National Barn Dance* from 1930-37 and the *Renfro Valley Show* from 1937-39. Hosted the *Ozark Jubilee* series on ABC-TV from 1954-60. Regular on TV's *Mr. Smith Goes To Washington*. **Pat Boone** married his daughter Shirley in 1953.

OPRY: 1946

DEBUT	PEAK	WKS	GOLD	Country Chart Hit	Songwriter	Label (& Number)
8/26/44	❶[13]	27		1 **Smoke On The Water /**	*Zeke Clements/Earl Nunn*	
9/30/44	5	1		2 **There's A Blue Star Shining Bright** (In A Window Tonight)	*Ira Bastow/Jack Foy/George Howard/John Ravencroft*	Decca 6102
6/23/45	4	2		3 **Hang Your Head In Shame /**	*Ed Nelson/Steve Nelson/Fred Rose*	
6/23/45	5	1		4 **I'll Never Let You Worry My Mind**	*Red Foley/Earl Nunn*	Decca 6108
9/8/45	❶[1]	14		5 **Shame On You** *[w/ Lawrence Welk]* **/**	*Spade Cooley*	
11/10/45	3[1]	2		6 **At Mail Call Today** *[w/ Lawrence Welk]*	*Gene Autry/Fred Rose*	Decca 18698
5/4/46	4	1		7 **Harriet** *[w/ Roy Ross & His Ramblers]*	*Abel Baer/Paul Cunningham*	Decca 9003
11/30/46	5	1		8 **Have I Told You Lately That I Love You** *[w/ Roy Ross & His Ramblers]* — from the movie *Over The Trail*; also see #65 below	*Scott Wiseman*	Decca 46014
				RED FOLEY and The Cumberland Valley Boys:		
3/15/47	4	1		9 **That's How Much I Love You**	*Eddy Arnold/Wally Fowler*	Decca 46028
4/5/47	❶[2]	16		10 **New Jolie Blonde** (New Pretty Blonde)	*Al Miller/Syd Nathan*	Decca 46034
6/21/47	5	1		11 **Freight Train Boogie**	*Bob Nobar/Jim Scott*	Decca 46035
11/22/47	2[1]	13		12 **Never Trust A Woman**	*Jenny Lou Carson/Red Foley*	Decca 46074
10/2/48+	❶[1]	40		13 **Tennessee Saturday Night**	A:❶[1] / S:3 *Billy Hughes*	Decca 46136
				RED FOLEY:		
3/26/49	4	15		14 **Candy Kisses /**	J:4 / S:6 *George Morgan*	
4/2/49	3[1]	21		15 **Tennessee Border**	J:3 / S:4 *Jimmy Work*	Decca 46151
5/14/49	15	1		16 **Blues In My Heart** *[w/ Cumberland Valley Boys]*	S:15 *Jenny Lou Carson/Red Foley*	Decca 46136
6/25/49	4	13		17 **Tennessee Polka /**	J:4 / S:6 *Erwin King*	
7/23/49	11	2		18 **I'm Throwing Rice** (At The Girl I Love)	S:11 / J:14 *Eddy Arnold/Ed Nelson/Steve Nelson*	Decca 46170
8/6/49	8	4		19 **Two Cents, Three Eggs And A Postcard**	J:8 *Doris Barner/Mickey Barner/Larry Vincent*	Decca 46165
12/17/49+	3[2]	6		20 **Sunday Down In Tennessee**	J:3 / A:3 / S:10 *Beasley Smith*	Decca 46197
12/31/49+	2[2]	10		21 **Tennessee Border No. 2** *[w/ Ernest Tubb]*	S:2 / J:2 *Jimmy Work*	Decca 46200
1/7/50	10	1		22 **I Gotta Have My Baby Back /**	J:10 / S:13 *Floyd Tillman*	
1/14/50	8	1		23 **Careless Kisses**	J:8 / S:14 *Tim Spencer*	Decca 46201
1/21/50	❶[13]	20	●	24 **Chattanoogie Shoe Shine Boy**	A:❶[13] / J:❶[13] / S:❶[12] *Jack Stapp/Harry Stone*	Decca 46205
1/21/50	7	2		25 **Don't Be Ashamed Of Your Age** *[w/ Ernest Tubb]*	J:7 / A:9 *Cindy Walker/Bob Wills*	Decca 46200
2/18/50	4	11		26 **Sugarfoot Rag** — Hank "Sugarfoot" Garland (guitar solo)	J:4 / A:8 *Hank Garland/Vaughn Horton*	Decca 46205
5/6/50	9	1		27 **Steal Away**	S:9 *Eddie Brackett/Red Foley*	Decca Faith 9-14505
5/13/50	❶[4]	15		28 **Birmingham Bounce /**	S:❶[4] / J:❶[3] / A:4 *Sid Gunter*	
5/27/50	5	4		29 **Choc'late Ice Cream Cone** *[w/ The Dixie Dons]*	A:5 / J:8 / S:10 *Famous Lashua*	Decca 9-46234
6/3/50	❶[1]	14		30 **Mississippi** *[w/ The Dixie Dons]*	J:❶[1] / S:2 / A:3 *Billy Simmons/Curley Williams*	Decca 9-46241
7/22/50	9	5		31 **Just A Closer Walk With Thee** *[w/ The Jordanaires]*	S:9 *Red Foley*	Decca Faith 9-14505
8/12/50	❶[3]	15		32 **Goodnight Irene** *[w/ Ernest Tubb]* **/**	J:❶[3] / S:❶[2] / A:2 *Huddie Ledbetter/John Lomax*	
9/2/50	9	2		33 **Hillbilly Fever No. 2** *[w/ Ernest Tubb]*	J:9 *George Vaughn*	Decca 9-46255
9/9/50	2[1]	12		34 **Cincinnati Dancing Pig**	S:2 / J:3 / A:6 *Al Lewis/Guy Wood*	Decca 9-46261
11/4/50	8	4		35 **Our Lady Of Fatima**	S:8 *Gladys Gollahon*	Decca Faith 9-14526
2/17/51	6	1		36 **My Heart Cries For You** *[w/ Evelyn Knight]*	A:6 *Percy Faith/Carl Sigman*	Decca 9-27378
2/17/51	7	3		37 **Hot Rod Race**	S:7 / J:8 / A:10 *George Wilson*	Decca 9-46286
5/12/51	8	3		38 **Hobo Boogie**	J:8 *Al Lewis/Guy Wood*	Decca 9-46304
5/19/51	9	1		39 **The Strange Little Girl** *[w/ Ernest Tubb & Anita Kerr Singers]*	J:9 *Richard Adler/Jerry Ross*	Decca 9-46311
7/7/51	5	11	●	40 There'll Be **Peace In The Valley** For Me *[w/ The Sunshine Boys Quartet]*	A:5 / J:5 / S:7 *Thomas A. Dorsey*	Decca 9-46319
11/24/51	3[3]	16		41 **Alabama Jubilee** *[w/ The Nashville Dixielanders]*	J:3 / S:5 / A:6 *George Cobb/Jack Yellen*	Decca 9-27810
2/2/52	5	9		42 **Too Old To Cut The Mustard** *[w/ Ernest Tubb]*	S:5 / J:8 / A:10 *Bill Carlisle*	Decca 9-46387
3/8/52	8	3		43 **Milk Bucket Boogie /**	J:8 *W.G. Murray/Reece Shipley*	
3/29/52	8	2		44 **Salty Dog Rag**	J:8 *Edward Crowe/John Gordy*	Decca 9-27981
11/15/52+	❶[1]	11		45 **Midnight**	S:❶[1] / J:2 / A:5 *Chet Atkins/Boudleaux Bryant*	Decca 28420
1/10/53	8	2		46 **Don't Let The Stars Get In Your Eyes**	S:8 *Slim Willet*	Decca 28460
3/21/53	6	4		47 **Hot Toddy**	J:6 / S:10 *Ralph Flanagan/Herb Hendler*	Decca 28587
4/18/53	7	2		48 **No Help Wanted #2** *[w/ Ernest Tubb]*	S:7 / J:9 *Bill Carlisle*	Decca 28634
5/9/53	8	1		49 **Slaves Of A Hopeless Love Affair**	J:8 *Billy Wallace*	Decca 28567
10/10/53	6	4		50 **Shake A Hand** *[w/ Anita Kerr Singers]*	S:6 / J:7 / A:10 *Joe Morris*	Decca 28839
3/6/54	8	10		51 **As Far As I'm Concerned** *[w/ Betty Foley]*	J:8 / A:8 / S:11 *Dale Parker*	Decca 29000
5/8/54	7	4		52 **Jilted**	J:7 / S:9 *Robert Colby/Dick Manning*	Decca 29100
5/22/54	❶[1]	41		53 **One By One** *[w/ Kitty Wells]* **/**	J:❶[1] / S:2 / A:2 *Jack Anglin/Jim Anglin/Johnnie Wright*	
7/10/54	12	1		54 **I'm A Stranger In My Home** *[w/ Kitty Wells]*	A:12 / S:15 *Neal Burris/Pee Wee King/Redd Stewart*	Decca 29065
1/8/55	4	15		55 **Hearts Of Stone** *[w/ Anita Kerr Singers]*	A:4 / J:4 / S:6 *Rudy Jackson/Eddy Ray*	Decca 29375
2/26/55	3[1]	16		56 **As Long As I Live** *[w/ Kitty Wells]* **/**	J:3 / S:7 / A:8 *Roy Acuff*	
2/26/55	6	17		57 **Make Believe** ('Til We Can Make It Come True) *[w/ Kitty Wells]*	J:6 / S:7 / A:14 *Jerry Hamilton/Billy Walker*	Decca 29390

DEBUT	PEAK	WKS	GOLD	ARTIST / Country Chart Hit	Ranking / Songwriter	Label (& Number)
				FOLEY, Red — cont'd		
6/25/55	3^{1}	23		58 **Satisfied Mind** *[w/ Betty Foley]*	J:3 / S:4 / A:6 *Joe Hays/Jack Rhodes*	Decca 29526
1/28/56	3^{2}	31		59 **You And Me** *[w/ Kitty Wells]* /	S:3 / A:3 / J:6 *Jack Anglin/Jim Anglin/Johnnie Wright*	
2/4/56	flip	6		60 **No One But You** *[w/ Kitty Wells]*	S:flip / J:flip *Eddie Smith*	Decca 29740
6/29/59	29	1		61 **Travelin' Man**	*John D. Loudermilk/Marijohn Wilkin*	Decca 30882
5/6/67	43	11		62 **Happiness Means You** *[w/ Kitty Wells]* /	*Jim Anglin*	
6/3/67	60	5		63 **Hello Number One** *[w/ Kitty Wells]*	*Jim Anglin*	Decca 32126
12/30/67+	63	4		64 **Living As Strangers** *[w/ Kitty Wells]*	*Bill Phillips/Jean Stromatt*	Decca 32223
1/18/69	74	2		65 **Have I Told You Lately That I Love You?** *[w/ Kitty Wells]* — new version of #8 above	*Scott Wiseman* **[R]**	Decca 32427

Alabama Jubilee ['51]
As Far As I'm Concerned ['54]
As Long As I Live ['55]
At Mail Call Today ['45]
Birmingham Bounce ['50]
Blues In My Heart ['49]
Candy Kisses ['49]
Careless Kisses ['50]
Chattanoogie Shoe Shine Boy ['50]
Choc'late Ice Cream Cone ['50]
Cincinnati Dancing Pig ['50]
Don't Be Ashamed Of Your Age ['50]
Don't Let The Stars Get In Your Eyes ['53]
Freight Train Boogie ['47]
Goodnight Irene ['50]
Hang Your Head In Shame ['45]
Happiness Means You ['67]
Harriet ['46]
Have I Told You Lately That I Love You ['46 '69]
Hearts Of Stone ['55]
Hello Number One ['67]
Hillbilly Fever No. 2 ['50]
Hobo Boogie ['51]
Hot Rod Race ['51]
Hot Toddy ['53]
I Gotta Have My Baby Back ['50]
I'll Never Let You Worry My Mind ['45]
I'm A Stranger In My Home ['54]
I'm Throwing Rice (At The Girl I Love) ['49]
Jilted ['54]
Just A Closer Walk With Thee ['50]
Living As Strangers ['68]
Make Believe ('Til We Can Make It Come True) ['55]
Midnight ['53]
Milk Bucket Boogie ['52]
Mississippi ['50]
My Heart Cries For You ['51]
Never Trust A Woman ['47]
New Jolie Blonde (New Pretty Blonde) ['47]
No Help Wanted #2 ['53]
No One But You ['56]
One By One ['54]
Our Lady Of Fatima ['50]
Salty Dog Rag ['52]
Satisfied Mind ['55]
Shake A Hand ['53]
Shame On You ['45]
Slaves Of A Hopeless Love Affair ['53]
Smoke On The Water ['44]
Steal Away ['50]
Strange Little Girl ['51]
Sugarfoot Rag ['50]
Sunday Down In Tennessee ['50]
Tennessee Border ['49]
Tennessee Border No. 2 ['50]
Tennessee Polka ['49]
Tennessee Saturday Night ['49]
That's How Much I Love You ['47]
There'll Be Peace In The Valley For Me ['51]
There's A Blue Star Shining Bright (In A Window Tonight) ['44]
Too Old To Cut The Mustard ['52]
Travelin' Man ['59]
Two Cents, Three Eggs And A Postcard ['49]
You And Me ['56]

FORD, Joy

Born on 3/10/1946 in Brilliant, Alabama; raised in Chicago, Illinois, and Poplar Bluff, Missouri. Female singer.

DEBUT	PEAK	WKS	GOLD	Country Chart Hit	Songwriter	Label (& Number)
12/16/78+	87	4		1 **Love Isn't Love (Til You Give It Away)**	*Bobby Fischer/Ricci Mareno*	Country Int'l. 134
10/13/79	97	4		2 **Take My Love**	*Andy Badale/Virginia Johnson/Frank Stanton*	Country Int'l. 142
3/26/83	97	1		3 **You Are The Music In Time With My Heart**	*Wayne Carson/Ronnie Reno*	Country Int'l. 190
8/10/85	96	2		4 **Melted Down Memories**	*Buck Moore/A.L. "Doodle" Owens/Judi Tigert*	Country Int'l. 206
8/20/88	99	1		5 **Yesterday's Rain**	*Damon Black*	Country Int'l. 216

FORD, Shelley — see CHEVALIER, Jay

FORD, Tennessee Ernie — 1940s: #24 / 1950s: #17 / All-Time: #134 // HOF: 1990

Born on 2/13/1919 in Fordtown, Tennessee. Died of liver failure on 10/17/1991 (age 72). Male singer/songwriter. Worked as a DJ. Hosted own TV series from 1955-65. Known as "The Old Pea Picker."

DEBUT	PEAK	WKS	GOLD	Country Chart Hit	Ranking / Songwriter	Label (& Number)
				TENNESSEE ERNIE:		
4/30/49	8	1		1 **Tennessee Border**	J:8 / S:15 *Jimmy Work*	Capitol 15400
5/28/49	14	1		2 **Country Junction**	J:14 *Tennessee Ernie Ford/Cliffie Stone*	Capitol 15430
9/10/49	8	4		3 **Smokey Mountain Boogie**	S:8 / J:13 *Tennessee Ernie Ford/Cliffie Stone*	Capitol 40212
11/26/49	❶^{4}	10		4 **Mule Train** /	A:❶^{4} / J:3 / S:4 *Fred Glickman/Hy Heath/Johnny Lange*	
12/10/49	3^{3}	11		5 **Anticipation Blues**	A:3 / S:5 / J:8 *Tennessee Ernie Ford*	Capitol 40258
2/11/50	2^{2}	10		6 **The Cry Of The Wild Goose**	S:2 / A:3 / J:5 *Terry Gilkyson*	Capitol F40280
8/26/50	5	6		7 **Ain't Nobody's Business But My Own** *[w/ Kay Starr]* /	A:5 / J:10 *Irving Taylor*	
9/16/50	2^{1}	16		8 **I'll Never Be Free** *[w/ Kay Starr]*	A:2 / J:2 / S:4 *Bennie Benjamin/George Weiss*	Capitol F1124
12/16/50+	❶^{14}	25	●	9 **The Shot Gun Boogie**	J:❶^{14} / S:❶^{3} / A:❶^{1} *Tennessee Ernie Ford*	Capitol F1295
3/3/51	8	2		10 **Tailor Made Woman** *[w/ Joe "Fingers" Carr]*	J:8 *Jimmy Bryant/Bill Kemp*	Capitol F1349
6/16/51	2^{1}	7		11 **Mr. And Mississippi**	A:2 / S:4 / J:6 *Irving Gordon*	Capitol F1521
6/16/51	9	1		12 **The Strange Little Girl**	S:9 *Richard Adler/Jerry Ross*	Capitol F1470
9/20/52	6	7		13 **Blackberry Boogie**	J:6 / S:9 / A:9 *Tennessee Ernie Ford*	Capitol F2170
6/6/53	8	3		14 **Hey, Mr. Cotton Picker**	J:8 *Bob Mitchum/Doc Stanford*	Capitol 2443
				TENNESSEE ERNIE FORD:		
8/14/54	9	9		15 **River Of No Return** — from the movie starring **Robert Mitchum** and Marilyn Monroe	S:9 *Ken Darby/Lionel Newman*	Capitol 2810
3/26/55	4	16		16 **Ballad Of Davy Crockett** — from the ABC-TV *Disneyland* series starring Fess Parker as "Davy Crockett"	S:4 / J:5 / A:6 *Tom Blackburn/George Bruns*	Capitol 3058
7/9/55	13	2		17 **His Hands**	S:13 *Stuart Hamblen*	Capitol 3135
11/12/55	❶^{10}	21	●	18 **Sixteen Tons** — **Grammy: Hall of Fame**	S:❶^{10} / J:❶^{7} / A:❶^{3} *Merle Travis*	Capitol 3262
3/17/56	12	5		19 **That's All**	S:12 *Merle Travis*	Capitol 3343
6/26/65	9	16		20 **Hicktown**	*Scott Turner/Charlie Williams*	Capitol 5425
7/26/69	54	3		21 **Honey-Eyed Girl (That's You That's You)**	*Don Robertson*	Capitol 2522
4/24/71	58	9		22 **Happy Songs Of Love**	*Arthur Kent/Frank Stanton*	Capitol 3079
3/31/73	66	4		23 **Printers Alley Stars**	*J.C. Cunningham*	Capitol 3556
7/14/73	73	5		24 **Farther Down The River (Where The Fishin's Good)**	*Steve Stone/Charlie Williams*	Capitol 3631
9/22/73	70	7		25 **Colorado Country Morning**	*J.C. Cunningham/Robert Duncan*	Capitol 3704
1/4/75	52	8		26 **Come On Down**	*Jack Hayford/Steve Stone*	Capitol 3916
4/19/75	63	9		27 **Baby** *[w/ Andra Willis]*	*Ray Griff*	Capitol 4044

Billboard DEBUT	PEAK	WKS	GOLD	ARTIST Country Chart Hit	Ranking / Songwriter	Label (& Number)
				FORD, Tennessee Ernie — cont'd		
11/22/75	**96**	4	28	**The Devil Ain't A Lonely Woman's Friend**	*Dallas Frazier/Whitey Shafer*	Capitol 4160
7/31/76	**95**	3	29	**I Been To Georgia On A Fast Train**	*Billy Joe Shaver*	Capitol 4285
				FORD, Whitey "The Duke of Paducah"	**HOF: 1986**	
				Born Benjamin Ford on 5/12/1901 in DeSoto, Missouri. Died on 6/20/1986 (age 85). Legendary comedian. Starred on NBC radio's *Plantation Party* from 1938-42. Hosted TV's *Country Junction* from 1958-1965. The producers of TV's *Hee Haw* purchased his vast joke library and used many of them on the show. *OPRY: 1942*		

				FORESTER SISTERS, The	**All-Time: #178**	
				Family vocal group from Lookout Mountain, Georgia: Kathy Forester (born on 1/4/1955), June Forester (born on 9/22/1956), Kim Forester (born on 11/4/1960) and Christy Forester (born on 12/21/1962).		
1/26/85	**10**	22	1	(That's What You Do) **When You're In Love**	S:9 / A:12 *Ken Bell/Terry Skinner/J.L. Wallace*	Warner 29114
6/29/85	**❶[1]**	22	2	**I Fell In Love Again Last Night**	S:❶[1] / A:❶[1] *Paul Overstreet/Thom Schuyler*	Warner 28988
11/2/85+	**❶[1]**	20	3	**Just In Case**	S:❶[1] / A:❶[1] *Sonny Lemaire/J.P. Pennington*	Warner 28875
3/15/86	**❶[1]**	22	4	**Mama's Never Seen Those Eyes**	S:❶[1] / A:❶[1] *Terry Skinner/J.L. Wallace*	Warner 28795
7/5/86	**2[2]**	24	5	**Lonely Alone**	A:❶[1] / S:2 *John Jarrard/J.D. Martin*	Warner 28687
9/27/86	**❶[1]**	20	6	**Too Much Is Not Enough** *[w/ The Bellamy Brothers]*	S:❶[1] / A:❶[1] *David Bellamy/Ron Taylor*	Curb/MCA 52917
3/7/87	**5**	23	7	**Too Many Rivers**	S:8 / A:8 *Harlan Howard*	Warner 28442
6/27/87	**❶[1]**	24	8	**You Again**	S:6 *Paul Overstreet/Don Schlitz*	Warner 28368
10/31/87+	**5**	25	9	**Lyin' In His Arms Again**	S:11 *Terry Skinner/J.L. Wallace*	Warner 28208
6/25/88	**9**	24	10	**Letter Home**	S:23 *Wendy Waldman*	Warner 27839
11/5/88+	**8**	22	11	**Sincerely**	S:30 *Alan Freed/Harvey Fuqua*	Warner 27686
2/18/89	**7**	20	12	**Love Will**	*Byron Gallimore/Don Pfrimmer*	Warner 27575
6/24/89	**9**	18	13	**Don't You**	*Johnny Pierce/Otha Young*	Warner 22943
11/25/89+	**7**	26	14	**Leave It Alone**	*Radney Foster/Bill Lloyd*	Warner 22773
4/14/90	**63**	7	15	**Drive South** *[w/ The Bellamy Brothers]*	*John Hiatt*	Warner/Curb
8/25/90	**63**	3	16	**Nothing's Gonna Bother Me Tonight**	*Bernie Nelson/Allen Shamblin*	Warner
				above 2 from the album *Come Hold Me* on Warner 26141		
1/26/91	**8**	20	17	**Men**	*Robert Byrne/Alan Schulman*	Warner
6/29/91	**62**	5	18	**Too Much Fun**	*Robert Byrne/Alan Schulman*	Warner
				above 2 from the album *Talkin' 'Bout Men* on Warner 26500		
3/14/92	**74**	3	19	**What'll You Do About Me**	*Dennis Linde*	Warner
7/18/92	**58**	6	20	**I Got A Date**	*Dave Allen/Tim Bays*	Warner
				above 2 from the album *I Got A Date* on Warner 26821		
				FORMAN, Peggy		
				Born in Centerville, Louisiana. Female singer/songwriter.		
8/20/77	**98**	4	1	**The Danger Zone**	*Ted Harris*	MCA 40757
5/24/80	**89**	4	2	**There Ain't Nothing Like A Rainy Night**	*Peggy Forman*	Dimension 1006
8/2/80	**78**	5	3	**Burning Up Your Memory**	*Peggy Forman*	Dimension 1008
7/4/81	**70**	6	4	**You're More To Me** (Than He's Ever Been)	*Peggy Forman*	Dimension 1020
10/24/81	**54**	6	5	**I Wish You Could Have Turned My Head** (And Left My Heart Alone)	*Sonny Throckmorton*	Dimension 1023
2/27/82	**71**	6	6	**That's What Your Lovin' Does To Me**	*Jesse Shofner*	Dimension 1027
				FORREST, Sylvia		
				Born in Knoxville, Tennessee. Female singer/songwriter.		
9/23/89	**84**	2		**The Nights Are Never Long Enough With You**	*Sylvia Forrest*	Door Knob 319
				FOSTER, Jerry	**SW: #8**	
				Born on 11/19/1935 in Tallapoosa, Missouri. Male singer/songwriter/guitarist.		
8/18/73	**98**	3	1	**Copperhead**	*Jim Casey/Bob McDill*	Cinnamon 764
12/8/73+	**51**	13	2	**Looking Back**	*Brook Benton/Belford Hendricks/Clyde Otis*	Cinnamon 774
11/27/76	**86**	6	3	**I Knew You When**	*Jerry Foster/Bill Rice*	Hitsville 6043
7/15/78	**84**	3	4	**I Want To Love You** *[w/ Tennessee Tornado]*	*Jerry Foster/Bill Rice*	Monument 256
				FOSTER, Lloyd David		
				Born in 1952 in Wills Point, Texas. Male singer/guitarist.		
6/19/82	**32**	13	1	**Blue Rendezvous**	*Tim DuBois/Wood Newton*	MCA 52061
10/23/82	**65**	7	2	**Honky Tonk Magic**	*Danny Morrison/Johnny Slate*	MCA 52123
2/26/83	**32**	12	3	**Unfinished Business**	*Danny Morrison/Wood Newton*	MCA 52173
9/3/83	**60**	6	4	**You've Got That Touch**	*Tim DuBois/Dave Robbins*	MCA 52248
11/24/84+	**44**	15	5	**I'm Gonna Love You Right Out Of The Blues**	*Walt Aldridge/Tom Brasfield*	Columbia 04670
4/13/85	**55**	9	6	**I Can Feel The Fire Goin' Out**	*Troy Seals/Eddie Setser*	Columbia 04836
10/12/85	**68**	6	7	**I'm As Over You As I'm Ever Gonna Get**	*Bruce Burch/Gene Dobbins/Anthony Smith*	Columbia 05601

DEBUT	PEAK	WKS	GOLD	ARTIST / Ranking / Country Chart Hit	Songwriter	Label (& Number)
				FOSTER, Radney		
				Born on 7/20/1959 in Del Rio, Texas. Male singer/songwriter/guitarist. Half of **Foster & Lloyd** duo.		
8/15/92	**10**	20		1 **Just Call Me Lonesome**	*George Ducas/Radney Foster*	Arista
1/23/93	**2^2**	20		2 **Nobody Wins**	*Radney Foster/Kim Richey*	Arista
6/12/93	**20**	20		3 **Easier Said Than Done**	*Radney Foster*	Arista
10/9/93	**34**	11		4 **Hammer And Nails**	*Cindy Bullens/Radney Foster*	Arista
2/26/94	**59**	6		5 **Closing Time**	*Radney Foster/Mark Sager*	Arista
				above 5 from the album *Del Rio, TX 1959* on Arista 18713		
7/9/94	**58**	7		6 **Labor Of Love**	*Cindy Bullens/Radney Foster*	Arista
10/29/94	**64**	5		7 **The Running Kind**	*Merle Haggard*	Arista
				from the various artists album *Mama's Hungry Eyes-A Tribute To* ***Merle Haggard*** on Arista 18760		
4/1/95	**54**	8		8 **Willin' To Walk**	*Radney Foster*	Arista
9/2/95	**59**	5		9 **If It Were Me**	*Radney Foster/Kim Richey*	Arista
				#6, 8 & 9: from the album *Labor Of Love* on Arista 18757		
7/3/99	**74**	1		10 **Godspeed (Sweet Dreams)**	*Radney Foster*	Arista
				from the album *See What You Want To See* on Arista 18833		
6/30/01	**54**	9		11 **Texas In 1880** ***[w/ Pat Green]***	*Radney Foster* **[R]**	Dualtone
				new version of #3 under **Foster & Lloyd**; from the album *Are You Ready For The Big Show?* on Dualtone 1102		
7/27/02	**43**	19		12 **Everyday Angel**	*Radney Foster*	Dualtone
2/15/03	**52**	9		13 **Scary Old World** ***[w/ Chely Wright or Georgia Middleman]***	*Radney Foster/Harlan Howard*	Dualtone
				above 2 from Foster's album *Another Way To Go* on Dualtone 1128		
				FOSTER, Sally		
				Born on 3/31/1921 in Chicago, Illinois. Died in April 1995 (age 74). Female singer.		
1/26/46	**3^4**	10		**Someday (You'll Want Me To Want You)** ***[w/ Hoosier Hot Shots]***	*Jimmie Hodges* **[N]**	Decca 18738
				FOSTER & LLOYD		
				Duo of singers/songwriters/guitarists **Radney Foster** and Bill Lloyd. Foster was born on 7/20/1959 in Del Rio, Texas. Lloyd was born on 12/6/1955 in Bowling Green, Kentucky. Lloyd was also a member of **The Sky Kings**. Also see **Tomorrow's World**.		
7/4/87	**4**	21		1 **Crazy Over You**	S:7 *Radney Foster/Bill Lloyd*	RCA 5210
11/7/87+	**8**	21		2 **Sure Thing**	S:15 *Radney Foster/Bill Lloyd*	RCA 5281
4/9/88	**18**	17		3 **Texas In 1880**	S:29 *Radney Foster*	RCA 6900
				also see #11 under **Radney Foster**		
8/6/88	**6**	23		4 **What Do You Want From Me This Time**	S:17 *Radney Foster/Bill Lloyd*	RCA 8633
1/28/89	**5**	17		5 **Fair Shake**	*Guy Clark/Radney Foster/Bill Lloyd*	RCA 8795
6/3/89	**43**	11		6 **Before The Heartache Rolls In**	*Radney Foster/Bill Lloyd*	RCA 8942
8/19/89	**48**	8		7 **Suzette**	*Bill Lloyd*	RCA 9028
4/7/90	**43**	14		8 **Is It Love**	*Radney Foster/Bill Lloyd*	RCA
11/24/90+	**38**	12		9 **Can't Have Nothin'**	*Radney Foster/Bill Lloyd*	RCA
				above 2 from the album *Version Of The Truth* on RCA 2113		
				FOUR GUYS, The		
				Vocal group from Steubenville, Ohio: Brent Burkett (born on 7/28/1939), Sam Wellington (born on 3/20/1939), Gary Chadwick and Gary Buck (not to be confused with the solo singer). Buck was formerly married to **Louise Mandrell**. Buck was replaced by Laddie Cain (born on 11/22/1951) in 1980. Chadwick was replaced by John Frost (born on 12/3/1949) in 1981.		
				OPRY: 1967		
10/19/74	**88**	3		1 **Too Late To Turn Back Now**	*Allen Reynolds/Don Williams*	RCA Victor 10055
12/8/79	**93**	4		2 **Mama Rocked Us To Sleep (With Country Music)**	*Roger Murrah*	Collage 102
3/13/82	**85**	4		3 **Made In The U.S.A.**	*Bobby Emmons/Chips Moman*	J&B 1001
				4 RUNNER		
				Male vocal group: Craig Morris, Billy Simon, Lee Hilliard and Jim Chapman.		
3/18/95	**26**	20		1 **Cain's Blood**	S:6 *Mike Johnson/Jack Sundrud*	Polydor
7/1/95	**51**	10		2 **A Heart With 4 Wheel Drive**	*Billy Maddox/Paul Thorn*	Polydor
10/14/95	**65**	4		3 **Home Alone**	*Craig Morris/Dennis Wilson*	Polydor
1/20/96	**57**	9		4 **Ripples**	*Tony Haselden*	Polydor
				above 4 from the album *4 Runner* on Polydor 527379		
7/6/96	**54**	12		5 **That Was Him (This Is Now)**	*Vern Rust/Keith Urban*	A&M
				from the album *One For The Ages* on A&M 540602		
12/6/03	**59**	1		6 **Forrest County Line**	*Al Anderson/Craig Wiseman*	Fresh
				from the album *Getaway Car* on Fresh 146220		
				FOWLER, Ken		
				Born in Olive Branch, Mississippi. Male singer.		
2/8/86	**96**	2		**You're A Heartache To Follow**	*Johnny Cymbal/Ben Peters/Austin Roberts*	Deja Vu 111
				FOWLER, Kevin		
				Born in Amarillo, Texas. Male singer/songwriter/guitarist.		
7/10/04	**49**	20		**Ain't Drinkin' Anymore**	*Kevin Fowler*	Equity
				from the album *Loose, Loud & Crazy* on Equity 3003		
				FOWLER, Wally — see TENNESSEE VALLEY BOYS		
				FOX, Dolly		
				Born in Los Angeles, California. Female singer.		
12/9/78	**93**	2		**I've Got A Reason For Living**	*Steve O'Brien*	Artic 1025
				FOX, Kent		
				Born Walter Kent Fox on 10/16/1947 in Lexington, Kentucky. Male singer/songwriter.		
6/2/73	**73**	4		**New York Callin' Miami**	*Kent Fox/Bob Walker*	MCA 40038

DEBUT	PEAK	WKS	GOLD		ARTIST / Country Chart Hit	Songwriter	Label (& Number)
					FOXFIRE		
					Male vocal trio: Dave Hall, Russ Allison and Don Miller.		
6/9/79	**30**	10		1	**Fell Into Love**	*Russ Allison/Don Miller*	NSD 24
4/26/80	**38**	9		2	**I Can See Forever Loving You**	*Russ Allison/Don Miller*	Elektra 46625
11/15/80	**55**	8		3	**Whatever Happened To Those Drinking Songs**	*Ron Birmann/Dave Hall/Don Miller*	Elektra 47070
					FOXTON, Kelly		
					Born in Florida. Female singer/model. Known as "America's Military Pin-Up Queen."		
2/16/80	**78**	4			**Hasn't It Been Good Together** ***[w/ Hank Snow]***	*Linda Kaufman/Gloria Shayne*	RCA 11891
					FOXWORTHY, Jeff		
					Born on 9/6/1958 in Atlanta, Georgia; raised in Hapeville, Georgia. Stand-up comedian/actor. Starred in own TV sitcom, 1995-97. Began hosting own radio countdown show in April 1999.		
9/10/94	**67**	8		1	**Redneck Stomp**	S:8 *Jeff Foxworthy/Scott Rouse* **[C-L]**	Warner
7/8/95	**53**	17		2	**Party All Night** ***[w/ Little Texas]***	S:5 *Jeff Foxworthy/Scott Rouse* **[L-N]**	Warner
					from the album *Games Rednecks Play* on Warner 45856		
12/16/95+	**18**	5		3	**Redneck 12 Days Of Christmas**	S:❶^{9} *Jeff Foxworthy* **[X-N]**	Warner
6/8/96	**42**	12		4	**Redneck Games** ***[w/ Alan Jackson]***	S:2 *Jeff Foxworthy/Scott Rouse/Ronny Scaife* **[L-N]**	Warner
12/14/96+	**39**	5		5	**Redneck 12 Days Of Christmas**	*Jeff Foxworthy* **[X-N-R]**	Warner
1/4/97	**67**	2		6	**'Twas The Night After Christmas**	*(traditional)/Jeff Foxworthy* **[X-C]**	Warner
12/27/97+	**39**	3		7	**Redneck 12 Days Of Christmas**	*Jeff Foxworthy* **[X-C-R]**	Warner
					#1 & 3-7: from the album *Crank It Up - The Music Album* on Warner 46361		
5/2/98	**70**	6		8	**Totally Committed**	*Jeff Foxworthy/Jim Hollihan* **[N]**	Warner
					from the album *Totally Committed* on Warner 46861		
1/2/99	**37**	2		9	**Redneck 12 Days Of Christmas**	*Jeff Foxworthy* **[X-N-R]**	Warner
12/25/99+	**35**	3		10	**Redneck 12 Days Of Christmas**	*Jeff Foxworthy* **[X-N-R]**	Warner
					above 2 from the album *Crank It Up - The Music Album* on Warner 46361		
4/15/00	**63**	6		11	**The Blue Collar Dollar Song** ***[w/ Bill Engvall & Marty Stuart]***	*Bill Engvall/Jeff Foxworthy/ Doug Grau/Porter Howell* **[N]**	DreamWorks
					from the album *Big Funny* on DreamWorks 50200		
					FRADY, Garland		
					Born on 1/11/1941 in Lexington, North Carolina. Died on 5/27/2004 (age 63). Male singer/songwriter/guitarist.		
8/18/73	**89**	7			**The Barrooms Have Found You**	*Tim Darby/Garland Frady*	Countryside 45104
					FRANCIS, Cleve		
					Born Cleveland Francis on 4/22/1945 in Jennings, Louisiana. Black male singer. Worked as a cardiologist in Alexandria, Virginia.		
1/18/92	**52**	11		1	**Love Light**	*Glen Castleberry/Bill Graham*	Liberty
5/2/92	**47**	14		2	**You Do My Heart Good**	*Mike Lantrip/Tom Paden*	Liberty
9/19/92	**74**	2		3	**How Can I Hold You**	*Billy Dean/Tom Shapiro/Chris Waters*	Liberty
					above 3 from the album *Tourist In Paradise* on Liberty 96498		
5/8/93	**63**	8		4	**Walkin'**	*Tim Nichols/Will Robinson*	Liberty
					from the album *Walkin'* on Liberty 80033		
					FRANCIS, Connie		
					Born Concetta Rosa Maria Franconero on 12/12/1938 in Newark, New Jersey. Female pop singer.		
7/25/60	**24**	3	●	1	**Everybody's Somebody's Fool**	*Howard Greenfield/Jack Keller*	MGM 12899
3/1/69	**33**	10		2	**The Wedding Cake**	*Margaret Lewis/Mira Smith*	MGM 14034
3/12/83	**84**	3		3	**There's Still A Few Good Love Songs Left In Me**	*Howard Greenfield/Richard Leigh*	Polydor 810087
					FRANKS, Tillman		
					Born on 9/29/1920 in Stamps, Arkansas. Male singer/songwriter/guitarist. In the car crash which killed **Johnny Horton** in 1960.		
12/21/63	**30**	4		1	**Tadpole** ***[w/ the Cedar Grove Three]***	*Tillman Franks/Merle Kilgore* **[I]**	Starday 651
5/2/64	**30**	11		2	**When The World's On Fire**	*A.P. Carter/Tillman Franks*	Starday 670
					TILLMAN FRANKS SINGERS		
					FRAZIER, Brenda		
					Born in Dallas, Texas. Female singer.		
12/6/80	**92**	2			**I've Given Up Giving In To The Blues**	*Jim Dowell/Larry Shell*	Tyro 1004
					FRAZIER, Dallas	**SW: #6**	
					Born on 10/27/1939 in Spiro, Oklahoma; raised in Bakersfield, California. Male singer/songwriter/guitarist.		
11/11/67+	**28**	11		1	**Everybody Oughta Sing A Song**	*Dallas Frazier*	Capitol 2011
4/13/68	**43**	8		2	**The Sunshine Of My World**	*Dallas Frazier*	Capitol 2133
9/21/68	**59**	5		3	**I Hope I Like Mexico Blues**	*Dallas Frazier/A.L. "Doodle" Owens*	Capitol 2257
3/8/69	**63**	9		4	**The Conspiracy Of Homer Jones**	*Dallas Frazier/A.L. "Doodle" Owens* **[N]**	Capitol 2402
					parody of "Ode To Billy Joe" by **Bobbie Gentry** and "Harper Valley P.T.A." by **Jeannie C. Riley**		
11/8/69	**45**	10		5	**California Cotton Fields**	*Dallas Frazier/Earl Montgomery*	RCA Victor 0259
8/29/70	**45**	7		6	**The Birthmark Henry Thompson Talks About**	*Dallas Frazier/A.L. "Doodle" Owens*	RCA Victor 9881
2/27/71	**43**	8		7	**Big Mable Murphy**	*Dallas Frazier*	RCA Victor 9950
7/29/72	**42**	11		8	**North Carolina**	*Dallas Frazier/A.L. "Doodle" Owens*	RCA Victor 0748
					FRAZIER RIVER		
					Group from Cincinnati, Ohio: Danny Frazier, Chuck Adair, Jim Morris, Bob Wilson, Brian Braverman and Greg Amburgy.		
2/10/96	**57**	9		1	**She Got What She Deserves**	*Charlie Black/Bobby Fischer/Jenny Yates*	Decca
6/22/96	**67**	8		2	**Tangled Up In Texas**	*Billy Burnette/Larry Henley/Dennis W. Morgan*	Decca
					above 2 from the album *Frazier River* on MCA 11303		
					FREE, Johnny		
					Born in North Carolina. Male singer.		
4/28/79	**100**	1			**Borrowed Time**	*Olivia Newton-John*	Sabre 4509

Billboard DEBUT	PEAK	WKS	GOLD	ARTIST / Country Chart Hit	Ranking / Songwriter	Label (& Number)

FREEMAN, Ernie

Born on 8/16/1922 in Cleveland, Ohio. Died of a heart attack on 5/16/1981 (age 58). Male pianist.

DEBUT	PEAK	WKS	GOLD	Country Chart Hit	Songwriter	Label (& Number)
1/13/58	11	2		Raunchy	S:11 *Bill Justis/Sid Manker* **[I]**	Imperial 5474

FRICKE, Janie — 1980s: #22 / All-Time: #86

Born on 12/19/1947 in South Whitney, Indiana. Female singer. Former backing singer for RCA record label. Sang numerous commercial jingles. Later a regular on TNN's ***The Statler Brothers** Show*. Occasionally spells her name "Frickie."

CMA: Female Vocalist 1982 & 1983

DEBUT	PEAK	WKS	GOLD	Country Chart Hit	Songwriter	Label (& Number)
9/17/77	21	13		1 What're You Doing Tonight	*Bob McDill*	Columbia 10605
10/29/77+	4	16		2 Come A Little Bit Closer *[w/ Johnny Duncan]*	*Tommy Boyce/Wes Farrell/Bobby Hart*	Columbia 10634
3/4/78	21	12		3 Baby It's You	*Tom Gmeiner/John Greenebaum*	Columbia 10695
5/27/78	12	13		4 Please Help Me, I'm Falling (In Love With You)	*Hal Blair/Don Robertson*	Columbia 10743
10/7/78	❶[1]	14		5 On My Knees *[w/ Charlie Rich]*	*Charlie Rich*	Epic 50616
11/11/78+	22	12		6 Playin' Hard To Get	*John Thompson*	Columbia 10849
3/3/79	14	12		7 I'll Love Away Your Troubles For Awhile	*Johnny MacRae/Bob Morrison*	Columbia 10910
7/7/79	28	10		8 Let's Try Again	*Danny Steagall*	Columbia 11029
11/17/79+	26	13		9 But Love Me	*Kenny Nolan*	Columbia 11139
3/22/80	22	12		10 Pass Me By (If You're Only Passing Through)	*Hillman Hall*	Columbia 11224
7/12/80	17	14		11 He's Out Of My Life *[w/ Johnny Duncan]*	*Tom Bahler*	Columbia 11312
11/1/80+	2[1]	18		12 Down To My Last Broken Heart	*Chick Rains*	Columbia 11384
3/14/81	12	14		13 Pride	*Irene Stanton/Wayne Walker*	Columbia 60509
7/25/81	4	18		14 I'll Need Someone To Hold Me (When I Cry)	*Wayland Holyfield/Bob McDill*	Columbia 02197
12/12/81+	4	19		15 Do Me With Love	*John Schweers*	Columbia 02644
5/8/82	❶[1]	18		16 Don't Worry 'Bout Me Baby	*Deborah Allen/Bruce Channel/Kieran Kane*	Columbia 02859
9/18/82	❶[1]	19		17 It Ain't Easy Bein' Easy	*Mark Gray/Shawna Harrington/Les Taylor*	Columbia 03214
1/15/83	4	19		18 You Don't Know Love	*Beckie Foster/Don King*	Columbia 03498
5/21/83	❶[1]	20		19 He's A Heartache (Looking For A Place To Happen)	*Larry Henley/Jeff Silbar*	Columbia 03899
9/17/83	❶[1]	20		20 Tell Me A Lie	*Mickey Buckins/Barbara Wyrick*	Columbia 04091
1/14/84	❶[1]	18		21 Let's Stop Talkin' About It	*Deborah Allen/Rory Bourke/Rafe Van Hoy*	Columbia 04317
5/12/84	8	17		22 If The Fall Don't Get You	*Sam Lorber/Dave Robbins/Van Stephenson*	Columbia 04454
9/1/84	❶[1]	23		23 Your Heart's Not In It	S:❶[1] / A:❶[1] *Michael Garvin/Bucky Jones/Tom Shapiro*	Columbia 04578
10/27/84+	❶[1]	22		24 A Place To Fall Apart *[w/ Merle Haggard]*	S:❶[1] / A:❶[1] *Merle Haggard/Willie Nelson/Freddy Powers*	Epic 04663
1/5/85	7	19		25 The First Word In Memory Is Me	S:6 / A:7 *Pat Bunch/Mary Ann Kennedy/Pam Rose*	Columbia 04731
5/18/85	2[1]	22		26 She's Single Again	S:2 / A:2 *Charlie Craig/Peter McCann*	Columbia 04896
9/21/85	4	23		27 Somebody Else's Fire	S:4 / A:4 *Pat Bunch/Mary Ann Kennedy/Pam Rose*	Columbia 05617
2/1/86	5	22		28 Easy To Please	A:4 / S:5 *Rhonda Fleming/Kent Robbins*	Columbia 05781
				JANIE FRICKIE:		
6/28/86	❶[1]	22		29 Always Have Always Will	S:❶[1] / A:2 *Johnny Mears*	Columbia 06144
11/8/86+	20	16		30 When A Woman Cries	S:7 / A:20 *Buck Moore/Mentor Williams*	Columbia 06417
3/14/87	32	11		31 Are You Satisfied	S:24 *Homer Escamilla/Sheb Wooley*	Columbia 06985
5/9/87	21	12		32 From Time To Time (It Feels Like Love Again) *[w/ Larry Gatlin/Gatlin Brothers]*	S:18 *Larry Gatlin*	Columbia 07088
8/29/87	63	4		33 Baby You're Gone	*Steve Davis/Dennis W. Morgan*	Columbia 07353
4/16/88	54	8		34 Where Does Love Go (When It's Gone)	*Peter Rowan*	Columbia 07770
6/25/88	50	8		35 I'll Walk Before I'll Crawl	*Gidget Baird/Linda Buell*	Columbia 07927
9/24/88	64	4		36 Heart	*Paul Overstreet/Don Schlitz*	Columbia 08031
5/20/89	56	7		37 Love Is One Of Those Words	*Holly Dunn/Tom Shapiro/Chris Waters*	Columbia 68758
9/16/89	43	9		38 Give 'Em My Number	*Dave Loggins*	Columbia 69057

FRIEDMAN, Kinky

Born Richard Friedman on 10/31/1944 in Chicago, Illinois; raised in Austin, Texas. Male singer/songwriter/guitarist.

DEBUT	PEAK	WKS	GOLD	Country Chart Hit	Songwriter	Label (& Number)
7/14/73	69	8		Sold American	*Kinky Friedman*	Vanguard 35173

FRIZZELL, Allen

Born in El Dorado, Arkansas. Male singer/songwriter/guitarist. Younger brother of **Lefty Frizzell** and **David Frizzell**. Formerly married to **Shelly West**.

DEBUT	PEAK	WKS	GOLD	Country Chart Hit	Songwriter	Label (& Number)
5/16/81	86	4		1 Beer Joint Fever	*Whitey Shafer*	Sound Factory 429
8/29/81	81	3		2 She's Livin' It Up (And I'm Drinkin' 'Em Down)	*Buck Moore/Bill Taylor*	Sound Factory 447
6/8/85	73	3		3 It'll Be Love By Morning	*Allen Frizzell/Bo Roberts*	Epic 04870

Billboard			GOLD	ARTIST	Ranking	
DEBUT	PEAK	WKS		Country Chart Hit	Songwriter	Label (& Number)

FRIZZELL, David

All-Time: #199

Born on 9/26/1941 in El Dorado, Arkansas. Male singer/songwriter/guitarist. Younger brother of **Lefty Frizzell** and older brother of **Allen Frizzell**. Formed a duo with sister-in-law **Shelly West**.

CMA: Vocal Duo (with Shelly West) 1981 & 1982

DEBUT	PEAK	WKS	#	Country Chart Hit	Songwriter	Label (& Number)
6/20/70	67	3	1	**L.A. International Airport**	*Leanne Scott*	Columbia 45139
10/31/70	36	10	2	**I Just Can't Help Believing**	*Barry Mann/Cynthia Weil*	Columbia 45238
12/18/71	73	2	3	**Goodbye**	*Larry Butler/Buddy Killen*	Cartwheel 202
5/19/73	63	5	4	**Words Don't Come Easy**	*Mac Davis*	Capitol 3589
8/25/73	94	4	5	**Take Me One More Ride**	*Jack Lebsock*	Capitol 3684
10/2/76	100	1	6	**A Case Of You**	*Joni Mitchell*	RSO 856
1/17/81	❶[1]	17	7	**You're The Reason God Made Oklahoma** *[w/ Shelly West]* from the movie *Any Which Way You Can* starring **Clint Eastwood**	*Larry Collins/Sandy Pinkard*	Warner 49650
6/20/81	9	15	8	**A Texas State Of Mind** *[w/ Shelly West]*	*Cliff Crofford/John Durrill/Snuff Garrett*	Warner 49745
9/5/81	45	9	9	**Lefty** *[w/ Merle Haggard]*	*Larry Bastian*	Warner 49778
10/10/81	16	16	10	**Husbands And Wives** *[w/ Shelly West]*	*Roger Miller*	Warner 49825
2/6/82	8	18	11	**Another Honky-Tonk Night On Broadway** *[w/ Shelly West]*	*...Milton Brown/Steve Dorff/Snuff Garrett*	Warner 50007
5/29/82	❶[1]	23	12	**I'm Gonna Hire A Wino To Decorate Our Home**	*Dewayne Blackwell*	Warner 50063
7/17/82	4	18	13	**I Just Came Here To Dance** *[w/ Shelly West]*	*Ken Bell/Terry Skinner/J.L. Wallace*	Warner 29980
10/9/82+	5	20	14	**Lost My Baby Blues**	*Ben Peters*	Warner 29901
12/4/82+	43	11	15	**Please Surrender** *[w/ Shelly West]* from the movie *Honkytonk Man* starring **Clint Eastwood**	*Cliff Crofford/John Durrill/Snuff Garrett*	Warner 29850
3/26/83	52	10	16	**Cajun Invitation** *[w/ Shelly West]*	*Milton Brown/Steve Dorff/Snuff Garrett*	Warner 29756
5/28/83	10	16	17	**Where Are You Spending Your Nights These Days**	*...Milton Brown/Steve Dorff/Snuff Garrett/Dick Thorn*	Viva 29617
9/3/83	71	4	18	**Pleasure Island** *[w/ Shelly West]*	*Ron Hellard/Bucky Jones/Curly Putman*	Viva 29544
10/8/83	39	13	19	**A Million Light Beers Ago**	*Dewayne Blackwell*	Viva 29498
1/14/84	64	6	20	**Black And White**	*Kerry Chater/Gail Lopata*	Viva 29388
2/4/84	20	17	21	**Silent Partners** *[w/ Shelly West]*	*Kerry Chater/Austin Roberts/Tommy Rocco*	Viva 29404
4/28/84	60	6	22	**Who Dat**	*Milton Brown/Steve Dorff/Snuff Garrett*	Viva 29332
7/28/84	49	9	23	**When We Get Back To The Farm (That's When We Really Go To Town)**	*...Michael Garvin/Tom Shapiro/Chris Waters*	Viva 29232
9/15/84	13	20	24	**It's A Be Together Night** *[w/ Shelly West]*	S:8 / A:16 *Charlie Black/Tommy Rocco/John Schweers*	Viva 29187
12/1/84+	49	13	25	**No Way José**	*J.C. Cunningham/Steve Stone*	Viva 29158
3/2/85	63	7	26	**Country Music Love Affair**	*Jim Hurt/Billy Ray Reynolds*	Viva 29066
4/13/85	60	8	27	**Do Me Right** *[w/ Shelly West]*	*Bill Price*	Viva 29048
3/29/86	71	5	28	**Celebrity**	*Alex Harvey*	Nash. America 1002
5/9/87	74	7	29	**Beautiful Body**	*Wanda Mallette/Bob Morrison/Patti Ryan*	Compleat 168

FRIZZELL, Lefty

1950s: #16 / All-Time: #90 // HOF: 1982

Born William Orville Frizzell on 3/31/1928 in Corsicana, Texas; raised in El Dorado, Arkansas. Died of a stroke on 7/19/1975 (age 47). Male singer/songwriter/guitarist. Older brother of **Allen Frizzell** and **David Frizzell**.

OPRY: 1951

DEBUT	PEAK	WKS	#	Country Chart Hit	Songwriter	Label (& Number)
10/28/50	❶[3]	22	1	**If You've Got The Money I've Got The Time /** Grammy: Hall of Fame	J:❶[3] / S:2 / A:2 *Jim Beck/Lefty Frizzell*	
11/4/50+	❶[3]	32	2	**I Love You A Thousand Ways**	A:❶[3] / J:3 / S:5 *Lefty Frizzell*	Columbia 4-20739
3/3/51	4	12	3	**Look What Thoughts Will Do /**	A:4 / S:9 / J:9 *Jim Beck/Dub Dickerson/Lefty Frizzell*	
3/10/51	7	2	4	**Shine, Shave, Shower (It's Saturday)**	J:7 *Jim Beck/Lefty Frizzell*	Columbia 4-20772
4/14/51	❶[11]	27	5	**I Want To Be With You Always**	A:❶[11] / S:❶[6] / J:❶[5] *Jim Beck/Lefty Frizzell*	Columbia 4-20799
8/4/51	❶[12]	28	6	**Always Late (With Your Kisses) /**	S:❶[12] / A:❶[6] / J:❶[6] *Blackie Crawford/Lefty Frizzell*	
8/18/51	2[8]	29	7	**Mom And Dad's Waltz**	S:2 / A:2 / J:3 *Lefty Frizzell*	Columbia 4-20837
10/13/51	6	9	8	**Travellin' Blues**	S:6 / J:7 / A:8 *Jimmie Rodgers*	Columbia 4-20842
12/22/51+	❶[3]	21	9	**Give Me More, More, More (Of Your Kisses) /**	A:❶[3] / J:❶[3] / S:3 *Jim Beck/Lefty Frizzell/Ray Price*	
1/12/52	7	5	10	**How Long Will It Take (To Stop Loving You)**	A:7 *Lefty Frizzell*	Columbia 4-20885
4/12/52	2[1]	12	11	**Don't Stay Away (Till Love Grows Cold)**	S:2 / J:2 / A:4 *Lefty Frizzell/Loys Southerland*	Columbia 4-20911
9/27/52	6	5	12	**Forver (And Always)**	S:6 *Lefty Frizzell/A.M. Lyle*	Columbia 4-20997
12/6/52+	3[1]	9	13	**I'm An Old, Old Man (Tryin' To Live While I Can)**	S:3 / J:4 *Lefty Frizzell*	Columbia 21034
5/23/53	8	1	14	**(Honey, Baby, Hurry!) Bring Your Sweet Self Back To Me**	A:8 *Lefty Frizzell*	Columbia 21084
2/20/54	8	2	15	**Run 'Em Off**	J:8 *Tony Lee/Onie Wheeler*	Columbia 21194
1/15/55	11	4	16	**I Love You Mostly**	S:11 / A:13 *Bobby Adams/Lefty Frizzell*	Columbia 21328
11/24/58+	13	11	17	**Cigarettes And Coffee Blues**	*Marty Robbins*	Columbia 41268
6/8/59	6	15	18	**The Long Black Veil**	*Danny Dill/Marijohn Wilkin*	Columbia 41384
4/27/63	23	2	19	**Forbidden Lovers**	*Irene Stanton/Wayne Walker*	Columbia 42676

DEBUT	PEAK	WKS	GOLD	ARTIST / Ranking / Country Chart Hit	Songwriter	Label (& Number)
				FRIZZELL, Lefty — cont'd		
11/9/63	**30**	1		20 **Don't Let Her See Me Cry**	*Lefty Frizzell*	Columbia 42839
1/11/64	**❶[4]**	26		21 **Saginaw, Michigan**	*Bill Anderson/Don Wayne*	Columbia 42924
8/8/64	**28**	11		22 **The Nester**	*Don Wayne*	Columbia 43051
1/16/65	**50**	2		23 **'Gator Hollow**	*Mel Tillis*	Columbia 43169
5/1/65	**12**	15		24 **She's Gone Gone Gone**	*Harlan Howard*	Columbia 43256
10/16/65	**36**	5		25 **A Little Unfair /**	*Hank Cochran/Chuck Howard*	
11/13/65	**41**	4		26 **Love Looks Good On You**	*Jack Shook*	Columbia 43364
10/15/66	**51**	6		27 **I Just Couldn't See The Forest (For The Trees)**	*Bill Delaney/Lefty Frizzell*	Columbia 43747
3/25/67	**49**	10		28 **You Gotta Be Puttin' Me On**	*Mack Vickery*	Columbia 44023
9/2/67	**63**	4		29 **Get This Stranger Out Of Me**	*A.L. "Doodle" Owens*	Columbia 44205
8/10/68	**59**	3		30 **The Marriage Bit**	*Don Wayne*	Columbia 44563
3/22/69	**64**	4		31 **An Article From Life**	*Johnny Wilson*	Columbia 44738
8/22/70	**49**	10		32 **Watermelon Time In Georgia**	*Harlan Howard*	Columbia 45197
8/12/72	**59**	10		33 **You, Babe**	*Whitey Shafer*	Columbia 45652
9/22/73	**43**	13		34 **I Can't Get Over You To Save My Life**	*Lefty Frizzell/Whitey Shafer*	ABC 11387
2/16/74	**25**	12		35 **I Never Go Around Mirrors**	*Lefty Frizzell/Whitey Shafer*	ABC 11416
6/15/74	**52**	9		36 **Railroad Lady**	*Jimmy Buffett/Jerry Jeff Walker*	ABC 11442
9/21/74	**21**	14		37 **Lucky Arms**	*Lefty Frizzell/Whitey Shafer*	ABC 12023
2/22/75	**67**	7		38 **Life's Like Poetry**	*Merle Haggard*	ABC 12061
7/5/75	**50**	11		39 **Falling**	*A.L. "Doodle" Owens/Whitey Shafer*	ABC 12103
				FRUSHAY, Ray		
				Born Raymond Frusha on 3/1/1944 in San Diego, California; raised in Austin, Texas. Male singer/songwriter.		
9/8/79	**93**	2		1 **I Got Western Pride**	*Mack Jackson*	Western Pride 105
3/22/80	**90**	2		2 **Pickin' Up Love**	*Ray Frushay/Mack Jackson*	Western Pride 113
				FUHRMAN, Micki		
				Born in Coushatta, Louisiana. Female singer/songwriter.		
11/11/78	**93**	4		1 **Leave While I'm Sleeping**	*Roger Bowling/Micki Fuhrman*	Louisiana Hayride 785
7/28/79	**86**	3		2 **Blue River Of Tears**	*Randy Goodrum*	MCA 41057
11/22/80	**60**	7		3 **Hold Me, Thrill Me, Kiss Me**	*Harry Noble*	MCA 51005
2/18/84	**48**	10		4 **I Bet You Never Thought I'd Go This Far**	*Jerry Gillespie/Stan Webb*	MCA 52321
				FULLER, Jerry		
				Born Jerrell Lee Fuller on 11/19/1938 in Fort Worth, Texas. Male singer/songwriter/producer.		
1/13/79	**98**	1		1 **Salt On The Wound**	*Jerry Fuller*	ABC 12436
6/2/79	**90**	4		2 **Lines**	*Jerry Fuller*	MCA 41022

G

DEBUT	PEAK	WKS	GOLD	ARTIST / Ranking / Country Chart Hit	Songwriter	Label (& Number)
				GABRIEL		
				Born Gabriel Farago in Hungary; at four months old, fled with family to Innsbruck, Austria. Emmigrated to Buffalo, New York, at age four. Male singer/songwriter.		
1/24/81	**85**	3		1 **I Think I Could Love You (Better Than He Did)**	*Debbie Hupp/Bob Morrison*	NSD 70
4/18/81	**93**	2		2 **Friends Before Lovers**	*Gabriel Farago*	Ridgetop 01381
				GAINES, Chris — see BROOKS, Garth		
				GALLIMORE, Byron		
				Born in Puryear, Tennessee. Male singer/songwriter.		
6/14/80	**93**	2		**No Ordinary Woman**	*Byron Gallimore*	Little Giant 025
				GALLION, Bob		
				Born on 4/22/1924 in Ashland, Kentucky. Died on 8/20/1999 (age 75). Male singer/songwriter/guitarist.		
11/3/58	**28**	1		1 **That's What I Tell My Heart**	*Luke McDaniel*	MGM 12700
5/18/59	**18**	9		2 **You Take The Table And I'll Take The Chairs**	*John D. Loudermilk*	MGM 12777
11/28/60+	**7**	22		3 **Loving You (Was Worth This Broken Heart)**	*Helen Carter*	Hickory 1130
6/19/61	**20**	4		4 **One Way Street**	*Don Gibson*	Hickory 1145
12/4/61	**20**	2		5 **Sweethearts Again**	*Bob Gallion*	Hickory 1154
11/10/62	**5**	15		6 **Wall To Wall Love**	*Helen Carter/June Carter*	Hickory 1181
8/31/63	**23**	2		7 **Ain't Got Time For Nothin'**	*Harlan Howard*	Hickory 1220
7/20/68	**71**	2		8 **Pick A Little Happy Song**	*Jerry Chesnut*	United Artists 50309
9/8/73	**99**	2		9 **Love By Appointment** *[w/ Pati Powell]*	*Bob Gallion/June Patrick/David Schwartz/Sybil Tarpley*	Metromedia 0037
				GALWAY, James		
				Born on 12/8/1939 in Belfast, Ireland. Classical flutist.		
2/19/83	**57**	11		**The Wayward Wind** *[w/ Sylvia]*	*Stan Lebowsky/Herb Newman*	RCA 13441
				GARNER, Kristin		
				Born in Owego, New York. Female singer.		
5/19/01	**59**	1		**Let's Burn It Down**	*Roger Ferris*	Atlantic
				GARNETT, Gale		
				Born on 7/17/1942 in Auckland, New Zealand. Female singer/songwriter/actress.		
12/5/64	**43**	3		**We'll Sing In The Sunshine**	*Gale Garnett*	RCA Victor 8388

Billboard DEBUT	PEAK	WKS	GOLD	ARTIST / Ranking / Country Chart Hit	Songwriter	Label (& Number)
				GARRETT, Pat		
				Born Patrick Sickafus in Lebanon, Pennsylvania. Male singer/bassist.		
11/12/77	**98**	1		1 **A Little Something On The Side**	*Pat Garrett*	Kansa 3000
8/2/80	**80**	5		2 **Sexy Ole Lady**	*Pat Garrett*	Gold Dust 101
10/18/80	**89**	3		3 **Your Magic Touch**	*Pat Garrett*	Gold Dust 102
11/7/81	**73**	5		4 **Everlovin' Woman**	*Dan Devaney/Dennis Linde*	Gold Dust 104
9/13/86	**74**	6		5 **Rockin' My Country Heart**	*Pat Garrett/Harry Price*	Compleat 157
10/3/87	**82**	3		6 **Suck It In**	*Pat Garrett*	MDJ 73087
				GARRISON, Al		
				Born in Macon, Georgia. Male singer.		
9/26/87	**87**	2		**Where Do I Go From Here**	*Jerry Foster/Roger Lavoie/Johnny Morris*	Motion 1032
				GARRISON, Glen		
				Born on 6/13/1941 in Slarcy, Arkansas. Male singer.		
11/4/67	**72**	2		1 **Goodbye Swingers**	*Ronnie Self*	Imperial 66257
6/22/68	**48**	6		2 **I'll Be Your Baby Tonight**	*Bob Dylan*	Imperial 66300
				GARRON, Jess		
				Born in San Diego, California. Male singer.		
3/31/79	**30**	11		1 **Lo Que Sea (What Ever May The Future Be)**	*Rafael Ruiz*	Charta 131
8/4/79	**65**	6		2 **It's Summer Time**	*Charles Fields*	Charta 136

GATLIN, Larry, & The Gatlin Brothers — **1980s: #39 / All-Time: #84**

Trio of brothers: Larry Gatlin (born on 5/2/1948 in Seminole, Texas), Steve Gatlin (born on 4/4/1951 in Olney, Texas) and Rudy Gatlin (born on 8/20/1952 in Olney, Texas). Larry is the chief singer/songwriter with Steve (guitar) and Rudy (bass) providing the harmony vocals. Worked as a gospel trio and had their own TV series in Abilene, Texas.

OPRY: 1976

DEBUT	PEAK	WKS	GOLD	Country Chart Hit	Songwriter	Label (& Number)
				LARRY GATLIN:		
10/20/73	**40**	13		1 **Sweet Becky Walker**	*Larry Gatlin*	Monument 8584
3/16/74	**45**	12		2 **Bitter They Are Harder They Fall**	*Larry Gatlin*	Monument 8602
9/7/74	**14**	15		3 **Delta Dirt**	*Larry Gatlin*	Monument 8622
8/23/75	**71**	7		4 **Let's Turn The Lights On**	*Larry Gatlin*	Monument 8657
				LARRY GATLIN with Family & Friends:		
12/27/75+	**5**	19		5 **Broken Lady** Grammy: Song	*Larry Gatlin*	Monument 8680
6/12/76	**43**	9		6 **Warm And Tender**	*Larry Gatlin*	Monument 8696
10/30/76+	**5**	16		7 **Statues Without Hearts**	*Larry Gatlin*	Monument 201
2/26/77	**12**	11		8 **Anything But Leavin'**	*Larry Gatlin*	Monument 212
5/28/77	**3**[2]	16		9 **I Don't Wanna Cry**	*Larry Gatlin*	Monument 221
9/10/77	**3**[2]	14		10 **Love Is Just A Game**	*Larry Gatlin*	Monument 226
12/10/77+	**❶**[1]	16		11 **I Just Wish You Were Someone I Love**	*Larry Gatlin*	Monument 234
				LARRY GATLIN:		
4/15/78	**2**[2]	14		12 **Night Time Magic**	*Larry Gatlin*	Monument 249
8/12/78	**13**	11		13 **Do It Again Tonight**	*Larry Gatlin*	Monument 259
11/11/78+	**7**	14		14 **I've Done Enough Dyin' Today**	*Larry Gatlin*	Monument 270
				LARRY GATLIN & THE GATLIN BROTHERS BAND:		
8/25/79	**❶**[2]	15		15 **All The Gold In California**	*Larry Gatlin*	Columbia 11066
1/5/80	**43**	8		16 **The Midnight Choir**	*Larry Gatlin*	Columbia 11169
3/8/80	**12**	12		17 **Taking Somebody With Me When I Fall**	*Larry Gatlin*	Columbia 11219
6/14/80	**18**	13		18 **We're Number One**	*Larry Gatlin*	Columbia 11282
10/4/80	**5**	17		19 **Take Me To Your Lovin' Place**	*Larry Gatlin*	Columbia 11369
2/21/81	**25**	11		20 **It Don't Get No Better Than This**	*Larry Gatlin*	Columbia 11438
6/6/81	**20**	12		21 **Wind Is Bound To Change**	*Larry Gatlin*	Columbia 02123
10/3/81	**4**	17		22 **What Are We Doin' Lonesome**	*Larry Gatlin*	Columbia 02522
2/6/82	**15**	13		23 **In Like With Each Other**	*Larry Gatlin*	Columbia 02698
5/29/82	**19**	12		24 **She Used To Sing On Sunday**	*Larry Gatlin*	Columbia 02910
9/11/82	**5**	19		25 **Sure Feels Like Love**	*Larry Gatlin*	Columbia 03159
1/29/83	**20**	15		26 **Almost Called Her Baby By Mistake**	*Larry Gatlin*	Columbia 03517
5/21/83	**32**	11		27 **Easy On The Eye**	*Larry Gatlin*	Columbia 03885
9/24/83	**❶**[2]	22		28 **Houston (Means I'm One Day Closer To You)**	*Larry Gatlin*	Columbia 04105
3/24/84	**7**	18		29 **Denver**	*Larry Gatlin*	Columbia 04395
				LARRY GATLIN & THE GATLIN BROTHERS:		
7/21/84	**3**[1]	24		30 **The Lady Takes The Cowboy Everytime** S:3 / A:3	*Larry Gatlin*	Columbia 04533
10/12/85	**43**	13		31 **Runaway Go Home**	*Larry Gatlin*	Columbia 05632
1/18/86	**12**	21		32 **Nothing But Your Love Matters** S:12 / A:13	*Larry Gatlin*	Columbia 05764

Billboard DEBUT	PEAK	WKS	GOLD	ARTIST / Country Chart Hit	Ranking / Songwriter	Label (& Number)
				LARRY, STEVE, RUDY: THE GATLIN BROTHERS:		
8/23/86	2^{1}	22		33 She Used To Be Somebody's Baby	S:2 / A:2 *Larry Gatlin*	Columbia 06252
12/27/86+	4	21		34 Talkin' To The Moon	S:3 / A:4 *Larry Gatlin*	Columbia 06592
5/9/87	21	12		35 From Time To Time (It Feels Like Love Again) *[w/ Janie Fricke]*	S:18 *Larry Gatlin*	Columbia 07088
8/15/87	16	15		36 Changin' Partners	S:15 *Larry Gatlin*	Columbia 07320
3/26/88	4	21		37 Love Of A Lifetime	S:8 *Larry Gatlin*	Columbia 07747
8/13/88	34	13		38 Alive And Well	S:24 *Larry Gatlin*	Columbia 07998
				LARRY GATLIN AND THE GATLIN BROTHERS:		
2/25/89	54	7		39 When She Holds Me	*Larry Gatlin*	Universal 53501
5/6/89	37	10		40 I Might Be What You're Lookin' For	*Larry Gatlin*	Universal 66005
9/2/89	51	8		41 #1 Heartache Place	*Larry Gatlin*	Universal 66021
8/4/90	65	6		42 Boogie And Beethoven from the album *Cookin' Up A Storm* on Capitol 93954	*Larry Gatlin*	Capitol

GATTIS, Keith

Born on 5/26/1971 in Georgetown, Texas. Singer/songwriter/guitarist.

DEBUT	PEAK	WKS	GOLD	Country Chart Hit	Songwriter	Label (& Number)
3/30/96	53	9		Little Drops Of My Heart from the album *Keith Gattis* on RCA 66834	*Keith Gattis*	RCA

GAULT, Lenny

Born on 8/16/1942 in Oregon. Male singer.

DEBUT	PEAK	WKS	GOLD	Country Chart Hit	Songwriter	Label (& Number)
9/30/78	87	3		1 Turn On The Bright Lights	*Ray Pennington*	MRC 1020
1/6/79	78	4		2 I Just Need A Coke (To Get The Whiskey Down)	*Dave Kirby/Glenn Martin*	MRC 1024
4/7/79	89	3		3 The Honky-Tonks Are Calling Me Again	*Ray Pennington*	King Coal 03

GAYLE, Crystal — 1970s: #44 / 1980s: #15 / All-Time: #45

Born Brenda Gail Webb on 1/9/1951 in Paintsville, Kentucky; raised in Wabash, Indiana. Female singer/songwriter. Sister of **Loretta Lynn**, **Peggy Sue** and **Jay Lee Webb**; distant cousin of **Patty Loveless**. Known for her trademark ankle-length hair.

CMA: Female Vocalist 1977 & 1978

DEBUT	PEAK	WKS	GOLD	Country Chart Hit	Songwriter	Label (& Number)
9/19/70	23	13		1 I've Cried (The Blues Right Out Of My Eyes) also see #14 below	*Loretta Lynn*	Decca 32721
3/11/72	70	2		2 Everybody Oughta Cry	*Theresa Beaty/Sylvia Richey*	Decca 32925
7/1/72	49	5		3 I Hope You're Havin' Better Luck Than Me	*Ted Harris*	Decca 32969
5/25/74	39	12		4 Restless	*Ed Bruce/Patsy Bruce*	United Artists 428
10/26/74+	6	21		5 Wrong Road Again	*Allen Reynolds*	United Artists 555
3/29/75	27	11		6 Beyond You	*Bill Gatzimos/Crystal Gayle*	United Artists 600
7/26/75	21	15		7 This Is My Year For Mexico	*Vince Matthews*	United Artists 680
11/29/75+	8	16		8 Somebody Loves You	*Allen Reynolds*	United Artists 740
4/3/76	❶^{1}	18		9 I'll Get Over You	*Richard Leigh*	United Artists 781
8/21/76	31	9		10 One More Time (Karneval)	*Bryan Blackburn*	United Artists 838
11/6/76+	❶^{1}	16		11 You Never Miss A Real Good Thing (Till He Says Goodbye)	*Bob McDill*	United Artists 883
3/26/77	2^{2}	15		12 I'll Do It All Over Again	*Wayland Holyfield/Bob McDill*	United Artists 948
7/9/77	❶^{4}	18	●	13 Don't It Make My Brown Eyes Blue Grammy: Song & Female Vocal	*Richard Leigh*	United Artists 1016
12/10/77+	40	11		14 I've Cried (The Blues Right Out Of My Eyes) [R] same version as #1 above	*Loretta Lynn*	MCA 40837
2/11/78	❶^{1}	14		15 Ready For The Times To Get Better	*Allen Reynolds*	United Artists 1136
6/17/78	❶^{2}	16		16 Talking In Your Sleep	*Roger Cook/Bobby Wood*	United Artists 1214
12/2/78+	❶^{2}	14		17 Why Have You Left The One You Left Me For	*Mark True*	United Artists 1259
4/14/79	3^{2}	13		18 When I Dream	*Sandy Theoret*	United Artists 1288
7/21/79	7	13		19 Your Kisses Will	*Van Stephenson*	United Artists 1306
9/1/79	2^{3}	15		20 Half The Way	*Ralph Murphy/Bobby Wood*	Columbia 11087
12/8/79+	5	14		21 Your Old Cold Shoulder	*Richard Leigh*	United Artists 1329
2/9/80	❶^{1}	14		22 It's Like We Never Said Goodbye	*Roger Greenaway/Geoff Stephens*	Columbia 11198
5/3/80	64	6		23 River Road	*Sylvia Tyson*	United Artists 1347
5/10/80	8	15		24 The Blue Side	*David Lasley/Allee Willis*	Columbia 11270
7/26/80	58	7		25 Heart Mender	*Milton Blackford/Richard Leigh*	United Artists 1362
9/13/80	❶^{1}	18		26 If You Ever Change Your Mind	*Robert Gundry/Jerry McGee*	Columbia 11359
2/7/81	17	14		27 Take It Easy	*Delbert McClinton*	Columbia 11436
5/23/81	❶^{1}	17		28 Too Many Lovers	*Sam Hogin/Ted Lindsay/Mark True*	Columbia 02078
10/10/81	3^{3}	18		29 The Woman In Me	*Susan Thomas*	Columbia 02523
2/20/82	5	19		30 You Never Gave Up On Me	*Leslie Pearl*	Columbia 02718
8/7/82	9	15		31 Livin' In These Troubled Times	*Roger Cook/Phil Donnelly/Sam Hogin*	Columbia 03048
10/9/82	❶^{1}	19		32 You And I *[w/ Eddie Rabbitt]*	*Frank J. Myers*	Elektra 69936
11/20/82+	❶^{1}	22		33 'Til I Gain Control Again	*Rodney Crowell*	Elektra 69893
4/2/83	❶^{1}	16		34 Our Love Is On The Faultline	*Reece Kirk*	Warner 29719
7/16/83	❶^{1}	19		35 Baby, What About You	*Josh Leo/Wendy Waldman*	Warner 29582
9/24/83	49	9		36 Keepin' Power	*Roger Cook/Bobby Wood*	Columbia 04093
10/29/83+	❶^{1}	21		37 The Sound Of Goodbye	*Hugh Prestwood*	Warner 29452

DEBUT	PEAK	WKS	GOLD	ARTIST / Ranking / Country Chart Hit	Songwriter	Label (& Number)
				GAYLE, Crystal — cont'd		
2/25/84	2^{2}	19		38 I Don't Wanna Lose Your Love	*Joey Carbone*	Warner 29356
7/7/84	❶^{1}	20		39 Turning Away	S:30 *Tim Krekel*	Warner 29254
10/27/84+	4	23		40 Me Against The Night	A:2 / S:4 *Pat Bunch/Mary Ann Kennedy/Pam Rose*	Warner 29151
3/23/85	3^{1}	21		41 Nobody Wants To Be Alone	A:3 / S:4 *Rhonda Fleming/Michael Masser*	Warner 29050
8/10/85	5	18		42 A Long And Lasting Love	A:4 / S:5 *Gerry Goffin/Michael Masser*	Warner 28963
11/23/85+	❶^{1}	19		43 Makin' Up For Lost Time (The Dallas Lovers' Song) *[w/ Gary Morris]* from the TV series *Dallas* starring Larry Hagman	S:❶^{1} / A:❶^{1} *Dave Loggins/Gary Morris*	Warner 28856
7/26/86	❶^{1}	19		44 Cry	S:❶^{1} / A:❶^{1} *Churchill Kohlman*	Warner 28689
11/22/86+	❶^{1}	22		45 Straight To The Heart	A:❶^{1} / S:10 *Terry Britten/Graham Lyle*	Warner 28518
4/25/87	4	18		46 Another World *[w/ Gary Morris]* theme from the TV soap opera	S:5 / A:29 *John Leffler/Ralph Schuckett*	Warner 28373
7/18/87	26	15		47 Nobody Should Have To Love This Way	*Charlie Black/Rory Bourke/Tommy Rocco*	Warner 28409
10/24/87+	11	18		48 Only Love Can Save Me Now	*Bucky Jones/Tom Shapiro/Chris Waters*	Warner 28209
2/13/88	26	15		49 All Of This & More *[w/ Gary Morris]*	*Becky Foster/Jennifer Kimball/Greg Prestopino*	Warner 28106
8/27/88	22	15		50 Nobody's Angel	*Karen Brooks/Randy Sharp*	Warner 27811
1/7/89	44	9		51 Tennessee Nights	*Jan Buckingham/Shawna Harrington*	Warner 27682
9/15/90	72	2		52 Never Ending Song Of Love from the album *Ain't Gonna Worry* on Capitol 94301	*Delaney Bramlett*	Capitol
				GEARING, Ashley Born in 1991 in Springfield, Massachusetts. Female singer.		
6/21/03	36	16		Can You Hear Me When I Talk To You?	S:3 *Jimmy Harnen/Rick Manwiller*	Lyric Street
				GEEZINSLAW BROTHERS, The Novelty duo from Austin, Texas: Sam Allred (born on 5/5/1938) and DeWayne "Son" Smith (born on 9/17/1946).		
10/15/66	66	3		1 You Wouldn't Put The Shuck On Me	*Sam Allred* [N]	Capitol 5722
7/15/67	57	6		2 Change Of Wife	*Sam Allred* [N]	Capitol 5918
10/21/67	48	8		3 Chubby (Please Take Your Love To Town) parody of "Ruby, Don't Take Your Love To Town" by **Kenny Rogers**	*Dick Miles/Mel Tillis* [N]	Capitol 2002
8/22/92	56	13		4 Help, I'm White And I Can't Get Down *[The Geezinslaws]* from the album *Feelin' Good, Gittin' Up, Gittin' Down* on Step One 0074	*Roger Ball/Clinton Gregory* [N]	Step One
				GENTRY, Bobbie Born Roberta Streeter on 7/27/1944 in Chickasaw County, Mississippi; raised in Greenwood, Mississippi. Female singer/songwriter/guitarist. Formerly married to **Jim Stafford**. Won the 1967 Best New Artist Grammy Award.		
9/9/67	17	8	●	1 Ode To Billie Joe **Grammy: Hall of Fame / RS500**	*Bobbie Gentry*	Capitol 5950
6/1/68	72	4		2 Louisiana Man	*Doug Kershaw*	Capitol 2147
11/23/68	44	7		3 Less Of Me *[w/ Glen Campbell]*	*Glen Campbell*	Capitol 2314
2/8/69	14	14		4 Let It Be Me *[w/ Glen Campbell]*	*Gilbert Becaud/Mann Curtis*	Capitol 2387
12/13/69+	26	12		5 Fancy	*Bobbie Gentry*	Capitol 2675
2/21/70	6	13		6 All I Have To Do Is Dream *[w/ Glen Campbell]*	*Boudleaux Bryant*	Capitol 2745
				GENTRY, Gary Born in Athens, Texas. Male singer/songwriter.		
4/25/81	84	2		1 I Sold All Of Tom T's Songs Last Night	*Gary Gentry/Sonny Hall* [N]	Elektra 47122
12/19/81	83	4		2 (s.o.b.) Same Old Boy	*Mitchell Crawford/Gary Gentry/Sonny Hall/Jim Kent*	Elektra 47238
				GENTRY, Montgomery — see MONTGOMERY GENTRY		
				GHOST TRAIN — see TAYLOR, Chip		
				GIBBS, Terri Born on 6/15/1954 in Miami, Florida; raised in Augusta, Georgia. Female singer/songwriter/pianist. Blind since birth. ***CMA: Horizon 1981***		
10/11/80+	8	20		1 Somebody's Knockin'	*Jerry Gillespie/Ed Penney*	MCA 41309
6/6/81	19	12		2 Rich Man	*Ed Mattson*	MCA 51119
9/26/81	38	10		3 I Wanna Be Around	*Johnny Mercer/Sadie Vimmerstedt*	MCA 51180
12/26/81+	12	17		4 Mis'ry River	*Glenn Worf*	MCA 51225
5/1/82	19	13		5 Ashes To Ashes	*Jerry McBee/Ed Penney*	MCA 52040
8/14/82	45	8		6 Some Days It Rains All Night Long	*Ed Penney*	MCA 52088
11/13/82+	33	14		7 Baby I'm Gone	*Glenn Worf*	MCA 52134
8/13/83	17	17		8 Anybody Else's Heart But Mine	*Walt Aldridge*	MCA 52252
12/3/83	65	8		9 Tell Mama	*Clarence Carter/Marcus Daniel/Wilber Terrell*	MCA 52308
3/30/85	43	12		10 A Few Good Men **Kathy Mattea** (harmony vocal)	*Ken Bell/Mickey Buckins*	Warner 29056
7/6/85	70	5		11 Rockin' In A Brand New Cradle	*Joe Chambers/Larry Jenkins*	Warner 28993
11/2/85	70	5		12 Someone Must Be Missing You Tonight	*Paula Breedlove/Johnny MacRae/Bob Morrison*	Warner 28895
10/24/87	87	3		13 Turn Around	*Jimmy Payne*	Horizon 2963

Billboard DEBUT	PEAK	WKS	GOLD	ARTIST / Country Chart Hit	Ranking / Songwriter	Label (& Number)

GIBSON, Don   1950s: #22 / 1960s: #18 / 1970s: #23 / All-Time: #38 // HOF: 2001

Born on 4/3/1928 in Shelby, North Carolina. Died on 11/17/2003 (age 75). Male singer/songwriter/guitarist. Worked local clubs and radio while still in high school. Moved to Knoxville in 1953 and worked on the WNOX *Barn Dance* radio series.

OPRY: 1958

DEBUT	PEAK	WKS	GOLD	Country Chart Hit	Songwriter	Label (& Number)
8/11/56	9	1		1 **Sweet Dreams** (also see #15 below)	A:9 *Don Gibson*	MGM 12194
2/17/58	❶^{8}	34		2 **Oh Lonesome Me /**	S:❶^{8} / A:❶^{8} *Don Gibson*	
3/17/58	7	14		3 **I Can't Stop Lovin' You**	A:7 *Don Gibson*	RCA Victor 7133
6/9/58	❶^{2}	24		4 **Blue Blue Day**	S:❶^{2} / A:2 *Don Gibson*	RCA Victor 7010
9/29/58	5	19		5 **Give Myself A Party /**	S:5 / A:12 *Don Gibson*	
10/6/58	8	9		6 **Look Who's Blue**	A:8 *Don Gibson*	RCA Victor 7330
2/2/59	3^{4}	16		7 **Who Cares /**	*Don Gibson*	
2/23/59	27	2		8 **A Stranger To Me**	*Don Gibson*	RCA Victor 7437
5/11/59	11	13		9 **Lonesome Old House**	*Don Gibson*	RCA Victor 7505
8/17/59	5	16		10 **Don't Tell Me Your Troubles**	*Don Gibson*	RCA Victor 7566
12/7/59+	14	9		11 **I'm Movin' On /**	*Hank Snow*	
1/4/60	29	1		12 **Big Hearted Me**	*Don Gibson*	RCA Victor 7629
3/7/60	2^{1}	21		13 **Just One Time**	*Don Gibson*	RCA Victor 7690
8/8/60	11	11		14 **Far, Far Away** (also see #48 below)	*Don Gibson*	RCA Victor 7762
11/28/60+	6	16		15 **Sweet Dreams** (new version of #1 above)	*Don Gibson* **[R]**	RCA Victor 7805
3/13/61	22	6		16 **What About Me**	*Don Gibson*	RCA Victor 7841
6/19/61	2^{1}	26		17 **Sea Of Heartbreak**	*Hal David/Paul Hampton*	RCA Victor 7890
12/18/61+	2^{1}	21		18 **Lonesome Number One**	*Don Gibson*	RCA Victor 7959
5/19/62	5	14		19 **I Can Mend Your Broken Heart**	*Don Gibson*	RCA Victor 8017
11/17/62	22	4		20 **So How Come** (No One Loves Me)	*Boudleaux Bryant/Felice Bryant*	RCA Victor 8085
4/6/63	12	10		21 **Head Over Heels In Love With You**	*Lester Flatt*	RCA Victor 8144
8/31/63	22	5		22 **Anything New Gets Old** (Except My Love For You)	*Don Gibson*	RCA Victor 8192
11/28/64+	23	16		23 **Cause I Believe In You**	*Don Gibson*	RCA Victor 8456
7/3/65	19	13		24 **Again**	*Don Gibson*	RCA Victor 8589
10/9/65	10	13		25 **Watch Where You're Going**	*Don Gibson*	RCA Victor 8678
1/22/66	12	12		26 **A Born Loser**	*Don Gibson*	RCA Victor 8732
5/7/66	6	17		27 (Yes) **I'm Hurting**	*Don Gibson*	RCA Victor 8812
11/5/66+	8	17		28 **Funny, Familiar, Forgotten, Feelings**	*Mickey Newbury*	RCA Victor 8975
6/3/67	51	4		29 **Lost Highway**	*Leon Payne*	RCA Victor 9177
8/26/67	23	12		30 **All My Love**	*Don Gibson*	RCA Victor 9266
3/23/68	37	7		31 **Ashes Of Love /**	*Jack Anglin/Jim Anglin/Johnny Wright*	
6/1/68	71	3		32 **Good Morning, Dear**	*Mickey Newbury*	RCA Victor 9460
7/13/68	12	14		33 **It's A Long, Long Way To Georgia**	*Larry Murray*	RCA Victor 9563
11/23/68+	30	9		34 **Ever Changing Mind**	*Joe Melson/Susie Melson*	RCA Victor 9663
2/22/69	2^{1}	17		35 **Rings Of Gold** *[w/ Dottie West]*	*Gene Thomas*	RCA Victor 9715
5/3/69	28	9		36 **Solitary**	*Leon Payne*	RCA Victor 0143
7/12/69	32	10		37 **Sweet Memories** *[w/ Dottie West]*	*Mickey Newbury*	RCA Victor 0178
9/6/69	21	8		38 **I Will Always**	*Don Gibson*	RCA Victor 0219
12/13/69+	7	13		39 **There's A Story** (Goin' 'Round) *[w/ Dottie West]*	*Don Gibson*	RCA Victor 0291
3/14/70	17	12		40 **Don't Take All Your Loving**	*Don Gibson*	Hickory 1559
6/27/70	16	13		41 **A Perfect Mountain**	*Gene Thomas*	Hickory 1571
7/18/70	46	10		42 **Til I Can't Take It Anymore** *[w/ Dottie West]*	*Dorian Burton/Clyde Otis*	RCA Victor 9867
10/10/70	37	12		43 **Someway**	*Don Gibson*	Hickory 1579
1/23/71	19	13		44 **Guess Away The Blues**	*Don Gibson*	Hickory 1588
5/22/71	29	11		45 (I Heard That) **Lonesome Whistle**	*Jimmie Davis/Hank Williams*	Hickory 1598
8/28/71	50	8		46 **The Two Of Us Together** *[w/ Sue Thompson]*	*Don Gibson*	Hickory 1607
10/23/71	5	17		47 **Country Green**	*Eddy Raven*	Hickory 1614
2/19/72	12	13		48 **Far, Far Away** (new version of #14 above)	*Don Gibson* **[R]**	Hickory 1623
4/22/72	71	3		49 **Did You Ever Think** *[w/ Sue Thompson]*	*Don Gibson*	Hickory 1629
6/10/72	❶^{1}	18		50 **Woman** (Sensuous Woman)	*Gary S. Paxton*	Hickory 1638
8/12/72	37	11		51 **I Think They Call It Love** *[w/ Sue Thompson]*	*Bobby Bond*	Hickory 1646
10/21/72	11	13		52 **Is This The Best I'm Gonna Feel**	*Don Gibson*	Hickory 1651
12/23/72	64	5		53 **Cause I Love You** *[w/ Sue Thompson]*	*Don Gibson*	Hickory 1654
2/17/73	26	11		54 **If You're Goin' Girl**	*Bobby Bond*	Hickory 1661
3/17/73	52	6		55 **Go With Me** *[w/ Sue Thompson]*	*Gene Thomas*	Hickory 1665
5/26/73	6	14		56 **Touch The Morning**	*Eddy Raven*	Hickory 1671
9/15/73	53	9		57 **Warm Love** *[w/ Sue Thompson]*	*Don Gibson*	Hickory/MGM 303
10/6/73	30	11		58 **That's What I'll Do**	*Don Gibson*	Hickory/MGM 306
12/29/73+	12	13		59 **Snap Your Fingers**	*Grady Martin/Alex Zanetis*	Hickory/MGM 312
5/4/74	8	15		60 **One Day At A Time**	*Gary S. Paxton*	Hickory/MGM 318

Billboard			G O L D	ARTIST	Ranking	
DEBUT	PEAK	WKS		Country Chart Hit	Songwriter	Label (& Number)

GIBSON, Don — cont'd

DEBUT	PEAK	WKS	GOLD	Country Chart Hit	Songwriter	Label (& Number)
8/10/74	**31**	12		61 **Good Old Fashioned Country Love** ***[w/ Sue Thompson]***	*Glenn Barber/Jim Mundy*	Hickory/MGM 324
8/31/74	**9**	17		62 **Bring Back Your Love To Me**	*Don Gibson*	Hickory/MGM 327
1/18/75	**27**	12		63 **I'll Sing For You**	*Bobby Bond*	Hickory/MGM 338
4/19/75	**24**	11		64 **(There She Goes) I Wish Her Well**	*Don Gibson*	Hickory/MGM 345
7/19/75	**36**	11		65 **Oh, How Love Changes** ***[w/ Sue Thompson]***	*DeWayne Orender/K. Phyllis Powell*	Hickory/MGM 350
8/16/75	**43**	11		66 **Don't Stop Loving Me**	*Don Gibson*	Hickory/MGM 353
12/6/75+	**76**	8		67 **I Don't Think I'll Ever (Get Over You)**	*Don Gibson*	Hickory/MGM 361
3/13/76	**79**	5		68 **You've Got To Stop Hurting Me Darling**	*Don Gibson*	Hickory/MGM 365
4/3/76	**98**	2		69 **Get Ready-Here I Come** ***[w/ Sue Thompson]***	*DeWayne Orender/K. Phyllis Powell*	Hickory/MGM 367
5/29/76	**39**	10		70 **Doing My Time**	*Jimmie Skinner*	Hickory/MGM 372
11/6/76	**23**	12		71 **I'm All Wrapped Up In You**	*Don Gibson*	ABC/Hickory 54001
3/12/77	**30**	10		72 **Fan The Flame, Feed The Fire**	*Eddy Raven*	ABC/Hickory 54010
7/2/77	**16**	13		73 **If You Ever Get To Houston (Look Me Down)**	*Mickey Newbury*	ABC/Hickory 54014
10/22/77	**67**	5		74 **When Do We Stop Starting Over**	*Mickey Newbury*	ABC/Hickory 54019
2/11/78	**16**	14		75 **Starting All Over Again**	*Phillip Mitchell*	ABC/Hickory 54024
6/3/78	**22**	10		76 **The Fool**	*Naomi Ford/Lee Hazlewood*	ABC/Hickory 54029
10/7/78	**61**	7		77 **Oh, Such A Stranger /**	*Don Gibson*	
10/7/78	**flip**	7		78 **I Love You Because**	*Leon Payne*	ABC/Hickory 54036
12/23/78+	**26**	12		79 **Any Day Now**	*Burt Bacharach/Bob Hilliard*	ABC/Hickory 54039
6/9/79	**37**	10		80 **Forever One Day At A Time**	*Eddy Raven*	MCA 41031
3/29/80	**42**	7		81 **Sweet Sensuous Sensations**	*Kenny Walker*	Warner/Curb 49193
12/13/80+	**80**	6		82 **Love Fires**	*Kenny Walker*	Warner/Curb 49602

Again ['65]
All My Love ['67]
Any Day Now ['79]
Anything New Gets Old (Except My Love For You) ['63]
Ashes Of Love ['68]
Big Hearted Me ['60]
Blue Blue Day ['58]
Born Loser ['66]
Bring Back Your Love To Me ['74]
Cause I Believe In You ['65]
Cause I Love You ['72]
Country Green ['71]
Did You Ever Think ['72]
Doing My Time ['76]
Don't Stop Loving Me ['75]
Don't Take All Your Loving ['70]
Don't Tell Me Your Troubles ['59]
Ever Changing Mind ['69]
Fan The Flame, Feed The Fire ['77]
Far, Far Away ['60]
Far, Far Away ['72]
Fool ['78]
Forever One Day At A Time ['79]
Funny, Familiar, Forgotten, Feelings ['67]
Get Ready-Here I Come ['76]
Give Myself A Party ['58]
Go With Me ['73]
Good Morning, Dear ['68]
Good Old Fashioned Country Love ['74]
Guess Away The Blues ['71]
Head Over Heels In Love With You ['63]
I Can Mend Your Broken Heart ['62]
I Can't Stop Lovin' You ['58]
I Don't Think I'll Ever (Get Over You) ['76]
(I Heard That) Lonesome Whistle ['71]
I Love You Because ['78]
I Think They Call It Love ['72]
I Will Always ['69]
I'll Sing For You ['75]
I'm All Wrapped Up In You ['76]
I'm Movin' On ['60]
If You Ever Get To Houston (Look Me Down) ['77]
If You're Goin' Girl ['73]
Is This The Best I'm Gonna Feel ['72]
It's A Long, Long Way To Georgia ['68]
Just One Time ['60]
Lonesome Number One ['62]
Lonesome Old House ['59]
Look Who's Blue ['58]
Lost Highway ['67]
Love Fires ['81]
Oh, How Love Changes ['75]
Oh Lonesome Me ['58]
Oh, Such A Stranger ['78]
One Day At A Time ['74]
Perfect Mountain ['70]
Rings Of Gold ['69]
Sea Of Heartbreak ['61]
Snap Your Fingers ['74]
So How Come (No One Loves Me) ['62]
Solitary ['69]
Someway ['70]
Starting All Over Again ['78]
Stranger To Me ['59]
Sweet Dreams ['56]
Sweet Dreams ['61]
Sweet Memories ['69]
Sweet Sensuous Sensations ['80]
That's What I'll Do ['73]
(There She Goes) I Wish Her Well ['75]
There's A Story (Goin' 'Round) ['70]
Til I Can't Take It Anymore ['70]
Touch The Morning ['73]
Two Of Us Together ['71]
Warm Love ['73]
Watch Where You're Going ['65]
What About Me ['61]
When Do We Stop Starting Over ['77]
Who Cares ['59]
Woman (Sensuous Woman) ['72]
(Yes) I'm Hurting ['66]
You've Got To Stop Hurting Me Darling ['76]

GIBSON, Hal

Born in San Antonio, Texas. Male singer.

DEBUT	PEAK	WKS	GOLD	Country Chart Hit	Songwriter	Label (& Number)
12/16/89	**87**	3		**The Love She Found In Me**	*Dennis Linde/Bob Morrison*	Sundial 163

GIBSON/MILLER BAND

Group led by singer/songwriter Dave Gibson (born on 10/1/1956) and guitarist Bill "Blue" Miller (born on 7/15/1952). Includes Mike Daly (steel guitar; born on 6/11/1955), Bryan Grassmeyer (bass; born on 6/6/1954) and Steve Grossman (drums; born on 4/3/1962).

DEBUT	PEAK	WKS	GOLD	Country Chart Hit	Songwriter	Label (& Number)
11/14/92+	**37**	20		1 **Big Heart**	*Dave Gibson/Blue Miller/Freddy Weller*	Epic
2/13/93	**20**	20		2 **High Rollin'**	*Dave Gibson/Blue Miller*	Epic
6/12/93	**22**	20		3 **Texas Tattoo**	*Dave Gibson/Blue Miller*	Epic
9/25/93	**46**	11		4 **Small Price**	*Austin Cunningham/Thom McHugh*	Epic
1/22/94	**40**	13		5 **Stone Cold Country** above 5 from the album *Where There's Smoke* on Epic 52980	*Dave Gibson/Blue Miller*	Epic
5/28/94	**49**	10		6 **Mammas Don't Let Your Babies Grow Up To Be Cowboys** from the movie *The Cowboy Way* starring Woody Harrelson	*Ed Bruce/Patsy Bruce*	Epic
9/24/94	**59**	7		7 **Red, White And Blue Collar** above 2 from the album *Red, White And Blue Collar* on Epic 57627	*Dave Gibson/Blue Miller*	Epic

GILKYSON, Terry

Born Hamilton Gilkyson on 6/17/1916 in Mont Clare, Pennsylvania. Died of an aneurysm on 10/15/1999 (age 83). Male folk singer/guitarist.

DEBUT	PEAK	WKS	GOLD	Country Chart Hit	Songwriter	Label (& Number)
6/2/51	**8**	2	●	**On Top Of Old Smoky** ***[w/ The Weavers]***	J:8 *Pete Seeger*	Decca 9-27515

GILL, Vince

1990s: #6 / All-Time: #46

Born on 4/12/1957 in Norman, Oklahoma. Male singer/songwriter/guitarist. Member of **Pure Prairie League** from 1979-83. Married to Janis Oliver of **Sweethearts Of The Rodeo** from 1980-97. Married Amy Grant on 3/10/2000. Member of **The Notorious Cherry Bombs**. Also see **America The Beautiful**, **Hope** and **Tomorrow's World**.

CMA: Male Vocalist 1991, 1992, 1993, 1994 & 1995 / Entertainer 1993 & 1994 // OPRY: 1991

DEBUT	PEAK	WKS	GOLD	Country Chart Hit	Songwriter	Label (& Number)
2/11/84	**40**	13		1 **Victim Of Life's Circumstances**	*Delbert McClinton*	RCA 13731
5/19/84	**38**	11		2 **Oh Carolina**	*Randy Albright/Jim Elliott/Mark D. Sanders*	RCA 13809
9/22/84	**39**	15		3 **Turn Me Loose**	*Vince Gill*	RCA 13860
3/16/85	**32**	17		4 **True Love**	S:26 *Vince Gill*	RCA 14020

DEBUT	PEAK	WKS	GOLD	ARTIST / Country Chart Hit	Ranking / Songwriter	Label (& Number)
				GILL, Vince — cont'd		
7/13/85	**10**	18		5 **If It Weren't For Him** *[w/ Rosanne Cash]* A:6 / S:10	*Rosanne Cash/Vince Gill*	RCA 14140
11/23/85+	**9**	25		6 **Oklahoma Borderline** S:9 / A:9	*Guy Clark/Rodney Crowell/Vince Gill*	RCA 14216
6/7/86	**33**	15		7 **With You** A:32	*Vince Gill*	RCA 14371
5/2/87	**5**	21		8 **Cinderella** S:11	*Reed Nielsen*	RCA 5131
9/19/87	**16**	16		9 **Let's Do Something** S:25	*Vince Gill/Reed Nielsen*	RCA 5257
1/30/88	**11**	17		10 **Everybody's Sweetheart** S:20	*Vince Gill*	RCA 5331
6/4/88	**39**	10		11 **The Radio**	*Vince Gill/Reed Nielsen*	RCA 8301
9/16/89	**22**	20		12 **Never Alone**	*Rosanne Cash/Vince Gill*	MCA 53717
1/20/90	**13**	26		13 **Oklahoma Swing** *[w/ Reba McEntire]*	*Tim DuBois/Vince Gill*	MCA
5/26/90	**2^{2}**	21		14 **When I Call Your Name**	*Tim DuBois/Vince Gill*	MCA
				Grammy: Male Vocal / CMA: Single & Song; **Patty Loveless** (backing vocal)		
9/29/90	**3^{2}**	20		15 **Never Knew Lonely**	*Vince Gill*	MCA
				above 3 from the album *When I Call Your Name* on MCA 42321		
2/16/91	**7**	20		16 **Pocket Full Of Gold**	*Brian Allsmiller/Vince Gill*	MCA
3/30/91	**25**	20		17 **Restless** *[w/ Mark O'Connor/Ricky Skaggs/Steve Wariner]*	*Carl Perkins*	Warner
				Grammy: Vocal Collaboration / CMA: Vocal Event; from O'Connor's album *The New Nashville Cats* on Warner 26509		
6/15/91	**7**	20		18 **Liza Jane**	*Vince Gill/Reed Nielsen*	MCA
9/21/91+	**4**	20		19 **Look At Us**	*Max D. Barnes/Vince Gill*	MCA
				CMA: Song		
2/1/92	**2^{2}**	20		20 **Take Your Memory With You**	*Vince Gill*	MCA
				#16 & 18-20: from the album *Pocket Full Of Gold* on MCA 10140		
7/4/92	**❶^{2}**	20		21 **I Still Believe In You**	*Vince Gill/John Jarvis*	MCA
				Grammy: Song & Male Vocal		
10/17/92	**❶^{3}**	20		22 **Don't Let Our Love Start Slippin' Away**	*Vince Gill/Pete Wasner*	MCA
2/20/93	**❶^{2}**	20		23 **The Heart Won't Lie** *[w/ Reba McEntire]*	*Kim Carnes/Donna Weiss*	MCA
				from McEntire's album *It's Your Call* on MCA 10673		
4/10/93	**3^{1}**	20		24 **No Future In The Past**	*Vince Gill/Carl Jackson*	MCA
7/31/93	**❶^{1}**	20		25 **One More Last Chance**	*Vince Gill/Gary Nicholson*	MCA
10/30/93	**42**	20		26 **I Can't Tell You Why**	*Glenn Frey/Don Henley/Timothy B. Schmit*	Giant
				from the various artists album *Common Thread: Songs Of The* ***Eagles*** on Giant 24531		
12/18/93+	**52**	4		27 **Have Yourself A Merry Little Christmas**	*Ralph Blane/Hugh Martin* **[X]**	MCA
				from the album *Let There Be Peace On Earth* on MCA 10877		
1/8/94	**❶^{1}**	20		28 **Tryin' To Get Over You**	*Vince Gill*	MCA
				#21, 22, 24, 25 & 28: from the album *I Still Believe In You* on MCA 10630		
4/16/94	**2^{3}**	20		29 **Whenever You Come Around**	*Vince Gill/Pete Wasner*	MCA
7/9/94	**2^{2}**	20		30 **What The Cowgirls Do**	*Vince Gill/Reed Nielsen*	MCA
10/15/94	**3^{3}**	20		31 **When Love Finds You**	*Vince Gill/Michael Omartian*	MCA
				Grammy: Male Vocal		
12/24/94+	**54**	3		32 **Have Yourself A Merry Little Christmas**	*Ralph Blane/Hugh Martin* **[X-R]**	MCA
1/7/95	**74**	1		33 **It Won't Be The Same This Year**	*Vince Gill* **[X]**	MCA
				above 2 from the album *Let There Be Peace On Earth* on MCA 10877		
2/4/95	**4**	20		34 **Which Bridge To Cross (Which Bridge To Burn)**	*Bill Anderson/Vince Gill*	MCA
5/13/95	**2^{1}**	20		35 **You Better Think Twice**	*Vince Gill/Reed Nielsen*	MCA
9/2/95	**14**	20		36 **Go Rest High On That Mountain**	*Vince Gill*	MCA
				Grammy: Song & Male Vocal; #29-31 & 34-36: from the album *When Love Finds You* on MCA 11047		
9/16/95	**15**	20		37 **I Will Always Love You** *[w/ Dolly Parton]*	*Dolly Parton*	Columbia
				CMA: Vocal Event; from Parton's album *Something Special* on Columbia 67140		
4/13/96	**12**	20		38 **High Lonesome Sound** *[w/ Alison Krauss]*	*Vince Gill*	MCA
				Grammy: Vocal Collaboration		
7/20/96	**5**	20		39 **Worlds Apart**	*Bob DiPiero/Vince Gill*	MCA
				Grammy: Male Vocal		
11/9/96+	**2^{1}**	20		40 **Pretty Little Adriana**	*Vince Gill*	MCA
				Grammy: Male Vocal		
3/29/97	**2^{1}**	20		41 **A Little More Love** S:21	*Vince Gill*	MCA
7/19/97	**8**	20		42 **You And You Alone**	*Vince Gill*	MCA
				above 5 from the album *High Lonesome Sound* on MCA 11422		
12/13/97+	**34**	13		43 **It's Not Over** *[w/ Mark Chesnutt & Alison Krauss]*	*Larry Kingston/Mark Wright*	Decca
				from Chesnutt's album *Thank God For Believers* on Decca 70006		
1/3/98	**64**	2		44 **Have Yourself A Merry Little Christmas**	*Ralph Blane/Hugh Martin* **[X-R]**	MCA
				from the album *Let There Be Peace On Earth* on MCA 10877		
5/30/98	**5**	20		45 **If You Ever Have Forever In Mind** S:6	*Vince Gill/Troy Seals*	MCA Nashville
				Grammy: Male Vocal		
10/10/98	**33**	12		46 **Kindly Keep It Country**	*Vince Gill*	MCA Nashville
1/9/99	**74**	1		47 **Blue Christmas**	*Billy Hayes/Jay Johnson* **[X]**	MCA Nashville
				from the album *Breath of Heaven* on MCA Nashville 70038		
1/23/99	**27**	19		48 **Don't Come Cryin' To Me**	*Vince Gill/Reed Nielsen*	MCA Nashville
5/29/99	**27**	20		49 **My Kind Of Woman/My Kind Of Man** *[w/ Patty Loveless]*	*Vince Gill*	MCA Nashville
				CMA: Vocal Event; #45, 46, 48 & 49: from the album *The Key* on MCA Nashville 70017		
10/23/99	**62**	10		50 **If You Ever Leave Me** *[w/ Barbra Streisand]*	*Richard Marx*	Columbia
				from Streisand's album *A Love Like Ours* on Columbia 69601		
1/29/00	**20**	20		51 **Let's Make Sure We Kiss Goodbye**	*Vince Gill*	MCA Nashville
5/20/00	**6**	32		52 **Feels Like Love**	*Vince Gill*	MCA Nashville
1/20/01	**31**	16		53 **Shoot Straight From Your Heart**	*Vince Gill*	MCA Nashville
				above 3 from the album *Let's Make Sure We Kiss Goodbye* on MCA Nashville 70098		
11/9/02+	**17**	20		54 **Next Big Thing**	*Al Anderson/Vince Gill/John Hobbs*	MCA Nashville
				Grammy: Male Vocal		
3/29/03	**31**	17		55 **Someday**	*Vince Gill/Richard Marx*	MCA Nashville
10/11/03	**44**	11		56 **Young Man's Town**	*Vince Gill*	MCA Nashville

DEBUT	PEAK	WKS	GOLD	ARTIST / Ranking / Country Chart Hit	Songwriter	Label (& Number)

GILL, Vince — cont'd

DEBUT	PEAK	WKS	#	Country Chart Hit	Songwriter	Label (& Number)
3/20/04	51	7	57	In These Last Few Days	*Vince Gill*	MCA Nashville
				above 4 from the album *Next Big Thing* on MCA Nashville 70286		
12/11/04+	47	20	58	Not Me *[w/ Keni Thomas & Emmylou Harris]*	*Brent Maher/Billy Montana/Keni Thomas*	Moraine
				from Thomas's album *Flags Of Our Fathers* on Moraine 2350		

GILLETTE, Steve

Born in California. Male singer/songwriter.

DEBUT	PEAK	WKS	#	Country Chart Hit	Songwriter	Label (& Number)
2/23/80	76	5		Lost The Good Thing *[w/ Jennifer Warnes]*	*Steve Gillette/David McKechnie*	Regency 45002

GILLEY, Mickey **1970s: #47 / 1980s: #23 / All-Time: #55**

Born on 3/9/1936 in Natchez, Mississippi; raised in Ferriday, Lousiana. Male singer/songwriter/pianist. Co-owner with Sherwood Cryer of Gilleys nightclub in Pasadena, Texas, from 1971-89. Gilley and the club were featured in the movie *Urban Cowboy*. Cousin of **Jerry Lee Lewis** and Reverend Jimmy Swaggart.

DEBUT	PEAK	WKS	#	Country Chart Hit	Songwriter	Label (& Number)
10/19/68	68	6	1	Now I Can Live Again	*Jack Clement*	Paula 1200
4/20/74	❶[1]	16	2	Room Full Of Roses	*Tim Spencer*	Playboy 50056
8/10/74	❶[1]	18	3	I Overlooked An Orchid	*Shirley Lyn/Carl Smith/Carl Story*	Playboy 6004
12/7/74+	❶[1]	12	4	City Lights	*Bill Anderson*	Playboy 6015
3/15/75	❶[1]	15	5	Window Up Above	*George Jones*	Playboy 6031
7/5/75	11	13	6	Bouquet Of Roses	*Bob Hilliard/Steve Nelson*	Playboy 6041
10/18/75	32	9	7	Roll You Like A Wheel *[w/ Barbi Benton]*	*Vic McAlpin*	Playboy 6045
11/22/75+	7	13	8	Overnight Sensation	*Bob McDill*	Playboy 6055
2/21/76	❶[1]	16	9	Don't The Girls All Get Prettier At Closing Time	*Baker Knight*	Playboy 6063
6/26/76	❶[1]	14	10	Bring It On Home To Me	*Sam Cooke*	Playboy 6075
10/16/76	3[1]	14	11	Lawdy Miss Clawdy	*Lloyd Price*	Playboy 6089
2/19/77	❶[1]	17	12	She's Pulling Me Back Again	*Jerry Foster/Bill Rice*	Playboy 6100
6/11/77	4	14	13	Honky Tonk Memories	*Rory Bourke/Gene Dobbins/Johnny Wilson*	Playboy 5807
11/5/77	9	14	14	Chains Of Love	*Ahmet Ertegun/Van Walls*	Playboy 5818
3/18/78	8	13	15	The Power Of Positive Drinkin'	*Rick Klang/Don Pfrimmer*	Playboy 5826
7/29/78	9	14	16	Here Comes The Hurt Again	*Jerry Foster/Bill Rice*	Epic 50580
11/18/78+	13	15	17	The Song We Made Love To	*Ken Wahle*	Epic 50631
3/17/79	10	14	18	Just Long Enough To Say Goodbye	*Jerry Foster/Bill Rice*	Epic 50672
7/21/79	8	14	19	My Silver Lining	*Roger Murrah/Tina Murrah*	Epic 50740
11/17/79+	17	14	20	A Little Getting Used To	*Jerry Taylor*	Epic 50801
5/10/80	❶[1]	16	21	True Love Ways	*Buddy Holly/Norman Petty*	Epic 50876
5/31/80	❶[1]	17	22	Stand By Me	*Ben E. King/Jerry Leiber/Mike Stoller*	Full Moon 46640
				from the movie *Urban Cowboy* starring John Travolta		
10/18/80	❶[1]	16	23	That's All That Matters	*Hank Cochran*	Epic 50940
2/14/81	❶[1]	15	24	A Headache Tomorrow (Or A Heartache Tonight)	*Chick Rains*	Epic 50973
7/4/81	❶[1]	16	25	You Don't Know Me	*Eddy Arnold/Cindy Walker*	Epic 02172
11/7/81+	❶[1]	18	26	Lonely Nights	*Stewart Harris/Keith Stegall*	Epic 02578
3/20/82	3[2]	18	27	Tears Of The Lonely	*Wayland Holyfield*	Epic 02774
7/31/82	❶[1]	16	28	Put Your Dreams Away	*Wayland Holyfield/Richard Leigh*	Epic 03055
11/13/82+	❶[1]	18	29	Talk To Me	*Joe Seneca*	Epic 03326
4/2/83	❶[1]	18	30	Fool For Your Love	*Don Singleton*	Epic 03783
7/16/83	❶[1]	22	31	Paradise Tonight *[w/ Charly McClain]*	*Bill Kenner/Mark Wright*	Epic 04007
9/3/83	5	21	32	Your Love Shines Through	*Wayland Holyfield/Gary Nicholson*	Epic 04018
1/7/84	2[1]	20	33	You've Really Got A Hold On Me	*Smokey Robinson*	Epic 04269
2/18/84	5	18	34	Candy Man *[w/ Charly McClain]*	*Fred Neil/Beverly Ross*	Epic 04368
6/16/84	14	17	35	The Right Stuff *[w/ Charly McClain]*	*Bobby Fischer/Rick Giles/Billy Haynes*	Epic 04489
9/1/84	4	22	36	Too Good To Stop Now (S:4 / A:4)	*Rory Bourke/Bob McDill*	Epic 04563
2/2/85	10	17	37	I'm The One Mama Warned You About (A:9 / S:10)	*Mickey James/Gayle Zeiler*	Epic 04746
5/4/85	12	17	38	It Ain't Gonna Worry My Mind *[w/ Ray Charles]* (A:11 / S:12)	*Richard Leigh*	Columbia 04860
8/24/85	10	22	39	You've Got Something On Your Mind (A:9 / S:10)	*Don Gibson/Roger Murrah/Norro Wilson*	Epic 05460
12/21/85+	5	21	40	Your Memory Ain't What It Used To Be (S:2 / A:6)	*Dickey Betts/Mary Fielder/Kim Morrison*	Epic 05744
7/26/86	6	19	41	Doo-Wah Days (S:6 / A:6)	*Doug Gilmore/Ed Hunnicutt/Gene Vincent*	Epic 06184
4/4/87	16	14	42	Full Grown Fool (S:15 / A:28)	*Allen Reynolds/Kay Taylor*	Epic 07009
7/16/88	49	8	43	I'm Your Puppet	*Spooner Oldham/Dan Penn*	Airborne 10002
10/29/88+	23	19	44	She Reminded Me Of You (S:28)	*Wayland Holyfield/Peter McCann*	Airborne 10008
4/15/89	62	5	45	You Still Got A Way With My Heart	*Ron Moore/Marty Parker*	Airborne 10016
7/15/89	53	8	46	There! I've Said It Again	*Redd Evans/Dave Mann*	Airborne 75740

GILMAN, Billy

Born on 5/24/1988 in Westerly, Rhode Island; raised in Hope Valley, Rhode Island. Male singer.

DEBUT	PEAK	WKS	#	Country Chart Hit	Songwriter	Label (& Number)
5/27/00	20	20	1	One Voice (S:❶[5])	*Don Cook/David Malloy*	Epic
10/14/00+	33	21	2	Oklahoma (S:2)	*John Allen/D. Vincent Williams*	Epic
				above 2 from the album *One Voice* on Epic 62086		
12/9/00+	50	5	3	Warm & Fuzzy	*Don Cook/David Malloy* [X]	Epic
				from the album *Classic Christmas* on Epic 61594		

DEBUT	PEAK	WKS	GOLD	ARTIST / Ranking / Country Chart Hit	Songwriter	Label (& Number)
				GILMAN, Billy — cont'd		
6/2/01	**50**	7		4 **She's My Girl**	*Brian Baker/Zack Turner/Lonnie Wilson*	Epic
9/22/01	**56**	2		5 **Elisabeth**	*Kim Patton/Liz Rose*	Epic
				above 2 from the album *Dare To Dream* on Epic 62087		
				GILMORE, Jimmie Dale		
				Born on 5/6/1945 in Tulia, Texas. Male singer/guitarist.		
8/27/88	**72**	5		1 **White Freight Liner Blues**	*Townes Van Zandt*	Hightone 504
6/10/89	**85**	2		2 **Honky Tonk Song**	*Buck Peddy/Mel Tillis*	Hightone 510
				GIMBLE, Johnny, & The Texas Swing Band		
				Born on 5/30/1926 in Tyler, Texas. Male fiddler. Prolific session musician. Member of the **Nashville Superpickers**.		
				CMA: Musician 1975, 1986, 1987, 1989 & 1990		
1/15/83	**70**	6		1 **One Fiddle, Two Fiddle** *[w/ Ray Price]* /	*Cliff Crofford/John Durrill/Snuff Garrett*	
1/15/83	**flip**	6		2 **San Antonio Rose** *[w/ Ray Price]*	*Bob Wills*	Warner 29830
				above 2 from the movie *Honkytonk Man* starring **Clint Eastwood**		
				GINO THE NEW GUY		
				Born Gino Ruberto on 10/14/1963 in Wabasha, Minnesota; raised in Lake City, Minnesota. Morning show producer at Minneapolis radio station KEEY-FM.		
8/12/95	**56**	11		**Any Gal Of Mine**	*Mutt Lange/Gino Ruberto/Shania Twain* **[N]**	(no label)
				parody of "Any Man Of Mine" by **Shania Twain**; from his homemade album *Any Gal Of Mine* (no label or number)		
				GIRLS NEXT DOOR		
				Female vocal group: Doris King (born on 2/13/1957), Diane Williams (born on 8/9/1959), Cindy Nixon (born on 8/3/1958) and Tammy Stephens (born on 4/13/1961).		
2/1/86	**14**	21		1 **Love Will Get You Through Times With No Money**	S:11 / A:16 *Tim DuBois/Sam Lorber/Jeff Silbar*	MTM 72059
6/14/86	**8**	21		2 **Slow Boat To China**	S:6 / A:8 *Mike Ragogna*	MTM 72068
11/1/86	**26**	14		3 **Baby I Want It**	A:26 *Beth Nielsen Chapman*	MTM 72078
2/7/87	**28**	13		4 **Walk Me In The Rain**	A:28 *Tony Romeo*	MTM 72084
7/4/87	**43**	9		5 **What A Girl Next Door Could Do**	*Roger Ferris*	MTM 72088
10/17/87	**57**	6		6 **Easy To Find**	*Roger Ferris*	MTM 72095
9/10/88	**73**	4		7 **Love And Other Fairy Tales**	*Charlie Black/Buzz Cason/Austin Roberts*	MTM 72106
12/2/89+	**54**	7		8 **He's Gotta Have Me**	*Chapin Hartford/Don Pfrimmer*	Atlantic 88791
9/1/90	**71**	1		9 **How 'Bout Us**	*Dana Walden*	Atlantic
				from the album *How 'Bout Us* on Atlantic 82068		
				GLASER, Chuck		
				Born on 2/27/1936 in Spalding, Nebraska. Male singer/guitarist. Member of **The Glaser Brothers**.		
1/5/74	**81**	7		**Gypsy Queen**	*Greg Quill/Kerryn Tolhurst*	MGM 14663
				GLASER, Jim — **All-Time: #262**		
				Born on 12/16/1937 in Spalding, Nebraska. Male singer/songwriter/guitarist. Member of **The Glaser Brothers**.		
8/31/68	**32**	8		1 **God Help You Woman**	*Jim Glaser*	RCA Victor 9587
1/4/69	**40**	10		2 **Please Take Me Back**	*Jim Glaser/Jimmy Payne*	RCA Victor 9696
5/10/69	**52**	7		3 **I'm Not Through Loving You**	*Jim Glaser/Jimmy Payne*	RCA Victor 0142
10/11/69	**53**	5		4 **Molly**	*Alex Harvey*	RCA Victor 0231
9/1/73	**67**	12		5 **I See His Love All Over You**	*Jim Glaser/Jimmy Payne*	MGM 14590
6/15/74	**68**	8		6 **Fool Passin' Through**	*Bill Holmes/Peggy Russell*	MGM 14713
12/21/74+	**51**	12		7 **Forgettin' 'Bout You**	*Allen Reynolds/Don Williams*	MGM 14758
5/31/75	**88**	5		8 **One, Two, Three (Never Gonna Fall In Love Again)**	*Bob McDill*	MGM 14798
11/15/75	**43**	10		9 **Woman, Woman**	*Jim Glaser/Jimmy Payne*	MGM 14834
11/6/76	**66**	10		10 **She's Free But She's Not Easy**	*Jim Glaser/Jimmy Payne*	MCA 40636
7/23/77	**88**	4		11 **Chasin' My Tail**	*Jim Glaser/Jimmy Payne*	MCA 40742
11/26/77	**86**	4		12 **Don't Let My Love Stand In Your Way**	*Ken Jones*	MCA 40813
11/20/82+	**16**	22		13 **When You're Not A Lady**	*Pat McManus/Lefty Pedroski*	Noble Vision 101
4/2/83	**28**	13		14 **You Got Me Running**	*Parker McGee*	Noble Vision 102
8/27/83	**17**	21		15 **The Man In The Mirror**	*Tony Arata*	Noble Vision 103
1/28/84	**10**	24		16 **If I Could Only Dance With You**	*Pat McManus*	Noble Vision 104
6/9/84	**❶**[1]	24		17 **You're Gettin' To Me Again**	*Woody Bomar/Pat McManus*	Noble Vision 105
11/17/84+	**16**	19		18 **Let Me Down Easy**	S:15 / A:18 *Larry Lafferty/John Michael*	Noble Vision 107
6/29/85	**54**	8		19 **I'll Be Your Fool Tonight**	*Tony Arata*	MCA 52619
9/14/85	**27**	18		20 **In Another Minute**	A:25 / S:28 *Mike Kosser/Curly Putman*	MCA 52672
12/28/85+	**53**	9		21 **If I Don't Love You**	*Fred Knipe*	MCA 52748
4/26/86	**40**	11		22 **The Lights Of Albuquerque**	A:37 *Bucky Jones/Dickey Lee/Bob McDill*	MCA 52808
				GLASER, Tompall		
				Born Thomas Paul Glaser on 9/3/1933 in Spalding, Nebraska. Male singer/songwriter/guitarist. Lead singer of **The Glaser Brothers**.		
10/6/73	**77**	7		1 **Bad, Bad, Bad Cowboy**	*Tompall Glaser*	MGM 14622
3/23/74	**96**	5		2 **Texas Law Sez**	*Judy Riley*	MGM 14701
9/14/74	**63**	8		3 **Musical Chairs**	*Shel Silverstein*	MGM 14740
5/24/75	**21**	19		4 **Put Another Log On The Fire (Male Chauvinist National Anthem)** *[Tompall]*	*Shel Silverstein* **[N]**	MGM 14800
4/24/76	**36**	9		5 **T For Texas** *[w/ His Outlaw Band]*	*Jimmie Rodgers*	Polydor 14314
4/9/77	**45**	9		6 **It'll Be Her**	*Billy Ray Reynolds*	ABC 12261
				also see #20 under **Tompall & The Glaser Brothers**		
12/3/77	**91**	3		7 **It Never Crossed My Mind**	*Bill Chappell*	ABC 12309
2/25/78	**79**	6		8 **Drinking Them Beers**	*Bill Chappell*	ABC 12329

Billboard DEBUT	PEAK	WKS	GOLD		ARTIST / Country Chart Hit	Ranking / Songwriter	Label (& Number)

GLASER BROTHERS, Tompall & The — All-Time: #243

Family trio from Spalding, Nebraska: brothers **Tompall Glaser**, **Chuck Glaser** and **Jim Glaser**. Opened own recording studio in Nashville in 1969 which was a hangout for the budding "outlaw" music movement. Trio split up in 1973. Reunited in 1979 and then split up once again in 1982.

CMA: Vocal Group 1970 // OPRY: 1966

DEBUT	PEAK	WKS	GOLD	#	Country Chart Hit	Songwriter	Label (& Number)
12/31/66+	24	15		1	**Gone, On The Other Hand**	*Jack Clement*	MGM 13611
7/22/67	27	16		2	**Through The Eyes Of Love**	*Mitt Addington/Jack Clement*	MGM 13754
2/24/68	42	9		3	**The Moods Of Mary**	*Jack Clement/Allen Reynolds*	MGM 13880
7/27/68	36	10		4	**One Of These Days**	*Vince Matthews*	MGM 13954
3/22/69	11	16		5	**California Girl (And The Tennessee Square)**	*Jack Clement*	MGM 14036
7/19/69	24	11		6	**Wicked California**	*Jack Clement*	MGM 14064
12/27/69+	30	9		7	**Walk Unashamed**	*Tompall Glaser*	MGM 14096
4/11/70	33	11		8	**All That Keeps Ya Goin'** from the movie *...tick...tick...tick...* starring George Kennedy	*Bill Hoover*	MGM 14113
10/24/70	23	11		9	**Gone Girl**	*Jack Clement*	MGM 14169
6/12/71	22	9		10	**Faded Love** ***[w/ Leon McAuliffe & The Cimarron Boys]***	*Bob Wills/Johnnie Lee Wills*	MGM 14249
8/28/71	7	15		11	**Rings**	*Alex Harvey/Eddie Reeves*	MGM 14291
1/15/72	23	13		12	**Sweet, Love Me Good Woman**	*Bill Holmes/Larry Kennedy*	MGM 14339
6/17/72	15	15		13	**Ain't It All Worth Living For** ***[w/ The Nashville Studio Band]***	*Sammy King*	MGM 14390
1/20/73	46	9		14	**A Girl Like You**	*Tompall Glaser*	MGM 14462
5/12/73	47	8		15	**Charlie**	*Tompall Glaser*	MGM 14516
4/19/80	43	8		16	**Weight Of My Chains**	*Jimmy Payne*	Elektra 46595
11/8/80	34	11		17	**Sweet City Woman**	*Rich Dodson*	Elektra 47056
5/2/81	2^{2}	16		18	**Lovin' Her Was Easier (Than Anything I'll Ever Do Again)**	*Kris Kristofferson*	Elektra 47134
9/19/81	17	14		19	**Just One Time**	*Don Gibson*	Elektra 47193
2/13/82	19	13		20	**It'll Be Her** [R] new version of #6 under **Tompall Glaser**	*Billy Ray Reynolds*	Elektra 47405
6/12/82	28	10		21	**I Still Love You (After All These Years)**	*Mickey Newbury*	Elektra 47461
11/6/82	88	3		22	**Maria Consuela**	*Tim Henderson*	Elektra 69947

GLENN, Darrell

Born on 12/7/1935 in Waco, Texas. Died of cancer on 4/9/1990 (age 54). Male singer.

DEBUT	PEAK	WKS	GOLD	#	Country Chart Hit	Songwriter	Label (& Number)
7/25/53	4	13			**Crying In The Chapel**	A:4 / J:4 / S:7 *Artie Glenn*	Valley 105

GLENN, Howdy

Born in Texas. Black male singer.

DEBUT	PEAK	WKS	GOLD	#	Country Chart Hit	Songwriter	Label (& Number)
9/17/77	62	6		1	**Touch Me**	*Willie Nelson*	Warner 8447
7/29/78	72	5		2	**You Mean The World To Me**	*Billy Sherrill/Glenn Sutton*	Warner 8616

GODFREY, Ray

Born Arnold Godfrey in Copperville, Tennessee. Male singer.

DEBUT	PEAK	WKS	GOLD	#	Country Chart Hit	Songwriter	Label (& Number)
6/27/60	8	15		1	**The Picture**	*Max D. Barnes/Kent Westberry*	Savoy 3021
12/29/62+	20	6		2	**Better Times A Comin'**	*Cal Veale*	Sims 130

GOLDEN, Jeff

Born in Atlanta, Georgia. Male singer/songwriter.

DEBUT	PEAK	WKS	GOLD	#	Country Chart Hit	Songwriter	Label (& Number)
9/10/88	91	2		1	**Southern And Proud Of It**	*Jeff Golden*	MGA 30274
11/26/88	91	2		2	**This Old World Ain't The Same**	*Jeff Golden*	MGA 30275
3/18/89	80	3		3	**That Newsong (They're Playin)**	*Jeff Golden*	Soundwaves 4816
6/24/89	87	3		4	**Singing The Blues**	*Melvin Endsley*	MGA 104

GOLDEN, William Lee

Born on 1/12/1939 in Brewton, Alabama. Male singer. Member of the **Oak Ridge Boys**. Father of **The Goldens**. Also see **Tomorrow's World**.

DEBUT	PEAK	WKS	GOLD	#	Country Chart Hit	Songwriter	Label (& Number)
6/21/86	53	7		1	**Love Is The Only Way Out**	*Larry Boone/Gene Nelson/Paul Nelson*	MCA 52819
11/1/86	72	4		2	**You Can't Take It With You**	*Steve Bogard/Rick Giles*	MCA 52944

GOLDENS, The

Duo of brothers from Brewton, Alabama: Rusty Golden (born on 1/3/1959) and Chris Golden (born on 10/17/1962). Sons of **William Lee Golden**. Chris a member of **Cedar Creek**. Rusty was a member of The Boys Band.

DEBUT	PEAK	WKS	GOLD	#	Country Chart Hit	Songwriter	Label (& Number)
3/5/88	55	6		1	**Put Us Together Again**	*Gerard McMahon*	Epic 07716
7/2/88	63	6		2	**Sorry Girls**	*Rusty Golden*	Epic 07928
5/4/91	67	3		3	**Keep The Faith** from the album *Rush For Gold* on Capitol/SBK 94395	*Jim Sales/Keith Stegall*	Capitol/SBK

GOLDSBORO, Bobby — All-Time: #257

Born on 1/18/1941 in Marianna, Florida. Male singer/songwriter/guitarist. Hosted own syndicated TV show from 1972-75.

DEBUT	PEAK	WKS	GOLD	#	Country Chart Hit	Songwriter	Label (& Number)
3/9/68	56	5		1	**I Just Wasted The Rest** ***[w/ Del Reeves]***	*Hugh X. Lewis*	United Artists 50243
3/30/68	❶^{3}	15	●	2	**Honey**	*Bobby Russell*	United Artists 50283
7/13/68	15	11		3	**Autumn Of My Life**	*Bobby Goldsboro*	United Artists 50318
10/26/68	37	10		4	**The Straight Life**	*Sonny Curtis*	United Artists 50461
3/15/69	49	5		5	**Glad She's A Woman**	*Bodie Chandler*	United Artists 50497
5/3/69	22	11		6	**I'm A Drifter**	*Bobby Goldsboro*	United Artists 50525
8/30/69	15	10		7	**Muddy Mississippi Line**	*Bobby Goldsboro*	United Artists 50565
11/1/69	31	10		8	**Take A Little Good Will Home** ***[w/ Del Reeves]***	*Jerry Chesnut*	United Artists 50591
12/20/69+	56	7		9	**Mornin Mornin**	*Dennis Linde*	United Artists 50614
5/16/70	71	2		10	**Can You Feel It**	*Bobby Goldsboro*	United Artists 50650

DEBUT	PEAK	WKS	GOLD	ARTIST / Country Chart Hit	Ranking / Songwriter	Label (& Number)
				GOLDSBORO, Bobby — cont'd		
1/2/71	**7**	15		11 **Watching Scotty Grow**	*Mac Davis*	United Artists 50727
5/29/71	**48**	7		12 **And I Love You So**	*Don McLean*	United Artists 50776
8/4/73	**100**	2		13 **Summer (The First Time)**	*Bobby Goldsboro*	United Artists 251
1/19/74	**52**	10		14 **Marlena**	*Bobby Goldsboro*	United Artists 371
5/11/74	**62**	6		15 **I Believe The South Is Gonna Rise Again** ***[w/ The TSU Chorus]***	*Bobby Braddock*	United Artists 422
9/7/74	**79**	5		16 **Hello Summertime**	*Bill Backer/Roger Cook/Roquel Davis/Roger Greenaway*	United Artists 529
5/15/76	**22**	14		17 **A Butterfly For Bucky**	*Don Cox/Bobby Goldsboro*	United Artists 793
3/19/77	**82**	5		18 **Me And The Elephants**	*Benny Whitehead*	Epic 50342
7/9/77	**85**	4		19 **The Cowboy And The Lady**	*Bobby Goldsboro*	Epic 50413
10/25/80+	**17**	15		20 **Goodbye Marie**	*Dennis Linde/Mel McDaniel*	Curb 5400
3/7/81	**20**	12		21 **Alice Doesn't Love Here Anymore**	*Bobby Goldsboro*	Curb 70052
7/4/81	**19**	14		22 **Love Ain't Never Hurt Nobody**	*Bobby Goldsboro*	Curb 02117
11/14/81	**31**	11		23 **The Round-Up Saloon**	*Bobby Goldsboro*	Curb 02583
2/20/82	**49**	9		24 **Lucy And The Stranger**	*Bobby Goldsboro*	Curb 02726
				GOODNIGHT, Gary		
				Born in 1954 in Immokalee, Florida. Male singer.		
11/8/80	**90**	3		1 **I Have To Break The Chains That Bind Me**	*Greg Trampe*	Door Knob 138
1/24/81	**91**	2		2 **Make Me Believe**	*Chris Isenberg*	Door Knob 141
3/21/81	**90**	3		3 **Get Me High, Off This Low**	*Steve Clark*	Door Knob 149
5/16/81	**75**	5		4 **Tell Me So**	*Vince Guzzetta*	Door Knob 155
8/8/81	**72**	5		5 **Let Me Fill For You A Fantasy**	*Lloyd Schoonmaker*	Door Knob 159
11/28/81	**90**	3		6 **Losin' Myself In You**	*Lloyd Schoonmaker*	Door Knob 166
1/16/82	**67**	7		7 **Lady, Lay Down (Lay Down On My Pillow)**	*Jane Johnson*	Door Knob 169
7/17/82	**64**	7		8 **Bringing Out The Fool In Me**	*Troy Seals/Eddie Setser*	Soundwaves 4675
				GOODSON, Lloyd		
				Born Cecil Lloyd Goodson on 2/13/1937 in Texas. Male singer/songwriter. Also recorded as **C.L. Goodson**.		
9/13/75	**93**	4		1 **18 Yellow Roses** ***[C.L. Goodson]***	*Bobby Darin*	Island 030
12/11/76	**80**	6		2 **Jesus Is The Same In California**	*Lloyd Goodson/Don Lee*	United Artists 891
				GOODSON, Mitch		
				Born in Dothan, Alabama. Male singer.		
2/9/80	**95**	3		1 **Draggin' Leather**	*Bill Emerson/Jodie Emerson*	Partridge 002
4/12/80	**70**	6		2 **Do You Wanna Spend The Night**	*Eddy Raven*	Partridge 011
				GOODWIN, Bill		
				Born on 6/2/1930 in Cumberland City, Tennessee. Male singer.		
5/11/63	**17**	8		**Shoes Of A Fool**	*James Coleman/Jimmy Day*	Vee Jay 501
				GORDON, Luke		
				Born on 4/15/1932 in Quincy, Kentucky. Male singer.		
12/22/58+	**13**	7		**Dark Hollow**	*Bill Browning*	Island 0640
				GORDON, Noah		
				Born on 9/19/1971 in Sparta, Illinois. Male singer/songwriter/guitarist.		
1/14/95	**68**	3		**The Blue Pages** from the album *I Need A Break* on Patriot 81221	*Noah Gordon/Marvin Morrow*	Patriot
				GORDON, Robert		
				Born in 1947 in Washington DC. Male singer.		
3/31/79	**99**	1		1 **It's Only Make Believe**	*Jack Nance/Conway Twitty*	RCA 11471
6/23/79	**98**	1		2 **Walk On By**	*Kendall Hayes*	RCA 11608
				GORME, Eydie		
				Born on 8/16/1931 in the Bronx, New York. Female singer. Married singer Steve Lawrence on 12/29/1957.		
8/11/73	**94**	5		**Take One Step**	*Robert Allen/Arthur Kent*	MGM 14563
				GOSDIN, Rex		
				Born Equen Gosdin on 5/19/1938 in Woodland, Alabama. Died on 5/23/1983 (age 45). Male singer/songwriter/guitarist. Brother of **Vern Gosdin**. Member of **The Gosdin Bros.**		
7/14/79	**94**	3		1 **We're Making Up For Lost Time**	*Rex Gosdin/V.L. Haywood*	MRC 10589
5/31/80	**51**	10		2 **Just Give Me What You Think Is Fair** ***[w/ Tommy Jennings]***	*Rex Gosdin/V.L. Haywood/Jeff Tweel*	Sabre 4520
11/8/80	**92**	2		3 **Lovin' You Is Music To My Mind**	*Rex Gosdin/Vernon Reed*	Grape Vine 12046
6/11/83	**90**	3		4 **That Old Time Feelin'**	*Rex Gosdin/Carole Halupke*	Sun 1178

GOSDIN, Vern — **1980s: #47 / All-Time: #94**

Born on 8/5/1934 in Woodland, Alabama. Male singer/songwriter/guitarist. Joined the Gosdin Family radio show from Birmingham in the early 1950s. Moved to California in 1960 and formed The Golden State Boys with his brother **Rex Gosdin**; they later recorded together as **The Gosdin Bros.**

DEBUT	PEAK	WKS	GOLD	Country Chart Hit	Songwriter	Label (& Number)
10/30/76+	**16**	15		1 **Hangin' On /**	*Ira Allen/Buddy Mize*	
3/5/77	**9**	15		2 **Yesterday's Gone** **Emmylou Harris** (harmony vocal, above 2)	*Wayne Bradford*	Elektra 45353

DEBUT	PEAK	WKS	GOLD	ARTIST / Country Chart Hit	Ranking / Songwriter	Label (& Number)
				GOSDIN, Vern — cont'd		
6/25/77	7	15		3 Till The End	*Cathy Gosdin*	Elektra 45411
10/22/77	17	13		4 Mother Country Music	*Joe Nixon*	Elektra 45436
1/21/78	23	11		5 It Started All Over Again	*Ken Lusk/Shirl Milete/Gary S. Paxton*	Elektra 45411
5/20/78	9	12		6 Never My Love	*Dick Addrisi/Don Addrisi*	Elektra 45483
10/7/78	13	11		7 Break My Mind	*John D. Loudermilk*	Elektra 45532
3/17/79	16	13		8 You've Got Somebody, I've Got Somebody	*Mike Johnson*	Elektra 46021
7/7/79	21	14		9 All I Want And Need Forever	*Dennis Payne*	Elektra 46052
11/3/79	57	6		10 Sarah's Eyes	*Vern Gosdin/Shirl Melete*	Elektra 46550
1/24/81	28	11		11 Too Long Gone	*Max D. Barnes*	Ovation 1163
5/16/81	7	17		12 Dream Of Me	*Buddy Cannon/Jimmy Darrell/Raleigh Squires*	Ovation 1171
1/16/82	28	15		13 Don't Ever Leave Me Again	*Max D. Barnes*	AMI 1302
7/10/82	22	13		14 Your Bedroom Eyes	*Rich Landers*	AMI 1307
10/23/82+	10	19		15 Today My World Slipped Away	*Vern Gosdin/Mark Wright*	AMI 1310
2/12/83	5	21		16 If You're Gonna Do Me Wrong (Do It Right)	*Max D. Barnes/Vern Gosdin*	Compleat 102
2/12/83	49	7		17 Friday Night Feelin'	*Rich Landers*	AMI 1312
6/4/83	5	22		18 Way Down Deep	*Max D. Barnes/Max T. Barnes*	Compleat 108
10/1/83	10	21		19 I Wonder Where We'd Be Tonight	*Vern Gosdin/Jim Sales*	Compleat 115
3/31/84	❶[1]	25		20 I Can Tell By The Way You Dance (You're Gonna Love Me Tonight)	*Sandy Pinkard/Robert Strandlund*	Compleat 122
7/21/84	10	20		21 What Would Your Memories Do	S:26 *Hank Cochran/Dean Dillon*	Compleat 126
12/1/84+	10	20		22 Slow Burning Memory	A:9 / S:10 *Max D. Barnes/Vern Gosdin*	Compleat 135
5/4/85	20	17		23 Dim Lights, Thick Smoke (And Loud, Loud Music)	S:19 / A:22 *Max Fidler/Joe Maphis/Rose Lee Maphis*	Compleat 142
8/31/85	35	13		24 I Know The Way To You By Heart	*Tony Laiolo*	Compleat 145
3/22/86	68	8		25 It's Only Love Again	*Tim Krekel*	Compleat 153
6/7/86	61	10		26 Was It Just The Wine	*Buddy Cannon/Vern Gosdin*	Compleat 155
9/13/86	51	8		27 Time Stood Still	*Robert Jones*	Compleat 158
11/7/87+	4	23		28 Do You Believe Me Now	S:2 *Max D. Barnes/Vern Gosdin*	Columbia 07627
4/9/88	❶[1]	22		29 Set 'Em Up Joe tribute to **Ernest Tubb**	S:❶[2] *Buddy Cannon/Hank Cochran/Dean Dillon/Vern Gosdin*	Columbia 07762
8/27/88	6	23		30 Chiseled In Stone	S:2 *Max D. Barnes/Vern Gosdin*	Columbia 08003
1/7/89	2[1]	22		31 Who You Gonna Blame It On This Time	*Hank Cochran/Vern Gosdin*	Columbia 08528
5/27/89	❶[1]	22		32 I'm Still Crazy	*Buddy Cannon/Stephen Gosdin/Vern Gosdin*	Columbia 68888
9/30/89+	4	26		33 That Just About Does It	*Max D. Barnes/Vern Gosdin*	Columbia 69084
2/3/90	10	26		34 Right In The Wrong Direction	*Hank Cochran/Vern Gosdin/Mack Vickery*	Columbia
6/23/90	75	1		35 Tanqueray above 2 from the album *Alone* on Columbia 45104	*Hank Cochran/Vern Gosdin/Jim Vest/Mack Vickery*	Columbia
9/1/90	14	20		36 This Ain't My First Rodeo	*Max D. Barnes/Hank Cochran/Vern Gosdin*	Columbia
12/8/90+	10	20		37 Is It Raining At Your House above 2 from the album *10 Years Of Greatest Hits - Newly Recorded* on Columbia 45409	*Hank Cochran/Dean Dillon/Vern Gosdin*	Columbia
5/25/91	64	8		38 I Knew My Day Would Come	*Max D. Barnes/Vern Gosdin*	Columbia
8/24/91	51	12		39 The Garden	*Bobby Fischer/Freddy Weller*	Columbia
11/30/91+	54	13		40 A Month Of Sundays above 3 from the album *Out Of My Heart* on Columbia 47051	*Buddy Cannon/Vern Gosdin/John Northrup*	Columbia
4/10/93	67	5		41 Back When from the album *Nickels And Dimes And Love* on Columbia 52994	*Hugh Prestwood*	Columbia
				GOSDIN BROS., The Duo from Woodland, Alabama: **Vern Gosdin** and **Rex Gosdin**. Rex died on 5/23/1983 (age 45).		
10/7/67	37	11		Hangin' On	*Ira Allen/Buddy Mize*	Bakersfield Int'l. 1002
				GRACIN, Josh Born on 10/18/1980 in Westland, Michigan. Male singer/songwriter. Placed fourth on the second season of TV's *American Idol*. Served as a lance corporal in the United States Marines.		
3/13/04	4	26		1 I Want To Live	*Brett James/Rivers Rutherford*	Lyric Street
9/11/04+	❶[1]	36		2 Nothin' To Lose	*Marcel Chagnon/Kevin Savigar*	Lyric Street
4/30/05	11↑	22↑		3 Stay With Me (Brass Bed) above 3 from the album *Josh Gracin* on Lyric Street 165045	*Jedd Hughes/Brett James/Terry McBride*	Lyric Street
				GRAHAM, Tammy Born on 2/7/1968 in Little Rock, Arkansas. Female singer/pianist.		
5/11/96	63	8		1 Tell Me Again	*Walt Aldridge/Terry McBride*	Career
3/22/97	37	15		2 A Dozen Red Roses	S:4 *Carrie Folks/John Greenebaum/Archie Jordan*	Career
8/2/97	59	4		3 Cool Water above 3 from the album *Tammy Graham* on Career 18842	*Bob DiPiero/Wendell Mobley*	Career
				GRAMMER, Billy Born on 8/28/1925 in Benton, Illinois. Male singer/songwriter/guitarist. ***OPRY: 1959***		
1/5/59	5	13		1 Gotta Travel On based on 19th-century tune that originated in the British Isles	*Paul Clayton/Larry Ehrlich/Ronnie Gilbert/Lee Hays/Fred Hellerman/Dave Lazer/Pete Seeger*	Monument 400
1/19/63	18	5		2 I Wanna Go Home song also known as "Detroit City"	*Danny Dill/Mel Tillis*	Decca 31449
1/11/64	43	2		3 I'll Leave The Porch Light A-Burning	*Jerry Key/Larry Key*	Decca 31562
8/27/66	35	3		4 Bottles	*L.L. Favortie/Eddie Rabbitt*	Epic 10052
12/31/66+	30	12		5 The Real Thing	*Roy Baham*	Epic 10103

Billboard DEBUT	PEAK	WKS	GOLD	ARTIST / Ranking / Country Chart Hit	Songwriter	Label (& Number)
				GRAMMER, Billy — cont'd		
9/23/67	**48**	11		6 **Mabel (You Have Been A Friend To Me)**	*Tom T. Hall*	Rice 5025
8/31/68	**70**	4		7 **The Ballad Of John Dillinger**	*Tom T. Hall*	Mercury 72836
10/18/69	**66**	5		8 **Jesus Is A Soul Man**	*Jack Cardwell/Lawrence Reynolds*	Stop 321
				GRAND, Gil		
				Born on 1/8/1968 in Sudbury, Ontario, Canada. Male singer/songwriter.		
5/16/98	**73**	3		1 **Famous First Words**	*Byron Hill/J.B. Rudd*	Monument
2/13/99	**55**	8		2 **Let's Start Livin'**	*Gil Grand/Steve Rice*	Monument
5/22/99	**70**	1		3 **I Already Fell**	*Gil Grand/Byron Hill*	Monument
				above 3 from the album *Famous First Words* on Monument 68200		
				GRANT, Barry		
				Born in West Palm Beach, Florida. Male singer. Also recorded as **Amarillo** and **Breakfast Barry**.		
9/29/79	**95**	2		1 **We're In For Hard Times** *[Breakfast Barry]*	*Joe Stocks*	Countrystock 1602
12/15/79	**91**	5		2 **Out With The Boys /**	*Waylon Jennings*	
4/26/80	**89**	3		3 **Pretty Poison**	*Eddy Raven*	CSI 001
				AMARILLO:		
12/27/80+	**82**	4		4 **That's The Way My Woman Loves**	*Paul Harrison*	NSD 72
3/21/81	**87**	3		5 **How Long Has This Been Going On /**	*Lamar Morris*	
6/13/81	**70**	5		6 **Somehow, Someway And Someday**	*Don Jackson*	NSD 81
10/10/81	**86**	4		7 **A Little Bit Crazy**	*Tim DuBois/Wood Newton/Dan Tyler*	NSD 104
				GRANT, Tom		
				Born on 8/28/1950 in Milwaukee, Wisconsin. Male singer. Member of **Trinity Lane**.		
1/27/79	**40**	8		1 **If You Could See You Through My Eyes**	*Larry Henley/Jim Hurt*	Republic 036
6/30/79	**63**	5		2 **We've Gotta Get Away From It All**	*David Rogers/Kent Westberry*	Republic 043
9/8/79	**16**	11		3 **Sail On**	*Lionel Richie*	Republic 045
10/16/82	**76**	4		4 **I'm Gonna Love You Right Out Of This World**	*Dave Burgess/Don Pfrimmer*	Elektra 69961
8/10/85	**63**	8		5 **Everyday People** *[w/ Margo Smith]*	*Max D. Barnes/Troy Seals*	Bermuda Dunes 110
				GRASCALS, The		
				Bluegrass group formed in Nashville, Tennessee: Jamie Johnson (vocals), Terry Eldredge (vocals, guitar), Danny Roberts (guitar), Jimmy Mattingly (fiddle), David Talbot (banjo) and Terry Smith (bass).		
12/4/04	**3**[1S]	33		**Viva Las Vegas** *[w/ Dolly Parton]*	*Doc Pomus/Mort Shuman*	Rounder
				from the album *The Grascals* on Rounder 610549		
				GRAY, Billy		
				Born on 12/29/1924 in Paris, Texas. Died of heart failure on 3/27/1975 (age 50). Male singer/songwriter/guitarist. Member of **Hank Thompson**'s Brazos Valley Boys.		
7/24/54	**8**	8		**You Can't Have My Love** *[w/ Wanda Jackson]*	...S:8 / A:8 / J:10 *Billy Gray/Chuck Harding/Hank Thompson*	Decca 29140
				GRAY, Claude — **All-Time: #238**		
				Born on 1/25/1932 in Henderson, Texas. Male singer/songwriter/guitarist. Nicknamed "The Tall Texan."		
3/21/60	**10**	13		1 **Family Bible**	*Willie Nelson*	D 1118
1/9/61	**4**	23		2 **I'll Just Have A Cup Of Coffee (Then I'll Go)**	*Bill Brock*	Mercury 71732
6/26/61	**3**[3]	19		3 **My Ears Should Burn (When Fools Are Talked About)**	*Roger Miller*	Mercury 71826
1/13/62	**26**	1		4 **Let's End It Before It Begins**	*Jimmy Isle/Jay Rainwater*	Mercury 71898
10/20/62	**20**	5		5 **Daddy Stopped In**	*Joe Dowell*	Mercury 72001
2/9/63	**18**	6		6 **Knock Again, True Love**	*Wayne Walker*	Mercury 72063
3/21/64	**43**	12		7 **Eight Years (And Two Children Later)**	*Don Wayne*	Mercury 72236
7/30/66	**22**	10		8 **Mean Old Woman**	*Dallas Frazier*	Columbia 43614
11/26/66+	**9**	18		9 **I Never Had The One I Wanted**	*Claude Gray/Jimmy Louis/Sheb Wooley*	Decca 32039
				also see #25 below		
6/3/67	**45**	9		10 **Because Of Him /**	*Lorene Allen/Walter Haynes*	
6/24/67	**67**	3		11 **If I Ever Need A Lady (I'll Call You)**	*Gene Chrysler*	Decca 32122
				also see #24 below		
9/23/67	**12**	14		12 **How Fast Them Trucks Can Go**	*Casey Anderson*	Decca 32180
5/18/68	**31**	12		13 **Night Life**	*Walt Breeland/Paul Buskirk/Willie Nelson*	Decca 32312
11/9/68	**68**	2		14 **The Love Of A Woman**	*Chuck Rogers*	Decca 32393
5/3/69	**41**	11		15 **Don't Give Me A Chance**	*John West*	Decca 32456
10/25/69	**34**	10		16 **Take Off Time**	*Autry Inman*	Decca 32566
4/11/70	**54**	6		17 **The Cleanest Man In Cincinnati**	*Shel Silverstein*	Decca 32648
7/18/70	**40**	8		18 **Everything Will Be Alright**	*Jack Reno/Joe Wright*	Decca 32697
3/27/71	**41**	9		19 **Angel**	*Claude Gray/Ken Maranell*	Decca 32786
9/2/72	**66**	7		20 **What Every Woman Wants To Hear**	*Joe Wright*	Million 18
1/20/73	**58**	8		21 **Woman Ease My Mind**	*Johnny Nace*	Million 31
10/16/76	**88**	5		22 **Rockin' My Memories (To Sleep)**	*Vern Stovall*	Granny White 10001
1/22/77	**92**	4		23 **We Fell In Love That Way**	*Aaron Allen*	Granny White 10002
6/3/78	**68**	7		24 **If I Ever Need A Lady**	*Gene Chrysler* **[R]**	Granny White 10006
				new version of #11 above		
1/13/79	**78**	6		25 **I Never Had The One I Wanted**	*Claude Gray/Jimmy Louis/Sheb Wooley* **[R]**	Granny White 10007
				new version of #9 above		
2/6/82	**68**	6		26 **Let's Go All The Way** *[w/ Norma Jean]*	*Dusty Rose*	Granny White 10009
2/22/86	**77**	4		27 **Sweet Caroline**	*Neil Diamond*	Country Int'l. 208

DEBUT	PEAK	WKS	GOLD	ARTIST / Country Chart Hit	Ranking / Songwriter	Label (& Number)

GRAY, Damon

Born in Belen, New Mexico. Male singer/songwriter/guitarist.

DEBUT	PEAK	WKS	GOLD	Country Chart Hit	Songwriter	Label (& Number)
2/12/00	**75**	1		**I'm Lookin' For Trouble**	*Kelly Delaney/Dave Gillon/Ronnie Godfrey*	Broken Bow
				from the album *Lookin' For Trouble* on Broken Bow 7777		

GRAY, Dobie

Born Lawrence Brown on 7/26/1940 in Brookshire, Texas. Black male singer.

DEBUT	PEAK	WKS	GOLD	Country Chart Hit	Songwriter	Label (& Number)
3/22/86	**35**	13		1 **That's One To Grow On**	*Jerry Fuller*	Capitol 5562
7/12/86	**42**	9		2 **The Dark Side Of Town**	*Dobie Gray/Troy Seals/Eddie Setser*	Capitol 5596
11/15/86	**67**	9		3 **From Where I Stand**	*Jennifer Kimball/Thom Schuyler*	Capitol 5647
11/21/87	**82**	2		4 **Take It Real Easy**	*Larry Butler/Dean Dillon*	Capitol 44087

GRAY, Jan

Born in Oneida, Kentucky. Female singer.

DEBUT	PEAK	WKS	GOLD	Country Chart Hit	Songwriter	Label (& Number)
11/15/80	**80**	3		1 **No Love At All**	*Wayne Carson/Johnny Christopher*	Paid 106
8/21/82	**85**	3		2 **There I Go Dreamin' Again**	*Johnny MacRae/Bob Morrison/Johnny Wilson*	Jamex 006
11/6/82	**89**	3		3 **Closer To Crazy**	*DeWayne Orender/Woodrow Wright*	Jamex 008
6/18/83	**49**	11		4 **No Fair Fallin' In Love**	*John Scott Sherrill*	Jamex 010
10/15/83	**55**	7		5 **Before We Knew It**	*Lewis Anderson/Fred Koller*	Jamex 011
1/21/84	**51**	9		6 **Bad Night For Good Girls**	*Mitch Johnson/Harry Shannon*	Jamex 012
5/10/86	**64**	6		7 **Cross My Heart**	*Deborah Nash/Jill Wood*	Cypress 8510

GRAY, Mark

Born on 10/24/1952 in Vicksburg, Mississippi. Male singer/songwriter/pianist. Member of **Exile** from 1979-82.

DEBUT	PEAK	WKS	GOLD	Country Chart Hit	Songwriter	Label (& Number)
5/28/83	**25**	20		1 **It Ain't Real (If It Ain't You)**	*Mark Gray/Eddie Setser*	Columbia 03893
10/15/83+	**18**	18		2 **Wounded Hearts**	*Mark Gray/Shawna Harrington*	Columbia 04137
1/28/84	**10**	22		3 **Left Side Of The Bed**	*Mark Gray/Sonny Lemaire/Brian Woods*	Columbia 04324
5/26/84	**9**	23		4 **If All The Magic Is Gone**	*Chester Lester*	Columbia 04464
9/29/84	**9**	21		5 **Diamond In The Dust**	A:8 / S:9 *Mark Gray/Sonny Lemaire*	Columbia 04610
2/23/85	**6**	22		6 **Sometimes When We Touch** *[w/ Tammy Wynette]*	A:5 / S:6 *Dan Hill/Barry Mann*	Columbia 04782
7/27/85	**43**	13		7 **Smooth Sailing (Rock In The Road)**	*Mark Gray/Steve Pippin/Johnny Slate*	Columbia 05403
11/23/85+	**7**	21		8 **Please Be Love**	S:7 / A:7 *J.D. Martin/Jim Photoglo*	Columbia 05695
4/12/86	**14**	17		9 **Back When Love Was Enough**	S:13 / A:15 *Mike Reid/Troy Seals*	Columbia 05857
5/28/88	**69**	5		10 **Song In My Heart** *[w/ Bobbi Lace]*	*Benny Berry*	615 1014
12/17/88+	**70**	5		11 **It's Gonna Be Love** *[w/ Bobbi Lace]*	*Benny Berry*	615 1016

GRAYGHOST

Group from Arkansas led by Bill White. Formerly known as **Razorback**.

RAZORBACK:

DEBUT	PEAK	WKS	GOLD	Country Chart Hit	Songwriter	Label (& Number)
4/11/87	**70**	3		1 **As Long As I've Been Loving You**	*Todd Cerney/Carmen Daily*	Compleat 166
6/13/87	**61**	7		2 **Make A Living Out Of Loving You**	*Joe Gayden/Mac Gayden/Sam Hogin*	Compleat 174
11/28/87	**66**	7		3 **This Ole House**	*Dennis W. Morgan/Frank J. Myers/Don Pfrimmer*	Compleat 184
9/17/88	**70**	4		4 **Where Were You When I Was Blue**	*Lacey Schaffer/Tom Ware*	Mercury 870633

GRAYGHOST:

DEBUT	PEAK	WKS	GOLD	Country Chart Hit	Songwriter	Label (& Number)
6/10/89	**70**	5		5 **Let's Sleep On It**	*Leroy Anderson/Cyril Rawson*	Mercury 874194
9/23/89	**69**	4		6 **If This Ain't Love (There Ain't No Such Thing)**	*Bob McDill/Jim Weatherly*	Mercury 876240

GRAYSON, Jack

Born **Jack Lebsock** in Texas. Male singer/songwriter. Legally changed his name to Jack Grayson.

JACK LEBSOCK:

DEBUT	PEAK	WKS	GOLD	Country Chart Hit	Songwriter	Label (& Number)
8/11/73	**94**	3		1 **For Lovers Only**	*Jack Lebsock*	Capitol 3665
1/5/74	**76**	6		2 **Lovin' Comes Easy**	*Jack Lebsock*	Capitol 3751

"BLACKJACK" JACK GRAYSON:

DEBUT	PEAK	WKS	GOLD	Country Chart Hit	Songwriter	Label (& Number)
4/14/79	**92**	3		3 **I Ain't Never Been To Heaven (But I've Spent The Night With You)**	*Jack Lebsock/Joe Sun*	Churchill 7729
12/22/79+	**65**	8		4 **Tonight I'm Feelin' You (All Over Again)**	*Jack Lebsock/Joe Sun*	Hitbound 4501
				also see #11 below		
6/14/80	**70**	6		5 **The Stores Are Full Of Roses**	*Jack Lebsock/Ted Purvin*	Hitbound 4503
8/30/80	**59**	7		6 **The Devil Stands Only Five Foot Five**	*Jack Lebsock/Ted Purvin*	Hitbound 4504

JACK GRAYSON and Blackjack:

DEBUT	PEAK	WKS	GOLD	Country Chart Hit	Songwriter	Label (& Number)
12/13/80+	**37**	14		7 **A Loser's Night Out**	*Jack Lebsock/Ted Purvin*	Koala 328
4/4/81	**56**	6		8 **Magic Eyes**	*John Gray/Jack Lebsock/Ted Purvin*	Koala 331
7/25/81	**45**	9		9 **My Beginning Was You**	*Jack Lebsock/Ted Purvin*	Koala 334
12/19/81+	**18**	17		10 **When A Man Loves A Woman**	*Calvin Lewis/Andrew Wright*	Koala 340

JACK GRAYSON:

DEBUT	PEAK	WKS	GOLD	Country Chart Hit	Songwriter	Label (& Number)
5/22/82	**38**	11		11 **Tonight I'm Feeling You (All Over Again)**	*Jack Lebsock/Joe Sun* **[R]**	Joe-Wes 81000
				new version of #4 above		
8/14/82+	**68**	6		12 **I Ain't Giving Up On Her Yet**	*Jack Lebsock*	Joe-Wes 81006
1/14/84	**77**	4		13 **Lean On Me**	*Bill Withers*	AMI 1318

GRAYSON, Kim

Born in Dallas, Texas; raised in Plano, Texas. Female singer/actress.

DEBUT	PEAK	WKS	GOLD	Country Chart Hit	Songwriter	Label (& Number)
8/1/87	**74**	3		1 **Love's Slippin' Up On Me**	*Bob McDill*	Soundwaves 4787
12/5/87	**62**	7		2 **If You Only Knew**	*Jane Mariash/Diana Rae*	Soundwaves 4795
4/16/88	**65**	6		3 **Missin' Texas**	*Roger Brown*	Soundwaves 4800

DEBUT	PEAK	WKS	GOLD	ARTIST / Country Chart Hit	Ranking / Songwriter	Label (& Number)
				GREAT DIVIDE, The		
				Group from Stillwater, Oklahoma: Mike McClure (vocals), Scott Lester (guitar), Kelley Green (bass) and J.J. Lester (drums).		
4/18/98	74	1		1 Never Could	*Mike McClure/Mike Shannon*	Atlantic
8/15/98	59	8		2 Pour Me A Vacation	*Mike McClure/Randy Taylor*	Atlantic
				above 2 from the album *Break In The Storm* on Atlantic 83086		
				GREAT PLAINS		
				Group of Nashville session musicians: Jack Sundrud (vocals, guitar), Russ Pahl (guitar), Denny Dadmun-Bixby (bass) and Michael Young (drums). Pahl and Young left in 1993. Lex Browning (guitar) joined in 1996.		
10/5/91	63	7		1 A Picture Of You	*Gary Burr/Jack Sundrud*	Columbia
1/11/92	41	15		2 Faster Gun	*Gary Burr/Jack Sundrud*	Columbia
5/23/92	63	6		3 Iola	*Sue Braswell/Keith Miles/Jack Sundrud*	Columbia
				above 3 from the album *Great Plains* on Columbia 48651		
5/25/96	58	9		4 Dancin' With The Wind	*Craig Bickhardt/Jack Sundrud*	Magnatone
				from the album *Homeland* on Magnatone 105		
				GREEN, Bill		
				Born in Athens, Alabama. Male singer.		
9/18/76	94	3		1 Texas On A Saturday Night	*David Price*	Phono 2629
12/9/78	98	1		2 Fool Such As I	*William Trader*	NSD 11
				GREEN, Jerry		
				Born in Austin, Texas. Male singer/songwriter.		
10/15/77	96	1		1 I Know The Feeling	*Jerry Green*	Concorde 152
12/10/77	96	4		2 Genuine Texas Good Guy	*Jeff Walker/Dave Woodward*	Concorde 154
				GREEN, Lloyd		
				Born on 10/4/1937 in Mobile, Alabama. Male session steel guitarist.		
2/10/73	36	10		1 I Can See Clearly Now	*Johnny Nash* [I]	Monument 8562
6/30/73	73	3		2 Here Comes The Sun	*George Harrison* [I]	Monument 8574
12/25/76+	92	6		3 You And Me	*George Richey/Billy Sherrill* [I]	October 1002
				GREEN, Pat	**2000s: #41**	
				Born on 4/5/1972 in San Antonio, Texas; raised in Waco, Texas. Male singer/songwriter/guitarist.		
4/7/01	60	2		1 Texas On My Mind *[w/ Cory Morrow]*	*Django Walker*	Write On
				from the album *Songs We Wish We'd Written* on Write On 2000		
6/30/01	54	9		2 Texas In 1880 *[w/ Radney Foster]*	*Radney Foster*	Dualtone
				from Foster's album *Are You Ready For The Big Show?* on Dualtone 1102		
9/15/01	35	14		3 Carry On	*Pat Green/Walt Wilkins*	Republic
1/26/02	36	20		4 Three Days	*Radney Foster/Pat Green*	Republic
				above 2 from the album *Three Days* on Republic 016016		
5/31/03	3^2	32		5 Wave On Wave	*Pat Green/David Neuhauser/Justin Pollard*	Republic
12/27/03+	31	20		6 Guy Like Me	*Pat Green/Dave Neuhauser*	Republic
				above 2 from the album *Wave On Wave* on Republic 000562		
12/27/03+	43	3		7 Winter Wonderland	*Felix Bernard/Richard Smith* [X]	Lost Highway
				from the various artists album *A Very Special Acoustic Christmas* on Lost Highway 001038		
8/21/04	21	24		8 Don't Break My Heart Again	*Wade Bowen/Pat Green*	Republic
1/15/05	42	20		9 Somewhere Between Texas And Mexico	*Irene Kelley/Trent Sumnar*	Republic
3/5/05	21	20		10 Baby Doll	*Pat Green/Robert Thomas*	Republic
				above 3 from the album *Lucky Ones* on Republic 003522		

GREENE, Jack — **1960s: #42 / All-Time: #123**

Born on 1/7/1930 in Maryville, Tennessee. Male singer/songwriter/guitarist. Drummer with **Ernest Tubb**'s group from 1962-64. Nicknamed the "Jolly Green Giant."

CMA: Male Vocalist 1967 // OPRY: 1967

DEBUT	PEAK	WKS	GOLD	Country Chart Hit	Songwriter	Label (& Number)
12/25/65+	37	7		1 Ever Since My Baby Went Away	*Marty Robbins*	Decca 31856
10/22/66	❶⁷	23		2 There Goes My Everything	*Dallas Frazier*	Decca 32023
				CMA: Single		
4/22/67	❶⁵	20		3 All The Time /	*Mel Tillis/Wayne Walker*	
5/13/67	63	5		4 Wanting You But Never Having You	*Dallas Frazier*	Decca 32123
9/30/67	2^4	20		5 What Locks The Door	*Vic McAlpin*	Decca 32190
2/17/68	❶¹	15		6 You Are My Treasure	*Cindy Walker*	Decca 32261
7/20/68	4	16		7 Love Takes Care Of Me	*Jimmy Peppers*	Decca 32352
12/14/68+	❶²	17		8 Until My Dreams Come True	*Dallas Frazier*	Decca 32423
5/10/69	❶²	18		9 Statue Of A Fool	*Jan Crutchfield*	Decca 32490
10/4/69	4	14		10 Back In The Arms Of Love /	*Dallas Frazier*	
10/25/69	66	2		11 The Key That Fits Her Door	*Dallas Frazier*	Decca 32558
11/15/69+	2^2	16		12 Wish I Didn't Have To Miss You *[w/ Jeannie Seely]*	*Hank Cochran/Dave Kirby*	Decca 32580
3/14/70	16	11		13 Lord Is That Me	*Dallas Frazier/Whitey Shafer*	Decca 32631
7/18/70	14	14		14 The Whole World Comes To Me /	*Betty Walker*	
7/18/70	flip	14		15 If This Is Love	*Dallas Frazier/A.L. "Doodle" Owens*	Decca 32699

Billboard DEBUT	PEAK	WKS	GOLD	ARTIST / Country Chart Hit	Ranking / Songwriter	Label (& Number)

GREENE, Jack — cont'd

DEBUT	PEAK	WKS	#	Country Chart Hit	Songwriter	Label (& Number)
11/14/70	15	12	16	**Something Unseen** /	*Hank Cochran*	
11/14/70	45	12	17	**What's The Use**	*Jerry Foster/Bill Rice*	Decca 32755
4/10/71	13	14	18	**There's A Whole Lot About A Woman** (A Man Don't Know) /	*Bill Eldridge/Walter Haynes/Gary Stewart*	
4/10/71	flip	13	19	**Makin' Up His Mind**	*Paul Craft*	Decca 32823
9/4/71	26	12	20	**Hanging Over Me**	*Hank Cochran/Red Lane*	Decca 32863
12/11/71+	15	13	21	**Much Oblige** *[w/ Jeannie Seely]*	*George Deaton/Luke Fulford/Gene Simmons*	Decca 32898
3/25/72	31	11	22	**If You Ever Need My Love**	*Lindy Leigh/Marie Wilson*	Decca 32939
8/12/72	19	12	23	**What In The World Has Gone Wrong With Our Love** *[w/ Jeannie Seely]*	*Hank Cochran/Johnny Slate*	Decca 32991
12/9/72+	17	12	24	**Satisfaction**	*Hank Cochran/Red Lane*	Decca 33008
4/14/73	40	12	25	**The Fool I've Been Today**	*Ted Harris*	MCA 40035
8/18/73	11	16	26	**I Need Somebody Bad**	*Ben Peters*	MCA 40108
2/9/74	13	13	27	**It's Time To Cross That Bridge**	*Ben Peters*	MCA 40179
7/27/74	66	9	28	**Sing For The Good Times**	*Ron Fraser*	MCA 40263
11/22/75	88	5	29	**He Little Thing'd Her Out Of My Arms**	*Hank Cochran*	MCA 40481
1/5/80	28	11	30	**Yours For The Taking**	*Red Lane/Danny Morrison*	Frontline 704
5/17/80	48	7	31	**The Rock I'm Leaning On**	*V.L. Haywood/Chris Ryder*	Frontline 706
11/1/80	63	6	32	**Devil's Den**	*Bob Jenkins*	Firstline 709
3/5/83	98	2	33	**The Jukebox Never Plays Home Sweet Home**	*Dan Mitchell*	EMH 0016
6/11/83	92	3	34	**From Cotton To Satin**	*David Chamberlain/Jim Vest*	EMH 0019
7/14/84	93	3	35	**Dying To Believe**	*Steve Chandler/Fred Knipe*	EMH 0031
11/17/84	81	5	36	**If It's Love** (Then Bet It All)	*J.R. Cochran*	EMH 0035

GREENE, Lorne

Born on 2/12/1914 in Ottawa, Ontario, Canada. Died of heart failure on 9/11/1987 (age 73). Acted in several movies and TV shows. Best known as "Ben Cartwright" on TV's *Bonanza*.

DEBUT	PEAK	WKS	#	Country Chart Hit	Songwriter	Label (& Number)
12/5/64	21	10	1	**Ringo**	*Hal Blair/Don Robertson* [S]	RCA Victor 8444
8/13/66	50	2	2	**Waco** (title song from the movie starring Howard Keel)	*Hal Blair/Jimmie Haskell* [S]	RCA Victor 8901

GREEN RIVER BOYS, The — see CAMPBELL, Glen

GREENWOOD, Lee

1980s: #25 / All-Time: #98

Born Melvin Lee Greenwood on 10/27/1942 in Los Angeles, California. Male singer/songwriter. Worked as a blackjack dealer in Las Vegas casinos from 1973-77. Married former Miss Tennessee, Kimberly Payne, on 4/11/1992.

CMA: Male Vocalist 1983 & 1984

DEBUT	PEAK	WKS	#	Country Chart Hit	Songwriter	Label (& Number)
9/19/81+	17	22	1	**It Turns Me Inside Out**	*Jan Crutchfield*	MCA 51159
3/27/82	5	18	2	**Ring On Her Finger, Time On Her Hands**	*Don Goodman/Mary Ann Kennedy/Pam Rose*	MCA 52026
8/7/82	7	17	3	**She's Lying**	*Jan Crutchfield*	MCA 52087
12/11/82+	7	21	4	**Ain't No Trick** (It Takes Magic)	*Jim Hurt/Steve Pippin*	MCA 52150
4/9/83	6	20	5	**I.O.U.** (Grammy: Male Vocal)	*Kerry Chater/Austin Roberts*	MCA 52199
8/20/83	❶[1]	22	6	**Somebody's Gonna Love You**	*Don Cook/Rafe Van Hoy*	MCA 52257
12/17/83+	❶[1]	19	7	**Going, Going, Gone**	*Jan Crutchfield*	MCA 52322
5/26/84	7	17	8	**God Bless The USA** (also see #34 below)	*Lee Greenwood*	MCA 52386
7/21/84	3[2]	20	9	**To Me** *[w/ Barbara Mandrell]*	S:15 / A:23 *Mack David/Mike Reid*	MCA 52415
8/18/84	3[1]	25	10	**Fool's Gold**	S:2 / A:3 *Don Roth/Timmy Tappan*	MCA 52426
12/22/84+	9	19	11	**You've Got A Good Love Comin'**	A:7 / S:10 *Danny Morrison/Jeff Silbar/Van Stephenson*	MCA 52509
2/2/85	19	15	12	**It Should Have Been Love By Now** *[w/ Barbara Mandrell]*	A:18 / S:20 *Jan Crutchfield/Paul Harrison*	MCA 52525
4/20/85	❶[1]	20	13	**Dixie Road**	S:❶[1] / A:❶[1] *Don Goodman/Mary Ann Kennedy/Pam Rose*	MCA 52564
8/31/85	❶[1]	23	14	**I Don't Mind The Thorns** (If You're The Rose)	S:❶[1] / A:❶[1] *Jan Buckingham/Linda Young*	MCA 52656
12/28/85+	❶[1]	20	15	**Don't Underestimate My Love For You**	S:❶[1] / A:❶[1] *Steve Diamond/Steve Dorff/Dave Loggins*	MCA 52741
4/19/86	❶[1]	22	16	**Hearts Aren't Made To Break** (They're Made To Love)	S:❶[1] / A:❶[1] *Steve Dean/Roger Murrah*	MCA 52807
8/9/86	10	18	17	**Didn't We**	S:8 / A:10 *Graham Lyle/Troy Seals*	MCA 52896
11/29/86+	❶[1]	24	18	**Mornin' Ride**	A:❶[1] / S:8 *Steve Bogard/Jeff Tweel*	MCA 52984
5/9/87	5	17	19	**Someone**	S:7 *Charlie Black/Steve Dorff/Austin Roberts*	MCA 53096
8/29/87	9	19	20	**If There's Any Justice**	S:21 *Tony Colton/Mike Nobel/Michael Spriggs*	MCA 53156
12/26/87+	5	22	21	**Touch And Go Crazy**	S:11 *Michael Garvin/Bucky Jones/Tom Shapiro*	MCA 53234
4/30/88	12	18	22	**I Still Believe**	S:22 *Doug Johnson*	MCA 53312
8/20/88	20	17	23	**You Can't Fall In Love When You're Cryin'**	S:24 *Lee Greenwood*	MCA 53386
1/28/89	16	17	24	**I'll Be Lovin' You**	*Paul Overstreet/Don Schlitz*	MCA 53475
6/3/89	43	11	25	**I Love The Way He Left You**	*Tom Brasfield/Robert Byrne*	MCA 53655
9/16/89	55	5	26	**I Go Crazy**	*Paul Davis*	MCA 53716
7/7/90	2[1]	21	27	**Holdin' A Good Hand**	*Rob Crosby/Johnny Few*	Capitol
10/27/90+	14	20	28	**We've Got It Made**	*Sandy Ramos/Bob Regan*	Capitol
3/2/91	52	8	29	**Just Like Me** (above 3 from the album *Holdin' A Good Hand* on Capitol 94153)	*Debbie Hupp/Bob Morrison*	Capitol

DEBUT	PEAK	WKS	GOLD	ARTIST / Ranking / Country Chart Hit	Songwriter	Label (& Number)
				GREENWOOD, Lee — cont'd		
5/11/91	**12**	20		30 **Hopelessly Yours** *[w/ Suzy Bogguss]*	*Curly Putman/Keith Whitley*	Capitol
				from Greenwood's album *A Perfect 10* on Capitol 95541		
10/5/91	**46**	11		31 **Between A Rock And A Heartache**	*Larry Clark/Ron Irving/Dave Simmonds*	Capitol
2/8/92	**58**	6		32 **If You'll Let This Fool Back In**	*John Jarrard/S. Alan Taylor*	Capitol
				above 2 from the album *When You're In Love* on Capitol 95527		
8/22/92	**73**	2		33 **Before I'm Ever Over You**	*Sandy Ramos/Jerry Vandiver*	Liberty
				from the album *Love's On The Way* on Liberty 98834		
9/29/01	**16**	20		34 **God Bless The USA**	S:❶[10] *Lee Greenwood* **[R]**	Curb
				new version of #8 above; from the album *Best of Lee Greenwood: God Bless The USA* on Curb 77862		
				GREGG, Ricky Lynn		
				Born on 8/22/1961 in Longview, Texas. Male singer/songwriter/guitarist.		
3/13/93	**36**	20		1 **If I Had A Cheatin' Heart**	*Wayland Holyfield/Al Turney*	Liberty
7/24/93	**58**	9		2 **Can You Feel It**	*Ricky Lynn Gregg/Don Sampson*	Liberty
				above 2 from the album *Ricky Lynn Gregg* on Liberty 80135		
8/13/94	**73**	2		3 **Get A Little Closer**	*Kent Blazy/Neil Thrasher/Kim Williams*	Liberty
				from the album *Get A Little Closer* on Liberty 28580		
				GREGORY, Clinton		
				Born on 3/1/1966 in Martinsville, Virginia. Male singer/fiddle player.		
1/5/91	**64**	7		1 **Couldn't Love Have Picked A Better Place To Die**	*Bucky Jones/Curly Putman*	Step One
				from the album *Music 'N Me* on Step One 0057		
4/6/91	**26**	20		2 **(If It Weren't For Country Music) I'd Go Crazy**	*Alan Syms*	Step One
7/13/91	**51**	11		3 **One Shot At A Time**	*Curt Ryle*	Step One
11/2/91	**53**	15		4 **Satisfy Me And I'll Satisfy You**	*Bill Dees*	Step One
				above 3 from the album *(If It Weren't For Country Music) I'd Go Crazy* on Step One 0064		
2/15/92	**25**	20		5 **Play, Ruby, Play**	*Tony Brown/Troy Seals*	Step One
7/4/92	**50**	13		6 **She Takes The Sad Out Of Saturday Night**	*Billy Henderson/Curt Ryle*	Step One
9/26/92	**29**	20		7 **Who Needs It**	*Brent Mason/Judy Mehaffey*	Step One
3/6/93	**65**	5		8 **Look Who's Needing Who**	*Kevin Grantt/Clinton Gregory/Randy Hardison*	Step One
				above 4 from the album *Freeborn Man* on Step One 0070		
6/12/93	**52**	7		9 **Standing On The Edge Of Love**	*J.P. Pennington/Troy Seals*	Step One
9/25/93	**59**	5		10 **Master Of Illusion**	*Curt Ryle/Sonny Tillis*	Step One
				above 2 from the album *Master Of Illusion* on Step One 0075		
3/4/95	**68**	4		11 **You Didn't Miss A Thing**	*Bill Rice/Mary Sharon Rice*	Polydor
				from the album *Clinton Gregory* on Polydor 823862		
				GREGORY, Terry		
				Born Teresa Gregory Burdine on 4/30/1956 in Takoma Park, Maryland. Female singer/songwriter.		
5/2/81	**16**	15		1 **Just Like Me**	*Dene Anton/Ron Wilkins*	Handshake 70071
9/5/81	**59**	6		2 **Cinderella**	*Linda Kimball/Mark Sherrill/Josh Whitmore*	Handshake 02442
11/14/81+	**30**	13		3 **I Can't Say Goodbye To You**	*Becky Hobbs*	Handshake 02563
3/13/82	**44**	11		4 **I Never Knew The Devil's Eyes Were Blue**	*Lee Dresser*	Handshake 02736
6/26/82	**48**	7		5 **I'm Takin' A Heart Break**	*Linda Kimball/Mark Sherrill/Josh Whitmore*	Handshake 02959
4/21/84	**75**	5		6 **Cowgirl In A Coupe DeVille**	*John Brandes/Rob Brandes/Mark Burdine/Terry Gregory/Chuck Pyle*	Scotti Brothers 04410
2/2/85	**66**	7		7 **Pardon Me, But This Heart's Taken**	*Kin Vassy/Justin Wilde*	Scotti Brothers 04735
				GRIFF, Ray **All-Time: #283 / SW: #90**		
				Born John Raymond Griff on 4/22/1940 in Vancouver, British Columbia, Canada; raised in Winfield, Alberta, Canada. Male singer/songwriter/guitarist.		
12/23/67+	**49**	9		1 **Your Lily White Hands**	*Ray Griff*	MGM 13855
4/27/68	**50**	7		2 **The Sugar From My Candy**	*Ray Griff*	Dot 17082
10/3/70	**26**	9		3 **Patches**	*Ronald Dunbar/General Johnson*	Royal American 19
11/20/71+	**14**	15		4 **The Mornin' After Baby Let Me Down**	*Ray Griff*	Royal American 46
12/2/72	**62**	6		5 **It Rains Just The Same In Missouri**	*Ray Griff*	Dot 17440
4/28/73	**66**	3		6 **A Song For Everyone**	*Ray Griff*	Dot 17456
8/25/73	**46**	10		7 **What Got To You** (Before It Got To Me) /	*Ray Griff*	
11/24/73+	**42**	11		8 **Darlin'**	*Ray Griff*	Dot 17471
5/11/74	**65**	7		9 **That Doesn't Mean** (I Don't Love My God)	*Ray Griff*	Dot 17501
10/12/74	**91**	2		10 **The Hill**	*Ray Griff*	Dot 17519
3/8/75	**65**	9		11 **If That's What It Takes**	*Ray Griff*	ABC/Dot 17542
9/6/75	**16**	16		12 **You Ring My Bell**	*Ray Griff*	Capitol 4126
1/24/76	**11**	15		13 **If I Let Her Come In**	*Ray Griff*	Capitol 4208
5/22/76	**40**	10		14 **I Love The Way That You Love Me**	*Ray Griff*	Capitol 4266
8/28/76	**24**	12		15 **That's What I Get** (For Doin' My Own Thinkin')	*Ray Griff*	Capitol 4320
12/18/76+	**27**	11		16 **The Last Of The Winfield Amateurs** /	*Ray Griff*	
1/22/77	**flip**	6		17 **You Put The Bounce Back Into My Step**	*Ray Griff*	Capitol 4368
4/23/77	**28**	10		18 **A Passing Thing**	*Ray Griff*	Capitol 4415
7/30/77	**69**	5		19 **A Cold Day In July**	*Ray Griff*	Capitol 4446
10/22/77	**52**	9		20 **Raymond's Place**	*Ray Griff*	Capitol 4492
11/7/81	**87**	3		21 **Draw Me A Line**	*Ray Griff*	Vision 440
7/3/82	**95**	2		22 **Things That Songs Are Made Of**	*Ray Griff*	Vision 442
5/7/83	**86**	3		23 **If Tomorrow Never Comes**	*Ray Griff*	RCA 50722
4/19/86	**71**	5		24 **What My Woman Does To Me**	*Ray Griff*	RCA 50846

DEBUT	PEAK	WKS	GOLD	ARTIST / Country Chart Hit	Ranking / Songwriter	Label (& Number)
				GRIFFITH, Glenda		
				Born in California; raised in Wichita, Kansas. Female singer.		
1/7/78	**96**	4		**Don't Worry ('Bout Me)**	*Marty Robbins*	Ariola America 7680
				GRIFFITH, Nanci		
				Born on 7/16/1954 in Seguin, Texas; raised in Austin, Texas. Female singer/songwriter/guitarist.		
6/21/86	**85**	3		1 **Once In A Very Blue Moon**	*Pat Alger/Eugene Levine*	Philo 1096
1/17/87	**36**	14		2 **Lone Star State Of Mind**	*Pat Alger/Fred Koller/Gene Levine*	MCA 53008
4/25/87	**57**	7		3 **Trouble In The Fields**	*Nanci Griffith/Rick West*	MCA 53082
8/1/87	**64**	6		4 **Cold Hearts/Closed Minds**	*Nanci Griffith*	MCA 53147
12/5/87	**58**	7		5 **Never Mind**	*Harlan Howard*	MCA 53184
4/9/88	**37**	13		6 **I Knew Love**	*Roger Brown*	MCA 53306
7/23/88	**64**	5		7 **Anyone Can Be Somebody's Fool**	*Nanci Griffith*	MCA 53374
				GRIGGS, Andy	**2000s: #33 / All-Time: #285**	
				Born on 8/13/1973 in Moore, Louisiana. Male singer/songwriter/guitarist.		
12/12/98+	**2^{2}**	36		1 **You Won't Ever Be Lonely**	S:5 *Andy Griggs/Brett Jones*	RCA
7/17/99	**10**	22		2 **I'll Go Crazy**	*Andy Griggs/Zack Turner/Lonnie Wilson*	RCA
12/25/99+	**2^{5}**	30		3 **She's More**	*Rob Crosby/Liz Hengber*	RCA
3/4/00	**50**	10		4 **Grow Young With You** *[w/ Coley McCabe]*	*Austin Cunningham/Hillary Lindsey*	RCA
				from the movie *Where The Heart Is* starring Natalie Portman (soundtrack on RCA 67963)		
7/29/00	**50**	7		5 **Waitin' On Sundown**	*Gary Nicholson/Russell Smith*	RCA
9/30/00+	**19**	22		6 **You Made Me That Way**	*Gary Burr/David Malloy*	RCA
				#1-3, 5 & 6: from the album *You Won't Ever Be Lonely* on RCA 67596		
5/19/01	**22**	22		7 **How Cool Is That**	*Andy Griggs/Wendell Mobley/Neil Thrasher*	RCA
2/2/02	**7**	32		8 **Tonight I Wanna Be Your Man**	*Rivers Rutherford/Troy Verges*	RCA
9/21/02	**33**	20		9 **Practice Life** *[w/ Martina McBride]*	*Andy Griggs/Brett James*	RCA
				above 3 from the album *Freedom* on RCA 67006		
2/28/04	**5**	33		10 **She Thinks She Needs Me**	*Sonny Lemaire/Clay Mills/Shane Minor*	RCA
10/16/04+	**5**	33		11 **If Heaven**	*Gretchen Peters*	RCA
				above 2 from the album *This I Gotta See* on RCA 59630		
				GRIGSBY TWINS, The		
				The Grigsby Twins are actually **Kenny Chesney**'s mother (Karen Chesney) and aunt (Sharon Chesney).		
1/10/04	**57**	1		**Silent Night** *[w/ Kenny Chesney]*	*Franz Gruber/Josef Mohr* **[X]**	BNA
				from Chesney's album *All I Want For Christmas Is A Real Good Tan* on BNA 51808		
				GROCE, Larry		
				Born on 4/22/1948 in Dallas, Texas. Male singer/songwriter.		
1/31/76	**61**	8		**Junk Food Junkie**	*Larry Groce* **[L-N]**	Warner/Curb 8165
				recorded at McCabe's guitar shop in Santa Monica		
				GROOMS, Sherry		
				Born in Caruthersville, Missouri; raised in West Memphis, Arkansas. Female singer.		
10/15/77	**97**	1		1 **The King Of Country Music Meets The Queen Of Rock & Roll** *[w/ Even Stevens]*	*Shel Silverstein*	Elektra 45430
9/9/78	**87**	4		2 **Me**	*David Malloy/Even Stevens/Dan Tyler*	Parachute 514
				GROOVEGRASS BOYZ, The		
				Studio group assembled by producer Scott Rouse. Vocalists include **Doc Watson** and **Mac Wiseman**.		
11/23/96	**70**	5		**Macarena**	S:6 *Antonio Romero/Rafael Ruiz* **[N]**	Imprint
				GROVES, Edgel		
				Born in Atlanta, Georgia. Male singer.		
5/9/81	**42**	9		**Footprints In The Sand**	*Jerry Buckner/Gary Garcia* **[S]**	Silver Star 20
				GUITAR, Bonnie		
				Born Bonnie Buckingham on 3/25/1923 in Seattle, Washington. Female singer/songwriter/guitarist. Owner of Dolphin/Dolton record labels.		
6/10/57	**14**	1		1 **Dark Moon**	A:14 *Ned Miller*	Dot 15550
11/11/57	**15**	1		2 **Mister Fire Eyes**	A:15 *Bonnie Guitar/Ned Miller*	Dot 15612
3/5/66	**9**	16		3 **I'm Living In Two Worlds**	*Jan Crutchfield*	Dot 16811
7/23/66	**14**	9		4 **Get Your Lie The Way You Want It**	*Buddy Mize*	Dot 16872
10/15/66	**24**	10		5 **The Tallest Tree**	*Richard Antonio*	Dot 16919
2/25/67	**64**	5		6 **The Kickin' Tree**	*Richard Antonio/Bonnie Guitar*	Dot 16987
4/29/67	**33**	11		7 **You Can Steal Me**	*Fred Lehner*	Dot 17007
8/12/67	**4**	16		8 **A Woman In Love**	*Casey Anderson*	Dot 17029
12/23/67+	**13**	16		9 **Stop The Sun**	*Bonnie Guitar*	Dot 17057
6/8/68	**10**	14		10 **I Believe In Love**	*Charles Anderson*	Dot 17097
9/28/68	**41**	10		11 **Leaves Are The Tears Of Autumn**	*Leon Carr/Earl Shuman*	Dot 17150
7/5/69	**55**	5		12 **A Truer Love You'll Never Find (Than Mine)** *[w/ Buddy Killen]*	*Red Lane*	Paramount 0004
8/23/69	**36**	7		13 **That See Me Later Look**	*Eddie Miller/Curly Putman*	Dot 17276
10/24/70	**70**	3		14 **Allegheny**	*Chris Gantry*	Paramount 0045
8/5/72	**54**	7		15 **Happy Everything**	*Helen Cornelius*	Columbia 45643
12/14/74+	**95**	6		16 **From This Moment On**	*Bonnie Guitar*	MCA 40306
4/19/80	**92**	3		17 **Honey On The Moon**	*Bonnie Guitar*	4 Star 1041
12/2/89	**79**	3		18 **Still The Same**	*Bob Seger*	Playback 75714

Billboard DEBUT	PEAK	WKS	GOLD	ARTIST Ranking / Country Chart Hit	Songwriter	Label (& Number)

GUNN, J.W.

Born John Wesley Gunn in Texas. Male singer/songwriter.

DEBUT	PEAK	WKS	GOLD	Country Chart Hit	Songwriter	Label (& Number)
11/27/82	**87**	3		**Love Me Today, Love Me Forever**	*J.W. Gunn/Mike Hahn*	Primero 1013

GURLEY, Randy

Born Eleanor Rand Gurley on 11/29/1953 in Salem, Massachusetts; raised in Burbank, California. Female singer.

DEBUT	PEAK	WKS	GOLD	Country Chart Hit	Songwriter	Label (& Number)
9/2/78	**77**	5		1 **True Love Ways**	*Buddy Holly/Norman Petty*	ABC 12392
7/14/79	**97**	2		2 **Don't Treat Me Like A Stranger**	*Dave Loggins*	RCA 11611
10/27/79	**92**	3		3 **If I Ever**	*Otha Young*	RCA 11726

GUTHRIE, Jack, and his Oklahomans

Born Leon Guthrie on 11/13/1915 in Olive, Oklahoma. Died of tuberculosis on 1/15/1948 (age 32). Singer/songwriter/guitarist. Cousin of Woody Guthrie.

DEBUT	PEAK	WKS	GOLD	Country Chart Hit	Songwriter	Label (& Number)
7/7/45	**❶[6]**	19		1 **Oklahoma Hills /**	*Jack Guthrie*	
7/21/45	**5**	2		2 **I'm A Brandin' My Darlin' With My Heart**	*Lewis Bellin/Jack Kenney*	Capitol 201
3/1/47	**3[1]**	3		3 **Oakie Boogie**	*Johnny Tyler*	Capitol 341

GUY & RALNA

Husband-and-wife vocal duo of Guy Hovis (born on 9/24/1941 in Tupelo, Mississippi) and Ralna English (born in Spur, Texas). Regulars on **Lawrence Welk**'s TV show from 1970-82. Married from 1968-84.

DEBUT	PEAK	WKS	GOLD	Country Chart Hit	Songwriter	Label (& Number)
7/26/75	**95**	3		**We've Got It All Together Now**	*Glenn Sutton*	Ranwood 1029

H

HADDOCK, Durwood

Born on 8/16/1934 in Lamasco, Texas. Male singer/songwriter/fiddler.

DEBUT	PEAK	WKS	GOLD	Country Chart Hit	Songwriter	Label (& Number)
11/23/74+	**67**	8		1 **Angel In An Apron**	*Ron Hellard/Gary S. Paxton*	Caprice 2004
3/12/77	**98**	1		2 **Low Down Time** also see #5 below	*Durwood Haddock*	Eagle Int'l. 1137
6/17/78	**75**	9		3 **The Perfect Love Song**	*Jim McGowan*	Country Int'l. 132
11/4/78	**87**	4		4 **Everynight Sensation**	*Durwood Haddock/Jim McGowan*	Eagle Int'l. 1148
5/12/79	**96**	2		5 **Low Down Time** same version as #2 above	*Durwood Haddock* **[R]**	Country Int'l. 140
10/25/80	**89**	3		6 **It Sure Looks Good On You**	*Bobby Fischer*	Eagle Int'l. 1161

HAGER, Charley

Born in Tampa, Florida. Male singer.

DEBUT	PEAK	WKS	GOLD	Country Chart Hit	Songwriter	Label (& Number)
1/14/89	**88**	2		**Men With Broken Hearts**	*Hank Williams*	Killer 114

HAGERS, The

Identical twin brothers Jim Hager and John Hager. Born on 8/30/1946 in Chicago, Illinois. Regulars on TV's *Hee Haw*.

DEBUT	PEAK	WKS	GOLD	Country Chart Hit	Songwriter	Label (& Number)
11/8/69	**41**	8		1 **Gotta Get To Oklahoma ('Cause California's Gettin' To Me)**	*Rodney Lay/Buck Owens*	Capitol 2647
4/4/70	**74**	2		2 **Loneliness Without You**	*Jim Hager/Shannon Lindell*	Capitol 2740
5/23/70	**50**	6		3 **Goin' Home To Your Mother**	*Ted Anderson*	Capitol 2803
9/12/70	**59**	8		4 **Silver Wings**	*Merle Haggard*	Capitol 2887
1/23/71	**47**	6		5 **I'm Miles Away**	*Robert McCoy*	Capitol 3012

HAGGARD, Marty

Born on 6/18/1958 in Bakersfield, California. Male singer/guitarist. Son of **Merle Haggard**; brother of **Noel Haggard**.

DEBUT	PEAK	WKS	GOLD	Country Chart Hit	Songwriter	Label (& Number)
3/7/81	**85**	3		1 **Charleston Cotton Mill**	*Dave Kirby/Red Lane*	Dimension 1016
9/13/86	**62**	7		2 **Talkin' Blue Eyes**	*John Jarrard/Charles Quillen*	MTM 72073
3/21/87	**75**	6		3 **Weekend Cowboys**	*Mickey Carroll*	MTM 72085
3/26/88	**57**	8		4 **Trains Make Me Lonesome**	*Paul Overstreet/Thom Schuyler*	MTM 72103
6/25/88	**70**	5		5 **Now You See 'Em, Now You Don't**	*Sterling Whipple*	MTM 72107

HAGGARD, Merle — 1960s: #19 / 1970s: #2 / 1980s: #3 / All-Time: #4 // HOF: 1994

Born on 4/6/1937 in Bakersfield, California. Male singer/songwriter/guitarist. Served nearly three years in San Quentin prison for burglary, from 1957-60. Granted full pardon by Governor Ronald Reagan on 3/14/1972. Formed his backing band, The Strangers, in 1965. Acted in several movies and TV shows. Formerly married to singers **Bonnie Owens** and **Leona Williams**. Father of **Marty Haggard** and **Noel Haggard**. Also see **Same Old Train**.

CMA: Male Vocalist 1970 / Entertainer 1970 / Vocal Duo (with Willie Nelson) 1983

DEBUT	PEAK	WKS	GOLD	Country Chart Hit	Songwriter	Label (& Number)
12/28/63+	**19**	3		1 **Sing A Sad Song**	*Wynn Stewart*	Tally 155
6/6/64	**45**	5		2 **Sam Hill**	*Tommy Collins*	Tally 178
9/12/64	**28**	26		3 **Just Between The Two Of Us** *[w/ Bonnie Owens]*	*Liz Anderson*	Tally 181
1/2/65	**10**	22		4 **(My Friends Are Gonna Be) Strangers**	*Liz Anderson*	Tally 179
9/18/65	**42**	4		5 **I'm Gonna Break Every Heart I Can**	*Merle Haggard*	Capitol 5460
				MERLE HAGGARD And The Strangers:		
4/9/66	**5**	27		6 **Swinging Doors**	*Merle Haggard*	Capitol 5600
8/27/66	**3[1]**	20		7 **The Bottle Let Me Down**	*Merle Haggard*	Capitol 5704
12/17/66+	**❶[1]**	18		8 **The Fugitive /**	*Casey Anderson/Liz Anderson*	
12/31/66+	**32**	11		9 **Someone Told My Story**	*Merle Haggard*	Capitol 5803
3/18/67	**2[2]**	18		10 **I Threw Away The Rose**	*Merle Haggard*	Capitol 5844

DEBUT	PEAK	WKS	GOLD	ARTIST Ranking / Country Chart Hit	Songwriter	Label (& Number)
				MERLE HAGGARD And The Strangers:		
7/8/67	❶[1]	16		11 Branded Man	*Merle Haggard*	Capitol 5931
11/18/67+	❶[2]	20		12 Sing Me Back Home	*Merle Haggard*	Capitol 2017
3/9/68	❶[2]	15		13 The Legend Of Bonnie And Clyde	*Merle Haggard*	Capitol 2123
7/27/68	❶[4]	15		14 Mama Tried	*Merle Haggard*	Capitol 2219
				Grammy: Hall of Fame; from the movie *Killers Three* starring Haggard		
11/9/68+	3[3]	16		15 I Take A Lot Of Pride In What I Am	*Merle Haggard*	Capitol 2289
2/22/69	❶[1]	17		16 Hungry Eyes	*Merle Haggard*	Capitol 2383
7/5/69	❶[1]	15		17 Workin' Man Blues	*Merle Haggard*	Capitol 2503
10/11/69	❶[4]	16		18 Okie From Muskogee	*Eddie Burris/Merle Haggard*	Capitol 2626
				CMA: Single		
2/7/70	❶[3]	14		19 The Fightin' Side Of Me	*Merle Haggard*	Capitol 2719
4/18/70	9	13		20 Street Singer	*Roy Nichols* [I]	Capitol 2778
6/13/70	3[1]	14		21 Jesus, Take A Hold	*Merle Haggard*	Capitol 2838
10/10/70	3[3]	17		22 I Can't Be Myself /	*Merle Haggard*	
10/17/70	flip	16		23 Sidewalks Of Chicago	*Dave Kirby*	Capitol 2891
2/20/71	3[2]	13		24 Soldier's Last Letter	*Henry Stewart/Ernest Tubb*	Capitol 3024
7/3/71	2[2]	15		25 Someday We'll Look Back	*Merle Haggard*	Capitol 3112
10/16/71	❶[2]	14		26 Daddy Frank (The Guitar Man)	*Merle Haggard*	Capitol 3198
12/4/71+	❶[3]	16		27 Carolyn	*Tommy Collins*	Capitol 3222
3/25/72	❶[2]	15		28 Grandma Harp /	*Merle Haggard*	
4/29/72	flip	10		29 Turnin' Off A Memory	*Merle Haggard*	Capitol 3294
9/2/72	❶[1]	14		30 It's Not Love (But It's Not Bad)	*Hank Cochran/Glenn Martin*	Capitol 3419
12/9/72+	❶[1]	14		31 I Wonder If They Ever Think Of Me	*Merle Haggard*	Capitol 3488
3/10/73	3[1]	14		32 The Emptiest Arms In The World	*Merle Haggard*	Capitol 3552
6/30/73	❶[2]	16		33 Everybody's Had The Blues	*Merle Haggard* [L]	Capitol 3641
10/27/73	❶[4]	17		34 If We Make It Through December *[Merle Haggard]*	*Merle Haggard* [X]	Capitol 3746
3/2/74	❶[1]	15		35 Things Aren't Funny Anymore	*Merle Haggard*	Capitol 3830
6/29/74	❶[1]	14		36 Old Man From The Mountain	*Merle Haggard*	Capitol 3900
11/9/74+	❶[1]	15		37 Kentucky Gambler	*Dolly Parton*	Capitol 3974
2/15/75	❶[2]	14		38 Always Wanting You	*Merle Haggard*	Capitol 4027
5/24/75	❶[1]	15		39 Movin' On	*Merle Haggard*	Capitol 4085
				theme from the TV series starring Claude Akins		
10/4/75	❶[1]	15		40 It's All In The Movies	*Kelli Haggard/Merle Haggard*	Capitol 4141
1/17/76	❶[1]	14		41 The Roots Of My Raising	*Tommy Collins*	Capitol 4204
5/22/76	10	11		42 Here Comes The Freedom Train	*Stephen Lemberg*	Capitol 4267
9/11/76	❶[1]	13		43 Cherokee Maiden /	*Cindy Walker*	
9/11/76	flip	13		44 What Have You Got Planned Tonight Diana	*Dave Kirby*	Capitol 4326
				MERLE HAGGARD:		
4/2/77	2[2]	14		45 If We're Not Back In Love By Monday	*Glenn Martin/Sonny Throckmorton*	MCA 40700
7/2/77	2[2]	14		46 Ramblin' Fever /	*Merle Haggard*	
7/16/77	flip	12		47 When My Blue Moon Turns To Gold Again	*Gene Sullivan/Wiley Walker*	MCA 40743
9/3/77	16	13		48 A Working Man Can't Get Nowhere Today	*Merle Haggard*	Capitol 4477
10/8/77	4	15		49 From Graceland To The Promised Land	*Merle Haggard*	MCA 40804
				The Jordanaires (backing vocals); tribute to **Elvis Presley**		
1/14/78	12	12		50 Running Kind /	*Merle Haggard*	
2/4/78	flip	9		51 Making Believe	*Jimmy Work*	Capitol 4525
3/18/78	2[2]	16		52 I'm Always On A Mountain When I Fall	*Chuck Howard*	MCA 40869
7/8/78	91	4		53 Willie *[w/ Hank Cochran]*	*Glenn Martin*	Capitol 4585
8/12/78	2[3]	13		54 It's Been A Great Afternoon /	*Merle Haggard*	
9/23/78	flip	7		55 Love Me When You Can	*Merle Haggard*	MCA 40936
10/28/78	8	12		56 The Bull And The Beaver *[w/ Leona Williams]*	*Merle Haggard/Leona Williams*	MCA 40962
10/28/78	82	4		57 The Way It Was In '51 *[w/ The Strangers]*	*Merle Haggard*	Capitol 4636
				recorded in 1975		
4/14/79	4	13		58 Red Bandana /	*Merle Haggard*	
4/14/79	flip	13		59 I Must Have Done Something Bad	*Red Lane*	MCA 41007
9/15/79	4	13		60 My Own Kind Of Hat /	*Merle Haggard/Red Lane*	
9/15/79	flip	13		61 Heaven Was A Drink Of Wine	*Whitey Shafer*	MCA 41112
10/13/79	31	9		62 Walkin' The Floor Over You *[w/ Ernest Tubb]*	*Ernest Tubb*	Cachet 4507
3/15/80	2[2]	14		63 The Way I Am	*Sonny Throckmorton*	MCA 41200
5/17/80	❶[1]	16		64 Bar Room Buddies *[w/ Clint Eastwood]*	*Milton Brown/Cliff Crofford/Steve Dorff/Snuff Garrett*	Elektra 46634
7/5/80	3[1]	15		65 Misery And Gin	*John Durrill/Snuff Garrett*	MCA 41255
				above 2 from the movie *Bronco Billy* starring **Clint Eastwood**		
10/25/80+	❶[1]	17		66 I Think I'll Just Stay Here And Drink	*Merle Haggard*	MCA 51014
2/14/81	9	14		67 Leonard	*Merle Haggard*	MCA 51048
				tribute to **Tommy Collins** (real name: Leonard Sipes)		
3/28/81	41	8		68 I Can't Hold Myself In Line *[w/ Johnny Paycheck]*	*Merle Haggard*	Epic 51012
6/6/81	4	16		69 Rainbow Stew	*Merle Haggard*	MCA 51120
9/5/81	45	9		70 Lefty *[w/ David Frizzell]*	*Larry Bastian*	Warner 49778
9/19/81	❶[1]	17		71 My Favorite Memory	*Merle Haggard*	Epic 02504
1/16/82	❶[1]	19		72 Big City	*Merle Haggard/Dean Holloway*	Epic 02686
				Leona Williams (harmony vocal)		
4/17/82	49	10		73 Dealing With The Devil	*Eddy Raven/Whitey Shafer*	MCA 52020

DEBUT	PEAK	WKS	GOLD	ARTIST Ranking Country Chart Hit	Songwriter	Label (& Number)
				HAGGARD, Merle — cont'd		
5/15/82	2[2]	18		74 **Are The Good Times Really Over** (I Wish A Buck Was Still Silver)	*Merle Haggard*	Epic 02894
8/7/82	❶[1]	15		75 **Yesterday's Wine** *[w/ George Jones]*	*Willie Nelson*	Epic 03072
10/23/82+	❶[1]	21		76 **Going Where The Lonely Go**	*Merle Haggard*	Epic 03315
12/4/82+	10	19		77 **C.C. Waterback** *[w/ George Jones]*	*Merle Haggard*	Epic 03405
1/15/83	6	18		78 **Reasons To Quit** *[w/ Willie Nelson]*	*Merle Haggard*	Epic 03494
3/12/83	❶[1]	18		79 **You Take Me For Granted**	*Leona Williams*	Epic 03723
4/30/83	❶[1]	21		80 **Pancho And Lefty** *[w/ Willie Nelson]*	*Townes Van Zandt*	Epic 03842
5/28/83	42	14		81 **We're Strangers Again** *[w/ Leona Williams]*	*Merle Haggard/Leona Williams*	Mercury 812214
7/16/83	3[1]	20		82 **What Am I Gonna Do** (With The Rest Of My Life)	*Merle Haggard*	Epic 04006
10/8/83	54	10		83 **It's All In The Game**	*Charles Dawes/Carl Sigman*	MCA 52276
11/19/83+	❶[1]	21		84 **That's The Way Love Goes**	*Lefty Frizzell/Whitey Shafer*	Epic 04226
				Grammy: Male Vocal; also see #107 below		
3/24/84	❶[1]	21		85 **Someday When Things Are Good**	*Leona Williams*	Epic 04402
7/14/84	❶[1]	18		86 **Let's Chase Each Other Around The Room**	*Merle Haggard/Freddy Powers/Sheril Rodgers*	Epic 04512
10/27/84+	❶[1]	22		87 **A Place To Fall Apart** *[w/ Janie Fricke]* S:❶[1] / A:❶[1]	*Merle Haggard/Willie Nelson/Freddy Powers*	Epic 04663
3/16/85	❶[1]	19		88 **Natural High** S:❶[1] / A:❶[1]	*Freddy Powers*	Epic 04830
				Janie Frickie (harmony vocal)		
6/15/85	55	10		89 **Make-Up And Faded Blue Jeans**	*Merle Haggard*	MCA 52595
				recorded in 1980		
7/6/85	10	17		90 **Kern River** S:10 / A:10	*Merle Haggard*	Epic 05426
10/5/85	36	15		91 **Amber Waves Of Grain**	*Merle Haggard*	Epic 05659
12/14/85	60	11		92 **American Waltz**	*John Greenebaum/Troy Seals/Eddie Setser*	Epic 05734
1/25/86	5	20		93 **I Had A Beautiful Time** S:4 / A:5	*Merle Haggard*	Epic 05782
5/31/86	9	23		94 **A Friend In California** S:6 / A:7	*Freddy Powers*	Epic 06097
10/18/86	21	15		95 **Out Among The Stars** S:18 / A:22	*Adam Mitchell*	Epic 06344
4/18/87	58	8		96 **Almost Persuaded**	*Billy Sherrill/Glenn Sutton*	Epic 07036
9/19/87	58	5		97 **If I Could Only Fly** *[w/ Willie Nelson]*	*Waylon Jennings*	Epic 07400
11/21/87+	❶[1]	22		98 **Twinkle, Twinkle Lucky Star** S:❶[3]	*Merle Haggard*	Epic 07631
3/19/88	9	19		99 **Chill Factor** S:6	*Merle Haggard*	Epic 07754
7/9/88	22	18		100 **We Never Touch At All** S:14	*Hank Cochran*	Epic 07944
11/19/88+	23	17		101 **You Babe** S:19	*Whitey Shafer*	Epic 08111
4/8/89	18	18		102 **5:01 Blues**	*Michael Garvin/Jeff Tweel*	Epic 68598
7/22/89	4	26		103 **A Better Love Next Time**	*Johnny Christopher/Bobby Wood*	Epic 68979
12/2/89+	23	16		104 **If You Want To Be My Woman**	*Merle Haggard*	Epic 73076
9/1/90	60	6		105 **When It Rains It Pours**	*John Cody Carter*	Curb
				from the album *Blue Jungle* on Curb 77313		
1/29/94	58	12		106 **In My Next Life**	*Max D. Barnes*	Curb
				from the album *Merle Haggard 1994* on Curb 77636		
9/18/99	56	7		107 **That's The Way Love Goes** *[w/ Jewel]*	*Lefty Frizzell/Whitey Shafer* **[R]**	BNA
				new version of #84 above; from the album *For The Record - 43 Legendary Hits* on BNA 67844		

Almost Persuaded ['87]
Always Wanting You ['75]
Amber Waves Of Grain ['85]
American Waltz ['85]
Are The Good Times Really Over (I Wish A Buck Was Still Silver) ['82]
Bar Room Buddies ['80]
Better Love Next Time ['89]
Big City ['82]
Bottle Let Me Down ['66]
Branded Man ['67]
Bull And The Beaver ['78]
C.C. Waterback ['83]
Carolyn ['72]
Cherokee Maiden ['76]
Chill Factor ['88]
Daddy Frank (The Guitar Man) ['71]
Dealing With The Devil ['82]
Emptiest Arms In The World ['73]
Everybody's Had The Blues ['73]
Fightin' Side Of Me ['70]
5:01 Blues ['89]
Friend In California ['86]
From Graceland To The Promised Land ['77]
Fugitive ['67]
Going Where The Lonely Go ['83]
Grandma Harp ['72]
Heaven Was A Drink Of Wine ['79]
Here Comes The Freedom Train ['76]
Hungry Eyes ['69]
I Can't Be Myself ['70]
I Can't Hold Myself In Line ['81]
I Had A Beautiful Time ['86]
I Must Have Done Something Bad ['79]
I Take A Lot Of Pride In What I Am ['69]
I Think I'll Just Stay Here And Drink ['81]
I Threw Away The Rose ['67]
I Wonder If They Ever Think Of Me ['73]
I'm Always On A Mountain When I Fall ['78]
I'm Gonna Break Every Heart I Can ['65]
If I Could Only Fly ['87]
If We Make It Through December ['73]
If We're Not Back In Love By Monday ['77]
If You Want To Be My Woman ['90]
In My Next Life ['94]
It's All In The Game ['83]
It's All In The Movies ['75]
It's Been A Great Afternoon ['78]
It's Not Love (But It's Not Bad) ['72]
Jesus, Take A Hold ['70]
Just Between The Two Of Us ['64]
Kentucky Gambler ['75]
Kern River ['85]
Lefty ['81]
Legend Of Bonnie And Clyde ['68]
Leonard ['81]
Let's Chase Each Other Around The Room ['84]
Love Me When You Can ['78]
Make-Up And Faded Blue Jeans ['85]
Making Believe ['78]
Mama Tried ['68]
Misery And Gin ['80]
Movin' On ['75]
My Favorite Memory ['81]
(My Friends Are Gonna Be) Strangers ['65]
My Own Kind Of Hat ['79]
Natural High ['85]
Okie From Muskogee ['69]
Old Man From The Mountain ['74]
Out Among The Stars ['86]
Pancho And Lefty ['83]
Place To Fall Apart ['85]
Rainbow Stew ['81]
Ramblin' Fever ['77]
Reasons To Quit ['83]
Red Bandana ['79]
Roots Of My Raising ['76]
Running Kind ['78]
Sam Hill ['64]
Sidewalks Of Chicago ['70]
Sing A Sad Song ['64]
Sing Me Back Home ['68]
Soldier's Last Letter ['71]
Someday We'll Look Back ['71]
Someday When Things Are Good ['84]
Someone Told My Story ['67]
Street Singer ['70]
Swinging Doors ['66]
That's The Way Love Goes ['84]
That's The Way Love Goes ['99]
Things Aren't Funny Anymore ['74]
Turnin' Off A Memory ['72]
Twinkle, Twinkle Lucky Star ['88]
Walkin' The Floor Over You ['79]
Way I Am ['80]
Way It Was In '51 ['78]
We Never Touch At All ['88]
We're Strangers Again ['83]
What Am I Gonna Do (With The Rest Of My Life) ['83]
What Have You Got Planned Tonight Diana ['76]
When It Rains It Pours ['90]
When My Blue Moon Turns To Gold Again ['77]
Willie ['78]
Workin' Man Blues ['69]
Working Man Can't Get Nowhere Today ['77]
Yesterday's Wine ['82]
You Babe ['89]
You Take Me For Granted ['83]

DEBUT	PEAK	WKS	GOLD	ARTIST Ranking Country Chart Hit	Songwriter	Label (& Number)
				HAGGARD, Noel		
				Born on 4/4/1963 in Bakersfield, California. Male singer/guitarist. Son of **Merle Haggard**; brother of **Marty Haggard**.		
2/1/97	75	1		1 **Once You Learn**	*Billy Livsey/Don Schlitz*	Atlantic
8/9/97	75	1		2 **Tell Me Something Bad About Tulsa**	*Red Lane*	Atlantic
				above 2 from the album *One Lifetime* on Atlantic 82877		
				HALL, Buck		
				Born in Arlington, Texas. Male singer.		
9/23/89	87	2		**Swinging Doors**	*Merle Haggard*	Track 206

Billboard DEBUT	PEAK	WKS	GOLD	ARTIST Ranking / Country Chart Hit	Songwriter	Label (& Number)

HALL, Connie

Born on 6/24/1929 in Walden, Kentucky; raised in Cincinnati, Ohio. Female singer/songwriter.

DEBUT	PEAK	WKS	#	Country Chart Hit	Songwriter	Label (& Number)
2/15/60	21	4	1	The Bottle Or Me	*Bill Franks/Jimmie Skinner*	Mercury 71540
10/10/60	25	2	2	The Poison In Your Hand /	*Connie Hall*	
10/17/60	17	2	3	It's Not Wrong	*Warner MacPherson/Webb Pierce*	Decca 31130
				answer to "Is It Wrong (For Loving You)" by **Warner Mack**		
4/24/61	20	5	4	Sleep, Baby, Sleep	*Bill Anderson/Buddy Killen/Curly Putnam*	Decca 31208
1/20/62	23	5	5	What A Pleasure	*Ray Lunsford*	Decca 31310
1/5/63	14	3	6	Fool Me Once	*Bill Anderson/Moneen Carpenter*	Decca 31438

HALL, Rebecca

Born in Rustburg, Virginia. Female singer.

DEBUT	PEAK	WKS	#	Country Chart Hit	Songwriter	Label (& Number)
8/3/85	83	3		Heartbeat	*Jamie O'Hara/Kevin Welch*	Capitol 5486

HALL, Sammy

Born in North Carolina. Male singer.

DEBUT	PEAK	WKS	#	Country Chart Hit	Songwriter	Label (& Number)
4/28/84	88	3		Anything For Your Love	*Stewart Harris/Roger Murrah*	Dream 300

HALL, Tom T. — 1970s: #15 / All-Time: #69

Born Thomas Hall on 5/25/1936 in Olive Hill, Kentucky. Male singer/songwriter/guitarist. Worked as a DJ on WMOR-Morehead, Kentucky. Added "T." to his name when he began singing career. Hosted *Pop Goes The Country* TV series. Known as "The Storyteller."

OPRY: 1980

DEBUT	PEAK	WKS	#	Country Chart Hit	Songwriter	Label (& Number)
8/5/67	30	10	1	I Washed My Face In The Morning Dew	*Tom T. Hall*	Mercury 72700
5/11/68	66	3	2	The World The Way I Want It	*Tom T. Hall*	Mercury 72786
9/14/68	68	4	3	Ain't Got The Time	*Tom T. Hall*	Mercury 72835
11/16/68+	4	18	4	Ballad Of Forty Dollars	*Tom T. Hall*	Mercury 72863
5/10/69	40	8	5	Strawberry Farms	*Tom T. Hall*	Mercury 72913
8/23/69	5	15	6	Homecoming	*Tom T. Hall*	Mercury 72951
12/20/69+	❶[2]	15	7	A Week In A Country Jail	*Tom T. Hall*	Mercury 72998
4/4/70	8	14	8	Shoeshine Man	*Tom T. Hall*	Mercury 73039
7/11/70	8	13	9	Salute To A Switchblade	*Tom T. Hall*	Mercury 73078
11/14/70	23	13	10	Day Drinkin' *[w/ Dave Dudley]*	*Tom T. Hall*	Mercury 73139
12/26/70+	14	12	11	One Hundred Children	*Tom T. Hall*	Mercury 73140
4/3/71	21	11	12	Ode To A Half A Pound Of Ground Round	*Tom T. Hall*	Mercury 73189
7/10/71	❶[2]	20	13	The Year That Clayton Delaney Died	*Tom T. Hall*	Mercury 73221
3/18/72	8	15	14	Me And Jesus	*Tom T. Hall*	Mercury 73278
				The Mt. Pisgah United Methodist Church Choir (backing vocals)		
7/8/72	11	12	15	The Monkey That Became President	*Tom T. Hall*	Mercury 73297
10/7/72	26	9	16	More About John Henry	*Tom T. Hall*	Mercury 73327
12/2/72+	❶[1]	15	17	(Old Dogs-Children And) Watermelon Wine	*Tom T. Hall*	Mercury 73346
12/16/72+	14	12	18	Hello We're Lonely *[w/ Patti Page]*	*Tom T. Hall*	Mercury 73347
5/5/73	3[2]	13	19	Ravishing Ruby	*Tom T. Hall*	Mercury 73377
6/30/73	16	11	20	Watergate Blues /	*Tom T. Hall* **[N]**	
6/30/73	flip	11	21	Spokane Motel Blues	*Tom T. Hall*	Mercury 73394
11/10/73+	❶[2]	18	22	I Love	*Tom T. Hall*	Mercury 73436
6/1/74	2[2]	15	23	That Song Is Driving Me Crazy	*Tom T. Hall*	Mercury 73488
9/14/74	❶[1]	16	24	Country Is	*Tom T. Hall*	Mercury 73617
12/21/74	69	16	25	Sneaky Snake /	*Tom T. Hall*	
12/28/74+	❶[1]	15	26	I Care	*Tom T. Hall*	Mercury 73641
5/31/75	8	15	27	Deal	*Tom T. Hall*	Mercury 73686
9/6/75	4	16	28	I Like Beer	*Tom T. Hall*	Mercury 73704
1/10/76	❶[1]	16	29	Faster Horses (The Cowboy And The Poet)	*Tom T. Hall*	Mercury 73755
5/15/76	24	12	30	Negatory Romance	*Tom T. Hall*	Mercury 73795
10/16/76	9	14	31	Fox On The Run	*Tony Hazzard*	Mercury 73850
4/9/77	4	16	32	Your Man Loves You, Honey	*Tom T. Hall*	Mercury 73899
8/6/77	12	12	33	It's All In The Game	*Charles Dawes/Carl Sigman*	Mercury 55001
12/3/77+	13	14	34	May The Force Be With You Always	*Tom T. Hall*	RCA 11158
				inspired by the movie *Star Wars*		
4/8/78	13	13	35	I Wish I Loved Somebody Else	*Tom T. Hall*	RCA 11253
				Bonnie Brown and **Maxine Brown** (backing vocals, above 2)		
9/16/78	9	13	36	What Have You Got To Lose	*Tom T. Hall*	RCA 11376
1/20/79	14	12	37	Son Of Clayton Delaney	*Tom T. Hall*	RCA 11453
5/12/79	20	10	38	There Is A Miracle In You	*Tom T. Hall*	RCA 11568
9/29/79	11	14	39	You Show Me Your Heart (And I'll Show You Mine)	*Tom T. Hall*	RCA 11713
1/5/80	9	13	40	The Old Side Of Town /	*Tom T. Hall*	
1/5/80	flip	13	41	Jesus On The Radio (Daddy On The Phone)	*Tom T. Hall*	RCA 11888
5/24/80	51	7	42	Soldier Of Fortune	*Gary Sefton*	RCA 12005
8/16/80	36	10	43	Back When Gas Was Thirty Cents A Gallon	*Tom T. Hall*	RCA 12066
5/2/81	41	8	44	The All New Me	*Tom T. Hall*	RCA 12219

DEBUT	PEAK	WKS	GOLD	ARTIST / Country Chart Hit	Ranking / Songwriter	Label (& Number)
				HALL, Tom T. — cont'd		
5/22/82	**77**	4		45 **There Ain't No Country Music On This Jukebox** *[w/ Earl Scruggs]*	*Tom T. Hall*	Columbia 02858
7/31/82	**72**	5		46 **Song Of The South** *[w/ Earl Scruggs]*	*Bob McDill*	Columbia 03033
7/30/83	**42**	10		47 **Everything From Jesus To Jack Daniels**	*Tom T. Hall*	Mercury 812835
7/14/84	**81**	3		48 **Famous In Missouri**	*Jerome Clark/Robin Williams*	Mercury 880030
9/8/84	**8**	21		49 **P.S. I Love You**	S:8 / A:8 *Gordon Jenkins/Johnny Mercer*	Mercury 880216
5/25/85	**40**	9		50 **A Bar With No Beer**	*Tom T. Hall*	Mercury 880690
8/31/85	**42**	11		51 **Down In The Florida Keys**	*Tom T. Hall*	Mercury 884017
7/19/86	**52**	8		52 **Susie's Beauty Shop /**	*Tom T. Hall*	
10/4/86	**79**	3		53 **Love Letters In The Sand**	*J. Fred Coots/Charles Kenny/Nick Kenny*	Mercury 884850
12/6/86	**65**	7		54 **Down At The Mall**	*Roger Murrah/John Schweers*	Mercury 888155
				HALLMAN, Victoria Born in Mobile, Alabama. Female singer/actress. Regular on TV's *Hee Haw* from 1980-90.		
8/22/87	**92**	2		**Next Time I Marry** Those Hallman Girls (backing vocals)	*R.C. Bannon*	Evergreen 1055
				HALLMARK, Roger — see THRASHER BROTHERS		
				HAMBLEN, Stuart Born Carl Stuart Hamblen on 10/20/1908 in Kellyville, Texas. Died of a brain tumor on 3/8/1989 (age 80). Male singer/songwriter/actor. Moved to Hollywood in the early 1930s and appeared in many western movies and on radio with own band. Ran for president on Prohibition Party ticket in 1952.	**1950s: #43**	
11/12/49+	**3**^{2}	7		1 (I Won't Go Huntin', Jake) **But I'll Go Chasin' Women**	J:3 / S:9 *Stuart Hamblen*	Columbia 20625
8/5/50	**2**^{9}	26		2 (Remember Me) **I'm The One Who Loves You**	A:2 / S:3 / J:4 *Stuart Hamblen*	Columbia 4-20714
1/6/51	**8**	2		3 **It's No Secret**	A:8 *Stuart Hamblen*	Columbia 4-20724
8/21/54	**2**^{1}	30		4 **This Ole House**	A:2 / S:3 / J:5 *Stuart Hamblen*	RCA Victor 5739
				**HAMILTON, George IV** Born on 7/19/1937 in Winston-Salem, North Carolina. Male singer/songwriter/guitarist. Own TV series on ABC in 1959, and in Canada in the late 1970s. Father of **George Hamilton V**. Also see **Some Of Chet's Friends**. ***OPRY: 1960***	**1960s: #24 / All-Time: #122**	
10/10/60	**4**	17		1 **Before This Day Ends**	*Roy Drusky/Vic McAlpin/Marie Wilson*	ABC-Paramount 10125
6/12/61	**9**	13		2 **Three Steps To The Phone** (Millions of Miles)	*Harlan Howard*	RCA Victor 7881
11/13/61	**13**	8		3 **To You And Yours** (From Me And Mine)	*Bill Anderson*	RCA Victor 7934
6/16/62	**22**	2		4 **China Doll**	*Cindy Walker*	RCA Victor 8001
8/25/62	**6**	14		5 **If You Don't Know I Ain't Gonna Tell You**	*George Hamilton IV*	RCA Victor 8062
1/19/63	**21**	5		6 **In This Very Same Room**	*Harlan Howard*	RCA Victor 8118
6/15/63	❶^{4}	24		7 **Abilene**	*John D. Loudermilk*	RCA Victor 8181
1/18/64	**21**	8		8 **There's More Pretty Girls Than One**	*Arthur Smith*	RCA Victor 8250
3/28/64	**25**	8		9 **Linda With The Lonely Eyes /**	*John D. Loudermilk*	
4/18/64	**28**	6		10 **Fair And Tender Ladies**	*Maybelle Carter*	RCA Victor 8304
8/29/64	**9**	14		11 **Fort Worth, Dallas Or Houston**	*John D. Loudermilk*	RCA Victor 8392
12/5/64+	**11**	18		12 **Truck Driving Man**	*Terry Fell*	RCA Victor 8462
7/10/65	**18**	16		13 **Walking The Floor Over You**	*Ernest Tubb*	RCA Victor 8608
12/4/65+	**16**	12		14 **Write Me A Picture**	*Vance Bulla*	RCA Victor 8690
4/23/66	**15**	17		15 **Steel Rail Blues**	*Gordon Lightfoot*	RCA Victor 8797
9/3/66	**9**	16		16 **Early Morning Rain**	*Gordon Lightfoot*	RCA Victor 8924
1/21/67	**7**	21		17 **Urge For Going**	*Joni Mitchell*	RCA Victor 9059
7/1/67	**6**	17		18 **Break My Mind**	*John D. Loudermilk*	RCA Victor 9239
12/23/67+	**18**	13		19 **Little World Girl**	*John D. Loudermilk*	RCA Victor 9385
6/1/68	**50**	8		20 **It's My Time**	*John D. Loudermilk*	RCA Victor 9519
10/19/68	**38**	10		21 **Take My Hand For Awhile**	*Buffy Sainte-Marie*	RCA Victor 9637
3/15/69	**26**	10		22 **Back To Denver**	*Bobby Bond*	RCA Victor 0100
6/21/69	**25**	13		23 **Canadian Pacific**	*Ray Griff*	RCA Victor 0171
11/8/69	**29**	9		24 **Carolina In My Mind**	*James Taylor*	RCA Victor 0256
5/2/70	**3**^{2}	16		25 **She's A Little Bit Country**	*Harlan Howard*	RCA Victor 9829
8/29/70	**16**	12		26 **Back Where It's At**	*Bobby Bond*	RCA Victor 9886
9/26/70	**65**	2		27 **Let's Get Together** *[w/ Skeeter Davis]*	*Chet Powers*	RCA Victor 9893
1/30/71	**13**	12		28 **Anyway**	*Bobby Bond*	RCA Victor 9945
5/22/71	**35**	11		29 **Countryfied**	*Dick Damron*	RCA Victor 0469
9/18/71	**23**	12		30 **West Texas Highway**	*Boomer Castleman/Michael Murphey*	RCA Victor 0531
2/5/72	**33**	10		31 **10 Degrees & Getting Colder**	*Gordon Lightfoot*	RCA Victor 0622
5/13/72	**63**	8		32 **Country Music In My Soul**	*Bobby Bond*	RCA Victor 0697
9/9/72	**52**	9		33 **Travelin' Light**	*Gary S. Paxton*	RCA Victor 0776
12/23/72+	**22**	13		34 **Blue Train** (Of The Heartbreak Line)	*John D. Loudermilk*	RCA Victor 0854
5/19/73	**38**	10		35 **Dirty Old Man**	*Bob Ruzicka*	RCA Victor 0948
9/22/73	**50**	7		36 **Second Cup Of Coffee**	*Gordon Lightfoot*	RCA Victor 0084
1/26/74	**59**	9		37 **Claim On Me**	*Lee Clayton*	RCA Victor 0203

DEBUT	PEAK	WKS	GOLD	ARTIST Ranking / Country Chart Hit	Songwriter	Label (& Number)
				HAMILTON, George IV — cont'd		
4/9/77	**81**	5		38 **I Wonder Who's Kissing Her Now**	*Frank Adams/Bill Hough/Joe Howard*	ABC/Dot 17687
10/15/77	**93**	2		39 **Everlasting (Everlasting Love)**	*Danny Flowers*	ABC/Dot 17723
4/1/78	**81**	4		40 **Only The Best**	*Jim Rooney*	ABC 12342
				HAMILTON, George V		
				Born on 11/11/1960 in Nashville, Tennessee. Male singer/songwriter/guitarist. Son of **George Hamilton IV**.		
2/20/88	**75**	3		**She Says**	*George Hamilton V*	MTM 72101
				HAMILTON, Penny		
				Born in Boulder, Colorado. Female singer.		
8/4/79	**94**	4		**You Lit The Fire, Now Fan The Flame**	*Dave Gibson*	Door Knob 096
				HAMPTON THE HAMPSTER		
				Hampton is a cartoon hampster. Created by producers Robert DeBoer and Anthony Grace. Based on a real hampster owned by Deidre LeCarte.		
8/26/00	**70**	1		**The Hampsterdance Song**	*Robert DeBoer/Anthony Grace/Paul Grace/Roger Miller* **[I-N]**	Koch
				samples "Whistle Stop" by **Roger Miller**; from the album *Hampsterdance - The Album* on Koch 8212		
				HANDY, Cheryl		
				Born in 1969 in Virginia; raised in Goodlettsville, Tennessee. Female singer.		
4/14/84	**83**	4		1 **Here I Go Again**	*Ted Harris*	Audiograph 475
1/24/87	**67**	5		2 **One Of The Boys**	*Phil Barnhart/Kent Blazy*	RCM 00105
8/8/87	**56**	6		3 **Will You Still Love Me Tomorrow?**	*Gerry Goffin/Carole King*	Compleat 176
				HANKS, Kamryn		
				Born in Oklahoma. Female singer.		
10/21/89	**85**	2		**Eyes Never Lie**	*Rory Bourke/Jeff Tweel*	Country Pride 0025
				HANNA-McEUEN		
				Duo of cousins from Evergreen, Colorado: Jaime Hanna and Jonathan McEuen. Sons of Jeff Hanna and John McEuen of the **Nitty Gritty Dirt Band**.		
3/12/05	**38**	20		**Something Like A Broken Heart**	*Jaime Hanna/Alan Miller/Robert Reynolds*	MCA Nashville
				from the album *Hanna-McEuen* on DreamWorks 001399		
				HANSON, Connie		
				Born in Houston, Texas. Female singer/actress. Played "Marshalene" in the movie *Urban Cowboy*.		
12/25/82+	**64**	9		**There's Still A Lot Of Love In San Antone** ***[w/ Darrell McCall]***	*A.L. "Doodle" Owens/Lou Rochelle*	Soundwaves 4692
				HANSON, Jennifer		
				Born in Whittier, California; raised in La Habra, California. Female singer/songwriter.		
8/3/02+	**16**	32		1 **Beautiful Goodbye**	S:❶[1] *Jennifer Hanson/Kim Patton*	Capitol
4/19/03	**42**	12		2 **This Far Gone**	*Tony Martin/Mark Nesler*	Capitol
8/2/03	**40**	13		3 **Half A Heart Tattoo**	*Jennifer Hanson/Mike Heeney/A.J. Masters*	Capitol
				above 3 from the album *Jennifer Hanson* on Capitol 35247		
				HARDEN, Arlene		
				Born Ava Harden on 3/1/1945 in England, Arkansas. Female singer. Member of **The Harden Trio**.		
7/15/67	**48**	9		1 **Fair Weather Love**	*Jan Crutchfield/Wayne Walker*	Columbia 44133
12/9/67+	**49**	7		2 **You're Easy To Love**	*Dave Burgess*	Columbia 44310
4/6/68	**32**	11		3 **He's A Good Ole Boy**	*Harlan Howard*	Columbia 44461
8/17/68	**41**	9		4 **What Can I Say**	*Ray Griff*	Columbia 44581
5/3/69	**45**	9		5 **Too Much Of A Man (To Be Tied Down)**	*Larry Kingston*	Columbia 44783
12/20/69+	**63**	4		6 **My Friend**	*Bill Dees/Roy Orbison*	Columbia 45016
4/25/70	**13**	14		7 **Lovin' Man (Oh Pretty Woman)**	*Bill Dees/Roy Orbison*	Columbia 45120
8/29/70	**28**	11		8 **Crying**	*Joe Melson/Roy Orbison*	Columbia 45203
1/9/71	**22**	11		9 **True Love Is Greater Than Friendship**	*Carl Perkins*	Columbia 45287
				from the movie *Little Fauss And Big Halsy* starring Robert Redford		
5/1/71	**25**	11		10 **Married To A Memory**	*Alex Harvey*	Columbia 45365
7/31/71	**49**	9		11 **Congratulations (You Sure Made A Man Out Of Him)**	*Jim Barr*	Columbia 45420
12/18/71+	**46**	9		12 **Ruby Gentry's Daughter**	*Curly Putman*	Columbia 45489
4/15/72	**29**	12		13 **A Special Day**	*Bobby Harden*	Columbia 45577
11/4/72	**45**	8		14 **It Takes A Lot Of Tenderness**	*Alex Harvey*	Columbia 45708
6/30/73	**21**	13		15 **Would You Walk With Me Jimmy**	*A.L. "Doodle" Owens/Whitey Shafer*	Columbia 45845
				ARLEEN HARDEN:		
7/20/74	**72**	8		16 **Leave Me Alone (Ruby Red Dress)**	*Linda Laurie*	Capitol 3911
10/29/77	**100**	2		17 **A Place Where Love Has Been**	*Dennis Linde/Mel McDaniel*	Elektra 45434
4/1/78	**74**	4		18 **You're Not Free And I'm Not Easy**	*Herb Coleman/Bob Morrison*	Elektra 45463
				HARDEN, Bobby		
				Born on 6/27/1942 in England, Arkansas. Male singer. Member of **The Harden Trio**.		
3/15/75	**48**	8		**One Step**	*Larry Keith/Steve Pippin*	United Artists 597
				HARDEN TRIO, The		
				Family trio from England, Arkansas: **Bobby Harden** and sisters Robbie Harden and **Arlene Harden**.		
2/12/66	**2^{1}**	21		1 **Tippy Toeing**	*Bobby Harden*	Columbia 43463
11/5/66	**28**	11		2 **Seven Days Of Crying (Makes One Weak)**	*Jerry Smith*	Columbia 43844
4/22/67	**16**	14		3 **Sneaking 'Cross The Border**	*Bobby Harden*	Columbia 44059
2/10/68	**56**	4		4 **He Looks A Lot Like You**	*Paul Johnson/Walt Johnson*	Columbia 44420

DEBUT	PEAK	WKS	GOLD	ARTIST / Ranking / Country Chart Hit / Songwriter	Label (& Number)
				HARDEN TRIO, The — cont'd	
6/29/68	**47**	7		5 **Everybody Wants To Be Somebody Else** ... *Ed Hamilton/Bob Tubert/Dale Ward*	Columbia 44552
12/7/68+	**64**	6		6 **Who Loves You** ... *Curly Putman*	Columbia 44675
				THE HARDENS (ARLENE & ROBBIE)	
				HARDIN, Gus	
				Born Carolyn Ann Blankenship on 4/9/1945 in Tulsa, Oklahoma. Died in a car crash on 2/18/1996 (age 50). Female singer.	
2/19/83	**10**	16		1 **After The Last Goodbye** ... *Billy Henderson/Bud McGuire/Eddie Moore/George Pearce*	RCA 13445
5/28/83	**26**	14		2 **If I Didn't Love You** ... *Deborah Allen/Rafe Van Hoy*	RCA 13532
9/24/83	**32**	12		3 **Loving You Hurts** ... *Ava Aldridge/Cindy Richardson*	RCA 13597
12/24/83+	**41**	12		4 **Fallen Angel (Flying High Tonight)** ... *Walt Aldridge/Billy Henderson/Billy Maddox*	RCA 13704
3/24/84	**43**	11		5 **I Pass** ... *Michael Garvin/David Rosson/Tom Shapiro*	RCA 13751
6/23/84	**52**	8		6 **How Are You Spending My Nights** ... *Richard Carpenter/Kent Robbins*	RCA 13814
11/10/84+	**8**	21		7 **All Tangled Up In Love** ***[w/ Earl Thomas Conley]*** S:5 / A:8 *Bob McDill/Jim Weatherly*	RCA 13938
4/20/85	**79**	4		8 **My Mind Is On You** ... *Dave Loggins/Don Schlitz*	RCA 14040
8/17/85	**72**	7		9 **Just As Long As I Have You** ***[w/ Dave Loggins]*** ... *Dave Loggins/J.D. Martin*	RCA 14159
1/11/86	**73**	7		10 **What We Gonna Do** ... *Richard Feldman/Pat Robinson*	RCA 14255
				HARDING, Gayle	
				Born in Belmont, California. Female singer.	
11/11/78	**92**	2		1 **Sexy Eyes** ... *Bob Jenkins*	Robchris 1008
1/27/79	**84**	3		2 **I'm Lovin' The Lovin' Out Of You** ... *Bob Jenkins*	Robchris 1009
				HARDY, Johnny	
				Born in Rockmont, Georgia. Male singer.	
2/13/61	**17**	10		**In Memory Of Johnny Horton** ... *Jim Howell*	J&J 003
				HARGROVE, Danny	
				Born in Detroit, Michigan. Male singer/songwriter/guitarist.	
5/13/78	**73**	7		1 **Sweet Mary** ... *Steve Jablecki*	50 States 61
9/23/78	**98**	2		2 **I Wanna Be Her #1** ... *Danny Hargrove*	50 States 64
				HARGROVE, Linda	
				Born on 2/3/1949 in Tallahassee, Florida. Female singer/songwriter/pianist.	
10/19/74	**98**	2		1 **Blue Jean Country Queen** ... *Linda Hargrove*	Elektra 45204
12/28/74+	**82**	4		2 **I've Never Loved Anyone More** ... *Linda Hargrove/Michael Nesmith*	Elektra 45215
11/8/75+	**39**	13		3 **Love Was (Once Around The Dance Floor)** ... *Linda Hargrove*	Capitol 4153
3/6/76	**86**	5		4 **Love, You're The Teacher** ... *Pete Drake/Linda Hargrove*	Capitol 4228
7/24/76	**86**	4		5 **Fire At First Sight** ... *Linda Hargrove*	Capitol 4283
4/2/77	**91**	3		6 **Down To My Pride** ... *Pete Drake/Linda Hargrove*	Capitol 4390
9/24/77	**61**	9		7 **Mexican Love Songs** ... *Pete Drake/Linda Hargrove*	Capitol 4447
10/14/78	**93**	4		8 **You Are Still The One** ... *Linda Hargrove*	RCA 11378
				HARLESS, Ogden	
				Born William Harless in 1949 in Hattiesburg, Mississippi. Male singer.	
9/19/87	**84**	2		1 **Somebody Ought To Tell Him That She's Gone** ... *Bobby Braddock/David Chamberlain/Bucky Jones/Curley Putman*	Door Knob 283
11/28/87	**74**	3		2 **Walk On Boy** ... *Charles Weathers*	Door Knob 287
1/16/88	**64**	5		3 **I Wish We Were Strangers** ... *Bill Rice/Mary Sharon Rice*	Door Knob 293
4/23/88	**82**	3		4 **Down On The Bayou** ... *Charles Weathers*	Door Knob 297
8/27/88	**92**	2		5 **Together Alone** ... *Bobby Braddock*	MSC 188
				HARLING, Keith	
				Born on 5/8/1963 in Greenwood, South Carolina; raised in Chattanooga, Tennessee. Male singer/songwriter/guitarist.	
3/7/98	**24**	20		1 **Papa Bear** ... *Keith Harling*	MCA Nashville
8/1/98	**39**	17		2 **Coming Back For You** ... *John Rich/Tom Shapiro/Chris Waters*	MCA Nashville
12/19/98+	**61**	6		3 **Write It In Stone** ... *Keith Harling*	MCA Nashville
2/20/99	**58**	4		4 **There Goes The Neighborhood** ... *Keith Harling*	MCA Nashville
				above 4 from the album *Write It In Stone* on MCA Nashville 70024	
11/6/99+	**52**	12		5 **Bring It On** ... *Rivers Rutherford*	Giant
12/25/99+	**60**	3		6 **Santa's Got A Semi** ... *Pat Bunch/Doug Johnson* **[X]**	Giant
12/9/00+	**60**	5		7 **Santa's Got A Semi** ... *Pat Bunch/Doug Johnson* **[X-R]**	Giant
				above 3 from the album *Bring It On* on Giant 24732	
				HARMS, Joni	
				Born on 11/5/1959 in Canby, Oregon. Female singer/songwriter.	
3/11/89	**34**	11		1 **I Need A Wife** ... *Joni Harms/Dan Tyler*	Universal 53492
6/24/89	**54**	8		2 **The Only Thing Bluer Than His Eyes** ... *Bill Brookshire/Jackson Hale*	Universal 66012
				HARRELL & SCOTT	
				Vocal duo: Tony Harrell and Leland Scott.	
9/23/89	**96**	2		1 **Weak Men Break** ... *Connie Harrell/Tony Harrell/Leland Scott*	Associated Artists 503
12/16/89+	**75**	5		2 **Darkness Of The Light** ... *Tony Harrell/Leland Scott*	Associated Artists 505
				HARRINGTON, Carly	
				Born in Knoxville, Tennessee. Female singer.	
8/6/88	**64**	6		**Badland Preacher** ... *David Featherstone*	Oak 1055

DEBUT	PEAK	WKS	GOLD	ARTIST / Ranking / Country Chart Hit	Songwriter	Label (& Number)

HARRIS, Donna

Born in Tennessee. Female singer.

DEBUT	PEAK	WKS	GOLD	Country Chart Hit	Songwriter	Label (& Number)
10/1/66	45	8		**He Was Almost Persuaded** answer to "Almost Persuaded" by **David Houston**	*Billy Sherrill/Glenn Sutton*	ABC 10839

HARRIS, Emmylou — 1980s: #20 / All-Time: #62

Born on 4/2/1947 in Birmingham, Alabama. Female singer/songwriter/guitarist. Worked as a folk singer in Washington DC in the late 1960s. First recorded for Jubilee in 1969. Married to producer Brian Ahern from 1977-84. Married to British songwriter/producer Paul Kennerley from 1985-93. Also see **Same Old Train**.

CMA: Female Vocalist 1980 // OPRY: 1992

DEBUT	PEAK	WKS	GOLD	Country Chart Hit	Songwriter	Label (& Number)
4/19/75	73	8		1 **Too Far Gone** also see #13 below	*Billy Sherrill*	Reprise 1326
7/5/75	4	17		2 **If I Could Only Win Your Love** **Herb Pedersen** (harmony vocal)	*Charlie Louvin/Ira Louvin*	Reprise 1332
12/27/75	99	1		3 **Light Of The Stable** **Dolly Parton**, **Linda Ronstadt** and **Neil Young** (backing vocals)	*Elizabeth Rhymer/Steven Rhymer* **[X]**	Reprise 1341
1/3/76	12	12		4 **The Sweetest Gift** ***[w/ Linda Ronstadt]***	*J.B. Coats*	Asylum 45295
3/6/76	❶[1]	14		5 **Together Again**	*Buck Owens*	Reprise 1346
6/5/76	3[2]	16		6 **One Of These Days**	*Earl Montgomery*	Reprise 1353
10/23/76	❶[2]	14		7 **Sweet Dreams**	*Don Gibson*	Reprise 1371
2/26/77	6	13		8 **(You Never Can Tell) C'est La Vie**	*Chuck Berry*	Warner 8329
5/28/77	8	14		9 **Making Believe** **Herb Pedersen** (harmony vocal)	*Jimmy Work*	Warner 8388
12/3/77+	3[1]	15		10 **To Daddy**	*Dolly Parton*	Warner 8498
4/15/78	❶[1]	14		11 **Two More Bottles Of Wine**	*Delbert McClinton*	Warner 8553
8/5/78	12	11		12 **Easy From Now On**	*Carlene Carter/Susanna Clark*	Warner 8623
2/3/79	13	13		13 **Too Far Gone** same version as #1 above	*Billy Sherrill* **[R]**	Warner 8732
5/12/79	11	13		14 **Play Together Again Again** ***[w/ Buck Owens]***	*Jerry Abbott/Buck Owens/Charles Stewart*	Warner 8830
6/2/79	4	14		15 **Save The Last Dance For Me**	*Doc Pomus/Mort Shuman*	Warner 8815
9/8/79	91	6		16 **Love Don't Care** ***[w/ Charlie Louvin]***	*Hal Bynum/Don Wayne*	Little Darlin' 7922
9/22/79	6	12		17 **Blue Kentucky Girl** **Grammy: Female Vocal**	*Johnny Mullins*	Warner 49056
3/1/80	❶[1]	14		18 **Beneath Still Waters**	*Dallas Frazier*	Warner 49164
5/31/80	7	15		19 **Wayfaring Stranger**	*Brian Ahern*	Warner 49239
6/28/80	6	15		20 **That Lovin' You Feelin' Again** ***[w/ Roy Orbison]*** **Grammy: Vocal Duo**; from the movie *Roadie* starring Meat Loaf	*Roy Orbison/Chris Price*	Warner 49262
9/13/80	13	11		21 **The Boxer**	*Paul Simon*	Warner 49551
3/7/81	10	12		22 **Mister Sandman**	*Pat Ballard*	Warner 49684
6/13/81	44	8		23 **I Don't Have To Crawl**	*Rodney Crowell*	Warner 49739
9/19/81	3[1]	17		24 **If I Needed You** ***[w/ Don Williams]***	*Townes Van Zandt*	Warner 49809
1/16/82	9	16		25 **Tennessee Rose**	*Karen Brooks/Hank DeVito*	Warner 49892
5/29/82	3[2]	17		26 **Born To Run**	*Paul Kennerley*	Warner 29993
10/16/82+	❶[1]	20		27 **(Lost His Love) On Our Last Date**	*Floyd Cramer/Conway Twitty*	Warner 29898
3/19/83	5	17		28 **I'm Movin' On**	*Hank Snow*	Warner 29729
7/2/83	28	13		29 **So Sad (To Watch Good Love Go Bad)**	*Don Everly*	Warner 29583
7/9/83	14	19		30 **Wild Montana Skies** ***[w/ John Denver]***	*John Denver*	RCA 13562
11/19/83+	26	13		31 **Drivin' Wheel**	*T-Bone Burnett/Billy Swan*	Warner 29443
3/24/84	9	21		32 **In My Dreams** **Grammy: Female Vocal**	*Paul Kennerley*	Warner 29329
8/11/84	9	22		33 **Pledging My Love**	S:9 / A:9 *Don Robey/Ferdinand Washington*	Warner 29218
11/24/84+	26	18		34 **Someone Like You**	S:23 *Dickey Lee/Bob McDill*	Warner 29138
3/30/85	14	17		35 **White Line**	S:12 / A:14 *Emmylou Harris/Paul Kennerley*	Warner 29041
7/20/85	44	11		36 **Rhythm Guitar**	*Emmylou Harris/Paul Kennerley*	Warner 28952
8/3/85	14	19		37 **Thing About You** ***[w/ Southern Pacific]***	S:13 / A:14 *Tom Petty*	Warner 28943
11/30/85	55	9		38 **Timberline**	*Emmylou Harris/Paul Kennerley*	Warner 28852
3/1/86	60	6		39 **I Had My Heart Set On You**	*Rodney Crowell/Paul Kennerley*	Warner 28770
5/3/86	43	13		40 **Today I Started Loving You Again**	*Merle Haggard/Bonnie Owens*	Warner 28714
2/21/87	❶[1]	19		41 **To Know Him Is To Love Him** ***[w/ Dolly Parton & Linda Ronstadt]***	S:❶[1] / A:❶[1] *Phil Spector*	Warner 28492
5/30/87	3[1]	18		42 **Telling Me Lies** ***[w/ Dolly Parton & Linda Ronstadt]***	S:10 *Betsy Cook/Linda Thompson*	Warner 28371
7/11/87	60	7		43 **Someday My Ship Will Sail**	*Allen Reynolds*	Warner 28302
9/26/87	5	22		44 **Those Memories Of You** ***[w/ Dolly Parton & Linda Ronstadt]***	S:10 *Alan O'Bryant*	Warner 28248
12/12/87+	53	13		45 **Back In Baby's Arms** from the movie *Planes, Trains & Automobiles* starring Steve Martin and John Candy	*Bob Montgomery*	Hughes/MCA 53236
3/26/88	6	18		46 **Wildflowers** ***[w/ Dolly Parton & Linda Ronstadt]***	S:13 *Dolly Parton*	Warner 27970
7/2/88	❶[1]	21		47 **We Believe In Happy Endings** ***[w/ Earl Thomas Conley]***	S:3 *Bob McDill*	RCA 8632
12/17/88+	8	22		48 **Heartbreak Hill**	*Emmylou Harris/Paul Kennerley*	Reprise 27635
4/29/89	16	21		49 **Heaven Only Knows**	*Paul Kennerley*	Reprise 22999
8/26/89	51	6		50 **I Still Miss Someone**	*Johnny Cash/Roy Cash*	Reprise 22850
1/19/91	71	3		51 **Wheels Of Love** from the album *Brand New Dance* on Reprise 26309	*Marjorie Plant*	Reprise

DEBUT	PEAK	WKS	GOLD	ARTIST / Country Chart Hit	Ranking / Songwriter	Label (& Number)

HARRIS, Emmylou — cont'd

DEBUT	PEAK	WKS	GOLD	Country Chart Hit	Songwriter	Label (& Number)
10/16/93	**63**	8		52 **High Powered Love**	*Tony Joe White*	Asylum
1/29/94	**65**	5		53 **Thanks To You**	*Jesse Winchester*	Asylum
				above 2 from the album *Cowgirl's Prayer* on Asylum 61541		
12/11/04+	**47**	20		54 **Not Me** ***[w/ Keni Thomas & Vince Gill]***	*Brent Maher/Billy Montana/Keni Thomas*	Moraine
				from Thomas's album *Flags Of Our Fathers* on Moraine 2350		

HARRISON, B.J.

Born in Marshalltown, Iowa. Male singer.

DEBUT	PEAK	WKS	GOLD	Country Chart Hit	Songwriter	Label (& Number)
5/24/80	**93**	2		**I Need A Little More Time**	*Carol Schelton/Troy Shondell*	TeleSonic 801

HARRISON, Dixie

Born on 8/17/1953 in Faulkner County, Arkansas. Female singer.

DEBUT	PEAK	WKS	GOLD	Country Chart Hit	Songwriter	Label (& Number)
10/23/82	**98**	2		**Yes Mam (He Found Me In A Honky Tonk)**	*Roy Acuff/Barber/Fred Rose*	Air Int'l. 10078

HART, Clay

Born Henry Clay Hart on 7/1/1942 in Providence, Rhode Island. Male singer. Regular on **Lawrence Welk**'s TV show from 1969-75. Married Sally Flynn, another regular on the Welk show, on 12/6/1974.

DEBUT	PEAK	WKS	GOLD	Country Chart Hit	Songwriter	Label (& Number)
5/31/69	**30**	11		1 **Spring**	*John Tipton*	Metromedia 119
9/20/69	**25**	9		2 **Another Day, Another Mile, Another Highway**	*John Tipton*	Metromedia 140
1/31/70	**73**	3		3 **Face Of A Dear Friend**	*John Tipton*	Metromedia 158
5/2/70	**62**	7		4 **If I'd Only Come And Gone**	*Shel Silverstein*	Metromedia 172

HART, Freddie

1970s: #16 / All-Time: #79

Born Frederick Segrest on 12/21/1926 in Lochapoka, Alabama. Male singer/songwriter/guitarist. Served in U.S. Marines during World War II. Moved to Phoenix in 1950 and worked with **Lefty Frizzell** from 1951-52. Appeared on *Home Town Jamboree* TV series. Later operated a trucking company and school for handicapped children in Burbank, California.

DEBUT	PEAK	WKS	GOLD	Country Chart Hit	Songwriter	Label (& Number)
4/20/59	**24**	4		1 **The Wall**	*Harlan Howard*	Columbia 41345
11/16/59	**17**	4		2 **Chain Gang**	*Harlan Howard*	Columbia 41456
5/2/60	**18**	11		3 **The Key's In The Mailbox**	*Harlan Howard*	Columbia 41597
1/9/61	**27**	2		4 **Lying Again**	*Harlan Howard*	Columbia 41805
11/6/61	**23**	2		5 **What A Laugh!**	*Freddie Hart/Harlan Howard*	Columbia 42146
10/30/65	**23**	12		6 **Hank Williams' Guitar** ***[w/ The Heartbeats]***	*Eddie Dean/Freddie Hart*	Kapp 694
5/7/66	**45**	4		7 **Why Should I Cry Over You** ***[w/ The Heartbeats]***	*Zeke Clements*	Kapp 743
7/8/67	**63**	5		8 **I'll Hold You In My Heart**	*Eddy Arnold/Tommy Dilbeck*	Kapp 820
12/30/67+	**24**	15		9 **Togetherness**	*Freddie Hart*	Kapp 879
6/8/68	**21**	15		10 **Born A Fool**	*Alex Zanetis*	Kapp 910
				also see #21 below		
11/23/68	**70**	2		11 **Don't Cry Baby**	*Alex Zanetis*	Kapp 944
1/3/70	**27**	10		12 **The Whole World Holding Hands**	*Freddie Hart*	Capitol 2692
4/11/70	**48**	9		13 **One More Mountain To Climb**	*Freddie Hart/David Ingles*	Capitol 2768
7/4/70	**41**	11		14 **Fingerprints**	*Freddie Hart/Ken Hunt*	Capitol 2839
11/21/70	**68**	4		15 **California Grapevine**	*Homer Joy*	Capitol 2933
7/10/71	**❶[3]**	24	●	16 **Easy Loving**	*Freddie Hart*	Capitol 3115
1/29/72	**❶[6]**	19		17 **My Hang-Up Is You**	*Freddie Hart*	Capitol 3261

FREDDIE HART And The Heartbeats:

DEBUT	PEAK	WKS	GOLD	Country Chart Hit	Songwriter	Label (& Number)
6/24/72	**❶[2]**	14		18 **Bless Your Heart**	*Freddie Hart/Jack Lebsock*	Capitol 3353
10/14/72	**❶[3]**	17		19 **Got The All Overs For You (All Over Me)**	*Freddie Hart*	Capitol 3453
2/3/73	**❶[1]**	14		20 **Super Kind Of Woman**	*Jack Lebsock*	Capitol 3524
5/19/73	**41**	10		21 **Born A Fool** ***[Freddie Hart]***	*Alex Zanetis* **[R]**	MCA 40011
				same version as #10 above		
6/2/73	**❶[1]**	16		22 **Trip To Heaven**	*Freddie Hart*	Capitol 3612
10/6/73	**3[2]**	16		23 **If You Can't Feel It (It Ain't There)**	*Freddie Hart*	Capitol 3730
2/23/74	**2[1]**	12		24 **Hang In There Girl** ***[Freddie Hart]***	*Freddie Hart*	Capitol 3827
6/22/74	**3[1]**	14		25 **The Want-To's**	*Freddie Hart*	Capitol 3898
11/2/74+	**3[1]**	16		26 **My Woman's Man**	*Ben Peters/George Richey*	Capitol 3970
3/1/75	**5**	15		27 **I'd Like To Sleep Til I Get Over You**	*Roger Bowling*	Capitol 4031
6/28/75	**2[2]**	16		28 **The First Time**	*Jack Lebsock*	Capitol 4099
10/18/75	**6**	15		29 **Warm Side Of You**	*Freddie Hart*	Capitol 4152
1/31/76	**11**	11		30 **You Are The Song (Inside Of Me)**	*Ben Peters/George Richey*	Capitol 4210
4/10/76	**12**	14		31 **She'll Throw Stones At You**	*Alan Cartee/Vic Dana/George Soulé*	Capitol 4251
8/21/76	**11**	14		32 **That Look In Her Eyes**	*Ben Peters*	Capitol 4313
12/4/76+	**8**	14		33 **Why Lovers Turn To Strangers**	*Bobby Fender/Freddie Hart*	Capitol 4363

FREDDIE HART:

DEBUT	PEAK	WKS	GOLD	Country Chart Hit	Songwriter	Label (& Number)
4/16/77	**11**	11		34 **Thank God She's Mine**	*Mike Kosser/Curly Putman/Sonny Throckmorton*	Capitol 4409
7/16/77	**13**	12		35 **The Pleasure's Been All Mine /**	*Joe Nixon*	
7/30/77	**flip**	10		36 **It's Heaven Loving You**	*Freddie Hart/Jack Lebsock*	Capitol 4448
11/5/77	**43**	10		37 **The Search** ***[w/ The Heartbeats]***	*Sheb Wooley*	Capitol 4498
1/21/78	**27**	11		38 **So Good, So Rare, So Fine**	*Harry Shannon/Steve Stone*	Capitol 4530
4/22/78	**34**	10		39 **Only You**	*Buck Ram/Ande Rand*	Capitol 4561

Billboard DEBUT	PEAK	WKS	GOLD	ARTIST Ranking Country Chart Hit	Songwriter	Label (& Number)
				HART, Freddie — cont'd		
8/19/78	**21**	12		40 **Toe To Toe**	*Jerry Fuller*	Capitol 4609
2/24/79	**40**	8		41 **My Lady**	*Don Goodman/Bud Reneau/Rick Schulman*	Capitol 4684
5/26/79	**28**	12		42 **Wasn't It Easy Baby**	*Jack Lebsock/Bob Morris*	Capitol 4720
6/7/80	**15**	12		43 **Sure Thing**	*Earl Thomas Conley/Nelson Larkin*	Sunbird 7550
9/13/80	**33**	10		44 **Rose's Are Red**	*Nelson Larkin/Dan Willis*	Sunbird 7553
4/18/81	**31**	10		45 **You're Crazy Man**	*Freddie Hart/Charlie Owens*	Sunbird 7560
9/12/81	**38**	9		46 **You Were There**	*Johnny MacRae/Bob Morrison*	Sunbird 7565
6/29/85	**81**	4		47 **I Don't Want To Lose You**	*David Brewer/Faye Brewer/Freddie Hart*	El Dorado 101
9/5/87	**77**	4		48 **Best Love I Never Had**	*Kent Blazy/Jim Dowell*	Fifth Street 1091
				HART, J.D.		
				Born in Albemarle, North Carolina. Male singer.		
11/4/89	**79**	3		**Come Back Brenda**	*Even Stevens/Marty Stuart*	Universal 66017
				HART, Rod		
				Born in Beulah, Michigan. Male singer/songwriter.		
11/27/76+	**23**	11		**C.B. Savage**	*Rod Hart* **[N]**	Plantation 144
				"gay" answer to "Convoy" by **C.W. McCall**		
				HART, Sally June		
				Born in Atlanta, Georgia. Female singer.		
9/20/75	**91**	3		**Takin' What I Can Get**	*J.C. Cunningham*	Buddah 479
				HART, Tara Lyn		
				Born in Roblin, Manitoba, Canada. Female singer/songwriter.		
10/16/99	**67**	1		1 **Stuff That Matters**	*David Martin*	Columbia
3/18/00	**65**	1		2 **Don't Ever Let Me Go** S:22	*Beth Nielsen Chapman/Bill LaBounty/Annie Roboff*	Columbia
6/17/00	**68**	1		3 **That's When You Came Along**	*Tara Lyn Hart/Steve Moccio*	Columbia
				above 3 from the album *Tara Lyn Hart* on Columbia 69602		
				HARTER, J. Michael		
				Born in 1979 in Tempe, Arizona. Male singer/guitarist.		
6/15/02	**45**	16		**Hard Call To Make**	*Steve Seskin/Mark Alan Springer*	Broken Bow
				from the album *Unexpected Change* on Broken Bow 7099		
				HARTFORD, Chapin		
				Born Paula Hartford Foster on 5/15/1944 in Boston, Massachusetts. Female singer/songwriter.		
8/26/78	**91**	3		**I Knew The Mason**	*Chapin Hartford*	LS 165
				HARTFORD, John		
				Born on 12/30/1937 in Brooklyn, New York; raised in St. Louis, Missouri. Died of cancer on 6/4/2001 (age 63). Male singer/songwriter/banjo player. Regular on TV's *The Smothers Brothers Comedy Hour.*		
5/27/67	**60**	7		1 **Gentle On My Mind**	*John Hartford*	RCA Victor 9175
8/18/84	**81**	3		2 **Piece Of My Heart**	*Bert Berns/Jerry Ragovoy*	Flying Fish 4013
				HARTSOOK, Jimmy		
				Born on 8/10/1959 in Lenoir City, Tennessee. Male singer.		
1/26/74	**94**	5		**Anything To Prove My Love To You**	*Bob Morrison*	RCA Victor 0202
				HARTT, Dolly		
				Born in Nashville, Tennessee. Female singer.		
2/13/88	**85**	3		**Here Comes The Night**	*Ronnie Gossett/Vicki Gossett*	Kass 1015
				HARVELL, Nate		
				Born on 8/17/1954 in Alabama. Male singer.		
7/15/78	**23**	13		1 **Three Times A Lady**	*Lionel Richie*	Republic 025
12/2/78	**73**	5		2 **One In A Million**	*Randy Barlow/Fred Kelly*	Republic 033
				HARVICK, Kerry		
				Born on 9/10/1974 in Commanche, Texas. Female singer.		
10/2/04	**45**	8		**Cowgirls**	*Hillary Lindsey/Angelo Petraglia/Ryan Tyler*	Lyric Street
				HATFIELD, Vince and Dianne		
				Husband-and-wife duo from Memphis, Tennessee.		
8/1/81	**83**	4		1 **I Won't Last A Day Without You**	*Roger Nichols/Paul Williams*	Soundwaves 4638
5/1/82	**81**	3		2 **Back In My Baby's Arms**	*Kye Fleming/Dennis W. Morgan*	Soundwaves 4668
7/2/83	**90**	2		3 **Love Has Made A Woman Out Of You**	*Rory Bourke/Kerry Chater/Dickey Lee*	Soundwaves 4704
				HAUSER, Bruce		
				Born in Kansas. Male singer. **Sawmill Creek** was his backing band.		
10/24/81	**90**	3		1 **Barely Gettin' By** ***[Sawmill Creek]***	*John Hart*	Cowboy 1045
12/21/85	**77**	6		2 **I Just Came Back (To Break My Heart Again)** ***[w/ Sawmill Creek Band]***	*J.P. Pennington*	Cowboy 200
7/19/86	**81**	3		3 **Bidding America Goodbye (The Auction)** ***[w/ Sawmill Creek]***	*Jamie O'Hara*	Cowboy 202
				HAVENS, Bobby, and Country Company		
				Born on 3/13/1948 in Baird, Texas. Male singer/songwriter/guitarist.		
12/9/78	**100**	2		**Hey You**	*Bobby Havens*	Cin Kay 043
				HAWKINS, Brad		
				Born on 1/13/1974 in Dallas, Texas. Male singer/guitarist.		
2/28/98	**68**	6		**We Lose**	*Rick Bowles/Randy Scruggs*	Curb

DEBUT	PEAK	WKS	GOLD	ARTIST / Country Chart Hit	Ranking / Songwriter	Label (& Number)
				HAWKINS, Debi		
				Born Deborah Kaye Hawkins in Paso Robles, California. Female singer.		
3/22/75	**61**	9		1 **Making Believe**	*John Hobson/Jimmy Work*	Warner 8076
7/26/75	**80**	5		2 **What I Keep Sayin', Is A Lie**	*Marvin Moore/Bernie Wayne*	Warner 8104
11/8/75	**88**	3		3 **When I Stop Dreaming**	*Charlie Louvin/Ira Louvin*	Warner 8140
3/27/76	**97**	2		4 **Walnut Street Wrangler**	*Dan Darst/Carmol Taylor*	Warner 8188
6/18/77	**57**	8		5 **Love Letters**	*Edward Heyman/Victor Young*	Warner 8394
				HAWKINS, Erskine, and his Orchestra		
				Born on 7/26/1914 in Birmingham, Alabama. Died on 11/11/1993 (age 79). Black trumpeter/bandleader/composer.		
2/5/44	**6**	1		**Don't Cry, Baby**	*Sam Lowe/Jimmy Mitchell*	Bluebird 30-0813
				Jimmy Mitchelle (vocal)		
				HAWKINS, Hawkshaw	**1940s: #46**	
				Born Harold Franklin Hawkins on 12/22/1921 in Huntington, West Virginia. Died in a plane crash on 3/5/1963 (age 41) near Camden, Tennessee (with **Patsy Cline** and **Cowboy Copas**). Male singer/songwriter/guitarist. Married **Jean Shepard** on 11/26/1960.		
				OPRY: 1955		
5/1/48	**9**	4		1 **Pan American**	J:9 *Hank Williams*	King 689
8/21/48	**6**	15		2 **Dog House Boogie**	J:6 / S:12 *Hawkshaw Hawkins/Boothe Woodall*	King 720
12/24/49	**15**	1		3 **I Wasted A Nickel**	S:15 *Shorty Long/Bob Newman*	King 821
3/17/51	**8**	1		4 **I Love You A Thousand Ways**	A:8 *Lefty Frizzell*	King 918
10/13/51	**8**	2		5 **I'm Waiting Just For You**	A:8 *Henry Glover/Carolyn Leigh*	King 45-969
12/8/51+	**7**	4		6 **Slow Poke**	J:7 / S:8 *Pee Wee King/Chilton Price/Redd Stewart*	King 45-998
8/10/59	**15**	7		7 **Soldier's Joy**	*Jimmie Driftwood*	Columbia 41419
3/2/63	❶^4	25		8 **Lonesome 7-7203**	*Justin Tubb*	King 5712
				HAWKS, Mickey		
				Born in High Point, North Carolina. Male singer.		
9/23/89	**94**	2		**Me And My Harley-Davidson**	*Danny Caldwell*	C-Horse 589
				HAY, George D.	**HOF: 1966**	
				Born George Dewey Hay on 11/9/1895 in Attica, Indiana. Died on 5/8/1968 (age 72). Founder and first announcer of radio's *Grand Ole Opry*. Nicknamed "The Solemn Ole Judge." Head of the *Grand Ole Opry* from first broadcast on 11/28/1925 until 1930 (replaced by Harry Stone); stayed on as the program's announcer until September 1947.		
				OPRY: 1925		
				HAYES, Wade	**All-Time: #274**	
				Born on 4/20/1969 in Bethel Acres, Oklahoma. Male singer/songwriter/guitarist. One-half of **McHayes** duo.		
11/19/94+	❶^2	20		1 **Old Enough To Know Better**	*Wade Hayes/Chick Rains*	Columbia
3/18/95	**4**	20		2 **I'm Still Dancin' With You**	S:3 *Wade Hayes/Chick Rains*	Columbia
7/15/95	**10**	20		3 **Don't Stop**	S:16 *Chick Rains/Tom Shapiro*	Columbia
10/28/95+	**5**	20		4 **What I Meant To Say**	S:6 *Don Cook/Sam Hogin/Jim McBride*	Columbia
				above 4 from the album *Old Enough To Know Better* on Columbia 66412		
5/11/96	**2**^{2}	20		5 **On A Good Night**	S:11 *Larry Boone/Don Cook/Paul Nelson*	Columbia
10/5/96	**42**	9		6 **Where Do I Go To Start All Over**	*Wade Hayes/Chick Rains*	Columbia
12/21/96+	**46**	11		7 **It's Over My Head**	*Wade Hayes/Chick Rains*	Columbia
				above 3 from the album *On A Good Night* on Columbia 67563		
8/9/97	**55**	8		8 **Wichita Lineman**	S:18 *Jimmy Webb*	Columbia
11/1/97+	**5**	25		9 **The Day That She Left Tulsa (In A Chevy)**	S:8 *Steve Diamond/Mark D. Sanders*	Columbia
4/11/98	**50**	10		10 **When The Wrong One Loves You Right**	*Leslie Satcher*	Columbia
7/4/98	**13**	24		11 **How Do You Sleep At Night**	*Jim McBride/Jerry Salley*	Columbia
1/16/99	**57**	8		12 **Tore Up From The Floor Up**	*Bob Regan/J.B. Rudd*	Columbia
				above 4 from the album *When The Wrong One Loves You Right* on Columbia 68037		
2/5/00	**48**	12		13 **Up North (Down South, Back East, Out West)**	S:11 *Danny Wells/Jill Wood*	Monument
5/6/00	**45**	14		14 **Goodbye Is The Wrong Way To Go**	S:19 *Shawn Camp/Will Smith*	Monument
				above 2 from the album *Highways And Heartaches* on Monument 69955		
				HAZARD		
				Vocal trio from Hazard, Kentucky: Wayne Davis, Bernie Faulkner and Bruce Dees. Faulkner was a member of **Exile**.		
4/2/83	**69**	5		**Love Letters**	*Edward Heyman/Victor Young*	Warner 29755
				HAZARD, Donna		
				Born in Nashville, Tennessee. Female singer. Session vocalist with **The Concrete Cowboy Band**.		
1/17/81	**45**	9		1 **My Turn**	*Len Chiriacka/Jay Huguely*	Excelsior 1004
5/2/81	**55**	7		2 **Go Home And Go To Pieces**	*Don Roth*	Excelsior 1009
7/11/81	**54**	8		3 **Love Never Hurt So Good**	*Mary Fielder/Bob Whitaker*	Excelsior 1016
12/26/81+	**76**	5		4 **Slow Texas Dancing**	*Donna Hazard/Ed Keeley/Steve Vining*	Excelsior 1020
				HEAD, Roy	**All-Time: #297**	
				Born on 9/1/1941 in Three Rivers, Texas. Male singer/songwriter/guitarist.		
10/19/74	**66**	9		1 **Baby's Not Home**	*Mickey Newbury*	Mega 1219
4/5/75	**19**	14		2 **The Most Wanted Woman In Town**	*Bucky Jones/Royce Porter/Dan Wilson*	Shannon 829
8/16/75	**47**	10		3 **Help Yourself To Me**	*Bucky Jones/Royce Porter*	Shannon 833
11/22/75+	**55**	8		4 **I'll Take It**	*Bobby Abshire*	Shannon 838
2/7/76	**28**	11		5 **The Door I Used To Close**	*Dallas Frazier/Earl Montgomery*	ABC/Dot 17608
6/5/76	**50**	8		6 **Bridge For Crawling Back**	*Bucky Jones/Royce Porter*	ABC/Dot 17629
9/4/76	**51**	8		7 **One Night**	*Dave Bartholomew/Pearl King*	ABC/Dot 17650

DEBUT	PEAK	WKS	GOLD	ARTIST / Country Chart Hit	Ranking / Songwriter	Label (& Number)
				HEAD, Roy — cont'd		
12/25/76+	57	8		8 Angel With A Broken Wing	Don Goodman/Bud Reneau/Mark Sherrill	ABC/Dot 17669
7/2/77	79	6		9 Julianne	Roger Bowling/Bill Emerson	ABC/Dot 17706
10/8/77+	16	20		10 Come To Me	Gene Price	ABC/Dot 17722
4/1/78	19	13		11 Now You See 'Em, Now You Don't	Sterling Whipple	ABC 12346
7/22/78	28	10		12 Tonight's The Night (It's Gonna Be Alright)	Rod Stewart	ABC 12383
11/4/78	45	7		13 Love Survived	Jerry Foster/Bill Rice	ABC 12418
3/24/79	74	5		14 Kiss You And Make It Better	Mac Davis	ABC 12462
11/10/79	79	4		15 In Our Room	Max D. Barnes/Troy Seals	Elektra 46549
2/2/80	65	4		16 The Fire Of Two Old Flames	Max D. Barnes/Troy Seals	Elektra 46582
7/5/80	59	6		17 Long Drop	Pix Pickford	Elektra 46653
9/27/80	70	5		18 Drinkin' Them Long Necks	Danny Morrison/John Wesley Ryles/Johnny Slate	Elektra 47029
10/24/81	75	5		19 After Texas	J. Martin Johnson/Bucky Jones	Churchill 7778
5/29/82	89	3		20 Play Another Gettin' Drunk And Take Somebody Home Song	George Soulé	NSD 129
9/11/82	64	7		21 The Trouble With Hearts	Jerry Davis/Lathan Hudson/Larry Kingston	NSD 146
1/8/83	85	4		22 Your Mama Don't Dance	Kenny Loggins/Jim Messina	NSD 156
12/10/83	79	5		23 Where Did He Go Right	Walt Aldridge/Tom Brasfield	Avion 105
9/7/85	93	2		24 Break Out The Good Stuff	Michael Garvin/Ron Hellard/Bucky Jones	Texas Crude 614
				HEAP, Jimmy, and The Melody Masters		
				Born on 3/3/1922 in Taylor, Texas. Died on 12/4/1977 (age 55). Male singer/guitarist. Leader of swing band, The Melody Masters, which featured lead singer Houston "Perk" Williams. Father of Jimmy Heap, Jr., of **The Drifting Cowboys**.		
1/9/54	5	13		Release Me *[w/ Perk Williams]*	S:5 / J:8 / A:10 *Eddie Miller/W.S. Stevenson*	Capitol 2518
				HEARTLAND		
				Group from Kansas. Led by singer/songwriter Mark Carman.		
9/24/88	79	3		1 New River	Mark Carman	Tra-Star 1221
12/17/88	82	3		2 Making Love To Dixie	Joe Henderson/Dan Mitchell	Tra-Star 1222
3/18/89	61	5		3 Keep The Faith	Jim Sales/Keith Stegall	Tra-Star 1223
				HEART OF NASHVILLE		
				The Heart of Nashville Foundation was founded to benefit the nation's hungry and homeless. Some of the singers participating in this recording include **Roy Acuff**, **Lynn Anderson**, **Eddy Arnold**, **Bobby Bare**, **Sonny James**, **George Jones**, **Webb Pierce**, **Jerry Reed**, **Tanya Tucker**, **Porter Wagoner** and **Faron Young**.		
6/8/85	61	9		One Big Family	Ronnie McDowell/Mike Reid/Troy Seals	Compleat 679001
				HEATH, Boyd		
				Born on 3/2/1910 in Buffalo, New York. Died on 8/4/1994 (age 84). Male singer. Emcee of the NBC-TV show *Saturday Night Jamboree* in 1949.		
5/5/45	7	1		Smoke On The Water	Zeke Clements/Earl Nunn	Bluebird 33-0522
				HEATHERLY, Eric		
				Born on 2/21/1970 in Chattanooga, Tennessee. Male singer/songwriter/guitarist.		
2/26/00	6	28		1 Flowers On The Wall	S:7 *Lew DeWitt*	Mercury
9/16/00	46	10		2 Swimming In Champagne	Richard E. Carpenter/Eric Heatherly	Mercury
11/4/00+	32	21		3 Wrong Five O' Clock	Richard E. Carpenter/Eric Heatherly	Mercury
				above 3 from the album *Swimming In Champagne* on Mercury 170124		
7/6/02	36	17		4 The Last Man Committed	Eric Heatherly	DreamWorks
				HEAVENER, David		
				Born on 12/22/1953 in Louisville, Kentucky. Male singer/songwriter.		
11/28/81	73	4		1 Cheat On Him Tonight	David Heavener	Brent 1017
2/20/82	70	4		2 Honky Tonk Tonight	David Heavener	Brent 1019
7/31/82	86	3		3 I Am The Fire	David Heavener	Brent 1020
				HECKEL, Beverly		
				Born in Elkins, West Virginia. Member of **The Heckels**. Married **Johnny Russell** in 1977. Female singer.		
6/11/77	88	5		1 Don't Hand Me No Hand Me Down Love	Rory Bourke/Charles Silver	RCA 10981
9/16/78	56	7		2 Bluer Than Blue	Randy Goodrum	RCA 11360
				HECKELS, The		
				Family vocal trio from Elkins, West Virginia: sisters Susie Heckel and **Beverly Heckel**, with Susie's husband Denny Franks.		
6/26/76	91	5		A Cowboy Like You	Tompall Glaser	RCA Victor 10685
				HELMS, Bobby	**1950s: #35 / All-Time: #300**	
				Born on 8/15/1935 in Bloomington, Indiana. Died of emphysema on 6/19/1997 (age 61). Male singer/guitarist.		
3/30/57	❶[4]	52		1 Fraulein	A:❶[4] / S:❶[3] / J:9 *Lawton Williams*	Decca 30194
10/14/57	❶[4]	26	●	2 My Special Angel	S:❶[4] / A:❶[1] *Jimmy Duncan*	Decca 30423
12/23/57	13	1	●	3 Jingle Bell Rock	A:13 *Joe Beal/Jim Boothe* [X]	Decca 30513
				also see #13 below		
3/3/58	10	9		4 Just A Little Lonesome	S:10 / A:12 *Cindy Walker*	Decca 30557
5/12/58	5	12		5 Jacqueline	S:5 *Mort Garson/Bob Hilliard*	Decca 30619
				from the movie *The Case Against Brooklyn* starring Darren McGavin		
3/30/59	26	3		6 New River Train	Maggie Andrews	Decca 30831
10/24/60	16	4		7 Lonely River Rhine	Betty Sue Perry	Decca 31148
6/24/67	46	7		8 He Thought He'd Die Laughing	Joe Poovey	Little Darlin' 0030
12/30/67+	60	6		9 The Day You Stop Loving Me	Ray Buzzeo	Little Darlin' 0034
4/20/68	53	9		10 I Feel You, I Love You	Ray Buzzeo	Little Darlin' 0041
8/2/69	43	9		11 So Long	Merrill St. John	Little Darlin' 0062

DEBUT	PEAK	WKS	GOLD	ARTIST / Ranking / Country Chart Hit	Songwriter	Label (& Number)
				HELMS, Bobby — cont'd		
6/27/70	41	9		12 **Mary Goes 'Round**	*Mervin Shiner/Kent Westberry*	Certron 10002
1/4/97	60	2		13 **Jingle Bell Rock**	*Joe Beal/Jim Boothe* **[X-R]**	TVT
				same version as #3 above; from the movie *Jingle All The Way* starring Arnold Schwarzenegger (soundtrack on TVT 8070)		
				HENDERSON, Brice		
				Born on 1/4/1954 in Frederick, Maryland. Male singer.		
1/22/83	61	7		1 **Lonely Eyes**	*Bob McDill*	Union Station 1000
4/30/83	55	8		2 **Lovers Again**	*Dave Gillon*	Union Station 1001
9/17/83	64	5		3 **Flames**	*Mark True*	Union Station 1003
				HENDERSON, Mike		
				Born on 7/14/1953 in Independence, Missouri. Male singer/songwriter.		
2/5/94	69	4		**Hillbilly Jitters**	*Mike Henderson/Walt Wilson*	RCA
				from the album *Country Music Made Me Do It* on RCA 66324		
				HENHOUSE FIVE PLUS TOO — see STEVENS, Ray		
				HENLEY, Don		
				Born on 7/22/1947 in Gilmer, Texas. Rock singer/songwriter/drummer. Member of the **Eagles**. Married model Sharon Summerall on 5/20/1995.		
11/7/92+	2[1]	20		1 **Walkaway Joe** *[w/ Trisha Yearwood]*	*Greg Barnhill/Vince Melamed*	MCA
				from Yearwood's album *Hearts In Armor* on MCA 10641		
10/28/00	61	6		2 **For My Wedding**	*Larry John McNally*	Warner
				from the album *Inside Job* on Warner 47083		
12/1/01+	31	19		3 **Inside Out** *[w/ Trisha Yearwood]*	*Bryan Adams/Gretchen Peters*	MCA Nashville
				from Yearwood's album *Inside Out* on MCA Nashville 70200		
				HENRY, Audie		
				Born in Brazil; raised in Canada. Female singer.		
1/19/85	97	3		1 **You'll Never Find A Good Man (Playing In A Country Band)**	*Stan Ratliff*	Canyon Creek 2025
4/27/85	91	2		2 **Being A Fool Again**	*Helen Cornelius*	Canyon Creek 2008
7/27/85	73	5		3 **Heaven Knows**	*Jimmy Darrell/Raleigh Squires/Billy Williams*	Canyon Creek 5020
10/19/85	71	5		4 **Sweet Salvation**	*Don Cook/Chip Hardy*	Canyon Creek 8019
				HENSLEY, Tari		
				Born Tari Hodges on 3/6/1953 in Independence, Missouri. Female singer.		
4/9/83	86	3		1 **Falling In Love**	*Bob McDill*	Mercury 76197
9/8/84	69	4		2 **Love Isn't Love ('Til You Give It Away)**	*Don Roth/Timmy Tappan*	Mercury 880054
2/9/85	61	6		3 **I'm The One Who's Breaking Up**	*Bruce Burch/Gene Dobbins/Pat McManus*	Mercury 880424
7/27/85	64	6		4 **Hard Baby To Rock**	*Mark Collie/David Luttrell/Phil Thomas*	Mercury 880801
4/5/86	57	7		5 **Oh Yes I Can**	*Susanna Clark/John Reid*	Mercury 884484
7/26/86	52	10		6 **I've Cried A Mile**	*Tompall Glaser/Harlan Howard*	Mercury 884852
				HERMAN, Woody		
				Born on 5/16/1913 in Milwaukee, Wisconsin. Died of heart failure on 10/29/1987 (age 74). Legendary big band saxophonist/clarinetist. Won Grammy's Lifetime Achievement Award in 1987.		
5/12/79	69	4		**My Blue Heaven** *[w/ Mac Wiseman]*	*Walter Donaldson/George Whiting*	Churchill 7735
				HERNDON, Ty — **All-Time: #240**		
				Born Boyd Tyrone Herndon on 5/2/1962 in Meridian, Mississippi; raised in Butler, Alabama. Male singer/guitarist.		
2/25/95	❶[1]	20		1 **What Mattered Most**	S:4 *Gary Burr/Vince Melamed*	Epic
6/10/95	7	20		2 **I Want My Goodbye Back**	S:22 *Dave Berg/Pat Bunch/Doug Johnson*	Epic
10/14/95+	21	20		3 **Heart Half Empty** *[w/ Stephanie Bentley]*	S:10 *Gary Burr/Desmond Child*	Epic
3/30/96	63	2		4 **In Your Face**	*Annette Cotter/Kim Tribble*	Epic
				above 4 from the album *What Mattered Most* on Epic 66397		
6/29/96	❶[1]	20		5 **Living In A Moment**	S:8 *Pat Bunch/Doug Johnson*	Epic
11/2/96+	21	20		6 **She Wants To Be Wanted Again**	S:20 *Billy Henderson/Steven Jones*	Epic
3/22/97	2[2]	20		7 **Loved Too Much**	*Billy Livsey/Don Schlitz*	Epic
9/20/97	17	20		8 **I Have To Surrender**	*Pat Bunch/Doug Johnson*	Epic
				above 4 from the album *Living In A Moment* on Epic 67564		
3/28/98	5	23		9 **A Man Holdin' On (To A Woman Lettin' Go)**	S:11 *Gene Dobbins/John Ramey/Bobby Taylor*	Epic
8/15/98	❶[1]	26		10 **It Must Be Love**	*Craig Bickhardt/Jack Sundrud*	Epic
12/26/98+	5	26		11 **Hands Of A Working Man**	*Jim Collins/D. Vincent Williams*	Epic
				above 3 from the album *Big Hopes* on Epic 68167		
8/21/99	18	20		12 **Steam**	S:3 *Lewis Anderson/Bob Regan*	Epic
1/15/00	72	2		13 **You Can Leave Your Hat On**	*Randy Newman*	Epic
1/22/00	26	20		14 **No Mercy**	S:6 *Todd Cerney/Steve Davis/Dennis W. Morgan*	Epic
7/15/00	58	9		15 **A Love Like That**	*Marc Beeson/Don Pfrimmer*	Epic
				above 4 from the album *Steam* on Epic 79269		
12/29/01+	37	19		16 **Heather's Wall**	*Rick Giles/Gilles Godard/Tim Nichols*	Epic
7/6/02	55	3		17 **A Few Short Years**	*Sonny Tillis/Bobby Tomberlin*	Epic
				from the album *This Is Ty Herndon: Greatest Hits* on Epic 86642		
				HERRING, Red		
				Born in Tennessee. Male singer/songwriter.		
7/4/60	27	2		**Wasted Love**	*Red Herring*	Country Jubilee 533
				HESTER, Hoot		
				Born Hubert Hester on 8/13/1951 in Louisville, Kentucky. Male singer.		
4/21/79	95	3		**I Still Love Her Memory**	*Duane Hester*	Little Darlin' 7911

Billboard DEBUT	PEAK	WKS	GOLD	ARTIST / Country Chart Hit	Ranking / Songwriter	Label (& Number)

HEWITT, Dolph

Born on 7/15/1914 in West Finley, Pennsylvania. Died on 12/10/1996 (age 82). Male singer/guitarist. Regular on the WLS *National Barn Dance* from 1946-60.

DEBUT	PEAK	WKS	GOLD	Country Chart Hit	Songwriter	Label (& Number)
12/17/49	8	1		I Wish I Knew ... A:8	*Ellen Endsley/Melvin Endsley*	RCA Victor 21-0107

HIATT, John

Born on 8/20/1952 in Indianapolis, Indiana. Rock singer/songwriter/guitarist.

DEBUT	PEAK	WKS	GOLD	Country Chart Hit	Songwriter	Label (& Number)
3/3/90	63	6		One Step Over The Line *[w/ The Nitty Gritty Dirt Band & Rosanne Cash]*	*John Hiatt*	Universal

HICKEY, Sara "Honeybear"

Born in Exeter, California. Female singer. Won the 1977 Miss California Rodeo contest.

DEBUT	PEAK	WKS	GOLD	Country Chart Hit	Songwriter	Label (& Number)
6/25/83	82	2		This Ain't Tennessee And He Ain't You	*Larry Bastian/Jim Shaw*	PCM 203

HICKS, Jeanette

Born in 1934 in Dothan, Alabama. Female singer.

DEBUT	PEAK	WKS	GOLD	Country Chart Hit	Songwriter	Label (& Number)
1/26/57	10	1		Yearning *[w/ George Jones]* ... J:10	*Eddie Eddings/George Jones*	Starday 279

HICKS, Laney — see SMALLWOOD, Laney

HIGGINS, Bertie

Born Elbert Higgins on 12/8/1944 in Tarpon Springs, Florida. Male singer/songwriter.

DEBUT	PEAK	WKS	GOLD	Country Chart Hit	Songwriter	Label (& Number)
3/13/82	50	10	●	1 Key Largo inspired by the movie starring Humphrey Bogart and Lauren Bacall	*Bertie Higgins/Sonny Limbo*	Kat Family 02524
6/19/82	90	3		2 Just Another Day In Paradise	*Bertie Higgins/Columbia Jones/Sonny Limbo*	Kat Family 02839
9/3/88	72	5		3 You Blossom Me	*Buddy Buie/Ronnie Hammond*	Southern Tracks 2000
1/21/89	75	5		4 Homeless People	*Buddy Buie/Bertie Higgins/Sonny Limbo*	Southern Tracks 2005

HIGHFILL, George

Born in Fort Smith, Arkansas; raised in Stigler, Oklahoma. Male singer/songwriter.

DEBUT	PEAK	WKS	GOLD	Country Chart Hit	Songwriter	Label (& Number)
7/18/87	69	4		1 Waitin' Up	*George Highfill*	Warner 28312
10/31/87	72	4		2 Mad Money	*George Highfill*	Warner 28177

HIGHWAY 101 — **All-Time: #205**

Group formed in Los Angeles, California: **Paulette Carlson** (vocals, guitar; born on 10/11/1953), Jack Daniels (guitar; born on 10/27/1949), Curtis Stone (bass; born on 4/3/1950) and Scott "Cactus" Moser (drums; born on 5/3/1957). Stone is the son of **Cliffie Stone**. Carlson left in late 1990; replaced by Nikki Nelson (born on 1/3/1969). Also see **Tomorrow's World**.

CMA: Vocal Group 1988 & 1989

DEBUT	PEAK	WKS	GOLD	Country Chart Hit	Songwriter	Label (& Number)
1/10/87	4	24		1 The Bed You Made For Me ... S:4 / A:4	*Paulette Carlson*	Warner 28483
5/23/87	2[1]	23		2 Whiskey, If You Were A Woman ... S:❶[1]	*Mary Francis/Johnny MacRae/Bob Morrison*	Warner 28372
9/26/87	❶[2]	23		3 Somewhere Tonight ... S:3	*Rodney Crowell/Harlan Howard*	Warner 28223
2/13/88	❶[1]	19		4 Cry, Cry, Cry ... S:2	*Don Devaney/John Scott Sherrill*	Warner 28105
6/18/88	❶[1]	20		5 (Do You Love Me) Just Say Yes ... S:2	*Bob DiPiero/Dennis Robbins/John Sherrill*	Warner 27867
10/22/88+	5	19		6 All The Reasons Why ... S:6	*Paulette Carlson/Beth Nielsen Chapman*	Warner 27735
2/11/89	7	18		7 Setting Me Up	*Mark Knopfler*	Warner 27581
6/17/89	6	21		8 Honky Tonk Heart	*Jim Photoglo/Russell Smith*	Warner 22955
10/7/89+	❶[1]	26		9 Who's Lonely Now	*Kix Brooks/Don Cook*	Warner 22779
2/10/90	4	26		10 Walkin', Talkin', Cryin', Barely Beatin' Broken Heart	*Roger Miller/Justin Tubb*	Warner
5/26/90	11	21		11 This Side Of Goodbye above 2 from the album *Paint The Town* on Warner 25992	*Cactus Moser/Mike Noble/Jeff Pennig*	Warner
9/22/90	14	20		12 Someone Else's Trouble Now from the album *Greatest Hits* on Warner 26253	*Gary Nicholson/Pam Tillis*	Warner
4/13/91	14	20		13 Bing Bang Boom	*Hugh Prestwood*	Warner
9/14/91	31	20		14 The Blame	*Cactus Moser/Gene Nelson/Paul Nelson*	Warner
1/11/92	22	20		15 Baby, I'm Missing You	*Nancy Montgomery/Steve Seskin*	Warner
5/23/92	54	7		16 Honky Tonk Baby above 4 from the album *Bing Bang Boom* on Warner 26588	*Mike Henderson/Mark Irwin*	Warner
10/2/93	67	2		17 You Baby You from the album *The New Frontier* on Liberty 81351	*Gary Mallaber/Chris McCarty*	Liberty

HILKA

Born Hilka Cornelius in Germany; raised in Salt Lake City, Utah. Female singer/songwriter. Member of **Dandy**.

DEBUT	PEAK	WKS	GOLD	Country Chart Hit	Songwriter	Label (& Number)
10/13/79	89	3		1 I Just Wonder Where He Could Be Tonight *[w/ Jebry Lee Briley]*	*Hilka Cornelius*	IBC 0004
2/9/80	96	2		2 (I'm Just The) Cuddle Up Kind	*Lee Morgan*	IBC 0006

HILL, Billy — see BILLY HILL

HILL, Faith — **1990s: #25 / 2000s: #18 / All-Time: #93**

Born on 9/21/1967 in Jackson, Mississippi. Adopted at less than a week old and raised as Audrey Faith Perry in Star, Mississippi. Female singer. Began singing in church at age three. Moved to Nashville in 1987. Briefly married to musician Daniel Hill in the late 1980s (took his last name). Married **Tim McGraw** on 10/6/1996. Played "Sarah Sunderson" in the movie *The Stepford Wives*. Also see **Hope** and **One Heart At A Time**.

CMA: Female Vocalist 2000

DEBUT	PEAK	WKS	GOLD	Country Chart Hit	Songwriter	Label (& Number)
10/16/93+	❶[4]	20		1 Wild One	*Pat Bunch/Jamie Kyle/Will Rambeaux*	Warner
2/12/94	❶[1]	20		2 Piece Of My Heart	*Bert Berns/Jerry Ragovoy*	Warner
6/4/94	35	12		3 But I Will	*Troy Seals/Eddie Setser/Larry Stewart*	Warner

DEBUT	PEAK	WKS	GOLD	#	ARTIST / Country Chart Hit	Ranking / Songwriter	Label (& Number)
					HILL, Faith — cont'd		
9/24/94	**2^{2}**	20		4	**Take Me As I Am**	*Bob DiPiero/Karen Staley*	Warner
					above 4 from the album *Take Me As I Am* on Warner 45389		
8/5/95	**5**	20		5	**Let's Go To Vegas**	S:8 *Karen Staley*	Warner
11/11/95+	**❶^{3}**	20		6	**It Matters To Me**	S:❶^{10} *Ed Hill/Mark D. Sanders*	Warner
2/24/96	**3^{1}**	20		7	**Someone Else's Dream**	*Karen Staley*	Warner
7/13/96	**6**	20		8	**You Can't Lose Me**	*Trey Bruce/Thom McHugh*	Warner
10/19/96+	**8**	20		9	**I Can't Do That Anymore**	*Alan Jackson*	Warner
					above 5 from the album *It Matters To Me* on Warner 45872		
5/10/97	**❶^{6}**	20	▲	10	**It's Your Love** *[w/ Tim McGraw]*	S:❶^{12} *Stephony Smith*	Curb
					CMA: Vocal Event; from McGraw's album *Everywhere* on Curb 77886		
2/28/98	**❶^{3}**	25	▲	11	**This Kiss**	S:❶^{21} *Beth Nielsen Chapman/Robin Lerner/Annie Roboff*	Warner
5/30/98	**3^{2}**	20		12	**Just To Hear You Say That You Love Me** *[w/ Tim McGraw]*	*Diane Warren*	Warner
9/12/98	**❶^{1}**	21		13	**Let Me Let Go**	*Steve Diamond/Dennis W. Morgan*	Warner
1/16/99	**12**	20		14	**Love Ain't Like That**	*Tim Gaetano/A.J. Masters*	Warner
5/8/99	**4**	24		15	**The Secret Of Life**	*Gretchen Peters*	Warner
					above 5 from the album *Faith* on Warner 46790		
10/9/99	**❶^{6}**	28	●	16	**Breathe**	S:❶^{12} *Stephanie Bentley/Holly Lamar*	Warner
					Grammy: Female Vocal		
11/20/99+	**6**	45		17	**Let's Make Love** *[w/ Tim McGraw]*	*Marv Green/Chris Lindsey/Bill Luther/Aimee Mayo*	Warner/Curb
					Grammy: Vocal Collaboration; also from McGraw's album *Greatest Hits* on Curb 77978		
11/27/99+	**❶^{4}**	38		18	**The Way You Love Me**	S:❶^{15} *Mike Delaney/Keith Follese*	Warner
11/27/99+	**63**	4		19	**I Got My Baby**	*Bob DiPiero/Annie Roboff*	Warner
11/27/99	**68**	1		20	**It Will Be Me**	*Gordon Kennedy/Wayne Kirkpatrick*	Warner
11/27/99	**74**	1		21	**If I'm Not In Love**	*Dawn Thomas*	Warner
10/28/00+	**36**	17		22	**There Will Come A Day**	*Chris Lindsey/Bill Luther/Aimee Mayo*	Warner
12/9/00+	**26**	6		23	**Where Are You Christmas?**	*Mariah Carey/James Horner/Will Jennings* **[X]**	Interscope
					from the movie *Dr. Seuss' How The Grinch Stole Christmas* starring Jim Carrey (soundtrack on Interscope 490765)		
1/13/01	**3^{1}**	20		24	**If My Heart Had Wings**	*Fred Knoblock/Annie Roboff*	Warner
					#16-22 & 24: from the album *Breathe* on Warner 47373		
5/26/01	**11**	20		25	**There You'll Be**	S:10 *Diane Warren*	Warner
					from the movie *Pearl Harbor* starring Ben Affleck (soundtrack on Warner 48113)		
9/29/01	**35**	13		26	**The Star Spangled Banner**	*Francis Scott Key* **[L]**	Warner
					recorded at the 2000 Super Bowl		
8/24/02	**12**	20		27	**Cry**	*Angie Aparo*	Warner
					Grammy: Female Vocal		
11/23/02+	**26**	20		28	**When The Lights Go Down**	*Rivers Rutherford/Jeffrey Steele/Craig Wiseman*	Warner
5/10/03	**28**	16		29	**You're Still Here**	S:6 *Matraca Berg/Aimee Mayo*	Warner
					above 3 from the album *Cry* on Warner 48001		
5/28/05	**❶^{2}**	18↑		30	**Mississippi Girl**	*John Rich/Adam Shoenfield*	Warner
					from the album *Fireflies* on Warner 48794		
					HILL, Goldie	**1950s: #46**	
					Born Argolda Voncile Hill on 1/11/1933 in Karnes County, Texas. Died of cancer on 2/24/2005 (age 72). Married **Carl Smith** on 9/19/1957. Known as "The Golden Hillbilly."		
					OPRY: 1953		
1/10/53	**❶^{3}**	9		1	**I Let The Stars Get In My Eyes**	J:❶^{3} / S:4 *Goldie Hill/Virginia Suber/Slim Willet*	Decca 28473
					answer to "Don't Let The Stars Get In Your Eyes" by **Slim Willet**		
7/3/54	**4**	21		2	**Looking Back To See** *[w/ Justin Tubb]*	J:4 / S:5 / A:5 *Jim Ed Brown/Maxine Brown*	Decca 29145
1/8/55	**11**	2		3	**Sure Fire Kisses** *[w/ Justin Tubb]*	A:11 / S:13 *George Mysels/Jack Perry/Michael Philips/Harry Sims*	Decca 29349
3/26/55	**14**	2		4	**Are You Mine** *[w/ Red Sovine]*	S:14 *Jim Amadeo/Don Grashey/Myrna Lorrie*	Decca 29411
2/23/59	**17**	4		5	**Yankee, Go Home**	*Harlan Howard*	Decca 30826
					Red Sovine (narration)		
4/6/68	**73**	2		6	**Lovable Fool** *[Goldie Hill Smith]*	*Harlan Howard*	Epic 10296
					HILL, Kim		
					Born on 12/30/1963 in Starkville, Mississippi. Female singer.		
4/2/94	**68**	6			**Janie's Gone Fishin'**	*Wayne Kirkpatrick*	BNA
					from the album *So Far, So Good* on BNA 66332		
					HILL, Tiny		
					Born Harry Hill on 7/19/1906 in Sullivan Township, Illinois. Died in 1972 (age 66). Male novelty singer. Nicknamed "Tiny" because of his weight (350 pounds).		
					EARLY HITS: Doodle Doo Doo (1939) / Angry (1939)		
1/26/46	**3^{2}**	4		1	**Sioux City Sue**	*Ray Freedman/Dick Thomas* **[N]**	Mercury 2024
1/10/48	**5**	1		2	**Never Trust A Woman** *[w/ The Cactus Cutups]*	*Jenny Lou Carson* **[N]**	Mercury 6062
2/3/51	**7**	2		3	**Hot Rod Race**	S:7 *George Wilson* **[N]**	Mercury 5547-X45
					original version of **Charlie Ryan**'s 1960 hit "Hot Rod Lincoln"		
3/24/51	**10**	1		4	**I'll Sail My Ship Alone**	J:10 *Henry Bernard/Morry Burns/Lois Mann/Henry Thurston*	Mercury 5508-X45
					HILL CITY		
					Group from Fort Worth, Texas.		
8/10/85	**86**	3			**I'd Do It In A Heartbeat**	*Rick Giles/Gary Harrison*	Moon Shine 3040

DEBUT	PEAK	WKS	GOLD	ARTIST / Ranking / Country Chart Hit / Songwriter	Label (& Number)
				HILLMAN, Chris	
				Born on 12/4/1944 in Los Angeles, California. Male singer/songwriter/guitarist. Member of The Byrds from 1964-68 and the **Flying Burrito Brothers** from 1968-72. Formed **The Desert Rose Band** in 1986.	
9/29/84	**81**	6		1 **Somebody's Back In Town** ... *Don Helms/Doyle Wilburn/Teddy Wilburn*	Sugar Hill 4105
4/27/85	**77**	5		2 **Running The Roadblocks** ... *Chris Hillman/Pete Knobler*	Sugar Hill 4106
4/29/89	**6**	21		3 **You Ain't Going Nowhere** ***[w/ Roger McGuinn]*** ... *Bob Dylan*	Universal 66006
				HILTON, Denny	
				Born in Missouri. Male singer.	
3/28/81	**84**	2		1 **Layin' Low** ... *Brenda Libby*	Oak 1027
2/13/82	**92**	2		2 **How'd You Get So Good** ... *Michael Garvin/Chris Waters*	Rosebridge 0014
2/5/83	**88**	2		3 **Sharing The Night Together** ... *Ava Aldridge/Eddie Struzick*	Rosebridge 010
				HINOJOSA, Tish	
				Born Leticia Hinojosa on 2/6/1955 in San Antonio, Texas. Female singer/songwriter.	
6/14/86	**80**	3		1 **I'll Pull You Through** ***[w/ Craig Dillingham]*** ... *Joe Lubinsky/Howard Pfeifer*	MCA/Curb 52823
12/23/89+	**75**	4		2 **Til U Love Me Again** ... *Tish Hinojosa*	A&M 1468
				HITCHCOCK, Stan	
				Born on 3/21/1936 in Kansas City, Missouri. Male singer. Worked as a DJ on KWTO and KTTS in Springfield, Missouri. Moved to Nashville in 1962. Own TV series in the mid-1960s. Former program director for Country Music Television.	
9/16/67	**54**	6		1 **She's Looking Good** ... *Autry Inman*	Epic 10182
12/9/67	**66**	2		2 **Rings** ... *Ray Pennington/Billy Sherrill*	Epic 10246
5/18/68	**57**	8		3 **I'm Easy To Love** ... *Curly Putman*	Epic 10307
10/19/68	**60**	4		4 **The Phoenix Flash** ... *Red Lane/Curly Putman*	Epic 10388
10/11/69	**17**	11		5 **Honey, I'm Home** *Jerry Foster/Bill Rice*	Epic 10525
4/18/70	**46**	6		6 **Call Me Gone** ... *Jerry Foster*	Epic 10586
10/17/70	**54**	7		7 **Dixie Belle** ... *Jerry Foster/Bill Rice*	GRT 23
3/13/71	**59**	7		8 **At Least Part Of The Way** ... *Jerry Foster/Bill Rice*	GRT 39
7/14/73	**65**	7		9 **The Same Old Way** ... *Jerry Foster/Bill Rice*	Cinnamon 759
12/8/73	**91**	4		10 **Half-Empty Bed** ... *Bob McDill/Allen Reynolds*	Cinnamon 770
3/9/74	**80**	7		11 **I'm Free** ... *Jerry Foster/Bill Rice*	Cinnamon 782
6/3/78	**100**	2		12 **Falling** ... *Lenny LeBlanc/Eddie Struzick*	MMI 1024
3/10/79	**85**	3		13 **Finders Keepers Losers Weepers** ***[w/ Sue Richards]*** ... *Murry Kellum/Pearly Mitchell*	MMI 1028
4/11/81	**81**	4		14 **She Sings Amazing Grace** ... *Jerry Foster/Bill Rice*	Ramblin' 1711
				HOBBS, Becky	
				Born Rebecca Ann Hobbs on 1/24/1950 in Bartlesville, Oklahoma. Female singer/songwriter/guitarist.	
12/23/78+	**95**	5		1 **The More I Get The More I Want** ... *Becky Hobbs/Ben Raleigh*	Mercury 55049
6/30/79	**44**	11		2 **I Can't Say Goodbye To You** ... *Becky Hobbs*	Mercury 55062
12/8/79+	**52**	9		3 **Just What The Doctor Ordered** ... *Becky Hobbs*	Mercury 57010
5/3/80	**79**	6		4 **I'm Gonna Love You Tonight (Like There's No Tomorrow)** ... *Becky Hobbs*	Mercury 57020
10/11/80	**87**	2		5 **I Learned All About Cheatin' From You** ... *Becky Hobbs*	Mercury 57033
2/7/81	**84**	4		6 **Honky-Tonk Saturday Night** ... *Becky Hobbs/Michael Martin*	Mercury 57041
6/25/83	**10**	18		7 **Let's Get Over Them Together** ***[w/ Moe Bandy]*** *Charlie Craig/Keith Stegall*	Columbia 03970
6/2/84	**46**	10		8 **Oklahoma Heart** ... *Byron Gallimore/Becky Hobbs/Blake Mevis/Bill Shore*	Liberty 1520
9/8/84	**64**	6		9 **Pardon Me (Haven't We Loved Somewhere Before)** ... *Becky Hobbs/Candy Parton*	EMI America 8224
12/8/84	**77**	6		10 **Wheels In Emotion** ... *Randy Albright/John Greenebaum/Becky Hobbs*	EMI America 8247
6/22/85	**37**	12		11 **Hottest "Ex" In Texas** ... *James Blackmon/Leigh Traughber/Carl Vipperman*	EMI America 8273
3/5/88	**31**	19		12 **Jones On The Jukebox** ... S:13 *Don Goodman/Becky Hobbs/Mack Vickery*	MTM 72104
7/9/88	**43**	10		13 **They Always Look Better When They're Leavin'** ... S:18 *Becky Hobbs*	MTM 72109
10/8/88	**53**	9		14 **Are There Any More Like You (Where You Came From)** ... *Becky Hobbs*	MTM 72114
8/5/89	**39**	11		15 **Do You Feel The Same Way Too?** ... *Becky Hobbs*	RCA 8974
				HOBBS, Bud, with His Trail Herders	
				Born in San Francisco, California. Male singer/guitarist.	
9/25/48	**13**	1		1 **Lazy Mazy** ... J:13 *Sheb Wooley*	MGM 10206
1/29/49	**12**	4		2 **I Heard About You** ... J:12 / S:13 *Sheb Wooley*	MGM 10305
5/21/49	**12**	1		3 **Candy Kisses** ... J:12 / S:13 *George Morgan*	MGM 10366
				HOBBS, Lou	
				Born in Cape Girardeau, Missouri. Male singer.	
3/7/81	**79**	3		1 **Loving You Was All I Ever Needed** ... *Stan Kesler/Bobby Wood*	Kik 902
9/5/81	**93**	2		2 **We're Building Our Love On A Rock** ... *Jim McBride/Roger Murrah*	Kik 911
				HOBBS, Pam	
				Born in West Memphis, Arkansas. Female singer.	
2/7/81	**85**	4		1 **Have You Ever Seen The Rain** ... *John Fogerty*	50 States 79
5/2/81	**88**	2		2 **I Thought I Heard You Calling My Name** ... *Lee Emerson*	50 States 81
9/26/81	**93**	2		3 **You're The Only Dancer** ... *Jackie DeShannon*	50 States 84
				HOFFMAN, Billy	
				Born in Arkansas; raised in Poteau, Oklahoma. Male singer/guitarist.	
6/17/00	**69**	1		1 **Perfect Night** ... *Helen Hamm/Tony Stampley*	Critter
12/2/00	**75**	1		2 **You're The Ticket** ... *Jess Brown/Keith Follese/Wade Kirby*	Critter
				above 2 from the album *All I Wanted Was You* on Critter 10012	

Billboard DEBUT	PEAK	WKS	GOLD	ARTIST / Country Chart Hit	Ranking / Songwriter	Label (& Number)
				HOGSED, Roy		
				Born on 12/24/1919 in Flippin, Arkansas. Died in March 1978 (age 58). Male singer.		
8/21/48	**15**	1		**Cocaine Blues** J:15	*Woody Guthrie/Cisco Houston*	Capitol 40120
				HOKUM, Suzi Jane		
				Born in Los Angeles, California. Female singer.		
9/9/67	**51**	7		1 **Here We Go Again** ***[w/ Virgil Warner]***	*Don Lanier/Red Steagall*	LHI 17018
2/24/68	**65**	4		2 **Storybook Children** ***[w/ Virgil Warner]***	*Chip Taylor/Billy Vera*	LHI 1204
8/30/69	**75**	2		3 **Reason To Believe**	*Tim Hardin*	LHI 14
				HOLDEN, Rebecca		
				Born on 6/12/1958 in San Antonio, Texas. Female singer/actress. Played "April Curtis" on TV's *Knight Rider.*		
11/25/89	**82**	2		1 **The Truth Doesn't Always Rhyme**	*Bill Anderson/Lari White*	Tra-Star 1229
12/16/89	**78**	4		2 **License To Steal**	*Mike Anthony/Ron Moore*	Tra-Star 1234
				HOLLADAY, Dave		
				Born David Blanchette in 1958 in Charleston, South Carolina. Committed suicide on 9/19/2002 (age 44). Male singer/guitarist.		
12/13/86	**83**	4		**Now She's In Paris**	*Wade Kirby/Jesse Shofner*	Step One 365
				HOLLAND, Greg		
				Born on 2/22/1967 in Douglas, Georgia. Male singer.		
8/6/94	**63**	5		1 **Let Me Drive**	*Bob DiPiero/Gerry House*	Warner
11/12/94	**66**	5		2 **When I Come Back (I Wanna Be My Dog)**	*Al Anderson/Craig Wiseman*	Warner
				above 2 from the album *Let Me Drive* on Warner 45638		
				HOLLIER, Jill		
				Born in Port Arthur, Texas. Female singer.		
11/15/86	**79**	2		1 **Sweet Time**	*Gary Baker/Susan Longacre/Quentin Powers*	Warner 28559
8/12/89	**83**	3		2 **If It Wasn't For The Heartache**	*Kix Brooks/Chris Waters*	Warner 22966
				from the movie *Pink Cadillac* starring **Clint Eastwood**		
12/23/89+	**81**	4		3 **Mama's Daily Bread**	*Toni Dae/Mike Lantrip*	Warner 22700
				HOLLOWELL, Terri		
				Born on 7/2/1956 in Jeffersonville, Indiana. Female singer.		
6/17/78	**81**	4		1 **Happy Go Lucky Morning**	*Scott Summer*	Con Brio 134
9/23/78	**76**	4		2 **Strawberry Fields Forever**	*John Lennon/Paul McCartney*	Con Brio 139
12/23/78+	**76**	6		3 **Just Stay With Me**	*Lori Parker*	Con Brio 144
3/24/79	**35**	11		4 **May I**	*Ken Bowman*	Con Brio 150
7/21/79	**56**	8		5 **It's Too Soon To Say Goodbye**	*Joe Ashley*	Con Brio 156
				HOLLY, Doyle		
				Born Doyle Hendricks on 6/30/1936 in Perkins, Oklahoma. Male singer/bassist. Member of **The Buckaroos** from 1963-70.		
11/18/72	**63**	6		1 **My Heart Cries For You**	*Percy Faith/Carl Sigman*	Barnaby 5004
6/16/73	**29**	14		2 **Queen Of The Silver Dollar**	*Shel Silverstein*	Barnaby 5018
10/6/73	**17**	13		3 **Lila**	*Bob Millsap*	Barnaby 5027
3/2/74	**58**	9		4 **Lord How Long Has This Been Going On** ***[w/ The Vanishing Breed]***	*Lee Morris*	Barnaby 5030
6/15/74	**75**	8		5 **A Rainbow In My Hand**	*Bob Millsap/Coke Sams*	Barnaby 602
9/7/74	**69**	6		6 **Just Another Cowboy Song**	*Dennis Coats*	Barnaby 605
11/16/74+	**53**	11		7 **Richard And The Cadillac Kings**	*Elwood Simpson/Stephen K. Smith*	Barnaby 608
				HOLM, Johnny		
				Born in Fargo, North Dakota. Male singer/guitarist.		
10/1/77	**100**	2		**Lightnin' Bar Blues**	*Hoyt Axton*	ASI 1012
				HOLMES, Monty		
				Born in Lubbock, Texas. Male singer.		
1/21/89	**82**	3		1 **A Way To Survive**	*Moneen Carpenter/Hank Cochran*	Ashley 1001
5/16/98	**43**	16		2 **Why'd You Start Lookin' So Good**	*Paul Davis*	Bang II
8/29/98	**53**	12		3 **Alone**	*Barry Gibb/Maurice Gibb/Robin Gibb*	Bang II
11/14/98	**59**	5		4 **Leave My Mama Out Of This**	*Kent Blazy/Monty Holmes/Royal Wade Kimes*	Bang II
				above 3 from the album *All I Ever Wanted* on Bang II 2000		
				HOLT, Darrell		
				Born in Tennessee. Male singer/songwriter. Former singer with the group **Sweetwater**.		
12/12/87+	**57**	10		1 **Catch 22**	*Norma Gelin/Darrell Holt*	Anoka 222
3/26/88	**58**	9		2 **I Can't Take Her Anywhere**	*Walt Aldridge/John Jarrard*	Anoka 221
10/1/88	**66**	6		3 **I'd Throw It All Away**	*Darrell Holt*	Anoka 224
2/11/89	**71**	5		4 **Only The Strong Survive**	*Jerry Butler/Kenny Gamble/Leon Huff*	Anoka 225
				HOLY, Steve	**2000s: #40**	
				Born on 2/23/1972 in Dallas, Texas. Male singer.		
10/16/99+	**29**	20		1 **Don't Make Me Beg**	*Frank Rogers*	Curb
4/22/00	**24**	24		2 **Blue Moon** S:9	*Gary Leach/Mark Tinney*	Curb
11/11/00+	**24**	25		3 **The Hunger**	*David Flint/Billy Montana*	Curb
7/28/01+	**❶[5]**	41		4 **Good Morning Beautiful**	*Todd Cerney/Zack Lyle*	Curb
				above 4 from the album *Blue Moon* on Curb 77972		
9/7/02	**27**	20		5 **I'm Not Breakin'**	*Marc Christian/John Foster*	Curb
2/8/03	**37**	14		6 **Rock-A-Bye Heart**	*Dennis Matkosky/Arnie Roman*	Curb
5/22/04	**26**	21		7 **Put Your Best Dress On**	*Bill Austin/Dillon Dixon/Don Pfrimmer/Dave Williams*	Curb
4/30/05	**49**	11		8 **Go Home**	*Jim Collins/Curtis Wright*	Curb

Billboard DEBUT	PEAK	WKS	GOLD	ARTIST / Country Chart Hit	Ranking / Songwriter	Label (& Number)

HOMER AND JETHRO — HOF: 2001

Comedy duo from Knoxville, Tennessee: Henry "Homer" Haynes (guitar) and Kenneth "Jethro" Burns (mandolin). Homer was born on 7/27/1920; died of a heart attack on 8/7/1971 (age 51). Jethro was born on 3/10/1920; died of cancer on 2/4/1989 (age 68). Regulars on the WLS *National Barn Dance* from 1950-58. Also see **Some Of Chet's Friends**.

DEBUT	PEAK	WKS	Country Chart Hit	Songwriter	Label (& Number)
3/26/49	**14**	1	1 **I Feel That Old Age Creeping On**	J:14 *Jethro Burns/Homer Haynes* **[N]**	King 749
8/27/49	**9**	1	2 **Baby, It's Cold Outside** *[w/ June Carter]*	S:9 *Frank Loesser* **[N]**	RCA Victor 48-0075
			from the movie *Neptune's Daughter* starring Esther Williams		
11/5/49	**14**	1	3 **Tennessee Border-No. 2**	J:14 *Jimmy Work* **[N]**	RCA Victor 21-0110
			parody of "Tennessee Border" by **Red Foley**		
5/23/53	**2**[2]	9	4 **(How Much Is) That Hound Dog In The Window**	S:2 / J:3 / A:10 *Bob Merrill* **[N]**	RCA Victor 5280
			parody of "The Doggie In The Window" by **Patti Page**		
8/14/54	**14**	1	5 **Hernando's Hideaway**	S:14 *Richard Adler/Jerry Ross* **[N]**	RCA Victor 5788
10/19/59	**26**	3	6 **The Battle Of Kookamonga**	*Jimmie Driftwood/J.J. Reynolds* **[N]**	RCA Victor 7585
			parody of "The Battle Of New Orleans" by **Johnny Horton**		
4/18/64	**49**	1	7 **I Want To Hold Your Hand**	*John Lennon/Paul McCartney* **[N]**	RCA Victor 8345

HOMESTEADERS, The

Trio formed in Nashville, Tennessee: Jack Boles, Jerry Rivers and Floyd Robinson. Rivers, also a member of **The Drifting Cowboys**, died of cancer on 10/4/1996 (age 68).

DEBUT	PEAK	WKS	Country Chart Hit	Songwriter	Label (& Number)
10/15/66	**44**	7	1 **Show Me The Way To The Circus**	*Johnny MacRae*	Little Darlin' 0010
8/3/68	**67**	2	2 **Gonna Miss Me**	*Bill Irwin*	Little Darlin' 0045

HOMETOWN NEWS

Duo of Ron Kingery (from Carmi, Illinois) and Scott Whitehead (from Montgomery City, Missouri).

DEBUT	PEAK	WKS	Country Chart Hit	Songwriter	Label (& Number)
3/16/02	**37**	19	1 **Minivan**	*Ron Kingery/Scott Whitehead*	VFR
9/14/02	**47**	9	2 **Wheels**	*Ron Kingery*	VFR
			above 2 from the album *Wheels* on VFR 734760		

HOOD, Bobby

Born in Alabama. Male singer/songwriter.

DEBUT	PEAK	WKS	Country Chart Hit	Songwriter	Label (& Number)
4/1/78	**91**	3	1 **Come On In**	*Bobby Hood*	Plantation 169
8/5/78	**60**	7	2 **I've Got An Angel (That Loves Me Like The Devil)**	*Bobby Hood*	Chute 101
10/14/78	**87**	3	3 **Come To Me**	*Bobby Hood*	Chute 102
2/24/79	**85**	3	4 **Slow Tunes And Promises**	*Jack Wilkerson*	Chute 004
8/11/79	**45**	8	5 **Easy**	*Jerry Fuller*	Chute 008
12/8/79	**72**	5	6 **It Takes One To Know One**	*Jerry Fuller*	Chute 009
3/22/80	**75**	4	7 **When She Falls**	*Jerry Foster/Bill Rice*	Chute 010
9/13/80	**85**	3	8 **Mexico Winter**	*Buck Moore/Jim Mundy*	Chute 015
11/29/80	**89**	3	9 **Pick Up The Pieces Joanne**	*Fred MacRae/Bob Morrison*	Chute 016
9/26/81	**74**	4	10 **Woman In My Heart**	*Ava Aldridge*	Chute 018

HOOD, Ray

Born in Alabama. Male singer/songwriter/guitarist.

DEBUT	PEAK	WKS	Country Chart Hit	Songwriter	Label (& Number)
5/4/96	**73**	3	1 **Freedom**	*Mike Lawler/Bill Rice/Mary Sharon Rice*	Caption/Curb
			from the album *Back To Back Heartaches* on Caption/Curb 5561		
11/11/00	**67**	1	2 **Critical List**	*Ray Hood*	Caption
			from the album *Ray Hood* on Caption 5570		

HOOSIER HOT SHOTS — 1940s: #33

Novelty group from Fort Wayne, Indiana: brothers Paul "Hezzie" (song whistle, washboard, drums, alto horn; born on 4/11/1905; died on 4/27/1980, age 75) and Kenneth "Rudy" Triesch (banjo, bass horn; born on 9/13/1903; died on 9/17/1987, age 84), with Charles Otto "Gabe" Ward (clarinet, saxophone, fife; born on 11/26/1904; died on 1/14/1992, age 87) and Frank Kettering (banjo, guitar, flute, piano, bass fiddle; born on 1/1/1909; died in June 1973, age 64). Gil Taylor replaced Kettering late 1943. Regulars on the WLS *National Barn Dance* from 1933-42. Also appeared in several western movies.

EARLY HITS: Breezin' Along With The Breeze (1937) / Red Hot Fannie (1938) / The Man With The Whiskers (1938) / Annabelle (1939)

DEBUT	PEAK	WKS	Country Chart Hit	Songwriter	Label (& Number)
6/17/44	**3**[1]	2	1 **She Broke My Heart In Three Places**	*Milton Drake/Al Hoffman/Jerry Livingston* **[N]**	Decca 4442
1/26/46	**3**[4]	10	2 **Someday (You'll Want Me To Want You)** *[w/ Sally Foster]*	*Jimmie Hodges* **[N]**	Decca 18738
2/9/46	**2**[1]	16	3 **Sioux City Sue** *[w/ Two Ton Baker]*	*Ray Freedman/Dick Thomas* **[N]**	Decca 18745

HOPE

All-star collaboration for the T.J. Martell Foundation (cancer research): **John Berry**, **Terri Clark**, **Vince Gill**, **Faith Hill**, **Tracy Lawrence**, **Little Texas**, **Neal McCoy**, **Tim McGraw**, **Lorrie Morgan**, **Marty Stuart**, **Travis Tritt** and **Trisha Yearwood**.

DEBUT	PEAK	WKS	Country Chart Hit	Songwriter	Label (& Number)
5/4/96	**57**	4	**Hope**	S:17 *Gerry Beckley*	Giant

HORN, DeAnne

Born in Clearwater, Florida. Female singer.

DEBUT	PEAK	WKS	Country Chart Hit	Songwriter	Label (& Number)
2/18/78	**97**	2	1 **I Just Want To Love You**	*Randy Sharp*	Chartwheel 102
7/8/78	**100**	1	2 **I Know**	*Barbara George*	Chartwheel 108

HORN, James T.

Born on 8/29/1966 in Foreman, Arkansas. Male singer/guitarist.

DEBUT	PEAK	WKS	Country Chart Hit	Songwriter	Label (& Number)
11/8/97	**72**	1	**Texas Diary**	*Bob DiPiero/Gerry House*	Curb/Universal

HORNSBY, Bruce, And The Range

Born on 11/23/1954 in Williamsburg, Virginia. Male singer/songwriter/pianist. Won the 1986 Best New Artist Grammy Award.

DEBUT	PEAK	WKS	Country Chart Hit	Songwriter	Label (& Number)
3/14/87	**38**	10	**Mandolin Rain**	*Bruce Hornsby/John Hornsby*	RCA 5087

HORTON, Billie Jean

Born Billie Jean Jones Eshlimar in Bossier City, Louisiana. Female singer. Married to **Hank Williams** from 10/18/1952 until his death on 1/1/1953. Married to **Johnny Horton** from 9/26/1953 until his death on 11/5/1960.

DEBUT	PEAK	WKS	GOLD	#	Country Chart Hit	Songwriter	Label (& Number)
8/28/61	**29**	3			**Ocean Of Tears**	*Bill Franks/Russell Sims*	20th Fox 266

HORTON, Johnny — 1950s: #24 / All-Time: #250

Born on 4/30/1925 in Los Angeles, California; raised in Tyler, Texas. Died in a car crash on 11/5/1960 (age 35). Male singer/songwriter/guitarist. Known as "The Singing Fisherman." Joined the *Louisiana Hayride* in 1951. Married to **Billie Jean Horton**, widow of **Hank Williams**, from 9/26/1953 until his death.

DEBUT	PEAK	WKS	GOLD	#	Country Chart Hit	Songwriter	Label (& Number)
5/5/56	**9**	12		1	**Honky-Tonk Man** A:9 / S:14 — also see #13 below	*Tillman Franks/Howard Hausey/Johnny Horton*	Columbia 21504
9/8/56	**7**	13		2	**I'm A One-Woman Man** A:7 / S:9 / J:9	*Tillman Franks/Johnny Horton*	Columbia 21538
2/23/57	**11**	5		3	**I'm Coming Home** A:11 / S:15	*Franks/Johnny Horton*	Columbia 40813
5/27/57	**9**	1		4	**The Woman I Need** J:9	*Carl Adams/Tommy Blake/Eddie Hall*	Columbia 40919
9/29/58	**8**	8		5	**All Grown Up** A:8 — also see #14 below	*Howard Hausey*	Columbia 41210
1/12/59	**❶[1]**	23		6	**When It's Springtime In Alaska (It's Forty Below)**	*Tillman Franks*	Columbia 41308
4/27/59	**❶[10]**	21	●	7	**The Battle Of New Orleans** — **Grammy: Single & Hall of Fame**; original melody written in celebration of the final battle of the War of 1812	*Jimmie Driftwood*	Columbia 41339
9/7/59	**10**	9		8	**Johnny Reb /**	*Merle Kilgore*	
9/7/59	**19**	7		9	**Sal's Got A Sugar Lip**	*Jimmie Driftwood*	Columbia 41437
3/28/60	**6**	15		10	**Sink The Bismarck** — inspired by the movie starring Kenneth Moore, which is based on the sinking of the German battleship in World War II	*Tillman Franks/Johnny Horton*	Columbia 41568
11/14/60+	**❶[5]**	22		11	**North To Alaska** — from the movie starring John Wayne	*Mike Phillips*	Columbia 41782
4/24/61	**9**	8		12	**Sleepy-Eyed John**	*Tex Atchison*	Columbia 41963
4/14/62	**11**	12		13	**Honky-Tonk Man** [R] — new version of #1 above	*Tillman Franks/Howard Hausey/Johnny Horton*	Columbia 42302
2/9/63	**26**	5		14	**All Grown Up** [R] — same version as #5 above	*Howard Hausey*	Columbia 42653

HORTON, Steven Wayne

Born in Memphis, Tennessee. Male singer/guitarist.

DEBUT	PEAK	WKS	GOLD	#	Country Chart Hit	Songwriter	Label (& Number)
8/19/89	**68**	5			**Roll Over**	*Billy Joe Burnette/Steve Cropper*	Capitol 44350

HOSFORD, Larry

Born on 9/9/1943 in Salinas, California. Male singer/songwriter/guitarist.

DEBUT	PEAK	WKS	GOLD	#	Country Chart Hit	Songwriter	Label (& Number)
12/7/74+	**62**	8		1	**Long Distance Kisses**	*Larry Hosford*	Shelter 40312
4/26/75	**78**	6		2	**Everything's Broken Down**	*Larry Hosford*	Shelter 40381

HOT APPLE PIE

Group formed in Nashville, Tennessee: **Brady Seals** (vocals, guitar), Mark "Sparky" Matekja (guitar), Keith Horne (bass) and Trey Landry (drums). Seals was leader of **Little Texas**.

DEBUT	PEAK	WKS	GOLD	#	Country Chart Hit	Songwriter	Label (& Number)
3/19/05	**26**	24			**Hillbillies** — from the album *Hot Apple Pie* on DreamWorks 003866	*Greg McDowell/Kizzy Plush/Brady Seals*	DreamWorks

HOUSE, David

Born in Lubbock, Texas. Male singer/songwriter.

DEBUT	PEAK	WKS	GOLD	#	Country Chart Hit	Songwriter	Label (& Number)
6/26/82	**96**	2		1	**Everything's All Right**	*David House/Jerry Manuel*	Door Knob 177
10/9/82	**88**	2		2	**Little White Lies**	*David House*	Door Knob 183

HOUSE, James

Born on 3/22/1955 in Sacromento, California. Male singer/songwriter/guitarist.

DEBUT	PEAK	WKS	GOLD	#	Country Chart Hit	Songwriter	Label (& Number)
3/25/89	**25**	14		1	**Don't Quit Me Now**	*James House/Wendy Waldman*	MCA 53510
7/15/89	**52**	6		2	**That'll Be The Last Thing**	*Dave Gibson/James House/Craig Karp*	MCA 53669
10/21/89	**48**	11		3	**Hard Times For An Honest Man**	*James House/Rick Seratte*	MCA 53731
12/8/90	**60**	9		4	**You Just Get Better All The Time** — from the album *Hard Times For An Honest Man* on MCA 10026	*Johnny Christopher/Tony Joe White*	MCA
8/27/94	**52**	8		5	**A Real Good Way To Wind Up Lonesome**	*Dale Dodson/James House/John Jarrard*	Epic
11/26/94+	**25**	20		6	**Little By Little**	*Rick Bowles/James House*	Epic
4/29/95	**6**	20		7	**This Is Me Missing You** S:16	*Debi Cochran/James House/Monty Powell*	Epic
9/16/95	**49**	11		8	**Anything For Love** — above 4 from the album *Days Gone By* on Epic 57501	*Phil Barnhart/Sam Hogin/James House*	Epic
8/24/96	**69**	1		9	**Little Deuce Coupe** ***[w/ The Beach Boys]*** — from **The Beach Boys**' album *Stars And Stripes Vol. 1* on River North 1205	*Roger Christian/Brian Wilson*	River North

HOUSTON, David — 1960s: #17 / 1970s: #22 / All-Time: #51

Born on 12/9/1938 in Bossier City, Louisiana. Died of a brain aneurysm on 11/30/1993 (age 54). Male singer/songwriter/guitarist. Acted in the movies *Cottonpickin' Chicken-Pluckers* and *Horse Soldiers*.

OPRY: 1972

DEBUT	PEAK	WKS	GOLD	#	Country Chart Hit	Songwriter	Label (& Number)
10/19/63	**2[1]**	18		1	**Mountain Of Love**	*Venita Del Rio/Laura Martin*	Epic 9625
3/7/64	**37**	6		2	**Passing Through /**	*Richard Blakeslee/David Houston*	
3/28/64	**17**	15		3	**Chickashay**	*Tillman Franks/David Houston*	Epic 9658

DEBUT	PEAK	WKS	GOLD	ARTIST / Ranking / Country Chart Hit	Songwriter	Label (& Number)
				HOUSTON, David — cont'd		
7/11/64	11	17		4 **One If For Him, Two If For Me**	*Gene Davis*	Epic 9690
10/10/64	17	14		5 **Love Looks Good On You**	*Chips Moman/Paul Richey*	Epic 9720
1/30/65	18	17		6 **Sweet, Sweet Judy**	*David Houston*	Epic 9746
9/11/65	3^{2}	18		7 **Livin' In A House Full Of Love**	*Billy Sherrill/Glenn Sutton*	Epic 9831
3/5/66	47	2		8 **Sammy**	*Don Wayne*	Epic 9884
6/25/66	❶^{9}	25		9 **Almost Persuaded**	*Billy Sherrill/Glenn Sutton*	Epic 10025
				Grammy: Single, Song & Male Vocal		
12/10/66+	14	12		10 **Where Could I Go? (But To Her)** /	*Billy Sherrill/Glenn Sutton*	
12/24/66+	3^{2}	16		11 **A Loser's Cathedral**	*Billy Sherrill/Glenn Sutton*	Epic 10102
4/29/67	❶^{1}	18		12 **With One Exception**	*Billy Sherrill/Glenn Sutton*	Epic 10154
7/15/67	❶^{2}	18		13 **My Elusive Dreams** *[w/ Tammy Wynette]*	*Curly Putman/Billy Sherrill*	Epic 10194
9/23/67	❶^{2}	17		14 **You Mean The World To Me**	*Billy Sherrill/Glenn Sutton*	Epic 10224
1/20/68	11	14		15 **It's All Over** *[w/ Tammy Wynette]*	*Billy Sherrill/Glenn Sutton*	Epic 10274
3/9/68	❶^{1}	14		16 **Have A Little Faith**	*Billy Sherrill/Glenn Sutton*	Epic 10291
6/15/68	❶^{1}	16		17 **Already It's Heaven**	*Billy Sherrill/Glenn Sutton*	Epic 10338
10/19/68	2^{2}	14		18 **Where Love Used To Live**	*Billy Sherrill/Glenn Sutton*	Epic 10394
1/18/69	4	17		19 **My Woman's Good To Me**	*Billy Sherrill/Glenn Sutton*	Epic 10430
6/28/69	3^{1}	16		20 **I'm Down To My Last "I Love You"**	*Billy Sherrill/Glenn Sutton*	Epic 10488
11/8/69+	❶^{4}	17		21 **Baby, Baby (I Know You're A Lady)**	*Alex Harvey/Norro Wilson*	Epic 10539
4/4/70	3^{2}	17		22 **I Do My Swinging At Home**	*Billy Sherrill*	Epic 10596
8/8/70	6	15		23 **Wonders Of The Wine**	*Webber Parrish/Billy Sherrill/Norro Wilson*	Epic 10643
10/3/70	6	14		24 **After Closing Time** *[w/ Barbara Mandrell]*	*Billy Sherrill/Danny Walls/Norro Wilson*	Epic 10656
1/9/71	2^{4}	16		25 **A Woman Always Knows**	*Billy Sherrill*	Epic 10696
6/12/71	9	13		26 **Nashville**	*Don Wayne*	Epic 10748
9/25/71	32	16		27 **Home Sweet Home**	*Larry Butler/Billy Sherrill*	Epic 10778
10/2/71	20	12		28 **We've Got Everything But Love** *[w/ Barbara Mandrell]*	*Carmol Taylor*	Epic 10779
10/9/71	10	14		29 **Maiden's Prayer**	*David Houston/Billy Sherrill*	Epic 10778
2/19/72	18	13		30 **The Day That Love Walked In**	*Billy Sherrill/Glenn Sutton*	Epic 10830
6/10/72	8	12		31 **Soft, Sweet And Warm**	*Carmol Taylor/Norro Wilson*	Epic 10870
9/16/72	24	13		32 **A Perfect Match** *[w/ Barbara Mandrell]*	*Ben Peters/Glenn Sutton*	Epic 10908
10/14/72	41	9		33 **I Wonder How John Felt (When He Baptized Jesus)**	*Billy Sherrill/Carmol Taylor/Norro Wilson*	Epic 10911
12/30/72+	2^{2}	16		34 **Good Things**	*Billy Sherrill/Carmol Taylor/Norro Wilson*	Epic 10939
6/2/73	3^{2}	14		35 **She's All Woman**	*Carmol Taylor*	Epic 10995
11/3/73	22	11		36 **The Lady Of The Night**	*Earl Montgomery/George Richey*	Epic 11048
12/22/73+	6	16		37 **I Love You, I Love You** *[w/ Barbara Mandrell]*	*Sammy Lyons/Danny Walls/Norro Wilson*	Epic 11068
3/30/74	33	12		38 **That Same Ol' Look Of Love**	*George Richey/Carmol Taylor/Norro Wilson*	Epic 11096
5/25/74	40	12		39 **Lovin' You Is Worth It** *[w/ Barbara Mandrell]*	*Quinton Claunch/Carmol Taylor*	Epic 11120
8/10/74	14	16		40 **Ten Commandments Of Love** *[w/ Barbara Mandrell]*	*Marshall Paul*	Epic 20005
9/14/74	9	15		41 **Can't You Feel It**	*George Richey/Carmol Taylor/Norro Wilson*	Epic 50009
3/1/75	36	10		42 **A Man Needs Love**	*George Richey/Carmol Taylor/Norro Wilson*	Epic 50066
6/14/75	40	10		43 **I'll Be Your Steppin' Stone**	*Bozo Darnell/Major Luper*	Epic 50113
9/27/75	69	6		44 **Sweet Molly** *[w/ Calvin Crawford]*	*Anne Young*	Epic 50134
11/1/75	35	10		45 **The Woman On My Mind**	*David Houston/George Richey/Carmol Taylor/Norro Wilson*	Epic 50156
2/7/76	51	9		46 **What A Night**	*Carmol Taylor/Norro Wilson*	Epic 50186
9/25/76	24	12		47 **Come On Down (To Our Favorite Forget-About-Her Place)**	*Billy Sherrill/Norro Wilson*	Epic 50275
4/30/77	33	9		48 **So Many Ways**	*Bobby Stevenson*	Gusto 156
8/6/77	68	6		49 **Ain't That Lovin' You Baby**	*Jimmy Reed*	Gusto 162
11/19/77	98	1		50 **The Twelfth Of Never**	*Jerry Livingston/Paul Francis Webster*	Gusto 168
12/24/77+	56	9		51 **It Started All Over Again**	*Ken Lusk/Shirl Milete/Gary S. Paxton*	Gusto 172
4/8/78	72	5		52 **No Tell Motel**	*Bob Jenkins/Larry Shell*	Gusto 184
6/24/78	51	9		53 **Waltz Of The Angels**	*Dick Reynolds/Jack Rhoades*	Colonial 101
12/9/78+	46	10		54 **Best Friends Make The Worst Enemies**	*Lewis Anderson/Julie Didier/Casey Kelly*	Elektra 45552
4/21/79	33	10		55 **Faded Love And Winter Roses**	*Fred Rose*	Elektra 46028
8/18/79	57	8		56 **Let Your Love Fall Back On Me**	*Jonathan Lee*	Derrick 126
11/10/79	60	8		57 **Here's To All The Too Hard Working Husbands (In The World)**	*Pat Bunch/Pearly Mitchell*	Derrick 127
5/31/80	64	7		58 **You're The Perfect Reason**	*Buck Moore*	Country Int'l. 145
9/13/80	78	4		59 **Sad Love Song Lady**	*Buck Moore/Don Wayne*	Country Int'l. 148
5/9/81	69	6		60 **Texas Ida Red**	*Phil Baugh/Shirl Milete*	Excelsior 1012
4/22/89	85	2		61 **A Penny For Your Thoughts Tonight Virginia**	*Buck Moore*	Country Int'l. 220

After Closing Time ['70]
Ain't That Lovin' You Baby ['77]
Almost Persuaded ['66]
Already It's Heaven ['68]
Baby, Baby (I Know You're A Lady) ['70]
Best Friends Make The Worst Enemies ['79]
Can't You Feel It ['74]
Chickashay ['64]
Come On Down (To Our Favorite Forget-About-Her Place) ['76]
Day That Love Walked In ['72]
Faded Love And Winter Roses ['79]
Good Things ['73]
Have A Little Faith ['68]
Here's To All The Too Hard Working Husbands (In The World) ['79]
Home Sweet Home ['71]
I Do My Swinging At Home ['70]
I Love You, I Love You ['74]
I Wonder How John Felt (When He Baptized Jesus) ['72]
I'll Be Your Steppin' Stone ['75]
I'm Down To My Last "I Love You" ['69]
It Started All Over Again ['78]
It's All Over ['68]
Lady Of The Night ['73]
Let Your Love Fall Back On Me ['79]
Livin' In A House Full Of Love ['65]
Loser's Cathedral ['67]
Love Looks Good On You ['64]
Lovin' You Is Worth It ['74]
Maiden's Prayer ['71]
Man Needs Love ['75]
Mountain Of Love ['63]
My Elusive Dreams ['67]
My Woman's Good To Me ['69]
Nashville ['71]
No Tell Motel ['78]
One If For Him, Two If For Me ['64]
Passing Through ['64]
Penny For Your Thoughts Tonight Virginia ['89]
Perfect Match ['72]
Sad Love Song Lady ['80]
Sammy ['66]
She's All Woman ['73]
So Many Ways ['77]
Soft, Sweet And Warm ['72]
Sweet Molly ['75]
Sweet, Sweet Judy ['65]
Ten Commandments Of Love ['74]
Texas Ida Red ['81]
That Same Ol' Look Of Love ['74]
Twelfth Of Never ['77]
Waltz Of The Angels ['78]
We've Got Everything But Love ['71]
What A Night ['76]
Where Could I Go? (But To Her) ['67]
Where Love Used To Live ['68]
With One Exception ['67]
Woman Always Knows ['71]
Woman On My Mind ['75]
Wonders Of The Wine ['70]
You Mean The World To Me ['67]
You're The Perfect Reason ['80]

Billboard DEBUT	PEAK	WKS	GOLD	ARTIST / Country Chart Hit	Songwriter	Label (& Number)

HOWARD, Chuck

Born in Flat Fork, Kentucky. Died on 8/15/1983 (age 45). Male singer/songwriter.

DEBUT	PEAK	WKS	GOLD	Country Chart Hit	Songwriter	Label (& Number)
8/23/80	**66**	7		**I've Come Back (To Say I Love You One More Time)**	*Chuck Howard*	Warner/Curb 49509

HOWARD, Eddy

Born on 9/12/1914 in Woodland, California. Died on 5/23/1963 (age 48). Male singer.

DEBUT	PEAK	WKS	GOLD	Country Chart Hit	Songwriter	Label (& Number)
8/9/47	**5**	1		**Ragtime Cowboy Joe** — from the movie *Hello Frisco, Hello* starring Alice Faye	*Maurice Abrahams/Grant Clarke/Lewis Muir*	Majestic 1155

HOWARD, Harlan — HOF: 1997 / SW: #1

Born on 9/8/1927 in Lexington, Kentucky; raised in Detroit, Michigan. Died of a heart attack on 3/3/2002 (age 74). Male singer/songwriter. Married to **Jan Howard** from 1957-67.

DEBUT	PEAK	WKS	GOLD	Country Chart Hit	Songwriter	Label (& Number)
4/10/71	**38**	15		**Sunday Morning Christian**	*Harlan Howard/Lawrence Reynolds*	Nugget 1058

HOWARD, Jan — 1960s: #46 / All-Time: #177

Born Lula Grace Johnson on 3/13/1930 in West Plains, Missouri. Female singer/songwriter. Married to **Harlan Howard** from 1957-67. Toured with **Bill Anderson**, **Johnny Cash** and **Tammy Wynette**.

OPRY: 1971

DEBUT	PEAK	WKS	GOLD	Country Chart Hit	Songwriter	Label (& Number)
1/11/60	**13**	12		1 **The One You Slip Around With**	*Harlan Howard/Fuzzy Owen*	Challenge 59059
5/30/60	**26**	2		2 **Wrong Company** *[w/ Wynn Stewart]*	*Harlan Howard*	Challenge 9071
11/16/63	**27**	3		3 **I Wish I Was A Single Girl Again**	*Harlan Howard*	Capitol 5035
1/16/65	**25**	13		4 **What Makes A Man Wander?**	*Harlan Howard*	Decca 31701
2/19/66	**29**	8		5 **I Know You're Married (But I Love You Still)** *[w/ Bill Anderson]* /	*Mack Magaha/Don Reno*	
3/12/66	**44**	1		6 **Time Out** *[w/ Bill Anderson]*	*Harlan Howard/Richard Johnson*	Decca 31884
4/23/66	**5**	20		7 **Evil On Your Mind**	*Harlan Howard*	Decca 31933
10/8/66	**10**	13		8 **Bad Seed**	*Bill Anderson*	Decca 32016
3/11/67	**32**	11		9 **Any Old Way You Do**	*Harlan Howard*	Decca 32096
7/22/67	**26**	10		10 **Roll Over And Play Dead**	*Enslo Rich*	Decca 32154
10/28/67	**❶[4]**	20		11 **For Loving You** *[w/ Bill Anderson]*	*Steve Karliski* [S]	Decca 32197
3/9/68	**16**	13		12 **Count Your Blessings, Woman**	*Bill Anderson*	Decca 32269
8/10/68	**27**	11		13 **I Still Believe In Love**	*Bill Anderson*	Decca 32357
11/23/68+	**15**	14		14 **My Son**	*Jan Howard*	Decca 32407
3/8/69	**24**	11		15 **When We Tried**	*Jerry Chesnut*	Decca 32447
9/20/69	**20**	9		16 **We Had All The Good Things Going**	*Jerry Monday/Mervin Shiner*	Decca 32543
11/15/69+	**2[1]**	15		17 **If It's All The Same To You** *[w/ Bill Anderson]*	*Bill Anderson*	Decca 32511
3/21/70	**26**	10		18 **Rock Me Back To Little Rock**	*Lola Jean Dillon*	Decca 32636
6/20/70	**4**	15		19 **Someday We'll Be Together** *[w/ Bill Anderson]*	*Jackey Beavers/Johnny Bristol/Harvey Fuqua*	Decca 32689
11/14/70	**64**	5		20 **The Soul You Never Had**	*Bill Anderson*	Decca 32743
2/13/71	**56**	10		21 **Baby Without You** /	*Mike Settle*	
3/27/71	**flip**	2		22 **Marriage Has Ruined More Good Love Affairs**	*Jan Howard*	Decca 32778
10/9/71	**4**	15		23 **Dis-Satisfied** *[w/ Bill Anderson]*	*Bill Anderson/Carter Howard/Jan Howard*	Decca 32877
12/25/71+	**36**	14		24 **Love Is Like A Spinning Wheel**	*Bill Owens*	Decca 32905
5/6/72	**43**	10		25 **Let Him Have It**	*Ben Peters*	Decca 32955
3/31/73	**74**	2		26 **Too Many Ties That Bind**	*Ben Peters*	MCA 40020
11/9/74	**96**	4		27 **Seein' Is Believin'**	*Glenn Martin*	GRT 010
4/30/77	**70**	6		28 **I'll Hold You In My Heart (Till I Can Hold You In My Arms)**	*Eddy Arnold/Tommy Dilbeck/Hal Harton*	Con Brio 118
10/1/77	**65**	7		29 **Better Off Alone**	*Scott Summer*	Con Brio 125
4/22/78	**93**	3		30 **To Love A Rolling Stone**	*Don King*	Con Brio 132

HOWARD, Jim

Born James Helton in Texas. Male singer/songwriter.

DEBUT	PEAK	WKS	GOLD	Country Chart Hit	Songwriter	Label (& Number)
7/18/64	**38**	9		**Meet Me Tonight Outside Of Town**	*Jim Howard*	Del-Mar 1013

HOWARD, Randy

Born on 5/9/1950 in Macon, Georgia. Male singer/songwriter/guitarist.

DEBUT	PEAK	WKS	GOLD	Country Chart Hit	Songwriter	Label (& Number)
4/9/83	**84**	4		1 **All-American Redneck**	*Randy Howard* [L]	Warner 29781
1/9/88	**66**	5		2 **Ring Of Fire**	*June Carter/Merle Kilgore*	Atlantic Amer. 99387

HOWARD, Rebecca Lynn

Born on 4/24/1979 in Salyersville, Kentucky. Female singer/songwriter.

DEBUT	PEAK	WKS	GOLD	Country Chart Hit	Songwriter	Label (& Number)
7/17/99	**65**	8		1 **When My Dreams Come True**	S:14 *Trey Bruce/J.D. Martin*	MCA Nashville
2/26/00	**54**	12		2 **Out Here In The Water**	*Robin Lee Bruce/Trey Bruce/Rebecca Lynn Howard*	MCA Nashville
9/9/00	**71**	4		3 **I Don't Paint Myself Into Corners** — above 3 from the album *Rebecca Lynn Howard* on MCA Nashville 170091	*Trey Bruce/Rebecca Lynn Howard*	MCA Nashville
5/11/02	**12**	30		4 **Forgive** — from the album *Forgive* on MCA Nashville 170288	*Trey Bruce/Rebecca Lynn Howard*	MCA Nashville
7/26/03	**43**	10		5 **What A Shame**	*Holly Butler/Tom Damphier/David Frasier*	MCA Nashville
11/1/03	**49**	16		6 **I Need A Vacation**	*Rebecca Lynn Howard/Leslie Satcher*	MCA Nashville
4/23/05	**48**	8		7 **No One'll Ever Love Me**	*Christi Baker/Shari Baker/Kelly Shiver*	Arista Nashville

DEBUT	PEAK	WKS	GOLD		ARTIST / Country Chart Hit	Songwriter	Label (& Number)
					HUBBLE, Hal		
					Born in 1940 in Indianapolis, Indiana. Male singer/songwriter.		
11/25/78	**76**	6			**My Pulse Pumps Passions**	*Hal Hubble*	50 States 66
					HUDSON, Helen		
					Born on 1/19/1953 in Sydney, Australia. Female singer/songwriter.		
5/26/79	**91**	5			**Nothing But Time**	*Helen Hudson*	Cyclone 102
					HUDSON, Larry G.		
					Born on 12/19/1949 in Hawkinsville, Georgia; raised in Unadilla, Georgia. Female singer/songwriter/guitarist.		
6/12/76	**89**	4		1	**Singing A Happy Song**	*DeWayne Orender/K. Phyllis Powell*	Aquarian 605
10/14/78	**37**	10		2	**Just Out Of Reach Of My Two Open Arms**	*Virgil Stewart*	Lone Star 702
1/27/79	**31**	10		3	**Loving You Is A Natural High**	*Larry G. Hudson*	Lone Star 706
3/15/80	**34**	10		4	**I Can't Cheat**	*Larry G. Hudson*	Mercury 57015
8/16/80	**39**	9		5	**I'm Still In Love With You**	*Byron Hill/Chick Rains*	Mercury 57029
					HUGHES, Hollie		
					Born on 6/9/1975 in Carrollton, Texas. Female singer. Daughter of Luv Records owner Kent Hughes.		
2/14/87	**75**	3			**67 Miles To Cow Town**	*Steve Saunders*	Luv 130
					HUGHES, Jedd		
					Born in 1982 in Quorn, Australia. Male singer/songwriter/guitarist.		
5/29/04	**54**	7		1	**High Lonesome** S:8	*Billy Burnette/Jedd Hughes/Terry McBride*	MCA Nashville
2/19/05	**60**	3		2	**Soldier For The Lonely**	*Jedd Hughes/Jennifer Kimball/Terry McBride*	MCA Nashville
					above 2 from the album *Transcontinental* on MCA Nashville 190302		
					HUGHES, Joel		
					Born on 10/2/1955 in Jenkins, Kentucky. Male singer.		
3/13/82	**75**	4			**Handy Man**	*Otis Blackwell/Jimmy Jones*	Sunbird 7569
					HUMMERS, The		
					Studio vocal group asssembled by songwriters Dan Dalton and Larry Road.		
7/21/73	**38**	7		1	**Old Betsy Goes Boing, Boing, Boing**	*Dan Dalton/Larry Road* **[N]**	Capitol 3646
					adapted from a Mazda jingle		
6/1/74	**91**	4		2	**Julianna**	*Jim Cellura*	Capitol 3870
					HUMMON, Marcus		
					Born on 12/28/1960 in Fort Wayne, Indiana. Male singer/songwriter.		
3/16/96	**73**	6			**God's Country**	*Butch Curry/Marcus Hummon*	Epic
					from the album *All In Good Time* on Epic 66124		
					HUMPERDINCK, Engelbert		
					Born Arnold Dorsey on 5/2/1936 in Madras, India; raised in Leicester, England. Male pop singer. Starred in his own musical variety TV series in 1970.		
1/8/77	**40**	12	●	1	**After The Lovin'**	*Ritchie Adams/Alan Bernstein*	Epic/MAM 50270
7/2/77	**93**	3		2	**Goodbye My Friend**	*Ritchie Adams/Alan Bernstein*	Epic/MAM 50365
1/27/79	**93**	4		3	**This Moment In Time**	*Ritchie Adams/Alan Bernstein*	Epic/MAM 50632
5/14/83	**39**	14		4	**Til You And Your Lover Are Lovers Again**	*Jan Buckingham/Mark Gray*	Epic 03817
					HUNLEY, Con — **All-Time: #246**		
					Born Conrad Hunley on 4/9/1945 in Fountain City, Tennessee. Male singer/songwriter/pianist.		
1/29/77	**96**	4		1	**Pick Up The Pieces**	*Mike Martin*	Prairie Dust 7608
4/16/77	**75**	6		2	**I'll Always Remember That Song**	*Charlie Daniels*	Prairie Dust 7614
7/23/77	**67**	7		3	**Breaking Up Is Hard To Do**	*Con Hunley*	Prairie Dust 7618
2/4/78	**34**	10		4	**Cry Cry Darling**	*Joe Miller/Jimmy Newman*	Warner 8520
5/13/78	**13**	12		5	**Week-End Friend**	*Troy Seals/Eddie Setser*	Warner 8572
10/7/78	**14**	13		6	**You've Still Got A Place In My Heart**	*Leon Payne*	Warner 8671
1/27/79	**14**	14		7	**I've Been Waiting For You All Of My Life**	*Linda Kimball/Mark Sherrill*	Warner 8723
5/26/79	**20**	12		8	**Since I Fell For You**	*Buddy Johnson*	Warner 8812
11/3/79+	**20**	14		9	**I Don't Want To Lose You**	*Steve Davis/Billy Sherrill/Norro Wilson*	Warner 49090
3/8/80	**19**	12		10	**You Lay A Whole Lot Of Love On Me**	*Hank Beach/Forest Borders*	Warner 49187
8/16/80	**19**	13		11	**They Never Lost You**	*Charles Quillen/David Wills*	Warner 49528
12/20/80+	**11**	16		12	**What's New With You**	*Dean Dillon/Charles Quillen*	Warner 49613
8/29/81	**17**	15		13	**She's Steppin' Out**	*Walt Aldridge/Tom Brasfield*	Warner 49800
1/9/82	**20**	14		14	**No Relief In Sight**	*Rory Bourke/Gene Dobbins/Johnny Wilson*	Warner 49887
5/22/82	**12**	15		15	**Oh Girl**	*Eugene Record*	Warner 50058
					Oak Ridge Boys (backing vocals)		
10/9/82	**43**	9		16	**Confidential**	*Dorinda Morgan*	Warner 29902
4/30/83	**42**	10		17	**Once You Get The Feel Of It**	*Larry Butler/Dean Dillon*	MCA 52208
9/3/83	**84**	4		18	**Satisfied Mind**	*Joe Hayes/Jack Rhodes*	MCA 52259
					Porter Wagoner (guest vocal)		
3/17/84	**75**	7		19	**Deep In The Arms Of Texas**	*Kelly Bach*	Prairie Dust 84110
12/15/84+	**57**	11		20	**All American Country Boy**	*Charlie Craig/Keith Stegall*	Capitol 5428
3/16/85	**54**	8		21	**I'd Rather Be Crazy**	*Byron Gallimore/Don Pfrimmer/Paul Worley*	Capitol 5457
7/13/85	**49**	9		22	**Nobody Ever Gets Enough Love**	*Steve Davis/Dennis W. Morgan*	Capitol 5485
11/30/85+	**48**	15		23	**What Am I Gonna Do About You**	*Jim Allison/Doug Gilmore/Bob Simon*	Capitol 5525
5/31/86	**49**	13		24	**Blue Suede Blues**	*Richard Fagan/Ralph James/Patti Ryan*	Capitol 5586
9/27/86	**55**	9		25	**Quittin' Time**	*Michael Garvin/Ron Hellard/Bucky Jones*	Capitol 5631

Billboard DEBUT	PEAK	WKS	GOLD	ARTIST / Country Chart Hit	Ranking / Songwriter	Label (& Number)

HUNNICUTT, Ed

Born on 7/29/1951 in Troy, New York; raised in Columbia, South Carolina. Male singer/songwriter.

DEBUT	PEAK	WKS	GOLD	Country Chart Hit	Songwriter	Label (& Number)
5/21/83	**69**	6		1 **Fade To Blue**	*Dave Burgess/Ed Hunnicutt/Dennis Knutson*	MCA 52207
10/8/83	**59**	7		2 **My Angel's Got The Devil In Her Eyes**	*Dave Burgess/Eddie Burton/Dennis Knutson*	MCA 52262
3/17/84	**41**	9		3 **In Real Life**	*Kent Robbins*	MCA 52353

HUNT, John — see BACKTRACK

HUNTER, Jesse

Born on 1/14/1959 in Shelby County, Tennessee. Male singer/songwriter.

DEBUT	PEAK	WKS	GOLD	Country Chart Hit	Songwriter	Label (& Number)
3/5/94	**56**	9		1 **Born Ready**	*Dave Gibson/Allen Shamblin*	BNA
6/18/94	**65**	8		2 **By The Way She's Lookin'**	*Rory Bourke/Jesse Hunter*	BNA
10/22/94	**42**	15		3 **Long Legged Hannah (From Butte Montana)**	*Jesse Hunter*	BNA

above 3 from the album *A Man Like Me* on BNA 66220

HUNTER, Tommy

Born on 3/20/1937 in London, Ontario, Canada. Male singer/guitarist. Regular on CBC-TV series *Country Hoedown* from 1956-65. Hosted own CBC-TV series from 1965-89. Known as "Canada's Country Gentleman."

DEBUT	PEAK	WKS	GOLD	Country Chart Hit	Songwriter	Label (& Number)
9/9/67	**66**	3		**Mary In The Morning**	*Johnny Cymbal/Mike Lendell*	Columbia 44234

HURLEY, Libby

Born in Clarksville, Arkansas. Female singer.

DEBUT	PEAK	WKS	GOLD	Country Chart Hit	Songwriter	Label (& Number)
10/3/87	**60**	6		1 **Don't Get Me Started**	*Ted Hewitt/Sandy Ramos*	Epic 07366
1/16/88	**43**	10		2 **You Just Watch Me**	*Rick Giles/Bob Regan*	Epic 07650
4/23/88	**59**	8		3 **Don't Talk To Me**	*Bill Rice/Mary Sharon Rice*	Epic 07771

HURT, Charlotte

Born in Memphis, Tennessee. Female singer.

DEBUT	PEAK	WKS	GOLD	Country Chart Hit	Songwriter	Label (& Number)
9/16/78	**85**	5		**The Price Of Borrowed Love Is Just To High**	*SheLeah Jenson*	Compass 0020

HURT, Cindy

Born in 1956 in Mundelein, Illinois. Female singer/actress. Toured with the musical *Sophisticated Ladies* in 1980.

DEBUT	PEAK	WKS	GOLD	Country Chart Hit	Songwriter	Label (& Number)
3/21/81	**74**	5		1 **Single Girl**	*Martha Sharpe*	Churchill 7767
6/6/81	**56**	8		2 **Headin' For A Heartache**	*Byron Hill/J. Remington Wilde*	Churchill 7772
9/5/81	**46**	10		3 **Dreams Can Come In Handy**	*Bob Millsap*	Churchill 7777
1/30/82	**28**	13		4 **Don't Come Knockin**	*Mike Heeney/Francy Matan*	Churchill 94000
6/12/82	**35**	10		5 **Talk To Me Loneliness**	*John Gulley*	Churchill 94004
11/20/82	**67**	8		6 **What's Good About Goodbye**	*Charlie Craig*	Churchill 94010
7/2/83	**65**	6		7 **I'm In Love All Over Again**	*Layng Martine Jr.*	Churchill 94013

HUSKEY, Kenni

Born Nora Carolyn Huskey on 12/2/1954 in Newport, Arkansas. Female singer.

DEBUT	PEAK	WKS	GOLD	Country Chart Hit	Songwriter	Label (& Number)
10/23/71	**71**	6		1 **A Living Tornado**	*Ike Cargill*	Capitol 3184
1/29/72	**74**	2		2 **Within My Loving Arms**	*Buck Owens*	Capitol 3229

HUSKY, Ferlin — 1950s: #18 / 1960s: #31 / All-Time: #74

Born on 12/3/1925 in Flat River, Missouri. Male singer/songwriter/guitarist. Spent five years in U.S. Merchant Marines during World War II. After discharge, worked clubs in Bakersfield. Recorded as "Terry Preston" in the early 1950s. Acted in several movies. Also recorded as **Simon Crum**. Also see **Jean Shepard**.

OPRY: 1957

DEBUT	PEAK	WKS	GOLD	Country Chart Hit	Songwriter	Label (& Number)
7/25/53	❶^{6}	23		1 **A Dear John Letter** *[w/ Jean Shepard]*	S:❶^{6} / J:❶^{4} / A:2 *Fuzzy Owen/Lewis Tally*	Capitol 2502
10/10/53	**4**	7		2 **Forgive Me John** *[w/ Jean Shepard]*	S:4 / J:6 / A:8 *Billy Barton/Jean Shepard*	Capitol 2586
1/15/55	**6**	10		3 **I Feel Better All Over (More Than Anywhere's Else)** *[Ferlin Huskey]* /	...A:6 / S:15 *Ken Rogers/Leon Smith*	
1/15/55	**7**	8		4 **Little Tom** *[Ferlin Huskey]*	A:7 *Clyde Wilson*	Capitol 3001
4/16/55	**5**	15		5 **Cuzz Yore So Sweet** *[Simon Crum]*	A:5 *John Kane* [N]	Capitol 3063
5/28/55	**14**	1		6 **I'll Baby Sit With You** *[w/ His Hush Puppies]*	S:14 *Clyde Wilson*	Capitol 3097
2/23/57	❶^{10}	27		7 **Gone**	S:❶^{10} / A:❶^{9} / J:❶^{5} *Smokey Rogers*	Capitol 3628
				originally recorded by Husky in 1952 as by Terry Preston on Capitol 2298		
7/1/57	**8**	13		8 **A Fallen Star** /	S:8 / A:8 *James Joiner*	
7/15/57	**12**	1		9 **Prize Possession**	A:12 *David Hill*	Capitol 3742
10/27/58	**23**	1		10 **I Will**	*Roy Drusky/Ferlin Husky/Lester Vanadore*	Capitol 4046
11/3/58+	**2**^{3}	24		11 **Country Music Is Here To Stay** *[Simon Crum]*	*Ferlin Husky* [N]	Capitol 4073
2/16/59	**14**	12		12 **My Reason For Living**	*Gertrude Cox/Ferlin Husky*	Capitol 4123
6/1/59	**11**	10		13 **Draggin' The River**	*Vic McAlpin*	Capitol 4186
11/16/59	**21**	8		14 **Black Sheep**	*Ferlin Husky/Jack Rhodes*	Capitol 4278
9/5/60	❶^{10}	36		15 **Wings Of A Dove**	*Bob Ferguson*	Capitol 4406
10/9/61	**23**	1		16 **Willow Tree**	*Bettie Husky*	Capitol 4594
1/27/62	**13**	10		17 **The Waltz You Saved For Me**	*Emil Flindt/Gus Kahn/Wayne King*	Capitol 4650
5/26/62	**16**	11		18 **Somebody Save Me**	*Alex Zanetis*	Capitol 4721
9/22/62	**28**	1		19 **Stand Up**	*Cliff Crofford*	Capitol 4779
12/1/62	**21**	2		20 **It Was You**	*Johnnie Bailes/Ferlin Husky/George Sherry/Wayne Walker*	Capitol 4853
2/22/64	**13**	21		21 **Timber I'm Falling**	*Ferlin Husky/Dalton Timbur*	Capitol 5111

DEBUT	PEAK	WKS	GOLD	#	ARTIST / Country Chart Hit	Songwriter	Label (& Number)
					HUSKY, Ferlin — cont'd		
4/10/65	**46**	7		22	**True True Lovin'**	*Gerald Nelson/Chuck Taylor*	Capitol 5355
					also see #42 below		
12/11/65	**48**	2		23	**Money Greases The Wheels**	*Dallas Frazier*	Capitol 5522
6/4/66	**27**	5		24	**I Could Sing All Night**	*Tommy Collins/Ferlin Husky*	Capitol 5615
7/9/66	**17**	12		25	**I Hear Little Rock Calling**	*Dallas Frazier*	Capitol 5679
12/3/66+	**4**	17		26	**Once**	*Ted Harris*	Capitol 5775
					FERLIN HUSKY And The Hushpuppies:		
4/1/67	**37**	11		27	**What Am I Gonna Do Now**	*Jimmy Peppers*	Capitol 5852
7/15/67	**14**	15		28	**You Pushed Me Too Far**	*Bobby Braddock*	Capitol 5938
12/23/67+	**4**	18		29	**Just For You** *[Ferlin Husky]*	*Larry Butler/Curly Putman*	Capitol 2048
5/25/68	**26**	10		30	**I Promised You The World**	*Curly Putman*	Capitol 2154
10/19/68	**25**	10		31	**White Fences And Evergreen Trees**	*Dallas Frazier*	Capitol 2288
3/15/69	**33**	10		32	**Flat River, MO.**	*Dallas Frazier*	Capitol 2411
6/21/69	**16**	14		33	**That's Why I Love You So Much**	*Jerry Foster/Bill Rice*	Capitol 2512
					FERLIN HUSKY:		
11/22/69	**21**	10		34	**Every Step Of The Way**	*Curly Putman*	Capitol 2666
5/16/70	**11**	13		35	**Heavenly Sunshine**	*George Richey/Glenn Sutton*	Capitol 2793
9/12/70	**45**	9		36	**Your Sweet Love Lifted Me**	*George Richey/Glenn Sutton*	Capitol 2882
12/26/70+	**14**	11		37	**Sweet Misery**	*Jan Crutchfield/Wayne Walker*	Capitol 2999
3/27/71	**28**	11		38	**One More Time**	*Larry Butler/Jan Crutchfield/Buddy Killen*	Capitol 3069
9/11/71	**45**	9		39	**Open Up The Book (And Take A Look)**	*Ferlin Husky/Paul Johnson/Tommy Stough/Lester Vanadore*	Capitol 3165
4/22/72	**39**	10		40	**Just Plain Lonely**	*Jerry Foster/Bill Rice*	Capitol 3308
9/9/72	**53**	8		41	**How Could You Be Anything But Love**	*Dallas Frazier/A.L. "Doodle" Owens*	Capitol 3415
1/13/73	**35**	10		42	**True True Lovin'**	*Gerald Nelson/Chuck Taylor* **[R]**	ABC 11345
					new version of #22 above		
4/28/73	**46**	9		43	**Between Me And Blue**	*Gayle Barnhill/Rory Bourke*	ABC 11360
8/11/73	**75**	4		44	**Baby's Blue**	*Gayle Barnhill/Rory Bourke*	ABC 11381
11/3/73+	**17**	13		45	**Rosie Cries A Lot**	*Jerry Foster/Bill Rice*	ABC 11395
5/4/74	**26**	15		46	**Freckles And Polliwog Days**	*Dallas Frazier/A.L. "Doodle" Owens*	ABC 11432
9/21/74	**60**	7		47	**A Room For A Boy...Never Used**	*Dick Feller*	ABC 12021
12/28/74+	**34**	11		48	**Champagne Ladies And Blue Ribbon Babies**	*Dallas Frazier/A.L. "Doodle" Owens*	ABC 12048
4/19/75	**37**	11		49	**Burning**	*Jerry Foster/Bill Rice*	ABC 12085
9/27/75	**90**	6		50	**An Old Memory (Got In My Eye) /**	*Jerry Foster/Bill Rice*	
10/4/75	**74**	5		51	**She's Not Yours Anymore**	*Jerry Foster/Bill Rice*	ABC/Dot 17574
					HUTCHENS, The		
					Trio of brothers from Sandy Rudge, North Carolina: Barry Hutchens, Bill Hutchens and Bryan Hutchens.		
10/7/95	**56**	7			**Knock, Knock**	*Jerry Salley/Jeff Stevens*	Atlantic
					HUTCHINS, Loney		
					Born on 11/7/1946 in Sullivan County, Tennessee. Male singer/songwriter.		
7/4/87	**92**	2			**Still Dancing**	*Loney Hutchins*	ARC 0005

I

DEBUT	PEAK	WKS	GOLD	#	ARTIST / Country Chart Hit	Songwriter	Label (& Number)
					IFIELD, Frank		
					Born on 11/30/1937 in Coventry, Warwickshire, England; raised in New South Wales, Australia. Pop singer/songwriter/actor.		
8/27/66	**42**	6		1	**No One Will Ever Know**	*Mel Foree/Fred Rose*	Hickory 1397
10/22/66	**28**	14		2	**Call Her Your Sweetheart**	*Leon Payne*	Hickory 1411
12/23/67+	**68**	4		3	**Oh, Such A Stranger**	*Don Gibson*	Hickory 1486
10/5/68	**67**	3		4	**Good Morning, Dear**	*Mickey Newbury*	Hickory 1514
					IGLESIAS, Julio		
					Born on 9/23/1943 in Madrid, Spain. Latin singer.		
					CMA: Vocal Duo (with Willie Nelson) 1984		
3/10/84	**❶**[2]	20	▲	1	**To All The Girls I've Loved Before** *[w/ Willie Nelson]*	*Hal David/Albert Hammond*	Columbia 04217
9/17/88	**8**	19		2	**Spanish Eyes** *[w/ Willie Nelson]*	S:2 *Bert Kaempfert/Charles Singleton/Eddie Snyder*	Columbia 08066
					INDIANA		
					Group from Florida. Led by singer/songwriter Tom Hamilton.		
4/18/87	**85**	2			**Midnite Rock**	*Tommy Dee/Tom Hamilton*	Killer 1005
					INGLE, Red, & The Natural Seven		
					Born Ernest Ingle on 11/7/1906 in Toledo, Ohio. Died on 9/7/1965 (age 58). Comic singer/violinist/clarinetist/saxophonist. Formed group The Natural Seven: Luke "Red" Roundtree (guitar), Noel Boggs (steel guitar), Herman "The Hermit" Snyder (banjo), Art Wenzel (accordion), Joseph "Country" Washbourne (suitcase), Rull Hall (bass) and Ray Hagan (drums).		
6/21/47	**2**[11]	18			**Temptation (Tim-Tayshun)**	*Nacio Herb Brown/Arthur Freed* **[N]**	Capitol 412
					Cinderella G. Stump (**Jo Stafford**) and Red Ingle (vocals)		
					INGLES, David		
					Born in Cleveland, Oklahoma; raised in Bristow, Oklahoma. Male singer/songwriter.		
11/29/69	**72**	2			**Johnny Let The Sunshine In**	*David Ingles*	Capitol 2648

DEBUT	PEAK	WKS	GOLD	ARTIST / Country Chart Hit	Songwriter	Label (& Number)
				INGRAM, Jack		
				Born on 11/15/1970 in Houston, Texas. Male singer/guitarist.		
7/19/97	**51**	10		1 **Flutter**	*Colin Boyd*	Rising Tide
				from the album *Livin' Or Dyin'* on Rising Tide 53046		
10/23/99	**64**	1		2 **How Many Days**	*Jim Lauderdale/Terry McBride*	Lucky Dog
				from the album *Hey You* on Lucky Dog 69850		
				INGRAM, James		
				Born on 2/16/1956 in Akron, Ohio. Black male singer/songwriter/pianist.		
11/10/84	**70**	10		**What About Me?** ***[w/ Kenny Rogers & Kim Carnes]***	*David Foster/Richard Marx/Kenny Rogers*	RCA 13899
				INMAN, Autry		
				Born Robert Autry Inman on 1/6/1929 in Florence, Alabama. Died on 9/6/1988 (age 59). Male singer/songwriter/guitarist.		
7/11/53	**4**	4		1 **That's All Right**	J:4 *Autry Inman*	Decca 28629
4/13/63	**22**	3		2 **The Volunteer**	*Autry Inman*	Sims 131
11/2/68	**14**	15		3 **Ballad Of Two Brothers**	*Bobby Braddock/Buddy Killen/Curly Putman*	Epic 10389
				INMAN, Jerry		
				Born in 1946 in Billings, Montana. Male singer.		
12/28/74+	**95**	2		1 **You're The One**	*Bob Morrison*	Chelsea 3006
8/26/78	**95**	2		2 **Why, Baby, Why**	*Darrell Edwards/George Jones*	Elektra 45508
2/17/79	**94**	2		3 **Why Don't We Lie Down And Talk It Over**	*Robert Jones/Jim Shaw*	Elektra 46006
				IRBY, Jerry, And His Texas Ranchers		
				Born on 10/20/1917 in New Braunfels, Texas. Died in December 1983 (age 66). Male singer/songwriter/guitarist.		
6/19/48	**11**	2		1 **Cryin' In My Beer**	J:11 *Jerry Irby*	MGM 10151
7/3/48	**10**	1		2 **Great Long Pistol**	J:10 *Jerry Irby*	MGM 10188
				IRVING, Lonnie		
				Born on 6/11/1932 in Stoneville, North Carolina. Died of leukemia on 12/2/1960 (age 28). Male singer/songwriter.		
3/14/60	**13**	15		**Pinball Machine**	*Lonnie Irving*	Starday 486
				ISAACS, Sonya		
				Born on 7/22/1974 in LaFollette, Tennessee. Female singer/songwriter/guitarist.		
8/21/99	**54**	10		1 **On My Way To You**	*Sonya Isaacs/Tim Mensy*	Lyric Street
1/22/00	**46**	18		2 **I've Forgotten How You Feel**	S:15 *Sonya Isaacs/Keith Sewell*	Lyric Street
8/19/00	**64**	6		3 **Barefoot In The Grass**	*Ken Harrell/Shaye Smith*	Lyric Street
				above 3 from the album *Sonya Isaacs* on Lyric Street 65004		
1/12/02	**59**	1		4 **What Do You See**	*Sonya Isaacs*	Lyric Street
11/15/03+	**36**	17		5 **No Regrets Yet**	*Darrell Brown/Sonya Isaacs*	Lyric Street
				ISAACSON, Peter		
				Born in Vermont. Male singer.		
7/23/83	**76**	5		1 **Froze In Her Line Of Fire**	*Eric Butler/Bill Delaney/Ted Lindsay*	Union Station 1002
11/26/83	**61**	6		2 **Don't Take Much**	*Jack Murray*	Union Station 1004
3/24/84	**93**	2		3 **No Survivors**	*Arthur Fixel/Bobby Wood*	Union Station 1005
5/12/84	**71**	5		4 **It's A Cover Up**	*Arthur Fixel/Ellen McQueary*	Union Station 1006
				IVES, Burl		
				Born on 6/14/1909 in Huntington Township, Illinois. Died of cancer on 4/14/1995 (age 85). Actor/singer. Acted in several movies.		
2/12/49	**13**	1		1 **Lavender Blue (Dilly Dilly)** ***[w/ Captain Stubby & The Buccaneers]***	S:13 *Eliot Daniel/Larry Morey*	Decca 24547
5/21/49	**8**	5		2 **Riders In The Sky (Cowboy Legend)**	J:8 / S:15 *Stan Jones*	Columbia 38445
7/26/52	**6**	4		3 **Wild Side Of Life** ***[w/ Grady Martin]***	J:6 / S:10 *Arlie Carter/William Warren*	Decca 9-28055
2/3/62	**2**[2]	17		4 **A Little Bitty Tear**	*Hank Cochran*	Decca 31330
4/28/62	**9**	13		5 **Funny Way Of Laughin'**	*Hank Cochran*	Decca 31371
				Grammy: Single		
8/11/62	**3**[1]	11		6 **Call Me Mr. In-Between**	*Harlan Howard*	Decca 31405
12/1/62+	**12**	7		7 **Mary Ann Regrets**	*Harlan Howard*	Decca 31433
9/17/66	**47**	6		8 **Evil Off My Mind**	*Harlan Howard*	Decca 31997
2/4/67	**72**	2		9 **Lonesome 7-7203**	*Justin Tubb*	Decca 32078
				IVIE, Roger — see SILVER CREEK		
				IVORY JACK		
				Born in Kentucky. Male singer.		
2/9/80	**78**	4		1 **Made In The USA**	*Bobby Emmons/Chips Moman*	NSD 36
5/9/81	**81**	4		2 **Love Signs**	*Fred Kelly*	Country Int'l. 154

J

DEBUT	PEAK	WKS	GOLD	ARTIST / Country Chart Hit	Songwriter	Label (& Number)
				JACK AND TRINK		
				Husband-and-wife duo of Jack Ruthven and Trink Ruthven.		
9/9/78	**93**	4		**I'm Tired Of Being Me**	*Jack Ruthven*	NSD 4

Billboard DEBUT	PEAK	WKS	GOLD	ARTIST / Country Chart Hit	Ranking / Songwriter	Label (& Number)

JACKSON, Alan

1990s: #3 / 2000s: #4 / All-Time: #22

Born on 10/17/1958 in Newnan, Georgia. Male singer/songwriter/guitarist. Former car salesman and construction worker. Formed own band, Dixie Steel. Signed to **Glen Campbell**'s publishing company in 1985.

CMA: Entertainer 1995, 2002 & 2003 / Male Vocalist 2002 & 2003 // OPRY: 1991

DEBUT	PEAK	WKS	GOLD	Country Chart Hit	Songwriter	Label (& Number)
10/21/89	45	12		1 **Blue Blooded Woman**	*Alan Jackson/Roger Murrah/Keith Stegall*	Arista 9892
1/13/90	3^{2}	26		2 **Here In The Real World**	*Mark Irwin/Alan Jackson*	Arista
6/23/90	3^{1}	21		3 **Wanted**	*Charlie Craig/Alan Jackson*	Arista
10/6/90	2^{2}	20		4 **Chasin' That Neon Rainbow**	*Alan Jackson/Jim McBride*	Arista
1/19/91	❶^{2}	20		5 **I'd Love You All Over Again**	*Alan Jackson*	Arista
				above 4 from the album *Here In The Real World* on Arista 8623		
5/18/91	❶^{3}	20		6 **Don't Rock The Jukebox**	*Alan Jackson/Roger Murrah/Keith Stegall*	Arista
8/31/91	❶^{1}	20		7 **Someday**	*Alan Jackson/Jim McBride*	Arista
12/14/91+	41	6		8 **I Only Want You For Christmas**	*Tim Nichols/Zack Turner* **[X]**	Arista
				from the album *Honky Tonk Christmas* on Arista 18736		
1/11/92	❶^{1}	20		9 **Dallas**	*Alan Jackson/Keith Stegall*	Arista
4/25/92	3^{2}	20		10 **Midnight In Montgomery**	*Alan Jackson/Don Sampson*	Arista
7/25/92	❶^{2}	20		11 **Love's Got A Hold On You**	*Carson Chamberlain/Keith Stegall*	Arista
				#6, 7 & 9-11: from the album *Don't Rock The Jukebox* on Arista 8681		
10/24/92	❶^{1}	20		12 **She's Got The Rhythm (And I Got The Blues)**	*Alan Jackson/Randy Travis*	Arista
2/6/93	4	20		13 **Tonight I Climbed The Wall**	*Alan Jackson*	Arista
5/15/93	❶^{4}	20	●	14 **Chattahoochee**	*Alan Jackson/Jim McBride*	Arista
				CMA: Single		
8/28/93	75	1		15 **Tropical Depression**	*Charlie Craig/Alan Jackson/Jim McBride*	Arista
9/18/93	2^{1}	20		16 **Mercury Blues**	*K.C. Douglas/Robert Geddins*	Arista
				tune later used for a Ford truck commercial		
10/30/93	64	17		17 **Tequila Sunrise**	*Glenn Frey/Don Henley*	Giant
				from the various artists album *Common Thread: The Songs Of The* ***Eagles*** on Giant 24531		
12/18/93+	53	4		18 **Honky Tonk Christmas**	*Buddy Brock/Zack Turner/Kim Williams* **[X]**	Arista
				from the album *Honky Tonk Christmas* on Arista 18736		
1/29/94	4	20		19 **(Who Says) You Can't Have It All**	*Alan Jackson/Jim McBride*	Arista
				#12-16 & 19: from the album *A Lot About Livin' (And A Little 'Bout Love)* on Arista 18711		
6/18/94	❶^{3}	20		20 **Summertime Blues**	*Jerry Capehart/Eddie Cochran*	Arista
8/27/94+	❶^{1}	26		21 **Gone Country**	*Bob McDill*	Arista
9/3/94	❶^{3}	20		22 **Livin' On Love**	*Alan Jackson*	Arista
11/12/94	56	7		23 **A Good Year For The Roses** ***[w/ George Jones]***	*Jerry Chesnut*	MCA
				from Jones's album *The Bradley Barn Sessions* on MCA 11096		
1/7/95	59	1		24 **Honky Tonk Christmas**	*Buddy Brock/Zack Turner/Kim Williams* **[X-R]**	Arista
				from the album *Honky Tonk Christmas* on Arista 18736		
2/11/95	6	20		25 **Song For The Life**	*Rodney Crowell*	Arista
5/13/95	❶^{1}	20		26 **I Don't Even Know Your Name**	*Alan Jackson/William Jackson/Daniel Loftin*	Arista
				#20-22, 25 & 26: from the album *Who I Am* on Arista 18759		
10/21/95	❶^{2}	20		27 **Tall, Tall Trees**	*George Jones/Roger Miller*	Arista
12/23/95+	48	4		28 **I Only Want You For Christmas**	*Tim Nichols/Zack Turner* **[X-R]**	Arista
				from the album *Honky Tonk Christmas* on Arista 18736		
12/30/95+	❶^{1}	20		29 **I'll Try**	*Alan Jackson*	Arista
4/20/96	3^{1}	20		30 **Home**	*Alan Jackson*	Arista
				#27, 29 & 30: from the album *The Greatest Hits Collection* on Arista 18801		
6/8/96	42	12		31 **Redneck Games** ***[w/ Jeff Foxworthy]***	S:2 *Jeff Foxworthy/Scott Rouse/Ronny Scaife* **[L-N]**	Warner
				from Foxworthy's album *Crank It Up - The Music Album* on Warner 46361		
10/26/96	❶^{3}	20		32 **Little Bitty**	S:❶^{7} *Tom T. Hall*	Arista Nashville
12/28/96+	56	3		33 **Rudolph The Red-Nosed Reindeer**	*Johnny Marks* **[X]**	Arista Nashville
				from the various artists album *Star Of Wonder - A Country Christmas Collection* on Arista Nashville 18822		
1/18/97	9	20		34 **Everything I Love**	*Harley Allen/Carson Chamberlain*	Arista Nashville
4/12/97	2^{2}	20		35 **Who's Cheatin' Who**	S:15 *Jerry Hayes*	Arista Nashville
7/12/97	❶^{1}	20		36 **There Goes**	*Alan Jackson*	Arista Nashville
10/11/97+	2^{1}	20		37 **Between The Devil And Me**	*Harley Allen/Carson Chamberlain*	Arista Nashville
12/27/97+	51	3		38 **A Holly Jolly Christmas**	*Johnny Marks* **[X]**	Arista Nashville
				introduced by **Burl Ives** in the 1964 animated TV special *Rudolph The Red-Nosed Reindeer*		
1/3/98	48	2		39 **I Only Want You For Christmas**	*Tim Nichols/Zack Turner* **[X-R]**	Arista Nashville
				above 2 from the album *Honky Tonk Christmas* on Arista 18736		
1/24/98	18	15		40 **A House With No Curtains**	*Alan Jackson/Jim McBride*	Arista Nashville
				#32, 34-37 & 40: from the album *Everything I Love* on Arista Nashville 18813		
8/1/98	3^{1}	20		41 **I'll Go On Loving You**	*Kieran Kane*	Arista Nashville
10/17/98+	❶^{1}	20		42 **Right On The Money**	*Charlie Black/Phil Vassar*	Arista Nashville
2/6/99	4	20		43 **Gone Crazy**	*Alan Jackson*	Arista Nashville
5/29/99	3^{1}	23		44 **Little Man**	*Alan Jackson*	Arista Nashville
				above 4 from the album *High Mileage* on Arista Nashville 18864		
10/9/99	6	20		45 **Pop A Top**	*Nat Stuckey*	Arista Nashville
11/6/99	63	3		46 **Margaritaville** ***[w/ Jimmy Buffett]***	*Jimmy Buffett*	Arista Nashville
11/13/99	71	1		47 **My Own Kind Of Hat**	*Merle Haggard/Red Lane*	Arista Nashville
11/13/99	72	1		48 **She Just Started Liking Cheatin' Songs**	*Kent Robbins*	Arista Nashville

DEBUT	PEAK	WKS	GOLD	ARTIST / Country Chart Hit	Ranking / Songwriter	Label (& Number)
				JACKSON, Alan — cont'd		
2/19/00	**37**	15		49 **The Blues Man**	*Hank Williams Jr.*	Arista Nashville
3/11/00	**38**	20		50 **Murder On Music Row** ***[w/ George Strait]***	*Larry Cordle/Larry Shell*	MCA Nashville
				CMA: Vocal Event; from Strait's album *Latest Greatest Straitest Hits* on MCA Nashville 70100		
4/29/00	❶^{1}	27		51 **It Must Be Love**	*Bob McDill*	Arista Nashville
				#45-49 & 51: from the album *Under The Influence* on Arista Nashville 18892		
10/7/00	**6**	20		52 **www.memory**	*Alan Jackson*	Arista Nashville
11/25/00+	❶^{3}	26		53 **Where I Come From**	*Alan Jackson*	Arista Nashville
11/25/00+	**53**	10		54 **It's Alright To Be A Redneck**	*Bill Kenner/Pat McLaughlin*	Arista Nashville
11/25/00	**72**	1		55 **Three Minute Positive Not Too Country Up-Tempo Love Song**	*Alan Jackson*	Arista Nashville
3/10/01	**5**	21		56 **When Somebody Loves You**	*Alan Jackson*	Arista Nashville
				above 5 from the album *When Somebody Loves You* on Arista Nashville 69335		
11/24/01	❶^{5}	20		57 **Where Were You (When The World Stopped Turning)**	*Alan Jackson*	Arista Nashville
				Grammy: Song / CMA: Single & Song; written after the 9/11 terrorist attacks		
1/19/02	**44**	8		58 **Designated Drinker** ***[w/ George Strait]***	*Alan Jackson*	Arista Nashville
2/2/02	❶^{4}	31		59 **Drive (For Daddy Gene)**	*Alan Jackson*	Arista Nashville
6/29/02	**3^{2}**	25		60 **Work In Progress**	*Alan Jackson*	Arista Nashville
12/14/02+	**37**	5		61 **Let It Be Christmas**	*Alan Jackson* **[X]**	Arista Nashville
				from the album *Let It Be Christmas* on Arista Nashville 67062		
12/21/02+	**2^{1}**	24		62 **That'd Be Alright**	*Tim Nichols/Mark D. Sanders/Tia Sillers*	Arista Nashville
				#57-60 & 62: from the album *Drive* on Arista Nashville 67039		
1/11/03	**58**	1		63 **Jingle Bells**	*James Pierpont* **[X]**	Arista Nashville
				from the album *Let It Be Christmas* on Arista Nashville 67062		
6/21/03	❶^{8}	27		64 **It's Five O'Clock Somewhere** ***[w/ Jimmy Buffett]***	*Jim Brown/Don Rollins*	Arista Nashville
				Grammy: Song / CMA: Vocal Event		
11/8/03+	❶^{2}	25		65 **Remember When**	*Alan Jackson*	Arista Nashville
				above 2 from the album *Greatest Hits Volume II and Some Other Stuff* on Arista Nashville 53097		
1/3/04	**51**	2		66 **Just Put A Ribbon In Your Hair**	*Hoss Burns/Don Huber* **[X]**	Lost Highway
				from the various artists album *A Very Special Acoustic Christmas* on Lost Highway 001038		
5/29/04	**8**	20		67 **Hey Good Lookin'** ***[w/ Jimmy Buffett/Clint Black/Kenny Chesney/Toby Keith/George Strait]***		
				from Buffett's album *License To Chill* on RCA 62270	*...Hank Williams*	RCA
6/26/04	**5**	20		68 **Too Much Of A Good Thing**	*Alan Jackson*	Arista Nashville
10/16/04+	**5**	22		69 **Monday Morning Church**	*Brent Baxter/Erin Enderlin*	Arista Nashville
4/2/05	**18**	20		70 **The Talkin' Song Repair Blues**	*Dennis Linde*	Arista Nashville
				above 3 from the album *What I Do* on Arista Nashville 63103		

Between The Devil And Me ['98]
Blue Blooded Woman ['89]
Blues Man ['00]
Chasin' That Neon Rainbow ['90]
Chattahoochee ['93]
Dallas ['92]
Designated Drinker ['02]
Don't Rock The Jukebox ['91]
Drive (For Daddy Gene) ['02]
Everything I Love ['97]
Gone Country ['95]
Gone Crazy ['99]
Good Year For The Roses ['94]
Here In The Real World ['90]
Hey Good Lookin' ['04]
Holly Jolly Christmas ['98]
Home ['96]
Honky Tonk Christmas ['94, '95]
House With No Curtains ['98]
I Don't Even Know Your Name ['95]
I Only Want You For Christmas ['92, '96, '98]
I'd Love You All Over Again ['91]
I'll Go On Loving You ['98]
I'll Try ['96]
It Must Be Love ['00]
It's Alright To Be A Redneck ['01]
It's Five O'Clock Somewhere ['03]
Jingle Bells ['03]
Just Put A Ribbon In Your Hair ['04]
Let It Be Christmas ['03]
Little Bitty ['96]
Little Man ['99]
Livin' On Love ['94]
Love's Got A Hold On You ['92]
Margaritaville ['99]
Mercury Blues ['93]
Midnight In Montgomery ['92]
Monday Morning Church ['05]
Murder On Music Row ['00]
My Own Kind Of Hat ['99]
Pop A Top ['99]
Redneck Games ['96]
Remember When ['04]
Right On The Money ['99]
Rudolph The Red-Nosed Reindeer ['97]
She Just Started Liking Cheatin' Songs ['99]
She's Got The Rhythm (And I Got The Blues) ['92]
Someday ['91]
Song For The Life ['95]
Summertime Blues ['94]
Talkin' Song Repair Blues ['05]
Tall, Tall Trees ['95]
Tequila Sunrise ['93]
That'd Be Alright ['03]
There Goes ['97]
Three Minute Positive Not Too Country Up-Tempo Love Song ['00]
Tonight I Climbed The Wall ['93]
Too Much Of A Good Thing ['04]
Tropical Depression ['93]
Wanted ['90]
When Somebody Loves You ['01]
Where I Come From ['01]
Where Were You (When The World Stopped Turning) ['01]
(Who Says) You Can't Have It All ['94]
Who's Cheatin' Who ['97]
Work In Progress ['02]
www.memory ['00]

JACKSON, Carl

Born on 9/18/1953 in Louisville, Mississippi. Male singer/songwriter/banjo player.

DEBUT	PEAK	WKS	GOLD	Country Chart Hit	Songwriter	Label (& Number)
11/3/84	**44**	15		1 **She's Gone, Gone, Gone**	*Harlan Howard*	Columbia 04647
3/2/85	**70**	7		2 **All That's Left For Me**	*Carl Jackson*	Columbia 04786
6/1/85	**45**	9		3 **Dixie Train**	*Carl Jackson/Jim Weatherly*	Columbia 04926
1/25/86	**85**	7		4 **You Are The Rock (And I'm A Rolling Stone)**	*Irene Kelley*	Columbia 05645

JACKSON, Lolita

Born in Texas. Female singer.

DEBUT	PEAK	WKS	GOLD	Country Chart Hit	Songwriter	Label (& Number)
3/18/89	**89**	2		**Every Time You Walk In The Room**	*Sandy Myers*	Oak 1069

JACKSON, Nisha

Born in Tennessee. Black female singer.

DEBUT	PEAK	WKS	GOLD	Country Chart Hit	Songwriter	Label (& Number)
10/24/87	**81**	3		**Alive And Well**	*Michael Garvin/Bucky Jones*	Capitol 44064

JACKSON, Stonewall — 1950s: #49 / 1960s: #14 / All-Time: #103

Born on 11/6/1932 in Emerson, North Carolina. Male singer/songwriter/guitarist. Served in the U.S. Army in 1948; served in The U.S. Navy from 1949-54. Had own log-trucking company in Georgia in 1955. Descendent of General Thomas Jonathan "Stonewall" Jackson.

DEBUT	PEAK	WKS	GOLD	Country Chart Hit	Songwriter	Label (& Number)
11/3/58+	**2^{1}**	23		1 **Life To Go**	*George Jones*	Columbia 41257
6/8/59	❶^{5}	19		2 **Waterloo /**	*John D. Loudermilk/Marijohn Wilkin*	
6/29/59	**24**	5		3 **Smoke Along The Track**	*Don Helms/Alan Rose*	Columbia 41393

DEBUT	PEAK	WKS	G O L D	ARTIST / Country Chart Hit	Ranking / Songwriter	Label (& Number)
				JACKSON, Stonewall — cont'd		
11/23/59	**29**	1		4 **Igmoo** (The Pride Of South Central High)	*Cindy Walker/Marijohn Wilkin*	Columbia 41488
1/18/60	**12**	12		5 **Mary Don't You Weep**	*Mel Tillis/Marijohn Wilkin*	Columbia 41533
4/4/60	**6**	17		6 **Why I'm Walkin'** /	*Stonewall Jackson*	
4/25/60	**15**	5		7 **Life Of A Poor Boy**	*Johnny Mosby/Jonie Mosby*	Columbia 41591
11/7/60	**13**	15		8 **A Little Guy Called Joe**	*Wayne Walker/Marijohn Wilkin*	Columbia 41785
3/13/61	**26**	6		9 **Greener Pastures**	*Marijohn Wilkin*	Columbia 41932
8/7/61	**27**	2		10 **Hungry For Love**	*Mel Tillis*	Columbia 42028
1/20/62	**3**[2]	22		11 **A Wound Time Can't Erase** /	*William Johnson*	
2/3/62	**18**	3		12 **Second Choice**	*Irene Stanton/Wayne Walker*	Columbia 42229
6/30/62	**11**	10		13 **One Look At Heaven** /	*Marijohn Wilkin*	
7/21/62	**9**	7		14 **Leona**	*Cindy Walker*	Columbia 42426
1/26/63	**11**	10		15 **Can't Hang Up The Phone**	*John D. Loudermilk*	Columbia 42628
5/18/63	**8**	14		16 **Old Showboat**	*Fred Burch/Marijohn Wilkin*	Columbia 42765
11/9/63	**15**	8		17 **Wild Wild Wind**	*Roy Botkin*	Columbia 42846
12/7/63+	**❶**[1]	22		18 **B.J. The D.J.**	*Hugh X. Lewis*	Columbia 42889
4/25/64	**24**	13		19 **Not My Kind Of People**	*Benny Joy/Hugh X. Lewis*	Columbia 43011
8/22/64	**4**	25		20 **Don't Be Angry**	*Wade Jackson*	Columbia 43076
2/27/65	**8**	19		21 **I Washed My Hands In Muddy Water**	*Joe Babcock*	Columbia 43197
7/17/65	**30**	9		22 **Trouble And Me** /	*Jimmy Rule*	
8/14/65	**22**	7		23 **Lost In The Shuffle**	*Ray Griff*	Columbia 43304
11/6/65	**44**	3		24 **Poor Red Georgia Dirt** /	*Fred Burch/Gary Stewart*	
11/27/65+	**24**	12		25 **If This House Could Talk**	*Hugh X. Lewis*	Columbia 43411
4/30/66	**24**	8		26 **The Minute Men** (Are Turning In Their Graves)	*Harlan Howard*	Columbia 43552
8/6/66	**12**	15		27 **Blues Plus Booze** (Means I Lose)	*Elkin Brown*	Columbia 43718
2/4/67	**5**	17		28 **Stamp Out Loneliness**	*Carl Belew/Van Givens*	Columbia 43966
6/10/67	**15**	15		29 **Promises And Hearts** (Were Made To Break)	*Bobby Dyson/Larry Lee*	Columbia 44121
10/7/67	**27**	12		30 **This World Holds Nothing** (Since You're Gone)	*Jake Schneider/Claude Southall*	Columbia 44283
2/17/68	**39**	10		31 **Nothing Takes The Place Of Loving You**	*Ben Peters*	Columbia 44416
6/8/68	**31**	9		32 **I Believe In Love**	*Juanita Jackson/Stonewall Jackson*	Columbia 44501
9/28/68	**16**	15		33 **Angry Words**	*Hugh X. Lewis*	Columbia 44625
3/1/69	**52**	7		34 **Somebody's Always Leaving**	*Jack Schneider/Claude Southall*	Columbia 44726
6/14/69	**25**	9		35 **"Never More" Quote The Raven**	*Cy Coben*	Columbia 44863
10/4/69	**19**	10		36 **Ship In The Bottle**	*Hugh X. Lewis/Glenn Sutton*	Columbia 44976
3/7/70	**72**	2		37 **Better Days For Mama**	*Hugh King*	Columbia 45075
7/4/70	**72**	2		38 **Born That Way**	*Hugh X. Lewis/Glenn Sutton*	Columbia 45151
10/10/70	**63**	4		39 **Oh, Lonesome Me**	*Don Gibson*	Columbia 45217
5/22/71	**7**	13		40 **Me And You And A Dog Named Boo**	*Lobo*	Columbia 45381
3/11/72	**51**	9		41 **That's All This Old World Needs** *[w/ Brentwood Children's Choir]*	*Demetriss Tapp/Bob Tubert*	Columbia 45546
7/29/72	**71**	5		42 **Torn From The Pages Of Life**	*Carmol Taylor/Agnes Wilson*	Columbia 45632
1/27/73	**70**	3		43 **I'm Not Strong Enough** (To Build Another Dream)	*Dallas Frazier/A.L. "Doodle" Owens*	Columbia 45738
7/28/73	**41**	9		44 **Herman Schwartz**	*Jerry Foster/Bill Rice*	MGM 14569

JACKSON, Wanda — **1960s: #48 / All-Time: #196**

Born on 10/20/1937 in Maud, Oklahoma; raised in Bakersfield, California, and Oklahoma City, Oklahoma. Female singer/songwriter/guitarist/pianist. Own radio show on KLPR-Oklahoma City in 1950. Recorded with **Hank Thompson** in 1954. Had three solo records released while still in high school. Worked with **Red Foley**'s *Ozark Jubilee* from 1955-62; toured with **Elvis Presley** in 1955 and 1956.

DEBUT	PEAK	WKS	G O L D	Country Chart Hit	Songwriter	Label (& Number)
7/24/54	**8**	8		1 **You Can't Have My Love** *[w/ Billy Gray]* S:8 / A:8 / J:10	*Billy Gray/Chuck Harding/Hank Thompson*	Decca 29140
10/20/56	**15**	1		2 **I Gotta Know** A:15	*Thelma Blackman*	Capitol 3485
7/31/61	**9**	14		3 **Right Or Wrong**	*Wanda Jackson*	Capitol 4553
11/20/61+	**6**	15		4 **In The Middle Of A Heartache**	*Laurie Christienson/Pat Franzese/Wanda Jackson*	Capitol 4635
6/9/62	**28**	1		5 **If I Cried Every Time You Hurt Me**	*Harlan Howard*	Capitol 4723
1/25/64	**46**	1		6 **Slippin'**	*Fuzzy Owen*	Capitol 5072
3/28/64	**36**	11		7 **The Violet And A Rose**	*Bud Auge/John Reinfield/Mel Tillis*	Capitol 5142
2/26/66	**18**	11		8 **The Box It Came In**	*Vic McAlpin*	Capitol 5559
6/25/66	**28**	7		9 **Because It's You**	*Bobby George/Vern Stoval*	Capitol 5645
9/3/66	**46**	10		10 **This Gun Don't Care**	*Larry Lee*	Capitol 5712
12/17/66+	**11**	18		11 **Tears Will Be The Chaser For Your Wine**	*LeRoy Coates/Dale David*	Capitol 5789
				WANDA JACKSON And The Party Timers:		
4/22/67	**21**	12		12 **Both Sides Of The Line**	*Marian Francis*	Capitol 5863
8/19/67	**51**	7		13 **My Heart Gets All The Breaks** /	*Justin Tubb*	
8/19/67	**64**	2		14 **You'll Always Have My Love**	*Yvonne Devaney*	Capitol 5960
11/25/67+	**22**	12		15 **A Girl Don't Have To Drink To Have Fun**	*Joe Nixon/Charlie Williams*	Capitol 2021
1/27/68	**46**	6		16 **By The Time You Get To Phoenix** — answer to "By The Time I Get To Phoenix" by **Glen Campbell**	*Jimmy Webb*	Capitol 2085
5/4/68	**34**	10		17 **My Baby Walked Right Out On Me**	*Curtis Wayne*	Capitol 2151
9/7/68	**46**	6		18 **Little Boy Soldier**	*Curly Putman*	Capitol 2245
11/16/68+	**51**	9		19 **I Wish I Was Your Friend**	*Harlan Howard*	Capitol 2315

Billboard DEBUT	PEAK	WKS	GOLD	ARTIST / Ranking / Country Chart Hit	Songwriter	Label (& Number)
				WANDA JACKSON:		
2/8/69	**41**	10		20 **If I Had A Hammer**	*Lee Hays/Pete Seeger*	Capitol 2379
7/12/69	**48**	7		21 **Everything's Leaving**	*Red Lane*	Capitol 2524
9/27/69	**20**	11		22 **My Big Iron Skillet**	*Bryan Creswell/Wilda Creswell*	Capitol 2614
1/3/70	**35**	10		23 **Two Separate Bar Stools**	*Bill Graham*	Capitol 2693
4/4/70	**17**	11		24 **A Woman Lives For Love**	*George Richey/Glenn Sutton/Norris Wilson*	Capitol 2761
9/12/70	**50**	7		25 **Who Shot John**	*Jerry Hadli*	Capitol 2872
12/12/70+	**13**	11		26 **Fancy Satin Pillows**	*Jan Crutchfield/Dee Moeller*	Capitol 2986
8/7/71	**25**	12		27 **Back Then**	*Jerry Crutchfield*	Capitol 3143
11/27/71+	**35**	11		28 **I Already Know (What I'm Getting For My Birthday)**	*Red Williams*	Capitol 3218
4/8/72	**57**	7		29 **I'll Be Whatever You Say**	*Jamie Rogers*	Capitol 3293
1/26/74	**98**	4		30 **Come On Home (To This Lonely Heart)**	*Colbert Croft/Joyce Croft*	Myrrh 125
				JACOBS, Lori		
				Born in Ann Arbor, Michigan. Female singer/songwriter.		
3/15/80	**94**	2		**Tugboat Annie**	*Lori Jacobs*	Neostat 102
				JACQUES, Rick		
				Born in Nashville, Tennessee. Male singer/songwriter.		
5/6/78	**89**	2		**Song Man**	*Rick Jacques*	Caprice 2046
				JAMES, Atlanta — see VICKERY, Mack		
				JAMES, Brett		
				Born on 6/5/1968 in Columbia, Missouri. Male singer/songwriter/guitarist.		
7/15/95	**60**	6		1 **Female Bonding**	*Brett James*	Career
10/21/95	**68**	5		2 **If I Could See Love**	*Steve Bogard/Brett James*	Career
1/20/96	**73**	2		3 **Worth The Fall**	*Brett James*	Career
				above 3 from the album *Brett James* on Career 18789		
4/6/02	**34**	17		4 **Chasin' Amy**	*Brett James/Troy Verges*	Arista Nashville
2/15/03	**39**	13		5 **After All**	*Chris Davis/Brett James*	Arista Nashville
				JAMES, Dusty		
				Born in Oklahoma City, Oklahoma. Male singer.		
7/14/79	**76**	4		**You're All The Woman I'll Ever Need**	*Lee Dresser*	SCR 172
				JAMES, George		
				Born in 1958 in Rockford, Illinois. Male singer.		
5/12/79	**94**	3		1 **It's Gotta Be Magic**	*Linda Kimball/Mark Sherrill/Josh Whitmore*	Janc 10417
10/20/79	**95**	2		2 **When Our Love Began (Cowboys And Indians)**	*Bud Reneau/Mark Sherrill*	Janc 103
				JAMES, Jesseca		
				Born Kathy Jenkins in 1960 in Oklahoma. Female singer. Daughter of **Conway Twitty**. Also recorded as **Kathy Twitty**.		
10/2/76	**87**	4		1 **Johnny One Time**	*Dallas Frazier/A.L. "Doodle" Owens*	MCA 40613
4/30/77	**93**	3		2 **My First Country Song**	*Conway Twitty*	MCA 40703
1/12/85	**82**	5		3 **Green Eyes** *[Kathy Twitty]*	*Mary Fielder/Kim Morrison*	Permian 82009
				JAMES, Mary Kay		
				Born Mary Kay Mulkey in Atlanta, Georgia. Female singer/guitarist.		
5/4/74	**78**	6		1 **Please Help Me Say No**	*Jim Rushing*	JMI 38
9/14/74	**48**	13		2 **It Amazes Me (Sweet Lovin' Time)**	*Wayland Holyfield/Allen Reynolds*	JMI 46
1/25/75	**57**	8		3 **The Crossroad**	*Allen Reynolds*	Avco 605
5/3/75	**76**	7		4 **I Think I'll Say Goodbye**	*Marshall Chapman/Jim Rushing*	Avco 610

JAMES, Sonny **1950s: #26 / 1960s: #12 / 1970s: #10 / All-Time: #21**

Born James Hugh Loden on 5/1/1929 in Hackleburg, Alabama. Male singer/songwriter/guitarist. Sang with his four sisters as The Loden Family. Served in the U.S. Army from 1950-52. Acted in the movies *Second Fiddle To A Steel Guitar*, *Nashville Rebel*, *Las Vegas Hillbillies* and *Hillbillys In A Haunted House*. Known as "The Southern Gentleman." Also see **Heart Of Nashville**.

OPRY: 1965

DEBUT	PEAK	WKS	GOLD	Country Chart Hit	Songwriter	Label (& Number)
2/7/53	**9**	1		1 **That's Me Without You**	A:9 *Joe Miller*	Capitol 2259
11/20/54	**14**	1		2 **She Done Give Her Heart To Me**	A:14 *Sonny James*	Capitol 2906
3/24/56	**7**	11		3 **For Rent (One Empty Heart)**	A:7 / J:8 / S:12 *Sonny James/Jack Morrow*	Capitol 3357
6/30/56	**11**	6		4 **Twenty Feet Of Muddy Water**	A:11 *Bill Smith*	Capitol 3441
11/10/56	**12**	1		5 **The Cat Came Back**	A:12 *Sonny James*	Capitol 3542
12/22/56+	**❶[9]**	24	●	6 **Young Love /**	A:❶[9] / S:❶[7] / J:❶[3] *Ric Cartey/Carole Joyner*	
1/26/57	**6**	12		7 **You're The Reason I'm In Love**	A:6 *Jack Morrow*	Capitol 3602
4/13/57	**9**	9		8 **First Date, First Kiss, First Love**	S:9 / A:9 *Mary Stovall/Dan Welch*	Capitol 3674
8/12/57	**15**	1		9 **Lovesick Blues**	A:15 *Cliff Friend/Irving Mills/Hank Williams*	Capitol 3734
1/6/58	**8**	5		10 **Uh-Huh-mm**	A:8 / S:14 *Sylvester Bradford/Al Lewis*	Capitol 3840
5/9/60	**22**	6		11 **Jenny Lou**	*Mark McIntyre/William Olofson*	NRC 050
7/20/63	**9**	15		12 **The Minute You're Gone**	*Jimmy Gateley*	Capitol 4969
12/21/63	**17**	9		13 **Going Through The Motions (Of Living)**	*Jean Chapel*	Capitol 5057
3/28/64	**6**	17		14 **Baltimore**	*Boudleaux Bryant/Felice Bryant*	Capitol 5129

DEBUT	PEAK	WKS	GOLD	ARTIST / Country Chart Hit	Ranking / Songwriter	Label (& Number)
				JAMES, Sonny — cont'd		
7/18/64	27	6		15 Sugar Lump /	Joe Thomas	
8/8/64	19	13		16 Ask Marie	Anna Carter/Fred Carter	Capitol 5197
11/14/64+	❶^{4}	25		17 **You're The Only World I Know**	Sonny James/Bob Tubert	Capitol 5280
4/3/65	2^{1}	20		18 I'll Keep Holding On (Just To Your Love)	Bob Tubert	Capitol 5375
8/14/65	❶^{3}	22		19 **Behind The Tear**	Ned Miller/Sue Miller	Capitol 5454
12/11/65+	3^{3}	18		20 True Love's A Blessing	Sonny James/Carole Smith	Capitol 5536
4/9/66	❶^{2}	20		21 **Take Good Care Of Her**	Arthur Kent/Ed Warren	Capitol 5612
8/13/66	2^{2}	20		22 Room In Your Heart	Sonny James/Frances Long	Capitol 5690
2/25/67	❶^{2}	18		23 **Need You**	Johnny Blackburn/Teepee Mitchell/Lew Porter	Capitol 5833
6/10/67	❶^{4}	17		24 **I'll Never Find Another You**	Tom Springfield	Capitol 5914
9/23/67	❶^{5}	18		25 **It's The Little Things**	Arlie Duff	Capitol 5987
1/20/68	❶^{3}	17		26 **A World Of Our Own**	Tom Springfield	Capitol 2067
					Cindy Walker	Capitol 2155
					Don Robertson	Capitol 2271
					Joe Melson/Roy Orbison	Capitol 2370
					J.P. Richardson	Capitol 2486
					Ivory Joe Hunter	Capitol 2595
					Brook Benton/Belford Hendricks/Clyde Otis	Capitol 2700
					Tony Hatch	Capitol 2782
					Sonny James/Carole Smith	Capitol 2834
					Brook Benton/Clyde Otis	Capitol 2914
					Ivory Joe Hunter	Capitol 3015
					Jimmy Reed	Capitol 3114
					Sonny James/Carole Smith	Capitol 3174
					Burt Bacharach/Hal David	Capitol 3232
					Kelso Herston/Jack Morrow	Capitol 3322
				...s	Ernest Bader/Larry Kusick/Hans Last/Eddie Snyder	Columbia 45644
					Buddy Buie/J.R. Cobb/Emory Gordy	Capitol 3398
					Charles Matthews	Columbia 45706
					Ted Riedel	Capitol 3475
				...yday	Don Robertson	Columbia 45770
				...h Me	Richard Hollingsworth/Sonny James	Capitol 3564
				...ou	Allen Reynolds/Don Williams	Columbia 45871
					Sonny James/Carole Smith	Capitol 3653
					Ben Peters/Carole Smith	Capitol 3779
					Warner Mack	Columbia 46003
				...ife With Love)	Sonny James/Carole Smith	Columbia 10001
					Sonny James/Carole Smith	Columbia 10072
					James Gilreath	Columbia 10121
				... You	Jack Scott	Columbia 10184
					Juan Carlos Calderon [I]	Columbia 10249
					Guy Massey	
					Gene Autry/Ray Whitley	Columbia 10276
				... My Baby	Isaac Hayes/David Porter	Columbia 10335
					Sonny James/Carole Smith	Columbia 10392
					Lou Herscher/Don Robertson	Columbia 10466
					Jimmie Rodgers [L]	Columbia 10551
					John D. Loudermilk [L]	Columbia 10628
				...**State Prison Band** (above 2)		
					Bobby Lee Springfield/Luther Wood	Columbia 10703
					Mitchell Torok	Columbia 10764
					Arlie Duff	Columbia 10852
					Joe Tex	Monument 280
					Fred Foster/Gunther-Eric Thoner	Monument 288
				...outhern Gentlemen:		
					Sonny James/Carole Smith	Dimension 1026
					Ron Miller/Bryan Wells	Dimension 1033
				...R:		
					Sonny James/Virgil True	Dimension 1036
					Randy Goodrum/Dave Loggins	Dimension 1040
					Sonny James/Carole Smith	Dimension 1045

DEBUT	PEAK	WKS	GOLD	ARTIST / Ranking / Country Chart Hit	Songwriter	Label (& Number)
				JAMES, Sonny — cont'd		

True Love's A Blessing ['66]
Twenty Feet Of Muddy Water ['56]
Uh-Huh-mm ['58]
What In The World's Come Over You ['75]
When Something Is Wrong With My Baby ['76]
When The Snow Is On The Roses ['72]
White Silver Sands ['72]
World Of Our Own ['68]
You're Free To Go ['77]
You're The Only World I Know ['65]
You're The Reason I'm In Love ['57]
Young Love ['57]

DEBUT	PEAK	WKS	GOLD	ARTIST / Ranking / Country Chart Hit	Songwriter	Label (& Number)
				JAMES, Tommy		
				Born Thomas Jackson on 4/29/1947 in Dayton, Ohio; raised in Niles, Michigan. Pop singer/songwriter.		
3/15/80	**93**	2		**Three Times In Love**	*Tommy James/Rick Serota*	Millennium 11785
				JAMESON, Cody		
				Born in Manhattan, New York. Female pop singer.		
4/16/77	**64**	7		**Brooklyn**	*Lefty Pedroski*	Atco 7073
				JAN & MALCOLM		
				Female-male duo from Dallas, Texas.		
3/12/77	**99**	2		**Rainbow In Your Eyes (Love's Got A Hold On Me)**	*Leon Russell*	Paula 421
				JANÉT, Joanna		
				Born in Baton Rouge, Louisiana. Female singer.		
4/13/02	**55**	3		**Since I've Seen You Last**	*Ashley Gorley/Bryan Simpson*	DreamWorks
				JANO		
				Born Jano Bourland. Male singer/songwriter.		
10/20/79	**94**	2		**Sundown Sideshow**	*Jano Bourland*	SCR 180
				JANSKY, Clifton		
				Born in 1956 in Pleasanton, Texas. Male singer/songwriter/guitarist.		
4/13/85	**97**	2		**Will You Love Me In The Morning**	*Clifton Jansky*	Axbar 6033
				JAYE, Jerry		
				Born Gerald Jaye Hatley on 10/19/1937 in Manila, Arkansas. Male singer.		
8/9/75	**53**	8		1 **It's All In The Game**	*Charles Dawes/Carl Sigman*	Columbia 10170
6/12/76	**32**	13		2 **Honky Tonk Women Love Red Neck Men**	*Danny Hogan/Ronny Scaife/Bob Tucker*	Hi 2310
11/20/76	**78**	9		3 **Hot And Still Heatin'**	*Don Scaife/Ronny Scaife*	Hi 2318
				JEAN — see NORMA JEAN		
				JED ZEPPELIN		
				All-star group: **Diamond Rio**, **Lee Roy Parnell** and **Steve Wariner**. Group name is a pun on Led Zeppelin.		
12/10/94+	**48**	15		**Workin' Man Blues**	*Merle Haggard*	Arista
				from the various artists album *Mama's Hungry Eyes: A Tribute To **Merle Haggard*** on Arista 18760		
				JEFFERSON, Paul		
				Born on 8/15/1961 in Woodside, California. Male singer/songwriter/guitarist.		
5/18/96	**50**	10		1 **Check Please**	*Paul Jefferson/Jon Michaels*	Almo Sounds
8/17/96	**73**	1		2 **Fear Of A Broken Heart**	*Paul Jefferson/Steve McClintock/Billy Spencer*	Almo Sounds
10/19/96	**73**	1		3 **I Might Just Make It**	*Paul Jefferson/David Vincent*	Almo Sounds
				above 3 from the album *Paul Jefferson* on Almo Sounds 80007		
				JENKINS, The		
				Female vocal trio from Sebastopol, California: mother Nancy Jenkins, with her daughters Kacie Jenkins and Brodie Jenkins.		
3/27/04	**34**	17		1 **Blame It On Mama**	S:2 *Dennis Hysom/Nancy Jenkins/Christine Walker*	Capitol
8/14/04	**38**	12		2 **Getaway Car**	S:❶^{3} *Gary Haase/Billy Mann*	Capitol
				JENKINS, Bob		
				Born in Oklahoma. Male singer/songwriter.		
2/6/82	**76**	3		1 **The Cube** *[w/ daughter Mandy]*	*Bob Jenkins* **[N]**	Liberty 1448
				a song about Rubick's Cube		
2/19/83	**86**	3		2 **Workin' In A Coalmine**	*Bob Jenkins*	Picap 009
				JENKINS, Bobby		
				Born in 1942 in Corpus Christi, Texas. Male singer/songwriter.		
6/16/84	**69**	5		1 **Blackjack Whiskey**	*Bobby Jenkins*	Zone 7 40984
8/25/84	**82**	3		2 **Louisiana Heatwave**	*Bobby Jenkins*	Zone 7 61884
5/11/85	**85**	3		3 **Me And Margarita**	*Bobby Jenkins*	Zone 7 30185
				JENKINS, Larry		
				Born in West Helena, Arkansas. Male singer/songwriter. Nephew of **Conway Twitty**.		
10/30/82	**76**	6		1 **I'm So Tired Of Going Home Drunk**	*Joe Chambers/Larry Jenkins*	Capitol 5167
7/28/84	**87**	3		2 **You're The Best I Never Had**	*Joe Chambers/Larry Jenkins*	MCA 52396
				JENKINS, Matt		
				Born in Aledo, Texas. Male singer/songwriter/guitarist.		
6/25/05	**51**	11		**King Of The Castle**	*Matt Jenkins*	Universal South
				JENNINGS, Bob		
				Born on 9/26/1924 in Liberty, Tennessee. Died of a self-inflicted gunshot on 4/19/1984 (age 59). Male singer.		
5/9/64	**32**	13		1 **The First Step Down (Is The Longest)**	*Ray Pennington*	Sims 161
11/14/64	**34**	8		2 **Leave A Little Play (In The Chain Of Love)**	*Jimmy Dickens/Larry Kirby*	Sims 202

Billboard | ARTIST | Ranking

DEBUT	PEAK	WKS	GOLD	Country Chart Hit	Songwriter	Label (& Number)

JENNINGS, Shooter

Born Waylon Albright Jennings in 1979 in Nashville, Tennessee. Male singer/songwriter/guitarist. Son of **Waylon Jennings** and **Jessi Colter**.

DEBUT	PEAK	WKS	GOLD	Country Chart Hit	Songwriter	Label (& Number)
4/23/05	**26**↑	23↑		**4th Of July** *[w/ George Jones]* from Jennings' album *Put The O Back In Country* on Universal South 003816	*Shooter Jennings*	Universal South

JENNINGS, Tommy

Born on 8/8/1938 in Littlefield, Texas. Male singer/guitarist. Brother of **Waylon Jennings**.

DEBUT	PEAK	WKS	GOLD	Country Chart Hit	Songwriter	Label (& Number)
8/2/75	**96**	4		1 **Make It Easy On Yourself**	*Paul Huffman/Joane Keller*	Paragon 102
4/15/78	**71**	7		2 **Don't You Think It's Time**	*Mitch Johnson/Billy Lee Morris/Harold Shedd*	Monument 248
5/31/80	**51**	10		3 **Just Give Me What You Think Is Fair** *[w/ Rex Gosdin]*	*Rex Gosdin/V.L. Haywood/Jeff Tweel*	Sabre 4520

JENNINGS, Waylon 1960s: #37 / 1970s: #9 / 1980s: #9 / All-Time: #12 // HOF: 2001

Born on 6/15/1937 in Littlefield, Texas. Died of diabetes on 2/13/2002 (age 64). Male singer/songwriter/guitarist. Brother of **Tommy Jennings**; father of **Shooter Jennings**. Played bass for Buddy Holly on the ill-fated "Winter Dance Party" tour in 1959. Gave up his seat to the Big Bopper on the plane, which crashed on 2/3/1959, killing Holly, Ritchie Valens and the Big Bopper. Established himself in the mid-1970s as a leader of the "outlaw" music movement. Married **Jessi Colter** on 10/26/1969. Acted in the movies *Nashville Rebel* and *MacKintosh And T.J.* Narrator for TV's *The Dukes Of Hazzard.* Also see **Some Of Chet's Friends**.

CMA: Male Vocalist 1975 / Vocal Duo (with Willie Nelson) 1976

DEBUT	PEAK	WKS	GOLD	Country Chart Hit	Songwriter	Label (& Number)
8/21/65	**49**	2		1 **That's The Chance I'll Have To Take**	*Jackson King*	RCA Victor 8572
9/25/65	**16**	13		2 **Stop The World** (And Let Me Off)	*Carl Belew/W.S. Stevenson*	RCA Victor 8652
1/15/66	**17**	15		3 **Anita, You're Dreaming**	*Don Bowman/Waylon Jennings*	RCA Victor 8729
6/4/66	**17**	13		4 **Time To Bum Again**	*Harlan Howard*	RCA Victor 8822
9/3/66	**9**	18		5 (That's What You Get) **For Lovin' Me**	*Gordon Lightfoot*	RCA Victor 8917
12/17/66+	**11**	15		6 **Green River** from the movie *Nashville Rebel* starring Jennings	*Harlan Howard*	RCA Victor 9025
4/1/67	**12**	16		7 **Mental Revenge**	*Mel Tillis*	RCA Victor 9146
8/19/67	**8**	17		8 **The Chokin' Kind** *[w/ The Waylors]* /	*Harlan Howard*	
9/9/67	**67**	5		9 **Love Of The Common People** *[w/ The Waylors]*	*John Hurley/Ronnie Wilkins*	RCA Victor 9259
1/27/68	**5**	16		10 **Walk On Out Of My Mind**	*Red Lane*	RCA Victor 9414
3/30/68	**4**	15		11 **I Got You** *[w/ Anita Carter]*	*Gordon Galbraith/Ricci Mareno*	RCA Victor 9480
7/13/68	**2^{5}**	18		12 **Only Daddy That'll Walk The Line**	*Jimmy Bryant*	RCA Victor 9561
11/16/68+	**5**	17		13 **Yours Love**	*Harlan Howard*	RCA Victor 9642
3/8/69	**19**	12		14 **Something's Wrong In California**	*Wayne Carson/Rodney Lay*	RCA Victor 0105
5/24/69	**20**	12		15 **The Days Of Sand And Shovels** /	*Bud Reneau*	
5/31/69	**37**	6		16 **Delia's Gone**	*Caperton Henley*	RCA Victor 0157
8/23/69	**23**	11		17 **MacArthur Park** *[w/ The Kimberlys]* **Grammy: Vocal Group**	*Jimmy Webb*	RCA Victor 0210
11/29/69+	**3^{2}**	15		18 **Brown Eyed Handsome Man**	*Chuck Berry*	RCA Victor 0281
4/18/70	**12**	14		19 **Singer Of Sad Songs**	*Alex Zanetis*	RCA Victor 9819
8/29/70	**5**	15		20 **The Taker**	*Kris Kristofferson/Shel Silverstein*	RCA Victor 9885
11/14/70	**25**	10		21 **Suspicious Minds** *[w/ Jessi Colter]* also see #40 below	*Mark James*	RCA Victor 9920
12/5/70+	**16**	12		22 (Don't Let The Sun Set On You) **Tulsa**	*Wayne Carson*	RCA Victor 9925
4/3/71	**14**	14		23 **Mississippi Woman**	*Red Lane*	RCA Victor 9967
6/19/71	**39**	8		24 **Under Your Spell Again** *[w/ Jessi Colter]*	*Buck Owens/Dusty Rhodes*	RCA Victor 9992
8/7/71	**12**	15		25 **Cedartown, Georgia**	*Charles Cobble/Jimmy Peters/Sammi Smith/Mack Vickery*	RCA Victor 1003
1/8/72	**3^{1}**	18		26 **Good Hearted Woman** also see #39 below	*Waylon Jennings/Willie Nelson*	RCA Victor 0615
6/10/72	**7**	13		27 **Sweet Dream Woman**	*Al Gorgoni/Chip Taylor*	RCA Victor 0716
10/21/72	**6**	15		28 **Pretend I Never Happened**	*Willie Nelson*	RCA Victor 0808
2/17/73	**7**	14		29 **You Can Have Her**	*Bill Cook*	RCA Victor 0886
5/26/73	**28**	10		30 **We Had It All**	*Donnie Fritts/Troy Seals*	RCA Victor 0961
10/6/73	**8**	15		31 **You Ask Me To**	*Waylon Jennings/Billy Joe Shaver*	RCA Victor 0086
4/27/74	**❶^{1}**	13		32 **This Time**	*Waylon Jennings*	RCA Victor 0251
8/10/74	**❶^{1}**	13		33 **I'm A Ramblin' Man**	*Ray Pennington*	RCA Victor 10020
12/21/74+	**2^{1}**	15		34 **Rainy Day Woman** /	*Waylon Jennings*	
1/11/75	**flip**	12		35 **Let's All Help The Cowboys** (Sing The Blues)	*Jack Clement*	RCA Victor 10142
5/3/75	**10**	14		36 **Dreaming My Dreams With You**	*Allen Reynolds*	RCA Victor 10270
9/6/75	**❶^{1}**	16		37 **Are You Sure Hank Done It This Way** /	*Waylon Jennings*	
9/13/75	**flip**	15		38 **Bob Wills Is Still The King**	*Waylon Jennings*	RCA Victor 10379
12/27/75+	**❶^{3}**	17		39 **Good Hearted Woman** *[w/ Willie Nelson]* **CMA: Single**; new duet version of #26 above	*Waylon Jennings/Willie Nelson* **[L-R]**	RCA Victor 10529
5/1/76	**2^{1}**	14		40 **Suspicious Minds** *[w/ Jessi Colter]* same version as #21 above	*Mark James* **[R]**	RCA Victor 10653
7/31/76	**4**	14		41 **Can't You See** /	*Toy Caldwell*	
9/11/76	**flip**	8		42 **I'll Go Back To Her**	*Waylon Jennings*	RCA Victor 10721
11/20/76+	**7**	14		43 **Are You Ready For The Country** /	*Neil Young*	
11/27/76+	**flip**	13		44 **So Good Woman**	*Waylon Jennings*	RCA 10842
4/16/77	**❶^{6}**	18		45 **Luckenbach, Texas** (Back To The Basics Of Love) **Willie Nelson** (ending vocal)	*Bobby Emmons/Chips Moman*	RCA 10924
5/7/77	**69**	6		46 **You Are My Sunshine** *[w/ Duane Eddy/Willie Nelson/Kin Vassy/Deed Eddy]*	*...Jimmie Davis/Charles Mitchell*	Elektra 45359

Billboard DEBUT	PEAK	WKS	GOLD		ARTIST Country Chart Hit	Ranking Songwriter	Label (& Number)
					JENNINGS, Waylon — cont'd		
10/8/77	❶^{2}	16		47	**The Wurlitzer Prize** (I Don't Want To Get Over You) /	*Bobby Emmons/Chips Moman*	
10/8/77	flip	16		48	**Lookin' For A Feeling**	*Waylon Jennings*	RCA 11118
1/21/78	❶^{4}	16		49	**Mammas Don't Let Your Babies Grow Up To Be Cowboys** *[w/ Willie Nelson] /* Grammy: Vocal Duo	*...Ed Bruce/Patsy Bruce*	
1/28/78	flip	15		50	**I Can Get Off On You** *[w/ Willie Nelson]*	*Waylon Jennings/Willie Nelson*	RCA 11198
5/20/78	2^{2}	13		51	**There Ain't No Good Chain Gang** *[w/ Johnny Cash]*	*Hal Bynum/Dave Kirby*	Columbia 10742
7/29/78	❶^{3}	13		52	**I've Always Been Crazy**	*Waylon Jennings*	RCA 11344
					WAYLON:		
10/28/78	5	13		53	**Don't You Think This Outlaw Bit's Done Got Out Of Hand /**	*Waylon Jennings*	
11/11/78	flip	11		54	**Girl I Can Tell** (You're Trying To Work It Out)	*Fred Carter/Waylon Jennings*	RCA 11390
5/19/79	❶^{3}	14		55	**Amanda**	*Bob McDill*	RCA 11596
9/22/79	❶^{2}	13		56	**Come With Me**	*Chuck Howard*	RCA 11723
11/17/79+	22	12		57	**I Wish I Was Crazy Again**	*Bob McDill*	Columbia 10742
1/5/80	❶^{1}	15		58	**I Ain't Living Long Like This**	*Rodney Crowell*	RCA 11898
5/31/80	7	13		59	**Clyde**	*J.J. Cale*	RCA 12007
8/23/80	❶^{1}	17	●	60	**Theme From The Dukes Of Hazzard** (Good Ol' Boys) from the TV series starring **John Schneider** and **Tom Wopat**	*Waylon Jennings*	RCA 12067
2/21/81	17	12		61	**Storms Never Last** *[w/ Jessi Colter]*	*Jessi Colter*	RCA 12176
6/6/81	10	13		62	**Wild Side Of Life/It Wasn't God Who Made Honky Tonk Angels** *[w/ Jessi Colter]*	*...Arlie Carter/Joe Miller/William Warren*	RCA 12245
11/21/81+	5	19		63	**Shine** from the movie *The Pursuit Of D.B. Cooper* starring Robert Duvall	*Waylon Jennings*	RCA 12367
3/13/82	❶^{2}	18		64	**Just To Satisfy You** *[w/ Willie Nelson]*	*Don Bowman/Waylon Jennings*	RCA 13073
6/26/82	4	16		65	**Women Do Know How To Carry On**	*Bobby Emmons/Waylon Jennings*	RCA 13257
10/23/82	13	15		66	(Sittin' On) **The Dock Of The Bay** *[w/ Willie Nelson]*	*Steve Cropper/Otis Redding*	RCA 13319
3/19/83	❶^{1}	16		67	**Lucille** (You Won't Do Your Daddy's Will)	*Albert Collins/Richard Penniman*	RCA 13465
					WAYLON JENNINGS:		
6/4/83	6	16		68	**Leave Them Boys Alone** *[w/ Hank Williams, Jr. & Ernest Tubb]*	*...Dean Dillon/Gary Stewart/Tanya Tucker/Hank Williams Jr.*	Warner/Curb 29633
7/2/83	10	18		69	**Breakin' Down**	*Joe Rainey*	RCA 13543
8/6/83	20	14		70	**Hold On, I'm Comin'** *[w/ Jerry Reed]*	*Isaac Hayes/David Porter*	RCA 13580
10/8/83	8	19		71	**Take It To The Limit** *[w/ Willie Nelson]*	*Don Henley/Randy Meisner*	Columbia 04131
10/22/83	15	16		72	**The Conversation** *[w/ Hank Williams, Jr.]*	*Richie Albright/Waylon Jennings/Hank Williams Jr.*	RCA 13631
3/3/84	4	20		73	**I May Be Used** (But Baby I Ain't Used Up)	*Bob McDill*	RCA 13729
6/16/84	6	18		74	**Never Could Toe The Mark**	*Waylon Jennings*	RCA 13827
9/29/84	6	21		75	**America**	S:5 / A:6 *Sammy Johns*	RCA 13908
1/19/85	10	19		76	**Waltz Me To Heaven**	S:9 / A:9 *Dolly Parton*	RCA 13984
5/18/85	❶^{1}	20		77	**Highwayman** *[w/ Willie Nelson/Johnny Cash/Kris Kristofferson]* Grammy: Song	S:❶^{1} / A:❶^{1} *Jimmy Webb*	Columbia 04881
6/22/85	2^{2}	21		78	**Drinkin' And Dreamin'**	S:❶^{1} / A:2 *Max D. Barnes/Troy Seals*	RCA 14094
9/14/85	15	18		79	**Desperados Waiting For A Train** *[w/ Willie Nelson/Johnny Cash/Kris Kristofferson]*	...S:15 / A:16 *Guy Clark*	Columbia 05594
11/16/85+	13	18		80	**The Devil's On The Loose**	S:11 / A:13 *Larry Willoughby*	RCA 14215
2/15/86	7	19		81	**Working Without A Net**	S:6 / A:8 *Don Cook/John Jarvis/Gary Nicholson*	MCA 52776
5/17/86	5	19		82	**Will The Wolf Survive**	A:6 / S:6 *David Hidalgo/Louie Perez*	MCA 52830
5/17/86	35	11		83	**Even Cowgirls Get The Blues** *[w/ Johnny Cash]*	A:34 *Rodney Crowell*	Columbia 05896
9/20/86	8	21		84	**What You'll Do When I'm Gone**	S:8 / A:8 *Larry Butler*	MCA 52915
1/31/87	❶^{1}	19		85	**Rose In Paradise**	A:❶^{1} / S:12 *Stewart Harris/Jim McBride*	MCA 53009
5/16/87	8	19		86	**Fallin' Out**	S:16 *Dennis Lile*	MCA 53088
9/12/87	6	22		87	**My Rough And Rowdy Days**	S:14 *Waylon Jennings/Roger Murrah*	MCA 53158
12/5/87+	23	15		88	**Somewhere Between Ragged And Right** *[w/ John Anderson]*	*...Waylon Jennings/Roger Murrah*	MCA 53226
1/23/88	16	16		89	**If Ole Hank Could Only See Us Now** (Chapter Five...Nashville)	...S:29 *Shooter Jennings/Waylon Jennings/Roger Murrah*	MCA 53243
3/26/88	14	19		90	**High Ridin' Heroes** *[w/ David Lynn Jones]*	S:27 *David Lynn Jones*	Mercury 870128
9/24/88	38	9		91	**How Much Is It Worth To Live In L.A.**	*Waylon Jennings/Roger Murrah*	MCA 53314
1/7/89	28	16		92	**Which Way Do I Go** (Now That I'm Gone)	*Stephen Clark/Johnny MacRae*	MCA 53476
5/20/89	61	5		93	**Trouble Man**	*Waylon Jennings/Tony Joe White*	MCA 53634
9/2/89	59	6		94	**You Put The Soul In The Song**	*John Detterline/Tim Gaetano/Don Goodman*	MCA 53710
3/3/90	25	14		95	**Silver Stallion** *[w/ Willie Nelson/Johnny Cash/Kris Kristofferson]* from their album *Highwayman 2* on Columbia 45240	*Lee Clayton*	Columbia
5/26/90	5	21		96	**Wrong**	*Andre Pessis/Steve Seskin*	Epic
10/13/90	67	6		97	**Where Corn Don't Grow**	*Mark Allan/Roger Murrah*	Epic
1/12/91	66	4		98	**What Bothers Me Most**	*Max D. Barnes/Troy Seals*	Epic
2/9/91	22	12		99	**The Eagle** above 4 from the album *The Eagle* on Epic 46104	*Hank Cochran/Red Lane/Mack Vickery*	Epic
6/15/91	51	10		100	**If I Can Find A Clean Shirt** *[w/ Willie Nelson]* from their album *Clean Shirt* on Epic 47462	*Waylon Jennings/Troy Seals*	Epic

Billboard DEBUT	PEAK	WKS	GOLD	ARTIST / Country Chart Hit	Ranking / Songwriter	Label (& Number)

JENNINGS, Waylon — cont'd

I Can Get Off On You ['78]
I Got You ['68]
I May Be Used (But Baby I Ain't Used Up) ['84]
I Wish I Was Crazy Again ['80]
I'll Go Back To Her ['76]
I'm A Ramblin' Man ['74]
I've Always Been Crazy ['78]
If I Can Find A Clean Shirt ['91]
If Ole Hank Could Only See Us Now ['88]
Just To Satisfy You ['82]
Leave Them Boys Alone ['83]
Let's All Help The Cowboys (Sing The Blues) ['75]
Lookin' For A Feeling ['77]
Love Of The Common People ['67]
Lucille (You Won't Do Your Daddy's Will) ['83]
Luckenbach, Texas (Back To The Basics Of Love) ['77]
MacArthur Park ['69]
Mammas Don't Let Your Babies Grow Up To Be Cowboys ['78]
Mental Revenge ['67]
Mississippi Woman ['71]
My Rough And Rowdy Days ['87]
Never Could Toe The Mark ['84]
Only Daddy That'll Walk The Line ['68]
Pretend I Never Happened ['72]
Rainy Day Woman ['75]
Rose In Paradise ['87]
Shine ['82]
Silver Stallion ['90]
Singer Of Sad Songs ['70]
(Sittin' On) The Dock Of The Bay ['82]
So Good Woman ['77]
Something's Wrong In California ['69]
Somewhere Between Ragged And Right ['88]
Stop The World (And Let Me Off) ['65]
Storms Never Last ['81]
Suspicious Minds ['70, '76]
Sweet Dream Woman ['72]
Take It To The Limit ['83]
Taker ['70]
That's The Chance I'll Have To Take ['65]
(That's What You Get) For Lovin' Me ['66]
Theme From The Dukes Of Hazzard (Good Ol' Boys) ['80]
There Ain't No Good Chain Gang ['78]
This Time ['74]
Time To Burn Again ['66]
Trouble Man ['89]
Under Your Spell Again ['71]
Walk On Out Of My Mind ['68]
Waltz Me To Heaven ['85]
We Had It All ['73]
What Bothers Me Most ['91]
What You'll Do When I'm Gone ['86]
Where Corn Don't Grow ['90]
Which Way Do I Go (Now That I'm Gone) ['89]
Wild Side Of Life/It Wasn't God Who Made Honky Tonk Angels ['81]
Will The Wolf Survive ['86]
Women Do Know How To Carry On ['82]
Working Without A Net ['86]
Wrong ['90]
Wurlitzer Prize (I Don't Want To Get Over You) ['77]
You Are My Sunshine ['77]
You Ask Me To ['73]
You Can Have Her ['73]
You Put The Soul In The Song ['89]
Yours Love ['69]

JEREMIAH

Born in California. Male singer.

DEBUT	PEAK	WKS	GOLD	Country Chart Hit	Songwriter	Label (& Number)
10/8/88	**96**	1		**To Be Loved**	*Tyran Carlo/Berry Gordy*	Chariot 1921

JERRICO, Sherri

Born in Buda, Texas. Female singer.

DEBUT	PEAK	WKS	GOLD	Country Chart Hit	Songwriter	Label (& Number)
10/8/77	**95**	2		**Thanks For Leaving, Lucille** — answer to "Lucille" by **Kenny Rogers**	*Jerry Hale/Jim Warford*	Gusto 164

JEWEL

Born Jewel Kilcher on 5/23/1974 in Payson, Utah; raised in Homer, Alaska. Adult Alternative singer/songwriter/guitarist. Wrote own book of poetry. Played "Sue Lee Shelley" in the movie *Ride With The Devil*.

DEBUT	PEAK	WKS	GOLD	Country Chart Hit	Songwriter	Label (& Number)
9/18/99	**56**	7		**That's The Way Love Goes** ***[w/ Merle Haggard]***	*Lefty Frizzell/Whitey Shafer*	BNA

JEWELL, Buddy

Born on 4/2/1961 in Lepanto, Arkansas. Male singer/songwriter. Winner of TV's first *Nashville Star* talent series.

DEBUT	PEAK	WKS	GOLD	Country Chart Hit	Songwriter	Label (& Number)
5/24/03	**3^{1}**	24		1 **Help Pour Out The Rain (Lacey's Song)**	S:❶^{2} *Buddy Jewell*	Columbia
11/1/03+	**3^{4}**	30		2 **Sweet Southern Comfort**	*Rodney Clawson/Brad Crisler*	Columbia
6/12/04	**38**	13		3 **One Step At A Time** — above 3 from the album *Buddy Jewell* on Columbia 90131	*Burton Collins/Stacy Widelitz*	Columbia
2/12/05	**27**	22		4 **If She Were Any Other Woman** — from the album *Times Like These* on Columbia 92873	S:❶^{15} *Brett Beavers/Connie Harrington/Kelley Lovelace*	Columbia

JIM & JESSE

Duo of brothers from Carfax, Virginia: Jim McReynolds (born on 2/13/1927; died on 12/31/2002, age 75; guitar) and Jesse McReynolds (born on 7/9/1929; mandolin).

OPRY: 1964

DEBUT	PEAK	WKS	GOLD	Country Chart Hit	Songwriter	Label (& Number)
7/18/64	**43**	2		1 **Cotton Mill Man**	*Joe Langston*	Epic 9676
12/19/64+	**39**	6		2 **Better Times A-Coming** ***[w/ The Virginia Boys]***	*Cal Veale*	Epic 9729
4/1/67	**18**	16		3 **Diesel On My Tail** ***[w/ The Virginia Boys]***	*Jim Fagan*	Epic 10138
9/23/67	**44**	4		4 **Ballad Of Thunder Road**	*Robert Mitchum/Don Raye*	Epic 10213
1/27/68	**49**	6		5 **Greenwich Village Folk Song Salesman**	*Tom T. Hall*	Epic 10263
9/7/68	**56**	6		6 **Yonder Comes A Freight Train**	*Ray Pennington*	Epic 10370
1/10/70	**38**	9		7 **The Golden Rocket**	*Hank Snow*	Epic 10563
2/13/71	**41**	9		8 **Freight Train**	*Paul James/Fred Williams*	Capitol 3026
6/5/82	**56**	9		9 **North Wind** ***[w/ Charlie Louvin]***	*Don Pfrimmer/Charles Quillen*	Soundwaves 4671
9/27/86	**78**	3		10 **Oh Louisiana**	*Ken Wesley*	MSR 198310

JIMMY & JOHNNY

Duo of Jimmy Lee Fautheree (born in 1934 in El Dorado, Arkansas; died of cancer on 6/29/2004, age 70) and **Country Johnny Mathis** (born on 9/28/1933 in Maud, Texas).

DEBUT	PEAK	WKS	GOLD	Country Chart Hit	Songwriter	Label (& Number)
9/25/54	**3^{1}**	18		**If You Don't Somebody Else Will**	J:3 / A:5 / S:6 *Geraldine Hamilton/Jimmy Lee/Johnny Mathis*	Chess 4859

JJ WHITE

Duo of sisters from California: Janice White and Jayne White.

DEBUT	PEAK	WKS	GOLD	Country Chart Hit	Songwriter	Label (& Number)
7/20/91	**69**	4		1 **The Crush**	*John Hiatt*	Curb
1/4/92	**73**	1		2 **Heart Break Train**	*J.D. Martin/Roger Murrah*	Curb
4/25/92	**63**	4		3 **Jezebel Kane** — above 3 from the album *Janice & Jayne* on Curb 77492	*Andre Pessis/Janice White/Jayne White*	Curb
9/12/92	**64**	3		4 **One Like That**	*Tim Nichols/Janice White/Jayne White*	Curb

JOE BOB'S NASHVILLE SOUND COMPANY

Studio group led by Joe Bob Barnhill (born on 10/14/33 in Turkey, Texas). Father of **Joe Barnhill**.

DEBUT	PEAK	WKS	GOLD	Country Chart Hit	Songwriter	Label (& Number)
5/17/75	**84**	6		**In The Mood**	*Joe Garland/Andy Razaf* **[I]**	Capitol 4059

JOHN DEER

Studio creation of singers/songwriters Larry O'Keefe and Jerry Wright.

DEBUT	PEAK	WKS	GOLD	Country Chart Hit	Songwriter	Label (& Number)
10/10/70	**57**	7		**Waxahachie Woman**	*Larry O'Keefe/Jerry Wright*	Royal American 21

Billboard DEBUT	PEAK	WKS	GOLD	ARTIST / Country Chart Hit	Ranking / Songwriter	Label (& Number)
				JOHNNIE & JACK	**1950s: #20 / All-Time: #265**	
				Duo formed in Tennessee: **Johnnie Wright** (born on 5/13/1914) and Jack Anglin (born on 5/13/1916; died in a car crash on 3/7/1963, age 46). Duo were regulars on the *Louisiana Hayride* from 1948-52.		
				OPRY: 1947		
				JOHNNIE and JACK and Their Tennessee Mountain Boys:		
1/20/51	**4**	17		1 **Poison Love**	A:4 / S:5 / J:9 *Elmer Laird*	RCA Victor 48-0377
7/21/51	**5**	11		2 **Cryin' Heart Blues**	J:5 / A:6 / S:10 *John Brown*	RCA Victor 48-0478
5/10/52	**7**	5		3 **Three Ways Of Knowing**	J:7 *Jimmie Davis/Nelson King*	RCA Victor 47-4555
				JOHNNIE and JACK (The Tennessee Mountain Boys):		
4/10/54	**❶[2]**	18		4 **(Oh Baby Mine) I Get So Lonely**	A:❶[2] / S:5 *Pat Ballard*	RCA Victor 5681
7/17/54	**3[1]**	17		5 **Goodnight, Sweetheart, Goodnight** /	A:3 / S:4 / J:4 *Calvin Carter/James Hudson*	
8/7/54	**15**	1		6 **Honey, I Need You**	A:15 *Jack Anglin/Jim Anglin/Johnnie Wright*	RCA Victor 5775
11/13/54	**9**	10		7 **Beware Of "It"** /	S:9 / J:9 / A:10 *Cy Coben*	
11/27/54+	**7**	4		8 **Kiss-Crazy Baby**	J:7 / S:13 *Dave Coleman*	RCA Victor 5880
5/21/55	**14**	3		9 **No One Dear But You**	A:14 *Bud Deckelman*	RCA Victor 6094
12/17/55	**15**	1		10 **S.O.S.**	A:15 *Jack Anglin/Jim Anglin/Johnnie Wright*	RCA Victor 6295
3/3/56	**13**	3		11 **I Want To Be Loved** *[w/ Ruby Wells]*	A:13 *Johnnie Bailes/Walter Bailes*	RCA Victor 6395
				JOHNNIE AND JACK:		
2/24/58	**7**	18		12 **Stop The World (And Let Me Off)**	S:7 / A:9 *Carl Belew/W.S. Stevenson*	RCA Victor 7137
10/20/58	**18**	3		13 **Lonely Island Pearl**	*Buck Peddy/Mel Tillis*	RCA Victor 7324
8/10/59	**16**	12		14 **Sailor Man**	*Jimmie Driftwood*	RCA Victor 7545
8/11/62	**17**	4		15 **Slow Poison** *[Johnny And Jack]*	*Walter Hirsch/Pat McCarthy/Lee Pearl*	Decca 31397
				JOHNS, Sammy		
				Born on 2/7/1946 in Charlotte, North Carolina. Pop singer/songwriter/guitarist.		
11/30/74+	**79**	7		1 **Early Morning Love**	*Sammy Johns*	GRC 2021
9/19/81	**50**	7		2 **Common Man**	*Sammy Johns*	Elektra 47189
9/3/88	**80**	6		3 **Chevy Van**	*Sammy Johns*	MCA 53398
				JOHNS, Sarah		
				Born on 2/3/1953 in Jacksonville, Illinois. Female singer/songwriter.		
8/30/75	**75**	3		1 **I'm Ready To Love You Now**	*Sarah Johns/Bud Reneau*	RCA Victor 10333
1/10/76	**97**	4		2 **Feelings**	*Albert Morris*	RCA Victor 10465
3/27/76	**86**	3		3 **Let The Big Wheels Roll**	*Don Goodman/Mentor Williams*	RCA Victor 10590
				JOHNS, Tricia		
				Born in Austin, Texas. Female singer/songwriter.		
5/14/77	**100**	1		1 **The Heat Is On**	*Baker Knight*	Warner 8357
12/27/80+	**90**	3		2 **Did We Fall Out Of Love**	*Tricia Johns*	Elektra 47057
8/8/81	**57**	8		3 **Cathy's Clown**	*Don Everly/Phil Everly*	Elektra 47172
				JOHNSON, Buddy, And His Orchestra		
				Born Woodrow Wilson Johnson on 1/10/1915 in Darlington, South Carolina. Died of a brain tumor on 2/9/1977 (age 62). Black orchestra leader/songwriter/pianist.		
3/11/44	**2[2]**	7		**When My Man Comes Home** Ella Johnson (vocal)	*Buddy Johnson/J. Mayo Williams*	Decca 8655
				JOHNSON, Carolyn Dawn		
				Born on 4/30/1971 in Grand Prairie, Alberta, Canada. Female singer/songwriter/guitarist. Also see **America The Beautiful**.		
9/16/00+	**25**	23		1 **Georgia** **Martina McBride** (backing vocal)	S:7 *Carolyn Dawn Johnson/Troy Verges*	Arista Nashville
4/21/01	**5**	32		2 **Complicated**	*Carolyn Dawn Johnson/Shaye Smith*	Arista Nashville
12/15/01+	**7**	29		3 **I Don't Want You To Go**	*Carolyn Dawn Johnson/Tommy Polk*	Arista Nashville
7/20/02	**24**	21		4 **One Day Closer To You** above 4 from the album *Room With A View* on Arista Nashville 69336	*Mary Danna/Carolyn Dawn Johnson*	Arista Nashville
11/29/03+	**13**	25		5 **Simple Life**	*Chris Lindsey/Hillary Lindsey/Aimee Mayo/Troy Verges*	Arista Nashville
6/12/04	**52**	4		6 **Die Of A Broken Heart** above 2 from the album *Dress Rehearsal* on Arista Nashville 57500	*Carolyn Dawn Johnson/Shaye Smith*	Arista Nashville
				JOHNSON, Lois		
				Born in Knoxville, Tennessee. Female singer. Worked on local radio from age 11. Regular appearances on WWVA-Wheeling *Jamboree*. Toured with **Hank Williams Jr.** from 1970-73.		
1/25/69	**74**	3		1 **Softly And Tenderly**	*Buddy Lackey/Jack Rhodes*	Columbia 44725
7/4/70	**23**	12		2 **Removing The Shadow** *[w/ Hank Williams, Jr.]*	*Eddie Pleasant/Hank Williams Jr.*	MGM 14136
10/3/70	**12**	13		3 **So Sad (To Watch Good Love Go Bad)** *[w/ Hank Williams, Jr.]*	*Don Everly*	MGM 14164
12/5/70+	**48**	9		4 **When He Touches Me (Nothing Else Matters)**	*Carolyn Varga*	MGM 14186
2/27/71	**65**	2		5 **From Warm To Cool To Cold**	*Gene Dobbins*	MGM 14217
4/1/72	**14**	14		6 **Send Me Some Lovin'** *[w/ Hank Williams, Jr.]*	*John Marascalco/Leo Price*	MGM 14356
7/15/72	**63**	8		7 **Rain-Rain**	*Gary S. Paxton*	MGM 14401
11/18/72+	**22**	11		8 **Whole Lotta Loving** *[w/ Hank Williams, Jr.]*	*Dave Bartholomew/Fats Domino*	MGM 14443
11/17/73	**97**	2		9 **Love Will Stand**	*Jerry Foster/Bill Rice*	MGM 14638
7/20/74	**19**	19		10 **Come On In And Let Me Love You**	*Don Silvers*	20th Century 2106
12/28/74+	**6**	15		11 **Loving You Will Never Grow Old**	*Don Silvers*	20th Century 2151
5/17/75	**48**	8		12 **You Know Just What I'd Do**	*Jerry Foster/Bill Rice*	20th Century 2187
9/13/75	**95**	4		13 **Hope For The Flowers**	*Warren Keith/Don Silvers*	20th Century 2223
10/11/75	**70**	8		14 **The Door's Always Open**	*Dickey Lee/Bob McDill*	20th Century 2242

Billboard DEBUT	PEAK	WKS	GOLD	ARTIST / Country Chart Hit	Ranking / Songwriter	Label (& Number)
				JOHNSON, Lois — cont'd		
7/24/76	**87**	2		15 **Weep No More My Baby**	*Don Silvers*	Polydor 14328
1/15/77	**20**	13		16 **Your Pretty Roses Came Too Late**	*Jerry Foster/Bill Rice*	Polydor 14371
5/14/77	**40**	8		17 **I Hate Goodbyes**	*Jerry Foster/Bill Rice*	Polydor 14392
11/19/77	**97**	3		18 **All The Love We Threw Away** ***[w/ Bill Rice]***	*Jerry Foster/Bill Rice*	Polydor 14435
5/20/78	**63**	7		19 **When I Need You**	*Albert Hammond/Carole Bayer Sager*	Polydor 14476
6/2/84	**89**	3		20 **It Won't Be Easy**	*Don Silvers*	EMH 0030
				JOHNSON, Michael		
				Born on 8/8/1944 in Alamosa, Colorado; raised in Denver, Colorado. Male singer/songwriter/guitarist.		
11/16/85+	**9**	25		1 **I Love You By Heart** ***[w/ Sylvia]***	A:9 / S:10 *Jerry Gillespie/Stan Webb*	RCA 14217
4/26/86	**12**	20		2 **Gotta Learn To Love Without You**	S:8 / A:13 *Michael Johnson/Kent Robbins*	RCA 14294
9/27/86+	**❶**[1]	23		3 **Give Me Wings**	S:❶[1] / A:2 *Rhonda Fleming/Don Schlitz*	RCA 14412
1/31/87	**❶**[1]	26		4 **The Moon Is Still Over Her Shoulder**	A:❶[1] / S:7 *Hugh Prestwood*	RCA 5091
6/13/87	**26**	13		5 **Ponies**	*Jeff Bullock*	RCA 5171
10/17/87+	**4**	20		6 **Crying Shame**	S:17 *Michael Johnson/Brent Maher/Don Schlitz*	RCA 5279
4/2/88	**7**	22		7 **I Will Whisper Your Name**	S:17 *Randy Vanwarmer*	RCA 6833
8/27/88	**9**	20		8 **That's That**	S:23 *Hugh Prestwood*	RCA 8650
12/17/88+	**52**	8		9 **Roller Coaster Run (Up Too Slow, Down Too Fast)**	*Hugh Prestwood*	RCA 8748
				JOHNSON, Roland		
				Born on 10/9/1921 in Cullman, Alabama. Male singer/songwriter.		
3/2/59	**25**	3		**I Traded Her Love (For Deep Purple Wine)**	*Roland Johnson/Junior Robertson*	Brunswick 55110
				JOHNSON, Tim		
				Born in Pennsylvania. Male singer.		
9/19/87	**78**	3		**Hard Headed Heart**	*Jim Allison/Dan Chauvin*	Sundial 135
				JOHNSTON, Day		
				Born in New Mexico. Female singer/songwriter.		
9/3/88	**82**	3		**What Cha' Doin' To Me**	*Day Johnston*	Roadrunner 4639
				JOHNSTONS, The		
				Family vocal group from Colorado.		
2/28/87	**82**	5		**Two-Name Girl**	*Rafe Van Hoy/Eric Wrobbel*	Hidden Valley 1286
				JOLIE & THE WANTED		
				Group from Omaha, Nebraska: Jolie Edwards (vocals), Phil Symonds (guitar), Jon Trebing (guitar), Steve King (keyboards), Ethan Pilzer (bass) and Andy Hull (drums).		
9/16/00	**55**	7		1 **I Would**	*Brett James/Troy Verges*	DreamWorks
2/10/01	**55**	1		2 **Boom**	*Shara Johnson/John Rich*	DreamWorks
				above 2 from the album *Jolie & The Wanted* on DreamWorks 50243		
				JON AND LYNN		
				Husband-and-wife duo from Cincinnati, Ohio: Jon Hargis and Lynn Hargis. Married in 1975.		
12/19/81+	**59**	7		1 **Let The Good Times Roll**	*Leonard Lee*	Soundwaves 4656
8/21/82	**86**	3		2 **(What A Day For A) Day Dream**	*John Sebastian*	Soundwaves 4677
				JONES, Ann		
				Born Ann Matthews in 1920 in Hutchison, Kansas; raised in Enid, Oklahoma. Female singer/songwriter.		
10/15/49	**15**	1		**Give Me A Hundred Reasons**	J:15 *Ann Jones*	Capitol 15414
				JONES, Anthony Armstrong		
				Born Ronnie Jones on 6/2/1949 in Ada, Oklahoma. Male singer/guitarist. Took stage name from the British photographer who married Princess Margaret.		
6/28/69	**22**	13		1 **Proud Mary**	*John Fogerty*	Chart 5017
10/18/69	**28**	8		2 **New Orleans**	*Frank Guida/Joseph Royster*	Chart 5033
1/10/70	**8**	11		3 **Take A Letter Maria**	*R.B. Greaves*	Chart 5045
5/23/70	**56**	5		4 **Lead Me Not Into Temptation**	*Richard Hollingsworth*	Chart 5064
7/25/70	**38**	11		5 **Sugar In The Flowers**	*Janice Deckard/Jimbeau Hinson*	Chart 5083
11/21/70	**40**	9		6 **Sweet Caroline**	*Neil Diamond*	Chart 5100
4/14/73	**70**	3		7 **I'm Right Where I Belong**	*Glenn Sutton*	Epic 10970
7/7/73	**33**	10		8 **Bad, Bad Leroy Brown**	*Jim Croce*	Epic 11002
11/17/73	**69**	8		9 **I've Got Mine**	*Kenny O'Dell*	Epic 11042
5/3/86	**74**	5		10 **Those Eyes**	*Larry Byrom/Paul Overstreet/Thom Schuyler*	AIR 103
				JONES, David Lynn		
				Born on 1/15/1950 in Bexar, Arkansas. Male singer/songwriter/bassist.		
8/22/87	**10**	20		1 **Bonnie Jean (Little Sister)**	S:15 *David Lynn Jones*	Mercury 888733
3/26/88	**14**	19		2 **High Ridin' Heroes** ***[w/ Waylon Jennings]***	S:27 *David Lynn Jones*	Mercury 870128
7/30/88	**36**	10		3 **The Rogue**	*David Lynn Jones*	Mercury 870525
11/12/88	**66**	6		4 **Tonight In America**	*Jimmy Everett/David Lynn Jones*	Mercury 872054

Billboard DEBUT	PEAK	WKS	GOLD	ARTIST / Country Chart Hit	Ranking	Songwriter	Label (& Number)

JONES, George

1950s: #21 / 1960s: #2 / 1970s: #8 / 1980s: #17 / All-Time: #2 // HOF: 1992

Born on 9/12/1931 in Saratoga, Texas. Male singer/songwriter/guitarist. Started singing on radio stations KTXJ in Jasper, Texas, and KRIC in Beaumont, Texas. Served in the U.S. Marines from 1950-52. Recorded rockabilly as Thumper Jones and Hank Smith. Married to **Tammy Wynette** from 1969-75. Known as "No Show Jones" (due to several missed shows in the late 1970s) and "Possum." Also see **Heart Of Nashville**.

CMA: Male Vocalist 1980 & 1981 // OPRY: 1956

DEBUT	PEAK	WKS	GOLD	#	Country Chart Hit	Charts	Songwriter	Label (& Number)
10/29/55	4	18		1	**Why Baby Why**	J:4 / S:4 / A:4	*Darrell Edwards/George Jones*	Starday 202
1/28/56	7	7		2	**What Am I Worth**	J:7 / A:10 / S:14	*Darrell Edwards/George Jones*	Starday 216
7/14/56	7	8		3	**You Gotta Be My Baby**	J:7 / A:10	*George Jones*	Starday 247
10/20/56	3[1]	11		4	**Just One More** /	J:3	*George Jones*	
11/10/56	flip	5		5	**Gonna Come Get You**	J:flip	*George Jones*	Starday 264
1/26/57	10	1		6	**Yearning** *[w/ Jeanette Hicks]*	J:10	*Eddie Eddings/George Jones*	Starday 279
3/9/57	10	2		7	**Don't Stop The Music** /	J:10 / S:15 / A:15	*George Jones*	
3/16/57	flip	1		8	**Uh, Uh, No**	J:flip	*George Jones*	Mercury 71029
6/10/57	13	6		9	**Too Much Water**	S:13	*Sonny James/George Jones*	Mercury 71096
4/14/58	7	10		10	**Color Of The Blues**	A:7 / S:18	*George Jones/Lawton Williams*	Mercury 71257
11/17/58	6	16		11	**Treasure Of Love** /		*George Jones/J.P. Richardson*	
12/8/58	29	1		12	**If I Don't Love You (Grits Ain't Groceries)**		*George Jones/J.P. Richardson*	Mercury 71373
3/9/59	❶[5]	22		13	**White Lightning**		*J.P. Richardson*	Mercury 71406
7/20/59	7	13		14	**Who Shot Sam**		*Darrell Edwards/Raymond Jackson/George Jones*	Mercury 71464
11/23/59+	15	12		15	**Money To Burn** /		*Johnny Nelms*	
11/23/59	19	12		16	**Big Harlan Taylor**		*Roger Miller*	Mercury 71514
4/4/60	16	12		17	**Accidently On Purpose** /		*Darrell Edwards/George Jones*	
4/25/60	30	1		18	**Sparkling Brown Eyes**		*Billy Cox*	Mercury 71583
8/22/60	25	2		19	**Out Of Control**		*Darrell Edwards/George Jones/Herby Treece*	Mercury 71641
11/7/60+	2[1]	34		20	**The Window Up Above**		*George Jones*	Mercury 71700
5/29/61	16	2		21	**Family Bible**		*Walt Breeland/Paul Buskirk/Claude Gray*	Mercury 71721
6/19/61	❶[7]	32		22	**Tender Years**		*Darrell Edwards*	Mercury 71804
9/18/61	15	3		23	**Did I Ever Tell You** *[w/ Margie Singleton]*		*Jerry Kennedy/Margie Singleton*	Mercury 71856
2/24/62	5	12		24	**Aching, Breaking Heart**		*Roe Hall*	Mercury 71910
4/14/62	❶[6]	23		25	**She Thinks I Still Care** / Grammy: Hall of Fame		*Dickey Lee*	
4/28/62	17	5		26	**Sometimes You Just Can't Win** also see #77 below		*Smokey Stover*	United Artists 424
6/16/62	11	10		27	**Waltz Of The Angels** *[w/ Margie Singleton]*		*Dick Reynolds/Jack Rhodes*	Mercury 71955
7/21/62	13	11		28	**Open Pit Mine**		*D.T. Gentry*	United Artists 462
8/25/62	28	1		29	**You're Still On My Mind**		*Luke McDaniel*	Mercury 72010
10/6/62	3[4]	18		30	**A Girl I Used To Know** *[w/ The Jones Boys]* /		*Jack Clement*	
10/13/62	13	9		31	**Big Fool Of The Year** *[w/ The Jones Boys]*		*Justin Tubb*	United Artists 500
2/9/63	7	18		32	**Not What I Had In Mind** *[w/ The Jones Boys]* /		*Jack Clement*	
4/6/63	29	1		33	**I Saw Me** *[w/ The Jones Boys]*		*June Davis/George Jones*	United Artists 528
5/4/63	3[1]	28		34	**We Must Have Been Out Of Our Minds** *[w/ Melba Montgomery]*		*Melba Montgomery*	United Artists 575
7/13/63	5	22		35	**You Comb Her Hair**		*Hank Cochran/Harlan Howard*	United Artists 578
11/30/63	20	5		36	**What's In Our Heart** *[w/ Melba Montgomery]* /		*George Jones/Johnny Mathis*	
12/7/63	17	7		37	**Let's Invite Them Over** *[w/ Melba Montgomery]*		*Onie Wheeler*	United Artists 635
2/1/64	5	18		38	**Your Heart Turned Left (And I Was On The Right)** /		*Harlan Howard*	
2/8/64	15	9		39	**My Tears Are Overdue**		*Freddie Hart*	United Artists 683
3/28/64	39	3		40	**The Last Town I Painted**		*Buddy Word*	Mercury 72233
6/6/64	31	7		41	**Something I Dreamed** /		*Harlan Howard*	
6/20/64	10	16		42	**Where Does A Little Tear Come From**		*Marge Barton/Fred MacRae*	United Artists 724
9/5/64	31	5		43	**Please Be My Love** *[w/ Melba Montgomery]*		*Monroe Fields/Carl Sauceman*	United Artists 732
9/26/64	3[6]	28		44	**The Race Is On**		*Don Rollins*	United Artists 751
12/12/64+	25	15		45	**Multiply The Heartaches** *[w/ Melba Montgomery]*		*Kathy Dee*	United Artists 784
1/30/65	15	15		46	**Least Of All**		*Sonny James/Carole Smith*	United Artists 804
3/13/65	9	21		47	**Things Have Gone To Pieces**		*Leon Payne*	Musicor 1067
4/24/65	16	10		48	**I've Got Five Dollars And It's Saturday Night** *[w/ Gene Pitney]*		*Ted Daffan*	Musicor 1066
6/5/65	14	12		49	**Wrong Number**		*George Jones/Dick Overbey*	United Artists 858
7/3/65	25	7		50	**Louisiana Man** *[w/ Gene Pitney]*		*Doug Kershaw*	Musicor 1097
8/28/65	6	18		51	**Love Bug**		*Wayne Kemp/Curtis Wayne*	Musicor 1098
10/9/65	40	3		52	**What's Money**		*B.J. Horton/George Jones*	United Artists 901
11/6/65+	8	18		53	**Take Me** also see #80 below		*George Jones/Leon Payne*	Musicor 1117
11/20/65	50	2		54	**Big Job** *[w/ Gene Pitney]*		*Hank Mills*	Musicor 1115
3/12/66	6	17		55	**I'm A People**		*Dallas Frazier*	Musicor 1143
3/12/66	46	3		56	**World's Worse Loser**		*Autry Inman*	United Artists 965
6/4/66	47	3		57	**That's All It Took** *[w/ Gene Pitney]*		*Darrell Edwards/Charlotte Grier/George Jones*	Musicor 1165
6/25/66	30	7		58	**Old Brush Arbors**		*Gordon Ardis/Darrell Edwards*	Musicor 1174
7/30/66	5	16		59	**Four-O-Thirty Three**		*George Jones/Earl Montgomery*	Musicor 1181
11/19/66	70	3		60	**Close Together (As You And Me)** *[w/ Melba Montgomery]*		*Earl Montgomery*	Musicor 1204
1/21/67	❶[2]	22		61	**Walk Through This World With Me**		*Kay Savage/Sandra Seamons*	Musicor 1226

DEBUT	PEAK	WKS	GOLD	#	ARTIST / Country Chart Hit	Songwriter	Label (& Number)
					JONES, George — cont'd		
5/20/67	**5**	17		62	**I Can't Get There From Here**	*Dallas Frazier*	Musicor 1243
9/9/67	**24**	10		63	**Party Pickin'** *[w/ Melba Montgomery]*	*Alex Zanetis*	Musicor 1238
10/7/67	**7**	18		64	**If My Heart Had Windows**	*Dallas Frazier*	Musicor 1267
2/3/68	**8**	14		65	**Say It's Not You**	*Dallas Frazier*	Musicor 1289
4/13/68	**35**	11		66	**Small Time Laboring Man**	*George Jones/Earl Montgomery*	Musicor 1297
7/6/68	**3**[1]	13		67	**As Long As I Live**	*Alex Zanetis*	Musicor 1298
9/28/68	**12**	12		68	**Milwaukee, Here I Come** *[w/ Brenda Carter]*	*Lee Fikes*	Musicor 1325
11/23/68+	**2**[2]	17		69	**When The Grass Grows Over Me**	*Don Chapel*	Musicor 1333
3/29/69	**2**[2]	18		70	**I'll Share My World With You**	*Ben Wilson*	Musicor 1351
7/19/69	**6**	14		71	**If Not For You**	*Jerry Chesnut*	Musicor 1366
11/15/69+	**6**	14		72	**She's Mine /**	*Jack Ripley*	
11/22/69	**72**	13		73	**No Blues Is Good News**	*Eddie Noack*	Musicor 1381
3/14/70	**28**	10		74	**Where Grass Won't Grow**	*Earl Montgomery*	Musicor 1392
7/4/70	**13**	14		75	**Tell Me My Lying Eyes Are Wrong** *[w/ The Jones Boys]*	*Dallas Frazier/Whitey Shafer*	Musicor 1408
11/21/70+	**2**[1]	15		76	**A Good Year For The Roses** also see #156 below	*Jerry Chesnut*	Musicor 1425
3/20/71	**10**	13		77	**Sometimes You Just Can't Win** new version of #26 above	*Smokey Stover* **[R]**	Musicor 1432
6/12/71	**7**	14		78	**Right Won't Touch A Hand**	*Earl Montgomery*	Musicor 1440
10/2/71	**13**	12		79	**I'll Follow You** (Up To Our Cloud)	*David Turner*	Musicor 1446
12/25/71+	**9**	13		80	**Take Me** *[w/ Tammy Wynette]* new version of #53 above	*George Jones/Leon Payne* **[R]**	Epic 10815
2/12/72	**6**	14		81	**We Can Make It**	*Billy Sherrill/Glenn Sutton*	Epic 10831
2/12/72	**30**	8		82	**A Day In The Life Of A Fool**	*Eddie Noack*	RCA Victor 0625
5/20/72	**2**[1]	14		83	**Loving You Could Never Be Better**	*Charlene Montgomery/Earl Montgomery/Betty Tate*	Epic 10858
7/8/72	**6**	15		84	**The Ceremony** *[w/ Tammy Wynette]*	*Billy Sherrill/Jenny Strickland/Carmol Taylor*	Epic 10881
10/14/72	**46**	7		85	**Wrapped Around Her Finger**	*George Jones/Tammy Wynette*	RCA Victor 0792
10/28/72	**5**	16		86	**A Picture Of Me** (Without You)	*George Richey/Norro Wilson*	Epic 10917
11/25/72+	**38**	9		87	**Old Fashioned Singing** *[w/ Tammy Wynette]*	*Earl Montgomery/Tammy Wynette*	Epic 10923
3/3/73	**6**	14		88	**What My Woman Can't Do**	*George Jones/Earl Montgomery/Billy Sherrill*	Epic 10959
4/7/73	**32**	9		89	**Let's Build A World Together** *[w/ Tammy Wynette]*	*George Richey/Carmol Taylor/Norro Wilson*	Epic 10963
6/23/73	**7**	13		90	**Nothing Ever Hurt Me** (Half As Bad As Losing You)	*Bobby Braddock*	Epic 11006
9/1/73	**❶**[2]	17		91	**We're Gonna Hold On** *[w/ Tammy Wynette]*	*George Jones/Earl Montgomery*	Epic 11031
11/24/73+	**3**[1]	16		92	**Once You've Had The Best**	*Johnny Paycheck*	Epic 11053
2/9/74	**15**	13		93	(We're Not) **The Jet Set** *[w/ Tammy Wynette]*	*Bobby Braddock*	Epic 11083
4/6/74	**25**	12		94	**The Telephone Call** *[w/ stepdaughter Tina]*	*Billy Sherrill/Carmol Taylor*	Epic 11099
6/8/74	**❶**[1]	17		95	**The Grand Tour**	*George Richey/Carmol Taylor/Norro Wilson*	Epic 11122
7/27/74	**8**	12		96	**We Loved It Away** *[w/ Tammy Wynette]*	*George Richey/Carmol Taylor*	Epic 11151
10/26/74+	**❶**[1]	13		97	**The Door**	*Billy Sherrill/Norro Wilson*	Epic 50038
3/22/75	**10**	14		98	**These Days** (I Barely Get By)	*George Jones/Tammy Wynette*	Epic 50088
5/17/75	**25**	13		99	**God's Gonna Get'cha** (For That)	*E.E. Collins*	Epic 50099
7/26/75	**21**	11		100	**Memories Of Us /**	*Dave Kirby/Glenn Martin*	
11/1/75	**92**	4		101	**I Just Don't Give A Damn**	*George Jones/Jimmy Peppers*	Epic 50127
2/7/76	**16**	12		102	**The Battle**	*Linda Kimball/George Richey/Norro Wilson*	Epic 50187
5/22/76	**37**	9		103	**You Always Look Your Best** (Here In My Arms)	*Mike Kosser/Steve Pippin/Curly Putman*	Epic 50227
6/5/76	**❶**[1]	15		104	**Golden Ring** *[w/ Tammy Wynette]*	*Bobby Braddock/Rafe Van Hoy*	Epic 50235
9/4/76	**3**[2]	16		105	**Her Name Is...**	*Bobby Braddock*	Epic 50271
12/11/76+	**❶**[2]	16		106	**Near You** *[w/ Tammy Wynette]*	*Francis Craig/Kermit Goell*	Epic 50314
5/21/77	**34**	8		107	**Old King Kong**	*Sammy Lyons*	Epic 50385
7/16/77	**5**	13		108	**Southern California** *[w/ Tammy Wynette]*	*Roger Bowling/George Richey/Billy Sherrill*	Epic 50418
8/13/77	**24**	10		109	**If I Could Put Them All Together** (I'd Have You)	*Even Stevens*	Epic 50423
1/7/78	**6**	14		110	**Bartender's Blues** **James Taylor** (harmony vocal)	*James Taylor*	Epic 50495
7/1/78	**11**	13		111	**I'll Just Take It Out In Love**	*Bob McDill*	Epic 50564
12/9/78+	**7**	13		112	**Mabellene** *[w/ Johnny Paycheck]*	*Chuck Berry/Russ Frato/Alan Freed*	Epic 50647
5/26/79	**14**	11		113	**You Can Have Her** *[w/ Johnny Paycheck]*	*Bill Cook*	Epic 50708
6/30/79	**22**	11		114	**Someday My Day Will Come**	*V.L. Haywood/Earl Montgomery/Chris Ryder*	Epic 50684
3/1/80	**2**[1]	14		115	**Two Story House** *[w/ Tammy Wynette]*	*David Lindsey/Glenn Tubb/Tammy Wynette*	Epic 50849
4/12/80	**❶**[1]	18		116	**He Stopped Loving Her Today** **Grammy: Male Vocal / CMA: Single / RS500**	*Bobby Braddock/Curly Putman*	Epic 50867
6/21/80	**31**	9		117	**When You're Ugly Like Us** (You Just Naturally Got To Be Cool) *[w/ Johnny Paycheck]*	*...Don Goodman/Rick Schulman*	Epic 50891
8/23/80	**2**[1]	17		118	**I'm Not Ready Yet**	*Tom T. Hall*	Epic 50922
9/6/80	**19**	11		119	**A Pair Of Old Sneakers** *[w/ Tammy Wynette]*	*Larry Kingston/Glenn Sutton*	Epic 50930
12/13/80+	**18**	12		120	**You Better Move On** *[w/ Johnny Paycheck]*	*Arthur Alexander*	Epic 50949
1/17/81	**8**	15		121	**If Drinkin' Don't Kill Me** (Her Memory Will)	*Rich Beresford/Harlan Sanders*	Epic 50968
10/3/81	**❶**[1]	17		122	**Still Doin' Time**	*Mike Heeney/John Moffatt*	Epic 02526
2/6/82	**5**	19		123	**Same Ole Me** **Oak Ridge Boys** (backing vocals)	*Paul Overstreet*	Epic 02696
8/7/82	**❶**[1]	15		124	**Yesterday's Wine** *[w/ Merle Haggard]*	*Willie Nelson*	Epic 03072
12/4/82+	**10**	19		125	**C.C. Waterback** *[w/ Merle Haggard]*	*Merle Haggard*	Epic 03405
1/15/83	**3**[2]	19		126	**Shine On** (Shine All Your Sweet Love On Me)	*Johnny MacRae/Robert Morrison*	Epic 03489
5/7/83	**❶**[1]	18		127	**I Always Get Lucky With You**	*Gary Church/Merle Haggard/Freddy Powers/Tex Whitson*	Epic 03883

DEBUT	PEAK	WKS	GOLD	ARTIST / Ranking / Country Chart Hit	Songwriter	Label (& Number)
				JONES, George — cont'd		
9/10/83	2^{1}	22		128 **Tennessee Whiskey**	*Dean Dillon/Linda Hargrove*	Epic 04082
12/17/83+	6	18		129 **We Didn't See A Thing** ***[w/ Ray Charles & Chet Atkins]***	*Gary Gentry*	Columbia 04297
4/7/84	3^{2}	19		130 **You've Still Got A Place In My Heart**	*Leon Payne*	Epic 04413
9/22/84	2^{3}	23		131 **She's My Rock**	S:❶^{2} / A:2 *Sharon Dobbins*	Epic 04609
12/22/84+	15	16		132 **Hallelujah, I Love You So** ***[w/ Brenda Lee]***	A:13 / S:15 *Ray Charles*	Epic 04723
4/27/85	19	18		133 **Size Seven Round (Made Of Gold)** ***[w/ Lacy J. Dalton]***	S:17 / A:19 *Monroe Fields/Gary Lumpkin*	Epic 04876
8/3/85	3^{1}	20		134 **Who's Gonna Fill Their Shoes**	S:2 / A:5 *Max D. Barnes/Troy Seals*	Epic 05439
11/23/85+	3^{2}	22		135 **The One I Loved Back Then (The Corvette Song)**	S:❶^{1} / A:3 *Gary Gentry*	Epic 05698
4/19/86	9	21		136 **Somebody Wants Me Out Of The Way**	S:5 / A:11 *Dennis Knutson/A.L. "Doodle" Owens*	Epic 05862
9/13/86	10	23		137 **Wine Colored Roses**	S:7 / A:11 *Dennis Knutson*	Epic 06296
1/17/87	8	20		138 **The Right Left Hand**	S:2 / A:8 *Dennis Knutson/A.L. "Doodle" Owens*	Epic 06593
5/16/87	26	18		139 **I Turn To You**	S:14 *Max D. Barnes/Curly Putman*	Epic 07107
12/19/87+	26	14		140 **The Bird**	S:9 *Dennis Knutson/A.L. "Doodle" Owens*	Epic 07655
3/26/88	52	10		141 **I'm A Survivor**	*Jim McBride/Keith Stegall*	Epic 07748
6/4/88	63	6		142 **The Old Man No One Loves**	*Wyman Asbill*	Epic 07913
9/3/88	43	10		143 **If I Could Bottle This Up** ***[w/ Shelby Lynne]***	S:22 *Dean Dillon/Paul Overstreet*	Epic 08011
12/17/88+	5	20		144 **I'm A One Woman Man**	*Tillman Franks/Johnny Horton*	Epic 08509
4/29/89	26	13		145 **The King Is Gone (So Are You)**	*Roger Ferris*	Epic 68743
7/29/89	31	16		146 **Writing On The Wall**	*Bobby Fischer/Freddy Weller*	Epic 68991
11/11/89	62	6		147 **Radio Lover**	*Ron Hellard/Bucky Jones/Curly Putman*	Epic 73070
9/8/90	8	20		148 **A Few Ole Country Boys** ***[w/ Randy Travis]*** — from Travis's album *Heroes And Friends* on Warner 26310	*Troy Seals/Mentor Williams*	Warner
8/31/91	32	20		149 **You Couldn't Get The Picture**	*Chuck Harter*	MCA
1/11/92	55	14		150 **She Loved A Lot In Her Time**	*Randy Boudreaux/Sam Hogin/Kim Williams*	MCA
4/11/92	60	7		151 **Honky Tonk Myself To Death** — above 3 from the album *And Along Came Jones* on MCA 10398	*Max D. Barnes/Max T. Barnes*	MCA
10/17/92+	34	20		152 **I Don't Need Your Rockin' Chair** — **CMA: Vocal Event; Vince Gill, Mark Chesnutt, Garth Brooks, Travis Tritt, Joe Diffie, Alan Jackson, Pam Tillis, T. Graham Brown, Patty Lovless** and **Clint Black** (guest vocals)	*Frank Dycus/Kerry Kurt Phillips/Billy Yates*	MCA
3/20/93	65	6		153 **Wrong's What I Do Best** — above 2 from the album *Walls Can Fall* on MCA 10652	*Mike Campbell/Dickey Lee/Freddy Weller*	MCA
11/13/93+	24	20		154 **High-Tech Redneck**	*Byron Hill/Zack Turner*	MCA
3/12/94	52	10		155 **Never Bit A Bullet Like This** ***[w/ Sammy Kershaw]*** — above 2 from the album *High-Tech Redneck* on MCA 10910	*Jim Foster/Mark Petersen*	MCA
11/12/94	56	7		156 **A Good Year For The Roses** ***[w/ Alan Jackson]*** — from the album *The Bradley Barn Sessions* on MCA 11096; new version of #76 above	*Jerry Chesnut* **[R]**	MCA
7/1/95	69	4		157 **One** ***[w/ Tammy Wynette]*** — from their album *One* on MCA 11248	*Ed Bruce/Judith Bruce/Ron Peterson*	MCA
9/14/96	66	6		158 **Honky Tonk Song** — from the album *I Lived To Tell It All* on MCA 11478	*Frank J. Myers/Billy Yates*	MCA
9/20/97	14	20		159 **You Don't Seem To Miss Me** ***[w/ Patty Loveless]*** — **CMA: Vocal Event**; from Loveless's album *Long Stretch Of Lonesome* on Epic 67997	S:9 *Jim Lauderdale*	Epic
5/8/99	30	20		160 **Choices** — **Grammy: Male Vocal**	*Michael Curtis/Billy Yates*	Asylum
11/6/99+	45	20		161 **The Cold Hard Truth**	*Jamie O'Hara*	Asylum
11/20/99+	30	13		162 **A Country Boy Can Survive** ***[w/ Chad Brock & Hank Williams, Jr.]*** — from Brock's album *Yes!* on Warner 47659	S:2 *Hank Williams Jr.*	Warner
5/13/00	55	12		163 **Sinners & Saints** — #160, 161 & 163: from the album *Cold Hard Truth* on Asylum 62368	*J.B. Rudd/Carl Vipperman/Darryl Worley*	Asylum
8/4/01	47	9		164 **The Man He Was**	*Harley Allen/John Wiggins*	Bandit
10/13/01	24	20		165 **Beer Run** ***[w/ Garth Brooks]***	*Keith Anderson/Kent Blazy/George Ducas/Amanda Williams/Kim Williams*	Bandit
3/30/02	55	1		166 **50,000 Names** — above 3 from the album *The Rock: Stone Cold Country 2001* on Bandit 67029	*Jamie O'Hara*	Bandit
4/23/05	26↑	23↑		167 **4th Of July** ***[w/ Shooter Jennings]*** — from Jennings' album *Put The O Back In Country* on Universal South 003816	*Shooter Jennings*	Universal South

Accidently On Purpose ['60]
Aching, Breaking Heart ['62]
As Long As I Live ['68]
Bartender's Blues ['78]
Battle ['76]
Beer Run ['01]
Big Fool Of The Year ['62]
Big Harlan Taylor ['59]
Big Job ['65]
Bird ['88]
C.C. Waterback ['83]
Ceremony ['72]
Choices ['99]
Close Together (As You And Me) ['66]
Cold Hard Truth ['00]
Color Of The Blues ['58]
Country Boy Can Survive ['00]
Day In The Life Of A Fool ['72]
Did I Ever Tell You ['61]
Don't Stop The Music ['57]
Door ['75]
Family Bible ['61]
Few Ole Country Boys ['90]
50,000 Names ['02]
Four-O-Thirty Three ['66]
4th Of July ['00]
Girl I Used To Know ['62]
God's Gonna Get'cha (For That) ['75]
Golden Ring ['76]
Gonna Come Get You ['56]
Good Year For The Roses ['71, '94]
Grand Tour ['74]
Hallelujah, I Love You So ['85]
He Stopped Loving Her Today ['80]
Her Name Is... ['76]
High-Tech Redneck ['94]
Honky Tonk Myself To Death ['92]
Honky Tonk Song ['96]
I Always Get Lucky With You ['83]
I Can't Get There From Here ['67]
I Don't Need Your Rockin' Chair ['93]
I Just Don't Give A Damn ['75]
I Saw Me ['63]
I Turn To You ['87]
I'll Follow You (Up To Our Cloud) ['71]
I'll Just Take It Out In Love ['78]
I'll Share My World With You ['69]
I'm A One Woman Man ['89]
I'm A People ['66]
I'm A Survivor ['88]
I'm Not Ready Yet ['80]
I've Got Five Dollars And It's Saturday Night ['65]
If Drinkin' Don't Kill Me (Her Memory Will) ['81]
If I Could Bottle This Up ['88]
If I Could Put Them All Together (I'd Have You) ['77]
If I Don't Love You (Grits Ain't Groceries) ['58]
If My Heart Had Windows ['67]
If Not For You ['69]
Just One More ['56]
King Is Gone (So Are You) ['89]
Last Town I Painted ['64]
Least Of All ['65]
Let's Build A World Together ['73]
Let's Invite Them Over ['63]
Louisiana Man ['65]
Love Bug ['65]
Loving You Could Never Be Better ['72]
Mabellene ['79]
Man He Was ['01]
Memories Of Us ['75]
Milwaukee, Here I Come ['68]
Money To Burn ['60]
Multiply The Heartaches ['65]
My Tears Are Overdue ['64]
Near You ['77]
Never Bit A Bullet Like This ['94]
No Blues Is Good News ['69]
Not What I Had In Mind ['63]
Nothing Ever Hurt Me (Half As Bad As Losing You) ['73]
Old Brush Arbors ['66]
Old Fashioned Singing ['73]
Old King Kong ['77]
Old Man No One Loves ['88]
Once You've Had The Best ['74]
One I Loved Back Then (The Corvette Song) ['86]
One ['95]
Open Pit Mine ['62]
Out Of Control ['60]
Pair Of Old Sneakers ['80]
Party Pickin' ['67]
Picture Of Me (Without You) ['72]
Please Be My Love ['64]
Race Is On ['64]
Radio Lover ['89]
Right Left Hand ['87]
Right Won't Touch A Hand ['71]
Same Ole Me ['82]
Say It's Not You ['68]
She Loved A Lot In Her Time ['92]
She Thinks I Still Care ['62]
She's Mine ['70]
She's My Rock ['84]
Shine On (Shine All Your Sweet Love On Me) ['83]
Sinners & Saints ['00]
Size Seven Round (Made Of Gold) ['85]
Small Time Laboring Man ['68]
Somebody Wants Me Out Of The Way ['86]
Someday My Day Will Come ['79]
Something I Dreamed ['64]
Sometimes You Just Can't Win ['62, '71]
Southern California ['77]
Sparkling Brown Eyes ['60]
Still Doin' Time ['81]
Take Me ['66, '72]
Telephone Call ['74]
Tell Me My Lying Eyes Are Wrong ['70]
Tender Years ['61]
Tennessee Whiskey ['83]
That's All It Took ['66]
These Days (I Barely Get By) ['75]
Things Have Gone To Pieces ['65]
Too Much Water ['57]
Treasure Of Love ['58]
Two Story House ['80]
Uh, Uh, No ['57]
Walk Through This World With Me ['67]
Waltz Of The Angels ['62]
We Can Make It ['72]

JONES, George — cont'd

We Didn't See A Thing ['84]
We Loved It Away ['74]
We Must Have Been Out Of Our Minds ['63]
We're Gonna Hold On ['73]
(We're Not) The Jet Set ['74]
What Am I Worth ['56]
What My Woman Can't Do ['73]
What's In Our Heart ['63]
What's Money ['65]
When The Grass Grows Over Me ['69]
When You're Ugly Like Us (You Just Naturally Got To Be Cool) ['80]
Where Does A Little Tear Come From ['64]
Where Grass Won't Grow ['70]
White Lightning ['59]
Who Shot Sam ['59]
Who's Gonna Fill Their Shoes ['85]
Why Baby Why ['55]
Window Up Above ['61]
Wine Colored Roses ['86]
World's Worse Loser ['66]
Wrapped Around Her Finger ['72]
Writing On The Wall ['89]
Wrong Number ['65]
Wrong's What I Do Best ['93]
Yearning ['57]
Yesterday's Wine ['82]
You Always Look Your Best (Here In My Arms) ['76]
You Better Move On ['81]
You Can Have Her ['79]
You Comb Her Hair ['63]
You Couldn't Get The Picture ['91]
You Don't Seem To Miss Me ['97]
You Gotta Be My Baby ['56]
You're Still On My Mind ['62]
You've Still Got A Place In My Heart ['84]
Your Heart Turned Left (And I Was On The Right) ['64]

JONES, Grandpa — **HOF: 1978**

Born Louis Marshall Jones on 10/20/1913 in Niagra, Kentucky; raised in Akron, Ohio. Died of a stroke on 2/19/1998 (age 84). Male singer/banjo player. Began appearing as "Grandpa" in 1935. Regular on TV's *Hee-Haw.*

EARLY HIT: Mountain Dew (1942) // OPRY: 1946

DEBUT	PEAK	WKS		Country Chart Hit	Songwriter	Label (& Number)
2/23/59	21	2	1	The All-American Boy	*Orville Lunsford/Bill Parsons*	Decca 30823
12/15/62+	5	16	2	T For Texas	*Jimmie Rodgers*	Monument 801

JONES, Harrison

Born on 2/13/1947 in Corbin, Kentucky. Male singer.

DEBUT	PEAK	WKS		Country Chart Hit	Songwriter	Label (& Number)
6/22/74	72	7		But Tonight I'm Gonna Love You	*David Connors/Steve Monahan*	GRT 004

JONES, JC

Born in 1973 in Los Angeles, California. Male singer.

DEBUT	PEAK	WKS		Country Chart Hit	Songwriter	Label (& Number)
1/17/98	61	6		One Night from the album *One Night* on Rising Tide 53049	*Janis Carnes/Rick Carnes/Lewis Storey*	Rising Tide

JONES, Kacey

Born in San Francisco, California. Female singer/songwriter.

DEBUT	PEAK	WKS		Country Chart Hit	Songwriter	Label (& Number)
4/7/01	14[S]	1		Till Dale Earnhardt Wins Cup #8	*Kacey Jones/Sharyn Lane*	IGO

JONES, Mickey

Born on 6/10/1941 in Houston, Texas. Male singer. Member of **Kenny Rogers & The First Edition**.

DEBUT	PEAK	WKS		Country Chart Hit	Songwriter	Label (& Number)
3/3/79	94	5	1	She Loves My Troubles Away	*Rayburn Anthony/Max D. Barnes*	Bayshore 100
9/2/89	85	3	2	A Song A Day Keeps The Blues Away	*Randy Haspel/Jim Hurt/Bob Simon*	Stop Hunger 1102
11/25/89	80	3	3	Bigger Man Than Me!	*Curtis Wayne*	Stop Hunger 1103

JONES, Tom

Born Thomas Jones Woodward on 6/7/1940 in Pontypridd, South Wales. Male pop singer. Won the 1965 Best New Artist Grammy Award. Hosted own TV variety series from 1969-71.

DEBUT	PEAK	WKS		Country Chart Hit	Songwriter	Label (& Number)
12/25/76+	❶[1]	17	1	Say You'll Stay Until Tomorrow	*Roger Greenaway/Barry Mason*	Epic/MAM 50308
6/4/77	87	3	2	Take Me Tonight adapted from Tchaikovsky's *Pathetique Symphony*	*Roy Alfred/Wally Gold/Aaron Schroeder*	Epic/MAM 50382
11/19/77	71	8	3	What A Night	*Carmol Taylor/Norro Wilson*	Epic/MAM 50468
4/18/81	19	14	4	Darlin'	*Oscar Blandemer*	Mercury 76100
8/8/81	25	11	5	What In The World's Come Over You	*Jack Scott*	Mercury 76115
11/28/81+	26	14	6	Lady Lay Down	*Don Cook/Rafe Van Hoy*	Mercury 76125
9/18/82	16	18	7	A Woman's Touch	*Jerry Fuller*	Mercury 76172
2/26/83	4	18	8	Touch Me (I'll Be Your Fool Once More)	*Al Downing*	Mercury 810445
7/2/83	34	12	9	It'll Be Me	*Jack Clement*	Mercury 812631
12/10/83+	13	22	10	I've Been Rained On Too	*Jonathan Philibert*	Mercury 814820
4/28/84	30	14	11	This Time	*Roger Greenaway/Bobby Whitlock*	Mercury 818801
9/1/84	53	9	12	All The Love Is On The Radio	*Leon Russell/Doug Snider*	Mercury 880173
12/8/84+	67	9	13	I'm An Old Rock And Roller (Dancin' To A Different Beat)	*Carroll Baker/Terry Frewer*	Mercury 880402
3/2/85	48	9	14	Give Her All The Roses (Don't Wait Until Tomorrow)	*Terry Dempsey/Les Reed*	Mercury 880569
9/14/85	76	6	15	Not Another Heart Song	*Steve Bogard/Rory Bourke/Jeff Tweel*	Mercury 884039
11/23/85+	36	13	16	It's Four In The Morning	*Jerry Chesnut*	Mercury 884252

JONES, Zona

Born in 1961 in Kingsville, Texas; raised in Valentine, Texas. Male singer/songwriter/guitarist.

DEBUT	PEAK	WKS		Country Chart Hit	Songwriter	Label (& Number)
2/21/04	53	1	1	House Of Negotiable Affections	*Bobby Braddock/Kim Williams*	D/Quarterback
1/1/05	47	20	2	Two Hearts above 2 from the album *Harleys & Horses* on D/Quarterback 9002	*Ed Hill/A.J. Masters*	D/Quarterback

JORDAN, Jill

Born Jill Galehouse in Wooster, Ohio. Female singer. Grandfather was pro baseball pitcher Denny Galehouse.

DEBUT	PEAK	WKS		Country Chart Hit	Songwriter	Label (& Number)
2/20/88	68	5	1	Calendar Blues	*Karren Pell/Dan Strimer*	Maxx 822
6/11/88	72	4	2	I Did It For Love	*Karren Pell/Mike Woody*	Maxx 823

JORDAN, Louis, And His Tympany Five — **1940s: #28**

Born on 7/8/1908 in Brinkley, Arkansas. Died of a heart attack on 2/4/1975 (age 66). Black singer/saxophonist. Inducted into the Rock and Roll Hall of Fame in 1987.

DEBUT	PEAK	WKS		Country Chart Hit	Songwriter	Label (& Number)
1/15/44	❶[3]	13	1	Ration Blues /	*Collenane Clark/Anthonio Cosey/Louis Jordan*	
1/29/44	7	1	2	Deacon Jones	*Hy Heath/Johnny Lange/Richard Loring*	Decca 8654
7/1/44	❶[5]	9	3	Is You Is Or Is You Ain't (Ma' Baby) from the movie *Follow The Boys* starring Marlene Dietrich	*Billy Austin/Louis Jordan*	Decca 8659

JOY, Homer

Born in Arkansas; later based in Bakersfield, California. Male singer/songwriter.

DEBUT	PEAK	WKS		Country Chart Hit	Songwriter	Label (& Number)
3/23/74	80	5		John Law	*Homer Joy*	Capitol 3834

DEBUT	PEAK	WKS	GOLD	ARTIST / Country Chart Hit	Ranking / Songwriter	Label (& Number)

JOYCE, Brenda

Born in 1955 in Indianapolis, Indiana. Female singer.

DEBUT	PEAK	WKS	Country Chart Hit	Songwriter	Label (& Number)
9/15/79	**96**	1	**Don't Touch Me**	*Hank Cochran*	Western Pacific 107

JUAN, Don — see DON JUAN

JUDD, Cledus T.

Born Barry Poole on 12/18/1964 in Crowe Springs, Georgia. Novelty singer specializing in song parodies.

DEBUT	PEAK	WKS	Country Chart Hit	Songwriter	Label (& Number)
5/29/99	**16^{S}**	10	1 **Everybody's Free (To Get Sunburned)** parody of "Everybody's Free (To Wear Sunscreen)" by Baz Luhrmann	*Bruce Burch/Heidi Campbell/Chris Clark/Cledus T. Judd/Scott Rouse* [C]	Razor & Tie
8/26/00	**61**	9	2 **My Cellmate Thinks I'm Sexy** parody of "She Thinks My Tractor's Sexy" by **Kenny Chesney**	S:4 *Chris Clark/Jim Collins/Cledus T. Judd/Paul Overstreet* [N]	Monument
12/2/00	**67**	2	3 **How Do You Milk A Cow** parody of "How Do You Like Me Now" by **Toby Keith**; above 2 from the album *Just Another Day In Parodies* on Monument 85106	*Chuck Cannon/Toby Keith* [N]	Monument
10/18/03	**55**	4	4 **Martie, Emily & Natalie** parody of "Celebrity" by **Brad Paisley**; from the album *The Original Dixie Hick* on Audium 8194	*Cledus T. Judd/Brad Paisley* [N]	Audium
9/4/04	**48**	6	5 **I Love NASCAR** parody of "I Love This Bar" by **Toby Keith** (Toby contributes a cameo vocal)	*Scotty Emerick/Toby Keith* [N]	Koch
12/18/04	**58**	1	6 **Bake Me A Country Ham** parody of "Paint Me A Birmingham" by **Tracy Lawrence**; above 2 from the album *Bipolar And Proud* on Koch 9809	*Gary Duffy/Buck Moore* [N]	Koch

JUDD, Wynonna — see WYNONNA

JUDDS, The — 1980s: #38 / All-Time: #114

Family duo from Ashland, Kentucky: Naomi Judd (born Diana Ellen Judd on 1/11/1946) and her daughter **Wynonna** Judd (born Christina Ciminella on 5/30/1964). Moved to Hollywood in 1968. Moved to Nashville in 1979. Naomi's chronic hepatitis forced duo to split at the end of 1991. Naomi's daughter and Wynonna's half-sister is actress Ashley Judd.

CMA: Horizon 1984 / Vocal Group 1985, 1986 & 1987 / Vocal Duo 1988, 1989, 1990 & 1991

THE JUDDS (Wynonna & Naomi):

DEBUT	PEAK	WKS	Country Chart Hit	Songwriter	Label (& Number)
12/17/83+	**17**	18	1 **Had A Dream (For The Heart)**	*Dennis Linde*	RCA/Curb 13673
4/28/84	**❶^{1}**	23	2 **Mama He's Crazy** Grammy: Vocal Duo	*Kenny O'Dell*	RCA/Curb 13772
10/6/84	**❶^{2}**	22	3 **Why Not Me** Grammy: Vocal Duo / CMA: Single	A:❶^{2} / S:2 *Harlan Howard/Brent Maher/Sonny Throckmorton*	RCA/Curb 13923
2/2/85	**❶^{1}**	22	4 **Girls Night Out**	S:❶^{1} / A:❶^{1} *Jeff Bullock/Brent Maher*	RCA/Curb 13991
6/8/85	**❶^{1}**	21	5 **Love Is Alive**	S:❶^{1} / A:❶^{1} *Kent Robbins*	RCA/Curb 14093
10/5/85	**❶^{2}**	22	6 **Have Mercy**	A:❶^{2} / S:2 *Paul Kennerley*	RCA/Curb 14193
2/15/86	**❶^{1}**	20	7 **Grandpa (Tell Me 'Bout The Good Old Days)** Grammy: Song & Vocal Duo	S:❶^{1} / A:❶^{1} *Jamie O'Hara*	RCA/Curb 14290
5/24/86	**❶^{1}**	18	8 **Rockin' With The Rhythm Of The Rain**	S:❶^{1} / A:❶^{1} *Brent Maher/Don Schlitz*	RCA/Curb 14362
10/18/86+	**❶^{1}**	20	9 **Cry Myself To Sleep**	A:❶^{1} / S:2 *Paul Kennerley*	RCA/Curb 5000
2/14/87	**10**	13	10 **Don't Be Cruel**	S:6 / A:10 *Otis Blackwell/Elvis Presley*	RCA/Curb 5094
5/9/87	**❶^{1}**	19	11 **I Know Where I'm Going**	S:❶^{2} *Craig Bickhardt/Brent Maher/Don Schlitz*	RCA/Curb 5164
8/22/87	**❶^{1}**	22	12 **Maybe Your Baby's Got The Blues**	S:3 *Graham Lyle/Troy Seals*	RCA/Curb 5255
1/16/88	**❶^{1}**	17	13 **Turn It Loose**	S:3 *Craig Bickhardt/Brent Maher/Don Schlitz*	RCA/Curb 5329
6/11/88	**2^{2}**	17	14 **Give A Little Love** Grammy: Vocal Duo	S:4 *Paul Kennerley*	RCA/Curb 8300

THE JUDDS:

DEBUT	PEAK	WKS	Country Chart Hit	Songwriter	Label (& Number)
10/22/88+	**❶^{1}**	20	15 **Change Of Heart**	S:2 *Naomi Judd*	RCA/Curb 8715
2/25/89	**❶^{1}**	21	16 **Young Love**	*Paul Kennerley/Kent Robbins*	Curb/RCA 8820
7/8/89	**❶^{1}**	21	17 **Let Me Tell You About Love**	*Paul Kennerley/Brent Maher/Carl Perkins*	Curb/RCA 8947
11/25/89+	**8**	26	18 **One Man Woman**	*Paul Kennerley*	Curb/RCA 9077
3/31/90	**16**	21	19 **Guardian Angels** from the album *River Of Time* on Curb/RCA 9595	*John Jarvis/Naomi Judd/Don Schlitz*	Curb/RCA
8/11/90	**5**	21	20 **Born To Be Blue**	*Mack David/Brent Maher/Mike Reid*	Curb/RCA
12/8/90+	**5**	20	21 **Love Can Build A Bridge** Grammy: Song & Vocal Duo	*John Jarvis/Naomi Judd/Paul Overstreet*	Curb/RCA
4/13/91	**6**	20	22 **One Hundred And Two**	*Wynonna Judd/Paul Kennerley/Don Potter*	Curb/RCA
9/14/91	**29**	16	23 **John Deere Tractor** above 4 from the album *Love Can Build A Bridge* on Curb/RCA 2070	*Lawrence Hammond*	Curb/RCA
1/10/98	**68**	1	24 **Silver Bells** from the album *Christmas Time with The Judds* on RCA/Curb 6422	*Ray Evans/Jay Livingston* [X]	RCA/Curb
2/19/00	**26**	18	25 **Stuck In Love** from the album *New Day Dawning [Bonus CD]* on Curb 541067	*Gary Nicholson/Kim Patton*	Curb

JURGENS, Dick, and his Orchestra

Born on 1/9/1910 in Sacramento, California. Died of cancer on 10/5/1995 (age 85). Male orchestra leader.

DEBUT	PEAK	WKS	Country Chart Hit	Songwriter	Label (& Number)
3/8/47	**4**	2	**(Oh Why, Oh Why, Did I Ever Leave) Wyoming** Jimmy Castle, Al Galante and Band (vocals)	*Morey Amsterdam*	Columbia 37210

JUSTIN, Dean

Born in Minnesota. Country singer/guitarist.

DEBUT	PEAK	WKS	Country Chart Hit	Songwriter	Label (& Number)
7/19/03	**4^{S}**	11	**Carry The Flag**	*LaSalle Gabriel/Jon Tesar*	SLR

DEBUT	PEAK	WKS	GOLD	ARTIST / Country Chart Hit	Ranking / Songwriter	Label (& Number)
				JUSTIS, Bill, and His Orchestra		
				Born on 10/14/1926 in Birmingham, Alabama. Died on 7/15/1982 (age 55). Session saxophonist/arranger/producer.		
11/25/57+	**6**	16	●	**Raunchy**	S:6 / A:14 *Bill Justis/Sid Manker* **[I]**	Phillips 3519
				Grammy: Hall of Fame; Sid Manker (guitar); Bill Justis (sax)		

K

DEBUT	PEAK	WKS	GOLD	ARTIST / Country Chart Hit	Ranking / Songwriter	Label (& Number)
				KALIN TWINS		
				White vocal duo of twins Herbert Kalin and Harold Kalin. Born on 2/16/1934 in Port Jervis, New York.		
8/4/58	**13**	7	●	**When**	S:13 *Paul Evans/Jack Reardon*	Decca 30642
				KANDY, Jim		
				Born in Tennessee. Male singer.		
9/4/65	**29**	6		**I'm The Man**	*Bernard Spurlock*	K-Ark 647
				KANE, Kieran		
				Born on 10/7/1949 in Queens, New York. Male singer/songwriter. Member of **The O'Kanes**.		
3/21/81	**80**	4		1 **The Baby**	*Kieran Kane*	Elektra 47111
6/20/81	**14**	16		2 **You're The Best**	*Bruce Channel/Kieran Kane*	Elektra 47148
11/7/81+	**16**	18		3 **It's Who You Love**	*Charlie Black/Rory Bourke/Kieran Kane*	Elektra 47228
3/6/82	**26**	14		4 **I Feel It With You**	*Kieran Kane/Richard Kane*	Elektra 47415
7/10/82	**26**	12		5 **I'll Be Your Man Around The House**	*Kieran Kane*	Elektra 47478
10/30/82	**45**	8		6 **Gonna Have A Party**	*Bruce Channel/Cliff Cochran/Kieran Kane*	Elektra 69943
4/30/83	**30**	12		7 **It's You**	*Bruce Channel/Kieran Kane/Richard Kane*	Warner 29711
3/17/84	**28**	14		8 **Dedicate**	*Kieran Kane*	Warner 29336
				KANTER, Hillary		
				Born in Cincinnati, Ohio. Female singer/pianist.		
8/18/84	**51**	9		1 **Good Night For Falling In Love**	*David Malloy/Eddie Rabbitt/Even Stevens*	RCA 13835
12/1/84+	**54**	18		2 **Hey**	*Ramon Arcusa/Mario Balducci/Giovanni Belfiore/Julio Iglesias*	RCA 13935
5/4/85	**50**	9		3 **We Work**	*David Malloy/Even Stevens/Kin Vassy/Billy Joe Walker*	RCA 14053
				KAY, Melissa		
				Born in Winter Garden, Florida. Female singer.		
2/6/88	**75**	3		1 **Don't Forget Your Way Home**	*J.R. Brannen/Ed Hunnicutt*	Reed 1115
8/6/88	**79**	3		2 **After Lovin' You**	*Kelly Delaney/Dave Gillon*	Reed 1119
5/6/89	**87**	3		3 **Poison Sugar**	*Dennis Knutson/A.L. "Doodle" Owens*	Reed 1123
				KAYE, Angela		
				Born in 1966 in Kentucky. Female singer.		
10/10/81	**81**	5		**Catching Fire**	*Janis Carnes/Rick Carnes*	Yatahey 804
				KAYE, Barry		
				Born on 4/24/1946 in Los Angeles, California. Male singer.		
3/11/78	**89**	5		**Easy**	*Lionel Richie*	MCA 40868
				KAYE, Debbie Lori		
				Born on 5/6/1950 in New York. Female singer.		
6/22/68	**68**	3		**Come On Home**	*Jack Rhodes/George Richey*	Columbia 44538
				KAYE, Lois		
				Born Lois Kaye Edmiston on 12/8/1950 in Knox, Indiana; raised in Beecher, Indiana. Female singer.		
11/3/79	**96**	2		**Drown In The Flood**	*Gail Davies*	Ovation 1130
				KAYE, Sandra		
				Born Sandra Kaye Van Auken in Longview, Washington. Female singer.		
7/29/78	**52**	7		1 **This Magic Moment**	*Doc Pomus/Mort Shuman*	Door Knob 068
10/21/78	**80**	5		2 **One More Time**	*Chris Isenberg*	Door Knob 075
12/23/78+	**84**	5		3 **I'll Still Love You In My Dreams**	*Andrew Inglese*	Door Knob 088
3/3/79	**83**	5		4 **I've Seen It All**	*Ronnie Nelms*	Door Knob 093
8/18/79	**95**	4		5 **You Broke My Heart So Gently (It Almost Didn't Break)**	*John Allingham/Gerry Stone*	Door Knob 097
				KAYLE, Kortney		
				Born on 2/8/1979 in Ayr, Ontario, Canda. Female singer.		
3/24/01	**60**	1		1 **Don't Let Me Down**	*Zack Turner/Lonnie Wilson*	Lyric Street
6/9/01	**50**	12		2 **Unbroken By You**	S:5 *Jack Blades/Trey Bruce/Gary Burr*	Lyric Street
				KEARNEY, Ramsey		
				Born William Ramsey Kearney on 10/30/1933 in Bolivar, Tennessee. Male singer.		
8/24/85	**96**	1		1 **King Of Oak Street**	*Alex Harvey*	Safari 114
9/10/88	**97**	1		2 **One Time Thing**	*J.D. Johnson*	Safari 117

Billboard DEBUT	PEAK	WKS	GOLD	ARTIST / Country Chart Hit	Ranking / Songwriter	Label (& Number)

KEITH, Toby

1990s: #31 / 2000s: #1 / All-Time #56

Born Toby Keith Covel on 7/8/1961 in Clinton, Oklahoma; raised in Moore, Oklahoma. Male singer/songwriter/guitarist. Former oil field worker, rodeo hand and defensive end for the Oklahoma Drillers semipro football team. Lead singer of group Easy Money from 1984-88. Also see **America The Beautiful**.

CMA: 2001 Male Vocalist

DEBUT	PEAK	WKS	GOLD	Country Chart Hit	Songwriter	Label (& Number)
3/6/93	❶^{2}	20		1 **Should've Been A Cowboy**	*Toby Keith*	Mercury
7/3/93	**5**	20		2 **He Ain't Worth Missing**	*Toby Keith*	Mercury
11/13/93+	**2**^{1}	20		3 **A Little Less Talk And A Lot More Action**	*Keith Hinton/Jimmy Stewart*	Mercury
3/19/94	**2**^{1}	20		4 **Wish I Didn't Know Now**	*Toby Keith*	Mercury
				above 4 from the album *Toby Keith* on Mercury 514421		
7/30/94	❶^{1}	20		5 **Who's That Man**	*Toby Keith*	Polydor
12/3/94+	**10**	20		6 **Upstairs Downtown**	*Carl Goff/Toby Keith*	Polydor
3/25/95	**2**^{3}	20		7 **You Ain't Much Fun**	S:9 *Carl Goff/Toby Keith*	Polydor
7/15/95	**15**	20		8 **Big Ol' Truck**	*Toby Keith*	Polydor
				above 4 from the album *Boomtown* on Polydor 523407		
12/16/95+	**50**	5		9 **Santa I'm Right Here**	*Ronald Reynolds* **[X]**	Mercury
				from the album *Christmas To Christmas* on Mercury 527909		
3/9/96	**2**^{2}	20		10 **Does That Blue Moon Ever Shine On You**	S:3 *Toby Keith*	A&M
7/13/96	**6**	20		11 **A Woman's Touch**	*Toby Keith/Wayne Perry*	A&M
11/23/96+	❶^{1}	20		12 **Me Too**	*Chuck Cannon/Toby Keith*	A&M
				above 3 from the album *Blue Moon* on A&M 531192		
6/14/97	**2**^{2}	20		13 **We Were In Love**	S:11 *Chuck Cannon/Allen Shamblin*	Mercury
10/11/97+	**2**^{1}	20		14 **I'm So Happy I Can't Stop Crying** ***[w/ Sting]***	S:7 *Sting*	Mercury
1/31/98	**5**	20		15 **Dream Walkin'**	*Chuck Cannon/Toby Keith*	Mercury
5/23/98	**40**	10		16 **Double Wide Paradise**	*Billy Maddox/Paul Thorn*	Mercury
				above 4 from the album *Dream Walkin'* on Mercury 534836		
9/12/98	**18**	20		17 **Getcha Some**	*Chuck Cannon/Toby Keith*	Mercury
2/20/99	**44**	9		18 **If A Man Answers**	*Chuck Cannon/Toby Keith*	Mercury
				above 2 from the album *Greatest Hits Volume One* on Mercury 558962		
10/2/99	**44**	10		19 **When Love Fades**	*Chuck Cannon/Toby Keith*	DreamWorks
11/20/99+	❶^{5}	42		20 **How Do You Like Me Now?!**	S:4 *Chuck Cannon/Toby Keith*	DreamWorks
5/27/00	**4**	24		21 **Country Comes To Town**	*Toby Keith*	DreamWorks
10/28/00+	❶^{3}	34		22 **You Shouldn't Kiss Me Like This**	*Toby Keith*	DreamWorks
				above 4 from the album *How Do You Like Me Now?!* on DreamWorks 450209		
12/30/00+	**57**	2		23 **Old Toy Trains**	*Roger Miller* **[X]**	DreamWorks
5/26/01	❶^{1}	22		24 **I'm Just Talkin' About Tonight**	*Scotty Emerick/Toby Keith*	DreamWorks
8/25/01	❶^{5}	28		25 **I Wanna Talk About Me**	*Bobby Braddock*	DreamWorks
12/22/01+	❶^{5}	31		26 **My List**	*Rand Bishop/Tim James*	DreamWorks
				CMA: Single; above 3 from the album *Pull My Chain* on DreamWorks 450297		
5/25/02	❶^{1}	20		27 **Courtesy Of The Red, White And Blue (The Angry American)**	*Toby Keith*	DreamWorks
8/3/02+	❶^{6}	39		28 **Beer For My Horses** ***[w/ Willie Nelson]***	*Scotty Emerick/Toby Keith*	DreamWorks
8/17/02	❶^{1}	29		29 **Who's Your Daddy?**	*Toby Keith*	DreamWorks
1/18/03	**13**	20		30 **Rock You Baby**	*Scotty Emerick/Toby Keith*	DreamWorks
				above 4 from the album *Unleashed* on DreamWorks 450254		
7/26/03	**24**	23		31 **I Can't Take You Anywhere** ***[w/ Scotty Emerick]***	S:2 *Scotty Emerick/Toby Keith*	DreamWorks
				from Emerick's album *The Coast Is Clear* on DreamWorks 450434		
8/30/03	❶^{5}	24		32 **I Love This Bar**	*Scotty Emerick/Toby Keith*	DreamWorks
11/22/03+	❶^{4}	23		33 **American Soldier**	*Chuck Cannon/Toby Keith*	DreamWorks
3/20/04	❶^{1}	20		34 **Whiskey Girl**	*Scotty Emerick/Toby Keith*	DreamWorks
				above 3 from the album *Shock'n Y'all* on DreamWorks 450435		
5/29/04	**8**	20		35 **Hey Good Lookin'** ***[w/ Jimmy Buffett/Clint Black/Kenny Chesney/Alan Jackson/George Strait]*** from Buffett's album *License To Chill* on RCA 62270	*Hank Williams*	RCA
8/14/04	**3**^{1}	20		36 **Stays In Mexico**	*Toby Keith*	DreamWorks
11/27/04+	**27**	14		37 **Mockingbird** ***[w/ daughter Krystal]***	*Charlie Foxx/Inez Foxx*	DreamWorks
				above 2 from the album *Greatest Hits 2* on DreamWorks 002323		
2/12/05	**8**	20		38 **Honkytonk U**	*Toby Keith*	DreamWorks
5/21/05	❶^{6}	19↑		39 **As Good As I Once Was**	*Scotty Emerick/Toby Keith*	DreamWorks
				above 2 from the album *Honkytonk University* on DreamWorks 004300		

KELLER, Joanie

Born in Wayne, Nebraska. Female singer/guitarist.

DEBUT	PEAK	WKS	GOLD	Country Chart Hit	Songwriter	Label (& Number)
3/25/00	**66**	1		**Three Little Teardrops**	*Buck Moore/Frank Myers J.*	Broken Bow
				from the album *Sparks Are Gonna Fly* on Broken Bow 7773		

KELLEY, John

Born in Little Rock, Arkansas; raised in Indiana. Male singer.

DEBUT	PEAK	WKS	GOLD	Country Chart Hit	Songwriter	Label (& Number)
7/24/82	**81**	4		**This Morning I Woke Up In New York City**	*Marty Yonts*	ComStar 8201

KELLUM, Murry

Born on 12/31/1942 in Jackson, Tennessee; raised in Plain, Texas. Died in a plane crash on 9/30/1990 (age 47). Male singer/songwriter.

DEBUT	PEAK	WKS	GOLD	Country Chart Hit	Songwriter	Label (& Number)
6/19/71	**26**	10		1 **Joy To The World**	*Hoyt Axton*	Epic 10741
11/20/71	**74**	2		2 **Train Train (Carry Me Away)**	*Bill Graham/Freddy Weller*	Epic 10784

DEBUT	PEAK	WKS	GOLD	ARTIST / Country Chart Hit ... Songwriter	Label (& Number)
				KELLUM, Murry — cont'd	
2/2/74	**55**	9		3 **Lovely Lady** ... *Murry Kellum/Sonny Ledet*	Cinnamon 777
5/25/74	**98**	2		4 **Girl Of My Life** ... *Murry Kellum/Sonny Ledet*	Cinnamon 794
				KELLY, Irene	
				Born in Latrobe, Pennsylvania. Female singer.	
12/2/89	**67**	7		**Love Is A Hard Road** ... *Nancy Montgomery/Marshall Morgan*	MCA 53756
				KELLY, Jerri	
				Born on 10/11/1947 in Phoenix, Arizona; raised in Stephenville, Texas. Female singer/songwriter.	
1/18/75	**65**	10		1 **I Can't Help Myself (Sugar Pie, Honey Bunch)** ***[w/ Price Mitchell]*** ... *Lamont Dozier/Brian Holland/Eddie Holland*	GRT 016
1/26/80	**90**	2		2 **For A Slow Dance With You** ... *Mick Lloyd/Steve Whisenhunt*	Little Giant 021
8/2/80	**66**	9		3 **Fallin' For You** ... *Karolyn Freeman*	Little Giant 026
11/8/80	**85**	3		4 **Forsaking All The Rest** ... *Jerri Kelly*	Little Giant 030
1/31/81	**85**	3		5 **Be My Lover, Be My Friend** ***[w/ Mick Lloyd]*** ... *Mick Lloyd*	Little Giant 040
8/8/81	**85**	4		6 **Sweet Natural Love** ***[w/ Mick Lloyd]*** ... *Tommy Faia*	Little Giant 046
8/14/82	**56**	8		7 **Walk Me 'Cross The River** ... *Dick Stockard*	Carrere 03017
				KELLY, Karen	
				Born in Los Angeles, California. Female singer.	
9/19/70	**75**	2		**Let Me Go, Lover** ... *Jenny Lou Carson/Al Hill*	Capitol 2883
				KEMP, Dave	
				Born in Tennessee. Male singer/songwriter/guitarist.	
5/28/83	**75**	4		**Ain't That The Way It Goes** ... *John Jarrard/Mark D. Sanders*	Soundwaves 4702
				KEMP, Wayne	
				Born on 6/1/1941 in Greenwood, Arkansas. Male singer/songwriter. Auto racer while a teenager.	
2/1/69	**61**	6		1 **Won't You Come Home (And Talk To A Stranger)** ... *Wayne Kemp*	Decca 32422
9/27/69	**73**	2		2 **Bar Room Habits** ... *Wayne Kemp*	Decca 32534
1/9/71	**57**	8		3 **Who'll Turn Out The Lights** ... *Wayne Kemp/Mack Vickery*	Decca 32767
5/29/71	**52**	9		4 **Award To An Angel** ... *Wayne Kemp/Mack Vickery*	Decca 32824
12/18/71	**72**	2		5 **Did We Have To Come This Far (To Say Goodbye)** ... *Dallas Frazier/A.L. "Doodle" Owens*	Decca 32891
6/3/72	**53**	5		6 **Darlin'** ... *Ray Griff*	Decca 32946
3/17/73	**17**	14		7 **Honky Tonk Wine** ... *Mack Vickery*	MCA 40019
9/1/73	**53**	10		8 **Kentucky Sunshine** ... *Charles Arrington*	MCA 40112
2/2/74	**32**	11		9 **Listen** ... *Ray Griff/Jay Marshall*	MCA 40176
7/6/74	**57**	11		10 **Harlan County** ... *Bill Emerson/Billy Large*	MCA 40249
6/12/76	**72**	7		11 **Waiting For The Tables To Turn** ... *Wayne Kemp/Mack Vickery*	United Artists 805
8/28/76	**71**	5		12 **I Should Have Watched That First Step** ... *Wayne Kemp*	United Artists 850
5/21/77	**91**	3		13 **Leona Don't Live Here Anymore** ... *Curly Putnam/Sonny Throckmorton*	United Artists 980
8/27/77	**76**	6		14 **I Love It (When You Love All Over Me)** ... *Buddy Killen/Sheb Wooley*	United Artists 1031
7/12/80	**62**	6		15 **Love Goes To Hell When It Dies** ... *Wayne Kemp/Sammy Lyons*	Mercury 57023
11/15/80	**47**	10		16 **I'll Leave This World Loving You** ... *Wayne Kemp*	Mercury 57035
4/4/81	**35**	12		17 **Your Wife Is Cheatin' On Us Again** ... *Wayne Kemp/Warren Robb*	Mercury 57047
7/25/81	**46**	7		18 **Just Got Back From No Man's Land** ... *Danny Walls*	Mercury 57053
11/14/81	**75**	5		19 **Why Am I Doing Without** ... *Dave Kirby/Red Lane*	Mercury 57060
4/10/82	**78**	4		20 **Sloe Gin And Fast Women** ... *Dave Hall/Danny Walls*	Mercury 76139
9/4/82	**64**	6		21 **She Only Meant To Use Him** ... *Dallas Cody/Charles Quillen*	Mercury 76165
7/16/83	**55**	10		22 **Don't Send Me No Angels** ... *Wayne Kemp*	Door Knob 200
6/30/84	**75**	4		23 **I've Always Wanted To** ... *Danny Walls/Bobby Warren*	Door Knob 211
3/8/86	**70**	4		24 **Red Neck And Over Thirty** ***[w/ Bobby G. Rice]*** ... *Buffalo Jones*	Door Knob 243

KENDALLS, The — **All-Time: #127**

Father-and-daughter duo from St. Louis, Missouri: Royce Kendall (born on 9/25/1934; died of a heart attack on 5/22/1998, age 63) and Jeannie Kendall (born on 11/30/1954). Real last name: Kuykendall. Royce played with his brother Floyce as the Austin Brothers; became regulars on TV's *Town Hall Party* in the 1950s.

DEBUT	PEAK	WKS	GOLD	Country Chart Hit ... Songwriter	Label (& Number)
7/25/70	**52**	6		1 **Leaving On A Jet Plane** ... *John Denver*	Stop 373
2/12/72	**53**	9		2 **Two Divided By Love** ... *Marty Kupps/Dennis Lambert/Brian Potter*	Dot 17405
7/1/72	**66**	4		3 **Everything I Own** ... *David Gates*	Dot 17422
4/2/77	**80**	7		4 **Makin' Believe** ... *Jimmy Work*	Ovation 1101
8/6/77	**❶⁴**	20		5 **Heaven's Just A Sin Away** ... *Jerry Gillespie*	Ovation 1103
				Grammy: Vocal Duo / CMA: Single	
2/11/78	**2²**	15		6 **It Don't Feel Like Sinnin' To Me** ... *Mike Kosser/Curly Putman*	Ovation 1106
5/27/78	**6**	14		7 **Pittsburgh Stealers** ... *Larry Kingston/Jim Rushing*	Ovation 1109
9/23/78	**❶¹**	15		8 **Sweet Desire /** ... *Jeannie Kendall*	
9/23/78	**flip**	15		9 **Old Fashioned Love** ... *Mitch Johnson/Mike Martin*	Ovation 1112
1/13/79	**5**	14		10 **I Had A Lovely Time** ... *Don Cook/Sonny Throckmorton*	Ovation 1119
5/5/79	**11**	11		11 **Just Like Real People** ... *Bob McDill*	Ovation 1125

DEBUT	PEAK	WKS	GOLD	ARTIST / Ranking / Country Chart Hit	Songwriter	Label (& Number)
				KENDALLS, The — cont'd		
8/18/79	**16**	11		12 **I Don't Do Like That No More /**	*Sonny Throckmorton/Rafe Van Hoy*	
8/18/79	**flip**	11		13 **Never My Love**	*Jerry Foster/Bill Rice*	Ovation 1129
11/17/79+	**5**	15		14 **You'd Make An Angel Wanna Cheat**	*Bob Morrison/Bill Zerface/Jim Zerface*	Ovation 1136
4/5/80	**5**	13		15 **I'm Already Blue**	*Bob McDill*	Ovation 1143
8/2/80	**9**	15		16 **Put It Off Until Tomorrow**	*Bill Owens/Dolly Parton*	Ovation 1154
3/28/81	**26**	11		17 **Heart Of The Matter**	*Jim Rushing/Don Schlitz*	Ovation 1169
8/22/81	**7**	16		18 **Teach Me To Cheat**	*Ken Bell/Terry Skinner/J.L. Wallace*	Mercury 57055
12/12/81+	**10**	19		19 **If You're Waiting On Me (You're Backing Up)**	*Ken Bell/Terry Skinner/J.L. Wallace*	Mercury 76131
6/5/82	**30**	12		20 **Cheater's Prayer**	*Lewis Anderson*	Mercury 76155
9/18/82	**35**	10		21 **That's What I Get For Thinking**	*Ken Bell/Terry Skinner/J.L. Wallace*	Mercury 76178
5/28/83	**19**	14		22 **Precious Love**	*Byron Walls*	Mercury 812300
				Emmylou Harris (harmony vocal)		
8/27/83	**20**	19		23 **Movin' Train**	*Charlie Black/Tommy Rocco*	Mercury 814195
1/14/84	**❶**[1]	23		24 **Thank God For The Radio**	*Max D. Barnes/Robert Jones*	Mercury 818056
6/2/84	**15**	17		25 **My Baby's Gone**	*Hazel Houser*	Mercury 822203
10/27/84+	**20**	17		26 **I'd Dance Every Dance With You**	S:16 / A:21 *Mark Paden/Kevin Welch*	Mercury 880306
3/2/85	**27**	14		27 **Four Wheel Drive**	S:21 / A:26 *Mack Watkins*	Mercury 880588
6/1/85	**26**	14		28 **If You Break My Heart**	S:21 / A:25 *Michael Garvin/Bucky Jones/Tom Shapiro*	Mercury 880828
10/12/85	**45**	8		29 **Two Heart Harmony**	*Glynn Fought/Rick Giles/Gary Harrison/Bernadette McMaken*	Mercury 884140
6/28/86	**42**	9		30 **Too Late**	*Todd Cerney/Nancy Montgomery*	MCA/Curb 52850
9/27/86	**60**	7		31 **Fire At First Sight**	*Terry Skinner/J.L. Wallace*	MCA/Curb 52933
12/6/86+	**46**	9		32 **Little Doll**	*Mack Watkins*	MCA/Curb 52983
5/2/87	**54**	8		33 **Routine**	*Bob Regan*	Step One 371
7/11/87	**51**	8		34 **Dancin' With Myself Tonight**	*Chuck Burns/Don Huber*	Step One 374
12/12/87+	**62**	7		35 **Still Pickin' Up After You**	*Larry Bastian/Dewayne Blackwell*	Step One 379
4/16/88	**57**	7		36 **The Rhythm Of Romance**	*Steve Bogard/Rick Giles*	Step One 384
6/24/89	**69**	6		37 **Blue Blue Day**	*Don Gibson*	Epic 68933
				KENNARD AND JOHN		
				Duo of Phillip Kennard and Ron John.		
11/18/89	**73**	4		**Thrill Of Love**	*Ron John/Philip Kennard*	Curb/MCA 10563
				KENNEDY, Gene, & Karen Jeglum		
				Husband-and-wife duo. Gene was born Kenneth Kennedy on 10/3/1933 in Florence, South Carolina. Karen was born in Blanchardville, Wisconsin. Co-owners of the Door Knob record label.		
2/28/81	**80**	4		1 **I Want To See Me In Your Eyes**	*Arthur Kent/Frank Stanton*	Door Knob 145
4/25/81	**84**	4		2 **I'd Rather Be The Stranger In Your Eyes**	*Charlie Craig/L.E. White*	Door Knob 151
7/18/81	**87**	2		3 **Easier To Go /**	*Betsy Smith/Ray Webster*	
3/20/82	**49**	9		4 **A Thing Or Two On My Mind**	*Max Fagan*	Door Knob 173
7/24/82	**80**	4		5 **What About Tonight (We Might Find Something Beautiful Tonight)**	*Doug Barnes*	Door Knob 179
4/23/83	**86**	3		6 **Be Happy For Me**	*Mark Gibbons/Jerry Winn*	Door Knob 192
8/2/86	**78**	4		7 **My Wife's House** *[Gene Kennedy]*	*Bob Jennings/Lorene Mann*	Society 110
				KENNEDY, Larry Wayne		
				Born in Little Rock, Arkansas. Male singer.		
11/30/85	**83**	3		**She Almost Makes Me Forget About You**	*Lewis Anderson/Brent Mason*	Jere 1001
				KENNEDY, Ray		
				Born on 5/13/1954 in Buffalo, New York. Male singer/songwriter/guitarist.		
11/17/90+	**10**	20		1 **What A Way To Go**	*Bobby David/Ray Kennedy/Jim Rushing*	Atlantic
4/13/91	**58**	10		2 **Scars**	*Bobby David/Don Henry/Ray Kennedy*	Atlantic
8/10/91	**74**	1		3 **I Like The Way It Feels**	*Bobby David/Ray Kennedy/Red Lane*	Atlantic
				above 3 from the album *What A Way To Go* on Atlantic 82109		
11/7/92	**70**	5		4 **No Way Jose**	*Paul Battle/Michael Garvin*	Atlantic
				from the album *Guitar Man* on Atlantic 82422		
				KENNY G		
				Born Kenny Gorelick on 7/6/1956 in Seattle, Washington. Soprano/tenor saxophonist.		
1/15/00	**49**	1		**Auld Lang Syne (The Millennium Mix)**	*(traditional)* **[I-S]**	Arista
				contains audioclips from dozens of historical events of the last 100 years; from the album *Faith - A Holiday Album* on Arista 19090		
				KENNY O.		
				Born Kenny O. Smith in Tennessee. Male singer.		
8/22/81	**83**	3		**Old Fangled Country Songs**	*Jerry Duncan/Betty Jo Gibson*	Rhinestone 1002
				KENT, George		
				Born on 6/12/1935 in Dallas, Texas. Male singer.		
12/13/69+	**26**	15		1 **Hello, I'm A Jukebox**	*Tom T. Hall* **[S]**	Mercury 72985
				Diana Duke (female vocal)		
7/4/70	**70**	3		2 **Doogie Ray**	*Jack Key/Rick Key*	Mercury 73066
12/5/70+	**62**	7		3 **Mama Bake A Pie (Daddy Kill A Chicken)**	*Tom T. Hall*	Mercury 73127
5/18/74	**48**	9		4 **Take My Life And Shape It With Your Love**	*Bucky Jones/Royce Porter*	Shannon 818
12/28/74+	**65**	6		5 **Whole Lotta Difference In Love**	*Bucky Jones/Royce Porter*	Shannon 824
11/22/75	**97**	3		6 **She'll Wear It Out Leaving Town**	*Bucky Jones/George Kent/Joe Winchell*	Shannon 834
3/13/76	**75**	6		7 **Shake 'Em Up and Let 'Em Roll**	*Jerry Leiber/Mike Stoller*	Shannon 840
2/26/77	**89**	5		8 **Low Class Reunion**	*Sterling Whipple*	Soundwaves 4542

Billboard			G O L D	ARTIST Ranking		
DEBUT	PEAK	WKS		Country Chart Hit	Songwriter	Label (& Number)

KENTUCKY HEADHUNTERS, The

Country-rock group from Edmonton, Kentucky: brothers Ricky Lee Phelps (vocals; born on 10/8/1953) and Doug Phelps (bass; born on 2/16/1960), brothers Richard Young (guitar; born on 1/27/1955) and Fred Young (drums; born on 7/8/1958), and their cousin Greg Martin (guitar; born on 3/31/1954). The Phelps brothers left in 1992 to form **Brother Phelps**; replaced by Mark Orr (vocals; born on 11/16/1949) and Anthony Kenney (bass; born on 10/8/1953). Doug Phelps (vocals) returned in 1996, replacing Orr.

CMA: Vocal Group 1990 & 1991

DEBUT	PEAK	WKS		Country Chart Hit	Songwriter	Label (& Number)
9/30/89	**25**	21	1	**Walk Softly On This Heart Of Mine**	*Jake Landers/Bill Monroe*	Mercury 874744
2/24/90	**15**	26	2	**Dumas Walker**	*Greg Martin/Doug Phelps/Ricky Lee Phelps/Fred Young/Richard Young*	Mercury
6/2/90	**8**	21	3	**Oh Lonesome Me**	*Don Gibson*	Mercury
10/13/90	**23**	20	4	**Rock 'N' Roll Angel**	*Richard Young*	Mercury
				above 3 from the album *Pickin' On Nashville* on Mercury 838744		
3/30/91	**49**	11	5	**The Ballad Of Davy Crockett**	*Tom Blackburn/George Bruns*	Mercury
6/22/91	**56**	9	6	**With Body And Soul**	*Virginia Stauffer*	Mercury
9/21/91	**63**	6	7	**It's Chitlin' Time**	*Greg Martin/Doug Phelps/Ricky Lee Phelps/Fred Young/Richard Young*	Mercury
11/23/91	**60**	7	8	**Only Daddy That'll Walk The Line**	*Jimmy Bryant*	Mercury
				above 4 from the album *Electric Barnyard* on Mercury 848054		
2/20/93	**54**	6	9	**Honky Tonk Walkin'**	*Anthony Kenney/Greg Martin/Mark Orr/Fred Young/Richard Young*	Mercury
5/22/93	**71**	4	10	**Dixie Fried**	*Howard Griffin/Carl Perkins*	Mercury
				above 2 from the album *Rave On!!* on Mercury 512568		
3/22/97	**70**	3	11	**Singin' The Blues**	*Melvin Endsley*	BNA
				from the album *Stompin' Grounds* on BNA 67461		
10/28/00	**66**	1	12	**Too Much To Lose**	*Vern Grissom/Anthony Kenney/Greg Martin/Doug Phelps/Fred Young/Richard Young*	Audium
				from the album *Songs From The Grass String Ranch* on Audium 8117		

KENYON, Joe

Pseudonym for producer/guitarist Jerry Kennedy and pianist David Briggs.

DEBUT	PEAK	WKS		Country Chart Hit	Songwriter	Label (& Number)
6/27/87	**33**	15		**Hymne**	*Vangelis* **[I]**	Mercury 888642
				tune featured in Gallo Wine commercials		

KERSH, David

Born on 12/9/1970 in Humble, Texas. Male singer.

DEBUT	PEAK	WKS		Country Chart Hit	Songwriter	Label (& Number)
5/4/96	**65**	5	1	**Breaking Hearts And Taking Names**	*Porter Howell/Tony Martin/Reese Wilson*	Curb
8/3/96	**6**	22	2	**Goodnight Sweetheart**	S:7 *Randy Boudreaux/L. David Lewis/Kim Williams*	Curb
1/18/97	**3**[1]	20	3	**Another You**	*Brad Paisley*	Curb
5/31/97	**11**	20	4	**Day In, Day Out**	*Marv Green/Thom McHugh*	Curb
				above 4 from the album *Goodnight Sweetheart* on Curb 77848		
12/6/97+	**3**[2]	25	5	**If I Never Stop Loving You**	S:4 *Skip Ewing/Donny Kees*	Curb
3/14/98	**29**	23	6	**Wonderful Tonight**	*Eric Clapton*	Curb
9/26/98	**46**	16	7	**Something To Think About**	*Tony Martin/Tim Nichols*	Curb
				above 3 from the album *If I Never Stop Loving You* on Curb 77895		

KERSHAW, Doug

Born on 1/24/1936 in Tiel Ridge, Louisiana. Male singer/songwriter/fiddler. Teamed with brother Russell "Rusty" Kershaw in duo **Rusty & Doug**. Acted in the movies *Zachariah, Medicine Ball Caravan* and *Days Of Heaven.* Third cousin of **Sammy Kershaw**.

DEBUT	PEAK	WKS		Country Chart Hit	Songwriter	Label (& Number)
10/11/69	**70**	3	1	**Diggy Liggy Lo**	*Joe Miller* **[R]**	Warner 7329
				new version of #5 under **Rusty & Doug**		
2/2/74	**77**	9	2	**Mama's Got The Know How**	*Doug Kershaw*	Warner 7763
5/1/76	**76**	6	3	**It Takes All Day To Get Over Night**	*Doug Kershaw*	Warner 8195
5/21/77	**96**	3	4	**I'm Walkin'**	*Dave Bartholomew/Fats Domino*	Warner 8374
6/27/81	**29**	13	5	**Hello Woman**	*Doug Kershaw*	Scotti Brothers 02137
8/27/88	**52**	7	6	**Cajun Baby** ***[w/ Hank Williams, Jr.]***	*Hank Williams/Hank Williams Jr.*	BGM 81588
3/11/89	**66**	6	7	**Boogie Queen**	*Dave Green/Bobby Jenkins*	BGM 12989

KERSHAW, Sammy **1990s: #22 / All-Time: #131**

Born on 2/24/1958 in Abbeville, Louisiana; raised in Kaplan, Louisiana. Male singer/songwriter/guitarist. Third cousin of **Doug Kershaw**. Acted in the 1995 movie *Fall Time.* Married **Lorrie Morgan** on 9/29/2001.

DEBUT	PEAK	WKS		Country Chart Hit	Songwriter	Label (& Number)
10/12/91+	**3**[2]	20	1	**Cadillac Style**	*Mark Petersen*	Mercury
2/8/92	**12**	20	2	**Don't Go Near The Water**	*James Foster/Chapin Hartford*	Mercury
6/13/92	**17**	20	3	**Yard Sale**	*Larry Bastian/Dewayne Blackwell*	Mercury
10/3/92+	**10**	20	4	**Anywhere But Here**	*Buddy Cannon/Bob DiPiero/John Scott Sherrill*	Mercury
				above 4 from the album *Don't Go Near The Water* on Mercury 510161		
2/13/93	**❶**[1]	20	5	**She Don't Know She's Beautiful**	*Paul Harrison/Bob McDill*	Mercury
5/8/93	**9**	20	6	**Haunted Heart**	*Buddy Brock/Kim Williams*	Mercury
9/4/93	**7**	20	7	**Queen Of My Double Wide Trailer**	*Dennis Linde*	Mercury
1/15/94	**3**[1]	20	8	**I Can't Reach Her Anymore**	*Mark Petersen/Bruce Theien*	Mercury
				above 4 from the album *Haunted Heart* on Mercury 514332		
3/12/94	**52**	10	9	**Never Bit A Bullet Like This** ***[w/ George Jones]***	*Jim Foster/Mark Petersen*	MCA
				from Jones's album *High-Tech Redneck* on MCA 10910		
5/21/94	**2**[1]	20	10	**National Working Woman's Holiday**	*J.D. Hicks/Roger Murrah/William Terry*	Mercury

DEBUT	PEAK	WKS	GOLD	ARTIST / Country Chart Hit	Ranking / Songwriter	Label (& Number)
				KERSHAW, Sammy — cont'd		
8/27/94	**2^{2}**	20		11 **Third Rate Romance**	*Howard Smith*	Mercury
12/3/94+	**27**	16		12 **Southbound**	*Mac McAnally*	Mercury
12/24/94+	**50**	3		13 **Christmas Time's A Comin'**	*Tex Logan* **[X]**	Mercury
				from the album *Christmas Time's A Comin'* on Mercury 522638		
3/18/95	**18**	20		14 **If You're Gonna Walk, I'm Gonna Crawl**	*Larry Bastian/Buddy Cannon*	Mercury
				#10-12 & 14: from the album *Feelin' Good Train* on Mercury 522125		
8/26/95	**47**	8		15 **Your Tattoo**	*Kostas/Jack Tempchin*	Mercury
				from the album *The Hits, Chapter One* on Mercury 528536		
3/23/96	**5**	20		16 **Meant To Be**	S:14 *Rick Bowles/Chris Waters*	Mercury
7/27/96	**10**	20		17 **Vidalia**	*Tim Nichols/Mark D. Sanders*	Mercury
11/9/96+	**28**	20		18 **Politics, Religion And Her**	*Byron Hill/Tony Martin*	Mercury
4/12/97	**29**	20		19 **Fit To Be Tied Down**	*Wynn Varble/Charles Victor*	Mercury
				above 4 from the album *Politics, Religion And Her* on Mercury 528893		
10/25/97+	**2^{2}**	26		20 **Love Of My Life**	S:8 *Dan Hill/Keith Stegall*	Mercury
1/3/98	**53**	2		21 **Christmas Time's A Comin'**	*Tex Logan* **[X-R]**	Mercury
				from the album *Christmas Time's A Comin'* on Mercury 522638		
3/14/98	**22**	20		22 **Matches**	*Skip Ewing/Roger Springer*	Mercury
6/27/98	**31**	20		23 **Honky Tonk America**	S:17 *Bob McDill*	Mercury
10/10/98+	**35**	20		24 **One Day Left To Live**	*Randy Boudreaux/Dean Dillon/John Northrop*	Mercury
				#20 & 22-24: from the album *Labor Of Love* on Mercury 536318		
2/27/99	**17**	20		25 **Maybe Not Tonight** ***[w/ Lorrie Morgan]***	*Dan Hill/Keith Stegall*	BNA/Mercury
				also from Morgan's album *My Heart* on BNA 67763		
8/14/99	**37**	15		26 **When You Love Someone**	*Dan Hill/Keith Stegall*	Mercury
11/27/99+	**35**	17		27 **Me And Maxine**	*Gordon Bradberry/Michael Lunn*	Mercury
				above 3 from the album *Maybe Not Tonight* on Mercury 538889		
2/17/01	**39**	17		28 **He Drinks Tequila** ***[w/ Lorrie Morgan]***	*Shawn Camp/Michele McCord*	RCA
				from their album *I Finally Found Someone* on RCA 67004		
1/25/03	**33**	20		29 **I Want My Money Back**	*Dave Berg/Annie Tate/Sam Tate*	Audium
8/16/03	**58**	3		30 **I've Never Been Anywhere**	*Jim Collins/Dean Dillon*	Audium
				above 2 from the album *I Want My Money Back* on Audium 8167		

KETCHUM, Hal — All-Time: #258

Born on 4/9/1953 in Greenwich, New York. Male singer/songwriter/guitarist.

OPRY: 1994

DEBUT	PEAK	WKS	GOLD	Country Chart Hit	Songwriter	Label (& Number)
5/11/91	**2^{1}**	21		1 **Small Town Saturday Night**	*Pat Alger/Hank DeVito*	Curb
10/26/91+	**13**	20		2 **I Know Where Love Lives**	*Hal Ketchum*	Curb
2/15/92	**2^{1}**	20		3 **Past The Point Of Rescue**	*Mick Hanly*	Curb
5/30/92	**16**	20		4 **Five O'Clock World**	*Allen Reynolds*	Curb
				above 4 from the album *Past The Point Of Rescue* on Curb 77450		
9/26/92+	**3^{1}**	20		5 **Sure Love**	*Gary Burr/Pete Wasner*	Curb
2/20/93	**2^{1}**	20		6 **Hearts Are Gonna Roll**	*Hal Ketchum/Ronny Scaife*	Curb
6/19/93	**8**	20		7 **Mama Knows The Highway**	*Charles Quatro/Pete Wasner*	Curb
10/9/93	**24**	20		8 **Someplace Far Away (Careful What You're Dreamin')**	*Hal Ketchum*	Curb
				above 4 from the album *Sure Love* on Curb 77581		
4/23/94	**20**	20		9 **(Tonight We Just Might) Fall In Love Again**	*Al Anderson/Hal Ketchum*	Curb
9/24/94	**22**	19		10 **That's What I Get (For Losin' You)**	*Al Anderson/Hal Ketchum*	Curb
2/11/95	**8**	20		11 **Stay Forever**	S:15 *Hal Ketchum/Benmont Tench*	Curb
8/26/95	**49**	8		12 **Every Little Word**	*Marcus Hummon/Hal Ketchum*	Curb
11/18/95	**56**	7		13 **Veil Of Tears**	*Hal Ketchum/Mike Nobel/Jeff Pennig*	Curb
				above 5 from the album *Every Little Word* on Curb 77660		
2/28/98	**36**	20		14 **I Saw The Light**	S:23 *Todd Rundgren*	Curb
				from the album *I Saw The Light* on Curb 77895		
12/2/00+	**40**	16		15 **She Is**	*Hal Ketchum*	Curb
				from the album *Lucky Man* on Curb 78707		
8/7/04	**60**	1		16 **My Love Will Not Change**	*Billy Burnette/Shawn Camp*	Curb

KID ROCK

Born Robert Ritchie on 1/17/1971 in Romeo, Michigan. White hip-hop/rock singer.

DEBUT	PEAK	WKS	GOLD	Country Chart Hit	Songwriter	Label (& Number)
10/12/02+	**21**	33	●	1 **Picture** ***[w/ Sheryl Crow or Allison Moorer]***	S:❶^{52} *Robert Ritchie*	Lava
				commercial single features Moorer; the vast majority of radio stations played the original album version featuring Crow; from the album *Cocky* on Lava 83482		
6/19/04	**50**	11		2 **Single Father**	*David Allan Coe/Robert Ritchie*	Top Dog
				from the album *Kid Rock* on Top Dog 83685		

KILGORE, Jerry

Born in Tillamook, Oregon. Male singer/songwriter.

DEBUT	PEAK	WKS	GOLD	Country Chart Hit	Songwriter	Label (& Number)
8/7/99	**36**	20		1 **Love Trip**	*Gil Grand/Brett Jones/Jerry Kilgore*	Virgin
1/15/00	**49**	9		2 **The Look**	*Tim Nichols/Jeff Stevens*	Virgin
8/5/00	**73**	1		3 **Cactus In A Coffee Can**	*Steve Seskin/Allen Shamblin*	Virgin
				above 3 from the album *Love Trip* on Virgin 47828		

KILGORE, Merle

Born Wyatt Merle Kilgore on 9/8/1934 in Chickasha, Oklahoma; raised in Shreveport, Louisiana. Male singer/songwriter.

DEBUT	PEAK	WKS	GOLD	Country Chart Hit	Songwriter	Label (& Number)
2/1/60	**12**	13		1 **Dear Mama**	*Merle Kilgore*	Starday 469
7/4/60	**10**	11		2 **Love Has Made You Beautiful /**	*Merle Kilgore*	
7/18/60	**29**	1		3 **Getting Old Before My Time**	*Merle Kilgore*	Starday 497
				recitation by Jimmy Jay		
10/21/67	**71**	3		4 **Fast Talking Louisiana Man**	*Merle Kilgore*	Columbia 44279

KILGORE, Merle — cont'd

DEBUT	PEAK	WKS	GOLD	Country Chart Hit	Songwriter	Label (& Number)
8/24/74	95	4		5 Montgomery Mable	*Bobby Emmons/Chips Moman*	Warner 7831
1/16/82	54	7		6 Mister Garfield **Johnny Cash** and **Hank Williams, Jr.** (backing vocals)	*Jack Elliott*	Elektra 47252
7/14/84	74	4		7 Just Out Of Reach	*Virgil Stewart*	Warner 29267
5/11/85	92	4		8 Guilty	*Alex Zanetis*	Warner 29062

KILLEN, Buddy

Born William Killen on 11/13/1932 in Lexington, Alabama. Male singer/musician/producer. Owner of the Tree Publishing Company.

DEBUT	PEAK	WKS	GOLD	Country Chart Hit	Songwriter	Label (& Number)
7/5/69	55	5		A Truer Love You'll Never Find (Than Mine) *[w/ Bonnie Guitar]*	*Red Lane*	Paramount 0004

KIMBERLYS, The

Vocal group from Oklahoma: brothers Harold and Carl Kimberly, with their spouses, sisters Verna and Vera Kimberly. Their children recorded as **Kimberly Springs**.

DEBUT	PEAK	WKS	GOLD	Country Chart Hit	Songwriter	Label (& Number)
8/23/69	23	11		MacArthur Park *[w/ Waylon Jennings]* **Grammy: Vocal Group**	*Jimmy Webb*	RCA Victor 0210

KIMBERLY SPRINGS

Family vocal group from Oklahoma: four sisters and brothers, and a cousin (children of **The Kimberlys**).

DEBUT	PEAK	WKS	GOLD	Country Chart Hit	Songwriter	Label (& Number)
6/23/84	49	10		1 Slow Dancin'	*Jerry Fuller/John Hobbs*	Capitol 5366
10/20/84	74	5		2 Old Memories Are Hard To Lose	*Jerry Fuller/Jerry Self*	Capitol 5404

KIMES, Royal Wade

Born on 3/4/1951 in Arkansas. Male singer/songwriter/guitarist.

DEBUT	PEAK	WKS	GOLD	Country Chart Hit	Songwriter	Label (& Number)
1/3/04	60	1		Mile High Honey from the album *A Dyin' Breed* on Wonderment 1002	*Larry Crowley/Leslie Easterbrook/Royal Wade Kimes*	Wonderment

KING, Claude — **1960s: #29 / All-Time: #168**

Born on 2/5/1933 in Shreveport, Louisiana. Male singer/songwriter/guitarist. Attended University of Idaho on a baseball scholarship. Worked on the *Louisiana Hayride* from 1952. First recorded for Gotham in 1952. Acted in the movies *Swamp Girl* and *Year of The Yahoo*, and in the TV miniseries *The Blue And The Gray*.

DEBUT	PEAK	WKS	GOLD	Country Chart Hit	Songwriter	Label (& Number)
7/3/61	7	16		1 Big River, Big Man	*Mike Phillips*	Columbia 42043
11/13/61+	7	15		2 The Comancheros inspired by the movie starring John Wayne	*Tillman Franks*	Columbia 42196
5/5/62	❶[9]	26	●	3 Wolverton Mountain	*Merle Kilgore/Claude King*	Columbia 42352
10/20/62	10	7		4 The Burning Of Atlanta	*Chuck Taylor*	Columbia 42581
12/22/62+	11	9		5 I've Got The World By The Tail	*Claude King*	Columbia 42630
3/9/63	12	9		6 Sheepskin Valley	*Merle Kilgore/Claude King*	Columbia 42688
6/29/63	12	5		7 Building A Bridge	*Claude King*	Columbia 42782
8/17/63	13	5		8 Hey Lucille!	*Fred Burch/Jimmy Newman/Marijohn Wilkin*	Columbia 42833
2/29/64	33	7		9 That's What Makes The World Go Around	*Claude King*	Columbia 42959
8/15/64	11	18		10 Sam Hill	*Tommy Collins*	Columbia 43083
12/26/64+	47	3		11 Whirlpool (Of Your Love)	*Don Christopher/Merle Kilgore/Claude King*	Columbia 43157
6/26/65	6	18		12 Tiger Woman	*Merle Kilgore/Claude King*	Columbia 43298
11/27/65+	17	11		13 Little Buddy	*Claude King*	Columbia 43416
3/12/66	13	15		14 Catch A Little Raindrop	*Dorsey Burnette/Joe Osborn*	Columbia 43510
11/26/66+	50	12		15 Little Things That Every Girl Should Know	*Claude King*	Columbia 43867
4/29/67	32	10		16 The Watchman	*Claude King/Mack Vickery*	Columbia 44035
8/26/67	50	10		17 Laura (What's He Got That I Ain't Got)	*Leon Ashley/Margie Singleton*	Columbia 44237
12/9/67	59	2		18 Yellow Haired Woman	*Shel Silverstein*	Columbia 44340
6/8/68	67	3		19 Parchman Farm Blues	*Mose Allison*	Columbia 44504
10/19/68	48	6		20 The Power Of Your Sweet Love	*Cliff Crofford*	Columbia 44642
3/1/69	52	7		21 Sweet Love On My Mind	*Claude King*	Columbia 44749
5/17/69	9	15		22 All For The Love Of A Girl	*Johnny Horton*	Columbia 44833
11/8/69	18	10		23 Friend, Lover, Woman, Wife	*Mac Davis*	Columbia 45015
5/30/70	33	10		24 I'll Be Your Baby Tonight	*Bob Dylan*	Columbia 45142
11/7/70+	17	15		25 Mary's Vineyard	*Wayne Carson/Bob Wilkins*	Columbia 45248
4/10/71	23	13		26 Chip 'N' Dale's Place	*Dan Hoffman/Norro Wilson*	Columbia 45340
9/18/71	54	5		27 When You're Twenty-One	*Claude King*	Columbia 45441
2/5/72	57	6		28 Darlin' Raise The Shade (Let The Sun Shine In)	*Claude King/Carmol Taylor/Norro Wilson*	Columbia 45515
11/4/72	48	8		29 He Ain't Country	*Jimmy Mullins/Roy Stamps*	Columbia 45704
5/28/77	94	3		30 Cotton Dan	*Dan Tyler*	True 103

KING, Don

Born on 5/1/1954 in Freemont, Nebraska. Male singer/songwriter/guitarist.

DEBUT	PEAK	WKS	GOLD	Country Chart Hit	Songwriter	Label (& Number)
9/11/76	78	5		1 Cabin High (In The Blue Ridge Mountains)	*Lori Parker*	Con Brio 112
2/19/77	16	13		2 I've Got You (To Come Home To)	*Don King/Dave Woodward*	Con Brio 116
6/4/77	17	13		3 She's The Girl Of My Dreams	*Don King/Jeff Walker*	Con Brio 120
10/8/77	41	9		4 I Must Be Dreaming	*Don King/Dave Woodward*	Con Brio 126
1/28/78	29	9		5 Music Is My Woman	*Scott Summer*	Con Brio 129

DEBUT	PEAK	WKS	GOLD		ARTIST / Country Chart Hit	Ranking / Songwriter	Label (& Number)
					KING, Don — cont'd		
5/13/78	29	10		6	**Don't Make No Promises (You Can't Keep)**	*Don King/Dave Woodward*	Con Brio 133
8/5/78	26	11		7	**The Feelings So Right Tonight**	*Don King/Jeff Walker*	Con Brio 137
11/25/78+	28	13		8	**You Were Worth Waiting For**	*Jeanine Walker*	Con Brio 142
3/10/79	39	8		9	**Live Entertainment**	*Don King*	Con Brio 149
6/23/79	73	3		10	**I've Got Country Music In My Soul**	*Don King/Dave Woodward*	Con Brio 153
2/16/80	40	9		11	**Lonely Hotel**	*Stewart Harris/Keith Stegall*	Epic 50840
5/24/80	32	12		12	**Here Comes That Feeling Again**	*Stewart Harris/Keith Stegall*	Epic 50877
9/27/80	44	8		13	**Take This Heart**	*Dwight Batteau*	Epic 50928
5/9/81	38	11		14	**I Still Miss Someone**	*Johnny Cash/Roy Cash*	Epic 02046
9/19/81	27	12		15	**The Closer You Get**	*Mark Gray/J.P. Pennington*	Epic 02468
1/16/82	40	9		16	**Running On Love**	*Stewart Harris/Keith Stegall*	Epic 02674
10/2/82	64	6		17	**Maximum Security (To Minimum Wage)**	*Don King/Dave Woodward*	Epic 03155
3/15/86	71	6		18	**All We Had Was One Another**	*Don King/Mark Sameth*	Bench Mark 8601
10/15/88	86	2		19	**Can't Stop The Music**	*Don King/Dave Woodward*	615 1015
					KING, Donny		
					Born Joseph Mier in Crowley, Louisiana. Male singer/guitarist.		
3/1/75	20	11		1	**Mathilda**	*George Khoury/Huey Thierry*	Warner 8074
11/8/75	72	6		2	**I'm A Fool To Care**	*Ted Daffan*	Warner 8145
7/31/76	91	4		3	**Stop The World (And Let Me Off)**	*Carl Belew/W.S. Stevenson*	Warner 8229
					KING, Jill		
					Born on 4/2/1974 in Arab, Alabama. Female singer/guitarist.		
3/1/03	60	1		1	**One Mississippi**	*Jess Leary/Craig Wiseman*	Blue Diamond
1/24/04	56	1		2	**98.6° And Fallin'**	*Matraca Berg/Harlan Howard*	Blue Diamond
					above 2 from the album *Jillbilly* on Blue Diamond 1513		
					KING, Matt		
					Born on 9/28/1966 in Asheville, North Carolina. Male singer/songwriter/guitarist.		
8/23/97	54	11		1	**A Woman Like You**	*Dave Gibson/Craig Karp/Matt King*	Atlantic
11/8/97	70	4		2	**I Wrote The Book**	*Matt King/Steve McElroy*	Atlantic
2/21/98	46	15		3	**A Woman's Tears**	*Marc Christian/Jack Hargrove/Matt King*	Atlantic
					above 3 from the album *Five O'Clock Hero* on Atlantic 82981		
5/22/99	54	12		4	**From Your Knees**	*Leslie Satcher*	Atlantic
7/17/99	54	9		5	**Rub It In**	*Layng Martine Jr.*	Atlantic
					above 2 from the album *Hard Country* on Atlantic 83194		
					KING, Pee Wee	**1940s: #37 / 1950s: #29 / All-Time: #270 // HOF: 1974**	
					Born Julius Kuczynski on 2/18/1914 in Abrams, Wisconsin; raised in Milwaukee, Wisconsin. Died of a heart attack on 3/7/2000 (age 86). Male singer/songwriter/accordionist/fiddler. Led own band, the Golden West Cowboys, from 1936. Own radio and TV series on WAVE-Louisville from 1947-57.		
					OPRY: 1937		
					PEE WEE KING and his Golden West Cowboys:		
4/3/48	3^{2}	35		1	**Tennessee Waltz**	S:3 / J:4 *Pee Wee King/Redd Stewart*	RCA Victor 20-2680
					also see #5 below		
6/18/49	12	2		2	**Tennessee Tears**	S:12 *Erwin King/Ernie Lee*	RCA Victor 21-0037
					Dave Denney (vocal)		
9/10/49	3^{1}	3		3	**Tennessee Polka**	J:3 *Erwin King*	RCA Victor 21-0086
1/21/50	10	1		4	**Bonaparte's Retreat**	A:10 *Pee Wee King*	RCA Victor 48-0114
2/17/51	6	4		5	**Tennessee Waltz**	A:6 / J:7 *Pee Wee King/Redd Stewart* [R]	RCA Victor 48-0407
					same version as #1 above		
9/15/51	❶^{15}	31	●	6	**Slow Poke**	J:❶^{15} / S:❶^{14} / A:❶^{9} *Pee Wee King/Chilton Price/Redd Stewart*	RCA Victor 48-0489
					PEE WEE KING and his Band featuring Redd Stewart:		
2/16/52	5	14		7	**Silver And Gold**	S:5 / J:5 / A:7 *Bob Crosby/Henry Prichard/Del Sharbutt*	RCA Victor 47-4458
5/17/52	8	3		8	**Busybody**	J:8 / A:9 *Roy Brodsky/Sid Tepper*	RCA Victor 47-4655
1/2/54	4	10		9	**Changing Partners /**	A:4 *Larry Coleman/Joe Darion*	
1/23/54	9	2		10	**Bimbo**	J:9 / S:10 / A:10 *Rod Morris*	RCA Victor 5537
7/10/54	15	1		11	**Backward, Turn Backward**	A:15 *Dave Coleman*	RCA Victor 5694
					Redd Stewart (vocal, all of above - except #2)		
					KING, Sherri		
					Born on 9/4/1953 in Knoxville, Tennessee. Female singer.		
10/2/76	95	2			**Almost Persuaded**	*Billy Sherrill/Glenn Sutton*	United Artists 855
					KING COLE TRIO — see COLE, Nat "King"		
					KING EDWARD IV AND THE KNIGHTS		
					Born Edward Smith on 7/13/1931 in Cincinnati, Ohio. Died on 3/24/1981 (age 49). Male guitarist/songwriter. The Knights featured male singer Cary Len and female singer Gigi.		
9/3/77	90	5		1	**Greenback Shuffle**	*Edward Smith*	Soundwaves 4550
3/11/78	87	5		2	**Wipe You From My Eyes (Gettin' Over You)**	*Cary Lynn Rutledge*	Soundwaves 4563
7/22/78	68	8		3	**Baby Blue**	*Johannes Bouwens*	Soundwaves 4573
5/26/79	89	3		4	**A Couple More Years**	*Dennis Locorriere/Shel Silverstein*	Soundwaves 4583
4/26/80	91	2		5	**A Song For Noel**	*Edward Smith*	Soundwaves 4597
1/31/81	48	9		6	**Dixie Road**	*Don Goodman/Mary Ann Kennedy/Pam Rose*	Soundwaves 4626
5/30/81	49	8		7	**Keep On Movin'**	*Cary Lynn Rutledge/Edward Smith*	Soundwaves 4635

DEBUT	PEAK	WKS	GOLD	ARTIST / Country Chart Hit	Ranking / Songwriter	Label (& Number)
				KING SISTERS, The		
				Family vocal group from Salt Lake City, Utah: sisters Alyce, Yvonne, Donna and Louise Driggs. Group hosted own TV series. Louise married orchestra leader Alvino Rey. Alyce died on 8/21/1996 (age 80). Louise died on 8/4/1997 (age 83).		
12/28/46	**5**	1		**Divorce Me C.O.D.**	*Cliffie Stone/Merle Travis*	Victor 20-2018
				Buddy Cole (orch.)		
				KINGSTON, Larry		
				Born on 8/10/1941 in Lafayette, Indiana. Died on 2/20/2005 (age 63). Male singer/songwriter.		
4/6/74	**61**	10		1 **Good Morning Loving**	*Larry Kingston*	JMI 37
12/13/75	**91**	4		2 **Good Morning Lovin'**	*Larry Kingston* [R]	Warner 8139
				above 2 are the same version		
				KINLEYS, The		
				Vocal duo of identical twin sisters Heather Kinley and Jennifer Kinley (born on 11/5/1970 in Philadelphia, Pennsylvania).		
8/2/97	**7**	22		1 **Please**	S:4 *Tony Haselden*	Epic
12/20/97+	**12**	20		2 **Just Between You And Me**	S:20 *Heather Kinley/Jennifer Kinley/Debbie Zavitson/Russell Zavitson*	Epic
5/2/98	**49**	10		3 **Dance In The Boat**	*Craig Bickhardt/Tony Haselden*	Epic
7/11/98	**48**	13		4 **You Make It Seem So Easy**	*Heather Kinley/Jennifer Kinley/Jon McElroy*	Epic
				above 4 from the album *Just Between You And Me* on Epic 67965		
10/24/98+	**19**	22		5 **Somebody's Out There Watching**	S:4 *Steve Booker/Franne Golde/Robin Lerner*	Epic
				from the TV series *Touched By An Angel* starring Roma Downey (soundtrack on Epic 68971)		
8/7/99	**63**	2		6 **My Heart Is Still Beating**	*Bobby Braddock*	Epic
4/1/00	**34**	21		7 **She Ain't The Girl For You**	S:9 *Jon McElroy/Vince Melamed*	Epic
10/28/00+	**35**	22		8 **I'm In**	S:9 *Radney Foster/Georgia Middleman*	Epic
				above 3 from the album *II* on Epic 69593		
				KIRBY, Dave		
				Born on 7/10/1938 in Brady, Texas. Died of cancer on 4/17/2004 (age 65). Singer/songwriter. Married **Leona Williams** in 1985.		
11/8/69	**67**	4		1 **Her And The Car And The Mobile Home**	*Dave Kirby/Don Stock*	Monument 1168
5/16/81	**37**	11		2 **North Alabama**	*Joe Allen/Dave Kirby*	Dimension 1019
9/12/81	**64**	5		3 **Moccasin Man**	*Joe Allen/Dave Kirby*	Dimension 1022
				KIRK, Eddie		
				Born on 3/21/1919 in Greeley, Colorado. Died on 6/27/1997 (age 78). Male singer/songwriter. National Yodeling Champion in 1935 and 1936. On the **Gene Autry** radio shows and *Town Hall Party* in Compton, California during the late 1940s. Appeared in several western movies.		
10/2/48	**9**	6		1 **The Gods Were Angry With Me**	J:9 / S:10 *Bill Mackintosh/Roma Mackintosh*	Capitol 15176
				Tex Ritter (recitation)		
3/12/49	**9**	3		2 **Candy Kisses**	S:9 / J:10 *George Morgan*	Capitol 15391
				KIRK, Red		
				Born on 5/24/1925 in Knoxville, Tennessee. Died on 5/13/1999 (age 73). Worked on WNOX-Knoxville and WIMA-Lima, Ohio. Known as "The Voice Of The Country."		
6/25/49	**14**	1		1 **Lovesick Blues**	J:14 *(traditional)*	Mercury 6189
7/22/50	**7**	7		2 **Lose Your Blues**	A:7 *Hal Miller*	Mercury 6257
				Jerry Byrd (lead vocal)		
				KNIGHT, Evelyn		
				Born in 1920 in Reedsville, Virginia. Femlae singer. Known as "The Lass With The Delicate Air."		
2/17/51	**6**	1		**My Heart Cries For You** *[w/ Red Foley]*	A:6 *Percy Faith/Carl Sigman*	Decca 9-27378
				KNOBLOCK, Fred		
				Born J. Fred Knobloch on 4/28/1953 in Jackson, Mississippi. Male singer/songwriter. Member of **Schuyler, Knobloch & Overstreet**.		
8/2/80	**30**	11		1 **Why Not Me**	*Fred Knoblock/Carson Whitsett*	Scotti Brothers 518
10/18/80	**53**	6		2 **Let Me Love You**	*Fred Knoblock*	Scotti Brothers 607
11/29/80+	**10**	18		3 **Killin' Time** *[w/ Susan Anton]*	*Jeff Harrington/Jeff Pennig*	Scotti Brothers 609
8/22/81	**10**	14		4 **Memphis**	*Chuck Berry*	Scotti Brothers 02434
3/20/82	**33**	10		5 **I Had It All**	*Steve Allen/Fred Knoblock/Terry Moretti*	Scotti Brothers 02752
				KNOX, Buddy		
				Born on 7/20/1933 in Happy, Texas. Died of cancer on 2/14/1999 (age 65). Male singer/guitarist.		
6/22/68	**64**	6		**Gypsy Man**	*Sonny Curtis*	United Artists 50301
				KOLANDER, Steve		
				Born on 11/15/1961 in Lake Charles, Louisiana; raised in Austin, Texas. Male singer/songwriter/guitarist.		
11/26/94	**63**	5		1 **Listen To Your Woman**	*Steve Kolander/Ed Tree*	River North
3/11/95	**70**	5		2 **Black Dresses**	*Steve Kolander*	River North
				above 2 from the album *Steve Kolander* on River North 61098		
				KRAMER, Rex		
				Born in Smackover, Arkansas; raised in Baytown, Texas. Had own surf-rock band, The Coastliners, in the mid-1960s. Played banjo with The New Christy Minstrels in the late 1960s.		
3/6/76	**100**	2		**You Oughta Be Against The Law**	*Rex Kramer*	Columbia 10286

DEBUT	PEAK	WKS	GOLD	ARTIST / Country Chart Hit	Ranking / Songwriter	Label (& Number)

KRAUSS, Alison, & Union Station

Born on 7/23/1971 in Champaign, Illinois. Female singer/songwriter/bluegrass fiddler. Union Station is her backing band: Dan Tyminski (guitar; lead voice of **The Soggy Bottom Boys**), Ron Block (banjo), Adam Steffey (mandolin) and Barry Bales (bass). Also see **The Red Hots** and **Same Old Train**.

CMA: Horizon 1995 / Female Vocalist 1995 // OPRY: 1993

DEBUT	PEAK	WKS	GOLD	Country Chart Hit	Songwriter	Label (& Number)
9/21/91	73	1		1 **Steel Rails** from the album *I've Got That Old Feeling* on Rounder 0275	*Louisa Branscomb*	Rounder
12/3/94+	7	20		2 **Somewhere In The Vicinity Of The Heart** ***[w/ Shenandoah]*** **Grammy: Vocal Collaboration / CMA: Vocal Event**; from the album *In The Vicinity Of The Heart* on Liberty 31109	*Rick Chudacoff/Bill LaBounty*	Liberty
2/25/95	3^{1}	20		3 **When You Say Nothing At All** **CMA: Single**; from the various artists album ***Keith Whitley*** *: A Tribute Album* on BNA 66416	S:2 *Paul Overstreet/Don Schlitz*	BNA
7/15/95	49	13		4 **Baby, Now That I've Found You** **Grammy: Female Vocal**; above 2 from the album *Now That I've Found You: A Collection* on Rounder 0325	S:15 *Tony MacAulay/John MacLeod*	Rounder
4/13/96	12	20		5 **High Lonesome Sound** ***[w/ Vince Gill]*** **Grammy: Vocal Collaboration**; from Gill's album *High Lonesome Sound* on MCA 11422	*Vince Gill*	MCA
5/24/97	73	2		6 **Find My Way Back To My Heart** from the album *So Long So Wrong* on Rounder 0365	*Alison Krauss/Mark Simos*	Rounder
12/13/97+	34	13		7 **It's Not Over** ***[w/ Mark Chesnutt & Vince Gill]*** from Chesnutt's album *Thank God For Believers* on Decca 70006	*Larry Kingston/Mark Wright*	Decca
7/17/99	67	4		8 **Forget About It** from the album *Forget About It* on Rounder 0465	*Robert Castleman*	Rounder
10/30/99+	❶^{1}	37		9 **Buy Me A Rose** ***[w/ Kenny Rogers & Billy Dean]*** from Rogers' album *She Rides Wild Horses* on DreamCatcher 004	*Jim Funk/Erik Hickenlooper*	Dreamcatcher
10/20/01+	46	16		10 **The Lucky One** **Grammy: Song & Vocal Group**; from the album *New Favorite* on Rounder 610495	*Robert Castleman*	Rounder
12/13/03	57	2		11 **Coat Of Many Colors** ***[w/ Shania Twain]*** from the various artists album *Just Because I'm A Woman: Songs Of* ***Dolly Parton*** on Sugar Hill 3980	*Dolly Parton*	Sugar Hill
4/10/04	3^{3}	24		12 **Whiskey Lullaby** ***[w/ Brad Paisley]*** **CMA: Musical Event**; from Paisley's album *Mud On The Tires* on Arista Nashville 50605	*Bill Anderson/Jon Randall*	Arista Nashville
11/20/04+	36	20		13 **Restless** from the album *Lonely Runs Both Ways* on Rounder 610525	S:❶^{2} *Robert Castleman*	Rounder
1/8/05	58	1		14 **Shimmy Down The Chimney** from the various artists album *Shimmy Down The Chimney: A Country Christmas* on Capitol 71143	*Alison Krauss/Victor Krauss* **[X]**	Capitol

KRISTOFFERSON, Kris — HOF: 2004

Born on 6/22/1936 in Brownsville, Texas. Male singer/songwriter/guitarist. Attended England's Oxford University on a Rhodes scholarship. Married to **Rita Coolidge** from 1973-80. Wrote numerous hit songs. Starred in many movies.

DEBUT	PEAK	WKS	GOLD	Country Chart Hit	Songwriter	Label (& Number)
4/22/72	70	2		1 **Josie**	*Kris Kristofferson*	Monument 8536
4/7/73	❶^{1}	20	●	2 **Why Me** **Rita Coolidge** and **Larry Gatlin** (backing vocals)	*Kris Kristofferson*	Monument 8571
12/22/73+	92	5		3 **A Song I'd Like To Sing** ***[w/ Rita Coolidge]***	*Kris Kristofferson*	A&M 1475
3/23/74	98	2		4 **Loving Arms** ***[w/ Rita Coolidge]***	*Tom Jans*	A&M 1498
12/28/74+	87	4		5 **Rain** ***[w/ Rita Coolidge]***	*Larry Gatlin*	Monument 8630
1/5/80	91	5		6 **Prove It To You One More Time Again**	*Kris Kristofferson*	Columbia 11160
4/18/81	68	7		7 **Nobody Loves Anybody Anymore**	*Kris Kristofferson/Billy Swan*	Columbia 60507
11/3/84	46	11		8 **How Do You Feel About Foolin' Around** ***[w/ Willie Nelson]***	...*Steve Bruton/Kris Kristofferson/Michael Utley*	Columbia 04652
5/18/85	❶^{1}	20		9 **Highwayman** ***[w/ Waylon Jennings/Willie Nelson/Johnny Cash]*** **Grammy: Song**	S:❶^{1} / A:❶^{1} *Jimmy Webb*	Columbia 04881
9/14/85	15	18		10 **Desperados Waiting For A Train** ***[w/ Waylon Jennings/Willie Nelson/Johnny Cash]***	...S:15 / A:16 *Guy Clark*	Columbia 05594
2/28/87	67	6		11 **They Killed Him**	*Kris Kristofferson*	Mercury 888345
3/3/90	25	14		12 **Silver Stallion** ***[w/ Waylon Jennings/Willie Nelson/Johnny Cash]*** from their album *Highwayman 2* on Columbia 45240	*Lee Clayton*	Columbia

KUNKEL, Leah

Born Leah Cohen in 1948 in Baltimore, Maryland. Female singer/songwriter. Sister of Mama Cass Elliott. Formerly married to session drummer Russ Kunkel.

DEBUT	PEAK	WKS	GOLD	Country Chart Hit	Songwriter	Label (& Number)
10/22/88	94	2		**Loving Arms** ***[w/ Livingston Taylor]***	*Tom Jans*	Critique 99275

L

LaBEEF, Sleepy

Born Thomas LaBeff on 7/20/1935 in Smackover, Arkansas. Male singer/guitarist.

DEBUT	PEAK	WKS	GOLD	Country Chart Hit	Songwriter	Label (& Number)
4/13/68	73	3		1 **Every Day**	*Elizabeth Russell*	Columbia 44455
6/19/71	67	5		2 **Blackland Farmer**	*Frankie Miller*	Plantation 74

LACE

Female vocal trio from Canada: Beverly Mahood, Corbi Dyann and Giselle Brohman.

DEBUT	PEAK	WKS	GOLD	Country Chart Hit	Songwriter	Label (& Number)
8/28/99	65	3		1 **I Want A Man**	S:19 *Rick Giles/Gilles Godard/Tim Nichols*	143/Warner
2/19/00	71	1		2 **You Could've Had Me** above 2 from the album *Lace* on 143/Warner 47449	*Stephanie Bentley/Eric Silver*	143/Warner

LACE, Bobbi

Born Laura Smith in Florida. Female singer/actress.

DEBUT	PEAK	WKS	GOLD	Country Chart Hit	Songwriter	Label (& Number)
3/29/86	94	2		1 **You've Been My Rock For Ages**	*Mark Miller*	GBS 730
6/13/87	79	4		2 **Skin Deep**	*Brian Nash*	615 1008

Billboard DEBUT	PEAK	WKS	GOLD	ARTIST / Ranking / Country Chart Hit	Songwriter	Label (& Number)
				LACE, Bobbi — cont'd		
12/19/87	**88**	3		3 **There's A Real Woman In Me**	*Melissa Javors*	615 1010
3/5/88	**89**	2		4 **Another Woman's Man**	*Michelle Hunt/Gayle Matthis/Kerry Tolley*	615 1011
5/28/88	**69**	5		5 **Song In My Heart** *[w/ Mark Gray]*	*Benny Berry*	615 1014
8/20/88	**77**	3		6 **If Hearts Could Talk**	*Berni Nash/Anthony Smith*	615 1012
12/17/88+	**70**	5		7 **It's Gonna Be Love** *[w/ Mark Gray]*	*Benny Berry*	615 1016
6/24/89	**95**	2		8 **Son Of A Preacher Man**	*John Hurley/Ronnie Wilkins*	615 1017
				LA COSTA		
				Born LaCosta Tucker on 4/6/1951 in Seminole, Texas. Female singer. Sister of **Tanya Tucker**.		
4/20/74	**25**	15		1 **I Wanta Get To You**	*George Richey/Carmol Taylor/Norro Wilson*	Capitol 3856
9/14/74	**3^{2}**	17		2 **Get On My Love Train**	*Carmol Taylor/Norro Wilson*	Capitol 3945
2/15/75	**10**	13		3 **He Took Me For A Ride**	*Shirley Tackett/Carmol Taylor/Norro Wilson*	Capitol 4022
6/7/75	**19**	12		4 **This House Runs On Sunshine**	*Brian Bennett/Mike Redway*	Capitol 4082
9/27/75	**11**	14		5 **Western Man**	*Doug Owen*	Capitol 4139
1/31/76	**28**	9		6 **I Just Got A Feeling**	*Steve Davis/Sammy Lyons*	Capitol 4209
5/15/76	**23**	12		7 **Lovin' Somebody On A Rainy Night**	*Dave Loggins*	Capitol 4264
9/11/76	**37**	10		8 **What'll I Do**	*Helen Cornelius/Jerry Crutchfield*	Capitol 4327
5/7/77	**75**	7		9 **We're All Alone**	*Boz Scaggs*	Capitol 4414
11/26/77	**100**	1		10 **Jessie And The Light**	*Buzz Cason/Bobby Russell*	Capitol 4495
2/25/78	**79**	7		11 **Even Cowgirls Get The Blues**	*Sonny Curtis*	Capitol 4541
6/3/78	**94**	3		12 **#1 With A Heartache**	*Howard Greenfield/Neil Sedaka*	Capitol 4577
5/17/80	**68**	6		13 **Changing All The Time**	*Mike Chapman/Nicky Chinn*	Capitol 4830
2/27/82	**48**	9		14 **Love Take It Easy On Me** *[LaCosta Tucker]*	*Dennis Linde/Alan Rush*	Elektra 47414
				LaFLEUR, Don		
				Born in California. Male singer/songwriter.		
10/8/88	**97**	2		**Beggars Can't Be Choosers**	*Chris Hillman/Don LaFleur/T.J. Worth*	Worth 102
				LAMAR, Holly		
				Born in Atlanta, Georgia; raised in Cairo, Georgia. Female singer/songwriter.		
9/7/02	**51**	7		1 **These Are The Days**	*Stephanie Bentley/Holly Lamar*	Universal South
2/22/03	**59**	1		2 **Unkissed**	*Barry Alfonso/Holly Lamar*	Universal South
				above 2 from the album *Unkissed* on Universal South 170293		
				LaMASTER, Don		
				Born in Dallas, Texas. Male singer.		
3/11/89	**94**	1		**My Rose Is Blue**	*John Capps*	K-Ark 1046
				LAMBERT, Miranda		
				Born on 11/10/1983 in Lindale, Texas. Female singer/songwriter/guitarist.		
10/23/04+	**27**	23		1 **Me And Charlie Talking**	*Miranda Lambert/Rick Lambert/Heather Little*	Epic
4/16/05	**32**	20		2 **Bring Me Down**	*Travis Howard/Miranda Lambert*	Epic
				above 2 from the album *Kerosene* on Epic 92026		
				LANA RAE — see RAE		
				LANCE, Lynda K.		
				Born in 1949 in Smithfield, Pennsylvania. Female singer.		
11/1/69	**59**	5		1 **A Woman's Side Of Love**	*Dick Heard/Eddie Rabbitt*	Royal American 290
1/30/71	**46**	6		2 **My Guy**	*Smokey Robinson*	Royal American 24
8/21/71	**74**	2		3 **Will You Love Me Tomorrow**	*Gerry Goffin/Carole King*	Royal American 35
8/11/73	**77**	5		4 **You, You, You**	*Robert Mellin/Lotar Olias*	Triune 7207
10/23/76	**93**	5		5 **Say You Love Me**	*Christine McVie*	Gar-Pax 081
1/13/79	**78**	4		6 **I Hate The Way Our Love Is** *[w/ Jimmy Peters]*	*Ava Aldridge*	Vista 101
4/28/79	**98**	3		7 **First Class Fool** *[w/ Jimmie Peters]*	*Billy Larkin/Richard Larkin*	Vista 106
				LANDERS, Dave		
				Born in St. Louis, Missouri. Male singer/guitarist. Uncle of **Rich Landers**.		
7/9/49	**10**	7		**Before You Call**	S:10 / J:12 *Fred Rose*	MGM 10427
				LANDERS, Rich		
				Born in St. Louis, Missouri. Male singer/songwriter/guitarist. Nephew of **Dave Landers**.		
3/28/81	**41**	10		1 **Friday Night Feelin'**	*Rich Landers*	Ovation 1166
7/11/81	**40**	9		2 **Hold On**	*Rich Landers*	Ovation 1173
12/19/81+	**52**	9		3 **Lay Back Down And Love Me**	*Jimmie Young*	AMI 1301
6/12/82	**74**	5		4 **Pull My String**	*Rich Landers*	AMI 1305
1/29/83	**40**	10		5 **Take It All**	*Rich Landers*	AMI 1311
9/10/83	**68**	5		6 **Every Breath You Take**	*Sting*	AMI 1316
				LANE, Cristy — **All-Time: #254**		
				Born Eleanor Johnston on 1/8/1940 in Peoria, Illinois. Female singer/songwriter. Married Lee Stoller in 1960. Stoller started the LS record label in 1976.		
2/12/77	**52**	10		1 **Tryin' To Forget About You**	*Boudleaux Bryant*	LS 110
6/4/77	**53**	7		2 **Sweet Deceiver**	*Boudleaux Bryant/Felice Bryant*	LS 121
8/20/77	**7**	16		3 **Let Me Down Easy**	*Lobo*	LS 131
12/17/77+	**16**	13		4 **Shake Me I Rattle**	*Hal Hackady/Charles Naylor*	LS 148
4/1/78	**10**	14		5 **I'm Gonna Love You Anyway**	*Layng Martine Jr.*	LS 156
7/22/78	**7**	14		6 **Penny Arcade**	*Boudleaux Bryant/Felice Bryant*	LS 167

DEBUT	PEAK	WKS	GOLD	ARTIST / Country Chart Hit	Songwriter	Label (& Number)
				LANE, Cristy — cont'd		
12/2/78+	**5**	16		7 **I Just Can't Stay Married To You**	*Charlie Black/Rory Bourke/Jerry Gillespie*	LS 169
5/5/79	**10**	14		8 **Simple Little Words**	*Doug Johnson*	United Artists 1304
8/25/79	**17**	11		9 **Slippin' Up, Slippin' Around**	*Terry Woodford/Barbara Wyrick*	United Artists 1314
12/15/79+	**16**	13		10 **Come To My Love**	*Sam Lorber/Jeff Silbar*	United Artists 1328
3/29/80	❶[1]	18		11 **One Day At A Time**	*Kris Kristofferson/Marijohn Wilkin*	United Artists 1342
8/16/80	**8**	14		12 **Sweet Sexy Eyes**	*Bob Jenkins*	United Artists 1369
1/17/81	**17**	14		13 **I Have A Dream**	*Benny Andersson/Bjorn Ulvaeus*	Liberty 1396
5/2/81	**21**	13		14 **Love To Love You**	*David Heavener*	Liberty 1406
10/10/81	**38**	10		15 **Cheatin' Is Still On My Mind**	*Bob Jenkins*	Liberty 1432
1/9/82	**22**	14		16 **Lies On Your Lips**	*Jim Dowell/Larry Shell*	Liberty 1443
5/8/82	**52**	8		17 **Fragile--Handle With Care**	*Don Huber/Rick Kelley*	Liberty 1461
11/13/82	**81**	3		18 **The Good Old Days**	*Linda Lance/Ron Oates*	Liberty 1483
7/23/83	**63**	7		19 **I've Come Back (To Say I Love You One More Time)**	*Chuck Howard*	Liberty 1501
10/29/83	**80**	4		20 **Footprints In The Sand**	*Diana Willis* [S]	Liberty 1508
5/9/87	**88**	2		21 **I Wanna Wake Up With You /**	*Ben Peters*	
5/9/87	**flip**	2		22 **He's Got The Whole World In His Hands**	*(traditional)*	LS 1987
				LANE, Jerry "Max" Born on 2/19/1943 in Fort Worth, Texas. Male singer/songwriter/guitarist.		
7/1/67	**49**	6		1 **Keeping Up Appearances** *[w/ Lynn Anderson]*	*Liz Anderson*	Chart 1425
11/16/74	**63**	8		2 **Right Out Of This World**	*Eddie Rabbitt/Even Stevens*	ABC 12031
6/14/75	**81**	5		3 **I've Got A Lotta Missin' You To Do**	*Jerry "Max" Lane*	ABC 12091
4/23/83	**87**	2		4 **When The Music Stops**	*Jerry "Max" Lane*	Stockyard 1000
12/17/83	**96**	3		5 **I've Got A Lot Of Missin' You To Do** new version of #3 above	*Jerry "Max" Lane* [R]	Stockyard 1003
				LANE, Red — **SW: #60** Born Hollis DeLaughter on 2/9/1939 in Bogalusa, Louisiana. Male singer/songwriter/guitarist.		
4/24/71	**32**	11		1 **The World Needs A Melody**	*Larry Henley/Red Lane/Johnny Slate*	RCA Victor 9970
10/30/71	**68**	2		2 **Set The World On Fire (With Love)**	*Larry Henley/Red Lane/Johnny Slate*	RCA Victor 0534
1/22/72	**66**	5		3 **Throw A Rope Around The Wind** from the movie *Going Home* starring **Robert Mitchum**	*Larry Henley/Red Lane*	RCA Victor 0616
7/8/72	**65**	3		4 **It Was Love While It Lasted**	*Red Lane*	RCA Victor 0721
				LANE, Terri Born in Joelton, Tennessee. Female singer.		
3/24/73	**37**	11		1 **Daisy May (And Daisy May Not)**	*Bill Goodwin/Teri Lynn*	Monument 8565
10/20/73	**98**	2		2 **Be Certain**	*Bobby Barker/Johnny Koonse*	Monument 8582
5/25/74	**94**	3		3 **Mockingbird** *[w/ Jimmy Nall]*	*Charlie Foxx/Inez Foxx*	Monument 8610
				LANE, Trinity — see TRINITY		
				LANE BROTHERS, The Pop vocal trio from Brooklyn, New York: brothers Pete Loconto, Frank Loconto and Art Loconto.		
3/28/81	**83**	4		**Marianne** new version of their #64 Pop hit from 1957	*Richard Dehr/Terry Gilkyson/Frank Miller*	FXL 0026
				lang, k.d. Born Kathryn Dawn Lang on 11/2/1961 in Consort, Alberta, Canada. Eclectic female singer.		
12/5/87+	**42**	13		1 **Crying** *[w/ Roy Orbison]* **Grammy: Vocal Collaboration**; from the movie *Hiding Out* starring Jon Cryer	*Joe Melson/Roy Orbison*	Virgin 99388
5/14/88	**21**	17		2 **I'm Down To My Last Cigarette**	S:16 *Harlan Howard/Billy Walker*	Sire 27919
9/17/88	**53**	8		3 **Lock, Stock And Teardrops**	*Roger Miller*	Sire 27813
7/1/89	**22**	16		4 **Full Moon Full Of Love** *[w/ the reclines]*	*Leroy Preston/Jeannie Smith*	Sire 22932
11/11/89	**55**	5		5 **Three Days** *[w/ the reclines]*	*Willie Nelson*	Sire 22734
				LANG, Kelly Born on 1/10/1967 in Oklahoma City, Oklahoma; raised in Hendersonville, Tennessee. Female singer.		
9/25/82	**88**	2		**Lady, Lady**	*Stewart Harris*	Soundwaves 4681
				LANSDOWNE, Jerry Born in California. Male singer/songwriter.		
4/29/89	**98**	2		**She Had Every Right To Do You Wrong**	*Jerry Lansdowne/Tony Marty*	Step One 400
				LaPOINTE, Perry Born in Orange, Texas. Male singer/guitarist.		
6/21/86	**64**	5		1 **New Shade Of Blue**	*Johnette Burton/Fred Horton*	Door Knob 249
10/18/86	**92**	2		2 **You're A Better Man Than I**	*Johnette Burton/Fred Horton*	Door Knob 252
12/27/86+	**73**	5		3 **Chosen**	*Randy Boone/Larry Schmid*	Door Knob 260
4/11/87	**73**	4		4 **Walk On By**	*Kendall Hayes*	Door Knob 270
8/1/87	**72**	4		5 **The Power Of A Woman**	*Lorna Bright/Danny Thompson*	Door Knob 281
9/17/88	**76**	4		6 **Clean Livin' Folk** *[w/ Bobby G. Rice]*	*Julia Farkas*	Door Knob 307
3/25/89	**68**	4		7 **Open For Suggestions**	*Wyndi Harp*	Door Knob 303
10/14/89	**79**	3		8 **Sweet Memories Of You**	*Larry Heath*	Door Knob 333
				LARGE, Billy Born in Oklahoma. Male singer.		
10/15/66	**62**	6		**The Goodie Wagon**	*Bud Logan/Charles Snoddy*	Columbia 43741

DEBUT	PEAK	WKS	GOLD	ARTIST / Country Chart Hit	Ranking / Songwriter	Label (& Number)
				LARKIN, Billy		
				Born on 1/27/1950 in Huntland, Tennessee. Male singer/guitarist.		
1/11/75	**22**	13		1 **Leave It Up To Me**	*Earl Thomas Conley*	Bryan 1010
5/3/75	**23**	12		2 **The Devil In Mrs. Jones**	*Earl Thomas Conley/Mary Larkin*	Bryan 1018
9/6/75	**34**	10		3 **Indian Giver**	*Earl Thomas Conley*	Bryan 1026
6/5/76	**66**	7		4 **#1 With A Heartache**	*Howard Greenfield/Neil Sedaka*	Casino 053
8/28/76	**36**	9		5 **Kiss And Say Goodbye**	*Winfred Lovett*	Casino 076
12/18/76+	**88**	4		6 **Here's To The Next Time**	*John Carter/Geoff Stephens*	Casino 097
10/7/78	**67**	4		7 **My Side Of Town**	*Debbie Hupp/Bob Morrison*	Mercury 55040
4/19/80	**72**	4		8 **I Can't Stop Now**	*James Coleman/Moe Lytle*	Sunbird 107
1/10/81	**35**	13		9 **20/20 Hindsight**	*Wade Conklin/Tom Gmeiner/John Greenebaum*	Sunbird 7557
5/30/81	**24**	13		10 **Longing For The High**	*O.B. McClinton/Steve McCovey*	Sunbird 7562
				LARRATT, Iris		
				Born in Lloydminster, Saskatchewan, Canada; raised in Prince George, British Columbia, Canada. Female singer.		
7/21/79	**100**	1		**You Can't Make Love To A Memory**	*Ron Jankowski*	Infinity 50,015
				LARSEN, Blaine		
				Born in 1986 in Buckley, Washington. Male singer/songwriter/guitarist.		
6/5/04	**60**	1		1 **In My High School**	*Tim Johnson/Blaine Larsen*	BNA
11/13/04+	**18**	24		2 **How Do You Get That Lonely**	*Rory Lee Feek/Jamie Teachenor*	BNA
5/28/05	**36**	18↑		3 **The Best Man**	*Rory Lee Feek/Tim Johnson/Blaine Larsen*	BNA
				above 3 from the album *Off To Join The World* on BNA 66012		
				LARSON, Nicolette		
				Born on 7/17/1952 in Helena, Montana; raised in Kansas City, Missouri. Died of a cerebral edema on on 12/16/1997 (age 45). Female singer/songwriter/guitarist.		
2/9/85	**42**	12		1 **Only Love Will Make It Right**	*Bob McDill*	MCA 52528
5/4/85	**46**	11		2 **When You Get A Little Lonely**	*Nicolette Larson/Josh Leo/Wendy Waldman*	MCA 52571
9/21/85	**72**	8		3 **Building Bridges**	*Hank DeVito/Larry Willoughby*	MCA 52653
3/22/86	**63**	5		4 **Let Me Be The First**	*Deborah Allen/Kix Brooks/Rafe Van Hoy*	MCA 52797
6/7/86	**9**	23		5 **That's How You Know When Love's Right** ***[w/ Steve Wariner]***	...A:9 / S:11 *Craig Bickhardt/Wendy Waldman*	MCA 52839
10/11/86	**49**	8		6 **That's More About Love (Than I Wanted To Know)**	*Bucky Jones/Dickey Lee/Bob McDill*	MCA 52937
				LATHAM, Buddy		
				Born in Cookville, Tennessee. Male singer/drummer.		
9/3/88	**97**	2		**(She Likes) Warm Summer Days**	*Richard Burt/Patricia Hommel*	Prairie Dust 8853
				LAUDERDALE, Jim		
				Born on 4/11/1957 in Troutman, North Carolina. Male singer/songwriter.		
12/17/88	**86**	3		**Stay Out Of My Arms**	*Jim Lauderdale*	Epic 08113
				**LAWRENCE, Tracy**	**1990s: #18 / 2000s: #44 / All-Time: #102**	
				Born on 1/27/1968 in Atlanta, Texas; raised in Foreman, Arkansas. Male singer/songwriter/guitarist. Wounded in a 1991 shooting incident in Nashville (fully recovered). Also see **Hope**.		
11/9/91+	**❶[1]**	20		1 **Sticks And Stones**	*Roger Dillon/Elbert West*	Atlantic
2/8/92	**3[2]**	20		2 **Today's Lonely Fool**	*Kenny Beard/Stan Davis*	Atlantic
6/20/92	**4**	20		3 **Runnin' Behind**	*Ed Hill/Mark D. Sanders*	Atlantic
10/10/92+	**8**	20		4 **Somebody Paints The Wall**	*Charles Browder/Elroy Kahanek/Nelson Larkin/Tommy Smith*	Atlantic
				above 4 from the album *Sticks And Stones* on Atlantic 82326		
2/20/93	**❶[2]**	20		5 **Alibis**	*Randy Boudreaux*	Atlantic
6/5/93	**❶[1]**	20		6 **Can't Break It To My Heart**	*Earl Clark/Tracy Lawrence/Kirk Roth/Elbert West*	Atlantic
9/4/93	**❶[1]**	20		7 **My Second Home**	*Kenny Beard/Tracy Lawrence/Paul Nelson*	Atlantic
2/5/94	**❶[2]**	20		8 **If The Good Die Young**	*Paul Nelson/Craig Wiseman*	Atlantic
				above 4 from the album *Alibis* on Atlantic 82483		
5/28/94	**7**	20		9 **Renegades, Rebels And Rogues**	*Larry Boone/Earl Clark/Paul Nelson*	Atlantic
				from the movie *Maverick* starring Mel Gibson and Jodie Foster (soundtrack on Atlantic 82595)		
9/10/94	**2[1]**	20		10 **I See It Now**	*Larry Boone/Woody Lee/Paul Nelson*	Atlantic
12/31/94+	**2[2]**	20		11 **As Any Fool Can See**	*Kenny Beard/Paul Nelson*	Atlantic
4/15/95	**❶[1]**	20		12 **Texas Tornado**	S:25 *Bobby Braddock*	Atlantic
7/29/95	**2[1]**	20		13 **If The World Had A Front Porch**	*Kenny Beard/Tracy Lawrence/Paul Nelson*	Atlantic
				above 4 from the album *I See It Now* on Atlantic 82656		
12/16/95+	**4**	20		14 **If You Loved Me**	*Paul Nelson/Tom Shapiro*	Atlantic
3/23/96	**❶[3]**	20		15 **Time Marches On**	*Bobby Braddock*	Atlantic
7/27/96	**2[1]**	20		16 **Stars Over Texas**	S:13 *Larry Boone/Tracy Lawrence/Paul Nelson*	Atlantic
11/2/96+	**2[2]**	20		17 **Is That A Tear**	S:7 *Kenny Beard/John Jarrard*	Atlantic
				above 4 from the album *Time Marches On* on Atlantic 82866		
2/22/97	**2[1]**	20		18 **Better Man, Better Off**	S:4 *Stan Davis/Bill Jones*	Atlantic
5/31/97	**4**	20		19 **How A Cowgirl Says Goodbye**	*Larry Boone/Tracy Lawrence/Paul Nelson*	Atlantic
9/20/97	**26**	13		20 **The Coast Is Clear**	*Jim Brown/Bill Jones*	Atlantic

DEBUT	PEAK	WKS	GOLD	ARTIST / Country Chart Hit	Ranking / Songwriter	Label (& Number)
				LAWRENCE, Tracy — cont'd		
7/25/98	**46**	8		21 **While You Sleep**	*Larry Boone/Tracy Lawrence/Paul Nelson*	Atlantic
				above 4 from the album *The Coast Is Clear* on Atlantic 82985		
11/6/99+	**3^3**	29		22 **Lessons Learned**	*Larry Boone/Tracy Lawrence/Paul Nelson*	Atlantic
2/26/00	**24^S**	1		23 **I'll Never Pass This Way Again**	*Jack Murphy/Frank Wildhorn*	Atlantic
				from the various artists album *The Civil War: The Nashville Sessions* on Atlantic 83090		
5/27/00	**18**	21		24 **Lonely**	*Robin Lee Bruce/Roxie Dean*	Atlantic
3/24/01	**35**	12		25 **Unforgiven**	*Larry Boone/Paul Nelson/Bobby Pinson*	Atlantic
				#22, 24 & 25: from the album *Lessons Learned* on Atlantic 83269		
9/1/01	**36**	15		26 **Life Don't Have To Be So Hard**	*Casey Beathard/Kenny West*	Atlantic
2/2/02	**53**	7		27 **What A Memory**	*Jeff Bates/Kenny Beard*	Atlantic
				above 2 from the album *Tracy Lawrence* on Atlantic 48187		
11/1/03+	**4**	32		28 **Paint Me A Birmingham**	*Gary Duffy/Buck Moore*	DreamWorks
6/26/04	**36**	13		29 **It's All How You Look At It**	*Dave Berg/Georgia Middleman/Rivers Rutherford*	DreamWorks
10/9/04	**46**	7		30 **Sawdust On Her Halo**	*Monty Criswell/Rick Huckaby*	DreamWorks
				above 3 from the album *Strong* on DreamWorks 001032		
				LAWRENCE, Vicki		
				Born on 5/26/1949 in Inglewood, California. Female actress/singer. Regular on Carol Burnett's CBS-TV series from 1967-78. Also starred in TV's *Mama's Family*, 1982-87. Married to songwriter/singer **Bobby Russell** from 1972-74.		
4/28/73	**36**	8	●	**The Night The Lights Went Out In Georgia**	*Bobby Russell*	Bell 45,303
				LAWSON, Janet		
				Born in Baltimore, Maryland. Female singer.		
7/25/70	**74**	2		**Two Little Rooms**	*Jim Woods*	United Artists 50671
				LAWSON, Shannon		
				Born in Taylorsville, Kentucky. Male singer/songwriter/guitarist.		
2/9/02	**28**	20		1 **Goodbye On A Bad Day**	*Shannon Lawson/Mark A. Peters*	MCA Nashville
8/10/02	**45**	7		2 **Dream Your Way To Me**	*Shannon Lawson/Tim Nichols*	MCA Nashville
				above 2 from the album *Chase The Sun* on MCA Nashville 170233		
4/10/04	**53**	7		3 **Smokin' Grass**	*Shannon Lawson/Billy Yates*	Equity
6/19/04	**48**	10		4 **Just Like A Redneck**	*Del Gray/Shannon Lawson*	Equity
				above 2 from the album *The Big Yee-Haw* on Equity 3002		
				LAY, Rodney, and The Wild West		
				Born on 2/13/1940 in Coffeyville, Kansas. Male singer/bassist. Regular on TV's *Hee Haw* from 1980-87. Musical director for **Roy Clark** from 1980-87. The Wild West consisted of Vernon Sandusky (guitar), Troy Klontz (steel guitar), Shelby Eicher and Kenny Putnam (fiddles), John French (keyboards) and Terrell Glaze (drums).		
5/30/81	**85**	4		1 **Seven Days Come Sunday** *[Rodney Lay]*	*Gil Francis/Bob House*	Sun 1164
4/24/82	**72**	5		2 **Happy Country Birthday Darling**	*Ronnie Rogers*	Churchill 94001
8/14/82	**45**	11		3 **I Wish I Had A Job To Shove**	*Ronnie Rogers*	Churchill 94005
1/8/83	**53**	8		4 **You Could've Heard A Heart Break**	*Marc Rossi*	Churchill 94012
5/14/83	**64**	5		5 **Marylee**	*Stewart Harris/Keith Stegall*	Churchill 94020
11/29/86	**79**	3		6 **Walk Softly On The Bridges** *[Rodney Lay]*	*Dallas Frazier/A.L. "Doodle" Owens*	Evergreen 1046
				LEAPY LEE		
				Born Lee Graham on 7/2/1942 in Eastbourne, England. Male singer/actor.		
10/19/68	**11**	15		1 **Little Arrows**	*Albert Hammond/Mike Hazlewood*	Decca 32380
3/21/70	**55**	4		2 **Good Morning**	*Tat Meager*	Decca 32625
11/8/75	**82**	5		3 **Every Road Leads Back To You**	*Barry Mason/Keith Potger*	MCA 40470
				LEATHERWOOD, Bill		
				Born in Canton, North Carolina. Male singer/songwriter.		
7/11/60	**11**	13		**The Long Walk**	*Bill Leatherwood*	Country Jubilee 539
				LEATHERWOOD, Patti		
				Born Patti DiAngelo on 9/1/1950 in Cleveland, Ohio. Female singer.		
12/18/76+	**79**	7		1 **It Should Have Been Easy**	*Bob McDill*	Epic 50303
7/30/77	**98**	1		2 **Feels So Much Better**	*Johnny Christopher/Layng Martine Jr.*	Epic 50409
				LeBEAU, Tim		
				Born in Lexington, South Carolina. Male singer.		
10/22/88	**98**	1		**Playing With Matches**	*Danny Walls/Bobby Warren*	Rose Hill 001
				LEBSOCK, Jack — see GRAYSON, Jack		
				LEDFORD, Susan		
				Born in Fort Payne, Alabama. Female singer.		
8/5/89	**81**	4		**Ancient History**	*Irene Stanton/Wayne Walker*	Project One 6189
				LeDOUX, Chris		
				Born on 10/2/1948 in Biloxi, Mississippi; raised in Austin, Texas. Died of liver cancer on 3/9/2005 (age 56). Male singer/songwriter/guitarist. Also a successful rodeo performer.		
4/14/79	**99**	1		1 **Lean, Mean And Hungry**	*Chris LeDoux*	Lucky Man 10270
11/17/79	**98**	3		2 **Cabello Diablo (Devil Horse)**	*Charlie Daniels*	Lucky Man 6520
8/23/80	**96**	2		3 **Ten Seconds In The Saddle**	*Terry Smith*	Lucky Man 6834
7/6/91	**63**	10		4 **This Cowboy's Hat**	*Jake Brooks*	Capitol
1/4/92	**69**	5		5 **Workin' Man's Dollar**	*Chris LeDoux*	Capitol
5/23/92	**72**	2		6 **Riding For A Fall**	*Chris LeDoux*	Liberty
				above 3 from the album *Western Underground* on Capitol 96499		

LeDOUX, Chris — cont'd

DEBUT	PEAK	WKS	GOLD	Country Chart Hit	Songwriter	Label (& Number)
7/25/92	7	20		7 Whatcha Gonna Do With A Cowboy	Garth Brooks/Mark D. Sanders	Liberty
				Garth Brooks (backing vocal)		
11/7/92+	18	20		8 Cadillac Ranch	Chuck Jones/Chris Waters	Liberty
2/20/93	52	10		9 Look At You Girl	Lanty Ross	Liberty
				above 3 from the album *Whatcha Gonna Do With A Cowboy* on Liberty 98818		
6/26/93	54	6		10 Under This Old Hat	Mike Anthony/Larry Cordle	Liberty
9/11/93	61	6		11 Every Time I Roll The Dice	Max D. Barnes/Troy Seals	Liberty
12/25/93+	50	13		12 For Your Love	Joe Ely	Liberty
				above 3 from the album *Under This Old Hat* on Liberty 80892		
8/27/94	71	3		13 Honky Tonk World	Paul Nelson/Craig Wiseman	Liberty
1/21/95	67	8		14 Tougher Than The Rest	Bruce Springsteen	Liberty
7/1/95	68	3		15 Dallas Days And Fort Worth Nights	Kris Bergsnes/Gordon Eatherly	Liberty
				above 3 from the album *Haywire* on Liberty 28770		
4/20/96	71	9		16 Gravitational Pull	Butch Curry/Ray Methvin	Capitol
2/8/97	65	1		17 When I Say Forever	Dennis Linde	Capitol
				above 2 from the album *Stampede* on Capitol 34071		
6/20/98	62	9		18 Runaway Love	Mike Caruso/Tamara Champlin/Dennis Matkosky	Capitol
10/3/98	68	5		19 Bang A Drum *[w/ Jon Bon Jovi]*	Jon Bon Jovi	Capitol
5/8/99	64	9		20 Life Is A Highway	Tom Cochrane	Capitol
				above 3 from the album *One Road Man* on Capitol 21942		
10/16/99	66	4		21 Stampede	Chris LeDoux	Capitol
				from the album *20 Greatest Hits* on Capitol 99781		
8/19/00	65	4		22 Silence On The Line	Sterling Whipple	Capitol
				from the album *Cowboy* on Capitol 26601		
2/7/04	56	5		23 Horsepower	Mac McAnally	Capitol
				from the album *Horsepower* on Capitol 81580		

LEE, Billy — see NUNN, Earl

LEE, Brenda — **All-Time: #164 // HOF: 1997**

Born Brenda Mae Tarpley on 12/11/1944 in Lithonia, Georgia. Female singer. Known as "Little Miss Dynamite." Inducted into the Rock and Roll Hall of Fame in 2002. Also see **America The Beautiful**.

DEBUT	PEAK	WKS	GOLD	Country Chart Hit	Songwriter	Label (& Number)
4/6/57	15	1		1 One Step At A Time	S:15 Hugh Ashley	Decca 30198
2/15/69	50	11		2 Johnny One Time	Dallas Frazier/A.L. "Doodle" Owens	Decca 32428
8/7/71	30	13		3 If This Is Our Last Time	Dallas Frazier	Decca 32848
1/29/72	37	12		4 Misty Memories	Ben Peters	Decca 32918
7/8/72	45	10		5 Always On My Mind	Wayne Carson/Johnny Christopher/Mark James	Decca 32975
2/17/73	5	15		6 Nobody Wins	Kris Kristofferson	MCA 40003
8/18/73	6	15		7 Sunday Sunrise	Mark James	MCA 40107
1/12/74	6	15		8 Wrong Ideas	Shel Silverstein	MCA 40171
7/13/74	4	14		9 Big Four Poster Bed	Shel Silverstein	MCA 40262
11/2/74+	6	14		10 Rock On Baby	Gene Dobbins/Johnny Wilson	MCA 40318
4/12/75	8	13		11 He's My Rock	Sharon Dobbins	MCA 40385
8/9/75	23	12		12 Bringing It Back	Greg Gordon	MCA 40442
2/7/76	38	9		13 Find Yourself Another Puppet	Jimbeau Hinson	MCA 40511
7/17/76	77	5		14 Brother Shelton	Bill Anthony/Bob Morrison	MCA 40584
11/13/76	41	9		15 Takin' What I Can Get	J.C. Cunningham	MCA 40640
3/19/77	78	5		16 Ruby's Lounge	Milton Brown/Steve Dorff	MCA 40683
6/17/78	62	6		17 Left-Over Love	Terry Woodford/Barbara Wyrick	Elektra 45492
10/20/79	8	15		18 Tell Me What It's Like	Ben Peters	MCA 41130
2/16/80	10	12		19 The Cowgirl And The Dandy	Bobby Goldsboro	MCA 41187
7/12/80	49	7		20 Don't Promise Me Anything (Do It)	Jimbeau Hinson	MCA 41270
9/20/80	9	14		21 Broken Trust	Jimbeau Hinson	MCA 41322
				The Oak Ridge Boys (backing vocals)		
1/31/81	26	10		22 Every Now And Then	Shayne Dolan/Rock Killough	MCA 51047
6/6/81	67	5		23 Fool, Fool	Max D. Barnes/Jerry McBee/Troy Seals	MCA 51113
8/15/81	75	5		24 Enough For You	Kris Kristofferson	MCA 51154
10/24/81	32	13		25 Only When I Laugh	Richard Maltby Jr./David Shire	MCA 51195
				from the movie starring Marsha Mason		
1/30/82	33	11		26 From Levis To Calvin Klein Jeans	Bucky Jones/Rick Lathrop/Rich Runyeon	MCA 51230
6/19/82	70	6		27 Keeping Me Warm For You	Johnny Christopher/Kermit Goell	MCA 52060
11/6/82	78	4		28 Just For The Moment	Michael Foster/Jimbeau Hinson	MCA 52124
				The Oak Ridge Boys (backing vocals)		
4/9/83	43	9		29 You're Gonna Love Yourself (In The Morning) *[w/ Willie Nelson]*	Donnie Fritts	Monument 03781
9/24/83	75	4		30 Didn't We Do It Good	Bill Rice/Mary Sharon Rice	MCA 52268
8/11/84	22	16		31 A Sweeter Love (I'll Never Know)	Jerry Crutchfield	MCA 52394
12/22/84+	15	16		32 Hallelujah, I Love You So *[w/ George Jones]*	A:13 / S:15 Ray Charles	Epic 04723
8/24/85	54	9		33 I'm Takin' My Time	Pat Alger/Rich Beresford	MCA 52654
12/21/85+	50	12		34 Why You Been Gone So Long	Mickey Newbury	MCA 52720
1/3/98	62	2		35 Rockin' Around The Christmas Tree	Johnny Marks [X]	MCA

Billboard DEBUT	PEAK	WKS	GOLD	ARTIST Ranking / Country Chart Hit	Songwriter	Label (& Number)

LEE, Chandy

Born in Brandon, Mississippi. Female singer.

DEBUT	PEAK	WKS	GOLD	Country Chart Hit	Songwriter	Label (& Number)
7/7/79	100	2		**She's Still Around**	*Bob McDill*	ODC 548

LEE, Dickey — **All-Time: #192**

Born Royden Dickey Lipscombe on 9/21/1936 in Memphis, Tennessee; later based in Beaumont, Texas. Male singer/songwriter/guitarist. First recorded for Sun Records in 1957.

DEBUT	PEAK	WKS	GOLD	Country Chart Hit	Songwriter	Label (& Number)
6/19/71	55	8		1 **The Mahogany Pulpit**	*Wallace Hyde/Joe Keene*	RCA Victor 9988
9/18/71	8	14		2 **Never Ending Song Of Love**	*Delaney Bramlett*	RCA Victor 1013
1/22/72	25	13		3 **I Saw My Lady**	*Richard Gove*	RCA Victor 0623
6/17/72	15	13		4 **Ashes Of Love**	*Jack Anglin/Jim Anglin/Johnny Wright*	RCA Victor 0710
10/7/72	31	11		5 **Baby, Bye Bye**	*Don Williams*	RCA Victor 0798
3/10/73	43	11		6 **Crying Over You**	*Danny Flowers*	RCA Victor 0892
6/30/73	30	7		7 **Put Me Down Softly**	*Bob McDill/Allen Reynolds*	RCA Victor 0980
9/22/73	49	9		8 **Sparklin' Brown Eyes**	*Billy Cox*	RCA Victor 0082
2/23/74	46	11		9 **I Use The Soap**	*David Gates*	RCA Victor 0227
8/17/74	90	4		10 **Give Me One Good Reason**	*Wayland Holyfield*	RCA Victor 10014
11/30/74+	22	13		11 **The Busiest Memory In Town**	*Geoffrey Morgan*	RCA Victor 10091
8/23/75	❶^{1}	18		12 **Rocky**	*Jay Stevens*	RCA Victor 10361
1/31/76	9	14		13 **Angels, Roses, And Rain**	*Bob Morrison/Bill Zerface/Jim Zerface*	RCA Victor 10543
6/5/76	35	10		14 **Makin' Love Don't Always Make Love Grow**	*Sterling Whipple*	RCA Victor 10684
9/11/76	3^{2}	18		15 **9,999,999 Tears**	*Razzy Bailey*	RCA 10764
3/19/77	20	13		16 **If You Gotta Make A Fool Of Somebody**	*Rudy Clark*	RCA 10914
7/2/77	22	11		17 **Virginia, How Far Will You Go**	*Wayland Holyfield/Bob House*	RCA 11009
10/15/77	21	14		18 **Peanut Butter**	*Razzy Bailey*	RCA 11125
2/4/78	27	11		19 **Love Is A Word**	*Otha Young*	RCA 11191
7/15/78	49	6		20 **My Heart Won't Cry Anymore**	*Ava Aldridge/Pam Byer*	RCA 11294
10/21/78	58	6		21 **It's Not Easy**	*Barry Mann/Cynthia Weil*	RCA 11389
7/28/79	58	9		22 **I'm Just A Heartache Away**	*Wayland Holyfield/Dickey Lee*	Mercury 55068
11/10/79	94	3		23 **He's An Old Rock 'N' Roller**	*Jay Stevens*	Mercury 57005
3/29/80	61	5		24 **Don't Look Back**	*Bob McDill*	Mercury 57017
7/26/80	30	12		25 **Workin' My Way To Your Heart**	*Layng Martine Jr.*	Mercury 57027
11/8/80+	30	12		26 **Lost In Love** *[w/ Kathy Burdick]*	*Graham Russell*	Mercury 57036
6/27/81	37	10		27 **Honky Tonk Hearts**	*Bob McDill*	Mercury 57052
10/3/81	53	7		28 **I Wonder If I Care As Much**	*Don Everly*	Mercury 57056
1/30/82	56	6		29 **Everybody Loves A Winner**	*Bob McDill*	Mercury 76129

LEE, Don

Born in Louisiana. Singer/songwriter/guitarist.

DEBUT	PEAK	WKS	GOLD	Country Chart Hit	Songwriter	Label (& Number)
9/11/82	86	3		**16 Lovin' Ounces To The Pound**	*Robert Duncan/J.R. Halper/Bob Jones/Don Lee*	Crescent 103

LEE, Harold

Born in Oklahoma. Male singer/songwriter.

DEBUT	PEAK	WKS	GOLD	Country Chart Hit	Songwriter	Label (& Number)
4/6/68	56	6		1 **The Two Sides Of Me**	*Harold Lee*	Columbia 44458
9/25/71	74	3		2 **Mountain Woman**	*Bob Millsap*	Cartwheel 198

LEE, Johnny — **1980s: #41 / All-Time: #135**

Born John Lee Ham on 7/3/1946 in Texas City, Texas; raised in Alta Loma, Texas. Male singer/songwriter/guitarist. Played in rock bands in the early 1960s. Own band, the Road Runners, in high school. Married to actress Charlene Tilton from 1982-84.

DEBUT	PEAK	WKS	GOLD	Country Chart Hit	Songwriter	Label (& Number)
12/27/75+	59	9		1 **Sometimes**	*Gene Thomas*	ABC/Dot 17603
7/31/76	22	12		2 **Red Sails In The Sunset**	*Jimmy Kennedy/Hugh Williams*	GRT 065
12/4/76+	37	10		3 **Ramblin' Rose**	*Joe Sherman/Noel Sherman*	GRT 096
5/21/77	15	13		4 **Country Party** — same tune as "Garden Party" by **Rick Nelson** with new lyrics	*Rick Nelson*	GRT 125
10/29/77	58	7		5 **Dear Alice**	*Lewis Anderson*	GRT 137
3/4/78	43	8		6 **This Time**	*Chips Moman*	GRT 144
7/19/80	❶^{3}	14	●	7 **Lookin' For Love** — from the movie *Urban Cowboy* starring John Travolta	*Wanda Mallette/Bob Morrison/Patti Ryan*	Full Moon 47004
10/25/80	❶^{2}	16		8 **One In A Million**	*Chick Rains*	Asylum 47076
2/14/81	3^{2}	14		9 **Pickin' Up Strangers**	*Byron Hill*	Asylum 47105

Billboard			GOLD	ARTIST / Ranking		
DEBUT	PEAK	WKS		Country Chart Hit	Songwriter	Label (& Number)
				LEE, Johnny — cont'd		
4/25/81	**52**	6		10 **Rode Hard And Put Up Wet**	*Marshall Chapman*	Full Moon/Epic 02012
				from the movie *Urban Cowboy* starring John Travolta		
5/30/81	**3[1]**	16		11 **Prisoner Of Hope**	*Gerald Metcalf/Sterling Whipple*	Asylum 47138
10/3/81	**❶[1]**	15		12 **Bet Your Heart On Me**	*Jim McBride*	Full Moon/Asy. 47215
1/23/82	**10**	15		13 **Be There For Me Baby**	*Charlie Black/Tommy Rocco*	Asylum 47301
5/15/82	**14**	13		14 **When You Fall In Love**	*Steve Earle/John Scott Sherrill*	Full Moon/Asy. 47444
10/9/82	**10**	18		15 **Cherokee Fiddle**	*Michael Murphey*	Full Moon/Asy. 69945
				Charlie Daniels and **Michael Martin Murphey** (backing vocals)		
2/5/83	**6**	18		16 **Sounds Like Love**	*Charlie Black/Tommy Rocco*	Full Moon/Asy. 69848
6/11/83	**2[2]**	22		17 **Hey Bartender**	*Floyd Dickson*	Full Moon 29605
10/8/83	**23**	16		18 **My Baby Don't Slow Dance**	*Bill Lamb/Peter Wood*	Warner 29486
2/4/84	**❶[1]**	22		19 **The Yellow Rose** *[w/ Lane Brody]* /	*Lane Brody/Johnny Lee*	
				same melody as "The Yellow Rose Of Texas" with new lyrics; from the TV series starring Cybill Shepherd		
2/4/84	**flip**	3		20 **Say When**	*Gary Nicholson/Kevin Welch*	Warner 29375
5/26/84	**42**	12		21 **One More Shot**	*Doug Hauseman/Ron Moore*	Warner 29270
8/25/84	**❶[1]**	24		22 **You Could've Heard A Heart Break**	S:❶[1] / A:❶[1] *Marc Rossi*	Warner 29206
1/5/85	**9**	20		23 **Rollin' Lonely**	S:8 / A:9 *Gary Harrison/J.D. Martin*	Warner 29110
5/11/85	**12**	18		24 **Save The Last Chance**	A:11 / S:12 *Walt Aldridge/Robert Byrne*	Warner 29021
10/5/85	**19**	18		25 **They Never Had To Get Over You**	A:17 / S:19 *Bud McGuire/Mike McGuire*	Warner 28901
1/25/86	**56**	9		26 **The Loneliness In Lucy's Eyes (The Life Sue Ellen Is Living)**	*David Allan Coe*	Warner 28839
				from the TV series *Dallas* starring Larry Hagman		
4/5/86	**50**	8		27 **I Could Get Used To This** *[w/ Lane Brody]*	*Jan Buckingham/Bruce Miller*	Warner 28747
6/3/89	**59**	6		28 **Maybe I Won't Love You Anymore**	*Barbara Hart/Buzz Hart*	Curb/MCA 10536
8/19/89	**69**	5		29 **I'm Not Over You**	*Sam Neely*	Curb/MCA 10552
10/14/89	**53**	8		30 **I Can Be A Heartbreaker, Too**	*Tommy Johnson/Lee Satterfield*	Curb/MCA 10564
12/23/89+	**66**	4		31 **You Can't Fly Like An Eagle**	*Tom Dennis/Chris Gantry/Barrett King/Tony Vincent*	Curb 10573
				LEE, Joni		
				Born Joni Lee Jenkins in 1957 in Arkansas; raised in Oklahoma. Female singer. Daughter of **Conway Twitty**.		
8/16/75	**4**	13		1 **Don't Cry Joni** *[w/ Conway Twitty]*	*Conway Twitty*	MCA 40407
12/13/75+	**16**	12		2 **I'm Sorry Charlie**	*Conway Twitty*	MCA 40501
5/15/76	**42**	9		3 **Angel On My Shoulder**	*Shelby Flint*	MCA 40553
7/31/76	**62**	6		4 **Baby Love**	*Lamont Dozier/Brian Holland/Eddie Holland*	MCA 40592
4/23/77	**97**	2		5 **The Reason Why I'm Here**	*Conway Twitty*	MCA 40687
1/7/78	**94**	4		6 **I Love How You Love Me**	*Larry Kolber/Barry Mann*	MCA 40826
				LEE, Leapy — see LEAPY LEE		
				LEE, Robin		
				Born Robin Lee Irwin on 11/7/1953 in Nashville, Tennessee. Female singer/songwriter/pianist.		
2/26/83	**87**	3		1 **Turning Back The Covers (Don't Turn Back The Time)**	*Karen Gloria/Peter Gloria/Joyce Goodwin*	Evergreen 1003
6/11/83	**81**	3		2 **Heart For A Heart**	*Lobo/Jeff Raymond*	Evergreen 1006
1/7/84	**54**	10		3 **Angel In Your Arms**	*Tom Brasfield/Herbert Ivey/Terry Woodford*	Evergreen 1016
4/28/84	**63**	7		4 **Want Ads**	*General Johnson/Barney Perkins/Greg Perry*	Evergreen 1018
8/11/84	**62**	5		5 **Cold In July**	*Michael Bird*	Evergreen 1023
12/1/84	**71**	7		6 **I Heard It On The Radio**	*Buzz Cason/Dickey Lee*	Evergreen 1026
6/29/85	**49**	7		7 **Paint The Town Blue** *[w/ Lobo]*	*Roger Lavoie*	Evergreen 1033
11/16/85	**44**	10		8 **Safe In The Arms Of Love**	*Bucky Jones/Bob McDill/Tommy Rocco*	Evergreen 1037
3/29/86	**37**	12		9 **I'll Take Your Love Anytime**	*Charlie Black/Tommy Rocco*	Evergreen 1039
8/2/86	**48**	8		10 **If You're Anything Like Your Eyes**	*Terry Skinner/J.L. Wallace*	Evergreen 1043
4/23/88	**52**	8		11 **This Old Flame**	*Bobby Borchers/Pam Wolfe*	Atlantic Amer. 99353
8/20/88	**56**	7		12 **Shine A Light On A Lie**	*Don Goodman/Randy Howard/Nelson Larkin*	Atlantic Amer. 99307
11/26/88	**51**	8		13 **Before You Cheat On Me Once (You Better Think Twice)**	...*Don Goodman/Mary Larkin/Nelson Larkin/Pal Rakes*	Atlantic Amer. 99264
3/10/90	**12**	25		14 **Black Velvet**	*David Tyson/Chris Ward*	Atlantic
9/1/90	**70**	2		15 **How About Goodbye**	*Thom Schuyler*	Atlantic
11/10/90	**67**	3		16 **Love Letter**	*Bonnie Hayes*	Atlantic
				above 3 from the album *Black Velvet* on Atlantic 82085		
7/6/91	**51**	9		17 **Nothin' But You**	*Steve Earle*	Atlantic
				from the album *Heart On A Chain* on Atlantic 82259		
2/5/94	**71**	1		18 **When Love Comes Callin'**	*Trey Bruce/Robin Lee*	Atlantic
				LEE, T.L. — see BLIXSETH, Tim		
				LEE, Vicki		
				Born in Pensacola, Florida. Female singer.		
11/1/86	**93**	2		**Bluemonia**	*Don Cook/Jamie O'Hara*	Sunshine 1400
				LEE, Wilma — see COOPER, Stoney		
				LEE, Woody		
				Born on 4/1/1968 in Garland, Texas. Male singer/guitarist.		
3/25/95	**46**	18		1 **Get Over It**	*Stephanie Bentley/Adrienne Follese/Keith Follese*	Atlantic
7/15/95	**58**	7		2 **I Like The Sound Of That**	*Andre Pessis/Steve Seskin*	Atlantic
				above 2 from the album *Get Over It* on Atlantic 82767		

DEBUT	PEAK	WKS	GOLD	ARTIST / Country Chart Hit	Ranking / Songwriter	Label (& Number)

LeGARDES, The

Duo of twin brothers Ted LeGarde and Tom LeGarde. Born on 3/15/1931 in MacKay, Australia. Moved to the U.S. in 1957. Worked on **Doye O'Dell**'s *Western Varieties* TV shows in Hollywood. Hosted own TV series on KTLA in Los Angeles.

DEBUT	PEAK	WKS	#	Country Chart Hit	Songwriter	Label (& Number)
6/3/78	**88**	3	1	**True Love**	*Cole Porter*	Raindrop 012
3/24/79	**82**	4	2	**I Can Almost Touch The Feelin'**	*Jim Lusk/Shirl Milete/Gary S. Paxton*	4 Star 1037
10/18/80	**92**	3	3	**Daddy's Makin' Records In Nashville** ***[LeGarde Twins]***	*Paul Clements*	Invitation 101
8/27/88	**92**	1	4	**Crocodile Man (From Walk-About-Creek)** ***[LeGarde Twins]***	*Tom Kelly*	Bear 194

LEHR, Zella

Born on 3/14/1951 in Burbank, California. Female singer. Regular on TV's *Hee-Haw*.

DEBUT	PEAK	WKS	#	Country Chart Hit	Songwriter	Label (& Number)
12/17/77+	**7**	18	1	**Two Doors Down**	*Dolly Parton*	RCA 11174
5/27/78	**31**	10	2	**When The Fire Gets Hot**	*Tom Benjamin*	RCA 11265
8/26/78	**20**	12	3	**Danger, Heartbreak Ahead**	*Deborah Allen/Don Cook*	RCA 11359
1/6/79	**24**	10	4	**Play Me A Memory**	*Milton Blackford/Richard Leigh*	RCA 11433
5/5/79	**59**	5	5	**Only Diamonds Are Forever**	*Chip Hardy/Richard Leigh*	RCA 11543
7/14/79	**34**	10	6	**Once In A Blue Moon**	*Sam Lorber/Jeff Silbar*	RCA 11648
12/15/79+	**26**	12	7	**Love Has Taken Its' Time**	*Ronnie Brooks/Dan Keen/John Pritchard*	RCA 11754
4/12/80	**25**	12	8	**Rodeo Eyes**	*John Beland*	RCA 11953
10/11/80	**34**	10	9	**Love Crazy Love**	*Deborah Allen/Rafe Van Hoy*	RCA 12073
8/15/81	**16**	15	10	**Feedin' The Fire**	*Becky Hobbs*	Columbia 02431
1/23/82	**56**	6	11	**Blue Eyes Don't Make An Angel**	*Peter Dibbens/Mike Shepstone*	Columbia 02677
9/25/82	**85**	2	12	**What A Way To Spend The Night**	*Troy Seals/Mark Sherrill*	Columbia 03164
3/19/83	**86**	4	13	**Haven't We Loved Somewhere Before**	*Becky Hobbs/Candy Parton*	Columbia 03593
9/29/84	**72**	5	14	**All Heaven Is About To Break Loose**	*Charlie Black/Steve Bogard/Tommy Rocco*	Compleat 129
2/9/85	**66**	6	15	**You Bring Out The Lover In Me**	*Charlie Black/Layng Martine Jr.*	Compleat 136

LEIGH, Bonnie

Born in Ashland, Maine. Female singer.

DEBUT	PEAK	WKS	#	Country Chart Hit	Songwriter	Label (& Number)
12/6/86	**76**	3	1	**Runaway**	*Max Crook/Del Shannon*	R.C.P. 010
7/25/87	**80**	3	2	**That's When (You Can Call Me Your Own)**	*Paula Edwards*	R.C.P. 016
12/19/87	**77**	3	3	**Moon Walking**	*Dickie Brown*	R.C.P. 020

LEIGH, Danni

Born on 2/9/1970 in Strasburg, Virginia. Female singer.

DEBUT	PEAK	WKS	#	Country Chart Hit	Songwriter	Label (& Number)
9/12/98	**57**	10	1	**If The Jukebox Took Teardrops** from the album *29 Nights* on MCA 70032	*Mike Henderson/Mark Irwin*	Decca
3/25/00	**59**	7	2	**Honey I Do**	S:19 *Al Anderson/Stacy Dean Campbell*	Monument
7/8/00	**56**	5	3	**I Don't Feel That Way** above 2 from the album *A Shot Of Whiskey & A Prayer* on Monument 63764	*Charlie Robison*	Monument

LEIGH, Richard

Born on 5/26/1951 in McLean, Virginia. Male singer/songwriter.

DEBUT	PEAK	WKS	#	Country Chart Hit	Songwriter	Label (& Number)
8/13/83	**65**	5		**Ain't Gonna Worry My Mind**	*Richard Leigh*	Capitol 5247

LEIGH, Shannon

Born in Kentucky. Female singer.

DEBUT	PEAK	WKS	#	Country Chart Hit	Songwriter	Label (& Number)
10/2/82	**90**	2		**Rock N' Roll Stories**	*Bucky Jones/Mike Kosser*	AMI 1308

LEMMON, Dave

Born in Preston, Idaho. Male singer.

DEBUT	PEAK	WKS	#	Country Chart Hit	Songwriter	Label (& Number)
1/29/83	**89**	2		**Too Good To Be Through**	*Steve Eaton/Chris Waters*	SCP 9781

LESTER, Chester

Born in Mammouth, West Virginia. Male singer/songwriter.

DEBUT	PEAK	WKS	#	Country Chart Hit	Songwriter	Label (& Number)
2/10/79	**86**	4		**Mama, Make Up My Room**	*Chester Lester*	Con Brio 148

LEWIS, Bobby — All-Time: #260

Born on 5/9/1942 in Hodgenville, Kentucky. Male singer/songwriter/lute player.

DEBUT	PEAK	WKS	#	Country Chart Hit	Songwriter	Label (& Number)
10/15/66	**6**	18	1	**How Long Has It Been**	*David Snyder/Sonny Throckmorton*	United Artists 50067
3/25/67	**49**	7	2	**Two Of The Usual**	*Fred Carter*	United Artists 50133
6/17/67	**12**	14	3	**Love Me And Make It All Better**	*Eddie Rabbitt*	United Artists 50161
10/21/67	**26**	12	4	**I Doubt It**	*Johnny MacRae*	United Artists 50208
3/23/68	**29**	10	5	**Ordinary Miracle**	*Sonny Throckmorton*	United Artists 50263
7/27/68	**10**	16	6	**From Heaven To Heartache**	*Ben Peters*	United Artists 50327
12/28/68+	**27**	13	7	**Each And Every Part Of Me**	*George Fischoff/Doc Pomus*	United Artists 50476
5/31/69	**41**	8	8	**Til Something Better Comes Along**	*Jerry Chesnut*	United Artists 50528
9/13/69	**25**	10	9	**Things For You And I**	*Jerry Chesnut/Earl Sinks*	United Artists 50573
1/17/70	**41**	10	10	**I'm Going Home**	*Sonny Throckmorton*	United Artists 50620
5/30/70	**14**	16	11	**Hello Mary Lou**	*Gene Pitney*	United Artists 50668
11/14/70	**67**	3	12	**Simple Days And Simple Ways**	*Alex Harvey/Scott Turner*	United Artists 50719
7/31/71	**51**	7	13	**If I Had You**	*Jerry Chesnut*	United Artists 50791
11/27/71	**45**	9	14	**Today's Teardrops**	*Gene Pitney/Aaron Schroeder*	United Artists 50850
7/14/73	**95**	4	15	**Here With You**	*Bobby Lewis*	Ace of Hearts 0466
10/6/73	**21**	15	16	**Too Many Memories**	*Gayle Barnhill/Rory Bourke*	Ace of Hearts 0472
2/16/74	**32**	10	17	**I Never Get Through Missing You**	*Biff Collie/Arthur Kent/Frank Stanton*	Ace of Hearts 0480
4/27/74	**47**	12	18	**Lady Lover**	*Gene Kennedy/Bobby Lewis*	GRT 007
10/12/74	**78**	8	19	**I See Love**	*Chuck Rogers*	GRT 008

DEBUT	PEAK	WKS	GOLD	ARTIST / Ranking / Country Chart Hit	Songwriter	Label (& Number)

LEWIS, Bobby — cont'd

DEBUT	PEAK	WKS	GOLD	#	Country Chart Hit	Songwriter	Label (& Number)
6/21/75	**71**	8		20	**Let Me Take Care Of You**	*Arthur Kent/Frank Stanton*	Ace of Hearts 0502
11/22/75	**79**	5		21	**It's So Nice To Be With You**	*Jim Gold*	Ace of Hearts 7503
9/11/76	**52**	7		22	**For Your Love**	*Ed Townsend*	RPA 7603
1/8/77	**74**	5		23	**I'm Getting High Remembering**	*Ray Griff*	RPA 7613
5/7/77	**81**	6		24	**What A Diff'rence A Day Made**	*Stanley Adams/Maria Grever*	RPA 7622
4/21/79	**39**	10		25	**She's Been Keepin' Me Up Nights**	*Sam Lorber/John Potts/Jeff Silbar*	Capricorn 0318
7/6/85	**91**	3		26	**Love Is An Overload**	*Bill Rice/Mary Sharon Rice*	HME 04853

LEWIS, Hugh X.

Born Hubert Brad Lewis on 12/7/1932 in Yeaddiss, Kentucky. Male singer/songwriter/guitarist. Acted in the movies *40-Acre Feud, Gold Guitar* and *Cottonpickin' Chicken-Pluckers.*

DEBUT	PEAK	WKS	GOLD	#	Country Chart Hit	Songwriter	Label (& Number)
12/26/64+	**21**	16		1	**What I Need Most**	*Hugh X. Lewis*	Kapp 622
9/4/65	**32**	6		2	**Out Where The Ocean Meets The Sky**	*Fred Burch/Mel Tillis*	Kapp 673
12/18/65+	**30**	10		3	**I'd Better Call The Law On Me**	*Hugh X. Lewis*	Kapp 717
6/25/66	**45**	2		4	**I'm Losing You (I Can Tell)**	*Hugh X. Lewis*	Kapp 757
10/15/66	**61**	2		5	**Wish Me A Rainbow** from the movie *This Property Is Condemned* starring Robert Redford	*Ray Evans/Jay Livingston*	Kapp 771
7/1/67	**38**	11		6	**You're So Cold (I'm Turning Blue)**	*Harlan Howard/Tony Senn*	Kapp 830
12/9/67+	**49**	9		7	**Wrong Side Of The World**	*Alex Zanetis*	Kapp 868
3/23/68	**36**	10		8	**Evolution And The Bible**	*Hugh X. Lewis*	Kapp 895
1/4/69	**69**	5		9	**Tonight We're Calling It A Day**	*Harlan Howard*	Kapp 955
3/29/69	**72**	6		10	**All Heaven Broke Loose**	*Hugh X. Lewis/Glenn Sutton*	Kapp 978
7/26/69	**74**	2		11	**Restless Melissa**	*Darrell Statler*	Kapp 2020
1/17/70	**56**	6		12	**Everything I Love**	*Hugh X. Lewis/Glenn Sutton*	Columbia 45047
11/28/70	**68**	4		13	**Blues Sells A Lot Of Booze**	*Hugh X. Lewis/Glenn Sutton*	GRT 28
7/22/78	**93**	4		14	**Love Don't Hide From Me**	*Hugh X. Lewis*	Little Darlin' 7803
4/21/79	**92**	5		15	**What Can I Do (To Make You Love Me)**	*Hugh X. Lewis*	Little Darlin' 7913

LEWIS, J.D.

Born James David Lewis in Georgia. Male singer/songwriter.

DEBUT	PEAK	WKS	GOLD	#	Country Chart Hit	Songwriter	Label (& Number)
12/9/89	**82**	2			**My Heart's On Hold**	*J.D. Lewis/Mike Novotny*	Sing Me 43

LEWIS, Jerry Lee **1950s: #37 / 1970s: #17 / All-Time: #48**

Born on 9/29/1935 in Ferriday, Louisiana. Male singer/songwriter/pianist. Married to Myra Gale Brown, his 13-year-old cousin, from 1958-71. Known as "The Killer." Survived several personal setbacks and serious illnesses. Cousin of singer **Mickey Gilley** and former TV evangelist Jimmy Swaggart. Brother of **Linda Gail Lewis**. Inducted into the Rock and Roll Hall of Fame in 1986. Early career was documented in the 1989 movie *Great Balls Of Fire* starring Dennis Quaid as Lewis.

DEBUT	PEAK	WKS	GOLD	#	Country Chart Hit	Songwriter	Label (& Number)
6/17/57	❶^{2}	23	●	1	**Whole Lot Of Shakin' Going On** **Grammy: Hall of Fame / RS500**	S:❶^{2} / A:6 *Sunny David/Dave Williams*	Sun 267
12/2/57+	❶^{2}	19	●	2	**Great Balls Of Fire /** **Grammy: Hall of Fame / RS500**	S:❶^{2} / A:4 *Otis Blackwell/Jack Hammer*	
12/23/57+	**4**	10		3	**You Win Again**	A:4 / S:flip *Hank Williams*	Sun 281
3/17/58	**4**	13		4	**Breathless**	S:4 / A:12 *Otis Blackwell*	Sun 288
6/9/58	**9**	10		5	**High School Confidential** title song from the movie starring Russ Tamblyn (song introduced by Lewis in the movie)	S:9 *Ron Hargrave*	Sun 296
10/13/58	**19**	1		6	**I'll Make It All Up To You**	S:19 *Charlie Rich*	Sun 303
5/8/61	**27**	1		7	**What'd I Say**	*Ray Charles*	Sun 356
8/7/61	**22**	5		8	**Cold Cold Heart** also see #51 below	*Hank Williams*	Sun 364
2/1/64	**36**	2		9	**Pen And Paper**	*Diane Kilroy/Eddie Kilroy*	Smash 1857
3/9/68	**4**	17		10	**Another Place Another Time**	*Jerry Chesnut*	Smash 2146
6/8/68	**2**^{2}	16		11	**What's Made Milwaukee Famous (Has Made A Loser Out Of Me)**	*Glenn Sutton*	Smash 2164
9/28/68	**2**^{2}	12		12	**She Still Comes Around (To Love What's Left Of Me)**	*Glenn Sutton*	Smash 2186
12/28/68+	❶^{1}	15		13	**To Make Love Sweeter For You**	*Jerry Kennedy/Glenn Sutton*	Smash 2202
5/24/69	**9**	11		14	**Don't Let Me Cross Over** ***[w/ Linda Gail Lewis]***	*Penny Jay*	Smash 2220
5/31/69	**3**^{3}	15		15	**One Has My Name (The Other Has My Heart)**	*Hal Blair/Dearest Dean/Eddie Dean*	Smash 2224
8/16/69	**6**	12		16	**Invitation To Your Party** recorded on 8/28/1963	*Bill Taylor*	Sun 1101
10/4/69	**2**^{2}	13		17	**She Even Woke Me Up To Say Goodbye**	*Doug Gilmore/Mickey Newbury*	Smash 2244
11/29/69+	**2**^{2}	16		18	**One Minute Past Eternity** recorded on 8/28/1963	*Stan Kesler/Bill Taylor*	Sun 1107
1/10/70	**71**	2		19	**Roll Over Beethoven** ***[w/ Linda Gail Lewis]***	*Chuck Berry*	Smash 2254
2/21/70	**2**^{2}	14		20	**Once More With Feeling**	*Kris Kristofferson/Shel Silverstein*	Smash 2257
4/25/70	**7**	15		21	**I Can't Seem To Say Goodbye** recorded on 8/28/1963	*Don Robertson*	Sun 1115
8/22/70	❶^{2}	15		22	**There Must Be More To Love Than This**	*William Taylor/LaVerne Thomas*	Mercury 73099
11/21/70+	**11**	12		23	**Waiting For A Train (All Around The Watertank)** recorded on 6/5/1962	*Jimmie Rodgers*	Sun 1119
1/30/71	**48**	8		24	**In Loving Memories**	*Cecil Harrelson/Linda Gail Lewis*	Mercury 73155
3/27/71	**3**^{1}	16		25	**Touching Home**	*Dallas Frazier/A.L. "Doodle" Owens*	Mercury 73192

DEBUT	PEAK	WKS	GOLD		ARTIST / Country Chart Hit	Songwriter	Label (& Number)
					LEWIS, Jerry Lee — cont'd		
6/26/71	**31**	9		26	**Love On Broadway**	*Ronnie Self*	Sun 1125
					recorded on 8/27/1963		
7/24/71	**11**	13		27	**When He Walks On You** (Like You Have Walked On Me)	*Dallas Frazier/A.L. "Doodle" Owens*	Mercury 73227
11/6/71+	**❶[1]**	17		28	**Would You Take Another Chance On Me /**	*Jerry Foster/Bill Rice*	
11/20/71+	**flip**	15		29	**Me And Bobby McGee**	*Fred Foster/Kris Kristofferson*	Mercury 73248
3/11/72	**❶[3]**	15		30	**Chantilly Lace /**	*J.P. Richardson*	
3/11/72	**flip**	15		31	**Think About It Darlin'**	*Jerry Foster/Bill Rice*	Mercury 73273
6/17/72	**11**	11		32	**Lonely Weekends**	*Charlie Rich*	Mercury 73296
10/7/72	**14**	13		33	**Who's Gonna Play This Old Piano**	*Ray Griff*	Mercury 73328
2/17/73	**19**	10		34	**No More Hanging On**	*Jerry Chesnut*	Mercury 73361
4/21/73	**20**	11		35	**Drinking Wine Spo-Dee O'Dee**	*Granville McGhee*	Mercury 73374
8/4/73	**60**	6		36	**No Headstone On My Grave**	*Charlie Rich*	Mercury 73402
9/29/73	**6**	14		37	**Sometimes A Memory Ain't Enough**	*Stan Kesler*	Mercury 73423
2/9/74	**21**	12		38	**I'm Left, You're Right, She's Gone**	*Stan Kesler/Bill Taylor*	Mercury 73452
6/22/74	**18**	12		39	**Tell Tale Signs**	*Alex Zanetis*	Mercury 73491
10/19/74	**8**	12		40	**He Can't Fill My Shoes**	*Frank Dycus/Larry Kingston*	Mercury 73618
2/22/75	**13**	12		41	**I Can Still Hear The Music In The Restroom**	*Tom T. Hall*	Mercury 73661
6/28/75	**24**	13		42	**Boogie Woogie Country Man**	*Troy Seals*	Mercury 73685
12/6/75	**68**	5		43	**A Damn Good Country Song**	*Donnie Fritts*	Mercury 73729
2/14/76	**58**	6		44	**Don't Boogie Woogie**	*Layng Martine Jr.*	Mercury 73763
8/7/76	**6**	15		45	**Let's Put It Back Together Again**	*Jerry Foster/Bill Rice*	Mercury 73822
12/18/76+	**27**	11		46	**The Closest Thing To You**	*Bob McDill*	Mercury 73872
10/29/77+	**4**	18		47	**Middle Age Crazy**	*Sonny Throckmorton*	Mercury 55011
3/11/78	**10**	12		48	**Come On In**	*Bobby Braddock*	Mercury 55021
6/24/78	**10**	12		49	**I'll Find It Where I Can**	*Michael Clark/Douglas Van Arsdale*	Mercury 55028
12/16/78+	**26**	13		50	**Save The Last Dance For Me**	*Doc Pomus/Mort Shuman*	Sun 1139
					recorded on 6/12/1961		
4/7/79	**84**	3		51	**Cold, Cold Heart**	*Hank Williams* **[R]**	Sun 1141
					same recording as #8 above; **Orion** (dubbed-in vocals, above 2)		
4/7/79	**18**	11		52	**Rockin' My Life Away /**	*Mack Vickery*	
4/7/79	**flip**	11		53	**I Wish I Was Eighteen Again**	*Sonny Throckmorton*	Elektra 46030
7/21/79	**20**	11		54	**Who Will The Next Fool Be**	*Charlie Rich*	Elektra 46067
2/9/80	**11**	12		55	**When Two Worlds Collide**	*Bill Anderson/Roger Miller*	Elektra 46591
5/24/80	**28**	12		56	**Honky Tonk Stuff**	*Jerry Chesnut*	Elektra 46642
9/6/80	**10**	12		57	**Over The Rainbow**	*Harold Arlen/E.Y. Harburg*	Elektra 47026
					first heard in the 1939 movie *The Wizard Of Oz* starring Judy Garland		
1/17/81	**4**	15		58	**Thirty Nine And Holding**	*Jerry Foster/Bill Rice*	Elektra 47095
4/24/82	**43**	11		59	**I'm So Lonesome I Could Cry**	*Hank Williams*	Mercury 76148
9/25/82	**52**	7		60	**I'd Do It All Again**	*Jerry Foster/Bill Rice*	Elektra 69962
12/18/82+	**44**	10		61	**My Fingers Do The Talkin'**	*Buck Moore/Bill Taylor*	MCA 52151
3/19/83	**66**	6		62	**Come As You Were**	*Paul Craft*	MCA 52188
7/9/83	**69**	5		63	**Why You Been Gone So Long**	*Mickey Newbury*	MCA 52233
8/23/86	**61**	6		64	**Sixteen Candles**	*Luther Dixon/Allyson Khent*	America/Sm. 884934
1/14/89	**50**	7		65	**Never Too Old To Rock 'N' Roll** ***[w/ Ronnie McDowell]***	*...Ronnie McDowell/Joe Meador/Richard Young*	Curb 10521

Another Place Another Time ['68]
Boogie Woogie Country Man ['75]
Breathless ['58]
Chantilly Lace ['72]
Closest Thing To You ['77]
Cold Cold Heart ['61, '79]
Come As You Were ['83]
Come On In ['78]
Damn Good Country Song ['75]
Don't Boogie Woogie ['76]
Don't Let Me Cross Over ['69]
Drinking Wine Spo-Dee O'Dee ['73]
Great Balls Of Fire ['58]
He Can't Fill My Shoes ['74]
High School Confidential ['58]
Honky Tonk Stuff ['80]
I Can Still Hear The Music In The Restroom ['75]
I Can't Seem To Say Goodbye ['70]
I Wish I Was Eighteen Again ['79]
I'd Do It All Again ['82]
I'll Find It Where I Can ['78]
I'll Make It All Up To You ['58]
I'm Left, You're Right, She's Gone ['74]
I'm So Lonesome I Could Cry ['82]
In Loving Memories ['71]
Invitation To Your Party ['69]
Let's Put It Back Together Again ['76]
Lonely Weekends ['72]
Love On Broadway ['71]
Me And Bobby McGee ['72]
Middle Age Crazy ['78]
My Fingers Do The Talkin' ['83]
Never Too Old To Rock 'N' Roll ['89]
No Headstone On My Grave ['73]
No More Hanging On ['73]
Once More With Feeling ['70]
One Has My Name (The Other Has My Heart) ['69]
One Minute Past Eternity ['70]
Over The Rainbow ['80]
Pen And Paper ['64]
Rockin' My Life Away ['79]
Roll Over Beethoven ['70]
Save The Last Dance For Me ['79]
She Even Woke Me Up To Say Goodbye ['69]
She Still Comes Around (To Love What's Left Of Me) ['68]
Sixteen Candles ['86]
Sometimes A Memory Ain't Enough ['73]
Tell Tale Signs ['74]
There Must Be More To Love Than This ['70]
Think About It Darlin' ['72]
Thirty Nine And Holding ['81]
To Make Love Sweeter For You ['69]
Touching Home ['71]
Waiting For A Train (All Around The Watertank) ['71]
What'd I Say ['61]
What's Made Milwaukee Famous (Has Made A Loser Out Of Me) ['68]
When He Walks On You (Like You Have Walked On Me) ['71]
When Two Worlds Collide ['80]
Who Will The Next Fool Be ['79]
Who's Gonna Play This Old Piano ['72]
Whole Lot Of Shakin' Going On ['57]
Why You Been Gone So Long ['83]
Would You Take Another Chance On Me ['72]
You Win Again ['58]

DEBUT	PEAK	WKS	GOLD		ARTIST / Country Chart Hit	Songwriter	Label (& Number)
					LEWIS, Linda Gail		
					Born on 7/18/1947 in Ferriday, Louisiana. Female singer. Sister of **Jerry Lee Lewis**.		
5/24/69	**9**	11		1	**Don't Let Me Cross Over** ***[w/ Jerry Lee Lewis]***	*Penny Jay*	Smash 2220
1/10/70	**71**	2		2	**Roll Over Beethoven** ***[w/ Jerry Lee Lewis]***	*Chuck Berry*	Smash 2254
8/19/72	**39**	8		3	**Smile, Somebody Loves You**	*Tony Austin*	Mercury 73316
					LEWIS, Margaret		
					Born in West Virginia. Female singer.		
6/29/68	**74**	3			**Honey** (I Miss You Too)	*Bobby Russell*	SSS Int'l. 741
					answer to "Honey" by **Bobby Goldsboro**		
					LEWIS, Melissa		
					Born on 10/16/1964 in Exeter, New Hampshire; raised in New Hope, North Carolina. Male singer.		
3/1/80	**75**	5		1	**The First Time**	*Ophelia Casper/Mac Phillips/Doug Zepp*	Door Knob 122
5/17/80	**71**	6		2	**One Good Reason**	*Mac Phillips/Tom Webb/Doug Zepp*	Door Knob 129

DEBUT	PEAK	WKS	GOLD	ARTIST / Ranking / Country Chart Hit	Songwriter	Label (& Number)
				LEWIS, Ross		
				Born in Dallas, Texas. Male singer.		
12/17/88	**89**	4		1 **Hold Your Fire**	*Robert Alley/Dennis W. Morgan*	Wolf Dog 4
1/28/89	**70**	5		2 **Love In Motion**	*Rick Giles/Frank J. Myers*	Wolf Dog 5
4/1/89	**67**	5		3 **The Chance You Take**	*Rick Giles/Gary Harrison/Frank J. Myers*	Wolf Dog 6
9/23/89	**91**	2		4 **Of All The Foolish Things To Do**	*Roger Greenaway/Dennis W. Morgan*	Wolf Dog 7
				LEWIS, Texas Jim, And His Lone Star Cowboys		
				Born on 10/15/1909 in Meigs, Georgia. Died on 1/23/1990 (age 80). Singer/guitarist/actor. Appeared in several western movies.		
9/2/44	**3**[2]	6		**Too Late To Worry Too Blue To Cry**	*Al Dexter*	Decca 6099
				LIBBY, Brenda		
				Born in Missouri. Female singer.		
11/26/83	**97**	1		**Give It Back**	*Brenda Barnett/Charlie Chalmers/Lisa Palas/Sandra Rhodes*	Comstock 1726
				LIGHTFOOT, Gordon		
				Born on 11/17/1938 in Orilla, Ontario, Canada. Folk-pop singer/songwriter/guitarist.		
6/1/74	**13**	15	●	1 **Sundown**	*Gordon Lightfoot*	Reprise 1194
10/19/74	**81**	6		2 **Carefree Highway**	*Gordon Lightfoot*	Reprise 1309
4/5/75	**47**	7		3 **Rainy Day People**	*Gordon Lightfoot*	Reprise 1328
10/9/76	**50**	11		4 **The Wreck Of The Edmund Fitzgerald**	*Gordon Lightfoot*	Reprise 1369
				true story of the shipwreck in Lake Superior on 11/10/1975		
2/25/78	**92**	4		5 **The Circle Is Small (I Can See It In Your Eyes)**	*Gordon Lightfoot*	Warner 8518
9/2/78	**100**	2		6 **Dreamland**	*Gordon Lightfoot*	Warner 8644
5/24/80	**80**	5		7 **Dream Street Rose**	*Gordon Lightfoot*	Warner 49230
8/30/86	**71**	9		8 **Anything For Love**	*David Foster/Gordon Lightfoot*	Warner 28655
				LINCOLN COUNTY		
				Vocal trio from Lincoln County, Mississippi.		
4/11/81	**84**	4		**Making The Night The Best Part Of My Day**	*Wayland Holyfield/Ben Peters*	Soundwaves 4629
				LINDSEY, Bennie		
				Born in Tennessee. Male singer.		
11/13/76	**100**	2		**Save The Last Dance**	*Doc Pomus/Mort Shuman*	Phono 2633
				LINDSEY, Judy		
				Born in Arlington, Texas. Female singer.		
1/28/89	**83**	3		**Wrong Train**	*Jerry McBee/Ed Penney*	Gypsy 83881
				LINDSEY, LaWanda		
				Born on 1/12/1953 in Tampa, Florida; raised in Savannah, Georgia. Female singer.		
1/4/69	**58**	9		1 **Eye To Eye** *[w/ Kenny Vernon]*	*Jimmy Day/John Owen*	Chart 1063
12/20/69	**48**	10		2 **Partly Bill**	*Steve Allen/Vance Bulla*	Chart 5042
3/21/70	**27**	14		3 **Pickin' Wild Mountain Berries** *[w/ Kenny Vernon]*	*Bob McRee/Clifton Thomas/Edward Thomas*	Chart 5055
7/25/70	**63**	6		4 **We'll Sing In The Sunshine**	*Gale Garnett*	Chart 5076
9/19/70	**51**	9		5 **Let's Think About Where We're Going** *[w/ Kenny Vernon]*	*Bob Yarbrough*	Chart 5090
2/27/71	**42**	9		6 **The Crawdad Song** *[w/ Kenny Vernon]*	*Connie Eaton/Noel Gibson*	Chart 5114
2/26/72	**60**	7		7 **Wish I Was A Little Boy Again**	*D.J. Edwards/Glenn Sutton*	Chart 5153
7/14/73	**38**	10		8 **Today Will Be The First Day Of The Rest Of My Life**	*Buddy Alan/Jim Shaw*	Capitol 3652
11/17/73	**87**	5		9 **Sunshine Feeling**	*Jim Shaw*	Capitol 3739
2/23/74	**62**	8		10 **Hello Trouble**	*Orville Couch/Eddie McDuff*	Capitol 3819
6/1/74	**28**	14		11 **Hello Out There**	*Wayne Walker/Kent Westberry*	Capitol 3875
9/28/74	**67**	7		12 **I Ain't Hangin' 'Round**	*Rocky Topp*	Capitol 3950
4/2/77	**76**	5		13 **Walk Right Back**	*Sonny Curtis*	Mercury 73889
10/7/78	**85**	4		14 **I'm A Woman In Love**	*Terry Skinner/J.L. Wallace*	Mercury 55041
				LINES, Aaron		
				Born in 1978 in Fort McMurray, Alberta, Canada. Male singer/songwriter/guitarist.		
8/17/02+	**4**	32		1 **You Can't Hide Beautiful**	*Michael Dulaney/Jason Sellers*	RCA
4/19/03	**39**	15		2 **Love Changes Everything**	*Chris Farren/Aaron Lines*	RCA
				above 2 from the album *Living Out Loud* on RCA 67057		
2/12/05	**36**	18		3 **Waitin' On The Wonderful**	*Dave Berg/Hillary Lindsey/Angelo Petraglia*	BNA
				from the album *Waitin' On The Wonderful* on BNA 66999		
				LINTON, Sherwin		
				Born on 7/28/1939 in Volga, South Dakota; raised in Hazel, South Dakota. Male singer/songwriter/pianist.		
10/22/77	**88**	3		**Jesse I Wanted That Award**	*Sherwin Linton*	Soundwaves 4556
				LIPTON, Holly		
				Born on 9/14/1950 in Manhattan, New York. Female singer.		
10/21/89	**89**	2		**At This Moment**	*Billy Vera*	Evergreen 1096
				LITTLE, Peggy		
				Born on 8/8/1945 in Marlin, Texas; raised in Waco, Texas. Female singer. Regular on TV's *The Mike Douglas Show.*		
3/15/69	**40**	10		1 **Son Of A Preacher Man**	*John Hurley/Ronnie Wilkins*	Dot 17199
6/21/69	**43**	10		2 **Sweet Baby Girl**	*Carl Kidd/Keni Lewis/Darrell Statler*	Dot 17259
10/18/69	**44**	9		3 **Put Your Lovin' Where Your Mouth Is**	*Darrell Statler*	Dot 17308
2/21/70	**37**	11		4 **Mama, I Won't Be Wearing A Ring**	*Dallas Frazier/A.L. "Doodle" Owens*	Dot 17338
8/8/70	**59**	3		5 **I Knew You'd Be Leaving**	*Billy Ray Reynolds*	Dot 17353

DEBUT	PEAK	WKS	GOLD	ARTIST / Country Chart Hit	Songwriter	Label (& Number)
				LITTLE, Peggy — cont'd		
5/1/71	**75**	2		6 **I've Got To Have You**	*Kris Kristofferson*	Dot 17371
4/14/73	**70**	2		7 **Listen, Spot**	*Gene Chrysler*	Epic 10968
8/18/73	**37**	10		8 **Sugarman**	*George Richey/Carmol Taylor/Norro Wilson*	Epic 11028

LITTLE BIG TOWN

Vocal group from Georgia: Karen Fairchild, Kimberly Roads, Phillip Sweet and Jimi Westbrook.

DEBUT	PEAK	WKS	GOLD	Country Chart Hit	Songwriter	Label (& Number)
3/2/02	**33**	19		1 **Don't Waste My Time**	*Karen Fairchild/Irene Kelley/Clay Mills/Kimberly Roads/Phillip Sweet/Jimi Westbrook*	Monument
7/13/02	**42**	9		2 **Everything Changes** — above 2 from the album *Little Big Town* on Monument 85374	*Karen Fairchild/Tommy Lee James/Jennifer Kimball/Kimberly Roads/Phillip Sweet/Jimi Westbrook*	Monument
6/4/05	**30↑**	17↑		3 **Boondocks** — from the album *Looking For A Reason* from Equity 3010	*Karen Fairchild/Wayne Kirkpatrick/Kimberly Roads/Phillip Sweet/Jimi Westbrook*	Equity

LITTLE TEXAS — 1990s: #40 / All-Time: #219

Group from Arlington, Texas: **Tim Rushlow** (vocals; born on 10/6/1966), Porter Howell (guitar; born on 6/21/1964), Dwayne O'Brien (guitar; born on 6/30/1963), **Brady Seals** (keyboards; born on 3/29/1969), Duane Propes (bass; born on 12/17/1966) and Del Gray (drums; born on 5/8/1968). Jeff Huskins (born on 4/26/1966) replaced Seals in 1995. Seals later formed **Hot Apple Pie**. Also see **Hope**.

DEBUT	PEAK	WKS	GOLD	Country Chart Hit	Songwriter	Label (& Number)
9/14/91	**8**	20		1 **Some Guys Have All The Love**	*Porter Howell/Dwayne O'Brien*	Warner
2/8/92	**13**	20		2 **First Time For Everything**	*Porter Howell/Dwayne O'Brien*	Warner
6/20/92	**5**	20		3 **You And Forever And Me**	*Stewart Harris/Porter Howell*	Warner
10/10/92+	**17**	20		4 **What Were You Thinkin'**	*Christy DiNapoli/Porter Howell/Dwayne O'Brien/Brady Seals*	Warner
1/30/93	**16**	20		5 **I'd Rather Miss You** — above 5 from the album *First Time For Everything* on Warner 26820	*Porter Howell/Dwayne O'Brien*	Warner
5/29/93	**2^{1}**	20		6 **What Might Have Been**	*Porter Howell/Dwayne O'Brien/Brady Seals*	Warner
7/17/93	**4**	24		7 **God Blessed Texas**	*Porter Howell/Brady Seals*	Warner
12/11/93	**73**	4		8 **Peaceful Easy Feeling** — from the various artists album *Common Thread: Songs Of The* ***Eagles*** on Giant 24531	*Jack Tempchin*	Giant
1/15/94	**❶^{2}**	20		9 **My Love**	*Tommy Barnes/Porter Howell/Brady Seals*	Warner
5/21/94	**14**	20		10 **Stop On A Dime** — #6, 7, 9 & 10: from the album *Big Time* on Warner 45276	*Porter Howell/Dwayne O'Brien/Brady Seals*	Warner
8/27/94	**5**	20		11 **Kick A Little**	*Porter Howell/Dwayne O'Brien/Brady Seals*	Warner
12/24/94+	**4**	20		12 **Amy's Back In Austin**	*Steve Davis/Brady Seals*	Warner
4/29/95	**27**	16		13 **Southern Grace** — above 3 from the album *Kick A Little* on Warner 45739	*Stewart Harris/Porter Howell/Brady Seals*	Warner
7/8/95	**53**	17		14 **Party All Night** ***[w/ Jeff Foxworthy]*** — from Foxworthy's album *Games Rednecks Play* on Warner 45856	S:5 *Jeff Foxworthy/Scott Rouse* **[L-N]**	Warner
9/2/95	**5**	20		15 **Life Goes On**	*Keith Follese/Del Gray/Thom McHugh*	Warner
12/30/95+	**44**	13		16 **Country Crazy** — above 2 from the album *Greatest Hits* on Warner 46017	*Porter Howell/Chuck Jones*	Warner
10/19/96+	**52**	20		17 **Kiss The Girl** — from the 1989 animated movie *The Little Mermaid* ; from the various artists album *The Best Of Country Sing The Best Of Disney* on Walt Disney 60902	*Howard Ashman/Alan Menken*	Walt Disney
3/1/97	**45**	10		18 **Bad For Us**	*Porter Howell/Dwayne O'Brien/Tom Shapiro*	Warner
5/17/97	**64**	5		19 **Your Mama Won't Let Me**	*Keith Follese/Del Gray/Thom McHugh*	Warner
9/20/97	**71**	2		20 **The Call** — above 3 from the album *Little Texas* on Warner 46501	*Walt Aldridge/Tim Rushlow*	Warner

LLOYD, Mick

Born in California. Male singer/songwriter/producer.

DEBUT	PEAK	WKS	GOLD	Country Chart Hit	Songwriter	Label (& Number)
1/31/81	**85**	3		1 **Be My Lover, Be My Friend** ***[w/ Jerri Kelly]***	*Mick Lloyd*	Little Giant 040
8/8/81	**85**	4		2 **Sweet Natural Love** ***[w/ Jerry Kelly]***	*Tommy Faia*	Little Giant 046

LOBO

Born Roland Kent Lavoie on 7/31/1943 in Tallahassee, Florida. Male singer/songwriter/guitarist. Started own Lobo record label in 1981. Member of **The Wolfpack**.

DEBUT	PEAK	WKS	GOLD	Country Chart Hit	Songwriter	Label (& Number)
12/5/81+	**40**	12		1 **I Don't Want To Want You**	*Roger Lavoie*	Lobo 1
3/27/82	**63**	7		2 **Come Looking For Me**	*Lobo*	Lobo 4
9/4/82	**88**	3		3 **Living My Life Without You**	*Lobo/Jeff Raymond*	Lobo 10
3/9/85	**57**	5		4 **Am I Going Crazy (Or Just Out Of My Mind)**	*Billy Aerts/Lobo/Will Robinson*	Evergreen 1028
6/29/85	**49**	7		5 **Paint The Town Blue** ***[w/ Robin Lee]***	*Roger Lavoie*	Evergreen 1033

LOCKLIN, Hank — 1950s: #36 / 1960s: #33 / All-Time: #141

Born Lawrence Hankins Locklin on 2/15/1918 in McLellan, Florida. Male singer/songwriter/guitarist. Regular performer in 1942 on radio station WCOA in Pensacola, Florida. Joined the *Louisiana Hayride* in the late 1940s. Once known as "The Rocky Mountain Boy." Also see **Some Of Chet's Friends**.

OPRY: 1960

DEBUT	PEAK	WKS	GOLD	Country Chart Hit	Songwriter	Label (& Number)
6/25/49	**8**	5		1 **The Same Sweet Girl**	J:8 / S:15 *Hank Locklin*	4 Star 1313
9/5/53	**❶^{3}**	32		2 **Let Me Be The One**	A:❶^{3} / J:❶^{2} / S:2 *Paul Blevins/Joseph Hobson/W.S. Stevenson*	4 Star 1641
3/24/56	**9**	1		3 **Why Baby Why**	A:9 *Darrell Edwards/George Jones*	RCA Victor 6347
8/19/57	**4**	39		4 **Geisha Girl /**	S:4 / A:6 *Lawton Williams*	
11/11/57	**flip**	6		5 **Livin' Alone**	*Wayne Walker*	RCA Victor 6984
3/31/58	**5**	35		6 **Send Me The Pillow You Dream On**	A:5 / S:5 *Hank Locklin*	RCA Victor 7127

DEBUT	PEAK	WKS	GOLD	ARTIST / Country Chart Hit	Ranking / Songwriter	Label (& Number)
				LOCKLIN, Hank — cont'd		
4/28/58	3[2]	23		7 **It's A Little More Like Heaven /**	A:3 / S:8 *Jim Atkins/Hoyt Johnson*	
6/2/58	flip	7		8 **Blue Glass Skirt**	*Lawton Williams*	RCA Victor 7203
3/7/60	❶[14]	36		9 **Please Help Me, I'm Falling**	*Hal Blair/Don Robertson*	RCA Victor 7692
				also see #30 below		
12/31/60+	14	12		10 **One Step Ahead Of My Past**	*Hal Blair/Don Robertson*	RCA Victor 7813
6/5/61	12	7		11 **From Here To There To You**	*Pete McKinlay*	RCA Victor 7871
9/11/61	14	12		12 **You're The Reason /**	*Bobby Edwards/Terry Fell/Fred Henley/Mildred Imes*	
10/2/61	7	14		13 **Happy Birthday To Me**	*Bill Anderson*	RCA Victor 7921
1/13/62	10	14		14 **Happy Journey**	*Fred Jay/Charles Nowa*	RCA Victor 7965
6/23/62	14	11		15 **We're Gonna Go Fishin'**	*Tex Atchison*	RCA Victor 8034
4/20/63	23	4		16 **Flyin' South**	*Cindy Walker*	RCA Victor 8156
				also see #31 below		
1/18/64	41	4		17 **Wooden Soldier**	*Lawton Williams*	RCA Victor 8248
3/21/64	15	17		18 **Followed Closely By My Teardrops**	*Paul Evans/Fred Tobias*	RCA Victor 8318
5/15/65	32	9		19 **Forty Nine, Fifty One**	*Jack Barlow/Moneen Carpenter*	RCA Victor 8560
12/25/65+	35	9		20 **The Girls Get Prettier (Every Day)**	*Harlan Howard*	RCA Victor 8695
4/9/66	48	2		21 **Insurance**	*Lawton Williams*	RCA Victor 8783
10/15/66	69	2		22 **The Best Part Of Loving You**	*Ann Prince*	RCA Victor 8928
3/4/67	41	10		23 **Hasta Luego (See You Later)**	*Johnny Hicks*	RCA Victor 9092
7/1/67	73	4		24 **Nashville Women**	*Harlan Howard*	RCA Victor 9218
10/21/67+	8	20		25 **The Country Hall Of Fame**	*Karl Davis*	RCA Victor 9323
3/30/68	40	8		26 **Love Song For You**	*Neal Merritt*	RCA Victor 9476
8/24/68	57	5		27 **Everlasting Love**	*Buzz Cason/Mac Gayden*	RCA Victor 9582
11/2/68	62	6		28 **Lovin' You (The Way I Do)**	*Ben Peters*	RCA Victor 9646
2/1/69	34	10		29 **Where The Blue Of The Night Meets The Gold Of The Day**	*Roy Turk*	RCA Victor 9710
1/3/70	68	3		30 **Please Help Me, I'm Falling** *[w/ Danny Davis]*	*Blair/Don Robertson* **[R]**	RCA Victor 0287
				new version of #9 above		
6/27/70	56	6		31 **Flying South** *[w/ Danny Davis]*	*Cindy Walker* **[R]**	RCA Victor 9849
				new version of #16 above		
10/10/70	68	4		32 **Bless Her Heart...I Love Her**	*Hank Cochran/Danny Davis*	RCA Victor 9894
3/13/71	61	4		33 **She's As Close As I Can Get To Loving You**	*Dallas Frazier/A.L. "Doodle" Owens*	RCA Victor 9955
				LOFTIS, Bobby Wayne		
				Born in Battle Creek, Michigan. Male singer/pianist.		
8/14/76	85	6		1 **See The Big Man Cry**	*Ed Bruce Jr.*	Charta 100
12/25/76+	54	11		2 **Poor Side Of Town**	*Lou Adler/Johnny Rivers*	Charta 104
6/11/77	75	6		3 **You're So Good For Me (And That's Bad)**	*Tim Christian/Charles Fields/Don Riis*	Charta 108
3/4/78	87	5		4 **Can't Shake You Off My Mind**	*Charles Fields*	Charta 118
4/21/79	89	2		5 **Small Time Picker**	*Bucky Lindsey/Ronnie Rogers*	Charta 132
				LOGAN, Bud		
				Born in Tennessee. Male singer/bassist. Former member of **The Blue Boys** (backing group for **Jim Reeves**).		
12/22/73+	14	17		1 **Wake Me Into Love** *[w/ Wilma Burgess]*	*Red Lane/Tom McKeon/Royce Porter*	Shannon 816
7/6/74	53	10		2 **The Best Day Of The Rest Of Our Love** *[w/ Wilma Burgess]*	*Bucky Jones/Royce Porter*	Shannon 820
				LOGAN, Josh		
				Born in Richmond, Kentucky. Male singer/guitarist.		
12/10/88+	58	9		1 **Everytime I Get To Dreamin'**	*John Capps/John Detterline/Don Goodman*	Curb 10519
6/3/89	62	7		2 **Somebody Paints The Wall**	*Charles Browder/Elroy Kahanek/Nelson Larkin/Tommy Smith*	Curb/MCA 10528
9/2/89	75	4		3 **I Was Born With A Broken Heart**	*Jim McBride/Aaron Tippin*	Curb/MCA 10553
				LOGGINS, Dave	**SW: #84**	
				Born on 11/10/1947 in Mountain City, Tennessee. Male singer/songwriter. Cousin of Kenny Loggins (of **Loggins & Messina**).		
9/8/84	❶[1]	22		1 **Nobody Loves Me Like You Do** *[w/ Anne Murray]*	S:❶[1] / A:❶[1] *James Dunne/Pamela Phillips*	Capitol 5401
8/17/85	72	7		2 **Just As Long As I Have You** *[w/ Gus Hardin]*	*Dave Loggins/J.D. Martin*	RCA 14159
				LOGGINS & MESSINA		
				Duo of Kenny Loggins and Jim Messina. Loggins was born on 1/7/1947 in Everett, Washington; raised in Alhambra, California. Messina was born on 12/5/1947 in Maywood, California; raised in Harlingen, Texas. Former member of **Poco**.		
12/20/75+	92	6		**Oh, Lonesome Me**	*Don Gibson*	Columbia 10222
				LONDON, Eddie		
				Born Kenneth Edward London on 7/31/1956 to an American military family in Dreux, France. Male singer/bassist.		
7/6/91	41	19		**If We Can't Do It Right**	*Ronnie Rogers/Mark Wright*	RCA
				LONESOME STRANGERS, The		
				Vocal group from Los Angeles, California: Jeff Rymes, Randy Weeks, Lorne Rall and Mike McLean.		
2/11/89	32	13		1 **Goodbye Lonesome, Hello Baby Doll**	*Lee Emerson*	Hightone 508
6/24/89	66	5		2 **Just Can't Cry No More**	*Jeff Rymes*	Hightone 511

Billboard DEBUT	PEAK	WKS	GOLD	ARTIST / Country Chart Hit	Ranking / Songwriter	Label (& Number)

LONESTAR

1990s: #49 / 2000s: #7 / All-Time: #99

Group from Nashville, Tennessee: **Richie McDonald** (vocals, guitar; born on 2/6/1962), **John Rich** (vocals, bass; born on 1/7/1974), Michael Britt (guitar; born on 6/15/1966), Dean Sams (keyboards; born on 8/3/1966) and Keech Rainwater (drums; born on 1/24/1963). Rich left in January 1998; later formed **Big & Rich**. Also see **America The Beautiful**.

CMA: Vocal Group 2001

DEBUT	PEAK	WKS	GOLD	#	Country Chart Hit	Songwriter	Label (& Number)
8/19/95	8	20		1	**Tequila Talkin'**	*Bill LaBounty/Chris Waters*	BNA
1/13/96	❶[3]	20		2	**No News**	S:5 *Phil Barnhart/Sam Hogin/Mark D. Sanders*	BNA
5/25/96	8	20		3	**Runnin' Away With My Heart**	*Michael Britt/Sam Hogin/Mark D. Sanders*	BNA
9/28/96	45	15		4	**When Cowboys Didn't Dance**	*Kyle Green/Richie McDonald*	BNA
12/7/96+	18	20		5	**Heartbroke Every Day**	*Cam King/Bill LaBounty/Ricky Vincent*	BNA
					above 5 from the album *Lonestar* on BNA 66642		
1/11/97	75	1		6	**I'll Be Home For Christmas**	*Kim Gannon/Walter Kent/Buck Ram* **[X]**	BNA
					from the various artists album *Country Cares For Kids* on BNA 67518		
5/3/97	❶[2]	20		7	**Come Cryin' To Me**	S:18 *John Rich/Mark D. Sanders/Wally Wilson*	BNA
8/30/97+	12	22		8	**You Walked In**	S:8 *Bryan Adams/Mutt Lange*	BNA
1/31/98	13	21		9	**Say When**	*Larry Boone/Paul Nelson/John Rich*	BNA
7/4/98	2[1]	26		10	**Everything's Changed**	*Larry Boone/Richie McDonald/Paul Nelson*	BNA
					above 4 from the album *Crazy Nights* on BNA 67422		
1/2/99	59	2		11	**I'll Be Home For Christmas**	*Kim Gannon/Walter Kent/Buck Ram* **[X-R]**	BNA
					from the various artists album *Country Cares For Kids* on BNA 67518		
1/9/99	61	1		12	**All My Love For Christmas**	*Billy Lawson/Wally Wilson* **[X]**	RCA
					from the various artists album *Country Christmas Classics* on RCA 67698		
2/6/99	47	12		13	**Saturday Night**	*Chuck Cannon/Jimmy Stewart*	BNA
4/10/99	❶[8]	41	●	14	**Amazed**	S:❶[6] *Marv Green/Chris Lindsey/Aimee Mayo*	BNA
9/18/99+	❶[1]	31		15	**Smile**	*Keith Follese/Chris Lindsey*	BNA
4/15/00	❶[4]	36		16	**What About Now**	*Aaron Barker/Ron Harbin/Anthony Smith*	BNA
9/16/00+	❶[2]	26		17	**Tell Her**	*Mark McClendon/Craig Wiseman*	BNA
					above 5 from the album *Lonely Grill* on BNA 60321		
12/23/00+	46	4		18	**Little Drummer Boy**	*Katherine Davis/Henry Onorati/Harry Simeone* **[X]**	BNA
12/30/00+	67	2		19	**Santa Claus Is Comin' To Town**	*J. Fred Coots/Haven Gillespie* **[X]**	BNA
12/30/00+	71	2		20	**Have Yourself A Merry Little Christmas**	*Ralph Blane/Hugh Martin* **[X]**	BNA
12/30/00	72	2		21	**Winter Wonderland**	*Felix Bernard/Richard Smith* **[X]**	BNA
					above 4 from the album *This Christmas Time* on BNA 67975		
4/14/01	❶[6]	26		22	**I'm Already There**	*Gary Baker/Richie McDonald/Frank J. Myers*	BNA
7/14/01+	12	27		23	**Unusually Unusual**	*Mark McGuinn*	BNA
8/18/01	10	23		24	**With Me**	*Brett James/Troy Verges*	BNA
1/26/02	3[4]	30		25	**Not A Day Goes By**	*Maribeth Derry/Steve Diamond*	BNA
					above 4 from the album *I'm Already There* on BNA 67011		
3/15/03	❶[1]	32		26	**My Front Porch Looking In**	*Richie McDonald/Frank J. Myers/Don Pfrimmer*	BNA
8/16/03	8	20		27	**Walking In Memphis**	*Marc Cohn*	BNA
					above 2 from the album *From There To Here: Greatest Hits* on BNA 67076		
3/6/04	4	21		28	**Let's Be Us Again**	*Maribeth Derry/Tommy Lee James/Richie McDonald*	BNA
5/22/04	53	2		29	**Somebody's Someone**	*Richie McDonald*	BNA
7/24/04	❶[2]	28		30	**Mr. Mom**	*Ron Harbin/Richie McDonald/Don Pfrimmer*	BNA
1/22/05	16	20		31	**Class Reunion (That Used To Be Us)**	*Richie McDonald/Frank J. Myers/Don Pfrimmer*	BNA
					above 4 from the album *Let's Be Us Again* on BNA 59751		
6/18/05	16↑	15↑		32	**You're Like Comin' Home**	*Brandon Kinney/Brian Maher/Jeremy Stover*	BNA
					from the album *Coming Home* on BNA 70394		

LONG, Shorty, And The Santa Fe Rangers

Born Emidio Vagnoni on 10/31/1923 in Reading, Pennsylvania. Died on 10/25/1991 (age 67). Male singer. Not to be confused with the R&B singer of the same name.

DEBUT	PEAK	WKS	GOLD	#	Country Chart Hit	Songwriter	Label (& Number)
10/30/48	12	1			**Sweeter Than The Flowers**	S:12 *Morry Burns/Lois Mann/Ervin Rouse*	Decca 46139

LONZO & OSCAR

Comedy duo: Ken "Lonzo" Marvin (born Lloyd George on 6/27/1924 in Haleyville, Alabama; died on 10/16/1991, age 67) and Rollin "Oscar" Sullivan (born on 1/19/1919 in Edmonton, Kentucky). Marvin was replaced in 1950 by Rollin's brother, John "Lonzo" Sullivan (born on 7/7/1917 in Edmonton, Kentucky; died on 6/5/1967, age 49). They were often joined on-stage by Clell "Cousin Jody" Summey (born on 12/11/1919; died on 8/18/1975, age 55). After John Sullivan's death, Rollin continued the duo with David "Lonzo" Hooten (born on 2/4/1935 in St. Claire, Missouri).

OPRY: 1947

DEBUT	PEAK	WKS	GOLD	#	Country Chart Hit	Songwriter	Label (& Number)
1/31/48	5	7		1	**I'm My Own Grandpa**	J:5 *Moe Jaffe/Dwight Latham* **[N]**	Victor 20-2563
					LONZO & OSCAR with the Winston County Pea Pickers		
6/5/61	26	1		2	**Country Music Time**	*Curly Henson* **[N]**	Starday 543
1/12/74	29	12		3	**Traces Of Life**	*Paul Huffman/Joane Keller*	GRC 1006

LORD, Bobby

Born on 1/6/1934 in Sanford, Florida. Male singer/songwriter/guitarist. Hosted own syndicated TV show in 1966.

OPRY: 1960

DEBUT	PEAK	WKS	GOLD	#	Country Chart Hit	Songwriter	Label (& Number)
9/8/56	10	2		1	**Without Your Love**	J:10 / A:15 *Wanda Jackson*	Columbia 21539
1/11/64	21	10		2	**Life Can Have Meaning**	*John D. Loudermilk*	Hickory 1232
4/6/68	44	11		3	**Live Your Life Out Loud**	*Ted Harris*	Decca 32277
9/14/68	49	5		4	**The True And Lasting Kind**	*Ted Harris*	Decca 32373
2/15/69	40	9		5	**Yesterday's Letters**	*Ted Harris*	Decca 32431

DEBUT	PEAK	WKS	GOLD	ARTIST / Country Chart Hit	Ranking / Songwriter	Label (& Number)
				LORD, Bobby — cont'd		
11/22/69+	**28**	11		6 **Rainbow Girl**	*Ted Harris*	Decca 32578
5/2/70	**15**	13		7 **You And Me Against The World**	*Ted Harris*	Decca 32657
8/22/70	**21**	14		8 **Wake Me Up Early In The Morning**	*Ted Harris*	Decca 32718
3/27/71	**75**	2		9 **Goodbye Jukebox**	*Ted Harris*	Decca 32797
				LORD, Mike Born in San Antonio, Texas. Male singer/drummer.		
6/27/87	**94**	2		**Just Try Texas**	*Dave Kirby/Warren Robb*	NSD 230
				LORIE ANN Born in Texas. Female singer.		
9/3/88	**81**	3		1 **Down On Market Street**	*Cliff Buckosh/Dave Richardson*	Sing Me 34
1/14/89	**78**	3		2 **Say The Part About I Love You**	*Eddy Raven*	Sing Me 37
6/24/89	**98**	1		3 **Just Because You're Leavin'**	*Max T. Barnes/Dave Richardson*	Sing Me 41
				LORRIE, Myrna, & Buddy DeVal Lorrie was born Myrna Petrunke on 8/6/1940 in Fort William, Ontario, Canada. Female singer/songwriter. DeVal was born on 4/15/1915 in Port Arthur, Ontario, Canada. Male singer.		
1/1/55	**6**	14		**Are You Mine**	A:6 / J:7 / S:12 *Jim Amadeo/Don Grashey/Myrna Lorrie*	Abbott 172
				LOS LOBOS Rock group from Los Angeles, California: David Hildago (vocals), Cesar Rosas (guitar), Steve Berlin (saxophone), Conrad Lozano (bass) and Louie Perez (drums).		
8/22/87	**57**	8		1 **La Bamba** from the movie starring Lou Diamond Phillips	*Ritchie Valens* **[F]**	Slash 28336
3/19/88	**55**	10		2 **One Time One Night**	*David Hidalgo/Louie Perez*	Slash 28464
				LOS LONELY BOYS Rock trio of brothers from Texas: Henry Garza (guitar), Joey "JoJo" Garza (bass) and Ringo Garza (drums). All share vocals.		
7/31/04	**46**	20		**Heaven** from the album *Los Lonely Boys* on Epic 80305	*Henry Garza/Joey Garza/Ringo Garza*	Epic
				LOU, Bonnie — see BONNIE LOU		
				LOUDERMILK, John D. Born on 3/31/1934 in Durham, North Carolina. Male singer/songwriter. First cousin of **The Louvin Brothers**. Also see **Some Of Chet's Friends**.	**SW: #74**	
6/29/63	**23**	4		1 **Bad News**	*John D. Loudermilk*	RCA Victor 8154
3/7/64	**44**	7		2 **Blue Train** (Of The Heartbreak Line)	*John D. Loudermilk*	RCA Victor 8308
9/26/64	**45**	5		3 **Th' Wife**	*John D. Loudermilk* **[N]**	RCA Victor 8389
7/3/65	**20**	11		4 **That Ain't All**	*John D. Loudermilk*	RCA Victor 8579
6/17/67	**51**	5		5 **It's My Time**	*John D. Loudermilk*	RCA Victor 9189
				LOUVIN, Charlie Born Charlie Loudermilk on 7/7/1927 in Section, Alabama. Male singer/songwriter/guitarist. Half of **The Louvin Brothers**. First cousin of **John D. Loudermilk**. *OPRY: 1955*	**All-Time: #204**	
6/20/64	**4**	27		1 **I Don't Love You Anymore**	*Bill Anderson*	Capitol 5173
12/12/64+	**27**	15		2 **Less And Less**	*Roger Miller*	Capitol 5296
3/27/65	**7**	17		3 **See The Big Man Cry**	*Ed Bruce*	Capitol 5369
10/23/65	**26**	8		4 **Think I'll Go Somewhere And Cry Myself To Sleep**	*Bill Anderson*	Capitol 5475
12/18/65+	**15**	12		5 **You Finally Said Something Good** (When You Said Goodbye)	*Gene Strasser/George Winters*	Capitol 5550
10/15/66	**58**	5		6 **The Proof Is In The Kissing**	*Larry Lee/Charlie Louvin*	Capitol 5729
12/24/66+	**38**	11		7 **Off And On**	*Bill Anderson*	Capitol 5791
4/22/67	**44**	10		8 **On The Other Hand**	*Fred Massey/Billy J. Smith*	Capitol 5872
8/5/67	**46**	9		9 **I Forgot To Cry**	*A.L. "Doodle" Owens*	Capitol 5948
11/4/67+	**36**	12		10 **The Only Way Out** (Is To Walk Over Me)	*Neal Merritt*	Capitol 2007
3/9/68	**20**	14		11 **Will You Visit Me On Sundays?**	*Dallas Frazier*	Capitol 2106
8/17/68	**15**	12		12 **Hey Daddy**	*Gene Chrysler*	Capitol 2231
12/21/68+	**19**	13		13 **What Are Those Things** (With Big Black Wings)	*Dallas Frazier/A.L. "Doodle" Owens*	Capitol 2350
4/19/69	**27**	11		14 **Let's Put Our World Back Together**	*Jimmy Peppers*	Capitol 2448
9/27/69	**29**	9		15 **Little Reasons**	*Ed Bruce*	Capitol 2612
1/17/70	**42**	9		16 **Here's A Toast To Mama**	*Buck Owens/Gene Price*	Capitol 2703
7/4/70	**47**	8		17 **Come And Get It Mama**	*Sonny Throckmorton*	Capitol 2824
10/24/70	**18**	14		18 **Something To Brag About** *[w/ Melba Montgomery]*	*Bobby Braddock*	Capitol 2915
11/28/70+	**54**	7		19 **Sittin' Bull**	*Lorene Allen/Loretta Lynn*	Capitol 2972
2/13/71	**26**	12		20 **Did You Ever** *[w/ Melba Montgomery]*	*Bobby Braddock*	Capitol 3029
6/12/71	**30**	10		21 **Baby, You've Got What It Takes** *[w/ Melba Montgomery]*	*Clyde Otis/Murray Stein*	Capitol 3111
11/27/71	**60**	5		22 **I'm Gonna Leave You** *[w/ Melba Montgomery]*	*Rayburn Anthony*	Capitol 3208
5/20/72	**70**	2		23 **Just In Time** (To Watch Love Die)	*David Allan Coe/Jimmy Townsend*	Capitol 3319
8/19/72	**66**	4		24 **Baby, What's Wrong With Us** *[w/ Melba Montgomery]*	*Larry Kingston*	Capitol 3388
1/20/73	**59**	6		25 **A Man Likes Things Like That** *[w/ Melba Montgomery]*	*Lorene Allen/Jim Owen*	Capitol 3508
1/5/74	**36**	13		26 **You're My Wife, She's My Woman**	*Al Broughton/David Wilkins*	United Artists 368
6/15/74	**76**	8		27 **It Almost Felt Like Love**	*Sonny Throckmorton*	United Artists 430
9/8/79	**91**	6		28 **Love Don't Care** *[w/ Emmylou Harris]*	*Hal Bynum/Don Wayne*	Little Darlin' 7922
6/5/82	**56**	9		29 **North Wind** *[w/ Jim & Jesse]*	*Don Pfrimmer/Charles Quillen*	Soundwaves 4671
6/17/89	**87**	2		30 **The Precious Jewel** *[w/ Roy Acuff]*	*Roy Acuff*	Hal Kat 63058

Billboard DEBUT	PEAK	WKS	GOLD	ARTIST / Country Chart Hit	Ranking / Songwriter	Label (& Number)

LOUVIN, Ira

Born Ira Loudermilk on 4/21/1924 in Section, Alabama. Died in a car crash on 6/20/1965 (age 41). Male singer/songwriter/mandolin player. Half of **The Louvin Brothers**. First cousin of **John D. Loudermilk**.

DEBUT	PEAK	WKS	GOLD	Country Chart Hit	Songwriter	Label (& Number)
8/14/65	**44**	4		**Yodel, Sweet Molly**	*Anne Young*	Capitol 5428

LOUVIN BROTHERS, The — 1950s: #31 // HOF: 2001

Duo of brothers from Section, Alabama: **Charlie Louvin** (vocals, guitar; born on 7/7/1927) and **Ira Louvin** (vocals, mandolin; born on 4/21/1924; died in a car crash on 6/20/1965, age 41). Charlie remained a member of the *Grand Ole Opry* as a solo artist.

OPRY: 1955

DEBUT	PEAK	WKS	GOLD	Country Chart Hit	Ranking / Songwriter	Label (& Number)
9/10/55	**8**	13		1 **When I Stop Dreaming**	A:8 / S:13 *Charlie Louvin/Ira Louvin*	Capitol 3177
1/14/56	**❶[2]**	24		2 **I Don't Believe You've Met My Baby**	A:❶[2] / S:5 / J:5 *Autry Inman*	Capitol 3300
5/26/56	**7**	10		3 **Hoping That You're Hoping**	A:7 / S:8 *Betty Harrison*	Capitol 3413
10/6/56	**7**	12		4 **You're Running Wild /**	S:7 / A:11 *Ray Edenton/Don Winters*	
10/6/56	**7**	11		5 **Cash On The Barrel Head**	S:7 / A:10 *Charlie Louvin/Ira Louvin*	Capitol 3523
3/9/57	**11**	4		6 **Don't Laugh**	A:11 *Rebe Gosdin*	Capitol 3630
7/15/57	**14**	1		7 **Plenty Of Everything But You**	A:14 *Charlie Louvin/Ira Louvin*	Capitol 3715
10/20/58+	**9**	22		8 **My Baby's Gone**	*Hazel Houser*	Capitol 4055
2/16/59	**19**	7		9 **Knoxville Girl**	*Charlie Louvin/Ira Louvin*	Capitol 4117
3/13/61	**12**	14		10 **I Love You Best Of All**	*Charlie Louvin/Ira Louvin*	Capitol 4506
9/25/61	**26**	1		11 **How's The World Treating You**	*Chet Atkins/Boudleaux Bryant*	Capitol 4628
11/17/62	**21**	6		12 **Must You Throw Dirt In My Face**	*Bill Anderson*	Capitol 4822

LOVELESS, Patty — 1990s: #16 / All-Time: #73

Born Patricia Ramey on 1/4/1957 in Pikeville, Kentucky. Female singer/songwriter/guitarist. Married record producer Emory Gordy Jr. on 2/6/1989. Distant cousin of **Loretta Lynn**, **Crystal Gayle**, **Peggy Sue** and **Jay Lee Webb**. Also see **Same Old Train**.

CMA: Female Vocalist 1996 // OPRY: 1988

DEBUT	PEAK	WKS	GOLD	Country Chart Hit	Ranking / Songwriter	Label (& Number)
12/7/85+	**46**	10		1 **Lonely Days, Lonely Nights**	*Karen Staley*	MCA 52694
11/29/86+	**49**	10		2 **Wicked Ways**	*Karen Staley*	MCA 52969
3/14/87	**56**	8		3 **I Did**	*Patty Loveless*	MCA 53040
6/20/87	**43**	10		4 **After All**	*Jimbeau Hinson/Harry Stinson*	MCA 53097
10/31/87	**43**	11		5 **You Saved Me**	*Curtis Wright*	MCA 53179
2/6/88	**10**	20		6 **If My Heart Had Windows**	S:14 *Dallas Frazier*	MCA 53270
6/4/88	**2[1]**	20		7 **A Little Bit In Love**	S:11 *Steve Earle*	MCA 53333
10/8/88+	**4**	20		8 **Blue Side Of Town**	S:5 *Hank DeVito/Paul Kennerley*	MCA 53418
2/4/89	**5**	20		9 **Don't Toss Us Away**	*Bryan MacLean*	MCA 53477
5/27/89	**❶[1]**	20		10 **Timber, I'm Falling In Love**	*Kostas*	MCA 53641
9/9/89	**6**	26		11 **The Lonely Side Of Love**	*Kostas*	MCA 53702
1/6/90	**❶[1]**	26		12 **Chains** from the album *Honky Tonk Angel* on MCA 42223	*Hal Bynum/Bud Reneau*	MCA
5/19/90	**5**	21		13 **On Down The Line**	*Kostas*	MCA
9/22/90	**20**	20		14 **The Night's Too Long**	*Lucinda Williams*	MCA
1/12/91	**5**	20		15 **I'm That Kind Of Girl**	*Matraca Berg/Ronnie Samoset*	MCA
5/11/91	**22**	20		16 **Blue Memories** above 4 from the album *On Down The Line* on MCA 6401	*Karen Brooks/Paul Kennerley*	MCA
9/7/91	**3[1]**	20		17 **Hurt Me Bad (In A Real Good Way)**	*Deborah Allen/Rafe Van Hoy*	MCA
1/4/92	**13**	20		18 **Jealous Bone**	*Steve Bogard/Rick Giles*	MCA
4/25/92	**30**	20		19 **Can't Stop Myself From Loving You** above 3 from the album *Up Against My Heart* on MCA 10336	*Dean Folkvord/Kostas*	MCA
8/8/92	**47**	10		20 **Send A Message To My Heart** ***[w/ Dwight Yoakam]*** from Yoakam's album *If There Was A Way* on Reprise 26344	*Kostas/Kelly Louvin*	Reprise
4/3/93	**❶[2]**	20		21 **Blame It On Your Heart**	*Harlan Howard/Kostas*	Epic
7/17/93	**20**	20		22 **Nothin' But The Wheel**	*John Scott Sherrill*	Epic
11/20/93+	**6**	20		23 **You Will**	*Mary Ann Kennedy/Pam Rose/Randy Sharp*	Epic
3/19/94	**3[2]**	20		24 **How Can I Help You Say Goodbye** above 4 from the album *Only What I Feel* on Epic 53236	*Burton Collins/Karen Taylor-Good*	Epic
7/30/94	**3[1]**	20		25 **I Try To Think About Elvis**	*Gary Burr*	Epic
11/12/94+	**4**	20		26 **Here I Am**	*Tony Arata*	Epic
3/18/95	**5**	20		27 **You Don't Even Know Who I Am**	S:4 *Gretchen Peters*	Epic
7/8/95	**6**	20		28 **Halfway Down** above 4 from the album *When Fallen Angels Fly* on Epic 64188	*Jim Lauderdale*	Epic
12/30/95+	**❶[2]**	20		29 **You Can Feel Bad**	S:12 *Matraca Berg/Tim Krekel*	Epic
4/13/96	**13**	20		30 **A Thousand Times A Day**	*Gary Burr/Gary Nicholson*	Epic
8/24/96	**❶[1]**	20		31 **Lonely Too Long**	*Mike Lawler/Bill Rice/Mary Sharon Rice*	Epic
12/21/96+	**4**	20		32 **She Drew A Broken Heart**	*Jon McElroy/Ned McElroy*	Epic
4/26/97	**15**	20		33 **The Trouble With The Truth** above 5 from the album *The Trouble With The Truth* on Epic 67269	*Gary Nicholson*	Epic
9/20/97	**14**	20		34 **You Don't Seem To Miss Me** ***[w/ George Jones]*** **CMA: Vocal Event**	S:9 *Jim Lauderdale*	Epic

DEBUT	PEAK	WKS	GOLD	ARTIST / Ranking / Country Chart Hit	Songwriter	Label (& Number)
				LOVELESS, Patty — cont'd		
1/31/98	**12**	20		35 **To Have You Back Again**	*Annie Roboff/Arnie Roman*	Epic
6/6/98	**20**	20		36 **High On Love**	*Jeff Hanna/Kostas*	Epic
10/17/98	**57**	5		37 **Like Water Into Wine**	*Gretchen Peters*	Epic
				above 4 from the album *Long Stretch Of Lonesome* on Epic 67997		
1/16/99	**21**	20		38 **Can't Get Enough**	*Kent Blazy/Blair Daly/Will Rambeaux*	Epic
				from the album *Classics* on Epic 69809		
5/29/99	**27**	20		39 **My Kind Of Woman/My Kind Of Man** ***[w/ Vince Gill]***	*Vince Gill*	MCA Nashville
				CMA: Vocal Event; from Gill's album *The Key* on MCA Nashville 70017		
6/10/00	**13**	28		40 **That's The Kind Of Mood I'm In**	S:8 *Rick Giles/Gilles Godard/Tim Nichols*	Epic
1/6/01	**20**	21		41 **The Last Thing On My Mind**	*Al Anderson/Craig Wiseman*	Epic
				above 2 from the album *Strong Heart* on Epic 69880		
6/14/03	**18**	20		42 **Lovin' All Night**	S:10 *Rodney Crowell*	Epic
11/8/03+	**29**	20		43 **On Your Way Home**	*Matraca Berg/Ronnie Samoset*	Epic
5/8/04	**60**	1		44 **I Wanna Believe**	*Jessi Alexander/Al Anderson/Gary Nicholson*	Epic
				above 3 from the album *On Your Way Home* on Epic 86620		
				LOVETT, Lyle		
				Born on 11/1/1957 in Klein, Texas. Male singer/songwriter/guitarist. Acted in several movies. Married to actress Julia Roberts from 1993-95. No relation to Ruby Lovett.		
7/12/86	**21**	19		1 **Farther Down The Line**	S:14 / A:24 *Lyle Lovett*	Curb/MCA 52818
11/1/86+	**10**	19		2 **Cowboy Man**	S:7 / A:10 *Lyle Lovett*	Curb/MCA 52951
2/21/87	**18**	14		3 **God Will**	A:19 *Lyle Lovett*	Curb/MCA 53030
6/6/87	**15**	14		4 **Why I Don't Know**	*Lyle Lovett*	Curb/MCA 53102
10/3/87	**13**	18		5 **Give Back My Heart**	S:19 *Lyle Lovett*	Curb/MCA 53157
1/30/88	**17**	16		6 **She's No Lady**	S:14 *Lyle Lovett*	Curb/MCA 53246
5/21/88	**24**	14		7 **I Loved You Yesterday**	S:27 *Lyle Lovett*	Curb/MCA 53316
9/17/88	**66**	4		8 **If I Had A Boat**	*Lyle Lovett*	Curb/MCA 53401
12/10/88+	**45**	9		9 **I Married Her Just Because She Looks Like You**	*Lyle Lovett*	Curb/MCA 53471
3/4/89	**82**	3		10 **Stand By Your Man**	*Billy Sherrill/Tammy Wynette*	Curb/MCA 53611
6/17/89	**84**	2		11 **Nobody Knows Me**	*Lyle Lovett*	Curb/MCA 53650
9/23/89	**49**	7		12 **If I Were The Man You Wanted**	*Lyle Lovett*	Curb/MCA 53703
9/28/96	**68**	2		13 **Don't Touch My Hat**	*Lyle Lovett*	Curb/MCA
1/18/97	**72**	1		14 **Private Conversation**	*Lyle Lovett*	Curb/MCA
				above 2 from the album *The Road To Ensenada* on Curb/MCA 11409		
				LOVETT, Ruby		
				Born on 2/16/1967 in Laurel, Mississippi. Female singer/songwriter. No relation to Lyle Lovett.		
10/4/97	**73**	1		**Look What Love Can Do**	*Hunter Davis/Ruby Lovett/Pie Taylor*	Curb
				from the album *Ruby Lovett* on Curb 77857		
				LOWE, Jim		
				Born on 5/7/1927 in Springfield, Missouri. Male singer/songwriter/pianist.		
5/20/57	**8**	3		1 **Talkin' To The Blues /**	S:8 *Jim Lowe/Marvin Moore*	
				from the TV series *Modern Romances*		
7/8/57	**flip**	1		2 **Four Walls**	*George Campbell/Marvin Moore*	Dot 15569
				LOWES, The		
				Family vocal group from Texas.		
7/19/86	**61**	5		1 **Good And Lonesome**	*Ron Hellard/Bucky Jones/Curly Putnam*	Soundwaves 4775
11/8/86	**84**	4		2 **Cry Baby**	*Don Cook/Jamie O'Hara/Curly Putnam*	API 1001
1/17/87	**70**	5		3 **I Ain't Never**	*Webb Pierce/Mel Tillis*	API 1002
				LOWRY, Ron		
				Born in Arizona. Male singer.		
2/28/70	**39**	11		1 **Marry Me**	*Sandy Mason/Les Reed*	Republic 1409
8/22/70	**65**	6		2 **Oh How I Waited**	*Les Reed/Geoff Stephens*	Republic 1415
				LUCAS, Lauren		
				Born in Columbia, South Carolina. Female singer.		
4/16/05	**52**	4		**What You Ain't Gonna Get**	*Marcus Hummon/Tom Shapiro*	Warner
				LUCAS, Tammy		
				Born in Georgia. Female singer.		
2/11/89	**75**	4		**9,999,999 Tears**	*Razzy Bailey*	SOA 005
				LUKE THE DRIFTER, JR. — see WILLIAMS, Hank Jr.		
				LULU BELLE & SCOTTY		
				Popular wife-and-husband duo. Myrtle "Lulu Belle" Cooper (guitar) was born on 12/24/1913 in Boone, North Carolina. Died on 2/8/1999 (age 85). Scotty Wiseman (banjo) was born on 11/8/1909 in Ingalls, North Carolina. Died on 1/31/1981 (age 71). Known as the "Hayloft Sweethearts" and the "Sweethearts of Country Music." Stars of the WLS radio *National Barn Dance* from 1933-58. Appeared in several movies. Married on 12/13/1934.		

Billboard DEBUT	PEAK	WKS	GOLD	ARTIST / Country Chart Hit	Songwriter	Label (& Number)

LUMAN, Bob

All-Time: #159

Born on 4/15/1937 in Nacogdoches, Texas. Died of pneumonia on 12/27/1978 (age 41). Male singer/songwriter/guitarist. Joined the *Louisiana Hayride* in 1956. First recorded for Imperial in 1957. Appeared in the 1957 movie *Carnival Rock*.

OPRY: 1965

DEBUT	PEAK	WKS	Country Chart Hit	Songwriter	Label (& Number)
10/10/60	**9**	10	1 **Let's Think About Living**	*Boudleaux Bryant* [N]	Warner 5172
2/22/64	**24**	14	2 **The File**	*John D. Loudermilk*	Hickory 1238
1/29/66	**39**	5	3 **Five Miles From Home (Soon I'll See Mary)**	*Mickey Newbury*	Hickory 1355
6/4/66	**39**	5	4 **Poor Boy Blues**	*Carl Perkins*	Hickory 1382
9/24/66	**42**	11	5 **Come On And Sing**	*Mel Tillis*	Hickory 1410
2/18/67	**59**	6	6 **Hardly Anymore**	*Doug Kershaw*	Hickory 1430
7/22/67	**61**	2	7 **If You Don't Love Me (Then Why Don't You Leave Me Alone)**	*Mickey Newbury*	Hickory 1460
5/11/68	**19**	14	8 **Ain't Got Time To Be Unhappy**	*Glenn Sutton*	Epic 10312
9/28/68	**50**	7	9 **I Like Trains**	*Glenn Sutton*	Epic 10381
2/22/69	**24**	12	10 **Come On Home And Sing The Blues To Daddy**	*Bob Corbin*	Epic 10439
6/7/69	**65**	5	11 **It's All Over (But The Shouting)**	*Joe Luman*	Hickory 1536
6/28/69	**23**	13	12 **Every Day I Have To Cry Some**	*Arthur Alexander*	Epic 10480
11/29/69+	**60**	9	13 **The Gun**	*Glenn Sutton*	Epic 10535
3/28/70	**56**	5	14 **Gettin' Back To Norma**	*Ray Griff*	Epic 10581
5/9/70	**56**	8	15 **Still Loving You** also see #26 below	*Troy Shondell*	Hickory 1564
7/11/70	**22**	14	16 **Honky Tonk Man**	*Tillman Franks/Howard Hausey/Johnny Horton*	Epic 10631
11/28/70+	**44**	10	17 **What About The Hurt**	*Jerry Foster/Bill Rice*	Epic 10667
3/27/71	**60**	5	18 **Is It Any Wonder That I Love You**	*Jerry Foster/Bill Rice*	Epic 10699
7/17/71	**40**	9	19 **I Got A Woman**	*Ray Charles*	Epic 10755
11/6/71	**30**	10	20 **A Chain Don't Take To Me**	*Dallas Frazier*	Epic 10786
1/29/72	**6**	17	21 **When You Say Love**	*Jerry Foster/Bill Rice*	Epic 10823
6/3/72	**21**	10	22 **It Takes You**	*Jerry Foster/Bill Rice*	Epic 10869
9/2/72	**4**	19	23 **Lonely Women Make Good Lovers**	*Spooner Oldham/Freddy Weller*	Epic 10905
1/27/73	**7**	14	24 **Neither One Of Us**	*Jim Weatherly*	Epic 10943
6/9/73	**23**	11	25 **A Good Love Is Like A Good Song**	*Casey Kelly*	Epic 10994
10/20/73+	**7**	15	26 **Still Loving You** new version of #15 above	*Troy Shondell* [R]	Epic 11039
3/9/74	**23**	11	27 **Just Enough To Make Me Stay**	*Jim Weatherly*	Epic 11087
7/13/74	**25**	11	28 **Let Me Make The Bright Lights Shine For You**	*Waylon Jennings/Troy Seals*	Epic 11138
2/8/75	**22**	13	29 **Proud Of You Baby**	*Billy Sherrill/Norro Wilson*	Epic 50065
9/13/75	**48**	12	30 **Shame On Me**	*Bill Enis/Lawton Williams*	Epic 50136
2/7/76	**41**	9	31 **A Satisfied Mind**	*Joe Hayes/Jack Rhodes*	Epic 50183
5/8/76	**82**	4	32 **The Man From Bowling Green**	*Max D. Barnes/Troy Seals*	Epic 50216
8/7/76	**89**	4	33 **How Do You Start Over**	*Bill Dees/Roy Orbison*	Epic 50247
11/27/76	**94**	4	34 **Labor Of Love**	*Steve Wariner*	Epic 50297
1/22/77	**63**	8	35 **He's Got A Way With Women**	*Steve Wariner*	Epic 50323
8/6/77	**33**	9	36 **I'm A Honky-Tonk Woman's Man**	*Jerry Foster/Bill Rice*	Polydor 14408
10/8/77	**13**	16	37 **The Pay Phone**	*Glenn Martin*	Polydor 14431
12/24/77	**92**	3	38 **A Christmas Tribute**	*Jerry Foster/Wilburn Rice* [X]	Polydor 14444
2/11/78	**47**	8	39 **Proud Lady**	*Sonny Throckmorton*	Polydor 14454

LUNSFORD, Mike

Born on 6/30/1950 in Guyman, Oklahoma. Male singer/songwriter/guitarist.

DEBUT	PEAK	WKS	Country Chart Hit	Songwriter	Label (& Number)
3/1/75	**56**	12	1 **While The Feelings Good**	*Roger Bowling/Freddie Hart*	Gusto 124
11/8/75	**87**	5	2 **Sugar Sugar**	*Jeff Barry/Andy Kim*	Starday 133
7/31/76	**16**	12	3 **Honey Hungry**	*James Coleman/Moe Lytle*	Starday 143
11/20/76+	**28**	11	4 **Stealin' Feelin'**	*James Coleman/Moe Lytle*	Starday 146
2/26/77	**61**	7	5 **If There Ever Comes A Day**	*Mike Lunsford/Bill Mercer*	Starday 149
7/16/77	**71**	5	6 **I Can't Stop Now**	*James Coleman/Moe Lytle*	Starday 160
5/27/78	**85**	4	7 **The Reason Why I'm Here**	*Conway Twitty*	Starday 187
11/18/78	**91**	5	8 **I Wish I'd Never Borrowed Anybody's Angel**	*Moe Lytle/A.L. "Doodle" Owens*	Gusto 9013
5/26/79	**82**	4	9 **I Still Believe In You**	*Charlie Craig*	Gusto 9018
2/23/80	**93**	3	10 **Is It Wrong**	*Warner Mack*	Gusto 9024
4/23/88	**89**	2	11 **Tonight She Went Crazy Without Me**	*Charlie Black/Austin Roberts/Tommy Rocco*	Evergreen 1068

LYERLY, Bill

Born on 2/28/1953 in Richmond, Virginia. Male singer/songwriter/guitarist.

DEBUT	PEAK	WKS	Country Chart Hit	Songwriter	Label (& Number)
6/20/81	**53**	7	**My Baby's Coming Home Again Today**	*Bill Lyerly*	RCA 12255

LYNDELL, Liz

Born Elizabeth Jones Tidwell in Fairview, Tennessee. Female singer. Acted in the movie *That's Country*.

DEBUT	PEAK	WKS	Country Chart Hit	Songwriter	Label (& Number)
10/11/80	**88**	2	1 **Undercover Man**	*Linda Kimball/John Riggs/Mark Sherrill*	Koala 326
3/7/81	**78**	4	2 **I'm Gonna Let Go (And Love Somebody)**	*Jack Lebsock*	Koala 330
7/11/81	**85**	3	3 **Right In The Wrong Direction**	*Robert Jones/Jerry Taylor*	Koala 332

Billboard DEBUT	PEAK	WKS	GOLD	ARTIST Ranking / Country Chart Hit	Songwriter	Label (& Number)

LYNDEN, Tracy

Born in Montana. Female singer.

DEBUT	PEAK	WKS	GOLD	Country Chart Hit	Songwriter	Label (& Number)
5/25/85	**80**	5		**Straight Laced Lady**	*R.C. Bannon/Keith McGregor*	RCA 14059

LYNN, Jenny

Born in Alabama. Female singer.

DEBUT	PEAK	WKS	GOLD	Country Chart Hit	Songwriter	Label (& Number)
9/23/78	**86**	3		**Taste Of Love**	*David Heavener*	Colonial 102

LYNN, Judy

Born Judy Lynn Voiten on 4/12/1936 in Boise, Idaho. Singer/songwriter. Retired in 1980 to become an ordained minister.

DEBUT	PEAK	WKS	GOLD	Country Chart Hit	Songwriter	Label (& Number)
8/18/62	**7**	16		1 **Footsteps Of A Fool**	*Don Carter/Danny Harrison*	United Artists 472
1/26/63	**29**	1		2 **My Secret**	*Judy Lynn*	United Artists 519
4/6/63	**16**	15		3 **My Father's Voice**	*Judy Lynn*	United Artists 571
5/15/71	**74**	2		4 **Married To A Memory**	*Alex Harvey*	Amaret 131
1/18/75	**92**	5		5 **Padre**	*Alan Romans/Paul Francis Webster*	Warner 8059

LYNN, Loretta — 1960s: #15 / 1970s: #5 / All-Time: #20 // HOF: 1988

Born Loretta Webb on 4/14/1935 in Butcher Holler, Kentucky. Female singer/songwriter/guitarist. Married to Oliver "Mooney" Lynn from 1/10/1948 until his death on 8/22/1996 (age 69). Her autobiography and movie called *Coal Miner's Daughter* (which starred **Sissy Spacek** as Lynn). Sister of **Crystal Gayle**, **Peggy Sue** and **Jay Lee Webb**; distant cousin of **Patty Loveless**. Her son **Ernest Rey** and daughters Patsy and Peggy (as **The Lynns**) also recorded.

CMA: Female Vocalist 1967, 1972 & 1973 / Entertainer 1972 / Vocal Duo (with Conway Twitty) 1972, 1973, 1974 & 1975 // OPRY: 1962

DEBUT	PEAK	WKS	GOLD	Country Chart Hit	Songwriter	Label (& Number)
6/13/60	**14**	9		1 **I'm A Honky Tonk Girl**	*Loretta Lynn*	Zero 107
7/7/62	**6**	16		2 **Success**	*Johnny Mullins*	Decca 31384
6/8/63	**13**	11		3 **The Other Woman**	*Betty Sue Perry*	Decca 31471
11/16/63+	**4**	25		4 **Before I'm Over You**	*Betty Sue Perry*	Decca 31541
5/2/64	**3^{3}**	24		5 **Wine Women And Song**	*Betty Sue Perry*	Decca 31608
7/25/64	**11**	23		6 **Mr. And Mrs. Used To Be** *[w/ Ernest Tubb]*	*Joe Deaton*	Decca 31643
12/5/64+	**3^{2}**	23		7 **Happy Birthday**	*Ron Kitson*	Decca 31707
5/22/65	**7**	18		8 **Blue Kentucky Girl**	*Johnny Mullins*	Decca 31769
7/24/65	**24**	11		9 **Our Hearts Are Holding Hands** *[w/ Ernest Tubb]*	*Bill Anderson*	Decca 31793
9/18/65	**10**	16		10 **The Home You're Tearin' Down**	*Betty Sue Perry*	Decca 31836
2/5/66	**4**	14		11 **Dear Uncle Sam**	*Loretta Lynn*	Decca 31893
6/4/66	**2^{2}**	23		12 **You Ain't Woman Enough**	*Loretta Lynn*	Decca 31966
11/12/66+	**❶^{1}**	19		13 **Don't Come Home A'Drinkin' (With Lovin' On Your Mind)**	*Loretta Lynn/Peggy Sue Wells*	Decca 32045
2/25/67	**45**	9		14 **Sweet Thang** *[w/ Ernest Tubb]*	*Nat Stuckey*	Decca 32091
5/13/67	**7**	17		15 **If You're Not Gone Too Long /**	*Wanda Ballman*	
6/10/67	**72**	2		16 **A Man I Hardly Know**	*Loretta Lynn*	Decca 32127
9/23/67	**5**	17		17 **What Kind Of Girl (Do You Think I Am?)**	*Loretta Lynn/Teddy Wilburn*	Decca 32184
2/24/68	**❶^{1}**	17		18 **Fist City**	*Loretta Lynn*	Decca 32264
6/15/68	**2^{1}**	16		19 **You've Just Stepped In (From Stepping Out On Me)**	*Don Trowbridge*	Decca 32332
10/26/68	**3^{3}**	16		20 **Your Squaw Is On The Warpath**	*Loretta Lynn*	Decca 32392
2/22/69	**❶^{1}**	16		21 **Woman Of The World (Leave My World Alone)**	*Sharon Higgins*	Decca 32439
6/14/69	**18**	10		22 **Who's Gonna Take The Garbage Out** *[w/ Ernest Tubb]*	*Lucille Cosenza/Johnny Tillotson/Teddy Wilburn*	Decca 32496
7/19/69	**3^{3}**	15		23 **To Make A Man (Feel Like A Man)**	*Loretta Lynn*	Decca 32513
11/29/69+	**11**	16		24 **Wings Upon Your Horns**	*Loretta Lynn*	Decca 32586
3/7/70	**4**	14		25 **I Know How**	*Loretta Lynn*	Decca 32637
6/27/70	**6**	15		26 **You Wanna Give Me A Lift**	*Loretta Lynn*	Decca 32693
10/31/70	**❶^{1}**	15		27 **Coal Miner's Daughter** Grammy: Hall of Fame	*Loretta Lynn*	Decca 32749
2/6/71	**❶^{2}**	14		28 **After The Fire Is Gone** *[w/ Conway Twitty]* Grammy: Vocal Duo	*L.E. White*	Decca 32776
3/27/71	**3^{2}**	15		29 **I Wanna Be Free**	*Loretta Lynn*	Decca 32796
7/31/71	**5**	16		30 **You're Lookin' At Country**	*Loretta Lynn*	Decca 32851
10/2/71	**❶^{1}**	17		31 **Lead Me On** *[w/ Conway Twitty]*	*Leon Copeland*	Decca 32873
12/11/71+	**❶^{2}**	16		32 **One's On The Way**	*Shel Silverstein*	Decca 32900
7/8/72	**3^{2}**	15		33 **Here I Am Again**	*Shel Silverstein*	Decca 32974
12/9/72+	**❶^{1}**	16		34 **Rated "X"**	*Loretta Lynn*	Decca 33039
5/19/73	**❶^{2}**	15		35 **Love Is The Foundation**	*William Hall*	MCA 40058
6/23/73	**❶^{1}**	14		36 **Louisiana Woman, Mississippi Man** *[w/ Conway Twitty]*	*Becki Bluefield/Jim Owen*	MCA 40079
11/17/73+	**3^{1}**	16		37 **Hey Loretta**	*Shel Silverstein*	MCA 40150
4/27/74	**4**	15		38 **They Don't Make 'Em Like My Daddy**	*Jerry Chesnut*	MCA 40223
6/15/74	**❶^{1}**	15		39 **As Soon As I Hang Up The Phone** *[w/ Conway Twitty]*	*Conway Twitty*	MCA 40251
9/7/74	**❶^{1}**	17		40 **Trouble In Paradise**	*Kenny O'Dell*	MCA 40283
2/15/75	**5**	12		41 **The Pill**	*Lorene Allen/T.D. Bayless/Don McHan*	MCA 40358
6/21/75	**❶^{1}**	16		42 **Feelins'** *[w/ Conway Twitty]*	*Don Goodman/Will Jennings/Troy Seals*	MCA 40420
8/2/75	**10**	14		43 **Home**	*Bobby Harden*	MCA 40438
11/15/75+	**2^{1}**	14		44 **When The Tingle Becomes A Chill**	*Lola Jean Dillon*	MCA 40484
4/10/76	**20**	10		45 **Red, White And Blue**	*Loretta Lynn*	MCA 40541

Billboard DEBUT	PEAK	WKS	GOLD	ARTIST / Ranking / Country Chart Hit	Songwriter	Label (& Number)
				LYNN, Loretta — cont'd		
6/19/76	**3**^{2}	12		46 **The Letter** *[w/ Conway Twitty]*	*Charles Haney/Conway Twitty*	MCA 40572
9/11/76	❶^{2}	17		47 **Somebody Somewhere** (Don't Know What He's Missin' Tonight)	*Lola Jean Dillon*	MCA 40607
2/26/77	❶^{1}	17		48 **She's Got You**	*Hank Cochran*	MCA 40679
6/4/77	**2**^{3}	14		49 **I Can't Love You Enough** *[w/ Conway Twitty]*	*Max D. Barnes/Troy Seals*	MCA 40728
8/6/77	**7**	13		50 **Why Can't He Be You**	*Hank Cochran*	MCA 40747
12/3/77+	❶^{2}	15		51 **Out Of My Head And Back In My Bed**	*Peggy Forman*	MCA 40832
5/27/78	**12**	11		52 **Spring Fever**	*Lola Jean Dillon*	MCA 40910
6/24/78	**6**	11		53 **From Seven Till Ten** *[w/ Conway Twitty]* /	*Max D. Barnes/Troy Seals*	
7/8/78	**flip**	9		54 **You're The Reason Our Kids Are Ugly** *[w/ Conway Twitty]*	*Lola Jean Dillon/L.E. White*	MCA 40920
11/4/78	**10**	13		55 **We've Come A Long Way, Baby**	*Shirl Milete/L.E. White*	MCA 40954
5/5/79	**3**^{1}	14		56 **I Can't Feel You Anymore**	*Theresa Beaty/Meredith Stewart*	MCA 41021
10/13/79	**5**	14		57 **I've Got A Picture Of Us On My Mind**	*Bobby Harden*	MCA 41129
11/10/79+	**9**	14		58 **You Know Just What I'd Do** *[w/ Conway Twitty]* /	*Jerry Foster/Bill Rice*	
11/10/79+	**flip**	14		59 **The Sadness Of It All** *[w/ Conway Twitty]*	*Rusty Wolfe*	MCA 41141
3/1/80	**35**	8		60 **Pregnant Again**	*Lee Pockriss/Mark Sameth*	MCA 41185
5/10/80	**5**	15		61 **It's True Love** *[w/ Conway Twitty]*	*Randy Goodrum*	MCA 41232
6/7/80	**30**	11		62 **Naked In The Rain**	*Buddy Cannon/Kenny Starr*	MCA 41250
10/25/80	**20**	13		63 **Cheatin' On A Cheater**	*Woody Bomar/Johnny Wilson*	MCA 51015
1/31/81	**7**	15		64 **Lovin' What Your Lovin' Does To Me** *[w/ Conway Twitty]*	*Jane Crouch/Toni Dae*	MCA 51050
2/28/81	**20**	12		65 **Somebody Led Me Away**	*Lola Jean Dillon*	MCA 51058
5/30/81	**2**^{2}	18		66 **I Still Believe In Waltzes** *[w/ Conway Twitty]*	*Michael Hughes/Johnny MacRae/Bob Morrison*	MCA 51114
1/23/82	**9**	19		67 **I Lie**	*Tom Damphier*	MCA 52005
8/14/82	**19**	16		68 **Making Love From Memory**	*Nilda Daniel/Sid Linard*	MCA 52092
1/22/83	**39**	12		69 **Breakin' It** /	*Mark Germino*	
1/22/83	**flip**	12		70 **There's All Kinds Of Smoke** (In The Barroom)	*Don Wayne*	MCA 52158
5/28/83	**53**	10		71 **Lyin', Cheatin', Woman Chasin', Honky Tonkin', Whiskey Drinkin' You**	...*Gene Dobbins/Pat McManus*	MCA 52219
11/26/83	**59**	9		72 **Walking With My Memories**	*Fred Koller/Mike Pace*	MCA 52289
7/20/85	**19**	18		73 **Heart Don't Do This To Me** S:19 / A:22	*Kin Vassy/Justin Wilde*	MCA 52621
11/9/85	**72**	5		74 **Wouldn't It Be Great**	*Loretta Lynn*	MCA 52706
2/8/86	**81**	5		75 **Just A Woman**	*Stewart Harris/Carlotta McKee*	MCA 52766
4/16/88	**57**	12		76 **Who Was That Stranger**	*Max D. Barnes/Don Cook/Curly Putman*	MCA 53320
12/25/93+	**68**	2		77 **Silver Threads And Golden Needles** *[w/ Dolly Parton & Tammy Wynette]* from their album *Honky Tonky Angels* on Columbia 53414	...*Dick Reynolds/Jack Rhodes*	Columbia
9/23/00	**72**	1		78 **Country In My Genes** from the album *Still Country* on Audium 8119	*Larry Cordle/Betty Key/Larry Shell*	Audium

After The Fire Is Gone ['71]
As Soon As I Hang Up The Phone ['74]
Before I'm Over You ['64]
Blue Kentucky Girl ['65]
Breakin' It ['83]
Cheatin' On A Cheater ['80]
Coal Miner's Daughter ['70]
Country In My Genes ['00]
Dear Uncle Sam ['66]
Don't Come Home A'Drinkin' (With Lovin' On Your Mind) ['67]
Feelins' ['75]
Fist City ['68]
From Seven Till Ten ['78]
Happy Birthday ['65]
Heart Don't Do This To Me ['85]
Here I Am Again ['72]
Hey Loretta ['74]
Home ['75]
Home You're Tearin' Down ['65]
I Can't Feel You Anymore ['79]
I Can't Love You Enough ['77]
I Know How ['70]
I Lie ['82]
I Still Believe In Waltzes ['81]
I Wanna Be Free ['71]
I'm A Honky Tonk Girl ['60]
I've Got A Picture Of Us On My Mind ['79]
If You're Not Gone Too Long ['67]
It's True Love ['80]
Just A Woman ['86]
Lead Me On ['71]
Letter ['76]
Louisiana Woman, Mississippi Man ['73]
Love Is The Foundation ['73]
Lovin' What Your Lovin' Does To Me ['81]
Lyin', Cheatin', Woman Chasin', Honky Tonkin', Whiskey Drinkin' You ['83]
Making Love From Memory ['82]
Man I Hardly Know ['67]
Mr. And Mrs. Used To Be ['64]
Naked In The Rain ['80]
One's On The Way ['72]
Other Woman ['63]
Our Hearts Are Holding Hands ['65]
Out Of My Head And Back In My Bed ['78]
Pill ['75]
Pregnant Again ['80]
Rated "X" ['73]
Red, White And Blue ['76]
Sadness Of It All ['80]
She's Got You ['77]
Silver Threads And Golden Needles ['94]
Somebody Led Me Away ['81]
Somebody Somewhere (Don't Know What He's Missin' Tonight) ['76]
Spring Fever ['78]
Success ['62]
Sweet Thang ['67]
There's All Kinds Of Smoke (In The Barroom) ['83]
They Don't Make 'Em Like My Daddy ['74]
To Make A Man (Feel Like A Man) ['69]
Trouble In Paradise ['74]
Walking With My Memories ['83]
We've Come A Long Way, Baby ['78]
What Kind Of Girl (Do You Think I Am?) ['67]
When The Tingle Becomes A Chill ['76]
Who Was That Stranger ['88]
Who's Gonna Take The Garbage Out ['69]
Why Can't He Be You ['77]
Wine Women And Song ['64]
Wings Upon Your Horns ['70]
Woman Of The World (Leave My World Alone) ['69]
Wouldn't It Be Great ['85]
You Ain't Woman Enough ['66]
You Know Just What I'd Do ['80]
You Wanna Give Me A Lift ['70]
You're Lookin' At Country ['71]
You're The Reason Our Kids Are Ugly ['78]
You've Just Stepped In (From Stepping Out On Me) ['68]
Your Squaw Is On The Warpath ['68]

LYNN, Marcia

Born Marcia Lynne Dickinson on 11/19/1963 in North Adams, Massachusetts. Female singer.

DEBUT	PEAK	WKS	GOLD	Country Chart Hit	Songwriter	Label (& Number)
3/14/87	**77**	5		1 **You've Got That Leaving Look In Your Eye**	*Jerry Gropp/Shirl Milete*	Soundwaves 4784
12/26/87+	**62**	8		2 **Don't Start The Fire**	*Tommy Rocco/Terry Skinner/J.L. Wallace*	Evergreen 1063

LYNN, Michelle

Born in West Virginia. Female singer.

DEBUT	PEAK	WKS	GOLD	Country Chart Hit	Songwriter	Label (& Number)
1/14/89	**92**	2		1 **The Letter**	*Gary Heyde/Carolyn Swilly*	Master 07
6/3/89	**88**	2		2 **Brand New Week**	*Gayla Dewan/Dan Mitchell*	Master 11

LYNN, Rebecca

Born on 11/17/1952 in Dallas, Texas. Female singer.

DEBUT	PEAK	WKS	GOLD	Country Chart Hit	Songwriter	Label (& Number)
7/8/78	**39**	8		1 **Music, Music, Music**	*Bernie Baum/Stephan Weiss*	Scorpion 0550
10/14/78	**69**	5		2 **Minstrel Man**	*Neil Levenson*	Scorpion 0559
2/24/79	**83**	5		3 **Goody Goody**	*Matty Malneck/Johnny Mercer*	Scorpion 0573
6/2/79	**82**	3		4 **Disco Girl Go Away** /	*Mike Borchetta/Sally Hamilton*	
7/21/79	**69**	6		5 **Make Believe You Love Me**	*Norman Sallitt*	Scorpion 0581
3/1/80	**87**	3		6 **Fairytale**	*Anita Pointer/Bonnie Pointer*	Sunbird 106

DEBUT	PEAK	WKS	GOLD		ARTIST / Country Chart Hit	Ranking / Songwriter	Label (& Number)
					LYNN, Trisha		
					Born in Kentucky. Female singer.		
7/2/88	**76**	2		1	**I Go To Pieces**	*Del Shannon*	Oak 1053
5/13/89	**82**	3		2	**Kiss Me Darling**	*Stephanie Winslow*	Oak 1072
7/29/89	**69**	5		3	**Not Fade Away** *[Trish Lynn]*	*Buddy Holly/Norman Petty*	Oak 1062
10/28/89	**65**	4		4	**I Can't Help Myself**	*Lamont Dozier/Brian Holland/Eddie Holland*	Oak 1083
					LYNNE, Shelby		
					Born Shelby Lynn Moorer on 10/22/1968 in Quantico, Virginia; raised in Jackson, Alabama. Female singer. Older sister of **Allison Moorer**. Won the 2000 Best New Artist Grammy Award. Also see **Tomorrow's World**.		
9/3/88	**43**	10		1	**If I Could Bottle This Up** *[w/ George Jones]*	S:22 *Dean Dillon/Paul Overstreet*	Epic 08011
3/18/89	**93**	1		2	**Under Your Spell Again**	*Buck Owens*	Epic 68584
6/24/89	**38**	11		3	**The Hurtin' Side**	*Rory Bourke/Mike Reid*	Epic 68942
10/21/89	**62**	7		4	**Little Bits And Pieces**	*Hank Cochran/Dean Dillon*	Epic 73032
6/30/90	**26**	17		5	**I'll Lie Myself To Sleep**	*Tony Haselden/Tim Mensy*	Epic
10/27/90+	**23**	20		6	**Things Are Tough All Over**	*Trey Bruce/Lisa Silver*	Epic
3/23/91	**45**	16		7	**What About The Love We Made**	*John Rotch*	Epic
					above 3 from the album *Tough All Over* on Epic 46066		
7/27/91	**50**	9		8	**The Very First Lasting Love** *[w/ Les Taylor]*	*Paul Hollowell/Les Taylor/Lonnie Wilson*	Epic
11/9/91	**54**	13		9	**Don't Cross Your Heart**	*Tony Haselden/Tim Mensy*	Epic
					above 2 from the album *Soft Talk* on Epic 47388		
7/17/93	**69**	6		10	**Feelin' Kind Of Lonely Tonight**	*Brent Maher/Jamie O'Hara*	Morgan Creek
					from the album *Temptation* on Morgan Creek 20018		
6/24/95	**59**	8		11	**Slow Me Down**	*Stephanie Davis/Shelby Lynne/Brett Maher*	Magnatone
					from the album *Restless* on Magnatone 102		
					LYNNS, The		
					Identical twin daughters of **Loretta Lynn**: Peggy Lynn and Patsy Lynn (born on 8/6/1964 in Hurricane Mills, Tennessee).		
10/25/97	**48**	10		1	**Nights Like These**	*Patsy Lynn/Peggy Lynn*	Reprise
2/28/98	**43**	10		2	**Woman To Woman**	S:14 *Patsy Lynn/Peggy Lynn/Philip Russell*	Reprise
					above 2 from the album *The Lynns* on Reprise 46754		

M

DEBUT	PEAK	WKS	GOLD		ARTIST / Country Chart Hit	Ranking / Songwriter	Label (& Number)
					MAC, Jimmy		
					Born in Washington. Male singer.		
6/23/84	**93**	1			**You Really Know How To Break A Heart**	*David Lynn Jones*	AV 924
					MacGREGOR, Byron		
					Born Gary Mack in 1948 in Calgary, Alberta, Canada. Died on 1/3/1995 (age 46). News director at radio station CKLW in Detroit when he did the narration for "Americans."		
1/26/74	**59**	5	●		**Americans**	*Gordon Sinclair* **[S]**	Westbound 222
					background music: "America The Beautiful"		
					MacGREGOR, Mary		
					Born on 5/6/1948 in St. Paul, Minnesota. Female singer/songwriter.		
1/8/77	3^{2}	16	●	1	**Torn Between Two Lovers**	*Phil Jarrell/Peter Yarrow*	Ariola America 7638
4/23/77	**36**	10		2	**This Girl (Has Turned Into A Woman)**	*Mary MacGregor/Peter Yarrow*	Ariola America 7662
8/6/77	**86**	3		3	**For A While**	*Kevin Hunter/Peter Yarrow*	Ariola America 7667
					MACK, Bobby		
					Born in Austin, Texas. Male singer/guitarist.		
8/18/73	**79**	6			**Love Will Come Again (Just Like The Roses)**	*Alda Calongne/Jean Chapel*	Ace of Hearts 0467
					MACK, Gary		
					Born in Odessa, Texas. Male singer.		
3/20/76	**94**	2		1	**To Be With You Again**	*Marvis Harris*	Soundwaves 4528
6/26/76	**95**	2		2	**One Love Down**	*Don Earl/Rick Klang*	Soundwaves 4532
4/2/83	**90**	2		3	**I've Been Out Of Love Too Long**	*Buddy Brock/Phil Lister*	Grand Prize 5205
					MACK, Warner	**1960s: #43 / All-Time: #189**	
					Born Warner MacPherson on 4/2/1935 in Nashville, Tennessee; raised in Vicksburg, Mississippi. Male singer/songwriter/guitarist. Regular on the *Louisiana Hayride* and the *Ozark Jubilee*. Involved in a serious car accident on 11/29/1964 near Princeton, Indiana.		
8/12/57+	**9**	36		1	**Is It Wrong (For Loving You)**	S:9 / A:11 *Warner Mack*	Decca 30301
1/11/64	**34**	7		2	**Surely**	*Peggy Whittington*	Decca 31559
11/28/64+	**4**	24		3	**Sittin' In An All Nite Cafe**	*Jim Glaser*	Decca 31684
5/29/65	❶^{1}	23		4	**The Bridge Washed Out**	*Jimmy Louis/Mart Melshee/Sandra Smith*	Decca 31774
11/6/65+	3^{1}	19		5	**Sittin' On A Rock (Crying In A Creek)**	*Jimmy Louis/Mart Melshee*	Decca 31853
3/26/66	3^{1}	20		6	**Talkin' To The Wall**	*Warner Mack/Bill Montague*	Decca 31911

DEBUT	PEAK	WKS	GOLD	ARTIST / Ranking / Country Chart Hit	Songwriter	Label (& Number)
				MACK, Warner — cont'd		
9/3/66	**4**	17		7 **It Takes A Lot Of Money**	*Bob Morris*	Decca 32004
2/11/67	**8**	17		8 **Drifting Apart**	*Hal Gurnee*	Decca 32082
6/24/67	**4**	17		9 **How Long Will It Take**	*Warner Mack*	Decca 32142
11/11/67+	**11**	16		10 **I'd Give The World (To Be Back Loving You)**	*Warner Mack*	Decca 32211
5/18/68	**7**	16		11 **I'm Gonna Move On**	*Warner Mack*	Decca 32308
11/23/68+	**23**	19		12 **Don't Wake Me I'm Dreaming**	*Warner Mack*	Decca 32394
5/3/69	**6**	15		13 **Leave My Dream Alone**	*Warner Mack*	Decca 32473
9/27/69	**8**	13		14 **I'll Still Be Missing You**	*Warner Mack*	Decca 32547
4/4/70	**19**	12		15 **Love Hungry**	*Warner Mack*	Decca 32646
9/12/70	**16**	13		16 **Live For The Good Times**	*Warner Mack*	Decca 32725
2/20/71	**34**	11		17 **You Make Me Feel Like A Man**	*Warner Mack*	Decca 32781
8/28/71	**53**	9		18 **I Wanna Be Loved Completely**	*Warner Mack*	Decca 32858
2/26/72	**45**	9		19 **Draggin' The River**	*Warner Mack*	Decca 32926
8/5/72	**59**	6		20 **You're Burnin' My House Down**	*Warner Mack*	Decca 32982
1/27/73	**54**	7		21 **Some Roads Have No Ending**	*Warner Mack*	Decca 33045
11/10/73+	**91**	7		22 **Goodbyes Don't Come Easy**	*Warner Mack*	MCA 40137
11/19/77	**87**	5		23 **These Crazy Thoughts (Run Through My Mind)**	*Warner Mack*	Pageboy 31
				MACKEY, Bobby		
				Born on 3/25/1948 in Concord, Kentucky. Male singer/guitarist.		
6/12/82	**57**	8		**Pepsi Man**	*Bill Addison*	Moon Shine 3007
				MACON, Uncle Dave **HOF: 1966**		
				Born on 10/7/1870 in Warren County, Tennessee. Died on 3/22/1952 (age 81). Legendary singer/songwriter/banjo player. Worked with the **Delmore Brothers**, **Roy Acuff** and **Bill Monroe**.		
				OPRY: 1925		
				MADDOX, Rose		
				Born Roselea Arbana Brogdon on 8/15/1925 in Boaz, Alabama; raised in Bakersfield, California. Died of kidney failure on 4/15/1998 (age 72). Female singer/songwriter/fiddle player.		
5/18/59	**22**	3		1 **Gambler's Love**	*Billy Hodges/Jack Shults*	Capitol 4177
1/30/61	**14**	13		2 **Kissing My Pillow /**	*Wally Lewis/Fuzzy Owens*	
2/13/61	**15**	7		3 **I Want To Live Again**	*Fuzzy Owens*	Capitol 4487
5/15/61	**8**	12		4 **Mental Cruelty** *[w/ Buck Owens]* /	*Dixie Davis/Larry Davis/Buck Owens*	
5/22/61	**4**	14		5 **Loose Talk** *[w/ Buck Owens]*	*Freddie Hart/Ann Lucas*	Capitol 4550
8/14/61	**14**	6		6 **Conscience, I'm Guilty**	*Dick Reynolds/Jack Rhodes*	Capitol 4598
11/10/62+	**3**[1]	18		7 **Sing A Little Song Of Heartache**	*Del Reeves*	Capitol 4845
3/16/63	**18**	8		8 **Lonely Teardrops**	*Lee Ross*	Capitol 4905
6/15/63	**18**	13		9 **Down To The River**	*Buck Owens*	Capitol 4975
8/3/63	**15**	6		10 **We're The Talk Of The Town** *[w/ Buck Owens]* /	*Buck Owens/Rollie Weber*	
8/10/63	**19**	6		11 **Sweethearts In Heaven** *[w/ Buck Owens]*	*Buck Owens*	Capitol 4992
11/23/63	**18**	6		12 **Somebody Told Somebody**	*Eddie Miller*	Capitol 5038
3/7/64	**44**	6		13 **Alone With You**	*Roy Drusky/Lester Vanadore/Faron Young*	Capitol 5110
8/1/64	**30**	8		14 **Blue Bird Let Me Tag Along**	*Rose Maddox/Skeets McDonald*	Capitol 5186
				MAGGARD, Cledus, And The Citizen's Band		
				Born Jay Huguely on 9/21/1947 in Quick Sand, Kentucky. Novelty singer/songwriter. Recorded "The White Knight" while working at Leslie Advertising in Greenville, South Carolina.		
12/20/75+	**❶**[1]	14		1 **The White Knight**	*Jay Huguely* **[N]**	Mercury 73751
4/17/76	**42**	7		2 **Kentucky Moonrunner**	*Jay Huguely/Jerry Kennedy* **[N]**	Mercury 73789
8/14/76	**73**	4		3 **Virgil And The $300 Vacation** *[Cledus Maggard]*	*Jay Huguely/Jerry Kennedy* **[N]**	Mercury 73823
7/15/78	**82**	4		4 **The Farmer** *[Cledus Maggard]*	*Jay Huguely/Jerry Kennedy* **[N]**	Mercury 55033
				MAINES BROTHERS BAND, The		
				Family group from Texas: Kenny Maines (guitar, harmonica), Steve Maines (guitar), Lloyd Maines (steel guitar) and Donnie Maines (drums). With Richard Bowden (fiddle), Cary Banks (keyboards) and Jerry Brownlow (bass). Lloyd is the father of Natalie Maines (lead singer of the **Dixie Chicks**).		
12/3/83	**72**	6		1 **Louisiana Anna**	*Ken Bell/Terry Skinner/J.L. Wallace*	Mercury 814561
3/24/84	**85**	3		2 **You Are A Miracle**	*Cary Banks/Jerry Brownlow*	Mercury 818346
2/9/85	**24**	16		3 **Everybody Needs Love On Saturday Night** S:21 / A:23	*Ken Bell/Terry Skinner/J.L. Wallace*	Mercury 880536
8/10/85	**84**	4		4 **When My Blue Moon Turns To Gold Again**	*Gene Sullivan/Wiley Walker*	Mercury 880995
11/23/85	**72**	8		5 **Some Of Shelly's Blues**	*Michael Nesmith*	Mercury 884228
3/15/86	**59**	7		6 **Danger Zone**	*Terry Skinner/J.L. Wallace*	Mercury 884483
				MALCHAK, Tim		
				Born on 6/25/1957 in Binghamton, New York. Male singer/songwriter/guitarist. Half of **Malchak & Rucker** duo.		
11/22/86	**68**	7		1 **Easy Does It**	*Tim Malchak/Deborah Stern*	Alpine 004
3/7/87	**37**	13		2 **Colorado Moon**	*Tim Malchak*	Alpine 006
8/1/87	**39**	11		3 **Restless Angel**	*Tim Malchak*	Alpine 007
1/30/88	**35**	14		4 **It Goes Without Saying**	*John Jarrard/Lisa Palas/Mark D. Sanders*	Alpine 008
10/1/88	**43**	11		5 **Not A Night Goes By**	*Steve Diamond/Jim Weatherly*	Alpine 009
4/15/89	**70**	4		6 **Not Like This**	*Austin Gardner/Tim Malchak*	Universal 66004
8/5/89	**54**	6		7 **If You Had A Heart**	*Tim Malchak/Bernie Nelson*	Universal 66013

DEBUT	PEAK	WKS	GOLD	#	ARTIST / Country Chart Hit	Songwriter	Label (& Number)

MALCHAK & RUCKER

Duo of **Tim Malchak** and Dwight Rucker. White singer Malchak was born on 6/25/1957 in Binghamton, New York. Black singer Rucker was born on 3/21/1952 in Oxford, New York.

DEBUT	PEAK	WKS	GOLD	#	Country Chart Hit	Songwriter	Label (& Number)
11/10/84	**92**	2		1	**Just Like That**	*Paul Battle/Don Cook/Sonny Throckmorton*	Revolver 004
3/23/85	**67**	5		2	**Why Didn't I Think Of That**	*Jamie O'Hara/John Potts*	Revolver 007
11/2/85	**69**	6		3	**I Could Love You In A Heartbeat**	*Richard Brannan/Thom Schuyler*	Alpine 001
5/3/86	**67**	5		4	**Let Me Down Easy**	*Tim Malchak*	Alpine 002
8/2/86	**64**	6		5	**Slow Motion**	*Bob DiPiero/Pat McManus*	Alpine 003

MALENA, Don

Born in Bakersfield, California. Male singer/guitarist.

DEBUT	PEAK	WKS	GOLD	#	Country Chart Hit	Songwriter	Label (& Number)
1/10/87	**72**	4		1	**Ready Or Not**	*Mitch Johnson/S. Alan Taylor*	Maxima 1256
6/27/87	**76**	4		2	**Moonwalkin'**	*Jackson Leap*	Maxima 1277
1/23/88	**75**	4		3	**Dance For Me**	*Denny Henson/Bill Johnson*	Maxima 1311

MALIBU STORM

Bluegrass trio from Los Angeles, California: identical twin sisters Dana (banjo) and Lauren (fiddle), with younger brother Michael (bass). All share vocals.

DEBUT	PEAK	WKS	GOLD	#	Country Chart Hit	Songwriter	Label (& Number)
6/26/04+	**2^{2S}**	21			**Photograph** from the album *Malibu Storm* on Rounder 0486	*Steve Clark/Joe Elliott/Mutt Lange/Rick Savage/Pete Willis*	Rounder

MALLORY, Doug

Born in Nova Scotia, Canada. Male singer.

DEBUT	PEAK	WKS	GOLD	#	Country Chart Hit	Songwriter	Label (& Number)
2/20/88	**52**	8			**Perfect Strangers** ***[w/ Anne Murray]***	*Astor Anderson/Jonas Field/John Sareussen/Markus Spiro*	Capitol 44134

MANCINI, Henry

Born on 4/16/1924 in Cleveland, Ohio; raised in Aliquippa, Pennsylvania. Died of cancer on 6/14/1994 (age 70). Prolific movie and TV composer/arranger/conductor. Won Grammy's Lifetime Achievement Award in 1995.

DEBUT	PEAK	WKS	GOLD	#	Country Chart Hit	Songwriter	Label (& Number)
2/19/72	**2^{2}**	15			**All His Children** ***[w/ Charley Pride]*** from the movie *Sometimes A Great Notion* starring Paul Newman	*Alan Bergman/Marilyn Bergman/Henry Mancini*	RCA Victor 0624

MANDRELL, Barbara — 1970s: #31 / 1980s: #28 / All-Time: #52

Born on 12/25/1948 in Houston, Texas; raised in Oceanside, California. Female singer/multi-instrumentalist. Sister of **Louise Mandrell**. Hosted own TV series from 1980-82; acted on TV's *Sunset Beach* in 1997.

CMA: Female Vocalist 1979 & 1981 / Entertainer 1980 & 1981 // OPRY: 1972

DEBUT	PEAK	WKS	GOLD	#	Country Chart Hit	Songwriter	Label (& Number)
9/13/69	**55**	7		1	**I've Been Loving You Too Long (To Stop Now)**	*Otis Redding*	Columbia 44955
5/23/70	**18**	12		2	**Playin' Around With Love**	*Billy Sherrill*	Columbia 45143
10/3/70	**6**	14		3	**After Closing Time** ***[w/ David Houston]***	*Billy Sherrill/Danny Walls/Norro Wilson*	Epic 10656
1/30/71	**17**	12		4	**Do Right Woman - Do Right Man**	*Chips Moman/Dan Penn*	Columbia 45307
6/26/71	**12**	12		5	**Treat Him Right**	*Roy Head*	Columbia 45391
10/2/71	**20**	12		6	**We've Got Everything But Love** ***[w/ David Houston]***	*Carmol Taylor*	Epic 10779
12/11/71+	**10**	13		7	**Tonight My Baby's Coming Home**	*Billy Sherrill/Glenn Sutton*	Columbia 45505
4/15/72	**11**	13		8	**Show Me**	*Joe Tex*	Columbia 45580
9/16/72	**24**	13		9	**A Perfect Match** ***[w/ David Houston]***	*Ben Peters/Glenn Sutton*	Epic 10908
11/4/72	**27**	12		10	**Holdin' On (To The Love I Got)**	*Carmol Taylor/Norro Wilson/Tammy Wynette*	Columbia 45702
4/21/73	**24**	11		11	**Give A Little, Take A Little**	*Mike Kosser/Steve Pippin*	Columbia 45819
8/18/73	**7**	17		12	**The Midnight Oil**	*Joe Allen*	Columbia 45904
12/22/73+	**6**	16		13	**I Love You, I Love You** ***[w/ David Houston]***	*Sammy Lyons/Danny Walls/Norro Wilson*	Epic 11068
5/25/74	**40**	12		14	**Lovin' You Is Worth It** ***[w/ David Houston]***	*Quinton Claunch/Carmol Taylor*	Epic 11120
6/15/74	**12**	16		15	**This Time I Almost Made It**	*Billy Sherrill*	Columbia 46054
8/10/74	**14**	16		16	**Ten Commandments Of Love** ***[w/ David Houston]***	*Marshall Paul*	Epic 20005
2/22/75	**39**	9		17	**Wonder When My Baby's Comin' Home**	*Kermit Goell/Arthur Kent*	Columbia 10082
12/20/75+	**5**	17		18	**Standing Room Only**	*Susan Manchester/Charles Silver*	ABC/Dot 17601
5/8/76	**16**	13		19	**That's What Friends Are For**	*Rob Parsons/Ed Penney*	ABC/Dot 17623
8/14/76	**24**	12		20	**Love Is Thin Ice**	*Geoffrey Morgan*	ABC/Dot 17644
12/18/76+	**16**	12		21	**Midnight Angel**	*Bill Anthony/Bob Morrison*	ABC/Dot 17668
4/2/77	**3^{2}**	17		22	**Married But Not To Each Other**	*Denise LaSalle/Frankie Miller*	ABC/Dot 17688
9/3/77	**12**	14		23	**Hold Me**	*Glenn Ray*	ABC/Dot 17716
12/24/77+	**4**	16		24	**Woman To Woman**	*James Banks/Eddie Marion/Henderson Thigpen*	ABC/Dot 17736
5/20/78	**5**	13		25	**Tonight**	*Don Cook/Rafe Van Hoy*	ABC 12362
9/9/78	❶^{3}	15		26	**Sleeping Single In A Double Bed**	*Kye Fleming/Dennis W. Morgan*	ABC 12403
2/17/79	❶^{1}	14		27	**(If Loving You Is Wrong) I Don't Want To Be Right**	*Homer Banks/Carl Hampton/Raymond Jackson*	MCA 12451
8/11/79	**4**	14		28	**Fooled By A Feeling**	*Kye Fleming/Dennis W. Morgan*	MCA 41077
12/15/79+	❶^{1}	15		29	**Years**	*Kye Fleming/Dennis W. Morgan*	MCA 41162
6/21/80	**3^{1}**	16		30	**Crackers**	*Kye Fleming/Dennis W. Morgan*	MCA 41263
10/11/80	**6**	17		31	**The Best Of Strangers**	*Kye Fleming/Dennis W. Morgan*	MCA 51001
2/7/81	**13**	13		32	**Love Is Fair /**	*Kye Fleming/Dennis W. Morgan*	
2/7/81	**flip**	13		33	**Sometime, Somewhere, Somehow**	*Brant Beene/Jack Turner*	MCA 51062
5/9/81	❶^{1}	13		34	**I Was Country When Country Wasn't Cool** **[L]** **George Jones** (guest vocal)	*Kye Fleming/Dennis W. Morgan*	MCA 51107
9/5/81	**2^{1}**	16		35	**Wish You Were Here** **[L]**	*Kye Fleming/Dennis W. Morgan*	MCA 51171

Billboard DEBUT	PEAK	WKS	GOLD	ARTIST / Country Chart Hit	Ranking / Songwriter	Label (& Number)
				MANDRELL, Barbara — cont'd		
5/1/82	❶[1]	19		36 'Till You're Gone	*Walt Aldridge/Tom Brasfield*	MCA 52038
9/4/82	9	15		37 Operator, Long Distance Please	*Kye Fleming/Dennis W. Morgan*	MCA 52111
4/23/83	4	19		38 In Times Like These	*Rhonda Fleming/Dennis W. Morgan*	MCA 52206
8/27/83	❶[1]	21		39 One Of A Kind Pair Of Fools	*R.C. Bannon/John Bettis*	MCA 52258
2/18/84	3[1]	21		40 Happy Birthday Dear Heartache	*Mack David/Archie Jordan*	MCA 52340
6/9/84	2[1]	21		41 Only A Lonely Heart Knows	*Steve Davis/Dennis W. Morgan*	MCA 52397
7/21/84	3[2]	20		42 To Me *[w/ Lee Greenwood]*	S:15 / A:23 *Mack David/Mike Reid*	MCA 52415
10/6/84	11	20		43 Crossword Puzzle	A:9 / S:12 *Steve Dean/Frank J. Myers*	MCA 52465
2/2/85	19	15		44 It Should Have Been Love By Now *[w/ Lee Greenwood]*	A:18 / S:20 *Jan Crutchfield/Paul Harrison*	MCA 52525
3/9/85	7	20		45 There's No Love In Tennessee	S:5 / A:8 *Steve Davis/Dennis W. Morgan*	MCA 52537
8/24/85	8	18		46 Angel In Your Arms	A:8 / S:8 *Tom Brasfield/Herbert Ivey/Terry Woodford*	MCA 52645
12/7/85+	4	19		47 Fast Lanes And Country Roads	S:3 / A:4 *Steve Dean/Roger Murrah*	MCA 52737
3/29/86	20	14		48 When You Get To The Heart *[w/ Oak Ridge Boys]*	A:20 / S:21 *Tony Brown/Wayland Holyfield/Norro Wilson*	MCA 52802
8/16/86	6	22		49 No One Mends A Broken Heart Like You	A:6 / S:8 *John Schweers*	MCA 52900
7/4/87	13	17		50 Child Support	S:7 *Thom Schuyler*	EMI America 43032
12/5/87	48	11		51 Sure Feels Good	*Frederick Knight/Carson Whitsett*	EMI America 50102
3/12/88	49	11		52 Angels Love Bad Men **Waylon Jennings** (guest vocal)	*Waylon Jennings/Roger Murrah*	EMI America 43042
8/20/88	5	22		53 I Wish That I Could Fall In Love Today	S:9 *Harlan Howard*	Capitol 44220
2/4/89	19	16		54 My Train Of Thought	*Bruce Burch/Mike Woody*	Capitol 44276
7/1/89	49	8		55 Mirror Mirror	*Bobby Barker/Phil Thomas*	Capitol 44383

MANDRELL, Louise — All-Time: #208

Born on 7/13/1954 in Corpus Christi, Texas. Female singer/multi-instrumentalist. Sister of **Barbara Mandrell**. Formerly married to **R.C. Bannon** and Gary Buck (of **The Four Guys**).

DEBUT	PEAK	WKS	GOLD	Country Chart Hit	Songwriter	Label (& Number)
8/26/78	77	5		1 Put It On Me	*Mike Kosser/Steve Pippin/Curly Putman*	Epic 50565
1/6/79	69	5		2 Everlasting Love	*Buzz Cason/Mac Gayden*	Epic 50651
3/10/79	46	8		3 I Thought You'd Never Ask *[w/ R.C. Bannon]*	*Don Cook/Curly Putman*	Epic 50668
6/2/79	13	12		4 Reunited *[w/ R.C. Bannon]*	*Dino Fekaris/Freddie Perren*	Epic 50717
9/1/79	72	5		5 I Never Loved Anyone Like I Love You	*R.C. Bannon*	Epic 50752
11/17/79	48	8		6 We Love Each Other *[w/ R.C. Bannon]*	*Buddy Killen*	Epic 50789
3/29/80	63	5		7 Wake Me Up	*Mike Kosser/Curly Putman*	Epic 50856
7/19/80	82	4		8 Beggin' For Mercy	*Mike Kosser/Curly Putman*	Epic 50896
9/27/80	61	6		9 Love Insurance	*R.C. Bannon/John Schweers*	Epic 50935
11/28/81+	35	11		10 Where There's Smoke There's Fire *[w/ R.C. Bannon]*	*Kye Fleming/Dennis W. Morgan*	RCA 12359
2/13/82	35	12		11 (You Sure Know Your Way) Around My Heart	*Charlie Black/Rory Bourke/Tommy Rocco*	RCA 13039
6/5/82	56	7		12 Our Wedding Band *[w/ R.C. Bannon]* /	*Don Pfrimmer/Charles Quillen*	
6/5/82	flip	7		13 Just Married *[w/ R.C. Bannon]*	*Jack Clement/Carol Hall*	RCA 13095
7/24/82	20	15		14 Some Of My Best Friends Are Old Songs	*Bobby Borchers/Don Goodman/Jeff Raymond/Mack Vickery*	RCA 13278
11/6/82+	22	16		15 Romance	*Joe Huffman/Chris Waters*	RCA 13373
12/11/82+	35	7		16 Christmas Is Just A Song For Us This Year *[w/ R.C. Bannon]*	*R.C. Bannon* [X]	RCA 13358
2/26/83	6	17		17 Save Me	*R.C. Bannon/Guy Fletcher/Doug Flett*	RCA 13450
7/16/83	10	19		18 Too Hot To Sleep	*R.C. Bannon/John Bettis*	RCA 13567
11/5/83+	13	17		19 Runaway Heart	*Steve Pippin/Michael Spriggs*	RCA 13649
3/24/84	7	20		20 I'm Not Through Loving You Yet	*Holly Dunn/Tom Shapiro/Chris Waters*	RCA 13752
8/18/84	24	15		21 Goodbye Heartache	S:19 / A:25 *R.C. Bannon/Michael Spriggs*	RCA 13850
12/8/84+	52	12		22 This Bed's Not Big Enough	*Jim McBride/Charlie Monk*	RCA 13954
3/30/85	8	19		23 Maybe My Baby	S:8 / A:10 *Eric Carmen*	RCA 14039
8/17/85	5	21		24 I Wanna Say Yes	S:4 / A:5 *R.C. Bannon*	RCA 14151
12/14/85+	22	17		25 Some Girls Have All The Luck	S:20 / A:23 *Jeff Fortgang*	RCA 14251
6/28/86	35	11		26 I Wanna Hear It From Your Lips	A:39 *Eric Carmen/Dean Pitchford*	RCA 14364
2/28/87	28	13		27 Do I Have To Say Goodbye	A:28 *Jim McBride/Peter McCann*	RCA 5115
11/21/87	74	3		28 Tender Time	*Ronnie Rogers*	RCA 5208
4/9/88	51	9		29 As Long As We Got Each Other *[w/ Eric Carmen]* from the TV series *Growing Pains* starring Alan Thicke and Joanna Kerns	*John Bettis/Steve Dorff*	RCA 20288

MANN, Carl

Born on 8/24/1942 in Huntingdon, Tennessee. Rockabilly singer/pianist. Member of the **Carl Perkins** band from 1962-64.

DEBUT	PEAK	WKS	GOLD	Country Chart Hit	Songwriter	Label (& Number)
5/15/76	100	1		Twilight Time	*Al Nevins/Morty Nevins/Buck Ram*	ABC/Dot 17621

MANN, Lorene

Born on 1/4/1937 in Huntland, Tennessee. Female singer/songwriter.

DEBUT	PEAK	WKS	GOLD	Country Chart Hit	Songwriter	Label (& Number)
10/2/65	23	9		1 Hurry, Mr. Peters *[w/ Justin Tubb]* answer to "Yes, Mr. Peters" by **Roy Drusky** & **Priscilla Mitchell**	*Steve Karliski/Larry Kolber*	RCA Victor 8659
7/30/66	44	2		2 We've Gone Too Far, Again *[w/ Justin Tubb]*	*Bobby Bare*	RCA Victor 8834
1/7/67	47	11		3 Don't Put Your Hands On Me	*Lorene Mann*	RCA Victor 9045
5/20/67	50	8		4 Have You Ever Wanted To?	*Lorene Mann*	RCA Victor 9183
9/23/67	63	6		5 You Love Me Too Little	*Lorene Mann*	RCA Victor 9288
1/6/68	24	15		6 The Dark End Of The Street *[w/ Archie Campbell]*	*Chips Moman/Dan Penn*	RCA Victor 9401
6/29/68	31	10		7 Tell It Like It Is *[w/ Archie Campbell]*	*George Davis/Lee Diamond*	RCA Victor 9549
9/28/68	57	8		8 Warm And Tender Love *[w/ Archie Campbell]*	*Bobby Robinson*	RCA Victor 9615
1/4/69	36	9		9 My Special Prayer *[w/ Archie Campbell]*	*Wini Scott*	RCA Victor 9691

Billboard			G O L D	ARTIST	Ranking	
DEBUT	PEAK	WKS		Country Chart Hit	Songwriter	Label (& Number)
				MANNERS, Zeke, and his Band	**1940s: #42**	
				Born Leo Manness on 10/10/1911 in San Francisco, California. Died of heart failure on 10/14/2000 (age 89). Male pianist/accordionist. Former member of the **Beverly Hill Billies**.		
2/16/46	**2^9**	19		1 **Sioux City Sue**	*Ray Freedman/Dick Thomas* **[N]**	Victor 20-1797
				Curly Gribbs (vocal)		
12/14/46	**5**	2		2 **Inflation**	*Lester Lee/Zeke Manners* **[N]**	Victor 20-2013
				MANNING, Linda		
				Born in Cullman, Arkansas. Female singer.		
12/28/68+	**54**	8		**Since They Fired The Band Director (At Murphy High)**	*Tom T. Hall*	Mercury 72875
				MANNING, Rhonda		
				Born in Nashville, Tennessee. Female singer.		
12/19/87	**87**	3		1 **Out With The Boys**	*Larry Kingston/Paul Richey*	Soundwaves 4792
6/11/88	**73**	3		2 **You Really Know How To Break A Heart**	*David Lynn Jones*	Soundwaves 4799
				MANTELLI, Steve		
				Born in Texas. Male singer.		
10/9/82	**94**	2		1 **I'll Baby You**	*Bob Jenkins*	Picap 008
1/8/83	**84**	4		2 **You're A Keep Me Wondering Kind Of Woman**	*Bob Jenkins/Mike Spivey*	Picap 005
				MARCEL		
				Born Marcel Chagnon in Grosse Pointe, Michigan. Male singer/songwriter/guitarist.		
5/18/02	**46**	8		**Country Rock Star**	*Marcel Chagnon/Kevin Savigar*	Mercury
				from the album *You, Me And The Windshield* on Mercury 170303		
				MARCY BROS., The		
				Vocal trio of brothers from Hay Springs, Nebraska: Kevin Marcy, Kris Marcy and Kendal Marcy.		
5/7/88	**68**	5		1 **The Things I Didn't Say**	*Shel Silverstein*	Warner 27938
2/11/89	**52**	9		2 **Threads Of Gold**	*Don King/Allen Shamblin*	Warner 27573
5/20/89	**34**	10		3 **Cotton Pickin' Time**	*Paul Overstreet/Even Stevens*	Warner 22956
11/4/89	**70**	4		4 **You're Not Even Crying**	*Sandy Knox/Steve Seskin*	Warner 22753
1/13/90	**79**	1		5 **Missing You**	*Lee Johnson/Becky Ryan*	Warner
				from the album *Missing You* on Warner 26051		
8/24/91	**71**	2		6 **She Can**	*Austin Gardner/Steve Seskin*	Atlantic
				from the album *The Marcy Brothers* on Atlantic 82213		
				MARIE SISTERS		
				Duo from Lewisville, Texas: sisters Chaz Marie and Kessie Marie.		
4/20/02	**46**	11		**Real Bad Mood**	*Don Poythress/Leslie Satcher*	Republic
				from the album *Marie Sisters* on Republic 017819		
				MARIPAT		
				Born Maripat Davis in California. Female singer.		
6/24/89	**97**	1		**No One To Talk To But The Blues**	*Wayne Walker-Sherry*	Oak 1073
				MARLIN SISTERS, The		
				Vocal duo from Pennsylvania: sisters Trudy Marlin and Gloria Marlin. Also known as the Beaver Valley Sweethearts. Recorded vocals for **The Pinetoppers**.		
4/30/49	**7**	7	●	**Blue Skirt Waltz** *[w/ Frankie Yankovic]*	S:7 / J:10 *Vaclav Blaha/Mitchell Parish*	Columbia 12394
				MARNEY, Ben		
				Born in Jackson, Mississippi. Male singer/guitarist.		
7/18/81	**92**	2		**Where Cheaters Go**	*Tim Hardin*	Southern Biscuit 107
				MARR, Leah		
				Born in California. Female singer.		
10/1/88	**83**	3		1 **Sealed With A Kiss**	*Gary Geld/Peter Udell*	Oak 1060
9/23/89	**80**	3		2 **Half Heaven Half Heartache**	*George Goehring/Wally Gold/Aaron Schroeder*	Oak 1071
12/16/89+	**76**	4		3 **I've Been A Fool**	*Stephanie Winslow*	Oak 1084
				MARRIOTT, John		
				Born in Arizona. Male singer/songwriter.		
12/9/89	**92**	4		**Modern Day Cowboy**	*John Marriott*	Phoenix 152
				MARSHALL, Roger		
				Born in Arkansas. Male singer.		
7/16/88	**73**	4		1 **Hocus Pocus**	*Roger Murrah/Larry Shell*	AVM 17
11/19/88	**99**	1		2 **Take A Letter Maria**	*R.B. Greaves*	Master 05
				MARSHALL DYLLON		
				Vocal group from San Antonio, Texas: brothers Paul Martin and Michael Martin, Todd Sansom, Jess Littleton and Daniel Cahoon.		
9/30/00+	**37**	20		1 **Live It Up**	*Robert Byrne/Phil Vassar*	Dreamcatcher
3/17/01	**47**	7		2 **You**	*Jimmy Olander/Will Robinson/Aaron Sain*	Dreamcatcher
7/14/01	**44**	9		3 **She Ain't Gonna Cry**	*Chris Farren/Joel Feeney*	Dreamcatcher
				above 3 from the album *Enjoy The Ride* on Dreamcatcher 101		

DEBUT	PEAK	WKS	GOLD	ARTIST / Country Chart Hit	Songwriter	Label (& Number)
				MARSHALL TUCKER BAND, The		
				Southern-rock group from Spartanburg, South Carolina: Doug Gray (vocals; born on 5/22/1948), brothers Toy (guitar; born on 11/13/1947) and Tommy Caldwell (bass; born on 11/9/1949), George McCorkle (guitar; born on 10/11/1946), Jerry Eubanks (sax, flute; born on 3/19/1950) and Paul Riddle (drums; born in 1953). Tommy Caldwell died in a car crash on 4/28/1980 (age 30); replaced by Franklin Wilkie. Toy Caldwell left in 1985; died of respiratory failure on 2/25/1993 (age 45). Marshall Tucker was the owner of the band's rehearsal hall.		
3/13/76	**82**	3		1 **Searchin' For A Rainbow**	*Toy Caldwell*	Capricorn 0251
9/4/76	**63**	7		2 **Long Hard Ride**	*Toy Caldwell*	Capricorn 0258
4/16/77	**51**	10		3 **Heard It In A Love Song**	*Toy Caldwell*	Capricorn 0270
6/25/83	**62**	7		4 **A Place I've Never Been**	*Toy Caldwell*	Warner 29619
9/5/87	**44**	11		5 **Hangin' Out In Smokey Places**	*Larry Butler/Dean Dillon*	Mercury 888775
1/16/88	**79**	3		6 **Once You Get The Feel Of It**	*Larry Butler/Dean Dillon*	Mercury 870050
12/19/92+	**68**	6		7 **Driving You Out Of My Mind** (from the album *Still Smokin* on Cabin Fever 913)	*Tim Lawter*	Cabin Fever
6/26/93	**71**	1		8 **Walk Outside The Lines** (from the album *Walk Outside The Lines* on Cabin Fever 929)	*Garth Brooks/Charley Stefl*	Cabin Fever
				MARTEL, Marty		
				Born Donald Martel on 3/9/1939 in Ogdensburg, New York. Male singer.		
11/17/79	**96**	2		**First Step**	*Jerry McBee*	Ridgetop 00679
				MARTELL, Linda		
				Born on 6/4/1941 in Leesville, South Carolina. Black female singer.		
8/2/69	**22**	10		1 **Color Him Father**	*Richard Spencer*	Plantation 24
12/13/69+	**33**	8		2 **Before The Next Teardrop Falls**	*Vivian Keith/Ben Peters*	Plantation 35
3/28/70	**58**	6		3 **Bad Case Of The Blues**	*Margaret Lewis/Myra Smith*	Plantation 46
				MARTIN, Benny		
				Born on 5/8/1928 in Sparta, Tennessee. Died of heart failure on 3/13/2001 (age 72). Bluegrass singer/fiddle player.		
5/25/63	**28**	1		1 **Rosebuds And You**	*Tommy Scott*	Starday 623
1/8/66	**46**	3		2 **Soldier's Prayer In Viet Nam** ***[w/ Don Reno]***	*Benny Martin/Don Reno* **[S]**	Monument 912
				MARTIN, Betty		
				Born in Powhatan, Virginia. Female singer/songwriter.		
10/7/78	**77**	4		**Don't You Feel It Now**	*Ronnie Nelms*	Door Knob 071
				MARTIN, Bobbi		
				Born Barbara Martin on 11/29/1938 in Brooklyn, New York; raised in Baltimore, Maryland. Died of cancer on 5/2/2000 (age 61). Female singer.		
10/15/66	**64**	3		**Oh, Lonesome Me**	*Don Gibson*	Coral 62488
				MARTIN, Brad		
				Born on 5/3/1973 in Greenfield, Ohio. Male singer/songwriter/guitarist.		
2/16/02	**15**	29		1 **Before I Knew Better**	*David Lee/Bryan Simpson*	Epic
10/12/02	**51**	8		2 **Rub Me The Right Way** (above 2 from the album *Wings Of A Honky Tonk Angel* on Epic 85115)	*Mike Geiger/Brad Martin/John Ramey*	Epic
4/19/03	**50**	9		3 **One Of Those Days**	*Tim James/Craig Wiseman*	Epic
				MARTIN, Dean		
				Born Dino Crocetti on 6/7/1917 in Steubenville, Ohio. Died of respiratory failure on 12/25/1995 (age 78). Male singer/actor. Teamed with comedian Jerry Lewis from 1946-56. Martin starred in several movies with and without Lewis. Hosted own TV variety show from 1965-74.		
7/9/83	**35**	12		**My First Country Song** (**Conway Twitty** (guest vocal))	*Conway Twitty*	Warner 29584
				MARTIN, Grady, & His Slew Foot Five		
				Born Thomas Grady Martin on 1/17/1929 in Chapel Hill, Tennessee. Died of a heart attack on 12/3/2001 (age 72). Popular session musician.		
7/26/52	**6**	4		1 **Wild Side Of Life** ***[w/ Burl Ives]***	J:6 / S:10 *Arlie Carter/William Warren*	Decca 9-28055
8/30/52	**10**	1		2 **Till The End Of The World** ***[w/ Bing Crosby]***	J:10 *Vaughn Horton*	Decca 9-28265
				MARTIN, Gypsy		
				Born in Knoxville, Tennessee. Female singer.		
10/10/81	**93**	2		**This Ain't Tennessee And He Ain't You**	*Larry Bastian/Jim Shaw*	Omni 61581
				MARTIN, J.D.		
				Born Jerald Derstine Martin in Harrisonburg, Virginia. Male singer/songwriter.		
5/10/86	**72**	6		1 **Running Out Of Reasons To Run**	*J.D. Martin/Jim Rushing*	Capitol 5573
9/6/86	**77**	5		2 **Wrap Me Up In Your Love**	*John Jarrard/J.D. Martin*	Capitol 5606
				MARTIN, Jerry		
				Born in Texas. Male singer/songwriter.		
3/16/91	**71**	1		**Letter To Saddam Hussein**	*Jerry Martin* **[S]**	Desert Storm
				MARTIN, Jimmy		
				Born on 8/10/1927 in Sneedville, Tennessee. Died of cancer on 5/14/2005 (age 77). Bluegrass singer/songwriter/guitarist/mandolin player. Member of **Bill Monroe**'s Bluegrass Boys from 1949-53.		
12/8/58	**14**	6		1 **Rock Hearts**	*Bill Otis*	Decca 30703
5/25/59	**26**	3		2 **Night**	*Jimmy Martin*	Decca 30877
2/8/64	**19**	15		3 **Widow Maker**	*Penny Jay/Buddy Wilson*	Decca 31558
5/7/66	**49**	2		4 **I Can't Quit Cigarettes**	*Jerry Crutchfield/Billy Kitchens* **[N]**	Decca 31921

DEBUT	PEAK	WKS	GOLD	ARTIST / Country Chart Hit	Ranking / Songwriter	Label (& Number)
				MARTIN, Jimmy — cont'd		
5/18/68	72	2		5 Tennessee	*Jimmy Martin/Doyle Neikirk*	Decca 32300
8/4/73	97	2		6 Grand Ole Opry Song *[w/ Nitty Gritty Dirt Band]*	*Hylo Brown*	United Artists 247
				MARTIN, Joey		
				Born in Georgia. Male singer/actor.		
10/14/78	92	1		I've Been A Long Time Leaving (But I'll Be A Long Time Gone)	*Roger Miller*	Nickolodean 1002
				MARTIN, Leland		
				Born on 2/20/1957 in Success, Missouri. Male singer/songwriter/guitarist.		
10/12/02	60	1		1 If I Had Long Legs (Like Alan Jackson)	*Leland Martin* [N]	IGO
3/1/03	59	1		2 Hey Love, No Fair	*Charles Mendosa/Doug Wayne*	IGO
				above 2 from the album *Simply Traditional* on IGO 3841		
				MARTIN, Mike — see DELRAY, Martin		
				MARTINDALE, Wink		
				Born Winston Martindale on 12/4/1933 in Jackson, Tennessee. Worked as a DJ and hosted several TV game shows.		
10/19/59	11	10	●	Deck Of Cards	*"T" Texas Tyler* [S]	Dot 15968
				MARTINE, Layng Jr.		
				Born on 3/24/1942 in Greenwich, Connecticut. Male singer/songwriter.		
8/28/76	93	2		Summertime Lovin'	*Layng Martine Jr.*	Playboy 6081
				MARTINEZ, John Arthur		
				Born in Austin, Texas. Male singer/songwriter/guitarist.		
2/21/04	56	1		Home Made Of Stone	*John Arthur Martinez/Ande Rasmussen/Steve Seskin*	Dualtone
				from the album *Lone Starry Night* on Dualtone 1154		
				MARTINO, Al		
				Born Alfred Cini on 10/7/1927 in Philadelphia, Pennsylvania. Pop singer. Played "Johnny Fontaine" in movie *The Godfather.*		
12/20/69+	69	3		I Started Loving You Again	*Merle Haggard*	Capitol 2674
				MARVELL, James		
				Born in Tampa, Florida. Male singer/songwriter/guitarist. Member of the groups Mercy and **The Country Cavaleers**.		
3/14/81	94	2		1 Urban Cowboys, Outlaws, Cavaleers /	*Buddy Good/James Marvell*	
5/30/81	90	3		2 Love (Can Make You Happy)	*Jack Sigler*	Cavaleer 117
				MASON, Dona		
				Born in Huntsville, Alabama. Female singer.		
10/10/87	62	5		Green Eyes (Cryin' Those Blue Tears) *[w/ Danny Davis]*	*Mary Fielder/Kim Morrison*	Jaroco 8742
				MASON, Mila		
				Born on 8/22/1963 in Dawson Springs, Kentucky. Female singer.		
8/17/96	18	20		1 That's Enough Of That	*Randy Albright/Mark D. Sanders/Lisa Silver*	Atlantic
2/8/97	21	20		2 Dark Horse	S:15 *Amanda Marshall/Dean McTaggart/David Tyson*	Atlantic
6/28/97	59	8		3 That's The Kinda Love (That I'm Talkin' About)	*Lewellyn Bakey*	Atlantic
				above 3 from the album *That's Enough Of That* on Atlantic 82923		
11/29/97+	31	20		4 Closer To Heaven	*Bill Luther/Aimee Mayo*	Atlantic
5/23/98	57	6		5 The Strong One	*Byron Hill/Cyril Rawson*	Atlantic
				above 2 from the album *The Strong One* on Atlantic 83059		
				MASON, Sandy		
				Born Sandy Theoret in Birdville, Pennsylvania. Female singer.		
5/13/67	64	5		There You Go	*Audrey Allison*	Hickory 1442
				MASON DIXON		
				Trio formed in Beaumont, Texas: Frank Gilligan (vocals, bass; born on 11/2/1955), Jerry Dengler (guitar, banjo; born on 5/29/1955) and Rick Henderson (guitar; born on 3/29/1953).		
10/22/83	69	7		1 Every Breath You Take	*Sting*	Texas 5502
4/21/84	51	11		2 I Never Had A Chance With You	*Dan Mitchell*	Texas 5556
9/22/84	49	15		3 Gettin' Over You	*Cary Lynn Rutledge*	Texas 5557
2/23/85	47	10		4 Only A Dream Away	S:27 *Paul Detmer*	Texas 5558
8/31/85	76	9		5 Houston Heartache	*Joe Henderson/Johnny McCollum/Dan Mitchell*	Texas 5508
1/11/86	72	10		6 Got My Heart Set On You	*Dobie Gray/Bud Reneau*	Texas 5510
8/2/86	53	10		7 Home Grown	*Murry Kellum/Dan Mitchell*	Premier One 101
4/18/87	39	14		8 3935 West End Avenue	*W.T. Davidson/Steve Dean/Frank J. Myers*	Premier One 112
10/10/87	51	8		9 Don't Say No Tonight	*Robert Barry/Dan Mitchell/Lorin Reyzek*	Premier One 115
8/6/88	62	5		10 Dangerous Road	*Rory Bourke/Mike Reid*	Capitol 44189
11/5/88	49	13		11 When Karen Comes Around	*Dewayne Blackwell/Fischer/Earl Lee/Robert Ellis Orrall*	Capitol 44249
2/11/89	35	13		12 Exception To The Rule	*Bucky Jones/Tom Shapiro/Chris Waters*	Capitol 44331
6/17/89	52	7		13 A Mountain Ago	*Paul Overstreet/Don Schlitz*	Capitol 44381
				MASSEY, Louise, & The Westerners		
				Born Victoria Louise Massey on 8/10/1902 in Midland, Texas. Died on 6/20/1983 (age 80). One of the most popular groups of the 1930s and 1940s. The Westerners consisted of Louise's brothers Curtis Massey (died on 10/20/1991, age 81) and Allen Massey (died on 3/3/1983, age 75), Louise's husband Milt Mabie (died in September 1973, age 73) and accordianist Larry Wellington. Group starred on radio's *National Barn Dance* from 1933-36.		
				EARLY HITS: Rock And Rye Polka (1940) / Beer And Skittles (1941) / My Adobe Hacienda (1941) / Honey, I'm In Love With You (1943)		

DEBUT	PEAK	WKS	GOLD	ARTIST / Country Chart Hit	Ranking / Songwriter	Label (& Number)
				MASSEY, Wayne		
				Born in Glendale, California. Male singer/actor. Played "Johnny Drummond" on TV's *One Life To Live* (1980-84). Married **Charly McClain** in July 1984.		
1/17/81	**82**	3		1 **Diamonds And Teardrops**	*Barbara Morrison/Bob Morrison*	Polydor 2147
5/21/83	**71**	6		2 **Lover In Disguise**	*Jim Dowell/Blake Mevis*	MCA 52211
8/6/83	**57**	7		3 **Say You'll Stay**	*Kent Blazy/Jim Dowell/Tim DuBois*	MCA 52246
7/6/85	**5**	22		4 **With Just One Look In Your Eyes** ***[w/ Charly McClain]***	S:5 / A:6 *Steve Davis/Dennis W. Morgan*	Epic 05398
11/16/85+	**10**	20		5 **You Are My Music, You Are My Song** ***[w/ Charly McClain]***	S:9 / A:10 *Jim Carter/Jodie Erwin*	Epic 05693
3/29/86	**17**	15		6 **When It's Down To Me And You** ***[w/ Charly McClain]***	S:16 / A:17 *Steve Davis/Dennis W. Morgan*	Epic 05842
12/6/86	**74**	6		7 **When Love Is Right** ***[w/ Charly McClain]***	*John Greenebaum/Gene Nelson/Paul Nelson*	Epic 06433
2/11/89	**81**	3		8 **Shoot The Moon**	*Mark Allan*	Mercury 870994
				MASTERS, A.J.		
				Born Arthur John Masters in Walden, New York. Male singer/songwriter/bassist.		
11/16/85	**98**	1		1 **Lonely Together**	*Jerry Lansdowne/Tony Marty/A.J. Masters*	Bermuda Dunes 111
3/8/86	**48**	9		2 **Back Home**	*Jerry Lansdowne/A.J. Masters*	Bermuda Dunes 112
7/26/86	**54**	9		3 **Love Keep Your Distance**	*Jerry Lansdowne/A.J. Masters*	Bermuda Dunes 114
11/8/86	**65**	5		4 **I Don't Mean Maybe**	*A.J. Masters/Dave Moordigian/Bill Thornbury*	Bermuda Dunes 115
1/17/87	**58**	6		5 **Take A Little Bit Of It Home**	*Craig Dillingham/Mark Sherrill*	Bermuda Dunes 104
4/18/87	**70**	4		6 **In It Again**	*Jerry Lansdowne/A.J. Masters*	Bermuda Dunes 116
8/15/87	**67**	7		7 **255 Harbor Drive /**	*Don Goodman/A.J. Masters/Mark Sherrill*	
11/21/87	**77**	3		8 **Our Love Is Like The South**	*Bobby Borchers/Don Goodman/A.J. Masters*	Bermuda Dunes 117
				MATA, Billy		
				Born in San Antonio, Texas. Male singer.		
1/30/88	**82**	3		1 **Macon Georgia Love**	*Russell Summerville*	BGM 92087
1/7/89	**89**	2		2 **Photographic Memory**	*Bobby Boyd*	BGM 70188
				MATHIS, Country Johnny		
				Born on 9/28/1933 in Maud, Texas. Male singer/songwriter. One-half of **Jimmy & Johnny** duo.		
3/9/63	**14**	13		**Please Talk To My Heart**	*Jimmy Fautheree/Johnny Mathis*	United Artists 536
				MATHIS, Joel		
				Born in Valdosta, Georgia. Male singer.		
6/8/74	**89**	3		1 **Ann**	*Wes Helm*	Chart 5217
1/28/78	**89**	2		2 **The Farmer's Song (We Ain't Gonna Work For Peanuts) /**	*Jerry Duncan/Lenore Gibson*	
1/28/78	**flip**	2		3 **Dirt Farming Man**	*Jerry Duncan*	Soundwaves 4562

DEBUT	PEAK	WKS	GOLD	ARTIST / Country Chart Hit	Ranking / Songwriter	Label (& Number)
				MATTEA, Kathy	**1990s: #47 / All-Time: #101**	
				Born on 6/21/1959 in Cross Lanes, West Virginia. Female singer/songwriter/guitarist. Attended West Virginia University in 1977. Discovered in 1983 while working as a waitress in Nashville. Also see **The Red Hots**. ***CMA: Female Vocalist 1989 & 1990***		
10/8/83	**25**	18		1 **Street Talk**	*Leland Domann/Ralph Whiteway*	Mercury 814375
2/25/84	**26**	16		2 **Someone Is Falling In Love**	*Leland Domann/Pebe Sebert*	Mercury 818289
6/16/84	**44**	10		3 **You've Got A Soft Place To Fall**	*Kerry Chater/Bob McDill/Hunter Moore*	Mercury 822218
9/15/84	**50**	11		4 **That's Easy For You To Say**	*Debbie Clifford/David Hodges*	Mercury 880192
3/16/85	**34**	14		5 **It's Your Reputation Talkin'**	*Mitch Johnson/Harry Shannon*	Mercury 880595
7/6/85	**22**	19		6 **He Won't Give In**	S:19 / A:22 *Johnny Pierce*	Mercury 880867
11/2/85	**46**	11		7 **Heart Of The Country**	*Donny Lowery/Wendy Waldman*	Mercury 884177
4/12/86	**3^1**	22		8 **Love At The Five & Dime**	A:3 / S:4 *Nanci Griffith*	Mercury 884573
9/13/86	**10**	24		9 **Walk The Way The Wind Blows**	S:7 / A:12 *Tim O'Brien*	Mercury 884978
2/7/87	**5**	25		10 **You're The Power**	S:❶^1 / A:5 *Craig Bickhardt/F.C. Collins*	Mercury 888319
5/23/87	**6**	20		11 **Train Of Memories**	S:4 *Anderson Byrd/Jimbeau Hinson*	Mercury 888574
10/17/87+	**❶^1**	24		12 **Goin' Gone**	S:3 *Pat Alger/Bill Dale/Fred Koller*	Mercury 888874
3/12/88	**❶^2**	20		13 **Eighteen Wheels And A Dozen Roses** CMA: Single	S:❶^2 *Gene Nelson/Paul Nelson*	Mercury 870148
7/9/88	**4**	19		14 **Untold Stories**	S:8 *Tim O'Brien*	Mercury 870476
11/12/88+	**4**	22		15 **Life As We Knew It**	S:17 *Walter Carter/Fred Koller*	Mercury 872082
4/15/89	**❶^1**	20		16 **Come From The Heart**	*Susanna Clark/Richard Leigh*	Mercury 872766
8/19/89	**❶^1**	21		17 **Burnin' Old Memories**	*Larry Boone/Gene Nelson/Paul Nelson*	Mercury 874672
11/25/89+	**10**	26		18 **Where've You Been** Grammy: Song & Female Vocal	*Don Henry/Jon Vezner*	Mercury 876262
4/7/90	**2^1**	21		19 **She Came From Fort Worth** from the album *Willow In The Wind* on Mercury 836950	*Pat Alger/Fred Koller*	Mercury
7/21/90	**9**	20		20 **The Battle Hymn Of Love** ***[w/ Tim O'Brien]***	*Paul Overstreet/Don Schlitz*	Mercury
11/10/90+	**9**	20		21 **A Few Good Things Remain** above 2 from the album *A Collection Of Hits* on Mercury 842230	*Pat Alger/Jon Vezner*	Mercury
3/9/91	**7**	20		22 **Time Passes By**	*Susan Longacre/Jon Vezner*	Mercury
7/6/91	**18**	20		23 **Whole Lotta Holes**	*Don Henry/Jon Vezner*	Mercury
10/19/91+	**27**	20		24 **Asking Us To Dance** above 3 from the album *Time Passes By* on Mercury 846975	*Hugh Prestwood*	Mercury

Billboard DEBUT	PEAK	WKS	GOLD	ARTIST / Country Chart Hit	Ranking / Songwriter	Label (& Number)
				MATTEA, Kathy — cont'd		
9/26/92	**11**	20		25 **Lonesome Standard Time**	*Larry Cordle/Jim Rushing*	Mercury
1/23/93	**19**	20		26 **Standing Knee Deep In A River (Dying Of Thirst)**	*Bucky Jones/Dickey Lee/Bob McDill*	Mercury
2/13/93	**27**	20		27 **Romeo** ***[w/ Dolly Parton/Mary-Chapin Carpenter/Billy Ray Cyrus/Pam Tillis/Tanya Tucker]*** from Parton's album *Slow Dancing With The Moon* on Columbia 53199	*...Dolly Parton*	Columbia
5/29/93	**50**	9		28 **Seeds**	*Pat Alger/Ralph Murphy*	Mercury
8/21/93	**64**	4		29 **Listen To The Radio**	*Nanci Griffith*	Mercury
				#25, 26, 28 & 29: from the album *Lonesome Standard Time* on Mercury 512567		
3/26/94	**3^{2}**	20		30 **Walking Away A Winner**	*Bob DiPiero/Tom Shapiro*	Mercury
7/23/94	**13**	20		31 **Nobody's Gonna Rain On Our Parade**	*Brad Parker/Will Rambeaux*	Mercury
11/12/94+	**34**	15		32 **Maybe She's Human**	*Layng Martine Jr./Kent Robbins*	Mercury
4/1/95	**20**	15		33 **Clown In Your Rodeo**	*Wayne Kirkpatrick*	Mercury
				above 4 from the album *Walking Away A Winner* on Mercury 518852		
1/18/97	**21**	20		34 **455 Rocket**	*David Rawlings/Gillian Welch*	Mercury
8/16/97	**39**	16		35 **Love Travels**	*Bob Halligan/Linda Halligan*	Mercury
				above 2 from the album *Love Travels* on Mercury 532899		
3/27/99	**73**	1		36 **Among The Missing** ***[w/ Michael McDonald]***	S:16 *Peter McCann*	BNA
4/22/00	**53**	8		37 **Trouble With Angels**	*Terry Wilson*	Mercury
7/8/00	**63**	4		38 **BFD**	*Craig Carothers/Don Henry*	Mercury
				above 2 from the album *The Innocent Years* on Mercury 170130		
				MATTHEWS, WRIGHT & KING		
				Vocal trio: Raymond Matthews (born on 10/13/1956 in Alabama), Woody Wright (born on 10/10/1957 in Tennessee) and Tony King (born on 6/27/1957 in North Carolina). Wright was a member of **Memphis**. King was a member of **The Tennesseans**.		
4/4/92	**41**	19		1 **The Power Of Love**	*Walt Aldridge*	Columbia
8/22/92	**55**	7		2 **Mother's Eyes**	*Gary Harrison/Karen Staley*	Columbia
11/28/92	**68**	4		3 **House Huntin'**	*Bob DiPiero/John Jarrard/Mark D. Sanders*	Columbia
				above 3 from the album *Power Of Love* on Columbia 48797		
6/19/93	**45**	19		4 **I Got A Love**	*Jackson Leap*	Columbia
10/16/93	**74**	2		5 **One Of These Days**	*Billy Livsey/Don Schlitz*	Columbia
				above 2 from the album *Dream Seekers* on Columbia 53198		
				MAVERICKS, The		
				Group from Miami, Florida: Raul Malo (vocals, guitar; born on 8/7/1965), David Lee Holt (guitar), Robert Reynolds (bass; born on 4/30/1962) and Paul Deakin (drums; born on 9/2/1959). Holt was replaced by Nick Kane (born on 8/21/1954) in 1995. Reynolds was married to **Trisha Yearwood** from 1994-99.		
				CMA: Vocal Group 1995 & 1996		
6/20/92	**74**	1		1 **Hey Good Lookin'** from the album *From Hell To Paradise* on MCA 10544	*Hank Williams*	MCA
1/1/94	**25**	20		2 **What A Crying Shame**	*Kostas/Raul Malo*	MCA
5/14/94	**18**	20		3 **O What A Thrill**	*Jesse Winchester*	MCA
10/1/94	**20**	20		4 **There Goes My Heart**	*Kostas/Raul Malo*	MCA
1/28/95	**30**	16		5 **I Should Have Been True**	*Stan Lynch/Raul Malo*	MCA
5/13/95	**49**	12		6 **All That Heaven Will Allow**	*Bruce Springsteen*	MCA
				above 5 from the album *What A Crying Shame* on MCA 10961		
8/19/95	**22**	20		7 **Here Comes The Rain** **Grammy: Vocal Group**	*Kostas/Raul Malo*	MCA
1/20/96	**13**	20		8 **All You Ever Do Is Bring Me Down**	*Al Anderson/Raul Malo*	MCA
6/22/96	**54**	10		9 **Missing You**	*Al Anderson/Raul Malo*	MCA
				above 3 from the album *Music For All Occasions* on MCA 11257		
11/16/96	**65**	5		10 **I Don't Care (If You Love Me Anymore)** from the movie *Michael* starring John Travolta (soundtrack on Revolution 24666)	*Raul Malo*	Revolution
2/7/98	**51**	12		11 **To Be With You**	*James House/Raul Malo*	MCA
6/6/98	**63**	7		12 **Dance The Night Away**	*Raul Malo*	MCA
				above 2 from the album *Trampoline* on MCA 70018		
10/16/99	**42**	20		13 **Here Comes My Baby** from the album *The Best Of The Mavericks* on Mercury 170112	*Cat Stevens*	Mercury
2/14/04	**59**	1		14 **Air That I Breathe** from the album *The Mavericks* on Sanctuary 84612	*Albert Hammond/Mike Hazlewood*	Sanctuary
				MAY, Ralph		
				Born in Cincinnati, Ohio. Male singer.		
5/2/81	**93**	2		1 **Cajun Lady**	*Bobby Charles/Fred Koller*	Soundwaves 4630
2/20/82	**83**	3		2 **In A Stranger's Eyes** ***[w/ The Ohio River Band]***	*Chick Rains*	AMI 1901
8/28/82	**88**	3		3 **Here Comes That Feelin' Again**	*Chick Rains*	Primero 1006
2/19/83	**57**	8		4 **Angels Get Lonely Too**	*Richard Leigh/Jeff Tweel*	Primero 1021
1/17/87	**73**	4		5 **Memory Attack** ***[w/ The Ohio River Band]***	*Steve Bogard/Jeff Tweel*	Evergreen 1048
				McALYSTER		
				Vocal group formed in Pensacola, Florida: Josh Walther, Cody Collins, Leigh Usilton and Valerie Gillis.		
11/25/00	**69**	1		**I Know How The River Feels**	S:8 *Steven Jones/Amy Powers*	MCA
				McANALLY, Mac		
				Born Lyman McAnally on 7/15/1957 in Red Bay, Alabama. Male singer/songwriter/guitarist.		
2/3/90	**14**	21		1 **Back Where I Come From**	*Mac McAnally*	Warner
7/7/90	**70**	5		2 **Down The Road**	*Mac McAnally*	Warner
				above 2 from the album *Simple Life* on Warner 26136		
5/9/92	**62**	6		3 **Live And Learn**	*Mac McAnally*	MCA

DEBUT	PEAK	WKS	GOLD	#	ARTIST / Country Chart Hit	Songwriter	Label (& Number)
					McANALLY, Mac — cont'd		
9/19/92	**72**	3		4	**The Trouble With Diamonds**	*Mac McAnally*	MCA
1/9/93	**72**	2		5	**Junk Cars**	*Mac McAnally*	MCA
					above 3 from the album *Live And Learn* on MCA 10543		

McANALLY, Shane

Born on 10/12/1974 in Mineral Wells, Texas. Male singer/songwriter.

DEBUT	PEAK	WKS	GOLD	#	Country Chart Hit	Songwriter	Label (& Number)
1/23/99	**41**	20		1	**Say Anything**	*Rich Herring/Shane McAnally*	Curb
7/17/99	**31**	20		2	**Are Your Eyes Still Blue**	S:10 *Steve Mandile/Shane McAnally/Julie Wood*	Curb
8/5/00	**50**	11		3	**Run Away**	*Rich Herring/Shane McAnally*	Curb
					above 3 from the album *Shane McAnally* on Curb 77818		

McAULIFFE, Leon

Born William Leon McAuliffe on 1/3/1917 in Houston, Texas. Died on 8/20/1988 (age 71). Male singer/steel guitarist. Member of **Bob Wills & His Texas Playboys** from 1935-42. Appeared in several western movies.

DEBUT	PEAK	WKS	GOLD	#	Country Chart Hit	Songwriter	Label (& Number)
6/4/49	**6**	5		1	**Panhandle Rag** ***[w/ his Western Swing Band]***	S:6 / J:10 *Leon McAuliffe* **[I]**	Columbia 20546
8/21/61	**16**	15		2	**Cozy Inn**	*Harlan Howard*	Cimarron 4050
12/22/62+	**22**	11		3	**Faded Love**	*Bob Wills/John Wills* **[I]**	Cimarron 4057
					also see #6 below		
1/11/64	**35**	1		4	**Shape Up Or Ship Out /**	*Eugene Grace*	
2/8/64	**47**	1		5	**I Don't Love Nobody**	*Harlan Howard*	Capitol 5066
6/12/71	**22**	9		6	**Faded Love** ***[w/ Tompall & The Glaser Brothers]***	*Bob Wills/Johnnie Lee Wills* **[R]**	MGM 14249
					new version of #3 above		

McBEE, Jerry

Born in Kentucky. Male singer/songwriter. Member of **Bluestone**.

DEBUT	PEAK	WKS	GOLD	#	Country Chart Hit	Songwriter	Label (& Number)
4/12/80	**86**	4			**That's The Chance We'll Have To Take**	*Jerry McBee*	Dimension 1004

McBRIDE, Dale

Born on 12/18/1936 in Bell County, Texas; raised in Lampasas, Texas. Died of a brain tumor on 11/30/1992 (age 55). Male singer/songwriter/guitarist. Father of Terry McBride (of **McBride & The Ride**).

DEBUT	PEAK	WKS	GOLD	#	Country Chart Hit	Songwriter	Label (& Number)
3/27/71	**70**	2		1	**Corpus Christi Wind**	*Dale McBride*	Thunderbird 539
5/22/76	**90**	6		2	**Getting Over You Again**	*Eddie Rabbitt*	Con Brio 109
					also see #12 below		
11/20/76+	**26**	13		3	**Ordinary Man**	*Jack Ruthven*	Con Brio 114
3/12/77	**60**	8		4	**I'm Savin' Up Sunshine**	*Sid Linard*	Con Brio 117
7/9/77	**53**	7		5	**Love I Need You**	*Dale McBride/Fran Powers*	Con Brio 121
9/24/77	**73**	6		6	**My Girl**	*Dale McBride*	Con Brio 124
12/10/77+	**37**	10		7	**Always Lovin Her Man**	*Harold Kinman*	Con Brio 127
3/18/78	**56**	8		8	**A Sweet Love Song The World Can Sing**	*Don King/Dave Woodward*	Con Brio 131
7/15/78	**45**	7		9	**I Don't Like Cheatin' Songs**	*Don King/Dave Woodward*	Con Brio 135
10/21/78	**72**	5		10	**Let's Be Lonely Together**	*Scott Summer*	Con Brio 140
2/3/79	**66**	5		11	**It's Hell To Know She's Heaven**	*Jim Hsieh/Mike Kosser*	Con Brio 145
5/12/79	**67**	7		12	**Getting Over You Again**	*Eddie Rabbitt* **[R]**	Con Brio 151
					same version as #2 above		
9/22/79	**61**	7		13	**Get Your Hands On Me Baby**	*Dale McBride*	Con Brio 158

McBRIDE, Martina — 1990s: #23 / 2000s: #10 / All-Time: #75

Born Martina Schiff on 7/29/1966 in Medicine Lodge, Kansas; raised in Sharon, Kansas. Female singer/songwriter. Married sound technician John McBride on 5/15/1988. Sold T-shirts for **Garth Brooks**'s 1991 concert tour. Signed to RCA in early 1992. Also see **America The Beautiful**.

CMA: Female Vocalist 1999, 2002, 2003 & 2004 // OPRY: 1995

DEBUT	PEAK	WKS	GOLD	#	Country Chart Hit	Songwriter	Label (& Number)
5/2/92	**23**	20		1	**The Time Has Come**	*Susan Longacre/Lonnie Wilson*	RCA
8/22/92	**43**	15		2	**That's Me**	*Bob Alan/Tony Haselden*	RCA
12/5/92+	**44**	15		3	**Cheap Whiskey**	*Emory Gordy Jr./Jim Rushing*	RCA
					above 3 from the album *The Time Has Come* on RCA 66002		
7/31/93	**2^1**	21		4	**My Baby Loves Me**	*Gretchen Peters*	RCA
1/8/94	**6**	20		5	**Life #9**	*Kostas/Tony Perez*	RCA
5/7/94	**12**	20		6	**Independence Day**	*Gretchen Peters*	RCA
10/22/94+	**21**	20		7	**Heart Trouble**	*Paul Kennerley*	RCA
3/11/95	**49**	9		8	**Where I Used To Have A Heart**	*Craig Bickhardt*	RCA
					above 5 from the album *The Way That I Am* on RCA 66288		
7/29/95	**4**	20		9	**Safe In The Arms Of Love**	S:20 *Pat Bunch/Mary Ann Kennedy/Pam Rose*	RCA
12/2/95+	**❶^1**	20		10	**Wild Angels**	S:15 *Matraca Berg/Gary Harrison/Harry Stinson*	RCA
4/6/96	**28**	19		11	**Phones Are Ringin' All Over Town**	*Marc Beeson/David MacKechnie/Kin Vassy*	RCA
8/31/96	**38**	15		12	**Swingin' Doors**	*Bobby Boyd/Jim Foster/Chapin Hartford*	RCA
1/11/97	**74**	1		13	**O Holy Night**	*Adolphe Adam/John Dwight* **[X]**	RCA
					from the album *White Christmas* on RCA 67654		
1/25/97	**26**	16		14	**Cry On The Shoulder Of The Road**	*Matraca Berg/Tim Krekel*	RCA
					#9-12 & 14: from the album *Wild Angels* on RCA 66509		
2/22/97+	**9**	20		15	**Valentine** ***[w/ Jim Brickman]***	*Jim Brickman/Jack Kugell*	RCA
6/14/97	**11**	20		16	**Still Holding On** ***[w/ Clint Black]***	*Matraca Berg/Clint Black/Marty Stuart*	RCA
					from Black's album *Nothin' But The Taillights* on RCA 67515		

Billboard DEBUT	PEAK	WKS	GOLD		ARTIST / Country Chart Hit	Ranking / Songwriter	Label (& Number)
					McBRIDE, Martina — cont'd		
9/13/97+	❶[1]	25		17	**A Broken Wing**	S:4 *Phil Barnhart/Sam Hogin/James House*	RCA
1/10/98	67	1		18	**O Holy Night**	*Adolphe Adam/John Dwight* **[X-R]**	RCA
					from the album *White Christmas* on RCA 67654		
4/25/98	2[2]	22		19	**Happy Girl**	*Beth Nielsen Chapman/Annie Roboff*	RCA
5/9/98	55	7		20	**This Small Divide** ***[w/ Jason Sellers]***	*Gary Burr/Jason Sellers*	BNA
					from Sellers' album *I'm Your Man* on BNA 67517		
9/19/98+	❶[1]	26		21	**Wrong Again**	S:15 *Tommy Lee James/Cynthia Weil*	RCA
1/2/99	49	2		22	**O Holy Night**	*Adolphe Adam/John Dwight* **[X-R]**	RCA
1/2/99	54	2		23	**Have Yourself A Merry Little Christmas**	*Ralph Blane/Hugh Martin* **[X]**	RCA
1/2/99	64	2		24	**Let It Snow, Let It Snow, Let It Snow**	*Sammy Cahn/Jule Styne* **[X]**	RCA
					above 3 from the album *White Christmas* on RCA 67654		
3/6/99	2[1]	27		25	**Whatever You Say**	*Ed Hill/Tony Martin*	RCA
					#15, 17, 19, 21 & 25: from the album *Evolution* on RCA 67516		
7/31/99	❶[5]	33		26	**I Love You**	*Adrienne Follese/Keith Follese/Tammy Hyler*	RCA
11/20/99+	3[2]	28		27	**Love's The Only House**	*Buzz Cason/Tom Douglas*	RCA
1/1/00	75	1		28	**White Christmas**	*Irving Berlin* **[X]**	RCA
1/8/00	53	1		29	**Have Yourself A Merry Little Christmas**	*Ralph Blane/Hugh Martin* **[X-R]**	RCA
1/8/00	57	1		30	**O Holy Night**	*Adolphe Adam/John Dwight* **[X-R]**	RCA
1/8/00	73	1		31	**Let It Snow, Let It Snow, Let It Snow**	*Sammy Cahn/Jule Styne* **[X-R]**	RCA
					above 4 from the album *White Christmas* on RCA 67654		
5/6/00	10	29		32	**There You Are**	*Bob DiPiero/Ed Hill/Mark D. Sanders*	RCA
12/9/00+	59	6		33	**Have Yourself A Merry Little Christmas**	*Ralph Blane/Hugh Martin* **[X-R]**	RCA
12/16/00+	62	4		34	**White Christmas**	*Irving Berlin* **[X-R]**	RCA
					above 2 from the album *White Christmas* on RCA 67654		
12/23/00+	11	21		35	**It's My Time**	*Billy Crain/Tammy Hyler/Kim Tribble*	RCA
					#26, 27, 32 & 35: from the album *Emotion* on RCA 67824		
12/23/00+	41	4		36	**O Holy Night**	*Adolphe Adam/John Dwight* **[X-R]**	RCA
12/23/00	67	3		37	**The Christmas Song (Chestnuts Roasting On An Open Fire)**	*Mel Torme/Robert Wells* **[X]**	RCA
					above 2 from the album *White Christmas* on RCA 67654		
6/30/01	8	20		38	**When God-Fearin' Women Get The Blues**	*Leslie Satcher*	RCA
11/3/01+	❶[2]	32		39	**Blessed**	*Brett James/Hillary Lindsey/Troy Verges*	RCA
5/11/02	3[2]	30		40	**Where Would You Be**	*Rick Farrell/Rachel Proctor*	RCA
9/21/02	33	20		41	**Practice Life** ***[w/ Andy Griggs]***	*Andy Griggs/Brett James*	RCA
					from Griggs's album *Freedom* on RCA 67006		
11/30/02+	5	26		42	**Concrete Angel**	*Martina McBride/Paul Worley*	RCA
					#38-40 & 42: from the album *Greatest Hits* on RCA 67012		
6/21/03	3[2]	23		43	**This One's For The Girls**	*Chris Lindsey/Hillary Lindsey/Aimee Mayo*	RCA
					backing vocalists include **Faith Hill**, **Carolyn Dawn Johnson** and McBride's daughters Delaney and Emma		
11/22/03+	4	20		44	**In My Daughter's Eyes**	*James Slater*	RCA
4/17/04	12	20		45	**How Far**	*Ed Hill/Jamie O'Neal/Shaye Smith*	RCA
9/4/04	20	20		46	**Trip Around The Sun** ***[w/ Jimmy Buffett]***	*Al Anderson/Steve Bruton/Sharon Vaughn*	Mailboat
					from Buffett's album *License To Chill* on Mailboat 62270		
12/4/04+	16	21		47	**God's Will**	*Barry Dean/Tom Douglas*	RCA
					#43-45 & 47: from the album *Martina* on RCA 54207		
					McBRIDE & THE RIDE		
					Group of Nashville session musicians: Terry McBride (vocals, bass; born on 9/16/1958 in Taylor, Texas), Ray Herndon (guitar) and Billy Thomas (drums). Herndon and Thomas left in 1993; Kenny Vaughn (guitar), Randy Frazier (bass) and Keith Edwards (drums) joined. Gary Morse and Jeff Roach also joined by 1994. McBride is the son of **Dale McBride**.		
3/16/91	15	20		1	**Can I Count On You**	*Bill Carter/Ruth Ellsworth/Terry McBride*	MCA
8/3/91	28	20		2	**Same Old Star**	*Bill Carter/Ruth Ellsworth/Terry McBride/Gary Nicholson*	MCA
					above 2 from the album *Burnin' Up The Road* on MCA 42343		
3/14/92	2[2]	20		3	**Sacred Ground**	*Kix Brooks/Vern Rust*	MCA
7/18/92	5	20		4	**Going Out Of My Mind**	*Kostas/Terry McBride*	MCA
11/14/92+	5	20		5	**Just One Night**	*Terry McBride*	MCA
					above 3 from the album *Sacred Ground* on MCA 10540		
3/27/93	3[1]	20		6	**Love On The Loose, Heart On The Run**	*Anna Graham/Kostas*	MCA
7/31/93	17	20		7	**Hurry Sundown**	*Denny Henson/Brent Mason/Keith Stegall*	MCA
					above 2 from the album *Hurry Sundown* on MCA 10787		
11/27/93+	26	20		8	**No More Cryin'**	*Josh Leo/Terry McBride*	MCA
					from the movie *8 Seconds* starring Luke Perry (soundtrack on MCA 10927)		
					TERRY McBRIDE & THE RIDE:		
7/2/94	45	12		9	**Been There**	*Billy Livsey/Don Schlitz*	MCA
11/5/94	72	3		10	**High Hopes And Empty Pockets**	*Anderson Byrd/Jim Robinson*	MCA
2/18/95	57	7		11	**Somebody Will**	*Walt Aldridge/Brad Crisler/Steven Jones*	MCA
					above 3 from the album *Terry McBride & The Ride* on MCA 11049		
4/6/02	50	3		12	**Anything That Touches You**	*Steve Bogard/Marv Green/Terry McBride*	Dualtone
					from the album *Amarillo Sky* on Dualtone 1122		
					McCABE, Coley		
					Born in McConnellsburg, Pennsylvania; raised in Hedgesville, West Virginia. Female singer.		
3/4/00	50	10		1	**Grow Young With You** ***[w/ Andy Griggs]***	*Austin Cunningham/Hillary Lindsey*	RCA
					from the movie *Where The Heart Is* starring Natalie Portman (soundtrack on RCA 67963)		
6/23/01	56	5		2	**Who I Am To You**	*Shaye Smith/Craig Wiseman*	RCA

Billboard DEBUT	PEAK	WKS	GOLD	ARTIST / Ranking / Country Chart Hit	Songwriter	Label (& Number)
				McCALL, C.W.		
				Born William Fries on 11/15/1928 in Audubon, Iowa. Male singer/songwriter. Was working for the Bozell and Jacobs advertising agency when he created the "C.W. McCall" character. Elected mayor of Ouray, Colorado, in the early 1980s.		
7/13/74	**19**	11		1 **Old Home Filler-Up An' Keep On-A-Truckin' Cafe**	*Chip Davis/Bill Fries* [N]	MGM 14738
12/7/74+	**12**	16		2 **Wolf Creek Pass**	*Chip Davis/Bill Fries* [N]	MGM 14764
5/10/75	**13**	12		3 **Classified**	*Chip Davis/Bill Fries* [N]	MGM 14801
9/20/75	**24**	11		4 **Black Bear Road**	*Chip Davis/Bill Fries* [N]	MGM 14825
11/29/75	**❶**[6]	15	●	5 **Convoy**	*Chip Davis/Bill Fries* [N]	MGM 14839
				also see #9 below		
3/27/76	**19**	10		6 **There Won't Be No Country Music (There Won't Be No Rock 'N' Roll)**	*Chip Davis/Bill Fries* [S]	Polydor 14310
7/4/76	**32**	9		7 **Crispy Critters**	*Chip Davis/Bill Fries/C.W. McCall* [N]	Polydor 14331
10/16/76	**88**	4		8 **Four Wheel Cowboy**	*Chip Davis/Bill Fries/C.W. McCall* [N]	Polydor 14352
12/18/76+	**40**	8		9 **'Round The World With The Rubber Duck**	*Chip Davis/Bill Fries* [N]	Polydor 14365
				sequel to #5 above		
2/26/77	**56**	7		10 **Audubon**	*Chip Davis/Bill Fries/C.W. McCall* [N]	Polydor 14377
9/17/77	**2**[2]	16		11 **Roses For Mama**	*Gene Dobbins/Wayne Sharpe/Johnny Wilson* [S]	Polydor 14420
1/20/79	**81**	4		12 **Outlaws And Lone Star Beer**	*Robert Duncan/John Durrill*	Polydor 14527
				McCALL, Darrell		
				Born on 4/30/1940 in New Jasper, Ohio. Male singer/songwriter/guitarist. Acted in the movies *Nashville Rebel*, *Road To Nashville* and *What Am I Bid.*		
1/12/63	**17**	8		1 **A Stranger Was Here** *[w/ The Milestones]*	*Bob Forshee*	Philips 40079
4/27/68	**67**	5		2 **I'd Love To Live With You Again**	*Dick Overbey*	Wayside 1011
8/17/68	**60**	8		3 **Wall Of Pictures**	*Richie Johnson/Darrell McCall*	Wayside 1021
7/12/69	**53**	9		4 **Hurry Up**	*Darrell McCall*	Wayside 003
2/7/70	**62**	4		5 **The Arms Of My Weakness**	*J. Martin Johnson*	Wayside 008
4/27/74	**48**	9		6 **There's Still A Lot Of Love In San Antone**	*A.L. "Doodle" Owens/Lou Rochelle*	Atlantic 4019
3/20/76	**52**	8		7 **Pins And Needles (In My Heart)**	*Fred Rose*	Columbia 10296
3/12/77	**32**	13		8 **Lily Dale** *[w/ Willie Nelson]*	*Tim Moore/B.J. Wills*	Columbia 10480
7/16/77	**35**	10		9 **Dreams Of A Dreamer**	*Jug Brown*	Columbia 10576
1/7/78	**59**	9		10 **Down The Roads Of Daddy's Dreams**	*Don Goodman/Mark Sherrill*	Columbia 10653
5/13/78	**91**	5		11 **The Weeds Outlived The Roses**	*Earl Thomas Conley*	Columbia 10723
3/1/80	**89**	5		12 **San Antonio Medley** *[w/ Curtis Potter]*	*Floyd Jenkins/A.L. "Doodle" Owens/Lou Rochelle/Bob Wills*	Hillside 01
8/9/80	**43**	9		13 **Long Line Of Empties**	*Patti Ferguson/Gene Rowe*	RCA 12033
12/25/82+	**64**	9		14 **There's Still A Lot Of Love In San Antone** *[w/ Connie Hanson]*	*A.L. "Doodle" Owens/Lou Rochelle*	Soundwaves 4692
6/9/84	**79**	4		15 **Memphis In May**	*Bobby Keel*	Indigo 304
				McCANN, Lila		
				Born on 12/4/1981 in Steilacoom, Washington. Female singer.		
5/17/97	**28**	20		1 **Down Came A Blackbird**	*Michael Smotherman/Markus Spiro*	Asylum
9/27/97+	**3**[3]	29		2 **I Wanna Fall In Love**	*Buddy Brock/Markus Spiro*	Asylum
3/7/98	**42**	12		3 **Almost Over You**	*Jennifer Kimball/Cindy Richardson*	Asylum
7/4/98	**63**	5		4 **Yippy Ky Yay**	*Andrew Gold/Markus Spiro*	Asylum
				above 4 from the album *Lila* on Asylum 62042		
1/30/99	**9**	26		5 **With You**	S:❶[1] *Robin Lee Bruce/Matt Hendrix*	Asylum
7/31/99	**41**	20		6 **Crush**	*Cathy Majeski/Sunny Russ/Stephony Smith*	Asylum
11/27/99+	**47**	13		7 **I Will Be**	*Bob Farrell/Tanya Leah*	Asylum
3/11/00	**60**	10		8 **Kiss Me Now**	*Gary Burr/Markus Spiro*	Asylum
				above 4 from the album *Something In The Air* on Asylum 62355		
5/5/01	**43**	11		9 **Come A Little Closer**	S:5 *Philip Douglas/Tony Marty/Jennifer Sherrill*	Warner
				from the album *Complete* on Warner 48002		
2/5/05	**53**	10		10 **Go Easy On Me**	*Marc Beeson/Jim Collins*	Broken Bow
				McCARTERS, The		
				Vocal trio of sisters from Sevierville, Tennessee: Jennifer McCarter (born on 3/1/1964) and twins Lisa McCarter and Teresa McCarter (born on 11/11/1966).		
1/16/88	**5**	20		1 **Timeless And True Love**	S:12 *Charlie Black/Buzz Cason/Austin Roberts*	Warner 28125
6/11/88	**4**	20		2 **The Gift**	S:14 *Nancy Montgomery*	Warner 27868
10/8/88	**28**	15		3 **I Give You Music**	*Dennis Adkins*	Warner 27721
4/15/89	**9**	20		4 **Up And Gone**	*Bill Caswell/Verlon Thompson*	Warner 22991
				JENNIFER McCARTER and THE McCARTERS:		
10/28/89+	**26**	15		5 **Quit While I'm Behind**	*Bill Caswell/Verlon Thompson*	Warner 22763
3/31/90	**73**	2		6 **Better Be Home Soon**	*Neil Finn*	Warner
6/9/90	**73**	2		7 **Shot Full Of Love**	*Bob McDill*	Warner
				above 2 from the album *Better Be Home Soon* on Warner ??		
				McCARTNEY, Paul, & Wings		
				Born on 6/18/1942 in Allerton, Liverpool, England. Male singer/songwriter/bassist. Founding member of The Beatles. Formed group Wings with wife Linda (keyboards, backing vocals). They married on 3/12/1969; Linda died of cancer on 4/17/1998 (age 55). Married ex-model Heather Mills on 6/11/2002. Won Grammy's Lifetime Achievement Award in 1990.		
12/21/74+	**51**	10		**Sally G**	*Paul McCartney*	Apple 1875

DEBUT	PEAK	WKS	G O L D	ARTIST / Country Chart Hit	Ranking / Songwriter	Label (& Number)

McCLAIN, Charly

1980s: #34 / All-Time: #112

Born Charlotte McClain on 3/26/1956 in Jackson, Tennessee; raised in Memphis, Tennessee. Female singer/songwriter. Regular on local Memphis show *Mid-South Jamboree* from 1973-75. Married **Wayne Massey** in July 1984.

DEBUT	PEAK	WKS	GOLD	Country Chart Hit	Songwriter	Label (& Number)
10/23/76	67	11		1 **Lay Down**	*Danny Hogan/Ronny Scaife*	Epic 50285
3/5/77	82	5		2 **Lay Something On My Bed Besides A Blanket**	*Danny Hogan/Gladys Scaife/Ronny Scaife*	Epic 50338
5/14/77	87	4		3 **It's Too Late To Love Me Now**	*Rory Bourke/Gene Dobbins/Johnny Wilson*	Epic 50378
10/1/77	73	5		4 **Make The World Go Away**	*Hank Cochran*	Epic 50436
4/8/78	13	16		5 **Let Me Be Your Baby**	*Johnny MacRae/Bob Morrison*	Epic 50525
9/16/78	8	14		6 **That's What You Do To Me**	*Johnny MacRae/Bob Morrison*	Epic 50598
1/27/79	24	11		7 **Take Me Back**	*Charly McClain/Larry Rogers/Red Williams*	Epic 50653
5/19/79	11	14		8 **When A Love Ain't Right**	*Bob Morrison/Johnny Wilson*	Epic 50706
9/15/79	20	12		9 **You're A Part Of Me**	*Kim Carnes*	Epic 50759
10/20/79	16	14		10 **I Hate The Way I Love It** ***[w/ Johnny Rodriguez]***	*Ava Aldridge*	Epic 50791
1/12/80	7	15		11 **Men**	*Jerry Hayes/Ronny Scaife*	Epic 50825
5/3/80	23	13		12 **Let's Put Our Love In Motion**	*Johnny MacRae/Bob Morrison*	Epic 50873
8/9/80	18	13		13 **Women Get Lonely**	*R.C. Bannon/Larry Rogers*	Epic 50916
11/29/80+	❶[1]	17		14 **Who's Cheatin' Who**	*Jerry Hayes*	Epic 50948
4/11/81	5	18		15 **Surround Me With Love**	*Wayland Holyfield/Norro Wilson*	Epic 01045
8/22/81	4	16		16 **Sleepin' With The Radio On**	*Steve Davis*	Epic 02421
12/26/81+	5	18		17 **The Very Best Is You**	*Larry Shell/Frank Stephens*	Epic 02656
6/26/82	3[2]	20		18 **Dancing Your Memory Away**	*Eddie Burton/Tom Grant*	Epic 02975
10/23/82+	7	21		19 **With You**	*Ron Muir/Larry Shell*	Epic 03308
4/9/83	20	15		20 **Fly Into Love**	*Lewis Anderson/Mark Wright*	Epic 03808
7/16/83	❶[1]	22		21 **Paradise Tonight** ***[w/ Mickey Gilley]***	*Bill Kenner/Mark Wright*	Epic 04007
11/5/83+	3[2]	21		22 **Sentimental Ol' You**	*Bob DiPiero/Pat McManus*	Epic 04172
2/18/84	5	18		23 **Candy Man** ***[w/ Mickey Gilley]***	*Fred Neil/Beverly Ross*	Epic 04368
4/7/84	22	15		24 **Band Of Gold**	*Lamont Dozier/Ronald Dunbar/Brian Holland/Eddie Holland*	Epic 04423
6/16/84	14	17		25 **The Right Stuff** ***[w/ Mickey Gilley]***	*Bobby Fischer/Rick Giles/Billy Haynes*	Epic 04489
9/22/84	25	18		26 **Some Hearts Get All The Breaks**	A:22 / S:30 *Buck Moore/Jeff Raymond*	Epic 04586
2/16/85	❶[1]	23		27 **Radio Heart**	S:❶[1] / A:❶[1] *Steve Davis/Dennis W. Morgan*	Epic 04777
7/6/85	5	22		28 **With Just One Look In Your Eyes** ***[w/ Wayne Massey]***	S:5 / A:6 *Steve Davis/Dennis W. Morgan*	Epic 05398
11/16/85+	10	20		29 **You Are My Music, You Are My Song** ***[w/ Wayne Massey]***	S:9 / A:10 *Jim Carter/Jodie Erwin*	Epic 05693
3/29/86	17	15		30 **When It's Down To Me And You** ***[w/ Wayne Massey]***	S:16 / A:17 *Steve Davis/Dennis W. Morgan*	Epic 05842
8/16/86	41	11		31 **So This Is Love**	*Steve Davis/Dennis W. Morgan*	Epic 06167
12/6/86	74	6		32 **When Love Is Right** ***[w/ Wayne Massey]***	*John Greenebaum/Gene Nelson/Paul Nelson*	Epic 06433
3/7/87	20	24		33 **Don't Touch Me There**	S:18 / A:22 *Mike Heeney*	Epic 06980
8/22/87	51	9		34 **And Then Some**	*Tom Damphier/Kent Robbins*	Epic 07244
2/6/88	60	5		35 **Still I Stay**	*Mike Heeney/Pat McManus*	Epic 07670
8/20/88	55	7		36 **Sometimes She Feels Like A Man**	*Rick Bowles/Paul Harrison*	Mercury 870508
11/12/88	58	6		37 **Down The Road**	*Kent Blazy/J.R. Roper*	Mercury 872036
2/4/89	50	6		38 **One In Your Heart One On Your Mind**	*Mike Heeney/Jackson Leap*	Mercury 872506
7/29/89	65	5		39 **You Got The Job**	*Layng Martine Jr.*	Mercury 872998

McCLINTON, Delbert

Born on 11/4/1940 in Lubbock, Texas. Male singer/harmonica player.

DEBUT	PEAK	WKS	GOLD	Country Chart Hit	Songwriter	Label (& Number)
4/17/93	4	20		1 **Tell Me About It** ***[w/ Tanya Tucker]*** from Tucker's album *Can't Run From Yourself* on Liberty 98987	*Bill LaBounty/Pat McLaughlin*	Liberty
11/29/97+	65	9		2 **Sending Me Angels** from the album *One Of The Fortunate Few* on Curb/Rising Tide 53042	*Francis Miller/Jerry Williams*	Curb/Rising Tide

McCLINTON, O.B.

Born Obie Burnett McClinton on 4/25/1940 in Senatobia, Mississippi. Died of cancer on 9/23/1987 (age 47). Black singer/songwriter/guitarist. Known as "The Chocolate Cowboy."

DEBUT	PEAK	WKS	GOLD	Country Chart Hit	Songwriter	Label (& Number)
7/1/72	70	6		1 **Six Pack Of Trouble**	*Jerry Ward*	Enterprise 9051
11/4/72+	37	13		2 **Don't Let The Green Grass Fool You**	*Jerry Akines/Johnnie Bellmon/Victor Drayton/Reginald Turner*	Enterprise 9059
3/10/73	36	8		3 **My Whole World Is Falling Down**	*Bettye Crutcher/Booker T. Jones*	Enterprise 9062
6/30/73	67	6		4 **I Wish It Would Rain**	*Roger Penzabene/Barrett Strong/Norman Whitfield*	Enterprise 9070
3/16/74	62	9		5 **Something Better**	*Mike Kosser/Rafe Van Hoy*	Enterprise 9091
6/29/74	86	6		6 **If You Loved Her That Way**	*Ben Peters*	Enterprise 9100
1/4/75	77	6		7 **Yours And Mine**	*Al Middelton*	Enterprise 9108
5/1/76	100	1		8 **It's So Good Lovin' You**	*O.B. McClinton*	Mercury 73777
7/8/78	90	4		9 **Hello, This Is Anna** ***[w/ Peggy Jo Adams]***	*Ron Crick/Nate Herman*	Epic 50563
12/2/78	82	5		10 **Natural Love**	*Razzy Bailey*	Epic 50620
5/19/79	79	5		11 **The Real Thing**	*O.B. McClinton*	Epic 50698
8/25/79	58	8		12 **Soap**	*O.B. McClinton*	Epic 50749
10/4/80	62	5		13 **Not Exactly Free**	*Dave Hall/Gary Lumpkin*	Sunbird 7554
6/9/84	69	5		14 **Honky Tonk Tan**	*Randy Hatch/O.B. McClinton/Josh Whitmore*	Moon Shine 3024
3/14/87	61	6		15 **Turn The Music On**	*O.B. McClinton*	Epic 6682

DEBUT	PEAK	WKS	GOLD	ARTIST / Ranking / Country Chart Hit	Songwriter	Label (& Number)

McCOMAS, Brian

Born on 5/23/1972 in Bethesda, Maryland; raised in Harrison, Arkansas. Male singer/songwriter.

DEBUT	PEAK	WKS	GOLD	Country Chart Hit	Songwriter	Label (& Number)
8/25/01	**41**	16		1 **Night Disappear With You**	S:4 *Brian McComas*	Lyric Street
1/26/02	**46**	10		2 **I Could Never Love You Enough**	*Brian McComas*	Lyric Street
3/8/03	**10**	27		3 **99.9% Sure (I've Never Been Here Before)**	*Billy Austin/Greg Barnhill*	Lyric Street
10/4/03+	**21**	30		4 **You're In My Head**	*Shane Minor/Jeffrey Steele/Chris Wallin*	Lyric Street
				above 4 from the album *Brian McComas* on Lyric Street 165025		
3/19/05	**43**	8		5 **The Middle Of Nowhere**	*Brian McComas*	Lyric Street

McCORD, Cali

Born in Springfield, Ohio. Female singer.

DEBUT	PEAK	WKS	GOLD	Country Chart Hit	Songwriter	Label (& Number)
12/12/87+	**46**	10		1 **Bad Day For A Break Up**	*Randy Barlow/Fred Kelly*	Gazelle 011
4/16/88	**60**	6		2 **All In My Mind**	*Maxine Brown/Fred Johnson/Leroy Kirkland*	Gazelle 012

McCORISON, Dan

Born in Denver, Colorado; raised in Detroit, Michigan. Male singer/guitarist.

DEBUT	PEAK	WKS	GOLD	Country Chart Hit	Songwriter	Label (& Number)
6/25/77	**96**	3		**That's The Way My Woman Loves Me**	*Paul Harrison*	MCA 40729

McCOY, Charlie

Born on 3/28/1941 in Oak Hill, West Virginia. Songwriter/harmonica player. Prolific session musician. Member of the **Nashville Superpickers**.

DEBUT	PEAK	WKS	GOLD	Country Chart Hit	Songwriter	Label (& Number)
2/5/72	**16**	15		1 **I Started Loving You Again**	*Merle Haggard/Buck Owens* [I]	Monument 8529
7/8/72	**23**	12		2 **I'm So Lonesome I Could Cry**	*Hank Williams* [I]	Monument 8546
11/4/72	**19**	11		3 **I Really Don't Want To Know**	*Howard Barnes/Don Robertson* [I]	Monument 8554
3/10/73	**26**	10		4 **Orange Blossom Special**	*Ervin Rouse* [I]	Monument 8566
7/14/73	**33**	9		5 **Shenandoah**	*Charlie McCoy* [I]	Monument 8576
10/20/73	**33**	13		6 **Release Me**	*Eddie Miller/W.S. Stevenson* [I]	Monument 8589
3/2/74	**68**	6		7 **Silver Threads And Golden Needles**	*Dick Reynolds/Jack Rhodes* [I]	Monument 8600
6/1/74	**22**	13		8 **Boogie Woogie (a/k/a T.D.'s Boogie Woogie)** *[w/ Barefoot Jerry]*	*Clarence "Pine Top" Smith* [I]	Monument 8611
8/14/76	**97**	2		9 **Wabash Cannonball**	*A.P. Carter* [I]	Monument 8703
2/5/77	**98**	3		10 **Summit Ridge Drive** *[w/ Barefoot Jerry]*	*Artie Shaw* [I]	Monument 45210
8/12/78	**30**	10		11 **Fair And Tender Ladies**	*Maybelle Carter*	Monument 258
12/16/78	**96**	3		12 **Drifting Lovers**	*Charlie Craig*	Monument 272
4/28/79	**94**	3		13 **Midnight Flyer**	*Paul Craft*	Monument 282
9/8/79	**94**	2		14 **Ramblin' Music Man**	*Russ Hicks*	Monument 289
12/19/81	**92**	3		15 **Until The Nights** *[w/ Laney Smallwood]*	*Billy Joel*	Monument 21001
4/16/83	**74**	4		16 **The State Of Our Union** *[w/ Laney Hicks]*	*Chip Hardy/Jim Rushing*	Monument 03518

McCOY, Neal — 1990s: #34 / All-Time: #155

Born Hubert Neal McGauhey on 7/30/1958 in Jacksonville, Texas (of Irish and Filipino parents). Male singer. Also recorded as **Neal McGoy** (the phonetic spelling of his surname). Began singing in Texas clubs in the late 1970s. Regularly opened shows for **Charley Pride** from 1981-87. Also see **Hope** and **One Heart At A Time**.

DEBUT	PEAK	WKS	GOLD	Country Chart Hit	Songwriter	Label (& Number)
8/27/88	**85**	2		1 **That's How Much I Love You** *[Neal McGoy]*	*Bobby Lee Springfield*	16th Avenue 70417
1/5/91	**48**	10		2 **If I Built You A Fire**	*Monty Holmes/Don Sampson*	Atlantic
9/7/91	**50**	10		3 **This Time I Hurt Her More (Than She Loves Me)**	*Earl Thomas Conley/Mary Larkin*	Atlantic
				above 2 from the album *At This Moment* on Atlantic 82171		
5/9/92	**40**	14		4 **Where Forever Begins**	*Trey Bruce/Thom McHugh*	Atlantic
9/5/92	**57**	8		5 **There Ain't Nothin' I Don't Like About You**	*Mark Irwin/Katherine Wallace*	Atlantic
2/13/93	**26**	16		6 **Now I Pray For Rain**	*Lee Satterfield/George Teren*	Atlantic
				above 3 from the album *Where Forever Begins* on Atlantic 82396		
12/18/93+	**❶**[2]	20		7 **No Doubt About It**	*Steve Seskin/John Scott Sherrill*	Atlantic
4/23/94	**❶**[4]	20		8 **Wink**	*Bob DiPiero/Tom Shapiro*	Atlantic
8/6/94	**5**	20		9 **The City Put The Country Back In Me**	*Mike Geiger/Mike Huffman/Woody Mullis*	Atlantic
				above 3 from the album *No Doubt About It* on Atlantic 82568		
12/17/94+	**3**[2]	20		10 **For A Change**	S:24 *Steve Seskin/John Scott Sherrill*	Atlantic
4/29/95	**3**[3]	20		11 **They're Playin' Our Song**	*Bob DiPiero/John Jarrard/Mark D. Sanders*	Atlantic
8/12/95	**16**	20		12 **If I Was A Drinkin' Man**	*Byron Hill/J.B. Rudd*	Atlantic
1/6/96	**3**[1]	20		13 **You Gotta Love That**	S:15 *Jess Brown/Brett Jones*	Atlantic
				above 4 from the album *You Gotta Love That!* on Atlantic 82727		
5/18/96	**4**	20		14 **Then You Can Tell Me Goodbye**	S:3 *John D. Loudermilk*	Atlantic
7/20/96	**71**	3		15 **Hillbilly Rap**	*William Attaway/Irving Burgie/Bernard Edwards/Paul Henning/Nile Rodgers*	Atlantic
9/28/96	**35**	11		16 **Going, Going, Gone**	*Steve Cropper/Bob DiPiero/John Scott Sherrill*	Atlantic
12/14/96+	**35**	17		17 **That Woman Of Mine**	*Don Cook/Tim Mensy*	Atlantic
				above 4 from the album *Neal McCoy* on Atlantic 82907		
5/24/97	**5**	21		18 **The Shake**	*Butch Carr/Jon McElroy*	Atlantic
				from the album *Greatest Hits* on Atlantic 83011		
10/18/97+	**22**	20		19 **If You Can't Be Good (Be Good At It)**	*Bill Miller/Troy Seals*	Atlantic
3/28/98	**50**	8		20 **Party On**	*Karen Taylor-Good/Paul Williams*	Atlantic
6/27/98	**29**	20		21 **Love Happens Like That**	*Aaron Barker/Ron Harbin/Anthony Smith*	Atlantic
				above 3 from the album *Be Good At It* on Atlantic 83057		
2/13/99	**37**	17		22 **I Was**	*Charlie Black/Phil Vassar*	Atlantic

DEBUT	PEAK	WKS	Gold	#	ARTIST / Country Chart Hit	Ranking / Songwriter	Label (& Number)
					McCOY, Neal — cont'd		
6/12/99	**42**	13		23	**The Girls Of Summer**	*Randy Boudreaux/Bobby Carmichael*	Atlantic
					above 2 from the album *The Life Of The Party* on Atlantic 83170		
3/18/00	**38**	16		24	**Forever Works For Me (Monday, Tuesday, Wednesday, Thursday)**	S:17 *Steve Bogard/Rick Giles*	Giant
9/2/00	**37**	21		25	**Every Man For Himself**	*Mark Elliott/Tim Johnson*	Giant
9/2/00	**59**	12		26	**Now That's Awesome!** ***[w/ Bill Engvall/Tracy Byrd/T. Graham Brown]*** from Engvall's album *Now That's Awesome!* on BNA 69311	S:13 *Bill Engvall/Porter Howell* **[N]**	BNA
1/6/01	**74**	1		27	**I'll Be Home For Christmas/Have Yourself A Merry Little Christmas**	*Ralph Blane/Kim Gannon/Walter Kent/Hugh Martin/Buck Ram* **[X]**	Warner
					from the various artists album *Believe: A Christmas Collection* on Warner 24750		
2/17/01	**41**	9		28	**Beatin' It In**	*Brett Beavers/Kelly Garrett*	Giant
					#24, 25 & 28: from the album *24-7-365* on Giant 24748		
10/12/02	**46**	9		29	**The Luckiest Man In The World**	S:7 *Monty Powell/Eric Silver*	Warner
					from the album *The Luckiest Man In The World* on Warner 48343		
4/16/05	**20**↑	21↑		30	**Billy's Got His Beer Goggles On**	*Michael Mobley/Phillip White*	903 Records
					from the album *That's Life* on 903 Records 1001		
					McCRARY, Renee		
					Born in Baton Rouge, Louisiana. Female singer.		
2/22/03	**57**	1			**Angel**	*Sarah McLachlan*	Mamalike
					McCREADY, Mindy		
					Born Malinda McCready on 11/30/1975 in Fort Myers, Florida. Female singer. Formerly engaged to actor Dean Cain.		
2/3/96	**6**	23		1	**Ten Thousand Angels**	S:4 *Billy Henderson/Steven Jones*	BNA
6/8/96	❶[1]	20		2	**Guys Do It All The Time**	S:2 *Kim Tribble/Bobby Whiteside*	BNA
10/12/96+	**18**	20		3	**Maybe He'll Notice Her Now** ***[w/ Richie McDonald]***	*Tim Johnson*	BNA
3/1/97	**4**	20		4	**A Girl's Gotta Do (What A Girl's Gotta Do)**	S:5 *Rick Bowles/Robert Byrne*	BNA
					above 4 from the album *Ten Thousand Angels* on BNA 66806		
9/20/97	**26**	18		5	**What If I Do**	S:8 *Mark D. Sanders*	BNA
1/17/98	**19**	20		6	**You'll Never Know**	S:9 *Angelo Petraglia/Kim Richey*	BNA
6/6/98	**41**	12		7	**The Other Side Of This Kiss**	S:23 *Bob DiPiero/David Malloy/Mark D. Sanders*	BNA
					above 3 from the album *If I Don't Stay The Night* on BNA 67504		
10/24/98	**68**	1		8	**Let's Talk About Love**	*Pound Lamb*	BNA
					from the various artists album *Country Cares For Kids* on BNA 67518		
6/12/99	**57**	6		9	**One In A Million**	*Beth Nielsen Chapman/Annie Roboff*	BNA
8/21/99	**57**	9		10	**All I Want Is Everything**	*Matraca Berg/Marshall Chapman*	BNA
					above 2 from the album *I'm Not So Tough* on BNA 67765		
11/11/00+	**46**	13		11	**Scream**	*Helen Darling/Tammy Wagoner*	Capitol
2/2/02	**49**	9		12	**Maybe, Maybe Not**	*Jim Collins/Mila Mason*	Capitol
					above 2 from the album *Mindy McCready* on Capitol 25931		
					McCREADY, Rich		
					Born on 2/9/1970 in Seneca, Missouri. Male singer/songwriter/guitarist.		
1/27/96	**58**	10		1	**Hangin' On**	*Kevin Hurley/David Ingram/Brian Maher/Rich McCready*	Magnatone
4/27/96	**53**	6		2	**Thinkin' Strait**	*Brian Maher/Rich McCready/Billy Montana*	Magnatone
					above 2 from the album *Rich McCready* on Magnatone 104		
5/10/97	**74**	1		3	**That Just About Covers It**	*Brett Beavers/Larry Boone*	Magnatone
					from the album *That Just About Covers It* on Magnatone 1115		
					McCULLA, Paula		
					Born in Nashville, Tennessee. Female singer/songwriter.		
2/6/88	**69**	5			**Thanks For Leavin' Him (For Me)**	*Joyce Goodwin/Paula McCulla*	Rivermark 1001
					McCULLOUGH, Gary		
					Born in Missouri. Male singer.		
5/23/87	**80**	2			**I'd Know A Lie**	*Naomi Martin/Jimmy Payne*	Soundwaves 4786
					McDANIEL, Mel	**1980s: #44 / All-Time: #124**	
					Born on 9/6/1942 in Checotah, Oklahoma. Male singer/songwriter/guitarist. Began performing in 1957. Formed first group in early 1960s. Worked clubs in Alaska from 1971-73. ***OPRY: 1986***		
5/8/76	**51**	10		1	**Have A Dream On Me**	*Bob Morrison*	Capitol 4249
9/18/76	**70**	7		2	**I Thank God She Isn't Mine**	*Johnny MacRae/Bob Morrison*	Capitol 4324
1/22/77	**39**	11		3	**All The Sweet**	*Bob Morrison/Bill Zerface/Jim Zerface*	Capitol 4373
6/4/77	**18**	14		4	**Gentle To Your Senses**	*Larry Williams*	Capitol 4430
9/17/77	**27**	11		5	**Soul Of A Honky Tonk Woman**	*Herb Coleman/Bob Morrison*	Capitol 4481
12/17/77+	**11**	16		6	**God Made Love**	*Dennis Linde/Johnny MacRae/Mel McDaniel/Lendell Pollard*	Capitol 4520
5/20/78	**80**	5		7	**The Farm**	*Dennis Linde*	Capitol 4569
8/19/78	**26**	11		8	**Bordertown Woman**	*Max D. Barnes*	Capitol 4597
3/17/79	**33**	10		9	**Love Lies**	*Skippy Barrett/Charlie Black*	Capitol 4691
6/30/79	**24**	13		10	**Play Her Back To Yesterday**	*Michael Hughes/Bob Morrison*	Capitol 4740
10/20/79	**27**	11		11	**Lovin' Starts Where Friendship Ends**	*Dennis Linde/Alan Rush*	Capitol 4784
7/5/80	**39**	9		12	**Hello Daddy, Good Morning Darling**	*Scott Anders/Wayne Dunn/Sid Linard/Roger Murrah/Keith Stegall*	Capitol 4886

Billboard DEBUT	PEAK	WKS	GOLD	ARTIST / Country Chart Hit	Ranking / Songwriter	Label (& Number)
				McDANIEL, Mel — cont'd		
11/29/80+	**23**	14		13 **Countryfied**	*Danny Hogan/Ronny Scaife*	Capitol 4949
3/28/81	**7**	14		14 **Louisiana Saturday Night**	*Bob McDill*	Capitol 4983
7/18/81	**10**	16		15 **Right In The Palm Of Your Hand**	*Bob McDill*	Capitol 5022
11/14/81+	**19**	16		16 **Preaching Up A Storm**	*Scott Anders/Roger Murrah*	Capitol 5059
3/20/82	**10**	16		17 **Take Me To The Country** ***[Mel McDaniels]***	*Larry Rogers/Ronny Scaife/Don Singleton*	Capitol 5095
7/3/82	**4**	18		18 **Big Ole Brew**	*Russell Smith*	Capitol 5138
11/6/82+	**20**	16		19 **I Wish I Was In Nashville**	*Bob McDill*	Capitol 5169
4/9/83	**22**	15		20 **Old Man River (I've Come To Talk Again)**	*Danny Hogan/Ronny Scaife*	Capitol 5218
7/30/83	**39**	12		21 **Hot Time In Old Town Tonight**	*Herb McCullough*	Capitol 5259
11/5/83+	**9**	20		22 **I Call It Love**	*Bob McDill*	Capitol 5298
3/10/84	**49**	9		23 **Where'd That Woman Go** ***[w/ Oklahoma Wind]***	*Alex Harvey/Harlan Howard*	Capitol 5333
5/19/84	**59**	8		24 **Most Of All I Remember You** ***[w/ Oklahoma Wind]***	*Ronny Scaife/Phil Thomas*	Capitol 5349
7/28/84	**64**	6		25 **All Around The Water Tank** ***[w/ Oklahoma Wind]***	*Bob Miller*	Capitol 5371
11/10/84+	**❶[1]**	28		26 **Baby's Got Her Blue Jeans On**	S:❶[1] / A:❶[1] *Bob McDill*	Capitol 5418
3/16/85	**6**	21		27 **Let It Roll (Let It Rock)**	S:6 / A:6 *Chuck Berry*	Capitol 5458
9/14/85	**5**	21		28 **Stand Up**	S:4 / A:5 *Bruce Channel/Ricky Rector/Sonny Throckmorton*	Capitol 5513
1/25/86	**22**	16		29 **Shoe String**	A:19 / S:21 *Dave Gillon/Sam Hogin*	Capitol 5544
5/31/86	**53**	9		30 **Doctor's Orders**	S:37 *Rory Bourke/Bruce Channel/Kieran Kane*	Capitol 5587
9/27/86	**12**	19		31 **Stand On It**	A:11 / S:12 *Bruce Springsteen*	Capitol 5620
2/7/87	**56**	7		32 **Oh What A Night**	*Dickey Lee/Bob McDill*	Capitol 5682
5/16/87	**49**	17		33 **Anger & Tears**	*Carol Chase/Russell Smith*	Capitol 5705
8/15/87	**60**	8		34 **Love Is Everywhere**	*Dennis Linde*	Capitol 44052
11/21/87	**64**	8		35 **Now You're Talkin'**	*Ronny Scaife/Phil Thomas*	Capitol 44106
2/13/88	**58**	7		36 **Ride This Train**	*Tricia Walker*	Capitol 44127
5/14/88	**9**	21		37 **Real Good Feel Good Song**	S:18 *Larry Alderman/Richard Fagan*	Capitol 44158
10/22/88	**62**	6		38 **Henrietta**	*Richard Fagan/Rich Grissom/Shelby Kennedy*	Capitol 44244
2/4/89	**54**	7		39 **Walk That Way**	*Rich Grissom/Stan Munsey*	Capitol 44303
4/29/89	**70**	4		40 **Blue Suede Blues**	*Richard Fagan/Ralph James/Patti Ryan*	Capitol 44358
10/21/89	**80**	3		41 **You Can't Play The Blues (In An Air-Conditioned Room)** from the album *Rock-A-Billy Boy* on Capitol 93882	*Richard Fagan/Gordon Kennedy*	Capitol
				McDONALD, Michael Born on 2/12/1952 in St. Louis, Missouri. Male singer/songwriter/keyboardist. Former lead singer of The Doobie Brothers. Also see **One Heart At A Time**.		
3/27/99	**73**	1		**Among The Missing** ***[w/ Kathy Mattea]***	S:16 *Peter McCann*	BNA
				McDONALD, Richie Born on 2/6/1962 in Lubbock, Texas. Male singer/songwriter/guitarist. Lead singer of **Lonestar**.		
10/12/96+	**18**	20		**Maybe He'll Notice Her Now** ***[w/ Mindy McCready]*** from McCready's album *Ten Thousand Angels* on BNA 66806	*Tim Johnson*	BNA
				McDONALD, Skeets Born Enos McDonald on 10/1/1915 in Greenway, Arkansas. Died of a heart attack on 3/31/1968 (age 52). Male singer/songwriter/guitarist.		
10/25/52	**❶[3]**	18		1 **Don't Let The Stars Get In Your Eyes**	J:❶[3] / S:2 / A:3 *Slim Willet*	Capitol F2216
10/24/60	**21**	6		2 **This Old Heart**	*Eddie Miller/Bob Morris*	Columbia 41773
9/28/63	**9**	18		3 **Call Me Mr. Brown**	*Barbara Miller*	Columbia 42807
12/25/65+	**29**	5		4 **Big Chief Buffalo Nickel (Desert Blues)**	*Jimmie Rodgers*	Columbia 43425
1/7/67	**28**	11		5 **Mabel**	*Skeets McDonald/Eddie Miller*	Columbia 43946

McDOWELL, Ronnie — **1980s: #40 / All-Time: #117**

Born on 3/26/1950 in Fountain Head, Tennessee; raised in Portland, Tennessee. Male singer/songwriter/guitarist. Began his singing career in 1968 while in the U.S. Navy. Worked as a commercial sign painter in Tennessee during the early 1970s.

DEBUT	PEAK	WKS	GOLD	Country Chart Hit	Songwriter	Label (& Number)
9/10/77	**13**	9	●	1 **The King Is Gone** tribute to **Elvis Presley**	*Ronnie McDowell/Lee Morgan*	Scorpion 135
12/24/77+	**5**	17		2 **I Love You, I Love You, I Love You**	*Ronnie McDowell*	Scorpion 149
4/29/78	**15**	12		3 **Here Comes The Reason I Live**	*Ben Peters*	Scorpion 159
7/29/78	**59**	5		4 **I Just Wanted You To Know** ***[w/ the Jordanaires]*** /	*Ronnie McDowell*	
7/29/78	**68**	5		5 **Animal** ***[w/ the Jordanaires]***	*Ronnie McDowell*	Scorpion 0553
10/7/78	**39**	8		6 **This Is A Holdup**	*Bill Wence/Daniel Wence*	Scorpion 0560
1/13/79	**68**	4		7 **He's A Cowboy From Texas**	*Ronnie McDowell*	Scorpion 0569
4/28/79	**18**	14		8 **World's Most Perfect Woman**	*Ronnie McDowell*	Epic 50696
8/25/79	**26**	11		9 **Love Me Now** /	*Paul Kelly*	
1/5/80	**29**	10		10 **Never Seen A Mountain So High**	*Buddy Killen/Ronnie McDowell*	Epic 50753
3/29/80	**37**	8		11 **Lovin' A Livin' Dream**	*Buddy Killen/Ronnie McDowell*	Epic 50857
7/5/80	**80**	4		12 **How Far Do You Want To Go**	*Buddy Killen/Ronnie McDowell*	Epic 50895
8/23/80	**36**	11		13 **Gone**	*Smokey Rogers*	Epic 50925
12/27/80+	**2[1]**	17		14 **Wandering Eyes**	*Jamie O'Hara*	Epic 50962

DEBUT	PEAK	WKS	GOLD	ARTIST / Country Chart Hit	Ranking / Songwriter	Label (& Number)
				McDOWELL, Ronnie — cont'd		
6/27/81	❶[1]	16		15 **Older Women**	*Jamie O'Hara*	Epic 02129
11/14/81+	4	18		16 **Watchin' Girls Go By**	*Buddy Killen/Ronnie McDowell*	Epic 02614
5/8/82	11	19		17 **I Just Cut Myself**	*Chance Jones/Mike Lantrip*	Epic 02884
9/11/82	7	17		18 **Step Back**	*Craig Morris*	Epic 03203
1/29/83	10	19		19 **Personally**	*Paul Kelly*	Epic 03526
6/11/83	❶[1]	22		20 **You're Gonna Ruin My Bad Reputation**	*Jeff Crossan*	Epic 03946
10/15/83+	3[1]	23		21 **You Made A Wanted Man Of Me**	*Jeff Crossan*	Epic 04167
2/25/84	7	19		22 **I Dream Of Women Like You**	*Troy Seals*	Epic 04367
6/23/84	8	21		23 **I Got A Million Of 'Em**	*Michael Garvin/Ron Hellard/Bucky Jones*	Epic 04499
2/23/85	5	23		24 **In A New York Minute**	A:4 / S:5 *Michael Garvin/Tom Shapiro/Chris Waters*	Epic 04816
7/20/85	9	20		25 **Love Talks**	S:7 / A:9 *Michael Garvin/Bucky Jones/Tom Shapiro*	Epic 05404
5/3/86	6	18		26 **All Tied Up**	S:4 / A:7 *Buddy Killen/Ronnie McDowell/Joe Meador*	Curb/MCA 52816
9/6/86	37	14		27 **When You Hurt, I Hurt**	*Ronnie McDowell*	Curb/MCA 52907
12/13/86+	30	14		28 **Lovin' That Crazy Feelin'**	A:30 *Bill Conn/Ronnie McDowell/Joe Meador*	Curb/MCA 52994
6/20/87	55	8		29 **Make Me Late For Work Today**	*Ronnie McDowell/Curly Putman*	Curb/MCA 53126
12/26/87+	8	23		30 **It's Only Make Believe** **Conway Twitty** (guest vocal)	S:6 *Jack Nance/Conway Twitty*	Curb 10501
5/28/88	36	12		31 **I'm Still Missing You /**	*Ronnie McDowell/Joe Meador/Steve Sheppard*	
7/16/88	27	14		32 **Suspicion**	*Doc Pomus/Mort Shuman*	Curb 10508
1/14/89	50	7		33 **Never Too Old To Rock 'N' Roll** *[w/ Jerry Lee Lewis]*	*Ronnie McDowell/Joe Meador/Richard Young*	Curb 10521
4/1/89	39	12		34 **Sea Of Heartbreak**	*Hal David/Paul Hampton*	Curb 10525
7/8/89	69	6		35 **Who'll Turn Out The Lights**	*Ronnie McDowell*	Curb 10544
12/2/89+	50	15		36 **She's A Little Past Forty**	*Buddy Killen/Ronnie McDowell/J.P. Pennington*	Curb 10558
12/8/90+	26	20		37 **Unchained Melody**	*Alex North/Hy Zaret*	Curb

McENTIRE, Pake

Born Dale McEntire in 6/23/1953 in Chockie, Oklahoma. Male singer/guitarist. Brother of **Reba McEntire**.

DEBUT	PEAK	WKS	GOLD	Country Chart Hit	Songwriter	Label (& Number)
1/18/86	20	16		1 **Every Night**	S:14 / A:21 *Layng Martine Jr.*	RCA 14220
5/10/86	3[1]	22		2 **Savin' My Love For You**	A:3 / S:3 *Michael Clark*	RCA 14336
10/11/86	12	19		3 **Bad Love**	S:10 / A:11 *Dennis Linde*	RCA 5004
2/21/87	25	12		4 **Heart Vs. Heart** **Reba McEntire** (harmony vocal)	A:25 *Don Henry/Marty Parker*	RCA 5092
6/6/87	46	11		5 **Too Old To Grow Up Now**	*Alex Harvey/Peter McCann*	RCA 5207
9/26/87	29	21		6 **Good God, I Had It Good**	*Reed Nielsen/Mark Wright*	RCA 5256
2/27/88	62	6		7 **Life In The City**	*Buddy Cannon*	RCA 5332

McENTIRE, Reba   1980s: #10 / 1990s: #5 / 2000s: #24 / All-Time: #13

Born on 3/28/1955 in Chockie, Oklahoma. Female singer/actress. Sister of **Pake McEntire**. Competed in rodeos as a horseback barrel rider. Married to rodeo champion Charlie Battles from 1976-87. Married her manager, Narvel Blackstock, in 1989. Acted in the movies *Tremors* and *North*; starred on Broadway in *Annie Get Your Gun*; starred in TV sitcom *Reba* since 2001. Seven members of her band (including **Chris Austin** and **Paula Kay Evans**) and her tour manager were killed in a plane crash on 3/16/1991.

CMA: Female Vocalist 1984, 1985, 1986 & 1987 / Entertainer 1986 // OPRY: 1986

DEBUT	PEAK	WKS	GOLD	Country Chart Hit	Songwriter	Label (& Number)
5/8/76	88	5		1 **I Don't Want To Be A One Night Stand**	*Layng Martine Jr.*	Mercury 73788
2/12/77	86	4		2 (There's Nothing Like The Love) **Between A Woman And A Man**	*Danny Hice/Ruby Hice*	Mercury 73879
8/6/77	88	4		3 **Glad I Waited Just For You**	*Bucky Jones/Royce Porter*	Mercury 73929
5/20/78	20	12		4 **Three Sheets In The Wind** *[w/ Jacky Ward]* **/**	*Randall Thompson/Sharon Thompson*	
5/27/78	flip	11		5 **I'd Really Love To See You Tonight** *[w/ Jacky Ward]*	*Parker McGee*	Mercury 55026
9/2/78	28	12		6 **Last Night, Ev'ry Night**	*Bob Morrison/Bill Zerface/Jim Zerface*	Mercury 55036
4/21/79	36	10		7 **Runaway Heart**	*Paul Harrison*	Mercury 55058
7/7/79	26	11		8 **That Makes Two Of Us** *[w/ Jacky Ward]*	*Jerry Fuller*	Mercury 55054
9/22/79	19	12		9 **Sweet Dreams**	*Don Gibson*	Mercury 57003
1/5/80	40	8		10 (I Still Long To Hold You) **Now And Then**	*Jerry Fuller*	Mercury 57014
6/14/80	8	15		11 (You Lift Me) **Up To Heaven**	*Johnny MacRae/Bob Morrison/Bill Zerface/Jim Zerface*	Mercury 57025
10/18/80	18	14		12 **I Can See Forever In Your Eyes**	*Bob DiPiero*	Mercury 57034
3/14/81	13	16		13 **I Don't Think Love Ought To Be That Way**	*Richard Mainegra/Layng Martine Jr.*	Mercury 57046
7/4/81	5	19		14 **Today All Over Again**	*Lola Jean Dillon/Bobby Harden*	Mercury 57054
11/21/81+	13	18		15 **Only You** (And You Alone)	*Buck Ram/Ande Rand*	Mercury 57062
6/5/82	3[2]	19		16 **I'm Not That Lonely Yet**	*Bill Rice/Mary Sharon Rice*	Mercury 76157
10/2/82+	❶[1]	22		17 **Can't Even Get The Blues**	*Rick Carnes/Tom Damphier*	Mercury 76180
2/5/83	❶[1]	21		18 **You're The First Time I've Thought About Leaving**	*Kerry Chater/Dickey Lee*	Mercury 810338
7/30/83	7	18		19 **Why Do We Want** (What We Know We Can't Have)	*Don King/Dave Woodward*	Mercury 812632
12/3/83+	12	22		20 **There Ain't No Future In This**	*Bill Rice/Mary Sharon Rice*	Mercury 814629
3/17/84	5	19		21 **Just A Little Love**	*Steve Davis/Dennis W. Morgan*	MCA 52349
6/23/84	15	20		22 **He Broke Your Mem'ry Last Night**	*Bucky Jones/Dickey Lee*	MCA 52404
10/13/84+	❶[1]	23		23 **How Blue**	S:❶[1] / A:❶[1] *John Moffat*	MCA 52468
2/16/85	❶[1]	22		24 **Somebody Should Leave**	S:❶[1] / A:❶[1] *Harlan Howard/Chick Rains*	MCA 52527
6/15/85	6	19		25 **Have I Got A Deal For You**	S:5 / A:7 *Mike Heeney/Jackson Leap*	MCA 52604
10/5/85	5	24		26 **Only In My Mind**	S:5 / A:5 *Reba McEntire*	MCA 52691

DEBUT	PEAK	WKS	GOLD		ARTIST / Country Chart Hit	Ranking / Songwriter	Label (& Number)
					McENTIRE, Reba — cont'd		
2/22/86	❶[1]	23		27	**Whoever's In New England**	S:❶[1] / A:❶[1] *Kendal Franceschi/Quentin Powers*	MCA 52767
					Grammy: Female Vocal		
6/28/86	❶[1]	19		28	**Little Rock**	A:❶[1] / S:2 *Bob DiPiero/Gerry House/Pat McManus*	MCA 52848
10/11/86	❶[2]	19		29	**Mind Your Own Business** *[w/ Hank Williams, Jr./Willie Nelson/Tom Petty/Reverend Ike]*	...S:❶[2] / A:❶[2] *Hank Williams*	Warner/Curb 28581
10/11/86+	❶[1]	22		30	**What Am I Gonna Do About You**	A:❶[2] / S:❶[1] *Jim Allison/Doug Gilmore/Bob Simon*	MCA 52922
2/7/87	4	17		31	**Let The Music Lift You Up**	A:4 / S:8 *Troy Seals/Eddie Setser*	MCA 52990
5/23/87	❶[1]	21		32	**One Promise Too Late**	S:❶[1] *Dave Loggins/Don Schlitz/Lisa Silver*	MCA 53092
9/19/87	❶[1]	22		33	**The Last One To Know**	S:❶[1] *Matraca Berg/Jane Mariash*	MCA 53159
1/23/88	❶[1]	20		34	**Love Will Find Its Way To You**	S:4 *Dave Loggins/J.D. Martin*	MCA 53244
5/14/88	5	16		35	**Sunday Kind Of Love**	S:3 *Barbara Belle/Anita Leonard/Louis Prima/Stan Rhodes*	MCA 53315
9/10/88	❶[1]	22		36	**I Know How He Feels**	S:3 *Rick Bowles/Will Robinson*	MCA 53402
12/24/88+	❶[1]	21		37	**New Fool At An Old Game**	*Steve Bogard/Rick Giles/Sheila Stephen*	MCA 53473
5/13/89	❶[1]	19		38	**Cathy's Clown**	*Don Everly/Phil Everly*	MCA 53638
9/2/89	4	26		39	**'Til Love Comes Again**	*Ed Hill/Bob Regan*	MCA 53694
12/23/89+	7	26		40	**Little Girl**	*Kendal Franceschi/Quentin Powers*	MCA 53763
4/14/90	2[2]	21		41	**Walk On**	*Steve Dean/Lonnie Williams*	MCA
					from the album *Sweet Sixteen* on MCA 6294		
8/25/90	❶[1]	20		42	**You Lie**	*Charlie Black/Bobby Fischer/Austin Roberts*	MCA
12/1/90+	3[1]	20		43	**Rumor Has It**	*Bruce Burch/Vern Dant/Larry Shell*	MCA
3/2/91	8	20		44	**Fancy**	*Bobbie Gentry*	MCA
5/25/91	2[1]	20		45	**Fallin' Out Of Love**	*Jon Ims*	MCA
					above 4 from the album *Rumor Has It* on MCA 10016		
10/12/91	❶[2]	20		46	**For My Broken Heart**	*Liz Hengber/Keith Palmer*	MCA
1/25/92	❶[2]	20		47	**Is There Life Out There**	*Rick Giles/Susan Longacre*	MCA
4/25/92	12	20		48	**The Night The Lights Went Out In Georgia**	*Bobby Russell*	MCA
8/15/92	3[1]	20		49	**The Greatest Man I Never Knew**	*Richard Leigh/Layng Martine Jr.*	MCA
					above 4 from the album *For My Broken Heart* on MCA 10400		
11/21/92+	5	20		50	**Take It Back**	*Kristy Jackson*	MCA
2/20/93	❶[2]	20		51	**The Heart Won't Lie** *[w/ Vince Gill]*	*Kim Carnes/Donna Weiss*	MCA
5/15/93	5	20		52	**It's Your Call**	*Bruce Burch/Shawna Burkhart/Liz Hengber*	MCA
					above 3 from the album *It's Your Call* on MCA 10673		
8/28/93	❶[1]	20		53	**Does He Love You** *[w/ Linda Davis]*	*Sandy Knox/Billy Stritch*	MCA
					Grammy: Vocal Collaboration / CMA: Vocal Event		
12/18/93+	7	20		54	**They Asked About You**	*Bill Nash/Kim Nash/Freddy Weller*	MCA
					above 2 from the album *Greatest Hits Volume Two* on MCA 10906		
2/26/94	72	6		55	**If I Had Only Known**	*Craig Morris/Jana Stanfield*	MCA
					from the movie *8 Seconds* starring Luke Perry (soundtrack on MCA 10927)		
4/9/94	5	20		56	**Why Haven't I Heard From You**	*Sandy Knox/Terry Welborn*	MCA
7/30/94	15	20		57	**She Thinks His Name Was John**	*Sandy Knox/Steve Rosen*	MCA
11/5/94+	2[1]	20		58	**Till You Love Me**	*Gary Burr/Bob DiPiero*	MCA
2/18/95	❶[1]	20		59	**The Heart Is A Lonely Hunter**	*Ed Hill/Mark D. Sanders/Kim Williams*	MCA
5/27/95	2[1]	20		60	**And Still**	*Liz Hengber/Tommy Lee James*	MCA
					above 5 from the album *Read My Mind* on MCA 10994		
9/16/95	20	12		61	**On My Own**	*Don Goodman/Mary Ann Kennedy/Pam Rose*	MCA
					Linda Davis, **Martina McBride** and **Trisha Yearwood** (backing vocals)		
11/11/95+	9	20		62	**Ring On Her Finger, Time On Her Hands**	*Don Goodman/Mary Ann Kennedy/Pam Rose*	MCA
3/30/96	19	20		63	**Starting Over Again**	*Bruce Sudano/Donna Summer*	MCA
					above 3 from the album *Starting Over* on MCA 11264		
10/5/96	2[3]	20		64	**The Fear Of Being Alone**	*Walt Aldridge/Bruce Miller*	MCA
12/28/96+	❶[1]	20		65	**How Was I To Know**	*Cathy Majeski/Sunny Russ/Stephony Smith*	MCA
1/4/97	63	2		66	**The Christmas Song (Chestnuts Roasting On An Open Fire)**	*Mel Torme/Robert Wells* **[X]**	MCA
					from the album *Merry Christmas To You* on MCA 42031		
4/12/97	2[1]	20		67	**I'd Rather Ride Around With You**	*Tim Nichols/Mark D. Sanders*	MCA
9/6/97	15	20		68	**What If It's You**	*Cathy Majeski/Robert Ellis Orrall*	MCA
					#64, 65, 67 & 68: from the album *What If It's You* on MCA 11500		
12/20/97+	23	15		69	**What If**	S:3 *Diane Warren*	MCA Nashville
					all proceeds from this single donated to the Salvation Army		
5/2/98	❶[2]	20		70	**If You See Him/If You See Her** *[w/ Brooks & Dunn]*	...*Tommy Lee James/Jennifer Kimball/Terry McBride*	Arista Nashville
7/25/98	4	20		71	**Forever Love**	*Nancy Bryant/Liz Hengber/Pamela Russ*	MCA Nashville
11/14/98+	6	20		72	**Wrong Night**	*Rick Bowles/Josh Leo*	MCA Nashville
1/2/99	68	2		73	**I'll Be Home For Christmas**	*Kim Gannon/Walter Kent/Buck Ram* **[X]**	MCA
1/9/99	73	1		74	**Away In A Manger**	*John McFarland/James Murray* **[X]**	MCA
					above 2 from the album *Merry Christmas To You* on MCA 42031		
3/20/99	7	20		75	**One Honest Heart**	*Gary Baker/David Malloy/Frank J. Myers*	MCA Nashville
					#70-72 & 75: from the album *If You See Him* on MCA Nashville 70019		
9/18/99+	3[3]	26		76	**What Do You Say**	*Michael Dulaney/Neil Thrasher*	MCA Nashville
12/4/99+	58	5		77	**The Secret Of Giving**	*Rick Bowles/Sunny Russ* **[X]**	MCA Nashville
					from the album *Secret Of Giving - A Christmas Collection* on MCA Nashville 170092		
12/4/99	70	1		78	**'Til I Said It To You**	*Tom Shapiro/Sharon Vaughn/Wally Wilson*	MCA Nashville
12/4/99	75	1		79	**I'm Not Your Girl**	*Shelly Peiken/Eric Silver*	MCA Nashville
12/18/99+	50	3		80	**I Saw Mama Kissing Santa Claus**	*Tommy Connor* **[X]**	MCA Nashville
					from the album *Secret Of Giving - A Christmas Collection* on MCA Nashville 170092		

DEBUT	PEAK	WKS	GOLD		ARTIST / Country Chart Hit	Ranking / Songwriter	Label (& Number)
					McENTIRE, Reba — cont'd		
2/12/00	4	24		81	I'll Be	*Diane Warren*	MCA Nashville
9/9/00	20	21		82	We're So Good Together	*Bob DiPiero/Annie Roboff/John Scott Sherrill*	MCA Nashville
					#76, 78, 79, 81 & 82: from the album *So Good Together* on MCA Nashville 170119		
7/28/01	3[1]	21		83	I'm A Survivor	*Shelby Kennedy/Phillip White*	MCA Nashville
1/26/02	36	11		84	Sweet Music Man	*Kenny Rogers*	MCA Nashville
					above 2 from the album *Greatest Hits Volume III - I'm A Survivor* on MCA Nashville 170202		
8/30/03	14	21		85	I'm Gonna Take That Mountain	*Melissa Peirce/Jerry Salley*	MCA Nashville
1/17/04	❶[1]	32		86	Somebody	*Dave Berg/Annie Tate/Sam Tate*	MCA Nashville
9/4/04+	7	27		87	He Gets That From Me	*Steven Jones/Phillip White*	MCA Nashville
3/19/05	16	20		88	My Sister	*Bonnie Baker/Amy Dalley/Roxie Dean*	MCA Nashville
					above 4 from the album *Room To Breathe* on MCA Nashville 000451		

And Still ['95]
Away In A Manger ['99]
Can't Even Get The Blues ['83]
Cathy's Clown ['89]
Christmas Song (Chestnuts Roasting On An Open Fire) ['97]
Does He Love You ['93]
Fallin' Out Of Love ['91]
Fancy ['91]
Fear Of Being Alone ['96]
For My Broken Heart ['91]
Forever Love ['98]
Glad I Waited Just For You ['77]
Greatest Man I Never Knew ['92]
Have I Got A Deal For You ['85]
He Broke Your Mem'ry Last Night ['84]
He Gets That From Me ['05]
Heart Is A Lonely Hunter ['95]
Heart Won't Lie ['93]
How Blue ['85]
How Was I To Know ['97]
I Can See Forever In Your Eyes ['80]
I Don't Think Love Ought To Be That Way ['81]
I Don't Want To Be A One Night Stand ['76]
I Know How He Feels ['88]
I Saw Mama Kissing Santa Claus ['00]
(I Still Long To Hold You) Now And Then ['80]
I'd Rather Ride Around With You ['97]
I'd Really Love To See You Tonight ['78]
I'll Be Home For Christmas ['99]
I'll Be ['00]
I'm A Survivor ['01]
I'm Gonna Take That Mountain ['03]
I'm Not That Lonely Yet ['82]
I'm Not Your Girl ['99]
If I Had Only Known ['94]
If You See Him/If You See Her ['98]
Is There Life Out There ['92]
It's Your Call ['93]
Just A Little Love ['84]
Last Night, Ev'ry Night ['78]
Last One To Know ['87]
Let The Music Lift You Up ['87]
Little Girl ['90]
Little Rock ['86]
Love Will Find Its Way To You ['88]
Mind Your Own Business ['86]
My Sister ['05]
New Fool At An Old Game ['89]
Night The Lights Went Out In Georgia ['92]
On My Own ['95]
One Honest Heart ['99]
One Promise Too Late ['87]
Only In My Mind ['85]
Only You (And You Alone) ['82]
Ring On Her Finger, Time On Her Hands ['96]
Rumor Has It ['91]
Runaway Heart ['79]
Secret Of Giving ['00]
She Thinks His Name Was John ['94]
Somebody Should Leave ['85]
Somebody ['04]
Starting Over Again ['96]
Sunday Kind Of Love ['88]
Sweet Dreams ['79]
Sweet Music Man ['02]
Take It Back ['93]
That Makes Two Of Us ['79]
There Ain't No Future In This ['84]
(There's Nothing Like The Love) Between A Woman And A Man ['77]
They Asked About You ['94]
Three Sheets In The Wind ['78]
'Til I Said It To You ['99]
'Til Love Comes Again ['89]
Till You Love Me ['95]
Today All Over Again ['81]
Walk On ['90]
We're So Good Together ['00]
What Am I Gonna Do About You ['87]
What Do You Say ['00]
What If It's You ['97]
What If ['98]
Whoever's In New England ['86]
Why Do We Want (What We Know We Can't Have) ['83]
Why Haven't I Heard From You ['94]
Wrong Night ['99]
You Lie ['90]
(You Lift Me) Up To Heaven ['80]
You're The First Time I've Thought About Leaving ['83]

McEUEN, John

Born on 12/19/1945 in Oakland, California. Male singer/songwriter/banjo player. Founding member of the **Nitty Gritty Dirt Band**.

DEBUT	PEAK	WKS	GOLD		Country Chart Hit	Songwriter	Label (& Number)
4/6/85	81	4			Blue Days Black Nights	*Ben Hall*	Warner 29047

McGILL, Tony

Born in Pearl, Mississippi. Male singer.

DEBUT	PEAK	WKS	GOLD		Country Chart Hit	Songwriter	Label (& Number)
1/17/87	76	4		1	Like An Oklahoma Morning	*Tommy Dee/Ann J. Morton*	Killer 1004
6/27/87	82	3		2	Taming My Mind	*Tommy Dee*	Killer 1006
1/9/88	78	4		3	For Your Love	*Ed Townsend*	Killer 1008

McGOVERN, Maureen

Born on 7/27/1949 in Youngstown, Ohio. Female singer/actress. Acted in the movies *The Towering Inferno* and *Airplane*. Starred in Broadway's *Pirates Of Penzance*.

DEBUT	PEAK	WKS	GOLD		Country Chart Hit	Songwriter	Label (& Number)
3/3/79	93	3			Can You Read My Mind	*Leslie Bricusse/John Williams*	Warner/Curb 8750
					love theme from the movie *Superman* starring Christopher Reeves		

McGRAW, Tim — 1990s: #9 / 2000s: #2 / All-Time: #40

Born Samuel Timothy McGraw on 5/1/1967 in Delhi, Louisiana; raised in Start, Louisiana. Male singer/songwriter/guitarist. Son of former Major League baseball pitcher Tug McGraw. Married **Faith Hill** on 10/6/1996. Acted in the movies *Black Cloud* and *Friday Night Lights*. Also see **Hope**.

CMA: Male Vocalist 1999 & 2000 / Entertainer 2001

DEBUT	PEAK	WKS	GOLD		Country Chart Hit	Songwriter	Label (& Number)
10/10/92	47	15		1	Welcome To The Club	*Andre Pessis/Steve Seskin*	Curb
4/10/93	60	7		2	Memory Lane	*Joe Diffie/Lonnie Wilson*	Curb
7/24/93	71	2		3	Two Steppin' Mind	*Buddy Brock/John Northrup*	Curb
					above 3 from the album *Tim McGraw* on Curb 77603		
1/22/94	8	20	●	4	Indian Outlaw	*Tommy Barnes/John D. Loudermilk/Gene Simmons*	Curb
					includes a verse from the 1971 #1 Pop hit "Indian Reservation" by the Raiders		
4/2/94	❶[2]	20	●	5	Don't Take The Girl	S:16 *Larry Johnson/Craig Martin*	Curb
7/16/94	2[3]	20		6	Down On The Farm	*Jerry Laseter/Kerry Kurt Phillips*	Curb
10/29/94+	❶[2]	20		7	Not A Moment Too Soon	S:11 *Joe Bob Barnhill/Wayne Perry*	Curb
2/25/95	5	20		8	Refried Dreams	*James Foster/Mark Petersen*	Curb
					above 5 from the album *Not A Moment Too Soon* on Curb 77659		
8/12/95	❶[5]	20	●	9	I Like It, I Love It	S:❶[19] *Jeb Stuart Anderson/Steve Dukes/Markus Hall*	Curb
10/7/95	2[2]	20		10	Can't Be Really Gone	S:4 *Gary Burr*	Curb
11/4/95+	5	21		11	All I Want Is A Life	*Tony Mullins/Stan Munsey/Don Pfrimmer*	Curb
6/22/96	❶[2]	20		12	She Never Lets It Go To Her Heart	*Tom Shapiro/Chris Waters*	Curb
10/12/96+	4	20		13	Maybe We Should Just Sleep On It	*Jerry Laseter/Kerry Kurt Phillips*	Curb
					above 5 from the album *All I Want* on Curb 77800		
5/10/97	❶[6]	20	▲	14	It's Your Love *[w/ Faith Hill]*	S:❶[12] *Stephony Smith*	Curb
					CMA: Vocal Event		
7/5/97	❶[2]	26		15	Everywhere	*Mike Reid/Craig Wiseman*	Curb
8/9/97+	❶[6]	42		16	Just To See You Smile	*Tony Martin/Mark Nesler*	Curb

Billboard DEBUT	PEAK	WKS	GOLD	ARTIST / Ranking / Country Chart Hit	Songwriter	Label (& Number)

McGRAW, Tim — cont'd

DEBUT	PEAK	WKS	GOLD	Country Chart Hit	Songwriter	Label (& Number)
3/7/98	**75**	2		17 **You Turn Me On**	*Billy Lawson*	Curb
3/14/98	**2**[1]	20		18 **One Of These Days**	S:9 *Marcus Hummon/Monty Powell/Kip Raines*	Curb
5/30/98	**3**[2]	20		19 **Just To Hear You Say That You Love Me** *[w/ Faith Hill]*	*Diane Warren*	Warner
				from Hill's album *Faith* on Warner 46790		
7/11/98	❶[4]	32		20 **Where The Green Grass Grows**	*Jess Leary/Craig Wiseman*	Curb
11/7/98+	**2**[1]	20		21 **For A Little While**	*Steve Mandile/Jeff Vandiver/Phil Vassar*	Curb
				#14-18, 20 & 21: from the album *Everywhere* on Curb 77886		
3/20/99	❶[5]	24		22 **Please Remember Me**	S:❶[13] *Rodney Crowell/Will Jennings*	Curb
				Patty Loveless (backing vocal)		
5/15/99	❶[5]	39		23 **Something Like That**	*Rick Ferrell/Keith Follese*	Curb
5/15/99+	❶[2]	37		24 **My Best Friend**	*Bill Luther/Aimee Mayo*	Curb
5/15/99+	**64**	15		25 **Seventeen**	*Chris Lindsey/Bill Luther/Aimee Mayo*	Curb
5/15/99	**66**	5		26 **The Trouble With Never**	*Tony Martin/Mark Nesler*	Curb
5/22/99	**74**	1		27 **Senorita Margarita**	*Bob DiPiero/George Teren*	Curb
11/20/99+	**6**	45		28 **Let's Make Love** *[w/ Faith Hill]*	*Marv Green/Chris Lindsey/Bill Luther/Aimee Mayo*	Warner/Curb
				Grammy: Vocal Collaboration; from McGraw's album *Greatest Hits* on Curb 77978 and from Hill's album *Breathe* on Warner 47373		
4/8/00	❶[5]	46		29 **My Next Thirty Years**	*Phil Vassar*	Curb
4/15/00	**7**	20		30 **Some Things Never Change**	*Walt Aldridge/Brad Crisler*	Curb
				#22-27, 29 & 30: from the album *A Place In The Sun* on Curb 77942		
11/4/00+	**32**	21		31 **Things Change**	*Marv Green/Chris Lindsey/Bill Luther/Aimee Mayo*	Curb
3/24/01	❶[1]	20		32 **Grown Men Don't Cry**	*Tom Douglas/Steve Seskin*	Curb
5/12/01	**52**	18		33 **Telluride**	*Brett James/Troy Verges*	Curb
7/28/01	❶[2]	22		34 **Angry All The Time**	*Bruce Robison*	Curb
9/15/01+	❶[1]	33		35 **Bring On The Rain** *[w/ Jo Dee Messina]*	*Helen Darling/Billy Montana*	Curb
				from Messina's album *Burn* on Curb 77977		
12/1/01+	❶[1]	23		36 **The Cowboy In Me**	*Al Anderson/Jeffrey Steele/Craig Wiseman*	Curb
5/25/02	❶[1]	21		37 **Unbroken**	*Holly Lamar/Annie Roboff*	Curb
				#31-34, 36 & 37: from the album *Set This Circus Down* on Curb 78711		
9/21/02	**5**	20		38 **Red Rag Top**	*Jason White*	Curb
11/30/02+	**49**	15		39 **Tiny Dancer**	*Elton John/Bernie Taupin*	Curb
12/14/02+	**2**[3]	22		40 **She's My Kind Of Rain**	*Tommy Lee James/Robin Lerner*	Curb
5/17/03	❶[2]	27		41 **Real Good Man**	*Rivers Rutherford/George Teren*	Curb
11/1/03+	❶[2]	25		42 **Watch The Wind Blow By**	*Dylan Altman/Anders Osborne*	Curb
				above 5 from the album *Tim McGraw And The Dancehall Doctors* on Curb 78746		
6/5/04	❶[7]	21		43 **Live Like You Were Dying**	*Tim Nichols/Craig Wiseman*	Curb
				Grammy: Song & Male Vocal / CMA: Single & Song		
9/4/04	❶[1]	24		44 **Back When**	*Stan Lynch/Stephony Smith/Jeff Stevens*	Curb
1/29/05	**14**	20		45 **Drugs Or Jesus**	*Brett James/Chris Lindsey/Aimee Mayo/Troy Verges*	Curb
5/28/05	**5**	18↑		46 **Do You Want Fries With That**	*Casey Beathard/Kerry Kurt Phillips*	Curb
				above 4 from the album *Live Like You Were Dying* on Curb 78858		

McGUFFEY LANE

Country-rock group from Columbus, Ohio: Bob McNelley (vocals), John Schwab (guitar), Terry Efaw (steel guitar), Stephen Douglass (keyboards), Stephen Reis (bass) and Dave Rangeler (drums). Group name taken from a street in Athens, Ohio. Douglass died in a car crash on 1/12/1984 (age 33). McNelley died of a self-inflicted gunshot wound on 1/7/1987 (age 36).

DEBUT	PEAK	WKS	GOLD	Country Chart Hit	Songwriter	Label (& Number)
11/20/82+	**44**	13		1 **Making A Living's Been Killing Me**	*Nancy Montgomery/Marshall Morgan/Zack Van Arsdale*	Atco 99959
3/26/83	**62**	6		2 **Doing It Right**	*Wood Newton/Dan Tyler*	Atco 99908
5/12/84	**44**	12		3 **Day By Day**	*Bob McNelley/John Schwab*	Atlantic Amer. 99778
9/1/84	**63**	8		4 **The First Time**	*Stephen Douglass/Bob McNelley/John Schwab/Dan Tyler*	Atlantic Amer. 99717

McGUINN, Mark

Born in 1969 in Greensboro, North Carolina. Singer/songwriter/guitarist.

DEBUT	PEAK	WKS	GOLD	Country Chart Hit	Songwriter	Label (& Number)
1/20/01	**6**	20		1 **Mrs. Steven Rudy**	S:❶[4] *Shane Decker/Mark McGuinn*	VFR
6/23/01	**25**	20		2 **That's A Plan**	*Bobby Byrd/David Leone*	VFR
12/8/01+	**29**	20		3 **She Doesn't Dance**	*Shane Decker/Mark McGuinn/Don Pfrimmer*	VFR
				above 3 from the album *Mark McGuinn* on VFR 734757		
7/20/02	**54**	2		4 **More Beautiful Today**	*Billy Davidson/Mark McGuinn/John Reynolds*	VFR

McGUINN, Roger

Born James McGuinn on 7/13/1942 in Chicago, Illinois. Rock singer/songwriter/guitarist. Lead singer of The Byrds.

DEBUT	PEAK	WKS	GOLD	Country Chart Hit	Songwriter	Label (& Number)
4/29/89	**6**	21		**You Ain't Going Nowhere** *[w/ Chris Hillman]*	*Bob Dylan*	Universal 66006

McGUIRE, Doug

Born in Oklahoma. Male singer.

DEBUT	PEAK	WKS	GOLD	Country Chart Hit	Songwriter	Label (& Number)
7/26/80	**64**	6		**Stranger, I'm Married**	*Fred Kelly*	Multi-Media 7

McHAYES

Duo formed in Nashville, Tennessee: Mark McClurg and **Wade Hayes**.

DEBUT	PEAK	WKS	GOLD	Country Chart Hit	Songwriter	Label (& Number)
4/19/03	**41**	15		**It Doesn't Mean I Don't Love You**	S:❶[1] *Bobby Pinson/Jeremy Spillman/Trent Willmon*	Universal South

McKUHEN, Lanier

Born in Macon, Georgia. Male singer.

DEBUT	PEAK	WKS	GOLD	Country Chart Hit	Songwriter	Label (& Number)
4/25/87	**75**	4		**Searching** (For Someone Like You)	*Murphy Maddux*	Soundwaves 4785

DEBUT	PEAK	WKS	GOLD	ARTIST / Ranking / Country Chart Hit	Songwriter	Label (& Number)
				McLEAN, Don		
				Born on 10/2/1945 in New Rochelle, New York. Male singer/songwriter/guitarist.		
1/31/81	**6**	14		1 **Crying**	*Joe Melson/Roy Orbison*	Millennium 11799
5/9/81	**68**	6		2 **Since I Don't Have You**	*James Beaumont/Walter Lester/Joseph Rock/John Taylor/ Joseph Verscharen/Janet Vogel*	Millennium 11804
4/18/87	**73**	4		3 **He's Got You**	*Hank Cochran*	EMI America 8375
				male version of "She's Got You" by **Patsy Cline**		
11/14/87	**49**	8		4 **You Can't Blame The Train**	*Terri Sharp*	Capitol 44098
7/30/88	**65**	4		5 **Love In The Heart**	*Michael Brewer*	Capitol 44186
				McMILLAN, Jimmy		
				Born in Fort Worth, Texas. Male singer.		
12/20/80	**92**	3		1 **Footsteps**	*Russ Hanson/Sheb Wooley*	Blum 001
3/14/81	**96**	2		2 **Her Empty Pillow (Lying Next To Mine)**	*John Kinsey*	Blum 767
				McMILLAN, Terry		
				Born on 10/12/1953 in Lexington, North Carolina. Male singer/harmonica player.		
12/11/82	**85**	4		**Love Is A Full Time Thing**	*Alan Rhody*	RCA 13360
				McPHERSON, Wyley		
				Born Paul Richardson in Arkansas. Male singer/songwriter. Brother of producer George Richey (former husband of **Tammy Wynette**).		
8/7/82	**89**	2		1 **Jedediah Jones**	*Dennis Knutson/Paul Richey/Jerry Taylor*	i.e. 007
10/9/82	**81**	3		2 **The Devil Inside**	*Larry Bastian*	i.e. 009
				McQUAIG, Scott		
				Born on 1/27/1960 in Meridian, Mississippi. Male singer/songwriter.		
8/12/89	**56**	8		1 **Honky Tonk Amnesia**	*A.L. "Doodle" Owens/Whitey Shafer*	Universal 66001
11/4/89	**54**	7		2 **Johnny And The Dreamers**	*Tony Colton/Scott McQuaig*	Universal 66028
				McVICKER, Dana		
				Born in Baltimore, Maryland; raised in Phillipe, West Virginia. Female singer.		
3/14/87	**64**	6		1 **I'd Rather Be Crazy**	*Bobby Braddock*	EMI America 8371
6/27/87	**64**	5		2 **Call Me A Fool**	*Dave Loggins*	EMI America 43017
5/28/88	**65**	5		3 **Rock-A-Bye Heart**	*Skip Ewing/Michael White*	Capitol 44155
10/22/88	**88**	2		4 **I'm Loving The Wrong Man Again**	*Harlan Howard/Ron Peterson*	Capitol 44223
				MEADE, Donna		
				Born in 1953 in Chase City, Virginia. Female singer. Married **Jimmy Dean** on 10/27/1991.		
1/9/88	**63**	8		1 **Be Serious**	*Clifford Curry/Randy Layne*	Mercury 888993
5/7/88	**50**	9		2 **Love's Last Stand**	*Jimmy Jay/Donny Kees/Tommy Riggs*	Mercury 870283
7/30/88	**69**	4		3 **Congratulations**	*Michael Garvin/Ron Hellard/Walt Wilson*	Mercury 870527
10/29/88	**78**	3		4 **Leavin' On Your Mind**	*Webb Pierce/Wayne Walker*	Mercury 872010
6/3/89	**57**	7		5 **When He Leaves You**	*Mike Reid/Kent Robbins*	Mercury 874280
10/7/89	**61**	4		6 **Cry Baby**	*Don Cook/Jamie O'Hara/Curly Putman*	Mercury 874806
				MEDLEY, Bill		
				Born on 9/19/1940 in Santa Ana, California. Male singer. One-half of The Righteous Brothers duo.		
1/6/79	**91**	3		1 **Statue Of A Fool**	*Jan Crutchfield*	United Artists 1270
12/10/83+	**28**	18		2 **Till Your Memory's Gone**	*Bill Rice/Mary Sharon Rice*	RCA 13692
4/14/84	**17**	18		3 **I Still Do**	*John Jarrard/J.D. Martin*	RCA 13753
8/4/84	**26**	14		4 **I've Always Got The Heart To Sing The Blues**	*Graham Lyle/Troy Seals*	RCA 13851
3/2/85	**47**	9		5 **Is There Anything I Can Do**	*Wayland Holyfield/Gary Nicholson*	RCA 14021
5/11/85	**55**	7		6 **Women In Love**	*Bob McDill*	RCA 14081
				MELLENCAMP, John Cougar		
				Born on 10/7/1951 in Seymour, Indiana. Rock singer/songwriter/producer. Director/star of the movie *Falling from Grace*; leader of the **Buzzin' Cousins** who appeared in the movie. Married model Elaine Irwin on 9/5/1992.		
8/12/89	**82**	5		1 **Jackie Brown**	*John Mellencamp*	Mercury 874644
9/11/04	**21**	20		2 **What Say You** ***[w/ Travis Tritt]***	*Michael Bradford/Frank J. Myers*	Columbia
				from Tritt's album *My Honky Tonk History* on Columbia 92084		
				MELLONS, Ken		
				Born on 7/10/1965 in Kingsport, Tennessee; raised in Nashville, Tennessee. Male singer/songwriter/guitarist.		
4/2/94	**55**	9		1 **Lookin' In The Same Direction**	*Dale Dodson/Ken Mellons/Jimmy Melton*	Epic
7/30/94	**8**	20		2 **Jukebox Junkie**	*Jerry Cupit/Janice Honeycutt/Ken Mellons*	Epic
12/17/94+	**42**	14		3 **I Can Bring Her Back**	*Dale Dodson/Ken Mellons/Gene Simmons*	Epic
3/25/95	**40**	12		4 **Workin' For The Weekend**	*Jerry Cupit/Janice Honeycutt/Ken Mellons*	Epic
				above 4 from the album *Ken Mellons* on Epic 53746		
9/30/95	**39**	20		5 **Rub-A-Dubbin'**	*Stan Davis/Don Goodman/Becky Hobbs*	Epic
4/27/96	**55**	8		6 **Stranger In Your Eyes**	*Max D. Barnes/Joe Chambers/Larry Jenkins*	Epic
				above 2 from the album *Where Forever Begins* on Epic 66965		
1/3/04	**54**	3		7 **Paint Me A Birmingham**	*Gary Duffy/Buck Moore*	Home
				from the album *Sweet* on Home 776150		
				MELTON, Terri		
				Born in Knoxville, Tennessee. Female singer/pianist.		
9/9/78	**76**	4		1 **If You Think I Love You Now** ***[w/ Jim Mundy]***	*Jim Mundy*	MCM 100
1/6/79	**87**	2		2 **Kiss You All Over** ***[w/ Jim Mundy]***	*Mike Chapman/Nicky Chinn*	MCM 101

Billboard DEBUT	PEAK	WKS	GOLD	ARTIST / Country Chart Hit	Ranking / Songwriter	Label (& Number)

MEMPHIS

Group from Memphis, Tennessee. Led by Woody Wright (later a member of **Matthews, Wright & King**).

DEBUT	PEAK	WKS		Country Chart Hit	Songwriter	Label (& Number)
8/25/84	**85**	4		**We've Got To Start Meeting Like This**	*Ken Bell/Terry Skinner/J.L. Wallace*	MPI 1691

MENSY, Tim

Born Timothy Menzies on 8/25/1959 in Mechanicsville, Virginia. Male singer/songwriter/guitarist. Member of **Bandana**.

DEBUT	PEAK	WKS		Country Chart Hit	Songwriter	Label (& Number)
4/15/89	**67**	5	1	**Hometown Advantage**	*Tony Haselden/Tim Mensy*	Columbia 68676
8/19/89	**60**	7	2	**Stone By Stone**	*Gene Dobbins/Tim Mensy/Glenn Ray*	Columbia 69007
1/13/90	**82**	1	3	**You Still Love Me In My Dreams** from the album *Stone By Stone* on Columbia 45088	*Tim Mensy*	Columbia
7/11/92	**53**	9	4	**This Ol' Heart**	*Tim Mensy*	Giant
10/31/92	**52**	14	5	**That's Good**	*Tony Haselden/Tim Mensy*	Giant
2/27/93	**74**	2	6	**She Dreams** above 3 from the album *This Ol' Heart* on Giant 24463	*Gary Harrison/Tim Mensy*	Giant

MERCYME

Christian pop group from Lakeland, Florida: Bart Millard (vocals), Mike Scheuchzer (guitar), Nathan Cochran (bass) and Robby Shaffer (drums).

DEBUT	PEAK	WKS		Country Chart Hit	Songwriter	Label (& Number)
12/27/03+	**52**	16		**I Can Only Imagine** from the album *Almost There* on INO/Curb 85725	*Bart Millard*	INO/Curb

MEREDITH, Buddy

Born William Meredith on 4/13/1926 in Beaver Falls, Pennsylvania; later based in South Dakota. Male singer.

DEBUT	PEAK	WKS		Country Chart Hit	Songwriter	Label (& Number)
5/12/62	**27**	2		**I May Fall Again**	*Bob Forshee*	Nashville 5042

MERRILL AND JESSICA

Vocal duo: Merrill Osmond (born on 4/30/1953; member of the **Osmond Brothers**) and **Jessica Boucher**.

DEBUT	PEAK	WKS		Country Chart Hit	Songwriter	Label (& Number)
5/9/87	**62**	6		**You're Here To Remember (I'm Here To Forget)**	*Carol Chase/Wayland Holyfield*	EMI America 8388

MERRITT, Tift

Born in 1975 in Houston, Texas; raised in Bynum, North Carolina. Female singer/songwriter/guitarist.

DEBUT	PEAK	WKS		Country Chart Hit	Songwriter	Label (& Number)
2/26/05	**60**	1		**Good Hearted Man** from the album *Tambourine* on Lost Highway 002528	*Tift Merritt*	Lost Highway

MESSINA, Jo Dee — 2000s: #15 / All-Time: #160

Born on 8/25/1970 in Framingham, Massachusetts; raised in Holliston, Massachusetts. Female singer. Began singing professionally in 1985.

CMA: Horizon 1999

DEBUT	PEAK	WKS		Country Chart Hit	Songwriter	Label (& Number)
1/27/96	**2**[1]	20	1	**Heads Carolina, Tails California**	S:3 *Tim Nichols/Mark D. Sanders*	Curb
7/6/96	**7**	20	2	**You're Not In Kansas Anymore**	*Tim Nichols/Zack Turner*	Curb
11/16/96	**53**	13	3	**Do You Wanna Make Something Of It**	*Terry Anderson/Bob DiPiero*	Curb
5/3/97	**64**	5	4	**He'd Never Seen Julie Cry** above 4 from the album *Jo Dee Messina* on Curb 77820	*Max T. Barnes/Leslie Satcher*	Curb
1/17/98	**❶**[2]	30	5	**Bye-Bye**	*Rory Bourke/Phil Vassar*	Curb
5/23/98	**❶**[3]	30	6	**I'm Alright**	S:2 *Phil Vassar*	Curb
10/10/98+	**❶**[3]	32	7	**Stand Beside Me**	*Steve Davis*	Curb
5/1/99	**2**[7]	34	8	**Lesson In Leavin'**	*Randy Goodrum/Brent Maher*	Curb
10/23/99+	**8**	27	9	**Because You Love Me**	*Kostas/John Scott Sherrill*	Curb
3/18/00	**75**	1	10	**No Time For Tears** above 6 from the album *I'm Alright* on Curb 77904	*Steven Jones/Jo Dee Messina*	Curb
5/20/00	**❶**[4]	27	11	**That's The Way**	S:2 *Holly Lamar/Annie Roboff*	Curb
10/14/00+	**2**[1]	26	12	**Burn**	*Tina Arena/Pam Reswick/Steve Werfel*	Curb
4/14/01	**5**	23	13	**Downtime**	*Phillip Coleman/Carolyn Dawn Johnson*	Curb
9/15/01+	**❶**[1]	33	14	**Bring On The Rain** *[w/ Tim McGraw]*	*Helen Darling/Billy Montana*	Curb
5/11/02	**23**	20	15	**Dare To Dream** above 5 from the album *Burn* on Curb 77977	*Jane Bach/Adrienne Follese*	Curb
1/18/03	**21**	20	16	**Was That My Life**	*Marv Green/Bill Luther*	Curb
7/26/03	**15**	28	17	**I Wish** above 2 from the album *Greatest Hits* on Curb 78790	*Ed Hill/Tommy Lee James*	Curb
1/1/05	**❶**[2]	25	18	**My Give A Damn's Busted**	*Joe Diffie/Tony Martin/Tom Shapiro*	Curb
6/25/05	**23**↑	14↑	19	**Delicious Surprise (I Believe It)** above 2 from the album *Delicious Surprise* on Curb 78770	*Glen Burtnick/Beth Hart*	Curb

MESSNER, Bud, & His Sky Line Boys

Born Norman Messner on 10/9/1917 in Luray, Virginia. Died on 5/5/2001 (age 83). Male singer. His Sky Line Boys included Buddy Allen, Jack Throckmorton, Jimmy Throckmorton and Ray Ingram.

DEBUT	PEAK	WKS		Country Chart Hit	Songwriter	Label (& Number)
6/3/50	**7**	6		**Slippin' Around With Jole Blon** Bill Franklin (vocal); same melody as the 1949 hit "Slippin' Around"	J:7 / S:9 *Bill Franklin*	Abbey 15004

MEYERS, Augie

Born on 5/31/1940 in San Antonio, Texas. Male singer/keyboardist/accordionist. Member of the Sir Douglas Quintet and the Texas Tornados.

DEBUT	PEAK	WKS		Country Chart Hit	Songwriter	Label (& Number)
2/20/88	**86**	3		**Kep Pa So**	*Augie Meyers*	Atlantic Amer. 99382

DEBUT	PEAK	WKS	GOLD	ARTIST / Country Chart Hit	Songwriter	Label (& Number)
				MEYERS, Michael		
				Born in Florida. Male singer.		
1/16/82	**94**	2		**I'm Just The Leavin' Kind**	*Jim West*	MBP 1980
				MICHAELS, Bret		
				Born Bret Michael Sychak on 3/15/1963 in Harrisburg, Pennsylvania. Male singer/songwriter. Lead singer of hard-rock group Poison.		
10/9/04	**45**	16		**All I Ever Needed** ***[w/ Jessica Andrews]***	*Bret Michaels*	Poor Boy
				MICHAELS, Jill		
				Born in Hollywood, California. Female singer.		
7/2/83	**57**	6		**Are You Lonesome Tonight** ***[w/ John Schneider]***	*Lou Handman/Roy Turk*	Scotti Brothers 03945
				MIDDLEMAN, Georgia		
				Born on 12/27/1967 in Houston, Texas. Female singer/songwriter.		
7/15/00	**53**	10		1 **No Place Like Home**	*A.J. Masters/Karen Rochelle*	Giant
11/18/00	**60**	3		2 **Kick Down The Door**	*Kristy Jackson/Georgia Middleman*	Giant
				above 2 from the album *Endless Possibilities* on Giant 24718		
2/15/03	**52**	9		3 **Scary Old World** ***[w/ Radney Foster]***	*Radney Foster/Harlan Howard*	Dualtone
				version with Middleman was released as a promotional single only		
				MIDDLETON, Eddie		
				Born in Albany, Georgia. Male singer.		
6/11/77	**87**	6		1 **Midnight Train To Georgia**	*Jim Weatherly*	Epic 50388
9/10/77	**38**	10		2 **Endlessly**	*Brook Benton/Clyde Otis*	Epic 50431
12/10/77+	**44**	10		3 **What Kind Of Fool (Do You Think I Am)**	*Ray Whitley*	Epic 50481
				MILES, Dick		
				Born in LaGrange, Georgia. Male singer/songwriter.		
3/16/68	**17**	10		**The Last Goodbye**	*Kelso Herston/Dick Miles/Bob Prather* **[S]**	Capitol 2113
				MILLER, Carl		
				Born in Broadway, Virginia. Male singer/songwriter.		
6/18/83	**84**	3		**Life Of The Party**	*Carl Miller*	Country Bach 0004
				MILLER, Dean		
				Born on 10/15/1965 in Santa Fe, New Mexico. Male singer/songwriter/guitarist. Son of **Roger Miller**.		
7/26/97	**54**	7		1 **Nowhere, USA**	*Dean Miller*	Capitol
11/8/97	**67**	1		2 **My Heart's Broke Down (But My Mind's Made Up)**	*Sarah Majors/Dean Miller*	Capitol
2/21/98	**57**	6		3 **Wake Up And Smell The Whiskey**	*Brett James/Dean Miller*	Capitol
				above 3 from the album *Dean Miller* on Capitol 31559		
7/13/02	**58**	1		4 **Love Is A Game**	*Sean McGraw/Dean Miller*	Universal South
				from the album *Just Me* on Universal South 30011		
				MILLER, Ellen Lee		
				Born in Nevada. Female singer.		
2/11/89	**92**	2		**You Only Love Me When I'm Leavin'**	*Darlene Austin/Don Goodman/Pal Rakes*	Golden Trumpet 103
				MILLER, Frankie		
				Born on 12/17/1930 in Victoria, Texas. Male singer/songwriter/guiatrist.		
4/13/59	**5**	19		1 **Black Land Farmer**	*Frankie Miller*	Starday 424
10/5/59	**7**	21		2 **Family Man**	*J.A. Balthrop*	Starday 457
5/23/60	**15**	14		3 **Baby Rocked Her Dolly**	*Merle Kilgore*	Starday 496
7/17/61	**16**	5		4 **Black Land Farmer**	*Frankie Miller* **[R]**	Starday 424
				same version as #1 above		
2/15/64	**34**	6		5 **A Little South Of Memphis**	*Tommy Hill/Frankie Miller*	Starday 655
				MILLER, Jody — **All-Time: #227**		
				Born Myrna Joy Brooks on 11/29/1941 in Phoenix, Arizona; raised in Blanchard, Oklahoma. Female singer.		
5/29/65	**5**	11		1 **Queen Of The House**	*Roger Miller/Mary Taylor*	Capitol 5402
				Grammy: Female Vocal; answer to "King Of The Road" by **Roger Miller**		
11/9/68	**73**	2		2 **Long Black Limousine**	*Bobby George/Vern Stovall*	Capitol 2290
8/15/70	**21**	13		3 **Look At Mine**	*Tony Hatch/Jackie Trent*	Epic 10641
1/2/71	**19**	13		4 **If You Think I Love You Now (I've Just Started)**	*Curly Putman/Billy Sherrill*	Epic 10692
6/12/71	**5**	15		5 **He's So Fine**	*Ronnie Mack*	Epic 10734
10/9/71	**5**	14		6 **Baby, I'm Yours**	*Van McCoy*	Epic 10785
3/25/72	**15**	13		7 **Be My Baby**	*Jeff Barry/Ellie Greenwich/Phil Spector*	Epic 10835
5/27/72	**13**	11		8 **Let's All Go Down To The River** ***[w/ Johnny Paycheck]***	*Earl Montgomery/Sue Richards*	Epic 10863
6/17/72	**4**	14		9 **There's A Party Goin' On**	*Billy Sherrill/Glenn Sutton*	Epic 10878
11/4/72	**18**	11		10 **To Know Him Is To Love Him**	*Phil Spector*	Epic 10916
3/17/73	**9**	12		11 **Good News**	*George Richey/Billy Sherrill/Norro Wilson*	Epic 10960
7/14/73	**5**	13		12 **Darling, You Can Always Come Back Home**	*Jerry Foster/Bill Rice*	Epic 11016
11/24/73+	**29**	13		13 **The House Of The Rising Sun**	*Alan Price*	Epic 11056
3/16/74	**55**	9		14 **Reflections**	*Nancy Johnston/Red Lane/Royce Porter*	Epic 11094
6/22/74	**46**	11		15 **Natural Woman**	*Gerry Goffin/Carole King/Jerry Wexler*	Epic 11134
11/16/74+	**41**	10		16 **Country Girl**	*Peter Gosing/Alan Hawkshaw*	Epic 50042
3/15/75	**78**	9		17 **The Best In Me**	*Dave Hall*	Epic 50079
7/12/75	**67**	9		18 **Don't Take It Away**	*Max D. Barnes/Troy Seals*	Epic 50117
11/8/75	**69**	8		19 **Will You Love Me Tomorrow?**	*Gerry Goffin/Carole King*	Epic 50158

DEBUT	PEAK	WKS	GOLD	ARTIST / Ranking / Country Chart Hit	Songwriter	Label (& Number)
				MILLER, Jody — cont'd		
3/27/76	**48**	9		20 **Ashes Of Love**	*Jack Anglin/Jim Anglin/Johnny Wright*	Epic 50203
12/4/76+	**25**	12		21 **When The New Wears Off Our Love**	*Paul Craft*	Epic 50304
4/9/77	**71**	7		22 **Spread A Little Love Around**	*Richard Leigh*	Epic 50360
9/17/77	**76**	5		23 **Another Lonely Night**	*Larry Butler/Jerry Crutchfield*	Epic 50432
4/15/78	**97**	2		24 **Soft Lights And Slow Sexy Music**	*Lee Dresser*	Epic 50512
7/15/78	**67**	6		25 (I Wanna) **Love My Life Away**	*Gene Pitney*	Epic 50568
10/7/78	**65**	4		26 **Kiss Away**	*Billy Sherrill/Glenn Sutton*	Epic 50612
7/7/79	**97**	2		27 **Lay A Little Lovin' On Me**	*Jeff Barry/Jim Cretecos/Robin McNamara*	Epic 50734
				MILLER, Mary K.		
				Born in 1957 in Houston, Texas. Female singer.		
7/30/77	**89**	5		1 **I Fall To Pieces** *[Mary Miller]*	*Hank Cochran*	Inergi 300
10/8/77	**54**	8		2 **You Just Don't Know**	*Bobby Darin*	Inergi 302
12/24/77+	**33**	10		3 **The Longest Walk**	*Eddie Polop/Fred Spielman*	Inergi 304
3/4/78	**41**	9		4 **Right Or Wrong**	*Wanda Jackson*	Inergi 306
6/3/78	**28**	8		5 **I Can't Stop Loving You**	*Don Gibson*	Inergi 307
9/16/78	**19**	11		6 **Handcuffed To A Heartache**	*Bobby David/Jim Rushing*	Inergi 310
12/9/78+	**45**	9		7 **Going, Going, Gone**	*Kim Morrison*	Inergi 311
3/10/79	**17**	14		8 **Next Best Feeling**	*Chip Hardy/Danny Hice*	Inergi 312
7/28/79	**47**	7		9 **Guess Who Loves You**	*Deborah Allen/Rafe Van Hoy*	RCA 11665
4/5/80	**85**	3		10 **Say A Long Goodbye**	*Mitch Johnson/Harry Shannon*	Inergi 315
				MILLER, Ned		
				Born Henry Ned Miller on 4/12/1925 in Raines, Utah. Male singer/songwriter/guitarist.		
12/15/62+	**2**[4]	19		1 **From A Jack To A King**	*Ned Miller*	Fabor 114
5/25/63	**27**	3		2 **One Among The Many**	*Ned Miller*	Fabor 116
9/14/63	**28**	1		3 **Another Fool Like Me**	*Ned Miller/Sue Miller*	Fabor 121
4/25/64	**13**	22		4 **Invisible Tears**	*Ned Miller/Sue Miller*	Fabor 128
1/16/65	**7**	20		5 **Do What You Do Do Well**	*Ned Miller*	Fabor 137
8/14/65	**28**	8		6 **Whistle Walkin'**	*Ned Miller*	Capitol 5431
6/18/66	**39**	8		7 **Summer Roses**	*Ned Miller*	Capitol 5661
10/15/66	**44**	9		8 **Teardrop Lane**	*Ned Miller*	Capitol 5742
5/13/67	**53**	6		9 **Hobo**	*Ned Miller*	Capitol 5868
2/17/68	**61**	5		10 **Only A Fool**	*Ned Miller*	Capitol 2074
4/25/70	**39**	9		11 **The Lover's Song**	*Ned Miller*	Republic 1411

MILLER, Roger **1960s: #20 / All-Time: #108 // HOF: 1995**

Born on 1/2/1936 in Fort Worth, Texas; raised in Erick, Oklahoma. Died of cancer on 10/25/1992 (age 56). Male singer/songwriter/guitarist. Father of **Dean Miller**. With **Faron Young** as writer/drummer in 1962. Hosted own TV show in 1966. Wrote the Broadway musical *Big River*.

DEBUT	PEAK	WKS	GOLD	Country Chart Hit	Songwriter	Label (& Number)
10/31/60+	**14**	16		1 **You Don't Want My Love**	*Roger Miller*	RCA Victor 7776
6/5/61	**6**	18		2 **When Two Worlds Collide**	*Bill Anderson/Roger Miller*	RCA Victor 7878
6/1/63	**26**	1		3 **Lock, Stock And Teardrops**	*Roger Miller*	RCA Victor 8175
6/6/64	**❶**[6]	25		4 **Dang Me**	*Roger Miller* [N]	Smash 1881
				Grammy: Single, Song, Male Vocal & Hall of Fame		
9/19/64	**3**[2]	17		5 **Chug-A-Lug**	*Roger Miller* [N]	Smash 1926
12/12/64+	**15**	11		6 **Do-Wacka-Do**	*Roger Miller* [N]	Smash 1947
2/13/65	**❶**[5]	20	●	7 **King Of The Road**	*Roger Miller*	Smash 1965
				Grammy: Single, Song, Male Vocal & Hall of Fame		
5/22/65	**2**[2]	18		8 **Engine Engine #9**	*Roger Miller*	Smash 1983
7/24/65	**10**	12		9 **One Dyin' And A Buryin'**	*Roger Miller*	Smash 1994
10/2/65	**7**	13		10 **Kansas City Star**	*Roger Miller* [N]	Smash 1998
11/20/65+	**3**[1]	16		11 **England Swings**	*Roger Miller*	Smash 2010
2/26/66	**5**	14		12 **Husbands And Wives /**	*Roger Miller*	
2/26/66	**13**	10		13 **I've Been A Long Time Leavin'** (But I'll Be A Long Time Gone)	*Roger Miller*	Smash 2024
7/9/66	**35**	5		14 **You Can't Roller Skate In A Buffalo Herd**	*Roger Miller* [N]	Smash 2043
9/24/66	**39**	9		15 **My Uncle Used To Love Me But She Died**	*Roger Miller* [N]	Smash 2055
11/19/66	**55**	3		16 **Heartbreak Hotel**	*Mae Boren Axton/Thomas Durden/Elvis Presley*	Smash 2066
4/1/67	**7**	17		17 **Walkin' In The Sunshine**	*Roger Miller*	Smash 2081
10/28/67	**27**	11		18 **The Ballad Of Waterhole #3** (Code Of The West)	*Dave Grusin/Robert Wells*	Smash 2121
				from the movie *Waterhole #3* starring James Coburn		
3/9/68	**6**	13		19 **Little Green Apples**	*Bobby Russell*	Smash 2148
				Grammy: Song		
12/14/68+	**15**	12		20 **Vance**	*Bobby Russell*	Smash 2197
7/5/69	**12**	16		21 **Me And Bobby McGee**	*Fred Foster/Kris Kristofferson*	Smash 2230
10/18/69	**14**	10		22 **Where Have All The Average People Gone**	*Dennis Linde*	Smash 2246
3/14/70	**36**	7		23 **The Tom Green County Fair**	*Dennis Linde*	Smash 2258

Billboard DEBUT	PEAK	WKS	GOLD	ARTIST Country Chart Hit	Songwriter	Label (& Number)

MILLER, Roger — cont'd

DEBUT	PEAK	WKS	GOLD	Country Chart Hit	Songwriter	Label (& Number)
8/29/70	15	12		24 South /	Bobby Russell	
8/29/70	flip	12		25 Don't We All Have The Right	Roger Miller	Mercury 73102
4/17/71	11	14		26 Tomorrow Night In Baltimore	Kenny Price	Mercury 73190
8/7/71	28	11		27 Loving Her Was Easier (Than Anything I'll Ever Do Again)	Kris Kristofferson	Mercury 73230
3/25/72	34	11		28 We Found It In Each Other's Arms /	Hank Cochran/Red Lane	
3/25/72	63	11		29 Sunny Side Of My Life	David Brown	Mercury 73268
9/9/72	41	11		30 Rings For Sale	John Hadley	Mercury 73321
12/30/72+	42	8		31 Hoppy's Gone	Larry Henley/Red Lane/Johnny Slate	Mercury 73354
7/14/73	14	14		32 Open Up Your Heart	Buddy Killen/Roger Miller	Columbia 45873
11/17/73+	24	11		33 I Believe In The Sunshine	Roger Miller	Columbia 45948
3/9/74	86	3		34 Whistle Stop from the animated movie *Robin Hood*	Roger Miller	Columbia 46000
12/7/74+	44	10		35 Our Love	Roger Miller	Columbia 10052
4/12/75	57	10		36 I Love A Rodeo	Roger Miller	Columbia 10107
9/10/77	68	6		37 Baby Me Baby	Roger Miller	Windsong 11072
10/27/79	98	2		38 The Hat	Roger Miller	20th Century 2421
10/10/81	36	10		39 Everyone Gets Crazy Now And Then	Kevin Welch	Elektra 47192
6/5/82	19	16		40 Old Friends *[w/ Willie Nelson & Ray Price]*	Roger Miller	Columbia 02681
10/5/85	36	12		41 River In The Rain from the Broadway musical *Big River* starring Daniel H. Jenkins	Roger Miller	MCA 52663
8/2/86	81	8		42 Some Hearts Get All The Breaks	Grant Boatwright/Roger Miller	MCA 52855

MILLINDER, Lucky, And His Orchestra

Born Lucius Millinder on 8/8/1900 in Anniston, Alabama; raised in Chicago, Illinois. Died on 9/28/1966 (age 66). Black bandleader.

DEBUT	PEAK	WKS	GOLD	Country Chart Hit	Songwriter	Label (& Number)
1/15/44	4	5		1 Sweet Slumber Trevor Bacon (vocal)	Lucky Millinder/Al Neiburg/Henri Woode	Decca 18569
7/29/44	4	2		2 Hurry, Hurry Wynonie "Mr. Blues" Harris (vocal)	Benny Carter/Richard Larkin	Decca 18609

MILLS, Frank

Born on 6/27/1942 in Toronto, Ontario, Canada. Male pianist/composer/producer/arranger.

DEBUT	PEAK	WKS	GOLD	Country Chart Hit	Songwriter	Label (& Number)
2/24/79	44	14	●	Music Box Dancer	Frank Mills [I]	Polydor 14517

MILLS BROTHERS

R&B family vocal trio from Piqua, Ohio: Herbert Mills (born on 4/2/1912; died on 4/12/1989, age 77), Harry Mills (born on 8/19/1913; died on 6/28/1982, age 68) and Donald Mills (born on 4/29/1915; died on 11/13/1999, age 84). Won Grammy's Lifetime Achievement Award in 1998.

DEBUT	PEAK	WKS	GOLD	Country Chart Hit	Songwriter	Label (& Number)
3/21/70	64	3		It Ain't No Big Thing	Shorty Hall/Alice Joy/Alice Merritt	Dot 17321

MILSAP, Ronnie **1970s: #25 / 1980s: #6 / All-Time: #25**

Born on 1/16/1943 in Robbinsville, North Carolina. Male singer/songwriter/pianist. Blind since birth. Formed the Apparitions while in high school. Joined J.J. Cale's band. Played session keyboards for **Elvis Presley** in 1969.

CMA: Male Vocalist 1974, 1976 & 1977 / Entertainer 1977 // OPRY: 1976

DEBUT	PEAK	WKS	GOLD	Country Chart Hit	Songwriter	Label (& Number)
6/30/73	10	14		1 I Hate You /	Dan Penn	
6/30/73	flip	14		2 (All Together Now) Let's Fall Apart	Johnny Koonse	RCA Victor 0969
11/3/73+	11	18		3 That Girl Who Waits On Tables	Bobby Barker	RCA Victor 0097
3/30/74	❶[1]	15		4 Pure Love	Eddie Rabbitt	RCA Victor 0237
7/20/74	❶[2]	14		5 Please Don't Tell Me How The Story Ends **Grammy: Male Vocal**	Kris Kristofferson	RCA Victor 0313
11/30/74+	❶[1]	13		6 (I'd Be) A Legend In My Time	Don Gibson	RCA Victor 10112
3/15/75	6	14		7 Too Late To Worry, Too Blue To Cry	Al Dexter	RCA Victor 10228
7/19/75	❶[2]	16		8 Daydreams About Night Things	John Schweers	RCA Victor 10335
9/20/75	15	13		9 She Even Woke Me Up To Say Goodbye recorded in 1970	Doug Gilmore/Mickey Newbury	Warner 8127
10/25/75+	4	16		10 Just In Case	Hugh Moffatt	RCA Victor 10420
12/27/75+	77	6		11 A Rose By Any Other Name recorded in 1970	Irwin Levine/Toni Wine	Warner 8160
3/20/76	❶[1]	14		12 What Goes On When The Sun Goes Down	John Schweers	RCA Victor 10593
6/19/76	79	5		13 Crying recorded in 1970	Joe Melson/Roy Orbison	Warner 8218
7/10/76	❶[2]	14		14 (I'm A) Stand By My Woman Man **Grammy: Male Vocal**	Kent Robbins	RCA Victor 10724
11/27/76+	❶[1]	15		15 Let My Love Be Your Pillow	John Schweers	RCA 10843
5/28/77	❶[3]	18		16 It Was Almost Like A Song	Hal David/Archie Jordan	RCA 10976
11/19/77+	❶[1]	16		17 What A Difference You've Made In My Life	Archie Jordan	RCA 11146
6/3/78	❶[3]	13		18 Only One Love In My Life	R.C. Bannon/John Bettis	RCA 11270
9/2/78	❶[1]	12		19 Let's Take The Long Way Around The World	Archie Jordan/Naomi Martin	RCA 11369
12/16/78+	2[3]	15		20 Back On My Mind Again /	Conrad Pierce/Charles Quillen	
12/16/78+	flip	15		21 Santa Barbara	Hal David/Archie Jordan	RCA 11421

DEBUT	PEAK	WKS	GOLD	#	ARTIST / Country Chart Hit	Ranking / Songwriter	Label (& Number)
					MILSAP, Ronnie — cont'd		
4/28/79	❶^{1}	15		22	**Nobody Likes Sad Songs**	*Wayland Holyfield/Bob McDill*	RCA 11553
8/18/79	6	13		23	**In No Time At All /**	*Archie Jordan/Richard Leigh*	
8/18/79	flip	13		24	**Get It Up**	*Tom Brasfield/Robert Byrne*	RCA 11695
1/12/80	❶^{1}	15		25	**Why Don't You Spend The Night**	*Bob McDill*	RCA 11909
4/12/80	❶^{3}	15		26	**My Heart /**	*Don Pfrimmer/Charles Quillen*	
4/12/80	flip	15		27	**Silent Night** (After The Fight)	*John Schweers*	RCA 11952
6/21/80	❶^{1}	16		28	**Cowboys And Clowns /** from the movie *Bronco Billy* starring **Clint Eastwood**	*Steve Dorff/Snuff Garrett/Gary Harju/Larry Herbstritt*	
6/21/80	flip	16		29	**Misery Loves Company**	*Jerry Reed*	RCA 12006
10/11/80	❶^{1}	14		30	**Smoky Mountain Rain**	*Kye Fleming/Dennis W. Morgan*	RCA 12084
3/21/81	❶^{1}	14		31	**Am I Losing You**	*Jim Reeves*	RCA 12194
7/4/81	❶^{2}	15		32	**(There's) No Gettin' Over Me** Grammy: Male Vocal	*Walt Aldridge/Tom Brasfield*	RCA 12264
10/31/81+	❶^{1}	16		33	**I Wouldn't Have Missed It For The World**	*Kye Fleming/Dennis W. Morgan/Charles Quillen*	RCA 12342
5/1/82	❶^{1}	17		34	**Any Day Now**	*Burt Bacharach/Bob Hilliard*	RCA 13216
8/7/82	❶^{1}	18		35	**He Got You**	*Ralph Murphy/Bobby Wood*	RCA 13286
11/20/82+	❶^{1}	19		36	**Inside /**	*Mike Reid*	
11/27/82+	flip	18		37	**Carolina Dreams**	*Kye Fleming/Dennis W. Morgan/Marie Tomlinson*	RCA 13362
4/2/83	5	18		38	**Stranger In My House** Grammy: Song	*Mike Reid*	RCA 13470
7/23/83	❶^{1}	19		39	**Don't You Know How Much I Love You**	*Michael Stewart/Dan Williams*	RCA 13564
11/12/83+	❶^{1}	19		40	**Show Her**	*Mike Reid*	RCA 13658
5/19/84	❶^{1}	19		41	**Still Losing You**	*Mike Reid*	RCA 13805
9/1/84	6	19		42	**Prisoner Of The Highway**	S:6 / A:7 *Mike Reid*	RCA 13847
4/6/85	❶^{1}	20		43	**She Keeps The Home Fires Burning**	S:❶^{1} / A:❶^{1} *Dennis W. Morgan/Don Pfrimmer/Mike Reid*	RCA 14034
7/13/85	❶^{2}	23		44	**Lost In The Fifties Tonight** (In The Still Of The Night) Grammy: Male Vocal	A:❶^{2} / S:❶^{1} *Fred Parris/Mike Reid/Troy Seals*	RCA 14135
3/8/86	❶^{1}	20		45	**Happy, Happy Birthday Baby**	S:❶^{1} / A:❶^{1} *Gilbert Lopez/Margo Sylvia*	RCA 14286
7/5/86	❶^{1}	20		46	**In Love**	A:❶^{2} / S:❶^{1} *Bruce Dees/Mike Reid*	RCA 14365
11/22/86+	❶^{1}	21		47	**How Do I Turn You On**	S:❶^{1} / A:❶^{1} *Robert Byrne/Mike Reid*	RCA 5033
5/23/87	❶^{1}	19		48	**Snap Your Fingers**	S:❶^{1} *Grady Martin/Alex Zanetis*	RCA 5169
6/27/87	❶^{1}	17		49	**Make No Mistake, She's Mine** *[w/ Kenny Rogers]* Grammy: Vocal Collaboration	S:3 *Kim Carnes*	RCA 5209
10/24/87+	❶^{1}	20		50	**Where Do The Nights Go**	S:2 *Rory Bourke/Mike Reid*	RCA 5259
3/5/88	2^{1}	21		51	**Old Folks** *[w/ Mike Reid]*	S:5 *Mike Reid*	RCA 6896
7/23/88	4	18		52	**Button Off My Shirt**	S:4 *Billy Livsey/Graham Lyle*	RCA 8389
12/24/88+	❶^{1}	20		53	**Don't You Ever Get Tired** (Of Hurting Me)	*Hank Cochran*	RCA 8746
4/29/89	4	21		54	**Houston Solution**	*Paul Overstreet/Don Schlitz*	RCA 8868
9/23/89	❶^{2}	26		55	**A Woman In Love**	*Doug Millett/Curtis Wright*	RCA 9027
2/10/90	2^{2}	26		56	**Stranger Things Have Happened** from the album *Stranger Things Have Happened* on RCA 9588	*Roger Murrah/Keith Stegall*	RCA
3/9/91	3^{2}	20		57	**Are You Lovin' Me Like I'm Lovin' You**	*J.C. Cunningham/Steve Stone*	RCA
7/13/91	6	20		58	**Since I Don't Have You**	*James Beaumont/Joseph Rock*	RCA
12/7/91+	4	20		59	**Turn That Radio On**	*Paul Davis/Archie Jordan*	RCA
3/28/92	11	20		60	**All Is Fair In Love And War** above 4 from the album *Back To The Grindstone* on RCA 2375	*Robert Byrne/Tim Nichols*	RCA
9/12/92	45	9		61	**L.A. To The Moon** from the album *Greatest Hits Volume 3* on RCA 66048	*Susan Longacre/Lonnie Wilson*	RCA
7/10/93	30	15		62	**True Believer** from the album *True Believer* on Liberty 80805	*John Hiatt*	Liberty
7/1/00	57	7		63	**Time, Love & Money** from the album *40 #1 Hits* on Virgin 48871	*Sherrié Austin/Dave Berg/Will Rambeaux*	Virgin

All Is Fair In Love And War ['92]
(All Together Now) Let's Fall Apart ['73]
Am I Losing You ['81]
Any Day Now ['82]
Are You Lovin' Me Like I'm Lovin' You ['91]
Back On My Mind Again ['79]
Button Off My Shirt ['88]
Carolina Dreams ['83]
Cowboys And Clowns ['80]
Crying ['76]
Daydreams About Night Things ['75]
Don't You Ever Get Tired (Of Hurting Me) ['89]
Don't You Know How Much I Love You ['83]
Get It Up ['79]
Happy, Happy Birthday Baby ['86]
He Got You ['82]
Houston Solution ['89]
How Do I Turn You On ['87]
I Hate You ['73]
I Wouldn't Have Missed It For The World ['82]
(I'd Be) A Legend In My Time ['75]
(I'm A) Stand By My Woman Man ['76]
In Love ['86]
In No Time At All ['79]
Inside ['83]
It Was Almost Like A Song ['77]
Just In Case ['76]
L.A. To The Moon ['92]
Let My Love Be Your Pillow ['77]
Let's Take The Long Way Around The World ['78]
Lost In The Fifties Tonight (In The Still Of The Night) ['85]
Make No Mistake, She's Mine ['87]
Misery Loves Company ['80]
My Heart ['80]
Nobody Likes Sad Songs ['79]
Old Folks ['88]
Only One Love In My Life ['78]
Please Don't Tell Me How The Story Ends ['74]
Prisoner Of The Highway ['84]
Pure Love ['74]
Rose By Any Other Name ['76]
Santa Barbara ['79]
She Even Woke Me Up To Say Goodbye ['75]
She Keeps The Home Fires Burning ['85]
Show Her ['84]
Silent Night (After The Fight) ['80]
Since I Don't Have You ['91]
Smoky Mountain Rain ['80]
Snap Your Fingers ['87]
Still Losing You ['84]
Stranger In My House ['83]
Stranger Things Have Happened ['90]
That Girl Who Waits On Tables ['74]
(There's) No Gettin' Over Me ['81]
Time, Love & Money ['00]
Too Late To Worry, Too Blue To Cry ['75]
True Believer ['93]
Turn That Radio On ['92]
What A Difference You've Made In My Life ['78]
What Goes On When The Sun Goes Down ['76]
Where Do The Nights Go ['88]
Why Don't You Spend The Night ['80]
Woman In Love ['89]

MINNIE PEARL — HOF: 1975

Born Sarah Ophelia Colley on 10/25/1912 in Centerville, Tennessee. Died of a stroke on 3/4/1996 (age 83). Female comedian. Regular on TV's *Hee-Haw*. Trademark was her straw hat with its $1.98 price tag still attached.

OPRY: 1940

DEBUT	PEAK	WKS	GOLD	#	Country Chart Hit	Songwriter	Label (& Number)
3/5/66	10	12			**Giddyup Go - Answer** answer to "Giddyup Go" by **Red Sovine**	*Tommy Hill* [S]	Starday 754

DEBUT	PEAK	WKS	GOLD	ARTIST / Country Chart Hit	Ranking	Songwriter	Label (& Number)
				MINOR, Shane			
				Born on 5/3/1968 in Modesto, California. Male singer.			
3/6/99	**20**	20		**Slave To The Habit**	1	S:23 *Chuck Cannon/Toby Keith/Kostas*	Mercury
7/24/99	**24**	20		**Ordinary Love**	2	*Bob DiPiero/Dan Truman/Craig Wiseman*	Mercury
2/5/00	**44**	11		**I Think You're Beautiful**	3	*Maribeth Derry/Steve Diamond*	Mercury
				above 3 from the album *Shane Minor* on Mercury 538346			
				MINTER, Pat			
				Born on 8/9/1935 in Texas. Died on 5/18/2001 (age 65). Male singer/bassist.			
12/9/89	**84**	2		**Whiskey River You Win**		*James Ross*	Killer 121
				MITCHELL, Charles, and his Orchestra			
				Born on 8/30/1903 in Louisiana. Died in February 1974 (age 70). Male singer/songwriter/steel guitarist.			
4/29/44	**4**	1		**If It's Wrong To Love You**		*Bonnie Dodd/Charles Mitchell*	Bluebird 33-0508
				MITCHELL, Charlie			
				Born in Texas. Male singer/songwriter.			
11/12/88	**81**	4		**I'm Goin' Nowhere**		*Charlie Mitchell*	Soundwaves 4810
				MITCHELL, Guy			
				Born Al Cernik on 2/27/1927 in Detroit, Michigan. Died on 7/1/1999 (age 72). Male pop singer.			
11/4/67	**51**	8		**Traveling Shoes**	1	*Wayne Walker*	Starday 819
2/24/68	**61**	5		**Alabam**	2	*Cowboy Copas*	Starday 828
12/14/68	**71**	3		**Frisco Line**	3	*Bob Davis/Dexter Shaffer*	Starday 846
				MITCHELL, Marty			
				Born in Birmingham, Alabama. Male singer.			
6/15/74	**64**	7		**Midnight Man**	1	*Jerry House*	Atlantic 4023
12/11/76	**87**	4		**My Eyes Adored You**	2	*Bob Crewe/Kenny Nolan*	Hitsville 6044
2/18/78	**34**	10		**You Are The Sunshine Of My Life**	3	*Stevie Wonder*	MC/Curb 5005
				MITCHELL, Price			
				Born in Mississippi. Male singer.			
1/18/75	**65**	10		**I Can't Help Myself (Sugar Pie, Honey Bunch)** ***[w/ Jerri Kelly]***	1	*Lamont Dozier/Brian Holland/Eddie Holland*	GRT 016
4/19/75	**29**	11		**Personality**	2	*Llloyd Price*	GRT 020
2/7/76	**83**	5		**Seems Like I Can't Live With You, But I Can't Live Without You**	3	*Burton Cummings/Domenic Troiano*	GRT 037
5/29/76	**75**	5		**Tra-La-La-La Suzy**	4	*Brenda Jones/Welton Young*	GRT 050
9/4/76	**75**	4		**You're The Reason I'm Living**	5	*Bobby Darin*	GRT 067
1/5/80	**45**	9		**Mr. & Mrs. Untrue** ***[w/ Rene Sloane]***	6	*Irwin Levine/Toni Wine*	Sunbird 101
				MITCHELL, Priscilla			
				Born on 9/18/1941 in Marietta, Georgia. Female singer. Married to **Jerry Reed** since 1959.			
5/29/65	❶^2	23		**Yes, Mr. Peters** ***[w/ Roy Drusky]***	1	*Steve Karliski/Larry Kolber*	Mercury 72416
12/4/65	**45**	2		**Slippin' Around** ***[w/ Roy Drusky]***	2	*Floyd Tillman*	Mercury 72497
3/25/67	**61**	5		**I'll Never Tell On You** ***[w/ Roy Drusky]***	3	*Steve Karliski/Larry Kolber*	Mercury 72650
6/17/67	**53**	4		**He's Not For Real**	4	*Jerry Reed*	Mercury 72681
2/3/68	**73**	3		**Your Old Handy Man**	5	*Dolly Parton*	Mercury 72757
				MITCHUM, Robert			
				Born on 8/6/1917 in Bridgeport, Connecticut. Died of cancer on 7/1/1997 (age 79). Legendary actor.			
5/13/67	**9**	17		**Little Old Wine Drinker Me**	1	*Dick Jennings/Hank Mills*	Monument 1006
10/21/67	**55**	7		**You Deserve Each Other**	2	*John D. Loudermilk*	Monument 1025
				MIZE, Billy			
				Born on 4/29/1929 in Arkansas City, Kansas; raised in California. Male singer/songwriter/steel guitarist.			
10/15/66	**57**	5		**You Can't Stop Me** ***[w/ The Jordanaires]***	1	*Billy Mize*	Columbia 43770
9/28/68	**58**	7		**Walking Through The Memories Of My Mind**	2	*Eddie Miller*	Columbia 44621
4/26/69	**40**	9		**Make It Rain**	3	*Billy Mize*	Imperial 66365
9/13/69	**43**	9		**While I'm Thinkin' About It**	4	*Charlie Williams*	Imperial 66403
6/20/70	**71**	2		**If This Was The Last Song**	5	*Jimmy Webb*	Imperial 66447
11/14/70	**49**	7		**Beer Drinking, Honky Tonkin' Blues**	6	*Mickey Newbury*	United Artists 50717
9/2/72	**66**	5		**Take It Easy**	7	*Jackson Browne/Glenn Frey*	United Artists 50945
7/28/73	**99**	2		**California Is Just Mississippi**	8	*Jay Ramsey*	United Artists 265
2/16/74	**79**	5		**Thank You For The Feeling**	9	*Larry Henley/Red Lane/Johnny Slate*	United Artists 372
9/25/76	**31**	13		**It Hurts To Know The Feeling's Gone**	10	*A.L. "Doodle" Owens/Warren Robb*	Zodiac 1011
2/12/77	**68**	5		**Livin' Her Life In A Song**	11	*Cliff Crofford*	Zodiac 1014
				MOEBAKKEN, Dick			
				Born on 8/26/1941 in Minneapolis, Minnesota. Later played bass for **Sherwin Linton**'s band.			
9/30/78	**98**	3		**Heaven Is Being Good To Me**		*Bruce Bednarchuk/Terry Jensen*	ASI 1016
				an impression of **Walter Brennan** to the tune of "Old Rivers"			
				MOFFATT, Hugh			
				Born on 11/10/1948 in Fort Worth, Texas. Male singer/guitarist. Brother of **Katy Moffatt**.			
5/6/78	**95**	2		**The Gambler**		*Don Schlitz*	Mercury 55024

DEBUT	PEAK	WKS	GOLD	ARTIST / Country Chart Hit	Ranking / Songwriter	Label (& Number)
				MOFFATT, Katy		
				Born in 1950 in Fort Worth, Texas. Female singer/guitarist. Sister of **Hugh Moffatt**.		
1/17/76	**83**	5		1 **I Can Almost See Houston From Here**	*Ray Willis*	Columbia 10271
7/4/81	**83**	3		2 **Take It As It Comes** ***[w/ Michael Murphey]***	*Michael Murphey*	Epic 02075
11/5/83	**66**	6		3 **Under Loved And Over Lonely**	*Max D. Barnes/Kent Westberry*	Permian 82002
2/11/84	**82**	4		4 **Reynosa**	*Amanda McBroom*	Permian 82004
5/5/84	**66**	6		5 **This Ain't Tennessee And He Ain't You**	*Larry Bastian/Jim Shaw*	Permian 82005
				MOLLY & THE HEYMAKERS		
				Group from Hayward, Wisconsin: Martha "Molly" Scheer (vocals, fiddle, rhythm guitar), Andy Dee (lead guitar), Jeff Nelson (bass) and Joe Lindzius (drums).		
12/22/90+	**50**	15		1 **Chasin' Something Called Love**	*Gary Burr/Molly Scheer*	Reprise
5/18/91	**59**	6		2 **He Comes Around**	*Gary Burr/Molly Scheer*	Reprise
5/16/92	**69**	5		3 **Jimmy McCarthy's Truck**	*Sam Hogin/Molly Scheer*	Reprise
				MONDAY, Carla		
				Born on 7/31/1952 in California. Female singer.		
10/24/87	**79**	3		**No One Can Touch Me**	*Lisa Angelle/Sam Hogan/Craig Karp*	MCM 001
				MONROE, Bill, and His Blue Grass Boys	**1940s: #22 // HOF: 1970**	
				Born on 9/13/1911 in Rosine, Kentucky. Died of a stroke on 9/9/1996 (age 84). Singer/songwriter/mandolin player. Known as "The Father Of Bluegrass." Formed the Blue Grass Boys which incldued **Flatt & Scruggs**. Won Grammy's Lifetime Achievement Award in 1993. Inducted into the Rock and Roll Hall of Fame in 1997.		
				EARLY HITS: Blue Moon Of Kentucky (1945; NRR) / Uncle Pen (1945) // OPRY: 1939		
3/23/46	**3^1**	6		1 **Kentucky Waltz**	*Bill Monroe*	Columbia 36907
12/7/46	**5**	4		2 **Footprints In The Snow**	*Boyd Lane*	Columbia 37151
6/19/48	**11**	1		3 **Sweetheart, You Done Me Wrong**	J:11 *Lester Flatt/Bill Monroe*	Columbia 38172
11/6/48	**13**	1		4 **Wicked Path Of Sin**	S:13 *Bill Monroe*	Columbia 20503
11/27/48	**11**	5		5 **Little Community Church** ***[w/ his Blue Grass Quartet]***	S:11 / J:12 *Bill Monroe*	Columbia 20488
4/16/49	**12**	2		6 **Toy Heart**	S:12 *Bill Monroe*	Columbia 20552
8/6/49	**12**	1		7 **When You Are Lonely**	J:12 *Lester Flatt/Bill Monroe*	Columbia 20526
11/3/58	**27**	1		8 **Scotland** ***[Bill Monroe]***	*Bill Monroe* **[I]**	Decca 30739
3/2/59	**15**	6		9 **Gotta Travel On**	*Paul Clayton/Larry Ehrlich/Ronnie Gilbert/Lee Hays/Fred Hellerman/Dave Lazer/Pete Seeger*	Decca 30809
				MONROE, Vaughn		
				Born on 10/7/1911 in Akron, Ohio. Died on 5/21/1973 (age 61). Pop singer/bandleader/trumpeter.		
5/14/49	**2^1**	5	●	**Riders In The Sky** **(A Cowboy Legend)**	S:2 / J:10 *Stan Jones*	RCA Victor 47-2902
				MONTANA		
				Group from Reno, Nevada. Entire group killed in a plane crash on 7/4/1987 near Flathead Lake, Montana.		
11/14/81	**83**	3		**The Shoe's On The Other Foot Tonight**	*Rich Bean*	Waterhouse 15005
				MONTANA SLIM — CARTER, Wilf		
				MONTANA, Billy, & The Long Shots		
				Born William Schlappi on 9/28/1959 in Voorheesville, New York. Male singer/songwriter/bassist. The Long Shots: Bobby Kendall (guitar), Kyle Montana (guitar), Dave Flint (fiddle) and Doug Bernhard (drums).		
3/21/87	**46**	9		1 **Crazy Blue**	*Michael Clark/Tim DuBois*	Warner 28426
8/22/87	**40**	11		2 **Baby I Was Leaving Anyhow**	*Harlan Howard*	Warner 28256
8/20/88	**48**	9		3 **Oh Jenny**	*Vern Dant/Nancy Montgomery/Marshall Morgan*	Warner 27809
				BILLY MONTANA:		
4/8/95	**55**	11		4 **Didn't Have You**	*Billy Montana/James Watson*	Magnatone
8/19/95	**58**	7		5 **Rain Through The Roof**	*Billy Montana/James Watson*	Magnatone
11/11/95	**70**	1		6 **No Yesterday**	*Billy Montana/Joy Swinea*	Magnatone
				above 3 from the album *No Yesterday* on Magnatone 101		
				MONTANA, Patsy	**HOF: 1996**	
				Born Ruby Blevins on 10/30/1908 in Hope, Arkansas. Died on 5/3/1996 (age 87). The first commercially successful female country singer.		
				EARLY HIT: I Wanna Be A Cowboy's Sweetheart (1936)		
				MONTANA SKYLINE		
				Group from Missoula, Montana.		
12/26/81+	**87**	4		**Full Moon - Empty Pockets**	*Robert Jones/Mike Kosser*	Snow 2022
				**MONTGOMERY, John Michael**	**1990s: #17 / 2000s: #39 / All-Time: #87**	
				Born on 1/20/1965 in Danville, Kentucky. Male singer/songwriter/guitarist. Younger brother of Eddie Montgomery (of **Montgomery Gentry**). Began playing with local bands in 1980.		
				CMA: Horizon 1994		
10/3/92+	**4**	20		1 **Life's A Dance**	*Steve Seskin/Allen Shamblin*	Atlantic
3/13/93	**❶[3]**	20		2 **I Love The Way You Love Me**	*Chuck Cannon/Victoria Shaw*	Atlantic
7/10/93	**21**	20		3 **Beer And Bones**	*Whitey Shafer/Lonnie Williams*	Atlantic
				above 3 from the album *Life's A Dance* on Atlantic 82420		

Billboard DEBUT	PEAK	WKS	GOLD		ARTIST / Country Chart Hit	Ranking / Songwriter	Label (& Number)
					MONTGOMERY, John Michael — cont'd		
12/18/93+	❶^{4}	20	●	4	**I Swear**	*Gary Baker/Frank J. Myers*	Atlantic
					Grammy: Song / CMA: Single		
3/19/94	**4**	20		5	**Rope The Moon**	*Aggie Brown/Jess Brown/Jim Denton*	Atlantic
4/9/94	**72**	2		6	**Kick It Up**	*Anderson Byrd/Jim Robinson*	Atlantic
5/7/94	❶^{2}	20		7	**Be My Baby Tonight**	*Richard Fagan/Ed Hill*	Atlantic
9/24/94	❶^{1}	20		8	**If You've Got Love**	*Mark D. Sanders/Steve Seskin*	Atlantic
					above 5 from the album *Kickin' It Up* on Atlantic 82559		
3/4/95	❶^{3}	20		9	**I Can Love You Like That**	*Maribeth Derry/Steve Diamond/Jennifer Kimball*	Atlantic
5/6/95	❶^{3}	20		10	**Sold (The Grundy County Auction Incident)**	*Richard Fagan/Robb Royer*	Atlantic
8/26/95	**3**^{2}	20		11	**No Man's Land**	S:5 *Steve Seskin/John Scott Sherrill*	Atlantic
11/18/95+	**4**	20		12	**Cowboy Love**	*Bill Douglas/Jeff Wood*	Atlantic
3/2/96	**4**	20		13	**Long As I Live**	*Rick Bowles/Will Robinson*	Atlantic
					above 5 from the album *John Michael Montgomery* on Atlantic 82728		
9/14/96	**15**	19		14	**Ain't Got Nothin' On Us**	S:9 *Wendell Mobley/Jim Robinson*	Atlantic
10/19/96+	**2**^{3}	20		15	**Friends**	S:❶^{3} *Jerry Holland*	Atlantic
3/1/97	**6**	20		16	**I Miss You A Little**	S:4 *Mike Anthony/Richard Fagin/John Michael Montgomery*	Atlantic
6/14/97	**2**^{1}	20		17	**How Was I To Know**	*Blair Daly/Will Rambeaux*	Atlantic
					above 4 from the album *What I Do Best* on Atlantic 82947		
8/16/97	**56**	5		18	**Warning Signs** *[w/ Bill Engvall]*	S:21 *Bill Engvall/Scott Rouse/Ronny Scaife* **[C]**	Warner
					from Engvall's album *Warning Signs* on Warner 43934		
10/4/97+	**4**	21		19	**Angel In My Eyes**	*Blair Daly/Tony Mullins*	Atlantic
					from the album *Greatest Hits* on Atlantic 83060		
3/14/98	**14**	20		20	**Love Working On You**	S:23 *Jim Collins/Craig Wiseman*	Atlantic
5/30/98	**3**^{1}	21		21	**Cover You In Kisses**	S:9 *Jess Brown/Brett Jones/Jerry Kilgore*	Atlantic
10/10/98+	**4**	25		22	**Hold On To Me**	S:6 *Blair Daly/Will Rambeaux*	Atlantic
					above 3 from the album *Leave A Mark* on Atlantic 83104		
3/27/99	**15**	20		23	**Hello L.O.V.E.**	*Jeffrey Steele/Danny Wells*	Atlantic
7/17/99	**2**^{1}	28		24	**Home To You**	*Sara Light/Arlos Smith*	Atlantic
1/22/00	**50**	10		25	**Nothing Catches Jesus By Surprise**	*Tom Douglas/Waylon Jennings*	Atlantic
3/4/00	**48**	16		26	**You Are**	*Steve Dean/Noah Gordon/Wil Nance*	Atlantic
					above 4 from the album *Home To You* on Atlantic 83185		
8/19/00	❶^{3}	23		27	**The Little Girl**	*Harley Allen*	Atlantic
1/20/01	**44**	11		28	**That's What I Like About You**	*Larry Alderman/Richard Fagan*	Atlantic
6/16/01	**59**	1		29	**Even Then**	*Pat Bunch/Shane Teeters*	Atlantic
					above 3 from the album *Brand New Me* on Atlantic 83378		
7/27/02	**19**	26		30	**'Til Nothing Comes Between Us**	*Rebecca Marshall/Tony Marty/Kerry Singletary*	Warner
2/8/03	**45**	8		31	**Country Thang**	*Kenny Beard/Lonnie Wilson/Jimmy Yeary*	Warner
6/7/03	**52**	5		32	**Four-Wheel Drive**	*Kevin Harris*	Warner
					above 3 from the album *Pictures* on Warner 48341		
1/31/04	**2**^{4}	25		33	**Letters From Home**	*Tony Lane/David Lee*	Warner
7/17/04	**51**	9		34	**Goes Good With Beer**	*Casey Beathard/Ed Hill*	Warner
					above 2 from the album *Letters From Home* on Warner 48729		

MONTGOMERY, Melba — **All-Time: #207**

Born on 10/14/1938 in Iron City, Tennessee; raised in Florence, Alabama. Female singer/songwriter/guitarist/fiddle player. Won the *Grand Ole Opry*'s 1958 Pet Milk Amateur Contest. Toured as a member of **Roy Acuff**'s troupe from 1958-62.

DEBUT	PEAK	WKS	GOLD		Country Chart Hit	Songwriter	Label (& Number)
5/4/63	**3**^{1}	28		1	**We Must Have Been Out Of Our Minds** *[w/ George Jones]*	*Melba Montgomery*	United Artists 575
8/24/63	**26**	6		2	**Hall Of Shame**	*George Riddle*	United Artists 576
11/30/63	**20**	5		3	**What's In Our Heart** *[w/ George Jones]* /	*George Jones/Johnny Mathis*	
12/7/63	**17**	7		4	**Let's Invite Them Over** *[w/ George Jones]*	*Onie Wheeler*	United Artists 635
12/7/63+	**22**	9		5	**The Greatest One Of All**	*George Riddle*	United Artists 652
9/5/64	**31**	5		6	**Please Be My Love** *[w/ George Jones]*	*Monroe Fields/Carl Sauceman*	United Artists 732
12/12/64+	**25**	15		7	**Multiply The Heartaches** *[w/ George Jones]*	*Kathy Dee*	United Artists 784
1/15/66	**15**	12		8	**Baby Ain't That Fine** *[w/ Gene Pitney]*	*Dallas Frazier*	Musicor 1135
11/19/66	**70**	3		9	**Close Together** (As You And Me) *[w/ George Jones]*	*Earl Montgomery*	Musicor 1204
7/8/67	**61**	3		10	**What Can I Tell The Folks Back Home**	*Dallas Frazier*	Musicor 1241
9/9/67	**24**	10		11	**Party Pickin'** *[w/ George Jones]*	*Alex Zanetis*	Musicor 1238
10/24/70	**18**	14		12	**Something To Brag About** *[w/ Charlie Louvin]*	*Bobby Braddock*	Capitol 2915
2/13/71	**26**	12		13	**Did You Ever** *[w/ Charlie Louvin]*	*Bobby Braddock*	Capitol 3029
6/12/71	**30**	10		14	**Baby, You've Got What It Takes** *[w/ Charlie Louvin]*	*Clyde Otis/Murray Stein*	Capitol 3111
6/19/71	**61**	4		15	**He's My Man**	*Jerry Crutchfield*	Capitol 3091
11/27/71	**60**	5		16	**I'm Gonna Leave You** *[w/ Charlie Louvin]*	*Rayburn Anthony*	Capitol 3208
8/19/72	**66**	4		17	**Baby, What's Wrong With Us** *[w/ Charlie Louvin]*	*Larry Kingston*	Capitol 3388
1/20/73	**59**	6		18	**A Man Likes Things Like That** *[w/ Charlie Louvin]*	*Lorene Allen/Jim Owen*	Capitol 3508
10/6/73	**38**	11		19	**Wrap Your Love Around Me**	*Melba Montgomery/Jack Solomon*	Elektra 45866
1/12/74	**58**	9		20	**He'll Come Home**	*Danny Samson/Ruby Van Noy*	Elektra 45875
3/16/74	❶^{1}	16		21	**No Charge**	*Harlan Howard*	Elektra 45883
7/20/74	**67**	8		22	**Your Pretty Roses Came Too Late**	*Jerry Foster/Bill Rice*	Elektra 45894
10/19/74	**59**	10		23	**If You Want The Rainbow**	*Harlan Howard*	Elektra 45211
2/1/75	**15**	12		24	**Don't Let The Good Times Fool You**	*Gary S. Paxton*	Elektra 45229
5/24/75	**45**	9		25	**Searchin'** (For Someone Like You)	*Murphy Maddux*	Elektra 45247
1/10/76	**67**	7		26	**Love Was The Wind**	*Michael Clark*	Elektra 45296
7/16/77	**83**	4		27	**Never Ending Love Affair**	*Roger Bowling/Larry Butler/Steve Tutsie*	United Artists 1008
12/10/77+	**22**	14		28	**Angel Of The Morning**	*Chip Taylor*	United Artists 1115

Billboard DEBUT	PEAK	WKS	GOLD	ARTIST / Country Chart Hit	Ranking / Songwriter	Label (& Number)
				MONTGOMERY, Melba — cont'd		
10/25/80	**92**	2		29 **The Star**	*Lee Bach*	Kari 111
8/30/86	**79**	4		30 **Straight Talkin**	*Buddy Cannon/Harold Shedd/Larry Shell*	Compass 45-7
				MONTGOMERY, Nancy		
				Born in San Francisco, California. Female singer.		
7/4/81	**85**	2		**All I Have To Do Is Dream**	*Boudleaux Bryant*	Ovation 1172
				MONTGOMERY GENTRY	**2000s: #13 / All-Time: #226**	
				Vocal duo of Eddie Montgomery and Troy Gentry. Montgomery was born Gerald Edward Montgomery on 9/30/1963 in Danville, Kentucky; raised in Nicholasville, Kentucky. Older brother of **John Michael Montgomery**. Gentry was born on 4/5/1967 in Lexington, Kentucky.		
				CMA: Vocal Duo 2000		
2/13/99	**13**	20		1 **Hillbilly Shoes**	S:3 *Mike Geiger/Woody Mullis/Bobby Taylor*	Columbia
6/5/99	**5**	26		2 **Lonely And Gone**	S:4 *Greg Crowe/Dave Gibson/Bill McCorvey*	Columbia
11/20/99+	**17**	21		3 **Daddy Won't Sell The Farm**	*Robin Branda/Steve Fox*	Columbia
4/22/00	**31**	20		4 **Self Made Man**	*Jay Knowles/Wynn Varble*	Columbia
9/23/00	**31**	21		5 **All Night Long** ***[w/ Charlie Daniels]*** above 5 from the album *Tattoos & Scars* on Columbia 69156	S:7 *Bruce Brown/Charlie Daniels/Joe DiGregorio/ Jack Gavin/Charles Hayward*	Columbia
12/16/00+	**38**	4		6 **Merry Christmas From The Family**	S:8 *Robert Earl Keen* **[X-N]**	Columbia
2/10/01	**2^{3}**	33		7 **She Couldn't Change Me**	S:3 *Chris Knight/Gary Nicholson*	Columbia
8/25/01+	**23**	22		8 **Cold One Comin' On** above 2 from the album *Carrying On* on Columbia 62167	*Mike Geiger/Mike Huffman/Woody Mullis*	Columbia
3/16/02	**45**	7		9 **Didn't I** from the movie *We Were Soldiers* starring Mel Gibson (soundtrack on Columbia 86403)	*Anthony Smith*	Columbia
6/8/02	**5**	30		10 **My Town**	*Reed Nielson/Jeffrey Steele*	Columbia
12/28/02+	**5**	33		11 **Speed**	S:3 *Jeffrey Steele/Chris Wallin*	Columbia
7/26/03	**4**	26		12 **Hell Yeah** above 3 from the album *My Town* on Columbia 86520	*Jeffrey Steele/Craig Wiseman*	Columbia
2/7/04	❶^{1}	26		13 **If You Ever Stop Loving Me**	*Bob DiPiero/Rivers Rutherford/Tom Shapiro*	Columbia
7/24/04	**22**	20		14 **You Do Your Thing**	*Casey Beathard/Ed Hill*	Columbia
11/27/04+	**3^{2}**	28		15 **Gone**	*Bob DiPiero/Jeffrey Steele*	Columbia
5/21/05	❶^{2}	22↑		16 **Something To Be Proud Of** above 4 from the album *You Do Your Thing* on Columbia 90558	*Jeffrey Steele/Chris Wallin*	Columbia
				MOODY, Clyde		
				Born on 9/19/1915 in Cherokee, North Carolina; raised in Marion, North Carolina. Died on 4/7/1989 (age 73). Male singer/songwriter/guitarist. Known as "The Hillbilly Waltz King."		
6/19/48	**15**	1		1 **Carolina Waltz /**	S:15 *Clyde Moody*	
8/14/48	**8**	1		2 **Red Roses Tied In Blue**	S:8 *Wally Fowler*	King 706
3/11/50	**8**	2		3 **I Love You Because**	A:8 *Leon Payne*	King 837
				MOORE, Beth		
				Born on 11/27/1944 in Michigan. Female singer.		
1/23/71	**61**	8		**Put Your Hand In The Hand**	*Gene MacLellan*	Capitol 3013
				MOORE, Jim, & Sidewinder		
				Born in Phoenix, Arizona. Male singer.		
9/3/88	**88**	2		**Ain't She Shinin' Tonight**	*Don Goodman/Johnny Neel/Pal Rakes*	Willow Wind 0511
				MOORE, Lattie		
				Born on 10/17/1924 in Scotsville, Kentucky. Male rockabilly singer/songwriter/guitarist.		
1/30/61	**25**	3		**Drunk Again**	*Autry Inman*	King 5413
				MOORER, Allison		
				Born on 6/21/1972 in Frankville, Alabama. Female singer/songwriter. Younger sister of **Shelby Lynne**.		
6/20/98	**73**	1		1 **A Soft Place To Fall** from the movie *The Horse Whisperer* starring Robert Redford (soundtrack on MCA 70025)	*Allison Moorer/Gwil Owen*	MCA
9/5/98	**72**	2		2 **Set You Free** from the album *Alabama Song* on MCA Nashville 70028	*Allison Moorer/Doyle Primm*	MCA Nashville
7/22/00	**66**	1		3 **Send Down An Angel**	*Allison Moorer/Doyle Primm*	MCA Nashville
12/2/00+	**57**	5		4 **Think It Over** above 2 from the album *The Hardest Part* on MCA Nashville 170114	*Allison Moorer/Doyle Primm*	MCA Nashville
				MOREY, Sean		
				Born in Boston, Massachusetts; later based in Los Angeles, California. Male comedian.		
7/4/98	**70**	11		**The Man Song** from the album *He's The Man* on Banjo 1197	*Sean Morey* **[N]**	Banjo
				MORGAN, Al		
				Born in Cincinnati, Ohio; later based in Chicago, Illinois. Male singer/pianist. Hosted own TV series from 1949-51. Known as "Mr. Flying Fingers."		
9/17/49	**8**	1		**Jealous Heart**	S:8 *Jenny Lou Carson*	London 30001
				MORGAN, Billie		
				Born on 12/13/1922 in Nashville, Tennessee. Died on 1/19/2000 (age 77). Female singer/songwriter.		
3/23/59	**22**	3		**Life To Live**	*Billie Morgan/Dale Potter*	Starday 420

DEBUT	PEAK	WKS	GOLD	ARTIST / Country Chart Hit ... Songwriter	Ranking	Label (& Number)
				MORGAN, Craig	**2000s: #35**	
				Born Craig Morgan Greer on 7/17/1964 in Kingston Springs, Tennessee. Male singer/songwriter.		
2/26/00	**38**	20		1 **Something To Write Home About** ...S:24 *Craig Morgan/Tony Ramey*		Atlantic
6/10/00	**46**	20		2 **Paradise** ...*Harley Allen/Craig Morgan*		Atlantic
12/16/00	**68**	3		3 **The Kid In Me** ...*Dave Clark/Dan Dean/Don Koch* **[X]**		
4/7/01	**51**	3		4 **I Want Us Back** ...*Buddy Cannon/Marla Cannon/Dean Dillon* #1, 2 & 4: from the album *Craig Morgan* on Atlantic 83299		Atlantic
12/15/01+	**49**	9		5 **God, Family And Country** ...*Lance McDaniel/Craig Morgan/Craig Morris*		Broken Bow
10/19/02+	**6**	37		6 **Almost Home** ...*Craig Morgan/Kerry Kurt Phillips*		Broken Bow
8/16/03+	**25**	27		7 **Every Friday Afternoon** ...*Neal Coty/Jimmy Melton*		Broken Bow
5/1/04	**27**	22		8 **Look At Us** ...*Larry Bastian/Buddy Cannon/Craig Morgan* above 4 from the album *I Love It* on Broken Bow 75672		Broken Bow
11/6/04+	**❶**[4]	36		9 **That's What I Love About Sunday** *Adam Dorsey/Mark Narmore*		Broken Bow
5/21/05	**6**↑	19↑		10 **Redneck Yacht Club** ...*Tom Shepherd/Steve Williams* above 2 from the album *My Kind Of Livin'* on Broken Bow 75472		Broken Bow
				MORGAN, David		
				Born on 8/13/1953 in Dallas, Texas. Male singer.		
11/1/97	**72**	1		**Those Who Couldn't Wait** ...*Max T. Barnes/Gene Cotton* from the album *The Well* on Stage Coach 0326		Stage Coach

				MORGAN, George	**1940s: #20 / 1950s: #40 / All-Time: #144 // HOF: 1998**	
				Born on 6/28/1924 in Waverly, Tennessee; raised in Barberton, Ohio. Died of a heart attack on 7/7/1975 (age 51). Male singer/songwriter/guitarist. Father of **Lorrie Morgan**. ***OPRY: 1948***		
2/26/49	**❶**[3]	23		1 **Candy Kisses /** S:❶[3] / J:2 *George Morgan*		
3/19/49	**4**	14		2 **Please Don't Let Me Love You** ...S:4 / J:4 *Ralph Jones*		Columbia 20547
4/30/49	**8**	6		3 **Rainbow In My Heart /** ...S:8 / J:10 *George Morgan*		
5/7/49	**11**	1		4 **All I Need Is Some More Lovin'** ...S:11 *Johnny Daume*		Columbia 20563
7/23/49	**4**	12		5 **Room Full Of Roses** ...S:4 / J:10 *Tim Spencer*		Columbia 20594
10/29/49	**5**	9		6 **Cry-Baby Heart /** ...S:5 / J:6 / A:7 *Leon Payne*		
12/10/49	**4**	4		7 **I Love Everything About You** ...A:4 / S:14 *Cindy Walker*		Columbia 20627
4/19/52	**2**[6]	23		8 **Almost** ...S:2 / A:2 / J:2 *Vic McAlpin/Jack Toombs*		Columbia 4-20906
3/7/53	**10**	1		9 (I Just Had A Date) **A Lover's Quarrel** ...J:10 *Vic McAlpin*		Columbia 21070
1/26/57	**15**	1		10 **There Goes My Love** ...A:15 *Buck Owens*		Columbia 40792
2/16/59	**3**[2]	23		11 **I'm In Love Again** ...*Vic McAlpin/George Morgan*		Columbia 41318
8/17/59	**20**	9		12 **Little Dutch Girl /** ...*Mel Tillis/Wayne Walker*		
8/24/59	**26**	1		13 **The Last Thing I Want To Know** ...*Vic McAlpin/George Morgan/Roy Wiggins*		Columbia 41420
1/11/60	**4**	20		14 **You're The Only Good Thing** (That's Happened To Me) ...*Jack Toombs*		Columbia 41523
1/18/64	**23**	7		15 **One Dozen Roses** (And Our Love) / ...*Benny Joy*		
3/7/64	**45**	2		16 **All Right** (I'll Sign The Papers) ...*Mel Tillis*		Columbia 42882
5/9/64	**23**	17		17 **Slipping Around** *[w/ Marion Worth]* ...*Floyd Tillman*		Columbia 43020
9/26/64	**37**	9		18 **Tears And Roses** ...*Dick Heard/Hank Hunter*		Columbia 43098
12/11/65+	**27**	10		19 **A Picture That's New** ...*Imogene Woods*		Columbia 43393
4/15/67	**40**	12		20 **I Couldn't See** ...*Tommy Hill/George Morgan*		Starday 804
8/19/67	**58**	5		21 **Shiny Red Automobile** ...*Dixie Dean/Ray King*		Starday 814
1/13/68	**55**	6		22 **Barbara** ...*A.L. "Doodle" Owens*		Starday 825
4/27/68	**56**	7		23 **Living** ...*Tommy Hill/George Morgan*		Starday 834
8/31/68	**31**	10		24 **Sounds Of Goodbye** ...*Dick Heard/Eddie Rabbitt*		Starday 850
4/19/69	**30**	9		25 **Like A Bird** ...*Larry Kingston*		Stop 252
4/18/70	**17**	13		26 **Lilacs And Fire** ...*Frank Dycus/Larry Kingston*		Stop 365
12/11/71	**68**	3		27 **Gentle Rains Of Home** ...*Jean Chapel*		Decca 32886
				GEORGE MORGAN Featuring "Little" Roy Wiggins:		
1/20/73	**62**	7		28 **Makin' Heartaches** ...*George Morgan*		Decca 33037
6/30/73	**56**	9		29 **Mr. Ting-A-Ling** (Steel Guitar Man) ...*George Morgan*		MCA 40069
12/15/73+	**21**	14		30 **Red Rose From The Blue Side Of Town** *[George Morgan]* ...*Betty Jean Robinson/Hank Snow*		MCA 40159
6/1/74	**66**	6		31 **Somewhere Around Midnight** ...*Max Powell*		MCA 40227
11/2/74	**82**	6		32 **A Candy Mountain Melody** ...*Sun Child/Crystal Lady*		MCA 40298
2/22/75	**65**	9		33 **In The Misty Moonlight** ...*Cindy Walker*		4 Star 1001
7/5/75	**62**	11		34 **From This Moment On** ...*Bonnie Guitar*		4 Star 1009
11/24/79	**93**	3		35 **I'm Completely Satisfied With You** *[w/ Lorrie Morgan]* ...*Betty Jean Robinson*		4 Star 1040
				MORGAN, Jane		
				Born Jane Currier in 1920 in Boston, Massachusetts; raised in Florida. Female singer.		
5/30/70	**61**	5		1 **A Girl Named Johnny Cash** ...*Martin Mull* **[N]** answer to "A Boy Named Sue" by **Johnny Cash**		RCA Victor 9839
11/7/70	**70**	2		2 **The First Day** ...*Nat Stuckey*		RCA Victor 9901

MORGAN, Lorrie

1990s: #19 / All-Time: #104

Born Loretta Lynn Morgan on 6/27/1959 in Nashville, Tennessee. Female singer. Daughter of **George Morgan**. Married to **Keith Whitley** from 1986 until his death in 1989. Married to **Jon Randall** from 1996-99. Married **Sammy Kershaw** on 9/29/2001. Also see **Hope**.

OPRY: 1984

Billboard DEBUT	PEAK	WKS	GOLD	ARTIST / Country Chart Hit	Songwriter	Label (& Number)
3/10/79	**75**	5		1 **Two People In Love**	*Eddy Raven*	ABC/Hickory 54041
7/28/79	**88**	3		2 **Tell Me I'm Only Dreaming**	*Liz Anderson*	MCA 41052
11/24/79	**93**	3		3 **I'm Completely Satisfied With You** ***[w/ George Morgan]***	*Betty Jean Robinson*	4 Star 1040
3/17/84	**69**	5		4 **Don't Go Changing**	*Lewis Anderson/Casey Kelly*	MCA 52331
12/10/88+	**20**	19		5 **Trainwreck Of Emotion**	*Allen Kohnhorst/Jon Vezner*	RCA 8638
4/15/89	**9**	22		6 **Dear Me**	*Scott Mateer/Carson Whitsett*	RCA 8866
9/9/89	**2**[3]	26		7 **Out Of Your Shoes**	*Patti Ryan/Sharon Spivey/Jill Wood*	RCA 9016
2/3/90	**❶**[1]	26		8 **Five Minutes**	*Beth Nielsen Chapman*	RCA
5/26/90	**4**	21		9 **He Talks To Me**	*Rory Bourke/Mike Reid*	RCA
				above 2 from the album *Leave The Light On* on RCA 9594		
7/28/90	**13**	20		10 **'Til A Tear Becomes A Rose** ***[w/ Keith Whitley]***	*Bill Rice/Mary Sharon Rice*	RCA
				CMA: Vocal Event; from Whitley's album *Greatest Hits* on RCA 2277		
3/30/91	**3**[2]	20		11 **We Both Walk**	*Tom Shapiro/Chris Waters*	RCA
8/3/91	**9**	20		12 **A Picture Of Me (Without You)**	*George Richey/Norro Wilson*	RCA
12/14/91+	**4**	20		13 **Except For Monday**	*Reed Nielsen*	RCA
5/9/92	**14**	20		14 **Something In Red**	*Angela Kaset*	RCA
				above 4 from the album *Something In Red* on RCA 3021		
9/5/92	**2**[2]	20		15 **Watch Me**	*Gary Burr/Tom Shapiro*	BNA
12/19/92+	**❶**[3]	20		16 **What Part Of No**	*Wayne Perry/Gerald Smith*	BNA
4/3/93	**14**	20		17 **I Guess You Had To Be There**	*Barbara Cloyd/Jon Robbin*	BNA
7/31/93	**8**	20		18 **Half Enough**	*Reed Nielsen/Wendy Waldman*	BNA
				above 4 from the album *Watch Me* on BNA 66047		
11/27/93	**59**	6		19 **Crying Time**	*Buck Owens*	Fox/RCA
				from the movie *The Beverly Hillbillies* starring Jim Varney (soundtrack on Fox/RCA 66313)		
1/8/94	**64**	1		20 **My Favorite Things**	*Oscar Hammerstein/Richard Rodgers* **[X]**	BNA
				from the album *Merry Christmas From London* on BNA 66282		
3/19/94	**31**	12		21 **My Night To Howl**	*Charlie Black/Rick Giles/Austin Roberts*	BNA
5/21/94	**51**	11		22 **If You Came Back From Heaven**	*Richard Landis/Lorrie Morgan*	BNA
8/13/94	**39**	13		23 **Heart Over Mind**	*Bob Alan/Stan Munsey*	BNA
				above 3 from the album *War Paint* on BNA 66379		
5/6/95	**❶**[1]	20		24 **I Didn't Know My Own Strength**	S:12 *Rick Bowles/Robert Byrne*	BNA
9/2/95	**4**	20		25 **Back In Your Arms Again**	S:15 *Paul Davis/Fred Knoblock*	BNA
12/23/95+	**32**	17		26 **Standing Tall**	*Larry Butler/Ben Peters*	BNA
				above 3 from the album *Greatest Hits* on BNA 66508		
1/6/96	**67**	1		27 **Sleigh Ride**	*Leroy Anderson/Mitchell Parish* **[X]**	BNA
				from the album *Merry Christmas From London* on BNA 66282		
4/6/96	**18**	20		28 **By My Side** ***[w/ Jon Randall]***	S:4 *Dawn Thomas*	BNA
8/10/96	**45**	12		29 **I Just Might Be**	*John Moffat*	BNA
9/7/96	**73**	1		30 **Don't Worry Baby** ***[w/ The Beach Boys]***	*Roger Christian/Brian Wilson*	River North
				from The Beach Boys album *Stars And Stripes Vol. 1* on River North 1205		
12/28/96+	**64**	3		31 **Sleigh Ride**	*Leroy Anderson/Mitchell Parish* **[X-R]**	BNA
				from the album *Merry Christmas From London* on BNA 66282		
1/25/97	**4**	20		32 **Good As I Was To You**	*Billy Livsey/Don Schlitz*	BNA
				#28, 29 & 32: from the album *Greater Need* on BNA 66847		
7/5/97	**3**[1]	20		33 **Go Away**	S:6 *Cathy Majeski/Sunny Russ/Stephony Smith*	BNA
11/8/97+	**14**	20		34 **One Of Those Nights Tonight**	*Rick Giles/Susan Longacre*	BNA
4/4/98	**49**	7		35 **I'm Not That Easy To Forget**	*Stephanie Bentley/George Teren/Chris Waters*	BNA
8/8/98	**66**	3		36 **You'd Think He'd Know Me Better**	*Bobbie Cryner*	BNA
				above 4 from the album *Shakin' Things Up* on BNA 67499		
2/27/99	**17**	20		37 **Maybe Not Tonight** ***[w/ Sammy Kershaw]***	*Dan Hill/Keith Stegall*	BNA/Mercury
				also from Kershaw's album *Maybe Not Tonight* on Mercury 538889		
7/31/99	**72**	3		38 **Here I Go Again**	*Kim Richey*	BNA
				above 2 from the album *My Heart* on BNA 67763		
12/11/99+	**42**	5		39 **Sleigh Ride**	*Leroy Anderson/Mitchell Parish* **[X-R]**	BNA
12/11/99	**69**	2		40 **My Favorite Things**	*Oscar Hammerstein/Richard Rodgers* **[X-R]**	BNA
				above 2 from the album *Merry Christmas From London* on BNA 66282		
1/22/00	**63**	5		41 **To Get To You**	*Brett James/Holly Lamar*	BNA
				from the album *To Get To You: Greatest Hits Collection* on BNA 67919		
2/17/01	**39**	17		42 **He Drinks Tequila** ***[w/ Sammy Kershaw]***	*Shawn Camp/Michele McCord*	RCA
				from their album *I Finally Found Someone* on RCA 67004		
10/11/03+	**50**	12		43 **Do You Still Want To Buy Me That Drink (Frank)**	*Roxie Dean/Buffy Lawson/P.J. Matthews*	Image
				from the album *Show Me How* on Image 0609		

MORGAN, Misty — see BLANCHARD, Jack

Billboard DEBUT	PEAK	WKS	GOLD	ARTIST / Country Chart Hit	Ranking / Songwriter	Label (& Number)

MORI, Miki

Born in Nephi, Utah. Female singer.

DEBUT	PEAK	WKS	GOLD	Country Chart Hit	Songwriter	Label (& Number)
6/30/79	91	1		1 **Tell All Your Troubles To Me** *[Mickie Mori]*	*Johnny Rodriguez*	Red Feather 2280
10/20/79	79	4		2 **The Part Of Me That Needs You Most**	*Mike Chapman/Nicky Chinn*	Oak 1002
2/2/80	48	7		3 **Driftin Away**	*Johnny Rodriguez*	Oak 1010
7/19/80	51	8		4 **The Last Farewell**	*Joe Eagan*	NSD 49
1/10/81	59	6		5 **Rainin' In My Eyes**	*Pat Garrett*	Starcom 1001

MORRIS, Bob

Born on 2/3/1930 in Hasty, Arkansas. Died of cancer on 12/3/1981 (age 51). Male singer/songwriter.

DEBUT	PEAK	WKS	GOLD	Country Chart Hit	Songwriter	Label (& Number)
2/25/67	62	5		**Fishin' On The Mississippi**	*Bob Morris*	Tower 307

MORRIS, Gary — 1980s: #35 / All-Time: #136

Born on 12/7/1948 in Fort Worth, Texas. Male singer/songwriter/guitarist/actor. Acted in Broadway's *Les Miserables* and *La Boheme*. Portrayed "Wayne Masterson" on TV's *The Colbys*.

DEBUT	PEAK	WKS	GOLD	Country Chart Hit	Songwriter	Label (& Number)
10/18/80	40	13		1 **Sweet Red Wine**	*Randy DuBois/Tim DuBois*	Warner 49564
3/7/81	40	10		2 **Fire In Your Eyes**	*Gary Morris/Kevin Welch*	Warner 49668
10/17/81	8	17		3 **Headed For A Heartache**	*Kent Blazy/Jim Dowell*	Warner 49829
2/27/82	12	17		4 **Don't Look Back**	*Gary Morris/Eddie Setser*	Warner 50017
7/10/82	15	15		5 **Dreams Die Hard**	*Chick Rains*	Warner 29967
11/27/82+	9	19		6 **Velvet Chains**	*Ron Hellard/Kevin Welch*	Warner 29853
4/16/83	5	20		7 **The Love She Found In Me**	*Dennis Linde/Bob Morrison*	Warner 29683
8/6/83	4	25		8 **The Wind Beneath My Wings**	*Larry Henley/Jeff Silbar*	Warner 29532
11/26/83+	4	19		9 **Why Lady Why**	*Gary Morris/Eddie Setser*	Warner 29450
12/17/83+	9	23		10 **You're Welcome To Tonight** *[w/ Lynn Anderson]*	*Grant Boatwright/Larry Henley/Jim Hurt*	Permian 82003
4/7/84	7	18		11 **Between Two Fires**	*Jan Buckingham/Sam Lorber/J.D. Martin*	Warner 29321
7/28/84	7	19		12 **Second Hand Heart**	A:19 / S:21 *Mark Gray/Craig Karp/Harold Tipton*	Warner 29230
11/24/84+	❶[1]	20		13 **Baby Bye Bye**	S:❶[1] / A:❶[1] *Jamie Brantley/Gary Morris*	Warner 29131
5/4/85	9	20		14 **Lasso The Moon** — from the movie *Rustler's Rhapsody* starring Tom Berenger	A:8 / S:9 *Milton Brown/Steve Dorff*	Warner 29028
8/24/85	❶[1]	23		15 **I'll Never Stop Loving You**	A:❶[1] / S:2 *Dave Loggins/J.D. Martin*	Warner 28947
11/23/85+	❶[1]	19		16 **Makin' Up For Lost Time (The Dallas Lovers' Song)** *[w/ Crystal Gayle]* — from the TV series *Dallas* starring Larry Hagman	S:❶[1] / A:❶[1] *Dave Loggins/Gary Morris*	Warner 28856
1/11/86	❶[1]	20		17 **100% Chance Of Rain**	S:❶[1] / A:2 *Charlie Black/Austin Roberts*	Warner 28823
5/17/86	28	12		18 **Anything Goes**	A:27 / S:32 *Gary Morris/Eddie Setser*	Warner 28713
7/12/86	27	13		19 **Honeycomb**	S:21 / A:28 *Bob Merrill*	Warner 28654
11/1/86+	❶[1]	21		20 **Leave Me Lonely**	A:❶[1] / S:4 *Gary Morris*	Warner 28542
2/28/87	9	20		21 **Plain Brown Wrapper**	A:9 / S:24 *Gary Morris/Kevin Welch*	Warner 28468
4/25/87	4	18		22 **Another World** *[w/ Crystal Gayle]* — theme from the TV serial	S:5 / A:29 *John Leffler/Ralph Schuckett*	Warner 28373
10/10/87	64	5		23 **Finishing Touches**	*Gary Morris/Kevin Welch*	Warner 28218
2/13/88	26	15		24 **All Of This & More** *[w/ Crystal Gayle]*	*Becky Foster/Jennifer Kimball/Greg Prestopino*	Warner 28106
5/27/89	48	12		25 **Never Had A Love Song**	*Jamie Brantley/Gary Morris*	Universal 66011
10/21/89	60	5		26 **The Jaws Of Modern Romance**	*Michael Cody*	Universal 66026
2/9/91	47	19		27 **Miles Across The Bedroom** — from the album *These Days* on Capitol 94103	*Lester Moore/Jeffrey Rea*	Capitol

MORRIS, Lamar

Born in Andalusia, Alabama. Male singer/songwriter. Member of **The Bama Band**.

DEBUT	PEAK	WKS	GOLD	Country Chart Hit	Songwriter	Label (& Number)
11/12/66	69	2		1 **Send Me A Box Of Kleenex**	*Lamar Morris/Mack Vickery*	MGM 13586
1/13/68	46	10		2 **The Great Pretender**	*Buck Ram*	MGM 13866
6/13/70	74	3		3 **She Came To Me**	*Warren Keith/Lamar Morris*	MGM 14114
1/2/71	59	6		4 **You're The Reason I'm Living**	*Bobby Darin*	MGM 14187
4/17/71	27	12		5 **If You Love Me (Really Love Me)**	*Marguerite Monnot/Geoffrey Parsons*	MGM 14236
11/27/71	74	3		6 **Near You**	*Francis Craig/Kermit Goell*	MGM 14289
2/17/73	71	3		7 **You Call Everybody Darling**	*Sam Martin/Ben Trace/Clem Watts*	MGM 14448

MORRISON, Kathy — see WILBOURNE, Bill

MORROW, Cory

Born on 5/1/1972 in Houston, Texas. Male singer/songwriter/guitarist.

DEBUT	PEAK	WKS	GOLD	Country Chart Hit	Songwriter	Label (& Number)
4/7/01	60	2		**Texas On My Mind** *[w/ Pat Green]* — from the album *Songs We Wish We'd Written* on Write On 2000	*Django Walker*	Write On

MORTON, Ann J.

Born Anna Jane White on 4/4/1943 in Muldrow, Oklahoma. Female singer/songwriter. Sister of **Jim Mundy** and **Bill White**.

DEBUT	PEAK	WKS	GOLD	Country Chart Hit	Songwriter	Label (& Number)
11/6/76	82	7		1 **Poor Wilted Rose**	*Ann J. Morton*	Prairie Dust 7606
3/26/77	63	10		2 **You Don't Have To Be A Baby To Cry**	*Bob Merrill/Terry Shand*	Prairie Dust 7613
7/16/77	86	4		3 **Don't Want To Take A Chance (On Loving You)**	*Wayne Johnston*	Prairie Dust 7617
10/1/77	72	6		4 **Blueberry Hill**	*Al Lewis/Vincent Rose/Larry Stock*	Prairie Dust 7619

DEBUT	PEAK	WKS	GOLD	ARTIST / Country Chart Hit	Ranking / Songwriter	Label (& Number)

MORTON, Ann J. — cont'd

DEBUT	PEAK	WKS	GOLD	Country Chart Hit	Songwriter	Label (& Number)
2/18/78	**83**	3		5 **Black And Blue Heart**	*Dennis W. Morgan*	Prairie Dust 7621
9/30/78	**83**	4		6 **Share Your Love Tonight**	*Jerry Foster/Bill Rice*	Prairie Dust 7627
1/27/79	**59**	6		7 **I'm Not In The Mood** (For Love)	*Kelly Bach*	Prairie Dust 7629
6/16/79	**86**	3		8 **Don't Stay On Your Side Of The Bed Tonight**	*Ann J. Morton/Eddie Rager*	Prairie Dust 7631
8/18/79	**42**	10		9 **My Empty Arms**	*Kelly Bach*	Prairie Dust 7632
1/26/80	**63**	5		10 (We Used To Kiss Each Other On The Lips But It's) **All Over Now** /	*Ann J. Morton/Eddie Rager*	
1/26/80	**flip**	5		11 **I Like Being Lonely**	*Kelly Bach/Sheryl McCament*	Prairie Dust 7633
2/14/81	**89**	3		12 **You've Got The Devil In Your Eyes**	*Bill Ellis/Shirl Milete*	Prairie Dust 8004

MOSBY, Johnny and Jonie

Husband-and-wife team of Johnny Mosby (born on 4/26/1933 in Fort Smith, Arkansas) and Jonie Mosby (born Janice Irene Shields on 8/10/1940 in Van Nuys, California). Married from 1958-73.

DEBUT	PEAK	WKS	GOLD	Country Chart Hit	Songwriter	Label (& Number)
5/18/63	**13**	9		1 **Don't Call Me From A Honky Tonk**	*Harlan Howard*	Columbia 42668
10/12/63+	**12**	16		2 **Trouble In My Arms** /	*Mike Anthony/Paul Kaufman*	
11/2/63	**27**	1		3 **Who's Been Cheatin' Who**	*Ned Miller/Sue Miller*	Columbia 42841
4/18/64	**16**	13		4 **Keep Those Cards And Letters Coming In**	*Harlan Howard*	Columbia 43005
10/10/64	**21**	11		5 **How The Other Half Lives**	*Norman Owens/Beverly Stewart/Wynn Stewart*	Columbia 43100
10/7/67	**36**	12		6 **Make A Left And Then A Right**	*Johnny Mosby/Jonie Mosby*	Capitol 5980
2/17/68	**53**	6		7 **Mr. & Mrs. John Smith**	*Johnny Mosby*	Capitol 2087
6/22/68	**58**	5		8 **Our Golden Wedding Day**	*Johnny Mosby/Jonie Mosby*	Capitol 2179
2/15/69	**12**	15		9 **Just Hold My Hand**	*Bill Barberis/Teddy Randazzo/Ben Weinstein*	Capitol 2384
6/21/69	**38**	12		10 **Hold Me, Thrill Me, Kiss Me**	*Harry Noble*	Capitol 2505
10/25/69	**26**	9		11 **I'll Never Be Free**	*Bennie Benjamin/George Weiss*	Capitol 2608
2/28/70	**34**	8		12 **Third World**	*Roy Bennett/Arthur Kent*	Capitol 2730
5/9/70	**18**	13		13 **I'm Leavin' It Up To You**	*Don Harris/Dewey Terry*	Capitol 2796
9/5/70	**47**	7		14 **My Happiness**	*Borney Bergantine/Betty Peterson*	Capitol 2865
3/6/71	**41**	9		15 **Oh, Love Of Mine**	*Pat Floyd*	Capitol 3039
12/18/71+	**70**	3		16 **Just One More Time**	*J.C. Cunningham*	Capitol 3219
1/6/73	**72**	2		17 **I've Been There** *[Jonie Mosby]*	*Robert Duncan*	Capitol 3454

MOWREY, Dude

Born Daniel Mowrey on 2/10/1972 in Ft. Lauderdale; raised in Ocala, Florida. Male singer/songwriter/guitarist.

DEBUT	PEAK	WKS	GOLD	Country Chart Hit	Songwriter	Label (& Number)
8/24/91	**65**	3		1 **Cowboys Don't Cry** from the album *Honky Tonk* on Capitol 95085	*Jim Allison/Doug Gilmore/Jeff Raymond/Bob Simon*	Capitol
4/17/93	**57**	8		2 **Maybe You Were The One**	*Robert Landis/Hunter Moore*	Arista
8/14/93	**69**	4		3 **Hold On, Elroy**	*Dennis Linde*	Arista
2/12/94	**57**	7		4 **Somewhere In Between** above 3 from the album *Dude Mowrey* on Arista 18678	*Allen Shamblin/Jon Vezner*	Arista

MULLEN, Bruce

Born in California. Male singer/songwriter.

DEBUT	PEAK	WKS	GOLD	Country Chart Hit	Songwriter	Label (& Number)
5/25/74	**88**	3		**Auctioneer Love**	*Bonnie Guitar/Bruce Mullen*	Chart 5215

MULLICAN, Moon — **1940s: #34 / 1950s: #47**

Born Aubrey Mullican on 3/29/1909 in Corrigan, Texas. Died of a heart attack on 1/1/1967 (age 57). Male singer/songwriter/pianist. Known as the "King Of The Hillbilly Piano Players."

OPRY: 1951

DEBUT	PEAK	WKS	GOLD	Country Chart Hit	Songwriter	Label (& Number)
2/8/47	**2**[1]	15		1 **New Pretty Blonde** (Jole Blon) ***[w/ the Showboys]***	*Moon Mullican/Syd Nathan*	King 578
7/26/47	**4**	1		2 **Jole Blon's Sister**	*Morry Burns/Syd Nathan*	King 632
5/15/48	**3**[1]	26		3 **Sweeter Than The Flowers**	S:3 / J:3 *Morry Burns/Lois Mann/Ervin Rouse*	King 673
3/18/50	**❶**[4]	36		4 **I'll Sail My Ship Alone**	J:❶[4] / S:❶[1] / A:2 *Henry Bernard/Morry Burns/Lois Mann/Henry Thurston*	King 830
8/26/50	**4**	11		5 **Mona Lisa** / from the movie *Captain Carey, U.S.A.* starring Alan Ladd	J:4 / A:7 / S:8 *Ray Evans/Jay Livingston*	
8/26/50	**5**	7		6 **Goodnight Irene**	J:5 / S:10 / A:10 *Huddie Ledbetter/Alan Lomax*	King 886
8/4/51	**7**	2		7 **Cherokee Boogie** (Eh-Oh-Aleena)	S:7 / J:10 *Moon Mullican/Chief William Redbird*	King 965
5/29/61	**15**	4		8 **Ragged But Right**	*George Jones*	Starday 545

MULLINS, Dee

Born on 4/7/1937 in Gafford, Texas. Died on 3/13/1991 (age 53). Male singer.

DEBUT	PEAK	WKS	GOLD	Country Chart Hit	Songwriter	Label (& Number)
2/10/68	**64**	3		1 **I Am The Grass**	*Margaret Lewis/Myra Smith*	SSS Int'l. 728
7/13/68	**51**	7		2 **Texas Tea**	*Ben Peters*	SSS Int'l. 745
4/26/69	**53**	6		3 **The Big Man**	*Gary McFarland/Carol Stivers/Jerry Teifer*	Plantation 17
1/9/71	**71**	2		4 **Remember Bethlehem**	*Jake Thackery* **[X]**	Plantation 68
4/14/73	**61**	9		5 **Circle Me**	*Jerry McBee*	Triune 7205

MUNDY, Jim

Born James White on 2/8/1934 in Muldrow, Oklahoma. Male singer/songwriter. Brother of **Ann J. Morton** and **Bill White**.

DEBUT	PEAK	WKS	GOLD	Country Chart Hit	Songwriter	Label (& Number)
12/1/73+	**13**	15		1 **The River's Too Wide**	*Bob Morrison*	ABC 11400
4/13/74	**49**	11		2 **Come Home**	*Jim Mundy*	ABC 11428
9/7/74	**71**	5		3 **She's No Ordinary Woman** (Ordinarily)	*Glenn Barber/Jim Mundy*	ABC 12001
4/19/75	**37**	9		4 **She's Already Gone**	*Jim Mundy*	ABC 12074
8/30/75	**81**	8		5 **Blue Eyes And Waltzes**	*Tony Austin*	ABC 12120
4/17/76	**86**	4		6 **I'm Knee Deep In Loving You**	*Sonny Throckmorton*	ABC/Dot 17617
8/7/76	**94**	4		7 **I Never Met A Girl I Didn't Like**	*Jim Mundy*	ABC/Dot 17638
7/30/77	**70**	6		8 **Summertime Blues**	*Jerry Capehart/Eddie Cochran*	Hill Country 778

DEBUT	PEAK	WKS	GOLD	ARTIST / Country Chart Hit	Ranking / Songwriter	Label (& Number)
				MUNDY, Jim — cont'd		
9/9/78	76	4		9 If You Think I Love You Now *[w/ Terri Melton]*	*Jim Mundy*	MCM 100
1/6/79	87	2		10 Kiss You All Over *[w/ Terri Melton]*	*Mike Chapman/Nicky Chinn*	MCM 101
				MUNDY, Marilyn		
				Born in Bokoshe, Oklahoma; raised in Flower Hill, Oklahoma. Female singer.		
6/17/89	85	2		1 I Still Love You Babe	*Linda Easterling*	Door Knob 322
1/6/90	85	2		2 Feelings For Each Other	*Henry Gray/Marion Walton*	Door Knob 336
				MURPHEY, Mark		
				Born in Nevada. Male singer/songwriter.		
5/6/89	96	1		California Wine	*Mark Murphey*	Traveler Ent. 106

MURPHEY, Michael Martin — 1980s: #46 / All-Time: #156

Born on 3/14/1945 in Oak Cliff, Texas. Male singer/songwriter/guitarist. Member of the Texas Twosome while still in high school. Toured as "Travis Lewis" of The Lewis & Clarke Expedition in 1967. Worked as a staff writer for Screen Gems. Acted in the movies *Take This Job And Shove It* and *Hard Country*.

DEBUT	PEAK	WKS	GOLD	ARTIST / Country Chart Hit	Ranking / Songwriter	Label (& Number)
				MICHAEL MURPHEY:		
2/21/76	36	10		1 A Mansion On The Hill	*Fred Rose/Hank Williams*	Epic 50184
1/22/77	58	8		2 Cherokee Fiddle	*Michael Murphey*	Epic 50319
4/28/79	93	3		3 Chain Gang	*Sam Cooke*	Epic 50686
8/18/79	92	3		4 Backslider's Wine	*Michael Murphey*	Epic 50739
7/4/81	83	3		5 Take It As It Comes *[w/ Katy Moffatt]*	*Michael Murphey*	Epic 02075
3/27/82	44	10		6 The Two-Step Is Easy	*Michael Murphey*	Liberty 1455
6/19/82	❶[1]	24		7 What's Forever For	*Rafe Van Hoy*	Liberty 1466
11/13/82+	3[1]	20		8 Still Taking Chances	*Michael Murphey*	Liberty 1486
3/26/83	11	17		9 Love Affairs	*Mike D'Abo/Michael Murphey*	Liberty 1494
9/10/83	9	21		10 Don't Count The Rainy Days	*Jerry Careaga/Wayland Holyfield*	Liberty 1505
1/28/84	7	18		11 Will It Be Love By Morning	*Lewis Anderson/Fred Koller*	Liberty 1514
				MICHAEL MARTIN MURPHEY:		
5/12/84	12	17		12 Disenchanted	*Michael Murphey/Jim Ed Norman/Chick Rains*	Liberty 1517
8/25/84	19	16		13 Radio Land	A:17 / S:21 *Michael Murphey/Jim Ed Norman/Chick Rains*	Liberty 1523
12/1/84+	8	23		14 What She Wants	S:7 / A:8 *Renee Armand/Kerry Chater*	EMI America 8243
5/25/85	9	20		15 Carolina In The Pines	A:9 / S:10 *Michael Murphey*	EMI America 8265
2/8/86	26	14		16 Tonight We Ride	S:24 / A:27 *Michael Murphey/Jim Ed Norman*	Warner 28797
5/24/86	15	16		17 Rollin' Nowhere	S:14 / A:15 *Michael Murphey*	Warner 28694
8/30/86	40	14		18 Fiddlin' Man	*Michael Murphey/Jim Ed Norman/Chick Rains*	Warner 28598
2/7/87	4	21		19 A Face In The Crowd *[w/ Holly Dunn]*	A:4 / S:15 *Gary Harrison/Karen Staley*	Warner 28471
5/23/87	❶[1]	23		20 A Long Line Of Love	S:9 *Paul Overstreet/Thom Schuyler*	Warner 28370
11/21/87+	3[1]	27		21 I'm Gonna Miss You, Girl	S:7 *Jesse Winchester*	Warner 28168
4/16/88	4	20		22 Talkin' To The Wrong Man *[w/ son Ryan Murphey]*	S:5 *Michael Murphey*	Warner 27947
9/10/88	29	13		23 Pilgrims On The Way (Matthew's Song)	*Marcus Hummon*	Warner 27810
12/17/88+	3[1]	27		24 From The Word Go	*Michael Garvin/Chris Waters*	Warner 27668
5/20/89	9	22		25 Never Givin' Up On Love from the movie *Pink Cadillac* starring **Clint Eastwood**	*Michael Smotherman*	Warner 22970
10/7/89	48	11		26 Family Tree	*Thom Schuyler*	Warner 22765
1/6/90	67	3		27 Route 66 from the album *Land Of Enchantment* on Warner 25894	*Bobby Troup*	Warner
9/8/90	52	11		28 Cowboy Logic	*Don Cook/Chick Rains*	Warner
3/16/91	74	1		29 Let The Cowboy Dance above 2 from the album *Cowboy Songs* on Warner 26308	*Don Cook/Michael Murphey/Chick Rains*	Warner
				MURPHY, David Lee — All-Time: #288		
				Born on 1/7/1959 in Herrin, Illinois. Male singer/songwriter/guitarist.		
3/5/94	36	20		1 Just Once from the movie *8 Seconds* starring Luke Perry (soundtrack on MCA 10927)	*David Lee Murphy/Kim Tribble*	MCA
8/20/94	52	7		2 Fish Ain't Bitin'	*David Lee Murphy*	MCA
3/18/95	6	22		3 Party Crowd	S:5 *Jimbeau Hinson/David Lee Murphy*	MCA
8/12/95	❶[2]	20		4 Dust On The Bottle	S:13 *David Lee Murphy*	MCA
11/25/95+	13	20		5 Out With A Bang above 4 from the album *Out With A Bang* on MCA 11044	*David Lee Murphy/Kim Tribble*	MCA
3/23/96	2[1]	20		6 Every Time I Get Around You	*David Lee Murphy*	MCA
8/3/96	5	20		7 The Road You Leave Behind	*David Lee Murphy*	MCA
1/25/97	53	5		8 Genuine Rednecks	*David Lee Murphy*	MCA
3/15/97	51	7		9 Breakfast In Birmingham above 4 from the album *Gettin' Out The Good Stuff* on MCA 11423	*David Lee Murphy/Kim Tribble*	MCA
7/5/97	25	20		10 All Lit Up In Love	*David Lee Murphy*	MCA
11/15/97+	37	20		11 Just Don't Wait Around Til She's Leavin' above 2 from the album *We Can't All Be Angels* on MCA 70002	*David Lee Murphy*	MCA
1/17/04	5	28		12 Loco	*David Lee Murphy/Kim Tribble*	Audium
10/16/04	46	16		13 Inspiration *[w/ Lee Roy Parnell]* above 2 from Murphy's album *Tryin' To Get There* on Koch 8189	*David Lee Murphy*	Koch

Billboard

DEBUT	PEAK	WKS	GOLD		ARTIST / Country Chart Hit	Songwriter	Label (& Number)

MURPHY, Jimmy

Born in Philadelphia, Pennsylvania. Male singer.

DEBUT	PEAK	WKS	GOLD		Country Chart Hit	Songwriter	Label (& Number)
10/25/86	**74**	4		1	**Two Sides**	*Scott Davis*	Encore 10033
1/31/87	**51**	9		2	**Keep The Faith**	*Jim Sales/Keith Stegall*	Encore 10036

MURPHY, Tim

Born in California. Male singer/songwriter/guitarist.

DEBUT	PEAK	WKS	GOLD		Country Chart Hit	Songwriter	Label (& Number)
1/3/04	**59**	1			**Bert & Bobby's Auto Body Shop**	*Max T. Barnes/Keith Follese*	Labeless

MURRAY, Anne — 1970s: #45 / 1980s: #32 / All-Time: #59

Born Morna Anne Murray on 6/20/1945 in Springhill, Nova Scotia, Canada. Female singer. High school gym teacher for one year after college. With CBC-TV show *Sing Along Jubilee*. First recorded for Arc in 1968. Regular on **Glen Campbell**'s TV series.

CMA: Vocal Duo (with Dave Loggins) 1985

DEBUT	PEAK	WKS	GOLD		Country Chart Hit	Songwriter	Label (& Number)
7/25/70	**10**	19	●	1	**Snowbird**	*Gene MacLellan*	Capitol 2738
1/16/71	**53**	5		2	**Sing High - Sing Low**	*Brent Titcomb*	Capitol 2988
3/20/71	**27**	12		3	**A Stranger In My Place** also see #14 below	*Kenny Rogers/Kin Vassy*	Capitol 3059
5/22/71	**67**	2		4	**Put Your Hand In The Hand**	*Gene MacLellan*	Capitol 3082
10/30/71	**40**	8		5	**I Say A Little Prayer/By The Time I Get To Phoenix** ***[w/ Glen Campbell]***	*Burt Bacharach/Hal David/Jimmy Webb*	Capitol 3200
1/22/72	**11**	15		6	**Cotton Jenny**	*Gordon Lightfoot*	Capitol 3260
12/23/72+	**10**	17		7	**Danny's Song**	*Kenny Loggins*	Capitol 3481
6/2/73	**20**	10		8	**What About Me**	*Scott MacKenzie*	Capitol 3600
8/25/73	**79**	7		9	**Send A Little Love My Way** from the movie *Oklahoma Crude* starring George C. Scott	*Hal David/Henry Mancini*	Capitol 3648
12/22/73+	**5**	15		10	**Love Song** **Grammy: Female Vocal**	*Dona Lynn George/Kenny Loggins*	Capitol 3776
4/27/74	❶^{2}	17		11	**He Thinks I Still Care**	*Dickey Lee*	Capitol 3867
9/28/74	**5**	16		12	**Son Of A Rotten Gambler**	*Chip Taylor*	Capitol 3955
2/15/75	**28**	10		13	**Uproar**	*Paul Grady*	Capitol 4025
6/7/75	**79**	6		14	**A Stranger In My Place** same version as #3 above	*Kenny Rogers/Kin Vassy* **[R]**	Capitol 4072
10/25/75	**49**	9		15	**Sunday Sunrise**	*Mark James*	Capitol 4142
2/7/76	**19**	14		16	**The Call**	*Gene MacLellan*	Capitol 4207
5/29/76	**41**	8		17	**Golden Oldie**	*Brenda Russell/Brian Russell*	Capitol 4265
9/11/76	**22**	12		18	**Things**	*Bobby Darin*	Capitol 4329
2/5/77	**57**	8		19	**Sunday School To Broadway**	*Danny Hice/Ruby Hice*	Capitol 4375
1/21/78	**4**	16		20	**Walk Right Back**	*Sonny Curtis*	Capitol 4527
5/13/78	**4**	18	●	21	**You Needed Me**	*Randy Goodrum*	Capitol 4574
1/27/79	❶^{3}	15		22	**I Just Fall In Love Again**	*Steve Dorff/Larry Herbstritt/Harry Lloyd/Gloria Sklerov*	Capitol 4675
5/19/79	❶^{1}	15		23	**Shadows In The Moonlight**	*Charlie Black/Rory Bourke*	Capitol 4716
9/29/79	❶^{1}	14		24	**Broken Hearted Me**	*Randy Goodrum*	Capitol 4773
1/5/80	**3^{2}**	14		25	**Daydream Believer**	*John Stewart*	Capitol 4813
4/5/80	**9**	14		26	**Lucky Me**	*Charlie Black/Rory Bourke*	Capitol 4848
6/28/80	**23**	11		27	**I'm Happy Just To Dance With You**	*John Lennon/Paul McCartney*	Capitol 4878
9/6/80	❶^{1}	16		28	**Could I Have This Dance** **Grammy: Female Vocal**; from the movie *Urban Cowboy* starring John Travolta	*Wayland Holyfield/Bob House*	Capitol 4920
4/4/81	❶^{1}	14		29	**Blessed Are The Believers**	*Charlie Black/Rory Bourke/Sandy Pinkard*	Capitol 4987
7/4/81	**16**	13		30	**We Don't Have To Hold Out**	*Gordon Adams/Aidan Mason*	Capitol 5013
9/12/81	**9**	15		31	**It's All I Can Do**	*Archie Jordan/Richard Leigh*	Capitol 5023
1/16/82	**4**	18		32	**Another Sleepless Night**	*Charlie Black/Rory Bourke*	Capitol 5083
7/31/82	**7**	16		33	**Hey! Baby!**	*Bruce Channel/Margaret Cobb*	Capitol 5145
11/20/82+	**7**	19		34	**Somebody's Always Saying Goodbye**	*Bob McDill*	Capitol 5183
9/17/83	❶^{1}	20		35	**A Little Good News** **Grammy: Female Vocal / CMA: Single**	*Charlie Black/Rory Bourke/Tommy Rocco*	Capitol 5264
2/4/84	**46**	12		36	**That's Not The Way (It's S'posed To Be)**	*Phil Galdston/Andy Goldmark*	Capitol 5305
4/28/84	❶^{1}	20		37	**Just Another Woman In Love**	*Wanda Mallette/Patti Ryan*	Capitol 5344
9/8/84	❶^{1}	22		38	**Nobody Loves Me Like You Do** ***[w/ Dave Loggins]***	S:❶^{1} / A:❶^{1} *James Dunne/Pamela Phillips*	Capitol 5401
1/19/85	**2^{1}**	22		39	**Time Don't Run Out On Me**	S:2 / A:3 *Gerry Goffin/Carole King*	Capitol 5436
5/18/85	**7**	20		40	**I Don't Think I'm Ready For You** from the movie *Stick* starring **Burt Reynolds**	A:6 / S:7 *Milton Brown/Steve Dorff/Snuff Garrett/Allen Reynolds*	Capitol 5472
1/25/86	❶^{1}	19		41	**Now And Forever (You And Me)**	S:❶^{1} / A:2 *David Foster/Randy Goodrum/Jim Vallance*	Capitol 5547
5/24/86	**62**	9		42	**Who's Leaving Who**	*Markus Spiro/Jack White*	Capitol 5576
8/23/86	**26**	15		43	**My Life's A Dance**	A:24 *Markus Spiro/Jack White*	Capitol 5610
12/27/86+	**23**	14		44	**On And On**	A:23 *Jerry Buckner*	Capitol 5655
5/9/87	**20**	23		45	**Are You Still In Love With Me**	S:12 *Karl Porter/Markus Spiro/Jack White*	Capitol 44005
8/29/87	**27**	13		46	**Anyone Can Do The Heartbreak**	*Amanda McBroom/Tom Snow*	Capitol 44053
2/20/88	**52**	8		47	**Perfect Strangers** ***[w/ Doug Mallory]***	*Astor Anderson/Jonas Field/John Sareussen/Markus Spiro*	Capitol 44134
9/3/88	**52**	7		48	**Flying On Your Own**	*Rita MacNeil*	Capitol 44219

DEBUT	PEAK	WKS	GOLD	ARTIST / Ranking / Country Chart Hit	Songwriter	Label (& Number)
				MURRAY, Anne — cont'd		
11/26/88+	**36**	12		49 **Slow Passin' Time**	*Charlie Black/Rory Bourke/Tommy Rocco*	Capitol 44272
3/25/89	**55**	9		50 **Who But You**	*Charlie Black/Rory Bourke/K.T. Oslin*	Capitol 44341
9/30/89	**28**	15		51 **If I Ever Fall In Love Again** ***[w/ Kenny Rogers]***	*Steve Dorff/Gloria Sklerov*	Capitol 44432
8/25/90	**5**	20		52 **Feed This Fire**	*Hugh Prestwood*	Capitol
12/8/90+	**39**	19		53 **Bluebird**	*Ron Irving*	Capitol
				above 2 from the album *You Will* on Capitol 94102		
10/5/91	**56**	11		54 **Everyday**	*Richard Brannan/David Malloy*	Capitol
				from the album *Yes I Do* on Capitol 96310		
				MUSIC ROW		
				Duo of Glen Gill and Bill Pippin.		
3/7/81	**86**	4		1 **There Ain't A Song**	*Wes Helm*	Debut 8013
5/16/81	**92**	2		2 **Lady's Man**	*Wes Helm/Bill Pippin*	Debut 8115
6/27/81	**88**	3		3 **It's Not The Rain**	*Ronny Hughes/Bill Pippin*	Debut 8116
				MYERS, Frank		
				Born in Snowdoun, Alabama; raised in Montgomery, Alabama. Male singer.		
8/3/74	**82**	7		**Hangin' On To What I've Got**	*Bob Millsap*	Caprice 1999
				MYLES, Heather		
				Born in Riverside, California. Female singer.		
1/30/99	**75**	1		**Love Me A Little Bit Longer**	*Heather Myles*	Rounder/Mercury
				from the album *Highways & Honky Tonks* on Rounder/Mercury 3147		

N

DEBUT	PEAK	WKS	GOLD	ARTIST / Ranking / Country Chart Hit	Songwriter	Label (& Number)
				NAIL, David		
				Born in Kennett, Missouri. Male singer/songwriter.		
5/18/02	**52**	7		**Memphis**	*David Nail*	Mercury
				NAIL, Linda		
				Born Linda Naile on 1/19/1954 in Wabash, Arkansas. Female singer.		
12/9/78+	**58**	9		1 **Me Touchin' You**	*Bobby Bond*	Ridgetop 00178
3/10/79	**67**	5		2 **There Hangs His Hat**	*Andy Badale/Jenny Johnson/Frank Stanton*	Ridgetop 00279
2/5/83	**85**	2		3 **You're A Part Of Me** ***[w/ Danny White]***	*Kim Carnes*	Grand Prix 2
5/14/83	**80**	4		4 **Reminiscing**	*Travis Wammack*	Grand Prix 3
				NAILL, Jerry		
				Born in 1948 in Sugar Land, Texas. Male singer/songwriter/guitarist.		
2/2/80	**92**	4		**Her Cheatin Heart (Made A Drunken Fool Of Me)**	*Dave Kirby/Jerry Naill/Judy Okonski*	El Dorado 156
				NALL, Jimmy		
				Born in Texas. Male singer/guitarist.		
5/25/74	**94**	3		**Mockingbird** ***[w/ Terri Lane]***	*Charlie Foxx/Inez Foxx*	Monument 8610
				NASH, Bill		
				Born in Pharr, Texas. Male singer.		
7/4/81	**79**	4		1 **Burning Bridges**	*Walter Scott*	Liberty 1410
10/17/81	**61**	6		2 **Slippin' Out, Slippin' In**	*Dave Burgess*	Liberty 1433
5/22/82	**65**	6		3 **Survivor**	*Dennis Knutson*	Liberty 1463
				NASH, Linda		
				Born in Canada. Female singers.		
10/27/73	**83**	10		**Country Boogie Woogie**	*Jim Owen*	Ace of Hearts 0473
				NASHVILLE BRASS — see DAVIS, Danny		
				NASHVILLE NIGHTSHIFT		
				Studio group formed in Nashville, Tennessee.		
8/31/85	**89**	2		**Nightshift**	*Franne Golde/Dennis Lambert/Walter Orange*	NCA 133737
				tribute to **Marty Robbins**		
				NASHVILLE SUPERPICKERS		
				Group of top session musicians: **Phil Baugh** (guitar), Buddy Emmons (steel guitar), **Charlie McCoy** (harmonica), **Johnny Gimble** (fiddle), **Hargus "Pig" Robbins** (piano), Russ Hicks (guitar), Henry Strzelecki (bass) and Buddy Harman (drums).		
2/7/81	**83**	2		**New York Cowboy**	*Roger Murrah*	Sound Factory 426
				NAYLOR, Jerry		
				Born on 3/6/1939 in Stephenville, Texas. Male singer/bassist.		
1/25/75	**27**	12		1 **Is This All There Is To A Honky Tonk?**	*Robert Duncan/Don Lee*	Melodyland 6003
10/2/76	**94**	2		2 **The Bad Part Of Me**	*Porter Jordon/Jerry Styner*	Hitsville 6041
12/4/76+	**50**	9		3 **The Last Time You Love Me**	*Porter Jordan/Jerry Styner*	Hitsville 6046
2/4/78	**37**	9		4 **If You Don't Want To Love Her**	*Oskar Solomon*	MC/Curb 5004
5/27/78	**80**	4		5 **Rave On /**	*Norman Petty/Bill Tilghman/Sunny West*	
6/10/78	**flip**	2		6 **Lady, Would You Like To Dance**	*Jerry Blanton*	MC/Curb 5010
3/24/79	**54**	5		7 **But For Love**	*Terry Cashman/Gene Pistilli/Tommy West*	Warner/Curb 8767
7/7/79	**72**	4		8 **She Wears It Well**	*Oskar Solomon*	Warner/Curb 8881
11/17/79	**69**	4		9 **Don't Touch Me** ***[w/ Kelli Warren]***	*Hank Cochran*	Jeremiah 1002

Billboard DEBUT	PEAK	WKS	GOLD	ARTIST / Ranking / Country Chart Hit	Songwriter	Label (& Number)

NAYLOR, Jerry — cont'd

DEBUT	PEAK	WKS	GOLD	Country Chart Hit	Songwriter	Label (& Number)
3/8/80	**61**	5		10 **Cheating Eyes**	*Dick Davidson*	Oak 1014
11/29/86	**75**	4		11 **For Old Time Sake**	*Ron Johnson*	West 723

NEEL, Jo Anna

Born in Buckeye, Arizona. Female singer/songwriter.

DEBUT	PEAK	WKS	GOLD	Country Chart Hit	Songwriter	Label (& Number)
11/13/71	**68**	5		1 **Daddy Was A Preacher But Mama Was A Go-Go Girl**	*Bob Neel/Jo Anna Neel*	Decca 32865
4/22/72	**44**	10		2 **One More Time**	*Michael Fennelly*	Decca 32950

NEELY, Sam

Born on 8/22/1948 in Cuero, Texas. Male singer/guitarist.

DEBUT	PEAK	WKS	GOLD	Country Chart Hit	Songwriter	Label (& Number)
9/14/74	**49**	12		1 **You Can Have Her**	*Bill Cook*	A&M 1612
2/1/75	**61**	8		2 **I Fought The Law**	*Sonny Curtis*	A&M 1651
9/10/77	**98**	3		3 **Sail Away**	*Rafe Van Hoy*	Elektra 45419
3/12/83	**78**	4		4 **The Party's Over (Everybody's Gone)** tribute to the final episode of TV's *M*A*S*H* which aired on 2/28/1983	*Lobo/Jeff Raymond*	MCA 52194
6/18/83	**77**	5		5 **When You Leave That Way You Can Never Go Back**	*Stephen Clark/Johnny MacRae*	MCA 52226
1/21/84	**81**	3		6 **Old Photographs**	*Ken Beal/Kix Brooks/Bill McClelland*	MCA 52323

NELSON, Bonnie

Born in 1949 in Denver, Colorado. Female singer.

DEBUT	PEAK	WKS	GOLD	Country Chart Hit	Songwriter	Label (& Number)
12/6/86	**83**	3		1 **Don't Let It Go To Your Heart**	*Bob Stamper*	Door Knob 257
5/23/87	**84**	2		2 **More Than Friendly Persuasion**	*Larry Clark/Steve Younger*	Door Knob 264

NELSON, Nikki

Born on 1/3/1969 in San Diego, California; raised in Topaz City, Nevada. Female singer. Former lead singer of **Highway 101**.

DEBUT	PEAK	WKS	GOLD	Country Chart Hit	Songwriter	Label (& Number)
3/15/97	**62**	5		**Too Little Too Much**	*Gayla Borders/Jeff Borders/Chapin Hartford*	Columbia

NELSON, Ricky — 1950s: #48

Born Eric Hilliard Nelson on 5/8/1940 in Teaneck, New Jersey. Died on 12/31/1985 (age 45) in a plane crash in DeKalb, Texas. Male singer/songwriter/guitarist. Son of bandleader Ozzie Nelson and vocalist Harriet Hilliard. Rick and brother David appeared on Nelson's radio show from March 1949; later on TV from 1952-66. Formed own Stone Canyon Band in 1969. In movies *Rio Bravo*, *The Wackiest Ship In The Army* and *Love And Kisses*. Married Kristin Harmon (sister of actor Mark Harmon) in 1963; divorced in 1982. Their daughter Tracy is an actress. Their twin sons, Matthew and Gunnar, began recording as Nelson in 1990. Inducted into the Rock and Roll Hall of Fame in 1987.

DEBUT	PEAK	WKS	GOLD	Country Chart Hit	Songwriter	Label (& Number)
1/20/58	**8**	12	●	1 **Stood Up /**	S:8 *Willis Dickerson/Erma Herrold*	
1/20/58	**12**	6		2 **Waitin' In School**	S:12 *Dorsey Burnette/Johnny Burnette*	Imperial 5483
4/14/58	**10**	11		3 **My Bucket's Got A Hole In It /**	S:10 *Clarence Williams*	
4/14/58	**10**	10	●	4 **Believe What You Say**	S:10 *Dorsey Burnette/Johnny Burnette*	Imperial 5503
7/7/58	**3^{1}**	15	●	5 **Poor Little Fool**	S:3 / A:8 *Sharon Sheeley*	Imperial 5528
				RICK NELSON:		
6/10/67	**58**	5		6 **Take A City Bride**	*Gib Gilbeau*	Decca 32120
9/16/72	**44**	9	●	7 **Garden Party** ***[w/ Stone Canyon Band]***	*Rick Nelson*	Decca 32980
5/11/74	**89**	2		8 **One Night Stand** ***[w/ Stone Canyon Band]***	*Dennis Larden*	MCA 40214
4/21/79	**59**	9		9 **Dream Lover**	*Bobby Darin*	Epic 50674
7/12/86	**88**	7		10 **Dream Lover** above 2 are the same version	*Bobby Darin* **[R]**	Epic 06066

NELSON, Terry — C COMPANY

NELSON, Willie — 1970s: #14 / 1980s: #1 / All-Time: #7 // HOF: 1993

Born on 4/30/1933 in Abbott, Texas. Male singer/songwriter/guitarist/actor. Played bass for **Ray Price**'s band. Acted in the several movies. Formerly married to **Shirley Collie**. Won Grammy's Lifetime Achievement Award in 2000. Also see **Some Of Chet's Friends** and **USA For Africa**.

CMA: Vocal Duo (with Waylon Jennings) 1976 / Entertainer 1979 / Vocal Duo (with Merle Haggard) 1983 / Vocal Duo (with Julio Iglesias) 1984 // OPRY: 1964

DEBUT	PEAK	WKS	GOLD	Country Chart Hit	Songwriter	Label (& Number)
3/17/62	**10**	13		1 **Willingly** ***[w/ Shirley Collie]***	*Hank Cochran*	Liberty 55403
5/26/62	**7**	13		2 **Touch Me**	*Willie Nelson*	Liberty 55439
4/6/63	**25**	5		3 **Half A Man**	*Willie Nelson*	Liberty 55532
1/18/64	**33**	3		4 **You Took My Happy Away**	*Willie Nelson*	Liberty 55638
5/8/65	**43**	5		5 **She's Not For You**	*Willie Nelson*	RCA Victor 8519
10/16/65	**48**	2		6 **I Just Can't Let You Say Goodbye**	*Willie Nelson*	RCA Victor 8682
10/1/66	**19**	13		7 **One In A Row**	*Willie Nelson*	RCA Victor 8933
3/4/67	**24**	16		8 **The Party's Over**	*Willie Nelson*	RCA Victor 9100
6/24/67	**21**	11		9 **Blackjack County Chain**	*Red Lane*	RCA Victor 9202
10/21/67	**50**	9		10 **San Antonio**	*Jerry Blanton*	RCA Victor 9324
2/10/68	**22**	11		11 **Little Things**	*Shirley Nelson/Willie Nelson*	RCA Victor 9427
6/15/68	**44**	8		12 **Good Times** also see #70 below	*Willie Nelson*	RCA Victor 9536
9/7/68	**36**	7		13 **Johnny One Time**	*Dallas Frazier/A.L. "Doodle" Owens*	RCA Victor 9605
12/21/68+	**13**	14		14 **Bring Me Sunshine**	*Sylvia Dee/Arthur Kent*	RCA Victor 9684
12/13/69+	**36**	9		15 **I Hope So** recorded in 1963	*Shirley Nelson*	Liberty 56143

Billboard DEBUT	PEAK	WKS	GOLD	ARTIST Ranking Country Chart Hit	Songwriter	Label (& Number)
				NELSON, Willie — cont'd		
3/14/70	42	9		16 **Once More With Feeling**	*Shirley Nelson*	RCA Victor 9798
11/28/70	68	2		17 **Laying My Burdens Down**	*Willie Nelson*	RCA Victor 9903
2/6/71	28	11		18 **I'm A Memory**	*Willie Nelson*	RCA Victor 9951
				also see #39 below		
10/23/71	62	7		19 **Yesterday's Wine /**	*Willie Nelson*	
11/13/71	flip	4		20 **Me And Paul**	*Willie Nelson*	RCA Victor 0542
				also see #96 below		
2/19/72	73	2		21 **The Words Don't Fit The Picture**	*Willie Nelson*	RCA Victor 0635
7/14/73	60	5		22 **Shotgun Willie**	*Willie Nelson*	Atlantic 2968
9/29/73	22	13		23 **Stay All Night (Stay A Little Longer)**	*Tommy Duncan/Bob Wills*	Atlantic 2979
2/16/74	51	5		24 **I Still Can't Believe You're Gone**	*Willie Nelson*	Atlantic 3008
4/6/74	17	13		25 **Bloody Mary Morning**	*Willie Nelson*	Atlantic 3020
8/17/74	17	11		26 **After The Fire Is Gone** ***[w/ Tracy Nelson]***	*L.E. White*	Atlantic 4028
12/7/74	93	3		27 **Sister's Coming Home**	*Willie Nelson*	Atlantic 3228
7/19/75	❶^{2}	18		28 **Blue Eyes Crying In The Rain**	*Fred Rose*	Columbia 10176
				Grammy: Male Vocal / RS500		
11/15/75+	29	11		29 **Fire And Rain**	*James Taylor*	RCA Victor 10429
12/27/75+	❶^{3}	17		30 **Good Hearted Woman** ***[w/ Waylon Jennings]***	*Waylon Jennings/Willie Nelson* **[L]**	RCA Victor 10529
				CMA: Single		
1/3/76	2^{1}	15		31 **Remember Me**	*"T" Texas Tyler*	Columbia 10275
3/27/76	46	7		32 **The Last Letter**	*Rex Griffin*	United Artists 771
4/17/76	55	6		33 **I Gotta Get Drunk**	*Willie Nelson* **[L]**	RCA Victor 10591
5/1/76	11	13		34 **I'd Have To Be Crazy**	*Steve Fromholz*	Columbia 10327
7/24/76	❶^{1}	15		35 **If You've Got The Money I've Got The Time**	*Jim Beck/Lefty Frizzell*	Columbia 10383
12/18/76+	4	14		36 **Uncloudy Day**	*Willie Nelson*	Columbia 10453
3/12/77	32	13		37 **Lily Dale** ***[w/ Darrell McCall]***	*Tim Moore/B.J. Wills*	Columbia 10480
5/7/77	69	6		38 **You Are My Sunshine** ***[w/ Duane Eddy/Waylon Jennings/Kin Vassy/Deed Eddy]***	*...Jimmie Davis/Charles Mitchell*	Elektra 45359
5/14/77	22	11		39 **I'm A Memory**	*Willie Nelson* **[R]**	RCA 10969
				same version as #18 above		
7/30/77	9	12		40 **I Love You A Thousand Ways**	*Jim Beck/Lefty Frizzell*	Columbia 10588
9/10/77	16	13		41 **You Ought To Hear Me Cry**	*Willie Nelson*	RCA 11061
11/19/77+	9	16		42 **Something To Brag About** ***[w/ Mary Kay Place]***	*Bobby Braddock*	Columbia 10644
1/21/78	❶^{4}	16		43 **Mammas Don't Let Your Babies Grow Up To Be Cowboys** ***[w/ Waylon Jennings] /***	*...Ed Bruce/Patsy Bruce*	
				Grammy: Vocal Duo		
1/28/78	flip	15		44 **I Can Get Off On You** ***[w/ Waylon Jennings]***	*Waylon Jennings/Willie Nelson*	RCA 11198
3/18/78	5	15		45 **If You Can Touch Her At All**	*Lee Clayton*	RCA 11235
3/25/78	❶^{1}	16		46 **Georgia On My Mind**	*Hoagy Carmichael/Stuart Gorrell*	Columbia 10704
				Grammy: Male Vocal		
7/15/78	❶^{1}	13		47 **Blue Skies**	*Irving Berlin*	Columbia 10784
10/14/78	77	5		48 **Ain't Life Hell** ***[w/ Hank Cochran]***	*Hank Cochran*	Capitol 4635
10/21/78	3^{3}	14		49 **All Of Me**	*Gerald Marks/Seymour Simons*	Columbia 10834
10/28/78	67	5		50 **Will You Remember Mine**	*Willie Nelson*	Lone Star 703
11/25/78	86	3		51 **There'll Be No Teardrops Tonight**	*Nelson King/Hank Williams*	United Artists 1254
12/23/78+	12	12		52 **Whiskey River**	*Johnny Bush* **[L]**	Columbia 10877
2/10/79	4	14		53 **Sweet Memories**	*Mickey Newbury*	RCA 11465
4/14/79	15	12		54 **September Song**	*Maxwell Anderson/Kurt Weill*	Columbia 10929
7/7/79	❶^{1}	13		55 **Heartbreak Hotel** ***[w/ Leon Russell]***	*Mae Boren Axton/Thomas Durden/Elvis Presley*	Columbia 11023
8/18/79	16	13		56 **Crazy Arms**	*Ralph Mooney/Chuck Seals*	RCA 11673
11/10/79+	4	14		57 **Help Me Make It Through The Night**	*Kris Kristofferson*	Columbia 11126
1/12/80	❶^{2}	14		58 **My Heroes Have Always Been Cowboys**	*Sharon Vaughn*	Columbia 11186
				from the movie *The Electric Horseman* starring Robert Redford		
2/2/80	20	12		59 **Night Life** ***[w/ Danny Davis & The Nashville Brass]***	*Walt Breeland/Paul Buskirk/Willie Nelson*	RCA 11893
5/3/80	6	15		60 **Midnight Rider**	*Gregg Allman*	Columbia 11257
5/17/80	41	8		61 **Funny How Time Slips Away** ***[w/ Danny Davis]***	*Willie Nelson*	RCA 11999
8/9/80	3^{2}	15		62 **Faded Love** ***[w/ Ray Price]***	*Bob Wills/Johnnie Lee Wills*	Columbia 11329
8/30/80	❶^{1}	16		63 **On The Road Again**	*Willie Nelson*	Columbia 11351
				Grammy: Song / RS500; from the movie *Honeysuckle Rose* starring Nelson		
10/4/80	92	2		64 **Family Bible**	*Walt Breeland/Paul Buskirk/Claude Gray*	Songbird 41313
11/8/80	57	9		65 **A Little Bitty Tear** ***[w/ Hank Cochran]***	*Hank Cochran*	Elektra 47062
12/6/80+	11	14		66 **Don't You Ever Get Tired (Of Hurting Me)** ***[w/ Ray Price]***	*Hank Cochran*	Columbia 11405
1/10/81	❶^{1}	14		67 **Angel Flying Too Close To The Ground**	*Willie Nelson*	Columbia 11418
				from the movie *Honeysuckle Rose* starring Nelson		
2/28/81	65	6		68 **There's A Crazy Man** ***[w/ Jody Payne]***	*Mentor Williams*	Kari 117
4/18/81	11	12		69 **Mona Lisa**	*Ray Evans/Jay Livingston*	Columbia 02000
6/27/81	25	12		70 **Good Times**	*Willie Nelson* **[R]**	RCA 12254
				same version as #12 above		
7/25/81	26	11		71 **I'm Gonna Sit Right Down And Write Myself A Letter**	*Fred Ahlert/Joe Young*	Columbia 02187
10/3/81	23	12		72 **Mountain Dew**	*Bascom Lunsford/Scott Wiseman*	RCA 12328
11/14/81	39	10		73 **Heartaches Of A Fool**	*Walt Breeland/Paul Buskirk/Willie Nelson*	Columbia 02558
3/6/82	❶^{2}	21	▲	74 **Always On My Mind**	*Wayne Carson/Johnny Christopher/Mark James*	Columbia 02741
				Grammy: Song & Male Vocal / CMA: Single		
3/13/82	❶^{2}	18		75 **Just To Satisfy You** ***[w/ Waylon Jennings]***	*Don Bowman/Waylon Jennings*	RCA 13073
6/5/82	19	16		76 **Old Friends** ***[w/ Roger Miller & Ray Price]***	*Roger Miller*	Columbia 02681
8/14/82	2^{2}	17		77 **Let It Be Me**	*Gilbert Becaud/Mann Curtis/Pierre Delanoe*	Columbia 03073

DEBUT	PEAK	WKS	GOLD		ARTIST / Country Chart Hit	Songwriter	Label (& Number)
					NELSON, Willie — cont'd		
10/9/82	72	5		78	**In The Jailhouse Now** *[w/ Webb Pierce]*	*Jimmie Rodgers*	Columbia 03231
10/23/82	13	15		79	**(Sittin' On) The Dock Of The Bay** *[w/ Waylon Jennings]*	*Steve Cropper/Otis Redding*	RCA 13319
12/4/82+	2^{2}	20		80	**Last Thing I Needed First Thing This Morning**	*Donna Farar/Gary Nunn*	Columbia 03385
12/11/82+	7	20		81	**Everything's Beautiful (In It's Own Way)** *[w/ Dolly Parton]*	*Dolly Parton*	Monument 03408
1/15/83	6	18		82	**Reasons To Quit** *[w/ Merle Haggard]*	*Merle Haggard*	Epic 03494
3/12/83	10	16		83	**Little Old Fashioned Karma**	*Willie Nelson*	Columbia 03674
4/9/83	43	9		84	**You're Gonna Love Yourself (In The Morning)** *[w/ Brenda Lee]*	*Donnie Fritts*	Monument 03781
4/30/83	❶^{1}	21		85	**Pancho And Lefty** *[w/ Merle Haggard]*	*Townes Van Zandt*	Epic 03842
6/18/83	3^{1}	21		86	**Why Do I Have To Choose**	*Willie Nelson*	Columbia 03965
10/8/83	8	19		87	**Take It To The Limit** *[w/ Waylon Jennings]*	*Don Henley/Randy Meisner*	Columbia 04131
12/24/83+	11	16		88	**Without A Song**	*Ed Eliscu/Billy Rose/Vince Youmans*	Columbia 04263
3/10/84	❶^{2}	20	▲	89	**To All The Girls I've Loved Before** *[w/ Julio Iglesias]*	*Hal David/Albert Hammond*	Columbia 04217
8/18/84	❶^{1}	25		90	**City Of New Orleans** **Grammy: Song**	A:❶^{2} / S:❶^{1} *Steve Goodman*	Columbia 04568
10/27/84	91	2		91	**Wabash Cannonball** *[w/ Hank Wilson]*	*Leon Russell*	Paradise 629
11/3/84	46	11		92	**How Do You Feel About Foolin' Around** *[w/ Kris Kristofferson]*	*Steve Bruton/Kris Kristofferson/Michael Utley*	Columbia 04652
12/15/84+	❶^{1}	27		93	**Seven Spanish Angels** *[w/ Ray Charles]*	S:❶^{1} / A:❶^{1} *Troy Seals/Eddie Setser*	Columbia 04715
4/13/85	❶^{1}	22		94	**Forgiving You Was Easy**	S:❶^{1} / A:❶^{1} *Willie Nelson*	Columbia 04847
5/18/85	❶^{1}	20		95	**Highwayman** *[w/ Waylon Jennings/JohnnyCash/Kristofferson]* **Grammy: Song**	S:❶^{1} / A:❶^{1} *Jimmy Webb*	Columbia 04881
9/14/85	14	19		96	**Me And Paul** new version of #20 above	A:11 / S:14 *Willie Nelson* **[R]**	Columbia 05597
9/14/85	15	18		97	**Desperados Waiting For A Train** *[w/ Waylon Jennings/Johnny Cash/Kris Kristofferson]*	S:15 / A:16 *Guy Clark*	Columbia 05594
3/29/86	❶^{1}	20		98	**Living In The Promiseland**	A:❶^{1} / S:2 *David Lynn Jones*	Columbia 05834
8/2/86	56	8		99	**I've Already Cheated On You** *[w/ David Allan Coe]*	S:29 *David Allan Coe/Willie Nelson*	Columbia 06227
8/9/86	21	17		100	**I'm Not Trying To Forget You**	A:21 / S:28 *Willie Nelson*	Columbia 06246
10/11/86	❶^{2}	19		101	**Mind Your Own Business** *[w/ Hank Williams, Jr./Reba McEntire/Tom Petty/Reverend Ike]*	S:❶^{2} / A:❶^{2} *Hank Williams*	Warner/Curb 28581
12/6/86+	24	13		102	**Partners After All**	S:17 / A:24 *Bobby Emmons/Chips Moman*	Columbia 06530
3/21/87	44	11		103	**Heart Of Gold**	*Neil Young*	Columbia 07007
7/11/87	27	12		104	**Island In The Sea**	S:20 *Willie Nelson*	Columbia 07202
9/19/87	58	5		105	**If I Could Only Fly** *[w/ Merle Haggard]*	*Waylon Jennings*	Epic 07400
1/9/88	82	3		106	**Nobody There But Me**	*Charles Hayden/Bruce Hornsby/John Hornsby*	Columbia 07636
9/17/88	8	19		107	**Spanish Eyes** *[w/ Julio Iglesias]*	S:2 *Bert Kaempfert/Charles Singleton/Eddie Snyder*	Columbia 08066
1/21/89	41	8		108	**Twilight Time**	*Al Nevins/Morty Nevins/Buck Ram*	Columbia 08541
6/10/89	❶^{1}	21		109	**Nothing I Can Do About It Now**	*Beth Nielsen Chapman*	Columbia 68923
10/7/89+	8	26		110	**There You Are**	*Kye Fleming/Mike Reid*	Columbia 73015
2/24/90	52	13		111	**The Highway** from the album *A Horse Called Music* on Columbia 45046	*Tommy Conners/Richard Wesley*	Columbia
3/3/90	25	14		112	**Silver Stallion** *[w/ Waylon Jennings/Johnny Cash/Kris Kristofferson]* from their album *Highwayman 2* on Columbia 45240	*Lee Clayton*	Columbia
9/29/90	17	20		113	**Ain't Necessarily So**	*Beth Nielsen Chapman*	Columbia
1/19/91	70	3		114	**The Piper Came Today**	*Chester Lester*	Columbia
3/16/91	45	12		115	**Ten With A Two** above 3 from the album *Born For Trouble* on Columbia 45492	*Jack Mack/Bill Nosworthy/Bo Roberts/Mack Vickery*	Columbia
6/15/91	51	10		116	**If I Can Find A Clean Shirt** *[w/ Waylon Jennings]* from their album *Clean Shirt* on Epic 47462	*Waylon Jennings/Troy Seals*	Epic
6/26/93	70	1		117	**Graceland** from the album *Across The Borderline* on Columbia 52752	*Paul Simon*	Columbia
1/26/02	22	20		118	**Mendocino County Line** *[w/ Lee Ann Womack]* **Grammy: Vocal Collaboration / CMA: Vocal Event**	*Matt Serletic/Bernie Taupin*	Lost Highway
7/13/02	41	12		119	**Maria (Shut Up And Kiss Me)** above 2 from the album *Stars & Guitars* on Lost Highway 170340	*Rob Thomas*	Lost Highway
8/3/02+	❶^{6}	39		120	**Beer For My Horses** *[w/ Toby Keith]* from Keith's album *Unleashed* on DreamWorks 540254	*Scotty Emerick/Toby Keith*	DreamWorks
1/3/04	50	2		121	**Please Come Home For Christmas** from the various artists album *A Very Special Acoustic Christmas* on Lost Highway 001038	*Charles Brown/Gene Redd* **[X]**	Lost Highway
1/10/04	45	1		122	**Pretty Paper** *[w/ Kenny Chesney]* from Chesney's album *All I Want For Christmas Is A Real Good Tan* on BNA 51808	*Willie Nelson* **[X]**	BNA

Billboard DEBUT	PEAK	WKS	GOLD	ARTIST / Country Chart Hit	Ranking / Songwriter	Label (& Number)

NELSON, Willie — cont'd

Please Come Home For Christmas ['04]
Pretty Paper ['04]
Reasons To Quit ['83]
Remember Me ['76]
San Antonio ['67]
September Song ['79]
Seven Spanish Angels ['85]
She's Not For You ['65]
Shotgun Willie ['73]
Silver Stallion ['90]
Sister's Coming Home ['74]
(Sittin' On) The Dock Of The Bay ['82]
Something To Brag About ['78]
Spanish Eyes ['88]
Stay All Night (Stay A Little Longer) ['73]
Sweet Memories ['79]
Take It To The Limit ['83]
Ten With A Two ['91]
There You Are ['90]
There'll Be No Teardrops Tonight ['78]
There's A Crazy Man ['81]
To All The Girls I've Loved Before ['84]
Touch Me ['62]
Twilight Time ['89]
Uncloudy Day ['77]
Wabash Cannonball ['84]
Whiskey River ['79]
Why Do I Have To Choose ['83]
Will You Remember Mine ['78]
Willingly ['62]
Without A Song ['84]
Words Don't Fit The Picture ['72]
Yesterday's Wine ['71]
You Are My Sunshine ['77]
You Ought To Hear Me Cry ['77]
You Took My Happy Away ['64]
You're Gonna Love Yourself (In The Morning) ['83]

NESBITT, Jim

Born on 12/1/1931 in Bishopville, South Carolina. Novelty singer/songwriter. Known as "The 'Lasses Sopper."

DEBUT	PEAK	WKS	#	Country Chart Hit	Songwriter	Label (& Number)
4/3/61	**11**	7	1	**Please Mr. Kennedy**	*Jim Nesbitt* [N]	Dot 16197
2/2/63	**28**	1	2	**Livin' Offa Credit**	*Jim Nesbitt* [N]	Dot 16424
3/21/64	**7**	24	3	**Looking For More In '64**	*Bill Moore* [N]	Chart 1065
9/26/64	**20**	13	4	**Mother-In-Law**	*Linda Casper* [N]	Chart 1100
1/30/65	**15**	13	5	**A Tiger In My Tank**	*Jim Nesbitt* [N]	Chart 1165
6/26/65	**34**	6	6	**Still Alive In '65**	*Jim Nesbitt* [N]	Chart 1200
8/14/65	**21**	11	7	**The Friendly Undertaker**	*Jim Nesbitt* [N]	Chart 1240
1/1/66	**49**	2	8	**You Better Watch Your Friends**	*Jim Nesbitt* [N]	Chart 1290
8/27/66	**38**	9	9	**Heck Of A Fix In 66**	*Jim Nesbitt* [N]	Chart 1350
12/17/66+	**60**	8	10	**Stranded**	*Jim Nesbitt* [N]	Chart 1410
6/10/67	**74**	2	11	**Husbands-In-Law**	*Jim Nesbitt* [N]	Chart 1445
3/16/68	**63**	7	12	**Truck Drivin' Cat With Nine Wives**	*Jim Nesbitt* [N]	Chart 1018
2/28/70	**20**	12	13	**Runnin' Bare**	*Jim Nesbitt* [N]	Chart 5052

NESLER, Mark

Born on 1/5/1961 in Beaumont, Texas. Male singer/songwriter/guitarist.

DEBUT	PEAK	WKS	#	Country Chart Hit	Songwriter	Label (& Number)
6/6/98	**47**	15	1	**Used To The Pain**	*Tony Martin/Mark Nesler*	Asylum
10/3/98+	**46**	19	2	**Slow Down**	*Tony Martin/Mark Nesler*	Asylum
3/13/99	**62**	5	3	**Baby Ain't Rocking Me Right**	*Tony Martin/Mark Nesler*	Asylum
				above 3 from the album *I'm Just That Way* on Asylum 62223		

NETTLES, Bill, and his Dixie Blue Boys

Born on 3/13/1903 in Natchitoches, Louisiana. Died of a heart attack on 4/5/1967 (age 64). Male singer/songwriter.

DEBUT	PEAK	WKS	#	Country Chart Hit	Songwriter	Label (& Number)
6/25/49	**9**	6		**Hadacol Boogie**	J:9 *Bill Nettles*	Mercury 6190

NEVILLE, Aaron

Born on 1/24/1941 in New Orleans, Louisiana. Black singer. Member of The Neville Brothers.

DEBUT	PEAK	WKS	#	Country Chart Hit	Songwriter	Label (& Number)
7/31/93	**38**	20	1	**The Grand Tour**	*George Richey/Carmol Taylor/Norro Wilson*	A&M
				from the album *The Grand Tour* on A&M 540086		
6/4/94	**72**	2	2	**I Fall To Pieces** ***[w/ Trisha Yearwood]***	*Hank Cochran/Harlan Howard*	MCA
				Grammy: Vocal Collaboration; from the various artists album *Rhythm Country & Blues* on MCA 10965		

NEWBURY, Mickey

Born Milton Newbury on 5/19/1940 in Houston, Texas. Died on 9/28/2002 (age 62). Male singer/songwriter.

DEBUT	PEAK	WKS	#	Country Chart Hit	Songwriter	Label (& Number)
6/23/73	**53**	8	1	**Sunshine**	*Mickey Newbury*	Elektra 45853
2/5/77	**94**	3	2	**Hand Me Another Of Those**	*Mickey Newbury*	ABC/Hickory 54006
4/8/78	**94**	3	3	**Gone To Alabama**	*Mickey Newbury*	ABC/Hickory 54025
3/24/79	**82**	4	4	**Looking For The Sunshine**	*Mickey Newbury*	ABC/Hickory 54042
6/16/79	**81**	4	5	**Blue Sky Shinin'**	*Mickey Newbury*	MCA/Hickory 41032
2/9/80	**82**	3	6	**America The Beautiful**	*Katherine Lee Bates*	Hickory 1673
10/15/88	**93**	2	7	**An American Trilogy**	*Mickey Newbury*	Airborne 10005

NEW GRASS REVIVAL

Group of session musicians: John Cowan (vocals, bass; born on 8/24/1952), Sam Bush (fiddle, mandolin; born on 4/15/1952), Pat Flynn (guitar; born on 5/17/1952) and Béla Fleck (banjo; born on 7/10/1959). Cowan was later a member of **The Sky Kings**.

DEBUT	PEAK	WKS	#	Country Chart Hit	Songwriter	Label (& Number)
7/5/86	**78**	5	1	**What You Do To Me**	*Johanna Hall/John Hall*	EMI America 8329
9/20/86	**53**	8	2	**Ain't That Peculiar**	*Warren Moore/Smokey Robinson/R. Rogers/Marvin Tarplin*	EMI America 8347
10/3/87	**44**	9	3	**Unconditional Love**	*Roger Cook/Gary Nicholson*	Capitol 44078
3/5/88	**45**	11	4	**Can't Stop Now**	*Gary Nicholson/Wendy Waldman*	Capitol 44128
5/27/89	**37**	13	5	**Callin' Baton Rouge**	*Dennis Linde*	Capitol 44357
10/7/89	**58**	9	6	**You Plant Your Fields**	*Donny Lowery/Wendy Waldman*	Capitol 44453

NEWMAN, Jack

Born in San Antonio, Texas. Male singer/songwriter/guitarist.

DEBUT	PEAK	WKS	#	Country Chart Hit	Songwriter	Label (& Number)
8/24/59	**24**	1		**House Of Blue Lovers**	*Jack Newman*	TNT 170

NEWMAN, Jimmy — 1950s: #23 / 1960s: #35 / All-Time: #140

Born Jimmy Yves Newman on 8/27/1927 in High Point, Louisiana. Male singer/songwriter/guitarist. Regular on the *Louisiana Hayride*. The "C" in his stage name stands for Cajun.

OPRY: 1956

DEBUT	PEAK	WKS	#	Country Chart Hit	Songwriter	Label (& Number)
5/22/54	**4**	11	1	**Cry, Cry, Darling**	A:4 / J:8 / S:9 *Joe Miller/Jimmy Newman*	Dot 1195
3/26/55	**7**	7	2	**Daydreamin'**	J:7 / A:9 / S:13 *Bill Cantrell/Quinton Claunch/Bud Deckelman*	Dot 1237

DEBUT	PEAK	WKS	GOLD	ARTIST / Country Chart Hit	Ranking / Songwriter	Label (& Number)
				NEWMAN, Jimmy — cont'd		
7/9/55	7	10		3 **Blue Darlin'**	A:7 / J:8 / S:13 *Lessie Lyles*	Dot 1260
12/17/55+	9	2		4 **God Was So Good**	A:9 *Georgia Miller*	Dot 1270
4/7/56	9	6		5 **Seasons Of My Heart**	J:9 / A:10 *Darrell Edwards/George Jones*	Dot 1278
7/7/56	13	4		6 **Come Back To Me**	A:13 *Jimmy Newman*	Dot 1283
5/20/57	2[2]	21		7 **A Fallen Star**	A:2 / S:4 / J:9 *James Joiner*	Dot 1289
11/3/58+	7	16		8 **You're Makin' A Fool Out Of Me**	*Tompall Glaser*	MGM 12707
4/13/59	19	4		9 **So Soon**	*Mel Tillis/Wayne Walker*	MGM 12749
6/22/59	30	1		10 **Lonely Girl**	*Roger Miller*	MGM 12790
7/27/59	9	13		11 **Grin And Bear It**	*John D. Loudermilk/Marijohn Wilkin*	MGM 12812
11/2/59	29	1		12 **Walkin' Down The Road**	*John D. Loudermilk*	MGM 12830
3/7/60	21	7		13 **I Miss You Already**	*Marvin Rainwater/Faron Young*	MGM 12864
6/20/60	6	14		14 **A Lovely Work Of Art**	*James Joiner*	MGM 12894
11/7/60	11	18		15 **Wanting You With Me Tonight**	*Roye Lee*	MGM 12945
4/17/61	14	8		16 **Everybody's Dying For Love**	*Marijohn Wilkin*	Decca 31217
12/25/61+	22	2		17 **Alligator Man**	*Floyd Chance/Jimmy Newman*	Decca 31324
12/22/62+	12	9		18 **Bayou Talk**	*Jimmy Newman*	Decca 31440
12/14/63+	9	19		19 **D.J. For A Day**	*Tom T. Hall*	Decca 31553
5/16/64	34	3		20 **Angel On Leave /**	*Jimmy Key*	
5/30/64	34	3		21 **Summer Skies And Golden Sands**	*Peter Bartholomew/Paul Friswell/Laurie Mason*	Decca 31609
				JIMMY "C" NEWMAN (above 4)		
4/10/65	37	7		22 **City Of The Angels /**	*Tom T. Hall/Jimmy Newman*	
4/24/65	13	16		23 **Back In Circulation**	*Tom T. Hall*	Decca 31745
9/25/65	8	21		24 **Artificial Rose**	*Tom T. Hall*	Decca 31841
3/26/66	10	16		25 **Back Pocket Money**	*Tom T. Hall*	Decca 31916
10/8/66	25	8		26 **Bring Your Heart Home**	*Tom T. Hall*	Decca 31994
1/14/67	32	11		27 **Dropping Out Of Sight**	*Tom T. Hall*	Decca 32067
5/27/67	24	12		28 **Louisiana Saturday Night**	*Tom T. Hall/Jimmy Newman*	Decca 32130
10/28/67+	11	17		29 **Blue Lonely Winter**	*Roy Baham/Jimmy Newman*	Decca 32202
4/13/68	47	8		30 **Sunshine And Bluebirds**	*Roy Baham/Jimmy Newman*	Decca 32285
8/31/68	20	13		31 **Born To Love You**	*Cindy Walker*	Decca 32366
5/31/69	31	8		32 **Boo Dan**	*Tom T. Hall*	Decca 32484
11/28/70	65	6		33 **I'm Holding Your Memory (But He's Holding You)**	*Carl Belew/Van Givens*	Decca 32740

NEWMAN, Randy

Born on 11/28/1943 in New Orleans, Louisiana. Male singer/songwriter/pianist.

DEBUT	PEAK	WKS	GOLD	Country Chart Hit	Songwriter	Label (& Number)
8/19/78	78	4		**Rider In The Rain**	*Randy Newman*	Warner 8630

NEWMAN, Terri Sue

Born in 1954 in Levelland, Texas. Female singer/pianist/guitarist.

DEBUT	PEAK	WKS	GOLD	Country Chart Hit	Songwriter	Label (& Number)
1/13/79	43	10		**Gypsy Eyes**	*Eugene Smith*	Texas Soul 71378

NEWSONG

Christian pop group formed in Kennesaw, Georgia: Eddie Carswell (vocals), Billy Goodwin (guitar), Leonard Ahlstrom (guitar), Scotty Wilbanks (sax, keyboards), Mark Clay (bass) and Jack Pumphrey (drums).

DEBUT	PEAK	WKS	GOLD	Country Chart Hit	Songwriter	Label (& Number)
12/16/00+	31	5		**The Christmas Shoes** — from the album *Sheltering Tree* on Benson 83327	*Leonard Ahlstrom/Eddie Carswell* [X]	Benson

NEWTON, Juice — All-Time: #171

Born Judy Kay Newton on 2/18/1952 in Lakehurst, New Jersey; raised in Virginia Beach. Female singer/guitarist. Formed group Dixie Peach, which later evolved into Silver Spur. Eventually adopted "Juice" as her legal name.

DEBUT	PEAK	WKS	GOLD	Country Chart Hit	Songwriter	Label (& Number)
2/21/76	88	6		1 **Love Is A Word** *[w/ Silver Spur]*	*Otha Young*	RCA Victor 10538
2/10/79	37	9		2 **Let's Keep It That Way**	*Curly Putnam/Rafe Van Hoy*	Capitol 4679
5/26/79	80	4		3 **Lay Back In The Arms Of Someone**	*Mike Chapman/Nicky Chinn*	Capitol 4714
9/15/79	81	4		4 **Any Way That You Want Me**	*Chip Taylor*	Capitol 4768
11/10/79	42	8		5 **Until Tonight**	*Steve McClintock/Kathleen Parker*	Capitol 4793
2/2/80	35	10		6 **Sunshine**	*Jonathan Edwards*	Capitol 4818
4/26/80	41	10		7 **You Fill My Life**	*Otha Young*	Capitol 4856
3/7/81	22	11	●	8 **Angel Of The Morning**	*Chip Taylor*	Capitol 4976
6/13/81	14	16	●	9 **Queen Of Hearts**	*Hank DeVito*	Capitol 4997
10/24/81+	❶[1]	19		10 **The Sweetest Thing (I've Ever Known)**	*Otha Young*	Capitol 5046
5/22/82	30	10		11 **Love's Been A Little Bit Hard On Me**	*Gary Burr*	Capitol 5120
8/28/82	2[2]	19		12 **Break It To Me Gently** — Grammy: Female Vocal	*Diane Lampert/Joe Seneca*	Capitol 5148
12/11/82+	53	11		13 **Heart Of The Night**	*John Bettis/Michael Clark*	Capitol 5192
9/3/83	45	13		14 **Stranger At My Door**	*Charlie Black/Rory Bourke/Kerry Chater*	Capitol 5265
6/23/84	64	9		15 **A Little Love**	*Danny Douma/Richard Feldman/Todd Sharp*	RCA 13823
8/18/84	32	13		16 **Ride 'Em Cowboy**	*Paul Davis*	Capitol 5379
10/20/84	57	7		17 **Restless Heart**	*Tim DuBois/Dave Robbins/Van Stephenson*	RCA 13907

DEBUT	PEAK	WKS	GOLD	ARTIST / Country Chart Hit	Ranking / Songwriter	Label (& Number)
				NEWTON, Juice — cont'd		
7/20/85	❶^{1}	22		18 **You Make Me Want To Make You Mine**	S:❶^{1} / A:❶^{1} *Dave Loggins*	RCA 14139
11/9/85+	❶^{1}	24		19 **Hurt**	S:❶^{1} / A:❶^{1} *Jimmie Crane/Al Jacobs*	RCA 14199
4/5/86	**5**	21		20 **Old Flame**	A:3 / S:5 *Reed Nielsen*	RCA 14295
7/12/86	❶^{1}	20		21 **Both To Each Other** (Friends & Lovers) *[w/ Eddie Rabbitt]*	S:❶^{1} / A:❶^{1} *Paul Gordon/Jay Gruska*	RCA 14377
8/23/86	**9**	18		22 **Cheap Love**	S:8 / A:9 *Del Shannon*	RCA 14417
12/13/86+	**9**	20		23 **What Can I Do With My Heart**	A:9 / S:19 *Otha Young*	RCA 5068
7/18/87	**24**	15		24 **First Time Caller**	*Reed Nielsen*	RCA 5170
11/14/87+	**8**	22		25 **Tell Me True**	S:19 *Paul Kennerley/Brent Maher*	RCA 5283
5/6/89	**40**	12		26 **When Love Comes Around The Bend**	*Josh Leo/Pam Tillis/Mark Wright*	RCA 8815
				NEWTON, Wayne Born on 4/3/1942 in Roanoke, Virginia. Male singer/multi-instrumentalist.		
7/15/72	**55**	8	●	1 **Daddy Don't You Walk So Fast**	*Peter Callander/Geoff Stephens*	Chelsea 0100
10/7/89	**63**	5		2 **While The Feeling's Good** *[w/ Tammy Wynette]*	*Roger Bowling/Freddie Hart*	Curb 10559
				NEWTON, Wood Born in Hampton, Arkansas. Male singer/songwriter.		
10/28/78	**52**	7		1 **Last Exit For Love**	*Even Stevens/Dan Tyler*	Elektra 45528
3/3/79	**44**	8		2 **Lock, Stock, & Barrel**	*B,J, Bourgoin/Even Stevens*	Elektra 46013
7/7/79	**81**	4		3 **Julie** (Do I Ever Cross Your Mind?)	*Randy DuBois/Tim DuBois/Wood Newton*	Elektra 46059
				NEWTON-JOHN, Olivia Born on 9/26/1948 in Cambridge, England; raised in Melbourne, Australia. Female singer/actress. Acted in the movies *Grease*, *Xanadu* and *Two Of A Kind*. Also see **One Heart At A Time**. ***CMA: Female Vocalist 1974***	**All-Time: #268**	
8/25/73	**7**	22	●	1 **Let Me Be There** **Grammy: Female Vocal**	*John Rostill*	MCA 40101
4/13/74	**2^{2}**	18	●	2 **If You Love Me** (Let Me Know)	*John Rostill*	MCA 40209
8/24/74	**6**	17	●	3 **I Honestly Love You** also see #16 below	*Peter Allen/Jeff Barry*	MCA 40280
2/1/75	**3^{1}**	14	●	4 **Have You Never Been Mellow**	*John Farrar*	MCA 40349
6/14/75	**5**	15	●	5 **Please Mr. Please**	*John Rostill/Bruce Welch*	MCA 40418
9/27/75	**19**	12		6 **Something Better To Do**	*John Farrar*	MCA 40459
12/6/75+	**5**	12		7 **Let It Shine**	*Linda Hargrove*	MCA 40495
3/13/76	**5**	13		8 **Come On Over**	*Barry Gibb/Robin Gibb*	MCA 40525
8/14/76	**14**	10		9 **Don't Stop Believin'**	*John Farrar*	MCA 40600
10/30/76	**21**	11		10 **Every Face Tells A Story**	*Mike Allison/Don Black/Peter Sills*	MCA 40642
1/29/77	**40**	10		11 **Sam**	*Don Black/John Farrar/Hank Marvin*	MCA 40670
7/22/78	**20**	13	●	12 **Hopelessly Devoted To You** from the movie *Grease* starring Newton-John and John Travolta	*John Farrar*	RSO 903
1/6/79	**94**	3	●	13 **A Little More Love**	*John Farrar*	MCA 40975
5/5/79	**87**	5		14 **Deeper Than The Night**	*Tom Snow/Johnny Vastano*	MCA 41009
8/4/79	**29**	11		15 **Dancin' 'Round And 'Round**	*Adam Mitchell*	MCA 41074
5/30/98	**16^{S}**	17		16 **I Honestly Love You** new version of #3 above	*Peter Allen/Jeff Barry* **[R]**	MCA Nashville
				NEYMAN, June Born in Missouri. Female singer.		
11/11/78	**93**	2		1 **He Ain't Heavy, He's My Brother**	*Bobby Scott*	Starship 101
2/17/79	**97**	3		2 **You're Gonna Miss Me**	*Eddie Curtis*	Starship 110
				NICHOLS, Joe Born on 11/26/1976 in Rogers, Arkansas. Male singer/songwriter. ***CMA: Horizon 2003***	**2000s: #32**	
3/23/02	**3^{3}**	36		1 **The Impossible**	S:❶^{5} *Kelley Lovelace/Lee Miller*	Universal South
11/2/02+	❶^{1}	32		2 **Brokenheartsville**	S:4 *Randy Boudreaux/Clint Daniels/Donny Kees/Blake Mevis*	Universal South
5/3/03	**17**	20		3 **She Only Smokes When She Drinks**	*Connie Harrington/Tony Martin/Tim Nichols*	Universal South
9/27/03+	**18**	25		4 **Cool To Be A Fool** above 4 from the album *Man With A Memory* on Universal South 170285	*Steve Dean/Wil Nance/Joe Nichols*	Universal South
3/27/04	**10**	33		5 **If Nobody Believed In You**	*Harley Allen*	Universal South
11/20/04+	**4**	31		6 **What's A Guy Gotta Do** above 2 from the album *Revelation* on Universal South 002514	*Kelley Lovelace/Joe Nichols/Don Sampson*	Universal South
12/11/04+	**37**	5		7 **Let It Snow! Let It Snow! Let It Snow!**	*Sammy Cahn/Jule Styne* **[X]**	Universal South
1/1/05	**60**	1		8 **The Christmas Song**	*Mel Torme/Robert Wells* **[X]**	Universal South
1/8/05	**56**	1		9 **I'll Be Home For Christmas**	*Kim Gannon/Walter Kent/Buck Ram* **[X]**	Universal South
1/8/05	**57**	1		10 **Have Yourself A Merry Little Christmas** above 4 from the album *A Traditional Christmas* on Universal South 002588	*Ralph Blane/Hugh Martin* **[X]**	Universal South
				NICKEL CREEK Bluegrass trio from Los Angeles, California: brother-and-sister Sean Watkins (guitar) and Sara Watkins (fiddle), with Chris Thile (mandolin).		
6/16/01	**48**	13		1 **When You Come Back Down**	*Tim O'Brien/Danny O'Keefe*	Sugar Hill
3/9/02	**49**	11		2 **The Lighthouse's Tale** above 2 from the album *Nickel Creek* on Sugar Hill 3909	*Adam McKenzie/Chris Thile*	Sugar Hill
8/31/02	**56**	7		3 **This Side** from the album *This Side* on Sugar Hill 3941	*Sean Watkins*	Sugar Hill

Billboard DEBUT	PEAK	WKS	GOLD	ARTIST / Country Chart Hit	Ranking / Songwriter	Label (& Number)

NICKS, Stevie

Born Stephanie Nicks on 5/26/1948 in Phoenix, Arizona; raised in San Francisco, California. Female singer/songwriter. Member of Fleetwood Mac.

DEBUT	PEAK	WKS	GOLD	Country Chart Hit	Songwriter	Label (& Number)
6/19/82	70	5		After The Glitter Fades	*Stevie Nicks*	Modern 7405

NIELSEN, Shaun

Born Sherrill Nielsen. Male singer.

DEBUT	PEAK	WKS	GOLD	Country Chart Hit	Songwriter	Label (& Number)
3/15/80	88	3		Lights Of L.A.	*Jerry McBee*	Adonda 79022

NIELSEN WHITE BAND, The

Group of former rock musicians: Gary Nielsen (of The Trashmen), Jack White (of McKendree Spring), Tom Eckhoff (of the Dillman Band) and Lonnie Knight.

DEBUT	PEAK	WKS	GOLD	Country Chart Hit	Songwriter	Label (& Number)
12/20/86+	67	6		1 Somethin' You Got	*Sonny Lemaire/J.P. Pennington*	Vision 122574
5/2/87	56	7		2 I Got The One I Wanted	*Donny Lowery*	Vision 122575

NIGHTSTREETS

Vocal trio: Rick Taylor, Jerry Taylor and Joyce Hawthorne. Also recorded as **Streets**.

DEBUT	PEAK	WKS	GOLD	Country Chart Hit	Songwriter	Label (& Number)
1/26/80	32	10		1 Love In The Meantime *[Streets]*	*Robert Jones/Jerry Taylor*	Epic 50827
6/14/80	74	5		2 Falling Together	*Max D. Barnes/Robert Jones*	Epic 50886
11/15/80	81	5		3 If I Had It My Way	*Robert Jones/Jerry Taylor*	Epic 50944
3/21/81	72	4		4 (Lookin' At Things) In A Different Light	*Jerry Taylor*	Epic 51004

NILLES, Lynn — see BRODY, Lane

NITTY GRITTY DIRT BAND — 1980s: #42 / All-Time: #128

Country-folk-rock group from Long Beach, California. Led by Jeff Hanna (vocals, guitar; born on 7/11/1947) and **John McEuen** (banjo, mandolin; born on 12/19/1945). Various members included Jimmie Fadden (harmonica; born on 3/9/1948), Jim Ibbotson (guitar; born on 1/21/1947), Al Garth (violin) and Bernie Leadon (guitar; **Eagles**; born on 7/19/1947), who replaced McEuen briefly in early 1987. In the movies *For Singles Only* and *Paint Your Wagon*. Hanna married **Matraca Berg**. Jeff and John's sons recorded as **Hanna-McEuen**.

DEBUT	PEAK	WKS	GOLD	Country Chart Hit	Songwriter	Label (& Number)
11/27/71	56	6		1 I Saw The Light *[w/ Roy Acuff]*	*Hank Williams*	United Artists 50849
8/4/73	97	2		2 Grand Ole Opry Song *[w/ Jimmy Martin]*	*Hylo Brown*	United Artists 247
7/12/75	79	7		3 (All I Have To Do Is) Dream	*Boudleaux Bryant*	United Artists 655
2/9/80	58	9		4 An American Dream *[The Dirt Band]* — **Linda Ronstadt** (harmony vocal)	*Rodney Crowell*	United Artists 1330
8/2/80	77	4		5 Make A Little Magic *[The Dirt Band]* — **Nicolette Larson** (backing vocal)	*Robert Carpenter/Jeff Hanna/Richard Hathaway*	United Artists 1356
6/11/83	19	18		6 Shot Full Of Love	*Bob McDill*	Liberty 1499
10/1/83	9	23		7 Dance Little Jean	*Jim Ibbotson*	Liberty 1507
1/7/84	93	2		8 Colorado Christmas	*Steve Goodman* **[X]**	Liberty 1513
5/26/84	❶^{1}	20		9 Long Hard Road (The Sharecropper's Dream)	*Rodney Crowell*	Warner 29282
9/22/84	3^{2}	24		10 I Love Only You	S:3 / A:3 *Dave Loggins/Don Schlitz*	Warner 29203
1/12/85	2^{2}	20		11 High Horse	S:2 / A:2 *Jim Ibbotson*	Warner 29099
6/8/85	❶^{1}	21		12 Modern Day Romance	S:❶^{1} / A:❶^{1} *Kix Brooks/Dan Tyler*	Warner 29027
10/12/85+	3^{1}	21		13 Home Again In My Heart	S:3 / A:3 *Josh Leo/Wendy Waldman*	Warner 28897
3/1/86	6	19		14 Partners, Brothers And Friends	A:6 / S:7 *Jeff Hanna/Jim Ibbotson*	Warner 28780
6/21/86	5	21		15 Stand A Little Rain	A:5 / S:7 *Donny Lowery/Don Schlitz*	Warner 28690
11/15/86+	7	20		16 Fire In The Sky	A:7 / S:14 *Bob Carpenter/Jeff Hanna*	Warner 28547
3/28/87	2^{1}	17		17 Baby's Got A Hold On Me	S:4 / A:11 *Bob Carpenter/Jeff Hanna/Josh Leo*	Warner 28443
7/11/87	❶^{1}	23		18 Fishin' In The Dark	S:2 *Jim Photoglo/Wendy Waldman*	Warner 28311
11/14/87+	5	22		19 Oh What A Love	S:12 *Jim Ibbotson*	Warner 28173
4/16/88	4	18		20 Workin' Man (Nowhere To Go)	S:9 *Jimmie Fadden*	Warner 27940
9/3/88	2^{1}	22		21 I've Been Lookin'	S:6 *Jeff Hanna/Jim Ibbotson*	Warner 27750
12/24/88+	6	20		22 Down That Road Tonight	*Jeff Hanna/Josh Leo/Wendy Waldman*	Warner 27679
5/13/89	27	15		23 Turn Of The Century	*Fred Knoblock/Dan Tyler*	Universal 66009
5/27/89	14	23		24 And So It Goes *[w/ John Denver]*	*Paul Overstreet/Don Schlitz*	Universal 66008
10/7/89+	10	26		25 When It's Gone	*Jimmie Fadden/Don Schlitz*	Universal 66023
3/3/90	63	6		26 One Step Over The Line *[w/ Rosanne Cash & John Hiatt]* — from Nitty Gritty Dirt Band's album *Will The Circle Be Unbroken Volume II* on Universal 12500	*John Hiatt*	Universal
5/26/90	65	9		27 From Small Things (Big Things One Day Come)	*Bruce Springsteen*	MCA
9/1/90	60	19		28 You Made Life Good Again — above 2 from the album *The Rest Of The Dream* on MCA 6407	*Bob DiPiero/Steve Seskin*	MCA
7/25/92	66	3		29 I Fought The Law	*Sonny Curtis*	Liberty
12/12/92	74	2		30 One Good Love — above 2 from the album *Not Fade Away* on Liberty 98564	*Radney Foster/Jeff Hanna*	Liberty
2/28/98	52	9		31 Bang, Bang, Bang	*Al Anderson/Craig Wiseman*	DreamWorks
6/19/99	63	5		32 Bang, Bang, Bang — above 2 from the album *Bang, Bang, Bang* on DreamWorks 50125	*Al Anderson/Craig Wiseman* **[R]**	DreamWorks

NIX, Tom

Born in Denver, Colorado. Male singer.

DEBUT	PEAK	WKS	GOLD	Country Chart Hit	Songwriter	Label (& Number)
1/10/81	79	4		Home Along The Highway	*Lee Bach*	RMA 6009

NIXON, Nick

Born Hershel Nixon on 3/20/1941 in Poplar Bluff, Missouri. Male singer.

DEBUT	PEAK	WKS	GOLD	Country Chart Hit	Songwriter	Label (& Number)
8/10/74	90	3		1 I'm Turning You Loose	*Curly Putman/Sonny Throckmorton*	Mercury 73467
10/5/74	63	7		2 A Habit I Can't Break	*Gene Price*	Mercury 73506

Billboard DEBUT	PEAK	WKS	GOLD	ARTIST / Ranking / Country Chart Hit	Songwriter	Label (& Number)
				NIXON, Nick — cont'd		
3/8/75	**55**	9		3 **It's Only A Barroom**	*Eddie Rabbitt/Even Stevens*	Mercury 73654
7/12/75	**38**	12		4 **I'm Too Use To Loving You**	*Ben Peters*	Mercury 73691
11/29/75	**64**	10		5 **She's Just An Old Love Turned Memory**	*John Schweers*	Mercury 73726
3/13/76	**28**	13		6 **Rocking In Rosalee's Boat**	*Bob McDill*	Mercury 73772
1/8/77	**83**	5		7 **Neon Lights**	*Larry Ballard*	Mercury 73866
7/2/77	**51**	10		8 **Love Songs And Romance Magazines**	*Byron Wallis*	Mercury 73930
11/5/77+	**34**	13		9 **I'll Get Over You**	*Ben Peters*	Mercury 55010
8/12/78	**87**	4		10 **She's Lying Next To Me**	*Bill Haney*	Mercury 55035
6/2/79	**79**	4		11 **What're We Doing, Doing This Again**	*Bob McDill*	MCA 41030
9/29/79	**86**	4		12 **San Francisco Is A Lonely Town**	*Ben Peters*	MCA 41100
				NOACK, Eddie		
				Born Armona Noack on 4/29/1930 in Houston, Texas. Died of a cerebral hemorrhage on 2/5/1978 (age 47). Male singer/songwriter.		
12/15/58	**14**	2		**Have Blues--Will Travel**	*Eddie Noack/Wayne Walker*	D 1019
				NOBLE, Nick		
				Born Nicholas Valkan on 6/21/1936 in Chicago, Illinois. Male singer/songwriter.		
8/26/78	**40**	10		1 **Stay With Me**	*Lew Douglas/Nick Noble*	Churchill 7713
4/14/79	**36**	10		2 **The Girl On The Other Side**	*Lew Douglas/Nick Noble*	TMS 601
9/22/79	**72**	5		3 **I Wanna Go Back**	*Phil Coulter/Bill Martin*	TMS 612
2/9/80	**35**	10		4 **Big Man's Cafe**	*Lew Douglas/Nick Noble*	Churchill 7755
				NOEL		
				Born Noel Haughey in Salina, California. Female singer/songwriter.		
12/25/82	**90**	3		1 **One Tear (At A Time)**	*Noel Haughey*	Deep South 706
10/5/85	**86**	3		2 **P.S.**	*Noel Haughey*	Madd Cash 1045
				NOLEN, Gabbie		
				Born on 7/7/1982 in La Grange, Texas. Female singer.		
4/6/02	**45**	7		**Almost There** S:❶[1]	*Jason Greene/Dick Kaiser/Les Rawlins*	Republic
				NORMA JEAN — **1960s: #45 / All-Time: #259**		
				Born Norma Jean Beasler on 1/30/1938 in Wellston, Oklahoma. Female singer/guitarist. Regular on **Porter Wagoner**'s TV series from 1960-67. Also see **Some Of Chet's Friends**.		
				OPRY: 1965		
1/4/64	**11**	19		1 **Let's Go All The Way** (also see #22 below)	*Dusty Rose*	RCA Victor 8261
5/30/64	**32**	11		2 **I'm A Walkin' Advertisement (For The Blues)** /	*Cy Coben*	
6/20/64	**25**	16		3 **Put Your Arms Around Her**	*Bob Morris*	RCA Victor 8328
10/10/64	**8**	22		4 **Go Cat Go**	*Harlan Howard*	RCA Victor 8433
4/10/65	**21**	8		5 **I Cried All The Way To The Bank**	*Liz Anderson*	RCA Victor 8518
7/31/65	**8**	14		6 **I Wouldn't Buy A Used Car From Him**	*Harlan Howard*	RCA Victor 8623
2/19/66	**41**	3		7 **You're Driving Me Out Of My Mind** /	*Gayle Smith*	
3/5/66	**48**	1		8 **Then Go Home To Her**	*Hank Cochran/Jeannie Seely*	RCA Victor 8720
4/16/66	**28**	8		9 **The Shirt**	*Bill Anderson/George Bailey/Mel Strickland*	RCA Victor 8790
8/13/66	**28**	11		10 **Pursuing Happiness**	*Harlan Howard*	RCA Victor 8887
10/15/66	**5**	17		11 **The Game Of Triangles** *[w/ Bobby Bare & Liz Anderson]*	*Cy Coben*	RCA Victor 8963
11/19/66+	**24**	13		12 **Don't Let That Doorknob Hit You**	*Vic McAlpin*	RCA Victor 8989
4/1/67	**48**	10		13 **Conscience Keep An Eye On Me**	*Glen Goza/Jack Rhodes*	RCA Victor 9147
8/19/67	**38**	10		14 **Jackson Ain't A Very Big Town**	*Vic McAlpin*	RCA Victor 9258
11/18/67+	**18**	14		15 **Heaven Help The Working Girl**	*Harlan Howard*	RCA Victor 9362
3/30/68	**53**	6		16 **Truck Driving Woman**	*Roland Pike/Johnny Wilson*	RCA Victor 9466
7/20/68	**35**	10		17 **You Changed Everything About Me But My Name**	*Hank Cochran/Jeanne Seely*	RCA Victor 9558
11/30/68	**61**	5		18 **One Man Band**	*Rayburn Anthony/Tony Austin/Gene Dobbins*	RCA Victor 9645
4/12/69	**44**	8		19 **Dusty Road**	*Larry Brinkley/Dave Kirby/Vic McAlpin/Howard White*	RCA Victor 0115
10/10/70	**48**	9		20 **Whiskey-Six Years Old**	*Glenn Martin/Johnny Slate*	RCA Victor 9900
1/30/71	**42**	9		21 **The Kind Of Needin' I Need**	*Bill Anderson*	RCA Victor 9946
2/6/82	**68**	6		22 **Let's Go All The Way** *[w/ Claude Gray]* (new version of #1 above)	*Dusty Rose* **[R]**	Granny White 10009
				NORMAN, Jim		
				Born in Texas. Male singer.		
11/18/78	**98**	2		**The Love In Me**	*Rick Klang*	Republic 030
				NORWOOD, Daron		
				Born on 9/30/1965 in Lubbock, Texas; raised in Tahoka, Texas. Male singer/pianist.		
11/27/93+	**26**	20		1 **If It Wasn't For Her I Wouldn't Have You**	*Terry Skinner/J.L. Wallace*	Giant
4/16/94	**24**	19		2 **Cowboys Don't Cry**	*Jim Allison/Doug Gilmore/Jeff Raymond/Bob Simon*	Giant
8/6/94	**48**	9		3 **If I Ever Love Again** (above 3 from the album *Daron Norwood* on Giant 24527)	*Bill Spencer/Curtis Wright*	Giant
1/7/95	**75**	1		4 **The Working Elf Blues** (parody of "Workin' Man Blues" by **Merle Haggard**; from the various artists album *Giant Country Christmas Volume 1* on Giant 24573)	*Ken Forsythe/Tim Johnson/Jim Moran* **[X]**	Giant
2/4/95	**50**	9		5 **Bad Dog, No Biscuit**	*Rick Ferrell/Billy Kitchens*	Giant
6/3/95	**58**	9		6 **My Girl Friday** (above 2 from the album *Ready, Willing And Able* on Giant 24610)	*Carl Jackson/Curtis Wright*	Giant

Billboard DEBUT	PEAK	WKS	GOLD	ARTIST / Country Chart Hit	Ranking / Songwriter	Label (& Number)

NOTORIOUS CHERRY BOMBS, The

All-star group: **Rodney Crowell** (vocals, guitar), **Vince Gill** (vocals, banjo), Richard Bennett (guitar), Hank DeVito (steel guitar), Tony Brown (piano), John Hobbs (organ), Michael Rhodes (bass) and Eddie Bayers (drums).

DEBUT	PEAK	WKS	GOLD	Country Chart Hit	Songwriter	Label (& Number)
7/24/04	47	7		**It's Hard To Kiss The Lips At Night That Chew Your Ass Out All Day Long** from the album *The Notorious Cherry Bombs* on Universal South 002530	*...Rodney Crowell/Vince Gill*	Universal South

***NSYNC**

Male teen vocal group formed in Orlando, Florida: Chris Kirkpatrick, Josh ("JC") Chasez, Joey Fatone, Justin Timberlake and Lance Bass. Timberlake and Chasez were regulars on TV's *The Mickey Mouse Club*. Fatone appeared in the 2002 movie *My Big Fat Greek Wedding*.

DEBUT	PEAK	WKS	GOLD	Country Chart Hit	Songwriter	Label (& Number)
5/1/99	3[3]	23		**God Must Have Spent A Little More Time On You** *[w/ Alabama]*...S:3 from Alabama's album *Twentieth Century* on RCA 67793	*Evan Rogers/Carl Sturken*	RCA

NUNLEY, Bill

Born in Virginia. Male singer.

DEBUT	PEAK	WKS	GOLD	Country Chart Hit	Songwriter	Label (& Number)
4/2/88	74	3		1 **I'll Know The Good Times** COUNTRY BILL NUNLEY	*Sonny Bailey/Danny Morrison/Todd Morrison*	Cannery 0402
8/27/88	98	2		2 **The Way You Got Over Me**	*Michael John*	Cannery 0525

NUNN, Earl, and His Alabama Ramblers Featuring Billy Lee

Born in Alabama. Male singer.

DEBUT	PEAK	WKS	GOLD	Country Chart Hit	Songwriter	Label (& Number)
4/9/49	13	1		**Double Talkin' Woman** ...J:13	*Jim Suhler*	Specialty 701

NUTTER, Mayf

Born Mayfred Nutter Adamson on 10/19/1941 in Jane Lew, West Virginia. Male singer/songwriter/guitarist.

DEBUT	PEAK	WKS	GOLD	Country Chart Hit	Songwriter	Label (& Number)
2/14/70	65	5		1 **Hey There Johnny** *[w/ Hugh Jarrett Singers]*	*John Capps/Albertus Johnson*	Reprise 0882
10/16/71	57	6		2 **Never Ending Song Of Love**	*Delaney Bramlett*	Capitol 3181
12/18/71+	58	7		3 **Never Had A Doubt**	*Mayf Nutter*	Capitol 3226
4/15/72	59	7		4 **The Sing-Along Song**	*Mayf Nutter*	Capitol 3296
10/27/73	78	10		5 **Green Door**	*Bob Davis/Marvin Moore*	Capitol 3734
5/8/76	87	5		6 **Sweet Southern Lovin'**	*Kenny Walker*	GNP Crescendo 805
1/15/77	99	2		7 **Goin' Skinny Dippin'**	*Mayf Nutter* **[N]**	GNP Crescendo 809

O

OAK RIDGE BOYS — **1980s: #7 / All-Time: #53**

Vocal group formed in Oak Ridge, Tennessee: Duane Allen (lead; born on 4/29/1943), **Joe Bonsall** (tenor; born on 5/18/1948), **William Lee Golden** (baritone; born on 1/12/1939) and Richard Sterban (bass; born on 4/24/1943). All had previously sung in gospel groups. Steve Sanders (born on 9/17/1952) replaced Golden from 1987 until Golden returned in 1996. Sanders died of a self-inflicted gunshot wound on 6/10/1998 (age 45).

CMA: Vocal Group 1978

DEBUT	PEAK	WKS	GOLD	Country Chart Hit	Songwriter	Label (& Number)
8/4/73	57	7		1 **Praise The Lord And Pass The Soup** *[w/ Johnny Cash & The Carter Family]*	*...Albert Hammond/Mike Hazlewood*	Columbia 45890
6/26/76	83	5		2 **Family Reunion**	*David Allan Coe*	Columbia 10349
7/16/77	3[1]	18		3 **Y'All Come Back Saloon**	*Sharon Vaughn*	ABC/Dot 17710
12/3/77+	2[2]	16		4 **You're The One**	*Bob Morrison*	ABC/Dot 17732
4/15/78	❶[1]	15		5 **I'll Be True To You**	*Alan Rhody*	ABC 12350
9/2/78	3[1]	13		6 **Cryin' Again**	*Don Cook/Rafe Van Hoy*	ABC 12397
12/9/78+	3[2]	15		7 **Come On In**	*Michael Clark*	ABC 12434
4/7/79	2[2]	13		8 **Sail Away**	*Rafe Van Hoy*	MCA 12463
6/23/79	94	1		9 **Rhythm Guitar** recorded in 1975	*T.A. Hill*	Columbia 11009
8/18/79	7	13		10 **Dream On**	*Dennis Lambert/Brian Potter*	MCA 41078
12/1/79+	❶[1]	15		11 **Leaving Louisiana In The Broad Daylight**	*Donivan Cowart/Rodney Crowell*	MCA 41154
4/19/80	❶[1]	15		12 **Trying To Love Two Women**	*Sonny Throckmorton*	MCA 41217
7/19/80	3[1]	16		13 **Heart Of Mine**	*Michael Foster*	MCA 41280
11/15/80+	3[2]	17		14 **Beautiful You**	*Dave Hanner*	MCA 51022
4/4/81	❶[1]	14	▲	15 **Elvira** Grammy: Vocal Group / CMA: Single	*Dallas Frazier*	MCA 51084
9/5/81	❶[1]	15		16 **Fancy Free**	*Dan August/Jimbeau Hinson*	MCA 51169
1/23/82	❶[1]	15		17 **Bobbie Sue**	*Wood Newton/Adell Tyler/Dan Tyler*	MCA 51231
6/5/82	22	10		18 **So Fine**	*Johnny Otis*	MCA 52065
7/31/82	2[2]	19		19 **I Wish You Could Have Turned My Head (And Left My Heart Alone)**	*Sonny Throckmorton*	MCA 52095
11/20/82+	3[2]	16		20 **Thank God For Kids**	*Eddy Raven* **[X]**	MCA 52145
2/26/83	❶[1]	16		21 **American Made**	*Bob DiPiero/Pat McManus*	MCA 52179
6/4/83	❶[1]	18		22 **Love Song**	*Steve Runkle*	MCA 52224
10/22/83+	5	19		23 **Ozark Mountain Jubilee**	*Scott Anders/Roger Murrah*	MCA 52288
2/25/84	❶[1]	22		24 **I Guess It Never Hurts To Hurt Sometimes**	*Randy Vanwarmer*	MCA 52342
7/14/84	❶[1]	21		25 **Everyday** S:27	*Dave Loggins/J.D. Martin*	MCA 52419
11/10/84+	❶[1]	21		26 **Make My Life With You** S:❶[1] / A:❶[1]	*Gary Burr*	MCA 52488
3/30/85	❶[1]	20		27 **Little Things** S:❶[1] / A:❶[1]	*Billy Barber*	MCA 52556
8/3/85	❶[1]	21		28 **Touch A Hand, Make A Friend** S:❶[1] / A:❶[1]	*Homer Banks/Carl Hampton/Raymond Jackson*	MCA 52646
11/23/85+	3[1]	19		29 **Come On In (You Did The Best You Could Do)** ...S:3 / A:3	*Rick Giles/George Green*	MCA 52722

DEBUT	PEAK	WKS	GOLD	ARTIST / Ranking / Country Chart Hit	Songwriter	Label (& Number)
				OAK RIDGE BOYS — cont'd		
3/22/86	**15**	15		30 **Juliet**	S:14 / A:15 *John Hall/Larry Hoppen*	MCA 52801
3/29/86	**20**	14		31 **When You Get To The Heart** ***[w/ Barbara Mandrell]***	...A:20 / S:21 *Tony Brown/Wayland Holyfield/Norro Wilson*	MCA 52802
7/12/86	**24**	15		32 **You Made A Rock Of A Rolling Stone**	A:24 *Kix Brooks/Chris Waters*	MCA 52873
2/21/87	**❶[1]**	24		33 **It Takes A Little Rain (To Make Love Grow)**	A:3 / S:6 *Steve Dean/J.D. Hicks/Roger Murrah*	MCA 53010
6/13/87	**❶[1]**	23		34 **This Crazy Love**	S:11 *J.D. Hicks/Roger Murrah*	MCA 53023
10/10/87	**17**	15		35 **Time In**	*Rich Alves/J.D. Hicks/Roger Murrah*	MCA 53175
2/27/88	**5**	22		36 **True Heart**	S:20 *Michael Clark/Don Schlitz*	MCA 53272
7/30/88	**❶[1]**	21		37 **Gonna Take A Lot Of River**	S:❶[1] *Mark Henley/John Kurhajetz*	MCA 53381
12/3/88+	**10**	20		38 **Bridges And Walls**	*Roger Murrah/Randy Vanwarmer*	MCA 53460
4/1/89	**7**	22		39 **Beyond Those Years**	*Troy Seals/Eddie Setser*	MCA 53625
8/19/89	**4**	25		40 **An American Family**	*Bob Corbin*	MCA 53705
12/16/89+	**❶[1]**	26		41 **No Matter How High**	*Joey Scarbury/Even Stevens*	MCA 53757
5/19/90	**71**	3		42 **Baby, You'll Be My Baby** from the album *American Dreams* on MCA 42311	*Gene Pistilli/Troy Seals*	MCA
12/1/90+	**31**	15		43 (You're My) **Soul And Inspiration** from the movie *My Heroes Have Always Been Cowboys* starring Scott Glenn (soundtrack on RCA 2338)	*Barry Mann/Cynthia Weil*	RCA
3/23/91	**6**	20		44 **Lucky Moon**	*Doug Johnson/Mark Wright*	RCA
8/10/91	**70**	5		45 **Change My Mind**	*Jason Blume/A.J. Masters*	RCA
10/5/91	**44**	13		46 **Baby On Board** above 3 from the album *Unstoppable* on RCA 3023	*J.C. Crowley/Jeff Silbar*	RCA
6/27/92	**69**	4		47 **Fall** from the album *The Long Haul* on RCA 66004	*Don Von Tress*	RCA
10/16/99	**71**	1		48 **Ain't No Short Way Home** from the album *Voices* on Platinum 9355	*Bob DiPiero/Jim Photoglo*	Platinum
				O'BRIEN, Tim Born on 3/16/1954 in Wheeling, West Virginia. Bluegrass singer/songwriter/guitarist.		
7/21/90	**9**	20		**The Battle Hymn Of Love** ***[w/ Kathy Mattea]***	*Paul Overstreet/Don Schlitz*	Mercury
				O'CONNOR, Mark Born on 8/5/1961 in Seattle, Washington. Male fiddle player. Member of rock group The Dregs in early 1980s. ***CMA: Musician 1991, 1992, 1993, 1994, 1995 & 1996***		
3/30/91	**25**	20		1 **Restless** ***[w/ Vince Gill/Ricky Skaggs/Steve Wariner]*** **Grammy: Vocal Collaboration / CMA: Vocal Event**	*Carl Perkins*	Warner
8/3/91	**71**	3		2 **Now It Belongs To You** ***[w/ Steve Wariner]*** above 2 from the album *The New Nashville Cats* on Warner 26509	*Steve Wariner*	Warner
12/25/93+	**54**	10		3 **The Devil Comes Back To Georgia** ***[w/ Charlie Daniels/Johnny Cash/Marty Stuart/Travis Tritt]*** from O'Connor's album *Heroes* on Warner 45257	...*Tom Crain/Charlie Daniels/Joe DiGregorio/Fred Edwards/Charles Hayward/Jim Marshall*	Warner
				O'DAY, Tommy Born in Fresno, California. Male singer/songwriter.		
1/28/78	**96**	3		1 **Mr. Sandman**	*Pat Ballard*	Nu-Trayl 916
4/8/78	**82**	4		2 **Memories Are Made Of This**	*Richard Dehr/Terry Gilkyson/Frank Miller*	Nu-Trayl 919
8/12/78	**97**	2		3 **When A Woman Cries**	*Betty Duke/Sammy Lyons*	Nu-Trayl 923
12/23/78+	**93**	4		4 **I Heard A Song Today**	*Tommy O'Day*	Nu-Trayl 926
5/5/79	**89**	2		5 **Accentuate The Positive**	*Harold Arlen/Johnny Mercer*	Nu-Trayl 929
7/14/79	**99**	2		6 **Your Other Love**	*Doc Pomus/Mort Shuman*	Nu-Trayl 930
				O'DELL, Doye Born Allen Doye O'Dell on 11/22/1912 in Gustine, Texas. Died on 1/3/2001 (age 88). Male singer/songwriter. Appeared in several western movies. Hosted own kiddie TV show in California.		
7/24/48	**12**	3		**Dear Oakie**	J:12 / S:13 *Doye O'Dell/Rudy Sooter*	Exclusive 33
				O'DELL, Kenny Born Kenneth Gist in 1942 in Oklahoma. Male singer/songwriter/guitarist.		
3/9/74	**58**	10		1 **You Bet Your Sweet, Sweet Love**	*Kenny O'Dell*	Capricorn 0038
1/18/75	**18**	13		2 **Soulful Woman**	*Kenny O'Dell*	Capricorn 0219
5/31/75	**37**	10		3 **My Honky Tonk Ways**	*Kenny O'Dell*	Capricorn 0233
7/8/78	**9**	14		4 **Let's Shake Hands And Come Out Lovin'**	*Kenny O'Dell*	Capricorn 0301
11/4/78+	**12**	15		5 **As Long As I Can Wake Up In Your Arms**	*Larry Henley/Kenny O'Dell*	Capricorn 0309
3/10/79	**32**	10		6 **Medicine Woman**	*Kenny O'Dell*	Capricorn 0317
				ODESSA Born in Indiana. Female singer.		
4/8/89	**89**	2		**Hooked On You**	*Chris Ward*	Sing Me 40
				ODOM, Donna Born on 8/14/1944 in Ebbwvale, South Wales. Female singer/songwriter.		
1/20/68	**65**	5		**She Gets The Roses (I Get The Tears)**	*Donna Odom*	Decca 32214
				O'DONNAL, Karen Born in Pennsylvania. Female singer.		
12/9/72+	**40**	10		**We Know It's Over** ***[w/ Dave Dudley]***	*Randy Rogers*	Mercury 73345

DEBUT	PEAK	WKS	GOLD	ARTIST / Country Chart Hit	Ranking / Songwriter	Label (& Number)
				O'DONNELL, Rosie		
				Born on 3/21/1962 in Commack, New York. Acted in several movies. Hosted own TV talk show.		
12/25/99	**72**	1		**Santa On The Rooftop** ***[w/ Trisha Yearwood]***	*Annie Roboff/Arnie Roman* **[X]**	Columbia
				from O'Donnell's album *A Rosie Christmas* on Columbia 63685		
				O'DOSKI, Gail		
				Born in 1940 in Bartow, Florida. Male singer.		
12/26/87+	**73**	4		1 **First Came The Feelin'**	*Jeff Hess/John Volinkaty*	Door Knob 288
5/28/88	**77**	4		2 **(Just An) Old Wives' Tale**	*Jim Cox/Adrienne Leisten/Rick Wingerter*	Door Knob 300
				O'GWYNN, James		
				Born on 1/26/1928 in Winchester, Mississippi; raised in Hattiesburg, Mississippi. Male singer/songwriter. Known as "The Smilin' Irishman."		
10/20/58	**16**	3		1 **Talk To Me Lonesome Heart**	*James O'Gwynn*	D 1006
12/29/58	**28**	3		2 **Blue Memories**	*James O'Gwynn/Paul Williams*	D 1022
4/27/59	**13**	4		3 **How Can I Think Of Tomorrow**	*Roy Crocker/James O'Gwynn*	Mercury 71419
12/21/59+	**26**	4		4 **Easy Money**	*James O'Gwynn/Glen Paul*	Mercury 71513
2/20/61	**21**	6		5 **House Of Blue Lovers**	*Jack Newman*	Mercury 71731
4/21/62	**7**	10		6 **My Name Is Mud**	*Bill Anderson*	Mercury 71935
				O'KANES, The		
				Duo of Jamie O'Hara (born on 8/8/1950 in Toledo, Ohio) and **Kieran Kane** (born on 10/7/1949 in Queens, New York).		
9/20/86	**10**	25		1 **Oh Darlin'**	S:6 / A:11 *Kieran Kane/Jamie O'Hara*	Columbia 06242
2/7/87	**❶**[1]	22		2 **Can't Stop My Heart From Loving You**	S:2 / A:2 *Kieran Kane/Jamie O'Hara*	Columbia 06606
6/27/87	**9**	18		3 **Daddies Need To Grow Up Too**	S:7 *Kieran Kane/Jamie O'Hara*	Columbia 07187
10/17/87+	**5**	25		4 **Just Lovin' You**	S:2 *Kieran Kane/Jamie O'Hara*	Columbia 07611
3/5/88	**4**	20		5 **One True Love**	S:3 *Kieran Kane/Jamie O'Hara*	Columbia 07736
7/9/88	**10**	20		6 **Blue Love**	S:2 *Kieran Kane/Jamie O'Hara*	Columbia 07943
11/12/88	**71**	5		7 **Rocky Road**	*Kieran Kane/Jamie O'Hara*	Columbia 08099
				O'KEEFE, Danny		
				Born in 1943 in Wenatchee, Washington. Pop singer/songwriter.		
10/28/72	**63**	6		**Good Time Charlie's Got The Blues**	*Danny O'Keefe*	Signpost 70006
				O'NEAL, Austin		
				Born in North Carolina. Male singer.		
8/27/83	**93**	2		**Nights Like Tonight**	*Paul Harrison/Mickey Salter*	Project One 002
				O'NEAL, Coleman		
				Born in Philadelphia, Pennsylvania. Male singer/songwriter.		
1/5/63	**8**	16		**Mr. Heartache, Move On**	*Coleman O'Neal*	Chancellor 108
				O'NEAL, Jamie	**2000s: #38**	
				Born Jamie Murphy on 6/3/1968 in Sydney, Australia; raised in Hawaii and Nevada. Female singer/songwriter. Also see **America The Beautiful**.		
8/12/00+	**❶**[1]	35		1 **There Is No Arizona**	*Lisa Drew/Jamie O'Neal/Shaye Smith*	Mercury
3/31/01	**❶**[1]	29		2 **When I Think About Angels**	*Roxie Dean/Jamie O'Neal/Sonny Tillis*	Mercury
9/8/01	**21**	20		3 **Shiver**	*Lisa Drew/Jamie O'Neal/Shaye Smith*	Mercury
12/1/01+	**31**	20		4 **I'm Not Gonna Do Anything Without You** ***[w/ Mark Wills]***	*Rich Alves/Randy Vanwarmer*	Mercury
				from Wills' album *Loving Every Minute* on Mercury 170209		
3/16/02	**41**	11		5 **Frantic**	*Lisa Drew/Jamie O'Neal/Shaye Smith*	Mercury
				#1-3 & 5: from the album *Shiver* on Mercury 170132		
5/24/03	**34**	16		6 **Every Little Thing**	*Roxie Dean/Jamie O'Neal/Sonny Tillis*	Mercury
10/9/04+	**18**	24		7 **Trying To Find Atlantis**	*Zack Turner/Chris Waters*	Capitol
4/9/05	**8**↑	25↑		8 **Somebody's Hero**	*Ed Hill/Jamie O'Neal/Shaye Smith*	Capitol
				above 2 from the album *Brave* on Capitol 79894		
				ONE HEART AT A TIME		
				All-star group: **Garth Brooks**, **Billy Dean**, **Faith Hill**, **Neal McCoy**, **Michael McDonald**, **Olivia Newton-John**, **Victoria Shaw** and **Bryan White**.		
5/30/98	**69**	5		**One Heart At A Time**	S:5 *Victoria Shaw*	Atlantic
				ORBISON, Roy		
				Born on 4/23/1936 in Vernon, Texas. Died of a heart attack on 12/6/1988 (age 52). Pop-rock singer/songwriter/guitarist. Inducted into the Rock and Roll Hall of Fame in 1987. Won Grammy's Lifetime Achievement Award in 1998.		
6/28/80	**6**	15		1 **That Lovin' You Feelin' Again** ***[w/ Emmylou Harris]***	*Roy Orbison/Chris Price*	Warner 49262
				Grammy: Vocal Duo; from the movie *Roadie* starring Meat Loaf		
10/10/87	**75**	4		2 **In Dreams**	*Roy Orbison*	Virgin 99434
				new version of his #7 Pop hit from 1963; from the movie *Blue Velvet* starring Kyle McLachlan		
12/5/87+	**42**	13		3 **Crying** ***[w/ k.d. lang]***	*Joe Melson/Roy Orbison*	Virgin 99388
				Grammy: Vocal Collaboration; from the movie *Hiding Out* starring Jon Cryer		
2/4/89	**7**	20		4 **You Got It**	*Jeff Lynne/Roy Orbison/Tom Petty*	Virgin 99245
6/24/89	**51**	13		5 **California Blue**	*Jeff Lynne/Roy Orbison/Tom Petty*	Virgin 99202
12/23/89	**89**	4		6 **Oh Pretty Woman**	*Bill Dees/Roy Orbison* **[L]**	Virgin 99159
				recorded in September 1987 at the Coconut Grove in Los Angeles; new version of his #1 Pop hit from 1964		
				ORDGE, Jimmy Arthur		
				Born in Donalda, Alberta, Canada. Male singer.		
7/11/81	**89**	3		**Stay Away From Jim**	*George Fischoff*	Dore 969

DEBUT	PEAK	WKS	GOLD	ARTIST / Country Chart Hit	Ranking / Songwriter	Label (& Number)
				ORENDER, DeWayne		
				Born in Tennessee. Male singer/songwriter.		
11/27/76	**53**	9		1 **If You Want To Make Me Feel At Home**	*Ronny Hughes/Lamar Morris*	RCA 10813
4/23/77	**87**	3		2 **To Make A Good Love Die**	*Lamar Morris/DeWayne Orender*	RCA 10936
8/27/77	**97**	2		3 **Love Me Into Heaven Again**	*Lamar Morris/DeWayne Orender*	RCA 11039
5/6/78	**51**	7		4 **Brother**	*DeWayne Orender*	Nu-Trayl 920
12/23/78+	**92**	4		5 **Better Than Now**	*Phil Everly/Terry Slater*	Volunteer 102
				ORIGINAL TEXAS PLAYBOYS		
				Veterans of **Bob Wills**' longtime band: **Leon Rausch** (vocals), Bob Kizer (guitar), **Leon McAuliffe** (steel guitar), Rudy Martin (clarinet), Jack Stidham and Bob Boatwright (fiddles), Al Stricklin (piano), Joe Ferguson (bass) and Smokey Dacus (drums).		
				CMA: Instrumental Group 1977		
4/2/77	**94**	3		**Gambling Polka Dot Blues**	*Jimmie Rodgers*	Capitol 4401
				ORION		
				Born Jimmy Bell (later adopted by the Ellis family) on 2/26/1945 in Orrville, Alabama. Shot to death during an attempted robbery on 12/12/1998 (age 53). Based his masked character on the novel *Orion* by Gail Brewer-Giorgio. Many people speculated that it was actually **Elvis Presley** under the mask. Also see **Jerry Lee Lewis**.		
6/23/79	**89**	6		1 **Ebony Eyes /**	*John D. Loudermilk*	
6/23/79	**flip**	6		2 **Honey**	*Bobby Russell*	Sun 1142
4/26/80	**69**	5		3 **A Stranger In My Place**	*Kenny Rogers/Kin Vassy*	Sun 1152
7/19/80	**68**	6		4 **Texas Tea**	*Ben Peters*	Sun 1153
10/11/80	**65**	9		5 **Am I That Easy To Forget**	*Carl Belew/Shelby Singleton/W.S. Stevenson*	Sun 1156
1/10/81	**63**	6		6 **Rockabilly Rebel**	*Steve Bloomfield*	Sun 1159
3/21/81	**79**	4		7 **Crazy Little Thing Called Love**	*Freddie Mercury*	Sun 1162
6/27/81	**76**	5		8 **Born**	*Fred Burch/Willie Young*	Sun 1165
12/12/81	**83**	4		9 **Some You Win, Some You Lose**	*Jesse Brady/Orion Darnell*	Sun 1170
7/10/82	**69**	6		10 **Morning, Noon And Night /**	*Jack Ward*	
7/10/82	**70**	4		11 **Honky Tonk Heaven**	*Billy Burnette/Larry Henley*	Sun 1175
				ORLEANS		
				Pop-rock group from New York: brothers Lawrence Hoppen (vocals, guitar) and Lance Hoppen (bass), Bob Leinback (keyboards), R.A. Martin (horns) and Wells Kelly (drums). Kelly died on 10/29/1984 (age 35).		
11/15/86	**59**	6		**You're Mine**	*Johanna Hall/John Hall*	MCA 52963
				ORRALL, Robert Ellis		
				Born on 5/4/1955 in Winthrop, Massachusetts. Male singer/songwriter. One-half of **Orrall & Wright** duo.		
11/14/92+	**19**	20		1 **Boom! It Was Over**	*Bill Lloyd/Robert Ellis Orrall*	RCA
3/20/93	**31**	20		2 **A Little Bit Of Her Love**	*Robert Ellis Orrall/Lonnie Wilson*	RCA
7/24/93	**64**	5		3 **Every Day When I Get Home**	*Gary Cotton/Robert Ellis Orrall*	RCA
				above 3 from the album *Flying Colors* on RCA 66090		
				ORRALL & WRIGHT		
				Duo of **Robert Ellis Orrall** and **Curtis Wright**.		
7/2/94	**47**	11		1 **She Loves Me Like She Means It**	*Robert Ellis Orrall/Angelo Petraglia/Billy Spencer*	Giant
10/15/94	**70**	2		2 **If You Could Say What I'm Thinking**	*Robert Ellis Orrall/Curtis Wright*	Giant
				above 2 from the album *Orrall & Wright* on Giant 24561		
				ORTEGA, Gilbert		
				Born in Gallup, New Mexico. Male singer.		
1/28/78	**91**	3		1 **Is It Wrong**	*Warner Mack*	LRJ 1050
5/20/78	**93**	4		2 **I Don't Believe I'll Fall In Love Today**	*Harlan Howard*	Ortega 1051
				ORVILLE AND IVY		
				Duo of prolific session guitarists Wesley Webb "Speedy" West (born on 1/25/1924 in Springfield, Missouri; died on 11/15/2003, age 79) and Ivy "Jimmy" Bryant (born on 3/5/1925 in Moultrie, Georgia; died on 9/22/1980, age 55).		
4/1/67	**73**	2		**Shinbone**	*Billy Liebert/Scott Turner* **[I]**	Imperial 66219
				OSBORNE, Jimmie		
				Born on 4/8/1923 in Winchester, Kentucky. Committed suicide on 12/26/1957 (age 34). Male singer/songwriter/guitarist.		
7/10/48	**10**	2		1 **My Heart Echoes**	J:10 *Johnnie Bailes*	King 715
6/25/49	**7**	6		2 **The Death Of Little Kathy Fiscus**	S:7 *Jimmie Osborne*	King 788
10/7/50	**9**	3		3 **God Please Protect America**	A:9 *Jimmie Osborne*	King 893
				OSBORNE BROTHERS, The		
				Bluegrass duo of brothers from Hyden, Kentucky: Bobby Osborne (born on 12/7/1931; mandolin) and Sonny Osborne (born on 10/29/1937; banjo).		
				CMA: Vocal Group 1971 // OPRY: 1964		
3/24/58	**13**	2		1 **Once More** *[w/ Red Allen]*	A:13 *Dusty Owens*	MGM 12583
3/12/66	**41**	4		2 **Up This Hill And Down**	*Richard Staedtler*	Decca 31886
12/17/66+	**33**	10		3 **The Kind Of Woman I Got**	*Danny Walls*	Decca 32052
7/22/67	**66**	3		4 **Roll Muddy River**	*Betty Sue Perry*	Decca 32137
2/3/68	**33**	10		5 **Rocky Top**	*Boudleaux Bryant/Felice Bryant*	Decca 32242
				also see #19 below		
6/15/68	**60**	7		6 **Cut The Cornbread, Mama**	*Dana Ferris*	Decca 32325
10/19/68	**58**	6		7 **Son Of A Sawmill Man**	*Pete Goble/Bobby Osborne*	Decca 32382
8/9/69	**28**	11		8 **Tennessee Hound Dog**	*Boudleaux Bryant/Felice Bryant*	Decca 32516
1/17/70	**58**	6		9 **Ruby, Are You Mad**	*Cynthia Carver*	Decca 32598

DEBUT	PEAK	WKS	GOLD	ARTIST / Ranking / Country Chart Hit	Songwriter	Label (& Number)
				OSBORNE BROTHERS, The — cont'd		
12/5/70	**69**	2		10 **My Old Kentucky Home (Turpentine And Dandelion Wine)**	*Randy Newman*	Decca 32746
3/13/71	**37**	10		11 **Georgia Pineywoods**	*Boudleaux Bryant/Felice Bryant*	Decca 32794
9/11/71	**62**	7		12 **Muddy Bottom**	*Boudleaux Bryant/Felice Bryant*	Decca 32864
1/6/73	**74**	2		13 **Midnight Flyer**	*Paul Craft*	Decca 33028
4/28/73	**66**	2		14 **Lizzie Lou**	*Boudleaux Bryant/Felice Bryant*	MCA 40028
9/1/73	**64**	6		15 **Blue Heartache**	*Paul Craft*	MCA 40113
1/31/76	**86**	4		16 **Don't Let Smokey Mountain Smoke Get In Your Eyes**	*Cecil Null*	MCA 40509
10/13/79	**95**	3		17 **Shackles And Chains** *[w/ Mac Wiseman]*	*Jimmie Davis*	CMH 1522
4/26/80	**75**	5		18 **I Can Hear Kentucky Calling Me**	*Boudleaux Bryant/Felice Bryant*	CMH 1524
11/9/96+	**2**^{2S}	151↑		19 **Rocky Top** — new version of #5 above	*Boudleaux Bryant/Felice Bryant* **[R]**	Decca
				O'SHEA, Cathy — Born Catherine Herbsleb on 7/20/1941 in Kansas City, Missouri. Female singer.		
8/26/78	**94**	4		**Roses Ain't Red**	*Diane Pfeifer*	MCA 40934
				O'SHEA, Shad, & The 18 Wheelers — Born Howard Lovdal in San Diego, California. Male singer/songwriter. Started the Fraternity Records label in 1975.		
3/27/76	**85**	3		**Colorado Call**	*Shad O'Shea* **[N]**	Private Stock 45,071
				OSLIN, K.T. — **All-Time: #251** — Born Kay Toinette Oslin on 5/15/1941 in Crossett, Arkansas; raised in Mobile, Alabama. Female singer/songwriter/pianist/actress. Acted in the touring musicals *Hello Dolly*, *West Side Story* and *Promises Promises*. Also see **Alabama**. *CMA: Female Vocalist 1988*		
5/16/81	**72**	4		1 **Clean Your Own Tables** *[Kay T. Oslin]*	*Chip Taylor*	Elektra 47132
1/10/87	**40**	15		2 **Wall Of Tears**	*Richard Leigh/Peter McCann*	RCA 5066
4/25/87	**7**	21		3 **80's Ladies** — Grammy: Female Vocal	S:13 *K.T. Oslin*	RCA 5154
9/12/87	**❶**^{1}	25		4 **Do Ya'**	S:❶^{1} *K.T. Oslin*	RCA 5239
1/30/88	**❶**^{1}	21		5 **I'll Always Come Back**	S:3 *K.T. Oslin*	RCA 5330
7/9/88	**13**	15		6 **Money**	S:12 *K.T. Oslin*	RCA 8388
10/15/88+	**❶**^{1}	20		7 **Hold Me** — Grammy: Song & Female Vocal	S:❶^{2} *K.T. Oslin*	RCA 8725
2/11/89	**2**^{1}	19		8 **Hey Bobby**	*K.T. Oslin*	RCA 8865
6/10/89	**5**	18		9 **This Woman**	*K.T. Oslin*	RCA 8943
10/21/89	**23**	13		10 **Didn't Expect It To Go Down This Way**	*K.T. Oslin*	RCA 9029
7/7/90	**73**	3		11 **Two Hearts** — from the album *80's Ladies* on RCA 5924	*Rory Bourke/K.T. Oslin*	RCA
9/29/90	**❶**^{2}	20		12 **Come Next Monday**	*Charlie Black/Rory Bourke/K.T. Oslin*	RCA
2/16/91	**28**	13		13 **Mary And Willie**	*K.T. Oslin*	RCA
7/6/91	**69**	2		14 **You Call Everybody Darling**	*Sam Martin/Ben Trace/Clem Watts*	RCA
9/14/91	**63**	3		15 **Cornell Crawford** — above 4 from the album *Love In A Small Town* on RCA 2365	*Joe Miller/K.T. Oslin*	RCA
5/1/93	**64**	3		16 **New Way Home** — from the album *Greatest Hits: Songs From An Aging Sex Bomb* on RCA 66227	*K.T. Oslin*	RCA
8/31/96	**64**	5		17 **Silver Tongue And Goldplated Lies** — from the album *My Roots Are Showing...* on BNA 66920	*John Hutchison*	BNA
3/17/01	**53**	9		18 **Live Close By, Visit Often** — from the album *Live Close By, Visit Often* on BNA 69026	S:25 *Kostas/Raul Malo/K.T. Oslin*	BNA
				OSMOND, Donny And Marie — Brother-and-sister vocal duo from Ogden, Utah: Donny (born on 12/9/1957) and **Marie Osmond**. Co-hosted of own musical/variety TV series from 1976-78. Starred in the movie *Goin' Coconuts*.		
7/27/74	**17**	13	●	1 **I'm Leaving It (All) Up To You**	*Don Harris/Dewey Terry*	MGM/Kolob 14735
6/21/75	**71**	6		2 **Make The World Go Away**	*Hank Cochran*	MGM/Kolob 14807
				OSMOND, Marie — **All-Time: #245** — Born Olive Marie Osmond on 10/13/1959 in Ogden, Utah. Sister of **The Osmond Brothers**. Co-hosted TV series *Donny & Marie* from 1976-78. Hosted own TV series from 1980-81. Co-hosted TV's *Ripley's Believe It Or Not* from 1985-86. Starred in the 1995 TV series *Maybe This Time*. *CMA: Vocal Duo (with Dan Seals) 1986*		
9/8/73	**❶**^{2}	16	●	1 **Paper Roses**	*Fred Spielman/Janice Torre*	MGM/Kolob 14609
8/10/74	**33**	11		2 **In My Little Corner Of The World**	*Bob Hilliard/Lee Pockriss*	MGM/Kolob 14694
3/1/75	**29**	10		3 **Who's Sorry Now**	*Bert Kalmar/Harry Ruby/Ted Snyder*	MGM/Kolob 14786
8/7/76	**85**	4		4 **"A" My Name Is Alice**	*Joel Hirschhorn/Al Kasha*	Polydor 14333
3/20/82	**74**	6		5 **I've Got A Bad Case Of You**	*Walt Aldridge/Tom Brasfield*	Elektra/Curb 47430
8/14/82	**58**	7		6 **Back To Believing Again**	*Rory Bourke/Bob McDill*	Elektra/Curb 69995
3/24/84	**82**	4		7 **Who's Counting**	*Kye Fleming/Dennis W. Morgan*	RCA/Curb 13680
2/9/85	**54**	8		8 **Until I Fall In Love Again**	*Larry Boone/Dave Gibson*	Curb/Capitol 5445
7/6/85	**❶**^{1}	23		9 **Meet Me In Montana** *[w/ Dan Seals]*	S:❶^{1} / A:❶^{1} *Paul Davis*	Curb/Capitol 5478
11/9/85+	**❶**^{1}	21		10 **There's No Stopping Your Heart**	S:❶^{1} / A:❶^{1} *Michael Brook/Craig Karp*	Curb/Capitol 5521
3/29/86	**4**	21		11 **Read My Lips**	S:4 / A:4 *Marc Blatte/Larry Gottlieb*	Curb/Capitol 5563
8/30/86	**❶**^{1}	21		12 **You're Still New To Me** *[w/ Paul Davis]*	S:❶^{1} / A:❶^{1} *Paul Davis/Paul Overstreet*	Curb/Capitol 5613
12/27/86+	**14**	18		13 **I Only Wanted You**	S:3 / A:14 *Michael Garvin/Bucky Jones/Tom Shapiro*	Curb/Capitol 5663
4/11/87	**24**	13		14 **Everybody's Crazy 'Bout My Baby**	S:29 *Mike Reid*	Curb/Capitol 5703

Billboard DEBUT	PEAK	WKS	GOLD	#	ARTIST / Country Chart Hit	Ranking / Songwriter	Label (& Number)
					OSMOND, Marie — cont'd		
7/25/87	50	12		15	Cry Just A Little	*Paul Davis*	Curb/Capitol 44044
5/28/88	50	10		16	Without A Trace	*Katerina Kitridge/Sonny Throckmorton*	Curb/Capitol 44176
8/20/88	47	8		17	Sweet Life *[w/ Paul Davis]*	*Susan Collins/Paul Davis*	Curb/Capitol 44215
12/17/88+	59	8		18	I'm In Love And He's In Dallas	*Richard Leigh/Kent Robbins*	Curb/Capitol 44269
8/26/89	70	5		19	Steppin' Stone	*Gary Scruggs/Kevin Welch*	Curb/Capitol 44412
11/18/89	75	4		20	Slowly But Surely	*Michael Garvin/Bucky Jones/Jim Weatherly*	Curb/Capitol 44468
10/13/90	57	10		21	Like A Hurricane from the album *The Best Of Marie Osmond* on Curb 77263	*Michael Clark*	Curb
2/11/95	75	1		22	What Kind Of Man (Walks On A Woman)	*Gary Baker/Frank J. Myers*	Curb
					OSMOND BROTHERS, The Family vocal group from Ogden, Utah: Alan Osmond, Wayne Osmond, Merrill Osmond and Jay Osmond. Brothers of **Donny And Marie Osmond**. Also see **Merrill And Jessica**.		
5/1/82	17	15		1	I Think About Your Lovin' *[The Osmonds]*	*Diana Trask*	Elektra/Curb 47438
9/4/82	28	12		2	It's Like Falling In Love (Over And Over)	*Rich Alves/Scott Anders/Roger Murrah*	Elektra/Curb 69969
12/25/82+	43	10		3	Never Ending Song Of Love	*Delaney Bramlett*	Elektra/Curb 69883
6/11/83	67	8		4	She's Ready For Someone To Love Her	*Charlie Black/Jerry Gillespie/Tommy Rocco*	Warner/Curb 29594
1/21/84	43	11		5	Where Does An Angel Go When She Cries	*Kerry Chater/Tommy Rocco*	Warner/Curb 29387
5/5/84	39	12		6	If Every Man Had A Woman Like You	*Bobby Lee Springfield*	Warner/Curb 29312
6/8/85	54	9		7	Any Time	*Herb Lawson*	Warner/Curb 28982
12/14/85+	56	11		8	Baby When Your Heart Breaks Down	*Kix Brooks*	Curb/EMI Amer. 8298
3/15/86	45	13		9	Baby Wants	*Jerry Gillespie/Stan Webb*	Curb/EMI Amer. 8313
6/21/86	69	5		10	You Look Like The One I Love	*Deborah Allen/Rafe Van Hoy*	Curb/EMI Amer. 8325
11/1/86	70	7		11	Looking For Suzanne	*Paul Kennerley*	Curb/EMI Amer. 8360
					OTT, Paul Born Paul Ott Carruth on 9/25/1934 in McComb, Mississippi. Male singer/songwriter.		
6/30/79	87	2			A Salute To The Duke tribute to John Wayne	*Fred Foster/Paul Ott* [S]	Elektra 46066
					OTTO, James Born in Fort Lewis, Washington. Male singer/songwriter/guitarist.		
6/22/02	45	15		1	The Ball	*P.J. Matthews/James Otto/Kerry Kurt Phillips*	Mercury
10/4/03+	33	20		2	Days Of Our Lives	S:3 *James Otto/Bobby Terry*	Mercury
4/3/04	58	2		3	Sunday Morning And Saturday Night above 3 from the album *Days Of Our Lives* on Mercury 002110	*Tim Nichols/Jeffrey Steele*	Mercury
					OVERSTREET, Paul Born on 3/17/1955 in Antioch, Mississippi. Male singer/songwriter/guitarist. Member of **Schuyler, Knobloch & Overstreet**. Married to Freida Parton (sister of **Dolly Parton**) from 1975-76. No relation to Tommy Overstreet.	**All-Time: #249**	
5/8/82	76	5		1	Beautiful Baby	*Paul Overstreet/Even Stevens*	RCA 13042
11/21/87+	❶[1]	24		2	I Won't Take Less Than Your Love *[w/ Tanya Tucker & Paul Davis]*	S:2 *Paul Overstreet/Don Schlitz*	Capitol 44100
9/24/88	3[3]	21		3	Love Helps Those	S:7 *Paul Overstreet*	MTM 72113
4/8/89	9	21		4	Sowin' Love	*Paul Overstreet/Don Schlitz*	RCA 8919
8/26/89	5	26		5	All The Fun	*Taylor Dunn/Paul Overstreet*	RCA 9015
1/6/90	2[1]	26		6	Seein' My Father In Me	*Taylor Dunn/Paul Overstreet*	RCA
5/19/90	3[1]	21		7	Richest Man On Earth above 2 from the album *Sowin' Love* on RCA 9717	*Paul Overstreet/Don Schlitz*	RCA
11/24/90+	❶[1]	20		8	Daddy's Come Around	*Paul Overstreet/Don Schlitz*	RCA
3/16/91	4	20		9	Heroes	*Claire Cloninger/Paul Overstreet*	RCA
7/20/91	5	20		10	Ball And Chain	*Paul Overstreet/Don Schlitz*	RCA
11/23/91+	30	18		11	If I Could Bottle This Up	*Dean Dillon/Paul Overstreet*	RCA
3/14/92	57	9		12	Billy Can't Read above 5 from the album *Heroes* on RCA 2459	*Buddy Brock/Aaron Tippin*	RCA
7/11/92	22	19		13	Me And My Baby	*Paul Davis/Paul Overstreet*	RCA
11/7/92	57	11		14	Still Out There Swinging	*Paul Overstreet*	RCA
4/3/93	60	7		15	Take Another Run above 3 from the album *Love Is Strong* on RCA 66029	*Paul Overstreet/Don Schlitz*	RCA
1/20/96	73	2		16	We've Got To Keep On Meeting Like This from the album *Time* on Scarlet Moon 873	*Archie Jordan/Paul Overstreet*	Scarlet Moon

OVERSTREET, Tommy — **1970s: #42 / All-Time: #148**

Born on 9/10/1937 in Oklahoma City, Oklahoma. Male singer/songwriter/guitarist. On TV in Houston in the early 1960s. Worked with **Slim Willet** in the mid-1960s; own band thereafter. Managed the Nashville office of Dot Records from 1967-74. Cousin of 1920s singing star Gene Austin. Uncle of **Susan St. Marie**. No relation to Paul Overstreet.

DEBUT	PEAK	WKS	GOLD	#	Country Chart Hit	Songwriter	Label (& Number)
10/11/69	73	2		1	Rocking A Memory (That Won't Go To Sleep)	*Dallas Frazier/A.L. "Doodle" Owens*	Dot 17281
12/12/70+	56	7		2	If You're Looking For A Fool	*Bob McRee/Clifton Thomas/Edward Thomas*	Dot 17357
4/24/71	5	16		3	Gwen (Congratulations)	*Jerry Gillespie/Ricci Mareno*	Dot 17375
8/14/71	5	16		4	I Don't Know You (Anymore)	*Charlie Black/Ricci Mareno*	Dot 17387

DEBUT	PEAK	WKS	GOLD	ARTIST / Ranking / Country Chart Hit / Songwriter	Label (& Number)
				OVERSTREET, Tommy — cont'd	
1/1/72	2^1	16		5 Ann (Don't Go Runnin') — *Buzz Cason*	Dot 17402
5/20/72	16	14		6 A Seed Before The Rose — *Jerry Gillespie/Ricci Mareno*	Dot 17418
9/23/72	3^2	18		7 Heaven Is My Woman's Love — *Sharon Dobbins*	Dot 17428
4/21/73	7	15		8 Send Me No Roses — *Charlie Black/Ricci Mareno*	Dot 17455
9/15/73	7	17		9 I'll Never Break These Chains — *Skippy Barrett/Charlie Black/Ricci Mareno*	Dot 17474
2/16/74	3^1	16		10 (Jeannie Marie) You Were A Lady — *Charlie Black/Ricci Mareno*	Dot 17493
7/27/74	8	16		11 If I Miss You Again Tonight — *Charlie Black/Marianne Mareno/Ricci Mareno*	Dot 17515
12/14/74+	9	14		12 I'm A Believer — *Skippy Barrett/Ricci Mareno*	ABC/Dot 17533
5/10/75	6	16		13 That's When My Woman Begins — *Jerry Gillespie*	ABC/Dot 17552
10/11/75	16	12		14 From Woman To Woman — *Jerry Gillespie/Ricci Mareno*	ABC/Dot 17580
6/12/76	15	13		15 Here Comes That Girl Again — *Rory Bourke/Gene Dobbins/Johnny Wilson*	ABC/Dot 17630
10/2/76	29	11		16 Young Girl — *Jerry Fuller*	ABC/Dot 17657
12/25/76+	11	15		17 If Love Was A Bottle Of Wine — *Sterling Whipple*	ABC/Dot 17672
5/7/77	5	14		18 Don't Go City Girl On Me — *Mike Kosser/Rafe Van Hoy*	ABC/Dot 17697
9/17/77	20	12		19 This Time I'm In It For The Love — *Bob McDill*	ABC/Dot 17721
1/21/78	12	12		20 Yes Ma'am — *Sonny Throckmorton*	ABC/Dot 17737
6/10/78	20	12		21 Better Me — *Sterling Whipple*	ABC 12367
9/30/78	11	12		22 Fadin' In, Fadin' Out — *Bobby Braddock/Sonny Throckmorton*	ABC 12408
1/27/79	91	3		23 Tears (There's Nowhere Else To Hide) *[w/ The Nashville Express]* — *Tommy Overstreet/Dale Vest*	Tina 523
3/3/79	45	7		24 Cheater's Kit — *Rory Bourke/Gene Dobbins/Johnny Wilson*	ABC 12456
5/5/79	27	11		25 I'll Never Let You Down — *Dennis Payne*	Elektra 46023
8/25/79	23	10		26 What More Could A Man Need — *Chick Rains*	Elektra 46516
11/17/79+	36	11		27 Fadin' Renegade — *Coke Sams*	Elektra 46564
3/22/80	41	9		28 Down In The Quarter — *Sonny Tackett*	Elektra 46600
6/28/80	47	7		29 Sue — *Alfred Little*	Elektra 46658
10/4/80	72	5		30 Me And The Boys In The Band — *Bob Millsap*	Elektra 47041
7/30/83	69	7		31 Dream Maker — *Byron Hill/J. Remington Wilde*	AMI 1314
12/3/83	84	3		32 Heart Of Dixie — *Bob McDill*	AMI 1317
5/19/84	87	3		33 I Still Love Your Body — *Robert Smith/Bobby Lee Springfield*	Gervasi 665
6/28/86	74	5		34 Next To You — *Jerry Fuller*	Silver Dollar 0002
				OWEN, Jim	
				Born on 4/21/1941 in Robards, Kentucky. Singer/songwriter/guitarist/actor. Starred as **Hank Williams** in a one-man show.	
1/28/78	97	2		1 Lovesick Blues *[w/ The Drifting Cowboys]* — *Cliff Friend/Irving Mills*	Epic 50498
11/29/80	82	4		2 Ten Anniversary Presents — *Jim Owen* [S]	Sun 1157
1/30/82	82	3		3 Hell Yes, I Cheated — *Larry Cheshier/Royce Sutton*	Sun 1171
				OWEN BROTHERS	
				Vocal duo of brothers from Georgia: Bill Owen and Marty Owen.	
12/25/82	95	3		1 Nights Out At The Days End — *Roger Ball/Jerry Fox/Lonnie Wilson*	Audiograph 445
9/17/83	86	3		2 Southern Women — *Kent Blazy/Mickey Hiter/John Mohead*	Audiograph 470
				OWENS, A.L. "Doodle" **SW: #43**	
				Born Arthur Leo Owens on 11/28/1930 in Waco, Texas. Died on 10/4/1999 (age 68). Male singer/songwriter.	
1/14/78	78	4		Honky Tonk Toys — *A.L. "Doodle" Owens/Judy Vowell*	Raindrop 010
				OWENS, Bonnie	
				Born Bonnie Campbell on 10/1/1932 in Blanchard, Oklahoma. Female singer/songwriter/guitarist. Married to **Buck Owens** from 1948-53. Married to **Merle Haggard** from 1965-78. Mother of **Buddy Alan**.	
6/22/63	25	1		1 Why Don't Daddy Live Here Anymore — *Dallas Frazier/Fuzzy Owens*	Tally 149
4/4/64	27	6		2 Don't Take Advantage Of Me — *Bobby Morris/Bonnie Owens*	Tally 156
9/12/64	28	26		3 Just Between The Two Of Us *[w/ Merle Haggard]* — *Liz Anderson*	Tally 181
9/18/65	41	4		4 Number One Heel — *Bonnie Owens/Buck Owens*	Capitol 5459
11/19/66	69	4		5 Consider The Children *[w/ The Strangers]* — *Merle Haggard/Dean Holloway*	Capitol 5755
2/15/69	68	4		6 Lead Me On *[w/ The Strangers]* — *Leon Copeland*	Capitol 2340

OWENS, Buck **1960s: #1 / 1970s: #26 / All-Time: #11 // HOF: 1996**

Born Alvis Edgar Owens on 8/12/1929 in Sherman, Texas; raised in Mesa, Arizona. Male singer/songwriter/guitarist. Married to **Bonnie Owens** from 1948-53. Moved to Bakersfield, California, in 1951. Played lead guitar for **Tommy Collins** in the mid-1950s. Co-host of TV's *Hee-Haw* from 1969-86. Father of **Buddy Alan**. Backing group: **The Buckaroos**.

DEBUT	PEAK	WKS	GOLD	ARTIST / Ranking / Country Chart Hit / Songwriter	Label (& Number)
5/11/59	24	2		1 Second Fiddle — *Buck Owens*	Capitol 4172
10/5/59	4	22		2 Under Your Spell Again — *Buck Owens*	Capitol 4245
3/7/60	3^4	30		3 Above And Beyond — *Harlan Howard*	Capitol 4337
9/19/60	2^3	24		4 Excuse Me (I Think I've Got A Heartache) / — *Harlan Howard/Buck Owens*	
10/24/60	25	3		5 I've Got A Right To Know — *Buck Owens*	Capitol 4412
1/30/61	2^8	26		6 Foolin' Around / — *Harlan Howard/Buck Owens*	
3/27/61	27	1		7 High As The Mountains — *Buck Owens*	Capitol 4496
5/15/61	8	12		8 Mental Cruelty *[w/ Rose Maddox]* / — *Dixie Davis/Larry Davis/Buck Owens*	
5/22/61	4	14		9 Loose Talk *[w/ Rose Maddox]* — *Freddie Hart/Ann Lucas*	Capitol 4550

DEBUT	PEAK	WKS	GOLD	Ranking	ARTIST / Country Chart Hit	Songwriter	Label (& Number)
					OWENS, Buck — cont'd		
8/7/61	2[1]	24		10	Under The Influence Of Love	Harlan Howard/Buck Owens	Capitol 4602
2/24/62	11	16		11	Nobody's Fool But Yours	Buck Owens	Capitol 4679
7/28/62	11	11		12	Save The Last Dance For Me	Walter Hirsch/Frank Magine/Phil Spitalny	Capitol 4765
10/27/62	8	8		13	Kickin' Our Hearts Around /	Wanda Jackson	
10/27/62	17	5		14	I Can't Stop (My Lovin' You)	Buck Owens/Don Rich	Capitol 4826
12/29/62+	10	14		15	You're For Me /	Tommy Collins/Buck Owens	
1/5/63	24	3		16	House Down The Block	Buck Owens	Capitol 4872
4/13/63	❶[4]	28		17	Act Naturally	Voni Morrison/Johnny Russell	Capitol 4937
					also see #89 below		
8/3/63	15	6		18	We're The Talk Of The Town *[w/ Rose Maddox]* /	Buck Owens/Rollie Weber	
8/10/63	19	6		19	Sweethearts In Heaven *[w/ Rose Maddox]*	Buck Owens	Capitol 4992
9/21/63	❶[16]	30		20	Love's Gonna Live Here	Buck Owens	Capitol 5025
3/28/64	❶[7]	26		21	My Heart Skips A Beat /	Buck Owens	
4/4/64	❶[2]	27		22	Together Again	Buck Owens	Capitol 5136
8/29/64	❶[6]	27		23	I Don't Care (Just As Long As You Love Me) /	Buck Owens	
10/10/64	33	9		24	Don't Let Her Know	Bonnie Owens/Buck Owens/Don Rich	Capitol 5240
1/23/65	❶[5]	20		25	I've Got A Tiger By The Tail	Harlan Howard/Buck Owens	Capitol 5336
					Grammy: Hall of Fame		
5/15/65	❶[6]	20		26	Before You Go	Buck Owens/Don Rich	Capitol 5410
7/31/65	❶[1]	19		27	Only You (Can Break My Heart) /	Buck Owens	
7/31/65	10	14		28	Gonna Have Love	Buck Owens/Red Simpson	Capitol 5465
					also see #90 below		
					BUCK OWENS & THE BUCKAROOS:		
10/30/65	❶[2]	17		29	Buckaroo /	Bob Morris [I]	
12/11/65+	24	9		30	If You Want A Love	Bonnie Owens/Buck Owens/Don Rich	Capitol 5517
1/22/66	❶[7]	19		31	Waitin' In Your Welfare Line /	Buck Owens/Don Rich/Nat Stuckey	
2/26/66	43	2		32	In The Palm Of Your Hand	Buck Owens	Capitol 5566
					also see #60 below		
5/21/66	❶[6]	21		33	Think Of Me	Estrella Olson/Don Rich	Capitol 5647
9/3/66	❶[4]	20		34	Open Up Your Heart	Buck Owens	Capitol 5705
1/14/67	❶[4]	16		35	Where Does The Good Times Go	Buck Owens	Capitol 5811
4/1/67	❶[3]	16		36	Sam's Place	Buck Owens/Red Simpson	Capitol 5865
7/15/67	❶[1]	16		37	Your Tender Loving Care	Buck Owens	Capitol 5942
10/14/67+	2[1]	18		38	It Takes People Like You (To Make People Like Me)	Buck Owens	Capitol 2001
1/27/68	❶[1]	15		39	How Long Will My Baby Be Gone	Buck Owens	Capitol 2080
4/20/68	2[1]	15		40	Sweet Rosie Jones	Buck Owens	Capitol 2142
7/27/68	7	15		41	Let The World Keep On A Turnin' *[w/ Buddy Alan]*	Buck Owens	Capitol 2237
10/26/68	5	15		42	I've Got You On My Mind Again	Buck Owens	Capitol 2300
2/1/69	❶[2]	15		43	Who's Gonna Mow Your Grass	Buck Owens	Capitol 2377
5/24/69	❶[2]	15		44	Johnny B. Goode	Chuck Berry [L]	Capitol 2485
8/9/69	❶[1]	15		45	Tall Dark Stranger	Buck Owens	Capitol 2570
11/15/69	5	13		46	Big In Vegas	Buck Owens/Terry Stafford	Capitol 2646
2/21/70	13	11		47	We're Gonna Get Together *[w/ Susan Raye]*	Buck Owens	Capitol 2731
5/9/70	12	12		48	Togetherness *[w/ Susan Raye]*	Freddie Hart	Capitol 2791
6/6/70	2[2]	15		49	The Kansas City Song	Buck Owens/Red Simpson	Capitol 2783
8/29/70	8	13		50	The Great White Horse *[w/ Susan Raye]*	Buck Owens/Leanne Scott	Capitol 2871
11/7/70	9	13		51	I Wouldn't Live In New York City (If They Gave Me The Whole Dang Town)	Buck Owens	Capitol 2947
2/6/71	9	13		52	Bridge Over Troubled Water	Paul Simon	Capitol 3023
5/1/71	3[4]	17		53	Ruby (Are You Mad)	Cynthia Carver	Capitol 3096
9/4/71	2[2]	14		54	Rollin' In My Sweet Baby's Arms	Buck Owens	Capitol 3164
12/4/71+	29	10		55	Too Old To Cut The Mustard *[w/ Buddy Alan]*	Bill Carlisle	Capitol 3215
2/12/72	8	12		56	I'll Still Be Waiting For You	Buck Owens	Capitol 3262
4/29/72	❶[1]	15		57	Made In Japan	Bob Morris/Faye Morris	Capitol 3314
7/15/72	13	14		58	Looking Back To See *[w/ Susan Raye]*	Jim Ed Brown/Maxine Brown	Capitol 3368
9/16/72	13	14		59	You Ain't Gonna Have Ol' Buck To Kick Around No More	Buck Owens [L]	Capitol 3429
12/30/72+	23	10		60	In The Palm Of Your Hand	Buck Owens [R]	Capitol 3504
					new version of #32 above		
3/31/73	14	11		61	Ain't It Amazing, Gracie	Glenn Garrison/Buck Owens	Capitol 3563
6/16/73	35	8		62	The Good Old Days (Are Here Again) *[w/ Susan Raye]*	Buck Owens	Capitol 3601
					BUCK OWENS:		
8/18/73	27	11		63	Arms Full Of Empty	Buck Owens	Capitol 3688
12/1/73+	8	12		64	Big Game Hunter	Buck Owens	Capitol 3769
3/23/74	9	13		65	On The Cover Of The Music City News	Buck Owens/Jim Shaw [N]	Capitol 3841
7/20/74	6	13		66	(It's A) Monsters' Holiday	Buck Owens [N]	Capitol 3907
11/30/74+	8	15		67	Great Expectations	Buck Owens	Capitol 3976
3/29/75	19	11		68	41st Street Lonely Hearts' Club /	Dennis Knutson/Jim Shaw	
4/26/75	flip	7		69	Weekend Daddy	Dennis Knutson/Buck Owens/Danny Shatswell	Capitol 4043
7/5/75	20	13		70	Love Is Strange *[w/ Susan Raye]*	Mickey Baker/Bo Diddley/Sylvia Robinson	Capitol 4100
10/4/75	51	7		71	The Battle Of New Orleans	Jimmie Driftwood	Capitol 4138
6/26/76	44	9		72	Hollywood Waltz	Glenn Frey/Don Henley/Bernie Leadon	Warner 8223
9/25/76	43	8		73	California Okie	Robert Jones	Warner 8255

DEBUT	PEAK	WKS	GOLD	ARTIST / Ranking / Country Chart Hit	Songwriter	Label (& Number)

OWENS, Buck — cont'd

DEBUT	PEAK	WKS	GOLD	Country Chart Hit	Songwriter	Label (& Number)
2/26/77	90	4		74 **World Famous Holiday Inn**	*Dennis Knutson/Jim Shaw*	Warner 8316
7/16/77	100	1		75 **It's Been A Long, Long Time**	*Perry Jones/Dennis Knutson*	Warner 8395
9/10/77	91	3		76 **Our Old Mansion**	*George Richey/Carmol Taylor/Norro Wilson*	Warner 8433
8/19/78	27	12		77 **Nights Are Forever Without You**	*Parker McGee*	Warner 8614
12/23/78+	80	5		78 **Do You Wanna Make Love**	*Peter McCann*	Warner 8701
5/12/79	11	13		79 **Play Together Again Again** *[w/ Emmylou Harris]*	*Jerry Abbott/Buck Owens/Charles Stewart*	Warner 8830
9/8/79	30	10		80 **Hangin' In And Hangin' On**	*Buck Owens*	Warner 49046
12/15/79+	22	13		81 **Let Jesse Rob The Train**	*Buck Owens*	Warner 49118
4/5/80	42	9		82 **Love Is A Warm Cowboy**	*Buck Owens*	Warner 49200
7/26/80	72	4		83 **Moonlight And Magnolia**	*Rory Bourke/Len Chiriacka*	Warner 49278
5/30/81	92	2		84 **Without You**	*Buck Owens/Gene Price*	Warner 49651
7/16/88	❶[1]	18		85 **Streets Of Bakersfield** *[w/ Dwight Yoakam]* S:❶[3]	*Homer Joy*	Reprise 27964
10/22/88	46	9		86 **Hot Dog**	*Denny Dedmon/Buck Owens*	Capitol 44248
1/28/89	54	6		87 **A-11**	*Hank Cochran*	Capitol 44295
4/8/89	60	7		88 **Put A Quarter In The Jukebox**	*Buck Owens*	Capitol 44356
7/15/89	27	11		89 **Act Naturally** *[w/ Ringo Starr]* [R] new version of #17 above	*Voni Morrison/Johnny Russell*	Capitol 44409
10/14/89	76	7		90 **Gonna Have Love** [R] new version of #28 above; from the album *Act Naturally* on Capitol 92893	*Buck Owens/Red Simpson*	Capitol

A-11 ['89]
Above And Beyond ['60]
Act Naturally ['63]
Act Naturally ['89]
Ain't It Amazing, Gracie ['73]
Arms Full Of Empty ['73]
Battle Of New Orleans ['75]
Before You Go ['65]
Big Game Hunter ['74]
Big In Vegas ['69]
Bridge Over Troubled Water ['71]
Buckaroo ['65]
California Okie ['76]
Do You Wanna Make Love ['79]
Don't Let Her Know ['64]
Excuse Me (I Think I've Got A Heartache) ['60]
Foolin' Around ['61]
41st Street Lonely Hearts' Club ['75]
Gonna Have Love ['65]
Gonna Have Love ['89]
Good Old Days (Are Here Again) ['73]
Great Expectations ['75]
Great White Horse ['70]
Hangin' In And Hangin' On ['79]
High As The Mountains ['61]
Hollywood Waltz ['76]
Hot Dog ['88]
House Down The Block ['63]
How Long Will My Baby Be Gone ['68]
I Can't Stop (My Lovin' You) ['62]
I Don't Care (Just As Long As You Love Me) ['64]
I Wouldn't Live In New York City (If They Gave Me The Whole Dang Town) ['70]
I'll Still Be Waiting For You ['72]
I've Got A Right To Know ['60]
I've Got A Tiger By The Tail ['65]
I've Got You On My Mind Again ['68]
If You Want A Love ['66]
In The Palm Of Your Hand ['66]
In The Palm Of Your Hand ['73]
It Takes People Like You (To Make People Like Me) ['68]
(It's A) Monsters' Holiday ['74]
It's Been A Long, Long Time ['77]
Johnny B. Goode ['69]
Kansas City Song ['70]
Kickin' Our Hearts Around ['62]
Let Jesse Rob The Train ['80]
Let The World Keep On A Turnin' ['68]
Looking Back To See ['72]
Loose Talk ['61]
Love Is A Warm Cowboy ['80]
Love Is Strange ['75]
Love's Gonna Live Here ['63]
Made In Japan ['72]
Mental Cruelty ['61]
Moonlight And Magnolia ['80]
My Heart Skips A Beat ['64]
Nights Are Forever Without You ['78]
Nobody's Fool But Yours ['62]
On The Cover Of The Music City News ['74]
Only You (Can Break My Heart) ['65]
Open Up Your Heart ['66]
Our Old Mansion ['77]
Play Together Again Again ['79]
Put A Quarter In The Jukebox ['89]
Rollin' In My Sweet Baby's Arms ['71]
Ruby (Are You Mad) ['71]
Sam's Place ['67]
Save The Last Dance For Me ['62]
Second Fiddle ['59]
Streets Of Bakersfield ['88]
Sweet Rosie Jones ['68]
Sweethearts In Heaven ['63]
Tall Dark Stranger ['69]
Think Of Me ['66]
Together Again ['64]
Togetherness ['70]
Too Old To Cut The Mustard ['72]
Under The Influence Of Love ['61]
Under Your Spell Again ['59]
Waitin' In Your Welfare Line ['66]
We're Gonna Get Together ['70]
We're The Talk Of The Town ['63]
Weekend Daddy ['75]
Where Does The Good Times Go ['67]
Who's Gonna Mow Your Grass ['69]
Without You ['81]
World Famous Holiday Inn ['77]
You Ain't Gonna Have Ol' Buck To Kick Around No More ['72]
You're For Me ['63]
Your Tender Loving Care ['67]

OWENS, Marie

Born in 1956 in Virginia. Female singer.

DEBUT	PEAK	WKS	GOLD	Country Chart Hit	Songwriter	Label (& Number)
2/23/74	44	9		1 **J. John Jones**	*K. Phyllis Powell/Billy Ray Reynolds*	MCA 40184
6/8/74	71	8		2 **Release Me**	*Eddie Miller/W.S. Stevenson*	MCA 40241
11/16/74	71	7		3 **I Want To Lay Down Beside You**	*Tim Drummond*	MCA 40308
10/25/75	84	4		4 **Someone Loves You Honey**	*Don Devaney*	4 Star 1019
2/12/77	92	4		5 **When Your Good Love Was Mine**	*Jerry Foster/Bill Rice*	MMI 1012
5/7/77	88	4		6 **Burning**	*Jerry Foster/Bill Rice*	MMI 1015
8/13/77	80	5		7 **Ease My Mind On You**	*Chuck Riddle*	Sing Me 12

OXFORD, Vernon

Born on 6/8/1941 in Larue, Arkansas; raised in Wichita, Kansas. Male singer/songwriter/fiddle player.

DEBUT	PEAK	WKS	GOLD	Country Chart Hit	Songwriter	Label (& Number)
12/6/75+	54	12		1 **Shadows Of My Mind**	*E.E. Collins*	RCA Victor 10442
4/3/76	83	6		2 **Your Wanting Me Is Gone**	*J.R. Cochran*	RCA Victor 10595
6/12/76	17	12		3 **Redneck! (The Redneck National Anthem)**	*Ramona Redd/Mitchell Torok*	RCA Victor 10693
10/16/76	60	7		4 **Clean Your Own Tables**	*Chip Taylor*	RCA 10787
1/29/77	55	6		5 **A Good Old Fashioned Saturday Night Honky Tonk Barroom Brawl**	*Tim DuBois/John Ragsdale*	RCA 10872
5/7/77	87	3		6 **Only The Shadows Know**	*Curly Putman*	RCA 10952
7/23/77	95	2		7 **Redneck Roots**	*Ramona Redd/Mitchell Torok*	RCA 11020

OZARK MOUNTAIN DAREDEVILS

Country-rock group from Springfield, Missouri: Larry Lee (vocals, drums), John Dillon (guitar), Steve Cash (harmonica) and Michael "Supe" Granda (bass).

DEBUT	PEAK	WKS	GOLD	Country Chart Hit	Songwriter	Label (& Number)
5/8/76	84	4		**You Made It Right**	*Elizabeth Dillon/John Dillon*	A&M 1809

P

PACIFIC STEEL CO. Featuring Jay Dee Maness

Steel guitar instrumental duo: Jay Dee Maness and Junior "Red" Rhodes.

DEBUT	PEAK	WKS	GOLD	Country Chart Hit	Songwriter	Label (& Number)
12/6/80	88	5		**Fat 'N Sassy** [I]	*Jay Dee Maness*	Pacific Arts 111

PACK, Bob

Born in Danville, California. Male singer/songwriter.

DEBUT	PEAK	WKS	GOLD	Country Chart Hit	Songwriter	Label (& Number)
7/23/88	74	4		**The Request**	*Bob Pack*	Oak 1051

DEBUT	PEAK	WKS	GOLD	ARTIST / Country Chart Hit / Ranking / Songwriter	Label (& Number)

PACK, Ray

Born in West Virginia. Male singer.

DEBUT	PEAK	WKS	GOLD	Country Chart Hit ... Songwriter	Label (& Number)
2/11/89	**91**	2		**Where Was I** ... *Eddie Burton/Tom Grant*	Happy Man 818

PAGE, Patti — All-Time: #291

Born Clara Ann Fowler on 11/8/1927 in Muskogee, Oklahoma; raised in Tulsa, Oklahoma. Female pop singer. Hosted own TV series from 1955-58 and *The Big Record* from 1957-58. Acted in the 1960 movie *Elmer Gantry*.

DEBUT	PEAK	WKS	GOLD	Country Chart Hit ... Songwriter	Label (& Number)
5/7/49	**15**	1		1 **Money, Marbles And Chalk** ... J:15 *Pop Eckler*	Mercury 5251
12/30/50+	**2^{3}**	12	●	2 **The Tennessee Waltz** J:2 / S:5 / A:5 *Pee Wee King/Redd Stewart* Grammy: Hall of Fame	Mercury 5534-X45
7/17/61	**21**	3		3 **Mom And Dad's Waltz** ... *Lefty Frizzell*	Mercury 71823
2/17/62	**13**	15		4 **Go On Home** ... *Hank Cochran*	Mercury 71906
5/30/70	**22**	10		5 **I Wish I Had A Mommy Like You** ... *Billy Sherrill/Danny Walls/Norro Wilson*	Columbia 45159
1/16/71	**24**	10		6 **Give Him Love** ... *Jerry Foster/Bill Rice*	Mercury 73162
5/8/71	**37**	8		7 **Make Me Your Kind Of Woman** ... *Emily Mitchell/Norro Wilson*	Mercury 73199
8/14/71	**63**	4		8 **I'd Rather Be Sorry** ... *Kris Kristofferson*	Mercury 73222
11/20/71	**38**	9		9 **Think Again /** ... *Jerry Foster/Bill Rice*	
12/4/71	**flip**	3		10 **A Woman Left Lonely** ... *Spooner Oldham/Dan Penn*	Mercury 73249
12/16/72+	**14**	12		11 **Hello We're Lonely** *[w/ Tom T. Hall]* ... *Tom T. Hall*	Mercury 73347
9/8/73	**42**	11		12 **I Can't Sit Still** ... *Carmol Taylor/Norro Wilson*	Epic 11032
12/29/73+	**29**	11		13 **You're Gonna Hurt Me (One More Time)** ... *George Richey/Carmol Taylor/Norro Wilson*	Epic 11072
5/18/74	**59**	7		14 **Someone Came To See Me (In The Middle Of The Night)** ... *Tupper Saussy*	Epic 11109
11/30/74+	**70**	7		15 **I May Not Be Lovin' You** ... *George Richey/Billy Sherrill/Norro Wilson*	Avco 603
7/26/75	**67**	7		16 **Less Than The Song** ... *Hoyt Axton*	Avco 613
3/21/81	**39**	8		17 **No Aces** ... *Walt Cunningham/Bob House*	Plantation 197
7/18/81	**76**	2		18 **On The Inside /** ... *David Caswell* from the TV series *Prisoner: Cell Block H* starring Patsy King	
8/1/81	**66**	4		19 **A Poor Man's Roses** ... *Milton DeLugg/Bob Hilliard*	Plantation 201
5/8/82	**80**	4		20 **My Man Friday** ... *Ken Barken/Jay Hungerford*	Plantation 208

PAIGE, Allison

Born on 5/27/1982 in Refugio, Texas. Female singer.

DEBUT	PEAK	WKS	GOLD	Country Chart Hit ... Songwriter	Label (& Number)
5/13/00	**72**	5		**The End Of The World** ... *Sylvia Dee/Arthur Kent* from the album *It's My Party* on Capitol 66463	Capitol

PAISLEY, Brad — 2000s: #11 / All-Time: #198

Born on 10/28/1972 in Glen Dale, West Virginia. Male singer/songwriter/guitarist. Married actress Kimberly Williams on 3/15/2003.

CMA: Horizon 2000 // OPRY: 2001

DEBUT	PEAK	WKS	GOLD	Country Chart Hit ... Songwriter	Label (& Number)
2/6/99	**12**	31		1 **Who Needs Pictures** ... S:6 *Chris DuBois/Brad Paisley/Frank Rogers*	Arista Nashville
9/4/99	**❶^{1}**	30		2 **He Didn't Have To Be** *Kelley Lovelace/Brad Paisley*	Arista Nashville
2/12/00	**18**	20		3 **Me Neither** ... *Chris DuBois/Brad Paisley/Frank Rogers*	Arista Nashville
7/1/00	**❶^{2}**	32		4 **We Danced** *Chris DuBois/Brad Paisley* above 4 from the album *Who Needs Pictures* on Arista Nashville 18871	Arista Nashville
10/14/00	**68**	2		5 **Hard To Be A Husband, Hard To Be A Wife** *[w/ Chely Wright]* ... *Brad Paisley/Chely Wright* from the various artists album *75 Years Of The WSM Grand Ole Opry Volume Two* on MCA Nashville 170176	MCA Nashville
3/24/01	**4**	21		6 **Two People Fell In Love** ... *Kelley Lovelace/Tim Owens/Brad Paisley*	Arista Nashville
8/18/01	**58**	1		7 **Too Country** ... *Bill Anderson/Chuck Cannon* **CMA: Vocal Event**; **George Jones**, **Bill Anderson** and **Buck Owens** (guest vocals)	Arista Nashville
9/1/01+	**2^{3}**	31		8 **Wrapped Around** ... *Chris DuBois/Kelley Lovelace/Brad Paisley*	Arista Nashville
3/2/02	**❶^{2}**	25		9 **I'm Gonna Miss Her (The Fishin' Song)** *Brad Paisley/Frank Rogers*	Arista Nashville
8/17/02+	**7**	30		10 **I Wish You'd Stay** ... *Chris DuBois/Brad Paisley* above 5 from the album *Part II* on Arista Nashville 67008	Arista Nashville
3/22/03	**3^{4}**	29		11 **Celebrity** ... *Brad Paisley*	Arista Nashville
9/6/03+	**2^{1}**	32		12 **Little Moments** ... *Chris DuBois/Brad Paisley*	Arista Nashville
4/10/04	**3^{3}**	24		13 **Whiskey Lullaby** *[w/ Alison Krauss]* ... *Bill Anderson/Jon Randall* **CMA: Musical Event**	Arista Nashville
9/18/04+	**❶^{1}**	30		14 **Mud On The Tires** *Chris DuBois* above 4 from the album *Mud On The Tires* on Arista Nashville 50605	Arista Nashville
5/7/05	**4**	21↑		15 **Alcohol** ... *Brad Paisley* from the album *Time Well Wasted* on Arista Nashville 69642	Arista Nashville

PALMER, Keith

Born on 6/23/1957 in Hayatt, Missouri; raised in Corning, Arkansas. Died on 6/13/1996 (age 38). Male singer/songwriter.

DEBUT	PEAK	WKS	GOLD	Country Chart Hit ... Songwriter	Label (& Number)
9/28/91	**54**	17		1 **Don't Throw Me In The Briarpatch** ... *Kix Brooks/Chris Waters*	Epic
1/25/92	**60**	8		2 **Forgotten But Not Gone** ... *Buzz Cason/Johnny MacRae* above 2 from the album *Keith Palmer* on Epic 48611	Epic

PALOMINO ROAD

Group of Nashville session musicians: Ronnie Guilbeau (vocals), Randy Frazier, J.T. Corenflos and Chip Lewis. Guilbeau is the son of Gib Guilbeau (of the **Burrito Brothers**).

DEBUT	PEAK	WKS	GOLD	Country Chart Hit ... Songwriter	Label (& Number)
1/16/93	**46**	15		**Why Baby Why** ... *Darrell Edwards/George Jones* from the album *Palomino Road* on Liberty 80476	Liberty

Billboard DEBUT	PEAK	WKS	GOLD	ARTIST / Country Chart Hit	Ranking / Songwriter	Label (& Number)
				PAPA JOE'S MUSIC BOX — see SMITH, Jerry		
				PARIS, Jack		
				Born in Ottumwa, Iowa. Male singer/songwriter.		
2/14/76	**94**	3		1 **It Sets Me Free**	*Jack Paris*	2-J 201
3/19/77	**98**	2		2 **Gypsy River**	*Charles Fields/Don Riis*	50 States 49
12/10/77+	**75**	7		3 **Mississippi**	*John Phillips*	50 States 57
3/4/78	**86**	4		4 **Lay Down Sally**	*Eric Clapton/Marcy Levy/George Terry*	50 States 58
8/19/78	**98**	3		5 (It's Gonna Be A) **Happy Day**	*Dale Davis*	50 States 62
				PARKER, Billy		
				Born on 7/19/1937 in Okemah, Oklahoma; raised in Tulsa, Oklahoma. Male singer/guitarist. DJ on KVOO-Tulsa. Member of **Ernest Tubb**'s band from 1968-70.		
9/18/76	**79**	8		1 **It's Bad When You're Caught** (With The Goods)	*Tommy Overstreet/Dale Vest*	SCR 133
1/22/77	**71**	8		2 **Lord, If I Make It To Heaven Can I Bring My Own Angel Along**	*Tommy Overstreet/Dale Vest*	SCR 136
6/4/77	**75**	6		3 **What Did I Promise Her Last Night**	*Ron McCown*	SCR 144
10/1/77	**94**	3		4 **If You Got To Have It Your Way** (I'll Go Mine)	*Tommy Overstreet/Dale Vest*	SCR 148
1/7/78	**62**	9		5 **You Read Between The Lines**	*Ron McCown*	SCR 153
4/29/78	**81**	4		6 **If There's One Angel Missing** (She's Here In My Arms Tonight)	*Wayne Morse*	SCR 157
8/26/78	**50**	7		7 **Until The Next Time**	*Oskar Solomon*	SCR 160
12/23/78+	**73**	6		8 **Pleasin' My Woman /**	*Don Devaney*	
3/10/79	**98**	1		9 **Thanks E.T. Thanks A Lot** — tribute to **Ernest Tubb**	*Tommy Williamson*	SCR 162
8/11/79	**80**	4		10 **Thanks A Lot**	*Eddie Miller/Don Sessions*	SCR 177
12/22/79+	**82**	6		11 **Tough Act To Follow**	*Billy Palmer/Vern Stovall*	SCR 181
2/14/81	**74**	3		12 **Better Side Of Thirty**	*John McFarland*	Oak 47565
8/22/81	**53**	7		13 **I'll Drink To That**	*Alice Merritt*	Soundwaves 4643
1/9/82	**51**	10		14 **I See An Angel Every Day**	*James Forst*	Soundwaves 4659
5/1/82	**41**	11		15 (Who's Gonna Sing) **The Last Country Song**	*Buddy Brock*	Soundwaves 4670
7/31/82	**53**	8		16 **If I Ever Need A Lady** — **Darrell McCall** (harmony vocal, above 2)	*Gene Chrysler*	Soundwaves 4678
10/30/82	**68**	6		17 **Too Many Irons In The Fire** *[w/ Cal Smith]*	*James Forst*	Soundwaves 4686
3/26/83	**68**	6		18 **Who Said Love Was Fair**	*Rick Gibson*	Soundwaves 4699
7/9/83	**59**	8		19 **Love Don't Know A Lady** (From A Honky Tonk Girl)	*Merrill Lane*	Soundwaves 4708
2/13/88	**72**	5		20 **You Are My Angel**	*Danny Byram*	Canyon Creek 1208
10/22/88	**81**	4		21 **She's Sittin' Pretty**	*Bart Barton*	Canyon Creek 0801
5/27/89	**87**	4		22 **It's Time For Your Dreams To Come True**	*Stan Ratliff*	Canyon Creek 0315
				PARKER, Caryl Mack		
				Born in Abilene, Texas. Female singer/songwriter/guitarist.		
10/26/96	**67**	5		1 **Better Love Next Time**	*Caryl Mack Parker/Kim Patton*	Magnatone
3/22/97	**66**	4		2 **One Night Stand** — above 2 from the album *Caryl Mack Parker* on Magnatone 112	*Lisa Drew/Caryl Mack Parker/Scott Parker*	Magnatone
				PARKER, Gary Dale		
				Born on 7/6/1958 in Nashville, Tennessee. Male singer.		
1/13/90	**87**	1		**Once And For Always**	*Jackson Leap*	615 Records 1022
				PARKER, Lori		
				Born in California. Female singer/songwriter.		
11/13/76	**92**	3		1 **Steppin' Out Tonight**	*Lori Parker*	Con Brio 113
9/3/77	**89**	4		2 **I Like Everything About Loving You**	*Cile David/Billy Deaton*	Con Brio 122
				PARKS, Michael		
				Born on 4/4/1938 in Corona, California. Male singer/actor. Played "Jim Bronson" on TV's *Then Came Bronson*.		
3/21/70	**41**	9		**Long Lonesome Highway** — from the TV series *Then Came Bronson* starring Parks	*James Hendricks*	MGM 14104
				PARKS, P.J.		
				Born in Denver, Colorado. Male singer.		
1/10/81	**86**	4		1 **The Way You Are**	*Jerry Foster/Bill Rice*	Kik 901
4/4/81	**85**	3		2 **Falling In**	*Karen Bell/Terry Skinner/J.L. Wallace*	Kik 903
				PARNELL, Lee Roy	**1990s: #42 / All-Time: #211**	
				Born on 12/21/1956 in Stephenville, Texas. Male singer/songwriter/guitarist. Also see **Jed Zeppelin**.		
3/17/90	**59**	8		1 **Crocodile Tears**	*Lee Roy Parnell/Leroy Preston*	Arista
6/30/90	**54**	13		2 **Oughta Be A Law**	*Gary Nicholson/Dan Penn*	Arista
10/27/90	**73**	1		3 **Family Tree** — above 3 from the album *Lee Roy Parnell* on Arista 8625	*David Durocher/Jeanne Smith*	Arista
2/22/92	**50**	20		4 **The Rock**	*Russell Smith/Jim Varsos*	Arista
5/16/92	**2^{2}**	20		5 **What Kind Of Fool Do You Think I Am**	*Alan Carmichael/Gary Griffin*	Arista
10/3/92+	**8**	20		6 **Love Without Mercy**	*Don Pfrimmer/Mike Reid*	Arista
3/6/93	**2^{1}**	20		7 **Tender Moment** — above 4 from the album *Love Without Mercy* on Arista 18684	*Rory Bourke/Lewis Moore/Lee Roy Parnell*	Arista
8/21/93	**6**	20		8 **On The Road**	*Bob McDill*	Arista
1/8/94	**3^{1}**	20		9 **I'm Holding My Own**	*Tony Arata*	Arista
5/21/94	**17**	20		10 **Take These Chains From My Heart**	*Hy Heath/Fred Rose*	Arista
10/1/94	**51**	9		11 **The Power Of Love** — above 4 from the album *On The Road* on Arista 18739	*Don Cook/Gary Nicholson*	Arista

DEBUT	PEAK	WKS	GOLD	ARTIST / Country Chart Hit	Ranking / Songwriter	Label (& Number)
				PARNELL, Lee Roy — cont'd		
5/20/95	2[1]	20		12 **A Little Bit Of You**	*Trey Bruce/Craig Wiseman*	Career
9/9/95+	12	20		13 **When A Woman Loves A Man**	*Mark Luna/Rafe Van Hoy*	Career
1/20/96	3[2]	20		14 **Heart's Desire**	*Lewis Moore/Lee Roy Parnell*	Career
5/18/96	12	20		15 **Givin' Water To A Drowning Man**	*Gary Nicholson/Lee Roy Parnell*	Career
9/21/96	46	15		16 **We All Get Lucky Sometimes**	*Gary Nicholson/Jimmy Scott*	Career
				above 5 from the album *We All Get Lucky Sometimes* on Career 18790		
1/11/97	71	1		17 **Please Come Home For Christmas**	*Charles Brown/Gene Redd* [X]	Arista
				from the album *Star Of Wonder* on Arista 18822		
4/19/97	35	18		18 **Lucky Me, Lucky You**	*Gary Nicholson/Lee Roy Parnell*	Arista Nashville
8/16/97	39	13		19 **You Can't Get There From Here**	*Bob DiPiero/Wendell Mobley*	Arista Nashville
2/14/98	50	8		20 **All That Matters Anymore**	*Gary Nicholson/Lee Roy Parnell*	Arista Nashville
				above 3 from the album *Every Night's A Saturday Night* on Arista Nashville 18841		
7/24/99	57	8		21 **She Won't Be Lonely Long**	*Bob McDill*	Arista Nashville
				from the album *Hits And Highways Ahead* on Arista Nashville 18889		
10/16/04	46	16		22 **Inspiration** *[w/ David Lee Murphy]*	*David Lee Murphy*	Koch
				from Murphy's album *Tryin' To Get There* on Koch 8189		
				PARSONS, Rob		
				Born in Traverse City, Michigan. Male singer/songwriter.		
1/9/82	74	4		**Shadow Of Love**	*Rob Parsons*	MCA 51202

PARTON, Dolly **1970s: #4 / 1980s: #11 / All-Time: #8 // HOF: 1999**

Born on 1/19/1946 in Locust Ridge, Tennessee. Female singer/songwriter/guitarist/actress. Regular on **Porter Wagoner**'s TV show from 1967-74. Starred in the movies *9 To 5, The Best Little Whorehouse In Texas, Steel Magnolias* and *Straight Talk.* In 1986, opened Dollywood theme park in the Smoky Mountains. Hosted own TV variety show in 1987. Sister of **Randy Parton** and **Stella Parton**.

CMA: Vocal Group (with Porter Wagoner) 1968 / Vocal Duo (with Porter Wagoner) 1970 & 1971 / Female Vocalist 1975 & 1976 / Entertainer 1978 // OPRY: 1969

DEBUT	PEAK	WKS	GOLD	Country Chart Hit	Songwriter	Label (& Number)
1/21/67	24	14		1 **Dumb Blonde**	*Curly Putman*	Monument 982
6/10/67	17	12		2 **Something Fishy**	*Dolly Parton*	Monument 1007
12/2/67+	7	17		3 **The Last Thing On My Mind** *[w/ Porter Wagoner]*	*Tom Paxton*	RCA Victor 9369
4/13/68	7	16		4 **Holding On To Nothin'** *[w/ Porter Wagoner]*	*Jerry Chesnut*	RCA Victor 9490
6/29/68	17	14		5 **Just Because I'm A Woman**	*Dolly Parton*	RCA Victor 9548
7/27/68	5	13		6 **We'll Get Ahead Someday** *[w/ Porter Wagoner]* /	*Mack Magaha*	
10/5/68	51	6		7 **Jeannie's Afraid Of The Dark** *[w/ Porter Wagoner]*	*Dolly Parton*	RCA Victor 9577
11/16/68	25	11		8 **In The Good Old Days (When Times Were Bad)**	*Dolly Parton*	RCA Victor 9657
3/8/69	9	14		9 **Yours Love** *[w/ Porter Wagoner]*	*Harlan Howard*	RCA Victor 0104
4/12/69	40	10		10 **Daddy**	*Dolly Parton*	RCA Victor 0132
6/21/69	16	11		11 **Always, Always** *[w/ Porter Wagoner]*	*Joyce McCord*	RCA Victor 0172
7/26/69	50	8		12 **In The Ghetto**	*Mac Davis*	RCA Victor 0192
10/18/69	45	8		13 **My Blue Ridge Mountain Boy**	*Dolly Parton*	RCA Victor 0243
10/25/69	5	16		14 **Just Someone I Used To Know** *[w/ Porter Wagoner]*	*Jack Clement*	RCA Victor 0247
1/31/70	40	8		15 **Daddy Come And Get Me**	*Dorothy Jo Hope/Dolly Parton*	RCA Victor 9784
2/14/70	9	15		16 **Tomorrow Is Forever** *[w/ Porter Wagoner]*	*Dolly Parton*	RCA Victor 9799
7/4/70	3[2]	16		17 **Mule Skinner Blues (Blue Yodel No. 8)**	*Jimmie Rodgers/George Vaughn*	RCA Victor 9863
8/1/70	7	15		18 **Daddy Was An Old Time Preacher Man** *[w/ Porter Wagoner]*	*Dorothy Jo Hope/Dolly Parton*	RCA Victor 9875
12/12/70+	❶[1]	15		19 **Joshua**	*Dolly Parton*	RCA Victor 9928
2/27/71	7	13		20 **Better Move It On Home** *[w/ Porter Wagoner]*	*Ray Griff*	RCA Victor 9958
4/10/71	23	12		21 **Comin' For To Carry Me Home**	*Dolly Parton*	RCA Victor 9971
6/26/71	14	12		22 **The Right Combination** *[w/ Porter Wagoner]*	*Porter Wagoner*	RCA Victor 9994
7/17/71	17	12		23 **My Blue Tears**	*Dolly Parton*	RCA Victor 9999
10/30/71	4	16		24 **Coat Of Many Colors**	*Dolly Parton*	RCA Victor 0538
11/13/71+	11	13		25 **Burning The Midnight Oil** *[w/ Porter Wagoner]*	*Porter Wagoner*	RCA Victor 0565
3/11/72	6	14		26 **Touch Your Woman**	*Dolly Parton*	RCA Victor 0662
4/8/72	9	14		27 **Lost Forever In Your Kiss** *[w/ Porter Wagoner]*	*Dolly Parton*	RCA Victor 0675
8/12/72	20	9		28 **Washday Blues**	*Porter Wagoner*	RCA Victor 0757
9/2/72	14	13		29 **Together Always** *[w/ Porter Wagoner]*	*Dolly Parton*	RCA Victor 0773
1/6/73	15	13		30 **My Tennessee Mountain Home**	*Dolly Parton*	RCA Victor 0868
3/3/73	30	9		31 **We Found It** *[w/ Porter Wagoner]*	*Porter Wagoner*	RCA Victor 0893
5/19/73	20	11		32 **Traveling Man**	*Dolly Parton*	RCA Victor 0950
6/23/73	3[2]	17		33 **If Teardrops Were Pennies** *[w/ Porter Wagoner]*	*Carl Butler*	RCA Victor 0981
11/3/73+	❶[1]	19		34 **Jolene**	*Dolly Parton*	RCA Victor 0145
				RS500		
4/6/74	❶[1]	15		35 **I Will Always Love You**	*Dolly Parton*	RCA Victor 0234
				also see #65 and #101 below		
8/3/74	❶[1]	17		36 **Please Don't Stop Loving Me** *[w/ Porter Wagoner]*	*Dolly Parton/Porter Wagoner*	RCA Victor 10010
8/31/74	❶[1]	17		37 **Love Is Like A Butterfly**	*Dolly Parton*	RCA Victor 10031
1/25/75	❶[1]	13		38 **The Bargain Store**	*Dolly Parton*	RCA Victor 10164
6/7/75	2[1]	16		39 **The Seeker**	*Dolly Parton*	RCA Victor 10310
7/12/75	5	17		40 **Say Forever You'll Be Mine** *[w/ Porter Wagoner]*	*Dolly Parton*	RCA Victor 10328
9/27/75	9	14		41 **We Used To**	*Dolly Parton*	RCA Victor 10396
2/28/76	19	11		42 **Hey, Lucky Lady**	*Dolly Parton*	RCA Victor 10564

DEBUT	PEAK	WKS	GOLD		ARTIST / Country Chart Hit	Ranking / Songwriter	Label (& Number)
					PARTON, Dolly — cont'd		
5/15/76	8	14		43	Is Forever Longer Than Always *[w/ Porter Wagoner]*	*Frank Dycus/Porter Wagoner*	RCA Victor 10652
7/31/76	3^{1}	15		44	All I Can Do	*Dolly Parton*	RCA Victor 10730
4/9/77	11	13		45	Light Of A Clear Blue Morning	*Dolly Parton*	RCA 10935
10/15/77	❶^{5}	19	●	46	Here You Come Again	*Barry Mann/Cynthia Weil*	RCA 11123
					Grammy: Female Vocal		
3/18/78	❶^{2}	14		47	It's All Wrong, But It's All Right /	*Dolly Parton*	
4/1/78	flip	12		48	Two Doors Down	*Dolly Parton*	RCA 11240
8/19/78	❶^{3}	13		49	Heartbreaker	*Carole Bayer Sager/David Wolfert*	RCA 11296
11/25/78+	❶^{1}	14		50	I Really Got The Feeling /	*Billy Vera*	
11/25/78	48	14		51	Baby I'm Burnin'	*Dolly Parton*	RCA 11420
6/9/79	❶^{2}	14		52	You're The Only One	*Bruce Roberts/Carole Bayer Sager*	RCA 11577
9/1/79	7	13		53	Sweet Summer Lovin' /	*Blaise Tosti*	
9/1/79	flip	13		54	Great Balls Of Fire	*Otis Blackwell/Jack Hammer*	RCA 11705
3/22/80	❶^{1}	14		55	Starting Over Again	*Bruce Sudano/Donna Summer*	RCA 11926
6/21/80	2^{2}	17		56	Making Plans *[w/ Porter Wagoner]*	*Voni Morrison/Johnny Russell*	RCA 11983
7/19/80	❶^{1}	16		57	Old Flames Can't Hold A Candle To You	*Hugh Moffatt/Pebe Sebert*	RCA 12040
11/8/80+	12	14		58	If You Go, I'll Follow You *[w/ Porter Wagoner]*	*Dolly Parton/Porter Wagoner*	RCA 12119
11/29/80+	❶^{1}	14	●	59	9 To 5	*Dolly Parton*	RCA 12133
					Grammy: Song & Female Vocal; from the movie starring Parton		
4/11/81	❶^{1}	17		60	But You Know I Love You	*Mike Settle*	RCA 12200
8/29/81	14	13		61	The House Of The Rising Sun /	*Alan Price*	
8/29/81	flip	1		62	Working Girl	*Dolly Parton*	RCA 12282
2/27/82	8	17		63	Single Women	*Michael O'Donoghue*	RCA 13057
5/29/82	7	15		64	Heartbreak Express	*Dolly Parton*	RCA 13234
7/31/82	❶^{1}	19		65	I Will Always Love You /	*Dolly Parton* [R]	
					new version of #35 above; from the movie *The Best Little Whorehouse In Texas* starring Parton		
7/31/82	flip	19		66	Do I Ever Cross Your Mind	*Dolly Parton*	RCA 13260
11/6/82+	8	17		67	Hard Candy Christmas	*Carol Hall* [X]	RCA 13361
					from the movie *The Best Little Whorehouse In Texas* starring Parton		
12/11/82+	7	20		68	Everything's Beautiful (In It's Own Way) *[w/ Willie Nelson]*	*Dolly Parton*	Monument 03408
4/30/83	20	16		69	Potential New Boyfriend	*Steve Kipner/John Parker*	RCA 13514
9/3/83	❶^{2}	23	▲	70	Islands In The Stream *[w/ Kenny Rogers]*	*Barry Gibb/Maurice Gibb/Robin Gibb*	RCA 13615
12/24/83+	3^{1}	19		71	Save The Last Dance For Me	*Doc Pomus/Mort Shuman*	RCA 13703
4/7/84	36	10		72	Downtown	*Tony Hatch*	RCA 13756
6/9/84	❶^{1}	20		73	Tennessee Homesick Blues	*Dolly Parton*	RCA 13819
9/15/84	10	20		74	God Won't Get You	S:10 / A:11 *Dolly Parton*	RCA 13883
					above 2 from the movie *Rhinestone* starring Parton		
12/15/84+	53	7		75	The Greatest Gift Of All *[w/ Kenny Rogers]*	*John Jarvis* [X]	RCA 13945
1/26/85	3^{1}	22		76	Don't Call It Love	A:3 / S:4 *Dean Pitchford/Tom Snow*	RCA 13987
5/25/85	❶^{1}	20		77	Real Love *[w/ Kenny Rogers]*	S:❶^{1} / A:❶^{1} *Richard Brannan/David Malloy/Randy McCormick*	RCA 14058
11/30/85+	❶^{1}	22		78	Think About Love	S:❶^{1} / A:❶^{1} *Richard Brannan/Tom Campbell*	RCA 14218
5/3/86	17	15		79	Tie Our Love (In A Double Knot)	A:15 / S:17 *John Reid/Jeff Silbar*	RCA 14297
9/6/86	31	13		80	We Had It All	S:28 / A:29 *Donnie Fritts/Troy Seals*	RCA 5001
2/21/87	❶^{1}	19		81	To Know Him Is To Love Him *[w/ Linda Ronstadt & Emmylou Harris]*	S:❶^{1} / A:❶^{1} *Phil Spector*	Warner 28492
5/30/87	3^{1}	18		82	Telling Me Lies *[w/ Linda Ronstadt & Emmylou Harris]*	S:10 *Betsy Cook/Linda Thompson*	Warner 28371
9/26/87	5	22		83	Those Memories Of You *[w/ Linda Ronstadt & Emmylou Harris]*	S:10 *Alan O'Bryant*	Warner 28248
12/19/87+	63	8		84	The River Unbroken	*David Batteau/Darrell Brown*	Columbia 07665
3/26/88	6	18		85	Wildflowers *[w/ Linda Ronstadt & Emmylou Harris]*	S:13 *Dolly Parton*	Warner 27970
5/6/89	❶^{1}	20		86	Why'd You Come In Here Lookin' Like That	*Bob Carlisle/Randy Thomas*	Columbia 68760
8/26/89	❶^{1}	26		87	Yellow Roses	*Dolly Parton*	Columbia 69040
12/9/89+	39	8		88	He's Alive	*Don Francisco*	Columbia 73200
2/3/90	39	11		89	Time For Me To Fly	*Kevin Cronin*	Columbia
5/12/90	29	12		90	White Limozeen	*Mac Davis/Dolly Parton*	Columbia
					above 2 from the album *White Limozeen* on Columbia 44384		
8/18/90	21	20		91	Love Is Strange *[w/ Kenny Rogers]*	*Mickey Baker/Bo Diddley/Sylvia Robinson*	Reprise
					from Rogers' album *Love Is Strange* on Reprise 26289		
3/2/91	❶^{1}	20		92	Rockin' Years *[w/ Ricky Van Shelton]*	*Floyd Parton*	Columbia
6/8/91	15	20		93	Silver And Gold	*Carl Perkins/Greg Perkins/Stan Perkins*	Columbia
10/19/91	33	20		94	Eagle When She Flies	*Dolly Parton*	Columbia
1/25/92	46	10		95	Country Road	*Dolly Parton/Gary Scruggs*	Columbia
					above 4 from the album *Eagle When She Flies* on Columbia 46882		
4/11/92	64	5		96	Straight Talk	*Dolly Parton*	Hollywood
					from the movie starring Parton (soundtrack on Hollywood 61303)		
2/13/93	27	20		97	Romeo *[w/ Mary-Chapin Carpenter/Billy Ray Cyrus/Kathy Mattea/Pam Tillis/Tanya Tucker]*	*...Dolly Parton*	Columbia
5/1/93	58	9		98	More Where That Came From	*Dolly Parton*	Columbia
					above 2 from the album *Slow Dancing With The Moon* on Columbia 53199		
12/25/93+	68	2		99	Silver Threads And Golden Needles *[w/ Tammy Wynette & Loretta Lynn]*		
					from their album *Honky Tonk Angels* on Columbia 53414	*...Dick Reynolds/Jack Rhodes*	Columbia
10/15/94	70	4		100	PMS Blues	*Dolly Parton*	Columbia
					from the album *Heartsongs - Live From Home* on Columbia 66123		
9/16/95	15	20		101	I Will Always Love You *[w/ Vince Gill]*	*Dolly Parton* [R]	Columbia
					CMA: Vocal Event; from the album *Something Special* on Columbia 67140; new version of #35 and #65 above		

Billboard DEBUT	PEAK	WKS	GOLD	ARTIST / Country Chart Hit	Ranking / Songwriter	Label (& Number)
				PARTON, Dolly — cont'd		
10/5/96	**62**	10		102 **Just When I Needed You Most** from the album *Treasures* on Rising Tide 53041	*Randy Vanwarmer*	Rising Tide
7/19/97	**8^{S}**	12		103 **Peace Train** Ladysmith Black Mambazo (backing vocals)	*Cat Stevens*	Flip It
1/3/98	**73**	2		104 **Hard Candy Christmas** from the various artists album *Country Christmas, Volume 2* on RCA 4809; same version as #67 above	*Carol Hall* **[X-R]**	RCA
9/5/98	**74**	2		105 **Honky Tonk Songs** from the album *Hungry Again* on Decca 70041	*Dolly Parton*	Decca
12/26/98+	**70**	2		106 **Winter Wonderland/Sleigh Ride** from the album *Country Christmas Classics* on RCA 67698	*Leroy Anderson/Felix Bernard/Mitchell Parish/Richard Smith* **[X]**	RCA
11/23/02	**60**	1		107 **Hello God** from the album *Halos & Horns* on Blue Eye 3946	*Dolly Parton*	Blue Eye
12/4/04	**3^{1S}**	33		108 **Viva Las Vegas** ***[w/ The Grascals]*** from the album *The Grascals* on Rounder 610549	*Doc Pomus/Mort Shuman*	Rounder

All I Can Do ['76]
Always, Always ['69]
Baby I'm Burnin' ['78]
Bargain Store ['75]
Better Move It On Home ['71]
Burning The Midnight Oil ['72]
But You Know I Love You ['81]
Coat Of Many Colors ['71]
Comin' For To Carry Me Home ['71]
Country Road ['92]
Daddy Come And Get Me ['70]
Daddy Was An Old Time Preacher Man ['70]
Daddy ['69]
Do I Ever Cross Your Mind ['82]
Don't Call It Love ['85]
Downtown ['84]
Dumb Blonde ['67]
Eagle When She Flies ['91]
Everything's Beautiful (In It's Own Way) ['83]
God Won't Get You ['84]
Great Balls Of Fire ['79]
Greatest Gift Of All ['85]
Hard Candy Christmas ['83]
Hard Candy Christmas ['98]
He's Alive ['90]
Heartbreak Express ['82]
Heartbreaker ['78]
Hello God ['02]
Here You Come Again ['77]
Hey, Lucky Lady ['76]
Holding On To Nothin' ['68]
Honky Tonk Songs ['98]
House Of The Rising Sun ['81]
I Really Got The Feeling ['79]
I Will Always Love You ['74]
I Will Always Love You ['82]
I Will Always Love You ['95]
If Teardrops Were Pennies ['73]
If You Go, I'll Follow You ['81]
In The Ghetto ['69]
In The Good Old Days (When Times Were Bad) ['68]
Is Forever Longer Than Always ['76]
Islands In The Stream ['83]
It's All Wrong, But It's All Right ['78]
Jeannie's Afraid Of The Dark ['68]
Jolene ['74]
Joshua ['71]
Just Because I'm A Woman ['68]
Just Someone I Used To Know ['69]
Just When I Needed You Most ['96]
Last Thing On My Mind ['68]
Light Of A Clear Blue Morning ['77]
Lost Forever In Your Kiss ['72]
Love Is Like A Butterfly ['74]
Love Is Strange ['90]
Making Plans ['80]
More Where That Came From ['93]
Mule Skinner Blues (Blue Yodel No. 8) ['70]
My Blue Ridge Mountain Boy ['69]
My Blue Tears ['71]
My Tennessee Mountain Home ['73]
9 To 5 ['81]
Old Flames Can't Hold A Candle To You ['80]
PMS Blues ['94]
Peace Train ['97]
Please Don't Stop Loving Me ['74]
Potential New Boyfriend ['83]
Real Love ['85]
Right Combination ['71]
River Unbroken ['88]
Rockin' Years ['91]
Romeo ['93]
Save The Last Dance For Me ['84]
Say Forever You'll Be Mine ['75]
Seeker ['75]
Silver And Gold ['91]
Silver Threads And Golden Needles ['94]
Single Women ['82]
Something Fishy ['67]
Starting Over Again ['80]
Straight Talk ['92]
Sweet Summer Lovin' ['79]
Telling Me Lies ['87]
Tennessee Homesick Blues ['84]
Think About Love ['86]
Those Memories Of You ['87]
Tie Our Love (In A Double Knot) ['86]
Time For Me To Fly ['90]
To Know Him Is To Love Him ['87]
Together Always ['72]
Tomorrow Is Forever ['70]
Touch Your Woman ['72]
Traveling Man ['73]
Two Doors Down ['78]
Viva Las Vegas ['04]
Washday Blues ['72]
We Found It ['73]
We Had It All ['86]
We Used To ['75]
We'll Get Ahead Someday ['68]
White Limozeen ['90]
Why'd You Come In Here Lookin' Like That ['89]
Wildflowers ['88]
Winter Wonderland/Sleigh Ride ['99]
Working Girl ['81]
Yellow Roses ['89]
You're The Only One ['79]
Yours Love ['69]

PARTON, Randy

Born on 12/15/1955 in Sevier County, Tennessee. Brother of **Dolly Parton** and **Stella Parton**.

DEBUT	PEAK	WKS	GOLD	Country Chart Hit	Songwriter	Label (& Number)
3/7/81	**30**	12		1 **Hold Me Like You Never Had Me**	*Tom Brasfield/Robert Byrne*	RCA 12137
8/1/81	**30**	10		2 **Shot Full Of Love**	*Bob McDill*	RCA 12271
12/19/81	**80**	4		3 **Don't Cry Baby**	*David Finnerty*	RCA 12351
5/1/82	**76**	4		4 **Oh, No**	*Lionel Richie*	RCA 13087
10/22/83	**92**	2		5 **A Stranger In Her Bed**	*Blake Mevis/Bill Shore/David Wills*	RCA 13608

PARTON, Stella

Born on 5/4/1949 in Sevier County, Tennessee. Sister of **Dolly Parton** and **Randy Parton**.

DEBUT	PEAK	WKS	GOLD	Country Chart Hit	Songwriter	Label (& Number)
5/24/75	**9**	18		1 **I Want To Hold You In My Dreams Tonight**	*Bob Dean/Stella Parton*	Country Soul 039
9/27/75	**56**	10		2 **It's Not Funny Anymore**	*Bob Dean/Paul Overstreet*	Soul Country 088
1/8/77	**87**	5		3 **Neon Women** ***[w/ Carmol Taylor]***	*Bobbi Cole/Toni Dae/Carmol Taylor*	Elektra 45367
3/19/77	**60**	9		4 **I'm Not That Good At Goodbye**	*Bob McDill/Don Williams*	Elektra 45383
7/30/77	**15**	13		5 **The Danger Of A Stranger**	*Shel Silverstein/Even Stevens*	Elektra 45410
11/12/77+	**14**	15		6 **Standard Lie Number One**	*Dennis Wilson*	Elektra 45437
3/25/78	**20**	10		7 **Four Little Letters**	*Even Stevens/Dan Tyler*	Elektra 45468
7/1/78	**28**	9		8 **Undercover Lovers**	*Sherry Grooms/Even Stevens*	Elektra 45490
10/14/78	**21**	10		9 **Stormy Weather**	*Leo Sayer/Tom Snow*	Elektra 45533
4/21/79	**26**	11		10 **Steady As The Rain**	*Dolly Parton*	Elektra 46029
7/28/79	**36**	9		11 **The Room At The Top Of The Stairs**	*Even Stevens/Dan Tyler*	Elektra 46502
3/6/82	**65**	7		12 **I'll Miss You**	*Bob Teague*	Town House 1056
7/24/82	**75**	5		13 **Young Love**	*Ric Cartey/Carole Joyner*	Town House 1058
3/21/87	**86**	3		14 **Cross My Heart**	*Rachel Dennison/Frank Dycus/Randy Parton*	Luv 132
4/1/89	**74**	3		15 **I Don't Miss You Like I Used To**	*Jan Buckingham/Curtis Stone*	Airborne 10015

PASTELL, James

Born James Futch in 1940 in El Dorado, Arkansas. Male singer.

DEBUT	PEAK	WKS	GOLD	Country Chart Hit	Songwriter	Label (& Number)
9/10/77	**95**	5		**Hell Yes I Cheated**	*Larry Cheshier/Glenn Sutton*	Paula 425

PAUL, Buddy

Born in Shreveport, Louisiana. Male singer/songwriter.

DEBUT	PEAK	WKS	GOLD	Country Chart Hit	Songwriter	Label (& Number)
8/1/60	**22**	4		**This Old Town**	*Buddy Paul*	Murco 1018

PAUL, Joyce

Born in Tulsa, Oklahoma. Female singer.

DEBUT	PEAK	WKS	GOLD	Country Chart Hit	Songwriter	Label (& Number)
6/22/68	**36**	10		**Phone Call To Mama**	*Jerry Chesnut/Norro Wilson*	United Artists 50315

PAUL, Les, and Mary Ford

Pop duo. Paul was born Lester Polsfuss on 6/9/1915 in Waukesha, Wisconsin. Innovator in electric guitar and multi-track recordings. Mary Ford was born Colleen Summers on 7/7/1924 in Pasadena, California. Died on 9/30/1977 (age 53). They were married from 1949-63.

DEBUT	PEAK	WKS	GOLD	Country Chart Hit	Songwriter	Label (& Number)
3/10/51	**7**	1	●	**Mockin' Bird Hill**	A:7 *Vaughn Horton*	Capitol F1373

Billboard DEBUT	PEAK	WKS	GOLD	ARTIST / Country Chart Hit	Ranking / Songwriter	Label (& Number)

PAXTON, Gary S.

Born in Mesa, Arizona. Male singer/songwriter/guitarist.

DEBUT	PEAK	WKS	GOLD	Country Chart Hit	Songwriter	Label (& Number)
2/7/76	85	5		Too Far Gone (To Care What You Do To Me)	*Karen Adams/Gary S. Paxton*	RCA Victor 10449

PAYCHECK, Johnny — 1970s: #35 / All-Time: #76

Born Donald Eugene Lytle on 5/31/1938 in Greenfield, Ohio. Died of emphysema on 2/18/2003 (age 64). Male singer/songwriter/guitarist. Played in the backing bands for **Porter Wagoner**, **Faron Young**, **Ray Price** and **George Jones**. First recorded solo as Donny Young. Served two years in prison for a 1985 barroom shooting incident.

OPRY: 1997

DEBUT	PEAK	WKS	GOLD	Country Chart Hit	Songwriter	Label (& Number)
10/16/65	26	12		1 A-11	*Hank Cochran*	Hilltop 3007
2/26/66	40	2		2 Heartbreak Tennessee	*Jack Clement*	Hilltop 3009
6/4/66	8	19		3 The Lovin' Machine	*Larry Kingston*	Little Darlin' 008
11/5/66+	13	15		4 Motel Time Again	*Bobby Bare*	Little Darlin' 0016
4/8/67	15	15		5 Jukebox Charlie	*Aubrey Mayhew/Johnny Paycheck*	Little Darlin' 0020
9/2/67	32	10		6 The Cave	*Larry Kingston*	Little Darlin' 0032
12/23/67+	41	11		7 Don't Monkey With Another Monkey's Monkey	*Dale Morris*	Little Darlin' 0035
4/27/68	59	7		8 (It Won't Be Long) And I'll Be Hating You	*Aubrey Mayhew/Johnny Paycheck*	Little Darlin' 0042
8/17/68	66	4		9 My Heart Keeps Running To You	*Ray Buzzeo*	Little Darlin' 0046
12/14/68	73	4		10 If I'm Gonna Sink	*Aubrey Mayhew/Johnny Paycheck*	Little Darlin' 0052
6/28/69	31	13		11 Wherever You Are	*Aubrey Mayhew/Johnny Paycheck*	Little Darlin' 0060
10/9/71	2^{1}	19		12 She's All I Got	*Gary Anderson/Jerry Williams*	Epic 10783
3/11/72	4	14		13 Someone To Give My Love To	*Jerry Foster/Bill Rice*	Epic 10836
5/27/72	13	11		14 Let's All Go Down To The River *[w/ Jody Miller]*	*Earl Montgomery/Sue Richards*	Epic 10863
6/24/72	12	11		15 Love Is A Good Thing	*Jerry Foster/Bill Rice*	Epic 10876
10/7/72	21	12		16 Somebody Loves Me	*Jerry Foster/Bill Rice*	Epic 10912
2/24/73	10	12		17 Something About You I Love	*Jerry Foster/Bill Rice*	Epic 10947
6/9/73	2^{3}	15		18 Mr. Lovemaker	*Johnny Paycheck*	Epic 10999
11/3/73+	8	15		19 Song And Dance Man	*Jerry Foster/Bill Rice*	Epic 11046
3/16/74	19	12		20 My Part Of Forever	*Jerry Foster/Bill Rice*	Epic 11090
7/6/74	23	11		21 Keep On Lovin' Me	*Will Jennings/Troy Seals*	Epic 11142
11/2/74+	12	15		22 For A Minute There	*Jerry Foster/Bill Rice*	Epic 50040
3/1/75	26	11		23 Loving You Beats All I've Ever Seen	*Johnny Paycheck*	Epic 50073
5/31/75	38	12		24 I Don't Love Her Anymore	*Red Lane/Danny Morrison*	Epic 50111
9/27/75	23	12		25 All-American Man	*Gary Adams/Johnny Paycheck*	Epic 50146
2/21/76	56	8		26 The Feminine Touch	*Frank Dycus/Larry Kingston*	Epic 50193
5/8/76	49	8		27 Gone At Last *[w/ Charnissa]*	*Paul Simon*	Epic 50215
7/24/76	34	10		28 11 Months And 29 Days	*Johnny Paycheck/Billy Sherrill*	Epic 50249
10/23/76	44	8		29 I Can See Me Lovin' You Again	*Jerry Foster/Bill Rice*	Epic 50291
2/12/77	7	16		30 Slide Off Of Your Satin Sheets	*Wayne Carson/Donn Tankersley*	Epic 50334
6/11/77	8	16		31 I'm The Only Hell (Mama Ever Raised)	*Bobby Borchers/Wayne Kemp/Mack Vickery*	Epic 50391
11/5/77+	❶^{2}	18		32 Take This Job And Shove It /	*David Allan Coe*	
1/28/78	50	10		33 Colorado Kool-Aid	*Phil Thomas* [S]	Epic 50469
4/15/78	17	10		34 Georgia In A Jug /	*Bobby Braddock*	
4/15/78	33	10		35 Me And The I.R.S.	*Don Scaife/Gladys Scaife/Ronny Scaife/Phil Thomas*	Epic 50539
10/21/78	7	12		36 Friend, Lover, Wife	*Johnny Paycheck/Billy Sherrill*	Epic 50621
12/9/78+	7	13		37 Mabellene *[w/ George Jones]*	*Chuck Berry/Russ Frato/Alan Freed*	Epic 50647
1/27/79	27	11		38 The Outlaw's Prayer	*Billy Sherrill/Glenn Sutton*	Epic 50655
1/27/79	94	4		39 Down On The Corner At A Bar Called Kelly's recorded in 1967	*Aubrey Mayhew/Mike McGivern/Johnny Paycheck*	Little Darlin' 7808
5/26/79	14	11		40 You Can Have Her *[w/ George Jones]*	*Bill Cook*	Epic 50708
10/13/79	49	6		41 (Stay Away From) The Cocaine Train	*Johnny Paycheck*	Epic 50777
12/22/79+	17	13		42 Drinkin' And Drivin'	*Gary Gentry*	Epic 50818
4/5/80	40	9		43 Fifteen Beers	*Brenda Davis/Steve Davis*	Epic 50863
6/21/80	31	9		44 When You're Ugly Like Us (You Just Naturally Got To Be Cool) *[w/ George Jones]*	*Don Goodman/Rick Schulman*	Epic 50891
9/6/80	22	11		45 In Memory Of A Memory	*Russ Pate/Johnny Paycheck*	Epic 50923
12/13/80+	18	12		46 You Better Move On *[w/ George Jones]*	*Arthur Alexander*	Epic 50949
3/28/81	41	8		47 I Can't Hold Myself In Line *[w/ Merle Haggard]*	*Merle Haggard*	Epic 51012
7/4/81	57	7		48 Yesterday's News (Just Hit Home Today)	*Merle Haggard*	Epic 02144
1/23/82	75	4		49 The Highlight Of '81	*Michael Garvin/Ron Hellard*	Epic 02684
4/24/82	69	5		50 No Way Out	*Johnny Paycheck*	Epic 02817
8/14/82	88	4		51 D.O.A. (Drunk On Arrival)	*Mike Heeney/Ed Hudson/Larry Lee*	Epic 03052
12/1/84+	30	18		52 I Never Got Over You	S:27 / A:30 *Tommy Jennings*	A.M.I. 1322
4/6/85	47	10		53 You're Every Step I Take	*Ronnie Friend*	A.M.I. 1323
12/7/85	63	8		54 Everything Is Changing	*Wade Kirby/Jesse Shofner*	A.M.I. 1327
5/17/86	21	22		55 Old Violin	S:12 / A:25 *Johnny Paycheck*	Mercury 884720
11/8/86	49	10		56 Don't Bury Me 'Til I'm Ready	*John Moffat*	Mercury 888088
2/28/87	56	7		57 Come To Me	*Hilka Cornelius*	Mercury 888341

DEBUT	PEAK	WKS	GOLD	ARTIST / Ranking / Country Chart Hit	Songwriter	Label (& Number)

PAYCHECK, Johnny — cont'd

DEBUT	PEAK	WKS	Ranking	Country Chart Hit	Songwriter	Label (& Number)
7/11/87	72	5	58	**I Grow Old Too Fast** (And Smart Too Slow)	*John Long*	Mercury 888651
4/9/88	81	2	59	**Out Of Beer**	*Holly Darwin/Mike Darwin*	Desperado 1001
2/18/89	90	2	60	**Scars**	*Billy Burns*	Damascus 2001

A-11 ['65]
All-American Man ['75]
Cave ['67]
Colorado Kool-Aid ['78]
Come To Me ['87]
D.O.A. (Drunk On Arrival) ['82]
Don't Bury Me 'Til I'm Ready ['86]
Don't Monkey With Another Monkey's Monkey ['68]
Down On The Corner At A Bar Called Kelly's ['79]
Drinkin' And Drivin' ['80]
11 Months And 29 Days ['76]
Everything Is Changing ['85]
Feminine Touch ['76]
Fifteen Beers ['80]
For A Minute There ['75]
Friend, Lover, Wife ['78]
Georgia In A Jug ['78]
Gone At Last ['76]
Heartbreak Tennessee ['66]
Highlight Of '81 ['82]
I Can See Me Lovin' You Again ['76]
I Can't Hold Myself In Line ['81]
I Don't Love Her Anymore ['75]
I Grow Old Too Fast (And Smart Too Slow) ['87]
I Never Got Over You ['85]
I'm The Only Hell (Mama Ever Raised) ['77]
If I'm Gonna Sink ['68]
In Memory Of A Memory ['80]
(It Won't Be Long) And I'll Be Hating You ['68]
Jukebox Charlie ['67]
Keep On Lovin' Me ['74]
Let's All Go Down To The River ['72]
Love Is A Good Thing ['72]
Lovin' Machine ['66]
Loving You Beats All I've Ever Seen ['75]
Mabellene ['79]
Me And The I.R.S. ['78]
Motel Time Again ['67]
Mr. Lovemaker ['73]
My Heart Keeps Running To You ['68]
My Part Of Forever ['74]
No Way Out ['82]
Old Violin ['86]
Out Of Beer ['88]
Outlaw's Prayer ['79]
Scars ['89]
She's All I Got ['71]
Slide Off Of Your Satin Sheets ['77]
Somebody Loves Me ['72]
Someone To Give My Love To ['72]
Something About You I Love ['73]
Song And Dance Man ['74]
(Stay Away From) The Cocaine Train ['79]
Take This Job And Shove It ['78]
When You're Ugly Like Us (You Just Naturally Got To Be Cool) ['80]
Wherever You Are ['69]
Yesterday's News (Just Hit Home Today) ['81]
You Better Move On ['81]
You Can Have Her ['79]
You're Every Step I Take ['85]

PAYNE, Dennis

Born in Bakersfield, California. Male singer.

DEBUT	PEAK	WKS	Ranking	Country Chart Hit	Songwriter	Label (& Number)
2/20/88	66	5	1	**I Can't Hang On Anymore**	*Ted Irwin/Gene Pistilli*	True 88
10/29/88	94	2	2	**That's Why You Haven't Seen Me**	*Bobby Reed/Conley White*	True 93

PAYNE, Jimmy

Born on 4/12/1936 in Leachville, Arkansas. Male singer/guitarist.

DEBUT	PEAK	WKS	Ranking	Country Chart Hit	Songwriter	Label (& Number)
4/19/69	60	6	1	**L.A. Angels**	*Dick Feller*	Epic 10444
11/3/73	79	5	2	**Ramblin' Man**	*Dickey Betts*	Cinnamon 772
8/1/81	80	4	3	**Turnin' My Love On**	*Bob Millsap*	Kik 907

PAYNE, Jody

Born in 1936 in Garrard County, Kentucky. Male singer/harmonica player. Member of **Willie Nelson**'s band.

DEBUT	PEAK	WKS	Ranking	Country Chart Hit	Songwriter	Label (& Number)
2/28/81	65	6		**There's A Crazy Man** ***[w/ The Willie Nelson Family Band]***	*Mentor Williams*	Kari 117

PAYNE, Leon

Born on 6/15/1917 in Alba, Texas. Died of a heart attack on 9/11/1969 (age 52). Blind since early childhood. Male singer/songwriter/guitarist/pianist/drummer.

DEBUT	PEAK	WKS	Ranking	Country Chart Hit	Songwriter	Label (& Number)
11/5/49+	❶^{2}	32		**I Love You Because**	A:❶^{2} / S:4 / J:10 *Leon Payne*	Capitol 40238

PEARCE, Kevin

Born in 1960 in Lake Alfred, Florida. Male singer.

DEBUT	PEAK	WKS	Ranking	Country Chart Hit	Songwriter	Label (& Number)
1/14/84	91	2	1	**It's Gonna Be A Heartache**	*Roger Murrah*	Orlando 108
1/18/86	92	2	2	**Pink Cadillac**	*Bruce Springsteen*	Orlando 111
10/31/87	90	2	3	**The Bigger The Love**	*Billy Burnette/Larry Henley/Larry Keith*	Evergreen 1057
2/27/88	66	6	4	**Love Ain't Made For Fools**	*Terry Skinner/J.L. Wallace*	Evergreen 1067
6/25/88	68	6	5	**Took It Like A Man, Cried Like A Baby**	*Charlie Black/Rory Bourke/Tommy Rocco*	Evergreen 1074

PEARL, Minnie — see MINNIE

PEARL RIVER

Group from Mississippi: Jeff Stewart (vocals), Chuck Ethredge, Ken Fleming, Bryan Culpepper, Joe Morgan and Derek George.

DEBUT	PEAK	WKS	Ranking	Country Chart Hit	Songwriter	Label (& Number)
5/1/93	62	8		**Fool To Fall**	*Wood Newton/Larry Stewart*	Liberty

from the album *Find Out What's Happening* on Liberty 80478

PEDERSEN, Herb

Born on 4/27/1944 in Berkeley, California. Male singer/songwriter/banjo player. Member of **The Desert Rose Band**.

DEBUT	PEAK	WKS	Ranking	Country Chart Hit	Songwriter	Label (& Number)
1/15/77	56	7		**Our Baby's Gone**	*Herb Pedersen*	Epic 50309

PEEK, Everett

Born in Iowa. Male singer.

DEBUT	PEAK	WKS	Ranking	Country Chart Hit	Songwriter	Label (& Number)
5/7/77	94	3		**Sea Cruise**	*Huey Smith/John Vincent*	Commercial 00016

PEEL, Dave

Born on 4/27/1945 in Nashville, Tennessee. Male singer/actor. Played "Bud Hamilton" in the movie *Nashville*.

DEBUT	PEAK	WKS	Ranking	Country Chart Hit	Songwriter	Label (& Number)
11/15/69	66	4	1	**I'm Walkin'**	*Dave Bartholomew/Fats Domino*	Chart 5037
3/14/70	62	7	2	**Wax Museum**	*Grant King*	Chart 5054
5/23/70	44	9	3	**Hit The Road Jack** ***[w/ Connie Eaton]***	*Percy Mayfield*	Chart 5066
11/7/70	56	7	4	**It Takes Two** ***[w/ Connie Eaton]***	*Sylvia Moy/William Stevenson*	Chart 5099
1/23/71	56	4	5	(You've Got To) **Move Two Mountains**	*Berry Gordy*	Chart 5109

PEGGY SUE

Born Peggy Sue Webb on 3/24/1947 in Butcher Holler, Kentucky. Female singer/songwriter. Sister of **Loretta Lynn**, **Crystal Gayle** and **Jay Lee Webb**; distant cousin of **Patty Loveless**. Married to **Sonny Wright**.

DEBUT	PEAK	WKS	Ranking	Country Chart Hit	Songwriter	Label (& Number)
6/7/69	28	11	1	**I'm Dynamite**	*Loretta Lynn*	Decca 32485
11/1/69	30	10	2	**I'm Gettin' Tired Of Babyin' You**	*Loretta Lynn/Peggy Sue Wells*	Decca 32571
4/18/70	65	3	3	**After The Preacher's Gone**	*Sammy Lyon/Danny Walls*	Decca 32640
7/11/70	37	11	4	**All American Husband**	*Julie Ann Beisbier*	Decca 32698
12/12/70	58	4	5	**Apron Strings**	*Maxine Kelton/Jean Nelson*	Decca 32754
5/15/71	68	5	6	**I Say, "Yes, Sir"**	*Jean Henderson/Vincent Poole*	Decca 32812
1/15/77	34	10	7	**Every Beat Of My Heart**	*Johnny Otis*	Door Knob 021
4/9/77	51	9	8	**I Just Came In Here** (To Let A Little Hurt Out)	*McKay Phillips/Doug Zepp*	Door Knob 029
7/2/77	81	4	9	**Good Evening Henry**	*Claude Branz*	Door Knob 036
10/22/77	100	1	10	**If This Is What Love's All About** ***[w/ Sonny Wright]***	*Dave Hall/Danny Walls*	Door Knob 038

DEBUT	PEAK	WKS	GOLD	ARTIST / Country Chart Hit	Songwriter	Label (& Number)
				PEGGY SUE — cont'd		
2/4/78	**85**	5		11 **To Be Loved**	*Tyran Carlo/Berry Gordy*	Door Knob 045
6/10/78	**87**	2		12 **Let Me Down Easy**	*Andy Badale/Ginny Johnson/Frank Stanton*	Door Knob 052
9/2/78	**80**	5		13 **All Night Long**	*Andy Badale/Ginny Johnson/Frank Stanton*	Door Knob 069
11/18/78+	**37**	12		14 **How I Love You In The Morning**	*Ed Jones/Elaine Rhoades*	Door Knob 079
3/24/79	**30**	10		15 **I Want To See Me In Your Eyes**	*Arthur Kent/Frank Stanton*	Door Knob 094
6/30/79	**51**	6		16 **The Love Song And The Dream Belong To Me**	*Andy Badale/Gene Kennedy/Frank Stanton*	Door Knob 102
11/10/79	**86**	5		17 **Gently Hold Me** *[w/ Sonny Wright]*	*Mack Jackson*	Door Knob 113
3/29/80	**80**	4		18 **For As Long As You Want Me**	*Arthur Kent/Frank Stanton*	Door Knob 121
7/12/80	**93**	3		19 **Why Don't You Go To Dallas**	*Buddy Landon/Janis Landon*	Door Knob 131
				PENN, Bobby		
				Born in Houston, Texas. Male singer.		
7/3/71	**51**	11		1 **You Were On My Mind**	*Sylvia Fricker*	50 States 1
9/7/74	**88**	5		2 **Watch Out For Lucy**	*Lonnie Mack*	50 States 29
7/4/76	**100**	1		3 **Little Weekend Warriors**	*Bob Zimmerman*	50 States 42
				PENNINGTON, J.P.		
				Born James Preston Pennington on 1/22/1949 in Berea, Kentucky. Male singer/songwriter. Former member of **Exile**.		
3/23/91	**45**	19		1 **Whatever It Takes**	*Robert Byrne/Will Robinson*	MCA
8/3/91	**72**	1		2 **You Gotta Get Serious**	*J.P. Pennington/Troy Seals/Eddie Setser*	MCA
				above 2 from the album *Whatever It Takes* on MCA 10213		
				PENNINGTON, Ray		
				Born Ramon Pennington 1933 in Clay County, Kentucky. Male singer/songwriter/guitarist. Member of **Bluestone** and **The Swing Shift Band**.		
11/5/66	**43**	9		1 **Who's Been Mowing The Lawn (While I Was Gone)**	*Ray Pennington*	Capitol 5751
5/6/67	**29**	8		2 **Ramblin' Man**	*Ray Pennington*	Capitol 5855
11/18/67	**65**	3		3 **Who's Gonna Walk The Dog (And Put Out The Cat)**	*Ray Pennington*	Capitol 2006
7/5/69	**70**	6		4 **What Eva Doesn't Have**	*Ray Pennington*	Monument 1145
12/6/69	**69**	5		5 **This Song Don't Care Who Sings It**	*Ray Pennington*	Monument 1170
5/2/70	**61**	7		6 **You Don't Know Me**	*Eddy Arnold/Cindy Walker*	Monument 1194
8/8/70	**74**	2		7 **The Other Woman**	*Don Rollins*	Monument 1208
1/2/71	**68**	5		8 **Bubbles In My Beer**	*Tommy Duncan/Cindy Walker*	Monument 1231
11/18/78	**79**	4		9 **She Wanted A Little Bit More**	*Ray Pennington*	MRC 1022
				PENNY, Hank		
				Born Herbert Penny on 9/18/1918 in Birmingham, Alabama. Died of heart failure on 4/17/1992 (age 73). Male singer/songwriter/banjo player. Worked as a comedian on **Spade Cooley**'s TV series in Los Angeles, California. Married to **Sue Thompson** from 1953-63.		
6/15/46	**4**	6		1 **Steel Guitar Stomp**	*Hank Penny* **[I]**	King 528
9/14/46	**4**	4		2 **Get Yourself A Red Head**	*Tommy Duncan/Hank Penny*	King 540
2/25/50	**4**	12		3 **Bloodshot Eyes**	J:4 *Ruth Hall/Hank Penny*	King 828
				PENNY, Joe		
				Born Joseph Pennington on 1/15/1928 in Plant City, Florida. Male singer/songwriter.		
7/18/64	**41**	7		**Frosty Window Pane**	*Joe Penny*	Sims 173
				PEPPER, Brenda		
				Born in Chicago, Illinois. Female singer.		
6/21/75	**97**	4		**You Bring Out The Best In Me**	*Linda Darrell*	Playboy 6038
				PEREZ, Tony		
				Born in New Mexico. Male singer.		
3/4/89	**79**	3		1 **Oh How I Love You (Como Te Quiero)**	*Bob DiPiero/Tony Perez/John Scott Sherrill*	Reprise 27591
10/14/89	**78**	4		2 **Take Another Run**	*Paul Overstreet/Don Schlitz*	Reprise 22838
				PERFECT STRANGER		
				Group from Carthage, Texas: Steve Murray (vocals), Richard Raines (guitar), Shayne Morrison (bass) and Andy Ginn (drums).		
4/15/95	**4**	22		1 **You Have The Right To Remain Silent**	S:2 *Brenda Sweat/Calvin Sweat*	Curb
9/30/95	**52**	10		2 **I'm A Stranger Here Myself**	*Michael Keith/Dave Lindsey/Matt Lindsey*	Curb
2/17/96	**56**	10		3 **Remember The Ride**	*Michael Harrell/Kim Williams*	Curb
				above 3 from the album *You Have The Right To Remain Silent* on Curb 77799		
3/29/97	**62**	7		4 **Fire When Ready**	*Tony Martin/Tom Shapiro*	Curb
1/16/99	**66**	7		5 **A Little Bit More Of Your Love**	*Jason Deere/Kelly Garrett*	Pacific/Curb
				above 2 from the album *The Hits* on Curb 78718		
4/15/00	**75**	1		6 **Coming Up Short Again**	*Bob DiPiero/Vince Gill*	Pacific/ Curb
				PERKINS, Carl — **1950s: #44**		
				Born on 4/9/1932 near Tiptonville, Tennessee. Died of a stroke on 1/19/1998 (age 65). Rockabilly singer/guitarist/songwriter. Member of **Johnny Cash**'s touring band from 1965-75. Inducted into the Rock and Roll Hall of Fame in 1987.		
2/18/56	**❶^3**	24		1 **Blue Suede Shoes**	J:❶^3 / S:2 / A:2 *Carl Perkins*	Sun 234
				Grammy: Hall of Fame / RS500		
6/30/56	**7**	6		2 **Boppin' The Blues**	J:7 / S:9 *Curly Griffin/Carl Perkins*	Sun 243
10/6/56	**10**	2		3 **Dixie Fried /**	S:10 *Howard Griffin/Carl Perkins*	
				also see #13 below		
10/6/56	**flip**	2		4 **I'm Sorry, I'm Not Sorry**	*Wanda Ballman*	Sun 249
3/9/57	**13**	8		5 **Your True Love**	S:13 *Carl Perkins*	Sun 261
3/31/58	**17**	9		6 **Pink Pedal Pushers**	S:17 *Carl Perkins*	Columbia 41131

DEBUT	PEAK	WKS	GOLD	ARTIST / Ranking / Country Chart Hit ... Songwriter	Label (& Number)
				PERKINS, Carl — cont'd	
12/17/66+	**22**	15		7 **Country Boy's Dream** ... *Eddie Newton*	Dollie 505
5/20/67	**40**	8		8 **Shine, Shine, Shine** ... *Carl Perkins/Roger Sovine*	Dollie 508
1/4/69	**20**	15		9 **Restless** ... *Carl Perkins*	Columbia 44723
5/29/71	**65**	5		10 **Me Without You** ... *Carl Perkins*	Columbia 45347
12/11/71+	**53**	7		11 **Cotton Top** ... *Carl Perkins*	Columbia 45466
5/6/72	**60**	5		12 **High On Love** ... *Carl Perkins*	Columbia 45582
10/13/73	**61**	7		13 **(Let's Get) Dixiefried** ... *Howard Griffin/Carl Perkins* [R] new version of #3 above	Mercury 73425
6/7/86	**31**	14		14 **Birth Of Rock And Roll** ... S:26 / A:29 *Carl Perkins/Greg Perkins*	America Sm. 884760
3/28/87	**83**	3		15 **Class Of '55** ... *Bobby Emmons/Chips Moman*	America Sm. 888142
				PERKINS, Dal Born in Abilene, Texas. Male singer.	
1/13/68	**73**	3		**Helpless** ... *Bob Morris*	Columbia 44343
				PERRY, Brenda Kaye Born in Waynesboro, Virginia. Female singer.	
10/22/77	**64**	9		1 **Ringgold Georgia** *[w/ Billy Walker]* ... *Jerry McBee*	MRC 1005
1/21/78	**35**	11		2 **Deeper Water** ... *Jerry McBee*	MRC 1010
4/22/78	**37**	9		3 **I Can't Get Up By Myself** ... *Ray Pennington*	MRC 1013
10/14/78	**78**	5		4 **My Daddy Was A Travelin' Man** ... *Ray Pennington*	MRC 1021
2/17/79	**90**	3		5 **Make Me Your Woman** ... *Bucky Jones/Royce Porter*	MRC 1026
				PETERS, Ben **SW: #24** Born on 6/20/1933 in Hollandale, Mississippi. Died of pneumonia on 5/25/2005 (age 71). Male singer/songwriter. Father of **Debbie Peters**.	
7/19/69	**46**	9		1 **San Francisco Is A Lonely Town** ... *Ben Peters*	Liberty 56114
9/1/73	**92**	4		2 **Would You Still Love Me** ... *Ben Peters*	Capitol 3687
				PETERS, Debbie Born in 1959 in Mississippi. Female singer. Daughter of **Ben Peters**.	
3/15/80	**84**	2		**It Can't Wait** ... *Ben Peters*	Oak 1012
				PETERS, Doug Born Doug Volchko on 8/4/1959 in Chicago, Illinois. Male singer/songwriter.	
8/6/88	**85**	2		**My Heart's Way Behind** ... *Doug Peters*	Comstock 1895
				PETERS, Gretchen Born on 11/14/1962 in Bronxville, New York; raised in Boulder, Colorado. Female singer/songwriter.	
4/20/96	**68**	3		1 **When You Are Old** ... *Gretchen Peters* from the album *The Secret Of Life* on Imprint 10000	Imprint
1/15/00	**55**	1		2 **New Year's Eve 1999** *[w/ Alabama]* ... *Gretchen Peters*	RCA
				PETERS, Jimmie Born on 10/12/1938 in Whiteface, Texas. Male singer/bassist.	
5/28/77	**59**	7		1 **Somebody Took Her Love (And Never Gave It Back)** ... *Mickey McNair/Jimmie Peters*	Mercury 73911
10/8/77	**73**	6		2 **Lipstick Traces** ... *Naomi Neville*	Mercury 55005
2/18/78	**75**	4		3 **634-5789** ... *Steve Cropper/Eddie Floyd*	Mercury 55016
6/3/78	**84**	4		4 **I Will Always Love You** ... *Dolly Parton*	Mercury 55025
1/13/79	**78**	4		5 **I Hate The Way Our Love Is** *[w/ Lynda K. Lance]* ... *Ava Aldridge*	Vista 101
4/28/79	**98**	3		6 **First Class Fool** *[w/ Linda K. Lance]* ... *Billy Larkin/Richard Larkin*	Vista 106
3/1/80	**75**	4		7 **Hearts** ... *Kelly Gordon/Robert Paxton*	Sunbird 105
				PETERS & LEE Pop duo from England: Lennie Peters (who was blind) and Dianne Lee. Duo split in 1980. Peters died of cancer on 10/10/1992 (age 59).	
3/16/74	**79**	8		**Welcome Home** ... *Stanislaus Beldone/Bryan Blackburn/Jean Dupre*	Philips 40729
				PETERSON, Colleen Born on 11/14/1950 in Peterboro, Canada. Died of cancer on 10/9/1996 (age 45). Female singer/songwriter.	
11/27/76	**100**	2		**Souvenirs** ... *Colleen Peterson*	Capitol 4349
				PETERSON, Michael Born on 8/7/1959 in Tucson, Arizona. Male singer/songwriter/guitarist.	
5/17/97	**3**[1]	20		1 **Drink, Swear, Steal & Lie** ... S:4 *Paula Carpenter/Michael Peterson*	Reprise
9/13/97	**❶**[1]	22		2 **From Here To Eternity** *Robert Ellis Orrall/Michael Peterson*	Reprise
1/31/98	**8**	20		3 **Too Good To Be True** ... *Michael Peterson/Gene Pistilli*	Reprise
5/30/98	**37**	14		4 **When The Bartender Cries** ... *Hunter Davis/Michael Peterson*	Reprise
9/26/98+	**19**	22		5 **By The Book** ... *Robert Ellis Orrall/Michael Peterson* above 5 from the album *Michael Peterson* on Reprise 46618	Reprise
3/13/99	**45**	17		6 **Somethin' 'Bout A Sunday** ... *Tim Nichols/Craig Wiseman*	Reprise
6/26/99	**39**	20		7 **Sure Feels Real Good** ... S:20 *Michael Peterson/Gene Pistilli* above 2 from the album *Being Human* on Warner 47373	Reprise
8/10/02	**44**	9		8 **Modern Man** ... *Franne Golde/Michael Peterson/Bruce Roberts*	AGR
11/2/02	**58**	1		9 **Lesson In Goodbye** ... *John Bettis/Bruce Robison/Monte Warden* above 2 from the album *Modern Man* on AGR 2010	AGR

DEBUT	PEAK	WKS	GOLD	ARTIST / Country Chart Hit ... Songwriter	Label (& Number)
				PETRONE, Shana	
				Born on 5/8/1972 in Parkridge, Illinois; raised in Fort Lauderdale, Florida. Former dance singer.	
6/27/98	**60**	5		1 **Heaven Bound** ... *Chuck Jones/Keith Stegall*	Epic
6/12/99	**45**	13		2 **This Time** ... S:24 *Gordon Kennedy/Phil Maderia/Bill Owsley*	Epic
10/30/99	**66**	6		3 **Something Real** ... *Bill Luther/Aimee Mayo*	Epic
				PETTY, Tom	
				Born on 10/20/1950 in Gainesville, Florida. Rock singer/songwriter/guitarist. Leader of The Heartbreakers. Group inducted into the Rock and Roll Hall of Fame in 2002.	
10/11/86	**❶**[2]	19		**Mind Your Own Business** ***[w/ Hank Williams Jr./Reba McEntire/Willie Nelson/Reverend Ike]*** ...S:❶[2] / A:❶[2] *Hank Williams*	Warner/Curb 28581
				PFEIFER, Diane	
				Born on 11/4/1950 in St. Louis, Missouri. Female singer/songwriter.	
3/1/80	**85**	3		1 **Free To Be Lonely Again** ... *Diane Pfeifer*	Capitol 4823
5/17/80	**59**	7		2 **Roses Ain't Red** ... *Diane Pfeifer*	Capitol 4858
10/4/80	**83**	3		3 **Wishful Drinkin'** ... *Diane Pfeifer*	Capitol 4916
11/28/81+	**35**	10		4 **Play Something We Could Love To** ... *Diane Pfeifer*	Capitol 5060
6/12/82	**85**	3		5 **Something To Love For Again** ... *Diane Pfeifer*	Capitol 5116
9/25/82	**76**	4		6 **Let's Get Crazy Again** ... *Michael Clark/Troy Seals*	Capitol 5154
				PHELPS, Brother — see BROTHER PHELPS	
				PHILLIPS, Bill **All-Time: #298**	
				Born on 1/28/1936 in Canton, North Carolina. Male singer/guitarist. Known as "Tater."	
8/24/59	**27**	2		1 **Sawmill** ***[w/ Mel Tillis]*** ... *Mel Tillis/Horace Whatley*	Columbia 41416
2/8/60	**24**	4		2 **Georgia Town Blues** ***[w/ Mel Tillis]*** ... *Buck Peddy/Mel Tillis*	Columbia 41530
3/14/64	**22**	18		3 **I Can Stand It (As Long As She Can)** ... *Ramona Redd/Mitchell Torok*	Decca 31584
10/17/64	**26**	10		4 **Stop Me** ... *Roy Botkin*	Decca 31648
4/2/66	**6**	18		5 **Put It Off Until Tomorrow** *Bill Owens/Dolly Parton*	Decca 31901
				Dolly Parton (harmony vocal)	
8/13/66	**8**	19		6 **The Company You Keep** ... *Bill Owens/Dolly Parton*	Decca 31996
1/21/67	**10**	15		7 **The Words I'm Gonna Have To Eat** ... *Liz Anderson*	Decca 32074
7/22/67	**39**	7		8 **I Learn Something New Everyday** ... *Betty Gary/Bill Hayes*	Decca 32141
11/18/67+	**25**	13		9 **Love's Dead End** ... *Bill Phillips/Bobby Sykes*	Decca 32207
3/15/69	**54**	10		10 **I Only Regret** ... *Bill Owens/Dolly Parton*	Decca 32432
10/18/69	**10**	14		11 **Little Boy Sad** ... *Wayne Walker*	Decca 32565
3/28/70	**43**	7		12 **She's Hungry Again** ... *Cecil Null*	Decca 32638
8/22/70	**46**	9		13 **Same Old Story, Same Old Lie** ... *Betty Jean Robinson*	Decca 32707
2/27/71	**56**	6		14 **Big Rock Candy Mountain** ... *Dorsey Burnette/Barry DeVorzon*	Decca 32782
3/18/72	**66**	8		15 **I Am, I Said** ... *Neil Diamond*	United Artists 50879
8/11/73	**91**	3		16 **It's Only Over Now And Then** ... *Whitey Shafer*	United Artists 266
6/24/78	**90**	3		17 **Divorce Suit (You Were Named Co-Respondent)** ... *Sonny Throckmorton*	Soundwaves 4570
2/3/79	**89**	3		18 **You're Gonna Make A Cheater Out Of Me** ... *Sonny Throckmorton*	Soundwaves 4579
7/7/79	**85**	3		19 **At The Moonlite** ... *Don Cook/Rafe Van Hoy*	Soundwaves 4587
				PHILLIPS, Charlie	
				Born on 7/2/1937 in Clovis, New Mexico. Male singer/guitarist.	
4/14/62	**9**	7		1 **I Guess I'll Never Learn** ... *Fred Carter*	Columbia 42289
10/12/63	**30**	1		2 **This Is The House** ... *John Hathcock/Ray Winkler*	Columbia 42851
				PHILLIPS, John	
				Born on 8/30/1935 in Paris Island, South Carolina. Died of heart failure on 3/18/2001 (age 65). Male singer/songwriter/guitarist. Co-founder of The Mamas & The Papas. Formerly married to actress Michele Phillips. Father of actress MacKenzie Phillips and singer Chynna Phillips (of Wilson Phillips).	
7/4/70	**58**	7		**Mississippi** ... *John Phillips*	Dunhill/ABC 4236
				PHILLIPS, Stu	
				Born on 1/19/1933 in Montreal, Quebec, Canada. Male singer/guitarist. Known as "The Western Gentleman."	
				OPRY: 1967	
4/30/66	**39**	5		1 **Bracero** ... *Leon Payne*	RCA Victor 8771
8/20/66	**32**	11		2 **The Great El Tigre (The Tiger)** ... *Cy Coben*	RCA Victor 8868
2/4/67	**44**	8		3 **Walk Me To The Station** ... *Stu Phillips*	RCA Victor 9066
6/17/67	**21**	14		4 **Vin Rosé** ... *Stu Phillips/Cindy Walker*	RCA Victor 9219
10/21/67	**13**	12		5 **Juanita Jones** ... *Paul Evans/Paul Parnes*	RCA Victor 9333
4/20/68	**62**	6		6 **The Note In Box Number 9** ... *Paul Evans/Paul Parnes*	RCA Victor 9481
7/13/68	**53**	7		7 **The Top Of The World** ... *Bill Irwin*	RCA Victor 9557
12/21/68+	**68**	6		8 **Bring Love Back Into Our World** ... *Joe Melson/Susie Melson*	RCA Victor 9673
				PIANO RED	
				Born William Lee Perryman on 10/19/1911 in Hampton, Georgia; raised in Atlanta, Georgia. Died of cancer on 7/25/1985 (age 73). Boogie woogie singer/pianist.	
2/16/85	**93**	5		**Yo Yo (The Right String, But The Wrong Yo Yo)** ***[w/ Danny Shirley]*** ... *William Perryman*	Amor 1006

Billboard DEBUT	PEAK	WKS	GOLD	ARTIST / Country Chart Hit	Ranking	Songwriter	Label (& Number)

PIERCE, Webb

1950s: #1 / 1960s: #7 / All-Time: #9 // HOF: 2001

Born on 8/8/1921 in West Monroe, Louisiana. Died of heart failure on 2/24/1991 (age 69). Male singer/songwriter/guitarist. Hosted own radio show on KMLB in West Monroe in 1937. Served in the U.S. Army from 1940-43. Joined the *Louisiana Hayride* in 1950. Co-owner of Cedarwood music publishing company. Acted in the movies *Buffalo Guns, Music City USA* and *Road To Nashville*. His daughter Debbie was a member of **Chantilly**. Also see **Heart Of Nashville**.

OPRY: 1955

DEBUT	PEAK	WKS	#	Country Chart Hit	Ranking	Songwriter	Label (& Number)
1/5/52	❶^{4}	27	1	**Wondering**	A:❶^{4} / J:4 / S:4	*Joe Werner*	Decca 9-46364
6/7/52	❶^{3}	20	2	**That Heart Belongs To Me**	A:❶^{3} / J:2 / S:5	*Webb Pierce*	Decca 9-28091
10/4/52	❶^{4}	23	3	**Back Street Affair**	A:❶^{4} / J:❶^{3} / S:❶^{2}	*Billy Wallace*	Decca 9-28369
1/31/53	4	7	4	**I'll Go On Alone /**	J:4 / S:7 / A:8	*Marty Robbins*	
2/14/53	4	6	5	**That's Me Without You**	A:4 / J:4 / S:9	*Joe Miller*	Decca 28534
3/28/53	4	14	6	**The Last Waltz /**	S:4 / A:5 / J:5	*Myrna Freeman/Webb Pierce*	
4/18/53	5	6	7	**I Haven't Got The Heart**	J:5 / A:6	*Webb Pierce*	Decca 28594
7/4/53	❶^{8}	22	8	**It's Been So Long /**	A:❶^{8} / S:❶^{6} / J:❶^{1}	*Audrey Grisham*	
				melody is the same as "I've Got Five Dollars And It's Saturday Night" by **Faron Young**			
7/4/53	9	2	9	**Don't Throw Your Life Away**	J:9	*Webb Pierce/Billy Wallace*	Decca 28725
10/24/53	❶^{12}	27	10	**There Stands The Glass /**	S:❶^{12} / J:❶^{9} / A:❶^{6}	*Audrey Grisham/Russ Hull/Mary Shurtz*	
10/24/53+	3^{1}	17	11	**I'm Walking The Dog**	J:3 / A:4 / S:6	*Cliff Grimsley/Tex Grimsley*	Decca 28834
2/6/54	❶^{17}	36	12	**Slowly**	S:❶^{17} / J:❶^{17} / A:❶^{15}	*Tommy Hill/Webb Pierce*	Decca 28991
6/5/54	❶^{2}	31	13	**Even Tho /**	A:❶^{2} / J:2 / S:3	*Willie Jones/Curt Peeples*	
6/12/54	4	18	14	**Sparkling Brown Eyes** ***[w/ Wilburn Brothers]***	S:4 / A:4 / J:4	*Billy Cox*	Decca 29107
10/9/54	❶^{10}	29	15	**More And More /**	J:❶^{10} / S:❶^{9} / A:❶^{8}	*Merle Kilgore*	
10/9/54	4	12	16	**You're Not Mine Anymore**	A:4 / S:8	*Webb Pierce/Teddy Wilburn*	Decca 29252
2/5/55	❶^{21}	37	17	**In The Jailhouse Now /**	J:❶^{21} / S:❶^{20} / A:❶^{15}	*Jimmie Rodgers*	
				Wilburn Brothers (harmony vocals); also see #96 below			
2/12/55	10	2	18	**I'm Gonna Fall Out Of Love With You**	A:10 / S:14	*Randy Hughes/Martha Taylor*	Decca 29391
6/18/55	❶^{12}	32	19	**I Don't Care /**	S:❶^{12} / A:❶^{12} / J:❶^{12}	*Webb Pierce/Cindy Walker*	
6/25/55	flip	6	20	**Your Good For Nothing Heart**	A:flip / J:flip	*Pat Noto/Webb Pierce/Edward Scalzi/George Williams*	Decca 29480
9/24/55	❶^{13}	32	21	**Love, Love, Love /**	A:❶^{13} / J:❶^{9} / S:❶^{8}	*Ted Jarrett*	
10/29/55	7	5	22	**If You Were Me**	A:7 / S:flip / J:flip	*Frank Miller/Webb Pierce*	Decca 29662
12/17/55+	❶^{4}	25	23	**Why Baby Why** ***[w/ Red Sovine]***	A:❶^{4} / S:❶^{1} / J:❶^{1}	*Darrell Edwards/George Jones*	Decca 29755
3/3/56	2^{7}	21	24	**Yes I Know Why /**	A:2 / J:3 / S:3	*Webb Pierce*	
3/10/56	3^{1}	13	25	**'Cause I Love You**	J:3 / S:5 / A:12	*Danny Hill/Webb Pierce*	Decca 29805
4/21/56	5	14	26	**Little Rosa** ***[w/ Red Sovine]***	S:5 / A:5 / J:5	*Webb Pierce/Red Sovine* **[S]**	Decca 29876
7/21/56	7	11	27	**Any Old Time /**	A:7 / J:7 / S:10	*Jimmie Rodgers*	
7/21/56	flip	6	28	**We'll Find A Way**	J:flip / S:flip	*Webb Pierce*	Decca 29974
10/13/56	10	8	29	**Teenage Boogie /**	S:10 / A:15	*Webb Pierce*	
10/13/56	flip	5	30	**I'm Really Glad You Hurt Me**	S:flip	*Webb Pierce*	Decca 30045
1/5/57	3^{1}	22	31	**I'm Tired /**	S:3 / A:4 / J:4	*Buck Peddy/Ray Price/Mel Tillis*	
2/2/57	flip	4	32	**It's My Way**		*Webb Pierce/Wayne Walker*	Decca 30155
3/30/57	❶^{1}	22	33	**Honky Tonk Song**	A:❶^{1} / S:2 / J:7	*Buck Peddy/Mel Tillis*	Decca 30255
4/6/57	8	9	34	**Oh' So Many Years** ***[w/ Kitty Wells]***	A:8	*Frankie Bailes*	Decca 30183
4/13/57	12	2	35	**Someday**	S:12 / A:12 / J:flip	*Sonny Curtis/Webb Pierce*	Decca 30255
5/27/57	7	15	36	**Bye Bye, Love /**	A:7 / S:8	*Boudleaux Bryant/Felice Bryant*	
6/10/57	7	12	37	**Missing You**	A:7 / S:13	*Dale Noe/Red Sovine*	Decca 30321
9/30/57	3^{1}	17	38	**Holiday For Love /**	A:3 / S:6	*Webb Pierce/Mel Tillis/Wayne Walker*	
11/18/57	12	1	39	**Don't Do It Darlin'**	A:12	*Webb Pierce*	Decca 30419
1/20/58	12	1	40	**One Week Later** ***[w/ Kitty Wells]***	A:12	*Gary Walker*	Decca 30489
5/5/58	3^{1}	17	41	**Cryin' Over You /**	A:3 / S:12	*Mark Dee/Al Peshoff*	
6/2/58	10	4	42	**You'll Come Back**	A:10 / S:flip	*Billy Barton/Webb Pierce*	Decca 30623
9/29/58	10	12	43	**Falling Back To You /**	A:10 / S:18	*Billy Phillips/Webb Pierce*	
10/20/58	7	10	44	**Tupelo County Jail**		*Webb Pierce/Mel Tillis*	Decca 30711
1/19/59	22	3	45	**I'm Letting You Go**		*Roy Drusky/Webb Pierce/Lester Vanadore*	Decca 30789
4/6/59	6	16	46	**A Thousand Miles Ago**		*Webb Pierce/Mel Tillis*	Decca 30858
7/20/59	2^{9}	25	47	**I Ain't Never**		*Webb Pierce/Mel Tillis*	Decca 30923
12/21/59+	4	18	48	**No Love Have I**		*Mel Tillis*	Decca 31021
4/11/60	17	10	49	(Doin' The) **Lovers Leap /**		*Lee Emerson/Webb Pierce*	
5/23/60	11	8	50	**Is It Wrong** (For Loving You)		*Warner Mack*	Decca 31058
9/12/60	11	8	51	**Drifting Texas Sand**		*Buster Coward*	Decca 31118
11/14/60	4	18	52	**Fallen Angel**		*Wayne Walker/Marijohn Wilkin*	Decca 31165
2/20/61	5	15	53	**Let Forgiveness In**		*Webb Pierce*	Decca 31197
5/29/61	3^{2}	21	54	**Sweet Lips**		*Webb Pierce/Doug Tubb/Wayne Walker*	Decca 31249
9/25/61	5	22	55	**Walking The Streets /**		*Gene Evans/Jimmy Fields/Jimmy Littlejohn*	
10/2/61	7	19	56	**How Do You Talk To A Baby**		*Webb Pierce/Wayne Walker*	Decca 31298
2/10/62	5	16	57	**Alla My Love**		*Harold Donny/Jimmy Gateley*	Decca 31347
5/26/62	8	13	58	**Crazy Wild Desire /**		*Webb Pierce/Mel Tillis*	
6/2/62	7	13	59	**Take Time**		*Harry Hart/Mel Tillis/Marijohn Wilkin*	Decca 31380
10/6/62	5	15	60	**Cow Town /**		*Hal Burns/Tex Ritter*	
10/13/62	19	10	61	**Sooner Or Later**		*Webb Pierce/Mel Tillis*	Decca 31421

DEBUT	PEAK	WKS	GOLD	#	ARTIST / Country Chart Hit	Songwriter	Label (& Number)
					PIERCE, Webb — cont'd		
1/5/63	**25**	3		62	**How Come Your Dog Don't Bite Nobody But Me** *[w/ Mel Tillis]*	*Mel Tillis/Wayne Walker*	Decca 31445
3/2/63	**15**	8		63	**Sawmill /**	*Horace Whitley*	
4/6/63	**21**	3		64	**If I Could Come Back**	*Buck Peddy/Webb Pierce/Mel Tillis*	Decca 31451
6/22/63	**7**	15		65	**Sands Of Gold**	*Hal Eddy/Cliff Parman/Webb Pierce*	Decca 31488
10/26/63+	**13**	15		66	**If The Back Door Could Talk /**	*Grady Martin/Webb Pierce*	
11/9/63	**9**	13		67	**Those Wonderful Years**	*Webb Pierce/Don Schroeder*	Decca 31544
2/15/64	**25**	13		68	**Waiting A Lifetime**	*Webb Pierce*	Decca 31582
5/23/64	**2**[1]	23		69	**Memory #1**	*Max Powell/Wayne Walker*	Decca 31617
9/26/64	**9**	15		70	**Finally** *[w/ Kitty Wells]*	*Mel Tillis/Wayne Walker*	Decca 31663
1/30/65	**26**	14		71	**That's Where My Money Goes /**	*Buck Peddy/Mel Tillis*	
2/6/65	**46**	5		72	**Broken Engagement**	*Max Powell/Mary Rhodes/Wayne Walker*	Decca 31704
3/20/65	**22**	14		73	**Loving You Then Losing You**	*Max Powell/Wayne Walker*	Decca 31737
8/14/65	**13**	14		74	**Who Do I Think I Am /**	*Jerry "Max" Lane/Webb Pierce/Max Powell*	
8/21/65	**50**	2		75	**Hobo And The Rose**	*Vince Matthews/Don Vinson*	Decca 31816
4/16/66	**46**	6		76	**You Ain't No Better Than Me**	*Max Powell/Wayne Walker*	Decca 31924
8/27/66	**25**	10		77	**Love's Something** (I Can't Understand)	*Webb Pierce/Max Powell/Wayne Walker*	Decca 31982
10/29/66	**14**	17		78	**Where'd Ya Stay Last Night**	*Joe Hudgins*	Decca 32033
3/18/67	**39**	15		79	**Goodbye City, Goodbye Girl**	*John Lopshonsky/Max Powell*	Decca 32098
8/5/67	**6**	18		80	**Fool Fool Fool**	*Max Powell/Wayne Walker*	Decca 32167
1/27/68	**24**	13		81	**Luzianna**	*DeWayne Phillips/Webb Pierce/Max Powell*	Decca 32246
7/6/68	**26**	9		82	**Stranger In A Strange, Strange City /**	*Webb Pierce/Max Powell*	
8/3/68	**74**	2		83	**In Another World**	*Alex Zanetis*	Decca 32339
10/26/68	**22**	10		84	**Saturday Night**	*Sue Brewer/Webb Pierce/Max Powell*	Decca 32388
2/22/69	**32**	10		85	**If I Had Last Night To Live Over**	*Webb Pierce/Max Powell*	Decca 32438
7/5/69	**14**	13		86	**This Thing**	*Sylvia Fisher/Audrey Grisham*	Decca 32508
11/29/69+	**38**	9		87	**Love Ain't Never Gonna Be No Better**	*Rusty Adams/Cecil Null*	Decca 32577
3/28/70	**71**	3		88	**Merry-Go-Round World**	*Sylvia Fisher/Webb Pierce*	Decca 32641
8/1/70	**56**	5		89	**The Man You Want Me To Be**	*Webb Pierce*	Decca 32694
12/26/70+	**73**	3		90	**Showing His Dollar**	*Rusty Adams/Webb Pierce*	Decca 32762
3/13/71	**31**	11		91	**Tell Him That You Love Him**	*Pat Benson*	Decca 32787
9/18/71	**73**	2		92	**Someone Stepped In** (And Stole Me Blind)	*Webb Pierce*	Decca 32855
7/15/72	**54**	8		93	**I'm Gonna Be A Swinger**	*Webb Pierce/Eugene Ward*	Decca 32973
11/22/75	**57**	9		94	**The Good Lord Giveth** (And Uncle Sam Taketh Away)	*Sylvia Fisher/Webb Pierce*	Plantation 131
3/13/76	**82**	5		95	**I've Got Leaving On My Mind**	*Webb Pierce/Wayne Walker*	Plantation 136
10/9/82	**72**	5		96	**In The Jailhouse Now** *[w/ Willie Nelson]* new version of #17 above	*Jimmie Rodgers* **[R]**	Columbia 03231

Alla My Love ['62]
Any Old Time ['56]
Back Street Affair ['52]
Broken Engagement ['65]
Bye Bye, Love ['57]
'Cause I Love You ['56]
Cow Town ['62]
Crazy Wild Desire ['62]
Cryin' Over You ['58]
(Doin' The) Lovers Leap ['60]
Don't Do It Darlin' ['57]
Don't Throw Your Life Away ['53]
Drifting Texas Sand ['60]
Even Tho ['54]
Fallen Angel ['60]
Falling Back To You ['58]
Finally ['64]
Fool Fool Fool ['67]
Good Lord Giveth (And Uncle Sam Taketh Away) ['75]
Goodbye City, Goodbye Girl ['67]
Hobo And The Rose ['65]
Holiday For Love ['57]
Honky Tonk Song ['57]
How Come Your Dog Don't Bite Nobody But Me ['63]
How Do You Talk To A Baby ['61]
I Ain't Never ['59]
I Don't Care ['55]
I Haven't Got The Heart ['53]
I'll Go On Alone ['53]
I'm Gonna Be A Swinger ['72]
I'm Gonna Fall Out Of Love With You ['55]
I'm Letting You Go ['59]
I'm Really Glad You Hurt Me ['56]
I'm Tired ['57]
I'm Walking The Dog ['54]
I've Got Leaving On My Mind ['76]
If I Could Come Back ['63]
If I Had Last Night To Live Over ['69]
If The Back Door Could Talk ['64]
If You Were Me ['55]
In Another World ['68]
In The Jailhouse Now ['55]
In The Jailhouse Now ['82]
Is It Wrong (For Loving You) ['60]
It's Been So Long ['53]
It's My Way ['57]
Last Waltz ['53]
Let Forgiveness In ['61]
Little Rosa ['56]
Love Ain't Never Gonna Be No Better ['70]
Love, Love, Love ['55]
Love's Something (I Can't Understand) ['66]
Loving You Then Losing You ['65]
Luzianna ['68]
Man You Want Me To Be ['70]
Memory #1 ['64]
Merry-Go-Round World ['70]
Missing You ['57]
More And More ['54]
No Love Have I ['60]
Oh' So Many Years ['57]
One Week Later ['58]
Sands Of Gold ['63]
Saturday Night ['68]
Sawmill ['63]
Showing His Dollar ['71]
Slowly ['54]
Someday ['57]
Someone Stepped In (And Stole Me Blind) ['71]
Sooner Or Later ['62]
Sparkling Brown Eyes ['54]
Stranger In A Strange, Strange City ['68]
Sweet Lips ['61]
Take Time ['62]
Teenage Boogie ['56]
Tell Him That You Love Him ['71]
That Heart Belongs To Me ['52]
That's Me Without You ['53]
That's Where My Money Goes ['65]
There Stands The Glass ['53]
This Thing ['69]
Those Wonderful Years ['63]
Thousand Miles Ago ['59]
Tupelo County Jail ['58]
Waiting A Lifetime ['64]
Walking The Streets ['61]
We'll Find A Way ['56]
Where'd Ya Stay Last Night ['66]
Who Do I Think I Am ['65]
Why Baby Why ['56]
Wondering ['52]
Yes I Know Why ['56]
You Ain't No Better Than Me ['66]
You'll Come Back ['58]
You're Not Mine Anymore ['54]
Your Good For Nothing Heart ['55]

PILLOW, Ray

Born on 7/4/1937 in Lynchburg, Virginia. Male singer/songwriter/guitarist.

OPRY: 1966

DEBUT	PEAK	WKS	GOLD	#	Country Chart Hit	Songwriter	Label (& Number)
2/13/65	**49**	4		1	**Take Your Hands Off My Heart**	*Fred Carter*	Capitol 5323
12/25/65+	**17**	10		2	**Thank You Ma'am**	*Joe Langston*	Capitol 5518
4/23/66	**32**	6		3	**Common Colds And Broken Hearts**	*Carol Barton*	Capitol 5597
5/14/66	**9**	15		4	**I'll Take The Dog** *[w/ Jean Shepard]*	*Marge Barton/Johnny MacRae*	Capitol 5633
10/8/66	**26**	11		5	**Volkswagen**	*Lee Emerson/Bill O'Brien*	Capitol 5735
11/26/66+	**25**	11		6	**Mr. Do-It-Yourself** *[w/ Jean Shepard]*	*Johnny MacRae*	Capitol 5769
8/12/67	**56**	6		7	**I Just Want To Be Alone**	*Bill Irwin*	Capitol 5953
12/9/67	**62**	2		8	**Gone With The Wine**	*Tony Moon*	Capitol 2030
9/14/68	**51**	8		9	**Wonderful Day**	*Ted Harris*	ABC 11114
8/23/69	**38**	8		10	**Reconsider Me**	*Margaret Lewis/Myra Smith*	Plantation 25
2/5/72	**62**	3		11	**Since Then**	*Johnny Wilson*	Mega 0055
5/13/72	**66**	7		12	**She's Doing It To Me Again**	*Gene Dobbins/Johnny Wilson*	Mega 0072
1/5/74	**80**	8		13	**Countryfied**	*Danny Hogan/Ronny Scaife*	Mega 1202
12/21/74+	**77**	4		14	**Livin' In The Sunshine Of Your Love**	*Betty Duke/Dave Hall*	ABC/Dot 17526
12/27/75	**100**	1		15	**Roll On, Truckers**	*Otha Young*	ABC/Dot 17589
5/13/78	**97**	3		16	**Who's Gonna Tie My Shoes**	*Bill Emerson*	Hilltop 130

Billboard DEBUT	PEAK	WKS	GOLD	Ranking	ARTIST / Country Chart Hit	Songwriter	Label (& Number)
					PILLOW, Ray — cont'd		
7/21/79	82	4		17	Super Lady	*Larry McFaden/Ray Pillow*	MCA 41047
7/18/81	82	3		18	One Too Many Memories	*Kent Westberry*	First Generation 011
					PINETOPPERS, The		
					Group from Broad Top, Pennsylvania: brothers Roy Horton (died on 9/23/2003, age 89) and Vaughn Horton (died on 2/29/1988, age 76), Ray Smith, Rusty Keefer and Johnny Browers. Vocals by **The Marlin Sisters**. Roy Horton was elected to the Country Music Hall of Fame in 1982.		
12/23/50+	3^4	13			Mockin' Bird Hill (J:3 / A:4 / S:5)	*Vaughn Horton*	Coral 9-64061
					PINK, Celinda		
					Born in Tuscaloosa, Alabama; raised in Birmingham. Female singer.		
4/24/93	68	4			Pack Your Lies And Go	*Alan Syms*	Step One
					PINKARD & BOWDEN		
					Novelty duo. Pinkard was born James Pinkard on 1/16/1947 in Abbeville, Louisiana. Bowden was born Richard Bowden on 9/30/1945 in Linden, Texas.		
3/3/84	64	8		1	Adventures In Parodies [N] **side one:** Help Me Make It Through The Yard/Daddy Sang Bass/Delta Dawg/Somebody Done Somebody's Song Wrong/Drivin' My Wife Away; **side two:** Three Mile Island (Wolverton Mountain)/Blue Hairs Driving In My Lane/What's A W-4 (What's Forever For)	*Larry Butler/Larry Collins/Alex Harvey/Merle Kilgore/Claude King/Carl Perkins/ Kris Kristofferson/David Malloy/Chips Moman/Eddie Rabbitt/Fred Rose/Even Stevens/Rafe Van Hoy*	Warner 29370
9/15/84	39	9		2	Mama, She's Lazy [N] parody of "Mama He's Crazy" by **The Judds**	*Kenny O'Dell*	Warner 29205
8/16/86	92	3		3	She Thinks I Steal Cars [N] parody of "She Thinks I Still Care" by **George Jones**	*Richard Bowden/Dickey Lee/Sandy Pinkard/Jim Sales*	Warner 2526
6/4/88	87	2		4	Arab, Alabama [N] melody based on "Good Hearted Woman" by **Waylon Jennings**	*Richard Bowden/Sandy Pinkard/Tim Wilson*	Warner 27909
4/15/89	79	4		5	Libyan On A Jet Plane (Leavin' On A Jet Plane) [N] parody of "Leaving On A Jet Plane" by Peter, Paul & Mary	*Richard Bowden/John Denver/ Sandy Pinkard/Tim Wilson*	Warner 22987
					PINMONKEY		
					Group formed in Nashville, Tennessee: brothers Chad Jeffers (guitar) and Michael Jeffers (bass), Michael Reynolds (vocals) and Rick Schell (drums). Group name taken from an episode of TV's *The Simpsons*.		
4/13/02	25	20		1	Barbed Wire And Roses	*Sean Locke/Mark Selby/Tia Sillers*	BNA
11/16/02+	36	20		2	I Drove All Night above 2 from the album *Pinmonkey* on BNA 67049	*Tom Kelly/Billy Steinberg*	BNA
3/27/04	44	9		3	Let's Kill Saturday Night	*Robbie Fulks*	BNA
					PINSON, Bobby		
					Born in Panhandle, Texas. Male singer/songwriter/guitarist.		
2/19/05	16	21			Don't Ask Me How I Know from the album *Man Like Me* on RCA 68173	*Bart Butler/Brett Jones/Bobby Pinson*	RCA
					PIRATES OF THE MISSISSIPPI		
					Group from Montgomery, Alabama: "Wild" Bill McCorvey (vocals; born on 7/4/1959), Rich "Dude" Alves (guitar; born on 5/25/1953), Pat Severs (steel guitar; born on 11/10/1952), Dean Townson (bass; born on 4/2/1959) and Jimmy Lowe (drums; born on 8/2/1955).		
7/28/90	26	20		1	Honky Tonk Blues	*Hank Williams Sr.*	Capitol
11/17/90+	49	14		2	Rollin' Home	*Rich Alves/Gary Harrison/Bill McCorvey*	Capitol
3/16/91	15	20		3	Feed Jake	*Danny Mayo*	Capitol
7/27/91	29	20		4	Speak Of The Devil above 4 from the album *Pirates Of The Mississippi* on Capitol 94389	*Rich Alves/Danny Mayo/Bill McCorvey*	Capitol
11/2/91	41	20		5	Fighting For You	*Bill McCorvey/Roger Murrah*	Capitol
2/29/92	22	20		6	Til I'm Holding You Again	*Rich Alves/Larry Gottlieb/Bill McCorvey*	Liberty
6/27/92	36	19		7	Too Much above 3 from the album *Walk The Plank* on Capitol 95798	*Guy Clark/Lee Roy Parnell*	Liberty
10/10/92	56	8		8	A Street Man Named Desire from the album *A Street Man Named Desire* on Liberty 98781	*Rich Alves/Gary Harrison/Bill McCorvey*	Liberty
10/30/93	63	7		9	Dream You from the album *Dream You* on Liberty 80379	*Jerry Phillips/Craig Wiseman*	Liberty
					PITNEY, Gene		
					Born on 2/17/1941 in Hartford, Connecticut; raised in Rockville, Connecticut. Male singer/songwriter/guitarist. Inducted into the Rock and Roll Hall of Fame in 2002.		
4/24/65	16	10		1	I've Got Five Dollars And It's Saturday Night *[w/ George Jones]*	*Ted Daffan*	Musicor 1066
7/3/65	25	7		2	Louisiana Man *[w/ George Jones]*	*Doug Kershaw*	Musicor 1097
11/20/65	50	2		3	Big Job *[w/ George Jones]*	*Hank Mills*	Musicor 1115
1/15/66	15	12		4	Baby Ain't That Fine *[w/ Melba Montgomery]*	*Dallas Frazier*	Musicor 1135
6/4/66	47	3		5	That's All It Took *[w/ George Jones]*	*Darrell Edwards/Charlotte Grier/George Jones*	Musicor 1165
					PLACE, Mary Kay		
					Born on 8/23/1947 in Tulsa, Oklahoma. Female singer/songwriter/actress. Played "Loretta Haggers" on TV's *Mary Hartman, Mary Hartman* from 1976-78. Also acted in several other movies and TV shows.		
10/16/76	3^3	16		1	Baby Boy	*Mary Kay Place*	Columbia 10422
4/9/77	72	5		2	Vitamin L **MARY KAY PLACE as LORETTA HAGGERS** (above 2)	*Mary Kay Place*	Columbia 10510
11/19/77+	9	16		3	Something To Brag About *[w/ Willie Nelson]*	*Bobby Braddock*	Columbia 10644
					PLEASANT VALLEY BOYS — see CROW, Alvin		
					PLOWMAN, Linda		
					Born on 12/31/1956 in Tuscaloosa, Alabama. Female singer.		
1/30/71	75	3		1	I'm So Lonesome I Could Cry	*Hank Williams*	Janus 146
9/8/73	93	3		2	Nobody But You	*Theresa Beaty/Paul Richey*	Columbia 45905

DEBUT	PEAK	WKS	GOLD	ARTIST / Country Chart Hit	Songwriter	Label (& Number)
				POACHER		
				Group from Warrington, Cheshire, England: Tim Flaherty (vocals), Adrian Hart (guitar), Pete Allen (steel guitar), Pete Longbottom (banjo), Allan Crookes (bass) and Stan Bennett (drums).		
11/4/78	**86**	3		**Darling**	*Oscar Blandemer*	Republic 028
				POCO		
				Pop-folk-rock group from Los Angeles, California. Numerous personnel changes. Lineup in 1979: Paul Cotton (vocals, guitar), Rusty Young (steel guitar), Kim Bullard (keyboards), Charlie Harrison (bass) and Steve Chapman (drums). Young was later a member of **The Sky Kings**.		
2/10/79	**95**	2		1 **Crazy Love**	*Rusty Young*	ABC 12439
6/30/79	**96**	4		2 **Heart Of The Night**	*Paul Cotton*	MCA 41023
				POE, Michelle		
				Born in Toledo, Ohio; raised in Florida. Female singer.		
8/28/04+	**3^{1S}**	5		**Just One Of The Boys**	*Shaunna Bolton/Adrienne Follese/Tammy Hyler*	DreamWorks
				POINTER, Anita		
				Born on 1/23/1948 in Oakland, California. Member of the **Pointer Sisters**.		
8/2/86	**2^{1}**	20		**Too Many Times** ***[w/ Earl Thomas Conley]*** ..S:❶[1] / A:2	*Tony McShear/Scott Page/Micheal Smotherman*	RCA 14380
				POINTER SISTERS		
				Black female vocal group from Oakland, California: sisters Ruth Pointer, Bonnie Pointer, June Pointer and **Anita Pointer**.		
7/27/74	**37**	16		**Fairytale**	*Anita Pointer/Bonnie Pointer*	ABC/Blue Thumb 254
				Grammy: Vocal Group		
				POLLARD, Chuck		
				Born in Shreveport, Louisiana. Male singer/songwriter. Cousin of **Gene Wyatt**.		
8/5/78	**56**	7		1 **You Should Win An Oscar Every Night**	*Chuck Pollard*	MCA 40944
11/11/78	**71**	5		2 **The Other Side Of Jeannie**	*Chuck Pollard*	MCA 40965
				POMSL, Pat		
				Born in Arkansas. Female singer.		
2/3/79	**97**	1		**Let My Fingers Do The Walking**	*Narvel Felts*	ASI 1017
				POOLE, Cheryl		
				Born in Tyler, Texas. Female singer.		
8/10/68	**39**	10		1 **Three Playing Love**	*Don Crawford*	Paula 309
2/1/69	**70**	3		2 **The Skin's Gettin' Closer To The Bone**	*Weldon Myrick*	Paula 1207
7/12/69	**57**	9		3 **Walk Among The People**	*Bill Scally*	Paula 1214
2/14/70	**70**	2		4 **Everybody's Gotta Hurt**	*Mike Cain*	Paula 1219
				POSEY, Sandy		
				Born on 6/18/1944 in Jasper, Alabama; raised in West Memphis, Arkansas. Female singer.		
10/30/71+	**18**	14		1 **Bring Him Safely Home To Me**	*Larry Butler/Billy Sherrill*	Columbia 45458
5/27/72	**51**	11		2 **Why Don't We Go Somewhere And Love**	*Larry Henley/Kenny O'Dell*	Columbia 45596
10/28/72	**36**	8		3 **Happy, Happy Birthday Baby**	*Gilbert Lopez/Margo Sylvia*	Columbia 45703
5/5/73	**39**	8		4 **Don't**	*Jerry Leiber/Mike Stoller*	Columbia 45828
6/19/76	**99**	3		5 **Trying To Live Without You Kind Of Days**	*Don Goodman/Bud Reneau*	Monument 8698
12/18/76	**93**	3		6 **It's Midnight (Do You Know Where Your Baby Is?)**	*Bobby Emmons*	Warner 8289
3/11/78	**21**	12		7 **Born To Be With You**	*Don Robertson*	Warner 8540
8/5/78	**26**	10		8 **Love, Love, Love/Chapel Of Love**	*Jeff Barry/Mack David/Ellie Greenwich/ Ted McCrae/Phil Spector/Sid Wyche*	Warner 8610
2/10/79	**26**	12		9 **Love Is Sometimes Easy**	*Sandy Posey*	Warner 8731
6/30/79	**82**	3		10 **Try Home**	*Allen Chapman/Jeff Tweel*	Warner 8852
2/26/83	**88**	3		11 **Can't Get Used To Sleeping Without You**	*Ray Davis/Billy Robinson/Ronnie Rodgers*	Audiograph 449
				POTTER, Curtis		
				Born on 4/18/1940 in Cross Plains, Texas; raised in Abilene, Texas. Male singer.		
5/12/79	**92**	3		1 **Fraulein (The Texas National Anthem)**	*Lawton Williams*	Hillside 03
				Darrell McCall (harmony vocal)		
3/1/80	**89**	5		2 **San Antonio Medley** ***[w/ Darrell McCall]***	*Floyd Jenkins/A.L. "Doodle" Owens/Lou Rochelle/Bob Wills*	Hillside 01
				POWELL, Pati		
				Born in Findlay, Ohio. Female singer.		
9/8/73	**99**	2		**Love By Appointment** ***[w/ Bob Gallion]***	*Bob Gallion/June Patrick/David Schwartz/Sybil Tarpley*	Metromedia 0037
				POWELL, Sandy		
				Born in Alabama. Female singer.		
10/31/81	**48**	8		**Slip Away** ***[w/ Mel Street]***	*Joe Deaton*	Sunbird 7568
				POWELL, Sue		
				Born in Gallatin, Tennessee; raised in Sellersburg, Indiana. Member of **Dave & Sugar** from 1977-80. Co-host of TV's *Nashville On The Road* in 1982.		
5/16/81	**57**	7		1 **Midnite Flyer**	*Paul Craft*	RCA 12227
10/31/81	**49**	6		2 **(There's No Me) Without You**	*Kye Fleming/Dennis W. Morgan*	RCA 12287
				PRADO, Perez, And His Orchestra		
				Born Damaso Perez Prado on 12/11/1916 in Mantanzas, Cuba. Died of a stroke on 9/14/1989 (age 72). Latin bandleader. Known as "The King of The Mambo."		
8/18/58	**18**	1	●	**Patricia** S:18	*Bob Marcus/Perez Prado* **[I]**	RCA Victor 7245

DEBUT	PEAK	WKS	GOLD		ARTIST / Country Chart Hit	Ranking / Songwriter	Label (& Number)

PRAIRIE OYSTER

Group from Toronto, Ontario, Canada: Russell DeCarle (vocals, bass), Keith Glass (guitar), Denis Delorme (steel guitar), Joan Besen (piano), John P. Allen (fiddle) and Bruce Moffet (drums).

DEBUT	PEAK	WKS	GOLD	#	Country Chart Hit	Songwriter	Label (& Number)
3/24/90	**62**	9		1	**Goodbye, So Long, Hello**	*Willie Bennett/Russell DeCarle*	RCA
6/9/90	**70**	8		2	**I Don't Hurt Anymore**	*Don Robertson/Jack Rollins*	RCA
					above 2 from the album *Different Kind Of Fire* on RCA 2049		
12/21/91+	**51**	9		3	**One Precious Love**	*Joan Besen*	RCA
					from the album *Everybody Knows* on RCA 61013		

PRATHER, Colt

Born on 12/10/1975 in El Paso, Texas; raised in Pinon, New Mexico. Male singer/songwriter.

DEBUT	PEAK	WKS	GOLD	#	Country Chart Hit	Songwriter	Label (& Number)
2/28/04	**48**	7			**I Won't Go On And On**	*Tucker Looney/Colt Prather*	Epic

PRESLEY, Elvis **1950s: #8 / 1970s: #34 / All-Time: #36 // HOF: 1998**

Born on 1/8/1935 in Tupelo, Mississippi. Died of heart failure on 8/16/1977 (age 42). Known as "The King of Rock & Roll." First recorded for Sun in 1954. Signed to RCA Records on 11/22/1955. In U.S. Army from 1958-1960. Starred in 33 movies (beginning with *Love Me Tender* in 1956). NBC-TV special in 1968. Married to Priscilla Beaulieu from 1967-73. Priscilla pursued acting in the 1980s with roles in TV's *Dynasty* and the *Naked Gun* movies. Their only child, Lisa Marie, was married to Michael Jackson from 1994-96. Elvis won Grammy's Lifetime Achievement Award in 1971. Inducted into the Rock and Roll Hall of Fame in 1986.

DEBUT	PEAK	WKS	GOLD	#	Country Chart Hit	Songwriter	Label (& Number)
7/16/55	**5**	15		1	**Baby Let's Play House /**	A:5 / S:10 *Arthur Gunter*	
					NRR		
8/6/55	**flip**	3		2	**I'm Left, You're Right, She's Gone**	S:flip *Stan Kesler/Bill Taylor*	Sun 217
					NRR		
9/17/55+	❶^{5}	39		3	**I Forgot To Remember To Forget /**	J:❶^{5} / S:❶^{2} / A:4 *Charlie Feathers/Stanley Kesler*	
					NRR		
9/17/55+	**10**	4		4	**Mystery Train**	J:10 / S:11 / A:11 *Junior Parker/Sam Phillips*	Sun 223
					RS500 / NRR		
3/3/56	❶^{17}	27	▲^{2}	5	**Heartbreak Hotel /**	S:❶^{17} / J:❶^{13} / A:❶^{12} *Mae Boren Axton/Thomas Durden/Elvis Presley*	
					Grammy: Hall of Fame / RS500		
3/31/56	**8**	6		6	**I Was The One**	A:8 / S:flip / J:flip *Hal Blair/Claude DeMetrius/Bill Peppers/Aaron Schroeder*	RCA Victor 47-6420
					also see #83 below		
6/2/56	❶^{2}	20	▲	7	**I Want You, I Need You, I Love You /**	S:❶^{2} / J:❶^{1} / A:5 *Ira Kosloff/Maurice Mysels*	
6/2/56	**13**	13		8	**My Baby Left Me**	S:13 / J:flip *Arthur Crudup*	RCA Victor 47-6540
8/4/56	❶^{10}	28	▲^{4}	9	**Hound Dog /**	J:❶^{10} / S:❶^{5} / A:6 *Jerry Leiber/Mike Stoller*	
					Grammy: Hall of Fame / RS500		
8/11/56	❶^{10}	28		10	**Don't Be Cruel**	J:❶^{10} / S:❶^{5} / A:2 *Otis Blackwell/Elvis Presley*	RCA Victor 47-6604
					Grammy: Hall of Fame / RS500		
10/20/56	**3**^{2}	18	▲^{3}	11	**Love Me Tender /**	S:3 / J:4 / A:4 *Vera Matson/Elvis Presley*	
					RS500; from the movie starring Presley; adapted from the 1861 tune "Aura Lee"		
11/10/56	**flip**	6		12	**Anyway You Want Me (That's How I Will Be)**	S:flip *Cliff Owens/Aaron Schroeder*	RCA Victor 47-6643
12/29/56	**10**	3		13	**Love Me**	A:10 / J:10 *Jerry Leiber/Mike Stoller* **[EP]**	RCA Victor EPA-992
					from the EP *Elvis, Volume 1*; the other cuts on the EP are "When My Blue Moon Turns To Gold Again," "Paralyzed" and "Rip It Up"		
2/2/57	**3**^{2}	14	▲	14	**Too Much /**	J:3 / S:5 / A:6 *Lee Rosenberg/Bernard Weinman*	
3/2/57	**8**	1		15	**Playing For Keeps**	J:8 *Stan Kesler*	RCA Victor 47-6800
4/13/57	❶^{1}	16	▲^{2}	16	**All Shook Up**	J:❶^{1} / S:3 / A:3 *Otis Blackwell/Elvis Presley*	RCA Victor 47-6870
					RS500		
7/1/57	❶^{1}	20	▲^{2}	17	**(Let Me Be Your) Teddy Bear**	S:❶^{1} / A:4 *Bernie Lowe/Kal Mann*	RCA Victor 47-7000
					also see #72 below		
8/19/57	**11**	2		18	**Mean Woman Blues**	A:11 *Claude DeMetrius* **[EP]**	RCA Victor 2-1515
					from the EP *Loving You, Vol. II*; above 3 from the movie *Loving You* starring Presley		
9/16/57	**15**	2		19	**Loving You**	A:15 *Jerry Leiber/Mike Stoller*	RCA Victor 47-7000
10/14/57	❶^{1}	24	▲^{2}	20	**Jailhouse Rock /**	S:❶^{1} / A:3 *Jerry Leiber/Mike Stoller*	
					RS500		
10/28/57	**11**	4		21	**Treat Me Nice**	A:11 *Jerry Leiber/Mike Stoller*	RCA Victor 47-7035
					above 2 from the movie *Jailhouse Rock* starring Presley		
2/3/58	**2**^{5}	18	▲	22	**Don't /**	S:2 / A:3 *Jerry Leiber/Mike Stoller*	
2/3/58	**4**	13		23	**I Beg Of You**	S:4 / A:5 *Rose Marie McCoy/Kelly Owens*	RCA Victor 47-7150
4/21/58	**3**^{4}	15	▲	24	**Wear My Ring Around Your Neck /**	S:3 / A:4 *Bert Carroll/Russell Moody*	
					also see #84 below		
5/12/58	**flip**	2		25	**Doncha' Think It's Time**	S:flip *Willie Dixon/Clyde Otis*	RCA Victor 47-7240
6/30/58	**2**^{2}	16	▲	26	**Hard Headed Woman /**	S:2 / A:8 *Claude DeMetrius*	
7/21/58	**flip**	3		27	**Don't Ask Me Why**	S:flip *Ben Weisman/Fred Wise*	RCA Victor 47-7280
					above 2 from the movie *King Creole* starring Presley		
12/22/58	**24**	3	▲	28	**One Night**	*Dave Bartholomew/Pearl King*	RCA Victor 47-7410
5/30/60	**27**	2	▲	29	**Stuck On You**	*J. Leslie McFarland/Aaron Schroeder*	RCA Victor 47-7740
					recorded 15 days after Presley's Army discharge		
12/12/60+	**22**	6	▲^{2}	30	**Are You Lonesome To-night?**	*Lou Handman/Roy Turk*	RCA Victor 47-7810
4/6/68	**55**	6		31	**U.S. Male**	*Jerry Reed*	RCA Victor 47-9465
6/29/68	**50**	8		32	**Your Time Hasn't Come Yet, Baby**	*Joel Hirschhorn/Al Kasha*	RCA Victor 47-9547
					ELVIS PRESLEY with The Jordanaires (#14-19, 22-27, 29-32)		
					from the movie *Speedway* starring Presley		
4/19/69	**56**	2		33	**Memories**	*Mac Davis/Billy Strange*	RCA Victor 47-9731
					from the NBC-TV special *Elvis*		
6/14/69	**60**	7	▲	34	**In The Ghetto**	*Mac Davis*	RCA Victor 47-9741

DEBUT	PEAK	WKS	GOLD	ARTIST / Country Chart Hit	Songwriter	Label (& Number)
				PRESLEY, Elvis — cont'd		
8/16/69	**74**	3	●	35 **Clean Up Your Own Back Yard**	*Mac Davis/Billy Strange*	RCA Victor 47-9747
				from the movie *The Trouble With Girls (and how to get into it)* starring Presley		
12/20/69+	**13**	12	▲	36 **Don't Cry Daddy**	*Mac Davis*	RCA Victor 47-9768
2/28/70	**31**	10	●	37 **Kentucky Rain**	*Dick Heard/Eddie Rabbitt*	RCA Victor 47-9791
6/6/70	**37**	10	●	38 **The Wonder Of You**	*Baker Knight* **[L]**	RCA Victor 47-9835
8/29/70	**57**	6	●	39 **I've Lost You** /	*Alan Blaikley/Ken Howard*	
8/29/70	**flip**	6		40 **The Next Step Is Love**	*Paul Evans/Paul Parnes*	RCA Victor 47-9873
12/5/70	**56**	5	●	41 **You Don't Have To Say You Love Me**	*Pino Donaggio/Simon Napier-Bell/Vito Pallavicini/Vicki Wickham*	RCA Victor 47-9916
				above 3 from the movie *Elvis-That's The Way It Is*		
1/9/71	**9**	13		42 **There Goes My Everything** /	*Dallas Frazier*	
				also see #81 below		
1/9/71	**23**	13	●	43 **I Really Don't Want To Know**	*Howard Barnes/Don Robertson*	RCA Victor 47-9960
3/27/71	**55**	8		44 **Where Did They Go, Lord**	*Dallas Frazier/A.L. "Doodle" Owens*	RCA Victor 47-9980
6/5/71	**34**	8		45 **Life**	*Shirl Milete*	RCA Victor 47-9985
3/4/72	**68**	2		46 **Until It's Time For You To Go**	*Buffy Sainte-Marie*	RCA Victor 74-0619
9/9/72	**36**	13	▲	47 **It's A Matter Of Time**	*Clive Westlake*	RCA Victor 74-0769
12/9/72+	**16**	13	●	48 **Always On My Mind** /	*Wayne Carson/Johnny Christopher/Mark James*	
12/16/72+	**flip**	12	●	49 **Separate Ways**	*Richard Mainegra/Red West*	RCA Victor 74-0815
				from the movie *Elvis on Tour*		
4/28/73	**31**	10		50 **Fool** /	*James Last/Carl Sigman*	
4/28/73	**flip**	10		51 **Steamroller Blues**	*James Taylor* **[L]**	RCA Victor 74-0910
				from the TV special *Aloha from Hawaii via Satellite*		
10/6/73	**42**	10		52 **For Ol' Times Sake**	*Tony Joe White*	RCA Victor 0088
2/16/74	**4**	13		53 **I've Got A Thing About You Baby** /	*Tony Joe White*	
2/16/74	**flip**	13		54 **Take Good Care Of Her**	*Arthur Kent/Ed Warren*	RCA Victor 0196
6/8/74	**6**	15		55 **Help Me** /	*Larry Gatlin*	
6/8/74	**flip**	15		56 **If You Talk In Your Sleep**	*Johnny Christopher/Red West*	RCA Victor 0280
10/26/74+	**9**	14		57 **It's Midnight** /	*Jerry Chesnut/Billy Edd Wheeler*	
12/28/74+	**flip**	5		58 **Promised Land**	*Chuck Berry*	RCA Victor 10074
2/8/75	**14**	10		59 **My Boy**	*Jean-Pierre Boutayre/Phil Coulter/Claude Francois/Bill Martin*	RCA Victor 10191
5/17/75	**11**	13		60 **T-R-O-U-B-L-E**	*Jerry Chesnut*	RCA Victor 10278
10/18/75	**33**	10		61 **Pieces Of My Life**	*Troy Seals*	RCA Victor 10401
4/10/76	**6**	13		62 **Hurt** /	*Jimmie Crane/Al Jacobs*	
4/10/76	**45**	13		63 **For The Heart**	*Dennis Linde*	RCA Victor 10601
12/25/76+	**❶[1]**	16		64 **Moody Blue** /	*Mark James*	
12/25/76+	**flip**	16		65 **She Thinks I Still Care**	*Dickey Lee*	RCA 10857
6/25/77	**❶[1]**	17	▲	66 **Way Down** /	*Layng Martine Jr.*	
6/25/77	**flip**	17		67 **Pledging My Love**	*Don Robey/Ferdinand Washington*	RCA 10998
11/19/77+	**2[1]**	15	●	68 **My Way**	*Paul Anka/Claude Francois/Jacques Revaux* **[L]**	RCA 11165
				from the CBS-TV special *Elvis In Concert*; based on the French standard "Comme D'Habitude"		
3/25/78	**6**	11		69 **Unchained Melody** /	*Alex North/Hy Zaret*	
3/25/78	**flip**	11		70 **Softly, As I Leave You**	*Giorgio Calabrese/Antonio DeVita/Harold Shaper* **[L-S]**	RCA 11212
				Elvis narrates, with vocal by Sherrill Neilsen		
8/12/78	**78**	4		71 **Puppet On A String** *[w/ The Jordanaires]* /	*Roy Bennett/Sid Tepper*	
8/12/78	**flip**	4		72 **(Let Me Be Your) Teddy Bear** *[w/ The Jordanaires]*	*Bernie Lowe/Kal Mann* **[R]**	RCA 11320
				same version as #17 above		
4/21/79	**10**	12		73 **Are You Sincere** /	*Wayne Walker*	
4/21/79	**flip**	12		74 **Solitaire**	*Philip Cody/Neil Sedaka*	RCA 11533
8/11/79	**6**	13		75 **There's A Honky Tonk Angel (Who Will Take Me Back In)** /	*Denny Rice/Troy Seals*	
8/11/79	**flip**	13		76 **I Got A Feelin' In My Body**	*Dennis Linde*	RCA 11679
1/17/81	**❶[1]**	13		77 **Guitar Man**	*Jerry Reed*	RCA 12158
				Jerry Reed (guitar); remix by Felton Jarvis (died on 1/3/1981) of Presley's #43 Pop hit from 1968		
4/18/81	**8**	15		78 **Lovin' Arms** /	*Tom Jans*	
4/18/81	**flip**	15		79 **You Asked Me To**	*Waylon Jennings/Billy Joe Shaver*	RCA 12205
2/27/82	**73**	4		80 **You'll Never Walk Alone** *[w/ The Jordanaires]* /	*Oscar Hammerstein/Richard Rodgers*	
2/27/82	**flip**	4		81 **There Goes My Everything**	*Dallas Frazier* **[R]**	RCA 13058
				same version as #42 above		
11/6/82	**31**	12		82 **The Elvis Medley**	*Otis Blackwell/Mark James/Jerry Leiber/Dennis Linde/ Bernie Lowe/Kal Mann/Elvis Presley/Mike Stoller*	RCA 13351
				Jailhouse Rock/Teddy Bear/Hound Dog/Don't Be Cruel/Burning Love/ Suspicious Minds		
5/7/83	**92**	2		83 **I Was The One** /	*Hal Blair/Claude DeMetrius/Bill Peppers/Aaron Schroeder* **[R]**	
				same version (with newly added overdubs) of #6 above		
5/7/83	**flip**	2		84 **Wear My Ring Around Your Neck**	*Bert Carroll/Russell Moody* **[R]**	RCA 13500
				same version (with newly added overdubs) of #24 above		
1/3/98	**55**	2		85 **Blue Christmas**	*Billy Hayes/Jay Johnson* **[X]**	RCA
				recorded in 1957; from the album *Blue Christmas* on RCA 5486		

All Shook Up ['57]
Always On My Mind ['73]
Anyway You Want Me (That's How I Will Be) ['56]
Are You Lonesome To-night? ['61]
Are You Sincere ['79]
Baby Let's Play House ['55]
Blue Christmas ['98]
Clean Up Your Own Back Yard ['69]
Don't ['58]
Don't Ask Me Why ['58]
Don't Be Cruel ['56]
Don't Cry Daddy ['70]
Doncha' Think It's Time ['58]
Elvis Medley ['82]
Fool ['73]
For Ol' Times Sake ['73]
For The Heart ['76]
Guitar Man ['81]
Hard Headed Woman ['58]
Heartbreak Hotel ['56]
Help Me ['74]
Hound Dog ['56]
Hurt ['76]
I Beg Of You ['58]
I Forgot To Remember To Forget ['56]
I Got A Feelin' In My Body ['79]
I Really Don't Want To Know ['71]
I Want You, I Need You, I Love You ['56]
I Was The One ['56, '83]
I'm Left, You're Right, She's Gone ['55]
I've Got A Thing About You Baby ['74]
I've Lost You ['70]
If You Talk In Your Sleep ['74]
In The Ghetto ['69]
It's A Matter Of Time ['72]
It's Midnight ['75]
Jailhouse Rock ['57]
Kentucky Rain ['70]
(Let Me Be Your) Teddy Bear ['57, '78]
Life ['71]
Love Me ['56]
Love Me Tender ['56]
Lovin' Arms ['81]
Loving You ['57]
Mean Woman Blues ['57]
Memories ['69]
Moody Blue ['77]
My Baby Left Me ['56]
My Boy ['75]
My Way ['78]
Mystery Train ['56]
Next Step Is Love ['70]
One Night ['58]
Pieces Of My Life ['75]
Playing For Keeps ['57]
Pledging My Love ['77]
Promised Land ['75]
Puppet On A String ['78]
Separate Ways ['73]
She Thinks I Still Care ['77]
Softly, As I Leave You ['78]

DEBUT	PEAK	WKS	GOLD	ARTIST / Country Chart Hit	Ranking / Songwriter	Label (& Number)

PRESLEY, Elvis — cont'd

Solitaire ['79]
Steamroller Blues ['73]
Stuck On You ['60]
Take Good Care Of Her ['74]
There Goes My Everything ['71]
There Goes My Everything ['82]
There's A Honky Tonk Angel (Who Will Take Me Back In) ['79]
Too Much ['57]
Treat Me Nice ['57]
T-R-O-U-B-L-E ['75]
U.S. Male ['68]
Unchained Melody ['78]
Until It's Time For You To Go ['72]
Way Down ['77]
Wear My Ring Around Your Neck ['58, '83]
Where Did They Go, Lord ['71]
Wonder Of You ['70]
You Asked Me To ['81]
You Don't Have To Say You Love Me ['70]
You'll Never Walk Alone ['82]
Your Time Hasn't Come Yet, Baby ['68]

PRESTON, Eddie

Born Edward Preston Snyder in San Diego, California. Male singer/songwriter/pianist. Former member of the pop group The Cascades.

DEBUT	PEAK	WKS		Country Chart Hit	Songwriter	Label (& Number)
4/22/89	**87**	3		1 **When Did You Stop**	*Eddie Preston*	Platinum 101
9/9/89	**71**	4		2 **Long Time Comin'**	*Eddie Preston*	Platinum 102

PRICE, Chuck

Born in Chicago, Illinois. Male singer.

DEBUT	PEAK	WKS		Country Chart Hit	Songwriter	Label (& Number)
11/2/74	**75**	6		1 **Slow Down**	*Kris Kristofferson*	Playboy 6010
11/22/75	**54**	8		2 **Last Of The Outlaws**	*Bobby Borchers/Mack Vickery*	Playboy 6052
4/3/76	**97**	2		3 **Cadillac Johnson**	*Ken McDuffie*	Playboy 6067
5/29/76	**48**	8		4 **I Don't Want It**	*Jerry Chesnut*	Playboy 6072
10/23/76	**81**	3		5 **Rye Whiskey**	*(traditional)/Tex Ritter*	Playboy 6087
2/26/77	**91**	4		6 **Is Anybody Goin' To San Antone**	*Dave Kirby/Glenn Martin*	Playboy 6099

PRICE, David

Born in Odessa, Texas. Male singer.

DEBUT	PEAK	WKS		Country Chart Hit	Songwriter	Label (& Number)
2/8/64	**29**	8		**The World Lost A Man** — tribute to John F. Kennedy	*Tom T. Hall*	Rice 1001

PRICE, Denise

Born Denise Davis in Russellville, Alabama. Female singer.

DEBUT	PEAK	WKS		Country Chart Hit	Songwriter	Label (& Number)
12/25/82	**94**	3		**Two Hearts Can't Be Wrong**	*Jerry Barlow/Dennis Knutson*	Dimension 1037

PRICE, Kenny

All-Time: #186

Born on 5/27/1931 in Florence, Kentucky. Died of a heart attack on 8/4/1987 (age 56). Male singer. Had own radio show on WZIP in Cincinnati in 1945. Served in the U.S. Army from 1952-54. Regular on TV's *Hee-Haw*. Known as "The Round Mound of Sound."

DEBUT	PEAK	WKS		Country Chart Hit	Songwriter	Label (& Number)
8/20/66	**7**	18		1 **Walking On New Grass**	*Ray Pennington*	Boone 1042
12/24/66+	**7**	17		2 **Happy Tracks**	*Ray Pennington*	Boone 1051
5/13/67	**26**	12		3 **Pretty Girl, Pretty Clothes, Pretty Sad**	*Harlan Howard*	Boone 1056
9/9/67	**24**	12		4 **Grass Won't Grow On A Busy Street**	*Ray Pennington*	Boone 1063
12/16/67+	**11**	15		5 **My Goal For Today**	*Chuck Howard*	Boone 1067
4/27/68	**31**	8		6 **Going Home For The Last Time**	*Ray Pennington/Johnny Slate*	Boone 1070
9/7/68	**37**	8		7 **Southern Bound**	*Ray Pennington*	Boone 1075
12/7/68	**59**	6		8 **It Don't Mean A Thing To Me**	*Ray Pennington*	Boone 1081
5/10/69	**64**	5		9 **Who Do I Know In Dallas**	*Hank Cochran/Willie Nelson*	Boone 1085
12/6/69	**62**	4		10 **Atlanta Georgia Stray**	*Christopher Cedzich*	RCA Victor 0260
1/31/70	**17**	12		11 **Northeast Arkansas Mississippi County Bootlegger**	*Ed Bruce*	RCA Victor 9787
7/18/70	**10**	14		12 **Biloxi**	*Larry Kingston*	RCA Victor 9869
12/19/70+	**8**	14		13 **The Sheriff Of Boone County**	*Frank Marusa/Elson Smith*	RCA Victor 9932
5/1/71	**55**	7		14 **Tell Her You Love Her**	*Scott Wiseman*	RCA Victor 9973
9/18/71	**38**	11		15 **Charlotte Fever**	*Larry Kingston*	RCA Victor 1015
1/15/72	**37**	10		16 **Super Sideman**	*Bobby Bond*	RCA Victor 0617
4/29/72	**44**	11		17 **You Almost Slipped My Mind**	*Tilden Back/Delbert Barker/Don Goodman/Troy Seals*	RCA Victor 0686
9/16/72	**24**	11		18 **Sea Of Heartbreak**	*Hal David/Paul Hampton*	RCA Victor 0781
1/20/73	**53**	8		19 **Don't Tell Me Your Troubles**	*Don Gibson*	RCA Victor 0872
5/12/73	**52**	7		20 **30 California Women**	*Doc Richardson/Bun Wilson*	RCA Victor 0936
9/22/73	**52**	11		21 **You're Wearin' Me Down**	*Ray Griff*	RCA Victor 0083
12/29/73+	**29**	12		22 **Turn On Your Light** (And Let It Shine)	*Ray Pennington*	RCA Victor 0198
4/27/74	**69**	6		23 **Que Pasa**	*Eddie Rabbitt/Even Stevens*	RCA Victor 0256
8/31/74	**42**	11		24 **Let's Truck Together**	*Donna Price*	RCA Victor 10039
1/4/75	**67**	10		25 **Easy Look**	*Curly Putman/Sonny Throckmorton*	RCA Victor 10141
5/3/75	**65**	8		26 **Birds And Children Fly Away**	*Ray Pennington*	RCA Victor 10260
1/10/76	**60**	8		27 **Too Big A Price To Pay**	*Rollin Bennett*	RCA Victor 10460
6/4/77	**60**	6		28 **I'd Buy You Chattanooga**	*Ray Pennington*	MRC 1001
9/17/77	**74**	5		29 **Leavin'**	*Joey Davis*	MRC 1004
12/24/77+	**50**	9		30 **Afraid You'd Come Back**	*Dave Kirby*	MRC 1007
4/8/78	**74**	6		31 **Sunshine Man**	*Ray Pennington*	MRC 1012
1/20/79	**67**	7		32 **Hey There**	*Richard Adler/Jerry Ross*	MRC 1025
2/23/80	**60**	5		33 **Well Rounded Traveling Man**	*Ray Pennington/Troy Seals*	Dimension 1003
9/13/80	**79**	4		34 **She's Leavin'** (And I'm Almost Gone)	*Fred Lehner/Jerry McBee/Ray Pennington*	Dimension 1010

Billboard DEBUT	PEAK	WKS	GOLD	ARTIST / Country Chart Hit	Ranking / Songwriter	Label (& Number)

PRICE, Ray 1950s: #12 / 1960s: #9 / 1970s: #37 / All-Time: #10 // HOF: 1996

Born on 1/12/1926 in Perryville, Texas; raised in Dallas, Texas. Male singer/songwriter/guitarist. Served in the U.S. Marines from 1944-46. Began radio singing career in 1948 on KRBC in Abilene, Texas. Joined the *Big D Jamboree* in Dallas in 1949. Known as "The Cherokee Cowboy."

OPRY: 1952

DEBUT	PEAK	WKS	#	Country Chart Hit	Songwriter	Label (& Number)
5/17/52	3^{2}	11	1	**Talk To Your Heart**	A:3 / J:6 / S:10 *C.M. Bradley/Louise Ulrich*	Columbia 4-20913
11/8/52	4	9	2	**Don't Let The Stars Get In Your Eyes**	S:4 / A:6 / J:7 *Slim Willet*	Columbia 4-21025
3/6/54	2^{2}	19	3	**I'll Be There** (If You Ever Want Me) /	S:2 / A:2 / J:3 *Rusty Gabbard/Ray Price*	
4/10/54	6	13	4	**Release Me**	J:6 / S:7 *Eddie Miller/William Stevenson*	Columbia 21214
6/26/54	13	4	5	**Much Too Young To Die**	S:13 / A:13 *Rusty Gabbard*	Columbia 21249
10/30/54	8	13	6	**If You Don't, Somebody Else Will** ***[w/ His Cherokee Cowboys]***	S:8 / J:10 / A:14 *Geraldine Hamilton/Jimmy Lee/Johnny Mathis*	Columbia 21315
1/7/56	5	11	7	**Run Boy**	A:5 / J:10 / S:15 *Hy Heath*	Columbia 21474
5/26/56	❶^{20}	45	8	**Crazy Arms** /	A:❶^{20} / S:❶^{11} / J:❶^{1} *Ralph Mooney/Chuck Seals*	
				Grammy: Hall of Fame		
6/9/56	7	7	9	**You Done Me Wrong**	A:7 / S:flip / J:flip *George Jones/Ray Price*	Columbia 21510
11/10/56	2^{2}	21	10	**I've Got A New Heartache** /	A:2 / J:2 / S:3 *Wayne Walker*	
11/17/56	4	21	11	**Wasted Words**	S:4 / A:6 / J:9 *Don Gibson*	Columbia 21562
6/10/57	12	4	12	**I'll Be There** (When You Get Lonely)	A:12 / S:13 *Dave Burgess*	Columbia 40889
7/29/57	❶^{4}	37	13	**My Shoes Keep Walking Back To You**	A:❶^{4} / S:3 *Lee Ross/Bob Wills*	Columbia 40951
3/3/58	3^{2}	18	14	**Curtain In The Window** /	A:3 / S:6 *Lee Ross*	
4/7/58	flip	4	15	**It's All Your Fault**	*Wayne Walker*	Columbia 41105
7/14/58	❶^{13}	34	16	**City Lights** /	A:2 / S:4 *Bill Anderson*	
7/21/58	3^{1}	19	17	**Invitation To The Blues**	A:3 / S:8 *Roger Miller*	Columbia 41191
1/5/59	7	19	18	**That's What It's Like To Be Lonesome**	*Bill Anderson*	Columbia 41309
5/11/59	2^{1}	40	19	**Heartaches By The Number**	*Harlan Howard*	Columbia 41374
10/12/59	❶^{2}	30	20	**The Same Old Me** /	*Fuzzy Owen*	
11/23/59	5	15	21	**Under Your Spell Again**	*Buck Owens/Dusty Rhodes*	Columbia 41477
4/4/60	2^{8}	27	22	**One More Time**	*Mel Tillis*	Columbia 41590
10/3/60	5	17	23	**I Wish I Could Fall In Love Today** /	*Harlan Howard*	
10/24/60	23	3	24	**I Can't Run Away From Myself**	*Hank Cochran/Ray Price*	Columbia 41767
3/20/61	5	21	25	**Heart Over Mind** /	*Mel Tillis*	
3/27/61	13	11	26	**The Twenty-Fourth Hour**	*Ray Price*	Columbia 41947
10/9/61	3^{1}	23	27	**Soft Rain** /	*Ray Price*	
11/13/61	26	2	28	**Here We Are Again**	*Wayne Walker*	Columbia 42132
6/2/62	12	8	29	**I've Just Destroyed The World** (I'm Living In) /	*Willie Nelson/Ray Price*	
6/2/62	22	1	30	**Big Shoes**	*Justin Tubb*	Columbia 42310
9/22/62	5	15	31	**Pride**	*Irene Stanton/Wayne Walker*	Columbia 42518
2/9/63	7	20	32	**Walk Me To The Door** /	*Conway Twitty*	
3/2/63	11	16	33	**You Took Her Off My Hands** (Now Please Take Her Off My Mind)	*Harlan Howard/Skeets McDonald/Wynn Stewart*	Columbia 42658
8/10/63	2^{1}	21	34	**Make The World Go Away** /	*Hank Cochran*	
10/5/63	28	2	35	**Night Life**	*Walt Breeland/Paul Buskirk/Willie Nelson*	Columbia 42827
3/14/64	2^{4}	27	36	**Burning Memories** /	*Mel Tillis/Wayne Walker*	
4/4/64	34	9	37	**That's All That Matters**	*Hank Cochran*	Columbia 42971
9/5/64	7	17	38	**Please Talk To My Heart**	*Jimmy Fautheree*	Columbia 43086
1/9/65	38	4	39	**A Thing Called Sadness**	*Chuck Howard*	Columbia 43162
5/8/65	2^{2}	24	40	**The Other Woman**	*Don Rollins*	Columbia 43264
11/27/65+	11	14	41	**Don't You Ever Get Tired Of Hurting Me**	*Hank Cochran*	Columbia 43427
				also see #83 below		
4/23/66	7	18	42	**A Way To Survive** /	*Moneen Carpenter/Hank Cochran*	
6/11/66	28	6	43	**I'm Not Crazy Yet**	*Don Rollins*	Columbia 43560
10/15/66	3^{2}	18	44	**Touch My Heart**	*Aubrey Mayhew/Donny Young*	Columbia 43795
3/25/67	9	17	45	**Danny Boy**	*Fred Weatherly*	Columbia 44042
7/22/67	6	18	46	**I'm Still Not Over You** /	*Willie Nelson*	
8/19/67	73	1	47	**Crazy**	*Willie Nelson*	Columbia 44195
12/30/67+	8	15	48	**Take Me As I Am** (Or Let Me Go)	*Boudleaux Bryant*	Columbia 44374
5/4/68	11	16	49	**I've Been There Before**	*Paul Anka/Bobby Gosh*	Columbia 44505
10/5/68	6	14	50	**She Wears My Ring**	*Boudleaux Bryant/Felice Bryant*	Columbia 44628
3/1/69	51	4	51	**Set Me Free**	*Curly Putman*	Columbia 44747
3/8/69	11	15	52	**Sweetheart Of The Year**	*Van Givens/Clyde Pitts*	Columbia 44761
8/16/69	14	12	53	**Raining In My Heart**	*Boudleaux Bryant/Felice Bryant*	Columbia 44931
11/22/69	14	11	54	**April's Fool**	*Dave Kirby/Glenn Martin*	Columbia 45005
3/7/70	8	15	55	**You Wouldn't Know Love**	*Hank Cochran/Dave Kirby*	Columbia 45095
6/27/70	❶^{1}	26	56	**For The Good Times** /	*Kris Kristofferson*	
				Grammy: Male Vocal		
7/11/70	flip	18	57	**Grazin' In Greener Pastures**	*Ray Pennington*	Columbia 45178
3/20/71	❶^{3}	19	58	**I Won't Mention It Again**	*Cam Mullins*	Columbia 45329
8/7/71	2^{1}	17	59	**I'd Rather Be Sorry**	*Kris Kristofferson*	Columbia 45425

Billboard DEBUT	PEAK	WKS	GOLD	ARTIST / Ranking / Country Chart Hit	Songwriter	Label (& Number)
				PRICE, Ray — cont'd		
4/15/72	2[1]	14		60 **The Lonesomest Lonesome /**	*Mac Davis*	
4/15/72	66	14		61 **That's What Leaving's About**	*Tom Lazaros*	Columbia 45583
11/4/72	❶[3]	16		62 **She's Got To Be A Saint**	*Mario DiNapoli/Joseph Paulini*	Columbia 45724
7/28/73	❶[1]	16		63 **You're The Best Thing That Ever Happened To Me**	*Jim Weatherly*	Columbia 45889
3/16/74	25	13		64 **Storms Of Troubled Times**	*Jim Weatherly*	Columbia 46015
8/17/74	15	11		65 **Like A First Time Thing**	*Jim Weatherly*	Columbia 10006
10/26/74+	4	15		66 **Like Old Times Again**	*Jim Weatherly*	Myrrh 146
2/8/75	3[1]	14		67 **Roses And Love Songs**	*Jim Weatherly*	Myrrh 150
5/31/75	17	13		68 **Farthest Thing From My Mind**	*Jim Weatherly*	ABC 12095
8/9/75	31	11		69 **If You Ever Change Your Mind**	*Jim Weatherly*	Columbia 10150
11/8/75	40	12		70 **Say I Do**	*Ray Hildebrand*	ABC/Dot 17588
3/27/76	34	9		71 **That's All She Wrote**	*Jerry Fuller*	ABC/Dot 17616
7/24/76	41	10		72 **To Make A Long Story Short /**	*Jerry Fuller*	
7/24/76	47	10		73 **We're Getting There**	*Jerry Fuller*	ABC/Dot 17637
12/4/76+	14	15		74 **A Mansion On The Hill**	*Fred Rose/Hank Williams*	ABC/Dot 17666
3/26/77	38	9		75 **Help Me**	*Larry Gatlin*	Columbia 10503
5/28/77	28	11		76 **Different Kind Of Flower** ***[w/ The Cherokee Cowboys]***	*Gary Sefton*	ABC/Dot 17690
10/1/77	21	12		77 **Born To Love Me**	*Bob Morrison*	ABC/Dot 17718
10/28/78+	19	13		78 **Feet**	*Jerry Fuller*	Monument 267
3/3/79	30	12		79 **There's Always Me**	*Don Robertson*	Monument 277
6/9/79	18	13		80 **That's The Only Way To Say Good Morning**	*Wayne Carson*	Monument 283
11/24/79+	43	9		81 **Misty Morning Rain**	*Don Chappell*	Monument 290
8/9/80	3[2]	15		82 **Faded Love** ***[w/ Willie Nelson]***	*Bob Wills/Johnnie Lee Wills*	Columbia 11329
12/6/80+	11	14		83 **Don't You Ever Get Tired (Of Hurting Me)** ***[w/ Willie Nelson]*** new version of #41 above	*Hank Cochran* **[R]**	Columbia 11405
3/28/81	28	13		84 **Getting Over You Again**	*Dave Kirby/Warren Robb*	Dimension 1018
7/18/81	6	17		85 **It Don't Hurt Me Half As Bad**	*Joe Allen/Deoin Lay/Bucky Lindsey*	Dimension 1021
11/14/81+	9	18		86 **Diamonds In The Stars**	*Jesse Shofner*	Dimension 1024
4/3/82	18	15		87 **Forty And Fadin'**	*Buck Moore/Jim Mundy/Don Tucker/Karen Tucker*	Dimension 1031
6/5/82	19	16		88 **Old Friends** ***[w/ Roger Miller & Willie Nelson]***	*Roger Miller*	Columbia 02681
8/7/82	62	7		89 **Wait Till Those Bridges Are Gone**	*Dave Kirby/Warren Robb*	Dimension 1035
12/4/82+	55	9		90 **Somewhere In Texas**	*Ray Pennington*	Dimension 1038
1/15/83	70	6		91 **One Fiddle, Two Fiddle /**	*Cliff Crofford/John Durrill/Snuff Garrett*	
1/15/83	flip	6		92 **San Antonio Rose** **RAY PRICE with Johnny Gimble & The Texas Swing Band** (above 2) above 2 from the movie *Honkytonk Man* starring **Clint Eastwood**	*Bob Wills*	Warner 29830
5/7/83	72	6		93 **Willie, Write Me A Song**	*Cliff Crofford*	Warner 29691
8/27/83	70	5		94 **Scotch And Soda**	*Dave Guard*	Viva 29543
6/23/84	87	4		95 **A New Place To Begin** ***[w/ The Cherokee Cowboys]***	*Dave Kirby/Warren Robb*	Viva 29277
9/8/84	73	6		96 **Better Class Of Loser** ***[w/ The Cherokee Cowboys]***	*Harlan Howard/Ron Peterson*	Viva 29217
11/17/84	77	7		97 **What Am I Gonna Do Without You** ***[w/ The Cherokee Cowboys]***	*Larry Bastian*	Viva 29147
5/25/85	77	6		98 **(She's Got A Hold Of Me Where It Hurts) She Won't Let Go**	*Lee Bach*	Step One 341
8/31/85	81	7		99 **I'm Not Leaving (I'm Just Getting Out Of Your Way)**	*Hank Cochran/Dean Dillon/Royce Porter*	Step One 344
12/21/85+	67	7		100 **Five Fingers**	*Dave Kirby/Ray Pennington*	Step One 350
3/15/86	60	8		101 **You're Nobody Till Somebody Loves You**	*James Cavanaugh/Russ Morgan/Larry Stock*	Step One 352
6/21/86	73	5		102 **All The Way**	S:36 *Sammy Cahn/James Van Heusen*	Step One 355
9/27/86	86	3		103 **Please Don't Talk About Me When I'm Gone**	*Sid Clare/Sam Stept*	Step One 361
12/27/86+	55	8		104 **When You Gave Your Love To Me**	*Jesse Shofner*	Step One 366
10/24/87	52	11		105 **Just Enough Love**	*Matraca Berg/Jane Mariash*	Step One 378
3/12/88	68	5		106 **Big Ole Teardrops**	*Dave Kirby/Warren Robb*	Step One 383
7/9/88	55	7		107 **Don't The Morning Always Come Too Soon**	*Fred Lehner/Jerry McBee*	Step One 388
12/10/88	83	4		108 **I'd Do It All Over Again**	*Jerry Fuller*	Step One 393
11/18/89	79	3		109 **Love Me Down To Size**	*Lobo Loggins/Johnny McCollum/Don Rollins*	Step One 410

All The Way ['86]
April's Fool ['69]
Better Class Of Loser ['84]
Big Ole Teardrops ['88]
Big Shoes ['62]
Born To Love Me ['77]
Burning Memories ['64]
City Lights ['58]
Crazy Arms ['56]
Crazy ['67]
Curtain In The Window ['58]
Danny Boy ['67]
Diamonds In The Stars ['82]
Different Kind Of Flower ['77]
Don't Let The Stars Get In Your Eyes ['52]
Don't The Morning Always Come Too Soon ['88]
Don't You Ever Get Tired Of Hurting Me ['66]
Don't You Ever Get Tired (Of Hurting Me) ['81]
Faded Love ['80]
Farthest Thing From My Mind ['75]
Feet ['79]
Five Fingers ['86]
For The Good Times ['70]
Forty And Fadin' ['82]
Getting Over You Again ['81]
Grazin' In Greener Pastures ['70]
Heart Over Mind ['61]
Heartaches By The Number ['59]
Help Me ['77]
Here We Are Again ['61]
I Can't Run Away From Myself ['60]
I Wish I Could Fall In Love Today ['60]
I Won't Mention It Again ['71]
I'd Do It All Over Again ['88]
I'd Rather Be Sorry ['71]
I'll Be There (If You Ever Want Me) ['54]
I'll Be There (When You Get Lonely) ['57]
I'm Not Crazy Yet ['66]
I'm Not Leaving (I'm Just Getting Out Of Your Way) ['85]
I'm Still Not Over You ['67]
I've Been There Before ['68]
I've Got A New Heartache ['56]
I've Just Destroyed The World (I'm Living In) ['62]
If You Don't, Somebody Else Will ['54]
If You Ever Change Your Mind ['75]
Invitation To The Blues ['58]
It Don't Hurt Me Half As Bad ['81]
It's All Your Fault ['58]
Just Enough Love ['87]
Like A First Time Thing ['74]
Like Old Times Again ['75]
Lonesomest Lonesome ['72]
Love Me Down To Size ['89]
Make The World Go Away ['63]
Mansion On The Hill ['77]
Misty Morning Rain ['80]
Much Too Young To Die ['54]
My Shoes Keep Walking Back To You ['57]
New Place To Begin ['84]
Night Life ['63]
Old Friends ['82]
One Fiddle, Two Fiddle ['83]
One More Time ['60]
Other Woman ['65]
Please Don't Talk About Me When I'm Gone ['86]
Please Talk To My Heart ['64]
Pride ['62]
Raining In My Heart ['69]
Release Me ['54]
Roses And Love Songs ['75]
Run Boy ['56]
Same Old Me ['59]
San Antonio Rose ['83]
Say I Do ['75]
Scotch And Soda ['83]
Set Me Free ['69]
She Wears My Ring ['68]
(She's Got A Hold Of Me Where It Hurts) She Won't Let Go ['85]
She's Got To Be A Saint ['72]
Soft Rain ['61]
Somewhere In Texas ['83]
Storms Of Troubled Times ['74]
Sweetheart Of The Year ['69]
Take Me As I Am (Or Let Me Go) ['68]
Talk To Your Heart ['52]
That's All She Wrote ['76]
That's All That Matters ['64]
That's The Only Way To Say Good Morning ['79]
That's What It's Like To Be Lonesome ['59]
That's What Leaving's About ['72]
There's Always Me ['79]
Thing Called Sadness ['65]
To Make A Long Story Short ['76]
Touch My Heart ['66]
Twenty-Fourth Hour ['61]
Under Your Spell Again ['59]
Wait Till Those Bridges Are Gone ['82]
Walk Me To The Door ['63]
Wasted Words ['56]
Way To Survive ['66]
We're Getting There ['76]
What Am I Gonna Do Without You ['84]
When You Gave Your Love To Me ['87]
Willie, Write Me A Song ['83]
You Done Me Wrong ['56]
You Took Her Off My Hands (Now Please Take Her Off My Mind) ['63]
You Wouldn't Know Love ['70]
You're Nobody Till Somebody Loves You ['86]
You're The Best Thing That Ever Happened To Me ['73]

Billboard DEBUT	PEAK	WKS	GOLD	ARTIST / Ranking / Country Chart Hit	Songwriter	Label (& Number)
				PRICE, Toni		
				Born in Tennessee. Female singer/actress. Had a bit part in the movie *Sweet Dreams.*		
1/25/86	**59**	9		1 **Mississippi Break Down**	*Curtis King/Chuck Wadley*	Luv 114
9/27/86	**71**	6		2 **How Much Do I Owe You**	*Dan Haley/Steve Karol*	Master 01
9/26/87	**80**	3		3 **I Want To Be Wanted**	*Kim Gannon/Pino Spotti*	Prairie Dust 8744

PRIDE, Charley **1970s: #3 / 1980s: #31 / All-Time: #19 // HOF: 2000**

Born on 3/18/1938 in Sledge, Mississippi. Black singer/guitarist. Played baseball with the Detroit Eagles and Memphis Red Sox of the Negro American League; also played in the Pioneer League. One of his most famous recordings, "Crystal Chandelier," was never released as a commercial single.

CMA: Male Vocalist 1971 & 1972/ Entertainer 1971 // OPRY: 1993

DEBUT	PEAK	WKS	GOLD	Country Chart Hit	Songwriter	Label (& Number)
12/3/66+	**9**	19		1 **Just Between You And Me**	*Jack Clement*	RCA Victor 9000
4/29/67	**6**	19		2 **I Know One**	*Jack Clement*	RCA Victor 9162
9/2/67	**4**	19		3 **Does My Ring Hurt Your Finger**	*Doris Clement/John Crutchfield/Don Robertson*	RCA Victor 9281
				COUNTRY CHARLEY PRIDE (above 3)		
1/6/68	**4**	17		4 **The Day The World Stood Still**	*Jerry Foster/Bill Rice*	RCA Victor 9403
5/18/68	**2^{2}**	15		5 **The Easy Part's Over**	*Jerry Foster/Bill Rice*	RCA Victor 9514
10/5/68	**4**	14		6 **Let The Chips Fall**	*Jack Clement*	RCA Victor 9622
2/1/69	**3^{3}**	16		7 **Kaw-Liga**	*Fred Rose/Hank Williams* **[L]**	RCA Victor 9716
6/14/69	❶^{1}	17		8 **All I Have To Offer You** (Is Me)	*Dallas Frazier/A.L. "Doodle" Owens*	RCA Victor 0167
11/8/69	❶^{3}	16		9 **(I'm So) Afraid Of Losing You Again**	*Dallas Frazier/A.L. "Doodle" Owens*	RCA Victor 0265
3/7/70	❶^{2}	17		10 **Is Anybody Goin' To San Antone**	*Dave Kirby/Glenn Martin*	RCA Victor 9806
6/13/70	❶^{2}	17		11 **Wonder Could I Live There Anymore**	*Bill Rice*	RCA Victor 9855
9/26/70	❶^{2}	16		12 **I Can't Believe That You've Stopped Loving Me**	*Dallas Frazier/A.L. "Doodle" Owens*	RCA Victor 9902
2/6/71	❶^{3}	14		13 **I'd Rather Love You**	*Johnny Duncan*	RCA Victor 9952
4/24/71	**21**	10		14 **Let Me Live /**	*Ben Peters*	
4/24/71	**70**	10		15 **Did You Think To Pray**	*Jack Johnson/Charley Pride*	RCA Victor 9974
6/26/71	❶^{4}	16		16 **I'm Just Me**	*Glenn Martin*	RCA Victor 9996
10/23/71	❶^{5}	19	●	17 **Kiss An Angel Good Mornin'**	*Ben Peters*	RCA Victor 0550
				Grammy: Song		
2/19/72	**2^{2}**	15		18 **All His Children** ***[w/ Henry Mancini]***	*Alan Bergman/Marilyn Bergman/Henry Mancini*	RCA Victor 0624
				from the movie *Sometimes A Great Notion* starring Paul Newman		
6/3/72	❶^{3}	16		19 **It's Gonna Take A Little Bit Longer**	*Ben Peters*	RCA Victor 0707
10/7/72	❶^{3}	16		20 **She's Too Good To Be True**	*Johnny Duncan*	RCA Victor 0802
2/10/73	❶^{1}	14		21 **A Shoulder To Cry On**	*Merle Haggard*	RCA Victor 0884
5/12/73	❶^{1}	15		22 **Don't Fight The Feelings Of Love**	*John Schweers*	RCA Victor 0942
10/13/73	❶^{1}	16		23 **Amazing Love**	*John Schweers*	RCA Victor 0073
4/20/74	**3^{1}**	14		24 **We Could**	*Felice Bryant*	RCA Victor 0257
8/24/74	**3^{2}**	17		25 **Mississippi Cotton Picking Delta Town**	*Harold Dorman/Wiley Gann*	RCA Victor 10030
12/14/74+	❶^{1}	12		26 **Then Who Am I**	*Dallas Frazier/A.L. "Doodle" Owens*	RCA Victor 10126
3/29/75	**6**	14		27 **I Ain't All Bad**	*Johnny Duncan*	RCA Victor 10236
8/9/75	❶^{1}	14		28 **Hope You're Feelin' Me** (Like I'm Feelin' You)	*Bobby David/Jim Rushing*	RCA Victor 10344
12/6/75+	**3^{2}**	14		29 **The Happiness Of Having You**	*Ted Harris*	RCA Victor 10455
3/13/76	❶^{1}	14		30 **My Eyes Can Only See As Far As You**	*Naomi Martin/Jimmy Payne*	RCA Victor 10592
8/28/76	**2^{2}**	15		31 **A Whole Lotta Things To Sing About**	*Ben Peters*	RCA 10757
1/29/77	❶^{1}	14		32 **She's Just An Old Love Turned Memory**	*John Schweers*	RCA 10875
5/21/77	❶^{1}	14		33 **I'll Be Leaving Alone**	*Wayland Holyfield/Dickey Lee*	RCA 10975
9/17/77	❶^{1}	14		34 **More To Me**	*Ben Peters*	RCA 11086
2/11/78	❶^{2}	15		35 **Someone Loves You Honey**	*Don Devaney*	RCA 11201
6/24/78	**3^{2}**	15		36 **When I Stop Leaving** (I'll Be Gone)	*Kent Robbins*	RCA 11287
10/21/78	**2^{3}**	14		37 **Burgers And Fries**	*Ben Peters*	RCA 11391
2/24/79	❶^{1}	15		38 **Where Do I Put Her Memory**	*Jim Weatherly*	RCA 11477
7/14/79	❶^{1}	15		39 **You're My Jamaica**	*Kent Robbins*	RCA 11655
10/27/79	**89**	2		40 **Dallas Cowboys**	*John Schweers*	RCA 11736
11/3/79+	**2^{1}**	15		41 **Missin' You**	*Kye Fleming/Dennis W. Morgan*	RCA 11751
2/16/80	❶^{1}	13		42 **Honky Tonk Blues**	*Hank Williams*	RCA 11912
5/10/80	❶^{1}	15		43 **You Win Again**	*Hank Williams*	RCA 12002
9/27/80	**4**	18		44 **You Almost Slipped My Mind**	*Tilden Back/Delbert Barker/Don Goodman/Troy Seals*	RCA 12100
3/7/81	**7**	13		45 **Roll On Mississippi**	*Kye Fleming/Dennis W. Morgan*	RCA 12178
8/22/81	❶^{2}	15		46 **Never Been So Loved** (In All My Life)	*Wayland Holyfield/Norro Wilson*	RCA 12294
12/26/81+	❶^{1}	18		47 **Mountain Of Love**	*Harold Dorman*	RCA 13014
4/24/82	**2^{2}**	18		48 **I Don't Think She's In Love Anymore**	*Kent Robbins*	RCA 13096
8/28/82	❶^{1}	17		49 **You're So Good When You're Bad**	*Ben Peters*	RCA 13293
12/4/82+	❶^{1}	19		50 **Why Baby Why**	*Darrell Edwards/George Jones*	RCA 13397
3/5/83	**7**	16		51 **More And More**	*Merle Kilgore/Webb Pierce*	RCA 13451
6/25/83	❶^{1}	21		52 **Night Games**	*Blake Mevis/Norro Wilson*	RCA 13542
10/15/83+	**2^{1}**	20		53 **Ev'ry Heart Should Have One**	*Byron Gallimore/Bill Shore*	RCA 13648

Billboard DEBUT	PEAK	WKS	GOLD	ARTIST / Country Chart Hit	Ranking / Songwriter	Label (& Number)
				PRIDE, Charley — cont'd		
6/9/84	**9**	20		54 **The Power Of Love**	*Don Cook/Gary Nicholson*	RCA 13821
11/3/84	**32**	13		55 **Missin' Mississippi**	*Byron Gallimore/Blake Mevis/Bill Shore*	RCA 13936
4/13/85	**25**	13		56 **Down On The Farm**	S:24 / A:27 *John Greenebaum/Eddie Seals/Troy Seals*	RCA 14045
7/6/85	**34**	11		57 **Let A Little Love Come In**	*Bob McDill*	RCA 14134
1/18/86	**75**	5		58 **The Best There Is**	*Randy Goodrum/Wayland Holyfield*	RCA 14265
4/5/86	**74**	7		59 **Love On A Blue Rainy Day**	*Richard Carpenter/Kent Robbins*	RCA 14296
3/21/87	**14**	22		60 **Have I Got Some Blues For You**	S:❶[1] / A:19 *David Chamberlain*	16th Avenue 70400
7/18/87	**31**	15		61 **If You Still Want A Fool Around**	*Kent Robbins*	16th Avenue 70402
12/12/87+	**5**	23		62 **Shouldn't It Be Easier Than This**	S:❶[1] *Rick Giles/John Jarrard*	16th Avenue 70408
5/7/88	**13**	19		63 **I'm Gonna Love Her On The Radio**	S:7 *Tom Brasfield/Mac McAnally*	16th Avenue 70414
10/15/88	**49**	13		64 **Where Was I**	*Stephen Clark/Rich Peoples*	16th Avenue 70420
2/25/89	**49**	7		65 **White Houses**	*J.C. Cunningham*	16th Avenue 70425
7/1/89	**77**	4		66 **The More I Do**	*Gidget Baird/Byron Gallimore*	16th Avenue 70429
11/4/89+	**28**	17		67 **Amy's Eyes**	*Terry Brown/Jaima Hunt*	16th Avenue 70435

All His Children ['72]
All I Have To Offer You (Is Me) ['69]
Amazing Love ['73]
Amy's Eyes ['90]
Best There Is ['86]
Burgers And Fries ['78]
Dallas Cowboys ['79]
Day The World Stood Still ['68]
Did You Think To Pray ['71]
Does My Ring Hurt Your Finger ['67]
Don't Fight The Feelings Of Love ['73]
Down On The Farm ['85]
Easy Part's Over ['68]
Ev'ry Heart Should Have One ['84]
Happiness Of Having You ['76]
Have I Got Some Blues For You ['87]
Honky Tonk Blues ['80]
Hope You're Feelin' Me (Like I'm Feelin' You) ['75]
I Ain't All Bad ['75]
I Can't Believe That You've Stopped Loving Me ['70]
I Don't Think She's In Love Anymore ['82]
I Know One ['67]
I'd Rather Love You ['71]
I'll Be Leaving Alone ['77]
I'm Gonna Love Her On The Radio ['88]
I'm Just Me ['71]
(I'm So) Afraid Of Losing You Again ['69]
If You Still Want A Fool Around ['87]
Is Anybody Goin' To San Antone ['70]
It's Gonna Take A Little Bit Longer ['72]
Just Between You And Me ['67]
Kaw-Liga ['69]
Kiss An Angel Good Mornin' ['71]
Let A Little Love Come In ['85]
Let Me Live ['71]
Let The Chips Fall ['68]
Love On A Blue Rainy Day ['86]
Missin' Mississippi ['84]
Missin' You ['80]
Mississippi Cotton Picking Delta Town ['74]
More And More ['83]
More I Do ['89]
More To Me ['77]
Mountain Of Love ['82]
My Eyes Can Only See As Far As You ['76]
Never Been So Loved (In All My Life) ['81]
Night Games ['83]
Power Of Love ['84]
Roll On Mississippi ['81]
She's Just An Old Love Turned Memory ['77]
She's Too Good To Be True ['72]
Shoulder To Cry On ['73]
Shouldn't It Be Easier Than This ['88]
Someone Loves You Honey ['78]
Then Who Am I ['75]
We Could ['74]
When I Stop Leaving (I'll Be Gone) ['78]
Where Do I Put Her Memory ['79]
Where Was I ['88]
White Houses ['89]
Whole Lotta Things To Sing About ['76]
Why Baby Why ['83]
Wonder Could I Live There Anymore ['70]
You Almost Slipped My Mind ['80]
You Win Again ['80]
You're My Jamaica ['79]
You're So Good When You're Bad ['82]

PROCTOR, Paul

Born in Arlington, Texas. Male singer.

DEBUT	PEAK	WKS		Country Chart Hit	Songwriter	Label (& Number)
12/20/86	**74**	4		1 **Not Tonight**	*Kix Brooks/Tom Shapiro/Chris Waters*	Aurora 1003
2/21/87	**79**	4		2 **He's Not Good Enough**	*Paul Davis/Jennifer Kimball/Joe Wilson*	Aurora 1005
7/25/87	**62**	6		3 **Ain't We Got Love**	*Charlie Craig/Keith Stegall*	19th Avenue 1009
11/19/88	**96**	1		4 **Tied To The Wheel Of A Runaway Heart**	*Mark Collie/Bobby Neal/Ronny Scaife/Phil Thomas*	19th Avenue 1012

PROCTOR, Rachel

Born in Charleston, West Virginia. Female singer/songwriter.

DEBUT	PEAK	WKS		Country Chart Hit	Songwriter	Label (& Number)
5/17/03	**24**	21		1 **Days Like This**	*Odie Blackmon/Rachel Proctor*	BNA
12/27/03+	**43**	11		2 **Didn't I**	*Kris Bergsnes/Brian Nash/Mike Post*	BNA
3/13/04	**18**	22		3 **Me And Emily**	*Rachel Proctor/Chris Tompkins*	BNA
9/25/04	**37**	11		4 **Where I Belong**	*Chris Lindsey/Hillary Lindsey/Aimee Mayo/Troy Verges*	BNA
				above 4 from the album *Where I Belong* on BNA 51217		

PROPHET, Ronnie

Born on 12/26/1938 in Calumet, Quebec, Canada. Male singer/guitarist. Hosted own TV series in Canada and England.

DEBUT	PEAK	WKS		Country Chart Hit	Songwriter	Label (& Number)
8/23/75	**26**	12		1 **Sanctuary**	*Rory Bourke*	RCA Victor 50027
12/27/75+	**36**	10		2 **Shine On**	*Rory Bourke*	RCA Victor 50136
5/1/76	**50**	7		3 **It's Enough**	*Rory Bourke*	RCA Victor 50205
10/9/76	**82**	5		4 **Big Big World**	*Fred Burch/Gerald Nelson/Red West*	RCA 50273
10/15/77	**99**	2		5 **It Ain't Easy Lovin' Me**	*Jeff Barry/Cynthia Weil*	RCA 50391

PROSSER, James

Born in Mound Valley, Kansas. Male singer.

DEBUT	PEAK	WKS		Country Chart Hit	Songwriter	Label (& Number)
2/27/99	**59**	6		1 **Life Goes On**	*Steven Jones*	Warner
6/26/99	**66**	4		2 **Angels Don't Fly**	*John Fountain/Bill Webb*	Warner
				above 2 from the album *Life Goes On* on Warner 47254		

PRUETT, Jeanne — All-Time: #255

Born Norma Jean Bowman on 1/30/1937 in Pell City, Alabama. Female singer/songwriter/guitarist.

OPRY: 1973

DEBUT	PEAK	WKS		Country Chart Hit	Songwriter	Label (& Number)
9/18/71	**66**	6		1 **Hold On To My Unchanging Love**	*Jeanne Pruett*	Decca 32857
3/11/72	**34**	12		2 **Love Me**	*Jeanne Pruett*	Decca 32929
				also see #23 below		
8/5/72	**64**	3		3 **Call On Me**	*Jeanne Pruett*	Decca 32977
11/4/72	**60**	6		4 **I Forgot More Than You'll Ever Know (About Him)**	*Cecil Null*	Decca 33013
3/31/73	**❶[3]**	18		5 **Satin Sheets**	*John Volinkaty*	MCA 40015
				also see #17 below		
9/15/73	**8**	14		6 **I'm Your Woman**	*Bob Johnston*	MCA 40116
3/23/74	**15**	14		7 **You Don't Need To Move A Mountain**	*Wayland Holyfield/Jim Rushing*	MCA 40207
8/31/74	**22**	15		8 **Welcome To The Sunshine (Sweet Baby Jane)**	*Ray Willis*	MCA 40284
1/18/75	**25**	12		9 **Just Like Your Daddy**	*John Adrian*	MCA 40340
5/10/75	**41**	9		10 **Honey On His Hands**	*Max D. Barnes/Troy Seals*	MCA 40395
7/26/75	**24**	13		11 **A Poor Man's Woman**	*Jeanne Pruett*	MCA 40440
12/13/75+	**77**	7		12 **My Baby's Gone**	*Hazel Houser*	MCA 40490
10/2/76	**41**	8		13 **I've Taken**	*Walter Haynes/Jeanne Pruett*	MCA 40605

DEBUT	PEAK	WKS	GOLD	#	ARTIST / Country Chart Hit	Songwriter	Label (& Number)
					PRUETT, Jeanne — cont'd		
2/19/77	**30**	10		14	**I'm Living A Lie**	*Wayland Holyfield*	MCA 40678
5/21/77	**85**	4		15	**She's Still All Over You**	*Wayland Holyfield/Bob McDill*	MCA 40723
2/25/78	**94**	3		16	**I'm A Woman**	*Wayland Holyfield/Bob McDill*	Mercury 55017
8/11/79	**54**	8		17	**Please Sing Satin Sheets For Me**	*Jeanne Pruett/John Volinkaty*	IBC 0002
					final 20 seconds of recording features a refrain of #5 above		
11/24/79+	**6**	16		18	**Back To Back**	*Jerry McBee/Jeanne Pruett*	IBC 0005
3/15/80	**5**	15		19	**Temporarily Yours**	*Bobby Fischer/Sonny Throckmorton*	IBC 0008
7/5/80	**9**	14		20	**It's Too Late**	*Rory Bourke/Gene Dobbins/Johnny Wilson*	IBC 0010
3/14/81	**81**	3		21	**Sad Ole Shade Of Gray**	*Glenn Martin/Sonny Throckmorton*	Paid 118
6/6/81	**72**	4		22	**I Ought To Feel Guilty**	*Bob Morrison/Bill Zerface/Jim Zerface*	Paid 136
4/16/83	**58**	8		23	**Love Me** ***[w/ Marty Robbins]***	*Jeanne Pruett* **[R]**	Audiograph 454
					new version of #2 above		
7/9/83	**73**	4		24	**Lady Of The Eighties**	*David Bellamy*	Audiograph 467
8/22/87	**81**	3		25	**Rented Room**	*Jeanne Pruett*	MSR 1956
					PRUITT, Lewis		
					Born on 10/30/1923 in Atlanta, Georgia. Died on 1/28/2003 (age 79). Male singer/songwriter/guitarist.		
12/7/59+	**10**	21		1	**Timbrook**	*Jim Howell/Don Pierce*	Peach 725
6/27/60	**4**	17		2	**Softly And Tenderly (I'll Hold You In My Arms)**	*Red Bailey/Jim Howell*	Decca 31095
4/3/61	**11**	9		3	**Crazy Bullfrog**	*Lewis Pruitt*	Decca 31201
					PRYOR, Cactus, and his Pricklypears		
					Born Richard Pryor in Austin, Texas. DJ at KTBC in Austin. Member of the Country Music DJ Hall of Fame. Appeared in the John Wayne movies *Hellfighters* and *The Green Berets*.		
6/3/50	**7**	1			**Cry Of The Dying Duck In A Thunder-Storm**	A:7 *Cactus Pryor* **[N]**	4 Star 1459
					parody of "The Cry Of The Wild Goose" by **Tennessee Ernie Ford**		
					PRYSOCK, Arthur		
					Born on 1/2/1929 in Spartanburg, South Carolina. Died on 6/14/1997 (age 68). Black male singer.		
9/29/79	**74**	5			**Today I Started Loving You Again**	*Merle Haggard/Bonnie Owens*	Gusto 9023
					PUCKETT, Jerry		
					Born in Deleware. Male singer/songwriter/guitarist.		
8/27/83	**81**	3			**Heart On The Run**	*John Crocker/Jerry Puckett*	Atlantic Amer. 99860
					PUCKETT, Riley		
					Born George Puckett on 5/7/1894 in Alpharetta, Georgia. Died of blood poisoning on 7/13/1946 (age 52). Highly influential guitarist/banjo player. Blinded shortly after birth. Founding member of the Skillet Lickers stringband.		
					EARLY HIT: My Carolina Home (1927)		
					PULLINS, Leroy		
					Born Carl Leroy Pullins on 11/12/1940 in Elgin, Illinois. Male singer/songwriter/guitarist.		
6/25/66	**18**	11			**I'm A Nut**	*Leroy Pullins* **[N]**	Kapp 758
					PUMP BOYS AND DINETTES		
					From original cast recording of the Broadway musical *Pump Boys And Dinettes*. Featuring cast members Jim Wann and Cass Morgan.		
3/19/83	**67**	5			**The Night Dolly Parton Was Almost Mine**	*Jim Wann*	CBS 03549
					PURE PRAIRIE LEAGUE		
					Country-pop-rock group from Cincinnati, Ohio. Numerous personnel changes. Lineup in 1976: George Ed Powell (vocals, guitar), Larry Goshorn (guitar), Michael Connor (keyboards), Mike Reilly (bass) and Billy Hinds (drums). **Vince Gill** was lead singer from 1979-83.		
6/19/76	**96**	2			**That'll Be The Day**	*Jerry Allison/Buddy Holly/Norman Petty*	RCA Victor 10679
					PUTMAN, Curly **SW: #18**		
					Born Claude Putman on 11/20/1930 in Princeton, Alabama. Male singer/songwriter.		
2/29/60	**23**	1		1	**The Prison Song**	*Curly Putman*	Cherokee 504
7/8/67	**41**	9		2	**My Elusive Dreams**	*Curly Putman/Billy Sherrill*	ABC 10934
11/4/67	**67**	3		3	**Set Me Free**	*Curly Putman*	ABC 10984
					PYLE, Chuck		
					Born in Pittsburgh, Pennsylvania; raised in Newton, Iowa. Male singer/songwriter.		
9/28/85	**60**	6		1	**Drifter's Wind**	*Chuck Pyle*	Urban Sound 786
1/18/86	**81**	6		2	**Breathless In The Night**	*Chuck Pyle*	Urban Sound 782

Q

DEBUT	PEAK	WKS	GOLD	#	ARTIST / Country Chart Hit	Songwriter	Label (& Number)
					QUIST, Jack		
					Born on 4/17/1954 in Salt Lake City, Utah. Male singer/songwriter.		
9/11/82	**52**	9		1	**Memory Machine**	*Ted Harris*	Memory Machine 1015
9/9/89	**77**	3		2	**Where Does Love Go (When It Dies)**	*Stan Garland/Cal Gillen/Jack Quist/Anne Reeves*	Grudge 4756

Billboard DEBUT	PEAK	WKS	GOLD	ARTIST / Country Chart Hit	Ranking / Songwriter	Label (& Number)

R

RABBITT, Eddie — 1980s: #27 / All-Time: #58

Born on 11/27/1941 in Brooklyn, New York; raised in East Orange, New Jersey. Died of cancer on 5/7/1998 (age 56). Male singer/songwriter/guitarist. First recorded for 20th Century in 1964. Became established after **Elvis Presley** recorded his song "Kentucky Rain."

DEBUT	PEAK	WKS	GOLD	Country Chart Hit	Songwriter	Label (& Number)
8/31/74	34	14		1 You Get To Me	*Eddie Rabbitt*	Elektra 45895
3/22/75	12	17		2 Forgive And Forget	*Eddie Rabbitt/Even Stevens*	Elektra 45237
8/30/75	11	14		3 I Should Have Married You	*Eddie Rabbitt/Even Stevens*	Elektra 45269
2/7/76	❶[1]	16		4 Drinkin' My Baby (Off My Mind)	*Eddie Rabbitt/Even Stevens*	Elektra 45301
6/5/76	5	15		5 Rocky Mountain Music /	*Eddie Rabbitt*	
6/5/76	flip	15		6 Do You Right Tonight	*Eddie Rabbitt/Even Stevens*	Elektra 45315
11/6/76+	3[2]	16		7 Two Dollars In The Jukebox	*Eddie Rabbitt*	Elektra 45357
4/2/77	2[1]	16		8 I Can't Help Myself	*Eddie Rabbitt/Even Stevens*	Elektra 45390
8/20/77	6	15		9 We Can't Go On Living Like This	*Eddie Rabbitt/Even Stevens*	Elektra 45418
2/18/78	2[2]	16		10 Hearts On Fire	*Eddie Rabbitt/Even Stevens/Dan Tyler*	Elektra 45461
6/10/78	❶[1]	14		11 You Don't Love Me Anymore	*Alan Ray/Jeff Raymond*	Elektra 45488
9/30/78	❶[1]	14		12 I Just Want To Love You	*David Malloy/Eddie Rabbitt/Even Stevens*	Elektra 45531
12/23/78+	❶[3]	15		13 Every Which Way But Loose from the movie starring **Clint Eastwood**	*Milton Brown/Steve Dorff/Snuff Garrett*	Elektra 45554
6/16/79	❶[1]	14		14 Suspicions	*David Malloy/Randy McCormick/Eddie Rabbitt/Even Stevens*	Elektra 46053
11/3/79+	5	15		15 Pour Me Another Tequilla	*David Malloy/Eddie Rabbitt/Even Stevens*	Elektra 46558
3/15/80	❶[1]	14		16 Gone Too Far	*David Malloy/Eddie Rabbitt/Even Stevens*	Elektra 46613
6/21/80	❶[1]	15	●	17 Drivin' My Life Away from the movie *Roadie* starring Meat Loaf	*David Malloy/Eddie Rabbitt/Even Stevens*	Elektra 46656
11/8/80+	❶[1]	17	●	18 I Love A Rainy Night	*David Malloy/Eddie Rabbitt/Even Stevens*	Elektra 47066
8/1/81	❶[1]	16		19 Step By Step	*David Malloy/Eddie Rabbitt/Even Stevens*	Elektra 47174
11/21/81+	❶[1]	17		20 Someone Could Lose A Heart Tonight	*David Malloy/Eddie Rabbitt/Even Stevens*	Elektra 47239
4/10/82	2[3]	16		21 I Don't Know Where To Start	*Thom Schuyler*	Elektra 47435
10/9/82	❶[1]	19		22 You And I *[w/ Crystal Gayle]*	*Frank J. Myers*	Elektra 69936
4/2/83	❶[1]	17		23 You Can't Run From Love	*David Malloy/Eddie Rabbitt/Even Stevens*	Warner 29712
9/3/83	10	18		24 You Put The Beat In My Heart	*Rick Giles/Don Pfrimmer*	Warner 29512
12/17/83+	10	15		25 Nothing Like Falling In Love	*Jim Schnaars/Thom Schuyler*	Warner 29431
5/19/84	3[1]	18		26 B-B-B-Burnin' Up With Love	*Eddie Rabbitt/Even Stevens/Billy Joe Walker*	Warner 29279
10/6/84+	❶[1]	23		27 The Best Year Of My Life	S:❶[1] / A:❶[1] *Eddie Rabbitt/Even Stevens*	Warner 29186
2/23/85	4	19		28 Warning Sign	S:3 / A:4 *Eddie Rabbitt/Even Stevens*	Warner 29089
7/13/85	6	21		29 She's Comin' Back To Say Goodbye	A:5 / S:6 *Eddie Rabbitt/Even Stevens*	Warner 28976
10/12/85	10	18		30 A World Without Love	S:10 / A:10 *Phil Galdston/Eddie Rabbitt/Even Stevens*	RCA 14192
3/22/86	4	19		31 Repetitive Regret	S:4 / A:4 *Reed Nielsen/Mark Wright*	RCA 14317
7/12/86	❶[1]	20		32 Both To Each Other (Friends & Lovers) *[w/ Juice Newton]*	S:❶[1] / A:❶[1] *Paul Gordon/Jay Gruska*	RCA 14377
11/1/86+	9	20		33 Gotta Have You	A:9 / S:10 *Richard Landis/Reed Nielsen/Eddie Rabbitt*	RCA 5012
1/16/88	❶[1]	20		34 I Wanna Dance With You	S:7 *Eddie Rabbitt/Billy Joe Walker*	RCA 5238
5/28/88	❶[1]	18		35 The Wanderer	S:2 *Ernie Maresca*	RCA 8306
10/8/88	7	22		36 We Must Be Doin' Somethin' Right	S:9 *Reed Nielsen/Eddie Rabbitt*	RCA 8716
5/13/89	66	10		37 That's Why I Fell In Love With You	*Eddie Rabbitt/Even Stevens/Billy Joe Walker*	RCA 8819
12/9/89+	❶[2]	26		38 On Second Thought	*Eddie Rabbitt*	Universal 66025
4/7/90	8	21		39 Runnin' With The Wind	*Reed Nielsen/Eddie Rabbitt*	Capitol
8/4/90	32	9		40 It's Lonely Out Tonite	*Reed Nielsen/Eddie Rabbitt*	Capitol
9/29/90	11	20		41 American Boy	*Eddie Rabbitt*	Capitol
3/2/91	58	9		42 Tennessee Born And Bred above 4 from the album *Jersey Boy* on Capitol 93882	*Reed Nielsen/Eddie Rabbitt*	Capitol
8/17/91	50	14		43 Hang Up The Phone from the album *Ten Rounds* on Capitol 95955	*Eddie Rabbitt*	Capitol

RABBITT, Jimmy, And Renegade

Born Edward Payne in Holdenville, Oklahoma; raised in Tyler, Texas. Male singer/songwriter/guitarist. Worked as a DJ on many radio stations since 1964.

DEBUT	PEAK	WKS	GOLD	Country Chart Hit	Songwriter	Label (& Number)
5/8/76	80	4		Ladies Love Outlaws	*Lee Clayton*	Capitol 4257

RAE, Lana

Born in Oklahoma. Female singer.

DEBUT	PEAK	WKS	GOLD	Country Chart Hit	Songwriter	Label (& Number)
2/19/72	26	14		You're My Shoulder To Lean On	*Warner Mack*	Decca 32927

RAINES, Leon

Born in Mobile, Alabama. Male singer.

DEBUT	PEAK	WKS	GOLD	Country Chart Hit	Songwriter	Label (& Number)
4/30/83	79	4		1 I'll Be Seeing You	*Sammy Fain/Irving Kahal*	American Spotlite 103
7/7/84	91	2		2 Don't Give Up On Her Now	*Frank Knapp/Alan Rhody*	American Spotlite 107
11/24/84	81	3		3 Biloxi Lady	*Stewart Harris/Keith Stegall*	Atlantic Amer. 99700
3/9/85	83	2		4 It Happens Every Time	*Milton Brown/Steve Dorff*	Atlantic Amer. 99670
12/26/87+	71	5		5 Most Of All	*Buddy Buie/J.R. Cobb*	Southern Tracks 1089

Billboard DEBUT	PEAK	WKS	GOLD	ARTIST / Country Chart Hit	Ranking / Songwriter	Label (& Number)
				RAINFORD, Tina		
				Born on 12/25/1946 in Berlin, Germany. Female singer.		
4/9/77	**25**	14		1 **Silver Bird**	*Ron Vaplus*	Epic 50340
10/15/77	**91**	4		2 **Big Silver Angel**	*Wayne Carson*	Epic 50455
				RAINSFORD, Willie		
				Born in Nashville, Tennessee. Male singer/pianist.		
3/26/77	**98**	2		1 **No Relief In Sight**	*Rory Bourke/Gene Dobbins/Johnny Wilson*	Louisiana Hay. 7615
8/13/77	**85**	5		2 **Cheater's Kit**	*Rory Bourke/Gene Dobbins/Johnny Wilson*	Louisiana Hay. 7629
				RAINWATER, Jack		
				Born in Detroit, Michigan. Male singer/guitarist. No relation to Marvin Rainwater.		
11/12/77	**96**	3		**All I Want Is To Love You**	*Alfred Cardillo*	Laurie 3658
				RAINWATER, Marvin		
				Born Marvin Percy on 7/2/1925 in Wichita, Kansas. Male singer/songwriter/guitarist. No relation to Jack Rainwater.		
4/6/57	**3**^{3}	28	●	1 **Gonna Find Me A Bluebird /**	S:3 / A:3 / J:5 *Marvin Rainwater*	
7/29/57	**flip**	1		2 **So You Think You've Got Troubles**	S:flip *Marvin Rainwater*	MGM 12412
4/14/58	**15**	3		3 **Whole Lotta Woman**	S:15 *Marvin Rainwater*	MGM 12609
9/15/58	**11**	1		4 **Nothin' Needs Nothin' (Like I Need You)**	A:11 *Claude DeMetruis/Aaron Schroeder*	MGM 12701
7/6/59	**16**	6		5 **Half-Breed**	*John D. Loudermilk*	MGM 12803
				RAINWOOD, Michael		
				Born in Texas. Male singer/songwriter/guitarist.		
10/9/99	**21**^{S}	1		**I Want It All**	*Michael Rainwood*	Atomik
				RAITT, Bonnie		
				Born on 11/8/1949 in Burbank, California. Blues-rock singer/guitarist. Daugher of Broadway actor/singer John Raitt. Married to actor Michael O'Keefe from 1991-99.		
10/4/80	**42**	8		**Don't It Make Ya Wanna Dance**	*Rusty Wier*	Full Moon 47033
				from the movie *Urban Cowboy* starring John Travolta		
				RAKES, Pal		
				Born Palmer Rakes in Tampa, Florida. Male singer/songwriter/guitarist.		
4/2/77	**24**	12		1 **That's When The Lyin' Stops (And The Lovin' Starts)**	*Russ Faith/Pal Rakes/Norro Wilson*	Warner 8340
7/30/77	**31**	10		2 **'Til I Can't Take It Anymore**	*Dorian Burton/Clyde Otis*	Warner 8416
1/7/78	**46**	10		3 **If I Ever Come Back**	*Russ Faith/Pal Rakes*	Warner 8506
10/28/78	**81**	3		4 **Till Then**	*Sol Marcus/Eddie Seiler/Guy Wood*	Warner 8656
3/17/79	**92**	3		5 **You And Me And The Green Grass**	*Ray Griff*	Warner 8765
10/29/88	**71**	5		6 **I'm Only Lonely For You**	*Donny Kees/Richard Ross*	Atlantic Amer. 99276
6/24/89	**73**	5		7 **All You're Takin' Is My Love**	*Travis Wammack*	Atlantic Amer. 99214
11/4/89	**66**	3		8 **We Did It Once (We Can Do It Again)**	*Randy Howard/Donny Kees/Nelson Larkin/Pal Rakes*	Atlantic 88800
				RAMBLING ROGUE — see ROSE, Fred		
				RANCH, The		
				Trio from Australia: **Keith Urban** (vocals, guitar), Jerry Flowers (bass) and Peter Clarke (drums).		
9/27/97	**50**	13		1 **Walkin' The Country**	*Vern Rust/Keith Urban*	Capitol
3/14/98	**61**	5		2 **Just Some Love**	*Scott Phelps/Cyril Rawson*	Capitol
				above 2 from the album *The Ranch* on Capitol 55400		
				RANDALL, Jon		
				Born Jon Randall Stewart on 2/17/1969 in Dallas, Texas. Male singer/songwriter/guitarist. Married to **Lorrie Morgan** from 1996-99.		
7/16/94	**74**	3		1 **This Heart**	*Tony Haselden/Tim Mensy*	RCA
				from the album *What You Don't Know* on RCA 66407		
4/6/96	**18**	20		2 **By My Side** *[w/ Lorrie Morgan]*	S:4 *Dawn Thomas*	BNA
				from Morgan's album *Greater Need* on BNA 66847		
3/20/99	**71**	3		3 **Cold Coffee Morning**	*Bill Anderson/Jon Randall*	Asylum
				from the album *Cold Coffee Morning* on Asylum 62276		
				RANDOLPH, Robert		
				Born in Newark, New Jersey. Black singer/steel guitarist.		
12/11/04	**55**	5		**Mission Temple Fireworks Stand** *[w/ Sawyer Brown]*	*Billy Maddox/Paul Thorn*	Curb
				from Sawyer Brown's album *Mission Temple Fireworks Stand* on Curb 78879		
				RANEY, Wayne	**1940s: #38**	
				Born on 8/17/1920 in Wolf Bayou, Arkansas. Died of cancer on 1/23/1993 (age 72). Male singer/songwriter/harmonica player.		
10/30/48	**11**	1		1 **Lost John Boogie**	J:11 / S:14 *Wayne Raney*	King 719
11/20/48	**13**	2		2 **Jack And Jill Boogie**	J:13 *Mac Luna/Norman Luna*	King 732
7/30/49	**❶**^{3}	22		3 **Why Don't You Haul Off And Love Me**	J:❶^{3} / S:❶^{2} / A:5 *Lonnie Glosson/Wayne Raney*	King 791
				RASCAL FLATTS	**2000s: #9 / All-Time: #203**	
				Vocal trio formed in Columbus, Ohio: Gary LeVox (born on 7/10/1970), Jay DeMarcus (born on 4/26/1971) and Joe Don Rooney (born on 9/13/1975).		
				CMA: Horizon 2002 / Vocal Group 2003 & 2004		
3/4/00	**3**^{2}	31		1 **Prayin' For Daylight**	S:5 *Steve Bogard/Rick Giles*	Lyric Street
8/12/00+	**9**	30		2 **This Everyday Love**	*Gene Nelson/Danny Wells*	Lyric Street
12/2/00	**73**	2		3 **Long Slow Beautiful Dance**	*Kevin Fisher/Fred Wilhelm*	Lyric Street
3/31/01	**7**	24		4 **While You Loved Me**	*Marty Dodson/Danny Wells/Kim Williams*	Lyric Street

Billboard DEBUT	PEAK	WKS	GOLD	ARTIST / Country Chart Hit	Ranking / Songwriter	Label (& Number)
				RASCAL FLATTS — cont'd		
10/13/01+	4	34		5 **I'm Movin' On**	*Phillip White/D. Vincent Williams*	Lyric Street
				above 5 from the album *Rascal Flatts* on Lyric Street 165011		
6/29/02	❶^{3}	36		6 **These Days**	*Steve Robson/Jeffrey Steele/Danny Wells*	Lyric Street
1/25/03	3^{3}	25		7 **Love You Out Loud**	*Brett James/Lonnie Wilson*	Lyric Street
7/12/03	2^{3}	25		8 **I Melt**	*Gary LeVox/Wendell Mobley/Neil Thrasher*	Lyric Street
1/3/04	❶^{1}	25		9 **Mayberry**	*Arlos Smith*	Lyric Street
				above 4 from the album *Melt* on Lyric Street 165031		
6/26/04	9	20		10 **Feels Like Today**	*Wayne Hector/Steve Robson*	Lyric Street
11/6/04+	❶^{5}	26		11 **Bless The Broken Road**	*Bobby Boyd/Jeff Hanna/Marcus Hummon*	Lyric Street
				also see #15 below		
1/15/05	19↑	26↑		12 **Skin** (Sarabeth)	*Joe Henry/Doug Johnson*	Lyric Street
1/29/05	53	6		13 **Oklahoma-Texas Line**	*Jay DeMarcus/Gary LeVox/Joe Dan Rooney*	Lyric Street
3/26/05	❶^{3}	25		14 **Fast Cars And Freedom**	*Gary LeVox/Wendell Mobley/Neil Thrasher*	Lyric Street
				above 5 from the album *Feels Like Today* on Lyric Street 165049		
6/11/05	50	1		15 **Bless The Broken Road** ***[w/ Carrie Underwood]***	*Bobby Boyd/Jeff Hanna/Marcus Hummon* **[R]**	Arista
				new version of #11 above; only available as a paid download		
				RATTLESNAKE ANNIE		
				Born Rosan Gallimore on 12/26/1941 in Puryear, Tennessee. Female singer/guitarist.		
5/2/87	79	3		1 **Callin' Your Bluff**	*Max D. Barnes/Lonnie Mack*	Columbia 07024
1/9/88	79	3		2 **Somewhere South Of Macon**	*Marshall Chapman/Jim Rushing*	Columbia 07634
				RAUSCH, Leon		
				Born Edgar Leon Rausch on 10/2/1927 in Springfield, Missouri. Male singer/guitarist. Member of the **Original Texas Playboys**.		
1/17/76	99	1		1 **Through The Bottom Of The Glass**	*Paul Craft*	Derrick 105
8/21/76	91	5		2 **She's The Trip That I've Been On**	*Dallas Frazier/Whitey Shafer*	Derrick 107
6/10/78	89	5		3 **I'm Satisfied With You**	*Fred Rose*	Derrick 119
10/21/78	95	4		4 **Let's Have A Heart To Heart Talk**	*Billy Austin/Eddie Brent/Paul Sanders*	Derrick 122
10/20/79	91	4		5 **You Can Be Replaced**	*Bill Anderson/Jerry Crutchfield*	Derrick 124
12/15/79+	81	6		6 **Palimony**	*Jim Mundy*	Derrick 128

RAVEN, Eddy — **1980s: #29 / All-Time: #96**

Born Edward Garvin Futch on 8/19/1944 in Lafayette, Louisiana. Male singer/songwriter/guitarist. First recorded for Cosmos label in 1962. Worked as staff writer for Acuff-Rose publishing company.

DEBUT	PEAK	WKS	GOLD	Country Chart Hit	Songwriter	Label (& Number)
3/16/74	63	10		1 **The Last Of The Sunshine Cowboys**	*Eddy Raven*	ABC 11421
11/23/74+	46	13		2 **Ain't She Somethin' Else**	*Jerry Foster/Bill Rice*	ABC 12037
4/19/75	27	11		3 **Good News, Bad News**	*Parke Richards*	ABC 12083
8/2/75	68	10		4 **You're My Rainy Day Woman**	*Jerry Foster/Bill Rice*	ABC 12111
12/20/75+	34	10		5 **Free To Be**	*Eddy Raven*	ABC/Dot 17595
4/10/76	87	5		6 **I Wanna Live**	*John D. Loudermilk*	ABC/Dot 17618
8/28/76	94	3		7 **The Curse Of A Woman**	*Sterling Whipple*	ABC/Dot 17646
12/11/76	90	4		8 **I'm Losing It All**	*Curly Putman/Rafe Van Hoy*	ABC/Dot 17663
9/2/78	71	5		9 **You're A Dancer**	*Eddy Raven*	Monument 260
12/8/79+	44	11		10 **Sweet Mother Texas**	*Eddy Raven/Whitey Shafer*	Dimension 003
3/15/80	25	11		11 **Dealin' With The Devil**	*Eddy Raven/Whitey Shafer*	Dimension 1005
6/7/80	30	11		12 **You've Got Those Eyes**	*David Powelson/Eddy Raven*	Dimension 1007
9/20/80	34	11		13 **Another Texas Song**	*Eddy Raven*	Dimension 1011
1/24/81	23	12		14 **Peace Of Mind**	*Eddy Raven*	Dimension 1017
5/23/81	13	15		15 **I Should've Called**	*Eddy Raven*	Elektra 47136
10/17/81+	11	18		16 **Who Do You Know In California**	*Eddy Raven*	Elektra 47216
2/20/82	14	18		17 **A Little Bit Crazy**	*Eddy Raven*	Elektra 47413
6/19/82	10	16		18 **She's Playing Hard To Forget**	*Elroy Kahanek/Keith Stegall*	Elektra 47469
11/6/82+	25	17		19 **San Antonio Nights**	*Eddy Raven*	Elektra 69929
3/17/84	❶^{1}	22		20 **I Got Mexico**	*Frank J. Myers/Eddy Raven*	RCA 13746
7/21/84	9	18		21 **I Could Use Another You**	*Bucky Jones/Tom Shapiro/Chris Waters*	RCA 13839
11/10/84+	9	23		22 **She's Gonna Win Your Heart**	S:7 / A:7 *Billy Burnette/Mentor Williams*	RCA 13939
4/20/85	9	21		23 **Operator, Operator**	A:6 / S:10 *Janet Willoughby/Larry Willoughby*	RCA 14044
8/3/85	8	24		24 **I Wanna Hear It From You**	A:7 / S:8 *Rick Giles/Nancy Montgomery*	RCA 14164
12/7/85+	3^{1}	23		25 **You Should Have Been Gone By Now**	S:3 / A:3 *Frank J. Myers/Don Pfrimmer/Eddy Raven*	RCA 14250
5/31/86	3^{1}	22		26 **Sometimes A Lady**	A:3 / S:4 *Frank J. Myers/Eddy Raven*	RCA 14319
11/15/86+	3^{1}	24		27 **Right Hand Man**	A:3 / S:6 *Gary Scruggs*	RCA 5032
3/28/87	3^{1}	21		28 **You're Never Too Old For Young Love**	S:8 / A:15 *Rick Giles/Frank J. Myers*	RCA 5128
7/25/87	❶^{1}	24		29 **Shine, Shine, Shine**	S:12 *Ken Bell/Bud McQuire*	RCA 5221
2/13/88	❶^{1}	21		30 **I'm Gonna Get You**	S:2 *Dennis Linde*	RCA 6831
6/18/88	❶^{1}	21		31 **Joe Knows How To Live**	S:3 *Max D. Barnes/Graham Lyle/Troy Seals*	RCA 8303
12/3/88+	4	21		32 **'Til You Cry**	*Steve Bogard/Rick Giles*	RCA 8798
4/22/89	❶^{1}	21		33 **In A Letter To You**	*Dennis Linde*	Universal 66003

Billboard | **GOLD** | **ARTIST** Ranking | **Country Chart Hit**.......**Songwriter** | **Label (& Number)**

RAVEN, Eddy — cont'd

DEBUT	PEAK	WKS	GOLD	#	Country Chart Hit	Songwriter	Label (& Number)
8/19/89	❶^{1}	26		34	**Bayou Boys**	*Frank J. Myers/Eddy Raven/Troy Seals*	Universal 66016
12/23/89+	**6**	26		35	**Sooner Or Later**	*Beckie Foster/Bill LaBounty/Susan Longacre*	Capitol 44528
4/21/90	**10**	21		36	**Island**	*Eddy Raven/Troy Seals*	Capitol
9/22/90	**56**	7		37	**Zydeco Lady**	*Eddy Raven/Troy Seals*	Capitol
					above 2 from the album *Temporary Sanity* on Capitol 90289		
3/30/91	**60**	7		38	**Rock Me In The Rhythm Of Your Love**	*Robert Earl Keen/Lisa Silver*	Capitol
6/29/91	**58**	8		39	**Too Much Candy For A Dime**	*Dave Powelson/Eddy Raven*	Capitol
					above 2 from the album *Right For The Flight* on Capitol 94258		
3/10/01	**60**	1		40	**Cowboys Don't Cry**	*Eddy Raven/Jason Winfield*	Row Music Group
					from the album *Living In Black And White* on Row Music Group 88194		

RAY, Mundo — see EARWOOD, Mundo

RAYBON, Marty

Born on 12/8/1959 in Greenville, Alabama. Former lead singer of **Shenandoah** and the **Raybon Bros.**

DEBUT	PEAK	WKS	GOLD	#	Country Chart Hit	Songwriter	Label (& Number)
1/29/00	**63**	9			**Cracker Jack Diamond**	*Ronny Scaife/Neil Thrasher*	Tri Chord
					from the album *Marty Raybon* on Tri Chrod 33001		

RAYBON BROS.

Vocal duo from Greenville, Alabama: **Marty Raybon** and Tim Raybon.

DEBUT	PEAK	WKS	GOLD	#	Country Chart Hit	Songwriter	Label (& Number)
5/31/97	**37**	20	●	1	**Butterfly Kisses**	S:2 *Bob Carlisle/Randy Thomas*	MCA
8/16/97	**64**	4		2	**The Way She's Lookin'**	*Don Cook/Billy Lawson*	MCA
					above 2 from the album *Raybon Bros.* on MCA 70014		

RAYE, Collin — 1990s: #12 / All-Time: #95

Born Floyd Collin Wray on 8/22/1959 in DeQueen, Arkansas. Male singer/songwriter/guitarist. His mother, Lois Wary, was a regional singing star in Arkansas. Moved to Oregon in 1980 where he formed **The Wrays** (as "Bubba Wray").

DEBUT	PEAK	WKS	GOLD	#	Country Chart Hit	Songwriter	Label (& Number)
6/8/91	**29**	20		1	**All I Can Be (Is A Sweet Memory)**	*Harlan Howard*	Epic
10/19/91+	❶^{3}	20		2	**Love, Me**	*Max T. Barnes/Skip Ewing*	Epic
2/29/92	**2**^{1}	20		3	**Every Second**	*Wayne Perry/Gerald Smith*	Epic
7/4/92	**74**	1		4	**It Could've Been So Good**	*Chris Waters/Lonnie Wilson*	Epic
					above 4 from the album *All I Can Be* on Epic 47468		
8/1/92	❶^{2}	20		5	**In This Life**	*Mike Reid/Allen Shamblin*	Epic
12/5/92+	**7**	20		6	**I Want You Bad (And That Ain't Good)**	*Jackson Leap*	Epic
4/3/93	**5**	20		7	**Somebody Else's Moon**	*Paul Nelson/Tom Shapiro*	Epic
8/7/93	**4**	20		8	**That Was A River**	*Rick Giles/Susan Longacre*	Epic
					above 4 from the album *In This Life* on Epic 48983		
12/11/93+	**6**	20		9	**That's My Story**	*Tony Haselden/Lee Roy Parnell*	Epic
4/9/94	**2**^{1}	20		10	**Little Rock**	*Tom Douglas*	Epic
8/6/94	**8**	20		11	**Man Of My Word**	*Gary Burr/Allen Shamblin*	Epic
12/3/94+	❶^{1}	20		12	**My Kind Of Girl**	*Debi Cochran/John Jarrard/Monty Powell*	Epic
4/8/95	**4**	20		13	**If I Were You**	*Chris Farren/John Hobbs*	Epic
					above 5 from the album *Extremes* on Epic 53952		
7/29/95	**2**^{2}	20		14	**One Boy, One Girl**	S:2 *Shaye Smith/Mark Alan Springer*	Epic
11/18/95+	**3**^{1}	20		15	**Not That Different**	S:5 *Joie Scott/Karen Taylor-Good*	Epic
11/25/95	**57**	11		16	**What If Jesus Comes Back Like That**	*Pat Bunch/Doug Johnson*	Epic
3/9/96	**3**^{4}	20		17	**I Think About You**	*Don Schlitz/Steve Seskin*	Epic
7/13/96	**12**	20		18	**Love Remains**	*Jim Daddario/Tom Douglas*	Epic
11/9/96+	**21**	11		19	**What If Jesus Comes Back Like That**	*Pat Bunch/Doug Johnson* [R]	Epic
2/22/97	**2**^{2}	20		20	**On The Verge**	*Hugh Prestwood*	Epic
					# 14-20: from the album *I Think About You* on Epic 67033		
6/7/97	**2**^{1}	20		21	**What The Heart Wants**	*Michael Dulaney*	Epic
9/6/97	**70**	6		22	**Open Arms**	*Jonathan Cain/Steve Perry/Neal Schon*	Epic
10/25/97	**51**	11		23	**The Gift** *[w/ Jim Brickman & Susan Ashton]*	*Jim Brickman/Tom Douglas* [X]	Epic
12/13/97+	**3**^{3}	22		24	**Little Red Rodeo**	*Charlie Black/Rory Bourke/Phil Vassar*	Epic
					above 4 from the album *The Best Of Collin Raye: Direct Hits* on Epic 67893		
4/25/98	❶^{2}	26		25	**I Can Still Feel You**	*Tammy Hyler/Kim Tribble*	Epic
8/22/98	**3**^{1}	25		26	**Someone You Used To Know**	S:6 *Tim Johnson/Rory Lee*	Epic
1/30/99	**4**	24		27	**Anyone Else**	*Radney Foster*	Epic
7/17/99	**39**	17		28	**Start Over Georgia**	*Collin Raye/Scott Wray*	Epic
					above 4 from the album *The Walls Came Down* on Epic 68876		
2/5/00	**3**^{2}	25		29	**Couldn't Last A Moment**	S:4 *Jeffrey Steele/Danny Wells*	Epic
6/24/00	**50**	17		30	**Tired Of Loving This Way** *[w/ Bobbie Eakes]*	*Gene Lesage/Allison Mellon*	Epic
11/11/00+	**43**	13		31	**She's All That**	*Collin Raye/Scott Wray*	Epic
3/10/01	**47**	6		32	**You Still Take Me There**	*Del Gray/Brett James/Thom McHugh*	Epic
					above 4 from the album *Tracks* on Epic 69995		
8/11/01	**43**	12		33	**Ain't Nobody Gonna Take That From Me**	*Rivers Rutherford/Annie Tate/Sam Tate*	Epic
					from the album *Can't Back Down* on Epic 85794		

DEBUT	PEAK	WKS	GOLD	#	ARTIST Ranking / Country Chart Hit	Songwriter	Label (& Number)

RAYE, Susan — 1970s: #48 / All-Time: #180

Born on 10/18/1944 in Eugene, Oregon. Female singer. Appeared on the *Hoedown* TV show in Portland. Worked with **Buck Owens** from 1968-76. Regular on TV's *Hee-Haw*. Acted in the movie *From Nashville With Music*.

DEBUT	PEAK	WKS	#	Country Chart Hit	Songwriter	Label (& Number)
1/10/70	**30**	11	1	**Put A Little Love In Your Heart**	*Jackie DeShannon/Jimmy Holiday/Randy Myers*	Capitol 2701
2/21/70	**13**	11	2	**We're Gonna Get Together** *[w/ Buck Owens]*	*Buck Owens*	Capitol 2731
5/9/70	**12**	12	3	**Togetherness** *[w/ Buck Owens]*	*Freddie Hart*	Capitol 2791
7/4/70	**35**	11	4	**One Night Stand**	*Buck Owens*	Capitol 2833
8/29/70	**8**	13	5	**The Great White Horse** *[w/ Buck Owens]*	*Buck Owens/Leanne Scott*	Capitol 2871
11/14/70+	**10**	13	6	**Willy Jones**	*Buck Owens*	Capitol 2950
2/20/71	**9**	16	7	**L.A. International Airport**	*Leanne Scott*	Capitol 3035
7/17/71	**6**	16	8	**Pitty, Pitty, Patter**	*Bob Morris*	Capitol 3129
11/13/71+	**3^1**	14	9	**(I've Got A) Happy Heart**	*Pat Levely/Buck Owens*	Capitol 3209
4/1/72	**44**	8	10	**A Song To Sing**	*Buddy Alan*	Capitol 3289
5/27/72	**10**	12	11	**My Heart Has A Mind Of Its Own**	*Howard Greenfield/Jack Keller*	Capitol 3327
7/15/72	**13**	14	12	**Looking Back To See** *[w/ Buck Owens]*	*Jim Ed Brown/Maxine Brown*	Capitol 3368
9/30/72	**16**	11	13	**Wheel Of Fortune**	*Bennie Benjamin/George Weiss*	Capitol 3438
12/23/72+	**17**	14	14	**Love Sure Feels Good In My Heart**	*Buddy Alan*	Capitol 3499
4/7/73	**18**	12	15	**Cheating Game**	*Bonnie Guitar/Dennis Knutson*	Capitol 3569
6/16/73	**35**	8	16	**The Good Old Days (Are Here Again)** *[w/ Buck Owens]*	*Buck Owens*	Capitol 3601
9/8/73	**23**	12	17	**Plastic Trains, Paper Planes**	*Buck Owens*	Capitol 3699
12/15/73+	**57**	9	18	**When You Get Back From Nashville**	*Buck Owens*	Capitol 3782
4/6/74	**18**	14	19	**Stop The World (And Let Me Off)**	*Carl Belew/W.S. Stevenson*	Capitol 3850
8/3/74	**49**	11	20	**You Can Sure See It From Here**	*Jim Shaw/Rocky Topp*	Capitol 3927
11/23/74+	**9**	16	21	**Whatcha Gonna Do With A Dog Like That**	*Bob Morris*	Capitol 3980
5/24/75	**58**	7	22	**Ghost Story**	*Joe Allen*	Capitol 4063
7/5/75	**20**	13	23	**Love Is Strange** *[w/ Buck Owens]*	*Mickey Baker/Bo Diddley/Sylvia Robinson*	Capitol 4100
10/16/76	**87**	5	24	**Ozark Mountain Lullaby**	*Robert Jones*	United Artists 870
2/19/77	**64**	6	25	**Mr. Heartache**	*Kent Robbins*	United Artists 934
4/30/77	**53**	8	26	**Saturday Night To Sunday Quiet**	*John Schweers*	United Artists 976
8/13/77	**51**	9	27	**It Didn't Have To Be A Diamond**	*Roger Bowling/Robert Jones/George Richey*	United Artists 1026
11/3/84	**76**	5	28	**Put Another Notch In Your Belt /**	*Mac Davis*	
2/15/86	**68**	5	29	**I Just Can't Take The Leaving Anymore**	*Bud McGuire/Eddie Moore*	Westexas America 1

RAZORBACK — see GRAYGHOST

REBEL HEARTS

Vocal trio from Reno, Nevada: Laura Angelini, Darren Castle and Don McDowell.

DEBUT	PEAK	WKS	Country Chart Hit	Songwriter	Label (& Number)
9/9/00	**75**	1	**When Will I Be Loved**	*Phil Everly*	House Of Tunes

RECORD, Donnie

Born on 3/31/1952 in Enid, Oklahoma. Male singer/guitarist.

DEBUT	PEAK	WKS	Country Chart Hit	Songwriter	Label (& Number)
8/6/83	**95**	1	**One More Goodbye, One More Hello**	*Deborah Allen/Rafe Van Hoy*	BriarRose 1001

REDDY, Helen

Born on 10/25/1941 in Melbourne, Australia. Female singer/actress.

DEBUT	PEAK	WKS	Country Chart Hit	Songwriter	Label (& Number)
10/22/77	**98**	1	**Laissez Les Bontemps Rouler**	*Julie Didier/Casey Kelly*	Capitol 4487

title is French for "Let The Good Times Roll"

RED HOTS, The

All-star group: **Suzy Boggus**, **Alison Krauss**, **Kathy Mattea** and **Crosby, Stills & Nash**.

DEBUT	PEAK	WKS	Country Chart Hit	Songwriter	Label (& Number)
10/22/94	**75**	1	**Teach Your Children**	*Graham Nash*	Mercury

from the various artists album *Red Hot + Country* on Mercury 522639

REDMON & VALE

Female vocal duo: Allison Redmon (from Georgia) and Tina Vale (from Iowa).

DEBUT	PEAK	WKS	#	Country Chart Hit	Songwriter	Label (& Number)
5/29/99	**65**	3	1	**If I Had A Nickel (One Thin Dime)**	*Rick Bowles/Tom Shapiro*	DreamWorks
9/11/99	**74**	1	2	**Squeezin' The Love Outta You**	*Carolyn Dawn Johnson/Steve Mandile/Troy Verges*	DreamWorks

above 2 from the album *Redmon & Vale* on DreamWorks 50057

REDMOND, Robb

Born in Sherman Oaks, California. Male singer.

DEBUT	PEAK	WKS	Country Chart Hit	Songwriter	Label (& Number)
3/5/77	**87**	4	**Lunch Time Lovers**	*Bobby Borchers/Mack Vickery*	NBC 001

RED, WHITE & BLUE (GRASS)

Bluegrass group from Birmingham, Alabama: husband-and-wife Ginger Boatwright (vocals, guitar) and Grant Boatwright (guitar), Dale Whitcomb (fiddle), Dave Sebolt (bass) and Michael Barnett (drums).

DEBUT	PEAK	WKS	Country Chart Hit	Songwriter	Label (& Number)
12/22/73+	**71**	9	**July You're A Woman**	*John Stewart*	GRC 1009

RED WILLOW BAND

Group from Beardon, South Dakota: Chris Gage, Hank Harris, Kenny Putnam, Marley Forman and Barry Carpenter.

DEBUT	PEAK	WKS	Country Chart Hit	Songwriter	Label (& Number)
6/2/79	**97**	1	**I Wish I Had Your Arms Around Me**	*Chris Gage*	Lost 1288

DEBUT	PEAK	WKS	GOLD	ARTIST / Country Chart Hit	Songwriter	Label (& Number)

REECE, Ben

Born in New York. Male singer/songwriter.

DEBUT	PEAK	WKS	GOLD	Country Chart Hit	Songwriter	Label (& Number)
9/6/75	**41**	12		1 **Mirror, Mirror**	*Ben Reece*	20th Century 2227
1/3/76	**87**	5		2 **It Don't Bother Me**	*Tommy Hammond/Virginia Hammond*	20th Century 2262
7/10/76	**83**	6		3 **Even If It's Wrong**	*Milton Blackford/Richard Mainegra*	Polydor 14329
11/13/76	**89**	4		4 **Honky Tonk Fool**	*Milton Blackford/Richard Mainegra*	Polydor 14356

REED, Bobby

Born in Rockford, Illinois. Male singer/songwriter.

DEBUT	PEAK	WKS	GOLD	Country Chart Hit	Songwriter	Label (& Number)
3/5/83	**90**	2		**If I Just Had My Woman**	*Bobby Reed*	CBO 132

REED, Jerry

1970s: #38 / All-Time: #81

Born Jerry Reed Hubbard on 3/20/1937 in Atlanta, Georgia. Male singer/songwriter/guitarist/actor. Known as "The Guitar Man." Acted in several movies. Regular on TV's *Concrete Cowboys*. Married to **Priscilla Mitchell** since 1959. Also see **Heart Of Nashville** and **Some Of Chet's Friends**.

CMA: Musician 1970 & 1971

DEBUT	PEAK	WKS	GOLD	Country Chart Hit	Songwriter	Label (& Number)
5/20/67	**53**	9		1 **Guitar Man** — Reed played guitar on **Elvis Presley**'s version in 1968	*Jerry Reed*	RCA Victor 9152
11/4/67+	**15**	15		2 **Tupelo Mississippi Flash**	*Jerry Reed*	RCA Victor 9334
4/13/68	**14**	15		3 **Remembering** — also see #28 below	*Jerry Reed*	RCA Victor 9493
9/28/68	**48**	10		4 **Alabama Wild Man** — also see #16 below	*Jerry Reed*	RCA Victor 9623
1/18/69	**60**	6		5 **Oh What A Woman!**	*Jerry Reed*	RCA Victor 9701
4/5/69	**20**	10		6 **There's Better Things In Life**	*Jerry Reed*	RCA Victor 0124
8/30/69	**11**	13		7 **Are You From Dixie** (Cause I'm From Dixie Too)	*George Cobb/Jack Yellen*	RCA Victor 0211
3/7/70	**14**	12		8 **Talk About The Good Times**	*Jerry Reed*	RCA Victor 9804
8/8/70	**16**	11		9 **Georgia Sunshine**	*Jerry Reed*	RCA Victor 9870
10/24/70	**16**	18	●	10 **Amos Moses** /	*Jerry Reed* **[N]**	
11/14/70	**flip**	11		11 **The Preacher And The Bear**	*Jerry Reed* **[N]**	RCA Victor 9904
5/8/71	**❶[5]**	15		12 **When You're Hot, You're Hot** — **Grammy: Male Vocal**	*Jerry Reed* **[N]**	RCA Victor 9976
9/11/71	**11**	13		13 **Ko-Ko Joe**	*Jerry Reed*	RCA Victor 1011
1/1/72	**27**	11		14 **Another Puff**	*Earl Jarrett/Jerry Reed* **[N]**	RCA Victor 0613
4/1/72	**24**	11		15 **Smell The Flowers**	*Jerry Reed*	RCA Victor 0667
7/15/72	**22**	12		16 **Alabama Wild Man** — new version of #4 above	*Jerry Reed* **[R]**	RCA Victor 0738
12/23/72+	**18**	10		17 **You Took All The Ramblin' Out Of Me**	*Jerry Reed*	RCA Victor 0857
5/26/73	**❶[1]**	15		18 **Lord, Mr. Ford**	*Dick Feller* **[N]**	RCA Victor 0960
12/15/73+	**25**	10		19 **The Uptown Poker Club**	*Jean Havez/Bill Vodery/Bert Williams*	RCA Victor 0194
2/9/74	**13**	10		20 **The Crude Oil Blues**	*Jerry Reed* **[N]**	RCA Victor 0224
5/11/74	**12**	14		21 **A Good Woman's Love**	*Cy Coben*	RCA Victor 0273
10/5/74	**72**	6		22 **Boogie Woogie Rock And Roll**	*Eddy Raven*	RCA Victor 10063
12/14/74+	**18**	12		23 **Let's Sing Our Song**	*Jerry Reed*	RCA Victor 10132
4/5/75	**64**	9		24 **Mind Your Love**	*Jerry Reed*	RCA Victor 10247
7/12/75	**65**	9		25 **The Telephone**	*Jim Owen* **[N]**	RCA Victor 10325
10/4/75	**60**	8		26 **You Got A Lock On Me**	*Jerry Reed*	RCA Victor 10389
7/4/76	**54**	8		27 **Gator** — from the movie starring **Burt Reynolds**	*Jerry Reed*	RCA Victor 10717
10/9/76	**57**	7		28 **Remembering** — new version of #3 above	*Jerry Reed* **[R]**	RCA 10784
3/5/77	**19**	12		29 **Semolita**	*Lally Stott*	RCA 10893
7/2/77	**68**	5		30 **With His Pants In His Hand**	*Carson Parks*	RCA 11008
8/13/77	**2[2]**	16		31 **East Bound And Down** / — from the movie *Smokey & The Bandit* starring **Burt Reynolds**	*Dick Feller/Jerry Reed*	
9/3/77	**flip**	13		32 (I'm Just A) **Redneck In A Rock And Roll Bar**	*Bill Anthony/Bob Morrison*	RCA 11056
12/24/77+	**20**	12		33 **You Know What** *[w/ Seidina Reed]*	*Jerry Reed*	RCA 11164
3/25/78	**39**	9		34 **Sweet Love Feelings**	*Jerry Reed*	RCA 11232
6/10/78	**10**	12		35 (I Love You) **What Can I Say** /	*Dick Feller*	
7/15/78	**flip**	7		36 **High Rollin'** — from the movie *High-Ballin'* starring Reed	*Dick Feller/Jerry Reed*	RCA 11281
11/11/78+	**14**	14		37 **Gimme Back My Blues**	*Billy Edd Wheeler*	RCA 11407
2/24/79	**18**	11		38 **Second-Hand Satin Lady** (And A Bargain Basement Boy)	*Dick Feller*	RCA 11472
6/16/79	**40**	7		39 (Who Was The Man Who Put) **The Line In Gasoline**	*Dick Feller* **[N]**	RCA 11638
9/8/79	**67**	5		40 **Hot Stuff** — from the movie starring Reed	*Jerry Reed*	RCA 11698
12/1/79+	**12**	14		41 **Sugar Foot Rag**	*Hank Garland/Vaughn Horton*	RCA 11764
3/29/80	**36**	10		42 **Age** /	*Jim Croce*	
3/29/80	**flip**	10		43 **Workin' At The Carwash Blues**	*Jim Croce*	RCA 11944
7/12/80	**64**	6		44 **The Friendly Family Inn**	*Barry Grant/Lee Likes*	RCA 12034

Billboard DEBUT	PEAK	WKS	GOLD		ARTIST / Country Chart Hit	Ranking / Songwriter	Label (& Number)

REED, Jerry — cont'd

DEBUT	PEAK	WKS	GOLD		Country Chart Hit	Songwriter	Label (& Number)
8/30/80	**26**	12		45	**Texas Bound And Flyin'** from the movie *Smokey & The Bandit II* starring **Burt Reynolds**	*Jerry Reed*	RCA 12083
1/10/81	**80**	4		46	**Caffein, Nicotine, Benzedrine (And Wish Me Luck)**	*Bill Hayes/Bill Howard/Betty Mackey*	RCA 12157
5/9/81	**87**	3		47	**The Testimony Of Soddy Hoe**	*Dick Feller/Jerry Reed*	RCA 12210
7/4/81	**84**	2		48	**Good Friends Make Good Lovers**	*Troy Seals*	RCA 12253
9/26/81	**30**	12		49	**Patches**	*Ronald Dunbar/General Johnson*	RCA 12318
4/17/82	**32**	13		50	**The Man With The Golden Thumb**	*Billy Henderson/Bud McGuire*	RCA 13081
7/10/82	**❶**^{2}	17		51	**She Got The Goldmine (I Got The Shaft)**	*Tim DuBois* **[N]**	RCA 13268
10/16/82	**2**^{3}	16		52	**The Bird** impressions of **Willie Nelson**'s "Whiskey River" and "On The Road Again" and **George Jones**'s "He Stopped Loving Her Today"	*Hal Coleman/Barry Etris* **[N]**	RCA 13355
1/29/83	**13**	15		53	**Down On The Corner**	*John Fogerty*	RCA 13422
5/21/83	**16**	17		54	**Good Ole Boys /**	*Ken Bell/Terry Skinner/J.L. Wallace*	
5/21/83	**flip**	17		55	**She's Ready For Someone To Love Her**	*Charlie Black/Jerry Gillespie/Tommy Rocco*	RCA 13527
8/6/83	**20**	14		56	**Hold On, I'm Comin'** ***[w/ Waylon Jennings]***	*Isaac Hayes/David Porter*	RCA 13580
11/12/83	**58**	6		57	**I'm A Slave**	*Jerry Reed*	RCA 13663

REEVES, Del

1960s: #30 / All-Time: #105

Born Franklin Delano Reeves on 7/14/1933 in Sparta, North Carolina. Male singer/songwriter/multi-instrumentalist. Hosted the *Country Carnival* TV show. Acted in the movies *Second Fiddle To A Steel Guitar*, *Sam Whiskey*, *Cotton Pickin' Chicken-Pluckers* and *Forty-Acre Feud*.

OPRY: 1966

DEBUT	PEAK	WKS	GOLD		Country Chart Hit	Songwriter	Label (& Number)
11/6/61	**9**	17		1	**Be Quiet Mind**	*Liz Anderson*	Decca 31307
10/27/62	**11**	11		2	**He Stands Real Tall**	*Cal Veale*	Decca 31417
4/27/63	**13**	14		3	**The Only Girl I Can't Forget**	*Del Reeves*	Reprise 20158
8/8/64	**41**	12		4	**Talking To The Night Lights**	*Lynn Cramer*	Columbia 43044
3/13/65	**❶**^{2}	20		5	**Girl On The Billboard**	*Walter Haynes/Hank Mills* **[N]**	United Artists 824
8/14/65	**4**	17		6	**The Belles Of Southern Bell**	*Don Wayne*	United Artists 890
12/4/65+	**9**	13		7	**Women Do Funny Things To Me**	*Larry Kingston*	United Artists 940
4/16/66	**42**	7		8	**One Bum Town**	*Hank Mills*	United Artists 50001
7/2/66	**37**	5		9	**Gettin' Any Feed For Your Chickens**	*Neal Merritt*	United Artists 50035
10/29/66	**27**	12		10	**This Must Be The Bottom**	*Del Reeves/Ellen Reeves*	United Artists 50081
3/18/67	**45**	9		11	**Blame It On My Do Wrong**	*Dallas Frazier*	United Artists 50128
6/17/67	**33**	10		12	**The Private**	*Jack Barlow/Curly Putman*	United Artists 50157
10/7/67	**12**	18		13	**A Dime At A Time**	*Jerry Chesnut*	United Artists 50210
3/9/68	**56**	5		14	**I Just Wasted The Rest** ***[w/ Bobby Goldsboro]***	*Hugh X. Lewis*	United Artists 50243
3/30/68	**18**	13		15	**Wild Blood**	*Jerry Chesnut*	United Artists 50270
8/17/68	**5**	14		16	**Looking At The World Through A Windshield**	*Jerry Chesnut/Mike Hoyer*	United Artists 50332
12/28/68+	**3**^{1}	17		17	**Good Time Charlie's**	*Jerry Chesnut*	United Artists 50487
5/24/69	**5**	14		18	**Be Glad**	*Justin Tubb/Kent Westberry*	United Artists 50531
10/11/69	**12**	11		19	**There Wouldn't Be A Lonely Heart In Town**	*Scott Fishbein/Ira Kosloff*	United Artists 50564
11/1/69	**31**	10		20	**Take A Little Good Will Home** ***[w/ Bobby Goldsboro]***	*Jerry Chesnut*	United Artists 50591
2/7/70	**14**	12		21	**A Lover's Question** ***[w/ The Goodtime Charlies]***	*Brook Benton/Jimmy Williams*	United Artists 50622
5/23/70	**41**	11		22	**Son Of A Coal Man**	*Billy Edd Wheeler*	United Artists 50667
5/30/70	**20**	12		23	**Land Mark Tavern** ***[w/ Penny DeHaven]***	*Jerry Chesnut*	United Artists 50669
10/3/70	**22**	10		24	**Right Back Loving You Again**	*Jerry Chesnut*	United Artists 50714
1/9/71	**30**	11		25	**Bar Room Talk**	*Jerry Chesnut*	United Artists 50743
4/10/71	**33**	12		26	**Working Like The Devil (For The Lord)**	*Carl Belew/Van Givens*	United Artists 50763
7/10/71	**9**	12		27	**The Philadelphia Fillies**	*Jim Mundy*	United Artists 50802
10/23/71	**31**	10		28	**A Dozen Pairs Of Boots**	*Red Steagall*	United Artists 50840
1/22/72	**29**	12		29	**The Best Is Yet To Come**	*Glenn Martin*	United Artists 50877
6/10/72	**62**	6		30	**No Rings--No Strings**	*Gary S. Paxton*	United Artists 50906
6/24/72	**54**	6		31	**Crying In The Rain** ***[w/ Penny DeHaven]***	*Howard Greenfield/Carole King*	United Artists 50829
11/11/72	**47**	6		32	**Before Goodbye**	*George Martin*	United Artists 50964
2/24/73	**54**	5		33	**Trucker's Paradise**	*Jerry Allison*	United Artists 51106
6/9/73	**44**	10		34	**Mm-Mm Good**	*Mike Kosser/Steve Pippin/Curly Putman*	United Artists 249
9/8/73	**22**	15		35	**Lay A Little Lovin' On Me**	*Charlie Craig/Anne Reeves*	United Artists 308
2/23/74	**70**	8		36	**What A Way To Go**	*Jerry Chesnut*	United Artists 378
5/11/74	**62**	7		37	**Prayer From A Mobile Home**	*Hank Mills*	United Artists 427
9/21/74	**89**	4		38	**She Likes Country Bands**	*Charlie Craig*	United Artists 532
12/14/74+	**65**	8		39	**Pour It All On Me**	*Roger Bowling/William Cross/Paul Richey*	United Artists 564
2/15/75	**65**	9		40	**But I Do**	*Paul Gayten/Robert Guidry*	United Artists 593
6/14/75	**74**	5		41	**Puttin' In Overtime At Home**	*Ben Peters*	United Artists 639
10/18/75	**92**	3		42	**You Comb Her Hair Every Morning**	*Hank Cochran/Harlan Howard*	United Artists 702
2/14/76	**51**	9		43	**I Ain't Got Nobody**	*Roger Bowling/Larry Butler*	United Artists 760
5/1/76	**29**	11		44	**On The Rebound** ***[w/ Billie Jo Spears]***	*Larry Atwood/Charlie Craig*	United Artists 797
8/7/76	**42**	8		45	**Teardrops Will Kiss The Morning Dew** ***[w/ Billie Jo Spears]***	*Paul Craft*	United Artists 832
11/20/76	**79**	4		46	**My Better Half**	*Bobby Braddock*	United Artists 885
6/4/77	**78**	5		47	**Ladies Night**	*Roger Bowling/Steve Tutsie*	United Artists 989

DEBUT	PEAK	WKS	GOLD	ARTIST / Country Chart Hit	Ranking / Songwriter	Label (& Number)
				REEVES, Del — cont'd		
5/6/78	**93**	3		48 **When My Angel Turns Into A Devil**	*Ben Peters*	United Artists 1191
9/2/78	**79**	5		49 **Dig Down Deep**	*Bobby Fischer/Don Wayne*	United Artists 1230
4/12/80	**82**	6		50 **Take Me To Your Heart**	*Rory Bourke/Gene Dobbins/Rick Klang*	Koala 584
9/6/80	**90**	3		51 **What Am I Gonna Do?**	*Jerry Foster/Bill Rice*	Koala 594
6/6/81	**67**	4		52 **Swinging Doors**	*Merle Haggard*	Koala 333
9/5/81	**53**	7		53 **Slow Hand**	*John Bettis/Michael Clark*	Koala 336
1/23/82	**67**	5		54 **Ain't Nobody Gonna Get My Body But You**	*Jim Calhoun*	Koala 339
4/26/86	**95**	3		55 **The Second Time Around**	*Rocky Priolo*	Playback 1103

REEVES, Jim **1950s: #14 / 1960s: #3 / All-Time: #17 // HOF: 1967**

Born on 8/20/1923 in Panola County, Texas. Died in a plane crash in Nashville on 7/31/1964 (age 40). Male singer/songwriter/guitarist. Known as "Gentleman Jim." Uncle of **John Rex Reeves**. Worked as a DJ at KWKH in Shreveport, Louisiana. Joined the *Louisiana Hayride* in 1953. Played "Jim Madison" in the movie *Kimberley Jim*.

OPRY: 1955

DEBUT	PEAK	WKS	GOLD	Country Chart Hit	Ranking / Songwriter	Label (& Number)
3/28/53	**❶[9]**	26		1 **Mexican Joe** *[w/ The Circle O Ranch Boys]*	J:❶[9] / A:❶[7] / S:❶[6] *Mitchell Torok*	Abbott 116
12/5/53+	**❶[3]**	21		2 **Bimbo**	A:❶[3] / S:2 / J:2 *Rod Morris*	Abbott 148
1/9/54	**3[1]**	22		3 **I Love You** *[w/ Ginny Wright]*	A:3 / J:7 / S:8 *Billy Barton*	Fabor 101
6/26/54	**15**	1		4 **Then I'll Stop Loving You**	A:15 *Jim Reeves*	Abbott 160
10/23/54+	**5**	12		5 **Penny Candy**	J:5 / A:8 *Cal Veale*	Abbott 170
4/30/55	**9**	1		6 **Drinking Tequila**	J:9 *Bob Center*	Abbott 178
8/20/55	**4**	20		7 **Yonder Comes A Sucker /**	J:4 / A:6 / S:8 *Jim Reeves*	
9/3/55	**flip**	2		8 **I'm Hurtin' Inside**	J:flip *Cy Coben*	RCA Victor 6200
6/23/56	**8**	13		9 **My Lips Are Sealed**	A:8 / J:8 / S:10 *Hal Blair/Bill Peppers/Ben Weisman*	RCA Victor 6517
9/29/56	**4**	19		10 **According To My Heart /**	A:4 / S:9 / J:10 *Gary Walker*	
11/3/56	**flip**	1		11 **The Mother Of A Honky Tonk Girl**	S:flip *Shorty Long/Bob Newman*	RCA Victor 6620
1/12/57	**3[2]**	18		12 **Am I Losing You /** also see #30 below	A:3 / J:3 / S:8 *Jim Reeves*	
2/23/57	**flip**	5		13 **Waitin' For A Train**	J:flip *Jimmie Rodgers*	RCA Victor 6749
4/29/57	**❶[8]**	26		14 **Four Walls**	A:❶[8] / S:2 / J:4 *George Campbell/Marvin Moore*	RCA Victor 6874
8/19/57	**9**	6		15 **Two Shadows On Your Window /**	A:9 / S:flip *Mickey Baker/Joe Robinson*	
8/26/57	**12**	1		16 **Young Hearts**	S:12 / A:14 *Roy Bennett/Sid Tepper*	RCA Victor 6973
12/2/57+	**3[7]**	18		17 **Anna Marie**	A:3 / S:10 *Cindy Walker*	RCA Victor 7070
4/21/58	**10**	3		18 **Overnight /**	A:10 / S:flip *J. Leslie McFarland*	
5/12/58	**8**	7		19 **I Love You More**	A:8 / S:14 *Marlin Greene*	RCA Victor 7171
7/14/58	**2[3]**	22		20 **Blue Boy**	A:2 / S:4 *Boudleaux Bryant*	RCA Victor 7266
11/10/58+	**❶[5]**	25		21 **Billy Bayou /**	*Roger Miller*	
11/17/58+	**18**	7		22 **I'd Like To Be**	*Hugh Ashley*	RCA Victor 7380
3/30/59	**2[4]**	20		23 **Home**	*Roger Miller*	RCA Victor 7479
7/27/59	**5**	16		24 **Partners /**	*Danny Dill*	
8/17/59	**17**	7		25 **I'm Beginning To Forget You**	*Willie Phelps*	RCA Victor 7557
12/7/59+	**❶[14]**	34	●	26 **He'll Have To Go** **Grammy: Hall of Fame**	*Audrey Allison/Joe Allison*	RCA Victor 7643
7/18/60	**3[1]**	18		27 **I'm Gettin' Better /**	*Jim Reeves*	
7/25/60	**6**	16		28 **I Know One**	*Jack Clement*	RCA Victor 7756
10/31/60	**3[8]**	25		29 **I Missed Me /**	*Bill Anderson*	
11/21/60	**8**	14		30 **Am I Losing You** new version of #12 above	*Jim Reeves* **[R]**	RCA Victor 7800
3/27/61	**4**	12		31 **The Blizzard**	*Harlan Howard*	RCA Victor 7855
7/17/61	**15**	11		32 **What Would You Do? /**	*Jim Reeves*	
10/2/61	**16**	6		33 **Stand At Your Window**	*Jim Carroll*	RCA Victor 7905
12/11/61+	**2[2]**	21		34 **Losing Your Love /**	*Bill Anderson/Buddy Killen*	
12/11/61+	**7**	16		35 **(How Can I Write On Paper) What I Feel In My Heart**	*...Don Carter/Danny Harrison/George Kent/Jim Reeves*	RCA Victor 7950
5/19/62	**20**	3		36 **A Letter To My Heart /**	*Cindy Walker*	
5/26/62	**2[9]**	21		37 **Adios Amigo**	*Ralph Freed/Jerry Livingston*	RCA Victor 8019
9/1/62	**2[3]**	21		38 **I'm Gonna Change Everything /**	*Alex Zanetis*	
9/8/62	**18**	3		39 **Pride Goes Before A Fall**	*Leon Payne*	RCA Victor 8080
2/9/63	**3[5]**	23		40 **Is This Me?**	*Bill West/Dottie West*	RCA Victor 8127
7/13/63	**3[3]**	18		41 **Guilty /**	*Alex Zanetis*	
7/27/63	**11**	18		42 **Little Ole You**	*Dave Burgess/Jim Reeves*	RCA Victor 8193
1/25/64	**2[2]**	26		43 **Welcome To My World /**	*John Hathcock/Ray Winkler*	
2/1/64	**43**	2		44 **Good Morning Self**	*Jimmy Key*	RCA Victor 8289
3/28/64	**7**	21		45 **Love Is No Excuse** *[w/ Dottie West]*	*Justin Tubb*	RCA Victor 8324
7/11/64	**❶[7]**	26		46 **I Guess I'm Crazy**	*Werly Fairburn*	RCA Victor 8383
11/28/64+	**3[3]**	19		47 **I Won't Forget You**	*Harlan Howard*	RCA Victor 8461
3/6/65	**❶[3]**	23		48 **This Is It**	*Cindy Walker*	RCA Victor 8508
7/24/65	**❶[3]**	21		49 **Is It Really Over?**	*Jim Reeves*	RCA Victor 8625
1/8/66	**2[3]**	17		50 **Snow Flake**	*Ned Miller* **[X]**	RCA Victor 47-8719

DEBUT	PEAK	WKS	GOLD	ARTIST / Country Chart Hit	Songwriter	Label (& Number)
				REEVES, Jim — cont'd		
4/2/66	❶[4]	21		51 **Distant Drums**	*Cindy Walker*	RCA Victor 8789
8/13/66	❶[1]	19		52 **Blue Side Of Lonesome**	*Leon Payne*	RCA Victor 8902
1/21/67	❶[1]	16		53 **I Won't Come In While He's There**	*Gene Davis*	RCA Victor 9057
7/1/67	**16**	14		54 **The Storm**	*Jim Reeves/Alex Zanetis*	RCA Victor 9238
11/4/67+	**9**	17		55 **I Heard A Heart Break Last Night**	*Leon Payne*	RCA Victor 9343
3/9/68	**9**	13		56 **That's When I See The Blues (In Your Pretty Brown Eyes)**	*Carl Belew/Tommy Blake/W.S. Stevenson*	RCA Victor 9455
9/21/68	**7**	15		57 **When You Are Gone**	*Dean Manuel*	RCA Victor 9614
4/12/69	**6**	14		58 **When Two Worlds Collide**	*Bill Anderson/Roger Miller*	RCA Victor 0135
12/6/69+	**10**	14		59 **Nobody's Fool /**	*Hal Bynum*	
12/13/69+	**flip**	13		60 **Why Do I Love You (Melody Of Love)**	*Hans Engelmann/Tom Glazer* [S]	RCA Victor 0286
8/15/70	**4**	15		61 **Angels Don't Lie**	*Dale Noe*	RCA Victor 9880
4/10/71	**16**	12		62 **Gypsy Feet**	*Leona Butram/Nelli Smith*	RCA Victor 9969
1/29/72	**15**	14		63 **The Writing's On The Wall**	*Alex Zanetis*	RCA Victor 0626
7/29/72	**8**	16		64 **Missing You**	*Dale Noe/Red Sovine*	RCA Victor 0744
6/2/73	**12**	14		65 **Am I That Easy To Forget**	*Carl Belew/W.S. Stevenson*	RCA Victor 0963
4/20/74	**19**	14		66 **I'd Fight The World**	*Joe Allison/Hank Cochran*	RCA Victor 0255
6/21/75	**54**	11		67 **You Belong To Me**	*Pee Wee King/Chilton Price/Redd Stewart*	RCA Victor 10299
11/8/75	**71**	6		68 **You'll Never Know**	*Mack Gordon/Harry Warren*	RCA Victor 10418
2/21/76	**54**	9		69 **I Love You Because**	*Leon Payne*	RCA Victor 10557
4/23/77	**14**	13		70 **It's Nothin' To Me**	*Pat Patterson*	RCA 10956
8/27/77	**23**	11		71 **Little Ole Dime**	*Jim Carroll*	RCA 11060
2/4/78	**29**	11		72 **You're The Only Good Thing (That's Happened To Me)**	*Jack Toombs*	RCA 11187
6/23/79	**10**	14		73 **Don't Let Me Cross Over** ***[w/ Deborah Allen]***	*Penny Jay*	RCA 11564
11/3/79+	**6**	15		74 **Oh, How I Miss You Tonight** ***[w/ Deborah Allen]***	*Joe Burke/Benny Davis/Mark Fisher*	RCA 11737
4/12/80	**10**	16		75 **Take Me In Your Arms And Hold Me** ***[w/ Deborah Allen]***	*Cindy Walker*	RCA 11946
11/22/80+	**35**	11		76 **There's Always Me**	*Don Robertson*	RCA 12118
11/7/81+	**5**	17		77 **Have You Ever Been Lonely (Have You Ever Been Blue)** ***[w/ Patsy Cline]***	*George Brown/Peter DeRose*	RCA 12346
6/5/82	**54**	8		78 **I Fall To Pieces** ***[w/ Patsy Cline]***	*Hank Cochran/Harlan Howard*	MCA 52052
1/8/83	**46**	9		79 **The Jim Reeves Medley** Four Walls/I Missed Me/He'll Have To Go/Oh, How I Miss You Tonight	*Audrey Allison/Joe Allison/Bill Anderson/Joe Burke/ George Campbell/Benny Davis/Mark Fisher/Marvin Moore*	RCA 13410
1/21/84	**70**	6		80 **The Image Of Me**	*Harlan Howard*	RCA 13693

According To My Heart ['56]
Adios Amigo ['62]
Am I Losing You ['57, '60]
Am I That Easy To Forget ['73]
Angels Don't Lie ['70]
Anna Marie ['58]
Billy Bayou ['59]
Bimbo ['54]
Blizzard ['61]
Blue Boy ['58]
Blue Side Of Lonesome ['66]
Distant Drums ['66]
Don't Let Me Cross Over ['79]
Drinking Tequila ['55]
Four Walls ['57]
Good Morning Self ['64]
Guilty ['63]
Gypsy Feet ['71]
Have You Ever Been Lonely (Have You Ever Been Blue) ['82]
He'll Have To Go ['60]
Home ['59]
(How Can I Write On Paper) What I Feel In My Heart ['62]
I Fall To Pieces ['82]
I Guess I'm Crazy ['64]
I Heard A Heart Break Last Night ['68]
I Know One ['60]
I Love You ['54]
I Love You Because ['76]
I Love You More ['58]
I Missed Me ['60]
I Won't Come In While He's There ['67]
I Won't Forget You ['65]
I'd Fight The World ['74]
I'd Like To Be ['59]
I'm Beginning To Forget You ['59]
I'm Gettin' Better ['60]
I'm Gonna Change Everything ['62]
I'm Hurtin' Inside ['55]
Image Of Me ['84]
Is It Really Over? ['65]
Is This Me? ['63]
It's Nothin' To Me ['77]
Jim Reeves Medley ['83]
Letter To My Heart ['62]
Little Ole Dime ['77]
Little Ole You ['63]
Losing Your Love ['62]
Love Is No Excuse ['64]
Mexican Joe ['53]
Missing You ['72]
Mother Of A Honky Tonk Girl ['56]
My Lips Are Sealed ['56]
Nobody's Fool ['70]
Oh, How I Miss You Tonight ['80]
Overnight ['58]
Partners ['59]
Penny Candy ['55]
Pride Goes Before A Fall ['62]
Snow Flake ['66]
Stand At Your Window ['61]
Storm ['67]
Take Me In Your Arms And Hold Me ['80]
That's When I See The Blues (In Your Pretty Brown Eyes) ['68]
Then I'll Stop Loving You ['54]
There's Always Me ['81]
This Is It ['65]
Two Shadows On Your Window ['57]
Waitin' For A Train ['57]
Welcome To My World ['64]
What Would You Do? ['61]
When Two Worlds Collide ['69]
When You Are Gone ['68]
Why Do I Love You (Melody Of Love) ['70]
Writing's On The Wall ['72]
Yonder Comes A Sucker ['55]
You Belong To Me ['75]
You'll Never Know ['75]
You're The Only Good Thing (That's Happened To Me) ['78]
Young Hearts ['57]

REEVES, John Rex

Born in Panola County, Texas. Male singer. Nephew of **Jim Reeves**.

DEBUT	PEAK	WKS	GOLD	Country Chart Hit	Songwriter	Label (& Number)
2/21/81	**93**	2		1 **What Would You Do**	*Jim Reeves*	Soc-A-Gee 109
8/1/81	**90**	2		2 **You're The Reason**	*Bobby Edwards/Terry Fell/Fred Henley/Mildred Imes*	Soc-A-Gee 110

REEVES, Julie

Born in 1974 in Ashland, Kentucky. Female singer.

DEBUT	PEAK	WKS	GOLD	Country Chart Hit	Songwriter	Label (& Number)
3/6/99	**51**	9		1 **It's About Time**	*Ed Hill/Mark D. Sanders*	Virgin
6/12/99	**39**	17		2 **Trouble Is A Woman**	S:19 *Tim Johnson/David Malloy/Kim Williams*	Virgin
11/27/99+	**38**	20		3 **What I Need** above 3 from the album *It's About Time* on Virgin 33091	*Marv Green*	Virgin

REEVES, Ronna

Born on 9/21/1966 in Big Springs, Texas. Female singer.

DEBUT	PEAK	WKS	GOLD	Country Chart Hit	Songwriter	Label (& Number)
3/7/92	**49**	11		1 **The More I Learn (The Less I Understand About Love)**	*Steve Dean/Karen Staley*	Mercury
7/18/92	**70**	4		2 **What If You're Wrong**	*Austin Cunningham/Denise Davis*	Mercury
11/7/92	**71**	2		3 **We Can Hold Our Own** above 3 from the album *The More I Learn* on Mercury 510847	*Paul Harrison*	Mercury
6/26/93	**73**	2		4 **Never Let Him See Me Cry**	*Jennifer Kimball/Kim Richey*	Mercury
9/25/93	**74**	2		5 **He's My Weakness** above 2 from the album *What Comes Naturally* on Mercury 514710	*Gloria Sklerov/Robin Tapp*	Mercury

REGAN, Bob, & Lucille Starr — see CANADIAN SWEETHEARTS, The

REGINA REGINA

Vocal duo of Regina Nicks (from Houston, Texas) and Regina Leigh (from North Carolina).

DEBUT	PEAK	WKS	GOLD	Country Chart Hit	Songwriter	Label (& Number)
1/18/97	**53**	8		**More Than I Wanted To Know** from the album *Regina Regina* on Giant 24662	*Mike Noble/Bob Regan*	Giant

DEBUT	PEAK	WKS	GOLD	#	ARTIST / Country Chart Hit	Ranking / Songwriter	Label (& Number)

REID, Mike

Born on 5/24/1947 in Alquippa, Pennsylvania. Male singer/songwriter/pianist. Pro football player with the Cincinnati Bengals from 1970-75.

DEBUT	PEAK	WKS	GOLD	#	Country Chart Hit	Songwriter	Label (& Number)
3/5/88	2[1]	21		1	**Old Folks** *[w/ Ronnie Milsap]*	S:5 *Mike Reid*	RCA 6896
11/24/90+	❶[2]	20		2	**Walk On Faith**	*Mike Reid/Allen Shamblin*	Columbia
3/30/91	17	20		3	**Till You Were Gone**	*Rory Bourke/Mike Reid*	Columbia
7/13/91	14	20		4	**As Simple As That**	*Mike Reid/Allen Shamblin*	Columbia
11/9/91+	23	20		5	**I'll Stop Loving You**	*Robert Byrne/Mike Reid*	Columbia
4/18/92	54	7		6	**I Got A Life**	*Rory Bourke/Mike Reid*	Columbia
					above 5 from the album *Turning For Home* on Columbia 46141		
8/29/92	45	11		7	**Keep On Walkin'**	*Amanda McBroom/Mike Reid*	Columbia
11/21/92+	43	13		8	**Call Home**	*Mike Reid/Troy Seals*	Columbia
					above 2 from the album *Twilight Town* on Columbia 48967		

REMINGTON, Rita

Born Rita Unruh in McPherson, Kansas. Female singer.

DEBUT	PEAK	WKS	GOLD	#	Country Chart Hit	Songwriter	Label (& Number)
9/8/73	99	3		1	**I've Never Been This Far Before**	*Conway Twitty*	Plantation 103
					female version of "You've Never Been This Far Before" by **Conway Twitty**		
1/14/78	86	5		2	**Don't Let The Flame Burn Out**	*Jackie DeShannon*	Plantation 167
4/8/78	100	3		3	**To Each His Own**	*Ray Evans/Jay Livingston*	Plantation 171
10/24/81	80	4		4	**Don't We Belong In Love** *[w/ The Smokey Valley Symphony]*	*Michael Garvin/Tom Shapiro*	Plantation 202
3/20/82	76	5		5	**The Flame**	*Bucky Lindsey/Larry Shell*	Plantation 207

REMINGTONS, The

Trio of Jimmy Griffin (**Black Tie**), Richard Mainegra and Rick Yancey (both of Cymarron). Yancey left in 1992; replaced by Denny Henson.

DEBUT	PEAK	WKS	GOLD	#	Country Chart Hit	Songwriter	Label (& Number)
10/12/91+	10	20		1	**A Long Time Ago**	*Richard Mainegra*	BNA
2/15/92	33	20		2	**I Could Love You (With My Eyes Closed)**	*Richard Mainegra/Rick Yancey*	BNA
6/6/92	18	20		3	**Two-Timin' Me**	*Jimmy Griffin/Richard Mainegra/Rick Yancey*	BNA
					above 3 from the album *Blue Frontier* on BNA 61045		
2/6/93	52	6		4	**Nobody Loves You When You're Free**	*Jimmy Griffin/Richard Mainegra/Rick Yancey*	BNA
7/10/93	69	1		5	**Wall Around Her Heart**	*Denny Henson/Steve Wilson*	BNA
					above 2 from the album *Aim For The Heart* on BNA 66152		

RENO, Don

Born on 2/21/1927 in Spartanburg, South Carolina. Died on 10/16/1984 (age 57). Male singer/songwriter/banjo player. Teamed with Red Smiley as **Reno & Smiley**. Father of Dale, Don Wayne and **Ronnie Reno** (**Reno Brothers**).

DEBUT	PEAK	WKS	GOLD	#	Country Chart Hit	Songwriter	Label (& Number)
1/8/66	46	3			**Soldier's Prayer In Viet Nam** *[w/ Benny Martin]*	*Benny Martin/Don Reno* **[S]**	Monument 912

RENO, Jack

Born on 11/30/1935 in Bloomfield, Iowa. Male singer/guitarist. Worked as a DJ on several radio stations since 1958.

DEBUT	PEAK	WKS	GOLD	#	Country Chart Hit	Songwriter	Label (& Number)
12/9/67+	10	17		1	**Repeat After Me**	*Glenn Tubb*	JAB 9009
5/11/68	41	11		2	**How Sweet It Is (To Be In Love With You)**	*Bobby Braddock*	JAB 9015
11/16/68+	19	14		3	**I Want One**	*Bobby Braddock*	Dot 17169
5/10/69	34	11		4	**I'm A Good Man (In A Bad Frame Of Mind)**	*Red Lane*	Dot 17233
9/20/69	22	9		5	**We All Go Crazy**	*Jack Moran*	Dot 17293
4/18/70	67	3		6	**That's The Way I See It**	*Bob Millsap*	Dot 17340
10/9/71	12	15		7	**Hitchin' A Ride**	*Peter Callander/Mitch Murray*	Target 0137
1/22/72	26	14		8	**Heartaches By The Numbers**	*Harlan Howard*	Target 0141
5/27/72	38	10		9	**Do You Want To Dance**	*Bobby Freeman*	Target 0150
8/25/73	67	8		10	**Beautiful Sunday**	*Daniel Boone/Rod McQueen*	United Artists 299
2/9/74	57	10		11	**Let The Four Winds Blow**	*Dave Bartholomew/Fats Domino*	United Artists 374
8/31/74	70	7		12	**Jukebox**	*Jack Reno/Tommy Williamson*	United Artists 502

RENO, Ronnie

Born on 9/28/1947 in Buffalo, South Carolina. Male singer/songwriter/guitarist. Son of **Don Reno**. Member of **Merle Haggard**'s Strangers from 1971-78.

DEBUT	PEAK	WKS	GOLD	#	Country Chart Hit	Songwriter	Label (& Number)
1/22/83	86	3		1	**Homemade Love**	*Wayne Carson/Ronnie Reno*	EMH 0010
9/24/83	76	4		2	**The Letter**	*Wayne Carson*	EMH 0024

RENO AND SMILEY

Duo of **Don Reno** and Red Smiley. Reno was born on 2/21/1927 in Spartanburg, South Carolina; died on 10/16/1984 (age 57). Smiley was born Arthur Lee Smiley on 5/17/1925 in Asheville, North Carolina; died on 1/2/1972 (age 46). Duo also recorded as **Chick And His Hot Rods**.

DEBUT	PEAK	WKS	GOLD	#	Country Chart Hit	Songwriter	Label (& Number)
5/29/61	14	10		1	**Don't Let Your Sweet Love Die**	*Clarke Van Ness*	King 5469
8/28/61	23	5		2	**Love Oh Love, Oh Please Come Home**	*Leon Jackson*	King 5520
9/18/61	27	2		3	**Jimmy Caught The Dickens (Pushing Ernest In The Tub)** **CHICK AND HIS HOT RODS**	*...Russ Easter/Charlton Heney/Don Reno* **[N]**	King 5537

RENO BROTHERS

Bluegrass trio from Roanoke, Virginia: brothers Dale Reno (born on 2/6/1961), Don Wayne Reno (born on 2/8/1963) and **Ronnie Reno** (born on 9/28/1947). Sons of **Don Reno**.

DEBUT	PEAK	WKS	GOLD	#	Country Chart Hit	Songwriter	Label (& Number)
7/2/88	77	2		1	**Yonder Comes A Freight Train**	*Ray Pennington*	Step One 387
4/1/89	84	2		2	**Love Will Never Be The Same**	*Wayne Carson/Ronnie Reno*	Step One 398

Billboard DEBUT	PEAK	WKS	GOLD	ARTIST / Country Chart Hit	Ranking / Songwriter	Label (& Number)

RESTLESS HEART — All-Time: #130

Group formed in Nashville, Tennessee: **Larry Stewart** (vocals, guitar, keyboards; born on 3/2/1959), Dave Innis (guitar, keyboards; born on 4/9/1959), Greg Jennings (guitar; born on 10/2/1954), Paul Gregg (bass; born on 12/3/1954) and John Dittrich (drums; born on 4/7/1951). Stewart went solo in early 1992. Innis left in early 1993. The remaining three continued with two backing musicians. Dittrich later formed **The Buffalo Club**.

DEBUT	PEAK	WKS	#	Country Chart Hit	Songwriter	Label (& Number)
1/26/85	**23**	16	1	**Let The Heartache Ride** ...S:23 / A:23	*Tim DuBois/Dave Robbins/Van Stephenson*	RCA 13969
6/1/85	**10**	18	2	**I Want Everyone To Cry** ...S:9 / A:10	*Wood Newton/Mike Noble*	RCA 14086
10/26/85+	**7**	19	3	(Back To The) **Heartbreak Kid** ...S:7 / A:8	*Tim DuBois/Van Stephenson*	RCA 14190
3/15/86	**10**	20	4	**Til I Loved You** ...A:8 / S:11	*Dave Robbins/Jeff Silbar/Van Stephenson*	RCA 14292
8/9/86	**❶[1]**	23	5	**That Rock Won't Roll** S:❶[1] / A:❶[1]	*Bob DiPiero/John Scott Sherrill*	RCA 14376
12/20/86+	**❶[1]**	25	6	**I'll Still Be Loving You** A:❶[1] / S:7	*Pat Bunch/Todd Cerney/Mary Ann Kennedy/Pam Rose*	RCA 5065
5/30/87	**❶[1]**	25	7	**Why Does It Have To Be (Wrong Or Right)** S:5	*Donny Lowery/Randy Sharp*	RCA 5132
10/31/87+	**❶[1]**	23	8	**Wheels** S:5	*Dave Loggins*	RCA 5280
5/21/88	**❶[1]**	21	9	**Bluest Eyes In Texas** S:2	*Tim DuBois/Dave Robbins/Van Stephenson*	RCA 8386
9/24/88	**❶[1]**	23	10	**A Tender Lie** S:❶[1]	*Randy Sharp*	RCA 8714
2/25/89	**3[1]**	18	11	**Big Dreams In A Small Town**	*Tim DuBois/Dave Robbins/Van Stephenson*	RCA 8816
7/29/89	**4**	20	12	**Say What's In Your Heart**	*Donny Lowery/Don Schlitz*	RCA 9034
12/16/89+	**4**	26	13	**Fast Movin' Train**	*Dave Loggins*	RCA 9115
4/21/90	**5**	21	14	**Dancy's Dream**	*Tim DuBois/Greg Jennings/Monty Powell*	RCA
9/1/90	**21**	16	15	**When Somebody Loves You**	*Rick Giles/Johnny Neel*	RCA
12/22/90+	**16**	20	16	**Long Lost Friend**	*Steve Bogard/Dave Robbins/Larry Stewart*	RCA
				above 3 from the album *Fast Movin' Train* on RCA 9961		
10/19/91+	**3[1]**	20	17	**You Can Depend On Me**	*Jimmy Griffin/Ronnie Rogers*	RCA
2/29/92	**40**	15	18	**Familiar Pain**	*Walt Aldridge/Susan Longacre*	RCA
				above 2 from the album *The Best Of Restless Heart* on RCA 61041		
9/12/92	**9**	20	19	**When She Cries**	*Marc Beeson/Sonny Lemaire*	RCA
1/23/93	**13**	20	20	**Mending Fences**	*Anderson Byrd/Jim Robinson*	RCA
5/22/93	**11**	20	21	**We Got The Love**	*Steve Bogard/Rick Giles*	RCA
11/6/93	**72**	2	22	**Big Iron Horses**	*John Dittrich/Dave Innis/Vince Melamed*	RCA
				above 4 from the album *Big Iron Horses* on RCA 66049		
4/30/94	**52**	9	23	**Baby Needs New Shoes**	*Billy Crain/Ronnie Guilbeau/Thom McHugh*	RCA
				from the album *Matters Of The Heart* on RCA 66397		
5/16/98	**33**	17	24	**No End To This Road**	*Kent Blazy/Michael Dulaney/Neil Thrasher*	RCA
9/12/98	**64**	2	25	**For Lack Of Better Words**	*Dillon Dixon/Joie Scott/Kim Tribble*	RCA
				above 2 from the album *Greatest Hits* on RCA 67628		
1/9/99	**58**	1	26	**Little Drummer Boy** [X]	*Katherine Davis/Henry Onorati/Harry Simeone*	RCA
				from the various artists album *Country Christmas Classics* on RCA 67698		
7/24/04	**29**	17	27	**Feel My Way To You**	*Danny Orton/Jennifer Schott*	Koch
				from the album *Still Restless* on Koch 9821		

REVEREND IKE

Born Frederick Eikerenkoetter on 6/1/1935 in Ridgeland, South Carolina. Popular black preacher.

DEBUT	PEAK	WKS	#	Country Chart Hit	Songwriter	Label (& Number)
10/11/86	**❶[2]**	19		**Mind Your Own Business** ***[w/ Hank Williams Jr./Reba McEntire/Willie Nelson/Tom Petty]*** ...S:❶[2] / A:❶[2]	*Hank Williams*	Warner/Curb 28581

REX, Tim, and Oklahoma

Born in Oklahoma. Male singer.

DEBUT	PEAK	WKS	#	Country Chart Hit	Songwriter	Label (& Number)
11/8/80	**87**	3	1	**Arizona Highway**	*Mike Rabon*	Dee Jay 103
12/13/80+	**46**	12	2	**Gettin' Over You**	*Cary Lynn Rutledge*	Dee Jay 107
4/11/81	**43**	10	3	**Spread My Wings**	*Robin Harris/Carl Hendricks/Jerry Sisk/Greg Stevens*	Dee Jay 111

REY, Ernest

Born in Nashville, Tennessee. Male singer. Son of **Loretta Lynn**.

DEBUT	PEAK	WKS	#	Country Chart Hit	Songwriter	Label (& Number)
3/17/79	**97**	1		**Mama's Sugar**	*Sonny Throckmorton*	MCA 40991

REYNOLDS, Allen

Born on 8/18/1938 in North Little Rock, Arkansas; raised in Memphis, Tennessee. Male singer/songwriter/producer.

DEBUT	PEAK	WKS	#	Country Chart Hit	Songwriter	Label (& Number)
5/20/78	**95**	5		**Wrong Road Again**	*Allen Reynolds*	Triple I 496

REYNOLDS, Burt

Born on 2/11/1936 in Waycross, Georgia. Popular actor. Starred in several movies and the TV series *Evening Shade*.

DEBUT	PEAK	WKS	#	Country Chart Hit	Songwriter	Label (& Number)
10/25/80	**51**	7		**Let's Do Something Cheap And Superficial**	*Richard Levinson*	MCA 51004
				from the movie *Smokey & The Bandit II* starring Reynolds		

RHOADS, Randy

Born in Missouri. Male singer/guitarist.

DEBUT	PEAK	WKS	#	Country Chart Hit	Songwriter	Label (& Number)
1/13/90	**89**	1		**Honey Do Weekend**	*Bennie Wade*	Blue Ridge 001

RICE, Bill — SW: #5

Born in Gallo, Arkansas. Male singer/songwriter/producer.

DEBUT	PEAK	WKS	#	Country Chart Hit	Songwriter	Label (& Number)
3/20/71	**33**	10	1	**Travelin' Minstrel Man**	*Jerry Foster/Bill Rice*	Capitol 3049
9/11/71	**51**	9	2	**Honky-Tonk Stardust Cowboy**	*Darrell Statler*	Capitol 3156
4/8/72	**74**	2	3	**A Girl Like Her Is Hard To Find**	*Jerry Foster/Bill Rice*	Epic 10833
7/1/72	**63**	5	4	**Something To Call Mine**	*Jerry Foster/Bill Rice*	Epic 10877

DEBUT	PEAK	WKS	GOLD		ARTIST / Country Chart Hit	Songwriter	Label (& Number)
					RICE, Bill — cont'd		
11/19/77	**97**	3		5	**All The Love We Threw Away** *[w/ Lois Johnson]*	*Jerry Foster/Bill Rice*	Polydor 14435
3/11/78	**100**	2		6	**Beggars And Choosers**	*Jerry Foster/Bill Rice*	Polydor 14453

RICE, Bobby G. — All-Time: #230

Born Robert Gene Rice on 7/11/1944 in Boscobel, Wisconsin. Male singer/songwriter/guitarist.

DEBUT	PEAK	WKS	GOLD		Country Chart Hit	Songwriter	Label (& Number)
4/25/70	**32**	8		1	**Sugar Shack**	*Faye Boss/Keith McCormack*	Royal American 6
8/8/70	**35**	11		2	**Hey Baby**	*Bruce Channel/Margaret Cobb*	Royal American 18
1/9/71	**46**	9		3	**Lover Please**	*Billy Swan*	Royal American 27
5/22/71	**20**	15		4	**Mountain Of Love**	*Harold Dorman*	Royal American 32
1/1/72	**33**	11		5	**Suspicion**	*Doc Pomus/Mort Shuman*	Royal American 48
12/23/72+	**3**[1]	16		6	**You Lay So Easy On My Mind** (also see #28 below)	*Charles Fields/Bobby G. Rice/Don Riis*	Metromedia 902
5/5/73	**8**	15		7	**You Give Me You**	*Tony Moon*	Metromedia 0107
9/22/73	**13**	14		8	**The Whole World's Making Love Again Tonight**	*Charles Fields/Bobby G. Rice/Don Riis*	Metromedia 0075
9/28/74	**30**	14		9	**Make It Feel Like Love Again**	*Earl Thomas Conley/Dick Heard*	GRT 009
1/11/75	**9**	14		10	**Write Me A Letter**	*Tim Martin/Walt Meskell*	GRT 014
5/3/75	**10**	14		11	**Freda Comes, Freda Goes**	*Roger Cook/Roger Greenaway/Mike Hazlewood*	GRT 021
8/30/75	**64**	11		12	**I May Never Be Your Lover (But I'll Always Be Your Friend)**	*Teddy Gentry*	GRT 028
1/3/76	**35**	11		13	**Pick Me Up On Your Way Down**	*Harlan Howard*	GRT 036
7/24/76	**53**	9		14	**You Are My Special Angel** (same tune as "My Special Angel" by **Bobby Helms**)	*Jimmy Duncan*	GRT 061
11/13/76	**54**	9		15	**Woman Stealer**	*Gary Paxton Jr./Gary S. Paxton/Steve Paxton*	GRT 084
7/9/77	**66**	7		16	**Just One Kiss Magdelena**	*A.B. Clyde/David Fisher/Mike Holm/Rainer Pietsch*	GRT 120
7/22/78	**57**	6		17	**Whisper It To Me**	*Rick Klang/Don Pfrimmer*	Republic 023
11/11/78	**30**	10		18	**The Softest Touch In Town**	*R.C. Bannon/Harlan Sanders/Kent Westberry*	Republic 031
6/9/79	**49**	8		19	**Oh Baby Mine (I Get So Lonely)**	*Pat Ballard*	Republic 041
12/1/79	**67**	8		20	**You Make It So Easy**	*Earl Thomas Conley*	Sunset 102
5/3/80	**53**	9		21	**The Man Who Takes You Home**	*Earl Thomas Conley*	Sunbird 108
2/7/81	**86**	2		22	**Livin' Together (Lovin' Apart)**	*Bob Morrison/Mary Welch*	Sunbird 7558
10/10/81	**63**	5		23	**Pardon My French**	*Johnny Duncan/Betty Jo Gibson*	Charta 166
6/8/85	**95**	2		24	**New Tradition**	*Steve Chiasson*	Door Knob 230
3/8/86	**70**	4		25	**Red Neck And Over Thirty** *[w/ Wayne Kemp]*	*Buffalo Jones*	Door Knob 243
9/13/86	**70**	5		26	**You've Taken Over My Heart**	*Bobby G. Rice*	Door Knob 251
6/27/87	**85**	2		27	**Rachel's Room**	*Ann Williams*	Door Knob 274
10/3/87	**79**	3		28	**You Lay So Easy On My Mind** (new version of #6 above)	*Charles Fields/Bobby G. Rice/Don Riis* [R]	Door Knob 285
3/5/88	**70**	5		29	**A Night Of Love Forgotten**	*Dave Graham*	Door Knob 295
9/17/88	**76**	4		30	**Clean Livin' Folk** *[w/ Perry LaPointe]*	*Julia Farkas*	Door Knob 307

RICH, Charlie — 1970s: #12 / All-Time: #83

Born on 12/14/1932 in Colt, Arkansas. Died of an acute blood clot on 7/25/1995 (age 62). Male singer/songwriter/pianist. First played jazz and blues. Own jazz group, the Velvetones, mid-1950s, while in U.S. Air Force. Session work with Sun Records in 1958. Known as "The Silver Fox."

CMA: Male Vocalist 1973 / Entertainer 1974

DEBUT	PEAK	WKS	GOLD		Country Chart Hit	Songwriter	Label (& Number)
3/9/68	**44**	8		1	**Set Me Free**	*Curly Putman*	Epic 10287
8/24/68	**45**	8		2	**Raggedy Ann**	*Dallas Frazier/A.L. "Doodle" Owens*	Epic 10358
8/9/69	**41**	11		3	**Life's Little Ups And Downs**	*Margaret Rich*	Epic 10492
2/28/70	**67**	5		4	**Who Will The Next Fool Be** (recorded in January 1959)	*Charlie Rich*	Sun 1110
3/28/70	**47**	6		5	**July 12, 1939**	*Norro Wilson*	Epic 10585
10/24/70	**37**	12		6	**Nice 'N' Easy**	*Alan Bergman/Marilyn Bergman/Lew Spence*	Epic 10662
8/14/71	**72**	2		7	**A Woman Left Lonely**	*Spooner Oldham/Dan Penn*	Epic 10745
11/27/71+	**35**	13		8	**A Part Of Your Life**	*Margaret Rich*	Epic 10809
8/26/72	**6**	17		9	**I Take It On Home**	*Kenny O'Dell*	Epic 10867
2/10/73	**❶**[2]	20	▲	10	**Behind Closed Doors** (**Grammy: Song, Male Vocal & Hall of Fame / CMA: Single**)	*Kenny O'Dell*	Epic 10950
7/14/73	**29**	11		11	**Tomorrow Night**	*Sam Coslow/Will Grosz*	RCA Victor 0983
9/22/73	**❶**[3]	18	●	12	**The Most Beautiful Girl**	*Rory Bourke/Billy Sherrill/Norro Wilson*	Epic 11040
12/22/73+	**❶**[2]	17		13	**There Won't Be Anymore**	*Charlie Rich*	RCA Victor 0195
2/23/74	**❶**[3]	14		14	**A Very Special Love Song** (**Grammy: Song**)	*Billy Sherrill/Norro Wilson*	Epic 11091
5/4/74	**❶**[1]	13		15	**I Don't See Me In Your Eyes Anymore**	*Bennie Benjamin/George Weiss*	RCA Victor 0260
6/22/74	**23**	12		16	**A Field Of Yellow Daisies**	*Margaret Rich*	Mercury 73498
8/10/74	**❶**[1]	15		17	**I Love My Friend**	*Billy Sherrill/Norro Wilson*	Epic 20006
9/28/74	**❶**[1]	15		18	**She Called Me Baby**	*Harlan Howard*	RCA Victor 10062
12/28/74+	**71**	5		19	**Something Just Came Over Me**	*Margaret Rich*	Mercury 73646
2/1/75	**3**[1]	12		20	**My Elusive Dreams**	*Curly Putman/Billy Sherrill*	Epic 50064
4/12/75	**23**	12		21	**It's All Over Now**	*Charlie Rich*	RCA Victor 10256
5/24/75	**3**[1]	17		22	**Every Time You Touch Me (I Get High)**	*Charlie Rich/Billy Sherrill*	Epic 50103

DEBUT	PEAK	WKS	GOLD	ARTIST Ranking / Country Chart Hit	Songwriter	Label (& Number)

RICH, Charlie — cont'd

DEBUT	PEAK	WKS	GOLD	Country Chart Hit	Songwriter	Label (& Number)
9/20/75	**4**	14		23 **All Over Me**	*Ben Peters*	Epic 50142
12/20/75+	**56**	7		24 **Now Everybody Knows**	*Don Bowman*	RCA Victor 10458
12/27/75+	**10**	13		25 **Since I Fell For You**	*Buddy Johnson*	Epic 50182
4/24/76	**22**	10		26 **America, The Beautiful (1976)**	*Kermit Goell/Billy Sherrill*	Epic 50222
9/4/76	**27**	9		27 **Road Song**	*Paul Clements*	Epic 50268
1/8/77	**24**	12		28 **My Mountain Dew** all of above RCA and Mercury hits were recorded from 1963-66	*Charlie Rich*	RCA 10859
2/5/77	**12**	13		29 **Easy Look**	*Curly Putman/Sonny Throckmorton*	Epic 50328
5/28/77	**❶[2]**	19		30 **Rollin' With The Flow**	*Jerry Hayes*	Epic 50392
4/8/78	**8**	14		31 **Puttin' In Overtime At Home**	*Ben Peters*	United Artists 1193
7/1/78	**10**	13		32 **Beautiful Woman**	*Steve Davis/Billy Sherrill/Norro Wilson*	Epic 50562
7/22/78	**46**	8		33 **I Still Believe In Love**	*Jacob Mayer*	United Artists 1223
10/7/78	**❶[1]**	14		34 **On My Knees** *[w/ Janie Fricke]*	*Charlie Rich*	Epic 50616
1/6/79	**3[2]**	14		35 **I'll Wake You Up When I Get Home** from the movie *Every Which Way But Loose* starring **Clint Eastwood**	*Milton Brown/Steve Dorff*	Elektra 45553
1/6/79	**45**	8		36 **The Fool Strikes Again**	*George Cobb/Steve Davis/Mark Sherrill*	United Artists 1269
3/10/79	**26**	11		37 **I Lost My Head**	*Larry Keith/Steve Pippin/Johnny Slate*	United Artists 1280
5/12/79	**20**	13		38 **Spanish Eyes**	*Bert Kaempfert/Charles Singleton/Eddie Snyder*	Epic 50701
8/18/79	**84**	4		39 **Life Goes On**	*Margaret Rich*	United Artists 1307
11/24/79+	**22**	13		40 **You're Gonna Love Yourself In The Morning**	*Donnie Fritts*	United Artists 1325
3/8/80	**74**	5		41 **I'd Build A Bridge**	*Mike Settle*	United Artists 1340
5/3/80	**61**	7		42 **Even A Fool Would Let Go**	*Kerry Chater/Tom Snow*	Epic 50869
10/11/80	**12**	14		43 **A Man Just Don't Know What A Woman Goes Through**	*...Bob Brabham/Linda Brown/Archie Jordan*	Elektra 47047
2/14/81	**26**	11		44 **Are We Dreamin' The Same Dream**	*Billy Burnette/Johnny Christopher*	Elektra 47104
5/23/81	**47**	7		45 **You Made It Beautiful** from the movie *Take This Job And Shove It* starring Art Carney	*Steve Davis/Billy Sherrill/Glenn Sutton*	Epic 02058

RICH, Debbie

Born Debra Sue Rathjen in Levenworth, Washington; raised in Napa Valley, California. Female singer.

DEBUT	PEAK	WKS	GOLD	Country Chart Hit	Songwriter	Label (& Number)
12/3/88	**87**	2		1 **I Ain't Gonna Take This Layin' Down**	*Bob Stamper*	Door Knob 311
2/25/89	**71**	4		2 **Don't Be Surprised If You Get It**	*Gigi Selman*	Door Knob 318
4/22/89	**74**	4		3 **I've Had Enough Of You**	*Johnette Burton*	Door Knob 321
9/2/89	**68**	5		4 **Do It Again (I Think I Saw Diamonds)**	*Ann Williams*	Door Knob 327

RICH, Don — see ALAN, Buddy

RICH, John

Born on 1/7/1974 in Amarillo, Texas. Former singer/bassist of **Lonestar**. One-half of **Big & Rich** duo.

DEBUT	PEAK	WKS	GOLD	Country Chart Hit	Songwriter	Label (& Number)
7/8/00	**53**	20		1 **I Pray For You**	S:20 *Kenny Alphin/John Rich*	BNA
4/7/01	**46**	8		2 **Forever Loving You**	*Kenny Alphin/Vicky McGeehe/John Rich*	BNA

RICHARDS, Earl

Born Henry Earl Sinks in Amarillo, Texas. Male singer. Owned the Ace of Hearts record label.

DEBUT	PEAK	WKS	GOLD	Country Chart Hit	Songwriter	Label (& Number)
9/6/69	**39**	10		1 **The House Of Blue Lights**	*Don Raye/Freddie Slack*	United Artists 50561
1/31/70	**73**	2		2 **Corrine, Corrina**	*Bo Chapman/Mitchell Parish/J. Mayo Williams*	United Artists 50619
10/10/70	**57**	4		3 **Sunshine**	*Mickey Newbury*	United Artists 50704
1/13/73	**23**	12		4 **Margie, Who's Watching The Baby**	*Mack David/R.B. Greaves*	Ace of Hearts 0461
4/28/73	**66**	6		5 **Things Are Kinda Slow At The House**	*Larry Kingston*	Ace of Hearts 0465
7/21/73	**58**	11		6 **The Sun Is Shining (On Everybody But Me)**	*Chuck Deal/Don Deal*	Ace of Hearts 0470
12/22/73+	**85**	5		7 **How Can I Tell Her /**	*Lobo*	
3/2/74	**83**	7		8 **Walkin' In Teardrops**	*Bill Emerson/Jodie Emerson*	Ace of Hearts 0477
10/18/75	**91**	5		9 **My Babe**	*Willie Dixon*	Ace of Hearts 7502

RICHARDS, Sue

Born Maggie Sue Wimberly on 11/26/1946 in Muscle Shoals, Alabama. Female singer/songwriter.

DEBUT	PEAK	WKS	GOLD	Country Chart Hit	Songwriter	Label (& Number)
3/27/71	**56**	8		1 **Feel Free To Go**	*Bill Anderson*	Epic 10709
1/12/74	**48**	13		2 **I Just Had You On My Mind**	*Sue Richards*	Dot 17481
7/20/74	**93**	5		3 **Ease Me To The Ground**	*Bud Reneau*	Dot 17508
5/3/75	**99**	2		4 **Homemade Love**	*Richard Mainegra*	ABC/Dot 17547
9/6/75	**32**	12		5 **Tower Of Strength**	*Burt Bacharach/Bob Hilliard*	ABC/Dot 17572
1/17/76	**25**	11		6 **Sweet Sensuous Feelings**	*Ava Aldridge/Roy Aldridge*	ABC/Dot 17600
5/1/76	**50**	10		7 **Please Tell Him That I Said Hello**	*Peter Dibbens/Mike Shepstone*	ABC/Dot 17622
8/21/76	**70**	6		8 **I'll Never See Him Again**	*Milton Blackford/Richard Mainegra*	ABC/Dot 17645
11/26/77	**94**	3		9 **Someone Loves Him**	*David Chamberlain/Jim Vest*	Epic 50465
7/15/78	**94**	4		10 **Hey, What Do You Say (We Fall In Love)**	*Lee Dresser*	Epic 50546
3/10/79	**85**	3		11 **Finders Keepers Losers Weepers** *[w/ Stan Hitchcock]*	*Murry Kellum/Pearly Mitchell*	MMI 1028

RICHEY, Kim

Born on 12/1/1956 in Zanesville, Ohio. Female singer/songwriter.

DEBUT	PEAK	WKS	GOLD	Country Chart Hit	Songwriter	Label (& Number)
6/24/95	**47**	12		1 **Just My Luck**	*Angelo Petraglia/Kim Richey*	Mercury
10/7/95	**59**	12		2 **Those Words We Said**	*Angelo Petraglia/Kim Richey*	Mercury
4/20/96	**66**	3		3 **From Where I Stand** above 3 from the album *Kim Richey* on Mercury 526812	*Kim Richey/Tia Sillers*	Mercury
5/10/97	**72**	2		4 **I Know** from the album *Bitter Sweet* on Mercury 534255	*John Leventhal/Kim Richey*	Mercury

DEBUT	PEAK	WKS	GOLD	ARTIST / Country Chart Hit	Ranking / Songwriter	Label (& Number)

RICHIE, Lionel

Born on 6/20/1949 in Tuskegee, Alabama. Black singer/songwriter/pianist. Former lead singer of the Commodores. Also see **USA For Africa**.

DEBUT	PEAK	WKS	GOLD	Country Chart Hit	Songwriter	Label (& Number)
7/21/84	**24**	18		1 **Stuck On You**	*Lionel Richie*	Motown 1746
12/6/86+	**10**	15		2 **Deep River Woman** ***[w/ Alabama]***	S:❶[1] / A:10 *Lionel Richie*	Motown 1873

RICHMOND, Rashell

Born in Georgia. Female singer.

DEBUT	PEAK	WKS	GOLD	Country Chart Hit	Songwriter	Label (& Number)
6/20/81	**55**	6		**Daddy** ***[w/ Billy Edd Wheeler]***	*Jerry Duncan/Betty Gibson/Billy Edd Wheeler*	NSD 94

RICKS, Steve

Born in Little Rock, Arkansas. Male singer.

DEBUT	PEAK	WKS	GOLD	Country Chart Hit	Songwriter	Label (& Number)
6/14/86	**81**	4		**Private Clown**	*Bill McCord*	Southwind 8205

RICOCHET — All-Time: #280

Group formed in Texas: Perry "Heath" Wright (vocals, guitar; born on 4/22/1967), Teddy Carr (guitar; born on 7/4/1960), brothers Duane "Junior" Bryant (fiddle; born on 10/23/1968) and Jeff Bryant (drums; born on 12/27/1962), Eddie Kilgallon (keyboards; born on 5/12/1965) and Greg Cook (bass; born on 1/28/1965).

DEBUT	PEAK	WKS	GOLD	Country Chart Hit	Songwriter	Label (& Number)
12/9/95+	**5**	21		1 **What Do I Know**	S:14 *Cathy Majeski/Sunny Russ/Stephony Smith*	Columbia
4/27/96	**❶[2]**	20		2 **Daddy's Money**	S:7 *Bob DiPiero/Mark D. Sanders/Steve Seskin*	Columbia
7/20/96	**58**	1		3 **The Star Spangled Banner**	*Francis Scott Key*	Columbia
8/17/96	**9**	20		4 **Love Is Stronger Than Pride**	*Rick Bowles/Doug Johnson*	Columbia
12/14/96+	**43**	5		5 **Let It Snow, Let It Snow, Let It Snow**	*Sammy Cahn/Jule Styne* **[X]**	Columbia
1/18/97	**20**	16		6 **Ease My Troubled Mind**	*Michael Garvin/Tom Shapiro/Chris Waters*	Columbia
				#1, 2, 4 & 6: from the album *Ricochet* on Columbia 67223		
5/3/97	**18**	20		7 **He Left A Lot To Be Desired**	S:15 *Larry Boone/Rick Bowles*	Columbia
9/13/97	**39**	13		8 **Blink Of An Eye**	*Rick Bowles/Josh Leo*	Columbia
12/13/97+	**44**	5		9 **Let It Snow, Let It Snow, Let It Snow**	*Sammy Cahn/Jule Style* **[X-R]**	Columbia
2/7/98	**44**	10		10 **Connected At The Heart**	*Skip Ewing/Donny Kees*	Columbia
				#7, 8 & 10: from the album *Blink Of An Eye* on Columbia 67773		
8/1/98	**58**	4		11 **Honky Tonk Baby**	*Melba Montgomery/Billy Yates*	Columbia
11/21/98+	**52**	15		12 **Can't Stop Thinkin' 'Bout That**	*Marty Dodson/Dusty Drake/Sam Mullins*	Columbia
12/12/98+	**41**	5		13 **Let It Snow, Let It Snow, Let It Snow**	*Sammy Cahn/Jule Styne* **[X-R]**	Columbia
4/24/99	**48**	15		14 **Seven Bridges Road**	*Steve Young*	Columbia
12/25/99+	**39**	3		15 **Let It Snow, Let It Snow, Let It Snow**	*Sammy Cahn/Jule Styne* **[X-R]**	Columbia
4/1/00	**45**	15		16 **Do I Love You Enough**	S:15 *Richard Fagan/Lisa Palas*	Columbia
8/19/00	**48**	16		17 **She's Gone**	*Michael Dulaney/John Hobbs/Jeffrey Steele*	Columbia
				#14, 16 & 17: from the album *What You Leave Behind* on Columbia 69198		

RIDDLE, Allan

Born on 5/16/1929 in Spartanburg, South Carolina. Male singer/guitarist.

DEBUT	PEAK	WKS	GOLD	Country Chart Hit	Songwriter	Label (& Number)
11/7/60	**16**	12		**The Moon Is Crying**	*Jimmie Edwards*	Plaid 1001

RIDE THE RIVER

Group led by singer/guitarist Danny Stockard.

DEBUT	PEAK	WKS	GOLD	Country Chart Hit	Songwriter	Label (& Number)
2/21/87	**63**	5		1 **You Left Her Lovin' You**	*Jim Cunningham/Nina Taylor*	Advantage 165
6/13/87	**55**	7		2 **The First Cut Is The Deepest**	*Cat Stevens*	Advantage 169
10/31/87	**57**	7		3 **It's Such A Heartache**	*Hillary Kanter/Even Stevens*	Advantage 182
2/6/88	**51**	9		4 **After Last Night's Storm**	*J. Charles Kelly*	Advantage 189

RILEY, Dan

Born in California. Male singer/songwriter.

DEBUT	PEAK	WKS	GOLD	Country Chart Hit	Songwriter	Label (& Number)
12/22/79+	**78**	5		**Lily**	*Barry Kaye/Dan Riley*	Armada 103

RILEY, Jeannie C. — All-Time: #241

Born Jeanne Carolyn Stephenson on 10/19/1945 in Anson, Texas. Female singer/guitarist.

DEBUT	PEAK	WKS	GOLD	Country Chart Hit	Songwriter	Label (& Number)
8/24/68	**❶[3]**	14	●	1 **Harper Valley P.T.A.**	*Tom T. Hall*	Plantation 3
				Grammy: Female Vocal / CMA: Single		
12/7/68+	**6**	15		2 **The Girl Most Likely**	*Margaret Lewis/Myra Smith*	Plantation 7
1/25/69	**35**	9		3 **The Price I Pay To Stay**	*Ed Bruce*	Capitol 2378
3/29/69	**5**	13		4 **There Never Was A Time**	*Margaret Lewis/Myra Smith*	Plantation 16
6/28/69	**32**	9		5 **The Rib**	*Margaret Lewis/Myra Smith*	Plantation 22
10/4/69	**33**	11		6 **The Back Side Of Dallas /**	*Jerry Foster/Bill Rice*	
10/25/69	**34**	8		7 **Things Go Better With Love**	*Naomi Martin*	Plantation 29
1/31/70	**7**	12		8 **Country Girl**	*Margaret Lewis/Myra Smith*	Plantation 44
6/27/70	**21**	11		9 **Duty Not Desire**	*Becki Bluefield*	Plantation 59
12/12/70	**60**	4		10 **My Man /**	*Margaret Lewis/Myra Smith*	
12/12/70	**62**	4		11 **The Generation Gap**	*Betty Craig/Charlie Craig/Jim Hayner*	Plantation 65
4/3/71	**4**	15		12 **Oh, Singer**	*Margaret Lewis/Myra Smith*	Plantation 72
7/3/71	**7**	15		13 **Good Enough To Be Your Wife**	*Ralph Murphy*	Plantation 75
10/23/71	**15**	13		14 **Roses And Thorns**	*Naomi Martin*	Plantation 79
11/20/71	**47**	8		15 **Houston Blues**	*Bobby Bond*	MGM 14310
1/15/72	**12**	12		16 **Give Myself A Party**	*Don Gibson*	MGM 14341
5/20/72	**30**	11		17 **Good Morning Country Rain**	*Eddy Raven*	MGM 14382
10/28/72	**57**	6		18 **One Night**	*Dave Bartholomew/Pearl King*	MGM 14427
3/10/73	**44**	7		19 **When Love Has Gone Away**	*Bud Johnston*	MGM 14495

DEBUT	PEAK	WKS	GOLD		ARTIST / Country Chart Hit	Ranking / Songwriter	Label (& Number)

RILEY, Jeannie C. — cont'd

DEBUT	PEAK	WKS	GOLD	#	Country Chart Hit	Songwriter	Label (& Number)
7/14/73	51	7		20	**Hush**	*Joe South*	MGM 14554
11/10/73	57	9		21	**Another Football Year**	*Barney Ashner/Marlene Ashner/Howard White*	MGM 14666
9/28/74	89	6		22	**Plain Vanilla** ***[w/ The Red River Symphony]***	*Jeannie C. Riley*	Mercury 73616
7/17/76	94	4		23	**The Best I've Ever Had**	*Jeannie C. Riley*	Warner 8226

RILEY, Larry

Born in Scottsdale, Arizona. Male singer.

DEBUT	PEAK	WKS	GOLD	#	Country Chart Hit	Songwriter	Label (& Number)
1/17/81	90	2		1	**Cheater's Last Chance**	*Christopher Blake/Bobby Fischer/Andre Pessis*	F&L 507
5/30/81	93	2		2	**Code-A-Phone**	*Christopher Blake/Bobby Fischer*	F&L 509

RIMES, LeAnn — 2000s: #31 / All-Time: #175

Born Margaret LeAnn Rimes on 8/28/1982 in Jackson, Mississippi; raised in Garland, Texas. Female singer/songwriter. Won her first talent show in 1987. Winner on TV's *Star Search* in 1990. Hosted TV talent show *Nashville Star*. Married actor Dean Sheremet on 2/23/2002. Won the 1996 Best New Artist Grammy Award.

CMA: Horizon 1997

DEBUT	PEAK	WKS	GOLD	#	Country Chart Hit	Songwriter	Label (& Number)
5/25/96	10	20	●	1	**Blue** — Grammy: Song & Female Vocal	S:❶^{20} *Bill Mack*	Curb
7/27/96	43	10		2	**Hurt Me**	*Deborah Allen/Bobby Braddock/Rafe Van Hoy*	MCG/Curb
9/28/96	❶^{2}	20		3	**One Way Ticket (Because I Can)**	*Keith Hinton/Judy Rodman*	MCG/Curb
12/21/96+	3^{1}	20		4	**Unchained Melody**	*Alex North/Hy Zaret*	Curb
12/28/96+	51	3		5	**Put A Little Holiday In Your Heart** **[X]** — above 2 available only as a bonus CD single with the purchase of her album *Blue* at Target stores during the 1996 holiday season	*Greg Wojahn/Roger Wojahn/Scott Wojahn*	Curb
3/22/97	5	20		6	**The Light In Your Eyes** — #1-3 & 6: from the album *Blue* on Curb 77821	*Dan Tyler*	Curb
6/14/97	43	20	▲^{3}	7	**How Do I Live** — from the movie *Con Air* starring Nicolas Cage; spent a record-setting 309 weeks on the Country Sales chart	S:❶^{32} *Diane Warren*	Curb
8/23/97	48	7	●	8	**You Light Up My Life**	S:2 *Joe Brooks*	Curb
10/11/97+	4	21		9	**On The Side Of Angels** — above 3 from the album *You Light Up My Life - Inspirational Songs* on Curb 77885	*Gary Burr/Gerry House*	Curb
12/27/97+	71	2		10	**Put A Little Holiday In Your Heart** **[X-R]**	*Greg Wojahn/Roger Wojahn/Scott Wojahn*	Curb
3/28/98	4	20	●	11	**Commitment**	S:2 *Tony Colton/Tony Marty/Bobby Wood*	Curb
8/1/98	10	20		12	**Nothin' New Under The Moon**	*Rick Bowles/Josh Leo/Tom Shapiro*	Curb
11/28/98+	41	14		13	**These Arms Of Mine** — above 3 from the album *Sittin' On Top Of The World* on Curb 77901	*Jeff Tweel/Susan Tweel*	Curb
9/4/99+	6	25		14	**Big Deal** — from the album *LeAnn Rimes* on Curb 77947	S:❶^{11} *Al Anderson/Jeffrey Steele*	Curb
12/25/99	18^{S}	2		15	**Cattle Call** ***[w/ Eddy Arnold]***	*Tex Owens*	Curb
4/15/00	8	31		16	**I Need You** — from the TV movie *Jesus* starring Jeremy Sisto	S:❶^{6} *Ty Lacy/Dennis Matkosky*	Curb/Capitol
10/21/00	61	8		17	**Can't Fight The Moonlight**	*Diane Warren*	Curb
2/24/01	18	20		18	**But I Do Love You** — above 2 from the movie *Coyote Ugly* starring Piper Perabo (soundtrack on Curb 78703); above 3 from the album *I Need You* on Curb 77979	S:❶^{37} *Diane Warren*	Curb
10/27/01	51	2		19	**God Bless America** — from the album *God Bless America* on Curb 78726	S:3 *Irving Berlin*	Curb
11/16/02	60	1		20	**Life Goes On**	*Andreas Carlsson/Desmond Child/LeAnn Rimes*	Curb
3/8/03	43	15		21	**Suddenly** — above 2 from the album *Twisted Angel* on Curb 78747	*Andreas Carlsson/Desmond Child*	Curb
12/13/03+	37	16		22	**This Love** — from the album *Greatest Hits* on Curb 78829	*Marc Beeson/Jim Collins*	Asylum-Curb
9/4/04+	5	27		23	**Nothin 'Bout Love Makes Sense**	*Gary Burr/Joel Feeney/Kylie Sackley*	Asylum-Curb
12/25/04+	50	3		24	**A Different Kind Of Christmas** **[X]**	*Peter Amato/Jud Friedman/Allan Rich/LeAnn Rimes*	Asylum-Curb
1/1/05	48	2		25	**Rockin' Around The Christmas Tree** **[X]**	*Johnny Marks*	Asylum-Curb
1/8/05	60	1		26	**Have Yourself A Merry Little Christmas** **[X]** — above 3 from the album *What A Wonderful World* on Asylum-Curb 78779	*Ralph Blane/Hugh Martin*	Asylum-Curb
4/2/05	14↑	26↑		27	**Probably Wouldn't Be This Way** — #23 & 27: from the album *This Woman* on Asylum-Curb 78859	*John Kennedy/Tammi Kidd*	Asylum-Curb

RISHARD, Rod

Born in Nederland, Texas. Male singer/guitarist.

DEBUT	PEAK	WKS	GOLD	#	Country Chart Hit	Songwriter	Label (& Number)
8/20/83	77	5		1	**You'd Better Believe It**	*Devon Dickson*	Soundwaves 4715
11/19/83	74	5		2	**How Do You Tell Someone You Love**	*Jimmy Payne/Jim Swanson*	Soundwaves 4717
3/24/84	89	3		3	**The More I Go Blind**	*Keith Durham*	Soundwaves 4724
7/28/84	84	3		4	**Midnight Angel Of Mercy**	*Joe Gibson/Roger Gore/Jimmy Payne*	Soundwaves 4734

Billboard DEBUT	PEAK	WKS	GOLD	ARTIST / Country Chart Hit	Ranking / Songwriter	Label (& Number)

RITTER, Tex — 1940s: #8 / All-Time: #158 // HOF: 1964

Born Maurice Woodward Ritter on 1/12/1905 in Murvaul, Texas. Died of a heart attack on 1/2/1974 (age 68). Male singer/songwriter/guitarist/actor. Acted in several western movies from 1936-45. Co-host of *Town Hall Party* radio and TV series from 1953-60. Father of actor John Ritter (died 9/11/2003, age 54).

OPRY: 1965

DEBUT	PEAK	WKS	#	Country Chart Hit	Songwriter	Label (& Number)
				TEX RITTER and His Texans:		
11/11/44	❶^{6}	20	1	**I'm Wastin' My Tears On You /**	*Frank Harford/Tex Ritter*	
11/11/44+	2^{1}	22	2	**There's A New Moon Over My Shoulder**	*Lee Blastic/Jimmie Davis/Ekko Whelan*	Capitol 174
12/16/44+	2^{2}	23	3	**Jealous Heart**	*Jenny Lou Carson*	Capitol 179
8/4/45	❶^{11}	20	4	**You Two Timed Me One Time Too Often**	*Jenny Lou Carson*	Capitol 206
				TEX RITTER:		
12/8/45+	❶^{3}	7	5	**You Will Have To Pay /**	*Sarah Jane Cooper/Bonnie Dodd/Tex Ritter*	
12/29/45+	2^{1}	3	6	**Christmas Carols By The Old Corral**	*Archie Gottler/Johnny Lange* [X]	Capitol 223
5/18/46	5	6	7	**Long Time Gone**	*Frank Harford/Tex Ritter*	Capitol 253
10/19/46	3^{1}	10	8	**When You Leave Don't Slam The Door /**	*Joe Allison*	
12/7/46	3^{1}	2	9	**Have I Told You Lately That I Love You**	*Scott Wiseman*	Capitol 296
3/13/48	9	1	10	**Rye Whiskey**	*(traditional)*	Capitol Amer. 40084
6/12/48	10	7	11	**Deck Of Cards**	S:10 / J:13 *"T" Texas Tyler* [S]	Capitol Amer. 40114
6/12/48	15	1	12	**Pecos Bill** *[w/ Andy Parker & The Plainsmen]* — from the movie *Melody Time* starring **Roy Rogers**	J:15 *Eliot Daniel/Johnny Lange*	Capitol Amer. 40106
7/10/48	5	7	13	**Rock And Rye**	S:5 / J:8 *Edith Bergdahl/Frank Harford/Tex Ritter* [N]	Capitol 15119
11/18/50	6	3	14	**Daddy's Last Letter** — an actual letter from Private First Class John H. McCormick, a soldier killed in the Korean War	A:6 / S:8 *John McCormick* [S]	Capitol F1267
6/19/61	5	21	15	**I Dreamed Of A Hill-Billy Heaven**	*Eddie Dean/Hal Southern* [S]	Capitol 4567
3/5/66	50	1	16	**The Men In My Little Girl's Life**	*Mary Candy/Eddie Deane/Gloria Shayne* [S]	Capitol 5574
3/25/67	13	15	17	**Just Beyond The Moon**	*Jeremy Slate*	Capitol 5839
9/30/67	59	3	18	**A Working Man's Prayer**	*Ed Bruce*	Capitol 5966
8/17/68	69	4	19	**Texas**	*Cindy Walker*	Capitol 2232
2/8/69	53	6	20	**A Funny Thing Happened (On The Way To Miami)**	*Bobby Braddock/Curly Putman*	Capitol 2388
7/26/69	39	10	21	**Growin' Up**	*Alex Barris*	Capitol 2541
6/6/70	57	8	22	**Green Green Valley**	*Bill Anderson*	Capitol 2815
9/18/71	67	3	23	**Fall Away**	*Boudleaux Bryant/Felice Bryant*	Capitol 3154
11/18/72	67	5	24	**Comin' After Jinny**	*Shel Silverstein*	Capitol 3457
1/26/74	35	8	25	**The Americans (A Canadian's Opinion)**	*Gordon Sinclair* [S]	Capitol 3814

RIVER ROAD

Group from Louisiana: Steve Grisaffe (vocals, bass), Tony Ardoin (guitar), Charles Ventre (keyboards), Richard Comeaux (steel guitar) and Mike Burch (drums).

DEBUT	PEAK	WKS	#	Country Chart Hit	Songwriter	Label (& Number)
5/10/97	48	14	1	**I Broke It, I'll Fix It**	*Buzz Cason/Byron Hill*	Capitol
8/23/97	37	17	2	**Nickajack**	S:23 *Steve Bogard/Steve Cumutte/Matt Maher*	Capitol
12/13/97+	51	10	3	**Somebody Will** — above 3 from the album *River Road* on Capitol 53052	*Walt Aldridge/Brad Crisler/Steven Jones*	Capitol
3/18/00	45	14	4	**Breathless** — from the album *Somethin' In The Water* on Virgin 48962	S:24 *Kent Blazy/Kelly Shiver/Neil Thrasher*	Virgin

RIVERS, Eddie

Born in Beaver Dam, Wisconsin. Male singer/guitarist.

DEBUT	PEAK	WKS	#	Country Chart Hit	Songwriter	Label (& Number)
4/30/77	98	2	1	**Open Up Your Door**	*Charles Fields/Don Riis*	Charta 102
6/10/89	93	1	2	**You Won The Battle**	*Doug Erickson/Joan Walker*	Charta 218

RIVERS, Jack

Born on 12/16/1917 in Los Angeles, California. Died on 2/11/1989 (age 71). Male singer/guitarist.

DEBUT	PEAK	WKS	#	Country Chart Hit	Songwriter	Label (& Number)
9/18/48	12	2		**Dear Oakie**	J:12 *Doye O'Dell/Rudy Sooter*	Capitol 15169

RIVERS, Johnny

Born John Ramistella on 11/7/1942 in Brooklyn, New York; raised in Baton Rouge, Louisiana. Singer/songwriter/guitarist.

DEBUT	PEAK	WKS	#	Country Chart Hit	Songwriter	Label (& Number)
6/29/74	58	8		**Six Days On The Road**	*Earl Green/Carl Montgomery*	Atlantic 3028

ROBBINS, Dennis

Born in Hazelwood, North Carolina. Male singer/songwriter/guitarist. Former member of the rock group Rockets. Lead singer of **Billy Hill**.

DEBUT	PEAK	WKS	#	Country Chart Hit	Songwriter	Label (& Number)
1/17/87	63	8	1	**Long Gone Lonesome Blues**	*Hank Williams Sr.*	MCA 52987
10/3/87	71	9	2	**Two Of A Kind (Workin' On A Full House)**	*Bobby Boyd/Warren Haynes/Dennis Robbins*	MCA 53143
5/9/92	34	20	3	**Home Sweet Home**	*Dennis Robbins*	Giant
9/5/92	59	6	4	**My Side Of Town** — above 2 from album *Man With A Plan* on Giant 24458	*Bob DiPiero/Dennis Robbins/John Scott Sherrill*	Giant
1/15/94	68	4	5	**Mona Lisa On Cruise Control** — from the album *Born Ready* on Giant 24543	*Michael Ehmig/Dennis Robbins/John Scott Sherrill*	Giant

Billboard DEBUT	PEAK	WKS	GOLD	#	ARTIST / Country Chart Hit	Ranking	Songwriter	Label (& Number)

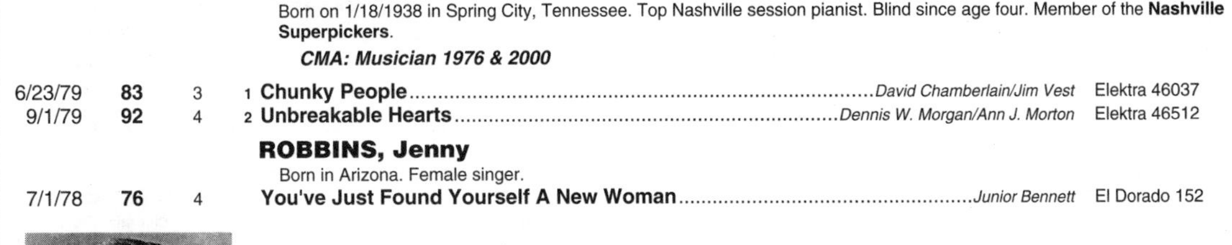

ROBBINS, Hargus "Pig"

Born on 1/18/1938 in Spring City, Tennessee. Top Nashville session pianist. Blind since age four. Member of the **Nashville Superpickers**.

CMA: Musician 1976 & 2000

DEBUT	PEAK	WKS	GOLD	#	Country Chart Hit		Songwriter	Label (& Number)
6/23/79	**83**	3		1	**Chunky People**		*David Chamberlain/Jim Vest*	Elektra 46037
9/1/79	**92**	4		2	**Unbreakable Hearts**		*Dennis W. Morgan/Ann J. Morton*	Elektra 46512

ROBBINS, Jenny

Born in Arizona. Female singer.

DEBUT	PEAK	WKS	GOLD	#	Country Chart Hit		Songwriter	Label (& Number)
7/1/78	**76**	4			**You've Just Found Yourself A New Woman**		*Junior Bennett*	El Dorado 152

ROBBINS, Marty   1950s: #15 / 1960s: #6 / 1970s: #28 / All-Time: #14 // HOF: 1982

Born Martin David Robinson on 9/26/1925 in Glendale, Arizona. Died of heart failure on 12/8/1982 (age 57). Male singer/songwriter/guitarist. Father of **Ronny Robbins**. Served in the U.S. Navy from 1944-47. Hosted *Western Caravan* TV show in Phoenix in 1951. Acted in the movies *Road To Nashville* and *Guns Of A Stranger*. Hosted TV's *Marty Robbins' Spotlight* in 1977.

OPRY: 1953

DEBUT	PEAK	WKS	GOLD	#	Country Chart Hit	Chart	Songwriter	Label (& Number)
12/20/52+	❶^{2}	18		1	**I'll Go On Alone**	A:❶^{2} / S:10	*Marty Robbins*	Columbia 21022
3/28/53	**5**	11		2	**I Couldn't Keep From Crying**	J:5 / S:6 / A:6	*Marty Robbins*	Columbia 21075
7/3/54	**12**	3		3	**Pretty Words**	A:12 / S:14	*Marty Robbins*	Columbia 21246
11/20/54	**14**	1		4	**Call Me Up** (And I'll Come Calling On You)	A:14	*Marty Robbins*	Columbia 21291
1/8/55	**14**	1		5	**Time Goes By**	A:14	*Marty Robbins*	Columbia 21324
2/12/55	**7**	11		6	**That's All Right**	A:7 / S:9	*Arthur Crudup*	Columbia 21351
10/1/55	**9**	7		7	**Maybelline**	A:9	*Chuck Berry/Russ Frato/Alan Freed*	Columbia 21446
9/22/56	❶^{13}	30		8	**Singing The Blues /**	S:❶^{13} / J:❶^{13} / A:❶^{11}	*Melvin Endsley*	
10/6/56	**7**	10		9	**I Can't Quit** (I've Gone Too Far)	A:7	*Marty Robbins*	Columbia 21545
2/2/57	**3**^{1}	15		10	**Knee Deep In The Blues /**	A:3 / S:5 / J:7	*Melvin Endsley*	
3/2/57	**14**	2		11	**The Same Two Lips**	A:14 / S:flip / J:flip	*Marty Robbins*	Columbia 40815
4/20/57	❶^{5}	22	●	12	**A White Sport Coat** (And A Pink Carnation)	S:❶^{5} / J:❶^{5} / A:❶^{1}	*Marty Robbins*	Columbia 40864
9/9/57	**11**	3		13	**Please Don't Blame Me /**	S:11	*Marty Robbins*	
9/9/57	**15**	3		14	**Teen-Age Dream**	S:15 / A:15	*Marty Robbins*	Columbia 40969
11/25/57+	❶^{4}	23		15	**The Story Of My Life**	S:❶^{4} / A:❶^{4}	*Burt Bacharach/Hal David*	Columbia 41013
4/7/58	❶^{2}	25		16	**Just Married /**	A:❶^{2} / S:3	*Al Allen/Barry DeVorzon*	
4/7/58	**2**^{2}	25		17	**Stairway Of Love**	S:2 / A:8	*Roy Bennett/Sid Tepper*	Columbia 41143
8/18/58	**4**	10		18	**She Was Only Seventeen** (He Was One Year More)	S:4 / A:13	*Marty Robbins*	Columbia 41208
12/15/58	**23**	5		19	**Ain't I The Lucky One**		*Melvin Endsley*	Columbia 41282
3/9/59	**15**	9		20	**The Hanging Tree** from the movie starring Gary Cooper		*Mack David/Jerry Livingston*	Columbia 41325
11/9/59	❶^{7}	26		21	**El Paso** **Grammy: Single & Hall of Fame**; also see #73 below		*Marty Robbins*	Columbia 41511
3/21/60	**5**	14		22	**Big Iron**		*Marty Robbins*	Columbia 41589
9/26/60	**26**	4		23	**Five Brothers**		*Tompall Glaser*	Columbia 41771
2/6/61	❶^{10}	19		24	**Don't Worry**		*Marty Robbins*	Columbia 41922
6/5/61	**24**	4		25	**Jimmy Martinez**		*Marty Robbins*	Columbia 42008
9/18/61	**3**^{5}	20		26	**It's Your World**		*Marty Robbins*	Columbia 42065
2/3/62	**12**	13		27	**Sometimes I'm Tempted**		*Marty Robbins*	Columbia 42246
6/2/62	**12**	9		28	**Love Can't Wait**		*Marty Robbins*	Columbia 42375
8/4/62	❶^{8}	21		29	**Devil Woman**		*Marty Robbins*	Columbia 42486
12/8/62+	❶^{1}	14		30	**Ruby Ann**		*Roberta Bellamy*	Columbia 42614
3/23/63	**14**	9		31	**Cigarettes And Coffee Blues**		*Marty Robbins*	Columbia 42701
9/7/63	**13**	11		32	**Not So Long Ago**		*Marty Robbins*	Columbia 42831
11/30/63+	❶^{3}	23		33	**Begging To You**		*Marty Robbins*	Columbia 42890
3/7/64	**15**	11		34	**Girl From Spanish Town**		*Marty Robbins*	Columbia 42968
6/20/64	**3**^{8}	21		35	**The Cowboy In The Continental Suit**		*Marty Robbins*	Columbia 43049
10/31/64	**8**	17		36	**One Of These Days**		*Marty Robbins*	Columbia 43134
4/17/65	❶^{1}	21		37	**Ribbon Of Darkness**		*Gordon Lightfoot*	Columbia 43258
11/13/65	**50**	1		38	**Old Red**		*Marty Robbins*	Columbia 43377
12/4/65+	**21**	10		39	**While You're Dancing**		*Bobby Braddock*	Columbia 43428
2/19/66	**14**	11		40	**Count Me Out /**		*Jeanne Pruett*	
3/5/66	**21**	7		41	**Private Wilson White**		*Marty Robbins*	Columbia 43500
7/9/66	**3**^{1}	18		42	**The Shoe Goes On The Other Foot Tonight**		*Buddy Mize*	Columbia 43680
11/19/66+	**16**	14		43	**Mr. Shorty**		*Marty Robbins*	Columbia 43870
2/4/67	**16**	12		44	**No Tears Milady /**		*Marty Robbins*	
2/25/67	**34**	11		45	**Fly Butterfly Fly**		*Marty Robbins*	Columbia 43845
6/3/67	❶^{1}	16		46	**Tonight Carmen**		*Marty Robbins*	Columbia 44128
9/16/67	**9**	14		47	**Gardenias In Her Hair**		*Joy Byers/Bob Tubert*	Columbia 44271
5/4/68	**10**	15		48	**Love Is In The Air**		*Marty Robbins*	Columbia 44509
10/5/68	❶^{2}	15		49	**I Walk Alone**		*Herbert Wilson*	Columbia 44633
2/8/69	**5**	14		50	**It's A Sin**		*Fred Rose/Zeb Turner*	Columbia 44739

DEBUT	PEAK	WKS	GOLD	#	ARTIST / Country Chart Hit	Ranking / Songwriter	Label (& Number)
					ROBBINS, Marty — cont'd		
7/5/69	8	14		51	**I Can't Say Goodbye**	*Joy Byers/Rink Hardin*	Columbia 44895
11/22/69+	10	13		52	**Camelia**	*Marty Robbins*	Columbia 45024
2/21/70	❶[1]	17		53	**My Woman, My Woman, My Wife** Grammy: Song	*Marty Robbins*	Columbia 45091
9/12/70	7	14		54	**Jolie Girl**	*Greg Fowler*	Columbia 45215
12/19/70+	5	12		55	**Padre**	*Alan Romans/Paul Francis Webster*	Columbia 45273
5/22/71	7	13		56	**The Chair /**	*Marty Robbins*	
6/12/71	flip	8		57	**Seventeen Years**	*Marty Robbins*	Columbia 45377
10/2/71	9	14		58	**Early Morning Sunshine**	*Jay Marshall*	Columbia 45442
1/1/72	6	16		59	**The Best Part Of Living**	*Bill Johnson*	Columbia 45520
9/9/72	32	9		60	**I've Got A Woman's Love**	*Marty Robbins*	Columbia 45668
9/23/72	11	15		61	**This Much A Man**	*Marty Robbins*	Decca 33006
2/17/73	60	7		62	**Laura (What's He Got That I Ain't Got)**	*Leon Ashley/Margie Singleton*	Columbia 45775
3/3/73	6	15		63	**Walking Piece Of Heaven**	*Marty Robbins*	MCA 40012
6/23/73	40	8		64	**A Man And A Train** from the movie *Emperor of The North Pole* starring Lee Marvin	*Hal David/Frank DeVol*	MCA 40067
10/13/73	9	14		65	**Love Me /** also see #93 below	*Jeanne Pruett*	
11/3/73	flip	11		66	**Crawling On My Knees**	*Marty Robbins*	MCA 40134
1/26/74	10	14		67	**Twentieth Century Drifter**	*Marty Robbins*	MCA 40172
5/25/74	12	15		68	**Don't You Think**	*Marty Robbins*	MCA 40236
10/5/74	39	11		69	**Two Gun Daddy**	*Marty Robbins*	MCA 40296
1/18/75	23	12		70	**Life /**	*Marty Robbins*	
5/31/75	76	4		71	**It Takes Faith**	*Marty Robbins*	MCA 40342
7/19/75	55	9		72	**Shotgun Rider**	*Dennis Winters/Don Winters*	MCA 40425
4/17/76	❶[2]	16		73	**El Paso City** sequel to #21 above	*Marty Robbins*	Columbia 10305
9/4/76	❶[1]	14		74	**Among My Souvenirs**	*Edgar Leslie/Horatio Nicholls*	Columbia 10396
2/5/77	4	13		75	**Adios Amigo**	*Ray Girado/Bobby Vinton*	Columbia 10472
5/21/77	10	13		76	**I Don't Know Why (I Just Do)**	*Fred Ahlert/Roy Turk*	Columbia 10536
10/15/77	6	15		77	**Don't Let Me Touch You**	*Marty Robbins/Billy Sherrill*	Columbia 10629
1/28/78	6	13		78	**Return To Me**	*Danny DiMinno/Carmen Lombardo*	Columbia 10673
11/4/78	17	12		79	**Please Don't Play A Love Song**	*Steve Davis/Billy Sherrill*	Columbia 10821
2/17/79	15	13		80	**Touch Me With Magic**	*Steve Bogard/Michael Utley*	Columbia 10905
6/23/79	16	12		81	**All Around Cowboy**	*Marty Robbins*	Columbia 11016
10/13/79	25	10		82	**Buenos Dias Argentina**	*Udo Jurgens/Ben Raleigh*	Columbia 11102
4/12/80	37	9		83	**She's Made Of Faith**	*Marty Robbins*	Columbia 11240
7/12/80	72	5		84	**One Man's Trash (Is Another Man's Treasure)**	*Dennis Winters/Don Winters*	Columbia 11291
11/1/80	28	12		85	**An Occasional Rose**	*Dave Burgess*	Columbia 11372
2/7/81	47	7		86	**Completely Out Of Love**	*Marty Robbins*	Columbia 11425
9/26/81	83	4		87	**Jumper Cable Man**	*Marty Robbins*	Columbia 02444
11/21/81	45	9		88	**Teardrops In My Heart**	*Vaughn Horton*	Columbia 02575
5/22/82	10	18		89	**Some Memories Just Won't Die**	*Bobby Lee Springfield*	Columbia 02854
10/2/82	24	16		90	**Tie Your Dream To Mine**	*Tim DuBois/Sam Lorber/Jeff Silbar/Van Stephenson*	Columbia 03236
12/25/82+	10	17		91	**Honkytonk Man** from the movie starring **Clint Eastwood**	*Dewayne Blackwell*	Warner 29847
3/26/83	48	9		92	**Change Of Heart**	*Randy Sharp*	Columbia 03789
4/16/83	58	8		93	**Love Me** ***[w/ Jeanne Pruett]*** new version of #65 above	*Jeanne Pruett* **[R]**	Audiograph 454
6/11/83	57	9		94	**What If I Said I Love You**	*Charlie Black/Tommy Rocco*	Columbia 03927

Adios Amigo ['77]
Ain't I The Lucky One ['58]
All Around Cowboy ['79]
Among My Souvenirs ['76]
Begging To You ['64]
Best Part Of Living ['72]
Big Iron ['60]
Buenos Dias Argentina ['79]
Call Me Up (And I'll Come Calling On You) ['54]
Camelia ['70]
Chair ['71]
Change Of Heart ['83]
Cigarettes And Coffee Blues ['63]
Completely Out Of Love ['81]
Count Me Out ['66]
Cowboy In The Continental Suit ['64]
Crawling On My Knees ['73]
Devil Woman ['62]
Don't Let Me Touch You ['77]
Don't Worry ['61]
Don't You Think ['74]
Early Morning Sunshine ['71]
El Paso City ['76]
El Paso ['59]
Five Brothers ['60]
Fly Butterfly Fly ['67]
Gardenias In Her Hair ['67]
Girl From Spanish Town ['64]
Hanging Tree ['59]
Honkytonk Man ['83]
I Can't Quit (I've Gone Too Far) ['56]
I Can't Say Goodbye ['69]
I Couldn't Keep From Crying ['53]
I Don't Know Why (I Just Do) ['77]
I Walk Alone ['68]
I'll Go On Alone ['53]
I've Got A Woman's Love ['72]
It Takes Faith ['75]
It's A Sin ['69]
It's Your World ['61]
Jimmy Martinez ['61]
Jolie Girl ['70]
Jumper Cable Man ['81]
Just Married ['58]
Knee Deep In The Blues ['57]
Laura (What's He Got That I Ain't Got) ['73]
Life ['75]
Love Can't Wait ['62]
Love Is In The Air ['68]
Love Me ['73]
Love Me ['83]
Man And A Train ['73]
Maybelline ['55]
Mr. Shorty ['67]
My Woman, My Woman, My Wife ['70]
No Tears Milady ['67]
Not So Long Ago ['63]
Occasional Rose ['80]
Old Red ['65]
One Man's Trash (Is Another Man's Treasure) ['80]
One Of These Days ['64]
Padre ['71]
Please Don't Blame Me ['57]
Please Don't Play A Love Song ['78]
Pretty Words ['54]
Private Wilson White ['66]
Return To Me ['78]
Ribbon Of Darkness ['65]
Ruby Ann ['63]
Same Two Lips ['57]
Seventeen Years ['71]
She Was Only Seventeen (He Was One Year More) ['58]
She's Made Of Faith ['80]
Shoe Goes On The Other Foot Tonight ['66]
Shotgun Rider ['75]
Singing The Blues ['56]
Some Memories Just Won't Die ['82]
Sometimes I'm Tempted ['62]
Stairway Of Love ['58]
Story Of My Life ['58]
Teardrops In My Heart ['81]
Teen-Age Dream ['57]
That's All Right ['55]
This Much A Man ['72]
Tie Your Dream To Mine ['82]
Time Goes By ['55]
Tonight Carmen ['67]
Touch Me With Magic ['79]
Twentieth Century Drifter ['74]
Two Gun Daddy ['74]
Walking Piece Of Heaven ['73]
What If I Said I Love You ['83]
While You're Dancing ['66]
White Sport Coat (And A Pink Carnation) ['57]

DEBUT	PEAK	WKS	GOLD	#	ARTIST / Country Chart Hit	Ranking / Songwriter	Label (& Number)
					ROBBINS, Ronny Born Ronald Robinson on 7/16/1949 in Phoenix, Arizona. Male singer. Son of **Marty Robbins**.		
11/11/78	99	1		1	**The Last Lie I Told Her**	*Paul Melton*	Artic 878
2/24/79	95	1		2	**Why'd The Last Time Have To Be The Best**	*Willis Williams/Reggie Young*	Artic 8782
11/17/79	91	2		3	**I Know I'm Not Your Hero Anymore**	*Frank Dycus/Larry Kingston*	TRC 081
7/21/84	62	7		4	**Those You Lose**	*Sterling Whipple*	Columbia 04506

Billboard DEBUT	PEAK	WKS	GOLD	ARTIST Ranking / Country Chart Hit	Songwriter	Label (& Number)

ROBERTS, Julie

Born on 2/1/1979 in Lancaster, South Carolina. Female singer.

DEBUT	PEAK	WKS	GOLD	Country Chart Hit	Songwriter	Label (& Number)
2/21/04	18	32		1 Break Down Here	S:❶[16] Jess Brown/P.J. Matthews	Mercury
11/6/04	47	9		2 The Chance	Deanna Bryant/Liz Hengber	Mercury
2/19/05	46	8		3 Wake Up Older	Lisa Carver	Mercury

above 3 from the album *Julie Roberts* on Mercury 001902

ROBERTS, Kenny — 1940s: #48

Born George Kingsbury on 10/14/1926 in Lenoir City, Tennessee; raised in Greenfield, Massachusetts. Male singer/songwriter/guitarist. Known for his yodeling.

DEBUT	PEAK	WKS	GOLD	Country Chart Hit	Songwriter	Label (& Number)
9/17/49	4	11	●	1 I Never See Maggie Alone /	J:4 / S:5 Everett Lynton/Harry Tilsley	
10/8/49	15	1		2 Wedding Bells	J:15 Claude Boone	Coral 64012
11/19/49	14	1		3 Jealous Heart	J:14 Jenny Lou Carson	Coral 64021
5/13/50	8	4		4 Choc'late Ice Cream Cone	A:8 / J:10 Famous Lashua	Coral 64032

ROBERTS, Pat

Born on 7/23/1948 in Seattle, Washington. Male singer.

DEBUT	PEAK	WKS	GOLD	Country Chart Hit	Songwriter	Label (& Number)
10/21/72	34	12		1 Rhythm Of The Rain	John Gummoe	Dot 17434
3/3/73	59	8		2 Thanks For Lovin' Me	Ben Peters/George Richey	Dot 17451
7/14/73	79	4		3 Here Comes My Little Baby	Theresa Beaty/Sylvia Richey	Dot 17465
11/3/73	81	5		4 I'm Gonna Keep Searching	George Richey/Carmol Taylor/Norro Wilson	Dot 17478
4/6/74	77	6		5 You Got Everything That You Want	Bobby Fischer/Ricci Mareno	Dot 17495

ROBERTSON, Eck

Born Alexander Robertson on 11/20/1887 in Madison County, Arkansas; raised in Hamlin, Texas. Died on 2/17/1975 (age 87). Folk fiddler. One of the first to record a commercial country music record.

EARLY HITS: Arkansas Traveler (1922; NRR) / Sallie Gooden (1922; NRR)

ROBERTSON, Jack

Born in Houston, Texas. Male singer.

DEBUT	PEAK	WKS	GOLD	Country Chart Hit	Songwriter	Label (& Number)
7/9/88	66	5		It's Not Easy	Chisai Childs	Soundwaves 4808

ROBERTSON, Texas Jim, and The Panhandle Punchers — 1940s: #44

Born on 2/27/1909 in Batesville, Texas. Died on 11/11/1966 (age 57). Male singer/guitarist.

DEBUT	PEAK	WKS	GOLD	Country Chart Hit	Songwriter	Label (& Number)
12/28/46	5	1		1 Filipino Baby /	Billy Cox/Clarke Van Ness	
2/15/47	5	1		2 Rainbow At Midnight	John Miller	RCA Victor 20-1975
2/28/48	8	1		3 Signed, Sealed And Delivered	Cowboy Copas/Lois Mann	RCA Victor 20-2651
1/7/50	13	1		4 Slipping Around	S:13 Floyd Tillman	RCA Victor 48-0071

ROBEY, Loretta

Born on 7/14/1943 in Oviedo, Florida. Female singer/songwriter.

DEBUT	PEAK	WKS	GOLD	Country Chart Hit	Songwriter	Label (& Number)
6/11/77	100	1		Sophisticated Country Lady	Loretta Robey	Soundwaves 4545

ROBIN & CRUISER

Duo of brothers from Tennessee: Robin Gordon and Cruiser Gordon.

DEBUT	PEAK	WKS	GOLD	Country Chart Hit	Songwriter	Label (& Number)
10/24/87	79	4		Rings Of Gold	Gene Thomas	16th Avenue 70404

ROBINSON, Betty Jean

Born in Hyden, Kentucky. Female singer/songwriter.

DEBUT	PEAK	WKS	GOLD	Country Chart Hit	Songwriter	Label (& Number)
4/24/71	51	10		1 All I Need Is You *[w/ Carl Belew]*	Betty Jean Robinson	Decca 32802
11/23/74+	49	10		2 On The Way Home	Betty Jean Robinson	MCA 40300
4/5/75	87	4		3 God Is Good	Billy Burns/Betty Jean Robinson	4 Star 1004

ROBINSON, Sharon

Born in Kansas. Female singer.

DEBUT	PEAK	WKS	GOLD	Country Chart Hit	Songwriter	Label (& Number)
12/26/87	86	4		Have You Hurt Any Good Ones Lately	Walt Aldridge/Stan Paulk	Nightfall 001

ROBISON, Carson — 1940s: #50

Born on 8/4/1890 in Oswego, Kansas. Died on 3/24/1957 (age 66). Singer/songwriter/guitarist. Known as "The Kansas Jaybird."

EARLY HITS: Way Down Home [w/ Gene Austin] (1925) / My Carolina Home (1927) / When Your Hair Has Turned To Silver [w/ Frank Luther] (1931) / Mussolini's Letter To Hitler (1942)

DEBUT	PEAK	WKS	GOLD	Country Chart Hit	Songwriter	Label (& Number)
6/30/45	5	1		1 Hitler's Last Letter To Hirohito	Carson Robison [N]	Victor 20-1665
8/14/48	3[2]	28		2 Life Gits Tee-Jus Don't It *[w/ His Pleasant Valley Boys]*	S:3 / J:3 Carson Robison [N]	MGM 10224

ROBISON, Charlie

Born in Houston, Texas; raised in Bandera, Texas. Male singer/songwriter/guitarist. Married Emily Erwin of the **Dixie Chicks** on 5/1/1999.

DEBUT	PEAK	WKS	GOLD	Country Chart Hit	Songwriter	Label (& Number)
1/16/99	60	20		1 Barlight	Charlie Robison	Lucky Dog
11/20/99+	65	13		2 My Hometown	Charlie Robison	Lucky Dog
4/8/00	67	1		3 Poor Man's Son	Charlie Robison	Lucky Dog
				above 3 from the album *Life Of The Party* on Lucky Dog 69327		
3/31/01	35	20		4 I Want You Bad	S:8 Terry Adams/Phil Crandon	Columbia
				from the album *Step Right Up* on Columbia 61404		
5/17/03	58	1		5 Walter	Jay Knowles/Cory Mayo	Columbia
				from the album *Live* on Columbia 86787		

ROCKINHORSE

Group from Oakland, Minnesota. Led by female singer Toni Rose.

DEBUT	PEAK	WKS	GOLD	Country Chart Hit	Songwriter	Label (& Number)
8/30/86	68	6		1 Have I Got A Heart For You	Marvin Morrow/Keith Stegall	Long Shot 1002
12/6/86	86	3		2 Let A Little Love In (Tennessee Saturday Night)	Don Hair	Long Shot 1003

DEBUT	PEAK	WKS	GOLD	ARTIST / Country Chart Hit ... Songwriter	Label (& Number)

ROCKIN' SIDNEY

Born Sidney Simien on 4/9/1938 in Lebeau, Louisiana. Died of cancer on 2/25/1998 (age 59). Black singer/songwriter/accordianist.

DEBUT	PEAK	WKS	GOLD	Country Chart Hit ... Songwriter	Label (& Number)
6/22/85	**19**	20		**My Toot-Toot** ... S:8 / A:23 *Sidney Simien*	Epic 05430

RODGERS, Jimmie — 1950s: #45 // HOF: 1961

Born on 9/8/1897 in Meridian, Mississippi. Died of tuberculosis on 5/26/1933 (age 35). Male singer/songwriter/guitarist. Known as "America's Blue Yodeler," "The Singing Brakeman," and "The Father of Country Music." Inducted into the Rock and Roll Hall of Fame in 1986 as an early influence of rock and roll.

EARLY HITS: Blue Yodel [T For Texas] (1927; NRR) / In The Jail House Now (1928) / The Brakeman's Blues (1928) / Waiting For A Train (1929) / Blue Yodel No. 8 [Mule Skinner Blues] (1931)

DEBUT	PEAK	WKS	GOLD	Country Chart Hit ... Songwriter	Label (& Number)
5/14/55	**7**	12		**In The Jailhouse Now No. 2** ... J:7 / S:8 / A:9 *Jimmie Rodgers* **JIMMIE RODGERS and the Rainbow Ranch Boys** recorded in 1930 on Victor 22523; new overdubbed backing includes **Chet Atkins** and **Hank Snow**	RCA Victor 6092

RODGERS, Jimmie

Born on 9/18/1933 in Camas, Washington. Male singer/guitarist. Hosted own TV series in 1959 and 1969.

DEBUT	PEAK	WKS	GOLD	Country Chart Hit ... Songwriter	Label (& Number)
10/14/57	**7**	13	●	1 **Honeycomb** ... S:7 / A:11 *Bob Merrill*	Roulette 4015
12/2/57	**6**	16	●	2 **Kisses Sweeter Than Wine** ... S:6 / A:8 *Ronnie Gilbert/Lee Hays/Fred Hellerman/Huddie Ledbetter/Pete Seeger*	Roulette 4031
3/3/58	**5**	11	●	3 **Oh-Oh, I'm Falling In Love Again** S:5 / A:15 *Al Hoffman/Dick Manning/Mark Markwell*	Roulette 4045
5/19/58	**5**	17	●	4 **Secretly** / ... S:5 / A:14 *Al Hoffman/Dick Manning/Mark Markwell* also see #9 below	
5/19/58	**flip**	9		5 **Make Me A Miracle** ... S:flip *Al Hoffman/Dick Manning/Mark Markwell*	Roulette 4070
8/25/58	**13**	8		6 **Are You Really Mine** ... S:13 *Al Hoffman/Dick Manning/Mark Markwell*	Roulette 4090
10/29/77	**67**	10		7 **A Good Woman Likes To Drink With The Boys** ... *Dave Ellingson*	ScrimShaw 1313
2/11/78	**74**	5		8 **Everytime I Sing A Love Song** ... *Phyllis Molinary/Gloria Sklerov*	ScrimShaw 1314
9/23/78	**65**	5		9 **Secretly** ... *Al Hoffman/Dick Manning/Mark Markwell* **[R]** new version of #4 above	ScrimShaw 1318
3/17/79	**89**	4		10 **Easy To Love** / ... *Ed Martinez/Ron Wilkins*	
3/17/79	**flip**	4		11 **Easy** *[w/ Michele]* ... *Jerry Fuller*	ScrimShaw 1319

RODMAN, Judy

Born Judy Mae Robbins on 5/23/1951 in Riverside, California; raised in Miami and Jacksonville, Florida. Female singer/songwriter/guitarist. Former jingle and session singer.

DEBUT	PEAK	WKS	GOLD	Country Chart Hit ... Songwriter	Label (& Number)
3/23/85	**40**	14		1 **I've Been Had By Love Before** ... *Tom Damphier*	MTM 72050
8/10/85	**33**	14		2 **You're Gonna Miss Me When I'm Gone** ... *Hugh Prestwood*	MTM 72054
11/16/85+	**30**	17		3 **I Sure Need Your Lovin'** ... A:29 *Billy Aerts/Judy Rodman*	MTM 72061
4/5/86	❶^{1}	25		4 **Until I Met You** A:❶^{1} / S:2 *Hank Riddle*	MTM 72065
10/4/86+	**9**	21		5 **She Thinks That She'll Marry** ... S:9 / A:10 *DeWayne Orender/Judy Rodman*	MTM 72076
2/21/87	**7**	17		6 **Girls Ride Horses Too** ... S:2 / A:7 *Alice Randall/Mark D. Sanders*	MTM 72083
6/20/87	**5**	27		7 **I'll Be Your Baby Tonight** ... S:3 *Bob Dylan*	MTM 72089
10/31/87+	**18**	21		8 **I Want A Love Like That** ... S:19 *Janis Ian/Thom Schuyler*	MTM 72092
5/21/88	**43**	9		9 **Goin' To Work** ... *Bill Lloyd/Pam Tillis*	MTM 72105
8/13/88	**45**	9		10 **I Can Love You** ... *Gary Scruggs*	MTM 72112

RODRIGUEZ, Johnny — 1970s: #29 / All-Time: #80

Born Juan Rodriguez on 12/10/1951 in Sabinal, Texas. Male singer/songwriter/guitarist. Performed with high school rock band in the late 1960s. Worked with the **Tom T. Hall** band from 1971-72. First recorded solo in 1972. Also see **Tomorrow's World**.

DEBUT	PEAK	WKS	GOLD	Country Chart Hit ... Songwriter	Label (& Number)
11/11/72+	**9**	18		1 **Pass Me By (If You're Only Passing Through)** ... *Hillman Hall*	Mercury 73334
3/31/73	❶^{1}	16		2 **You Always Come Back (To Hurting Me)** *Tom T. Hall/Johnny Rodriguez*	Mercury 73368
8/18/73	❶^{2}	17		3 **Ridin' My Thumb To Mexico** *Johnny Rodriguez*	Mercury 73416
12/29/73+	❶^{1}	14		4 **That's The Way Love Goes** *Lefty Frizzell/Whitey Shafer*	Mercury 73446
3/30/74	**6**	14		5 **Something** ... *George Harrison*	Mercury 73471
7/13/74	**2^{1}**	13		6 **Dance With Me (Just One More Time)** ... *Johnny Rodriguez*	Mercury 73493
10/19/74	**3^{2}**	13		7 **We're Over** ... *Barry Mann/Cynthia Weil*	Mercury 73621
2/8/75	❶^{1}	12		8 **I Just Can't Get Her Out Of My Mind** *Larry Gatlin*	Mercury 73659
5/24/75	❶^{1}	18		9 **Just Get Up And Close The Door** *Linda Hargrove*	Mercury 73682
10/4/75	❶^{1}	15		10 **Love Put A Song In My Heart** *Ben Peters*	Mercury 73715
2/28/76	**3^{2}**	15		11 **I Couldn't Be Me Without You** ... *Billy Joe Shaver*	Mercury 73769
7/10/76	**2^{2}**	13		12 **I Wonder If I Ever Said Goodbye** ... *Mickey Newbury*	Mercury 73815
10/9/76	**5**	14		13 **Hillbilly Heart** ... *Johnny Christopher/Dan Penn*	Mercury 73855
1/15/77	**5**	14		14 **Desperado** ... *Glenn Frey/Don Henley*	Mercury 73878
5/14/77	**5**	13		15 **If Practice Makes Perfect** ... *Larry Gatlin*	Mercury 73914
9/3/77	**25**	10		16 **Eres Tu** ... *Juan Carlos Calderon* **[F]**	Mercury 55004
11/5/77	**14**	13		17 **Savin' This Love Song For You** ... *Linda Hargrove*	Mercury 55012
2/25/78	**7**	14		18 **We Believe In Happy Endings** ... *Bob McDill*	Mercury 55020
7/8/78	**7**	13		19 **Love Me With All Your Heart (Cuando Calienta El Sol)** ... *Carlos Rigual/Mario Rigual/Michael Vaughn*	Mercury 55029
12/16/78+	**16**	13		20 **Alibis** ... *Pat Killough/Rock Killough*	Mercury 55050

DEBUT	PEAK	WKS	GOLD	ARTIST Ranking Country Chart Hit	Songwriter	Label (& Number)

RODRIGUEZ, Johnny — cont'd

DEBUT	PEAK	WKS	GOLD	#	Country Chart Hit	Songwriter	Label (& Number)
3/10/79	**6**	14		21	**Down On The Rio Grande**	*Bill Boling/Johnny Rodriguez/Doug Teasley*	Epic 50671
7/7/79	**17**	13		22	**Fools For Each Other**	*Bill Boling/Johnny Rodriguez*	Epic 50735
10/20/79	**16**	14		23	**I Hate The Way I Love It** *[w/ Charly McClain]*	*Ava Aldridge*	Epic 50791
11/24/79+	**19**	14		24	**What'll I Tell Virginia**	*Bob McDill*	Epic 50808
4/5/80	**29**	11		25	**Love, Look At Us Now**	*Mickey Newbury*	Epic 50859
9/20/80	**17**	16		26	**North Of The Border**	*Steve Davis/Billy Sherrill*	Epic 50932
4/11/81	**22**	13		27	**I Want You Tonight**	*Steve Davis*	Epic 01033
8/8/81	**30**	11		28	**Trying Not To Love You**	*Merle Haggard*	Epic 02411
12/5/81	**73**	7		29	**It's Not The Same Old You /**	*Richard Kerr/Troy Seals*	
2/13/82	**66**	6		30	**Born With The Blues**	*Johnny Rodriguez*	Epic 02638
11/27/82	**89**	3		31	**He's Not Entitled To Your Love**	*Steve Davis/Sam Hogin/Bobby Whitlock*	Epic 03275
2/26/83	**4**	20		32	**Foolin'**	*Ralph Mooney*	Epic 03598
7/9/83	**6**	21		33	**How Could I Love Her So Much**	*Hugh Moffatt*	Epic 03972
11/19/83+	**35**	12		34	**Back On Her Mind Again**	*Johnny Rodriguez*	Epic 04206
1/28/84	**15**	17		35	**Too Late To Go Home**	*Len Chera*	Epic 04336
5/19/84	**30**	15		36	**Let's Leave The Lights On Tonight**	*Rory Bourke/Bob McDill*	Epic 04460
8/18/84	**63**	7		37	**First Time Burned**	*Jim McBride*	Epic 04562
10/13/84	**60**	8		38	**Rose Of My Heart**	*Hugh Moffatt*	Epic 04628
4/6/85	**69**	7		39	**Here I Am Again**	*Shel Silverstein*	Epic 04838
12/28/85+	**51**	15		40	**She Don't Cry Like She Used To**	*Frank Saulino/Jim Valentini*	Epic 05732
12/12/87+	**12**	26		41	**I Didn't** (Every Chance I Had) S:25	*Bobby Barker/Keith Palmer*	Capitol 44071
7/16/88	**41**	15		42	**I Wanta Wake Up With You**	*Ben Peters*	Capitol 44204
10/15/88	**44**	10		43	**You Might Want To Use Me Again**	*Bobby Barker/Keith Palmer*	Capitol 44245
2/18/89	**72**	4		44	**No Chance To Dance**	*Bob DiPiero/Dennis Robbins/John Scott Sherrill*	Capitol 44325
8/5/89	**78**	3		45	**Back To Stay**	*Johnny Rodriguez/Keith Stegall*	Capitol 44403

ROE, Marlys

Born in Brookings, South Dakota. Female singer.

DEBUT	PEAK	WKS	GOLD	#	Country Chart Hit	Songwriter	Label (& Number)
8/11/73	**71**	9			**Carry Me Back**	*Dan Hoffman/Chuck Woolery*	GRC 1002

ROE, Tommy

Born on 5/9/1942 in Atlanta, Georgia. Male singer/songwriter/guitarist.

DEBUT	PEAK	WKS	GOLD	#	Country Chart Hit	Songwriter	Label (& Number)
6/9/73	**73**	2		1	**Working Class Hero**	*Tommy Roe*	MGM South 7013
5/19/79	**77**	3		2	**Massachusetts**	*Barry Gibb/Maurice Gibb/Robin Gibb*	Warner/Curb 8800
10/27/79	**70**	4		3	**You Better Move On**	*Arthur Alexander*	Warner/Curb 49085
6/21/80	**87**	3		4	**Charlie, I Love Your Wife**	*Joel Hirschhorn/Al Kasha/Michael Lloyd*	Warner/Curb 49235
11/16/85	**57**	11		5	**Some Such Foolishness**	*Roger Wade*	Curb/MCA 52711
3/1/86	**51**	7		6	**Radio Romance**	*Ken Bell/Mickey Buckins*	Curb/MCA 52778
12/20/86+	**38**	14		7	**Let's Be Fools Like That Again**	*Lewis Anderson*	Mercury 888206
5/23/87	**67**	5		8	**Back When It Really Mattered**	*Jerry Careaga/John Jarvis*	Mercury 888497

ROGERS, Dann

Born in Houston, Texas. Male singer/songwriter. Nephew of **Kenny Rogers**.

DEBUT	PEAK	WKS	GOLD	#	Country Chart Hit	Songwriter	Label (& Number)
9/5/87	**78**	3			**Just A Kid From Texas**	*Steve Diamond/Dann Rogers/Russell Smith*	MCA 53133

ROGERS, David **All-Time: #172**

Born on 3/27/1936 in Atlanta, Georgia. Died on 8/10/1993 (age 57). Male singer/songwriter/guitarist. Worked clubs in Atlanta from 1952-67 (including six years at the Egyptian Ballroom). Worked on the WWVA-Wheeling *Jamboree* in 1967.

DEBUT	PEAK	WKS	GOLD	#	Country Chart Hit	Songwriter	Label (& Number)
3/2/68	**69**	5		1	**I'd Be Your Fool Again**	*Jimmy Lewallen/David Rogers*	Columbia 44430
7/20/68	**38**	11		2	**I'm In Love With My Wife**	*Hank Mills*	Columbia 44561
11/16/68+	**37**	13		3	**You Touched My Heart**	*Merle Kilgore/Bob Tubert*	Columbia 44668
5/17/69	**59**	7		4	**Dearly Beloved**	*Vic McAlpin*	Columbia 44796
11/22/69+	**23**	12		5	**A World Called You**	*Rhett Davis*	Columbia 45007
5/9/70	**46**	9		6	**So Much In Love With You**	*Vic McAlpin*	Columbia 45111
10/17/70	**26**	11		7	**I Wake Up In Heaven**	*Larry Kingston*	Columbia 45226
5/29/71	**19**	15		8	**She Don't Make Me Cry**	*Sorrells Pickard*	Columbia 45383
11/13/71+	**21**	13		9	**Ruby You're Warm**	*Dave Kirby*	Columbia 45478
2/26/72	**9**	15		10	**Need You**	*Buddy Wheeler*	Columbia 45551
8/5/72	**38**	9		11	**Goodbye**	*Bobby Russell*	Columbia 45642
11/11/72	**35**	11		12	**All Heaven Breaks Loose**	*Gayle Barnhill/Rory Bourke*	Columbia 45714
4/28/73	**17**	12		13	**Just Thank Me**	*Doug Ashdown/Jimmy Stewart*	Atlantic 2957
8/25/73	**22**	12		14	**It'll Be Her**	*Billy Ray Reynolds*	Atlantic 4005
1/5/74	**9**	14		15	**Loving You Has Changed My Life**	*Jerry Foster/Bill Rice*	Atlantic 4012
5/25/74	**21**	13		16	**Hey There Girl**	*Jerry Foster/Bill Rice*	Atlantic 4022
9/28/74	**59**	7		17	**I Just Can't Help Believin'**	*Barry Mann/Cynthia Weil*	Atlantic 4204
4/12/75	**60**	8		18	**It Takes A Whole Lotta Livin' In A House**	*Gary S. Paxton*	United Artists 617
8/7/76	**66**	7		19	**Whispers And Grins**	*Larry Shoberg*	Republic 256
11/6/76	**84**	6		20	**Mahogany Bridge**	*Rick Klang/Don Pfrimmer*	Republic 311

DEBUT	PEAK	WKS	GOLD	Ranking	ARTIST / Country Chart Hit	Songwriter	Label (& Number)
					ROGERS, David — cont'd		
1/15/77	**21**	12		21	**I'm Gonna Love You Right Out Of This World**	*Dave Burgess/Don Pfrimmer*	Republic 343
4/30/77	**76**	4		22	**The Lady And The Baby**	*Rick Klang/Don Pfrimmer*	Republic 382
6/18/77	**49**	7		23	**I Love What My Woman Does To Me**	*Rick Klang/Billy Thunderkloud*	Republic 001
9/3/77	**47**	8		24	**Do You Hear My Heart Beat**	*Dave Burgess/Don Pfrimmer*	Republic 006
11/26/77+	**24**	12		25	**You And Me Alone**	*Rick Klang/Don Pfrimmer*	Republic 011
2/25/78	**22**	12		26	**I'll Be There (When You Get Lonely)**	*Dave Burgess*	Republic 015
5/27/78	**32**	10		27	**Let's Try To Remember**	*Don Pfrimmer/David Rogers*	Republic 020
9/9/78	**31**	9		28	**When A Woman Cries**	*Betty Duke/Sammy Lyons*	Republic 029
3/3/79	**18**	14		29	**Darlin'**	*Oscar Blandemer*	Republic 038
7/14/79	**36**	8		30	**You Are My Rainbow**	*R.C. Bannon/Harlan Sanders*	Republic 042
12/15/79+	**39**	9		31	**You're Amazing**	*Tom Grant*	Republic 048
5/23/81	**88**	3		32	**Houston Blue**	*Jim McBride*	Kari 120
11/6/82	**92**	2		33	**Crown Prince Of The Barroom**	*Harold Shields*	Music Master 012
2/19/83	**67**	7		34	**Hold Me**	*Vince Rundus/Harold Shields*	Music Master 1004
6/4/83	**71**	5		35	**You've Still Got Me**	*Harold Shields*	Mr. Music 016
11/12/83	**87**	4		36	**The Devil Is A Woman**	*Bobby Borchers/Howard Goff*	Mr. Music 018
3/3/84	**72**	4		37	**I'm A Country Song**	*Jonmark Stone*	Hal Kat Kountry 2083
					ROGERS, James Born on 12/22/1949 in Chattanooga, Tennessee; raised in Fort Oglethorpe, Georgia. Male singer/songwriter.		
12/9/89	**72**	5			**Something's Got A Hold On Me**	*James Rogers*	Soundwaves 4830
					ROGERS, Jesse, and his '49ers Born on 3/5/1911 in Waynesboro, Mississippi. Died in December 1973 (age 62). Male singer.		
9/10/49	**15**	1			**Wedding Bells**	J:15 *Claude Boone*	Bluebird 32-0002

ROGERS, Kenny **1980s: #4 / 2000s: #45 / All-Time: #27**

Born on 8/21/1938 in Houston, Texas. Male singer/songwriter/guitarist/actor. Member of the Kirby Stone Four and The New Christy Minstrels in the mid-1960s. Formed **The First Edition** in 1967. Went solo in 1973. Starred in the movie *Six Pack* and several TV movies including *The Gambler*, *Coward Of The County*, *Wild Horses* and *Rio Diablo*. Formerly married to Marianne Gordon of TV's *Hee-Haw*. Uncle of **Dann Rogers**. Also see **America The Beautiful** and **USA For Africa**.

CMA: Vocal Duo (with Dottie West) 1978 & 1979 / Male Vocalist 1979

DEBUT	PEAK	WKS	GOLD	Ranking	ARTIST / Country Chart Hit	Songwriter	Label (& Number)
					KENNY ROGERS AND THE FIRST EDITION:		
7/19/69	**39**	11		1	**Ruby, Don't Take Your Love To Town**	*Mel Tillis*	Reprise 0829
10/25/69	**46**	8		2	**Ruben James**	*Barry Etris/Alex Harvey*	Reprise 0854
7/14/73	**69**	6		3	**Today I Started Loving You Again**	*Merle Haggard/Bonnie Owens*	Jolly Rogers 1004
					KENNY ROGERS:		
12/13/75+	**19**	13		4	**Love Lifted Me**	*William Rowe*	United Artists 746
6/26/76	**46**	12		5	**While The Feeling's Good**	*Roger Bowling/Freddie Hart*	United Artists 812
10/9/76	**19**	13		6	**Laura (What's He Got That I Ain't Got?)**	*Leon Ashley/Margie Singleton*	United Artists 868
1/29/77	❶[2]	20	●	7	**Lucille** Grammy: Male Vocal / CMA: Single	*Roger Bowling/Hal Bynum*	United Artists 929
8/6/77	❶[1]	14		8	**Daytime Friends**	*Ben Peters*	United Artists 1027
10/22/77	**9**	15		9	**Sweet Music Man**	*Kenny Rogers*	United Artists 1095
2/18/78	❶[2]	17		10	**Every Time Two Fools Collide** *[w/ Dottie West]*	*Jan Dyer/Jeff Tweel*	United Artists 1137
6/3/78	❶[1]	14		11	**Love Or Something Like It**	*Steve Glassmeyer/Kenny Rogers*	United Artists 1210
9/2/78	**2**[1]	14		12	**Anyone Who Isn't Me Tonight** *[w/ Dottie West]*	*Julie Didier/Casey Kelly*	United Artists 1234
10/28/78	❶[3]	16		13	**The Gambler** Grammy: Song & Male Vocal	*Don Schlitz*	United Artists 1250
2/17/79	❶[1]	15		14	**All I Ever Need Is You** *[w/ Dottie West]*	*Jimmy Holiday/Eddie Reeves*	United Artists 1276
4/21/79	❶[2]	16	●	15	**She Believes In Me**	*Steve Gibb*	United Artists 1273
7/7/79	**3**[1]	15		16	**Til I Can Make It On My Own** *[w/ Dottie West]*	*George Richey/Billy Sherrill/Tammy Wynette*	United Artists 1299
9/15/79	❶[2]	12		17	**You Decorated My Life** Grammy: Song	*Debbie Hupp/Bob Morrison*	United Artists 1315
11/17/79+	❶[3]	15	●	18	**Coward Of The County**	*Roger Bowling/Billy Edd Wheeler*	United Artists 1327
4/5/80	**3**[3]	14		19	**Don't Fall In Love With A Dreamer** *[w/ Kim Carnes]*	*Kim Carnes/Dave Ellingson*	United Artists 1345
6/28/80	**4**	14		20	**Love The World Away** from the movie *Urban Cowboy* starring John Travolta	*Bob Morrison/Johnny Wilson*	United Artists 1359
10/11/80	❶[1]	14	●	21	**Lady**	*Lionel Richie*	Liberty 1380
4/4/81	❶[1]	15		22	**What Are We Doin' In Love** *[w/ Dottie West]*	*Randy Goodrum*	Liberty 1404
6/20/81	❶[2]	15		23	**I Don't Need You**	*Rick Christian*	Liberty 1415
9/12/81	**5**	14		24	**Share Your Love With Me**	*Al Braggs/Deadric Malone*	Liberty 1430
11/14/81+	**9**	16		25	**Blaze Of Glory**	*Larry Keith/Danny Morrison/Johnny Slate*	Liberty 1441
1/30/82	**5**	16		26	**Through The Years**	*Steve Dorff/Marty Panzer*	Liberty 1444
7/10/82	❶[1]	16		27	**Love Will Turn You Around** from the movie *Six Pack* starring Rogers	*David Malloy/Kenny Rogers/Thom Schuyler/Even Stevens*	Liberty 1471
10/16/82	**3**[3]	17		28	**A Love Song**	*Lee Greenwood*	Liberty 1485
1/29/83	❶[1]	17		29	**We've Got Tonight** *[w/ Sheena Easton]*	*Bob Seger*	Liberty 1492
5/7/83	**13**	17		30	**All My Life**	*Dave Robbins/Jeff Silbar/Van Stephenson*	Liberty 1495
7/30/83	**5**	18		31	**Scarlet Fever**	*Mike Dekle*	Liberty 1503

Billboard DEBUT	PEAK	WKS	GOLD		ARTIST Country Chart Hit	Ranking Songwriter	Label (& Number)
					ROGERS, Kenny — cont'd		
9/3/83	❶[2]	23	▲	32	**Islands In The Stream** *[w/ Dolly Parton]*	*Barry Gibb/Maurice Gibb/Robin Gibb*	RCA 13615
11/19/83+	**20**	17		33	**You Were A Good Friend**	*Kim Carnes/Dave Ellingson*	Liberty 1511
1/14/84	**3**[1]	17		34	**Buried Treasure**	*Barry Gibb/Maurice Gibb/Robin Gibb*	RCA 13710
3/24/84	**19**	15		35	**Together Again** *[w/ Dottie West]*	*Buck Owens*	Liberty 1516
4/21/84	**30**	13		36	**Eyes That See In The Dark**	*Barry Gibb/Maurice Gibb*	RCA 13774
6/30/84	**11**	19		37	**Evening Star /**	*Barry Gibb/Maurice Gibb*	
8/4/84	**flip**	14		38	**Midsummer Nights**	*Albhy Galuten/Barry Gibb*	RCA 13832
11/10/84	**70**	10		39	**What About Me?** *[w/ Kim Carnes & James Ingram]*	*David Foster/Richard Marx/Kenny Rogers*	RCA 13899
12/15/84+	**53**	7		40	**The Greatest Gift Of All** *[w/ Dolly Parton]*	*John Jarvis* **[X]**	RCA 13945
12/22/84+	❶[1]	21		41	**Crazy**	S:❶[1] / A:❶[1] *Richard Marx/Kenny Rogers*	RCA 13975
4/13/85	**37**	12		42	**Love Is What We Make It**	*Roger Murrah/Keith Stegall*	Liberty 1524
5/25/85	❶[1]	20		43	**Real Love** *[w/ Dolly Parton]*	S:❶[1] / A:❶[1] *Richard Brannan/David Malloy/Randy McCormick*	RCA 14058
7/20/85	**57**	8		44	**Twentieth Century Fool**	*Brian Neary/Jim Photoglo*	Liberty 1525
10/12/85+	❶[1]	22		45	**Morning Desire**	S:❶[3] / A:❶[1] *Dave Loggins*	RCA 14194
1/18/86	**47**	9		46	**Goodbye Marie**	*Dennis Linde/Mel McDaniel*	Liberty 1526
2/22/86	❶[1]	20		47	**Tomb Of The Unknown Love**	S:❶[1] / A:❶[1] *Michael Smotherman*	RCA 14298
6/14/86	**46**	12		48	**The Pride Is Back** *[w/ Nickie Ryder]*	S:29 *Marc Blatte/Larry Gottlieb/Alan Monde*	RCA 14384
					tune used for a Chrysler jingle		
10/18/86	**53**	12		49	**They Don't Make Them Like They Used To**	*Burt Bacharach/Carole Bayer Sager*	RCA 5016
					from the movie *Tough Guys* starring Burt Lancaster and Kirk Douglas		
12/27/86+	**2**[2]	21		50	**Twenty Years Ago**	A:2 / S:5 *Wood Newton/Mike Noble/Christopher Spriggs/Dan Tyler*	RCA 5078
6/27/87	❶[1]	17		51	**Make No Mistake, She's Mine** *[w/ Ronnie Milsap]*	S:3 *Kim Carnes*	RCA 5209
					Grammy: Vocal Collaboration		
10/10/87	**2**[2]	19		52	**I Prefer The Moonlight**	S:5 *Gary Chapman/Mark Wright*	RCA 5258
3/5/88	**6**	16		53	**The Factory**	S:12 *Bud McGuire*	RCA 6832
8/13/88	**26**	15		54	**When You Put Your Heart In It**	S:25 *James Dunne/Austin Roberts*	Reprise 27812
9/3/88+	**86**	5		55	**I Don't Call Him Daddy**	*Reed Nielsen*	RCA 8390
5/27/89	**30**	12		56	**Planet Texas**	*John Parks*	Reprise 27690
8/26/89	**8**	26		57	**The Vows Go Unbroken (Always True To You)**	*Gary Burr/Eric Kaz*	Reprise 22828
9/30/89	**28**	15		58	**If I Ever Fall In Love Again** *[w/ Anne Murray]*	*Steve Dorff/Gloria Sklerov*	Capitol 44432
2/17/90	**25**	13		59	**Maybe** *[w/ Holly Dunn]*	*Bill Rice/Mary Sharon Rice*	Reprise
					from the album *Something Inside So Strong* on Reprise 25792		
8/18/90	**21**	20		60	**Love Is Strange** *[w/ Dolly Parton]*	*Mickey Baker/Bo Diddley/Sylvia Robinson*	Reprise
2/2/91	**69**	4		61	**Lay My Body Down**	*Joe Henry/Bob Morrison*	Reprise
					above 2 from the album *Love Is Strange* on Reprise 26289		
11/30/91+	**11**	20		62	**If You Want To Find Love**	*Max D. Barnes/Skip Ewing/Kenny Rogers*	Reprise
					Linda Davis (backing vocal); from the album *Back Home Again* on Reprise 26740		
1/4/97	**55**	2		63	**Mary, Did You Know** *[w/ Wynonna]*	*Buddy Greene/Mark Lowry* **[X]**	Magnatone
					from the album *The Gift* on Magnatone 108		
4/17/99	**26**	20		64	**The Greatest**	*Don Schlitz*	Dreamcatcher
9/11/99	**67**	5		65	**Slow Dance More**	*Pat Bunch/Doug Johnson*	Dreamcatcher
10/30/99+	❶[1]	37		66	**Buy Me A Rose** *[w/ Alison Krauss & Billy Dean]*	*Jim Funk/Erik Hickenlooper*	Dreamcatcher
					above 3 from Rogers' album *She Rides Wild Horses* on Dreamcatcher 004		
7/1/00	**32**	20		67	**He Will, She Knows**	*Steve Leslie/Frank Rogers*	Dreamcatcher
1/27/01	**26**	23		68	**There You Go Again**	*Tommy Lee James/Jennifer Kimball/Terry McBride*	Dreamcatcher
8/18/01	**47**	9		69	**Beautiful (All That You Could Be)**	*Rory Bourke/Mike Reid*	Dreamcatcher
11/3/01	**39**	17		70	**Homeland**	*Keith Miles/Jack Sundrud*	Dreamcatcher
					above 4 from the album *There You Go Again* on Dreamcatcher 006		
3/30/02	**47**	13		71	**Harder Cards**	*Mike Henderson/Craig Wiseman*	Dreamcatcher
5/31/03	**49**	6		72	**I'm Missing You**	*Billy Kirsch/Steve Wariner*	Dreamcatcher
10/18/03	**40**	17		73	**Handprints On The Wall**	*Nelson Blanchard/Scott Innes/Claude Parish*	Dreamcatcher
					above 3 from the album *Back To The Well* on Dreamcatcher 008		
7/31/04	**60**	1		74	**My World Is Over** *[w/ Whitney Duncan]*	*Whitney Duncan/Brian Nash/Mike Post*	Capitol
					from Rogers' album *42 Ultimate Hits* on Capitol 98794		

All I Ever Need Is You ['79]
All My Life ['83]
Anyone Who Isn't Me Tonight ['78]
Beautiful (All That You Could Be) ['01]
Blaze Of Glory ['82]
Buried Treasure ['84]
Buy Me A Rose ['00]
Coward Of The County ['80]
Crazy ['85]
Daytime Friends ['77]
Don't Fall In Love With A Dreamer ['80]
Evening Star ['84]
Every Time Two Fools Collide ['78]
Eyes That See In The Dark ['84]
Factory ['88]
Gambler ['78]
Goodbye Marie ['86]
Greatest Gift Of All ['85]
Greatest ['99]
Handprints On The Wall ['03]
Harder Cards ['02]
He Will, She Knows ['00]
Homeland ['01]
I Don't Call Him Daddy ['89]
I Don't Need You ['81]
I Prefer The Moonlight ['87]
I'm Missing You ['03]
If I Ever Fall In Love Again ['89]
If You Want To Find Love ['92]
Islands In The Stream ['83]
Lady ['80]
Laura (What's He Got That I Ain't Got?) ['76]
Lay My Body Down ['91]
Love Is Strange ['90]
Love Is What We Make It ['85]
Love Lifted Me ['76]
Love Or Something Like It ['78]
Love Song ['82]
Love The World Away ['80]
Love Will Turn You Around ['82]
Lucille ['77]
Make No Mistake, She's Mine ['87]
Mary, Did You Know ['97]
Maybe ['90]
Midsummer Nights ['84]
Morning Desire ['86]
My World Is Over ['04]
Planet Texas ['89]
Pride Is Back ['86]
Real Love ['85]
Ruben James ['69]
Ruby, Don't Take Your Love To Town ['69]
Scarlet Fever ['83]
Share Your Love With Me ['81]
She Believes In Me ['79]
Slow Dance More ['99]
Sweet Music Man ['77]
There You Go Again ['01]
They Don't Make Them Like They Used To ['86]
Through The Years ['82]
Til I Can Make It On My Own ['79]
Today I Started Loving You Again ['73]
Together Again ['84]
Tomb Of The Unknown Love ['86]
Twentieth Century Fool ['85]
Twenty Years Ago ['87]
Vows Go Unbroken (Always True To You) ['89]
We've Got Tonight ['83]
What About Me? ['84]
What Are We Doin' In Love ['81]
When You Put Your Heart In It ['88]
While The Feeling's Good ['76]
You Decorated My Life ['79]
You Were A Good Friend ['84]

ROGERS, Randy, Band

Born in San Marcos, Texas. Male singer/songwriter/guitarist. His band: Geoffrey Hill (guitar), Brady Black (fiddle), Jon Richardson (bass) and Les Lawless (drums).

DEBUT	PEAK	WKS	Country Chart Hit	Songwriter	Label (& Number)
1/15/05	**43**	20	**Tonight's Not The Night**	*Radney Foster/Randy Rogers*	Smith Music Group

DEBUT	PEAK	WKS	GOLD	ARTIST / Country Chart Hit	Ranking / Songwriter	Label (& Number)
				ROGERS, Ronnie		
				Born Randall Rogers in Nashville, Tennessee. Male singer/songwriter.		
11/21/81+	**39**	11		1 **Gonna Take My Angel Out Tonight**	*Ronnie Rogers*	Lifesong 45094
3/20/82	**37**	9		2 **My Love Belongs To You**	*Ronnie Rogers*	Lifesong 45095
6/12/82	**54**	8		3 **First Time Around**	*Ronnie Rogers*	Lifesong 45116
9/25/82	**86**	3		4 **Happy Country Birthday /**	*Ronnie Rogers*	
10/16/82	**86**	3		5 **Takin' It Back To The Hills**	*Ronnie Rogers*	Lifesong 45118
6/25/83	**66**	7		6 **Inside Story**	*Ronnie Rogers*	Epic 03953
9/19/87	**57**	8		7 **Good Timin' Shoes**	*Ronnie Rogers*	MTM 72094
8/6/88	**82**	2		8 **Let's Be Bad Tonight**	*Ronnie Rogers*	MTM 72110
				ROGERS, Roy	**1940s: #35 // HOF: 1988**	
				Born Leonard Franklin Slye on 11/5/1911 in Cincinnati, Ohio. Died of heart failure on 7/6/1998 (age 86). Popular "singing cowboy" who starred in several movies. Formed the Pioneer Trio, in 1934 with Bob Nolan and Tim Spencer, which evolved into the **Sons Of The Pioneers**; group appeared in several movies. Went solo in 1937; briefly known as "Dick Weston." By 1938, known as "Roy Rogers." Married actress Dale Evans on 12/31/1947; stars of *The Roy Rogers Show* TV show (1951-57) and *The Roy Rogers & Dale Evans Show* in 1962.		
7/6/46	**7**	1		1 **A Little White Cross On The Hill**	*Fred Rose*	RCA Victor 20-1872
3/15/47	**4**	1		2 **My Chickashay Gal**	*Spade Cooley/Smokey Rogers*	RCA Victor 20-2124
6/12/48	**6**	14		3 **Blue Shadows On The Trail /**	S:6 / J:7 *Eliot Daniel/Johnny Lange*	
6/12/48	**13**	4		4 **(There'll Never Be Another) Pecos Bill** **ROY ROGERS and The Sons Of The Pioneers** (above 2) above 2 from the movie *Melody Time* starring Rogers	S:13 *Eliot Daniel/Johnny Lange*	RCA Victor 20-2780
2/4/50	**8**	1		5 **Stampede** **The Sons Of The Pioneers** (backing vocals)	A:8 *Darol Rice/Foy Willing*	RCA Victor 48-0161
9/26/70	**35**	10		6 **Money Can't Buy Love**	*Betty Craig*	Capitol 2895
1/30/71	**12**	11		7 **Lovenworth**	*Jerry Crutchfield/Don Earl/Nick Nixon*	Capitol 3016
6/26/71	**47**	11		8 **Happy Anniversary**	*Bill Eldridge/Gary Stewart*	Capitol 3117
2/26/72	**73**	4		9 **These Are The Good Old Days**	*Jean Chapel/Bob Jennings*	Capitol 3263
12/21/74+	**15**	13		10 **Hoppy, Gene And Me** tribute to Hopalong Cassidy, **Gene Autry** and **Roy Rogers**	*Milton Brown/Steve Dorff/Snuff Garrett* **[N]**	20th Century 2154
8/23/80	**80**	4		11 **Ride Concrete Cowboy, Ride** **ROY ROGERS And The Sons Of The Pioneers** from the movie *Smokey & The Bandit II* starring **Burt Reynolds**	*Cliff Crofford/John Durrill/Snuff Garrett*	MCA 41294
11/2/91	**42**	10		12 **Hold On Partner** ***[w/ Clint Black]*** from Rogers' album *Roy Rogers Tribute* on RCA 3024	*Bobby Paine/Larsen Paine*	RCA
				ROGERS, Smokey		
				Born Eugene Rogers on 3/23/1917 in McMinnville, Tennessee. Died on 11/23/1993 (age 76). Male singer/banjo player.		
1/1/49	**8**	4		**A Little Bird Told Me**	J:8 *Harvey Brooks*	Capitol 15326
				ROHRS, Donnie		
				Born in 1946 in Covina, California. Male singer/songwriter/guitarist.		
12/16/78	**95**	3		1 **Hey Baby**	*Bruce Channel/Margaret Cobb*	Ad-Korp 1258
5/2/81	**85**	6		2 **Waltzes And Western Swing**	*Charles Duvall/Donnie Rohrs*	Pacific Chall. 4504
				ROLAND, Adrian		
				Born in Lamarque, Texas. Male singer/songwriter.		
9/19/60	**19**	4		**Imitation Of Love**	*Howard Gregory/Adrian Roland*	Allstar 7207
				RONE, Roger		
				Born in Illinois. Male singer.		
8/26/89	**83**	3		**Holdin' On To Nothin'**	*Allan Phillips/Bobby Reed*	True 98
				RONICK, Holly		
				Born in Tennessee. Female singer.		
11/4/89	**86**	2		**Ain't No One Like Me In Tennessee**	*Kevin Thomas*	Happy Man 822

DEBUT	PEAK	WKS	GOLD	ARTIST / Country Chart Hit	Ranking / Songwriter	Label (& Number)
				RONSTADT, Linda	**All-Time: #173**	
				Born on 7/15/1946 in Tucson, Arizona. Female singer/songwriter/actress. While in high school formed folk trio The Three Ronstadts (with sister and brother). To Los Angeles in 1964. Formed the Stone Poneys with Bobby Kimmel (guitar) and Ken Edwards (keyboards); recorded for Sidewalk in 1966. Went solo in 1968. In 1971 formed backing band with Glenn Frey, **Don Henley**, Randy Meisner and Bernie Leadon (later became the **Eagles**). Acted in the movie *Pirates Of Penzance.*		
3/2/74	**20**	12		1 **Silver Threads And Golden Needles**	*Dick Reynolds/Jack Rhodes*	Asylum 11032
3/30/74	**10**	15		2 **When The Morning Comes** ***[w/ Hoyt Axton]***	*Hoyt Axton*	A&M 1497
12/21/74+	**2**[1]	17		3 **I Can't Help It (If I'm Still In Love With You)** **Grammy: Female Vocal**	*Hank Williams*	Capitol 3990
4/19/75	**❶**[1]	15		4 **When Will I Be Loved**	*Phil Everly*	Capitol 4050
5/10/75	**57**	7		5 **Lion In The Winter** ***[w/ Hoyt Axton]***	*Hoyt Axton*	A&M 1683
9/13/75	**54**	7		6 **It Doesn't Matter Anymore**	*Paul Anka*	Capitol 4050
9/13/75	**5**	15		7 **Love Is A Rose**	*Neil Young*	Asylum 45282
1/3/76	**11**	12		8 **Tracks Of My Tears /**	*Warren Moore/Smokey Robinson/Marvin Tarplin*	
1/3/76	**12**	12		9 **The Sweetest Gift** ***[w/ Emmylou Harris]***	*J.B. Coats*	Asylum 45295
9/4/76	**27**	11		10 **That'll Be The Day**	*Jerry Allison/Buddy Holly/Norman Petty*	Asylum 45340

DEBUT	PEAK	WKS	GOLD	ARTIST / Country Chart Hit	Ranking / Songwriter	Label (& Number)
				RONSTADT, Linda — cont'd		
12/18/76+	6	15		11 Crazy	*Willie Nelson*	Asylum 45361
9/17/77	2^2	19	▲	12 Blue Bayou	*Joe Melson/Roy Orbison*	Asylum 45431
11/12/77	81	6		13 It's So Easy	*Buddy Holly/Norman Petty*	Asylum 45438
2/18/78	46	9		14 Poor Poor Pitiful Me	*Warren Zevon*	Asylum 45462
5/13/78	8	13		15 I Never Will Marry	*Fred Hellerman*	Asylum 45479
9/2/78	41	8		16 Back In The U.S.A.	*Chuck Berry*	Asylum 45519
12/2/78	85	5		17 Ooh Baby Baby	*Warren Moore/Smokey Robinson*	Asylum 45546
3/10/79	59	6		18 Love Me Tender	*Vera Matson/Elvis Presley*	Asylum 46011
3/1/80	42	8		19 Rambler Gambler	*Linda Ronstadt*	Asylum 46602
10/16/82	27	12		20 Sometimes You Just Can't Win ***[w/ John David Souther]***	*Smokey Stover*	Asylum 69948
1/29/83	84	3		21 I Knew You When	*Joe South*	Asylum 69853
2/21/87	❶^1	19		22 To Know Him Is To Love Him ***[w/ Dolly Parton & Emmylou Harris]***	S:❶^1 / A:❶^1 *Phil Spector*	Warner 28492
5/30/87	3^1	18		23 Telling Me Lies ***[w/ Dolly Parton & Emmylou Harris]***	S:10 *Betsy Cook/Linda Thompson*	Warner 28371
9/26/87	5	22		24 Those Memories Of You ***[w/ Dolly Parton & Emmylou Harris]***	S:10 *Alan O'Bryant*	Warner 28248
3/26/88	6	18		25 Wildflowers ***[w/ Dolly Parton & Emmylou Harris]***	S:13 *Dolly Parton*	Warner 27970
4/29/95	61	9		26 Walk On from the album *Feels Like Home* on Elektra 61703	*Matraca Berg/Ronnie Samoset*	Elektra
				ROOFTOP SINGERS, The Folk trio from New York: Erik Darling, Lynne Taylor and Willard Svanoe. Taylor died in 1982 (age 54).		
2/23/63	23	4	●	Walk Right In	*Gus Cannon/Hosie Woods*	Vanguard 35017
				ROSE, Fred Born on 8/24/1898 in Evansville, Indiana. Died of a heart attack on 12/1/1954 (age 56). Male singer/songwriter. Formed Acuff-Rose music publishing company with **Roy Acuff** in 1942; they also formed the Hickory record label in 1953. Recorded as **The Rambling Rogue**.	**HOF: 1961 / SW: #46**	
10/27/45	5	1		Tender Hearted Sue ***[The Rambling Rogue]***	*Fred Rose*	Okeh 6747
				ROSE, Pam Born Pamela Rose Thacker in Chattanooga; raised in Eau Gallie, Florida. Female singer. Member of **Calamity Jane**.		
7/23/77	83	5		1 Midnight Flight	*Mike McClellan*	Capitol 4440
11/19/77	93	3		2 Runaway Heart	*Paul Harrison*	Capitol 4491
1/5/80	52	7		3 It's Not Supposed To Be That Way **Willie Nelson** (guest vocal)	*Willie Nelson*	Epic 50819
4/19/80	60	6		4 I'm Not Through Loving You Yet	*Conway Twitty/L.E. White*	Epic 50861
				ROSE, Richard and Gary Duo of brothers from Houston, Texas.		
2/13/88	81	3		Younger Man, Older Woman	*Gary Rose/Richard Rose*	Capitol 44118
				ROSS, Charlie Born in Greenville, Mississippi. Male singer.		
2/28/76	13	12		1 Without Your Love (Mr. Jordan)	*Perry Cone/Paul Vance*	Big Tree 16056
6/5/82	33	13		2 The High Cost Of Loving	*Walt Aldridge/Tom Brasfield*	Town House 1057
9/18/82	45	9		3 Are We In Love (Or Am I)	*Don Pfrimmer/Charles Quillen*	Town House 1061
1/8/83	70	5		4 The Name Of The Game Is Cheating	*Tim DuBois/Wood Newton*	Town House 1063
				ROSS, Jeris Born in East Alton, Illinois. Female singer.		
3/11/72	75	2		1 Brand New Key	*Melanie Safka*	Cartwheel 206
6/24/72	58	12		2 Old Fashioned Love Song	*Paul Williams*	Cartwheel 214
12/22/73+	58	7		3 Moontan	*Bobby Braddock*	ABC 11397
4/26/75	17	14		4 Pictures On Paper	*Gary S. Paxton*	ABC 12064
10/11/75	66	8		5 I'd Rather Be Picked Up Here (Than Be Put Down At Home)	*George Morgan*	ABC/Dot 17573
10/29/77	77	6		6 I Think I'll Say Goodbye	*Marshall Chapman/Jim Rushing*	Gazelle 431
9/15/79	94	4		7 Little Bit More	*Bobby Gosh*	Door Knob 108
1/26/80	75	5		8 You Win Again	*Hank Williams*	Door Knob 117
				ROSS, Roy, & His Ramblers Born in New York. Male bandleader.		
5/4/46	4	1		1 Harriet ***[w/ Red Foley]***	*Abel Baer/Paul Cunningham*	Decca 9003
11/30/46	5	1		2 Have I Told You Lately That I Love You ***[w/ Red Foley]***	*Scott Wiseman*	Decca 46014
				ROVERS, The Irish-born folk group formed in Calgary, Alberta, Canada: Jimmy Ferguson (vocals), brothers Will Millar (vocals, guitar) and George Millar (guitar), their cousin Joe Millar (bass) and Wilcil McDowell (accordian). First known as The Irish Rovers. Ferguson died in October 1997 (age 57).		
2/28/81	45	11		1 Wasn't That A Party	*Tom Paxton*	Epic 51007
3/13/82	77	4		2 Pain In My Past	*Max D. Barnes/Frank Dycus*	Epic 02728
				ROWE, Stacey Born in Albany, Georgia. Female singer.		
6/30/79	96	2		I Couldn't Live Without Your Love	*Tony Hatch/Jackie Trent*	Sabre 4510

DEBUT	PEAK	WKS	GOLD	ARTIST / Ranking / Country Chart Hit	Songwriter	Label (& Number)
				ROWELL, Ernie		
				Born in Auburn, Alabama. Male singer/songwriter/guitarist.		
7/24/71	74	2		1 **Going Back To Louisiana**	*Robert Osborn*	Prize 08
9/29/79	91	4		2 **I'm Leavin' You Alone**	*Ernie Rowell*	Grass 05
5/9/81	59	6		3 **Music In The Mountains**	*Cleo Anderson/Ernie Rowell/Virgil Warner*	Grass 07
10/3/87	86	3		4 **You Left My Heart For Broke**	*Kerry O'Neil/Will Robinson*	Revolver 016
				ROWLAND, Dave — see DAVE & SUGAR		
				ROY, Bobbie		
				Born Barbara Elaine Roy on 7/27/1953 in Landstuhl, Germany (U.S. Army base); raised in Elkins, West Virginia. Female singer.		
6/3/72	32	9		1 **One Woman's Trash (Another Woman's Treasure)**	*Red Lane*	Capitol 3301
9/23/72	58	8		2 **Leavin' On Your Mind**	*Webb Pierce/Wayne Walker*	Capitol 3428
12/16/72+	62	5		3 **I Like Everything About Loving You**	*Cile David*	Capitol 3477
1/27/73	51	5		4 **I Am Woman**	*Ray Burton/Helen Reddy*	Capitol 3513
				ROYAL, Billy Joe — **All-Time: #261**		
				Born on 4/3/1942 in Valdosta, Georgia; raised in Marietta, Georgia. Male singer/songwriter/guitarist/pianist/drummer.		
10/26/85+	10	22		1 **Burned Like A Rocket**	S:6 / A:11 *Gary Burr*	Atlantic Amer. 99599
5/3/86	41	16		2 **Boardwalk Angel**	S:25 *John Cafferty*	Atlantic Amer. 99555
8/23/86	14	24		3 **I Miss You Already**	S:9 / A:17 *Marvin Rainwater/Faron Young*	Atlantic Amer. 99519
2/7/87	11	26		4 **Old Bridges Burn Slow**	S:❶^{1} / A:11 *Sanford Brown/Jerry Meaders/Joe South*	Atlantic Amer. 99485
6/27/87	23	15		5 **Members Only** *[w/ Donna Fargo]*	S:21 *Larry Addison*	Mercury 888680
10/17/87+	5	23		6 **I'll Pin A Note On Your Pillow**	S:❶^{2} *Carol Berzas/Don Goodman/Nelson Larkin*	Atlantic Amer. 99404
3/12/88	10	22		7 **Out Of Sight And On My Mind**	S:❶^{1} *Bruce Burch/Rich Peoples*	Atlantic Amer. 99364
8/27/88	17	17		8 **It Keeps Right On Hurtin'**	S:❶^{1} *Johnny Tillotson*	Atlantic Amer. 99295
2/4/89	2^{2}	17		9 **Tell It Like It Is**	*George Davis/Lee Diamond*	Atlantic Amer. 99242
5/20/89	4	24		10 **Love Has No Right**	*Nelson Larkin/Billy Joe Royal/Randy Scruggs*	Atlantic Amer. 99217
9/30/89+	2^{1}	26		11 **Till I Can't Take It Anymore**	*Dorian Burton/Clyde Otis*	Atlantic 88815
5/12/90	17	21		12 **Searchin' For Some Kind Of Clue**	*Donny Kees/Nelson Larkin/Pal Rakes*	Atlantic
9/15/90	33	20		13 **Ring Where A Ring Used To Be**	*Kris Bergsnes/Gordon Eatherly/Bob Moulds*	Atlantic
				above 2 from the album *Out Of The Shadows* on Atlantic 82104		
1/26/91	29	14		14 **If The Jukebox Took Teardrops**	*Wyatt Easterling/Don Goodman/Mike Graham/Nelson Larkin*	Atlantic
3/21/92	51	8		15 **I'm Okay (And Gettin' Better)**	*Max T. Barnes/Skip Ewing*	Atlantic
				from the album *Billy Joe Royal* on Atlantic 82327		
				RUCKER, Dwight — see MALCHAK, Tim		
				RUE, Arnie		
				Born Arnold Amaru in Massachusetts; raised in California. Male singer/songwriter.		
5/5/79	56	6		1 **Spare A Little Lovin' (On A Fool)**	*Arnie Rue*	NSD 19
11/17/79	74	4		2 **Rodle-Odeo-Home**	*Arnie Rue*	NSD 32
				RUSHING, Jim		
				Born in Lubbock, Texas. Male singer/songwriter.		
9/27/80	81	2		1 **Dixie Dirt**	*Danny Morrison/Jim Rushing*	Ovation 1153
12/27/80+	56	8		2 **I've Loved Enough To Know**	*Fred Koller/Jim Rushing*	Ovation 1161
				RUSHLOW, Tim		
				Born on 10/6/1966 in Midwest City, Oklahoma; raised in Arlington, Texas. Male singer/songwriter. Former lead singer of **Little Texas**. Formed own **Rushlow** group with cousin Doni Harris (guitar), Kurt Allison (guitar), Billy Welch (keyboards), Tully Kennedy (bass) and Rich Redmond (drums).		
4/1/00	60	5		1 **When You Love Me**	*Porter Howell/David Malloy/Tim Rushlow*	Atlantic
11/4/00+	8	28		2 **She Misses Him**	*Tim Johnson*	Atlantic
7/21/01	43	15		3 **Crazy Life**	S:24 *Kevin Fisher*	Atlantic
12/29/01+	52	8		4 **Love, Will (The Package)**	*Tim Rushlow*	Atlantic
				above 4 from the album *Tim Rushlow* on Atlantic 83326		
5/10/03	16	30		5 **I Can't Be Your Friend** *[Rushlow]*	*Rodney Clawson/Brad Crisler*	Lyric Street
5/15/04	42	11		6 **Sweet Summer Rain** *[Rushlow]*	*Jim Collins/Danny Orton*	Lyric Street
				above 2 from the album *Right Now* on Lyric Street 165039		
				RUSSELL, Bobby		
				Born on 4/19/1941 in Nashville, Tennessee. Died of a heart attack on 11/19/1992 (age 51). Male singer/songwriter. Married to **Vicki Lawrence** from 1972-74.		
11/9/68	64	8		1 **1432 Franklin Pike Circle Hero**	*Bobby Russell*	Elf 90,020
3/1/69	66	3		2 **Carlie**	*Bobby Russell*	Elf 90,023
8/16/69	34	9		3 **Better Homes And Gardens**	*Bobby Russell*	Elf 90,031
7/10/71	24	13		4 **Saturday Morning Confusion**	*Bobby Russell* **[N]**	United Artists 50788
8/18/73	93	3		5 **Mid American Manufacturing Tycoon**	*Bobby Russell*	Columbia 45901
				RUSSELL, Clifford		
				Born in Knoxville, Tennessee. Male singer.		
2/12/83	97	2		**She Feels Like A New Man Tonight**	*Chester Lester*	Sugartree 0509
				RUSSELL, Jimmy		
				Born in New Jersey. Male singer.		
12/18/76	99	4		**You've Got To Move Two Mountains**	*Berry Gordy*	Charta 103

Billboard			GOLD	ARTIST / Country Chart Hit	Ranking / Songwriter	Label (& Number)
DEBUT	PEAK	WKS				

RUSSELL, Johnny

All-Time: #242

Born on 1/23/1940 in Moorhead, Mississippi; raised in Fresno, California. Died of diabetes on 7/3/2001 (age 61). Male singer/songwriter/guitarist. Married **Beverly Heckel** in 1977.

OPRY: 1985

DEBUT	PEAK	WKS	Country Chart Hit	Songwriter	Label (& Number)
8/21/71	64	3	1 Mr. And Mrs. Untrue	*Irwin Levine/Toni Wine*	RCA Victor 1000
12/11/71+	57	9	2 What A Price	*Fats Domino/Jack Jessup/Pee Wee Maddux*	RCA Victor 0570
4/1/72	59	7	3 Mr. Fiddle Man	*Johnny Russell/Linda Watts*	RCA Victor 0665
7/1/72	36	12	4 Rain Falling On Me	*Jimmy Peppers*	RCA Victor 0729
11/11/72+	12	15	5 Catfish John	*Bob McDill/Allen Reynolds*	RCA Victor 0810
3/24/73	31	10	6 Chained	*Jerry Foster/Bill Rice*	RCA Victor 0908
8/4/73	4	19	7 Rednecks, White Socks And Blue Ribbon Beer	*Wayland Holyfield/Bob McDill/Chuck Neese*	RCA Victor 0021
11/10/73+	14	13	8 The Baptism Of Jesse Taylor	*Dallas Frazier/Whitey Shafer*	RCA Victor 0165
4/13/74	39	10	9 She's In Love With A Rodeo Man	*Bob McDill*	RCA Victor 0248
9/14/74	38	10	10 She Burn't The Little Roadside Tavern Down	*Bill Howard*	RCA Victor 10038
12/21/74+	23	11	11 That's How My Baby Builds A Fire	*Jim Foster*	RCA Victor 10135
4/26/75	13	17	12 Hello I Love You	*Ronnie Rogers*	RCA Victor 10258
10/11/75	45	10	13 Our Marriage Was A Failure	*Bob McDill/Johnny Russell*	RCA Victor 10403
2/21/76	57	9	14 I'm A Trucker	*Jerry Foster/Bill Rice*	RCA Victor 10563
5/22/76	45	8	15 This Man And Woman Thing	*Johnny Russell/Jerry Strickland*	RCA Victor 10667
12/25/76+	32	10	16 The Son Of Hickory Holler's Tramp /	*Dallas Frazier*	
12/25/76+	flip	10	17 I Wonder How She's Doing Now	*Johnny Russell*	RCA 10853
6/25/77	91	3	18 Obscene Phone Call **Beverly Heckel** (female vocal)	*John Schweers*	RCA 10984
12/10/77+	64	9	19 Leona	*Jack Hall/Jimmy Hall*	RCA 11160
5/13/78	24	12	20 You'll Be Back (Every Night In My Dreams)	*Wayland Holyfield/Johnny Russell*	Polydor 14475
11/25/78+	29	12	21 How Deep In Love Am I?	*Bob McDill*	Mercury 55045
5/19/79	57	6	22 I Might Be Awhile In New Orleans	*Wayland Holyfield*	Mercury 55060
11/17/79	56	7	23 Ain't No Way To Make A Bad Love Grow	*Sonny Throckmorton*	Mercury 57008
3/15/80	57	6	24 While The Choir Sang The Hymn (I Thought Of Her)	*Lola Jean Dillon/Bobby Harden*	Mercury 57016
6/21/80	59	7	25 We're Back In Love Again	*Glenn Martin/Sonny Throckmorton*	Mercury 57026
12/13/80+	57	9	26 Song Of The South	*Bob McDill*	Mercury 57038
4/18/81	49	9	27 Here's To The Horses	*Rory Bourke/Gene Dobbins/Hugh Moffatt*	Mercury 57050
7/25/87	72	4	28 Butterbeans *[w/ Little David Wilkins]*	*Charlie Colvin*	16th Avenue 70401

RUSSELL, Leon

Born Claude Russell Bridges on 4/2/1942 in Lawton, Oklahoma. Male singer/songwriter/multi-instrumentalist. Prolific studio musician. Also recorded as **Hank Wilson**.

DEBUT	PEAK	WKS	Country Chart Hit	Songwriter	Label (& Number)
9/29/73	57	11	1 Roll In My Sweet Baby's Arms *[Hank Wilson]*	*Lester Flatt*	Shelter 7336
1/12/74	68	8	2 A Six Pack To Go *[Hank Wilson]*	*Dick Hart/Johnny Lowe/Hank Thompson*	Shelter 7338
7/7/79	❶[1]	13	3 Heartbreak Hotel *[w/ Willie Nelson]*	*Mae Boren Axton/Thomas Durden/Elvis Presley*	Columbia 11023
7/28/84	63	12	4 Good Time Charlie's Got The Blues	*Danny O'Keefe*	Paradise 628
10/27/84	91	2	5 Wabash Cannonball *[w/ Willie Nelson]*	*Leon Russell*	Paradise 629

RUSTY & DOUG

Duo of brothers from Tiel Ridge, Louisiana: Russell Lee "Rusty" (born on 2/2/1938; died of a heart attack on 10/23/2001, age 63) and **Doug Kershaw** (born on 1/24/1936).

OPRY: 1957

DEBUT	PEAK	WKS	Country Chart Hit	Songwriter	Label (& Number)
8/13/55	14	2	1 So Lovely, Baby	A:14 *Doug Kershaw/Joe Miller*	Hickory 1027
9/23/57	14	1	2 Love Me To Pieces	A:14 *Melvin Endsley*	Hickory 1068
10/20/58	22	2	3 Hey Sheriff	*Boudleaux Bryant/Felice Bryant*	Hickory 1083
2/6/61	10	15	4 Louisiana Man	*Doug Kershaw*	Hickory 1137
8/21/61	14	10	5 Diggy Liggy Lo also see #1 under **Doug Kershaw**	*Joe Miller*	Hickory 1151

RUTTAN, Deric

Born in Bracebridge, Ontario, Canada. Male singer/songwriter/guitarist.

DEBUT	PEAK	WKS	Country Chart Hit	Songwriter	Label (& Number)
6/14/03	46	12	When You Come Around	*Steve Bogard/Deric Ruttan*	Lyric Street

RUUD, Nancy

Born on 3/23/1958 in Montana. Female singer.

DEBUT	PEAK	WKS	Country Chart Hit	Songwriter	Label (& Number)
7/12/80	88	3	1 A Good Love Is Like A Good Song	*Casey Kelly*	Calico 16425
10/18/80	90	3	2 Always, Sometimes, Never	*Bob Morrison*	Calico 16493
4/4/81	87	2	3 I'm Gonna Hang Up This Heartache	*Johnny MacRae/Bob Morrison*	C&R 101
6/20/81	83	2	4 Blue As The Blue In Your Eyes	*Bob DiPiero/John Scott Sherrill*	C&R 102

RYAN, Charlie, and The Timberline Riders

Born on 12/19/1915 in Graceville, Minnesota; raised in Montana. Male singer/songwriter/guitarist.

DEBUT	PEAK	WKS	Country Chart Hit	Songwriter	Label (& Number)
9/5/60	14	6	Hot Rod Lincoln	*Charlie Ryan/W.S. Stevenson* [N-S]	4 Star 1733

RYAN, Jamey

Born in Texas. Female singer.

DEBUT	PEAK	WKS	Country Chart Hit	Songwriter	Label (& Number)
8/19/67	62	3	1 You're Lookin' For A Plaything	*Howard Crockett*	Columbia 44169
5/23/70	75	2	2 Holy Cow	*Allen Toussaint*	Show Biz 232
8/11/73	88	2	3 Keep On Loving Me	*Will Jennings/Troy Seals*	Atlantic 4001

RYAN, Tim

Born Tim Ryan Roullier on 2/4/1964 in Montana. Male singer/songwriter/guitarist.

DEBUT	PEAK	WKS	GOLD	#	Country Chart Hit	Songwriter	Label (& Number)
8/4/90	**42**	17		1	**Dance In Circles**	*Alex Harvey/Tim Ryan*	Epic
12/22/90+	**69**	6		2	**Breakin' All The Way**	*Hutson Brock/Red Lane*	Epic
					above 2 from the album *Tim Ryan* on Epic 45270		
9/21/91	**68**	3		3	**Seventh Direction**	*Donny Lowery/Wood Newton*	Epic
1/18/92	**65**	4		4	**I Will Love You Anyhow**	*Radney Foster/Bill Lloyd*	Epic
					above 2 from the album *Seasons Of The Heart* on Epic 47842		
1/23/93	**71**	4		5	**Idle Hands**	*Reed Nielsen*	BNA
					from the album *Idle Hands* on BNA 66122		

RYAN, Wesley

Born in Texas. Male singer.

DEBUT	PEAK	WKS	GOLD	#	Country Chart Hit	Songwriter	Label (& Number)
7/25/81	**82**	4			**Nothin' To Do But Just Lie**	*Curly Putman/Sterling Whipple*	NSD 93

RYDER, Nickie

Born in Houston, Texas. Female singer.

DEBUT	PEAK	WKS	GOLD	#	Country Chart Hit	Songwriter	Label (& Number)
6/14/86	**46**	12			**The Pride Is Back** ***[w/ Kenny Rogers]***	S:29 *Marc Blatte/Larry Gottlieb/Alan Monde*	RCA 14384
					tune used for a Chrysler jingle		

RYLES, John Wesley

All-Time: #248

Born on 12/2/1950 in Bastrop, Louisiana. Male singer/songwriter/guitarist.

DEBUT	PEAK	WKS	GOLD	#	Country Chart Hit	Songwriter	Label (& Number)
					JOHN WESLEY RYLES I:		
12/7/68+	**9**	17		1	**Kay**	*Hank Mills*	Columbia 44682
					also see #12 below		
5/17/69	**55**	8		2	**Heaven Below**	*Jerry Fuller*	Columbia 44819
12/13/69+	**57**	7		3	**The Weakest Kind Of Man**	*John Wesley Ryles*	Columbia 45018
5/2/70	**17**	10		4	**I've Just Been Wasting My Time**	*Jerry Foster/Bill Rice*	Columbia 45119
11/20/71	**39**	10		5	**Reconsider Me**	*Margaret Lewis/Myra Smith*	Plantation 81
					JOHN WESLEY RYLES:		
1/24/76	**83**	7		6	**Tell It Like It Is**	*George Davis/Lee Diamond*	Music Mill 214
7/10/76	**72**	6		7	**When A Man Loves A Woman**	*Calvin Lewis/Andrew Wright*	Music Mill 240
3/26/77	**18**	17		8	**Fool**	*Terry Skinner*	ABC/Dot 17679
8/13/77	**5**	16		9	**Once In A Lifetime Thing**	*Jerry Foster/Bill Rice*	ABC/Dot 17698
12/24/77+	**13**	12		10	**Shine On Me (The Sun Still Shines When It Rains)**	*Terry Skinner/J.L. Wallace*	ABC/Dot 17733
4/15/78	**63**	6		11	**Easy**	*Terry Skinner*	ABC 12348
7/15/78	**50**	7		12	**Kay**	*Hank Mills* **[R]**	ABC 12375
					new version of #1 above		
10/7/78	**45**	7		13	**Someday You Will**	*Jerry Foster/Bill Rice*	ABC 12410
12/23/78+	**33**	11		14	**Love Ain't Made For Fools**	*Terry Skinner/J.L. Wallace*	ABC 12432
6/2/79	**14**	14		15	**Liberated Woman**	*Wayne Carson*	MCA 41033
10/13/79	**20**	12		16	**You Are Always On My Mind**	*Wayne Carson/Johnny Christopher/Mark James*	MCA 41124
2/23/80	**24**	10		17	**Perfect Strangers**	*Sam Lorber/Jeff Silbar*	MCA 41184
7/19/80	**52**	8		18	**May I Borrow Some Sugar From You**	*Bobby Emmons/Chips Moman*	MCA 41278
11/8/80	**54**	10		19	**Cheater's Trap**	*Scott Anders/Roger Murrah*	MCA 51013
4/4/81	**80**	3		20	**Somewhere To Come When It Rains**	*Red Lane*	MCA 51080
7/18/81	**78**	3		21	**Mathilda**	*George Khoury/Huey Thierry*	MCA 51128
6/26/82	**76**	4		22	**We've Got To Start Meeting Like This**	*Ken Bell/Terry Skinner/J.L. Wallace*	Primero 1004
12/4/82	**80**	3		23	**Just Once**	*Barry Mann/Cynthia Weil*	Primero 1016
8/25/84	**78**	4		24	**She Took It Too Well**	*Lobo/D. Lowery*	16th Avenue 500
5/9/87	**36**	15		25	**Midnight Blue**	*Don Goodman/John Wesley Ryles*	Warner 28377
12/5/87+	**20**	16		26	**Louisiana Rain**	*Rich Alves/Roger Murrah*	Warner 28228
6/4/88	**53**	7		27	**Nobody Knows**	*Don Goodman/Pal Rakes/Jeff Raymond/John Wesley Ryles*	Warner 27869

S

SADLER, Sammy

Born 8/23/1967 in Memphis, Tennessee; raised in Bonham, Texas. Male singer.

DEBUT	PEAK	WKS	GOLD	#	Country Chart Hit	Songwriter	Label (& Number)
1/7/89	**70**	4		1	**Tell It Like It Is**	*George Davis/Lee Diamond*	Evergreen 1088
7/1/89	**89**	3		2	**You Made It Easy**	*Don Goodman/Johnny Morris/Pal Rakes*	Evergreen 1093
1/13/90	**86**	1		3	**Once In A Lifetime Thing**	*Jerry Foster/Wilburn Rice*	Evergreen 1106

SADLER, SSgt Barry

Born on 11/1/1940 in Carlsbad, New Mexico. Died of heart failure on 11/5/1989 (age 49). Male singer/songwriter. Staff Sergeant of U.S. Army Special Forces (aka Green Berets). Served in Vietnam until leg injury.

DEBUT	PEAK	WKS	GOLD	#	Country Chart Hit	Songwriter	Label (& Number)
2/19/66	$\mathbf{2^{2}}$	14	●	1	**The Ballad Of The Green Berets**	*Robin Moore/Barry Sadler*	RCA Victor 8739
5/28/66	**46**	4		2	**The "A" Team**	*Phyllis Landsberg/Barry Sadler/Leonard Whitcup*	RCA Victor 8804

SAHM, Doug, & The Texas Tornados

Born on 11/5/1941 in San Antonio, Texas. Died of heart failure on 11/18/1999 (age 58). Male singer/songwriter/guitarist. Formed the Sir Douglas Quintet in 1965. Formed a new Texas Tornados group with all-star lineup in 1990.

DEBUT	PEAK	WKS	GOLD	#	Country Chart Hit	Songwriter	Label (& Number)
10/16/76	**100**	1			**Cowboy Peyton Place**	*Doug Sahm*	ABC/Dot 17656

Billboard DEBUT	PEAK	WKS	GOLD	ARTIST / Country Chart Hit	Ranking / Songwriter	Label (& Number)

ST. JOHN, Tommy

Born on 3/23/1962 in Oak Ridge, Tennessee. Male singer.

DEBUT	PEAK	WKS	#	Country Chart Hit	Songwriter	Label (& Number)
1/8/83	55	9	1	The Light Of My Life (Has Gone Out Tonight)	*Dick Brady/Elizabeth Haynes/Robert Thames*	RCA 13405
4/16/83	78	4	2	Where'd Ya Stay Last Night	*Joe Hudgins*	RCA 13475
7/23/83	86	2	3	Stars On The Water	*Rodney Crowell*	RCA 13561

ST. MARIE, Susan

Born in Oklahoma. Female singer. Niece of **Tommy Overstreet**.

DEBUT	PEAK	WKS	#	Country Chart Hit	Songwriter	Label (& Number)
11/3/73	91	4	1	All Or Nothing With Me	*Jerry Foster/Bill Rice*	Cinnamon 768
11/19/77	91	7	2	It's The Love In You	*Bobby Lee Springfield/Van Stephenson*	Pinnacle 101

SAME OLD TRAIN

Collaboration of artists: **Clint Black**, **Joe Diffie**, **Merle Haggard**, **Emmylou Harris**, **Alison Krauss**, **Patty Loveless**, **Earl Scruggs**, **Ricky Skaggs**, **Marty Stuart**, **Pam Tillis**, **Randy Travis**, **Travis Tritt**, and **Dwight Yoakam**.

DEBUT	PEAK	WKS	#	Country Chart Hit	Songwriter	Label (& Number)
9/19/98	59	5		Same Old Train	*Marty Stuart*	Columbia

Grammy: Vocal Collaboration; from the various artists album *Tribute To Tradition* on Columbia 68073

SAMI JO

Born Sami Jo Cole in Batesville, Arkansas. Female singer.

DEBUT	PEAK	WKS	#	Country Chart Hit	Songwriter	Label (& Number)
2/9/74	52	12	1	Tell Me A Lie	*Mickey Buckins/Barbara Wyrick*	MGM South 7029
7/6/74	61	9	2	It Could Have Been Me	*Harry Lloyd/Gloria Sklerov*	MGM South 7034
1/4/75	62	9	3	I'll Believe Anything You Say	*Jerry Andrick*	MGM 14773
5/15/76	91	4	4	God Loves Us (When We All Sing Together)	*Larry Bowie/Sonny Limbo*	Polydor 14315
9/4/76	67	6	5	Take Me To Heaven	*Richard Mainegra/Susan Taylor*	Polydor 14341
5/2/81	76	4	6	One Love Over Easy *[Sami Jo Cole]*	*Pamela Phillips/Gloria Sklerov*	Elektra 47127
10/31/81	82	3	7	I Can't Help Myself (Here Comes The Feeling) *[Sami Jo Cole]*	*Eddie Rabbitt/Even Stevens*	Elektra 47211

SAMONE, Stephany

Born in Pleasant Grove, Texas. Female singer. Represented Texas in the 1987 Miss America pagent.

DEBUT	PEAK	WKS	#	Country Chart Hit	Songwriter	Label (& Number)
6/7/80	68	6	1	Do That To Me One More Time	*Toni Tenille*	MDJ 1004
11/22/80	65	7	2	Somebody's Gotta Do The Losing	*Jackie Dixon/Harold Shedd*	MDJ 1006

SAMPLES, Junior

Born Alvin Samples on 8/10/1926 in Cumming, Georgia. Died of a heart attack on 11/13/1983 (age 57). Comedian. Regular on TV's *Hee Haw*.

DEBUT	PEAK	WKS	#	Country Chart Hit	Songwriter	Label (& Number)
7/22/67	52	4		World's Biggest Whopper	*Jim Morrison* [S]	Chart 1460

Jim Morrison (interviewer)

SANDERS, Ben (The 5th Ave. Country Boy)

Born in Dallas, Texas. Male singer.

DEBUT	PEAK	WKS	#	Country Chart Hit	Songwriter	Label (& Number)
11/19/88	100	1		I'm Leavin' You	*Floyd Huddleston*	Luv 129

SANDERS, Debbie

Born in Florida. Female singer/songwriter.

DEBUT	PEAK	WKS	#	Country Chart Hit	Songwriter	Label (& Number)
4/15/89	91	2		No Time At All	*Debbie Sanders*	K-Ark 1050

SANDERS, Mack

Born in Wichita, Kansas. Male singer/songwriter. Married to **Sherry Bryce**; together they owned the Pilot label.

DEBUT	PEAK	WKS	#	Country Chart Hit	Songwriter	Label (& Number)
1/21/78	89	3		Sweet Country Girl	*Mack Sanders*	Pilot 45101

SANDERS, Ray

Born Raymon Sanders on 10/1/1935 in St. John, Kentucky. Male singer/songwriter/guitarist.

DEBUT	PEAK	WKS	#	Country Chart Hit	Songwriter	Label (& Number)
10/31/60	18	11	1	A World So Full Of Love	*Roger Miller*	Liberty 55267
4/3/61	20	8	2	Lonelyville	*Mac McKeel*	Liberty 55304
5/24/69	22	13	3	Beer Drinkin' Music	*Red Steagall*	Imperial 66366
10/25/69	73	2	4	Three Tears (For The Sad, Hurt, And Blue)	*Jerry Fuller*	Imperial 66408
8/1/70	36	11	5	Blame It On Rosey	*Bill Hervey*	United Artists 50689
12/26/70+	38	9	6	Judy	*Shel Silverstein*	United Artists 50732
5/29/71	56	9	7	Walk All Over Georgia	*Red Steagall*	United Artists 50774
10/2/71	18	16	8	All I Ever Need Is You	*Jimmy Holiday/Eddie Reeves*	United Artists 50827
5/20/72	69	5	9	A Rose By Any Other Name (Is Still A Rose)	*Irwin Levine/Toni Wine*	United Artists 50886
9/9/72	67	4	10	Lucius Grinder	*Don Goodman/Troy Seals*	United Artists 50933
5/5/73	75	2	11	Another Way To Say Goodbye	*Alda Calongne/Jean Chapel*	United Artists 201
8/6/77	56	7	12	I Don't Want To Be Alone Tonight	*Daryl Hall/Ray Sanders*	Republic 003
1/21/78	91	3	13	Tennessee	*Rick Klang/Don Pfrimmer*	Republic 013
11/29/80	93	2	14	You're A Pretty Lady, Lady	*Gene Cleamer*	Hillside 05

SANDERS, The

Brother-and-sister duo from Alaska: Dale Sanders and Vicki Sanders.

DEBUT	PEAK	WKS	#	Country Chart Hit	Songwriter	Label (& Number)
8/20/88	76	3	1	You Fit Right Into My Heart	*Fred Knoblock/Paul Overstreet/Thom Schuyler*	Airborne 10001
2/11/89	64	7	2	Grandma's Old Wood Stove	*Billy Stone*	Airborne 10013
5/27/89	73	5	3	Who Needs You	*Curtis Wright*	Airborne 10019

SAN FERNANDO VALLEY MUSIC BAND

Group from St. Paul, Minnesota. Led by Brian Murphy (vocals) and Jeff Stephens (guitar).

DEBUT	PEAK	WKS	#	Country Chart Hit	Songwriter	Label (& Number)
6/30/79	83	8		Taken To The Line	*Jeff Stephens*	C&S 017

SANTA FE — see CHAPMAN, Cee Cee

DEBUT	PEAK	WKS	GOLD	ARTIST / Country Chart Hit	Ranking / Songwriter	Label (& Number)
				SANZ, Victor		
				Born on 10/13/1973 in Wasco, California. Male singer/guitarist.		
6/10/00	68	4		1 **I'm Gonna Be There**	*Mark Elliott/Roy Hurd*	Gramac
9/23/00	68	1		2 **Destination Unknown**	*Tom Botkin/Les Rawlins/Don Skaggs*	Gramac
				above 2 from the album *Destination Unknown* on Gramac 7777		
12/18/04	60	1		3 **Tell Me What You Wanna Do**	*Steve Bogard/Marv Green/Bill Luther*	WCI
				from the album *Hey Country* on WCI 8604		
				SARAH		
				Born in Pennsylvania; raised in California. Female singer/songwriter. Wife of H.L. Vogt, owner of Hub label.		
9/19/87	81	2		1 **Lyin' Eyes**	*Sarah Lou Vogt*	Hub 45
6/4/88	81	3		2 **Chains**	*Gerry Goffin/Carole King*	Hub 46
10/15/88	77	4		3 **Don't Send Me Roses**	*Sarah Lou Vogt*	Hub 48
				SARGEANTS, Gary		
				Born Gary Lusk in Miami, Florida. Male singer/drummer.		
12/15/73+	55	11		1 **Ode To Jole Blon**	*Tom T. Hall*	Mercury 73440
10/5/74	72	7		2 **Day Time Lover**	*Tom T. Hall*	Mercury 73608
				SASKIA & SERGE		
				Husband-and-wife duo from Schagen, Holland. Saskia was born Trudy van den Berg on 4/23/1947. Serge was born Ruud Schaap on 3/2/1946. First recorded in 1966 as Trudy & Ruud. Changed name to Saskia & Serge in 1969.		
1/7/78	88	5		**Jambalaya (On The Bayou)**	*Hank Williams*	ABC/Hickory 54020
				SAULS, Corkey		
				Born Grady Sauls in Tennessee. Male singer/songwriter.		
2/10/79	96	1		**There Goes That Smile Again**	*Corkey Sauls*	Sand Mountain 822
				SAVANNAH		
				Group from Brunswick, Georgia. Led by brothers Jay Willis and Gene Willis.		
10/29/83	87	5		1 **Backstreet Ballet**	*Sonny Limbo/Gene Willis/Jay Willis*	Mercury 814360
7/21/84	73	5		2 **My Girl**	*Smokey Robinson/Ronnie White*	Mercury 880037
				SAWMILL CREEK — see HAUSER, Bruce		
				SAWYER, Ray		
				Born on 2/1/1937 in Chickasaw, Alabama. Male singer/songwriter. Eye-patch wearing member of **Dr. Hook**.		
11/6/76	28	12		1 **(One More Year Of) Daddy's Little Girl**	*Hazel Smith*	Capitol 4344
2/16/80	80	4		2 **I Don't Feel Much Like Smilin'**	*Dennis Locorriere/Ray Sawyer*	Capitol 4820

SAWYER BROWN — **1990s: #21 / All-Time: #67**

Group formed in Nashville, Tennessee: Mark Miller (vocals; born on 10/25/1958), Bobby Randall (guitar; born on 9/16/1952), Gregg Hubbard (keyboards; born on 10/4/1960), Jim Scholten (bass; born on 4/18/1952) and Joe Smyth (drums; born on 9/6/1957). Won first prize on TV's *Star Search* in 1984. Duncan Cameron (of **Amazing Rhythm Aces**; born on 7/27/1956) replaced Randall in 1991.

CMA: Horizon 1985

DEBUT	PEAK	WKS	GOLD	ARTIST / Country Chart Hit	Ranking / Songwriter	Label (& Number)
10/6/84+	16	22		1 **Leona**	S:10 / A:19 *Bill Shore/David Wills*	Capitol/Curb 5403
2/9/85	❶^{1}	21		2 **Step That Step**	S:❶^{1} / A:❶^{1} *Mark Miller*	Capitol/Curb 5446
6/8/85	3^{2}	21		3 **Used To Blue**	S:3 / A:3 *Fred Knoblock/Bill LaBounty*	Capitol/Curb 5477
10/5/85	5	20		4 **Betty's Bein' Bad**	S:5 / A:5 *Marshall Chapman*	Capitol/Curb 5517
2/1/86	14	18		5 **Heart Don't Fall Now**	S:14 / A:14 *Beckie Foster/Bill LaBounty/Carolyn Swilley*	Capitol/Curb 5548
5/10/86	15	16		6 **Shakin'**	S:14 / A:16 *Mark Miller/Randy Scruggs*	Capitol/Curb 5585
9/13/86	11	18		7 **Out Goin' Cattin'** ***[w/ "Cat" Joe Bonsall]***	A:11 / S:12 *Mark Miller/Randy Scruggs*	Capitol/Curb 5629
1/17/87	25	13		8 **Gypsies On Parade**	S:21 / A:25 *Mark Miller*	Capitol/Curb 5677
5/23/87	58	9		9 **Savin' The Honey For The Honeymoon**	*Jeff Barry/Rick Vito*	Capitol/Curb 44007
8/22/87	29	13		10 **Somewhere In The Night**	S:29 *Don Cook/Rafe Van Hoy*	Capitol/Curb 44054
12/5/87+	2^{1}	22		11 **This Missin' You Heart Of Mine**	S:13 *Mike Geiger/Woody Mullis*	Capitol/Curb 44108
4/23/88	27	13		12 **Old Photographs**	*Ken Beal/Kix Brooks/Bill McClelland*	Capitol/Curb 44143
10/1/88	11	17		13 **My Baby's Gone**	S:20 *Dennis Linde*	Capitol/Curb 44218
12/10/88+	51	7		14 **It Wasn't His Child**	*Skip Ewing* **[X]**	Capitol/Curb 44282
2/25/89	50	9		15 **Old Pair Of Shoes**	*Mark Miller*	Capitol/Curb 44332
9/2/89	5	26		16 **The Race Is On**	*Don Rollins*	Capitol/Curb 44431
3/3/90	33	13		17 **Did It For Love**	*Mark Miller*	Capitol/Curb
5/26/90	33	13		18 **Puttin' The Dark Back Into The Night**	*Mark Miller*	Capitol/Curb
				above 2 from the album *The Boys Are Back* on Capitol/Curb 92358		
10/6/90	40	17		19 **When Love Comes Callin'**	*Mark Miller/Randy Scruggs*	Curb/Capitol
				from the album *Greatest Hits* on Curb/Capitol 94259		
2/9/91	70	3		20 **One Less Pony**	*Mark Miller*	Curb/Capitol
4/6/91	68	6		21 **Mama's Little Baby Loves Me**	*Gregg Hubbard/Mark Miller*	Curb/Capitol
7/20/91	2^{1}	20		22 **The Walk**	*Mark Miller*	Curb/Capitol
				above 3 from the album *Buick* on Curb/Capitol 94260		
11/23/91+	3^{1}	20		23 **The Dirt Road**	*Gregg Hubbard/Mark Miller*	Curb/Capitol
3/7/92	❶^{1}	20		24 **Some Girls Do**	*Mark Miller*	Curb/Capitol
				above 2 from the album *The Dirt Road* on Curb/Capitol 95624		
8/8/92	5	20		25 **Cafe On The Corner**	*Mac McAnally*	Curb
11/28/92+	3^{1}	20		26 **All These Years**	*Mac McAnally*	Curb

DEBUT	PEAK	WKS	GOLD	ARTIST / Country Chart Hit	Ranking / Songwriter	Label (& Number)
				SAWYER BROWN — cont'd		
3/27/93	**5**	20		27 **Trouble On The Line**	*Mark Miller/Bill Shore*	Curb
				above 3 from the album *Cafe On The Corner* on Curb 77574		
7/3/93	**❶^{2}**	20		28 **Thank God For You**	*Mac McAnally/Mark Miller*	Curb
10/16/93+	**4**	20		29 **The Boys And Me**	*Mac McAnally/Mark Miller*	Curb
2/19/94	**40**	11		30 **Outskirts Of Town**	*Duncan Cameron/Gregg Hubbard*	Curb
6/25/94	**5**	20		31 **Hard To Say**	*Mark Miller*	Curb
				above 4 from the album *Outskirts Of Town* on Curb 77626		
11/19/94+	**2^{2}**	20		32 **This Time**	*Mac McAnally/Mark Miller*	Curb
3/18/95	**4**	20		33 **I Don't Believe In Goodbye**	S:25 *Scotty Emerick/Mark Miller/Bryan White*	Curb
				above 2 from the album *Greatest Hits 1990-1995* on Curb 77689		
7/22/95	**11**	20		34 (This Thing Called) **Wantin' And Havin' It All**	S:17 *Dave Loggins/Ronnie Samoset*	Curb
11/25/95+	**19**	20		35 **'Round Here**	*Scotty Emerick/Gregg Hubbard/Mark Miller*	Curb
3/23/96	**3^{2}**	21		36 **Treat Her Right**	S:10 *Ava Aldridge/Lenny LeBlanc*	Curb
8/17/96	**46**	10		37 **She's Gettin' There**	*Scotty Emerick/Mark Miller/John Northrup/Mary Potts*	Curb
				above 4 from the album *This Thing Called Wantin' And Havin' It All* on Curb 77785		
3/1/97	**13**	20		38 **Six Days On The Road**	*Earl Green/Carl Montgomery*	Curb
6/28/97	**6**	20		39 **This Night Won't Last Forever**	S:8 *Ron Freeland/Bill LaBounty*	Curb
2/14/98	**55**	7		40 **Another Side**	*Mark Miller*	Curb
4/11/98	**60**	6		41 **Small Talk**	*Mac McAnally/Mark Miller*	Curb
				above 4 from the album *Six Days On The Road* on Curb 77883		
11/14/98+	**6**	28		42 **Drive Me Wild**	S:7 *Gregg Hubbard/Mike Lawler/Mark Miller*	Curb
5/29/99	**47**	13		43 **I'm In Love With Her**	*Chuck Cannon/Allen Shamblin*	Curb
1/29/00	**40**	17		44 **800 Pound Jesus**	*Billy Maddox/Paul Thorn*	Curb
6/24/00	**50**	12		45 **Perfect World**	*Chuck Cannon/Billy Maddox/Mark Miller/Paul Thorn*	Curb
				above 4 from the album *Drive Me Wild* on Curb 77902		
11/25/00+	**44**	17		46 **Lookin' For Love**	*Wanda Mallette/Bob Morrison/Patti Ryan* **[L]**	Curb
				from the album *The Hits Live* on Curb 77976		
2/2/02	**45**	10		47 **Circles**	*Marv Green/Dave Loggins*	Curb
5/4/02	**57**	1		48 **Can You Hear Me Now**	*Dave Loggins/Mark Miller*	Curb
				above 2 from the album *Can You Hear Me Now* on Curb 78737		
8/2/03	**48**	9		49 **I'll Be Around**	*Tim Nichols/Craig Wiseman*	Lyric Street
12/11/04	**55**	5		50 **Mission Temple Fireworks Stand** ***[w/ Robert Randolph]***	*Billy Maddox/Paul Thorn*	Curb
				from Sawyer Brown's album *Mission Temple Fireworks Stand* on Curb 78879		
				SAYER, Leo		
				Born Gerard Sayer on 5/21/1948 in Shoreham, Sussex, England. Male pop singer.		
10/21/78	**63**	6		**Raining In My Heart**	*Boudleaux Bryant/Felice Bryant*	Warner 8682
				SCARBURY, Joey		
				Born on 6/7/1955 in Ontario, California. Male pop singer.		
10/20/84	**76**	7		**The River's Song**	*Stephen Geyer/Mike Post*	RCA 13913
				from the movie *The River Rat* starring Tommy Lee Jones		
				SCHAFFER, Norm		
				Born in Dallas, Texas. Male singer.		
3/12/88	**77**	4		**Dallas Darlin'**	*Milton Brown/Steve Dorff*	DSP 8712
				SCHEREE		
				Born in Boston, Massachusetts. Female singer.		
8/25/79	**94**	3		**I'm In Another World**	*Chuck Deal/Don Sanders*	Compass 0027
				SCHLITZ, Don	**SW: #12**	
				Born on 8/29/1952 in Durham, North Carolina. Male singer/songwriter.		
5/6/78	**65**	7		1 **The Gambler**	*Don Schlitz*	Capitol 4576
3/31/79	**91**	3		2 **You're The One Who Rewrote My Life Story**	*Tom Benjamin*	Capitol 4661
				SCHMUCKER, Paul		
				Born in Des Plaines, Illinois. Male singer/songwriter.		
11/25/78	**69**	6		1 **The Giver**	*Carol Schelton/Troy Shondell*	Star-Fox 378
3/3/79	**72**	4		2 **Makin' Love** (Is A Beautiful Thing To Do)	*Paul Schmucker*	Star-Fox 578
6/2/79	**74**	5		3 **Steal Away**	*Carol Shelton/Troy Shondell*	Star-Fox 279
				Joni Dolson (backing vocal)		
8/11/79	**83**	5		4 **Rainy Days And Rainbows**	*Troy Shondell*	Star-Fox 779
				all of above produced by **Troy Shondell**		
				SCHNEIDER, John	**All-Time: #235**	
				Born on 4/8/1954 in Mount Kisco, New York. Male singer/actor. Acted in several TV shows and movies. Best-known as "Bo Duke" on TV's *The Dukes of Hazzard*.		
6/13/81	**4**	17		1 **It's Now Or Never**	*Wally Gold/Aaron Schroeder*	Scotti Brothers 02105
				adapted from the Italian song "O Sole Mio" of 1899		
10/3/81	**13**	16		2 **Them Good Ol' Boys Are Bad**	*Kim Espy/Jeff Harrington/Jeff Pennig*	Scotti Brothers 02489
5/22/82	**32**	9		3 **Dreamin'**	*Barry DeVorzon/Ted Ellis*	Scotti Brothers 02889
8/21/82	**56**	7		4 **In The Driver's Seat**	*Jeff Harrington/Jeff Pennig*	Scotti Brothers 03062
7/2/83	**57**	6		5 **Are You Lonesome Tonight** ***[w/ Jill Michaels]***	*Lou Handman/Roy Turk*	Scotti Brothers 03945
10/1/83	**81**	3		6 **If You Believe**	*Mike Stanton*	Scotti Brothers 04064
7/28/84	**❶^{1}**	28		7 **I've Been Around Enough To Know**	S:❶^{1} / A:2 *Dickey Lee/Bob McDill*	MCA 52407
1/5/85	**❶^{1}**	23		8 **Country Girls**	S:❶^{1} / A:❶^{1} *Troy Seals/Eddie Setser*	MCA 52510
4/20/85	**10**	20		9 **It's A Short Walk From Heaven To Hell**	S:7 / A:11 *Ken Bell/Terry Skinner/J.L. Wallace*	MCA 52567

Billboard DEBUT	PEAK	WKS	GOLD	ARTIST Ranking / Country Chart Hit	Songwriter	Label (& Number)
				SCHNEIDER, John — cont'd		
8/10/85	10	20		10 I'm Going To Leave You Tomorrow ....S:9 / A:11	Tim Daniels/Gene Dobbins/Johnny Wilson	MCA 52648
12/14/85+	❶[1]	24		11 What's A Memory Like You (Doing In A Love Like This) S:❶[1] / A:❶[1]	John Jarrard/Charles Quillen	MCA 52723
5/10/86	❶[1]	20		12 You're The Last Thing I Needed Tonight S:❶[1] / A:❶[1]	Don Pfrimmer/David Wills	MCA 52827
8/30/86	5	23		13 At The Sound Of The Tone .....S:5 / A:5	Max T. Barnes/David Richardson	MCA 52901
12/20/86+	10	21		14 Take The Long Way Home .....A:10 / S:16	Doug Crider/Johnny Neel	MCA 52989
4/4/87	6	20		15 Love, You Ain't Seen The Last Of Me .....S:9 / A:24	Kendal Franceschi	MCA 53069
7/18/87	32	15		16 When The Right One Comes Along	John Hooker/Russell Smith	MCA 53144
11/7/87	59	6		17 If It Was Anyone But You	Don Schlitz/Lisa Silver	MCA 53199
				SCHUTT, Dawn		
				Born in Crown Point, Indiana. Female singer.		
3/18/89	96	2		Take Time	Kent Blazy/Allen Estes/Chris Hill	Master 10
				SCHUYLER, Thom		
				Born on 6/10/1952 in Bethlehem, Pennsylvania. Male singer/songwriter. Member of **Schuyler, Knobloch & Overstreet**.		
7/16/83	49	10		1 A Little At A Time	Larry Byrom/Thom Schuyler	Capitol 5239
10/22/83	43	11		2 Brave Heart	Thom Schuyler	Capitol 5281
				SCHUYLER, KNOBLOCH & OVERSTREET		
				Trio of prolific songwriters: **Thom Schuyler**, **Fred Knoblock** and **Paul Overstreet**. Also known as **S-K-O**. Overstreet replaced by **Craig Bickhardt** in 1987.		
7/12/86	9	29		1 You Can't Stop Love .....A:7 / S:11	Paul Overstreet/Thom Schuyler	MTM 72071
				S-K-O:		
12/6/86+	❶[1]	22		2 Baby's Got A New Baby S:❶[1] / A:❶[1]	Fred Knoblock/Dan Tyler	MTM 72081
4/18/87	16	14		3 American Me S:16	Fred Knoblock/Thom Schuyler	MTM 72086
				SCHUYLER, KNOBLOCH AND BICKHARDT:		
8/15/87	19	17		4 No Easy Horses	Fred Knoblock/Don Schlitz/Thom Schuyler	MTM 72090
11/28/87+	24	18		5 This Old House S:18	Craig Bickhardt/Thom Schuyler	MTM 72100
4/23/88	8	22		6 Givers And Takers S:14	Craig Bickhardt	MTM 72099
10/22/88	44	11		7 Rigamarole	Fred Knoblock/Dan Tyler	MTM 72115
				SCOTT, Earl		
				Born Earl Batdorf on 9/9/1936 in Youngstown, Ohio. Male singer. Father of rock singer John Batdorf (of Batdorf & Rodney).		
11/3/62	8	10		1 Then A Tear Fell	Warner Mack	Kapp 854
7/27/63	23	7		2 Loose Lips	Joe Poovey	Mercury 72110
1/4/64	30	1		3 Restless River	Steve Karliski/Larry Kolber	Mercury 72190
1/23/65	30	14		4 I'll Wander Back To You	Fred Burch/Danny Dill/Mel Tillis	Decca 31693
11/23/68	71	3		5 Too Rough On Me	Jean Chapel	Decca 32397
				SCOTT, Jack		
				Born Jack Scafone on 1/28/1936 in Windsor, Ontario, Canada. Male singer/guitarist.		
7/6/74	92	4		You're Just Gettin' Better	Ron Hellard/Gary S. Paxton	Dot 17504
				SCOTT, Lang		
				Born in Sumter, South Carolina; raised in Harleyville, South Carolina. Male singer. Married to **Linda Davis**.		
4/21/84	68	6		1 Run Your Sweet Love By Me One More Time /	Roy Dockery Jr./Dave Gibson	
8/18/84	91	2		2 It's Been One Of Those Days	Tim DuBois/Chester Lester/Mike Seals	MCA 52359
				SCRUGGS, Earl		
				Born on 1/6/1924 in Flint Hill, North Carolina. Banjo player. Half of **Flatt & Scruggs** duo. His revue consisted of sons Gary Scruggs (vocals, bass), **Randy Scruggs** (guitar) and Steve Scruggs (keyborads), with Jim Murphey (steel guitar) and Jody Maphis (drums). Steve Scruggs murdered his wife, then killed himself on 9/23/1992. Also see **Same Old Train**.		
10/24/70	74	2		1 Nashville Skyline Rag written and first recorded by Bob Dylan on his 1969 *Nashville Skyline* album	Bob Dylan [I]	Columbia 45218
				EARL SCRUGGS REVUE:		
7/7/79	30	11		2 I Could Sure Use The Feeling	Dennis Linde/Mel McDaniel	Columbia 10992
11/3/79	82	4		3 Play Me No Sad Songs	Roger Bowling/Larry Butler/Mack Jackson	Columbia 11106
1/19/80	46	9		4 Blue Moon Of Kentucky	Bill Monroe	Columbia 11176
				TOM T. HALL & EARL SCRUGGS:		
5/22/82	77	4		5 There Ain't No Country Music On This Jukebox	Tom T. Hall	Columbia 02858
7/31/82	72	5		6 Song Of The South	Bob McDill	Columbia 03033
				SCRUGGS, Randy		
				Born on 8/3/1953 in Nashville, Tennessee. Male guitarist/songwriter. Son of **Earl Scruggs**. ***CMA: Musician 1999 & 2003***		
12/19/98	67	9		It's Only Love *[w/ Mary Chapin Carpenter]* from the album *Crown Of Jewels* on Reprise 46930	Mary-Chapin Carpenter/Randy Scruggs	Reprise
				SEA, Johnny		
				Born John Seay on 7/15/1940 in Gulfport, Mississippi. Male singer/guitarist.		
4/20/59	13	9		1 Frankie's Man, Johnny	(traditional)	NRC 019
2/8/60	13	8		2 Nobody's Darling But Mine	Jimmie Davis	NRC 049
5/23/64	27	10		3 My Baby Walks All Over Me	Billy Mize	Philips 40164
4/10/65	19	16		4 My Old Faded Rose	June Carter/Johnny Cash	Philips 40267
6/11/66	14	11		5 Day For Decision	Allen Peltier [S]	Warner 5820
4/1/67	61	4		6 Nothin's Bad As Bein' Lonely	Bobby Goldsboro	Warner 5889

Billboard DEBUT	PEAK	WKS	GOLD	ARTIST / Country Chart Hit	Ranking / Songwriter	Label (& Number)
				JOHNNY SEAY:		
3/30/68	**68**	2		7 **Going Out To Tulsa**	*C.E. Daniels*	Columbia 44423
10/19/68	**32**	11		8 **Three Six Packs, Two Arms And A Juke Box**	*Red Lane/Curly Putman*	Columbia 44634
				SEAL, Jim		
				Born in Los Angeles, California. Male singer.		
10/25/80	**79**	5		**Bourbon Cowboy**	*David Hodges/Jim Hodges/Lewis Moore*	NSD 66
				SEALS, Brady		
				Born on 3/29/1969 in Hamilton, Ohio. Male singer/songwriter/guitarist. Former member of **Little Texas**; later formed **Hot Apple Pie**. Related to **Johnny Duncan**, **Dan Seals** and **Troy Seals**.		
9/7/96+	**32**	20		1 **Another You, Another Me**	S:3 *Will Jennings/Troy Seals*	Reprise
2/22/97	**69**	6		2 **Still Standing Tall**	*Tommy Barnes/Brady Seals*	Reprise
8/23/97	**74**	1		3 **Natural Born Lovers**	*Brady Seals/Troy Seals/Eddie Setser*	Reprise
				above 3 from the album *The Truth* on Reprise 46258		
6/13/98	**55**	12		4 **I Fell**	*Tommy Barnes*	Warner
10/24/98	**66**	2		5 **Whole Lotta Hurt**	*Jamie O'Hara/Brady Seals*	Warner
7/10/99	**74**	2		6 **The Best Is Yet To Come**	*Rodney Crowell/Brady Seals*	Warner
				above 3 from the album *Brady Seals* on Warner 46939		

SEALS, Dan — **1980s: #43 / All-Time: #126**

Born on 2/8/1950 in McCamey, Texas; raised in Iraan and Rankin, Texas. Male singer/songwriter/guitarist. Brother of Jim Seals (of pop duo Seals & Crofts). Member of England Dan & John Ford Coley duo. Related to **Johnny Duncan**, **Brady Seals** and **Troy Seals**. Also see **Tomorrow's World**.

CMA: Vocal Duo (with Marie Osmond) 1986

DEBUT	PEAK	WKS	GOLD	Country Chart Hit	Songwriter	Label (& Number)
4/30/83	**18**	17		1 **Everybody's Dream Girl**	*Dave Robbins/Dan Seals/Van Stephenson*	Liberty 1496
8/13/83	**28**	14		2 **After You**	*Paul Battle/Bucky Jones/Chris Waters*	Liberty 1504
11/19/83+	**37**	16		3 **You Really Go For The Heart**	*Charlie Black/Jerry Gillespie/Tommy Rocco*	Liberty 1512
2/25/84	**10**	21		4 **God Must Be A Cowboy**	*Dan Seals*	Liberty 1515
7/28/84	**9**	23		5 (You Bring Out) **The Wild Side Of Me**	S:9 / A:12 *Dan Seals*	EMI America 8220
11/24/84+	**2**^{2}	21		6 **My Baby's Got Good Timing**	A:2 / S:2 *Bob McDill/Dan Seals*	EMI America 8245
3/30/85	**9**	19		7 **My Old Yellow Car**	S:7 / A:10 *Thom Schuyler*	EMI America 8261
7/6/85	❶^{1}	23		8 **Meet Me In Montana** ***[w/ Marie Osmond]***	S:❶^{1} / A:❶^{1} *Paul Davis*	Curb/Capitol 5478
10/26/85+	❶^{1}	27		9 **Bop**	S:❶^{1} / A:❶^{1} *Paul Davis/Jennifer Kimball*	EMI America 8289
				CMA: Single		
4/5/86	❶^{1}	23		10 **Everything That Glitters** (Is Not Gold)	S:❶^{2} / A:❶^{1} *Bob McDill/Dan Seals*	EMI America 8311
10/25/86+	❶^{1}	22		11 **You Still Move Me**	S:❶^{1} / A:❶^{1} *Dan Seals*	EMI America 8343
3/7/87	❶^{1}	19		12 **I Will Be There**	S:❶^{2} / A:5 *Jennifer Kimball/Tom Snow*	EMI America 8377
6/27/87	❶^{1}	21		13 **Three Time Loser**	S:❶^{1} *Dan Seals*	EMI America 43023
10/17/87+	❶^{1}	26		14 **One Friend**	S:❶^{1} *Dan Seals*	Capitol 44077
6/18/88	❶^{1}	22		15 **Addicted**	S:4 *Cheryl Wheeler*	Capitol 44130
11/12/88+	❶^{1}	21		16 **Big Wheels In The Moonlight**	S:22 *Bob McDill/Dan Seals*	Capitol 44267
3/18/89	**5**	24		17 **They Rage On**	*Bob McDill/Dan Seals*	Capitol 44345
2/17/90	❶^{3}	26		18 **Love On Arrival**	*Dan Seals*	Capitol
6/9/90	❶^{2}	21		19 **Good Times**	*Sam Cooke*	Capitol
10/13/90	**49**	10		20 **Bordertown**	*Bob McDill/Dan Seals*	Capitol
2/2/91	**57**	6		21 **Water Under The Bridge**	*Bruce Burch/John Porter McMeans*	Capitol
				above 4 from the album *On Arrival* on Capitol 91782		
11/2/91	**62**	10		22 **Sweet Little Shoe**	*Jesse Winchester*	Warner
4/25/92	**43**	13		23 **Mason Dixon Line**	*Dan Seals*	Warner
7/25/92	**51**	9		24 **When Love Comes Around The Bend**	*Josh Leo/Pam Tillis/Mark Wright*	Warner
				above 3 from the album *Walking The Wire* on Warner 26770		
7/2/94	**66**	6		25 **All Fired Up**	*Steve Davis/Dennis W. Morgan/Bobby Lee Springfield*	Warner
				from the album *Fired Up* on Warner 45628		
				SEALS, Troy	**SW: #17**	
				Born on 11/16/1938 in Big Hill, Kentucky; raised in Ohio. Male singer/songwriter/guitarist. Recorded with wife **Jo Ann Campbell** as Jo Ann & Troy in the mid-1960s. Related to **Johnny Duncan**, **Brady Seals** and **Dan Seals**.		
8/11/73	**93**	4		1 **I Got A Thing About You Baby**	*Tony Joe White*	Atlantic 4004
1/19/74	**96**	7		2 **You Can't Judge A Book By The Cover** /	*Willie Dixon*	
2/2/74	**78**	5		3 **Star Of The Bar**	*Jo Ann Campbell/Troy Seals*	Atlantic 4013
5/11/74	**81**	6		4 **Honky-Tonkin'**	*John Bettis/Dave Gillon/Don Goodman/Troy Seals*	Atlantic 4020
7/19/75	**76**	7		5 **Easy**	*Don Goodman/Troy Seals*	Columbia 10173
3/27/76	**88**	5		6 **Sweet Dreams**	*Don Gibson*	Columbia 10303
4/23/77	**93**	2		7 **Grand Ole Blues**	*Troy Seals/Billy Sherrill*	Columbia 10511
2/16/80	**85**	3		8 **One Night Honeymoon**	*Tom Daey/Troy Seals*	Elektra 46573
				SEARS, Dawn		
				Born in East Grand Forks, Minnesota. Female singer.		
5/7/94	**62**	7		**Runaway Train**	*Terry Burns/Kim Richey*	Decca
				from the album *Nothing But Good* on Decca 11056		

DEBUT	PEAK	WKS	GOLD	ARTIST / Country Chart Hit	Ranking / Songwriter	Label (& Number)
				SEBASTIAN, John		
				Born on 3/17/1944 in Brooklyn, New York. Pop-rock singer/songwriter. Lead singer of The Lovin' Spoonful.		
5/15/76	**93**	2	●	**Welcome Back**	*John Sebastian*	Reprise 1349
				from the TV series *Welcome Back, Kotter* starring Gabriel Kaplan		
				SEELY, Jeannie	**All-Time: #224**	
				Born Marilyn Jeanne Seely on 7/6/1940 in Titusville, Pennsylvania; raised in Townville, Pennsylvania. Female singer/songwriter. Formerly married to **Hank Cochran**.		
				OPRY: 1967		
4/16/66	2^3	21		1 **Don't Touch Me**	*Hank Cochran*	Monument 933
				Grammy: Female Vocal		
9/10/66	**15**	15		2 **It's Only Love**	*Hank Cochran*	Monument 965
12/17/66+	**13**	13		3 **A Wanderin' Man**	*Hank Cochran*	Monument 987
3/18/67	**39**	10		4 **When It's Over**	*Hank Cochran*	Monument 999
7/8/67	**42**	8		5 **These Memories**	*Hank Cochran*	Monument 1011
10/28/67+	**10**	15		6 **I'll Love You More (Than You Need)**	*Hank Cochran*	Monument 1029
2/24/68	**24**	12		7 **Welcome Home To Nothing**	*Hank Cochran*	Monument 1054
6/22/68	**23**	10		8 **How Is He?**	*Marijohn Wilkin*	Monument 1075
3/22/69	**43**	11		9 **Just Enough To Start Me Dreamin'**	*Hank Cochran*	Decca 32452
11/15/69+	2^2	16		10 **Wish I Didn't Have To Miss You** *[w/ Jack Greene]*	*Hank Cochran/Dave Kirby*	Decca 32580
3/7/70	**46**	6		11 **Please Be My New Love**	*Hank Cochran*	Decca 32628
12/5/70	**58**	5		12 **Tell Me Again**	*Jerry Crutchfield*	Decca 32757
7/17/71	**71**	5		13 **You Don't Understand Him Like I Do**	*Jackie DeShannon/Randy Newman*	Decca 32838
11/20/71+	**42**	10		14 **Alright I'll Sign The Papers**	*Mel Tillis*	Decca 32882
12/11/71+	**15**	13		15 **Much Oblige** *[w/ Jack Greene]*	*George Deaton/Luke Fulford/Gene Simmons*	Decca 32898
6/17/72	**47**	9		16 **Pride**	*Irene Stanton/Wayne Walker*	Decca 32964
8/12/72	**19**	12		17 **What In The World Has Gone Wrong With Our Love** *[w/ Jack Greene]*	*...Hank Cochran/Johnny Slate*	Decca 32991
1/20/73	**72**	4		18 **Farm In Pennsyltucky /**	*Jeannie Seely*	
1/27/73	**flip**	3		19 **Between The King And I**	*Red Lane*	Decca 33042
7/7/73	**6**	18		20 **Can I Sleep In Your Arms**	*Hank Cochran*	MCA 40074
12/15/73+	**11**	13		21 **Lucky Ladies**	*Hank Cochran*	MCA 40162
5/18/74	**37**	10		22 **I Miss You**	*Cliff Cochran/Hank Cochran*	MCA 40225
9/21/74	**26**	14		23 **He Can Be Mine**	*Jeannie Seely*	MCA 40287
7/19/75	**59**	9		24 **Take My Hand**	*Hank Cochran*	MCA 40428
4/17/76	**96**	3		25 **Since I Met You Boy**	*Cliff Cochran/J.R. Cochran*	MCA 40528
6/11/77	**80**	5		26 **We're Still Hangin' In There Ain't We Jessi**	*Jeanne Seely*	Columbia 10550
1/28/78	**97**	1		27 **Take Me To Bed**	*Hank Cochran/Glenn Martin*	Columbia 10664
				SEEVERS, Les		
				Born in West Virginia. Male singer.		
3/8/69	**57**	9		**What Kind Of Magic**	*Bernard Chianco*	Decca 32434
				SEGER, Bob, & The Silver Bullet Band		
				Born on 5/6/1945 in Dearborn, Michigan; raised in Detroit, Michigan. Rock singer/songwriter. Inducted into the Rock and Roll Hall of Fame in 2004.		
1/22/83	**15**	14		**Shame On The Moon**	*Rodney Crowell*	Capitol 5187
				SEGO BROTHERS AND NAOMI, The		
				Group from Macon, Georgia. Included James Sego (died on 7/24/1979, age 51) and his wife Naomi.		
2/1/64	**50**	1		**Sorry I Never Knew You**	*Sherman Branch*	Songs of Faith 8032
				SEINER, Barbara		
				Born in Tennessee. Female singer.		
3/3/79	**87**	3		**Jealous Heart**	*Jenny Lou Carson*	Starship 109
				SELF, Ted		
				Born on 7/5/1925 in Utah. Died on 7/31/1996 (age 71). Male singer/songwriter/guitarist.		
7/4/60	**20**	10		**Little Angel (Come Rock Me To Sleep)**	*Ted Self*	Plaid 115
				SELLARS, Marilyn		
				Born on 12/31/1950 in Northfield, Minnesota. Female singer.		
4/20/74	**19**	17		1 **One Day At A Time**	*Kris Kristofferson/Marijohn Wilkin*	Mega 1205
12/14/74+	**39**	14		2 **He's Everywhere**	*Gene Dobbins/Jean Whitehead*	Mega 1221
5/24/75	**84**	4		3 **Gather Me**	*Tony Austin/Gene Dobbins*	Mega 1230
1/24/76	**91**	3		4 **The Door I Used To Close**	*Dallas Frazier/Earl Montgomery*	Mega 1242
				SELLERS, Jason		
				Born on 3/4/1971 in Gilmer, Texas. Male singer/songwriter. Married to **Lee Ann Womack** from 1991-97.		
8/2/97	**37**	14		1 **I'm Your Man**	*Austin Cunningham/Mark D. Sanders*	BNA
11/22/97+	**46**	14		2 **That Does It**	*Austin Cunningham/Jason Sellers*	BNA
5/9/98	**55**	7		3 **This Small Divide** *[w/ Martina McBride]*	*Gary Burr/Jason Sellers*	BNA
				above 3 from the album *I'm Your Man* on BNA 67517		
7/10/99	**33**	20		4 **A Matter Of Time**	S:14 *Annie Roboff/Jason Sellers/Craig Wiseman*	BNA
3/4/00	**64**	5		5 **Can't Help Calling Your Name**	*Josh Bernard/Tim Mathews*	BNA
				above 2 from the album *A Matter Of Time* on BNA 67764		

Billboard DEBUT	PEAK	WKS	GOLD	ARTIST / Country Chart Hit	Ranking / Songwriter	Label (& Number)
				SELLERS, Shane		
				Born in Erath, Louisiana. Male singer.		
5/12/01	**58**	1		**Matthew, Mark, Luke and Earnhardt** S:7	*Randy Boudreaux/Dennis Knutson/Roger Wade*	DreamWorks
				a tribute to Dale Earnhardt, who was killed while racing at the Daytona 500 on 2/18/2001		
				SEMINOLE		
				Duo of brothers from Florida: Jimmy Myers and Donald "Butch" Myers.		
8/16/97	**69**	6		**She Knows Me By Heart**	*Donnie Myers/Bill Shore/Rick West*	Curb/Universal
				SERRATT, Kenny		
				Born on 10/20/1947 in Manila, Arkansas; raised in Dyess, Arkansas. Male singer. Nicknamed "Country Kin."		
12/9/72+	**56**	9		1 **Goodbyes Come Hard For Me**	*Tommy Collins*	MGM 14435
				KENNY SERRATT and The Messengers:		
5/5/73	**68**	3		2 **This Just Ain't No Good Day For Leavin'**	*Dallas Frazier/Whitey Shafer*	MGM 14517
9/29/73	**70**	13		3 **Love And Honor**	*Merle Haggard*	MGM 14636
				above 3 produced by **Merle Haggard**		
				KENNY SERATT:		
8/2/75	**88**	6		4 **If I Could Have It Any Other Way**	*Gary Branson*	Melodyland 6014
8/21/76	**72**	6		5 **I've Been There Too**	*Joe Nixon/Charlie Williams*	Hitsville 6039
2/12/77	**54**	8		6 **Daddy, They're Playin' A Song About You**	*Harry Shannon/Steve Stone*	Hitsville 6049
12/15/79	**82**	4		7 **Never Gonna' Be A Country Star /**	*Geray Hanley*	
12/15/79	**flip**	4		8 **A Damn Good Drinking Song**	*Kenny Seratt/Steve Stone*	MDJ 1001
5/3/80	**54**	8		9 **Saturday Night In Dallas**	*Dewey Groom/Vern Stovall*	MDJ 1003
9/13/80	**39**	8		10 **Until The Bitter End**	*Skippy Barrett/Tim Daniels/Gene Dobbins*	MDJ 1005
5/2/81	**70**	7		11 **Sidewalks Are Grey**	*Tommy Collins*	MDJ 1008
				SESSIONS, Ronnie		
				Born on 12/7/1948 in Henrietta, Oklahoma; raised in Bakersfield, California. Male singer/songwriter/guitarist.		
8/5/72	**36**	10		1 **Never Been To Spain**	*Hoyt Axton*	MGM 14394
11/18/72	**59**	6		2 **Tossin' And Turnin'**	*Ritchie Adams/Malou Rene*	MGM 14445
6/23/73	**66**	5		3 **She Feels So Good I Hate To Put Her Down**	*Larry Henley/Kenny O'Dell*	MGM 14528
				also released as "I Just Can't Put Her Down"		
9/29/73	**87**	7		4 **If That Back Door Could Talk**	*Hank Cochran*	MGM 14619
10/4/75	**61**	10		5 **Makin' Love**	*Floyd Robinson*	MCA 40462
7/17/76	**81**	4		6 **Support Your Local Honky Tonks**	*Ray Willis/Tom Willis*	MCA 40581
10/30/76+	**16**	17		7 **Wiggle Wiggle**	*Layng Martine Jr.*	MCA 40624
4/9/77	**15**	13		8 **Me And Millie (Stompin' Grapes And Gettin' Silly)**	*Bobby Goldsboro*	MCA 40705
8/6/77	**30**	10		9 **Ambush**	*Layng Martine Jr.*	MCA 40758
12/10/77+	**57**	9		10 **I Like To Be With You**	*Johnny Christopher/Bobby Wood*	MCA 40831
3/25/78	**72**	7		11 **Cash On The Barrelhead**	*Charlie Louvin/Ira Louvin*	MCA 40875
7/15/78	**96**	2		12 **I Never Go Around Mirrors**	*Lefty Frizzell/Whitey Shafer*	MCA 40917
10/7/78	**25**	9		13 **Juliet And Romeo**	*Tim Krekel*	MCA 40952
6/30/79	**94**	3		14 **Do You Want To Fly**	*Bill Holmes/Wayne Marshall*	MCA 41038
12/1/79	**84**	5		15 **Honky Tonkin'**	*John Bettis/Dave Gillon/Don Goodman/Troy Seals*	MCA 41142
12/27/86+	**78**	5		16 **I Bought The Shoes That Just Walked Out On Me**	*Red Simpson/Steve Stone*	Compleat 161
				SEXTON, Mark		
				Born in Reno, Nevada. Male singer.		
11/24/79	**97**	2		**Don't Say No To Me Tonight**	*Dick Addrisi/Don Addrisi*	Sun-De-Mar 79101
				SHAFER, Whitey	**SW: #65**	
				Born Sanger Shafer on 10/24/1934 in Whitney, Texas. Male singer/songwriter.		
12/13/80+	**48**	9		1 **You Are A Liar**	*Whitey Shafer*	Elektra 47063
4/11/81	**67**	3		2 **If I Say I Love You (Consider Me Drunk)**	*Whitey Shafer*	Elektra 47117
				SHAMBLIN, Michael		
				Born in Chattanooga, Tennessee. Male singer.		
3/8/86	**77**	3		1 **Foreign Affairs**	*Bobby Fischer/Dan Mitchell*	F&L 548
6/7/86	**83**	2		2 **Wishful Dreamin'**	*Bobby Fischer/Rick Giles*	F&L 549
				SHANE, Michael		
				Born in Dallas, Texas. Male singer.		
2/11/89	**93**	2		1 **What's The Matter Baby**	*Adrianna Appel/Joanna Jacobs*	Regal 1988
7/1/89	**99**	1		2 **Broken Dreams And Memories**	*Adrianna Appel/Michael Shane*	Regal 9891
				SHANNON, Bonnie		
				Born Bonnie Shannon Belt in Willits, California. Female singer/songwriter.		
12/20/80	**88**	4		**Lovin' You Lightly**	*Bonnie Shannon*	Door Knob 139
				SHANNON, Del		
				Born Charles Westover on 12/30/1934 in Coopersville, Michigan. Died of a self-inflicted gunshot wound on 2/8/1990 (age 55). Male pop singer/songwriter.		
3/9/85	**56**	6		**In My Arms Again**	*Del Shannon*	Warner 29098
				SHANNON, Guy		
				Born in Arizona. Male singer/pianist.		
7/7/73	**69**	5		1 **Naughty Girl**	*Mac Davis*	Cinnamon 758
10/6/73	**63**	11		2 **Soul Deep**	*Wayne Carson*	Cinnamon 769

DEBUT	PEAK	WKS	GOLD	ARTIST / Country Chart Hit	Ranking / Songwriter	Label (& Number)

SHARP, Kevin

Born on 12/10/1970 in Weiser, Idaho; raised in Sacramento, California. Male singer. Survived a battle with bone cancer from 1988-91.

DEBUT	PEAK	WKS	GOLD	Country Chart Hit	Songwriter	Label (& Number)
9/28/96+	❶[4]	22		1 **Nobody Knows**	*Don DuBose/Joe Richards*	Asylum
2/8/97	**3**[1]	21		2 **She's Sure Taking It Well**	*Tim Buppert/Don Pfrimmer/George Teren*	143/Asylum
7/26/97	**4**	20		3 **If You Love Somebody**	*Chris Farren/Jeffrey Steele*	143/Asylum
11/22/97+	**43**	13		4 **There's Only You**	*Skip Ewing/Donny Kees*	143/Asylum
				above 4 from the album *Measure Of A Man* on Asylum 61930		
3/21/98	**51**	8		5 **Love Is All That Really Matters**	*Annie Roboff/Arnie Roman*	143/Asylum
6/27/98	**61**	9		6 **If She Only Knew**	*Gordon Chambers/Chris Farren*	143/Asylum
				above 2 from the album *Love Is* on Asylum 62165		

SHARP, Rosemary

Born in Fort Worth, Texas. Female singer.

DEBUT	PEAK	WKS	GOLD	Country Chart Hit	Songwriter	Label (& Number)
2/28/87	**85**	3		1 **Didn't You Go And Leave Me**	*Barry Brown*	Canyon Creek 1226
8/8/87	**76**	4		2 **Real Good Heartache**	*Michael Garvin/Craig Morris*	Canyon Creek 0401
10/31/87	**67**	6		3 **If You're Gonna Tell Me Lies (Tell Me Good Ones)**	*Doug Atkin/Larry Whinnery*	Canyon Creek 0908
4/9/88	**68**	5		4 **The Stairs**	*Pamela Brown/Dave Roberts*	Canyon Creek 0210

SHARPE, Sunday

Born in 1946 in Orlando, Florida. Female singer/songwriter.

DEBUT	PEAK	WKS	GOLD	Country Chart Hit	Songwriter	Label (& Number)
8/17/74	**11**	14		1 **I'm Having Your Baby**	*Paul Anka*	United Artists 507
				female version of "(You're) Having My Baby" by Paul Anka		
12/21/74+	**47**	9		2 **Mr. Songwriter**	*Thomas Boyce/Mel Powers*	United Artists 571
3/29/75	**48**	8		3 **Put Your Head On My Shoulder**	*Paul Anka*	United Artists 602
2/14/76	**80**	5		4 **Find A New Love, Girl**	*Milton Blackford/Sunday Sharpe*	United Artists 758
11/6/76	**18**	12		5 **A Little At A Time**	*Jerry Foster/Bill Rice*	Playboy 6090
6/18/77	**62**	5		6 **I'm Not The One You Love (I'm The One You Make Love To)**	*Jerry Foster/Bill Rice*	Playboy 5806
8/27/77	**45**	7		7 **Hold On Tight**	*Rory Bourke/Gene Dobbins/Johnny Wilson*	Playboy 5813

SHATSWELL, Danny

Born on 3/7/1953 in Oklahoma. Died on 10/1/1994 (age 41). Male singer/guitarist.

DEBUT	PEAK	WKS	GOLD	Country Chart Hit	Songwriter	Label (& Number)
6/17/78	**97**	2		**I'm A Mender**	*Dennis Knutson*	Mercury 55027

SHAVER, Billy Joe

Born on 8/16/1939 in Corsicana, Texas; raised in Waco, Texas. Male singer/songwriter.

DEBUT	PEAK	WKS	GOLD	Country Chart Hit	Songwriter	Label (& Number)
9/15/73	**88**	3		1 **I Been To Georgia On A Fast Train**	*Billy Joe Shaver*	Monument 8580
3/11/78	**80**	5		2 **You Asked Me To**	*Waylon Jennings/Billy Joe Shaver*	Capricorn 0286

SHAW, Brian

Born on 12/3/1949 in Grove City, Pennsylvania. Male singer/bassist.

DEBUT	PEAK	WKS	GOLD	Country Chart Hit	Songwriter	Label (& Number)
9/8/73	**55**	8		1 **The Devil Is A Woman**	*Bobby Borchers/Howard Goff*	RCA Victor 0058
12/15/73+	**62**	11		2 **Good Enough To Be Your Man**	*Dave Kirby*	RCA Victor 0186
4/6/74	**50**	9		3 **Friend Named Red**	*Gene Taylor/Sam Weedman*	RCA Victor 0230
10/12/74	**17**	15		4 **Here We Go Again**	*Sonny Throckmorton*	RCA Victor 10071
10/16/76	**97**	2		5 **Showdown**	*Jerry Fuller*	Republic 306
3/12/77	**97**	2		6 **What Kind Of Fool (Does That Make Me)**	*Mike Kosser/Curly Putnam*	Republic 360

SHAW, Ron

Born in Anaheim, California. Male singer/songwriter. Former member of The Hillside Singers.

DEBUT	PEAK	WKS	GOLD	Country Chart Hit	Songwriter	Label (& Number)
6/25/77	**94**	4		1 **Hurtin' Kind Of Love**	*Ron Shaw*	Pacific Chall. 1511
				also see #7 below		
7/8/78	**79**	7		2 **Goin' Home**	*Ron Shaw*	Pacific Chall. 1522
10/7/78	**36**	9		3 **Save The Last Dance For Me**	*Doc Pomus/Mort Shuman*	Pacific Chall. 1631
1/20/79	**68**	7		4 **I Cry Instead**	*John Lennon/Paul McCartney*	Pacific Chall. 1633
7/28/79	**93**	3		5 **One And One Make Three**	*Ron Shaw*	Pacific Chall. 1635
9/22/79	**90**	4		6 **What The World Needs Now (Is Love Sweet Love)**	*Burt Bacharach/Hal David*	Pacific Chall. 1636
3/22/80	**91**	4		7 **Hurtin' Kind Of Love**	*Ron Shaw* **[R]**	Pacific Chall. 1637
				same version as #1 above		
8/16/80	**94**	2		8 **The Legend Of Harry And The Mountain**	*Lula Belle Garland*	Pacific Chall. 1638
2/7/81	**78**	4		9 **Reachin' For Freedom**	*Robert Lee Smith*	Pacific Chall. 1639
				RON SHAW & The Desert Wind Band (above 2)		

SHAW, Victoria

Born on 7/13/1962 in Manhattan, New York; raised in Los Angeles, California. Female singer/songwriter. Also see **One Heart At A Time**.

DEBUT	PEAK	WKS	GOLD	Country Chart Hit	Songwriter	Label (& Number)
2/25/84	**61**	10		1 **Break My Heart**	*Angela Kaset/Howard Tipton*	MPB 5008
5/7/94	**57**	9		2 **Cry Wolf**	*Jess Leary/Victoria Shaw*	Reprise
9/3/94	**74**	2		3 **Tears Dry**	*Victoria Shaw/Jon Vezner*	Reprise
6/10/95	**58**	7		4 **Forgiveness**	*Bob DiPiero/Victoria Shaw*	Reprise
				above 3 from the album *In Full View* on Reprise 45592		

SHAY, Dorothy

Born Dorothy Sims on 4/11/1921 in Jacksonville, Florida. Died of a heart attack on 10/22/1978 (age 57). Female singer/actress. Known as "The Park Avenue Hillbillie." Acted in the movie *Comin' 'Round The Mountain.*

DEBUT	PEAK	WKS	GOLD	Country Chart Hit	Songwriter	Label (& Number)
8/16/47	**4**	7		**Feudin' And Fightin'**	*Al Dubin/Burton Lane*	Columbia 37189
				from the Broadway musical *Laffing Room Only* starring Betty Garrett		

DEBUT	PEAK	WKS	GOLD		ARTIST / Country Chart Hit	Ranking / Songwriter	Label (& Number)

SHeDAISY — 2000s: #22 / All-Time: #271

Vocal trio from Magna, Utah: sisters Kristyn Osborn (born on 8/24/1970), Kelsi Osborn (born on 11/21/1974) and Kassidy Osborn (born on 10/30/1976).

DEBUT	PEAK	WKS	GOLD	#	Country Chart Hit	Songwriter	Label (& Number)
2/27/99	3^{1}	32		1	**Little Good-Byes**	S:5 *Jason Deere/Kenny Greenberg/Kristyn Osborn*	Lyric Street
9/4/99+	9	31		2	**This Woman Needs**	*Bonnie Baker/Connie Harrington/Kristyn Osborn*	Lyric Street
12/11/99+	40	5		3	**Deck The Halls**	S:❶^{3} *(traditional)* [X]	Lyric Street
1/15/00	2^{3}	44		4	**I Will...But**	*Jason Deere/Kristyn Osborn*	Lyric Street
9/23/00+	11	27		5	**Lucky 4 You (Tonight I'm Just Me)**	*Jason Deere/Coley McCabe/Kristyn Osborn*	Lyric Street
12/9/00+	37	6		6	**Deck The Halls**	*(traditional)* [X-R]	Lyric Street
12/9/00+	44	6		7	**Jingle Bells**	*James Pierpont* [X]	Lyric Street
					#3, 6 & 7: from the album *Brand New Year* on Lyric Street 65007		
4/21/01	27	20		8	**Still Holding Out For You**	*Richard Marx/Kristyn Osborn*	Lyric Street
					#1, 2, 4, 5 & 8: from the album *The Whole SheBang* on Lyric Street 65002		
3/9/02	27	14		9	**Get Over Yourself**	*Marcus Hummon/Kristyn Osborn*	Lyric Street
5/25/02	28	20		10	**Mine All Mine**	*Kristyn Osborn/Hollie Poole*	Lyric Street
					featured in the movie *Sweet Home Alabama* starring Reese Witherspoon; above 2 from the album *Knock On The Sky* on Lyric Street 165015		
2/7/04	12	20		11	**Passenger Seat**	*Connie Harrington/Kristyn Osborn*	Lyric Street
7/10/04	14	25		12	**Come Home Soon**	*Kristyn Osborn/John Shanks*	Lyric Street
2/5/05	7	30		13	**Don't Worry 'Bout A Thing**	*Jason Deere/Kristyn Osborn*	Lyric Street
					above 3 from the album *Sweet Right Here* on Lyric Street 165044		

SHELTON, Blake — 2000s: #23

Born on 6/18/1976 in Ada, Oklahoma. Male singer/songwriter/guitarist.

DEBUT	PEAK	WKS	GOLD	#	Country Chart Hit	Songwriter	Label (& Number)
4/28/01	❶^{5}	27		1	**Austin**	S:❶^{8} *David Kent/Kirsti Manna*	Warner
10/20/01+	18	21		2	**All Over Me**	*Earl Thomas Conley/Mike Pyle/Blake Shelton*	Warner
3/30/02	14	26		3	**Ol' Red**	*James Bohan/Don Goodman/Mark Sherrill*	Warner
					above 3 from the album *Blake Shelton* on Warner 24731		
11/2/02+	❶^{3}	24		4	**The Baby**	*Harley Allen/Michael White*	Warner
4/26/03	32	13		5	**Heavy Liftin'**	*Boyd Houston/Rivers Rutherford/George Teren/Robert Teren*	Warner
7/12/03	24	20		6	**Playboys Of The Southwestern World**	*Neal Coty/Randy Vanwarmer*	Warner
					above 3 from the album *The Dreamer* on Warner 48237		
3/13/04	37	12		7	**When Somebody Knows You That Well**	*Harley Allen/Jimmy Melton*	Warner
8/7/04	❶^{4}	30		8	**Some Beach**	*Rory Lee Feek/Paul Overstreet*	Warner
2/5/05	10	27		9	**Goodbye Time**	*J.D. Hicks/Roger Murrah*	Warner
					above 3 from the album *Blake Shelton's Barn & Grill* on Warner 48728		

SHELTON, Ricky Van — 1990s: #38 / All-Time: #119

Born on 1/12/1952 in Danville, Virginia; raised in Grit, Virginia. Male singer/songwriter/guitarist. Van is his middle name. Worked as a pipefitter prior to his music career.

CMA: Horizon 1988 / Male Vocalist 1989 // OPRY: 1988

DEBUT	PEAK	WKS	GOLD	#	Country Chart Hit	Songwriter	Label (& Number)
12/20/86+	24	18		1	**Wild-Eyed Dream**	A:24 *Alan Rhody*	Columbia 06542
4/18/87	7	19		2	**Crime Of Passion**	S:2 *Walt Aldridge/Mac McAnally*	Columbia 07025
8/22/87	❶^{1}	25		3	**Somebody Lied**	S:❶^{2} *Joe Chambers/Larry Jenkins*	Columbia 07311
1/9/88	❶^{1}	23		4	**Life Turned Her That Way**	S:❶^{3} *Harlan Howard*	Columbia 07672
5/7/88	❶^{1}	20		5	**Don't We All Have The Right**	S:❶^{2} *Roger Miller*	Columbia 07798
9/10/88	❶^{2}	21		6	**I'll Leave This World Loving You**	S:❶^{2} *Wayne Kemp*	Columbia 08022
1/7/89	❶^{1}	16		7	**From A Jack To A King**	*Ned Miller*	Columbia 08529
4/22/89	4	16		8	**Hole In My Pocket**	*Boudleaux Bryant/Felice Bryant*	Columbia 68694
7/22/89	❶^{1}	22		9	**Living Proof**	*Stephen Clark/Johnny MacRae*	Columbia 68994
11/25/89+	2^{2}	26		10	**Statue Of A Fool**	*Jan Crutchfield*	Columbia 73077
3/10/90	❶^{1}	25		11	**I've Cried My Last Tear For You**	*Tony King/Chris Waters*	Columbia
6/30/90	2^{2}	21		12	**I Meant Every Word He Said**	*Joe Chambers/Bucky Jones/Curly Putman*	Columbia
10/27/90+	4	20		13	**Life's Little Ups And Downs**	*Margaret Rich*	Columbia
					above 3 from the album *RVS III* on Columbia 45250		
3/2/91	❶^{1}	20		14	**Rockin' Years** ***[w/ Dolly Parton]***	*Floyd Parton*	Columbia
					from Parton's album *Eagle When She Flies* on Columbia 46882		
5/4/91	❶^{1}	20		15	**I Am A Simple Man**	*Walt Aldridge*	Columbia
8/24/91	❶^{2}	20		16	**Keep It Between The Lines**	*Kathy Louvin/Russell Smith*	Columbia
11/30/91+	13	20		17	**After The Lights Go Out**	*Warner Mack*	Columbia
3/21/92	2^{1}	20		18	**Backroads**	*Charlie Majors*	Columbia
					above 4 from the album *Backroads* on Columbia 46855		
7/25/92	26	20		19	**Wear My Ring Around Your Neck**	*Bert Carroll/Russell Moody*	Epic Soundtrax
					from the movie *Honeymoon In Vegas* starring James Caan and Nicolas Cage (soundtrack on Epic Soundtrax 52845)		
10/24/92+	5	20		20	**Wild Man**	*Rick Giles/Susan Longacre*	Columbia
3/13/93	26	20		21	**Just As I Am**	*Larry Boone/Paul Nelson*	Columbia
					above 2 from the album *Greatest Hits Plus* on Columbia 52753		
8/21/93	44	12		22	**A Couple Of Good Years Left**	*Gary Burr*	Columbia
1/15/94	20	20		23	**Where Was I**	*Gary Burr/Harry Stinson*	Columbia
					above 2 from the album *A Bridge I Didn't Burn* on Columbia 48992		
9/24/94	49	10		24	**Wherever She Is**	*James House/John Jarrard*	Columbia

Billboard DEBUT	PEAK	WKS	GOLD	ARTIST / Country Chart Hit	Ranking / Songwriter	Label (& Number)

SHELTON, Ricky Van — cont'd

DEBUT	PEAK	WKS	GOLD	Country Chart Hit	Songwriter	Label (& Number)
1/28/95	62	5		25 Lola's Love above 2 from the album *Love And Honor* on Columbia 66153	*Dennis Linde*	Columbia
6/24/00	71	1		26 The Decision from the album *Fried Green Tomatoes* on Audium 8116	*Ricky Van Shelton/Jerry Thompson*	Audium

SHENANDOAH — **1990s: #37 / All-Time: #133**

Group formed in Muscle Shoals, Alabama: **Marty Raybon** (vocals; born on 12/8/1959), Jim Seales (guitar; born on 3/20/1954), Stan Thorn (keyboards; born on 3/16/1959), Ralph Ezell (bass; born on 6/26/1953) and Mike McGuire (drums; born on 12/28/1958). Seales was guitarist for the R&B group Funkadelic. McGuire married actress Teresa Blake (of TV soap *All My Children*) on 7/9/1994. Rocky Thacker replaced Ezell in 1995. Thorn left in 1996.

DEBUT	PEAK	WKS	GOLD	Country Chart Hit	Songwriter	Label (& Number)
8/1/87	54	7		1 They Don't Make Love Like We Used To	*J.R. Adkins/Billy Henderson*	Columbia 07128
12/12/87+	28	18		2 Stop The Rain	*Wayland Holyfield/Richard Leigh*	Columbia 07654
4/23/88	9	24		3 She Doesn't Cry Anymore	S:13 *Robert Byrne/Will Robinson*	Columbia 07779
10/1/88	5	21		4 Mama Knows	S:5 *Tony Haselden/Tim Mensy*	Columbia 08042
1/28/89	❶[2]	21		5 The Church On Cumberland Road	*Bob DiPiero/Dave Robbins/John Scott Sherrill*	Columbia 68550
5/20/89	❶[1]	24		6 Sunday In The South	*Jay Booker*	Columbia 68892
9/16/89	❶[1]	26		7 Two Dozen Roses	*Robert Byrne/Mac McAnally*	Columbia 69061
2/17/90	6	26		8 See If I Care from the album *The Road Not Taken* on Columbia 44468	*Walt Aldridge/Robert Byrne*	Columbia
6/9/90	❶[3]	21		9 Next To You, Next To Me	*Robert Ellis Orrall/Curtis Wright*	Columbia
10/6/90	5	20		10 Ghost In This House	*Hugh Prestwood*	Columbia
1/19/91	7	20		11 I Got You	*Robert Byrne/Greg Fowler/Teddy Gentry*	Columbia
5/4/91	9	20		12 The Moon Over Georgia	*Mark Narmore*	Columbia
9/7/91	38	11		13 When You Were Mine above 5 from the album *Extra Mile* on Columbia 45490	*Robert Byrne/Gene Nelson*	Columbia
4/4/92	2[1]	20		14 Rock My Baby	*Billy Spencer/Phil Whitley/Curtis Wright*	RCA
8/8/92	28	18		15 Hey Mister (I Need This Job)	*Renee Armand/Kerry Chater*	RCA
11/28/92+	15	20		16 Leavin's Been A Long Time Comin' above 3 from the album *Long Time Comin'* on RCA 66001	*Charlie Craig/Stowe Dailey/Mike McGuire*	RCA
6/5/93	15	20		17 Janie Baker's Love Slave	*Dennis Linde*	RCA
10/9/93+	3[1]	20		18 I Want To Be Loved Like That	*Phil Barnhart/Sam Hogin/Bill LaBounty*	RCA
2/12/94	❶[1]	20		19 If Bubba Can Dance (I Can Too)	*Bob McDill/Mike McGuire/Marty Raybon*	RCA
6/25/94	46	11		20 I'll Go Down Loving You above 4 from the album *Under The Kudzu* on RCA 66267	*Chapin Hartford/Sam Hogin/Monty Powell*	RCA
12/3/94+	7	20		21 Somewhere In The Vicinity Of The Heart *[w/ Alison Krauss]* **Grammy: Vocal Collaboration / CMA: Vocal Event**	*Rick Chudacoff/Bill LaBounty*	Liberty
4/22/95	4	20		22 Darned If I Don't (Danged If I Do)	*Dean Dillon/Ronnie Dunn*	Liberty
8/5/95	24	20		23 Heaven Bound (I'm Ready)	*Dennis Linde*	Liberty
11/4/95+	40	20		24 Always Have, Always Will above 4 from the album *In The Vicinity Of The Heart* on Liberty 31109	*Larry Boone/Woody Lee/Paul Nelson*	Liberty
2/24/96	43	12		25 All Over But The Shoutin' from the album *Now And Then* on Capitol 35352	*Richard Fagan/Michael Smotherman*	Capitol
9/9/00	65	1		26 What Children Believe from the album *2000* on Free Falls 7012	*Jim Elliott/Brent Lamb/Jerry Salley*	Free Falls

SHEPARD, Jean — **1950s: #32 / All-Time: #109**

Born Ollie Imogene Shepard on 11/21/1933 in Paul's Valley, Oklahoma; raised in Visalia, California. Female singer/songwriter/bassist. Formed all-girl band, the Melody Ranch Girls, in the late 1940s. Discovered by **Hank Thompson**. Worked with **Red Foley**'s *Ozark Jubilee* from 1955-57. Married **Hawkshaw Hawkins** on 11/26/1960.

OPRY: 1955

DEBUT	PEAK	WKS	GOLD	Country Chart Hit	Songwriter	Label (& Number)
7/25/53	❶[6]	23		1 A Dear John Letter *[w/ Ferlin Huskey]*	S:❶[6] / J:❶[4] / A:2 *Fuzzy Owen/Lewis Tally*	Capitol 2502
10/10/53	4	7		2 Forgive Me John *[w/ Ferlin Huskey]*	S:4 / J:6 / A:8 *Billy Barton/Jean Shepard*	Capitol 2586
6/25/55	4	22		3 A Satisfied Mind /	J:4 / S:4 / A:10 *Joe Hayes/Jack Rhodes*	
7/16/55	13	1		4 Take Possession	A:13 / S:flip / J:flip *Tom Glazer/Helen Martell*	Capitol 3118
10/8/55	4	19		5 Beautiful Lies /	S:4 / J:4 / A:12 *Jack Rhodes*	
10/22/55	10	3		6 I Thought Of You	A:10 / S:flip / J:flip *Jimmy Rollins*	Capitol 3222
12/22/58	18	2		7 I Want To Go Where No One Knows Me	*Ken Grant/Jerry Jericho*	Capitol 4068
4/20/59	30	1		8 Have Heart, Will Love	*Roy Bennett/Sid Tepper*	Capitol 4129
5/30/64	5	24		9 Second Fiddle (To An Old Guitar)	*Betty Amos/Vic Willis*	Capitol 5169
1/9/65	38	11		10 A Tear Dropped By	*Rusty Adams/Larry Lee*	Capitol 5304
6/5/65	30	7		11 Someone's Gotta Cry	*Don Bowman*	Capitol 5392
3/5/66	13	16		12 Many Happy Hangovers To You	*Johnny MacRae*	Capitol 5585
5/14/66	9	15		13 I'll Take The Dog *[w/ Ray Pillow]*	*Marge Barton/Johnny MacRae*	Capitol 5633
7/16/66	10	18		14 If Teardrops Were Silver	*Dan Wayne*	Capitol 5681
11/26/66+	25	11		15 Mr. Do-It-Yourself *[w/ Ray Pillow]*	*Johnny MacRae*	Capitol 5769
1/28/67	12	15		16 Heart, We Did All That We Could	*Ned Miller*	Capitol 5822
5/27/67	17	12		17 Your Forevers (Don't Last Very Long)	*Wes Buchanan/Steve Stone/Scott Turner*	Capitol 5899
9/30/67	40	8		18 I Don't See How I Can Make It	*George Richey*	Capitol 5983
2/10/68	52	6		19 An Old Bridge	*Hank Mills*	Capitol 2073
6/15/68	36	8		20 A Real Good Woman	*Johnny Mosby/Jonie Mosby*	Capitol 2180

DEBUT	PEAK	WKS	GOLD		ARTIST / Country Chart Hit	Ranking / Songwriter	Label (& Number)
					SHEPARD, Jean — cont'd		
10/5/68	62	8		21	Everyday's A Happy Day For Fools	*Dallas Frazier*	Capitol 2273
5/3/69	69	4		22	I'm Tied Around Your Finger	*John Paul Jones/Patsy Jones*	Capitol 2425
9/6/69	18	11		23	Seven Lonely Days	*Marshall Brown/Alden Shuman/Earl Shuman*	Capitol 2585
1/3/70	8	14		24	Then He Touched Me	*George Richey/Norro Wilson*	Capitol 2694
4/25/70	23	11		25	A Woman's Hand	*Jan Crutchfield*	Capitol 2779
8/15/70	22	12		26	I Want You Free	*Martha Sharpe*	Capitol 2847
11/7/70	12	14		27	Another Lonely Night	*Larry Butler/Jerry Crutchfield*	Capitol 2941
2/20/71	24	10		28	With His Hand In Mine	*Lorene Allen/Larry Butler/Ruth Butler*	Capitol 3033
9/18/71	55	2		29	Just As Soon As I Get Over Loving You	*Ben Peters/George Richey*	Capitol 3153
1/8/72	55	8		30	Safe In These Lovin' Arms Of Mine	*Emily Mitchell/Billy Sherrill/Norro Wilson*	Capitol 3238
6/3/72	68	4		31	Virginia	*Don Reid*	Capitol 3315
8/19/72	46	10		32	Just Like Walkin' In The Sunshine	*Neal Merritt/Mary Woodward*	Capitol 3395
6/9/73	4	18		33	Slippin' Away	*Bill Anderson*	United Artists 248
11/24/73+	36	11		34	Come On Phone	*Larry Henley/Johnny Slate*	United Artists 317
2/23/74	13	13		35	At The Time	*Bill Anderson*	United Artists 384
6/29/74	17	12		36	I'll Do Anything It Takes (To Stay With You)	*Larry Butler/Jan Crutchfield/Curly Putman*	United Artists 442
10/26/74+	14	13		37	Poor Sweet Baby	*Bill Anderson*	United Artists 552
2/22/75	16	13		38	The Tip Of My Fingers	*Bill Anderson*	United Artists 591
8/30/75	49	10		39	I'm A Believer (In A Whole Lot Of Lovin')	*Ken Jones*	United Artists 701
12/20/75+	44	9		40	Another Neon Night	*Chuck Howard/Joanne Spain*	United Artists 745
4/10/76	49	8		41	Mercy	*Bill Anderson*	United Artists 776
6/26/76	41	10		42	Ain't Love Good	*Larry Butler/Ben Peters*	United Artists 818
12/4/76+	74	7		43	I'm Giving You Denver	*Dave Kirby*	United Artists 899
4/16/77	82	5		44	Hardly A Day Goes By	*Robert Jones*	United Artists 956
4/15/78	85	6		45	The Real Thing	*Ronnie McDowell*	Scorpion 157

SHEPPARD, T.G. — 1980s: #19 / All-Time: #64

Born William Browder on 7/20/1944 in Humbolt, Tennessee. Male singer/songwriter/guitarist. Worked as backup singer with Travis Wammack's band. Recorded as Brian Stacey for Atlantic in 1966. Invented his stage name; initials do not signify "The German Sheppard" or "The Good Sheppard," as commonly thought.

DEBUT	PEAK	WKS	GOLD		Country Chart Hit	Songwriter	Label (& Number)
11/30/74+	❶^{1}	19		1	Devil In The Bottle	*Bobby David*	Melodyland 6002
4/12/75	❶^{1}	15		2	Tryin' To Beat The Morning Home	*Elroy Kahanek/T.G. Sheppard/Red Williams*	Melodyland 6006
8/16/75	14	16		3	Another Woman	*Buzz Cason/Dan Penn*	Melodyland 6016
12/27/75+	7	15		4	Motels And Memories	*Ron Birmann/Don Miller*	Melodyland 6028
5/29/76	14	13		5	Solitary Man	*Neil Diamond*	Hitsville 6032
9/18/76	8	14		6	Show Me A Man	*Sterling Whipple*	Hitsville 6040
12/25/76+	37	8		7	May I Spend Every New Years With You	*Don Goodman/Bud Reneau/Mark Sherrill*	Hitsville 6048
3/5/77	20	10		8	Lovin' On	*Ben Peters*	Hitsville 6053
11/12/77+	13	14		9	Mister D.J.	*Gil Francis/Bob House*	Warner/Curb 8490
2/18/78	13	13		10	Don't Ever Say Good-Bye	*Paul Dempsey*	Warner/Curb 8525
5/27/78	5	13		11	When Can We Do This Again	*Curly Putman/Sonny Throckmorton*	Warner/Curb 8593
9/23/78	7	11		12	Daylight	*Robert John Jones/Mike Kosser*	Warner/Curb 8678
12/16/78+	8	14		13	Happy Together	*Garry Bonner/Alan Gordon*	Warner/Curb 8721
4/21/79	4	13		14	You Feel Good All Over	*Sonny Throckmorton*	Warner/Curb 8808
8/4/79	❶^{2}	14		15	Last Cheater's Waltz	*Sonny Throckmorton*	Warner/Curb 49024
12/1/79+	❶^{2}	15		16	I'll Be Coming Back For More	*Curly Putman/Sterling Whipple*	Warner/Curb 49110
4/5/80	6	16		17	Smooth Sailin'	*Curly Putman/Sonny Throckmorton*	Warner/Curb 49214
8/2/80	❶^{1}	15		18	Do You Wanna Go To Heaven	*Bucky Jones/Curly Putman*	Warner/Curb 49515
12/6/80+	❶^{1}	13		19	I Feel Like Loving You Again	*Bobby Braddock/Sonny Throckmorton*	Warner/Curb 49615
3/14/81	❶^{1}	15		20	I Loved 'Em Every One	*Phil Sampson*	Warner/Curb 49690
7/18/81	❶^{1}	16		21	Party Time	*Bruce Channel*	Warner/Curb 49761
11/21/81+	❶^{1}	19		22	Only One You	*Michael Garvin/Bucky Jones*	Warner/Curb 49858
4/3/82	❶^{1}	16		23	Finally	*Gary Chapman*	Warner/Curb 50041
9/4/82	❶^{1}	19		24	War Is Hell (On The Homefront Too)	*Bucky Jones/Curly Putman/Dan Wilson*	Warner/Curb 29934
11/20/82+	❶^{1}	20		25	Faking Love *[w/ Karen Brooks]*	*Matraca Berg/Bobby Braddock*	Warner/Curb 29854
4/9/83	12	15		26	Without You	*Tom Evans/Pete Ham*	Warner/Curb 29695
10/15/83+	❶^{1}	21		27	Slow Burn	*Charlie Black/Tommy Rocco*	Warner/Curb 29469
2/18/84	12	15		28	Make My Day *[w/ Clint Eastwood]* from the movie *Sudden Impact* starring **Clint Eastwood**	*Dewayne Blackwell* [N]	Warner/Curb 29343
6/2/84	3^{2}	21		29	Somewhere Down The Line	*Lewis Anderson/Casey Kelly*	Warner/Curb 29369
9/29/84	57	9		30	Home Again *[w/ Judy Collins]*	*Gerry Goffin/Michael Masser*	Elektra 69697
11/10/84+	4	22		31	One Owner Heart	A:4 / S:5 *Walt Aldridge/Tom Brasfield/Mac McAnally*	Warner/Curb 29167
3/9/85	10	17		32	You're Going Out Of My Mind	S:10 / A:12 *Wayland Holyfield/Jerry McBee*	Warner/Curb 29071
5/11/85	21	18		33	Fooled Around And Fell In Love	A:18 / S:23 *Elvin Bishop*	Columbia 04890
9/7/85	8	20		34	Doncha?	S:5 / A:9 *Walt Aldridge*	Columbia 05591
12/28/85+	9	18		35	In Over My Heart	S:8 / A:9 *Walt Aldridge/Tom Brasfield/Jim Rutledge*	Columbia 05747

DEBUT	PEAK	WKS	GOLD	ARTIST / Country Chart Hit	Ranking / Songwriter	Label (& Number)

SHEPPARD, T.G. — cont'd

DEBUT	PEAK	WKS	GOLD	Country Chart Hit	Songwriter	Label (& Number)
5/17/86	❶^{1}	23		36 **Strong Heart**	S:❶^{1} / A:❶^{1} *Charlie Black/Austin Roberts/Tommy Rocco*	Columbia 05905
10/11/86+	2^{2}	26		37 **Half Past Forever (Till I'm Blue In The Heart)**	A:2 / S:2 *Tom Brasfield/Robert Byrne*	Columbia 06347
3/21/87	2^{1}	20		38 **You're My First Lady**	S:5 / A:13 *Mac McAnally*	Columbia 06999
9/5/87	2^{1}	24		39 **One For The Money**	S:2 *Buck Moore/Mentor Williams*	Columbia 07312
9/24/88	48	7		40 **Don't Say It With Diamonds (Say It With Love)**	*Randy Boudreaux/Michael Garvin*	Columbia 08029
11/26/88+	14	20		41 **You Still Do**	*Casey Kelly/Lonnie Wilson*	Columbia 08119
3/30/91	63	6		42 **Born In A High Wind**	*Walt Aldridge/Gary Baker/Susan Longacre*	Curb/Capitol

SHERLEY, Glen

Born on 3/9/1936 in Oklahoma; raised in California. Died of a self-inflicted gunshot on 5/11/1978 (age 42). Male singer/songwriter/guitarist. Was an inmate at the California State Prison in Vacaville when he recorded song below.

DEBUT	PEAK	WKS	GOLD	Country Chart Hit	Songwriter	Label (& Number)
7/10/71	63	4		**Greystone Chapel** recorded at Folsom Prison on 1/31/1971	*Glen Sherley* **[L]**	Mega 0027

SHIBLEY, Arkie, and his Mountain Dew Boys

Born Arleigh Shibley on 2/26/1915 in Van Buren, Arkansas. Died on 4/29/1993 (age 78). Male singer. His Mountain Dew Boys consisted of Leon Kelly, Jack Hays and Phil Fregon.

DEBUT	PEAK	WKS	GOLD	Country Chart Hit	Songwriter	Label (& Number)
12/30/50+	5	7		**Hot Rod Race**	A:5 / J:6 *George Wilson* **[N]**	Gilt-Edge 5021

SHINER, Mervin

Born on 2/20/1921 in Bethlehem, Pennsylvania. Male singer/guitarist.

DEBUT	PEAK	WKS	GOLD	Country Chart Hit	Songwriter	Label (& Number)
10/8/49	5	11		1 **Why Don't You Haul Off And Love Me**	J:5 / S:11 *Lonnie Glosson/Wayne Raney*	Decca 46178
4/1/50	6	3	●	2 **Peter Cottontail**	A:6 / S:7 *Steve Nelson/Jack Rollins*	Decca 9-46221
5/27/67	73	4		3 **Big Brother** *[Murv Shiner]*	*Jack Clement/Dickey Lee/Allen Reynolds*	MGM 13704
1/4/69	50	10		4 **Too Hard To Say I'm Sorry** *[Murv Shiner]*	*Jack Clement/Jack Johnson*	MGM 14007

SHIRLEY, Danny

Born on 8/12/1956 in Chattanooga, Tennessee. Lead singer of **Confederate Railroad**.

DEBUT	PEAK	WKS	GOLD	Country Chart Hit	Songwriter	Label (& Number)
10/20/84	72	5		1 **Love And Let Love**	*Del Gray/Bud Reneau*	Amor 1002
2/16/85	93	5		2 **Yo Yo (The Right String, But The Wrong Yo Yo)** *[w/ Piano Red]*	*William Perryman*	Amor 1006
8/29/87	82	3		3 **Deep Down (Everybody Wants To Be From Dixie)**	*Dennis Knutson/Roger Wade*	Amor 2001
12/5/87	81	2		4 **Going To California**	*Roger Bullocks/Randall Ott*	Amor 2002
2/20/88	76	7		5 **I Make The Living (She Makes The Living Worthwhile)**	*Ken Bell/Bobby Keel*	Amor 2004

SHIRLEY & SQUIRRELY

Studio group assembled by producer Bob Milsap.

DEBUT	PEAK	WKS	GOLD	Country Chart Hit	Songwriter	Label (& Number)
6/5/76	28	11		**Hey Shirley (This Is Squirrely)**	*Jimmie Green/Danny Wolfe* **[N]**	GRT 054

SHONDELL, Troy

Born Gary Schelton on 5/14/1939 in Fort Wayne, Indiana. Male singer/multi-instrumentalist.

DEBUT	PEAK	WKS	GOLD	Country Chart Hit	Songwriter	Label (& Number)
10/6/79	95	2		1 **Still Loving You**	*Troy Shondell*	Star-Fox 77
11/8/80	83	4		2 **(Sittin' Here) Lovin' You**	*John Sebastian*	TeleSonic 804
5/14/88	79	2		3 **(I'm Looking For Some) New Blue Jeans**	*Ray Sanders/Spanky Scott/Troy Shondell*	AVM 14

SHOOTERS, The

Group from Muscle Shoals, Alabama: Walt Aldridge (vocals), Barry Billings (guitar), Chalmers Davis (keyboards), Gary Baker (bass; **Baker & Myers**) and Michael Dillon (drums).

DEBUT	PEAK	WKS	GOLD	Country Chart Hit	Songwriter	Label (& Number)
1/24/87	21	15		1 **They Only Come Out At Night**	A:21 *Walt Aldridge/John Jarrard/Lisa Palas*	Epic 06623
6/6/87	41	11		2 **'Til The Old Wears Off**	*Walt Aldridge*	Epic 07131
9/26/87	34	13		3 **Tell It To Your Teddy Bear**	*Walt Aldridge/Gary Baker/Susan Longacre*	Epic 07367
1/30/88	31	15		4 **I Taught Her Everything She Knows About Love**	*Walt Aldridge/Greg Fowler/Teddy Gentry/John Jarrard*	Epic 07684
10/22/88+	13	21		5 **Borderline**	*Walt Aldridge*	Epic 08082
3/4/89	17	19		6 **If I Ever Go Crazy**	*Sheila Aldridge/Walt Aldridge*	Epic 68587
7/15/89	39	9		7 **You Just Can't Lose 'Em All**	*Walt Aldridge/John Jarrard/Lisa Palas*	Epic 68955

SHOPPE, The

Group from Dallas, Texas: Mark Cathey and Kevin Bailey (vocals), Roger Ferguson (guitar), Clarke Wilcox (banjo), Mike Caldwell (harmonica), Jack Wilcox (bass) and Lou Chavez (drums).

DEBUT	PEAK	WKS	GOLD	Country Chart Hit	Songwriter	Label (& Number)
4/19/80	76	5		1 **Three Way Love**	*J. Clarke Wilcox*	Rainbow Sound 8019
8/30/80	78	4		2 **Star Studded Nights**	*Sonny Throckmorton*	Rainbow Sound 8022
2/21/81	33	10		3 **Doesn't Anybody Get High On Love Anymore**	*Johnny Cymbal/Austin Roberts*	NSD 80
5/23/81	61	7		4 **Dream Maker**	*Byron Hill/J. Remington Wilde*	NSD 90
11/17/84	74	5		5 **If You Think I Love You Now**	*Jim Mundy*	American Country 2
2/16/85	79	6		6 **Hurts All Over**	*Charles Stewart/Ronnie Weiss*	American Country 3
9/14/85	56	8		7 **Holdin' The Family Together**	*Frank J. Myers/Don Pfrimmer*	MTM 72056
12/21/85+	47	11		8 **While The Moon's In Town**	*Bob DiPiero/Pat McManus*	MTM 72063

SHRUM, Walter, and his Colorado Hillbillies

Born on 10/16/1896 in Denver, Colorado. Died in February 1971 (age 74). Male singer. Appeared in several western movies.

DEBUT	PEAK	WKS	GOLD	Country Chart Hit	Songwriter	Label (& Number)
10/6/45	3^{1}	1		**Triflin' Gal**	*Cindy Walker*	Coast 2010

SHUPE, Ryan, & The RubberBand

Born in Provo, Utah. Male singer/songwriter/fiddler. The RubberBand: Roger Archibald (guitar), Craig Miner (banjo), Colin Botts (bass) and Bart Olson (drums).

DEBUT	PEAK	WKS	GOLD	Country Chart Hit	Songwriter	Label (& Number)
4/16/05	27↑	23↑		**Dream Big** from the album *Dream Big* on Capitol 37369	S:2 *Ryan Shupe*	Capitol

DEBUT	PEAK	WKS	GOLD	ARTIST / Country Chart Hit ..... Songwriter	Label (& Number)
				SHURFIRE	
				Vocal group from Calgary, Alberta, Canada.	
7/4/87	**54**	7		1 **Bringin' The House Down** ..... *Billy Dean/Jim Dowell*	AIR 173
11/21/87	**49**	9		2 **Roll The Dice** ..... *Larry Boone/Paul Nelson*	AIR 180
3/12/88	**57**	6		3 **First In Line** ..... *Butch Baker/Wade Kirby*	AIR 181
				SHYLO	
				Vocal trio from Texas: Danny Hogan, Ronny Scaife and Perry York.	
2/14/76	**75**	8		1 **Dog Tired Of Cattin' Around** ..... *Danny Hogan/Ronny Scaife*	Columbia 10267
6/12/76	**75**	7		2 **Livin' On Love Street** ..... *Danny Hogan/Ronny Scaife*	Columbia 10343
9/25/76	**86**	5		3 **Ol' Man River (I've Come To Talk Again)** ..... *Danny Hogan/Ronny Scaife*	Columbia 10398
1/8/77	**63**	8		4 **Drinkin' My Way Back Home** ..... *Don Scaife/Ronny Scaife/Phil Thomas*	Columbia 10456
5/28/77	**87**	4		5 **(I'm Coming Home To You) Dixie** ..... *Danny Hogan/Ronny Scaife*	Columbia 10534
12/17/77+	**91**	5		6 **Gotta Travel On** ... *Paul Clayton/Larry Ehrlich/Ronnie Gilbert/Lee Hays/Fred Hellerman/Dave Lazer/Pete Seeger*	Columbia 10647
3/10/79	**79**	6		7 **Freckles** ..... *Sterling Whipple*	Columbia 10918
9/15/79	**92**	2		8 **I'm Puttin' My Love Inside You** ..... *Larry Rogers/Ronny Scaife/Red Williams*	Columbia 11048
5/22/82	**89**	3		9 **Crime In The Sheets** ..... *Jerry Hayes/Ronny Scaife/Don Singleton*	Mercury 76151
				SIDE OF THE ROAD GANG	
				Group from Dallas, Texas.	
8/14/76	**98**	2		**Suitcase Life** ..... *Richie Supa*	Capitol 4298
				SIERRA	
				Vocal group from Virginia: E.J. Harris (lead), William Arney (tenor), Rodney Painter (baritone) and David Mangum (bass).	
2/5/83	**58**	8		1 **Keep On Playin' That Country Music** ..... *Keith Stegall*	Musicom 52701
5/14/83	**87**	3		2 **I'd Do It In A Heart Beat** ..... *Jerry Duncan/Bob Ham*	Musicom 52702
11/5/83	**93**	2		3 **Old Fashioned Lovin'** ..... *Dave Gibson*	Cardinal 052
3/17/84	**70**	6		4 **Branded Man** ..... *Bradley Palmer/Stewart Palmer*	Awesome 101
6/23/84	**68**	6		5 **Love Is The Reason** ..... *Verlon Thompson*	Awesome 106
2/9/85	**68**	6		6 **The Almighty Lover** ..... *Auby Aldridge/Ava Aldridge*	Awesome 110
				SILVER CITY BAND	
				Group from Memphis, Tennessee.	
10/1/77	**99**	2		1 **If You Really Want Me To I'll Go** ..... *Delbert McClinton*	Columbia 10601
7/29/78	**95**	2		2 **I'm Still Missing You** ..... *Don Singleton*	Columbia 10759
				SILVER CREEK	
				Bluegrass group from Oklahoma: Roger Ivie (vocals, guitar), Bobby Dee (guitar), Sam Edwards (steel guitar) and Larry Miller (fiddle).	
9/12/81	**94**	2		1 **You And Me And Tennessee** ..... *Rayburn Anthony*	Cardinal 8102
				ROGER IVIE And SILVERCREEK	
11/21/81	**64**	7		2 **Lonely Women** ..... *Roger Ivie*	Cardinal 8103
				SIMMONS, Gene	
				Born in 1933 in Tupelo, Mississippi. Known as "Jumpin' Gene." Not to be confused with the lead singer of Kiss.	
9/10/77	**88**	3		**Why Didn't I Think Of That** ..... *Roger Bowling*	Deltune 1201
				SIMON, Carly	
				Born on 6/25/1945 in Manhattan, New York. Pop singer/songwriter/pianist. Won the 1971 Best New Artist Grammy Award. Married to **James Taylor** from 1972-83.	
9/9/78	**33**	10		**Devoted To You** *[w/ James Taylor]* ..... *Boudleaux Bryant*	Elektra 45506
				SIMON & VERITY	
				Vocal duo from England.	
2/16/85	**78**	4		1 **We've Still Got Love** ..... *Sonny Lemaire/J.P. Pennington*	EMI America 8257
5/18/85	**91**	3		2 **Your Eyes** ..... *Wayne Perkins/Terry Skinner/J.L. Wallace*	EMI America 8264
				SIMPSON, Jenny	
				Born in 1973 in Nashville, Tennessee. Female singer.	
10/24/98	**54**	7		**Ticket Out Of Kansas** ..... *Tia Sillers*	Mercury
				from the album *Jenny Simpson* on Polygram 538038	
				SIMPSON, Red	
				Born Joseph Simpson on 3/6/1934 in Higley, Arizona. Male singer/songwriter/guitarist.	
4/2/66	**38**	4		1 **Roll Truck Roll** ..... *Tommy Collins*	Capitol 5577
6/4/66	**39**	3		2 **The Highway Patrol** ..... *Dennis Payne/Alan Rush/Red Simpson*	Capitol 5637
12/24/66+	**41**	8		3 **Diesel Smoke, Dangerous Curves** ..... *Cal Martin*	Capitol 5783
12/4/71+	**4**	17		4 **I'm A Truck** ..... *Bob Stanton*	Capitol 3236
4/22/72	**62**	5		5 **Country Western Truck Drivin' Singer** ..... *Red Simpson*	Capitol 3298
6/30/73	**63**	5		6 **Awful Lot To Learn About Truck Drivin'** ..... *Glen Goza*	Capitol 3616
9/18/76	**92**	4		7 **Truck Driver's Heaven** ..... *Eddie Dean/Red Simpson/Hal Southern*	Warner 8259
				same tune as "I Dreamed Of A Hillbilly Heaven" by **Eddie Dean**	
10/27/79	**99**	2		8 **The Flying Saucer Man And The Truck Driver** ..... *Red Simpson*	K.E.Y. 108
				SINATRA, Nancy	
				Born on 6/8/1940 in Jersey City, New Jersey; raised in Los Angeles, California. Female singer/actress. Daughter of **Frank Sinatra**. Appeared in several movies.	
7/11/81	**23**	12		1 **Texas Cowboy Night** *[w/ Mel Tillis]* ..... *Buddy Cannon/Raleigh Squires/Mel Tillis*	Elektra 47157
12/26/81+	**43**	8		2 **Play Me Or Trade Me** *[w/ Mel Tillis]* / ..... *Owen Davis/Mike Huffman*	
12/26/81+	**flip**	8		3 **Where Would I Be** *[w/ Mel Tillis]* ..... *Judy Mehaffey*	Elektra 47247

DEBUT	PEAK	WKS	GOLD	ARTIST Country Chart Hit	Ranking Songwriter	Label (& Number)

SINGLETARY, Daryle

Born on 3/10/1971 in Cairo, Georgia. Male singer/songwriter.

DEBUT	PEAK	WKS	GOLD	Country Chart Hit	Songwriter	Label (& Number)
4/8/95	**39**	13		1 **I'm Living Up To Her Low Expectations**	*Bob McDill/Tommy Rocco*	Giant
7/29/95	**2**[1]	20		2 **I Let Her Lie**	S:21 *Tim Johnson*	Giant
12/9/95+	**4**	20		3 **Too Much Fun**	*Thomas Knight/Curtis Wright*	Giant
5/11/96	**50**	10		4 **Workin' It Out**	*Tim Johnson/Brett Jones*	Giant
				above 4 from the album *Daryle Singletary* on Giant 24606		
10/12/96+	**2**[1]	23		5 **Amen Kind Of Love**	*Trey Bruce/Wayne Tester*	Giant
3/15/97	**48**	10		6 **The Used To Be's**	*Mike Huffman/Donny Kees/Bob Morrison*	Giant
7/26/97	**68**	3		7 **Even The Wind**	*Hank Cochran/Tim Johnson*	Giant
				above 3 from the album *All Because Of You* on Giant 24660		
11/8/97+	**28**	20		8 **The Note**	S:9 *Buck Moore/Michele Ray*	Giant
4/4/98	**49**	10		9 **That's Where You're Wrong**	*Jeff Crossan*	Giant
7/11/98	**44**	12		10 **My Baby's Lovin'**	*Michael Lunn/Delbert McClinton*	Giant
				above 3 from the album *Ain't It The Truth* on Giant 24696		
7/1/00	**55**	20		11 **I Knew I Loved You**	*Darren Hayes/Daniel Jones*	Audium
12/16/00	**70**	1		12 **I've Thought Of Everything**	*Trey Matthews/Daryle Singletary/Kerry Singletary*	Audium
				above 2 from the album *Now And Again* on Audium 8125		
6/15/02	**47**	12		13 **That's Why I Sing This Way**	*Max D. Barnes*	Audium
9/28/02	**43**	19		14 **I'd Love To Lay You Down**	*Fred MacRae*	Audium
				above 2 from the album *That's Why I Sing This Way* on Audium 8151		

SINGLETON, Margie

Born Margaret Ebey on 10/5/1935 in Coushatta, Louisiana. Female singer/songwriter/guitarist. Formerly married to music executive Shelby Singleton. Married **Leon Ashley** in 1965.

DEBUT	PEAK	WKS	GOLD	Country Chart Hit	Songwriter	Label (& Number)
8/3/59	**25**	5		1 **Nothin' But True Love**	*Shelby Singleton/Paul Williams*	Starday 443
2/1/60	**12**	14		2 **The Eyes Of Love**	*Margie Singleton/Shelby Singleton*	Starday 472
9/18/61	**15**	3		3 **Did I Ever Tell You** ***[w/ George Jones]***	*Jerry Kennedy/Margie Singleton*	Mercury 71856
6/16/62	**11**	10		4 **Waltz Of The Angels** ***[w/ George Jones]***	*Dick Reynolds/Jack Rhodes*	Mercury 71955
12/28/63+	**11**	14		5 **Old Records**	*Merle Kilgore/Arthur Thomas*	Mercury 72213
3/14/64	**5**	23		6 **Keeping Up With The Joneses** ***[w/ Faron Young]*** /	*Justin Tubb*	
3/28/64	**40**	6		7 **No Thanks, I Just Had One** ***[w/ Faron Young]***	*Bill Anderson*	Mercury 72237
12/5/64	**38**	8		8 **Another Woman's Man - Another Man's Woman** ***[w/ Faron Young]***	...*Marlin Greene/Dan Pennington*	Mercury 72312
9/9/67	**39**	8		9 **Ode To Billie Joe**	*Bobbie Gentry*	Ashley 2011
11/11/67	**54**	7		10 **Hangin' On** ***[w/ Leon Ashley]***	*Ira Allen/Buddy Mize*	Ashley 2015
3/2/68	**52**	8		11 **Wandering Mind**	*Leon Ashley/Merle Kilgore/Margie Singleton*	Ashley 2050
5/11/68	**55**	6		12 **You'll Never Be Lonely Again** ***[w/ Leon Ashley]***	*Leon Ashley/Margie Singleton*	Ashley 3000

SIXWIRE

Group formed in Nashville, Tennessee: **Andy Childs** (vocals, guitar), Steve Mandile and Robb Houston (guitars), John Howard (bass) and Chuck Tilley (drums).

DEBUT	PEAK	WKS	GOLD	Country Chart Hit	Songwriter	Label (& Number)
4/20/02	**30**	20		1 **Look At Me Now**	*Steve Mandile/Steve McClintock*	Warner
11/9/02	**55**	4		2 **Way Too Deep**	*Andy Childs/Steve Mandile*	Warner
				above 2 from the album *Sixwire* on Warner 48312		

SKAGGS, Ricky

1980s: #21 / All-Time: #85

Born on 7/18/1954 in Cordell, Kentucky. Male singer/songwriter/mandolin player. Played mandolin from age five. Member of the Clinch Mountain Boys (1969) and **The Country Gentlemen** (1974). Married **Sharon White** in 1982. Also see **Same Old Train**.

CMA: Horizon 1982 / Male Vocalist 1982 / Entertainer 1985 / Vocal Duo (with Sharon White) 1987 // OPRY: 1982

DEBUT	PEAK	WKS	GOLD	Country Chart Hit	Songwriter	Label (& Number)
4/19/80	**86**	4		1 **I'll Take The Blame**	*Carter Stanley*	Sugar Hill 3706
5/2/81	**16**	16		2 **Don't Get Above Your Raising**	*Lester Flatt/Earl Scruggs*	Epic 02034
9/12/81	**9**	17		3 **You May See Me Walkin'**	*Albert Uhr*	Epic 02499
1/23/82	❶[1]	23		4 **Crying My Heart Out Over You**	*Carl Butler/Louise Certain/George Sherry/Gladys Stacey*	Epic 02692
5/29/82	❶[1]	18		5 **I Don't Care**	*Webb Pierce/Cindy Walker*	Epic 02931
9/18/82	❶[1]	17		6 **Heartbroke**	*Guy Clark*	Epic 03212
12/25/82+	❶[1]	20		7 **I Wouldn't Change You If I Could**	*Paul Jones/Arthur Smith*	Epic 03482
4/30/83	❶[1]	19		8 **Highway 40 Blues**	*Larry Cordle*	Epic 03812
8/13/83	**2**[1]	19		9 **You've Got A Lover**	*Shake Russell*	Epic 04044
12/3/83+	❶[1]	20		10 **Don't Cheat In Our Hometown**	*Roy Marcum/Ray Pennington*	Sugar Hill/Epic 04245
3/24/84	❶[1]	18		11 **Honey** (Open That Door)	*Mel Tillis*	Sugar Hill/Epic 04394
7/21/84	❶[1]	19		12 **Uncle Pen**	S:7 / A:20 *Bill Monroe*	Sugar Hill/Epic 04527
11/3/84+	**2**[1]	22		13 **Something In My Heart**	S:❶[1] / A:3 *Wayland Patton*	Epic 04668
3/23/85	❶[1]	19		14 **Country Boy**	S:❶[1] / A:❶[1] *Tony Colton/Albert Lee/Ray Smith*	Epic 04831
9/14/85	**7**	23		15 **You Make Me Feel Like A Man**	S:7 / A:8 *Peter Rowan*	Epic 05585
1/11/86	❶[1]	20		16 **Cajun Moon**	S:❶[1] / A:❶[1] *Jim Rushing*	Epic 05748
5/24/86	**10**	18		17 **I've Got A New Heartache**	S:7 / A:10 *Ray Price/Wayne Walker*	Epic 05898
10/4/86	**4**	20		18 **Love's Gonna Get You Someday**	S:3 / A:4 *Carl Chambers*	Epic 06327
2/14/87	**30**	11		19 **I Wonder If I Care As Much**	S:19 / A:30 *Don Everly*	Epic 06650

DEBUT	PEAK	WKS	GOLD	ARTIST / Ranking / Country Chart Hit	Songwriter	Label (& Number)
				SKAGGS, Ricky — cont'd		
5/2/87	**10**	23		20 **Love Can't Ever Get Better Than This** *[w/ Sharon White]* S:5	*Irene Kelley/Nancy Montgomery*	Epic 07060
10/17/87+	**18**	20		21 **I'm Tired** S:12	*Buck Peddy/Ray Price/Mel Tillis*	Epic 07416
2/27/88	**33**	13		22 **(Angel On My Mind) That's Why I'm Walkin'** S:16	*Melvin Endsley/Stonewall Jackson*	Epic 07721
				same tune as "Why I'm Walkin'" by **Stonewall Jackson**		
6/11/88	**17**	16		23 **Thanks Again** S:11	*Jim Rushing*	Epic 07924
10/15/88	**30**	15		24 **Old Kind Of Love** S:19	*Paul Overstreet*	Epic 08063
4/8/89	**❶**[1]	21		25 **Lovin' Only Me**	*Hillary Kanter/Even Stevens*	Epic 68693
8/5/89	**5**	26		26 **Let It Be You**	*Harry Stinson/Kevin Welch*	Epic 68995
12/9/89+	**13**	26		27 **Heartbreak Hurricane**	*Larry Cordle/Jim Rushing*	Epic 73078
4/21/90	**20**	16		28 **Hummingbird**	*Tim DuBois/Greg Jennings*	Epic
9/1/90	**25**	20		29 **He Was On To Somethin' (So He Made You)**	*Sonny Curtis*	Epic
				above 2 from the album *Kentucky Thunder* on Epic 45027		
3/30/91	**25**	20		30 **Restless** *[w/ Mark O'Connor/Vince Gill/Steve Wariner]*	*Carl Perkins*	Warner
				Grammy: Vocal Collaboration / CMA: Vocal Event; from O'Connor's album *The New Nashville Cats* on Warner 26509		
8/17/91	**37**	18		31 **Life's Too Long (To Live Like This)**	*Don Cook/John Jarvis/Dan Wilson*	Epic
12/21/91+	**12**	20		32 **Same Ol' Love**	*Chris Austin/Greg Barnhill*	Epic
5/16/92	**43**	10		33 **From The Word Love**	*Keith Sewell*	Epic
				above 3 from the album *My Father's Son* on Epic 47389		
11/25/95+	**57**	14		34 **Solid Ground**	*Gary Owens*	Atlantic
4/20/96	**45**	11		35 **Cat's In The Cradle**	*Harry Chapin/Sandy Chapin*	Atlantic
				above 2 from the album *Solid Ground* on Atlantic 82834		
7/27/02	**56**	1		36 **Halfway Home Cafe**	*Paul Barranco/Paul Overstreet*	Skaggs Family
				from the album *History Of The Future* on Skaggs Family 901003		
				SKINNER, Jimmie		
				Born on 4/27/1909 in Blue Lick, Ohio. Died of a heart attack on 10/28/1979 (age 70). Male singer/songwriter/guitarist.		
4/30/49	**15**	1		1 **Tennessee Border** S:15	*Jimmy Work*	Radio Artist 244
11/4/57+	**5**	17		2 **I Found My Girl In The USA** ..... A:5 / S:9	*Jimmie Skinner*	Mercury 71192
				answer to "Fraulein" by **Bobby Helms** and "Geisha Girl" by **Hank Locklin**		
3/24/58	**8**	8		3 **What Makes A Man Wander** ..... A:8 / S:14	*Jimmie Helms/Jay Rainwater/Jimmie Skinner*	Mercury 71256
1/12/59	**21**	8		4 **Walkin' My Blues Away /**	*Bill Anderson/Jimmie Skinner*	
1/19/59	**7**	10		5 **Dark Hollow**	*Bill Browning*	Mercury 71387
8/3/59	**17**	11		6 **John Wesley Hardin**	*Jimmie Skinner*	Mercury 71470
1/18/60	**14**	11		7 **Riverboat Gambler**	*Sammy Lyons/Jimmie Skinner*	Mercury 71539
5/16/60	**21**	4		8 **Lonesome Road Blues**	*Jimmie Skinner*	Mercury 71606
8/29/60	**13**	8		9 **Reasons To Live**	*Ted Mullins/Jimmie Skinner*	Mercury 71663
12/19/60	**30**	1		10 **Careless Love**	*Jimmie Skinner*	Mercury 71704
				SKIP AND LINDA		
				Duo of Skip Eaton and **Linda Davis**.		
8/21/82	**63**	7		1 **If You Could See You Through My Eyes**	*Larry Henley/Jim Hurt*	MDJ 68178
10/23/82	**73**	5		2 **I Just Can't Turn Temptation Down**	*Don Cusic*	MDJ 68179
12/18/82	**89**	4		3 **This Time**	*Roger Murrah/Tina Murrah*	MDJ 68180
				S-K-O — see SCHUYLER, KNOBLOCH & OVERSTREET		
				SKY KINGS, The		
				All-star trio: John Cowan (**New Grass Revival**), Bill Lloyd (**Foster & Lloyd**) and Rusty Young (**Poco**).		
4/20/96	**52**	7		**Picture Perfect**	*John Northrup/Robert Ellis Orrall*	Warner
				SLATER, David		
				Born on 11/22/1962 in Dallas, Texas. Male singer. Winner on TV's *Star Search* in 1987.		
3/26/88	**36**	13		1 **I'm Still Your Fool**	*Byron Hill/Preston Sullivan*	Capitol 44129
6/25/88	**30**	17		2 **The Other Guy**	*Graham Goble*	Capitol 44184
10/22/88	**63**	8		3 **We Were Meant To Be Lovers**	*Brian Neary/Jim Photoglo*	Capitol 44257
5/13/89	**65**	6		4 **She Will**	*Jeff Tweel/Dan Tyler*	Capitol 44359
9/23/89	**75**	3		5 **Whatcha Gonna Do About Her**	*Gary Baker/Mac McAnally/Freddy Powers*	Capitol 44433
				SLEDD, Patsy		
				Born Patricia Randolph on 1/29/1944 in Falcon, Missouri. Female singer/pianist.		
9/9/72	**68**	6		1 **Nothing Can Stop My Loving You**	*George Jones/Roger Miller*	Mega 0085
1/5/74	**33**	12		2 **Chip Chip**	*Jeff Barry/Cliff Crawford/Artie Resnick*	Mega 1203
				#10 Pop hit for Gene McDaniels in 1962		
12/7/74+	**72**	9		3 **See Saw**	*Billy Davis/Harry Pratt/Charles Sutton*	Mega 1217
2/7/76	**90**	5		4 **The Cowboy And The Lady**	*Peggy Russell*	Mega 1244
11/28/87	**79**	3		5 **Don't Stay If You Don't Love Me**	*Eddie Pleasant*	Showtime 1007
				SLEWFOOT		
				Bluegrass group from Myrtle Beach, South Carolina: Jake Wiegandt (vocals, guitar), Jay Swanigan (banjo), Chris Kennedy (dobro), Arek Parsley (bass) and Nate Benbow (drums).		
9/13/86	**85**	3		**Nice To Be With You**	*Jim Gold*	Step One 360
				SLIGO STUDIO BAND		
				Group from Norfolk, Virginia.		
4/18/81	**94**	2		**You're The Reason**	*Ernie Bivens*	GBS 708
				SLOANE, Rene		
				Born in Tennessee. Female singer.		
1/5/80	**45**	9		**Mr. & Mrs. Untrue** *[w/ Price Mitchell]*	*Irwin Levine/Toni Wine*	Sunbird 101

Billboard DEBUT	PEAK	WKS	GOLD	ARTIST / Country Chart Hit	Ranking / Songwriter	Label (& Number)

SLYE, Carrie

Born on 2/28/1960 in Grants, New Mexico; raised in Gurden, Arkansas. Female singer.

DEBUT	PEAK	WKS	GOLD	Country Chart Hit	Songwriter	Label (& Number)
7/23/83	**78**	4		Ease The Fever	*Bob Morrison/Bill Zerface/Jim Zerface*	Friday 42683

SMALLWOOD, Laney

Born in Denver, Colorado. Female singer. Also recorded as **Laney Hicks**.

DEBUT	PEAK	WKS	GOLD	Country Chart Hit	Songwriter	Label (& Number)
7/1/78	**57**	6		1 That "I Love You, You Love Me Too" Love Song	*Lewis Anderson/Becky Hobbs*	Monument 255
12/19/81	**92**	3		2 Until The Nights *[w/ Charlie McCoy]*	*Billy Joel*	Monument 21001
4/16/83	**74**	4		3 The State Of Our Union **CHARLIE McCOY & LANEY HICKS**	*Chip Hardy/Jim Rushing*	Monument 03518

SMART, Jimmy

Born in Terrell, Texas. Male singer/guitarist.

DEBUT	PEAK	WKS	GOLD	Country Chart Hit	Songwriter	Label (& Number)
10/10/60	**18**	2		1 Broken Dream	*Randy Starr/Dick Wolfe*	Allstar 7211
3/13/61	**16**	7		2 Shorty	*Jim Howell*	Plaid 1004

SMILEY, Red — see RENO & SMILEY

SMITH, Andy Lee

Born in St. Louis, Missouri. Female singer.

DEBUT	PEAK	WKS	GOLD	Country Chart Hit	Songwriter	Label (& Number)
11/11/89	**71**	3		Invitation To The Blues	*Roger Miller*	615 Records 1024

SMITH, Anthony

Born in Oneida, Tennessee. Male singer/songwriter/guitarist.

DEBUT	PEAK	WKS	GOLD	Country Chart Hit	Songwriter	Label (& Number)
4/27/02	**26**	20		1 If That Ain't Country	*Anthony Smith/Jeffrey Steele*	Mercury
10/5/02	**40**	16		2 John J. Blanchard	*Anthony Smith/Chris Wallin*	Mercury
2/8/03	**40**	12		3 Half A Man above 3 from the album *If That Ain't Country* on Mercury 170292	*Anthony Smith*	Mercury

SMITH, Arthur "Guitar Boogie" — 1940s: #47

Born on 4/1/1921 in Clinton, South Carolina. Male guitarist/songwriter.

DEBUT	PEAK	WKS	GOLD	Country Chart Hit	Songwriter	Label (& Number)
9/25/48	**9**	2		1 Banjo Boogie	J:9 *Arthur Smith* [I]	MGM 10229
12/25/48+	**8**	7		2 Guitar Boogie /	J:8 *Arthur Smith* [I]	
1/1/49	**8**	4		3 Boomerang **ARTHUR "Guitar Boogie" SMITH and His Cracker-Jacks** (above 3)	J:8 *Arthur Smith* [I]	MGM 10293
10/19/63	**29**	3		4 Tie My Hunting Dog Down, Jed parody of "Tie Me Kangaroo Down, Sport" by Rolf Harris	*Rolf Harris* [N]	Starday 642

SMITH, Bobby

Born in 1946 in Balch Springs, Texas. Male singer.

DEBUT	PEAK	WKS	GOLD	Country Chart Hit	Songwriter	Label (& Number)
5/7/77	**70**	8		1 Do You Wanna Make Love	*Peter McCann*	Autumn 398
8/22/81	**30**	11		2 Just Enough Love (For One Woman)	*Dave Kirby/Danny Morrison*	Liberty 1417
11/28/81+	**40**	10		3 Too Many Hearts In The Fire	*Tim DuBois/Jim Hurt/Wood Newton*	Liberty 1439
2/20/82	**47**	9		4 And Then Some	*Mark Gray/Larry Henley/Johnny Slate*	Liberty 1452
10/2/82	**68**	5		5 It's Been One Of Those Days	*Tim DuBois/Chester Lester/Mike Seals*	Liberty 1480

SMITH, Cal — All-Time: #176

Born Calvin Grant Shofner on 4/7/1932 in Gans, Oklahoma; raised in Oakland, California. Male singer/guitarist. Worked clubs and as a DJ in San Jose. Regular member of the *California Hayride*. Worked with **Ernest Tubb** from 1962-68.

DEBUT	PEAK	WKS	GOLD	Country Chart Hit	Songwriter	Label (& Number)
1/28/67	**58**	10		1 The Only Thing I Want	*Johnny Russell*	Kapp 788
8/19/67	**61**	2		2 I'll Never Be Lonesome With You	*Johnny Dillingham*	Kapp 834
2/24/68	**60**	5		3 Destination Atlanta G.A.	*Bill Hayes/Bill Howard*	Kapp 884
6/22/68	**58**	7		4 Jacksonville	*Walter Haynes/Jimmy Rule*	Kapp 913
10/5/68	**35**	7		5 Drinking Champagne	*Warner Mack*	Kapp 938
6/14/69	**51**	8		6 It Takes All Night Long	*Bill Eldridge/Gary Stewart*	Kapp 994
9/27/69	**55**	4		7 You Can't Housebreak A Tomcat	*Bill Eldridge/Gary Stewart*	Kapp 2037
1/3/70	**47**	2		8 Heaven Is Just A Touch Away	*Carl Knight*	Kapp 2059
4/25/70	**70**	2		9 The Difference Between Going And Really Gone	*Jimmie Helms/Grant Townsley*	Kapp 2076
1/16/71	**58**	7		10 That's What It's Like To Be Lonesome	*Bill Anderson*	Decca 32768
5/6/72	**4**	15		11 I've Found Someone Of My Own	*Frank Robinson*	Decca 32959
9/16/72	**58**	8		12 For My Baby	*Brook Benton/Clyde Otis*	Decca 33003
12/16/72+	**❶**[1]	17		13 The Lord Knows I'm Drinking	*Bill Anderson*	Decca 33040
5/26/73	**25**	11		14 I Can Feel The Leavin' Coming On /	*Shel Silverstein*	
6/23/73	**flip**	7		15 I've Loved You All Over The World	*Glenn Johnson*	MCA 40061
10/13/73	**63**	9		16 Bleep You /	*Bobby Braddock*	
10/27/73	**flip**	7		17 An Hour And A Six-Pack	*Bill Anderson*	MCA 40136
3/9/74	**❶**[1]	15		18 Country Bumpkin **CMA: Single**	*Don Wayne*	MCA 40191
8/3/74	**11**	13		19 Between Lust And Watching TV	*Bill Anderson*	MCA 40265
12/7/74+	**❶**[1]	16		20 It's Time To Pay The Fiddler	*Walter Haynes/Don Wayne*	MCA 40335
4/26/75	**13**	13		21 She Talked A Lot About Texas	*Don Wayne*	MCA 40394

DEBUT	PEAK	WKS	GOLD	ARTIST / Ranking / Country Chart Hit	Songwriter	Label (& Number)
				SMITH, Cal — cont'd		
10/25/75	**12**	14		22 **Jason's Farm**	*John Adrian*	MCA 40467
2/14/76	**33**	10		23 **Thunderstorms**	*Sterling Whipple*	MCA 40517
6/5/76	**43**	9		24 **MacArthur's Hand**	*Don Wayne*	MCA 40563
10/9/76	**38**	10		25 **Woman Don't Try To Sing My Song**	*Don Wayne*	MCA 40618
1/22/77	**15**	14		26 **I Just Came Home To Count The Memories**	*Glenn Ray*	MCA 40671
4/30/77	**23**	10		27 **Come See About Me**	*Conway Twitty*	MCA 40714
9/24/77	**53**	8		28 **Helen**	*Jim Mundy*	MCA 40789
12/17/77+	**51**	9		29 **Throwin' Memories On The Fire**	*Bobby Bond*	MCA 40839
2/25/78	**73**	4		30 **I'm Just A Farmer**	*Sonny Throckmorton*	MCA 40864
6/24/78	**68**	5		31 **Bits And Pieces Of Life**	*Charlie Williams*	MCA 40911
1/6/79	**71**	6		32 **The Rise And Fall Of The Roman Empire**	*Bobby Fischer/Don Wayne*	MCA 40982
4/14/79	**91**	2		33 **One Little Skinny Rib**	*Ted Harris*	MCA 41001
11/3/79	**92**	2		34 **The Room At The Top Of The Stairs**	*Lola Jean Dillon*	MCA 41128
10/30/82	**68**	6		35 **Too Many Irons In The Fire** *[w/ Billy Parker]*	*James Forst*	Soundwaves 4686
9/6/86	**75**	5		36 **King Lear**	*Mel Holt*	Step One 358

SMITH, Carl 1950s: #4 / 1960s: #21 / All-Time: #26 // HOF: 2003

Born on 3/15/1927 in Maynardville, Tennessee. Male singer/songwriter/guitarist. Began singing on radio station WROL in Knoxville. Served in the U.S. Navy from 1945-47. Played bass in Skeets Williamson's band. Married to **June Carter** from 1952-56; their daughter is **Carlene Carter**. Married **Goldie Hill** on 9/19/1957.

OPRY: 1950

DEBUT	PEAK	WKS	GOLD	Country Chart Hit	Songwriter	Label (& Number)
6/2/51	**2^{1}**	20		1 **Let's Live A Little**	A:2 / S:3 / J:3 *Ruth Coletharp*	Columbia 4-20796
8/4/51	**4**	17		2 **Mr. Moon /**	A:4 / J:5 / S:8 *Autry Inman/Shirley Lyn/Carl Smith*	
8/4/51	**8**	3		3 **If Teardrops Were Pennies**	J:8 / S:9 / A:9 *Carl Butler*	Columbia 4-20825
10/27/51	**❶^{8}**	33		4 **Let Old Mother Nature Have Her Way**	J:❶^{8} / S:❶^{6} / A:❶^{3} *Louie Clark/Loys Southerland*	Columbia 4-20862
3/1/52	**❶^{8}**	24		5 **(When You Feel Like You're In Love) Don't Just Stand There**	...A:❶^{8} / S:❶^{5} / J:❶^{3} *Jack Henley/Ernest Tubb*	Columbia 4-20893
5/24/52	**❶^{1}**	19		6 **Are You Teasing Me /**	A:❶^{1} / J:2 / S:2 *Charlie Louvin/Ira Louvin*	
5/31/52	**5**	10		7 **It's A Lovely, Lovely World**	A:5 / S:8 / J:9 *Boudleaux Bryant*	Columbia 4-20922
10/25/52	**6**	6		8 **Our Honeymoon**	A:6 / J:6 / S:7 *Boudleaux Bryant/Carl Smith*	Columbia 4-21008
1/31/53	**9**	1		9 **That's The Kind Of Love I'm Looking For**	J:9 *John Masters*	Columbia 21051
5/2/53	**7**	3		10 **Just Wait 'Til I Get You Alone /**	A:7 / J:7 / S:9 *Boudleaux Bryant/Felice Bryant*	
5/9/53	**4**	6		11 **Orchids Mean Goodbye**	J:4 / S:7 / A:7 *Boudleaux Bryant/Mark Webb*	Columbia 21087
7/4/53	**2^{2}**	10		12 **Trademark /**	S:2 / J:5 / A:6 *Porter Wagoner/Gary Walker*	
7/18/53	**6**	1		13 **Do I Like It?**	A:6 *Cy Coben*	Columbia 21119
7/25/53	**❶^{8}**	26		14 **Hey Joe!**	J:❶^{8} / A:❶^{4} / S:❶^{2} *Boudleaux Bryant*	Columbia 21129
11/7/53	**7**	6		15 **Satisfaction Guaranteed**	S:7 / A:7 / J:8 *Kay Twomey/Ben Weisman/Fred Wise*	Columbia 21166
2/13/54	**7**	4		16 **Dog-Gone It, Baby, I'm In Love**	A:7 / S:8 *Jack Amway/Arrett Keefer*	Columbia 21197
5/1/54	**2^{1}**	16		17 **Back Up Buddy**	A:2 / S:4 / J:4 *Boudleaux Bryant*	Columbia 21226
8/7/54	**4**	11		18 **Go, Boy, Go**	S:4 / A:7 / J:9 *Floyd Wilson*	Columbia 21266
11/6/54+	**❶^{7}**	32		19 **Loose Talk /**	S:❶^{7} / A:❶^{6} / J:❶^{4} *Freddie Hart/Ann Lucas*	
11/6/54+	**5**	10		20 **More Than Anything Else In The World**	A:5 / S:15 *Leon Payne*	Columbia 21317
1/22/55	**5**	16		21 **Kisses Don't Lie /**	S:5 / J:7 / A:8 *Pearl Butler/George Sherry*	
1/29/55	**13**	2		22 **No, I Don't Believe I Will**	S:13 / A:15 / J:flip *Jean Crowe*	Columbia 21340
4/23/55	**12**	3		23 **Wait A Little Longer Please, Jesus**	A:12 *Hazel Houser/Chester Smith*	Columbia 21368
5/14/55	**3^{3}**	25		24 **There She Goes /**	A:3 / S:5 / J:8 *Durwood Haddock/Eddie Miller/W.S. Stevenson*	
5/14/55	**11**	7		25 **Old Lonesome Times**	S:11 / A:13 *Carl Smith*	Columbia 21382
10/15/55	**11**	4		26 **Don't Tease Me**	A:11 / S:13 *Carl Smith*	Columbia 21429
12/3/55+	**6**	14		27 **You're Free To Go /**	S:6 / J:6 / A:7 *Lou Herscher/Don Robertson*	
12/3/55+	**7**	15		28 **I Feel Like Cryin'**	S:7 / J:9 / A:11 *Werly Fairburn*	Columbia 21462
3/31/56	**11**	3		29 **I've Changed**	A:11 / S:14 *Danny Dill*	Columbia 21493
6/23/56	**4**	23		30 **You Are The One** *[w/ The Tunesmiths]* **/**	A:4 / J:5 / S:6 *Pat Patterson*	
8/4/56	**6**	6		31 **Doorstep To Heaven** *[w/ The Tunesmiths]*	S:6 *Leon Payne*	Columbia 21522
10/13/56	**6**	12		32 **Before I Met You** *[w/ The Tunesmiths]* **/**	J:6 / A:7 / S:9 *Joe Lewis/Charles Seitz*	
10/20/56	**9**	10		33 **Wicked Lies**	S:9 / J:flip *Joe Brewster/Pearl Jones/Carl Smith*	Columbia 21552
3/2/57	**15**	1		34 **You Can't Hurt Me Anymore**	S:15 *Lee Emerson*	Columbia 40823
9/16/57	**2^{2}**	19		35 **Why, Why**	A:2 / S:7 *Mel Tillis/Wayne Walker*	Columbia 40984
3/3/58	**6**	14		36 **Your Name Is Beautiful**	A:6 / S:9 *John Gluck/Diane Lampert*	Columbia 41092
12/15/58	**28**	1		37 **Walking The Slow Walk**	*Mel Tillis*	Columbia 41243
1/19/59	**15**	11		38 **The Best Years Of Your Life**	*Keith Lloyd*	Columbia 41290
6/1/59	**19**	3		39 **It's All My Heartache**	*Bill Phillips/Mel Tillis*	Columbia 41344
7/20/59	**5**	12		40 **Ten Thousand Drums**	*Carl Smith/Mel Tillis*	Columbia 41417
12/14/59	**24**	4		41 **Tomorrow Night**	*Will Grosz/Sam Koslow*	Columbia 41489

Billboard DEBUT	PEAK	WKS	GOLD	Ranking	ARTIST / Country Chart Hit	Songwriter	Label (& Number)
					SMITH, Carl — cont'd		
3/21/60	**30**	1		42	**Make The Waterwheel Roll**	*Mel Tillis/Marijohn Wilkin*	Columbia 41557
6/20/60	**28**	2		43	**Cut Across Shorty**	*Wayne Walker/Marijohn Wilkin*	Columbia 41642
2/20/61	**29**	2		44	**You Make Me Live Again**	*Ray Price/Wayne Walker*	Columbia 41819
7/10/61	**11**	9		45	**Kisses Never Lie**	*Wayne Walker*	Columbia 42042
1/13/62	**11**	15		46	**Air Mail To Heaven /**	*Kent Westberry*	
1/27/62	**24**	2		47	**Things That Mean The Most**	*Marijohn Wilkin*	Columbia 42222
5/12/62	**16**	7		48	**The Best Dressed Beggar (In Town)**	*Houston Turner*	Columbia 42349
4/20/63	**28**	1		49	**Live For Tomorrow**	*Wayne Walker*	Columbia 42686
8/24/63	**17**	8		50	**In The Back Room Tonight**	*Roy Botkin*	Columbia 42768
11/9/63+	**23**	5		51	**I Almost Forgot Her Today /**	*Del Reeves/Ellen Reeves*	
12/21/63+	**16**	11		52	**Triangle**	*Jean Chapel*	Columbia 42858
2/22/64	**17**	14		53	**The Pillow That Whispers**	*Cal Veale*	Columbia 42949
6/20/64	**15**	20		54	**Take My Ring Off Your Finger**	*Benny Joy/Hugh X. Lewis*	Columbia 43033
10/17/64	**14**	15		55	**Lonely Girl /**	*Carl Smith/Mel Tillis/Wayne Walker*	
12/12/64+	**26**	9		56	**When It's Over**	*Carl Belew/Clyde Pitts*	Columbia 43124
2/13/65	**32**	11		57	**She Called Me Baby**	*Harlan Howard*	Columbia 43200
6/12/65	**42**	3		58	**Keep Me Fooled /**	*Roy Botkin*	
6/26/65	**33**	8		59	**Be Good To Her**	*Marvin Rainwater*	Columbia 43266
10/16/65	**36**	6		60	**Let's Walk Away Strangers**	*Benny Joy/Mel Tillis*	Columbia 43361
3/12/66	**45**	4		61	**Why Do I Keep Doing This To Us /**	*Benny Joy/Kent Westberry*	
3/19/66	**49**	1		62	**Why Can't You Feel Sorry For Me**	*Merle Kilgore/Marvin Rainwater*	Columbia 43485
9/17/66	**42**	5		63	**Man With A Plan**	*Baker Knight/Oscar Smith*	Columbia 43753
12/3/66+	**52**	8		64	**You Better Be Better To Me /**	*Dallas Frazier*	
1/14/67	**65**	3		65	**It's Only A Matter Of Time**	*Rubye Glasgow/Joan Hager*	Columbia 43866
4/22/67	**68**	3		66	**Mighty Day /**	*Johnny Russell*	
5/13/67	**54**	7		67	**I Should Get Away Awhile (From You)**	*Danny Dill/Mel Tillis*	Columbia 44034
8/26/67	**10**	18		68	**Deep Water**	*Fred Rose*	Columbia 44233
1/13/68	**18**	11		69	**Foggy River**	*Fred Rose*	Columbia 44396
5/18/68	**43**	9		70	**You Ought To Hear Me Cry**	*Willie Nelson*	Columbia 44486
9/21/68	**48**	5		71	**There's No More Love**	*Johnny Mathis*	Columbia 44620
1/4/69	**25**	13		72	**Faded Love And Winter Roses**	*Fred Rose*	Columbia 44702
4/26/69	**18**	13		73	**Good Deal, Lucille**	*Joe Miller/Al Terry/Charles Theriot*	Columbia 44816
8/16/69	**14**	12		74	**I Love You Because**	*Leon Payne*	Columbia 44939
12/6/69+	**35**	8		75	**Heartbreak Avenue**	*Mel Foree*	Columbia 45031
3/14/70	**18**	10		76	**Pull My String And Wind Me Up**	*Jim Mundy*	Columbia 45086
7/11/70	**46**	8		77	**Pick Me Up On Your Way Down /**	*Harlan Howard*	
8/8/70	**flip**	4		78	**Bonaparte's Retreat**	*Pee Wee King*	Columbia 45177
10/3/70	**20**	12		79	**How I Love Them Old Songs**	*Mickey Newbury*	Columbia 45225
2/13/71	**44**	10		80	**Don't Worry 'Bout The Mule (Just Load The Wagon)**	*Glenn Barber*	Columbia 45293
6/5/71	**43**	8		81	**Lost It On The Road**	*Jack Fisher*	Columbia 45382
9/11/71	**21**	13		82	**Red Door**	*Bobby Bond*	Columbia 45436
12/11/71+	**34**	12		83	**Don't Say You're Mine**	*Cam Mullins*	Columbia 45497
5/13/72	**46**	11		84	**Mama Bear**	*Wiley Smith*	Columbia 45558
8/5/72	**54**	9		85	**If This Is Goodbye**	*Cam Mullins*	Columbia 45648
9/29/73	**76**	6		86	**I Need Help**	*Gene Davis*	Columbia 45923
1/25/75	**67**	9		87	**The Way I Lose My Mind**	*Dallas Frazier/Whitey Shafer*	Hickory/MGM 337
11/15/75	**97**	2		88	**Roly Poly**	*Fred Rose*	Hickory/MGM 357
5/29/76	**97**	3		89	**If You Don't, Somebody Else Will**	*Jimmy Fautheree/Geraldine Hamilton/Johnny Mathis*	Hickory/MGM 371
12/11/76	**98**	4		90	**A Way With Words**	*Eddy Raven*	ABC/Hickory 54004
4/9/77	**96**	4		91	**Show Me A Brick Wall**	*Steve Collom*	ABC/Hickory 54009
9/3/77	**84**	4		92	**This Kinda Love Ain't Meant For Sunday School**	*Jimmy Walker*	ABC/Hickory 54016
2/4/78	**81**	4		93	**This Lady Loving Me**	*Eddy Raven*	ABC/Hickory 54022

Air Mail To Heaven ['62]
Are You Teasing Me ['52]
Back Up Buddy ['54]
Be Good To Her ['65]
Before I Met You ['56]
Best Dressed Beggar (In Town) ['62]
Best Years Of Your Life ['59]
Bonaparte's Retreat ['70]
Cut Across Shorty ['60]
Deep Water ['67]
Do I Like It? ['53]
Dog-Gone It, Baby, I'm In Love ['54]
Don't Say You're Mine ['72]
Don't Tease Me ['55]
Don't Worry 'Bout The Mule (Just Load The Wagon) ['71]
Doorstep To Heaven ['56]
Faded Love And Winter Roses ['69]
Foggy River ['68]
Go, Boy, Go ['54]
Good Deal, Lucille ['69]
Heartbreak Avenue ['70]
Hey Joe! ['53]
How I Love Them Old Songs ['70]
I Almost Forgot Her Today ['64]
I Feel Like Cryin' ['56]
I Love You Because ['69]
I Need Help ['73]
I Should Get Away Awhile (From You) ['67]
I've Changed ['56]
If Teardrops Were Pennies ['51]
If This Is Goodbye ['72]
If You Don't, Somebody Else Will ['76]
In The Back Room Tonight ['63]
It's A Lovely, Lovely World ['52]
It's All My Heartache ['59]
It's Only A Matter Of Time ['67]
Just Wait 'Til I Get You Alone ['53]
Keep Me Fooled ['65]
Kisses Don't Lie ['55]
Kisses Never Lie ['61]
Let Old Mother Nature Have Her Way ['51]
Let's Live A Little ['51]
Let's Walk Away Strangers ['65]
Live For Tomorrow ['63]
Lonely Girl ['64]
Loose Talk ['55]
Lost It On The Road ['71]
Make The Waterwheel Roll ['60]
Mama Bear ['72]
Man With A Plan ['66]
Mighty Day ['67]
More Than Anything Else In The World ['55]
Mr. Moon ['51]
No, I Don't Believe I Will ['55]
Old Lonesome Times ['55]
Orchids Mean Goodbye ['53]
Our Honeymoon ['52]
Pick Me Up On Your Way Down ['70]
Pillow That Whispers ['64]
Pull My String And Wind Me Up ['70]
Red Door ['71]
Roly Poly ['75]
Satisfaction Guaranteed ['53]
She Called Me Baby ['65]
Show Me A Brick Wall ['77]
Take My Ring Off Your Finger ['64]
Ten Thousand Drums ['59]
That's The Kind Of Love I'm Looking For ['53]
There She Goes ['55]
There's No More Love ['68]
Things That Mean The Most ['62]
This Kinda Love Ain't Meant For Sunday School ['77]
This Lady Loving Me ['78]
Tomorrow Night ['59]
Trademark ['53]
Triangle ['64]
Wait A Little Longer Please, Jesus ['55]
Walking The Slow Walk ['58]
Way I Lose My Mind ['75]
Way With Words ['76]
When It's Over ['65]
(When You Feel Like You're In Love) Don't Just Stand There ['52]
Why Can't You Feel Sorry For Me ['66]
Why Do I Keep Doing This To Us ['66]
Why, Why ['57]
Wicked Lies ['56]
You Are The One ['56]
You Better Be Better To Me ['67]
You Can't Hurt Me Anymore ['57]
You Make Me Live Again ['61]
You Ought To Hear Me Cry ['68]
You're Free To Go ['56]
Your Name Is Beautiful ['58]

Billboard DEBUT	PEAK	WKS	GOLD	ARTIST / Country Chart Hit	Ranking / Songwriter	Label (& Number)

SMITH, Connie — 1960s: #28 / 1970s: #43 / All-Time: #78

Born Constance June Meador on 8/14/1941 in Elkhart, Indiana; raised in Hinton, West Virginia, and Warner, Ohio. Female singer/songwriter. Acted in the movies *Las Vegas Hillbillies*, *Road To Nashville* and *Second Fiddle To A Steel Guitar*. Married **Marty Stuart** on 7/8/1997. Also see **Some Of Chet's Friends**.

OPRY: 1965

DEBUT	PEAK	WKS	#	Country Chart Hit	Songwriter	Label (& Number)
9/26/64	❶[8]	28	1	**Once A Day**	*Bill Anderson*	RCA Victor 8416
1/23/65	4	24	2	**Then And Only Then /**	*Bill Anderson*	
2/6/65	25	17	3	**Tiny Blue Transistor Radio**	*Bill Anderson*	RCA Victor 8489
6/5/65	9	16	4	**I Can't Remember**	*Bette Anderson/Bill Anderson*	RCA Victor 8551
9/25/65	4	19	5	**If I Talk To Him**	*Dolores Edgin/Priscilla Mitchell*	RCA Victor 8663
2/12/66	4	17	6	**Nobody But A Fool (Would Love You)**	*Bill Anderson*	RCA Victor 8746
6/11/66	2[2]	17	7	**Ain't Had No Lovin'**	*Dallas Frazier*	RCA Victor 8842
10/15/66	3[3]	19	8	**The Hurtin's All Over**	*Harlan Howard*	RCA Victor 8964
3/11/67	10	15	9	**I'll Come Runnin'**	*Connie Smith*	RCA Victor 9108
6/24/67	4	15	10	**Cincinnati, Ohio**	*Bill Anderson*	RCA Victor 9214
10/28/67	5	15	11	**Burning A Hole In My Mind**	*Cy Coben*	RCA Victor 9335
1/27/68	7	14	12	**Baby's Back Again**	*Betty Robinson*	RCA Victor 9413
5/18/68	10	15	13	**Run Away Little Tears**	*Dallas Frazier*	RCA Victor 9513
9/28/68	20	11	14	**Cry, Cry, Cry**	*Shirley Wood*	RCA Victor 9624
3/1/69	13	14	15	**Ribbon Of Darkness**	*Gordon Lightfoot*	RCA Victor 0101
7/5/69	20	11	16	**Young Love** *[w/ Nat Stuckey]*	*Ric Cartey/Carole Joyner*	RCA Victor 0181
11/8/69	6	15	17	**You And Your Sweet Love**	*Bill Anderson*	RCA Victor 0258
3/14/70	59	4	18	**If God Is Dead (Who's That Living In My Soul)** *[w/ Nat Stuckey]*	*Lawrence Reynolds*	RCA Victor 9805
5/16/70	5	15	19	**I Never Once Stopped Loving You**	*Bill Anderson/Jan Howard*	RCA Victor 9832
9/12/70	14	11	20	**Louisiana Man**	*Doug Kershaw*	RCA Victor 9887
1/2/71	11	14	21	**Where Is My Castle**	*Dallas Frazier*	RCA Victor 9938
5/8/71	2[2]	17	22	**Just One Time**	*Don Gibson*	RCA Victor 9981
10/16/71	14	15	23	**I'm Sorry If My Love Got In Your Way**	*Dallas Frazier/Whitey Shafer*	RCA Victor 0535
3/4/72	5	15	24	**Just For What I Am**	*Dallas Frazier/A.L. "Doodle" Owens*	RCA Victor 0655
8/5/72	7	15	25	**If It Ain't Love (Let's Leave It Alone)**	*Dallas Frazier*	RCA Victor 0752
12/23/72+	8	14	26	**Love Is The Look You're Looking For**	*Rose Lee Maphis*	RCA Victor 0860
3/31/73	21	12	27	**You've Got Me (Right Where You Want Me)**	*George Richey/Connie Smith*	Columbia 45816
6/23/73	23	10	28	**Dream Painter**	*Dallas Frazier/Whitey Shafer*	RCA Victor 0971
11/10/73+	10	14	29	**Ain't Love A Good Thing**	*Dallas Frazier*	Columbia 45954
3/23/74	35	11	30	**Dallas**	*Lawton Williams*	Columbia 46008
6/29/74	13	13	31	**I Never Knew (What That Song Meant Before)**	*Whitey Shafer*	Columbia 46058
11/16/74+	13	12	32	**I've Got My Baby On My Mind**	*Whitey Shafer*	Columbia 10051
2/22/75	30	10	33	**I Got A Lot Of Hurtin' Done Today**	*Whitey Shafer*	Columbia 10086
5/17/75	15	13	34	**Why Don't You Love Me**	*Hank Williams*	Columbia 10135
10/4/75	29	11	35	**The Song We Fell In Love To**	*Ray Baker/Tupper Saussy*	Columbia 10210
1/31/76	10	15	36	**('Til) I Kissed You**	*Don Everly*	Columbia 10277
6/5/76	31	10	37	**So Sad (To Watch Good Love Go Bad)**	*Don Everly*	Columbia 10345
8/28/76	13	14	38	**I Don't Wanna Talk It Over Anymore**	*Eddy Raven*	Columbia 10393
3/26/77	42	8	39	**The Latest Shade Of Blue**	*Eddy Raven*	Columbia 10501
5/28/77	58	7	40	**Coming Around**	*Red Lane*	Monument 219
11/5/77+	14	15	41	**I Just Want To Be Your Everything**	*Barry Gibb*	Monument 231
2/25/78	34	10	42	**Lovin' You Baby**	*Jo Ann Campbell/Troy Seals*	Monument 241
5/27/78	68	6	43	**There'll Never Be Another For Me**	*John Ford Coley/Parker McGee/Dan Seals*	Monument 252
11/4/78	68	5	44	**Smooth Sailin'**	*Curly Putman/Sonny Throckmorton*	Monument 266
4/7/79	88	3	45	**Lovin' You, Lovin' Me /**	*Sonny Throckmorton*	
4/7/79	flip	3	46	**Ten Thousand And One**	*Pat Bunch/Dan Mitchell*	Monument 281
6/23/79	93	2	47	**Don't Say Love**	*Jim Glaser/Jimmy Payne*	Monument 284
7/27/85	71	6	48	**A Far Cry From You**	*Steve Earle/Jimbeau Hinson*	Epic 05414

SMITH, Darden

Born on 3/11/1962 in Brenham, Texas. Male singer/songwriter.

DEBUT	PEAK	WKS	#	Country Chart Hit	Songwriter	Label (& Number)
2/20/88	56	8	1	**Little Maggie**	*Darden Smith*	Epic 07709
5/28/88	59	6	2	**Day After Tomorrow**	*Darden Smith*	Epic 07906

SMITH, David

Born in Dallas, Texas. Male singer.

DEBUT	PEAK	WKS	Country Chart Hit	Songwriter	Label (& Number)
10/20/79	64	5	**Heroes And Idols (Don't Come Easy)**	*Jack Eubanks/Pete Ray/Harold Shedd*	MDJ 1004

SMITH, Dennis

Born in Arkansas. Male singer.

DEBUT	PEAK	WKS	Country Chart Hit	Songwriter	Label (& Number)
3/1/80	94	2	**California Calling**	*Bill Wence/Dan Willis*	Adonda 79021

DEBUT	PEAK	WKS	GOLD	ARTIST / Country Chart Hit ... Songwriter	Label (& Number)
				SMITH, Jerry, and His Pianos	
				Born in Philadelphia, Pennsylvania. Male pianist/songwriter. Prolific session musician. Also recorded as **Papa Joe's Music Box**.	
5/17/69	44	10		1 **Truck Stop** ... *Jerry Smith* [I]	ABC 11162
8/16/69	63	5		2 **Sweet 'N' Sassy** ... *Jerry Smith* [I]	ABC 11230
12/20/69	62	3		3 **Papa Joe's Thing** *[Papa Joe's Music Box]* ... *Jerry Smith* [I]	ABC 11246
6/6/70	44	9		4 **Drivin' Home** ... *Jerry Smith* [I]	Decca 32679
10/3/70	60	7		5 **Steppin' Out** ... *Jerry Smith* [I]	Decca 32730
				SMITH, Kate	
				Born on 5/1/1907 in Greenville, Virginia. Died on 6/17/1986 (age 79). Popular soprano. Hosted own radio and TV shows.	
10/30/48	10	1		**Foggy River** ... S:10 *Fred Rose*	MGM 30059
				SMITH, Logan	
				Born in Kentucky. Male singer/songwriter.	
1/19/74	63	11		**Little Man** ... *Logan Smith* [N]	Brand X 6
				SMITH, Lou	
				Born in Cincinnati, Ohio. Male singer/guitarist.	
8/15/60	9	17		1 **Cruel Love** ... *Arthur Smiley*	KRCO 105
4/17/61	21	5		2 **I'm Wondering** ... *Bob Beckham/Harry Bryant/Wayne Walker*	Salvo 2862

SMITH, Margo — **All-Time: #195**

Born Betty Lou Miller on 4/9/1942 in Dayton, Ohio. Female singer/songwriter. Sang with the Apple Sisters vocal group while in high school. Taught kindergarden during the 1960s. Formed a gospel duo with her daughter Holly in the 1990s.

DEBUT	PEAK	WKS	GOLD	ARTIST / Country Chart Hit ... Songwriter	Label (& Number)
4/5/75	8	18		1 **There I Said It** ... *Margo Smith*	20th Century 2172
9/13/75	30	12		2 **Paper Lovin'** ... *Margo Smith*	20th Century 2222
12/20/75+	51	8		3 **Meet Me Later** ... *Margo Smith*	20th Century 2255
5/29/76	10	14		4 **Save Your Kisses For Me** ... *Tony Hiller/Martin Lee/Lee Sheridan*	Warner 8213
10/2/76	7	16		5 **Take My Breath Away** ... *Margo Smith/Norro Wilson*	Warner 8261
3/12/77	12	12		6 **Love's Explosion** ... *Margo Smith/Norro Wilson*	Warner 8339
6/25/77	23	10		7 **My Weakness** ... *Margo Smith/Norro Wilson*	Warner 8399
8/20/77	43	8		8 **So Close Again** *[w/ Norro Wilson]* ... *Jim Shaw/Margo Smith/Norro Wilson*	Warner 8427
12/17/77+	❶[2]	18		9 **Don't Break The Heart That Loves You** *Benny Davis/Ted Murray*	Warner 8508
4/29/78	❶[1]	15		10 **It Only Hurts For A Little While** *Mack David/Fred Spielman*	Warner 8555
9/9/78	3[2]	14		11 **Little Things Mean A Lot** ... *Edith Lindeman/Carl Stutz*	Warner 8653
1/20/79	7	13		12 **Still A Woman** ... *Mack David/Margo Smith/Norro Wilson*	Warner 8726
5/5/79	10	13		13 **If I Give My Heart To You** ... *Jimmy Brewster/Jimmie Crane/Al Jacobs*	Warner 8806
9/8/79	27	9		14 **Baby My Baby** ... *Mack David/Margo Smith/Norro Wilson* [S]	Warner 49038
12/8/79+	13	13		15 **The Shuffle Song** ... *Mack David/Margo Smith/Norro Wilson*	Warner 49109
7/5/80	43	9		16 **My Guy** ... *Smokey Robinson*	Warner 49250
10/11/80	52	7		17 **He Gives Me Diamonds, You Give Me Chills** ... *Don Goodman/Mary Ann Kennedy*	Warner 49569
12/20/80+	12	14		18 **Cup Of Tea** *[w/ Rex Allen, Jr.]* ... *Harlan White*	Warner 49626
4/25/81	72	4		19 **My Heart Cries For You** ... *Percy Faith/Carl Sigman*	Warner 49701
6/13/81	26	12		20 **While The Feeling's Good** *[w/ Rex Allen, Jr.]* ... *Roger Bowling/Freddie Hart*	Warner 49738
5/8/82	64	7		21 **Either You're Married Or You're Single** ... *Gene Dobbins/Tommy Rocco*	AMI 1304
8/21/82	70	5		22 **Could It Be I Don't Belong Here Anymore** ... *Mack Phillips/Doug Zepp*	AMI 1309
12/10/83	78	4		23 **Wedding Bells** ... *Claude Boone*	Moon Shine 3019
1/28/84	63	7		24 **Please Tell Him That I Said Hello** ... *Peter Dibbens/Shep Stone*	Moon Shine 3021
6/22/85	82	2		25 **All I Do Is Dream Of You** ... *Nacio Herb Brown/Alan Freed*	Bermuda Dunes 106
8/10/85	63	8		26 **Everyday People** *[w/ Tom Grant]* ... *Max D. Barnes/Troy Seals*	Bermuda Dunes 110
4/23/88	77	4		27 **Echo Me** ... *Jerry Fuller*	Playback 1300
				SMITH, Rick	
				Born in Louisville, Kentucky. Male singer/songwriter.	
9/11/76	99	2		1 **The Way I Loved Her** ... *Rick Smith*	Cin Kay 110
10/23/76	58	7		2 **Daddy How'm I Doin'** ... *Herb Coleman*	Cin Kay 114
				SMITH, Russell	
				Born Howard Russell Smith on 6/17/1949 in Nashville, Tennessee. Male singer/songwriter. Former lead singer of the **Amazing Rhythm Aces**.	
2/4/84	74	6		1 **Where Did We Go Right** ... *Dave Loggins/Don Schlitz*	Capitol 5293
5/14/88	53	8		2 **Three Piece Suit** ... *Dereama Sherrill/Lisa Silver/Russell Smith*	Epic 07789
7/23/88	49	8		3 **Betty Jean** ... *Lisa Silver/Russell Smith*	Epic 07972
3/18/89	37	14		4 **I Wonder What She's Doing Tonight** ... *John Jarrard/Gary Nicholson*	Epic 68615
7/22/89	61	8		5 **Anger And Tears** ... *Carol Chase/Russell Smith*	Epic 68964

DEBUT	PEAK	WKS	GOLD	ARTIST / Country Chart Hit	Songwriter	Label (& Number)

SMITH, Sammi — All-Time: #162

Born Jewel Fay Smith on 8/5/1943 in Orange, California; raised in Oklahoma. Died of emphysema on 2/12/2005 (age 61). Female singer/songwriter. Performing since age 11. Moved to Dallas in 1973 and became part of the "outlaw" movement.

DEBUT	PEAK	WKS	GOLD	Country Chart Hit	Songwriter	Label (& Number)
1/27/68	69	2		1 **So Long, Charlie Brown, Don't Look For Me Around**	*Harold Lee*	Columbia 44370
6/8/68	53	7		2 **Why Do You Do Me Like You Do**	*John Hartford*	Columbia 44523
8/16/69	58	6		3 **Brownville Lumberyard**	*Tom Hartman*	Columbia 44905
9/5/70	25	13		4 **He's Everywhere**	*Gene Dobbins/Jean Whitehead*	Mega 0001
12/19/70+	❶^{3}	20	●	5 **Help Me Make It Through The Night** Grammy: Song, Female Vocal & Hall of Fame / CMA: Single	*Kris Kristofferson*	Mega 0015
5/15/71	10	14		6 **Then You Walk In**	*David Malloy/Johnny Wilson*	Mega 0026
9/18/71	27	12		7 **For The Kids**	*Shel Silverstein*	Mega 0039
1/1/72	38	10		8 **Kentucky**	*Sammi Smith*	Mega 0056
4/22/72	36	8		9 **Girl In New Orleans**	*Don Goodman/Troy Seals*	Mega 0068
6/17/72	13	15		10 **I've Got To Have You**	*Kris Kristofferson*	Mega 0079
12/23/72+	51	8		11 **The Toast Of '45**	*Jim Casey/Vince Matthews*	Mega 0097
5/19/73	62	8		12 **I Miss You Most When You're Here**	*John Virgin*	Mega 0109
9/29/73	44	12		13 **City Of New Orleans**	*Steve Goodman*	Mega 0118
1/19/74	16	12		14 **The Rainbow In Daddy's Eyes**	*Dallas Frazier/Whitey Shafer*	Mega 1204
6/1/74	75	7		15 **Never Been To Spain**	*Hoyt Axton*	Mega 1210
9/7/74	26	13		16 **Long Black Veil**	*Danny Dill/Marijohn Wilkin*	Mega 1214
2/1/75	33	11		17 **Cover Me**	*Wayne Carson*	Mega 1222
9/13/75	9	15		18 **Today I Started Loving You Again**	*Merle Haggard/Bonnie Owens*	Mega 1236
12/20/75+	81	7		19 **Huckelberry Pie** *[w/ Even Stevens]*	*Even Stevens*	Elektra 45292
1/10/76	51	6		20 **My Window Faces The South**	*Jerry Livingston/Mitchell Parish/Abner Silver*	Mega 1246
2/21/76	43	9		21 **As Long As There's A Sunday**	*Justin Tubb*	Elektra 45300
5/29/76	60	6		22 **I'll Get Better**	*Eddie Rabbitt/Even Stevens*	Elektra 45320
7/17/76	29	11		23 **Sunday School To Broadway**	*Danny Hice/Ruby Hice*	Elektra 45334
7/31/76	71	6		24 **Just You 'N' Me**	*James Pankow*	Zodiac 1005
2/5/77	19	12		25 **Loving Arms**	*Tom Jans*	Elektra 45374
5/14/77	27	11		26 **I Can't Stop Loving You**	*Don Gibson*	Elektra 45398
9/17/77	23	11		27 **Days That End In "Y"**	*Jim Malloy/Even Stevens*	Elektra 45429
4/29/78	48	8		28 **It Just Won't Feel Like Cheating** (With You)	*David Chamberlain/Jim Vest*	Elektra 45476
8/5/78	73	4		29 **Norma Jean**	*J.C. Cunningham*	Elektra 45504
3/10/79	16	14		30 **What A Lie**	*Terry Skinner/J.L. Wallace*	Cyclone 100
7/21/79	27	11		31 **The Letter**	*Wayne Carson*	Cyclone 104
11/29/80+	36	13		32 **I Just Want To Be With You**	*Roger Murrah*	Sound Factory 425
3/7/81	16	13		33 **Cheatin's A Two Way Street**	*Murl Bernard/Charles Duvall*	Sound Factory 427
8/8/81	34	11		34 **Sometimes I Cry When I'm Alone**	*Larry Bastian*	Sound Factory 446
3/27/82	69	5		35 **Gypsy And Joe**	*Bonnie Guitar*	Sound Factory 433
7/20/85	76	4		36 **You Just Hurt My Last Feeling**	*Hank Cochran/Royce Porter*	Step One 342
3/1/86	80	4		37 **Love Me All Over**	*Gene Dobbins/Tommy Rocco*	Step One 351

SMITH, Warren

Born on 2/7/1932 in Humphreys County, Mississippi. Died of a heart attack on 1/30/1980 (age 47). Rockabilly singer.

DEBUT	PEAK	WKS	GOLD	Country Chart Hit	Songwriter	Label (& Number)
9/5/60	5	17		1 **I Don't Believe I'll Fall In Love Today**	*Harlan Howard*	Liberty 55248
2/20/61	7	15		2 **Odds And Ends** (Bits And Pieces)	*Harlan Howard*	Liberty 55302
9/11/61	23	3		3 **Why, Baby, Why** *[w/ Shirley Collie]*	*Darrell Edwards/George Jones*	Liberty 55361
9/11/61	26	3		4 **Call Of The Wild**	*Billly Mize/Buddy Mize*	Liberty 55336
11/2/63	25	4		5 **That's Why I Sing In A Honky Tonk /**	*Ned Miller/Sue Miller*	
1/11/64	41	2		6 **Big City Ways**	*Eddie Miller*	Liberty 55615
8/1/64	41	8		7 **Blue Smoke**	*Bob Morris/Dean Seals*	Liberty 55699

SMOKIN' ARMADILLOS

Group from Bakersfield, California: Rick Russell (vocals), Josh Graham and Scott Meeks (guitars), Jason Theiste (fiddle), Aaron Casida (bass) and Darin Kirkindoll (drums).

DEBUT	PEAK	WKS	GOLD	Country Chart Hit	Songwriter	Label (& Number)
1/13/96	53	10		1 **Let Your Heart Lead Your Mind**	*Scott Meeks/Jason Theiste*	MCG/Curb
5/11/96	68	4		2 **Thump Factor** S:21 above 2 from the album *Smokin' Armadillos* on MCG/Curb 77748	*Tony Martin/Scott Meeks*	MCG/Curb
1/24/98	64	6		3 **I Don't Want No Part Of It** from the album *I Don't Want No Part Of It* on MCG/Curb 73037	*Max T. Barnes/Keith Follese*	MCG/Curb

SNODGRASS, Elmer

Born on 4/28/1914 in West Virginia. Died in September 1982 (age 68). Male comedian/emcee/songwriter. The Musical Pioneers: Chuck Atha (male vocals), Helen Farmer (female vocals), brothers Bob Still and Gene Still (guitars) and Stanford Lee (fiddle).

DEBUT	PEAK	WKS	GOLD	Country Chart Hit	Songwriter	Label (& Number)
1/18/60	20	10		1 **Until Today** *[w/ The Musical Pioneers]*	*Elmer Snodgrass*	Decca 31048
1/30/61	25	1		2 **What A Terrible Feeling**	*Chuck Atha*	Decca 31145

Billboard DEBUT	PEAK	WKS	GOLD	#	ARTIST / Country Chart Hit	Ranking / Songwriter	Label (& Number)

SNOW, Hank **1950s: #3 / 1960s: #26 / All-Time: #24 // HOF: 1979**

Born Clarence Snow on 5/9/1914 in Liverpool, Nova Scotia, Canada. Died of heart failure on 12/20/1999 (age 85). Male singer/songwriter/guitarist. Hosted own radio shows on CNHS in Halifax, CBC in Montreal and CKCW in Mocton, Canada. Backing group: The Rainbow Ranch Boys. Known as "The Singing Ranger." Also see **Some Of Chet's Friends**.

OPRY: 1950

DEBUT	PEAK	WKS	#	Country Chart Hit	Chart	Songwriter	Label (& Number)
				HANK SNOW, The Singing Ranger and his Rainbow Ranch Boys:			
12/31/49	10	1	1	Marriage Vow	S:10	*Jenny Lou Carson*	RCA Victor 48-0056
7/1/50	❶[21]	44	2	I'm Moving On	S:❶[21] / A:❶[18] / J:❶[14]	*Hank Snow*	RCA Victor 48-0328
				Grammy: Hall of Fame; also see #78 below			
11/25/50+	❶[2]	23	3	The Golden Rocket	S:❶[2] / A:❶[1] / J:2	*Hank Snow*	RCA Victor 48-0400
3/3/51	❶[8]	27	4	The Rhumba Boogie	S:❶[8] / J:❶[5] / A:❶[2]	*Hank Snow*	RCA Victor 48-0431
4/21/51	4	11	5	Bluebird Island *[w/ Anita Carter]* /	S:4 / J:7	*Hank Snow*	
5/12/51	2[1]	14	6	Down The Trail Of Achin' Hearts *[w/ Anita Carter]*	J:2 / S:7 / A:7	*Jimmy Kennedy/Nat Simon*	RCA Victor 48-0441
9/15/51	6	6	7	Unwanted Sign Upon Your Heart	S:6 / A:9	*Hank Snow*	RCA Victor 48-0498
12/15/51+	4	9	8	Music Makin' Mama From Memphis	J:4 / A:5 / S:6	*Hank Snow*	RCA Victor 47-4346
4/5/52	2[3]	18	9	The Gold Rush Is Over	J:2 / S:4 / A:4	*Cindy Walker*	RCA Victor 47-4522
7/5/52	2[1]	14	10	Lady's Man /	S:2 / J:5 / A:6	*Cy Coben*	
7/26/52	8	3	11	Married By The Bible, Divorced By The Law	J:8 / S:10	*John Rector/Neva Starns*	RCA Victor 47-4733
9/27/52	3[1]	11	12	I Went To Your Wedding	J:3 / A:4 / S:4	*Jessie Mae Robinson*	RCA Victor 47-4909
12/13/52+	4	10	13	The Gal Who Invented Kissin' /	S:4 / J:5 / A:9	*Earl Griswold/Charles Orr*	
12/27/52+	3[1]	16	14	(Now And Then, There's) A Fool Such As I	A:3 / J:3 / S:4	*William Trader*	RCA Victor 5034
4/4/53	9	2	15	Honeymoon On A Rocket Ship	S:9 / A:9 / J:9	*Johnny Masters*	RCA Victor 5155
6/6/53	3[1]	11	16	Spanish Fire Ball	S:3 / J:4 / A:5	*Dan Welch*	RCA Victor 5296
10/3/53	10	1	17	For Now And Always	A:10	*Leon Payne*	RCA Victor 5380
11/28/53	6	6	18	When Mexican Joe Met Jole Blon	S:6 / J:9	*Sheb Wooley*	RCA Victor 5490
5/29/54	❶[20]	41	19	I Don't Hurt Anymore	S:❶[20] / J:❶[20] / A:❶[18]	*Don Robertson/Jack Rollins*	RCA Victor 5698
12/4/54	10	6	20	That Crazy Mambo Thing	J:10 / S:11	*Cy Coben*	RCA Victor 5912
12/25/54+	❶[2]	16	21	Let Me Go, Lover!	A:❶[2] / J:2 / S:3	*Jenny Lou Carson*	RCA Victor 5960
1/1/55	15	1	22	The Next Voice You Hear	S:15	*Cindy Walker*	RCA Victor 5912
4/2/55	15	1	23	Silver Bell *[w/ Chet Atkins]*	S:15	*Edward Madden/Percy Wenrich* [I]	RCA Victor 5995
4/9/55	3[9]	27	24	Yellow Roses /	J:3 / S:3 / A:3	*Ken Devine*	
4/16/55	3[1]	17	25	Would You Mind?	A:3 / J:4 / S:flip	*Cy Coben*	RCA Victor 6057
7/23/55	7	8	26	Cryin', Prayin', Waitin', Hopin' /	J:7 / S:9 / A:10	*Stan Jones*	
7/23/55	7	2	27	I'm Glad I Got To See You Once Again	J:7 / S:12	*Don Gibson*	RCA Victor 6154
11/5/55	5	8	28	Mainliner (The Hawk With Silver Wings) /	J:5 / S:8	*Stuart Hamblen*	
11/5/55	5	9	29	Born To Be Happy	J:5 / A:10 / S:14	*Stuart Hamblen*	RCA Victor 6269
2/4/56	5	10	30	These Hands /	J:5 / A:6 / S:8	*Eddie Noack*	
2/18/56	11	4	31	I'm Moving In	S:11 / J:flip	*Hank Snow*	RCA Victor 6379
8/4/56	4	22	32	Conscience I'm Guilty /	J:4 / S:8 / A:9	*Dick Reynolds/Jack Rhodes*	
8/4/56	5	4	33	Hula Rock	J:5 / S:flip	*Betty Rose/Dusty Rose*	RCA Victor 6578
12/15/56+	7	9	34	Stolen Moments	J:7 / S:8 / A:9	*Joe Sherman/Sid Wayne*	RCA Victor 6715
				HANK SNOW:			
7/22/57	4	19	35	Tangled Mind /	A:4 / S:9	*Ted Daffan/Herman Shoss*	
7/22/57	8	14	36	My Arms Are A House	A:8 / S:13	*Alex Alstone/Jim Kennedy*	RCA Victor 6955
3/31/58	15	1	37	Whispering Rain	A:15 / S:18	*Jack Newman*	RCA Victor 7154
6/23/58	7	9	38	Big Wheels	A:7 / S:18	*Clovis Yarnall*	RCA Victor 7233
11/3/58	16	5	39	A Woman Captured Me		*Ted Daffan*	RCA Victor 7325
3/16/59	19	6	40	Doggone That Train		*Jimmie Davis*	RCA Victor 7448
6/1/59	6	11	41	Chasin' A Rainbow *[w/ The Rainbow Ranch Boys]*		*Ted Harris*	RCA Victor 7524
10/19/59	3[2]	20	42	The Last Ride		*Ted Daffan/Robert Halcomb*	RCA Victor 7586
4/11/60	22	5	43	Rockin', Rollin' Ocean		*Ted Daffan/Theda Roush*	RCA Victor 7702
7/18/60	9	15	44	Miller's Cave		*Jack Clement*	RCA Victor 7748
5/15/61	5	20	45	Beggar To A King		*J.P. Richardson*	RCA Victor 7869
10/9/61	11	9	46	The Restless One		*Hank Snow*	RCA Victor 7933
6/2/62	15	10	47	You Take The Future (And I'll Take The Past)		*Jim Glaser*	RCA Victor 8009
9/15/62	❶[2]	22	48	I've Been Everywhere		*Geoff Mack*	RCA Victor 8072
4/27/63	9	11	49	The Man Who Robbed The Bank At Santa Fe		*Jerry Leiber/Mike Stoller/Billy Edd Wheeler*	RCA Victor 8151
10/26/63	2[3]	22	50	Ninety Miles An Hour (Down A Dead End Street)		*Hal Blair/Don Robertson*	RCA Victor 8239
4/11/64	11	15	51	Breakfast With The Blues /		*Martin David/Vic McAlpin*	
				also see #79 below			
7/4/64	21	12	52	I Stepped Over The Line		*Don Robertson*	RCA Victor 8334
2/13/65	7	19	53	The Wishing Well (Down In The Well)		*Peter Hiscock*	RCA Victor 8488
10/30/65	28	5	54	The Queen Of Draw Poker Town		*Don Robertson/Jack Rollins*	RCA Victor 8655
12/25/65+	18	14	55	I've Cried A Mile		*Tompall Glaser/Harlan Howard*	RCA Victor 8713
5/7/66	22	11	56	The Count Down		*Hank Snow*	RCA Victor 8808
12/10/66+	21	14	57	Hula Love		*Dave Alldred/Jimmy Bowen/Buddy Knox/Don Lanier*	RCA Victor 9012
5/13/67	18	14	58	Down At The Pawn Shop *[w/ Anita Carter]*		*Don Deal*	RCA Victor 9188
9/23/67	20	15	59	Learnin' A New Way Of Life		*Jim Fagan*	RCA Victor 9300

DEBUT	PEAK	WKS	GOLD	ARTIST / Ranking / Country Chart Hit	Songwriter	Label (& Number)
				SNOW, Hank — cont'd		
2/24/68	**69**	3		60 **Who Will Answer? (Aleluya No. 1) /**	*Gutierrez Aute/Sheila Davis*	
4/6/68	**70**	5		61 **I Just Wanted To Know (How The Wind Was Blowing)**	*Cindy Walker*	RCA Victor 9433
6/8/68	**20**	13		62 **The Late And Great Love (Of My Heart)**	*Cindy Walker*	RCA Victor 9523
12/28/68+	**16**	16		63 **The Name Of The Game Was Love**	*Cy Coben*	RCA Victor 9685
5/31/69	**26**	9		64 **Rome Wasn't Built In A Day**	*Yvonne Devaney*	RCA Victor 0151
11/1/69	**53**	5		65 **That's When The Hurtin' Sets In**	*Jim Maxwell*	RCA Victor 0251
7/11/70	**52**	7		66 **Vanishing Breed**	*Bill Eldridge/Gary Stewart*	RCA Victor 9856
11/7/70	**57**	5		67 **Come The Morning**	*Dick Feller*	RCA Victor 9907
4/21/73	**71**	3		68 **North To Chicago**	*Les Pouliot*	RCA Victor 0915
2/9/74	**❶**[1]	15		69 **Hello Love**	*Aileen Muich/Betty Jean Robinson*	RCA Victor 0215
6/29/74	**36**	11		70 **That's You And Me**	*Jerry Weaver*	RCA Victor 0307
11/16/74+	**26**	11		71 **Easy To Love**	*Dave Burgess*	RCA Victor 10108
3/22/75	**47**	10		72 **Merry-Go-Round Of Love**	*Robert Floyd*	RCA Victor 10225
8/2/75	**79**	6		73 **Hijack**	*Jack Cloe*	RCA Victor 10338
11/29/75	**95**	2		74 **Colorado Country Morning**	*J.C. Cunningham/Robert Duncan*	RCA Victor 10439
5/29/76	**87**	4		75 **Who's Been Here Since I've Been Gone**	*Hank Snow*	RCA Victor 10681
11/27/76	**98**	1		76 **You're Wondering Why**	*Ray Griff*	RCA 10804
7/16/77	**81**	4		77 **Trouble In Mind**	*Richard Jones*	RCA 11021
9/24/77	**80**	4		78 **I'm Still Movin' On** sequel to #2 above	*Shel Silverstein/Hank Snow*	RCA 11080
12/3/77	**96**	2		79 **Breakfast With The Blues** new version of #51 above	*Louie Dunn/Vic McAlpin* **[R]**	RCA 11153
7/1/78	**93**	4		80 **Nevertheless**	*Bert Kalmar/Harry Ruby*	RCA 11276
10/7/78	**93**	4		81 **Ramblin' Rose**	*Joe Sherman/Noel Sherman*	RCA 11377
3/31/79	**80**	3		82 **The Mysterious Lady From St. Martinique**	*Ramona Redd/Mitchell Torok*	RCA 11487
7/21/79	**91**	3		83 **A Good Gal Is Hard To Find**	*Eddie Johnson*	RCA 11622
11/10/79	**98**	2		84 **It Takes Too Long**	*Buddy Cannon/Jimmy Darrell*	RCA 11734
2/16/80	**78**	4		85 **Hasn't It Been Good Together** ***[w/ Kelly Foxton]***	*Linda Kaufman/Gloria Shayne*	RCA 11891

Beggar To A King ['61]
Big Wheels ['58]
Bluebird Island ['51]
Born To Be Happy ['55]
Breakfast With The Blues ['64, '77]
Chasin' A Rainbow ['59]
Colorado Country Morning ['75]
Come The Morning ['70]
Conscience I'm Guilty ['56]
Count Down ['66]
Cryin', Prayin', Waitin', Hopin' ['55]
Doggone That Train ['59]
Down At The Pawn Shop ['67]
Down The Trail Of Achin' Hearts ['51]
Easy To Love ['75]
For Now And Always ['53]
Gal Who Invented Kissin' ['53]
Gold Rush Is Over ['52]
Golden Rocket ['51]
Good Gal Is Hard To Find ['79]
Hasn't It Been Good Together ['80]
Hello Love ['74]
Hijack ['75]
Honeymoon On A Rocket Ship ['53]
Hula Love ['67]
Hula Rock ['56]
I Don't Hurt Anymore ['54]
I Just Wanted To Know (How The Wind Was Blowing) ['68]
I Stepped Over The Line ['64]
I Went To Your Wedding ['52]
I'm Glad I Got To See You Once Again ['55]
I'm Moving In ['56]
I'm Moving On ['50]
I'm Still Movin' On ['77]
I've Been Everywhere ['62]
I've Cried A Mile ['66]
It Takes Too Long ['79]
Lady's Man ['52]
Last Ride ['59]
Late And Great Love (Of My Heart) ['68]
Learnin' A New Way Of Life ['67]
Let Me Go, Lover! ['55]
Mainliner (The Hawk With Silver Wings) ['55]
Man Who Robbed The Bank At Santa Fe ['63]
Marriage Vow ['49]
Married By The Bible, Divorced By The Law ['52]
Merry-Go-Round Of Love ['75]
Miller's Cave ['60]
Music Makin' Mama From Memphis ['52]
My Arms Are A House ['57]
Mysterious Lady From St. Martinique ['79]
Name Of The Game Was Love ['69]
Nevertheless ['78]
Next Voice You Hear ['55]
Ninety Miles An Hour (Down A Dead End Street) ['63]
North To Chicago ['73]
(Now And Then, There's) A Fool Such As I ['53]
Queen Of Draw Poker Town ['65]
Ramblin' Rose ['78]
Restless One ['61]
Rhumba Boogie ['51]
Rockin', Rollin' Ocean ['60]
Rome Wasn't Built In A Day ['69]
Silver Bell ['55]
Spanish Fire Ball ['53]
Stolen Moments ['57]
Tangled Mind ['57]
That Crazy Mambo Thing ['54]
That's When The Hurtin' Sets In ['69]
That's You And Me ['74]
These Hands ['56]
Trouble In Mind ['77]
Unwanted Sign Upon Your Heart ['51]
Vanishing Breed ['70]
When Mexican Joe Met Jole Blon ['53]
Whispering Rain ['58]
Who Will Answer? (Aleluya No. 1) ['68]
Who's Been Here Since I've Been Gone ['76]
Wishing Well (Down In The Well) ['65]
Woman Captured Me ['58]
Would You Mind? ['55]
Yellow Roses ['55]
You Take The Future (And I'll Take The Past) ['62]
You're Wondering Why ['76]

SNUFF

Group from Virginia: Jim Bowling (vocals), Robbie House and Chuck Larson (guitars), Cecil Hooker (fiddle), C. Scott Trabue (bass) and Michael Johnson (drums).

DEBUT	PEAK	WKS	GOLD	Country Chart Hit	Songwriter	Label (& Number)
8/7/82	**71**	6		**(So This Is) Happy Hour**	*Steve Gillette/David MacKechnie*	Elektra/Curb 69996

SNYDER, Jimmy

Born in Wheeling, West Virginia. Male singer.

DEBUT	PEAK	WKS	GOLD	Country Chart Hit	Songwriter	Label (& Number)
2/14/70	**30**	9		1 **The Chicago Story**	*Tom T. Hall*	Wayside 009
8/16/80	**71**	7		2 **Just To Prove My Love To You**	*David Allan Coe*	e.i.o. 1126

SNYDER, Rick

Born in California. Male singer.

DEBUT	PEAK	WKS	GOLD	Country Chart Hit	Songwriter	Label (& Number)
7/23/88	**66**	4		**Losing Somebody You Love**	*Rich Grissom/Donny Kees*	Capitol 44185

SOGGY BOTTOM BOYS, The

Fictitious bluegrass group created for the movie *O Brother, Where Art Thou?* George Clooney is "Ulysses", John Turturro is "Pete" and Tim Blake Nelson is "Delmar." Actual recording is performed by studio musicians, including lead vocal by Dan Tyminski of **Alison Krauss & Union Station**.

DEBUT	PEAK	WKS	GOLD	Country Chart Hit	Songwriter	Label (& Number)
3/17/01+	**35**	25		**I Am A Man Of Constant Sorrow** **Grammy: Vocal Collaboration / CMA: Single**; from the movie *O Brother, Where Art Thou?* starring George Clooney (soundtrack on Mercury 170069)	*(traditional)*	Mercury

SOLID GOLD BAND

Group from Galina, Kansas: Jim Rowland, John Green, Mike Bartlett, Tyler Ogle and Buddy Burr.

DEBUT	PEAK	WKS	GOLD	Country Chart Hit	Songwriter	Label (& Number)
11/28/81+	**47**	9		1 **Cherokee Country**	*Robert Russell*	NSD 110
2/20/82	**65**	6		2 **I Never Had The One That I Wanted /**	*Claude Gray/Jimmy Louis/Sheb Wooley*	
2/20/82	**flip**	6		3 **Bandera, Texas**	*Robert Russell*	NSD 121
7/17/82	**68**	6		4 **Country Fiddles**	*Robert Russell*	NSD 138

DEBUT	PEAK	WKS	GOLD	ARTIST / Country Chart Hit	Songwriter	Label (& Number)

SOME OF CHET'S FRIENDS

Group of RCA recording artists: **Eddy Arnold**, **Bobby Bare**, **Don Bowman**, **Jim Ed Brown**, **Archie Campbell**, **Floyd Cramer**, **Skeeter Davis**, **Jimmy Dean**, **George Hamilton IV**, **Homer & Jethro**, **Waylon Jennings**, **Hank Locklin**, **John D. Loudermilk**, **Willie Nelson**, **Norma Jean**, **Jerry Reed**, **Connie Smith**, **Hank Snow**, **Porter Wagoner** and **Dottie West**.

DEBUT	PEAK	WKS	Country Chart Hit	Songwriter	Label (& Number)
6/24/67	38	9	Chet's Tune (tribute to **Chet Atkins**)	*Cy Coben*	RCA Victor 9229

SONNIER, Jo-el

Born Joel Sonnier on 10/2/1946 in Rayne, Louisiana. Male singer/songwriter/accordianist. Once known as "The Cajun Valentino."

DEBUT	PEAK	WKS	Country Chart Hit	Songwriter	Label (& Number)
10/4/75	78	7	1 I've Been Around Enough To Know	*Dickey Lee/Bob McDill*	Mercury 73702
3/6/76	99	1	2 Always Late (With Your Kisses)	*Blackie Crawford/Lefty Frizzell*	Mercury 73754
6/5/76	100	1	3 He's Still All Over You	*Wayland Holyfield/Bob McDill*	Mercury 73796
11/28/87+	39	14	4 Come On Joe	*Tony Romeo*	RCA 5282
2/20/88	7	22	5 No More One More Time	S:14 *Dave Kirby/Troy Seals*	RCA 6895
7/16/88	9	19	6 Tear-Stained Letter	S:12 *Richard Thompson*	RCA 8304
11/19/88+	35	12	7 Rainin' In My Heart	*James Moore/Jerry West*	RCA 8726
5/6/89	47	10	8 (Blue, Blue, Blue) Blue, Blue	*Troy Seals/Eddie Setser*	RCA 8918
10/28/89+	24	17	9 If Your Heart Should Ever Roll This Way Again	*Austin Cunningham/Mark Irwin*	RCA 9014
4/7/90	65	6	10 The Scene Of The Crime (from the album *Have A Little Faith* on RCA 9718)	*Dennis Linde*	RCA

SONS OF THE DESERT

Group from Waco, Texas: brothers Drew Womack (vocals) and Tim Womack (guitar), Scott Saunders (keyboards), Doug Virden (bass) and Brian Westrum (drums). Also see **Lee Ann Womack**.

DEBUT	PEAK	WKS	Country Chart Hit	Songwriter	Label (& Number)
3/8/97	10	21	1 Whatever Comes First	S:22 *Walt Aldridge/Brad Crisler/Drew Womack*	Epic
8/30/97	33	17	2 Hand Of Fate	*Michael Lunn/Mike Noble*	Epic
1/17/98	31	19	3 Leaving October (above 3 from the album *Whatever Comes First* on Epic 67619)	*Tom Douglas/Drew Womack*	Epic
2/20/99	45	11	4 What About You	*Tony Mullins/Tony Toliver*	Epic
6/26/99	58	10	5 Albuquerque	*Chris Lindsey/Stephonie Seekel*	Epic
3/11/00	45	19	6 Change	*Mark Selby/Craig Wiseman*	MCA Nashville
8/12/00	42	15	7 Everybody's Gotta Grow Up Sometime	*Chris Lindsey/Stephonie Seekel*	MCA Nashville
2/10/01	22	30	8 What I Did Right (above 3 from the album *Change* on MCA Nashville 170131)	*Sonny Lemaire/Drew Womack*	MCA Nashville

SONS OF THE PIONEERS — 1940s: #12 // HOF: 1980

Originally a trio consisting of Robert "Bob Nolan" Nobles (born on 4/1/1908; died on 6/16/1980, age 72), Leonard "**Roy Rogers**" Slye (born on 11/5/1911; died on 7/6/1998, age 86) and Vernon "Tim" Spencer (born on 7/13/1908; died on 4/26/1974, age 65). Formed in 1934 and first called the Pioneers; recorded for Decca in 1934. Brothers Karl Farr (born on 4/25/1909; died on 9/20/1961, age 52) and Thomas "Hugh" Farr (born on 12/6/1903; died on 3/17/1980, age 76) were added in 1936. Group appeared in numerous western movies. Rogers and Spencer left in 1937; replaced by Lloyd Perryman (born on 1/29/1917; died on 5/31/1977, age 60) and Pat Brady. Spencer returned shortly thereafter.

DEBUT	PEAK	WKS	Country Chart Hit	Songwriter	Label (& Number)
10/6/45	4	2	1 Stars And Stripes On Iwo Jima	*Cliff Johnson/Bob Wills*	RCA Victor 20-1724
6/29/46	6	1	2 No One To Cry To	*Sid Robin/Foy Williams*	RCA Victor 20-1868
2/15/47	5	1	3 Baby Doll	*Bob Newman*	RCA Victor 20-2086
3/8/47	4	1	4 Cool Water (**Grammy: Hall of Fame**; recorded in 1941; also see #10 below)	*Bob Nolan*	Decca 46027
7/12/47	5	1	5 Cigareetes, Whusky, And Wild, Wild Women	*Tim Spencer*	RCA Victor 20-2199
7/26/47	4	2	6 Teardrops In My Heart	*Vaughn Horton*	RCA Victor 20-2276
6/12/48	6	14	7 Blue Shadows On The Trail *[w/ Roy Rogers]* /	S:6 / J:7 *Eliot Daniel/Johnny Lange*	
6/12/48	13	4	8 (There'll Never Be Another) Pecos Bill *[w/ Roy Rogers]*	S:13 *Eliot Daniel/Johnny Lange*	RCA Victor 20-2780
8/21/48	11	1	9 Tumbling Tumbleweeds (original version released in 1934 on Decca 5047)	J:11 *Bob Nolan*	RCA Victor 20-1904
9/4/48	7	11	10 Cool Water (same version as #4 above)	S:7 / J:11 *Bob Nolan* **[R]**	Decca 46027
2/19/49	12	1	11 My Best To You	J:12 *Isham Jones/Gene Willadsen*	RCA Victor 20-2199
9/10/49	10	1	12 Room Full Of Roses	J:10 *Tim Spencer*	RCA Victor 48-0060
8/23/80	80	4	13 Ride Concrete Cowboy, Ride *[w/ Roy Rogers]* (from the movie *Smokey & The Bandit II* starring **Burt Reynolds**)	*Cliff Crofford/John Durrill/Snuff Garrett*	MCA 41294

SOSEBEE, Tommy

Born Bud Thomas Sosebee on 5/23/1923 in Duncan, South Carolina. Died on 10/23/1967 (age 44). Male singer. Known as "The Voice Of The Hills."

DEBUT	PEAK	WKS	Country Chart Hit	Songwriter	Label (& Number)
3/14/53	7	2	Till I Waltz Again With You	A:7 *Sidney Prosen*	Coral 60916

SOUTH, Joe

Born Joe Souter on 2/28/1940 in Atlanta, Georgia. Male singer/songwriter/guitarist.

DEBUT	PEAK	WKS	Country Chart Hit	Songwriter	Label (& Number)
8/28/61	16	6	1 You're The Reason	*Bobby Edwards/Terry Fell/Fred Henley/Mildred Imes*	Fairlane 21006
10/4/69	27	9	2 Don't It Make You Want To Go Home *[w/ The Believers]*	*Joe South*	Capitol 2592
1/31/70	56	5	3 Walk A Mile In My Shoes *[w/ The Believers]*	*Joe South*	Capitol 2704

SOUTHER, J.D.

Born John David Souther on 11/2/1945 in Detroit, Michigan; raised in Amarillo, Texas. Male singer/songwriter.

DEBUT	PEAK	WKS	Country Chart Hit	Songwriter	Label (& Number)
12/1/79+	60	10	1 You're Only Lonely	*J.D. Souther*	Columbia 11079
10/16/82	27	12	2 Sometimes You Just Can't Win *[w/ Linda Ronstadt]*	*Smokey Stover*	Asylum 69948

DEBUT	PEAK	WKS	GOLD	ARTIST / Country Chart Hit	Ranking / Songwriter	Label (& Number)

SOUTHERN ASHE

Group from Columbus, Georgia: Jeff Frederick (vocals, guitar), Mike McLain and Rudd King (guitars), Tony Stephens (keyboards), Jimmy Pope (bass) and Alan Hussey (drums).

DEBUT	PEAK	WKS		Country Chart Hit	Songwriter	Label (& Number)
8/15/81	**80**	3		**Paradise**	*Jackson Leap*	Soundwaves 4641

SOUTHERN PACIFIC — All-Time: #276

Group formed in Los Angeles, California: Tim Goodman (vocals, guitar), John McFee (guitar, fiddle; The Doobie Brothers), Kurt Howell (keyboards), Stu Cook (bass; **Creedence Clearwater Revival**) and Keith Knudsen (drums; The Doobie Brothers). Goodman replaced by David Jenkins (formerly with Pablo Cruise) in 1986. Jenkins left in early 1989. Group disbanded in 1991. Howell later joined **Burnin' Daylight**. Knudsen died on 2/8/2005 (age 56).

DEBUT	PEAK	WKS		Country Chart Hit	Songwriter	Label (& Number)
6/1/85	**60**	6	1	**Someone's Gonna Love Me Tonight**	*Tim Goodman/Bruce Gowdy*	Warner 29020
8/3/85	**14**	19	2	**Thing About You** *[w/ Emmylou Harris]*	S:13 / A:14 *Tom Petty*	Warner 28943
11/16/85+	**18**	19	3	**Perfect Stranger**	A:17 / S:18 *Tim Goodman/John McFee*	Warner 28870
4/19/86	**9**	17	4	**Reno Bound**	A:8 / S:9 *John McFee/Andre Pessis*	Warner 28722
8/9/86	**17**	17	5	**A Girl Like Emmylou**	A:17 / S:19 *Stu Cook/Tim Goodman/Keith Knudsen/John McFee*	Warner 28647
12/6/86+	**37**	13	6	**Killbilly Hill**	*Tim Goodman/John McFee*	Warner 28554
3/21/87	**26**	14	7	**Don't Let Go Of My Heart**	S:26 *Kurt Howell/Harry Maslin*	Warner 28408
4/9/88	**14**	18	8	**Midnight Highway**	S:18 *Kurt Howell/John McFee*	Warner 27952
8/6/88	**2^{2}**	24	9	**New Shade Of Blue**	S:11 *John McFee/Andre Pessis*	Warner 27790
12/10/88+	**5**	19	10	**Honey I Dare You**	*Stu Cook/Dave Gibson/David Jenkins/Craig Karp/John McFee*	Warner 27691
5/27/89	**4**	19	11	**Any Way The Wind Blows** from the movie *Pink Cadillac* starring **Clint Eastwood**	*John McFee/Andre Pessis*	Warner 22965
12/2/89+	**26**	18	12	**Time's Up** *[w/ Carlene Carter]*	*Harry Stinson/Wendy Waldman/Kevin Welch*	Warner 22714
4/7/90	**31**	14	13	**I Go To Pieces**	*Del Shannon*	Warner
8/11/90	**32**	16	14	**Reckless Heart** above 2 from the album *County Line* on Warner 25895	*John McFee/Andre Pessis*	Warner

SOUTHERN REIGN

Group led by singers Patsy McKeehan and Jeff Crocker.

DEBUT	PEAK	WKS		Country Chart Hit	Songwriter	Label (& Number)
11/1/86	**80**	3	1	**The Auction**	*Don Goodman/Claude Hendricks/Bill Lancaster/Mark Sherrill*	Regal 1
1/10/87	**62**	7	2	**15 to 33**	*Frank Dycus/Don Goodman/John Wesley Ryles/Mark Sherrill*	Regal 2
5/2/87	**79**	4	3	**Summer On The Mississippi**	*Billy Aerts/Don Goodman/David Winter*	Regal 3
9/19/87	**61**	6	4	**Cheap Motels (And One Night Stands)**	*Ritchie Adams/Gloria Nissenson*	Step One 377
5/28/88	**60**	5	5	**Please Don't Leave Me Now**	*Skip Ewing/Don Sampson*	Step One 385
10/15/88	**80**	3	6	**There's A Telephone Ringing (In An Empty House)**	*Kix Brooks/Alan Layne/Kyle Young*	Step One 391

SOUTH SIXTY FIVE

Vocal group from Nashville, Tennessee: brothers Brent Parker and Stephen Parker, with Lance Leslie, Doug Urie and Jeremy Koeltzow.

DEBUT	PEAK	WKS		Country Chart Hit	Songwriter	Label (& Number)
12/12/98+	**55**	10	1	**A Random Act Of Senseless Kindness**	*Gary Baker/Frank J. Myers/Jerry Williams*	Atlantic
3/6/99	**56**	5	2	**No Easy Goodbye**	*Jerry Holland*	Atlantic
8/14/99	**60**	12	3	**Baby's Got My Number** above 3 from the album *South Sixty Five* on Atlantic 83124	*Roger Cook/Anthony Smith*	Atlantic
6/3/00	**72**	1	4	**Love Bug (Bite Me)**	*Tony Mullins/Stan Munsey/Russell Zavitson*	Atlantic
2/10/01	**54**	11	5	**The Most Beautiful Girl** from the album *Dream Large* on Atlantic 83379	S:8 *Rory Bourke/Billy Sherrill/Norro Wilson*	Atlantic

SOVINE, Red — 1950s: #42 / All-Time: #179

Born Woodrow Wilson Sovine on 7/17/1918 in Charleston, West Virginia. Died of a heart attack (while driving his car) on 4/4/1980 (age 61). Male singer/songwriter/guitarist. Father of **Roger Sovine**. Once known as "The Old Syrup Sopper."

OPRY: 1954

DEBUT	PEAK	WKS		Country Chart Hit	Songwriter	Label (& Number)
3/26/55	**14**	2	1	**Are You Mine** *[w/ Goldie Hill]*	S:14 *Jim Amadeo/Don Grashey/Myrna Lorrie*	Decca 29411
12/17/55+	**❶^{4}**	25	2	**Why Baby Why** *[w/ Webb Pierce]*	A:❶^{4} / S:❶^{1} / J:❶^{1} *Darrell Edwards/George Jones*	Decca 29755
3/24/56	**15**	1	3	**If Jesus Came To Your House**	A:15 *Clyde Chesser/Bill Hamby*	Decca 29825
4/21/56	**5**	14	4	**Little Rosa** *[w/ Webb Pierce]* /	S:5 / A:5 / J:5 *Webb Pierce/Red Sovine* **[S]**	
5/19/56	**5**	8	5	**Hold Everything (Till I Get Home)**	J:5 / S:flip *Buddy Dee/Joe Hayes*	Decca 29876
1/11/64	**22**	12	6	**Dream House For Sale**	*Wayne Walker* **[S]**	Starday 650
11/20/65+	**❶^{6}**	22	7	**Giddyup Go**	*Tommy Hill/Red Sovine* **[S]**	Starday 737
4/30/66	**47**	2	8	**Long Night**	*Tommy Hill/Red Sovine*	Starday 757
11/12/66	**44**	8	9	**Class Of 49**	*Red Sovine/Benny Whitehead*	Starday 779
2/18/67	**17**	12	10	**I Didn't Jump The Fence**	*Gene Crysler*	Starday 794
7/1/67	**33**	10	11	**In Your Heart** /	*Wayne Walker*	
7/29/67	**9**	16	12	**Phantom 309** also see #22 below	*Tommy Faile* **[S]**	Starday 811
12/9/67+	**33**	13	13	**Tell Maude I Slipped**	*Jerry Crutchfield*	Starday 823
7/20/68	**63**	2	14	**Loser Making Good**	*Shirl Milete*	Starday 842
10/12/68	**61**	6	15	**Normally, Norma Loves Me**	*Mel Tillis*	Starday 852
8/2/69	**62**	7	16	**Who Am I**	*Frank Dycus/Larry Kingston*	Starday 872
4/18/70	**52**	10	17	**I Know You're Married But I Love You Still**	*Mack Magaha/Don Reno*	Starday 889
7/25/70	**54**	7	18	**Freightliner Fever**	*Truman Lankford*	Starday 896

Billboard DEBUT	PEAK	WKS	GOLD	ARTIST / Country Chart Hit	Ranking / Songwriter	Label (& Number)
				SOVINE, Red — cont'd		
7/6/74	**16**	16		19 **It'll Come Back**	*Glenn Martin*	Chart 5220
				also see #31 below		
11/2/74	**58**	9		20 **Can I Keep Him Daddy**	*Ellen Greer/Red Sovine*	Chart 5230
8/30/75	**91**	4		21 **Daddy's Girl** *[w/ The Girls]*	*Glenn Martin*	Chart 7507
12/27/75+	**47**	10		22 **Phantom 309**	*Tommy Faile* **[S-R]**	Starday 101
				same version as #12 above		
6/19/76	**❶[3]**	13	●	23 **Teddy Bear**	*Billy Joe Burnette/Tommy Hill/Dale Royal/Red Sovine* **[S]**	Starday 142
9/18/76	**45**	5		24 **Little Joe**	*James Coleman/John Hill/Moe Lytle* **[S]**	Starday 144
12/11/76	**96**	2		25 **Last Goodbye**	*Kelso Herston/Dick Miles/Bob Prather* **[S]**	Starday 147
2/19/77	**98**	2		26 **Just Gettin' By**	*A.L. "Doodle" Owens/Gene Vowell*	Starday 148
12/3/77	**92**	5		27 **Woman Behind The Man Behind The Wheel**	*Gordon Grills/Red Sovine*	Gusto 169
3/11/78	**70**	5		28 **Lay Down Sally**	*Eric Clapton/Marcy Levy/George Terry*	Gusto 180
5/27/78	**77**	5		29 **The Days Of Me And You**	*Charlie Craig*	Gusto 188
4/12/80	**74**	5		30 **The Little Family Soldier**	*Tommy Hill* **[S]**	Gusto 9028
7/12/80	**89**	3		31 **It'll Come Back**	*Glenn Martin* **[R]**	Gusto 9030
				new version of #19 above		

SOVINE, Roger

Born on 2/17/1943 in Eleanor, West Virginia. Male singer/songwriter. Son of **Red Sovine**.

DEBUT	PEAK	WKS	GOLD	Country Chart Hit	Songwriter	Label (& Number)
5/4/68	**47**	8		1 **Culman, Alabam**	*Roger Sovine*	Imperial 66291
11/8/69	**68**	5		2 **Little Bitty Nitty Gritty Dirt Town**	*Roger Sovine*	Imperial 66398

SPACEK, Sissy

Born Mary Elizabeth Spacek on 12/25/1949 in Quitman, Texas. Female actress/singer. Acted in several movies and TV shows. Won Academy Award portraying **Loretta Lynn** in the movie *Coal Miner's Daughter.*

DEBUT	PEAK	WKS	GOLD	Country Chart Hit	Songwriter	Label (& Number)
4/26/80	**24**	11		1 **Coal Miner's Daughter**	*Loretta Lynn*	MCA 41221
				title song from the movie starring Spacek		
8/20/83	**15**	17		2 **Lonely But Only For You**	*Charlie Black/Rory Bourke/K.T. Oslin*	Atlantic Amer. 99847
1/21/84	**57**	9		3 **If I Can Just Get Through The Night**	*Peter Anders*	Atlantic Amer. 99801
5/5/84	**79**	3		4 **If You Could Only See Me Now**	*Keith Sykes*	Atlantic Amer. 99773

SPEARS, Billie Jo — All-Time: #150

Born Billie Jean Spears on 1/14/1937 in Beaumont, Texas. Female singer. Worked on the *Louisiana Hayride* in 1950. First recorded for Abbott in 1953 as "Billie Jean Moore." Very popular in England since 1977.

DEBUT	PEAK	WKS	GOLD	Country Chart Hit	Songwriter	Label (& Number)
11/30/68+	**48**	10		1 **He's Got More Love In His Little Finger**	*Ronnie Friend/Mack Vickery*	Capitol 2331
4/19/69	**4**	13		2 **Mr. Walker, It's All Over**	*Gene Crysler*	Capitol 2436
9/13/69	**43**	7		3 **Stepchild**	*Dallas Frazier*	Capitol 2593
12/20/69+	**40**	10		4 **Daddy, I Love You**	*Jerry Foster/Bill Rice*	Capitol 2690
7/25/70	**17**	14		5 **Marty Gray**	*Walt Woodward*	Capitol 2844
11/28/70	**30**	9		6 **I Stayed Long Enough**	*Tammy Wynette*	Capitol 2964
3/20/71	**23**	12		7 **It Could 'A Been Me**	*Jerry Chesnut/Walt Woodward*	Capitol 3055
2/12/72	**68**	3		8 **Souvenirs And California Mem'rys**	*Oris Clarke/David Allan Coe*	Capitol 3258
10/5/74	**80**	5		9 **See The Funny Little Clown**	*Bobby Goldsboro*	United Artists 549
2/1/75	**❶[1]**	17		10 **Blanket On The Ground**	*Roger Bowling*	United Artists 584
7/12/75	**20**	14		11 **Stay Away From The Apple Tree**	*Roger Bowling/Larry Butler*	United Artists 653
11/1/75+	**20**	15		12 **Silver Wings And Golden Rings**	*Molly-Ann Leikin/Gloria Sklerov*	United Artists 712
2/28/76	**5**	16		13 **What I've Got In Mind**	*Kenny O'Dell*	United Artists 764
5/1/76	**29**	11		14 **On The Rebound** *[w/ Del Reeves]*	*Larry Atwood/Charlie Craig*	United Artists 797
6/19/76	**5**	16		15 **Misty Blue**	*Bob Montgomery*	United Artists 813
8/7/76	**42**	8		16 **Teardrops Will Kiss The Morning Dew** *[w/ Del Reeves]*	*Paul Craft*	United Artists 832
10/23/76	**18**	12		17 **Never Did Like Whiskey**	*Kenny O'Dell*	United Artists 880
1/29/77	**11**	13		18 **I'm Not Easy**	*David Chamberlain/Jim Vest*	United Artists 935
5/7/77	**8**	13		19 **If You Want Me**	*Ben Peters*	United Artists 985
8/20/77	**18**	13		20 **Too Much Is Not Enough**	*Kenny O'Dell*	United Artists 1041
1/14/78	**18**	11		21 **Lonely Hearts Club**	*Roger Bowling/Larry Butler/Gene Simmons*	United Artists 1127
4/15/78	**17**	12		22 **I've Got To Go**	*Roger Bowling/Larry Butler*	United Artists 1190
8/12/78	**16**	12		23 **'57 Chevrolet**	*Roger Bowling*	United Artists 1229
11/11/78+	**24**	13		24 **Love Ain't Gonna Wait For Us**	*Larry Butler/Ben Peters*	United Artists 1251
2/24/79	**60**	6		25 **Yesterday**	*John Lennon/Paul McCartney*	United Artists 1274
4/21/79	**21**	11		26 **I Will Survive**	*Dino Fekaris/Freddie Perren*	United Artists 1292
8/4/79	**23**	12		27 **Livin' Our Love Together**	*Ben Peters*	United Artists 1309
11/3/79+	**21**	14		28 **Rainy Days And Stormy Nights**	*Charlie Craig*	United Artists 1326
2/23/80	**15**	13		29 **Standing Tall**	*Larry Butler/Ben Peters*	United Artists 1336
6/28/80	**39**	9		30 **Natural Attraction**	*Dennis Linde/Alan Rush*	United Artists 1358
1/10/81	**13**	13		31 **Your Good Girl's Gonna Go Bad**	*Billy Sherrill/Glenn Sutton*	Liberty 1395
5/2/81	**58**	5		32 **What The World Needs Now Is Love**	*Burt Bacharach/Hal David*	Liberty 1409
1/7/84	**39**	13		33 **Midnight Blue /**	*Rich Gillinson*	
4/7/84	**51**	8		34 **Midnight Love**	*Buck Moore*	Parliament 1801

DEBUT	PEAK	WKS	GOLD		ARTIST / Country Chart Hit	Songwriter	Label (& Number)
					SPEARS, Bobby		
					Born in Maryland. Male singer.		
4/29/78	87	4			(There's Nothing Like The Love) **Between A Woman And A Man** *[w/ Linda Cassady]*	*Danny Hice/Ruby Hice*	Cin Kay 129
					SPEEGLE, David		
					Born in Tampa, Florida. Male singer/guitarist.		
12/9/89	83	4			**Tie Me Up** (Hold Me Down)	*Kieran Kane/Jamie O'Hara*	Bitter Creek 07789
					SPEEKS, Ronnie		
					Born in Chicago, Illinois. Male singer.		
1/17/81	93	2			**Baby Loved Me**	*Joe Bob Barnhill/James Bilin*	Dimension 1014
					SPELLING ON THE STONE		
					Song refers to the spelling of **Elvis Presley**'s middle name on his grave stone. The artist has never been identified.		
12/24/88+	82	4			**Spelling On The Stone**	*Tony Crowe/Lee Stoller/Jimmy Young*	Curb 10522
					SPENCER, Teddy		
					Born in California. Male singer/songwriter.		
8/20/88	82	3			**Grass Is Greener**	*Teddy Spencer*	Oak 1052
					SPITZ, Michele		
					Born on 11/22/1961 in Saginaw, Michigan. Female singer/guitarist.		
7/25/81	93	2			**Old Fashioned Lover** (In A Brand New Love Affair)	*Mike Heeney/John Moffat*	50 States 83
					SPRINGER, Roger		
					Born on 6/15/1962 in Caddo, Oklahoma. Singer/songwriter/guitarist.		
5/23/92	69	2		1	**The Right One Left**	*Jackson Leap*	MCA
10/24/98	64	4		2	**Don't Try To Find Me**	*Anna Graham/Tony Martin*	Giant
					from the album *The Roger Springer Band* on Giant 24711		
					SPRINGER BROTHERS		
					Duo of brothers from Illinois: Bob Springer and Josh Springer.		
2/2/80	87	5		1	**What's A Nice Girl Like You** (Doin' In A Love Like This)	*Kenny Walker*	Elektra 46575
5/10/80	89	2		2	**Cathy's Clown**	*Don Everly/Phil Everly*	Elektra 46622
					SPRINGFIELD, Bobby Lee		
					Born in 1953 in Amarillo, Texas. Male singer/songwriter.		
3/26/83	86	3		1	**A Different Woman Every Night** *[Bobby Springfield]*	*Bobby Lee Springfield*	Kat Family 03562
6/13/87	75	5		2	**Hank Drank**	*Steve Davis/Dennis W. Morgan/Bobby Lee Springfield*	Epic 07110
9/5/87	66	5		3	**Chain Gang**	*Steve Davis/Dennis W. Morgan/Bobby Lee Springfield*	Epic 07310
					SPRINGFIELDS, The		
					Folk trio from England: Dusty Springfield (born on 4/16/1939; died on 3/2/1999, age 59), with her brother Tom Springfield and Tim Feild.		
8/25/62	16	10			**Silver Threads And Golden Needles**	*Dick Reynolds/Jack Rhodes*	Philips 40038
					SPURZZ		
					Group from Nashville, Tennessee. Member Tony Ingram later joined **Atlanta**.		
8/23/80	76	4			**Cowboy Stomp!**	*Buzz Cason/Freddy Weller*	Epic 50911
					STACK, Billy		
					Born in Clinton, Mississippi. Male singer.		
2/25/78	82	5		1	**Love Can Make The Children Sing**	*Joe Hunter/Roger LeBlanc*	Caprice 2045
6/24/78	100	1		2	**Boogiewoogieitis**	*Joe Hunter/Roger LeBlanc*	Caprice 2048
5/12/79	83	3		3	**No Greater Love**	*Don Lewis*	Caprice 2058
					STAFF, Bobbi		
					Born Barbara Grindstaff in 1946 in Kingston, North Carolina. Female singer.		
6/25/66	31	6			**Chicken Feed**	*Vance Bulla*	RCA Victor 8833
					STAFFORD, Jim		
					Born on 1/16/1944 in Eloise, Florida. Male singer/songwriter/guitarist. Co-hosted TV's *Those Amazing Animals* from 1980-81. Formerly married to **Bobbie Gentry**.		
3/2/74	66	8	●	1	**Spiders & Snakes**	*David Bellamy/Jim Stafford*	MGM 14648
5/18/74	64	7		2	**My Girl Bill**	*Jim Stafford* [N]	MGM 14718
8/17/74	57	6		3	**Wildwood Weed**	*Don Bowman* [N]	MGM 14737
1/10/81	65	6		4	**Cow Patti**	*Jim Stafford* [N]	Viva/Warner 49611
					from the movie *Any Which Way You Can* starring **Clint Eastwood**		
11/20/82	61	8		5	**What Mama Don't Know**	*John Hadley/Jim Stafford* [N]	Town House 1062
2/4/84	67	9		6	**Little Bits And Pieces**	*John Hadley*	Columbia 04339
					STAFFORD, Jo — **1940s: #41**		
					Born on 11/12/1917 in Coalinga, California. Female pop singer. Married orchestra leader Paul Weston. Also see **Red Ingle**.		
6/21/47	2^{11}	18		1	**Temptation** (Tim-Tayshun)	*Nacio Herb Brown/Arthur Freed* [N]	Capitol 412
9/20/47	5	2		2	**Feudin' And Fightin'**	*Al Dubin/Burton Lane* [N]	Capitol 443
					Paul Weston (orch.); from the Broadway musical *Laffing Room Only* starring Betty Garrett		

Billboard			G O L D	ARTIST	Ranking	
DEBUT	PEAK	WKS		Country Chart Hit	Songwriter	Label (& Number)

STAFFORD, Terry

Born on 11/22/1941 in Hollis, Oklahoma; raised in Amarillo, Texas. Died on 3/17/1996 (age 54). Male singer/songwriter.

DEBUT	PEAK	WKS	GOLD	Country Chart Hit	Songwriter	Label (& Number)
8/25/73	**35**	12		1 **Say, Has Anybody Seen My Sweet Gypsy Rose /**	*L. Russell Brown/Irwin Levine*	
12/1/73+	**31**	14		2 **Amarillo By Morning**	*Paul Fraser/Terry Stafford*	Atlantic 4006
3/23/74	**24**	13		3 **Captured**	*Rory Bourke/Eddie Rabbitt*	Atlantic 4015
8/24/74	**69**	6		4 **Stop If You Love Me**	*Rory Bourke*	Atlantic 4026
3/12/77	**94**	4		5 **It Sure Is Bad To Love Her**	*Terry Stafford*	Casino 113
2/18/89	**89**	3		6 **Lonestar Lonesome**	*J.C. Cunningham/Steve Stone*	Player 134

STALEY, Karen

Born in Pennsylvania. Female singer/songwriter.

DEBUT	PEAK	WKS	GOLD	Country Chart Hit	Songwriter	Label (& Number)
12/24/88+	**86**	4		1 **So Good To Be In Love**	*Karen Staley*	MCA 53470
5/13/89	**85**	2		2 **Now And Then**	*Gary Harrison/Karen Staley*	MCA 53632

STAMPLEY, Joe — 1970s: #20 / 1980s: #49 / All-Time: #60

Born on 6/6/1943 in Springhill, Louisiana. Male singer/songwriter/pianist. First recorded for Imperial in 1957. Lead singer of The Uniques in the mid-1960s. Worked as a staff writer for Gallico Music.

CMA: Vocal Duo (with Moe Bandy) 1980

DEBUT	PEAK	WKS	GOLD	Country Chart Hit	Songwriter	Label (& Number)
2/20/71	**74**	2		1 **Take Time To Know Her**	*Steve Davis*	Dot 17363
2/12/72	**75**	2		2 **Hello Operator**	*Joe Stampley/Carmol Taylor/Norro Wilson*	Dot 17400
6/17/72	**9**	17		3 **If You Touch Me (You've Got To Love Me)**	*Joe Stampley/Carmol Taylor/Norro Wilson*	Dot 17421
11/11/72+	**❶[1]**	15		4 **Soul Song**	*George Richey/Billy Sherrill/Norro Wilson*	Dot 17442
3/24/73	**7**	14		5 **Bring It On Home (To Your Woman)**	*Joe Stampley/Carmol Taylor/Norro Wilson*	Dot 17452
8/18/73	**12**	16		6 **Too Far Gone**	*Billy Sherrill*	Dot 17469
12/8/73+	**3[1]**	17		7 **I'm Still Loving You**	*George Richey/Glenn Sutton*	Dot 17485
5/4/74	**11**	13		8 **How Lucky Can One Man Be**	*Joe Stampley*	Dot 17502
9/14/74	**5**	16		9 **Take Me Home To Somewhere**	*George Richey/Carmol Taylor/Norro Wilson*	Dot 17522
1/18/75	**8**	11		10 **Penny**	*Steve Davis/Grace Lane*	ABC/Dot 17537
3/1/75	**❶[1]**	14		11 **Roll On Big Mama**	*Dan Darst*	Epic 50075
5/10/75	**41**	11		12 **Unchained Melody**	*Alex North/Hy Zaret*	ABC/Dot 17551
6/7/75	**11**	13		13 **Dear Woman**	*Steve Davis/Mark Sherrill/Joe Stampley*	Epic 50114
8/30/75	**70**	8		14 **Cry Like A Baby**	*Spooner Oldham/Dan Penn*	ABC/Dot 17575
9/20/75	**12**	13		15 **Billy, Get Me A Woman**	*Joe Stampley/Carmol Taylor/Norro Wilson*	Epic 50147
12/20/75+	**25**	10		16 **She's Helping Me Get Over Loving You**	*Dan Darst/Carmol Taylor*	Epic 50179
1/3/76	**61**	8		17 **You Make Life Easy**	*Joe Stampley/Carmol Taylor*	ABC/Dot 17599
3/13/76	**43**	8		18 **Sheik Of Chicago**	*Tom Wheeler*	Epic 50199
4/24/76	**❶[1]**	16		19 **All These Things** also see #43 below	*Naomi Neville*	ABC/Dot 17624
5/22/76	**43**	9		20 **Was It Worth It**	*Marvin Moore/Bernie Wayne*	Epic 50224
7/24/76	**16**	11		21 **The Night Time And My Baby**	*Joe Stampley/Carmol Taylor/Norro Wilson*	ABC/Dot 17642
8/7/76	**18**	14		22 **Whiskey Talkin'**	*Dan Darst/Joe Stampley/Carmol Taylor*	Epic 50259
10/30/76	**12**	12		23 **Everything I Own**	*David Gates*	ABC/Dot 17654
12/25/76+	**11**	15		24 **There She Goes Again**	*Alan Hawkshaw*	Epic 50316
4/2/77	**26**	12		25 **She's Long Legged**	*Dan Darst/Norro Wilson*	Epic 50361
7/2/77	**15**	13		26 **Baby, I Love You So**	*Billy Sherrill/Norro Wilson*	Epic 50410
10/22/77	**14**	13		27 **Everyday I Have To Cry Some**	*Arthur Alexander*	Epic 50453
3/18/78	**6**	16		28 **Red Wine And Blue Memories**	*Billy Sherrill/Mark Sherrill/Carmol Taylor*	Epic 50517
7/15/78	**6**	14		29 **If You've Got Ten Minutes (Let's Fall In Love)**	*Mike Dukes/Jerry Penrod*	Epic 50575
11/4/78+	**5**	16		30 **Do You Ever Fool Around**	*Don Giffin/Jerry Strickland*	Epic 50626
4/28/79	**12**	14		31 **I Don't Lie**	*Darrell Puett/David Rosson*	Epic 50694
7/14/79	**❶[1]**	16		32 **Just Good Ol' Boys** *[w/ Moe Bandy]*	*Ansley Fleetwood*	Columbia 11027
9/1/79	**9**	14		33 **Put Your Clothes Back On**	*Steve Davis/Billy Sherrill*	Epic 50754
11/17/79+	**7**	14		34 **Holding The Bag** *[w/ Moe Bandy]*	*Pat Bunch/Buck Moore*	Columbia 11147
3/15/80	**17**	12		35 **After Hours**	*Janis Carnes/Margo Pendarvis*	Epic 50854
4/12/80	**11**	15		36 **Tell Ole I Ain't Here, He Better Get On Home** *[w/ Moe Bandy]*	*Wayne Kemp*	Columbia 11244
6/28/80	**32**	11		37 **Haven't I Loved You Somewhere Before**	*David Hodges/Jim Hodges/Lewis Moore*	Epic 50893
10/4/80	**18**	15		38 **There's Another Woman**	*Joe Stampley*	Epic 50934
1/24/81	**9**	15		39 **I'm Gonna Love You Back To Loving Me Again**	*Larry Cheshier/Murry Kellum*	Epic 50972
3/14/81	**10**	15		40 **Hey Joe (Hey Moe)** *[w/ Moe Bandy]*	*Boudleaux Bryant*	Columbia 60508
5/23/81	**18**	15		41 **Whiskey Chasin'**	*Buddy Cannon*	Epic 02097
8/1/81	**12**	14		42 **Honky Tonk Queen** *[w/ Moe Bandy]*	*Robby Hicks*	Columbia 02198
10/24/81	**62**	5		43 **All These Things /** new version of #19 above	*Naomi Neville* **[R]**	
12/5/81+	**41**	10		44 **Let's Get Together And Cry**	*Johnny Koonse*	Epic 02533
3/20/82	**18**	17		45 **I'm Goin' Hurtin'**	*Justin Dickens*	Epic 02791
7/17/82	**30**	12		46 **I Didn't Know You Could Break A Broken Heart**	*John Curry/Justin Dickens*	Epic 03016
10/16/82+	**25**	15		47 **Backslidin'**	*Lewis Anderson/Paul Craft*	Epic 03290
2/19/83	**24**	14		48 **Finding You**	*Justin Dickens/Ansley Fleetwood*	Epic 03558

Billboard DEBUT	PEAK	WKS	GOLD	ARTIST Ranking	Country Chart Hit	Songwriter	Label (& Number)
					STAMPLEY, Joe — cont'd		
6/18/83	**12**	18		49	**Poor Side Of Town**	*Lou Adler/Johnny Rivers*	Epic 03966
10/29/83+	**8**	20		50	**Double Shot** (Of My Baby's Love)	*Don Smith/Cyril Vetter*	Epic 04173
2/11/84	**29**	16		51	**Brown Eyed Girl**	*Van Morrison*	Epic 04366
5/5/84	**39**	10		52	**Memory Lane** *[w/ Jessica Boucher]*	*Dave McComb/David Rosson/Tony Stampley*	Epic 04446
6/2/84	**8**	16		53	**Where's The Dress** *[w/ Moe Bandy]*	*George Cummings/Bucky Lindsey/Tony Stampley* [N]	Columbia 04477
10/13/84	**36**	10		54	**The Boy's Night Out** *[w/ Moe Bandy]*	*David Rosson/Joe Stampley/Tony Stampley*	Columbia 04601
1/26/85	**48**	10		55	**Daddy's Honky Tonk** *[w/ Moe Bandy]*	*Bobby Keel/Buck Moore*	Columbia 04756
4/20/85	**58**	8		56	**Still On A Roll** *[w/ Moe Bandy]*	*John Greenebaum/Becky Hobbs/Blake Mevis*	Columbia 04843
7/6/85	**67**	7		57	**When Something Is Wrong With My Baby**	*Isaac Hayes/David Porter*	Epic 05405
9/21/85	**47**	10		58	**I'll Still Be Loving You**	*David Rosson/Tony Stampley*	Epic 05592
2/1/86	**72**	6		59	**When You Were Blue And I Was Green**	*Earl Thomas Conley*	Epic 05758
7/30/88	**56**	6		60	**Cry Baby**	*Jerry Foster/Roger Lavoie/Johnny Morris*	Evergreen 1075
5/20/89	**89**	3		61	**You Sure Got This Ol' Redneck Feelin' Blue**	*Dean Dillon/Buzz Rabin*	Evergreen 1081
8/12/89	**59**	9		62	**If You Don't Know Me By Now**	*Kenny Gamble/Leon Huff*	Evergreen 1100

After Hours ['80]
All These Things ['76, '81]
Baby, I Love You So ['77]
Backslidin' ['83]
Billy, Get Me A Woman ['75]
Boy's Night Out ['84]
Bring It On Home (To Your Woman) ['73]
Brown Eyed Girl ['84]
Cry Baby ['88]
Cry Like A Baby ['75]
Daddy's Honky Tonk ['85]
Dear Woman ['75]
Do You Ever Fool Around ['79]
Double Shot (Of My Baby's Love) ['84]
Everyday I Have To Cry Some ['77]
Everything I Own ['76]
Finding You ['83]
Haven't I Loved You Somewhere Before ['80]
Hello Operator ['72]
Hey Joe (Hey Moe) ['81]
Holding The Bag ['80]
Honky Tonk Queen ['81]
How Lucky Can One Man Be ['74]
I Didn't Know You Could Break A Broken Heart ['82]
I Don't Lie ['79]
I'll Still Be Loving You ['85]
I'm Goin' Hurtin' ['82]
I'm Gonna Love You Back To Loving Me Again ['81]
I'm Still Loving You ['74]
If You Don't Know Me By Now ['89]
If You Touch Me (You've Got To Love Me) ['72]
If You've Got Ten Minutes (Let's Fall In Love) ['78]
Just Good Ol' Boys ['79]
Let's Get Together And Cry ['82]
Memory Lane ['84]
Night Time And My Baby ['76]
Penny ['75]
Poor Side Of Town ['83]
Put Your Clothes Back On ['79]
Red Wine And Blue Memories ['78]
Roll On Big Mama ['75]
She's Helping Me Get Over Loving You ['76]
She's Long Legged ['77]
Sheik Of Chicago ['76]
Soul Song ['73]
Still On A Roll ['85]
Take Me Home To Somewhere ['74]
Take Time To Know Her ['71]
Tell Ole I Ain't Here, He Better Get On Home ['80]
There She Goes Again ['77]
There's Another Woman ['80]
Too Far Gone ['73]
Unchained Melody ['75]
Was It Worth It ['76]
When Something Is Wrong With My Baby ['85]
When You Were Blue And I Was Green ['86]
Where's The Dress ['84]
Whiskey Chasin' ['81]
Whiskey Talkin' ['76]
You Make Life Easy ['76]
You Sure Got This Ol' Redneck Feelin' Blue ['89]

STANLEY BROTHERS

Bluegrass duo from Stratton, Virginia: Carter Stanley (born on 8/27/1925; died on 12/1/1966, age 41) and Ralph Stanley (born on 2/25/1927). Formed The Clinch Mountain Boys in 1946. Ralph joined the *Grand Ole Opry* in 2000.

DEBUT	PEAK	WKS	GOLD	#	Country Chart Hit	Songwriter	Label (& Number)
3/21/60	**17**	12			**How Far To Little Rock**	*Ruby Rakes* [N]	King 5306

STARCHER, Buddy

Born Oby Starcher on 3/16/1906 in Ripley, West Virginia. Died on 11/2/2001 (age 95). Male singer/songwriter/DJ.

DEBUT	PEAK	WKS	GOLD	#	Country Chart Hit	Songwriter	Label (& Number)
2/12/49	**8**	1		1	**I'll Still Write Your Name In The Sand**	J:8 *Buddy Starcher*	4 Star 1145
4/9/66	**2^{1}**	15		2	**History Repeats Itself** — an accounting of "coincidental" parallels between the careers and deaths of Presidents Lincoln and Kennedy	*Buddy Starcher* [S]	Boone 1038

STARK, Donna

Born in Albuquerque, New Mexico. Female singer.

DEBUT	PEAK	WKS	GOLD	#	Country Chart Hit	Songwriter	Label (& Number)
6/7/80	**92**	2			**Why Don't You Believe Me**	*Lew Douglas/Luther Lanley/Leroy Rodde*	RCI 2344

STARLAND VOCAL BAND

Pop group formed in Washington DC: two husband-and-wife teams: Bill Danoff and Kathy "Taffy" Nivert, with John Carroll and Margot Chapman.

DEBUT	PEAK	WKS	GOLD	#	Country Chart Hit	Songwriter	Label (& Number)
7/17/76	**94**	2	●		**Afternoon Delight**	*Bill Danoff*	Windsong 10588

STARR, Kay

Born Katherine Starks on 7/21/1922 in Dougherty, Oklahoma; raised in Dallas, Texas, and Memphis, Tennessee. Female pop singer. Acted in the movies *Make Believe Ballroom* and *When You're Smiling*.

DEBUT	PEAK	WKS	GOLD	#	Country Chart Hit	Songwriter	Label (& Number)
8/26/50	**5**	6		1	**Ain't Nobody's Business But My Own** *[w/ Tennessee Ernie Ford]* /	A:5 / J:10 *Irving Taylor*	
9/16/50	**2^{1}**	16		2	**I'll Never Be Free** *[w/ Tennessee Ernie Ford]*	A:2 / J:2 / S:4 *Bennie Benjamin/George Weiss*	Capitol F1124

STARR, Kenny

Born Kenneth Trebbe on 9/21/1952 in Topeka, Kansas; raised in Burlingame, Kansas. Male singer/guitarist.

DEBUT	PEAK	WKS	GOLD	#	Country Chart Hit	Songwriter	Label (& Number)
4/7/73	**56**	6		1	**That's A Whole Lotta Lovin'** (You Give Me)	*Mike Kosser/Steve Pippin*	MCA 40023
10/20/73	**97**	4		2	**Ev'ryday Woman**	*Bob Morrison*	MCA 40124
3/1/75	**89**	3		3	**Put Another Notch In Your Belt**	*Mac Davis*	MCA 40350
11/8/75+	**2^{2}**	15		4	**The Blind Man In The Bleachers**	*Sterling Whipple*	MCA 40474
3/13/76	**26**	10		5	**Tonight I'll Face The Man** (Who Made It Happen)	*Bill Anthony/Bob Morrison*	MCA 40524
7/4/76	**73**	5		6	**The Calico Cat** /	*Sterling Whipple*	
8/21/76	**75**	3		7	**Victims**	*Rory Bourke/Gene Dobbins/Johnny Wilson*	MCA 40580
11/13/76	**58**	8		8	**I Just Can't** (Turn My Habit Into Love)	*Michael Smotherman*	MCA 40637
2/12/77	**43**	8		9	**Me And The Elephant**	*Benny Whitehead*	MCA 40672
8/27/77	**64**	7		10	**Old Time Lovin'**	*Gerry House*	MCA 40769
11/19/77+	**25**	14		11	**Hold Tight**	*David Gates*	MCA 40817
4/22/78	**72**	5		12	**The Rest Of My Life**	*Richard Mainegra*	MCA 40880
7/1/78	**70**	6		13	**Slow Drivin'**	*Sterling Whipple*	MCA 40922

STARR, Lucille

Born Lucille Savoie in St. Boniface, Manitoba, Canada. Female singer. Recorded with husband Bob Regan as **The Canadian Sweethearts**.

DEBUT	PEAK	WKS	GOLD	#	Country Chart Hit	Songwriter	Label (& Number)
9/30/67	**72**	2		1	**Too Far Gone**	*Billy Sherrill*	Epic 10205
6/8/68	**63**	5		2	**Is It Love?**	*Ray Buzzeo*	Epic 10317

STARR, Penny — see DeHAVEN, Penny

DEBUT	PEAK	WKS	GOLD	ARTIST / Country Chart Hit	Ranking / Songwriter	Label (& Number)

STARR, Ringo

Born Richard Starkey on 7/7/1940 in Dingle, Liverpool, England. Male singer/songwriter/drummer. Member of The Beatles. Appeared in several movies. Married actress Barbara Bach on 4/27/1981.

DEBUT	PEAK	WKS	GOLD	Country Chart Hit	Songwriter	Label (& Number)
7/15/89	**27**	11		**Act Naturally** *[w/ Buck Owens]*	*Voni Morrison/Johnny Russell*	Capitol 44409

STATLER, Darrell

Born on 12/27/1940 in Llano, Texas. Male singer/songwriter.

DEBUT	PEAK	WKS	GOLD	Country Chart Hit	Songwriter	Label (& Number)
9/6/69	**40**	7		**Blue Collar Job**	*Darrell Statler*	Dot 17275

STATLER BROTHERS, The — 1980s: #24 / All-Time: #41

Vocal group from Staunton, Virginia: brothers Don Reid (born on 6/5/1945) and Harold Reid (born on 8/21/1939), Philip Balsley (born on 8/8/1939) and **Lew DeWitt** (born on 3/8/1938; died on 8/15/1990, age 52). Worked with **Johnny Cash** from 1963-71. Jimmy Fortune (born on 3/11/1955) replaced DeWitt in 1983. Hosted their own variety show on TNN.

CMA: Vocal Group 1972, 1973, 1974, 1975, 1976, 1977, 1979, 1980 & 1984

DEBUT	PEAK	WKS	GOLD	Country Chart Hit	Songwriter	Label (& Number)
9/25/65+	**2**^{4}	27		1 **Flowers On The Wall**	*Lew DeWitt*	Columbia 43315
6/18/66	**30**	11		2 **The Right One**	*Jack Clement*	Columbia 43624
11/26/66+	**37**	10		3 **That'll Be The Day**	*Don Reid*	Columbia 43868
5/13/67	**10**	14		4 **Ruthless**	*Bobby Braddock*	Columbia 44070
9/2/67	**10**	14		5 **You Can't Have Your Kate And Edith, Too**	*Bobby Braddock/Curly Putman*	Columbia 44245
4/27/68	**60**	3		6 **Jump For Joy**	*Bobby Braddock*	Columbia 44480
10/19/68	**75**	2		7 **Sissy /**	*Don Reid*	
1/4/69	**60**	3		8 **I'm The Boy**	*Lew DeWitt*	Columbia 44608
11/21/70+	**9**	17		9 **Bed Of Rose's**	*Harold Reid*	Mercury 73141
4/24/71	**19**	13		10 **New York City**	*Don Reid*	Mercury 73194
8/21/71	**13**	14		11 **Pictures**	*Lew DeWitt/Don Reid*	Mercury 73229
12/11/71+	**23**	13		12 **You Can't Go Home**	*Don Reid*	Mercury 73253
3/11/72	**2**^{4}	15		13 **Do You Remember These**	*Larry Lee/Don Reid/Harold Reid*	Mercury 73275
8/19/72	**6**	15		14 **The Class Of '57** Grammy: Vocal Group	*Don Reid/Harold Reid*	Mercury 73315
2/3/73	**20**	11		15 **Monday Morning Secretary**	*Don Reid*	Mercury 73360
6/9/73	**29**	9		16 **Woman Without A Home**	*Don Reid*	Mercury 73392
9/15/73	**26**	12		17 **Carry Me Back**	*Don Reid/Harold Reid*	Mercury 73415
1/12/74	**22**	11		18 **Whatever Happened To Randolph Scott**	*Don Reid/Harold Reid*	Mercury 73448
6/8/74	**31**	13		19 **Thank You World**	*Lew DeWitt/Don Reid*	Mercury 73485
11/9/74+	**15**	14		20 **Susan When She Tried**	*Don Reid*	Mercury 73625
3/1/75	**31**	11		21 **All American Girl**	*Don Reid/Harold Reid*	Mercury 73665
6/21/75	**3**^{1}	19		22 **I'll Go To My Grave Loving You**	*Don Reid*	Mercury 73687
1/3/76	**39**	9		23 **How Great Thou Art**	*S.K. Hine*	Mercury 73732
4/17/76	**13**	13		24 **Your Picture In The Paper**	*Don Reid*	Mercury 73785
10/2/76	**10**	14		25 **Thank God I've Got You**	*Don Reid*	Mercury 73846
1/15/77	**10**	13		26 **The Movies**	*Lew DeWitt*	Mercury 73877
4/30/77	**8**	13		27 **I Was There**	*Don Reid*	Mercury 73906
8/13/77	**18**	12		28 **Silver Medals And Sweet Memories**	*Don Reid*	Mercury 55000
12/3/77+	**17**	13		29 **Some I Wrote**	*Don Reid/Harold Reid*	Mercury 55013
3/18/78	**❶**^{2}	17		30 **Do You Know You Are My Sunshine**	*Don Reid/Harold Reid*	Mercury 55022
8/5/78	**3**^{2}	14		31 **Who Am I To Say**	*Kim Reid*	Mercury 55037
11/18/78+	**5**	15		32 **The Official Historian On Shirley Jean Berrell**	*Don Reid/Harold Reid*	Mercury 55048
3/31/79	**7**	12		33 **How To Be A Country Star**	*Don Reid/Harold Reid*	Mercury 55057
7/7/79	**11**	13		34 **Here We Are Again**	*Don Reid*	Mercury 55066
10/27/79	**10**	13		35 **Nothing As Original As You**	*Don Reid*	Mercury 57007
1/19/80	**8**	14		36 **(I'll Even Love You) Better Than I Did Then**	*Don Reid/Harold Reid*	Mercury 57012
7/12/80	**5**	16		37 **Charlotte's Web** from the movie *Smokey & The Bandit II* starring **Burt Reynolds**	*Cliff Crofford/John Durrill/Snuff Garrett*	Mercury 57031
11/8/80+	**13**	14		38 **Don't Forget Yourself**	*Don Reid*	Mercury 57037
3/28/81	**35**	9		39 **In The Garden**	*(traditional)*	Mercury 57048
6/13/81	**5**	18		40 **Don't Wait On Me** also see #64 below	*Don Reid/Harold Reid*	Mercury 57051
10/24/81+	**12**	16		41 **Years Ago**	*Don Reid*	Mercury 57059
3/13/82	**3**^{2}	18		42 **You'll Be Back (Every Night In My Dreams)**	*Wayland Holyfield/Johnny Russell*	Mercury 76142
7/3/82	**7**	16		43 **Whatever**	*Don Reid/Harold Reid*	Mercury 76162
10/23/82+	**17**	16		44 **A Child Of The Fifties**	*Don Reid*	Mercury 76184
4/16/83	**2**^{1}	19		45 **Oh Baby Mine (I Get So Lonely)**	*Pat Ballard*	Mercury 811488
8/13/83	**9**	17		46 **Guilty**	*Don Reid/Harold Reid*	Mercury 812988
12/10/83+	**❶**^{1}	23		47 **Elizabeth**	*Jimmy Fortune*	Mercury 814881
4/21/84	**3**^{1}	21		48 **Atlanta Blue**	*Don Reid*	Mercury 818700
8/18/84	**8**	23		49 **One Takes The Blame**	S:6 / A:8 *Don Reid*	Mercury 880130
12/8/84+	**❶**^{1}	20		50 **My Only Love**	S:❶^{1} / A:❶^{1} *Jimmy Fortune*	Mercury 880411
4/20/85	**3**^{1}	20		51 **Hello Mary Lou**	S:3 / A:3 *Gene Pitney*	Mercury 880685
8/24/85	**❶**^{1}	25		52 **Too Much On My Heart**	S:❶^{2} / A:❶^{1} *Jimmy Fortune*	Mercury 884016
1/11/86	**8**	21		53 **Sweeter And Sweeter**	S:7 / A:9 *Don Reid/Harold Reid*	Mercury 884317

DEBUT	PEAK	WKS	GOLD	ARTIST / Country Chart Hit	Ranking / Songwriter	Label (& Number)
				STATLER BROTHERS, The — cont'd		
5/17/86	**5**	24		54 **Count On Me**	S:3 / A:5 *Don Reid*	Mercury 884721
9/27/86	**36**	12		55 **Only You**	*Buck Ram/Ande Rand*	Mercury 888042
12/13/86+	**7**	21		56 **Forever**	S:❶² / A:7 *Jimmy Fortune*	Mercury 888219
6/13/87	**10**	20		57 **I'll Be The One**	S:9 *Debo Reid/Don Reid*	Mercury 888650
10/31/87	**42**	13		58 **Maple Street Mem'ries**	*Don Reid*	Mercury 888920
2/20/88	**15**	23		59 **The Best I Know How**	S:19 *Kim Reid*	Mercury 870164
6/11/88	**27**	19		60 **Am I Crazy?**	S:29 *Jimmy Fortune*	Mercury 870442
10/15/88+	**12**	22		61 **Let's Get Started If We're Gonna Break My Heart**	S:14 *Debo Reid/Don Reid/Harold Reid*	Mercury 870681
2/18/89	**36**	10		62 **Moon Pretty Moon**	*Kim Reid*	Mercury 872604
5/13/89	**6**	20		63 **More Than A Name On A Wall**	*Jimmy Fortune/John Rimel*	Mercury 874196
10/7/89	**67**	5		64 **Don't Wait On Me** new version of #40 above	*Don Reid/Harold Reid* **[L-R]**	Mercury 891014
11/18/89	**56**	7		65 **A Hurt I Can't Handle**	*Jimmy Fortune*	Mercury 876112
7/28/90	**54**	8		66 **Small Small World** from the album *Music, Memories And You* on Mercury 842518	*Thom Schuyler/Gary Scruggs*	Mercury

All American Girl ['75]
Am I Crazy? ['88]
Atlanta Blue ['84]
Bed Of Rose's ['71]
Best I Know How ['88]
Carry Me Back ['73]
Charlotte's Web ['80]
Child Of The Fifties ['83]
Class Of '57 ['72]
Count On Me ['86]
Do You Know You Are My Sunshine ['78]
Do You Remember These ['72]
Don't Forget Yourself ['81]
Don't Wait On Me ['81, '89]
Elizabeth ['84]
Flowers On The Wall ['66]
Forever ['87]
Guilty ['83]
Hello Mary Lou ['85]
Here We Are Again ['79]
How Great Thou Art ['76]
How To Be A Country Star ['79]
Hurt I Can't Handle ['89]
I Was There ['77]
I'll Be The One ['87]
(I'll Even Love You) Better Than I Did Then ['80]
I'll Go To My Grave Loving You ['75]
I'm The Boy ['69]
In The Garden ['81]
Jump For Joy ['68]
Let's Get Started If We're Gonna Break My Heart ['89]
Maple Street Mem'ries ['87]
Monday Morning Secretary ['73]
Moon Pretty Moon ['89]
More Than A Name On A Wall ['89]
Movies ['77]
My Only Love ['85]
New York City ['71]
Nothing As Original As You ['79]
Official Historian On Shirley Jean Berrell ['79]
Oh Baby Mine (I Get So Lonely) ['83]
One Takes The Blame ['84]
Only You ['86]
Pictures ['71]
Right One ['66]
Ruthless ['67]
Silver Medals And Sweet Memories ['77]
Sissy ['68]
Small Small World ['90]
Some I Wrote ['78]
Susan When She Tried ['75]
Sweeter And Sweeter ['86]
Thank God I've Got You ['76]
Thank You World ['74]
That'll Be The Day ['67]
Too Much On My Heart ['85]
Whatever ['82]
Whatever Happened To Randolph Scott ['74]
Who Am I To Say ['78]
Woman Without A Home ['73]
Years Ago ['82]
You Can't Go Home ['72]
You Can't Have Your Kate And Edith, Too ['67]
You'll Be Back (Every Night In My Dreams) ['82]
Your Picture In The Paper ['76]

STEAGALL, Red — All-Time: #289

Born Russell Steagall on 12/22/1937 in Gainesville, Texas. Male singer/songwriter/guitarist.

DEBUT	PEAK	WKS	GOLD	Country Chart Hit	Songwriter	Label (& Number)
1/15/72	**31**	11		1 **Party Dolls And Wine** *[Red Stegall]*	*Joe Bob Barnhill*	Capitol 3244
11/25/72+	**22**	12		2 **Somewhere, My Love**	*Maurice Jarre/Paul Francis Webster*	Capitol 3461
4/14/73	**51**	5		3 **True Love**	*Cole Porter*	Capitol 3562
7/14/73	**41**	8		4 **If You've Got The Time**	*Bill Backer*	Capitol 3651
10/6/73	**87**	7		5 **The Fiddle Man**	*Red Steagall*	Capitol 3724
1/26/74	**93**	5		6 **This Just Ain't My Day (For Lettin' Darlin' Down)**	*Dallas Frazier/A.L. "Doodle" Owens*	Capitol 3797
3/2/74	**54**	10		7 **I Gave Up Good Mornin' Darling**	*Sid Linard/Red Steagall*	Capitol 3825
7/20/74	**52**	9		8 **Finer Things In Life**	*Jim Weatherly*	Capitol 3913
10/26/74+	**17**	17		9 **Someone Cares For You**	*Red Steagall/Glenn Sutton*	Capitol 3965
3/22/75	**62**	9		10 **She Worshipped Me**	*Glenn Sutton*	Capitol 4042
2/28/76	**11**	15		11 **Lone Star Beer And Bob Wills Music**	*Red Steagall/Glenn Sutton*	ABC/Dot 17610
6/19/76	**29**	11		12 **Truck Drivin' Man**	*Terry Fell*	ABC/Dot 17634
9/25/76	**45**	9		13 **Rosie (Do You Wanna Talk It Over)**	*Sonny Throckmorton*	ABC/Dot 17653
12/25/76+	**59**	8		14 **Her L-O-V-E's Gone**	*Larry Cheshier/Glenn Sutton*	ABC/Dot 17670
3/12/77	**53**	8		15 **I Left My Heart In San Francisco**	*George Cory/Doug Cross*	ABC/Dot 17684
8/13/77	**90**	4		16 **Freckles Brown**	*Red Steagall*	ABC/Dot 17709
11/12/77	**72**	8		17 **The Devil Ain't A Lonely Woman's Friend**	*Dallas Frazier/Whitey Shafer*	ABC/Dot 17726
3/11/78	**63**	9		18 **Hang On Feelin' /**	*Mike Kosser/Richard Mainegra*	
4/15/78	**flip**	4		19 **Bob's Got A Swing Band In Heaven** tribute to **Bob Wills**	*Red Steagall*	ABC 12337
9/22/79	**41**	9		20 **Goodtime Charlie's Got The Blues**	*Danny O'Keefe*	Elektra 46527
2/9/80	**31**	9		21 **3 Chord Country Song**	*Danny Steagall/Red Steagall*	Elektra 46590
5/10/80	**49**	8		22 **Dim The Lights And Pour The Wine**	*Jay Harris/Bob Morrison*	Elektra 46633
8/23/80	**30**	12		23 **Hard Hat Days And Honky Tonk Nights**	*Eddie Kilroy/Dave Kirby*	Elektra 47014

STEARNS, June

Born Agnes June Stearns on 4/5/1939 in Albany, New York. Female singer/guitarist.

DEBUT	PEAK	WKS	GOLD	Country Chart Hit	Songwriter	Label (& Number)
4/27/68	**47**	12		1 **Empty House**	*Wayne Walker*	Columbia 44483
9/14/68	**57**	5		2 **Where He Stops Nobody Knows**	*Kris Kristofferson*	Columbia 44575
10/19/68	**21**	8		3 **Jackson Ain't A Very Big Town** *[w/ Johnny Duncan]*	*Vic McAlpin*	Columbia 44656
1/4/69	**53**	6		4 **Walking Midnight Road**	*Frank Hobson*	Columbia 44695
3/15/69	**74**	3		5 **Back To Back (We're Strangers)** *[w/ Johnny Duncan]*	*Marian Francis*	Columbia 44752
6/7/69	**70**	4		6 **What Makes You So Different**	*Vic McAlpin*	Columbia 44852
12/27/69	**58**	4		7 **Drifting Too Far (From Your Arms)**	*Vic McAlpin*	Columbia 45042
9/26/70	**41**	6		8 **Tyin' Strings**	*Harlan Howard*	Decca 32726
6/12/71	**57**	8		9 **Sweet Baby On My Mind**	*Jim Owen*	Decca 32828
10/16/71	**56**	8		10 **Your Kind Of Lovin'**	*Harlan Howard*	Decca 32876

STEEL, Ric

Born in El Paso, Texas. Male singer/songwriter.

DEBUT	PEAK	WKS	GOLD	Country Chart Hit	Songwriter	Label (& Number)
12/5/87+	**57**	9		1 **The Radio Song**	*Dan Lenzini/Ric Steel*	Panache 1001
6/18/88	**59**	7		2 **Whose Baby Are You**	*Joe Scaife/Ronny Scaife*	Panache 1002

Billboard DEBUT	PEAK	WKS	GOLD	ARTIST / Country Chart Hit	Ranking / Songwriter	Label (& Number)

STEELE, Jeffrey — SW: #77

Born Jeffrey LeVasseur on 8/27/1961 in Burbank, California; raised in North Hollywood. Male singer/songwriter/bassist. Former lead singer of **Boy Howdy**.

DEBUT	PEAK	WKS	GOLD	Country Chart Hit	Songwriter	Label (& Number)
3/22/97	**60**	4		1 **A Girl Like You**	*Chris Farren/Jeffrey Steele*	Curb
				from the album *Jeffrey Steele* on Curb 77849		
9/1/01	**33**	21		2 **Somethin' In The Water**	S:4 *Al Anderson/Bob DiPiero/Jeffrey Steele*	Monument
6/1/02	**49**	7		3 **Good To Go**	*Jeffrey Steele/Craig Wiseman*	Monument
				above 2 from the album *You Gotta Start Somwhere* on Monument 86131		
3/20/04	**54**	2		4 **Good Year For The Outlaw**	*Al Anderson/Bob DiPiero/Jeffrey Steele*	3 Ring Circus
				from the album *Outlaw* on 3 Ring Circus 9003		

STEELE, Larry

Born on 12/5/1937 in Colorado. Died on 3/6/2003 (age 65). Male singer/songwriter.

DEBUT	PEAK	WKS	GOLD	Country Chart Hit	Songwriter	Label (& Number)
1/15/66	**43**	3		1 **I Ain't Crying Mister**	*Larry Steele*	K-Ark 659
4/6/68	**75**	2		2 **Hard Times** ***[w/ The Wranglers]***	*Larry Steele*	K-Ark 802
11/9/74	**90**	5		3 **Daylight Losing Time**	*Larry Lee*	Air Stream 004

STEFFIN SISTERS

Vocal group from West Monroe, Louisiana: sisters Jenny Steffin, Marianne Steffin, Beth Steffin and Kathy Steffin.

DEBUT	PEAK	WKS	GOLD	Country Chart Hit	Songwriter	Label (& Number)
5/27/89	**88**	2		**I Still Need You**	*Mickey James*	Windward 7

STEGALL, Keith — SW: #71

Born Robert Keith Stegall on 11/1/1954 in Wichita Falls, Texas. Male singer/songwriter/guitarist/pianist. Acted in the movies *Killing At Hell's Gate* and *Country Gold*.

DEBUT	PEAK	WKS	GOLD	Country Chart Hit	Songwriter	Label (& Number)
3/1/80	**58**	6		1 **The Fool Who Fooled Around**	*Elroy Kahanek/Keith Stegall*	Capitol 4835
2/21/81	**55**	7		2 **Anything That Hurts You (Hurts Me)**	*Howard Lee/Charlie Monk*	Capitol 4967
9/12/81	**65**	5		3 **Won't You Be My Baby**	*Stewart Harris/Keith Stegall*	Capitol 5034
3/13/82	**64**	5		4 **In Love With Loving You**	*Charlie Monk/Keith Stegall*	EMI America 8107
5/12/84	**25**	16		5 **I Want To Go Somewhere**	*Donny Lowery/Mac McAnally*	Epic 04442
9/22/84	**19**	21		6 **Whatever Turns You On**	S:11 / A:21 *Donny Lowery/Keith Stegall*	Epic 04590
2/16/85	**13**	18		7 **California**	S:13 / A:18 *Charlie Craig/Jim McBride/Keith Stegall*	Epic 04771
6/15/85	**10**	22		8 **Pretty Lady**	A:9 / S:12 *Keith Stegall*	Epic 04934
11/2/85	**45**	10		9 **Feed The Fire**	*John Jarrard/Brent Mason*	Epic 05643
3/1/86	**36**	13		10 **I Think I'm In Love**	*Charlie Craig/Keith Stegall*	Epic 05815
11/15/86	**52**	9		11 **Ole Rock And Roller (With A Country Heart)**	*J.D. Hicks/Roger Murrah/Keith Stegall*	Epic 06418
1/27/96	**43**	13		12 **1969**	*Gary Harrison/Denny Henson/Keith Stegall*	Mercury
5/18/96	**75**	1		13 **Fifty-Fifty**	*Keith Stegall*	Mercury
				above 2 from the album *Passages* on Polygram 528437		

STEINER, Tommy Shane

Born in 1973 in Austin, Texas. Male singer.

DEBUT	PEAK	WKS	GOLD	Country Chart Hit	Songwriter	Label (& Number)
12/22/01+	**2^1**	28		1 **What If She's An Angel**	*Brian Wayne*	RCA
6/22/02	**43**	8		2 **Tell Me Where It Hurts**	*Diane Warren*	RCA
10/12/02	**43**	11		3 **What We're Gonna Do About It** ***[w/ Bridgette Wilson-Sampras]***	*Chris DuBois/Lee Miller*	RCA
				above 3 from the album *Then Came The Night* on RCA 67041		

STENMARK-MUELLER BAND

Duo from Salt Lake City, Utah: K.J. Stenmark and LynnDee Mueller.

DEBUT	PEAK	WKS	GOLD	Country Chart Hit	Songwriter	Label (& Number)
11/14/87	**95**	1		**Lover To Lover**	*Jerry Fuller/John Hobbs*	Envelope 7004

STEPHENS, Ott

Born on 9/21/1941 in Ringold, Georgia. Male singer/guitarist.

DEBUT	PEAK	WKS	GOLD	Country Chart Hit	Songwriter	Label (& Number)
1/19/63	**15**	7		1 **Robert E. Lee**	*Liz Anderson*	Chancellor 107
6/13/64	**23**	15		2 **Be Quiet Mind**	*Liz Anderson*	Reprise 0272
6/12/65	**36**	12		3 **Enough Man For You**	*James Hood*	Chart 1205

STEVENS, Even — SW: #50

Born in Lewiston, Ohio; raised in Cincinnati, Ohio. Male singer/songwriter.

DEBUT	PEAK	WKS	GOLD	Country Chart Hit	Songwriter	Label (& Number)
6/21/75	**38**	13		1 **Let The Little Boy Dream**	*Even Stevens*	Elektra 45254
12/20/75+	**81**	7		2 **Huckelberry Pie** ***[w/ Sammi Smith]***	*Even Stevens*	Elektra 45292
10/15/77	**97**	1		3 **The King Of Country Music Meets The Queen Of Rock & Roll** ***[w/ Sherry Grooms]***	*Shel Silverstein*	Elektra 45430

STEVENS, Geraldine

Born Geraldine Ann Pasquale on 2/17/1946 in Chicago, Illinois. Female singer. Better known as Dodie Stevens. Charted the pop hit "Pink Shoe Laces" in 1959.

DEBUT	PEAK	WKS	GOLD	Country Chart Hit	Songwriter	Label (& Number)
9/13/69	**57**	3		**Billy, I've Got To Go To Town**	*Vic Dana/Mel Tillis*	World Pacific 77927
				answer to "Ruby, Don't Take Your Love To Town" by **Kenny Rogers**		

STEVENS, Jeff, and The Bullets

Family trio from Alum Creek, West Virginia: brothers Jeff Stevens (vocals, guitar; born on 6/15/1959) and Warren Stevens (bass), with cousin Terry Dotson (drums).

DEBUT	PEAK	WKS	GOLD	Country Chart Hit	Songwriter	Label (& Number)
12/27/86+	**69**	8		1 **Darlington County**	*Bruce Springsteen*	Atlantic Amer. 99494
3/28/87	**61**	6		2 **You're In Love Alone**	*Ron Reynolds*	Atlantic Amer. 99475
7/18/87	**53**	8		3 **Geronimo's Cadillac**	*Michael Murphey/Charles Quarto*	Atlantic Amer. 99433
4/22/89	**70**	5		4 **Johnny Lucky And Suzi 66**	*Steve Davis/Don Goodman*	Atlantic Amer. 99259

STEVENS, Lee J.

Born in England. Male singer.

DEBUT	PEAK	WKS	GOLD	Country Chart Hit	Songwriter	Label (& Number)
1/14/89	**92**	2		**You'll Be The First To Know**	*Hank Cochran/Dean Dillon/Roy Porter*	Regal 01

DEBUT	PEAK	WKS	GOLD	ARTIST / Country Chart Hit	Ranking / Songwriter	Label (& Number)

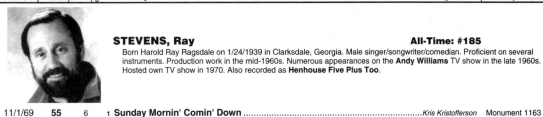

STEVENS, Ray — All-Time: #185

Born Harold Ray Ragsdale on 1/24/1939 in Clarksdale, Georgia. Male singer/songwriter/comedian. Proficient on several instruments. Production work in the mid-1960s. Numerous appearances on the **Andy Williams** TV show in the late 1960s. Hosted own TV show in 1970. Also recorded as **Henhouse Five Plus Too**.

DEBUT	PEAK	WKS	GOLD	#	Country Chart Hit	Songwriter	Label (& Number)
11/1/69	55	6		1	**Sunday Mornin' Comin' Down**	*Kris Kristofferson*	Monument 1163
12/27/69+	63	2		2	**Have A Little Talk With Myself**	*Ray Stevens*	Monument 1171
5/2/70	39	6	●	3	**Everything Is Beautiful**	*Ray Stevens*	Barnaby 2011
12/4/71+	17	13		4	**Turn Your Radio On**	*Albert Brumley*	Barnaby 2048
7/14/73	37	11		5	**Nashville**	*Ray Stevens*	Barnaby 5020
4/13/74	3[2]	13	●	6	**The Streak**	*Ray Stevens* [N]	Barnaby 600
11/30/74+	37	10		7	**Everybody Needs A Rainbow**	*Layng Martine Jr.*	Barnaby 610
3/22/75	3[2]	17		8	**Misty**	*Johnny Burke/Erroll Garner*	Barnaby 614
9/27/75	38	11		9	**Indian Love Call**	*Rudolf Friml/Oscar Hammerstein/Otto Harbach*	Barnaby 616
1/3/76	48	8		10	**Young Love**	*Ric Cartey/Carole Joyner*	Barnaby 618
5/1/76	16	13		11	**You Are So Beautiful**	*Bruce Fisher/Billy Preston*	Warner 8198
8/7/76	27	10		12	**Honky Tonk Waltz**	*Paul Craft*	Warner 8237
1/8/77	39	7		13	**In The Mood** *[Henhouse Five Plus Too]*	*Joe Garland/Andy Razaf* [N]	Warner 8301
2/19/77	81	6		14	**Get Crazy With Me**	*Ray Stevens*	Warner 8318
6/11/77	44	9		15	**Dixie Hummingbird**	*Ray Stevens*	Warner 8393
8/12/78	36	10		16	**Be Your Own Best Friend**	*Ray Stevens*	Warner 8603
4/14/79	85	3		17	**I Need Your Help Barry Manilow**	*Dale Gonyea* [N]	Warner 8785
2/9/80	7	12		18	**Shriner's Convention**	*Ray Stevens* [N]	RCA 11911
9/13/80	20	13		19	**Night Games**	*Cyrus Kalb*	RCA 12069
2/14/81	33	10		20	**One More Last Chance**	*Hal Bynum/Bud Reneau*	RCA 12170
2/6/82	35	10		21	**Written Down In My Heart**	*W.T. Davidson*	RCA 13038
5/22/82	63	7		22	**Where The Sun Don't Shine**	*Doug Gilmore/Mike Leath/Randy Sharp*	RCA 13207
2/11/84	64	8		23	**My Dad**	*Dale Gonyea*	Mercury 818057
12/8/84+	20	14		24	**Mississippi Squirrel Revival**	S:12 / A:28 *Carlene Kalb/Cyrus Kalb* [N]	MCA 52492
3/23/85	74	6		25	**It's Me Again, Margaret**	*Paul Craft* [N]	MCA 52548
9/14/85	45	14		26	**The Haircut Song**	*Cyrus Kalb/Mike Neun/Ray Stevens* [N]	MCA 52657
1/25/86	50	10		27	**The Ballad Of The Blue Cyclone**	S:26 *Larry Cheshier/Glenn Sutton* [N]	MCA 52771
9/13/86	70	7		28	**People's Court**	*Cyrus Kalb/Dave Slater/Jack White* [N]	MCA 52924
11/1/86	63	6		29	**Southern Air** — **Jerry Clower** and **Minnie Pearl** (guest vocals)	S:27 *Stuart Dill/Brent Holmes* [N]	MCA 52906
5/9/87	41	9		30	**Would Jesus Wear A Rolex**	S:15 *Margaret Archer/Chet Atkins* [N]	MCA 53101
10/8/88	88	2		31	**The Day I Tried To Teach Charlene MacKenzie How To Drive**	*Cyrus Kalb* [N]	MCA 53423
7/6/91	62	10		32	**Working For The Japanese**	*Ron DeLacy* [N]	Curb/Capitol
3/14/92	72	2		33	**Power Tools** — above 2 from the album *#1 With A Bullet* on Curb/Capitol 95914	*Cyrus Kalb* [N]	Curb/Capitol
12/29/01	48	5		34	**Osama-Yo' Mama** — from the album *Osama-Yo' Mama* on Curb 78733	S:2 *Cyrus Kalb/Ray Stevens* [N]	Curb

STEWART, Gary — All-Time: #216

Born on 5/28/1944 in Letcher County, Kentucky; raised in Fort Pierce, Florida. Committed suicide on 12/16/2003 (age 59). Male singer/songwriter/guitarist. Member of rock groups the Tomcats and the Amps in the early 1960s. First recorded solo for the Cory label in 1964.

DEBUT	PEAK	WKS	GOLD	#	Country Chart Hit	Songwriter	Label (& Number)
11/17/73	63	7		1	**Ramblin' Man**	*Dickey Betts*	RCA Victor 0144
6/1/74	10	18		2	**Drinkin' Thing**	*Wayne Carson*	RCA Victor 0281
10/19/74+	4	16		3	**Out Of Hand**	*Jeff Barry/Tom Jans*	RCA Victor 10061
3/8/75	❶[1]	13		4	**She's Actin' Single (I'm Drinkin' Doubles)**	*Wayne Carson*	RCA Victor 10222
6/21/75	15	15		5	**You're Not The Woman You Use To Be**	*Bill Eldridge/Gary Stewart*	MCA 40414
10/11/75	20	12		6	**Flat Natural Born Good-Timin' Man**	*Gary Stewart*	RCA Victor 10351
1/31/76	23	13		7	**Oh, Sweet Temptation**	*Wayne Carson*	RCA Victor 10550
5/22/76	15	14		8	**In Some Room Above The Street**	*Sterling Whipple*	RCA Victor 10680
11/20/76+	11	13		9	**Your Place Or Mine**	*Carol Anderson/Mary Beth Anderson/Rory Bourke*	RCA 10833
5/21/77	16	12		10	**Ten Years Of This**	*Wayne Carson/Gary Stewart*	RCA 10957
10/22/77	26	13		11	**Quits**	*Danny O'Keefe*	RCA 11131
3/11/78	16	12		12	**Whiskey Trip**	*Wayne Carson/Donn Tankersley*	RCA 11224
7/22/78	36	8		13	**Single Again**	*Gary Stewart*	RCA 11297
11/25/78+	41	9		14	**Stone Wall (Around Your Heart)**	*Pat Twitty*	RCA 11416
4/14/79	66	5		15	**Shady Streets**	*Dickey Betts/Billy Ray Reynolds/Dan Toler*	RCA 11534
7/14/79	75	3		16	**Mazelle**	*Russ Kirkpatrick*	RCA 11623
6/14/80	48	9		17	**Cactus And A Rose**	*Bobby Emmons/Chips Moman*	RCA 11960
9/27/80	66	4		18	**Are We Dreamin' The Same Dream /**	*Billy Burnette/Johnny Christopher*	
9/27/80	flip	4		19	**Roarin'**	*Johnny Cobb/Mike Lawler*	RCA 12081
4/11/81	72	4		20	**Let's Forget That We're Married**	*Jim Lewis/Gary Stewart/Sonny Tackett*	RCA 12203
11/7/81	36	11		21	**She's Got A Drinking Problem**	*Tim DuBois/Danny Morrison/Wood Newton*	RCA 12343
4/10/82	41	11		22	**Brotherly Love** *[w/ Dean Dillon]*	*Dean Dillon/Gary Stewart*	RCA 13049
7/24/82	83	4		23	**She Sings Amazing Grace**	*Jerry Foster/Bill Rice*	RCA 13261

DEBUT	PEAK	WKS	GOLD	ARTIST / Ranking / Country Chart Hit / Songwriter	Label (& Number)
				STEWART, Gary — cont'd	
1/8/83	**47**	12		24 **Those Were The Days** *[w/ Dean Dillon]* ... *Dean Dillon/Rex Huston/Gary Stewart*	RCA 13401
4/16/83	**71**	4		25 **Smokin' In The Rockies** *[w/ Dean Dillon]* ... *Buddy Cannon/Dean Dillon/Frank Dycus/Gary Stewart*	RCA 13472
4/14/84	**75**	7		26 **Hey, Bottle Of Whiskey** ... *Don Singleton*	Red Ash 8403
8/11/84	**64**	7		27 **I Got A Bad Attitude** ... *W.T. Davidson*	Red Ash 8406
10/1/88	**63**	7		28 **Brand New Whiskey** ... *Gary Stewart/Mary Lou Stewart*	Hightone 506
12/3/88+	**64**	9		29 **An Empty Glass** ... *Dean Dillon/Gary Stewart*	Hightone 507
3/18/89	**77**	3		30 **Rainin', Rainin', Rainin'** ... *Don Smith/Gary Stewart/Mary Lou Stewart*	Hightone 509
				STEWART, Larry	
				Born on 3/2/1959 in Paducah, Kentucky. Male singer/songwriter. Lead singer of **Restless Heart** from 1986-91.	
3/6/93	**5**	20		1 **Alright Already** ... *Byron Hill/J.B. Rudd*	RCA
7/3/93	**34**	17		2 **I'll Cry Tomorrow** ... *Steve Bogard/Rick Giles*	RCA
11/6/93	**62**	6		3 **We Can Love** ... *Marc Beeson/Jill Colucci*	RCA
				above 3 from the album *Down The Road* on RCA 66210	
8/20/94	**43**	11		4 **Heart Like A Hurricane** ... *Trey Bruce/Craig Wiseman*	Columbia
12/3/94+	**46**	16		5 **Losing Your Love** ... *Hank DeVito/Kye Fleming/Vince Gill*	Columbia
4/8/95	**56**	9		6 **Rockin' The Rock** ... *Gary Burr*	Columbia
				above 3 from the album *Heart Like A Hurricane* on Columbia 66411	
7/6/96	**46**	15		7 **Why Can't You** ... *R.C. Bannon/Larry Stewart*	Columbia
1/25/97	**70**	4		8 **Always A Woman** ... *Fred Knoblock/Steve O'Brien*	Columbia
				abvoe 2 from the album *Why Can't You* on Columbia 67410	
				STEWART, Lisa	
				Born on 8/6/1968 in Louisville, Mississippi. Female singer. Became co-host of TNN's *This Week In Country Music* in 1997.	
10/31/92	**61**	7		1 **Somebody's In Love** ... *Steve Bogard/Michael Clark*	BNA
3/20/93	**72**	3		2 **Drive Time** ... *Annette Cotter/Kim Tribble*	BNA
				above 2 from the album *Lisa Stewart* on BNA 66040	
				STEWART, Vernon	
				Born on 3/31/1927 in Russellville, Arkansas. Died in September 1981 (age 54). Male singer.	
1/12/63	**17**	6		**The Way It Feels To Die** ... *Liz Anderson*	Chart 501

DEBUT	PEAK	WKS	GOLD	ARTIST / Ranking / Country Chart Hit / Songwriter	Label (& Number)
				STEWART, Wynn — **1960s: #47 / All-Time: #174**	
				Born Wynnford Stewart on 6/7/1934 in Morrisville, Missouri. Died of a heart attack on 7/17/1985 (age 51). Male singer/songwriter/guitarist. Worked on KWTO in Springfield, Missouri, in 1947. Moved to California in 1949 and recorded for the Intro label at age 16. Own club and TV series in Las Vegas in the late 1950s.	
7/21/56	**14**	1		1 **The Waltz Of The Angels** ... A:14 *Dick Reynolds/Jack Rhodes*	Capitol 3408
12/28/59+	**5**	22		2 **Wishful Thinking** ... *Wynn Stewart*	Challenge 9061
5/30/60	**26**	2		3 **Wrong Company** *[w/ Jan Howard]* ... *Harlan Howard*	Challenge 9071
12/25/61	**18**	7		4 **Big, Big Love** ... *Ray Carroll/Wynn Stewart*	Challenge 9121
11/24/62	**27**	3		5 **Another Day, Another Dollar** ... *Bobby Austin/Wynn Stewart*	Challenge 9164
11/21/64	**30**	15		6 **Half Of This, Half Of That** ... *Don Sessions/Wynn Stewart*	Capitol 5271
10/16/65	**43**	7		7 **I Keep Forgettin' That I Forgot About You** ... *Liz Anderson*	Capitol 5485
2/25/67	**❶**[2]	22		8 **It's Such A Pretty World Today** *Dale Noe*	Capitol 5831
7/15/67	**9**	16		9 **'Cause I Have You /** ... *Don Sessions/Wynn Stewart*	
8/5/67	**68**	3		10 **That's The Only Way To Cry** ... *Cliff Massey/Wynn Stewart*	Capitol 5937
				WYNN STEWART And The Tourists:	
11/11/67+	**7**	16		11 **Love's Gonna Happen To Me** ... *Jimmy Stewart*	Capitol 2012
4/20/68	**10**	13		12 **Something Pretty** ... *Buddy Wayne/Charlie Williams*	Capitol 2137
8/24/68	**16**	11		13 **In Love** ... *Bobby George*	Capitol 2240
12/14/68+	**29**	11		14 **Strings** ... *Bobby Bishop/Wynn Stewart*	Capitol 2341
4/5/69	**20**	12		15 **Let The Whole World Sing It With Me** ... *Dale Noe*	Capitol 2421
7/26/69	**19**	10		16 **World-Wide Travelin' Man** ... *Vern Stovall*	Capitol 2549
11/15/69	**47**	9		17 **Yours Forever** ... *Red Simpson*	Capitol 2657
4/11/70	**55**	4		18 **You Don't Care What Happens To Me** ... *Fred Rose*	Capitol 2751
				WYNN STEWART:	
9/12/70	**13**	13		19 **It's A Beautiful Day** ... *Tracy Pendarvis*	Capitol 2888
1/2/71	**32**	10		20 **Heavenly** ... *Earl Ball/Chris Roberts/Steve Stone*	Capitol 3000
5/1/71	**55**	6		21 **Baby, It's Yours** ... *Cheryl Hickman*	Capitol 3080
9/18/71	**53**	5		22 **Hello Little Rock** ... *Ronnie Mack*	Capitol 3157
11/11/72	**49**	8		23 **Paint Me A Rainbow** ... *Bill Brooks/Greg Stevens*	RCA Victor 0819
7/14/73	**51**	9		24 **Love Ain't Worth a Dime Unless It's Free** ... *Wynn Stewart*	RCA Victor 0004
10/27/73	**62**	9		25 **It's Raining In Seattle** ... *Roger Murrah*	RCA Victor 0114
6/14/75	**80**	9		26 **Lonely Rain** ... *Don Earl*	Playboy 6035
7/31/76	**8**	14		27 **After The Storm** ... *Dale Noe*	Playboy 6080
11/20/76+	**19**	11		28 **Sing A Sad Song** ... *Wynn Stewart*	Playboy 6091
12/23/78+	**37**	11		29 **Eyes Big As Dallas** ... *Gary McCray*	WIN 126
6/9/79	**59**	5		30 **Could I Talk You Into Loving Me Again** ... *Len Green/Wynn Stewart*	WIN'S 127
8/24/85	**98**	1		31 **Wait Till I Get My Hands On You** ... *Ron McCown*	Pretty World 001

DEBUT	PEAK	WKS	GOLD	ARTIST / Country Chart Hit	Ranking / Songwriter	Label (& Number)

STING

Born Gordon Sumner on 10/2/1951 in Wallsend, England. Pop singer/songwriter/bassist. Lead singer of The Police. Appeared in several movies. Married actress/producer Trudie Styler on 8/20/1992. Recipient of *Billboard's* Century Award in 2003.

DEBUT	PEAK	WKS		Country Chart Hit	Songwriter	Label (& Number)
10/11/97+	2[1]	20		**I'm So Happy I Can't Stop Crying** *[w/ Toby Keith]* S:7	*Sting*	Mercury
				from Keith's album *Dream Walkin'* on Mercury 534836		

STOCKTON, Shane

Born on 3/18/1974 in Breckenridge, Texas. Male singer/songwriter/guitarist.

DEBUT	PEAK	WKS		Country Chart Hit	Songwriter	Label (& Number)
3/28/98	54	10	1	**What If I'm Right**	*Shane Stockton*	Decca
6/27/98	51	7	2	**Gonna Have To Fall**	*Shane Stockton*	Decca

STONE, Cliffie, And His Orchestra — 1940s: #43 // HOF: 1989

Born Clifford Snyder on 3/1/1917 in Burbank, California. Died of a heart attack on 1/17/1998 (age 80). Male singer/songwriter/bassist/bandleader. Popular radio/TV personality in Los Angeles, hosting *Hollywood Barn Dance*, *Lucky Stars* and *Dinner Bell Roundup* (later known as *Hometown Jamboree*). Worked as an A&R executive for Capitol Records.

DEBUT	PEAK	WKS		Country Chart Hit	Songwriter	Label (& Number)
3/15/47	4	1	1	**Silver Stars, Purple Sage, Eyes Of Blue**	*Denver Darling*	Capitol 354
3/6/48	4	8	2	**Peepin' Thru The Keyhole (Watching Jole Blon)** *[w/ His Barn Dance Band]*	*Sheb Wooley*	Capitol Amer. 40083
8/28/48	11	3	3	**When My Blue Moon Turns To Gold Again** J:11	*Gene Sullivan/Wiley Walker*	Capitol 15108
10/15/66	30	7	4	**Little Pink Mack** *[w/ Kay Adams]*	*Chris Roberts/Jim Thornton/Scott Turner*	Tower 269

STONE, Doug — 1990s: #28 / All-Time: #161

Born Douglas Brooks on 6/19/1956 in Marietta, Georgia; raised in Newnan, Georgia. Male singer/songwriter/guitarist. Began performing in 1963. Formed own groups: Impact, Image and Main Street. Changed name to avoid confusion with Garth Brooks. Starred in the 1995 movie *Gordy*; did voiceovers for several animated shows.

DEBUT	PEAK	WKS		Country Chart Hit	Songwriter	Label (& Number)
3/10/90	4	25	1	**I'd Be Better Off (In A Pine Box)**	*Stephen Clark/Johnny MacRae*	Epic
7/14/90	6	21	2	**Fourteen Minutes Old**	*Dennis Knutson/A.L. "Doodle" Owens*	Epic
11/10/90+	5	20	3	**These Lips Don't Know How To Say Goodbye**	*Harlan Howard*	Epic
3/16/91	❶[1]	20	4	**In A Different Light**	*Bucky Jones/Dickey Lee/Bob McDill*	Epic
				above 4 from the album *Doug Stone* on Epic 45303		
7/20/91	4	20	5	**I Thought It Was You**	*Gary Harrison/Tim Mensy*	Epic
11/16/91+	❶[2]	20	6	**A Jukebox With A Country Song**	*Gene Nelson/Ronnie Samoset*	Epic
3/21/92	3[1]	20	7	**Come In Out Of The Pain**	*Frank J. Myers/Don Pfrimmer*	Epic
				above 3 from the album *I Thought It Was You* on Epic 47357		
7/11/92	4	20	8	**Warning Labels**	*Oscar Turman/Kim Williams*	Epic
11/7/92+	❶[1]	20	9	**Too Busy Being In Love**	*Gary Burr/Victoria Shaw*	Epic
2/27/93	6	20	10	**Made For Lovin' You**	*Curly Putman/Sonny Throckmorton*	Epic
6/19/93	❶[1]	20	11	**Why Didn't I Think Of That**	*Paul Harrison/Bob McDill*	Epic
				above 4 from the album *From The Heart* on Epic 52436		
10/23/93+	2[2]	20	12	**I Never Knew Love**	*Larry Boone/Will Robinson*	Epic
2/26/94	4	20	13	**Addicted To A Dollar**	*Ray Hood/Ray Maddox/Doug Stone/Kim Tribble*	Epic
6/18/94	6	20	14	**More Love**	*Gary Burr/Doug Stone*	Epic
				above 3 from the album *More Love* on Epic 57271		
10/29/94+	7	20	15	**Little Houses**	*Mickey Cates/Skip Ewing*	Epic
				from the album *Greatest Hits Volume 1* on Epic 66803		
3/4/95	13	20	16	**Faith In Me, Faith In You** S:25	*Trey Bruce/Dave Loggins*	Columbia
6/24/95	41	11	17	**Sometimes I Forget**	*Billy Kirsch/Bob Regan*	Columbia
9/23/95+	12	20	18	**Born In The Dark**	*Chet Hinesley*	Columbia
				above 3 from the album *Faith In Me, Faith In You* on Columbia 64330		
6/20/98	48	8	19	**Gone Out Of My Mind**	*Gene Dobbins/Mike Huffman/Bob Morrison*	Columbia
				from the various artists album *A Tribute To Tradition* on Columbia 68073		
4/24/99	19	26	20	**Make Up In Love**	*Danny Orton/Tony Ramey*	Atlantic
10/30/99+	45	13	21	**Take A Letter Maria**	*R.B. Greaves*	Atlantic
4/22/00	64	1	22	**Surprise**	*Tony Haselden*	Atlantic
				above 3 from the album *Make Up In Love* on Atlantic 83206		

STONEMAN, Ernest "Pop"

Born on 5/25/1893 in Monarat, Virginia. Died on 6/14/1968 (age 75). Pioneering bluegrass singer/musician. Founder of family group **The Stonemans**.

EARLY HIT: The Titanic (1925)

STONEMANS, The

Family group from Monorat, Virginia: **Ernest "Pop" Stoneman** (see bio above), Calvin "Scotty" Stoneman (fiddle; born on 8/4/1932; died on 3/4/1973, age 40), Van Stoneman (guitar; born on 12/31/1940; died on 6/3/1995, age 54), Donna Stoneman (mandolin; born on 2/7/1934), Veronica "Roni" Stoneman (banjo; born on 5/5/1938) and Oscar "Jim" Stoneman (bass; born on 3/8/1937; died on 9/22/2002, age 65). All shared vocals. Roni was a regular on TV's *Hee-Haw.*

CMA: Vocal Group 1967

DEBUT	PEAK	WKS		Country Chart Hit	Songwriter	Label (& Number)
6/4/66	40	3	1	**Tupelo County Jail**	*Webb Pierce/Mel Tillis*	MGM 13466
10/8/66	21	11	2	**The Five Little Johnson Girls**	*Jack Clement*	MGM 13557
3/25/67	40	12	3	**Back To Nashville, Tennessee**	*Jack Clement*	MGM 13667
8/5/67	49	7	4	**West Canterbury Subdivision Blues**	*Jack Clement*	MGM 13755
7/20/68	41	8	5	**Christopher Robin**	*Vince Matthews*	MGM 13945

Billboard DEBUT	PEAK	WKS	GOLD	ARTIST / Country Chart Hit	Ranking / Songwriter	Label (& Number)

STOREY, Lewis

Born in Casa Grande, Arizona. Male singer/songwriter.

DEBUT	PEAK	WKS	#	Country Chart Hit	Songwriter	Label (& Number)
2/8/86	**48**	8	1	**Ain't No Tellin'**	*Lewis Storey*	Epic 05786
5/17/86	**60**	6	2	**Katie, Take Me Dancin'**	*Lewis Storey*	Epic 05890

STORIE, James

Born in Los Angeles, California. Male singer.

DEBUT	PEAK	WKS	#	Country Chart Hit	Songwriter	Label (& Number)
10/22/88	**100**	1		**Lost Highway**	*Leon Payne*	GMC 1001

STOVALL, Vern

Born on 10/3/1928 in Altus, Oklahoma; raised in Vian, Oklahoma. Male singer/songwriter.

DEBUT	PEAK	WKS	#	Country Chart Hit	Songwriter	Label (& Number)
6/12/65	**16**	15	1	**Country Guitar** *[w/ Phil Baugh]*	*Phil Baugh/Vern Stovall* **[N]**	Longhorn 559
9/23/67	**58**	8	2	**Dallas**	*Dewey Groom/Dan Stovall*	Longhorn 581

STRAIT, George — 1980s: #13 / 1990s: #2 / 2000s: #6 / All-Time: #6

Born on 5/18/1952 in Poteet, Texas; raised in Pearsall, Texas. Male singer/guitarist. Served in the U.S. Army from 1972-74. Graduated from Southwest Texas State with a degree in agriculture. Formed the Ace In The Hole band in 1975. Starred in the movie *Pure Country.*

CMA: Male Vocalist 1985, 1986, 1996, 1997 & 1998 / Entertainer 1989 & 1990

DEBUT	PEAK	WKS	#	Country Chart Hit	Songwriter	Label (& Number)
5/16/81	**6**	18	1	**Unwound**	*Dean Dillon/Frank Dycus*	MCA 51104
9/12/81	**16**	17	2	**Down And Out**	*Dean Dillon/Frank Dycus*	MCA 51170
1/30/82	**3**^{2}	22	3	**If You're Thinking You Want A Stranger (There's One Coming Home)**	*Blake Mevis/David Wills*	MCA 51228
6/19/82	❶^{1}	18	4	**Fool Hearted Memory**	*Byron Hill/Blake Mevis*	MCA 52066
				from the movie *The Soldier* starring Klaus Kinski		
10/9/82+	**6**	19	5	**Marina Del Rey**	*Dean Dillon/Frank Dycus*	MCA 52120
2/12/83	**4**	17	6	**Amarillo By Morning**	*Paul Fraser/Terry Stafford*	MCA 52162
6/11/83	❶^{1}	23	7	**A Fire I Can't Put Out**	*Darrell Statler*	MCA 52225
10/8/83+	❶^{1}	23	8	**You Look So Good In Love**	*Glen Ballard/Rory Bourke/Kerry Chater*	MCA 52279
2/11/84	❶^{1}	23	9	**Right Or Wrong**	*Paul Biese/Haven Gillespie/Arthur Sizemore*	MCA 52337
6/2/84	❶^{1}	21	10	**Let's Fall To Pieces Together**	*Dickey Lee/Tommy Rocco/Johnny Russell*	MCA 52392
9/29/84+	❶^{1}	23	11	**Does Fort Worth Ever Cross Your Mind**	S:❶^{1} / A:❶^{1} *Darlene Shafer/Whitey Shafer*	MCA 52458
2/2/85	**5**	20	12	**The Cowboy Rides Away**	S:4 / A:5 *Casey Kelly/Sonny Throckmorton*	MCA 52526
6/1/85	**5**	18	13	**The Fireman**	S:4 / A:5 *Wayne Kemp/Mack Vickery*	MCA 52586
9/21/85	❶^{1}	22	14	**The Chair**	S:❶^{1} / A:❶^{1} *Hank Cochran/Dean Dillon*	MCA 52667
1/18/86	**4**	21	15	**You're Something Special To Me**	S:4 / A:4 *David Anthony*	MCA 52764
5/17/86	❶^{1}	22	16	**Nobody In His Right Mind Would've Left Her**	S:❶^{1} / A:❶^{1} *Dean Dillon*	MCA 52817
9/13/86	❶^{1}	22	17	**It Ain't Cool To Be Crazy About You**	S:❶^{1} / A:❶^{1} *Dean Dillon/Royce Porter*	MCA 52914
1/17/87	❶^{1}	21	18	**Ocean Front Property**	S:❶^{4} / A:❶^{1} *Hank Cochran/Dean Dillon/Royce Porter*	MCA 53021
5/2/87	❶^{1}	16	19	**All My Ex's Live In Texas**	S:❶^{2} / A:25 *Lyndia Shafer/Whitey Shafer*	MCA 53087
8/22/87	❶^{1}	18	20	**Am I Blue**	S:❶^{3} *David Chamberlain*	MCA 53165
2/6/88	❶^{1}	19	21	**Famous Last Words Of A Fool**	S:❶^{2} *Dean Dillon/Rex Huston*	MCA 53248
5/21/88	❶^{1}	19	22	**Baby Blue**	S:❶^{2} *Aaron Barker*	MCA 53340
9/17/88	❶^{1}	20	23	**If You Ain't Lovin' (You Ain't Livin')**	S:❶^{2} *Tommy Collins*	MCA 53400
1/21/89	❶^{1}	18	24	**Baby's Gotten Good At Goodbye**	*Tony Martin/Troy Martin*	MCA 53486
4/29/89	❶^{1}	20	25	**What's Going On In Your World**	*David Chamberlain/Royce Porter*	MCA 53648
8/12/89	❶^{1}	21	26	**Ace In The Hole**	*Dennis Adkins*	MCA 53693
12/2/89+	**8**	26	27	**Overnight Success /**	*Whitey Shafer*	
3/24/90	**67**	5	28	**Hollywood Squares**	*Larry Cordle/Wayland Patton/Jeff Tanguay*	MCA
				above 2 from the album *Beyond The Blue Neon* on MCA 42266		
4/28/90	❶^{5}	21	29	**Love Without End, Amen**	*Aaron Barker*	MCA
8/11/90	**4**	21	30	**Drinking Champagne**	*Bill Mack*	MCA
11/3/90	❶^{5}	20	31	**I've Come To Expect It From You**	*Buddy Cannon/Dean Dillon*	MCA
				above 3 from the album *Livin' It Up* on MCA 6415		
3/23/91	❶^{2}	20	32	**If I Know Me**	*Pam Belford/Dean Dillon*	MCA
6/15/91	❶^{3}	20	33	**You Know Me Better Than That**	*Anna Graham/Tony Haselden*	MCA
10/5/91	**3**^{1}	20	34	**The Chill Of An Early Fall**	*Green Daniel/Gretchen Peters*	MCA
1/18/92	**24**	20	35	**Lovesick Blues**	*Cliff Friend/Irving Mills*	MCA
				above 4 from the album *Chill Of An Early Fall* on MCA 10204		
4/18/92	**5**	20	36	**Gone As A Girl Can Get**	*Jerry "Max" Lane*	MCA
7/11/92	**3**^{1}	20	37	**So Much Like My Dad**	*Bobby Emmons/Chips Moman*	MCA
				above 2 from the album *Holding My Own* on MCA 10532		
10/3/92	❶^{2}	20	38	**I Cross My Heart**	*Steve Dorff/Eric Kaz*	MCA
11/14/92	**70**	3	39	**Overnight Male**	*Richard Fagan/Ron Harbin/Kim Williams*	MCA
1/2/93	❶^{1}	20	40	**Heartland**	*John Bettis/Steve Dorff*	MCA
5/1/93	**6**	20	41	**When Did You Stop Loving Me**	*Monty Holmes/Donny Kees*	MCA
				above 4 from the movie *Pure Country* starring Strait (soundtrack on MCA 10651)		
8/21/93	❶^{2}	20	42	**Easy Come, Easy Go**	*Aaron Barker/Dean Dillon*	MCA
12/4/93+	**3**^{1}	20	43	**I'd Like To Have That One Back**	*Aaron Barker/Bill Shore/Roy West*	MCA
1/22/94	**8**	20	44	**Lovebug**	*Wayne Kemp/Curtis Wayne*	MCA

Billboard DEBUT	PEAK	WKS	GOLD		ARTIST / Country Chart Hit	Ranking / Songwriter	Label (& Number)
					STRAIT, George — cont'd		
6/25/94	4	20		45	The Man In Love With You	*Steve Dorff/Gary Harju*	MCA
					above 4 from the album *Easy Come, Easy Go* on MCA 10907		
10/8/94	❶[1]	20		46	The Big One	*Gerry House/Devon O'Day*	MCA
12/24/94+	❶[1]	20		47	You Can't Make A Heart Love Somebody	*Stephen Clark/Johnny MacRae*	MCA
3/25/95	3[1]	20		48	Adalida	*Mike Geiger/Mike Huffman/Woody Mullis*	MCA
6/24/95	7	20		49	Lead On	*Dean Dillon/Teddy Gentry*	MCA
					above 4 from the album *Lead On* on MCA 11092		
9/23/95	❶[4]	20		50	Check Yes Or No	*Dana Oglesby/Danny Wells*	MCA
					CMA: Single		
12/23/95+	5	20		51	I Know She Still Loves Me	*Aaron Barker/Monty Holmes*	MCA
					above 2 from the album *Strait Out Of The Box* on MCA 11263		
1/6/96	73	1		52	Santa Claus Is Coming To Town	*J. Fred Coots/Haven Gillespie* [X]	MCA
					from the album *Merry Christmas Strait To You* on MCA 5800		
4/6/96	❶[2]	20		53	Blue Clear Sky	*Bob DiPiero/John Jarrard/Mark D. Sanders*	MCA
5/18/96	❶[3]	20		54	Carried Away	*Steve Bogard/Jeff Stevens*	MCA
8/24/96	4	20		55	I Can Still Make Cheyenne	*Aaron Barker/Erv Woolsey*	MCA
12/21/96+	19	13		56	King Of The Mountain	*Larry Boone/Paul Nelson*	MCA
2/8/97	69	6		57	Do The Right Thing	*Jim Lauderdale/Gary Nicholson*	MCA
					above 5 from the album *Blue Clear Sky* on MCA 11428		
3/15/97	❶[5]	20		58	One Night At A Time	S:2 *Roger Cook/Eddy Kilgallon/Earl Lee*	MCA
5/3/97	❶[4]	21		59	Carrying Your Love With Me	*Steve Bogard/Jeff Stevens*	MCA
5/3/97+	❶[2]	20		60	Round About Way	*Steve Dean/Wil Nance*	MCA
5/3/97	70	1		61	Won't You Come Home (And Talk To A Stranger)	*Wayne Kemp*	MCA
9/6/97	3[1]	20		62	Today My World Slipped Away	*Vern Gosdin/Mark Wright*	MCA
					above 5 from the album *Carrying Your Love With Me* on MCA 11584		
1/3/98	58	2		63	Merry Christmas Strait To You	*Bob Kelly* [X]	MCA
1/3/98	69	2		64	Santa Claus Is Coming To Town	*J. Fred Coots/Haven Gillespie* [X-R]	MCA
					above 2 from the album *Merry Christmas Strait To You* on MCA 5800		
4/18/98	❶[3]	21		65	I Just Want To Dance With You	S:6 *Roger Cook/John Prine*	MCA Nashville
5/2/98	2[4]	25		66	True	*Marv Green/Jeff Stevens*	MCA Nashville
5/2/98	4	23		67	We Really Shouldn't Be Doing This	*Jim Lauderdale*	MCA Nashville
5/2/98+	59	15		68	You Haven't Left Me Yet	*Dana Oglesby/Kent Robbins*	MCA Nashville
					above 4 from the album *Carrying Your Love With Me* on MCA Nashville 11584		
1/9/99	4	20		69	Meanwhile	S:2 *Wayland Holyfield/Fred Knoblock*	MCA Nashville
3/13/99	❶[4]	37		70	Write This Down	*Dana Hunt/Kent Robbins*	MCA Nashville
3/13/99	4	24		71	What Do You Say To That	*Jim Lauderdale/Melba Montgomery*	MCA Nashville
3/13/99	69	2		72	Always Never The Same	*Marv Green/Terry McBride*	MCA Nashville
3/13/99	73	1		73	One Of You	*Kostas/Jim Lauderdale*	MCA Nashville
3/13/99	74	2		74	Peace Of Mind	*Aaron Barker/Dean Dillon*	MCA Nashville
3/13/99	75	1		75	I Look At You	*Steve Bogard/Jeff Stevens*	MCA Nashville
					#69-75: from the album *Always Never The Same* on MCA Nashville 70050		
12/18/99	72	2		76	Let It Snow, Let It Snow, Let It Snow	*Sammy Cahn/Jule Styne* [X]	MCA Nashville
12/18/99	73	2		77	I Know What I Want For Christmas	*Charlie Black/Dana Hunt* [X]	MCA Nashville
1/1/00	❶[3]	29		78	The Best Day	*Carson Chamberlain/Dean Dillon*	MCA Nashville
1/1/00	69	2		79	Jingle Bell Rock	*Joe Beal/Jim Boothe* [X]	MCA Nashville
					#76, 77 & 79: from the album *Merry Christmas Wherever You Are* on MCA Nashville 70093		
3/11/00	38	20		80	Murder On Music Row *[w/ Alan Jackson]*	*Larry Cordle/Larry Shell*	MCA Nashville
					CMA: Vocal Event; #78 & 80: from the album *Latest Greatest Straitest Hits* on MCA Nashville 70100		
7/29/00	2[3]	22		81	Go On	*Tony Martin/Mark Nesler*	MCA Nashville
10/21/00+	17	25		82	Don't Make Me Come Over There And Love You	*Jim Lauderdale/Carter Wood*	MCA Nashville
12/23/00	62	3		83	Old Time Christmas	*Aaron Barker/John Jarvis* [X]	MCA Nashville
					from the album *Merry Christmas Wherever You Are* on MCA 70093		
3/3/01	5	21		84	If You Can Do Anything Else	*Billy Livsey/Don Schlitz*	MCA Nashville
					#81, 82 & 84: from the album *George Strait* on MCA Nashville 170143		
10/13/01	2[4]	23		85	Run	*Tony Lane/Anthony Smith*	MCA Nashville
12/15/01+	33	5		86	Christmas Cookies	*Aaron Barker* [X]	MCA Nashville
					from the various artists album *Christmas Cookies* on MCA Nashville 170232		
1/19/02	44	8		87	Designated Drinker *[w/ Alan Jackson]*	*Alan Jackson*	Arista Nashville
					from Jackson's album *Drive* on Arista Nashville 67039		
2/16/02	❶[2]	32		88	Living And Living Well	*Tony Martin/Mark Nesler/Tom Shapiro*	MCA Nashville
7/27/02	50	11		89	Stars On The Water	*Rodney Crowell*	MCA Nashville
9/7/02	❶[2]	28		90	She'll Leave You With A Smile	*Odie Blackmon/Jay Knowles*	MCA Nashville
3/22/03	60	1		91	The Real Thing	*Chip Taylor*	MCA Nashville
					#85 & 88-91: from the album *The Road Less Traveled* on MCA Nashville 170220		
4/12/03	11	20		92	Tell Me Something Bad About Tulsa	*Red Lane*	MCA Nashville
8/9/03	2[2]	25		93	Cowboys Like Us	*Bob DiPiero/Anthony Smith*	MCA Nashville
1/17/04	6	22		94	Desperately	*Bruce Robison/Monte Warden*	MCA Nashville
1/17/04	45	8		95	Honk If You Honky Tonk	*Dean Dillon/Ken Mellons/John Northrup*	MCA Nashville
					above 4 from the album *Honkytonkville* on MCA Nashville 000114		
5/29/04	8	20		96	Hey Good Lookin' *[w/ Jimmy Buffett/Clint Black/Kenny Chesney/Alan Jackson/Toby Keith]*		
					from Buffett's album *License To Chill* on RCA 62270	*...Hank Williams*	RCA
7/17/04	❶[2]	20		97	I Hate Everything	*Gary Harrison/Keith Stegall*	MCA Nashville
					from the album *50 Number Ones* on MCA Nashville 000459		
4/9/05	4	20		98	You'll Be There	*Cory Mayo*	MCA Nashville
					from the album *Somewhere Down In Texas* on MCA Nashville 004446		

Billboard DEBUT	PEAK	WKS	GOLD	ARTIST / Ranking / Country Chart Hit	Songwriter	Label (& Number)

STRAIT, George — cont'd

Ace In The Hole ['89]
Adalida ['95]
All My Ex's Live In Texas ['87]
Always Never The Same ['99]
Am I Blue ['87]
Amarillo By Morning ['83]
Baby Blue ['88]
Baby's Gotten Good At Goodbye ['89]
Best Day ['00]
Big One ['94]
Blue Clear Sky ['96]
Carried Away ['96]
Carrying Your Love With Me ['97]
Chair ['85]
Check Yes Or No ['95]
Chill Of An Early Fall ['91]
Christmas Cookies ['02]
Cowboy Rides Away ['85]
Cowboys Like Us ['03]
Designated Drinker ['02]
Desperately ['04]
Do The Right Thing ['97]
Does Fort Worth Ever Cross Your Mind ['85]
Don't Make Me Come Over There And Love You ['01]
Down And Out ['81]
Drinking Champagne ['90]
Easy Come, Easy Go ['93]
Famous Last Words Of A Fool ['88]
Fire I Can't Put Out ['83]
Fireman ['85]
Fool Hearted Memory ['82]
Go On ['00]
Gone As A Girl Can Get ['92]
Heartland ['93]
Hey Good Lookin' ['04]
Hollywood Squares ['90]
Honk If You Honky Tonk ['04]
I Can Still Make Cheyenne ['96]
I Cross My Heart ['92]
I Hate Everything ['04]
I Just Want To Dance With You ['98]
I Know She Still Loves Me ['96]
I Know What I Want For Christmas ['99]
I Look At You ['99]
I'd Like To Have That One Back ['94]
I've Come To Expect It From You ['90]
If I Know Me ['91]
If You Ain't Lovin' (You Ain't Livin') ['88]
If You Can Do Anything Else ['01]
If You're Thinking You Want A Stranger (There's One Coming Home) ['82]
It Ain't Cool To Be Crazy About You ['86]
Jingle Bell Rock ['00]
King Of The Mountain ['97]
Lead On ['95]
Let It Snow, Let It Snow, Let It Snow ['99]
Let's Fall To Pieces Together ['84]
Living And Living Well ['02]
Love Without End, Amen ['90]
Lovebug ['94]
Lovesick Blues ['92]
Man In Love With You ['94]
Marina Del Rey ['83]
Meanwhile ['99]
Merry Christmas Strait To You ['98]
Murder On Music Row ['00]
Nobody In His Right Mind Would've Left Her ['86]
Ocean Front Property ['87]
Old Time Christmas ['00]
One Night At A Time ['97]
One Of You ['99]
Overnight Male ['92]
Overnight Success ['90]
Peace Of Mind ['99]
Real Thing ['03]
Right Or Wrong ['84]
Round About Way ['98]
Run ['01]
Santa Claus Is Coming To Town ['96, '98]
She'll Leave You With A Smile ['02]
So Much Like My Dad ['92]
Stars On The Water ['02]
Tell Me Something Bad About Tulsa ['03]
Today My World Slipped Away ['97]
True ['98]
Unwound ['81]
We Really Shouldn't Be Doing This ['98]
What Do You Say To That ['99]
What's Going On In Your World ['89]
When Did You Stop Loving Me ['93]
Won't You Come Home (And Talk To A Stranger) ['97]
Write This Down ['99]
You Can't Make A Heart Love Somebody ['95]
You Haven't Left Me Yet ['99]
You Know Me Better Than That ['91]
You Look So Good In Love ['84]
You'll Be There ['05]
You're Something Special To Me ['86]

STREET, Mel — All-Time: #220

Born King Malachi Street on 10/21/1933 in Grundy, Virginia. Died of a self-inflicted gunshot on 10/21/1978 (age 45). Singer/songwriter/guitarist. Worked as a contruction worker, an electrician and car mechanic prior to his music career.

Debut	Peak	Wks	Gold	#	Country Chart Hit	Songwriter	Label (& Number)
5/27/72	7	17		1	**Borrowed Angel**	*Mel Street*	Royal American 64
11/4/72+	5	16		2	**Lovin' On Back Streets**	*Hugh King*	Metromedia 901
3/17/73	11	15		3	**Walk Softly On The Bridges**	*Dallas Frazier/A.L. "Doodle" Owens*	Metromedia 906
7/28/73	38	10		4	**The Town Where You Live**	*Mel Street*	Metromedia 0018
11/10/73+	11	13		5	**Lovin' On Borrowed Time**	*Dick Heard/Eddie Rabbitt/Mel Street*	Metromedia 0143
5/11/74	15	15		6	**You Make Me Feel More Like A Man**	*John Riggs*	GRT 002
11/2/74+	16	13		7	**Forbidden Angel**	*John Riggs/Mel Street*	GRT 012
3/1/75	13	14		8	**Smokey Mountain Memories**	*Earl Thomas Conley/Richmond Devereux*	GRT 017
6/28/75	17	14		9	**Even If I Have To Steal**	*Ralph Carter*	GRT 025
10/11/75	23	11		10	(This Ain't Just Another) **Lust Affair**	*Earl Thomas Conley*	GRT 030
2/7/76	32	10		11	**The Devil In Your Kisses** (And The Angel In Your Eyes)	*Layng Martine Jr.*	GRT 043
6/12/76	10	14		12	**I Met A Friend Of Your's Today**	*Wayland Holyfield/Bob McDill*	GRT 057
10/23/76	24	13		13	**Looking Out My Window Through The Pain**	*John Schweers*	GRT 083
3/19/77	56	7		14	**Rodeo Bum**	*Dick Heard/Sharon Vaughn*	GRT 116
6/25/77	19	12		15	**Barbara Don't Let Me Be The Last To Know**	*Wayland Holyfield/Bob McDill*	Polydor 14399
9/24/77	15	12		16	**Close Enough For Lonesome**	*Bob McDill*	Polydor 14421
1/14/78	9	13		17	**If I Had A Cheating Heart**	*Wayland Holyfield/Al Turney*	Polydor 14448
4/22/78	24	10		18	**Shady Rest**	*Bob McDill*	Polydor 14468
10/21/78	68	5		19	**Just Hangin' On**	*Wayland Holyfield*	Mercury 55043
10/6/79	17	11		20	**The One Thing My Lady Never Puts Into Words**	*Mike Huffman*	Sunset 100
1/26/80	30	10		21	**Tonight Let's Sleep On It Baby**	*Mel Street*	Sunbird 103
11/1/80	36	12		22	**Who'll Turn Out The Lights**	*Wayne Kemp/Mack Vickery*	Sunbird 7555
10/31/81	48	8		23	**Slip Away** *[w/ Sandy Powell]*	*Joe Deaton*	Sunbird 7568

STREETFEET

Studio group assembled by songwriter/producer Rick Anderson.

Debut	Peak	Wks	Gold	#	Country Chart Hit	Songwriter	Label (& Number)
2/12/83	78	4			**Where Do You Go**	*Rick Anderson*	Triple T 2001

STREETS — see NIGHTSTREETS

STREISAND, Barbra

Born on 4/24/1942 in Brooklyn, New York. Popular singer/actress/director/producer. Starred in several movies and Broadway shows. Married to actor Elliott Gould from 1963-71. Married actor James Brolin on 7/1/1998. Won Grammy's Lifetime Achievement Award in 1995.

Debut	Peak	Wks	Gold	#	Country Chart Hit	Songwriter	Label (& Number)
11/25/78	70	8	▲	1	**You Don't Bring Me Flowers** *[w/ Neil Diamond]*	*Alan Bergman/Marilyn Bergman/Neil Diamond*	Columbia 10840
10/23/99	62	10		2	**If You Ever Leave Me** *[w/ Vince Gill]* — from Streisand's album *A Love Like Ours* on Columbia 69601	*Richard Marx*	Columbia

STRINGBEAN — see AKEMAN, David

STRODE, Lance

Born in Memphis, Tennessee. Male singer/songwriter.

Debut	Peak	Wks	Gold	#	Country Chart Hit	Songwriter	Label (& Number)
4/8/89	92	1			**Dangerous Ground**	*Lance Strode*	Bootstrap 0416

STROMAN, Gene

Born on 2/19/1961 in Terrell, Texas. Male singer.

Debut	Peak	Wks	Gold	#	Country Chart Hit	Songwriter	Label (& Number)
1/17/87	53	8		1	**Goodbye Song**	*Fred Knoblock*	Capitol 5662
8/15/87	74	5		2	**I Don't Feel Much Like A Cowboy Tonight**	*Michael Garvin/Bucky Jones/Tom Shapiro*	Capitol 44015

STRUNK, Jud

Born Justin Strunk on 6/11/1936 in Jamestown, New York; raised in Farmington, Maine. Died in a plane crash on 10/15/1981 (age 45). Male singer/songwriter/banjo player. Regular on TV's *Laugh-In*.

Debut	Peak	Wks	Gold	#	Country Chart Hit	Songwriter	Label (& Number)
2/24/73	33	14		1	**Daisy A Day**	*Jud Strunk*	MGM 14463
7/21/73	86	4		2	**Next Door Neighbor's Kid**	*Jud Strunk*	MGM 14572
8/9/75	51	6		3	**The Biggest Parakeets In Town**	*Jud Strunk* **[C-L]**	Melodyland 6015
2/7/76	88	5		4	**Pamela Brown**	*Tom T. Hall*	Melodyland 6027

DEBUT	PEAK	WKS	GOLD	ARTIST / Country Chart Hit	Ranking / Songwriter	Label (& Number)

STUART, Marty — **1990s: #43 / All-Time: #165**

Born John Marty Stuart on 9/30/1958 in Philadelphia, Mississippi. Male singer/songwriter/guitarist. Toured with Lester Flatt (**Flatt & Scruggs**) and Nashville Grass from age 13. Toured with the **Johnny Cash** Band from 1979-85. Once married to Cash's daughter Cindy. Married **Connie Smith** on 7/8/1997. Also see **Hope** and **Same Old Train**.

OPRY: 1992

DEBUT	PEAK	WKS		Country Chart Hit	Songwriter	Label (& Number)
12/28/85+	**19**	18		1 **Arlene** S:13 / A:22	*Curtis Allen*	Columbia 05724
5/31/86	**59**	6		2 **Honky Tonker**	*Steve Forbert*	Columbia 05897
8/9/86	**39**	12		3 **All Because Of You**	*Steve Forbert*	Columbia 06230
11/22/86	**59**	8		4 **Do You Really Want My Lovin'**	*Steve Goodman/Marty Stuart*	Columbia 06425
3/19/88	**56**	7		5 **Mirrors Don't Lie**	*Merle Haggard*	Columbia 07729
6/4/88	**66**	6		6 **Matches**	*Charlie Craig/Keith Stegall*	Columbia 07914
8/19/89	**32**	12		7 **Cry Cry Cry**	*Johnny Cash*	MCA 53687
11/18/89+	**42**	11		8 **Don't Leave Her Lonely Too Long**	*Kostas/Marty Stuart*	MCA 53751
4/28/90	**8**	21		9 **Hillbilly Rock**	*Paul Kennerley*	MCA
9/1/90	**20**	20		10 **Western Girls** above 2 from the album *Hillbilly Rock* on MCA 42312	*Paul Kennerley/Marty Stuart*	MCA
12/22/90+	**8**	20		11 **Little Things**	*Paul Kennerley/Marty Stuart*	MCA
4/20/91	**12**	20		12 **Till I Found You**	*Hank DeVito/Paul Kennerley*	MCA
8/17/91	**5**	20		13 **Tempted**	*Paul Kennerley/Marty Stuart*	MCA
11/23/91+	**2**[1]	20		14 **The Whiskey Ain't Workin'** ***[w/ Travis Tritt]*** **Grammy: Vocal Collaboration**; from the album *It's All About To Change* on Warner 26589	*Ronny Scaife/Marty Stuart*	Warner
2/8/92	**7**	20		15 **Burn Me Down** #11-13 & 15: from the album *Tempted* on MCA 10106	*Eddie Miller*	MCA
6/6/92	**7**	20		16 **This One's Gonna Hurt You (For A Long, Long Time)** ***[w/ Travis Tritt]***	*Marty Stuart*	MCA
9/12/92	**18**	20		17 **Now That's Country**	*Marty Stuart*	MCA
12/12/92+	**24**	20		18 **High On A Mountain Top**	*Alex Campbell/Ola Belle Reed*	MCA
4/17/93	**38**	15		19 **Hey Baby** above 4 from the album *This One's Gonna Hurt You* on MCA 10596	*Paul Kennerley/Marty Stuart*	MCA
12/25/93+	**54**	10		20 **The Devil Comes Back To Georgia** ***[w/ Mark O'Connor/Charlie Daniels/Johnny Cash/Travis Tritt]*** from O'Connor's album *Heroes* on Warner 45257	*...Tom Crain/Charlie Daniels/Joe DiGregorio/Fred Edwards/Charles Hayward/Jim Marshall*	Warner
1/22/94	**26**	19		21 **Kiss Me, I'm Gone**	*Bob DiPiero/Marty Stuart*	MCA
6/25/94	**54**	8		22 **Love And Luck**	*Bob DiPiero/Marty Stuart*	MCA
9/24/94	**68**	5		23 **That's What Love's About** above 3 from the album *Love And Luck* on MCA 10880	*Marty Stuart*	MCA
4/1/95	**58**	8		24 **The Likes Of Me**	*Larry Boone/Rick Bowles*	MCA
6/24/95	**46**	18		25 **If I Ain't Got You** above 2 from the album *The Marty Party Hit Pack* on MCA 11204	*Trey Bruce/Craig Wiseman*	MCA
4/20/96	**23**	20		26 **Honky Tonkin's What I Do Best** ***[w/ Travis Tritt]*** **CMA: Vocal Event**	*Marty Stuart*	MCA
8/17/96	**50**	10		27 **Thanks To You**	*Gary Nicholson/Marty Stuart*	MCA
10/26/96+	**26**	20		28 **You Can't Stop Love** above 3 from the album *Honky Tonkin's What I Do Best* on MCA 11429	*Kostas/Marty Stuart*	MCA
6/5/99	**69**	2		29 **Red, Red Wine And Cheatin' Songs** from the album *The Pilgrim* on MCA Nashville 70057	*Marty Stuart*	MCA Nashville
4/15/00	**63**	6		30 **The Blue Collar Dollar Song** ***[w/ Jeff Foxworthy & Bill Engvall]*** from Foxworthy's album *Big Funny* on DreamWorks 50200	*Bill Engvall/Jeff Foxworthy/ Doug Grau/Porter Howell* **[N]**	DreamWorks
7/12/03	**41**	11		31 **If There Ain't There Ought'a Be**	*Trey Bruce/Bobby Pinson*	Columbia
12/6/03	**54**	2		32 **Too Much Month (At The End Of The Money)** **MARTY STUART and His Fabulous Superlatives** (above 2) above 2 from the album *Country Music* on Columbia 87063	*Bob DiPiero/Dennis Robbins/John Scott Sherrill*	Columbia
1/10/04	**55**	1		33 **Even Santa Claus Gets The Blues** from the various artists album *A Very Special Acoustic Christmas* on Lost Highway 001038	*Marty Stuart* **[X]**	Lost Highway

STUBBY AND THE BUCCANEERS — see CAPTAIN STUBBY

STUCKEY, Nat — **All-Time: #151**

Born Nathan Stuckey on 12/17/1933 in Cass County, Texas. Died of cancer on 8/24/1988 (age 54). Male singer/songwriter/guitarist. Graduated from Arlington State College with a radio and TV degree. Worked as a DJ in Texas and Louisiana. Sang on numerous TV commercials in the 1980s.

DEBUT	PEAK	WKS		Country Chart Hit	Songwriter	Label (& Number)
9/10/66	**4**	18		1 **Sweet Thang**	*Nat Stuckey*	Paula 243
1/7/67	**17**	13		2 **Oh! Woman**	*Nat Stuckey*	Paula 257
4/15/67	**27**	12		3 **All My Tomorrows /**	*Nat Stuckey*	
4/29/67	**67**	3		4 **You're Puttin' Me On**	*Nat Stuckey*	Paula 267
9/2/67	**41**	8		5 **Adorable Women**	*Nat Stuckey*	Paula 276
12/23/67+	**17**	14		6 **My Can Do Can't Keep Up With My Want To**	*Nat Stuckey*	Paula 287
5/18/68	**63**	5		7 **Leave This One Alone**	*Faye Bradshaw*	Paula 300
10/12/68	**9**	16		8 **Plastic Saddle**	*Vic McAlpin*	RCA Victor 9631

DEBUT	PEAK	WKS	GOLD	Ranking	ARTIST / Country Chart Hit	Songwriter	Label (& Number)
					STUCKEY, Nat — cont'd		
2/15/69	**13**	11		9	**Joe And Mabel's 12th Street Bar And Grill**	*Bobby Braddock*	RCA Victor 9720
6/7/69	**15**	13		10	**Cut Across Shorty**	*Wayne Walker/Marijohn Wilkin*	RCA Victor 0163
7/5/69	**20**	11		11	**Young Love** *[w/ Connie Smith]*	*Ric Cartey/Carole Joyner*	RCA Victor 0181
10/4/69	**8**	11		12	**Sweet Thang And Cisco**	*Bill Eldridge/Gary Stewart*	RCA Victor 0238
1/10/70	**33**	10		13	**Sittin' In Atlanta Station**	*Ron Peterson/Van Trevor*	RCA Victor 9786
3/14/70	**59**	4		14	**If God Is Dead (Who's That Living In My Soul)** *[w/ Connie Smith]*	*Lawrence Reynolds*	RCA Victor 9805
5/16/70	**31**	8		15	**Old Man Willis**	*Tony Joe White*	RCA Victor 9833
9/5/70	**31**	9		16	**Whiskey, Whiskey**	*Tom Ghent*	RCA Victor 9884
12/12/70+	**11**	15		17	**She Wakes Me With A Kiss Every Morning (And She Loves Me To Sleep Every Night)**	*Dallas Frazier/A.L. "Doodle" Owens*	RCA Victor 9929
4/24/71	**24**	12		18	**Only A Woman Like You**	*Bill Eldridge/Gary Stewart*	RCA Victor 9977
9/4/71	**17**	13		19	**I'm Gonna Act Right**	*Mel Tillis*	RCA Victor 1010
12/11/71+	**16**	14		20	**Forgive Me For Calling You Darling**	*Dallas Frazier/A.L. "Doodle" Owens*	RCA Victor 0590
4/22/72	**26**	12		21	**Is It Any Wonder That I Love You**	*Jerry Foster/Bill Rice*	RCA Victor 0687
8/19/72	**18**	13		22	**Don't Pay The Ransom**	*Dalton Roberts*	RCA Victor 0761
2/3/73	**10**	14		23	**Take Time To Love Her**	*Jerry Foster/Bill Rice*	RCA Victor 0879
6/16/73	**22**	12		24	**I Used It All On You**	*Tom Crum*	RCA Victor 0973
10/20/73	**14**	12		25	**Got Leaving On Her Mind**	*Jack Clement*	RCA Victor 0115
2/23/74	**31**	11		26	**You Never Say You Love Me Anymore**	*Gayle Barnhill/Johnny Christopher*	RCA Victor 0222
6/1/74	**42**	13		27	**It Hurts To Know The Feeling's Gone**	*A.L. "Doodle" Owens/Warren Robb*	RCA Victor 0288
11/9/74+	**36**	12		28	**You Don't Have To Go Home**	*Nat Stuckey/Paul Wassell/Bob Younts*	RCA Victor 10090
7/5/75	**85**	7		29	**Boom Boom Barroom Man**	*Max D. Barnes/Troy Seals*	RCA Victor 10307
2/28/76	**13**	13		30	**Sun Comin' Up**	*Nat Stuckey*	MCA 40519
6/12/76	**46**	10		31	**The Way He's Treated You**	*Gary Price*	MCA 40568
9/4/76	**42**	9		32	**That's All She Ever Said Except Goodbye**	*Nat Stuckey*	MCA 40608
12/11/76+	**48**	8		33	**The Shady Side Of Charlotte**	*Gene Mabry/Harlan Sanders/Kent Westberry*	MCA 40658
7/23/77	**63**	6		34	**Buddy, I Lied**	*Glenn Martin*	MCA 40752
10/29/77	**62**	6		35	**I'm Coming Home To Face The Music**	*Don Goodman/Mark Sherrill*	MCA 40808
3/18/78	**66**	6		36	**That Lucky Old Sun (Just Rolls Around Heaven All Day)**	*Haven Gillespie/Beasley Smith*	MCA 40855
7/8/78	**26**	10		37	**The Days Of Sand And Shovels**	*Doyle Marsh/Bud Reneau*	MCA 40923
					SUDDERTH, Anna		
					Born in New Mexico. Female singer/songwriter.		
5/10/80	**90**	4			**Not A Day Goes By**	*Anna Sudderth/Barney Sudderth*	Verite 801
					SUGARLAND		
					Trio from Atlanta, Georgia: Jennifer Nettles (vocals), Kristen Hall (guitar) and Kristian Bush (mandolin).		
7/24/04+	**2^{2}**	46		1	**Baby Girl**	S:2 *Troy Bieser/Kristian Bush/Kristen Hall/Jennifer Nettles*	Mercury
4/16/05	**2^{5}**	24↑		2	**Something More**	*Kristian Bush/Kristen Hall/Jennifer Nettles*	Mercury
					above 2 from the album *Twice The Speed Of Life* on Mercury 002172		
					SULLIVAN, Gene		
					Born on 11/16/1914 in Carbon Hill, Alabama. Died on 10/24/1984 (age 69). Male singer/songwriter. One-half of **Wiley & Gene**.		
12/9/57+	**9**	8			**Please Pass The Biscuits**	A:9 / S:16 *Gene Sullivan* **[N]**	Columbia 40971
					SULLIVAN, Phil		
					Born in Texas. Male singer.		
6/8/59	**26**	6			**Hearts Are Lonely**	*Shorty Sullivan*	Starday 437
					SUMMAR, Trent, and the New Row Mob		
					Born in Tennessee. Male singer. The New Row Mob: Kenny Vaughan and Phil Wallace (guitars), Jerry McFadden (keyboards), Jared Reynolds (bass) and David Kennedy (drums).		
12/30/00	**74**	1			**It Never Rains In Southern California**	*Albert Hammond/Mike Hazlewood*	VFR
					from the album *Trent Summar & The New Row Mob* on VFR 734756		
					SUMMER, Scott		
					Born in Fort Smith, Kansas. Male singer/songwriter.		
2/3/79	**80**	4		1	**Flip Side Of Today**	*Scott Summer*	Con Brio 146
5/26/79	**92**	3		2	**I Don't Wanna Want You**	*Scott Summer/Colin Walker*	Con Brio 152
					SUN, Joe		
					Born James Joseph Paulson on 9/25/1943 in Rochester, Minnesota. Male singer/songwriter/guitarist.		
6/24/78	**14**	16		1	**Old Flames (Can't Hold A Candle To You)**	*Hugh Moffatt/Pebe Sebert*	Ovation 1107
11/4/78	**20**	12		2	**High And Dry**	*Mike Kosser/Curly Putman*	Ovation 1117
3/24/79	**27**	11		3	**On Business For The King /**	*Joel Hemphill/Joe Sun*	
3/24/79	**flip**	11		4	**Blue Ribbon Blues**	*Wayland Holyfield/Jim Rushing*	Ovation 1122
9/15/79	**20**	11		5	**I'd Rather Go On Hurtin'**	*Don Goodman/Bud Reneau*	Ovation 1127
12/8/79+	**34**	11		6	**Out Of Your Mind**	*Byron Hill/Dennis Knutson*	Ovation 1137
1/26/80	**48**	7		7	**What I Had With You** *[w/ Sheila Andrews]*	*Curly Putman/Sonny Throckmorton*	Ovation 1138
3/22/80	**23**	12		8	**Shotgun Rider**	*Larry Henley/Jim Hurt/Johnny Slate*	Ovation 1141
8/16/80	**21**	11		9	**Bombed, Boozed, And Busted**	*Dennis Knutson/Joe Sun*	Ovation 1152
12/27/80+	**43**	11		10	**Ready For The Times To Get Better**	*Allen Reynolds*	Ovation 1162
3/20/82	**40**	9		11	**Holed Up In Some Honky Tonk**	*Dean Dillon/Frank Dycus/Blake Mevis*	Elektra 47417
6/19/82	**57**	7		12	**Fraulein** *[w/ Shotgun]*	*Lawton Williams*	Elektra 47467
10/2/82	**85**	2		13	**You Make Me Want To Sing**	*Candy Hemphill*	Elektra 69954
7/14/84	**73**	5		14	**Bad For Me**	*Max D. Barnes/Joe Sun*	AMI 1319
1/26/85	**77**	3		15	**Why Would I Want To Forget**	*Pebe Sebert*	AMI 1321

Billboard DEBUT	PEAK	WKS	GOLD		ARTIST / Country Chart Hit	Ranking / Songwriter	Label (& Number)
					SUNSHINE RUBY		
					Born Ruby Bateman in 1940 in Texas. Female singer.		
6/20/53	4	1			**Too Young To Tango**	A:4 *Sheb Wooley*	RCA Victor 5250
					Sonny James (fiddle)		
					SUPER GRIT COWBOY BAND		
					Group from North Carolina. Led by singers/guitarists **Curtis Wright** and Bill Ellis. **Don Cox** was once a member.		
8/1/81	71	6		1	**If You Don't Know Me By Now**	*Bill Ellis*	Hoodswamp 8002
10/24/81	64	6		2	**Carolina By The Sea**	*Clyde Mattocks*	Hoodswamp 8003
3/6/82	83	3		3	**Semi Diesel Blues**	*Jerry Dunbar*	Hoodswamp 8004
7/10/82	48	9		4	**She Is The Woman**	*Curtis Wright*	Hoodswamp 8005
4/23/83	79	4		5	**I Bought The Shoes (That Just Walked Out On Me)**	*Red Simpson/Steve Stone*	Hoodswamp 8006
					SUPERNAW, Doug		
					Born on 9/26/1960 in Bryan, Texas. Male singer/songwriter/guitarist.		
2/20/93	50	13		1	**Honky Tonkin' Fool**	*Aaron Barker*	BNA
5/22/93	4	20		2	**Reno**	*Tim Buckley/Don Crider/Joe DeLeon/Allen Huff/Ken King/Doug Supernaw/Justin White*	BNA
10/2/93	❶[2]	20		3	**I Don't Call Him Daddy**	*Reed Nielsen*	BNA
2/5/94	23	20		4	**Red And Rio Grande**	*Lonnie Atkinson/Doug Supernaw*	BNA
					above 4 from the album *Red And Rio Grande* on BNA 66133		
7/2/94	55	9		5	**State Fair**	*Mickey Cates*	BNA
9/3/94	60	7		6	**You Never Even Call Me By My Name**	*Steve Goodman*	BNA
1/14/95	16	20		7	**What'll You Do About Me**	*Dennis Linde*	BNA
					above 3 from the album *Deep Thoughts From A Shallow Mind* on BNA 66396		
10/14/95+	3[1]	21		8	**Not Enough Hours In The Night**	S:13 *Aaron Barker/Ron Harbin/Kim Williams*	Giant
3/9/96	51	10		9	**She Never Looks Back**	S:21 *Frank Dycus/Jim Lauderdale*	Giant
6/8/96	53	9		10	**You Still Got Me**	*Ken King/Doug Supernaw*	Giant
					above 3 from the album *You Still Got Me* on Giant 24639		
10/12/96	69	1		11	**Long Tall Texan** *[w/ The Beach Boys]*	*Henry Strzelecki*	River North
					from The Beach Boys' album *Stars And Stripes Vol. 1* on River North 1205		
					SUTHERLAND, Christy		
					Born in Houston, Texas; raised in Port Lavaca, Texas. Female singer/songwriter/guitarist.		
8/28/04	53	5			**Freedom**	*Gordon Bradberry/Christy Sutherland*	Epic
					SUTTON, Glenn	**SW: #19**	
					Born Royce Glenn Sutton on 9/28/1937 in Hodge, Louisiana; raised in Henderson, Texas. Male singer/songwriter. Married to **Lynn Anderson** from 1968-77.		
1/6/79	55	5		1	**The Football Card**	*Glenn Sutton* **[N]**	Mercury 55052
9/15/79	73	4		2	**Red Neck Disco**	*Lee Dresser* **[N]**	Mercury 57001
10/11/86	74	4		3	**I'll Go Steppin' Too**	*Tom James*	Mercury 884974
					SWAMPWATER		
					Group led by guitarist Floyd "Gib" Guilbeau (later played fiddle with the **Burrito Brothers**).		
6/12/71	72	2			**Take A City Bride**	*Floyd Guilbeau*	King 6376
					SWAN, Billy		
					Born on 5/12/1942 in Cape Girardeau, Missouri. Male singer/songwriter/pianist. Member of **Black Tie**.		
10/12/74	❶[2]	14	●	1	**I Can Help**	*Billy Swan*	Monument 8621
8/30/75	17	14		2	**Everything's The Same (Ain't Nothing Changed)**	*Billy Swan*	Monument 8661
3/20/76	45	9		3	**Just Want To Taste Your Wine** *[w/ The Jordanaires]*	*Bobby Emmons*	Monument 8682
9/11/76	75	5		4	**You're The One**	*Slim Corbin/Buddy Holly/Waylon Jennings*	Monument 8706
12/11/76	95	2		5	**Shake, Rattle And Roll**	*Charles Calhoun*	Columbia 10443
6/24/78	30	15		6	**Hello! Remember Me**	*Huey Meaux*	A&M 2046
12/2/78	97	3		7	**No Way Around It (It's Love)**	*Billy Swan*	A&M 2103
4/4/81	18	13		8	**Do I Have To Draw A Picture**	*Guy Clark/Billy Swan*	Epic 51000
7/25/81	18	13		9	**I'm Into Lovin' You**	*Billy Swan*	Epic 02196
11/28/81+	19	14		10	**Stuck Right In The Middle Of Your Love**	*Johnny MacRae/Bob Morrison*	Epic 02601
4/10/82	32	13		11	**With Their Kind Of Money And Our Kind Of Love**	*Don Robertson/Billy Swan*	Epic 02841
10/9/82	56	9		12	**Your Picture Still Loves Me (And I Still Love You)**	*Johnny Crutchfield/Don Robertson/Billy Swan*	Epic 03226
1/29/83	39	10		13	**Rainbows And Butterflies**	*John Flynn*	Epic 03505
6/4/83	67	8		14	**Yes**	*Don Robertson/Billy Swan*	Epic 03917
4/26/86	45	10		15	**You Must Be Lookin' For Me**	*Billy Swan*	Mercury 884668
2/7/87	63	6		16	**I'm Gonna Get You**	*Dennis Linde*	Mercury 888320
					SWEAT, Isaac Payton		
					Born in 1945 in Port Arthur, Texas; raised in Nederland, Texas. Died on 6/23/1990 (age 45). Male singer.		
9/9/78	91	4			**Shed So Many Tears**	*Elton Anderson/Eddie Shuler*	Gusto 9010
					SWEET, Rachel		
					Born on 7/28/1962 in Akron, Ohio. Female pop singer.		
6/19/76	96	4			**We Live In Two Different Worlds**	*Fred Rose*	Derrick 1000
					SWEETHEARTS OF THE RODEO		
					Duo of sisters from Manhattan Beach, California: Janis Oliver (guitar, vocals; born on 11/28/1955) and Kristine Oliver (vocals; born on 3/1/1957). Janis was married to **Vince Gill** from 1980-97.		
4/5/86	21	15		1	**Hey Doll Baby**	S:12 / A:25 *Titus Turner*	Columbia 05824
7/26/86	7	22		2	**Since I Found You**	S:7 / A:7 *Radney Foster/Bill Lloyd*	Columbia 06166

DEBUT	PEAK	WKS	GOLD	#	ARTIST / Country Chart Hit	Ranking / Songwriter	Label (& Number)
					SWEETHEARTS OF THE RODEO — cont'd		
11/29/86+	**4**	22		3	**Midnight Girl/Sunset Town**	S:3 / A:4 *Don Schlitz*	Columbia 06525
4/4/87	**4**	17		4	**Chains Of Gold**	S:3 / A:17 *Paul Kennerley*	Columbia 07023
9/12/87	**10**	18		5	**Gotta Get Away**	S:11 *Janis Gill*	Columbia 07314
4/2/88	**5**	20		6	**Satisfy You**	S:2 *Janis Gill/Don Schlitz*	Columbia 07757
8/6/88	**5**	20		7	**Blue To The Bone**	S:❶^{1} *Michael Garvin/Bucky Jones*	Columbia 07985
12/3/88+	**9**	22		8	**I Feel Fine**	S:29 *John Lennon/Paul McCartney*	Columbia 08504
4/15/89	**39**	11		9	**If I Never See Midnight Again**	*Craig Bickhardt/Don Schlitz*	Columbia 68684
1/13/90	**25**	15		10	**This Heart** from the album *Buffalo Zone* on Columbia 45373	*Tony Haselden/Tim Mensy*	Columbia
8/24/91	**63**	4		11	**Hard-Headed Man**	*Cynthia Landis/Don Schlitz*	Columbia
11/9/91	**74**	1		12	**Devil And Your Deep Blue Eyes** above 2 from the album *Sisters* on Columbia 47658	*Lee Roy Parnell/Russell Smith*	Columbia
					SWEETWATER Gospel-based group led by Willie Wynn of **The Tennesseans**. Member **Darrell Holt** went solo in 1987.		
8/8/81	**84**	4		1	**Antioch Church House Choir /**	*Darrell Holt*	
10/17/81	**75**	4		2	**I'd Throw It All Away**	*Darrell Holt*	Faucet 1592
					SWING SHIFT BAND, The Group features Buddy Emmons and **Ray Pennington**.		
11/12/88	**76**	3			**(Turn Me Loose And) Let Me Swing**	*Ray Pennington*	Step One 392

SYLVIA — **All-Time: #193**

Born Sylvia Kirby on 12/9/1956 in Kokomo, Indiana. Female singer/songwriter. Sang in church choir from age three. Worked as a secretary for producer Tom Collins. Did session backup vocals. Made stage debut as a soloist in the fall of 1979.

DEBUT	PEAK	WKS	GOLD	#	Country Chart Hit	Songwriter	Label (& Number)
10/13/79	**36**	10		1	**You Don't Miss A Thing**	*Kye Fleming/Dennis W. Morgan*	RCA 11735
4/26/80	**35**	11		2	**It Don't Hurt To Dream**	*Dan Pate/Jean Pate/Charles Quillen*	RCA 11958
9/6/80	**10**	16		3	**Tumbleweed**	*Kye Fleming/Dennis W. Morgan*	RCA 12077
1/17/81	❶^{1}	14		4	**Drifter**	*Archie Jordan/Don Pfrimmer*	RCA 12164
4/25/81	**7**	16		5	**The Matador**	*Bob Morris/Don Pfrimmer*	RCA 12214
9/12/81	**8**	15		6	**Heart On The Mend**	*Kye Fleming/Dennis W. Morgan*	RCA 12302
1/16/82	**12**	15		7	**Sweet Yesterday**	*Kye Fleming/Dennis W. Morgan*	RCA 13020
6/5/82	❶^{1}	24	●	8	**Nobody**	*Kye Fleming/Dennis W. Morgan*	RCA 13223
10/30/82+	**2^{2}**	20		9	**Like Nothing Ever Happened**	*Kye Fleming/Dennis W. Morgan*	RCA 13330
2/19/83	**57**	11		10	**The Wayward Wind** ***[w/ James Galway]***	*Stan Lebowsky/Herb Newman*	RCA 13441
5/7/83	**5**	18		11	**Snapshot**	*Rhonda Fleming/Dennis W. Morgan*	RCA 13501
8/27/83	**18**	17		12	**The Boy Gets Around**	*Rhonda Fleming/Dennis W. Morgan*	RCA 13589
12/3/83+	**3^{2}**	19		13	**I Never Quite Got Back (From Loving You)**	*Don Pfrimmer/Mike Reid*	RCA 13689
4/7/84	**24**	14		14	**Victims Of Goodbye**	*Dennis W. Morgan/Don Pfrimmer*	RCA 13755
7/7/84	**36**	13		15	**Love Over Old Times**	*Lisa Angelle/Mike Reid*	RCA 13838
2/16/85	**2^{2}**	22		16	**Fallin' In Love**	S:2 / A:2 *Randy Goodrum/Brent Maher*	RCA 13997
6/29/85	**9**	18		17	**Cry Just A Little Bit**	A:8 / S:9 *Bob Heatlie*	RCA 14107
11/16/85+	**9**	25		18	**I Love You By Heart** ***[w/ Michael Johnson]***	A:9 / S:10 *Jerry Gillespie/Stan Webb*	RCA 14217
7/5/86	**33**	15		19	**Nothin' Ventured Nothin' Gained**	*Brent Maher/Don Potter/Don Schlitz*	RCA 14375
5/16/87	**66**	6		20	**Straight From My Heart**	*Jimmy Fortune/Sylvia Rutledge*	RCA 5127
					SYLVIE & HER SILVER DOLLAR BAND Group from Miami, Florida.		
7/1/89	**95**	2			**Where You Gonna Hang Your Hat**	*Jim Cox*	Playback 75711

T

DEBUT	PEAK	WKS	GOLD	#	Country Chart Hit	Songwriter	Label (& Number)
					TACKETT, Marlow Born in Dorton, Kentucky. Male singer/songwriter/guitarist.		
1/19/80	**95**	2		1	**Would You Know Love**	*Sonny Tackett*	Palace 1006
4/26/80	**93**	2		2	**Midnight Fire**	*Sonny Tackett*	Palace 1008
11/15/80	**92**	3		3	**Ride That Bull (Big Bertha)**	*John Gilbert/Marlow Tackett*	Kari 114
7/10/82	**67**	6		4	**Ever-Lovin' Woman**	*Dan Devaney/Dennis Linde*	RCA 13255
10/23/82	**54**	9		5	**634-5789**	*Steve Cropper/Eddie Floyd*	RCA 13347
4/23/83	**67**	6		6	**I Know My Way To You By Heart**	*Tony Laiolo*	RCA 13471
8/6/83	**56**	8		7	**I Spent The Night In The Heart Of Texas**	*Blake Mevis/Don Pfrimmer/David Wills*	RCA 13579
					TAFF, Russ Born on 11/11/1953 in Farmersville, California. Contemporary Christian singer/songwriter.		
1/14/95	**53**	9		1	**Love Is Not A Thing**	*Mark Cawley/Kye Fleming/Mary Ann Kennedy*	Reprise
4/1/95	**51**	10		2	**One And Only Love**	*Steven Jones/Bobby Tomberlin*	Reprise
7/29/95	**66**	4		3	**Bein' Happy** above 3 from the album *Winds Of Change* on Reprise 45676	*Russ Taff/Tori Taff*	Reprise

DEBUT	PEAK	WKS	GOLD	ARTIST / Country Chart Hit	Ranking / Songwriter	Label (& Number)
				TALBERT, Bubba		
				Born in 1949 in Blanchard, Louisiana. Male singer/songwriter.		
4/9/83	**81**	3		1 **Easy Catch**	*Bubba Talbert*	Ranger 5734
7/23/83	**77**	3		2 **Downright Broke My Heart**	*Bubba Talbert*	Ranger 702
				TALL, Tom		
				Born Tommie Lee Guthrie on 12/17/1937 in Amarillo, Texas. Male singer.		
1/1/55	**2^{3}**	26		1 **Are You Mine** ***[w/ Ginny Wright]***	A:2 / J:4 / S:5 *Jim Amadeo/Don Grashey/Myrna Lorrie*	Fabor 117
1/4/64	**25**	1		2 **Bad, Bad Tuesday**	*Del Reeves/Ellen Reeves*	Petal 1210
				TALLEY, James		
				Born on 11/9/1943 in Mehan, Oklahoma. Male singer/songwriter/guitarist.		
3/13/76	**75**	8		1 **Tryin' Like The Devil**	*James Talley*	Capitol 4218
7/24/76	**61**	9		2 **Are They Gonna Make Us Outlaws Again**	*James Talley*	Capitol 4297
4/23/77	**83**	4		3 **Alabama Summertime**	*James Talley*	Capitol 4410
				TAMMY JO		
				Born Tammy Jo Whitehead in Tennessee. Female singer.		
3/15/80	**88**	3		1 **I Go To Pieces**	*Del Shannon*	Ridgetop 00880
6/14/80	**76**	4		2 **Love Talking /**	*Chip Hardy/Sam Lorber*	
6/14/80	**flip**	4		3 **Wishing Well**	*Chip Hardy/Sam Lorber*	Ridgetop 00980
				TANNER, Fargo		
				Born in Little Rock, Arkansas; raised in Dallas, Texas. Male singer.		
6/7/75	**69**	11		**Don't Drop It**	*Terry Fell*	Avco 612
				TAPP, Demetriss		
				Born in North Carolina. Female singer.		
9/15/73	**97**	3		**Skinny Dippin'**	*Gary S. Paxton*	ABC 11383
				TATE, Michael		
				Born in California. Male singer.		
3/7/81	**93**	2		**Mexican Girl**	*Chris Nelson*	Oak 47102
				TAYLOR, Carmol	**SW: #56**	
				Born on 9/5/1931 in Brilliant, Alabama. Died of cancer on 12/5/1986 (age 55). Male singer/songwriter.		
6/28/75	**48**	11		1 **Back In The U.S.A.**	*Chuck Berry*	Elektra 45255
10/4/75	**91**	5		2 **Who Will I Be Loving Now**	*Carmol Taylor/Agnes Wilson*	Elektra 45277
2/14/76	**35**	12		3 **Play The Saddest Song On The Juke Box**	*Linda McGraw/Carmol Taylor*	Elektra 45299
5/8/76	**23**	11		4 **I Really Had A Ball Last Night**	*Wayne Kemp*	Elektra 45312
9/18/76	**53**	6		5 **That Little Difference**	*Monroe Fields/Carmol Taylor*	Elektra 45342
1/8/77	**87**	5		6 **Neon Women** ***[w/ Stella Parton]***	*Bobbi Cole/Toni Dae/Carmol Taylor*	Elektra 45367
1/22/77	**100**	1		7 **What Would I Do Then?**	*Carmol Taylor/Norro Wilson*	Elektra 45366
7/23/77	**80**	5		8 **Good Cheatin' Songs**	*David Malloy/Carmol Taylor*	Elektra 45409
				TAYLOR, Chet		
				Born in Dallas, Texas. Male singer.		
8/4/79	**92**	2		**Barefoot Angel**	*Alice Keister/Bob Morrison*	Vista 108
				TAYLOR, Chip		
				Born James Voigt in 1940 in Yonkers, New York. Male singer/songwriter. Brother of actor Jon Voigt.		
1/4/75	**80**	6		1 **Me As I Am**	*Chip Taylor*	Warner 8050
5/17/75	**28**	10		2 **Early Sunday Morning**	*Chip Taylor*	Warner 8090
9/13/75	**61**	7		3 **Big River**	*Johnny Cash*	Warner 8128
1/10/76	**92**	4		4 **Circle Of Tears**	*Chip Taylor*	Warner 8159
1/8/77	**93**	4		5 **Hello Atlanta** ***[w/ Ghost Train]***	*Chip Taylor*	Columbia 10446
				TAYLOR, Frank		
				Born in Philadelphia, Pennsylvania. Male singer.		
6/1/63	**28**	1		**Snow White Cloud**	*Ott Stephens/Slim Williamson*	Parkway 869
				TAYLOR, James		
				Born on 3/12/1948 in Boston, Massachusetts. Singer/songwriter/guitarist. Married to **Carly Simon** from 1972-83. Brother of **Livingston Taylor**. Recipient of *Billboard's* Century Award in 1998. Inducted into the Rock and Roll Hall of Fame in 2000.		
7/16/77	**88**	3		1 **Bartender's Blues**	*James Taylor*	Columbia 10557
9/9/78	**33**	10		2 **Devoted To You** ***[w/ Carly Simon]***	*Boudleaux Bryant*	Elektra 45506
12/7/85+	**26**	16		3 **Everyday**	S:25 / A:27 *Buddy Holly/Norman Petty*	Columbia 05681
3/15/86	**80**	9		4 **Only One**	*James Taylor*	Columbia 05785
				TAYLOR, Jim		
				Born in Chicago, Illinois. Male singer.		
8/5/78	**100**	1		1 **I'll Still Need You Mary Ann**	*Buddy Lee*	Checkmate 3069
12/9/78+	**68**	10		2 **Leave It To Love**	*Joe Hunter/Jim Whiting*	Checkmate 3106
				TAYLOR, Judy		
				Born in Murfreesboro, Tennessee. Female singer.		
1/9/82	**84**	3		1 **A Married Man**	*Bobby Braddock*	Warner 49859
5/22/82	**79**	4		2 **A Step In The Right Direction**	*Richard Grossman*	Warner 50061
9/25/82	**70**	4		3 **The End Of The World**	*Sylvia Dee/Arthur Kent*	Warner 29913

DEBUT	PEAK	WKS	GOLD	ARTIST / Country Chart Hit	Songwriter	Label (& Number)
				TAYLOR, Les		
				Born on 12/27/1948 in Oneida, Kentucky; raised in London, Kentucky. Male singer/songwriter. Member of **Exile** from 1979-89. Also see **Tomorrow's World**.		
11/25/89	**46**	11		1 **Shoulda, Coulda, Woulda Loved You**	*Ron Moore/Les Taylor/Lonnie Wilson*	Epic 73063
4/28/90	**58**	10		2 **Knowin' You Were Leavin'**	*Mike Reid/Tommy Rocco*	Epic
				from the album *That Old Desire* on Epic 45329		
3/9/91	**44**	12		3 **I Gotta Mind To Go Crazy**	*Ron Moore/Don Pfrimmer*	Epic
				from the album *Blue Kentucky Wind* on Epic 47096		
7/27/91	**50**	9		4 **The Very First Lasting Love** *[w/ Shelby Lynne]*	*Paul Hollowell/Les Taylor/Lonnie Wilson*	Epic
				from Lynne's album *Soft Talk* on Epic 47388		
				TAYLOR, Livingston		
				Born on 11/21/1950 in Boston, Massachusetts. Male singer/songwriter/guitarist. Younger brother of **James Taylor**.		
10/22/88	**94**	2		**Loving Arms** *[w/ Leah Kunkel]*	*Tom Jans*	Critique 99275
				TAYLOR, Mary		
				Born on 5/28/1945 in California. Female singer/songwriter. Regular on TV's *Hee Haw* from 1969-70.		
1/7/67	**72**	4		1 **Don't Waste Your Time**	*Mary Taylor*	Capitol 5776
6/22/68	**44**	8		2 **If I Don't Like The Way You Love Me**	*Mary Taylor*	Dot 17104
11/23/68	**51**	7		3 **Feed Me One More Lie**	*Dallas Frazier*	Dot 17168
				TAYLOR, R. Dean		
				Born in 1939 in Toronto, Ontario, Canada. Male singer/songwriter.		
1/15/83	**90**	2		**Let's Talk It Over**	*R. Dean Taylor*	Strummer 3748
				TAYLOR-GOOD, Karen		
				Born Karen Berke in El Paso, Texas. Female singer/songwriter.		
3/6/82	**38**	11		1 **Diamond In The Rough** *[Karen Taylor]*	*Taylor Sparks*	Mesa 1111
7/24/82	**67**	7		2 **Country Boy's Song** *[Karen Taylor]*	*John F. Dockery/Taylor Sparks*	Mesa 1112
11/20/82	**62**	9		3 **I'd Rather Be Doing Nothing With You**	*Taylor Sparks/Karen Taylor-Good*	Mesa 1113
3/5/83	**42**	11		4 **Tenderness Place**	*Larry Henley/Mark Mathis*	Mesa 1114
8/27/83	**62**	7		5 **Don't Call Me**	*Taylor Sparks/Karen Taylor-Good*	Mesa 1115
1/7/84	**62**	10		6 **Handsome Man**	*Patty Cloar/Bob Sargent/Jane Sargent/Taylor Sparks/Karen Taylor-Good*	Mesa 1116
9/8/84	**66**	7		7 **We Just Gotta Dance**	*Jerry Gillespie*	Mesa 1117
4/6/85	**61**	7		8 **Starlite**	*Taylor Sparks/Karen Taylor-Good*	Mesa 1118
10/5/85	**57**	8		9 **Up On Your Love**	*Kerry O'Neil/Will Robinson*	Mesa 1119
5/10/86	**79**	4		10 **Come In Planet Earth (Are You Listenin')**	*Kent MacDonald/Lanny Smith*	Mesa 2011
				TEBEY		
				Born in 1983 in Burlington, Ontario, Canada (Canadian mother; African father). Male singer. Name pronounced: Tay-Bay.		
1/18/03	**47**	9		**We Shook Hands (Man To Man)**	*Andre Pessis/Steve Seskin*	BNA
				TENNESSEANS, The		
				Group formed by Willie Wynn (later with **Sweetwater**). Included Tony King who was later with **Matthews, Wright & King**.		
12/2/78	**81**	5		**Nineteen-Sixty Something Songwriter Of The Year**	*John Adrian*	Capitol 4645
				TENNESSEE EXPRESS		
				Vocal group formed in Nashville, Tennessee. Consisted of two men and two women.		
8/15/81	**31**	11		1 **Big Like A River**	*Jerry Duncan/Aaron Wilburn*	RCA 12277
12/12/81	**75**	4		2 **Little Things**	*Bobby Goldsboro*	RCA 12362
4/3/82	**70**	4		3 **The Arms Of A Stranger**	*Alice Mills/Tommy Smith*	RCA 13078
7/24/82	**78**	5		4 **Operator /**	*William Spivery*	
7/24/82	**flip**	5		5 **Let Me In And Let Me Love You**	*Red Lane/Alice Mills*	RCA 13265
2/5/83	**62**	7		6 **How Long Will It Take**	*Warner Mack*	RCA 13423
6/4/83	**65**	6		7 **Cotton Fields**	*Huddie Ledbetter*	RCA 13526
				TENNESSEE PULLEYBONE		
				Group formed in Cookeville, Tennessee: Ken Smith (vocals, bass), Jerry Tuttle (vocals, guitar), Biff Watson (guitar) and John Wolters (drums). Wolters later joined **Dr. Hook**; died of cancer on 6/16/1997 (age 52).		
9/8/73	**75**	4		**The Door's Always Open**	*Dickey Lee/Bob McDill*	JMI 25
				TENNESSEE TORNADO — see FOSTER, Jerry		
				TENNESSEE VALLEY BOYS		
				Vocal group: Rick Baird, Jimmy Ponder, James Fulbright and Dan Britton. Assembled by Wally Fowler (born on 2/15/1917; died on 6/3/1994, age 77). Fowler also created the Oak Ridge Quartet (which evolved into the **Oak Ridge Boys**).		
4/14/84	**57**	10		**Lo And Behold**	*Don Goodman/Becky Hobbs/Johnny Rodriguez*	Nashwood 12684
				WALLY FOWLER'S TENNESSEE VALLEY BOYS		
				TENNISON, Chalee		
				Born on 4/11/1969 in Freeport, Texas. Female singer/songwriter.		
4/17/99	**46**	16		1 **Someone Else's Turn To Cry**	*Jim Robinson/Chalee Tennison*	Asylum
8/21/99	**64**	6		2 **Handful Of Water**	*Austin Cunningham/Allison Mellon/Jason Sellers*	Asylum
12/18/99+	**36**	19		3 **Just Because She Lives There**	*Dale Dodson/Billy Lawson*	Asylum
				above 3 from the album *Chalee Tennison* on Asylum 62371		
9/16/00	**56**	8		4 **Makin' Up With You**	*Jeremy Campbell/Phil O'Donnell*	Asylum
11/18/00+	**36**	21		5 **Go Back**	*Jeremy Campbell/Donny Hackett*	Asylum
				above 2 from the album *This Woman's Heart* on Warner 47820		
11/9/02	**54**	5		6 **Lonesome Road**	*Ashley Gorley/Melissa Pierce/Bryan Simpson*	DreamWorks
5/8/04	**5**[S]	1		7 **Easy Lovin' You**	*Amber White/Phillip White*	DreamWorks
				above 2 from the album *Parading In The Rain* on DreamWorks 450374		

Billboard DEBUT	PEAK	WKS	GOLD	ARTIST / Country Chart Hit	Ranking / Songwriter	Label (& Number)
				TERRY, Al		
				Born Allison Theriot on 1/14/1922 in Kaplan, Louisiana. Died on 11/23/1985 (age 63). Male singer/guitarist.		
4/24/54	**8**	5		1 **Good Deal, Lucille**	A:8 / J:8 *Joe Miller/Al Terry/Charles Theriot*	Hickory 1003
2/29/60	**28**	1		2 **Watch Dog**	*Bob Terry*	Hickory 1111
				TERRY, Gordon		
				Born on 10/7/1931 in Decatur, Alabama. Male singer/songwriter/fiddler.		
5/30/70	**62**	5		**The Ballad Of J.C.**	*Gordon Terry* [N]	Capitol 2792
				tribute to **Johnny Cash** to the tune of "The Ballad Of New Orleans"		
				TEXAS PLAYBOYS — see ORIGINAL TEXAS PLAYBOYS		
				TEXAS VOCAL COMPANY		
				Vocal trio from Dallas, Texas: Sandy Skinner, Dick Root and Dave Roth.		
4/30/83	**65**	5		1 **Two Hearts**	*Blake Mevis/Bill Shore/David Wills*	RCA 13504
10/8/83	**82**	3		2 **It Had To Be You**	*Blake Mevis/Bill Shore/David Wills*	RCA 13566
				THOMAS, B.J.	**All-Time: #266**	
				Born Billy Joe Thomas on 8/7/1942 in Hugo, Oklahoma; raised in Rosenberg, Texas. Male singer/songwriter.		
				OPRY: 1981		
2/22/75	**❶**[1]	16	●	1 **(Hey Won't You Play) Another Somebody Done Somebody Wrong Song** Grammy: Song	*Larry Butler/Chips Moman*	ABC 12054
10/4/75	**37**	10		2 **Help Me Make It (To My Rockin' Chair)**	*Bobby Emmons*	ABC 12121
5/14/77	**98**	1		3 **Home Where I Belong**	*Pat Terry*	Myrrh 166
1/28/78	**25**	13		4 **Everybody Loves A Rain Song**	*Mark James/Chips Moman*	MCA 40854
2/10/79	**86**	3		5 **We Could Have Been The Closest Of Friends**	*Steve Pippin/Johnny Slate*	MCA 40986
4/18/81	**27**	11		6 **Some Love Songs Never Die**	*Alice Kiester/Johnny MacRae/Bob Morrison*	MCA 51087
8/8/81	**22**	12		7 **I Recall A Gypsy Woman**	*Bob McDill/Allen Reynolds*	MCA 51151
2/12/83	**❶**[1]	21		8 **Whatever Happened To Old Fashioned Love**	*Lewis Anderson*	Cleveland Int'l. 03492
7/9/83	**❶**[1]	21		9 **New Looks From An Old Lover**	*Lathan Hudson/Red Lane/Gloria Thomas*	Columbia 03985
11/26/83+	**3**[1]	21		10 **Two Car Garage**	*Greg Harrison/J.D. Martin*	Cleveland Int'l 04237
4/14/84	**10**	19		11 **The Whole World's In Love When You're Lonely**	*Fred Knoblock/Dan Tyler*	Cleveland Int'l 04431
8/4/84	**14**	18		12 **Rock And Roll Shoes** *[w/ Ray Charles]*	S:14 / A:21 *Paul Kennerley/Graham Lyle*	Columbia 04531
10/20/84+	**17**	19		13 **The Girl Most Likely To**	S:17 / A:17 *Wood Newton/Steve Pippin*	Cleveland Int'l 04608
11/9/85	**61**	11		14 **The Part Of Me That Needs You Most**	*Mike Chapman/Nicky Chinn*	Columbia 05647
2/22/86	**62**	7		15 **America Is**	*Hal David/Joe Raposo*	Columbia 05771
10/4/86	**59**	6		16 **Night Life**	*Walt Breeland/Paul Buskirk/Willie Nelson*	Columbia 06314
7/29/00	**66**	1		17 **You Call That A Mountain**	*Michael Garvin/Bucky Jones*	Kardina
				from the album *You Call That A Mountain* on Kardina 241		
				THOMAS, Darrell		
				Born in 1952 in Melcher, Iowa. Male singer/songwriter.		
5/19/79	**99**	3		**Waylon, Sing To Mama**	*Darrell Thomas*	Ozark Opry 101
				THOMAS, Dick	**1940s: #29**	
				Born Richard Thomas Goldhahn on 9/4/1915 in Philadelphia, Pennsylvania. Died on 11/22/2003 (age 88). Male singer/songwriter/fiddler. Acted in several western movies.		
9/29/45	**❶**[4]	23		1 **Sioux City Sue**	*Ray Freedman/Dick Thomas*	National 5007
12/8/45	**4**	1		2 **Honestly**	*Johnny Fortis/Max Spickol*	National 5008
9/25/48	**13**	1		3 **The Beaut From Butte**	J:13 *Max Freedman/Dick Thomas*	Decca 46132
2/12/49	**12**	1		4 **The Sister Of Sioux City Sue**	J:12 / S:14 *Max Freedman/Dick Thomas*	Decca 46147
				DICK THOMAS And His Nashville Ramblers (above 2)		
				THOMAS, Jeff		
				Born in Reno, Nevada. Male singer.		
1/17/87	**85**	3		**Hollywood's Dream**	*Doug Hauseman/Ron Moore*	Revolver 014
				THOMAS, Keni		
				Born in Gainesville, Florida. Male singer/songwriter/guitarist.		
12/11/04+	**47**	20		**Not Me** *[w/ Vince Gill & Emmylou Harris]*	*Brent Maher/Billy Montana/Keni Thomas*	Moraine
				from Thomas's album *Flags Of Our Fathers* on Moraine 2350		

Billboard DEBUT	PEAK	WKS	GOLD	ARTIST / Country Chart Hit	Ranking / Songwriter	Label (& Number)
				THOMPSON, Hank	**1940s: #16 / 1950s: #11 / 1960s: #50 / All-Time: #42 // HOF: 1989**	
				Born on 9/3/1925 in Waco, Texas. Male singer/songwriter/guitarist. On WACO radio as a teenager, billed as "Hank, The Hired Hand." Served in the U.S. Navy during World War II. First recorded for Globe in 1946. Backing group: The Brazos Valley Boys.		
				HANK THOMPSON and His Brazos Valley Boys:		
1/31/48	**2**[2]	38		1 **Humpty Dumpty Heart**	J:2 / S:3 *Hank Thompson*	Capitol Amer. 40065
9/4/48	**12**	2		2 **Yesterday's Mail**	J:12 *Hank Thompson*	Capitol 15132
10/16/48	**7**	10		3 **Green Light**	J:7 / S:8 *Hank Thompson*	Capitol 15187
				also see #21 below		
2/5/49	**10**	1		4 **What Are We Gonna Do About The Moonlight**	J:10 *Hank Thompson*	Capitol 15132
2/5/49	**14**	1		5 **I Find You Cheatin' On Me /**	S:14 *Hank Thompson*	
2/12/49	**15**	1		6 **You Broke My Heart (In Little Bitty Pieces)**	J:15 *Hank Thompson*	Capitol 15345

DEBUT	PEAK	WKS	GOLD		ARTIST / Country Chart Hit	Ranking	Songwriter	Label (& Number)
					THOMPSON, Hank — cont'd			
10/1/49	6	7		7	Whoa Sailor	J:6 / S:8	*Hank Thompson*	Capitol 40218
10/1/49	10	1		8	Soft Lips /	J:10	*Walt McCoy*	
11/5/49	15	1		9	The Grass Looks Greener Over Yonder	J:15	*Hank Thompson*	Capitol 40211
3/15/52	❶[15]	30		10	The Wild Side Of Life	S:❶[15] / J:❶[15] / A:❶[8]	*Arlie Carter/William Warren*	Capitol F1942
					Grammy: Hall of Fame			
6/28/52	3[1]	15		11	Waiting In The Lobby Of Your Heart	J:3 / S:5 / A:7	*Billy Gray/Hank Thompson*	Capitol F2063
12/13/52	10	1		12	The New Wears Off Too Fast	J:10	*Billy Gray/Hank Thompson*	Capitol F2269
3/28/53	9	2		13	No Help Wanted	J:9 / S:10 / A:10	*Bill Carlisle*	Capitol 2376
5/23/53	❶[3]	20		14	Rub-A-Dub-Dub	J:❶[3] / A:2 / S:5	*Hank Thompson*	Capitol 2445
9/19/53	8	4		15	Yesterday's Girl	S:8 / A:8	*Billy Gray/Hank Thompson*	Capitol 2553
12/12/53+	❶[2]	19		16	Wake Up, Irene	J:❶[2] / S:3 / A:4	*Weldon Allard/John Hathcock*	Capitol 2646
					answer to "Goodnight, Irene" by **Red Foley** & **Ernest Tubb**			
5/8/54	10	2		17	Breakin' The Rules /	S:10	*Al Blasigame/Billy Gray/Hank Thompson*	
5/22/54	9	1		18	A Fooler, A Faker	J:9 / S:15	*Billy Gray/Hank Thompson*	Capitol 2758
7/3/54	9	12		19	Honky-Tonk Girl /	S:9 / J:10 / A:11	*Chuck Harding/Hank Thompson*	
					also see #72 below			
7/17/54	10	4		20	We've Gone Too Far	S:10 / A:15	*Billy Gray/Hank Thompson*	Capitol 2823
10/16/54	3[4]	20		21	The New Green Light	J:3 / S:7 / A:8	*Hank Thompson*	Capitol 2920
					new version of #3 above			
2/26/55	12	4		22	If Lovin' You Is Wrong /	S:12 / A:14	*Billy Gray/Hank Thompson*	
3/12/55	13	2		23	Annie Over	S:13	*Don Clay/Billy Gray/Hank Thompson*	Capitol 3030
6/4/55	5	9		24	Wildwood Flower *[w/ Merle Travis]* /	J:5 / S:8 / A:13	*A.P. Carter/Hank Thompson* [I]	
6/4/55	7	8		25	Breakin' In Another Heart	S:7	*Billy Gray/Dorothy Thompson/Hank Thompson*	Capitol 3106
8/20/55	6	11		26	Most Of All	A:6 / S:11	*Hank Thompson*	Capitol 3188
12/10/55	5	7		27	Don't Take It Out On Me /	S:5 / J:9 / A:13	*Hank Thompson*	
12/17/55	flip	5		28	Honey, Honey Bee Ball	S:flip / J:flip	*Jerry Hamilton*	Capitol 3275
3/24/56	4	22		29	The Blackboard Of My Heart /	A:4 / J:6 / S:6	*Lyle Gaston/Hank Thompson*	
3/24/56	14	5		30	I'm Not Mad, Just Hurt	S:14 / J:flip	*Lila DeRushe/Orville Proctor*	Capitol 3347
2/23/57	13	4		31	Rockin' In The Congo /	S:13	*Orville Proctor*	
					also see #78 below			
3/16/57	flip	2		32	I Was The First One	S:flip	*Dorothy Thompson/Hank Thompson*	Capitol 3623
10/14/57	14	2		33	Tears Are Only Rain	A:14	*Weldon Allard/John Hathcock*	Capitol 3781
6/9/58	11	3		34	How Do You Hold A Memory	A:11	*Lyle Gaston/Orville Proctor*	Capitol 3950
8/18/58	2[4]	22		35	Squaws Along The Yukon	J:5 / S:10	*Cam Smith*	Capitol 4017
12/1/58+	7	23		36	I've Run Out Of Tomorrows /		*Harry Compton/Vernon Mize/Orville Proctor*	
2/2/59	26	3		37	You're Going Back To Your Old Ways Again		*Billy Gray/Hank Thompson*	Capitol 4085
5/11/59	13	10		38	Anybody's Girl /		*Billy Gray/Hank Thompson*	
6/29/59	25	1		39	Total Strangers		*Hank Thompson*	Capitol 4182
11/9/59+	22	10		40	I Didn't Mean To Fall In Love		*Hank Thompson*	Capitol 4269
3/21/60	10	16		41	A Six Pack To Go		*Hank Thompson*	Capitol 4334
8/1/60	14	14		42	She's Just A Whole Lot Like You		*Hank Thompson*	Capitol 4386
5/29/61	7	11		43	Oklahoma Hills /		*Jack Guthrie/Woody Guthrie*	
5/29/61	25	2		44	Teach Me How To Lie		*Hank Thompson*	Capitol 4556
9/18/61	12	10		45	Hangover Tavern		*Johnny Lowe/Hank Thompson*	Capitol 4605
9/7/63	23	1		46	I Wasn't Even In The Running		*Hank Thompson*	Capitol 4968
9/28/63	22	5		47	Too In Love		*Ned Fairchild/Merle Travis*	Capitol 5008
1/11/64	45	2		48	Twice As Much		*Bob Blanchard/Billy Gray/Hank Thompson*	Capitol 5071
8/14/65	42	2		49	Then I'll Start Believing In You		*Will Penix/Hank Thompson*	Capitol 5422
10/22/66	15	14		50	Where Is The Circus		*Bobby Bishop/Hank Thompson*	Warner 5858
2/4/67	16	13		51	He's Got A Way With Women		*Rodney Lay/Hank Thompson*	Warner 5886
					HANK THOMPSON:			
7/13/68	7	15		52	On Tap, In The Can, Or In The Bottle		*Dick Hart/Hank Thompson*	Dot 17108
10/26/68+	5	15		53	Smoky The Bar		*Will Penix/Hank Thompson*	Dot 17163
3/8/69	47	9		54	I See Them Everywhere		*Tommy Higgins/Hank Thompson*	Dot 17207
7/12/69	46	9		55	The Pathway Of My Life		*Red Lane*	Dot 17262
10/18/69	60	6		56	Oklahoma Home Brew		*Will Penix/Hank Thompson*	Dot 17307
5/9/70	54	5		57	But That's All Right		*Red Lane*	Dot 17347
10/10/70	69	4		58	One Of The Fortunate Few		*Charlie Williams*	Dot 17354
3/6/71	15	14		59	Next Time I Fall In Love (I Won't)		*Ned Miller*	Dot 17365
7/17/71	18	16		60	The Mark Of A Heel		*Neal Merritt/Gene Wilson*	Dot 17385
12/4/71+	11	14		61	I've Come Awful Close		*Ann J. Morton*	Dot 17399
4/29/72	16	12		62	Cab Driver		*Carson Parks*	Dot 17410
9/23/72	53	8		63	Glow Worm		*Paul Lincke/Johnny Mercer/Lilla Robinson*	Dot 17430
3/17/73	70	2		64	Roses In The Wine		*Buckley Maxwell/Steve Stone*	Dot 17447
9/1/73	48	9		65	Kindly Keep It Country		*Paul Gailey/Hank Thompson*	Dot 17470
2/2/74	8	15		66	The Older The Violin, The Sweeter The Music		*Curly Putman*	Dot 17490
7/13/74	10	16		67	Who Left The Door To Heaven Open		*Betty Duke*	Dot 17512
1/25/75	29	10		68	Mama Don't 'Low		*Hank Thompson*	ABC/Dot 17535
6/28/75	70	8		69	That's Just My Truckin' Luck		*Bobby Barker/Johnny Koonse*	ABC/Dot 17556
3/6/76	72	6		70	Asphalt Cowboy		*Clark Bentley/Lawton Williams*	ABC/Dot 17612
9/4/76	86	3		71	Big Band Days		*Joe Allen*	ABC/Dot 17649

DEBUT	PEAK	WKS	GOLD	ARTIST / Ranking / Country Chart Hit	Songwriter	Label (& Number)
				THOMPSON, Hank — cont'd		
1/15/77	**91**	4		72 **Honky Tonk Girl** new version of #19 above	*Chuck Harding/Hank Thompson* **[R]**	ABC/Dot 17673
5/21/77	**92**	2		73 **Just An Old Flame**	*Bob Robinson/Hank Thompson*	ABC/Dot 17695
10/21/78	**92**	3		74 **I'm Just Gettin' By**	*Jerry Foster/Bill Rice*	ABC 12409
3/3/79	**88**	3		75 **Dance With Me Molly**	*Roger Bowling/Steve Tutsie*	ABC 12447
8/25/79	**29**	12		76 **I Hear The South Callin' Me**	*R.C. Bannon/John Bettis*	MCA 41079
2/2/80	**32**	9		77 **Tony's Tank-Up, Drive-In Cafe**	*Glenn Sutton*	MCA 41176
12/19/81+	**82**	5		78 **Rockin' In The Congo** new version of #31 above	*Hank Thompson* **[R]**	Churchill 7779
7/23/83	**82**	5		79 **Once In A Blue Moon**	*Marc Rossi*	Churchill 94026

Annie Over ['55]
Anybody's Girl ['59]
Asphalt Cowboy ['76]
Big Band Days ['76]
Blackboard Of My Heart ['56]
Breakin' In Another Heart ['55]
Breakin' The Rules ['54]
But That's All Right ['70]
Cab Driver ['72]
Dance With Me Molly ['79]
Don't Take It Out On Me ['55]
Fooler, A Faker ['54]
Glow Worm ['72]
Grass Looks Greener Over Yonder ['49]
Green Light ['48]
Hangover Tavern ['61]
He's Got A Way With Women ['67]
Honey, Honey Bee Ball ['55]
Honky-Tonk Girl ['54, '77]
How Do You Hold A Memory ['58]
Humpty Dumpty Heart ['48]
I Didn't Mean To Fall In Love ['60]
I Find You Cheatin' On Me ['49]
I Hear The South Callin' Me ['79]
I See Them Everywhere ['69]
I Was The First One ['57]
I Wasn't Even In The Running ['63]
I'm Just Gettin' By ['78]
I'm Not Mad, Just Hurt ['56]
I've Come Awful Close ['72]
I've Run Out Of Tomorrows ['59]
If Lovin' You Is Wrong ['55]
Just An Old Flame ['77]
Kindly Keep It Country ['73]
Mama Don't 'Low ['75]
Mark Of A Heel ['71]
Most Of All ['55]
New Green Light ['54]
New Wears Off Too Fast ['52]
Next Time I Fall In Love (I Won't) ['71]
No Help Wanted ['53]
Oklahoma Hills ['61]
Oklahoma Home Brew ['69]
Older The Violin, The Sweeter The Music ['74]
On Tap, In The Can, Or In The Bottle ['68]
Once In A Blue Moon ['83]
One Of The Fortunate Few ['70]
Pathway Of My Life ['69]
Rockin' In The Congo ['57, 82]
Roses In The Wine ['73]
Rub-A-Dub-Dub ['53]
She's Just A Whole Lot Like You ['60]
Six Pack To Go ['60]
Smoky The Bar ['69]
Soft Lips ['49]
Squaws Along The Yukon ['58]
Teach Me How To Lie ['61]
Tears Are Only Rain ['57]
That's Just My Truckin' Luck ['75]
Then I'll Start Believing In You ['65]
Tony's Tank-Up, Drive-In Cafe ['80]
Too In Love ['63]
Total Strangers ['59]
Twice As Much ['64]
Waiting In The Lobby Of Your Heart ['52]
Wake Up, Irene ['54]
We've Gone Too Far ['54]
What Are We Gonna Do About The Moonlight ['49]
Where Is The Circus ['66]
Who Left The Door To Heaven Open ['74]
Whoa Sailor ['49]
Wild Side Of Life ['52]
Wildwood Flower ['55]
Yesterday's Girl ['53]
Yesterday's Mail ['48]
You Broke My Heart (In Little Bitty Pieces) ['49]
You're Going Back To Your Old Ways Again ['59]

THOMPSON, J.W.

Born in Alexandria, Louisiana. Male singer.

DEBUT	PEAK	WKS	GOLD	Country Chart Hit	Songwriter	Label (& Number)
9/15/79	**90**	2		1 **The Visitor**	*Ted Hardan*	Southern Star 309
10/4/80	**56**	9		2 **Halftime**	*Phil Olive/Jim Santoro*	NSD 62
1/24/81	**72**	4		3 **Two Out Of Three Ain't Bad**	*Jerry Duncan*	NSD 75
10/22/83	**97**	1		4 **We've Got A Good Thing Goin'**	*Glenn Barber/J. Martin Johnson*	USA Country 1001
7/14/84	**91**	2		5 **Hello Josephine**	*Dave Bartholomew/Fats Domino*	Century 21 109

THOMPSON, Sue

Born Eva Sue McKee on 7/19/1926 in Nevada, Missouri; raised in San Jose, California. Female singer/guitarist. Married to **Hank Penny** from 1953-63.

DON GIBSON & SUE THOMPSON:

DEBUT	PEAK	WKS	GOLD	Country Chart Hit	Songwriter	Label (& Number)
8/28/71	**50**	8		1 **The Two Of Us Together**	*Don Gibson*	Hickory 1607
4/22/72	**71**	3		2 **Did You Ever Think**	*Don Gibson*	Hickory 1629
8/12/72	**37**	11		3 **I Think They Call It Love**	*Bobby Bond*	Hickory 1646
11/18/72	**72**	5		4 **Candy And Roses** *[Sue Thompson]*	*Jim Mundy*	Hickory 1652
12/23/72	**64**	5		5 **Cause I Love You**	*Don Gibson*	Hickory 1654
3/17/73	**52**	6		6 **Go With Me**	*Gene Thomas*	Hickory 1665
9/15/73	**53**	9		7 **Warm Love**	*Don Gibson*	Hickory/MGM 303
8/10/74	**31**	12		8 **Good Old Fashioned Country Love**	*Glenn Barber/Jim Mundy*	Hickory/MGM 324
7/19/75	**36**	11		9 **Oh, How Love Changes**	*DeWayne Orender/K. Phyllis Powell*	Hickory/MGM 350
9/6/75	**50**	9		10 **Big Mable Murphy** *[Sue Thompson]*	*Dallas Frazier*	Hickory/MGM 354
2/21/76	**95**	3		11 **Never Naughty Rosie** *[Sue Thompson]*	*Dallas Frazier*	Hickory/MGM 364
4/3/76	**98**	2		12 **Get Ready-Here I Come**	*DeWayne Orender/K. Phyllis Powell*	Hickory/MGM 367

THOMPSON, Uncle Jimmy

Born Jesse Thompson in 1848 in Smith County, Tennessee. Died on 2/17/1931 (age 83). Legendary fiddle player. The very first performer on the very first *Grand Ole Opry* radio show on 11/28/1925. Known for his white beard and cantankerous attitude.

OPRY: 1925

THOMPSON BROTHERS BAND, The

Trio from Norwell, Massachusetts: brothers Andy Thompson (vocals) and Matt Thompson (drums), with Mike Whitty (bass).

DEBUT	PEAK	WKS	GOLD	Country Chart Hit	Songwriter	Label (& Number)
11/15/97	**56**	8		1 **Drive Me Crazy**	*Ron Davies/Ron Kimbro/Mike Whitty*	RCA
2/28/98	**58**	11		2 **Back On The Farm** above 2 from the album *Blame It On The Dog* on RCA 67503	*Don Henry*	RCA

THOMSON, Cyndi

Born on 10/19/1976 in Tifton, Georgia. Female singer/songwriter.

DEBUT	PEAK	WKS	GOLD	Country Chart Hit	Songwriter	Label (& Number)
3/31/01	**❶**[3]	35		1 **What I Really Meant To Say** S:❶[8]	*Tommy Lee James/Cyndi Thomson/Chris Waters*	Capitol
11/10/01+	**21**	20		2 **I Always Liked That Best**	*Tommy Lee James/Jennifer Kimball/Cyndi Thomson*	Capitol
4/13/02	**31**	17		3 **I'm Gone** above 3 from the album *My World* on Capitol 26010	*Chuck Prophet/Kim Richey*	Capitol

THORNTON, Marsha

Born on 10/22/1964 in Killen, Alabama. Female singer.

DEBUT	PEAK	WKS	GOLD	Country Chart Hit	Songwriter	Label (& Number)
9/23/89	**62**	7		1 **Deep Water**	*Fred Rose*	MCA 53711
1/6/90	**59**	10		2 **A Bottle Of Wine And Patsy Cline** from the album *Marsha Thornton* on RCA 42319	*Lindy Gravelle/Tommy Rocco*	MCA
2/16/91	**73**	2		3 **Maybe The Moon Will Shine** from the album *Maybe The Moon Will Shine* on MCA 10142	*Mary Lyn Dias/Johnny Pierce*	MCA

Billboard DEBUT	PEAK	WKS	GOLD	ARTIST / Country Chart Hit	Ranking / Songwriter	Label (& Number)
				THOROGOOD, George		
				Born on 12/31/1952 in Wilmington, Deleware. Rock singer/guitarist.		
10/9/99	**66**	4		**Move It On Over** *[w/ Travis Tritt]*	*Hank Williams*	Elektra
				from the animated TV series *King Of The Hill* (soundtrack on Elektra 62441)		
				THRASHER BROTHERS		
				Vocal group of brothers Joe Thrasher (lead), Jim Thrasher (tenor) and Andy Thrasher (baritone), with John Gresham (bass) and **Roger Hallmark** (guitar, banjo, fiddle). Joe's son, Neil, formed **Thrasher Shiver** duo.		
12/15/79+	**72**	5		1 **A Message To Khomeini**	*Chance Jones/Sid Linard* **[N]**	Vulcan 10004
				ROGER HALLMARK and The Thrasher Brothers		
3/7/81	**83**	2		2 **Lovers Love**	*Blake Mevis/Don Pfrimmer*	MCA 51049
2/6/82	**62**	5		3 **Best Of Friends**	*Linda Creed/Barry DeVorzon*	MCA 51227
				from the TV series *Simon & Simon* starring Gerald McRaney and Jameson Parker		
9/11/82	**60**	6		4 **Still The One**	*Johanna Hall/John Hall*	MCA 52093
1/15/83	**81**	4		5 **Wherever You Are**	*Kent Robbins*	MCA 52153
12/10/83	**80**	8		6 **Whatcha Got Cookin' In Your Oven Tonight**	*Woody Bomar/Pat McManus*	MCA 52297
				THRASHER SHIVER		
				Duo of Neil Thrasher and Kelly Shiver. Neil's father, Joe, was lead singer of the **Thrasher Brothers**.		
8/10/96	**65**	6		1 **Goin', Goin', Gone**	*Mike Delaney/Neil Thrasher*	Asylum
2/22/97	**49**	10		2 **Be Honest**	*Archie Jordan/Kelly Shiver*	Asylum
				above 2 from the album *Thrasher Shiver* on Asylum 61929		
				3 OF HEARTS		
				Female vocal trio from Fort Worth, Texas: Blaire Stroud, Kayie McNeill and Deserea Wasdin.		
4/21/01	**43**	10		1 **Love Is Enough**	S:4 *Neil Thrasher/Jim Varsos*	RCA
8/18/01	**59**	1		2 **Arizona Rain**	*Vicky Banks*	RCA
				above 2 from the album *3 Of Hearts* on RCA 67916		
12/15/01+	**39**	5		3 **The Christmas Shoes**	S:7 *Leonard Ahlstrom/Eddie Carswell* **[X]**	RCA
				THREE SUNS, The		
				Instrumental trio from Philadelphia, Pennsylvania: brothers Al Nevins (guitar) and Morty Nevins (accordian), with cousin Artie Dunn (organ). Al Nevins died on 1/25/1965 (age 48). Morty Nevins died on 7/23/1990 (age 63). Dunn died on 1/15/1996 (age 73).		
2/4/50	**7**	4		**Beyond The Sunset** *[w/ Rosalie Allen & Elton Britt]*	A:7 *Blanche Brock/Virgil Brock*	RCA Victor 47-3105
				THROCKMORTON, Sonny	**SW: #34**	
				Born James Throckmorton on 4/2/1941 in Carlsbad, New Mexico. Male singer/songwriter.		
9/4/76	**76**	6		1 **Rosie**	*Sonny Throckmorton*	Starcrest 073
12/25/76+	**73**	7		2 **Lovin' You, Lovin' Me**	*Sonny Throckmorton*	Starcrest 094
9/16/78	**54**	8		3 **I Wish You Could Have Turned My Head (And Left My Heart Alone)**	*Sonny Throckmorton*	Mercury 55039
2/3/79	**47**	8		4 **Smooth Sailin'** /	*Curly Putman/Sonny Throckmorton*	
2/3/79	**flip**	8		5 **Last Cheater's Waltz**	*Sonny Throckmorton*	Mercury 55051
7/14/79	**66**	6		6 **Can't You Hear That Whistle Blow**	*Chris Dodson/Sonny Throckmorton*	Mercury 55061
4/5/80	**89**	3		7 **Friday Night Blues**	*Sonny Throckmorton/Rafe Van Hoy*	Mercury 57018
12/12/81	**77**	5		8 **A Girl Like You**	*Buzz Cason/Freddy Weller*	MCA 51214
				THUNDERKLOUD, Billy, & The Chieftones		
				Vocal group of Native Americans from Edmonton, Alberta, Canada: Vincent "Billy Thunderkloud" Clifford, Jack Wolf, Barry Littlestar and Richard Grayowl.		
5/17/75	**16**	12		1 **What Time Of Day**	*Ron McCown*	20th Century 2181
10/25/75	**37**	11		2 **Pledging My Love**	*Don Robey/Ferdinand Washington*	20th Century 2239
5/29/76	**74**	5		3 **Indian Nation (The Lament of the Cherokee Reservation Indian)**	*John D. Loudermilk*	Polydor 14321
8/7/76	**47**	8		4 **Try A Little Tenderness**	*Jimmy Campbell/Reg Connelly/Harry Woods*	Polydor 14338
12/11/76	**77**	6		5 **It's Alright**	*Jerry Foster/Bill Rice*	Polydor 14362
				THURSTON, Jamie Lee		
				Born in Montpeiler, Vermont; raised in Waterbury, Vermont. Male singer/songwriter/guitarist.		
2/1/03	**59**	2		**It Can All Be Gone**	*Tommy Conners/Stewart Harris/Jamie Lee Thurston*	View 2
				TIBOR BROTHERS, The		
				Vocal group of brothers from Hebron, North Dakota: Gerard Tibor, Francis Tibor, Harvey Tibor, Kurt Tibor and Larry Tibor.		
4/17/76	**95**	3		**It's So Easy Lovin' You**	*Gerard Tibor*	Ariola America 7615
				TIERNY, Patti		
				Born in California. Female singer.		
9/22/73	**90**	4		**Cryin' Eyes**	*Jimmy Bowen/Rafe Van Hoy*	MGM 14561
				**TILLIS, Mel**	**1970s: #6 / All-Time: #31**	
				Born Lonnie Melvin Tillis on 8/8/1932 in Tampa, Florida; raised in Pahokee, Florida. Singer/songwriter/guitarist/actor. Acted in the movies *W.W. & The Dixie Dancekings, Smokey & The Bandit II, Uphill All The Way* and *Murder In Music City*. Owned several music publishing companies. Backing band: The Statesiders. Father of **Pam Tillis**. Known for his stuttering speech.		
				CMA: Entertainer 1976		
11/10/58	**24**	4		1 **The Violet And A Rose**	*Bud Auge/John Reinfeld/Mel Tillis*	Columbia 41189
1/5/59	**28**	4		2 **Finally**	*Mel Walker/Wayne Walker*	Columbia 41277

Billboard DEBUT	PEAK	WKS	GOLD	ARTIST / Country Chart Hit	Ranking / Songwriter	Label (& Number)
				TILLIS, Mel — cont'd		
8/24/59	**27**	2		3 **Sawmill** *[w/ Bill Phillips]* — also see #33 below	*Mel Tillis/Horace Whatley*	Columbia 41416
2/8/60	**24**	4		4 **Georgia Town Blues** *[w/ Bill Phillips]*	*Buck Peddy/Mel Tillis*	Columbia 41530
1/5/63	**25**	3		5 **How Come Your Dog Don't Bite Nobody But Me** *[w/ Webb Pierce]*	*Mel Tillis/Wayne Walker*	Decca 31445
7/3/65	**14**	16		6 **Wine**	*Mel Tillis*	RIC 158
10/15/66	**17**	14		7 **Stateside**	*Mel Tillis*	Kapp 772
2/18/67	**11**	19		8 **Life Turned Her That Way**	*Harlan Howard*	Kapp 804
7/15/67	**20**	14		9 **Goodbye Wheeling**	*Mel Tillis*	Kapp 837
12/16/67	**71**	3		10 **Survival Of The Fittest**	*Mel Tillis*	Kapp 867
1/13/68	**26**	12		11 **All Right** (I'll Sign The Papers)	*Mel Tillis*	Kapp 881
5/11/68	**17**	15		12 **Something Special**	*Ray Griff*	Kapp 905
10/5/68	**31**	7		13 **Destroyed By Man**	*Jerry Hadli/Joe Hayes*	Kapp 941
12/21/68+	**10**	17		14 **Who's Julie**	*Wayne Carson*	Kapp 959
4/19/69	**13**	15		15 **Old Faithful**	*Mel Tillis*	Kapp 986
				MEL TILLIS And The Statesiders:		
8/16/69	**9**	15		16 **These Lonely Hands Of Mine**	*Lamar Morris/Charlie Norrell*	Kapp 2031
1/17/70	**10**	11		17 **She'll Be Hanging 'Round Somewhere**	*Damon Black*	Kapp 2072
4/25/70	**3**^{1}	17		18 **Heart Over Mind**	*Mel Tillis*	Kapp 2086
7/25/70	**5**	14		19 **Heaven Everyday**	*Jerry Foster/Bill Rice*	MGM 14148
10/17/70	**25**	11		20 **To Lonely, Too Long**	*Jim Owen*	Kapp 2103
11/7/70	**8**	13		21 **Commercial Affection**	*Mel Tillis*	MGM 14176
1/30/71	**4**	15		22 **The Arms Of A Fool**	*Ron McCown*	MGM 14211
5/8/71	**56**	9		23 **One More Drink**	*Jim Owen*	Kapp 2121
6/5/71	**8**	15		24 **Take My Hand** *[w/ Sherry Bryce]*	*Helen Acton/Les Acton/Shirley Price*	MGM 14255
7/31/71	**8**	16		25 **Brand New Mister Me**	*Ron McCown*	MGM 14275
10/30/71	**9**	14		26 **Living And Learning** *[w/ Sherry Bryce]*	*Terry Skinner*	MGM 14303
1/1/72	**14**	13		27 **Untouched**	*Carl Knight*	MGM 14329
4/8/72	**38**	10		28 **Anything's Better Than Nothing** *[w/ Sherry Bryce]*	*Marie Wilson*	MGM 14365
5/6/72	**12**	11		29 **Would You Want The World To End**	*Ron McCown*	MGM 14372
8/12/72	❶^{2}	15		30 **I Ain't Never**	*Webb Pierce/Mel Tillis*	MGM 14418
12/9/72+	**3**^{1}	16		31 **Neon Rose**	*Gayle Barnhill/Rory Bourke*	MGM 14454
4/28/73	**21**	13		32 **Thank You For Being You**	*Hal Harbour/Kent Westberry*	MGM 14522
8/25/73	**2**^{1}	17		33 **Sawmill** — new version of #3 above	*Mel Tillis/Horace Whatley* **[R]**	MGM 14585
11/17/73+	**26**	13		34 **Let's Go All The Way Tonight** *[w/ Sherry Bryce]*	*Mel Tillis*	MGM 14660
1/12/74	**2**^{1}	18		35 **Midnight, Me And The Blues**	*Jerry House*	MGM 14689
4/13/74	**11**	14		36 **Don't Let Go** *[w/ Sherry Bryce]*	*Jesse Stone*	MGM 14714
5/18/74	**3**^{1}	16		37 **Stomp Them Grapes**	*Ron McCown*	MGM 14720
10/5/74	**3**^{1}	14		38 **Memory Maker**	*Mel Tillis/Kent Westberry*	MGM 14744
1/4/75	**14**	13		39 **You Are The One** *[w/ Sherry Bryce]*	*Hal Harbour/Kent Westberry*	MGM 14776
2/1/75	**7**	16		40 **Best Way I Know How**	*Jerry Chesnut*	MGM 14782
5/17/75	**32**	13		41 **Mr. Right And Mrs. Wrong** *[w/ Sherry Bryce]*	*Hal Harbour/Kent Westberry*	MGM 14803
6/14/75	**4**	16		42 **Woman In The Back Of My Mind**	*Roger Jaudon/Ron McCown*	MGM 14804
11/1/75+	**16**	14		43 **Lookin' For Tomorrow** (And Findin' Yesterdays)	*David Alids/Billy Arr*	MGM 14835
3/20/76	**15**	10		44 **Mental Revenge**	*Mel Tillis*	MGM 14846
				MEL TILLIS:		
5/29/76	**11**	13		45 **Love Revival**	*Tom Gmeiner/John Greenebaum*	MCA 40559
10/2/76	❶^{2}	16		46 **Good Woman Blues**	*Ken McDuffie*	MCA 40627
1/15/77	❶^{1}	14		47 **Heart Healer**	*Tom Gmeiner/John Greenebaum*	MCA 40667
4/23/77	**9**	13		48 **Burning Memories**	*Mel Tillis/Wayne Walker*	MCA 40710
8/13/77	**3**^{2}	16		49 **I Got The Hoss**	*Jerry House*	MCA 40764
12/24/77+	**4**	16		50 **What Did I Promise Her Last Night**	*Ron McCown/Wayne Walker*	MCA 40836
5/13/78	❶^{1}	14		51 **I Believe In You**	*Buddy Cannon/Gene Dunlap*	MCA 40900
9/9/78	**4**	13		52 **Ain't No California**	*Sterling Whipple*	MCA 40946
1/13/79	**2**^{3}	14		53 **Send Me Down To Tucson** / — from the movie *Every Which Way But Loose* starring **Clint Eastwood**	*Cliff Crofford/Snuff Garrett*	
1/13/79	**flip**	14		54 **Charlie's Angel**	*Dee Gaskin*	MCA 40983
6/16/79	❶^{1}	15		55 **Coca Cola Cowboy** — from the movie *Every Which Way But Loose* starring **Clint Eastwood**	*Sam Atchley/Irving Dain/Steve Dorff/Sandy Pinkard*	MCA 41041
9/29/79	**6**	14		56 **Blind In Love**	*Bob Corbin*	Elektra 46536
1/19/80	**6**	13		57 **Lying Time Again**	*Chance Walker*	Elektra 46583
4/26/80	**3**^{1}	16		58 **Your Body Is An Outlaw**	*Buzz Rabin*	Elektra 46628
8/30/80	**9**	13		59 **Steppin' Out**	*Billy Starr*	Elektra 47015
12/13/80+	❶^{1}	16		60 **Southern Rains**	*Roger Murrah*	Elektra 47082
4/4/81	**8**	13		61 **A Million Old Goodbyes**	*Buzz Cason/Steve Gibb/Bobby Russell*	Elektra 47116
7/11/81	**23**	12		62 **Texas Cowboy Night** *[w/ Nancy Sinatra]*	*Buddy Cannon/Raleigh Squires/Mel Tillis*	Elektra 47157
9/5/81	**10**	16		63 **One-Night Fever**	*Johnny MacRae/Bob Morrison*	Elektra 47178
12/26/81+	**43**	8		64 **Play Me Or Trade Me** *[w/ Nancy Sinatra]* /	*Owen Davis/Mike Huffman*	
12/26/81+	**flip**	8		65 **Where Would I Be** *[w/ Nancy Sinatra]*	*Judy Mehaffey*	Elektra 47247
2/27/82	**36**	9		66 **It's A Long Way To Daytona**	*Mel Tillis*	Elektra 47412
5/29/82	**37**	9		67 **The One That Got Away**	*Steve Nobles*	Elektra 47453

TILLIS, Mel — cont'd

DEBUT	PEAK	WKS	#	Country Chart Hit	Songwriter	Label (& Number)
9/25/82	**17**	15	68	**Stay A Little Longer**	*Tommy Duncan/Bob Wills*	Elektra 69963
3/12/83	**10**	20	69	**In The Middle Of The Night**	*Bob Corbin*	MCA 52182
8/6/83	**49**	10	70	**A Cowboy's Dream**	*Jim Bowman/Cal Miller*	MCA 52247
10/29/83	**53**	10	71	**She Meant Forever When She Said Goodbye**	*Buddy Cannon*	MCA 52285
4/28/84	**10**	22	72	**New Patches**	*Tommy Collins*	MCA 52373
10/27/84	**47**	12	73	**Slow Nights** *[w/ Glen Campbell]*	*Bob Albright*	MCA 52474
6/1/85	**37**	12	74	**You Done Me Wrong**	*George Jones/Ray Price*	RCA 14061
9/7/85	**61**	7	75	**California Road**	*Sam Weedman*	RCA 14175
3/5/88	**31**	14	76	**You'll Come Back (You Always Do)**	*Andy Badale/Norman Mailer*	Mercury 870192
11/4/89	**67**	4	77	**City Lights**	*Bill Anderson*	Radio 001

Ain't No California ['78]
All Right (I'll Sign The Papers) ['68]
Anything's Better Than Nothing ['72]
Arms Of A Fool ['71]
Best Way I Know How ['75]
Blind In Love ['79]
Brand New Mister Me ['71]
Burning Memories ['77]
California Road ['85]
Charlie's Angel ['79]
City Lights ['89]
Coca Cola Cowboy ['79]
Commercial Affection ['70]
Cowboy's Dream ['83]
Destroyed By Man ['68]
Don't Let Go ['74]
Finally ['59]
Georgia Town Blues ['60]
Good Woman Blues ['76]
Goodbye Wheeling ['67]
Heart Healer ['77]
Heart Over Mind ['70]
Heaven Everyday ['70]
How Come Your Dog Don't Bite Nobody But Me ['63]
I Ain't Never ['72]
I Believe In You ['78]
I Got The Hoss ['77]
In The Middle Of The Night ['83]
It's A Long Way To Daytona ['82]
Let's Go All The Way Tonight ['74]
Life Turned Her That Way ['67]
Living And Learning ['71]
Lookin' For Tomorrow (And Findin' Yesterdays) ['76]
Love Revival ['76]
Lying Time Again ['80]
Memory Maker ['74]
Mental Revenge ['76]
Midnight, Me And The Blues ['74]
Million Old Goodbyes ['81]
Mr. Right And Mrs. Wrong ['75]
Neon Rose ['73]
New Patches ['84]
Old Faithful ['69]
One More Drink ['71]
One-Night Fever ['81]
One That Got Away ['82]
Play Me Or Trade Me ['82]
Sawmill ['59, '73]
Send Me Down To Tucson ['79]
She Meant Forever When She Said Goodbye ['83]
She'll Be Hanging 'Round Somewhere ['70]
Slow Nights ['84]
Something Special ['68]
Southern Rains ['81]
Stateside ['66]
Stay A Little Longer ['82]
Steppin' Out ['80]
Stomp Them Grapes ['74]
Survival Of The Fittest ['67]
Take My Hand ['71]
Texas Cowboy Night ['81]
Thank You For Being You ['73]
These Lonely Hands Of Mine ['69]
To Lonely, Too Long ['70]
Untouched ['72]
Violet And A Rose ['58]
What Did I Promise Her Last Night ['78]
Where Would I Be ['82]
Who's Julie ['69]
Wine ['65]
Woman In The Back Of My Mind ['75]
Would You Want The World To End ['72]
You Are The One ['75]
You Done Me Wrong ['85]
You'll Come Back (You Always Do) ['88]
Your Body Is An Outlaw ['80]

TILLIS, Pam

1990s: #24 / All-Time: #138

Born on 7/24/1957 in Plant City, Florida. Female singer/songwriter/guitarist. Daughter of **Mel Tillis**. Formerly married to Bob DiPiero of **Billy Hill**. Also see **Same Old Train** and **Tomorrow's World**.

CMA: Female Vocalist 1994 // OPRY: 2000

DEBUT	PEAK	WKS	#	Country Chart Hit	Songwriter	Label (& Number)
11/10/84	**71**	5	1	**Goodbye Highway**	*Mary Ann Kennedy/Pam Rose/Pam Tillis*	Warner 29155
1/25/86	**55**	8	2	**Those Memories Of You**	*Allan Bryant*	Warner 28806
7/5/86	**67**	4	3	**I Thought I'd About Had It With Love**	*Milton Brown/Beth Nielsen Chapman*	Warner 28676
2/21/87	**68**	6	4	**I Wish She Wouldn't Treat You That Way**	*Walker Igleheart/Kevin Welch*	Warner 28444
5/16/87	**71**	6	5	**There Goes My Love**	*Buck Owens*	Warner 28346
12/1/90+	**5**	20	6	**Don't Tell Me What To Do**	*Max D. Barnes/Harlan Howard*	Arista
4/6/91	**6**	20	7	**One Of Those Things**	*Paul Overstreet/Pam Tillis*	Arista
8/17/91	**11**	20	8	**Put Yourself In My Place**	*Carl Jackson/Pam Tillis*	Arista
12/14/91+	**3^{2}**	20	9	**Maybe It Was Memphis**	*Michael Anderson*	Arista
4/11/92	**21**	20	10	**Blue Rose Is**	*Jan Buckingham/Bob DiPiero/Pam Tillis*	Arista
				above 5 from the album *Put Yourself In My Place* on Arista 18642		
8/22/92	**3^{1}**	20	11	**Shake The Sugar Tree**	*Chapin Hartford*	Arista
1/2/93	**4**	20	12	**Let That Pony Run**	*Gretchen Peters*	Arista
2/13/93	**27**	20	13	**Romeo** *[w/ Dolly Parton/Mary-Chapin Carpenter/Billy Ray Cyrus/Kathy Mattea/Tanya Tucker]*		
				from Parton's album *Slow Dancing With The Moon* on Columbia 53199	...*Dolly Parton*	Columbia
5/1/93	**11**	20	14	**Cleopatra, Queen Of Denial**	*Jan Buckingham/Bob DiPiero/Pam Tillis*	Arista
8/28/93	**16**	20	15	**Do You Know Where Your Man Is**	*Carol Chase/Dave Gibson/Russell Smith*	Arista
				#11, 12, 14 & 15: from the album *Homeward Looking Angel* on Arista 18649		
3/26/94	**5**	20	16	**Spilled Perfume**	*Dean Dillon/Pam Tillis*	Arista
8/6/94	**2^{1}**	20	17	**When You Walk In The Room**	*Jackie DeShannon*	Arista
11/19/94+	**❶^{2}**	20	18	**Mi Vida Loca (My Crazy Life)**	*Jess Leary/Pam Tillis*	Arista
3/11/95	**16**	12	19	**I Was Blown Away**	*Layng Martine Jr.*	Arista
6/3/95	**3^{1}**	20	20	**In Between Dances**	*Barry Alfonso/Craig Bickhardt*	Arista
				above 5 from the album *Sweetheart's Dance* on Arista 18758		
10/7/95+	**6**	20	21	**Deep Down**	*Walt Aldridge/John Jarrard*	Arista
1/27/96	**8**	20	22	**The River And The Highway**	*Gerry House/Don Schlitz*	Arista
6/8/96	**14**	20	23	**It's Lonely Out There**	*Bob DiPiero/Pam Tillis*	Arista
10/12/96	**62**	4	24	**Betty's Got A Bass Boat**	*Bernie Nelson/Craig Wiseman*	Arista
				above 4 from the album *All Of This Love* on Arista 18799		
4/26/97	**4**	20	25	**All The Good Ones Are Gone**	*Dean Dillon/Bob McDill*	Arista Nashville
9/6/97	**5**	21	26	**Land Of The Living**	*Wayland Patton/Tia Sillers*	Arista Nashville
				above 2 from the album *Greatest Hits* on Arista Nashville 18836		
5/16/98	**12**	20	27	**I Said A Prayer**	S:12 *Leslie Satcher*	Arista Nashville
9/12/98	**38**	12	28	**Every Time**	*Tommy Lee James/Jennifer Kimball*	Arista Nashville
				above 2 from the album *Every Time* on Arista Nashville 18861		
8/28/99	**50**	9	29	**After A Kiss**	*Carolyn Dawn Johnson/Steven Jones*	Arista Nashville
				from the movie *Happy, Texas* starring Steve Zahn (soundtrack on Arista Nashville 18898)		
12/9/00+	**22**	22	30	**Please**	*Michael Dulaney/John Hobbs/Jeffrey Steele*	Arista Nashville
				from the album *Thunder & Roses* on Arista Nashville 67000		

DEBUT	PEAK	WKS	GOLD		ARTIST / Country Chart Hit	Ranking / Songwriter	Label (& Number)

TILLMAN, Floyd

Born on 12/8/1914 in Ryan, Oklahoma; raised in Post, Texas. Died of leukemia on 8/22/2003 (age 88). Male singer/songwriter/guitarist.

DEBUT	PEAK	WKS	#	Country Chart Hit	Songwriter	Label (& Number)
1/8/44	❶[1]	13	1	**They Took The Stars Out Of Heaven**	*Floyd Tillman*	Decca 6090
12/16/44	**5**	3	2	**G.I. Blues /**	*Floyd Tillman*	
12/30/44	**4**	8	3	**Each Night At Nine**	*Floyd Tillman*	Decca 6104
				FLOYD TILLMAN and His Favorite Playboys (above 3)		
8/3/46	**2**[1]	7	4	**Drivin' Nails In My Coffin**	*Jerry Irby*	Columbia 36998
7/10/48	**5**	19	5	**I Love You So Much, It Hurts**	J:5 / S:6 *Floyd Tillman*	Columbia 20430
1/29/49	**14**	1	6	**Please Don't Pass Me By**	S:14 *Floyd Tillman*	Columbia 20496
7/2/49	**5**	12	7	**Slipping Around**	S:5 / A:6 / J:6 *Floyd Tillman*	Columbia 20581
10/8/49	**6**	8	8	**I'll Never Slip Around Again**	S:6 / J:8 *Floyd Tillman*	Columbia 20615
12/31/49+	**4**	3	9	**I Gotta Have My Baby Back**	A:4 *Floyd Tillman*	Columbia 20641
12/19/60	**29**	1	10	**It Just Tears Me Up**	*Lawton Williams*	Liberty 55280

TILLOTSON, Johnny

Born on 4/20/1939 in Jacksonville, Florida; raised in Palatka, Florida. Male singer/songwriter.

DEBUT	PEAK	WKS	#	Country Chart Hit	Songwriter	Label (& Number)
6/23/62	**4**	13	1	**It Keeps Right On A-Hurtin'**	*Lorene Mann/Johnny Tillotson*	Cadence 1418
9/8/62	**11**	10	2	**Send Me The Pillow You Dream On**	*Hank Locklin*	Cadence 1424
11/11/67+	**48**	10	3	**You're The Reason**	*Bobby Edwards/Terry Fell/Fred Henley/Mildred Imes*	MGM 13829
2/17/68	**63**	6	4	**I Can Spot A Cheater**	*Glenn Sutton/Paul Tannen*	MGM 13888
6/18/77	**99**	1	5	**Toy Hearts**	*Richard Mainegra*	United Artists 986
3/31/84	**91**	2	6	**Lay Back (In The Arms Of Someone)**	*Mike Chapman/Nicky Chinn*	Reward 04346

TILTON, Sheila

Born in 1951 in Kailua, Hawaii. Female singer.

DEBUT	PEAK	WKS	#	Country Chart Hit	Songwriter	Label (& Number)
7/10/76	**23**	13		**Half As Much**	*Curley Williams*	Con Brio 110

TINY TIM

Born Herbert Khaury on 4/12/1930 in Brooklyn, New York. Died of heart failure on 11/30/1996 (age 66). Novelty singer/ukulele player.

DEBUT	PEAK	WKS	#	Country Chart Hit	Songwriter	Label (& Number)
4/16/88	**70**	5		**Leave Me Satisfied**	*Joe Henderson/Dan Mitchell*	NLT 1993

TIPPIN, Aaron — 1990s: #35 / 2000s: #42 / All-Time: #139

Born on 7/3/1958 in Pensacola, Florida; raised in Travelers Rest, South Carolina. Male singer/songwriter/guitarist. Worked as a corporate airline pilot before his singing career.

DEBUT	PEAK	WKS	#	Country Chart Hit	Songwriter	Label (& Number)
11/3/90+	**6**	20	1	**You've Got To Stand For Something**	*Buddy Brock/Aaron Tippin*	RCA
4/6/91	**40**	19	2	**I Wonder How Far It Is Over You**	*Buddy Brock/Aaron Tippin*	RCA
8/24/91	**54**	11	3	**She Made A Memory Out Of Me**	*Aaron Tippin*	RCA
				above 3 from the album *You've Got To Stand For Something* on RCA 2374		
2/15/92	❶[3]	20	4	**There Ain't Nothin' Wrong With The Radio**	*Buddy Brock/Aaron Tippin*	RCA
6/20/92	**5**	20	5	**I Wouldn't Have It Any Other Way**	*Butch Curry/Aaron Tippin*	RCA
10/24/92	**38**	13	6	**I Was Born With A Broken Heart**	*Jim McBride/Aaron Tippin*	RCA
1/30/93	**7**	20	7	**My Blue Angel**	*Philip Douglas/Aaron Tippin/Kim Williams*	RCA
				above 4 from the album *Read Between The Lines* on RCA 61129		
6/26/93	**7**	20	8	**Working Man's Ph.D.**	*Bobby Byrd/Philip Douglas/Aaron Tippin*	RCA
10/23/93+	**17**	20	9	**The Call Of The Wild**	*Buddy Brock/Mike Heeney/Aaron Tippin*	RCA
2/12/94	**47**	10	10	**Honky-Tonk Superman**	*Buddy Brock/Aaron Tippin*	RCA
4/23/94	**30**	20	11	**Whole Lotta Love On The Line**	*Donny Kees/Aaron Tippin*	RCA
				above 4 from the album *Call Of The Wild* on RCA 66251		
10/8/94+	**15**	20	12	**I Got It Honest**	*Bruce Burch/Marcus Johnson/Aaron Tippin*	RCA
2/25/95	**39**	11	13	**She Feels Like A Brand New Man Tonight**	*Mike Heeney/Aaron Tippin*	RCA
				above 2 from the album *Lookin' Back At Myself* on RCA 66420		
9/2/95	❶[2]	21	14	**That's As Close As I'll Get To Loving You**	S:3 *Sally Dworsky/Jan Leyers*	RCA
2/3/96	**22**	16	15	**Without Your Love**	*Al Anderson/Craig Wiseman*	RCA
6/1/96	**51**	11	16	**Everything I Own**	*Tony Martin/Reese Wilson*	RCA
10/19/96	**69**	2	17	**How's The Radio Know**	*Mike Heeney/Aaron Tippin*	RCA
				above 4 from the album *Tool Box* on RCA 66740		
2/15/97	**50**	7	18	**That's What Happens When I Hold You**	*Johnny Cymbal/Angela Kaset*	RCA
4/26/97	**65**	4	19	**A Door**	*Tim Nichols/Mark D. Sanders*	RCA
				above 2 from the album *Greatest Hits...And Then Some* on RCA 67427		
8/8/98+	**6**	29	20	**For You I Will**	S:3 *Tony Martin/Mark Nesler*	Lyric Street
1/30/99	**17**	20	21	**I'm Leaving**	*Aaron Barker/Ron Harbin/L. David Lewis*	Lyric Street
6/5/99	**33**	18	22	**Her**	*Jeffrey Steele/Craig Wiseman*	Lyric Street
10/23/99	**47**	9	23	**What This Country Needs**	*Donny Kees/Aaron Tippin*	Lyric Street
				above 4 from the album *What This Country Needs* on Lyric Street 65003		
5/27/00	❶[2]	33	24	**Kiss This**	*Philip Douglas/Aaron Tippin/Thea Tippin*	Lyric Street
1/13/01	**17**	21	25	**People Like Us**	*David Lee Murphy/Kim Tribble*	Lyric Street
8/11/01	**40**	9	26	**Always Was**	*Tony Colton/Bobby Wood*	Lyric Street
				above 3 from the album *People Like Us* on Lyric Street 65014		

DEBUT	PEAK	WKS	GOLD	ARTIST / Country Chart Hit	Ranking / Songwriter	Label (& Number)
				TIPPIN, Aaron — cont'd		
10/6/01+	**2^{1}**	23		27 **Where The Stars And Stripes And The Eagle Fly**	S:❶^{6} *Kenny Beard/Casey Beathard/Aaron Tippin*	Lyric Street
12/22/01+	**52**	4		28 **Jingle Bell Rock**	*Joe Beal/Jim Boothe* **[X]**	Lyric Street
				from the album *A December To Remember* on Lyric Street 165016		
4/27/02	**46**	10		29 **I'll Take Love Over Money**	*Bob DiPiero/Tony Mullins*	Lyric Street
8/10/02	**40**	15		30 **If Her Lovin' Don't Kill Me**	*Vicky McGehee/John Rich/Tim Womack*	Lyric Street
12/21/02+	**35**	19		31 **Love Like There's No Tomorrow** ***[w/ Thea Tippin]***	*Aaron Tippin/Thea Tippin*	Lyric Street
				#27 & 29-31: from the album *Stars & Stripes* on Lyric Street 165033		
				TODD, Dick		
				Born in Pennsylvania. Male singer.		
9/2/67	**52**	6		**Big Wheel Cannonball** ***[w/ The Appalachian Wildcats]***	*Vaughn Horton*	Decca 32168
				new lyrical version of **Roy Acuff**'s "Wabash Cannonball"		
				TOLIVER, Tony		
				Born on 7/4/1968 in Richards, Texas. Male singer/pianist.		
8/10/96	**71**	6		1 **Bettin' Forever On You**	*Paul Nelson/Tom Shapiro*	Curb/Rising Tide
1/18/97	**67**	2		2 **He's On The Way Home**	*Tony Martin/Reese Wilson*	Curb/Rising Tide
				above 2 from the album *Half Saint, Half Sinner* on Curb/Rising Tide 53040		
				TOMMY & DONNA		
				Husband-and-wife duo from California: Tommy Greene and Donna Greene.		
11/26/88	**72**	6		**Take It Slow With Me**	*Tommy Greene*	Oak 1067
				TOMORROW'S WORLD		
				All-star collaboration in honor of Earth Day: **Lynn Anderson**, **Butch Baker**, **Shane Barmby**, **Billy Hill**, **Suzy Bogguss**, **Kix Brooks**, **T. Graham Brown**, **The Burch Sisters**, **Holly Dunn**, **Foster & Lloyd**, **Vince Gill**, **William Lee Golden**, **Highway 101**, **Shelby Lynne**, **Johnny Rodriguez**, **Dan Seals**, **Les Taylor**, **Pam Tillis**, **Mac Wiseman** and **Kevin Welch**.		
5/5/90	**74**	1		**Tomorrow's World**	*Kix Brooks/Pam Tillis*	Warner
				TOMPALL — see GLASER BROTHERS		
				TOPEL & WARE		
				Duo of Michael Topel and James Ware.		
10/24/87	**93**	3		**Change Of Heart**	*Michael Topel/James Ware*	RCI 2406
				TOROK, Mitchell		
				Born on 10/28/1929 in Houston, Texas. Male singer/songwriter/guitarist.		
8/22/53	**❶^{2}**	24		1 **Caribbean**	J:❶^{2} / S:4 / A:5 *Mitchell Torok*	Abbott 140
1/23/54	**9**	3		2 **Hootchy Kootchy Henry (From Hawaii)**	J:9 *Mitchell Torok*	Abbott 150
2/18/67	**73**	3		3 **Instant Love**	*Ramona Redd/Mitchell Torok*	Reprise 0541
				TOUCH OF COUNTRY		
				Vocal group from Phoenix, Arizona.		
11/12/88	**85**	3		1 **I Won't Be Seeing Her No More**	*Hank Cochran/Dean Dillon*	OL 127
7/15/89	**87**	3		2 **Did I Leave My Heart At Your House**	*Max D. Barnes/Harlan Howard*	OL 130
				TOUPS, Wayne, & Zydecajun		
				Born on 10/2/1958 in Lafayette, Louisiana. Male singer/accordianist. Zydecajun: Wade Richard (guitar), Rick Lagneaux (keyboards), Mark Miller (bass) and Troy Gaspard (drums).		
3/6/99	**66**	5		**Free Me**	*Walt Aldridge*	BTM
				from the album *More Than Just A Little* on BTM 0002		
				TRACTORS, The		
				Country-rock group from Tulsa, Oklahoma: Casey Van Beek (vocals; born on 12/1/1942), Steve Ripley (guitar; born on 1/5/1950), Walt Richmond (keyboards; born on 4/18/1947), Ron Getman (bass; born on 12/13/1948) and Jamie Oldaker (drums; born on 9/5/1951).		
8/27/94	**11**	20		1 **Baby Likes To Rock It**	*Walt Richmond/Steve Ripley*	Arista
12/17/94+	**41**	4		2 **The Santa Claus Boogie**	*Steve Ripley* **[X]**	Arista
				from the album *Have Yourself A Tractors Christmas* on Arista 18805		
12/31/94+	**50**	11		3 **Tryin' To Get To New Orleans**	*Tim DuBois/Walt Richmond/Steve Ripley*	Arista
				#1 & 3: from the album *The Tractors* on Arista 18728		
12/16/95+	**43**	5		4 **Santa Claus Is Comin' (In A Boogie Woogie Choo Choo Train)**	*Walt Richmond/Steve Ripley* **[X]**	Arista
12/23/95+	**63**	3		5 **The Santa Claus Boogie**	*Steve Ripley* **[X-R]**	Arista
				above 2 from the album *Have Yourself A Tractors Christmas* on Arista 18805		
10/4/97	**75**	1		6 **The Last Time**	*Mick Jagger/Keith Richards*	Beyond Music
				from the various artists album *Stone Country* on Beyond Music 3055		
12/27/97+	**65**	3		7 **Santa Claus Is Comin' (In A Boogie Woogie Choo Choo Train)**	*Walt Richmond/Steve Ripley* **[X-R]**	Arista
				from the album *Have Yourself A Tractors Christmas* on Arista 18805		
11/21/98	**57**	10		8 **Shortenin' Bread**	*Don Keesee/Walt Richmond/Steve Ripley/Kasey Van Beek*	Arista
4/17/99	**72**	1		9 **I Wouldn't Tell You No Lie**	*Ron Getman/Steve Ripley*	Arista
				above 2 from the album *Farmers In A Changing World* on Arista 18878		
				TRADER-PRICE		
				Vocal group from Burns Flat, Oklahoma: brothers Dan, Chris and Erick Trader-Price, with Don Bell.		
8/12/89	**55**	7		1 **Sad Eyes**	*Robert John*	Universal 66022
12/23/89+	**64**	4		2 **Lately Rose**	*Chris Price/Dan Price/Erick Price*	Universal 66031
				TRAMMELL, Bobby Lee		
				Born in Jonesboro, Arkansas. Male singer.		
5/27/72	**52**	9		**Love Isn't Love (Till You Give It Away)**	*Bobby Fischer/Ricci Mareno*	Souncot 1135

Billboard DEBUT	PEAK	WKS	GOLD	ARTIST / Country Chart Hit	Ranking / Songwriter	Label (& Number)

TRASK, Diana

Born on 6/23/1940 in Warburton, Australia. Female singer/pianist.

DEBUT	PEAK	WKS	GOLD	Country Chart Hit	Songwriter	Label (& Number)
6/22/68	70	4		1 **Lock, Stock And Tear Drops**	*Roger Miller*	Dial 4077
11/23/68	59	6		2 **Hold What You've Got**	*Joe Tex*	Dot 17160
8/30/69	58	4		3 **Children**	*Cletus Haegert/Kathy Haegert*	Dot 17286
11/29/69+	37	7		4 **I Fall To Pieces**	*Hank Cochran/Harlan Howard*	Dot 17316
3/28/70	38	9		5 **Beneath Still Waters**	*Dallas Frazier*	Dot 17342
7/31/71	59	9		6 **The Chokin' Kind**	*Harlan Howard*	Dot 17384
1/22/72	30	14		7 **We've Got To Work It Out Between Us**	*Ann J. Morton*	Dot 17404
7/15/72	33	12		8 **It Meant Nothing To Me**	*Bobby Henry*	Dot 17424
3/3/73	15	13		9 **Say When**	*Dottie Bruce/Carmol Taylor/Norro Wilson*	Dot 17448
7/7/73	20	13		10 **It's A Man's World (If You Had A Man Like Mine)**	*Glenn Sutton/Carmol Taylor/Norro Wilson*	Dot 17467
12/8/73+	16	15		11 **When I Get My Hands On You**	*Carmol Taylor/Diana Trask/Norro Wilson*	Dot 17486
3/30/74	13	13		12 **Lean It All On Me**	*Josh Whitmore*	Dot 17496
8/17/74	32	10		13 (If You Wanna Hold On) **Hold On To Your Man**	*Tom Ewen/Diana Trask*	Dot 17520
1/11/75	21	14		14 **Oh Boy**	*Tony Romeo*	ABC/Dot 17536
6/28/75	82	5		15 **There Has To Be A Loser**	*Paul Anka*	ABC/Dot 17555
11/29/75	99	2		16 **Cry**	*Churchill Kohlman*	ABC/Dot 17587
6/13/81	62	6		17 **This Must Be My Ship**	*Scott Anders/Roger Murrah/Tina Murrah*	Kari 121
9/19/81	74	3		18 **Stirrin' Up Feelings**	*Jerry Foster/Bill Rice*	Kari 123

TRAVIS, Merle — 1940s: #10 / All-Time: #234 // HOF: 1977

Born on 11/29/1917 in Rosewood, Kentucky. Died on 10/20/1983 (age 65). Male singer/songwriter/guitarist. Father of **Tom Bresh**. Acted in the movie *From Here To Eternity*. Regular on TV's *Hometown Jamboree* and *Town Hall Party*.

DEBUT	PEAK	WKS	GOLD	Country Chart Hit	Songwriter	Label (& Number)
6/8/46	2^{4}	11		1 **Cincinnati Lou /**	*Shug Fisher/Merle Travis*	
6/15/46	3^{3}	9		2 **No Vacancy**	*Cliffie Stone/Merle Travis*	Capitol 258
9/21/46	❶^{14}	23		3 **Divorce Me C.O.D. /**	*Cliffie Stone/Merle Travis*	
1/11/47	5	2		4 **Missouri**	*Harry Duncan/Hank Penny*	Capitol 290
1/25/47	❶^{14}	22		5 **So Round, So Firm, So Fully Packed**	*Eddie Kirk/Cliffie Stone/Merle Travis*	Capitol 349
5/17/47	4	3		6 **Steel Guitar Rag /**	*Leon McAuliffe/Cliffie Stone/Merle Travis*	
5/24/47	4	4		7 **Three Times Seven**	*Cliffie Stone/Merle Travis*	Capitol 384
11/1/47	4	2		8 **Fat Gal /**	*Merle Travis*	
3/20/48	7	1		9 **Merle's Boogie Woogie**	*Merle Travis*	Capitol Amer. 40026
8/28/48	11	3		10 **Crazy Boogie**	J:11 / S:12 *Ike Cargill*	Capitol 15143
2/5/49	13	1		11 **What A Shame**	J:13 *Tex Atchison/Buck Nation/Merle Travis*	Capitol 15317
6/4/55	5	9		12 **Wildwood Flower** *[w/ Hank Thompson]*	J:5 / S:8 / A:13 *A.P. Carter/Hank Thompson* **[I]**	Capitol 3106
7/30/66	44	4		13 **John Henry, Jr.**	*Jack Triplett*	Capitol 5657

TRAVIS, Randy — 1990s: #15 / All-Time: #50

Born Randy Traywick on 5/4/1959 in Marshville, North Carolina. Male singer/songwriter/guitarist/actor. Married his manager, Lib Hatcher, on 5/31/1991. Appeared in several movies and TV shows. Also see **Same Old Train**.

CMA: Horizon 1986 / Male Vocalist 1987 & 1988 // OPRY: 1986

DEBUT	PEAK	WKS	GOLD	Country Chart Hit	Songwriter	Label (& Number)
1/6/79	91	4		1 **She's My Woman** *[Randy Traywick]*	*Jerry Tassel/Van Tassel*	Paula 431
8/31/85+	❶^{1}	35		2 **On The Other Hand**	S:❶^{2} / A:❶^{1} *Paul Overstreet/Don Schlitz*	Warner 28962
12/28/85+	6	24		3 **1982**	S:4 / A:7 *James Blackmon/Carl Vipperman*	Warner 28828
8/16/86	❶^{1}	21		4 **Diggin' Up Bones**	S:❶^{1} / A:❶^{1} *Albert Gore/Paul Overstreet*	Warner 28649
12/13/86+	2^{2}	21		5 **No Place Like Home**	A:2 / S:4 *Paul Overstreet*	Warner 28525
4/25/87	❶^{3}	22		6 **Forever And Ever, Amen** Grammy: Song / CMA: Single	S:❶^{2} / A:16 *Paul Overstreet/Don Schlitz*	Warner 28384
8/29/87	❶^{1}	22		7 **I Won't Need You Anymore (Always And Forever)**	S:❶^{1} *Max D. Barnes/Troy Seals*	Warner 28246
12/12/87+	❶^{1}	19		8 **Too Gone Too Long**	S:3 *Gene Pistilli*	Warner 28286
4/9/88	❶^{2}	18		9 **I Told You So**	S:❶^{2} *Randy Travis*	Warner 27969
7/30/88	❶^{1}	17		10 **Honky Tonk Moon**	S:❶^{2} *Dennis O'Rourke*	Warner 27833
11/19/88+	❶^{1}	18		11 **Deeper Than The Holler**	S:2 *Paul Overstreet/Don Schlitz*	Warner 27689
3/11/89	❶^{1}	17		12 **Is It Still Over?**	*Ken Bell/Larry Henley*	Warner 27551
7/1/89	17	15		13 **Promises**	*John Lindley/Randy Travis*	Warner 22917
9/23/89	❶^{1}	26		14 **It's Just A Matter Of Time**	*Brook Benton/Belford Hendricks/Clyde Otis*	Warner 22841
1/27/90	❶^{4}	26		15 **Hard Rock Bottom Of Your Heart**	*Hugh Prestwood*	Warner
5/12/90	2^{2}	21		16 **He Walked On Water** above 2 from the album *No Holdin' Back* on Warner 25988	*Allen Shamblin*	Warner
9/8/90	8	20		17 **A Few Ole Country Boys** *[w/ George Jones]*	*Troy Seals/Mentor Williams*	Warner
2/2/91	3^{2}	20		18 **Heroes And Friends** above 2 from the album *Heroes And Friends* on Warner 26310	*Don Schlitz/Randy Travis*	Warner
5/4/91	3^{2}	20		19 **Point Of Light**	*Don Schlitz/Thom Schuyler*	Warner
8/24/91	49	8		20 **We're Strangers Again** *[w/ Tammy Wynette]* from Wynette's album *Best Loved Hits* on Epic 48588	*Merle Haggard/Leona Williams*	Epic
9/28/91	❶^{1}	20		21 **Forever Together**	*Alan Jackson/Randy Travis*	Warner
12/21/91+	2^{3}	20		22 **Better Class Of Losers**	*Alan Jackson/Randy Travis*	Warner

DEBUT	PEAK	WKS	GOLD	ARTIST / Country Chart Hit	Ranking / Songwriter	Label (& Number)
				TRAVIS, Randy — cont'd		
4/4/92	**20**	20		23 **I'd Surrender All**	*Alan Jackson/Randy Travis*	Warner
				#19 & 21-23: from the album *High Lonesome* on Warner 26661		
8/15/92	**❶[1]**	20		24 **If I Didn't Have You**	*Max D. Barnes/Skip Ewing*	Warner
11/21/92+	**❶[2]**	20		25 **Look Heart, No Hands**	*Trey Bruce/Russell Smith*	Warner
				from the album *Greatest Hits Volume Two* on Warner 45045		
4/10/93	**21**	20		26 **An Old Pair Of Shoes**	*Jerry Foster/Art Masters/Johnny Morris*	Warner
				#24 & 26: from the album *Greatest Hits Volume One* on Warner 45044		
9/4/93	**46**	8		27 **Cowboy Boogie**	*Robert Blythe*	Warner
12/25/93+	**65**	6		28 **Wind In The Wire**	*Stewart MacDougall/David Wilkie*	Warner
				above 2 from the album *Wind In The Wire* on Warner 45319		
3/12/94	**2[1]**	20		29 **Before You Kill Us All**	*Max T. Barnes/Keith Follese*	Warner
6/11/94	**❶[1]**	20		30 **Whisper My Name**	*Trey Bruce*	Warner
10/22/94	**5**	20		31 **This Is Me**	*Thom McHugh/Tom Shapiro*	Warner
2/11/95	**7**	20		32 **The Box**	*Buck Moore/Randy Travis*	Warner
				above 4 from the album *This Is Me* on Warner 45501		
6/15/96	**24**	17		33 **Are We In Trouble Now**	*Mark Knopfler*	Warner
10/5/96	**25**	20		34 **Would I**	*Mark Winchester*	Warner
2/22/97	**60**	4		35 **Price To Pay**	*Trey Bruce/Craig Wiseman*	Warner
				above 3 from the album *Full Circle* on Warner 46328		
4/26/97	**51**	15		36 **King Of The Road**	*Roger Miller*	Asylum
				from the movie *Traveller* starring Mark Wahlberg and Bill Paxton (soundtrack on Asylum 62030)		
3/7/98	**2[1]**	20		37 **Out Of My Bones**	S:7 *Gary Burr/Robin Lerner/Sharon Vaughn*	DreamWorks
6/13/98	**9**	20		38 **The Hole**	S:14 *Skip Ewing/J.D. Hicks*	DreamWorks
10/10/98+	**2[1]**	21		39 **Spirit Of A Boy - Wisdom Of A Man**	*Trey Bruce/Glenn Burtnik*	DreamWorks
3/6/99	**16**	20		40 **Stranger In My Mirror**	*Skip Ewing/Kim Williams*	DreamWorks
				above 4 from the album *You And You Alone* on DreamWorks 50034		
8/14/99	**16**	20		41 **A Man Ain't Made Of Stone**	*Gary Burr/Franne Golde/Robin Lerner*	DreamWorks
1/29/00	**48**	10		42 **Where Can I Surrender**	*Rock Killough*	DreamWorks
4/29/00	**54**	10		43 **A Little Left Of Center**	*Billy Henderson/Steven Jones*	DreamWorks
8/19/00	**68**	1		44 **I'll Be Right Here Loving You**	*T.W. Hale/Jeffrey Steele*	DreamWorks
				above 4 from the album *A Man Ain't Made Of Stone* on DreamWorks 450119		
12/23/00	**75**	1		45 **Baptism**	*Michael Cates*	Warner
				from the album *Inspirational Journey* on Warner 47893		
10/27/01	**59**	2		46 **America Will Always Stand**	S:4 *Becki Bluefield/Michael Curtis/Yvonne Sanson/Randy Travis/Doc Walley*	Relentless
12/7/02+	**❶[1]**	34		47 **Three Wooden Crosses**	*Doug Johnson/Kim Williams*	Word-Curb/Warner
				CMA: Song		
7/26/03	**48**	14		48 **Pray For The Fish**	*Philip Moore/Dan Murph/Ray Scott*	Word-Curb/Warner
				above 2 from the album *Rise And Shine* on Word-Curb/Warner 886236		
11/20/04+	**46**	11		49 **Four Walls**	*Don Rollins/Harry Stinson/David Williams*	Word-Curb
				from the album *Passing Through* on Word-Curb 86348		
				TREVINO, Rick	**All-Time: #286**	
				Born Ricardo Trevino on 5/16/1971 in Austin, Texas. Male singer/songwriter/guitarist.		
9/18/93	**44**	20		1 **Just Enough Rope**	*Steve Dean/Karen Staley*	Columbia
2/12/94	**35**	19		2 **Honky Tonk Crowd**	*Marty Stuart*	Columbia
6/4/94	**3[1]**	20		3 **She Can't Say I Didn't Cry**	*Tony Martin/Troy Martin/Reese Wilson*	Columbia
10/8/94+	**5**	20		4 **Doctor Time**	*Susan Longacre/Lonnie Wilson*	Columbia
				above 4 from the album *Rick Trevino* on Columbia 53560		
2/11/95	**43**	12		5 **Looking For The Light**	*Liz Hengber/Tim Mensy*	Columbia
5/6/95	**6**	20		6 **Bobbie Ann Mason**	S:6 *Mark D. Sanders*	Columbia
9/9/95	**45**	11		7 **Save This One For Me**	*Mark D. Sanders/Verlon Thompson*	Columbia
				above 3 from the album *Looking For The Light* on Columbia 66771		
6/1/96	**2[2]**	20		8 **Learning As You Go**	*Larry Boone/Billy Lawson*	Columbia
10/26/96+	**❶[1]**	22		9 **Running Out Of Reasons To Run**	*Bob Regan/George Teren*	Columbia
3/22/97	**7**	22		10 **I Only Get This Way With You**	*Dave Loggins/Alan Ray*	Columbia
9/27/97	**44**	8		11 **See Rock City**	*Bob DiPiero/John Jarrard/Mark D. Sanders*	Columbia
				above 4 from the album *Learning As You Go* on Columbia 67452		
8/15/98	**52**	9		12 **Only Lonely Me**	*Larry Boone/Rick Bowles*	Columbia
6/21/03	**41**	20		13 **In My Dreams**	*Raul Malo/Alan Miller/Rick Trevino*	Warner
				from the album *In My Dreams* on Warner 48484		
				TREVOR, Van		
				Born on 11/12/1940 in Lewiston, Maine. Male singer/songwriter/producer.		
4/23/66	**22**	18		1 **Born To Be In Love With You**	*Hank Hunter/Van Trevor*	Band Box 367
11/19/66+	**27**	13		2 **Our Side**	*Van Trevor*	Band Box 371
9/9/67	**26**	15		3 **You've Been So Good To Me**	*Dick Heard/Van Trevor*	Date 1565
4/27/68	**31**	11		4 **Take Me Along With You**	*Dick Heard/Eddie Rabbitt*	Date 1594
2/1/69	**42**	9		5 **The Things That Matter**	*Don Sumner*	Royal American 280
5/10/69	**56**	7		6 **A Man Away From Home**	*Van Trevor*	Royal American 283
6/13/70	**42**	8		7 **Luziana River**	*Dick Heard/Eddie Rabbitt/Van Trevor*	Royal American 9
1/23/71	**54**	6		8 **Wish I Was Home Instead**	*Ron Peterson/Jim Shipp*	Royal American 23
				TRIBBLE, Mark		
				Born in Starkville, Mississippi. Male singer/bassist.		
5/6/89	**86**	2		**Lay Me Down Carolina**	*Rich Alves/Roger Murrah*	Paloma 5

DEBUT	PEAK	WKS	GOLD	ARTIST / Country Chart Hit	Ranking / Songwriter	Label (& Number)

TRICK PONY — 2000s: #47

Trio formed in Nashville, Tennessee: Heidi Newfield (vocals), Keith Burns (guitar, vocals) and Ira Dean (bass, vocals).

DEBUT	PEAK	WKS	GOLD	Country Chart Hit	Songwriter	Label (& Number)
10/21/00+	**12**	28		1 **Pour Me** S:2	*Rory Beighley/Keith Burns/Ira Dean/Heidi Newfield/Sammy Wedlock*	Warner
5/5/01	**4**	33		2 **On A Night Like This** S:3	*Doug Kahan/Karen Staley*	Warner
1/19/02	**13**	24		3 **Just What I Do**	*Keith Burns/Ira Dean*	Warner
				above 3 from the album *Trick Pony* on Warner 47927		
8/31/02+	**19**	24		4 **On A Mission**	*Ira Dean/David Lee Murphy/Kim Tribble*	Warner
4/5/03	**47**	10		5 **A Boy Like You**	*Heidi Newfield/Rivers Rutherford/Tom Shapiro*	Warner
				above 2 from the album *On A Mission* on Warner 48236		
7/3/04	**27**	20		6 **The Bride**	*Daryl Burgess/Lee Ann Burgess/Liz Hengber*	Asylum-Curb
2/12/05	**22**	28		7 **It's A Heartache**	*Ronnie Scott/Steve Wolfe*	Asylum-Curb
				above 2 from the album *R.I.D.E.* on Asylum-Curb 78864		

TRIGGS, Trini

Born on 8/8/1965 in Natchitoches, Louisiana. Black male singer.

DEBUT	PEAK	WKS	GOLD	Country Chart Hit	Songwriter	Label (& Number)
9/5/98	**47**	16		1 **Straight Tequila** S:17	*Jack Hargrove/Don Stafford*	Curb
1/30/99	**53**	19		2 **Horse To Mexico**	*Jon McElroy/Pebe Sebert*	Curb
2/26/00	**62**	3		3 **The Wreckin' Crew**	*David Flint/Billy Montana*	Curb
1/31/04	**59**	1		4 **Heaven On Earth**	*David Kersh/Arlos Smith*	Curb

TRINITY, Bobby

Born in Texas. Male singer.

DEBUT	PEAK	WKS	GOLD	Country Chart Hit	Songwriter	Label (& Number)
8/27/77	**95**	2		**I Love Everything I Get My Hands On**	*Roger Bowling/George Richey/Don Wayne*	GRT 128

TRINITY LANE

Trio of singer/songwriters: **Tom Grant**, Allen Estes and Sharon Anderson.

DEBUT	PEAK	WKS	GOLD	Country Chart Hit	Songwriter	Label (& Number)
4/23/88	**75**	4		1 **For A Song**	*Sharon Anderson/Allen Estes*	Curb 10507
8/13/88	**70**	3		2 **Someday, Somenight**	*Allen Estes/Chris Hill*	Curb 10511
11/5/88	**90**	2		3 **Ready To Take That Ride**	*Sharon Anderson/Allen Estes/Tom Grant/Chris Hill*	Curb 10515

TRIPP, Allen

Born in Fort Worth, Texas. Male singer.

DEBUT	PEAK	WKS	GOLD	Country Chart Hit	Songwriter	Label (& Number)
3/20/82	**39**	11		**Love Is**	*David Heavener*	Nashville 1001

TRITT, Travis — 1990s: #10 / 2000s: #21 / All-Time: #65

Born James Travis Tritt on 2/9/1963 in Marietta, Georgia. Male singer/songwriter/guitarist. Began singing in Atlanta nightclubs in 1981. Married model Theresa Nelson on 4/12/1997. Also see **Hope** and **Same Old Train**.

CMA: Horizon 1991 // OPRY: 1992

DEBUT	PEAK	WKS	GOLD	Country Chart Hit	Songwriter	Label (& Number)
9/2/89	**9**	26		1 **Country Club**	*Catesby Jones/Dennis Lord*	Warner 22882
2/24/90	**❶**[1]	26		2 **Help Me Hold On**	*Pat Terry/Travis Tritt*	Warner
6/16/90	**2**[1]	21		3 **I'm Gonna Be Somebody**	*Jill Colucci/Stewart Harris*	Warner
9/22/90	**28**	18		4 **Put Some Drive In Your Country**	*Travis Tritt*	Warner
2/16/91	**3**[1]	20		5 **Drift Off To Dream**	*Stewart Harris/Travis Tritt*	Warner
				above 4 from the album *Country Club* on Warner 26094		
6/1/91	**2**[1]	20		6 **Here's A Quarter (Call Someone Who Cares)**	*Travis Tritt*	Warner
9/14/91	**❶**[2]	20		7 **Anymore**	*Jill Colucci/Travis Tritt*	Warner
11/23/91+	**2**[1]	20		8 **The Whiskey Ain't Workin'** ***[w/ Marty Stuart]***	*Ronny Scaife/Marty Stuart*	Warner
				Grammy: Vocal Collaboration		
3/7/92	**4**	20		9 **Nothing Short Of Dying**	*Travis Tritt*	Warner
5/9/92	**72**	3		10 **Bible Belt** ***[w/ Little Feat]***	*Travis Tritt*	Warner
				from the movie *My Cousin Vinny* starring Joe Pesci; above 5 from the album *It's All About To Change* on Warner 26589		
6/6/92	**7**	20		11 **This One's Gonna Hurt You (For A Long, Long Time)** ***[w/ Marty Stuart]***	*Marty Stuart*	MCA
				from Stuart's album *This One's Gonna Hurt You* on MCA 10596		
8/29/92	**5**	20		12 **Lord Have Mercy On The Working Man**	*Kostas*	Warner
				Brooks & Dunn, **T. Graham Brown**, **George Jones**, **Little Texas**, **Dana McVicker**, **Tanya Tucker** and **Porter Wagoner** (guest vocals)		
12/5/92+	**❶**[2]	20		13 **Can I Trust You With My Heart**	*Stewart Harris/Travis Tritt*	Warner
12/12/92+	**13**	20		14 **T-R-O-U-B-L-E**	*Jerry Chesnut*	Warner
7/17/93	**11**	20		15 **Looking Out For Number One**	*Troy Seals/Travis Tritt*	Warner
10/30/93+	**21**	22		16 **Take It Easy**	*Jackson Browne/Glenn Frey*	Warner
				from the various artists album *Common Thread: Songs Of The* ***Eagles*** on Giant 24531		
10/30/93	**30**	17		17 **Worth Every Mile**	*Travis Tritt*	Warner
				#12-15 & 17: from the album *T-R-O-U-B-L-E* on Warner 45058		
12/25/93+	**54**	10		18 **The Devil Comes Back To Georgia** ***[w/ Mark O'Connor/Charlie Daniels/J. Cash/M. Stuart]***	*Tom Crain/Charlie Daniels/Joe DiGregorio/Fred Edwards/Charles Hayward/Jim Marshall*	Warner
				from O'Connor's album *Heroes* on Warner 45257		
4/23/94	**❶**[1]	20		19 **Foolish Pride**	*Travis Tritt*	Warner
8/6/94	**22**	16		20 **Ten Feet Tall And Bulletproof**	*Travis Tritt*	Warner
11/26/94+	**11**	20		21 **Between An Old Memory And Me**	*Charlie Craig/Keith Stegall*	Warner
4/15/95	**2**[1]	20		22 **Tell Me I Was Dreaming**	*Bruce Brown/Travis Tritt*	Warner
				above 4 from the album *Ten Feet Tall And Bulletproof* on Warner 45603		
8/19/95	**7**	20		23 **Sometimes She Forgets**	*Steve Earle*	Warner

DEBUT	PEAK	WKS	GOLD	ARTIST / #	Country Chart Hit	Ranking / Songwriter	Label (& Number)
					TRITT, Travis — cont'd		
1/20/96	**51**	8		24	**Only You (And You Alone)**	*Buck Ram/Ande Rand*	Warner
					above 2 from the album *Greatest Hits - From The Beginning* on Warner 46001		
4/20/96	**23**	20		25	**Honky Tonkin's What I Do Best** ***[w/ Marty Stuart]***	*Marty Stuart*	MCA
					CMA: Vocal Event; from Stuart's album *Honky Tonkin's What I Do Best* on MCA 11429		
7/27/96	**3**^{1}	20		26	**More Than You'll Ever Know**	S:6 *Travis Tritt*	Warner
11/23/96+	**6**	20		27	**Where Corn Don't Grow**	*Roger Murrah/Mark Alan Springer*	Warner
1/25/97	**29**	20	●	28	**Here's Your Sign (Get The Picture)** ***[w/ Bill Engvall]***	S:❶^{8} *Bill Engvall/Scott Rouse/Ronny Scaife* **[C]**	Warner
					from Engvall's album *Here's Your Sign* on Warner 46263		
4/19/97	**24**	20		29	**She's Going Home With Me**	*Travis Tritt*	Warner
7/26/97	**18**	20		30	**Helping Me Get Over You** ***[w/ Lari White]***	*Travis Tritt/Lari White*	Warner
11/22/97+	**23**	20		31	**Still In Love With You**	*Travis Tritt*	Warner
					#26, 27 & 29-31: from the album *The Restless Kind* on Warner 46304		
8/29/98	**29**	20		32	**If I Lost You**	S:3 *Stewart Harris/Travis Tritt*	Warner
1/2/99	**38**	17		33	**No More Looking Over My Shoulder**	S:19 *Michael Peterson/Craig Wiseman*	Warner
4/10/99	**52**	10		34	**Start The Car**	*Jude Cole*	Warner
					above 3 from the album *No More Looking Over My Shoulder* on Warner 47097		
10/9/99	**66**	4		35	**Move It On Over** ***[w/ George Thorogood]***	*Hank Williams*	Elektra
					from the animated TV series *King Of The Hill* (soundtrack on Elektra 62441)		
7/1/00	**❶**^{1}	34		36	**Best Of Intentions**	S:4 *Travis Tritt*	Columbia
12/16/00+	**2**^{4}	38		37	**It's A Great Day To Be Alive**	*Darrell Scott*	Columbia
6/16/01	**2**^{3}	32		38	**Love Of A Woman**	*Kevin Brandt*	Columbia
1/12/02	**8**	21		39	**Modern Day Bonnie And Clyde**	*Walt Aldridge/James LeBlanc*	Columbia
					above 4 from the album *Down The Road I Go* on Columbia 62165		
7/6/02	**13**	29		40	**Strong Enough To Be Your Man**	*Travis Tritt*	Columbia
1/25/03	**26**	20		41	**Country Ain't Country**	*Casey Beathard/Teresa Boaz/Carson Chamberlain*	Columbia
					above 2 from the album *Strong Enough* on Columbia 86660		
1/25/03	**51**	6		42	**Southern Boy** ***[w/ Charlie Daniels Band]***	*Charlie Daniels/Travis Tritt*	Blue Hat
					from Daniels' album *Redneck Fiddlin' Man* on Blue Hat 8159		
8/9/03	**50**	4		43	**Lonesome, On'ry And Mean**	*Steve Young*	RCA
					from the various artists album *I've Always Been Crazy: A Tribute To* ***Waylon Jennings*** on RCA 67064		
5/8/04	**28**	20		44	**The Girl's Gone Wild**	*Bob DiPiero/Rivers Rutherford*	Columbia
9/11/04	**21**	20		45	**What Say You** ***[w/ John Mellencamp]***	*Michael Bradford/Frank J. Myers*	Columbia
3/5/05	**32**	19		46	**I See Me**	*Casey Beathard/Chris Mohr*	Columbia
					above 3 from the album *My Honky Tonk History* on Columbia 92084		

TUBB, Ernest **1940s: #2 / 1950s: #7 / 1960s: #36 / All-Time: #18 // HOF: 1965**

Born on 2/9/1914 in Crisp, Texas. Died of emphysema on 9/6/1984 (age 70). Male singer/songwriter/guitarist. Known as "The Texas Troubadour." Acted in the movies *Fighting Buckaroo, Hollywood Barn Dance, Ridin' West* and *Jamboree.* Broadcast from his own Ernest Tubb Record Shop in Nashville beginning in 1947. Father of **Justin Tubb**.

EARLY HIT: Walking The Floor Over You (1941) // OPRY: 1943

DEBUT	PEAK	WKS	#	Country Chart Hit	Songwriter	Label (& Number)
1/8/44	**2**^{3}	17	1	**Try Me One More Time**	*Ernest Tubb*	Decca 6093
5/27/44	**❶**^{4}	29	2	**Soldier's Last Letter /**	*Henry Stewart/Ernest Tubb*	
6/3/44	**4**	3	3	**Yesterday's Tears**	*Ernest Tubb*	Decca 6098
3/17/45	**6**	1	4	**Keep My Mem'ry In Your Heart /**	*Ernest Tubb*	
3/31/45	**3**^{1}	14	5	**Tomorrow Never Comes**	*Johnny Bond/Ernest Tubb*	Decca 6106
8/4/45	**3**^{4}	8	6	**Careless Darlin'**	*Bob Shelton/Ernest Tubb/Lou Wayne*	Decca 6110
11/17/45	**❶**^{4}	13	7	**It's Been So Long Darling**	*Ernest Tubb*	Decca 6112
11/16/46+	**❶**^{2}	20	8	**Rainbow At Midnight**	*John Miller*	Decca 46018
11/16/46	**2**^{4}	12	9	**Filipino Baby /**	*Billy Cox/Clarke Van Ness*	
12/21/46	**5**	2	10	**Drivin' Nails In My Coffin**	*Jerry Irby*	Decca 46019
5/17/47	**4**	6	11	**Don't Look Now (But Your Broken Heart Is Showing) /**	*Ernest Tubb*	
6/28/47	**5**	1	12	**So Round, So Firm, So Fully Packed**	*Eddie Kirk/Cliffie Stone/Merle Travis*	Decca 46040
7/19/47	**4**	1	13	**I'll Step Aside**	*Johnny Bond*	Decca 46041
5/15/48	**5**	14	14	**Seaman's Blues**	S:5 / J:8 *Billy Tubb*	Decca 46119
7/17/48	**15**	1	15	**You Nearly Lose Your Mind**	J:15 *Ernest Tubb*	Decca 46125
8/7/48	**5**	13	16	**Forever Is Ending Today /**	S:5 / J:6 *Johnny Bond/Ike Cargill/Ernest Tubb*	
9/4/48	**9**	6	17	**That Wild And Wicked Look In Your Eye**	J:9 *Sam Nichols*	Decca 46134
12/11/48+	**2**^{1}	17	18	**Have You Ever Been Lonely? (Have You Ever Been Blue) /**	J:2 / S:9 *George Brown/Peter DeRose*	
12/11/48+	**5**	17	19	**Let's Say Goodbye Like We Said Hello**	S:5 / J:6 *Jimmie Skinner/Ernest Tubb*	Decca 46144
3/19/49	**4**	9	20	**Till The End Of The World**	J:4 / S:11 *Vaughn Horton*	Decca 46150
4/9/49	**2**^{1}	16	21	**I'm Bitin' My Fingernails And Thinking Of You** ***[w/ Andrews Sisters]*** **/**	J:2 / S:4 *Ernie Benedict/Lenny Sanders/Ernest Tubb/Roy West*	
4/16/49	**6**	5	22	**Don't Rob Another Man's Castle** ***[w/ Andrews Sisters]***	J:6 / S:10 *Jenny Lou Carson*	Decca 24592
5/7/49	**15**	1	23	**Daddy, When Is Mommy Coming Home**	J:15 *Troy Martin/Ernest Tubb*	Decca 46150
5/28/49	**6**	4	24	**Mean Mama Blues**	J:6 *Ernest Tubb*	Decca 46162
7/30/49	**❶**^{1}	20	25	**Slipping Around**	J:❶^{1} / S:4 *Floyd Tillman*	Decca 46173
9/3/49	**6**	10	26	**My Filipino Rose /**	J:6 / S:11 *Hank Snow*	
9/3/49	**8**	8	27	**Warm Red Wine**	S:8 / J:9 *Cindy Walker*	Decca 46175
9/17/49	**10**	3	28	**My Tennessee Baby**	J:10 *Ernest Tubb*	Decca 46173

DEBUT	PEAK	WKS	GOLD	#	ARTIST / Country Chart Hit	Ranking	Songwriter	Label (& Number)
					TUBB, Ernest — cont'd			
12/3/49+	❶^{1}	6		29	**Blue Christmas /** also see #43 and #48 below	J:❶^{1} / S:2 / A:2	*Billy Hayes/Jay Johnson* **[X]**	
12/24/49+	7	1		30	**White Christmas**	J:7 / S:15	*Irving Berlin* **[X]**	Decca 9-46186
12/31/49+	2^{2}	10		31	**Tennessee Border No. 2** ***[w/ Red Foley]*** /	S:2 / J:2	*Jimmy Work*	
1/21/50	7	2		32	**Don't Be Ashamed Of Your Age** ***[w/ Red Foley]***	J:7 / A:9	*Cindy Walker/Bob Wills*	Decca 46200
2/4/50	2^{1}	17		33	**Letters Have No Arms /**	J:2 / A:3 / S:5	*Arbie Gibson/Ernest Tubb*	
2/25/50	8	1		34	**I'll Take A Back Seat For You**	J:8	*Ernest Tubb*	Decca 46207
2/25/50	2^{1}	20		35	**I Love You Because /**	J:2 / S:4 / A:6	*Leon Payne*	
3/18/50	8	2		36	**Unfaithful One**	J:8	*Cliff Bruner*	Decca 46213
6/24/50	3^{3}	15		37	**Throw Your Love My Way /**	A:3 / J:4 / S:5	*Loys Southerland/Ernest Tubb*	
8/5/50	9	4		38	**Give Me A Little Old Fashioned Love**	J:9	*Ernest Tubb*	Decca 9-46243
8/12/50	❶^{3}	15		39	**Goodnight Irene** ***[w/ Red Foley & The Sunshine Trio]*** /	J:❶^{3} / S:❶^{2} / A:2	*Huddie Ledbetter/John Lomax*	
9/2/50	9	2		40	**Hillbilly Fever No. 2** ***[w/ Red Foley]***	J:9	*George Vaughn*	Decca 9-46255
10/28/50	10	2		41	**You Don't Have To Be A Baby To Cry**	J:10	*Bob Merrill/Terry Shand*	Decca 9-46257
11/4/50	5	9		42	**(Remember Me) I'm The One Who Loves You**	J:5 / S:7	*Stuart Hamblen*	Decca 9-46269
12/30/50+	9	1		43	**Blue Christmas**	A:9 / J:10	*Billy Hayes/Jay Johnson* **[X-R]**	Decca 9-46186
5/19/51	9	1		44	**The Strange Little Girl** ***[w/ Red Foley & Anita Kerr Singers]***	J:9	*Richard Adler/Jerry Ross*	Decca 9-46311
6/2/51	9	3		45	**Don't Stay Too Long**	A:9	*Ernest Tubb/Don Whitney*	Decca 9-46296
9/15/51	6	2		46	**Hey La La**	J:6	*Leonard McRight/Ray Price*	Decca 9-46338
12/15/51	7	2		47	**Driftwood On The River**	J:7	*John Klenner/Bob Miller*	Decca 9-46377
1/5/52	5	1		48	**Blue Christmas**	A:5	*Billy Hayes/Jay Johnson* **[X-R]**	Decca 9-46186
2/2/52	5	9		49	**Too Old To Cut The Mustard** ***[w/ Red Foley]***	S:5 / J:8 / A:10	*Bill Carlisle*	Decca 9-46387
2/9/52	3^{2}	11		50	**Missing In Action**	S:3 / A:5 / J:9	*Helen Kaye/Arthur Smith*	Decca 9-46389
5/17/52	9	2		51	**Somebody's Stolen My Honey**	J:9 / S:10	*Boudleaux Bryant*	Decca 9-28067
9/13/52	5	11		52	**Fortunes In Memories**	J:5 / A:7	*Charlie Walker/Lou Wayne*	Decca 9-28310
4/18/53	7	2		53	**No Help Wanted #2** ***[w/ Red Foley]***	S:7 / J:9	*Bill Carlisle*	Decca 28634
12/12/53	9	2		54	**Divorce Granted**	J:9	*Charlie Tebbetts*	Decca 28869
10/16/54	11	5		55	**Two Glasses, Joe**	S:11	*Cindy Walker*	Decca 29220
9/17/55	7	11		56	**The Yellow Rose Of Texas**	A:7 / S:13	*Don George*	Decca 29633
12/17/55	7	4		57	**Thirty Days (To Come Back Home)**	J:7 / A:10	*Chuck Berry*	Decca 29731
7/8/57	8	2		58	**Mister Love** ***[w/ The Wilburn Brothers]***	A:8	*Doug Kershaw/Rusty Kershaw*	Decca 30305
4/28/58	13	4		59	**House Of Glass**	A:13	*Jimmy Duncan*	Decca 30549
5/26/58	9	10		60	**Hey, Mr. Bluebird** ***[w/ The Wilburn Brothers]***	A:9 / S:14	*Cindy Walker*	Decca 30610
10/20/58	8	11		61	**Half A Mind /**		*Roger Miller*	
10/20/58	21	1		62	**The Blues**		*Cindy Walker*	Decca 30685
1/5/59	19	3		63	**What Am I Living For**		*Art Harris/Fred Jay*	Decca 30759
5/4/59	12	13		64	**I Cried A Tear**		*Fred Jay/Al Julia*	Decca 30872
9/28/59	14	14		65	**Next Time**		*Glenn Douglas*	Decca 30952
9/5/60	16	7		66	**Ev'rybody's Somebody's Fool**		*Howard Greenfield/Jack Keller*	Decca 31119
6/5/61	16	9		67	**Thoughts Of A Fool**		*Mel Tillis/Wayne Walker*	Decca 31241
11/13/61	14	11		68	**Through That Door**		*Hank Cochran*	Decca 31300
8/18/62	16	9		69	**I'm Looking High And Low For My Baby /**		*Art Gibson*	
9/8/62	30	1		70	**Show Her Lots Of Gold**		*Tommy Hill/Ray King*	Decca 31399
6/22/63	28	1		71	**Mr. Juke Box**		*Eddie Davis/Ralph Davis*	Decca 31476
9/28/63	3^{1}	23		72	**Thanks A Lot**		*Eddie Miller/Don Sessions*	Decca 31526
5/30/64	26	17		73	**Be Better To Your Baby**		*Justin Tubb*	Decca 31614
7/25/64	11	23		74	**Mr. And Mrs. Used To Be** ***[w/ Loretta Lynn]***		*Joe Deaton*	Decca 31643
12/26/64+	15	17		75	**Pass The Booze**		*Ray Butts/Gene Northington*	Decca 31706
3/6/65	29	12		76	**Do What You Do Do Well**		*Ned Miller*	Decca 31742
7/24/65	24	11		77	**Our Hearts Are Holding Hands** ***[w/ Loretta Lynn]***		*Bill Anderson*	Decca 31793
10/23/65	34	7		78	**Waltz Across Texas** ***[w/ His Texas Troubadours]*** also see #90 below		*Billy Tubb*	Decca 31824
1/1/66	48	2		79	**It's For God, And Country, And You Mom (That's Why I'm Fighting In Viet Nam)** ***[w/ His Texas Troubadours]***		*Dave McEnery*	Decca 31861
4/2/66	32	9		80	**Till My Getup Has Gotup And Gone** ***[w/ His Texas Troubadours]***		*Bud Logan/Charles Snoddy*	Decca 31908
10/15/66	16	16		81	**Another Story**		*Arlie Duff*	Decca 32022
2/25/67	45	9		82	**Sweet Thang** ***[w/ Loretta Lynn]***		*Nat Stuckey*	Decca 32091
2/3/68	55	5		83	**Too Much Of Not Enough**		*Jack Ripley*	Decca 32237
7/20/68	69	2		84	**I'm Gonna Make Like A Snake**		*Loretta Lynn*	Decca 32315
3/15/69	43	7		85	**Saturday Satan Sunday Saint**		*Wayne Walker*	Decca 32448
6/14/69	18	10		86	**Who's Gonna Take The Garbage Out** ***[w/ Loretta Lynn]***		*Lucille Cosenza/Johnny Tillotson/Teddy Wilburn*	Decca 32496
7/21/73	93	2		87	**I've Got All The Heartaches I Can Handle**		*Shel Silverstein*	MCA 40056
12/17/77+	79	7		88	**Sometimes I Do /**		*Jeannie Seely*	
12/17/77+	flip	7		89	**Half My Heart's In Texas**		*Linda Hargrove*	1st Generation 001
6/2/79	56	6		90	**Waltz Across Texas** **Willie Nelson** (guest vocal); new version of #78 above		*Billy Tubb* **[R]**	Cachet 4501
10/13/79	31	9		91	**Walkin' The Floor Over You** ***[w/ Merle Haggard]***		*Ernest Tubb*	Cachet 4507
6/4/83	6	16		92	**Leave Them Boys Alone** ***[w/ Hank Williams, Jr. & Waylon Jennings]***		*Dean Dillon/Gary Stewart/Tanya Tucker/Hank Williams Jr.*	Warner/Curb 29633

TUBB, Ernest — cont'd

Another Story ['66]
Be Better To Your Baby ['64]
Blue Christmas ['50, '51, '52]
Blues ['58]
Careless Darlin' ['45]
Daddy, When Is Mommy Coming Home ['49]
Divorce Granted ['53]
Do What You Do Do Well ['65]
Don't Be Ashamed Of Your Age ['50]
Don't Look Now (But Your Broken Heart Is Showing) ['47]
Don't Rob Another Man's Castle ['49]
Don't Stay Too Long ['51]
Driftwood On The River ['51]
Drivin' Nails In My Coffin ['46]
Ev'rybody's Somebody's Fool ['60]
Filipino Baby ['46]
Forever Is Ending Today ['48]
Fortunes In Memories ['52]
Give Me A Little Old Fashioned Love ['50]
Goodnight Irene ['50]
Half A Mind ['58]
Half My Heart's In Texas ['78]
Have You Ever Been Lonely? (Have You Ever Been Blue) ['49]
Hey La La ['51]
Hey, Mr. Bluebird ['58]
Hillbilly Fever No. 2 ['50]
House Of Glass ['58]
I Cried A Tear ['59]
I Love You Because ['50]
I'll Step Aside ['47]
I'll Take A Back Seat For You ['50]
I'm Bitin' My Fingernails And Thinking Of You ['49]
I'm Gonna Make Like A Snake ['68]
I'm Looking High And Low For My Baby ['62]
I've Got All The Heartaches I Can Handle ['73]
It's Been So Long Darling ['45]
It's For God, And Country, And You Mom (That's Why I'm Fighting In Viet Nam) ['66]
Keep My Mem'ry In Your Heart ['45]
Leave Them Boys Alone ['83]
Let's Say Goodbye Like We Said Hello ['49]
Letters Have No Arms ['50]
Mean Mama Blues ['49]
Missing In Action ['52]
Mister Love ['57]
Mr. And Mrs. Used To Be ['64]
Mr. Juke Box ['63]
My Filipino Rose ['49]
My Tennessee Baby ['49]
Next Time ['59]
No Help Wanted #2 ['53]
Our Hearts Are Holding Hands ['65]
Pass The Booze ['65]
Rainbow At Midnight ['47]
(Remember Me) I'm The One Who Loves You ['50]
Saturday Satan Sunday Saint ['69]
Seaman's Blues ['48]
Show Her Lots Of Gold ['62]
Slipping Around ['49]
So Round, So Firm, So Fully Packed ['47]
Soldier's Last Letter ['44]
Somebody's Stolen My Honey ['52]
Sometimes I Do ['78]
Strange Little Girl ['51]
Sweet Thang ['67]
Tennessee Border No. 2 ['50]
Thanks A Lot ['63]
That Wild And Wicked Look In Your Eye ['48]
Thirty Days (To Come Back Home) ['55]
Thoughts Of A Fool ['61]
Through That Door ['61]
Throw Your Love My Way ['50]
Till My Getup Has Gotup And Gone ['66]
Till The End Of The World ['49]
Tomorrow Never Comes ['45]
Too Much Of Not Enough ['68]
Too Old To Cut The Mustard ['52]
Try Me One More Time ['44]
Two Glasses, Joe ['54]
Unfaithful One ['50]
Walkin' The Floor Over You ['79]
Waltz Across Texas ['65, '79]
Warm Red Wine ['49]
What Am I Living For ['59]
White Christmas ['50]
Who's Gonna Take The Garbage Out ['69]
Yellow Rose Of Texas ['55]
Yesterday's Tears ['44]
You Don't Have To Be A Baby To Cry ['50]
You Nearly Lose Your Mind ['48]

TUBB, Justin

Born on 8/20/1935 in San Antonio, Texas. Died of a stomach aneurysm on 1/24/1998 (age 62). Male singer/songwriter/guitarist. Son of **Ernest Tubb**.

OPRY: 1955

DEBUT	PEAK	WKS	#	Country Chart Hit	Songwriter	Label (& Number)
7/3/54	4	21	1	**Looking Back To See** *[w/ Goldie Hill]* J:4 / S:5 / A:5	*Jim Ed Brown/Maxine Brown*	Decca 29145
1/8/55	11	2	2	**Sure Fire Kisses** *[w/ Goldie Hill]* A:11 / S:13	*George Mysels/Jack Perry/Michael Philips/Harry Sims*	Decca 29349
2/19/55	8	7	3	**I Gotta Go Get My Baby** A:8	*Marvin Rainwater*	Decca 29401
4/13/63	6	16	4	**Take A Letter, Miss Gray**	*Justin Tubb*	Groove 0017
10/2/65	23	9	5	**Hurry, Mr. Peters** *[w/ Lorene Mann]* — answer to "Yes, Mr. Peters" by **Roy Drusky** & **Priscilla Mitchell**	*Steve Karliski/Larry Kolber*	RCA Victor 8659
7/30/66	44	2	6	**We've Gone Too Far, Again** *[w/ Lorene Mann]*	*Bobby Bare*	RCA Victor 8834
2/25/67	63	7	7	**But Wait There's More**	*Justin Tubb*	RCA Victor 9082

TUCKER, Jerry Lee

Born in Arizona. Male singer.

DEBUT	PEAK	WKS	#	Country Chart Hit	Songwriter	Label (& Number)
11/12/88	93	2		**Livin' In Shadows**	*Lee Dresser*	Oak 1057

TUCKER, Jimmy

Born in California. Male singer.

DEBUT	PEAK	WKS	#	Country Chart Hit	Songwriter	Label (& Number)
5/19/79	98	2	1	**I'm Gonna Move to The Country (And Get Away To It All)**	*Barney Sudderth*	Gar-Pax 2715
12/8/79	85	4	2	**(You've Got That) Fire Goin' Again**	*Maury Pigg*	NSD 35
4/5/80	82	3	3	**The Reading Of The Will**	*Dave Hall/Gary Lumpkin*	NSD 40

TUCKER, La Costa — see LA COSTA

TUCKER, Rick

Born in California. Male singer/songwriter.

DEBUT	PEAK	WKS	#	Country Chart Hit	Songwriter	Label (& Number)
1/21/89	83	3		**Honey I'm Just Walking Out The Door**	*Rick Tucker*	Oak 1066

TUCKER, Tanya   1970s: #41 / 1980s: #45 / 1990s: #27 / All-Time: #32

Born on 10/10/1958 in Seminole, Texas; raised in Wilcox, Arizona. Female singer/songwriter/actress. Sister of **LaCosta**. Appeared on the *Lew King* TV series in Phoenix from 1969. Acted in the movies *Jeremiah Johnson* and *Hard Country*. Also see **Heart Of Nashville**.

CMA: Female Vocalist 1991

DEBUT	PEAK	WKS	#	Country Chart Hit	Songwriter	Label (& Number)
5/13/72	6	17	1	**Delta Dawn**	*Larry Collins/Alex Harvey*	Columbia 45588
11/18/72+	5	15	2	**Love's The Answer /**	*Emily Mitchell/Norro Wilson*	
12/2/72+	flip	13	3	**The Jamestown Ferry**	*Bobby Borchers/Mack Vickery*	Columbia 45721
3/24/73	❶[1]	17	4	**What's Your Mama's Name**	*Dallas Frazier/Earl Montgomery*	Columbia 45799
7/21/73	❶[1]	16	5	**Blood Red And Goin' Down**	*Curly Putman*	Columbia 45892
1/12/74	❶[1]	17	6	**Would You Lay With Me (In A Field Of Stone)**	*David Allan Coe*	Columbia 45991
6/8/74	4	14	7	**The Man That Turned My Mama On**	*Ed Bruce*	Columbia 46047
1/4/75	18	11	8	**I Believe The South Is Gonna Rise Again**	*Bobby Braddock*	Columbia 10069
4/26/75	❶[1]	15	9	**Lizzie And The Rainman**	*Larry Henley/Kenny O'Dell*	MCA 40402
6/14/75	18	15	10	**Spring**	*John Tipton*	Columbia 10127
8/23/75	❶[1]	15	11	**San Antonio Stroll**	*Peter Noah*	MCA 40444
11/8/75	23	10	12	**Greener Than The Grass (We Laid On)**	*David Allan Coe*	Columbia 10236
12/13/75+	4	15	13	**Don't Believe My Heart Can Stand Another You**	*Billy Ray Reynolds*	MCA 40497
4/17/76	3[2]	14	14	**You've Got Me To Hold On To**	*Dave Loggins*	MCA 40540
8/7/76	❶[1]	15	15	**Here's Some Love**	*Richard Mainegra/Jack Roberts*	MCA 40598
12/25/76+	12	12	16	**Ridin' Rainbows**	*Jan Crutchfield/Connie Ethridge/Susan Pugh*	MCA 40650
4/16/77	7	14	17	**It's A Cowboy Lovin' Night**	*Ronnie Rogers*	MCA 40708
7/23/77	40	8	18	**You Are So Beautiful**	*Bruce Fisher/Billy Preston*	Columbia 10577
8/13/77	16	11	19	**Dancing The Night Away**	*James H. Brown/Russell Smith*	MCA 40755

DEBUT	PEAK	WKS	GOLD	ARTIST / Ranking / Country Chart Hit	Songwriter	Label (& Number)
				TUCKER, Tanya — cont'd		
6/10/78	**86**	3		20 **Save Me**	*Jerry Goldstein/Tanya Tucker*	MCA 40902
11/25/78+	**5**	15		21 **Texas** (When I Die)	*Bobby Borchers/Ed Bruce/Patsy Bruce*	MCA 40976
4/7/79	**18**	13		22 **I'm The Singer, You're The Song**	*Jerry Goldstein/Tanya Tucker*	MCA 41005
8/23/80	**10**	14		23 **Pecos Promenade** — from the movie *Smokey & The Bandit II* starring **Burt Reynolds**	*Larry Collins/Snuff Garrett/Sandy Pinkard*	MCA 41305
9/27/80	**59**	6		24 **Dream Lover** ***[w/ Glen Campbell]***	*Bobby Darin*	MCA 41323
12/20/80+	**4**	15		25 **Can I See You Tonight**	*Deborah Allen/Rafe Van Hoy*	MCA 51037
4/11/81	**85**	4		26 **Why Don't We Just Sleep On It Tonight** ***[w/ Glen Campbell]***	*Glenn Riggs/Harry Shannon*	Capitol 4986
4/25/81	**40**	8		27 **Love Knows We Tried**	*Rory Bourke/Kerry Chater/Jan Crutchfield*	MCA 51096
7/4/81	**50**	7		28 **Should I Do It**	*Layng Martine Jr.*	MCA 51131
10/17/81	**83**	4		29 **Rodeo Girls**	*Joe Rainey/Tanya Tucker*	MCA 51184
10/16/82	**77**	4		30 **Cry /**	*Garth Murphy/Frank Musker*	
11/27/82+	**10**	23		31 **Feel Right**	*Larry Byrom*	Arista 0677
4/23/83	**41**	12		32 **Changes**	*Frank J. Myers/Eddy Raven/Tanya Tucker*	Arista 1053
7/23/83	**22**	15		33 **Baby I'm Yours**	*Van McCoy*	Arista 9046
2/15/86	**3**[2]	25		34 **One Love At A Time**	S:3 / A:4 *Paul Davis/Paul Overstreet*	Capitol 5533
7/12/86	**❶**[1]	24		35 **Just Another Love**	S:❶[1] / A:❶[1] *Paul Davis*	Capitol 5604
11/8/86+	**2**[1]	23		36 **I'll Come Back As Another Woman**	S:❶[1] / A:2 *Richard Carpenter/Kent Robbins*	Capitol 5652
3/28/87	**8**	25		37 **It's Only Over For You**	S:❶[1] / A:23 *Rory Bourke/Mike Reid*	Capitol 5694
7/25/87	**2**[2]	25		38 **Love Me Like You Used To**	S:❷[2] *Paul Davis/Bobby Emmons*	Capitol 44036
11/21/87+	**❶**[1]	24		39 **I Won't Take Less Than Your Love** ***[w/ Paul Davis & Paul Overstreet]***	...S:2 *Paul Overstreet/Don Schlitz*	Capitol 44100
4/2/88	**❶**[1]	20		40 **If It Don't Come Easy**	S:5 *Dave Gibson/Craig Karp*	Capitol 44142
7/16/88	**❶**[1]	23		41 **Strong Enough To Bend**	S:5 *Beth Nielsen Chapman/Don Schlitz*	Capitol 44188
12/3/88+	**2**[1]	19		42 **Highway Robbery**	*Michael Garvin/Bucky Jones/Tom Shapiro*	Capitol 44271
4/1/89	**4**	19		43 **Call On Me**	*Gary Scruggs*	Capitol 44348
7/22/89	**27**	15		44 **Daddy And Home**	*Jimmie Rodgers*	Capitol 44401
10/28/89+	**2**[2]	26		45 **My Arms Stay Open All Night**	*Paul Overstreet/Don Schlitz*	Capitol 44469
3/24/90	**3**[1]	23		46 **Walking Shoes**	*Paul Kennerley*	Capitol
6/23/90	**6**	21		47 **Don't Go Out** ***[w/ T. Graham Brown]***	*Radney Foster/Bill Lloyd*	Capitol
10/20/90+	**6**	20		48 **It Won't Be Me**	*Tom Shapiro/Chris Waters*	Capitol
2/23/91	**12**	20		49 **Oh What It Did To Me** — above 4 from the album *Tennessee Woman* on Capitol 91821	*Jerry Crutchfield*	Capitol
6/22/91	**2**[1]	20		50 **Down To My Last Teardrop**	*Paul Davis*	Capitol
10/12/91+	**2**[1]	20		51 (Without You) **What Do I Do With Me**	*David Chamberlain/David Lewis/Royce Porter*	Capitol
2/15/92	**3**[1]	20		52 **Some Kind Of Trouble**	*Brent Maher/Don Potter/Mike Reid*	Capitol
5/30/92	**4**	20		53 **If Your Heart Ain't Busy Tonight** — above 4 from the album *What Do I Do With Me* on Capitol 95562	*Tom Shapiro/Chris Waters*	Capitol
9/26/92	**2**[1]	20		54 **Two Sparrows In A Hurricane**	*Mark Alan Springer*	Liberty
1/16/93	**2**[2]	20		55 **It's A Little Too Late**	*Roger Murrah/Pat Terry*	Liberty
2/13/93	**27**	20		56 **Romeo** ***[w/ Dolly Parton/Mary-Chapin Carpenter/Billy Ray Cyrus/Kathy Mattea/Pam Tillis]*** — from Parton's album *Slow Dancing With The Moon* on Columbia 53199	...*Dolly Parton*	Columbia
4/17/93	**4**	20		57 **Tell Me About It** ***[w/ Delbert McClinton]*** — #54, 55 & 57: from the album *Can't Run From Yourself* on Liberty 98987	*Bill LaBounty/Pat McLaughlin*	Liberty
10/9/93	**2**[1]	20		58 **Soon**	*Casey Kelly/Bob Regan*	Liberty
11/20/93	**75**	2		59 **Already Gone** — from the various artists album *Common Thread: Songs Of The* ***Eagles*** on Giant 24531	*Robert Strandlund/Jack Tempchin*	Giant
1/15/94	**11**	20		60 **We Don't Have To Do This**	*Gary Burr/Victoria Shaw*	Liberty
5/28/94	**4**	20		61 **Hangin' In**	*Steve Bogard/Rick Giles*	Liberty
9/17/94	**20**	19		62 **You Just Watch Me** — #58 & 60-62: from the album *Soon* on Liberty 89048	*Rick Giles/Bob Regan*	Liberty
2/11/95	**27**	15		63 **Between The Two Of Them**	*Mickey Cates*	Liberty
5/27/95	**40**	11		64 **Find Out What's Happenin'** — above 2 from the album *Fire To Fire* on Liberty 28943	*Jerry Crutchfield*	Liberty
3/1/97	**9**	20		65 **Little Things**	S:9 *Michael Dulaney/Steven Jones*	Capitol
7/19/97	**45**	11		66 **Ridin' Out The Heartache** — above 2 from the album *Complicated* on Capitol 36885	*Cathy Majeski/Sunny Russ/Stephony Smith*	Capitol
8/24/02	**34**	22		67 **A Memory Like I'm Gonna Be**	*Jerry Laseter/Roger Murrah*	Tuckertime
3/8/03	**49**	9		68 **Old Weakness** (Coming On Strong) — above 2 from the album *Tanya* on Tuckertime 38827	*Bob DiPiero/Gary Nicholson*	Tuckertime

Already Gone ['93]
Baby I'm Yours ['83]
Between The Two Of Them ['95]
Blood Red And Goin' Down ['73]
Call On Me ['89]
Can I See You Tonight ['81]
Changes ['83]
Cry ['82]
Daddy And Home ['89]
Dancing The Night Away ['77]
Delta Dawn ['72]
Don't Believe My Heart Can Stand Another You ['76]
Don't Go Out ['90]
Down To My Last Teardrop ['91]
Dream Lover ['80]
Feel Right ['83]
Find Out What's Happenin' ['95]
Greener Than The Grass (We Laid On) ['75]
Hangin' In ['94]
Here's Some Love ['76]
Highway Robbery ['89]
I Believe The South Is Gonna Rise Again ['75]
I Won't Take Less Than Your Love ['88]
I'll Come Back As Another Woman ['87]
I'm The Singer, You're The Song ['79]
If It Don't Come Easy ['88]
If Your Heart Ain't Busy Tonight ['92]
It Won't Be Me ['91]
It's A Cowboy Lovin' Night ['77]
It's A Little Too Late ['93]
It's Only Over For You ['87]
Jamestown Ferry ['73]
Just Another Love ['86]
Little Things ['97]
Lizzie And The Rainman ['75]
Love Knows We Tried ['81]
Love Me Like You Used To ['87]
Love's The Answer ['73]
Man That Turned My Mama On ['74]
Memory Like I'm Gonna Be ['02]
My Arms Stay Open All Night ['90]
Oh What It Did To Me ['91]
Old Weakness (Coming On Strong) ['03]
One Love At A Time ['86]
Pecos Promenade ['80]
Ridin' Out The Heartache ['97]
Ridin' Rainbows ['77]
Rodeo Girls ['81]
Romeo ['93]
San Antonio Stroll ['75]
Save Me ['78]
Should I Do It ['81]
Some Kind Of Trouble ['92]
Soon ['93]
Spring ['75]
Strong Enough To Bend ['88]
Tell Me About It ['93]
Texas (When I Die) ['79]
Two Sparrows In A Hurricane ['92]
Walking Shoes ['90]
We Don't Have To Do This ['94]
What's Your Mama's Name ['73]
Why Don't We Just Sleep On It Tonight ['81]
(Without You) What Do I Do With Me ['92]
Would You Lay With Me (In A Field Of Stone) ['74]
You Are So Beautiful ['77]
You Just Watch Me ['94]
You've Got Me To Hold On To ['76]

DEBUT	PEAK	WKS	GOLD		ARTIST / Country Chart Hit	Songwriter	Label (& Number)

TURNER, Grant — HOF: 1981

Born Jesse Granderson Turner on 5/17/1912 in Abilene, Texas. Died on 10/19/1991 (age 79). Dean of the *Grand Ole Opry* announcers from 1945.

DEBUT	PEAK	WKS	GOLD		Country Chart Hit	Songwriter	Label (& Number)
10/24/64	48	1			The Bible In Her Hand	*Donna Veale*	Chart 1130

TURNER, Josh

Born on 11/20/1977 in Florence, South Carolina; raised in Hannah, South Carolina. Male singer/songwriter/guitarist.

DEBUT	PEAK	WKS	GOLD		Country Chart Hit	Songwriter	Label (& Number)
9/21/02	46	7		1	She'll Go On You	*Mark Narmore*	MCA Nashville
5/31/03+	13	44		2	Long Black Train	S:2 *Josh Turner*	MCA Nashville
4/17/04	31	20		3	What It Ain't	*Monty Criswell/Tim Mensy*	MCA Nashville
					above 3 from the album *Long Black Train* on MCA Nashville 000974		

TURNER, Lane

Born in Levelland, Texas. Male singer/songwriter.

DEBUT	PEAK	WKS	GOLD		Country Chart Hit	Songwriter	Label (& Number)
5/1/04	56	7			Always Wanting More (Breathless)	S:10 *Kent Blazy/Monty Holmes/Lane Turner*	Warner

TURNER, Mary Lou

Born on 6/13/1947 in Hazard, Kentucky; raised in Dayton, Ohio. Female singer.

DEBUT	PEAK	WKS	GOLD		Country Chart Hit	Songwriter	Label (& Number)
7/6/74	94	2		1	All That Keeps Me Goin'	*Bill Anderson*	MCA 40244
1/25/75	85	7		2	Come On Home	*Linda Darrell*	MCA 40343
11/29/75+	❶^{1}	16		3	Sometimes *[w/ Bill Anderson]*	*Bill Anderson*	MCA 40488
3/27/76	7	12		4	That's What Made Me Love You *[w/ Bill Anderson]*	*Larry Shoberg*	MCA 40533
6/12/76	25	12		5	It's Different With You	*Bill Anderson*	MCA 40566
10/2/76	30	10		6	Love It Away	*Linda Darrell*	MCA 40620
2/5/77	41	9		7	Cheatin' Overtime	*Peggy Forman*	MCA 40674
6/4/77	93	3		8	The Man Still Turns Me On	*Bill Anderson/David Byrd*	MCA 40727
7/16/77	18	12		9	Where Are You Going, Billy Boy *[w/ Bill Anderson]*	*Dave Kirby/Glenn Martin*	MCA 40753
12/10/77+	73	7		10	He Picked Me Up When You Let Me Down	*Bobby Braddock/Tommy Casassa*	MCA 40828
1/28/78	25	10		11	I'm Way Ahead Of You *[w/ Bill Anderson]*	*Curly Putman/Sonny Throckmorton*	MCA 40852
8/4/79	78	4		12	Yours And Mine	*Don Devaney/Johnny Wilson*	Churchill 7741
10/20/79	81	4		13	Caught With My Feelings Down /	*David Byrd/Mary Lou Turner*	
11/3/79	flip	2		14	You Can't Remember And I Can't Forget	*Ted Purvin*	Churchill 7744
2/9/80	91	2		15	I Wanna Love You Tonight	*Billy Troy*	Churchill 7751

TURNER, Zeb

Born William Grishaw on 6/23/1915 in Lynchburg, Virginia. Died of cancer on 1/10/1978 (age 62). Singer/songwriter/guitarist.

DEBUT	PEAK	WKS	GOLD		Country Chart Hit	Songwriter	Label (& Number)
9/17/49	11	1		1	Tennessee Boogie	J:11 *Zeb Turner*	King 790
4/21/51	8	2		2	Chew Tobacco Rag	J:8 / A:9 *Zeb Turner*	King 45-950

TURNER NICHOLS

Duo of South Carolina native Zack Turner and Missouri native Tim Nichols. Formed songwriting partnership in 1988.

DEBUT	PEAK	WKS	GOLD		Country Chart Hit	Songwriter	Label (& Number)
8/14/93	51	13		1	Moonlight Drive-In	*Billy Kirsch/Tim Nichols/Zack Turner*	BNA
12/11/93+	49	11		2	She Loves To Hear Me Rock	*Tim Nichols/Zack Turner*	BNA
					above 2 from the album *Turner Nichols* on BNA 66298		

TUTTLE, Wesley, And His Texas Stars

Born on 12/13/1917 in Lamar, Colorado. Died of heart failure on 9/29/2003 (age 85). Male singer/songwriter/guitarist. Acted in several western movies. Married actress Marilyn Myers in 1946.

DEBUT	PEAK	WKS	GOLD		Country Chart Hit	Songwriter	Label (& Number)
10/6/45	❶^{4}	14		1	With Tears In My Eyes	*Paul Howard*	Capitol 216
3/9/46	3^{1}	4		2	Detour /	*Paul Westmoreland*	
3/16/46	5	2		3	I Wish I Had Never Met Sunshine	*Gene Autry/Dale Evans/Oakley Haldeman*	Capitol 233
7/20/46	4	5		4	Tho' I Tried (I Can't Forget You)	*Gene Autry/Oakley Haldeman/Smokey Rogers*	Capitol 267
11/20/54	15	1		5	Never *[w/ Marilyn Tuttle]*	S:15 *Terry Fell*	Capitol 2850

TWAIN, Shania — 1990s: #30 / 2000s: #29 / All-Time: #113

Born Eileen Regina Edwards on 8/28/1965 in Windsor, Ontario, Canada; raised in Timmins, Ontario, Canada. Female singer/songwriter. Adopted the name Shania which means "I'm on my way" in the Ojibwa Indian language. Managed by **Mary Bailey** in the late 1980s. Married rock producer Robert John "Mutt" Lange on 12/28/1993.

CMA: Entertainer 1999

DEBUT	PEAK	WKS	GOLD		Country Chart Hit	Songwriter	Label (& Number)
3/27/93	55	18		1	What Made You Say That	*Tony Haselden/Stan Munsey*	Mercury
7/3/93	55	11		2	Dance With The One That Brought You	*Sam Hogin/Gretchen Peters*	Mercury
					above 2 from the album *Shania Twain* on Mercury 514422		
1/14/95	11	20		3	Whose Bed Have Your Boots Been Under?	*Mutt Lange/Shania Twain*	Mercury
5/13/95	❶^{2}	20	●	4	Any Man Of Mine	S:❶^{10} *Mutt Lange/Shania Twain*	Mercury
8/12/95	14	20		5	The Woman In Me (Needs The Man In You)	*Mutt Lange/Shania Twain*	Mercury
11/18/95+	❶^{2}	20		6	(If You're Not In It For Love) I'm Outta Here!	S:❶^{1} *Mutt Lange/Shania Twain*	Mercury
2/24/96	❶^{2}	20		7	You Win My Love	S:2 *Mutt Lange*	Mercury
5/11/96	❶^{1}	20		8	No One Needs To Know	*Mutt Lange/Shania Twain*	Mercury
8/10/96	28	14		9	Home Ain't Where His Heart Is (Anymore)	S:19 *Mutt Lange/Shania Twain*	Mercury
11/30/96+	48	9		10	God Bless The Child	S:❶^{1} *Mutt Lange/Shania Twain*	Mercury
					#3-10: from the album *The Woman In Me* on Mercury 522886		
10/4/97	❶^{5}	20	●	11	Love Gets Me Every Time	S:2 *Mutt Lange/Shania Twain*	Mercury

Billboard DEBUT	PEAK	WKS	GOLD	ARTIST / Country Chart Hit	Ranking / Songwriter	Label (& Number)
				TWAIN, Shania — cont'd		
11/15/97+	❶[1]	26		12 **Honey, I'm Home** S:❶[5]	*Mutt Lange/Shania Twain*	Mercury
11/15/97+	4	20		13 **Man! I Feel Like A Woman!**	*Mutt Lange/Shania Twain*	Mercury
				Grammy: Female Vocal		
11/15/97+	6	20		14 **Don't Be Stupid** (You Know I Love You) S:2	*Mutt Lange/Shania Twain*	Mercury
11/15/97+	6	20		15 **Come On Over**	*Mutt Lange/Shania Twain*	Mercury
				Grammy: Song		
11/15/97+	6	32		16 **From This Moment On** *[w/ Bryan White]*	*Mutt Lange/Shania Twain*	Mercury
1/24/98	❶[1]	24	▲	17 **You're Still The One** S:❶[22]	*Mutt Lange/Shania Twain*	Mercury
				Grammy: Song & Female Vocal		
12/12/98+	8	20		18 **That Don't Impress Me Much**	*Mutt Lange/Shania Twain*	Mercury
6/19/99	13	20		19 **You've Got A Way**	*Mutt Lange/Shania Twain*	Mercury
1/15/00	30	17		20 **Rock This Country!**	*Mutt Lange/Shania Twain*	Mercury
7/8/00	17	21		21 **I'm Holdin' On To Love** (To Save My Life)	*Mutt Lange/Shania Twain*	Mercury
				#11-21: from the album *Come On Over* on Mercury 536003		
10/19/02	7	20		22 **I'm Gonna Getcha Good!**	*Mutt Lange/Shania Twain*	Mercury
11/16/02+	12	20		23 **Up!**	*Mutt Lange/Shania Twain*	Mercury
12/7/02	60	1		24 **When You Kiss Me**	*Mutt Lange/Shania Twain*	Mercury
4/12/03	4	26		25 **Forever And For Always**	*Mutt Lange/Shania Twain*	Mercury
10/11/03+	9	20		26 **She's Not Just A Pretty Face**	*Mutt Lange/Shania Twain*	Mercury
12/13/03	57	2		27 **Coat Of Many Colors** *[w/ Alison Krauss & Union Station]*	*Dolly Parton*	Sugar Hill
				from the various artists album *Just Because I'm A Woman: Songs Of* **Dolly Parton** on Sugar Hill 3980		
2/21/04	18	20		28 **It Only Hurts When I'm Breathing**	*Mutt Lange/Shania Twain*	Mercury
				#22-26 & 28: from the album *Up!* on Mercury 170314		
9/18/04	7	20		29 **Party For Two** *[w/ Billy Currington]*	*Mutt Lange/Shania Twain*	Mercury
1/29/05	24	15		30 **Don't!**	*Mutt Lange/Shania Twain*	Mercury
5/21/05	45	8		31 **I Ain't No Quitter**	*Mutt Lange/Shania Twain*	Mercury
				above 3 from the album *Greatest Hits* on Mercury 003072		

TWISTER ALLEY

Group from area of Arkansas known as "Twister Alley": Shellee Morris (vocals), Amy Hitt, Steve Goins, Lance Blythe, Randy Loyd and Kevin King.

DEBUT	PEAK	WKS	GOLD	Country Chart Hit	Songwriter	Label (& Number)
11/6/93	61	7		1 **Nothing In Common But Love**	*Donny Lowery/Craig Wiseman*	Mercury
3/12/94	70	4		2 **Young Love**	*Ric Cartey/Carole Joyner*	Mercury
				above 2 from the album *Twister Alley* on Mercury 514927		

TWITTY, Conway — 1970s: #1 / 1980s: #2 / All-Time: #5 // HOF: 1999

Born Harold Lloyd Jenkins on 9/1/1933 in Friars Point, Mississippi; raised in Helena, Arkansas. Died of an abdominal aneurysm on 6/5/1993 (age 59). Male singer/songwriter/guitarist. Father of **Joni Lee** and **Jesseca James**. Uncle of **Larry Jenkins**. Changed name in 1957 (borrowed from Conway, Arkansas and Twitty, Texas). Acted in the movies *Sexpot Goes To College* and *College Confidential*. Owned the Twitty City tourist complex in Hendersonville, Tennessee.

CMA: Vocal Duo (with Loretta Lynn) 1972, 1973, 1974 & 1975

DEBUT	PEAK	WKS	GOLD	Country Chart Hit	Songwriter	Label (& Number)
3/26/66	18	12		1 **Guess My Eyes Were Bigger Than My Heart**	*Liz Anderson*	Decca 31897
9/17/66	36	10		2 **Look Into My Teardrops**	*Don Bowman/Harlan Howard*	Decca 31983
2/18/67	21	14		3 **I Don't Want To Be With Me**	*Mickey Jaco*	Decca 32081
7/8/67	32	12		4 **Don't Put Your Hurt In My Heart**	*Mickey Jaco*	Decca 32147
12/9/67	61	4		5 **Funny** (But I'm Not Laughing)	*Mickey Jaco*	Decca 32208
3/23/68	5	18		6 **The Image Of Me**	*Wayne Kemp*	Decca 32272
8/17/68	❶[1]	17		7 **Next In Line**	*Wayne Kemp/Curtis Wayne*	Decca 32361
12/28/68+	2[2]	17		8 **Darling, You Know I Wouldn't Lie**	*Wayne Kemp/Red Lane*	Decca 32424
5/10/69	❶[1]	17		9 **I Love You More Today**	*L.E. White*	Decca 32481
9/20/69	❶[1]	14		10 **To See My Angel Cry**	*Charles Haney/Conway Twitty/L.E. White*	Decca 32546
1/3/70	3[1]	14		11 **That's When She Started To Stop Loving You**	*Wayne Kemp*	Decca 32599
4/25/70	❶[4]	20		12 **Hello Darlin'**	*Conway Twitty*	Decca 32661
				Grammy: Hall of Fame		
10/10/70	❶[1]	18		13 **Fifteen Years Ago**	*Raymond Smith*	Decca 32742
2/6/71	❶[2]	14		14 **After The Fire Is Gone** *[w/ Loretta Lynn]*	*L.E. White*	Decca 32776
				Grammy: Vocal Duo		
2/6/71	59	6		15 **What Am I Living For**	*Stewart Harris/Fred Jay*	MGM 14205
3/20/71	❶[1]	17		16 **How Much More Can She Stand**	*Harry Compton*	Decca 32801
7/17/71	4	14		17 **I Wonder What She'll Think About Me Leaving**	*Merle Haggard*	Decca 32842
9/11/71	50	10		18 **What A Dream**	*Chuck Willis*	MGM 14274
10/2/71	❶[1]	17		19 **Lead Me On** *[w/ Loretta Lynn]*	*Leon Copeland*	Decca 32873
12/4/71+	4	16		20 **I Can't See Me Without You**	*Conway Twitty*	Decca 32895
4/1/72	❶[1]	15		21 (Lost Her Love) **On Our Last Date**	*Floyd Cramer/Conway Twitty*	Decca 32945
7/29/72	❶[1]	15		22 **I Can't Stop Loving You**	*Don Gibson*	Decca 32988
12/2/72+	❶[2]	15		23 **She Needs Someone To Hold Her** (When She Cries)	*Raymond Smith*	Decca 33033
3/31/73	2[1]	14		24 **Baby's Gone**	*Billy Parks/Conway Twitty*	MCA 40027
6/23/73	❶[1]	14		25 **Louisiana Woman, Mississippi Man** *[w/ Loretta Lynn]*	*Becki Bluefield/Jim Owen*	MCA 40079
7/21/73	❶[3]	19		26 **You've Never Been This Far Before**	*Conway Twitty*	MCA 40094
1/19/74	❶[1]	15		27 **There's A Honky Tonk Angel** (Who'll Take Me Back In)	*Denny Rice/Troy Seals*	MCA 40173
5/11/74	3[2]	15		28 **I'm Not Through Loving You Yet**	*Conway Twitty/L.E. White*	MCA 40224

Billboard DEBUT	PEAK	WKS	GOLD	Ranking	ARTIST / Country Chart Hit	Songwriter	Label (& Number)
					TWITTY, Conway — cont'd		
6/15/74	❶[1]	15		29	As Soon As I Hang Up The Phone *[w/ Loretta Lynn]*	*Conway Twitty*	MCA 40251
8/24/74	❶[2]	17		30	I See The Want To In Your Eyes	*Wayne Carson*	MCA 40282
1/11/75	❶[1]	14		31	Linda On My Mind	*Conway Twitty*	MCA 40339
5/24/75	❶[2]	13		32	Touch The Hand	*Ron Peterson/Conway Twitty*	MCA 40407
6/21/75	❶[1]	16		33	Feelins' *[w/ Loretta Lynn]*	*Don Goodman/Will Jennings/Troy Seals*	MCA 40420
8/16/75	4	13		34	Don't Cry Joni	*Conway Twitty*	MCA 40407
12/6/75+	❶[1]	14		35	This Time I've Hurt Her More Than She Loves Me	*Earl Thomas Conley/Mary Larkin*	MCA 40492
4/3/76	❶[1]	13		36	After All The Good Is Gone	*Conway Twitty*	MCA 40534
6/19/76	3[2]	12		37	The Letter *[w/ Loretta Lynn]*	*Charles Haney/Conway Twitty*	MCA 40572
8/21/76	❶[1]	13		38	The Games That Daddies Play	*Conway Twitty*	MCA 40601
11/20/76+	❶[1]	14		39	I Can't Believe She Gives It All To Me	*Conway Twitty*	MCA 40649
3/5/77	❶[1]	16		40	Play, Guitar Play	*Conway Twitty*	MCA 40682
6/4/77	2[3]	14		41	I Can't Love You Enough *[w/ Loretta Lynn]*	*Max D. Barnes/Troy Seals*	MCA 40728
7/23/77	❶[1]	15		42	I've Already Loved You In My Mind	*Conway Twitty*	MCA 40754
10/29/77	3[3]	15		43	Georgia Keeps Pulling On My Ring	*Tim Marshall/David Wilkins*	MCA 40805
2/18/78	16	10		44	The Grandest Lady Of Them All	*Mel McDaniel/Bob Morrison*	MCA 40857
6/24/78	6	11		45	From Seven Till Ten *[w/ Loretta Lynn]* /	*Max D. Barnes/Troy Seals*	
7/8/78	flip	9		46	You're The Reason Our Kids Are Ugly *[w/ Loretta Lynn]*	*Lola Jean Dillon/L.E. White*	MCA 40920
7/15/78	2[1]	14		47	Boogie Grass Band	*Ronnie Reno*	MCA 40929
11/18/78+	3[2]	15		48	Your Love Had Taken Me That High	*Jack Dunham/Galen Raye*	MCA 40963
3/17/79	❶[1]	14		49	Don't Take It Away	*Max D. Barnes/Troy Seals*	MCA 41002
7/14/79	❶[1]	15		50	I May Never Get To Heaven	*Bill Anderson/Buddy Killen*	MCA 41059
10/27/79	❶[3]	14		51	Happy Birthday Darlin'	*Chuck Howard*	MCA 41135
11/10/79+	9	14		52	You Know Just What I'd Do *[w/ Loretta Lynn]* /	*Jerry Foster/Bill Rice*	
11/10/79+	flip	14		53	The Sadness Of It All *[w/ Loretta Lynn]*	*Rusty Wolfe*	MCA 41141
2/2/80	❶[1]	13		54	I'd Just Love To Lay You Down	*Fred MacRae*	MCA 41174
5/10/80	5	15		55	It's True Love *[w/ Loretta Lynn]*	*Randy Goodrum*	MCA 41232
6/28/80	6	13		56	I've Never Seen The Likes Of You	*Wayland Holyfield/Bob McDill*	MCA 41271
10/18/80+	3[1]	17		57	A Bridge That Just Won't Burn	*Jim McBride/Roger Murrah*	MCA 51011
1/31/81	7	15		58	Lovin' What Your Lovin' Does To Me *[w/ Loretta Lynn]*	*Jane Crouch/Toni Dae*	MCA 51050
2/21/81	❶[1]	14		59	Rest Your Love On Me /	*Barry Gibb*	
3/7/81	flip	12		60	I Am The Dreamer (You Are The Dream)	*Russ Allison/Dallas Cody/David Hall*	MCA 51059
5/30/81	2[2]	18		61	I Still Believe In Waltzes *[w/ Loretta Lynn]*	*Michael Hughes/Johnny MacRae/Bob Morrison*	MCA 51114
7/11/81	❶[1]	16		62	Tight Fittin' Jeans	*Mike Huffman*	MCA 51137
10/31/81+	❶[1]	18		63	Red Neckin' Love Makin' Night	*Max D. Barnes/Troy Seals*	MCA 51199
1/30/82	❶[1]	17		64	The Clown	*Brenda Barnett/Wayne Carson/Charlie Chalmers/Sandra Rhodes*	Elektra 47302
4/24/82	❶[2]	16		65	Slow Hand	*John Bettis/Michael Clark*	Elektra 47443
5/8/82	69	7		66	Over Thirty (Not Over The Hill)	*Bucky Jones*	MCA 52032
9/18/82	2[2]	18		67	We Did But Now You Don't	*Woody Bomar/Berni Clifford/Pat McManus*	Elektra 69964
12/25/82+	❶[1]	19		68	The Rose	*Amanda McBroom*	Elektra 69854
4/2/83	44	11		69	We Had It All	*Donnie Fritts/Troy Seals*	MCA 52154
5/28/83	2[2]	21		70	Lost In The Feeling **Ricky Skaggs** (backing vocal)	*Lewis Anderson*	Warner 29636
9/24/83	6	19		71	Heartache Tonight	*Glenn Frey/Don Henley/Bob Seger/J.D. Souther*	Warner 29505
12/24/83+	7	18		72	Three Times A Lady	*Lionel Richie*	Warner 29395
4/14/84	❶[1]	19		73	Somebody's Needin' Somebody	*Len Chera*	Warner 29308
7/28/84	❶[1]	19		74	I Don't Know A Thing About Love (The Moon Song) **Joni Lee** (backing vocal)	S:❶[1] / A:❶[1] *Harlan Howard*	Warner 29227
11/10/84+	❶[1]	21		75	Ain't She Somethin' Else	A:❶[1] / S:2 *Jerry Foster/Bill Rice*	Warner 29137
3/16/85	❶[1]	20		76	Don't Call Him A Cowboy	S:❶[1] / A:❶[1] *Debbie Hupp/Johnny MacRae/Bob Morrison*	Warner 29057
7/6/85	3[1]	19		77	Between Blue Eyes And Jeans	S:3 / A:3 *Ken McDuffie*	Warner 28966
10/26/85	19	18		78	The Legend And The Man	S:16 / A:21 *Ron Hellard/Bucky Jones/Curly Putman*	Warner 28866
3/1/86	26	14		79	You'll Never Know How Much I Needed You Today	A:24 / S:29 *Jim Benton/Patty Linthicum/Jan Carlton Vinson*	Warner 28772
6/7/86	❶[1]	21		80	Desperado Love	S:❶[2] / A:❶[1] *Michael Garvin/Sammy Johns*	Warner 28692
10/18/86+	2[1]	25		81	Fallin' For You For Years	A:2 / S:3 *Mike Reid/Troy Seals*	Warner 28577
3/7/87	2[2]	23		82	Julia	S:3 / A:4 *Don Cook/John Jarvis*	MCA 53034
7/11/87	2[1]	24		83	I Want To Know You Before We Make Love	S:2 *Becky Hobbs/Candy Parton*	MCA 53134
11/14/87+	6	23		84	That's My Job	S:8 *Gary Burr*	MCA 53200
4/9/88	7	19		85	Goodbye Time	S:11 *J.D. Hicks/Roger Murrah*	MCA 53276
8/6/88	9	19		86	Saturday Night Special	S:8 *Larry Bastian/Dewayne Blackwell*	MCA 53373
11/26/88+	4	23		87	I Wish I Was Still In Your Dreams	S:30 *Don Cook/John Jarvis*	MCA 53456
4/22/89	2[1]	25		88	She's Got A Single Thing In Mind	*Walt Aldridge*	MCA 53633
8/26/89	19	15		89	House On Old Lonesome Road	*Dave Gibson/Bernie Nelson*	MCA 53688
12/9/89+	51	12		90	Who's Gonna Know	*Jimmy Griffin/Richard Mainegra/Rick Yancey*	MCA 53759
4/14/90	30	14		91	Fit To Be Tied Down from the album *Greatest Hits Volume III* on MCA 6391	*Walt Aldridge*	MCA
9/8/90	2[2]	20		92	Crazy In Love	*Randy McCormick/Even Stevens*	MCA
1/5/91	3[2]	20		93	I Couldn't See You Leavin'	*Rory Bourke/Ronny Scaife*	MCA
5/4/91	57	9		94	One Bridge I Didn't Burn above 3 from the album *Crazy In Love* on MCA 10027	*Steve Dean/Jim McBride*	MCA

DEBUT	PEAK	WKS	GOLD		ARTIST / Country Chart Hit	Songwriter	Label (& Number)
					TWITTY, Conway — cont'd		
8/24/91	22	20		95	**She's Got A Man On Her Mind**	*Billy Spencer/Curtis Wright*	MCA
12/7/91+	56	9		96	**Who Did They Think He Was**	*Richard Leigh/Pat McManus*	MCA
					above 2 from the album *Even Now* on MCA 10335		
8/14/93	62	5		97	**I'm The Only Thing (I'll Hold Against You)**	*Joe Diffie/Kim Williams/Lonnie Wilson*	MCA
					from the album *Final Touches* on MCA 10882		
6/26/04	57	6		98	**(I Wanna Hear) A Cheatin' Song** *[w/ Anita Cochran]*	*Anita Cochran*	Warner
					Twitty's vocals created from various snippets of his past recordings; from Cochran's album *God Created Woman* on Warner 48009		

After All The Good Is Gone ['76]
After The Fire Is Gone ['71]
Ain't She Somethin' Else ['85]
As Soon As I Hang Up The Phone ['74]
Baby's Gone ['73]
Between Blue Eyes And Jeans ['85]
Boogie Grass Band ['78]
Bridge That Just Won't Burn ['81]
Clown ['82]
Crazy In Love ['90]
Darling, You Know I Wouldn't Lie ['69]
Desperado Love ['86]
Don't Call Him A Cowboy ['85]
Don't Cry Joni ['75]
Don't Put Your Hurt In My Heart ['67]
Don't Take It Away ['79]
Fallin' For You For Years ['87]
Feelins' ['75]
Fifteen Years Ago ['70]
Fit To Be Tied Down ['90]
From Seven Till Ten ['78]
Funny (But I'm Not Laughing) ['67]
Games That Daddies Play ['76]
Georgia Keeps Pulling On My Ring ['77]
Goodbye Time ['88]
Grandest Lady Of Them All ['78]
Guess My Eyes Were Bigger Than My Heart ['66]
Happy Birthday Darlin' ['79]
Heartache Tonight ['83]
Hello Darlin' ['70]
House On Old Lonesome Road ['89]
How Much More Can She Stand ['71]
I Am The Dreamer (You Are The Dream) ['81]
I Can't Believe She Gives It All To Me ['77]
I Can't Love You Enough ['77]
I Can't See Me Without You ['72]
I Can't Stop Loving You ['72]
I Couldn't See You Leavin' ['91]
I Don't Know A Thing About Love (The Moon Song) ['84]
I Don't Want To Be With Me ['67]
I Love You More Today ['69]
I May Never Get To Heaven ['79]
I See The Want To In Your Eyes ['74]
I Still Believe In Waltzes ['81]
(I Wanna Hear) A Cheatin' Song ['04]
I Want To Know You Before We Make Love ['87]
I Wish I Was Still In Your Dreams ['89]
I Wonder What She'll Think About Me Leaving ['71]
I'd Just Love To Lay You Down ['80]
I'm Not Through Loving You Yet ['74]
I'm The Only Thing (I'll Hold Against You) ['93]
I've Already Loved You In My Mind ['77]
I've Never Seen The Likes Of You ['80]
Image Of Me ['68]
It's True Love ['80]
Julia ['87]
Lead Me On ['71]
Legend And The Man ['85]
Letter ['76]
Linda On My Mind ['75]
Look Into My Teardrops ['66]
(Lost Her Love) On Our Last Date ['72]
Lost In The Feeling ['83]
Louisiana Woman, Mississippi Man ['73]
Lovin' What Your Lovin' Does To Me ['81]
Next In Line ['68]
One Bridge I Didn't Burn ['91]
Over Thirty (Not Over The Hill) ['82]
Play, Guitar Play ['77]
Red Neckin' Love Makin' Night ['82]
Rest Your Love On Me ['81]
Rose ['83]
Sadness Of It All ['80]
Saturday Night Special ['88]
She Needs Someone To Hold Her (When She Cries) ['73]
She's Got A Man On Her Mind ['91]
She's Got A Single Thing In Mind ['89]
Slow Hand ['82]
Somebody's Needin' Somebody ['84]
That's My Job ['88]
That's When She Started To Stop Loving You ['70]
There's A Honky Tonk Angel (Who'll Take Me Back In) ['74]
This Time I've Hurt Her More Than She Loves Me ['76]
Three Times A Lady ['84]
Tight Fittin' Jeans ['81]
To See My Angel Cry ['69]
Touch The Hand ['75]
We Did But Now You Don't ['82]
We Had It All ['83]
What A Dream ['71]
What Am I Living For ['71]
Who Did They Think He Was ['92]
Who's Gonna Know ['90]
You Know Just What I'd Do ['80]
You'll Never Know How Much I Needed You Today ['86]
You're The Reason Our Kids Are Ugly ['78]
You've Never Been This Far Before ['73]
Your Love Had Taken Me That High ['79]

DEBUT	PEAK	WKS	GOLD		ARTIST / Country Chart Hit	Songwriter	Label (& Number)
					TWO HEARTS		
					Duo of sisters from Burbank, Oklahoma: Jama Bowen and Cathy Bowen.		
11/23/85	63	8		1	**Two Hearts Can't Be Wrong**	*Jerry Barlow/Dennis Knutson*	MDJ 5831
8/2/86	77	5		2	**Feel Like I'm Falling For You**	*Charlie Black/Johnny Cymbal/Tommy Rocco*	MDJ 5832
					TYLER, Bonnie		
					Born Gaynor Hopkins on 6/8/1953 in Swansea, Wales. Female pop singer.		
4/15/78	10	15	●	1	**It's A Heartache**	*Ronnie Scott/Steve Wolfe*	RCA 11249
2/24/79	86	3		2	**My Guns Are Loaded**	*Ronnie Scott/Steve Wolfe*	RCA 11468
					TYLER, Brad		
					Born on 12/29/1978 in Adrian, Michigan. Male singer.		
12/20/03	57	1			**Fridaynititus**	*Dan Mitchell*	Remuda
					TYLER, Kris		
					Born in Omaha, Nebraska. Female singer.		
4/12/97	68	5		1	**Keeping Your Kisses**	*Kris Tyler*	Rising Tide
11/8/97+	45	16		2	**What A Woman Knows**	*Gary Burr/Desmond Child/Kris Tyler*	Rising Tide
					above 2 from the album *What A Woman Knows* on Rising Tide 53045		
					TYLER, Ryan		
					Born on 10/6/1973 in Atlanta, Georgia; raised in Duluth, Georgia. Female singer/songwriter.		
8/16/03	36	20		1	**Run, Run, Run**	*Hunter Davis/Porter Howell/Kortney Kayle*	Arista Nashville
6/19/04	42	11		2	**The Last Thing She Said**	*Mickey Cones/Shaye Smith/Ryan Tyler*	Arista Nashville
					TYLER, "T" Texas — **1940s: #23**		
					Born David Luke Myrick on 6/20/1916 in Mena, Arkansas. Died of cancer on 1/23/1972 (age 55). Singer/songwriter/guitarist. Known as "The Man With A Million Friends." Acted in the movie *Horseman of The Sierras*. Hosted own *Range Round-Up* TV series in Los Angeles.		
8/24/46	5	1		1	**Filipino Baby** *[w/ his Oklahoma Melody Boys]*	*Billy Cox/Clarke Van Ness*	4 Star 1009
4/10/48	2^{1}	13		2	**Deck Of Cards** S:2 / J:3	*"T" Texas Tyler* **[S]**	4 Star 1228
7/3/48	10	2		3	**Dad Gave My Dog Away** S:10 / J:13	*Mary Shurtz/John Taylor/"T" Texas Tyler*	4 Star 1248
9/25/48	9	4		4	**Memories Of France /** J:9	*Al Dubin/J.R. Robinson*	
11/13/48	11	1		5	**Honky Tonk Gal** J:11	*Dusty Ellison*	4 Star 1249
11/26/49	4	5		6	**My Bucket's Got A Hole In It** J:4 / A:8	*Clarence Williams*	4 Star 1383
4/18/53	5	15		7	**Bumming Around** J:5 / S:5	*Pete Graves*	Decca 28579
7/17/54	3^{1}	19		8	**Courtin' In The Rain** *[w/ His Band]* A:3 / J:4	*"T" Texas Tyler*	4 Star 1660
					TYNDALL, Lynne		
					Born in Owensboro, Kentucky; raised in Nashville, Tennessee. Female singer.		
11/14/87	67	5		1	**Lovin' The Blue**	*Michael Bird*	Evergreen 1060
5/14/88	62	6		2	**This Is Me Leaving**	*John Gerrard/Karen Staley*	Evergreen 1071
11/5/88	83	4		3	**Love's Slippin' Up On Me**	*Bob McDill*	Evergreen 1079
6/10/89	74	3		4	**I Promise**	*Ron Hellard/Bucky Jones*	Evergreen 1091

Billboard DEBUT	PEAK	WKS	GOLD		ARTIST / Country Chart Hit	Ranking / Songwriter	Label (& Number)

U

ULISSE, Donna

Born in Hampton, Virginia. Female singer.

DEBUT	PEAK	WKS	GOLD		Country Chart Hit	Songwriter	Label (& Number)
2/2/91	**75**	3		1	**Things Are Mostly Fine**	*John Adrian*	Atlantic
4/13/91	**66**	5		2	**When Was The Last Time**	*Buck Moore/Frank J. Myers*	Atlantic

above 2 from the album *Trouble At The Door* on Atlantic 82282

UNCLE KRACKER

Born Matthew Shafer on 6/6/1974 in Mount Clemens, Michigan. White pop-rock singer/DJ. Member of **Kid Rock**'s posse.

DEBUT	PEAK	WKS	GOLD		Country Chart Hit	Songwriter	Label (& Number)
2/7/04	❶[5]	22			**When The Sun Goes Down** *[w/ Kenny Chesney]*	*Brett James*	BNA

from Chesney's album *When The Sun Goes Down* on BNA 58801

UNDERWOOD, Carrie

Born on 3/10/1983 in Checotah, Oklahoma. Female singer. Winner on the 2005 version of TV's *American Idol.*

DEBUT	PEAK	WKS	GOLD		Country Chart Hit	Songwriter	Label (& Number)
6/11/05	**50**	1			**Bless The Broken Road** *[w/ Rascal Flatts]*	*Bobby Boyd/Jeff Hanna/Marcus Hummon*	Arista

URBAN, Keith — 2000s: #8 / All-Time: #202

Born on 10/26/1967 in Whangarei, New Zealand; raised in Caboolture, Queensland, Australia. Male singer/songwriter. Former member of **The Ranch**. Also see **America The Beautiful**.

CMA: Horizon 2001 / Male Vocalist 2004

DEBUT	PEAK	WKS	GOLD		Country Chart Hit	Songwriter	Label (& Number)
8/28/99+	**18**	25		1	**It's A Love Thing**	*Monty Powell/Keith Urban*	Capitol
2/26/00	**4**	34		2	**Your Everything**	*Chris Lindsey/Bob Regan*	Capitol
10/7/00+	❶[1]	30		3	**But For The Grace Of God**	*Charlotte Caffey/Keith Urban/Jane Wiedlin*	Capitol
4/14/01	**3**[3]	27		4	**Where The Blacktop Ends**	*Allen Shamblin/Steve Wariner*	Capitol
					above 4 from the album *Keith Urban* on Capitol 97591		
7/6/02	❶[6]	41		5	**Somebody Like You**	*John Shanks/Keith Urban*	Capitol
11/30/02+	**3**[1]	30		6	**Raining On Sunday**	*Darrell Brown/Radney Foster*	Capitol
6/7/03	❶[1]	33		7	**Who Wouldn't Wanna Be Me**	*Monty Powell/Keith Urban*	Capitol
12/6/03+	❶[2]	28		8	**You'll Think Of Me**	*Darrell Brown/Ty Lacy/Dennis Matkosky*	Capitol
7/3/04	❶[4]	21		9	**Days Go By**	*Monty Powell/Keith Urban*	Capitol
7/10/04	**60**	1		10	**You Look Good In My Shirt**	*Tony Martin/Mark Nesler/Tom Shapiro*	Capitol
					#5-8 & 10: from the album *Golden Road* on Capitol 32936		
10/30/04+	**2**[5]	22		11	**You're My Better Half**	*John Shanks/Keith Urban*	Capitol
3/19/05	❶[5]	23		12	**Making Memories Of Us**	*Rodney Crowell*	Capitol

#9, 11 & 12: from the album *Be Here* on Capitol 77489

USA FOR AFRICA

All-star collaboration (USA: United Support of Artists) for starving people in Africa. Includes **Ray Charles**, **Kim Carnes**, **Willie Nelson**, **Lionel Richie** and **Kenny Rogers**.

DEBUT	PEAK	WKS	GOLD		Country Chart Hit	Songwriter	Label (& Number)
4/20/85	**76**	6	▲[4]		**We Are The World**	*Michael Jackson/Lionel Richie*	Columbia 04839

V

VALENTINO

Born Valentino Hernandez on 2/13/1960 in Toledo, Ohio. Male singer.

DEBUT	PEAK	WKS	GOLD		Country Chart Hit	Songwriter	Label (& Number)
8/1/81	**62**	6			**She Took The Place Of You**	*Sharon Vaughn*	RCA 12269

VANCE, Vince, & The Valiants

Born Andrew Stone in New Orleans, Louisiana. The Valiants: Kate Carlin, Gerra Adkins, Chrislynn Lee and Lisa Layne.

DEBUT	PEAK	WKS	GOLD		Country Chart Hit	Songwriter	Label (& Number)
12/25/93+	**55**	3		1	**All I Want For Christmas Is You**	*Troy Powers/Andy Stone* **[X]**	Waldoxy
12/24/94+	**52**	3		2	**All I Want For Christmas Is You**	*Troy Powers/Andy Stone* **[X-R]**	Waldoxy
12/23/95+	**52**	3		3	**All I Want For Christmas Is You**	*Troy Powers/Andy Stone* **[X-R]**	Waldoxy
12/28/96+	**49**	3		4	**All I Want For Christmas Is You**	*Troy Powers/Andy Stone* **[X-R]**	Waldoxy
12/27/97+	**43**	3		5	**All I Want For Christmas Is You**	*Troy Powers/Andy Stone* **[X-R]**	Waldoxy
12/11/99+	**31**	5		6	**All I Want For Christmas Is You**	*Troy Powers/Andy Stone* **[X-R]**	Waldoxy

all of above are the same version; from the album *All I Want For Christmas Is You* on Waldoxy 9289

VAN DYKE, Bruce

Born in 1953 in Medford, Oregon. Male singer/guitarist.

DEBUT	PEAK	WKS	GOLD		Country Chart Hit	Songwriter	Label (& Number)
5/6/89	**94**	1		1	**It's All In The Touch**	*Steve Bogard/Rory Bourke/Rick Giles*	Aria 51688
8/26/89	**73**	4		2	**Hard-Headed Heart**	*Jim Allison/Dan Chauvin*	Aria 51689

VAN DYKE, Leroy — All-Time: #267

Born on 10/4/1929 in Spring Fork, Missouri. Male singer/songwriter/guitarist. Acted in the movie *What Am I Bid.*

OPRY: 1962

DEBUT	PEAK	WKS	GOLD		Country Chart Hit	Songwriter	Label (& Number)
1/5/57	**9**	2		1	**Auctioneer**	A:9 / J:10 *Buddy Black/Leroy Van Dyke*	Dot 15503
9/4/61	❶[19]	37		2	**Walk On By**	*Kendall Hayes*	Mercury 71834
3/31/62	**3**[2]	12		3	**If A Woman Answers (Hang Up The Phone)**	*Barry Mann/Cynthia Weil*	Mercury 71926
12/29/62	**16**	7		4	**Black Cloud**	*Bill Black*	Mercury 72057
1/11/64	**50**	1		5	**Happy To Be Unhappy**	*Bobby Bare*	Mercury 72198
2/29/64	**45**	3		6	**Night People**	*Lee Morris*	Mercury 72232
1/9/65	**40**	5		7	**Anne Of A Thousand Days**	*Gene Nash*	Mercury 72360
10/15/66	**34**	9		8	**Roses From A Stranger**	*Boudleaux Bryant/Felice Bryant*	Warner 5841

DEBUT	PEAK	WKS	GOLD		ARTIST / Country Chart Hit	Ranking / Songwriter	Label (& Number)
					VAN DYKE, Leroy — cont'd		
4/15/67	**66**	4		9	**I've Never Been Loved**	*Boudleaux Bryant/Felice Bryant*	Warner 7001
1/6/68	**23**	11		10	**Louisville**	*Chuck Rogers*	Warner 7155
8/31/68	**69**	5		11	**You May Be Too Much For Memphis, Baby**	*Paul Hampton*	Kapp 931
11/1/69	**56**	4		12	**Crack In My World**	*Hermine Hilton/Dean Kay*	Kapp 2054
6/13/70	**63**	7		13	**An Old Love Affair, Now Showing**	*David Ingles*	Kapp 2091
12/12/70	**71**	2		14	**Mister Professor**	*Harlan Howard*	Decca 32756
9/18/71	**62**	5		15	**I Get Lonely When It Rains**	*Jerry Foster/Bill Rice*	Decca 32866
3/25/72	**69**	6		16	**I'd Rather Be Wantin' Love**	*Ted Harris*	Decca 32933
4/26/75	**79**	6		17	**Unfaithful Fools**	*Bobby Fischer*	ABC 12070
12/20/75+	**75**	7		18	**Who's Gonna Run The Truck Stop In Tuba City When I'm Gone?**	*Dolan Ellis*	ABC/Dot 17597
4/23/77	**77**	6		19	**Texas Tea**	*Ben Peters*	ABC/Dot 17691
					VANWARMER, Randy		
					Born Randall Van Wormer on 3/30/1955 in Indian Hills, Colorado. Died of leukemia on 1/12/2004 (age 48). Male singer/songwriter/guitarist.		
6/30/79	**71**	6	●	1	**Just When I Needed You Most**	*Randy Vanwarmer*	Bearsville 0334
2/20/88	**53**	8		2	**I Will Hold You**	*Roger Murrah/Randy Vanwarmer*	16th Avenue 70407
8/20/88	**72**	4		3	**Where The Rocky Mountains Touch The Morning Sun**	*Roger Murrah/Randy Vanwarmer*	16th Avenue 70418
					VAN ZANT		
					Duo from Jacksonville, Florida: brothers Donnie Van Zant and Johnny Van Zant. Donnie was lead singer of rock group 38 Special. Both are the younger brothers of former Lynyrd Skynyrd leader Ronnie Van Zant.		
3/26/05	**8**	26			**Help Somebody**	*Kip Raines/Jeffrey Steele*	Columbia
					from the album *Get Right With The Man* on Columbia 93500		
					VASSAR, Phil	**2000s: #17 / All-Time: #273**	
					Born on 5/28/1965 in Lynchburg, Virginia. Male singer/songwriter/pianist.		
10/30/99+	**5**	34		1	**Carlene**	*Charlie Black/Rory Bourke/Phil Vassar*	Arista Nashville
6/10/00	**❶[1]**	34		2	**Just Another Day In Paradise**	*Phil Vassar/Craig Wiseman*	Arista Nashville
1/20/01	**16**	20		3	**Rose Bouquet**	*Robert Byrne/Phil Vassar*	Arista Nashville
6/2/01	**9**	20		4	**Six-Pack Summer**	*Charlie Black/Tommy Rocco/Phil Vassar*	Arista Nashville
11/3/01+	**3[1]**	32		5	**That's When I Love You**	*Phil Vassar/Julie Wood-Vassar*	Arista Nashville
					above 5 from the album *Phil Vassar* on Arista Nashville 18891		
5/4/02	**5**	29		6	**American Child**	*Phil Vassar/Craig Wiseman*	Arista Nashville
1/11/03	**17**	19		7	**This Is God**	*Phil Vassar*	Arista Nashville
7/5/03	**41**	8		8	**Ultimate Love**	*Rodney Clawson/Phil Vassar/Julie Wood-Vassar*	Arista Nashville
					above 3 from the album *American Child* on Arista Nashville 67077		
5/1/04	**❶[2]**	32		9	**In A Real Love**	*Phil Vassar/Craig Wiseman*	Arista Nashville
11/27/04+	**17**	26		10	**I'll Take That As A Yes (The Hot Tub Song)**	*Jon McElroy/Vince Melamed*	Arista Nashville
6/25/05	**24↑**	14↑		11	**Good Ole Days**	*Phil Vassar/Craig Wiseman*	Arista Nashville
					above 3 from the album *Shaken Not Stirred* on Arista Nashville 61591		
					VASSY, Kin		
					Born Charles Kindred Vassy on 8/16/1943 in Atlanta, Georgia. Died of cancer on 6/15/1994 (age 50). Male singer. Former member of **The First Edition**.		
5/7/77	**69**	6		1	**You Are My Sunshine** ***[w/ Duane Eddy/Waylon Jennings/Willie Nelson/Deed Eddy]***	*Jimmie Davis/Charles Mitchell*	Elektra 45359
10/13/79	**85**	5		2	**Do I Ever Cross Your Mind**	*Dolly Parton*	ia 501
3/8/80	**67**	6		3	**Makes Me Wonder If I Ever Said Goodbye**	*Mickey Newbury*	ia 502
7/5/80	**88**	4		4	**There's Nobody Like You**	*Roger Miller*	ia 505
					above 2 produced by **Kenny Rogers**		
5/16/81	**39**	10		5	**Likin' Him And Lovin' You**	*Johnny MacRae/Bob Morrison*	Liberty 1407
8/15/81	**48**	8		6	**Sneakin' Around**	*Bob McDill*	Liberty 1427
12/12/81+	**21**	14		7	**When You Were Blue And I Was Green**	*Earl Thomas Conley*	Liberty 1440
5/1/82	**78**	4		8	**Cast The First Stone**	*Lonnie Ledford/J.L. Wallace*	Liberty 1458
8/21/82	**59**	8		9	**Women In Love**	*Bob McDill*	Liberty 1469
1/22/83	**80**	4		10	**Tryin' To Love Two**	*William Bell/Paul Mitchell*	Liberty 1488
					VAUGHN, Sammy		
					Born in Fort Worth, Texas. Male singer.		
8/19/78	**67**	5		1	**This Time Around**	*Oskar Solomon*	Oak 105
2/10/79	**98**	1		2	**Sunshine**	*Mickey Newbury*	Alpine 100
					VAUGHN, Sharon		
					Born in Florida. Female singer. Married Howard Bellamy (of the **Bellamy Brothers**) on 6/10/2002.		
4/27/74	**39**	11		1	**Until The End Of Time** ***[w/ Narvel Felts]***	*Jerry Foster/Bill Rice*	Cinnamon 793
8/10/74	**96**	4		2	**Never A Night Goes By**	*Jerry Foster/Bill Rice*	Cinnamon 799
12/6/75	**99**	2		3	**You And Me, Me And You**	*Will Jennings/Troy Seals*	ABC/Dot 17590
					VAUS, Steve		
					Born in San Diego, California. Male singer/songwriter/guitarist.		
8/8/92	**68**	2			**We Must Take America Back**	*Steve Vaus*	RCA
					VEACH, Gail		
					Born on 10/24/1954 in Bremerton, Washington. Female singer.		
8/1/87	**86**	2		1	**Would You Catch Me Baby (If I Fall For You)**	*Jerry McBee*	Prairie Dust 128
4/16/88	**93**	1		2	**Deepest Shade Of Blue**	*Larry Alderman/Richard Fagan*	Choice 101

Billboard DEBUT	PEAK	WKS	GOLD	Ranking	ARTIST / Country Chart Hit	Songwriter	Label (& Number)
					VEGA, Ray		
					Born on 7/28/1961 in Los Angeles, California; raised in El Paso, Texas. Singer/songwriter. Member of **The Vega Brothers**.		
11/16/96	**56**	12			**Remember When**	*John Bettis/Michael Clark/Ray Vega*	BNA
					from the album *Remember When* on BNA 64652		
					VEGA BROTHERS, The		
					Duo of brothers from El Paso, Texas: Robert Vega and **Ray Vega**.		
4/19/86	**54**	6			**Heartache The Size Of Texas**	*Ray Vega/Robert Vega*	MCA 52777
					VERA, Billy		
					Born William McCord on 5/28/1944 in Riverside, California; raised in Westchester County, New York. Male singer/songwriter. Acted in the movies *Buckaroo Banzai* and *The Doors*.		
1/24/87	**42**	13	●	1	**At This Moment** *[w/ The Beaters]*	*Billy Vera* [L]	Rhino 74403
4/25/87	**93**	2		2	**She Ain't Johnnie**	*L. Russell Brown/Billy Vera*	Macola 9812
					VERNON, Kenny		
					Born on 7/19/1940 in Jackson, Tennessee. Male singer/guitarist.		
10/1/66	**48**	2		1	**It Makes You Happy (To Know You Make Me Blue)**	*Gene Woods*	Caravan 123
1/4/69	**58**	9		2	**Eye To Eye** *[w/ LaWanda Lindsey]*	*Jimmy Day/John Owen*	Chart 1063
3/21/70	**27**	14		3	**Pickin' Wild Mountain Berries** *[w/ LaWanda Lindsey]*	*Bob McRee/Clifton Thomas/Edward Thomas*	Chart 5055
9/19/70	**51**	9		4	**Let's Think About Where We're Going** *[w/ LaWanda Lindsey]*	*Bob Yarbrough*	Chart 5090
2/27/71	**42**	9		5	**The Crawdad Song** *[w/ LaWanda Lindsey]*	*Connie Eaton/Noel Gibson*	Chart 5114
6/17/72	**56**	8		6	**That'll Be The Day**	*Jerry Allison/Buddy Holly/Norman Petty*	Capitol 3331
1/13/73	**55**	6		7	**Feel So Fine**	*Leonard Lee*	Capitol 3506
6/9/73	**66**	3		8	**Lady**	*Ray Griff*	Capitol 3590
1/5/74	**74**	8		9	**What Was Your Name Again?**	*Glenn Garrison*	Capitol 3785
					VICKERY, Mack		
					Born on 6/8/1938 in Town Creek, Alabama; raised in Adrianne, Michigan. Died of a heart attack on 12/21/2004 (age 66). Male singer/songwriter. Also recorded as **Atlanta James**.		
6/8/74	**95**	3		1	**That Kind Of Fool** *[Atlanta James]*	*Mack Vickery*	MCA 40233
5/28/77	**49**	7		2	**Ishabilly**	*Mack Vickery*	Playboy 5800
9/24/77	**94**	2		3	**Here's To The Horses**	*Rory Bourke/Gene Dobbins/Hugh Moffatt*	Playboy 5814
					VINCENT, Gene, and His Blue Caps		
					Born Vincent Eugene Craddock on 2/11/1935 in Norfolk, Virginia. Died of an ulcer on 10/12/1971 (age 36). Rock and roll singer/songwriter/guitarist.		
7/7/56	**5**	17			**Be-Bop-A-Lula**	J:5 / S:5 / A:9 *Tex Davis/Gene Vincent*	Capitol 3450
					Grammy: Hall of Fame / RS500		
					VINCENT, Rhonda		
					Born on 7/13/1962 in Kirksville, Missouri. Bluegrass singer/songwriter/guitarist.		
6/28/03	**58**	1		1	**You Can't Take It With You When You Go**	*T.J. Knight/Curtis Wright*	Rounder
					from the album *One Step Ahead* on Rounder 610497		
1/31/04	**48**	10		2	**If Heartaches Had Wings**	S:4 *Jody Alan Sweet*	Rounder
					VINCENT, Rick		
					Born in San Bernadino, California; raised in Bakersfield, California. Male singer/songwriter.		
12/12/92+	**39**	15		1	**The Best Mistakes I Ever Made**	*Rick Vincent*	Curb
5/22/93	**69**	4		2	**Ain't Been A Train Through Here In Years**	*Steve Hill/Rick Vincent*	Curb
					above 2 from the album *A Wanted Man* on Curb 77586		
					VINTON, Bobby		
					Born Stanley Robert Vinton on 4/16/1935 in Canonsburg, Pennsylvania. Hosted own TV variety series from 1975-76.		
2/28/70	**27**	9		1	**My Elusive Dreams**	*Curly Putman/Billy Sherrill*	Epic 10576
12/15/79	**86**	5		2	**Make Believe It's Your First Time**	*Bob Morrison/Johnny Wilson*	Tapestry 002
7/2/83	**87**	3		3	**You Are Love**	*Bobby Vinton*	Larc 81019
11/24/84	**91**	3		4	**Bed Of Roses**	*Rex Benson/Steve Gillette*	Tapestry 4009
12/24/88+	**63**	7		5	**The Last Rose**	*Coweta House*	Curb 10512
7/22/89	**70**	5		6	**Please Tell Her That I Said Hello**	*Peter Dibbens/Mike Shepstone*	Curb 10541
11/11/89	**64**	8		7	**It's Been One Of Those Days**	*Tim DuBois/Chester Lester/Mike Seals*	Curb 10560
					VON, Vicki Rae		
					Born in Marshalltown, Iowa; raised in Ankeny, Iowa. Female singer.		
4/11/87	**52**	10		1	**Not Tonight I've Got A Heartache**	*Walt Aldridge/Tom Brasfield*	Atlantic Amer. 99471
7/25/87	**53**	9		2	**Torn-Up**	*Charlie Black/Austin Roberts/Tommy Rocco*	Atlantic Amer. 99442

W

Billboard DEBUT	PEAK	WKS	GOLD	Ranking	ARTIST / Country Chart Hit	Songwriter	Label (& Number)
					WADE, Norman		
					Born in Columbus, Georgia. Male singer.		
11/17/79	**97**	2			**I'm A Long Gone Daddy**	*Hank Williams*	NSD 29
					WAGON, Chuck, And The Wheels		
					Vocal trio: Chuck Wagon, Carl Pyle and Sid Sequin.		
6/3/00	**75**	1			**Beauty's In The Eye Of The Beerholder**	*Randy Hardison/Chuck Wagon*	Lyric Street
					from the album *Off The Top Rope* on Lyric Street 65013		

Billboard DEBUT	PEAK	WKS	GOLD	ARTIST Ranking / Country Chart Hit	Songwriter	Label (& Number)

WAGONEERS

Group from Austin, Texas: Monte Warden (vocals, guitar), Brent Wilson (guitar), Craig Allan Pettigrew (bass) and Thomas Lewis (drums).

DEBUT	PEAK	WKS		Country Chart Hit	Songwriter	Label (& Number)
6/25/88	43	9		1 I Wanna Know Her Again	Monte Warden	A&M 1215
9/10/88	52	6		2 Every Step Of The Way	Monte Warden	A&M 1230
1/14/89	66	5		3 Help Me Get Over You	Monte Warden	A&M 1261
6/24/89	53	7		4 Sit A Little Closer	Mas Palermo/Monte Warden	A&M 1435

WAGONER, Porter

1950s: #33 / 1960s: #13 / 1970s: #30 / All-Time: #34 // HOF: 2002

Born on 8/12/1927 in West Plains, Missouri. Male singer/songwriter/guitarist. Hosted own TV series from 1960-79. Co-host of TNN's *Opry Backstage*. Also see **Heart Of Nashville** and **Some Of Chet's Friends**.

CMA: Vocal Group (with Dolly Parton) 1968 / Vocal Duo (with Dolly Parton) 1970 & 1971 // OPRY: 1957

DEBUT	PEAK	WKS		Country Chart Hit	Songwriter	Label (& Number)
10/30/54+	7	12		1 Company's Comin'	A:7 John Mullins	RCA Victor 5848
5/28/55	❶^{4}	33		2 A Satisfied Mind	A:❶^{4} / J:2 / S:2 Joe Hayes/Jack Rhodes	RCA Victor 6105
12/3/55+	3^{1}	22		3 Eat, Drink, And Be Merry (Tomorrow You'll Cry)	S:3 / J:3 / A:5 Celia Ferguson/Sandra Ferguson	RCA Victor 6289
3/31/56	8	11		4 What Would You Do? (If Jesus Came To Your House)	S:8 / A:14 Clyde Chesser/Bill Hamby	RCA Victor 6421
5/26/56	14	4		5 Uncle Pen	A:14 Bill Monroe	RCA Victor 6494
11/17/56	11	2		6 Tryin' To Forget The Blues	A:11 Boudleaux Bryant	RCA Victor 6598
8/19/57	11	3		7 I Thought I Heard You Calling My Name	A:11 Lee Emerson	RCA Victor 6964
5/4/59	29	1		8 Me And Fred And Joe And Bill	Paul Gilley/Billy Jack Hale	RCA Victor 7457
1/18/60	26	4		9 The Girl Who Didn't Need Love	Ron Isle	RCA Victor 7638
10/31/60	26	1		10 Falling Again /	John D. Loudermilk	
10/31/60	30	1		11 An Old Log Cabin For Sale	J.W. Payte	RCA Victor 7770
3/6/61	10	13		12 Your Old Love Letters	Johnny Bond	RCA Victor 7837
1/13/62	❶^{2}	29		13 Misery Loves Company	Jerry Reed	RCA Victor 7967
6/23/62	10	10		14 Cold Dark Waters	Don Owens	RCA Victor 8026
12/8/62+	7	15		15 I've Enjoyed As Much Of This As I Can Stand	Bill Anderson	RCA Victor 8105
6/22/63	20	7		16 My Baby's Not Here (In Town Tonight) /	C.C. Beam/C.L. Jiles/W.S. Stevenson	
7/20/63	29	1		17 In The Shadows Of The Wine	Dusty Rose	RCA Victor 8178
1/18/64	19	12		18 Howdy Neighbor Howdy	Jimmie Morris	RCA Victor 8257
4/25/64	5	23		19 Sorrow On The Rocks	Tony Moon	RCA Victor 8338
10/10/64	11	25		20 I'll Go Down Swinging	Bill Anderson	RCA Victor 8432
5/1/65	21	8		21 I'm Gonna Feed You Now (also see #73 below)	Bob Morris	RCA Victor 8524
7/31/65	4	19		22 Green, Green Grass Of Home	Curly Putman	RCA Victor 8622
12/25/65+	3^{1}	17		23 Skid Row Joe	Freddie Hart	RCA Victor 8723
5/7/66	21	12		24 I Just Came To Smell The Flowers	Vic McAlpin	RCA Victor 8800
11/5/66	48	4		25 Ole Slew-Foot (also see # 72 below)	Howard Hausey/Jay Webb	RCA Victor 8977
1/28/67	2^{1}	19		26 The Cold Hard Facts Of Life	Bill Anderson	RCA Victor 9067
7/15/67	15	16		27 Julie	Waylon Jennings	RCA Victor 9243
12/2/67+	7	17		28 The Last Thing On My Mind *[w/ Dolly Parton]*	Tom Paxton	RCA Victor 9369
12/16/67+	24	12		29 Woman Hungry	Gene Chrysler	RCA Victor 9379
4/13/68	7	16		30 Holding On To Nothin' *[w/ Dolly Parton]*	Jerry Chesnut	RCA Victor 9490
6/8/68	16	14		31 Be Proud Of Your Man	Betty Joe White/L.E. White	RCA Victor 9530
7/27/68	5	13		32 We'll Get Ahead Someday *[w/ Dolly Parton]* /	Mack Magaha	
10/5/68	51	6		33 Jeannie's Afraid Of The Dark *[w/ Dolly Parton]*	Dolly Parton	RCA Victor 9577
11/9/68+	2^{4}	21		34 The Carroll County Accident	Bob Ferguson	RCA Victor 9651
3/8/69	9	14		35 Yours Love *[w/ Dolly Parton]*	Harlan Howard	RCA Victor 0104
6/14/69	3^{2}	15		36 Big Wind	George McCormick/Wayne Walker/Alex Zanetis	RCA Victor 0168
6/21/69	16	11		37 Always, Always *[w/ Dolly Parton]*	Joyce McCord	RCA Victor 0172
10/25/69	5	16		38 Just Someone I Used To Know *[w/ Dolly Parton]*	Jack Clement	RCA Victor 0247
11/15/69	21	11		39 When You're Hot You're Hot	Curly Putman	RCA Victor 0267
2/14/70	9	15		40 Tomorrow Is Forever *[w/ Dolly Parton]*	Dolly Parton	RCA Victor 9799
3/14/70	41	5		41 You Got-ta Have A License	Tommy Collins	RCA Victor 9802
4/4/70	43	9		42 Little Boy's Prayer	Jim Owen	RCA Victor 9811
8/1/70	7	15		43 Daddy Was An Old Time Preacher Man *[w/ Dolly Parton]*	Dorothy Jo Hope/Dolly Parton	RCA Victor 9875
9/26/70	41	9		44 Jim Johnson	Bill Owens	RCA Victor 9895
1/2/71	18	16		45 The Last One To Touch Me	Dolly Parton	RCA Victor 9939
2/27/71	7	13		46 Better Move It On Home *[w/ Dolly Parton]*	Ray Griff	RCA Victor 9958
5/8/71	15	13		47 Charley's Picture	Frank Dycus/Larry Kingston	RCA Victor 9979
6/26/71	14	12		48 The Right Combination *[w/ Dolly Parton]*	Porter Wagoner	RCA Victor 9994
8/28/71	11	14		49 Be A Little Quieter	Porter Wagoner	RCA Victor 1007
11/13/71+	11	13		50 Burning The Midnight Oil *[w/ Dolly Parton]*	Porter Wagoner	RCA Victor 0565
2/26/72	8	14		51 What Ain't To Be, Just Might Happen	Porter Wagoner	RCA Victor 0648
4/8/72	9	14		52 Lost Forever In Your Kiss *[w/ Dolly Parton]*	Dolly Parton	RCA Victor 0675
8/5/72	14	13		53 A World Without Music	Porter Wagoner	RCA Victor 0753

DEBUT	PEAK	WKS	GOLD	#	ARTIST / Country Chart Hit	Songwriter	Label (& Number)
					WAGONER, Porter — cont'd		
9/2/72	**14**	13		54	**Together Always** *[w/ Dolly Parton]*	*Dolly Parton*	RCA Victor 0773
11/11/72	**16**	12		55	**Katy Did**	*Porter Wagoner*	RCA Victor 0820
3/3/73	**30**	9		56	**We Found It** *[w/ Dolly Parton]*	*Porter Wagoner*	RCA Victor 0893
4/21/73	**54**	7		57	**Lightening The Load**	*Porter Wagoner*	RCA Victor 0923
6/23/73	**3**[2]	17		58	**If Teardrops Were Pennies** *[w/ Dolly Parton]*	*Carl Butler*	RCA Victor 0981
7/14/73	**37**	9		59	**Wake Up, Jacob**	*Porter Wagoner*	RCA Victor 0013
12/15/73+	**43**	12		60	**George Leroy Chickashea**	*Porter Wagoner*	RCA Victor 0187
3/30/74	**46**	9		61	**Tore Down /**	*Porter Wagoner*	
3/30/74	**flip**	9		62	**Nothing Between**	*Porter Wagoner*	RCA Victor 0233
7/27/74	**15**	13		63	**Highway Headin' South**	*Porter Wagoner*	RCA Victor 0328
8/3/74	**❶**[1]	17		64	**Please Don't Stop Loving Me** *[w/ Dolly Parton]*	*Dolly Parton/Porter Wagoner*	RCA Victor 10010
12/14/74+	**19**	12		65	**Carolina Moonshiner**	*Dolly Parton*	RCA Victor 10124
7/12/75	**5**	17		66	**Say Forever You'll Be Mine** *[w/ Dolly Parton]*	*Dolly Parton*	RCA Victor 10328
11/8/75	**96**	2		67	**Indian Creek**	*Porter Wagoner*	RCA Victor 10411
5/15/76	**8**	14		68	**Is Forever Longer Than Always** *[w/ Dolly Parton]*	*Frank Dycus/Porter Wagoner*	RCA Victor 10652
11/13/76	**66**	5		69	**When Lea Jane Sang**	*Porter Wagoner*	RCA 10803
10/15/77	**76**	5		70	**I Haven't Learned A Thing** **Merle Haggard** (guest vocal)	*Sonny Throckmorton*	RCA 10974
1/7/78	**64**	6		71	**Mountain Music**	*Dolly Parton*	RCA 11186
11/18/78+	**31**	11		72	**Ole Slew-Foot /** new version of #25 above	*Howard Hausey/Jay Webb* **[R]**	
11/18/78+	**flip**	11		73	**I'm Gonna Feed 'Em Now** new version of #21 above	*Bob Morris* **[R]**	RCA 11411
3/17/79	**34**	8		74	**I Want To Walk You Home**	*Mac Gayden*	RCA 11491
8/11/79	**32**	9		75	**Everything I've Always Wanted**	*Johnny Marks*	RCA 11671
12/22/79+	**64**	7		76	**Hold On Tight**	*Porter Wagoner*	RCA 11771
5/24/80	**84**	4		77	**Is It Only Cause You're Lonely**	*Johnny Marks*	RCA 11998
6/21/80	**2**[2]	17		78	**Making Plans** *[w/ Dolly Parton]*	*Voni Morrison/Johnny Russell*	RCA 11983
11/8/80+	**12**	14		79	**If You Go, I'll Follow You** *[w/ Dolly Parton]*	*Dolly Parton/Porter Wagoner*	RCA 12119
11/13/82	**53**	8		80	**Turn The Pencil Over** from the movie *Honkytonk Man* starring **Clint Eastwood**	*Dewayne Blackwell*	Warner 29875
3/5/83	**35**	14		81	**This Cowboy's Hat**	*Jake Brooks*	Warner 29772

Always, Always ['69]
Be A Little Quieter ['71]
Be Proud Of Your Man ['68]
Better Move It On Home ['71]
Big Wind ['69]
Burning The Midnight Oil ['72]
Carolina Moonshiner ['75]
Carroll County Accident ['69]
Charley's Picture ['71]
Cold Dark Waters ['62]
Cold Hard Facts Of Life ['67]
Company's Comin' ['55]
Daddy Was An Old Time Preacher Man ['70]
Eat, Drink, And Be Merry (Tomorrow You'll Cry) ['56]
Everything I've Always Wanted ['79]
Falling Again ['60]
George Leroy Chickashea ['74]
Girl Who Didn't Need Love ['60]
Green, Green Grass Of Home ['65]
Highway Headin' South ['74]
Hold On Tight ['80]
Holding On To Nothin' ['68]
Howdy Neighbor Howdy ['64]
I Haven't Learned A Thing ['77]
I Just Came To Smell The Flowers ['66]
I Thought I Heard You Calling My Name ['57]
I Want To Walk You Home ['79]
I'll Go Down Swinging ['64]
I'm Gonna Feed 'Em Now ['79]
I'm Gonna Feed You Now ['65]
I've Enjoyed As Much Of This As I Can Stand ['63]
If Teardrops Were Pennies ['73]
If You Go, I'll Follow You ['81]
In The Shadows Of The Wine ['63]
Indian Creek ['75]
Is Forever Longer Than Always ['76]
Is It Only Cause You're Lonely ['80]
Jeannie's Afraid Of The Dark ['68]
Jim Johnson ['70]
Julie ['67]
Just Someone I Used To Know ['69]
Katy Did ['72]
Last One To Touch Me ['71]
Last Thing On My Mind ['68]
Lightening The Load ['73]
Little Boy's Prayer ['70]
Lost Forever In Your Kiss ['72]
Making Plans ['80]
Me And Fred And Joe And Bill ['59]
Misery Loves Company ['62]
Mountain Music ['78]
My Baby's Not Here (In Town Tonight) ['63]
Nothing Between ['74]
Old Log Cabin For Sale ['60]
Ole Slew-Foot ['66, '79]
Please Don't Stop Loving Me ['74]
Right Combination ['71]
Satisfied Mind ['55]
Say Forever You'll Be Mine ['75]
Skid Row Joe ['66]
Sorrow On The Rocks ['64]
This Cowboy's Hat ['83]
Together Always ['72]
Tomorrow Is Forever ['70]
Tore Down ['74]
Tryin' To Forget The Blues ['56]
Turn The Pencil Over ['82]
Uncle Pen ['56]
Wake Up, Jacob ['73]
We Found It ['73]
We'll Get Ahead Someday ['68]
What Ain't To Be, Just Might Happen ['72]
What Would You Do? (If Jesus Came To Your House) ['56]
When Lea Jane Sang ['76]
When You're Hot You're Hot ['69]
Woman Hungry ['68]
World Without Music ['72]
You Got-ta Have A License ['70]
Your Old Love Letters ['61]
Yours Love ['69]

WAKELY, Jimmy

1940s: #7 / 1950s: #28 / All-Time: #129

Born on 2/16/1914 in Mineola, Arkansas; raised in Oklahoma. Died on 9/23/1982 (age 68). Singer/songwriter/guitarist/pianist. Regular on **Gene Autry**'s *Melody Ranch* radio show in the early 1940s. Known as "The Melody Kid." Starred in several western movies. Hosted own radio show from 1952-57. Co-hosted TV's *Five Star Jubilee* in 1961.

EARLY HIT: There's A Star-Spangled Banner Waving Somewhere (1943)

DEBUT	PEAK	WKS	GOLD	#	Country Chart Hit	Songwriter	Label (& Number)
4/15/44	**2**[1]	4		1	**I'm Sending You Red Roses**	*Wally Fowler*	Decca 6095
4/3/48	**9**	6		2	**Signed, Sealed And Delivered**	S:9 / J:9 *Cowboy Copas/Lois Mann*	Capitol Amer. 40088
9/4/48	**❶**[11]	32		3	**One Has My Name** (The Other Has My Heart)	S:❶[11] / J:❶[7] *Hal Blair/Dearest Dean/Eddie Dean*	Capitol 15162
10/30/48+	**❶**[5]	28		4	**I Love You So Much It Hurts**	J:❶[5] / S:❶[4] *Floyd Tillman*	Capitol 15243
11/13/48+	**8**	5		5	**Mine All Mine**	J:8 *Lasses White*	Capitol 15236
2/5/49	**10**	1		6	**Forever More**	J:10 *Jimmy Wakely*	Capitol 15333
2/19/49	**9**	6		7	**Till The End Of The World**	S:9 / J:15 *Vaughn Horton*	Capitol 15368
5/14/49	**4**	9		8	**I Wish I Had A Nickel /**	J:4 / S:10 *William Barnhart/Tommy Sutton*	
6/18/49	**10**	3		9	**Someday You'll Call My Name**	J:10 *Jean Branch/Edith Hill*	Capitol 40153
8/6/49	**14**	2		10	**Tellin' My Troubles To My Old Guitar**	J:14 *Don Weston*	Capitol 40187
					MARGARET WHITING and JIMMY WAKELY:		
9/10/49	**❶**[17]	28	●	11	**Slipping Around /**	S:❶[17] / J:❶[12] / A:2 *Floyd Tillman*	
9/10/49	**6**	8		12	**Wedding Bells**	J:6 / S:7 *Jenny Lou Carson*	Capitol 40224
11/5/49	**2**[3]	13		13	**I'll Never Slip Around Again**	J:2 / S:2 / A:10 *Floyd Tillman*	Capitol 40246
2/11/50	**2**[1]	9		14	**Broken Down Merry-Go-Round /**	S:2 / J:3 / A:5 *Arthur Herbert/Fred Stryker*	
2/11/50	**3**[1]	7		15	**The Gods Were Angry With Me**	S:3 / J:4 *Bill Mackintosh/Roma Mackintosh*	Capitol F800

DEBUT	PEAK	WKS	GOLD		ARTIST / Country Chart Hit	Ranking / Songwriter	Label (& Number)
					MARGARET WHITING and JIMMY WAKELY:		
4/8/50	**7**	3		16	**Peter Cottontail** *[Jimmy Wakely]* A:7	*Steve Nelson/Jack Rollins*	Capitol 929
4/22/50	**2^{1}**	10		17	**Let's Go To Church** (Next Sunday Morning) S:2 / J:6 / A:6	*Steve Allen*	Capitol F960
9/23/50	**10**	1		18	**Mona Lisa** *[Jimmy Wakely]* A:10 from the movie *Captain Carey, U.S.A.* starring Alan Ladd	*Ray Evans/Jay Livingston*	Capitol F1151
11/18/50	**6**	1		19	**A Bushel And A Peck** S:6 / J:10 from the Broadway musical *Guys and Dolls* starring Robert Alda	*Frank Loesser*	Capitol F1234
1/20/51	**7**	1		20	**My Heart Cries For You** *[w/ Les Baxter]* S:7 / A:10	*Percy Faith/Carl Sigman*	Capitol F1328
3/17/51	**5**	12		21	**Beautiful Brown Eyes** *[w/ Les Baxter]* S:5 / J:5 / A:9	*Jerry Capehart/Alton Delmore/Arthur Smith*	Capitol F1393
6/2/51	**7**	2		22	**When You And I Were Young Maggie Blues** J:7	*Jack Frost/Jimmy McHugh*	Capitol F1500
12/8/51	**5**	5		23	**I Don't Want To Be Free** J:5	*Jimmy Wakely/George Wilson*	Capitol F1816

WALKER, Billy — **1960s: #22 / 1970s: #50 / All-Time: #71**

Born on 1/14/1929 in Ralls, Texas. Male singer/songwriter/guitarist. Regular on *Big D Jamboree* radio show in Dallas as "The Masked Singer" in 1949. Acted in the movies *Second Fiddle To A Steel Guitar* and *Red River Round Up*. Known as "The Tall Texan."

OPRY: 1960

DEBUT	PEAK	WKS	GOLD		Country Chart Hit	Ranking / Songwriter	Label (& Number)
6/26/54	**8**	13		1	**Thank You For Calling** A:8 / S:12	*Cindy Walker*	Columbia 21256
6/24/57	**12**	6		2	**On My Mind Again** A:12	*Dean Beard/Elmer Ray/Slim Willet*	Columbia 40920
11/7/60	**19**	8		3	**I Wish You Love**	*Carl Belew/Tommy Blake*	Columbia 41763
10/16/61	**23**	2		4	**Funny How Time Slips Away**	*Willie Nelson*	Columbia 42050
3/3/62	**❶^{2}**	23		5	**Charlie's Shoes**	*Roy Baham*	Columbia 42287
9/1/62	**5**	12		6	**Willie The Weeper**	*Freddie Hart/Billy Walker*	Columbia 42492
8/17/63	**21**	12		7	**Heart, Be Careful**	*Jay Bovington/Billy Walker*	Columbia 42794
12/28/63+	**22**	14		8	**The Morning Paper**	*Alex Zanetis*	Columbia 42891
4/25/64	**7**	24		9	**Circumstances** /	*Ronnie Self*	
5/9/64	**43**	4		10	**It's Lonesome**	*Hank Cochran*	Columbia 43010
10/10/64	**2^{2}**	22		11	**Cross The Brazos At Waco**	*Kay Arnold*	Columbia 43120
4/10/65	**8**	18		12	**Matamoros**	*Kay Arnold*	Columbia 43223
8/21/65	**16**	13		13	**If It Pleases You** /	*Wayne Walker*	
9/25/65	**45**	2		14	**I'm So Miserable Without You**	*Gene Strasser/George Winters*	Columbia 43327
6/4/66	**49**	2		15	**The Old French Quarter** (In New Orleans)	*Cindy Walker*	Monument 932
6/25/66	**2^{4}**	21		16	**A Million And One**	*Yvonne Devaney*	Monument 943
11/12/66+	**3^{2}**	17		17	**Bear With Me A Little Longer**	*Darrell Glenn*	Monument 980
3/4/67	**10**	15		18	**Anything Your Heart Desires**	*Billy Walker*	Monument 997
7/1/67	**18**	12		19	**In Del Rio**	*Billy Walker/Ray Wix*	Monument 1013
9/23/67	**11**	13		20	**I Taught Her Everything She Knows**	*Sylvia Dee/Arthur Kent*	Monument 1024
3/2/68	**18**	14		21	**Sundown Mary**	*Larry Baunach/Chris Gantry*	Monument 1055
7/13/68	**8**	10		22	**Ramona**	*Wolfe Gilbert/Mabel Wayne*	Monument 1079
11/2/68	**20**	10		23	**Age Of Worry**	*Billy Walker*	Monument 1098
2/8/69	**20**	13		24	**From The Bottle To The Bottom** *[w/ The Tennessee Walkers]*	*Kris Kristofferson*	Monument 1123
5/10/69	**12**	12		25	**Smoky Places**	*Abner Spector*	Monument 1140
9/6/69	**37**	7		26	**Better Homes And Gardens**	*Bobby Russell*	Monument 1154
12/6/69+	**9**	14		27	**Thinking 'Bout You, Babe**	*Harlan Howard*	Monument 1174
3/21/70	**23**	11		28	**Darling Days**	*Dallas Frazier/Whitey Shafer*	Monument 1189
6/27/70	**3^{1}**	18		29	**When A Man Loves A Woman** (The Way That I Love You)	*Bill Eldridge/Gary Stewart*	MGM 14134
10/24/70	**3^{1}**	15		30	**She Goes Walking Through My Mind**	*Bill Eldridge/Walter Haynes/Gary Stewart*	MGM 14173
1/23/71	**3^{1}**	14		31	**I'm Gonna Keep On Keep On Lovin' You**	*Rayburn Anthony/Gene Dobbins/Delores Whitehead*	MGM 14210
5/8/71	**28**	10		32	**It's Time To Love Her** from the movie *Lookin' Good* starring Robert Blake	*Bill Eldridge/Gary Stewart/Billy Walker*	MGM 14239
7/24/71	**22**	12		33	**Don't Let Him Make A Memory Out Of Me**	*Jerry McBee/A.L. "Doodle" Owens*	MGM 14268
11/13/71	**25**	10		34	**Traces Of A Woman**	*Bill Eldridge/Gary Stewart*	MGM 14305
5/27/72	**24**	11		35	**Gone** (Our Endless Love) *[w/ Mike Curb Congregation]*	*Darrell Glenn/Billy Walker*	MGM 14377
10/7/72	**3^{2}**	14		36	**Sing Me A Love Song To Baby**	*Rayburn Anthony/Gene Dobbins/Delores Whitehead*	MGM 14422
3/3/73	**34**	9		37	**My Mind Hangs On To You**	*Boudleaux Bryant/Felice Bryant*	MGM 14488
7/14/73	**52**	8		38	**The Hand Of Love**	*Jerry Foster/Bill Rice*	MGM 14565
11/10/73	**96**	3		39	**Too Many Memories**	*Gayle Barnhill/Rory Bourke*	MGM 14669
1/19/74	**39**	10		40	**I Changed My Mind**	*Conway Twitty*	MGM 14693
5/18/74	**74**	7		41	**How Far Our Love Goes**	*Jan Crutchfield/Buddy Killen/Curly Putman*	MGM 14717
9/7/74	**73**	9		42	**Fine As Wine**	*Eddie Rabbitt/Even Stevens*	MGM 14742
3/22/75	**10**	18		43	**Word Games**	*Bill Graham*	RCA Victor 10205
8/30/75	**25**	13		44	**If I'm Losing You**	*Gary S. Paxton*	RCA Victor 10345
12/20/75+	**19**	13		45	**Don't Stop In My World** (If You Don't Mean To Stay)	*Ray Pennington*	RCA Victor 10466
4/17/76	**41**	9		46	(Here I Am) **Alone Again**	*Ray Pennington*	RCA Victor 10613
7/31/76	**67**	6		47	**Love You All To Pieces**	*Joe Allen/Dave Kirby*	RCA Victor 10729
11/27/76+	**48**	9		48	**Instead Of Givin' Up** (I'm Givin' In)	*Billy Walker*	RCA 10821
7/2/77	**100**	1		49	(If You Can) **Why Can't I**	*Ray Pennington/Gene Vowell*	Casino 124
8/20/77	**86**	6		50	**It Always Brings Me Back Around To You**	*A.L. "Doodle" Owens/Gene Vowell*	MRC 1003

DEBUT	PEAK	WKS	GOLD	ARTIST / Country Chart Hit	Ranking / Songwriter	Label (& Number)
				WALKER, Billy — cont'd		
10/22/77	**64**	9		51 **Ringgold Georgia** *[w/ Brenda Kaye Perry]*	*Jerry McBee*	MRC 1005
1/14/78	**57**	7		52 **Carlena And José Gomez**	*Bobby Damron/Jay Jackson*	MRC 1009
5/6/78	**92**	2		53 **It's Not Over Till It's Over**	*Ray Pennington*	MRC 1014
8/26/78	**82**	4		54 **You're A Violin That Never Has Been Played**	*Dallas Harms*	Scorpion 0552
3/24/79	**72**	5		55 **Lawyers**	*John Riggs/Billy Walker*	Caprice 2056
6/23/79	**69**	6		56 **Sweet Lovin' Things /**	*Donn Tankersley*	
6/23/79	**flip**	6		57 **Rainbow And Roses**	*Barbara Lewis/Don Lewis*	Caprice 2057
9/29/79	**70**	6		58 **A Little Bit Short On Love (A Little Bit Long On Tears)**	*Billy Walker*	Caprice 2059
2/9/80	**48**	8		59 **You Turn My Love Light On**	*Billy Walker*	Caprice 2060
7/12/80	**74**	5		60 **Let Me Be The One** *[w/ Barbara Fairchild]*	*Jimbeau Henson*	Paid 102
10/11/80	**79**	3		61 **Love's Slipping Through Our Fingers (Leaving Time On Our Hands)** *[w/ Barbara Fairchild]* /	*John Riggs/Billy Walker*	
12/20/80+	**70**	7		62 **Bye Bye Love** *[w/ Barbara Fairchild]*	*Boudleaux Bryant/Felice Bryant*	Paid 107
4/2/83	**93**	2		63 **One Away From One Too Many**	*Ray Pennington*	Dimension 1042
12/7/85	**81**	5		64 **Coffee Brown Eyes**	*Stan Flaharty/Kent Westberry*	Tall Texan 57
7/30/88	**79**	3		65 **Wild Texas Rose**	*Billy Walker/Kent Westberry*	Tall Texan 60

Age Of Worry ['68]
Anything Your Heart Desires ['67]
Bear With Me A Little Longer ['67]
Better Homes And Gardens ['69]
Bye Bye Love ['81]
Carlena And José Gomez ['78]
Charlie's Shoes ['62]
Circumstances ['64]
Coffee Brown Eyes ['85]
Cross The Brazos At Waco ['64]
Darling Days ['70]
Don't Let Him Make A Memory Out Of Me ['71]
Don't Stop In My World (If You Don't Mean To Stay) ['76]
Fine As Wine ['74]
From The Bottle To The Bottom ['69]
Funny How Time Slips Away ['61]
Gone (Our Endless Love) ['72]
Hand Of Love ['73]
Heart, Be Careful ['63]
(Here I Am) Alone Again ['76]
How Far Our Love Goes ['74]
I Changed My Mind ['74]
I Taught Her Everything She Knows ['67]
I Wish You Love ['60]
I'm Gonna Keep On Keep On Lovin' You ['71]
I'm So Miserable Without You ['65]
If I'm Losing You ['75]
If It Pleases You ['65]
(If You Can) Why Can't I ['77]
In Del Rio ['67]
Instead Of Givin' Up (I'm Givin' In) ['77]
It Always Brings Me Back Around To You ['77]
It's Lonesome ['64]
It's Not Over Till It's Over ['78]
It's Time To Love Her ['71]
Lawyers ['79]
Let Me Be The One ['80]
Little Bit Short On Love (A Little Bit Long On Tears) ['79]
Love You All To Pieces ['76]
Love's Slipping Through Our Fingers (Leaving Time On Our Hands) ['80]
Matamoros ['65]
Million And One ['66]
Morning Paper ['64]
My Mind Hangs On To You ['73]
Old French Quarter (In New Orleans) ['66]
On My Mind Again ['57]
One Away From One Too Many ['83]
Rainbow And Roses ['79]
Ramona ['68]
Ringgold Georgia ['77]
She Goes Walking Through My Mind ['70]
Sing Me A Love Song To Baby ['72]
Smoky Places ['69]
Sundown Mary ['68]
Sweet Lovin' Things ['79]
Thank You For Calling ['54]
Thinking 'Bout You, Babe ['70]
Too Many Memories ['73]
Traces Of A Woman ['71]
When A Man Loves A Woman (The Way That I Love You) ['70]
Wild Texas Rose ['88]
Willie The Weeper ['62]
Word Games ['75]
You Turn My Love Light On ['80]
You're A Violin That Never Has Been Played ['78]

WALKER, Charlie — **All-Time: #247**

Born on 11/2/1926 in Copeville, Texas. Male singer/songwriter/guitarist. Worked as a DJ in the early 1950s. Acted in the movie *Country Music.*

OPRY: 1967

DEBUT	PEAK	WKS	GOLD	Country Chart Hit	Songwriter	Label (& Number)
1/28/56	**9**	2		1 **Only You, Only You**	J:9 *Jack Newman/Charlie Walker*	Decca 29715
10/20/58	**2**[4]	22		2 **Pick Me Up On Your Way Down**	*Harlan Howard*	Columbia 41211
6/8/59	**16**	9		3 **I'll Catch You When You Fall**	*Harlan Howard*	Columbia 41388
10/26/59	**22**	2		4 **When My Conscience Hurts The Most**	*Vic McAlpin/Lester Vanadore*	Columbia 41467
5/16/60	**11**	16		5 **Who Will Buy The Wine**	*Billy Mize*	Columbia 41633
2/6/61	**25**	3		6 **Facing The Wall**	*Hank Mills/Charlie Walker*	Columbia 41820
11/28/64+	**17**	16		7 **Close All The Honky Tonks**	*Red Simpson*	Epic 9727
6/5/65	**8**	18		8 **Wild As A Wildcat**	*Carmol Taylor*	Epic 9799
12/4/65+	**39**	7		9 **He's A Jolly Good Fellow**	*Billy Sherrill/Glenn Sutton*	Epic 9852
3/19/66	**37**	3		10 **The Man In The Little White Suit**	*Dallas Frazier*	Epic 9875
10/15/66	**56**	2		11 **Daddy's Coming Home (Next Week) /**	*Gene Crysler*	
10/29/66	**65**	5		12 **I'm Gonna Hang Up My Gloves**	*Merle Haggard*	Epic 10063
1/28/67	**38**	11		13 **The Town That Never Sleeps**	*Autry Inman*	Epic 10118
6/10/67	**8**	15		14 **Don't Squeeze My Sharmon**	*Carl Belew/Van Givens*	Epic 10174
11/4/67	**33**	10		15 **I Wouldn't Take Her To A Dogfight**	*Larry Kingston/Tom Snow*	Epic 10237
3/30/68	**54**	7		16 **Truck Drivin' Cat With Nine Wives**	*Jim Nesbitt*	Epic 10295
8/3/68	**31**	11		17 **San Diego**	*Dallas Frazier/A.L. "Doodle" Owens*	Epic 10349
3/1/69	**52**	10		18 **Honky-Tonk Season**	*Dallas Frazier*	Epic 10426
8/23/69	**44**	9		19 **Moffett, Oklahoma**	*Curtis Leach/Claude McBride*	Epic 10499
2/21/70	**56**	6		20 **Honky Tonk Women**	*Mick Jagger/Keith Richards*	Epic 10565
6/27/70	**52**	7		21 **Let's Go Fishin' Boys (The Girls Are Bitin')**	*Billy Arr*	Epic 10610
6/5/71	**71**	2		22 **My Baby Used To Be That Way**	*Johnny Carver*	Epic 10722
8/5/72	**74**	3		23 **I Don't Mind Goin' Under (If It'll Get Me Over You)**	*Dallas Frazier/A.L. "Doodle" Owens*	RCA Victor 0730
1/13/73	**65**	7		24 **Soft Lips And Hard Liquor**	*Lorene Allen/Walter Haynes*	RCA Victor 0870
8/17/74	**66**	8		25 **Odds And Ends (Bits And Pieces)**	*Harlan Howard*	Capitol 3922

WALKER, Cindy — **SW: #42**

Born on 7/20/1918 in Mart, Texas. Female singer/songwriter.

DEBUT	PEAK	WKS	GOLD	Country Chart Hit	Songwriter	Label (& Number)
11/4/44	**5**	1		**When My Blue Moon Turns To Gold Again**	*Gene Sullivan/Wiley Walker*	Decca 6103

Billboard DEBUT	PEAK	WKS	GOLD	ARTIST / Country Chart Hit	Ranking / Songwriter	Label (& Number)

WALKER, Clay

1990s: #26 / 2000s: #34 / All-Time: #111

Born Ernest Clayton Walker on 8/19/1969 in Beaumont, Texas. Male singer/songwriter/guitarist. Began playing professionally in bars around Texas in 1985. Studied business while attending college.

DEBUT	PEAK	WKS		Country Chart Hit	Songwriter	Label (& Number)
7/10/93	❶[1]	20	1	**What's It To You**	*Robert Ellis Orrall/Curtis Wright*	Giant
10/30/93+	❶[1]	20	2	**Live Until I Die**	*Clay Walker*	Giant
2/26/94	**11**	20	3	**Where Do I Fit In The Picture**	*Clay Walker*	Giant
4/30/94	**67**	3	4	**White Palace**	*Byron Hill/Zack Turner*	Giant
6/11/94	❶[1]	20	5	**Dreaming With My Eyes Open**	*Tony Arata*	Giant
				above 5 from the album *Clay Walker* on Giant 24511		
9/24/94	❶[1]	20	6	**If I Could Make A Living**	*Alan Jackson/Roger Murrah/Keith Stegall*	Giant
1/14/95	❶[2]	20	7	**This Woman And This Man**	*Michael Lunn/Jeff Pennig*	Giant
5/6/95	**16**	20	8	**My Heart Will Never Know**	S:10 *Steve Dorff/Billy Kirsch*	Giant
				above 3 from the album *If I Could Make A Living* on Giant 24582		
9/16/95	**2**[2]	20	9	**Who Needs You Baby**	S:4 *Randy Boudreaux/Clay Walker/Kim Williams*	Giant
1/13/96	**2**[1]	20	10	**Hypnotize The Moon**	S:❶[3] *Steve Dorff/Eric Kaz*	Giant
5/25/96	**5**	20	11	**Only On Days That End In "Y"**	*Richard Fagan*	Giant
9/28/96	**18**	19	12	**Bury The Shovel**	*Chris Arms/Chuck Jones*	Giant
				above 4 from the album *Hypnotize The Moon* on Giant 24640		
2/1/97	❶[2]	20	13	**Rumor Has It**	*Jason Greene/Clay Walker*	Giant
4/26/97	**18**	20	14	**One, Two, I Love You**	*Ed Hill/Bucky Jones*	Giant
8/9/97	**4**	20	15	**Watch This**	*Aaron Barker/Ron Harbin/Anthony Smith*	Giant
12/20/97+	**2**[1]	27	16	**Then What?**	S:4 *Randy Sharp/Jon Vezner*	Giant
				above 4 from the album *Rumor Has It* on Giant 24674		
4/18/98	**68**	9	17	**Holding Her And Loving You**	*Walt Aldridge/Tom Brasfield*	Giant
5/2/98	**35**	20	18	**Ordinary People**	S:20 *Ed Hill/Craig Wiseman*	Giant
8/22/98+	**2**[1]	27	19	**You're Beginning To Get To Me**	S:14 *Aaron Barker/Tom Shapiro*	Giant
				above 2 from the album *Greatest Hits* on Giant 24700		
2/20/99	**16**	22	20	**She's Always Right**	*Phil Barnhart/Ed Hill/Richie McDonald*	Giant
7/24/99+	**50**	18	21	**Once In A Lifetime Love**	*Jason Greene/Clay Walker*	Giant
8/7/99+	**11**	27	22	**Live, Laugh, Love**	*Gary Nicholson/Allen Shamblin*	Giant
11/6/99+	**3**[4]	34	23	**The Chain Of Love**	*Jonnie Barnett/Rory Lee*	Giant
				#17 & 20-23: from the album *Live, Laugh, Love* on Giant 24717		
12/9/00+	**51**	6	24	**Blue Christmas**	*Billy Hayes/Jay Johnson* **[X]**	Giant
1/6/01	**70**	1	25	**Cowboy Christmas**	*Jason Greene/Clay Walker/Lori Walker* **[X]**	Giant
				above 2 from the various artists album *Believe: A Christmas Collection* on Giant 24750		
2/24/01	**33**	13	26	**Say No More**	*Tom Shapiro/George Teren*	Giant
7/14/01	**27**	20	27	**If You Ever Feel Like Lovin' Me Again**	*Steve Bogard/Jerry Kilgore/Jeff Stevens*	Warner
				above 2 from the album *Say No More* on Giant 24759		
1/4/03	**49**	2	28	**Feliz Navidad**	*José Feliciano* **[X]**	Warner
				from the album *Christmas* on Warner 48235		
4/26/03	**9**	27	29	**A Few Questions**	*Phillip Moore/Ray Scott/Adam Wheeler*	RCA
12/13/03+	**9**	29	30	**I Can't Sleep**	*Clay Walker/Chely Wright*	RCA
7/17/04	**31**	15	31	**Jesus Was A Country Boy**	*Rivers Rutherford/Clay Walker*	RCA
				above 3 from the album *A Few Questions* on RCA 67068		

WALKER, Jerry Jeff

Born Ronald Clyde Crosby on 3/16/1942 in Oneonta, New York. Male singer/songwriter/guitarist.

DEBUT	PEAK	WKS		Country Chart Hit	Songwriter	Label (& Number)
12/6/75+	**54**	7	1	**Jaded Lover**	*Chuck Pyle*	MCA 40487
7/24/76	**88**	5	2	**It's A Good Night For Singing /**	*Robert Livingston*	
7/24/76	**flip**	5	3	**Dear John Letter Lounge**	*Rick Cardwell*	MCA 40570
8/6/77	**93**	4	4	**Mr. Bojangles**	*Jerry Jeff Walker*	MCA 40760
8/29/81	**82**	3	5	**Got Lucky Last Night**	*Jerry Jeff Walker*	SouthCoast 51146
7/8/89	**70**	6	6	**I Feel Like Hank Williams Tonight**	*Christopher Wall*	Tried & True 1692
10/14/89	**62**	6	7	**The Pickup Truck Song**	*Jerry Jeff Walker*	Tried & True 1695
12/9/89+	**63**	6	8	**Trashy Women**	*Christopher Wall*	Tried & True 1698

WALKER, Kathy

Born in Portland, Oregon. Female singer.

DEBUT	PEAK	WKS		Country Chart Hit	Songwriter	Label (& Number)
5/4/85	**91**	2	1	**It Can't Be Done**	*Tim Blixseth/Norman Saleet*	Compleat 141
				TIM BLIXSETH (with Kathy Walker)		
2/21/87	**78**	4	2	**A Silent Understanding**	*Edra Blixseth/Tim Blixseth*	Compleat 164
				T.L. LEE (with Kathy Walker)		

WALKER, Mike

Born in Columbus, Ohio; raised in Jackson, Tennessee. Male singer.

DEBUT	PEAK	WKS		Country Chart Hit	Songwriter	Label (& Number)
5/19/01	**42**	15		**Honey Do**	S:3 *Al Anderson/Kent Blazy/Jeffrey Steele*	DreamWorks
				from the album *Mike Walker* on DreamWorks 450303		

DEBUT	PEAK	WKS	GOLD	ARTIST / Country Chart Hit	Ranking / Songwriter	Label (& Number)

WALKER, Tamara

Born in Ohio; raised in Maryland. Female singer/songwriter.

DEBUT	PEAK	WKS		Country Chart Hit	Songwriter	Label (& Number)
3/4/00	**65**	2	1	**Askin' Too Much**	*Robin Lee Bruce/Roxie Dean/Sonny Tillis*	Curb
10/14/00	**69**	1	2	**Didn't We Love** S:10	*Tommy Lee James/Jennifer Kimball/Tamara Walker*	Curb
				from the movie *Coyote Ugly* starring Piper Perabo (soundtrack on Curb 78703)		

WALKER, Wiley — see WILEY & GENE

WALLACE, Jerry

All-Time: #167

Born on 12/15/1928 in Guilford, Missouri; raised in Glendale, Arizona. Male singer/guitarist. First recorded for Allied in 1951. Nicknamed "Mr. Smooth."

DEBUT	PEAK	WKS		Country Chart Hit	Songwriter	Label (& Number)
10/9/65	**23**	11	1	**Life's Gone And Slipped Away**	*Lucky Moeller/Webb Pierce/Max Powell*	Mercury 72461
4/9/66	**45**	2	2	**Diamonds And Horseshoes**	*Bert Pellish/Mitchell Tableporter*	Mercury 72529
7/9/66	**43**	7	3	**Wallpaper Roses**	*Don Robertson/Harold Spina*	Mercury 72589
10/15/66	**44**	7	4	**Not That I Care**	*Cindy Walker*	Mercury 72619
11/25/67+	**36**	13	5	**This One's On The House**	*Ramona Redd/Mitchell Torok*	Liberty 56001
5/18/68	**69**	3	6	**Another Time, Another Place, Another World**	*Eddie Dean/Buddy Landon*	Liberty 56028
9/14/68	**22**	10	7	**Sweet Child Of Sunshine**	*Gene Price*	Liberty 56059
4/5/69	**69**	6	8	**Son**	*Nancy Palmer/Scott Turner*	Liberty 56095
10/11/69	**71**	2	9	**Swiss Cottage Place**	*Mickey Newbury*	Liberty 56130
5/9/70	**74**	2	10	**Even The Bad Times Are Good**	*Carl Belew/Clyde Pitts*	Liberty 56155
2/13/71	**22**	14	11	**After You /**	*Joe Johnson/Dick Monda*	
2/13/71	**51**	14	12	**She'll Remember**	*Mavis Harris*	Decca 32777
8/21/71	**19**	14	13	**The Morning After**	*Jean Chapel*	Decca 32859
1/1/72	**12**	22	14	**To Get To You**	*Jean Chapel*	Decca 32914
7/22/72	**❶** [2]	17	15	**If You Leave Me Tonight I'll Cry**	*Hal Mooney/Gerald Sanford*	Decca 32989
				popularized due to play on TV's *Night Gallery* (the episode titled "The Tune In Dan's Cafe")		
12/2/72	**66**	7	16	**Thanks To You For Lovin' Me**	*Carl Belew/Van Givens*	United Artists 50971
12/9/72+	**2** [1]	15	17	**Do You Know What It's Like To Be Lonesome**	*Bert Pellish*	Decca 33036
4/14/73	**21**	12	18	**Sound Of Goodbye /**	*Vonny Baron*	
4/14/73	**flip**	12	19	**The Song Nobody Sings**	*Ed Penney*	MCA 40037
8/25/73	**3** [1]	16	20	**Don't Give Up On Me**	*Ben Peters*	MCA 40111
2/9/74	**18**	12	21	**Guess Who**	*Max Powell*	MCA 40183
6/15/74	**9**	14	22	**My Wife's House**	*Bob Jennings/Lorene Mann*	MCA 40248
11/16/74+	**20**	12	23	**I Wonder Whose Baby (You Are Now)**	*Max Powell*	MCA 40321
3/8/75	**32**	12	24	**Comin' Home To You**	*Kelly Bach/Jean Lane*	MGM 14788
7/19/75	**41**	9	25	**Wanted Man**	*Neal Davenport*	MGM 14809
11/1/75	**70**	6	26	**Georgia Rain**	*Willie Reinen*	MGM 14832
7/2/77	**26**	13	27	**I Miss You Already**	*Jerry Wallace/Kevin Young*	BMA 002
11/12/77+	**28**	12	28	**I'll Promise You Tomorrow**	*Andy Badale/Suzanne Shingler/Frank Stanton*	BMA 005
2/18/78	**24**	11	29	**At The End Of A Rainbow**	*Sid Jacobson/Jimmy Krondes*	BMA 006
6/3/78	**64**	6	30	**My Last Sad Song**	*Ron Muir*	BMA 008
10/14/78	**38**	8	31	**I Wanna Go To Heaven**	*Lorene Mann*	4 Star 1035
3/3/79	**67**	5	32	**Yours Love**	*Harlan Howard*	4 Star 1036
12/1/79+	**68**	8	33	**You've Still Got Me**	*Harry Shields*	Door Knob 116
4/5/80	**56**	7	34	**Cling To Me**	*Scotty Reed*	Door Knob 127
10/4/80	**80**	5	35	**If I Could Set My Love To Music**	*Dave Hall*	Door Knob 134

WALLACE, Ron

Born in Independence, Missouri. Male singer/guitarist.

DEBUT	PEAK	WKS		Country Chart Hit	Songwriter	Label (& Number)
9/2/95	**65**	6		**I'm Listening Now**	*Ed Hill/Bob Regan*	Columbia
				from the album *Bound And Determined* on Columbia 66117		

WALSH, David

Born in Syracuse, New York. Male singer/songwriter.

DEBUT	PEAK	WKS		Country Chart Hit	Songwriter	Label (& Number)
7/27/85	**91**	2	1	**Alice, Rita and Donna**	*Charles Fields*	Charta 196
10/26/85	**84**	3	2	**Tired Of The Same Old Thing**	*David Walsh*	Charta 198
10/29/88	**97**	1	3	**All The Things We Are Not**	*Mike Taylor*	Charta 212
2/18/89	**84**	3	4	**Somewhere In Canada**	*Joe Loiselle/Pat Monette/David Walsh*	Charta 215

WARD, Chris

Born in 1960 in New York. Male singer/guitarist.

DEBUT	PEAK	WKS		Country Chart Hit	Songwriter	Label (& Number)
8/17/96	**68**	2		**Fall Reaching**	*Josh Leo/Robert Ellis Orrall*	Giant

WARD, Dale

Born in Florida. Male singer.

DEBUT	PEAK	WKS		Country Chart Hit	Songwriter	Label (& Number)
11/9/68	**74**	2		**If Loving You Means Anything**	*Jerry Chesnut/Dale Ward*	Monument 1094

Billboard DEBUT	PEAK	WKS	GOLD	ARTIST / Country Chart Hit	Ranking / Songwriter	Label (& Number)

WARD, Jacky

All-Time: #237

Born on 11/18/1946 in Groveton, Texas. Male singer/guitarist.

DEBUT	PEAK	WKS	GOLD	Country Chart Hit	Songwriter	Label (& Number)
6/10/72	39	10		1 Big Blue Diamond	Kit Carson	Target 0146
7/14/73	88	3		2 Dream Weaver	Jerry Foster/Bill Rice	Mega 0112
4/19/75	50	12		3 Stealin'	Jerry Foster/Bill Rice	Mercury 73667
11/1/75+	38	13		4 Dance Her By Me (One More Time)	Danny Wolfe	Mercury 73716
4/17/76	92	4		5 She'll Throw Stones At You	Alan Cartee/Vic Dana/George Soulé	Mercury 73783
9/4/76	24	12		6 I Never Said It Would Be Easy	Jerry Foster/Bill Rice	Mercury 73826
2/5/77	31	12		7 Texas Angel	Jerry Foster/Bill Rice	Mercury 73880
6/25/77	69	6		8 Why Not Tonight	Jerry Foster/Bill Rice	Mercury 73918
9/10/77	9	19		9 Fools Fall In Love	Jerry Leiber/Mike Stoller	Mercury 55003
2/4/78	3^{1}	15		10 A Lover's Question	Brook Benton/Jimmy Williams	Mercury 55018
5/20/78	20	12		11 Three Sheets In The Wind *[w/ Reba McEntire]* /	Randall Thompson/Sharon Thompson	
5/27/78	flip	11		12 I'd Really Love To See You Tonight *[w/ Reba McEntire]*	Parker McGee	Mercury 55026
8/5/78	24	10		13 I Want To Be In Love	Layng Martine Jr.	Mercury 55038
11/4/78	11	13		14 Rhythm Of The Rain	John Gummoe	Mercury 55047
2/17/79	8	14		15 Wisdom Of A Fool	Roy Alfred/Abner Silver	Mercury 55055
7/7/79	26	11		16 That Makes Two Of Us *[w/ Reba McEntire]*	Jerry Fuller	Mercury 55054
9/22/79	14	12		17 You're My Kind Of Woman	Linda Kimball/Mark Sherrill/Josh Whitmore	Mercury 57004
1/5/80	32	10		18 I'd Do Anything For You	Julie Didier/Casey Kelly	Mercury 57013
5/24/80	8	16		19 Save Your Heart For Me	Bob McDill	Mercury 57022
9/13/80	7	15		20 That's The Way A Cowboy Rocks And Rolls	Tony Joe White	Mercury 57032
1/24/81	13	14		21 Somethin' On The Radio	Pat McManus	Mercury 57044
3/20/82	32	11		22 Travelin' Man	Jerry Fuller	Asylum 47424
7/3/82	57	7		23 Take The Mem'ry When You Go	Craig Bickhardt	Asylum 47468
3/5/83	85	3		24 The Night's Almost Over	Jacky Ward	Warner 69844
1/9/88	83	3		25 Can't Get To You From Here	Steve Chandler/Fred Knipe	Electric 105

WARINER, Steve

1980s: #18 / 1990s: #33 / All-Time: #44

Born on 12/25/1954 in Noblesville, Indiana. Male singer/songwriter/guitarist. Played bass while a teenager. Bassist with **Dottie West** from 1971-74. Worked with **Bob Luman** and **Chet Atkins**. Also see **Jed Zeppelin** and **Nicolette Larson**.

OPRY: 1996

DEBUT	PEAK	WKS	GOLD	Country Chart Hit	Songwriter	Label (& Number)
4/22/78	63	7		1 I'm Already Taken (also see #56 below)	Chet Atkins/Terry Ryan/Steve Wariner	RCA 11173
8/19/78	76	3		2 So Sad (To Watch Good Love Go Bad)	Don Everly	RCA 11336
1/27/79	94	2		3 Marie	Randy Newman	RCA 11447
8/4/79	60	7		4 Beside Me /	Randy Goodrum	
11/10/79	49	10		5 Forget Me Not	Al Byron/Paul Evans	RCA 11658
7/5/80	41	10		6 The Easy Part's Over	Jerry Foster/Bill Rice	RCA 12029
11/15/80+	7	17		7 Your Memory	Charles Quillen/John Schweers	RCA 12139
4/11/81	6	18		8 By Now	Dean Dillon/Don Pfrimmer/Charles Quillen	RCA 12204
9/26/81	❶^{1}	18		9 All Roads Lead To You	Kye Fleming/Dennis W. Morgan	RCA 12307
3/6/82	15	18		10 Kansas City Lights	Kye Fleming/Dennis W. Morgan	RCA 13072
9/4/82	30	11		11 Don't It Break Your Heart	Mack David/Archie Jordan	RCA 13308
11/27/82+	27	17		12 Don't Plan On Sleepin' Tonight	Sam Kunin/Gloria Sklerov	RCA 13395
5/7/83	23	13		13 Don't Your Mem'ry Ever Sleep At Night	Steve Dean/Randy Hatch	RCA 13515
8/13/83	5	18		14 Midnight Fire	Lewis Anderson/Dave Gibson	RCA 13588
12/10/83+	4	20		15 Lonely Women Make Good Lovers	Spooner Oldham/Freddy Weller	RCA 13691
4/7/84	12	18		16 Why Goodbye	Richard Leigh/Mark Wright	RCA 13768
9/22/84	49	10		17 Don't You Give Up On Love	Dave Gibson	RCA 13862
12/15/84+	3^{2}	25		18 What I Didn't Do	A:3 / S:3 Wood Newton/Mike Noble	MCA 52506
4/6/85	8	20		19 Heart Trouble	A:8 / S:9 Dave Gibson/Kent Robbins	MCA 52562
7/27/85	❶^{1}	22		20 Some Fools Never Learn	S:❶^{1} / A:❶^{1} John Scott Sherrill	MCA 52644
11/16/85+	❶^{1}	22		21 You Can Dream Of Me	A:❶^{1} / S:2 John Hall/Steve Wariner	MCA 52721
3/15/86	❶^{1}	24		22 Life's Highway	S:❶^{1} / A:❶^{1} Richard Leigh/Roger Murrah	MCA 52786
6/7/86	9	23		23 That's How You Know When Love's Right *[w/ Nicolette Larson]*	A:9 / S:11 Craig Bickhardt/Wendy Waldman	MCA 52839
8/16/86	4	19		24 Starting Over Again	S:3 / A:4 Don Goodman/John Wesley Ryles	MCA 52837
12/27/86+	❶^{1}	24		25 Small Town Girl	A:❶^{1} / S:9 Don Cook/John Jarvis	MCA 53006
4/25/87	❶^{1}	23		26 The Weekend	S:8 / A:30 Beckie Foster/Bill LaBounty	MCA 53068
5/30/87	6	28		27 The Hand That Rocks The Cradle *[w/ Glen Campbell]*	S:11 Ted Harris	MCA 53108
9/5/87	❶^{1}	23		28 Lynda	S:2 Bill LaBounty/Pat McLaughlin	MCA 53160
2/20/88	2^{1}	18		29 Baby I'm Yours	S:4 Guy Clark/Steve Wariner	MCA 53287
6/18/88	2^{2}	21		30 I Should Be With You	S:7 Steve Wariner	MCA 53347
10/15/88+	6	24		31 Hold On (A Little Longer)	S:15 Randy Hart/Steve Wariner	MCA 53419
3/4/89	❶^{1}	22		32 Where Did I Go Wrong	Steve Wariner	MCA 53504
7/1/89	❶^{1}	21		33 I Got Dreams	Bill LaBounty/Steve Wariner	MCA 53665

Billboard DEBUT	PEAK	WKS	GOLD	ARTIST Ranking Country Chart Hit	Songwriter	Label (& Number)
				WARINER, Steve — cont'd		
10/21/89+	**5**	26		34 **When I Could Come Home To You**	*Roger Murrah/Steve Wariner*	MCA 53738
3/17/90	**7**	24		35 **The Domino Theory**	*Beckie Foster/Bill LaBounty*	MCA
7/21/90	**8**	20		36 **Precious Thing**	*Mac McAnally/Steve Wariner*	MCA
11/10/90+	**17**	20		37 **There For Awhile**	*Anna Graham/Curtis Wright*	MCA
				above 3 from the album *Laredo* on MCA 42335		
3/30/91	**25**	20		38 **Restless** *[w/ Mark O'Connor/Vince Gill/Ricky Skaggs]*	*Carl Perkins*	Warner
				Grammy: Vocal Collaboration / CMA: Vocal Event		
8/3/91	**71**	3		39 **Now It Belongs To You** *[w/ Mark O'Connor]*	*Steve Wariner*	Warner
				above 2 from O'Connor's album *The New Nashville Cats* on Wariner 26509		
9/28/91+	**6**	20		40 **Leave Him Out Of This**	*Walt Aldridge/Susan Longacre*	Arista
2/8/92	**3**[1]	20		41 **The Tips Of My Fingers**	*Bill Anderson*	Arista
5/30/92	**9**	20		42 **A Woman Loves**	*Steve Bogard/Rick Giles*	Arista
9/12/92	**32**	15		43 **Crash Course In The Blues**	*Don Cook/John Jarvis/Steve Wariner*	Arista
2/20/93	**30**	14		44 **Like A River To The Sea**	*Steve Wariner*	Arista
				above 5 from the album *I Am Ready* on Arista 18691		
7/3/93	**8**	20		45 **If I Didn't Love You**	*Jon Vezner/Jack White*	Arista
11/13/93+	**24**	18		46 **Drivin' And Cryin'**	*Don Blake/Rick Giles*	Arista
4/9/94	**18**	20		47 **It Won't Be Over You**	*Trey Bruce/Thom McHugh*	Arista
9/17/94	**63**	4		48 **Drive**	*Bill LaBounty/Steve Wariner*	Arista
				above 4 from the album *Drive* on Arista 18721		
5/27/95	**72**	3		49 **Get Back**	*John Lennon/Paul McCartney*	Liberty
				from the various artists album *Come Together - America Salutes The Beatles* on Liberty 31712		
11/8/97+	**❶**[1]	23		50 **What If I Said** *[w/ Anita Cochran]*	S:3 *Anita Cochran*	Warner
				from Cochran's album *Back To You* on Warner 46395		
3/7/98	**2**[2]	21		51 **Holes In The Floor Of Heaven**	*Billy Kirsch/Steve Wariner*	Capitol
				CMA: Single		
5/9/98	**26**	20		52 **Burnin' The Roadhouse Down** *[w/ Garth Brooks]*	*Rick Carnes/Steve Wariner*	Capitol
6/27/98	**55**	4		53 **Road Trippin'**	*Marcus Hummon/Steve Wariner*	Capitol
10/17/98+	**36**	20		54 **Every Little Whisper**	*Billy Kirsch/Steve Wariner*	Capitol
				above 4 from the album *Burnin' The Roadhouse Down* on Capitol 94482		
2/20/99	**2**[1]	24		55 **Two Teardrops**	*Bill Anderson/Steve Wariner*	Capitol
7/3/99	**3**[3]	25		56 **I'm Already Taken**	*Terry Ryan/Steve Wariner* **[R]**	Capitol
				new version of #1 above; above 2 from the album *Two Teardrops* on Capitol 96139		
1/15/00	**5**	22		57 **Been There** *[w/ Clint Black]*	*Clint Black/Steve Wariner*	RCA
				from Black's album *D'lectrified* on RCA 67823		
3/18/00	**28**	19		58 **Faith In You**	*Bill Anderson/Steve Wariner*	Capitol
6/17/00	**22**	20		59 **Katie Wants A Fast One** *[w/ Garth Brooks]*	*Rick Carnes/Steve Wariner*	Capitol
				above 2 from Wariner's album *Faith In You* on Capitol 23503		
12/23/00	**65**	3		60 **Christmas In Your Arms**	*Bill Anderson/Steve Wariner* **[X]**	Capitol
				from the various artists album *Shimmy Down The Chimney: A Country Christmas* on Capitol 71143		
2/15/03	**52**	6		61 **Snowfall On The Sand**	*Billy Kirsch/Steve Wariner*	SelectOne
8/2/03	**58**	1		62 **I'm Your Man**	*Sam Hogin/Bob Regan/Steve Wariner*	SelectOne
				above 2 from the album *Steal Another Day* on SelectOne 11955		

All Roads Lead To You ['81]
Baby I'm Yours ['88]
Been There ['00]
Beside Me ['79]
Burnin' The Roadhouse Down ['98]
By Now ['81]
Christmas In Your Arms ['00]
Crash Course In The Blues ['92]
Domino Theory ['90]
Don't It Break Your Heart ['82]
Don't Plan On Sleepin' Tonight ['83]
Don't You Give Up On Love ['84]
Don't Your Mem'ry Ever Sleep At Night ['83]
Drive ['94]
Drivin' And Cryin' ['94]
Easy Part's Over ['80]
Every Little Whisper ['99]
Faith In You ['00]
Forget Me Not ['79]
Get Back ['95]
Hand That Rocks The Cradle ['87]
Heart Trouble ['85]
Hold On (A Little Longer) ['89]
Holes In The Floor Of Heaven ['98]
I Got Dreams ['89]
I Should Be With You ['88]
I'm Already Taken ['78, '99]
I'm Your Man ['03]
If I Didn't Love You ['93]
It Won't Be Over You ['94]
Kansas City Lights ['82]
Katie Wants A Fast One ['00]
Leave Him Out Of This ['92]
Life's Highway ['86]
Like A River To The Sea ['93]
Lonely Women Make Good Lovers ['84]
Lynda ['87]
Marie ['79]
Midnight Fire ['83]
Now It Belongs To You ['91]
Precious Thing ['90]
Restless ['91]
Road Trippin' ['98]
Small Town Girl ['87]
Snowfall On The Sand ['03]
So Sad (To Watch Good Love Go Bad) ['78]
Some Fools Never Learn ['85]
Starting Over Again ['86]
That's How You Know When Love's Right ['86]
There For Awhile ['91]
Tips Of My Fingers ['92]
Two Teardrops ['99]
Weekend ['87]
What I Didn't Do ['85]
What If I Said ['98]
When I Could Come Home To You ['90]
Where Did I Go Wrong ['89]
Why Goodbye ['84]
Woman Loves ['92]
You Can Dream Of Me ['86]
Your Memory ['81]

WARNER, Virgil

Born in Phoenix, Arizona. Male singer.

DEBUT	PEAK	WKS	GOLD	Country Chart Hit	Songwriter	Label (& Number)
9/9/67	**51**	7		1 **Here We Go Again** *[w/ Suzi Jane Hokum]*	*Don Lanier/Red Steagall*	LHI 17018
2/24/68	**65**	4		2 **Storybook Children** *[w/ Suzi Jane Hokum]*	*Chip Taylor/Billy Vera*	LHI 1204

WARNES, Jennifer

Born on 3/3/1947 in Seattle, Washington; raised in Orange County, California. Female singer.

DEBUT	PEAK	WKS	GOLD	Country Chart Hit	Songwriter	Label (& Number)
2/19/77	**17**	15		1 **Right Time Of The Night**	*Peter McCann*	Arista 0223
6/30/79	**10**	16		2 **I Know A Heartache When I See One**	*Charlie Black/Rory Bourke/Kerry Chater*	Arista 0430
1/12/80	**84**	3		3 **Don't Make Me Over**	*Burt Bacharach/Hal David*	Arista 0455
2/23/80	**76**	5		4 **Lost The Good Thing** *[w/ Steve Gillette]*	*Steve Gillette/David McKechnie*	Regency 45002
2/6/82	**57**	7		5 **Could It Be Love**	*Randy Sharp*	Arista 0611
2/28/87	**86**	4		6 **Ain't No Cure For Love**	*Leonard Cohen*	Cypress 661111

WARREN, Kelly

Born in Lamesa, Texas. Female singer.

DEBUT	PEAK	WKS	GOLD	Country Chart Hit	Songwriter	Label (& Number)
1/6/79	**85**	5		1 **One Man's Woman**	*Tom Brasfield/Barbara Wyrick*	RCA 11428
11/17/79	**69**	4		2 **Don't Touch Me** *[w/ Jerry Naylor]*	*Hank Cochran*	Jeremiah 1002

WARREN BROTHERS, The

Duo from Tampa, Florida: brothers Brad and Brett Warren. Starred in own *Barely Famous* reality TV series.

DEBUT	PEAK	WKS	GOLD	Country Chart Hit	Songwriter	Label (& Number)
8/29/98	**34**	20		1 **Guilty**	S:14 *Dave Berg/Brad Warren/Brett Warren*	BNA
1/16/99	**32**	20		2 **Better Man**	S:22 *Gary Nicholson/Brad Warren/Brett Warren*	BNA

WARREN BROTHERS, The — cont'd

DEBUT	PEAK	WKS		Country Chart Hit	Songwriter	Label (& Number)
5/29/99	**37**	16	3	**She Wants To Rock**	*Rob Stoney/Brad Warren/Brett Warren*	BNA
				above 3 from the album *Beautiful Day In The Cold Cruel World* on BNA 67678		
3/25/00	**22**	28	4	**That's The Beat Of A Heart** ***[w/ Sara Evans]***	*Tena Clark/Tim Heintz*	BNA
				from the movie *Where The Heart Is* starring Natalie Portman (soundtrack on RCA 67963)		
10/14/00+	**17**	25	5	**Move On**	*Brad Warren/Brett Warren/Danny Wilde*	BNA
6/2/01	**33**	16	6	**Where Does It Hurt**	*Brad Warren/Brett Warren*	BNA
				above 2 from the album *King Of Nothing* on BNA 67903		
4/5/03	**28**	10	7	**Hey Mr. President**	*Tom Douglas*	BNA
7/19/03	**54**	4	8	**Break The Record**	*Max T. Barnes/Cory Mayo*	BNA
9/13/03	**51**	12	9	**Sell A Lot Of Beer**	*Bill Anderson/Brad Warren/Brett Warren*	429 Records
				Tim McGraw (backing vocal); from the album *Well Deserved Obscurity* on 429 Records 17403		

WASHINGTON, Jon

Born in England. Male singer.

DEBUT	PEAK	WKS		Country Chart Hit	Songwriter	Label (& Number)
10/22/88	**73**	3	1	**One Dance Love Affair**	*Don Roth*	Door Knob 310
1/28/89	**73**	3	2	**Two Hearts**	*Stewart Harris/Keith Stegall*	Door Knob 315

WATERS, Chris — SW: #35

Born Christopher Dunn in San Antonio, Texas. Male singer/songwriter. Brother of **Holly Dunn**.

DEBUT	PEAK	WKS		Country Chart Hit	Songwriter	Label (& Number)
11/29/80	**82**	3	1	**My Lady Loves Me (Just As I Am)**	*Keith Stegall/Chris Waters*	Rio 1001
3/7/81	**89**	2	2	**It's Like Falling In Love (Over And Over Again)**	*Rich Alves/Scott Anders/Roger Murrah*	Rio 1002

WATERS, Joe

Born in Chillicothe, Ohio. Male singer/songwriter. Known as "Appalachia Joe."

DEBUT	PEAK	WKS		Country Chart Hit	Songwriter	Label (& Number)
9/26/81	**85**	3	1	**Livin' In The Light Of Her Love**	*Joe Waters*	New Colony 6811
12/12/81+	**47**	10	2	**Some Day My Ship's Comin' In**	*Joe Waters*	New Colony 6812
4/17/82	**75**	4	3	**The Queen Of Hearts Loves You**	*Joe Waters*	New Colony 6813
12/17/83+	**74**	6	4	**Harvest Moon**	*Joe Waters*	New Colony 6814
5/26/84	**90**	2	5	**Rise Above It All**	*Joe Waters*	New Colony 6815

WATSON, B.B.

Born Haskill Watson on 7/10/1953 in Tyler, Texas; raised in La Porte, Texas. Male singer. B.B. stands for Bad Boy.

DEBUT	PEAK	WKS		Country Chart Hit	Songwriter	Label (& Number)
8/10/91	**23**	21	1	**Light At The End Of The Tunnel**	*Richard Fagan/Kim Williams/Mack Williams*	BNA
2/1/92	**43**	12	2	**Lover Not A Fighter**	*Kent Blazy/Richard Fagan/Kim Williams*	BNA
				above 2 from the album *Light At The End Of The Tunnel* on BNA 61020		
4/15/00	**73**	1	3	**The Memory Is The Last Thing To Go**	*Don Pfrimmer/Don Skaggs*	SNA

WATSON, Clyde

Born on 7/25/1947 in Vermont. Male singer.

DEBUT	PEAK	WKS		Country Chart Hit	Songwriter	Label (& Number)
8/27/77	**99**	2		**The Touch Of Her Fingers**	*Troy Harbinson*	Groovy 100

WATSON, Doc & Merle

Father-and-son duo. Arthel "Doc" Watson was born on 3/2/1923 in Deep Gap, North Carolina. Blind singer/songwriter/guitarist/banjo player. Merle was born on 2/8/1949 in North Carolina. Died in a tractor accident on 10/23/1985 (age 36). Singer/banjo player. Also see **The Groovegrass Boyz**.

DEBUT	PEAK	WKS		Country Chart Hit	Songwriter	Label (& Number)
7/21/73	**71**	7	1	**Bottle Of Wine**	*Tom Paxton*	Poppy 276
9/2/78	**88**	5	2	**Don't Think Twice, It's All Right**	*Bob Dylan*	United Artists 1231

WATSON, Gene — 1980s: #36 / All-Time: #77

Born Gary Gene Watson on 10/11/1943 in Palestine, Texas; raised in Paris, Texas. Male singer/guitarist. Worked professionally since age 13. Own band, Gene Watson & The Other Four. First recorded for Tonka in 1965. Played for many years at the Dynasty Club in Houston.

DEBUT	PEAK	WKS		Country Chart Hit	Songwriter	Label (& Number)
1/25/75	**87**	7	1	**Bad Water**	*Jackie DeShannon/Jimmy Holiday/Randy Myers*	Resco 630
5/24/75	**3^{2}**	19	2	**Love In The Hot Afternoon**	*Vince Matthews/Kent Westberry*	Capitol 4076
10/11/75	**5**	15	3	**Where Love Begins**	*Ray Griff*	Capitol 4143
2/14/76	**10**	15	4	**You Could Know As Much About A Stranger**	*Nadine Bryant*	Capitol 4214
6/12/76	**20**	12	5	**Because You Believed In Me**	*Shorty Hall/A.L. "Doodle" Owens/Gene Vowell*	Capitol 4279
9/25/76	**52**	9	6	**Her Body Couldn't Keep You (Off My Mind)**	*Ray Griff*	Capitol 4331
1/29/77	**3^{3}**	17	7	**Paper Rosie**	*Dallas Harms*	Capitol 4378
8/13/77	**11**	15	8	**The Old Man And His Horn**	*Dallas Harms*	Capitol 4458
12/3/77+	**8**	16	9	**I Don't Need A Thing At All**	*Joe Allen*	Capitol 4513
4/8/78	**11**	14	10	**Cowboys Don't Get Lucky All The Time**	*Dallas Harms*	Capitol 4556
8/26/78	**8**	14	11	**One Sided Conversation**	*Joe Allen*	Capitol 4616
2/17/79	**5**	16	12	**Farewell Party**	*Lawton Williams*	Capitol 4680
6/9/79	**5**	15	13	**Pick The Wildwood Flower**	*Joe Allen*	Capitol 4723
9/15/79	**3^{1}**	13	14	**Should I Come Home (Or Should I Go Crazy)**	*Joe Allen*	Capitol 4772
1/5/80	**4**	14	15	**Nothing Sure Looked Good On You**	*Jim Rushing*	Capitol 4814
4/12/80	**18**	13	16	**Bedroom Ballad**	*Joe Allen*	Capitol 4854
8/2/80	**15**	12	17	**Raisin' Cane In Texas**	*Joe Allen/Deoin Lay*	Capitol 4898
11/1/80	**13**	14	18	**No One Will Ever Know**	*Mel Foree/Fred Rose*	Capitol 4940
2/7/81	**33**	8	19	**Any Way You Want Me**	*Leo Ofman*	Warner 49648
				from the movie *Any Which Way You Can* starring **Clint Eastwood**		

DEBUT	PEAK	WKS	GOLD	Ranking	ARTIST / Country Chart Hit	Songwriter	Label (& Number)
					WATSON, Gene — cont'd		
2/28/81	**17**	13		20	**Between This Time And The Next Time**	*Ray Griff*	MCA 51039
6/20/81	**23**	13		21	**Maybe I Should Have Been Listening**	*Buzz Rabin*	MCA 51127
10/3/81+	**❶[1]**	19		22	**Fourteen Carat Mind**	*Dallas Frazier/Larry Lee*	MCA 51183
2/27/82	**9**	18		23	**Speak Softly (You're Talking To My Heart)**	*Jessee Mendenhall/Steve Spurgin*	MCA 52009
7/3/82	**8**	18		24	**This Dream's On Me**	*Fred Koller*	MCA 52074
11/6/82+	**5**	21		25	**What She Don't Know Won't Hurt Her**	*Dave Lindsey/Ernie Rowell*	MCA 52131
3/19/83	**2[1]**	19		26	**You're Out Doing What I'm Here Doing Without**	*Allen Frizzell/Bo Roberts*	MCA 52191
7/23/83	**9**	18		27	**Sometimes I Get Lucky And Forget**	*Bob House/Ernie Rowell*	MCA 52243
11/26/83+	**10**	17		28	**Drinkin' My Way Back Home**	*Don Scaife/Ronny Scaife/Phil Thomas*	MCA 52309
3/31/84	**10**	17		29	**Forever Again**	*Dave Kirby/Warren Robb*	MCA 52356
6/30/84	**33**	14		30	**Little By Little**	*Larry Keith/Danny Morrison*	MCA 52410
10/13/84+	**7**	27		31	**Got No Reason Now For Goin' Home**	S:6 / A:6 *Johnny Russell*	Curb/MCA 52457
3/2/85	**43**	10		32	**One Hell Of A Heartache**	*Keith Palmer/Janet White*	Curb/MCA 52533
6/22/85	**24**	17		33	**Cold Summer Day In Georgia**	A:21 / S:24 *Dennis Knutson/A.L. "Doodle" Owens*	Epic 05407
10/19/85+	**5**	21		34	**Memories To Burn**	S:4 / A:5 *Dave Kirby/Warren Robb*	Epic 05633
3/1/86	**32**	15		35	**Carmen**	*Steve Spurgin*	Epic 05817
7/5/86	**50**	8		36	**Bottle Of Tears**	*Joe Allen/Deoin Lay/Jim Pasquale*	Epic 06057
9/13/86	**29**	14		37	**Everything I Used To Do**	S:23 / A:29 *Edwin Rowell*	Epic 06290
3/14/87	**43**	13		38	**Honky Tonk Crazy**	*Harlan Howard/Ron Peterson*	Epic 06987
8/15/87	**28**	16		39	**Everybody Needs A Hero**	S:23 *Max D. Barnes/Troy Seals*	Epic 07308
11/12/88+	**5**	22		40	**Don't Waste It On The Blues**	*Sandy Ramos/Jerry Vandiver*	Warner 27692
3/18/89	**20**	14		41	**Back In The Fire**	*Rory Bourke/Mike Reid*	Warner 27532
7/22/89	**24**	24		42	**The Jukebox Played Along**	*Ken Bell/Charles Quillen*	Warner 22912
11/25/89+	**41**	16		43	**The Great Divide**	*John Lindley/Randy Travis*	Warner 22751
2/23/91	**61**	7		44	**At Last**	*Mack Gordon/Harry Warren*	Warner
6/1/91	**67**	5		45	**You Can't Take It With You When You Go**	*Bert Colwell/Larry Cordle/Larry Shell*	Warner
					above 2 from the album *At Last* on Warner 26329		
1/2/93	**66**	5		46	**One And One And One**	*Buddy Cannon/John Northrup*	Broadland
1/25/97	**44**	18		47	**Change Her Mind**	*Larry Boone/Danny Mayo/Paul Nelson*	Step One
6/7/97	**73**	1		48	**No Goodbyes**	*Ray Pennington/David Smith*	Step One
					above 2 from the album *The Good Ole Days* on Step One 104		
					WAYNE, Bobby		
					Born Robert Wayne Edrington in Childress, Texas. Male singer/songwriter/guitarist. Member of **Merle Haggard**'s Strangers.		
2/6/71	**61**	7			**Harold's Super Service**	*Bobby Wayne*	Capitol 3025
					WAYNE, Jimmy		
					Born Jimmy Wayne Barber on 10/23/1972 in Bessemer City, North Carolina; raised in Gastonia, North Carolina. Country singer/songwriter.		
2/8/03	**3[3]**	28		1	**Stay Gone**	S:2 *Billy Kirsch/Jimmy Wayne*	DreamWorks
8/23/03+	**6**	32		2	**I Love You This Much**	*Charles DuBois/Don Sampson/Jimmy Wayne*	DreamWorks
12/27/03+	**40**	3		3	**Paper Angels**	*Don Sampson/Jimmy Wayne* **[X]**	DreamWorks
4/10/04	**18**	27		4	**You Are**	*Marv Green/Chris Lindsey/Aimee Mayo/Jimmy Wayne*	DreamWorks
11/13/04+	**18**	17		5	**Paper Angels**	*Don Sampson/Jimmy Wayne* **[X-R]**	DreamWorks
					all of above from the album *Jimmy Wayne* on DreamWorks 450355		
					WAYNE, Nancy		
					Born in Kentucky. Female singer.		
5/25/74	**55**	12		1	**The Back Door Of Heaven**	*Glen Ballantyne*	20th Century 2086
10/5/74	**34**	11		2	**Gone**	*Richard Burns*	20th Century 2124
4/26/75	**80**	7		3	**I Wanna Kiss You**	*Brian Richards*	20th Century 2184
					WEATHERLY, Jim		
					Born on 3/17/1943 in Pontotoc, Mississippi. Male singer/songwriter.		
2/1/75	**9**	13		1	**I'll Still Love You**	*Jim Weatherly*	Buddah 444
7/12/75	**58**	8		2	**It Must Have Been The Rain**	*Jim Weatherly*	Buddah 467
7/23/77	**27**	10		3	**All That Keeps Me Going**	*Jim Weatherly*	ABC 12288
11/3/79	**32**	11		4	**Smooth Sailin'**	*Jim Weatherly*	Elektra 46547
2/16/80	**34**	9		5	**Gift From Missouri**	*Jim Weatherly*	Elektra 46592
10/11/80	**82**	3		6	**Safe In The Arms Of Your Love (Cold In The Streets)**	*Jim Weatherly*	Elektra 47027
					WEAVERS, The		
					Highly influential folk group: Pete Seeger, Veronica "Ronnie" Gilbert, Lee Hays and Fred Kellerman. Hays died on 8/26/1981 (age 68).		
6/2/51	**8**	2	●		**On Top Of Old Smoky** *[w/ Terry Gilkyson]*	J:8 *Pete Seeger*	Decca 9-27515
					Vic Schoen (orch.); adaptation of a traditonal Southern Highlands folk song		
					WEBB, Jay Lee		
					Born Willie Lee Webb on 2/12/1937 in Van Lear, Kentucky. Died of cancer on 7/31/1996 (age 59). Male singer. Brother of **Loretta Lynn**, **Crystal Gayle** and **Peggy Sue**; distant cousin of **Patty Loveless**.		
2/11/67	**37**	6		1	**I Come Home A-Drinkin' (To A Worn-Out Wife Like You)** *[Jack Webb]* answer to **Loretta Lynn**'s "Don't Come Home A'Drinkin'"	*...Loretta Lynn/Peggy Sue Wells/Teddy Wilburn*	Decca 32087
2/1/69	**21**	13		2	**She's Lookin' Better By The Minute**	*Jimmie Helms/Grant Townsley*	Decca 32430
11/27/71	**69**	5		3	**The Happiness Of Having You**	*Ted Harris*	Decca 32887

DEBUT	PEAK	WKS	GOLD		ARTIST / Country Chart Hit	Ranking / Songwriter	Label (& Number)
					WEBB, June		
					Born on 9/22/1934 in L'Anse, Michigan. Female singer.		
11/3/58	**29**	3			**A Mansion On The Hill**	*Fred Rose/Hank Williams*	Hickory 1086
					WEBSTER, Chase		
					Born in Franklin, Tennessee. Male singer/songwriter.		
6/20/70	**68**	2			**Moody River**	*Chase Webster*	Show Biz 233
					WEISSBERG, Eric		
					Born in New York. Prominent session musician. Former member of The Tarriers.		
2/3/73	**5**	12	●	1	**Dueling Banjos** ***[w/ Steve Mandell]***	*Arthur Smith* **[I]**	Warner 7659
					Grammy: Instrumental; from the movie *Deliverance* starring **Burt Reynolds**		
3/29/75	**91**	4		2	**Yakety Yak** ***[w/ Deliverance]***	*Jerry Leiber/Mike Stoller*	Epic 50072
					WELCH, Ernie		
					Born in Decatur, Alabama. Male singer.		
5/20/89	**96**	1			**Who Have You Got To Lose**	*Don Parsons/Bill Terry*	Duck Tape 021
					WELCH, Kevin		
					Born on 8/17/1955 in Los Angeles, California; raised in Oklahoma. Male singer/songwriter. Also see **Tomorrow's World**.		
1/21/89	**41**	10		1	**Stay November**	*Thomas Cain/John Scott Sherrill*	Warner 27647
4/29/89	**64**	6		2	**I Came Straight To You**	*John Jarvis/Kevin Welch*	Warner 22972
5/26/90	**39**	11		3	**Till I See You Again**	*Kevin Welch*	Reprise
10/20/90	**49**	11		4	**Praying For Rain**	*Don Cook/Chris Waters*	Reprise
3/2/91	**54**	10		5	**True Love Never Dies**	*Gary Scruggs/Kevin Welch*	Reprise
					above 3 from the album *Kevin Welch* on Reprise 26171		
					WELK, Lawrence, And His Orchestra	**1940s: #45**	
					Born on 3/11/1903 in Strasburg, North Dakota. Died of pneumonia on 5/17/1992 (age 89). Polka bandleader/accordian player. Band's style labeled as "champagne music." Hosted own TV series from 1955-82.		
9/8/45	**❶[1]**	14		1	**Shame On You** ***[w/ Red Foley]*** /	*Spade Cooley*	
11/10/45	**3[1]**	2		2	**At Mail Call Today** ***[w/ Red Foley]***	*Gene Autry/Fred Rose*	Decca 18698

DEBUT	PEAK	WKS	GOLD		ARTIST / Country Chart Hit	Ranking / Songwriter	Label (& Number)
					WELLER, Freddy	**All-Time: #166**	
					Born Wilton Frederick Weller on 9/9/1947 in Atlanta, Georgia. Male singer/songwriter/guitarist. Began career on the *Atlanta Jubilee* in East Point, Georgia. Worked as a guitarist with **Billy Joe Royal** and **Joe South**. Member of Paul Revere & The Raiders from 1967-71.		
4/12/69	**2[2]**	17		1	**Games People Play**	*Joe South*	Columbia 44800
7/26/69	**5**	15		2	**These Are Not My People**	*Joe South*	Columbia 44916
11/22/69+	**25**	10		3	**Down In The Boondocks**	*Joe South*	Columbia 45026
4/11/70	**75**	2		4	**I Shook The Hand**	*James Banks*	Columbia 45087
12/12/70+	**3[2]**	18		5	**The Promised Land**	*Chuck Berry*	Columbia 45276
6/12/71	**3[2]**	14		6	**Indian Lake**	*Tony Romeo*	Columbia 45388
9/25/71	**5**	15		7	**Another Night Of Love**	*Spooner Oldham/Freddy Weller*	Columbia 45451
2/19/72	**26**	12		8	**Ballad Of A Hillbilly Singer**	*Curly Putman/Billy Sherrill*	Columbia 45542
6/24/72	**17**	12		9	**The Roadmaster**	*Spooner Oldham/Freddy Weller*	Columbia 45624
11/18/72+	**11**	13		10	**She Loves Me (Right Out Of My Mind)**	*Spooner Oldham/Freddy Weller*	Columbia 45723
4/21/73	**8**	14		11	**Too Much Monkey Business**	*Chuck Berry*	Columbia 45827
8/18/73	**13**	13		12	**The Perfect Stranger**	*Freddy Weller*	Columbia 45902
12/15/73+	**11**	15		13	**I've Just Got To Know (How Loving You Would Be)**	*Bill Emerson/Jodie Emerson*	Columbia 45968
5/18/74	**21**	14		14	**Sexy Lady**	*Freddy Weller*	Columbia 46040
9/14/74	**16**	15		15	**You're Not Getting Older (You're Getting Better)**	*Freddy Weller*	Columbia 10016
5/24/75	**64**	8		16	**Love You Back To Georgia**	*Layng Martine Jr.*	ABC/Dot 17554
9/20/75	**52**	9		17	**Stone Crazy**	*Jay Harris/Bob Morrison*	ABC/Dot 17577
3/20/76	**42**	9		18	**Ask Any Old Cheater Who Knows**	*Jerry Foster/Bill Rice*	Columbia 10300
7/4/76	**44**	9		19	**Liquor, Love And Life**	*Spooner Oldham/Freddy Weller*	Columbia 10352
10/9/76	**56**	8		20	**Room 269**	*Freddy Weller*	Columbia 10411
3/5/77	**79**	6		21	**Strawberry Curls**	*Richard Leigh*	Columbia 10482
5/28/77	**41**	9		22	**Merry-Go-Round**	*Tommy Roe/Freddy Weller*	Columbia 10539
9/10/77	**44**	9		23	**Nobody Cares But You**	*Freddy Weller*	Columbia 10598
2/25/78	**93**	4		24	**Let Me Fall Back In Your Arms**	*Spooner Oldham/Freddy Weller*	Columbia 10682
7/8/78	**32**	9		25	**Bar Wars**	*Buzz Cason*	Columbia 10769
10/21/78	**23**	12		26	**Love Got In The Way**	*Spooner Oldham/Freddy Weller*	Columbia 10837
1/27/79	**27**	11		27	**Fantasy Island**	*Buzz Cason/Freddy Weller*	Columbia 10890
5/19/79	**40**	8		28	**Nadine**	*Chuck Berry*	Columbia 10973
8/11/79	**44**	9		29	**That Run-Away Woman Of Mine**	*Don Cook/Curly Putman*	Columbia 11044
11/24/79+	**33**	11		30	**Go For The Night**	*Buzz Cason/Freddy Weller*	Columbia 11149
3/22/80	**66**	5		31	**A Million Old Goodbyes**	*Buzz Cason/Steve Gibb/Bobby Russell*	Columbia 11221
5/17/80	**45**	8		32	**Lost In Austin**	*Buzz Cason/Freddy Weller*	Columbia 11266

Billboard DEBUT	PEAK	WKS	GOLD		ARTIST / Country Chart Hit	Ranking / Songwriter	Label (& Number)

WELLMAN, Tiny

Born Paul Wellman in Flatwoods, Kentucky. Male singer/songwriter.

DEBUT	PEAK	WKS	GOLD	#	Country Chart Hit	Songwriter	Label (& Number)
6/25/88	85	2			Nothing Left To Lose	*Ron Durst/Tiny Wellman*	Lee Ann 7342

WELLS, Kitty — 1950s: #10 / 1960s: #11 / All-Time: #37 // HOF: 1976

Born Muriel Ellen Deason on 8/30/1919 in Nashville, Tennessee. Female singer/songwriter/guitarist. Married **Johnny Wright** on 10/30/1937. Mother of **Bobby Wright** and **Ruby Wright**. Member of the *Louisiana Hayride* from 1948-53. Won Grammy's Lifetime Achievement Award in 1991. Known as "The Queen of Country Music."

OPRY: 1952

DEBUT	PEAK	WKS	GOLD	#	Country Chart Hit	Songwriter	Label (& Number)
7/19/52	❶[6]	18		1	It Wasn't God Who Made Honky Tonk Angels	S:❶[6] / J:❶[5] / A:2 *Joe Miller*	Decca 9-28232
					Grammy: Hall of Fame; answer to "The Wild Side Of Life" by **Hank Thompson**; also see #81 below		
3/7/53	6	4		2	Paying For That Back Street Affair	S:6 / J:9 *Jimmy Rule/Billy Wallace*	Decca 28578
					answer to "Back Street Affair" by **Webb Pierce**		
9/12/53	8	2		3	Hey Joe	J:8 *Boudleaux Bryant*	Decca 28797
					answer to "Hey Joe!" by **Carl Smith**		
1/23/54	9	1		4	Cheatin's A Sin	J:9 *Billy Wallace*	Decca 28931
4/3/54	8	1		5	Release Me	J:8 *Eddie Miller/Dube Williams/Bob Younts*	Decca 29023
5/22/54	❶[1]	41		6	One By One *[w/ Red Foley]* /	J:❶[1] / S:2 / A:2 *Jack Anglin/Jim Anglin/Johnnie Wright*	
7/10/54	12	1		7	I'm A Stranger In My Home *[w/ Red Foley]*	A:12 / S:15 *Neal Burris/Pee Wee King/Redd Stewart*	Decca 29065
12/4/54	14	1		8	Thou Shalt Not Steal	S:14 *Don Everly*	Decca 29313
2/26/55	3[1]	16		9	As Long As I Live *[w/ Red Foley]* /	J:3 / S:7 / A:8 *Roy Acuff*	
2/26/55	6	17		10	Make Believe ('Til We Can Make It Come True) *[w/ Red Foley]*	J:6 / S:7 / A:14 *Jerry Hamilton/Billy Walker*	Decca 29390
3/12/55	2[15]	28		11	Makin' Believe /	S:2 / J:2 / A:2 *Jimmy Work*	
4/9/55	7	11		12	Whose Shoulder Will You Cry On	A:7 / S:flip / J:flip *Billy Wallace/Kitty Wells*	Decca 29419
7/30/55	9	13		13	There's Poison In Your Heart /	J:9 / S:11 *Zeke Clements*	
8/27/55	12	1		14	I'm In Love With You	A:12 / S:flip / J:flip *Benny Martin*	Decca 29577
12/17/55+	7	8		15	Lonely Side Of Town /	S:3 / J:7 *Roy Botkin*	
12/24/55	7	9		16	I've Kissed You My Last Time	S:7 / A:10 *Bill Carlisle/Tom Cutrer/Virginia Suber*	Decca 29728
1/28/56	3[2]	31		17	You And Me *[w/ Red Foley]* /	S:3 / A:3 / J:6 *Jack Anglin/Jim Anglin/Johnnie Wright*	
2/4/56	flip	6		18	No One But You *[w/ Red Foley]*	S:flip / J:flip *Eddie Smith*	Decca 29740
5/12/56	11	5		19	How Far Is Heaven *[w/ Carol Sue]*	A:11 / S:15 *Jimmie Davis/Tillman Franks*	Decca 29823
7/7/56	3[1]	34		20	Searching (For Someone Like You) /	J:3 / S:4 / A:4 *Murphy Maddux*	
9/22/56	13	1		21	I'd Rather Stay Home	A:13 / S:flip / J:flip *Boudleaux Bryant/Felice Bryant*	Decca 29956
12/1/56+	6	13		22	Repenting /	J:6 / S:9 / A:11 *Gary Walker*	
12/1/56+	flip	7		23	I'm Counting On You	S:flip / J:flip *Don Robertson*	Decca 30094
4/6/57	8	9		24	Oh' So Many Years *[w/ Webb Pierce]*	A:8 *Frankie Bailes*	Decca 30183
6/3/57	7	9		25	Three Ways (To Love You)	A:7 / S:15 *Julius Dixon/Eve Jay*	Decca 30288
9/23/57	10	6		26	(I'll Always Be Your) Fraulein	S:10 / A:13 *Roy Botkin/Wally Jarvis/Lawton Williams*	Decca 30415
					answer to "Fraulein" by **Bobby Helms**		
1/20/58	12	1		27	One Week Later *[w/ Webb Pierce]*	A:12 *Gary Walker*	Decca 30489
3/3/58	3[2]	19		28	I Can't Stop Loving You /	A:3 / S:8 *Don Gibson*	
3/31/58	flip	11		29	She's No Angel	S:flip *J.W. Arnold/Wanda Ballman*	Decca 30551
7/7/58	7	14		30	Jealousy	A:7 / S:11 *Jim Anglin*	Decca 30662
10/6/58	15	11		31	Touch And Go Heart /	*Rusty Gabbard*	
11/10/58	16	7		32	He's Lost His Love For Me	*Mel Tillis/Wayne Walker*	Decca 30736
2/16/59	5	14		33	Mommy For A Day /	*Harlan Howard/Buck Owens*	
3/9/59	18	2		34	All The Time	*Mel Tillis/Wayne Walker*	Decca 30804
7/6/59	12	10		35	Your Wild Life's Gonna Get You Down	*Bob Gallion*	Decca 30890
11/9/59+	5	25		36	Amigo's Guitar	*Roy Bodkin/John D. Loudermilk/Kitty Wells*	Decca 30987
4/18/60	5	22		37	Left To Right	*Lorene Mann*	Decca 31065
9/5/60	16	9		38	Carmel By The Sea	*Mel Tillis/Marijohn Wilkin*	Decca 31123
12/19/60	26	3		39	I Can't Tell My Heart That *[w/ Roy Drusky]*	*Jack Anglin/Jim Anglin/Johnnie Wright*	Decca 31164
3/6/61	19	10		40	The Other Cheek /	*Wayne Walker*	
3/20/61	29	2		41	Fickle Fun	*Bill Anderson*	Decca 31192
5/29/61	❶[4]	23		42	Heartbreak U.S.A. /	*Harlan Howard*	
6/26/61	20	5		43	There Must Be Another Way To Live	*Mel Tillis*	Decca 31246
12/4/61+	10	12		44	Day Into Night /	*Don Gibson*	
1/6/62	21	3		45	Our Mansion Is A Prison Now	*Don Gibson*	Decca 31313
3/3/62	5	14		46	Unloved Unwanted	*Irene Stanton/Wayne Walker*	Decca 31349
8/4/62	8	11		47	Will Your Lawyer Talk To God	*Harlan Howard/Richard Johnson*	Decca 31392
11/3/62	7	13		48	We Missed You	*Bill Anderson*	Decca 31422
3/30/63	13	9		49	Cold And Lonely (Is The Forecast For Tonight)	*Roy Bodkin*	Decca 31457
8/3/63	29	2		50	A Heartache For A Keepsake /	*Roger Miller*	
8/17/63	22	6		51	I Gave My Wedding Dress Away	*Hy Heath/Fred Rose*	Decca 31501
2/1/64	7	25		52	This White Circle On My Finger	*Margie Bainbridge/Dorothy Lewis*	Decca 31580
5/30/64	4	25		53	Password /	*Herman Phillips*	
6/20/64	34	4		54	I've Thought Of Leaving You	*Lee Emerson*	Decca 31622
9/26/64	9	15		55	Finally *[w/ Webb Pierce]*	*Mel Tillis/Wayne Walker*	Decca 31663

Billboard DEBUT	PEAK	WKS	GOLD	ARTIST / Country Chart Hit	Ranking / Songwriter	Label (& Number)
				WELLS, Kitty — cont'd		
12/26/64+	**8**	15		56 **I'll Repossess My Heart**	*Paul Yandell*	Decca 31705
3/20/65	**27**	14		57 **Six Lonely Hours** /	*James Coleman/Wayne Walker*	
4/17/65	**4**	17		58 **You Don't Hear**	*Tommy Cash/Jerry Huffman*	Decca 31749
8/14/65	**9**	16		59 **Meanwhile, Down At Joe's**	*Harlan Howard*	Decca 31817
2/5/66	**15**	13		60 **A Woman Half My Age**	*Virginia Kennedy*	Decca 31881
7/23/66	**14**	13		61 **It's All Over** (But The Crying)	*Harlan Howard/Jan Howard*	Decca 31957
10/15/66	**52**	9		62 **A Woman Never Forgets** /	*Bill Phillips/Johnny Wright*	
10/29/66	**49**	9		63 **Only Me And My Hairdresser Know**	*Arthur Thomas*	Decca 32024
2/18/67	**34**	16		64 **Love Makes The World Go Around**	*Jim Anglin*	Decca 32088
5/6/67	**43**	11		65 **Happiness Means You** *[w/ Red Foley]* /	*Jim Anglin*	
6/3/67	**60**	5		66 **Hello Number One** *[w/ Red Foley]*	*Jim Anglin*	Decca 32126
8/12/67	**28**	13		67 **Queen Of Honky Tonk Street**	*Jim Anglin*	Decca 32163
12/30/67+	**63**	4		68 **Living As Strangers** *[w/ Red Foley]*	*Bill Phillips/Jean Stromatt*	Decca 32223
1/27/68	**35**	10		69 **My Big Truck Drivin' Man**	*Hank Mills*	Decca 32247
5/11/68	**54**	8		70 **We'll Stick Together** *[w/ Johnny Wright]*	*Bill Phillips*	Decca 32294
7/27/68	**52**	8		71 **Gypsy King**	*Betty Mackey*	Decca 32343
11/16/68	**47**	7		72 **Happiness Hill**	*Roy Botkin*	Decca 32389
1/18/69	**74**	2		73 **Have I Told You Lately That I Love You?** *[w/ Red Foley]*	*Scott Wiseman*	Decca 32427
5/17/69	**61**	5		74 **Guilty Street**	*Cecil Null*	Decca 32455
8/15/70	**71**	4		75 **Your Love Is The Way**	*Bill Owens*	Decca 32700
4/17/71	**72**	2		76 **They're Stepping All Over My Heart**	*Shorty Long/Johnny Specca*	Decca 32795
7/24/71	**49**	9		77 **Pledging My Love**	*Don Robey/Ferdinand Washington*	Decca 32840
4/1/72	**72**	3		78 **Sincerely**	*Alan Freed/Harvey Fuqua*	Decca 32931
9/27/75	**94**	3		79 **Anybody Out There Wanna Be A Daddy**	*Dave Kirby/Curly Putman*	Capricorn 0240
8/25/79	**75**	6		80 **Thank You For The Roses**	*Jim Anglin*	Ruboca 122
10/6/79	**60**	6		81 **The Wild Side Of Life** *[w/ Rayburn Anthony]*	*Arlie Carter/William Warren*	Mercury 57006

All The Time ['59]
Amigo's Guitar ['60]
Anybody Out There Wanna Be A Daddy ['75]
As Long As I Live ['55]
Carmel By The Sea ['60]
Cheatin's A Sin ['54]
Cold And Lonely (Is The Forecast For Tonight) ['63]
Day Into Night ['62]
Fickle Fun ['61]
Finally ['64]
Guilty Street ['69]
Gypsy King ['68]
Happiness Hill ['68]
Happiness Means You ['67]
Have I Told You Lately That I Love You? ['69]
He's Lost His Love For Me ['58]
Heartache For A Keepsake ['63]
Heartbreak U.S.A. ['61]
Hello Number One ['67]
Hey Joe ['53]
How Far Is Heaven ['56]
I Can't Stop Loving You ['58]
I Can't Tell My Heart That ['60]
I Gave My Wedding Dress Away ['63]
I'd Rather Stay Home ['56]
(I'll Always Be Your) Fraulein ['57]
I'll Repossess My Heart ['65]
I'm A Stranger In My Home ['54]
I'm Counting On You ['57]
I'm In Love With You ['55]
I've Kissed You My Last Time ['55]
I've Thought Of Leaving You ['64]
It Wasn't God Who Made Honky Tonk Angels ['52]
It's All Over (But The Crying) ['66]
Jealousy ['58]
Left To Right ['60]
Living As Strangers ['68]
Lonely Side Of Town ['56]
Love Makes The World Go Around ['67]
Make Believe ('Til We Can Make It Come True) ['55]
Makin' Believe ['55]
Meanwhile, Down At Joe's ['65]
Mommy For A Day ['59]
My Big Truck Drivin' Man ['68]
No One But You ['56]
Oh' So Many Years ['57]
One By One ['54]
One Week Later ['58]
Only Me And My Hairdresser Know ['66]
Other Cheek ['61]
Our Mansion Is A Prison Now ['62]
Password ['64]
Paying For That Back Street Affair ['53]
Pledging My Love ['71]
Queen Of Honky Tonk Street ['67]
Release Me ['54]
Repenting ['57]
Searching (For Someone Like You) ['56]
She's No Angel ['58]
Sincerely ['72]
Six Lonely Hours ['65]
Thank You For The Roses ['79]
There Must Be Another Way To Live ['61]
There's Poison In Your Heart ['55]
They're Stepping All Over My Heart ['71]
This White Circle On My Finger ['64]
Thou Shalt Not Steal ['54]
Three Ways (To Love You) ['57]
Touch And Go Heart ['58]
Unloved Unwanted ['62]
We Missed You ['62]
We'll Stick Together ['68]
Whose Shoulder Will You Cry On ['55]
Wild Side Of Life ['79]
Will Your Lawyer Talk To God ['62]
Woman Half My Age ['66]
Woman Never Forgets ['66]
You And Me ['56]
You Don't Hear ['65]
Your Love Is The Way ['70]
Your Wild Life's Gonna Get You Down ['59]

WELLS, Mike

Born in 1964 in New Jersey. Male singer.

DEBUT	PEAK	WKS	GOLD	Country Chart Hit	Songwriter	Label (& Number)
2/22/75	**54**	9		1 **Sing A Love Song, Porter Wagoner**	*Linda Darrell*	Playboy 6029
2/7/76	**77**	7		2 **Wild World**	*Cat Stevens*	Playboy 6061

WELLS, Ruby

Born in Tennessee. Female singer.

DEBUT	PEAK	WKS	GOLD	Country Chart Hit	Songwriter	Label (& Number)
3/3/56	**13**	3		**I Want To Be Loved** *[w/ Johnnie & Jack]* A:13	*Johnnie Bailes/Walter Bailes*	RCA Victor 6395

WENCE, Bill

Born on 7/2/1942 in Salinas, California. Male singer/songwriter.

DEBUT	PEAK	WKS	GOLD	Country Chart Hit	Songwriter	Label (& Number)
9/15/79	**92**	4		1 **Quicksand**	*Bill Wence*	Rustic 1003
1/26/80	**85**	4		2 **Break Away**	*Bill Wence*	Rustic 1005
6/7/80	**63**	6		3 **I Wanna Do It Again**	*Bill Wence*	Rustic 1009
9/27/80	**85**	4		4 **Night Lies**	*Wayne Marshall/Bill Wence*	Rustic 1012

WEST, Dottie

1960s: #39 / 1970s: #39 / All-Time: #61

Born Dorothy Marie Marsh on 10/11/1932 in McMinnville, Tennessee. Died in a car crash on 9/4/1991 (age 58). Female singer/songwriter/guitarist. Mother of **Shelly West**. Acted in the movies *Second Fiddle To A Steel Guitar* and *There's A Still On The Hill*. Also see **Some Of Chet's Friends**.

CMA: Vocal Duo (with Kenny Rogers) 1978 & 1979 // OPRY: 1964

DEBUT	PEAK	WKS	GOLD	Country Chart Hit	Songwriter	Label (& Number)
11/30/63	**29**	2		1 **Let Me Off At The Corner**	*Larry Kronberg/Lou Meridith*	RCA Victor 8225
3/28/64	**7**	21		2 **Love Is No Excuse** *[w/ Jim Reeves]*	*Justin Tubb*	RCA Victor 8324
8/22/64	**10**	15		3 **Here Comes My Baby** — Grammy: Female Vocal	*Bill West/Dottie West*	RCA Victor 8374
2/27/65	**32**	8		4 **Didn't I**	*Dottie West*	RCA Victor 8467
5/22/65	**30**	10		5 **Gettin' Married Has Made Us Strangers**	*Gary Geld/Peter Udell*	RCA Victor 8525
8/21/65	**32**	5		6 **No Sign Of Living**	*Mirriam Eddy*	RCA Victor 8615

Billboard DEBUT	PEAK	WKS	GOLD	ARTIST Ranking Country Chart Hit	Songwriter	Label (& Number)
				WEST, Dottie — cont'd		
12/4/65+	22	14		7 **Before The Ring On Your Finger Turns Green**	*Boudleaux Bryant/Felice Bryant*	RCA Victor 8702
3/12/66	5	21		8 **Would You Hold It Against Me**	*Bill West/Dottie West*	RCA Victor 8770
8/13/66	24	10		9 **Mommy, Can I Still Call Him Daddy** *[w/ Dale West]*	*Bill West/Dottie West*	RCA Victor 8900
12/17/66+	17	13		10 **What's Come Over My Baby**	*Bill West/Dottie West*	RCA Victor 9011
3/18/67	8	16		11 **Paper Mansions**	*Ted Harris*	RCA Victor 9118
8/26/67	13	14		12 **Like A Fool**	*Yvonne Devaney*	RCA Victor 9267
12/16/67+	24	12		13 **Childhood Places**	*Sandy Mason/Les Reed*	RCA Victor 9377
4/27/68	15	12		14 **Country Girl**	*Red Lane/Dottie West*	RCA Victor 9497
9/7/68	19	12		15 **Reno**	*Ruby Allmond*	RCA Victor 9604
2/22/69	2[1]	17		16 **Rings Of Gold** *[w/ Don Gibson]*	*Gene Thomas*	RCA Victor 9715
7/12/69	32	10		17 **Sweet Memories** *[w/ Don Gibson]*	*Mickey Newbury*	RCA Victor 0178
10/4/69	47	6		18 **Clinging To My Baby's Hand**	*Red Lane/Dottie West*	RCA Victor 0239
12/13/69+	7	13		19 **There's A Story** (Goin' 'Round) *[w/ Don Gibson]*	*Don Gibson*	RCA Victor 0291
2/7/70	45	8		20 **I Heard Our Song**	*Sandy Mason*	RCA Victor 9792
7/18/70	46	10		21 **Til I Can't Take It Anymore** *[w/ Don Gibson]*	*Dorian Burton/Clyde Otis*	RCA Victor 9867
8/1/70	37	10		22 **It's Dawned On Me You're Gone**	*Hank Cochran/Red Lane*	RCA Victor 9872
10/31/70	21	12		23 **Forever Yours**	*Jimmy Peppers*	RCA Victor 9911
1/30/71	29	11		24 **Slowly** *[w/ Jimmy Dean]*	*Tommy Hill/Webb Pierce*	RCA Victor 9947
3/6/71	48	8		25 **Careless Hands**	*Bob Hilliard/Carl Sigman*	RCA Victor 9957
5/29/71	53	8		26 **Lonely Is**	*Jerry Foster/Bill Rice*	RCA Victor 9982
9/11/71	51	8		27 **Six Weeks Every Summer** (Christmas Every Other Year)	*Fran Powers*	RCA Victor 1012
6/3/72	52	9		28 **I'm Only A Woman**	*Ben Peters*	RCA Victor 0711
12/2/72+	28	11		29 **If It's All Right With You**	*Larry Henley/Kenny O'Dell*	RCA Victor 0828
4/28/73	44	9		30 **Just What I've Been Looking For** Larry Gatlin (backing vocal)	*Kenny O'Dell*	RCA Victor 0930
9/15/73	2[1]	15		31 **Country Sunshine**	*Billy Davis/Dottie West*	RCA Victor 0072
3/30/74	8	14		32 **Last Time I Saw Him**	*Michael Masser/Pamela Sawyer*	RCA Victor 0231
7/13/74	21	13		33 **House Of Love**	*Kenny O'Dell*	RCA Victor 0321
12/14/74+	35	10		34 **Lay Back Lover**	*Steve Pippin/Rafe Van Hoy*	RCA Victor 10125
5/10/75	65	10		35 **Rollin' In Your Sweet Sunshine**	*Jay Harris/Bob Morrison*	RCA Victor 10269
3/27/76	68	7		36 **Here Come The Flowers**	*Chips Moman/Toni Wine*	RCA Victor 10553
6/26/76	91	5		37 **If I'm A Fool For Loving You**	*Stan Kesler*	RCA Victor 10699
11/13/76+	19	15		38 **When It's Just You And Me**	*Kenny O'Dell*	United Artists 898
3/19/77	28	12		39 **Every Word I Write**	*Roger Bowling/Jan Crutchfield/George Richey*	United Artists 946
7/9/77	30	10		40 **Tonight You Belong To Me**	*Lee David/Billy Rose*	United Artists 1010
10/8/77	57	8		41 **That's All I Wanted To Know**	*Hugh Moffatt/Ed Penney*	United Artists 1084
2/18/78	❶[2]	17		42 **Every Time Two Fools Collide** *[w/ Kenny Rogers]*	*Jan Dyer/Jeff Tweel*	United Artists 1137
6/10/78	17	12		43 **Come See Me And Come Lonely**	*Red Lane*	United Artists 1209
9/2/78	2[1]	14		44 **Anyone Who Isn't Me Tonight** *[w/ Kenny Rogers]*	*Julie Didier/Casey Kelly*	United Artists 1234
12/2/78+	49	9		45 **Reaching Out To Hold You**	*Christina Carroll/Jay Loyd*	United Artists 1257
2/17/79	❶[1]	15		46 **All I Ever Need Is You** *[w/ Kenny Rogers]*	*Jimmy Holiday/Eddie Reeves*	United Artists 1276
7/7/79	3[1]	15		47 **Til I Can Make It On My Own** *[w/ Kenny Rogers]*	*George Richey/Billy Sherrill/Tammy Wynette*	United Artists 1299
10/20/79	12	15		48 **You Pick Me Up** (And Put Me Down)	*Randy Goodrum/Brent Maher*	United Artists 1324
2/9/80	❶[1]	15		49 **A Lesson In Leavin'**	*Randy Goodrum/Brent Maher*	United Artists 1339
6/7/80	13	14		50 **Leavin's For Unbelievers**	*Randy Goodrum/Brent Maher*	United Artists 1352
12/13/80+	❶[1]	16		51 **Are You Happy Baby?**	*Bob Stone*	Liberty 1392
4/4/81	❶[1]	15		52 **What Are We Doin' In Love** *[w/ Kenny Rogers]*	*Randy Goodrum*	Liberty 1404
7/11/81	16	14		53 (I'm Gonna) **Put You Back On The Rack**	*Randy Goodrum/Brent Maher*	Liberty 1419
9/19/81	80	4		54 **Once You Were Mine**	*Larry Gatlin*	RCA 12284
11/7/81+	16	14		55 **It's High Time**	*Randy Goodrum/Brent Maher*	Liberty 1436
2/20/82	26	13		56 **You're Not Easy To Forget**	*Tom Snow/Cynthia Weil*	Liberty 1451
9/11/82	29	11		57 **She Can't Get My Love Off The Bed**	*Debbie Hupp/Bob Morrison*	Liberty 1479
12/18/82+	63	7		58 **If It Takes All Night**	*David Rogers/Gloria Sklerov*	Liberty 1490
6/18/83	40	11		59 **Tulsa Ballroom**	*Dewayne Blackwell/John Durrill*	Liberty 1500
3/24/84	19	15		60 **Together Again** *[w/ Kenny Rogers]*	*Buck Owens*	Liberty 1516
9/15/84	77	7		61 **What's Good For The Goose** (Is Good For The Gander)	*Alex Harvey*	Permian 82006
12/1/84	67	8		62 **Let Love Come Lookin' For You**	*Jan Buckingham*	Permian 82007
5/25/85	53	8		63 **We Know Better Now**	*Steve Dean/Frank J. Myers*	Permian 82010

All I Ever Need Is You ['79]
Anyone Who Isn't Me Tonight ['78]
Are You Happy Baby? ['81]
Before The Ring On Your Finger Turns Green ['66]
Careless Hands ['71]
Childhood Places ['68]
Clinging To My Baby's Hand ['69]
Come See Me And Come Lonely ['78]
Country Girl ['68]
Country Sunshine ['73]
Didn't I ['65]
Every Time Two Fools Collide ['78]
Every Word I Write ['77]
Forever Yours ['70]
Gettin' Married Has Made Us Strangers ['65]
Here Come The Flowers ['76]
Here Comes My Baby ['64]
House Of Love ['74]
I Heard Our Song ['70]
(I'm Gonna) Put You Back On The Rack ['81]
I'm Only A Woman ['72]
If I'm A Fool For Loving You ['76]
If It Takes All Night ['83]
If It's All Right With You ['73]
It's Dawned On Me You're Gone ['70]
It's High Time ['82]
Just What I've Been Looking For ['73]
Last Time I Saw Him ['74]
Lay Back Lover ['75]
Leavin's For Unbelievers ['80]
Lesson In Leavin' ['80]
Let Love Come Lookin' For You ['84]
Let Me Off At The Corner ['63]
Like A Fool ['67]
Lonely Is ['71]
Love Is No Excuse ['64]
Mommy, Can I Still Call Him Daddy ['66]
No Sign Of Living ['65]
Once You Were Mine ['81]
Paper Mansions ['67]
Reaching Out To Hold You ['79]
Reno ['68]
Rings Of Gold ['69]
Rollin' In Your Sweet Sunshine ['75]
She Can't Get My Love Off The Bed ['82]
Six Weeks Every Summer (Christmas Every Other Year) ['71]
Slowly ['71]
Sweet Memories ['69]
That's All I Wanted To Know ['77]
There's A Story (Goin' 'Round) ['70]
Til I Can Make It On My Own ['79]
Til I Can't Take It Anymore ['70]
Together Again ['84]
Tonight You Belong To Me ['77]
Tulsa Ballroom ['83]
We Know Better Now ['85]
What Are We Doin' In Love ['81]
What's Come Over My Baby ['67]
What's Good For The Goose (Is Good For The Gander) ['84]
When It's Just You And Me ['77]
Would You Hold It Against Me ['66]
You Pick Me Up (And Put Me Down) ['79]
You're Not Easy To Forget ['82]

DEBUT	PEAK	WKS	GOLD	ARTIST / Country Chart Hit	Ranking / Songwriter	Label (& Number)

WEST, Elbert

Born in 1968 in Welch, West Virginia. Male singer.

DEBUT	PEAK	WKS	#	Country Chart Hit	Songwriter	Label (& Number)
6/9/01	56	3		**Diddley** — from the album *Livin' The Life* on Broken Bow 0004	*C.B. Carter/Joel Shapiro*	Broken Bow

WEST, Jim

Born in Georgia. Male singer/songwriter.

DEBUT	PEAK	WKS	#	Country Chart Hit	Songwriter	Label (& Number)
11/3/79	95	2	1	**Honky Tonk Disco**	*Jim West*	Macho 002
12/15/79	92	4	2	**Can't Love On Lies** *[w/ Carol Chase]*	*Jim West*	Macho 003
12/20/80	79	5	3	**Slip Away**	*Jim West*	Macho 008
3/14/81	83	3	4	**Lovin' Night** — **Stephanie Winslow** (backing vocal)	*Jim West*	Macho 009

WEST, Shelly — All-Time: #231

Born on 5/23/1958 in Cleveland, Ohio; raised in Nashville, Tennessee. Female singer/guitarist. Daughter of **Dottie West**. Married to **Allen Frizzell** from 1977-85. Formed a singing partnership with Allen's brother, **David Frizzell**.

CMA: Vocal Duo (with David Frizzell) 1981 & 1982

DAVID FRIZZELL & SHELLY WEST:

DEBUT	PEAK	WKS	#	Country Chart Hit	Songwriter	Label (& Number)
1/17/81	❶^{1}	17	1	**You're The Reason God Made Oklahoma** — from the movie *Any Which Way You Can* starring **Clint Eastwood**	*Larry Collins/Sandy Pinkard*	Warner 49650
6/20/81	9	15	2	**A Texas State Of Mind**	*Cliff Crofford/John Durrill/Snuff Garrett*	Warner 49745
10/10/81	16	16	3	**Husbands And Wives**	*Roger Miller*	Warner 49825
2/6/82	8	18	4	**Another Honky-Tonk Night On Broadway**	*Milton Brown/Steve Dorff/Snuff Garrett*	Warner 50007
7/17/82	4	18	5	**I Just Came Here To Dance**	*Ken Bell/Terry Skinner/J.L. Wallace*	Warner 29980
12/4/82+	43	11	6	**Please Surrender** — from the movie *Honkytonk Man* starring **Clint Eastwood**	*Cliff Crofford/John Durrill/Snuff Garrett*	Warner 29850

SHELLY WEST:

DEBUT	PEAK	WKS	#	Country Chart Hit	Songwriter	Label (& Number)
2/12/83	❶^{1}	23	7	**José Cuervo**	*Cindy Jordan*	Warner 29778
3/26/83	52	10	8	**Cajun Invitation** *[w/ David Frizzell]*	*Milton Brown/Steve Dorff/Snuff Garrett*	Warner 29756
7/2/83	4	18	9	**Flight 309 To Tennessee**	*Ronnie Scott*	Viva 29597
9/3/83	71	4	10	**Pleasure Island** *[w/ David Frizzell]*	*Ron Hellard/Bucky Jones/Curly Putman*	Viva 29544
11/5/83+	10	18	11	**Another Motel Memory**	*Charlie Black/Tommy Rocco*	Viva 29461
2/4/84	20	17	12	**Silent Partners** *[w/ David Frizzell]*	*Kerry Chater/Austin Roberts/Tommy Rocco*	Viva 29404
3/10/84	56	7	13	**Now I Lay Me Down To Cheat**	*Austin Roberts*	Viva 29353
6/2/84	34	14	14	**Somebody Buy This Cowgirl A Beer**	*Milton Brown/Steve Dorff/Snuff Garrett*	Viva 29265
9/15/84	13	20	15	**It's A Be Together Night** *[w/ David Frizzell]*	S:8 / A:16 *Charlie Black/Tommy Rocco/John Schweers*	Viva 29187
1/19/85	21	16	16	**Now There's You**	S:18 / A:21 *Len Chera/Bob Morrison/Rich Peoples*	Viva 29106
4/13/85	60	8	17	**Do Me Right** *[w/ David Frizzell]*	*Bill Price*	Viva 29048
6/15/85	46	10	18	**Don't Make Me Wait On The Moon**	*Jim McBride*	Warner 28997
9/7/85	64	7	19	**I'll Dance The Two Step**	*Randy Albright/John Greenebaum/Becky Hobbs*	Warner 28909
3/15/86	54	5	20	**What Would You Do**	*Michael Foster/David Thompson*	Warner 28769
9/6/86	55	10	21	**Love Don't Come Any Better Than This**	*Susan Longacre/Kent Robbins*	Warner 28648

WEST, Speedy — see ORVILLE & IVY

WESTERN FLYER

Group from Texas: Danny Myrick (vocals), Steve Charles, Chris Marion, Roger Helton, T.J. Klay and Bruce Gust. Named after the brand of bicycle.

DEBUT	PEAK	WKS	#	Country Chart Hit	Songwriter	Label (& Number)
7/23/94	61	9	1	**Western Flyer**	*Danny Myrick/Tony Wood*	Step One
10/29/94	62	8	2	**She Should've Been Mine**	*Kent Blazy/Rob Crosby/Jim Dowell*	Step One
7/22/95	71	3	3	**Friday Night Stampede**	*Marcus Hummon/Monty Powell*	Step One
11/11/95	74	1	4	**His Memory** — above 4 from the album *Western Flyer* on Step One 85	*Donny Kees/Rich Ross*	Step One
8/3/96	32	20	5	**What Will You Do With M-E** — from the album *Back In America* on Step One 98	S:24 *Craig Martin/Rick Tiger*	Step One

WESTERN UNION BAND, The

Group from Texas. Led by singer/guitarist Carl Kaye.

DEBUT	PEAK	WKS	#	Country Chart Hit	Songwriter	Label (& Number)
7/9/88	76	3	1	**Bed Of Roses**	*Rex Benson/Steve Gillette*	Shawn-Del 2201
10/8/88	81	3	2	**Rising Cost Of Loving You**	*Milton Wright*	Shawn-Del 2202

WHEELER, Billy Edd

Born on 12/9/1932 in Whitesville, West Virginia. Male singer/songwriter/guitarist.

DEBUT	PEAK	WKS	#	Country Chart Hit	Songwriter	Label (& Number)
11/28/64+	3^{2}	24	1	**Ode To The Little Brown Shack Out Back** — recorded "live" at The Mountain State Art & Craft Fair in Ripley, West Virginia	*Billy Edd Wheeler* **[L-N]**	Kapp 617
8/24/68	63	5	2	**I Ain't The Worryin' Kind**	*Billy Edd Wheeler*	Kapp 928
5/3/69	51	6	3	**West Virginia Woman**	*Billy Edd Wheeler*	United Artists 50507
9/13/69	62	7	4	**Fried Chicken And A Country Tune**	*Coleman Harwell*	United Artists 50579
7/29/72	71	3	5	**200 Lbs. O' Slingin' Hound**	*Billy Edd Wheeler*	RCA Victor 0739
11/17/79	94	2	6	**Duel Under The Snow**	*Billy Edd Wheeler*	Radio Cinema 001
6/20/81	55	6	7	**Daddy** *[w/ Rashell Richmond]*	*Jerry Duncan/Betty Gibson/Billy Edd Wheeler*	NSD 94

WHEELER, Karen

Born on 3/12/1947 in Sikeston, Missouri. Female singer/guitarist. Daughter of **Onie Wheeler**.

DEBUT	PEAK	WKS	#	Country Chart Hit	Songwriter	Label (& Number)
7/8/72	67	4	1	**The First Time For Us**	*Charlie Craig*	Chart 5166
3/9/74	31	12	2	**Born To Love And Satisfy**	*Jerry Foster/Bill Rice*	RCA Victor 0223
9/21/74	97	3	3	**What Can I Do (To Make You Happy)**	*Kent Robbins*	RCA Victor 10034

Billboard DEBUT	PEAK	WKS	GOLD	ARTIST / Country Chart Hit	Ranking / Songwriter	Label (& Number)

WHEELER, Onie

Born on 11/10/1921 in Senath, Missouri. Died onstage at the *Grand Ole Opry* on 5/27/1984 (age 62). Male singer/songwriter/harmonica player. Father of **Karen Wheeler**.

DEBUT	PEAK	WKS	#	Country Chart Hit	Songwriter	Label (& Number)
2/3/73	**53**	10		**John's Been Shucking My Corn**	*Onie Wheeler* **[N]**	Royal American 76

WHIPPLE, Sterling

Born on 7/14/1927 in Eugene, Oregon. Male singer/songwriter.

DEBUT	PEAK	WKS	#	Country Chart Hit	Songwriter	Label (& Number)
4/15/78	**26**	9	1	**Dirty Work**	*Sterling Whipple*	Warner 8552
10/14/78	**25**	10	2	**Then You'll Remember**	*Sterling Whipple*	Warner 8632
3/24/79	**84**	4	3	**Love Is Hours In The Making**	*Sterling Whipple*	Warner 8747

WHISPERING WILL

Novelty production assembled by writer/producer Nelson Larkin.

DEBUT	PEAK	WKS	#	Country Chart Hit	Songwriter	Label (& Number)
2/24/79	**89**	2		**Double W** parody of "Double S" by **Bill Anderson**	*Nelson Larkin* **[N]**	Vista 104

WHITE, Bill

Born in Muldrow, Oklahoma. Male singer. Brother of **Ann J. Morton** and **Jim Mundy**.

DEBUT	PEAK	WKS	#	Country Chart Hit	Songwriter	Label (& Number)
7/15/78	**79**	3		**Unbreakable Hearts**	*Dennis W. Morgan/Ann J. Morton*	Prairie Dust 7625

WHITE, Brian

Born in Los Angeles, California. Male singer/songwriter.

DEBUT	PEAK	WKS	#	Country Chart Hit	Songwriter	Label (& Number)
5/21/88	**70**	4		**It's Too Late To Love You Now**	*Brian White*	Oak 1050

WHITE, Bryan — All-Time: #232

Born on 2/17/1974 in Lawton, Oklahoma; raised in Oklahoma City, Oklahoma. Male singer/songwriter/guitarist. Began playing drums at age five. Moved to Nashville in 1992; worked as a staff writer at **Glen Campbell** Music. Married actress Erika Page on 10/14/2000. Also see **One Heart At A Time**.

CMA: Horizon 1996

DEBUT	PEAK	WKS	#	Country Chart Hit	Songwriter	Label (& Number)
10/8/94	**48**	9	1	**Eugene You Genius**	*Billy Lawson/Lonnie Wilson*	Asylum
12/24/94+	**24**	20	2	**Look At Me Now**	*Derek George/John Tirro/Bryan White*	Asylum
5/13/95	❶[1]	20	3	**Someone Else's Star**	S:5 *Skip Ewing/Jim Weatherly*	Asylum
10/7/95+	❶[1]	20	4	**Rebecca Lynn** above 4 from the album *Bryan White* on Asylum 61642	S:7 *Skip Ewing/Don Sampson*	Asylum
3/2/96	**4**	20	5	**I'm Not Supposed To Love You Anymore**	S:2 *Skip Ewing/Donny Kees*	Asylum
6/29/96	❶[2]	20	6	**So Much For Pretending**	S:6 *Derek George/John Tirro/Bryan White*	Asylum
10/19/96+	**15**	20	7	**That's Another Song**	*J.P. Daniel/Jule Medders/Doug Pincock/Monty Powell*	Asylum
3/1/97	❶[1]	20	8	**Sittin' On Go** above 4 from the album *Between Now And Forever* on Asylum 61880	*Rick Bowles/Josh Leo*	Asylum
8/2/97	**4**	20	9	**Love Is The Right Place**	S:7 *Marcus Hummon/Tommy Sims*	Asylum
11/15/97+	**6**	32	10	**From This Moment On** *[w/ Shania Twain]* from Twain's album *Come On Over* on Mercury 536003	*Mutt Lange/Shania Twain*	Mercury
11/29/97+	**16**	20	11	**One Small Miracle**	*Bill Anderson/Steve Wariner*	Asylum
4/11/98	**30**	11	12	**Bad Day To Let You Go**	*Bob DiPiero/Derek George/Bryan White*	Asylum
8/1/98	**45**	12	13	**Tree Of Hearts** #9 & 11-13: from the album *The Right Place* on Asylum 62047	*Skip Ewing/Don Sampson*	Asylum
6/19/99	**39**	20	14	**You're Still Beautiful To Me**	S:5 *Bryan Adams/Mutt Lange*	Asylum
10/23/99+	**40**	20	15	**God Gave Me You** above 2 from the album *How Lucky I Am* on Asylum 62278	*Andy Goldmark/J.D. Hicks/Jamie Houston*	Asylum
12/11/99	**62**	1	16	**Holiday Inn** from the album *Dreaming Of Christmas* on Asylum 62464	*Don Henry/Garry Schiera* **[X]**	Asylum
10/28/00	**56**	8	17	**How Long** from the album *Greatest Hits* on Asylum 47890	*Andrew Williams/David Williams*	Asylum

WHITE, Charley

Born in Montana. Male singer/songwriter.

DEBUT	PEAK	WKS	#	Country Chart Hit	Songwriter	Label (& Number)
6/30/79	**86**	2		**Rocket 'Til The Cows Come Home**	*Charley White* **[N]**	NSD 22

WHITE, Danny

Born Wilford Daniel White on 2/9/1952 in Mesa, Arizona. Pro football quarterback with the Dallas Cowboys from 1976-88.

DEBUT	PEAK	WKS	#	Country Chart Hit	Songwriter	Label (& Number)
2/5/83	**85**	2		**You're A Part Of Me** *[w/ Linda Nail]*	*Kim Carnes*	Grand Prix 2

WHITE, JJ — see JJ

WHITE, Joy

Born on 10/2/1961 in Turrell, Arkansas; raised in Mishawaka, Indiana. Female singer.

DEBUT	PEAK	WKS	#	Country Chart Hit	Songwriter	Label (& Number)
10/24/92	**68**	3	1	**Little Tears**	*Mike Henderson/Mark Irwin*	Columbia
1/30/93	**45**	14	2	**True Confessions**	*Kostas/Marty Stuart*	Columbia
6/12/93	**71**	3	3	**Cold Day In July** above 3 from the album *Between Midnight And Hindsight* on Columbia 48806	*Richard Leigh*	Columbia
7/9/94	**73**	5	4	**Wild Love** *[Joy Lynn White]* from the album *Wild Love* on Columbia 57444	*Blake Chancey/Dennis Linde/Paul Worley*	Columbia

WHITE, L.E., And Lola Jean Dillon

Duo of songwriters from Knoxville, Tennessee. White was born on 5/27/1930; died on 9/7/2004 (age 74). Father of **Michael White**.

DEBUT	PEAK	WKS	#	Country Chart Hit	Songwriter	Label (& Number)
6/18/77	**73**	7	1	**Home, Sweet Home**	*Lola Jean Dillon/L.E. White* **[N]**	Epic 50389
11/26/77	**90**	3	2	**You're The Reason Our Kids Are Ugly**	*Lola Jean Dillon/L.E. White* **[N]**	Epic 50474

DEBUT	PEAK	WKS	GOLD	ARTIST / Ranking / Country Chart Hit ... Songwriter	Label (& Number)
				WHITE, Lari	
				Born on 5/13/1965 in Dunedin, Florida. Female singer/songwriter/pianist.	
2/13/93	**44**	12		1 **What A Woman Wants** ... *Chuck Cannon/Lari White*	RCA
5/15/93	**47**	16		2 **Lead Me Not** ... *Lari White*	RCA
9/11/93	**68**	4		3 **Lay Around And Love On You** ... *Bobby David/Dave Gillon*	RCA
				above 3 from the album *Lead Me Not* on RCA 66117	
4/9/94	**10**	20		4 **That's My Baby** ... *Chuck Cannon/Lari White*	RCA
9/3/94	**5**	20		5 **Now I Know** ... *Don Cook/Cindy Greene/Chick Rains*	RCA
1/21/95	**10**	20		6 **That's How You Know (When You're In Love)** ... *Chuck Cannon/Lari White*	RCA
				above 3 from the album *Wishes* on RCA 66395	
12/16/95+	**20**	20		7 **Ready, Willing And Able** ... *Jess Leary/Jody Alan Sweet*	RCA
5/18/96	**52**	7		8 **Wild At Heart** ... *Al Anderson/Lari White*	RCA
				above 2 from the album *Don't Fence Me In* on RCA 66742	
7/26/97	**18**	20		9 **Helping Me Get Over You** ***[w/ Travis Tritt]*** ... *Travis Tritt/Lari White*	Warner
				from Tritt's album *The Restless Kind* on Warner 46304	
5/16/98	**16**	20		10 **Stepping Stone** ... S:7 *David Kent/Lari White/Craig Wiseman*	Lyric Street
10/3/98+	**32**	20		11 **Take Me** ... *Bob DiPiero/Stephony Smith*	Lyric Street
4/10/99	**64**	5		12 **John Wayne Walking Away** ... *Jerry Boonstra/Austin Cunningham/Doak Snead*	Lyric Street
				above 3 from the album *Stepping Stone* on Lyric Street 65001	
				WHITE, Mack	
				Born in Dothan, Georgia. Male singer/songwriter.	
12/1/73+	**34**	14		1 **Too Much Pride** ... *Mack White*	Commercial 1314
4/27/74	**66**	7		2 **Sweet And Tender Feeling** ... *Mack White*	Commercial 1315
10/19/74	**75**	10		3 **Ain't It All Worth Living For** ... *Sammy King*	Playboy 6016
2/28/76	**35**	13		4 **Let Me Be Your Friend** ... *DeWayne Orender/K. Phyllis Powell*	Commercial 1317
8/21/76	**34**	10		5 **Take Me As I Am (Or Let Me Go)** ... *Boudleaux Bryant*	Commercial 1319
11/27/76	**68**	8		6 **A Stranger To Me** ... *Don Gibson*	Commercial 1320
3/25/78	**77**	6		7 **Just Out Of Reach** ... *Virgil Stewart*	Commercial 00033
7/15/78	**83**	3		8 **Goodbyes Don't Come Easy** ... *Robert Lee Smith*	Commercial 00040
2/27/82	**88**	3		9 **Kiss The Hurt Away** ... *Mack White*	Commercial 121
				WHITE, Michael	
				Born in Knoxville, Tennessee; raised in Nashville, Tennessee. Male singer/songwriter. Son of **L.E. White**.	
12/21/91+	**32**	18		1 **Professional Fool** ... *Michael White*	Reprise
				from the album *Professional Fool* on Reprise 19128	
6/27/92	**43**	11		2 **Familiar Ground** ... *Tim Lancaster/Michael White*	Reprise
11/7/92	**63**	4		3 **She Likes To Dance** ... *Robert Bryne/Alan Schulman/Michael White*	Reprise
				above 2 from the album *She Likes To Dance* on Reprise 18694	
				WHITE, Roger	
				Born in Nashville, Tennessee. Male singer.	
10/14/67	**57**	4		**Mystery Of Tallahatchie Bridge** ... *Dick Heard*	Big A 103
				answer to "Ode To Billie Joe" by **Bobbie Gentry**	
				WHITE, Sharon	
				Born on 12/17/1953 in Abilene, Texas. Female singer. Member of **The Whites**. Married **Ricky Skaggs** in 1982.	
5/2/87	**10**	23		**Love Can't Ever Get Better Than This** ***[w/ Ricky Skaggs]*** ... S:5 *Irene Kelley/Nancy Montgomery*	Epic 07060
				WHITE, Tony Joe	
				Born on 7/23/1943 in Goodwill, Louisiana. Bayou-rock singer/songwriter.	
11/1/80	**91**	2		1 **Mama Don't Let Your Cowboys Grow Up To Be Babies** ... *LeAnn White/Tony Joe White*	Casablanca 2304
				Waylon Jennings (backing vocal); parody of "Mammas Don't Let Your Babies Grow Up To Be Cowboys" by **Waylon & Willie**	
11/26/83	**55**	10		2 **The Lady In My Life** ... *Tony Joe White*	Columbia 04134
3/3/84	**85**	3		3 **We Belong Together** ... *Tony Joe White*	Columbia 04356
				WHITEHEAD, Benny	
				Born in Dallas, Texas. Male singer.	
1/27/73	**61**	5		**Blue Eyed Jane** ... *Jimmie Rodgers/Lulu Belle White*	Reprise 1131
				WHITES, The — **All-Time: #294**	
				Family trio from Abilene, Texas: H.S. "Buck" White (guitar, mandolin, piano; born on 1/13/1930), with daughters Cheryl White (bass; born on 1/27/1955) and **Sharon White** (guitar; born on 12/17/1953). All share vocals. Sharon married **Ricky Skaggs** in 1982.	
				OPRY: 1984	
6/20/81	**66**	4		1 **Send Me The Pillow You Dream On** ... *Hank Locklin*	Capitol 5004
8/28/82	**10**	17		2 **You Put The Blue In Me** ... *Janis Carnes/Rick Carnes/Chip Hardy*	Elektra/Curb 69980
12/25/82+	**9**	19		3 **Hangin' Around** ... *Janis Carnes/Rick Carnes/Chip Hardy*	Elektra/Curb 69855
4/30/83	**9**	18		4 **I Wonder Who's Holding My Baby Tonight** ... *Donnie Clark/Vickie Clark/Joe Halterman*	Warner/Curb 29659
9/10/83	**25**	14		5 **When The New Wears Off Of Our Love** ... *Paul Craft*	Warner/Curb 29513
12/17/83+	**10**	19		6 **Give Me Back That Old Familiar Feeling** ... *Bill Graham*	Warner/Curb 29411
5/12/84	**14**	17		7 **Forever You** ... *John Beland*	MCA/Curb 52381
8/25/84	**10**	22		8 **Pins And Needles** ... S:8 / A:12 *Janis Carnes/Rick Carnes/Chip Hardy*	MCA/Curb 52432
3/9/85	**12**	17		9 **If It Ain't Love (Let's Leave It Alone)** ... S:11 / A:16 *Dallas Frazier*	MCA/Curb 52535
6/29/85	**27**	15		10 **Hometown Gossip** ... A:25 / S:27 *Richard Allen/Gail Davies*	MCA/Curb 52615
11/2/85	**33**	14		11 **I Don't Want To Get Over You** ... *Deborah Allen/Bobby Braddock/Rafe Van Hoy*	MCA/Curb 52697
5/24/86	**36**	12		12 **Love Won't Wait** ... A:35 *Lisa Palas/Will Robinson/Mark D. Sanders*	MCA/Curb 52825
11/8/86+	**30**	16		13 **It Should Have Been Easy** ... A:30 *Bob McDill*	MCA/Curb 52953

DEBUT	PEAK	WKS	GOLD	ARTIST / Country Chart Hit	Ranking / Songwriter	Label (& Number)

WHITES, The — cont'd

DEBUT	PEAK	WKS	GOLD	Country Chart Hit	Songwriter	Label (& Number)
3/7/87	58	7		14 There Ain't No Binds	*Bernie Nelson*	MCA/Curb 53038
4/8/89	82	2		15 Doing It By The Book	*Phil Barnhart/Bruce Carroll*	Canaan 689357

WHITE WATER JUNCTION

Group formed in Vermont.

DEBUT	PEAK	WKS	GOLD	Country Chart Hit	Songwriter	Label (& Number)
10/27/84	97	1		Sleeping Back To Back	*Kent Blazy/Mickey Hiter*	Jungle Rogue 1004

WHITING, Margaret — 1940s: #21 / 1950s: #38 / All-Time: #281

Born on 7/22/1924 in Detroit, Michigan; raised in Hollywood, California. Female pop singer.

MARGARET WHITING and JIMMY WAKELY:

DEBUT	PEAK	WKS	GOLD	Country Chart Hit	Songwriter	Label (& Number)
9/10/49	❶^{17}	28	●	1 Slipping Around /	S:❶^{17} / J:❶^{12} / A:2 *Floyd Tillman*	
9/10/49	6	8		2 Wedding Bells	J:6 / S:7 *Jenny Lou Carson*	Capitol 40224
11/5/49	2^{3}	13		3 I'll Never Slip Around Again	J:2 / S:2 / A:10 *Floyd Tillman*	Capitol 40246
2/11/50	2^{1}	9		4 Broken Down Merry-Go-Round /	S:2 / J:3 / A:5 *Arthur Herbert/Fred Stryker*	
2/11/50	3^{1}	7		5 The Gods Were Angry With Me	S:3 / J:4 *Bill Mackintosh/Roma Mackintosh*	Capitol F800
4/22/50	2^{1}	10		6 Let's Go To Church (Next Sunday Morning)	S:2 / J:6 / A:6 *Steve Allen*	Capitol F960
11/18/50	6	1		7 A Bushel And A Peck from the Broadway musical *Guys And Dolls* starring Robert Alda	S:6 / J:10 *Frank Loesser*	Capitol F1234
6/2/51	7	2		8 When You And I Were Young Maggie Blues	J:7 *Jack Frost/Jimmy McHugh*	Capitol F1500
12/8/51	5	5		9 I Don't Want To Be Free	J:5 *Jimmy Wakely/George Wilson*	Capitol F1816

WHITLEY, Keith — All-Time: #184

Born Jesse Keith Whitley on 7/1/1955 in Sandy Hook, Kentucky. Died of alcohol poisoning on 5/9/1989 (age 33). Male singer/songwriter/guitarist. Appeared with **Buddy Starcher** on radio in Charleston, West Virginia, at age eight. Formed the East Kentucky Mountain Boys with **Ricky Skaggs** in 1968. Played in Ralph Stanley's Clinch Mountain Boys in the mid-1970s. Married **Lorrie Morgan** in 1986.

DEBUT	PEAK	WKS	GOLD	Country Chart Hit	Songwriter	Label (& Number)
9/29/84	59	9		1 Turn Me To Love **Patty Loveless** (harmony vocal)	*Wayland Holyfield/Norro Wilson*	RCA 13810
2/23/85	76	7		2 A Hard Act To Follow	*David Chamberlain/Gary Nicholson*	RCA 13996
9/14/85	57	10		3 I've Got The Heart For You	*Larry Boone/John Greenebaum*	RCA 14173
11/2/85+	14	20		4 Miami, My Amy	S:13 / A:14 *Hank Cochran/Dean Dillon/Royce Porter*	RCA 14285
6/21/86	9	26		5 Ten Feet Away	A:8 / S:9 *Max D. Barnes/Troy Seals/Billy Sherrill*	RCA 14363
11/8/86+	9	23		6 Homecoming '63	A:9 / S:20 *Dean Dillon/Royce Porter*	RCA 5013
3/14/87	10	16		7 Hard Livin'	A:14 / S:15 *David Halley*	RCA 5116
8/29/87	36	17		8 Would These Arms Be In Your Way	*Hank Cochran/Vern Gosdin/Red Lane*	RCA 5237
11/14/87+	16	21		9 Some Old Side Road	*Roger Ferris*	RCA 5326
4/30/88	❶^{1}	23		10 Don't Close Your Eyes	S:5 *Bob McDill*	RCA 6901
9/17/88	❶^{2}	22		11 When You Say Nothing At All	S:5 *Paul Overstreet/Don Schlitz*	RCA 8637
1/21/89	❶^{2}	22		12 I'm No Stranger To The Rain **CMA: Single**	*Sonny Curtis/Ron Hellard*	RCA 8797
6/24/89	❶^{1}	19		13 I Wonder Do You Think Of Me	*Whitey Shafer*	RCA 8940
10/14/89+	❶^{1}	26		14 It Ain't Nothin'	*Tony Haselden*	RCA 9059
3/3/90	3^{1}	26		15 I'm Over You from the album *I Wonder Do You Think Of Me* on RCA 9809	*Tim Nichols/Zack Turner*	RCA
7/28/90	13	20		16 'Til A Tear Becomes A Rose ***[w/ Lorrie Morgan]*** **CMA: Vocal Event**; from Whitley's album *Greatest Hits* on RCA 2277	*Bill Rice/Mary Sharon Rice*	RCA
9/7/91	2^{1}	20		17 Brotherly Love ***[w/ Earl Thomas Conley]***	*Tim Nichols/Jimmy Stewart*	RCA
12/21/91+	15	20		18 Somebody's Doin' Me Right above 2 from the album *Kentucky Bluebird* on RCA 3156	*Fred Knoblock/Paul Overstreet/Dan Tyler*	RCA
11/4/95	75	1		19 Wherever You Are Tonight from the album *Wherever You Are Tonight* on BNA 66762	*Don Cook/Gary Nicholson/Keith Whitley*	BNA

WHITMAN, Slim — 1950s: #30 / All-Time: #146

Born Otis Dewey Whitman on 1/20/1924 in Tampa, Florida. Male singer/guitarist/yodeller. Served in the U.S. Navy from 1943-46. On radio station WDAE in Tampa in 1946; also worked local clubs. Regular on the *Louisiana Hayride* in 1950. Once known as "The Smilin' Star Duster."

DEBUT	PEAK	WKS	GOLD	Country Chart Hit	Songwriter	Label (& Number)
5/17/52	10	1		1 Love Song Of The Waterfall **SLIM WHITMAN (The Smilin' Star Duster)**	A:10 *Bob Nolan*	Imperial 45-8134
7/5/52	2^{3}	24	●	2 Indian Love Call	S:2 / J:2 / A:3 *Rudolf Friml/Oscar Hammerstein/Otto Harbach*	Imperial 45-8156
12/6/52+	3^{1}	13		3 Keep It A Secret /	A:3 / J:3 / S:5 *Jessie Mae Robinson*	
12/20/52	10	1		4 My Heart Is Broken In Three	J:10 *Ray Glaser*	Imperial 45-8169
11/14/53	8	5		5 North Wind	J:8 / S:8 / A:8 *Rod Morris*	Imperial 8208
1/23/54	2^{1}	18	●	6 Secret Love from the movie *Calamity Jane* starring Doris Day	A:2 / J:3 / S:3 *Sammy Fain/Paul Francis Webster*	Imperial 8223

DEBUT	PEAK	WKS	GOLD	ARTIST / Ranking / Country Chart Hit	Songwriter	Label (& Number)
				WHITMAN, Slim — cont'd		
5/1/54	**4**	23	●	7 **Rose-Marie** J:4 / S:5 / A:7	*Rudolf Friml/Oscar Hammerstein/Otto Harbach/Herbert Stothart*	Imperial 8236
11/6/54	**4**	3		8 **Singing Hills** J:4	*Mack David/Sammy Mysels/Dick Sanford*	Imperial 8267
1/15/55	**11**	2		9 **Cattle Call** S:11	*Tex Owens*	Imperial 8281
7/3/61	**30**	1		10 **The Bells That Broke My Heart**	*Jack Rollins/Mark Rollins*	Imperial 5746
2/29/64	**48**	1		11 **Tell Me Pretty Words**	*Ronald Mansfield*	Imperial 66012
10/30/65	**8**	17		12 **More Than Yesterday**	*Laura Dickens*	Imperial 66130
3/12/66	**17**	12		13 **The Twelfth Of Never**	*Jerry Livingston/Paul Francis Webster*	Imperial 66153
7/16/66	**49**	2		14 **I Remember You** also see #36 below	*Johnny Mercer/Victor Schertzinger*	Imperial 66181
12/3/66	**54**	6		15 **One Dream**	*Bobby Sykes*	Imperial 66212
3/11/67	**56**	8		16 **What's This World A-Comin' To**	*Alex Kramer/Randel Richardson/Willard Robison/Joan Whitney*	Imperial 66226
7/22/67	**61**	6		17 **I'm A Fool**	*Tommy Smith*	Imperial 66248
11/18/67	**65**	5		18 **The Keeper Of The Key**	*Ken Devine/Lance Guynes/Harlan Howard/Beverly Stewart*	Imperial 66262
3/16/68	**17**	14		19 **Rainbows Are Back In Style**	*Dave Burgess*	Imperial 66283
8/10/68	**22**	11		20 **Happy Street**	*Ben Peters*	Imperial 66311
11/30/68+	**43**	8		21 **Livin' On Lovin' (And Lovin' Livin' With You)**	*Dave Burgess*	Imperial 66337
4/19/69	**43**	4		22 **My Happiness**	*Borney Bergantine/Betty Peterson*	Imperial 66358
7/12/69	**61**	5		23 **Irresistible**	*Dave Burgess*	Imperial 66384
4/18/70	**27**	12		24 **Tomorrow Never Comes**	*Johnny Bond/Ernest Tubb*	Imperial 66441
8/8/70	**26**	12		25 **Shutters And Boards**	*Audie Murphy/Scott Turner*	United Artists 50697
12/12/70+	**7**	14		26 **Guess Who**	*Jesse Belvin/JoAnn Belvin*	United Artists 50731
5/1/71	**6**	15		27 **Something Beautiful (To Remember)**	*Moneen Carpenter*	United Artists 50775
8/14/71	**21**	13		28 **It's A Sin To Tell A Lie**	*Billy Mayhew*	United Artists 50806
12/11/71+	**56**	7		29 **Loveliest Night Of The Year**	*Irving Aaronson/Paul Francis Webster*	United Artists 50852
10/21/72	**51**	7		30 **(It's No) Sin**	*George Haven/Chester Shull*	United Artists 50952
3/3/73	**73**	4		31 **Hold Me**	*Ray Griff*	United Artists 178
7/14/73	**88**	5		32 **Where The Lilacs Grow**	*Mitch Bradley*	United Artists 269
4/20/74	**82**	5		33 **It's All In The Game**	*Charles Dawes/Carl Sigman*	United Artists 402
8/9/80	**15**	12		34 **When**	*Johannes Bouwens*	Cleveland Int'l 50912
11/22/80	**69**	5		35 **That Silver-Haired Daddy Of Mine**	*Gene Autry/Jimmy Long*	Cleveland Int'l 50946
2/7/81	**44**	8		36 **I Remember You** new version of #14 above	*Johnny Mercer/Victor Schertzinger* **[R]**	Cleveland Int'l 50971
8/15/81	**54**	7		37 **Can't Help Falling In Love With You**	*Luigi Creatore/Hugo Peretti/George Weiss*	Cleveland Int'l 02402
				WHITTAKER, Roger Born on 3/22/1936 in Nairobi, Kenya, Africa (of British parents). Adult Contemporary singer.		
12/17/83	**91**	4		**I Love You Because**	*Leon Payne*	Main Street 93016
				WICHITA LINEMEN, The Vocal group from Wichita, Kansas. Led by Greg Stevens.		
12/24/77	**100**	2		1 **Everyday Of My Life**	*Robin Harris/Carl Hendricks/Jerry Sisk/Greg Stevens*	Linemen 773
10/20/79	**93**	4		2 **You're A Pretty Lady, Lady** **THE WICHITA LINEMEN Featuring Greg Stevens**	*Gene Cleamer*	Linemen 10838
				WICKHAM, Lewie Born in New Mexico. Male singer/songwriter/guitarist.		
3/28/70	**36**	10		1 **Little Bit Late**	*Lewie Wickham* **[N]**	Starday 888
7/8/78	**59**	7		2 **$60 Duck**	*Lewie Wickham* **[N]**	MCA 40928
				WICKLINE Group from Fox Island, Washington. Led by husband-and-wife team of Bob Wickline and Lynda Wickline.		
3/28/81	**90**	3		1 **Do Fish Swim?**	*Bob Wickline*	Cascade Mt. 2325
9/10/83	**85**	3		2 **True Love's Getting Pretty Hard To Find**	*Bob Wickline*	Cascade Mt. 3030
2/4/84	**78**	7		3 **Ski Bumpus/Banjo Fantasy II** **WICKLINE BAND Featuring Scott Gavin**	*Scott Gavin/Wayne Shields* **[I]**	Cascade Mt. 4045
				WIER, Rusty Born in Corpus Christi, Texas; raised in Austin, Texas. Male singer/guitarist.		
4/25/87	**74**	4		1 **Close Your Eyes**	*James Taylor*	Black Hat 102
8/15/87	**70**	5		2 **(Lover Of The) Other Side Of The Hill**	*Chuck Pyle*	Black Hat 103
				WIGGINS, John & Audrey Brother-and-sister duo from Waynesville, North Carolina. John was born on 10/13/1962. Audrey was born on 12/26/1967.		
4/30/94	**47**	11		1 **Falling Out Of Love**	*John Wiggins*	Mercury
8/13/94	**22**	20		2 **Has Anybody Seen Amy**	*Don Henry/Jon Vezner*	Mercury
11/26/94	**58**	9		3 **She's In The Bedroom Crying** above 3 from the album *John & Audrey Wiggins* on Mercury 518853	*Chuck Cannon/Jimmy Stewart*	Mercury
4/5/97	**49**	12		4 **Somewhere In Love** from the album *The Dream* on Mercury 534286	*Chuck Leonard/Kerry Kurt Phillips*	Mercury
				WIGGINS, "Little" Roy Born Ivan Leroy Wiggins on 6/27/1926 in Nashville, Tennessee. Died on 8/3/1999 (age 73). Prolific session steel guitarist.		
				GEORGE MORGAN Featuring "Little" Roy Wiggins:		
1/20/73	**62**	7		1 **Makin' Heartaches**	*George Morgan*	Decca 33037
6/30/73	**56**	9		2 **Mr. Ting-A-Ling (Steel Guitar Man)**	*George Morgan*	MCA 40069
6/1/74	**66**	6		3 **Somewhere Around Midnight**	*Max Powell*	MCA 40227
11/2/74	**82**	6		4 **A Candy Mountain Melody**	*Sun Child/Crystal Lady*	MCA 40298

DEBUT	PEAK	WKS	GOLD	ARTIST / Ranking / Country Chart Hit	Songwriter	Label (& Number)

WIGGINS, "Little" Roy — cont'd

DEBUT	PEAK	WKS	#	Country Chart Hit	Songwriter	Label (& Number)
2/22/75	**65**	9	5	**In The Misty Moonlight**	*Cindy Walker*	4 Star 1001
7/5/75	**62**	11	6	**From This Moment On**	*Bonnie Guitar*	4 Star 1009

WILBOURN, Bill, & Kathy Morrison

Vocal duo. Wilbourn was born in Aliceville, Alabama. Morrison was born in California.

DEBUT	PEAK	WKS	#	Country Chart Hit	Songwriter	Label (& Number)
7/20/68	**65**	5	1	**The Lovers**	*Jean Chapel*	United Artists 50310
1/11/69	**44**	6	2	**Him And Her**	*Billy Edd Wheeler*	United Artists 50474
6/28/69	**52**	7	3	**Lovin' Season**	*Gene Thomas*	United Artists 50537
5/9/70	**34**	12	4	**A Good Thing**	*Jerry Chesnut*	United Artists 50660
10/31/70	**65**	6	5	**Look How Far We've Come**	*Jerry Chesnut*	United Artists 50718

WILBURN BROTHERS — 1950s: #27 / 1960s: #38 / All-Time: #143

Duo from Hardy, Arkansas: brothers Virgil "Doyle" Wilburn (born on 7/7/1930; died on 10/16/1982, age 52) and Thurman "Teddy" Wilburn (born on 11/30/1931; died on 11/24/2003, age 71). Regulars on the *Louisiana Hayride* from 1948-51. Doyle was once married to **Margie Bowes**.

OPRY: 1953

DEBUT	PEAK	WKS	#	Country Chart Hit	Songwriter	Label (& Number)
6/12/54	**4**	18	1	**Sparkling Brown Eyes** ***[w/ Webb Pierce]***	S:4 / A:4 / J:4 *Billy Cox*	Decca 29107
6/11/55	**13**	2	2	**I Wanna Wanna Wanna**	A:13 *Joe Miller*	Decca 29459
1/21/56	**13**	3	3	**You're Not Play Love**	A:13 *Jimmy Fautheree*	Decca 29747
8/11/56	**10**	8	4	**I'm So In Love With You**	A:10 *Sonny James/John Skye*	Decca 29887
12/1/56	**6**	11	5	**Go Away With Me**	A:6 *Dan Welch*	Decca 30087
7/8/57	**8**	2	6	**Mister Love** ***[w/ Ernest Tubb]***	A:8 *Doug Kershaw/Rusty Kershaw*	Decca 30305
5/26/58	**9**	10	7	**Hey, Mr. Bluebird** ***[w/ Ernest Tubb]***	A:9 / S:14 *Cindy Walker*	Decca 30610
1/5/59	**4**	19	8	**Which One Is To Blame /**	*Sunny Dull/Redd Stewart*	
1/19/59	**18**	4	9	**The Knoxville Girl**	*Doyle Wilburn/Teddy Wilburn*	Decca 30787
5/18/59	**6**	19	10	**Somebody's Back In Town**	*Don Helms/Doyle Wilburn/Teddy Wilburn*	Decca 30871
10/26/59	**9**	13	11	**A Woman's Intuition**	*Madelyn Burroughs*	Decca 30968
12/19/60	**27**	2	12	**The Best Of All My Heartaches**	*Tom Tall*	Decca 31152
7/31/61	**14**	6	13	**Blue Blue Day**	*Don Gibson*	Decca 31276
5/12/62	**4**	22	14	**Trouble's Back In Town**	*Dick Flood*	Decca 31363
11/17/62	**21**	5	15	**The Sound Of Your Footsteps**	*Jan Crutchfield*	Decca 31425
5/11/63	**4**	13	16	**Roll Muddy River**	*Betty Sue Perry*	Decca 31464
9/14/63	**10**	13	17	**Tell Her So**	*Glen Douglas*	Decca 31520
2/29/64	**34**	4	18	**Hangin' Around**	*Ben Hall/Weldon Myrick*	Decca 31578
11/14/64+	**19**	15	19	**I'm Gonna Tie One On Tonight**	*Lee Nichols*	Decca 31674
5/29/65	**30**	12	20	**I Had One Too Many**	*Lee McAlpin*	Decca 31764
9/18/65	**5**	20	21	**It's Another World**	*Darrell Statler*	Decca 31819
2/5/66	**8**	17	22	**Someone Before Me**	*Bob Hicks*	Decca 31894
7/9/66	**13**	14	23	**I Can't Keep Away From You**	*Darrell Statler*	Decca 31974
11/12/66+	**3^{1}**	20	24	**Hurt Her Once For Me /**	*Vince Finneran/Johnny Russell*	
2/11/67	**70**	3	25	**Just To Be Where You Are**	*Cindy Walker*	Decca 32038
4/29/67	**13**	14	26	**Roarin' Again**	*Don Ellis/Freda Reed/Gene Reed*	Decca 32117
9/9/67	**24**	14	27	**Goody, Goody Gumdrop**	*Shirl Milete*	Decca 32169
10/26/68	**43**	8	28	**We Need A Lot More Happiness**	*Joe Keene*	Decca 32386
3/15/69	**38**	11	29	**It Looks Like The Sun's Gonna Shine**	*Andrew Eddins*	Decca 32449
1/31/70	**37**	8	30	**Little Johnny From Down The Street**	*Larry Whitehead*	Decca 32608
3/4/72	**47**	9	31	**Arkansas**	*Damon Black*	Decca 32921

WILCOX, Harlow, and the Oakies

Born on 1/28/1943 in Norman, Oklahoma. Session guitarist.

DEBUT	PEAK	WKS	#	Country Chart Hit	Songwriter	Label (& Number)
9/20/69	**42**	13		**Groovy Grubworm**	*Bobby Warren/Harlow Wilcox* **[I]**	Plantation 28

WILD CHOIR

Group from Nashville, Tennessee: **Gail Davies**, Pete Pendras, Denny Bixby, Larry Chaney and Bob Mummert.

DEBUT	PEAK	WKS	#	Country Chart Hit	Songwriter	Label (& Number)
6/14/86	**51**	13	1	**Next Time**	*Gail Davies/Mary Ann Kennedy/Pam Rose*	RCA 14337
10/25/86	**40**	13	2	**Heart To Heart** **WILD CHOIR FEATURING GAIL DAVIES**	*John Hiatt/Fred Koller*	RCA 5011

WILD HORSES

Group from Texas: husband-and-wife Angela Rae (vocals) and Michael Mahler (guitar), with Joe Lee Koenig (guitar), Stephen Kellough (bass) and Ralph McCauley (drums).

DEBUT	PEAK	WKS	#	Country Chart Hit	Songwriter	Label (& Number)
10/20/01	**46**	11		**I Will Survive**	*Nancy Baxter/Stephanie Bentley/George Teren*	Epic

WILD ROSE

Female group: Pamela Gadd (vocals), Wanda Vick (guitar), Pam Perry (mandolin), Kathy Mac (bass) and Nancy Given Prout (drums). Prout was formerly married to Brian Prout of **Diamond Rio**.

DEBUT	PEAK	WKS	#	Country Chart Hit	Songwriter	Label (& Number)
9/16/89	**15**	17	1	**Breaking New Ground**	*Carl Jackson/Jerry Salley*	Universal 66018
1/13/90	**38**	15	2	**Go Down Swingin'** from the album *Breaking New Ground* on Universal 93885	*Sandy Ramos/Jerry Vandiver*	Universal
6/8/91	**73**	2	3	**Straight And Narrow** from the album *Straight And Narrow* on Capitol 94255	*Mike Noble/Monty Powell*	Capitol

DEBUT	PEAK	WKS	GOLD	ARTIST / Country Chart Hit	Ranking / Songwriter	Label (& Number)
				WILEY and GENE		
				Duo of Wiley Walker and **Gene Sullivan**. Walker was born on 11/17/1911 in Laurel Hill, Florida. Died on 5/17/1966 (age 54). Sullivan was born on 11/16/1914 in Carbon Hill, Alabama. Died on 10/24/1984 (age 69).		
1/5/46	2^{1}	1		Make Room In Your Heart For A Friend	*Gene Sullivan/Wiley Walker*	Columbia 36869
				WILKINS, Little David		
				Born on 5/18/1946 in Parsons, Tennessee. Male singer/songwriter/pianist.		
3/22/69	54	7		1 Just Blow In His Ear *[David Wilkins]*	*John Reynolds/Bill Way*	Plantation 11
6/23/73	63	4		2 Love In The Back Seat	*David Wilkins*	MCA 40034
9/22/73	41	12		3 Too Much Hold Back	*James Long/David Wilkins*	MCA 40115
3/30/74	50	9		4 Georgia Keeps Pulling On My Ring	*Tim Marshall/David Wilkins*	MCA 40200
10/26/74	77	8		5 Not Tonight	*Tim Marshall/David Wilkins*	MCA 40299
12/28/74+	14	15		6 Whoever Turned You On, Forgot To Turn You Off	*Tim Marshall/David Wilkins*	MCA 40345
7/19/75	11	14		7 One Monkey Don't Stop No Show	*Tim Marshall/David Wilkins*	MCA 40427
1/31/76	18	15		8 The Good Night Special	*Tim Marshall/David Wilkins*	MCA 40510
7/4/76	75	5		9 Disco-Tex /	*David Wilkins*	
7/10/76	flip	4		10 Half The Way In, Half The Way Out	*Tim Marshall/David Wilkins*	MCA 40579
11/20/76	88	5		11 The Greatest Show On Earth	*Tim Marshall/David Wilkins*	MCA 40646
1/22/77	21	12		12 He'll Play The Music (But You Can't Make Him Dance)	*Chic Doherty/Jody Johnson/David Wilkins*	MCA 40668
6/18/77	60	8		13 Is Everybody Ready	*David Wilkins*	MCA 40734
10/22/77	21	14		14 Agree To Disagree	*Ronny Hughes/Tommy Vernon*	Playboy 5822
3/4/78	68	6		15 Don't Stop The Music (You're Playing My Song)	*Jack Johnson/Tim Marshall/David Wilkins*	Playboy 5825
8/5/78	74	5		16 Motel Rooms	*Jerry Chesnut/Tommy Myracle/David Wilkins*	Epic 50571
7/12/86	79	3		17 Lady In Distress	*David Wilkins*	Jere 1003
7/25/87	72	4		18 Butterbeans *[w/ Johnny Russell]*	*Charlie Colvin*	16th Avenue 70401
				WILKINSONS, The		
				Family vocal trio from Belleville, Ontario, Canada, Ontario: father Steve Wilkinson (born on 8/18/1955) with children Amanda Wilkinson (born on 1/17/1982) and Tyler Wilkinson (born on 4/30/1984).		
6/13/98	3^{3}	22		1 26¢	S:2 *William Wallace/Steve Wilkinson*	Giant
10/24/98+	15	21		2 Fly (The Angel Song)	S:❶^{1} *Rory Bourke/Steve Wilkinson*	Giant
3/27/99	50	15		3 Boy Oh Boy	S:20 *Amanda Wilkinson/Steve Wilkinson*	Giant
7/10/99	45	15		4 The Yodelin' Blues	*Skip Ewing*	Giant
				above 4 from the album *Nothing But Love* on Giant 24699		
1/15/00	34	20		5 Jimmy's Got A Girlfriend	S:4 *Ron Harbin/Richie McDonald/Anthony Smith*	Giant
6/10/00	49	9		6 Shame On Me	*Gary Burr/Steve Wilkinson*	Giant
				above 2 from the album *Here And Now* on Giant 24736		
4/14/01	51	6		7 I Wanna Be That Girl	S:21 *Walt Aldridge/Brad Crisler*	Giant
				from the album *Shine* on Giant 24769		
				WILLCOX, Pete		
				Born in New York. Male singer/songwriter/actor. Professional **Elvis Presley** impersonator. Played "The King" on the TV's *The Last Precinct*.		
4/24/82	75	5		The King	*Pete Willcox*	M&M 503
				WILLET, Slim, With The Brush Cutters		
				Born Winston Lee Moore on 12/1/1919 in Victor, Texas. Died of a heart attack on 7/1/1966 (age 46). Singer/songwriter.		
9/27/52	❶^{1}	23		Don't Let The Stars (Get In Your Eyes)	A:❶^{1} / S:2 / J:2 *Slim Willet*	4 Star 1614
				WILLIAMS, Becky		
				Born in Corpus Christi, Texas. Female singer.		
7/9/88	75	4		Tie Me Up (Hold Me Down)	*Kieran Kane/Jamie O'Hara*	Country Pride 0011
				WILLIAMS, Beth		
				Born in Puerto Rico; raised in Texas. Female singer/songwriter.		
9/27/86	82	3		1 Wrong Train	*Jerry McBee/Ed Penney*	BGM 71086
11/29/86	64	7		2 These Eyes	*Beth Williams*	BGM 92486
3/28/87	58	6		3 Man At The Backdoor	*Beth Williams*	BGM 13087
				WILLIAMS, Cootie, and his Orchestra		
				Born Charles Melvin Williams on 7/24/1908 in Mobile, Alabama. Died on 9/15/1985 (age 77). Black jazz trumpeter.		
7/8/44	4	6		Red Blues	*Robert Haggart*	Hit 7084
				Eddie "Cleanhead" Vinson (vocal)		
				WILLIAMS, Diana		
				Born in Nashville, Tennessee. Female singer.		
8/28/76	53	6		Teddy Bear's Last Ride	*Billy Joe Burnette/Dale Royal* [S]	Capitol 4317
				answer to "Teddy Bear" by **Red Sovine**		

Billboard DEBUT	PEAK	WKS	GOLD	ARTIST Country Chart Hit	Ranking Songwriter	Label (& Number)

WILLIAMS, Don

1970s: #36 / 1980s: #14 / All-Time: #35

Born on 5/27/1939 in Floydada, Texas. Male singer/songwriter/guitarist. Made professional debut in 1957. Member of the Pozo-Seco Singers from 1964-71. Acted in the movies *W.W. & The Dixie Dancekings* and *Smokey & The Bandit II.*

CMA: Male Vocalist 1978 // OPRY: 1976

DEBUT	PEAK	WKS	GOLD	Country Chart Hit	Songwriter	Label (& Number)
12/16/72+	**14**	16		1 **The Shelter Of Your Eyes**	*Don Williams*	JMI 12
5/5/73	**12**	16		2 **Come Early Morning /**	*Bob McDill*	
7/28/73	**33**	11		3 **Amanda**	*Bob McDill*	JMI 24
11/17/73+	**13**	14		4 **Atta Way To Go**	*Don Williams*	JMI 32
3/2/74	**5**	15		5 **We Should Be Together**	*Allen Reynolds*	JMI 36
6/29/74	**62**	7		6 **Down The Road I Go**	*Don Williams*	JMI 42
7/6/74	**❶**[1]	17		7 **I Wouldn't Want To Live If You Didn't Love Me**	*Al Turney*	Dot 17516
12/14/74+	**4**	15		8 **The Ties That Bind**	*Vincent Corso/Clyde Otis*	ABC/Dot 17531
4/12/75	**❶**[1]	17		9 **You're My Best Friend**	*Wayland Holyfield*	ABC/Dot 17550
8/16/75	**❶**[1]	16		10 **(Turn Out The Light And) Love Me Tonight**	*Bob McDill*	ABC/Dot 17568
1/31/76	**❶**[1]	16		11 **Till The Rivers All Run Dry**	*Wayland Holyfield/Don Williams*	ABC/Dot 17604
6/12/76	**❶**[1]	14		12 **Say It Again**	*Bob McDill*	ABC/Dot 17631
10/16/76	**2**[2]	15		13 **She Never Knew Me**	*Wayland Holyfield/Bob McDill*	ABC/Dot 17658
3/12/77	**❶**[1]	16		14 **Some Broken Hearts Never Mend**	*Wayland Holyfield*	ABC/Dot 17683
9/3/77	**❶**[1]	15		15 **I'm Just A Country Boy**	*Marshall Baker/Fred Hellerman*	ABC/Dot 17717
2/11/78	**7**	14		16 **I've Got A Winner In You**	*Wayland Holyfield/Don Williams*	ABC 12332
7/1/78	**3**[1]	15		17 **Rake And Ramblin' Man**	*Bob McDill*	ABC 12373
11/4/78+	**❶**[1]	16		18 **Tulsa Time**	*Danny Flowers*	ABC 12425
3/17/79	**3**[3]	15		19 **Lay Down Beside Me**	*Don Williams*	MCA 12458
8/4/79	**❶**[1]	14		20 **It Must Be Love**	*Bob McDill*	MCA 41069
12/8/79+	**❶**[1]	16		21 **Love Me Over Again**	*Don Williams*	MCA 41155
2/16/80	**97**	2		22 **Could You Ever Really Love A Poor Boy**	*Don Williams*	Phono 2693
3/29/80	**2**[3]	15		23 **Good Ole Boys Like Me**	*Bob McDill*	MCA 41205
8/23/80	**❶**[2]	16		24 **I Believe In You**	*Roger Cook/Sam Hogin*	MCA 41304
2/21/81	**6**	16		25 **Falling Again**	*Bob McDill*	MCA 51065
7/4/81	**4**	15		26 **Miracles**	*Roger Cook*	MCA 51134
9/19/81	**3**[1]	17		27 **If I Needed You** ***[w/ Emmylou Harris]***	*Townes Van Zandt*	Warner 49809
11/21/81+	**❶**[1]	20		28 **Lord, I Hope This Day Is Good**	*Dave Hanner*	MCA 51207
4/17/82	**3**[1]	16		29 **Listen To The Radio**	*Fred Knipe*	MCA 52037
8/21/82	**3**[2]	17		30 **Mistakes**	*Richard Feldman*	MCA 52097
12/11/82+	**❶**[1]	20		31 **If Hollywood Don't Need You**	*Bob McDill*	MCA 52152
4/16/83	**❶**[1]	18		32 **Love Is On A Roll**	*Roger Cook/John Prine*	MCA 52205
7/30/83	**2**[1]	19		33 **Nobody But You**	*John Jarrard/J.D. Martin*	MCA 52245
12/3/83+	**❶**[1]	19		34 **Stay Young**	*Benny Gallagher/Graham Lyle*	MCA 52310
5/19/84	**❶**[1]	20		35 **That's The Thing About Love**	*Richard Leigh/Gary Nicholson*	MCA 52389
9/1/84	**11**	21		36 **Maggie's Dream**	A:10 / S:11 *Dave Loggins/Lisa Silver*	MCA 52448
1/5/85	**2**[1]	20		37 **Walkin' A Broken Heart**	S:2 / A:2 *Dennis Linde/Alan Rush*	MCA 52514
10/12/85	**20**	19		38 **It's Time For Love**	S:20 / A:20 *Bob McDill/Hunter Moore*	MCA 52692
1/18/86	**3**[2]	22		39 **We've Got A Good Fire Goin'**	S:2 / A:2 *Dave Loggins*	Capitol 5526
5/31/86	**❶**[1]	22		40 **Heartbeat In The Darkness**	A:❶[1] / S:2 *Dave Loggins/Russell Smith*	Capitol 5588
10/18/86+	**3**[1]	22		41 **Then It's Love**	A:3 / S:4 *Dennis Linde*	Capitol 5638
2/7/87	**9**	21		42 **Senorita**	A:9 / S:13 *Hank DeVito/Danny Flowers*	Capitol 5683
6/6/87	**4**	26		43 **I'll Never Be In Love Again**	S:❶[2] *Bob Corbin*	Capitol 44019
10/24/87+	**9**	26		44 **I Wouldn't Be A Man**	S:18 *Rory Bourke/Mike Reid*	Capitol 44066
3/12/88	**5**	23		45 **Another Place, Another Time**	S:16 *Paul Harrison/Bob McDill*	Capitol 44131
8/13/88	**7**	24		46 **Desperately**	S:22 *Jamie O'Hara/Kevin Welch*	Capitol 44216
1/7/89	**5**	21		47 **Old Coyote Town**	*Larry Boone/Gene Nelson/Paul Nelson*	Capitol 44274
4/22/89	**4**	24		48 **One Good Well**	*Mike Reid/Kent Robbins*	RCA 8867
9/16/89	**4**	26		49 **I've Been Loved By The Best**	*Paul Harrison/Bob McDill*	RCA 9017
1/27/90	**4**	26		50 **Just As Long As I Have You**	*Dave Loggins/J.D. Martin*	RCA
6/16/90	**22**	21		51 **Maybe That's All It Takes**	*Beth Nielsen Chapman*	RCA
				above 2 from the album *One Good Well* on RCA 9656		
9/15/90	**2**[2]	20		52 **Back In My Younger Days**	*Danny Flowers*	RCA
1/19/91	**4**	20		53 **True Love**	*Pat Alger*	RCA
5/18/91	**7**	20		54 **Lord Have Mercy On A Country Boy**	*Bob McDill*	RCA
				above 3 from the album *True Love* on RCA 2407		
2/15/92	**72**	3		55 **Too Much Love**	*Roger Cook/Roger Greenaway*	RCA
6/6/92	**73**	2		56 **It's Who You Love**	*Charlie Black/Rory Bourke/Kieran Kane*	RCA
				above 2 from the album *Currents* on RCA 61128		

Billboard DEBUT	PEAK	WKS	GOLD	ARTIST / Country Chart Hit	Ranking / Songwriter	Label (& Number)

WILLIAMS, Hank 1940s: #11 / 1950s: #6 / All-Time: #47 // HOF: 1961

Born Hiram King Williams on 9/17/1923 in Mount Olive, Alabama. Died of alcohol/drug abuse on 1/1/1953 (age 29). Male singer/songwriter/guitarist. Hosted own radio show on WSFA in Montgomery; billed as "The Singing Kid." Formed his own band, **The Drifting Cowboys**, as a teenager. Married Audrey Sheppard in 1944; their son is **Hank Williams, Jr.**; grandson is **Hank Williams III**. First recorded for Sterling in 1946. Regular on the *Louisiana Hayride* from 1948-49. In 1952, divorced Audrey, was fired from the Opry in August and married Billie Jean Jones Eshlimar (**Billie Jean Horton**) who later married **Johnny Horton**. Also recorded as Luke The Drifter. Won Grammy's Lifetime Achievement Award in 1987. Inducted into the Rock and Roll Hall of Fame in 1987 as a forefather of rock 'n' roll.

OPRY: 1949

HANK WILLIAMS With His Drifting Cowboys:

DEBUT	PEAK	WKS	GOLD	#	Country Chart Hit	Chart Peaks / Songwriter	Label (& Number)
8/9/47	4	3		1	Move It On Over	*Hank Williams*	MGM 10033
7/3/48	14	1		2	Honky Tonkin'	J:14 *Hank Williams*	MGM 10171
7/24/48	6	3		3	I'm A Long Gone Daddy	J:6 *Hank Williams*	MGM 10212
3/5/49	12	2		4	Mansion On The Hill	J:12 *Fred Rose/Hank Williams*	MGM 10328
3/5/49	❶^{16}	42	●	5	Lovesick Blues NRR	S:❶^{16} / J:❶^{10} *Cliff Friend/Irving Mills/Hank Williams*	MGM 10352
5/14/49	2^{2}	29		6	Wedding Bells	S:2 / J:2 *Claude Boone*	MGM 10401
7/9/49	6	2		7	Never Again (Will I Knock On Your Door)	J:6 *Hank Williams*	MGM 10352
7/23/49	5	11		8	Mind Your Own Business	J:5 / S:6 *Hank Williams*	MGM 10461
10/1/49	4	9		9	You're Gonna Change (Or I'm Gonna Leave) /	S:4 / J:8 *Hank Williams*	
10/8/49	12	3		10	Lost Highway	S:12 / J:14 *Leon Payne*	MGM 10506
11/26/49	2^{1}	12		11	My Bucket's Got A Hole In It	S:2 / J:2 / A:5 *Clarence Williams*	MGM 10560
2/18/50	5	5		12	I Just Don't Like This Kind Of Livin'	S:5 / J:5 / A:8 *Hank Williams*	MGM K10609
3/25/50	❶^{8}	21		13	Long Gone Lonesome Blues /	A:❶^{8} / S:❶^{5} / J:❶^{4} *Hank Williams*	
4/15/50	9	1		14	My Son Calls Another Man Daddy	J:9 *Jewell House/Hank Williams*	MGM K10645
5/27/50	❶^{10}	25		15	Why Don't You Love Me also see #41 below	A:❶^{10} / S:❶^{6} / J:❶^{5} *Hank Williams*	MGM K10696
10/7/50	5	6		16	They'll Never Take Her Love From Me /	A:5 *Leon Payne*	
10/14/50	9	1		17	Why Should We Try Anymore	S:9 *Hank Williams*	MGM K10760
11/18/50	❶^{1}	15		18	Moanin' The Blues /	A:❶^{1} / S:2 / J:3 *Hank Williams*	
11/18/50	9	4		19	Nobody's Lonesome For Me	A:9 *Hank Williams*	MGM K10832
3/3/51	8	4		20	Dear John /	J:8 / S:10 *Aubrey Gass/Tex Ritter*	
3/17/51	❶^{1}	46	●	21	Cold, Cold Heart	A:❶^{1} / S:2 / J:4 *Hank Williams*	MGM K10904
5/26/51	3^{1}	10		22	Howlin' At The Moon /	J:3 / S:4 / A:6 *Hank Williams*	
6/9/51	2^{2}	13		23	I Can't Help It (If I'm Still In Love With You)	A:2 / J:3 / S:6 *Hank Williams*	MGM K10961
7/14/51	❶^{8}	25		24	Hey, Good Lookin' Grammy: Hall of Fame	A:❶^{8} / J:2 / S:2 *Hank Williams*	MGM K11000
10/20/51	4	18		25	Crazy Heart /	J:4 / A:6 / S:7 *Maurice Murray/Fred Rose*	
10/20/51	9	2		26	Lonesome Whistle	A:9 *Jimmie Davis/Hank Williams*	MGM K11054
12/22/51+	4	15		27	Baby, We're Really In Love	J:4 / A:4 / S:8 *Hank Williams*	MGM K11100
3/1/52	2^{1}	12		28	Honky Tonk Blues	J:2 / S:7 / A:10 *Hank Williams*	MGM K11160
5/3/52	2^{2}	16		29	Half As Much	S:2 / J:4 / A:7 *Curley Williams*	MGM K11202
8/16/52	❶^{14}	29	●	30	Jambalaya (On The Bayou) Grammy: Hall of Fame	S:❶^{14} / A:❶^{14} / J:❶^{12} *Hank Williams*	MGM K11283
10/11/52	2^{1}	12		31	Settin' The Woods On Fire /	A:2 / J:4 / S:5 *Ed Nelson/Fred Rose*	
11/15/52	10	1		32	You Win Again	J:10 *Hank Williams*	MGM K11318
12/20/52+	❶^{1}	13		33	I'll Never Get Out Of This World Alive	S:❶^{1} / J:4 / A:7 *Fred Rose/Hank Williams*	MGM 11366
2/21/53	❶^{13}	19		34	Kaw-Liga /	S:❶^{13} / A:❶^{8} / J:❶^{8} *Fred Rose/Hank Williams*	
2/21/53	❶^{6}	23		35	Your Cheatin' Heart Grammy: Hall of Fame / RS500	A:❶^{6} / J:❶^{2} / S:2 *Hank Williams*	MGM 11416
5/16/53	❶^{4}	13		36	Take These Chains From My Heart	S:❶^{4} / J:2 / A:3 *Hy Heath/Fred Rose*	MGM 11479
7/25/53	4	9		37	I Won't Be Home No More	S:4 / J:4 / A:5 *Hank Williams*	MGM 11533
10/10/53	7	2		38	Weary Blues From Waitin'	S:7 / J:7 / A:9 *Hank Williams*	MGM 11574
4/30/55	9	3		39	Please Don't Let Me Love You	J:9 *Ralph Jones*	MGM 11928

HANK WILLIAMS:

DEBUT	PEAK	WKS	GOLD	#	Country Chart Hit	Songwriter	Label (& Number)
6/11/66	43	4		40	I'm So Lonesome I Could Cry Grammy: Hall of Fame / RS500; recorded in 1949; features new instrumental backing	*Hank Williams*	MGM 13489
10/9/76	61	7		41	Why Don't You Love Me same version as #15 above	*Hank Williams* [R]	MGM 14849
2/4/89	7	14		42	There's A Tear In My Beer *[w/ Hank Williams Jr.]* Grammy: Vocal Collaboration / CMA: Vocal Event	*Hank Williams*	Warner/Curb 27584

WILLIAMS, Hank Jr. 1960s: #49 / 1970s: #19 / 1980s: #8 / All-Time: #15

Born Randall Hank Williams on 5/26/1949 in Shreveport, Louisiana; raised in Nashville, Tennessee. Male singer/songwriter/guitarist. Son of **Hank Williams**; father of **Hank Williams III**. Injured in a mountain climbing accident on 8/8/1975 in Montana; returned to performing in 1977. Starred in movie *A Time To Sing*. His father gave him the nickname "Bocephus." Also recorded as **Luke The Drifter, Jr.**

CMA: Entertainer 1987 & 1988

DEBUT	PEAK	WKS	GOLD	#	Country Chart Hit	Songwriter	Label (& Number)
2/8/64	5	19		1	Long Gone Lonesome Blues	*Hank Williams*	MGM 13208
7/25/64	42	6		2	Guess What, That's Right, She's Gone	*Merle Kilgore/Glenn Sutton*	MGM 13253
12/26/64+	46	5		3	Endless Sleep	*Dolores Nance/Jody Reynolds*	MGM 13278

DEBUT	PEAK	WKS	GOLD	ARTIST / Country Chart Hit	Ranking / Songwriter	Label (& Number)
				WILLIAMS, Hank Jr. — cont'd		
5/28/66	5	19		4 **Standing In The Shadows**	*Hank Williams Jr.*	MGM 13504
12/24/66+	43	13		5 **I Can't Take It No Longer**	*Mack Vickery*	MGM 13640
6/17/67	60	4		6 **I'm In No Condition**	*Dolly Parton*	MGM 13730
8/26/67	46	8		7 **Nobody's Child**	*Cy Coben/Mel Foree*	MGM 13782
1/13/68	31	11		8 **I Wouldn't Change A Thing About You (But Your Name)**	*Hank Williams Jr.*	MGM 13857
6/1/68	51	6		9 **The Old Ryman**	*Buddy Lee/Eddie Sovine/Hank Williams Jr.*	MGM 13922
8/31/68	3^{2}	16		10 **It's All Over But The Crying**	*Hank Williams Jr.*	MGM 13968
				from the movie *A Time to Sing* starring Williams		
11/9/68	39	8		11 **I Was With Red Foley (The Night He Passed Away)** ***[Luke The Drifter, Jr.]***	*Hank Williams Jr.*	MGM 14002
1/18/69	14	12		12 **Custody** ***[Luke The Drifter, Jr.]***	*Steve Karliski/Larry Kolber*	MGM 14020
2/22/69	16	10		13 **A Baby Again**	*Billy Edd Wheeler*	MGM 14024
5/3/69	3^{3}	14		14 **Cajun Baby**	*Hank Williams/Hank Williams Jr.*	MGM 14047
				also see #82 below		
7/5/69	37	8		15 **Be Careful Of Stones That You Throw** ***[Luke The Drifter, Jr.]***	*Bonnie Dodd*	MGM 14062
9/13/69	4	14		16 **I'd Rather Be Gone**	*Merle Haggard/Hank Williams Jr.*	MGM 14077
1/3/70	36	8		17 **Something To Think About** ***[Luke The Drifter, Jr.]***	*Merle Kilgore/Lamar Morris/Hank Williams Jr.*	MGM 14095
3/7/70	12	13		18 **I Walked Out On Heaven**	*Hank Williams Jr.*	MGM 14107
5/23/70	36	9		19 **It Don't Take But One Mistake** ***[Luke The Drifter, Jr.]***	*Danny Walls/Hank Williams Jr.*	MGM 14120
7/4/70	23	12		20 **Removing The Shadow** ***[w/ Lois Johnson]***	*Eddie Pleasant/Hank Williams Jr.*	MGM 14136
8/1/70	❶^{2}	15		21 **All For The Love Of Sunshine** ***[w/ Mike Curb Cong.]***	*Mike Curb/Harley Hatcher/Lalo Schifrin*	MGM 14152
				from the movie *Kelly's Heroes* starring **Clint Eastwood**		
10/3/70	12	13		22 **So Sad (To Watch Good Love Go Bad)** ***[w/ Lois Johnson]***	*Don Everly*	MGM 14164
12/19/70+	3^{2}	15		23 **Rainin' In My Heart** ***[w/ Mike Curb Congregation]***	*Slim Harpo/Jerry West*	MGM 14194
4/24/71	6	14		24 **I've Got A Right To Cry**	*Joe Liggins*	MGM 14240
8/21/71	18	14		25 **After All They All Used To Belong To Me**	*Hank Williams Jr.*	MGM 14277
12/18/71+	7	14		26 **Ain't That A Shame** ***[w/ Mike Curb Congregation]***	*Dave Bartholomew/Fats Domino*	MGM 14317
4/1/72	14	14		27 **Send Me Some Lovin'** ***[w/ Lois Johnson]***	*John Marascalco/Leo Price*	MGM 14356
4/29/72	❶^{2}	16		28 **Eleven Roses**	*Darrell McCall/Lamar Morris*	MGM 14371
9/16/72	3^{2}	16		29 **Pride's Not Hard To Swallow**	*Jerry Chesnut*	MGM 14421
11/18/72+	22	11		30 **Whole Lotta Loving** ***[w/ Lois Johnson]***	*Dave Bartholomew/Fats Domino*	MGM 14443
2/24/73	23	13		31 **After You**	*Jerry Chesnut*	MGM 14486
6/16/73	12	14		32 **Hank**	*Don Wayne*	MGM 14550
10/20/73	4	18		33 **The Last Love Song**	*Hank Williams Jr.*	MGM 14656
3/9/74	13	12		34 **Rainy Night In Georgia**	*Tony Joe White*	MGM 14700
7/6/74	7	13		35 **I'll Think Of Something**	*Jerry Foster/Bill Rice*	MGM 14731
11/2/74	19	12		36 **Angels Are Hard To Find**	*Hank Williams Jr.*	MGM 14755
				also see #93 below		
4/12/75	26	10		37 **Where He's Going, I've Already Been /**	*Brent Cartee/Earl Montgomery/Hank Williams Jr.*	
5/24/75	flip	4		38 **The Kind Of Woman I Got**	*David Walls*	MGM 14794
7/5/75	29	13		39 **The Same Old Story**	*Warren Keith/Lamar Morris/Hank Williams Jr.*	MGM 14813
11/8/75	19	13		40 **Stoned At The Jukebox**	*Hank Williams Jr.*	MGM 14833
4/10/76	38	9		41 **Living Proof**	*Hank Williams Jr.*	MGM 14845
4/9/77	27	12		42 **Mobile Boogie**	*Norman King/Thomas Neeley*	Warner/Curb 8361
8/20/77	59	7		43 **I'm Not Responsible /**	*Merle Kilgore/Abe Mulkay*	
9/3/77	flip	5		44 **(Honey, Won't You) Call Me**	*Ed Villareal/Wanda Watkins*	Warner/Curb 8410
10/1/77	47	9		45 **One Night Stands**	*Baker Knight*	Warner/Curb 8451
1/7/78	38	9		46 **Feelin' Better**	*Hank Williams Jr.*	Warner/Curb 8507
5/13/78	76	4		47 **You Love The Thunder**	*Jackson Browne*	Warner/Curb 8564
8/12/78	15	12		48 **I Fought The Law**	*Sonny Curtis*	Warner/Curb 8641
11/25/78	54	6		49 **Old Flame, New Fire**	*Oskar Solomon*	Warner/Curb 8715
3/31/79	49	6		50 **To Love Somebody**	*Barry Gibb/Maurice Gibb/Robin Gibb*	Elektra/Curb 46018
6/9/79	4	15		51 **Family Tradition**	*Hank Williams Jr.*	Elektra/Curb 46046
10/6/79	2^{2}	14		52 **Whiskey Bent And Hell Bound**	*Hank Williams Jr.*	Elektra/Curb 46535
2/9/80	5	13		53 **Women I've Never Had**	*Hank Williams Jr.*	Elektra/Curb 46593
5/17/80	12	12		54 **Kaw-Liga**	*Fred Rose/Hank Williams*	Elektra/Curb 46636
8/30/80	6	13		55 **Old Habits**	*Hank Williams Jr.*	Elektra/Curb 47016
2/7/81	❶^{1}	13		56 **Texas Women**	*Hank Williams Jr.*	Elektra/Curb 47102
5/30/81	❶^{1}	14		57 **Dixie On My Mind**	*Hank Williams Jr.*	Elektra/Curb 47137
9/5/81	❶^{1}	19		58 **All My Rowdy Friends (Have Settled Down)**	*Hank Williams Jr.*	Elektra/Curb 47191
1/23/82	2^{3}	20		59 **A Country Boy Can Survive**	*Hank Williams Jr.*	Elektra/Curb 47257
				also see #99 below		
6/5/82	❶^{1}	15		60 **Honky Tonkin'**	*Hank Williams*	Elektra/Curb 47462
10/9/82	5	16		61 **The American Dream /**	*Hank Williams Jr.*	
10/9/82	flip	16		62 **If Heaven Ain't A Lot Like Dixie**	*Billy Maddox/Dave Moore*	Elektra/Curb 69960
1/29/83	4	18		63 **Gonna Go Huntin' Tonight**	*Hank Williams Jr.*	Elektra/Curb 69846
6/4/83	6	16		64 **Leave Them Boys Alone** ***[w/ Waylon Jennings & Ernest Tubb]***	*...Dean Dillon/Gary Stewart/Tanya Tucker/Hank Williams Jr.*	Warner/Curb 29633
10/1/83	5	21		65 **Queen Of My Heart**	*Hank Williams Jr.*	Warner/Curb 29500
10/22/83	15	16		66 **The Conversation** ***[w/ Waylon Jennings]***	*Richie Albright/Waylon Jennings/Hank Williams Jr.*	RCA 13631
2/18/84	3^{1}	18		67 **Man Of Steel**	*Hank Williams Jr.*	Warner/Curb 29382
6/16/84	5	18		68 **Attitude Adjustment**	*Hank Williams Jr.*	Warner/Curb 29253
10/6/84	10	19		69 **All My Rowdy Friends Are Coming Over Tonight**	S:8 / A:14 *Hank Williams Jr.*	Warner/Curb 29184
				opening theme for ABC's *Monday Night Football* (with new lyrics)		

DEBUT	PEAK	WKS	GOLD	ARTIST / Ranking / Country Chart Hit	Songwriter	Label (& Number)
				WILLIAMS, Hank Jr. — cont'd		
1/19/85	**10**	18		70 **Major Moves**	S:8 / A:9 *Hank Williams Jr.*	Warner/Curb 29095
5/11/85	**❶[1]**	23		71 **I'm For Love**	S:❶[1] / A:❶[1] *Hank Williams Jr.*	Warner/Curb 29022
8/31/85	**14**	17		72 **Two Old Cats Like Us** *[w/ Ray Charles]*	S:13 / A:17 *Troy Seals*	Columbia 05575
9/7/85	**4**	20		73 **This Ain't Dallas**	S:4 / A:4 *Hank Williams Jr.*	Warner/Curb 28912
2/22/86	**❶[1]**	18		74 **Ain't Misbehavin'**	S:❶[1] / A:❶[1] *Harry Brooks/Andy Razaf/Fats Waller*	Warner/Curb 28794
6/14/86	**2[2]**	21		75 **Country State Of Mind**	S:❶[1] / A:2 *Roger Wade/Hank Williams Jr.*	Warner/Curb 28691
10/11/86	**❶[2]**	19		76 **Mind Your Own Business** *[w/ Reba McEntire/Willie Nelson/Tom Petty/Reverend Ike]*	S:❶[2] / A:❶[2] *Hank Williams*	Warner/Curb 28581
2/21/87	**31**	11		77 **When Something Is Good (Why Does It Change)**	S:26 *Hank Williams Jr.*	Warner/Curb 28452
6/13/87	**❶[1]**	20		78 **Born To Boogie**	S:❶[2] *Hank Williams Jr.*	Warner/Curb 28369
10/10/87+	**4**	21		79 **Heaven Can't Be Found**	S:4 *Hank Williams Jr.*	Warner/Curb 28227
2/20/88	**2[1]**	21		80 **Young Country** **Butch Baker, T. Graham Brown, Steve Earle, Highway 101, Dana McVicker, Marty Stuart** and **Keith Whitley** (guest vocals)	S:❶[1] *Hank Williams Jr.*	Warner/Curb 28120
6/25/88	**8**	15		81 **If The South Woulda Won**	S:4 *Hank Williams Jr.*	Warner/Curb 27862
8/27/88	**52**	7		82 **Cajun Baby** *[w/ Doug Kershaw]* new version of #14 above	*Hank Williams/Hank Williams Jr.* **[R]**	BGM 81588
9/24/88	**21**	20		83 **That Old Wheel** *[w/ Johnny Cash]*	S:17 *Johnny Pierce*	Mercury 870688
11/5/88+	**14**	15		84 **Early In The Morning And Late At Night**	S:8 *Frank J. Myers/Troy Seals*	Warner/Curb 27722
2/4/89	**7**	14		85 **There's A Tear In My Beer** *[w/ Hank Williams Sr.]* **Grammy: Vocal Collaboration / CMA: Vocal Event**	*Hank Williams*	Warner/Curb 27584
7/8/89	**6**	20		86 **Finders Are Keepers**	*Hank Williams Jr.*	Warner/Curb 22945
2/10/90	**15**	18		87 **Ain't Nobody's Business**	*Porter Granger/Everette Robbins*	Warner/Curb
5/19/90	**10**	21		88 **Good Friends, Good Whiskey, Good Lovin'**	*Hank Williams Jr.*	Warner/Curb
9/1/90	**62**	6		89 **Man To Man**	*Tommy Barnes/Hank Williams Jr.*	Warner/Curb
9/15/90	**27**	6		90 **Don't Give Us A Reason** from the album *America (The Way I See It)* on Warner/Curb 26453	*Hank Williams Jr.*	Warner/Curb
1/5/91	**39**	13		91 **I Mean I Love You** #87-89 & 91: from the album *Lone Wolf* on Warner/Curb 26090	*Hank Williams Jr.*	Warner/Curb
5/4/91	**26**	19		92 **If It Will It Will**	*Hank Williams Jr.*	Warner/Curb
8/17/91	**59**	8		93 **Angels Are Hard To Find** new version of #36 above; above 2 from the album *Pure Hank* on Warner/Curb 26536	*Hank Williams Jr.* **[R]**	Warner/Curb
2/8/92	**54**	11		94 **Hotel Whiskey**	*Hank Williams Jr.*	Capricorn/Curb
5/23/92	**55**	8		95 **Come On Over To The Country** above 2 from the album *Maverick* on Capricorn/Curb 26806	*Hank Williams Jr.*	Capricorn/Curb
2/20/93	**62**	8		96 **Everything Comes Down To Money And Love** from the album *Out Of Left Field* on Capricorn/Curb 45225	*Dave Loggins/Gove Scrivenor*	Capricorn/Curb
12/24/94+	**62**	6		97 **I Ain't Goin' Peacefully**	*Hank Williams Jr.*	MCG/Curb
4/22/95	**74**	2		98 **Hog Wild** above 2 from the album *Hog Wild* on MCG/Curb 77690	S:26 *Rick Arnold/Hank Williams Jr.*	MCG/Curb
11/20/99+	**30**	13		99 **A Country Boy Can Survive** *[w/ Chad Brock & George Jones]* new version of #59 above; from Brock's album *Yes!* on Warner 47659	S:2 *Hank Williams Jr.*	Warner
11/10/01	**45**	7		100 **America Will Survive**	*Hank Williams Jr.*	Curb
11/2/02	**60**	1		101 **Outdoor Lovin' Man** above 2 from the album *Almeria Club* on Curb 78725	*Hank Williams Jr.*	Curb
8/2/03	**39**	11		102 **I'm One Of You**	*Neal Coty/Jimmy Melton*	Asylum-Curb
2/28/04	**36**	17		103 **Why Can't We All Just Get A Long Neck?**	*Chris Clark/Richard Fagan/Michael Smotherman*	Asylum-Curb
11/6/04	**59**	1		104 **Devil In The Bottle** above 3 from the album *I'm One Of You* on Asylum-Curb 78830	*Bobby David*	Asylum-Curb

After All They All Used To Belong To Me ['71]
After You ['73]
Ain't Misbehavin' ['86]
Ain't Nobody's Business ['90]
Ain't That A Shame ['72]
All For The Love Of Sunshine ['70]
All My Rowdy Friends Are Coming Over Tonight ['84]
All My Rowdy Friends (Have Settled Down) ['81]
America Will Survive ['01]
American Dream ['82]
Angels Are Hard To Find ['74, '91]
Attitude Adjustment ['84]
Baby Again ['69]
Be Careful Of Stones That You Throw ['69]
Born To Boogie ['87]
Cajun Baby ['69, '88]
Come On Over To The Country ['92]
Conversation ['83]
Country Boy Can Survive ['82, '00]
Country State Of Mind ['86]
Custody ['69]
Devil In The Bottle ['04]
Dixie On My Mind ['81]
Don't Give Us A Reason ['90]
Early In The Morning And Late At Night ['89]
Eleven Roses ['72]
Endless Sleep ['65]
Everything Comes Down To Money And Love ['93]
Family Tradition ['79]
Feelin' Better ['78]
Finders Are Keepers ['89]
Gonna Go Huntin' Tonight ['83]
Good Friends, Good Whiskey, Good Lovin' ['90]
Guess What, That's Right, She's Gone ['64]
Hank ['73]
Heaven Can't Be Found ['88]
Hog Wild ['95]
(Honey, Won't You) Call Me ['77]
Honky Tonkin' ['82]
Hotel Whiskey ['92]
I Ain't Goin' Peacefully ['95]
I Can't Take It No Longer ['67]
I Fought The Law ['78]
I Mean I Love You ['91]
I Walked Out On Heaven ['70]
I Was With Red Foley (The Night He Passed Away) ['68]
I Wouldn't Change A Thing About You (But Your Name) ['68]
I'd Rather Be Gone ['69]
I'll Think Of Something ['74]
I'm For Love ['85]
I'm In No Condition ['67]
I'm Not Responsible ['77]
I'm One Of You ['03]
I've Got A Right To Cry ['71]
If Heaven Ain't A Lot Like Dixie ['82]
If It Will It Will ['91]
If The South Woulda Won ['88]
It Don't Take But One Mistake ['70]
It's All Over But The Crying ['68]
Kaw-Liga ['80]
Kind Of Woman I Got ['75]
Last Love Song ['73]
Leave Them Boys Alone ['83]
Living Proof ['76]
Long Gone Lonesome Blues ['64]
Major Moves ['85]
Man Of Steel ['84]
Man To Man ['90]
Mind Your Own Business ['86]
Mobile Boogie ['77]
Nobody's Child ['67]
Old Flame, New Fire ['78]
Old Habits ['80]
Old Ryman ['68]
One Night Stands ['77]
Outdoor Lovin' Man ['02]
Pride's Not Hard To Swallow ['72]
Queen Of My Heart ['83]
Rainin' In My Heart ['71]
Rainy Night In Georgia ['74]
Removing The Shadow ['70]
Same Old Story ['75]
Send Me Some Lovin' ['72]
So Sad (To Watch Good Love Go Bad) ['70]
Something To Think About ['70]
Standing In The Shadows ['66]
Stoned At The Jukebox ['75]
Texas Women ['81]
That Old Wheel ['88]
There's A Tear In My Beer ['89]
This Ain't Dallas ['85]
To Love Somebody ['79]
Two Old Cats Like Us ['85]
When Something Is Good (Why Does It Change) ['87]
Where He's Going, I've Already Been ['75]
Whiskey Bent And Hell Bound ['79]
Whole Lotta Loving ['73]
Why Can't We All Just Get A Long Neck? ['04]
Women I've Never Had ['80]
You Love The Thunder ['78]
Young Country ['88]

DEBUT	PEAK	WKS	GOLD	ARTIST / Ranking / Country Chart Hit	Songwriter	Label (& Number)
				WILLIAMS, Hank III Born on 12/12/1972 in Houston, Texas. Male singer/guitarist. Son of **Hank Williams Jr.**; grandson of **Hank Williams**.		
11/18/00+	**50**	11		**I Don't Know** from the album *Risin' Outlaw* on Curb 77949	*Randy Howard*	Curb
				WILLIAMS, Jason D. Born in El Dorado, Arkansas. Male singer/pianist.		
5/20/89	**71**	5		1 **Where There's Smoke**	*Bobby Barker/Mark Collie*	RCA 8869
9/23/89	**70**	4		2 **Waitin' On Ice**	*Gary Nicholson/Wally Wilson*	RCA 9026

Billboard DEBUT	PEAK	WKS	GOLD	ARTIST / Country Chart Hit	Ranking / Songwriter	Label (& Number)

WILLIAMS, Johnny

Born in Goose Creek, Texas. Male singer.

DEBUT	PEAK	WKS	GOLD	Country Chart Hit	Songwriter	Label (& Number)
5/6/72	68	5		He Will Break Your Heart	*Jerry Butler/Calvin Carter/Curtis Mayfield*	Epic 10845

WILLIAMS, Lawton

Born on 7/24/1922 in Troy, Tennessee. Male singer/songwriter.

DEBUT	PEAK	WKS	GOLD	Country Chart Hit	Songwriter	Label (& Number)
10/23/61+	13	25		1 Anywhere There's People	*Steve Karliski*	Mercury 71867
9/19/64	40	4		2 Everything's O.K. On The LBJ	*Lawton Williams*	RCA Victor 8407

WILLIAMS, Leona

Born Leona Belle Helton on 1/7/1943 in Vienna, Missouri. Female singer/songwriter/guitarist. Married to **Merle Haggard** from 1978-83. Married **Dave Kirby** in 1985.

DEBUT	PEAK	WKS	GOLD	Country Chart Hit	Songwriter	Label (& Number)
5/31/69	66	5		1 Once More	*Dusty Owens*	Hickory 1532
8/21/71	52	9		2 Country Girl With Hot Pants On	*Jim Mundy*	Hickory 1606
9/22/73	93	3		3 Your Shoeshine Girl	*Eddy Raven/Barbara Sharp*	Hickory/MGM 304
10/28/78	8	12		4 The Bull And The Beaver ***[w/ Merle Haggard]***	*Merle Haggard/Leona Williams*	MCA 40962
2/17/79	92	2		5 The Baby Song /	*Charlie Black/Rory Bourke/Jerry Gillespie*	
2/17/79	flip	2		6 Call Me Crazy Lady	*Peggy Russell/Leona Williams*	MCA 40988
4/4/81	54	8		7 I'm Almost Ready	*Vince Gill*	Elektra 47114
11/14/81	84	3		8 Always Late With Your Kisses	*Blackie Crawford/Lefty Frizzell*	Elektra 47217
5/28/83	42	14		9 We're Strangers Again ***[w/ Merle Haggard]***	*Merle Haggard/Leona Williams*	Mercury 812214

WILLIAMS, Lois

Born in Tennessee. Female singer.

DEBUT	PEAK	WKS	GOLD	Country Chart Hit	Songwriter	Label (& Number)
9/20/69	74	3		A Girl Named Sam answer to "A Boy Named Sue" by **Johnny Cash**	*Bill Ellis/Charles Truett/Guy Willis* [N]	Starday 877

WILLIAMS, Otis

Born on 6/2/1936 in Cincinnati, Ohio. Black singer. Former leader of The Charms. Not to be confused with the same-named member of The Temptations.

DEBUT	PEAK	WKS	GOLD	Country Chart Hit	Songwriter	Label (& Number)
5/8/71	72	2		I Wanna Go Country ***[w/ The Midnight Cowboys]***	*Charlie Monk/Jim Owen*	Stop 388

WILLIAMS, Paul

Born on 9/19/1940 in Omaha, Nebraska. Male singer/songwriter/actor. Acted in several movies.

DEBUT	PEAK	WKS	GOLD	Country Chart Hit	Songwriter	Label (& Number)
12/12/81	93	4		Making Believe	*Jimmy Work*	Paid 146

WILLIAMS, Tex — 1940s: #9 / All-Time: #170

Born Sollie Paul Williams on 8/23/1917 in Ramsey, Illinois. Died of cancer on 10/11/1985 (age 68). Singer/songwriter/guitarist. Acted in many western movies. Worked as a singer with **Spade Cooley**'s band. Hosted own *Ranch Party* TV series in 1958.

TEX WILLIAMS And His Western Caravan:

DEBUT	PEAK	WKS	GOLD	Country Chart Hit	Songwriter	Label (& Number)
11/30/46	4	2		1 The California Polka	*Dale Fitzsimmons*	Capitol 302
7/5/47	❶[16]	23	●	2 Smoke! Smoke! Smoke! (That Cigarette) also see #19 below	*Merle Travis/Tex Williams* [N]	Capitol Amer. 40001
10/4/47	4	8		3 That's What I Like About The West new version of "That's What I Like About The South" by Phil Harris	*Edith Bergdahl/Robert McGimsey*	Capitol Amer. 40031
12/13/47	2[8]	15		4 Never Trust A Woman	*Jenny Lou Carson*	Capitol Amer. 40054
2/14/48	2[2]	11		5 Don't Telephone - Don't Telegraph (Tell A Woman)	*Al Stewart/Tex Williams*	Capitol Amer. 40081
5/15/48	4	12		6 Suspicion	S:4 / J:4 *Foster Carling/Les Paul*	Capitol 40109
6/19/48	5	15		7 Banjo Polka	J:5 / S:11 *Pedro DePaul/Andrew Soldi*	Capitol 15101
6/26/48	6	8		8 Who? Me? /	S:6 / J:11 *Riley Shepard*	
7/31/48	15	1		9 Foolish Tears	J:15 *Jenny Lou Carson*	Capitol 15113
9/11/48	6	5		10 Talking Boogie /	J:6 / S:12 *Cliffie Stone/Tex Williams*	
11/13/48	13	3		11 Just A Pair Of Blue Eyes	J:13 / S:14 *Ted Johnson/Dude Martin*	Capitol 15175
11/20/48	5	8		12 Life Gits Tee-Jus, Don't It?	J:5 / S:9 *Carson Robison* [N]	Capitol 15271
10/22/49	11	2		13 (There's A) Bluebird On Your Windowsill	J:11 / S:12 *Elizabeth Clarke*	Capitol 40225

TEX WILLIAMS:

DEBUT	PEAK	WKS	GOLD	Country Chart Hit	Songwriter	Label (& Number)
5/29/65	26	11		14 Too Many Tigers	*Larry Lee/Joe South*	Boone 1028
10/2/65	30	9		15 Big Tennessee	*Kenny Price*	Boone 1032
1/8/66	18	8		16 Bottom Of A Mountain	*Don McKinnon*	Boone 1036
9/24/66	44	2		17 Another Day, Another Dollar In The Hole	*Kenny Price*	Boone 1044
6/17/67	57	5		18 Black Jack County	*Red Lane*	Boone 1059
2/17/68	32	10		19 Smoke, Smoke, Smoke - '68 new version of #2 above	*Merle Travis/Tex Williams* [R]	Boone 1069
6/29/68	45	7		20 Here's To You And Me	*Liz Anderson*	Boone 1072
9/19/70	50	9		21 It Ain't No Big Thing	*Shorty Hall/Alice Merritt/Neal Merritt*	Monument 1216
8/28/71	29	14		22 The Night Miss Nancy Ann's Hotel For Single Girls Burned Down	*Dick Feller* [N]	Monument 8503
1/22/72	67	4		23 Everywhere I Go (He's Already Been There)	*Ray Pennington*	Monument 8533
6/29/74	70	8		24 Those Lazy, Hazy, Crazy Days Of Summer	*Hans Carste/Charles Tobias*	Granite 507

Billboard DEBUT	PEAK	WKS	GOLD	ARTIST / Country Chart Hit	Songwriter	Label (& Number)

WILLIAMS, Tucker
Born in Dallas, Texas. Male singer.

DEBUT	PEAK	WKS	GOLD	Country Chart Hit	Songwriter	Label (& Number)
1/19/80	**96**	2		**Donna-Earth Angel (Medley)**	*Jesse Belvin/Ritchie Valens*	Yatahey 999

WILLIAMS BROS.
Duo of brothers Jimmy Williams and Bobby Williams.

DEBUT	PEAK	WKS	GOLD	Country Chart Hit	Songwriter	Label (& Number)
6/15/63	**28**	1		**Bad Old Memories**	*Herb Price/Joyce Williams*	Del-Mar 1008

WILLING, Foy, And His Riders Of The Purple Sage
Born Foy Willingham on 5/14/1914 in Bosque County, Texas. Died on 6/24/1978 (age 64). Male singer/songwriter/guitarist. Acted in several western movies.

DEBUT	PEAK	WKS	GOLD	Country Chart Hit	Songwriter	Label (& Number)
7/15/44	**3**^{1}	5		1 **Texas Blues**	*Cottonseed Clark/Foy Willing*	Capitol 162
3/16/46	**6**	1		2 **Detour**	*Paul Westmoreland*	Decca 9000
12/14/46	**4**	1		3 **Have I Told You Lately (That I Love You)**	*Scott Wiseman*	Majestic 6000
6/19/48	**14**	2		4 **Anytime**	J:14 *Herb Lawson*	Capitol Amer. 40108
1/1/49	**15**	1		5 **Brush Those Tears From Your Eyes**	S:15 *Leland Gillette/Oakley Haldeman/Al Trace*	Capitol 15290

WILLIS, Andra
Female singer/actress. Regular on TV's *The Lawrence Welk Show* from 1967-69.

DEBUT	PEAK	WKS	GOLD	Country Chart Hit	Songwriter	Label (& Number)
2/24/73	**56**	7		1 **Down Home Lovin' Woman**	*Ed Villareal/Wanda Watkins*	Capitol 3525
8/4/73	**85**	5		2 **Til I Can't Take It Anymore**	*Dorian Burton/Clyde Otis*	Capitol 3666
4/19/75	**63**	9		3 **Baby** *[w/ Tennessee Ernie Ford]*	*Ray Griff*	Capitol 4044

WILLIS, Hal
Born Leonard Francis Gauthier in Roslyn, Quebec, Canada. Male singer/songwriter.

DEBUT	PEAK	WKS	GOLD	Country Chart Hit	Songwriter	Label (& Number)
10/31/64	**5**	16		1 **The Lumberjack**	*Ginger Willis/Hal Willis*	Sims 207
7/30/66	**45**	5		2 **Doggin' In The U.S. Mail**	*Ginger Willis/Hal Willis*	Sims 288

WILLIS, Kelly
Born on 10/1/1968 in Annandale, Virginia. Female singer/songwriter. Acted in the movie *Bob Roberts*.

DEBUT	PEAK	WKS	GOLD	Country Chart Hit	Songwriter	Label (& Number)
4/27/91	**51**	9		1 **Baby Take A Piece Of My Heart** from the album *Bang Bang* on MCA 10141	*Kostas/Kelly Willis*	MCA
7/31/93	**72**	2		2 **Whatever Way The Wind Blows**	*Marshall Crenshaw*	MCA
10/16/93	**63**	5		3 **Heaven's Just A Sin Away** above 2 from the album *Kelly Willis* on MCA 10789	*Jerry Gillespie*	MCA

WILLIS BROTHERS, The
Trio of brothers from Oklahoma: James "Guy" Willis (guitar; born on 7/5/1915; died on 4/13/1981, age 65), Charles "Skeeter" Willis (fiddle; born on 12/20/1917; died on 1/28/1976, age 58) and Richard "Vic" Willis (accordian; born on 5/31/1922; died on 1/15/1995, age 72).

OPRY: 1946

DEBUT	PEAK	WKS	GOLD	Country Chart Hit	Songwriter	Label (& Number)
9/5/64	**9**	20		1 **Give Me 40 Acres (To Turn This Rig Around)**	*Earl Green/John Green*	Starday 681
6/12/65	**41**	8		2 **A Six Foot Two By Four**	*Earl Green/John Green* **[N]**	Starday 713
2/25/67	**14**	15		3 **Bob**	*Jack Clement/Vince Matthews*	Starday 796
7/29/67	**62**	3		4 **Somebody Knows My Dog**	*Gene Crysler*	Starday 812

WILLMON, Trent
Born on 3/6/1973 in Afton, Texas. Male singer/songwriter/guitarist.

DEBUT	PEAK	WKS	GOLD	Country Chart Hit	Songwriter	Label (& Number)
4/3/04	**30**	18		1 **Beer Man**	*Casey Beathard/Trent Willmon*	Columbia
8/7/04	**36**	15		2 **Dixie Rose Deluxe's Honky Tonk, Feed Store, Gun Shop, Used Car, Beer, Bait, BBQ, Barber Shop, Laundromat**	S:2 *Mike Heeney/Trent Willmon*	Columbia
11/27/04+	**49**	12		3 **Home Sweet Holiday Inn**	*Jameson Clark/Chris Stapleton/Trent Willmon*	Columbia
1/15/05	**38**	21		4 **The Good Life** above 4 from the album *Trent Willmon* on Columbia 91257	*Bobby Pinson/Trent Willmon*	Columbia

WILLOUGHBY, Larry
Born in 1947 in Sherman, Texas. Male singer/songwriter/guitarist. Cousin of **Rodney Crowell**.

DEBUT	PEAK	WKS	GOLD	Country Chart Hit	Songwriter	Label (& Number)
11/12/83	**65**	5		1 **Heart On The Line (Operator, Operator)**	*Janet Willoughby/Larry Willoughby*	Atlantic Amer. 99826
2/4/84	**55**	8		2 **Building Bridges**	*Hank DeVito/Larry Willoughby*	Atlantic Amer. 99797
6/23/84	**82**	3		3 **Angel Eyes**	*Rodney Crowell*	Atlantic Amer. 99759

WILLS, Bob, and his Texas Playboys — 1940s: #3 / All-Time: #118 // HOF: 1968
Born James Robert Wills on 3/6/1905 in Kosse, Texas. Died of a stroke on 5/13/1975 (age 70). Male singer/songwriter/fiddler. Formed the Texas Playboys in 1933. Band featured **Tommy Duncan** (vocals) and **Leon McAuliffe** (steel guitar). Hosted own radio show on KVOO in Tulsa from 1934-58. Acted in several western movies. Known as "The King of Western Swing." Brother of **Johnnie Lee Wills**. His band recorded as the **Original Texas Playboys** in 1977. Inducted into the Rock and Roll Hall of Fame in 1999 as an early influence. **Tommy Duncan** performs the vocals on all songs below (unless noted).

EARLY HITS: Spanish Two Step (1935) / Maiden's Prayer (1938) / San Antonio Rose (1938) / Worried Mind (1941) / Ten Years (1942)

DEBUT	PEAK	WKS	GOLD	Country Chart Hit	Songwriter	Label (& Number)
1/8/44	**3**^{1}	1		1 **New San Antonio Rose** **Grammy: Hall of Fame / NRR**; recorded in 1940; vocal version of his original "San Antonio Rose" recording from 1938	*Bob Wills*	Okeh 5694
9/9/44	**2**^{5}	11		2 **We Might As Well Forget It /** Leon Huff (vocal)	*Johnny Bond*	
9/23/44	**2**^{2}	17		3 **You're From Texas** **Leon McAuliffe** (vocal); from the movie *A Tornado In The Saddle* starring Wills	*Cindy Walker*	Okeh 6722
3/24/45	❶^{2}	15		4 **Smoke On The Water /**	*Zeke Clements/Earl Nunn*	
3/24/45	**3**^{4}	18		5 **Hang Your Head In Shame**	*Ed Nelson/Steve Nelson/Fred Rose*	Okeh 6736

DEBUT	PEAK	WKS	GOLD	ARTIST / Country Chart Hit	Ranking / Songwriter	Label (& Number)
				WILLS, Bob, and his Texas Playboys — cont'd		
6/16/45	❶[1]	11		6 **Stars And Stripes On Iwo Jima /**	*Cliff Johnson/Bob Wills*	
7/21/45	5	4		7 **You Don't Care What Happens To Me**	*Fred Rose*	Okeh 6742
11/3/45+	2[1]	8		8 **Texas Playboy Rag /**	*Bob Wills* [I]	
11/17/45	❶[3]	14		9 **Silver Dew On The Blue Grass Tonight**	*Ed Burt*	Columbia 36841
12/29/45+	❶[1]	5		10 **White Cross On Okinawa**	*Bob Wills*	Columbia 36881
5/4/46	❶[16]	23		11 **New Spanish Two Step /**	*Tommy Duncan/Bob Wills*	
				vocal version of his 1935 instrumental hit		
5/11/46	3[8]	18		12 **Roly-Poly**	*Fred Rose*	Columbia 36966
11/30/46	2[2]	8		13 **Stay A Little Longer /**	*Tommy Duncan/Bob Wills*	
11/30/46	4	1		14 **I Can't Go On This Way**	*Fred Rose*	Columbia 37097
3/29/47	5	1		15 **I'm Gonna Be Boss From Now On**	*Bob Wills*	Columbia 37205
				Jesse Ashlock (vocal)		
5/17/47	❶[1]	6		16 **Sugar Moon**	*Cindy Walker/Bob Wills*	Columbia 37313
7/12/47	4	1		17 **Bob Wills Boogie**	*Bob Wills* [I]	Columbia 37357
1/31/48	4	17		18 **Bubbles In My Beer**	*Tommy Duncan/Cindy Walker/Bob Wills*	MGM 10116
7/3/48	8	2		19 **Keeper Of My Heart**	J:8 *Jerry Irby/Bob Wills*	MGM 10175
7/24/48	15	1		20 **Texarkana Baby**	S:15 *Cottonseed Clark/Fred Rose*	Columbia 38179
9/18/48	10	1		21 **Thorn In My Heart**	J:10 *Sam Martin/Bob Wills*	MGM 10236
1/21/50	10	1		22 **Ida Red Likes The Boogie**	J:10 *Tiny Moore/Bob Wills*	MGM K10570
				Tiny Moore (vocal); also see #26 below		
11/4/50	8	5		23 **Faded Love**	A:8 *Bob Wills/Johnnie Lee Wills*	MGM K10786
				Rusty McDonald and The Playboy Trio (vocals)		
8/8/60	5	17		24 **Heart To Heart Talk** ***[w/ Tommy Duncan]***	*Lee Ross*	Liberty 55260
1/23/61	26	1		25 **The Image Of Me** ***[w/ Tommy Duncan]***	*Harlan Howard/Wayne King*	Liberty 55264
10/16/76	99	1		26 **Ida Red**	*(traditional)/Bob Wills* [L]	Capitol 4332
				Leon Rausch (vocal); also see #22 above		
				WILLS, David		
				Born on 10/23/1951 in Pulaski, Tennessee. Male singer/songwriter/guitarist.		
11/16/74+	10	18		1 **There's A Song On The Jukebox**	*Billy Sherrill/Carmol Taylor*	Epic 50036
3/29/75	10	13		2 **From Barrooms To Bedrooms**	*David Wills*	Epic 50090
7/12/75	31	11		3 **The Barmaid**	*Tony Joe White*	Epic 50118
11/1/75	35	9		4 **She Deserves My Very Best**	*Robert Duncan*	Epic 50154
2/7/76	47	8		5 **Queen Of The Starlight Ballroom**	*Robert Duncan*	Epic 50188
5/22/76	55	7		6 **Woman**	*John Lennon/Paul McCartney*	Epic 50228
8/21/76	66	6		7 **(I'm Just Pouring Out) What She Bottled Up In Me**	*Doug Owen/Judy Vowell*	Epic 50260
5/21/77	52	9		8 **The Best Part Of My Days (Are My Nights With You)**	*Bob Zimmerman*	United Artists 988
9/17/77	91	4		9 **Cheatin' Turns Her On**	*Bill Holmes/Jimmy Payne*	United Artists 1042
11/19/77	82	5		10 **Do You Wanna Make Love**	*Peter McCann*	United Artists 1097
7/15/78	70	6		11 **You Snap Your Fingers (And I'm Back In Your Hands)**	*John Schweers*	United Artists 1196
2/17/79	50	7		12 **I'm Being Good**	*Archie Jordon/Naomi Martin*	United Artists 1271
10/6/79	82	4		13 **Endless**	*Gary Harrison/Don Pfrimmer*	United Artists 1319
5/31/80	91	5		14 **She's Hangin' In There (I'm Hangin' Out)**	*Dean Dillon/Charles Quillen/David Wills*	United Artists 1350
9/27/80	65	6		15 **The Light Of My Life (Has Gone Out Again Tonight)**	*Buzz Rabin*	United Artists 1375
3/12/83	52	7		16 **Those Nights, These Days**	*Ronnie Rogers*	RCA 13460
6/18/83	19	16		17 **The Eyes Of A Stranger**	*Steve Davis*	RCA 13541
11/12/83+	26	15		18 **Miss Understanding**	*Byron Gallimore/Blake Mevis/Bill Shore/David Wills*	RCA 13653
2/25/84	31	11		19 **Lady In Waiting**	*Bill Shore/David Wills*	RCA 13737
11/24/84	69	7		20 **Macon Love**	*Randy Albright/Jim Elliott/Mark D. Sanders*	RCA 13940
10/8/88	85	3		21 **Paper Thin Walls**	*Gordon Payne/David Wills*	Epic 08043
				WILLS, Johnnie Lee, And His Boys		
				Born on 9/2/1912 in Jewett, Texas. Died on 10/25/1984 (age 72). Male singer/songwriter/fiddler. Brother of **Bob Wills**.		
1/28/50	2[5]	11		1 **Rag Mop**	J:2 / S:2 / A:3 *Deacon Anderson/Johnnie Lee Wills*	Bullet 696
4/1/50	7	2		2 **Peter Cotton Tail**	J:7 / A:8 *Steve Nelson/Jack Rollins*	Bullet 700
				WILLS, Mark	**2000s: #30 / All-Time: #210**	
				Born Daryl Mark Williams on 8/8/1973 in Cleveland, Tennessee; raised in Blue Ridge, Georgia. Male singer/guitarist.		
6/8/96	6	20		1 **Jacob's Ladder**	S:13 *Tony Martin/Brenda Sweat/Calvin Sweat*	Mercury
10/12/96	33	18		2 **High Low And In Between**	*Harley Campbell/David Kent*	Mercury
3/1/97	5	21		3 **Places I've Never Been**	*Tony Martin/Amy Mayo/Reese Wilson*	Mercury
				above 3 from the album *Mark Wills* on Mercury 532116		
2/28/98	2[2]	25		4 **I Do [Cherish You]**	S:9 *Dan Hill/Keith Stegall*	Mercury
7/18/98	2[2]	28		5 **Don't Laugh At Me**	*Steve Seskin/Allen Shamblin*	Mercury
1/23/99	❶[1]	26		6 **Wish You Were Here**	*Bill Anderson/Skip Ewing/Debbie Moore*	Mercury
6/19/99	7	22		7 **She's In Love**	*Dan Hill/Keith Stegall*	Mercury
				above 4 from the album *Wish You Were Here* on Mercury 536317		
11/6/99+	2[1]	26		8 **Back At One**	*Brian McKnight*	Mercury
4/1/00	19	21		9 **Almost Doesn't Count**	*Shelly Peiken/Guy Roche*	Mercury
9/16/00	33	22		10 **I Want To Know (Everything There Is To Know About You)**	*Lewis Anderson/Bob Regan*	Mercury
				above 3 from the album *Permanently* on Mercury 546296		
4/28/01	18	26		11 **Loving Every Minute**	*Monty Criswell/Tom Shapiro/Michael White*	Mercury
12/1/01+	31	20		12 **I'm Not Gonna Do Anything Without You** ***[w/ Jamie O'Neal]***	*Rich Alves/Randy Vanwarmer*	Mercury
				above 2 from Wills's album *Loving Every Minute* on Mercury 170209		

DEBUT	PEAK	WKS	GOLD	ARTIST / Country Chart Hit	Songwriter	Label (& Number)
				WILLS, Mark — cont'd		
10/5/02+	❶[6]	34		13 **19 Somethin'**	*Chris DuBois/David Lee*	Mercury
3/1/03	28	20		14 **When You Think Of Me**	*Brett James/Troy Verges*	Mercury
				above 2 from the album *Greatest Hits* on Mercury 170313		
7/26/03	29	21		15 **And The Crowd Goes Wild**	*Jeffrey Steele/Craig Wiseman*	Mercury
11/15/03+	40	17		16 **That's A Woman**	*Steven Jones/Rivers Rutherford*	Mercury
				above 2 from the album *And The Crowd Goes Wild* on Mercury 001012		
				WILLS, Tommy		
				Born in Indianapolis, Indiana. Jazz saxophonist.		
1/13/79	100	1		**Wildwood Flower**	*A.P. Carter*	Golden Moon 004
				Marti Maes (vocal)		
				WILSON, Benny		
				Born in Young Harris, Georgia. Male singer.		
2/2/85	50	9		1 **Acres Of Diamonds**	*Waylon Caylor/Billy Henderson*	Columbia 04724
3/22/86	78	8		2 **If You Wanna Talk Love**	*Richard Brannan/Milton Brown*	Columbia 05829
				WILSON, Coleman		
				Born in Texas. Male singer/songwriter.		
7/31/61	23	5		**Passing Zone Blues**	*Coleman Wilson*	King 5512
				WILSON, Gretchen — **2000s: #48**		
				Born on 6/26/1973 in Granite City, Illinois; raised in Pocahontas, Illinois. Female singer/songwriter/guitarist.		
				CMA: Horizon 2004		
3/13/04	❶[5]	22		1 **Redneck Woman**	*John Rich/Gretchen Wilson*	Epic
				Grammy: Female Vocal		
6/19/04	3[1]	20		2 **Here For The Party**	*Kenny Alphin/John Rich/Gretchen Wilson*	Epic
10/30/04+	4	20		3 **When I Think About Cheatin'**	*Vicky McGehee/John Rich/Gretchen Wilson*	Epic
11/13/04	60	1		4 **Redbird Fever**	*John Rich/Gretchen Wilson*	Epic
				tribute to baseball's St. Louis Cardinals (new lyrics to the tune of "Redneck Woman"); only available as a paid download		
1/29/05	2[3]	20		5 **Homewrecker**	*Rivers Rutherford/George Teren/Gretchen Wilson*	Epic
				#1-3 & 5: from the album *Here For The Party* on Epic 90903		
				WILSON, Hank — see RUSSELL, Leon		
				WILSON, Jim		
				Born in Bowling Green, Kentucky. Male singer/songwriter.		
7/23/55	8	9		**Daddy, You Know What?**	A:8 *Jim Wilson*	Mercury 70635
				includes a short narration by Wilson's daughter June		
				WILSON, Larry Jon		
				Born on 10/7/1950 in Swainsboro, Georgia. Male singer.		
4/24/76	74	7		**Think I Feel A Hitchhike Coming On**	*Ray Whitley*	Monument 8692
				WILSON, Meri		
				Born on 6/15/1949 in Japan (father was a U.S. Air Force officer); raised in Marietta, Georgia. Died in a car crash on 12/28/2002 (age 53). Female singer/songwriter.		
6/18/77	50	8	●	**Telephone Man**	*Meri Wilson* [N]	GRT 127
				WILSON, Norro — **SW: #15**		
				Born Norris Wilson on 4/4/1938 in Scottsville, Kentucky. Male singer/songwriter.		
1/11/69	68	7		1 **Only You**	*Buck Ram/Ande Rand*	Smash 2192
4/5/69	44	8		2 **Love Comes But Once In A Lifetime**	*Mary Hughes*	Smash 2210
9/13/69	56	8		3 **Shame On Me**	*Bill Enis/Lawton Williams*	Smash 2236
7/4/70	20	13		4 **Do It To Someone You Love**	*Tom T. Hall*	Mercury 73077
11/28/70	53	9		5 **Old Enough To Want To (Fool Enough To Try)**	*Tom T. Hall*	Mercury 73125
11/18/72+	28	12		6 **Everybody Needs Lovin'**	*David Huston/Carmol Taylor/Norro Wilson*	RCA Victor 0824
3/31/73	64	4		7 **Darlin' Raise The Shade**	*Claude King/Carmol Taylor/Norro Wilson*	RCA Victor 0909
9/8/73	35	11		8 **Ain't It Good (To Feel This Way)**	*George Richey/Carmol Taylor/Norro Wilson*	RCA Victor 0062
7/6/74	96	2		9 **Loneliness (Can Break A Good Man Down)**	*George Richey/Carmol Taylor/Norro Wilson*	Capitol 3886
8/20/77	43	8		10 **So Close Again** ***[w/ Margo Smith]***	*Jim Shaw/Margo Smith/Norro Wilson*	Warner 8427
				WILSON, Tim		
				Born in Columbus, Georgia. Male comedian.		
3/27/93	70	2		1 **Garth Brooks Has Ruined My Life**	*Tim Wilson* [N]	Southern Tracks
				from the album *Songs For The Musically Disturbed* on Southern Tracks 77		
4/15/00	66	1		2 **The Ballad Of John Rocker**	*Tim Wilson* [N]	Capitol
				from the album *Hillbilly Homeboy* on Capitol 25930		
				WILSON-SAMPRAS, Bridgette		
				Born on 9/25/1973 in Gold Beach, Oregon. Female actress/singer. Appeared in several movies. Married pro tennis star Pete Sampras on 9/30/2000.		
10/12/02	43	11		**What We're Gonna Do About It** ***[w/ Tommy Shane Steiner]***	*Chris DuBois/Lee Miller*	RCA
				from Steiner's album *Then Came The Night* on RCA 67041		
				WINGS — see McCARTNEY, Paul		

WINSLOW, Stephanie

Born on 8/27/1956 in Yankton, South Dakota. Female singer/songwriter/fiddler. Formerly married to Ray Ruff (owner of the Oak record label).

DEBUT	PEAK	WKS	GOLD	Country Chart Hit	Songwriter	Label (& Number)
9/29/79	**10**	11		1 **Say You Love Me**	*Christine McVie*	Warner/Curb 49074
1/12/80	**14**	10		2 **Crying**	*Joe Melson/Roy Orbison*	Warner/Curb 49146
4/5/80	**38**	6		3 **I Can't Remember**	*Stephanie Winslow*	Warner/Curb 49201
6/21/80	**36**	10		4 **Try It On**	*Mike Chapman/Nicky Chinn*	Warner/Curb 49257
9/20/80	**35**	9		5 **Baby, I'm A Want You**	*David Gates*	Warner/Curb 49557
12/13/80+	**25**	13		6 **Anything But Yes Is Still A No**	*Leslie Pearl*	Warner/Curb 49628
3/21/81	**36**	7		7 **Hideaway Healing**	*Oskar Solomon/Stephanie Winslow*	Warner/Curb 49693
6/27/81	**39**	9		8 **I've Been A Fool /**	*Stephanie Winslow*	
6/27/81	**flip**	9		9 **Sometimes When We Touch**	*Dan Hill/Barry Mann*	Warner/Curb 49753
10/10/81	**29**	10		10 **When You Walk In The Room**	*Jackie DeShannon*	Warner/Curb 49831
5/1/82	**43**	10		11 **Slippin' And Slidin'**	*Richard Penniman*	Primero 1003
6/26/82	**40**	10		12 **Don't We Belong In Love**	*Michael Garvin/Tom Shapiro*	Primero 1007
9/18/82	**69**	5		13 **In Between Lovers**	*Bob Stone*	Primero/Curb 1012
5/14/83	**61**	6		14 **Nobody Else For Me**	*Stephanie Winslow*	Oak 1056
9/3/83	**25**	15		15 **Kiss Me Darling**	*Stephanie Winslow*	Curb/MCA 52291
1/7/84	**29**	12		16 **Dancin' With The Devil**	*Stephanie Winslow*	Curb/MCA 52327
4/7/84	**42**	9		17 **Baby, Come To Me**	*Rod Temperton*	Curb/MCA 52372

WINTERMUTE, Joann

Born in Dallas, Texas. Female singer/songwriter.

DEBUT	PEAK	WKS	GOLD	Country Chart Hit	Songwriter	Label (& Number)
3/11/89	**82**	3		1 **Two Old Flames One Cheatin' Fire**	*John Gulley/Don Miller*	Canyon Creek 1225
5/27/89	**81**	3		2 **I Wouldn't Trade Your Love**	*Joann Wintermute*	Door Knob 324
8/19/89	**78**	3		3 **How I Love You In The Morning**	*Ed Jones/Elaine Jones*	Door Knob 330

WINTERS, Don

Born on 4/17/1929 in Tampa, Florida. Died of cancer on 8/17/2002 (age 73). Male singer/songwriter.

DEBUT	PEAK	WKS	GOLD	Country Chart Hit	Songwriter	Label (& Number)
7/3/61	**10**	10		1 **Too Many Times /**	*Don Winters*	
7/17/61	**27**	2		2 **Shake Hands With A Loser**	*Don Winters*	Decca 31253

WISEMAN, Mac

Born Malcolm Wiseman on 5/23/1925 in Cremora, Virginia. Bluegrass singer/songwriter/banjo player. Also see **The Groovegrass Boyz** and **Tomorrow's World**.

DEBUT	PEAK	WKS	GOLD	Country Chart Hit	Songwriter	Label (& Number)
5/28/55	**10**	2		1 **The Ballad Of Davy Crockett** A:10	*Tom Blackburn/George Bruns*	Dot 1240
8/10/59	**5**	20		2 **Jimmy Brown The Newsboy**	*Mac Wiseman*	Dot 15946
9/21/63	**12**	8		3 **Your Best Friend And Me**	*Hank Cochran*	Capitol 5011
11/9/68	**54**	7		4 **Got Leavin' On Her Mind**	*Jack Clement*	MGM 13986
12/6/69+	**38**	9		5 **Johnny's Cash And Charley's Pride**	*Cy Coben* **[N]**	RCA Victor 0283
3/18/78	**78**	5		6 **Never Going Back Again**	*Lindsey Buckingham*	Churchill 7706
5/12/79	**69**	4		7 **My Blue Heaven** ***[w/ Woody Herman]***	*Walter Donaldson/George Whiting*	Churchill 7735
7/7/79	**88**	3		8 **Scotch And Soda**	*Dave Guard*	Churchill 7738
10/13/79	**95**	3		9 **Shackles And Chains** ***[w/ Osborne Bros.]***	*Jimmie Davis*	CMH 1522

WOFFORD, E.D.

Born in Tennessee. Male singer.

DEBUT	PEAK	WKS	GOLD	Country Chart Hit	Songwriter	Label (& Number)
7/1/78	**77**	4		**Baby, I Need Your Lovin'**	*Lamont Dozier/Brian Holland/Eddie Holland*	MC/Curb 5012

WOLF, Brad

Born in Caryville, Tennessee. Male singer/songwriter. Great-great-grandson of **Fiddlin' John Carson**.

DEBUT	PEAK	WKS	GOLD	Country Chart Hit	Songwriter	Label (& Number)
9/27/03	**58**	4		**Strictly Business**	*Phillip Moore/Brad Wolf*	Warner

WOLF, Gary

Born in 1948 in Richmond, Kentucky. Male singer/songwriter.

DEBUT	PEAK	WKS	GOLD	Country Chart Hit	Songwriter	Label (& Number)
7/17/82	**51**	9		1 **Love Never Dies**	*Joe Chambers/Larry Jenkins*	Columbia 02986
10/30/82	**64**	7		2 **The Perfect Picture (To Fit My Frame Of Mind)**	*Jim McBride/Roger Murrah*	Columbia 03272
2/19/83	**62**	7		3 **Livin' On Memories**	*Joe Chambers/Larry Jenkins*	Columbia 03493
7/7/84	**63**	8		4 **You Bring The Heartache (I'll Bring The Wine)**	*Joe Chambers/Larry Jenkins/Gary Wolf*	Mercury 822244
3/23/85	**73**	3		5 **It's My Life**	*Joe Doyle/Ray Shepherd/Gary Wolf*	Mercury 880564

WOLFPACK, The

All-star trio: **Kenny Earle**, **Narvel Felts** and **Lobo**.

DEBUT	PEAK	WKS	GOLD	Country Chart Hit	Songwriter	Label (& Number)
5/8/82	**88**	3		**Bull Smith Can't Dance The Cotton-Eyed Joe**	*Roger LaVoie/Lobo* **[N]**	Lobo 6

WOMACK, Lee Ann — 2000s: #27 / All-Time: #191

Born on 8/19/1966 in Jacksonville, Texas. Female singer. Married to **Jason Sellers** from 1991-97.

CMA: Female Vocalist 2001

DEBUT	PEAK	WKS	GOLD	Country Chart Hit	Songwriter	Label (& Number)
3/15/97	**23**	20		1 **Never Again, Again** S:9	*Monty Holmes/Barbie Isham*	Decca
6/21/97	**2**[1]	20		2 **The Fool**	*Marla Cannon/Gene Ellsworth/Charley Stefl*	Decca

DEBUT	PEAK	WKS	GOLD	ARTIST / Ranking / Country Chart Hit / Songwriter	Label (& Number)
				WOMACK, Lee Ann — cont'd	
11/1/97+	2[1]	22		3 **You've Got To Talk To Me** ... *Jamie O'Hara*	Decca
4/4/98	**27**	20		4 **Buckaroo** ... *Ed Hill/Mark D. Sanders*	Decca
				above 4 from the album *Lee Ann Womack* on Decca 11585	
8/8/98	2[3]	21		5 **A Little Past Little Rock** ... S:5 *Jess Brown/Brett Jones/Tony Lane*	Decca
12/26/98+	2[4]	25		6 **I'll Think Of A Reason Later** ... *Tony Martin/Tim Nichols*	Decca
6/5/99	**12**	20		7 **(Now You See Me) Now You Don't** ... *Jess Brown/Tony Lane/David Lee*	Decca
10/23/99	**56**	8		8 **Don't Tell Me** ... *Buddy Miller/Julie Miller*	Decca
				above 4 from the album *Some Things I Know* on Decca 70040	
3/25/00	❶[5]	32		9 **I Hope You Dance** S:❶[8] *Mark D. Sanders/Tia Sillers*	MCA Nashville
				Grammy: Song / CMA: Single; Sons Of The Desert (backing vocals)	
10/7/00+	**4**	26		10 **Ashes By Now** ... *Rodney Crowell*	MCA Nashville
4/7/01	**13**	21		11 **Why They Call It Falling** ... *Roxie Dean/Don Schlitz*	MCA Nashville
11/10/01+	**23**	20		12 **Does My Ring Burn Your Finger** ... *Buddy Miller/Julie Miller*	MCA Nashville
				above 4 from the album *I Hope You Dance* on MCA Nashville 170099	
1/26/02	**22**	20		13 **Mendocino County Line** *[w/ Willie Nelson]* ... *Matt Serletic/Bernie Taupin*	Lost Highway
				Grammy: Vocal Collaboration / CMA: Vocal Event; from Nelson's album *Stars & Guitars* on Lost Highway 170340	
6/1/02	**20**	20		14 **Something Worth Leaving Behind** ... *Brett Beavers/Tom Douglas*	MCA Nashville
10/26/02	**37**	17		15 **Forever Everyday** ... *Devon O'Day/Kim Patton*	MCA Nashville
				above 2 from the album *Something Worth Leaving Behind* on MCA Nashville 170287	
2/21/04	**24**	20		16 **The Wrong Girl** ... *Pat McLaughlin/Liz Rose*	MCA Nashville
				from the album *Greatest Hits* on MCA Nashville 001883	
10/23/04+	**10**	26		17 **I May Hate Myself In The Morning** ... *Odie Blackmon*	MCA Nashville
5/7/05	**22**↑	21↑		18 **He Oughta Know That By Now** ... *Clint Ingersoll/Jeremy Spillman*	MCA Nashville
				above 2 from the album *There's More Where That Came From* on MCA Nashville 003073	
				WOOD, Bobby	
				Born on 1/25/1941 in Memphis, Tennessee. Male singer/pianist.	
10/31/64	**46**	2		**That's All I Need To Know** ... *Stan Kesler*	Joy 288
				WOOD, Danny	
				Born in Grand Prairie, Texas. Male singer/songwriter/guitarist.	
10/23/76	**92**	4		1 **If This Is Freedom (I Want Out)** ... *Jerry Abbott/Charles Stewart*	London 242
4/2/77	**93**	2		2 **I Need Somethin' Easy Tonight** ... *Jerry Abbott/Charles Stewart*	London 248
6/21/80	**30**	10		3 **A Heart's Been Broken** ... *Charles Stewart/Danny Wood*	RCA 11968
12/6/80+	**37**	12		4 **It Took Us All Night Long To Say Goodbye** ... *Wayland Holyfield/Bob McDill*	RCA 12123
3/21/81	**58**	7		5 **Fool's Gold** ... *Jerry Abbott/Charles Stewart/Vic Stewart/Danny Wood*	RCA 12181
				WOOD, Del	
				Born Polly Adelaide Hendricks on 2/22/1920 in Nashville, Tennessee. Died on 10/3/1989 (age 69). Female pianist.	
				OPRY: 1953	
9/8/51	**5**	12	●	**Down Yonder** ... J:5 / A:7 / S:9 *Wolfe Gilbert* **[I]**	Tennessee 775
				WOOD, Jeff	
				Born on 5/10/1968 in Oklahoma City, Oklahoma. Male singer/songwriter.	
11/2/96+	**44**	18		1 **You Just Get One** ... *Vince Gill/Don Schlitz*	Imprint
3/15/97	**55**	10		2 **Use Mine** ... *Lisa Drew/Steve Seskin*	Imprint
6/7/97	**63**	8		3 **You Call That A Mountain** ... *Michael Garvin/Bucky Jones*	Imprint
				above 3 from the album *Between The Earth And The Stars* on Imprint 10006	
				WOOD, Nancy	
				Born Renate Kern in Germany; exchange student who lived in Janesville, Michigan. Female singer. Host of *Nancy's Country Drive-In* radio series in Germany.	
10/10/81	**79**	4		**Imagine That** ... *Byron Hill/J. Remington Wilde*	Montage 1202
				WOODRUFF, Bob	
				Born on 3/14/1961 in Suffern, New York. Male singer/songwriter.	
2/26/94	**70**	3		1 **Hard Liquor, Cold Women, Warm Beer** ... *Bob Woodruff*	Asylum
5/21/94	**74**	1		2 **Bayou Girl** ... *Bob Woodruff*	Asylum
				above 2 from the album *Dreams And Saturday Nights* on Asylum 61590	
				WOODS, Gene	
				Born in Chattanooga, Tennessee. Male singer.	
10/10/60	**7**	13		**The Ballad Of Wild River** ... *Marshall Pack*	HAP 1004
				WOODY, Bill	
				Born in 1959 in Jacksonville, Florida; raised in North Carolina. Male singer.	
4/21/79	**65**	9		1 **Just Between Us** ... *Mickey Newbury*	MCA 54043
8/4/79	**88**	4		2 **Love Wouldn't Leave Us Alone** ... *Dallas Frazier/A.L. "Doodle" Owens*	MCA 41070
				WOOLERY, Chuck	
				Born on 3/16/1942 in Ashland, Kentucky. Male singer/songwriter. Hosted TV's *Wheel Of Fortune* and *Love Connection*.	
7/9/77	**78**	5		1 **Painted Lady** ... *Linda Hargrove/Norro Wilson/Chuck Woolery*	Warner 8381
7/12/80	**94**	2		2 **The Greatest Love Affair** ... *Mack David/Billy Sherrill* **[S]**	Epic 50897
				WOOLEY, Amy	
				Born in Cleveland, Ohio. Male singer/guitarist.	
7/31/82	**51**	9		**If My Heart Had Windows** ... *Dallas Frazier*	MCA 52084

Billboard DEBUT	PEAK	WKS	GOLD	ARTIST / Country Chart Hit	Ranking / Songwriter	Label (& Number)

WOOLEY, Sheb

Born Shelby Wooley on 4/10/1921 in Erick, Oklahoma. Died of leukemia on 9/16/2003 (age 82). Singer/songwriter/actor. Played "Pete Nolan" on the TV series *Rawhide*. Also made comical recordings under pseudonym **Ben Colder**. Acted in the movies *High Noon, Rocky Mountain, Giant* and *Hoosiers*. Wrote *Hee Haw*'s theme song.

CMA: Comedian (as Ben Colder) 1968

DEBUT	PEAK	WKS	GOLD	Country Chart Hit	Songwriter	Label (& Number)
1/13/62	❶[1]	17		1 **That's My Pa**	*Sheb Wooley* **[N]**	MGM 13046
12/29/62	**18**	1		2 **Don't Go Near The Eskimos** ***[Ben Colder]*** — parody of "Don't Go Near The Indians" by **Rex Allen**	*Lorene Mann/Sheb Wooley* **[N]**	MGM 13104
3/2/63	**30**	2		3 **Hello Wall No. 2** ***[Ben Colder]*** — parody of "Hello Walls" by **Faron Young**	*Willie Nelson* **[N]**	MGM 13122
7/18/64	**33**	10		4 **Blue Guitar**	*Sheb Wooley*	MGM 13241
5/21/66	**34**	9		5 **I'll Leave The Singin' To The Bluebirds**	*Ray Griff*	MGM 13477
9/24/66	**6**	15		6 **Almost Persuaded No. 2** ***[Ben Colder]*** — parody of "Almost Persuaded" by **David Houston**	*Billy Sherrill/Glenn Sutton* **[N]**	MGM 13590
10/15/66	**70**	2		7 **Tonight's The Night My Angel's Halo Fell**	*Don Wright*	MGM 13556
6/29/68	**22**	12		8 **Tie A Tiger Down**	*Sheb Wooley*	MGM 13938
10/26/68	**24**	6		9 **Harper Valley P.T.A. (Later That Same Day)** ***[Ben Colder]*** — parody of "Harper Valley P.T.A." by **Jeannie C. Riley**	*...Jack Clement/Tom T. Hall/Sheb Wooley* **[N]**	MGM 13997
1/4/69	**65**	3		10 **Little Green Apples No. 2** ***[Ben Colder]*** — parody of "Little Green Apples" by **Roger Miller**	*Bobby Russell/Sheb Wooley* **[N]**	MGM 14015
1/11/69	**52**	9		11 **I Remember Loving You**	*Sheb Wooley*	MGM 14005
10/25/69	**63**	7		12 **The One Man Band**	*Sheb Wooley*	MGM 14085
2/13/71	**50**	6		13 **Fifteen Beers Ago** ***[Ben Colder]*** — parody of "Fifteen Years Ago" by **Conway Twitty**	*Raymond Smith/Sheb Wooley* **[N]**	MGM 14209

WOPAT, Tom

Born on 9/9/1951 in Lodi, Wisconsin. Male singer/songwriter/actor. Played "Luke Duke" on TV's *The Dukes of Hazzard.* Host of TNN's *Prime Time Country* in 1996.

DEBUT	PEAK	WKS	GOLD	Country Chart Hit	Songwriter	Label (& Number)
4/19/86	**39**	13		1 **True Love (Never Did Run Smooth)**	A:37 *Jim Rushing/Don Schlitz*	EMI America 8316
8/16/86	**44**	11		2 **I Won't Let You Down**	*Gary Burr*	EMI America 8334
12/20/86+	**16**	19		3 **The Rock And Roll Of Love**	A:15 / S:24 *Charlie Black/Bob McDill*	EMI America 8364
5/9/87	**28**	14		4 **Put Me Out Of My Misery**	*Lewis Anderson/Bob McDill*	EMI America 43010
8/29/87	**20**	17		5 **Susannah**	*Bill Rice/Mary Sharon Rice*	EMI America 43034
1/9/88	**18**	17		6 **A Little Bit Closer**	*Mary Ann Kennedy/Pam Rose/Thom Schuyler*	EMI-Manhattan 50112
6/11/88	**40**	10		7 **Hey Little Sister**	*Gary Scruggs*	Capitol 44144
10/8/88	**29**	16		8 **Not Enough Love**	*Chris Farren/Fred Knoblock*	Capitol 44243
6/29/91	**46**	15		9 **Too Many Honky Tonks (On My Way Home)**	*Tommy Barnes/Chiles Patrick/Bernard Shaw*	Epic
11/23/91	**51**	11		10 **Back To The Well** — above 2 from the album *Learning To Love* on Epic 47874	*Rick Bowles/Robert Byrne*	Epic

WORK, Jimmy

Born on 3/29/1924 in Akron, Ohio; raised in Dukedom, Tennessee. Male singer/songwriter/guitarist.

DEBUT	PEAK	WKS	GOLD	Country Chart Hit	Songwriter	Label (& Number)
2/19/55	**5**	13		1 **Making Believe**	J:5 / A:7 / S:11 *Jimmy Work*	Dot 1221
7/2/55	**6**	4		2 **That's What Makes The Juke Box Play**	J:6 *Jimmy Work*	Dot 1245

WORLEY, Darryl

2000s: #19 / All-Time: #279

Born on 10/31/1964 in Pyburn, Tennessee; raised in Savannah, Tennessee. Male singer/songwriter/guitarist.

DEBUT	PEAK	WKS	GOLD	Country Chart Hit	Songwriter	Label (& Number)
4/1/00	**15**	24		1 **When You Need My Love**	S:4 *Wynn Varble/Darryl Worley*	DreamWorks
10/7/00+	**12**	24		2 **A Good Day To Run**	*Bobby Tomberlin/Darryl Worley*	DreamWorks
4/7/01	**20**	20		3 **Second Wind**	*Steve Leslie/Darryl Worley*	DreamWorks
10/20/01	**41**	9		4 **Sideways** — above 4 from the album *Hard Rain Don't Last* on DreamWorks 450042	*J.B. Rudd/Carl Vipperman/Darryl Worley*	DreamWorks
3/23/02	❶[1]	32		5 **I Miss My Friend**	*Tony Martin/Mark Nesler/Tom Shapiro*	DreamWorks
10/19/02+	**26**	20		6 **Family Tree** — above 2 from the album *I Miss My Friend* on DreamWorks 50351	*Darrell Scott*	DreamWorks
3/8/03	❶[7]	20		7 **Have You Forgotten?**	*Wynn Varble/Darryl Worley*	DreamWorks
7/12/03	**31**	19		8 **Tennessee River Run**	*Steve Leslie/Darryl Worley*	DreamWorks
11/22/03	**57**	3		9 **I Will Hold My Ground** — above 3 from the album *Have You Forgotten* on DreamWorks 000064	*Frank Rogers/Darryl Worley*	DreamWorks
7/10/04+	❶[2]	33		10 **Awful, Beautiful Life**	*Harley Allen/Darryl Worley*	DreamWorks
3/5/05	**9**	21		11 **If Something Should Happen** — above 2 from the album *Darryl Worley* on DreamWorks 002322	*Jim Brown/Dan Demay/Dave Turnbull*	DreamWorks

WORTH, Marion

Born Mary Ann Ward on 7/4/1930 in Birmingham, Alabama. Died of emphysema on 12/19/1999 (age 69). Female singer/songwriter/guitarist.

OPRY: 1963

DEBUT	PEAK	WKS	GOLD	Country Chart Hit	Songwriter	Label (& Number)
10/19/59+	**12**	20		1 **Are You Willing, Willie**	*Marion Worth*	Cherokee 503
5/23/60	**5**	15		2 **That's My Kind Of Love**	*Marion Worth*	Guyden 2033
11/14/60	**7**	23		3 **I Think I Know**	*Curly Putman*	Columbia 41799
5/22/61	**21**	1		4 **There'll Always Be Sadness**	*Harlan Howard*	Columbia 41972
2/2/63	**14**	5		5 **Shake Me I Rattle (Squeeze Me I Cry)**	*Hal Hackady/Charles Naylor* **[X]**	Columbia 42640
6/8/63	**18**	3		6 **Crazy Arms**	*Ralph Mooney/Chuck Seals*	Columbia 42703
4/11/64	**33**	13		7 **You Took Him Off My Hands (Now Please Take Him Off My Mind)**	*...Harlan Howard/Skeets McDonald/Wynn Stewart*	Columbia 42992
5/9/64	**23**	17		8 **Slipping Around** ***[w/ George Morgan]***	*Floyd Tillman*	Columbia 43020

DEBUT	PEAK	WKS	GOLD	ARTIST / Ranking / Country Chart Hit	Songwriter	Label (& Number)
				WORTH, Marion — cont'd		
10/24/64	**25**	6		9 **The French Song**	*Lucille Starr*	Columbia 43119
12/11/65+	**32**	6		10 **I Will Not Blow Out The Light**	*Lucy Roberts/Gloria Shayne*	Columbia 43405
11/4/67	**64**	6		11 **A Woman Needs Love**	*Marion Worth*	Decca 32195
3/30/68	**45**	10		12 **Mama Sez**	*Marion Worth*	Decca 32278
				WRAYS, The		
				Group formed in Oregon: Bubba Wray, Jim Covert, Lynn Phillips, and Joe Dale Cleghorn. Bubba became better known as **Collin Raye**.		
3/19/83	**88**	3		1 **Reason To Believe**	*Tim Hardin*	CIS 3011
4/6/85	**93**	4		2 **Until We Meet Again**	*Collin Raye*	Sasparilla 0003
				THE WRAY BROTHERS BAND (above 2)		
5/10/86	**71**	5		3 **I Don't Want To Know Your Name**	*Michael Smotherman*	Mercury 884621
6/6/87	**48**	10		4 **You Lay A Lotta Love On Me**	*David Heavener*	Mercury 888542
				WREN, Larry		
				Born in Denver, Colorado. Male singer.		
5/21/77	**98**	3		1 **Lie To Me /**	*Brook Benton/Margie Singleton*	
5/21/77	**flip**	3		2 **It's Saturday Night**	*Richard Burt/Fred Niggler*	50 States 51
				WRIGHT, B.J.		
				Born Bobby Joe Wright in Gallatin, Tennessee. Male singer/songwriter.		
10/21/78	**96**	4		1 **Memory Bound**	*Marvin Jared/Bobby Wright*	Soundwaves 4577
3/24/79	**93**	2		2 **Leaning On Each Other**	*Bill Holmes/Jimmy Payne*	Soundwaves 4581
7/28/79	**61**	5		3 **I've Got A Right To Be Wrong**	*Bob House/Ernie Rowell*	Soundwaves 4589
12/22/79+	**87**	6		4 **Nobody's Darlin' But Mine**	*Jimmie Davis*	Soundwaves 4593
5/3/80	**36**	11		5 **J.R.**	*David Hall/Don Lee/Joe Meador/B.J. Wright*	Soundwaves 4604
				title refers to "J.R. Ewing" (Larry Hagman) of TV's *Dallas*		
8/2/80	**73**	5		6 **Lost Love Affair**	*Bernard Spurlock/B.J. Wright*	Soundwaves 4610
12/27/80+	**81**	6		7 **I Know An Ending (When It Comes)**	*Hank Cochran*	Soundwaves 4624
				WRIGHT, Bobby		
				Born John Robert Wright on 3/30/1942 in Charleston, West Virginia. Male singer/songwriter/guitarist/actor. Son of **Johnny Wright** and **Kitty Wells**; brother of **Ruby Wright**. Played "Willy Moss" on TV's *McHale's Navy*.		
4/29/67	**44**	12		1 **Lay Some Happiness On Me**	*Jean Chapel/Bob Jennings*	Decca 32107
12/2/67	**67**	3		2 **That See Me Later Look**	*Eddie Miller/Curly Putman*	Decca 32193
10/5/68	**70**	4		3 **Old Before My Time**	*Steve Karliski*	Decca 32367
5/17/69	**40**	10		4 **Upstairs In The Bedroom**	*Wayne Kemp/Dolores Tolbert*	Decca 32464
11/1/69	**70**	2		5 **Sing A Song About Love**	*Hank Million*	Decca 32564
3/8/70	**61**	4		6 **Take Me Back To The Goodtimes, Sally**	*Bud Johnston*	Decca 32633
8/1/70	**47**	9		7 **Hurry Home To Me**	*Jan Crutchfield/Ben Keith*	Decca 32705
4/24/71	**74**	2		8 **If You Want Me To I'll Go**	*Mickey Newbury*	Decca 32792
7/10/71	**13**	16		9 **Here I Go Again**	*Ted Harris*	Decca 32839
12/25/71+	**54**	8		10 **Search Your Heart**	*Ted Harris*	Decca 32903
8/12/72	**60**	5		11 **Just Because I'm Still In Love With You**	*Dallas Frazier/Whitey Shafer*	Decca 32985
1/27/73	**75**	1		12 **If Not For You**	*Bob Dylan*	Decca 33034
10/20/73	**39**	11		13 **Lovin' Someone On My Mind**	*Don Cook*	ABC 11390
2/23/74	**24**	12		14 **Seasons In The Sun**	*Jacques Brel/Rod McKuen*	ABC 11418
6/22/74	**56**	10		15 **Everybody Needs A Rainbow**	*Rory Bourke*	ABC 11443
10/5/74	**55**	11		16 **Baby's Gone**	*Bobby Goldsboro/Roy Orbison*	ABC 12028
3/8/75	**75**	7		17 **I Just Came Home To Count The Memories**	*Glenn Ray*	ABC 12062
1/8/77	**79**	6		18 **Neon Lady**	*Max D. Barnes/Ron Bledsoe/Troy Seals*	United Artists 913
9/24/77	**97**	1		19 **Playing With The Baby's Mama**	*Kenny O'Dell*	United Artists 1051
10/21/78	**100**	3		20 **Takin' A Chance**	*Joe Tex*	United Artists 1238
7/28/79	**77**	3		21 **I'm Turning You Loose**	*Curly Putman/Sonny Throckmorton*	United Artists 1300
				WRIGHT, Chely — **All-Time: #278**		
				Born Richelle Wright on 10/25/1970 in Kansas City, Missouri. Female singer/songwriter/guitarist.		
6/25/94	**58**	10		1 **He's A Good Ole Boy**	*Harlan Howard*	Polydor
10/22/94	**48**	14		2 **Till I Was Loved By You**	*Mark Irwin/Alan Jackson*	Polydor
2/4/95	**56**	8		3 **Sea Of Cowboy Hats**	*Dale Dodson/Jimmy Melton/Chely Wright*	Polydor
				above 3 from the album *Woman In The Moon* on Polydor 523225		
10/21/95	**66**	7		4 **Listenin' To The Radio**	*Sunny Russ/Stephony Smith*	Polydor
2/10/96	**41**	15		5 **The Love That We Lost**	*Gary Burr/Monty Powell*	Polydor
				above 2 from the album *Right In The Middle Of It* on Polydor 529553		
7/19/97	**14**	20		6 **Shut Up And Drive**	S:11 *Rivers Rutherford/Annie Tate/Sam Tate*	MCA
11/29/97+	**39**	15		7 **Just Another Heartache**	*Ed Hill/Mark D. Sanders*	MCA
3/28/98	**36**	20		8 **I Already Do**	*Gary Burr/Chely Wright*	MCA
				above 3 from the album *Let Me In* on MCA 70003		
3/13/99	**❶**[1]	31		9 **Single White Female**	S:3 *Carolyn Dawn Johnson/Shaye Smith*	MCA Nashville
10/9/99+	**11**	30		10 **It Was**	*Gary Burr/Mark Wright*	MCA Nashville
6/10/00	**49**	8		11 **She Went Out For Cigarettes**	*Ronnie Guilbeau/Jon McElroy*	MCA Nashville
				above 3 from the album *Single White Female* on MCA Nashville 70052		
10/14/00	**68**	2		12 **Hard To Be A Husband, Hard To Be A Wife** ***[w/ Brad Paisley]***	*Brad Paisley/Chely Wright*	MCA Nashville
				from the various artists album *75 Years Of The WSM Grand Ole Opry Volume Two* on MCA Nashville 170176		
6/2/01	**26**	20		13 **Never Love You Enough**	*Brett James/Angelo Petraglia*	MCA Nashville

DEBUT	PEAK	WKS	GOLD	ARTIST / Ranking / Country Chart Hit	Songwriter	Label (& Number)
				WRIGHT, Chely — cont'd		
12/22/01+	**23**	20		14 **Jezebel**	*Jay DeMarcus/Marcus Hummon*	MCA Nashville
				above 2 from the album *Never Love You Enough* on MCA Nashville 70210		
2/15/03	**52**	9		15 **Scary Old World** *[w/ Radney Foster]*	*Radney Foster/Harlan Howard*	Dualtone
				from Foster's album *Another Way To Go* on Dualtone 1128		
3/13/04	**40**	15		16 **Back Of The Bottom Drawer**	*Liz Rose/Chely Wright*	Painted Red
11/20/04+	**35**	19		17 **The Bumper Of My S.U.V.**	S:❶^{9} *Chely Wright*	Painted Red
				above 2 from the album *The Metropolitan Hotel* on Painted Red 12002		
				WRIGHT, Curtis		
				Born on 6/6/1955 in Huntington, Pennsylvania. Male singer/songwriter. Former member of the **Super Grit Cowboy Band** and **Orrall & Wright**.		
11/11/89	**38**	13		1 **She's Got A Man On Her Mind**	*Billy Spencer/Curtis Wright*	Airborne 75746
7/11/92	**59**	7		2 **Hometown Radio**	*Vern Rust*	Liberty
1/2/93	**53**	10		3 **If I Could Stop Lovin' You**	*Robert Ellis Orrall/Bill Spencer/Curtis Wright*	Liberty
				above 2 from the album *Curtis Wright* on Liberty 97825		
				WRIGHT, Ginny		
				Born in Twin City, Georgia. Female singer.		
1/9/54	**3^{1}**	22		1 **I Love You** *[w/ Jim Reeves]*	A:3 / J:7 / S:8 *Billy Barton*	Fabor 101
1/1/55	**2^{3}**	26		2 **Are You Mine** *[w/ Tom Tall]*	A:2 / J:4 / S:5 *Jim Amadeo/Don Grashey/Myrna Lorrie*	Fabor 117
				WRIGHT, Johnny		
				Born on 5/13/1914 in Mount Juliet, Tennessee; raised in Nashville, Tennessee. Male singer/songwriter/fiddler. Member of **Johnnie & Jack** duo. Married **Kitty Wells** in 1938. Father of **Bobby Wright** and **Ruby Wright**.		
5/2/64	**22**	15		1 **Walkin', Talkin', Cryin', Barely Beatin' Broken Heart**	*Roger Miller/Justin Tubb*	Decca 31593
				JOHNNY WRIGHT And The Tennessee Mountain Boys		
1/2/65	**37**	5		2 **Don't Give Up The Ship**	*Kendall Hayes*	Decca 31679
5/8/65	**28**	11		3 **Blame It On The Moonlight**	*Boudleaux Bryant/Felice Bryant*	Decca 31740
8/28/65	**❶^{3}**	21		4 **Hello Vietnam**	*Tom T. Hall*	Decca 31821
12/18/65+	**31**	10		5 **Keep The Flag Flying**	*Cecil Null*	Decca 31875
6/4/66	**31**	6		6 **Nickels, Quarters And Dimes**	*Bill Anderson/Jimmy Gateley*	Decca 31927
10/15/66	**53**	7		7 **I'm Doing This For Daddy**	*Gene Crysler*	Decca 32002
12/31/66+	**50**	11		8 **Mama's Little Jewel**	*Kermit Barrett/Hank Mills*	Decca 32061
8/12/67	**66**	5		9 **American Power**	*Jim Anglin*	Decca 32162
12/16/67	**69**	4		10 **Music To Cry By**	*Cecil Null*	Decca 32216
5/11/68	**54**	8		11 **We'll Stick Together** *[w/ Kitty Wells]*	*Bill Phillips*	Decca 32294
11/30/68	**66**	5		12 **(They Always Come Out) Smellin' Like A Rose**	*Ray Buzzeo/Wayne Manning*	Decca 32402
				WRIGHT, Justin		
				Born in 1961 in Springfield, Illinois; raised in Phoenix, Arizona. Male singer.		
2/4/89	**91**	2		**Settin' At The Kitchen Table**	*Lynda Shafer/Whitey Shafer*	Bear 195
				WRIGHT, Lee		
				Born in Arizona. Male singer/songwriter.		
12/23/78+	**86**	4		1 **Capricorn Kings**	*Ann J. Morton/Lee Wright*	Prairie Dust 7628
7/6/85	**90**	4		2 **The Eyes Have It**	*Bobby Fischer/Rick Giles*	Prairie Dust 5185
				WRIGHT, Michelle		
				Born on 7/1/1961 in Morpeth, Ontario, Canada. Female singer.		
6/2/90	**32**	21		1 **New Kind Of Love**	*Steve Bogard/Rick Giles*	Arista
10/13/90	**72**	5		2 **Woman's Intuition**	*Steve Bogard/Rick Giles*	Arista
5/11/91	**73**	2		3 **All You Really Wanna Do**	*Steve Bogard/Rick Giles*	Arista
				above 3 from the album *New Kind Of Love* on Arista 8627		
4/4/92	**10**	20		4 **Take It Like A Man**	*Tony Haselden*	Arista
7/25/92	**43**	19		5 **One Time Around**	*Chapin Hartford/Don Pfrimmer*	Arista
10/31/92	**31**	17		6 **He Would Be Sixteen**	*Charlie Black/Jill Colucci/Austin Roberts*	Arista
2/27/93	**55**	7		7 **The Change**	*Steve Bogard/Rick Giles*	Arista
				above 4 from the album *Now & Then* on Arista 18685		
7/30/94	**57**	8		8 **One Good Man**	*Steve Bogard/Rick Giles*	Arista
				from the album *The Reasons Why* on Arista 18753		
7/13/96	**50**	10		9 **Nobody's Girl**	*Gretchen Peters*	Arista
				from the album *For Me It's You* on Arista 18815		
1/22/00	**74**	2		10 **Your Love** *[w/ Jim Brickman]*	*Jim Brickman/Dane DeVillar/Sean Hosein*	Windham Hill
				from Brickman's album *Destiny* on Windham Hill 11396		
				WRIGHT, Randy		
				Born on 9/11/1956 in Troy, Missouri. Male singer/drummer.		
11/5/83	**86**	3		1 **There's Nobody Lovin' At Home**	*Charlie Black/Kerry Chater/Tommy Rocco*	MCA 52273
5/12/84	**77**	4		2 **If You're Serious About Cheating**	*R.C. Bannon/John Schweers*	MCA 52358
				WRIGHT, Ruby		
				Born on 10/27/1939 in Nashville, Tennessee. Female singer/songwriter. Daughter of **Kitty Wells** and **Johnny Wright**; sister of **Bobby Wright**.		
9/5/64	**13**	13		1 **Dern Ya**	*Roger Miller/Justin Tubb* **[N]**	RIC 126
				answer to "Dang Me" by **Roger Miller**		
11/5/66	**72**	2		2 **A New Place To Hang Your Hat**	*Curly Putman/Ruby Wright*	Epic 10055
5/27/67	**69**	7		3 **(I Can Find) A Better Deal Than That**	*Stu Basore*	Epic 10150

DEBUT	PEAK	WKS	GOLD	ARTIST / Country Chart Hit	Songwriter	Label (& Number)

WRIGHT, Sonny

Born Nathan Edward Wright on 2/2/1943 in Flagler, Colorado. Male singer. Married to **Peggy Sue**.

DEBUT	PEAK	WKS	GOLD	Country Chart Hit	Songwriter	Label (& Number)
10/22/77	100	1		1 **If This Is What Love's All About** *[w/ Peggy Sue]*	*Dave Hall/Danny Walls*	Door Knob 038
11/10/79	86	5		2 **Gently Hold Me** *[w/ Peggy Sue]*	*Mack Jackson*	Door Knob 113
4/26/80	91	4		3 **Molly (And The Texas Rain)**	*Fred Chaudier*	Door Knob 128

WRIGHT BROTHERS, The

Vocal trio from Bedford, Indiana: brothers Tom Wright and Tim Wright, with Karl Hinkle. John McDowell replaced Hinkle in early 1984.

DEBUT	PEAK	WKS	GOLD	Country Chart Hit	Songwriter	Label (& Number)
10/31/81	35	12		1 **Family Man**	*Alan Rhody*	Warner 49837
4/3/82	42	11		2 **When You Find Her, Keep Her**	*Michael Garvin/Tom Shapiro/Chris Waters*	Warner 50033
9/4/82	40	8		3 **Made In The U.S.A.**	*Bobby Emmons/Chips Moman*	Warner 29926
1/8/83	68	5		4 **So Easy To Love**	*Todd Cerney/Steve Diamond/Austin Roberts*	Warner 29839
3/31/84	33	13		5 **Southern Women**	*Kent Blazy/Mickey Hiter/John Mohead*	Mercury 818653
8/11/84	46	11		6 **So Close**	*Kent Blazy*	Mercury 880055
11/3/84	57	9		7 **Eight Days A Week**	*John Lennon/Paul McCartney*	Mercury 880316
3/30/85	48	10		8 **Fire In The Sky**	*Johnny Cymbal*	Mercury 880596
9/10/88	85	3		9 **Come On Rain**	*Dennis Linde*	Airborne 10006

WYATT, Gene

Born in 1937 in Shreveport, Louisiana. Died in 1979 (age 42). Male singer. Cousin of **Chuck Pollard**.

DEBUT	PEAK	WKS	GOLD	Country Chart Hit	Songwriter	Label (& Number)
3/23/68	74	2		1 **I Stole The Flowers From Your Garden**	*Jim Single*	Mercury 72752
8/17/68	69	3		2 **I Just Ain't Got (As Much As He's Got Going For Me)**	*Howard Hausey*	Paula 308

WYATT, Nina

Born in Waldorf, Maryland. Female singer.

DEBUT	PEAK	WKS	GOLD	Country Chart Hit	Songwriter	Label (& Number)
1/30/88	76	3		1 **Richer Now With You**	*R.J. Cannon*	Charta 207
8/20/88	88	2		2 **After The Passion Leaves**	*B.J. Sollenberger*	Charta 210

WYATT BROTHERS

Vocal duo: brothers Jerry Wyatt and Tim Wyatt.

DEBUT	PEAK	WKS	GOLD	Country Chart Hit	Songwriter	Label (& Number)
12/27/86+	79	5		**Wyatt Liquor**	*Jerry Wyatt/Tim Wyatt*	Wyatt 103

WYNETTE, Tammy — 1960s: #41 / 1970s: #7 / All-Time: #28 // HOF: 1998

Born Virginia Wynette Pugh on 5/5/1942 in Itawamba County, Mississippi. Died of a blood clot on 4/6/1998 (age 55). Female singer/songwriter. Married to **George Jones** from 1969-75. Married her manager George Richey (brother of **Wyley McPherson**) on 7/6/1978. Known as "The First Lady of Country Music."

CMA: Female Vocalist 1968, 1969 & 1970 // OPRY: 1970

DEBUT	PEAK	WKS	GOLD	Country Chart Hit	Songwriter	Label (& Number)
12/10/66+	44	9		1 **Apartment #9**	*Fern Foley/Fuzzy Owen/Johnny Paycheck*	Epic 10095
3/18/67	3[2]	21		2 **Your Good Girl's Gonna Go Bad**	*Billy Sherrill/Glenn Sutton*	Epic 10134
7/15/67	❶[2]	18		3 **My Elusive Dreams** *[w/ David Houston]*	*Curly Putman/Billy Sherrill*	Epic 10194
8/26/67	❶[3]	20		4 **I Don't Wanna Play House**	*Billy Sherrill/Glenn Sutton*	Epic 10211
				Grammy: Female Vocal		
1/6/68	❶[1]	17		5 **Take Me To Your World**	*Billy Sherrill/Glenn Sutton*	Epic 10269
1/20/68	11	14		6 **It's All Over** *[w/ David Houston]*	*Billy Sherrill/Glenn Sutton*	Epic 10274
5/18/68	❶[3]	17		7 **D-I-V-O-R-C-E**	*Bobby Braddock/Curly Putman*	Epic 10315
10/19/68	❶[3]	21		8 **Stand By Your Man**	*Billy Sherrill/Tammy Wynette*	Epic 10398
				Grammy: Female Vocal & Hall of Fame; also see #73 below		
4/12/69	❶[2]	14		9 **Singing My Song**	*Billy Sherrill/Glenn Sutton/Tammy Wynette*	Epic 10462
8/30/69	❶[2]	16		10 **The Ways To Love A Man**	*Billy Sherrill/Glenn Sutton/Tammy Wynette*	Epic 10512
1/31/70	2[2]	14		11 **I'll See Him Through**	*Billy Sherrill/Norro Wilson*	Epic 10571
5/23/70	❶[3]	16		12 **He Loves Me All The Way**	*Billy Sherrill/Carmol Taylor/Norro Wilson*	Epic 10612
9/12/70	❶[2]	15		13 **Run, Woman, Run**	*Ann Booth/Duke Goff/Dan Hoffman*	Epic 10653
11/28/70+	5	13		14 **The Wonders You Perform**	*Jerry Chesnut*	Epic 10687
3/6/71	2[3]	15		15 **We Sure Can Love Each Other**	*Billy Sherrill/Tammy Wynette*	Epic 10707
7/17/71	❶[2]	15		16 **Good Lovin' (Makes It Right)**	*Billy Sherrill*	Epic 10759
12/25/71+	9	13		17 **Take Me** *[w/ George Jones]*	*George Jones/Leon Payne*	Epic 10815
1/1/72	❶[1]	14		18 **Bedtime Story**	*Billy Sherrill/Glenn Sutton*	Epic 10818
5/20/72	2[2]	14		19 **Reach Out Your Hand**	*Billy Sherrill/Tammy Wynette*	Epic 10856
7/8/72	6	15		20 **The Ceremony** *[w/ George Jones]*	*Billy Sherrill/Jenny Strickland/Carmol Taylor*	Epic 10881
9/16/72	❶[1]	14		21 **My Man**	*Billy Sherrill/Carmol Taylor/Norro Wilson*	Epic 10909
11/25/72+	38	9		22 **Old Fashioned Singing** *[w/ George Jones]*	*Earl Montgomery/Tammy Wynette*	Epic 10923
12/30/72+	❶[1]	15		23 **'Til I Get It Right**	*Larry Henley/Red Lane*	Epic 10940
4/7/73	❶[1]	17		24 **Kids Say The Darndest Things**	*Billy Sherrill/Glenn Sutton*	Epic 10969
4/7/73	32	9		25 **Let's Build A World Together** *[w/ George Jones]*	*George Richey/Carmol Taylor/Norro Wilson*	Epic 10963
9/1/73	❶[2]	17		26 **We're Gonna Hold On** *[w/ George Jones]*	*George Jones/Earl Montgomery*	Epic 11031
12/29/73+	❶[2]	15		27 **Another Lonely Song**	*Billy Sherrill/Norro Wilson/Tammy Wynette*	Epic 11079
2/9/74	15	13		28 **(We're Not) The Jet Set** *[w/ George Jones]*	*Bobby Braddock*	Epic 11083

Billboard DEBUT	PEAK	WKS	GOLD	ARTIST / Country Chart Hit	Ranking / Songwriter	Label (& Number)
				WYNETTE, Tammy — cont'd		
7/27/74	**8**	12		29 **We Loved It Away** *[w/ George Jones]*	*George Richey/Carmol Taylor*	Epic 11151
8/17/74	**4**	16		30 **Woman To Woman**	*Billy Sherrill*	Epic 50008
2/15/75	**4**	16		31 **(You Make Me Want To Be) A Mother**	*Billy Sherrill/Norro Wilson*	Epic 50071
5/17/75	**25**	13		32 **God's Gonna Get'cha (For That)** *[w/ George Jones]*	*E.E. Collins*	Epic 50099
9/20/75	**13**	13		33 **I Still Believe In Fairy Tales**	*Glenn Martin*	Epic 50145
2/14/76	❶[1]	15		34 **'Til I Can Make It On My Own**	*George Richey/Billy Sherrill/Tammy Wynette*	Epic 50196
6/5/76	❶[1]	15		35 **Golden Ring** *[w/ George Jones]*	*Bobby Braddock/Rafe Van Hoy*	Epic 50235
8/21/76	❶[2]	16		36 **You And Me**	*George Richey/Billy Sherrill*	Epic 50264
12/11/76+	❶[2]	16		37 **Near You** *[w/ George Jones]*	*Francis Craig/Kermit Goell*	Epic 50314
3/19/77	**6**	14		38 **(Let's Get Together) One Last Time**	*George Richey/Billy Sherrill*	Epic 50349
7/16/77	**5**	13		39 **Southern California** *[w/ George Jones]*	*Roger Bowling/George Richey/Billy Sherrill*	Epic 50418
10/8/77	**6**	15		40 **One Of A Kind**	*Steve Davis/Billy Sherrill*	Epic 50450
4/22/78	**26**	11		41 **I'd Like To See Jesus (On The Midnight Special)**	*Robert Seay/Dorval Smith*	Epic 50538
7/15/78	**3**[2]	15		42 **Womanhood**	*Bobby Braddock*	Epic 50574
2/10/79	**6**	13		43 **They Call It Making Love**	*Bobby Braddock*	Epic 50661
6/9/79	**7**	14		44 **No One Else In The World**	*Steve Davis/Billy Sherrill*	Epic 50722
3/1/80	**2**[1]	14		45 **Two Story House** *[w/ George Jones]*	*David Lindsey/Glenn Tubb/Tammy Wynette*	Epic 50849
4/19/80	**17**	14		46 **He Was There (When I Needed You)**	*Sue Richards*	Epic 50868
8/9/80	**17**	13		47 **Starting Over**	*Bob McDill*	Epic 50915
9/6/80	**19**	11		48 **A Pair Of Old Sneakers** *[w/ George Jones]*	*Larry Kingston/Glenn Sutton*	Epic 50930
3/21/81	**21**	12		49 **Cowboys Don't Shoot Straight (Like They Used To)**	*Bobby Emmons/Chips Moman*	Epic 51011
9/5/81	**18**	14		50 **Crying In The Rain**	*Howard Greenfield/Carole King*	Epic 02439
3/27/82	**8**	17		51 **Another Chance**	*Bob Drawdy/Dennis Knutson/Jerry Taylor*	Epic 02770
8/14/82	**16**	16		52 **You Still Get To Me In My Dreams**	*A.L. "Doodle" Owens/Bill Shore*	Epic 03064
12/11/82+	**19**	15		53 **A Good Night's Love**	*Tim DuBois/Chester Lester*	Epic 03384
4/23/83	**46**	9		54 **I Just Heard A Heart Break (And I'm So Afraid It's Mine)**	*George Richey/Jerry Taylor/Tammy Wynette*	Epic 03811
7/9/83	**63**	7		55 **Unwed Fathers**	*Bobby Braddock/John Prine*	Epic 03971
10/1/83	**63**	6		56 **Still In The Ring**	*Michael Garvin/Bucky Jones*	Epic 04101
6/2/84	**40**	15		57 **Lonely Heart**	*Paul Overstreet*	Epic 04467
2/23/85	**6**	22		58 **Sometimes When We Touch** *[w/ Mark Gray]*	A:5 / S:6 *Dan Hill/Barry Mann*	Columbia 04782
7/13/85	**48**	9		59 **You Can Lead A Heart To Love (But You Can't Make It Fall)**	*Joe Chambers/Larry Jenkins/Mike Twitty*	Epic 05399
8/30/86	**53**	8		60 **Alive And Well**	*Michael Garvin/Bucky Jones*	Epic 06263
8/1/87	**12**	19		61 **Your Love**	S:7 *Beckie Foster/Tommy Rocco*	Epic 07226
				Ricky Skaggs (harmony vocal)		
12/5/87+	**16**	20		62 **Talkin' To Myself Again**	S:15 *Jamie O'Hara*	Epic 07635
				The O'Kanes (harmony vocals)		
5/7/88	**25**	15		63 **Beneath A Painted Sky**	S:24 *Joe Chambers/Bucky Jones*	Epic 07788
				Emmylou Harris (harmony vocal)		
2/18/89	**51**	11		64 **Next To You**	*Allen Estes/Chris Hill*	Epic 68570
5/27/89	**66**	6		65 **Thank The Cowboy For The Ride**	*Ed Bruce/Paul Richey*	Epic 68894
10/7/89	**63**	5		66 **While The Feeling's Good** *[w/ Wayne Newton]*	*Roger Bowling/Freddie Hart*	Curb 10559
9/1/90	**57**	8		67 **Let's Call It A Day Today**	*Byron Gallimore/Don Pfrimmer*	Epic
2/2/91	**56**	8		68 **What Goes With Blue**	*Dave Gibson/Paul Nelson*	Epic
				above 2 from the album *Heart Over Mind* on Epic 46238		
8/24/91	**49**	8		69 **We're Strangers Again** *[w/ Randy Travis]*	*Merle Haggard/Leona Williams*	Epic
				from Wynette's album *Best Loved Hits* on Epic 48588		
12/25/93+	**68**	2		70 **Silver Threads And Golden Needles** *[w/ Dolly Parton & Loretta Lynn]*		
				from their album *Honky Tonk Angels* on Columbia 53414	...*Dick Reynolds/Jack Rhodes*	Columbia
10/8/94	**67**	9		71 **Girl Thang** *[w/ Wynonna]*	*Keith Hinton/Michael Laybourn/Judy Rodman*	Epic
				from Wynette's album *Without Walls* on Epic 52481		
7/1/95	**69**	4		72 **One** *[w/ George Jones]*	*Ed Bruce/Judith Bruce/Ron Peterson*	MCA
				from their album *One* on MCA 11248		
4/25/98	**56**	1		73 **Stand By Your Man**	*Billy Sherrill/Tammy Wynette* **[R]**	Epic
				same version as #8 above; from the album *Super Hits* on Epic 67539		

Alive And Well ['86]
Another Chance ['82]
Another Lonely Song ['74]
Apartment #9 ['67]
Bedtime Story ['72]
Beneath A Painted Sky ['88]
Ceremony ['72]
Cowboys Don't Shoot Straight (Like They Used To) ['81]
Crying In The Rain ['81]
D-I-V-O-R-C-E ['68]
Girl Thang ['94]
God's Gonna Get'cha (For That) ['75]
Golden Ring ['76]
Good Lovin' (Makes It Right) ['71]
Good Night's Love ['83]
He Loves Me All The Way ['70]
He Was There (When I Needed You) ['80]
I Don't Wanna Play House ['67]
I Just Heard A Heart Break (And I'm So Afraid It's Mine) ['83]
I Still Believe In Fairy Tales ['75]
I'd Like To See Jesus (On The Midnight Special) ['78]
I'll See Him Through ['70]
It's All Over ['68]
Kids Say The Darndest Things ['73]
Let's Build A World Together ['73]
Let's Call It A Day Today ['90]
(Let's Get Together) One Last Time ['77]
Lonely Heart ['84]
My Elusive Dreams ['67]
My Man ['72]
Near You ['77]
Next To You ['89]
No One Else In The World ['79]
Old Fashioned Singing ['73]
One ['95]
One Of A Kind ['77]
Pair Of Old Sneakers ['80]
Reach Out Your Hand ['72]
Run, Woman, Run ['70]
Silver Threads And Golden Needles ['94]
Singing My Song ['69]
Sometimes When We Touch ['85]
Southern California ['77]
Stand By Your Man ['68, '98]
Starting Over ['80]
Still In The Ring ['83]
Take Me ['72]
Take Me To Your World ['68]
Talkin' To Myself Again ['88]
Thank The Cowboy For The Ride ['89]
They Call It Making Love ['79]
'Til I Can Make It On My Own ['76]
'Til I Get It Right ['73]
Two Story House ['80]
Unwed Fathers ['83]
Ways To Love A Man ['69]
We Loved It Away ['74]
We Sure Can Love Each Other ['71]
We're Gonna Hold On ['73]
(We're Not) The Jet Set ['74]
We're Strangers Again ['91]
What Goes With Blue ['91]
While The Feeling's Good ['89]
Woman To Woman ['74]
Womanhood ['78]
Wonders You Perform ['71]
You And Me ['76]
You Can Lead A Heart To Love (But You Can't Make It Fall) ['85]
(You Make Me Want To Be) A Mother ['75]
You Still Get To Me In My Dreams ['82]
Your Good Girl's Gonna Go Bad ['67]
Your Love ['87]

Billboard DEBUT	PEAK	WKS	GOLD	ARTIST Country Chart Hit	Ranking / Songwriter	Label (& Number)

WYNONNA

1990s: #32 / All-Time: #145

Born Christina Ciminella (her biological father was Charlie Jordan) on 5/30/1964 in Ashland, Kentucky. Female singer/guitarist. Began performing in 1977. Half of **The Judds** duo with her mother, Naomi, from 1983-91. Acted on TV's *Touched By An Angel*. Half-sister of actress Ashley Judd.

WYNONNA JUDD:

DEBUT	PEAK	WKS	GOLD	Country Chart Hit	Songwriter	Label (& Number)
2/15/92	❶[1]	20		1 **She Is His Only Need**	*Dave Loggins*	Curb/MCA
5/9/92	❶[3]	20		2 **I Saw The Light**	*Lisa Angelle/Andrew Gold*	Curb/MCA
8/15/92	❶[4]	20		3 **No One Else On Earth**	*Jill Colucci/Stewart Harris/Sam Lorber*	Curb/MCA
12/5/92+	4	20		4 **My Strongest Weakness**	*Naomi Judd/Mike Reid*	Curb/MCA
				above 4 from the album *Wynonna* on Curb/MCA 10529		
4/3/93	3[3]	20		5 **Tell Me Why**	*Karla Bonoff*	Curb/MCA
5/15/93	2[1]	20		6 **A Bad Goodbye** ***[w/ Clint Black]***	*Clint Black*	RCA
				from Black's album *No Time To Kill* on RCA 66239		
7/17/93	3[1]	20		7 **Only Love**	*Marcus Hummon/Roger Murrah*	Curb/MCA
10/30/93+	6	20		8 **Is It Over Yet**	*Billy Kirsch*	Curb/MCA
1/8/94	61	1		9 **Let's Make A Baby King**	*Jesse Winchester* **[X]**	Curb/MCA
2/19/94	2[1]	20		10 **Rock Bottom**	*Buddy Buie/J.R. Cobb*	Curb/MCA
6/4/94	10	20		11 **Girls With Guitars**	*Mary-Chapin Carpenter*	Curb/MCA
				#5 & 7-11: from the album *Tell Me Why* on Curb/MCA 10822		
10/8/94	67	9		12 **Girl Thang** ***[w/ Tammy Wynette]***	*Keith Hinton/Michael Laybourn/Judy Rodman*	Epic
				from Wynette's album *Without Walls* on Epic 52481		

WYNONNA:

DEBUT	PEAK	WKS	GOLD	Country Chart Hit	Songwriter	Label (& Number)
1/6/96	❶[1]	20		13 **To Be Loved By You**	*Gary Burr/Mike Reid*	Curb/MCA
4/27/96	14	20		14 **Heaven Help My Heart**	*Tina Arena/Dean McTaggart/David Tyson*	Curb/MCA
8/31/96	44	10		15 **My Angel Is Here**	*Mark Cawley/Billy Lawrie/Marie Lawrie*	Curb/MCA
11/16/96	55	6		16 **Somebody To Love You**	*Delbert McClinton/Gary Nicholson*	Curb/MCA
				above 4 from the album *Revelations* on Curb/MCA 11090		
1/4/97	55	2		17 **Mary, Did You Know** ***[w/ Kenny Rogers]***	*Buddy Greene/Mark Lowry* **[X]**	Magnatone
				from Rogers's album *The Gift* on Magnatone 108		
10/4/97	13	20		18 **When Love Starts Talkin'**	S:9 *Brent Maher/Gary Nicholson/Jamie O'Hara*	Curb/Universal
12/13/97+	14	20		19 **Come Some Rainy Day**	*Billy Kirsch/Bat McGrath*	Curb/Universal
4/25/98	45	10		20 **Always Will**	*John Hadley/Harry Stinson*	Curb/Universal
				above 3 from the album *The Other Side* on Curb/Universal 53061		
9/12/98	62	8		21 **Woman To Woman**	*Billy Sherrill*	Asylum
				from the various artists album ***Tammy Wynette*** *Remembered* on Asylum 62277		
12/5/98	68	4		22 **Freedom**	*Laythan Armor/Bunny Hull*	Curb/Universal
				from the various artists album *The Prince Of Egypt - Nashville* on DreamWorks 50045		
11/13/99+	31	20		23 **Can't Nobody Love You (Like I Do)**	S:6 *Cathy Majeski/Danny Orton*	Curb/Mercury
6/3/00	43	13		24 **Going Nowhere**	*Paul Begaud/Vanessa Corish/Kye Fleming*	Curb/Mercury
				above 2 from the album *New Day Dawning* on Curb/Mercury 541067		
5/10/03	14	20		25 **What The World Needs**	*Brett James/Holly Lamar*	Curb
9/13/03	37	15		26 **Heaven Help Me**	*Chuck Cannon/J.D. Hicks*	Asylum-Curb
1/24/04	33	18		27 **Flies On The Butter (You Can't Go Home Again)** ***[w/ Naomi Judd]***	*...Chuck Cannon/Austin Cunningham/Allen Shamblin*	Asylum-Curb
				above 3 from the album *What The World Needs Now Is Love* on Asylum-Curb 78811		

WYRICK, Jim, and Union Gold

Born in Maynardville, Tennessee. Male singer.

DEBUT	PEAK	WKS	GOLD	Country Chart Hit	Songwriter	Label (& Number)
2/26/83	85	2		**The Memory**	*Roger Bowling/Billy Edd Wheeler*	NSD 157

Y

YANKEE GREY

Group from Cincinnati, Ohio: Tim Hunt (vocals, guitar), Matt Basford (guitar), Joe Caverlee (fiddle), Jerry Hughes (keyboards), Dave Buchanan (bass) and Kevin Griffin (drums).

DEBUT	PEAK	WKS	GOLD	Country Chart Hit	Songwriter	Label (& Number)
6/26/99	8	33		1 **All Things Considered**	S:3 *Tim Hunt*	Monument
1/15/00	15	22		2 **Another Nine Minutes**	*Tim Buppert/Billy Crain/Tom Douglas*	Monument
7/1/00	43	14		3 **This Time Around**	*Joe Caverlee/Terry Clayton/Tim Hunt*	Monument
				above 3 from the album *Untamed* on Monument 69085		

YANKOVIC, Frankie, & His Yanks

1940s: #49

Born on 7/28/1915 in Davis, West Virginia; raised in Cleveland. Died on 10/14/1998 (age 83). Accordionist/polka bandleader. Known as "America's Polka King."

DEBUT	PEAK	WKS	GOLD	Country Chart Hit	Songwriter	Label (& Number)
5/8/48	7	1		1 **Just Because**	*Sid Robin/Bob Shelton/Joe Shelton*	Columbia 12359
1/1/49	13	1		2 **The Iron Range**	S:13 *John Pecon* **[I]**	Columbia 12381
4/30/49	7	7	●	3 **Blue Skirt Waltz** ***[w/ The Marlin Sisters]***	S:7 / J:10 *Vaclav Blaha/Mitchell Parish*	Columbia 12394

YARBROUGH, Bob

Born in 1940 in Chattanooga, Tennessee. Male singer.

DEBUT	PEAK	WKS	GOLD	Country Chart Hit	Songwriter	Label (& Number)
5/22/71	38	12		1 **You're Just More A Woman**	*Teresa Stamps*	Sugar Hill 013
4/17/76	85	5		2 **50 Ways To Leave Your Lover** ***[Bob Yarborough]***	*Paul Simon*	Music Mill 186

DEBUT	PEAK	WKS	GOLD	ARTIST / Country Chart Hit	Ranking / Songwriter	Label (& Number)
				YATES, Billy		
				Born on 3/13/1963 in Doniphan, Missouri. Male singer/songwriter.		
5/10/97	**69**	3		1 **I Smell Smoke**	*Monty Criswell/Lee Miller/Billy Yates*	Almo Sounds
5/24/97	**36**	16		2 **Flowers**	*Monty Criswell/Billy Yates*	Almo Sounds
10/4/97	**69**	1		3 **When The Walls Come Tumblin' Down**	*Monty Criswell/Billy Yates*	Almo Sounds
				above 3 from the album *Billy Yates* on Almo Sounds 80015		
11/18/00+	**53**	10		4 **What Do You Want From Me Now**	S:20 *Mike Geiger/Bobby Taylor/Billy Yates*	Columbia
				YATES, Jenny		
				Born in Phoenix, Arizona. Female singer/songwriter/guitarist.		
4/25/87	**80**	3		**A Whole Month Of Sundays**	*Dan Darst/Jenny Yates*	Mercury 888428
				YATES, Lori		
				Born in Toronto, Ontario, Canada. Female singer/songwriter.		
11/12/88	**77**	5		1 **Scene Of The Crime**	*Steve Buckingham/Don Schlitz/Lori Yates*	Columbia 08055
3/25/89	**78**	4		2 **Promises, Promises**	*Matraca Berg/Lori Yates*	Columbia 68596

DEBUT	PEAK	WKS	GOLD	ARTIST / Country Chart Hit	Ranking / Songwriter	Label (& Number)
				YEARWOOD, Trisha	**1990s: #14 / 2000s: #49 / All-Time: #89**	
				Born Patricia Lynn Yearwood on 9/19/1964 in Monticello, Georgia. Female singer. Majored in music business at Belmont University in Nashville. Married to fellow student Chris Latham from 1987-91. Married to Robert Reynolds of **The Mavericks** from 1994-99. Engaged to **Garth Brooks** on 5/25/2005. Also see **Hope**.		
				CMA: Female Vocalist 1997 & 1998 // OPRY: 1999		
5/18/91	**❶[2]**	20		1 **She's In Love With The Boy**	*Jon Ims*	MCA
9/14/91	**4**	20		2 **Like We Never Had A Broken Heart**	*Pat Alger/Garth Brooks*	MCA
12/21/91+	**8**	20		3 **That's What I Like About You**	*John Hadley/Kevin Welch/Wally Wilson*	MCA
3/28/92	**4**	20		4 **The Woman Before Me**	*Jude Johnstone*	MCA
				above 4 from the album *Trisha Yearwood* on MCA 10297		
8/8/92	**5**	20		5 **Wrong Side Of Memphis**	*Matraca Berg/Gary Harrison*	MCA
11/7/92+	**2[1]**	20		6 **Walkaway Joe** *[w/ Don Henley]*	*Greg Barnhill/Vince Melamed*	MCA
3/6/93	**12**	20		7 **You Say You Will**	*Beth Nielsen Chapman/Verlon Thompson*	MCA
6/12/93	**19**	20		8 **Down On My Knees**	*Beth Nielsen Chapman*	MCA
				above 4 from the album *Hearts In Armor* on MCA 10641		
10/16/93	**2[1]**	20		9 **The Song Remembers When**	*Hugh Prestwood*	MCA
2/5/94	**21**	20		10 **Better Your Heart Than Mine**	*Lisa Angelle/Andrew Gold*	MCA
				above 2 from the album *The Song Remembers When* on MCA 10911		
6/4/94	**72**	2		11 **I Fall To Pieces** *[w/ Aaron Neville]*	*Hank Cochran/Harlan Howard*	MCA
				Grammy: Vocal Collaboration; from the various artists album *Rhythm Country & Blues* on MCA 10965		
7/9/94	**❶[2]**	20		12 **XXX's And OOO's (An American Girl)**	*Matraca Berg/Alice Randall*	MCA
12/17/94+	**60**	4		13 **It Wasn't His Child**	*Skip Ewing* **[X]**	MCA
				from the album *The Sweetest Gift* on MCA 11091		
1/14/95	**❶[2]**	20		14 **Thinkin' About You**	*Bob Regan/Tom Shapiro*	MCA
4/29/95	**23**	15		15 **You Can Sleep While I Drive**	S:19 *Melissa Etheridge*	MCA
8/5/95	**9**	20		16 **I Wanna Go Too Far**	*Layng Martine Jr./Kent Robbins*	MCA
12/2/95+	**59**	8		17 **On A Bus To St. Cloud**	*Gretchen Peters*	MCA
				#12 & 14-17: from the album *Thinkin' About You* on MCA 11201		
7/13/96	**❶[2]**	20		18 **Believe Me Baby (I Lied)**	*Larry Gottlieb/Angelo Petraglia/Kim Richey*	MCA
11/9/96+	**3[1]**	20		19 **Everybody Knows**	*Matraca Berg/Gary Harrison*	MCA
3/1/97	**36**	13		20 **I Need You**	*Jess Brown/Wendell Mobley*	MCA
				above 3 from the album *Everybody Knows* on MCA 11477		
6/7/97	**2[1]**	20		21 **How Do I Live**	S:3 *Diane Warren*	MCA
				Grammy: Female Vocal; from the movie *Con Air* starring Nicolas Cage		
8/23/97	**2[2]**	20		22 **In Another's Eyes** *[w/ Garth Brooks]*	*Garth Brooks/John Peppard/Bobby Wood*	MCA
				Grammy: Vocal Collaboration		
1/17/98	**❶[2]**	20		23 **A Perfect Love**	*Sunny Russ/Stephony Smith*	MCA
				above 3 from the album *Songbook - A Collection Of Hits* on MCA 70011		
5/9/98	**2[1]**	23		24 **There Goes My Baby**	S:15 *Annie Roboff/Arnie Roman*	MCA Nashville
9/19/98	**18**	20		25 **Where Your Road Leads** *[w/ Garth Brooks]*	*Desmond Child/Victoria Shaw*	MCA Nashville
11/28/98+	**6**	20		26 **Powerful Thing**	*Al Anderson/Sharon Vaughn*	MCA Nashville
12/5/98	**65**	1		27 **Wild As The Wind** *[w/ Garth Brooks]*	*Charles Quatro/Pete Wasner*	Capitol
				from Brooks's album *Double Live* on Capitol 97424		
1/9/99	**63**	1		28 **Reindeer Boogie**	*Charlie Faircloth/Hank Snow/Cordia Volkmar* **[X]**	MCA
				from the album *The Sweetest Gift* on MCA 11091		
5/8/99	**10**	25		29 **I'll Still Love You More**	*Diane Warren*	MCA Nashville
				#24-26 & 29: from the album *Where Your Road Leads* on MCA Nashville 70023		
12/25/99	**72**	1		30 **Santa On The Rooftop** *[w/ Rosie O'Donnell]*	*Annie Roboff/Arnie Roman* **[X]**	Columbia
				from O'Donnell's album *A Rosie Christmas* on Columbia 63685		
1/15/00	**16**	20		31 **Real Live Woman**	*Bobbie Cryner*	MCA Nashville
2/12/00	**71**	1		32 **You're Where I Belong**	*Diane Warren*	Motown
				from the movie *Stuart Little* starring Geena Davis (soundtrack on Motown 542083)		
6/17/00	**45**	13		33 **Where Are You Now**	*Mary-Chapin Carpenter/Kim Richey*	MCA Nashville
				#31 & 33: from the album *Real Live Woman* on MCA Nashville 70102		
4/7/01	**4**	31		34 **I Would've Loved You Anyway**	*Mary Danna/Troy Verges*	MCA Nashville

Billboard DEBUT	PEAK	WKS	GOLD	ARTIST / Country Chart Hit	Ranking / Songwriter	Label (& Number)
				YEARWOOD, Trisha — cont'd		
12/1/01+	16	20		35 **Squeeze Me In** *[w/ Garth Brooks]*	*Delbert McClinton/Gary Nicholson*	Capitol
				from Brooks's album *Scarecrow* on Capitol 31330		
12/1/01+	31	19		36 **Inside Out** *[w/ Don Henley]*	*Bryan Adams/Gretchen Peters*	MCA Nashville
7/13/02	47	6		37 **I Don't Paint Myself Into Corners**	*Trey Bruce/Rebecca Lynn Howard*	MCA Nashville
				above 2 from the album *Inside Out* on MCA Nashville 70200		
4/30/05	15	22↑		38 **Georgia Rain**	*Ed Hill/Karyn Rochelle*	MCA Nashville
				from the album *Jasper County* on MCA Nashville 023260		

YOAKAM, Dwight — **1990s: #39 / All-Time: #110**

Born on 10/23/1956 in Pikeville, Kentucky. Male singer/songwriter/guitarist/actor. Played in southern Ohio before moving to Los Angeles in the early 1980s. First recorded for Oak Records. Member of the **Buzzin' Cousins**. Acted in the movies *Sling Blade*, *The Newton Boys* and *Panic Room*. Also see **Same Old Train**.

DEBUT	PEAK	WKS	GOLD	Country Chart Hit	Songwriter	Label (& Number)
3/1/86	3^{1}	24		1 **Honky Tonk Man**	S:3 / A:4 *Tillman Franks/Howard Hausey/Johnny Horton*	Reprise 28793
7/12/86	4	21		2 **Guitars, Cadillacs**	S:3 / A:4 *Dwight Yoakam*	Reprise 28688
11/15/86	31	15		3 **It Won't Hurt**	S:22 / A:30 *Dwight Yoakam*	Reprise 28565
4/11/87	7	16		4 **Little Sister**	S:4 / A:21 *Doc Pomus/Mort Shuman*	Reprise 28432
7/25/87	8	19		5 **Little Ways**	S:4 *Dwight Yoakam*	Reprise 28310
11/14/87+	6	19		6 **Please, Please Baby**	S:6 *Dwight Yoakam*	Reprise 28174
3/5/88	9	22		7 **Always Late With Your Kisses**	S:5 *Blackie Crawford/Lefty Frizzell*	Reprise 27994
7/16/88	❶^{1}	18		8 **Streets Of Bakersfield** *[w/ Buck Owens]*	S:❶^{3} *Homer Joy*	Reprise 27964
11/12/88+	❶^{1}	21		9 **I Sang Dixie**	S:18 *Dwight Yoakam*	Reprise 27715
3/4/89	5	19		10 **I Got You**	*Dwight Yoakam*	Reprise 27567
6/24/89	46	7		11 **Buenas Noches From A Lonely Room (She Wore Red Dresses)**	*Dwight Yoakam*	Reprise 22944
9/30/89	35	10		12 **Long White Cadillac**	*Dave Alvin*	Reprise 22799
10/20/90+	11	20		13 **Turn It On, Turn It Up, Turn Me Loose**	*Kostas/Wayland Patton*	Reprise
3/2/91	5	20		14 **You're The One**	*Dwight Yoakam*	Reprise
8/10/91	15	21		15 **Nothing's Changed Here**	*Kostas/Dwight Yoakam*	Reprise
12/21/91+	7	20		16 **It Only Hurts When I Cry**	*Roger Miller/Dwight Yoakam*	Reprise
4/25/92	18	20		17 **The Heart That You Own**	*Dwight Yoakam*	Reprise
8/8/92	47	10		18 **Send A Message To My Heart** *[w/ Patty Loveless]*	*Kostas/Kelly Louvin*	Reprise
				#13-18: from the album *If There Was Any Other Way* on Reprise 26344		
10/24/92	35	20		19 **Suspicious Minds**	*Mark James*	Epic Soundtrax
				from the movie *Honeymoon In Vegas* starring James Caan (soundtrack on Epic Soundtrax 52845)		
3/13/93	2^{3}	20		20 **Ain't That Lonely Yet**	*James House/Kostas*	Reprise
				Grammy: Male Vocal		
6/26/93	2^{1}	20		21 **A Thousand Miles From Nowhere**	*Dwight Yoakam*	Reprise
7/3/93+	2^{1}	20		22 **Fast As You**	*Dwight Yoakam*	Reprise
2/19/94	14	20		23 **Try Not To Look So Pretty**	*Kostas/Dwight Yoakam*	Reprise
7/2/94	22	20		24 **Pocket Of A Clown**	*Dwight Yoakam*	Reprise
				above 5 from the album *This Time* on Reprise 45241		
10/14/95	20	20		25 **Nothing**	S:19 *Kostas/Dwight Yoakam*	Reprise
2/3/96	51	8		26 **Gone (That'll Be Me)**	*Dwight Yoakam*	Reprise
4/20/96	59	5		27 **Sorry You Asked?**	*Dwight Yoakam*	Reprise
				above 3 from the album *Gone* on Reprise 46051		
7/12/97	47	10		28 **Claudette**	*Roy Orbison*	Reprise
				from the album *Under The Covers* on Reprise 46690		
1/3/98	60	2		29 **Santa Claus Is Back In Town**	*Jerry Leiber/Mike Stoller* **[X]**	Reprise
				from the album *Come On Christmas* on Warner 46683		
5/2/98	17	20		30 **Things Change**	*Dwight Yoakam*	Reprise
9/19/98	57	6		31 **These Arms**	*Dwight Yoakam*	Reprise
				above 2 from the album *A Long Way Home* on Reprise 46918		
5/1/99	12	20		32 **Crazy Little Thing Called Love**	*Freddie Mercury*	Reprise
9/4/99	54	8		33 **Thinking About Leaving**	*Rodney Crowell/Dwight Yoakam*	Reprise
				above 2 from the album *Last Chance For A Thousand Years* on Reprise 47389		
9/30/00+	26	23		34 **What Do You Know About Love**	*Dwight Yoakam*	Reprise
5/26/01	49	8		35 **I Want You To Want Me**	*Rick Nielsen*	Reprise
				above 2 from the album *Tomorrow's Sounds Today* on Reprise 47827		
6/21/03	52	6		36 **The Back Of Your Hand**	*Gregg Henry*	Audium
8/2/03	52	9		37 **The Late Great Golden State**	*Mike Stinson*	Audium
				above 2 from the album *Population: Me* on Audium 8176		

YOUNG, Cole

Born in Minneapolis, Minnesota. Male singer/songwriter.

DEBUT	PEAK	WKS	GOLD	Country Chart Hit	Songwriter	Label (& Number)
7/23/83	72	5		**Just Give Me One More Night**	*Don Goodman/Frank Green/Cole Young*	Evergreen 1008

Billboard			GOLD	ARTIST	Ranking	
DEBUT	PEAK	WKS		Country Chart Hit	Songwriter	Label (& Number)

YOUNG, Faron **1950s: #13 / 1960s: #10 / All-Time: #23 // HOF: 2000**

Born on 2/25/1932 in Shreveport, Louisiana. Died of a self-inflicted gunshot on 12/10/1996 (age 64). Male singer/songwriter/guitarist/actor. Joined the *Louisiana Hayride* in 1951. Served in the U.S. Army from 1952-54. Known as "The Young Sheriff." Acted in several movies. Founder and one-time publisher of the *Music City News* magazine. Also see **Heart Of Nashville**.

OPRY: 1954

DEBUT	PEAK	WKS	GOLD	Country Chart Hit	Songwriter	Label (& Number)
1/10/53	2^{1}	18		1 **Goin' Steady** (also see #66 below)	A:2 / J:7 / S:10 *Faron Young*	Capitol 2299
6/6/53	5	5		2 **I Can't Wait** (For The Sun To Go Down)	A:5 *Chet Atkins/Martha Carson/Sid Kessel*	Capitol 2461
9/4/54	8	9		3 **A Place For Girls Like You**	A:8 / S:13 *Joe Hayes*	Capitol 2859
11/20/54+	2^{3}	27		4 **If You Ain't Lovin'** (You Ain't Livin')	J:2 / A:2 / S:3 *Tommy Collins*	Capitol 2953
4/2/55	❶^{3}	22		5 **Live Fast, Love Hard, Die Young /**	A:❶^{3} / J:2 / S:3 *Joe Allison*	
4/9/55	flip	12		6 **Forgive Me, Dear**	J:flip *George Jones/Faron Young*	Capitol 3056
8/6/55	11	9		7 **Go Back You Fool /**	S:11 / J:flip *Hal Blair/Don Robertson*	
8/13/55	2^{4}	28		8 **All Right**	A:2 / J:3 / S:4 *Faron Young*	Capitol 3169
11/19/55+	5	13		9 **It's A Great Life** (If You Don't Weaken) **/**	A:5 / J:6 / S:7 *Audrey Allison/Joe Allison/Faron Young*	
12/17/55	flip	1		10 **For The Love Of A Woman Like You**	J:flip *Gertrude Cox/Jack Rhodes*	Capitol 3258
4/7/56	4	16		11 **I've Got Five Dollars And It's Saturday Night /**	J:4 / S:4 / A:10 *Ted Daffan*	
4/14/56	3^{1}	10		12 **You're Still Mine**	A:3 / S:5 / J:flip *Eddie Thorpe/Faron Young*	Capitol 3369
6/23/56	2^{1}	33		13 **Sweet Dreams /**	A:2 / J:4 / S:5 *Don Gibson*	
7/21/56	flip	3		14 **Until I Met You**	J:flip *George Jones/Faron Young*	Capitol 3443
11/10/56	9	6		15 **Turn Her Down /**	A:9 / S:13 *Ted Edlin/Faron Young*	
11/24/56	flip	1		16 **I'll Be Satisfied With Love**	S:flip *Gary Bryant/Wayne Walker*	Capitol 3549
2/23/57	5	13		17 **I Miss You Already** (And You're Not Even Gone) **/**	A:5 / S:8 *Marvin Rainwater/Faron Young*	
3/9/57	flip	1		18 **I'm Gonna Live Some Before I Die**	S:flip *Mae Boren Axton/Glenn Reeves*	Capitol 3611
5/20/57	15	1		19 **The Shrine Of St. Cecilia**	A:15 *Bert Carroll*	Capitol 3696
8/5/57	12	1		20 **Love Has Finally Come My Way**	A:12 *Lee Pockriss/Paul Vance*	Capitol 3753
6/23/58	❶^{13}	29		21 **Alone With You /**	A:❶^{13} / S:2 *Roy Drusky/Lester Vanadore/Faron Young*	
6/30/58	10	2		22 **Every Time I'm Kissing You**	A:10 *Carl Belew/Faron Young*	Capitol 3982
10/20/58	9	17		23 **That's The Way I Feel /**	*George Jones/Roger Miller*	
10/27/58	22	5		24 **I Hate Myself**	*Cliff Crofford*	Capitol 4050
1/26/59	20	10		25 **Last Night At A Party /**	*Roger Miller/Faron Young*	
2/2/59	16	9		26 **A Long Time Ago**	*Merle Kilgore/Faron Young*	Capitol 4113
4/13/59	14	8		27 **That's The Way It's Gotta Be**	*Roy Drusky*	Capitol 4164
7/20/59	❶^{4}	32		28 **Country Girl /**	*Roy Drusky*	
7/27/59	27	6		29 **I Hear You Talkin'**	*Faron Young*	Capitol 4233
11/16/59+	4	21		30 **Riverboat /**	*Bill Anderson*	
11/16/59+	10	18		31 **Face To The Wall**	*Bill Anderson/Faron Young*	Capitol 4291
4/11/60	5	17		32 **Your Old Used To Be**	*Faron Young*	Capitol 4351
10/24/60	21	5		33 **There's Not Any Like You Left**	*Faron Young*	Capitol 4410
12/26/60+	20	7		34 **Forget The Past /**	*Faron Young*	
1/16/61	28	3		35 **A World So Full Of Love**	*Roger Miller/Faron Young*	Capitol 4463
3/20/61	❶^{9}	23		36 **Hello Walls /** (**Grammy: Hall of Fame**)	*Willie Nelson*	
5/15/61	28	2		37 **Congratulations**	*Willie Nelson*	Capitol 4533
10/2/61	8	17		38 **Backtrack**	*Faron Young/Alex Zanetis*	Capitol 4616
3/24/62	7	13		39 **Three Days**	*Willie Nelson/Faron Young*	Capitol 4696
6/16/62	4	19		40 **The Comeback**	*Danny Dill*	Capitol 4754
12/22/62+	9	10		41 **Down By The River**	*Jan Crutchfield/Teddy Wilburn*	Capitol 4868
3/2/63	4	16		42 **The Yellow Bandana**	*Al Gorgoni/Steve Karliski/Larry Kobler*	Mercury 72085
6/1/63	30	1		43 **I've Come To Say Goodbye /**	*Hal Blair/Don Robertson*	
6/8/63	14	7		44 **Nightmare**	*Clint Ballard/Artie Rand*	Mercury 72114
10/26/63	13	7		45 **We've Got Something In Common**	*Jan Crutchfield*	Mercury 72167
12/21/63+	10	14		46 **You'll Drive Me Back** (Into Her Arms Again)	*Merle Kilgore/Miriam Lewis*	Mercury 72201
3/14/64	5	23		47 **Keeping Up With The Joneses** ***[w/ Margie Singleton]*** **/**	*Justin Tubb*	
3/28/64	40	6		48 **No Thanks, I Just Had One** ***[w/ Margie Singleton]***	*Bill Anderson*	Mercury 72237
7/25/64	48	2		49 **Old Courthouse /**	*Danny Dill/Wayne Walker*	
8/1/64	23	6		50 **Rhinestones**	*Merle Kilgore*	Mercury 72271
10/3/64	11	16		51 **My Friend On The Right**	*Red Lane/Faron Young*	Mercury 72313
12/5/64	38	8		52 **Another Woman's Man - Another Man's Woman** ***[w/ Margie Singleton]***	*Marlin Greene/Dan Pennington*	Mercury 72312
1/30/65	10	18		53 **Walk Tall**	*Don Wayne*	Mercury 72375
8/7/65	34	6		54 **Nothing Left To Lose**	*Dallas Frazier*	Mercury 72440
11/27/65+	14	13		55 **My Dreams**	*Herb Duncan*	Mercury 72490
10/15/66	7	16		56 **Unmitigated Gall**	*Mel Tillis*	Mercury 72617
4/8/67	48	8		57 **I Guess I Had Too Much To Dream Last Night**	*B.J. Moore/Ernie Rufty*	Mercury 72656
10/28/67+	14	16		58 **Wonderful World Of Women**	*Bobby Sykes/Wayne Walker*	Mercury 72728
3/9/68	14	16		59 **She Went A Little Bit Farther**	*Merle Kilgore/Mack Vickery*	Mercury 72774
8/3/68	8	16		60 **I Just Came To Get My Baby**	*Wayne Kemp*	Mercury 72827
3/1/69	25	13		61 **I've Got Precious Memories**	*Billy Deaton/Faron Young*	Mercury 72889

DEBUT	PEAK	WKS	GOLD	ARTIST / Ranking / Country Chart Hit	Songwriter	Label (& Number)
				YOUNG, Faron — cont'd		
7/12/69	2^{2}	16		62 **Wine Me Up**	*Billy Deaton/Faron Young*	Mercury 72936
11/1/69	4	14		63 **Your Time's Comin'**	*Kris Kristofferson/Shel Silverstein*	Mercury 72983
2/7/70	6	14		64 **Occasional Wife**	*Jim Kandy*	Mercury 73018
5/30/70	4	16		65 **If I Ever Fall In Love (With A Honky Tonk Girl)**	*Tom T. Hall*	Mercury 73065
10/10/70	5	12		66 **Goin' Steady** new version of #1 above	*Faron Young* **[R]**	Mercury 73112
3/27/71	6	17		67 **Step Aside**	*Ray Griff*	Mercury 73191
8/7/71	9	14		68 **Leavin' And Sayin' Goodbye**	*Jeannie Seely*	Mercury 73220
12/4/71+	❶^{2}	20		69 **It's Four In The Morning**	*Jerry Chesnut*	Mercury 73250
7/22/72	5	16		70 **This Little Girl Of Mine**	*Jan Crutchfield*	Mercury 73308
2/3/73	15	11		71 **She Fights That Lovin' Feeling**	*Jack Adams*	Mercury 73359
7/21/73	9	16		72 **Just What I Had In Mind**	*Ben Peters*	Mercury 73403
3/9/74	8	14		73 **Some Kind Of A Woman**	*Tommy Cash/Jimmy Peppers*	Mercury 73464
7/13/74	20	12		74 **The Wrong In Loving You**	*Toni Dae/Bobbi Odom*	Mercury 73500
11/30/74+	23	12		75 **Another You**	*Jimmy Peppers*	Mercury 73633
7/19/75	16	13		76 **Here I Am In Dallas**	*Ronny Hughes/Terry Ishmael/Lamar Morris*	Mercury 73692
12/13/75+	21	12		77 **Feel Again**	*John Virgin*	Mercury 73731
4/10/76	33	10		78 **I'd Just Be Fool Enough**	*Melvin Endsley*	Mercury 73782
10/9/76	30	11		79 **(The Worst You Ever Gave Me Was) The Best I Ever Had**	*Danny Hice/Ruby Hice*	Mercury 73847
7/9/77	25	11		80 **Crutches**	*Liz Anderson*	Mercury 73925
2/25/78	38	10		81 **Loving Here And Living There And Lying In Between**	*Tony Austin/Gene Dobbins/Johnny Wilson*	Mercury 55019
4/7/79	67	6		82 **The Great Chicago Fire**	*Bobby Fischer/Dave Kirby*	MCA 41004
7/14/79	70	5		83 **Second Hand Emotion /**	*Charlie Black/Rory Bourke*	
9/22/79	69	6		84 **That Over Thirty Look**	*Rick Klang*	MCA 41046
2/16/80	56	7		85 **(If I'd Only Known) It Was The Last Time**	*Archie Jordan/Naomi Martin*	MCA 41177
8/30/80	72	4		86 **Tearjoint**	*Donnie Fritts/Dan Penn*	MCA 41292
4/25/81	88	2		87 **Until The Bitter End**	*Tim Daniels/Gene Dobbins/Tommy Rocco*	MCA 51088
9/10/88	100	2		88 **Stop And Take The Time**	*Faron Young*	Step One 390
2/4/89	87	2		89 **Here's To You**	*Mel Holt*	Step One 397

All Right ['55]
Alone With You ['58]
Another Woman's Man - Another Man's Woman ['64]
Another You ['75]
Backtrack ['61]
Comeback ['62]
Congratulations ['61]
Country Girl ['59]
Crutches ['77]
Down By The River ['63]
Every Time I'm Kissing You ['58]
Face To The Wall ['60]
Feel Again ['76]
For The Love Of A Woman Like You ['55]
Forget The Past ['61]
Forgive Me, Dear ['55]
Go Back You Fool ['55]
Goin' Steady ['53, '70]
Great Chicago Fire ['79]
Hello Walls ['61]
Here I Am In Dallas ['75]
Here's To You ['89]
I Can't Wait (For The Sun To Go Down) ['53]
I Guess I Had Too Much To Dream Last Night ['67]
I Hate Myself ['58]
I Hear You Talkin' ['59]
I Just Came To Get My Baby ['68]
I Miss You Already (And You're Not Even Gone) ['57]
I'd Just Be Fool Enough ['76]
I'll Be Satisfied With Love ['56]
I'm Gonna Live Some Before I Die ['57]
I've Come To Say Goodbye ['63]
I've Got Five Dollars And It's Saturday Night ['56]
I've Got Precious Memories ['69]
If I Ever Fall In Love (With A Honky Tonk Girl) ['70]
(If I'd Only Known) It Was The Last Time ['80]
If You Ain't Lovin' (You Ain't Livin') ['55]
It's A Great Life (If You Don't Weaken) ['56]
It's Four In The Morning ['72]
Just What I Had In Mind ['73]
Keeping Up With The Joneses ['64]
Last Night At A Party ['59]
Leavin' And Sayin' Goodbye ['71]
Live Fast, Love Hard, Die Young ['55]
Long Time Ago ['59]
Love Has Finally Come My Way ['57]
Loving Here And Living There And Lying In Between ['78]
My Dreams ['66]
My Friend On The Right ['64]
Nightmare ['63]
No Thanks, I Just Had One ['64]
Nothing Left To Lose ['65]
Occasional Wife ['70]
Old Courthouse ['64]
Place For Girls Like You ['54]
Rhinestones ['64]
Riverboat ['60]
Second Hand Emotion ['79]
She Fights That Lovin' Feeling ['73]
She Went A Little Bit Farther ['68]
Shrine Of St. Cecilia ['57]
Some Kind Of A Woman ['74]
Step Aside ['71]
Stop And Take The Time ['88]
Sweet Dreams ['56]
Tearjoint ['80]
That Over Thirty Look ['79]
That's The Way I Feel ['58]
That's The Way It's Gotta Be ['59]
There's Not Any Like You Left ['60]
This Little Girl Of Mine ['72]
Three Days ['62]
Turn Her Down ['56]
Unmitigated Gall ['66]
Until I Met You ['56]
Until The Bitter End ['81]
Walk Tall ['65]
We've Got Something In Common ['63]
Wine Me Up ['69]
Wonderful World Of Women ['68]
World So Full Of Love ['61]
(Worst You Ever Gave Me Was) The Best I Ever Had ['76]
Wrong In Loving You ['74]
Yellow Bandana ['63]
You'll Drive Me Back (Into Her Arms Again) ['64]
You're Still Mine ['56]
Your Old Used To Be ['60]
Your Time's Comin' ['69]

YOUNG, Neil

Born on 11/12/1945 in Toronto, Ontario, Canada. Rock singer/songwriter/guitarist. Member of **Crosby, Stills, Nash & Young**. Inducted into the Rock and Roll Hall of Fame in 1995.

DEBUT	PEAK	WKS	Country Chart Hit	Songwriter	Label (& Number)
10/5/85	33	18	**Get Back To The Country**	A:29 *Neil Young*	Geffen 28883

YOUNG, Roger

Born in Yuma, Arizona. Male singer.

DEBUT	PEAK	WKS	Country Chart Hit	Songwriter	Label (& Number)
8/18/79	85	3	**Skip A Rope**	*Jack Moran/Glenn Tubb*	Dessa 79-2

YOUNG, Steve

Born on 7/12/1942 in Newnan, Georgia. Male singer/songwriter/guitarist.

DEBUT	PEAK	WKS	Country Chart Hit	Songwriter	Label (& Number)
2/5/77	84	5	**It's Not Supposed To Be That Way**	*Willie Nelson*	RCA 10868

YOUNGER, James & Michael

Duo of brothers from Edinburg, Texas: James Williams and Michael Williams.

DEBUT	PEAK	WKS	Country Chart Hit	Songwriter	Label (& Number)
			YOUNGER BROTHERS:		
4/24/82	68	5	1 **Lonely Hearts**	*Steve Davis*	MCA 52030
7/3/82	19	15	2 **Nothing But The Radio On**	*John Reid/Johnny Slate*	MCA 52076
12/11/82+	48	12	3 **There's No Substitute For You**	*W.T. Davidson/Mark Sameth*	MCA 52148
3/5/83	50	8	4 **Somewhere Down The Line**	*Lewis Anderson/Casey Kelly*	MCA 52183
			JAMES & MICHAEL YOUNGER:		
6/4/83	54	10	5 **A Taste Of The Wind**	*A. Michael Williams/James L. Williams*	MCA 52222
9/17/83	48	9	6 **Lovers On The Rebound**	*Fred Koller/Greg Timm*	MCA 52263
12/24/83+	65	8	7 **Shoot First, Ask Questions Later**	*Lewis Anderson*	MCA 52317
6/29/85	82	5	8 **My Special Angel**	*Jimmy Duncan*	Permian 82011
4/5/86	67	7	9 **Back On The Radio Again**	*Donnie Clark/Mike Daniel/A. Michael Williams/James L. Williams*	AIR 102
9/27/86	65	7	10 **She Wants To Marry A Cowboy**	*J.L. Williams*	AIR 106

DEBUT	PEAK	WKS	GOLD	ARTIST / Ranking / Country Chart Hit ... Songwriter	Label (& Number)
				YOUNGER BROTHERS BAND	
				Group from Leola, Pennsylvania. Led by Terry Gehman.	
9/8/84	**92**	2		**Making Love To Dixie** ... *Joe Henderson/Dan Mitchell*	ERP 04094

Z

DEBUT	PEAK	WKS	GOLD	ARTIST / Ranking / Country Chart Hit ... Songwriter	Label (& Number)
				ZACA CREEK	
				Group of brothers from Santa Ynez, California: Gates Foss (vocals), Scot Foss (guitar), Jeff Foss (keyboards) and James Foss (bass).	
9/23/89	**38**	11		1 **Sometimes Love's Not A Pretty Thing** ... *Charlie Black/Steve Bogard/Rory Bourke*	Columbia 69062
12/23/89+	**58**	6		2 **Ghost Town** ... *Charlie Black/Rory Bourke/Austin Roberts*	Columbia 73096
3/13/93	**70**	3		3 **Broken Heartland** ... *Bill LaBounty/Sam Lorber*	Giant
				from the album *Broken Heartland* on Giant 24491	
				ZADORA, Pia	
				Born Pia Schipani on 5/4/1954 in Hoboken, New Jersey. Female singer/actress. Appeared in several movies.	
3/31/79	**98**	1		1 **Tell Him** / ... *Bert Russell*	
4/28/79	**76**	3		2 **Bedtime Stories** ... *Van Stephenson*	Warner/Curb 8766
8/25/79	**65**	5		3 **I Know A Good Thing When I Feel It** ... *Bobby Lee Springfield*	Warner/Curb 49065
1/12/80	**55**	5		4 **Baby It's You** ... *Burt Bacharach/Mack David/Barney Williams*	Warner/Curb 49148
				ZEILER, Gayle	
				Born in Gilroy, California. Female singer. Ethel of **Ethel & The Shameless Hussies**.	
1/30/82	**78**	4		**No Place To Hide** ... *Kay Savage/Larry Stallings*	Equa 670

SONG TITLE SECTION

Lists, alphabetically, all titles from the Artist Section. The artist's name is listed with each title along with the highest position attained and the year the song peaked on the chart.

Some titles show the letter "**F**" as a position, indicating that the title was listed as a flip side and did not chart on its own.

A song with more than one charted version is listed once, with the artists' names listed below in chronological order. Many songs that have the <u>same title</u>, but are <u>different tunes</u>, are listed separately, with the highest peaking title listed first. This will make it easy to determine which songs are the same composition, the number of charted versions of a particular song, and which of these was the most popular.

Cross references have been used throughout to aid in finding a title.

Please keep the following in mind when searching for titles:

> Titles such as "I.O.U.," "P.T. 109," and "S.O.S." will be found at the beginning of their respective letters; however, titles such as "D-I-V-O-R-C-E" and "T-R-O-U-B-L-E," which are spellings of words, are listed with their regular spellings.
>
> Two-word titles that have the exact same spelling as one-word titles are listed together alphabetically whenever possible. ("Honky-Tonk Man" is listed directly before "Honkytonk Man.")
>
> Titles that are <u>identical</u>, except for an apostrophized word in one of the titles, are shown together whenever possible. ("Fallin' For You" appears immediately above "Falling For You.")

A

A-11
26/65 *Johnny Paycheck*
54/89 *Buck Owens*
85/76 **"A" My Name Is Alice** *Marie Osmond*
46/66 **"A" Team** *SSgt Barry Sadler*
Abilene
1/63 *George Hamilton IV*
24/77 *Sonny James*
Above And Beyond
3/60 *Buck Owens*
1/89 *Rodney Crowell*
16/98 **Absence Of The Heart** *Deana Carter*
16/81 **Acapulco** *Johnny Duncan*
89/79 **Accentuate The Positive** *Tommy O'Day*
16/60 **Accidently On Purpose** *George Jones*
4/56 **According To My Heart** *Jim Reeves*
1/89 **Ace In The Hole** *George Strait*
9/92 **Aces** *Suzy Bogguss*
5/62 **Aching, Breaking Heart** *George Jones*
Achy Breaky Heart
1/92 *Billy Ray Cyrus*
71/92 *Alvin & The Chipmunks*
50/85 **Acres Of Diamonds** *Benny Wilson*
86/90 **Across The Room From You** *Phil Cohron*
Act Naturally
1/63 *Buck Owens*
27/89 *Buck Owens & Ringo Starr*
3/95 **Adalida** *George Strait*
1/88 **Addicted** *Dan Seals*
4/94 **Addicted To A Dollar** *Doug Stone*
2/62 **Adios Amigo** *Jim Reeves*
4/77 **Adios Amigo** *Marty Robbins*
41/67 **Adorable Women** *Nat Stuckey*
64/84 **Adventures In Parodies** *Pinkard & Bowden*
14/49 **Afraid** *Rex Allen w/ Jerry Byrd*
22/73 **Afraid I'll Want To Love Her One More Time** *Billy "Crash" Craddock*
Afraid Of Losing You Again ..see: (I'm So)
50/78 **Afraid You'd Come Back** *Kenny Price*
50/99 **After A Kiss** *Pam Tillis*
4/84 **After All** *Ed Bruce*
39/03 **After All** *Brett James*
43/87 **After All** *Patty Loveless*
1/76 **After All The Good Is Gone** *Conway Twitty*
(After All These Years) ..see: I Still Love You
18/71 **After All They All Used To Belong To Me** *Hank Williams, Jr.*
1/89 **After All This Time** *Rodney Crowell*
6/70 **After Closing Time** *David Houston & Barbara Mandrell*
17/80 **After Hours** *Joe Stampley*
51/88 **After Last Night's Storm** *Ride The River*
79/88 **After Lovin' You** *Melissa Kay*
7/62 **After Loving You** *Eddy Arnold*
10/77 **(After Sweet Memories) Play Born To Lose Again** *Dottsy*
75/81 **After Texas** *Roy Head*
32/77 **After The Ball** *Johnny Cash*
After The Fire Is Gone
1/71 *Conway Twitty/Loretta Lynn*
17/74 *Willie Nelson & Tracy Nelson*
70/82 **After The Glitter Fades** *Stevie Nicks*
19/83 **After The Great Depression** *Razzy Bailey*
10/83 **After The Last Goodbye** *Gus Hardin*
13/92 **After The Lights Go Out** *Ricky Van Shelton*
16/82 **After The Love Slips Away** *Earl Thomas Conley*
40/77 **After The Lovin'** *Engelbert Humperdinck*
88/88 **After The Passion Leaves** *Nina Wyatt*
65/70 **After The Preacher's Gone** *Peggy Sue*
8/76 **After The Storm** *Wynn Stewart*
82/82 **After Tonight** *Deborah Allen*
22/71 **After You** *Jerry Wallace*
23/73 **After You** *Hank Williams, Jr.*
28/83 **After You** *Dan Seals*
Afternoon Delight
9/76 *Johnny Carver*
94/76 *Starland Vocal Band*
19/65 **Again** *Don Gibson*
66/92 **Against The Grain** *Garth Brooks*
53/00 **Against The Wind** *Brooks & Dunn*
36/80 **Age** *Jerry Reed*
20/68 **Age Of Worry** *Billy Walker*
21/77 **Agree To Disagree** *Little David Wilkins*
69/93 **Ain't Been A Train Through Here In Years** *Rick Vincent*
49/04 **Ain't Drinkin' Anymore** *Kevin Fowler*
65/99 **Ain't Enough Roses** *Lisa Brokop*
1/93 **Ain't Going Down (Til The Sun Comes Up)** *Garth Brooks*
55/69 **Ain't Gonna Worry** *Leon Ashley*
65/83 **Ain't Gonna Worry My Mind** *Richard Leigh*
15/96 **Ain't Got Nothin' On Us** *John Michael Montgomery*
68/68 **Ain't Got The Time** *Tom T. Hall*
23/63 **Ain't Got Time For Nothin'** *Bob Gallion*
19/68 **Ain't Got Time To Be Unhappy** *Bob Luman*
2/66 **Ain't Had No Lovin'** *Connie Smith*
23/58 **Ain't I The Lucky One** *Marty Robbins*
Ain't It All Worth Living For
15/72 *Tompall/Glaser Brothers*
75/74 *Mack White*
14/73 **Ain't It Amazing, Gracie** *Buck Owens*
97/76 **Ain't It Good To Be In Love Again** *Vicky Fletcher*
35/73 **Ain't It Good (To Feel This Way)** *Norro Wilson*
51/85 **Ain't It Just Like Love** *Billy Burnette*
77/78 **Ain't Life Hell** *Hank Cochran & Willie Nelson*
10/74 **Ain't Love A Good Thing** *Connie Smith*
41/76 **Ain't Love Good** *Jean Shepard*
1/86 **Ain't Misbehavin'** *Hank Williams, Jr.*
17/90 **Ain't Necessarily So** *Willie Nelson*
4/78 **Ain't No California** *Mel Tillis*
86/87 **Ain't No Cure For Love** *Jennifer Warnes*
74/76 **Ain't No Heartbreak** *Dorsey Burnette*
4/82 **Ain't No Money** *Rosanne Cash*
86/89 **Ain't No One Like Me In Tennessee** *Holly Ronick*
71/99 **Ain't No Short Way Home** *Oak Ridge Boys*
48/86 **Ain't No Tellin'** *Lewis Storey*
7/83 **Ain't No Trick (It Takes Magic)** *Lee Greenwood*
56/79 **Ain't No Way To Make A Bad Love Grow** *Johnny Russell*
67/82 **Ain't Nobody Gonna Get My Body But You** *Del Reeves*
43/01 **Ain't Nobody Gonna Take That From Me** *Collin Raye*
15/90 **Ain't Nobody's Business** *Hank Williams, Jr.*
5/50 **Ain't Nobody's Business But My Own** *Kay Starr & Tennessee Ernie Ford*
10/72 **Ain't Nothin' Shakin' (But The Leaves On The Trees)** *Billy "Crash" Craddock*
1/01 **Ain't Nothing 'Bout You** *Brooks & Dunn*
88/88 **Ain't She Shinin' Tonight** *Jim Moore & Sidewinder*
Ain't She Somethin' Else
46/75 *Eddy Raven*
1/85 *Conway Twitty*
7/72 **Ain't That A Shame** *Hank Williams, Jr.*
2/93 **Ain't That Lonely Yet** *Dwight Yoakam*
68/77 **Ain't That Lovin' You Baby** *David Houston*
53/86 **Ain't That Peculiar** *New Grass Revival*
75/83 **Ain't That The Way It Goes** *Dave Kemp*
62/87 **Ain't We Got Love** *Paul Proctor*
82/83 **Ain't Your Memory Got No Pride At All** *Ray Charles*
11/62 **Air Mail To Heaven** *Carl Smith*
Air That I Breathe
37/83 *Rex Allen, Jr.*
59/04 *Mavericks*
Alabam
1/60 *Cowboy Copas*
61/68 *Guy Mitchell*
46/05 **Alabama** *Cross Canadian Ragweed*
3/51 **Alabama Jubilee** *Red Foley*
83/77 **Alabama Summertime** *James Talley*
Alabama Wild Man
48/68 *Jerry Reed*
22/72 *Jerry Reed*
58/99 **Albuquerque** *Sons Of The Desert*
4↑/05 **Alcohol** *Brad Paisley*
1/93 **Alibis** *Tracy Lawrence*

Alibis
16/79 *Johnny Rodriguez*
81/84 *Lane Brody*
20/81 **Alice Doesn't Love Here Anymore** *Bobby Goldsboro*
69/82 **Alice In Dallas (Sweet Texas)** *Wyvon Alexander*
91/85 **Alice, Rita and Donna** *David Walsh*
18/75 **Alimony** *Bobby Bare*
34/88 **Alive And Well** *Gatlin Bros.*
Alive And Well
53/86 *Tammy Wynette*
81/87 *Nisha Jackson*
7/46 **All Alone In This World Without You** *Eddy Arnold*
21/59 **All-American Boy** *Grandpa Jones*
57/85 **All American Country Boy** *Con Hunley*
31/75 **All American Girl** *Statler Brothers*
37/70 **All American Husband** *Peggy Sue*
23/75 **All-American Man** *Johnny Paycheck*
84/83 **All-American Redneck** *Randy Howard*
16/79 **All Around Cowboy** *Marty Robbins*
67/74 **All Around Cowboy Of 1964** *Buddy Alan*
64/84 **All Around The Water Tank** *Mel McDaniel*
39/86 **All Because Of You** *Marty Stuart*
64/70 **All Day Sucker** *Liz Anderson*
66/94 **All Fired Up** *Dan Seals*
9/69 **All For The Love Of A Girl** *Claude King*
1/70 **All For The Love Of Sunshine** *Hank Williams, Jr.*
All Grown Up
8/58 *Johnny Horton*
26/63 *Johnny Horton*
35/72 **All Heaven Breaks Loose** *David Rogers*
72/69 **All Heaven Broke Loose** *Hugh X. Lewis*
72/84 **All Heaven Is About To Break Loose** *Zella Lehr*
2/72 **All His Children** *Charley Pride w/ Henry Mancini*
29/91 **All I Can Be (Is A Sweet Memory)** *Collin Raye*
3/76 **All I Can Do** *Dolly Parton*
82/85 **All I Do Is Dream Of You** *Margo Smith*
27/97 **All I Do Is Love Her** *James Bonamy*
All I Ever Need Is You
18/71 *Ray Sanders*
1/79 *Kenny Rogers & Dottie West*
45/04 **All I Ever Needed** *Bret Michaels w/ Jessica Andrews*
67/72 **All I Had To Do** *Jim Ed Brown*
All I Have To Do Is Dream
1/58 *Everly Brothers*
6/70 *Bobbie Gentry & Glen Campbell*
79/75 *Nitty Gritty Dirt Band*
85/81 *Nancy Montgomery*
1/69 **All I Have To Offer You (Is Me)** *Charley Pride*
11/49 **All I Need Is Some More Lovin'** *George Morgan*
51/71 **All I Need Is You** *Carl Belew & Betty Jean Robinson*
8/95 **All I Need To Know** *Kenny Chesney*
52/84 **All I Wanna Do (Is Make Love To You)** *Bandana*
21/79 **All I Want And Need Forever** *Vern Gosdin*
30/04 **All I Want For Christmas Is A Real Good Tan** *Kenny Chesney*
All I Want For Christmas Is You
55/94 *Vince Vance & The Valiants*
52/95 *Vince Vance & The Valiants*
52/96 *Vince Vance & The Valiants*
49/97 *Vince Vance & The Valiants*
43/98 *Vince Vance & The Valiants*
31/00 *Vince Vance & The Valiants*
5/96 **All I Want Is A Life** *Tim McGraw*
57/99 **All I Want Is Everything** *Mindy McCready*
96/77 **All I Want Is To Love You** *Jack Rainwater*
84/78 **All I Want To Do In Life** *Jack Clement*
67/71 **All I Want To Do Is Say I Love You** *Brian Collins*
30/82 **All I'm Missing Is You** *Eddy Arnold*
60/88 **All In My Mind** *Cali McCord*
13/73 **All In The Name Of Love** *Narvel Felts*
74/91 **All In The Name Of Love** *Bellamy Brothers*
11/92 **All Is Fair In Love And War** *Ronnie Milsap*
25/97 **All Lit Up In Love** *David Lee Murphy*
1/87 **All My Ex's Live In Texas** *George Strait*
9/70 **All My Hard Times** *Roy Drusky*
13/83 **All My Life** *Kenny Rogers*
23/67 **All My Love** *Don Gibson*
89/77 **All My Love** *Joe Ely*
61/99 **All My Love For Christmas** *Lonestar*
58/82 **All My Lovin** *Mundo Earwood*
10/84 **All My Rowdy Friends Are Coming Over Tonight** *Hank Williams, Jr.*
1/81 **All My Rowdy Friends (Have Settled Down)** *Hank Williams, Jr.*
27/67 **All My Tomorrows** *Nat Stuckey*
41/81 **All New Me** *Tom T. Hall*
31/00 **All Night Long** *Montgomery Gentry*
40/81 **All Night Long** *Johnny Duncan*
80/78 **All Night Long** *Peggy Sue*
All Of ..also see: Alla
3/78 **All Of Me** *Willie Nelson*
All Of Me Belongs To You
28/67 *Dick Curless*
70/67 *Hank Cochran*
46/97 **All Of The Above** *Ty England*
26/88 **All Of This & More** *Crystal Gayle/Gary Morris*
91/73 **All Or Nothing With Me** *Susan St. Marie*
4/58 **All Over Again** *Johnny Cash*
43/96 **All Over But The Shoutin'** *Shenandoah*
4/75 **All Over Me** *Charlie Rich*
18/02 **All Over Me** *Blake Shelton*
All Over Now ..see: (We Used To Kiss Each Other On The Lips But It's)
53/94 **All Over Town** *Don Cox*
2/55 **All Right** *Faron Young*
All Right (I'll Sign The Papers)
45/64 *George Morgan*
26/68 *Mel Tillis*
1/81 **All Roads Lead To You** *Steve Wariner*
1/57 **All Shook Up** *Elvis Presley*
8/85 **All Tangled Up In Love** *Gus Hardin w/ Earl Thomas Conley*
49/95 **All That Heaven Will Allow** *Mavericks*
27/77 **All That Keeps Me Going** *Jim Weatherly*
94/74 **All That Keeps Me Going** *Mary Lou Turner*
33/70 **All That Keeps Ya Goin'** *Tompall/Glaser Brothers*
50/98 **All That Matters Anymore** *Lee Roy Parnell*
70/85 **All That's Left For Me** *Carl Jackson*
5/89 **All The Fun** *Paul Overstreet*
1/79 **All The Gold In California** *Larry Gatlin/Gatlin Brothers*
50/88 **All The Good One's Are Taken** *Linda Davis*
4/97 **All The Good Ones Are Gone** *Pam Tillis*
20/76 **All The King's Horses** *Lynn Anderson*
5/72 **All The Lonely Women In The World** *Bill Anderson*
All The Love In The World ..see: (If You Add)
53/84 **All The Love Is On The Radio** *Tom Jones*
97/77 **All The Love We Threw Away** *Lois Johnson & Bill Rice*
73/75 **All The Love You'll Ever Need** *Cliff Cochran*
5/89 **All The Reasons Why** *Highway 101*
39/77 **All The Sweet** *Mel McDaniel*
97/88 **All The Things We Are Not** *David Walsh*
All The Time
18/59 *Kitty Wells*
1/67 *Jack Greene*
82/79 **All The Time In The World** *Dr. Hook*
73/86 **All The Way** *Ray Price*
All These Things
1/76 *Joe Stampley*
62/81 *Joe Stampley*
3/93 **All These Years** *Sawyer Brown*
8/99 **All Things Considered** *Yankee Grey*
72/90 **All Things Made New Again** *Suzy Bogguss*
6/86 **All Tied Up** *Ronnie McDowell*
F/73 **(All Together Now) Let's Fall Apart** *Ronnie Milsap*
71/86 **All We Had Was One Another** *Don King*
13/96 **All You Ever Do Is Bring Me Down** *Mavericks*

73/91 **All You Really Wanna Do**
Michelle Wright
73/89 **All You're Takin' Is My Love**
Pal Rakes
5/62 **Alla My Love** *Webb Pierce*
Allegheny
70/70 *Bonnie Guitar*
69/73 *Johnny Cash & June Carter Cash*
97/77 **Allegheny Lady** *Max D. Barnes*
22/62 **Alligator Man** *Jimmy Newman*
68/85 **Almighty Lover** *Sierra*
2/52 **Almost** *George Morgan*
11/96 **Almost A Memory Now**
BlackHawk
20/83 **Almost Called Her Baby By Mistake**
Larry Gatlin/Gatlin Brothers
19/00 **Almost Doesn't Count** *Mark Wills*
1/93 **Almost Goodbye** *Mark Chesnutt*
6/03 **Almost Home** *Craig Morgan*
22/99 **Almost Home**
Mary Chapin Carpenter
Almost Over You
86/84 *Sheena Easton*
42/98 *Lila McCann*
Almost Persuaded
1/66 *David Houston*
6/66 *Ben Colder [No. 2]*
95/76 *Sherri King*
F/77 *Maury Finney*
58/87 *Merle Haggard*
49/84 **Almost Saturday Night**
Burrito Brothers
45/02 **Almost There** *Gabbie Nolen*
53/98 **Alone** *Monty Holmes*
Alone Again ..also see: (Here I Am)
72/73 **Alone Again (Naturally)**
Brush Arbor
Alone With You
1/58 *Faron Young*
44/64 *Rose Maddox*
57/86 **Along For The Ride ('56 T-Bird)**
John Denver
75/93 **Already Gone** *Tanya Tucker*
1/68 **Already It's Heaven**
David Houston
5/93 **Alright Already** *Larry Stewart*
42/72 **Alright I'll Sign The Papers**
Jeannie Seely
18/80 **Always** *Patsy Cline*
70/97 **Always A Woman** *Larry Stewart*
16/69 **Always, Always**
Porter Wagoner & Dolly Parton
(Always And Forever) ..see: I Won't Need You Anymore
1/86 **Always Have Always Will**
Janie Frickie
40/96 **Always Have, Always Will**
Shenandoah
Always Late (With Your Kisses)
1/51 *Lefty Frizzell*
99/76 *Jo-el Sonnier*
84/81 *Leona Williams*
9/88 *Dwight Yoakam*
37/78 **Always Lovin Her Man**
Dale McBride
69/99 **Always Never The Same**
George Strait

Always On My Mind
45/72 *Brenda Lee*
16/73 *Elvis Presley*
20/79 *John Wesley Ryles*
1/82 *Willie Nelson*
6/71 **Always Remember** *Bill Anderson*
90/80 **Always, Sometimes, Never**
Nancy Ruud
Always Wanting More (Breathless) ..see: Breathless
1/75 **Always Wanting You**
Merle Haggard
40/01 **Always Was** *Aaron Tippin*
45/98 **Always Will** *Wynonna*
1/87 **Am I Blue** *George Strait*
27/88 **Am I Crazy?** *Statler Brothers*
57/85 **Am I Going Crazy (Or Just Out Of My Mind)** *Lobo*
Am I Losing You
3/57 *Jim Reeves*
8/60 *Jim Reeves*
1/81 *Ronnie Milsap*
Am I That Easy To Forget
9/59 *Carl Belew*
11/60 *Skeeter Davis*
12/73 *Jim Reeves*
65/80 *Orion*
Amanda
33/73 *Don Williams*
1/79 *Waylon Jennings*
Amarillo By Morning
31/74 *Terry Stafford*
4/83 *George Strait*
1/99 **Amazed** *Lonestar*
9/76 **Amazing Grace (Used To Be Her Favorite Song)**
Amazing Rhythm Aces
1/73 **Amazing Love** *Charley Pride*
36/85 **Amber Waves Of Grain**
Merle Haggard
30/77 **Ambush** *Ronnie Sessions*
2/97 **Amen Kind Of Love**
Daryle Singletary
6/84 **America** *Waylon Jennings*
73/93 **America, I Believe In You**
Charlie Daniels
62/86 **America Is** *B.J. Thomas*
America The Beautiful
22/76 *Charlie Rich [1976]*
82/80 *Mickey Newbury*
58/01 *America The Beautiful*
59/01 **America Will Always Stand**
Randy Travis
45/01 **America Will Survive**
Hank Williams, Jr.
85/79 **America's Sweetheart**
Corbin & Hanner
11/90 **American Boy** *Eddie Rabbitt*
5/02 **American Child** *Phil Vassar*
5/82 **American Dream**
Hank Williams, Jr.
58/80 **American Dream** *Dirt Band*
4/89 **American Family** *Oak Ridge Boys*
54/85 **American Farmer**
Charlie Daniels Band
(American Girl) ..see: XXX's And OOO's
1/93 **American Honky-Tonk Bar Association** *Garth Brooks*
1/83 **American Made** *Oak Ridge Boys*
88/88 **American Man** *Frank Burgess*

16/87 **American Me**
Schuyler, Knobloch & Overstreet
66/67 **American Power** *Johnny Wright*
1/04 **American Soldier** *Toby Keith*
93/88 **American Trilogy**
Mickey Newbury
60/85 **American Waltz** *Merle Haggard*
8/88 **Americana** *Moe Bandy*
Americans, The
35/74 *Tex Ritter*
59/74 *Byron MacGregor*
5/60 **Amigo's Guitar** *Kitty Wells*
68/98 **Amnesia** *Blake & Brian*
1/76 **Among My Souvenirs**
Marty Robbins
73/99 **Among The Missing** *Michael McDonald & Kathy Mattea*
16/70 **Amos Moses** *Jerry Reed*
4/95 **Amy's Back In Austin** *Little Texas*
28/90 **Amy's Eyes** *Charley Pride*
81/89 **Ancient History** *Susan Ledford*
48/71 **And I Love You So**
Bobby Goldsboro
And I'll Be Hating You ..see: (It Won't Be Long)
14/89 **And So It Goes** *John Denver & The Nitty Gritty Dirt Band*
2/95 **And Still** *Reba McEntire*
29/03 **And The Crowd Goes Wild**
Mark Wills
57/02 **And Then** *Dusty Drake*
47/82 **And Then Some** *Bobby Smith*
51/87 **And Then Some** *Charly McClain*
70/67 **And You Wonder Why**
Fred Carter, Jr.
41/71 **Angel** *Claude Gray*
57/03 **Angel** *Renee McCrary*
82/84 **Angel Eyes** *Larry Willoughby*
1/81 **Angel Flying Too Close To The Ground** *Willie Nelson*
67/75 **Angel In An Apron**
Durwood Haddock
1/84 **Angel In Disguise**
Earl Thomas Conley
4/98 **Angel In My Eyes**
John Michael Montgomery
Angel In Your Arms
71/77 *Vivian Bell*
54/84 *Robin Lee*
8/85 *Barbara Mandrell*
Angel Of The Morning
34/70 *Connie Eaton*
22/78 *Melba Montgomery*
22/81 *Juice Newton*
34/64 **Angel On Leave**
Jimmy "C" Newman
(Angel On My Mind) That's Why I'm Walkin' ..see: Why I'm Walkin'
42/76 **Angel On My Shoulder** *Joni Lee*
57/77 **Angel With A Broken Wing**
Roy Head
13/71 **Angel's Sunday** *Jim Ed Brown*
32/81 **Angela** *Mundo Earwood*
69/78 **Angelene** *Mundo Earwood*
60/79 **Angeline** *Ed Bruce*
Angels Among Us
51/94 *Alabama*
28/95 *Alabama*
Angels Are Hard To Find
19/74 *Hank Williams, Jr.*
59/91 *Hank Williams, Jr.*

66/99 **Angels Don't Fly** *James Prosser*
4/70 **Angels Don't Lie** *Jim Reeves*
57/83 **Angels Get Lonely Too** *Ralph May*
9/01 **Angels In Waiting** *Tammy Cochran*
49/88 **Angels Love Bad Men** *Barbara Mandrell*
9/76 **Angels, Roses, And Rain** *Dickey Lee*
35/99 **Angels Working Overtime** *Deana Carter*
Anger & Tears
49/87 *Mel McDaniel*
61/89 *Russell Smith*
1/01 **Angry All The Time** *Tim McGraw*
16/68 **Angry Words** *Stonewall Jackson*
68/78 **Animal** *Ronnie McDowell*
17/66 **Anita, You're Dreaming** *Waylon Jennings*
89/74 **Ann** *Joel Mathis*
2/72 **Ann (Don't Go Runnin')** *Tommy Overstreet*
95/89 **Anna ("Go With Him")** *Jack Denton*
28/68 **Anna, I'm Taking You Home** *Leon Ashley*
3/58 **Anna Marie** *Jim Reeves*
40/65 **Anne Of A Thousand Days** *Leroy Van Dyke*
13/55 **Annie Over** *Hank Thompson*
9/74 **Annie's Song** *John Denver*
2/60 **Another** *Roy Drusky*
28/63 **Another Bridge To Burn** *"Little" Jimmy Dickens*
8/82 **Another Chance** *Tammy Wynette*
27/62 **Another Day, Another Dollar** *Wynn Stewart*
44/66 **Another Day, Another Dollar In The Hole** *Tex Williams*
25/69 **Another Day, Another Mile, Another Highway** *Clay Hart*
61/72 **Another Day Of Loving** *Penny DeHaven*
25/79 **Another Easy Lovin' Night** *Randy Barlow*
21/78 **Another Fine Mess** *Glen Campbell*
28/63 **Another Fool Like Me** *Ned Miller*
57/73 **Another Football Year** *Jeannie C. Riley*
10/78 **Another Goodbye** *Donna Fargo*
31/74 **Another Goodbye Song** *Rex Allen, Jr.*
84/89 **Another Heart To Break The Fall** *Carrie Davis*
8/82 **Another Honky-Tonk Night On Broadway** *David Frizzell & Shelly West*
Another Lonely Night
12/70 *Jean Shepard*
76/77 *Jody Miller*
48/84 **Another Lonely Night With You** *Roy Clark*
1/74 **Another Lonely Song** *Tammy Wynette*
24/76 **Another Morning** *Jim Ed Brown*
10/84 **Another Motel Memory** *Shelly West*
44/76 **Another Neon Night** *Jean Shepard*
5/71 **Another Night Of Love** *Freddy Weller*
15/00 **Another Nine Minutes** *Yankee Grey*
45/97 **Another Perfect Day** *Blake & Brian*
4/68 **Another Place Another Time** *Jerry Lee Lewis*
5/88 **Another Place, Another Time** *Don Williams*
27/72 **Another Puff** *Jerry Reed*
Another Saturday Night
88/75 *Buddy Alan*
74/93 *Jimmy Buffett*
55/98 **Another Side** *Sawyer Brown*
4/82 **Another Sleepless Night** *Anne Murray*
Another Somebody Done Somebody Wrong Song ..see: (Hey Won't You Play)
16/66 **Another Story** *Ernest Tubb*
34/80 **Another Texas Song** *Eddy Raven*
69/68 **Another Time, Another Place, Another World** *Jerry Wallace*
75/73 **Another Way To Say Goodbye** *Ray Sanders*
Another Woman
14/75 *T.G. Sheppard*
92/78 *Billy "Crash" Craddock*
89/88 **Another Woman's Man** *Bobbi Lace*
38/64 **Another Woman's Man - Another Man's Woman** *Faron Young & Margie Singleton*
4/87 **Another World** *Crystal Gayle & Gary Morris*
3/97 **Another You** *David Kersh*
23/75 **Another You** *Faron Young*
32/97 **Another You, Another Me** *Brady Seals*
66/97 **Answer To My Prayer** *Skip Ewing*
3/49 **Anticipation Blues** *Tennessee Ernie Ford*
84/81 **Antioch Church House Choir** *Sweetwater*
Any Day Now
26/79 *Don Gibson*
1/82 *Ronnie Milsap*
56/95 **Any Gal Of Mine** *Gino The New Guy*
1/95 **Any Man Of Mine** *Shania Twain*
7/56 **Any Old Time** *Webb Pierce*
32/67 **Any Old Way You Do** *Jan Howard*
3/73 **Any Old Wind That Blows** *Johnny Cash*
71/93 **Any Road** *Corbin/Hanner*
Any Time ..see: Anytime
Any Way That You Want Me ..see: Anyway That You Want Me
4/89 **Any Way The Wind Blows** *Southern Pacific*
33/81 **Any Way You Want Me** *Gene Watson*
10/81 **Any Which Way You Can** *Glen Campbell*
17/83 **Anybody Else's Heart But Mine** *Terri Gibbs*
94/75 **Anybody Out There Wanna Be A Daddy** *Kitty Wells*
13/59 **Anybody's Girl** *Hank Thompson*
1/91 **Anymore** *Travis Tritt*
3/60 **Anymore** *Roy Drusky*
64/88 **Anyone Can Be Somebody's Fool** *Nanci Griffith*
27/87 **Anyone Can Do The Heartbreak** *Anne Murray*
4/99 **Anyone Else** *Collin Raye*
2/78 **Anyone Who Isn't Me Tonight** *Kenny Rogers & Dottie West*
12/77 **Anything But Leavin'** *Larry Gatlin*
1/05 **Anything But Mine** *Kenny Chesney*
25/81 **Anything But Yes Is Still A No** *Stephanie Winslow*
49/95 **Anything For Love** *James House*
71/86 **Anything For Love** *Gordon Lightfoot*
Anything For Your Love
80/84 *Brentwood*
88/84 *Sammy Hall*
28/86 **Anything Goes** *Gary Morris*
12/68 **Anything Leaving Town Today** *Dave Dudley*
22/63 **Anything New Gets Old (Except My Love For You)** *Don Gibson*
55/81 **Anything That Hurts You (Hurts Me)** *Keith Stegall*
50/02 **Anything That Touches You** *McBride & The Ride*
94/74 **Anything To Prove My Love To You** *Jimmy Hartsook*
10/67 **Anything Your Heart Desires** *Billy Walker*
38/72 **Anything's Better Than Nothing** *Mel Tillis & Sherry Bryce*
Anytime
1/48 *Eddy Arnold*
14/48 *Foy Willing*
73/69 *Patsy Cline*
54/85 *Osmond Brothers*
79/83 **Anytime You're Ready** *Narvel Felts*
13/71 **Anyway** *George Hamilton IV*
Anyway That You Want Me
81/79 *Juice Newton*
60/85 *Carlette*
54/95 **Anyway The Wind Blows** *Brother Phelps*
F/56 **Anyway You Want Me (That's How I Will Be)** *Elvis Presley*
10/93 **Anywhere But Here** *Sammy Kershaw*
F/81 **Anywhere There's A Jukebox** *Razzy Bailey*
13/62 **Anywhere There's People** *Lawton Williams*
63/69 **Anywhere U.S.A.** *Buckaroos*
72/77 **Apartment** *Johnny Carver*
Apartment #9
21/66 *Bobby Austin*
44/67 *Tammy Wynette*
57/67 **Apologize** *Buddy Cagle*
14/69 **April's Fool** *Ray Price*
58/70 **Apron Strings** *Peggy Sue*
87/88 **Arab, Alabama** *Pinkard & Bowden*
2/82 **Are The Good Times Really Over** *Merle Haggard*
53/88 **Are There Any More Like You (Where You Came From)** *Becky Hobbs*
61/76 **Are They Gonna Make Us Outlaws Again** *James Talley*

Are We Dreamin' The Same Dream
66/80 *Gary Stewart*
26/81 *Charlie Rich*
45/82 **Are We In Love (Or Am I)** *Charlie Ross*
24/96 **Are We In Trouble Now** *Randy Travis*
1/89 **Are You Ever Gonna Love Me** *Holly Dunn*
11/69 **Are You From Dixie (Cause I'm From Dixie Too)** *Jerry Reed*
1/81 **Are You Happy Baby?** *Dottie West*
Are You Lonesome To-night?
22/61 *Elvis Presley*
57/83 *John Schneider & Jill Michaels*
3/91 **Are You Lovin' Me Like I'm Lovin' You** *Ronnie Milsap*
Are You Mine
2/55 *Ginny Wright/Tom Tall*
6/55 *Myrna Lorrie & Buddy Deval*
14/55 *Red Sovine - Goldie Hill*
1/80 **Are You On The Road To Lovin' Me Again** *Debby Boone*
7/77 **Are You Ready For The Country** *Waylon Jennings*
13/58 **Are You Really Mine** *Jimmie Rodgers*
32/87 **Are You Satisfied** *Janie Frickie*
10/79 **Are You Sincere** *Elvis Presley*
20/87 **Are You Still In Love With Me** *Anne Murray*
1/75 **Are You Sure Hank Done It This Way** *Waylon Jennings*
1/52 **Are You Teasing Me** *Carl Smith*
12/60 **Are You Willing, Willie** *Marion Worth*
31/99 **Are Your Eyes Still Blue** *Shane McAnally*
87/80 **Arizona Highway** *Tim Rex & Oklahoma*
59/01 **Arizona Rain** *3 Of Hearts*
85/80 **Arizona Whiz** *George Burns*
47/72 **Arkansas** *Wilburn Brothers*
19/86 **Arlene** *Marty Stuart*
16/05 **Arlington** *Trace Adkins*
27/73 **Arms Full Of Empty** *Buck Owens*
4/71 **Arms Of A Fool** *Mel Tillis*
70/82 **Arms Of A Stranger** *Tennessee Express*
62/70 **Arms Of My Weakness** *Darrell McCall*
Around ..see: 'Round
Around My Heart ..see: (You Sure Know Your Way)
64/69 **Article From Life** *Lefty Frizzell*
8/65 **Artificial Rose** *Jimmy Newman*
2/95 **As Any Fool Can See** *Tracy Lawrence*
8/54 **As Far As I'm Concerned** *Red Foley & Betty Foley*
1/05 **As Good As I Once Was** *Toby Keith*
12/79 **As Long As I Can Wake Up In Your Arms** *Kenny O'Dell*
3/55 **As Long As I Live** *Red Foley & Kitty Wells*
3/68 **As Long As I Live** *George Jones*
1/84 **As Long As I'm Rockin' With You** *John Conlee*
70/87 **As Long As I've Been Loving You** *Razorback*
30/66 **As Long As The Wind Blows** *Johnny Darrell*
43/76 **As Long As There's A Sunday** *Sammi Smith*
83/88 **As Long As There's Women Like You** *Jerry Cooper*
51/88 **As Long As We Got Each Other** *Louise Mandrell w/ Eric Carmen*
68/92 **As Long As You Belong To Me** *Holly Dunn*
14/91 **As Simple As That** *Mike Reid*
1/74 **As Soon As I Hang Up The Phone** *Loretta Lynn/Conway Twitty*
Ashes By Now
78/80 *Rodney Crowell*
4/01 *Lee Ann Womack*
47/88 **Ashes In The Wind** *Moe Bandy*
Ashes Of Love
37/68 *Don Gibson*
15/72 *Dickey Lee*
48/76 *Jody Miller*
100/78 *Amazing Rhythm Aces*
26/87 *Desert Rose Band*
19/82 **Ashes To Ashes** *Terri Gibbs*
42/76 **Ask Any Old Cheater Who Knows** *Freddy Weller*
19/64 **Ask Marie** *Sonny James*
65/00 **Askin' Too Much** *Tamara Walker*
27/92 **Asking Us To Dance** *Kathy Mattea*
6/50 **A-Sleeping At The Foot Of The Bed** *"Little" Jimmy Dickens*
72/76 **Asphalt Cowboy** *Hank Thompson*
67/72 **Astrology** *Liz Anderson*
13/66 **At Ease Heart** *Ernie Ashworth*
61/91 **At Last** *Gene Watson*
59/71 **At Least Part Of The Way** *Stan Hitchcock*
At Mail Call Today
1/45 *Gene Autry*
3/45 *Lawrence Welk w/ Red Foley*
24/78 **At The End Of A Rainbow** *Jerry Wallace*
18/03 **At The End Of The Day** *Kellie Coffey*
85/79 **At The Moonlite** *Bill Phillips*
5/86 **At The Sound Of The Tone** *John Schneider*
13/74 **At The Time** *Jean Shepard*
At This Moment
42/87 *Billy Vera*
89/89 *Holly Lipton*
3/84 **Atlanta Blue** *Statler Brothers*
9/83 **Atlanta Burned Again Last Night** *Atlanta*
Atlanta Georgia Stray
36/68 *Sonny Curtis*
62/69 *Kenny Price*
6/46 **Atomic Power** *Buchanan Brothers*
13/74 **Atta Way To Go** *Don Williams*
5/84 **Attitude Adjustment** *Hank Williams, Jr.*
80/86 **Auction, The** *Southern Reign*
Auctioneer, The
9/57 *Leroy Van Dyke*
51/68 *Brenda Byers*
88/74 **Auctioneer Love** *Bruce Mullen*
56/77 **Audubon** *C.W. McCall*
49/00 **Auld Lang Syne (The Millennium Mix)** *Kenny G*
1/01 **Austin** *Blake Shelton*
84/80 **Autograph** *John Denver*
15/68 **Autumn Of My Life** *Bobby Goldsboro*
52/71 **Award To An Angel** *Wayne Kemp*
Away In A Manger
73/99 *Reba McEntire*
67/00 *Kenny Chesney*
1/05 **Awful, Beautiful Life** *Darryl Worley*
63/73 **Awful Lot To Learn About Truck Drivin'** *Red Simpson*
69/70 **Awful Lotta Lovin'** *Penny DeHaven*

B

3/84 **B-B-B-Burnin' Up With Love** *Eddie Rabbitt*
63/00 **BFD** *Kathy Mattea*
1/64 **B.J. The D.J.** *Stonewall Jackson*
1/03 **Baby, The** *Blake Shelton*
Baby
7/66 *Wilma Burgess*
63/75 *Tennessee Ernie Ford/Andra Willis*
80/81 **Baby, The** *Kieran Kane*
16/69 **Baby Again** *Hank Williams, Jr.*
62/99 **Baby Ain't Rocking Me Right** *Mark Nesler*
15/66 **Baby Ain't That Fine** *Gene Pitney & Melba Montgomery*
40/68 **Baby, Ain't That Love** *Jack Barlow*
1/70 **Baby, Baby (I Know You're A Lady)** *David Houston*
1/88 **Baby Blue** *George Strait*
68/78 **Baby Blue** *King Edward IV & The Knights*
3/76 **Baby Boy** *Mary Kay Place*
1/85 **Baby Bye Bye** *Gary Morris*
31/72 **Baby, Bye Bye** *Dickey Lee*
42/84 **Baby, Come To Me** *Stephanie Winslow*
5/47 **Baby Doll** *Sons Of The Pioneers*
6/74 **Baby Doll** *Barbara Fairchild*
21/05 **Baby Doll** *Pat Green*
26/72 **Baby Don't Get Hooked On Me** *Mac Davis*
75/89 **Baby Don't Go** *Dianne Davis*
23/77 **Baby, Don't Keep Me Hangin' On** *Susie Allanson*
65/92 **Baby Don't You Know** *Stacy Dean Campbell*
2/05 **Baby Girl** *Sugarland*
Baby I Lied
4/83 *Deborah Allen*
40/01 *Shannon Brown*
15/77 **Baby, I Love You So** *Joe Stampley*
77/78 **Baby, I Need Your Lovin'** *E.D. Wofford*
31/70 **Baby, I Tried** *Jim Ed Brown*
26/86 **Baby I Want It** *Girls Next Door*
40/87 **Baby I Was Leaving Anyhow** *Billy Montana*
35/80 **Baby, I'm A Want You** *Stephanie Winslow*
48/78 **Baby I'm Burnin'** *Dolly Parton*
33/83 **Baby I'm Gone** *Terri Gibbs*

22/92 **Baby, I'm Missing You** *Highway 101*
2/88 **Baby I'm Yours** *Steve Wariner*
Baby, I'm Yours
5/71 *Jody Miller*
33/78 *Debby Boone*
22/83 *Tanya Tucker*
9/49 **Baby, It's Cold Outside** *Homer & Jethro w/ June Carter*
21/78 **Baby It's You** *Janie Fricke*
55/80 **Baby It's You** *Pia Zadora*
55/71 **Baby, It's Yours** *Wynn Stewart*
62/99 **Baby Jesus Is Born** *Garth Brooks*
20/78 **Baby, Last Night Made My Day** *Susie Allanson*
80/74 **Baby Let Your Long Hair Down** *Don Adams*
5/55 **Baby Let's Play House** *Elvis Presley*
11/94 **Baby Likes To Rock It** *Tractors*
62/76 **Baby Love** *Joni Lee*
93/81 **Baby Loved Me** *Ronnie Speeks*
67/68 **Baby Me Baby** *Johnny Duncan*
68/77 **Baby Me Baby** *Roger Miller*
27/79 **Baby My Baby** *Margo Smith*
52/94 **Baby Needs New Shoes** *Restless Heart*
49/95 **Baby, Now That I've Found You** *Alison Krauss & Union Station*
44/91 **Baby On Board** *Oak Ridge Boys*
76/80 **Baby Ride Easy** *Carlene Carter w/ Dave Edmunds*
15/60 **Baby Rocked Her Dolly** *Frankie Miller*
28/61 **Baby Sittin' Boogie** *Buzz Clifford*
92/79 **Baby Song** *Leona Williams*
51/91 **Baby Take A Piece Of My Heart** *Kelly Willis*
36/90 **Baby, Walk On** *Matraca Berg*
45/86 **Baby Wants** *Osmond Bros.*
4/52 **Baby, We're Really In Love** *Hank Williams*
1/83 **Baby, What About You** *Crystal Gayle*
66/72 **Baby, What's Wrong With Us** *Charlie Louvin & Melba Montgomery*
Baby When Your Heart Breaks Down
73/83 *Kix Brooks*
56/86 *Osmond Bros.*
56/71 **Baby Without You** *Jan Howard*
22/77 **Baby, You Look Good To Me Tonight** *John Denver*
71/90 **Baby, You'll Be My Baby** *Oak Ridge Boys*
63/87 **Baby You're Gone** *Janie Frickie*
7/80 **Baby, You're Something** *John Conlee*
30/71 **Baby, You've Got What It Takes** *Charlie Louvin & Melba Montgomery*
7/68 **Baby's Back Again** *Connie Smith*
75/73 **Baby's Blue** *Ferlin Husky*
51/85 **Baby's Eyes** *Lane Brody*
2/73 **Baby's Gone** *Conway Twitty*
55/74 **Baby's Gone** *Bobby Wright*
2/87 **Baby's Got A Hold On Me** *Nitty Gritty Dirt Band*
1/87 **Baby's Got A New Baby** *S-K-O*
1/85 **Baby's Got Her Blue Jeans On** *Mel McDaniel*
60/99 **Baby's Got My Number** *South Sixty Five*
1/89 **Baby's Gotten Good At Goodbye** *George Strait*
66/74 **Baby's Not Home** *Roy Head*
12/72 **Baby's Smile, Woman's Kiss** *Johnny Duncan*
72/84 **Baby's Walkin'** *Chantilly*
2/00 **Back At One** *Mark Wills*
55/74 **Back Door Of Heaven** *Nancy Wayne*
48/86 **Back Home** *A.J. Masters*
1/74 **Back Home Again** *John Denver*
53/88 **Back In Baby's Arms** *Emmylou Harris*
13/65 **Back In Circulation** *Jimmy Newman*
39/82 **Back In Debbie's Arms** *Tom Carlile*
23/75 **Back In Huntsville Again** *Bobby Bare*
81/82 **Back In My Baby's Arms** *Vince & Dianne Hatfield*
2/90 **Back In My Younger Days** *Don Williams*
4/69 **Back In The Arms Of Love** *Jack Greene*
51/74 **Back In The Country** *Roy Acuff*
20/89 **Back In The Fire** *Gene Watson*
51/98 **Back In The Saddle** *Matraca Berg*
F/76 **Back In The Saddle Again** *Sonny James*
51/89 **Back In The Swing Again** *Linda Davis*
66/89 **Back In The Swing Of Things** *Dean Dillon*
48/87 **Back In The Swing Of Things Again** *Larry Boone*
Back In The U.S.A.
48/75 *Carmol Taylor*
41/78 *Linda Ronstadt*
4/95 **Back In Your Arms Again** *Lorrie Morgan*
41/96 **Back In My Arms Again** *Kenny Chesney*
40/04 **Back Of The Bottom Drawer** *Chely Wright*
52/03 **Back Of Your Hand** *Dwight Yoakam*
35/84 **Back On Her Mind Again** *Johnny Rodriguez*
2/79 **Back On My Mind Again** *Ronnie Milsap*
58/98 **Back On The Farm** *Thompson Brothers Band*
67/86 **Back On The Radio Again** *James & Michael Younger*
10/66 **Back Pocket Money** *Jimmy Newman*
33/69 **Back Side Of Dallas** *Jeannie C. Riley*
Back Street Affair
1/52 *Webb Pierce*
88/80 *Joe Douglas*
25/71 **Back Then** *Wanda Jackson*
6/80 **Back To Back** *Jeanne Pruett*
74/69 **Back To Back (We're Strangers)** *Johnny Duncan & June Stearns*
58/82 **Back To Believing Again** *Marie Osmond*
26/69 **Back To Denver** *George Hamilton IV*
60/03 **Back To Memphis** *Billy Ray Cyrus*
40/67 **Back To Nashville, Tennessee** *Stonemans*
78/89 **Back To Stay** *Johnny Rodriguez*
(Back To The Basics Of Love) **..see: Luckenbach, Texas**
7/86 **(Back To The) Heartbreak Kid** *Restless Heart*
17/78 **Back To The Love** *Susie Allanson*
51/91 **Back To The Well** *Tom Wopat*
84/75 **Back Up And Push** *Bill Black's Combo*
2/54 **Back Up Buddy** *Carl Smith*
1/04 **Back When** *Tim McGraw*
67/93 **Back When** *Vern Gosdin*
36/80 **Back When Gas Was Thirty Cents A Gallon** *Tom T. Hall*
67/87 **Back When It Really Mattered** *Tommy Roe*
14/86 **Back When Love Was Enough** *Mark Gray*
14/90 **Back Where I Come From** *Mac McAnally*
16/70 **Back Where It's At** *George Hamilton IV*
2/92 **Backroads** *Ricky Van Shelton*
16/03 **Backseat Of A Greyhound Bus** *Sara Evans*
1/79 **Backside Of Thirty** *John Conlee*
92/79 **Backslider's Wine** *Michael Murphey*
25/83 **Backslidin'** *Joe Stampley*
87/83 **Backstreet Ballet** *Savannah*
8/61 **Backtrack** *Faron Young*
15/54 **Backward, Turn Backward** *Pee Wee King*
77/73 **Bad, Bad, Bad Cowboy** *Tompall Glaser*
33/73 **Bad, Bad Leroy Brown** *Anthony Armstrong Jones*
25/64 **Bad, Bad Tuesday** *Tom Tall*
58/70 **Bad Case Of The Blues** *Linda Martell*
Bad Day For A Break Up
62/79 *Leslee Barnhill*
46/88 *Cali McCord*
30/98 **Bad Day To Let You Go** *Bryan White*
50/95 **Bad Dog, No Biscuit** *Daron Norwood*
73/84 **Bad For Me** *Joe Sun*
45/97 **Bad For Us** *Little Texas*
2/93 **Bad Goodbye** *Clint Black w/ Wynonna*
12/86 **Bad Love** *Pake McEntire*
79/89 **Bad Moon Rising** *Cerrito*
Bad News
23/63 *John D. Loudermilk*
8/64 *Johnny Cash*
36/82 *Boxcar Willie*
51/84 **Bad Night For Good Girls** *Jan Gray*
28/63 **Bad Old Memories** *Williams Bros.*
94/76 **Bad Part Of Me** *Jerry Naylor*
10/66 **Bad Seed** *Jan Howard*
87/75 **Bad Water** *Gene Watson*
64/88 **Badland Preacher** *Carly Harrington*
58/04 **Bake Me A Country Ham** *Cledus T. Judd*
45/02 **Ball, The** *James Otto*
5/91 **Ball And Chain** *Paul Overstreet*

26/72 **Ballad Of A Hillbilly Singer** *Freddy Weller*
Ballad Of A Teenage Queen
1/58 *Johnny Cash*
45/89 *Johnny Cash/Rosanne Cash/Everly Brothers*
Ballad Of Davy Crockett
4/55 *"Tennessee" Ernie Ford*
10/55 *Mac Wiseman*
49/91 *Kentucky Headhunters*
4/69 **Ballad Of Forty Dollars** *Tom T. Hall*
3/64 **Ballad Of Ira Hayes** *Johnny Cash*
62/70 **Ballad Of J.C.** *Gordon Terry*
1/63 **Ballad Of Jed Clampett** *Lester Flatt & Earl Scruggs*
70/68 **Ballad Of John Dillinger** *Billy Grammer*
66/00 **Ballad Of John Rocker** *Tim Wilson*
50/86 **Ballad Of The Blue Cyclone** *Ray Stevens*
2/66 **Ballad Of The Green Berets** *SSgt Barry Sadler*
44/67 **Ballad Of Thunder Road** *Jim & Jesse*
14/68 **Ballad Of Two Brothers** *Autry Inman*
27/67 **Ballad Of Waterhole #3 (Code Of The West)** *Roger Miller*
7/60 **Ballad Of Wild River** *Gene Woods*
32/81 **Bally-Hoo Days** *Eddy Arnold*
6/64 **Baltimore** *Sonny James*
22/84 **Band Of Gold** *Charly McClain*
F/82 **Bandera, Texas** *Solid Gold Band*
7/75 **Bandy The Rodeo Clown** *Moe Bandy*
68/98 **Bang A Drum** *Chris LeDoux w/ Jon Bon Jovi*
4/47 **Bang Bang** *Jimmie Davis*
52/98 **Bang, Bang, Bang** *Nitty Gritty Dirt Band*
9/48 **Banjo Boogie** *Arthur (Guitar Boogie) Smith*
Banjo Fantasy II ..see: Ski Bumpus
5/48 **Banjo Polka** *Tex Williams*
75/00 **Baptism** *Randy Travis*
14/74 **Baptism Of Jesse Taylor** *Johnny Russell*
1/80 **Bar Room Buddies** *Merle Haggard & Clint Eastwood*
73/69 **Bar Room Habits** *Wayne Kemp*
30/71 **Bar Room Talk** *Del Reeves*
32/78 **Bar Wars** *Freddy Weller*
40/85 **Bar With No Beer** *Tom T. Hall*
55/68 **Barbara** *George Morgan*
19/77 **Barbara Don't Let Me Be The Last To Know** *Mel Street*
25/02 **Barbed Wire And Roses** *Pinmonkey*
92/79 **Barefoot Angel** *Chwithet Taylor*
64/00 **Barefoot In The Grass** *Sonya Isaacs*
90/81 **Barely Gettin' By** *Sawmill Creek*
1/75 **Bargain Store** *Dolly Parton*
60/99 **Barlight** *Charlie Robison*
31/75 **Barmaid, The** *David Wills*
10/81 **Baron, The** *Johnny Cash*
63/66 **Baron, The** *Dick Curless*
65/82 **Barroom Games** *Mike Campbell*
41/75 **Barroom Pal, Goodtime Gals** *Jim Ed Brown*
45/85 **Barroom Roses** *Moe Bandy*
89/73 **Barrooms Have Found You** *Garland Frady*
Barstool Mountain
82/77 *Wayne Carson*
9/79 *Moe Bandy*
Bartender's Blues
88/77 *James Taylor*
6/78 *George Jones*
16/76 **Battle, The** *George Jones*
9/90 **Battle Hymn Of Love** *Kathy Mattea & Tim O'Brien*
49/71 **Battle Hymn Of Lt. Calley** *C Company*
26/59 **Battle Of Kookamonga** *Homer & Jethro*
Battle Of New Orleans
1/59 *Johnny Horton*
24/59 *Jimmie Driftwood*
51/75 *Buck Owens*
1/89 **Bayou Boys** *Eddy Raven*
74/94 **Bayou Girl** *Bob Woodruff*
12/63 **Bayou Talk** *Jimmy "C" Newman*
11/71 **Be A Little Quieter** *Porter Wagoner*
26/64 **Be Better To Your Baby** *Ernest Tubb*
Be-Bop-A-Lula
5/56 *Gene Vincent*
98/86 *Hank Chaney ["86"]*
37/69 **Be Careful Of Stones That You Throw** *Luke The Drifter, Jr.*
98/73 **Be Certain** *Terri Lane*
5/69 **Be Glad** *Del Reeves*
33/65 **Be Good To Her** *Carl Smith*
86/83 **Be Happy For Me** *Gene Kennedy & Karen Jeglum*
49/97 **Be Honest** *Thrasher Shiver*
92/75 **Be Honest With Me** *Kathy Barnes*
63/92 **Be My Angel** *Lionel Cartwright*
15/72 **Be My Baby** *Jody Miller*
1/94 **Be My Baby Tonight** *John Michael Montgomery*
85/81 **Be My Lover, Be My Friend** *Mick Lloyd & Jerri Kelly*
16/68 **Be Proud Of Your Man** *Porter Wagoner*
Be Quiet Mind
9/61 *Del Reeves*
23/64 *Ott Stephens*
63/88 **Be Serious** *Donna Meade*
10/82 **Be There For Me Baby** *Johnny Lee*
36/78 **Be Your Own Best Friend** *Ray Stevens*
1/96 **Beaches Of Cheyenne** *Garth Brooks*
3/67 **Bear With Me A Little Longer** *Billy Walker*
41/01 **Beatin' It In** *Neal McCoy*
13/48 **Beaut From Butte** *Dick Thomas*
47/01 **Beautiful (All That You Could Be)** *Kenny Rogers*
76/82 **Beautiful Baby** *Paul Overstreet*
74/87 **Beautiful Body** *David Frizzell*
5/51 **Beautiful Brown Eyes** *Jimmy Wakely & Les Baxter*
16/03 **Beautiful Goodbye** *Jennifer Hanson*
4/55 **Beautiful Lies** *Jean Shepard*
1/02 **Beautiful Mess** *Diamond Rio*
48/72 **Beautiful People** *Pat Daisy*
86/78 **Beautiful Song (For A Beautiful Lady)** *Lee Dresser*
67/73 **Beautiful Sunday** *Jack Reno*
10/78 **Beautiful Woman** *Charlie Rich*
3/81 **Beautiful You** *Oak Ridge Boys*
75/00 **Beauty's In The Eye Of The Beerholder** *Chuck Wagon & The Wheels*
Because ..also see: 'Cause
18/65 **Because I Cared** *Ernest Ashworth*
28/66 **Because It's You** *Wanda Jackson*
45/67 **Because Of Him** *Claude Gray*
73/79 **Because Of Losing You** *Narvel Felts*
65/86 **(Because Of You) The Things I've Done To Me** *Jim Collins*
74/75 **Because We Love** *Jack Blanchard & Misty Morgan*
20/76 **Because You Believed In Me** *Gene Watson*
8/00 **Because You Love Me** *Jo Dee Messina*
9/71 **Bed Of Rose's** *Statler Brothers*
Bed Of Roses
91/84 *Bobby Vinton*
76/87 *R.C. Coin*
76/88 *Western Union Band*
4/87 **Bed You Made For Me** *Highway 101*
24/80 **Bedroom, The** *Jim Ed Brown/Helen Cornelius*
18/80 **Bedroom Ballad** *Gene Watson*
18/78 **Bedroom Eyes** *Don Drumm*
36/81 **Bedtime Stories** *Jim Chesnut*
76/79 **Bedtime Stories** *Pia Zadora*
1/72 **Bedtime Story** *Tammy Wynette*
5/00 **Been There** *Clint Black w/ Steve Wariner*
45/94 **Been There** *McBride & The Ride*
21/93 **Beer And Bones** *John Michael Montgomery*
22/69 **Beer Drinkin' Music** *Ray Sanders*
58/82 **Beer Drinkin' Song** *Mac Davis*
49/70 **Beer Drinking, Honky Tonkin' Blues** *Billy Mize*
1/03 **Beer For My Horses** *Toby Keith w/ Willie Nelson*
86/81 **Beer Joint Fever** *Allen Frizzell*
30/04 **Beer Man** *Trent Willmon*
24/01 **Beer Run** *George Jones w/ Garth Brooks*
19/00 **Beer Thirty** *Brooks & Dunn*
55/80 **Beers To You** *Ray Charles & Clint Eastwood*
94/81 **Beethoven Was Before My Time** *Jerry Dycke*
47/72 **Before Goodbye** *Del Reeves*
63/96 **Before He Kissed Me** *Lisa Brokop*
80/82 **Before I Got To Know Her** *Brian Collins*
15/02 **Before I Knew Better** *Brad Martin*
6/56 **Before I Met You** *Carl Smith*
73/92 **Before I'm Ever Over You** *Lee Greenwood*
4/64 **Before I'm Over You** *Loretta Lynn*
2/79 **Before My Time** *John Conlee*
43/89 **Before The Heartache Rolls In** *Foster & Lloyd*

Before The Next Teardrop Falls
44/68 *Duane Dee*
33/70 *Linda Martell*
1/75 *Freddy Fender*
22/66 **Before The Ring On Your Finger Turns Green** *Dottie West*
Before This Day Ends
4/60 *George Hamilton IV*
23/61 *Eddy Arnold*
55/83 **Before We Knew It** *Jan Gray*
10/49 **Before You Call** *Dave Landers*
51/88 **Before You Cheat On Me Once (You Better Think Twice)** *Robin Lee*
1/65 **Before You Go** *Buck Owens*
2/94 **Before You Kill Us All** *Randy Travis*
5/61 **Beggar To A King** *Hank Snow*
100/78 **Beggars And Choosers** *Bill Rice*
97/88 **Beggars Can't Be Choosers** *Don Lafleur*
82/80 **Beggin' For Mercy** *Louise Mandrell*
1/64 **Begging To You** *Marty Robbins*
Behind Blue Eyes
57/72 *Mundo Earwood*
32/77 *Mundo Earwood*
Behind Closed Doors
1/73 *Charlie Rich*
64/98 *Joe Diffie*
1/65 **Behind The Tear** *Sonny James*
87/80 **Behind Your Eyes** *Charlie Daniels Band*
66/95 **Bein' Happy** *Russ Taff*
91/85 **Being A Fool Again** *Audie Henry*
1/96 **Believe Me Baby (I Lied)** *Trisha Yearwood*
10/58 **Believe What You Say** *Ricky Nelson*
Belleau Wood
41/98 *Garth Brooks*
65/99 *Garth Brooks*
4/65 **Belles Of Southern Bell** *Del Reeves*
30/61 **Bells That Broke My Heart** *Slim Whitman*
3/95 **Bend It Until It Breaks** *John Anderson*
25/88 **Beneath A Painted Sky** *Tammy Wynette*
Beneath Still Waters
38/70 *Diana Trask*
1/80 *Emmylou Harris*
55/89 **Beneath The Texas Moon** *J. C. Crowley*
59/04 **Bert & Bobby's Auto Body Shop** *Tim Murphy*
60/79 **Beside Me** *Steve Wariner*
54/81 **Best Bedroom In Town** *Judy Bailey*
1/00 **Best Day** *George Strait*
53/74 **Best Day Of The Rest Of Our Love** *Bud Logan & Wilma Burgess*
16/62 **Best Dressed Beggar (In Town)** *Carl Smith*
46/79 **Best Friends Make The Worst Enemies** *David Houston*
18↑/05 **Best I Ever Had** *Gary Allan*
15/88 **Best I Know How** *Statler Brothers*

94/76 **Best I've Ever Had** *Jeannie C. Riley*
78/75 **Best In Me** *Jody Miller*
29/72 **Best Is Yet To Come** *Del Reeves*
74/99 **Best Is Yet To Come** *Brady Seals*
77/87 **Best Love I Never Had** *Freddie Hart*
36/05 **Best Man** *Blaine Larsen*
39/93 **Best Mistakes I Ever Made** *Rick Vincent*
27/60 **Best Of All My Heartaches** *Wilburn Brothers*
45/84 **Best Of Families** *Big Al Downing*
62/82 **Best Of Friends** *Thrasher Brothers*
1/00 **Best Of Intentions** *Travis Tritt*
6/80 **Best Of Strangers** *Barbara Mandrell*
6/72 **Best Part Of Living** *Marty Robbins*
69/66 **Best Part Of Loving You** *Hank Locklin*
52/77 **Best Part Of My Days (Are My Nights With You)** *David Wills*
75/86 **Best There Is** *Charley Pride*
7/75 **Best Way I Know How** *Mel Tillis*
1/85 **Best Year Of My Life** *Eddie Rabbitt*
15/59 **Best Years Of Your Life** *Carl Smith*
1/81 **Bet Your Heart On Me** *Johnny Lee*
73/90 **Better Be Home Soon** *McCarters*
73/84 **Better Class Of Loser** *Ray Price*
2/92 **Better Class Of Losers** *Randy Travis*
72/70 **Better Days For Mama** *Stonewall Jackson*
Better Deal Than That ..see: (I Can Find) A
Better Homes And Gardens
34/69 *Bobby Russell*
37/69 *Billy Walker*
4/89 **Better Love Next Time** *Merle Haggard*
91/79 **Better Love Next Time** *Dr. Hook*
67/96 **Better Love Next Time** *Caryl Mack Parker*
1/89 **Better Man** *Clint Black*
32/99 **Better Man** *Warren Brothers*
2/97 **Better Man, Better Off** *Tracy Lawrence*
20/78 **Better Me** *Tommy Overstreet*
7/71 **Better Move It On Home** *Porter Wagoner & Dolly Parton*
65/77 **Better Off Alone** *Jan Howard*
75/83 **Better Off Blue** *Chantilly*
26/84 **Better Our Hearts Should Bend (Than Break)** *Bandana*
74/81 **Better Side Of Thirty** *Billy Parker*
75/98 **Better Than A Biscuit** *John Berry*
Better Than I Did Then ..see: (I'll Even Love You)
47/98 **Better Than It Used To Be** *Rhett Akins*
92/79 **Better Than Now** *DeWayne Orender*
3/95 **Better Things To Do** *Terri Clark*
Better Times A Comin'
20/63 *Ray Godfrey*
39/65 *Jim & Jesse*
64/97 **Better To Dream Of You** *Mary Chapin Carpenter*

21/94 **Better Your Heart Than Mine** *Trisha Yearwood*
71/96 **Bettin' Forever On You** *Tony Toliver*
49/88 **Betty Jean** *Russell Smith*
5/85 **Betty's Bein' Bad** *Sawyer Brown*
62/96 **Betty's Got A Bass Boat** *Pam Tillis*
91/77 **Betty's Song** *Roy Drusky*
46/91 **Between A Rock And A Heartache** *Lee Greenwood*
Between A Woman And A Man ..see: (There's Nothing Like The Love)
11/95 **Between An Old Memory And Me** *Travis Tritt*
3/85 **Between Blue Eyes And Jeans** *Conway Twitty*
11/74 **Between Lust And Watching TV** *Cal Smith*
46/73 **Between Me And Blue** *Ferlin Husky*
2/98 **Between The Devil And Me** *Alan Jackson*
F/73 **Between The King And I** *Jeannie Seely*
58/79 **Between The Lines** *Bobby Braddock*
27/95 **Between The Two Of Them** *Tanya Tucker*
17/81 **Between This Time And The Next Time** *Gene Watson*
7/84 **Between Two Fires** *Gary Morris*
Beverly Hillbillies ..see: Ballad Of Jed Clampett
9/54 **Beware Of "It"** *Johnnie & Jack*
81/76 **Beware Of The Woman** *Ruby Falls*
11/59 **Beyond The Shadow** *Browns*
7/50 **Beyond The Sunset** *Three Suns/ Elton Britt/Rosalie Allen*
7/89 **Beyond Those Years** *Oak Ridge Boys*
27/75 **Beyond You** *Crystal Gayle*
72/92 **Bible Belt** *Travis Tritt w/ Little Feat*
48/64 **Bible In Her Hand** *Grant Turner*
81/86 **Bidding America Goodbye (The Auction)** *Bruce Hauser/ Sawmill Creek Band*
22/74 **Biff, The Friendly Purple Bear** *Dick Feller*
1/61 **Big Bad John** *Jimmy Dean*
98/89 **Big Bad Mama** *Eddie Lee Carr*
86/76 **Big Band Days** *Hank Thompson*
24/62 **Big Battle** *Johnny Cash*
(Big Bertha) ..see: Ride That Bull
18/61 **Big, Big Love** *Wynn Stewart*
82/76 **Big Big World** *Ronnie Prophet*
59/69 **Big Black Bird (Spirit Of Our Love)** *Jack Blanchard & Misty Morgan*
39/72 **Big Blue Diamond** *Jacky Ward*
73/67 **Big Brother** *Murv Shiner*
29/66 **Big Chief Buffalo Nickel (Desert Blues)** *Skeets McDonald*
1/82 **Big City** *Merle Haggard*
41/64 **Big City Ways** *Warren Smith*
52/68 **Big Daddy** *Browns*
6/00 **Big Deal** *LeAnn Rimes*
3/89 **Big Dreams In A Small Town** *Restless Heart*
52/67 **Big Dummy** *Tommy Collins*

13/62 **Big Fool Of The Year** *George Jones*
70/67 **Big Foot** *Dick Curless*
4/74 **Big Four Poster Bed** *Brenda Lee*
8/74 **Big Game Hunter** *Buck Owens*
12/68 **Big Girls Don't Cry** *Lynn Anderson*
17/96 **Big Guitar** *BlackHawk*
19/59 **Big Harlan Taylor** *George Jones*
37/93 **Big Heart** *Gibson/Miller Band*
75/94 **Big Heart** *Rodney Crowell*
29/60 **Big Hearted Me** *Don Gibson*
5/69 **Big In Vegas** *Buck Owens*
5/60 **Big Iron** *Marty Robbins*
72/93 **Big Iron Horses** *Restless Heart*
50/65 **Big Job** *George Jones & Gene Pitney*
31/81 **Big Like A River** *Tennessee Express*
3/97 **Big Love** *Tracy Byrd*
5/89 **Big Love** *Bellamy Brothers*
Big Mable Murphy
43/71 *Dallas Frazier*
50/75 *Sue Thompson*
23/70 **Big Mama's Medicine Show** *Buddy Alan*
39/75 **Big Mamou** *Fiddlin' Frenchie Bourque*
53/69 **Big Man** *Dee Mullins*
35/80 **Big Man's Cafe** *Nick Noble*
4/59 **Big Midnight Special** *Wilma Lee & Stoney Cooper*
15/95 **Big Ol' Truck** *Toby Keith*
4/82 **Big Ole Brew** *Mel McDaniel*
68/88 **Big Ole Teardrops** *Ray Price*
1/94 **Big One** *George Strait*
66/98 **Big One** *Confederate Railroad*
48/68 **Big Rig Rollin' Man** *Johnny Dollar*
Big River
4/58 *Johnny Cash*
41/70 *Johnny Cash*
61/75 *Chip Taylor*
7/61 **Big River, Big Man** *Claude King*
56/71 **Big Rock Candy Mountain** *Bill Phillips*
22/62 **Big Shoes** *Ray Price*
91/77 **Big Silver Angel** *Tina Rainford*
2/03 **Big Star** *Kenny Chesney*
30/65 **Big Tennessee** *Tex Williams*
20/05 **Big Time** *Big & Rich*
27/98 **Big Time** *Trace Adkins*
38/85 **Big Train (From Memphis)** *John Fogerty*
Big Wheel Cannonball ..see: Wabash Cannonball
7/58 **Big Wheels** *Hank Snow*
1/89 **Big Wheels In The Moonlight** *Dan Seals*
65/69 **Big Wheels Sing For Me** *Johnny Dollar*
3/69 **Big Wind** *Porter Wagoner*
57/95 **Bigger Fish To Fry** *Boy Howdy*
80/89 **Bigger Man Than Me!** *Mickey Jones*
1/96 **Bigger Than The Beatles** *Joe Diffie*
58/85 **Bigger Than The Both Of Us** *Jimmy Buffett*
90/87 **Bigger The Love** *Kevin Pearce*
27/76 **Biggest Airport In The World** *Moe Bandy*
51/75 **Biggest Parakeets In Town** *Jud Strunk*
54/95 **Bill's Laundromat, Bar And Grill** *Confederate Railroad*
1/59 **Billy Bayou** *Jim Reeves*
57/92 **Billy Can't Read** *Paul Overstreet*
12/75 **Billy, Get Me A Woman** *Joe Stampley*
57/69 **Billy, I've Got To Go To Town** *Geraldine Stevens*
4/92 **Billy The Kid** *Billy Dean*
75/77 **Billy The Kid** *Charlie Daniels Band*
20↑/05 **Billy's Got His Beer Goggles On** *Neal McCoy*
10/70 **Biloxi** *Kenny Price*
81/84 **Biloxi Lady** *Leon Raines*
Bimbo
1/54 *Jim Reeves*
9/54 *Pee Wee King*
14/91 **Bing Bang Boom** *Highway 101*
2/82 **Bird, The** *Jerry Reed*
26/88 **Bird, The** *George Jones*
Bird Dog
1/58 *Everly Brothers*
86/78 *Bellamy Brothers*
47/01 **Bird Song** *Meredith Edwards*
65/75 **Birds And Children Fly Away** *Kenny Price*
63/86 **Birds Of A Feather** *Almost Brothers*
60/67 **Birmingham** *Tommy Collins*
55/69 **Birmingham Blues** *Jack Barlow*
1/50 **Birmingham Bounce** *Red Foley*
31/86 **Birth Of Rock And Roll** *Carl Perkins*
45/70 **Birthmark Henry Thompson Talks About** *Dallas Frazier*
68/78 **Bits And Pieces Of Life** *Cal Smith*
26/99 **Bitter End** *Deryl Dodd*
71/69 **Bitter Taste** *Elton Britt*
45/74 **Bitter They Are Harder They Fall** *Larry Gatlin*
83/78 **Black And Blue Heart** *Ann J. Morton*
37/89 **Black And White** *Rosanne Cash*
64/84 **Black And White** *David Frizzell*
24/75 **Black Bear Road** *C.W. McCall*
16/62 **Black Cloud** *Leroy Van Dyke*
15/90 **Black Coffee** *Lacy J. Dalton*
70/95 **Black Dresses** *Steve Kolander*
Black Jack ..see: Blackjack
Black Land Farmer
5/59 *Frankie Miller*
16/61 *Frankie Miller*
67/71 *Sleepy LaBeef*
1/83 **Black Sheep** *John Anderson*
21/59 **Black Sheep** *Ferlin Husky*
12/90 **Black Velvet** *Robin Lee*
6/52 **Blackberry Boogie** *Tennessee Ernie Ford*
41/76 **Blackbird (Hold Your Head High)** *Stoney Edwards*
4/56 **Blackboard Of My Heart** *Hank Thompson*
Blackjack County Chain
21/67 *Willie Nelson*
57/67 *Tex Williams*
69/84 **Blackjack Whiskey** *Bobby Jenkins*
Blackland Farmer ..see: Black Land
31/91 **Blame, The** *Highway 101*
34/04 **Blame It On Mama** *Jenkins*
45/67 **Blame It On My Do Wrong** *Del Reeves*
36/70 **Blame It On Rosey** *Ray Sanders*
5/91 **Blame It On Texas** *Mark Chesnutt*
28/65 **Blame It On The Moonlight** *Johnny Wright*
1/93 **Blame It On Your Heart** *Patty Loveless*
1/75 **Blanket On The Ground** *Billie Jo Spears*
9/82 **Blaze Of Glory** *Kenny Rogers*
63/73 **Bleep You** *Cal Smith*
68/70 **Bless Her Heart...I Love Her** *Hank Locklin*
Bless The Broken Road
42/98 *Melodie Crittenden*
1/05 *Rascal Flatts*
50/05 *Carrie Underwood w/ Rascal Flatts*
1/72 **Bless Your Heart** *Freddie Hart*
1/02 **Blessed** *Martina McBride*
1/81 **Blessed Are The Believers** *Anne Murray*
72/97 **Blessings, The** *Alabama*
6/79 **Blind In Love** *Mel Tillis*
2/76 **Blind Man In The Bleachers** *Kenny Starr*
83/80 **Blind Willie** *Chet Atkins*
39/97 **Blink Of An Eye** *Ricochet*
4/69 **Blistered** *Johnny Cash*
4/61 **Blizzard, The** *Jim Reeves*
1/73 **Blood Red And Goin' Down** *Tanya Tucker*
4/50 **Bloodshot Eyes** *Hank Penny*
17/74 **Bloody Mary Morning** *Willie Nelson*
59/88 **Blowin' Like A Bandit** *Asleep At The Wheel*
10/96 **Blue** *LeAnn Rimes*
48/82 **Blue And Broken Hearted Me** *Burrito Brothers*
83/81 **Blue As The Blue In Your Eyes** *Nancy Ruud*
27/80 **Blue Baby Blue** *Lynn Anderson*
2/77 **Blue Bayou** *Linda Ronstadt*
30/64 **Blue Bird Let Me Tag Along** *Rose Maddox*
45/89 **Blue Blooded Woman** *Alan Jackson*
47/89 **(Blue, Blue, Blue) Blue, Blue** *Jo-el Sonnier*
Blue Blue Day
1/58 *Don Gibson*
14/61 *Wilburn Brothers*
69/89 *Kendalls*
2/58 **Blue Boy** *Jim Reeves*
Blue Christmas
1/50 *Ernest Tubb*
9/51 *Ernest Tubb*
5/52 *Ernest Tubb*
55/98 *Elvis Presley*
74/99 *Vince Gill*
51/01 *Clay Walker*
1/96 **Blue Clear Sky** *George Strait*
40/81 **Blue Collar Blues** *Mundo Earwood*
63/00 **Blue Collar Dollar Song** *Jeff Foxworthy & Bill Engvall*
40/69 **Blue Collar Job** *Darrell Statler*
Blue Cyclone ..see: Ballad Of

Blue Darlin'
7/55 *Jimmy Newman*
F/78 *Narvel Felts*
81/85 **Blue Days Black Nights** *John McEuen*
61/73 **Blue Eyed Jane** *Benny Whitehead*
81/75 **Blue Eyes And Waltzes** *Jim Mundy*
Blue Eyes Crying In The Rain
1/75 *Willie Nelson*
73/77 *Ace Cannon*
56/82 **Blue Eyes Don't Make An Angel** *Zella Lehr*
F/58 **Blue Glass Skirt** *Hank Locklin*
33/64 **Blue Guitar** *Sheb Wooley*
Blue Heartache
64/73 *Osborne Brothers*
7/80 *Gail Davies*
15/85 **Blue Highway** *John Conlee*
98/74 **Blue Jean Country Queen** *Linda Hargrove*
Blue Kentucky Girl
7/65 *Loretta Lynn*
6/79 *Emmylou Harris*
11/68 **Blue Lonely Winter** *Jimmy Newman*
10/88 **Blue Love** *O'Kanes*
22/91 **Blue Memories** *Patty Loveless*
28/58 **Blue Memories** *James O'Gwynn*
24/00 **Blue Moon** *Steve Holy*
46/80 **Blue Moon Of Kentucky** *Earl Scruggs Revue*
1/82 **Blue Moon With Heartache** *Rosanne Cash*
68/95 **Blue Pages** *Noah Gordon*
32/82 **Blue Rendezvous** *Lloyd David Foster*
F/79 **Blue Ribbon Blues** *Joe Sun*
86/79 **Blue River Of Tears** *Micki Fuhrman*
21/92 **Blue Rose Is** *Pam Tillis*
6/48 **Blue Shadows On The Trail** *Roy Rogers*
8/80 **Blue Side** *Crystal Gayle*
1/66 **Blue Side Of Lonesome** *Jim Reeves*
4/89 **Blue Side Of Town** *Patty Loveless*
1/78 **Blue Skies** *Willie Nelson*
93/77 **Blue Skies And Roses** *Karon Blackwell*
7/49 **Blue Skirt Waltz** *Frankie Yankovic/Marlin Sisters*
81/79 **Blue Sky Shinin'** *Mickey Newbury*
41/64 **Blue Smoke** *Warren Smith*
Blue Suede Blues
49/86 *Con Hunley*
70/89 *Mel McDaniel*
1/56 **Blue Suede Shoes** *Carl Perkins*
6/46 **Blue Texas Moonlight** *Elton Britt*
5/88 **Blue To The Bone** *Sweethearts Of The Rodeo*
Blue Train (Of The Heartbreak Line)
44/64 *John D. Loudermilk*
22/73 *George Hamilton IV*
(Blue Yodel) ..see: Mule Skinner Blues / T For Texas
72/77 **Blueberry Hill** *Ann J. Morton*
4/46 **Blueberry Lane** *Elton Britt*
39/91 **Bluebird** *Anne Murray*
4/51 **Bluebird Island** *Hank Snow w/ Anita Carter*
Bluebird On Your Windowsill ..see: (There's A)
93/86 **Bluemonia** *Vicki Lee*
56/78 **Bluer Than Blue** *Beverly Heckel*
21/58 **Blues** *Ernest Tubb*
76/83 **Blues Don't Care Who's Got 'Em** *Eddy Arnold*
15/49 **Blues In My Heart** *Red Foley*
37/00 **Blues Man** *Alan Jackson*
12/66 **Blues Plus Booze (Means I Lose)** *Stonewall Jackson*
68/70 **Blues Sells A Lot Of Booze** *Hugh X. Lewis*
Blues Stay Away From Me
7/49 *Eddie Crosby*
1/50 *Delmore Brothers*
7/50 *Owen Bradley*
54/89 *Chris Austin*
1/88 **Bluest Eyes In Texas** *Restless Heart*
11/77 **Bluest Heartache Of The Year** *Kenny Dale*
39/66 **Boa Constrictor** *Johnny Cash*
41/86 **Boardwalk Angel** *Billy Joe Royal*
14/67 **Bob** *Willis Brothers*
69/74 **Bob, All The Playboys And Me** *Dorsey Burnette*
4/47 **Bob Wills Boogie** *Bob Wills*
F/75 **Bob Wills Is Still The King** *Waylon Jennings*
F/78 **Bob's Got A Swing Band In Heaven** *Red Steagall*
6/95 **Bobbie Ann Mason** *Rick Trevino*
1/82 **Bobbie Sue** *Oak Ridge Boys*
29/75 **Boilin' Cabbage** *Bill Black's Combo*
21/80 **Bombed, Boozed, And Busted** *Joe Sun*
Bonaparte's Retreat
10/50 *Pee Wee King*
F/70 *Carl Smith*
3/74 *Glen Campbell*
8/74 **Boney Fingers** *Hoyt Axton w/ Reneé Armand*
10/87 **Bonnie Jean (Little Sister)** *David Lynn Jones*
31/69 **Boo Dan** *Jimmy Newman*
65/90 **Boogie And Beethoven** *Gatlin Bros.*
53/87 **Boogie Back To Texas** *Asleep At The Wheel*
2/78 **Boogie Grass Band** *Conway Twitty*
51/04 **Boogie Man** *Clint Black*
66/89 **Boogie Queen** *Doug Kershaw*
22/74 **Boogie Woogie** *Charlie McCoy & Barefoot Jerry*
24/75 **Boogie Woogie Country Man** *Jerry Lee Lewis*
10/88 **Boogie Woogie Fiddle Country Blues** *Charlie Daniels Band*
72/74 **Boogie Woogie Rock And Roll** *Jerry Reed*
100/78 **Boogiewoogieitis** *Billy Stack*
55/01 **Boom** *Jolie & The Wanted*
85/75 **Boom Boom Barroom Man** *Nat Stuckey*
19/93 **Boom! It Was Over** *Robert Ellis Orrall*
8/49 **Boomerang** *Arthur "Guitar Boogie" Smith*
30↑/05 **Boondocks** *Little Big Town*
1/92 **Boot Scootin' Boogie** *Brooks & Dunn*
84/88 **Boots (These Boots Are Made For Walking)** *Brenda Cole*
1/86 **Bop** *Dan Seals*
7/56 **Boppin' The Blues** *Carl Perkins*
13/89 **Borderline** *Shooters*
49/90 **Bordertown** *Dan Seals*
26/78 **Bordertown Woman** *Mel McDaniel*
76/81 **Born** *Orion*
Born A Fool
21/68 *Freddie Hart*
41/73 *Freddie Hart*
12/77 **Born Believer** *Jim Ed Brown/Helen Cornelius*
2/92 **Born Country** *Alabama*
63/91 **Born In A High Wind** *T.G. Sheppard*
12/96 **Born In The Dark** *Doug Stone*
12/66 **Born Loser** *Don Gibson*
56/94 **Born Ready** *Jesse Hunter*
72/70 **Born That Way** *Stonewall Jackson*
5/90 **Born To Be Blue** *Judds*
52/68 **Born To Be By Your Side** *Jimmy Dean*
5/55 **Born To Be Happy** *Hank Snow*
22/66 **Born To Be In Love With You** *Van Trevor*
Born To Be With You
1/68 *Sonny James*
21/78 *Sandy Posey*
1/87 **Born To Boogie** *Hank Williams, Jr.*
1/01 **Born To Fly** *Sara Evans*
3/44 **Born To Lose** *Ted Daffan*
31/74 **Born To Love And Satisfy** *Karen Wheeler*
Born To Love Me
21/77 *Ray Price*
20/83 *Ray Charles*
6/93 **Born To Love You** *Mark Collie*
20/68 **Born To Love You** *Jimmy Newman*
40/84 **Born To Love You** *Karen Brooks*
3/82 **Born To Run** *Emmylou Harris*
66/82 **Born With The Blues** *Johnny Rodriguez*
17/86 **Born Yesterday** *Everly Brothers*
7/72 **Borrowed Angel** *Mel Street*
100/79 **Borrowed Time** *Johnny Free*
43/66 **Boston Jail** *Carl Belew*
Both Sides Of The Line
21/67 *Wanda Jackson*
58/74 *Josie Brown*
1/86 **Both To Each Other (Friends & Lovers)** *Eddie Rabbitt & Juice Newton*
13/67 **Bottle, Bottle** *Jim Ed Brown*
3/66 **Bottle Let Me Down** *Merle Haggard*
50/86 **Bottle Of Tears** *Gene Watson*
71/73 **Bottle Of Wine** *Doc & Merle Watson*
59/90 **Bottle Of Wine And Patsy Cline** *Marsha Thornton*
21/60 **Bottle Or Me** *Connie Hall*
35/66 **Bottles** *Billy Grammer*
18/66 **Bottom Of A Mountain** *Tex Williams*

Bouquet Of Roses
1/48 *Eddy Arnold*
11/75 *Mickey Gilley*
79/80 **Bourbon Cowboy** *Jim Seal*
33/72 **Bowling Green** *Hank Capps*
7/95 **Box, The** *Randy Travis*
18/66 **Box It Came In** *Wanda Jackson*
49/88 **Boxcar 109** *J. C. Crowley*
13/80 **Boxer, The** *Emmylou Harris*
18/83 **Boy Gets Around** *Sylvia*
47/03 **Boy Like You** *Trick Pony*
1/69 **Boy Named Sue** *Johnny Cash*
50/99 **Boy Oh Boy** *Wilkinsons*
36/84 **Boy's Night Out** *Moe Bandy & Joe Stampley*
4/94 **Boys And Me** *Sawyer Brown*
19/84 **Boys Like You** *Gail Davies*
39/66 **Bracero** *Stu Phillips*
75/72 **Brand New Key** *Jeris Ross*
1/91 **Brand New Man** *Brooks & Dunn*
8/71 **Brand New Mister Me** *Mel Tillis*
88/89 **Brand New Week** *Michelle Lynn*
63/88 **Brand New Whiskey** *Gary Stewart*
1/67 **Branded Man** *Merle Haggard*
70/84 **Branded Man** *Sierra*
(Brass Bed) ..see: Stay With Me
5/75 **Brass Buckles** *Barbi Benton*
43/83 **Brave Heart** *Thom Schuyler*
15/85 **Break Away** *Gail Davies*
85/80 **Break Away** *Bill Wence*
18/04 **Break Down Here** *Julie Roberts*
75/88 **Break Down The Walls** *De De Ames*
2/82 **Break It To Me Gently** *Juice Newton*
61/84 **Break My Heart** *Victoria Shaw*
Break My Mind
6/67 *George Hamilton IV*
13/78 *Vern Gosdin*
93/85 **Break Out The Good Stuff** *Roy Head*
54/03 **Break The Record** *Warren Brothers*
66/94 **Break These Chains** *Deborah Allen*
51/97 **Breakfast In Birmingham** *David Lee Murphy*
Breakfast With The Blues
11/64 *Hank Snow*
96/77 *Hank Snow*
69/91 **Breakin' All The Way** *Tim Ryan*
10/83 **Breakin' Down** *Waylon Jennings*
25/79 **Breakin' In A Brand New Broken Heart** *Debby Boone*
7/55 **Breakin' In Another Heart** *Hank Thompson*
39/83 **Breakin' It** *Loretta Lynn*
10/54 **Breakin' The Rules** *Hank Thompson*
65/96 **Breaking Hearts And Taking Names** *David Kersh*
15/89 **Breaking New Ground** *Wild Rose*
67/77 **Breaking Up Is Hard To Do** *Con Hunley*
1/99 **Breathe** *Faith Hill*
4/58 **Breathless** *Jerry Lee Lewis*
Breathless
45/00 *River Road*
56/04 *Lane Turner*
81/86 **Breathless In The Night** *Chuck Pyle*
12/48 **Breeze** *Cowboy Copas*
27/04 **Bride, The** *Trick Pony*
50/76 **Bridge For Crawling Back** *Roy Head*
45/81 **Bridge Over Broadway** *Capitals*
9/71 **Bridge Over Troubled Water** *Buck Owens*
3/81 **Bridge That Just Won't Burn** *Conway Twitty*
1/65 **Bridge Washed Out** *Warner Mack*
10/89 **Bridges And Walls** *Oak Ridge Boys*
11/65 **Bright Lights And Country Music** *Bill Anderson*
1/71 **Bright Lights, Big City** *Sonny James*
9/87 **Brilliant Conversationalist** *T. Graham Brown*
96/85 **Bring Back Love** *Lisa Angelle*
49/73 **Bring Back My Yesterday** *Glen Campbell*
9/74 **Bring Back Your Love To Me** *Don Gibson*
11/90 **Bring Back Your Love To Me** *Earl Thomas Conley*
18/72 **Bring Him Safely Home To Me** *Sandy Posey*
52/00 **Bring It On** *Keith Harling*
20/80 **Bring It On Home** *Big Al Downing*
1/76 **Bring It On Home To Me** *Mickey Gilley*
7/73 **Bring It On Home (To Your Woman)** *Joe Stampley*
68/69 **Bring Love Back Into Our World** *Stu Phillips*
32/05 **Bring Me Down** *Miranda Lambert*
13/69 **Bring Me Sunshine** *Willie Nelson*
1/02 **Bring On The Rain** *Jo Dee Messina w/ Tim McGraw*
80/85 **Bring On The Sunshine** *Dennis Bottoms*
25/66 **Bring Your Heart Home** *Jimmy Newman*
Bring Your Sweet Self Back To Me ..see: (Honey, Baby, Hurry!)
54/87 **Bringin' The House Down** *Shurfire*
23/75 **Bringing It Back** *Brenda Lee*
43/65 **Bringing Mary Home** *Country Gentlemen*
64/82 **Bringing Out The Fool In Me** *Gary Goodnight*
15/73 **Broad-Minded Man** *Jim Ed Brown*
62/93 **Broken** *Andy Childs*
94/76 **Broken Bones** *Tommy Cash*
1/77 **Broken Down In Tiny Pieces** *Billy "Crash" Craddock*
2/50 **Broken Down Merry-Go-Round** *Margaret Whiting & Jimmy Wakely*
18/60 **Broken Dream** *Jimmy Smart*
99/89 **Broken Dreams And Memories** *Michael Shane*
46/65 **Broken Engagement** *Webb Pierce*
1/79 **Broken Hearted Me** *Anne Murray*
70/93 **Broken Heartland** *Zaca Creek*
5/76 **Broken Lady** *Larry Gatlin*
10/92 **Broken Promise Land** *Mark Chesnutt*
Broken Road ..see: Bless The Broken Road
9/80 **Broken Trust** *Brenda Lee*
1/98 **Broken Wing** *Martina McBride*
1/03 **Brokenheartsville** *Joe Nichols*
64/77 **Brooklyn** *Cody Jameson*
51/78 **Brother** *DeWayne Orender*
Brother Juke-Box
96/77 *Don Everly*
1/91 *Mark Chesnutt*
75/70 **Brother River** *Johnny Darrell*
77/76 **Brother Shelton** *Brenda Lee*
Brotherly Love
53/89 *Moe Bandy*
2/91 *Keith Whitley & Earl Thomas Conley*
41/82 **Brotherly Love** *Gary Stewart/Dean Dillon*
29/84 **Brown Eyed Girl** *Joe Stampley*
3/70 **Brown Eyed Handsome Man** *Waylon Jennings*
58/69 **Brownville Lumberyard** *Sammi Smith*
41/73 **Brush Arbor Meeting** *Brush Arbor*
15/49 **Brush Those Tears From Your Eyes** *Foy Willing*
16/95 **Bubba Hyde** *Diamond Rio*
4/92 **Bubba Shot The Jukebox** *Mark Chesnutt*
Bubbles In My Beer
4/48 *Bob Wills*
68/71 *Ray Pennington*
1/65 **Buckaroo** *Buck Owens*
27/98 **Buckaroo** *Lee Ann Womack*
14/78 **Bucket To The South** *Ava Barber*
63/77 **Buddy, I Lied** *Nat Stuckey*
46/89 **Buenas Noches From A Lonely Room (She Wore Red Dresses)** *Dwight Yoakam*
25/79 **Buenos Dias Argentina** *Marty Robbins*
58/68 **Buffalo Nickel** *Rusty Draper*
16/93 **Bug, The** *Mary-Chapin Carpenter*
99/77 **Bugle Ann** *Wayne Carson*
12/63 **Building A Bridge** *Claude King*
Building Bridges
55/84 *Larry Willoughby*
72/85 *Nicolette Larson*
30/79 **Building Memories** *Sonny James*
8/78 **Bull And The Beaver** *Merle Haggard & Leona Williams*
66/80 **Bull Rider** *Johnny Cash*
88/82 **Bull Smith Can't Dance The Cotton-Eyed Joe** *Wolfpack*
Bumming Around
5/53 *Jimmie Dean*
5/53 *T. Texas Tyler*
31/76 **Bump Bounce Boogie** *Asleep At The Wheel*
35/05 **Bumper Of My S.U.V.** *Chely Wright*
4/52 **Bundle Of Southern Sunshine** *Eddy Arnold*
2/78 **Burgers And Fries** *Charley Pride*
3/84 **Buried Treasure** *Kenny Rogers*
2/01 **Burn** *Jo Dee Messina*
97/78 **Burn Atlanta Down** *Bobby Barnett*
43/01 **Burn Down The Trailer Park** *Billy Ray Cyrus*
80/84 **Burn Georgia Burn (There's A Fire In Your Soul)** *Butch Baker*
7/92 **Burn Me Down** *Marty Stuart*
4/92 **Burn One Down** *Clint Black*
10/86 **Burned Like A Rocket** *Billy Joe Royal*
71/87 **Burned Out** *Tina Danielle*

3/89 **Burnin' A Hole In My Heart** *Skip Ewing*
1/89 **Burnin' Old Memories** *Kathy Mattea*
26/98 **Burnin' The Roadhouse Down** *Steve Wariner w/ Garth Brooks*
31/75 **Burnin' Thing** *Mac Davis*
Burning
37/75 *Ferlin Husky*
88/77 *Marie Owens*
5/67 **Burning A Hole In My Mind** *Connie Smith*
Burning Bridges
18/67 *Glen Campbell*
79/81 *Bill Nash*
Burning Memories
2/64 *Ray Price*
9/77 *Mel Tillis*
10/62 **Burning Of Atlanta** *Claude King*
11/72 **Burning The Midnight Oil** *Porter Wagoner & Dolly Parton*
78/80 **Burning Up Your Memory** *Peggy Forman*
55/68 **Bury The Bottle With Me** *Dick Curless*
18/96 **Bury The Shovel** *Clay Walker*
21/71 **Bus Fare To Kentucky** *Skeeter Davis*
6/50 **Bushel And A Peck** *Margaret Whiting & Jimmy Wakely*
22/75 **Busiest Memory In Town** *Dickey Lee*
Busted
13/63 *Johnny Cash w/ Carter Family*
6/82 *John Conlee*
3/99 **Busy Man** *Billy Ray Cyrus*
8/52 **Busybody** *Pee Wee King*
But Alabama ..see: (Nothing Left Between Us)
But For Love
19/69 *Eddy Arnold*
54/79 *Jerry Naylor*
1/01 **But For The Grace Of God** *Keith Urban*
65/75 **But I Do** *Del Reeves*
18/01 **But I Do Love You** *LeAnn Rimes*
83/87 **But I Never Do** *Brenda Cole*
35/94 **But I Will** *Faith Hill*
30/82 **But It's Cheating** *Family Brown*
26/80 **But Love Me** *Janie Fricke*
68/89 **But, She Loves Me** *Roy Clark*
54/70 **But That's All Right** *Hank Thompson*
But Tonight I'm Gonna Love You
72/74 *Harrison Jones*
91/77 *Daniel*
63/67 **But Wait There's More** *Justin Tubb*
But You Know I Love You
2/69 *Bill Anderson*
1/81 *Dolly Parton*
16/60 **But You Use To** *Laverne Downs*
65/89 **But You Will** *Razzy Bailey*
72/87 **Butterbeans** *Johnny Russell & Little David Wilkins*
47/75 **Butterfly** *Eddy Arnold*
22/76 **Butterfly For Bucky** *Bobby Goldsboro*
Butterfly Kisses
37/97 *Raybon Bros.*
45/97 *Bob Carlisle*
66/97 *Jeff Carson*
4/88 **Button Off My Shirt** *Ronnie Milsap*
6/48 **Buttons And Bows** *Gene Autry*
1/00 **Buy Me A Rose** *Kenny Rogers*
18/96 **By My Side** *Lorrie Morgan & Jon Randall*
6/81 **By Now** *Steve Wariner*
19/99 **By The Book** *Michael Peterson*
By The Time I Get To Phoenix
2/68 *Glen Campbell*
40/71 *Glen Campbell & Anne Murray (medley)*
46/68 **By The Time You Get To Phoenix** *Wanda Jackson*
65/94 **By The Way She's Lookin'** *Jesse Hunter*
1/98 **Bye-Bye** *Jo Dee Messina*
96/79 **Bye, Bye, Baby** *Dan Dickey*
Bye Bye Love
1/57 *Everly Brothers*
7/57 *Webb Pierce*
70/81 *Billy Walker & Barbara Fairchild*

C

23/77 **C.B. Savage** *Rod Hart*
83/76 **C.B. Widow** *Linda Cassady*
10/83 **C.C. Waterback** *George Jones & Merle Haggard*
C'est La Vie ..see: (You Never Can Tell)
16/72 **Cab Driver** *Hank Thompson*
98/79 **Cabello Diablo (Devil Horse)** *Chris LeDoux*
78/76 **Cabin High (In The Blue Ridge Mountains)** *Don King*
9/59 **Cabin In The Hills** *Flatt & Scruggs*
48/80 **Cactus And A Rose** *Gary Stewart*
73/00 **Cactus In A Coffee Can** *Jerry Kilgore*
97/76 **Cadillac Johnson** *Chuck Price*
18/93 **Cadillac Ranch** *Chris LeDoux*
3/92 **Cadillac Style** *Sammy Kershaw*
30/02 **Cadillac Tears** *Kevin Denney*
5/92 **Cafe On The Corner** *Sawyer Brown*
80/81 **Caffein, Nicotine, Benzedrine** *Jerry Reed*
26/95 **Cain's Blood** *4 Runner*
Cajun Baby
3/69 *Hank Williams, Jr.*
52/88 *Doug Kershaw/Hank Williams Jr.*
52/83 **Cajun Invitation** *David Frizzell & Shelly West*
93/81 **Cajun Lady** *Ralph May*
1/86 **Cajun Moon** *Ricky Skaggs*
16/62 **Cajun Queen** *Jimmy Dean*
23/68 **Cajun Stripper** *Jim Ed Brown*
68/88 **Calendar Blues** *Jill Jordan*
73/76 **Calico Cat** *Kenny Starr*
11/48 **Calico Rag** *Al Dexter*
13/85 **California** *Keith Stegall*
45/79 **California** *Glen Campbell*
51/89 **California Blue** *Roy Orbison*
65/73 **California Blues (Blue Yodel No. 4)** *Compton Brothers*
94/80 **California Calling** *Dennis Smith*
45/69 **California Cotton Fields** *Dallas Frazier*
11/69 **California Girl (And The Tennessee Square)** *Tompall & The Glaser Brothers*
68/70 **California Grapevine** *Freddie Hart*
99/73 **California Is Just Mississippi** *Billy Mize*
31/77 **California Lady** *Randy Barlow*
43/76 **California Okie** *Buck Owens*
4/46 **California Polka** *Tex Williams*
61/85 **California Road** *Mel Tillis*
77/85 **California Sleeping** *Loy Blanton*
70/68 **California Sunshine** *Rusty Draper*
20/67 **California Up Tight Band** *Flatt & Scruggs*
96/89 **California Wine** *Mark Murphey*
19/76 **Call, The** *Anne Murray*
71/97 **Call, The** *Little Texas*
Call Her Your Sweetheart
9/52 *Eddy Arnold*
28/66 *Frank Ifield*
Call Home
52/86 *Glen Campbell*
43/93 *Mike Reid*
Call Me ..see: (Honey, Won't You)
64/87 **Call Me A Fool** *Dana McVicker*
55/02 **Call Me Claus** *Garth Brooks*
F/79 **Call Me Crazy Lady** *Leona Williams*
82/82 **Call Me Friend** *Vince Anthony*
46/70 **Call Me Gone** *Stan Hitchcock*
9/63 **Call Me Mr. Brown** *Skeets McDonald*
3/62 **Call Me Mr. In-Between** *Burl Ives*
14/54 **Call Me Up (And I'll Come Calling On You)** *Marty Robbins*
17/94 **Call Of The Wild** *Aaron Tippin*
26/61 **Call Of The Wild** *Warren Smith*
4/89 **Call On Me** *Tanya Tucker*
64/72 **Call On Me** *Jeanne Pruett*
Callin' Baton Rouge
37/89 *New Grass Revival*
2/94 *Garth Brooks*
79/87 **Callin' Your Bluff** *Rattlesnake Annie*
31/91 **Calloused Hands** *Mark Collie*
10/70 **Camelia** *Marty Robbins*
24/74 **Can I Come Home To You** *Bill Anderson*
64/92 **Can I Come On Home To You** *Bellamy Brothers*
15/91 **Can I Count On You** *McBride & The Ride*
58/74 **Can I Keep Him Daddy** *Red Sovine*
Can I See You Tonight
33/79 *Jewel Blanch*
4/81 *Tanya Tucker*
6/73 **Can I Sleep In Your Arms** *Jeannie Seely*
1/93 **Can I Trust You With My Heart** *Travis Tritt*
58/93 **Can You Feel It** *Ricky Lynn Gregg*
71/70 **Can You Feel It** *Bobby Goldsboro*
Can You Fool
16/78 *Glen Campbell*
72/84 *Paulette Carlson*
57/02 **Can You Hear Me Now** *Sawyer Brown*
36/03 **Can You Hear Me When I Talk To You?** *Ashley Gearing*
17/76 **Can You Hear Those Pioneers** *Rex Allen, Jr.*

93/79 **Can You Read My Mind** *Maureen McGovern*
2/95 **Can't Be Really Gone** *Tim McGraw*
1/93 **Can't Break It To My Heart** *Tracy Lawrence*
1/83 **Can't Even Get The Blues** *Reba McEntire*
61/00 **Can't Fight The Moonlight** *LeAnn Rimes*
21/99 **Can't Get Enough** *Patty Loveless*
83/88 **Can't Get To You From Here** *Jacky Ward*
88/83 **Can't Get Used To Sleeping Without You** *Sandy Posey*
11/63 **Can't Hang Up The Phone** *Stonewall Jackson*
38/91 **Can't Have Nothin'** *Foster & Lloyd*
64/00 **Can't Help Calling Your Name** *Jason Sellers*
54/81 **Can't Help Falling In Love With You** *Slim Whitman*
74/77 **Can't Help It** *Cates Sisters*
1/85 **Can't Keep A Good Man Down** *Alabama*
26/80 **Can't Keep My Mind Off Of Her** *Mundo Earwood*
92/79 **Can't Love On Lies** *Jim West w/ Carol Chase*
31/00 **Can't Nobody Love You (Like I Do)** *Wynonna*
87/78 **Can't Shake You Off My Mind** *Bobby Wayne Loftis*
1/87 **Can't Stop My Heart From Loving You** *O'Kanes*
30/92 **Can't Stop Myself From Loving You** *Patty Loveless*
45/88 **Can't Stop Now** *New Grass Revival*
86/88 **Can't Stop The Music** *Don King*
52/99 **Can't Stop Thinkin' 'Bout That** *Ricochet*
59/04 **Can't Tell Me Nothin'** *Brad Cotter*
9/74 **Can't You Feel It** *David Houston*
66/79 **Can't You Hear That Whistle Blow** *Sonny Throckmorton*
4/76 **Can't You See** *Waylon Jennings*
43/04 **Can't You Tell** *Diamond Rio*
25/69 **Canadian Pacific** *George Hamilton, IV*
Candle In The Wind ..see: (I'm Not) A
72/72 **Candy And Roses** *Sue Thompson*
Candy Kisses
1/49 *George Morgan*
4/49 *Elton Britt*
4/49 *Red Foley*
5/49 *Cowboy Copas*
9/49 *Eddie Kirk*
12/49 *Bud Hobbs*
5/84 **Candy Man** *Mickey Gilley & Charly McClain*
82/74 **Candy Mountain Melody** *George Morgan*
86/79 **Capricorn Kings** *Lee Wright*
24/74 **Captured** *Terry Stafford*
3/95 **Car, The** *Jeff Carson*
81/74 **Carefree Highway** *Gordon Lightfoot*
3/45 **Careless Darlin'** *Ernest Tubb*
48/71 **Careless Hands** *Dottie West*
8/50 **Careless Kisses** *Red Foley*
30/60 **Careless Love** *Jimmie Skinner*
Caribbean
1/53 *Mitchell Torok*
67/73 *Buddy Alan*
18/78 *Sonny James*
57/78 **Carlena And José Gomez** *Billy Walker*
5/00 **Carlene** *Phil Vassar*
66/69 **Carlie** *Bobby Russell*
16/60 **Carmel By The Sea** *Kitty Wells*
32/86 **Carmen** *Gene Watson*
64/81 **Carolina By The Sea** *Super Grit Cowboy Band*
F/83 **Carolina Dreams** *Ronnie Milsap*
44/81 **Carolina (I Remember You)** *Charlie Daniels Band*
29/69 **Carolina In My Mind** *George Hamilton, IV*
9/85 **Carolina In The Pines** *Michael Martin Murphey*
19/75 **Carolina Moonshiner** *Porter Wagoner*
15/48 **Carolina Waltz** *Clyde Moody*
Caroline's Still In Georgia
70/83 *Coulters*
76/84 *Mac Davis*
1/72 **Carolyn** *Merle Haggard*
88/75 **Carolyn At The Broken Wheel Inn** *Joe Allen*
6/87 **Carpenter, The** *John Conlee*
1/96 **Carried Away** *George Strait*
2/69 **Carroll County Accident** *Porter Wagoner*
26/73 **Carry Me Back** *Statler Brothers*
71/73 **Carry Me Back** *Marlys Roe*
35/01 **Carry On** *Pat Green*
4^{S}/03 **Carry The Flag** *Dean Justin*
74/90 **Carryin' On** *Canyon*
1/97 **Carrying Your Love With Me** *George Strait*
100/76 **Case Of You** *David Frizzell*
15/56 **Casey Jones (The Brave Engineer)** *Eddy Arnold*
Cash On The Barrel Head
7/56 *Louvin Brothers*
72/78 *Ronnie Sessions*
96/78 **Cashin' In (A Tribute To Luther Perkins)** *Bill Black's Combo*
78/82 **Cast The First Stone** *Kin Vassy*
12/56 **Cat Came Back** *Sonny James*
Cat's In The Cradle
97/75 *Compton Brothers*
45/96 *Ricky Skaggs*
13/66 **Catch A Little Raindrop** *Claude King*
49/81 **Catch Me If You Can** *Tom Carlile*
26/72 **Catch The Wind** *Jack Barlow*
50/77 **Catch The Wind** *Kathy Barnes*
57/88 **Catch 22** *Darrell Holt*
81/81 **Catching Fire** *Angela Kaye*
12/73 **Catfish John** *Johnny Russell*
Cathy's Clown
89/80 *Springer Brothers*
57/81 *Tricia Johns*
1/89 *Reba McEntire*
Cattle Call
1/55 *Eddy Arnold*
11/55 *Slim Whitman*
18^{S}/99 *Eddy Arnold w/ LeAnn Rimes*
81/79 **Caught With My Feelings Down** *Mary Lou Turner*
23/65 **Cause I Believe In You** *Don Gibson*
9/67 **'Cause I Have You** *Wynn Stewart*
3/56 **'Cause I Love You** *Webb Pierce*
64/72 **Cause I Love You** *Don Gibson & Sue Thompson*
32/67 **Cave, The** *Johnny Paycheck*
12/71 **Cedartown, Georgia** *Waylon Jennings*
3/03 **Celebrity** *Brad Paisley*
71/86 **Celebrity** *David Frizzell*
37/89 **Center Of My Universe** *Bellamy Brothers*
6/72 **Ceremony, The** *Tammy Wynette & George Jones*
12/65 **Certain** *Bill Anderson*
30/71 **Chain Don't Take To Me** *Bob Luman*
17/59 **Chain Gang** *Freddie Hart*
66/87 **Chain Gang** *Bobby Lee Springfield*
93/79 **Chain Gang** *Michael Murphey*
21/80 **Chain Gang Of Love** *Roy Clark*
3/00 **Chain Of Love** *Clay Walker*
31/73 **Chained** *Johnny Russell*
3/46 **Chained To A Memory** *Eddy Arnold*
1/90 **Chains** *Patty Loveless*
Chains
35/75 *Buddy Alan*
81/88 *Sarah*
4/87 **Chains Of Gold** *Sweethearts Of The Rodeo*
9/77 **Chains Of Love** *Mickey Gilley*
1/85 **Chair, The** *George Strait*
7/71 **Chair, The** *Marty Robbins*
22/80 **Champ, The** *Moe Bandy*
34/75 **Champagne Ladies And Blue Ribbon Babies** *Ferlin Husky*
11/98 **Chance, A** *Kenny Chesney*
47/04 **Chance, The** *Julie Roberts*
1/84 **Chance Of Lovin' You** *Earl Thomas Conley*
67/89 **Chance You Take** *Ross Lewis*
19/96 **Change, The** *Garth Brooks*
45/00 **Change** *Sons Of The Desert*
55/93 **Change, The** *Michelle Wright*
44/97 **Change Her Mind** *Gene Watson*
Change My Mind
70/91 *Oak Ridge Boys*
10/96 *John Berry*
1/89 **Change Of Heart** *Judds*
48/83 **Change Of Heart** *Marty Robbins*
93/87 **Change Of Heart** *Topel & Ware*
57/67 **Change Of Wife** *Geezinslaw Brothers*
41/83 **Changes** *Tanya Tucker*
24/77 **Changes In Latitudes, Changes In Attitudes** *Jimmy Buffett*
16/87 **Changin' Partners** *Gatlin Bros.*
4/54 **Changing Partners** *Pee Wee King*
68/80 **Changing All The Time** *La Costa*
1/72 **Chantilly Lace** *Jerry Lee Lewis*
Chapel Of Love ..see: Love, Love, Love
85/81 **Charleston Cotton Mill** *Marty Haggard*
16/67 **Charleston Railroad Tavern** *Bobby Bare*
57/75 **Charley Is My Name** *Johnny Duncan*
15/71 **Charley's Picture** *Porter Wagoner*
47/73 **Charlie** *Tompall/Glaser Brothers*

16/70 **Charlie Brown** *Compton Brothers*
87/80 **Charlie, I Love Your Wife** *Tommy Roe*
F/79 **Charlie's Angel** *Mel Tillis*
1/62 **Charlie's Shoes** *Billy Walker*
38/71 **Charlotte Fever** *Kenny Price*
5/80 **Charlotte's Web** *Statler Brothers*
6/59 **Chasin' A Rainbow** *Hank Snow*
34/02 **Chasin' Amy** *Brett James*
88/77 **Chasin' My Tail** *Jim Glaser*
50/91 **Chasin' Something Called Love** *Molly & The Heymakers*
2/90 **Chasin' That Neon Rainbow** *Alan Jackson*
1/93 **Chattahoochee** *Alan Jackson*
F/82 **Chattanooga City Limit Sign** *Johnny Cash*
1/50 **Chattanoogie Shoe Shine Boy** *Red Foley*
9/86 **Cheap Love** *Juice Newton*
61/87 **Cheap Motels (And One Night Stands)** *Southern Reign*
7/77 **Cheap Perfume And Candlelight** *Bobby Borchers*
13/94 **Cheap Seats** *Alabama*
45/83 **Cheap Thrills** *David Allan Coe*
44/93 **Cheap Whiskey** *Martina McBride*
46/79 **Cheaper Crude Or No More Food** *Bobby "Sofine" Butler*
73/81 **Cheat On Him Tonight** *David Heavener*
14/56 **Cheated Too** *Wilma Lee & Stoney Cooper*
94/80 **Cheater Fever** *Lynn Bailey*
Cheater's Kit
85/77 *Willie Rainsford*
45/79 *Tommy Overstreet*
90/81 **Cheater's Last Chance** *Larry Riley*
30/82 **Cheater's Prayer** *Kendalls*
54/80 **Cheater's Trap** *John Wesley Ryles*
15/76 **Cheatin' Is** *Barbara Fairchild*
38/81 **Cheatin' Is Still On My Mind** *Cristy Lane*
20/80 **Cheatin' On A Cheater** *Loretta Lynn*
52/98 **Cheatin' On Her Heart** *Jeff Carson*
41/77 **Cheatin' Overtime** *Mary Lou Turner*
61/82 **Cheatin' State Of Mind** *Bandana*
91/77 **Cheatin' Turns Her On** *David Wills*
9/54 **Cheatin's A Sin** *Kitty Wells*
16/81 **Cheatin's A Two Way Street** *Sammi Smith*
61/80 **Cheating Eyes** *Jerry Naylor*
18/73 **Cheating Game** *Susan Raye*
50/96 **Check Please** *Paul Jefferson*
1/95 **Check Yes Or No** *George Strait*
Cherokee Boogie
7/51 *Moon Mullican*
44/96 *BR5-49*
47/82 **Cherokee Country** *Solid Gold Band*
Cherokee Fiddle
58/77 *Michael Murphey*
10/82 *Johnny Lee*
1/76 **Cherokee Maiden** *Merle Haggard*
73/67 **Cherokee Strip** *Bob Beckham*
(Chestnuts Roasting On An Open Fire) ..see: Christmas Song
Chet Atkins ..see: Chit Akins
38/67 **Chet's Tune** *Some Of Chet's Friends*
80/88 **Chevy Van** *Sammy Johns*
8/51 **Chew Tobacco Rag** *Zeb Turner*
30/70 **Chicago Story** *Jimmy Snyder*
54/73 **Chick Inspector (That's Where My Money Goes)** *Dick Curless*
17/64 **Chickashay** *David Houston*
31/66 **Chicken Feed** *Bobbi Staff*
45/84 **Chicken In Black** *Johnny Cash*
69/67 **Chicken Pickin'** *Buckaroos*
8/81 **Chicken Truck** *John Anderson*
5/03 **Chicks Dig It** *Chris Cagle*
17/83 **Child Of The Fifties** *Statler Brothers*
13/87 **Child Support** *Barbara Mandrell*
24/68 **Childhood Places** *Dottie West*
30/73 **Children** *Johnny Cash*
58/69 **Children** *Diana Trask*
9/88 **Chill Factor** *Merle Haggard*
3/91 **Chill Of An Early Fall** *George Strait*
6/48 **Chime Bells** *Elton Britt*
22/62 **China Doll** *George Hamilton IV*
80/73 **China Nights (Shina No Yoru)** *Dick Curless*
33/74 **Chip Chip** *Patsy Sledd*
23/71 **Chip 'N' Dale's Place** *Claude King*
12/59 **Chip Off The Old Block** *Eddy Arnold*
6/88 **Chiseled In Stone** *Vern Gosdin*
14/64 **Chit Akins, Make Me A Star** *Don Bowman*
Choc'late Ice Cream Cone
5/50 *Red Foley*
8/50 *Kenny Roberts*
30/99 **Choices** *George Jones*
Chokin' Kind
8/67 *Waylon Jennings*
59/71 *Diana Trask*
87/83 *Freddy Fender*
69/75 **Choo Choo Ch'Boogie** *Asleep At The Wheel*
73/87 **Chosen** *Perry LaPointe*
7/49 **C-H-R-I-S-T-M-A-S** *Eddy Arnold*
12/55 **Christmas Can't Be Far Away** *Eddy Arnold*
Christmas Carol
68/96 *Skip Ewing*
60/98 *Skip Ewing*
2/46 **Christmas Carols By The Old Corral** *Tex Ritter*
33/02 **Christmas Cookies** *George Strait*
Christmas In Dixie
35/83 *Alabama*
47/98 *Alabama*
40/99 *Alabama*
37/00 *Alabama*
65/00 **Christmas In Your Arms** *Steve Wariner*
35/83 **Christmas Is Just A Song For Us This Year** *Louise Mandrell/RC Bannon*
Christmas Shoes
31/01 *Newsong*
39/02 *3 Of Hearts*
Christmas Song (Chestnuts Roasting On An Open Fire)
63/97 *Reba McEntire*
64/99 *Trace Adkins*
67/00 *Martina McBride*
60/05 *Joe Nichols*
57/95 **Christmas Time** *John Anderson*
Christmas Time's A Comin'
50/95 *Sammy Kershaw*
53/98 *Sammy Kershaw*
92/77 **Christmas Tribute** *Bob Luman*
54/05 **Christmas With You** *Clint Black*
41/68 **Christopher Robin** *Stonemans*
10/03 **Chrome** *Trace Adkins*
48/67 **Chubby (Please Take Your Love To Town)** *Geezinslaw Brothers*
3/64 **Chug-A-Lug** *Roger Miller*
83/79 **Chunky People** *Hargus "Pig" Robbins*
1/89 **Church On Cumberland Road** *Shenandoah*
5/47 **Cigareetes, Whusky, And Wild, Wild Women** *Sons Of The Pioneers*
Cigarettes And Coffee Blues
13/59 *Lefty Frizzell*
14/63 *Marty Robbins*
2/50 **Cincinnati Dancing Pig** *Red Foley*
2/46 **Cincinnati Lou** *Merle Travis*
4/67 **Cincinnati, Ohio** *Connie Smith*
5/87 **Cinderella** *Vince Gill*
45/72 **Cinderella** *Tony Booth*
59/81 **Cinderella** *Terry Gregory*
92/78 **Circle Is Small (I Can See It In Your Eyes)** *Gordon Lightfoot*
61/73 **Circle Me** *Dee Mullins*
49/96 **Circle Of Friends** *David Ball*
92/76 **Circle Of Tears** *Chip Taylor*
45/02 **Circles** *Sawyer Brown*
7/64 **Circumstances** *Billy Walker*
70/96 **Circus Leaving Town** *Philip Claypool*
City Lights
1/58 *Ray Price*
53/71 *Johnny Bush*
1/75 *Mickey Gilley*
67/89 *Mel Tillis*
City Of New Orleans
44/73 *Sammi Smith*
1/84 *Willie Nelson*
37/65 **City Of The Angels** *Jimmy Newman*
5/94 **City Put The Country Back In Me** *Neal McCoy*
59/74 **Claim On Me** *George Hamilton IV*
44/66 **Class Of 49** *Red Sovine*
83/87 **Class Of '55** *Carl Perkins*
6/72 **Class Of '57** *Statler Brothers*
16/05 **Class Reunion (That Used To Be Us)** *Lonestar*
Classic Cowboy ..see: (Great American)
13/75 **Classified** *C.W. McCall*
Claudette
15/58 *Everly Brothers*
41/72 *Compton Brothers*
47/97 *Dwight Yoakam*
76/88 **Clean Livin' Folk** *Bobby G. Rice & Perry LaPointe*
74/69 **Clean Up Your Own Back Yard** *Elvis Presley*
Clean Your Own Tables
77/75 *Stoney Edwards*
60/76 *Vernon Oxford*
72/81 *K.T. Oslin*
54/70 **Cleanest Man In Cincinnati** *Claude Gray*

11/93 **Cleopatra, Queen Of Denial** *Pam Tillis*
56/80 **Cling To Me** *Jerry Wallace*
47/69 **Clinging To My Baby's Hand** *Dottie West*
17/65 **Close All The Honky Tonks** *Charlie Walker*
15/77 **Close Enough For Lonesome** *Mel Street*
1/82 **Close Enough To Perfect** *Alabama*
81/74 **Close To Home** *Roy Drusky*
70/66 **Close Together (As You And Me)** *George Jones & Melba Montgomery*
74/87 **Close Your Eyes** *Rusty Wier*
89/82 **Closer To Crazy** *Jan Gray*
31/98 **Closer To Heaven** *Mila Mason*
40/82 **Closer To You** *Burrito Brothers*
Closer You Get
27/81 *Don King*
1/83 *Alabama*
66/69 **Closest Thing To Love (I've Ever Seen)** *Skeeter Davis*
27/77 **Closest Thing To You** *Jerry Lee Lewis*
59/94 **Closing Time** *Radney Foster*
1/82 **Clown, The** *Conway Twitty*
20/95 **Clown In Your Rodeo** *Kathy Mattea*
7/80 **Clyde** *Waylon Jennings*
Coal Miner's Daughter
1/70 *Loretta Lynn*
24/80 *Sissy Spacek*
26/97 **Coast Is Clear** *Tracy Lawrence*
47/04 **Coast Is Clear** *Scotty Emerick*
15/89 **Coast Of Colorado** *Skip Ewing*
Coat Of Many Colors
4/71 *Dolly Parton*
57/03 *Shania Twain w/ Alison Krauss*
1/79 **Coca Cola Cowboy** *Mel Tillis*
15/48 **Cocaine Blues** *Roy Hogsed*
Cocaine Train ..see: (Stay Away From) The
44/67 **Cockfight, The** *Archie Campbell*
72/77 **Coconut Grove** *Maury Finney*
93/81 **Code-A-Phone** *Larry Riley*
81/85 **Coffee Brown Eyes** *Billy Walker*
13/63 **Cold And Lonely (Is The Forecast For Tonight)** *Kitty Wells*
71/99 **Cold Coffee Morning** *Jon Randall*
Cold, Cold Heart
1/51 *Hank Williams*
22/61 *Jerry Lee Lewis*
84/79 *Jerry Lee Lewis*
10/62 **Cold Dark Waters** *Porter Wagoner*
Cold Day In July
71/93 *Joy White*
10/00 *Dixie Chicks*
69/77 **Cold Day In July** *Ray Griff*
2/67 **Cold Hard Facts Of Life** *Porter Wagoner*
45/00 **Cold Hard Truth** *George Jones*
64/87 **Cold Hearts/Closed Minds** *Nanci Griffith*
62/84 **Cold In July** *Robin Lee*
53/80 **Cold Lonesome Morning** *Johnny Cash*
23/02 **Cold One Comin' On** *Montgomery Gentry*
30/97 **Cold Outside** *Big House*
24/85 **Cold Summer Day In Georgia** *Gene Watson*
30/75 **Colinda** *Fiddlin' Frenchie Burke*
22/69 **Color Him Father** *Linda Martell*
38/72 **Color My World** *Barbara Fairchild*
7/58 **Color Of The Blues** *George Jones*
85/76 **Colorado Call** *Shad O'Shea*
93/84 **Colorado Christmas** *Nitty Gritty Dirt Band*
Colorado Country Morning
70/73 *Tennessee Ernie Ford*
95/75 *Hank Snow*
60/80 *Pat Boone*
50/78 **Colorado Kool-Aid** *Johnny Paycheck*
37/87 **Colorado Moon** *Tim Malchak*
70/70 **Columbus Stockade Blues** *Danny Davis*
7/62 **Comancheros, The** *Claude King*
4/78 **Come A Little Bit Closer** *Johnny Duncan w/ Janie Fricke*
43/01 **Come A Little Closer** *Lila McCann*
65/91 **Come A Little Closer** *Desert Rose Band*
47/70 **Come And Get It Mama** *Charlie Louvin*
20/59 **Come And Knock (On The Door Of My Heart)** *Roy Acuff*
Come As You Were
66/83 *Jerry Lee Lewis*
7/89 *T. Graham Brown*
79/89 **Come Back Brenda** *J.D. Hart*
13/56 **Come Back To Me** *Jimmy Newman*
1/97 **Come Cryin' To Me** *Lonestar*
12/73 **Come Early Morning** *Don Williams*
1/89 **Come From The Heart** *Kathy Mattea*
49/74 **Come Home** *Jim Mundy*
14/04 **Come Home Soon** *SheDaisy*
3/92 **Come In Out Of The Pain** *Doug Stone*
79/86 **Come In Planet Earth (Are You Listenin')** *Karen Taylor-Good*
6/58 **Come In Stranger** *Johnny Cash*
14/67 **Come Kiss Me Love** *Bobby Bare*
1/73 **Come Live With Me** *Roy Clark*
63/82 **Come Looking For Me** *Lobo*
58/74 **Come Monday** *Jimmy Buffett*
1/90 **Come Next Monday** *K.T. Oslin*
42/66 **Come On And Sing** *Bob Luman*
3/91 **Come On Back** *Carlene Carter*
52/75 **Come On Down** *Tennessee Ernie Ford*
24/76 **Come On Down (To Our Favorite Forget-About-Her Place)** *David Houston*
68/68 **Come On Home** *Debbie Lori Kaye*
76/84 **Come On Home** *Tony Arata*
85/75 **Come On Home** *Mary Lou Turner*
24/69 **Come On Home And Sing The Blues To Daddy** *Bob Luman*
98/74 **Come On Home (To This Lonely Heart)** *Wanda Jackson*
3/79 **Come On In** *Oak Ridge Boys*
8/76 **Come On In** *Sonny James*
10/78 **Come On In** *Jerry Lee Lewis*
91/78 **Come On In** *Bobby Hood*
19/74 **Come On In And Let Me Love You** *Lois Johnson*
3/86 **Come On In (You Did The Best You Could Do)** *Oak Ridge Boys*
39/88 **Come On Joe** *Jo-el Sonnier*
5/76 **Come On Over** *Olivia Newton-John*
6/99 **Come On Over** *Shania Twain*
55/92 **Come On Over To The Country** *Hank Williams, Jr.*
36/74 **Come On Phone** *Jean Shepard*
85/88 **Come On Rain** *Wright Brothers*
23/77 **Come See About Me** *Cal Smith*
17/78 **Come See Me And Come Lonely** *Dottie West*
37/67 **Come See What's Left Of Your Man** *Johnny Darrell*
14/98 **Come Some Rainy Day** *Wynonna*
7/71 **Come Sundown** *Bobby Bare*
57/70 **Come The Morning** *Hank Snow*
16/78 **Come To Me** *Roy Head*
56/87 **Come To Me** *Johnny Paycheck*
87/78 **Come To Me** *Bobby Hood*
16/80 **Come To My Love** *Cristy Lane*
4/59 **Come Walk With Me** *Wilma Lee & Stoney Cooper*
14/49 **Come Wet Your Mustache With Me** *Stubby & The Buccaneers*
1/79 **Come With Me** *Waylon Jennings*
4/62 **Comeback, The** *Faron Young*
67/72 **Comin' After Jinny** *Tex Ritter*
8/71 **Comin' Down** *Dave Dudley*
23/71 **Comin' For To Carry Me Home** *Dolly Parton*
32/75 **Comin' Home To You** *Jerry Wallace*
58/77 **Coming Around** *Connie Smith*
39/98 **Coming Back For You** *Keith Harling*
19/66 **Coming Back To You** *Browns*
50/69 **Coming Of The Roads** *Johnny Darrell & Anita Carger*
75/00 **Coming Up Short Again** *Perfect Stranger*
8/70 **Commercial Affection** *Mel Tillis*
4/98 **Commitment** *LeAnn Rimes*
32/66 **Common Colds And Broken Hearts** *Ray Pillow*
Common Man
50/81 *Sammy Johns*
1/83 *John Conlee*
43/94 **Company Time** *Linda Davis*
8/66 **Company You Keep** *Bill Phillips*
7/55 **Company's Comin'** *Porter Wagoner*
47/81 **Completely Out Of Love** *Marty Robbins*
5/01 **Complicated** *Carolyn Dawn Johnson*
5/03 **Concrete Angel** *Martina McBride*
59/91 **Concrete Cowboy** *Corbin/Hanner*
39/94 **Confessin' My Love** *Shawn Camp*
43/82 **Confidential** *Con Hunley*
28/61 **Congratulations** *Faron Young*
69/88 **Congratulations** *Donna Meade*
49/71 **Congratulations (You Sure Made A Man Out Of Him)** *Arlene Harden*
44/98 **Connected At The Heart** *Ricochet*
Conscience I'm Guilty
4/56 *Hank Snow*
14/61 *Rose Maddox*
48/67 **Conscience Keep An Eye On Me** *Norma Jean*

69/66 **Consider The Children**
Bonnie Owens
63/69 **Conspiracy Of Homer Jones**
Dallas Frazier
57/04 **Constantly**
Cross Canadian Ragweed
15/83 **Conversation, The** *Waylon Jennings w/ Hank Williams, Jr.*
1/75 **Convoy** *C.W. McCall*
18/04 **Cool To Be A Fool** *Joe Nichols*
Cool Water
4/47 *Sons Of The Pioneers*
7/48 *Sons Of The Pioneers*
59/97 **Cool Water** *Tammy Graham*
98/73 **Copperhead** *Jerry Foster*
63/91 **Cornell Crawford** *K.T. Oslin*
2/73 **Corner Of My Life** *Bill Anderson*
70/71 **Corpus Christi Wind**
Dale McBride
Corrine, Corrina
73/70 *Earl Richards*
73/94 *Asleep At The Wheel w/ Brooks & Dunn*
(Corvette Song) ..see: One I Loved Back Then
94/77 **Cotton Dan** *Claude King*
Cotton Fields
50/82 *Creedence Clearwater Revival*
65/83 *Tennessee Express*
11/72 **Cotton Jenny** *Anne Murray*
43/64 **Cotton Mill Man** *Jim & Jesse*
34/89 **Cotton Pickin' Time** *Marcy Bros.*
53/72 **Cotton Top** *Carl Perkins*
1/80 **Could I Have This Dance**
Anne Murray
59/79 **Could I Talk You Into Loving Me Again** *Wynn Stewart*
70/82 **Could It Be I Don't Belong Here Anymore** *Margo Smith*
57/82 **Could It Be Love** *Jennifer Warnes*
97/80 **Could You Ever Really Love A Poor Boy** *Don Williams*
26/81 **Could You Love Me (One More Time)** *John Conlee*
2/92 **Could've Been Me** *Billy Ray Cyrus*
15/80 **Couldn't Do Nothin' Right**
Rosanne Cash
3/00 **Couldn't Last A Moment**
Collin Raye
64/91 **Couldn't Love Have Picked A Better Place To Die**
Clinton Gregory
22/66 **Count Down** *Hank Snow*
5/97 **Count Me In** *Deana Carter*
14/66 **Count Me Out** *Marty Robbins*
5/86 **Count On Me** *Statler Brothers*
16/68 **Count Your Blessings, Woman**
Jan Howard
61/74 **Counterfeit Cowboy** *Dave Dudley*
44/87 **Countrified** *John Anderson*
23/96 **C-O-U-N-T-R-Y** *Joe Diffie*
26/03 **Country Ain't Country** *Travis Tritt*
97/73 **Country And Pop Music**
Urel Albert
83/73 **Country Boogie Woogie**
Linda Nash
1/85 **Country Boy** *Ricky Skaggs*
7/49 **Country Boy**
"Little" Jimmy Dickens
Country Boy Can Survive
2/82 *Hank Williams, Jr.*
30/00 *Chad Brock*

44/86 **Country Boy (Who Rolled The Rock Away)** *David Allan Coe*
3/75 **Country Boy (You Got Your Feet In L.A.)** *Glen Campbell*
22/67 **Country Boy's Dream**
Carl Perkins
67/82 **Country Boy's Song** *Karen Taylor*
1/74 **Country Bumpkin** *Cal Smith*
33/02 **Country By The Grace Of God**
Chris Cagle
9/89 **Country Club** *Travis Tritt*
4/00 **Country Comes To Town**
Toby Keith
44/96 **Country Crazy** *Little Texas*
36/75 **Country D.J.** *Bill Anderson*
68/82 **Country Fiddles** *Solid Gold Band*
1/59 **Country Girl** *Faron Young*
7/70 **Country Girl** *Jeannie C. Riley*
15/68 **Country Girl** *Dottie West*
41/75 **Country Girl** *Jody Miller*
61/73 **Country Girl (I Love You Still)**
Glenn Barber
96/88 **Country Girl In Paris** *John Denver*
52/71 **Country Girl With Hot Pants On**
Leona Williams
1/85 **Country Girls** *John Schneider*
5/71 **Country Green** *Don Gibson*
16/65 **Country Guitar**
Phil Baugh w/ Vern Stovall
8/68 **Country Hall Of Fame**
Hank Locklin
76/88 **Country Highways** *C.W. Ferrari*
72/00 **Country In My Genes**
Loretta Lynn
1/74 **Country Is** *Tom T. Hall*
87/81 **Country Is The Closest Thing To Heaven (You Can Hear)**
Concrete Cowboy Band
14/49 **Country Junction**
Tennessee Ernie Ford
23/78 **Country Lovin'** *Eddy Arnold*
27/74 **Country Lullabye** *Johnny Carver*
63/72 **Country Music In My Soul**
George Hamilton IV
2/59 **Country Music Is Here To Stay**
Simon Crum
63/85 **Country Music Love Affair**
David Frizzell
23/67 **Country Music Lover**
"Little" Jimmy Dickens
76/83 **Country Music Nightmare**
Boxcar Willie
26/61 **Country Music Time**
Lonzo & Oscar
15/77 **Country Party** *Johnny Lee*
31/87 **Country Rap** *Bellamy Brothers*
46/92 **Country Road** *Dolly Parton*
46/02 **Country Rock Star** *Marcel*
2/86 **Country State Of Mind**
Hank Williams, Jr.
2/73 **Country Sunshine** *Dottie West*
45/03 **Country Thang**
John Michael Montgomery
35/94 **Country 'Til I Die** *John Anderson*
62/72 **Country Western Truck Drivin' Singer** *Red Simpson*
Countryfied
80/74 *Ray Pillow*
23/81 *Mel McDaniel*
35/71 **Countryfied** *George Hamilton IV*

Couple More Years
51/76 *Dr. Hook*
89/79 *King Edward IV & The Knights*
44/93 **Couple Of Good Years Left**
Ricky Van Shelton
1/02 **Courtesy Of The Red, White And Blue (The Angry American)**
Toby Keith
3/54 **Courtin' In The Rain**
T. Texas Tyler
33/75 **Cover Me** *Sammi Smith*
3/98 **Cover You In Kisses**
John Michael Montgomery
65/81 **Cow Patti** *Jim Stafford*
5/62 **Cow Town** *Webb Pierce*
1/80 **Coward Of The County**
Kenny Rogers
13/76 **Cowboy** *Eddy Arnold*
82/81 **Cowboy** *Larry Dalton*
Cowboy And The Lady
85/77 *Bobby Goldsboro*
50/81 *John Denver*
Cowboy And The Lady
90/76 *Patsy Sledd*
63/77 *Tommy Cash*
(Cowboy And The Poet) ..see: Faster Horses
24/94 **Cowboy Band** *Billy Dean*
23/92 **Cowboy Beat** *Bellamy Brothers*
46/93 **Cowboy Boogie** *Randy Travis*
3/63 **Cowboy Boots** *Dave Dudley*
52/97 **Cowboy Cadillac** *Garth Brooks*
70/99 **Cowboy Cadillac**
Confederate Railroad
70/01 **Cowboy Christmas** *Clay Walker*
19/70 **Cowboy Convention**
Buddy Alan & Don Rich
36/89 **Cowboy Hat In Dallas**
Charlie Daniels Band
44/82 **Cowboy In A Three Piece Business Suit** *Rex Allen, Jr.*
1/02 **Cowboy In Me** *Tim McGraw*
3/64 **Cowboy In The Continental Suit**
Marty Robbins
91/76 **Cowboy Like You** *Heckels*
52/90 **Cowboy Logic**
Michael Martin Murphey
4/96 **Cowboy Love**
John Michael Montgomery
10/87 **Cowboy Man** *Lyle Lovett*
100/76 **Cowboy Peyton Place**
Doug Sahm
5/85 **Cowboy Rides Away**
George Strait
77/79 **Cowboy Singer** *Sonny Curtis*
76/80 **Cowboy Stomp!** *Spurzz*
1/00 **Cowboy Take Me Away**
Dixie Chicks
(Cowboy Tune) ..see: End Is Not In Sight
12/93 **Cowboy's Born With A Broken Heart** *Boy Howdy*
49/83 **Cowboy's Dream** *Mel Tillis*
13/77 **Cowboys Ain't Supposed To Cry**
Moe Bandy
1/80 **Cowboys And Clowns**
Ronnie Milsap
29/75 **Cowboys And Daddys**
Bobby Bare
(Cowboys And Indians) ..see: When Our Love Began

68/80 **Cowboys Are Common As Sin** *Max D. Barnes*
Cowboys Don't Cry
65/91 *Dude Mowrey*
24/94 *Daron Norwood*
60/01 **Cowboys Don't Cry** *Eddy Raven*
11/78 **Cowboys Don't Get Lucky All The Time** *Gene Watson*
21/81 **Cowboys Don't Shoot Straight (Like They Used To)** *Tammy Wynette*
2/03 **Cowboys Like Us** *George Strait*
10/80 **Cowgirl And The Dandy** *Brenda Lee*
75/84 **Cowgirl In A Coupe DeVille** *Terry Gregory*
45/04 **Cowgirls** *Kerry Harvick*
38/86 **Cowpoke** *Glen Campbell*
82/83 **Coyote Song** *Delia Bell*
16/61 **Cozy Inn** *Leon McAuliffe*
56/69 **Crack In My World** *Leroy Van Dyke*
63/00 **Cracker Jack Diamond** *Marty Raybon*
3/80 **Crackers** *Barbara Mandrell*
32/92 **Crash Course In The Blues** *Steve Wariner*
42/71 **Crawdad Song** *LaWanda Lindsey & Kenny Vernon*
F/73 **Crawling On My Knees** *Marty Robbins*
1/85 **Crazy** *Kenny Rogers*
Crazy
2/62 *Patsy Cline*
73/67 *Ray Price*
6/77 *Linda Ronstadt*
84/76 **Crazy Again** *Rayburn Anthony*
Crazy Arms
1/56 *Ray Price*
18/63 *Marion Worth*
16/79 *Willie Nelson*
46/87 **Crazy Blue** *Billy Montana*
17/79 **Crazy Blue Eyes** *Lacy J. Dalton*
11/48 **Crazy Boogie** *Merle Travis*
58/01 **Crazy 'Bout You Baby** *Billy Ray Cyrus*
11/61 **Crazy Bullfrog** *Lewis Pruitt*
4/47 **Crazy 'Cause I Love You** *Spade Cooley*
87/90 **Crazy Driver** *Dalice*
1/85 **Crazy For Your Love** *Exile*
3/87 **Crazy From The Heart** *Bellamy Brothers*
4/51 **Crazy Heart** *Hank Williams*
Crazy In Love
68/88 *Kim Carnes*
2/90 *Conway Twitty*
43/01 **Crazy Life** *Tim Rushlow*
97/77 **Crazy Little Mama (At My Front Door)** *Alvin Crow*
Crazy Little Thing Called Love
79/81 *Orion*
12/99 *Dwight Yoakam*
95/79 **Crazy Love** *Poco*
85/83 **Crazy Old Soldier** *David Allan Coe*
4/87 **Crazy Over You** *Foster & Lloyd*
8/62 **Crazy Wild Desire** *Webb Pierce*
10/74 **Credit Card Song** *Dick Feller*
89/82 **Crime In The Sheets** *Shylo*
7/87 **Crime Of Passion** *Ricky Van Shelton*

32/76 **Crispy Critters** *C.W. McCall*
67/00 **Critical List** *Ray Hood*
92/88 **Crocodile Man From Walk-About-Creek** *LeGarde Twins*
59/90 **Crocodile Tears** *Lee Roy Parnell*
14/89 **Cross My Broken Heart** *Suzy Bogguss*
64/86 **Cross My Heart** *Jan Gray*
86/87 **Cross My Heart** *Stella Parton*
2/64 **Cross The Brazos At Waco** *Billy Walker*
57/75 **Crossroad, The** *Mary Kay James*
11/84 **Crossword Puzzle** *Barbara Mandrell*
92/82 **Crown Prince Of The Barroom** *David Rogers*
13/74 **Crude Oil Blues** *Jerry Reed*
9/60 **Cruel Love** *Lou Smith*
41/99 **Crush** *Lila McCann*
69/91 **Crush, The** *JJ White*
25/77 **Crutches** *Faron Young*
Cry
3/72 *Lynn Anderson*
99/75 *Diana Trask*
1/86 *Crystal Gayle*
12/02 **Cry** *Faith Hill*
77/82 **Cry** *Tanya Tucker*
Cry Baby
52/83 *Narvel Felts*
56/88 *Joe Stampley*
Cry Baby
84/86 *Lowes*
61/89 *Donna Meade*
5/49 **Cry-Baby Heart** *George Morgan*
58/68 **Cry, Cry Again** *Liz Anderson*
1/88 **Cry, Cry, Cry** *Highway 101*
Cry! Cry! Cry!
14/55 *Johnny Cash*
32/89 *Marty Stuart*
20/68 **Cry, Cry, Cry** *Connie Smith*
Cry, Cry, Darling
4/54 *Jimmy Newman*
34/78 *Con Hunley*
67/78 *Glenn Barber*
50/87 **Cry Just A Little** *Marie Osmond*
9/85 **Cry Just A Little Bit** *Sylvia*
70/75 **Cry Like A Baby** *Joe Stampley*
1/87 **Cry Myself To Sleep** *Judds*
7/50 **Cry Of The Dying Duck In A Thunder-Storm** *Cactus Pryor*
2/50 **Cry Of The Wild Goose** *Tennessee Ernie Ford*
26/97 **Cry On The Shoulder Of The Road** *Martina McBride*
57/94 **Cry Wolf** *Victoria Shaw*
Cryin' ..also see: Crying
3/78 **Cryin' Again** *Oak Ridge Boys*
90/73 **Cryin' Eyes** *Patti Tierny*
56/98 **Cryin' Game** *Sara Evans*
5/51 **Cryin' Heart Blues** *Johnnie & Jack*
11/48 **Cryin' In My Beer** *Jerry Irby*
7/55 **Cryin', Prayin', Waitin', Hopin'** *Hank Snow*
56/03 **Cryin' Steel** *Jerry Burkhart*
Crying
28/70 *Arlene Harden*
79/76 *Ronnie Milsap*
14/80 *Stephanie Winslow*
6/81 *Don McLean*
42/88 *Roy Orbison & k.d. lang*

Crying In The Chapel
4/53 *Darrell Glenn*
4/53 *Rex Allen*
Crying In The Rain
54/72 *Del Reeves & Penny DeHaven*
18/81 *Tammy Wynette*
Crying My Heart Out Over You
21/60 *Flatt & Scruggs*
1/82 *Ricky Skaggs*
3/58 **Crying Over You** *Webb Pierce*
43/73 **Crying Over You** *Dickey Lee*
51/87 **Crying Over You** *Rosie Flores*
4/88 **Crying Shame** *Michael Johnson*
59/93 **Crying Time** *Lorrie Morgan*
12/65 **Crystal Chandelier** *Carl Belew*
76/82 **Cube, The** *Bob Jenkins*
2/50 **Cuddle Buggin' Baby** *Eddy Arnold*
Cuddle Up Kind ..see: (I'm Just The)
47/68 **Culman, Alabam** *Roger Sovine*
12/81 **Cup Of Tea** *Rex Allen, Jr. & Margo Smith*
59/67 **Cupid's Last Arrow** *Bobby Austin*
94/76 **Curse Of A Woman** *Eddy Raven*
3/58 **Curtain In The Window** *Ray Price*
14/69 **Custody** *Luke The Drifter, Jr.*
Cut Across Shorty
28/60 *Carl Smith*
15/69 *Nat Stuckey*
60/68 **Cut The Cornbread, Mama** *Osborne Brothers*
73/71 **Cute Little Waitress** *Stoney Edwards*
5/55 **Cuzz Yore So Sweet** *Simon Crum*

D

8/65 **DJ Cried** *Ernest Ashworth*
9/64 **D.J. For A Day** *Jimmy "C" Newman*
88/82 **D.O.A. (Drunk On Arrival)** *Johnny Paycheck*
10/48 **Dad Gave My Dog Away** *T. Texas Tyler*
9/87 **Daddies Need To Grow Up Too** *O'Kanes*
14/79 **Daddy** *Donna Fargo*
40/69 **Daddy** *Dolly Parton*
55/81 **Daddy** *Billy Edd Wheeler w/ Rashell Richmond*
27/89 **Daddy And Home** *Tanya Tucker*
85/74 **Daddy Bluegrass** *Stoney Edwards*
69/97 **Daddy Can You See Me** *Anita Cochran*
40/70 **Daddy Come And Get Me** *Dolly Parton*
55/72 **Daddy Don't You Walk So Fast** *Wayne Newton*
1/71 **Daddy Frank (The Guitar Man)** *Merle Haggard*
58/76 **Daddy How'm I Doin'** *Rick Smith*
40/70 **Daddy, I Love You** *Billie Jo Spears*
63/93 **Daddy Laid The Blues On Me** *Bobbie Cryner*
62/74 **Daddy Loves You Honey** *Dorsey Burnette*

9/94 **Daddy Never Was The Cadillac Kind** *Confederate Railroad*
45/74 **Daddy Number Two** *Glenn Barber*
93/80 **Daddy Played Harmonica** *Jerry Dycke*
1/69 **Daddy Sang Bass** *Johnny Cash*
20/62 **Daddy Stopped In** *Claude Gray*
54/77 **Daddy, They're Playin' A Song About You** *Kenny Seratt*
68/71 **Daddy Was A Preacher But Mama Was A Go-Go Girl** *Joanna Neel*
7/70 **Daddy Was An Old Time Preacher Man** *Porter Wagoner & Dolly Parton*
2/74 **Daddy What If** *Bobby Bare*
15/49 **Daddy, When Is Mommy Coming Home** *Ernest Tubb*
17/00 **Daddy Won't Sell The Farm** *Montgomery Gentry*
8/55 **Daddy, You Know What?** *Jim Wilson*
1/91 **Daddy's Come Around** *Paul Overstreet*
56/66 **Daddy's Coming Home (Next Week)** *Charlie Walker*
91/75 **Daddy's Girl** *Red Sovine*
7/86 **Daddy's Hands** *Holly Dunn*
48/85 **Daddy's Honky Tonk** *Moe Bandy & Joe Stampley*
6/50 **Daddy's Last Letter** *Tex Ritter*
42/97 **Daddy's Little Girl** *Kippi Brannon*
92/80 **Daddy's Makin' Records In Nashville** *LeGarde Twins*
1/96 **Daddy's Money** *Ricochet*
33/73 **Daisy A Day** *Jud Strunk*
37/73 **Daisy May (And Daisy May Not)** *Terri Lane*
66/73 **Dakota The Dancing Bear** *Johnny Darrell*
1/92 **Dallas** *Alan Jackson*
32/80 **Dallas** *Floyd Cramer*
35/74 **Dallas** *Connie Smith*
54/83 **Dallas** *Bama Band*
58/67 **Dallas** *Vern Stovall*
89/79 **Dallas Cowboys** *Charley Pride*
77/88 **Dallas Darlin'** *Norm Schaffer*
68/95 **Dallas Days And Fort Worth Nights** *Chris LeDoux*
(Dallas Lovers' Song) ..see: Makin' Up For Lost Time
71/90 **Dam These Tears** *Canyon*
68/75 **Damn Good Country Song** *Jerry Lee Lewis*
F/79 **Damn Good Drinking Song** *Kenny Seratt*
1/90 **Dance, The** *Garth Brooks*
75/88 **Dance For Me** *Don Malena*
38/76 **Dance Her By Me (One More Time)** *Jacky Ward*
42/90 **Dance In Circles** *Tim Ryan*
49/98 **Dance In The Boat** *Kinleys*
9/83 **Dance Little Jean** *Nitty Gritty Dirt Band*
63/98 **Dance The Night Away** *Mavericks*
23/81 **Dance The Two Step** *Susie Allanson*
2/74 **Dance With Me (Just One More Time)** *Johnny Rodriguez*
Dance With Me Molly
96/78 *Roger Bowling*
88/79 *Hank Thompson*
41/04 **Dance With My Father** *Kellie Coffey*
55/93 **Dance With The One That Brought You** *Shania Twain*
71/91 **Dance With Who Brung You** *Asleep At The Wheel*
1/80 **Dancin' Cowboys** *Bellamy Brothers*
72/87 **Dancin' In The Moonlight** *Durelle Ames*
29/79 **Dancin' 'Round And 'Round** *Olivia Newton-John*
3/97 **Dancin', Shaggin' On The Boulevard** *Alabama*
(Dancin' To A Different Beat) ..see: I'm An Old Rock And Roller
51/87 **Dancin' With Myself Tonight** *Kendalls*
29/84 **Dancin' With The Devil** *Stephanie Winslow*
58/96 **Dancin' With The Wind** *Great Plains*
16/77 **Dancing The Night Away** *Tanya Tucker*
3/82 **Dancing Your Memory Away** *Charly McClain*
5/90 **Dancy's Dream** *Restless Heart*
1/64 **Dang Me** *Roger Miller*
20/78 **Danger, Heartbreak Ahead** *Zella Lehr*
46/86 **Danger List (Give Me Someone I Can Love)** *Leon Everette*
15/77 **Danger Of A Stranger** *Stella Parton*
59/86 **Danger Zone** *Maines Brothers Band*
98/77 **Danger Zone** *Peggy Forman*
92/89 **Dangerous Ground** *Lance Strode*
62/88 **Dangerous Road** *Mason Dixon*
9/67 **Danny Boy** *Ray Price*
10/73 **Danny's Song** *Anne Murray*
23/02 **Dare To Dream** *Jo Dee Messina*
63/81 **Dare To Dream Again** *Phil Everly*
49/64 **Dark As A Dungeon** *Johnny Cash*
24/68 **Dark End Of The Street** *Archie Campbell & Lorene Mann*
76/86 **Dark Eyed Lady** *Bart Cameron*
Dark Hollow
7/59 *Jimmie Skinner*
13/59 *Luke Gordon*
21/97 **Dark Horse** *Mila Mason*
14/57 **Dark Moon** *Bonnie Guitar*
42/86 **Dark Side Of Town** *Dobie Gray*
75/90 **Darkness Of The Light** *Harrell & Scott*
1/88 **Darlene** *T. Graham Brown*
67/82 **Darlene** *Big Al Downing*
Darlin'
53/72 *Wayne Kemp*
42/74 *Ray Griff*
Darling
86/78 *Poacher*
18/79 *David Rogers*
19/81 *Tom Jones*
26/73 **Darlin' (Don't Come Back)** *Dorsey Burnette*
Darlin' Raise The Shade
57/72 *Claude King*
64/73 *Norro Wilson*
23/70 **Darling Days** *Billy Walker*
5/73 **Darling, You Can Always Come Back Home** *Jody Miller*
2/69 **Darling, You Know I Wouldn't Lie** *Conway Twitty*
69/87 **Darlington County** *Jeff Stevens & The Bullets*
4/95 **Darned If I Don't (Danged If I Do)** *Shenandoah*
4/47 **Daughter Of Jole Blon** *Johnny Bond*
Davy Crockett ..see: Ballad Of
59/88 **Day After Tomorrow** *Darden Smith*
44/84 **Day By Day** *McGuffey Lane*
Day Dream ..see: Daydream
23/70 **Day Drinkin'** *Dave Dudley & Tom T. Hall*
14/66 **Day For Decision** *Johnny Sea*
88/88 **Day I Tried To Teach Charlene MacKenzie How To Drive** *Ray Stevens*
11/97 **Day In, Day Out** *David Kersh*
30/72 **Day In The Life Of A Fool** *George Jones*
10/62 **Day Into Night** *Kitty Wells*
18/72 **Day That Love Walked In** *David Houston*
5/98 **Day That She Left Tulsa (In A Chevy)** *Wade Hayes*
4/68 **Day The World Stood Still** *Charley Pride*
72/74 **Day Time Lover** *Gary Sargeants*
60/68 **Day You Stop Loving Me** *Bobby Helms*
Daydream
86/82 *Jon & Lynn [What A Day For A]*
84/89 *Cerrito*
3/80 **Daydream Believer** *Anne Murray*
7/55 **Daydreamin'** *Jimmy Newman*
1/75 **Daydreams About Night Things** *Ronnie Milsap*
7/78 **Daylight** *T.G. Sheppard*
90/74 **Daylight Losing Time** *Larry Steele*
1/04 **Days Go By** *Keith Urban*
24/03 **Days Like This** *Rachel Proctor*
37/02 **Days Of America** *BlackHawk*
77/78 **Days Of Me And You** *Red Sovine*
33/04 **Days Of Our Lives** *James Otto*
Days Of Sand And Shovels
20/69 *Waylon Jennings*
26/78 *Nat Stuckey*
23/77 **Days That End In "Y"** *Sammi Smith*
1/77 **Daytime Friends** *Kenny Rogers*
59/71 **Dayton, Ohio** *Jack Barlow*
7/44 **Deacon Jones** *Louis Jordan*
19/60 **Dead Or Alive** *Bill Anderson*
8/75 **Deal** *Tom T. Hall*
Dealin' With The Devil
25/80 *Eddy Raven*
49/82 *Merle Haggard*
58/77 **Dear Alice** *Johnny Lee*
64/75 **Dear God** *Roy Clark*
9/62 **Dear Ivan** *Jimmy Dean*
7/53 **Dear Joan** *Jack Cardwell*
8/51 **Dear John** *Hank Williams*
Dear John Letter
1/53 *Jean Shepard w/ Ferlin Huskey*
11/65 *Skeeter Davis & Bobby Bare*
F/76 **Dear John Letter Lounge** *Jerry Jeff Walker*

12/60 **Dear Mama** *Merle Kilgore*
9/89 **Dear Me** *Lorrie Morgan*
88/80 **Dear Mr. President** *Max D. Barnes*
Dear Oakie
12/48 *Jack Rivers*
12/48 *Doye O'Dell*
4/66 **Dear Uncle Sam** *Loretta Lynn*
11/75 **Dear Woman** *Joe Stampley*
59/69 **Dearly Beloved** *David Rogers*
80/89 **Death And Taxes (And Me Lovin' You)** *Patsy Cole*
3/53 **Death Of Hank Williams** *Jack Cardwell*
7/49 **Death Of Little Kathy Fiscus** *Jimmie Osborne*
71/00 **Decision** *Ricky Van Shelton*
Deck Of Cards
2/48 *T. Texas Tyler*
10/48 *Tex Ritter*
11/59 *Wink Martindale*
60/91 *Bill Anderson*
Deck The Halls
40/00 *SheDaisy*
37/01 *SheDaisy*
28/84 **Dedicate** *Kieran Kane*
6/96 **Deep Down** *Pam Tillis*
82/87 **Deep Down (Everybody Wants To Be From Dixie)** *Danny Shirley*
75/84 **Deep In The Arms Of Texas** *Con Hunley*
10/87 **Deep River Woman** *Lionel Richie w/ Alabama*
Deep Water
10/67 *Carl Smith*
62/89 *Marsha Thornton*
1/89 **Deeper Than The Holler** *Randy Travis*
87/79 **Deeper Than The Night** *Olivia Newton-John*
35/78 **Deeper Water** *Brenda Kaye Perry*
93/88 **Deepest Shade Of Blue** *Gail Veach*
66/95 **Deja Blue** *Billy Ray Cyrus*
37/69 **Delia's Gone** *Waylon Jennings*
23↑/05 **Delicious Surprise (I Believe It)** *Jo Dee Messina*
17/79 **Della And The Dealer** *Hoyt Axton*
6/72 **Delta Dawn** *Tanya Tucker*
14/74 **Delta Dirt** *Larry Gatlin*
7/84 **Denver** *Gatlin Bros.*
13/64 **Dern Ya** *Ruby Wright*
(Desert Blues) ..see: Big Chief Buffalo Nickel
44/02 **Designated Drinker** *Alan Jackson w/ George Strait*
85/82 **Designer Jeans** *Glen Bailey*
Desperado
5/77 *Johnny Rodriguez*
54/93 *Clint Black*
1/86 **Desperado Love** *Conway Twitty*
15/85 **Desperados Waiting For A Train** *Waylon Jennings/Willie Nelson/ Johnny Cash/Kris Kristofferson*
6/04 **Desperately** *George Strait*
7/88 **Desperately** *Don Williams*
60/68 **Destination Atlanta G.A.** *Cal Smith*
68/00 **Destination Unknown** *Victor Sanz*
31/68 **Destroyed By Man** *Mel Tillis*

Detour
2/46 *Spade Cooley*
3/46 *Wesley Tuttle*
5/46 *Elton Britt*
6/46 *Foy Willing*
Detroit City
6/63 *Bobby Bare*
18/63 *Billy Grammer*
86/81 **Devil, The** *Hoyt Axton*
Devil Ain't A Lonely Woman's Friend
96/75 *Tennessee Ernie Ford*
72/77 *Red Steagall*
74/91 **Devil And Your Deep Blue Eyes** *Sweethearts Of The Rodeo*
54/94 **Devil Comes Back To Georgia** *Mark O'Connor w/ Charlie Daniels, Johnny Cash, Marty Stuart & Travis Tritt*
23/75 **Devil In Mrs. Jones** *Billy Larkin*
Devil In The Bottle
1/75 *T.G. Sheppard*
59/04 *Hank Williams, Jr.*
32/76 **Devil In Your Kisses (And The Angel In Your Eyes)** *Mel Street*
81/82 **Devil Inside** *Wyley McPherson*
Devil Is A Woman
55/73 *Brian Shaw*
87/83 *David Rogers*
59/80 **Devil Stands Only Five Foot Five** *"Blackjack" Jack Grayson*
Devil Went Down To Georgia
1/79 *Charlie Daniels Band*
60/98 *Charlie Daniels Band*
1/62 **Devil Woman** *Marty Robbins*
63/80 **Devil's Den** *Jack Greene*
13/86 **Devil's On The Loose** *Waylon Jennings*
Devoted To You
7/58 *Everly Brothers*
33/78 *Carly Simon & James Taylor*
9/84 **Diamond In The Dust** *Mark Gray*
38/82 **Diamond In The Rough** *Karen Taylor*
45/66 **Diamonds And Horseshoes** *Jerry Wallace*
82/81 **Diamonds And Teardrops** *Wayne Massey*
9/82 **Diamonds In The Stars** *Ray Price*
21/80 **Diane** *Ed Bruce*
15/61 **Did I Ever Tell You** *George Jones & Margie Singleton*
87/89 **Did I Leave My Heart At Your House** *Touch Of Country*
25/63 **Did I Miss You?** *Orville Couch*
25/97 **Did I Shave My Legs For This?** *Deana Carter*
74/85 **Did I Stay Too Long** *Dennis Bottoms*
33/90 **Did It For Love** *Sawyer Brown*
90/81 **Did We Fall Out Of Love** *Tricia Johns*
Did We Have To Come [Go] This Far (To Say Goodbye)
72/71 *Wayne Kemp*
80/82 *Donna Fargo*
26/71 **Did You Ever** *Charlie Louvin & Melba Montgomery*
71/72 **Did You Ever Think** *Don Gibson & Sue Thompson*
70/71 **Did You Think To Pray** *Charley Pride*

56/01 **Diddley** *Elbert West*
23/89 **Didn't Expect It To Go Down This Way** *K.T. Oslin*
55/95 **Didn't Have You** *Billy Montana*
32/65 **Didn't I** *Dottie West*
43/04 **Didn't I** *Rachel Proctor*
45/02 **Didn't I** *Montgomery Gentry*
10/86 **Didn't We** *Lee Greenwood*
75/83 **Didn't We Do It Good** *Brenda Lee*
69/00 **Didn't We Love** *Tamara Walker*
45/87 **Didn't We Shine** *Lynn Anderson*
85/87 **Didn't You Go And Leave Me** *Rosemary Sharp*
52/04 **Die Of A Broken Heart** *Carolyn Dawn Johnson*
18/67 **Diesel On My Tail** *Jim & Jesse*
41/67 **Diesel Smoke, Dangerous Curves** *Red Simpson*
69/83 **Diet Song** *Bobby Bare*
70/70 **Difference Between Going And Really Gone** *Cal Smith*
50/05 **Different Kind Of Christmas** *LeAnn Rimes*
28/77 **Different Kind Of Flower** *Ray Price*
80/89 **Different Situations** *Mack Abernathy*
86/83 **Different Woman Every Night** *Bobby Springfield*
79/78 **Dig Down Deep** *Del Reeves*
1/86 **Diggin' Up Bones** *Randy Travis*
Diggy Liggy Lo
14/61 *Rusty & Doug*
70/69 *Doug Kershaw*
20/85 **Dim Lights, Thick Smoke (And Loud, Loud Music)** *Vern Gosdin*
49/80 **Dim The Lights And Pour The Wine** *Red Steagall*
25/61 **Dime A Dozen** *Shirley Collie*
12/67 **Dime At A Time** *Del Reeves*
78/80 **Diplomat, The** *Roger Bowling*
F/78 **Dirt Farming Man** *Joel Mathis*
3/92 **Dirt Road** *Sawyer Brown*
38/73 **Dirty Old Man** *George Hamilton IV*
26/78 **Dirty Work** *Sterling Whipple*
4/71 **Dis-Satisfied** *Bill Anderson & Jan Howard*
90/79 **Disco Blues** *Jay Chevalier & Shelley Ford*
82/79 **Disco Girl Go Away** *Rebecca Lynn*
75/76 **Disco-Tex** *Little David Wilkins*
12/84 **Disenchanted** *Michael Martin Murphey*
81/79 **Disneyland Daddy** *Paul Evans*
1/66 **Distant Drums** *Jim Reeves*
86/78 **Divers Do It Deeper** *David Allan Coe*
77/88 **Divided** *Burbank Station*
1/68 **D-I-V-O-R-C-E** *Tammy Wynette*
9/53 **Divorce Granted** *Ernest Tubb*
Divorce Me C.O.D.
1/46 *Merle Travis*
5/46 *King Sisters*
4/47 *Johnny Bond*
90/78 **Divorce Suit (You Were Named Co-Respondent)** *Bill Phillips*
Dixie ..see: (I'm Coming Home To You)
54/70 **Dixie Belle** *Stan Hitchcock*
73/93 **Dixie Chicken** *Garth Brooks*

81/80 **Dixie Dirt** *Jim Rushing*
11/83 **Dixie Dreaming** *Atlanta*
Dixie Fried
10/56 *Carl Perkins*
61/73 *Carl Perkins [Let's Get]*
71/93 *Kentucky Headhunters*
44/77 **Dixie Hummingbird** *Ray Stevens*
45/74 **Dixie Lily** *Roy Drusky*
25/81 **Dixie Man** *Randy Barlow*
66/86 **Dixie Moon** *Ray Charles*
1/81 **Dixie On My Mind** *Hank Williams, Jr.*
Dixie Road
48/81 *King Edward IV & The Knights*
1/85 *Lee Greenwood*
36/04 **Dixie Rose Deluxe's Honky Tonk, Feed Store, Gun Shop, Used Car, Beer, Bait, BBQ, Barber Shop, Laundromat** *Trent Willmon*
45/85 **Dixie Train** *Carl Jackson*
1/83 **Dixieland Delight** *Alabama*
F/76 **Dixieland, You Will Never Die** *Lynn Anderson*
90/81 **Do Fish Swim?** *Wickline*
50/84 **Do I Ever Cross Your Mind** *Ray Charles*
Do I Ever Cross Your Mind
85/79 *Kin Vassy*
F/82 *Dolly Parton*
18/81 **Do I Have To Draw A Picture** *Billy Swan*
28/87 **Do I Have To Say Goodbye** *Louise Mandrell*
6/53 **Do I Like It?** *Carl Smith*
45/00 **Do I Love You Enough** *Ricochet*
2/78 **Do I Love You (Yes In Every Way)** *Donna Fargo*
55/97 **Do It Again** *Jeff Carson*
68/89 **Do It Again (I Think I Saw Diamonds)** *Debbie Rich*
13/78 **Do It Again Tonight** *Larry Gatlin*
77/87 **Do It For The Love Of It** *Bart Cameron*
42/79 **Do It In A Heartbeat** *Carlene Carter*
92/79 **Do It Or Die** *Atlanta Rhythm Section*
20/70 **Do It To Someone You Love** *Norro Wilson*
60/85 **Do Me Right** *David Frizzell & Shelly West*
4/82 **Do Me With Love** *Janie Fricke*
17/71 **Do Right Woman - Do Right Man** *Barbara Mandrell*
68/80 **Do That To Me One More Time** *Stephany Samone*
88/77 **Do The Buck Dance** *Ruby Falls*
69/97 **Do The Right Thing** *George Strait*
15/65 **Do-Wacka-Do** *Roger Miller*
Do What You Do Do Well
7/65 *Ned Miller*
29/65 *Ernest Tubb*
13/00 **Do What You Gotta Do** *Garth Brooks*
1/87 **Do Ya'** *K.T. Oslin*
4/88 **Do You Believe Me Now** *Vern Gosdin*
53/68 **Do You Believe This Town** *Roy Clark*
5/79 **Do You Ever Fool Around** *Joe Stampley*
39/89 **Do You Feel The Same Way Too?** *Becky Hobbs*
61/88 **Do You Have Any Doubts** *Alibi*
47/77 **Do You Hear My Heart Beat** *David Rogers*
2/73 **Do You Know What It's Like To Be Lonesome** *Jerry Wallace*
16/93 **Do You Know Where Your Man Is** *Pam Tillis*
1/78 **Do You Know You Are My Sunshine** *Statler Bros.*
1/81 **Do You Love As Good As You Look** *Bellamy Brothers*
1/88 **(Do You Love Me) Just Say Yes** *Highway 101*
72/86 **Do You Mind If I Step Into Your Dreams** *Cannons*
59/86 **Do You Really Want My Lovin'** *Marty Stuart*
86/80 **Do You Remember Roll Over Beethoven** *Sonny Curtis*
2/72 **Do You Remember These** *Statler Brothers*
F/76 **Do You Right Tonight** *Eddie Rabbitt*
50/04 **Do You Still Want To Buy Me That Drink (Frank)** *Lorrie Morgan*
73/87 **Do You Wanna Fall In Love** *Bandit Band*
1/80 **Do You Wanna Go To Heaven** *T.G. Sheppard*
Do You Wanna Make Love
70/77 *Bobby Smith*
82/77 *David Wills*
80/79 *Buck Owens*
53/96 **Do You Wanna Make Something Of It** *Jo Dee Messina*
70/80 **Do You Wanna Spend The Night** *Mitch Goodson*
5/05 **Do You Want Fries With That** *Tim McGraw*
38/72 **Do You Want To Dance** *Jack Reno*
94/79 **Do You Want To Fly** *Ronnie Sessions*
Dock Of The Bay ..see: (Sittin' On)
5/95 **Doctor Time** *Rick Trevino*
53/86 **Doctor's Orders** *Mel McDaniel*
1/85 **Does Fort Worth Ever Cross Your Mind** *George Strait*
32/84 **Does He Ever Mention My Name** *Rick & Janis Carnes*
1/93 **Does He Love You** *Reba McEntire w/ Linda Davis*
5/63 **Does He Mean That Much To You?** *Eddy Arnold*
23/02 **Does My Ring Burn Your Finger** *Lee Ann Womack*
4/67 **Does My Ring Hurt Your Finger** *Country Charley Pride*
20/81 **Does She Wish She Was Single Again** *Burrito Brothers*
2/96 **Does That Blue Moon Ever Shine On You** *Toby Keith*
33/81 **Doesn't Anybody Get High On Love Anymore** *Shoppe*
7/54 **Dog-Gone It, Baby, I'm In Love** *Carl Smith*
6/48 **Dog House Boogie** *Hawkshaw Hawkins*
64/95 **Dog On A Toolbox** *James Bonamy*
75/76 **Dog Tired Of Cattin' Around** *Shylo*
45/66 **Doggin' In The U.S. Mail** *Hal Willis*
19/59 **Doggone That Train** *Hank Snow*
61/91 **Doghouse** *John Conlee*
47/05 **Doin' It Right** *Steve Azar*
17/60 **(Doin' The) Lovers Leap** *Webb Pierce*
82/89 **Doing It By The Book** *Whites*
62/83 **Doing It Right** *McGuffey Lane*
39/76 **Doing My Time** *Don Gibson*
57/78 **Dolly** *R.W. Blackwood*
4/87 **Domestic Life** *John Conlee*
7/90 **Domino Theory** *Steve Wariner*
57/78 **Don Juan** *Billy "Crash" Craddock*
63/75 **Don Junior** *Jim Ed Brown*
Don't
2/58 *Elvis Presley*
39/73 *Sandy Posey*
24/05 **Don't!** *Shania Twain*
13/75 **Don't Anyone Make Love At Home Anymore** *Moe Bandy*
16/05 **Don't Ask Me How I Know** *Bobby Pinson*
F/58 **Don't Ask Me Why** *Elvis Presley*
Don't Be Angry
4/64 *Stonewall Jackson*
33/73 *Billy "Crash" Craddock*
3/77 *Donna Fargo*
7/50 **Don't Be Ashamed Of Your Age** *Ernest Tubb & Red Foley*
Don't Be Cruel
1/56 *Elvis Presley*
10/87 *Judds*
6/98 **Don't Be Stupid (You Know I Love You)** *Shania Twain*
71/89 **Don't Be Surprised If You Get It** *Debbie Rich*
4/76 **Don't Believe My Heart Can Stand Another You** *Tanya Tucker*
58/76 **Don't Boogie Woogie** *Jerry Lee Lewis*
13/81 **Don't Bother To Knock** *Jim Ed Brown/Helen Cornelius*
21/04 **Don't Break My Heart Again** *Pat Green*
1/78 **Don't Break The Heart That Loves You** *Margo Smith*
49/86 **Don't Bury Me 'Til I'm Ready** *Johnny Paycheck*
1/85 **Don't Call Him A Cowboy** *Conway Twitty*
3/85 **Don't Call It Love** *Dolly Parton*
62/83 **Don't Call Me** *Karen Taylor-Good*
13/63 **Don't Call Me From A Honky Tonk** *Johnny & Jonie Mosby*
42/71 **Don't Change On Me** *Penny DeHaven*
1/84 **Don't Cheat In Our Hometown** *Ricky Skaggs*
1/88 **Don't Close Your Eyes** *Keith Whitley*
27/99 **Don't Come Cryin' To Me** *Vince Gill*
1/67 **Don't Come Home A'Drinkin' (With Lovin' On Your Mind)** *Loretta Lynn*
28/82 **Don't Come Knockin** *Cindy Hurt*

9/83 **Don't Count The Rainy Days** *Michael Murphey*
54/91 **Don't Cross Your Heart** *Shelby Lynne*
6/44 **Don't Cry, Baby** *Erskine Hawkins*
70/68 **Don't Cry Baby** *Freddie Hart*
80/81 **Don't Cry Baby** *Randy Parton*
13/70 **Don't Cry Daddy** *Elvis Presley*
29/85 **Don't Cry Darlin'** *David Allan Coe*
4/75 **Don't Cry Joni** *Conway Twitty w/ Joni Lee*
12/57 **Don't Do It Darlin'** *Webb Pierce*
Don't Drop It
4/54 *Terry Fell*
69/75 *Fargo Tanner*
Don't Ever Leave Me Again
84/81 *Max D. Barnes*
28/82 *Vern Gosdin*
65/00 **Don't Ever Let Me Go** *Tara Lyn Hart*
13/78 **Don't Ever Say Good-Bye** *T.G. Sheppard*
3/80 **Don't Fall In Love With A Dreamer** *Kenny Rogers w/ Kim Carnes*
43/86 **Don't Fall In Love With Me** *Lacy J. Dalton*
33/79 **Don't Feel Like The Lone Ranger** *Leon Everette*
4/45 **Don't Fence Me In** *Gene Autry*
1/73 **Don't Fight The Feelings Of Love** *Charley Pride*
12/55 **Don't Forget** *Eddy Arnold*
44/74 **Don't Forget To Remember** *Skeeter Davis*
75/88 **Don't Forget Your Way Home** *Melissa Kay*
13/81 **Don't Forget Yourself** *Statler Brothers*
16/81 **Don't Get Above Your Raising** *Ricky Skaggs*
1/96 **Don't Get Me Started** *Rhett Akins*
60/87 **Don't Get Me Started** *Libby Hurley*
10/88 **Don't Give Candy To A Stranger** *Larry Boone*
41/69 **Don't Give Me A Chance** *Claude Gray*
91/84 **Don't Give Up On Her Now** *Leon Raines*
Don't Give Up On Me
3/73 *Jerry Wallace*
73/82 *Eddy Arnold*
90/76 **Don't Give Up On Me** *Stoney Edwards*
37/65 **Don't Give Up The Ship** *Johnny Wright*
27/90 **Don't Give Us A Reason** *Hank Williams, Jr.*
69/84 **Don't Go Changing** *Lorrie Morgan*
5/77 **Don't Go City Girl On Me** *Tommy Overstreet*
18/62 **Don't Go Near The Eskimos** *Ben Colder*
4/62 **Don't Go Near The Indians** *Rex Allen*
12/92 **Don't Go Near The Water** *Sammy Kershaw*
6/90 **Don't Go Out** *Tanya Tucker w/ T. Graham Brown*
1/87 **Don't Go To Strangers** *T. Graham Brown*
88/77 **Don't Hand Me No Hand Me Down Love** *Beverly Heckel*
4/45 **Don't Hang Around Me Anymore** *Gene Autry*
56/71 **Don't Hang No Halos On Me** *Connie Eaton*
1/01 **Don't Happen Twice** *Kenny Chesney*
30/82 **Don't It Break Your Heart** *Steve Wariner*
1/77 **Don't It Make My Brown Eyes Blue** *Crystal Gayle*
42/80 **Don't It Make Ya Wanna Dance** *Bonnie Raitt*
Don't It Make You Want To Go Home
27/69 *Joe South*
51/87 *Butch Baker*
Don't Just Stand There ..see: (When You Feel Like You're In Love)
1/70 **Don't Keep Me Hangin' On** *Sonny James*
11/57 **Don't Laugh** *Louvin Brothers*
2/98 **Don't Laugh At Me** *Mark Wills*
83/82 **Don't Lead Me On** *Wyvon Alexander*
42/90 **Don't Leave Her Lonely Too Long** *Marty Stuart*
67/83 **Don't Leave Me Lonely Loving You** *Randy Barlow*
44/64 **Don't Leave Me Lonely Too Long** *Kathy Dee*
11/74 **Don't Let Go** *Mel Tillis & Sherry Bryce*
26/87 **Don't Let Go Of My Heart** *Southern Pacific*
33/64 **Don't Let Her Know** *Buck Owens*
30/63 **Don't Let Her See Me Cry** *Lefty Frizzell*
22/71 **Don't Let Him Make A Memory Out Of Me** *Billy Walker*
83/86 **Don't Let It Go To Your Heart** *Bonnie Nelson*
Don't Let Me Cross Over
1/62 *Carl Butler & Pearl*
9/69 *Jerry Lee Lewis/Linda Gail Lewis*
10/79 *Jim Reeves w/ Deborah Allen*
60/01 **Don't Let Me Down** *Kortney Kayle*
6/77 **Don't Let Me Touch You** *Marty Robbins*
86/77 **Don't Let My Love Stand In Your Way** *Jim Glaser*
1/92 **Don't Let Our Love Start Slippin' Away** *Vince Gill*
86/76 **Don't Let Smokey Mountain Smoke Get In Your Eyes** *Osborne Brothers*
24/67 **Don't Let That Doorknob Hit You** *Norma Jean*
86/78 **Don't Let The Flame Burn Out** *Rita Remington*
15/75 **Don't Let The Good Times Fool You** *Melba Montgomery*
37/73 **Don't Let The Green Grass Fool You** *O.B. McClinton*
Don't Let The Stars (Get In Your Eyes)
1/52 *Slim Willet*
1/52 *Skeets McDonald*
4/52 *Ray Price*
8/53 *Red Foley*
16/71 **(Don't Let The Sun Set On You) Tulsa** *Waylon Jennings*
14/61 **Don't Let Your Sweet Love Die** *Reno & Smiley*
27/00 **Don't Lie** *Trace Adkins*
4/45 **Don't Live A Lie** *Gene Autry*
12/82 **Don't Look Back** *Gary Morris*
61/80 **Don't Look Back** *Dickey Lee*
60/03 **Don't Look Now** *Rodney Carrington*
11/81 **Don't Look Now (But We Just Fell In Love)** *Eddy Arnold*
4/47 **Don't Look Now (But Your Broken Heart Is Showing)** *Ernest Tubb*
17/97 **Don't Love Make A Diamond Shine** *Tracy Byrd*
1/84 **Don't Make It Easy For Me** *Earl Thomas Conley*
60/69 **Don't Make Love** *Mac Curtis*
29/00 **Don't Make Me Beg** *Steve Holy*
17/01 **Don't Make Me Come Over There And Love You** *George Strait*
51/95 **Don't Make Me Feel At Home** *Wesley Dennis*
F/57 **Don't Make Me Go** *Johnny Cash*
84/80 **Don't Make Me Over** *Jennifer Warnes*
46/85 **Don't Make Me Wait On The Moon** *Shelly West*
29/78 **Don't Make No Promises (You Can't Keep)** *Don King*
41/68 **Don't Monkey With Another Monkey's Monkey** *Johnny Paycheck*
18/72 **Don't Pay The Ransom** *Nat Stuckey*
27/83 **Don't Plan On Sleepin' Tonight** *Steve Wariner*
52/01 **Don't Play Any Love Songs** *Jameson Clark*
23/63 **Don't Pretend** *Bobby Edwards*
49/80 **Don't Promise Me Anything (Do It)** *Brenda Lee*
4/76 **Don't Pull Your Love (medley)** *Glen Campbell*
47/67 **Don't Put Your Hands On Me** *Lorene Mann*
32/67 **Don't Put Your Hurt In My Heart** *Conway Twitty*
25/89 **Don't Quit Me Now** *James House*
Don't Rob Another Man's Castle
1/49 *Eddy Arnold*
6/49 *Ernest Tubb & Andrews Sisters*
1/91 **Don't Rock The Jukebox** *Alan Jackson*
15/77 **Don't Say Goodbye** *Rex Allen, Jr.*
48/88 **Don't Say It With Diamonds (Say It With Love)** *T.G. Sheppard*
93/79 **Don't Say Love** *Connie Smith*
97/79 **Don't Say No To Me Tonight** *Mark Sexton*
51/87 **Don't Say No Tonight** *Mason Dixon*
76/83 **Don't Say You Love Me (Just Love Me Again)** *Mike Campbell*
34/72 **Don't Say You're Mine** *Carl Smith*
55/83 **Don't Send Me No Angels** *Wayne Kemp*
77/88 **Don't Send Me Roses** *Sarah*
2/72 **Don't She Look Good** *Bill Anderson*

8/67 **Don't Squeeze My Sharmon** *Charlie Walker*
62/88 **Don't Start The Fire** *Marcia Lynn*
2/52 **Don't Stay Away (Till Love Grows Cold)** *Lefty Frizzell*
79/87 **Don't Stay If You Don't Love Me** *Patsy Sledd*
86/79 **Don't Stay On Your Side Of The Bed Tonight** *Ann J. Morton*
9/51 **Don't Stay Too Long** *Ernest Tubb*
10/95 **Don't Stop** *Wade Hayes*
14/76 **Don't Stop Believin'** *Olivia Newton-John*
19/76 **Don't Stop In My World (If You Don't Mean To Stay)** *Billy Walker*
43/75 **Don't Stop Loving Me** *Don Gibson*
45/74 **Don't Stop Now** *Sherry Bryce*
10/57 **Don't Stop The Music** *George Jones*
68/78 **Don't Stop The Music (You're Playing My Song)** *Little David Wilkins*
27/64 **Don't Take Advantage Of Me** *Bonnie Owens*
17/70 **Don't Take All Your Loving** *Don Gibson*
Don't Take Her She's All I Got ..see: She's All I Got
Don't Take It Away
67/75 *Jody Miller*
1/79 *Conway Twitty*
5/55 **Don't Take It Out On Me** *Hank Thompson*
61/83 **Don't Take Much** *Peter Isaacson*
69/77 **Don't Take My Sunshine Away** *Ava Barber*
1/94 **Don't Take The Girl** *Tim McGraw*
1/59 **Don't Take Your Guns To Town** *Johnny Cash*
59/88 **Don't Talk To Me** *Libby Hurley*
11/55 **Don't Tease Me** *Carl Smith*
2/48 **Don't Telephone - Don't Telegraph (Tell A Woman)** *Tex Williams*
56/99 **Don't Tell Me** *Lee Ann Womack*
55/85 **Don't Tell Me Love Is Kind** *Almost Brothers*
5/91 **Don't Tell Me What To Do** *Pam Tillis*
Don't Tell Me Your Troubles
5/59 *Don Gibson*
53/73 *Kenny Price*
10/74 **Don't Tell (That Sweet Ole Lady Of Mine)** *Johnny Carver*
1/76 **Don't The Girls All Get Prettier At Closing Time** *Mickey Gilley*
55/88 **Don't The Morning Always Come Too Soon** *Ray Price*
88/78 **Don't Think Twice, It's All Right** *Doc & Merle Watson*
5/77 **Don't Throw It All Away** *Dave & Sugar*
54/91 **Don't Throw Me In The Briarpatch** *Keith Palmer*
9/53 **Don't Throw Your Life Away** *Webb Pierce*
5/89 **Don't Toss Us Away** *Patty Loveless*

Don't Touch Me
2/66 *Jeannie Seely*
12/66 *Wilma Burgess*
69/79 *Jerry Naylor/Kelli Warren*
96/79 *Brenda Joyce*
20/87 **Don't Touch Me There** *Charly McClain*
68/96 **Don't Touch My Hat** *Lyle Lovett*
97/79 **Don't Treat Me Like A Stranger** *Randy Gurley*
64/98 **Don't Try To Find Me** *Roger Springer*
1/86 **Don't Underestimate My Love For You** *Lee Greenwood*
Don't Wait On Me
5/81 *Statler Brothers*
67/89 *Statler Brothers*
23/69 **Don't Wake Me I'm Dreaming** *Warner Mack*
86/77 **Don't Want To Take A Chance (On Loving You)** *Ann J. Morton*
5/89 **Don't Waste It On The Blues** *Gene Watson*
33/02 **Don't Waste My Time** *Little Big Town*
72/67 **Don't Waste Your Time** *Mary Taylor*
Don't We All Have The Right
F/70 *Roger Miller*
1/88 *Ricky Van Shelton*
Don't We Belong In Love
80/81 *Rita Remington*
40/82 *Stephanie Winslow*
62/67 **Don't Wipe The Tears That You Cry For Him (On My Good White Shirt)** *Tommy Collins*
Don't Worry
1/61 *Marty Robbins*
96/78 *Glenda Griffith*
73/96 **Don't Worry Baby** *Beach Boys w/ Lorrie Morgan*
7/05 **Don't Worry 'Bout A Thing** *SheDaisy*
1/82 **Don't Worry 'Bout Me Baby** *Janie Fricke*
Don't Worry 'Bout The Mule (Just Load The Wagon)
41/68 *Glenn Barber*
44/71 *Carl Smith*
9/89 **Don't You** *Forester Sisters*
8/85 **Doncha?** *T.G. Sheppard*
62/91 **Don't You Even (Think About Leavin')** *Dean Dillon*
Don't You Ever Get Tired Of Hurting Me
11/66 *Ray Price*
92/77 *Connie Cato*
11/81 *Willie Nelson & Ray Price*
1/89 *Ronnie Milsap*
77/78 **Don't You Feel It Now** *Betty Martin*
49/84 **Don't You Give Up On Love** *Steve Wariner*
1/83 **Don't You Know How Much I Love You** *Ronnie Milsap*
12/74 **Don't You Think** *Marty Robbins*
71/78 **Don't You Think It's Time** *Tommy Jennings*
F/58 **Doncha' Think It's Time** *Elvis Presley*

5/78 **Don't You Think This Outlaw Bit's Done Got Out Of Hand** *Waylon Jennings*
23/83 **Don't Your Mem'ry Ever Sleep At Night** *Steve Wariner*
Doncha ..see: Don't You
96/80 **Donna-Earth Angel (Medley)** *Tucker Williams*
6/86 **Doo-Wah Days** *Mickey Gilley*
70/70 **Doogie Ray** *George Kent*
1/75 **Door, The** *George Jones*
65/97 **Door, A** *Aaron Tippin*
Door I Used To Close
28/76 *Roy Head*
91/76 *Marilyn Sellars*
Door Is Always Open
75/73 *Tennessee Pulleybone*
70/75 *Lois Johnson*
1/76 *Dave & Sugar*
88/75 **Door Number Three** *Jimmy Buffett*
6/56 **Doorstep To Heaven** *Carl Smith*
34/64 **Double Life** *Joe Carson*
30/78 **Double S** *Bill Anderson*
8/84 **Double Shot (Of My Baby's Love)** *Joe Stampley*
13/49 **Double Talkin' Woman** *Earl Nunn*
89/79 **Double W** *Whispering Will*
40/98 **Double Wide Paradise** *Toby Keith*
16/81 **Down And Out** *George Strait*
65/86 **Down At The Mall** *Tom T. Hall*
18/67 **Down At The Pawn Shop** *Hank Snow*
36/77 **Down At The Pool** *Johnny Carver*
4/47 **Down At The Roadside Inn** *Al Dexter*
2/91 **Down At The Twist And Shout** *Mary-Chapin Carpenter*
9/63 **Down By The River** *Faron Young*
28/97 **Down Came A Blackbird** *Lila McCann*
52/67 **Down, Down, Came The World** *Bobby Barnett*
1/91 **Down Home** *Alabama*
56/73 **Down Home Lovin' Woman** *Andra Willis*
10/95 **Down In Flames** *BlackHawk*
38/70 **Down In New Orleans** *Buddy Alan*
Down In Tennessee
12/86 *John Anderson*
23/95 *Mark Chesnutt*
Down In The Boondocks
37/69 *Penny DeHaven*
25/70 *Freddy Weller*
45/68 **Down In The Flood** *Flatt & Scruggs*
42/85 **Down In The Florida Keys** *Tom T. Hall*
68/88 **Down In The Orange Grove** *John Anderson*
41/80 **Down In The Quarter** *Tommy Overstreet*
81/88 **Down On Market Street** *Lorie Ann*
19/93 **Down On My Knees** *Trisha Yearwood*
82/88 **Down On The Bayou** *Ogden Harless*
13/83 **Down On The Corner** *Jerry Reed*
94/79 **Down On The Corner At A Bar Called Kelly's** *Johnny Paycheck*
2/94 **Down On The Farm** *Tim McGraw*
25/85 **Down On The Farm** *Charley Pride*

6/79 **Down On The Rio Grande** *Johnny Rodriguez*
6/89 **Down That Road Tonight** *Nitty Gritty Dirt Band*
58/88 **Down The Road** *Charly McClain*
70/90 **Down The Road** *Mac McAnally*
62/74 **Down The Road I Go** *Don Williams*
33/85 **Down The Road Mountain Pass** *Dan Fogelberg*
59/78 **Down The Roads Of Daddy's Dreams** *Darrell McCall*
2/51 **Down The Trail Of Achin' Hearts** *Hank Snow w/ Anita Carter*
16/79 **Down To Earth Woman** *Kenny Dale*
2/81 **Down To My Last Broken Heart** *Janie Fricke*
2/91 **Down To My Last Teardrop** *Tanya Tucker*
91/77 **Down To My Pride** *Linda Hargrove*
41/74 **Down To The End Of The Wine** *Jack Blanchard & Misty Morgan*
18/63 **Down To The River** *Rose Maddox*
5/51 **Down Yonder** *Del Wood*
32/73 **Downfall Of Me** *Sonny James*
64/79 **Downhill Stuff** *John Denver*
77/83 **Downright Broke My Heart** *Bubba Talbert*
5/01 **Downtime** *Jo Dee Messina*
36/84 **Downtown** *Dolly Parton*
31/71 **Dozen Pairs Of Boots** *Del Reeves*
37/97 **Dozen Red Roses** *Tammy Graham*
29/70 **Drag 'Em Off The Interstate, Sock It To 'Em, J.P. Blues** *Dick Curless*
95/80 **Draggin' Leather** *Mitch Goodson*
11/59 **Draggin' The River** *Ferlin Husky*
45/72 **Draggin' The River** *Warner Mack*
87/81 **Draw Me A Line** *Ray Griff*
Dream ..see: All I Have To Do Is
Dream Baby (How Long Must I Dream)
50/70 *Bob Regan & Lucille Starr*
7/71 *Glen Campbell*
9/83 *Lacy J. Dalton*
27↑/05 **Dream Big** *Ryan Shupe & The RubberBand*
22/64 **Dream House For Sale** *Red Sovine*
Dream Lover
5/71 *Billy "Crash" Craddock*
59/79 *Rick Nelson*
59/80 *Tanya Tucker & Glen Campbell*
88/86 *Rick Nelson*
94/84 **Dream Lover** *Susie Brading*
Dream Maker
61/81 *Shoppe*
69/83 *Tommy Overstreet*
47/73 **Dream Me Home** *Mac Davis*
40/79 **Dream Never Dies** *Bill Anderson*
7/81 **Dream Of Me** *Vern Gosdin*
7/79 **Dream On** *Oak Ridge Boys*
18/84 **Dream On Texas Ladies** *Rex Allen, Jr.*
23/73 **Dream Painter** *Connie Smith*
80/80 **Dream Street Rose** *Gordon Lightfoot*
5/98 **Dream Walkin'** *Toby Keith*
88/73 **Dream Weaver** *Jacky Ward*
63/93 **Dream You** *Pirates Of The Mississippi*
45/02 **Dream Your Way To Me** *Shannon Lawson*
32/82 **Dreamin'** *John Schneider*
32/79 **Dreamin's All I Do** *Earl Conley*
10/75 **Dreaming My Dreams With You** *Waylon Jennings*
1/94 **Dreaming With My Eyes Open** *Clay Walker*
100/78 **Dreamland** *Gordon Lightfoot*
9/86 **Dreamland Express** *John Denver*
46/81 **Dreams Can Come In Handy** *Cindy Hurt*
15/82 **Dreams Die Hard** *Gary Morris*
35/77 **Dreams Of A Dreamer** *Darrell McCall*
3/68 **Dreams Of The Everyday Housewife** *Glen Campbell*
8/73 **Drift Away** *Narvel Felts*
3/91 **Drift Off To Dream** *Travis Tritt*
1/81 **Drifter** *Sylvia*
60/85 **Drifter's Wind** *Chuck Pyle*
48/80 **Driftin Away** *Miki Mori*
8/67 **Drifting Apart** *Warner Mack*
96/78 **Drifting Lovers** *Charlie McCoy*
11/60 **Drifting Texas Sand** *Webb Pierce*
58/69 **Drifting Too Far (From Your Arms)** *June Stearns*
7/51 **Driftwood On The River** *Ernest Tubb*
F/70 **Drink Boys, Drink** *Jim Ed Brown*
59/69 **Drink Canada Dry** *Bobby Barnett*
25/80 **Drink It Down, Lady** *Rex Allen, Jr.*
3/97 **Drink, Swear, Steal & Lie** *Michael Peterson*
2/85 **Drinkin' And Dreamin'** *Waylon Jennings*
17/80 **Drinkin' And Drivin'** *Johnny Paycheck*
7/04 **Drinkin' Bone** *Tracy Byrd*
8/86 **Drinkin' My Baby Goodbye** *Charlie Daniels Band*
1/76 **Drinkin' My Baby (Off My Mind)** *Eddie Rabbitt*
Drinkin' My Way Back Home
63/77 *Shylo*
10/84 *Gene Watson*
70/80 **Drinkin' Them Long Necks** *Roy Head*
10/74 **Drinkin' Thing** *Gary Stewart*
Drinking Champagne
35/68 *Cal Smith*
4/90 *George Strait*
9/55 **Drinking Tequila** *Jim Reeves*
79/78 **Drinking Them Beers** *Tompall Glaser*
20/73 **Drinking Wine Spo-Dee O'Dee** *Jerry Lee Lewis*
63/94 **Drive** *Steve Wariner*
1/02 **Drive (For Daddy Gene)** *Alan Jackson*
56/97 **Drive Me Crazy** *Thompson Brothers Band*
6/99 **Drive Me Wild** *Sawyer Brown*
Drive South
63/90 *Forester Sisters w/ Bellamy Brothers*
2/93 *Suzy Bogguss*
72/93 **Drive Time** *Lisa Stewart*
24/94 **Drivin' And Cryin'** *Steve Wariner*
44/70 **Drivin' Home** *Jerry Smith*
50/04 **Drivin' Into The Sun** *Sherrié Austin*
Drivin' My Life Away
1/80 *Eddie Rabbitt*
56/98 *Rhett Akins*
Drivin' Nails In My Coffin
2/46 *Floyd Tillman*
5/46 *Ernest Tubb*
26/84 **Drivin' Wheel** *Emmylou Harris*
68/93 **Driving You Out Of My Mind** *Marshall Tucker Band*
17/76 **Dropkick Me, Jesus** *Bobby Bare*
Dropping Out Of Sight
32/67 *Jimmy Newman*
35/81 *Bobby Bare*
96/79 **Drown In The Flood** *Lois Kaye*
39/85 **Drowning In Memories** *T. Graham Brown*
14/05 **Drugs Or Jesus** *Tim McGraw*
25/61 **Drunk Again** *Lattie Moore*
(Drunk On Arrival) ..see: D.O.A.
94/79 **Duel Under The Snow** *Billy Edd Wheeler*
5/73 **Dueling Banjos** *Eric Weissberg & Steve Mandell*
(Dukes Of Hazzard) ..see: Theme From The
15/90 **Dumas Walker** *Kentucky Headhunters*
24/67 **Dumb Blonde** *Dolly Parton*
1/95 **Dust On The Bottle** *David Lee Murphy*
44/69 **Dusty Road** *Norma Jean*
21/70 **Duty Not Desire** *Jeannie C. Riley*
93/84 **Dying To Believe** *Jack Greene*

E

27/69 **Each And Every Part Of Me** *Bobby Lewis*
5/45 **Each Minute Seems A Million Years** *Eddy Arnold*
4/60 **Each Moment ('Spent With You)** *Ernest Ashworth*
4/44 **Each Night At Nine** *Floyd Tillman*
16/69 **Each Time** *Johnny Bush*
22/91 **Eagle, The** *Waylon Jennings*
53/94 **Eagle Over Angel** *Brother Phelps*
33/91 **Eagle When She Flies** *Dolly Parton*
35/70 **Early In The Morning** *Mac Curtis*
14/89 **Early In The Morning And Late At Night** *Hank Williams, Jr.*
79/75 **Early Morning Love** *Sammy Johns*
9/66 **Early Morning Rain** *George Hamilton IV*
9/71 **Early Morning Sunshine** *Marty Robbins*
28/75 **Early Sunday Morning** *Chip Taylor*
Earth Angel ..see: Donna
60/03 **Earthbound** *Rodney Crowell*
93/74 **Ease Me To The Ground** *Sue Richards*
80/77 **Ease My Mind On You** *Marie Owens*
20/97 **Ease My Troubled Mind** *Ricochet*
78/83 **Ease The Fever** *Carrie Slye*

Easier
61/83 *Sandy Croft*
91/84 *Sandy Croft*
20/93 **Easier Said Than Done** *Radney Foster*
87/81 **Easier To Go** *Gene Kennedy & Karen Jeglum*
2/77 **East Bound And Down** *Jerry Reed*
Easy
45/79 *Bobby Hood*
F/79 *Jimmie Rodgers & Michele*
63/78 **Easy** *John Wesley Ryles*
76/75 **Easy** *Troy Seals*
89/78 **Easy** *Barry Kaye*
69/95 **Easy As One, Two, Three** *John Bunzow*
2/75 **Easy As Pie** *Billy "Crash" Craddock*
81/83 **Easy Catch** *Bubba Talbert*
1/93 **Easy Come, Easy Go** *George Strait*
14/64 **Easy Come-Easy Go** *Bill Anderson*
68/86 **Easy Does It** *Tim Malchak*
27/01 **Easy For Me To Say** *Clint Black*
12/78 **Easy From Now On** *Emmylou Harris*
Easy Look
67/75 *Kenny Price*
12/77 *Charlie Rich*
5^{S}/04 **Easy Lovin' You** *Chalee Tennison*
1/71 **Easy Loving** *Freddie Hart*
26/60 **Easy Money** *James O'Gwynn*
32/83 **Easy On The Eye** *Gatlin Bros.*
1/52 **Easy On The Eyes** *Eddy Arnold*
Easy Part's Over
2/68 *Charley Pride*
41/80 *Steve Wariner*
57/87 **Easy To Find** *Girls Next Door*
26/75 **Easy To Love** *Hank Snow*
89/79 **Easy To Love** *Jimmie Rodgers*
5/86 **Easy To Please** *Janie Fricke*
3/56 **Eat, Drink, And Be Merry (Tomorrow You'll Cry)** *Porter Wagoner*
Ebony Eyes
25/61 *Everly Brothers*
89/79 *Orion*
77/88 **Echo Me** *Margo Smith*
2/49 **Echo Of Your Footsteps** *Eddy Arnold*
1/53 **Eddy's Song** *Eddy Arnold*
2/63 **8 X 10** *Bill Anderson*
57/84 **Eight Days A Week** *Wright Brothers*
40/00 **800 Pound Jesus** *Sawyer Brown*
43/64 **Eight Years (And Two Children Later)** *Claude Gray*
1/88 **Eighteen Wheels And A Dozen Roses** *Kathy Mattea*
93/75 **18 Yellow Roses** *C.L. Goodson*
7/87 **80's Ladies** *K.T. Oslin*
64/82 **Either You're Married Or You're Single** *Margo Smith*
1/59 **El Paso** *Marty Robbins*
1/76 **El Paso City** *Marty Robbins*
34/76 **11 Months And 29 Days** *Johnny Paycheck*
1/72 **Eleven Roses** *Hank Williams, Jr.*
56/01 **Elisabeth** *Billy Gilman*
1/84 **Elizabeth** *Statler Brothers*

Elvira
95/78 *Rodney Crowell*
1/81 *Oak Ridge Boys*
20/94 **Elvis And Andy** *Confederate Railroad*
31/82 **Elvis Medley** *Elvis Presley*
90/76 **Emmylou** *Brush Arbor*
10/97 **Emotional Girl** *Terri Clark*
3/73 **Emptiest Arms In The World** *Merle Haggard*
1/71 **Empty Arms** *Sonny James*
64/89 **Empty Glass** *Gary Stewart*
47/68 **Empty House** *June Stearns*
6/50 **Enclosed, One Broken Heart** *Eddy Arnold*
12/76 **End Is Not In Sight (The Cowboy Tune)** *Amazing Rhythm Aces*
End Of The World
2/63 *Skeeter Davis*
70/82 *Judy Taylor*
72/00 *Allison Paige*
82/79 **Endless** *David Wills*
46/65 **Endless Sleep** *Hank Williams, Jr.*
Endlessly
1/70 *Sonny James*
38/77 *Eddie Middleton*
13/68 **Enemy, The** *Jim Ed Brown*
2/65 **Engine Engine #9** *Roger Miller*
3/66 **England Swings** *Roger Miller*
75/81 **Enough For You** *Brenda Lee*
36/65 **Enough Man For You** *Ott Stephens*
Eres Tu (Touch The Wind)
67/76 *Sonny James*
25/77 *Johnny Rodriguez*
48/94 **Eugene You Genius** *Bryan White*
2/84 **Ev'ry Heart Should Have One** *Charley Pride*
Ev'rybody's Somebody's Fool ..see: Everybody's Somebody's Fool
97/73 **Ev'ryday Woman** *Kenny Starr*
37/80 **Evangelina** *Hoyt Axton*
51/98 **Evangeline** *Chad Brock*
61/80 **Even A Fool Would Let Go** *Charlie Rich*
Even Cowgirls Get The Blues
26/80 *Lynn Anderson*
35/86 *Johnny Cash & Waylon Jennings*
79/78 **Even Cowgirls Get The Blues** *La Costa*
17/75 **Even If I Have To Steal** *Mel Street*
41/96 **Even If I Tried** *Emilio*
68/97 **Even If It's Wrong** *BR5-49*
78/82 **Even If It's Wrong** *Jimmi Cannon*
83/76 **Even If It's Wrong** *Ben Reece*
16/91 **Even Now** *Exile*
55/04 **Even Santa Claus Gets The Blues** *Marty Stuart*
74/70 **Even The Bad Times Are Good** *Jerry Wallace*
5/92 **Even The Man In The Moon Is Crying** *Mark Collie*
68/97 **Even The Wind** *Daryle Singletary*
59/01 **Even Then** *John Michael Montgomery*
1/54 **Even Tho** *Webb Pierce*
55/72 **Evening** *Jim Ed Brown*
11/84 **Evening Star** *Kenny Rogers*
30/69 **Ever Changing Mind** *Don Gibson*
62/94 **Ever-Changing Woman** *Brother Phelps*

Ever-Lovin' Woman
73/81 *Pat Garrett*
67/82 *Marlow Tackett*
4/82 **Ever, Never Lovin' You** *Ed Bruce*
37/66 **Ever Since My Baby Went Away** *Jack Greene*
93/77 **Everlasting (Everlasting Love)** *George Hamilton IV*
Everlasting Love
14/79 *Narvel Felts*
69/79 *Louise Mandrell*
57/68 **Everlasting Love** *Hank Locklin*
34/77 **Every Beat Of My Heart** *Peggy Sue*
86/81 **Every Breath I Take** *Eme*
Every Breath You Take
68/83 *Rich Landers*
69/83 *Mason Dixon*
51/97 **Every Cowboy's Dream** *Rhett Akins*
Every Day ..see: Everyday
64/93 **Every Day When I Get Home** *Robert Ellis Orrall*
21/76 **Every Face Tells A Story** *Olivia Newton-John*
25/04 **Every Friday Afternoon** *Craig Morgan*
3/96 **Every Light In The House** *Trace Adkins*
3/93 **Every Little Thing** *Carlene Carter*
34/03 **Every Little Thing** *Jamie O'Neal*
36/99 **Every Little Whisper** *Steve Wariner*
49/95 **Every Little Word** *Hal Ketchum*
37/00 **Every Man For Himself** *Neal McCoy*
20/86 **Every Night** *Pake McEntire*
26/81 **Every Now And Then** *Brenda Lee*
34/76 **Every Now And Then** *Mac Davis*
2/94 **Every Once In A While** *BlackHawk*
12/02 **Every River** *Brooks & Dunn*
82/75 **Every Road Leads Back To You** *Leapy Lee*
2/92 **Every Second** *Collin Raye*
21/69 **Every Step Of The Way** *Ferlin Husky*
52/88 **Every Step Of The Way** *Wagoneers*
38/98 **Every Time** *Pam Tillis*
2/96 **Every Time I Get Around You** *David Lee Murphy*
61/93 **Every Time I Roll The Dice** *Chris LeDoux*
7/74 **Every Time I Turn The Radio On** *Bill Anderson*
10/58 **Every Time I'm Kissing You** *Faron Young*
34/96 **Every Time My Heart Calls Your Name** *John Berry*
57/96 **Every Time She Passes By** *George Ducas*
Every Time Two Fools Collide
99/77 *Lucky Clark*
1/78 *Kenny Rogers & Dottie West*
3/75 **Every Time You Touch Me (I Get High)** *Charlie Rich*
89/89 **Every Time You Walk In The Room** *Lolita Jackson*
1/79 **Every Which Way But Loose** *Eddie Rabbitt*
28/77 **Every Word I Write** *Dottie West*

3/62 **Everybody But Me** *Ernest Ashworth*
3/97 **Everybody Knows** *Trisha Yearwood*
54/71 **Everybody Knows** *Jimmy Dean*
17/66 **Everybody Loves A Nut** *Johnny Cash*
25/78 **Everybody Loves A Rain Song** *B.J. Thomas*
56/82 **Everybody Loves A Winner** *Dickey Lee*
5/82 **Everybody Makes Mistakes** *Lacy J. Dalton*
37/75 **Everybody Needs A Rainbow** *Ray Stevens*
56/74 **Everybody Needs A Rainbow** *Bobby Wright*
28/87 **Everybody Needs A Hero** *Gene Watson*
24/85 **Everybody Needs Love On Saturday Night** *Maines Brothers Band*
28/73 **Everybody Needs Lovin'** *Norro Wilson*
62/68 **Everybody Needs Somebody** *Compton Brothers*
70/72 **Everybody Oughta Cry** *Crystal Gayle*
28/68 **Everybody Oughta Sing A Song** *Dallas Frazier*
75/90 **Everybody Wants To Be Hank Williams** *Larry Boone*
47/68 **Everybody Wants To Be Somebody Else** *Harden Trio*
76/79 **Everybody Wants To Disco** *Glenn Barber*
52/69 **Everybody Wants To Get To Heaven** *Ed Bruce*
24/87 **Everybody's Crazy 'Bout My Baby** *Marie Osmond*
40/64 **Everybody's Darlin', Plus Mine** *Browns*
18/83 **Everybody's Dream Girl** *Dan Seals*
14/61 **Everybody's Dying For Love** *Jimmy Newman*
16S/99 **Everybody's Free (To Get Sunburned)** *Cledus T. Judd*
42/68 **Everybody's Got To Be Somewhere** *Johnny Dollar*
42/00 **Everybody's Gotta Grow Up Sometime** *Sons Of The Desert*
70/70 **Everybody's Gotta Hurt** *Cheryl Poole*
Everybody's Had The Blues
1/73 *Merle Haggard*
85/77 *Maury Finney*
20/72 **Everybody's Reaching Out For Someone** *Pat Daisy*
Everybody's Somebody's Fool
16/60 *Ernest Tubb*
24/60 *Connie Francis*
48/79 *Debby Boone*
11/88 **Everybody's Sweetheart** *Vince Gill*
Everyday ..also see: Ev'ryday
73/68 **Every Day** *Sleepy LaBeef*
1/84 **Everyday** *Oak Ridge Boys*
26/86 **Everyday** *James Taylor*
56/91 **Everyday** *Anne Murray*
43/02 **Everyday Angel** *Radney Foster*
70/71 **Everyday Family Man** *Jimmy Dickens*
60/03 **Everyday Girl** *Roxie Dean*
Everyday I Have To Cry Some
23/69 *Bob Luman*
14/77 *Joe Stampley*
76/88 **Everyday Man** *Gary Chapman*
100/77 **Everyday Of My Life** *Wichita Linemen*
63/85 **Everyday People** *Margo Smith & Tom Grant*
62/68 **Everyday's A Happy Day For Fools** *Jean Shepard*
87/78 **Everynight Sensation** *Durwood Haddock*
36/81 **Everyone Gets Crazy Now And Then** *Roger Miller*
46/82 **Everyone Knows I'm Yours** *Corbin/Hanner Band*
5/70 **Everything A Man Could Ever Need** *Glen Campbell*
42/02 **Everything Changes** *Little Big Town*
62/93 **Everything Comes Down To Money And Love** *Hank Williams, Jr.*
42/83 **Everything From Jesus To Jack Daniels** *Tom T. Hall*
9/97 **Everything I Love** *Alan Jackson*
56/70 **Everything I Love** *Hugh X. Lewis*
Everything I Own
66/72 *Kendalls*
12/76 *Joe Stampley*
51/96 **Everything I Own** *Aaron Tippin*
29/86 **Everything I Used To Do** *Gene Watson*
32/79 **Everything I've Always Wanted** *Porter Wagoner*
39/70 **Everything Is Beautiful** *Ray Stevens*
63/85 **Everything Is Changing** *Johnny Paycheck*
1/86 **Everything That Glitters (Is Not Gold)** *Dan Seals*
40/70 **Everything Will Be Alright** *Claude Gray*
98/76 **Everything You'd Never Want To Be** *Joe Brock*
Everything's A Waltz ..see: (When You Fall In Love)
96/82 **Everything's All Right** *David House*
7/83 **Everything's Beautiful (In It's Own Way)** *Dolly Parton & Willie Nelson*
78/75 **Everything's Broken Down** *Larry Hosford*
2/98 **Everything's Changed** *Lonestar*
93/76 **Everything's Coming Up Love** *Sherry Bryce*
48/69 **Everything's Leaving** *Wanda Jackson*
40/64 **Everything's O.K. On The LBJ** *Lawton Williams*
17/75 **Everything's The Same (Ain't Nothing Changed)** *Billy Swan*
12/99 **Everytime I Cry** *Terri Clark*
58/89 **Everytime I Get To Dreamin'** *Josh Logan*
74/78 **Everytime I Sing A Love Song** *Jimmie Rodgers*
Everytime Two Fools Collide ..see: Every Time
10/82 **Everytime You Cross My Mind (You Break My Heart)** *Razzy Bailey*
23/88 **Everytime You Go Outside I Hope It Rains** *Burch Sisters*
1/97 **Everywhere** *Tim McGraw*
67/72 **Everywhere I Go (He's Already Been There)** *Tex Williams*
24/81 **Evil Angel** *Ed Bruce*
47/66 **Evil Off My Mind** *Burl Ives*
5/66 **Evil On Your Mind** *Jan Howard*
36/68 **Evolution And The Bible** *Hugh X. Lewis*
4/92 **Except For Monday** *Lorrie Morgan*
35/89 **Exception To The Rule** *Mason Dixon*
2/60 **Excuse Me (I Think I've Got A Heartache)** *Buck Owens*
20/85 **Eye Of A Hurricane** *John Anderson*
58/69 **Eye To Eye** *LaWanda Lindsey & Kenny Vernon*
37/79 **Eyes Big As Dallas** *Wynn Stewart*
90/85 **Eyes Have It** *Lee Wright*
85/89 **Eyes Never Lie** *Kamryn Hanks*
19/83 **Eyes Of A Stranger** *David Wills*
12/60 **Eyes Of Love** *Margie Singleton*
30/84 **Eyes That See In The Dark** *Kenny Rogers*

F

4/87 **Face In The Crowd** *Michael Martin Murphey & Holly Dunn*
73/70 **Face Of A Dear Friend** *Clay Hart*
54/04 **Face Of God** *Billy Ray Cyrus*
1/88 **Face To Face** *Alabama*
92/77 **Face To Face** *David Allan Coe*
10/60 **Face To The Wall** *Faron Young*
25/61 **Facing The Wall** *Charlie Walker*
6/88 **Factory, The** *Kenny Rogers*
69/83 **Fade To Blue** *Ed Hunnicutt*
Faded Love
8/50 *Bob Wills*
7/63 *Patsy Cline*
22/63 *Leon McAuliffe*
22/71 *Tompall/Glaser Brothers*
3/80 *Willie Nelson & Ray Price*
Faded Love And Winter Roses
25/69 *Carl Smith*
33/79 *David Houston*
11/78 **Fadin' In, Fadin' Out** *Tommy Overstreet*
36/80 **Fadin' Renegade** *Tommy Overstreet*
Fair And Tender Ladies
28/64 *George Hamilton IV*
30/78 *Charlie McCoy*
5/89 **Fair Shake** *Foster & Lloyd*
48/67 **Fair Weather Love** *Arlene Harden*
Fairytale
37/74 *Pointer Sisters*
87/80 *Rebecca Lynn*
63/98 **Faith** *Big House*
13/95 **Faith In Me, Faith In You** *Doug Stone*
28/00 **Faith In You** *Steve Wariner*

51/99 **Faith Of The Heart** *Susan Ashton*

10/84 **Faithless Love** *Glen Campbell*

1/83 **Faking Love** *T.G. Sheppard & Karen Brooks*

69/92 **Fall** *Oak Ridge Boys*

67/71 **Fall Away** *Tex Ritter*

6/95 **Fall In Love** *Kenny Chesney*

Fall In Love Again ..see: (Tonight We Just Might)

10/79 **Fall In Love With Me Tonight** *Randy Barlow*

3/03 **Fall Into Me** *Emerson Drive*

68/96 **Fall Reaching** *Chris Ward*

91/78 **Fall Softly Snow** *Jim Ed Brown/Helen Cornelius*

4/60 **Fallen Angel** *Webb Pierce*

41/84 **Fallen Angel (Flyin' High Tonight)** *Gus Hardin*

Fallen Star

2/57 *Jimmy Newman*

8/57 *Ferlin Husky*

1/88 **Fallin' Again** *Alabama*

6/81 **Falling Again** *Don Williams*

26/60 **Falling Again** *Porter Wagoner*

66/80 **Fallin' For You** *Jerri Kelly*

90/89 **Falling For You** *Donnie Bowser*

2/87 **Fallin' For You For Years** *Conway Twitty*

2/85 **Fallin' In Love** *Sylvia*

86/83 **Falling In Love** *Tari Hensley*

Fallin' Never Felt So Good

39/93 *Shawn Camp*

52/00 *Mark Chesnutt*

8/87 **Fallin' Out** *Waylon Jennings*

2/91 **Fallin' Out Of Love** *Reba McEntire*

50/75 **Falling** *Lefty Frizzell*

100/78 **Falling** *Stan Hitchcock*

10/58 **Falling Back To You** *Webb Pierce*

85/81 **Falling In** *P.J. Parks*

99/88 **Falling In Love Right & Left** *Bear Creek Band*

86/80 **Falling In Trouble Again** *Sherry Brane*

47/94 **Falling Out Of Love** *John & Audrey Wiggins*

74/80 **Falling Together** *Nightstreets*

43/92 **Familiar Ground** *Michael White*

40/92 **Familiar Pain** *Restless Heart*

Family Bible

10/60 *Claude Gray*

16/61 *George Jones*

92/80 *Willie Nelson*

Family Inn ..see: Friendly Family Inn

7/59 **Family Man** *Frankie Miller*

35/81 **Family Man** *Wright Brothers*

92/76 **Family Man** *Al Bolt*

83/76 **Family Reunion** *Oak Ridge Boys*

4/79 **Family Tradition** *Hank Williams, Jr.*

26/03 **Family Tree** *Darryl Worley*

48/89 **Family Tree** *Michael Martin Murphey*

62/92 **Family Tree** *Lionel Cartwright*

73/90 **Family Tree** *Lee Roy Parnell*

73/98 **Famous First Words** *Gil Grand*

81/84 **Famous In Missouri** *Tom T. Hall*

Famous Last Words Of A Fool

67/83 *Dean Dillon*

1/88 *George Strait*

30/77 **Fan The Flame, Feed The Fire** *Don Gibson*

Fancy

26/70 *Bobbie Gentry*

8/91 *Reba McEntire*

1/81 **Fancy Free** *Oak Ridge Boys*

13/71 **Fancy Satin Pillows** *Wanda Jackson*

27/79 **Fantasy Island** *Freddy Weller*

71/85 **Far Cry From You** *Connie Smith*

Far, Far Away

11/60 *Don Gibson*

12/72 *Don Gibson*

5/79 **Farewell Party** *Gene Watson*

80/78 **Farm, The** *Mel McDaniel*

72/73 **Farm In Pennsyltucky** *Jeannie Seely*

82/78 **Farmer, The** *Cledus Maggard*

89/78 **Farmer's Song (We Ain't Gonna Work For Peanuts)** *Joel Mathis*

21/86 **Farther Down The Line** *Lyle Lovett*

73/73 **Farther Down The River (Where The Fishin's Good)** *Tennessee Ernie Ford*

17/75 **Farthest Thing From My Mind** *Ray Price*

2/94 **Fast As You** *Dwight Yoakam*

1/05 **Fast Cars And Freedom** *Rascal Flatts*

4/86 **Fast Lanes And Country Roads** *Barbara Mandrell*

4/90 **Fast Movin' Train** *Restless Heart*

71/67 **Fast Talking Louisiana Man** *Merle Kilgore*

41/92 **Faster Gun** *Great Plains*

1/76 **Faster Horses (The Cowboy And The Poet)** *Tom T. Hall*

75/95 **Fastest Horse In A One Horse Town** *Billy Ray Cyrus*

4/47 **Fat Gal** *Merle Travis*

88/80 **Fat 'N Sassy** *Pacific Steel Co.*

73/96 **Fear Of A Broken Heart** *Paul Jefferson*

2/96 **Fear Of Being Alone** *Reba McEntire*

71/88 **Fearless Heart** *Beards*

15/91 **Feed Jake** *Pirates Of The Mississippi*

51/68 **Feed Me One More Lie** *Mary Taylor*

45/85 **Feed The Fire** *Keith Stegall*

5/90 **Feed This Fire** *Anne Murray*

16/81 **Feedin' The Fire** *Zella Lehr*

84/82 **Feel** *Tom Carlile*

21/76 **Feel Again** *Faron Young*

56/71 **Feel Free To Go** *Sue Richards*

60/88 **Feel Like Foolin' Around** *Exile*

77/86 **Feel Like I'm Falling For You** *Two Hearts*

60/95 **Feel Like Makin' Love** *Philip Claypool*

29/04 **Feel My Way To You** *Restless Heart*

10/83 **Feel Right** *Tanya Tucker*

55/73 **Feel So Fine** *Kenny Vernon*

66/85 **Feel The Fire** *Family Brown*

38/78 **Feelin' Better** *Hank Williams, Jr.*

69/93 **Feelin' Kind Of Lonely Tonight** *Shelby Lynne*

2/86 **Feelin' The Feelin'** *Bellamy Brothers*

19/77 **Feeling's Right** *Narvel Felts*

97/76 **Feelings** *Sarah Johns*

1/75 **Feelins'** *Loretta Lynn/Conway Twitty*

96/83 **Feelings Feelin Right** *Lee Dresser*

85/90 **Feelings For Each Other** *Marilyn Mundy*

26/78 **Feelings So Right Tonight** *Don King*

6/00 **Feels Like Love** *Vince Gill*

9/04 **Feels Like Today** *Rascal Flatts*

98/77 **Feels So Much Better** *Patti Leatherwood*

1/81 **Feels So Right** *Alabama*

19/79 **Feet** *Ray Price*

49/03 **Feliz Navidad** *Clay Walker*

30/79 **Fell Into Love** *Foxfire*

48/89 **Fellow Travelers** *John Conlee*

60/95 **Female Bonding** *Brett James*

56/76 **Feminine Touch** *Johnny Paycheck*

Feudin' And Fightin'

4/47 *Dorothy Shay*

5/47 *Jo Stafford*

23/95 **Fever, The** *Garth Brooks*

43/85 **Few Good Men** *Terri Gibbs*

9/91 **Few Good Things Remain** *Kathy Mattea*

Few More Rednecks ..see: (What This World Needs Is) A

8/90 **Few Ole Country Boys** *Randy Travis & George Jones*

9/03 **Few Questions** *Clay Walker*

55/02 **Few Short Years** *Ty Herndon*

29/61 **Fickle Fun** *Kitty Wells*

87/73 **Fiddle Man** *Red Steagall*

75/73 **Fiddlin' Around** *Chet Atkins*

40/86 **Fiddlin' Man** *Michael Martin Murphey*

73/75 **Fiddlin' Of Jacques Pierre Bordeaux** *Fiddlin' Frenchie Burke*

23/74 **Field Of Yellow Daisies** *Charlie Rich*

40/80 **Fifteen Beers** *Johnny Paycheck*

50/71 **Fifteen Beers Ago** *Ben Colder*

24/67 **Fifteen Days** *Wilma Burgess*

62/87 **15 to 33** *Southern Reign*

1/70 **Fifteen Years Ago** *Conway Twitty*

75/96 **Fifty-Fifty** *Keith Stegall*

16/78 **'57 Chevrolet** *Billie Jo Spears*

55/02 **50,000 Names** *George Jones*

50 Ways To Leave Your Lover

85/76 *Bob Yarborough*

70/80 *Sonny Curtis*

1/70 **Fightin' Side Of Me** *Merle Haggard*

78/85 **Fightin' Fire With Fire** *Razzy Bailey*

27/92 **Fighting Fire With Fire** *Davis Daniel*

41/91 **Fighting For You** *Pirates Of The Mississippi*

24/64 **File, The** *Bob Luman*

Filipino Baby

2/46 *Ernest Tubb*

4/46 *Cowboy Copas*

5/46 *T. Texas Tyler*

5/46 *Texas Jim Robertson*

1/82 **Finally** *T.G. Sheppard*

Finally

28/59 *Mel Tillis*

9/64 *Kitty Wells & Webb Pierce*

80/76 **Find A New Love, Girl** *Sunday Sharpe*
73/97 **Find My Way Back To My Heart** *Alison Krauss & Union Station*
Find Out What's Happening
15/68 *Bobby Bare*
52/70 *Barbara Fairchild*
40/95 *Tanya Tucker*
38/76 **Find Yourself Another Puppet** *Brenda Lee*
6/89 **Finders Are Keepers** *Hank Williams, Jr.*
85/79 **Finders Keepers Losers Weepers** *Stan Hitchcock w/ Sue Richards*
24/83 **Finding You** *Joe Stampley*
73/74 **Fine As Wine** *Billy Walker*
52/75 **Fine Time To Get The Blues** *Jim Ed Brown*
52/74 **Finer Things In Life** *Red Steagall*
41/70 **Fingerprints** *Freddie Hart*
90/80 **Fingertips** *Johnny Carver*
19/95 **Finish What We Started** *Diamond Rio*
64/87 **Finishing Touches** *Gary Morris*
29/76 **Fire And Rain** *Willie Nelson*
1/81 **Fire & Smoke** *Earl Thomas Conley*
60/86 **Fire At First Sight** *Kendalls*
86/76 **Fire At First Sight** *Linda Hargrove*
Fire Goin' Again ..see: (You've Got That)
46/71 **Fire Hydrant #79** *Jack Blanchard & Misty Morgan*
1/83 **Fire I Can't Put Out** *George Strait*
84/81 **Fire In The Night** *Narvel Felts*
7/87 **Fire In The Sky** *Nitty Gritty Dirt Band*
48/85 **Fire In The Sky** *Wright Brothers*
40/81 **Fire In Your Eyes** *Gary Morris*
65/80 **Fire Of Two Old Flames** *Roy Head*
57/76 **Fire On The Bayou** *Bill Black Combo*
Fire On The Mountain ..see: (Frenchie Burke's)
62/97 **Fire When Ready** *Perfect Stranger*
21/75 **Fireball Rolled A Seven** *Dave Dudley*
5/85 **Fireman, The** *George Strait*
73/88 **First Came The Feelin'** *Gail O'Doski*
98/79 **First Class Fool** *Jimmie Peters/Linda K. Lance*
First Cut Is The Deepest
55/87 *Ride The River*
35/04 *Sheryl Crow*
9/57 **First Date, First Kiss, First Love** *Sonny James*
70/70 **First Day** *Jane Morgan*
84/78 **First Encounter Of A Close Kind** *Tom Bresh*
44/85 **First In Line** *Everly Brothers*
57/88 **First In Line** *Shurfire*
46/71 **First Love** *Penny DeHaven*
74/80 **First Love Feelings** *Glenn Barber*
5/95 **First Step** *Tracy Byrd*
96/79 **First Step** *Marty Martel*
32/64 **First Step Down (Is The Longest)** *Bob Jennings*
29/79 **First Thing Each Morning (Last Thing At Night)** *Cliff Cochran*
1/65 **First Thing Ev'ry Morning (And The Last Thing Ev'ry Night)** *Jimmy Dean*
2/75 **First Time** *Freddie Hart*
10/78 **First Time** *Billy "Crash" Craddock*
63/84 **First Time** *McGuffey Lane*
75/80 **First Time** *Melissa Lewis*
54/82 **First Time Around** *Ronnie Rogers*
63/84 **First Time Burned** *Johnny Rodriguez*
24/87 **First Time Caller** *Juice Newton*
13/92 **First Time For Everything** *Little Texas*
67/72 **First Time For Us** *Karen Wheeler*
51/67 **First Word** *Eddy Arnold*
7/85 **First Word In Memory Is Me** *Janie Fricke*
52/94 **Fish Ain't Bitin'** *David Lee Murphy*
1/87 **Fishin' In The Dark** *Nitty Gritty Dirt Band*
Fishin' On The Mississippi
62/67 *Bob Morris*
48/71 *Buddy Alan*
(Fishin' Song) ..see: I'm Gonna Miss Her
1/68 **Fist City** *Loretta Lynn*
29/97 **Fit To Be Tied Down** *Sammy Kershaw*
30/90 **Fit To Be Tied Down** *Conway Twitty*
26/60 **Five Brothers** *Marty Robbins*
14/59 **Five Feet High And Rising** *Johnny Cash*
67/86 **Five Fingers** *Ray Price*
5/64 **Five Little Fingers** *Bill Anderson*
21/66 **Five Little Johnson Girls** *Stonemans*
39/66 **Five Miles From Home (Soon I'll See Mary)** *Bob Luman*
1/90 **Five Minutes** *Lorrie Morgan*
16/92 **Five O'Clock World** *Hal Ketchum*
5/64 **500 Miles Away From Home** *Bobby Bare*
18/89 **5:01 Blues** *Merle Haggard*
76/82 **Flame, The** *Rita Remington*
45/83 **Flame In My Heart** *Delia Bell*
64/83 **Flames** *Brice Henderson*
18/76 **Flash Of Fire** *Hoyt Axton*
20/75 **Flat Natural Born Good-Timin' Man** *Gary Stewart*
33/69 **Flat River, MO.** *Ferlin Husky*
9/61 **Flat Top** *Cowboy Copas*
11/69 **Flattery Will Get You Everywhere** *Lynn Anderson*
1/71 **Flesh And Blood** *Johnny Cash*
33/04 **Flies On The Butter (You Can't Go Home Again)** *Wynonna w/ Naomi Judd*
4/83 **Flight 309 To Tennessee** *Shelly West*
80/79 **Flip Side Of Today** *Scott Summer*
78/81 **Flo's Yellow Rose** *Hoyt Axton*
8/68 **Flower Of Love** *Leon Ashley*
36/97 **Flowers** *Billy Yates*
Flowers On The Wall
2/66 *Statler Brothers*
6/00 *Eric Heatherly*
51/97 **Flutter** *Jack Ingram*
12/76 **Fly Away** *John Denver*
8/71 **Fly Away Again** *Dave Dudley*
34/67 **Fly Butterfly Fly** *Marty Robbins*
20/83 **Fly Into Love** *Charly McClain*
15/99 **Fly (The Angel Song)** *Wilkinsons*
Flyin' South
23/63 *Hank Locklin*
56/70 *Hank Locklin & Danny Davis*
52/88 **Flying On Your Own** *Anne Murray*
99/79 **Flying Saucer Man And The Truck Driver** *Red Simpson*
58/68 **Foggy Mountain Breakdown** *Flatt & Scruggs*
Foggy River
10/48 *Kate Smith*
18/68 *Carl Smith*
15/64 **Followed Closely By My Teardrops** *Hank Locklin*
10/81 **Following The Feeling** *Moe Bandy/Judy Bailey*
Folsom Prison Blues
4/56 *Johnny Cash*
1/68 *Johnny Cash*
74/68 *Don Bowman [#2]*
41/80 **Food Blues** *Bobby Bare*
2/97 **Fool, The** *Lee Ann Womack*
Fool, The
14/56 *Sanford Clark*
22/78 *Don Gibson*
Fool
18/77 *John Wesley Ryles*
52/84 *Narvel Felts*
31/73 **Fool** *Elvis Presley*
6/81 **Fool By Your Side** *Dave & Sugar*
67/81 **Fool, Fool** *Brenda Lee*
6/67 **Fool Fool Fool** *Webb Pierce*
1/83 **Fool For Your Love** *Mickey Gilley*
1/82 **Fool Hearted Memory** *George Strait*
32/99 **Fool, I'm A Woman** *Sara Evans*
40/73 **Fool I've Been Today** *Jack Greene*
33/83 **Fool In Me** *Sonny James*
4/72 **Fool Me** *Lynn Anderson*
14/63 **Fool Me Once** *Connie Hall*
68/74 **Fool Passin' Through** *Jim Glaser*
45/79 **Fool Strikes Again** *Charlie Rich*
Fool Such As I
3/53 *Hank Snow*
98/78 *Bill Green*
90/79 *Rodney Crowell*
5/90 *Baillie & the Boys*
72/81 **Fool That I Am** *Rita Coolidge*
62/93 **Fool To Fall** *Pearl River*
58/80 **Fool Who Fooled Around** *Keith Stegall*
3/84 **Fool's Gold** *Lee Greenwood*
58/81 **Fool's Gold** *Danny Wood*
81/82 **Fool's Gold** *Jimmi Cannon*
39/89 **Fool's Paradise** *Larry Boone*
44/98 **Fool's Progress** *Clint Daniels*
21/85 **Fooled Around And Fell In Love** *T.G. Sheppard*
25/79 **Fooled Around And Fell In Love** *Mundo Earwood*
4/79 **Fooled By A Feeling** *Barbara Mandrell*
9/54 **Fooler, A Faker** *Hank Thompson*
4/83 **Foolin'** *Johnny Rodriguez*
2/61 **Foolin' Around** *Buck Owens*
1/94 **Foolish Pride** *Travis Tritt*
15/48 **Foolish Tears** *Tex Williams*
Fools
19/72 *Johnny Duncan*
3/79 *Jim Ed Brown/Helen Cornelius*
9/77 **Fools Fall In Love** *Jacky Ward*

17/79 **Fools For Each Other**
Johnny Rodriguez
Fools For Each Other
96/79 *Guy Clark*
49/86 *Ed Bruce w/ Lynn Anderson*
55/79 **Football Card** *Glenn Sutton*
Footprints In The Sand
42/81 *Edgel Groves*
80/83 *Cristy Lane*
5/46 **Footprints In The Snow**
Bill Monroe
92/80 **Footsteps** *Jimmy McMillan*
7/62 **Footsteps Of A Fool** *Judy Lynn*
3/95 **For A Change** *Neal McCoy*
2/99 **For A Little While** *Tim McGraw*
12/75 **For A Minute There**
Johnny Paycheck
90/80 **For A Slow Dance With You**
Jerri Kelly
75/88 **For A Song** *Trinity Lane*
86/77 **For A While** *Mary MacGregor*
49/77 **For All The Right Reasons**
Barbara Fairchild
1/82 **For All The Wrong Reasons**
Bellamy Brothers
80/80 **For As Long As You Want Me**
Peggy Sue
13/91 **For Crying Out Loud** *Davis Daniel*
58/99 **For Crying Out Loud**
Anita Cochran
64/98 **For Lack Of Better Words**
Restless Heart
For Love's Own Sake
36/76 *Ed Bruce*
73/80 *Roy Clark*
94/73 **For Lovers Only** *Jack Lebsock*
For Loving Me ..see: (That's What You Get)
For Loving You
1/67 *Bill Anderson & Jan Howard*
72/68 *Skeeter Davis & Don Bowman*
58/72 **For My Baby** *Cal Smith*
1/91 **For My Broken Heart**
Reba McEntire
61/00 **For My Wedding** *Don Henley*
10/53 **For Now And Always** *Hank Snow*
42/73 **For Ol' Times Sake** *Elvis Presley*
75/86 **For Old Time Sake** *Jerry Naylor*
7/56 **For Rent (One Empty Heart)**
Sonny James
1/70 **For The Good Times** *Ray Price*
For The Heart ..see: Had A Dream
27/71 **For The Kids** *Sammi Smith*
F/55 **For The Love Of A Woman Like You** *Faron Young*
6/99 **For You I Will** *Aaron Tippin*
50/94 **For Your Love** *Chris LeDoux*
For Your Love
65/70 *Bobby Austin*
52/76 *Bobby Lewis*
78/88 *Tony McGill*
16/75 **Forbidden Angel** *Mel Street*
23/63 **Forbidden Lovers** *Lefty Frizzell*
23/64 **Forbidden Street**
Carl Butler & Pearl
12/48 **'Fore Day In The Morning**
Roy Brown
77/86 **Foreign Affairs** *Michael Shamblin*
7/87 **Forever** *Statler Brothers*
10/84 **Forever Again** *Gene Watson*
44/97 **Forever And A Day** *Gary Allan*

6/52 **Forever (And Always)**
Lefty Frizzell
1/87 **Forever And Ever, Amen**
Randy Travis
4/03 **Forever And For Always**
Shania Twain
37/02 **Forever Everyday**
Lee Ann Womack
15/61 **Forever Gone** *Ernest Ashworth*
73/79 **Forever In Blue Jeans**
Neil Diamond
5/48 **Forever Is Ending Today**
Ernest Tubb
4/98 **Forever Love** *Reba McEntire*
17/76 **Forever Lovers** *Mac Davis*
46/01 **Forever Loving You** *John Rich*
10/49 **Forever More** *Jimmy Wakely*
37/79 **Forever One Day At A Time**
Don Gibson
1/91 **Forever Together** *Randy Travis*
38/00 **Forever Works For Me (Monday, Tuesday, Wednesday, Thursday)** *Neal McCoy*
14/84 **Forever You** *Whites*
21/70 **Forever Yours** *Dottie West*
1/91 **Forever's As Far As I'll Go**
Alabama
67/99 **Forget About It** *Alison Krauss*
5/84 **Forget About Me**
Bellamy Brothers
49/79 **Forget Me Not** *Steve Wariner*
20/61 **Forget The Past** *Faron Young*
51/75 **Forgettin' 'Bout You** *Jim Glaser*
12/02 **Forgive** *Rebecca Lynn Howard*
12/75 **Forgive And Forget** *Eddie Rabbitt*
23/63 **Forgive Me** *Beverly Buff*
F/55 **Forgive Me, Dear** *Faron Young*
16/72 **Forgive Me For Calling You Darling** *Nat Stuckey*
4/53 **Forgive Me John**
Jean Shepard w/ Ferlin Huskey
58/95 **Forgiveness** *Victoria Shaw*
1/85 **Forgiving You Was Easy**
Willie Nelson
60/92 **Forgotten But Not Gone**
Keith Palmer
59/03 **Forrest County Line** *4 Runner*
85/80 **Forsaking All The Rest** *Jerri Kelly*
9/64 **Fort Worth, Dallas Or Houston**
George Hamilton IV
5/52 **Fortunes In Memories**
Ernest Tubb
18/82 **Forty And Fadin'** *Ray Price*
Forty Dollars ..see: Ballad Of
19/75 **41st Street Lonely Hearts' Club**
Buck Owens
1/85 **Forty Hour Week (For A Livin')**
Alabama
32/65 **Forty Nine, Fifty One**
Hank Locklin
21/97 **455 Rocket** *Kathy Mattea*
20/78 **Four Little Letters** *Stella Parton*
5/66 **Four-O-Thirty Three**
George Jones
67/91 **Four Scores And Seven Beers Ago** *Ray Benson*
3/65 **Four Strong Winds** *Bobby Bare*
21/96 **4 To 1 In Atlanta** *Tracy Byrd*
Four Walls
1/57 *Jim Reeves*
F/57 *Jim Lowe*
46/05 **Four Walls** *Randy Travis*

88/76 **Four Wheel Cowboy** *C.W. McCall*
27/85 **Four Wheel Drive** *Kendalls*
52/03 **Four-Wheel Drive**
John Michael Montgomery
1/82 **Fourteen Carat Mind**
Gene Watson
6/90 **Fourteen Minutes Old**
Doug Stone
64/68 **1432 Franklin Pike Circle Hero**
Bobby Russell
0/05 **4th Of July**
Shooter Jennings/George Jones
9/76 **Fox On The Run** *Tom T. Hall*
52/82 **Fragile--Handle With Care**
Cristy Lane
Frankie's Man, Johnny
9/59 *Johnny Cash*
13/59 *Johnny Sea*
41/02 **Frantic** *Jamie O'Neal*
Fraulein
1/57 *Bobby Helms*
92/79 *Curtis Potter*
57/82 *Joe Sun w/ Shotgun*
79/79 **Freckles** *Shylo*
26/74 **Freckles And Polliwog Days**
Ferlin Husky
90/77 **Freckles Brown** *Red Steagall*
10/75 **Freda Comes, Freda Goes**
Bobby G. Rice
4/53 **Free Home Demonstration**
Eddy Arnold
66/99 **Free Me** *Wayne Toups*
58/83 **Free Roamin' Mind** *Sonny James*
34/76 **Free To Be** *Eddy Raven*
Free To Be Lonely Again
14/80 *Debby Boone*
85/80 *Diane Pfeifer*
53/04 **Freedom** *Christy Sutherland*
68/98 **Freedom** *Wynonna*
73/96 **Freedom** *Ray Hood*
Freedom Ain't The Same As Bein' Free
87/73 *Archie Campbell*
53/77 *Eddy Arnold*
41/71 **Freight Train** *Jim & Jesse*
45/65 **Freight Train Blues** *Roy Acuff*
Freight Train Boogie
2/46 *Delmore Brothers*
5/47 *Red Foley*
54/70 **Freightliner Fever** *Red Sovine*
25/64 **French Song** *Marion Worth*
93/81 **(Frenchie Burke's) Fire On The Mountain**
Fiddlin' Frenchie Burke
Friday Night Blues
2/80 *John Conlee*
89/80 *Sonny Throckmorton*
Friday Night Feelin'
41/81 *Rich Landers*
49/83 *Vern Gosdin*
55/80 **Friday Night Fool** *Roger Bowling*
71/95 **Friday Night Stampede**
Western Flyer
39/91 **Friday Night's Woman**
Dean Dillon
57/03 **Fridaynititus** *Brad Tyler*
62/69 **Fried Chicken And A Country Tune** *Billy Edd Wheeler*
9/86 **Friend In California**
Merle Haggard
7/78 **Friend, Lover, Wife**
Johnny Paycheck

18/69 **Friend, Lover, Woman, Wife** *Claude King*
50/74 **Friend Named Red** *Brian Shaw*
68/97 **Friend To Me** *Garth Brooks*
Friendly Family Inn
64/80 *Jerry Reed*
95/80 *Hughie Burns*
78/84 **Friendly Game Of Hearts** *Penny DeHaven*
21/65 **Friendly Undertaker** *Jim Nesbitt*
1/81 **Friends** *Razzy Bailey*
2/97 **Friends** *John Michael Montgomery*
(Friends & Lovers) ..see: Both To Each Other
93/81 **Friends Before Lovers** *Gabriel*
68/96 **Friends Don't Drive Friends...** *Deryl Dodd*
1/90 **Friends In Low Places** *Garth Brooks*
71/68 **Frisco Line** *Guy Mitchell*
40/76 **Frog Kissin'** *Chet Atkins*
From A Jack To A King
2/63 *Ned Miller*
1/89 *Ricky Van Shelton*
10/75 **From Barrooms To Bedrooms** *David Wills*
92/83 **From Cotton To Satin** *Jack Greene*
4/77 **From Graceland To The Promised Land** *Merle Haggard*
From Heaven To Heartache
10/68 *Bobby Lewis*
22/70 *Eddy Arnold*
1/97 **From Here To Eternity** *Michael Peterson*
12/61 **From Here To There To You** *Hank Locklin*
33/82 **From Levis To Calvin Klein Jeans** *Brenda Lee*
(From Now On All My Friends Are Gonna Be) Strangers
6/65 *Roy Drusky*
10/65 *Merle Haggard*
6/78 **From Seven Till Ten** *Loretta Lynn/Conway Twitty*
65/90 **From Small Things (Big Things One Day Come)** *Nitty Gritty Dirt Band*
F/74 **From Tennessee To Texas** *Johnny Bush*
20/69 **From The Bottle To The Bottom** *Billy Walker*
60/99 **From The Inside Out** *Linda Davis*
3/89 **From The Word Go** *Michael Martin Murphey*
43/92 **From The Word Love** *Ricky Skaggs*
6/98 **From This Moment On** *Shania Twain w/ Bryan White*
From This Moment On
62/75 *George Morgan*
95/75 *Bonnie Guitar*
21/87 **From Time To Time** *Larry Gatlin & Janie Frickie*
65/71 **From Warm To Cool To Cold** *Lois Johnson*
From Where I Stand
66/96 *Kim Richey*
67/99 *Suzy Bogguss*
67/86 **From Where I Stand** *Dobie Gray*
43/97 **From Where I'm Sitting** *Gary Allan*
16/75 **From Woman To Woman** *Tommy Overstreet*
54/99 **From Your Knees** *Matt King*
51/89 **Frontier Justice** *Cee Cee Chapman & Santa Fe*
4/51 **Frosty The Snow Man** *Gene Autry*
41/64 **Frosty Window Pane** *Joe Penny*
76/83 **Froze In Her Line Of Fire** *Peter Isaacson*
90/81 **Frustration** *Wyvon Alexander*
11/67 **Fuel To The Flame** *Skeeter Davis*
1/67 **Fugitive, The** *Merle Haggard*
16/87 **Full Grown Fool** *Mickey Gilley*
87/82 **Full Moon - Empty Pockets** *Montana Skyline*
22/89 **Full Moon Full Of Love** *k.d. lang*
1/52 **Full Time Job** *Eddy Arnold*
31/00 **Fun Of Your Love** *Jennifer Day*
61/67 **Funny (But I'm Not Laughing)** *Conway Twitty*
1/72 **Funny Face** *Donna Fargo*
8/67 **Funny, Familiar, Forgotten, Feelings** *Don Gibson*
Funny How Time Slips Away
23/61 *Billy Walker*
12/75 *Narvel Felts*
41/80 *Danny Davis & Willie Nelson*
53/69 **Funny Thing Happened (On The Way To Miami)** *Tex Ritter*
9/62 **Funny Way Of Laughin'** *Burl Ives*
80/90 **Funny Ways Of Loving Me** *Steve Douglas*

G

5/44 **G.I. Blues** *Floyd Tillman*
4/53 **Gal Who Invented Kissin'** *Hank Snow*
58/67 **Gallant Men** *Senator Everett McKinley Dirksen*
1/69 **Galveston** *Glen Campbell*
Gambler, The
1/78 *Kenny Rogers*
65/78 *Don Schlitz*
95/78 *Hugh Moffatt*
6/53 **Gambler's Guitar** *Rusty Draper*
22/59 **Gambler's Love** *Rose Maddox*
Gamblin' Polka Dot Blues
8/49 *Tommy Duncan*
94/77 *Original Texas Playboys*
5/66 **Game Of Triangles** *Bobby Bare, Norma Jean, Liz Anderson*
2/69 **Games People Play** *Freddy Weller*
1/76 **Games That Daddies Play** *Conway Twitty*
51/91 **Garden, The** *Vern Gosdin*
44/72 **Garden Party** *Rick Nelson*
9/67 **Gardenias In Her Hair** *Marty Robbins*
70/93 **Garth Brooks Has Ruined My Life** *Tim Wilson*
84/75 **Gather Me** *Marilyn Sellars*
54/76 **Gator** *Jerry Reed*
50/65 **'Gator Hollow** *Lefty Frizzell*
4/57 **Geisha Girl** *Hank Locklin*
26/82 **General Lee** *Johnny Cash*
62/70 **Generation Gap** *Jeannie C. Riley*
86/76 **Gentle Fire** *Johnny Duncan*
Gentle On My Mind
30/67 *Glen Campbell*
60/67 *John Hartford*
44/68 *Glen Campbell*
68/71 **Gentle Rains Of Home** *George Morgan*
18/77 **Gentle To Your Senses** *Mel McDaniel*
Gently Hold Me
86/79 *Peggy Sue & Sonny Wright*
84/89 *Andi & The Brown Sisters*
53/97 **Genuine Rednecks** *David Lee Murphy*
96/77 **Genuine Texas Good Guy** *Jerry Green*
10/69 **George (And The North Woods)** *Dave Dudley*
43/74 **George Leroy Chickashea** *Porter Wagoner*
25/01 **Georgia** *Carolyn Dawn Johnson*
17/78 **Georgia In A Jug** *Johnny Paycheck*
Georgia Keeps Pulling On My Ring
50/74 *Little David Wilkins*
3/77 *Conway Twitty*
Georgia On A Fast Train
88/73 *Billy Joe Shaver [I Been To]*
95/76 *Tennessee Ernie Ford [I Been To]*
55/82 *Johnny Cash*
1/78 **Georgia On My Mind** *Willie Nelson*
37/71 **Georgia Pineywoods** *Osborne Brothers*
15/05 **Georgia Rain** *Trisha Yearwood*
70/75 **Georgia Rain** *Jerry Wallace*
16/70 **Georgia Sunshine** *Jerry Reed*
24/60 **Georgia Town Blues** *Mel Tillis & Bill Phillips*
83/82 **Georgiana** *Tommy Bell*
53/87 **Geronimo's Cadillac** *Jeff Stevens & The Bullets*
73/94 **Get A Little Closer** *Ricky Lynn Gregg*
Get A Little Dirt On Your Hands
14/62 *Bill Anderson*
46/80 *David Allan Coe & Bill Anderson*
72/95 **Get Back** *Steve Wariner*
57/78 **Get Back To Loving Me** *Jim Chesnut*
33/85 **Get Back To The Country** *Neil Young*
81/77 **Get Crazy With Me** *Ray Stevens*
56/77 **Get Down Country Music** *Brush Arbor*
65/93 **Get In Line** *Larry Boone*
21/82 **Get Into Reggae Cowboy** *Bellamy Brothers*
F/79 **Get It Up** *Ronnie Milsap*
73/81 **Get It While You Can** *Tom Carlile*
90/81 **Get Me High, Off This Low** *Gary Goodnight*
3/74 **Get On My Love Train** *La Costa*
90/89 **Get Out Of My Way** *Burbank Station*
46/95 **Get Over It** *Woody Lee*
27/02 **Get Over Yourself** *SheDaisy*
98/76 **Get Ready-Here I Come** *Don Gibson & Sue Thompson*

Get Rhythm
F/56 *Johnny Cash*
23/69 *Johnny Cash*
27/91 *Martin Delray*
(Get The Picture) ..see: Here's Your Sign
63/67 **Get This Stranger Out Of Me** *Lefty Frizzell*
34/70 **Get Together** *Gwen & Jerry Collins*
47/74 **Get Up I Think I Love You** *Jim Ed Brown*
5/67 **Get While The Gettin's Good** *Bill Anderson*
61/79 **Get Your Hands On Me Baby** *Dale McBride*
14/66 **Get Your Lie The Way You Want It** *Bonnie Guitar*
4/46 **Get Yourself A Red Head** *Hank Penny*
38/04 **Getaway Car** *Jenkins*
18/98 **Getcha Some** *Toby Keith*
37/66 **Gettin' Any Feed For Your Chickens** *Del Reeves*
56/70 **Gettin' Back To Norma** *Bob Luman*
43/02 **Gettin' Back To You** *Daisy Dern*
30/65 **Gettin' Married Has Made Us Strangers** *Dottie West*
Gettin' Over You
46/81 *Tim Rex & Oklahoma*
49/84 *Mason Dixon*
29/60 **Getting Old Before My Time** *Merle Kilgore*
28/81 **Getting Over You Again** *Ray Price*
Getting Over You Again
90/76 *Dale McBride*
67/79 *Dale McBride*
41/01 **Getting There** *Terri Clark*
5/90 **Ghost In This House** *Shenandoah*
(Ghost) Riders In The Sky ..see: Riders In The Sky
58/75 **Ghost Story** *Susan Raye*
58/90 **Ghost Town** *Zaca Creek*
49/66 **Giddyup Do-Nut** *Don Bowman*
1/66 **Giddyup Go** *Red Sovine*
10/66 **Giddyup Go - Answer** *Minnie Pearl*
4/88 **Gift, The** *McCarters*
51/97 **Gift, The** *Jim Brickman w/ Collin Raye & Susan Ashton*
34/80 **Gift From Missouri** *Jim Weatherly*
64/89 **Gift Of Love** *David Ball*
14/79 **Gimme Back My Blues** *Jerry Reed*
35/70 **Ginger Is Gentle And Waiting For Me** *Jim Ed Brown*
40/78 **Girl At The End Of The Bar** *John Anderson*
65/67 **Girl Crazy** *Carl Belew*
22/68 **Girl Don't Have To Drink To Have Fun** *Wanda Jackson*
15/64 **Girl From Spanish Town** *Marty Robbins*
58/94 **Girl From Yesterday** *Eagles*
F/78 **Girl I Can Tell (You're Trying To Work It Out)** *Waylon Jennings*
3/62 **Girl I Used To Know** *George Jones*
10[S]/02 **Girl In Love** *Robin English*
36/72 **Girl In New Orleans** *Sammi Smith*
17/86 **Girl Like Emmylou** *Southern Pacific*
74/72 **Girl Like Her Is Hard To Find** *Bill Rice*
46/73 **Girl Like You** *Tompall/Glaser Brothers*
60/97 **Girl Like You** *Jeffrey Steele*
77/81 **Girl Like You** *Sonny Throckmorton*
6/69 **Girl Most Likely** *Jeannie C. Riley*
17/85 **Girl Most Likely To** *B.J. Thomas*
61/70 **Girl Named Johnny Cash** *Jane Morgan*
74/69 **Girl Named Sam** *Lois Williams*
98/74 **Girl Of My Life** *Murry Kellum*
1/65 **Girl On The Billboard** *Del Reeves*
36/79 **Girl On The Other Side** *Nick Noble*
67/94 **Girl Thang** *Tammy Wynette w/ Wynonna*
26/60 **Girl Who Didn't Need Love** *Porter Wagoner*
26/70 **Girl Who'll Satisfy Her Man** *Barbara Fairchild*
28/04 **Girl's Gone Wild** *Travis Tritt*
4/97 **Girl's Gotta Do (What A Girl's Gotta Do)** *Mindy McCready*
35/66 **Girls Get Prettier (Every Day)** *Hank Locklin*
62/69 **Girls In Country Music** *Bobby Braddock*
1/04 **Girls Lie Too** *Terri Clark*
1/85 **Girls Night Out** *Judds*
42/99 **Girls Of Summer** *Neal McCoy*
7/87 **Girls Ride Horses Too** *Judy Rodman*
10/94 **Girls With Guitars** *Wynonna*
14/81 **Girls, Women And Ladies** *Ed Bruce*
2/88 **Give A Little Love** *Judds*
24/73 **Give A Little, Take A Little** *Barbara Mandrell*
13/87 **Give Back My Heart** *Lyle Lovett*
43/89 **Give 'Em My Number** *Janie Frickie*
48/85 **Give Her All The Roses (Don't Wait Until Tomorrow)** *Tom Jones*
24/71 **Give Him Love** *Patti Page*
97/83 **Give It Back** *Brenda Libby*
Give Me ..also see: Gimme
15/49 **Give Me A Hundred Reasons** *Ann Jones*
9/50 **Give Me A Little Old Fashioned Love** *Ernest Tubb*
52/94 **Give Me A Ring Sometime** *Lisa Brokop*
10/84 **Give Me Back That Old Familiar Feeling** *Whites*
9/64 **Give Me 40 Acres (To Turn This Rig Around)** *Willis Brothers*
3/89 **Give Me His Last Chance** *Lionel Cartwright*
1/52 **Give Me More, More, More (Of Your Kisses)** *Lefty Frizzell*
90/74 **Give Me One Good Reason** *Dickey Lee*
1/84 **Give Me One More Chance** *Exile*
3/95 **Give Me One More Shot** *Alabama*
60/96 **Give Me Some Wheels** *Suzy Bogguss*
(Give Me Someone I Can Love) ..see: Danger List
1/87 **Give Me Wings** *Michael Johnson*
41/99 **Give My Heart To You** *Billy Ray Cyrus*
13/57 **Give My Love To Rose** *Johnny Cash*
Give Myself A Party
5/58 *Don Gibson*
12/72 *Jeannie C. Riley*
69/78 **Giver, The** *Paul Schmucker*
8/88 **Givers And Takers** *Schuyler, Knobloch & Bickhardt*
12/96 **Givin' Water To A Drowning Man** *Lee Roy Parnell*
Giving Up Easy
81/79 *Leon Everette*
5/81 *Leon Everette*
88/77 **Glad I Waited Just For You** *Reba McEntire*
49/69 **Glad She's A Woman** *Bobby Goldsboro*
53/72 **Glow Worm** *Hank Thompson*
3/97 **Go Away** *Lorrie Morgan*
6/56 **Go Away With Me** *Wilburn Brothers*
36/01 **Go Back** *Chalee Tennison*
11/55 **Go Back You Fool** *Faron Young*
4/54 **Go, Boy, Go** *Carl Smith*
8/64 **Go Cat Go** *Norma Jean*
56/85 **Go Down Easy** *Dan Fogelberg*
38/90 **Go Down Swingin'** *Wild Rose*
53/05 **Go Easy On Me** *Lila McCann*
33/80 **Go For The Night** *Freddy Weller*
10/61 **Go Home** *Flatt & Scruggs*
49/05 **Go Home** *Steve Holy*
55/81 **Go Home And Go To Pieces** *Donna Hazard*
23/66 **Go Now Pay Later** *Liz Anderson*
2/00 **Go On** *George Strait*
13/62 **Go On Home** *Patti Page*
14/95 **Go Rest High On That Mountain** *Vince Gill*
72/99 **Go Tell It On The Mountain** *Garth Brooks*
52/73 **Go With Me** *Don Gibson & Sue Thompson*
51/01 **God Bless America** *LeAnn Rimes*
16/69 **God Bless America Again** *Bobby Bare*
48/97 **God Bless The Child** *Shania Twain*
God Bless The USA
7/84 *Lee Greenwood*
16/01 *Lee Greenwood*
4/93 **God Blessed Texas** *Little Texas*
49/02 **God, Family And Country** *Craig Morgan*
40/00 **God Gave Me You** *Bryan White*
32/68 **God Help You Woman** *Jim Glaser*
87/75 **God Is Good** *Betty Jean Robinson*
22/78 **God Knows** *Debby Boone*
91/76 **God Loves Us (When We All Sing Together)** *Sami Jo*
11/78 **God Made Love** *Mel McDaniel*
10/84 **God Must Be A Cowboy** *Dan Seals*
39/78 **God Must Have Blessed America** *Glen Campbell*
3/99 **God Must Have Spent A Little More Time On You** *Alabama w/ *NSYNC*
9/50 **God Please Protect America** *Jimmie Osborne*

69/00 **God Rest Ye Merry Gentlemen** *Garth Brooks*
9/56 **God Was So Good** *Jimmy Newman*
18/87 **God Will** *Lyle Lovett*
10/84 **God Won't Get You** *Dolly Parton*
73/96 **God's Country** *Marcus Hummon*
25/75 **God's Gonna Get'cha (For That)** *George Jones & Tammy Wynette*
16/05 **God's Will** *Martina McBride*
Gods Were Angry With Me
9/48 *Eddie Kirk*
3/50 *Margaret Whiting & Jimmy Wakely*
Godspeed (Sweet Dreams)
74/99 *Radney Foster*
48/03 *Dixie Chicks*
51/04 **Goes Good With Beer** *John Michael Montgomery*
69/90 **Goin' By The Book** *Johnny Cash*
5/83 **Goin' Down Hill** *John Anderson*
36/66 **Goin' Down The Road (Feelin' Bad)** *Skeeter Davis*
1/88 **Goin' Gone** *Kathy Mattea*
79/78 **Goin' Home** *Ron Shaw*
50/70 **Goin' Home To Your Mother** *Hagers*
99/77 **Goin' Skinny Dippin'** *Mayf Nutter*
Goin' Steady
2/53 *Faron Young*
5/70 *Faron Young*
2/95 **Goin' Through The Big D** *Mark Chesnutt*
43/88 **Goin' To Work** *Judy Rodman*
60/00 **Goin' Under Gettin' Over You** *Brooks & Dunn*
44/02 **Going Away** *Clark Family Experience*
74/71 **Going Back To Louisiana** *Ernie Rowell*
78/79 **Going Down Slow** *Cates Sisters*
65/96 **Goin', Goin', Gone** *Thrasher Shiver*
1/84 **Going, Going, Gone** *Lee Greenwood*
35/96 **Going, Going, Gone** *Neal McCoy*
45/79 **Going, Going, Gone** *Mary K. Miller*
31/68 **Going Home For The Last Time** *Kenny Price*
43/00 **Going Nowhere** *Wynonna*
5/92 **Going Out Of My Mind** *McBride & The Ride*
68/68 **Going Out To Tulsa** *Johnny Seay*
14/92 **Going Out Tonight** *Mary-Chapin Carpenter*
17/63 **Going Through The Motions (Of Living)** *Sonny James*
81/87 **Going To California** *Danny Shirley*
1/83 **Going Where The Lonely Go** *Merle Haggard*
93/81 **Gold Cadillac** *Tom Carlile*
2/52 **Gold Rush Is Over** *Hank Snow*
11/66 **Golden Guitar** *Bill Anderson*
41/76 **Golden Oldie** *Anne Murray*
1/76 **Golden Ring** *George Jones & Tammy Wynette*
Golden Rocket
1/51 *Hank Snow*
38/70 *Jim & Jesse*
1/79 **Golden Tears** *Dave & Sugar*
51/93 **Golden Years** *Holly Dunn*
Gone
1/57 *Ferlin Husky*
36/80 *Ronnie McDowell*
3/05 **Gone** *Montgomery Gentry*
34/74 **Gone** *Nancy Wayne*
5/92 **Gone As A Girl Can Get** *George Strait*
49/76 **Gone At Last** *Johnny Paycheck w/ Charnissa*
60/88 **Gone But Not Forgotten** *Cee Cee Chapman & Santa Fe*
1/95 **Gone Country** *Alan Jackson*
4/99 **Gone Crazy** *Alan Jackson*
Gone Girl
23/70 *Tompall/Glaser Brothers*
44/78 *Johnny Cash*
86/87 **Gone, Gone, Gone** *Brenda Cole*
(Gone Hillbilly Nuts) ..see: Little Ramona
24/67 **Gone, On The Other Hand** *Tompall/Glaser Brothers*
24/72 **Gone (Our Endless Love)** *Billy Walker*
48/98 **Gone Out Of My Mind** *Doug Stone*
51/96 **Gone (That'll Be Me)** *Dwight Yoakam*
94/78 **Gone To Alabama** *Mickey Newbury*
1/80 **Gone Too Far** *Eddie Rabbitt*
62/67 **Gone With The Wine** *Ray Pillow*
2/45 **Gonna Build A Big Fence Around Texas** *Gene Autry*
F/56 **Gonna Come Get You** *George Jones*
Gonna Find Me A Bluebird
3/57 *Marvin Rainwater*
12/57 *Eddy Arnold*
1/95 **Gonna Get A Life** *Mark Chesnutt*
Gonna Get Along Without You Now
8/64 *Skeeter Davis*
72/80 *Cates Sisters*
4/83 **Gonna Go Huntin' Tonight** *Hank Williams, Jr.*
45/82 **Gonna Have A Party** *Kieran Kane*
Gonna Have Love
10/65 *Buck Owens*
76/89 *Buck Owens*
51/98 **Gonna Have To Fall** *Shane Stockton*
67/68 **Gonna Miss Me** *Homesteaders*
1/88 **Gonna Take A Lot Of River** *Oak Ridge Boys*
39/82 **Gonna Take My Angel Out Tonight** *Ronnie Rogers*
61/86 **Good And Lonesome** *Lowes*
57/90 **Good As Gone** *Joe Barnhill*
4/97 **Good As I Was To You** *Lorrie Morgan*
80/77 **Good Cheatin' Songs** *Carmol Taylor*
25/63 **Good Country Song** *Hank Cochran*
12/01 **Good Day To Run** *Darryl Worley*
Good Deal, Lucille
8/54 *Al Terry*
18/69 *Carl Smith*
62/74 **Good Enough To Be Your Man** *Brian Shaw*
7/71 **Good Enough To Be Your Wife** *Jeannie C. Riley*
81/77 **Good Evening Henry** *Peggy Sue*
10/90 **Good Friends, Good Whiskey, Good Lovin'** *Hank Williams, Jr.*
84/81 **Good Friends Make Good Lovers** *Jerry Reed*
91/79 **Good Gal Is Hard To Find** *Hank Snow*
58/94 **Good Girls Go To Heaven** *Charlie Floyd*
29/87 **Good God, I Had It Good** *Pake McEntire*
60/05 **Good Hearted Man** *Tift Merritt*
Good Hearted Woman
3/72 *Waylon Jennings*
1/76 *Waylon Jennings & Willie Nelson*
65/99 **Good Idea Tomorrow** *Deryl Dodd*
38/05 **Good Life** *Trent Willmon*
11/04 **Good Little Girls** *Blue County*
57/75 **Good Lord Giveth (And Uncle Sam Taketh Away)** *Webb Pierce*
53/85 **Good Love Died Tonight** *Leon Everette*
Good Love Is Like A Good Song
23/73 *Bob Luman*
88/80 *Nancy Ruud*
1/71 **Good Lovin' (Makes It Right)** *Tammy Wynette*
21/80 **Good Lovin' Man** *Gail Davies*
27/71 **Good Man** *June Carter Cash*
55/70 **Good Morning** *Leapy Lee*
1/02 **Good Morning Beautiful** *Steve Holy*
30/72 **Good Morning Country Rain** *Jeannie C. Riley*
Good Morning, Dear
67/68 *Frank Ifield*
71/68 *Don Gibson*
Good Morning Loving
61/74 *Larry Kingston*
91/75 *Larry Kingston*
43/64 **Good Morning Self** *Jim Reeves*
37/77 **Good 'N' Country** *Kathy Barnes*
9/73 **Good News** *Jody Miller*
27/75 **Good News, Bad News** *Eddy Raven*
51/84 **Good Night For Falling In Love** *Hillary Kanter*
18/76 **Good Night Special** *Little David Wilkins*
19/83 **Good Night's Love** *Tammy Wynette*
(Good Ol' Boys) ..see: Good Ole Boys, & Theme From The Dukes Of Hazzard
47/97 **Good Ol' Fashioned Love** *Tracy Byrd*
15/81 **Good Ol' Girls** *Sonny Curtis*
81/82 **Good Old Days** *Cristy Lane*
35/73 **Good Old Days (Are Here Again)** *Buck Owens & Susan Raye*
31/74 **Good Old Fashioned Country Love** *Don Gibson & Sue Thompson*
55/77 **Good Old Fashioned Saturday Night Honky Tonk Barroom Brawl** *Vernon Oxford*
16/83 **Good Ole Boys** *Jerry Reed*
2/80 **Good Ole Boys Like Me** *Don Williams*

24↑/05 **Good Ole Days** *Phil Vassar*
1/94 **Good Run Of Bad Luck** *Clint Black*
1/02 **Good Stuff** *Kenny Chesney*
34/70 **Good Thing** *Bill Wilbourn & Kathy Morrison*
2/73 **Good Things** *David Houston*
49/03 **Good Time** *Jessica Andrews*
Good Time ..also see: Goodtime
3/69 **Good Time Charlie's** *Del Reeves*
1/90 **Good Times** *Dan Seals*
Good Times
44/68 *Willie Nelson*
25/81 *Willie Nelson*
50/00 **Good Times** *Anita Cochran*
57/87 **Good Timin' Shoes** *Ronnie Rogers*
49/02 **Good To Go** *Jeffrey Steele*
21/01 **Good Way To Get On My Bad Side** *Tracy Byrd & Mark Chesnutt*
1/76 **Good Woman Blues** *Mel Tillis*
67/77 **Good Woman Likes To Drink With The Boys** *Jimmie Rodgers*
12/74 **Good Woman's Love** *Jerry Reed*
54/04 **Good Year For The Outlaw** *Jeffrey Steele*
Good Year For The Roses
2/71 *George Jones*
56/94 *George Jones w/ Alan Jackson*
Goodbye
73/71 *David Frizzell*
19/74 *Rex Allen, Jr.*
22/79 *Eddy Arnold*
38/72 **Goodbye** *David Rogers*
39/67 **Goodbye City, Goodbye Girl** *Webb Pierce*
13/00 **Goodbye Earl** *Dixie Chicks*
86/80 **Goodbye Eyes** *Pebble Daniel*
24/84 **Goodbye Heartache** *Louise Mandrell*
70/92 **Goodbye Highway** *Darryl & Don Ellis*
71/84 **Goodbye Highway** *Pam Tillis*
45/00 **Goodbye Is The Wrong Way To Go** *Wade Hayes*
75/71 **Goodbye Jukebox** *Bobby Lord*
12/63 **Goodbye Kisses** *Cowboy Copas*
22/59 **Goodbye Little Darlin'** *Johnny Cash*
32/89 **Goodbye Lonesome, Hello Baby Doll** *Lonesome Strangers*
Goodbye Marie
17/81 *Bobby Goldsboro*
47/86 *Kenny Rogers*
93/77 **Goodbye My Friend** *Engelbert Humperdinck*
28/02 **Goodbye On A Bad Day** *Shannon Lawson*
11/94 **Goodbye Says It All** *BlackHawk*
62/90 **Goodbye, So Long, Hello** *Prairie Oyster*
53/87 **Goodbye Song** *Gene Stroman*
72/67 **Goodbye Swingers** *Glen Garrison*
Goodbye Time
7/88 *Conway Twitty*
10/05 *Blake Shelton*
20/67 **Goodbye Wheeling** *Mel Tillis*
8/87 **Goodbyes All We've Got Left** *Steve Earle*
56/73 **Goodbyes Come Hard For Me** *Kenny Serratt*
83/78 **Goodbyes Don't Come Easy** *Mack White*
91/74 **Goodbyes Don't Come Easy** *Warner Mack*
62/66 **Goodie Wagon** *Billy Large*
66/99 **Goodnight** *Suzy Bogguss*
Goodnight Irene
1/50 *Red Foley–Ernest Tubb*
5/50 *Moon Mullican*
53/76 **Goodnight My Love** *Randy Barlow*
6/96 **Goodnight Sweetheart** *David Kersh*
3/54 **Goodnight, Sweetheart, Goodnight** *Johnnie & Jack*
Goodtime Charlie's Got The Blues
63/72 *Danny O'Keefe*
41/79 *Red Steagall*
63/84 *Leon Russell*
83/79 **Goody Goody** *Rebecca Lynn*
24/67 **Goody, Goody Gumdrop** *Wilburn Brothers*
10/89 **Gospel According To Luke** *Skip Ewing*
Got Leaving On Her Mind
54/68 *Mac Wiseman*
14/73 *Nat Stuckey*
82/81 **Got Lucky Last Night** *Jerry Jeff Walker*
Got My Heart Set On You
1/86 *John Conlee*
72/86 *Mason Dixon*
7/85 **Got No Reason Now For Goin' Home** *Gene Watson*
1/72 **Got The All Overs For You (All Over Me)** *Freddie Hart*
10/87 **Gotta Get Away** *Sweethearts Of The Rodeo*
41/69 **Gotta Get To Oklahoma ('Cause California's Gettin' To Me)** *Hagers*
4/46 **Gotta Get Together With My Gal** *Elton Britt*
9/87 **Gotta Have You** *Eddie Rabbitt*
12/86 **Gotta Learn To Love Without You** *Michael Johnson*
4/78 **Gotta' Quit Lookin' At You Baby** *Dave & Sugar*
Gotta Travel On
5/59 *Billy Grammer*
15/59 *Bill Monroe*
91/78 *Shylo*
70/93 **Graceland** *Willie Nelson*
69/67 **Grain Of Salt** *Penny Starr*
93/77 **Grand Ole Blues** *Troy Seals*
97/73 **Grand Ole Opry Song** *Nitty Gritty Dirt Band w/ Jimmy Martin*
Grand Tour
1/74 *George Jones*
38/93 *Aaron Neville*
16/78 **Grandest Lady Of Them All** *Conway Twitty*
Grandma Got Run Over By A Reindeer
92/84 *Elmo & Patsy*
64/98 *Elmo & Patsy*
48/00 *Elmo & Patsy*
1/72 **Grandma Harp** *Merle Haggard*
(Grandma's Diary) ..see: Johnny, My Love
64/89 **Grandma's Old Wood Stove** *Sanders*
9/81 **Grandma's Song** *Gail Davies*
1/86 **Grandpa (Tell Me 'Bout The Good Old Days)** *Judds*
23/96 **Grandpa Told Me So** *Kenny Chesney*
82/88 **Grass Is Greener** *Teddy Spencer*
15/49 **Grass Looks Greener Over Yonder** *Hank Thompson*
24/67 **Grass Won't Grow On A Busy Street** *Kenny Price*
71/96 **Gravitational Pull** *Chris LeDoux*
F/70 **Grazin' In Greener Pastures** *Ray Price*
83/76 **(Great American) Classic Cowboy** *Penny DeHaven*
Great Balls Of Fire
1/58 *Jerry Lee Lewis*
F/79 *Dolly Parton*
67/79 **Great Chicago Fire** *Faron Young*
12/74 **Great Divide** *Roy Clark*
41/90 **Great Divide** *Gene Watson*
32/66 **Great El Tigre (The Tiger)** *Stu Phillips*
8/75 **Great Expectations** *Buck Owens*
58/73 **Great Filling Station Holdup** *Jimmy Buffett*
10/48 **Great Long Pistol** *Jerry Irby*
63/74 **Great Mail Robbery** *Rex Allen, Jr.*
46/68 **Great Pretender** *Lamar Morris*
8/70 **Great White Horse** *Buck Owens & Susan Raye*
26/99 **Greatest, The** *Kenny Rogers*
53/85 **Greatest Gift Of All** *Kenny Rogers & Dolly Parton*
94/80 **Greatest Love Affair** *Chuck Woolery*
3/92 **Greatest Man I Never Knew** *Reba McEntire*
22/64 **Greatest One Of All** *Melba Montgomery*
88/76 **Greatest Show On Earth** *Little David Wilkins*
Green Berets ..see: Ballad Of The
78/73 **Green Door** *Mayf Nutter*
95/81 **Green Eyed Girl** *Sean Morton Downey*
Green Eyes
37/82 *Tom Carlile*
62/87 *Danny Davis & Dona Mason*
82/85 **Green Eyes** *Kathy Twitty*
4/65 **Green, Green Grass Of Home** *Porter Wagoner*
57/70 **Green Green Valley** *Tex Ritter*
7/48 **Green Light** *Hank Thompson*
11/67 **Green River** *Waylon Jennings*
53/73 **Green Snakes On The Ceiling** *Johnny Bush*
90/77 **Greenback Shuffle** *King Edward IV & The Knights*
26/61 **Greener Pastures** *Stonewall Jackson*
23/75 **Greener Than The Grass (We Laid On)** *Tanya Tucker*
49/68 **Greenwich Village Folk Song Salesman** *Jim & Jesse*
63/71 **Greystone Chapel** *Glen Sherley*
4/46 **Grievin' My Heart Out For You** *Jimmie Davis*

9/59 **Grin And Bear It** *Jimmy Newman*
(Grits And Groceries) ..see: If I Don't Love You
42/69 **Groovy Grubworm** *Harlow Wilcox*
50/00 **Grow Young With You** *Coley McCabe*
39/69 **Growin' Up** *Tex Ritter*
1/01 **Grown Men Don't Cry** *Tim McGraw*
(Grundy County Auction Incident) ..see: Sold
16/90 **Guardian Angels** *Judds*
19/71 **Guess Away The Blues** *Don Gibson*
18/66 **Guess My Eyes Were Bigger Than My Heart** *Conway Twitty*
1/58 **Guess Things Happen That Way** *Johnny Cash*
42/64 **Guess What, That's Right, She's Gone** *Hank Williams, Jr.*
7/71 **Guess Who** *Slim Whitman*
18/74 **Guess Who** *Jerry Wallace*
47/79 **Guess Who Loves You** *Mary K. Miller*
Guilty
3/63 *Jim Reeves*
92/85 *Merle Kilgore*
9/83 **Guilty** *Statler Brothers*
34/98 **Guilty** *Warren Brothers*
37/82 **Guilty Eyes** *Bandana*
81/86 **Guilty Eyes** *Darlene Austin*
61/69 **Guilty Street** *Kitty Wells*
8/49 **Guitar Boogie** *Arthur "Guitar Boogie" Smith*
Guitar Man
53/67 *Jerry Reed*
1/81 *Elvis Presley*
Guitar Polka
1/46 *Al Dexter*
3/46 *Rosalie Allen*
7/86 **Guitar Town** *Steve Earle*
53/05 **Guitars And Tiki Bars** *Kenny Chesney*
4/86 **Guitars, Cadillacs** *Dwight Yoakam*
60/70 **Gun, The** *Bob Luman*
31/04 **Guy Like Me** *Pat Green*
1/96 **Guys Do It All The Time** *Mindy McCready*
5/71 **Gwen (Congratulations)** *Tommy Overstreet*
56/85 **Gypsies In The Palace** *Jimmy Buffett*
25/87 **Gypsies On Parade** *Sawyer Brown*
69/82 **Gypsy And Joe** *Sammi Smith*
43/79 **Gypsy Eyes** *Terri Sue Newman*
16/71 **Gypsy Feet** *Jim Reeves*
52/68 **Gypsy King** *Kitty Wells*
64/68 **Gypsy Man** *Buddy Knox*
81/74 **Gypsy Queen** *Chuck Glaser*
98/77 **Gypsy River** *Jack Paris*

H

63/74 **Habit I Can't Break** *Nick Nixon*
Had A Dream (For The Heart)
45/76 *Elvis Presley*
17/84 *Judds*
9/49 **Hadacol Boogie** *Bill Nettles*
45/85 **Haircut Song** *Ray Stevens*
40/03 **Half A Heart Tattoo** *Jennifer Hanson*
80/77 **Half A Love** *Roy Clark*
25/63 **Half A Man** *Willie Nelson*
40/03 **Half A Man** *Anthony Smith*
8/58 **Half A Mind** *Ernest Tubb*
Half As Much
2/52 *Hank Williams*
23/76 *Sheila Tilton*
16/59 **Half-Breed** *Marvin Rainwater*
91/73 **Half-Empty Bed** *Stan Hitchcock*
8/93 **Half Enough** *Lorrie Morgan*
80/89 **Half Heaven Half Heartache** *Leah Marr*
F/78 **Half My Heart's In Texas** *Ernest Tubb*
30/64 **Half Of This, Half Of That** *Wynn Stewart*
2/87 **Half Past Forever (Till I'm Blue In The Heart)** *T.G. Sheppard*
4/94 **Half The Man** *Clint Black*
2/79 **Half The Way** *Crystal Gayle*
F/76 **Half The Way In, Half The Way Out** *Little David Wilkins*
6/97 **Half Way Up** *Clint Black*
56/80 **Halftime** *J.W. Thompson*
6/95 **Halfway Down** *Patty Loveless*
56/02 **Halfway Home Cafe** *Ricky Skaggs*
26/63 **Hall Of Shame** *Melba Montgomery*
15/85 **Hallelujah, I Love You So** *George Jones w/ Brenda Lee*
22/68 **Hammer And Nails** *Jimmy Dean*
34/93 **Hammer And Nails** *Radney Foster*
70/00 **Hampsterdance Song** *Hampton The Hampster*
94/77 **Hand Me Another Of Those** *Mickey Newbury*
33/97 **Hand Of Fate** *Sons Of The Desert*
52/73 **Hand Of Love** *Billy Walker*
6/87 **Hand That Rocks The Cradle** *Glen Campbell w/ Steve Wariner*
11/61 **Hand You're Holding Now** *Skeeter Davis*
19/78 **Handcuffed To A Heartache** *Mary K. Miller*
64/99 **Handful Of Water** *Chalee Tennison*
65/73 **Handfull Of Dimes** *Jack Blanchard & Misty Morgan*
40/03 **Handprints On The Wall** *Kenny Rogers*
5/99 **Hands Of A Working Man** *Ty Herndon*
62/84 **Handsome Man** *Karen Taylor-Good*
75/82 **Handy Man** *Joel Hughes*
2/74 **Hang In There Girl** *Freddie Hart*
Hang On Feelin'
97/76 *Sherry Bryce*
63/78 *Red Steagall*
1/85 **Hang On To Your Heart** *Exile*
50/91 **Hang Up The Phone** *Eddie Rabbitt*
Hang Your Head In Shame
3/45 *Bob Wills*
4/45 *Red Foley*
9/83 **Hangin' Around** *Whites*
34/64 **Hangin' Around** *Wilburn Brothers*
4/94 **Hangin' In** *Tanya Tucker*
30/79 **Hangin' In And Hangin' On** *Buck Owens*
67/96 **Hangin' In And Hangin' On** *David Ball*
Hangin' On
37/67 *Gosdin Bros.*
54/67 *Leon Ashley & Margie Singleton*
16/77 *Vern Gosdin*
59/84 *Lane Brody*
58/96 **Hangin' On** *Rich McCready*
82/74 **Hangin' On To What I've Got** *Frank Myers*
44/87 **Hangin' Out In Smokey Places** *Marshall Tucker Band*
47/03 **Hangin' Round The Mistletoe** *Brooks & Dunn*
26/71 **Hanging Over Me** *Jack Greene*
15/59 **Hanging Tree** *Marty Robbins*
14/49 **Hangman's Boogie** *Cowboy Copas*
12/61 **Hangover Tavern** *Hank Thompson*
12/73 **Hank** *Hank Williams, Jr.*
39/73 **Hank And Lefty Raised My Country Soul** *Stoney Edwards*
75/87 **Hank Drank** *Bobby Lee Springfield*
23/65 **Hank Williams' Guitar** *Freddie Hart*
2/76 **Hank Williams, You Wrote My Life** *Moe Bandy*
93/84 **Hanky Panky** *Mike Dekle*
1/72 **Happiest Girl In The Whole U.S.A.** *Donna Fargo*
47/68 **Happiness Hill** *Kitty Wells*
63/69 **Happiness Lives In This House** *Mac Curtis*
43/67 **Happiness Means You** *Kitty Wells & Red Foley*
Happiness Of Having You
69/71 *Jay Lee Webb*
3/76 *Charley Pride*
47/71 **Happy Anniversary** *Roy Rogers*
3/65 **Happy Birthday** *Loretta Lynn*
1/79 **Happy Birthday Darlin'** *Conway Twitty*
3/84 **Happy Birthday Dear Heartache** *Barbara Mandrell*
7/61 **Happy Birthday To Me** *Hank Locklin*
Happy Country Birthday Darling
72/82 *Rodney Lay*
86/82 *Ronnie Rogers*
Happy Day ..see: (It's Gonna Be A)
89/78 **Happy Days** *Roy Clark*
68/99 **Happy Ever After** *T. Graham Brown*
54/72 **Happy Everything** *Bonnie Guitar*
2/98 **Happy Girl** *Martina McBride*
81/78 **Happy Go Lucky Morning** *Terri Hollowell*
Happy, Happy Birthday Baby
36/72 *Sandy Posey*
1/86 *Ronnie Milsap*
Happy Heart ..see: (I've Got A)
49/74 **Happy Hour** *Tony Booth*
10/62 **Happy Journey** *Hank Locklin*
92/79 **Happy Sax** *Maury Finney*
58/71 **Happy Songs Of Love** *Tennessee Ernie Ford*
2/68 **Happy State Of Mind** *Bill Anderson*
22/68 **Happy Street** *Slim Whitman*

Happy To Be Unhappy
11/63 *Gary Buck*
50/64 *Leroy Van Dyke*
9/66 **Happy To Be With You** *Johnny Cash*
8/79 **Happy Together** *T.G. Sheppard*
7/67 **Happy Tracks** *Kenny Price*
87/80 **Harbor Lights** *Rusty Draper*
76/85 **Hard Act To Follow** *Keith Whitley*
Hard Baby To Rock
64/85 *Tari Hensley*
71/89 *Susi Beatty*
45/02 **Hard Call To Make** *J. Michael Harter*
Hard Candy Christmas
8/83 *Dolly Parton*
73/98 *Dolly Parton*
36/92 **Hard Days And Honky Tonk Nights** *Earl Thomas Conley*
31/70 **Hard, Hard Traveling Man** *Dick Curless*
30/80 **Hard Hat Days And Honky Tonk Nights** *Red Steagall*
Hard Headed Heart
78/87 *Tim Johnson*
73/89 *Bruce Van Dyke*
63/91 **Hard-Headed Man** *Sweethearts Of The Rodeo*
2/58 **Hard Headed Woman** *Elvis Presley*
70/94 **Hard Liquor, Cold Women, Warm Beer** *Bob Woodruff*
10/87 **Hard Livin'** *Keith Whitley*
13/95 **Hard Lovin' Woman** *Mark Collie*
38/89 **Hard Luck Ace** *Lacy J. Dalton*
54/67 **Hard Luck Joe** *Johnny Duncan*
67/94 **Hard Luck Woman** *Garth Brooks*
1/90 **Hard Rock Bottom Of Your Heart** *Randy Travis*
59/05 **Hard Secret To Keep** *Mark Chesnutt*
7/80 **Hard Times** *Lacy J. Dalton*
75/68 **Hard Times** *Larry Steele*
48/89 **Hard Times For An Honest Man** *James House*
68/00 **Hard To Be A Husband, Hard To Be A Wife** *Brad Paisley & Chely Wright*
5/94 **Hard To Say** *Sawyer Brown*
11/93 **Hard Way** *Mary-Chapin Carpenter*
62/93 **Hard Way To Make An Easy Livin'** *Bellamy Brothers*
4/93 **Hard Workin' Man** *Brooks & Dunn*
47/02 **Harder Cards** *Kenny Rogers*
59/90 **Hardin County Line** *Mark Collie*
82/77 **Hardly A Day Goes By** *Jean Shepard*
59/67 **Hardly Anymore** *Bob Luman*
57/74 **Harlan County** *Wayne Kemp*
10/86 **Harmony** *John Conlee*
61/71 **Harold's Super Service** *Bobby Wayne*
1/68 **Harper Valley P.T.A.** *Jeannie C. Riley*
24/68 **Harper Valley P.T.A. (Later That Same Day)** *Ben Colder*
4/46 **Harriet** *Red Foley w/ Roy Ross*
74/84 **Harvest Moon** *Joe Waters*
35/65 **Harvest Of Sunshine** *Jimmy Dean*
68/70 **Harvey Harrington IV** *Johnny Carver*
22/94 **Has Anybody Seen Amy** *John & Audrey Wiggins*
78/80 **Hasn't It Been Good Together** *Hank Snow & Kelly Foxton*
41/67 **Hasta Luego (See You Later)** *Hank Locklin*
98/79 **Hat, The** *Roger Miller*
9/93 **Haunted Heart** *Sammy Kershaw*
11/69 **Haunted House** *Compton Brothers*
51/76 **Have A Dream On Me** *Mel McDaniel*
67/80 **Have A Good Day** *Henson Cargill*
1/68 **Have A Little Faith** *David Houston*
63/70 **Have A Little Talk With Myself** *Ray Stevens*
Have Another Drink
82/81 *Douglas*
73/84 *Doug Block*
14/58 **Have Blues--Will Travel** *Eddie Noack*
30/59 **Have Heart, Will Love** *Jean Shepard*
6/85 **Have I Got A Deal For You** *Reba McEntire*
Have I Got A Heart For You
60/83 *Chantilly*
68/86 *Rockin' Horse*
14/87 **Have I Got Some Blues For You** *Charley Pride*
47/64 **Have I Stayed Away Too Long** *Bobby Bare*
62/96 **Have I Told You Lately** *Emilio*
Have I Told You Lately That I Love You
3/46 *Gene Autry*
3/46 *Tex Ritter*
4/46 *Foy Willing*
5/46 *Red Foley w/ Roy Ross*
74/69 *Kitty Wells & Red Foley*
67/74 **Have It Your Way** *Dave Dudley*
1/85 **Have Mercy** *Judds*
57/96 **Have We Forgotten What Love Is** *Crystal Bernard*
Have You Ever Been Lonely? (Have You Ever Been Blue)
2/49 *Ernest Tubb*
5/82 *Jim Reeves & Patsy Cline*
85/81 **Have You Ever Seen The Rain** *Pam Hobbs*
50/67 **Have You Ever Wanted To?** *Lorene Mann*
1/03 **Have You Forgotten?** *Darryl Worley*
67/83 **Have You Heard** *Rick & Janis Carnes*
86/87 **Have You Hurt Any Good Ones Lately** *Sharon Robinson*
32/84 **Have You Loved Your Woman Today** *Craig Dillingham*
3/75 **Have You Never Been Mellow** *Olivia Newton-John*
Have Yourself A Merry Little Christmas
52/94 *Vince Gill*
54/95 *Vince Gill*
64/98 *Vince Gill*
54/99 *Martina McBride*
53/00 *Martina McBride*
59/01 *Martina McBride*
74/01 *Neal McCoy (medley)*
71/01 *Lonestar*
57/05 *Joe Nichols*
60/05 *LeAnn Rimes*
32/80 **Haven't I Loved You Somewhere Before** *Joe Stampley*
84/80 **Haven't I Loved You Somewhere Before** *Bluestone*
Haven't We Loved Somewhere Before ..see: Pardon Me (Haven't We Loved Somewhere Before)
He Ain't Country
51/68 *James Bell*
48/72 *Claude King*
93/78 **He Ain't Heavy, He's My Brother** *June Neyman*
5/93 **He Ain't Worth Missing** *Toby Keith*
19/77 **He Ain't You** *Lynn Anderson*
15/84 **He Broke Your Mem'ry Last Night** *Reba McEntire*
29/85 **He Burns Me Up** *Lane Brody*
23/64 **He Called Me Baby** *Patsy Cline*
26/74 **He Can Be Mine** *Jeannie Seely*
8/74 **He Can't Fill My Shoes** *Jerry Lee Lewis*
74/88 **He Cares** *Rosie Flores*
59/91 **He Comes Around** *Molly & The Heymakers*
1/99 **He Didn't Have To Be** *Brad Paisley*
He [She] Don't Make Me Cry
19/71 *David Rogers*
87/82 *Kippi Brannon*
39/01 **He Drinks Tequila** *Lorrie Morgan & Sammy Kershaw*
54/71 **He Even Woke Me Up To Say Goodbye** *Lynn Anderson*
68/93 **He Feels Guilty** *Bobbie Cryner*
7/05 **He Gets That From Me** *Reba McEntire*
52/80 **He Gives Me Diamonds, You Give Me Chills** *Margo Smith*
1/82 **He Got You** *Ronnie Milsap*
18/97 **He Left A Lot To Be Desired** *Ricochet*
88/75 **He Little Thing'd Her Out Of My Arms** *Jack Greene*
56/68 **He Looks A Lot Like You** *Harden Trio*
1/70 **He Loves Me All The Way** *Tammy Wynette*
77/75 **He Loves Me All To Pieces** *Ruby Falls*
22↑/05 **He Oughta Know That By Now** *Lee Ann Womack*
73/78 **He Picked Me Up When You Let Me Down** *Mary Lou Turner*
17/64 **He Says The Same Things To Me** *Skeeter Davis*
He Stands Real Tall
11/62 *Del Reeves*
21/65 *"Little" Jimmy Dickens*

1/80 **He Stopped Loving Her Today** *George Jones*
4/90 **He Talks To Me** *Lorrie Morgan*
2/94 **He Thinks He'll Keep Her** *Mary Chapin Carpenter*
He Thinks I Still Care ..see: She Thinks
46/67 **He Thought He'd Die Laughing** *Bobby Helms*
10/75 **He Took Me For A Ride** *La Costa*
13/75 **He Turns It Into Love Again** *Lynn Anderson*
2/90 **He Walked On Water** *Randy Travis*
45/66 **He Was Almost Persuaded** *Donna Harris*
25/90 **He Was On To Somethin' (So He Made You)** *Ricky Skaggs*
17/80 **He Was There (When I Needed You)** *Tammy Wynette*
68/72 **He Will Break Your Heart** *Johnny Williams*
32/00 **He Will, She Knows** *Kenny Rogers*
22/85 **He Won't Give In** *Kathy Mattea*
31/92 **He Would Be Sixteen** *Michelle Wright*
64/97 **He'd Never Seen Julie Cry** *Jo Dee Messina*
15/70 **He'd Still Love Me** *Lynn Anderson*
58/74 **He'll Come Home** *Melba Montgomery*
1/60 **He'll Have To Go** *Jim Reeves*
6/60 **He'll Have To Stay** *Jeanne Black*
21/77 **He'll Play The Music (But You Can't Make Him Dance)** *Little David Wilkins*
68/79 **He's A Cowboy From Texas** *Ronnie McDowell*
95/79 **He's A Good Man** *Judy Argo*
He's A Good Ole Boy
32/68 *Arlene Harden*
58/94 *Chely Wright*
1/83 **He's A Heartache (Looking For A Place To Happen)** *Janie Fricke*
39/66 **He's A Jolly Good Fellow** *Charlie Walker*
39/90 **He's Alive** *Dolly Parton*
94/79 **He's An Old Rock 'N' Roller** *Dickey Lee*
1/88 **He's Back And I'm Blue** *Desert Rose Band*
He's Everywhere
25/70 *Sammi Smith*
39/75 *Marilyn Sellars*
16/67 **He's Got A Way With Women** *Hank Thompson*
63/77 **He's Got A Way With Women** *Bob Luman*
48/69 **He's Got More Love In His Little Finger** *Billie Jo Spears*
F/87 **He's Got The Whole World In His Hands** *Cristy Lane*
2/98 **He's Got You** *Brooks & Dunn*
54/90 **He's Gotta Have Me** *Girls Next Door*
18/87 **He's Letting Go** *Baillie & The Boys*
16/58 **He's Lost His Love For Me** *Kitty Wells*
61/71 **He's My Man** *Melba Montgomery*
He's My Rock ..see: She's My Rock
74/93 **He's My Weakness** *Ronna Reeves*
89/82 **He's Not Entitled To Your Love** *Johnny Rodriguez*
53/67 **He's Not For Real** *Priscilla Mitchell*
79/87 **He's Not Good Enough** *Paul Proctor*
67/97 **He's On The Way Home** *Tony Toliver*
17/80 **He's Out Of My Life** *Johnny Duncan & Janie Fricke*
5/71 **He's So Fine** *Jody Miller*
He's Still All Over You ..see: She's Still
60/82 **He's Taken** *Lane Brody*
29/81 **He's The Fire** *Diana*
12/63 **Head Over Heels In Love With You** *Don Gibson*
7/77 **Head To Toe** *Bill Anderson*
1/81 **Headache Tomorrow (Or A Heartache Tonight)** *Mickey Gilley*
8/81 **Headed For A Heartache** *Gary Morris*
2/45 **Headin' Down The Wrong Highway** *Ted Daffan*
56/81 **Headin' For A Heartache** *Cindy Hurt*
2/96 **Heads Carolina, Tails California** *Jo Dee Messina*
Healin'
75/78 *Ava Barber*
23/79 *Bobby Bare*
51/77 **Heard It In A Love Song** *Marshall Tucker Band*
13/89 **Heart, The** *Lacy J. Dalton*
64/88 **Heart** *Janie Frickie*
77/87 **Heart** *Ronnie Dove*
21/63 **Heart, Be Careful** *Billy Walker*
73/92 **Heart Break Train** *JJ White*
19/85 **Heart Don't Do This To Me** *Loretta Lynn*
33/76 **Heart Don't Fail Me Now** *Randy Cornor*
14/86 **Heart Don't Fall Now** *Sawyer Brown*
81/83 **Heart For A Heart** *Robin Lee*
65/90 **Heart From A Stone** *Susi Beatty*
19/91 **Heart Full Of Love** *Holly Dunn*
62/67 **Heart Full Of Love** *Johnny Dallas*
1/48 **Heart Full Of Love (For A Handful Of Kisses)** *Eddy Arnold*
21/96 **Heart Half Empty** *Ty Herndon w/ Stephanie Bentley*
1/77 **Heart Healer** *Mel Tillis*
53/97 **Heart Hold On** *Buffalo Club*
1/95 **Heart Is A Lonely Hunter** *Reba McEntire*
43/94 **Heart Like A Hurricane** *Larry Stewart*
58/80 **Heart Mender** *Crystal Gayle*
84/83 **Heart Of Dixie** *Tommy Overstreet*
44/87 **Heart Of Gold** *Willie Nelson*
3/80 **Heart Of Mine** *Oak Ridge Boys*
Heart Of Stone ..see: (I Wish I Had A)
46/85 **Heart Of The Country** *Kathy Mattea*
26/81 **Heart Of The Matter** *Kendalls*
53/83 **Heart Of The Night** *Juice Newton*
96/79 **Heart Of The Night** *Poco*
Heart On The Line ..see: Operator, Operator
8/81 **Heart On The Mend** *Sylvia*
81/83 **Heart On The Run** *Jerry Puckett*
71/87 **Heart Out Of Control** *Joni Bishop*
Heart Over Mind
5/61 *Ray Price*
3/70 *Mel Tillis*
39/94 **Heart Over Mind** *Lorrie Morgan*
5/51 **Heart Strings** *Eddy Arnold*
18/92 **Heart That You Own** *Dwight Yoakam*
16/75 **Heart To Heart** *Roy Clark*
40/86 **Heart To Heart** *Wild Choir*
5/60 **Heart To Heart Talk** *Bob Wills*
8/85 **Heart Trouble** *Steve Wariner*
21/95 **Heart Trouble** *Martina McBride*
25/87 **Heart Vs. Heart** *Pake McEntire*
12/67 **Heart, We Did All That We Could** *Jean Shepard*
51/95 **Heart With 4 Wheel Drive** *4 Runner*
1/93 **Heart Won't Lie** *Reba McEntire & Vince Gill*
30/80 **Heart's Been Broken** *Danny Wood*
3/96 **Heart's Desire** *Lee Roy Parnell*
23/93 **Heartache** *Suzy Bogguss*
23/84 **Heartache And A Half** *Deborah Allen*
29/63 **Heartache For A Keepsake** *Kitty Wells*
54/86 **Heartache The Size Of Texas** *Vega Brothers*
6/83 **Heartache Tonight** *Conway Twitty*
Heartaches By The Number
2/59 *Ray Price*
26/72 *Jack Reno*
39/81 **Heartaches Of A Fool** *Willie Nelson*
83/85 **Heartbeat** *Rebecca Hall*
1/86 **Heartbeat In The Darkness** *Don Williams*
35/70 **Heartbreak Avenue** *Carl Smith*
7/82 **Heartbreak Express** *Dolly Parton*
8/89 **Heartbreak Hill** *Emmylou Harris*
Heartbreak Hotel
1/56 *Elvis Presley*
55/66 *Roger Miller*
1/79 *Willie Nelson & Leon Russell*
13/90 **Heartbreak Hurricane** *Ricky Skaggs*
Heartbreak Kid ..see: (Back To The)
40/66 **Heartbreak Tennessee** *Johnny Paycheck*
23/01 **Heartbreak Town** *Dixie Chicks*
1/61 **Heartbreak U.S.A.** *Kitty Wells*
1/78 **Heartbreaker** *Dolly Parton*
1/82 **Heartbroke** *Ricky Skaggs*
18/97 **Heartbroke Every Day** *Lonestar*
1/93 **Heartland** *George Strait*
75/80 **Hearts** *Jimmie Peters*
2/93 **Hearts Are Gonna Roll** *Hal Ketchum*
26/59 **Hearts Are Lonely** *Phil Sullivan*
1/86 **Hearts Aren't Made To Break (They're Made To Love)** *Lee Greenwood*
69/89 **Hearts In The Wind** *Gail Davies*
4/55 **Hearts Of Stone** *Red Foley*
2/78 **Hearts On Fire** *Eddie Rabbitt*

60/81 **Hearts (Our Hearts)**
Susie Allanson
100/77 **Heat Is On** *Tricia Johns*
37/02 **Heather's Wall** *Ty Herndon*
46/04 **Heaven** *Los Lonely Boys*
55/69 **Heaven Below** *John Wesley Ryles*
60/98 **Heaven Bound** *Shana Petrone*
24/95 **Heaven Bound (I'm Ready)**
Shenandoah
85/77 **Heaven Can Be Anywhere (Twin Pines Theme)**
Charlie Daniels Band
4/88 **Heaven Can't Be Found**
Hank Williams, Jr.
5/70 **Heaven Everyday** *Mel Tillis*
37/03 **Heaven Help Me** *Wynonna*
14/96 **Heaven Help My Heart** *Wynonna*
18/68 **Heaven Help The Working Girl**
Norma Jean
14/96 **Heaven In My Woman's Eyes**
Tracy Byrd
98/78 **Heaven Is Being Good To Me**
Dick Moebakken
47/70 **Heaven Is Just A Touch Away**
Cal Smith
3/72 **Heaven Is My Woman's Love**
Tommy Overstreet
73/85 **Heaven Knows** *Audie Henry*
88/80 **Heaven On A Freight Train**
Max D. Barnes
59/04 **Heaven On Earth** *Trini Triggs*
66/73 **Heaven On Earth** *Sonny James*
16/89 **Heaven Only Knows**
Emmylou Harris
1/68 **Heaven Says Hello** *Sonny James*
F/79 **Heaven Was A Drink Of Wine**
Merle Haggard
Heaven's Just A Sin Away
1/77 *Kendalls*
63/93 *Kelly Willis*
32/71 **Heavenly** *Wynn Stewart*
8/82 **Heavenly Bodies**
Earl Thomas Conley
11/70 **Heavenly Sunshine** *Ferlin Husky*
32/03 **Heavy Liftin'** *Blake Shelton*
38/66 **Heck Of A Fix In 66** *Jim Nesbitt*
53/77 **Helen** *Cal Smith*
1/86 **Hell And High Water**
T. Graham Brown
4/03 **Hell Yeah** *Montgomery Gentry*
Hell Yes I Cheated
95/77 *James Pastell*
82/82 *Jim Owen*
93/77 **Hello Atlanta**
Chip Taylor w/ Ghost Train
52/95 **Hello Cruel World** *George Ducas*
39/80 **Hello Daddy, Good Morning Darling** *Mel McDaniel*
1/70 **Hello Darlin'** *Conway Twitty*
4/61 **Hello Fool** *Ralph Emery*
60/02 **Hello God** *Dolly Parton*
13/75 **Hello I Love You** *Johnny Russell*
26/70 **Hello, I'm A Jukebox** *George Kent*
91/84 **Hello Josephine** *J.W. Thompson*
14/75 **Hello Little Bluebird** *Donna Fargo*
53/71 **Hello Little Rock** *Wynn Stewart*
1/74 **Hello Love** *Hank Snow*
15/99 **Hello L.O.V.E.**
John Michael Montgomery
Hello Mary Lou
14/70 *Bobby Lewis*
3/85 *Statler Brothers*

4/78 **Hello Mexico (And Adios Baby To You)** *Johnny Duncan*
60/67 **Hello Number One**
Kitty Wells & Red Foley
75/72 **Hello Operator** *Joe Stampley*
Hello Out There
8/62 *Carl Belew*
28/74 *LaWanda Lindsey*
30/78 **Hello! Remember Me** *Billy Swan*
79/74 **Hello Summertime**
Bobby Goldsboro
94/79 **Hello Texas** *Brian Collins*
90/78 **Hello, This Is Anna**
O.B. McClinton/Peggy Jo Adams
57/78 **Hello, This Is Joannie (The Telephone Answering Machine Song)** *Paul Evans*
Hello Trouble
5/63 *Orville Couch*
62/74 *LaWanda Lindsey*
11/89 *Desert Rose Band*
1/65 **Hello Vietnam** *Johnny Wright*
30/63 **Hello Wall No. 2** *Ben Colder*
1/61 **Hello Walls** *Faron Young*
14/73 **Hello We're Lonely**
Patti Page & Tom T. Hall
29/81 **Hello Woman** *Doug Kershaw*
56/92 **Help, I'm White And I Can't Get Down** *Geezinslaws*
Help Me
6/74 *Elvis Presley*
38/77 *Ray Price*
66/89 **Help Me Get Over You**
Wagoneers
1/90 **Help Me Hold On** *Travis Tritt*
Help Me Make It Through The Night
1/71 *Sammi Smith*
4/80 *Willie Nelson*
37/75 **Help Me Make It (To My Rockin' Chair)** *B.J. Thomas*
17/02 **Help Me Understand**
Trace Adkins
3/03 **Help Pour Out The Rain (Lacey's Song)** *Buddy Jewell*
8/05 **Help Somebody** *Van Zant*
Help Yourself To Me
47/75 *Roy Head*
97/75 *Debra Barber*
18/97 **Helping Me Get Over You**
Travis Tritt w/ Lari White
Helpless
19/64 *Joe Carson*
73/68 *Dal Perkins*
31/01 **Helplessly, Hopelessly**
Jessica Andrews
62/88 **Henrietta** *Mel McDaniel*
7/54 **Hep Cat Baby** *Eddy Arnold*
33/99 **Her** *Aaron Tippin*
67/69 **Her And The Car And The Mobile Home** *Dave Kirby*
52/76 **Her Body Couldn't Keep You (Off My Mind)** *Gene Watson*
92/80 **Her Cheatin Heart (Made A Drunken Fool Of Me)** *Jerry Naill*
96/81 **Her Empty Pillow (Lying Next To Mine)** *Jimmy McMillan*
59/77 **Her L-O-V-E's Gone** *Red Steagall*
7/97 **Her Man** *Gary Allan*
96/75 **Her Memory's Gonna Kill Me**
Jim Alley
3/76 **Her Name Is...** *George Jones*

59/71 **Here Come The Elephants**
Johnny Bond
68/76 **Here Come The Flowers**
Dottie West
2/68 **Here Comes Heaven** *Eddy Arnold*
1/71 **Here Comes Honey Again**
Sonny James
10/64 **Here Comes My Baby** *Dottie West*
42/99 **Here Comes My Baby** *Mavericks*
79/73 **Here Comes My Little Baby**
Pat Roberts
Here Comes Santa Claus (Down Santa Claus Lane)
4/48 *Gene Autry*
5/48 *Gene Autry*
8/50 *Gene Autry*
88/82 **Here Comes That Feelin' Again**
Ralph May
32/80 **Here Comes That Feeling Again**
Don King
15/76 **Here Comes That Girl Again**
Tommy Overstreet
65/89 **(Here Comes) That Old Familiar Feeling** *Lisa Childress*
80/76 **Here Comes That Rainy Day Feeling Again** *Connie Cato*
10/76 **Here Comes The Freedom Train**
Merle Haggard
9/78 **Here Comes The Hurt Again**
Mickey Gilley
85/88 **Here Comes The Night** *Dolly Hartt*
22/95 **Here Comes The Rain** *Mavericks*
4/68 **Here Comes The Rain, Baby**
Eddy Arnold
15/78 **Here Comes The Reason I Live**
Ronnie McDowell
73/73 **Here Comes The Sun**
Lloyd Green
38/73 **Here Comes The World Again**
Johnny Bush
3/04 **Here For The Party**
Gretchen Wilson
4/95 **Here I Am** *Patty Loveless*
Here I Am Again
3/72 *Loretta Lynn*
69/85 *Johnny Rodriguez*
41/76 **(Here I Am) Alone Again**
Billy Walker
Here I Am Drunk Again
13/60 *Clyde Beavers*
11/76 *Moe Bandy*
16/75 **Here I Am In Dallas** *Faron Young*
Here I Go Again
13/71 *Bobby Wright*
83/84 *Cheryl Handy*
72/99 **Here I Go Again** *Lorrie Morgan*
77/79 **Here I Go Again** *Dorsey Burnette*
20/78 **Here In Love** *Dottsy*
3/90 **Here In The Real World**
Alan Jackson
7/55 **Here Today And Gone Tomorrow**
Browns
2/91 **Here We Are** *Alabama*
11/79 **Here We Are Again**
Statler Brothers
26/61 **Here We Are Again** *Ray Price*
17/74 **Here We Go Again** *Brian Shaw*
Here We Go Again
51/67 *Virgil Warner & Suzi Jane Hokum*
66/72 *Johnny Duncan*
65/82 *Roy Clark*
95/73 **Here With You** *Bobby Lewis*

1/77 **Here You Come Again** *Dolly Parton*
2/91 **Here's A Quarter (Call Someone Who Cares)** *Travis Tritt*
42/70 **Here's A Toast To Mama** *Charlie Louvin*
1/76 **Here's Some Love** *Tanya Tucker*
64/97 **Here's The Deal** *Jeff Carson*
60/79 **Here's To All The Too Hard Working Husbands** *David Houston*
Here's To The Horses
94/77 *Mack Vickery*
49/81 *Johnny Russell*
88/77 **Here's To The Next Time** *Billy Larkin*
87/89 **Here's To You** *Faron Young*
45/68 **Here's To You And Me** *Tex Williams*
Here's Your Sign Christmas
39/99 *Bill Engvall*
46/00 *Bill Engvall*
29/97 **Here's Your Sign (Get The Picture)** *Bill Engvall w/ Travis Tritt*
41/73 **Herman Schwartz** *Stonewall Jackson*
14/54 **Hernando's Hideaway** *Homer And Jethro*
77/83 **Hero, The** *Lee Dresser*
4/91 **Heroes** *Paul Overstreet*
3/91 **Heroes And Friends** *Randy Travis*
64/79 **Heroes And Idols (Don't Come Easy)** *David Smith*
54/85 **Hey** *Hillary Kanter*
Hey Baby
35/70 *Bobby G. Rice*
95/78 *Donnie Rohrs*
7/82 *Anne Murray*
38/93 **Hey Baby** *Marty Stuart*
2/83 **Hey Bartender** *Johnny Lee*
2/89 **Hey Bobby** *K.T. Oslin*
75/84 **Hey, Bottle Of Whiskey** *Gary Stewart*
5/94 **Hey Cinderella** *Suzy Bogguss*
15/68 **Hey Daddy** *Charlie Louvin*
33/77 **Hey Daisy (Where Have All The Good Times Gone)** *Tom Bresh*
21/86 **Hey Doll Baby** *Sweethearts Of The Rodeo*
Hey, Good Lookin'
1/51 *Hank Williams*
74/92 *Mavericks*
8/04 *Jimmy Buffett*
58/89 **Hey Heart** *Dean Dillon*
56/04 **Hey Hollywood** *Donovan Chapman*
1/53 **Hey Joe!** *Carl Smith*
8/53 **Hey Joe** *Kitty Wells*
10/81 **Hey Joe (Hey Moe)** *Moe Bandy & Joe Stampley*
6/51 **Hey La La** *Ernest Tubb*
51/85 **Hey Lady** *Narvel Felts*
13/68 **Hey Little One** *Glen Campbell*
40/88 **Hey Little Sister** *Tom Wopat*
3/74 **Hey Loretta** *Loretta Lynn*
59/03 **Hey Love, No Fair** *Leland Martin*
13/63 **Hey Lucille!** *Claude King*
19/76 **Hey, Lucky Lady** *Dolly Parton*
9/58 **Hey, Mr. Bluebird** *Ernest Tubb & The Wilburn Brothers*
8/53 **Hey, Mr. Cotton Picker** *Tennessee Ernie Ford*
28/92 **Hey Mister (I Need This Job)** *Shenandoah*
28/03 **Hey Mr. President** *Warren Brothers*
22/58 **Hey Sheriff** *Rusty & Doug*
28/76 **Hey Shirley (This Is Squirrely)** *Shirley & Squirrely*
67/79 **Hey There** *Kenny Price*
21/74 **Hey There Girl** *David Rogers*
65/70 **Hey There Johnny** *Mayf Nutter*
94/78 **Hey, What Do You Say (We Fall In Love)** *Sue Richards*
1/75 **(Hey Won't You Play) Another Somebody Done Somebody Wrong Song** *B.J. Thomas*
100/78 **Hey You** *Bobby Havens*
9/65 **Hicktown** *Tennessee Ernie Ford*
15↑/05 **Hicktown** *Jason Aldean*
55/79 **Hide Me (In The Shadow Of Your Love)** *Judy Argo*
36/81 **Hideaway Healing** *Stephanie Winslow*
20/78 **High And Dry** *Joe Sun*
67/76 **High And Wild** *Earl Conley*
27/61 **High As The Mountains** *Buck Owens*
27/83 **High Cost Of Leaving** *Exile*
33/82 **High Cost Of Loving** *Charlie Ross*
1/89 **High Cotton** *Alabama*
72/94 **High Hopes And Empty Pockets** *McBride & The Ride*
2/85 **High Horse** *Nitty Gritty Dirt Band*
54/04 **High Lonesome** *Jedd Hughes*
12/96 **High Lonesome Sound** *Vince Gill w/ Alison Krauss*
33/96 **High Low And In Between** *Mark Wills*
24/93 **High On A Mountain Top** *Marty Stuart*
20/98 **High On Love** *Patty Loveless*
60/72 **High On Love** *Carl Perkins*
63/93 **High Powered Love** *Emmylou Harris*
14/88 **High Ridin' Heroes** *David Lynn Jones w/ Waylon Jennings*
20/93 **High Rollin'** *Gibson/Miller Band*
F/78 **High Rollin'** *Jerry Reed*
9/58 **High School Confidential** *Jerry Lee Lewis*
24/94 **High-Tech Redneck** *George Jones*
75/82 **Highlight Of '81** *Johnny Paycheck*
52/90 **Highway, The** *Willie Nelson*
1/83 **Highway 40 Blues** *Ricky Skaggs*
15/74 **Highway Headin' South** *Porter Wagoner*
Highway Patrol
39/66 *Red Simpson*
73/95 *Junior Brown*
2/89 **Highway Robbery** *Tanya Tucker*
55/02 **Highway Sunrise** *Rhett Akins*
1/85 **Highwayman** *Waylon Jennings/ Willie Nelson/Johnny Cash/ Kris Kristofferson*
79/75 **Hijack** *Hank Snow*
91/74 **Hill, The** *Ray Griff*
26/05 **Hillbillies** *Hot Apple Pie*
Hillbilly Fever
3/50 *"Little" Jimmy Dickens*
9/50 *Ernest Tubb-Red Foley [No. 2]*
8/81 **Hillbilly Girl With The Blues** *Lacy J. Dalton*
5/76 **Hillbilly Heart** *Johnny Rodriguez*
51/89 **Hillbilly Hell** *Bellamy Brothers*
37/86 **Hillbilly Highway** *Steve Earle*
69/94 **Hillbilly Jitters** *Mike Henderson*
71/96 **Hillbilly Rap** *Neal McCoy*
8/90 **Hillbilly Rock** *Marty Stuart*
13/99 **Hillbilly Shoes** *Montgomery Gentry*
Hillbilly Singer ..see: Ballad Of A
44/69 **Him And Her** *Bill Wilbourn & Kathy Morrison*
His And Hers
23/63 *Tony Douglas*
87/82 *Tony Douglas*
13/55 **His Hands** *"Tennessee" Ernie Ford*
74/95 **His Memory** *Western Flyer*
2/66 **History Repeats Itself** *Buddy Starcher*
43/89 **Hit The Ground Runnin'** *John Conlee*
44/70 **Hit The Road Jack** *Connie Eaton & Dave Peel*
12/71 **Hitchin' A Ride** *Jack Reno*
5/45 **Hitler's Last Letter To Hirohito** *Carson Robison*
53/67 **Hobo** *Ned Miller*
50/65 **Hobo And The Rose** *Webb Pierce*
8/51 **Hobo Boogie** *Red Foley*
73/88 **Hocus Pocus** *Roger Marshall*
74/95 **Hog Wild** *Hank Williams, Jr.*
5/56 **Hold Everything (Till I Get Home)** *Red Sovine*
1/89 **Hold Me** *K.T. Oslin*
12/77 **Hold Me** *Barbara Mandrell*
57/77 **Hold Me** *Rayburn Anthony*
67/83 **Hold Me** *David Rogers*
73/73 **Hold Me** *Slim Whitman*
30/81 **Hold Me Like You Never Had Me** *Randy Parton*
Hold Me, Thrill Me, Kiss Me
38/69 *Johnny & Jonie Mosby*
60/80 *Micki Fuhrman*
32/69 **Hold Me Tight** *Johnny Carver*
82/83 **Hold Me Till The Last Waltz Is Over** *Kathy Bauer*
5/86 **Hold On** *Rosanne Cash*
24/83 **Hold On** *Gail Davies*
40/81 **Hold On** *Rich Landers*
6/89 **Hold On (A Little Longer)** *Steve Wariner*
69/93 **Hold On, Elroy** *Dude Mowrey*
20/83 **Hold On, I'm Comin'** *Waylon Jennings & Jerry Reed*
42/91 **Hold On Partner** *Roy Rogers & Clint Black*
45/77 **Hold On Tight** *Sunday Sharpe*
64/80 **Hold On Tight** *Porter Wagoner*
4/99 **Hold On To Me** *John Michael Montgomery*
66/71 **Hold On To My Unchanging Love** *Jeanne Pruett*
Hold On To Your Man ..see: (If You Wanna Hold On)
25/78 **Hold Tight** *Kenny Starr*

Hold What You've Got
59/68 *Diana Trask*
36/79 *Sonny James*
89/88 **Hold Your Fire** *Ross Lewis*
4/97 **Holdin'** *Diamond Rio*
2/90 **Holdin' A Good Hand** *Lee Greenwood*
1/93 **Holdin' Heaven** *Tracy Byrd*
70/82 **Holdin' On** *Jessi Colter*
27/72 **Holdin' On (To The Love I Got)** *Barbara Mandrell*
6/96 **Holdin' Onto Somethin'** *Jeff Carson*
56/85 **Holdin' The Family Together** *Shoppe*
Holding Her And Loving You
1/83 *Earl Thomas Conley*
68/98 *Clay Walker*
83/89 **Holdin' On To Nothin'** *Roger Rone*
7/68 **Holding On To Nothin'** *Porter Wagoner & Dolly Parton*
7/80 **Holding The Bag** *Moe Bandy & Joe Stampley*
9/98 **Hole, The** *Randy Travis*
31/97 **Hole In My Heart** *BlackHawk*
4/89 **Hole In My Pocket** *Ricky Van Shelton*
Holed Up In Some Honky Tonk
40/82 *Joe Sun*
69/91 *Dean Dillon*
2/98 **Holes In The Floor Of Heaven** *Steve Wariner*
3/57 **Holiday For Love** *Webb Pierce*
62/99 **Holiday Inn** *Bryan White*
51/98 **Holly Jolly Christmas** *Alan Jackson*
82/88 **Hollywood Heroes** *Hunter Cain*
72/99 **Hollywood Indian Guides** *Bill Engvall*
80/80 **Hollywood Smiles** *Glen Campbell*
67/90 **Hollywood Squares** *George Strait*
44/76 **Hollywood Waltz** *Buck Owens*
85/87 **Hollywood's Dream** *Jeff Thomas*
75/70 **Holy Cow** *Jamey Ryan*
15/05 **Holy Water** *Big & Rich*
1/90 **Home** *Joe Diffie*
2/59 **Home** *Jim Reeves*
3/96 **Home** *Alan Jackson*
10/75 **Home** *Loretta Lynn*
57/84 **Home Again** *Judy Collins w/ T.G. Sheppard*
3/86 **Home Again In My Heart** *Nitty Gritty Dirt Band*
28/96 **Home Ain't Where His Heart Is (Anymore)** *Shania Twain*
65/95 **Home Alone** *4 Runner*
79/81 **Home Along The Highway** *Tom Nix*
53/86 **Home Grown** *Mason Dixon*
63/99 **Home In My Heart (North Carolina)** *Claudia Church*
Home Made Love
99/75 *Sue Richards*
6/76 *Tom Bresh*
86/83 **Homemade Love** *Ronnie Reno*
56/04 **Home Made Of Stone** *John Arthur Martinez*
3/57 **Home Of The Blues** *Johnny Cash*
49/05 **Home Sweet Holiday Inn** *Trent Willmon*
32/71 **Home Sweet Home** *David Houston*
34/92 **Home Sweet Home** *Dennis Robbins*
73/77 **Home, Sweet Home** *L.E. White & Lola Jean Dillon*
82/88 **Home Team** *Madonna Dolan*
2/99 **Home To You** *John Michael Montgomery*
98/77 **Home Where I Belong** *B.J. Thomas*
10/65 **Home You're Tearin' Down** *Loretta Lynn*
74/81 **Homebody** *Whispering Bill Anderson*
15/59 **Homebreaker** *Skeeter Davis*
5/69 **Homecoming** *Tom T. Hall*
9/87 **Homecoming '63** *Keith Whitley*
42/83 **Homegrown Tomatoes** *Guy Clark*
39/01 **Homeland** *Kenny Rogers*
75/89 **Homeless People** *Bertie Higgins*
Homemade ..see: Home Made
38/66 **Homesick** *Bobby Bare*
67/89 **Hometown Advantage** *Tim Mensy*
27/85 **Hometown Gossip** *Whites*
3/93 **Hometown Honeymoon** *Alabama*
59/92 **Hometown Radio** *Curtis Wright*
66/70 **Homeward Bound** *Brenda Byers*
2/05 **Homewrecker** *Gretchen Wilson*
4/45 **Honestly** *Dick Thomas*
4/04 **Honesty (Write Me A List)** *Rodney Atkins*
Honey
1/68 *Bobby Goldsboro*
F/79 *Orion*
64/68 **Honey** *Compton Brothers*
8/53 **(Honey, Baby, Hurry!) Bring Your Sweet Self Back To Me** *Lefty Frizzell*
2/70 **Honey Come Back** *Glen Campbell*
42/01 **Honey Do** *Mike Walker*
89/90 **Honey Do Weekend** *Randy Rhoads*
2/46 **Honey Do You Think It's Wrong** *Al Dexter*
43/70 **Honey, Don't** *Mac Curtis*
54/69 **Honey-Eyed Girl (That's You That's You)** *Tennessee Ernie Ford*
F/55 **Honey, Honey Bee Ball** *Hank Thompson*
16/76 **Honey Hungry** *Mike Lunsford*
5/89 **Honey I Dare You** *Southern Pacific*
Honey I Do
61/95 *Stacy Dean Campbell*
59/00 *Danni Leigh*
74/68 **Honey (I Miss You Too)** *Margaret Lewis*
15/54 **Honey, I Need You** *Johnnie & Jack*
17/69 **Honey, I'm Home** *Stan Hitchcock*
1/98 **Honey, I'm Home** *Shania Twain*
83/89 **Honey I'm Just Walking Out The Door** *Rick Tucker*
12/54 **Honey Love** *Carlisles*
41/75 **Honey On His Hands** *Jeanne Pruett*
92/80 **Honey On The Moon** *Bonnie Guitar*
1/84 **Honey (Open That Door)** *Ricky Skaggs*
F/77 **(Honey, Won't You) Call Me** *Hank Williams, Jr.*
Honeycomb
7/57 *Jimmie Rodgers*
27/86 *Gary Morris*
4/74 **Honeymoon Feelin'** *Roy Clark*
9/53 **Honeymoon On A Rocket Ship** *Hank Snow*
52/04 **Honeysuckle Sweet** *Jessi Alexander*
45/04 **Honk If You Honky Tonk** *George Strait*
31/98 **Honky Tonk America** *Sammy Kershaw*
Honky Tonk Amnesia
24/74 *Moe Bandy*
56/89 *Scott McQuaig*
5/93 **Honky Tonk Attitude** *Joe Diffie*
54/92 **Honky Tonk Baby** *Highway 101*
58/98 **Honky Tonk Baby** *Ricochet*
58/05 **Honky Tonk Badonk Adonk** *Trace Adkins*
Honky Tonk Blues
2/52 *Hank Williams*
1/80 *Charley Pride*
26/90 *Pirates Of The Mississippi*
Honky Tonk Christmas
53/94 *Alan Jackson*
59/95 *Alan Jackson*
43/87 **Honky Tonk Crazy** *Gene Watson*
97/83 **Honky Tonk Crazy** *Tommy Bell*
10/86 **Honky Tonk Crowd** *John Anderson*
35/94 **Honky Tonk Crowd** *Rick Trevino*
95/79 **Honky Tonk Disco** *Jim West*
89/76 **Honky Tonk Fool** *Ben Reece*
11/48 **Honky Tonk Gal** *T. Texas Tyler*
Honky-Tonk Girl
9/54 *Hank Thompson*
91/77 *Hank Thompson*
50/95 **Honky Tonk Healin'** *David Ball*
6/89 **Honky Tonk Heart** *Highway 101*
75/88 **Honky Tonk Heart (And A Hillbilly Soul)** *Clay Blaker*
37/81 **Honky Tonk Hearts** *Dickey Lee*
70/82 **Honky Tonk Heaven** *Orion*
65/91 **Honky Tonk Life** *Charlie Daniels*
65/82 **Honky Tonk Magic** *Lloyd David Foster*
Honky-Tonk Man
9/56 *Johnny Horton*
11/62 *Johnny Horton*
22/70 *Bob Luman*
3/86 *Dwight Yoakam*
10/83 **Honkytonk Man** *Marty Robbins*
4/77 **Honky Tonk Memories** *Mickey Gilley*
1/88 **Honky Tonk Moon** *Randy Travis*
60/92 **Honky Tonk Myself To Death** *George Jones*
12/81 **Honky Tonk Queen** *Moe Bandy & Joe Stampley*
84/81 **Honky-Tonk Saturday Night** *Becky Hobbs*
52/69 **Honky-Tonk Season** *Charlie Walker*
Honky Tonk Song
1/57 *Webb Pierce*
85/89 *Jimmie Dale Gilmore*
66/96 **Honky Tonk Song** *George Jones*
74/98 **Honky Tonk Songs** *Dolly Parton*

51/71 **Honky-Tonk Stardust Cowboy** *Bill Rice*
28/80 **Honky Tonk Stuff** *Jerry Lee Lewis*
47/94 **Honky-Tonk Superman** *Aaron Tippin*
69/84 **Honky Tonk Tan** *O.B. McClinton*
70/82 **Honky Tonk Tonight** *David Heavener*
78/78 **Honky Tonk Toys** *A.L. "Doodle" Owens*
3/97 **Honky Tonk Truth** *Brooks & Dunn*
54/93 **Honky Tonk Walkin'** *Kentucky Headhunters*
27/76 **Honky Tonk Waltz** *Ray Stevens*
17/73 **Honky Tonk Wine** *Wayne Kemp*
56/70 **Honky Tonk Women** *Charlie Walker*
32/76 **Honky Tonk Women Love Red Neck Men** *Jerry Jaye*
47/84 **Honky Tonk Women Make Honky Tonk Men** *Craig Dillingham*
71/94 **Honky Tonk World** *Chris LeDoux*
59/86 **Honky Tonker** *Marty Stuart*
Honky Tonkin'
14/48 *Hank Williams*
1/82 *Hank Williams, Jr.*
Honky-Tonkin'
81/74 *Troy Seals*
84/79 *Ronnie Sessions*
37/65 **Honky Tonkin' Again** *Buddy Cagle*
50/93 **Honky Tonkin' Fool** *Doug Supernaw*
23/96 **Honky Tonkin's What I Do Best** *Marty Stuart & Travis Tritt*
25/61 **Honky Tonkitis** *Carl Butler*
89/79 **Honky-Tonks Are Calling Me Again** *Lenny Gault*
Honkytonk ..also see: Honky Tonk
8/05 **Honkytonk U** *Toby Keith*
1/85 **Honor Bound** *Earl Thomas Conley*
2/81 **Hooked On Music** *Mac Davis*
89/89 **Hooked On You** *Odessa*
9/54 **Hootchy Kootchy Henry (From Hawaii)** *Mitchell Torok*
45/64 **Hootenanny Express** *Canadian Sweethearts*
57/96 **Hope** *Hope*
95/75 **Hope For The Flowers** *Lois Johnson*
1/75 **Hope You're Feelin' Me (Like I'm Feelin' You)** *Charley Pride*
47/97 **Hopechest Song** *Stephanie Bentley*
20/78 **Hopelessly Devoted To You** *Olivia Newton-John*
52/88 **Hopelessly Falling** *Jeff Chance*
Hopelessly Yours
67/89 *John Conlee*
12/91 *Lee Greenwood w/ Suzy Bogguss*
7/56 **Hoping That You're Hoping** *Louvin Brothers*
15/75 **Hoppy, Gene And Me** *Roy Rogers*
42/73 **Hoppy's Gone** *Roger Miller*
53/99 **Horse To Mexico** *Trini Triggs*
56/04 **Horsepower** *Chris LeDoux*
78/76 **Hot And Still Heatin'** *Jerry Jaye*
62/93 **Hot, Country And Single** *Dean Dillon*
46/88 **Hot Dog** *Buck Owens*
5/04 **Hot Mama** *Trace Adkins*
96/79 **Hot Mama** *Dan Dickey*
40/89 **Hot Nights** *Canyon*
61/87 **Hot Red Sweater** *Jay Booker*
Hot Rod Lincoln
14/60 *Charlie Ryan*
51/72 *Commander Cody*
65/88 *Asleep At The Wheel*
Hot Rod Race
5/51 *Arkie Shibley*
7/51 *Ramblin' Jimmie Dolan*
7/51 *Red Foley*
7/51 *Tiny Hill*
67/79 **Hot Stuff** *Jerry Reed*
59/80 **Hot Sunday Morning** *Wayne Armstrong*
39/83 **Hot Time In Old Town Tonight** *Mel McDaniel*
6/53 **Hot Toddy** *Red Foley*
54/92 **Hotel Whiskey** *Hank Williams, Jr.*
37/85 **Hottest "Ex" In Texas** *Becky Hobbs*
1/56 **Hound Dog** *Elvis Presley*
25/79 **Hound Dog Man** *Glen Campbell*
F/73 **Hour And A Six-Pack** *Cal Smith*
24/63 **House Down The Block** *Buck Owens*
68/92 **House Huntin'** *Matthews, Wright & King*
House Of Blue Lights
39/69 *Earl Richards*
17/87 *Asleep At The Wheel*
House Of Blue Lovers
24/59 *Jack Newman*
21/61 *James O'Gwynn*
21/95 **House Of Cards** *Mary Chapin Carpenter*
13/58 **House Of Glass** *Ernest Tubb*
21/74 **House Of Love** *Dottie West*
72/67 **House Of Memories** *Dick Curless*
53/04 **House Of Negotiable Affections** *Zona Jones*
House Of The Rising Sun
29/74 *Jody Miller*
14/81 *Dolly Parton*
19/89 **House On Old Lonesome Road** *Conway Twitty*
18/98 **House With No Curtains** *Alan Jackson*
88/81 **Houston Blue** *David Rogers*
47/71 **Houston Blues** *Jeannie C. Riley*
76/85 **Houston Heartache** *Mason Dixon*
20/74 **Houston (I'm Comin' To See You)** *Glen Campbell*
1/83 **Houston (Means I'm One Day Closer To You)** *Larry Gatlin/Gatlin Brothers*
4/89 **Houston Solution** *Ronnie Milsap*
4/97 **How A Cowgirl Says Goodbye** *Tracy Lawrence*
70/90 **How About Goodbye** *Robin Lee*
4/05 **How Am I Doin'** *Dierks Bentley*
52/84 **How Are You Spending My Nights** *Gus Hardin*
69/87 **How Beautiful You Are (To Me)** *Big Al Downing*
1/85 **How Blue** *Reba McEntire*
71/90 **How 'Bout Us** *Girls Next Door*
48/64 **How Can I Forget You** *Glenn Barber*
3/94 **How Can I Help You Say Goodbye** *Patty Loveless*
74/92 **How Can I Hold You** *Cleve Francis*
22/78 **How Can I Leave You Again** *John Denver*
85/74 **How Can I Tell Her** *Earl Richards*
13/59 **How Can I Think Of Tomorrow** *James O'Gwynn*
1/71 **How Can I Unlove You** *Lynn Anderson*
7/62 **(How Can I Write On Paper) What I Feel In My Heart** *Jim Reeves*
36/71 **How Can You Mend A Broken Heart** *Duane Dee*
74/75 **How Come It Took So Long (To Say Goodbye)** *Dave Dudley*
25/63 **How Come Your Dog Don't Bite Nobody But Me** *Webb Pierce & Mel Tillis*
22/01 **How Cool Is That** *Andy Griggs*
92/80 **How Could I Do This To Me** *Sam D. Bass*
6/83 **How Could I Love Her So Much** *Johnny Rodriguez*
53/72 **How Could You Be Anything But Love** *Ferlin Husky*
29/79 **How Deep In Love Am I?** *Johnny Russell*
19/89 **How Do** *Mary Chapin Carpenter*
1/97 **How Do I Get There** *Deana Carter*
59/98 **How Do I Let Go** *Lisa Brokop*
How Do I Live
2/97 *Trisha Yearwood*
43/97 *LeAnn Rimes*
1/87 **How Do I Turn You On** *Ronnie Milsap*
2/98 **How Do You Fall In Love** *Alabama*
46/84 **How Do You Feel About Foolin' Around** *Willie Nelson & Kris Kristofferson*
18/05 **How Do You Get That Lonely** *Blaine Larsen*
11/58 **How Do You Hold A Memory** *Hank Thompson*
1/00 **How Do You Like Me Now?!** *Toby Keith*
67/00 **How Do You Milk A Cow** *Cledus T. Judd*
13/98 **How Do You Sleep At Night** *Wade Hayes*
89/76 **How Do You Start Over** *Bob Luman*
How Do You Talk To A Baby
7/61 *Webb Pierce*
99/77 *Dugg Collins*
74/83 **How Do You Tell Someone You Love** *Rod Rishard*
12/04 **How Far** *Martina McBride*
80/80 **How Far Do You Want To Go** *Ronnie McDowell*
11/56 **How Far Is Heaven** *Kitty Wells*
74/74 **How Far Our Love Goes** *Billy Walker*
17/60 **How Far To Little Rock** *Stanley Brothers*
12/67 **How Fast Them Trucks Can Go** *Claude Gray*
1/99 **How Forever Feels** *Kenny Chesney*
39/76 **How Great Thou Art** *Statler Brothers*

3/70 **How I Got To Memphis** *Bobby Bare*
How I Love Them Old Songs
20/70 *Carl Smith*
57/72 *Jim Ed Brown*
91/77 *Danny Davis*
How I Love You In The Morning
37/79 *Peggy Sue*
78/89 *Joann Wintermute*
23/68 **How Is He?** *Jeannie Seely*
56/00 **How Long** *Bryan White*
1/98 **How Long Gone** *Brooks & Dunn*
6/66 **How Long Has It Been** *Bobby Lewis*
87/81 **How Long Has This Been Going On** *Amarillo*
How Long Will It Take
4/67 *Warner Mack*
62/83 *Tennessee Express*
7/52 **How Long Will It Take (To Stop Loving You)** *Lefty Frizzell*
1/68 **How Long Will My Baby Be Gone** *Buck Owens*
11/74 **How Lucky Can One Man Be** *Joe Stampley*
64/99 **How Many Days** *Jack Ingram*
69/89 **How Many Hearts** *Lynn Anderson*
71/86 **How Much Do I Owe You** *Toni Price*
38/88 **How Much Is It Worth To Live In L.A.** *Waylon Jennings*
2/53 **(How Much Is) That Hound Dog In The Window** *Homer & Jethro*
1/71 **How Much More Can She Stand** *Conway Twitty*
41/68 **How Sweet It Is (To Be In Love With You)** *Jack Reno*
21/64 **How The Other Half Lives** *Johnny & Jonie Mosby*
7/79 **How To Be A Country Star** *Statler Brothers*
69/68 **How To Catch An African Skeeter Alive** *Jimmy Dickens*
1/97 **How Was I To Know** *Reba McEntire*
2/97 **How Was I To Know** *John Michael Montgomery*
59/97 **How You Ever Gonna Know** *Garth Brooks*
1/97 **How Your Love Makes Me Feel** *Diamond Rio*
53/04 **How'd I Wind Up In Jamaica** *Tracy Byrd*
92/82 **How'd You Get So Good** *Denny Hilton*
69/96 **How's The Radio Know** *Aaron Tippin*
How's The World Treating You
4/53 *Eddy Arnold*
26/61 *Louvin Brothers*
19/64 **Howdy Neighbor Howdy** *Porter Wagoner*
3/51 **Howlin' At The Moon** *Hank Williams*
14/78 **Hubba Hubba** *Billy "Crash" Craddock*
81/76 **Huckelberry Pie** *Even Stevens/Sammi Smith*
21/67 **Hula Love** *Hank Snow*
5/56 **Hula Rock** *Hank Snow*
99/73 **Humming Bird** *Country Cavaleers*
20/90 **Hummingbird** *Ricky Skaggs*
5/70 **Humphrey The Camel** *Jack Blanchard & Misty Morgan*
2/48 **Humpty Dumpty Heart** *Hank Thompson*
24/01 **Hunger, The** *Steve Holy*
1/69 **Hungry Eyes** *Merle Haggard*
27/61 **Hungry For Love** *Stonewall Jackson*
73/71 **Hunter, The** *Alice Creech*
4/81 **Hurricane** *Leon Everette*
75/95 **Hurricane** *Carlene Carter*
47/70 **Hurry Home To Me** *Bobby Wright*
Hurry, Hurry!
2/44 *Benny Carter*
4/44 *Lucky Millinder*
23/65 **Hurry, Mr. Peters** *Justin Tubb & Lorene Mann*
81/85 **Hurry On Home** *Brooks Brothers Band*
17/93 **Hurry Sundown** *McBride & The Ride*
53/69 **Hurry Up** *Darrell McCall*
Hurt
14/75 *Connie Cato*
6/76 *Elvis Presley*
1/86 *Juice Newton*
56/03 **Hurt** *Johnny Cash*
100/78 **Hurt As Big As Texas** *Randy Cornor*
3/67 **Hurt Her Once For Me** *Wilburn Brothers*
56/89 **Hurt I Can't Handle** *Statler Brothers*
43/96 **Hurt Me** *LeAnn Rimes*
3/91 **Hurt Me Bad (In A Real Good Way)** *Patty Loveless*
59/82 **Hurtin' For Your Love** *Tom Carlile*
Hurtin' Kind Of Love
94/77 *Ron Shaw*
91/80 *Ron Shaw*
38/89 **Hurtin' Side** *Shelby Lynne*
3/66 **Hurtin's All Over** *Connie Smith*
79/85 **Hurts All Over** *Shoppe*
26/70 **Husband Hunting** *Liz Anderson*
Husbands And Wives
5/66 *Roger Miller*
16/81 *David Frizzell & Shelly West*
1/98 *Brooks & Dunn*
74/67 **Husbands-In-Law** *Jim Nesbitt*
51/73 **Hush** *Jeannie C. Riley*
33/87 **Hymne** *Joe Kenyon*
2/96 **Hypnotize The Moon** *Clay Walker*

I

6/83 **I.O.U.** *Lee Greenwood*
I.O.U.
9/76 *Jimmy Dean*
90/77 *Jimmy Dean*
77/83 *Jimmy Dean*
6/75 **I Ain't All Bad** *Charley Pride*
27/68 **I Ain't Buying** *Johnny Darrell*
43/66 **I Ain't Crying Mister** *Larry Steele*
68/79 **I Ain't Giving Up On Her Yet** *Jack Grayson*
62/95 **I Ain't Goin' Peacefully** *Hank Williams, Jr.*
87/88 **I Ain't Gonna Take This Layin' Down** *Debbie Rich*
10/79 **I Ain't Got No Business Doin' Business Today** *Razzy Bailey*
34/68 **I Ain't Got Nobody** *Dick Curless*
I Ain't Got Nobody
51/76 *Del Reeves*
60/81 *Roy Clark*
67/74 **I Ain't Hangin' 'Round** *LaWanda Lindsey*
1/80 **I Ain't Living Long Like This** *Waylon Jennings*
I Ain't Never
2/59 *Webb Pierce*
1/72 *Mel Tillis*
70/87 *Lowes*
92/79 **I Ain't Never Been To Heaven** *Jack Grayson*
73/79 **I Ain't No Fool** *Big Al Downing*
45/05 **I Ain't No Quitter** *Shania Twain*
41/04 **I Ain't Scared** *Carolina Rain*
63/68 **I Ain't The Worryin' Kind** *Billy Edd Wheeler*
23/64 **I Almost Forgot Her Today** *Carl Smith*
36/98 **I Already Do** *Chely Wright*
70/99 **I Already Fell** *Gil Grand*
35/72 **I Already Know (What I'm Getting For My Birthday)** *Wanda Jackson*
1/83 **I Always Get Lucky With You** *George Jones*
21/02 **I Always Liked That Best** *Cyndi Thomson*
35/02 **I Am A Man Of Constant Sorrow** *Soggy Bottom Boys*
1/91 **I Am A Simple Man** *Ricky Van Shelton*
66/72 **I Am, I Said** *Bill Phillips*
2/96 **I Am That Man** *Brooks & Dunn*
F/81 **I Am The Dreamer (You Are The Dream)** *Conway Twitty*
86/82 **I Am The Fire** *David Heavener*
64/68 **I Am The Grass** *Dee Mullins*
43/04 **I Am The Working Man** *Dusty Drake*
56/95 **I Am Who I Am** *Holly Dunn*
51/73 **I Am Woman** *Bobbie Roy*
I Been To Georgia On A Fast Train ..see: Georgia On A Fast Train
4/58 **I Beg Of You** *Elvis Presley*
1/03 **I Believe** *Diamond Rio*
99/76 **I Believe He's Gonna Drive That Rig To Glory** *Craig Donaldson*
10/68 **I Believe In Love** *Bonnie Guitar*
31/68 **I Believe In Love** *Stonewall Jackson*
24/74 **I Believe In The Sunshine** *Roger Miller*
1/78 **I Believe In You** *Mel Tillis*
1/80 **I Believe In You** *Don Williams*
I Believe The South Is Gonna Rise Again
62/74 *Bobby Goldsboro*
18/75 *Tanya Tucker*
48/84 **I Bet You Never Thought I'd Go This Far** *Micki Fuhrman*
I Bought The Shoes That Just Walked Out On Me
79/83 *Super Grit Cowboy Band*
78/87 *Ronnie Sessions*
78/78 **I Bow My Head (When They Say Grace)** *Daniel*

36/95 **I Brake For Brunettes** *Rhett Akins*
53/05 **I Break Things** *Erika Jo*
1/02 **I Breathe In, I Breathe Out** *Chris Cagle*
48/97 **I Broke It, I'll Fix It** *River Road*
9/84 **I Call It Love** *Mel McDaniel*
64/89 **I Came Straight To You** *Kevin Welch*
83/76 **I Can Almost See Houston From Here** *Katy Moffatt*
82/79 **I Can Almost Touch The Feelin'** *LeGardes*
53/89 **I Can Be A Heartbreaker, Too** *Johnny Lee*
42/95 **I Can Bring Her Back** *Ken Mellons*
47/64 **I Can Do That** *Tommy & Wanda Collins*
85/79 **I Can Feel Love** *Linda Calhoun*
55/85 **I Can Feel The Fire Goin' Out** *Lloyd David Foster*
25/73 **I Can Feel The Leavin' Coming On** *Cal Smith*
69/67 **(I Can Find) A Better Deal Than That** *Ruby Wright*
F/78 **I Can Get Off On You** *Waylon & Willie*
86/77 **I Can Give You Love** *Mundo Earwood*
I Can Hear Kentucky Calling Me
75/80 *Osborne Brothers*
83/80 *Chet Atkins*
1/74 **I Can Help** *Billy Swan*
45/88 **I Can Love You** *Judy Rodman*
7/98 **I Can Love You Better** *Dixie Chicks*
1/95 **I Can Love You Like That** *John Michael Montgomery*
5/62 **I Can Mend Your Broken Heart** *Don Gibson*
I Can Only Imagine
50/03 *Jeff Carson*
52/04 *Mercyme*
36/73 **I Can See Clearly Now** *Lloyd Green*
18/80 **I Can See Forever In Your Eyes** *Reba McEntire*
38/80 **I Can See Forever Loving You** *Foxfire*
97/85 **I Can See Him In Her Eyes** *Adam Baker*
44/76 **I Can See Me Lovin' You Again** *Johnny Paycheck*
63/68 **I Can Spot A Cheater** *Johnny Tillotson*
22/64 **I Can Stand It (As Long As She Can)** *Bill Phillips*
1/98 **I Can Still Feel You** *Collin Raye*
13/75 **I Can Still Hear The Music In The Restroom** *Jerry Lee Lewis*
4/96 **I Can Still Make Cheyenne** *George Strait*
1/84 **I Can Tell By The Way You Dance** *Vern Gosdin*
3/70 **I Can't Be Myself** *Merle Haggard*
16/03 **I Can't Be Your Friend** *Rushlow*
1/77 **I Can't Believe She Gives It All To Me** *Conway Twitty*
12/73 **I Can't Believe That It's All Over** *Skeeter Davis*
1/70 **I Can't Believe That You've Stopped Loving Me** *Charley Pride*

34/80 **I Can't Cheat** *Larry G. Hudson*
8/97 **I Can't Do That Anymore** *Faith Hill*
64/72 **I Can't Face The Bed Alone** *Henson Cargill*
3/79 **I Can't Feel You Anymore** *Loretta Lynn*
1/88 **I Can't Get Close Enough** *Exile*
5/80 **I Can't Get Enough Of You** *Razzy Bailey*
5/99 **I Can't Get Over You** *Brooks & Dunn*
29/83 **I Can't Get Over You (Getting Over Me)** *Bandana*
43/73 **I Can't Get Over You To Save My Life** *Lefty Frizzell*
5/67 **I Can't Get There From Here** *George Jones*
37/78 **I Can't Get Up By Myself** *Brenda Kaye Perry*
37/71 **I Can't Go On Loving You** *Roy Drusky*
4/46 **I Can't Go On This Way** *Bob Wills*
66/88 **I Can't Hang On Anymore** *Dennis Payne*
I Can't Help It (If I'm Still In Love With You)
2/51 *Hank Williams*
2/75 *Linda Ronstadt*
I Can't Help Myself (Here Comes The Feeling)
2/77 *Eddie Rabbitt*
82/81 *Sami Jo Cole*
I Can't Help Myself (Sugar Pie, Honey Bunch)
65/75 *Price Mitchell & Jerri Kelly*
65/89 *Trisha Lynn*
58/90 *Billy Hill*
68/86 **I Can't Help The Way I Don't Feel** *Kaylee Adams*
2/60 **(I Can't Help You) I'm Falling Too** *Skeeter Davis*
41/81 **I Can't Hold Myself In Line** *Johnny Paycheck & Merle Haggard*
13/66 **I Can't Keep Away From You** *Wilburn Brothers*
26/00 **I Can't Lie To Me** *Clay Davidson*
2/77 **I Can't Love You Enough** *Loretta Lynn/Conway Twitty*
86/76 **I Can't Quit Cheatin' On You** *Mundo Earwood*
49/66 **I Can't Quit Cigarettes** *Jimmy Martin*
7/56 **I Can't Quit (I've Gone Too Far)** *Marty Robbins*
3/94 **I Can't Reach Her Anymore** *Sammy Kershaw*
9/65 **I Can't Remember** *Connie Smith*
38/80 **I Can't Remember** *Stephanie Winslow*
23/60 **I Can't Run Away From Myself** *Ray Price*
8/69 **I Can't Say Goodbye** *Marty Robbins*
I Can't Say Goodbye To You
44/79 *Becky Hobbs*
30/82 *Terry Gregory*
2/44 **I Can't See For Lookin'** *King Cole Trio*
4/72 **I Can't See Me Without You** *Conway Twitty*

7/70 **I Can't Seem To Say Goodbye** *Jerry Lee Lewis*
42/73 **I Can't Sit Still** *Patti Page*
9/04 **I Can't Sleep** *Clay Walker*
14/63 **I Can't Stay Mad At You** *Skeeter Davis*
I Can't Stop Loving You
3/58 *Kitty Wells*
7/58 *Don Gibson*
1/72 *Conway Twitty*
27/77 *Sammi Smith*
28/78 *Mary K. Miller*
17/62 **I Can't Stop (My Lovin' You)** *Buck Owens*
I Can't Stop Now
71/77 *Mike Lunsford*
72/80 *Billy Larkin*
58/88 **I Can't Take Her Anywhere** *Darrell Holt*
43/67 **I Can't Take It No Longer** *Hank Williams, Jr.*
24/03 **I Can't Take You Anywhere** *Scotty Emerick w/ Toby Keith*
26/60 **I Can't Tell My Heart That** *Kitty Wells & Roy Drusky*
42/93 **I Can't Tell You Why** *Vince Gill*
9/90 **I Can't Turn The Tide** *Baillie & The Boys*
4/78 **I Can't Wait Any Longer** *Bill Anderson*
5/53 **I Can't Wait (For The Sun To Go Down)** *Faron Young*
1/87 **I Can't Win For Losin' You** *Earl Thomas Conley*
1/75 **I Care** *Tom T. Hall*
39/74 **I Changed My Mind** *Billy Walker*
1/79 **I Cheated Me Right Out Of You** *Moe Bandy*
4/78 **I Cheated On A Good Woman's Love** *Billy "Crash" Craddock*
37/67 **I Come Home A-Drinkin' (To A Worn-Out Wife Like You)** *Jack Webb*
7/90 **I Could Be Persuaded** *Bellamy Brothers*
50/86 **I Could Get Used To This** *Johnny Lee & Lane Brody*
1/86 **I Could Get Used To You** *Exile*
64/97 **I Could Love A Man Like That** *Anita Cochran*
69/85 **I Could Love You In A Heartbeat** *Malchak & Rucker*
33/92 **I Could Love You (With My Eyes Closed)** *Remingtons*
46/02 **I Could Never Love You Enough** *Brian McComas*
2/01 **I Could Not Ask For More** *Sara Evans*
27/66 **I Could Sing All Night** *Ferlin Husky*
30/79 **I Could Sure Use The Feeling** *Earl Scruggs Revue*
9/84 **I Could Use Another You** *Eddy Raven*
6/84 **I Could'a Had You** *Leon Everette*
3/76 **I Couldn't Be Me Without You** *Johnny Rodriguez*
4/47 **I Couldn't Believe It Was True** *Eddy Arnold*
5/53 **I Couldn't Keep From Crying** *Marty Robbins*

1/88 **I Couldn't Leave You If I Tried** *Rodney Crowell*
96/79 **I Couldn't Live Without Your Love** *Stacey Rowe*
40/67 **I Couldn't See** *George Morgan*
3/91 **I Couldn't See You Leavin'** *Conway Twitty*
12/59 **I Cried A Tear** *Ernest Tubb*
21/65 **I Cried All The Way To The Bank** *Norma Jean*
1/92 **I Cross My Heart** *George Strait*
18/02 **I Cry** *Tammy Cochran*
68/79 **I Cry Instead** *Ron Shaw*
56/87 **I Did** *Patty Loveless*
72/88 **I Did It For Love** *Jill Jordan*
12/88 **I Didn't (Every Chance I Had)** *Johnny Rodriguez*
17/67 **I Didn't Jump The Fence** *Red Sovine*
1/95 **I Didn't Know My Own Strength** *Lorrie Morgan*
30/82 **I Didn't Know You Could Break A Broken Heart** *Joe Stampley*
22/60 **I Didn't Mean To Fall In Love** *Hank Thompson*
2/96 **I Do** *Paul Brandt*
2/98 **I Do [Cherish You]** *Mark Wills*
3/70 **I Do My Swinging At Home** *David Houston*
53/00 **I Do Now** *Jessica Andrews*
I Don't Believe I'll Fall In Love Today
5/60 *Warren Smith*
93/78 *Gilbert Ortega*
4/95 **I Don't Believe In Goodbye** *Sawyer Brown*
1/56 **I Don't Believe You've Met My Baby** *Louvin Brothers*
I Don't Call Him Daddy
86/89 *Kenny Rogers*
1/93 *Doug Supernaw*
I Don't Care
1/55 *Webb Pierce*
1/82 *Ricky Skaggs*
65/96 **I Don't Care (If You Love Me Anymore)** *Mavericks*
1/64 **I Don't Care (Just as Long as You Love Me)** *Buck Owens*
16/79 **I Don't Do Like That No More** *Kendalls*
1/95 **I Don't Even Know Your Name** *Alan Jackson*
74/87 **I Don't Feel Much Like A Cowboy Tonight** *Gene Stroman*
80/80 **I Don't Feel Much Like Smilin'** *Ray Sawyer*
56/00 **I Don't Feel That Way** *Danni Leigh*
8/88 **I Don't Have Far To Fall** *Skip Ewing*
2/02 **I Don't Have To Be Me ('Til Monday)** *Steve Azar*
44/81 **I Don't Have To Crawl** *Emmylou Harris*
70/97 **I Don't Have To Wonder** *Garth Brooks*
I Don't Hurt Anymore
1/54 *Hank Snow*
37/77 *Narvel Felts*
92/77 *Linda Cassady*
70/90 *Prairie Oyster*
50/01 **I Don't Know** *Hank Williams III*
1/84 **I Don't Know A Thing About Love (The Moon Song)** *Conway Twitty*
46/95 **I Don't Know (But I've Been Told)** *Wesley Dennis*
2/82 **I Don't Know Where To Start** *Eddie Rabbitt*
10/77 **I Don't Know Why (I Just Do)** *Marty Robbins*
1/85 **I Don't Know Why You Don't Want Me** *Rosanne Cash*
5/71 **I Don't Know You (Anymore)** *Tommy Overstreet*
12/79 **I Don't Lie** *Joe Stampley*
45/78 **I Don't Like Cheatin' Songs** *Dale McBride*
38/75 **I Don't Love Her Anymore** *Johnny Paycheck*
52/86 **I Don't Love Her Anymore** *Almost Brothers*
47/64 **I Don't Love Nobody** *Leon McAuliff*
4/64 **I Don't Love You Anymore** *Charlie Louvin*
65/86 **I Don't Mean Maybe** *A.J. Masters*
74/72 **I Don't Mind Goin' Under (If It'll Get Me Over You)** *Charlie Walker*
1/85 **I Don't Mind The Thorns (If You're The Rose)** *Lee Greenwood*
74/89 **I Don't Miss You Like I Used To** *Stella Parton*
8/78 **I Don't Need A Thing At All** *Gene Watson*
1/81 **I Don't Need You** *Kenny Rogers*
34/93 **I Don't Need Your Rockin' Chair** *George Jones*
I Don't Paint Myself Into Corners
71/00 *Rebecca Lynn Howard*
47/02 *Trisha Yearwood*
43/74 **I Don't Plan On Losing You** *Brian Collins*
10/83 **I Don't Remember Loving You** *John Conlee*
40/67 **I Don't See How I Can Make It** *Jean Shepard*
1/74 **I Don't See Me In Your Eyes Anymore** *Charlie Rich*
2/96 **I Don't Think I Will** *James Bonamy*
76/76 **I Don't Think I'll Ever (Get Over You)** *Don Gibson*
7/85 **I Don't Think I'm Ready For You** *Anne Murray*
13/81 **I Don't Think Love Ought To Be That Way** *Reba McEntire*
2/82 **I Don't Think She's In Love Anymore** *Charley Pride*
I Don't Wanna ..also see: I Don't Want To
I Don't Wanna Cry
3/77 *Larry Gatlin*
88/78 *Maury Finney*
2/84 **I Don't Wanna Lose Your Love** *Crystal Gayle*
1/67 **I Don't Wanna Play House** *Tammy Wynette*
13/76 **I Don't Wanna Talk It Over Anymore** *Connie Smith*
92/79 **I Don't Wanna Want You** *Scott Summer*
48/76 **I Don't Want It** *Chuck Price*
64/98 **I Don't Want No Part Of It** *Smokin' Armadillos*
1/84 **I Don't Want To Be A Memory** *Exile*
88/76 **I Don't Want To Be A One Night Stand** *Reba McEntire*
56/77 **I Don't Want To Be Alone Tonight** *Ray Sanders*
5/51 **I Don't Want To Be Free** *Margaret Whiting & Jimmy Wakely*
I Don't Want To Be Right ..see: (If Loving You Is Wrong)
21/67 **I Don't Want To Be With Me** *Conway Twitty*
33/85 **I Don't Want To Get Over You** *Whites*
1/76 **I Don't Want To Have To Marry You** *Jim Ed Brown/Helen Cornelius*
I Don't Want To Know Your Name
54/81 *Glen Campbell*
71/86 *Wrays*
30/80 **I Don't Want To Lose** *Leon Everette*
20/80 **I Don't Want To Lose You** *Con Hunley*
81/85 **I Don't Want To Lose You** *Freddie Hart*
67/79 **I Don't Want To Love You Anymore** *Dandy*
45/89 **I Don't Want To Mention Any Names** *Burch Sisters*
1/99 **I Don't Want To Miss A Thing** *Mark Chesnutt*
68/87 **I Don't Want To Set The World On Fire** *Suzy Bogguss*
1/89 **I Don't Want To Spoil The Party** *Rosanne Cash*
40/82 **I Don't Want To Want You** *Lobo*
7/02 **I Don't Want You To Go** *Carolyn Dawn Johnson*
26/67 **I Doubt It** *Bobby Lewis*
7/84 **I Dream Of Women Like You** *Ronnie McDowell*
I Dreamed Of A Hill-Billy Heaven
10/55 *Eddie Dean*
5/61 *Tex Ritter*
92/76 *Red Simpson*
82/85 **I Dropped Your Name** *Danny Davis/The Nashville Brass*
36/03 **I Drove All Night** *Pinmonkey*
53/01 **I Drove Her To Dallas** *Tyler England*
I Fall To Pieces
1/61 *Patsy Cline*
37/70 *Diana Trask*
89/77 *Mary Miller*
61/81 *Patsy Cline*
54/82 *Patsy Cline/Jim Reeves*
72/94 *Aaron Neville & Trisha Yearwood*
6/55 **I Feel Better All Over (More Than Anywhere's Else)** *Ferlin Huskey*
I Feel Fine
59/70 *Penny DeHaven*
9/89 *Sweethearts Of The Rodeo*
26/82 **I Feel It With You** *Kieran Kane*
7/56 **I Feel Like Cryin'** *Carl Smith*
70/89 **I Feel Like Hank Williams Tonight** *Jerry Jeff Walker*
1/81 **I Feel Like Loving You Again** *T.G. Sheppard*

4/92 **I Feel Lucky** *Mary-Chapin Carpenter*
14/49 **I Feel That Old Age Creeping On** *Homer And Jethro*
34/85 **I Feel The Country Callin' Me** *Mac Davis*
53/68 **I Feel You, I Love You** *Bobby Helms*
55/98 **I Fell** *Brady Seals*
3/90 **I Fell In Love** *Carlene Carter*
1/85 **I Fell In Love Again Last Night** *Forester Sisters*
13/93 **I Fell In The Water** *John Anderson*
14/49 **I Find You Cheatin' On Me** *Hank Thompson*
I Forgot More Than You'll Ever Know
1/53 *Davis Sisters*
60/72 *Jeanne Pruett*
56/85 **I Forgot That I Don't Live Here Anymore** *Darrell Clanton*
46/67 **I Forgot To Cry** *Charlie Louvin*
1/56 **I Forgot To Remember To Forget** *Elvis Presley*
I Fought The Law
61/75 *Sam Neely*
15/78 *Hank Williams, Jr.*
66/92 *Nitty Gritty Dirt Band*
5/58 **I Found My Girl In The USA** *Jimmie Skinner*
10/53 **I Found Out More Than You Ever Knew** *Betty Cody*
F/70 **I Found You Just In Time** *Lynn Anderson*
22/63 **I Gave My Wedding Dress Away** *Kitty Wells*
54/74 **I Gave Up Good Mornin' Darling** *Red Steagall*
(I Gave You The Best Years Of My Life) ..see: Rock N' Roll
62/71 **I Get Lonely When It Rains** *Leroy Van Dyke*
I Get So Lonely ..see: (Oh Baby Mine)
1/66 **I Get The Fever** *Bill Anderson*
73/91 **I Get The Picture** *Skip Ewing*
28/88 **I Give You Music** *McCarters*
2/04 **I Go Back** *Kenny Chesney*
55/89 **I Go Crazy** *Lee Greenwood*
I Go To Pieces
88/80 *Tammy Jo*
39/88 *Dean Dillon*
76/88 *Trisha Lynn*
31/90 *Southern Pacific*
64/84 **I Got A Bad Attitude** *Gary Stewart*
58/92 **I Got A Date** *Forester Sisters*
5/04 **I Got A Feelin'** *Billy Currington*
F/79 **I Got A Feelin' In My Body** *Elvis Presley*
54/92 **I Got A Life** *Mike Reid*
30/75 **I Got A Lot Of Hurtin' Done Today** *Connie Smith*
45/93 **I Got A Love** *Matthews, Wright & King*
8/84 **I Got A Million Of 'Em** *Ronnie McDowell*
93/73 **I Got A Thing About You Baby** *Troy Seals*
40/71 **I Got A Woman** *Bob Luman*
1/89 **I Got Dreams** *Steve Wariner*
43/91 **I Got It Bad** *Matraca Berg*
15/95 **I Got It Honest** *Aaron Tippin*
1/84 **I Got Mexico** *Eddy Raven*
63/00 **I Got My Baby** *Faith Hill*
4/59 **I Got Stripes** *Johnny Cash*
3/77 **I Got The Hoss** *Mel Tillis*
56/87 **I Got The One I Wanted** *Nielsen White Band*
93/79 **I Got Western Pride** *Ray Frushay*
4/68 **I Got You** *Waylon Jennings & Anita Carter*
5/89 **I Got You** *Dwight Yoakam*
7/91 **I Got You** *Shenandoah*
88/79 **I Gotta Get Back The Feeling** *Sheila Andrews*
I Gotta Get Drunk (And I Shore Do Dread It)
27/63 *Joe Carson*
55/76 *Willie Nelson*
8/55 **I Gotta Go Get My Baby** *Justin Tubb*
I Gotta Have My Baby Back
4/50 *Floyd Tillman*
10/50 *Red Foley*
73/67 *Glen Campbell*
15/56 **I Gotta Know** *Wanda Jackson*
44/91 **I Gotta Mind To Go Crazy** *Les Taylor*
72/87 **I Grow Old Too Fast (And Smart Too Slow)** *Johnny Paycheck*
82/89 **I Guess By Now** *Big Al Downing*
48/67 **I Guess I Had Too Much To Dream Last Night** *Faron Young*
55/88 **I Guess I Just Missed You** *Canyon*
9/62 **I Guess I'll Never Learn** *Charlie Phillips*
I Guess I'm Crazy
13/55 *Tommy Collins*
1/64 *Jim Reeves*
1/84 **I Guess It Never Hurts To Hurt Sometimes** *Oak Ridge Boys*
14/93 **I Guess You Had To Be There** *Lorrie Morgan*
72/76 **I Guess You Never Loved Me Anyway** *Randy Cornor*
5/86 **I Had A Beautiful Time** *Merle Haggard*
63/87 **I Had A Heart** *Darlene Austin*
5/79 **I Had A Lovely Time** *Kendalls*
33/82 **I Had It All** *Fred Knoblock*
60/86 **I Had My Heart Set On You** *Emmylou Harris*
30/65 **I Had One Too Many** *Wilburn Brothers*
4/44 **I Hang My Head And Cry** *Gene Autry*
1/04 **I Hate Everything** *George Strait*
I Hate Goodbyes
25/73 *Bobby Bare*
40/77 *Lois Johnson*
22/58 **I Hate Myself** *Faron Young*
16/79 **I Hate The Way I Love It** *Johnny Rodriguez & Charly McClain*
78/79 **I Hate The Way Our Love Is** *Jimmy Peters & Lynda K. Lance*
10/73 **I Hate You** *Ronnie Milsap*
17/81 **I Have A Dream** *Cristy Lane*
26/77 **I Have A Dream, I Have A Dream** *Roy Clark*
I Have Loved You Girl (But Not Like This Before)
87/75 *Earl Thomas Conley*
2/83 *Earl Thomas Conley*
90/80 **I Have To Break The Chains That Bind Me** *Gary Goodnight*
17/97 **I Have To Surrender** *Ty Herndon*
7/88 **I Have You** *Glen Campbell*
5/53 **I Haven't Got The Heart** *Webb Pierce*
76/77 **I Haven't Learned A Thing** *Porter Wagoner*
54/67 **I Hear It Now** *Browns*
17/66 **I Hear Little Rock Calling** *Ferlin Husky*
I Hear The South Callin' Me
29/79 *Hank Thompson*
83/88 *Vassar Clements*
91/78 **I Hear You Coming Back** *Brent Burns*
27/59 **I Hear You Talkin'** *Faron Young*
9/68 **I Heard A Heart Break Last Night** *Jim Reeves*
93/79 **I Heard A Song Today** *Tommy O'Day*
12/49 **I Heard About You** *Bud Hobbs*
33/65 **I Heard From A Memory Last Night** *Jim Edward Brown*
71/84 **I Heard It On The Radio** *Robin Lee*
45/70 **I Heard Our Song** *Dottie West*
(I Heard That) Lonesome Whistle ..see: Lonesome Whistle
4/57 **I Heard The Bluebirds Sing** *Browns*
I Honestly Love You
6/74 *Olivia Newton-John*
16S/98 *Olivia Newton-John*
59/68 **I Hope I Like Mexico Blues** *Dallas Frazier*
36/70 **I Hope So** *Willie Nelson*
1/00 **I Hope You Dance** *Lee Ann Womack*
49/72 **I Hope You're Havin' Better Luck Than Me** *Crystal Gayle*
10/84 **I Hurt For You** *Deborah Allen*
69/68 **I Just Ain't Got (As Much As He's Got Going For Me)** *Gene Wyatt*
16/89 **I Just Called To Say Goodbye Again** *Larry Boone*
77/85 **I Just Came Back (To Break My Heart Again)** *Bruce Hauser/ Sawmill Creek Band*
4/82 **I Just Came Here To Dance** *David Frizzell & Shelly West*
I Just Came Home To Count The Memories
75/75 *Bobby Wright*
15/77 *Cal Smith*
7/82 *John Anderson*
I Just Came In Here (To Let A Little Hurt Out)
51/77 *Peggy Sue*
96/89 *Sandy Ellwanger*
8/68 **I Just Came To Get My Baby** *Faron Young*
21/66 **I Just Came To Smell The Flowers** *Porter Wagoner*
1/75 **I Just Can't Get Her Out Of My Mind** *Johnny Rodriguez*
I Just Can't Help Believing
36/70 *David Frizzell*
59/74 *David Rogers*
48/65 **I Just Can't Let You Say Goodbye** *Willie Nelson*

21/88 **I Just Can't Say No To You** *Moe Bandy*
63/95 **I Just Can't Stand To Be Unhappy** *Bobbie Cryner*
5/79 **I Just Can't Stay Married To You** *Cristy Lane*
68/86 **I Just Can't Take The Leaving Anymore** *Susan Raye*
58/76 **I Just Can't (Turn My Habit Into Love)** *Kenny Starr*
73/82 **I Just Can't Turn Temptation Down** *Skip & Linda*
40/72 **I Just Couldn't Let Her Walk Away** *Dorsey Burnette*
51/66 **I Just Couldn't See The Forest (For The Trees)** *Lefty Frizzell*
11/82 **I Just Cut Myself** *Ronnie McDowell*
92/75 **I Just Don't Give A Damn** *George Jones*
5/50 **I Just Don't Like This Kind Of Livin'** *Hank Williams*
1/79 **I Just Fall In Love Again** *Anne Murray*
28/76 **I Just Got A Feeling** *La Costa*
10/53 **(I Just Had A Date) A Lover's Quarrel** *George Morgan*
I Just Had You On My Mind
48/74 *Sue Richards*
21/78 *Dottsy*
22/80 *Billy "Crash" Craddock*
46/83 **I Just Heard A Heart Break** *Tammy Wynette*
63/76 **I Just Love Being A Woman** *Barbara Fairchild*
45/96 **I Just Might Be** *Lorrie Morgan*
78/79 **I Just Need A Coke (To Get The Whiskey Down)** *Lenny Gault*
11/81 **I Just Need You For Tonight** *Billy "Crash" Craddock*
17/74 **I Just Started Hatin' Cheatin' Songs Today** *Moe Bandy*
2/03 **I Just Wanna Be Mad** *Terri Clark*
43/79 **I Just Wanna Feel The Magic** *Bobby Borchers*
56/67 **I Just Want To Be Alone** *Ray Pillow*
36/81 **I Just Want To Be With You** *Sammi Smith*
14/78 **I Just Want To Be Your Everything** *Connie Smith*
1/98 **I Just Want To Dance With You** *George Strait*
1/78 **I Just Want To Love You** *Eddie Rabbitt*
97/78 **I Just Want To Love You** *DeAnne Horn*
70/68 **I Just Wanted To Know (How The Wind Was Blowing)** *Hank Snow*
1/94 **I Just Wanted You To Know** *Mark Chesnutt*
59/78 **I Just Wanted You To Know** *Ronnie McDowell*
56/68 **I Just Wasted The Rest** *Del Reeves & Bobby Goldsboro*
1/78 **I Just Wish You Were Someone I Love** *Larry Gatlin*
89/79 **I Just Wonder Where He Could Be Tonight** *Hilka & Jebry Lee Briley*
1/81 **I Keep Coming Back** *Razzy Bailey*
14/68 **I Keep Coming Back For More** *Dave Dudley*
43/65 **I Keep Forgettin' That I Forgot About You** *Wynn Stewart*
5/02 **I Keep Looking** *Sara Evans*
I Kissed You ..see: ('Til)
55/00 **I Knew I Loved You** *Daryle Singletary*
48/73 **I Knew Jesus (Before He Was A Star)** *Glen Campbell*
37/88 **I Knew Love** *Nanci Griffith*
64/91 **I Knew My Day Would Come** *Vern Gosdin*
91/78 **I Knew The Mason** *Chapin Hartford*
84/83 **I Knew You When** *Linda Ronstadt*
86/76 **I Knew You When** *Jerry Foster*
59/70 **I Knew You'd Be Leaving** *Peggy Little*
72/97 **I Know** *Kim Richey*
100/78 **I Know** *DeAnne Horn*
65/79 **I Know A Good Thing When I Feel It** *Pia Zadora*
10/79 **I Know A Heartache When I See One** *Jennifer Warnes*
81/81 **I Know An Ending (When It Comes)** *B.J. Wright*
4/70 **I Know How** *Loretta Lynn*
1/88 **I Know How He Feels** *Reba McEntire*
I Know How The River Feels
33/99 *Diamond Rio*
69/00 *McAlyster*
74/67 **I Know How To Do It** *Bobby Braddock*
91/79 **I Know I'm Not Your Hero Anymore** *Ronnie Robbins*
56/86 **I Know Love** *Everly Brothers*
67/83 **I Know My Way To You By Heart** *Marlow Tackett*
I Know One
6/60 *Jim Reeves*
6/67 *Charley Pride*
5/96 **I Know She Still Loves Me** *George Strait*
96/77 **I Know The Feeling** *Jerry Green*
35/85 **I Know The Way To You By Heart** *Vern Gosdin*
89/88 **I Know There's A Heart In There Somewhere** *Chris Austin*
73/99 **I Know What I Want For Christmas** *George Strait*
21/89 **I Know What I've Got** *J. C. Crowley*
1/87 **I Know Where I'm Going** *Judds*
13/92 **I Know Where Love Lives** *Hal Ketchum*
I Know You're Married (But I Love You Still)
29/66 *Bill Anderson & Jan Howard*
52/70 *Red Sovine*
39/67 **I Learn Something New Everyday** *Bill Phillips*
2/44 **I Learned A Lesson, I'll Never Forget** *5 Red Caps*
87/80 **I Learned All About Cheatin' From You** *Becky Hobbs*
53/77 **I Left My Heart In San Francisco** *Red Steagall*
2/97 **I Left Something Turned On At Home** *Trace Adkins*
42/73 **I Let Another Good One Get Away** *Dorsey Burnette*
2/95 **I Let Her Lie** *Daryle Singletary*
1/53 **I Let The Stars Get In My Eyes** *Goldie Hill*
9/82 **I Lie** *Loretta Lynn*
(I Lied) ..see: Believe Me Baby
4/75 **I Like Beer** *Tom T. Hall*
F/80 **I Like Being Lonely** *Ann J. Morton*
I Like Everything About Loving You
62/73 *Bobbie Roy*
89/77 *Lori Parker*
1/95 **I Like It, I Love It** *Tim McGraw*
23/78 **I Like Ladies In Long Black Dresses** *Bobby Borchers*
58/95 **I Like The Sound Of That** *Woody Lee*
74/91 **I Like The Way It Feels** *Ray Kennedy*
57/78 **I Like To Be With You** *Ronnie Sessions*
50/68 **I Like Trains** *Bob Luman*
70/69 **I Live To Love You** *Johnny Duncan*
75/99 **I Look At You** *George Strait*
3/00 **I Lost It** *Kenny Chesney*
26/79 **I Lost My Head** *Charlie Rich*
1/74 **I Love** *Tom T. Hall*
91/76 **I Love A Beautiful Guy** *Connie Cato*
1/81 **I Love A Rainy Night** *Eddie Rabbitt*
57/75 **I Love A Rodeo** *Roger Miller*
4/49 **I Love Everything About You** *George Morgan*
95/77 **I Love Everything I Get My Hands On** *Bobby Trinity*
4/83 **I Love Her Mind** *Bellamy Brothers*
I Love How You Love Me
94/78 *Joni Lee*
18/79 *Lynn Anderson*
17/83 *Glen Campbell*
76/77 **I Love It (When You Love All Over Me)** *Wayne Kemp*
1/74 **I Love My Friend** *Charlie Rich*
15/81 **I Love My Truck** *Glen Campbell*
48/04 **I Love NASCAR** *Cledus T. Judd*
3/84 **I Love Only You** *Nitty Gritty Dirt Band*
I Love That Woman (Like The Devil Loves Sin)
84/77 *Leon Everette*
28/80 *Leon Everette*
10/75 **I Love The Blues And The Boogie Woogie** *Billy "Crash" Craddock*
43/89 **I Love The Way He Left You** *Lee Greenwood*
40/76 **I Love The Way That You Love Me** *Ray Griff*
15/71 **I Love The Way That You've Been Lovin' Me** *Roy Drusky*
1/93 **I Love The Way You Love Me** *John Michael Montgomery*
1/03 **I Love This Bar** *Toby Keith*
4/64 **I Love To Dance With Annie** *Ernest Ashworth*
60/76 **I Love Us** *Skeeter Davis*
22/77 **I Love What Love Is Doing To Me** *Lynn Anderson*
49/77 **I Love What My Woman Does To Me** *David Rogers*

1/99 **I Love You** *Martina McBride*
3/54 **I Love You**
Ginny Wright/Jim Reeves
I Love You A Thousand Ways
1/51 *Lefty Frizzell*
8/51 *Hawkshaw Hawkins*
9/77 *Willie Nelson*
54/81 *John Anderson*
I Love You Because
1/50 *Leon Payne*
2/50 *Ernest Tubb*
8/50 *Clyde Moody*
20/60 *Johnny Cash*
14/69 *Carl Smith*
54/76 *Jim Reeves*
F/78 *Don Gibson*
91/83 *Roger Whittaker*
12/61 **I Love You Best Of All**
Louvin Brothers
9/86 **I Love You By Heart**
Sylvia & Michael Johnson
50/94 **I Love You 'Cause I Want To**
Carlene Carter
55/71 **I Love You Dear** *Eddy Arnold*
4/66 **I Love You Drops** *Bill Anderson*
6/74 **I Love You, I Love You** *David Houston & Barbara Mandrell*
5/78 **I Love You, I Love You, I Love You** *Ronnie McDowell*
(I Love You In Many Ways) ..see: Te' Quiero
8/58 **I Love You More** *Jim Reeves*
4/73 **I Love You More And More Everyday** *Sonny James*
1/69 **I Love You More Today**
Conway Twitty
11/55 **I Love You Mostly** *Lefty Frizzell*
I Love You So Much, It Hurts
5/48 *Floyd Tillman*
1/49 *Jimmy Wakely*
6/04 **I Love You This Much**
Jimmy Wayne
10/78 **(I Love You) What Can I Say**
Jerry Reed
1/81 **I Loved 'Em Every One**
T.G. Sheppard
24/88 **I Loved You Yesterday**
Lyle Lovett
64/68 **I Made The Prison Band**
Tommy Collins
76/88 **I Make The Living (She Makes The Living Worthwhile)**
Danny Shirley
45/89 **I Married Her Just Because She Looks Like You** *Lyle Lovett*
4/84 **I May Be Used (But Baby I Ain't Used Up)** *Waylon Jennings*
27/62 **I May Fall Again** *Buddy Meredith*
10/05 **I May Hate Myself In The Morning**
Lee Ann Womack
64/75 **I May Never Be Your Lover (But I'll Always Be Your Friend)**
Bobby G. Rice
1/79 **I May Never Get To Heaven**
Conway Twitty
70/75 **I May Not Be Lovin' You**
Patti Page
39/91 **I Mean I Love You**
Hank Williams, Jr.
2/90 **I Meant Every Word He Said**
Ricky Van Shelton
35/04 **I Meant To** *Brad Cotter*

39/97 **I Meant To Do That** *Paul Brandt*
2/03 **I Melt** *Rascal Flatts*
10/76 **I Met A Friend Of Your's Today**
Mel Street
57/79 **I Might Be Awhile In New Orleans**
Johnny Russell
37/89 **I Might Be What You're Lookin' For** *Larry Gatlin/Gatlin Brothers*
18/98 **I Might Even Quit Lovin' You**
Mark Chesnutt
73/96 **I Might Just Make It**
Paul Jefferson
74/94 **I Miss Her Missing Me**
Davis Daniel
59/04 **I Miss Me** *Brad Cotter*
1/02 **I Miss My Friend** *Darryl Worley*
37/74 **I Miss You** *Jeannie Seely*
6/97 **I Miss You A Little**
John Michael Montgomery
26/77 **I Miss You Already** *Jerry Wallace*
I Miss You Already (And You're Not Even Gone)
5/57 *Faron Young*
21/60 *Jimmy Newman*
14/86 *Billy Joe Royal*
62/73 **I Miss You Most When You're Here** *Sammi Smith*
(I Miss You Too) ..see: Honey
3/60 **I Missed Me** *Jim Reeves*
38/80 **I Must Be Crazy** *Susie Allanson*
89/89 **I Must Be Crazy** *Rick Arnold*
32/73 **I Must Be Doin' Something Right**
Roy Drusky
41/77 **I Must Be Dreaming** *Don King*
55/91 **I Must Have Been Crazy**
Matraca Berg
7/46 **I Must Have Been Wrong**
Bob Atcher
F/79 **I Must Have Done Something Bad**
Merle Haggard
77/80 **I Musta Died And Gone To Texas**
Amazing Rhythm Aces
77/88 **I Need A Good Woman Bad**
Lane Caudell
93/80 **I Need A Little More Time**
B.J. Harrison
57/91 **I Need A Miracle** *Larry Boone*
49/03 **I Need A Vacation**
Rebecca Lynn Howard
34/89 **I Need A Wife** *Joni Harms*
76/73 **I Need Help** *Carl Smith*
1/85 **I Need More Of You**
Bellamy Brothers
53/86 **I Need Some Good News Bad**
Chance
11/73 **I Need Somebody Bad**
Jack Greene
93/77 **I Need Somethin' Easy Tonight**
Danny Wood
65/87 **I Need To Be Loved Again**
Liz Boardo
8/00 **I Need You** *LeAnn Rimes*
36/97 **I Need You** *Trisha Yearwood*
22/77 **(I Need You) All The Time**
Eddy Arnold
40/00 **I Need You All The Time**
BlackHawk
85/79 **I Need Your Help Barry Manilow**
Ray Stevens
32/74 **I Never Get Through Missing You**
Bobby Lewis

I Never Go Around Mirrors
25/74 *Lefty Frizzell*
96/78 *Ronnie Sessions*
30/85 **I Never Got Over You**
Johnny Paycheck
46/69 **I Never Got Over You**
Carl Butler & Pearl
I Never Had A Chance With You
51/84 *Mason Dixon*
89/89 *Patsy Cole*
70/74 **I Never Had It So Good**
Buddy Alan
I Never Had The One I Wanted
9/67 *Claude Gray*
78/79 *Claude Gray*
65/82 *Solid Gold Band*
2/94 **I Never Knew Love** *Doug Stone*
44/82 **I Never Knew The Devil's Eyes Were Blue** *Terry Gregory*
13/74 **I Never Knew (What That Song Meant Before)** *Connie Smith*
72/79 **I Never Loved Anyone Like I Love You** *Louise Mandrell*
10/85 **I Never Made Love (Till I Made Love With You)** *Mac Davis*
89/78 **I Never Meant To Harm You**
Mike Ellis
94/76 **I Never Met A Girl I Didn't Like**
Jim Mundy
5/70 **I Never Once Stopped Loving You** *Connie Smith*
5/70 **I Never Picked Cotton** *Roy Clark*
3/84 **I Never Quite Got Back (From Loving You)** *Sylvia*
24/76 **I Never Said It Would Be Easy**
Jacky Ward
4/49 **I Never See Maggie Alone**
Kenny Roberts
50/96 **I Never Stopped Lovin' You**
Steve Azar
8/78 **I Never Will Marry** *Linda Ronstadt*
7/97 **I Only Get This Way With You**
Rick Trevino
54/69 **I Only Regret** *Bill Phillips*
I Only Want You For Christmas
41/92 *Alan Jackson*
48/96 *Alan Jackson*
48/98 *Alan Jackson*
14/87 **I Only Wanted You** *Marie Osmond*
72/81 **I Ought To Feel Guilty**
Jeanne Pruett
1/74 **I Overlooked An Orchid**
Mickey Gilley
72/88 **I Owe, I Owe (It's Off To Work I Go)** *David Chamberlain*
80/78 **I Owe It All To You** *Jerry Abbott*
43/84 **I Pass** *Gus Hardin*
48/05 **I Play Chicken With The Train**
Cowboy Troy
53/00 **I Pray For You** *John Rich*
2/87 **I Prefer The Moonlight**
Kenny Rogers
74/89 **I Promise** *Lynne Tyndall*
18/78 **I Promised Her A Rainbow**
Bobby Borchers
26/68 **I Promised You The World**
Ferlin Husky
42/03 **I Raq And Roll** *Clint Black*
I Really Don't Want To Know
1/54 *Eddy Arnold*
23/71 *Elvis Presley*
19/72 *Charlie McCoy*

1/79 **I Really Got The Feeling** *Dolly Parton*
23/76 **I Really Had A Ball Last Night** *Carmol Taylor*
I Recall A Gypsy Woman
16/73 *Tommy Cash*
22/81 *B.J. Thomas*
52/69 **I Remember Loving You** *Sheb Wooley*
86/87 **(I Remember When I Thought) Whiskey Was A River** *Bobby Borchers*
I Remember You
49/66 *Slim Whitman*
44/81 *Slim Whitman*
32/88 *Glen Campbell*
12/98 **I Said A Prayer** *Pam Tillis*
1/89 **I Sang Dixie** *Dwight Yoakam*
29/63 **I Saw Me** *George Jones*
I Saw Mommy Kissing Santa Claus
7/52 *Jimmy Boyd*
50/00 *Reba McEntire*
25/72 **I Saw My Lady** *Dickey Lee*
1/92 **I Saw The Light** *Wynonna*
36/98 **I Saw The Light** *Hal Ketchum*
56/71 **I Saw The Light** *Nitty Gritty Dirt Band w/ Roy Acuff*
40/71 **I Say A Little Prayer (medley)** *Glen Campbell/Anne Murray*
68/71 **I Say, "Yes, Sir"** *Peggy Sue*
51/82 **I See An Angel Every Day** *Billy Parker*
67/73 **I See His Love All Over You** *Jim Glaser*
2/94 **I See It Now** *Tracy Lawrence*
78/74 **I See Love** *Bobby Lewis*
99/78 **I See Love In Your Eyes** *Larry Booth*
32/05 **I See Me** *Travis Tritt*
1/74 **I See The Want To In Your Eyes** *Conway Twitty*
47/69 **I See Them Everywhere** *Hank Thompson*
75/70 **I Shook The Hand** *Freddy Weller*
4/02 **I Should Be Sleeping** *Emerson Drive*
2/88 **I Should Be With You** *Steve Wariner*
54/67 **I Should Get Away Awhile** *Carl Smith*
30/95 **I Should Have Been True** *Mavericks*
11/75 **I Should Have Married You** *Eddie Rabbitt*
71/76 **I Should Have Watched That First Step** *Wayne Kemp*
13/81 **I Should've Called** *Eddy Raven*
72/98 **I Should've Known** *Melodie Crittenden*
69/97 **I Smell Smoke** *Billy Yates*
84/81 **I Sold All Of Tom T's Songs Last Night** *Gary Gentry*
56/83 **I Spent The Night In The Heart Of Texas** *Marlow Tackett*
27/72 **I Start Thinking About You** *Johnny Carver*
I Started Loving You Again
69/70 *Al Martino*
16/72 *Charlie McCoy*
30/70 **I Stayed Long Enough** *Billie Jo Spears*

21/64 **I Stepped Over The Line** *Hank Snow*
12/88 **I Still Believe** *Lee Greenwood*
13/75 **I Still Believe In Fairy Tales** *Tammy Wynette*
27/68 **I Still Believe In Love** *Jan Howard*
46/78 **I Still Believe In Love** *Charlie Rich*
2/81 **I Still Believe In Waltzes** *Conway Twitty & Loretta Lynn*
1/89 **I Still Believe In You** *Desert Rose Band*
1/92 **I Still Believe In You** *Vince Gill*
82/79 **I Still Believe In You** *Mike Lunsford*
51/74 **I Still Can't Believe You're Gone** *Willie Nelson*
48/68 **I Still Didn't Have The Sense To Go** *Johnny Carver*
17/84 **I Still Do** *Bill Medley*
14/75 **I Still Feel The Same About You** *Bill Anderson*
40/80 **(I Still Long To Hold You) Now And Then** *Reba McEntire*
95/79 **I Still Love Her Memory** *Hoot Hester*
28/82 **I Still Love You (After All These Years)** *Tompall/Glaser Brothers*
85/89 **I Still Love You Babe** *Marilyn Mundy*
19/83 **I Still Love You In The Same Ol' Way** *Moe Bandy*
81/75 **I Still Love You (You Still Love Me)** *Mac Davis*
87/84 **I Still Love Your Body** *Tommy Overstreet*
I Still Miss Someone
43/65 *Flatt & Scruggs*
38/81 *Don King*
51/89 *Emmylou Harris*
88/89 **I Still Need You** *Steffin Sisters*
74/68 **I Stole The Flowers From Your Garden** *Gene Wyatt*
9/94 **I Sure Can Smell The Rain** *BlackHawk*
30/86 **I Sure Need Your Lovin'** *Judy Rodman*
1/94 **I Swear** *John Michael Montgomery*
3/69 **I Take A Lot Of Pride In What I Am** *Merle Haggard*
6/72 **I Take It On Home** *Charlie Rich*
2/94 **I Take My Chances** *Mary Chapin Carpenter*
I Take The Chance
2/56 *Browns*
7/63 *Ernest Ashworth*
89/87 *Kathy Edge*
52/87 **I Talked A Lot About Leaving** *Larry Boone*
11/67 **I Taught Her Everything She Knows** *Billy Walker*
31/88 **I Taught Her Everything She Knows About Love** *Shooters*
7/86 **I Tell It Like It Used To Be** *T. Graham Brown*
70/76 **I Thank God She Isn't Mine** *Mel McDaniel*
8/65 **I Thank My Lucky Stars** *Eddy Arnold*
4/95 **I Think About It All The Time** *John Berry*
3/96 **I Think About You** *Collin Raye*

17/82 **I Think About Your Lovin'** *Osmonds*
I Think I Could Love You Better Than She [He] Did
70/81 *Ava Barber*
85/81 *Gabriel*
7/60 **I Think I Know** *Marion Worth*
1/81 **I Think I'll Just Stay Here And Drink** *Merle Haggard*
I Think I'll Say Goodbye
76/75 *Mary Kay James*
77/77 *Jeris Ross*
36/86 **I Think I'm In Love** *Keith Stegall*
(I Think I've Got A Heartache) ..see: Excuse Me
37/72 **I Think They Call It Love** *Don Gibson & Sue Thompson*
56/96 **I Think We're On To Something** *Emilio*
43/03 **I Think You're Beautiful** *Amy Dalley*
44/00 **I Think You're Beautiful** *Shane Minor*
I Thought I Heard You Calling My Name
11/57 *Porter Wagoner*
29/76 *Jessi Colter*
88/81 *Pam Hobbs*
67/86 **I Thought I'd About Had It With Love** *Pam Tillis*
4/91 **I Thought It Was You** *Doug Stone*
10/55 **I Thought Of You** *Jean Shepard*
75/78 **I Thought You Were Easy** *Rayburn Anthony*
46/79 **I Thought You'd Never Ask** *Louise Mandrell & R.C. Bannon*
2/67 **I Threw Away The Rose** *Merle Haggard*
1/88 **I Told You So** *Randy Travis*
25/59 **I Traded Her Love (For Deep Purple Wine)** *Roland Johnson*
3/94 **I Try To Think About Elvis** *Patty Loveless*
26/87 **I Turn To You** *George Jones*
46/74 **I Use The Soap** *Dickey Lee*
22/73 **I Used It All On You** *Nat Stuckey*
26/70 **I Wake Up In Heaven** *David Rogers*
1/68 **I Walk Alone** *Marty Robbins*
1/56 **I Walk The Line** *Johnny Cash*
61/98 **I Walk The Line Revisited** *Rodney Crowell w/ Johnny Cash*
6/55 **I Walked Alone Last Night** *Eddy Arnold*
12/70 **I Walked Out On Heaven** *Hank Williams, Jr.*
59/85 **I Wanna Be A Cowboy 'Til I Die** *Jim Collins*
38/81 **I Wanna Be Around** *Terri Gibbs*
3/71 **I Wanna Be Free** *Loretta Lynn*
98/78 **I Wanna Be Her #1** *Danny Hargrove*
53/71 **I Wanna Be Loved Completely** *Warner Mack*
51/01 **I Wanna Be That Girl** *Wilkinsons*
78/77 **I Wanna Be With You Tonight** *Alabama*
60/04 **I Wanna Believe** *Patty Loveless*
33/79 **I Wanna' Come Over** *Alabama*
1/88 **I Wanna Dance With You** *Eddie Rabbitt*
63/80 **I Wanna Do It Again** *Bill Wence*

3/04 **I Wanna Do It All** *Terri Clark*
3/98 **I Wanna Fall In Love** *Lila McCann*
9/98 **I Wanna Feel That Way Again** *Tracy Byrd*
72/79 **I Wanna Go Back** *Nick Noble*
50/67 **I Wanna Go Bummin' Around** *Sonny Curtis*
72/71 **I Wanna Go Country** *Otis Williams*
I Wanna Go Home ..see: Detroit City
38/78 **I Wanna Go To Heaven** *Jerry Wallace*
9/95 **I Wanna Go Too Far** *Trisha Yearwood*
57/04 **(I Wanna Hear) A Cheatin' Song** *Anita Cochran w/ Conway Twitty*
8/85 **I Wanna Hear It From You** *Eddy Raven*
35/86 **I Wanna Hear It From Your Lips** *Louise Mandrell*
63/88 **(I Wanna Hear You) Say You Love Me Again** *Lisa Childress*
80/75 **I Wanna Kiss You** *Nancy Wayne*
43/88 **I Wanna Know Her Again** *Wagoneers*
I Wanna Live
1/68 *Glen Campbell*
87/76 *Eddy Raven*
67/78 **(I Wanna) Love My Life Away** *Jody Miller*
91/80 **I Wanna Love You Tonight** *Mary Lou Turner*
23/04 **I Wanna Make You Cry** *Jeff Bates*
1/51 **I Wanna Play House With You** *Eddy Arnold*
20/98 **I Wanna Remember This** *Linda Davis*
5/85 **I Wanna Say Yes** *Louise Mandrell*
22/93 **I Wanna Take Care Of You** *Billy Dean*
1/01 **I Wanna Talk About Me** *Toby Keith*
I Wanna Wake Up With You ..see: I Wanta
13/55 **I Wanna Wanna Wanna** *Wilburn Brothers*
59/05 **I Want A Cowboy** *Katrina Elam*
63/78 **I Want A Little Cowboy** *Jerry Abbott*
18/88 **I Want A Love Like That** *Judy Rodman*
65/99 **I Want A Man** *Lace*
10/85 **I Want Everyone To Cry** *Restless Heart*
21S/99 **I Want It All** *Michael Rainwood*
47/02 **I Want My Baby Back** *Mark Chesnutt*
7/95 **I Want My Goodbye Back** *Ty Herndon*
33/03 **I Want My Money Back** *Sammy Kershaw*
19/69 **I Want One** *Jack Reno*
83/80 **I Want That Feelin' Again** *Bill Anderson*
I Want To ..also see: I Wanna / I Want'a
I Want To Be A Cowboy's Sweetheart
5/46 *Rosalie Allen*
77/88 *Suzy Bogguss*
24/78 **I Want To Be In Love** *Jacky Ward*
13/56 **I Want To Be Loved** *Johnnie & Jack w/ Ruby Wells*
3/94 **I Want To Be Loved Like That** *Shenandoah*
4/45 **I Want To Be Sure** *Gene Autry*
80/87 **I Want To Be Wanted** *Toni Price*
1/51 **I Want To Be With You Always** *Lefty Frizzell*
35/97 **I Want To Be Your Girlfriend** *Mary Chapin Carpenter*
25/84 **I Want To Go Somewhere** *Keith Stegall*
18/58 **I Want To Go Where No One Knows Me** *Jean Shepard*
1/66 **I Want To Go With You** *Eddy Arnold*
9/75 **I Want To Hold You In My Dreams Tonight** *Stella Parton*
49/64 **I Want To Hold Your Hand** *Homer And Jethro*
33/00 **I Want To Know (Everything There Is To Know About You)** *Mark Wills*
2/87 **I Want To Know You Before We Make Love** *Conway Twitty*
71/74 **I Want To Lay Down Beside You** *Marie Owens*
4/04 **I Want To Live** *Josh Gracin*
15/61 **I Want To Live Again** *Rose Maddox*
84/78 **I Want To Love You** *Jerry Foster*
F/79 **I Want To Play My Horn On The Grand Ole' Opry** *Maury Finney*
I Want To See Me In Your Eyes
30/79 *Peggy Sue*
80/81 *Gene Kennedy & Karen Jeglum*
26/74 **I Want To Stay** *Narvel Felts*
34/79 **I Want To Walk You Home** *Porter Wagoner*
67/99 **I Want To With You** *David Ball*
51/01 **I Want Us Back** *Craig Morgan*
35/72 **I Want You** *Johnny Carver*
35/01 **I Want You Bad** *Charlie Robison*
7/93 **I Want You Bad (And That Ain't Good)** *Collin Raye*
22/70 **I Want You Free** *Jean Shepard*
1/56 **I Want You, I Need You, I Love You** *Elvis Presley*
49/01 **I Want You To Want Me** *Dwight Yoakam*
22/81 **I Want You Tonight** *Johnny Rodriguez*
25/74 **I Wanta Get To You** *La Costa*
I Wanta Wake Up With You
88/87 *Cristy Lane*
41/88 *Johnny Rodriguez*
37/99 **I Was** *Neal McCoy*
16/95 **I Was Blown Away** *Pam Tillis*
I Was Born With A Broken Heart
75/89 *Josh Logan*
38/92 *Aaron Tippin*
1/81 **I Was Country When Country Wasn't Cool** *Barbara Mandrell*
F/57 **I Was The First One** *Hank Thompson*
I Was The One
8/56 *Elvis Presley*
92/83 *Elvis Presley*
8/77 **I Was There** *Statler Brothers*
39/68 **I Was With Red Foley (The Night He Passed Away)** *Luke The Drifter, Jr.*
30/67 **I Washed My Face In The Morning Dew** *Tom T. Hall*
8/65 **I Washed My Hands In Muddy Water** *Stonewall Jackson*
23/63 **I Wasn't Even In The Running** *Hank Thompson*
15/49 **I Wasted A Nickel** *Hawkshaw Hawkins*
8/90 **I Watched It All (On My Radio)** *Lionel Cartwright*
19S/91 **I Wear Your Love** *Lisa Angelle*
9/61 **I Went Out Of My Way (To Make You Happy)** *Roy Drusky*
3/52 **I Went To Your Wedding** *Hank Snow*
23/58 **I Will** *Ferlin Husky*
80/77 **I Will** *Wendel Adkins*
21/69 **I Will Always** *Don Gibson*
I Will Always Love You
1/74 *Dolly Parton*
84/78 *Jimmie Peters*
1/82 *Dolly Parton*
15/95 *Dolly Parton w/ Vince Gill*
47/00 **I Will Be** *Lila McCann*
1/87 **I Will Be There** *Dan Seals*
28/99 **I Will Be There For You** *Jessica Andrews*
64/68 **I Will Bring You Water** *Browns*
2/00 **I Will...But** *SheDaisy*
45/85 **I Will Dance With You** *Karen Brooks w/ Johnny Cash*
46/71 **I Will Drink Your Wine** *Buddy Alan*
57/03 **I Will Hold My Ground** *Darryl Worley*
53/88 **I Will Hold You** *Randy Vanwarmer*
19/97 **I Will, If You Will** *John Berry*
50/01 **I Will Love You** *Lisa Angelle*
65/92 **I Will Love You Anyhow** *Tim Ryan*
45/72 **I Will Never Pass This Way Again** *Glen Campbell*
32/66 **I Will Not Blow Out The Light** *Marion Worth*
21/79 **I Will Rock And Roll With You** *Johnny Cash*
27/98 **I Will Stand** *Kenny Chesney*
49/93 **I Will Stand By You** *Corbin/Hanner*
21/79 **I Will Survive** *Billie Jo Spears*
46/01 **I Will Survive** *Wild Horses*
7/88 **I Will Whisper Your Name** *Michael Johnson*
15/03 **I Wish** *Jo Dee Messina*
28/66 **I Wish** *Ernest Ashworth*
(I Wish A Buck Was Still Silver) ..see: Are The Good Times Really Over
I Wish Her Well ..see: (There She Goes)
I Wish I Could Fall In Love Today
5/60 *Ray Price*
5/88 *Barbara Mandrell*
4/94 **I Wish I Could Have Been There** *John Anderson*
14/84 **I Wish I Could Write You A Song** *John Anderson*
4/89 **(I Wish I Had A) Heart Of Stone** *Baillie And The Boys*
45/82 **I Wish I Had A Job To Shove** *Rodney Lay*

22/70 **I Wish I Had A Mommy Like You** *Patti Page*
4/49 **I Wish I Had A Nickel** *Jimmy Wakely*
I Wish I Had Never Met Sunshine
3/46 *Gene Autry*
5/46 *Wesley Tuttle*
97/79 **I Wish I Had Your Arms Around Me** *Red Willow Band*
8/49 **I Wish I Knew** *Dolph Hewitt*
13/78 **I Wish I Loved Somebody Else** *Tom T. Hall*
27/63 **I Wish I Was A Single Girl Again** *Jan Howard*
22/80 **I Wish I Was Crazy Again** *Johnny Cash & Waylon Jennings*
I Wish I Was Eighteen Again
F/79 *Jerry Lee Lewis*
15/80 *George Burns*
20/83 **I Wish I Was In Nashville** *Mel McDaniel*
4/89 **I Wish I Was Still In Your Dreams** *Conway Twitty*
51/69 **I Wish I Was Your Friend** *Wanda Jackson*
91/78 **I Wish I'd Never Borrowed Anybody's Angel** *Mike Lunsford*
52/88 **I Wish It Was That Easy Going Home** *Jeff Dugan*
67/73 **I Wish It Would Rain** *O.B. McClinton*
68/87 **I Wish She Wouldn't Treat You That Way** *Pam Tillis*
I Wish That I Could Fall In Love Today ..see: I Wish I Could
3/86 **I Wish That I Could Hurt That Way Again** *T. Graham Brown*
19/74 **I Wish That I Had Loved You Better** *Eddy Arnold*
64/88 **I Wish We Were Strangers** *Ogden Harless*
I Wish You Could Have Turned My Head (And Left My Heart Alone)
54/78 *Sonny Throckmorton*
54/81 *Peggy Forman*
2/82 *Oak Ridge Boys*
24/73 **I Wish (You Had Stayed)** *Brian Collins*
19/60 **I Wish You Love** *Billy Walker*
7/03 **I Wish You'd Stay** *Brad Paisley*
4/53 **I Won't Be Home No More** *Hank Williams*
85/88 **I Won't Be Seeing Her No More** *Touch Of Country*
1/67 **I Won't Come In While He's There** *Jim Reeves*
3/65 **I Won't Forget You** *Jim Reeves*
3/50 **(I Won't Go Huntin', Jake) But I'll Go Chasin' Women** *Stuart Hamblen*
48/04 **I Won't Go On And On** *Colt Prather*
83/81 **I Won't Last A Day Without You** *Vince & Dianne Hatfield*
44/86 **I Won't Let You Down** *Tom Wopat*
58/98 **I Won't Lie** *Shannon Brown*
1/71 **I Won't Mention It Again** *Ray Price*
1/87 **I Won't Need You Anymore (Always And Forever)** *Randy Travis*
1/88 **I Won't Take Less Than Your Love** *Tanya Tucker/Paul Davis/ Paul Overstreet*
8/83 **I Wonder** *Rosanne Cash*
1/89 **I Wonder Do You Think Of Me** *Keith Whitley*
40/91 **I Wonder How Far It Is Over You** *Aaron Tippin*
41/72 **I Wonder How John Felt (When He Baptized Jesus)** *David Houston*
F/77 **I Wonder How She's Doing Now** *Johnny Russell*
I Wonder If I Care As Much
53/81 *Dickey Lee*
30/87 *Ricky Skaggs*
2/76 **I Wonder If I Ever Said Goodbye** *Johnny Rodriguez*
1/73 **I Wonder If They Ever Think Of Me** *Merle Haggard*
4/71 **I Wonder What She'll Think About Me Leaving** *Conway Twitty*
37/89 **I Wonder What She's Doing Tonight** *Russell Smith*
10/83 **I Wonder Where We'd Be Tonight** *Vern Gosdin*
9/83 **I Wonder Who's Holding My Baby Tonight** *Whites*
81/77 **I Wonder Who's Kissing Her Now** *George Hamilton IV*
20/75 **I Wonder Whose Baby (You Are Now)** *Jerry Wallace*
I Wore A Tie Today ..see: (Jim)
55/00 **I Would** *Jolie & The Wanted*
29/05 **I Would Cry** *Amy Dalley*
12/78 **I Would Like To See You Again** *Johnny Cash*
4/01 **I Would've Loved You Anyway** *Trisha Yearwood*
I Wouldn't Be A Man
9/88 *Don Williams*
45/96 *Billy Dean*
8/65 **I Wouldn't Buy A Used Car From Him** *Norma Jean*
31/68 **I Wouldn't Change A Thing About You (But Your Name)** *Hank Williams, Jr.*
1/83 **I Wouldn't Change You If I Could** *Ricky Skaggs*
5/92 **I Wouldn't Have It Any Other Way** *Aaron Tippin*
1/82 **I Wouldn't Have Missed It For The World** *Ronnie Milsap*
73/93 **I Wouldn't Know** *Andy Childs*
9/70 **I Wouldn't Live In New York City** *Buck Owens*
33/67 **I Wouldn't Take Her To A Dogfight** *Charlie Walker*
72/99 **I Wouldn't Tell You No Lie** *Tractors*
81/89 **I Wouldn't Trade Your Love** *Joann Wintermute*
1/74 **I Wouldn't Want To Live If You Didn't Love Me** *Don Williams*
70/97 **I Wrote The Book** *Matt King*
1/75 **(I'd Be) A Legend In My Time** *Ronnie Milsap*
4/90 **I'd Be Better Off (In A Pine Box)** *Doug Stone*
39/04 **I'd Be Lying** *Chris Cagle*
53/97 **I'd Be With You** *Kippi Brannon*
69/68 **I'd Be Your Fool Again** *David Rogers*
30/66 **I'd Better Call The Law On Me** *Hugh X. Lewis*
74/80 **I'd Build A Bridge** *Charlie Rich*
60/77 **I'd Buy You Chattanooga** *Kenny Price*
20/85 **I'd Dance Every Dance With You** *Kendalls*
32/80 **I'd Do Anything For You** *Jacky Ward*
94/88 **I'd Do Anything For You, Baby** *Andy & The Brown Sisters*
52/82 **I'd Do It All Again** *Jerry Lee Lewis*
83/88 **I'd Do It All Over Again** *Ray Price*
87/83 **I'd Do It In A Heart Beat** *Sierra*
86/85 **I'd Do It In A Heartbeat** *Hill City*
84/75 **I'd Do It With You** *Pat Boone w/ Shirley Boone*
I'd Fight The World
23/62 *Hank Cochran*
19/74 *Jim Reeves*
11/68 **I'd Give The World (To Be Back Loving You)** *Warner Mack*
I'd Go Crazy ..see: (If It Weren't For Country Music)
11/76 **I'd Have To Be Crazy** *Willie Nelson*
I'd Just Be Fool Enough
16/66 *Browns*
33/76 *Faron Young*
I'd Just Love To Lay You Down
1/80 *Conway Twitty*
43/02 *Daryle Singletary*
80/87 **I'd Know A Lie** *Gary McCullough*
18/59 **I'd Like To Be** *Jim Reeves*
3/94 **I'd Like To Have That One Back** *George Strait*
26/78 **I'd Like To See Jesus (On The Midnight Special)** *Tammy Wynette*
5/75 **I'd Like To Sleep Til I Get Over You** *Freddie Hart*
I'd Love To Lay You Down ..see: I'd Just Love To Lay You Down
67/68 **I'd Love To Live With You Again** *Darrell McCall*
1/91 **I'd Love You All Over Again** *Alan Jackson*
56/97 **I'd Love You To Love Me** *Emilio*
58/82 **I'd Love You To Want Me** *Narvel Felts*
54/85 **I'd Rather Be Crazy** *Con Hunley*
64/87 **I'd Rather Be Crazy** *Dana McVicker*
62/82 **I'd Rather Be Doing Nothing With You** *Karen Taylor-Good*
4/69 **I'd Rather Be Gone** *Hank Williams, Jr.*
66/75 **I'd Rather Be Picked Up Here (Than Be Put Down At Home)** *Jeris Ross*
I'd Rather Be Sorry
2/71 *Ray Price*
63/71 *Patti Page*
84/81 **I'd Rather Be The Stranger In Your Eyes** *Gene Kennedy & Karen Jeglum*
69/72 **I'd Rather Be Wantin' Love** *Leroy Van Dyke*
20/79 **I'd Rather Go On Hurtin'** *Joe Sun*

32/80 **I'd Rather Leave While I'm In Love** *Rita Coolidge*
10/61 **I'd Rather Loan You Out** *Roy Drusky*
1/71 **I'd Rather Love You** *Charley Pride*
16/93 **I'd Rather Miss You** *Little Texas*
2/97 **I'd Rather Ride Around With You** *Reba McEntire*
13/56 **I'd Rather Stay Home** *Kitty Wells*
F/78 **I'd Really Love To See You Tonight** *Jacky Ward & Reba McEntire*
67/83 **I'd Say Yes** *Paulette Carlson*
84/75 **I'd Still Be In Love With You** *Brian Collins*
20/92 **I'd Surrender All** *Randy Travis*
I'd Throw It All Away
75/81 *Sweetwater*
66/88 *Darrell Holt*
9/52 **I'd Trade All Of My Tomorrows (For Just One Yesterday)** *Eddy Arnold*
10/57 **(I'll Always Be Your) Fraulein** *Kitty Wells*
1/88 **I'll Always Come Back** *K.T. Oslin*
30/77 **I'll Always Love You** *Cates Sisters*
75/77 **I'll Always Remember That Song** *Con Hunley*
14/55 **I'll Baby Sit With You** *Ferlin Husky*
94/82 **I'll Baby You** *Steve Mantelli*
4/00 **I'll Be** *Reba McEntire*
48/03 **I'll Be Around** *Sawyer Brown*
7/45 **I'll Be Back** *Gene Autry*
1/80 **I'll Be Coming Back For More** *T.G. Sheppard*
67/74 **I'll Be Doggone** *Penny DeHaven*
I'll Be Home For Christmas
75/97 *Lonestar*
59/99 *Lonestar*
68/99 *Reba McEntire*
74/01 *Neal McCoy (medley)*
60/03 *Kenny Chesney*
56/05 *Joe Nichols*
1/77 **I'll Be Leaving Alone** *Charley Pride*
16/89 **I'll Be Lovin' You** *Lee Greenwood*
48/82 **I'll Be Loving You** *Big Al Downing*
68/00 **I'll Be Right Here Loving You** *Randy Travis*
91/73 **I'll Be Satisfied** *Don Adams*
F/56 **I'll Be Satisfied With Love** *Faron Young*
79/83 **I'll Be Seeing You** *Leon Raines*
10/87 **I'll Be The One** *Statler Brothers*
I'll Be There (If You Ever Want Me)
2/54 *Ray Price*
17/72 *Johnny Bush*
4/81 *Gail Davies*
I'll Be There (When You Get Lonely)
12/57 *Ray Price*
22/78 *David Rogers*
1/78 **I'll Be True To You** *Oak Ridge Boys*
57/72 **I'll Be Whatever You Say** *Wanda Jackson*
I'll Be Your Baby Tonight
48/68 *Glen Garrison*
33/70 *Claude King*
5/87 *Judy Rodman*
61/73 **I'll Be Your Bridge (Just Lay Me Down)** *Wilma Burgess*
54/85 **I'll Be Your Fool Tonight** *Jim Glaser*
26/82 **I'll Be Your Man Around The House** *Kieran Kane*
12/76 **I'll Be Your San Antone Rose** *Dottsy*
40/75 **I'll Be Your Steppin' Stone** *David Houston*
62/75 **I'll Believe Anything You Say** *Sami Jo*
16/59 **I'll Catch You When You Fall** *Charlie Walker*
2/87 **I'll Come Back As Another Woman** *Tanya Tucker*
10/67 **I'll Come Runnin'** *Connie Smith*
34/93 **I'll Cry Tomorrow** *Larry Stewart*
64/85 **I'll Dance The Two Step** *Shelly West*
17/74 **I'll Do Anything It Takes** *Jean Shepard*
2/77 **I'll Do It All Over Again** *Crystal Gayle*
53/81 **I'll Drink To That** *Billy Parker*
8/80 **(I'll Even Love You) Better Than I Did Then** *Statler Brothers*
60/87 **I'll Fall In Love Again** *Butch Baker*
10/78 **I'll Find It Where I Can** *Jerry Lee Lewis*
13/71 **I'll Follow You (Up To Our Cloud)** *George Jones*
88/87 **I'll Forget You** *Jerry Cooper*
3/44 **I'll Forgive You But I Can't Forget** *Roy Acuff*
60/76 **I'll Get Better** *Sammi Smith*
1/76 **I'll Get Over You** *Crystal Gayle*
34/78 **I'll Get Over You** *Nick Nixon*
6/88 **I'll Give You All My Love Tonight** *Bellamy Brothers*
F/76 **I'll Go Back To Her** *Waylon Jennings*
10/99 **I'll Go Crazy** *Andy Griggs*
46/94 **I'll Go Down Loving You** *Shenandoah*
11/64 **I'll Go Down Swinging** *Porter Wagoner*
I'll Go On Alone
1/53 *Marty Robbins*
4/53 *Webb Pierce*
3/98 **I'll Go On Loving You** *Alan Jackson*
74/86 **I'll Go Steppin' Too** *Glenn Sutton*
F/70 **I'll Go To A Stranger** *Johnny Bush*
3/75 **I'll Go To My Grave Loving You** *Statler Brothers*
68/74 **I'll Have To Say I Love You In A Song** *Jim Croce*
I'll Hold You In My Heart (Till I Can Hold You In My Arms)
1/47 *Eddy Arnold*
63/67 *Freddie Hart*
70/77 *Jan Howard*
4/61 **I'll Just Have A Cup Of Coffee (Then I'll Go)** *Claude Gray*
11/78 **I'll Just Take It Out In Love** *George Jones*
2/65 **I'll Keep Holding On (Just To Your Love)** *Sonny James*
74/88 **I'll Know The Good Times** *Bill Nunley*
43/64 **I'll Leave The Porch Light A-Burning** *Billy Grammer*
34/66 **I'll Leave The Singin' To The Bluebirds** *Sheb Wooley*
I'll Leave This World Loving You
47/80 *Wayne Kemp*
1/88 *Ricky Van Shelton*
26/90 **I'll Lie Myself To Sleep** *Shelby Lynne*
14/79 **I'll Love Away Your Troubles For Awhile** *Janie Fricke*
10/68 **I'll Love You More (Than You Need)** *Jeannie Seely*
11/70 **I'll Make Amends** *Roy Drusky*
19/58 **I'll Make It All Up To You** *Jerry Lee Lewis*
65/82 **I'll Miss You** *Stella Parton*
4/81 **I'll Need Someone To Hold Me (When I Cry)** *Janie Fricke*
I'll Never Be Free
2/50 *Kay Starr & Tennessee Ernie Ford*
26/69 *Johnny & Jonie Mosby*
11/78 *Jim Ed Brown/Helen Cornelius*
4/87 **I'll Never Be In Love Again** *Don Williams*
61/67 **I'll Never Be Lonesome With You** *Cal Smith*
7/73 **I'll Never Break These Chains** *Tommy Overstreet*
56/72 **I'll Never Fall In Love Again** *Liz Anderson*
1/67 **I'll Never Find Another You** *Sonny James*
6/95 **I'll Never Forgive My Heart** *Brooks & Dunn*
1/53 **I'll Never Get Out Of This World Alive** *Hank Williams*
27/79 **I'll Never Let You Down** *Tommy Overstreet*
5/45 **I'll Never Let You Worry My Mind** *Red Foley*
24S/00 **I'll Never Pass This Way Again** *Tracy Lawrence*
70/76 **I'll Never See Him Again** *Sue Richards*
I'll Never Slip Around Again
2/49 *Margaret Whiting & Jimmy Wakely*
6/49 *Floyd Tillman*
1/85 **I'll Never Stop Loving You** *Gary Morris*
61/67 **I'll Never Tell On You** *Roy Drusky & Priscilla Mitchell*
68/70 **I'll Paint You A Song** *Mac Davis*
5/88 **I'll Pin A Note On Your Pillow** *Billy Joe Royal*
28/78 **I'll Promise You Tomorrow** *Jerry Wallace*
80/86 **I'll Pull You Through** *Tish Hinojosa/Craig Dillingham*
8/65 **I'll Repossess My Heart** *Kitty Wells*
I'll Sail My Ship Alone
1/50 *Moon Mullican*
10/51 *Tiny Hill*
42/79 **I'll Say It's True** *Johnny Cash*

2/70 **I'll See Him Through** *Tammy Wynette*
2/69 **I'll Share My World With You** *George Jones*
22/63 **I'll Sign** *Beverly Buff*
27/75 **I'll Sing For You** *Don Gibson*
21/92 **I'll Start With You** *Paulette Carlson*
4/47 **I'll Step Aside** *Ernest Tubb*
1/87 **I'll Still Be Loving You** *Restless Heart*
45/81 **I'll Still Be Loving You** *Mundo Earwood*
47/85 **I'll Still Be Loving You** *Joe Stampley*
8/69 **I'll Still Be Missing You** *Warner Mack*
8/72 **I'll Still Be Waiting For You** *Buck Owens*
9/75 **I'll Still Love You** *Jim Weatherly*
84/79 **I'll Still Love You In My Dreams** *Sandra Kaye*
10/99 **I'll Still Love You More** *Trisha Yearwood*
100/78 **I'll Still Need You Mary Ann** *Jim Taylor*
8/49 **I'll Still Write Your Name In The Sand** *Buddy Starcher*
23/92 **I'll Stop Loving You** *Mike Reid*
8/50 **I'll Take A Back Seat For You** *Ernest Tubb*
75/84 **I'll Take As Much Of You As I Can Get** *Darrell Clanton*
55/76 **I'll Take It** *Roy Head*
46/02 **I'll Take Love Over Money** *Aaron Tippin*
17/05 **I'll Take That As A Yes (The Hot Tub Song)** *Phil Vassar*
86/80 **I'll Take The Blame** *Ricky Skaggs*
9/66 **I'll Take The Dog** *Jean Shepard & Ray Pillow*
47/99 **I'll Take Today** *Gary Allan*
37/86 **I'll Take Your Love Anytime** *Robin Lee*
2/99 **I'll Think Of A Reason Later** *Lee Ann Womack*
I'll Think Of Something
7/74 *Hank Williams, Jr.*
1/92 *Mark Chesnutt*
1/96 **I'll Try** *Alan Jackson*
6/74 **I'll Try A Little Bit Harder** *Donna Fargo*
59/05 **I'll Try Anything** *Amber Dotson*
2/45 **I'll Wait For You Dear** *Al Dexter*
3/79 **I'll Wake You Up When I Get Home** *Charlie Rich*
50/88 **I'll Walk Before I'll Crawl** *Janie Frickie*
30/65 **I'll Wander Back To You** *Earl Scott*
9/75 **I'm A Believer** *Tommy Overstreet*
49/75 **I'm A Believer (In A Whole Lot Of Lovin')** *Jean Shepard*
74/83 **I'm A Booger** *Roy Clark*
5/45 **I'm A Brandin' My Darlin' With My Heart** *Jack Guthrie*
7/45 **I'm A Convict With Old Glory In My Heart** *Elton Britt*
72/84 **I'm A Country Song** *David Rogers*
60/98 **I'm A Cowboy** *Bill Engvall*
22/69 **I'm A Drifter** *Bobby Goldsboro*
61/67 **I'm A Fool** *Slim Whitman*

I'm A Fool To Care
72/75 *Donny King*
91/78 *Marcia Ball*
34/69 **I'm A Good Man (In A Bad Frame Of Mind)** *Jack Reno*
14/60 **I'm A Honky Tonk Girl** *Loretta Lynn*
33/77 **I'm A Honky-Tonk Woman's Man** *Bob Luman*
I'm A Long Gone Daddy
6/48 *Hank Williams*
97/79 *Norman Wade*
9/70 **I'm A Lover (Not A Fighter)** *Skeeter Davis*
I'm A Memory
28/71 *Willie Nelson*
22/77 *Willie Nelson*
97/78 **I'm A Mender** *Danny Shatswell*
18/66 **I'm A Nut** *Leroy Pullins*
I'm A One-Woman Man
7/56 *Johnny Horton*
5/89 *George Jones*
6/66 **I'm A People** *George Jones*
1/74 **I'm A Ramblin' Man** *Waylon Jennings*
33/05 **I'm A Saint** *Mark Chesnutt*
58/83 **I'm A Slave** *Jerry Reed*
1/76 **(I'm A) Stand By My Woman Man** *Ronnie Milsap*
52/95 **I'm A Stranger Here Myself** *Perfect Stranger*
12/54 **I'm A Stranger In My Home** *Kitty Wells & Red Foley*
3/01 **I'm A Survivor** *Reba McEntire*
52/88 **I'm A Survivor** *George Jones*
57/89 **I'm A Survivor** *Lacy J. Dalton*
30/68 **I'm A Swinger** *Jimmy Dean*
4/72 **I'm A Truck** *Red Simpson*
57/76 **I'm A Trucker** *Johnny Russell*
32/64 **I'm A Walkin' Advertisement** *Norma Jean*
94/78 **I'm A Woman** *Jeanne Pruett*
85/78 **I'm A Woman In Love** *LaWanda Lindsey*
49/74 **(I'm A) YoYo Man** *Rick Cunha*
23/76 **I'm All Wrapped Up In You** *Don Gibson*
54/81 **I'm Almost Ready** *Leona Williams*
5/80 **I'm Already Blue** *Kendalls*
I'm Already Taken
63/78 *Steve Wariner*
3/99 *Steve Wariner*
1/01 **I'm Already There** *Lonestar*
1/98 **I'm Alright** *Jo Dee Messina*
20/70 **I'm Alright** *Lynn Anderson*
2/78 **I'm Always On A Mountain When I Fall** *Merle Haggard*
3/53 **I'm An Old, Old Man** *Lefty Frizzell*
67/85 **I'm An Old Rock And Roller (Dancin' To A Different Beat)** *Tom Jones*
68/85 **I'm As Over You As I'm Ever Gonna Get** *Lloyd David Foster*
64/75 **I'm Available** *Kathy Barnes*
17/59 **I'm Beginning To Forget You** *Jim Reeves*
50/79 **I'm Being Good** *David Wills*
2/49 **I'm Bitin' My Fingernails And Thinking Of You** *Andrews Sisters & Ernest Tubb*
38/68 **I'm Coming Back Home To Stay** *Buckaroos*

11/57 **I'm Coming Home** *Johnny Horton*
62/77 **I'm Coming Home To Face The Music** *Nat Stuckey*
87/77 **(I'm Coming Home To You) Dixie** *Shylo*
93/79 **I'm Completely Satisfied With You** *Lorrie & George Morgan*
F/57 **I'm Counting On You** *Kitty Wells*
50/00 **I'm Diggin' It** *Alecia Elliott*
53/66 **I'm Doing This For Daddy** *Johnny Wright*
21/88 **I'm Down To My Last Cigarette** *k.d. lang*
3/69 **I'm Down To My Last "I Love You"** *David Houston*
39/82 **I'm Drinkin' Canada Dry** *Burrito Brothers*
28/69 **I'm Dynamite** *Peggy Sue*
57/68 **I'm Easy To Love** *Stan Hitchcock*
I'm Falling Too ..see: (I Can't Help You)
1/85 **I'm For Love** *Hank Williams, Jr.*
80/74 **I'm Free** *Stan Hitchcock*
3/98 **I'm From The Country** *Tracy Byrd*
3/60 **I'm Gettin' Better** *Jim Reeves*
56/79 **I'm Gettin' Into Your Love** *Ruby Falls*
30/69 **I'm Gettin' Tired Of Babyin' You** *Peggy Sue*
10/77 **I'm Getting Good At Missing You (Solitaire)** *Rex Allen, Jr.*
74/77 **I'm Getting High Remembering** *Bobby Lewis*
74/77 **I'm Giving You Denver** *Jean Shepard*
7/55 **I'm Glad I Got To See You Once Again** *Hank Snow*
63/84 **I'm Glad You Couldn't Sleep Last Night** *Narvel Felts*
50/68 **I'm Goin' Back Home Where I Belong** *Buckaroos*
18/82 **I'm Goin' Hurtin'** *Joe Stampley*
81/88 **I'm Goin' Nowhere** *Charlie Mitchell*
63/86 **I'm Going Crazy** *Kenny Dale*
41/70 **I'm Going Home** *Bobby Lewis*
10/85 **I'm Going To Leave You Tomorrow** *John Schneider*
31/02 **I'm Gone** *Cyndi Thomson*
17/71 **I'm Gonna Act Right** *Nat Stuckey*
54/72 **I'm Gonna Be A Swinger** *Webb Pierce*
5/47 **I'm Gonna Be Boss From Now On** *Bob Wills*
2/90 **I'm Gonna Be Somebody** *Travis Tritt*
68/00 **I'm Gonna Be There** *Victor Sanz*
42/65 **I'm Gonna Break Every Heart I Can** *Merle Haggard*
2/62 **I'm Gonna Change Everything** *Jim Reeves*
10/55 **I'm Gonna Fall Out Of Love With You** *Webb Pierce*
I'm Gonna Feed You Now
21/65 *Porter Wagoner*
F/79 *Porter Wagoner*
I'm Gonna Get You
63/87 *Billy Swan*
1/88 *Eddy Raven*
7/02 **I'm Gonna Getcha Good!** *Shania Twain*

65/66 **I'm Gonna Hang Up My Gloves** *Charlie Walker*
87/81 **I'm Gonna Hang Up This Heartache** *Nancy Ruud*
1/82 **I'm Gonna Hire A Wino To Decorate Our Home** *David Frizzell*
I'm Gonna Hurt Her On The Radio ..see: I'm Gonna Love Her
3/71 **I'm Gonna Keep On Keep On Lovin' You** *Billy Walker*
81/73 **I'm Gonna Keep Searching** *Pat Roberts*
5/72 **I'm Gonna Knock On Your Door** *Billy "Crash" Craddock*
44/66 **I'm Gonna Leave You** *Anita Carter*
60/71 **I'm Gonna Leave You** *Charlie Louvin & Melba Montgomery*
78/81 **I'm Gonna Let Go (And Love Somebody)** *Liz Lyndell*
F/57 **I'm Gonna Live Some Before I Die** *Faron Young*
I'm Gonna Love [Hurt] Her On The Radio
52/85 *David Allan Coe*
13/88 *Charley Pride*
3/76 **I'm Gonna Love You** *Dave & Sugar*
13/79 **I'm Gonna Love You** *Glen Campbell*
10/78 **I'm Gonna Love You Anyway** *Cristy Lane*
36/00 **I'm Gonna Love You Anyway** *Trace Adkins*
9/81 **I'm Gonna Love You Back To Loving Me Again** *Joe Stampley*
I'm Gonna Love You Right Out Of This World
21/77 *David Rogers*
76/82 *Tom Grant*
44/85 **I'm Gonna Love You Right Out Of The Blues** *Lloyd David Foster*
17/80 **I'm Gonna Love You Tonight (In My Dreams)** *Johnny Duncan*
79/80 **I'm Gonna Love You Tonight (Like There's No Tomorrow)** *Becky Hobbs*
69/68 **I'm Gonna Make Like A Snake** *Ernest Tubb*
1/02 **I'm Gonna Miss Her (The Fishin' Song)** *Brad Paisley*
3/88 **I'm Gonna Miss You, Girl** *Michael Martin Murphey*
7/68 **I'm Gonna Move On** *Warner Mack*
98/79 **I'm Gonna Move To The Country (And Get Away To It All)** *Jimmy Tucker*
16/81 **(I'm Gonna) Put You Back On The Rack** *Dottie West*
26/81 **I'm Gonna Sit Right Down And Write Myself A Letter** *Willie Nelson*
14/03 **I'm Gonna Take That Mountain** *Reba McEntire*
19/65 **I'm Gonna Tie One On Tonight** *Wilburn Brothers*
28/71 **I'm Gonna Write A Song** *Tommy Cash*
14/64 **I'm Hanging Up The Phone** *Carl Butler & Pearl*
23/80 **I'm Happy Just To Dance With You** *Anne Murray*
11/74 **I'm Having Your Baby** *Sunday Sharpe*
68/76 **I'm High On You** *Jack Blanchard & Misty Morgan*
17/00 **I'm Holdin' On To Love (To Save My Life)** *Shania Twain*
3/94 **I'm Holding My Own** *Lee Roy Parnell*
65/70 **I'm Holding Your Memory (But He's Holding You)** *Jimmy Newman*
F/55 **I'm Hurtin' Inside** *Jim Reeves*
I'm Hurting ..see: (Yes)
35/01 **I'm In** *Kinleys*
1/92 **I'm In A Hurry (And Don't Know Why)** *Alabama*
94/79 **I'm In Another World** *Scheree*
47/72 **I'm In Love** *Buddy Alan*
3/59 **I'm In Love Again** *George Morgan*
65/83 **I'm In Love All Over Again** *Cindy Hurt*
59/89 **I'm In Love And He's In Dallas** *Marie Osmond*
21/95 **I'm In Love With A Capital "U"** *Joe Diffie*
48/03 **I'm In Love With A Married Woman** *Mark Chesnutt*
47/99 **I'm In Love With Her** *Sawyer Brown*
85/76 **I'm In Love With My Pet Rock** *Al Bolt*
38/68 **I'm In Love With My Wife** *David Rogers*
12/55 **I'm In Love With You** *Kitty Wells*
52/03 **I'm In Love With You** *Billy Dean*
60/67 **I'm In No Condition** *Hank Williams, Jr.*
48/02 **I'm In The Mood** *Alabama*
18/81 **I'm Into Lovin' You** *Billy Swan*
30/80 **I'm Into The Bottle** *Dean Dillon*
I'm Just A Country Boy
37/65 *Jim Edward Brown*
1/77 *Don Williams*
73/78 **I'm Just A Farmer** *Cal Smith*
35/03 **I'm Just A Girl** *Deana Carter*
58/79 **I'm Just A Heartache Away** *Dickey Lee*
F/77 **(I'm Just A) Redneck In A Rock And Roll Bar** *Jerry Reed*
4/81 **I'm Just An Old Chunk Of Coal** *John Anderson*
92/78 **I'm Just Gettin' By** *Hank Thompson*
1/71 **I'm Just Me** *Charley Pride*
66/76 **(I'm Just Pouring Out) What She Bottled Up In Me** *David Wills*
1/01 **I'm Just Talkin' About Tonight** *Toby Keith*
96/80 **(I'm Just The) Cuddle Up Kind** *Hilka*
94/82 **I'm Just The Leavin' Kind** *Michael Meyers*
71/79 **I'm Just Your Yesterday** *Dandy*
I'm Knee Deep In Loving You
86/76 *Jim Mundy*
2/77 *Dave & Sugar*
100/88 **I'm Leavin' You** *Ben Sanders*
91/79 **I'm Leavin' You Alone** *Ernie Rowell*
17/99 **I'm Leaving** *Aaron Tippin*
I'm Leavin' It (All) Up To You
18/70 *Johnny & Jonie Mosby*
17/74 *Donny & Marie Osmond*
26/78 *Freddy Fender*
I'm Left, You're Right, She's Gone
F/55 *Elvis Presley*
21/74 *Jerry Lee Lewis*
15/65 **I'm Letting You Go** *Eddy Arnold*
22/59 **I'm Letting You Go** *Webb Pierce*
65/95 **I'm Listening Now** *Ron Wallace*
30/77 **I'm Living A Lie** *Jeanne Pruett*
9/66 **I'm Living In Two Worlds** *Bonnie Guitar*
39/95 **I'm Living Up To Her Low Expectations** *Daryle Singletary*
75/00 **I'm Lookin' For Trouble** *Damon Gray*
79/88 **(I'm Looking For Some) New Blue Jeans** *Troy Shondell*
16/62 **I'm Looking High And Low For My Baby** *Ernest Tubb*
66/82 **I'm Looking Over The Rainbow** *Sonny James*
90/76 **I'm Losing It All** *Eddy Raven*
1/45 **I'm Losing My Mind Over You** *Al Dexter*
45/66 **I'm Losing You (I Can Tell)** *Hugh X. Lewis*
5/45 **I'm Lost Without You** *Al Dexter*
84/79 **I'm Lovin' The Lovin' Out Of You** *Gayle Harding*
88/88 **I'm Loving The Wrong Man Again** *Dana McVicker*
47/71 **I'm Miles Away** *Hagers*
49/03 **I'm Missing You** *Kenny Rogers*
11/56 **I'm Moving In** *Hank Snow*
I'm Moving On
1/50 *Hank Snow*
14/60 *Don Gibson*
5/83 *Emmylou Harris*
4/02 **I'm Movin' On** *Rascal Flatts*
5/48 **I'm My Own Grandpa** *Lonzo & Oscar*
1/89 **I'm No Stranger To The Rain** *Keith Whitley*
37/82 **(I'm Not) A Candle In The Wind** *Bobby Bare*
27/02 **I'm Not Breakin'** *Steve Holy*
34/93 **I'm Not Built That Way** *Billy Dean*
28/66 **I'm Not Crazy Yet** *Ray Price*
11/77 **I'm Not Easy** *Billie Jo Spears*
31/02 **I'm Not Gonna Do Anything Without You** *Mark Wills w/ Jamie O'Neal*
59/79 **I'm Not In The Mood (For Love)** *Ann J. Morton*
81/85 **I'm Not Leaving** *Ray Price*
1/75 **I'm Not Lisa** *Jessi Colter*
14/56 **I'm Not Mad, Just Hurt** *Hank Thompson*
69/89 **I'm Not Over You** *Johnny Lee*
I'm Not Ready Yet
58/68 *Blue Boys*
2/80 *George Jones*
59/77 **I'm Not Responsible** *Hank Williams, Jr.*
70/73 **I'm Not Strong Enough** *Stonewall Jackson*
2/95 **I'm Not Strong Enough To Say No** *BlackHawk*

4/96 **I'm Not Supposed To Love You Anymore** *Bryan White*
49/98 **I'm Not That Easy To Forget** *Lorrie Morgan*
60/77 **I'm Not That Good At Goodbye** *Stella Parton*
3/82 **I'm Not That Lonely Yet** *Reba McEntire*
F/84 **I'm Not That Way Anymore** *Alabama*
62/77 **I'm Not The One You Love** *Sunday Sharpe*
52/69 **I'm Not Through Loving You** *Jim Glaser*
I'm Not Through Loving You Yet
3/74 *Conway Twitty*
60/80 *Pam Rose*
7/84 **I'm Not Through Loving You Yet** *Louise Mandrell*
21/86 **I'm Not Trying To Forget You** *Willie Nelson*
75/99 **I'm Not Your Girl** *Reba McEntire*
51/92 **I'm Okay (And Gettin' Better)** *Billy Joe Royal*
79/85 **I'm On Fire** *Debonaires*
97/78 **I'm On My Way** *Captain & Tennille*
79/83 **I'm On The Outside Looking In** *Darlene Austin*
54/71 **I'm On The Road To Memphis** *Buddy Alan & Don Rich*
39/03 **I'm One Of You** *Hank Williams, Jr.*
52/72 **I'm Only A Woman** *Dottie West*
1/83 **I'm Only In It For The Love** *John Conlee*
71/88 **I'm Only Lonely For You** *Pal Rakes*
I'm Outta Here! ..see: (If You're Not In It For Love)
3/90 **I'm Over You** *Keith Whitley*
92/79 **I'm Puttin' My Love Inside You** *Shylo*
75/83 **I'm Ragged But I'm Right** *Johnny Cash*
(I'm Ready) ..see: Heaven Bound
75/75 **I'm Ready To Love You Now** *Sarah Johns*
F/56 **I'm Really Glad You Hurt Me** *Webb Pierce*
70/73 **I'm Right Where I Belong** *Anthony Armstrong Jones*
89/78 **I'm Satisfied With You** *Leon Rausch*
60/77 **I'm Savin' Up Sunshine** *Dale McBride*
9/63 **I'm Saving My Love** *Skeeter Davis*
53/91 **I'm Sending One Up For You** *T. Graham Brown*
2/44 **I'm Sending You Red Roses** *Jimmy Wakely*
(I'm So) Afraid Of Losing You Again
1/69 *Charley Pride*
76/90 *Ashley Evans*
2/98 **I'm So Happy I Can't Stop Crying** *Toby Keith w/ Sting*
10/56 **I'm So In Love With You** *Wilburn Brothers*

I'm So Lonesome I Could Cry
43/66 *Hank Williams*
75/71 *Linda Plowman*
23/72 *Charlie McCoy*
17/76 *Terry Bradshaw*
43/82 *Jerry Lee Lewis*
45/65 **I'm So Miserable Without You** *Billy Walker*
76/82 **I'm So Tired Of Going Home Drunk** *Larry Jenkins*
1/75 **I'm Sorry** *John Denver*
76/76 **I'm Sorry** *Connie Cato*
16/76 **I'm Sorry Charlie** *Joni Lee*
9/77 **I'm Sorry For You, My Friend** *Moe Bandy*
F/56 **I'm Sorry, I'm Not Sorry** *Carl Perkins*
14/71 **I'm Sorry If My Love Got In Your Way** *Connie Smith*
1/89 **I'm Still Crazy** *Vern Gosdin*
4/95 **I'm Still Dancin' With You** *Wade Hayes*
39/80 **I'm Still In Love With You** *Larry G. Hudson*
3/74 **I'm Still Loving You** *Joe Stampley*
36/88 **I'm Still Missing You** *Ronnie McDowell*
95/78 **I'm Still Missing You** *Silver City Band*
80/77 **I'm Still Movin' On** *Hank Snow*
6/67 **I'm Still Not Over You** *Ray Price*
36/88 **I'm Still Your Fool** *David Slater*
48/82 **I'm Takin' A Heart Break** *Terry Gregory*
54/85 **I'm Takin' My Time** *Brenda Lee*
5/91 **I'm That Kind Of Girl** *Patty Loveless*
60/69 **I'm The Boy** *Statler Brothers*
24/62 **(I'm The Girl On) Wolverton Mountain** *Jo Ann Campbell*
I'm The Man
29/65 *Jim Kandy*
92/77 *Dugg Collins*
28/72 **I'm The Man On Susie's Mind** *Glenn Barber*
10/85 **I'm The One Mama Warned You About** *Mickey Gilley*
I'm The One Who Loves You ..see: (Remember Me)
61/85 **I'm The One Who's Breaking Up** *Tari Hensley*
8/77 **I'm The Only Hell (Mama Ever Raised)** *Johnny Paycheck*
62/93 **I'm The Only Thing (I'll Hold Against You)** *Conway Twitty*
18/79 **I'm The Singer, You're The Song** *Tanya Tucker*
91/78 **I'm The South** *Eddy Arnold*
3/44 **I'm Thinking Tonight Of My Blue Eyes** *Gene Autry*
I'm Throwing Rice (At The Girl That I Love)
1/49 *Eddy Arnold*
11/49 *Red Foley*
69/69 **I'm Tied Around Your Finger** *Jean Shepard*
I'm Tired
3/57 *Webb Pierce*
18/88 *Ricky Skaggs*
93/78 **I'm Tired Of Being Me** *Jack And Trink*

38/75 **I'm Too Use To Loving You** *Nick Nixon*
6/01 **I'm Tryin'** *Trace Adkins*
I'm Turning You Loose
90/74 *Nick Nixon*
77/79 *Bobby Wright*
8/51 **I'm Waiting Just For You** *Hawkshaw Hawkins*
I'm Walkin'
66/69 *Dave Peel*
96/77 *Doug Kershaw*
3/54 **I'm Walking The Dog** *Webb Pierce*
12/49 **I'm Waltzing With Tears In My Eyes** *Cowboy Copas*
1/44 **I'm Wastin' My Tears On You** *Tex Ritter*
25/78 **I'm Way Ahead Of You** *Bill Anderson & Mary Lou Turner*
21/61 **I'm Wondering** *Lou Smith*
37/97 **I'm Your Man** *Jason Sellers*
58/03 **I'm Your Man** *Steve Wariner*
69/90 **I'm Your Man** *Skip Ewing*
49/88 **I'm Your Puppet** *Mickey Gilley*
(I'm Your Telephone Man) ..see: Let My Fingers Do The Walking
8/73 **I'm Your Woman** *Jeanne Pruett*
38/99 **I'm Yours** *Linda Davis*
56/86 **I've Already Cheated On You** *David Allan Coe & Willie Nelson*
1/77 **I've Already Loved You In My Mind** *Conway Twitty*
34/74 **I've Already Stayed Too Long** *Don Adams*
1/78 **I've Always Been Crazy** *Waylon Jennings*
26/84 **I've Always Got The Heart To Sing The Blues** *Bill Medley*
75/84 **I've Always Wanted To** *Wayne Kemp*
I've Been A Fool
39/81 *Stephanie Winslow*
76/90 *Leah Marr*
I've Been A Long Time Leavin' (But I'll Be A Long Time Gone)
13/66 *Roger Miller*
92/78 *Joey Martin*
I've Been Around Enough To Know
78/75 *Jo-el Sonnier*
1/84 *John Schneider*
I've Been Everywhere
1/62 *Hank Snow*
16/70 *Lynn Anderson*
40/85 **I've Been Had By Love Before** *Judy Rodman*
2/88 **I've Been Lookin'** *Nitty Gritty Dirt Band*
29/78 **I've Been Loved** *Cates Sisters*
4/89 **I've Been Loved By The Best** *Don Williams*
55/69 **I've Been Loving You Too Long (To Stop Now)** *Barbara Mandrell*
90/83 **I've Been Out Of Love Too Long** *Gary Mack*
13/84 **I've Been Rained On Too** *Tom Jones*
72/73 **I've Been There** *Jonie Mosby*
11/68 **I've Been There Before** *Ray Price*
72/76 **I've Been There Too** *Kenny Seratt*
2/55 **I've Been Thinking** *Eddy Arnold*

28/78 **I've Been Too Long Lonely Baby** *Billy "Crash" Craddock*
14/79 **I've Been Waiting For You All Of My Life** *Con Hunley*
2/84 **I've Been Wrong Before** *Deborah Allen*
11/56 **I've Changed** *Carl Smith*
70/86 **I've Changed My Mind** *Bama Band*
11/72 **I've Come Awful Close** *Hank Thompson*
I've Come Back (To Say I Love You One More Time)
66/80 *Chuck Howard*
63/83 *Cristy Lane*
1/90 **I've Come To Expect It From You** *George Strait*
30/63 **I've Come To Say Goodbye** *Faron Young*
I've Cried A Mile
18/66 *Hank Snow*
52/86 *Tari Hensley*
1/90 **I've Cried My Last Tear For You** *Ricky Van Shelton*
I've Cried (The Blues Right Out Of My Eyes)
23/70 *Crystal Gayle*
40/78 *Crystal Gayle*
7/79 **I've Done Enough Dyin' Today** *Larry Gatlin*
7/63 **I've Enjoyed As Much Of This As I Can Stand** *Porter Wagoner*
75/93 **I've Fallen In Love (And I Can't Get Up)** *Charlie Floyd*
46/00 **I've Forgotten How You Feel** *Sonya Isaacs*
4/72 **I've Found Someone Of My Own** *Cal Smith*
92/80 **I've Given Up Giving In To The Blues** *Brenda Frazier*
74/82 **I've Got A Bad Case Of You** *Marie Osmond*
62/78 **I've Got A Feelin' (Somebody Stealin')** *John Anderson*
3/72 **(I've Got A) Happy Heart** *Susan Raye*
I've Got A Lotta Missin' You To Do
81/75 *Jerry "Max" Lane*
96/83 *Jerry "Max" Lane*
I've Got A New Heartache
2/56 *Ray Price*
10/86 *Ricky Skaggs*
5/79 **I've Got A Picture Of Us On My Mind** *Loretta Lynn*
93/78 **I've Got A Reason For Living** *Dolly Fox*
61/79 **I've Got A Right To Be Wrong** *B.J. Wright*
6/71 **I've Got A Right To Cry** *Hank Williams, Jr.*
25/60 **I've Got A Right To Know** *Buck Owens*
4/74 **I've Got A Thing About You Baby** *Elvis Presley*
1/65 **I've Got A Tiger By The Tail** *Buck Owens*
7/78 **I've Got A Winner In You** *Don Williams*
32/72 **I've Got A Woman's Love** *Marty Robbins*
93/73 **I've Got All The Heartaches I Can Handle** *Ernest Tubb*
60/78 **I've Got An Angel (That Loves Me Like The Devil)** *Bobby Hood*
73/79 **I've Got Country Music In My Soul** *Don King*
I've Got Five Dollars And It's Saturday Night
4/56 *Faron Young*
16/65 *George Jones & Gene Pitney*
3/94 **I've Got It Made** *John Anderson*
82/76 **I've Got Leaving On My Mind** *Webb Pierce*
69/73 **I've Got Mine** *Anthony Armstrong Jones*
13/75 **I've Got My Baby On My Mind** *Connie Smith*
25/69 **I've Got Precious Memories** *Faron Young*
94/77 **I've Got Some Gettin' Over You To Do** *Benny Barnes*
57/85 **I've Got The Heart For You** *Keith Whitley*
11/63 **I've Got The World By The Tail** *Claude King*
17/78 **I've Got To Go** *Billie Jo Spears*
I've Got To Have You
75/71 *Peggy Little*
13/72 *Sammi Smith*
71/71 **I've Got To Sing** *Duane Dee*
64/87 **I've Got Ways Of Making You Talk** *Vicki Bird*
5/68 **I've Got You On My Mind Again** *Buck Owens*
16/77 **I've Got You (To Come Home To)** *Don King*
74/89 **I've Had Enough Of You** *Debbie Rich*
17/70 **I've Just Been Wasting My Time** *John Wesley Ryles*
12/62 **I've Just Destroyed The World (I'm Living In)** *Ray Price*
11/74 **I've Just Got To Know (How Loving You Would Be)** *Freddy Weller*
44/82 **I've Just Seen A Face** *Calamity Jane*
7/55 **I've Kissed You My Last Time** *Kitty Wells*
57/70 **I've Lost You** *Elvis Presley*
56/81 **I've Loved Enough To Know** *Jim Rushing*
15/76 **I've Loved You All Of The Way** *Donna Fargo*
F/73 **I've Loved You All Over The World** *Cal Smith*
58/03 **I've Never Been Anywhere** *Sammy Kershaw*
66/67 **I've Never Been Loved** *Leroy Van Dyke*
99/73 **I've Never Been This Far Before** *Rita Remington*
60/82 **I've Never Been To Me** *Charlene*
I've Never Loved Anyone More
14/75 *Lynn Anderson*
82/75 *Linda Hargrove*
6/80 **I've Never Seen The Likes Of You** *Conway Twitty*
65/76 **I've Rode With The Best** *Jim Ed Brown*
7/59 **I've Run Out Of Tomorrows** *Hank Thompson*
83/79 **I've Seen It All** *Sandra Kaye*
41/76 **I've Taken** *Jeanne Pruett*
4/45 **I've Taken All I'm Gonna Take From You** *Spade Cooley*
70/00 **I've Thought Of Everything** *Daryle Singletary*
34/64 **I've Thought Of Leaving You** *Kitty Wells*
99/76 **Ida Red** *Bob Wills*
10/50 **Ida Red Likes The Boogie** *Bob Wills*
71/93 **Idle Hands** *Tim Ryan*
44/99 **If A Man Answers** *Toby Keith*
70/90 **If A Man Could Live On Love Alone** *Skip Ewing*
3/62 **If A Woman Answers (Hang Up The Phone)** *Leroy Van Dyke*
9/84 **If All The Magic Is Gone** *Mark Gray*
42/64 **If Anyone Can Show Cause** *Glenn Barber*
1/94 **If Bubba Can Dance (I Can Too)** *Shenandoah*
8/81 **If Drinkin' Don't Kill Me (Her Memory Will)** *George Jones*
39/84 **If Every Man Had A Woman Like You** *Osmond Brothers*
13/79 **If Everyone Had Someone Like You** *Eddy Arnold*
59/70 **If God Is Dead (Who's That Living In My Soul)** *Nat Stuckey & Connie Smith*
48/04 **If Heartaches Had Wings** *Rhonda Vincent*
77/88 **If Hearts Could Talk** *Bobbi Lace*
5/05 **If Heaven** *Andy Griggs*
F/82 **If Heaven Ain't A Lot Like Dixie** *Hank Williams, Jr.*
40/02 **If Her Lovin' Don't Kill Me** *Aaron Tippin*
1/83 **If Hollywood Don't Need You** *Don Williams*
46/95 **If I Ain't Got You** *Marty Stuart*
48/91 **If I Built You A Fire** *Neal McCoy*
51/91 **If I Can Find A Clean Shirt** *Waylon Jennings & Willie Nelson*
57/84 **If I Can Just Get Through The Night** *Sissy Spacek*
72/76 **If I Can Make It (Through The Mornin')** *Tony Douglas*
If I Could Bottle This Up
43/88 *George Jones & Shelby Lynne*
30/92 *Paul Overstreet*
80/74 **(If I Could Climb) The Walls Of The Bottle** *David Allan Coe*
21/63 **If I Could Come Back** *Webb Pierce*
78/82 **If I Could Get You (into my Life)** *Gene Cotton*
88/75 **If I Could Have It Any Other Way** *Kenny Seratt*
1/94 **If I Could Make A Living** *Clay Walker*
50/04 **If I Could Only Bring You Back** *Joe Diffie*
10/84 **If I Could Only Dance With You** *Jim Glaser*
58/87 **If I Could Only Fly** *Merle Haggard & Willie Nelson*
4/75 **If I Could Only Win Your Love** *Emmylou Harris*

24/77 **If I Could Put Them All Together (I'd Have You)** *George Jones*
68/95 **If I Could See Love** *Brett James*
55/82 **If I Could See You Tonight** *Kippi Brannon*
80/80 **If I Could Set My Love To Music** *Jerry Wallace*
53/93 **If I Could Stop Lovin' You** *Curtis Wright*
4/79 **If I Could Write A Song As Beautiful As You** *Billy "Crash" Craddock*
28/62 **If I Cried Every Time You Hurt Me** *Wanda Jackson*
1/92 **If I Didn't Have You** *Randy Travis*
8/93 **If I Didn't Love You** *Steve Wariner*
26/83 **If I Didn't Love You** *Gus Hardin*
44/68 **If I Don't Like The Way You Love Me** *Mary Taylor*
29/58 **If I Don't Love You (Grits Ain't Groceries)** *George Jones*
53/86 **If I Don't Love You** *Jim Glaser*
92/79 **If I Ever** *Randy Gurley*
46/78 **If I Ever Come Back** *Pal Rakes*
4/70 **If I Ever Fall In Love** *Faron Young*
28/89 **If I Ever Fall In Love Again** *Anne Murray w/ Kenny Rogers*
17/89 **If I Ever Go Crazy** *Shooters*
28/80 **If I Ever Had To Say Goodbye To You** *Eddy Arnold*
48/94 **If I Ever Love Again** *Daron Norwood*
If I Ever Need A Lady
67/67 *Claude Gray*
68/78 *Claude Gray*
53/82 *Billy Parker*
3/01 **If I Fall You're Going Down With Me** *Dixie Chicks*
18/79 **If I Fell In Love With You** *Rex Allen, Jr.*
10/79 **If I Give My Heart To You** *Margo Smith*
66/88 **If I Had A Boat** *Lyle Lovett*
If I Had A Cheating Heart
9/78 *Mel Street*
36/93 *Ricky Lynn Gregg*
If I Had A Hammer
41/69 *Wanda Jackson*
29/72 *Johnny Cash & June Carter Cash*
65/99 **If I Had A Nickel (One Thin Dime)** *Redmon & Vale*
25/95 **If I Had Any Pride Left At All** *John Berry*
81/80 **If I Had It My Way** *Nightstreets*
2/76 **If I Had It To Do All Over Again** *Roy Clark*
60/78 **If I Had It To Do All Over Again** *Stoney Edwards*
32/69 **If I Had Last Night To Live Over** *Webb Pierce*
60/02 **If I Had Long Legs (Like Alan Jackson)** *Leland Martin*
72/94 **If I Had Only Known** *Reba McEntire*
1/89 **If I Had You** *Alabama*
51/71 **If I Had You** *Bobby Lewis*
90/83 **If I Just Had My Woman** *Bobby Reed*
11/81 **If I Keep On Going Crazy** *Leon Everette*
5/67 **If I Kiss You (Will You Go Away)** *Lynn Anderson*

93/75 **If I Knew Enough To Come Out Of The Rain** *Connie Eaton*
1/91 **If I Know Me** *George Strait*
11/76 **If I Let Her Come In** *Ray Griff*
88/89 **If I Live To Be A Hundred (I'll Die Young)** *Arne Benoni*
29/98 **If I Lost You** *Travis Tritt*
8/74 **If I Miss You Again Tonight** *Tommy Overstreet*
3/81 **If I Needed You** *Emmylou Harris & Don Williams*
39/89 **If I Never See Midnight Again** *Sweethearts Of The Rodeo*
3/98 **If I Never Stop Loving You** *David Kersh*
1/79 **If I Said You Have A Beautiful Body Would You Hold It Against Me** *Bellamy Brothers*
67/81 **If I Say I Love You (Consider Me Drunk)** *Whitey Shafer*
4/65 **If I Talk To Him** *Connie Smith*
16/95 **If I Was A Drinkin' Man** *Neal McCoy*
2/70 **If I Were A Carpenter** *Johnny Cash & June Carter*
49/89 **If I Were The Man You Wanted** *Lyle Lovett*
4/95 **If I Were You** *Collin Raye*
8/96 **If I Were You** *Terri Clark*
62/70 **If I'd Only Come And Gone** *Clay Hart*
56/80 **(If I'd Only Known) It Was The Last Time** *Faron Young*
91/76 **If I'm A Fool For Loving You** *Dottie West*
73/68 **If I'm Gonna Sink** *Johnny Paycheck*
25/75 **If I'm Losing You** *Billy Walker*
74/99 **If I'm Not In Love** *Faith Hill*
35/88 **If It Ain't Broke Don't Fix It** *John Anderson*
20/85 **If It Ain't Love** *Ed Bruce*
12/77 **If It Ain't Love By Now** *Jim Ed Brown/Helen Cornelius*
If It Ain't Love (Let's Leave It Alone)
7/72 *Connie Smith*
12/85 *Whites*
1/88 **If It Don't Come Easy** *Tanya Tucker*
14/72 **If It Feels Good Do It** *Dave Dudley*
16/65 **If It Pleases You** *Billy Walker*
63/83 **If It Takes All Night** *Dottie West*
68/85 **If It Was Any Better (I Couldn't Stand It)** *Narvel Felts*
59/87 **If It Was Anyone But You** *John Schneider*
19/83 **If It Was Easy** *Ed Bruce*
26/94 **If It Wasn't For Her I Wouldn't Have You** *Daron Norwood*
83/89 **If It Wasn't For The Heartache** *Jill Hollier*
59/95 **If It Were Me** *Radney Foster*
26/91 **(If It Weren't For Country Music) I'd Go Crazy** *Clinton Gregory*
10/85 **If It Weren't For Him** *Vince Gill*
26/91 **If It Will It Will** *Hank Williams, Jr.*
28/73 **If It's All Right With You** *Dottie West*
2/70 **If It's All The Same To You** *Bill Anderson & Jan Howard*

81/84 **If It's Love (Then Bet It All)** *Jack Greene*
4/44 **If It's Wrong To Love You** *Charles Mitchell*
91/76 **If It's Your Song You Sing It** *Linda Cassady*
6/90 **If Looks Could Kill** *Rodney Crowell*
69/87 **If Love Ever Made A Fool** *Razzy Bailey*
6/79 **If Love Had A Face** *Razzy Bailey*
11/77 **If Love Was A Bottle Of Wine** *Tommy Overstreet*
12/55 **If Lovin' You Is Wrong** *Hank Thompson*
(If Loving You Is Wrong) I Don't Want To Be Right
71/72 *Jackie Burns*
1/79 *Barbara Mandrell*
74/68 **If Loving You Means Anything** *Dale Ward*
If My Heart Had Windows
7/67 *George Jones*
51/82 *Amy Wooley*
10/88 *Patty Loveless*
3/01 **If My Heart Had Wings** *Faith Hill*
10/04 **If Nobody Believed In You** *Joe Nichols*
6/69 **If Not For You** *George Jones*
75/73 **If Not For You** *Bobby Wright*
26/77 **If Not You** *Dr. Hook*
16/88 **If Ole Hank Could Only See Us Now** *Waylon Jennings*
74/92 **If Only Your Eyes Could Lie** *Earl Thomas Conley*
5/77 **If Practice Makes Perfect** *Johnny Rodriguez*
9/97 **If She Don't Love You** *Buffalo Club*
15/73 **If She Just Helps Me Get Over You** *Sonny James*
61/98 **If She Only Knew** *Kevin Sharp*
27/05 **If She Were Any Other Woman** *Buddy Jewell*
27/82 **If Something Should Come Between Us (Let It Be Love)** *Burrito Brothers*
9/05 **If Something Should Happen** *Darryl Worley*
If Teardrops Were Pennies
8/51 *Carl Smith*
3/73 *Porter Wagoner & Dolly Parton*
10/66 **If Teardrops Were Silver** *Jean Shepard*
26/02 **If That Ain't Country** *Anthony Smith*
15/85 **If That Ain't Love** *Lacy J. Dalton*
87/73 **If That Back Door Could Talk** *Ronnie Sessions*
86/78 **If That's Not Loving You** *Ruby Falls*
65/75 **If That's What It Takes** *Ray Griff*
21/83 **If That's What You're Thinking** *Karen Brooks*
13/64 **If The Back Door Could Talk** *Webb Pierce*
1/91 **If The Devil Danced (In Empty Pockets)** *Joe Diffie*
8/84 **If The Fall Don't Get You** *Janie Fricke*
1/94 **If The Good Die Young** *Tracy Lawrence*

29/91 **If The Jukebox Took Teardrops** *Billy Joe Royal*
57/98 **If The Jukebox Took Teardrops** *Danni Leigh*
16/85 **If The Phone Doesn't Ring, It's Me** *Jimmy Buffett*
8/88 **If The South Woulda Won** *Hank Williams, Jr.*
If The Whole World Stopped Lovin'
12/67 *Roy Drusky*
56/73 *Eddy Arnold*
2/95 **If The World Had A Front Porch** *Tracy Lawrence*
6/78 **If The World Ran Out Of Love Tonight** *Jim Ed Brown/Helen Cornelius*
41/03 **If There Ain't There Ought'a Be** *Marty Stuart*
61/77 **If There Ever Comes A Day** *Mike Lunsford*
3/92 **If There Hadn't Been You** *Billy Dean*
21/80 **If There Were No Memories** *John Anderson*
48/80 **If There Were Only Time For Love** *Roy Clark*
9/87 **If There's Any Justice** *Lee Greenwood*
81/78 **If There's One Angel Missing (She's Here In My Arms Tonight)** *Billy Parker*
69/89 **If This Ain't Love (There Ain't No Such Thing)** *Grayghost*
24/66 **If This House Could Talk** *Stonewall Jackson*
92/76 **If This Is Freedom (I Want Out)** *Danny Wood*
54/72 **If This Is Goodbye** *Carl Smith*
45/78 **If This Is Just A Game** *David Allan Coe*
F/70 **If This Is Love** *Jack Greene*
30/71 **If This Is Our Last Time** *Brenda Lee*
100/77 **If This Is What Love's All About** *Peggy Sue & Sonny Wright*
71/70 **If This Was The Last Song** *Billy Mize*
1/89 **If Tomorrow Never Comes** *Garth Brooks*
86/83 **If Tomorrow Never Comes** *Ray Griff*
41/91 **If We Can't Do It Right** *Eddie London*
92/77 **If We Can't Do It Right** *Kathy & Larry Barnes*
1/73 **If We Make It Through December** *Merle Haggard*
2/77 **If We're Not Back In Love By Monday** *Merle Haggard*
69/75 **(If You Add) All The Love In The World** *Mac Davis*
31/82 **If You Ain't Got Nothin' (You Ain't Got Nothin' To Lose)** *Bobby Bare*
If You Ain't Lovin' (You Ain't Livin')
2/55 *Faron Young*
1/88 *George Strait*
81/83 **If You Believe** *John Schneider*
26/85 **If You Break My Heart** *Kendalls*
51/94 **If You Came Back From Heaven** *Lorrie Morgan*
41/00 **If You Can** *Tammy Cochran*
5/01 **If You Can Do Anything Else** *George Strait*
2/73 **If You Can Live With It (I Can Live Without It)** *Bill Anderson*
5/78 **If You Can Touch Her At All** *Willie Nelson*
100/77 **(If You Can) Why Can't I** *Billy Walker*
22/98 **If You Can't Be Good (Be Good At It)** *Neal McCoy*
7/66 **If You Can't Bite, Don't Growl** *Tommy Collins*
3/73 **If You Can't Feel It (It Ain't There)** *Freddie Hart*
1/88 **If You Change Your Mind** *Rosanne Cash*
6/90 **If You Could Only See Me Now** *T. Graham Brown*
79/84 **If You Could Only See Me Now** *Sissy Spacek*
70/94 **If You Could Say What I'm Thinking** *Orrall & Wright*
If You Could See You Through My Eyes
40/79 *Tom Grant*
63/82 *Skip & Linda*
6/62 **If You Don't Know I Ain't Gonna Tell You** *George Hamilton IV*
59/89 **If You Don't Know Me By Now** *Joe Stampley*
71/81 **If You Don't Know Me By Now** *Super Grit Cowboy Band*
11/77 **If You Don't Love Me (Why Don't You Just Leave Me Alone)** *Freddy Fender*
61/67 **If You Don't Love Me (Why Don't You Just Leave Me Alone)** *Bob Luman*
If You Don't Somebody Else Will
3/54 *Jimmy & Johnny*
8/54 *Ray Price*
97/76 *Carl Smith*
37/78 **If You Don't Want To Love Her** *Jerry Naylor*
1/80 **If You Ever Change Your Mind** *Crystal Gayle*
31/75 **If You Ever Change Your Mind** *Ray Price*
27/01 **If You Ever Feel Like Lovin' Me Again** *Clay Walker*
16/77 **If You Ever Get To Houston (Look Me Down)** *Don Gibson*
5/98 **If You Ever Have Forever In Mind** *Vince Gill*
62/99 **If You Ever Leave Me** *Barbra Streisand & Vince Gill*
31/72 **If You Ever Need My Love** *Jack Greene*
1/04 **If You Ever Stop Loving Me** *Montgomery Gentry*
12/81 **If You Go, I'll Follow You** *Porter Wagoner & Dolly Parton*
94/77 **If You Got To Have It Your Way** *Billy Parker*
20/77 **If You Gotta Make A Fool Of Somebody** *Dickey Lee*
54/89 **If You Had A Heart** *Tim Malchak*
1/72 **If You Leave Me Tonight I'll Cry** *Jerry Wallace*
If You Love Me (Let Me Know)
2/74 *Olivia Newton-John*
83/77 *Brian Collins*
27/71 **If You Love Me (Really Love Me)** *Lamar Morris*
4/97 **If You Love Somebody** *Kevin Sharp*
86/74 **If You Loved Her That Way** *O.B. McClinton*
4/96 **If You Loved Me** *Tracy Lawrence*
62/87 **If You Only Knew** *Kim Grayson*
99/77 **If You Really Want Me To I'll Go** *Silver City Band*
1/98 **If You See Him/If You See Her** *Reba McEntire/Brooks & Dunn*
73/70 **If You See My Baby** *Johnny Carver*
31/87 **If You Still Want A Fool Around** *Charley Pride*
F/74 **If You Talk In Your Sleep** *Elvis Presley*
74/84 **If You Think I Love You Now** *Shoppe*
76/78 **If You Think I Love You Now** *Jim Mundy & Terri Melton*
19/71 **If You Think I Love You Now (I've Just Started)** *Jody Miller*
F/77 **If You Think I'm Crazy Now** *Bobby Bare*
34/71 **If You Think That It's All Right** *Johnny Carver*
9/72 **If You Touch Me (You've Got To Love Me)** *Joe Stampley*
32/74 **(If You Wanna Hold On) Hold On To Your Man** *Diana Trask*
78/86 **If You Wanna Talk Love** *Benny Wilson*
24/66 **If You Want A Love** *Buck Owens*
8/77 **If You Want Me** *Billie Jo Spears*
2/91 **If You Want Me To** *Joe Diffie*
74/71 **If You Want Me To I'll Go** *Bobby Wright*
59/74 **If You Want The Rainbow** *Melba Montgomery*
23/90 **If You Want To Be My Woman** *Merle Haggard*
11/92 **If You Want To Find Love** *Kenny Rogers*
53/76 **If You Want To Make Me Feel At Home** *DeWayne Orender*
7/55 **If You Were Me** *Webb Pierce*
58/92 **If You'll Let This Fool Back In** *Lee Greenwood*
48/86 **If You're Anything Like Your Eyes** *Robin Lee*
26/73 **If You're Goin' Girl** *Don Gibson*
5/83 **If You're Gonna Do Me Wrong (Do It Right)** *Vern Gosdin*
68/77 **If You're Gonna Love (You Gotta Hurt)** *Dave Conway*
1/84 **If You're Gonna Play In Texas** *Alabama*
67/87 **If You're Gonna Tell Me Lies (Tell Me Good Ones)** *Rosemary Sharp*
18/95 **If You're Gonna Walk, I'm Gonna Crawl** *Sammy Kershaw*
If You're Looking For A Fool
56/71 *Tommy Overstreet*
34/78 *Freddy Fender*
7/67 **If You're Not Gone Too Long** *Loretta Lynn*

44/93 **If You're Not Gonna Love Me** *Deborah Allen*
1/96 **(If You're Not In It For Love) I'm Outta Here!** *Shania Twain*
If You're Serious About Cheatin'
61/80 *R.C. Bannon*
77/84 *Randy Wright*
3/82 **If You're Thinking You Want A Stranger** *George Strait*
10/82 **If You're Waiting On Me (You're Backing Up)** *Kendalls*
1/94 **If You've Got Love** *John Michael Montgomery*
6/78 **If You've Got Ten Minutes (Let's Fall In Love)** *Joe Stampley*
If You've Got The Money I've Got The Time
1/50 *Lefty Frizzell*
1/76 *Willie Nelson*
41/73 **If You've Got The Time** *Red Steagall*
4/92 **If Your Heart Ain't Busy Tonight** *Tanya Tucker*
24/90 **If Your Heart Should Ever Roll This Way Again** *Jo-el Sonnier*
70/83 **If Your Heart's A Rollin' Stone** *Helen Cornelius*
29/59 **Igmoo (The Pride Of South Central High)** *Stonewall Jackson*
5/68 **Image Of Me** *Conway Twitty*
Image Of Me
26/61 *Bob Wills*
70/84 *Jim Reeves*
4/98 **Imagine That** *Diamond Rio*
21/62 **Imagine That** *Patsy Cline*
79/81 **Imagine That** *Nancy Wood*
19/60 **Imitation Of Love** *Adrian Roland*
3/02 **Impossible, The** *Joe Nichols*
1/91 **In A Different Light** *Doug Stone*
61/91 **In A Different Light** *Linda Davis*
74/97 **In A Heartbeat** *Rodney Atkins*
1/89 **In A Letter To You** *Eddy Raven*
5/85 **In A New York Minute** *Ronnie McDowell*
1/04 **In A Real Love** *Phil Vassar*
83/82 **In A Stranger's Eyes** *Ralph May*
2/93 **In A Week Or Two** *Diamond Rio*
13/80 **In America** *Charlie Daniels Band*
13/90 **In Another Lifetime** *Desert Rose Band*
27/85 **In Another Minute** *Jim Glaser*
10/02 **In Another World** *Joe Diffie*
74/68 **In Another World** *Webb Pierce*
2/97 **In Another's Eyes** *Trisha Yearwood & Garth Brooks*
86/75 **In At Eight And Out At Ten** *Don Drumm*
3/95 **In Between Dances** *Pam Tillis*
69/82 **In Between Lovers** *Stephanie Winslow*
38/64 **In Case You Ever Change Your Mind** *Bill Anderson*
18/67 **In Del Rio** *Billy Walker*
75/87 **In Dreams** *Roy Orbison*
70/87 **In It Again** *A.J. Masters*
15/82 **In Like With Each Other** *Gatlin Bros.*
1/86 **In Love** *Ronnie Milsap*
16/68 **In Love** *Wynn Stewart*
48/86 **In Love With Her** *Adam Baker*
64/82 **In Love With Loving You** *Keith Stegall*
48/71 **In Loving Memories** *Jerry Lee Lewis*
22/80 **In Memory Of A Memory** *Johnny Paycheck*
17/61 **In Memory Of Johnny Horton** *Johnny Hardy*
61/78 **In Memory Of Your Love** *Debby Boone*
56/85 **In My Arms Again** *Del Shannon*
4/04 **In My Daughter's Eyes** *Martina McBride*
9/84 **In My Dreams** *Emmylou Harris*
41/03 **In My Dreams** *Rick Trevino*
1/84 **In My Eyes** *John Conlee*
12/90 **In My Eyes** *Lionel Cartwright*
60/04 **In My High School** *Blaine Larsen*
33/74 **In My Little Corner Of The World** *Marie Osmond*
58/94 **In My Next Life** *Merle Haggard*
19/94 **In My Own Backyard** *Joe Diffie*
6/79 **In No Time At All** *Ronnie Milsap*
79/79 **In Our Room** *Roy Head*
9/86 **In Over My Heart** *T.G. Sheppard*
4/95 **In Pictures** *Alabama*
41/84 **In Real Life** *Ed Hunnicutt*
15/76 **In Some Room Above The Street** *Gary Stewart*
17/63 **In The Back Room Tonight** *Carl Smith*
48/93 **In The Blood** *Rob Crosby*
56/82 **In The Driver's Seat** *John Schneider*
35/81 **In The Garden** *Statler Brothers*
In The Ghetto
50/69 *Dolly Parton*
60/69 *Elvis Presley*
25/68 **In The Good Old Days** *Dolly Parton*
3/93 **In The Heart Of A Woman** *Billy Ray Cyrus*
In The Jailhouse Now
1/55 *Webb Pierce*
8/62 *Johnny Cash*
15/77 *Sonny James*
72/82 *Willie Nelson & Webb Pierce*
7/55 **In The Jailhouse Now No. 2** *Jimmie Rodgers*
6/62 **In The Middle Of A Heartache** *Wanda Jackson*
23/64 **In The Middle Of A Memory** *Carl Belew*
10/83 **In The Middle Of The Night** *Mel Tillis*
54/88 **In The Middle Of The Night** *Canyon*
14/84 **In The Midnight Hour** *Razzy Bailey*
65/75 **In The Misty Moonlight** *George Morgan*
In The Mood
84/75 *Joe Bob's Nashville Sound Company*
39/77 *Henhouse Five Plus Too*
In The Palm Of Your Hand
43/66 *Buck Owens*
23/73 *Buck Owens*
34/66 **In The Same Old Way** *Bobby Bare*
29/63 **In The Shadows Of The Wine** *Porter Wagoner*
21/72 **In The Spring (The Roses Always Turn Red)** *Dorsey Burnette*
(In The Still Of The Night) ..see: Lost In The Fifties Tonight
51/04 **In These Last Few Days** *Vince Gill*
1/92 **In This Life** *Collin Raye*
21/63 **In This Very Same Room** *George Hamilton IV*
6/55 **In Time** *Eddy Arnold*
4/83 **In Times Like These** *Barbara Mandrell*
63/96 **In Your Face** *Ty Herndon*
33/67 **In Your Heart** *Red Sovine*
57/03 **In Your Love** *Rhett Akins*
12/94 **Independence Day** *Martina McBride*
96/75 **Indian Creek** *Porter Wagoner*
34/75 **Indian Giver** *Billy Larkin*
3/71 **Indian Lake** *Freddy Weller*
Indian Love Call
2/52 *Slim Whitman*
38/75 *Ray Stevens*
74/76 **Indian Nation** *Billy Thunderkloud*
8/94 **Indian Outlaw** *Tim McGraw*
72/75 **Indiana Girl** *Pat Boone*
5/46 **Inflation** *Zeke Manners*
68/98 **Innocent Bystander** *Billy Dean*
19/82 **Innocent Lies** *Sonny James*
74/98 **Innocent Man** *Sherrié Austin*
1/83 **Inside** *Ronnie Milsap*
31/02 **Inside Out** *Trisha Yearwood/Don Henley*
66/83 **Inside Story** *Ronnie Rogers*
46/04 **Inspiration** *David Lee Murphy w/ Lee Roy Parnell*
73/67 **Instant Love** *Mitchell Torok*
48/77 **Instead Of Givin' Up (I'm Givin' In)** *Billy Walker*
54/68 **Instinct For Survival** *Skeeter Davis*
48/66 **Insurance** *Hank Locklin*
93/82 **Intimate Strangers** *Terry Dale*
13/64 **Invisible Tears** *Ned Miller*
Invitation To The Blues
3/58 *Ray Price*
71/89 *Andy Lee Smith*
6/69 **Invitation To Your Party** *Jerry Lee Lewis*
63/92 **Iola** *Great Plains*
Ira Hayes ..see: Ballad Of
67/70 **Irma Jackson** *Tony Booth*
13/49 **Iron Range** *Frankie Yankovic*
61/69 **Irresistible** *Slim Whitman*
22/96 **Irresistible You** *Ty England*
Is Anybody Goin' To San Antone
1/70 *Charley Pride*
91/77 *Chuck Price*
60/77 **Is Everybody Ready** *Little David Wilkins*
8/76 **Is Forever Longer Than Always** *Porter Wagoner & Dolly Parton*
Is It Any Wonder That I Love You
60/71 *Bob Luman*
26/72 *Nat Stuckey*
5/92 **Is It Cold In Here** *Joe Diffie*
43/90 **Is It Love** *Foster & Lloyd*
63/68 **Is It Love?** *Lucille Starr*
84/80 **Is It Only Cause You're Lonely** *Porter Wagoner*
6/94 **Is It Over Yet** *Wynonna*

10/91 **Is It Raining At Your House** *Vern Gosdin*
1/65 **Is It Really Over?** *Jim Reeves*
1/89 **Is It Still Over?** *Randy Travis*
3/44 **Is It Too Late Now** *Jimmie Davis*
Is It Wrong (For Loving You)
9/58 *Warner Mack*
11/60 *Webb Pierce*
1/74 *Sonny James*
91/78 *Gilbert Ortega*
93/80 *Mike Lunsford*
2/97 **Is That A Tear** *Tracy Lawrence*
47/85 **Is There Anything I Can Do** *Bill Medley*
1/92 **Is There Life Out There** *Reba McEntire*
27/75 **Is This All There Is To A Honky Tonk?** *Jerry Naylor*
3/63 **Is This Me?** *Jim Reeves*
11/72 **Is This The Best I'm Gonna Feel** *Don Gibson*
1/44 **Is You Is Or Is You Ain't (Ma' Baby)** *Louis Jordan*
2/53 **Is Zat You, Myrtle** *Carlisles*
49/77 **Ishabilly** *Mack Vickery*
10/90 **Island** *Eddy Raven*
27/87 **Island In The Sea** *Willie Nelson*
1/83 **Islands In The Stream** *Kenny Rogers & Dolly Parton*
10/79 **Isn't It Always Love** *Lynn Anderson*
1/86 **It Ain't Cool To Be Crazy About You** *George Strait*
1/82 **It Ain't Easy Bein' Easy** *Janie Fricke*
99/77 **It Ain't Easy Lovin' Me** *Ronnie Prophet*
12/85 **It Ain't Gonna Worry My Mind** *Ray Charles w/ Mickey Gilley*
4/65 **It Ain't Me, Babe** *Johnny Cash & June Carter*
It Ain't No Big Thing
50/70 *Tex Williams*
64/70 *Mills Brothers*
1/90 **It Ain't Nothin'** *Keith Whitley*
25/83 **It Ain't Real (If It Ain't You)** *Mark Gray*
76/74 **It Almost Felt Like Love** *Charlie Louvin*
86/77 **It Always Brings Me Back Around To You** *Billy Walker*
95/85 **It Always Hurts Like The First Time** *Carroll Baker*
72/78 **It Amazes Me** *John Denver*
48/74 **It Amazes Me (Sweet Lovin' Time)** *Mary Kay James*
59/03 **It Can All Be Gone** *Jamie Lee Thurston*
91/85 **It Can't Be Done** *Tim Blixseth*
84/80 **It Can't Wait** *Debbie Peters*
23/71 **It Could 'A Been Me** *Billie Jo Spears*
61/74 **It Could Have Been Me** *Sami Jo*
74/92 **It Could've Been So Good** *Collin Raye*
1/77 **It Couldn't Have Been Any Better** *Johnny Duncan*
51/77 **It Didn't Have To Be A Diamond** *Susan Raye*
7/75 **It Do Feel Good** *Donna Fargo*
It Doesn't Matter Anymore
54/75 *Linda Ronstadt*
33/78 *R.C. Bannon*
41/03 **It Doesn't Mean I Don't Love You** *McHayes*
87/76 **It Don't Bother Me** *Ben Reece*
69/71 **It Don't Do No Good To Be A Good Girl** *Liz Anderson*
2/78 **It Don't Feel Like Sinnin' To Me** *Kendalls*
42/80 **It Don't Get Better Than This** *Sheila Andrews*
25/81 **It Don't Get No Better Than This** *Gatlin Bros.*
6/81 **It Don't Hurt Me Half As Bad** *Ray Price*
35/80 **It Don't Hurt To Dream** *Sylvia*
24/99 **It Don't Matter To The Sun** *Garth Brooks*
59/68 **It Don't Mean A Thing To Me** *Kenny Price*
70/92 **It Don't Take A Lot** *Mark Collie*
36/70 **It Don't Take But One Mistake** *Luke The Drifter, Jr.*
(It Feels Like Love Again) ..see: From Time To Time
88/78 **It Feels Like Love For The First Time** *Larry Curtis*
35/88 **It Goes Without Saying** *Tim Malchak*
82/83 **It Had To Be You** *Texas Vocal Company*
It Happens Every Time
85/74 *Dorsey Burnette*
83/85 *Leon Raines*
14/83 **It Hasn't Happened Yet** *Rosanne Cash*
It Hurts To Know The Feeling's Gone
42/74 *Nat Stuckey*
31/76 *Billy Mize*
53/94 **It Is No Secret** *Mark Collie*
29/60 **It Just Tears Me Up** *Floyd Tillman*
48/78 **It Just Won't Feel Like Cheating** *Sammi Smith*
It Keeps Right On A-Hurtin'
4/62 *Johnny Tillotson*
17/88 *Billy Joe Royal*
38/69 **It Looks Like The Sun's Gonna Shine** *Wilburn Brothers*
70/76 **It Makes Me Giggle** *John Denver*
48/66 **It Makes You Happy** *Kenny Vernon*
1/96 **It Matters To Me** *Faith Hill*
33/72 **It Meant Nothing To Me** *Diana Trask*
It Must Be Love
1/79 *Don Williams*
1/00 *Alan Jackson*
1/98 **It Must Be Love** *Ty Herndon*
74/93 **It Must Be The Rain** *Marty Brown*
58/75 **It Must Have Been The Rain** *Jim Weatherly*
91/77 **It Never Crossed My Mind** *Tompall Glaser*
74/00 **It Never Rains In Southern California** *Trent Summar*
1/78 **It Only Hurts For A Little While** *Margo Smith*
7/92 **It Only Hurts When I Cry** *Dwight Yoakam*
18/04 **It Only Hurts When I'm Breathing** *Shania Twain*
62/72 **It Rains Just The Same In Missouri** *Ray Griff*
94/76 **It Sets Me Free** *Jack Paris*
It Should Have Been Easy
22/77 *Dottsy*
79/77 *Patti Leatherwood*
30/87 *Whites*
19/85 **It Should Have Been Love By Now** *Barbara Mandrell/ Lee Greenwood*
It Started All Over Again
23/78 *Vern Gosdin*
56/78 *David Houston*
68/79 **It Started With A Smile** *Helen Cornelius*
94/77 **It Sure Is Bad To Love Her** *Terry Stafford*
1/93 **It Sure Is Monday** *Mark Chesnutt*
89/80 **It Sure Looks Good On You** *Durwood Haddock*
1/87 **It Takes A Little Rain (To Make Love Grow)** *Oak Ridge Boys*
4/66 **It Takes A Lot Of Money** *Warner Mack*
45/72 **It Takes A Lot Of Tenderness** *Arlene Harden*
60/75 **It Takes A Whole Lotta Livin' In A House** *David Rogers*
76/76 **It Takes All Day To Get Over Night** *Doug Kershaw*
51/69 **It Takes All Night Long** *Cal Smith*
76/75 **It Takes Faith** *Marty Robbins*
38/83 **It Takes Love** *Big Al Downing*
72/79 **It Takes One To Know One** *Bobby Hood*
2/68 **It Takes People Like You (To Make People Like Me)** *Buck Owens*
37/73 **It Takes Time** *Dave Dudley*
98/79 **It Takes Too Long** *Hank Snow*
56/70 **It Takes Two** *Connie Eaton & Dave Peel*
21/72 **It Takes You** *Bob Luman*
5/55 **It Tickles** *Tommy Collins*
31/84 **It Took A Lot Of Drinkin' (To Get That Woman Over Me)** *Moe Bandy*
37/81 **It Took Us All Night Long To Say Goodbye** *Danny Wood*
17/82 **It Turns Me Inside Out** *Lee Greenwood*
11/00 **It Was** *Chely Wright*
1/77 **It Was Almost Like A Song** *Ronnie Milsap*
7/75 **It Was Always So Easy (To Find An Unhappy Woman)** *Moe Bandy*
80/87 **It Was Love What It Was** *Bobby Borchers*
65/72 **It Was Love While It Lasted** *Red Lane*
It Was The Last Time ..see: (If I'd Only Known)
21/62 **It Was You** *Ferlin Husky*
37/81 **It Was You** *Billy "Crash" Craddock*

It Wasn't God Who Made Honky Tonk Angels
1/52 *Kitty Wells*
20/71 *Lynn Anderson*
10/81 *Waylon Jennings & Jessi Colter (medley)*
It Wasn't His Child
51/89 *Sawyer Brown*
60/95 *Trisha Yearwood*
56/91 **It Wasn't You, It Wasn't Me** *Daniele Alexander & Butch Baker*
68/99 **It Will Be Me** *Faith Hill*
41/03 **It Won't Be Christmas Without You** *Brooks & Dunn*
89/84 **It Won't Be Easy** *Lois Johnson*
59/68 **(It Won't Be Long) And I'll Be Hating You** *Johnny Paycheck*
6/91 **It Won't Be Me** *Tanya Tucker*
18/94 **It Won't Be Over You** *Steve Wariner*
74/95 **It Won't Be The Same This Year** *Vince Gill*
79/79 **It Won't Go Away** *Rayburn Anthony*
31/86 **It Won't Hurt** *Dwight Yoakam*
19/96 **It Works** *Alabama*
7/98 **It Would Be You** *Gary Allan*
7/96 **It Wouldn't Hurt To Have Wings** *Mark Chesnutt*
It'll Be Her [Him]
22/73 *David Rogers*
45/77 *Tompall Glaser*
89/78 *Johnny Cash*
46/81 *Debby Boone*
19/82 *Tompall/Glaser Brothers*
73/85 **It'll Be Love By Morning** *Allen Frizzell*
1/86 **It'll Be Me** *Exile*
34/83 **It'll Be Me** *Tom Jones*
It'll Come Back
16/74 *Red Sovine*
89/80 *Red Sovine*
43/03 **It'll Go Away** *Kevin Denney*
13/84 **It's A Be Together Night** *David Frizzell & Shelly West*
13/70 **It's A Beautiful Day** *Wynn Stewart*
38/00 **It's A Beautiful Thing** *Paul Brandt*
2/79 **It's A Cheating Situation** *Moe Bandy*
71/84 **It's A Cover Up** *Peter Isaacson*
7/77 **It's A Cowboy Lovin' Night** *Tanya Tucker*
30/83 **It's A Dirty Job** *Bobby Bare & Lacy J. Dalton*
88/76 **It's A Good Night For Singing** *Jerry Jeff Walker*
2/01 **It's A Great Day To Be Alive** *Travis Tritt*
5/56 **It's A Great Life (If You Don't Weaken)** *Faron Young*
It's A Heartache
10/78 *Bonnie Tyler*
32/81 *Dave & Sugar*
22/05 *Trick Pony*
3/58 **It's A Little More Like Heaven** *Hank Locklin*
1/97 **It's A Little Too Late** *Mark Chesnutt*
2/93 **It's A Little Too Late** *Tanya Tucker*
12/68 **It's A Long, Long Way To Georgia** *Don Gibson*
36/82 **It's A Long Way To Daytona** *Mel Tillis*
18/00 **It's A Love Thing** *Keith Urban*
It's A Lovely, Lovely World
5/52 *Carl Smith*
5/81 *Gail Davies*
20/73 **It's A Man's World** *Diana Trask*
36/72 **It's A Matter Of Time** *Elvis Presley*
6/74 **(It's A) Monsters' Holiday** *Buck Owens*
59/89 **It's A Natural Thing** *Jonathan Edwards*
10/85 **It's A Short Walk From Heaven To Hell** *John Schneider*
It's A Sin
1/47 *Eddy Arnold*
5/69 *Marty Robbins*
21/71 **It's A Sin To Tell A Lie** *Slim Whitman*
16/75 **It's A Sin When You Love Somebody** *Glen Campbell*
51/99 **It's About Time** *Julie Reeves*
36/04 **It's All How You Look At It** *Tracy Lawrence*
9/81 **It's All I Can Do** *Anne Murray*
It's All In The Game
82/74 *Slim Whitman*
53/75 *Jerry Jaye*
12/77 *Tom T. Hall*
54/83 *Merle Haggard*
72/93 **It's All In The Heart** *Stephanie Davis*
1/75 **It's All In The Movies** *Merle Haggard*
94/89 **It's All In The Touch** *Bruce Van Dyke*
15/96 **It's All In Your Head** *Diamond Rio*
19/59 **It's All My Heartache** *Carl Smith*
11/68 **It's All Over** *David Houston & Tammy Wynette*
41/76 **It's All Over** *Johnny Cash*
3/68 **It's All Over But The Crying** *Hank Williams, Jr.*
14/66 **It's All Over (But The Crying)** *Kitty Wells*
65/69 **It's All Over (But The Shouting)** *Bob Luman*
15/85 **It's All Over Now** *John Anderson*
23/75 **It's All Over Now** *Charlie Rich*
19/97 **It's All The Same To Me** *Billy Ray Cyrus*
1/78 **It's All Wrong, But It's All Right** *Dolly Parton*
F/58 **It's All Your Fault** *Ray Price*
7/65 **It's Alright** *Bobby Bare*
77/76 **It's Alright** *Billy Thunderkloud*
53/01 **It's Alright To Be A Redneck** *Alan Jackson*
11/89 **(It's Always Gonna Be) Someday** *Holly Dunn*
5/00 **It's Always Somethin'** *Joe Diffie*
60/83 **It's Another Silent Night** *Lane Brody*
5/65 **It's Another World** *Wilburn Brothers*
79/76 **It's Bad When You're Caught (With The Goods)** *Billy Parker*
2/78 **It's Been A Great Afternoon** *Merle Haggard*
100/77 **It's Been A Long, Long Time** *Buck Owens*
It's Been One Of Those Days
68/82 *Bobby Smith*
91/84 *Lang Scott*
64/89 *Bobby Vinton*
1/53 **It's Been So Long** *Webb Pierce*
1/45 **It's Been So Long Darling** *Ernest Tubb*
63/91 **It's Chitlin' Time** *Kentucky Headhunters*
37/70 **It's Dawned On Me You're Gone** *Dottie West*
25/76 **It's Different With You** *Mary Lou Turner*
66/91 **It's Easy To Tell** *Matraca Berg*
50/76 **It's Enough** *Ronnie Prophet*
1/03 **It's Five O'Clock Somewhere** *Alan Jackson & Jimmy Buffett*
48/66 **It's For God, And Country, And You Mom** *Ernest Tubb*
It's Four In The Morning
1/72 *Faron Young*
36/86 *Tom Jones*
1/05 **It's Getting Better All The Time** *Brooks & Dunn*
98/78 **(It's Gonna Be A) Happy Day** *Jack Paris*
91/84 **It's Gonna Be A Heartache** *Kevin Pearce*
70/89 **It's Gonna Be Love** *Mark Gray & Bobbie Lace*
1/72 **It's Gonna Take A Little Bit Longer** *Charley Pride*
55/87 **It's Goodbye And So-Long To You** *Lisa Childress*
94/79 **It's Gotta Be Magic** *George James*
44/84 **It's Great To Be Single Again** *David Allan Coe*
72/98 **It's Hard To Be A Parent** *Bill Engvall*
65/70 **It's Hard To Be A Woman** *Skeeter Davis*
10/80 **It's Hard To Be Humble** *Mac Davis*
40/82 **It's Hard To Be The Dreamer (When I Used To Be The Dream)** *Donna Fargo*
65/88 **It's Hard To Keep This Ship Together** *John Anderson*
47/04 **It's Hard To Kiss The Lips At Night That Chew Your Ass Out All Day Long** *Notorious Cherry Bombs*
F/77 **It's Heaven Loving You** *Freddie Hart*
66/79 **It's Hell To Know She's Heaven** *Dale McBride*
16/82 **It's High Time** *Dottie West*
It's In His Kiss ..see: Shoop Shoop Song
It's Just A Matter Of Time
1/70 *Sonny James*
7/86 *Glen Campbell*
1/89 *Randy Travis*
30/59 **It's Just About Time** *Johnny Cash*
46/85 **It's Just Another Heartache** *Bandana*
86/89 **It's Just The Whiskey Talkin'** *Ethel & The Shameless Hussies*

It's Like Falling In Love (Over And Over Again)
89/81 *Chris Waters*
28/82 *Osmond Brothers*
1/80 **It's Like We Never Said Goodbye** *Crystal Gayle*
14/96 **It's Lonely Out There** *Pam Tillis*
32/90 **It's Lonely Out Tonite** *Eddie Rabbitt*
43/64 **It's Lonesome** *Billy Walker*
61/89 **It's Love That Makes You Sexy** *Dean Dillon*
It's Me Again, Margaret
55/74 *Paul Craft*
74/85 *Ray Stevens*
9/75 **It's Midnight** *Elvis Presley*
5/96 **It's Midnight Cinderella** *Garth Brooks*
93/76 **It's Midnight (Do You Know Where Your Baby Is?)** *Sandy Posey*
11/76 **It's Morning (And I Still Love You)** *Jessi Colter*
73/85 **It's My Life** *Gary Wolf*
56/79 **It's My Party** *Sherry Brane*
11/01 **It's My Time** *Martina McBride*
It's My Time
51/67 *John D. Loudermilk*
50/68 *George Hamilton IV*
F/57 **It's My Way** *Webb Pierce*
8/51 **It's No Secret** *Stuart Hamblen*
51/72 **(It's No) Sin** *Slim Whitman*
58/78 **It's Not Easy** *Dickey Lee*
66/88 **It's Not Easy** *Jack Robertson*
56/75 **It's Not Funny Anymore** *Stella Parton*
1/72 **It's Not Love (But It's Not Bad)** *Merle Haggard*
34/98 **It's Not Over** *Mark Chesnutt*
92/78 **It's Not Over Till It's Over** *Billy Walker*
It's Not Supposed To Be That Way
84/77 *Steve Young*
52/80 *Pam Rose*
27/95 **It's Not The End Of The World** *Emilio*
88/81 **It's Not The Rain** *Music Row*
73/81 **It's Not The Same Old You** *Johnny Rodriguez*
17/60 **It's Not Wrong** *Connie Hall*
14/77 **It's Nothin' To Me** *Jim Reeves*
4/81 **It's Now Or Never** *John Schneider*
55/75 **It's Only A Barroom** *Nick Nixon*
65/67 **It's Only A Matter Of Time** *Carl Smith*
15/66 **It's Only Love** *Jeannie Seely*
67/98 **It's Only Love** *Randy Scruggs w/ Mary Chapin Carpenter*
68/86 **It's Only Love Again** *Vern Gosdin*
It's Only Make Believe
3/70 *Glen Campbell*
99/79 *Robert Gordon*
8/88 *Ronnie McDowell*
8/87 **It's Only Over For You** *Tanya Tucker*
91/73 **It's Only Over Now And Then** *Bill Phillips*
4/68 **It's Over** *Eddy Arnold*
14/80 **It's Over** *Rex Allen, Jr.*
46/97 **It's Over My Head** *Wade Hayes*
62/73 **It's Raining In Seattle** *Wynn Stewart*
57/81 **It's Really Love This Time** *Family Brown*
91/78 **It's Sad To Go To The Funeral (Of A Good Love That Has Died)** *Barbara Fairchild*
F/77 **It's Saturday Night** *Larry Wren*
62/82 **It's So Close To Christmas** *Bellamy Brothers*
81/77 **It's So Easy** *Linda Ronstadt*
95/76 **It's So Easy Lovin' You** *Tibor Brothers*
100/76 **It's So Good Lovin' You** *O.B. McClinton*
79/75 **It's So Nice To Be With You** *Bobby Lewis*
57/87 **It's Such A Heartache** *Ride The River*
1/67 **It's Such A Pretty World Today** *Wynn Stewart*
1/88 **It's Such A Small World** *Rodney Crowell & Rosanne Cash*
65/79 **It's Summer Time** *Jess Garron*
10/74 **It's That Time Of Night** *Jim Ed Brown*
87/75 **It's The Bible Against The Bottle** *Earl Conley*
1/67 **It's The Little Things** *Sonny James*
91/77 **It's The Love In You** *Susan St. Marie*
56/00 **It's The Most Wonderful Time Of The Year** *Garth Brooks*
20/85 **It's Time For Love** *Don Williams*
87/89 **It's Time For Your Dreams To Come True** *Billy Parker*
13/74 **It's Time To Cross That Bridge** *Jack Greene*
28/71 **It's Time To Love Her** *Billy Walker*
1/75 **It's Time To Pay The Fiddler** *Cal Smith*
12/79 **It's Time We Talk Things Over** *Rex Allen, Jr.*
It's Too Late To Love Me Now
87/77 *Charly McClain*
87/79 *Cher*
9/80 *Jeanne Pruett*
70/88 **It's Too Late To Love You Now** *Brian White*
56/79 **It's Too Soon To Say Goodbye** *Terri Hollowell*
5/80 **It's True Love** *Conway Twitty & Loretta Lynn*
3/46 **It's Up To You** *Al Dexter*
5/96 **It's What I Do** *Billy Dean*
It's Who You Love
16/82 *Kieran Kane*
73/92 *Don Williams*
59/83 **It's Written All Over Your Face** *Ronnie Dunn*
30/83 **It's You** *Kieran Kane*
5/90 **It's You Again** *Skip Ewing*
21/88 **It's You Again** *Exile*
55/84 **It's You Alone** *Gail Davies*
5/93 **It's Your Call** *Reba McEntire*
1/97 **It's Your Love** *Tim McGraw & Faith Hill*
34/85 **It's Your Reputation Talkin'** *Kathy Mattea*
9/98 **It's Your Song** *Garth Brooks*
3/61 **It's Your World** *Marty Robbins*

J

44/74 **J. John Jones** *Marie Owens*
J.C. ..see: Ballad Of
36/80 **J.R.** *B.J. Wright*
72/81 **Jacamo** *Donna Fargo*
49/68 **Jack And Jill** *Jim Ed Brown*
13/48 **Jack And Jill Boogie** *Wayne Raney*
72/79 **Jack Daniel's, If You Please** *David Allan Coe*
82/89 **Jackie Brown** *John Cougar Mellencamp*
2/67 **Jackson** *Johnny Cash & June Carter*
Jackson Ain't A Very Big Town
38/67 *Norma Jean*
21/68 *Johnny Duncan & June Stearns*
58/68 **Jacksonville** *Cal Smith*
6/96 **Jacob's Ladder** *Mark Wills*
5/58 **Jacqueline** *Bobby Helms*
54/76 **Jaded Lover** *Jerry Jeff Walker*
20/84 **Jagged Edge Of A Broken Heart** *Gail Davies*
1/57 **Jailhouse Rock** *Elvis Presley*
Jambalaya (On The Bayou)
1/52 *Hank Williams*
66/73 *Blue Ridge Rangers*
88/78 *Saskia & Serge*
F/73 **Jamestown Ferry** *Tanya Tucker*
15/93 **Janie Baker's Love Slave** *Shenandoah*
68/94 **Janie's Gone Fishin'** *Kim Hill*
34/72 **January, April And Me** *Dick Curless*
39/75 **January Jones** *Johnny Carver*
12/75 **Jason's Farm** *Cal Smith*
60/89 **Jaws Of Modern Romance** *Gary Morris*
13/92 **Jealous Bone** *Patty Loveless*
Jealous Heart
2/45 *Tex Ritter*
8/49 *Al Morgan*
14/49 *Kenny Roberts*
87/79 *Barbara Seiner*
12/64 **Jealous Hearted Me** *Eddy Arnold*
63/78 **Jealous Kind** *Rita Coolidge*
7/58 **Jealousy** *Kitty Wells*
3/74 **(Jeannie Marie) You Were A Lady** *Tommy Overstreet*
51/68 **Jeannie's Afraid Of The Dark** *Porter Wagoner & Dolly Parton*
Jed Clampett ..see: Ballad Of
89/82 **Jedediah Jones** *Wyley McPherson*
69/95 **Jenny Come Back** *Helen Darling*
22/60 **Jenny Lou** *Sonny James*
88/77 **Jesse I Wanted That Award** *Sherwin Linton*
100/77 **Jessie And The Light** *La Costa*
4/92 **Jesus And Mama** *Confederate Railroad*
66/69 **Jesus Is A Soul Man** *Billy Grammer*
80/76 **Jesus Is The Same In California** *Lloyd Goodson*
77/81 **Jesus Let Me Slide** *Dean Dillon*
F/80 **Jesus On The Radio (Daddy On The Phone)** *Tom T. Hall*
3/70 **Jesus, Take A Hold** *Merle Haggard*

31/04 **Jesus Was A Country Boy** *Clay Walker*
Jet Set ..see: (We're Not)
23/02 **Jezebel** *Chely Wright*
63/92 **Jezebel Kane** *JJ White*
7/54 **Jilted** *Red Foley*
74/71 **Jim Dandy** *Lynn Anderson*
27/61 **(Jim) I Wore A Tie Today** *Eddy Arnold*
56/70 **Jim, Jack, And Rose** *Johnny Bush*
41/70 **Jim Johnson** *Porter Wagoner*
46/83 **Jim Reeves Medley** *Jim Reeves*
26/68 **Jimmie Rodgers Blues** *Elton Britt*
5/59 **Jimmy Brown The Newsboy** *Mac Wiseman*
27/61 **Jimmy Caught The Dickens (Pushing Ernest In The Tub)** *Chick & His Hot Rods*
24/61 **Jimmy Martinez** *Marty Robbins*
69/92 **Jimmy McCarthy's Truck** *Molly & The Heymakers*
34/00 **Jimmy's Got A Girlfriend** *Wilkinsons*
Jingle Bell Rock
13/57 *Bobby Helms*
60/97 *Bobby Helms*
69/00 *George Strait*
52/02 *Aaron Tippin*
Jingle Bells
44/01 *SheDaisy*
58/03 *Alan Jackson*
49/04 *Kenny Chesney*
26/75 **Jo And The Cowboy** *Johnny Duncan*
24/68 **Jody And The Kid** *Roy Drusky*
13/69 **Joe And Mabel's 12th Street Bar And Grill** *Nat Stuckey*
1/88 **Joe Knows How To Live** *Eddy Raven*
29/83 **Jogger, The** *Bobby Bare*
5/94 **John Deere Green** *Joe Diffie*
29/91 **John Deere Tractor** *Judds*
John Dillinger ..see: Ballad Of
44/66 **John Henry, Jr.** *Merle Travis*
40/02 **John J. Blanchard** *Anthony Smith*
80/74 **John Law** *Homer Joy*
64/99 **John Roland Wood** *Deryl Dodd*
64/99 **John Wayne Walking Away** *Lari White*
17/59 **John Wesley Hardin** *Jimmie Skinner*
53/73 **John's Been Shucking My Corn** *Onie Wheeler*
54/89 **Johnny And The Dreamers** *Scott McQuaig*
1/69 **Johnny B. Goode** *Buck Owens*
72/69 **Johnny Let The Sunshine In** *David Ingles*
44/66 **Johnny Lose It All** *Johnny Darrell*
70/89 **Johnny Lucky And Suzi 66** *Jeff Stevens & The Bullets*
17/60 **Johnny, My Love (Grandma's Diary)** *Wilma Lee & Stoney Cooper*
Johnny One Time
36/68 *Willie Nelson*
50/69 *Brenda Lee*
87/76 *Jesseca James*
74/76 **Johnny Orphan** *Randy Barlow*
10/59 **Johnny Reb** *Johnny Horton*

38/70 **Johnny's Cash And Charley's Pride** *Mac Wiseman*
Jole Blon
4/47 *Roy Acuff [Our Own]*
4/47 *Harry Coates*
4/47 **Jole Blon's Sister** *Moon Mullican*
Jolene
1/74 *Dolly Parton*
55/01 *Sherrié Austin*
57/04 **Jolene** *Mickey Dimichele*
7/70 **Jolie Girl** *Marty Robbins*
31/88 **Jones On The Jukebox** *Becky Hobbs*
1/83 **José Cuervo** *Shelly West*
1/71 **Joshua** *Dolly Parton*
70/72 **Josie** *Kris Kristofferson*
26/71 **Joy To The World** *Murry Kellum*
13/67 **Juanita Jones** *Stu Phillips*
38/71 **Judy** *Ray Sanders*
41/71 **Juke Box Man** *Dick Curless*
61/86 **Juke Box Saturday Night** *Roy Clark*
70/74 **Jukebox** *Jack Reno*
15/67 **Jukebox Charlie** *Johnny Paycheck*
1/90 **Jukebox In My Mind** *Alabama*
8/94 **Jukebox Junkie** *Ken Mellons*
98/83 **Jukebox Never Plays Home Sweet Home** *Jack Greene*
24/89 **Jukebox Played Along** *Gene Watson*
1/92 **Jukebox With A Country Song** *Doug Stone*
2/87 **Julia** *Conway Twitty*
91/74 **Julianna** *Hummers*
79/77 **Julianne** *Roy Head*
15/67 **Julie** *Porter Wagoner*
81/79 **Julie (Do I Ever Cross Your Mind?)** *Wood Newton*
98/77 **Julieanne (Where Are You Tonight)?** *Wendel Adkins*
15/86 **Juliet** *Oak Ridge Boys*
25/78 **Juliet And Romeo** *Ronnie Sessions*
47/70 **July 12, 1939** *Charlie Rich*
July You're A Woman
71/74 *Red, White & Blue Grass*
77/74 *Ed Bruce*
100/76 **Jump Back Joe Joe** *Bill Black's Combo*
60/68 **Jump For Joy** *Statler Brothers*
83/81 **Jumper Cable Man** *Marty Robbins*
72/93 **Junk Cars** *Mac McAnally*
61/76 **Junk Food Junkie** *Larry Groce*
9/50 **Just A Closer Walk With Thee** *Red Foley*
35/81 **Just A Country Boy** *Rex Allen, Jr.*
78/87 **Just A Kid From Texas** *Dann Rogers*
Just A Little Bit ..see: Little Bit Of Lovin' (Goes A Long Long Way)
10/58 **Just A Little Lonesome** *Bobby Helms*
5/84 **Just A Little Love** *Reba McEntire*
1/48 **Just A Little Lovin' (Will Go A Long, Long Way)** *Eddy Arnold*
28/77 **Just A Little Thing** *Billy "Crash" Craddock*
13/48 **Just A Pair Of Blue Eyes** *Tex Williams*
81/86 **Just A Woman** *Loretta Lynn*

16/62 **Just Ain't** *Flatt & Scruggs*
63/67 **Just An Empty Place** *Ernie Ashworth*
92/77 **Just An Old Flame** *Hank Thompson*
77/88 **(Just An) Old Wives' Tale** *Gail O'Doski*
69/74 **Just Another Cowboy Song** *Doyle Holly*
1/00 **Just Another Day In Paradise** *Phil Vassar*
90/82 **Just Another Day In Paradise** *Bertie Higgins*
39/98 **Just Another Heartache** *Chely Wright*
73/92 **Just Another Hill** *Corbin/Hanner*
1/86 **Just Another Love** *Tanya Tucker*
68/89 **Just Another Miserable Day (Here In Paradise)** *Billy "Crash" Craddock*
35/78 **Just Another Rhinestone** *Don Drumm*
1/84 **Just Another Woman In Love** *Anne Murray*
26/93 **Just As I Am** *Ricky Van Shelton*
Just As Long As I Have You
72/85 *Gus Hardin & Dave Loggins*
4/90 *Don Williams*
11/56 **Just As Long As You Love Me** *Browns*
55/71 **Just As Soon As I Get Over Loving You** *Jean Shepard*
7/48 **Just Because** *Frankie Yankovic*
17/68 **Just Because I'm A Woman** *Dolly Parton*
60/72 **Just Because I'm Still In Love With You** *Bobby Wright*
36/00 **Just Because She Lives There** *Chalee Tennison*
98/89 **Just Because You're Leavin'** *Lorie Ann*
28/64 **Just Between The Two Of Us** *Merle Haggard & Bonnie Owens*
65/79 **Just Between Us** *Bill Woody*
9/67 **Just Between You And Me** *Charley Pride*
12/98 **Just Between You And Me** *Kinleys*
13/67 **Just Beyond The Moon** *Tex Ritter*
54/69 **Just Blow In His Ear** *David Wilkins*
2/55 **Just Call Me Lonesome** *Eddy Arnold*
10/92 **Just Call Me Lonesome** *Radney Foster*
66/89 **Just Can't Cry No More** *Lonesome Strangers*
37/98 **Just Don't Wait Around Til She's Leavin'** *David Lee Murphy*
52/87 **Just Enough Love** *Ray Price*
30/81 **Just Enough Love (For One Woman)** *Bobby Smith*
44/93 **Just Enough Rope** *Rick Trevino*
23/74 **Just Enough To Make Me Stay** *Bob Luman*
43/69 **Just Enough To Start Me Dreamin'** *Jeannie Seely*
56/74 **Just For Old Times Sake** *Eddy Arnold*
78/82 **Just For The Moment** *Brenda Lee*
5/72 **Just For What I Am** *Connie Smith*
4/68 **Just For You** *Ferlin Husky*

1/75 **Just Get Up And Close The Door** *Johnny Rodriguez*
98/77 **Just Gettin' By** *Red Sovine*
72/83 **Just Give Me One More Night** *Cole Young*
Just Give Me What You Think Is Fair
51/80 *Rex Gosdin w/ Tommy Jennings*
7/82 *Leon Everette*
1/79 **Just Good Ol' Boys** *Moe Bandy & Joe Stampley*
46/81 **Just Got Back From No Man's Land** *Wayne Kemp*
68/78 **Just Hangin' On** *Mel Street*
12/69 **Just Hold My Hand** *Johnny & Jonie Mosby*
Just Hooked On Country
42/82 *Albert Coleman's Atlanta Pops [Parts I & II]*
77/82 *Albert Coleman's Atlanta Pops [Part III]*
1/86 **Just In Case** *Forester Sisters*
4/76 **Just In Case** *Ronnie Milsap*
70/72 **Just In Time (To Watch Love Die)** *Charlie Louvin*
31/78 **Just Keep It Up** *Narvel Felts*
9/02 **Just Let Me Be In Love** *Tracy Byrd*
80/79 **Just Let Me Make Believe** *Jim Chesnut*
48/04 **Just Like A Redneck** *Shannon Lawson*
16/81 **Just Like Me** *Terry Gregory*
52/91 **Just Like Me** *Lee Greenwood*
11/79 **Just Like Real People** *Kendalls*
92/84 **Just Like That** *Malchak & Rucker*
5/93 **Just Like The Weather** *Suzy Bogguss*
46/72 **Just Like Walkin' In The Sunshine** *Jean Shepard*
25/75 **Just Like Your Daddy** *Jeanne Pruett*
10/79 **Just Long Enough To Say Goodbye** *Mickey Gilley*
5/88 **Just Lovin' You** *O'Kanes*
1/58 **Just Married** *Marty Robbins*
F/82 **Just Married** *Louise Mandrell & RC Bannon*
47/95 **Just My Luck** *Kim Richey*
36/94 **Just Once** *David Lee Murphy*
80/82 **Just Once** *John Wesley Ryles*
9/88 **Just One Kiss** *Exile*
66/77 **Just One Kiss Magdelena** *Bobby G. Rice*
3/56 **Just One More** *George Jones*
23/74 **Just One More Song** *Jack Blanchard & Misty Morgan*
70/72 **Just One More Time** *Johnny & Jonie Mosby*
5/93 **Just One Night** *McBride & The Ride*
67/87 **Just One Night Won't Do** *Big Al Downing*
3[S]/05 **Just One Of The Boys** *Michelle Poe*
Just One Time
2/60 *Don Gibson*
2/71 *Connie Smith*
17/81 *Tompall/Glaser Brothers*

Just Out Of Reach
100/76 *Perry Como*
37/78 *Larry G. Hudson*
77/78 *Mack White*
74/84 *Merle Kilgore*
84/86 **Just Out Riding Around** *Barbara Fairchild*
39/72 **Just Plain Lonely** *Ferlin Husky*
51/04 **Just Put A Ribbon In Your Hair** *Alan Jackson*
Just Say Yes ..see: (Do You Love Me)
61/98 **Just Some Love** *Ranch*
5/69 **Just Someone I Used To Know** *Porter Wagoner & Dolly Parton*
76/79 **Just Stay With Me** *Terri Hollowell*
17/73 **Just Thank Me** *David Rogers*
49/97 **Just The Same** *Terri Clark*
22/65 **Just Thought I'd Let You Know** *Carl Butler & Pearl*
70/67 **Just To Be Where You Are** *Wilburn Brothers*
3/98 **Just To Hear You Say That You Love Me** *Faith Hill w/ Tim McGraw*
Just To Prove My Love For [To] You
82/77 *David Allan Coe*
71/80 *Jimmy Snyder*
Just To Satisfy You
31/65 *Bobby Bare*
1/82 *Waylon Jennings & Willie Nelson*
1/98 **Just To See You Smile** *Tim McGraw*
94/87 **Just Try Texas** *Mike Lord*
7/53 **Just Wait 'Til I Get You Alone** *Carl Smith*
45/76 **Just Want To Taste Your Wine** *Billy Swan*
13/02 **Just What I Do** *Trick Pony*
9/73 **Just What I Had In Mind** *Faron Young*
44/73 **Just What I've Been Looking For** *Dottie West*
52/80 **Just What The Doctor Ordered** *Becky Hobbs*
Just When I Needed You Most
40/79 *Diana*
71/79 *Randy Vanwarmer*
62/96 *Dolly Parton*
71/76 **Just You 'N' Me** *Sammi Smith*

K

15/82 **Kansas City Lights** *Steve Wariner*
2/70 **Kansas City Song** *Buck Owens*
7/65 **Kansas City Star** *Roger Miller*
47/02 **Karma** *Jessica Andrews*
(Karneval) ..see: One More Time
2/72 **Kate** *Johnny Cash*
60/86 **Katie, Take Me Dancin'** *Lewis Storey*
22/00 **Katie Wants A Fast One** *Steve Wariner w/ Garth Brooks*
16/72 **Katy Did** *Porter Wagoner*
11/59 **Katy Too** *Johnny Cash*
Kaw-Liga
1/53 *Hank Williams*
3/69 *Charley Pride*
12/80 *Hank Williams, Jr.*

Kay
9/69 *John Wesley Ryles*
50/78 *John Wesley Ryles*
3/53 **Keep It A Secret** *Slim Whitman*
1/91 **Keep It Between The Lines** *Ricky Van Shelton*
17/90 **Keep It In The Middle Of The Road** *Exile*
42/65 **Keep Me Fooled** *Carl Smith*
1/73 **Keep Me In Mind** *Lynn Anderson*
51/01 **Keep Mom And Dad In Love** *Billy Dean & Suzy Bogguss*
6/45 **Keep My Mem'ry In Your Heart** *Ernest Tubb*
Keep On Lovin' Me
88/73 *Jamey Ryan*
23/74 *Johnny Paycheck*
49/81 **Keep On Movin'** *King Edward IV & The Knights*
58/83 **Keep On Playin' That Country Music** *Sierra*
70/82 **Keep On Rollin' Down The Line** *Boxcar Willie*
19/73 **Keep On Truckin'** *Dave Dudley*
45/92 **Keep On Walkin'** *Mike Reid*
53/73 **Keep Out Of My Dreams** *Dorsey Burnette*
Keep The Faith
51/87 *Jimmy Murphy*
61/89 *Heartland*
67/91 *Goldens*
31/66 **Keep The Flag Flying** *Johnny Wright*
16/64 **Keep Those Cards And Letters Coming In** *Johnny & Jonie Mosby*
8/48 **Keeper Of My Heart** *Bob Wills*
65/67 **Keeper Of The Key** *Slim Whitman*
2/95 **Keeper Of The Stars** *Tracy Byrd*
54/90 **Keepin' Me Up Nights** *Asleep At The Wheel*
49/83 **Keepin' Power** *Crystal Gayle*
99/76 **Keepin' Rosie Proud Of Me** *Razzy Bailey*
14/99 **Keepin' Up** *Alabama*
70/82 **Keeping Me Warm For You** *Brenda Lee*
58/97 **Keeping The Faith** *Mary Chapin Carpenter*
49/67 **Keeping Up Appearances** *Lynn Anderson & Jerry Lane*
5/64 **Keeping Up With The Joneses** *Faron Young & Margie Singleton*
68/97 **Keeping Your Kisses** *Kris Tyler*
6/05 **Keg In The Closet** *Kenny Chesney*
8/55 **Kentuckian Song** *Eddy Arnold*
38/72 **Kentucky** *Sammi Smith*
1/75 **Kentucky Gambler** *Merle Haggard*
20/62 **Kentucky Means Paradise** *Green River Boys/Glen Campbell*
42/76 **Kentucky Moonrunner** *Cledus Maggard*
31/70 **Kentucky Rain** *Elvis Presley*
53/73 **Kentucky Sunshine** *Wayne Kemp*
Kentucky Waltz
3/46 *Bill Monroe*
1/51 *Eddy Arnold*
26/77 **Kentucky Woman** *Randy Barlow*
86/88 **Kep Pa So** *Augie Meyers*
10/85 **Kern River** *Merle Haggard*

50/82 **Key Largo** *Bertie Higgins*
66/69 **Key That Fits Her Door** *Jack Greene*
Key's In The Mailbox
18/60 *Freddie Hart*
15/72 *Tony Booth*
5/94 **Kick A Little** *Little Texas*
60/00 **Kick Down The Door** *Georgia Middleman*
72/94 **Kick It Up** *John Michael Montgomery*
8/62 **Kickin' Our Hearts Around** *Buck Owens*
64/67 **Kickin' Tree** *Bonnie Guitar*
Kid, The
71/96 *Clint Black*
67/99 *Clint Black*
71/00 *Clint Black*
68/00 **Kid In Me** *Craig Morgan*
2/73 **Kid Stuff** *Barbara Fairchild*
1/87 **Kids Of The Baby Boom** *Bellamy Brothers*
1/73 **Kids Say The Darndest Things** *Tammy Wynette*
37/87 **Killbilly Hill** *Southern Pacific*
17/82 **Killin' Kind** *Bandana*
1/89 **Killin' Time** *Clint Black*
10/81 **Killin' Time** *Fred Knoblock & Susan Anton*
50/98 **Kind Of Heart That Breaks** *Chris Cummings*
42/71 **Kind Of Needin' I Need** *Norma Jean*
Kind Of Woman I Got
33/67 *Osborne Brothers*
F/75 *Hank Williams, Jr.*
33/98 **Kindly Keep It Country** *Vince Gill*
48/73 **Kindly Keep It Country** *Hank Thompson*
75/82 **King, The** *Pete Wilcox*
13/77 **King Is Gone** *Ronnie McDowell*
26/89 **King Is Gone (So Are You)** *George Jones*
75/86 **King Lear** *Cal Smith*
97/77 **King Of Country Music Meets The Queen Of Rock & Roll** *Even Stevens & Sherry Grooms*
96/85 **King Of Oak Street** *Ramsey Kearney*
51/05 **King Of The Castle** *Matt Jenkins*
19/97 **King Of The Mountain** *George Strait*
King Of The Road
1/65 *Roger Miller*
51/97 *Randy Travis*
49/96 **King Of The World** *BlackHawk*
1/71 **Kiss An Angel Good Mornin'** *Charley Pride*
36/76 **Kiss And Say Goodbye** *Billy Larkin*
65/78 **Kiss Away** *Jody Miller*
7/55 **Kiss-Crazy Baby** *Johnnie & Jack*
29/73 **Kiss It And Make It Better** *Mac Davis*
Kiss Me Darling
25/83 *Stephanie Winslow*
82/89 *Trisha Lynn*
26/94 **Kiss Me, I'm Gone** *Marty Stuart*
22/93 **Kiss Me In The Car** *John Berry*
79/83 **Kiss Me Just One More Time** *Floyd Brown*
60/00 **Kiss Me Now** *Lila McCann*
52/97 **Kiss The Girl** *Little Texas*
61/72 **Kiss The Hurt Away** *Ronnie Dove*
88/82 **Kiss The Hurt Away** *Mack White*
1/00 **Kiss This** *Aaron Tippin*
75/99 **Kiss This** *Lisa Angelle*
87/79 **Kiss You All Over** *Jim Mundy & Terri Melton*
74/79 **Kiss You And Make It Better** *Roy Head*
24/69 **Kissed By The Rain, Warmed By The Sun** *Glenn Barber*
5/55 **Kisses Don't Lie** *Carl Smith*
72/95 **Kisses Don't Lie** *George Ducas*
11/61 **Kisses Never Lie** *Carl Smith*
6/57 **Kisses Sweeter Than Wine** *Jimmie Rodgers*
14/61 **Kissing My Pillow** *Rose Maddox*
3/57 **Knee Deep In The Blues** *Marty Robbins*
18/63 **Knock Again, True Love** *Claude Gray*
56/95 **Knock, Knock** *Hutchens*
94/78 **Knock Knock Knock** *Frenchie Burke*
29/84 **Knock On Wood** *Razzy Bailey*
3/71 **Knock Three Times** *Billy "Crash" Craddock*
3/53 **Knothole** *Carlisles*
58/90 **Knowin' You Were Leavin'** *Les Taylor*
Knoxville Girl
18/59 *Wilburn Brothers*
19/59 *Louvin Brothers*
39/72 **Knoxville Station** *Bobby Austin*
11/71 **Ko-Ko Joe** *Jerry Reed*
4/47 **Kokomo Island** *Al Dexter*

L

60/69 **L.A. Angels** *Jimmy Payne*
L.A. International Airport
67/70 *David Frizzell*
9/71 *Susan Raye*
45/92 **L.A. To The Moon** *Ronnie Milsap*
57/87 **La Bamba** *Los Lobos*
58/94 **Labor Of Love** *Radney Foster*
79/89 **Labor Of Love** *Andi & The Brown Sisters*
94/76 **Labor Of Love** *Bob Luman*
80/76 **Ladies Love Outlaws** *Jimmy Rabbitt & Renegade*
78/77 **Ladies Night** *Del Reeves*
1/80 **Lady** *Kenny Rogers*
46/77 **Lady** *Johnny Cash*
66/73 **Lady** *Kenny Vernon*
79/77 **Lady Ain't For Sale** *Sherry Bryce*
76/77 **Lady And The Baby** *David Rogers*
14/75 **Lady Came From Baltimore** *Johnny Cash*
1/83 **Lady Down On Love** *Alabama*
79/86 **Lady In Distress** *Little David Wilkins*
55/83 **Lady In My Life** *Tony Joe White*
9/79 **Lady In The Blue Mercedes** *Johnny Duncan*
31/84 **Lady In Waiting** *David Wills*
88/82 **Lady, Lady** *Kelly Lang*
Lady Lay Down
1/79 *John Conlee*
26/82 *Tom Jones*
67/82 **Lady, Lay Down (Lay Down On My Pillow)** *Gary Goodnight*
4/85 **Lady Like You** *Glen Campbell*
47/74 **Lady Lover** *Bobby Lewis*
73/83 **Lady Of The Eighties** *Jeanne Pruett*
22/73 **Lady Of The Night** *David Houston*
31/83 **Lady, She's Right** *Leon Everette*
3/84 **Lady Takes The Cowboy Everytime** *Gatlin Bros.*
F/78 **Lady, Would You Like To Dance** *Jerry Naylor*
2/52 **Lady's Man** *Hank Snow*
64/96 **Lady's Man** *Rob Crosby*
92/81 **Lady's Man** *Music Row*
91/77 **Laid Back Country Picker** *Wendel Adkins*
82/83 **Laid Off** *Bill Anderson*
98/77 **Laissez Les Bontemps Rouler** *Helen Reddy*
(Lament Of Cherokee) ..see: Indian Reservation
20/70 **Land Mark Tavern** *Del Reeves & Penny DeHaven*
63/80 **Land Of Cotton** *Donna Fargo*
5/97 **Land Of The Living** *Pam Tillis*
2/02 **Landslide** *Dixie Chicks*
8/01 **Laredo** *Chris Cagle*
9/85 **Lasso The Moon** *Gary Morris*
65/73 **Last Blues Song** *Dick Curless*
Last Cheater's Waltz
1/79 *T.G. Sheppard*
F/79 *Sonny Throckmorton*
Last Country Song ..see: (Who's Gonna Sing)
12/80 **Last Cowboy Song** *Ed Bruce*
Last Date
11/61 *Floyd Cramer*
1/72 *Conway Twitty*
1/83 *Emmylou Harris*
7/64 **Last Day In The Mines** *Dave Dudley*
98/73 **Last Days Of Childhood** *Sam Durrence*
52/78 **Last Exit For Love** *Wood Newton*
51/80 **Last Farewell** *Miki Mori*
Last Goodbye
17/68 *Dick Miles*
96/76 *Red Sovine*
38/77 **Last Gunfighter Ballad** *Johnny Cash*
57/66 **Last Laugh** *Jim Edward Brown*
46/76 **Last Letter** *Willie Nelson*
99/78 **Last Lie I Told Her** *Ronnie Robbins*
43/78 **Last Love Of My Life** *Lynn Anderson*
4/73 **Last Love Song** *Hank Williams, Jr.*
36/02 **Last Man Committed** *Eric Heatherly*
20/59 **Last Night At A Party** *Faron Young*
28/78 **Last Night, Ev'ry Night** *Reba McEntire*
54/75 **Last Of The Outlaws** *Chuck Price*
43/82 **Last Of The Silver Screen Cowboys** *Rex Allen, Jr.*
63/74 **Last Of The Sunshine Cowboys** *Eddy Raven*
27/77 **Last Of The Winfield Amateurs** *Ray Griff*

21/04 **Last One Standing** *Emerson Drive*
1/87 **Last One To Know** *Reba McEntire*
18/71 **Last One To Touch Me** *Porter Wagoner*
4/88 **Last Resort** *T. Graham Brown*
3/59 **Last Ride** *Hank Snow*
63/89 **Last Rose** *Bobby Vinton*
2/83 **Last Thing I Needed First Thing This Morning** *Willie Nelson*
26/59 **Last Thing I Want To Know** *George Morgan*
7/68 **Last Thing On My Mind** *Porter Wagoner/Dolly Parton*
20/01 **Last Thing On My Mind** *Patty Loveless*
42/04 **Last Thing She Said** *Ryan Tyler*
75/97 **Last Time** *Tractors*
85/80 **Last Time** *Johnny Cash*
25/72 **Last Time I Called Somebody Darlin'** *Roy Drusky*
21/71 **Last Time I Saw Her** *Glen Campbell*
8/74 **Last Time I Saw Him** *Dottie West*
50/77 **Last Time You Love Me** *Jerry Naylor*
39/64 **Last Town I Painted** *George Jones*
69/67 **Last Train To Clarksville** *Ed Bruce*
80/82 **Last Train To Heaven** *Boxcar Willie*
4/53 **Last Waltz** *Webb Pierce*
52/73 **Last Will And Testimony (Of A Drinking Man)** *Howard Crockett*
73/81 **Last Word In Jesus Is Us** *Roy Clark*
Last Word In Lonesome Is Me
2/66 *Eddy Arnold*
90/76 *Terry Bradshaw*
20/68 **Late And Great Love (Of My Heart)** *Hank Snow*
52/03 **Late Great Golden State** *Dwight Yoakam*
38/03 **Lately (Been Dreamin' 'Bout Babies)** *Tracy Byrd*
49/77 **Lately I've Been Thinking Too Much Lately** *David Allan Coe*
64/90 **Lately Rose** *Trader-Price*
42/77 **Latest Shade Of Blue** *Connie Smith*
Laura (What's He Got That I Ain't Got)
1/67 *Leon Ashley*
50/67 *Claude King*
60/73 *Marty Robbins*
19/76 *Kenny Rogers*
13/49 **Lavender Blue (Dilly Dilly)** *Burl Ives w/ Captain Stubby*
3/76 **Lawdy Miss Clawdy** *Mickey Gilley*
9/72 **Lawrence Welk - Hee Haw Counter-Revolution Polka** *Roy Clark*
72/79 **Lawyers** *Billy Walker*
22/73 **Lay A Little Lovin' On Me** *Del Reeves*
97/79 **Lay A Little Lovin' On Me** *Jody Miller*
68/93 **Lay Around And Love On You** *Lari White*
52/82 **Lay Back Down And Love Me** *Rich Landers*
Lay Back In The Arms Of Someone
80/79 *Juice Newton*
13/80 *Randy Barlow*
91/84 *Johnny Tillotson*
35/75 **Lay Back Lover** *Dottie West*
67/76 **Lay Down** *Charly McClain*
3/79 **Lay Down Beside Me** *Don Williams*
Lay Down Sally
26/78 *Eric Clapton*
70/78 *Red Sovine*
86/78 *Jack Paris*
96/88 **Lay, Lady Lay** *Jim Bean*
86/89 **Lay Me Down Carolina** *Mark Tribble*
69/91 **Lay My Body Down** *Kenny Rogers*
44/67 **Lay Some Happiness On Me** *Bobby Wright*
82/77 **Lay Something On My Bed Besides A Blanket** *Charly McClain*
84/81 **Layin' Low** *Denny Hilton*
68/70 **Laying My Burdens Down** *Willie Nelson*
13/48 **Lazy Mazy** *Bud Hobbs*
47/93 **Lead Me Not** *Lari White*
56/70 **Lead Me Not Into Temptation** *Anthony Armstrong Jones*
Lead Me On
68/69 *Bonnie Owens*
1/71 *Loretta Lynn & Conway Twitty*
7/95 **Lead On** *George Strait*
13/74 **Lean It All On Me** *Diana Trask*
99/79 **Lean, Mean And Hungry** *Chris LeDoux*
55/77 **Lean On Jesus "Before He Leans On You"** *Paul Craft*
Lean On Me
91/75 *Paul Delicato*
77/84 *Jack Grayson*
93/79 **Leaning On Each Other** *B.J. Wright*
1/91 **Leap Of Faith** *Lionel Cartwright*
20/67 **Learnin' A New Way Of Life** *Hank Snow*
2/96 **Learning As You Go** *Rick Trevino*
59/91 **Learning The Game** *Black Tie*
2/93 **Learning To Live Again** *Garth Brooks*
28/81 **Learning To Live Again** *Bobby Bare*
15/65 **Least Of All** *George Jones*
34/64 **Leave A Little Play (In The Chain Of Love)** *Bob Jennings*
6/92 **Leave Him Out Of This** *Steve Wariner*
7/90 **Leave It Alone** *Forester Sisters*
68/79 **Leave It To Love** *Jim Taylor*
22/75 **Leave It Up To Me** *Billy Larkin*
72/74 **Leave Me Alone (Ruby Red Dress)** *Arleen Harden*
1/87 **Leave Me Lonely** *Gary Morris*
70/88 **Leave Me Satisfied** *Tiny Tim*
6/69 **Leave My Dream Alone** *Warner Mack*
59/98 **Leave My Mama Out Of This** *Monty Holmes*
6/83 **Leave Them Boys Alone** *Hank Williams, Jr. w/ Waylon Jennings & Ernest Tubb*
63/68 **Leave This One Alone** *Nat Stuckey*
93/78 **Leave While I'm Sleeping** *Micki Fuhrman*
41/68 **Leaves Are The Tears Of Autumn** *Bonnie Guitar*
74/77 **Leavin'** *Kenny Price*
82/85 **Leaving** *Charleston Express/Jesse Wales*
9/71 **Leavin' And Sayin' Goodbye** *Faron Young*
Leavin' On Your Mind
8/63 *Patsy Cline*
58/72 *Bobbie Roy*
92/80 *Karen Casey*
78/88 *Donna Meade*
75/81 **Leavin You Is Easier (Than Wishing You Were Gone)** *Joe Douglas*
15/93 **Leavin's Been A Long Time Comin'** *Shenandoah*
13/80 **Leavin's For Unbelievers** *Dottie West*
1/80 **Leaving Louisiana In The Broad Daylight** *Oak Ridge Boys*
31/98 **Leaving October** *Sons Of The Desert*
52/70 **Leaving On A Jet Plane** *Kendalls*
98/76 **Leaving Was Easy** *Mike Boyd*
64/73 **Leaving's Heavy On My Mind** *Sherry Bryce*
62/78 **Left-Over Love** *Brenda Lee*
10/84 **Left Side Of The Bed** *Mark Gray*
5/60 **Left To Right** *Kitty Wells*
45/81 **Lefty** *David Frizzell w/ Merle Haggard*
49/01 **Legacy** *Neal Coty*
19/85 **Legend And The Man** *Conway Twitty*
Legend In My Time ..see: (I'd Be) A
1/68 **Legend Of Bonnie And Clyde** *Merle Haggard*
94/80 **Legend Of Harry And The Mountain** *Ron Shaw/Desert Wind Band*
27/62 **Legend Of The Johnson Boys** *Flatt & Scruggs*
80/80 **Legend Of Wooley Swamp** *Charlie Daniels Band*
38/72 **Legendary Chicken Fairy** *Jack Blanchard & Misty Morgan*
9/62 **Leona** *Stonewall Jackson*
16/85 **Leona** *Sawyer Brown*
64/78 **Leona** *Johnny Russell*
91/77 **Leona Don't Live Here Anymore** *Wayne Kemp*
9/81 **Leonard** *Merle Haggard*
Leroy The Redneck Reindeer
33/96 *Joe Diffie*
46/97 *Joe Diffie*
54/98 *Joe Diffie*
27/65 **Less And Less** *Charlie Louvin*
44/68 **Less Of Me** *Bobbie Gentry & Glen Campbell*
67/75 **Less Than The Song** *Patti Page*
58/02 **Lesson In Goodbye** *Michael Peterson*
Lesson In Leavin'
1/80 *Dottie West*
2/99 *Jo Dee Messina*
3/00 **Lessons Learned** *Tracy Lawrence*

34/85 **Let A Little Love Come In** *Charley Pride*
86/86 **Let A Little Love In** *Rockin' Horse*
64/99 **Let 'Er Rip** *Dixie Chicks*
5/61 **Let Forgiveness In** *Webb Pierce*
6/93 **Let Go** *Brother Phelps*
7/93 **Let Go Of The Stone** *John Anderson*
18/91 **Let Her Go** *Mark Collie*
43/72 **Let Him Have It** *Jan Howard*
37/03 **Let It Be Christmas** *Alan Jackson*
Let It Be Me
14/69 *Glen Campbell & Bobbie Gentry*
2/82 *Willie Nelson*
5/89 **Let It Be You** *Ricky Skaggs*
57/89 **Let It Burn** *Jeff Chance*
78/88 **Let It Go** *Don Juan*
8/97 **Let It Rain** *Mark Chesnutt*
6/85 **Let It Roll (Let It Rock)** *Mel McDaniel*
5/76 **Let It Shine** *Olivia Newton-John*
Let It Snow, Let It Snow, Let It Snow
43/97 *Ricochet*
44/98 *Ricochet*
41/99 *Ricochet*
64/99 *Martina McBride*
72/99 *George Strait*
39/00 *Ricochet*
73/00 *Martina McBride*
37/05 *Joe Nichols*
22/80 **Let Jesse Rob The Train** *Buck Owens*
67/84 **Let Love Come Lookin' For You** *Dottie West*
59/04 **Let Me Be** *Deryl Dodd*
63/86 **Let Me Be The First** *Nicolette Larson*
1/53 **Let Me Be The One** *Hank Locklin*
74/80 **Let Me Be The One** *Billy Walker & Barbara Fairchild*
7/73 **Let Me Be There** *Olivia Newton-John*
13/78 **Let Me Be Your Baby** *Charly McClain*
35/76 **Let Me Be Your Friend** *Mack White*
(Let Me Be Your) Teddy Bear
1/57 *Elvis Presley*
F/78 *Elvis Presley*
7/77 **Let Me Down Easy** *Cristy Lane*
16/85 **Let Me Down Easy** *Jim Glaser*
67/86 **Let Me Down Easy** *Malchak & Rucker*
87/78 **Let Me Down Easy** *Peggy Sue*
63/94 **Let Me Drive** *Greg Holland*
93/78 **Let Me Fall Back In Your Arms** *Freddy Weller*
72/81 **Let Me Fill For You A Fantasy** *Gary Goodnight*
45/64 **Let Me Get Close To You** *Skeeter Davis*
Let Me Go, Lover!
1/55 *Hank Snow*
75/70 *Karen Kelly*
27/70 **Let Me Go (Set Me Free)** *Johnny Duncan*
23/80 **Let Me In** *Kenny Dale*
F/82 **Let Me In And Let Me Love You** *Tennessee Express*
11/97 **Let Me Into Your Heart** *Mary Chapin Carpenter*
1/98 **Let Me Let Go** *Faith Hill*
21/71 **Let Me Live** *Charley Pride*
53/80 **Let Me Love You** *Fred Knoblock*
99/77 **Let Me Love You Now** *Jim Chesnut*
22/77 **Let Me Love You Once Before You Go** *Barbara Fairchild*
69/76 **Let Me Love You Where It Hurts** *Jim Ed Brown*
25/74 **Let Me Make The Bright Lights Shine For You** *Bob Luman*
29/63 **Let Me Off At The Corner** *Dottie West*
Let Me Swing ..see: (Turn Me Loose And)
71/75 **Let Me Take Care Of You** *Bobby Lewis*
53/78 **Let Me Take You In My Arms Again** *James Darren*
1/89 **Let Me Tell You About Love** *Judds*
97/79 **Let My Fingers Do The Walking** *Pat Pomsl*
98/77 **Let My Fingers Do The Walking (I'm Your Telephone Man)** *Alan Cartee*
1/77 **Let My Love Be Your Pillow** *Ronnie Milsap*
78/73 **Let My Love Shine** *Marti Brown*
1/51 **Let Old Mother Nature Have Her Way** *Carl Smith*
10/84 **Let Somebody Else Drive** *John Anderson*
4/93 **Let That Pony Run** *Pam Tillis*
86/76 **Let The Big Wheels Roll** *Sarah Johns*
4/68 **Let The Chips Fall** *Charley Pride*
74/91 **Let The Cowboy Dance** *Michael Martin Murphey*
57/74 **Let The Four Winds Blow** *Jack Reno*
59/82 **Let The Good Times Roll** *Jon And Lynn*
23/85 **Let The Heartache Ride** *Restless Heart*
58/81 **Let The Little Bird Fly** *Dottsy*
38/75 **Let The Little Boy Dream** *Even Stevens*
4/87 **Let The Music Lift You Up** *Reba McEntire*
60/94 **Let The Picture Paint Itself** *Rodney Crowell*
20/69 **Let The Whole World Sing It With Me** *Wynn Stewart*
7/68 **Let The World Keep On A Turnin'** *Buck Owens & Buddy Alan*
8/05 **Let Them Be Little** *Billy Dean*
80/82 **Let Your Fingers Do The Walkin'** *Jebry Lee Briley*
53/96 **Let Your Heart Lead Your Mind** *Smokin' Armadillos*
57/79 **Let Your Love Fall Back On Me** *David Houston*
21/76 **Let Your Love Flow** *Bellamy Brothers*
13/72 **Let's All Go Down To The River** *Jody Miller & Johnny Paycheck*
F/75 **Let's All Help The Cowboys (Sing The Blues)** *Waylon Jennings*
82/88 **Let's Be Bad Tonight** *Ronnie Rogers*
38/87 **Let's Be Fools Like That Again** *Tommy Roe*
72/78 **Let's Be Lonely Together** *Dale McBride*
4/04 **Let's Be Us Again** *Lonestar*
32/73 **Let's Build A World Together** *George Jones & Tammy Wynette*
59/01 **Let's Burn It Down** *Kristin Garner*
92/78 **Let's Call It A Day** *Leslee Barnhill*
57/90 **Let's Call It A Day Today** *Tammy Wynette*
1/84 **Let's Chase Each Other Around The Room** *Merle Haggard*
16/87 **Let's Do Something** *Vince Gill*
51/80 **Let's Do Something Cheap And Superficial** *Burt Reynolds*
26/62 **Let's End It Before It Begins** *Claude Gray*
Let's Fall Apart ..see: (All Together Now)
1/84 **Let's Fall To Pieces Together** *George Strait*
64/83 **Let's Find Each Other Tonight** *Jose Feliciano*
72/81 **Let's Forget That We're Married** *Gary Stewart*
100/77 **Let's Get Acquainted Again** *Floyd Brown*
76/82 **Let's Get Crazy Again** *Diane Pfeifer*
(Let's Get) Dixiefried ..see: Dixie Fried
6/80 **Let's Get It While The Gettin's Good** *Eddy Arnold*
10/83 **Let's Get Over Them Together** *Moe Bandy/Becky Hobbs*
12/89 **Let's Get Started If We're Gonna Break My Heart** *Statler Brothers*
65/70 **Let's Get Together** *Skeeter Davis & George Hamilton IV*
41/82 **Let's Get Together And Cry** *Joe Stampley*
6/77 **(Let's Get Together) One Last Time** *Tammy Wynette*
Let's Go All The Way
11/64 *Norma Jean*
68/82 *Claude Gray & Norma Jean*
26/74 **Let's Go All The Way Tonight** *Mel Tillis & Sherry Bryce*
67/00 **Let's Go Chase Some Women** *Michael Chain*
52/70 **Let's Go Fishin' Boys (The Girls Are Bitin')** *Charlie Walker*
100/88 **Let's Go Party** *Kathy Bee*
70/94 **Let's Go Spend Your Money Honey** *Evangeline*
68/80 **Let's Go Through The Motions** *Cates Sisters*
2/50 **Let's Go To Church (Next Sunday Morning)** *Margaret Whiting & Jimmy Wakely*
5/95 **Let's Go To Vegas** *Faith Hill*
95/78 **Let's Have A Heart To Heart Talk** *Leon Rausch*
59/74 **Let's Hear It For Loneliness** *Mundo Earwood*
17/63 **Let's Invite Them Over** *George Jones & Melba Montgomery*
Let's Keep It That Way
37/79 *Juice Newton*
10/80 *Mac Davis*

44/04 **Let's Kill Saturday Night** *Pinmonkey*
30/84 **Let's Leave The Lights On Tonight** *Johnny Rodriguez*
2/51 **Let's Live A Little** *Carl Smith*
53/84 **Let's Live This Dream Together** *Narvel Felts*
52/75 **Let's Love While We Can** *Barbara Fairchild*
61/94 **Let's Make A Baby King** *Wynonna*
6/00 **Let's Make Love** *Faith Hill w/ Tim McGraw*
20/00 **Let's Make Sure We Kiss Goodbye** *Vince Gill*
6/76 **Let's Put It Back Together Again** *Jerry Lee Lewis*
23/80 **Let's Put Our Love In Motion** *Charly McClain*
27/69 **Let's Put Our World Back Together** *Charlie Louvin*
5/49 **Let's Say Goodbye Like We Said Hello** *Ernest Tubb*
9/78 **Let's Shake Hands And Come Out Lovin'** *Kenny O'Dell*
64/83 **Let's Sing About Love** *Big Al Downing*
18/75 **Let's Sing Our Song** *Jerry Reed*
70/89 **Let's Sleep On It** *Grayghost*
92/88 **Let's Start A Rumor Today** *Bobby Durham*
55/99 **Let's Start Livin'** *Gil Grand*
1/84 **Let's Stop Talkin' About It** *Janie Fricke*
1/78 **Let's Take The Long Way Around The World** *Ronnie Milsap*
27/79 **Let's Take The Time To Fall In Love Again** *Jim Chesnut*
68/98 **Let's Talk About Love** *Mindy McCready*
77/89 **Let's Talk About Us** *Shane Barmby*
90/83 **Let's Talk It Over** *R. Dean Taylor*
9/60 **Let's Think About Living** *Bob Luman*
51/70 **Let's Think About Where We're Going** *LaWanda Lindsey & Kenny Vernon*
42/74 **Let's Truck Together** *Kenny Price*
28/79 **Let's Try Again** *Janie Fricke*
32/78 **Let's Try To Remember** *David Rogers*
71/75 **Let's Turn The Lights On** *Larry Gatlin*
51/68 **Let's Wait A Little Longer** *Canadian Sweethearts*
36/65 **Let's Walk Away Strangers** *Carl Smith*
3/76 **Letter, The** *Loretta Lynn/Conway Twitty*
Letter, The
27/79 *Sammi Smith*
76/83 *Ronnie Reno*
92/89 **Letter, The** *Michelle Lynn*
56/03 **Letter (Almost Home)** *Clint Daniels*
9/88 **Letter Home** *Forester Sisters*
10/75 **Letter That Johnny Walker Read** *Asleep At The Wheel*
Letter To Home ..see: (Love Always)
20/62 **Letter To My Heart** *Jim Reeves*
71/91 **Letter To Saddam Hussein** *Jerry Martin*
2/04 **Letters From Home** *John Michael Montgomery*
2/50 **Letters Have No Arms** *Ernest Tubb*
6/92 **Letting Go** *Suzy Bogguss*
95/77 **Letting Go** *Tony Booth*
6/77 **Liars One, Believers Zero** *Bill Anderson*
14/79 **Liberated Woman** *John Wesley Ryles*
79/89 **Libyan On A Jet Plane (Leavin' On A Jet Plane)** *Pinkard & Bowden*
78/89 **License To Steal** *Rebecca Holden*
98/77 **Lie To Me** *Larry Wren*
2/85 **Lie To You For Your Love** *Bellamy Brothers*
22/82 **Lies On Your Lips** *Cristy Lane*
23/75 **Life** *Marty Robbins*
34/71 **Life** *Elvis Presley*
4/89 **Life As We Knew It** *Kathy Mattea*
21/64 **Life Can Have Meaning** *Bobby Lord*
36/01 **Life Don't Have To Be So Hard** *Tracy Lawrence*
4/95 **Life Gets Away** *Clint Black*
Life Gits Tee-Jus Don't It
3/48 *Carson Robison*
5/48 *Tex Williams*
5/95 **Life Goes On** *Little Texas*
59/99 **Life Goes On** *James Prosser*
60/02 **Life Goes On** *LeAnn Rimes*
84/79 **Life Goes On** *Charlie Rich*
20/02 **Life Happened** *Tammy Cochran*
62/88 **Life In The City** *Pake McEntire*
64/99 **Life Is A Highway** *Chris LeDoux*
6/94 **Life #9** *Martina McBride*
15/60 **Life Of A Poor Boy** *Stonewall Jackson*
84/83 **Life Of The Party** *Carl Miller*
2/59 **Life To Go** *Stonewall Jackson*
22/59 **Life To Live** *Billie Morgan*
Life Turned Her That Way
11/67 *Mel Tillis*
1/88 *Ricky Van Shelton*
4/93 **Life's A Dance** *John Michael Montgomery*
23/65 **Life's Gone And Slipped Away** *Jerry Wallace*
1/86 **Life's Highway** *Steve Wariner*
67/75 **Life's Like Poetry** *Lefty Frizzell*
Life's Little Ups And Downs
41/69 *Charlie Rich*
4/91 *Ricky Van Shelton*
98/78 **Life's Railway To Heaven** *Patsy Cline*
37/91 **Life's Too Long (To Live Like This)** *Ricky Skaggs*
4/94 **Lifestyles Of The Not So Rich And Famous** *Tracy Byrd*
71/70 **Lift Ring, Pull Open** *Jim Ed Brown*
23/91 **Light At The End Of The Tunnel** *B.B. Watson*
5/97 **Light In Your Eyes** *LeAnn Rimes*
11/77 **Light Of A Clear Blue Morning** *Dolly Parton*
55/83 **Light Of My Life (Has Gone Out Tonight)** *Tommy St. John*
65/80 **Light Of My Life (Has Gone Out Again Tonight)** *David Wills*
99/75 **Light Of The Stable** *Emmylou Harris*
70/84 **Light Up** *J.C. Cunningham*
35/88 **Light Years** *Glen Campbell*
54/73 **Lightening The Load** *Porter Wagoner*
90/89 **Lighter Shade Of Blue** *Andi & The Brown Sisters*
49/02 **Lighthouse's Tale** *Nickel Creek*
100/77 **Lightnin' Bar Blues** *Johnny Holm*
75/80 **Lightnin' Strikin'** *Cates*
19/99 **Lightning Does The Work** *Chad Brock*
40/86 **Lights Of Albuquerque** *Jim Glaser*
88/80 **Lights Of L.A.** *Shaun Nielsen*
30/69 **Like A Bird** *George Morgan*
15/74 **Like A First Time Thing** *Ray Price*
13/67 **Like A Fool** *Dottie West*
57/90 **Like A Hurricane** *Marie*
43/68 **Like A Merry-Go-Round** *Liz Anderson*
30/93 **Like A River To The Sea** *Steve Wariner*
58/68 **Like A Rolling Stone** *Flatt & Scruggs*
34/76 **Like A Sad Song** *John Denver*
76/87 **Like An Oklahoma Morning** *Tony McGill*
14/89 **Like Father Like Son** *Lionel Cartwright*
2/83 **Like Nothing Ever Happened** *Sylvia*
4/75 **Like Old Times Again** *Ray Price*
21/80 **Like Strangers** *Gail Davies*
1/96 **Like The Rain** *Clint Black*
3/96 **Like There Ain't No Yesterday** *BlackHawk*
57/98 **Like Water Into Wine** *Patty Loveless*
4/91 **Like We Never Had A Broken Heart** *Trisha Yearwood*
58/95 **Likes Of Me** *Marty Stuart*
39/81 **Likin' Him And Lovin' You** *Kin Vassy*
17/73 **Lila** *Doyle Holly*
17/70 **Lilacs And Fire** *George Morgan*
69/73 **Lilacs In Winter** *Ronnie Dove*
58/91 **Lillies White Lies** *Martin Delray*
78/80 **Lily** *Dan Riley*
32/77 **Lily Dale** *Darrell McCall & Willie Nelson*
92/74 **Lincoln Autry** *Connie Cato*
Lincoln Park Inn ..see: (Margie's At)
1/75 **Linda On My Mind** *Conway Twitty*
25/64 **Linda With The Lonely Eyes** *George Hamilton IV*
Line In Gasoline ..see: (Who Was The Man Who Put) The
90/79 **Lines** *Jerry Fuller*
57/75 **Lion In The Winter** *Hoyt Axton w/ Linda Ronstadt*
9/95 **Lipstick Promises** *George Ducas*
Lipstick Traces
73/77 *Jimmie Peters*
88/79 *Amazing Rhythm Aces*
44/76 **Liquor, Love And Life** *Freddy Weller*
24/72 **Listen** *Tommy Cash*
32/74 **Listen** *Wayne Kemp*
15/71 **Listen Betty** *Dave Dudley*

70/73 **Listen, Spot** *Peggy Little*
4/72 **Listen To A Country Song** *Lynn Anderson*
3/82 **Listen To The Radio** *Don Williams*
64/93 **Listen To The Radio** *Kathy Mattea*
63/94 **Listen To Your Woman** *Steve Kolander*
66/95 **Listenin' To The Radio** *Chely Wright*
20/60 **Little Angel (Come Rock Me To Sleep)** *Ted Self*
3/50 **Little Angel With The Dirty Face** *Eddy Arnold*
11/68 **Little Arrows** *Leapy Lee*
18/76 **Little At A Time** *Sunday Sharpe*
49/83 **Little At A Time** *Thom Schuyler*
5/75 **Little Band Of Gold** *Sonny James*
49/99 **Little Bird** *Sherrié Austin*
8/49 **Little Bird Told Me** *Smokey Rogers*
18/88 **Little Bit Closer** *Tom Wopat*
14/82 **Little Bit Crazy** *Eddy Raven*
86/81 **Little Bit Crazy** *Amarillo*
2/88 **Little Bit In Love** *Patty Loveless*
36/70 **Little Bit Late** *Lewie Wickham*
14/68 **Little Bit Later On Down The Line** *Bobby Bare*
94/79 **Little Bit More** *Jeris Ross*
66/99 **Little Bit More Of Your Love** *Perfect Stranger*
50/81 **Little Bit Of Heaven** *Roger Bowling*
76/87 **Little Bit Of Heaven** *Ray Charles*
31/93 **Little Bit Of Her Love** *Robert Ellis Orrall*
71/96 **Little Bit Of Honey** *Baker & Myers*
Little Bit Of Lovin' (Goes A Long Long Way)
63/87 *Diamonds*
61/88 *Vicki Bird*
2/95 **Little Bit Of You** *Lee Roy Parnell*
70/79 **Little Bit Short On Love (A Little Bit Long On Tears)** *Billy Walker*
6/75 **Little Bit South Of Saskatoon** *Sonny James*
62/89 **Little Bits And Pieces** *Shelby Lynne*
67/84 **Little Bits And Pieces** *Jim Stafford*
1/96 **Little Bitty** *Alan Jackson*
68/69 **Little Bitty Nitty Gritty Dirt Town** *Roger Sovine*
Little Bitty Tear
2/62 *Burl Ives*
57/80 *Hank Cochran w/ Willie Nelson*
10/62 **Little Black Book** *Jimmy Dean*
63/97 **Little Blue Dot** *James Bonamy*
10/69 **Little Boy Sad** *Bill Phillips*
46/68 **Little Boy Soldier** *Wanda Jackson*
43/70 **Little Boy's Prayer** *Porter Wagoner*
17/66 **Little Buddy** *Claude King*
25/95 **Little By Little** *James House*
33/84 **Little By Little** *Gene Watson*
11/48 **Little Community Church** *Bill Monroe*
69/96 **Little Deuce Coupe** *Beach Boys w/ James House*
46/87 **Little Doll** *Kendalls*
53/96 **Little Drops Of My Heart** *Keith Gattis*
Little Drummer Boy
24/60 *Johnny Cash*
58/99 *Restless Heart*
46/01 *Lonestar*
20/59 **Little Dutch Girl** *George Morgan*
74/80 **Little Family Soldier** *Red Sovine*
47/91 **Little Folks** *Charlie Daniels*
13/00 **Little Gasoline** *Terri Clark*
17/80 **Little Getting Used To** *Mickey Gilley*
1/00 **Little Girl** *John Michael Montgomery*
7/90 **Little Girl** *Reba McEntire*
31/74 **Little Girl Feeling** *Barbara Fairchild*
2/73 **Little Girl Gone** *Donna Fargo*
83/80 **Little Girls Need Daddies** *Sherry Brane*
3/99 **Little Good-Byes** *SheDaisy*
1/83 **Little Good News** *Anne Murray*
6/68 **Little Green Apples** *Roger Miller*
65/69 **Little Green Apples No. 2** *Ben Colder*
29/80 **Little Ground In Texas** *Capitals*
13/60 **Little Guy Called Joe** *Stonewall Jackson*
3/62 **Little Heartache** *Eddy Arnold*
7/95 **Little Houses** *Doug Stone*
45/97 **Little In Love** *Paul Brandt*
45/76 **Little Joe** *Red Sovine*
37/70 **Little Johnny From Down The Street** *Wilburn Brothers*
54/00 **Little Left Of Center** *Randy Travis*
2/94 **Little Less Talk And A Lot More Action** *Toby Keith*
64/84 **Little Love** *Juice Newton*
56/88 **Little Maggie** *Darden Smith*
3/99 **Little Man** *Alan Jackson*
63/74 **Little Man** *Logan Smith*
73/78 **Little Man's Got The Biggest Smile In Town** *Arthur Blanch*
21/61 **Little Miss Belong To No One** *Margie Bowes*
1/95 **Little Miss Honky Tonk** *Brooks & Dunn*
2/04 **Little Moments** *Brad Paisley*
2/97 **Little More Love** *Vince Gill*
94/79 **Little More Love** *Olivia Newton-John*
22/62 **Little Music Box** *Skeeter Davis*
10/83 **Little Old Fashioned Karma** *Willie Nelson*
9/67 **Little Old Wine Drinker Me** *Robert Mitchum*
23/77 **Little Ole Dime** *Jim Reeves*
11/63 **Little Ole You** *Jim Reeves*
2/98 **Little Past Little Rock** *Lee Ann Womack*
31/66 **Little Pedro** *Carl Butler & Pearl*
30/66 **Little Pink Mack** *Kay Adams w/ Cliffie Stone*
61/97 **Little Ramona (Gone Hillbilly Nuts)** *BR5-49*
29/69 **Little Reasons** *Charlie Louvin*
3/98 **Little Red Rodeo** *Collin Raye*
1/86 **Little Rock** *Reba McEntire*
2/94 **Little Rock** *Collin Raye*
5/56 **Little Rosa** *Red Sovine & Webb Pierce*
7/87 **Little Sister** *Dwight Yoakam*
98/77 **Little Something On The Side** *Pat Garrett*
34/64 **Little South Of Memphis** *Frankie Miller*
91/78 **Little Teardrops** *Linda Cassady*
68/92 **Little Tears** *Joy White*
1/85 **Little Things** *Oak Ridge Boys*
8/91 **Little Things** *Marty Stuart*
9/97 **Little Things** *Tanya Tucker*
22/68 **Little Things** *Willie Nelson*
75/81 **Little Things** *Tennessee Express*
Little Things Mean A Lot
79/77 *Linda Cassady*
3/78 *Margo Smith*
50/67 **Little Things That Every Girl Should Know** *Claude King*
7/55 **Little Tom** *Ferlin Husky*
36/65 **Little Unfair** *Lefty Frizzell*
8/87 **Little Ways** *Dwight Yoakam*
100/76 **Little Weekend Warriors** *Bobby Penn*
7/46 **Little White Cross On The Hill** *Roy Rogers*
88/82 **Little White Lies** *David House*
65/77 **Little White Moon** *Hoyt Axton*
18/68 **Little World Girl** *George Hamilton IV*
32/76 **Littlest Cowboy Rides Again** *Ed Bruce*
62/92 **Live And Learn** *Mac McAnally*
53/01 **Live Close By, Visit Often** *K.T. Oslin*
39/79 **Live Entertainment** *Don King*
1/55 **Live Fast, Love Hard, Die Young** *Faron Young*
16/70 **Live For The Good Times** *Warner Mack*
28/63 **Live For Tomorrow** *Carl Smith*
37/01 **Live It Up** *Marshall Dyllon*
11/00 **Live, Laugh, Love** *Clay Walker*
1/04 **Live Like You Were Dying** *Tim McGraw*
60/02 **Live Those Songs** *Kenny Chesney*
58/97 **Live To Love Again** *Burnin' Daylight*
1/94 **Live Until I Die** *Clay Walker*
44/68 **Live Your Life Out Loud** *Bobby Lord*
F/57 **Livin' Alone** *Hank Locklin*
68/77 **Livin' Her Life In A Song** *Billy Mize*
Livin' In A House Full Of Love
3/65 *David Houston*
70/91 *Glen Campbell*
43/97 *Gary Allan*
93/88 **Livin' In Shadows** *Jerry Lee Tucker*
85/81 **Livin' In The Light Of Her Love** *Joe Waters*
77/75 **Livin' In The Sunshine Of Your Love** *Ray Pillow*
9/82 **Livin' In These Troubled Times** *Crystal Gayle*
28/63 **Livin' Offa Credit** *Jim Nesbitt*
1/94 **Livin' On Love** *Alan Jackson*
75/76 **Livin' On Love Street** *Shylo*
43/69 **Livin' On Lovin' (And Lovin' Livin' With You)** *Slim Whitman*
62/83 **Livin' On Memories** *Gary Wolf*
23/79 **Livin' Our Love Together** *Billie Jo Spears*
46/81 **Livin' The Good Life** *Corbin/Hanner Band*

86/81 **Livin' Together (Lovin' Apart)** *Bobby G. Rice*
56/68 **Living** *George Morgan*
9/71 **Living And Learning** *Mel Tillis & Sherry Bryce*
1/02 **Living And Living Well** *George Strait*
63/68 **Living As Strangers** *Kitty Wells & Red Foley*
1/96 **Living In A Moment** *Ty Herndon*
1/86 **Living In The Promiseland** *Willie Nelson*
2/76 **Living It Down** *Freddy Fender*
55/87 **Living Like There's No Tomorrow** *John Conlee*
88/82 **Living My Life Without You** *Lobo*
29/77 **Living Next Door To Alice** *Johnny Carver*
1/89 **Living Proof** *Ricky Van Shelton*
38/76 **Living Proof** *Hank Williams, Jr.*
71/71 **Living Tornado** *Kenni Huskey*
F/70 **Living Under Pressure** *Eddy Arnold*
91/78 **Livingston Saturday Night** *Jimmy Buffett*
7/91 **Liza Jane** *Vince Gill*
1/75 **Lizzie And The Rainman** *Tanya Tucker*
66/73 **Lizzie Lou** *Osborne Brothers*
57/84 **Lo And Behold** *Wally Fowler's Tennessee Valley Boys*
30/79 **Lo Que Sea (What Ever May The Future Be)** *Jess Garron*
44/79 **Lock, Stock, & Barrel** *Wood Newton*
Lock, Stock And Teardrops
26/63 *Roger Miller*
70/68 *Diana Trask*
53/88 *k.d. lang*
5/04 **Loco** *David Lee Murphy*
23/69 **Lodi** *Buddy Alan*
62/95 **Lola's Love** *Ricky Van Shelton*
11/76 **Lone Star Beer And Bob Wills Music** *Red Steagall*
36/87 **Lone Star State Of Mind** *Nanci Griffith*
96/74 **Loneliness (Can Break A Good Man Down)** *Norro Wilson*
56/86 **Loneliness In Lucy's Eyes** *Johnny Lee*
74/70 **Loneliness Without You** *Hagers*
18/00 **Lonely** *Tracy Lawrence*
1/67 **Lonely Again** *Eddy Arnold*
2/86 **Lonely Alone** *Forester Sisters*
5/99 **Lonely And Gone** *Montgomery Gentry*
15/83 **Lonely But Only For You** *Sissy Spacek*
86/79 **Lonely Coming Down** *Keith Bradford*
46/86 **Lonely Days, Lonely Nights** *Patty Loveless*
Lonely Eyes
39/77 *Rayburn Anthony*
61/83 *Brice Henderson*
46/76 **Lonely Eyes** *Randy Barlow*
63/70 **Lonely For You** *Wilma Burgess*
14/64 **Lonely Girl** *Carl Smith*
30/59 **Lonely Girl** *Jimmy Newman*
Lonely Heart
81/83 *Cedar Creek*
40/84 *Tammy Wynette*

68/82 **Lonely Hearts** *Younger Brothers*
18/78 **Lonely Hearts Club** *Billie Jo Spears*
40/80 **Lonely Hotel** *Don King*
53/71 **Lonely Is** *Dottie West*
18/58 **Lonely Island Pearl** *Johnnie & Jack*
23/75 **Lonely Men, Lonely Women** *Connie Eaton*
1/82 **Lonely Nights** *Mickey Gilley*
38/72 **Lonely People** *Eddy Arnold*
83/78 **Lonely People** *Keith Bradford*
80/75 **Lonely Rain** *Wynn Stewart*
16/60 **Lonely River Rhine** *Bobby Helms*
6/89 **Lonely Side Of Love** *Patty Loveless*
76/78 **Lonely Side Of The Bed** *Linda Cassady*
7/56 **Lonely Side Of Town** *Kitty Wells*
Lonely Street
84/74 *Tony Booth*
8/78 *Rex Allen, Jr.*
5/76 **Lonely Teardrops** *Narvel Felts*
18/63 **Lonely Teardrops** *Rose Maddox*
41/79 **Lonely Together** *Diana*
98/85 **Lonely Together** *A.J. Masters*
1/96 **Lonely Too Long** *Patty Loveless*
11/72 **Lonely Weekends** *Jerry Lee Lewis*
75/80 **Lonely Wine** *Maury Finney*
64/81 **Lonely Women** *Silver Creek*
Lonely Women Make Good Lovers
4/72 *Bob Luman*
4/84 *Steve Wariner*
11/98 **Lonely Won't Leave Me Alone** *Trace Adkins*
13/66 **Lonelyville** *Dave Dudley*
20/61 **Lonelyville** *Ray Sanders*
Lonesome 7-7203
1/63 *Hawkshaw Hawkins*
72/67 *Burl Ives*
16/72 *Tony Booth*
24/84 *Darrell Clanton*
62/88 **Lonesome For You** *Chris Austin*
70/76 **Lonesome Is A Cowboy** *Mundo Earwood*
2/62 **Lonesome Number One** *Don Gibson*
11/59 **Lonesome Old House** *Don Gibson*
50/03 **Lonesome, On'ry And Mean** *Travis Tritt*
54/02 **Lonesome Road** *Chalee Tennison*
21/60 **Lonesome Road Blues** *Jimmie Skinner*
11/92 **Lonesome Standard Time** *Kathy Mattea*
Lonesome Whistle
9/51 *Hank Williams*
29/71 *Don Gibson*
Lonesomest Lonesome
2/72 *Ray Price*
49/73 *Pat Daisy*
73/81 **Lonestar Cowboy** *Donna Fargo*
89/89 **Lonestar Lonesome** *Terry Stafford*
5/85 **Long And Lasting Love** *Crystal Gayle*
52/80 **Long Arm Of The Law** *Roger Bowling*
4/96 **Long As I Live** *John Michael Montgomery*

73/68 **Long Black Limousine** *Jody Miller*
13/04 **Long Black Train** *Josh Turner*
Long Black Veil
6/59 *Lefty Frizzell*
26/74 *Sammi Smith*
62/75 **Long Distance Kisses** *Larry Hosford*
59/80 **Long Drop** *Roy Head*
61/78 **Long Gone Blues** *Cates Sisters*
Long Gone Lonesome Blues
1/50 *Hank Williams*
5/64 *Hank Williams, Jr.*
63/87 *Dennis Robbins*
1/02 **Long Goodbye** *Brooks & Dunn*
27/80 **Long Haired Country Boy** *Charlie Daniels Band*
51/96 **Long Hard Lesson Learned** *John Anderson*
63/76 **Long Hard Ride** *Marshall Tucker Band*
1/84 **Long Hard Road (The Sharecropper's Dream)** *Nitty Gritty Dirt Band*
6/67 **Long-Legged Guitar Pickin' Man** *Johnny Cash & June Carter*
42/94 **Long Legged Hannah (From Butte Montana)** *Jesse Hunter*
43/80 **Long Line Of Empties** *Darrell McCall*
1/87 **Long Line Of Love** *Michael Martin Murphey*
41/70 **Long Lonesome Highway** *Michael Parks*
5/70 **Long Long Texas Road** *Roy Drusky*
74/84 **Long Lost Causes** *Rick & Janis Carnes*
16/91 **Long Lost Friend** *Restless Heart*
47/66 **Long Night** *Red Sovine*
5/89 **Long Shot** *Baillie And The Boys*
73/00 **Long Slow Beautiful Dance** *Rascal Flatts*
17/05 **Long, Slow Kisses** *Jeff Bates*
69/96 **Long Tall Texan** *Beach Boys w/ Doug Supernaw*
10/92 **Long Time Ago** *Remingtons*
16/59 **Long Time Ago** *Faron Young*
71/89 **Long Time Comin'** *Eddie Preston*
Long Time Gone
5/46 *Tex Ritter*
2/02 *Dixie Chicks*
15/66 **Long Time Gone** *Dave Dudley*
55/97 **Long Trail Of Tears** *George Ducas*
11/60 **Long Walk** *Bill Leatherwood*
35/89 **Long White Cadillac** *Dwight Yoakam*
85/80 **Longer** *Dan Fogelberg*
35/69 **Longest Beer Of The Night** *Jim Ed Brown*
33/78 **Longest Walk** *Mary K. Miller*
17/76 **Longhaired Redneck** *David Allan Coe*
24/81 **Longing For The High** *Billy Larkin*
1/97 **Longneck Bottle** *Garth Brooks*
91/89 **Longneck Lone Star (And Two Step Dancin')** *Diana Sicily Currey*
75/67 **Longtime Traveling** *Buddy Cagle*
49/00 **Look, The** *Jerry Kilgore*
24/95 **Look At Me Now** *Bryan White*

30/02 **Look At Me Now** *Sixwire*
21/70 **Look At Mine** *Jody Miller*
59/68 **Look At The Laughter** *Wilma Burgess*
17/75 **Look At Them Beans** *Johnny Cash*
4/92 **Look At Us** *Vince Gill*
27/04 **Look At Us** *Craig Morgan*
52/93 **Look At You Girl** *Chris LeDoux*
1/93 **Look Heart, No Hands** *Randy Travis*
65/70 **Look How Far We've Come** *Bill Wilbourne & Kathy Morrison*
36/66 **Look Into My Teardrops** *Conway Twitty*
69/86 **Look Of A Lady In Love** *Johnny Duncan*
68/84 **Look Of A Lovin' Lady** *Wyvon Alexander*
11/95 **Look What Followed Me Home** *David Ball*
73/97 **Look What Love Can Do** *Ruby Lovett*
83/85 **Look What Love Did To Me** *Kenny Dale*
4/51 **Look What Thoughts Will Do** *Lefty Frizzell*
56/89 **Look What We Made (When We Made Love)** *Jonathan Edwards*
21/77 **Look Who I'm Cheating On Tonight** *Bobby Bare*
8/58 **Look Who's Blue** *Don Gibson*
65/93 **Look Who's Needing Who** *Clinton Gregory*
4/44 **Look Who's Talkin'** *Ted Daffan*
72/81 **(Lookin' At Things) In A Different Light** *Nightstreets*
F/77 **Lookin' For A Feeling** *Waylon Jennings*
Lookin' For Love
1/80 *Johnny Lee*
44/01 *Sawyer Brown*
16/76 **Lookin' For Tomorrow (And Findin' Yesterdays)** *Mel Tillis*
55/94 **Lookin' In The Same Direction** *Ken Mellons*
37/71 **Lookin' Out My Back Door** *Buddy Alan*
5/68 **Looking At The World Through A Windshield** *Del Reeves*
51/74 **Looking Back** *Jerry Foster*
Looking Back To See
4/54 *Goldie Hill - Justin Tubb*
8/54 *Browns*
13/72 *Buck Owens & Susan Raye*
7/64 **Looking For More In '64** *Jim Nesbitt*
30/76 **Looking For Space** *John Denver*
70/86 **Looking For Suzanne** *Osmond Bros.*
43/95 **Looking For The Light** *Rick Trevino*
82/79 **Looking For The Sunshine** *Mickey Newbury*
59/87 **Looking For You** *Rodney Crowell*
11/93 **Looking Out For Number One** *Travis Tritt*
24/76 **Looking Out My Window Through The Pain** *Mel Street*
35/90 **Looks Aren't Everything** *Mark Collie*
80/81 **Looks Like A Set-Up To Me** *Cedar Creek*
23/63 **Loose Lips** *Earl Scott*
Loose Talk
1/55 *Carl Smith*
4/61 *Buck Owens & Rose Maddox*
12/98 **Loosen Up My Strings** *Clint Black*
7/91 **Lord Have Mercy On A Country Boy** *Don Williams*
5/92 **Lord Have Mercy On The Working Man** *Travis Tritt*
58/74 **Lord How Long Has This Been Going On** *Doyle Holly*
1/82 **Lord, I Hope This Day Is Good** *Don Williams*
71/77 **Lord, If I Make It To Heaven Can I Bring My Own Angel Along** *Billy Parker*
16/70 **Lord Is That Me** *Jack Greene*
1/73 **Lord Knows I'm Drinking** *Cal Smith*
36/04 **Lord Loves The Drinkin' Man** *Mark Chesnutt*
1/73 **Lord, Mr. Ford** *Jerry Reed*
62/79 **Lorelei** *Sonny James*
7/50 **Lose Your Blues** *Red Kirk*
28/78 **Loser, The** *Kenny Dale*
63/68 **Loser Making Good** *Red Sovine*
3/67 **Loser's Cathedral** *David Houston*
36/71 **Loser's Cocktail** *Dick Curless*
90/78 **Loser's Just A Learner (On His Way To Better Things)** *Roger Bowling*
37/81 **Loser's Night Out** *Jack Grayson & Blackjack*
90/81 **Losin' Myself In You** *Gary Goodnight*
74/67 **Losing Kind** *Bobby Barnett*
14/80 **Losing Kind Of Love** *Lacy J. Dalton*
66/88 **Losing Somebody You Love** *Rick Snyder*
2/62 **Losing Your Love** *Jim Reeves*
46/95 **Losing Your Love** *Larry Stewart*
6/92 **Lost And Found** *Brooks & Dunn*
9/72 **Lost Forever In Your Kiss** *Porter Wagoner & Dolly Parton*
Lost Highway
12/49 *Hank Williams*
51/67 *Don Gibson*
100/88 *James Storie*
Lost His [Her] Love On Our Last Date ..see: Last Date
45/80 **Lost In Austin** *Freddy Weller*
84/88 **Lost In Austin** *Kenny Blair*
30/81 **Lost In Love** *Dickey Lee/Kathy Burdick*
Lost In The Feeling
2/83 *Conway Twitty*
59/00 *Mark Chesnutt*
1/85 **Lost In The Fifties Tonight (In The Still Of The Night)** *Ronnie Milsap*
22/65 **Lost In The Shuffle** *Stonewall Jackson*
62/99 **Lost In You** *Garth Brooks As Chris Gaines*
43/71 **Lost It On The Road** *Carl Smith*
11/48 **Lost John Boogie** *Wayne Raney*
73/80 **Lost Love Affair** *B.J. Wright*
5/83 **Lost My Baby Blues** *David Frizzell*
76/80 **Lost The Good Thing** *Steve Gillette w/ Jennifer Warnes*
15/58 **Lost To A Geisha Girl** *Skeeter Davis*
3/05 **Lot Of Leavin' Left To Do** *Dierks Bentley*
6/03 **Lot Of Things Different** *Kenny Chesney*
72/83 **Louisiana Anna** *Maines Brothers Band*
82/84 **Louisiana Heatwave** *Bobby Jenkins*
F/81 **Louisiana Joe** *Joe Douglas*
67/81 **Louisiana Lonely** *Narvel Felts*
Louisiana Man
10/61 *Rusty & Doug*
25/65 *George Jones & Gene Pitney*
72/68 *Bobbie Gentry*
14/70 *Connie Smith*
60/04 **Louisiana Melody** *David Ball*
20/88 **Louisiana Rain** *John Wesley Ryles*
7/81 **Louisiana Saturday Night** *Mel McDaniel*
24/67 **Louisiana Saturday Night** *Jimmy Newman*
1/73 **Louisiana Woman, Mississippi Man** *Loretta Lynn/Conway Twitty*
23/68 **Louisville** *Leroy Van Dyke*
75/90 **Louisville** *Jann Browne*
73/68 **Lovable Fool** *Goldie Hill Smith*
2/94 **Love A Little Stronger** *Diamond Rio*
11/83 **Love Affairs** *Michael Murphey*
71/97 **Love Ain't Easy** *Big House*
24/79 **Love Ain't Gonna Wait For Us** *Billie Jo Spears*
12/99 **Love Ain't Like That** *Faith Hill*
Love Ain't Made For Fools
33/79 *John Wesley Ryles*
66/88 *Kevin Pearce*
38/70 **Love Ain't Never Gonna Be No Better** *Webb Pierce*
19/81 **Love Ain't Never Hurt Nobody** *Bobby Goldsboro*
51/73 **Love Ain't Worth a Dime Unless It's Free** *Wynn Stewart*
14/85 **(Love Always) Letter To Home** *Glen Campbell*
80/78 **Love And Hate** *Mike Boyd*
70/73 **Love And Honor** *Kenny Serratt*
72/84 **Love And Let Love** *Danny Shirley*
54/94 **Love And Luck** *Marty Stuart*
73/88 **Love And Other Fairy Tales** *Girls Next Door*
3/86 **Love At The Five & Dime** *Kathy Mattea*
Love Bug
6/65 *George Jones*
8/94 *George Strait*
72/00 **Love Bug (Bite Me)** *South Sixty Five*
12/58 **Love Bug Crawl** *Jimmy Edwards*
28/82 **Love Busted** *Billy "Crash" Craddock*
99/73 **Love By Appointment** *Pati Powell & Bob Gallion*
5/91 **Love Can Build A Bridge** *Judds*
82/78 **Love Can Make The Children Sing** *Billy Stack*
90/81 **Love (Can Make You Happy)** *James Marvell*

10/87 **Love Can't Ever Get Better Than This** *Ricky Skaggs & Sharon White*
12/62 **Love Can't Wait** *Marty Robbins*
39/03 **Love Changes Everything** *Aaron Lines*
44/69 **Love Comes But Once In A Lifetime** *Norro Wilson*
34/80 **Love Crazy Love** *Zella Lehr*
58/94 **Love Didn't Do It** *Linda Davis*
13/81 **Love Dies Hard** *Randy Barlow*
86/77 **Love Doesn't Live Here Anymore** *Randy Cornor*
91/79 **Love Don't Care** *Charlie Louvin w/ Emmylou Harris*
1/85 **Love Don't Care (Whose Heart It Breaks)** *Earl Thomas Conley*
55/86 **Love Don't Come Any Better Than This** *Shelly West*
93/78 **Love Don't Hide From Me** *Hugh X. Lewis*
59/83 **Love Don't Know A Lady (From A Honky Tonk Girl)** *Billy Parker*
80/81 **Love Fires** *Don Gibson*
1/97 **Love Gets Me Every Time** *Shania Twain*
62/80 **Love Goes To Hell When It Dies** *Wayne Kemp*
73/85 **Love Gone Bad** *Jay Clark*
23/78 **Love Got In The Way** *Freddy Weller*
29/98 **Love Happens Like That** *Neal McCoy*
12/57 **Love Has Finally Come My Way** *Faron Young*
90/83 **Love Has Made A Woman Out Of You** *Vince & Dianne Hatfield*
10/60 **Love Has Made You Beautiful** *Merle Kilgore*
4/89 **Love Has No Right** *Billy Joe Royal*
26/80 **Love Has Taken Its' Time** *Zella Lehr*
3/88 **Love Helps Those** *Paul Overstreet*
19/70 **Love Hungry** *Warner Mack*
72/69 **Love, I Finally Found It** *Ernie Ashworth*
53/77 **Love I Need You** *Dale McBride*
98/78 **Love In Me** *Jim Norman*
70/89 **Love In Motion** *Ross Lewis*
63/73 **Love In The Back Seat** *Little David Wilkins*
1/81 **Love In The First Degree** *Alabama*
65/88 **Love In The Heart** *Don McLean*
3/75 **Love In The Hot Afternoon** *Gene Watson*
32/80 **Love In The Meantime** *Streets*
61/80 **Love Insurance** *Louise Mandrell*
39/82 **Love Is** *Allen Tripp*
85/82 **Love Is A Full Time Thing** *Terry McMillan*
58/02 **Love Is A Game** *Dean Miller*
69/69 **Love Is A Gentle Thing** *Barbara Fairchild*
12/72 **Love Is A Good Thing** *Johnny Paycheck*
67/89 **Love Is A Hard Road** *Irene Kelly*
64/89 **Love Is A Liar** *Cee Cee Chapman*
5/75 **Love Is A Rose** *Linda Ronstadt*
5/70 **Love Is A Sometimes Thing** *Bill Anderson*
68/76 **Love Is A Two-Way Street** *Dottsy*
42/80 **Love Is A Warm Cowboy** *Buck Owens*
Love Is A Word
88/76 *Juice Newton & Silver Spur*
27/78 *Dickey Lee*
1/85 **Love Is Alive** *Judds*
29/80 **Love Is All Around** *Sonny Curtis*
51/98 **Love Is All That Really Matters** *Kevin Sharp*
91/85 **Love Is An Overload** *Bobby Lewis*
51/68 **Love Is Ending** *Liz Anderson*
43/01 **Love Is Enough** *3 Of Hearts*
60/87 **Love Is Everywhere** *Mel McDaniel*
13/81 **Love Is Fair** *Barbara Mandrell*
53/99 **Love Is For Giving** *John Berry*
46/74 **Love Is Here** *Wilma Burgess*
84/79 **Love Is Hours In The Making** *Sterling Whipple*
10/68 **Love Is In The Air** *Marty Robbins*
3/77 **Love Is Just A Game** *Larry Gatlin*
57/69 **Love Is Just A State Of Mind** *Roy Clark*
44/81 **Love Is Knockin' At My Door** *Susie Allanson*
1/74 **Love Is Like A Butterfly** *Dolly Parton*
36/72 **Love Is Like A Spinning Wheel** *Jan Howard*
7/64 **Love Is No Excuse** *Jim Reeves & Dottie West*
53/95 **Love Is Not A Thing** *Russ Taff*
1/83 **Love Is On A Roll** *Don Williams*
47/89 **Love Is On The Line** *Canyon*
56/89 **Love Is One Of Those Words** *Janie Frickie*
47/76 **Love Is Only Love (When Shared By Two)** *Johnny Carver*
26/79 **Love Is Sometimes Easy** *Sandy Posey*
Love Is Strange
20/75 *Buck Owens & Susan Raye*
21/90 *Kenny Rogers & Dolly Parton*
9/96 **Love Is Stronger Than Pride** *Ricochet*
1/73 **Love Is The Foundation** *Loretta Lynn*
8/73 **Love Is The Look You're Looking For** *Connie Smith*
53/86 **Love Is The Only Way Out** *William Lee Golden*
68/84 **Love Is The Reason** *Sierra*
4/97 **Love Is The Right Place** *Bryan White*
24/76 **Love Is Thin Ice** *Barbara Mandrell*
37/85 **Love Is What We Make It** *Kenny Rogers*
69/84 **Love Isn't Love ('Til You Give It Away)** *Tari Hensley*
Love Isn't Love (Till You Give It Away)
52/72 *Bobby Lee Trammell*
93/76 *Eddie Bailes*
87/79 *Joy Ford*
30/76 **Love It Away** *Mary Lou Turner*
78/85 **Love, It's The Pits** *Lisa Angelle*
54/86 **Love Keep Your Distance** *A.J. Masters*
40/81 **Love Knows We Tried** *Tanya Tucker*
9/95 **Love Lessons** *Tracy Byrd*
67/90 **Love Letter** *Robin Lee*
Love Letters
57/77 *Debi Hawkins*
69/83 *Hazard*
79/86 **Love Letters In The Sand** *Tom T. Hall*
33/79 **Love Lies** *Mel McDaniel*
19/76 **Love Lifted Me** *Kenny Rogers*
52/92 **Love Light** *Cleve Francis*
58/00 **Love Like That** *Ty Herndon*
35/03 **Love Like There's No Tomorrow** *Aaron Tippin w/ Thea Tippin*
70/95 **Love Like This** *Carlene Carter*
29/80 **Love, Look At Us Now** *Johnny Rodriguez*
17/64 **Love Looks Good On You** *David Houston*
41/65 **Love Looks Good On You** *Lefty Frizzell*
1/55 **Love, Love, Love** *Webb Pierce*
26/78 **Love, Love, Love/Chapel Of Love** *Sandy Posey*
34/67 **Love Makes The World Go Around** *Kitty Wells*
1/92 **Love, Me** *Collin Raye*
Love Me
34/72 *Jeanne Pruett*
9/73 *Marty Robbins*
58/83 *Jeanne Pruett/Marty Robbins*
10/56 **Love Me** *Elvis Presley*
75/99 **Love Me A Little Bit Longer** *Heather Myles*
83/78 **Love Me Again** *Rita Coolidge*
80/86 **Love Me All Over** *Sammi Smith*
12/67 **Love Me And Make It All Better** *Bobby Lewis*
91/79 **Love Me Back To Sleep** *Jessi Colter*
79/89 **Love Me Down To Size** *Ray Price*
97/77 **Love Me Into Heaven Again** *DeWayne Orender*
24/79 **Love Me Like A Stranger** *Cliff Cochran*
2/87 **Love Me Like You Used To** *Tanya Tucker*
14/68 **Love Me, Love Me** *Bobby Barnett*
26/79 **Love Me Now** *Ronnie McDowell*
61/67 **Love Me Now (While I Am Living)** *Anita Carter*
1/80 **Love Me Over Again** *Don Williams*
Love Me Tender
3/56 *Elvis Presley*
59/79 *Linda Ronstadt*
14/57 **Love Me To Pieces** *Rusty & Doug*
87/82 **Love Me Today, Love Me Forever** *J.W. Gunn*
Love Me Tonight ..see: (Turn Out The Light And)
F/78 **Love Me When You Can** *Merle Haggard*
7/78 **Love Me With All Your Heart** *Johnny Rodriguez*
Love My Life Away ..see: (I Wanna)
42/82 **Love Never Comes Easy** *Helen Cornelius*
51/82 **Love Never Dies** *Gary Wolf*
54/81 **Love Never Hurt So Good** *Donna Hazard*
4/88 **Love Of A Lifetime** *Gatlin Bros.*
2/01 **Love Of A Woman** *Travis Tritt*
68/68 **Love Of A Woman** *Claude Gray*

2/98 **Love Of My Life** *Sammy Kershaw*
67/67 **Love Of The Common People** *Waylon Jennings*
23/61 **Love Oh Love, Oh Please Come Home** *Reno & Smiley*
74/86 **Love On A Blue Rainy Day** *Charley Pride*
1/90 **Love On Arrival** *Dan Seals*
31/71 **Love On Broadway** *Jerry Lee Lewis*
3/93 **Love On The Loose, Heart On The Run** *McBride & The Ride*
1/78 **Love Or Something Like It** *Kenny Rogers*
1/89 **Love Out Loud** *Earl Thomas Conley*
36/84 **Love Over Old Times** *Sylvia*
1/75 **Love Put A Song In My Heart** *Johnny Rodriguez*
12/96 **Love Remains** *Collin Raye*
6/87 **Love Reunited** *Desert Rose Band*
11/76 **Love Revival** *Mel Tillis*
30/00 **Love She Can't Live Without** *Clint Black*
Love She Found In Me
5/83 *Gary Morris*
87/89 *Hal Gibson*
81/81 **Love Signs** *Ivory Jack*
57/78 **Love Somebody To Death** *Ed Bruce*
2/87 **Love Someone Like Me** *Holly Dunn*
1/83 **Love Song** *Oak Ridge Boys*
3/82 **Love Song** *Kenny Rogers*
5/74 **Love Song** *Anne Murray*
8/03 **Love Song** *Jeff Bates*
40/80 **Love Song** *Dave Rowland & Sugar*
96/75 **Love Song** *Sherry Bryce*
51/79 **Love Song And The Dream Belong To Me** *Peggy Sue*
40/68 **Love Song For You** *Hank Locklin*
8/50 **Love Song In 32 Bars** *Johnny Bond*
10/52 **Love Song Of The Waterfall** *Slim Whitman*
99/77 **Love Song Sing Along** *Darrell Dodson*
51/77 **Love Songs And Romance Magazines** *Nick Nixon*
27/79 **Love Songs Just For You** *Glenn Barber*
51/76 **Love Still Makes The World Go 'Round** *Stoney Edwards*
Love Story ..see: Theme From
33/96 **Love Story In The Making** *Linda Davis*
17/73 **Love Sure Feels Good In My Heart** *Susan Raye*
45/78 **Love Survived** *Roy Head*
48/82 **Love Take It Easy On Me** *LaCosta Tucker*
58/71 **Love Takes A Lot Of My Time** *Skeeter Davis*
4/68 **Love Takes Care Of Me** *Jack Greene*
63/81 **Love Takes Two** *Roy Clark*
76/80 **Love Talking** *Tammy Jo*
9/85 **Love Talks** *Ronnie McDowell*
91/79 **Love Talks** *Dawn Chastain*
41/96 **Love That We Lost** *Chely Wright*

96/83 **Love The One You're With** *Brentwood*
4/80 **Love The World Away** *Kenny Rogers*
Love Theme From The Sandpiper ..see: Shadow Of Your Smile
72/96 **Love To Burn** *Mark Collie*
21/81 **Love To Love You** *Cristy Lane*
39/97 **Love Travels** *Kathy Mattea*
36/99 **Love Trip** *Jerry Kilgore*
30/82 **Love Was Born** *Randy Barlow*
39/76 **Love Was (Once Around The Dance Floor)** *Linda Hargrove*
67/76 **Love Was The Wind** *Melba Montgomery*
87/82 **Love Wheel** *Calamity Jane*
7/89 **Love Will** *Forester Sisters*
12/91 **Love Will Bring Her Around** *Rob Crosby*
79/73 **Love Will Come Again** *Bobby Mack*
1/88 **Love Will Find Its Way To You** *Reba McEntire*
14/86 **Love Will Get You Through Times With No Money** *Girls Next Door*
84/89 **Love Will Never Be The Same** *Reno Brothers*
69/87 **Love Will Never Slip Away** *Suzy Bogguss*
97/73 **Love Will Stand** *Lois Johnson*
52/02 **Love, Will (The Package)** *Tim Rushlow*
1/82 **Love Will Turn You Around** *Kenny Rogers*
1/90 **Love Without End, Amen** *George Strait*
8/93 **Love Without Mercy** *Lee Roy Parnell*
31/03 **Love Won't Let Me** *Tammy Cochran*
36/86 **Love Won't Wait** *Whites*
14/98 **Love Working On You** *John Michael Montgomery*
49/96 **Love Worth Fighting For** *Burnin' Daylight*
88/79 **Love Wouldn't Leave Us Alone** *Bill Woody*
Love, You Ain't Seen The Last Of Me
6/87 *John Schneider*
44/00 *Tracy Byrd*
67/76 **Love You All To Pieces** *Billy Walker*
38/96 **Love You Back** *Rhett Akins*
64/75 **Love You Back To Georgia** *Freddy Weller*
3/03 **Love You Out Loud** *Rascal Flatts*
86/76 **Love, You're The Teacher** *Linda Hargrove*
73/87 **Love'll Come Lookin' For You** *Cannons*
30/82 **Love's Been A Little Bit Hard On Me** *Juice Newton*
25/68 **Love's Dead End** *Bill Phillips*
12/77 **Love's Explosion** *Margo Smith*
13/82 **Love's Found You And Me** *Ed Bruce*
8/82 **Love's Gonna Fall Here Tonight** *Razzy Bailey*
4/86 **Love's Gonna Get You Someday** *Ricky Skaggs*

7/68 **Love's Gonna Happen To Me** *Wynn Stewart*
1/63 **Love's Gonna Live Here** *Buck Owens*
(Love's Got A Hold On Me) ..see: Rainbow In Your Eyes
1/92 **Love's Got A Hold On You** *Alan Jackson*
27/03 **Love's Got An Attitude (It Is What It Is)** *Amy Dalley*
50/88 **Love's Last Stand** *Donna Meade*
28/71 **Love's Old Song** *Barbara Fairchild*
Love's Slippin' Up On Me
74/87 *Kim Grayson*
83/88 *Lynne Tyndall*
79/80 **Love's Slipping Through Our Fingers** *Billy Walker & Barbara Fairchild*
25/66 **Love's Something (I Can't Understand)** *Webb Pierce*
5/73 **Love's The Answer** *Tanya Tucker*
3/00 **Love's The Only House** *Martina McBride*
Lovebug ..see: Love Bug
2/50 **Lovebug Itch** *Eddy Arnold*
2/97 **Loved Too Much** *Ty Herndon*
56/72 **Loveliest Night Of The Year** *Slim Whitman*
55/74 **Lovely Lady** *Murry Kellum*
65/80 **Lovely Lonely Lady** *R.C. Bannon*
6/60 **Lovely Work Of Art** *Jimmy Newman*
12/71 **Lovenworth** *Roy Rogers*
71/83 **Lover In Disguise** *Wayne Massey*
43/92 **Lover Not A Fighter** *B.B. Watson*
70/87 **(Lover Of The) Other Side Of The Hill** *Rusty Wier*
46/71 **Lover Please** *Bobby G. Rice*
70/82 **Lover (Right Where I Want You)** *Tom Carlile*
95/87 **Lover To Lover** *Stenmark-Mueller Band*
Lover's Leap ..see: (Doin' The)
Lover's Quarrel ..see: (I Just Had A Date)
Lover's Question
14/70 *Del Reeves*
3/78 *Jacky Ward*
39/70 **Lover's Song** *Ned Miller*
65/68 **Lovers, The** *Bill Wilbourne & Kathy Morrison*
55/83 **Lovers Again** *Brice Henderson*
3/80 **Lovers Live Longer** *Bellamy Brothers*
83/81 **Lovers Love** *Thrasher Brothers*
48/83 **Lovers On The Rebound** *James & Michael Younger*
Lovesick Blues
1/49 *Hank Williams*
14/49 *Red Kirk*
15/57 *Sonny James*
78/75 *Sonny Curtis*
97/78 *Jim Owen*
24/92 *George Strait*
Lovin' ..also see: Loving
37/80 **Lovin' A Livin' Dream** *Ronnie McDowell*
Lovin' All Night
10/92 *Rodney Crowell*
18/03 *Patty Loveless*
76/74 **Lovin' Comes Easy** *Jack Lebsock*

Lovin' Her Was Easier (Than Anything I'll Ever Do Again)
28/71 *Roger Miller*
2/81 *Tompall/Glaser Brothers*
8/66 **Lovin' Machine** *Johnny Paycheck*
Lovin' Man ..see: Oh Pretty Woman
83/81 **Lovin' Night** *Jim West*
96/73 **Lovin' Of Your Life** *Penny DeHaven*
Lovin' On
20/77 *T.G. Sheppard*
16/79 *Bellamy Brothers*
5/73 **Lovin' On Back Streets** *Mel Street*
11/74 **Lovin' On Borrowed Time** *Mel Street*
1/89 **Lovin' Only Me** *Ricky Skaggs*
84/82 **Lovin' Our Lives Away** *Dave Rowland*
52/69 **Lovin' Season** *Bill Wilbourn & Kathy Morrison*
23/76 **Lovin' Somebody On A Rainy Night** *La Costa*
39/73 **Lovin' Someone On My Mind** *Bobby Wright*
27/79 **Lovin' Starts Where Friendship Ends** *Mel McDaniel*
30/87 **Lovin' That Crazy Feelin'** *Ronnie McDowell*
67/87 **Lovin' The Blue** *Lynne Tyndall*
Lovin' Up A Storm ..see: Loving Up
7/81 **Lovin' What Your Lovin' Does To Me** *Conway Twitty & Loretta Lynn*
Lovin' You ..see: Loving You
34/00 **Lovin' You Against My Will** *Gary Allan*
34/78 **Lovin' You Baby** *Connie Smith*
92/80 **Lovin' You Is Music To My Mind** *Rex Gosdin*
40/74 **Lovin' You Is Worth It** *David Houston & Barbara Mandrell*
88/80 **Lovin' You Lightly** *Bonnie Shannon*
Lovin' You, Lovin' Me
73/77 *Sonny Throckmorton*
88/79 *Connie Smith*
39/78 **Lovin' You Off My Mind** *Cates Sisters*
62/68 **Lovin' You (The Way I Do)** *Hank Locklin*
Loving Arms
98/74 *Kris Kristofferson & Rita Coolidge*
19/77 *Sammi Smith*
8/81 *Elvis Presley*
94/88 *Livingston Taylor/Leah Kunkel*
14/63 **Loving Arms** *Carl Butler & Pearl*
1/91 **Loving Blind** *Clint Black*
18/01 **Loving Every Minute** *Mark Wills*
27/73 **Loving Gift** *Johnny Cash & June Carter Cash*
38/78 **Loving Here And Living There And Lying In Between** *Faron Young*
37/85 **Lovin' Up A Storm** *Bandana*
1/80 **Loving Up A Storm** *Razzy Bailey*
15/57 **Loving You** *Elvis Presley*
41/73 **Loving You** *Tony Booth*
26/75 **Loving You Beats All I've Ever Seen** *Johnny Paycheck*
2/72 **Loving You Could Never Be Better** *George Jones*
9/74 **Loving You Has Changed My Life** *David Rogers*
32/83 **Loving You Hurts** *Gus Hardin*
31/79 **Loving You Is A Natural High** *Larry G. Hudson*
73/82 **Loving You Is Always On My Mind** *Terry Dale*
33/71 **(Loving You Is) Sunshine** *Barbara Fairchild*
22/65 **Loving You Then Losing You** *Webb Pierce*
79/81 **Loving You Was All I Ever Needed** *Lou Hobbs*
7/61 **Loving You (Was Worth This Broken Heart)** *Bob Gallion*
6/75 **Loving You Will Never Grow Old** *Lois Johnson*
89/77 **Low Class Reunion** *George Kent*
31/79 **Low Dog Blues** *John Anderson*
Low Down Time
98/77 *Durwood Haddock*
96/79 *Durwood Haddock*
73/89 **Lower On The Hog** *John Anderson*
1/77 **Lucille** *Kenny Rogers*
1/83 **Lucille (You Won't Do Your Daddy's Will)** *Waylon Jennings*
67/72 **Lucius Grinder** *Ray Sanders*
1/77 **Luckenbach, Texas (Back to the Basics of Love)** *Waylon Jennings*
46/02 **Luckiest Man In The World** *Neal McCoy*
11/01 **Lucky 4 You (Tonight I'm Just Me)** *SheDaisy*
21/74 **Lucky Arms** *Lefty Frizzell*
34/97 **Lucky In Love** *Sherrié Austin*
11/74 **Lucky Ladies** *Jeannie Seely*
9/80 **Lucky Me** *Anne Murray*
35/97 **Lucky Me, Lucky You** *Lee Roy Parnell*
6/91 **Lucky Moon** *Oak Ridge Boys*
46/03 **Lucky One** *Alison Krauss*
62/72 **Lucy** *Eddy Arnold*
49/82 **Lucy And The Stranger** *Bobby Goldsboro*
5/64 **Lumberjack, The** *Hal Willis*
87/77 **Lunch Time Lovers** *Robb Redmond*
Lust Affair ..see: (This Ain't Just Another)
69/84 **Luther** *Boxcar Willie*
8/59 **Luther Played The Boogie** *Johnny Cash*
42/70 **Luziana River** *Van Trevor*
24/68 **Luzianna** *Webb Pierce*
53/83 **Lyin', Cheatin', Woman Chasin', Honky Tonkin', Whiskey Drinkin' You** *Loretta Lynn*
8/75 **Lyin' Eyes** *Eagles*
81/87 **Lyin' Eyes** *Sarah*
97/75 **Lyin' In Her Arms Again** *Dorsey Burnette*
5/88 **Lyin' In His Arms Again** *Forester Sisters*
27/61 **Lying Again** *Freddie Hart*
62/83 **Lying Here Lying** *Mac Davis*
2/79 **Lying In Love With You** *Jim Ed Brown/Helen Cornelius*
70/75 **Lying In My Arms** *Rex Allen, Jr.*
6/80 **Lying Time Again** *Mel Tillis*
1/87 **Lynda** *Steve Wariner*

M

28/67 **Mabel** *Skeets McDonald*
48/67 **Mabel (You Have Been A Friend To Me)** *Billy Grammer*
Mabellene
9/55 *Marty Robbins*
7/79 *George Jones & Johnny Paycheck*
23/69 **MacArthur Park** *Waylon Jennings*
43/76 **MacArthur's Hand** *Cal Smith*
70/96 **Macarena** *GrooveGrass Boyz*
82/88 **Macon Georgia Love** *Billy Mata*
69/84 **Macon Love** *David Wills*
6/64 **Mad** *Dave Dudley*
72/87 **Mad Money** *George Highfill*
6/93 **Made For Lovin' You** *Doug Stone*
1/72 **Made In Japan** *Buck Owens*
Made In The U.S.A.
78/80 *Ivory Jack*
40/82 *Wright Bros.*
85/82 *Four Guys*
11/84 **Maggie's Dream** *Don Williams*
56/81 **Magic Eyes** *Jack Grayson & Blackjack*
39/71 **Magnificent Sanctuary Band** *Roy Clark*
84/76 **Mahogany Bridge** *David Rogers*
55/71 **Mahogany Pulpit** *Dickey Lee*
10/71 **Maiden's Prayer** *David Houston*
84/76 **Maiden's Prayer** *Maury Finney*
5/55 **Mainliner (The Hawk With Silver Wings)** *Hank Snow*
10/85 **Major Moves** *Hank Williams, Jr.*
36/67 **Make A Left And Then A Right** *Johnny & Jonie Mosby*
77/80 **Make A Little Magic** *Dirt Band*
61/87 **Make A Living Out Of Loving You** *Razorback*
86/79 **Make Believe It's Your First Time** *Bobby Vinton*
6/55 **Make Believe ('Til We Can Make It Come True)** *Kitty Wells & Red Foley*
69/79 **Make Believe You Love Me** *Rebecca Lynn*
96/75 **Make It Easy On Yourself** *Tommy Jennings*
30/74 **Make It Feel Like Love Again** *Bobby G. Rice*
40/69 **Make It Rain** *Billy Mize*
57/79 **Make Love To Me** *Cates Sisters*
F/58 **Make Me A Miracle** *Jimmie Rodgers*
91/81 **Make Me Believe** *Gary Goodnight*
55/87 **Make Me Late For Work Today** *Ronnie McDowell*
57/04 **Make Me Stay Or Make Me Go** *Jessi Alexander*
37/71 **Make Me Your Kind Of Woman** *Patti Page*
90/79 **Make Me Your Woman** *Brenda Kaye Perry*
35/80 **Make Mine Night Time** *Bill Anderson*
12/84 **Make My Day** *T.G. Sheppard w/ Clint Eastwood*

1/85 **Make My Life With You** *Oak Ridge Boys*
1/87 **Make No Mistake, She's Mine** *Ronnie Milsap & Kenny Rogers*
2/46 **Make Room In Your Heart For A Friend** *Wiley & Gene*
30/60 **Make The Waterwheel Roll** *Carl Smith*
Make The World Go Away
2/63 *Ray Price*
1/65 *Eddy Arnold*
71/75 *Donny & Marie Osmond*
73/77 *Charly McClain*
55/85 **Make-Up And Faded Blue Jeans** *Merle Haggard*
19/99 **Make Up In Love** *Doug Stone*
4/96 **Maker Said Take Her** *Alabama*
67/80 **Makes Me Wonder If I Ever Said Goodbye** *Kin Vassy*
Makin' Believe ..see: Making
62/73 **Makin' Heartaches** *George Morgan*
61/75 **Makin' Love** *Ronnie Sessions*
35/76 **Makin' Love Don't Always Make Love Grow** *Dickey Lee*
72/79 **Makin' Love (Is A Beautiful Thing To Do)** *Paul Schmucker*
11/74 **Makin' The Best Of A Bad Situation** *Dick Feller*
1/86 **Makin' Up For Lost Time (The Dallas Lovers' Song)** *Crystal Gayle & Gary Morris*
F/71 **Makin' Up His Mind** *Jack Greene*
56/00 **Makin' Up With You** *Chalee Tennison*
44/83 **Making A Living's Been Killing Me** *McGuffey Lane*
Making Believe
2/55 *Kitty Wells*
5/55 *Jimmy Work*
61/75 *Debi Hawkins*
8/77 *Emmylou Harris*
80/77 *Kendalls*
F/78 *Merle Haggard*
93/81 *Paul Williams*
19/82 **Making Love From Memory** *Loretta Lynn*
Making Love To Dixie
92/84 *Younger Brothers Band*
82/88 *Heartland*
1/05 **Making Memories Of Us** *Keith Urban*
2/80 **Making Plans** *Porter Wagoner & Dolly Parton*
84/81 **Making The Night The Best Part Of My Day** *Lincoln County*
6/50 **Mama And Daddy Broke My Heart** *Eddy Arnold*
62/71 **Mama Bake A Pie (Daddy Kill A Chicken)** *George Kent*
46/72 **Mama Bear** *Carl Smith*
73/70 **Mama, Call Me Home** *Bob Dalton*
4/53 **Mama, Come Get Your Baby Boy** *Eddy Arnold*
68/70 **Mama Come'n Get Your Baby Boy** *Johnny Darrell*
9/92 **Mama Don't Forget To Pray For Me** *Diamond Rio*
13/96 **Mama Don't Get Dressed Up For Nothing** *Brooks & Dunn*
91/80 **Mama Don't Let Your Cowboys Grow Up To Be Babies** *Tony Joe White*
29/75 **Mama Don't 'Low** *Hank Thompson*
1/84 **Mama He's Crazy** *Judds*
37/70 **Mama, I Won't Be Wearing A Ring** *Peggy Little*
5/88 **Mama Knows** *Shenandoah*
8/93 **Mama Knows The Highway** *Hal Ketchum*
Mama Lou
34/69 *Penny DeHaven*
94/74 *Rita Coolidge*
86/79 **Mama, Make Up My Room** *Chester Lester*
93/79 **Mama Rocked Us To Sleep** *Four Guys*
1/62 **Mama Sang A Song** *Bill Anderson*
45/68 **Mama Sez** *Marion Worth*
39/84 **Mama, She's Lazy** *Pinkard & Bowden*
5/67 **Mama Spank** *Liz Anderson*
1/68 **Mama Tried** *Merle Haggard*
82/81 **Mama What Does Cheatin' Mean** *Carroll Baker*
81/90 **Mama's Daily Bread** *Jill Hollier*
77/74 **Mama's Got The Know How** *Doug Kershaw*
68/91 **Mama's Little Baby Loves Me** *Sawyer Brown*
50/67 **Mama's Little Jewel** *Johnny Wright*
1/86 **Mama's Never Seen Those Eyes** *Forester Sisters*
11/87 **Mama's Rockin' Chair** *John Conlee*
97/79 **Mama's Sugar** *Ernest Rey*
Mammas Don't Let Your Babies Grow Up To Be Cowboys
15/76 *Ed Bruce*
1/78 *Waylon Jennings & Willie Nelson*
49/94 *Gibson/Miller Band*
16/99 **Man Ain't Made Of Stone** *Randy Travis*
40/73 **Man And A Train** *Marty Robbins*
17/69 **Man And Wife Time** *Jim Ed Brown*
58/87 **Man At The Backdoor** *Beth Williams*
56/69 **Man Away From Home** *Van Trevor*
82/76 **Man From Bowling Green** *Bob Luman*
47/01 **Man He Was** *George Jones*
5/98 **Man Holdin' On (To A Woman Lettin' Go)** *Ty Herndon*
4/99 **Man! I Feel Like A Woman!** *Shania Twain*
72/67 **Man I Hardly Know** *Loretta Lynn*
44/84 **Man I Used To Be** *Boxcar Willie*
3/71 **Man In Black** *Johnny Cash*
4/94 **Man In Love With You** *George Strait*
37/66 **Man In The Little White Suit** *Charlie Walker*
17/83 **Man In The Mirror** *Jim Glaser*
12/80 **Man Just Don't Know What A Woman Goes Through** *Charlie Rich*
59/73 **Man Likes Things Like That** *Charlie Louvin & Melba Montgomery*
94/78 **Man Made Of Glass** *Ed Bruce*
36/75 **Man Needs Love** *David Houston*
18/01 **Man Of Me** *Gary Allan*
8/94 **Man Of My Word** *Collin Raye*
3/84 **Man Of Steel** *Hank Williams, Jr.*
30/75 **Man On Page 602** *Zoot Fenster*
70/98 **Man Song** *Sean Morey*
93/77 **Man Still Turns Me On** *Mary Lou Turner*
Man That Turned My Mama On
4/74 *Tanya Tucker*
70/78 *Ed Bruce*
1/97 **Man This Lonely** *Brooks & Dunn*
1/03 **Man To Man** *Gary Allan*
62/90 **Man To Man** *Hank Williams, Jr.*
(also see: We Shook Hands)
9/63 **Man Who Robbed The Bank At Santa Fe** *Hank Snow*
53/80 **Man Who Takes You Home** *Bobby G. Rice*
42/66 **Man With A Plan** *Carl Smith*
32/82 **Man With The Golden Thumb** *Jerry Reed*
56/70 **Man You Want Me To Be** *Webb Pierce*
60/02 **Man's Gotta Do** *Chad Brock*
28/70 **Man's Kind Of Woman** *Eddy Arnold*
38/87 **Mandolin Rain** *Bruce Hornsby*
6/72 **Manhattan Kansas** *Glen Campbell*
Mansion On The Hill
12/49 *Hank Williams*
29/58 *June Webb*
36/76 *Michael Murphey*
14/77 *Ray Price*
3/90 **Many A Long & Lonesome Highway** *Rodney Crowell*
13/66 **Many Happy Hangovers To You** *Jean Shepard*
34/89 **Many Mansions** *Moe Bandy*
10/49 **Many Tears Ago** *Eddy Arnold*
42/87 **Maple Street Mem'ries** *Statler Brothers*
Margaritaville
13/77 *Jimmy Buffett*
63/99 *Alan Jackson w/ Jimmy Buffett*
23/73 **Margie, Who's Watching The Baby** *Earl Richards*
4/69 **(Margie's At) The Lincoln Park Inn** *Bobby Bare*
88/82 **Maria Consuela** *Tompall/Glaser Brothers*
41/02 **Maria (Shut Up And Kiss Me)** *Willie Nelson*
83/81 **Marianne** *Lane Brothers*
94/79 **Marie** *Steve Wariner*
1/74 **Marie Laveau** *Bobby Bare*
6/83 **Marina Del Rey** *George Strait*
21/61 **Marines, Let's Go** *Rex Allen*
18/71 **Mark Of A Heel** *Hank Thompson*
52/74 **Marlena** *Bobby Goldsboro*
59/68 **Marriage Bit** *Lefty Frizzell*
F/71 **Marriage Has Ruined More Good Love Affairs** *Jan Howard*
10/53 **Marriage Of Mexican Joe** *Carolyn Bradshaw*
10/49 **Marriage Vow** *Hank Snow*
3/77 **Married But Not To Each Other** *Barbara Mandrell*
8/52 **Married By The Bible, Divorced By The Law** *Hank Snow*
84/82 **Married Man** *Judy Taylor*

Married To A Memory
25/71 *Arlene Harden*
74/71 *Judy Lynn*
33/81 **Married Women** *Sonny Curtis*
39/70 **Marry Me** *Ron Lowry*
55/03 **Martie, Emily & Natalie** *Cledus T. Judd*
17/70 **Marty Gray** *Billie Jo Spears*
28/91 **Mary And Willie** *K.T. Oslin*
12/63 **Mary Ann Regrets** *Burl Ives*
55/97 **Mary, Did You Know** *Kenny Rogers w/ Wynonna*
12/60 **Mary Don't You Weep** *Stonewall Jackson*
58/97 **Mary Go Round** *Skip Ewing*
41/70 **Mary Goes 'Round** *Bobby Helms*
66/67 **Mary In The Morning** *Tommy Hunter*
68/68 **Mary's Little Lamb** *Carl Belew*
17/71 **Mary's Vineyard** *Claude King*
64/83 **Marylee** *Rodney Lay*
43/92 **Mason Dixon Line** *Dan Seals*
77/79 **Massachusetts** *Tommy Roe*
59/93 **Master Of Illusion** *Clinton Gregory*
2/63 **Matador, The** *Johnny Cash*
7/81 **Matador** *Sylvia*
8/65 **Matamoros** *Billy Walker*
22/98 **Matches** *Sammy Kershaw*
66/88 **Matches** *Marty Stuart*
Mathilda
20/75 *Donny King*
78/81 *John Wesley Ryles*
33/99 **Matter Of Time** *Jason Sellers*
58/01 **Matthew, Mark, Luke and Earnhardt** *Shane Sellers*
(Matthew's Song) ..see: Pilgrims On The Way
64/82 **Maximum Security (To Minimum Wage)** *Don King*
35/79 **May I** *Terri Hollowell*
52/80 **May I Borrow Some Sugar From You** *John Wesley Ryles*
37/77 **May I Spend Every New Years With You** *T.G. Sheppard*
62/71 **May Old Acquaintance Be Forgot (Before I Lose My Mind)** *Compton Brothers*
1/65 **May The Bird Of Paradise Fly Up Your Nose** *"Little" Jimmy Dickens*
13/78 **May The Force Be With You Always** *Tom T. Hall*
8/51 **May The Good Lord Bless And Keep You** *Eddy Arnold*
68/75 **May You Rest In Peace** *Melody Allen*
25/90 **Maybe** *Kenny Rogers w/ Holly Dunn*
65/96 **Maybe** *Mandy Barnett*
7/78 **Maybe Baby** *Susie Allanson*
18/97 **Maybe He'll Notice Her Now** *Mindy McCready & Richie McDonald*
28/61 **Maybe I Do** *Dave Dudley*
48/91 **Maybe I Mean Yes** *Holly Dunn*
Maybe I [You] Should've Been Listening
31/78 *Rayburn Anthony*
45/78 *Jessi Colter*
23/81 *Gene Watson*
59/89 **Maybe I Won't Love You Anymore** *Johnny Lee*
82/79 **Maybe I'll Cry Over You** *Arthur Blanch*
3/92 **Maybe It Was Memphis** *Pam Tillis*
49/02 **Maybe, Maybe Not** *Mindy McCready*
8/85 **Maybe My Baby** *Louise Mandrell*
17/99 **Maybe Not Tonight** *Sammy Kershaw & Lorrie Morgan*
34/95 **Maybe She's Human** *Kathy Mattea*
22/90 **Maybe That's All It Takes** *Don Williams*
73/91 **Maybe The Moon Will Shine** *Marsha Thornton*
83/89 **Maybe There** *Lisa Childress*
4/97 **Maybe We Should Just Sleep On It** *Tim McGraw*
Maybe You Should've Been Listening ..see: Maybe I Should've
57/93 **Maybe You Were The One** *Dude Mowrey*
1/87 **Maybe Your Baby's Got The Blues** *Judds*
Maybelline ..see: Mabellene
1/04 **Mayberry** *Rascal Flatts*
75/79 **Mazelle** *Gary Stewart*
8/64 **Me** *Bill Anderson*
87/78 **Me** *Sherry Grooms*
4/85 **Me Against The Night** *Crystal Gayle*
Me And Bobby McGee
12/69 *Roger Miller*
F/72 *Jerry Lee Lewis*
27/05 **Me And Charlie Talking** *Miranda Lambert*
18/04 **Me And Emily** *Rachel Proctor*
29/59 **Me And Fred And Joe And Bill** *Porter Wagoner*
8/72 **Me And Jesus** *Tom T. Hall*
85/85 **Me And Margarita** *Bobby Jenkins*
35/00 **Me And Maxine** *Sammy Kershaw*
15/77 **Me And Millie** *Ronnie Sessions*
22/92 **Me And My Baby** *Paul Overstreet*
9/79 **Me And My Broken Heart** *Rex Allen, Jr.*
94/89 **Me And My Harley-Davidson** *Mickey Hawks*
12/76 **Me And Ole C.B.** *Dave Dudley*
Me And Paul
F/71 *Willie Nelson*
14/85 *Willie Nelson*
72/80 **Me And The Boys In The Band** *Tommy Overstreet*
Me And The Elephant
43/77 *Kenny Starr*
82/77 *Bobby Goldsboro*
33/78 **Me And The I.R.S.** *Johnny Paycheck*
2/96 **Me And You** *Kenny Chesney*
29/87 **Me And You** *Donna Fargo*
7/71 **Me And You And A Dog Named Boo** *Stonewall Jackson*
80/75 **Me As I Am** *Chip Taylor*
65/68 **Me, Me, Me, Me, Me** *Liz Anderson*
18/00 **Me Neither** *Brad Paisley*
72/79 **Me Plus You Equals Love** *Dawn Chastain*
1/97 **Me Too** *Toby Keith*
Me Touchin' You
58/79 *Linda Nail*
91/80 *Capitals*
65/71 **Me Without You** *Carl Perkins*
46/66 **Meadowgreen** *Browns*
30/60 **Mean Eyed Cat** *Johnny Cash*
6/49 **Mean Mama Blues** *Ernest Tubb*
22/66 **Mean Old Woman** *Claude Gray*
11/57 **Mean Woman Blues** *Elvis Presley*
79/80 **Mean Woman Blues** *Max D. Barnes*
5/96 **Meant To Be** *Sammy Kershaw*
4/99 **Meanwhile** *George Strait*
18/00 **Meanwhile Back At The Ranch** *Clark Family Experience*
9/65 **Meanwhile, Down At Joe's** *Kitty Wells*
32/79 **Medicine Woman** *Kenny O'Dell*
1/91 **Meet In The Middle** *Diamond Rio*
1/85 **Meet Me In Montana** *Marie Osmond w/ Dan Seals*
51/76 **Meet Me Later** *Margo Smith*
38/64 **Meet Me Tonight Outside Of Town** *Jim Howard*
(Melody of Love) ..see: Why Do I Love You
96/85 **Melted Down Memories** *Joy Ford*
23/87 **Members Only** *Donna Fargo & Billy Joe Royal*
73/89 **Mem'ries** *Vicki Bird*
56/69 **Memories** *Elvis Presley*
82/78 **Memories Are Made Of This** *Tommy O'Day*
9/48 **Memories Of France** *T. Texas Tyler*
21/75 **Memories Of Us** *George Jones*
5/86 **Memories To Burn** *Gene Watson*
85/83 **Memory, The** *Jim Wyrick*
73/87 **Memory Attack** *Ralph May*
96/78 **Memory Bound** *B.J. Wright*
91/76 **Memory Go Round** *R.W. Blackwood*
73/00 **Memory Is The Last Thing To Go** *B.B. Watson*
39/84 **Memory Lane** *Joe Stampley & Jessica Boucher*
60/93 **Memory Lane** *Tim McGraw*
34/02 **Memory Like I'm Gonna Be** *Tanya Tucker*
52/82 **Memory Machine** *Jack Quist*
3/74 **Memory Maker** *Mel Tillis*
2/64 **Memory #1** *Webb Pierce*
10/81 **Memphis** *Fred Knoblock*
52/02 **Memphis** *David Nail*
79/84 **Memphis In May** *Darrell McCall*
73/99 **Memphis Women & Chicken** *T. Graham Brown*
7/80 **Men** *Charly McClain*
8/91 **Men** *Forester Sisters*
23/04 **Men Don't Change** *Amy Dalley*
Men In My Little Girl's Life
16/66 *Archie Campbell*
50/66 *Tex Ritter*
60/94 **Men Will Be Boys** *Billy Dean*
88/89 **Men With Broken Hearts** *Charley Hager*
13/93 **Mending Fences** *Restless Heart*
22/02 **Mendocino County Line** *Willie Nelson w/ Lee Ann Womack*
8/61 **Mental Cruelty** *Buck Owens & Rose Maddox*
14/68 **Mental Journey** *Leon Ashley*
Mental Revenge
12/67 *Waylon Jennings*
15/76 *Mel Tillis*

2/93 **Mercury Blues** *Alan Jackson*
49/76 **Mercy** *Jean Shepard*
7/48 **Merle's Boogie Woogie** *Merle Travis*
55/00 **Merry Christmas From Texas Y'all** *Tracy Byrd*
38/01 **Merry Christmas From The Family** *Montgomery Gentry*
58/98 **Merry Christmas Strait To You** *George Strait*
41/77 **Merry-Go-Round** *Freddy Weller*
47/75 **Merry-Go-Round Of Love** *Hank Snow*
71/70 **Merry-Go-Round World** *Webb Pierce*
72/80 **Message To Khomeini** *Thrasher Brothers*
93/81 **Mexican Girl** *Michael Tate*
1/53 **Mexican Joe** *Jim Reeves*
61/77 **Mexican Love Songs** *Linda Hargrove*
94/85 **Mexico** *Backtrack/John Hunt*
4/44 **Mexico Joe** *Ivie Anderson w/ Ceele Burke*
85/80 **Mexico Winter** *Bobby Hood*
4/74 **Mi Esposa Con Amor (To My Wife With Love)** *Sonny James*
1/95 **Mi Vida Loca (My Crazy Life)** *Pam Tillis*
14/86 **Miami, My Amy** *Keith Whitley*
93/73 **Mid American Manufacturing Tycoon** *Bobby Russell*
Middle Age Crazy
4/78 *Jerry Lee Lewis*
58/03 *T. Graham Brown*
41/79 **Middle-Age Madness** *Earl Thomas Conley*
86/75 **Middle Of A Memory** *Eddy Arnold*
43/05 **Middle Of Nowhere** *Brian McComas*
1/53 **Midnight** *Red Foley*
16/77 **Midnight Angel** *Barbara Mandrell*
84/84 **Midnight Angel Of Mercy** *Rod Rishard*
36/87 **Midnight Blue** *John Wesley Ryles*
39/84 **Midnight Blue** *Billie Jo Spears*
76/82 **Midnight Cabaret** *Wyvon Alexander*
43/80 **Midnight Choir** *Gatlin Bros.*
5/83 **Midnight Fire** *Steve Wariner*
93/80 **Midnight Fire** *Marlow Tackett*
83/77 **Midnight Flight** *Pam Rose*
Midnight Flyer
74/73 *Osborne Brothers*
94/79 *Charlie McCoy*
4/87 **Midnight Girl/Sunset Town** *Sweethearts Of The Rodeo*
1/81 **Midnight Hauler** *Razzy Bailey*
14/88 **Midnight Highway** *Southern Pacific*
3/92 **Midnight In Montgomery** *Alan Jackson*
59/79 **Midnight Lace** *Big Al Downing*
51/84 **Midnight Love** *Billie Jo Spears*
93/82 **Midnight Magic** *Gary Buck*
64/74 **Midnight Man** *Marty Mitchell*
2/74 **Midnight, Me And The Blues** *Mel Tillis*
7/73 **Midnight Oil** *Barbara Mandrell*
6/80 **Midnight Rider** *Willie Nelson*
9/82 **Midnight Rodeo** *Leon Everette*
43/89 **Midnight Train** *Charlie Daniels Band*
87/77 **Midnight Train To Georgia** *Eddie Middleton*
57/81 **Midnite Flyer** *Sue Powell*
85/87 **Midnite Rock** *Indiana*
F/84 **Midsummer Nights** *Kenny Rogers*
68/67 **Mighty Day** *Carl Smith*
60/04 **Mile High Honey** *Royal Wade Kimes*
47/91 **Miles Across The Bedroom** *Gary Morris*
38/77 **Miles And Miles Of Texas** *Asleep At The Wheel*
8/52 **Milk Bucket Boogie** *Red Foley*
Miller's Cave
9/60 *Hank Snow*
4/64 *Bobby Bare*
2/66 **Million And One** *Billy Walker*
39/83 **Million Light Beers Ago** *David Frizzell*
Million Old Goodbyes
66/80 *Freddy Weller*
8/81 *Mel Tillis*
13/63 **Million Years Or So** *Eddy Arnold*
12/68 **Milwaukee, Here I Come** *George Jones & Brenda Carter*
51/93 **Mind Of Her Own** *John Berry*
64/75 **Mind Your Love** *Jerry Reed*
Mind Your Own Business
5/49 *Hank Williams*
35/64 *Jimmy Dean*
1/86 *Hank Williams, Jr. w/ Reba McEntire, Willie Nelson, Tom Petty & Reverend Ike*
8/49 **Mine All Mine** *Jimmy Wakely*
28/02 **Mine All Mine** *SheDaisy*
37/02 **Minivan** *Hometown News*
79/84 **Minstrel, The** *Mike Dekle*
69/78 **Minstrel Man** *Rebecca Lynn*
24/66 **Minute Men (Are Turning In Their Graves)** *Stonewall Jackson*
9/63 **Minute You're Gone** *Sonny James*
4/81 **Miracles** *Don Williams*
3/91 **Mirror Mirror** *Diamond Rio*
41/75 **Mirror, Mirror** *Ben Reece*
49/89 **Mirror Mirror** *Barbara Mandrell*
56/88 **Mirrors Don't Lie** *Marty Stuart*
12/82 **Mis'ry River** *Terri Gibbs*
3/80 **Misery And Gin** *Merle Haggard*
Misery Loves Company
1/62 *Porter Wagoner*
F/80 *Ronnie Milsap*
2/81 **Miss Emily's Picture** *John Conlee*
28↑/05 **Miss Me Baby** *Chris Cagle*
55/72 **Miss Pauline** *Billy Bob Bowman*
26/84 **Miss Understanding** *David Wills*
32/84 **Missin' Mississippi** *Charley Pride*
65/88 **Missin' Texas** *Kim Grayson*
3/52 **Missing In Action** *Ernest Tubb*
2/80 **Missin' You** *Charley Pride*
Missing You
7/57 *Webb Pierce*
8/72 *Jim Reeves*
15/99 **Missing You** *Brooks & Dunn*
54/96 **Missing You** *Mavericks*
79/90 **Missing You** *Marcy Bros.*
55/04 **Mission Temple Fireworks Stand** *Sawyer Brown w/ Robert Randolph*
1/50 **Mississippi** *Red Foley*
19/79 **Mississippi** *Charlie Daniels Band*
31/76 **Mississippi** *Barbara Fairchild*
Mississippi
58/70 *John Phillips*
75/78 *Jack Paris*
59/86 **Mississippi Break Down** *Toni Price*
3/74 **Mississippi Cotton Picking Delta Town** *Charley Pride*
1/05 **Mississippi Girl** *Faith Hill*
15/95 **Mississippi Moon** *John Anderson*
20/85 **Mississippi Squirrel Revival** *Ray Stevens*
14/71 **Mississippi Woman** *Waylon Jennings*
20/75 **Mississippi You're On My Mind** *Stoney Edwards*
5/47 **Missouri** *Merle Travis*
3/82 **Mistakes** *Don Williams*
Mister ..see: Mr.
3/75 **Misty** *Ray Stevens*
Misty Blue
4/66 *Wilma Burgess*
3/67 *Eddy Arnold*
5/76 *Billie Jo Spears*
37/72 **Misty Memories** *Brenda Lee*
77/86 **Misty Mississippi** *Rusty Budde*
43/80 **Misty Morning Rain** *Ray Price*
Misunderstanding ..see: Miss Understanding
44/73 **Mm-Mm Good** *Del Reeves*
Moanin' The Blues
1/50 *Hank Williams*
87/89 *Vicki Bird*
65/82 **Moanin The Blues** *Kenny Dale*
60/81 **Mobile Bay** *Johnny Cash*
27/77 **Mobile Boogie** *Hank Williams, Jr.*
64/81 **Moccasin Man** *Dave Kirby*
Mockin' Bird Hill
3/51 *Pinetoppers*
7/51 *Les Paul & Mary Ford*
9/77 *Donna Fargo*
Mockingbird
94/74 *Terri Lane & Jimmy Nall*
27/05 *Toby Keith w/ Krystal*
8/02 **Modern Day Bonnie And Clyde** *Travis Tritt*
75/86 **Modern Day Cowboy** *Jay Clark*
92/89 **Modern Day Cowboy** *John Marriott*
51/85 **Modern Day Marriages** *Razzy Bailey*
1/85 **Modern Day Romance** *Nitty Gritty Dirt Band*
44/02 **Modern Man** *Michael Peterson*
44/69 **Moffett, Oklahoma** *Charlie Walker*
5/64 **Molly** *Eddy Arnold*
53/69 **Molly** *Jim Glaser*
91/80 **Molly (And The Texas Rain)** *Sonny Wright*
10/48 **Molly Darling** *Eddy Arnold*
28/75 **Molly (I Ain't Gettin' Any Younger)** *Dorsey Burnette*
Mom And Dad's Waltz
2/51 *Lefty Frizzell*
21/61 *Patti Page*
43/79 **Moment By Moment** *Narvel Felts*
58/02 **Moment Like This** *Kelly Clarkson*
24/66 **Mommy, Can I Still Call Him Daddy** *Dottie West*
5/59 **Mommy For A Day** *Kitty Wells*

Mona Lisa
4/50 *Moon Mullican*
10/50 *Jimmy Wakely*
11/81 *Willie Nelson*
2/84 **Mona Lisa Lost Her Smile** *David Allan Coe*
68/94 **Mona Lisa On Cruise Control** *Dennis Robbins*
5/05 **Monday Morning Church** *Alan Jackson*
20/73 **Monday Morning Secretary** *Statler Brothers*
13/88 **Money** *K.T. Oslin*
15/57 **Money** *Browns*
35/70 **Money Can't Buy Love** *Roy Rogers*
74/89 **Money Don't Make A Man A Lover** *Dawnett Faucett*
48/65 **Money Greases The Wheels** *Ferlin Husky*
1/93 **Money In The Bank** *John Anderson*
Money, Marbles And Chalk
12/49 *Stubby & The Buccaneers*
15/49 *Patti Page*
50/02 **Money Or Love** *Clint Black*
15/60 **Money To Burn** *George Jones*
11/72 **Monkey That Became President** *Tom T. Hall*
Monsters' Holiday ..see: (It's A)
95/74 **Montgomery Mable** *Merle Kilgore*
54/92 **Month Of Sundays** *Vern Gosdin*
42/68 **Moods Of Mary** *Tompall/Glaser Brothers*
1/77 **Moody Blue** *Elvis Presley*
68/70 **Moody River** *Chase Webster*
16/60 **Moon Is Crying** *Allan Riddle*
1/87 **Moon Is Still Over Her Shoulder** *Michael Johnson*
9/91 **Moon Over Georgia** *Shenandoah*
36/89 **Moon Pretty Moon** *Statler Brothers*
(Moon Song) ..see: I Don't Know A Thing About Love
72/80 **Moonlight And Magnolia** *Buck Owens*
51/93 **Moonlight Drive-In** *Turner Nichols*
18/90 **Moonshadow Road** *T. Graham Brown*
58/74 **Moontan** *Jeris Ross*
76/87 **Moonwalkin'** *Don Malena*
77/87 **Moon Walking** *Bonnie Leigh*
10/00 **More** *Trace Adkins*
26/72 **More About John Henry** *Tom T. Hall*
More And More
1/54 *Webb Pierce*
7/83 *Charley Pride*
54/02 **More Beautiful Today** *Mark McGuinn*
77/89 **More I Do** *Charley Pride*
95/79 **More I Get The More I Want** *Becky Hobbs*
89/84 **More I Go Blind** *Rod Rishard*
49/92 **More I Learn (The Less I Understand About Love)** *Ronna Reeves*
6/94 **More Love** *Doug Stone*
61/82 **More Nights** *Lane Brody*
71/00 **More Of A Man** *Rodney Carrington*
51/80 **More Than A Bedroom Thing** *Bill Anderson*
6/89 **More Than A Name On A Wall** *Statler Brothers*
5/55 **More Than Anything Else In The World** *Carl Smith*
47/89 **More Than Enough** *Glen Campbell*
41/97 **More Than Everything** *Rhett Akins*
84/87 **More Than Friendly Persuasion** *Bonnie Nelson*
53/97 **More Than I Wanted To Know** *Regina Regina*
8/65 **More Than Yesterday** *Slim Whitman*
3/96 **More Than You'll Ever Know** *Travis Tritt*
1/77 **More To Me** *Charley Pride*
58/93 **More Where That Came From** *Dolly Parton*
14/72 **Mornin' After Baby Let Me Down** *Ray Griff*
56/70 **Mornin Mornin** *Bobby Goldsboro*
1/87 **Mornin' Ride** *Lee Greenwood*
4/70 **Morning** *Jim Ed Brown*
19/71 **Morning After** *Jerry Wallace*
5/80 **Morning Comes Too Early** *Jim Ed Brown/Helen Cornelius*
1/86 **Morning Desire** *Kenny Rogers*
88/74 **Morning Girl** *Duane Dee*
69/82 **Morning, Noon And Night** *Orion*
22/64 **Morning Paper** *Billy Walker*
Most Beautiful Girl
1/73 *Charlie Rich*
54/01 *South 65*
6/55 **Most Of All** *Hank Thompson*
41/84 **Most Of All** *Mac Davis*
71/88 **Most Of All** *Leon Raines*
59/84 **Most Of All I Remember You** *Mel McDaniel*
18/70 **Most Uncomplicated Goodbye I've Ever Heard** *Henson Cargill*
19/75 **Most Wanted Woman In Town** *Roy Head*
74/78 **Motel Rooms** *Little David Wilkins*
13/67 **Motel Time Again** *Johnny Paycheck*
7/76 **Motels And Memories** *T.G. Sheppard*
Mother ..see: (You Make Me Want To Be) A
17/77 **Mother Country Music** *Vern Gosdin*
20/64 **Mother-In-Law** *Jim Nesbitt*
21/68 **Mother, May I** *Liz Anderson & Lynn Anderson*
F/56 **Mother Of A Honky Tonk Girl** *Jim Reeves*
55/92 **Mother's Eyes** *Matthews, Wright & King*
52/89 **Mountain Ago** *Mason Dixon*
23/81 **Mountain Dew** *Willie Nelson*
1/82 **Mountain Music** *Alabama*
64/78 **Mountain Music** *Porter Wagoner*
Mountain Of Love
20/71 *Bobby G. Rice*
1/82 *Charley Pride*
2/63 **Mountain Of Love** *David Houston*
74/71 **Mountain Woman** *Harold Lee*
Move It On Over
4/47 *Hank Williams*
60/73 *Buddy Alan*
66/99 *Travis Tritt w/ George Thorogood*
17/01 **Move On** *Warren Brothers*
Move Two Mountains ..see: (You've Got To)
61/75 **Movie Magazine, Stars In Her Eyes** *Barbi Benton*
10/77 **Movies, The** *Statler Brothers*
1/75 **Movin' On** *Merle Haggard*
61/97 **Movin' Out To The Country** *Deryl Dodd*
20/83 **Movin' Train** *Kendalls*
2/51 **Mr. And Mississippi** *Tennessee Ernie Ford*
53/68 **Mr. & Mrs. John Smith** *Johnny & Jonie Mosby*
Mr. & Mrs. Untrue
64/71 *Johnny Russell*
45/80 *Price Mitchell/Rene Sloane*
11/64 **Mr. And Mrs. Used To Be** *Ernest Tubb & Loretta Lynn*
93/77 **Mr. Bojangles** *Jerry Jeff Walker*
13/78 **Mister D.J.** *T.G. Sheppard*
34/90 **Mister DJ** *Charlie Daniels Band*
25/67 **Mr. Do-It-Yourself** *Jean Shepard & Ray Pillow*
20/76 **Mr. Doodles** *Donna Fargo*
59/72 **Mr. Fiddle Man** *Johnny Russell*
15/57 **Mister Fire Eyes** *Bonnie Guitar*
Mister Garfield
15/65 *Johnny Cash*
54/82 *Merle Kilgore*
82/76 **Mr. Guitar** *Cates Sisters*
64/77 **Mr. Heartache** *Susan Raye*
8/63 **Mr. Heartache, Move On** *Coleman O'Neal*
20/79 **Mr. Jones** *Big Al Downing*
28/63 **Mr. Juke Box** *Ernest Tubb*
8/57 **Mister Love** *Ernest Tubb & Wilburn Brothers*
2/73 **Mr. Lovemaker** *Johnny Paycheck*
1/04 **Mr. Mom** *Lonestar*
4/51 **Mr. Moon** *Carl Smith*
44/81 **Mister Peepers** *Bill Anderson*
71/70 **Mister Professor** *Leroy Van Dyke*
32/75 **Mr. Right And Mrs. Wrong** *Mel Tillis & Sherry Bryce*
Mister Sandman
13/55 *Chet Atkins*
96/78 *Tommy O'Day*
10/81 *Emmylou Harris*
16/67 **Mr. Shorty** *Marty Robbins*
47/75 **Mr. Songwriter** *Sunday Sharpe*
56/73 **Mr. Ting-A-Ling (Steel Guitar Man)** *George Morgan*
4/69 **Mr. Walker, It's All Over** *Billie Jo Spears*
6/01 **Mrs. Steven Rudy** *Mark McGuinn*
15/72 **Much Oblige** *Jack Greene/Jeannie Seely*
13/54 **Much Too Young To Die** *Ray Price*
8/89 **Much Too Young (To Feel This Damn Old)** *Garth Brooks*
1/05 **Mud On The Tires** *Brad Paisley*
62/71 **Muddy Bottom** *Osborne Brothers*
15/69 **Muddy Mississippi Line** *Bobby Goldsboro*
Mule Skinner Blues
16/60 *Fendermen*
3/70 *Dolly Parton [Blue Yodel No. 8]*
1/49 **Mule Train** *Tennessee Ernie Ford*
25/65 **Multiply The Heartaches** *George Jones & Melba Montgomery*

38/00 **Murder On Music Row** *George Strait w/ Alan Jackson*
44/79 **Music Box Dancer** *Frank Mills*
92/78 **Music In My Life** *Mac Davis*
59/81 **Music In The Mountains** *Ernie Rowell*
29/78 **Music Is My Woman** *Don King*
4/52 **Music Makin' Mama From Memphis** *Hank Snow*
39/78 **Music, Music, Music** *Rebecca Lynn*
69/67 **Music To Cry By** *Johnny Wright*
63/74 **Musical Chairs** *Tompall Glaser*
29↑/05 **Must Be Doin' Somethin' Right** *Billy Currington*
Must You Throw Dirt In My Face
21/62 *Louvin Brothers*
60/78 *Roy Clark*
44/96 **My Angel Is Here** *Wynonna*
59/83 **My Angel's Got The Devil In Her Eyes** *Ed Hunnicutt*
63/90 **My Anniversary For Being A Fool** *Holly Dunn*
8/57 **My Arms Are A House** *Hank Snow*
2/90 **My Arms Stay Open All Night** *Tanya Tucker*
91/75 **My Babe** *Earl Richards*
23/83 **My Baby Don't Slow Dance** *Johnny Lee*
13/56 **My Baby Left Me** *Elvis Presley*
2/93 **My Baby Loves Me** *Martina McBride*
1/81 **My Baby Thinks He's A Train** *Rosanne Cash*
71/71 **My Baby Used To Be That Way** *Charlie Walker*
34/68 **My Baby Walked Right Out On Me** *Wanda Jackson*
27/64 **My Baby Walks All Over Me** *Johnny Sea*
53/81 **My Baby's Coming Home Again Today** *Bill Lyerly*
My Baby's Gone
9/59 *Louvin Brothers*
77/76 *Jeanne Pruett*
15/84 *Kendalls*
11/88 **My Baby's Gone** *Sawyer Brown*
2/85 **My Baby's Got Good Timing** *Dan Seals*
44/98 **My Baby's Lovin'** *Daryle Singletary*
20/63 **My Baby's Not Here (In Town Tonight)** *Porter Wagoner*
58/03 **My Beautiful America** *Charlie Daniels Band*
45/81 **My Beginning Was You** *Jack Grayson & Blackjack*
1/00 **My Best Friend** *Tim McGraw*
12/49 **My Best To You** *Sons Of The Pioneers*
79/76 **My Better Half** *Del Reeves*
20/69 **My Big Iron Skillet** *Wanda Jackson*
35/68 **My Big Truck Drivin' Man** *Kitty Wells*
7/93 **My Blue Angel** *Aaron Tippin*
69/79 **My Blue Heaven** *Mac Wiseman & Woody Herman*
45/69 **My Blue Ridge Mountain Boy** *Dolly Parton*
17/71 **My Blue Tears** *Dolly Parton*
14/75 **My Boy** *Elvis Presley*
My Bucket's Got A Hole In It
2/49 *Hank Williams*
4/49 *T. Texas Tyler*
10/58 *Ricky Nelson*
17/68 **My Can Do Can't Keep Up With My Want To** *Nat Stuckey*
61/00 **My Cellmate Thinks I'm Sexy** *Cledus T. Judd*
4/47 **My Chickashay Gal** *Roy Rogers*
(My Crazy Life) ..see: Mi Vida Loca
My Cup Runneth Over
63/67 *Blue Boys*
26/69 *Johnny Bush*
64/84 **My Dad** *Ray Stevens*
5/48 **My Daddy Is Only A Picture** *Eddy Arnold*
78/78 **My Daddy Was A Travelin' Man** *Brenda Kaye Perry*
14/66 **My Dreams** *Faron Young*
3/61 **My Ears Should Burn (When Fools Are Talked About)** *Claude Gray*
My Elusive Dreams
1/67 *David Houston & Tammy Wynette*
41/67 *Curly Putman*
70/67 *Rusty Draper*
73/67 *Johnny Darrell*
27/70 *Bobby Vinton*
3/75 *Charlie Rich*
42/79 **My Empty Arms** *Ann J. Morton*
7/54 **My Everything** *Eddy Arnold*
87/76 **My Eyes Adored You** *Marty Mitchell*
1/76 **My Eyes Can Only See As Far As You** *Charley Pride*
16/63 **My Father's Voice** *Judy Lynn*
1/81 **My Favorite Memory** *Merle Haggard*
My Favorite Things
64/94 *Lorrie Morgan*
69/99 *Lorrie Morgan*
6/49 **My Filipino Rose** *Ernest Tubb*
44/83 **My Fingers Do The Talkin'** *Jerry Lee Lewis*
My First Country Song
93/77 *Jesseca James*
35/83 *Dean Martin*
73/98 **My First, Last, One And Only** *Jim Collins*
6/83 **My First Taste Of Texas** *Ed Bruce*
63/70 **My Friend** *Arlene Harden*
11/64 **My Friend On The Right** *Faron Young*
(My Friends Are Gonna Be) Strangers ..see: (From Now On My Friends Are Gonna Be)
1/03 **My Front Porch Looking In** *Lonestar*
73/77 **My Girl** *Dale McBride*
73/84 **My Girl** *Savannah*
64/74 **My Girl Bill** *Jim Stafford*
58/95 **My Girl Friday** *Daron Norwood*
1/05 **My Give A Damn's Busted** *Jo Dee Messina*
11/68 **My Goal For Today** *Kenny Price*
20/77 **My Good Thing's Gone** *Narvel Felts*
14/69 **My Grass Is Green** *Roy Drusky*
86/79 **My Guns Are Loaded** *Bonnie Tyler*
My Guy
46/71 *Lynda K. Lance*
43/80 *Margo Smith*
1/72 **My Hang-Up Is You** *Freddie Hart*
My Happiness
43/69 *Slim Whitman*
47/70 *Johnny & Jonie Mosby*
1/80 **My Heart** *Ronnie Milsap*
My Heart Cries For You
6/51 *Evelyn Knight & Red Foley*
7/51 *Jimmy Wakely w/ Les Baxter*
63/72 *Doyle Holly*
72/81 *Margo Smith*
10/48 **My Heart Echoes** *Jimmie Osborne*
51/67 **My Heart Gets All The Breaks** *Wanda Jackson*
5/96 **My Heart Has A History** *Paul Brandt*
My Heart Has A Mind Of Its Own
10/72 *Susan Raye*
11/79 *Debby Boone*
64/85 **My Heart Holds On** *Holly Dunn*
10/52 **My Heart Is Broken In Three** *Slim Whitman*
5/02 **My Heart Is Lost To You** *Brooks & Dunn*
38/79 **My Heart Is Not My Own** *Mundo Earwood*
7/90 **My Heart Is Set On You** *Lionel Cartwright*
63/99 **My Heart Is Still Beating** *Kinleys*
66/68 **My Heart Keeps Running To You** *Johnny Paycheck*
1/64 **My Heart Skips A Beat** *Buck Owens*
80/84 **My Heart Will Always Belong To You** *Donna Fargo*
16/95 **My Heart Will Never Know** *Clay Walker*
49/78 **My Heart Won't Cry Anymore** *Dickey Lee*
10/49 **My Heart's Bouquet** *"Little" Jimmy Dickens*
67/97 **My Heart's Broke Down (But My Mind's Made Up)** *Dean Miller*
82/89 **My Heart's On Hold** *J.D. Lewis*
85/88 **My Heart's Way Behind** *Doug Peters*
1/80 **My Heroes Have Always Been Cowboys** *Willie Nelson*
17/80 **My Home's In Alabama** *Alabama*
65/00 **My Hometown** *Charlie Robison*
37/75 **My Honky Tonk Ways** *Kenny O'Dell*
42/04 **My Imagination** *Clint Black*
44/70 **My Joy** *Johnny Bush*
67/96 **My Kind Of Crazy** *John Anderson*
1/95 **My Kind Of Girl** *Collin Raye*
53/84 **My Kind Of Lady** *Burrito Brothers*
12/67 **My Kind Of Love** *Dave Dudley*
27/99 **My Kind Of Woman/My Kind Of Man** *Vince Gill w/ Patty Loveless*
40/79 **My Lady** *Freddie Hart*
My Lady Loves Me (Just As I Am)
82/80 *Chris Waters*
9/83 *Leon Everette*
5/61 **My Last Date (With You)** *Skeeter Davis*
37/73 **My Last Day** *Tony Douglas*
17/04 **My Last Name** *Dierks Bentley*
64/78 **My Last Sad Song** *Jerry Wallace*

1/69 **My Life (Throw It Away If I Want To)** *Bill Anderson*
26/86 **My Life's A Dance** *Anne Murray*
8/56 **My Lips Are Sealed** *Jim Reeves*
1/02 **My List** *Toby Keith*
1/70 **My Love** *Sonny James*
1/94 **My Love** *Little Texas*
15/59 **My Love And Little Me** *Margie Bowes*
37/82 **My Love Belongs To You** *Ronnie Rogers*
48/67 **My Love For You (Is Like A Mountain Range)** *Ernie Ashworth*
15/00 **My Love Goes On And On** *Chris Cagle*
53/73 **My Love Is Deep, My Love Is Wide** *Pat Daisy*
60/04 **My Love Will Not Change** *Hal Ketchum*
28/79 **My Mama Never Heard Me Sing** *Billy "Crash" Craddock*
1/72 **My Man** *Tammy Wynette*
60/70 **My Man** *Jeannie C. Riley*
80/82 **My Man Friday** *Patti Page*
1/96 **My Maria** *Brooks & Dunn*
34/73 **My Mind Hangs On To You** *Billy Walker*
79/85 **My Mind Is On You** *Gus Hardin*
24/77 **My Mountain Dew** *Charlie Rich*
44/05 **My Name** *George Canyon*
7/62 **My Name Is Mud** *James O'Gwynn*
1/91 **My Next Broken Heart** *Brooks & Dunn*
1/00 **My Next Thirty Years** *Tim McGraw*
31/94 **My Night To Howl** *Lorrie Morgan*
19/65 **My Old Faded Rose** *Johnny Sea*
My Old Kentucky Home
69/70 *Osborne Brothers*
42/75 *Johnny Cash*
36/02 **My Old Man** *Rodney Atkins*
9/85 **My Old Yellow Car** *Dan Seals*
1/85 **My Only Love** *Statler Brothers*
My Own Kind Of Hat
4/79 *Merle Haggard*
71/99 *Alan Jackson*
19/74 **My Part Of Forever** *Johnny Paycheck*
22/90 **My Past Is Present** *Rodney Crowell*
41/79 **My Pledge Of Love** *John Anderson*
14/76 **My Prayer** *Narvel Felts*
66/79 **My Prayer** *Glen Campbell*
76/78 **My Pulse Pumps Passions** *Hal Hubble*
14/59 **My Reason For Living** *Ferlin Husky*
94/89 **My Rose Is Blue** *Don Lamaster*
6/87 **My Rough And Rowdy Days** *Waylon Jennings*
40/64 **My Saro Jane** *Flatt & Scruggs*
1/93 **My Second Home** *Tracy Lawrence*
29/63 **My Secret** *Judy Lynn*
1/57 **My Shoes Keep Walking Back To You** *Ray Price*
59/92 **My Side Of Town** *Dennis Robbins*
67/78 **My Side Of Town** *Billy Larkin*
8/79 **My Silver Lining** *Mickey Gilley*
16/05 **My Sister** *Reba McEntire*
15/69 **My Son** *Jan Howard*
9/50 **My Son Calls Another Man Daddy** *Hank Williams*
76/81 **My Song Don't Sing The Same** *Kris Carpenter*
My Special Angel
1/57 *Bobby Helms*
53/76 *Bobby G. Rice*
82/85 *James & Michael Younger*
My Special Prayer
36/69 *Archie Campbell & Lorene Mann*
83/80 *Freddy Fender*
4/93 **My Strongest Weakness** *Wynonna*
57/85 **My Sweet-Eyed Georgia Girl** *Atlanta*
62/77 **My Sweet Lady** *John Denver*
38/89 **My Sweet Love Ain't Around** *Suzy Bogguss*
15/64 **My Tears Are Overdue** *George Jones*
36/64 **My Tears Don't Show** *Carl Butler & Pearl*
10/49 **My Tennessee Baby** *Ernest Tubb*
15/73 **My Tennessee Mountain Home** *Dolly Parton*
19/85 **My Toot-Toot** *Rockin' Sidney*
5/02 **My Town** *Montgomery Gentry*
19/89 **My Train Of Thought** *Barbara Mandrell*
45/81 **My Turn** *Donna Hazard*
39/66 **My Uncle Used To Love Me But She Died** *Roger Miller*
2/78 **My Way** *Elvis Presley*
49/66 **My Way Of Life** *Sonny Curtis*
23/77 **My Weakness** *Margo Smith*
36/73 **My Whole World Is Falling Down** *O.B. McClinton*
68/96 **My Wife Thinks You're Dead** *Junior Brown*
My Wife's House
9/74 *Jerry Wallace*
78/86 *Gene Kennedy*
51/76 **My Window Faces The South** *Sammi Smith*
15/81 **My Woman Loves The Devil Out Of Me** *Moe Bandy*
1/70 **My Woman, My Woman, My Wife** *Marty Robbins*
4/69 **My Woman's Good To Me** *David Houston*
68/70 **My Woman's Love** *Johnny Duncan*
3/75 **My Woman's Man** *Freddie Hart & The Heartbeats*
4/79 **My World Begins And Ends With You** *Dave & Sugar*
60/04 **My World Is Over** *Kenny Rogers w/ Whitney Duncan*
80/79 **Mysterious Lady From St. Martinique** *Hank Snow*
57/67 **Mystery Of Tallahatchie Bridge** *Roger White*
10/56 **Mystery Train** *Elvis Presley*

N

40/79 **Nadine** *Freddy Weller*
87/80 **Nag, Nag, Nag** *Bobby Braddock*
65/71 **Naked And Crying** *Henson Cargill*
30/80 **Naked In The Rain** *Loretta Lynn*
65/97 **Naked To The Pain** *James Bonamy*
70/83 **Name Of The Game Is Cheating** *Charlie Ross*
16/69 **Name Of The Game Was Love** *Hank Snow*
9/71 **Nashville** *David Houston*
37/73 **Nashville** *Ray Stevens*
61/75 **Nashville** *Hoyt Axton*
93/80 **Nashville Beer Garden** *Andy Badale*
54/67 **Nashville Cats** *Flatt & Scruggs*
74/70 **Nashville Skyline Rag** *Earl Scruggs*
73/67 **Nashville Women** *Hank Locklin*
77/82 **Natalie** *Dave Rowland*
2/94 **National Working Woman's Holiday** *Sammy Kershaw*
39/80 **Natural Attraction** *Billie Jo Spears*
74/97 **Natural Born Lovers** *Brady Seals*
1/85 **Natural High** *Merle Haggard*
20/82 **Natural Love** *Petula Clark*
82/78 **Natural Love** *O.B. McClinton*
46/74 **Natural Woman** *Jody Miller*
71/92 **Naturally** *Skip Ewing*
69/73 **Naughty Girl** *Guy Shannon*
Near You
74/71 *Lamar Morris*
1/77 *George Jones & Tammy Wynette*
34/87 **Need A Little Time Off For Bad Behavior** *David Allan Coe*
1/67 **Need You** *Sonny James*
9/72 **Need You** *David Rogers*
24/76 **Negatory Romance** *Tom T. Hall*
Neither One Of Us
7/73 *Bob Luman*
81/89 *Ronnie Bryant*
79/77 **Neon Lady** *Bobby Wright*
83/77 **Neon Lights** *Nick Nixon*
1/92 **Neon Moon** *Brooks & Dunn*
3/73 **Neon Rose** *Mel Tillis*
87/77 **Neon Women** *Carmol Taylor & Stella Parton*
28/64 **Nester, The** *Lefty Frizzell*
15/54 **Never** *Marilyn & Wesley Tuttle*
96/74 **Never A Night Goes By** *Sharon Vaughn*
23/97 **Never Again, Again** *Lee Ann Womack*
6/49 **Never Again (Will I Knock On Your Door)** *Hank Williams*
22/89 **Never Alone** *Vince Gill*
36/80 **Never Be Anyone Else** *R.C. Bannon*
1/86 **Never Be You** *Rosanne Cash*
29/99 **Never Been Kissed** *Sherrié Austin*
1/81 **Never Been So Loved (In All My Life)** *Charley Pride*
Never Been To Spain
36/72 *Ronnie Sessions*
75/74 *Sammi Smith*
52/94 **Never Bit A Bullet Like This** *George Jones /Sammy Kershaw*
36/75 **Never Coming Back Again** *Rex Allen, Jr.*
74/98 **Never Could** *Great Divide*
6/84 **Never Could Toe The Mark** *Waylon Jennings*
18/76 **Never Did Like Whiskey** *Billie Jo Spears*
83/77 **Never Ending Love Affair** *Melba Montgomery*

Never Ending Song Of Love
8/71 *Dickey Lee*
57/71 *Mayf Nutter*
43/83 *Osmond Brothers*
72/90 *Crystal Gayle*
9/89 **Never Givin' Up On Love** *Michael Martin Murphey*
78/78 **Never Going Back Again** *Mac Wiseman*
82/79 **Never Gonna' Be A Country Star** *Kenny Seratt*
58/72 **Never Had A Doubt** *Mayf Nutter*
48/89 **Never Had A Love Song** *Gary Morris*
8/89 **Never Had It So Good** *Mary Chapin Carpenter*
63/99 **Never In A Million Tears** *T. Graham Brown*
83/78 **Never Knew (How Much I Loved You 'Til I Lost You)** *Dawn Chastain*
3/90 **Never Knew Lonely** *Vince Gill*
73/93 **Never Let Him See Me Cry** *Ronna Reeves*
26/01 **Never Love You Enough** *Chely Wright*
58/87 **Never Mind** *Nanci Griffith*
25/69 **"Never More" Quote The Raven** *Stonewall Jackson*
9/78 **Never My Love** *Vern Gosdin*
F/79 **Never My Love** *Kendalls*
95/76 **Never Naughty Rosie** *Sue Thompson*
30/89 **Never Say Never** *T. Graham Brown*
29/80 **Never Seen A Mountain So High** *Ronnie McDowell*
50/89 **Never Too Old To Rock 'N' Roll** *Ronnie McDowell w/ Jerry Lee Lewis*
Never Trust A Woman
2/47 *Tex Williams*
2/47 *Red Foley*
5/48 *Tiny Hill*
93/78 **Nevertheless** *Hank Snow*
New Blue Jeans ..see: (I'm Looking For Some)
18/82 **New Cut Road** *Bobby Bare*
1/89 **New Fool At An Old Game** *Reba McEntire*
3/54 **New Green Light** *Hank Thompson*
39/68 **New Heart** *Ernie Ashworth*
New Jolie Blonde (New Pretty Blonde)
1/47 *Red Foley*
2/47 *Moon Mullican*
43/77 **New Kid In Town** *Eagles*
32/90 **New Kind Of Love** *Michelle Wright*
25/67 **New Lips** *Roy Drusky*
1/83 **New Looks From An Old Lover** *B.J. Thomas*
51/88 **New Never Wore Off My Sweet Baby** *Dean Dillon*
28/69 **New Orleans** *Anthony Armstrong Jones*
10/84 **New Patches** *Mel Tillis*
87/84 **New Place To Begin** *Ray Price*
72/66 **New Place To Hang Your Hat** *Ruby Wright*
New Pretty Blonde ..see: New Jolie Blonde
79/88 **New River** *Heartland*
26/59 **New River Train** *Bobby Helms*
3/44 **New San Antonio Rose** *Bob Wills*
2/88 **New Shade Of Blue** *Southern Pacific*
64/86 **New Shade Of Blue** *Perry LaPointe*
1/46 **New Spanish Two Step** *Bob WIlls*
5/46 **New Steel Guitar Rag** *Bill Boyd*
95/85 **New Tradition** *Bobby G. Rice*
64/93 **New Way Home** *K.T. Oslin*
17/82 **New Way Out** *Karen Brooks*
2/91 **New Way (To Light Up An Old Flame)** *Joe Diffie*
10/52 **New Wears Off Too Fast** *Hank Thompson*
62/82 **New Will Never Wear Off Of You** *Crash Craddock*
55/00 **New Year's Eve 1999** *Alabama w/ Gretchen Peters*
73/73 **New York Callin' Miami** *Kent Fox*
19/71 **New York City** *Statler Brothers*
83/81 **New York Cowboy** *Nashville Superpickers*
26/63 **New York Town** *Flatt & Scruggs*
18/80 **New York Wine And Tennessee Shine** *Dave & Sugar*
17/79 **Next Best Feeling** *Mary K. Miller*
17/03 **Next Big Thing** *Vince Gill*
86/73 **Next Door Neighbor's Kid** *Jud Strunk*
1/68 **Next In Line** *Conway Twitty*
9/57 **Next In Line** *Johnny Cash*
55/98 **Next Step** *Jim Collins*
F/70 **Next Step Is Love** *Elvis Presley*
16/92 **Next Thing Smokin'** *Joe Diffie*
14/59 **Next Time** *Ernest Tubb*
51/86 **Next Time** *Wild Choir*
15/71 **Next Time I Fall In Love (I Won't)** *Hank Thompson*
92/87 **Next Time I Marry** *Victoria Hallman*
51/89 **Next To You** *Tammy Wynette*
Next To You
78/85 *Craig Dillingham*
74/86 *Tommy Overstreet*
1/90 **Next To You, Next To Me** *Shenandoah*
15/55 **Next Voice You Hear** *Hank Snow*
37/70 **Nice 'N' Easy** *Charlie Rich*
85/86 **Nice To Be With You** *Slewfoot*
37/97 **Nickajack** *River Road*
80/83 **Nickel's Worth Of Heaven** *Brian Collins*
31/66 **Nickels, Quarters And Dimes** *Johnny Wright*
26/59 **Night** *Jimmy Martin*
77/75 **Night Atlanta Burned** *Atkins String Company*
41/01 **Night Disappear With You** *Brian McComas*
67/83 **Night Dolly Parton Was Almost Mine** *Pump Boys & Dinettes*
81/77 **Night Flying** *Roy Drusky*
1/83 **Night Games** *Charley Pride*
20/80 **Night Games** *Ray Stevens*
43/87 **Night Hank Williams Came To Town** *Johnny Cash*
58/85 **Night Has A Heart Of It's Own** *Lacy J. Dalton*
9/95 **Night Is Fallin' In My Heart** *Diamond Rio*
85/80 **Night Lies** *Bill Wence*
Night Life
28/63 *Ray Price*
31/68 *Claude Gray*
20/80 *Danny Davis & Willie Nelson*
59/86 *B.J. Thomas*
F/86 *Roy Clark*
29/71 **Night Miss Nancy Ann's Hotel For Single Girls Burned Down** *Tex Williams*
70/88 **Night Of Love Forgotten** *Bobby G. Rice*
45/64 **Night People** *Leroy Van Dyke*
Night The Lights Went Out In Georgia
36/73 *Vicki Lawrence*
12/92 *Reba McEntire*
Night They Drove Old Dixie Down
71/70 *Buckaroos*
33/71 *Alice Creech*
16/76 **Night Time And My Baby** *Joe Stampley*
2/78 **Night Time Magic** *Larry Gatlin*
83/79 **Night Time Music Man** *Judy Argo*
6/99 **Night To Remember** *Joe Diffie*
85/83 **Night's Almost Over** *Jacky Ward*
F/72 **Night's Not Over Yet** *Roy Drusky*
20/90 **Night's Too Long** *Patty Loveless*
14/63 **Nightmare** *Faron Young*
4/86 **Nights** *Ed Bruce*
27/78 **Nights Are Forever Without You** *Buck Owens*
84/89 **Nights Are Never Long Enough With You** *Sylvia Forrest*
48/97 **Nights Like These** *Lynns*
93/83 **Nights Like Tonight** *Austin O'Neal*
95/82 **Nights Out At The Days End** *Owen Brothers*
89/85 **Nightshift** *Nashville Nightshift*
1/81 **9 To 5** *Dolly Parton*
1/03 **19 Somethin'** *Mark Wills*
41/67 **Ninety Days** *Jimmy Dean*
56/04 **98.6° And Fallin'** *Jill King*
2/63 **Ninety Miles An Hour** *Hank Snow*
13/59 **Ninety-Nine** *Bill Anderson*
10/03 **99.9% Sure (I've Never Been Here Before)** *Brian McComas*
7/81 **1959** *John Anderson*
43/96 **1969** *Keith Stegall*
81/78 **Nineteen-Sixty Something Songwriter Of The Year** *Tennesseans*
6/86 **1982** *Randy Travis*
58/84 **1984** *Craig Dillingham*
9,999,999 Tears
3/76 *Dickey Lee*
75/89 *Tammy Lucas*
76/78 **Ninth Of September** *Jim Chesnut*
39/81 **No Aces** *Patti Page*
8/68 **No Another Time** *Lynn Anderson*
72/69 **No Blues Is Good News** *George Jones*
72/89 **No Chance To Dance** *Johnny Rodriguez*
1/74 **No Charge** *Melba Montgomery*
55/04 **No Depression In Heaven** *Sheryl Crow*
1/94 **No Doubt About It** *Neal McCoy*
56/99 **No Easy Goodbye** *South Sixty Five*
19/87 **No Easy Horses** *Schuyler, Knobloch & Bickhardt*
29/04 **No End In Sight** *Katrina Elam*

33/98 **No End To This Road** *Restless Heart*
49/83 **No Fair Fallin' In Love** *Jan Gray*
27/01 **No Fear** *Terri Clark*
3/93 **No Future In The Past** *Vince Gill*
No Gettin' Over Me ..see: (There's)
73/97 **No Goodbyes** *Gene Watson*
83/79 **No Greater Love** *Billy Stack*
60/73 **No Headstone On My Grave** *Jerry Lee Lewis*
No Help Wanted
1/53 *Carlisles*
9/53 *Hank Thompson*
7/53 **No Help Wanted #2** *Ernest Tubb - Red Foley*
13/55 **No, I Don't Believe I Will** *Carl Smith*
2/44 **No Letter Today** *Ted Daffan*
No Love At All
15/70 *Lynn Anderson*
80/80 *Jan Gray*
No Love Have I
4/60 *Webb Pierce*
26/78 *Gail Davies*
67/92 *Holly Dunn*
43/98 **No Man In His Wrong Heart** *Gary Allan*
3/95 **No Man's Land** *John Michael Montgomery*
1/90 **No Matter How High** *Oak Ridge Boys*
17/79 **No Memories Hangin' Round** *Rosanne Cash w/ Bobby Bare*
26/00 **No Mercy** *Ty Herndon*
26/94 **No More Cryin'** *McBride & The Ride*
19/73 **No More Hanging On** *Jerry Lee Lewis*
38/99 **No More Looking Over My Shoulder** *Travis Tritt*
No More One More Time
71/87 *Judy Byram*
7/88 *Jo-el Sonnier*
15/71 **No Need To Worry** *Johnny Cash & June Carter*
1/96 **No News** *Lonestar*
8/78 **No, No, No (I'd Rather Be Free)** *Rex Allen, Jr.*
F/56 **No One But You** *Kitty Wells & Red Foley*
79/87 **No One Can Touch Me** *Carla Monday*
14/55 **No One Dear But You** *Johnnie & Jack*
7/79 **No One Else In The World** *Tammy Wynette*
1/92 **No One Else On Earth** *Wynonna*
6/86 **No One Mends A Broken Heart Like You** *Barbara Mandrell*
1/96 **No One Needs To Know** *Shania Twain*
6/46 **No One To Cry To** *Sons Of The Pioneers*
97/89 **No One To Talk To But The Blues** *Maripat*
No One Will Ever Know
42/66 *Frank Ifield*
13/80 *Gene Watson*
48/05 **No One'll Ever Love Me** *Rebecca Lynn Howard*
10/67 **No One's Gonna Hurt You Anymore** *Bill Anderson*
78/87 **No Ordinary Memory** *Bill Anderson*
93/80 **No Ordinary Woman** *Byron Gallimore*
2/87 **No Place Like Home** *Randy Travis*
53/00 **No Place Like Home** *Georgia Middleman*
1/99 **No Place That Far** *Sara Evans*
78/82 **No Place To Hide** *Gayle Zeiler*
36/04 **No Regrets Yet** *Sonya Isaacs*
No Relief In Sight
98/77 *Willie Rainsford*
20/82 *Con Hunley*
62/72 **No Rings--No Strings** *Del Reeves*
57/82 **No Room To Cry** *Mike Campbell*
2/03 **No Shoes, No Shirt, No Problems** *Kenny Chesney*
32/65 **No Sign Of Living** *Dottie West*
58/92 **No Sir** *Darryl & Don Ellis*
10/78 **No Sleep Tonight** *Randy Barlow*
93/84 **No Survivors** *Peter Isaacson*
16/67 **No Tears Milady** *Marty Robbins*
72/78 **No Tell Motel** *David Houston*
40/64 **No Thanks, I Just Had One** *Margie Singleton & Faron Young*
No Thinkin' Thing ..see: (This Ain't)
91/89 **No Time At All** *Debbie Sanders*
75/00 **No Time For Tears** *Jo Dee Messina*
3/93 **No Time To Kill** *Clint Black*
3/46 **No Vacancy** *Merle Travis*
97/78 **No Way Around It (It's Love)** *Billy Swan*
70/92 **No Way Jose** *Ray Kennedy*
49/85 **No Way José** *David Frizzell*
53/96 **No Way Out** *Suzy Bogguss*
69/82 **No Way Out** *Johnny Paycheck*
53/80 **No Way To Drown A Memory** *Stoney Edwards*
70/95 **No Yesterday** *Billy Montana*
1/82 **Nobody** *Sylvia*
4/66 **Nobody But A Fool (Would Love You)** *Connie Smith*
2/83 **Nobody But You** *Don Williams*
43/69 **Nobody But You** *Buckaroos*
93/73 **Nobody But You** *Linda Plowman*
44/77 **Nobody Cares But You** *Freddy Weller*
61/83 **Nobody Else For Me** *Stephanie Winslow*
49/85 **Nobody Ever Gets Enough Love** *Con Hunley*
1/85 **Nobody Falls Like A Fool** *Earl Thomas Conley*
Nobody In His Right Mind Would've Left Her
25/81 *Dean Dillon*
1/86 *George Strait*
1/97 **Nobody Knows** *Kevin Sharp*
53/88 **Nobody Knows** *John Wesley Ryles*
84/89 **Nobody Knows Me** *Lyle Lovett*
1/79 **Nobody Likes Sad Songs** *Ronnie Milsap*
63/98 **Nobody Love, Nobody Gets Hurt** *Suzy Bogguss*
68/81 **Nobody Loves Anybody Anymore** *Kris Kristofferson*
1/84 **Nobody Loves Me Like You Do** *Anne Murray w/ Dave Loggins*
52/93 **Nobody Loves You When You're Free** *Remingtons*
26/87 **Nobody Should Have To Love This Way** *Crystal Gayle*
82/88 **Nobody There But Me** *Willie Nelson*
3/85 **Nobody Wants To Be Alone** *Crystal Gayle*
68/70 **Nobody Wants To Hear It Like It Is** *Jack Barlow*
2/93 **Nobody Wins** *Radney Foster*
5/73 **Nobody Wins** *Brenda Lee*
22/88 **Nobody's Angel** *Crystal Gayle*
46/67 **Nobody's Child** *Hank Williams, Jr.*
Nobody's Darling But Mine
13/60 *Johnny Sea*
87/80 *B.J. Wright*
10/70 **Nobody's Fool** *Jim Reeves*
24/81 **Nobody's Fool** *Deborah Allen*
11/62 **Nobody's Fool But Yours** *Buck Owens*
50/96 **Nobody's Girl** *Michelle Wright*
13/94 **Nobody's Gonna Rain On Our Parade** *Kathy Mattea*
55/00 **Nobody's Got It All** *John Anderson*
1/90 **Nobody's Home** *Clint Black*
9/50 **Nobody's Lonesome For Me** *Hank Williams*
2/90 **Nobody's Talking** *Exile*
8/69 **None Of My Business** *Henson Cargill*
73/78 **Norma Jean** *Sammi Smith*
2/92 **Norma Jean Riley** *Diamond Rio*
61/68 **Normally, Norma Loves Me** *Red Sovine*
37/81 **North Alabama** *Dave Kirby*
42/72 **North Carolina** *Dallas Frazier*
17/80 **North Of The Border** *Johnny Rodriguez*
1/61 **North To Alaska** *Johnny Horton*
71/73 **North To Chicago** *Hank Snow*
8/53 **North Wind** *Slim Whitman*
56/82 **North Wind** *Jim & Jesse & Charlie Louvin*
17/70 **Northeast Arkansas Mississippi County Bootlegger** *Kenny Price*
71/94 **Not** *Bellamy Brothers*
3/02 **Not A Day Goes By** *Lonestar*
90/80 **Not A Day Goes By** *Anna Sudderth*
1/95 **Not A Moment Too Soon** *Tim McGraw*
43/88 **Not A Night Goes By** *Tim Malchak*
76/85 **Not Another Heart Song** *Tom Jones*
2/90 **Not Counting You** *Garth Brooks*
3/96 **Not Enough Hours In The Night** *Doug Supernaw*
29/88 **Not Enough Love** *Tom Wopat*
62/80 **Not Exactly Free** *O.B. McClinton*
69/89 **Not Fade Away** *Trish Lynn*
70/89 **Not Like This** *Tim Malchak*
47/05 **Not Me** *Keni Thomas w/ Vince Gill & Emmylou Harris*
24/64 **Not My Kind Of People** *Stonewall Jackson*
87/84 **Not On The Bottom Yet** *Boxcar Willie*

1/95 **Not On Your Love** *Jeff Carson*
65/95 **Not So Different After All** *Brother Phelps*
13/63 **Not So Long Ago** *Marty Robbins*
3/96 **Not That Different** *Collin Raye*
44/66 **Not That I Care** *Jerry Wallace*
74/86 **Not Tonight** *Paul Proctor*
77/74 **Not Tonight** *Little David Wilkins*
52/87 **Not Tonight I've Got A Heartache** *Vicki Rae Von*
15/92 **Not Too Much To Ask** *Mary Chapin Carpenter w/ Joe Diffie*
7/63 **Not What I Had In Mind** *George Jones*
68/92 **Not With My Heart You Don't** *Paulette Carlson*
28/98 **Note, The** *Daryle Singletary*
62/68 **Note In Box Number 9** *Stu Phillips*
5/05 **Nothin 'Bout Love Makes Sense** *LeAnn Rimes*
38/05 **Nothin' But Cowboy Boots** *Blue County*
1/98 **Nothin' But The Taillights** *Clint Black*
20/93 **Nothin' But The Wheel** *Patty Loveless*
25/59 **Nothin' But True Love** *Margie Singleton*
Nothin' But You
70/83 *Steve Earle & The Dukes*
51/91 *Robin Lee*
26/97 **Nothin' Less Than Love** *Buffalo Club*
11/58 **Nothin' Needs Nothin' (Like I Need You)** *Marvin Rainwater*
10/98 **Nothin' New Under The Moon** *LeAnn Rimes*
35/76 **Nothin' Takes The Place Of You** *Asleep At The Wheel*
64/92 **Nothin' To Do (And All Night To Do It)** *Billy Burnette*
82/81 **Nothin' To Do But Just Lie** *Wesley Ryan*
1/05 **Nothin' To Lose** *Josh Gracin*
33/86 **Nothin' Ventured Nothin' Gained** *Sylvia*
61/67 **Nothin's Bad As Bein' Lonely** *Johnny Sea*
20/95 **Nothing** *Dwight Yoakam*
10/79 **Nothing As Original As You** *Statler Brothers*
26/82 **Nothing Behind You, Nothing In Sight** *John Conlee*
F/74 **Nothing Between** *Porter Wagoner*
19/82 **Nothing But The Radio On** *Younger Brothers*
91/79 **Nothing But Time** *Helen Hudson*
12/86 **Nothing But Your Love Matters** *Gatlin Bros.*
37/85 **Nothing Can Hurt Me Now** *Gail Davies*
68/72 **Nothing Can Stop My Loving You** *Patsy Sledd*
50/00 **Nothing Catches Jesus By Surprise** *John Michael Montgomery*
7/73 **Nothing Ever Hurt Me (Half As Bad As Losing You)** *George Jones*
1/89 **Nothing I Can Do About It Now** *Willie Nelson*
61/93 **Nothing In Common But Love** *Twister Alley*
87/84 **(Nothing Left Between Us) But Alabama** *Gordon Dee*
34/65 **Nothing Left To Lose** *Faron Young*
85/88 **Nothing Left To Lose** *Tiny Wellman*
10/84 **Nothing Like Falling In Love** *Eddie Rabbitt*
1/04 **Nothing On But The Radio** *Gary Allan*
4/92 **Nothing Short Of Dying** *Travis Tritt*
4/80 **Nothing Sure Looked Good On You** *Gene Watson*
39/68 **Nothing Takes The Place Of Loving You** *Stonewall Jackson*
15/91 **Nothing's Changed Here** *Dwight Yoakam*
63/90 **Nothing's Gonna Bother Me Tonight** *Forester Sisters*
3/90 **Nothing's News** *Clint Black*
41/04 **November** *Emerson Drive*
1/86 **Now And Forever (You And Me)** *Anne Murray*
85/89 **Now And Then** *Karen Staley*
(Now And Then There's) A ..see: Fool Such As I
56/76 **Now Everybody Knows** *Charlie Rich*
68/68 **Now I Can Live Again** *Mickey Gilley*
5/94 **Now I Know** *Lari White*
56/84 **Now I Lay Me Down To Cheat** *Shelly West*
62/82 **Now I Lay Me Down To Cheat** *David Allan Coe*
26/93 **Now I Pray For Rain** *Neal McCoy*
69/86 **Now I've Got A Heart Of Gold** *Sonny Curtis*
71/91 **Now It Belongs To You** *Mark O'Connor w/ Steve Wariner*
83/86 **Now She's In Paris** *Dave Holladay*
2/98 **Now That I Found You** *Terri Clark*
98/73 **Now That It's Over** *Brush Arbor*
38/81 **Now That The Feeling's Gone** *Billy "Crash" Craddock*
17/91 **Now That We're Alone** *Rodney Crowell*
43/96 **Now That's All Right With Me** *Mandy Barnett*
59/00 **Now That's Awesome!** *Bill Engvall*
18/92 **Now That's Country** *Marty Stuart*
21/85 **Now There's You** *Shelly West*
Now You See 'Em, Now You Don't
19/78 *Roy Head*
70/88 *Marty Haggard*
12/99 **(Now You See Me) Now You Don't** *Lee Ann Womack*
64/87 **Now You're Talkin'** *Mel McDaniel*
66/93 **Now You're Talkin'** *Dixiana*
7/92 **Nowhere Bound** *Diamond Rio*
20/87 **Nowhere Road** *Steve Earle*
54/97 **Nowhere, USA** *Dean Miller*
51/89 **#1 Heartache Place** *Larry Gatlin/Gatlin Brothers*
41/65 **Number One Heel** *Bonnie Owens*
#1 With A Heartache
66/76 *Billy Larkin*
94/78 *La Costa*
11/80 **Numbers** *Bobby Bare*
94/77 **Nyquil Blues** *Alvin Crow*

O

O Holy Night
55/96 *John Berry*
74/97 *Martina McBride*
63/98 *John Berry*
67/98 *Martina McBride*
49/99 *Martina McBride*
57/00 *Martina McBride*
41/01 *Martina McBride*
18/94 **O What A Thrill** *Mavericks*
3/47 **Oakie Boogie** *Jack Guthrie*
91/77 **Obscene Phone Call** *Johnny Russell*
28/80 **Occasional Rose** *Marty Robbins*
6/70 **Occasional Wife** *Faron Young*
1/87 **Ocean Front Property** *George Strait*
29/61 **Ocean Of Tears** *Billie Jean Horton*
Odds And Ends (Bits And Pieces)
7/61 *Warren Smith*
66/74 *Charlie Walker*
21/71 **Ode To A Half A Pound Of Ground Round** *Tom T. Hall*
Ode To Billie Joe
17/67 *Bobbie Gentry*
39/67 *Margie Singleton*
55/74 **Ode To Jole Blon** *Gary Sargeants*
3/65 **Ode To The Little Brown Shack Out Back** *Billy Edd Wheeler*
91/89 **Of All The Foolish Things To Do** *Ross Lewis*
22/97 **Of Course I'm Alright** *Alabama*
38/67 **Off And On** *Charlie Louvin*
F/76 **Off And Running** *Maury Finney*
5/79 **Official Historian On Shirley Jean Berrell** *Statler Brothers*
(Oh Baby Mine) I Get So Lonely
1/54 *Johnnie & Jack*
49/79 *Bobby G. Rice*
2/83 *Statler Brothers*
21/75 **Oh Boy** *Diana Trask*
38/84 **Oh Carolina** *Vince Gill*
10/86 **Oh Darlin'** *O'Kanes*
12/82 **Oh Girl** *Con Hunley*
25/70 **Oh Happy Day** *Glen Campbell*
9/87 **Oh Heart** *Baillie & The Boys*
70/74 **Oh, How Happy** *Sherry Bryce*
79/89 **Oh How I Love You (Como Te Quiero)** *Tony Perez*
6/80 **Oh, How I Miss You Tonight** *Jim Reeves w/ Deborah Allen*
65/70 **Oh How I Waited** *Ron Lowry*
36/75 **Oh, How Love Changes** *Don Gibson & Sue Thompson*
48/88 **Oh Jenny** *Billy Montana*
Oh Lonesome Me
1/58 *Don Gibson*
13/61 *Johnny Cash*
64/66 *Bobbi Martin*
63/70 *Stonewall Jackson*
92/76 *Loggins & Messina*
8/90 *Kentucky Headhunters*
78/86 **Oh Louisiana** *Jim & Jesse*
41/71 **Oh, Love Of Mine** *Johnny & Jonie Mosby*

5/93 **Oh Me, Oh My, Sweet Baby** *Diamond Rio*
42/64 **Oh No!** *Browns*
76/82 **Oh, No** *Randy Parton*
Oh-Oh, I'm Falling In Love Again
5/58 *Jimmie Rodgers*
29/73 *Eddy Arnold*
Oh Pretty Woman
13/70 *Arlene Harden (Lovin' Man)*
89/89 *Roy Orbison & Friends*
4/71 **Oh, Singer** *Jeannie C. Riley*
8/57 **Oh' So Many Years** *Kitty Wells & Webb Pierce*
Oh, Such A Stranger
68/68 *Frank Ifield*
61/78 *Don Gibson*
23/76 **Oh, Sweet Temptation** *Gary Stewart*
97/76 **Oh Those Texas Women** *Gene Davis*
5/88 **Oh What A Love** *Nitty Gritty Dirt Band*
56/87 **Oh What A Night** *Mel McDaniel*
60/69 **Oh What A Woman!** *Jerry Reed*
12/91 **Oh What It Did To Me** *Tanya Tucker*
4/47 **(Oh Why, Oh Why, Did I Ever Leave) Wyoming** *Dick Jurgens*
17/67 **Oh! Woman** *Nat Stuckey*
55/73 **Oh Woman** *Jack Barlow*
57/86 **Oh Yes I Can** *Tari Hensley*
1/69 **Okie From Muskogee** *Merle Haggard*
33/01 **Oklahoma** *Billy Gilman*
9/86 **Oklahoma Borderline** *Vince Gill*
49/82 **Oklahoma Crude** *Corbin/Hanner Band*
46/84 **Oklahoma Heart** *Becky Hobbs*
Oklahoma Hills
1/45 *Jack Guthrie*
7/61 *Hank Thompson*
60/69 **Oklahoma Home Brew** *Hank Thompson*
15/72 **Oklahoma Sunday Morning** *Glen Campbell*
86/76 **Oklahoma Sunshine** *Pat Boone*
13/90 **Oklahoma Swing** *Vince Gill*
53/05 **Oklahoma-Texas Line** *Rascal Flatts*
9/48 **Oklahoma Waltz** *Johnny Bond*
Ol' Man River ..see: Old Man River
14/02 **Ol' Red** *Blake Shelton*
70/68 **Old Before My Time** *Bobby Wright*
38/73 **Old Betsy Goes Boing, Boing, Boing** *Hummers*
48/86 **Old Blue Yodeler** *Razzy Bailey*
52/68 **Old Bridge** *Jean Shepard*
11/87 **Old Bridges Burn Slow** *Billy Joe Royal*
30/66 **Old Brush Arbors** *George Jones*
4/93 **Old Country** *Mark Chesnutt*
48/64 **Old Courthouse** *Faron Young*
5/89 **Old Coyote Town** *Don Williams*
1/73 **(Old Dogs-Children And) Watermelon Wine** *Tom T. Hall*
1/95 **Old Enough To Know Better** *Wade Hayes*
53/70 **Old Enough To Want To (Fool Enough To Try)** *Norro Wilson*
13/69 **Old Faithful** *Mel Tillis*
49/73 **Old Faithful** *Tony Booth*

86/81 **Old Familiar Feeling** *Wyvon Alexander*
83/81 **Old Fangled Country Songs** *Kenny O.*
F/78 **Old Fashioned Love** *Kendalls*
58/72 **Old Fashioned Love Song** *Jeris Ross*
93/81 **Old Fashioned Lover (In A Brand New Love Affair)** *Michele Spitz*
93/83 **Old Fashioned Lovin'** *Sierra*
38/73 **Old Fashioned Singing** *George Jones & Tammy Wynette*
1/81 **Old Flame** *Alabama*
5/86 **Old Flame** *Juice Newton*
46/89 **Old Flame, New Fire** *Burch Sisters*
54/78 **Old Flame, New Fire** *Hank Williams, Jr.*
Old Flames (Can't Hold A Candle To You)
14/78 *Joe Sun*
86/78 *Brian Collins*
1/80 *Dolly Parton*
5/92 **Old Flames Have New Names** *Mark Chesnutt*
2/88 **Old Folks** *Ronnie Milsap & Mike Reid*
49/66 **Old French Quarter (In New Orleans)** *Billy Walker*
19/82 **Old Friends** *Roger Miller/Willie Nelson/Ray Price*
6/80 **Old Habits** *Hank Williams, Jr.*
2/85 **Old Hippie** *Bellamy Brothers*
19/74 **Old Home Filler-Up An' Keep On-A-Truckin' Cafe** *C.W. McCall*
44/82 **Old Home Town** *Glen Campbell*
30/88 **Old Kind Of Love** *Ricky Skaggs*
34/77 **Old King Kong** *George Jones*
20/60 **Old Lamplighter** *Browns*
30/60 **Old Log Cabin For Sale** *Porter Wagoner*
11/55 **Old Lonesome Times** *Carl Smith*
63/70 **Old Love Affair, Now Showing** *Leroy Van Dyke*
11/77 **Old Man And His Horn** *Gene Watson*
1/74 **Old Man From The Mountain** *Merle Haggard*
63/88 **Old Man No One Loves** *George Jones*
Old Man River
86/76 *Shylo*
22/83 *Mel McDaniel*
31/70 **Old Man Willis** *Nat Stuckey*
Old Man's Back In Town
48/93 *Garth Brooks*
59/98 *Garth Brooks*
74/84 **Old Memories Are Hard To Lose** *Kimberly Springs*
90/75 **Old Memory (Got In My Eye)** *Ferlin Husky*
7/59 **Old Moon** *Betty Foley*
21/93 **Old Pair Of Shoes** *Randy Travis*
50/89 **Old Pair Of Shoes** *Sawyer Brown*
Old Photographs
81/84 *Sam Neely*
27/88 *Sawyer Brown*
11/64 **Old Records** *Margie Singleton*
50/65 **Old Red** *Marty Robbins*
3/62 **Old Rivers** *Walter Brennan*
51/68 **Old Ryman** *Hank Williams, Jr.*

5/86 **Old School** *John Conlee*
8/63 **Old Showboat** *Stonewall Jackson*
9/80 **Old Side Of Town** *Tom T. Hall*
9/51 **Old Soldiers Never Die** *Gene Autry*
64/95 **Old Stuff** *Garth Brooks*
62/00 **Old Time Christmas** *George Strait*
26/77 **Old Time Feeling** *Johnny Cash & June Carter Cash*
64/77 **Old Time Lovin'** *Kenny Starr*
97/74 **Old Time Sunshine Song** *Roy Acuff*
57/01 **Old Toy Trains** *Toby Keith*
21/86 **Old Violin** *Johnny Paycheck*
49/03 **Old Weakness (Coming On Strong)** *Tanya Tucker*
Old Wives' Tale ..see: (Just An)
3/52 **Older And Bolder** *Eddy Arnold*
8/74 **Older The Violin, The Sweeter The Music** *Hank Thompson*
1/81 **Older Women** *Ronnie McDowell*
52/86 **Ole Rock And Roller** *Keith Stegall*
Ole Slew-Foot
48/66 *Porter Wagoner*
31/79 *Porter Wagoner*
59/96 **On A Bus To St. Cloud** *Trisha Yearwood*
2/96 **On A Good Night** *Wade Hayes*
19/03 **On A Mission** *Trick Pony*
4/01 **On A Night Like This** *Trick Pony*
23/87 **On And On** *Anne Murray*
27/79 **On Business For The King** *Joe Sun*
5/90 **On Down The Line** *Patty Loveless*
71/99 **On Earth As It Is In Texas** *Deryl Dodd*
1/78 **On My Knees** *Charlie Rich w/ Janie Fricke*
12/57 **On My Mind Again** *Billy Walker*
20/95 **On My Own** *Reba McEntire*
54/99 **On My Way To You** *Sonya Isaacs*
1/90 **On Second Thought** *Eddie Rabbitt*
7/68 **On Tap, In The Can, Or In The Bottle** *Hank Thompson*
9/74 **On The Cover Of The Music City News** *Buck Owens*
76/81 **On The Inside** *Patti Page*
1/86 **On The Other Hand** *Randy Travis*
44/67 **On The Other Hand** *Charlie Louvin*
29/76 **On The Rebound** *Del Reeves & Billie Jo Spears*
6/93 **On The Road** *Lee Roy Parnell*
1/80 **On The Road Again** *Willie Nelson*
4/98 **On The Side Of Angels** *LeAnn Rimes*
69/91 **On The Surface** *Rosanne Cash*
2/97 **On The Verge** *Collin Raye*
49/75 **On The Way Home** *Betty Jean Robinson*
49/84 **On The Wings Of A Nightingale** *Everly Brothers*
85/83 **On The Wings Of My Victory** *Glen Campbell*
8/51 **On Top Of Old Smoky** *Weavers*
29/04 **On Your Way Home** *Patty Loveless*
4/67 **Once** *Ferlin Husky*
1/64 **Once A Day** *Connie Smith*
68/87 **Once A Fool, Always A Fool** *Jeff Dugan*

91/75 **Once Again I Go To Sleep With Lovin' On My Mind** *Melody Allen*
87/90 **Once And For Always** *Gary Dale Parker*
60/96 **Once I Was The Light Of Your Life** *Stephanie Bentley*
1/86 **Once In A Blue Moon** *Earl Thomas Conley*
34/79 **Once In A Blue Moon** *Zella Lehr*
82/83 **Once In A Blue Moon** *Hank Thompson*
50/00 **Once In A Lifetime Love** *Clay Walker*
Once In A Lifetime Thing
5/77 *John Wesley Ryles*
86/90 *Sammy Sadler*
85/86 **Once In A Very Blue Moon** *Nanci Griffith*
53/94 **Once In A While** *Billy Dean*
Once More
8/58 *Roy Acuff*
13/58 *Osborne Brothers & Red Allen*
66/69 *Leona Williams*
2/70 **Once More With Feeling** *Jerry Lee Lewis*
42/70 **Once More With Feeling** *Willie Nelson*
3/93 **Once Upon A Lifetime** *Alabama*
80/86 **Once Upon A Time** *Bobby Blue*
Once You Get The Feel Of It
42/83 *Con Hunley*
79/88 *Marshall Tucker Band*
75/97 **Once You Learn** *Noel Haggard*
80/81 **Once You Were Mine** *Dottie West*
3/74 **Once You've Had The Best** *George Jones*
3/02 **One, The** *Gary Allan*
69/95 **One** *George Jones & Tammy Wynette*
95/78 **One A.M. Alone** *Dave Dudley*
27/63 **One Among The Many** *Ned Miller*
66/93 **One And One And One** *Gene Watson*
93/79 **One And One Make Three** *Ron Shaw*
51/95 **One And Only Love** *Russ Taff*
93/83 **One Away From One Too Many** *Billy Walker*
85/80 **One Bar At A Time** *Stoney Edwards*
45/05 **One Believer** *Diamond Rio*
61/85 **One Big Family** *Heart Of Nashville*
2/95 **One Boy, One Girl** *Collin Raye*
57/91 **One Bridge I Didn't Burn** *Conway Twitty*
42/66 **One Bum Town** *Del Reeves*
1/54 **One By One** *Kitty Wells & Red Foley*
95/75 **One By One** *Jimmy Elledge*
73/88 **One Dance Love Affair** *Jon Washington*
One Day At A Time
19/74 *Marilyn Sellars*
1/80 *Cristy Lane*
8/74 **One Day At A Time** *Don Gibson*
55/05 **One Day At A Time** *Deana Carter*
24/02 **One Day Closer To You** *Carolyn Dawn Johnson*
35/99 **One Day Left To Live** *Sammy Kershaw*
72/82 **One Day Since Yesterday** *Colleen Camp*
23/64 **One Dozen Roses (And Our Love)** *George Morgan*
54/66 **One Dream** *Slim Whitman*
10/65 **One Dyin' And A Buryin'** *Roger Miller*
2/95 **One Emotion** *Clint Black*
70/83 **One Fiddle, Two Fiddle** *Ray Price*
75/82 **One Fine Morning** *Corbin/Hanner Band*
74/88 **One Fire Between Us** *Judy Byram*
2/87 **One For The Money** *T.G. Sheppard*
1/88 **One Friend** *Dan Seals*
74/92 **One Good Love** *Nitty Gritty Dirt Band*
57/94 **One Good Man** *Michelle Wright*
71/80 **One Good Reason** *Melissa Lewis*
4/89 **One Good Well** *Don Williams*
17/61 **One Grain Of Sand** *Eddy Arnold*
One Has My Name (The Other Has My Heart)
1/48 *Jimmy Wakely*
11/48 *Eddie Dean*
8/49 *Bob Eberly*
3/69 *Jerry Lee Lewis*
69/98 **One Heart At A Time** *One Heart At A Time*
43/85 **One Hell Of A Heartache** *Gene Watson*
One Hell Of A Woman ..see: (You Better Be)
7/99 **One Honest Heart** *Reba McEntire*
6/91 **One Hundred And Two** *Judds*
14/71 **One Hundred Children** *Tom T. Hall*
1/86 **100% Chance Of Rain** *Gary Morris*
3/86 **One I Loved Back Then (The Corvette Song)** *George Jones*
58/75 **One I Sing My Love Songs To** *Tommy Cash*
11/64 **One If For Him, Two If For Me** *David Houston*
1/80 **One In A Million** *Johnny Lee*
57/99 **One In A Million** *Mindy McCready*
73/78 **One In A Million** *Nate Harvell*
19/66 **One In A Row** *Willie Nelson*
50/89 **One In Your Heart One On Your Mind** *Charly McClain*
1/49 **One Kiss Too Many** *Eddy Arnold*
26/03 **One Last Time** *Dusty Drake*
33/73 **One Last Time** *Glen Campbell*
70/91 **One Less Pony** *Sawyer Brown*
64/92 **One Like That** *JJ White*
91/79 **One Little Skinny Rib** *Cal Smith*
11/62 **One Look At Heaven** *Stonewall Jackson*
33/91 **One Love** *Carlene Carter*
3/86 **One Love At A Time** *Tanya Tucker*
95/76 **One Love Down** *Gary Mack*
76/81 **One Love Over Easy** *Sami Jo Cole*
27/65 **One Man Band** *Phil Baugh*
42/86 **One Man Band** *Moe Bandy*
61/68 **One Man Band** *Norma Jean*
63/69 **One Man Band** *Sheb Wooley*
8/90 **One Man Woman** *Judds*
72/80 **One Man's Trash (Is Another Man's Treasure)** *Marty Robbins*
85/79 **One Man's Woman** *Kelly Warren*
2/70 **One Minute Past Eternity** *Jerry Lee Lewis*
60/03 **One Mississippi** *Jill King*
11/75 **One Monkey Don't Stop No Show** *Little David Wilkins*
1/01 **One More Day** *Diamond Rio*
56/71 **One More Drink** *Mel Tillis*
95/83 **One More Goodbye, One More Hello** *Donnie Record*
97/78 **One More Kiss** *Terri Bishop*
1/93 **One More Last Chance** *Vince Gill*
33/81 **One More Last Chance** *Ray Stevens*
12/69 **One More Mile** *Dave Dudley*
48/70 **One More Mountain To Climb** *Freddie Hart*
7/91 **One More Payment** *Clint Black*
42/84 **One More Shot** *Johnny Lee*
2/60 **One More Time** *Ray Price*
28/71 **One More Time** *Ferlin Husky*
44/72 **One More Time** *Jo Anna Neel*
65/74 **One More Time** *Skeeter Davis*
80/78 **One More Time** *Sandra Kaye*
31/76 **One More Time (Karneval)** *Crystal Gayle*
28/76 **(One More Year Of) Daddy's Little Girl** *Ray Sawyer*
One Night
24/58 *Elvis Presley*
57/72 *Jeannie C. Riley*
51/76 *Roy Head*
61/98 **One Night** *JC Jones*
7/94 **One Night A Day** *Garth Brooks*
1/97 **One Night At A Time** *George Strait*
10/81 **One-Night Fever** *Mel Tillis*
85/80 **One Night Honeymoon** *Troy Seals*
51/02 **One Night In New Orleans** *BlackHawk*
80/80 **One Night Led To Two** *Paul Evans*
39/71 **One Night Of Love** *Johnny Duncan*
35/70 **One Night Stand** *Susan Raye*
66/97 **One Night Stand** *Caryl Mack Parker*
89/74 **One Night Stand** *Rick Nelson*
47/77 **One Night Stands** *Hank Williams, Jr.*
82/82 **One Night Stanley** *Jerry Abbott*
71/88 **One Nite Stan** *Ethel & The Shameless Hussies*
6/77 **One Of A Kind** *Tammy Wynette*
13/80 **One Of A Kind** *Moe Bandy*
1/83 **One Of A Kind Pair Of Fools** *Barbara Mandrell*
28/60 **One Of Her Fools** *Paul Davis*
67/87 **One Of The Boys** *Cheryl Handy*
69/70 **One Of The Fortunate Few** *Hank Thompson*
3/76 **One Of These Days** *Emmylou Harris*
8/64 **One Of These Days** *Marty Robbins*
36/68 **One Of These Days** *Tompall/Glaser Brothers*
74/93 **One Of These Days** *Matthews, Wright & King*
2/98 **One Of These Days** *Tim McGraw*
50/03 **One Of Those Days** *Brad Martin*

64/95 **One Of Those Nights** *Lisa Brokop*
14/98 **One Of Those Nights Tonight** *Lorrie Morgan*
6/91 **One Of Those Things** *Pam Tillis*
73/99 **One Of You** *George Strait*
2/66 **One On The Right Is On The Left** *Johnny Cash*
4/85 **One Owner Heart** *T.G. Sheppard*
1/76 **One Piece At A Time** *Johnny Cash*
51/92 **One Precious Love** *Prairie Oyster*
1/87 **One Promise Too Late** *Reba McEntire*
26/78 **One Run For The Roses** *Narvel Felts*
51/91 **One Shot At A Time** *Clinton Gregory*
8/78 **One Sided Conversation** *Gene Watson*
52/84 **One Sided Love Affair** *Mike Campbell*
16/98 **One Small Miracle** *Bryan White*
41/97 **One Solitary Tear** *Sherrié Austin*
9/70 **One Song Away** *Tommy Cash*
48/75 **One Step** *Bobby Harden*
14/61 **One Step Ahead Of My Past** *Hank Locklin*
15/57 **One Step At A Time** *Brenda Lee*
38/04 **One Step At A Time** *Buddy Jewell*
90/83 **One Step Closer** *Cannons*
2/88 **One Step Forward** *Desert Rose Band*
63/90 **One Step Over The Line** *Nitty Gritty Dirt Band/Rosanne Cash/John Hiatt*
8/84 **One Takes The Blame** *Statler Brothers*
90/82 **One Tear (At A Time)** *Noel*
37/82 **One That Got Away** *Mel Tillis*
17/79 **One Thing My Lady Never Puts Into Words** *Mel Street*
43/92 **One Time Around** *Michelle Wright*
55/88 **One Time One Night** *Los Lobos*
97/88 **One Time Thing** *Ramsey Kearney*
54/72 **One Tin Soldier** *Skeeter Davis*
82/81 **One Too Many Memories** *Ray Pillow*
4/88 **One True Love** *O'Kanes*
18/97 **One, Two, I Love You** *Clay Walker*
88/75 **One, Two, Three (Never Gonna Fall In Love Again)** *Jim Glaser*
20/00 **One Voice** *Billy Gilman*
20/61 **One Way Street** *Bob Gallion*
1/96 **One Way Ticket (Because I Can)** *LeAnn Rimes*
12/58 **One Week Later** *Webb Pierce & Kitty Wells*
32/72 **One Woman's Trash (Another Woman's Treasure)** *Bobbie Roy*
61/83 **1 Yr 2 Mo 11 Days** *Wayne Carson*
38/72 **One You Say Good Mornin' To** *Jimmy Dean*
13/60 **One You Slip Around With** *Jan Howard*
1/72 **One's On The Way** *Loretta Lynn*
2/72 **Oney** *Johnny Cash*
47/85 **Only A Dream Away** *Mason Dixon*
61/68 **Only A Fool** *Ned Miller*
2/84 **Only A Lonely Heart Knows** *Barbara Mandrell*
24/71 **Only A Woman Like You** *Nat Stuckey*
Only Daddy That'll Walk The Line
2/68 *Waylon Jennings*
73/68 *Jim Alley*
60/91 *Kentucky Headhunters*
59/79 **Only Diamonds Are Forever** *Zella Lehr*
13/63 **Only Girl I Can't Forget** *Del Reeves*
23/03 **Only God (Could Stop Me Loving You)** *Emerson Drive*
3/91 **Only Here For A Little While** *Billy Dean*
12/83 **Only If There Is Another You** *Moe Bandy*
1/01 **Only In America** *Brooks & Dunn*
5/85 **Only In My Mind** *Reba McEntire*
52/98 **Only Lonely Me** *Rick Trevino*
3/93 **Only Love** *Wynonna*
Only Love Can Break A Heart
2/72 *Sonny James*
7/79 *Kenny Dale*
11/88 **Only Love Can Save Me Now** *Crystal Gayle*
42/85 **Only Love Will Make It Right** *Nicolette Larson*
49/66 **Only Me And My Hairdresser Know** *Kitty Wells*
5/96 **Only On Days That End In "Y"** *Clay Walker*
80/86 **Only One** *James Taylor*
1/78 **Only One Love In My Life** *Ronnie Milsap*
1/82 **Only One You** *T.G. Sheppard*
55/76 **Only Sixteen** *Dr. Hook*
81/78 **Only The Best** *George Hamilton IV*
1/69 **Only The Lonely** *Sonny James*
74/83 **Only The Names Have Been Changed** *Penny DeHaven*
87/77 **Only The Shadows Know** *Vernon Oxford*
71/89 **Only The Strong Survive** *Darrell Holt*
4/92 **Only The Wind** *Billy Dean*
54/89 **Only Thing Bluer Than His Eyes** *Joni Harms*
58/67 **Only Thing I Want** *Cal Smith*
36/68 **Only Way Out (Is To Walk Over Me)** *Charlie Louvin*
32/81 **Only When I Laugh** *Brenda Lee*
4/87 **Only When I Love** *Holly Dunn*
Only You
68/69 *Norro Wilson*
34/78 *Freddie Hart*
13/82 *Reba McEntire*
36/86 *Statler Brothers*
51/96 *Travis Tritt*
1/65 **Only You (Can Break My Heart)** *Buck Owens*
9/56 **Only You, Only You** *Charlie Walker*
85/78 **Ooh Baby Baby** *Linda Ronstadt*
70/97 **Open Arms** *Collin Raye*
68/89 **Open For Suggestions** *Perry LaPointe*
13/62 **Open Pit Mine** *George Jones*
45/71 **Open Up The Book (And Take A Look)** *Ferlin Husky*
98/77 **Open Up Your Door** *Eddie Rivers*
1/66 **Open Up Your Heart** *Buck Owens*
14/73 **Open Up Your Heart** *Roger Miller*
78/82 **Operator** *Tennessee Express*
9/82 **Operator, Long Distance Please** *Barbara Mandrell*
Operator, Operator
65/83 *Larry Willoughby*
9/85 *Eddy Raven*
10/61 **Optimistic** *Skeeter Davis*
Orange Blossom Special
3/65 *Johnny Cash*
26/73 *Charlie McCoy*
63/74 *Johnny Darrell*
4/53 **Orchids Mean Goodbye** *Carl Smith*
3/99 **Ordinary Life** *Chad Brock*
24/99 **Ordinary Love** *Shane Minor*
26/77 **Ordinary Man** *Dale McBride*
29/68 **Ordinary Miracle** *Bobby Lewis*
35/98 **Ordinary People** *Clay Walker*
52/74 **Orleans Parish Prison** *Johnny Cash*
48/01 **Osama-Yo' Mama** *Ray Stevens*
19/61 **Other Cheek** *Kitty Wells*
30/88 **Other Guy** *David Slater*
71/78 **Other Side Of Jeannie** *Chuck Pollard*
Other Side Of The Hill ..see: (Lover Of The)
72/78 **Other Side Of The Morning** *Barbara Fairchild*
41/98 **Other Side Of This Kiss** *Mindy McCready*
Other Woman
2/65 *Ray Price*
74/70 *Ray Pennington*
13/63 **Other Woman** *Loretta Lynn*
54/90 **Oughta Be A Law** *Lee Roy Parnell*
56/77 **Our Baby's Gone** *Herb Pedersen*
(Our Endless Love) ..see: Gone
58/68 **Our Golden Wedding Day** *Johnny & Jonie Mosby*
24/65 **Our Hearts Are Holding Hands** *Ernest Tubb & Loretta Lynn*
6/52 **Our Honeymoon** *Carl Smith*
18/69 **Our House Is Not A Home** *Lynn Anderson*
8/50 **Our Lady Of Fatima** *Red Foley*
64/89 **Our Little Corner** *Butch Baker*
44/75 **Our Love** *Roger Miller*
77/87 **Our Love Is Like The South** *A.J. Masters*
1/83 **Our Love Is On The Faultline** *Crystal Gayle*
43/92 **Our Love Was Meant To Be** *Boy Howdy*
21/62 **Our Mansion Is A Prison Now** *Kitty Wells*
45/75 **Our Marriage Was A Failure** *Johnny Russell*
91/77 **Our Old Mansion** *Buck Owens*
(Our Own) Jole Blon ..see: Jole Blon
42/65 **Our Ship Of Love** *Carl Butler & Pearl*
27/67 **Our Side** *Van Trevor*
33/64 **Our Things** *Margie Bowes*
56/82 **Our Wedding Band** *Louise Mandrell & RC Bannon*
21/86 **Out Among The Stars** *Merle Haggard*
9/54 **Out Behind The Barn** *"Little" Jimmy Dickens*

11/86 **Out Goin' Cattin'** *Sawyer Brown w/ "Cat" Joe Bonsall*
54/00 **Out Here In The Water** *Rebecca Lynn Howard*
81/88 **Out Of Beer** *Johnny Paycheck*
25/60 **Out Of Control** *George Jones*
4/75 **Out Of Hand** *Gary Stewart*
2/98 **Out Of My Bones** *Randy Travis*
1/78 **Out Of My Head And Back In My Bed** *Loretta Lynn*
50/77 **Out Of My Mind** *Cates*
10/88 **Out Of Sight And On My Mind** *Billy Joe Royal*
71/85 **Out Of Sight Out Of Mind** *Narvel Felts*
34/80 **Out Of Your Mind** *Joe Sun*
2/89 **Out Of Your Shoes** *Lorrie Morgan*
46/80 **Out Run The Sun** *Jim Chesnut*
32/65 **Out Where The Ocean Meets The Sky** *Hugh X. Lewis*
13/96 **Out With A Bang** *David Lee Murphy*
87/87 **Out With The Boys** *Rhonda Manning*
91/79 **Out With The Boys** *Barry Grant*
9/92 **Outbound Plane** *Suzy Bogguss*
60/02 **Outdoor Lovin' Man** *Hank Williams, Jr.*
27/79 **Outlaw's Prayer** *Johnny Paycheck*
81/79 **Outlaws And Lone Star Beer** *C.W. McCall*
91/89 **Outside Chance** *Larry Dean*
18/83 **Outside Lookin' In** *Bandana*
40/94 **Outskirts Of Town** *Sawyer Brown*
10/80 **Over** *Leon Everette*
62/98 **Over My Shoulder** *John Berry*
10/80 **Over The Rainbow** *Jerry Lee Lewis*
69/82 **Over Thirty (Not Over The Hill)** *Conway Twitty*
15/49 **Over Three Hills** *Ernie Benedict*
15/83 **Over You** *Lane Brody*
59/88 **Overdue** *Canyon*
10/58 **Overnight** *Jim Reeves*
70/92 **Overnight Male** *George Strait*
7/76 **Overnight Sensation** *Mickey Gilley*
8/90 **Overnight Success** *George Strait*
5/84 **Ozark Mountain Jubilee** *Oak Ridge Boys*
87/76 **Ozark Mountain Lullaby** *Susan Raye*

P

70/94 **PMS Blues** *Dolly Parton*
86/85 **P.S.** *Noel*
8/84 **P.S. I Love You** *Tom T. Hall*
3/62 **P.T. 109** *Jimmy Dean*
68/93 **Pack Your Lies And Go** *Celinda Pink*
Padre
5/71 *Marty Robbins*
92/75 *Judy Lynn*
34/86 **Pages Of My Mind** *Ray Charles*
77/82 **Pain In My Past** *Rovers*
Paint Me A Birmingham
4/04 *Tracy Lawrence*
54/04 *Ken Mellons*
49/72 **Paint Me A Rainbow** *Wynn Stewart*
13/89 **Paint The Town And Hang The Moon Tonight** *J. C. Crowley*
49/85 **Paint The Town Blue** *Robin Lee & Lobo*
52/68 **Painted Girls And Wine** *Ed Bruce*
78/77 **Painted Lady** *Chuck Woolery*
8/45 **Pair Of Broken Hearts** *Spade Cooley*
19/80 **Pair Of Old Sneakers** *George Jones & Tammy Wynette*
81/80 **Palimony** *Leon Rausch*
33/76 **Paloma Blanca** *George Baker Selection*
88/76 **Pamela Brown** *Jud Strunk*
9/48 **Pan American** *Hawkshaw Hawkins*
7/50 **Pan American Boogie** *Delmore Brothers*
1/83 **Pancho And Lefty** *Willie Nelson & Merle Haggard*
6/49 **Panhandle Rag** *Leon McAuliffe*
64/67 **Papa** *Bill Anderson*
24/98 **Papa Bear** *Keith Harling*
62/69 **Papa Joe's Thing** *Papa Joe's Music Box*
3/92 **Papa Loved Mama** *Garth Brooks*
16/71 **Papa Was A Good Man** *Johnny Cash*
Paper Angels
40/04 *Jimmy Wayne*
18/05 *Jimmy Wayne*
30/75 **Paper Lovin'** *Margo Smith*
8/67 **Paper Mansions** *Dottie West*
1/73 **Paper Roses** *Marie Osmond*
3/77 **Paper Rosie** *Gene Watson*
85/88 **Paper Thin Walls** *David Wills*
26/76 **Paradise** *Lynn Anderson*
26/96 **Paradise** *John Anderson*
46/00 **Paradise** *Craig Morgan*
80/81 **Paradise** *Southern Ashe*
54/82 **Paradise Knife And Gun Club** *Roy Clark*
1/83 **Paradise Tonight** *Charly McClain & Mickey Gilley*
67/68 **Parchman Farm Blues** *Claude King*
66/85 **Pardon Me, But This Heart's Taken** *Terry Gregory*
Pardon Me (Haven't We Loved Somewhere Before)
86/83 *Zella Lehr*
64/84 *Becky Hobbs*
63/81 **Pardon My French** *Bobby G. Rice*
49/71 **Part Of America Died** *Eddy Arnold*
Part Of Me That Needs You Most
79/79 *Miki Mori*
61/85 *B.J. Thomas*
35/72 **Part Of Your Life** *Charlie Rich*
68/69 **Parting (Is Such Sweet Sorrow)** *Wilma Burgess*
48/69 **Partly Bill** *LaWanda Lindsey*
38/81 **Partner Nobody Chose** *Guy Clark*
5/59 **Partners** *Jim Reeves*
24/87 **Partners After All** *Willie Nelson*
6/86 **Partners, Brothers And Friends** *Nitty Gritty Dirt Band*
53/95 **Party All Night** *Jeff Foxworthy w/ Little Texas & Scott Rouse*
6/95 **Party Crowd** *David Lee Murphy*
31/72 **Party Dolls And Wine** *Red Stegall*
7/04 **Party For Two** *Shania Twain*
50/98 **Party On** *Neal McCoy*
69/88 **Party People** *Butch Baker*
24/67 **Party Pickin'** *George Jones & Melba Montgomery*
1/81 **Party Time** *T.G. Sheppard*
24/67 **Party's Over** *Willie Nelson*
78/83 **Party's Over (Everybody's Gone)** *Sam Neely*
3/90 **Pass It On Down** *Alabama*
Pass Me By (If You're Only Passing Through)
9/73 *Johnny Rodriguez*
22/80 *Janie Fricke*
15/65 **Pass The Booze** *Ernest Tubb*
12/04 **Passenger Seat** *SheDaisy*
28/77 **Passing Thing** *Ray Griff*
67/69 **Passin' Through** *Ray Corbin*
37/64 **Passing Through** *David Houston*
23/61 **Passing Zone Blues** *Coleman Wilson*
4/93 **Passionate Kisses** *Mary-Chapin Carpenter*
4/64 **Password** *Kitty Wells*
2/92 **Past The Point Of Rescue** *Hal Ketchum*
Patches
26/70 *Ray Griff*
30/81 *Jerry Reed*
46/69 **Pathway Of My Life** *Hank Thompson*
18/58 **Patricia** *Perez Prado*
13/77 **Pay Phone** *Bob Luman*
6/53 **Paying For That Back Street Affair** *Kitty Wells*
Peace In The Valley ..see: (There'll Be)
23/81 **Peace Of Mind** *Eddy Raven*
74/99 **Peace Of Mind** *George Strait*
8S/97 **Peace Train** *Dolly Parton*
73/93 **Peaceful Easy Feeling** *Little Texas*
21/77 **Peanut Butter** *Dickey Lee*
10/76 **Peanuts And Diamonds** *Bill Anderson*
8/63 **Pearl Pearl Pearl** *Flatt & Scruggs*
Pecos Bill ..see: (There'll Never Be Another)
10/80 **Pecos Promenade** *Tanya Tucker*
8/64 **Peel Me A Nanner** *Roy Drusky*
4/48 **Peepin' Thru The Keyhole (Watching Jole Blon)** *Cliffie Stone*
36/64 **Pen And Paper** *Jerry Lee Lewis*
44/71 **Pencil Marks On The Wall** *Henson Cargill*
12/49 **Pennies For Papa** *"Little" Jimmy Dickens*
8/75 **Penny** *Joe Stampley*
7/78 **Penny Arcade** *Cristy Lane*
5/55 **Penny Candy** *Jim Reeves*
85/89 **Penny For Your Thoughts Tonight Virginia** *David Houston*
17/01 **People Like Us** *Aaron Tippin*
70/86 **People's Court** *Ray Stevens*
57/82 **Pepsi Man** *Bobby Mackey*
2/04 **Perfect** *Sara Evans*
Perfect
85/89 *Fairground Attraction*
23/90 *Baillie & the Boys*
23/81 **Perfect Fool** *Debby Boone*
1/98 **Perfect Love** *Trisha Yearwood*

75/78 **Perfect Love Song** *Durwood Haddock*
24/72 **Perfect Match** *David Houston & Barbara Mandrell*
16/70 **Perfect Mountain** *Don Gibson*
69/00 **Perfect Night** *Billy Hoffman*
64/82 **Perfect Picture (To Fit My Frame Of Mind)** *Gary Wolf*
13/73 **Perfect Stranger** *Freddy Weller*
18/86 **Perfect Stranger** *Southern Pacific*
24/80 **Perfect Strangers** *John Wesley Ryles*
52/88 **Perfect Strangers** *Anne Murray w/ Doug Mallory*
50/00 **Perfect World** *Sawyer Brown*
29/75 **Personality** *Price Mitchell*
10/83 **Personally** *Ronnie McDowell*
Peter Cottontail
3/50 *Gene Autry*
6/50 *Mervin Shiner*
7/50 *Johnnie Lee Wills*
7/50 *Jimmy Wakely*
14/64 **Petticoat Junction** *Flatt & Scruggs*
Phantom 309
9/67 *Red Sovine*
47/76 *Red Sovine*
9/71 **Philadelphia Fillies** *Del Reeves*
73/79 **Philodendron** *Mundo Earwood*
60/68 **Phoenix Flash** *Stan Hitchcock*
36/68 **Phone Call To Mama** *Joyce Paul*
28/96 **Phones Are Ringin' All Over Town** *Martina McBride*
2S/05 **Photograph** *Malibu Storm*
89/89 **Photographic Memory** *Billy Mata*
74/79 **Piano Picker** *George Fischoff*
71/68 **Pick A Little Happy Song** *Bob Gallion*
Pick Me Up On Your Way Down
2/58 *Charlie Walker*
46/70 *Carl Smith*
35/76 *Bobby G. Rice*
13/64 **Pick Of The Week** *Roy Drusky*
Pick The Wildwood Flower
34/74 *Johnny Cash/Mother Maybelle Carter*
5/79 *Gene Watson*
96/77 **Pick Up The Pieces** *Con Hunley*
89/80 **Pick Up The Pieces Joanne** *Bobby Hood*
90/80 **Pickin' Up Love** *Ray Frushay*
3/81 **Pickin' Up Strangers** *Johnny Lee*
61/67 **Pickin' Up The Mail** *Compton Brothers*
27/70 **Pickin' Wild Mountain Berries** *LaWanda Lindsey/Kenny Vernon*
8/05 **Pickin' Wildflowers** *Keith Anderson*
42/77 **Picking Up The Pieces Of My Life** *Mac Davis*
1/94 **Pickup Man** *Joe Diffie*
62/89 **Pickup Truck Song** *Jerry Jeff Walker*
8/60 **Picture, The** *Roy Godfrey*
21/03 **Picture** *Kid Rock w/ Sheryl Crow*
28/91 **Picture Me** *Davis Daniel*
Picture Of Me (Without You)
5/72 *George Jones*
9/91 *Lorrie Morgan*
63/91 **Picture Of You** *Great Plains*
52/96 **Picture Perfect** *Sky Kings*
27/66 **Picture That's New** *George Morgan*
13/71 **Pictures** *Statler Brothers*
35/84 **Pictures** *Atlanta*
17/75 **Pictures On Paper** *Jeris Ross*
Piece Of My Heart
68/85 *Sandy Croft*
1/94 *Faith Hill*
81/84 **Piece Of My Heart** *John Hartford*
33/75 **Pieces Of My Life** *Elvis Presley*
29/88 **Pilgrims On The Way (Matthew's Song)** *Michael Martin Murphey*
5/75 **Pill, The** *Loretta Lynn*
47/74 **Pillow, The** *Johnny Duncan*
17/64 **Pillow That Whispers** *Carl Smith*
13/60 **Pinball Machine** *Lonnie Irving*
65/71 **Pine Grove** *Compton Brothers*
15/67 **Piney Wood Hills** *Bobby Bare*
92/86 **Pink Cadillac** *Kevin Pearce*
17/58 **Pink Pedal Pushers** *Carl Perkins*
10/84 **Pins And Needles** *Whites*
52/76 **Pins And Needles (In My Heart)** *Darrell McCall*
70/91 **Piper Came Today** *Willie Nelson*
Pistol Packin' Mama
1/44 *Bing Crosby & Andrews Sisters*
1/44 *Al Dexter*
6/78 **Pittsburgh Stealers** *Kendalls*
6/71 **Pitty, Pitty, Patter** *Susan Raye*
62/85 **Pity Party** *Bill Anderson*
8/54 **Place For Girls Like You** *Faron Young*
62/83 **Place I've Never Been** *Marshall Tucker Band*
60/82 **Place In The Sun** *Sonny James*
1/85 **Place To Fall Apart** *Merle Haggard w/ Janie Fricke*
100/77 **Place Where Love Has Been** *Arleen Harden*
5/97 **Places I've Never Been** *Mark Wills*
9/87 **Plain Brown Wrapper** *Gary Morris*
89/74 **Plain Vanilla** *Jeannie C. Riley*
30/89 **Planet Texas** *Kenny Rogers*
9/68 **Plastic Saddle** *Nat Stuckey*
23/73 **Plastic Trains, Paper Planes** *Susan Raye*
89/82 **Play Another Gettin' Drunk And Take Somebody Home Song** *Roy Head*
17/80 **Play Another Slow Song** *Johnny Duncan*
Play Born To Lose Again ..see: (After Sweet Memories)
1/77 **Play, Guitar Play** *Conway Twitty*
24/79 **Play Her Back To Yesterday** *Mel McDaniel*
24/79 **Play Me A Memory** *Zella Lehr*
Play Me No Sad Songs
34/76 *Rex Allen, Jr.*
82/79 *Earl Scruggs Revue*
43/82 **Play Me Or Trade Me** *Mel Tillis & Nancy Sinatra*
25/92 **Play, Ruby, Play** *Clinton Gregory*
1/05 **Play Something Country** *Brooks & Dunn*
35/82 **Play Something We Could Love To** *Diane Pfeifer*
35/76 **Play The Saddest Song On The Juke Box** *Carmol Taylor*
74/82 **Play This Old Working Day Away** *Dean Dillon*
11/79 **Play Together Again Again** *Buck Owens w/ Emmylou Harris*
93/74 **Play With Me** *Penny DeHaven*
24/03 **Playboys Of The Southwestern World** *Blake Shelton*
18/70 **Playin' Around With Love** *Barbara Mandrell*
22/79 **Playin' Hard To Get** *Janie Fricke*
8/57 **Playing For Keeps** *Elvis Presley*
62/85 **Playing For Keeps** *Holly Dunn*
98/88 **Playing With Matches** *Tim LeBeau*
97/77 **Playing With The Baby's Mama** *Bobby Wright*
7/97 **Please** *Kinleys*
22/01 **Please** *Pam Tillis*
34/78 **Please** *Narvel Felts*
76/79 **Please Be Gentle** *Amy*
7/86 **Please Be Love** *Mark Gray*
31/64 **Please Be My Love** *George Jones & Melba Montgomery*
46/70 **Please Be My New Love** *Jeannie Seely*
50/86 **Please Bypass This Heart** *Jimmy Buffett*
Please Come Home For Christmas
70/97 *Gary Allan*
71/97 *Lee Roy Parnell*
50/04 *Willie Nelson*
75/75 **Please Come To Nashville** *Ronnie Dove*
69/74 **Please, Daddy** *John Denver*
11/57 **Please Don't Blame Me** *Marty Robbins*
10/69 **Please Don't Go** *Eddy Arnold*
60/88 **Please Don't Leave Me Now** *Southern Reign*
Please Don't Let Me Love You
4/49 *George Morgan*
9/55 *Hank Williams*
14/49 **Please Don't Pass Me By** *Floyd Tillman*
17/78 **Please Don't Play A Love Song** *Marty Robbins*
1/74 **Please Don't Stop Loving Me** *Porter Wagoner & Dolly Parton*
86/86 **Please Don't Talk About Me When I'm Gone** *Ray Price*
Please Don't Tell Me How The Story Ends
8/71 *Bobby Bare*
1/74 *Ronnie Milsap*
Please Help Me, I'm Falling
1/60 *Hank Locklin*
68/70 *Hank Locklin & Danny Davis*
12/78 *Janie Fricke*
78/74 **Please Help Me Say No** *Mary Kay James*
10/69 **Please Let Me Prove (My Love For You)** *Dave Dudley*
11/61 **Please Mr. Kennedy** *Jim Nesbitt*
5/75 **Please Mr. Please** *Olivia Newton-John*
9/58 **Please Pass The Biscuits** *Gene Sullivan*
92/80 **Please Play More Kenny Rogers** *Steven Lee Cook w/ The Jordanaires*
6/88 **Please, Please Baby** *Dwight Yoakam*

Please Remember Me
69/95 *Rodney Crowell*
1/99 *Tim McGraw*
54/79 **Please Sing Satin Sheets For Me** *Jeanne Pruett*
43/83 **Please Surrender** *David Frizzell & Shelly West*
40/69 **Please Take Me Back** *Jim Glaser*
Please Talk To My Heart
14/63 *Country Johnny Mathis*
7/64 *Ray Price*
82/80 *Freddy Fender*
Please Tell Him [Her] That I Said Hello
50/76 *Sue Richards*
63/84 *Margo Smith*
70/89 *Bobby Vinton*
73/79 **Pleasin' My Woman** *Billy Parker*
71/83 **Pleasure Island** *David Frizzell & Shelly West*
32/81 **Pleasure's All Mine** *Dave & Sugar*
13/77 **Pleasure's Been All Mine** *Freddie Hart*
Pledging My Love
49/71 *Kitty Wells*
37/75 *Billy Thunderkloud*
F/77 *Elvis Presley*
9/84 *Emmylou Harris*
14/57 **Plenty Of Everything But You** *Ira & Charley Louvin*
9/61 **Po' Folks** *Bill Anderson*
7/91 **Pocket Full Of Gold** *Vince Gill*
22/94 **Pocket Of A Clown** *Dwight Yoakam*
3/91 **Point Of Light** *Randy Travis*
25/60 **Poison In Your Hand** *Connie Hall*
Poison Love
4/51 *Johnnie & Jack*
27/78 *Gail Davies*
72/70 **Poison Red Berries** *Glenn Barber*
87/89 **Poison Sugar** *Melissa Kay*
28/97 **Politics, Religion And Her** *Sammy Kershaw*
12/61 **Polka On A Banjo** *Flatt & Scruggs*
26/87 **Ponies** *Michael Johnson*
1/70 **Pool Shark** *Dave Dudley*
30/83 **Poor Boy** *Razzy Bailey*
39/66 **Poor Boy Blues** *Bob Luman*
Poor Folks ..see: Po' Folks
61/71 **Poor Folks Stick Together** *Stoney Edwards*
51/83 **Poor Girl** *Rick & Janis Carnes*
3/58 **Poor Little Fool** *Ricky Nelson*
2/56 **Poor Man's Riches** *Benny Barnes*
55/93 **Poor Man's Rose** *Stacy Dean Campbell*
Poor Man's Roses (Or A Rich Man's Gold)
14/57 *Patsy Cline*
66/81 *Patti Page*
67/00 **Poor Man's Son** *Charlie Robison*
24/75 **Poor Man's Woman** *Jeanne Pruett*
43/98 **Poor Me** *Joe Diffie*
10/59 **Poor Old Heartsick Me** *Margie Bowes*
70/69 **Poor Old Ugly Gladys Jones** *Don Bowman*
85/77 **Poor People Of Paris** *Maury Finney*
Poor Poor Pitiful Me
46/78 *Linda Ronstadt*
5/96 *Terri Clark*
44/65 **Poor Red Georgia Dirt** *Stonewall Jackson*
Poor Side Of Town
54/77 *Bobby Wayne Loftis*
12/83 *Joe Stampley*
14/75 **Poor Sweet Baby** *Jean Shepard*
82/76 **Poor Wilted Rose** *Ann J. Morton*
Pop A Top
3/67 *Jim Ed Brown*
6/99 *Alan Jackson*
26/71 **Portrait Of My Woman** *Eddy Arnold*
37/97 **Postmarked Birmingham** *BlackHawk*
Potato ..see: 'Tater
20/83 **Potential New Boyfriend** *Dolly Parton*
65/75 **Pour It All On Me** *Del Reeves*
12/01 **Pour Me** *Trick Pony*
59/98 **Pour Me A Vacation** *Great Divide*
5/80 **Pour Me Another Tequilla** *Eddie Rabbitt*
72/87 **Power Of A Woman** *Perry LaPointe*
Power Of Love
9/84 *Charley Pride*
51/94 *Lee Roy Parnell*
41/92 **Power Of Love** *Matthews, Wright & King*
8/78 **Power Of Positive Drinkin'** *Mickey Gilley*
48/68 **Power Of Your Sweet Love** *Claude King*
72/92 **Power Tools** *Ray Stevens*
43/99 **Power Windows** *John Berry*
6/99 **Powerful Thing** *Trisha Yearwood*
33/02 **Practice Life** *Andy Griggs w/ Martina McBride*
57/73 **Praise The Lord And Pass The Soup** *Johnny Cash/ Carter Family/Oak Ridge Boys*
83/82 **Praise The Lord And Send Me The Money** *Bobby Bare*
48/03 **Pray For The Fish** *Randy Travis*
62/74 **Prayer From A Mobile Home** *Del Reeves*
3/00 **Prayin' For Daylight** *Rascal Flatts*
49/90 **Praying For Rain** *Kevin Welch*
F/70 **Preacher And The Bear** *Jerry Reed*
45/79 **Preacher Berry** *Donna Fargo*
19/82 **Preaching Up A Storm** *Mel McDaniel*
87/89 **Precious Jewel** *Charlie Louvin - Roy Acuff*
19/83 **Precious Love** *Kendalls*
44/73 **Precious Memories Follow Me** *Josie Brown*
8/90 **Precious Thing** *Steve Wariner*
35/80 **Pregnant Again** *Loretta Lynn*
6/72 **Pretend I Never Happened** *Waylon Jennings*
71/82 **Pretending Fool** *Michael Ballew*
26/67 **Pretty Girl, Pretty Clothes, Pretty Sad** *Kenny Price*
10/85 **Pretty Lady** *Keith Stegall*
2/97 **Pretty Little Adriana** *Vince Gill*
45/04 **Pretty Paper** *Kenny Chesney w/ Willie Nelson*
89/80 **Pretty Poison** *Barry Grant*
12/54 **Pretty Words** *Marty Robbins*
35/69 **Price I Pay To Stay** *Jeannie C. Riley*
85/78 **Price Of Borrowed Love Is Just To High** *Charlotte Hurt*
60/97 **Price To Pay** *Randy Travis*
Pride
5/62 *Ray Price*
47/72 *Jeannie Seely*
12/81 *Janie Fricke*
18/62 **Pride Goes Before A Fall** *Jim Reeves*
46/86 **Pride Is Back** *Kenny Rogers w/ Nickie Ryder*
(Pride Of South Central High) ..see: Igmoo
3/72 **Pride's Not Hard To Swallow** *Hank Williams, Jr.*
66/73 **Printers Alley Stars** *Tennessee Ernie Ford*
23/60 **Prison Song** *Curly Putman*
10/50 **Prison Without Walls** *Eddy Arnold*
3/81 **Prisoner Of Hope** *Johnny Lee*
6/84 **Prisoner Of The Highway** *Ronnie Milsap*
14/76 **Prisoner's Song** *Sonny James*
30/66 **Prissy** *Chet Atkins*
33/67 **Private, The** *Del Reeves*
81/86 **Private Clown** *Steve Ricks*
72/97 **Private Conversation** *Lyle Lovett*
21/66 **Private Wilson White** *Marty Robbins*
12/57 **Prize Possession** *Ferlin Husky*
14↑/05 **Probably Wouldn't Be This Way** *LeAnn Rimes*
17/59 **Problems** *Everly Brothers*
4/44 **Prodigal Son** *Roy Acuff*
32/92 **Professional Fool** *Michael White*
Promised Land
3/71 *Freddy Weller*
F/75 *Elvis Presley*
61/97 **Promised Land** *Joe Diffie*
17/89 **Promises** *Randy Travis*
82/78 **Promises** *Eric Clapton*
15/67 **Promises And Hearts (Were Made To Break)** *Stonewall Jackson*
4/68 **Promises, Promises** *Lynn Anderson*
78/89 **Promises, Promises** *Lori Yates*
58/66 **Proof Is In The Kissing** *Charlie Louvin*
3/93 **Prop Me Up Beside The Jukebox (If I Die)** *Joe Diffie*
47/78 **Proud Lady** *Bob Luman*
Proud Mary
22/69 *Anthony Armstrong Jones*
56/73 *Brush Arbor*
22/75 **Proud Of You Baby** *Bob Luman*
91/80 **Prove It To You One More Time Again** *Kris Kristofferson*
74/82 **Pull My String** *Rich Landers*
18/70 **Pull My String And Wind Me Up** *Carl Smith*
28/68 **Punish Me Tomorrow** *Carl Butler & Pearl*
78/78 **Puppet On A String** *Elvis Presley*
71/95 **Pure Bred Redneck** *Cooter Brown*
1/74 **Pure Love** *Ronnie Milsap*
28/66 **Pursuing Happiness** *Norma Jean*
11/65 **Pushed In A Corner** *Ernest Ashworth*

Put A Little Holiday In Your Heart
51/97 *LeAnn Rimes*
71/98 *LeAnn Rimes*
30/70 **Put A Little Love In Your Heart** *Susan Raye*
23/76 **Put A Little Lovin' On Me** *Bobby Bare*
60/89 **Put A Quarter In The Jukebox** *Buck Owens*
21/75 **Put Another Log On The Fire** *Tompall*
Put Another Notch In Your Belt
89/75 *Kenny Starr*
76/84 *Susan Raye*
Put It Off Until Tomorrow
6/66 *Bill Phillips*
9/80 *Kendalls*
77/78 **Put It On Me** *Louise Mandrell*
43/76 **Put Me Back Into Your World** *Eddy Arnold*
30/73 **Put Me Down Softly** *Dickey Lee*
99/78 **Put Me Out Of My Memory** *Johnny Bush*
28/87 **Put Me Out Of My Misery** *Tom Wopat*
28/90 **Put Some Drive In Your Country** *Travis Tritt*
55/88 **Put Us Together Again** *Goldens*
Put You Back On The Rack ..see: (I'm Gonna)
25/64 **Put Your Arms Around Her** *Norma Jean*
26/04 **Put Your Best Dress On** *Steve Holy*
9/79 **Put Your Clothes Back On** *Joe Stampley*
1/82 **Put Your Dreams Away** *Mickey Gilley*
11/00 **Put Your Hand In Mine** *Tracy Byrd*
Put Your Hand In The Hand
61/71 *Beth Moore*
67/71 *Anne Murray*
48/75 **Put Your Head On My Shoulder** *Sunday Sharpe*
34/98 **Put Your Heart Into It** *Sherrié Austin*
44/69 **Put Your Lovin' Where Your Mouth Is** *Peggy Little*
11/91 **Put Yourself In My Place** *Pam Tillis*
4/90 **Put Yourself In My Shoes** *Clint Black*
Puttin' In Overtime At Home
74/75 *Del Reeves*
8/78 *Charlie Rich*
33/90 **Puttin' The Dark Back Into The Night** *Sawyer Brown*
68/82 **Pyramid Of Cans** *Mundo Earwood*
85/80 **Pyramid Song** *J.C. Cunningham*

Q

69/74 **Que Pasa** *Kenny Price*
28/65 **Queen Of Draw Poker Town** *Hank Snow*
14/81 **Queen Of Hearts** *Juice Newton*
75/82 **Queen Of Hearts Loves You** *Joe Waters*
28/67 **Queen Of Honky Tonk Street** *Kitty Wells*
2/93 **Queen Of Memphis** *Confederate Railroad*
7/93 **Queen Of My Double Wide Trailer** *Sammy Kershaw*
5/83 **Queen Of My Heart** *Hank Williams, Jr.*
77/76 **Queen Of New Orleans** *Earl Conley*
83/75 **Queen Of Temptation** *Brian Collins*
5/65 **Queen Of The House** *Jody Miller*
Queen Of The Silver Dollar
29/73 *Doyle Holly*
25/76 *Dave & Sugar*
47/76 **Queen Of The Starlight Ballroom** *David Wills*
92/79 **Quicksand** *Bill Wence*
3/50 **Quicksilver** *Elton Britt & Rosalie Allen*
64/68 **Quiet Kind** *Mac Curtis*
36/87 **Quietly Crazy** *Ed Bruce*
26/90 **Quit While I'm Behind** *McCarters*
3/71 **Quits** *Bill Anderson*
26/77 **Quits** *Gary Stewart*
21/00 **Quittin' Kind** *Joe Diffie*
7/90 **Quittin' Time** *Mary-Chapin Carpenter*
55/86 **Quittin' Time** *Con Hunley*

R

Race Is On
3/64 *George Jones*
5/89 *Sawyer Brown*
85/87 **Rachel's Room** *Bobby G. Rice*
39/88 **Radio, The** *Vince Gill*
62/94 **Radio Active** *Bryan Austin*
1/85 **Radio Heart** *Charly McClain*
19/84 **Radio Land** *Michael Martin Murphey*
62/89 **Radio Lover** *George Jones*
51/86 **Radio Romance** *Tommy Roe*
53/90 **Radio Romance** *Canyon*
57/88 **Radio Song** *Ric Steel*
Rag Mop
2/50 *Johnnie Lee Wills*
90/78 *Drifting Cowboys*
19/78 **Ragamuffin Man** *Donna Fargo*
15/61 **Ragged But Right** *Moon Mullican*
31/74 **Ragged Old Flag** *Johnny Cash*
45/68 **Raggedy Ann** *Charlie Rich*
76/82 **Ragin' Cajun** *Charlie Daniels Band*
5/47 **Ragtime Cowboy Joe** *Eddy Howard*
52/74 **Railroad Lady** *Lefty Frizzell*
87/75 **Rain** *Kris Kristofferson & Rita Coolidge*
36/72 **Rain Falling On Me** *Johnny Russell*
63/72 **Rain-Rain** *Lois Johnson*
58/95 **Rain Through The Roof** *Billy Montana*
F/79 **Rainbow And Roses** *Billy Walker*
Rainbow At Midnight
5/46 *Carlisle Brothers*
1/47 *Ernest Tubb*
5/47 *Texas Jim Robertson*
28/70 **Rainbow Girl** *Bobby Lord*
16/74 **Rainbow In Daddy's Eyes** *Sammi Smith*
75/74 **Rainbow In My Hand** *Doyle Holly*
8/49 **Rainbow In My Heart** *George Morgan*
99/77 **Rainbow In Your Eyes** *Jan & Malcolm*
47/03 **Rainbow Man** *Jeff Bates*
77/89 **Rainbow Of Our Own** *Shane Barmby*
4/81 **Rainbow Stew** *Merle Haggard*
39/83 **Rainbows And Butterflies** *Billy Swan*
90/77 **Rainbows And Horseshoes** *R.C. Bannon*
20/66 **Rainbows And Roses** *Roy Drusky*
17/68 **Rainbows Are Back In Style** *Slim Whitman*
33/74 **Raindrops** *Narvel Felts*
55/83 **Rainin' Down In Nashville** *Tom Carlile*
59/81 **Rainin' In My Eyes** *Miki Mori*
77/89 **Rainin', Rainin', Rainin'** *Gary Stewart*
Rainin' In My Heart
3/71 *Hank Williams, Jr. w/ Mike Curb Congregation*
35/89 *Jo-el Sonnier*
Raining In My Heart
14/69 *Ray Price*
63/78 *Leo Sayer*
3/03 **Raining On Sunday** *Keith Urban*
4/77 **Rains Came** *Freddy Fender*
47/75 **Rainy Day People** *Gordon Lightfoot*
2/75 **Rainy Day Woman** *Waylon Jennings*
83/79 **Rainy Days And Rainbows** *Paul Schmucker*
21/80 **Rainy Days And Stormy Nights** *Billie Jo Spears*
13/74 **Rainy Night In Georgia** *Hank Williams, Jr.*
15/80 **Raisin' Cane In Texas** *Gene Watson*
3/78 **Rake And Ramblin' Man** *Don Williams*
42/80 **Rambler Gambler** *Linda Ronstadt*
2/77 **Ramblin' Fever** *Merle Haggard*
29/67 **Ramblin' Man** *Ray Pennington*
Ramblin' Man
63/73 *Gary Stewart*
79/73 *Jimmy Payne*
94/79 **Ramblin' Music Man** *Charlie McCoy*
Ramblin' Rose
37/77 *Johnny Lee*
93/78 *Hank Snow*
8/68 **Ramona** *Billy Walker*
55/99 **Random Act Of Senseless Kindness** *South Sixty Five*
1/73 **Rated "X"** *Loretta Lynn*
1/44 **Ration Blues** *Louis Jordan*
Raunchy
6/58 *Bill Justis*
11/58 *Ernie Freeman*
80/78 **Rave On** *Jerry Naylor*

3/73 **Ravishing Ruby** *Tom T. Hall*
52/77 **Raymond's Place** *Ray Griff*
2/72 **Reach Out Your Hand** *Tammy Wynette*
61/73 **Reach Out Your Hand And Touch Me** *Sonny James*
78/81 **Reachin' For Freedom** *Ron Shaw/Desert Wind Band*
49/79 **Reaching Out To Hold You** *Dottie West*
38/87 **Read Between The Lines** *Lynn Anderson*
4/86 **Read My Lips** *Marie Osmond*
82/80 **Reading Of The Will** *Jimmy Tucker*
Ready For The Times To Get Better
1/78 *Crystal Gayle*
43/81 *Joe Sun*
72/87 **Ready Or Not** *Don Malena*
2/99 **Ready To Run** *Dixie Chicks*
90/88 **Ready To Take That Ride** *Trinity Lane*
20/96 **Ready, Willing And Able** *Lari White*
46/02 **Real Bad Mood** *Marie Sisters*
38/80 **Real Buddy Holly Story** *Sonny Curtis*
20/80 **Real Cowboy (You Say You're)** *Billy "Crash" Craddock*
1/05 **Real Fine Place To Start** *Sara Evans*
67/86 **Real Good** *Bobby Bare*
9/88 **Real Good Feel Good Song** *Mel McDaniel*
76/87 **Real Good Heartache** *Rosemary Sharp*
1/03 **Real Good Man** *Tim McGraw*
52/94 **Real Good Way To Wind Up Lonesome** *James House*
36/68 **Real Good Woman** *Jean Shepard*
14/01 **Real Life (I Never Was The Same Again)** *Jeff Carson*
16/00 **Real Live Woman** *Trisha Yearwood*
1/85 **Real Love** *Dolly Parton w/ Kenny Rogers*
33/98 **Real Man** *Billy Dean*
69/89 **Real Old-Fashioned Broken Heart** *Bama Band*
30/67 **Real Thing** *Billy Grammer*
60/03 **Real Thing** *George Strait*
79/79 **Real Thing** *O.B. McClinton*
85/78 **Real Thing** *Jean Shepard*
Reason To Believe
75/69 *Suzi Jane Hokum*
88/83 *Wray Brothers Band*
Reason Why I'm Here
97/77 *Joni Lee*
85/78 *Mike Lunsford*
13/60 **Reasons To Live** *Jimmie Skinner*
6/83 **Reasons To Quit** *Merle Haggard & Willie Nelson*
1/96 **Rebecca Lynn** *Bryan White*
24/61 **Rebel - Johnny Yuma** *Johnny Cash*
17/58 **Rebel-'Rouser** *Duane Eddy*
9/88 **Rebels Without A Clue** *Bellamy Brothers*
1/93 **Reckless** *Alabama*
32/90 **Reckless Heart** *Southern Pacific*
Reconsider Me
38/69 *Ray Pillow*
39/71 *John Wesley Ryles*
2/75 *Narvel Felts*
23/94 **Red And Rio Grande** *Doug Supernaw*
4/79 **Red Bandana** *Merle Haggard*
4/44 **Red Blues** *Cootie Williams*
1/03 **Red Dirt Road** *Brooks & Dunn*
21/71 **Red Door** *Carl Smith*
17/78 **Red Hot Memory** *Kenny Dale*
70/86 **Red Neck And Over Thirty** *Wayne Kemp & Bobby G. Rice*
73/79 **Red Neck Disco** *Glenn Sutton*
85/77 **Red-Neck Hippie Romance** *Bobby Bare*
1/82 **Red Neckin' Love Makin' Night** *Conway Twitty*
5/02 **Red Rag Top** *Tim McGraw*
17/72 **Red Red Wine** *Roy Drusky*
69/99 **Red, Red Wine And Cheatin' Songs** *Marty Stuart*
21/74 **Red Rose From The Blue Side Of Town** *George Morgan*
60/75 **Red Roses For A Blue Lady** *Eddy Arnold*
8/48 **Red Roses Tied In Blue** *Clyde Moody*
22/76 **Red Sails In The Sunset** *Johnny Lee*
62/72 **Red Skies Over Georgia** *Henson Cargill*
49/95 **Red Strokes** *Garth Brooks*
20/76 **Red, White And Blue** *Loretta Lynn*
59/94 **Red, White And Blue Collar** *Gibson/Miller Band*
6/78 **Red Wine And Blue Memories** *Joe Stampley*
60/04 **Redbird Fever** *Gretchen Wilson*
42/96 **Redneck Games** *Jeff Foxworthy w/ Alan Jackson*
1/82 **Redneck Girl** *Bellamy Brothers*
Redneck In A Rock And Roll Bar ..see: (I'm Just A)
89/76 **Redneck Rock** *Bill Black's Combo*
95/77 **Redneck Roots** *Vernon Oxford*
55/96 **Redneck Son** *Ty England*
67/94 **Redneck Stomp** *Jeff Foxworthy*
17/76 **Redneck! (The Redneck National Anthem)** *Vernon Oxford*
Redneck 12 Days Of Christmas
18/96 *Jeff Foxworthy*
39/97 *Jeff Foxworthy*
39/98 *Jeff Foxworthy*
37/99 *Jeff Foxworthy*
35/00 *Jeff Foxworthy*
1/04 **Redneck Woman** *Gretchen Wilson*
6↑/05 **Redneck Yacht Club** *Craig Morgan*
4/73 **Rednecks, White Socks And Blue Ribbon Beer** *Johnny Russell*
55/74 **Reflections** *Jody Miller*
5/95 **Refried Dreams** *Tim McGraw*
87/80 **Regrets** *Carol Chase*
41/66 **Regular On My Mind** *Jim Edward Brown*
63/99 **Reindeer Boogie** *Trisha Yearwood*
Release Me
5/54 *Jimmy Heap/Perk Williams*
6/54 *Ray Price*
8/54 *Kitty Wells*
33/73 *Charlie McCoy*
71/74 *Marie Owens*
71/71 **Remember Bethlehem** *Dee Mullins*
(Remember Me) I'm The One Who Loves You
2/50 *Stuart Hamblen*
5/50 *Ernest Tubb*
2/76 *Willie Nelson*
56/96 **Remember The Ride** *Perfect Stranger*
1/04 **Remember When** *Alan Jackson*
56/96 **Remember When** *Ray Vega*
Remembering
14/68 *Jerry Reed*
57/76 *Jerry Reed*
80/83 **Reminiscing** *Linda Nail*
23/70 **Removing The Shadow** *Hank Williams, Jr. & Lois Johnson*
7/94 **Renegades, Rebels And Rogues** *Tracy Lawrence*
4/93 **Reno** *Doug Supernaw*
19/68 **Reno** *Dottie West*
76/85 **Reno And Me** *Bobby Bare*
9/86 **Reno Bound** *Southern Pacific*
81/87 **Rented Room** *Jeanne Pruett*
10/68 **Repeat After Me** *Jack Reno*
56/84 **Repeat After Me** *Family Brown*
6/57 **Repenting** *Kitty Wells*
4/86 **Repetitive Regret** *Eddie Rabbitt*
74/88 **Request, The** *Bob Pack*
4/97 **Rest Of Mine** *Trace Adkins*
72/78 **Rest Of My Life** *Kenny Starr*
86/80 **Rest Of Your Life** *Kay Austin*
Rest Your Love On Me
39/79 *Bee Gees*
1/81 *Conway Twitty*
Restless
20/69 *Carl Perkins*
25/91 *Mark O'Connor*
36/05 **Restless** *Alison Krauss & Union Station*
39/74 **Restless** *Crystal Gayle*
39/87 **Restless Angel** *Tim Malchak*
57/84 **Restless Heart** *Juice Newton*
74/69 **Restless Melissa** *Hugh X. Lewis*
11/61 **Restless One** *Hank Snow*
30/64 **Restless River** *Earl Scott*
6/78 **Return To Me** *Marty Robbins*
13/79 **Reunited** *Louise Mandrell & R.C. Bannon*
34/04 **Revenge Of A Middle-Aged Woman** *Tracy Byrd*
74/76 **Reverend Bob** *Barbi Benton*
71/82 **Reverend Mr. Black** *Johnny Cash*
82/84 **Reynosa** *Katy Moffatt*
1/75 **Rhinestone Cowboy** *Glen Campbell*
23/64 **Rhinestones** *Faron Young*
1/51 **Rhumba Boogie** *Hank Snow*
44/85 **Rhythm Guitar** *Emmylou Harris*
94/79 **Rhythm Guitar** *Oak Ridge Boys*
57/88 **Rhythm Of Romance** *Kendalls*
Rhythm Of The Rain
34/72 *Pat Roberts*
67/77 *Floyd Cramer*
11/78 *Jacky Ward*
32/69 **Rib, The** *Jeannie C. Riley*

Ribbon Of Darkness
1/65 *Marty Robbins*
13/69 *Connie Smith*
19/81 **Rich Man** *Terri Gibbs*
53/75 **Richard And The Cadillac Kings** *Doyle Holly*
76/88 **Richer Now With You** *Nina Wyatt*
10/55 **Richest Man (In the World)** *Eddy Arnold*
3/90 **Richest Man On Earth** *Paul Overstreet*
4/83 **Ride, The** *David Allan Coe*
80/80 **Ride Concrete Cowboy, Ride** *Roy Rogers*
85/82 **Ride Cowboy Ride** *Rex Allen, Jr.*
Ride 'Em Cowboy
47/75 *Paul Davis*
32/84 *Juice Newton*
48/84 *David Allan Coe*
73/94 **Ride 'em High, Ride 'em Low** *Brooks & Dunn*
11/73 **Ride Me Down Easy** *Bobby Bare*
36/67 **Ride, Ride, Ride** *Lynn Anderson*
92/80 **Ride That Bull (Big Bertha)** *Marlow Tackett*
58/88 **Ride This Train** *Mel McDaniel*
78/78 **Rider In The Rain** *Randy Newman*
Riders In The Sky
2/49 *Vaughn Monroe*
8/49 *Burl Ives*
27/73 *Roy Clark*
2/79 *Johnny Cash*
1/73 **Ridin' My Thumb To Mexico** *Johnny Rodriguez*
45/97 **Ridin' Out The Heartache** *Tanya Tucker*
12/77 **Ridin' Rainbows** *Tanya Tucker*
47/04 **Ridin' With The Legend** *Keith Bryant*
72/92 **Riding For A Fall** *Chris LeDoux*
2/01 **Riding With Private Malone** *David Ball*
44/88 **Rigamarole** *Schuyler, Knobloch & Bickhardt*
22/70 **Right Back Loving You Again** *Del Reeves*
65/82 **Right Back Loving You Again** *Chantilly*
14/71 **Right Combination** *Porter Wagoner & Dolly Parton*
1/87 **Right From The Start** *Earl Thomas Conley*
3/87 **Right Hand Man** *Eddy Raven*
10/81 **Right In The Palm Of Your Hand** *Mel McDaniel*
10/90 **Right In The Wrong Direction** *Vern Gosdin*
85/81 **Right In The Wrong Direction** *Liz Lyndell*
8/87 **Right Left Hand** *George Jones*
15/91 **Right Now** *Mary-Chapin Carpenter*
1/99 **Right On The Money** *Alan Jackson*
30/66 **Right One** *Statler Brothers*
69/92 **Right One Left** *Roger Springer*
Right Or Left At Oak Street
21/70 *Roy Clark*
83/75 *Molly Bee*
1/84 **Right Or Wrong** *George Strait*
Right Or Wrong
9/61 *Wanda Jackson*
41/78 *Mary K. Miller*
63/74 **Right Out Of This World** *Jerry "Max" Lane*
71/99 **Right Place** *Derailers*
Right String ..see: Yo Yo
14/84 **Right Stuff** *Charly McClain & Mickey Gilley*
17/77 **Right Time Of The Night** *Jennifer Warnes*
44/89 **Right Track, Wrong Train** *Canyon*
5/01 **Right Where I Need To Be** *Gary Allan*
7/71 **Right Won't Touch A Hand** *George Jones*
Ring Of Fire
1/63 *Johnny Cash*
66/88 *Randy Howard*
Ring On Her Finger, Time On Her Hands
5/82 *Lee Greenwood*
9/96 *Reba McEntire*
95/78 **Ring Telephone Ring** *Randy Cornor*
33/90 **Ring Where A Ring Used To Be** *Billy Joe Royal*
64/77 **Ringgold Georgia** *Billy Walker & Brenda Kaye Perry*
21/64 **Ringo** *Lorne Greene*
7/71 **Rings** *Tompall/Glaser Brothers*
66/67 **Rings** *Stan Hitchcock*
41/72 **Rings For Sale** *Roger Miller*
Rings Of Gold
2/69 *Dottie West & Don Gibson*
79/87 *Robin & Cruiser*
66/93 **Rip Off The Knob** *Bellamy Brothers*
57/96 **Ripples** *4 Runner*
90/84 **Rise Above It All** *Joe Waters*
71/79 **Rise And Fall Of The Roman Empire** *Cal Smith*
9/70 **Rise And Shine** *Tommy Cash*
73/87 **Rise And Shine** *Ronnie Dove*
44/78 **Rising Above It All** *Lynn Anderson*
81/88 **Rising Cost Of Loving You** *Western Union Band*
1/92 **River, The** *Garth Brooks*
8/96 **River And The Highway** *Pam Tillis*
23/69 **River Bottom** *Johnny Darrell*
36/85 **River In The Rain** *Roger Miller*
9/54 **River Of No Return** *"Tennessee" Ernie Ford*
64/80 **River Road** *Crystal Gayle*
63/88 **River Unbroken** *Dolly Parton*
76/84 **River's Song** *Joey Scarbury*
13/74 **River's Too Wide** *Jim Mundy*
4/60 **Riverboat** *Faron Young*
14/60 **Riverboat Gambler** *Jimmie Skinner*
27/76 **Road Song** *Charlie Rich*
55/98 **Road Trippin'** *Steve Wariner*
5/96 **Road You Leave Behind** *David Lee Murphy*
17/72 **Roadmaster, The** *Freddy Weller*
F/80 **Roarin'** *Gary Stewart*
13/67 **Roarin' Again** *Wilburn Brothers*
15/63 **Robert E. Lee** *Ott Stephens*
16/79 **Robinhood** *Billy "Crash" Craddock*
50/92 **Rock, The** *Lee Roy Parnell*
37/03 **Rock-A-Bye Heart** *Steve Holy*
65/88 **Rock-A-Bye Heart** *Dana McVicker*
Rock And Roll ..also see: Rock 'N' Roll / Rockin' Roll
Rock And Rye
5/48 *Tex Ritter*
14/48 *Al Dexter*
2/94 **Rock Bottom** *Wynonna*
14/58 **Rock Hearts** *Jimmy Martin*
48/80 **Rock I'm Leaning On** *Jack Greene*
35/70 **Rock Island Line** *Johnny Cash*
26/70 **Rock Me Back To Little Rock** *Jan Howard*
29/93 **Rock Me (In The Cradle Of Love)** *Deborah Allen*
60/91 **Rock Me In The Rhythm Of Your Love** *Eddy Raven*
2/92 **Rock My Baby** *Shenandoah*
2/94 **Rock My World (Little Country Girl)** *Brooks & Dunn*
29/75 **Rock N' Roll** *Mac Davis*
23/90 **Rock 'N' Roll Angel** *Kentucky Headhunters*
16/87 **Rock And Roll Of Love** *Tom Wopat*
14/84 **Rock And Roll Shoes** *Ray Charles w/ B.J. Thomas*
90/82 **Rock N' Roll Stories** *Shannon Leigh*
58/80 **Rock 'N' Roll To Rock Of Ages** *Bill Anderson*
6/75 **Rock On Baby** *Brenda Lee*
30/00 **Rock This Country!** *Shania Twain*
13/03 **Rock You Baby** *Toby Keith*
63/81 **Rockabilly Rebel** *Orion*
86/79 **Rocket 'Til The Cows Come Home** *Charley White*
Rockin' Around The Christmas Tree
62/98 *Brenda Lee*
64/00 *Alabama*
48/05 *LeAnn Rimes*
70/85 **Rockin' In A Brand New Cradle** *Terri Gibbs*
Rockin' In The Congo
13/57 *Hank Thompson*
82/82 *Hank Thompson*
63/86 **Rockin' In The Parkin' Lot** *Razzy Bailey*
57/03 **Rockin' Little Christmas** *Brooks & Dunn*
66/95 **Rockin' Little Christmas** *Carlene Carter*
70/86 **Rockin' My Angel** *Narvel Felts*
74/86 **Rockin' My Country Heart** *Pat Garrett*
18/79 **Rockin' My Life Away** *Jerry Lee Lewis*
88/76 **Rockin' My Memories (To Sleep)** *Claude Gray*
22/60 **Rockin', Rollin' Ocean** *Hank Snow*
56/95 **Rockin' The Rock** *Larry Stewart*
1/86 **Rockin' With The Rhythm Of The Rain** *Judds*
1/91 **Rockin' Years** *Dolly Parton w/ Ricky Van Shelton*
73/69 **Rocking A Memory (That Won't Go To Sleep)** *Tommy Overstreet*
28/76 **Rocking In Rosalee's Boat** *Nick Nixon*
1/75 **Rocky** *Dickey Lee*

5/76 **Rocky Mountain Music** *Eddie Rabbitt*
71/88 **Rocky Road** *O'Kanes*
Rocky Top
33/68 *Osborne Brothers*
17/70 *Lynn Anderson*
2S/04 *Osborne Brothers*
52/81 **Rode Hard And Put Up Wet** *Johnny Lee*
3/91 **Rodeo** *Garth Brooks*
56/77 **Rodeo Bum** *Mel Street*
37/82 **Rodeo Clown** *Mac Davis*
44/76 **Rodeo Cowboy** *Lynn Anderson*
25/80 **Rodeo Eyes** *Zella Lehr*
83/81 **Rodeo Girls** *Tanya Tucker*
10/82 **Rodeo Romeo** *Moe Bandy*
74/79 **Rodle-Odeo-Home** *Arnie Rue*
36/88 **Rogue, The** *David Lynn Jones*
77/80 **Rolaids, Doan's Pills And Preparation H** *Dave Dudley*
57/73 **Roll In My Sweet Baby's Arms** *Hank Wilson*
Roll Muddy River
4/63 *Wilburn Brothers*
66/67 *Osborne Brothers*
1/75 **Roll On Big Mama** *Joe Stampley*
1/84 **Roll On (Eighteen Wheeler)** *Alabama*
7/81 **Roll On Mississippi** *Charley Pride*
100/75 **Roll On, Truckers** *Ray Pillow*
68/89 **Roll Over** *Steven Wayne Horton*
26/67 **Roll Over And Play Dead** *Jan Howard*
Roll Over Beethoven
71/70 *Linda Gail Lewis & Jerry Lee Lewis*
64/82 *Narvel Felts*
49/87 **Roll The Dice** *Shurfire*
Roll Truck Roll
38/66 *Red Simpson*
67/71 *Tommy Cash*
32/75 **Roll You Like A Wheel** *Mickey Gilley & Barbi Benton*
84/87 **Roller Coaster** *Alibi*
52/89 **Roller Coaster Run** *Michael Johnson*
71/95 **Rollin'** *Garth Brooks*
49/91 **Rollin' Home** *Pirates Of The Mississippi*
Rollin' In My Sweet Baby's Arms
2/71 *Buck Owens*
76/76 *Maury Finney*
65/75 **Rollin' In Your Sweet Sunshine** *Dottie West*
9/85 **Rollin' Lonely** *Johnny Lee*
15/86 **Rollin' Nowhere** *Michael Martin Murphey*
47/73 **Rollin' Rig** *Dave Dudley*
1/77 **Rollin' With The Flow** *Charlie Rich*
Roly-Poly
3/46 *Bob Wills*
97/75 *Carl Smith*
65/00 *Asleep At The Wheel w/ Dixie Chicks*
22/83 **Romance** *Louise Mandrell*
59/86 **Romance** *Jim Collins*
26/69 **Rome Wasn't Built In A Day** *Hank Snow*

27/93 **Romeo** *Dolly Parton w/ Mary Chapin-Carpenter/ Billy Ray Cyrus/Kathy Mattea/Pam Tillis/ Tanya Tucker*
36/79 **Room At The Top Of The Stairs** *Stella Parton*
92/79 **Room At The Top Of The Stairs** *Cal Smith*
60/74 **Room For A Boy...Never Used** *Ferlin Husky*
Room Full Of Roses
4/49 *George Morgan*
10/49 *Sons Of The Pioneers*
1/74 *Mickey Gilley*
2/66 **Room In Your Heart** *Sonny James*
56/76 **Room 269** *Freddy Weller*
1/76 **Roots Of My Raising** *Merle Haggard*
4/94 **Rope The Moon** *John Michael Montgomery*
54/92 **Rosalee** *Stacy Dean Campbell*
1/44 **Rosalita** *Al Dexter*
2/68 **Rosanna's Going Wild** *Johnny Cash*
1/83 **Rose, The** *Conway Twitty*
16/01 **Rose Bouquet** *Phil Vassar*
Rose By Any Other Name (Is Still A Rose)
69/72 *Ray Sanders*
77/76 *Ronnie Milsap*
5/78 **Rose Colored Glasses** *John Conlee*
1/70 **Rose Garden** *Lynn Anderson*
1/87 **Rose In Paradise** *Waylon Jennings*
37/01 **Rose Is A Rose** *Meredith Edwards*
52/69 **Rose Is A Rose Is A Rose** *Jimmy Dean*
70/81 **Rose Is For Today** *Jim Chesnut*
4/54 **Rose-Marie** *Slim Whitman*
60/84 **Rose Of My Heart** *Johnny Rodriguez*
33/80 **Rose's Are Red** *Freddie Hart*
28/63 **Rosebuds And You** *Benny Martin*
Roses Ain't Red
94/78 *Cathy O'Shea*
59/80 *Diane Pfeifer*
3/75 **Roses And Love Songs** *Ray Price*
15/71 **Roses And Thorns** *Jeannie C. Riley*
2/77 **Roses For Mama** *C.W. McCall*
34/66 **Roses From A Stranger** *Leroy Van Dyke*
44/88 **Roses In December** *Larry Boone*
70/73 **Roses In The Wine** *Hank Thompson*
42/68 **Roses To Reno** *Bob Bishop*
17/74 **Rosie Cries A Lot** *Ferlin Husky*
Rosie (Do You Wanna Talk It Over)
45/76 *Red Steagall*
76/76 *Sonny Throckmorton*
13/04 **Rough & Ready** *Trace Adkins*
1/98 **Round About Way** *George Strait*
19/96 **'Round Here** *Sawyer Brown*
9/82 **'Round The Clock Lovin'** *Gail Davies*
40/77 **'Round The World With The Rubber Duck** *C.W. McCall*
31/81 **Round-Up Saloon** *Bobby Goldsboro*

Route 66
48/76 *Asleep At The Wheel*
67/90 *Michael Martin Murphey*
54/87 **Routine** *Kendalls*
11/68 **Row Row Row** *Henson Cargill*
1/53 **Rub-A-Dub-Dub** *Hank Thompson*
39/95 **Rub-A-Dubbin'** *Ken Mellons*
1/74 **Rub It In** *Billy "Crash" Craddock*
54/99 **Rub It In** *Matt King*
51/02 **Rub Me The Right Way** *Brad Martin*
46/69 **Ruben James** *Kenny Rogers & The First Edition*
1/63 **Ruby Ann** *Marty Robbins*
Ruby, Are You Mad
58/70 *Osborne Brothers*
3/71 *Buck Owens*
1/75 **Ruby, Baby** *Billy "Crash" Craddock*
Ruby, Don't Take Your Love To Town
9/67 *Johnny Darrell*
39/69 *Kenny Rogers & The First Edition*
46/72 **Ruby Gentry's Daughter** *Arlene Harden*
21/72 **Ruby You're Warm** *David Rogers*
78/77 **Ruby's Lounge** *Brenda Lee*
Rudolph, The Red-Nosed Reindeer
1/50 *Gene Autry*
5/50 *Gene Autry*
56/97 *Alan Jackson*
55/99 *Gene Autry*
60/00 *Gene Autry*
1/97 **Rumor Has It** *Clay Walker*
3/91 **Rumor Has It** *Reba McEntire*
2/01 **Run** *George Strait*
50/00 **Run Away** *Shane McAnally*
10/68 **Run Away Little Tears** *Connie Smith*
5/56 **Run Boy** *Ray Price*
8/54 **Run 'Em Off** *Lefty Frizzell*
36/03 **Run, Run, Run** *Ryan Tyler*
53/81 **Run To Her** *Susie Allanson*
1/70 **Run, Woman, Run** *Tammy Wynette*
68/84 **Run Your Sweet Love By Me One More Time** *Lang Scott*
Runaway
30/78 *Narvel Felts*
76/86 *Bonnie Leigh*
74/00 *Gary Allan*
43/85 **Runaway Go Home** *Gatlin Bros.*
13/84 **Runaway Heart** *Louise Mandrell*
Runaway Heart
93/77 *Pam Rose*
36/79 *Reba McEntire*
62/98 **Runaway Love** *Chris LeDoux*
1/88 **Runaway Train** *Rosanne Cash*
62/94 **Runaway Train** *Dawn Sears*
8/96 **Runnin' Away With My Heart** *Lonestar*
20/70 **Runnin' Bare** *Jim Nesbitt*
4/92 **Runnin' Behind** *Tracy Lawrence*
100/77 **Runnin' Out Again** *Paula Kay Evans*
8/90 **Runnin' With The Wind** *Eddie Rabbitt*
1/69 **Running Bear** *Sonny James*
24/85 **Running Down Memory Lane** *Rex Allen, Jr.*

70/70 **Running From A Memory**
Chaparral Brothers
Running Kind
12/78 *Merle Haggard*
64/94 *Radney Foster*
40/82 **Running On Love** *Don King*
1/97 **Running Out Of Reasons To Run**
Rick Trevino
72/86 **Running Out Of Reasons To Run**
J.D. Martin
77/85 **Running The Roadblocks**
Chris Hillman
14/79 **Rusty Old Halo** *Hoyt Axton*
10/67 **Ruthless** *Statler Brothers*
Rye Whiskey
9/48 *Tex Ritter*
81/76 *Chuck Price*

S

15/55 **S.O.S.** *Johnnie & Jack*
73/81 **S.O.S.** *Johnny Carver*
Sacred Ground
87/89 *Kix Brooks*
2/92 *McBride & The Ride*
70/88 **Sad Cliches** *Atlanta*
17/76 **Sad Country Love Song**
Tom Bresh
55/89 **Sad Eyes** *Trader-Price*
31/67 **Sad Face** *Ernie Ashworth*
2/97 **Sad Lookin' Moon** *Alabama*
78/80 **Sad Love Song Lady**
David Houston
81/81 **Sad Ole Shade Of Gray**
Jeanne Pruett
46/72 **Sad Situation** *Skeeter Davis*
59/86 **Sad State Of Affairs**
Leon Everette
F/80 **Sadness Of It All**
Conway Twitty/Loretty Lynn
4/95 **Safe In The Arms Of Love**
Martina McBride
44/85 **Safe In The Arms Of Love**
Robin Lee
82/80 **Safe In The Arms Of Your Love (Cold In The Streets)**
Jim Weatherly
55/72 **Safe In These Lovin' Arms Of Mine** *Jean Shepard*
1/64 **Saginaw, Michigan** *Lefty Frizzell*
Sail Away
98/77 *Sam Neely*
2/79 *Oak Ridge Boys*
16/79 **Sail On** *Tom Grant*
63/85 **Sailing Home To Me** *Loy Blanton*
16/59 **Sailor Man** *Johnnie And Jack*
16/02 **Saints & Angels** *Sara Evans*
19/59 **Sal's Got A Sugar Lip**
Johnny Horton
51/75 **Sally G** *Paul McCartney*
20/62 **Sally Was A Good Old Girl**
Hank Cochran
98/79 **Salt On The Wound** *Jerry Fuller*
8/52 **Salty Dog Rag** *Red Foley*
8/70 **Salute To A Switchblade**
Tom T. Hall
87/79 **Salute To The Duke** *Paul Ott*
40/77 **Sam** *Olivia Newton-John*

Sam Hill
11/64 *Claude King*
45/64 *Merle Haggard*
1/67 **Sam's Place** *Buck Owens*
12/92 **Same Ol' Love** *Ricky Skaggs*
83/81 **Same Old Boy** *Gary Gentry*
1/59 **Same Old Me** *Ray Price*
28/91 **Same Old Star**
McBride & The Ride
29/75 **Same Old Story** *Hank Williams, Jr.*
46/70 **Same Old Story, Same Old Lie**
Bill Phillips
59/98 **Same Old Train** *Same Old Train*
65/73 **Same Old Way** *Stan Hitchcock*
5/82 **Same Ole Me** *George Jones*
8/49 **Same Sweet Girl** *Hank Locklin*
14/57 **Same Two Lips** *Marty Robbins*
47/66 **Sammy** *David Houston*
50/67 **San Antonio** *Willie Nelson*
89/80 **San Antonio Medley**
Curtis Potter/Darrell McCall
25/83 **San Antonio Nights** *Eddy Raven*
San Antonio Rose
8/61 *Floyd Cramer*
F/83 *Ray Price*
San Antonio Stroll
1/75 *Tanya Tucker*
F/76 *Maury Finney*
31/68 **San Diego** *Charlie Walker*
San Francisco Is A Lonely Town
46/69 *Ben Peters*
86/79 *Nick Nixon*
26/75 **Sanctuary** *Ronnie Prophet*
7/63 **Sands Of Gold** *Webb Pierce*
F/79 **Santa Barbara** *Ronnie Milsap*
Santa Claus Boogie
41/95 *Tractors*
63/96 *Tractors*
71/99 **Santa Claus (I Still Believe In You)** *Alabama*
60/98 **Santa Claus Is Back In Town**
Dwight Yoakam
Santa Claus Is Comin' (In A Boogie Woogie Choo Choo Train)
43/96 *Tractors*
65/98 *Tractors*
Santa Claus Is Coming To Town
73/96 *George Strait*
69/98 *George Strait*
67/01 *Lonestar*
5/88 **Santa Fe** *Bellamy Brothers*
70/96 **Santa Got Lost In Texas**
Jeff Carson
50/96 **Santa I'm Right Here** *Toby Keith*
56/98 **Santa Looked A Lot Like Daddy**
Garth Brooks
72/99 **Santa On The Rooftop** *Trisha Yearwood & Rosie O'Donnell*
Santa's Got A Semi
60/00 *Keith Harling*
60/01 *Keith Harling*
57/70 **Santo Domingo** *Buddy Alan*
57/79 **Sarah's Eyes** *Vern Gosdin*
1/73 **Satin Sheets** *Jeanne Pruett*
17/73 **Satisfaction** *Jack Greene*
7/53 **Satisfaction Guaranteed**
Carl Smith

Satisfied Mind
1/55 *Porter Wagoner*
3/55 *Red Foley & Betty Foley*
4/55 *Jean Shepard*
25/73 *Roy Drusky*
41/76 *Bob Luman*
84/83 *Con Hunley*
Satisfy Me And I'll Satisfy You
83/74 *Josie Brown*
53/91 *Clinton Gregory*
5/88 **Satisfy You**
Sweethearts Of The Rodeo
24/71 **Saturday Morning Confusion**
Bobby Russell
22/68 **Saturday Night** *Webb Pierce*
47/99 **Saturday Night** *Lonestar*
54/80 **Saturday Night In Dallas**
Kenny Seratt
9/88 **Saturday Night Special**
Conway Twitty
53/77 **Saturday Night To Sunday Quiet**
Susan Raye
43/69 **Saturday Satan Sunday Saint**
Ernest Tubb
11/04 **Save A Horse (Ride A Cowboy)**
Big & Rich
6/83 **Save Me** *Louise Mandrell*
86/78 **Save Me** *Tanya Tucker*
12/85 **Save The Last Chance**
Johnny Lee
Save The Last Dance For Me
100/76 *Bennie Lindsey*
36/78 *Ron Shaw*
4/79 *Emmylou Harris*
26/79 *Jerry Lee Lewis*
3/84 *Dolly Parton*
11/62 **Save The Last Dance For Me**
Buck Owens
45/95 **Save This One For Me**
Rick Trevino
8/80 **Save Your Heart For Me**
Jacky Ward
10/76 **Save Your Kisses For Me**
Margo Smith
3/86 **Savin' My Love For You**
Pake McEntire
58/87 **Savin' The Honey For The Honeymoon** *Sawyer Brown*
14/77 **Savin' This Love Song For You**
Johnny Rodriguez
46/04 **Sawdust On Her Halo**
Tracy Lawrence
Sawmill
27/59 *Mel Tillis & Bill Phillips*
15/63 *Webb Pierce*
2/73 *Mel Tillis*
21/94 **Sawmill Road** *Diamond Rio*
85/80 **Say A Long Goodbye**
Mary K. Miller
41/99 **Say Anything** *Shane McAnally*
5/75 **Say Forever You'll Be Mine**
Porter Wagoner & Dolly Parton
35/73 **Say, Has Anybody Seen My Sweet Gypsy Rose**
Terry Stafford
38/96 **Say I** *Alabama*
40/75 **Say I Do** *Ray Price*
1/76 **Say It Again** *Don Williams*
31/91 **Say It's Not True** *Lionel Cartwright*
8/68 **Say It's Not You** *George Jones*
33/01 **Say No More** *Clay Walker*

78/89 **Say The Part About I Love You** *Lorie Ann*
4/89 **Say What's In Your Heart** *Restless Heart*
13/98 **Say When** *Lonestar*
15/73 **Say When** *Diana Trask*
F/84 **Say When** *Johnny Lee*
37/97 **Say Yes** *Burnin' Daylight*
Say You Love Me
93/76 *Lynda K. Lance*
10/79 *Stephanie Winslow*
Say You Love Me Again ..see: (I Wanna Hear You)
57/83 **Say You'll Stay** *Wayne Massey*
1/77 **Say You'll Stay Until Tomorrow** *Tom Jones*
2/77 **Saying Hello, Saying I Love You, Saying Goodbye** *Jim Ed Brown/Helen Cornelius*
5/83 **Scarlet Fever** *Kenny Rogers*
7/60 **Scarlet Ribbons (For Her Hair)** *Browns*
66/74 **Scarlet Water** *Johnny Duncan*
58/91 **Scars** *Ray Kennedy*
90/89 **Scars** *Johnny Paycheck*
52/03 **Scary Old World** *Radney Foster*
65/90 **Scene Of The Crime** *Jo-el Sonnier*
77/88 **Scene Of The Crime** *Lori Yates*
Scotch And Soda
88/79 *Mac Wiseman*
70/83 *Ray Price*
27/58 **Scotland** *Bill Monroe*
8/81 **Scratch My Back (And Whisper In My Ear)** *Razzy Bailey*
46/01 **Scream** *Mindy McCready*
Sea Cruise
94/77 *Everett Peek*
50/80 *Billy "Crash" Craddock*
56/95 **Sea Of Cowboy Hats** *Chely Wright*
Sea Of Heartbreak
2/61 *Don Gibson*
24/72 *Kenny Price*
33/79 *Lynn Anderson*
39/89 *Ronnie McDowell*
83/88 **Sealed With A Kiss** *Leah Marr*
5/48 **Seaman's Blues** *Ernest Tubb*
43/77 **Search, The** *Freddie Hart*
54/72 **Search Your Heart** *Bobby Wright*
82/76 **Searchin' For A Rainbow** *Marshall Tucker Band*
17/90 **Searchin' For Some Kind Of Clue** *Billy Joe Royal*
Searching (For Someone Like You)
3/56 *Kitty Wells*
45/75 *Melba Montgomery*
75/87 *Lanier McKuhen*
24/74 **Seasons In The Sun** *Bobby Wright*
Seasons Of My Heart
9/56 *Jimmy Newman*
10/60 *Johnny Cash*
90/79 **Second Best (Is Too Far Down The Line)** *Don Deal*
18/62 **Second Choice** *Stonewall Jackson*
50/73 **Second Cup Of Coffee** *George Hamilton IV*
24/59 **Second Fiddle** *Buck Owens*
5/64 **Second Fiddle (To An Old Guitar)** *Jean Shepard*
70/79 **Second Hand Emotion** *Faron Young*
7/84 **Second Hand Heart** *Gary Morris*
3/63 **Second Hand Rose** *Roy Drusky*
18/79 **Second-Hand Satin Lady (And A Bargain Basement Boy)** *Jerry Reed*
15/60 **Second Honeymoon** *Johnny Cash*
95/86 **Second Time Around** *Del Reeves*
5/86 **Second To No One** *Rosanne Cash*
60/72 **Second Tuesday In December** *Jack Blanchard & Misty Morgan*
20/01 **Second Wind** *Darryl Worley*
Secret Love
2/54 *Slim Whitman*
47/73 *Tony Booth*
1/75 *Freddy Fender*
58/00 **Secret Of Giving** *Reba McEntire*
4/99 **Secret Of Life** *Faith Hill*
Secretly
5/58 *Jimmie Rodgers*
65/78 *Jimmie Rodgers*
47/81 **Secrets** *Mac Davis*
6/90 **See If I Care** *Shenandoah*
44/97 **See Rock City** *Rick Trevino*
F/69 **See Ruby Fall** *Johnny Cash*
72/75 **See Saw** *Patsy Sledd*
See The Big Man Cry
7/65 *Charlie Louvin*
85/76 *Bobby Wayne Loftis*
80/74 **See The Funny Little Clown** *Billie Jo Spears*
51/96 **See Ya** *Confederate Railroad*
41/79 **See You In September** *Debby Boone*
18/76 **See You On Sunday** *Glen Campbell*
16/72 **Seed Before The Rose** *Tommy Overstreet*
50/93 **Seeds** *Kathy Mattea*
2/90 **Seein' My Father In Me** *Paul Overstreet*
Seeing Is Believing
96/74 *Jan Howard*
55/80 *Donna Fargo*
2/75 **Seeker, The** *Dolly Parton*
83/76 **Seems Like I Can't Live With You, But I Can't Live Without You** *Price Mitchell*
31/00 **Self Made Man** *Montgomery Gentry*
81/90 **Selfish Man** *Dwayne Crews*
51/03 **Sell A Lot Of Beer** *Warren Brothers*
83/82 **Semi Diesel Blues** *Super Grit Cowboy Band*
2/92 **Seminole Wind** *John Anderson*
19/77 **Semolita** *Jerry Reed*
79/73 **Send A Little Love My Way** *Anne Murray*
47/92 **Send A Message To My Heart** *Dwight Yoakam & Patty Loveless*
66/00 **Send Down An Angel** *Allison Moorer*
69/66 **Send Me A Box Of Kleenex** *Lamar Morris*
2/79 **Send Me Down To Tucson** *Mel Tillis*
7/73 **Send Me No Roses** *Tommy Overstreet*
14/72 **Send Me Some Lovin'** *Hank Williams, Jr./Lois Johnson*
61/81 **Send Me Somebody To Love** *Calamity Jane*
Send Me The Pillow You Dream On
5/58 *Hank Locklin*
23/60 *Browns*
11/62 *Johnny Tillotson*
66/81 *Whites*
65/98 **Sending Me Angels** *Delbert McClinton*
9/87 **Senorita** *Don Williams*
74/99 **Senorita Margarita** *Tim McGraw*
47/76 **Sentimental Journey** *Dave Dudley*
3/84 **Sentimental Ol' You** *Charly McClain*
F/73 **Separate Ways** *Elvis Presley*
September Song
40/69 *Roy Clark*
15/79 *Willie Nelson*
1/88 **Set 'Em Up Joe** *Vern Gosdin*
Set Him Free
5/59 *Skeeter Davis*
52/68 *Skeeter Davis*
Set Me Free
67/67 *Curly Putman*
44/68 *Charlie Rich*
51/69 *Ray Price*
68/71 **Set The World On Fire (With Love)** *Red Lane*
72/98 **Set You Free** *Allison Moorer*
91/89 **Settin' At The Kitchen Table** *Justin Wright*
2/52 **Settin' The Woods On Fire** *Hank Williams*
7/89 **Setting Me Up** *Highway 101*
Seven Bridges Road
55/81 *Eagles*
48/99 *Ricochet*
85/81 **Seven Days Come Sunday** *Rodney Lay*
28/66 **Seven Days Of Crying (Makes One Weak)** *Harden Trio*
Seven Lonely Days
7/53 *Bonnie Lou*
18/69 *Jean Shepard*
1/85 **Seven Spanish Angels** *Ray Charles w/ Willie Nelson*
1/81 **Seven Year Ache** *Rosanne Cash*
57/02 **17** *Cross Canadian Ragweed*
64/00 **Seventeen** *Tim McGraw*
F/71 **Seventeen Years** *Marty Robbins*
68/91 **Seventh Direction** *Tim Ryan*
Sexy Eyes ..see: Sweet Sexy Eyes
21/74 **Sexy Lady** *Freddy Weller*
80/80 **Sexy Ole Lady** *Pat Garrett*
48/80 **Sexy Song** *Carol Chase*
46/86 **Sexy Young Girl** *Mac Davis*
95/79 **Shackles And Chains** *Osborne Bros. & Mac Wiseman*
8/91 **Shadow Of A Doubt** *Earl Thomas Conley*
74/82 **Shadow Of Love** *Rob Parsons*
5/45 **Shadow On My Heart** *Ted Daffan*
1/79 **Shadows In The Moonlight** *Anne Murray*
28/79 **Shadows Of Love** *Rayburn Anthony*

Shadows Of My Mind
54/76 *Vernon Oxford*
15/83 *Leon Everette*
24/78 **Shady Rest** *Mel Street*
48/77 **Shady Side Of Charlotte** *Nat Stuckey*
66/79 **Shady Streets** *Gary Stewart*
5/97 **Shake, The** *Neal McCoy*
6/53 **Shake A Hand** *Red Foley*
15/54 **Shake-A-Leg** *Carlisles*
75/76 **Shake 'Em Up and Let 'Em Roll** *George Kent*
27/61 **Shake Hands With A Loser** *Don Winters*
Shake Me I Rattle (Squeeze Me I Cry)
14/63 *Marion Worth*
16/78 *Cristy Lane*
95/76 **Shake, Rattle And Roll** *Billy Swan*
3/92 **Shake The Sugar Tree** *Pam Tillis*
15/86 **Shakin'** *Sawyer Brown*
48/98 **Shame About That** *Sara Evans*
Shame On Me
18/62 *Bobby Bare*
56/69 *Norro Wilson*
48/75 *Bob Luman*
8/77 *Donna Fargo*
49/00 **Shame On Me** *Wilkinsons*
15/83 **Shame On The Moon** *Bob Seger*
Shame On You
1/45 *Spade Cooley*
1/45 *Lawrence Welk w/ Red Foley*
4/45 *Bill Boyd*
11/77 **Shame, Shame On Me** *Kenny Dale*
26/93 **Shame Shame Shame Shame** *Mark Collie*
1/91 **Shameless** *Garth Brooks*
35/64 **Shape Up Or Ship Out** *Leon McAuliff*
83/78 **Share Your Love Tonight** *Ann J. Morton*
5/81 **Share Your Love With Me** *Kenny Rogers*
15/79 **Sharing** *Kenny Dale*
Sharing The Night Together
50/78 *Dr. Hook*
88/83 *Denny Hilton*
44/01 **She Ain't Gonna Cry** *Marshall Dyllon*
93/87 **She Ain't Johnnie** *Billy Vera*
34/00 **She Ain't The Girl For You** *Kinleys*
2/95 **She Ain't Your Ordinary Girl** *Alabama*
83/85 **She Almost Makes Me Forget About You** *Larry Wayne Kennedy*
1/86 **She And I** *Alabama*
1/79 **She Believes In Me** *Kenny Rogers*
16/81 **She Belongs To Everyone But Me** *Burrito Brothers*
91/75 **She Brings Her Lovin' Home To Me** *Mundo Ray*
3/44 **She Broke My Heart In Three Places** *Hoosier Hot Shots*
38/74 **She Burn't The Little Roadside Tavern Down** *Johnny Russell*
She Called Me Baby
32/65 *Carl Smith*
55/72 *Dick Curless*
1/74 *Charlie Rich*
2/90 **She Came From Fort Worth** *Kathy Mattea*
74/70 **She Came To Me** *Lamar Morris*
71/91 **She Can** *Marcy Brothers*
1/78 **She Can Put Her Shoes Under My Bed** *Johnny Duncan*
29/82 **She Can't Get My Love Off The Bed** *Dottie West*
She Can't Give It Away
96/78 *Barbara Fairchild*
86/81 *Roy Clark*
48/95 **She Can't Love You** *Boy Howdy*
55/96 **She Can't Save Him** *Lisa Brokop*
3/94 **She Can't Say I Didn't Cry** *Rick Trevino*
2/80 **She Can't Say That Anymore** *John Conlee*
28/70 **She Cheats On Me** *Glenn Barber*
2/01 **She Couldn't Change Me** *Montgomery Gentry*
4/87 **She Couldn't Love Me Anymore** *T. Graham Brown*
63/71 **She Cried** *Roy Clark*
35/75 **She Deserves My Very Best** *David Wills*
8/89 **She Deserves You** *Baillie And The Boys*
73/82 **She Doesn't Belong To You** *Terry Aden*
9/88 **She Doesn't Cry Anymore** *Shenandoah*
29/02 **She Doesn't Dance** *Mark McGuinn*
51/86 **She Don't Cry Like She Used To** *Johnny Rodriguez*
1/93 **She Don't Know She's Beautiful** *Sammy Kershaw*
46/91 **She Don't Know That She's Perfect** *Bellamy Brothers*
3/89 **She Don't Love Nobody** *Desert Rose Band*
70/87 **She Don't Love You** *Susie Allanson*
She Don't Make Me Cry ..see: He [She] Don't Make Me Cry
14/54 **She Done Give Her Heart To Me** *Sonny James*
She Dreams
74/93 *Tim Mensy*
6/94 *Mark Chesnutt*
4/97 **She Drew A Broken Heart** *Patty Loveless*
She Even Woke Me Up To Say Goodbye
2/69 *Jerry Lee Lewis*
15/75 *Ronnie Milsap*
39/95 **She Feels Like A Brand New Man Tonight** *Aaron Tippin*
97/83 **She Feels Like A New Man Tonight** *Clifford Russell*
66/73 **She Feels So Good I Hate To Put Her Down** *Ronnie Sessions*
15/73 **She Fights That Lovin' Feeling** *Faron Young*
65/68 **She Gets The Roses (I Get The Tears)** *Donna Odom*
64/97 **She Gives** *Emilio*
3/70 **She Goes Walking Through My Mind** *Billy Walker*
1/82 **She Got The Goldmine (I Got The Shaft)** *Jerry Reed*
57/96 **She Got What She Deserves** *Frazier River*
98/89 **She Had Every Right To Do You Wrong** *Jerry Lansdowne*
40/01 **She Is** *Hal Ketchum*
56/03 **She Is** *Susan Ashton*
1/92 **She Is His Only Need** *Wynonna*
48/82 **She Is The Woman** *Super Grit Cowboy Band*
11/77 **She Just Loved The Cheatin' Out Of Me** *Moe Bandy*
89/78 **She Just Made Me Love You More** *Johnny Bush*
She Just Started Liking Cheatin' Songs
13/80 *John Anderson*
72/99 *Alan Jackson*
75/77 **She Keeps Hangin' On** *Rayburn Anthony*
1/85 **She Keeps The Home Fires Burning** *Ronnie Milsap*
55/74 **She Kept On Talkin'** *Molly Bee*
69/97 **She Knows Me By Heart** *Seminole*
1/82 **She Left Love All Over Me** *Razzy Bailey*
89/74 **She Likes Country Bands** *Del Reeves*
63/92 **She Likes To Dance** *Michael White*
97/88 **(She Likes) Warm Summer Days** *Buddy Latham*
55/92 **She Loved A Lot In Her Time** *George Jones*
47/94 **She Loves Me Like She Means It** *Orrall & Wright*
11/73 **She Loves Me (Right Out Of My Mind)** *Freddy Weller*
94/79 **She Loves My Troubles Away** *Mickey Jones*
71/87 **She Loves The Jerk** *Rodney Crowell*
49/94 **She Loves To Hear Me Rock** *Turner/Nichols*
54/91 **She Made A Memory Out Of Me** *Aaron Tippin*
53/83 **She Meant Forever When She Said Goodbye** *Mel Tillis*
21/74 **She Met A Stranger, I Met A Train** *Tommy Cash*
8/01 **She Misses Him** *Tim Rushlow*
1/73 **She Needs Someone To Hold Her (When She Cries)** *Conway Twitty*
27/94 **She Never Cried** *Confederate Railroad*
2/76 **She Never Knew Me** *Don Williams*
1/96 **She Never Lets It Go To Her Heart** *Tim McGraw*
51/96 **She Never Looks Back** *Doug Supernaw*
64/82 **She Only Meant To Use Him** *Wayne Kemp*
17/03 **She Only Smokes When She Drinks** *Joe Nichols*
59/84 **She Put The Sad In All His Songs** *Ronnie Dunn*
23/89 **She Reminded Me Of You** *Mickey Gilley*
57/97 **She Said, He Heard** *Suzy Bogguss*
17/96 **She Said Yes** *Rhett Akins*

75/88 **She Says** *George Hamilton V*
62/94 **She Should've Been Mine** *Western Flyer*
She Sings Amazing Grace
81/81 *Stan Hitchcock*
83/82 *Gary Stewart*
2/68 **She Still Comes Around** *Jerry Lee Lewis*
78/74 **She Still Comes To Me (To Pour The Wine)** *Henson Cargill*
3/84 **She Sure Got Away With My Heart** *John Anderson*
50/92 **She Takes The Sad Out Of Saturday Night** *Clinton Gregory*
13/75 **She Talked A Lot About Texas** *Cal Smith*
15/94 **She Thinks His Name Was John** *Reba McEntire*
92/86 **She Thinks I Steal Cars** *Pinkard & Bowden*
She [He] Thinks I Still Care
1/62 *George Jones*
1/74 *Anne Murray*
F/77 *Elvis Presley*
39/68 **She Thinks I'm On That Train** *Henson Cargill*
11/00 **She Thinks My Tractor's Sexy** *Kenny Chesney*
5/04 **She Thinks She Needs Me** *Andy Griggs*
9/87 **She Thinks That She'll Marry** *Judy Rodman*
30/85 **She Told Me Yes** *Chance*
37/92 **She Took It Like A Man** *Confederate Railroad*
78/84 **She Took It Too Well** *John Wesley Ryles*
11/77 **She Took More Than Her Share** *Moe Bandy*
62/81 **She Took The Place Of You** *Valentino*
59/02 **She Treats Her Body Like A Temple** *Confederate Railroad*
1/93 **She Used To Be Mine** *Brooks & Dunn*
2/86 **She Used To Be Somebody's Baby** *Gatlin Bros.*
11/85 **She Used To Love Me A Lot** *David Allan Coe*
19/82 **She Used To Sing On Sunday** *Gatlin Bros.*
11/71 **She Wakes Me With A Kiss Every Morning** *Nat Stuckey*
79/78 **She Wanted A Little Bit More** *Ray Pennington*
21/97 **She Wants To Be Wanted Again** *Ty Herndon*
65/86 **She Wants To Marry A Cowboy** *James & Michael Younger*
37/99 **She Wants To Rock** *Warren Brothers*
11/02 **She Was** *Mark Chesnutt*
4/58 **She Was Only Seventeen (He Was One Year More)** *Marty Robbins*
72/79 **She Wears It Well** *Jerry Naylor*
6/68 **She Wears My Ring** *Ray Price*
14/68 **She Went A Little Bit Farther** *Faron Young*
49/00 **She Went Out For Cigarettes** *Chely Wright*
65/89 **She Will** *David Slater*

57/99 **She Won't Be Lonely Long** *Lee Roy Parnell*
She Won't Let Go ..see: (She's Got A Hold Of Me Where It Hurts)
(She Wore Red Dresses) ..see: Buenas Noches From A Lonely Room
62/75 **She Worshipped Me** *Red Steagall*
53/92 **She Wrote The Book** *Rob Crosby*
4/94 **She'd Give Anything** *Boy Howdy*
10/70 **She'll Be Hanging 'Round Somewhere** *Mel Tillis*
46/02 **She'll Go On You** *Josh Turner*
1/02 **She'll Leave You With A Smile** *George Strait*
51/71 **She'll Remember** *Jerry Wallace*
She'll Throw Stones At You
12/76 *Freddie Hart*
92/76 *Jacky Ward*
97/75 **She'll Wear It Out Leaving Town** *George Kent*
67/81 **She's A Friend Of A Friend** *Burrito Brothers*
3/70 **She's A Little Bit Country** *George Hamilton IV*
50/90 **She's A Little Past Forty** *Ronnie McDowell*
1/85 **She's A Miracle** *Exile*
15/91 **She's A Natural** *Rob Crosby*
1/75 **She's Actin' Single (I'm Drinkin' Doubles)** *Gary Stewart*
She's All I Got
2/71 *Johnny Paycheck*
4/97 *Tracy Byrd [Don't Take Her]*
43/01 **She's All That** *Collin Raye*
3/73 **She's All Woman** *David Houston*
37/75 **She's Already Gone** *Jim Mundy*
16/99 **She's Always Right** *Clay Walker*
61/71 **She's As Close As I Can Get To Loving You** *Hank Locklin*
39/79 **She's Been Keepin' Me Up Nights** *Bobby Lewis*
6/85 **She's Comin' Back To Say Goodbye** *Eddie Rabbitt*
1/89 **She's Crazy For Leavin'** *Rodney Crowell*
66/72 **She's Doing It To Me Again** *Ray Pillow*
1/95 **She's Every Woman** *Garth Brooks*
66/76 **She's Free But She's Not Easy** *Jim Glaser*
46/96 **She's Gettin' There** *Sawyer Brown*
24/97 **She's Going Home With Me** *Travis Tritt*
48/00 **She's Gone** *Ricochet*
She's Gone Gone Gone
12/65 *Lefty Frizzell*
44/84 *Carl Jackson*
6/89 *Glen Campbell*
74/83 **She's Gone To L.A. Again** *Mickey Clark*
2/98 **She's Gonna Make It** *Garth Brooks*
9/85 **She's Gonna Win Your Heart** *Eddy Raven*
36/81 **She's Got A Drinking Problem** *Gary Stewart*
77/85 **(She's Got A Hold Of Me Where It Hurts) She Won't Let Go** *Ray Price*

She's Got A Man On Her Mind
38/89 *Curtis Wright*
22/91 *Conway Twitty*
26/96 **She's Got A Mind Of Her Own** *James Bonamy*
2/89 **She's Got A Single Thing In Mind** *Conway Twitty*
24/74 **She's Got Everything I Need** *Eddy Arnold*
1/97 **She's Got It All** *Kenny Chesney*
21/98 **She's Got That Look In Her Eyes** *Alabama*
1/92 **She's Got The Rhythm (And I Got The Blues)** *Alan Jackson*
1/72 **She's Got To Be A Saint** *Ray Price*
She's [He's] Got You
1/62 *Patsy Cline*
1/77 *Loretta Lynn*
73/87 *Don McLean*
91/80 **She's Hangin' In There (I'm Hangin' Out)** *David Wills*
25/76 **She's Helping Me Get Over Loving You** *Joe Stampley*
43/70 **She's Hungry Again** *Bill Phillips*
7/99 **She's In Love** *Mark Wills*
39/74 **She's In Love With A Rodeo Man** *Johnny Russell*
1/91 **She's In Love With The Boy** *Trisha Yearwood*
58/94 **She's In The Bedroom Crying** *John & Audrey Wiggins*
14/60 **She's Just A Whole Lot Like You** *Hank Thompson*
She's Just An Old Love Turned Memory
64/75 *Nick Nixon*
1/77 *Charley Pride*
79/80 **She's Leavin' (And I'm Almost Gone)** *Kenny Price*
37/71 **She's Leavin' (Bonnie, Please Don't Go)** *Jim Ed Brown*
81/81 **She's Livin' It Up (And I'm Drinkin' 'Em Down)** *Allen Frizzell*
26/77 **She's Long Legged** *Joe Stampley*
21/69 **She's Lookin' Better By The Minute** *Jay Lee Webb*
54/67 **She's Looking Good** *Stan Hitchcock*
7/82 **She's Lying** *Lee Greenwood*
87/78 **She's Lying Next To Me** *Nick Nixon*
37/80 **She's Made Of Faith** *Marty Robbins*
72/66 **She's Mighty Gone** *Johnny Darrell*
6/70 **She's Mine** *George Jones*
2/00 **She's More** *Andy Griggs*
50/01 **She's My Girl** *Billy Gilman*
2/03 **She's My Kind Of Rain** *Tim McGraw*
She's [He's] My Rock
20/73 *Stoney Edwards*
8/75 *Brenda Lee*
2/84 *George Jones*
91/79 **She's My Woman** *Randy Travis*
28/92 **She's Never Comin' Back** *Mark Collie*
F/58 **She's No Angel** *Kitty Wells*
17/88 **She's No Lady** *Lyle Lovett*
71/74 **She's No Ordinary Woman (Ordinarily)** *Jim Mundy*

6/93 **She's Not Cryin' Anymore** *Billy Ray Cyrus*
43/65 **She's Not For You** *Willie Nelson*
9/04 **She's Not Just A Pretty Face** *Shania Twain*
4/82 **She's Not Really Cheatin' (She's Just Gettin' Even)** *Moe Bandy*
1/94 **She's Not The Cheatin' Kind** *Brooks & Dunn*
74/75 **She's Not Yours Anymore** *Ferlin Husky*
10/82 **She's Playing Hard To Forget** *Eddy Raven*
1/77 **She's Pulling Me Back Again** *Mickey Gilley*
She's Ready For Someone To Love Her
67/83 *Osmond Brothers*
F/83 *Jerry Reed*
2/85 **She's Single Again** *Janie Fricke*
81/88 **She's Sittin' Pretty** *Billy Parker*
17/81 **She's Steppin' Out** *Con Hunley*
She's [He's] Still All Over You
100/76 *Jo-el Sonnier*
85/77 *Jeanne Pruett*
100/79 **She's Still Around** *Chandy Lee*
3/97 **She's Sure Taking It Well** *Kevin Sharp*
2/97 **She's Taken A Shine** *John Berry*
17/77 **She's The Girl Of My Dreams** *Don King*
She's The Trip That I've Been On
91/76 *Leon Rausch*
52/86 *Larry Boone*
69/67 **She's The Woman** *Barbara Cummings*
19/89 **She's There** *Daniele Alexander*
95/89 **She's Too Good To Be Cheated This Way** *Hunter Cain*
1/72 **She's Too Good To Be True** *Charley Pride*
1/87 **She's Too Good To Be True** *Exile*
91/78 **Shed So Many Tears** *Isaac Payton Sweat*
12/63 **Sheepskin Valley** *Claude King*
80/87 **Sheet Music** *Bill Anderson*
43/76 **Sheik Of Chicago** *Joe Stampley*
14/73 **Shelter Of Your Eyes** *Don Williams*
33/73 **Shenandoah** *Charlie McCoy*
8/71 **Sheriff Of Boone County** *Kenny Price*
94/75 **Shhh** *Kathy Barnes*
58/05 **Shimmy Down The Chimney** *Alison Krauss*
73/67 **Shinbone** *Orville And Ivy*
47/66 **Shindig In The Barn** *Tommy Collins*
5/82 **Shine** *Waylon Jennings*
56/88 **Shine A Light On A Lie** *Robin Lee*
36/76 **Shine On** *Ronnie Prophet*
49/98 **Shine On** *Jeff Carson*
13/78 **Shine On Me** *John Wesley Ryles*
3/83 **Shine On (Shine All Your Sweet Love On Me)** *George Jones*
7/51 **Shine, Shave, Shower (It's Saturday)** *Lefty Frizzell*
1/87 **Shine, Shine, Shine** *Eddy Raven*
40/67 **Shine, Shine, Shine** *Carl Perkins*
58/67 **Shiny Red Automobile** *George Morgan*

19/69 **Ship In The Bottle** *Stonewall Jackson*
5/92 **Ships That Don't Come In** *Joe Diffie*
28/66 **Shirt, The** *Norma Jean*
21/01 **Shiver** *Jamie O'Neal*
3/66 **Shoe Goes On The Other Foot Tonight** *Marty Robbins*
22/86 **Shoe String** *Mel McDaniel*
83/81 **Shoe's On The Other Foot Tonight** *Montana*
17/63 **Shoes Of A Fool** *Bill Goodwin*
1/98 **Shoes You're Wearing** *Clint Black*
8/70 **Shoeshine Man** *Tom T. Hall*
65/84 **Shoot First, Ask Questions Later** *James & Michael Younger*
31/01 **Shoot Straight From Your Heart** *Vince Gill*
81/89 **Shoot The Moon** *Wayne Massey*
57/71 **Short And Sweet** *Bobby Bare*
57/98 **Shortenin' Bread** *Tractors*
16/61 **Shorty** *Jimmy Smart*
Shot Full Of Love
30/81 *Randy Parton*
19/83 *Nitty Gritty Dirt Band*
73/90 *McCarters*
1/51 **Shot Gun Boogie** *Tennessee Ernie Ford*
30/84 **Shot In The Dark** *Leon Everette*
23/80 **Shotgun Rider** *Joe Sun*
55/75 **Shotgun Rider** *Marty Robbins*
60/73 **Shotgun Willie** *Willie Nelson*
Should I Come Home (Or Should I Go Crazy)
83/75 *Joe Allen*
3/79 *Gene Watson*
50/81 **Should I Do It** *Tanya Tucker*
10/58 **Should We Tell Him** *Everly Brothers*
3/95 **Should've Asked Her Faster** *Ty England*
1/93 **Should've Been A Cowboy** *Toby Keith*
46/89 **Shoulda, Coulda, Woulda Loved You** *Les Taylor*
71/00 **Shoulda Shut Up** *Bill Engvall*
1/73 **Shoulder To Cry On** *Charley Pride*
34/79 **Shoulder To Shoulder (Arm And Arm)** *Roy Clark*
5/88 **Shouldn't It Be Easier Than This** *Charley Pride*
1/84 **Show Her** *Ronnie Milsap*
30/62 **Show Her Lots Of Gold** *Ernest Tubb*
11/72 **Show Me** *Barbara Mandrell*
96/77 **Show Me A Brick Wall** *Carl Smith*
8/76 **Show Me A Man** *T.G. Sheppard*
56/78 **Show Me A Sign** *Jim Chesnut*
7/49 **Show Me The Way Back To Your Heart** *Eddy Arnold*
44/66 **Show Me The Way To The Circus** *Homesteaders*
81/76 **Show Me Where** *Ruby Falls*
71/85 **Showdown** *Carlette*
97/76 **Showdown** *Brian Shaw*
73/71 **Showing His Dollar** *Webb Pierce*
70/89 **Shows You What I Know** *Andi & The Brown Sisters*
15/57 **Shrine Of St. Cecilia** *Faron Young*
7/80 **Shriner's Convention** *Ray Stevens*

13/80 **Shuffle Song** *Margo Smith*
5/46 **Shut That Gate** *Ted Daffan*
14/97 **Shut Up And Drive** *Chely Wright*
1/94 **Shut Up And Kiss Me** *Mary Chapin Carpenter*
(also see: Maria)
26/70 **Shutters And Boards** *Slim Whitman*
46/04 **Sick And Tired** *Cross Canadian Ragweed*
7/51 **Sick, Sober And Sorry** *Johnny Bond*
70/81 **Sidewalks Are Grey** *Kenny Seratt*
F/70 **Sidewalks Of Chicago** *Merle Haggard*
41/01 **Sideways** *Darryl Worley*
72/83 **Sign Of The Times** *Donna Fargo*
Signed Sealed And Delivered
2/48 *Cowboy Copas*
6/48 *Bob Atcher*
8/48 *Texas Jim Robertson*
9/48 *Jimmy Wakely*
10/61 *Cowboy Copas*
Silence On The Line
29/80 *Henson Cargill*
65/00 *Chris LeDoux*
57/04 **Silent Night** *Kenny Chesney w/ The Grigsby Twins*
F/80 **Silent Night (After The Fight)** *Ronnie Milsap*
20/84 **Silent Partners** *David Frizzell & Shelly West*
7/81 **Silent Treatment** *Earl Thomas Conley*
78/87 **Silent Understanding** *T.L. Lee w/ Kathy Walker*
5/52 **Silver And Gold** *Pee Wee King*
15/91 **Silver And Gold** *Dolly Parton*
15/55 **Silver Bell** *Hank Snow & Chet Atkins*
Silver Bells
68/98 *Judds*
54/04 *Kenny Chesney*
25/77 **Silver Bird** *Tina Rainford*
1/45 **Silver Dew On The Blue Grass Tonight** *Bob Wills*
75/80 **Silver Eagle** *Atlanta Rhythm Section*
18/77 **Silver Medals And Sweet Memories** *Statler Brothers*
4/46 **Silver Spurs (On The Golden Stairs)** *Gene Autry*
25/90 **Silver Stallion** *Waylon Jennings/Willie Nelson/Johnny Cash/Kris Kristofferson*
4/47 **Silver Stars, Purple Sage, Eyes Of Blue** *Cliffie Stone*
Silver Threads And Golden Needles
16/62 *Springfields*
20/74 *Linda Ronstadt*
68/74 *Charlie McCoy*
68/94 *Dolly Parton/Tammy Wynette/ Loretta Lynn*
64/96 **Silver Tongue And Goldplated Lies** *K.T. Oslin*
59/70 **Silver Wings** *Hagers*
20/76 **Silver Wings And Golden Rings** *Billie Jo Spears*
67/70 **Simple Days And Simple Ways** *Bobby Lewis*

Simple I Love You
63/85 *Karen Brooks*
72/96 *Mandy Barnett*
13/04 **Simple Life** *Carolyn Dawn Johnson*
53/01 **Simple Life** *Mary Chapin Carpenter*
61/94 **Simple Life** *Andy Childs*
10/79 **Simple Little Words** *Cristy Lane*
12/90 **Simple Man** *Charlie Daniels Band*
45/71 **Simple Thing As Love** *Roy Clark*
Sin ..see: (It's No)
52/00 **Sin Wagon** *Dixie Chicks*
73/70 **Since December** *Eddy Arnold*
Since I Don't Have You
68/81 *Don McLean*
6/91 *Ronnie Milsap*
Since I Fell For You
10/76 *Charlie Rich*
20/79 *Con Hunley*
7/86 **Since I Found You** *Sweethearts Of The Rodeo*
Since I Met You, Baby
1/69 *Sonny James*
10/75 *Freddy Fender*
96/76 **Since I Met You Boy** *Jeannie Seely*
55/02 **Since I've Seen You Last** *Joanna Janét*
62/72 **Since Then** *Ray Pillow*
54/69 **Since They Fired The Band Director (At Murphy High)** *Linda Manning*
84/77 **Since You Broke My Heart** *Don Everly*
Sincerely
72/72 *Kitty Wells*
8/89 *Forester Sisters*
74/71 **Sing A Happy Song** *Connie Eaton*
3/63 **Sing A Little Song Of Heartache** *Rose Maddox*
54/75 **Sing A Love Song, Porter Wagoner** *Mike Wells*
Sing A Sad Song
26/63 *Buddy Cagle*
19/64 *Merle Haggard*
19/77 *Wynn Stewart*
70/69 **Sing A Song About Love** *Bobby Wright*
3/73 **Sing About Love** *Lynn Anderson*
37/02 **Sing Along** *Rodney Atkins*
59/72 **Sing-Along Song** *Mayf Nutter*
66/74 **Sing For The Good Times** *Jack Greene*
53/71 **Sing High - Sing Low** *Anne Murray*
3/72 **Sing Me A Love Song To Baby** *Billy Walker*
1/68 **Sing Me Back Home** *Merle Haggard*
12/70 **Singer Of Sad Songs** *Waylon Jennings*
29/75 **Singin' In The Kitchen** *Bobby Bare & The Family*
89/76 **Singing A Happy Song** *Larry G. Hudson*
4/54 **Singing Hills** *Slim Whitman*
18/71 **Singing In Viet Nam Talking Blues** *Johnny Cash*
1/69 **Singing My Song** *Tammy Wynette*

Singing The Blues
1/56 *Marty Robbins*
17/83 *Gail Davies*
87/89 *Jeff Golden*
70/97 *Kentucky Headhunters*
36/78 **Single Again** *Gary Stewart*
50/04 **Single Father** *Kid Rock*
74/81 **Single Girl** *Cindy Hurt*
1/99 **Single White Female** *Chely Wright*
8/82 **Single Women** *Dolly Parton*
6/60 **Sink The Bismarck** *Johnny Horton*
14/48 **Sinner's Death** *Roy Acuff*
55/00 **Sinners & Saints** *George Jones*
Sioux City Sue
1/45 *Dick Thomas*
2/46 *Zeke Manners*
2/46 *Hoosier Hot Shots & Two Ton Baker*
3/46 *Tiny Hill*
75/68 **Sissy** *Statler Brothers*
12/49 **Sister Of Sioux City Sue** *Dick Thomas*
93/74 **Sister's Coming Home** *Willie Nelson*
53/89 **Sit A Little Closer** *Wagoneers*
54/71 **Sittin' Bull** *Charlie Louvin*
83/80 **(Sittin' Here) Lovin' You** *Troy Shondell*
4/65 **Sittin' In An All Nite Cafe** *Warner Mack*
33/70 **Sittin' In Atlanta Station** *Nat Stuckey*
3/66 **Sittin' On A Rock (Crying In A Creek)** *Warner Mack*
1/97 **Sittin' On Go** *Bryan White*
13/82 **(Sittin' On) The Dock Of The Bay** *Waylon Jennings & Willie Nelson*
14/49 **Sittin' On The Doorstep** *Woody Carter*
Six Days On The Road
2/63 *Dave Dudley*
58/74 *Johnny Rivers*
29/88 *Steve Earle & The Dukes*
13/97 *Sawyer Brown*
41/65 **Six Foot Two By Four** *Willis Brothers*
27/65 **Six Lonely Hours** *Kitty Wells*
70/72 **Six Pack Of Trouble** *O.B. McClinton*
9/01 **Six-Pack Summer** *Phil Vassar*
Six Pack To Go
10/60 *Hank Thompson*
68/74 *Hank Wilson*
634-5789
75/78 *Jimmie Peters*
54/82 *Marlow Tackett*
12/65 **Six Times A Day (The Trains Came Down)** *Dick Curless*
66/00 **Six Tons Of Toys** *Paul Brandt*
51/71 **Six Weeks Every Summer (Christmas Every Other Year)** *Dottie West*
4/70 **Six White Horses** *Tommy Cash*
61/86 **Sixteen Candles** *Jerry Lee Lewis*
86/82 **16 Lovin' Ounces To The Pound** *Don Lee*
1/55 **Sixteen Tons** *Tennessee Ernie Ford*
7/82 **16th Avenue** *Lacy J. Dalton*
59/78 **$60 Duck** *Lewie Wickham*
75/87 **67 Miles To Cow Town** *Hollie Hughes*

19/85 **Size Seven Round (Made Of Gold)** *George Jones & Lacy J. Dalton*
78/84 **Ski Bumpus/Banjo Fantasy II** *Wickline Band*
3/66 **Skid Row Joe** *Porter Wagoner*
79/87 **Skin Deep** *Bobbi Lace*
19↑/05 **Skin (Sarabeth)** *Rascal Flatts*
70/69 **Skin's Gettin' Closer To The Bone** *Cheryl Poole*
97/73 **Skinny Dippin'** *Demetriss Tapp*
Skip A Rope
1/68 *Henson Cargill*
85/79 *Roger Young*
10/48 **Slap Her Down Again Paw** *Esmereldy*
20/99 **Slave To The Habit** *Shane Minor*
8/53 **Slaves Of A Hopeless Love Affair** *Red Foley*
57/76 **Sleep All Mornin'** *Ed Bruce*
20/61 **Sleep, Baby, Sleep** *Connie Hall*
11/78 **Sleep Tight, Good Night Man** *Bobby Bare*
4/81 **Sleepin' With The Radio On** *Charly McClain*
Sleeping ..also see: A-Sleeping
97/84 **Sleeping Back To Back** *White Water Junction*
1/78 **Sleeping Single In A Double Bed** *Barbara Mandrell*
73/76 **Sleeping With A Memory** *Kathy Barnes*
9/61 **Sleepy-Eyed John** *Johnny Horton*
Sleigh Ride
67/96 *Lorrie Morgan*
64/97 *Lorrie Morgan*
70/98 *Dolly Parton (medley)*
42/00 *Lorrie Morgan*
54/00 *Garth Brooks*
7/77 **Slide Off Of Your Satin Sheets** *Johnny Paycheck*
22/79 **Slip Away** *Dottsy*
48/81 **Slip Away** *Mel Street & Sandy Powell*
79/80 **Slip Away** *Jim West*
46/64 **Slippin'** *Wanda Jackson*
Slippin' And Slidin'
14/73 *Billy "Crash" Craddock*
43/82 *Stephanie Winslow*
7/50 **Slippin' Around With Jole Blon** *Bud Messner*
4/73 **Slippin' Away** *Jean Shepard*
19/78 **Slippin' Away** *Bellamy Brothers*
61/81 **Slippin' Out, Slippin' In** *Bill Nash*
17/79 **Slippin' Up, Slippin' Around** *Cristy Lane*
Slippin' Around
1/49 *Margaret Whiting & Jimmy Wakely*
1/49 *Ernest Tubb*
5/49 *Floyd Tillman*
13/50 *Texas Jim Robertson*
23/64 *Marion Worth & George Morgan*
45/65 *Roy Drusky & Priscilla Mitchell*
98/88 *Mack Abernathy*
78/82 **Sloe Gin And Fast Women** *Wayne Kemp*
10/78 **Slow And Easy** *Randy Barlow*
8/86 **Slow Boat To China** *Girls Next Door*
1/84 **Slow Burn** *T.G. Sheppard*

10/85 **Slow Burning Memory** *Vern Gosdin*
56/81 **Slow Country Dancin'** *Judy Bailey*
67/99 **Slow Dance More** *Kenny Rogers*
49/84 **Slow Dancin'** *Kimberly Springs*
6/79 **Slow Dancing** *Johnny Duncan*
13/82 **Slow Down** *Lacy J. Dalton*
46/99 **Slow Down** *Mark Nesler*
75/74 **Slow Down** *Chuck Price*
70/78 **Slow Drivin'** *Kenny Starr*
Slow Hand
53/81 *Del Reeves*
1/82 *Conway Twitty*
59/95 **Slow Me Down** *Shelby Lynne*
64/86 **Slow Motion** *Malchak & Rucker*
47/84 **Slow Nights** *Mel Tillis w/ Glen Campbell*
36/89 **Slow Passin' Time** *Anne Murray*
17/62 **Slow Poison** *Johnny & Jack*
Slow Poke
1/51 *Pee Wee King*
7/52 *Hawkshaw Hawkins*
76/82 **Slow Texas Dancing** *Donna Hazard*
85/79 **Slow Tunes And Promises** *Bobby Hood*
Slowly
1/54 *Webb Pierce*
29/71 *Jimmy Dean & Dottie West*
37/81 *Kippi Brannon*
75/89 **Slowly But Surely** *Marie Osmond*
46/93 **Small Price** *Gibson/Miller Band*
54/90 **Small Small World** *Statler Brothers*
24/00 **Small Stuff** *Alabama*
60/98 **Small Talk** *Sawyer Brown*
35/68 **Small Time Laboring Man** *George Jones*
89/79 **Small Time Picker** *Bobby Wayne Loftis*
44/97 **Small Town** *John Anderson*
1/87 **Small Town Girl** *Steve Wariner*
2/91 **Small Town Saturday Night** *Hal Ketchum*
50/03 **Smaller Pieces** *Dusty Drake*
24/72 **Smell The Flowers** *Jerry Reed*
Smellin' Like A Rose ..see: (They Always Come Out)
1/00 **Smile** *Lonestar*
15/74 **Smile For Me** *Lynn Anderson*
39/72 **Smile, Somebody Loves You** *Linda Gail Lewis*
13/60 **Smiling Bill McCall** *Johnny Cash*
24/59 **Smoke Along The Track** *Stonewall Jackson*
84/82 **Smoke Gets In Your Eyes** *Narvel Felts*
44/96 **Smoke In Her Eyes** *Ty England*
Smoke On The Water
1/44 *Red Foley*
1/45 *Bob Wills*
7/45 *Boyd Heath*
12/00 **Smoke Rings In The Dark** *Gary Allan*
Smoke! Smoke! Smoke! (That Cigarette)
1/47 *Tex Williams*
32/68 *Tex Williams ([68]*
97/73 *Commander Cody*
78/78 *Tom Bresh*
89/82 *Sammy Davis, Jr.*
8/49 **Smokey Mountain Boogie** *Tennessee Ernie Ford*
Smokey Mountain Memories
13/75 *Mel Street*
F/82 *Earl Thomas Conley*
53/04 **Smokin' Grass** *Shannon Lawson*
71/83 **Smokin' In The Rockies** *Gary Stewart & Dean Dillon*
1/80 **Smoky Mountain Rain** *Ronnie Milsap*
12/69 **Smoky Places** *Billy Walker*
5/69 **Smoky The Bar** *Hank Thompson*
Smooth Sailin'
68/78 *Connie Smith*
47/79 *Sonny Throckmorton*
6/80 *T.G. Sheppard*
32/79 **Smooth Sailin'** *Jim Weatherly*
43/85 **Smooth Sailing (Rock In The Road)** *Mark Gray*
94/79 **Smooth Southern Highway** *Don Cox*
77/76 **Snap, Crackle And Pop** *Johnny Carver*
Snap Your Fingers
40/71 *Dick Curless*
12/74 *Don Gibson*
1/87 *Ronnie Milsap*
5/83 **Snapshot** *Sylvia*
48/81 **Sneakin' Around** *Kin Vassy*
16/67 **Sneaking 'Cross The Border** *Harden Trio*
69/74 **Sneaky Snake** *Tom T. Hall*
2/66 **Snow Flake** *Jim Reeves*
28/63 **Snow White Cloud** *Frank Taylor*
10/70 **Snowbird** *Anne Murray*
52/03 **Snowfall On The Sand** *Steve Wariner*
46/84 **So Close** *Wright Brothers*
72/83 **So Close** *Backroads*
43/77 **So Close Again** *Margo Smith & Norro Wilson*
4/56 **So Doggone Lonesome** *Johnny Cash*
68/83 **So Easy To Love** *Wright Brothers*
64/88 **So Far Not So Good** *Jeff Chance*
22/82 **So Fine** *Oak Ridge Boys*
68/78 **So Good** *Jewel Blanch*
27/78 **So Good, So Rare, So Fine** *Freddie Hart*
86/89 **So Good To Be In Love** *Karen Staley*
F/77 **So Good Woman** *Waylon Jennings*
2/95 **So Help Me Girl** *Joe Diffie*
22/62 **So How Come (No One Loves Me)** *Don Gibson*
43/69 **So Long** *Bobby Helms*
69/68 **So Long, Charlie Brown, Don't Look For Me Around** *Sammi Smith*
1/44 **So Long Pal** *Al Dexter*
14/55 **So Lovely, Baby** *Rusty & Doug*
16/59 **So Many Times** *Roy Acuff*
So Many Ways
28/73 *Eddy Arnold*
33/77 *David Houston*
45/66 **So Much For Me, So Much For You** *Liz Anderson*
1/96 **So Much For Pretending** *Bryan White*
46/70 **So Much In Love With You** *David Rogers*
3/92 **So Much Like My Dad** *George Strait*
So Round, So Firm, So Fully Packed
1/47 *Merle Travis*
3/47 *Johnny Bond*
5/47 *Ernest Tubb*
So Sad (To Watch Good Love Go Bad)
12/70 *Hank Williams, Jr. & Lois Johnson*
31/76 *Connie Smith*
76/78 *Steve Wariner*
28/83 *Emmylou Harris*
19/59 **So Soon** *Jimmy Newman*
71/82 **(So This Is) Happy Hour** *Snuff*
20/71 **So This Is Love** *Tommy Cash*
41/86 **So This Is Love** *Charly McClain*
51/00 **So What** *Tammy Cochran*
14/62 **So Wrong** *Patsy Cline*
F/57 **So You Think You've Got Troubles** *Marvin Rainwater*
58/79 **Soap** *O.B. McClinton*
13/78 **Soft Lights And Hard Country Music** *Moe Bandy*
97/78 **Soft Lights And Slow Sexy Music** *Jody Miller*
10/49 **Soft Lips** *Hank Thompson*
65/73 **Soft Lips And Hard Liquor** *Charlie Walker*
73/98 **Soft Place To Fall** *Allison Moorer*
3/61 **Soft Rain** *Ray Price*
8/72 **Soft, Sweet And Warm** *David Houston*
30/78 **Softest Touch In Town** *Bobby G. Rice*
74/69 **Softly And Tenderly** *Lois Johnson*
4/60 **Softly And Tenderly (I'll Hold You In My Arms)** *Lewis Pruitt*
F/78 **Softly, As I Leave You** *Elvis Presley*
69/73 **Sold American** *Kinky Friedman*
29/76 **Sold Out Of Flagpoles** *Johnny Cash*
1/95 **Sold (The Grundy County Auction Incident)** *John Michael Montgomery*
71/91 **Soldier Boy** *Donna Fargo*
60/05 **Soldier For The Lonely** *Jedd Hughes*
51/80 **Soldier Of Fortune** *Tom T. Hall*
54/86 **Soldier Of Love** *Billy Burnette*
15/59 **Soldier's Joy** *Hawkshaw Hawkins*
Soldier's Last Letter
1/44 *Ernest Tubb*
3/71 *Merle Haggard*
46/66 **Soldier's Prayer In Viet Nam** *Don Reno & Benny Martin*
8S/05 **Soldier's Wife** *Roxie Dean*
57/96 **Solid Ground** *Ricky Skaggs*
F/79 **Solitaire** *Elvis Presley*
28/69 **Solitary** *Don Gibson*
14/76 **Solitary Man** *T.G. Sheppard*
1/04 **Some Beach** *Blake Shelton*
1/77 **Some Broken Hearts Never Mend** *Don Williams*
47/82 **Some Day My Ship's Comin' In** *Joe Waters*
10/81 **Some Days Are Diamonds (Some Days Are Stone)** *John Denver*
45/82 **Some Days It Rains All Night Long** *Terri Gibbs*

7/02 **Some Days You Gotta Dance** *Dixie Chicks*
1/85 **Some Fools Never Learn** *Steve Wariner*
52/03 **Some Gave All** *Billy Ray Cyrus*
1/92 **Some Girls Do** *Sawyer Brown*
22/86 **Some Girls Have All The Luck** *Louise Mandrell*
8/91 **Some Guys Have All The Love** *Little Texas*
25/84 **Some Hearts Get All The Breaks** *Charly McClain*
81/86 **Some Hearts Get All The Breaks** *Roger Miller*
17/78 **Some I Wrote** *Statler Brothers*
8/74 **Some Kind Of A Woman** *Faron Young*
3/92 **Some Kind Of Trouble** *Tanya Tucker*
68/91 **Some Kinda Woman** *Linda Davis*
27/81 **Some Love Songs Never Die** *B.J. Thomas*
10/82 **Some Memories Just Won't Die** *Marty Robbins*
61/82 **Some Never Stand A Chance** *Family Brown*
20/82 **Some Of My Best Friends Are Old Songs** *Louise Mandrell*
72/85 **Some Of Shelly's Blues** *Maines Brothers Band*
28/73 **Some Old California Memory** *Henson Cargill*
16/88 **Some Old Side Road** *Keith Whitley*
54/73 **Some Roads Have No Ending** *Warner Mack*
57/85 **Some Such Foolishness** *Tommy Roe*
13/96 **Some Things Are Meant To Be** *Linda Davis*
7/00 **Some Things Never Change** *Tim McGraw*
83/81 **Some You Win, Some You Lose** *Orion*
1/04 **Somebody** *Reba McEntire*
34/84 **Somebody Buy This Cowgirl A Beer** *Shelly West*
4/85 **Somebody Else's Fire** *Janie Fricke*
5/93 **Somebody Else's Moon** *Collin Raye*
10/76 **Somebody Hold Me (Until She Passes By)** *Narvel Felts*
69/97 **Somebody Knew** *Rhett Akins*
62/67 **Somebody Knows My Dog** *Willis Brothers*
20/81 **Somebody Led Me Away** *Loretta Lynn*
1/87 **Somebody Lied** *Ricky Van Shelton*
1/66 **Somebody Like Me** *Eddy Arnold*
66/93 **Somebody Like That** *Glen Campbell*
1/02 **Somebody Like You** *Keith Urban*
67/88 **Somebody Loses, Somebody Wins** *Rosie Flores*
21/72 **Somebody Loves Me** *Johnny Paycheck*
8/76 **Somebody Loves You** *Crystal Gayle*
9/93 **Somebody New** *Billy Ray Cyrus*
84/87 **Somebody Ought To Tell Him That She's Gone** *Ogden Harless*
Somebody Paints The Wall
62/89 *Josh Logan*
8/93 *Tracy Lawrence*
16/62 **Somebody Save Me** *Ferlin Husky*
1/85 **Somebody Should Leave** *Reba McEntire*
22/97 **Somebody Slap Me** *John Anderson*
1/76 **Somebody Somewhere** *Loretta Lynn*
6/79 **Somebody Special** *Donna Fargo*
33/98 **Somebody To Love** *Suzy Bogguss*
55/96 **Somebody To Love You** *Wynonna*
18/63 **Somebody Told Somebody** *Rose Maddox*
59/77 **Somebody Took Her Love (And Never Gave It Back)** *Jimmie Peters*
9/86 **Somebody Wants Me Out Of The Way** *George Jones*
Somebody Will
57/95 *McBride & The Ride*
51/98 *River Road*
52/69 **Somebody's Always Leaving** *Stonewall Jackson*
7/83 **Somebody's Always Saying Goodbye** *Anne Murray*
Somebody's Back In Town
6/59 *Wilburn Brothers*
81/84 *Chris Hillman*
2/51 **Somebody's Been Beatin' My Time** *Eddy Arnold*
32/81 **Somebody's Darling, Somebody's Wife** *Dottsy*
15/92 **Somebody's Doin' Me Right** *Keith Whitley*
64/78 **Somebody's Gonna Do It Tonight** *R.C. Bannon*
1/83 **Somebody's Gonna Love You** *Lee Greenwood*
65/80 **Somebody's Gotta Do The Losing** *Stephany Samone*
8↑/05 **Somebody's Hero** *Jamie O'Neal*
61/92 **Somebody's In Love** *Lisa Stewart*
8/81 **Somebody's Knockin'** *Terri Gibbs*
1/84 **Somebody's Needin' Somebody** *Conway Twitty*
19/99 **Somebody's Out There Watching** *Kinleys*
53/04 **Somebody's Someone** *Lonestar*
9/52 **Somebody's Stolen My Honey** *Ernest Tubb*
1/91 **Someday** *Alan Jackson*
12/57 **Someday** *Webb Pierce*
28/86 **Someday** *Steve Earle*
31/03 **Someday** *Vince Gill*
51/96 **Someday** *Steve Azar*
22/79 **Someday My Day Will Come** *George Jones*
60/87 **Someday My Ship Will Sail** *Emmylou Harris*
70/88 **Someday, Somenight** *Trinity Lane*
Someday Soon
39/76 *Kathy Barnes*
21/82 *Moe Bandy*
12/91 *Suzy Bogguss*
4/70 **Someday We'll Be Together** *Bill Anderson & Jan Howard*
2/71 **Someday We'll Look Back** *Merle Haggard*
1/84 **Someday When Things Are Good** *Merle Haggard*
45/78 **Someday You Will** *John Wesley Ryles*
10/49 **Someday You'll Call My Name** *Jimmy Wakely*
Someday (You'll Want Me To Want You)
2/46 *Elton Britt*
3/46 *Hoosier Hot Shots & Sally Foster*
4/46 *Gene Autry*
70/81 **Somehow, Someway And Someday** *Amarillo*
5/87 **Someone** *Lee Greenwood*
8/66 **Someone Before Me** *Wilburn Brothers*
59/74 **Someone Came To See Me (In The Middle Of The Night)** *Patti Page*
17/75 **Someone Cares For You** *Red Steagall*
1/82 **Someone Could Lose A Heart Tonight** *Eddie Rabbitt*
3/96 **Someone Else's Dream** *Faith Hill*
1/95 **Someone Else's Star** *Bryan White*
14/90 **Someone Else's Trouble Now** *Highway 101*
46/99 **Someone Else's Turn To Cry** *Chalee Tennison*
26/84 **Someone Is Falling In Love** *Kathy Mattea*
11/79 **Someone Is Looking For Someone Like You** *Gail Davies*
26/85 **Someone Like You** *Emmylou Harris*
94/77 **Someone Loves Him** *Sue Richards*
Someone Loves You Honey
84/75 *Marie Owens*
1/78 *Charley Pride*
70/85 **Someone Must Be Missing You Tonight** *Terri Gibbs*
73/71 **Someone Stepped In (And Stole Me Blind)** *Webb Pierce*
Someone To Give My Love To
4/72 *Johnny Paycheck*
42/93 *Tracy Byrd*
41/04 **Someone To Share It With** *Rodney Atkins*
32/67 **Someone Told My Story** *Merle Haggard*
3/98 **Someone You Used To Know** *Collin Raye*
60/85 **Someone's Gonna Love Me Tonight** *Southern Pacific*
30/65 **Someone's Gotta Cry** *Jean Shepard*
29/76 **Someone's With Your Wife Tonight, Mister** *Bobby Borchers*
24/93 **Someplace Far Away (Careful What You're Dreamin')** *Hal Ketchum*
45/99 **Somethin' 'Bout A Sunday** *Michael Peterson*
60/80 **Somethin' 'Bout You Baby I Like** *Glen Campbell & Rita Coolidge*
33/01 **Somethin' In The Water** *Jeffrey Steele*

40/97 **Somethin' Like This** *Joe Diffie*
13/81 **Somethin' On The Radio** *Jacky Ward*
67/87 **Somethin' You Got** *Nielsen White Band*
6/74 **Something** *Johnny Rodriguez*
10/73 **Something About You I Love** *Johnny Paycheck*
43/94 **Something Already Gone** *Carlene Carter*
6/71 **Something Beautiful (To Remember)** *Slim Whitman*
62/74 **Something Better** *O.B. McClinton*
19/75 **Something Better To Do** *Olivia Newton-John*
17/67 **Something Fishy** *Dolly Parton*
31/64 **Something I Dreamed** *George Jones*
2/85 **Something In My Heart** *Ricky Skaggs*
14/92 **Something In Red** *Lorrie Morgan*
71/75 **Something Just Came Over Me** *Charlie Rich*
38/05 **Something Like A Broken Heart** *Hanna-McEuen*
1/99 **Something Like That** *Tim McGraw*
2/05 **Something More** *Sugarland*
73/92 **Something Moving In Me** *Darryl & Don Ellis*
14/90 **Something Of A Dreamer** *Mary-Chapin Carpenter*
4/51 **Something Old, Something New** *Eddy Arnold*
53/74 **Something On Your Mind** *Jack Blanchard & Misty Morgan*
23/62 **Something Precious** *Skeeter Davis*
10/68 **Something Pretty** *Wynn Stewart*
66/99 **Something Real** *Shana Petrone*
17/68 **Something Special** *Mel Tillis*
2/97 **Something That We Do** *Clint Black*
1/05 **Something To Be Proud Of** *Montgomery Gentry*
81/78 **Something To Believe In** *Don Drumm*
Something To Brag About
18/70 *Charlie Louvin & Melba Montgomery*
9/78 *Mary Kay Place w/ Willie Nelson*
63/72 **Something To Call Mine** *Bill Rice*
85/82 **Something To Love For Again** *Diane Pfeifer*
36/70 **Something To Think About** *Luke The Drifter, Jr.*
46/98 **Something To Think About** *David Kersh*
38/00 **Something To Write Home About** *Craig Morgan*
15/70 **Something Unseen** *Jack Greene*
Something With A Ring To It
54/90 *Mark Collie*
68/98 *Garth Brooks*
20/02 **Something Worth Leaving Behind** *Lee Ann Womack*
81/78 **Something's Burning** *Kathy Barnes*
24/93 **Something's Gonna Change Her Mind** *Mark Collie*
72/89 **Something's Got A Hold On Me** *James Rogers*
60/69 **Something's Missing (It's You)** *Jackie Burns*
19/69 **Something's Wrong In California** *Waylon Jennings*
F/81 **Sometime, Somewhere, Somehow** *Barbara Mandrell*
10/74 **Sometime Sunshine** *Jim Ed Brown*
1/76 **Sometimes** *Bill Anderson & Mary Lou Turner*
21/01 **Sometimes** *Clay Davidson*
59/76 **Sometimes** *Johnny Lee*
3/86 **Sometimes A Lady** *Eddy Raven*
6/73 **Sometimes A Memory Ain't Enough** *Jerry Lee Lewis*
34/81 **Sometimes I Cry When I'm Alone** *Sammi Smith*
79/78 **Sometimes I Do** *Ernest Tubb*
41/95 **Sometimes I Forget** *Doug Stone*
9/83 **Sometimes I Get Lucky And Forget** *Gene Watson*
9/76 **Sometimes I Talk In My Sleep** *Randy Cornor*
12/62 **Sometimes I'm Tempted** *Marty Robbins*
67/79 **Sometimes Love** *Mundo Earwood*
38/89 **Sometimes Love's Not A Pretty Thing** *Zaca Creek*
55/88 **Sometimes She Feels Like A Man** *Charly McClain*
7/95 **Sometimes She Forgets** *Travis Tritt*
Sometimes When We Touch
F/81 *Stephanie Winslow*
6/85 *Mark Gray & Tammy Wynette*
Sometimes You Just Can't Win
17/62 *George Jones*
10/71 *George Jones*
27/82 *Linda Ronstadt & John David Souther*
37/70 **Someway** *Don Gibson*
66/74 **Somewhere Around Midnight** *George Morgan*
46/89 **Somewhere Between** *Suzy Bogguss*
2/74 **Somewhere Between Love And Tomorrow** *Roy Clark*
23/88 **Somewhere Between Ragged And Right** *John Anderson w/ Waylon Jennings*
1/82 **Somewhere Between Right And Wrong** *Earl Thomas Conley*
42/05 **Somewhere Between Texas And Mexico** *Pat Green*
Somewhere Down The Line
50/83 *Younger Brothers*
3/84 *T.G. Sheppard*
65/86 **Somewhere In America** *Mac Davis*
57/94 **Somewhere In Between** *Dude Mowrey*
84/89 **Somewhere In Canada** *David Walsh*
49/97 **Somewhere In Love** *John & Audrey Wiggins*
3/91 **Somewhere In My Broken Heart** *Billy Dean*
55/83 **Somewhere In Texas** *Ray Price*
29/87 **Somewhere In The Night** *Sawyer Brown*
7/95 **Somewhere In The Vicinity Of The Heart** *Shenandoah w/ Alison Krauss*
15/72 **Somewhere In Virginia In The Rain** *Jack Blanchard & Misty Morgan*
22/73 **Somewhere, My Love** *Red Steagall*
1/93 **Somewhere Other Than The Night** *Garth Brooks*
Somewhere South Of Macon
100/77 *Marshall Chapman*
79/88 *Rattlesnake Annie*
80/81 **Somewhere To Come When It Rains** *John Wesley Ryles*
1/87 **Somewhere Tonight** *Highway 101*
69/69 **Son** *Jerry Wallace*
41/70 **Son Of A Coal Man** *Del Reeves*
Son Of A Preacher Man
40/69 *Peggy Little*
95/89 *Bobbi Lace*
46/04 *Sherrié Austin*
5/74 **Son Of A Rotten Gambler** *Anne Murray*
58/68 **Son Of A Sawmill Man** *Osborne Brothers*
14/79 **Son Of Clayton Delaney** *Tom T. Hall*
Son Of Hickory Holler's Tramp
22/68 *Johnny Darrell*
32/77 *Johnny Russell*
71/83 **Son Of The South** *Bill Anderson*
85/89 **Song A Day Keeps The Blues Away** *Mickey Jones*
8/74 **Song And Dance Man** *Johnny Paycheck*
66/73 **Song For Everyone** *Ray Griff*
53/69 **Song For Jenny** *Ed Bruce*
91/80 **Song For Noel** *King Edward IV & The Knights*
6/95 **Song For The Life** *Alan Jackson*
92/74 **Song I'd Like To Sing** *Kris Kristofferson & Rita Coolidge*
69/88 **Song In My Heart** *Mark Gray & Bobbi Lace*
5/77 **Song In The Night** *Johnny Duncan*
89/78 **Song Man** *Rick Jacques*
69/73 **Songman** *Cashman & West*
F/73 **Song Nobody Sings** *Jerry Wallace*
54/80 **Song Of The Patriot** *Johnny Cash*
Song Of The South
57/81 *Johnny Russell*
72/82 *Tom T. Hall & Earl Scruggs*
1/89 *Alabama*
2/93 **Song Remembers When** *Trisha Yearwood*
37/71 **Song To Mama** *Carter Family w/ Johnny Cash*
44/72 **Song To Sing** *Susan Raye*
29/75 **Song We Fell In Love To** *Connie Smith*
13/79 **Song We Made Love To** *Mickey Gilley*
2/05 **Songs About Me** *Trace Adkins*
12/04 **Songs About Rain** *Gary Allan*
10/65 **Sons Of Katie Elder** *Johnny Cash*
2/93 **Soon** *Tanya Tucker*
53/77 **Soon As I Touched Her** *Dorsey Burnette*
6/90 **Sooner Or Later** *Eddy Raven*

19/62 **Sooner Or Later** *Webb Pierce*
100/77 **Sophisticated Country Lady** *Loretta Robey*
5/64 **Sorrow On The Rocks** *Porter Wagoner*
63/88 **Sorry Girls** *Goldens*
50/64 **Sorry I Never Knew You** *Sego Brothers And Naomi*
59/96 **Sorry You Asked?** *Dwight Yoakam*
Soul And Inspiration ..see: (You're My)
Soul Deep
22/70 *Eddy Arnold*
63/73 *Guy Shannon*
27/77 **Soul Of A Honky Tonk Woman** *Mel McDaniel*
10/82 **Soul Searchin'** *Leon Everette*
1/73 **Soul Song** *Joe Stampley*
64/70 **Soul You Never Had** *Jan Howard*
18/75 **Soulful Woman** *Kenny O'Dell*
1/84 **Sound Of Goodbye** *Crystal Gayle*
21/73 **Sound Of Goodbye** *Jerry Wallace*
21/62 **Sound Of Your Footsteps** *Wilburn Brothers*
6/83 **Sounds Like Love** *Johnny Lee*
Sounds Of Goodbye
31/68 *George Morgan*
41/68 *Tommy Cash*
15/70 **South** *Roger Miller*
41/99 **South Of Santa Fe** *Brooks & Dunn*
91/87 **South Of The Border** *Clay Blaker*
27/95 **Southbound** *Sammy Kershaw*
99/77 **Southbound** *R.C. Bannon*
71/88 **Southern Accent** *Bama Band*
63/86 **Southern Air** *Ray Stevens*
91/88 **Southern And Proud Of It** *Jeff Golden*
37/68 **Southern Bound** *Kenny Price*
51/03 **Southern Boy** *Charlie Daniels Band w/ Travis Tritt*
5/77 **Southern California** *George Jones & Tammy Wynette*
42/82 **Southern Fried** *Bill Anderson*
27/95 **Southern Grace** *Little Texas*
96/89 **Southern Lady** *Arne Benoni*
6/73 **Southern Loving** *Jim Ed Brown*
1/77 **Southern Nights** *Glen Campbell*
45/01 **Southern Rain** *Billy Ray Cyrus*
1/81 **Southern Rains** *Mel Tillis*
1/90 **Southern Star** *Alabama*
67/97 **Southern Streamline** *John Fogerty*
Southern Women
86/83 *Owen Brothers*
33/84 *Wright Brothers*
65/94 **Souvenirs** *Suzy Bogguss*
66/87 **Souvenirs** *Lane Caudell*
100/76 **Souvenirs** *Colleen Peterson*
68/72 **Souvenirs And California Mem'rys** *Billie Jo Spears*
9/89 **Sowin' Love** *Paul Overstreet*
Spanish Eyes
20/79 *Charlie Rich*
8/88 *Willie Nelson w/ Julio Iglesias)*
3/53 **Spanish Fire Ball** *Hank Snow*
56/79 **Spare A Little Lovin' (On A Fool)** *Arnie Rue*
Sparkling Brown Eyes
4/54 *Webb Pierce w/ Wilburn Brothers*
30/60 *George Jones*
49/73 *Dickey Lee*
10/51 **Sparrow In The Tree Top** *Rex Allen*
29/91 **Speak Of The Devil** *Pirates Of The Mississippi*
9/82 **Speak Softly** *Gene Watson*
29/72 **Special Day** *Arlene Harden*
5/03 **Speed** *Montgomery Gentry*
70/88 **Speed Of The Sound Of Loneliness** *Kim Carnes*
82/89 **Spelling On The Stone** *Spelling On The Stone*
16/04 **Spend My Time** *Clint Black*
66/74 **Spiders & Snakes** *Jim Stafford*
5/94 **Spilled Perfume** *Pam Tillis*
2/99 **Spirit Of A Boy - Wisdom Of A Man** *Randy Travis*
14/58 **Splish Splash** *Bobby Darin*
F/73 **Spokane Motel Blues** *Tom T. Hall*
71/77 **Spread A Little Love Around** *Jody Miller*
61/72 **Spread It Around** *Brian Collins*
43/81 **Spread My Wings** *Tim Rex & Oklahoma*
Spring
30/69 *Clay Hart*
18/75 *Tanya Tucker*
12/78 **Spring Fever** *Loretta Lynn*
2/58 **Squaws Along The Yukon** *Hank Thompson*
61/79 **Squeeze Box** *Freddy Fender*
16/02 **Squeeze Me In** *Garth Brooks w/ Trisha Yearwood*
74/99 **Squeezin' The Love Outta You** *Redmon & Vale*
68/88 **Stairs, The** *Rosemary Sharp*
2/58 **Stairway Of Love** *Marty Robbins*
5/67 **Stamp Out Loneliness** *Stonewall Jackson*
8/50 **Stampede** *Roy Rogers*
66/99 **Stampede** *Chris LeDoux*
5/86 **Stand A Little Rain** *Nitty Gritty Dirt Band*
16/61 **Stand At Your Window** *Jim Reeves*
1/99 **Stand Beside Me** *Jo Dee Messina*
10/66 **Stand Beside Me** *Jimmy Dean*
1/80 **Stand By Me** *Mickey Gilley*
Stand By My Woman Man ..see: (I'm A)
Stand By Your Man
1/68 *Tammy Wynette*
88/81 *David Allan Coe*
82/89 *Lyle Lovett*
56/98 *Tammy Wynette*
12/86 **Stand On It** *Mel McDaniel*
5/85 **Stand Up** *Mel McDaniel*
28/62 **Stand Up** *Ferlin Husky*
14/78 **Standard Lie Number One** *Stella Parton*
34/01 **Standin' Still** *Clark Family Experience*
65/68 **Standing In The Rain** *Chaparral Brothers*
5/66 **Standing In The Shadows** *Hank Williams, Jr.*
17/74 **Standing In Your Line** *Barbara Fairchild*
63/87 **Standing Invitation** *Adam Baker*
19/93 **Standing Knee Deep In A River (Dying Of Thirst)** *Kathy Mattea*
2/95 **Standing On The Edge Of Goodbye** *John Berry*
52/93 **Standing On The Edge Of Love** *Clinton Gregory*
50/92 **Standing On The Promises** *Lionel Cartwright*
3/94 **Standing Outside The Fire** *Garth Brooks*
5/76 **Standing Room Only** *Barbara Mandrell*
Standing Tall
15/80 *Billie Jo Spears*
32/96 *Lorrie Morgan*
75/86 **Standing Too Close To The Moon** *Tina Danielle*
92/80 **Star, The** *Melba Montgomery*
78/74 **Star Of The Bar** *Troy Seals*
(Star Of Wonder) ..see: We Three Kings
Star Spangled Banner
58/96 *Ricochet*
35/01 *Faith Hill*
Star-Studded Nights
54/77 *Ed Bruce*
78/80 *Shoppe*
61/85 **Starlite** *Karen Taylor-Good*
Stars And Stripes On Iwo Jima
1/45 *Bob Wills*
4/45 *Sons Of The Pioneers*
Stars On The Water
30/81 *Rodney Crowell*
86/83 *Tommy St. John*
50/02 *George Strait*
2/96 **Stars Over Texas** *Tracy Lawrence*
6/90 **Start All Over Again** *Desert Rose Band*
74/75 **Start All Over Again** *Johnny Carver*
39/99 **Start Over Georgia** *Collin Raye*
52/99 **Start The Car** *Travis Tritt*
41/93 **Startin' Over Blues** *Joe Diffie*
Starting All Over Again
16/78 *Don Gibson*
73/89 *Razzy Bailey*
17/80 **Starting Over** *Tammy Wynette*
Starting Over Again
1/80 *Dolly Parton*
19/96 *Reba McEntire*
4/86 **Starting Over Again** *Steve Wariner*
55/94 **State Fair** *Doug Supernaw*
2/94 **State Of Mind** *Clint Black*
70/97 **State Of Mind** *Crystal Bernard*
74/83 **State Of Our Union** *Charlie McCoy & Laney Hicks*
17/66 **Stateside** *Mel Tillis*
Statue Of A Fool
1/69 *Jack Greene*
10/74 *Brian Collins*
91/79 *Bill Medley*
2/90 *Ricky Van Shelton*
5/77 **Statues Without Hearts** *Larry Gatlin*
Stay A Little Longer
2/46 *Bob Wills*
22/73 *Willie Nelson*
17/82 *Mel Tillis*
89/81 **Stay Away From Jim** *Jimmy Arthur Ordge*
20/75 **Stay Away From The Apple Tree** *Billie Jo Spears*
49/79 **(Stay Away From) The Cocaine Train** *Johnny Paycheck*
8/95 **Stay Forever** *Hal Ketchum*

3/03 **Stay Gone** *Jimmy Wayne*
41/89 **Stay November** *Kevin Welch*
86/88 **Stay Out Of My Arms** *Jim Lauderdale*
7/70 **Stay There 'Til I Get There** *Lynn Anderson*
61/80 **Stay Until The Rain Stops** *Kathy Carllile*
Stay With Me
6/79 *Dave & Sugar*
57/79 *Dandy*
86/85 *Exile*
40/78 **Stay With Me** *Nick Noble*
89/83 **Stay With Me** *Tammy Chaparro*
11↑/05 **Stay With Me (Brass Bed)** *Josh Gracin*
1/84 **Stay Young** *Don Williams*
3/04 **Stays In Mexico** *Toby Keith*
65/95 **Steady As She Goes** *Mark Collie*
26/79 **Steady As The Rain** *Stella Parton*
9/50 **Steal Away** *Red Foley*
74/79 **Steal Away** *Paul Schmucker*
50/75 **Stealin'** *Jacky Ward*
28/77 **Stealin' Feelin'** *Mike Lunsford*
18/99 **Steam** *Ty Herndon*
F/73 **Steamroller Blues** *Elvis Presley*
4/47 **Steel Guitar Rag** *Merle Travis*
9/49 **Steel Guitar Ramble** *Cecil Campbell*
4/46 **Steel Guitar Stomp** *Hank Penny*
15/66 **Steel Rail Blues** *George Hamilton IV*
73/91 **Steel Rails** *Alison Krauss*
6/71 **Step Aside** *Faron Young*
7/82 **Step Back** *Ronnie McDowell*
1/81 **Step By Step** *Eddie Rabbitt*
79/82 **Step In The Right Direction** *Judy Taylor*
62/98 **Step Right Up** *Cactus Choir*
1/85 **Step That Step** *Sawyer Brown*
43/69 **Stepchild** *Billie Jo Spears*
9/80 **Steppin' Out** *Mel Tillis*
46/88 **Steppin' Out** *David Ball*
60/70 **Steppin' Out** *Jerry Smith*
92/76 **Steppin' Out Tonight** *Lori Parker*
70/89 **Steppin' Stone** *Marie Osmond*
16/98 **Stepping Stone** *Lari White*
1/92 **Sticks And Stones** *Tracy Lawrence*
1/63 **Still** *Bill Anderson*
7/79 **Still A Woman** *Margo Smith*
34/65 **Still Alive In '65** *Jim Nesbitt*
20/91 **Still Burnin' For You** *Rob Crosby*
92/87 **Still Dancing** *Loney Hutchins*
1/81 **Still Doin' Time** *George Jones*
48/92 **Still Got A Crush On You** *Davis Daniel*
11/97 **Still Holding On** *Clint Black & Martina McBride*
27/01 **Still Holding Out For You** *SheDaisy*
33/86 **Still Hurtin' Me** *Charlie Daniels Band*
60/88 **Still I Stay** *Charly McClain*
23/98 **Still In Love With You** *Travis Tritt*
56/86 **Still In The Picture** *Leon Everette*
63/83 **Still In The Ring** *Tammy Wynette*
1/84 **Still Losing You** *Ronnie Milsap*
Still Loving You
56/70 *Bob Luman*
7/74 *Bob Luman*
95/79 *Troy Shondell*
27/63 **Still Loving You** *Clyde Beavers*
58/85 **Still On A Roll** *Moe Bandy & Joe Stampley*
57/92 **Still Out There Swinging** *Paul Overstreet*
62/88 **Still Pickin' Up After You** *Kendalls*
69/97 **Still Standing Tall** *Brady Seals*
3/83 **Still Taking Chances** *Michael Murphey*
Still The One
11/77 *Bill Anderson*
60/82 *Thrasher Brothers*
79/89 **Still The Same** *Bonnie Guitar*
4/75 **Still Thinkin' 'Bout You** *Billy "Crash" Craddock*
5/88 **Still Within The Sound Of My Voice** *Glen Campbell*
74/81 **Stirrin' Up Feelings** *Diana Trask*
7/57 **Stolen Moments** *Hank Snow*
100/77 **Stolen Moments** *Daniel*
3/74 **Stomp Them Grapes** *Mel Tillis*
(Stompin' Grapes And Gettin' Silly) ..see: Me And Millie
87/82 **Stompin' On My Heart** *Glen Bailey*
59/97 **Stone, The** *John Berry*
60/89 **Stone By Stone** *Tim Mensy*
40/94 **Stone Cold Country** *Gibson/Miller Band*
75/88 **Stone Cold Love** *Beards*
52/75 **Stone Crazy** *Freddy Weller*
41/79 **Stone Wall (Around Your Heart)** *Gary Stewart*
19/75 **Stoned At The Jukebox** *Hank Williams, Jr.*
31/72 **Stonin' Around** *Dick Curless*
8/58 **Stood Up** *Ricky Nelson*
53/67 **Stood Up** *Floyd Cramer*
Stop And Smell The Roses
29/74 *Henson Cargill*
40/74 *Mac Davis*
100/88 **Stop And Take The Time** *Faron Young*
93/77 **Stop And Think It Over** *Mike Boyd*
69/74 **Stop If You Love Me** *Terry Stafford*
26/64 **Stop Me** *Bill Phillips*
48/88 **Stop Me (If You've Heard This One Before)** *Larry Boone*
14/94 **Stop On A Dime** *Little Texas*
28/88 **Stop The Rain** *Shenandoah*
15/66 **Stop The Start (Of Tears In My Heart)** *Johnny Dollar*
13/68 **Stop The Sun** *Bonnie Guitar*
Stop The World (And Let Me Off)
7/58 *Johnnie & Jack*
16/65 *Waylon Jennings*
18/74 *Susan Raye*
91/76 *Donny King*
70/80 **Stores Are Full Of Roses** *"Blackjack" Jack Grayson*
16/67 **Storm, The** *Jim Reeves*
33/94 **Storm In The Heartland** *Billy Ray Cyrus*
60/83 **Storm Of Love** *Chantilly*
Storms Never Last
17/75 *Dottsy*
17/81 *Waylon Jennings & Jessi Colter*
25/74 **Storms Of Troubled Times** *Ray Price*
21/78 **Stormy Weather** *Stella Parton*
33/80 **Story Behind The Story** *Big Al Downing*
10/90 **Story Of Love** *Desert Rose Band*
1/58 **Story Of My Life** *Marty Robbins*
65/68 **Storybook Children** *Virgil Warner & Suzi Jane Hokum*
16/60 **Straight A's In Love** *Johnny Cash*
73/91 **Straight And Narrow** *Wild Rose*
66/87 **Straight From My Heart** *Sylvia*
80/85 **Straight Laced Lady** *Tracy Lynden*
Straight Life
37/68 *Bobby Goldsboro*
45/68 *Sonny Curtis*
64/92 **Straight Talk** *Dolly Parton*
79/86 **Straight Talkin** *Melba Montgomery*
47/98 **Straight Tequila** *Trini Triggs*
1/92 **Straight Tequila Night** *John Anderson*
1/87 **Straight To The Heart** *Crystal Gayle*
1/44 **Straighten Up And Fly Right** *King Cole Trio*
60/67 **Stranded** *Jim Nesbitt*
26/79 **Stranded On A Dead End Street** *ETC Band*
Strange Little Girl
5/51 *Cowboy Copas*
9/51 *Tennessee Ernie Ford*
9/51 *Red Foley & Ernest Tubb*
4/76 **Stranger** *Johnny Duncan*
45/83 **Stranger At My Door** *Juice Newton*
64/80 **Stranger, I'm Married** *Doug McGuire*
26/68 **Stranger In A Strange, Strange City** *Webb Pierce*
92/83 **Stranger In Her Bed** *Randy Parton*
5/83 **Stranger In My House** *Ronnie Milsap*
16/99 **Stranger In My Mirror** *Randy Travis*
Stranger In My Place
27/71 *Anne Murray*
79/75 *Anne Murray*
69/80 *Orion*
55/96 **Stranger In Your Eyes** *Ken Mellons*
42/67 **Stranger On The Run** *Bill Anderson*
2/90 **Stranger Things Have Happened** *Ronnie Milsap*
64/86 **Stranger Things Have Happened** *Larry Boone*
Stranger To Me
27/59 *Don Gibson*
68/76 *Mack White*
17/63 **Stranger Was Here** *Darrell McCall*
Strangers ..see: (From Now On All My Friends Are Gonna Be)
7/88 **Strangers Again** *Holly Dunn*
54/76 **Strawberry Cake** *Johnny Cash*
79/77 **Strawberry Curls** *Freddy Weller*
40/69 **Strawberry Farms** *Tom T. Hall*
76/78 **Strawberry Fields Forever** *Terri Hollowell*
1/96 **Strawberry Wine** *Deana Carter*
3/74 **Streak, The** *Ray Stevens*

56/92 **Street Man Named Desire** *Pirates Of The Mississippi*
9/70 **Street Singer** *Merle Haggard*
25/83 **Street Talk** *Kathy Mattea*
1/88 **Streets Of Bakersfield** *Dwight Yoakam & Buck Owens*
5/66 **Streets Of Baltimore** *Bobby Bare*
18/03 **Streets Of Heaven** *Sherrié Austin*
73/96 **Strength Of A Woman** *Philip Claypool*
58/03 **Strictly Business** *Brad Wolf*
29/69 **Strings** *Wynn Stewart*
64/75 **Strings** *Johnny Carver*
65/83 **Stroker's Theme** *Charlie Daniels Band*
13/02 **Strong Enough To Be Your Man** *Travis Tritt*
1/88 **Strong Enough To Bend** *Tanya Tucker*
1/86 **Strong Heart** *T.G. Sheppard*
57/98 **Strong One** *Mila Mason*
15/83 **Strong Weakness** *Bellamy Brothers*
27/64 **Stronger Than Dirt** *Glenn Barber*
26/00 **Stuck In Love** *Judds*
24/84 **Stuck On You** *Lionel Richie*
27/60 **Stuck On You** *Elvis Presley*
19/82 **Stuck Right In The Middle Of Your Love** *Billy Swan*
36/00 **Stuff** *Diamond Rio*
67/99 **Stuff That Matters** *Tara Lyn Hart*
43/82 **Stumblin' In** *Chantilly*
6/62 **Success** *Loretta Lynn*
7/69 **Such A Fool** *Roy Drusky*
82/87 **Suck It In** *Pat Garrett*
43/03 **Suddenly** *LeAnn Rimes*
34/96 **Suddenly Single** *Terri Clark*
64/87 **Suddenly Single** *Bama Band*
1/04 **Suds In The Bucket** *Sara Evans*
47/80 **Sue** *Tommy Overstreet*
64/69 **Sugar Cane County** *Maxine Brown*
F/77 **Sugar Coated Love** *Freddy Fender*
1/80 **Sugar Daddy** *Bellamy Brothers*
Sugar Foot ..see: Sugarfoot
50/68 **Sugar From My Candy** *Ray Griff*
38/70 **Sugar In The Flowers** *Anthony Armstrong Jones*
27/64 **Sugar Lump** *Sonny James*
1/47 **Sugar Moon** *Bob Wills*
Sugar Shack
32/70 *Bobby G. Rice*
61/86 *Carlette*
87/75 **Sugar Sugar** *Mike Lunsford*
Sugarfoot Rag
4/50 *Red Foley*
12/80 *Jerry Reed*
37/73 **Sugarman** *Peggy Little*
98/76 **Suitcase Life** *Side Of The Road Gang*
Sukiyaki
21/63 *Clyde Beavers*
96/86 *Boots Clements*
68/73 **Summer Afternoons** *Buddy Alan*
55/94 **Summer In Dixie** *Confederate Railroad*
69/71 **Summer Man** *Anne Christine*
79/87 **Summer On The Mississippi** *Southern Reign*
39/66 **Summer Roses** *Ned Miller*
34/64 **Summer Skies And Golden Sands** *Jimmy "C" Newman*
100/73 **Summer (The First Time)** *Bobby Goldsboro*
2/88 **Summer Wind** *Desert Rose Band*
41/65 **Summer, Winter, Spring And Fall** *Roy Drusky*
1/95 **Summer's Comin'** *Clint Black*
Summertime Blues
70/77 *Jim Mundy*
1/94 *Alan Jackson*
75/97 **Summertime Girls** *Crawford/West*
93/76 **Summertime Lovin'** *Layng Martine, Jr.*
98/77 **Summit Ridge Drive** *Charlie McCoy & Barefoot Jerry*
13/76 **Sun Comin' Up** *Nat Stuckey*
30/65 **Sun Glasses** *Skeeter Davis*
62/77 **Sun In Dixie** *Kathy Barnes*
58/73 **Sun Is Shining (On Everybody But Me)** *Earl Richards*
42/79 **Sun Went Down In My World Tonight** *Leon Everette*
48/70 **Sun's Gotta' Shine** *Wilma Burgess*
32/76 **Sunday Afternoon Boatride In The Park On The Lake** *R.W. Blackwood*
3/50 **Sunday Down In Tennessee** *Red Foley*
68/82 **Sunday Go To Cheatin' Clothes** *Darlene Austin*
1/89 **Sunday In The South** *Shenandoah*
5/88 **Sunday Kind Of Love** *Reba McEntire*
58/04 **Sunday Morning And Saturday Night** *James Otto*
38/71 **Sunday Morning Christian** *Harlan Howard*
Sunday Morning Coming Down
55/69 *Ray Stevens*
1/70 *Johnny Cash*
Sunday School To Broadway
29/76 *Sammi Smith*
57/77 *Anne Murray*
Sunday Sunrise
6/73 *Brenda Lee*
49/75 *Anne Murray*
Sundown
13/74 *Gordon Lightfoot*
59/99 *Deryl Dodd*
18/68 **Sundown Mary** *Billy Walker*
94/79 **Sundown Sideshow** *Jano*
4/77 **Sunflower** *Glen Campbell*
63/72 **Sunny Side Of My Life** *Roger Miller*
12/61 **Sunny Tennessee** *Cowboy Copas*
Sunset Town ..see: Midnight Girl
35/80 **Sunshine** *Juice Newton*
Sunshine
57/70 *Earl Richards*
53/73 *Mickey Newbury*
98/79 *Sammy Vaughn*
47/68 **Sunshine And Bluebirds** *Jimmy Newman*
58/72 **Sunshine And Rainbows** *Roy Drusky*
87/73 **Sunshine Feeling** *LaWanda Lindsey*
Sunshine Man
54/68 *Mac Curtis*
74/78 *Kenny Price*
43/68 **Sunshine Of My World** *Dallas Frazier*
42/74 **Sunshine On My Shoulders** *John Denver*
1/73 **Super Kind Of Woman** *Freddie Hart*
73/74 **Super Kitten** *Connie Cato*
82/79 **Super Lady** *Ray Pillow*
14/86 **Super Love** *Exile*
37/72 **Super Sideman** *Kenny Price*
1/73 **Superman** *Donna Fargo*
33/74 **Superskirt** *Connie Cato*
81/76 **Support Your Local Honky Tonks** *Ronnie Sessions*
48/87 **Sure Feels Good** *Barbara Mandrell*
5/82 **Sure Feels Like Love** *Gatlin Bros.*
39/99 **Sure Feels Real Good** *Michael Peterson*
11/55 **Sure Fire Kisses** *Justin Tubb - Goldie Hill*
3/93 **Sure Love** *Hal Ketchum*
8/88 **Sure Thing** *Foster & Lloyd*
15/80 **Sure Thing** *Freddie Hart*
65/85 **Sure Thing** *Tony Arata*
34/64 **Surely** *Warner Mack*
73/66 **Surely Not** *Don Bowman*
64/00 **Surprise** *Doug Stone*
49/74 **Surprise, Surprise** *Sonny James*
5/81 **Surround Me With Love** *Charly McClain*
71/67 **Survival Of The Fittest** *Mel Tillis*
65/82 **Survivor** *Bill Nash*
15/75 **Susan When She Tried** *Statler Brothers*
20/87 **Susannah** *Tom Wopat*
52/86 **Susie's Beauty Shop** *Tom T. Hall*
4/48 **Suspicion** *Tex Williams*
Suspicion
33/72 *Bobby G. Rice*
27/88 *Ronnie McDowell*
1/79 **Suspicions** *Eddie Rabbitt*
Suspicious Minds
25/70 *Waylon Jennings & Jessi Colter*
2/76 *Waylon Jennings & Jessi Colter*
35/92 *Dwight Yoakam*
48/89 **Suzette** *Foster & Lloyd*
26/64 **Sweet Adorable You** *Eddy Arnold*
57/84 **Sweet And Easy To Love** *Mike Campbell*
66/74 **Sweet And Tender Feeling** *Mack White*
64/72 **Sweet Apple Wine** *Duane Dee*
43/69 **Sweet Baby Girl** *Peggy Little*
57/71 **Sweet Baby On My Mind** *June Stearns*
40/73 **Sweet Becky Walker** *Larry Gatlin*
Sweet Caroline
40/70 *Anthony Armstrong Jones*
77/86 *Claude Gray*
22/68 **Sweet Child Of Sunshine** *Jerry Wallace*
Sweet City Woman
48/77 *Johnny Carver*
34/80 *Tompall/Glaser Brothers*
89/78 **Sweet Country Girl** *Mack Sanders*
5/84 **Sweet Country Music** *Atlanta*
86/75 **Sweet Country Music** *Ruby Falls*

6/73 **Sweet Country Woman** *Johnny Duncan*
53/77 **Sweet Deceiver** *Cristy Lane*
1/78 **Sweet Desire** *Kendalls*
7/72 **Sweet Dream Woman** *Waylon Jennings*
Sweet Dreams
2/56 *Faron Young*
9/56 *Don Gibson*
6/61 *Don Gibson*
5/63 *Patsy Cline*
1/76 *Emmylou Harris*
88/76 *Troy Seals*
19/79 *Reba McEntire*
20/78 **Sweet Fantasy** *Bobby Borchers*
Sweet Home Alabama
94/81 *Charlie Daniels Band*
75/95 *Alabama*
Sweet Life
85/79 *Paul Davis*
47/88 *Marie Osmond w/ Paul Davis*
3/61 **Sweet Lips** *Webb Pierce*
94/78 **Sweet Little Devil** *Judy Allen*
62/91 **Sweet Little Shoe** *Dan Seals*
37/87 **Sweet Little '66** *Steve Earle & The Dukes*
69/85 **Sweet Love, Don't Cry** *Charleston Express/Jesse Wales*
39/78 **Sweet Love Feelings** *Jerry Reed*
23/72 **Sweet, Love Me Good Woman** *Tompall/Glaser Brothers*
52/69 **Sweet Love On My Mind** *Claude King*
56/78 **Sweet Love Song The World Can Sing** *Dale McBride*
86/75 **Sweet Lovin' Baby** *Wilma Burgess*
69/79 **Sweet Lovin' Things** *Billy Walker*
3/74 **Sweet Magnolia Blossom** *Billy "Crash" Craddock*
73/78 **Sweet Mary** *Danny Hargrove*
10/79 **Sweet Melinda** *Randy Barlow*
F/79 **Sweet Melinda** *John Denver*
Sweet Memories
32/69 *Dottie West & Don Gibson*
4/79 *Willie Nelson*
79/89 **Sweet Memories Of You** *Perry LaPointe*
Sweet Misery
16/67 *Jimmy Dean*
14/71 *Ferlin Husky*
69/75 **Sweet Molly** *David Houston & Calvin Crawford*
44/80 **Sweet Mother Texas** *Eddy Raven*
Sweet Music Man
9/77 *Kenny Rogers*
36/02 *Reba McEntire*
63/69 **Sweet 'N' Sassy** *Jerry Smith*
85/81 **Sweet Natural Love** *Mick Lloyd & Jerri Kelly*
40/80 **Sweet Red Wine** *Gary Morris*
44/84 **Sweet Rosanna** *Rex Allen, Jr.*
2/68 **Sweet Rosie Jones** *Buck Owens*
71/85 **Sweet Salvation** *Audie Henry*
25/76 **Sweet Sensuous Feelings** *Sue Richards*
42/80 **Sweet Sensuous Sensations** *Don Gibson*
Sweet Sexy Eyes
92/78 *Gayle Harding*
8/80 *Cristy Lane*
4/44 **Sweet Slumber** *Lucky Millinder*
3/04 **Sweet Southern Comfort** *Buddy Jewell*
52/81 **Sweet Southern Love** *Phil Everly*
87/76 **Sweet Southern Lovin'** *Mayf Nutter*
84/82 **Sweet Southern Moonlight** *Narvel Felts*
18/01 **Sweet Summer** *Diamond Rio*
7/79 **Sweet Summer Lovin'** *Dolly Parton*
42/04 **Sweet Summer Rain** *Rushlow*
7/75 **Sweet Surrender** *John Denver*
68/92 **Sweet Suzanne** *Buzzin' Cousins*
18/65 **Sweet, Sweet Judy** *David Houston*
8/78 **Sweet, Sweet Smile** *Carpenters*
23/76 **Sweet Talkin' Man** *Lynn Anderson*
Sweet Thang
4/66 *Nat Stuckey*
45/67 *Ernest Tubb & Loretta Lynn*
8/69 **Sweet Thang And Cisco** *Nat Stuckey*
79/86 **Sweet Time** *Jill Hollier*
26/69 **Sweet Wine** *Johnny Carver*
12/82 **Sweet Yesterday** *Sylvia*
8/86 **Sweeter And Sweeter** *Statler Brothers*
Sweeter Love (I'll Never Know)
53/72 *Barbara Fairchild*
22/84 *Brenda Lee*
Sweeter Than The Flowers
3/48 *Moon Mullican*
12/48 *Shorty Long*
12/76 **Sweetest Gift** *Linda Ronstadt & Emmylou Harris*
25/91 **Sweetest Thing** *Carlene Carter*
Sweetest Thing (I've Ever Known)
86/76 *Dottsy*
1/82 *Juice Newton*
11/69 **Sweetheart Of The Year** *Ray Price*
11/48 **Sweetheart, You Done Me Wrong** *Bill Monroe*
20/61 **Sweethearts Again** *Bob Gallion*
19/63 **Sweethearts In Heaven** *Buck Owens & Rose Maddox*
46/00 **Swimming In Champagne** *Eric Heatherly*
31/97 **Swing, The** *James Bonamy*
1/83 **Swingin'** *John Anderson*
38/96 **Swingin' Doors** *Martina McBride*
Swinging Doors
5/66 *Merle Haggard*
67/81 *Del Reeves*
87/89 *Buck Hall*
71/95 **Swinging On My Baby's Chain** *Philip Claypool*
71/69 **Swiss Cottage Place** *Jerry Wallace*
12/72 **Sylvia's Mother** *Bobby Bare*

T

T For Texas
5/63 *Grandpa Jones*
36/76 *Tompall & His Outlaw Band*
7/94 **T.L.C. A.S.A.P.** *Alabama*
30/63 **Tadpole** *Tillman Franks*
8/51 **Tailor Made Woman** *Tennessee Ernie Ford & Joe "Fingers" Carr*
5/54 **Tain't Nice (To Talk Like That)** *Carlisles*
Take A City Bride
58/67 *Rick Nelson*
72/71 *Swampwater*
Take A Letter Maria
8/70 *Anthony Armstrong Jones*
99/88 *Roger Marshall*
45/00 *Doug Stone*
6/63 **Take A Letter, Miss Gray** *Justin Tubb*
58/87 **Take A Little Bit Of It Home** *A.J. Masters*
31/69 **Take A Little Good Will Home** *Bobby Goldsboro & Del Reeves*
2/92 **Take A Little Trip** *Alabama*
71/68 **Take A Message To Mary** *Don Cherry*
83/83 **Take A Ride On A Riverboat** *Cedar Creek*
7/49 **Take An Old Cold 'Tater (And Wait)** *Jimmie Dickens*
Take Another Run
78/89 *Tony Perez*
60/93 *Paul Overstreet*
Take Good Care Of Her
1/66 *Sonny James*
F/74 *Elvis Presley*
73/79 **Take Good Care Of My Love** *Max Brown*
40/83 **Take It All** *Rich Landers*
83/81 **Take It As It Comes** *Michael Murphey w/ Katy Moffatt*
5/93 **Take It Back** *Reba McEntire*
17/81 **Take It Easy** *Crystal Gayle*
Take It Easy
66/72 *Billy Mize*
21/94 *Travis Tritt*
38/97 **Take It From Me** *Paul Brandt*
10/92 **Take It Like A Man** *Michelle Wright*
44/80 **Take It Like A Woman** *Debby Boone*
82/87 **Take It Real Easy** *Dobie Gray*
86/84 **Take It Slow** *Kenny Dale*
72/88 **Take It Slow With Me** *Tommy & Donna*
8/83 **Take It To The Limit** *Waylon Jennings & Willie Nelson*
Take Me
8/66 *George Jones*
9/72 *Tammy Wynette & George Jones*
32/99 **Take Me** *Lari White*
31/68 **Take Me Along With You** *Van Trevor*
2/94 **Take Me As I Am** *Faith Hill*
Take Me As I Am (Or Let Me Go)
8/68 *Ray Price*
34/76 *Mack White*
28/81 *Bobby Bare*
24/79 **Take Me Back** *Charly McClain*
76/81 **Take Me Back To The Country** *Baxter, Baxter & Baxter*
61/70 **Take Me Back To The Goodtimes, Sally** *Bobby Wright*
1/82 **Take Me Down** *Alabama*
50/71 **Take Me Home, Country Roads** *John Denver*
5/74 **Take Me Home To Somewhere** *Joe Stampley*
91/81 **Take Me Home With You** *Carl Chambers*

Take Me In Your Arms And Hold Me
1/50 *Eddy Arnold*
10/80 *Jim Reeves/Deborah Allen*
94/73 **Take Me One More Ride** *David Frizzell*
25/80 **Take Me, Take Me** *Rosanne Cash*
97/78 **Take Me To Bed** *Jeannie Seely*
67/76 **Take Me To Heaven** *Sami Jo*
10/82 **Take Me To The Country** *Mel McDaniel*
82/80 **Take Me To Your Heart** *Del Reeves*
5/80 **Take Me To Your Lovin' Place** *Gatlin Bros.*
1/68 **Take Me To Your World** *Tammy Wynette*
75/82 **Take Me Tonight** *Darlene Austin*
87/77 **Take Me Tonight** *Tom Jones*
43/00 **Take Me With You When You Go** *Tracy Byrd*
7/76 **Take My Breath Away** *Margo Smith*
8/71 **Take My Hand** *Mel Tillis & Sherry Bryce*
59/75 **Take My Hand** *Jeannie Seely*
38/68 **Take My Hand For Awhile** *George Hamilton IV*
48/74 **Take My Life And Shape It With Your Love** *George Kent*
97/79 **Take My Love** *Joy Ford*
98/78 **Take My Love To Rita** *Tommy Cash*
15/64 **Take My Ring Off Your Finger** *Carl Smith*
34/69 **Take Off Time** *Claude Gray*
94/73 **Take One Step** *Eydie Gorme*
13/55 **Take Possession** *Jean Shepard*
52/95 **Take That** *Lisa Brokop*
57/97 **Take The Keys To My Heart** *Garth Brooks*
10/87 **Take The Long Way Home** *John Schneider*
57/82 **Take The Mem'ry When You Go** *Jacky Ward*
Take These Chains From My Heart
1/53 *Hank Williams*
17/94 *Lee Roy Parnell w/ Brooks & Dunn*
44/80 **Take This Heart** *Don King*
1/78 **Take This Job And Shove It** *Johnny Paycheck*
7/62 **Take Time** *Webb Pierce*
96/89 **Take Time** *Dawn Schutt*
Take Time To Know Her
74/71 *Joe Stampley*
58/82 *David Allan Coe*
10/73 **Take Time To Love Her** *Nat Stuckey*
91/79 **Take Time To Smell The Flowers** *Max Brown*
49/65 **Take Your Hands Off My Heart** *Ray Pillow*
2/92 **Take Your Memory With You** *Vince Gill*
83/79 **Taken To The Line** *San Fernando Valley Music Band*
5/70 **Taker, The** *Waylon Jennings*
33/79 **Takes A Fool To Love A Fool** *Burton Cummings*
100/78 **Takin' A Chance** *Bobby Wright*
86/82 **Takin' It Back To The Hills** *Ronnie Rogers*
Takin' It Easy
94/78 *Joey Davis*
2/81 *Lacy J. Dalton*
41/98 **Takin' The Country Back** *John Anderson*
Takin' What I Can Get
91/75 *Sally June Hart*
41/76 *Brenda Lee*
12/80 **Taking Somebody With Me When I Fall** *Gatlin Bros.*
14/70 **Talk About The Good Times** *Jerry Reed*
1/63 **Talk Back Trembling Lips** *Ernest Ashworth*
26/66 **Talk Me Some Sense** *Bobby Bare*
63/94 **Talk Some** *Billy Ray Cyrus*
Talk To Me
13/78 *Freddy Fender*
1/83 *Mickey Gilley*
35/82 **Talk To Me Loneliness** *Cindy Hurt*
16/58 **Talk To Me Lonesome Heart** *James O'Gwynn*
3/52 **Talk To Your Heart** *Ray Price*
62/86 **Talkin' Blue Eyes** *Marty Haggard*
18/05 **Talkin' Song Repair Blues** *Alan Jackson*
16/88 **Talkin' To Myself Again** *Tammy Wynette*
8/57 **Talkin' To The Blues** *Jim Lowe*
4/87 **Talkin' To The Moon** *Gatlin Bros.*
Talkin' To The Wall
3/66 *Warner Mack*
7/74 *Lynn Anderson*
4/88 **Talkin' To The Wrong Man** *Michael Martin Murphey w/ Ryan Murphey*
18/73 **Talkin' With My Lady** *Johnny Duncan*
6/48 **Talking Boogie** *Tex Williams*
1/78 **Talking In Your Sleep** *Crystal Gayle*
41/64 **Talking To The Night Lights** *Del Reeves*
1/69 **Tall Dark Stranger** *Buck Owens*
1/95 **Tall, Tall Trees** *Alan Jackson*
24/66 **Tallest Tree** *Bonnie Guitar*
82/87 **Taming My Mind** *Tony McGill*
4/57 **Tangled Mind** *Hank Snow*
67/96 **Tangled Up In Texas** *Frazier River*
75/90 **Tanqueray** *Vern Gosdin*
62/87 **Tanya Montana** *David Allan Coe*
7/87 **Tar Top** *Alabama*
73/92 **Taste Of Freedom** *Aaron Barker*
23/66 **Taste Of Heaven** *Jim Edward Brown*
86/78 **Taste Of Love** *Jenny Lynn*
54/83 **Taste Of The Wind** *James & Michael Younger*
42/65 **'Tater Raisin' Man** *Dick Curless*
97/76 **Te' Quiero (I Love You In Many Ways)** *Country Cavaleers*
25/61 **Teach Me How To Lie** *Hank Thompson*
7/81 **Teach Me To Cheat** *Kendalls*
75/94 **Teach Your Children** *Red Hots*
72/99 **Team Of Destiny** *Kenny Chesney*
44/64 **Tear After Tear** *Rex Allen*
38/65 **Tear Dropped By** *Jean Shepard*
7/77 **Tear Fell** *Billy "Crash" Craddock*
9/88 **Tear-Stained Letter** *Jo-el Sonnier*
49/66 **Tear-Talk** *Johnny Dollar*
Tear Time
16/67 *Wilma Burgess*
1/78 *Dave & Sugar*
44/66 **Teardrop Lane** *Ned Miller*
38/94 **Teardrops** *George Ducas*
Teardrops In My Heart
4/47 *Sons Of The Pioneers*
18/76 *Rex Allen, Jr.*
45/81 *Marty Robbins*
84/78 **Teardrops In My Tequila** *Paul Craft*
42/76 **Teardrops Will Kiss The Morning Dew** *Del Reeves & Billie Jo Spears*
63/98 **Tearin' It Up (And Burnin' It Down)** *Garth Brooks*
72/80 **Tearjoint** *Faron Young*
37/64 **Tears And Roses** *George Morgan*
14/57 **Tears Are Only Rain** *Hank Thompson*
7/62 **Tears Broke Out On Me** *Eddy Arnold*
74/94 **Tears Dry** *Victoria Shaw*
3/82 **Tears Of The Lonely** *Mickey Gilley*
36/70 **Tears On Lincoln's Face** *Tommy Cash*
91/79 **Tears (There's Nowhere Else To Hide)** *Tommy Overstreet*
11/67 **Tears Will Be The Chaser For Your Wine** *Wanda Jackson*
1/76 **Teddy Bear** *Red Sovine*
1/73 **Teddy Bear Song** *Barbara Fairchild*
53/76 **Teddy Bear's Last Ride** *Diana Williams*
98/76 **Teddy Toad** *Bobby "Sofine" Butler*
15/57 **Teen-Age Dream** *Marty Robbins*
10/56 **Teenage Boogie** *Webb Pierce*
Teenage Queen ..see: Ballad Of
65/75 **Telephone, The** *Jerry Reed*
(Telephone Answering Machine Song) ..see: Hello, This Is Joannie
25/74 **Telephone Call** *George Jones*
50/77 **Telephone Man** *Meri Wilson*
91/79 **Tell All Your Troubles To Me** *Miki Mori*
45/84 **Tell 'Em I've Gone Crazy** *Ed Bruce*
1/01 **Tell Her** *Lonestar*
10/63 **Tell Her So** *Wilburn Brothers*
55/71 **Tell Her You Love Her** *Kenny Price*
98/79 **Tell Him** *Pia Zadora*
31/71 **Tell Him That You Love Him** *Webb Pierce*
Tell It Like It Is
31/68 *Archie Campbell & Lorene Mann*
83/76 *John Wesley Ryles*
2/89 *Billy Joe Royal*
70/89 *Sammy Sadler*
34/87 **Tell It To Your Teddy Bear** *Shooters*
65/83 **Tell Mama** *Terri Gibbs*
33/68 **Tell Maude I Slipped** *Red Sovine*
88/89 **Tell Me** *Kenny Carr*
Tell Me A Lie
52/74 *Sami Jo*
1/83 *Janie Fricke*

4/93 **Tell Me About It** *Tanya Tucker w/ Delbert McClinton*
58/70 **Tell Me Again** *Jeannie Seely*
63/96 **Tell Me Again** *Tammy Graham*
(Tell Me 'Bout The Good Old Days) ..see: Grandpa
47/01 **Tell Me How** *Chad Brock*
2/95 **Tell Me I Was Dreaming** *Travis Tritt*
88/79 **Tell Me I'm Only Dreaming** *Lorrie Morgan*
13/70 **Tell Me My Lying Eyes Are Wrong** *George Jones*
48/64 **Tell Me Pretty Words** *Slim Whitman*
75/81 **Tell Me So** *Gary Goodnight*
Tell Me Something Bad About Tulsa
75/97 *Noel Haggard*
11/03 *George Strait*
8/88 **Tell Me True** *Juice Newton*
8/79 **Tell Me What It's Like** *Brenda Lee*
60/04 **Tell Me What You Wanna Do** *Victor Sanz*
86/83 **Tell Me When I'm Hot** *Billy "Crash" Craddock*
43/02 **Tell Me Where It Hurts** *Tommy Shane Steiner*
3/93 **Tell Me Why** *Wynonna*
10/82 **Tell Me Why** *Earl Thomas Conley*
18/90 **Tell Me Why** *Jann Browne*
11/80 **Tell Ole I Ain't Here, He Better Get On Home** *Moe Bandy & Joe Stampley*
18/74 **Tell Tale Signs** *Jerry Lee Lewis*
14/49 **Tellin' My Troubles To My Old Guitar** *Jimmy Wakely*
3/87 **Telling Me Lies** *Dolly Parton, Linda Ronstadt, Emmylou Harris*
52/01 **Telluride** *Tim McGraw*
5/80 **Temporarily Yours** *Jeanne Pruett*
76/85 **Temptation** *Mike Martin*
2/47 **Temptation (Tim-Tayshun)** *Red Ingle*
5/91 **Tempted** *Marty Stuart*
82/80 **Ten Anniversary Presents** *Jim Owen*
14/74 **Ten Commandments Of Love** *David Houston & Barbara Mandrell*
33/72 **10 Degrees & Getting Colder** *George Hamilton IV*
9/86 **Ten Feet Away** *Keith Whitley*
22/94 **Ten Feet Tall And Bulletproof** *Travis Tritt*
2/65 **10 Little Bottles** *Johnny Bond*
1/02 **Ten Rounds With José Cuervo** *Tracy Byrd*
96/80 **Ten Seconds In The Saddle** *Chris LeDoux*
F/79 **Ten Thousand And One** *Connie Smith*
6/96 **Ten Thousand Angels** *Mindy McCready*
5/59 **Ten Thousand Drums** *Carl Smith*
45/91 **Ten With A Two** *Willie Nelson*
16/77 **Ten Years Of This** *Gary Stewart*
95/84 **Tenamock Georgia** *Charlie Bandy*
48/67 **Tender And True** *Ernie Ashworth*
5/45 **Tender Hearted Sue** *Rambling Rogue (Fred Rose)*
1/88 **Tender Lie** *Restless Heart*
72/83 **Tender Lovin' Lies** *Judy Bailey*
2/93 **Tender Moment** *Lee Roy Parnell*
74/87 **Tender Time** *Louise Mandrell*
6/95 **Tender When I Want To Be** *Mary Chapin Carpenter*
1/61 **Tender Years** *George Jones*
42/83 **Tenderness Place** *Karen Taylor-Good*
72/68 **Tennessee** *Jimmy Martin*
91/78 **Tennessee** *Ray Sanders*
1/70 **Tennessee Bird Walk** *Jack Blanchard & Misty Morgan*
11/49 **Tennessee Boogie** *Zeb Turner*
Tennessee Border
3/49 *Red Foley*
8/49 *Tennessee Ernie Ford*
12/49 *Bob Atcher*
15/49 *Jimmie Skinner*
Tennessee Border—No. 2
14/49 *Homer & Jethro*
2/50 *Red Foley & Ernest Tubb*
58/91 **Tennessee Born And Bred** *Eddie Rabbitt*
Tennessee Flat-Top Box
11/62 *Johnny Cash*
1/88 *Rosanne Cash*
1/84 **Tennessee Homesick Blues** *Dolly Parton*
28/69 **Tennessee Hound Dog** *Osborne Brothers*
7/48 **Tennessee Moon** *Cowboy Copas*
44/89 **Tennessee Nights** *Crystal Gayle*
Tennessee Polka
3/49 *Pee Wee King*
4/49 *Red Foley*
1/80 **Tennessee River** *Alabama*
31/03 **Tennessee River Run** *Darryl Worley*
9/82 **Tennessee Rose** *Emmylou Harris*
Tennessee Saturday Night
1/49 *Red Foley*
11/49 *Johnny Bond*
85/82 *Roy Clark*
5/59 **Tennessee Stud** *Eddy Arnold*
12/49 **Tennessee Tears** *Pee Wee King*
Tennessee Waltz
3/48 *Pee Wee King*
3/48 *Cowboy Copas*
12/48 *Roy Acuff*
2/51 *Patti Page*
6/51 *Pee Wee King*
18/80 *Lacy J. Dalton*
Tennessee Whiskey
77/81 *David Allan Coe*
2/83 *George Jones*
6/53 **Tennessee Wig Walk** *Bonnie Lou*
31/80 **Tequila Sheila** *Bobby Bare*
64/93 **Tequila Sunrise** *Alan Jackson*
8/95 **Tequila Talkin'** *Lonestar*
87/81 **Testimony Of Soddy Hoe** *Jerry Reed*
Texarkana Baby
1/48 *Eddy Arnold*
15/48 *Bob Wills*
36/76 **Texas** *Charlie Daniels Band*
69/68 **Texas** *Tex Ritter*
31/77 **Texas Angel** *Jacky Ward*
3/44 **Texas Blues** *Foy Willing*
26/80 **Texas Bound And Flyin'** *Jerry Reed*
23/81 **Texas Cowboy Night** *Mel Tillis & Nancy Sinatra*
72/97 **Texas Diary** *James T. Horn*
69/81 **Texas Ida Red** *David Houston*
Texas In 1880
18/88 *Foster & Lloyd*
54/01 *Radney Foster w/ Pat Green*
9/80 **Texas In My Rear View Mirror** *Mac Davis*
96/74 **Texas Law Sez** *Tompall Glaser*
75/78 **Texas Me & You** *Asleep At The Wheel*
81/86 **Texas Moon** *Johnny Duncan*
(Texas National Anthem) ..see: Fraulein
35/76 **Texas - 1947** *Johnny Cash*
94/76 **Texas On A Saturday Night** *Bill Green*
60/01 **Texas On My Mind** *Pat Green & Cory Morrow*
24/04 **Texas Plates** *Kellie Coffey*
2/46 **Texas Playboy Rag** *Bob Wills*
4/98 **Texas Size Heartache** *Joe Diffie*
9/81 **Texas State Of Mind** *David Frizzell & Shelly West*
22/93 **Texas Tattoo** *Gibson/Miller Band*
Texas Tea
51/68 *Dee Mullins*
77/77 *Leroy Van Dyke*
68/80 *Orion*
1/95 **Texas Tornado** *Tracy Lawrence*
5/79 **Texas (When I Die)** *Tanya Tucker*
34/76 **Texas Woman** *Pat Boone*
1/81 **Texas Women** *Hank Williams, Jr.*
6/70 **Thank God And Greyhound** *Roy Clark*
2/97 **Thank God For Believers** *Mark Chesnutt*
Thank God For Kids
3/83 *Oak Ridge Boys*
60/04 *Kenny Chesney*
1/84 **Thank God For The Radio** *Kendalls*
1/93 **Thank God For You** *Sawyer Brown*
Thank God I'm A Country Boy
1/75 *John Denver*
27/04 *Billy Dean*
10/76 **Thank God I've Got You** *Statler Brothers*
11/77 **Thank God She's Mine** *Freddie Hart*
66/89 **Thank The Cowboy For The Ride** *Tammy Wynette*
70/83 **Thank You Darling** *Bill Anderson*
33/80 **Thank You, Ever-Lovin'** *Kenny Dale*
21/73 **Thank You For Being You** *Mel Tillis*
8/54 **Thank You For Calling** *Billy Walker*
65/69 **Thank You For Loving Me** *Brenda Byers*
79/74 **Thank You For The Feeling** *Billy Mize*
75/79 **Thank You For The Roses** *Kitty Wells*
35/73 **Thank You For Touching My Life** *Tony Douglas*
17/66 **Thank You Ma'am** *Ray Pillow*
31/74 **Thank You World** *Statler Brothers*
24/75 **Thanks** *Bill Anderson*

Thanks A Lot
3/63 *Ernest Tubb*
80/79 *Billy Parker*
12/59 **Thanks A Lot** *Johnny Cash*
40/68 **Thanks A Lot For Tryin' Anyway** *Liz Anderson*
17/88 **Thanks Again** *Ricky Skaggs*
98/79 **Thanks E.T. Thanks A Lot** *Billy Parker*
69/88 **Thanks For Leavin' Him (For Me)** *Paula McCulla*
95/77 **Thanks For Leaving, Lucille** *Sherri Jerrico*
59/73 **Thanks For Lovin' Me** *Pat Roberts*
29/72 **Thanks For The Mem'ries** *Barbara Fairchild*
50/96 **Thanks To You** *Marty Stuart*
65/94 **Thanks To You** *Emmylou Harris*
66/72 **Thanks To You For Lovin' Me** *Jerry Wallace*
20/65 **That Ain't All** *John D. Loudermilk*
3/95 **That Ain't My Truck** *Rhett Akins*
61/70 **That Ain't No Stuff** *Compton Brothers*
1/94 **That Ain't No Way To Go** *Brooks & Dunn*
22/72 **That Certain One** *Tommy Cash*
53/04 **That Changed Me** *Chad Brock*
10/54 **That Crazy Mambo Thing** *Hank Snow*
1/55 **That Do Make It Nice** *Eddy Arnold*
46/98 **That Does It** *Jason Sellers*
65/74 **That Doesn't Mean (I Don't Love My God)** *Ray Griff*
8/99 **That Don't Impress Me Much** *Shania Twain*
11/74 **That Girl Who Waits On Tables** *Ronnie Milsap*
4/96 **That Girl's Been Spyin' On Me** *Billy Dean*
1/52 **That Heart Belongs To Me** *Webb Pierce*
That Hound Dog In The Window ..see: (How Much Is)
68/00 **That Hurts** *Paul Brandt*
57/78 **That "I Love You, You Love Me Too" Love Song** *Laney Smallwood*
68/84 **That It's All Over Feeling (All Over Again)** *Steve Clark*
74/97 **That Just About Covers It** *Rich McCready*
4/90 **That Just About Does It** *Vern Gosdin*
95/74 **That Kind Of Fool** *Atlanta James*
62/96 **That Last Mile** *Jeff Carson*
53/76 **That Little Difference** *Carmol Taylor*
11/76 **That Look In Her Eyes** *Freddie Hart*
72/70 **That Look Of Good-Bye** *Ernie Ashworth*
6/80 **That Lovin' You Feelin' Again** *Roy Orbison & Emmylou Harris*
66/78 **That Lucky Old Sun** *Nat Stuckey*
26/79 **That Makes Two Of Us** *Jacky Ward/Reba McEntire*
80/89 **That Newsong (They're Playin)** *Jeff Golden*
4/96 **That Ol' Wind** *Garth Brooks*
48/77 **That Old Cold Shoulder** *Tom Bresh*
That Old Familiar Feeling ..see: (Here Comes)
90/83 **That Old Time Feelin'** *Rex Gosdin*
21/88 **That Old Wheel** *Johnny Cash w/ Hank Williams, Jr.*
69/79 **That Over Thirty Look** *Faron Young*
50/73 **That Rain Makin' Baby Of Mine** *Roy Drusky*
40/95 **That Road Not Taken** *Joe Diffie*
1/86 **That Rock Won't Roll** *Restless Heart*
44/79 **That Run-Away Woman Of Mine** *Freddy Weller*
33/74 **That Same Ol' Look Of Love** *David Houston*
That See Me Later Look
67/67 *Bobby Wright*
36/69 *Bonnie Guitar*
69/80 **That Silver-Haired Daddy Of Mine** *Slim Whitman*
2/74 **That Song Is Driving Me Crazy** *Tom T. Hall*
1/93 **That Summer** *Garth Brooks*
53/05 **That Summer Song** *Blue County*
59/97 **That Train Don't Run** *Matraca Berg*
1/87 **That Was A Close One** *Earl Thomas Conley*
4/93 **That Was A River** *Collin Raye*
54/96 **That Was Him (This Is Now)** *4 Runner*
58/03 **That Was Us** *Chad Brock*
1/77 **That Was Yesterday** *Donna Fargo*
9/48 **That Wild And Wicked Look In Your Eye** *Ernest Tubb*
35/97 **That Woman Of Mine** *Neal McCoy*
2/03 **That'd Be Alright** *Alan Jackson*
(That'll Be Me) ..see: Gone
That'll Be The Day
56/72 *Kenny Vernon*
27/76 *Linda Ronstadt*
96/76 *Pure Prairie League*
37/67 **That'll Be The Day** *Statler Brothers*
52/89 **That'll Be The Last Thing** *James House*
2/69 **That's A No No** *Lynn Anderson*
25/01 **That's A Plan** *Mark McGuinn*
56/73 **That's A Whole Lotta Lovin' (You Give Me)** *Kenny Starr*
40/04 **That's A Woman** *Mark Wills*
12/56 **That's All** *"Tennessee" Ernie Ford*
46/64 **That's All I Need To Know** *Bobby Wood*
57/77 **That's All I Wanted To Know** *Dottie West*
47/66 **That's All It Took** *George Jones & Gene Pitney*
4/53 **That's All Right** *Autry Inman*
7/55 **That's All Right** *Marty Robbins*
42/76 **That's All She Ever Said Except Goodbye** *Nat Stuckey*
34/76 **That's All She Wrote** *Ray Price*
That's All That Matters
34/64 *Ray Price*
1/80 *Mickey Gilley*
51/72 **That's All This Old World Needs** *Stonewall Jackson*
15/97 **That's Another Song** *Bryan White*
1/95 **That's As Close As I'll Get To Loving You** *Aaron Tippin*
24/04 **That's Cool** *Blue County*
50/84 **That's Easy For You To Say** *Kathy Mattea*
18/96 **That's Enough Of That** *Mila Mason*
52/92 **That's Good** *Tim Mensy*
36/97 **That's How I Got To Memphis** *Deryl Dodd*
That's How Much I Love You
2/46 *Eddy Arnold*
4/47 *Red Foley*
85/88 **That's How Much I Love You** *Neal McCoy*
23/75 **That's How My Baby Builds A Fire** *Johnny Russell*
9/86 **That's How You Know When Love's Right** *Nicolette Larson w/ Steve Wariner*
10/95 **That's How You Know (When You're In Love)** *Lari White*
7/95 **That's Just About Right** *BlackHawk*
16/02 **That's Just Jessie** *Kevin Denney*
70/75 **That's Just My Truckin' Luck** *Hank Thompson*
42/01 **That's Just That** *Diamond Rio*
52/74 **That's Love** *Don Adams*
43/92 **That's Me** *Martina McBride*
That's Me Without You
4/53 *Webb Pierce*
9/53 *Sonny James*
49/86 **That's More About Love (Than I Wanted To Know)** *Nicolette Larson*
10/94 **That's My Baby** *Lari White*
6/88 **That's My Job** *Conway Twitty*
5/60 **That's My Kind Of Love** *Marion Worth*
1/62 **That's My Pa** *Sheb Wooley*
6/94 **That's My Story** *Collin Raye*
46/84 **That's Not The Way (It's S'posed To Be)** *Anne Murray*
35/86 **That's One To Grow On** *Dobie Gray*
9/88 **That's That** *Michael Johnson*
22/00 **That's The Beat Of A Heart** *Warren Brothers w/ Sara Evans*
49/65 **That's The Chance I'll Have To Take** *Waylon Jennings*
86/80 **That's The Chance We'll Have To Take** *Jerry McBee*
9/53 **That's The Kind Of Love I'm Looking For** *Carl Smith*
13/00 **That's The Kind Of Mood I'm In** *Patty Loveless*
59/97 **That's The Kinda Love (That I'm Talkin' About)** *Mila Mason*
68/67 **That's The Only Way To Cry** *Wynn Stewart*
18/79 **That's The Only Way To Say Good Morning** *Ray Price*
71/92 **That's The Thing About A Memory** *Tracy Byrd*
1/84 **That's The Thing About Love** *Don Williams*
That's The Truth
84/84 *Johnny Cash*
47/99 *Paul Brandt*
1/00 **That's The Way** *Jo Dee Messina*

7/80 **That's The Way A Cowboy Rocks And Rolls** *Jacky Ward*
9/58 **That's The Way I Feel** *Faron Young*
67/70 **That's The Way I See It** *Jack Reno*
14/59 **That's The Way It's Gotta Be** *Faron Young*
That's The Way Love Goes
1/74 *Johnny Rodriguez*
1/84 *Merle Haggard*
56/99 *Merle Haggard w/ Jewel*
60/91 **That's The Way Love Is** *Asleep At The Wheel*
That's The Way Love Should Be
23/75 *Brian Collins*
7/77 *Dave & Sugar*
That's The Way My Woman Loves Me
96/77 *Dan McCorison*
82/81 *Amarillo*
39/01 **That's What Brothers Do** *Confederate Railroad*
16/76 **That's What Friends Are For** *Barbara Mandrell*
50/97 **That's What Happens When I Hold You** *Aaron Tippin*
41/86 **That's What Her Memory Is For** *Butch Baker*
24/76 **That's What I Get (For Doin' My Own Thinkin')** *Ray Griff*
22/94 **That's What I Get (For Losin' You)** *Hal Ketchum*
4/96 **That's What I Get For Lovin' You** *Diamond Rio*
10/80 **That's What I Get For Loving You** *Eddy Arnold*
35/82 **That's What I Get For Thinking** *Kendalls*
4/47 **That's What I Like About The West** *Tex Williams*
8/92 **That's What I Like About You** *Trisha Yearwood*
44/01 **That's What I Like About You** *John Michael Montgomery*
1/05 **That's What I Love About Sunday** *Craig Morgan*
28/58 **That's What I Tell My Heart** *Bob Gallion*
30/73 **That's What I'll Do** *Don Gibson*
40/92 **That's What I'm Working On Tonight** *Dixiana*
2/04 **That's What It's All About** *Brooks & Dunn*
That's What It's Like To Be Lonesome
7/59 *Ray Price*
12/59 *Bill Anderson*
58/71 *Cal Smith*
66/72 **That's What Leaving's About** *Ray Price*
68/94 **That's What Love's About** *Marty Stuart*
7/76 **That's What Made Me Love You** *Bill Anderson & Mary Lou Turner*
That's What Makes The Juke Box Play
6/55 *Jimmy Work*
11/78 *Moe Bandy*
33/64 **That's What Makes The World Go Around** *Claude King*
6/04 **That's What She Gets For Loving Me** *Brooks & Dunn*
8/78 **That's What You Do To Me** *Charly McClain*
10/85 **(That's What You Do) When You're In Love** *Forester Sisters*
9/66 **(That's What You Get) For Lovin' Me** *Waylon Jennings*
5/88 **That's What Your Love Does To Me** *Holly Dunn*
71/82 **That's What Your Lovin' Does To Me** *Peggy Forman*
3/02 **That's When I Love You** *Phil Vassar*
9/68 **That's When I See The Blues (In Your Pretty Brown Eyes)** *Jim Reeves*
6/75 **That's When My Woman Begins** *Tommy Overstreet*
3/70 **That's When She Started To Stop Loving You** *Conway Twitty*
53/69 **That's When The Hurtin' Sets In** *Hank Snow*
24/77 **That's When The Lyin' Stops (And The Lovin' Starts)** *Pal Rakes*
68/00 **That's When You Came Along** *Tara Lyn Hart*
80/87 **That's When (You Can Call Me Your Own)** *Bonnie Leigh*
26/65 **That's Where My Money Goes** *Webb Pierce*
49/98 **That's Where You're Wrong** *Daryle Singletary*
66/89 **That's Why I Fell In Love With You** *Eddie Rabbitt*
1/72 **That's Why I Love You Like I Do** *Sonny James*
16/69 **That's Why I Love You So Much** *Ferlin Husky*
25/63 **That's Why I Sing In A Honky Tonk** *Warren Smith*
47/02 **That's Why I Sing This Way** *Daryle Singletary*
2/98 **That's Why I'm Here** *Kenny Chesney*
That's Why I'm Walkin' ..see: Why I'm Walkin'
94/88 **That's Why You Haven't Seen Me** *Dennis Payne*
36/74 **That's You And Me** *Hank Snow*
47/66 **That's You (And What's Left Of Me)** *Clyde Beavers*
74/79 **That's You, That's Me** *Dawn Chastain*
That's You That's You ..see: Honey-Eyed Girl
41/69 **That's Your Hang Up** *Johnny Carver*
13/81 **Them Good Ol' Boys Are Bad** *John Schneider*
1/80 **Theme From The Dukes Of Hazzard** *Waylon Jennings*
8/62 **Then A Tear Fell** *Earl Scott*
4/91 **Then Again** *Alabama*
4/65 **Then And Only Then** *Connie Smith*
48/66 **Then Go Home To Her** *Norma Jean*
8/70 **Then He Touched Me** *Jean Shepard*
2/49 **Then I Turned And Walked Slowly Away** *Eddy Arnold*
42/65 **Then I'll Start Believing In You** *Hank Thompson*
Then I'll Stop Loving You
15/54 *Jim Reeves*
12/64 *Browns*
3/87 **Then It's Love** *Don Williams*
31/70 **Then She's A Lover** *Roy Clark*
32/69 **Then The Baby Came** *Henson Cargill*
9/03 **Then They Do** *Trace Adkins*
2/98 **Then What?** *Clay Walker*
1/75 **Then Who Am I** *Charley Pride*
Then You Can Tell Me Goodbye
1/68 *Eddy Arnold*
4/76 *Glen Campbell (medley)*
4/96 *Neal McCoy*
10/71 **Then You Walk In** *Sammi Smith*
25/78 **Then You'll Remember** *Sterling Whipple*
86/81 **There Ain't A Song** *Music Row*
58/87 **There Ain't No Binds** *Whites*
77/82 **There Ain't No Country Music On This Jukebox** *Tom T. Hall & Earl Scruggs*
10/68 **There Ain't No Easy Run** *Dave Dudley*
12/84 **There Ain't No Future In This** *Reba McEntire*
2/78 **There Ain't No Good Chain Gang** *Johnny Cash & Waylon Jennings*
57/92 **There Ain't Nothin' I Don't Like About You** *Neal McCoy*
1/92 **There Ain't Nothin' Wrong With The Radio** *Aaron Tippin*
89/80 **There Ain't Nothing Like A Rainy Night** *Peggy Forman*
17/91 **There For Awhile** *Steve Wariner*
1/97 **There Goes** *Alan Jackson*
2/98 **There Goes My Baby** *Trisha Yearwood*
There Goes My Everything
1/66 *Jack Greene*
9/71 *Elvis Presley*
F/82 *Elvis Presley*
20/94 **There Goes My Heart** *Mavericks*
4/89 **There Goes My Heart Again** *Holly Dunn*
1/03 **There Goes My Life** *Kenny Chesney*
There Goes My Love
15/57 *George Morgan*
71/87 *Pam Tillis*
96/79 **There Goes That Smile Again** *Corkey Sauls*
58/99 **There Goes The Neighborhood** *Keith Harling*
67/79 **There Hangs His Hat** *Linda Nail*
82/75 **There Has To Be A Loser** *Diana Trask*
85/82 **There I Go Dreamin' Again** *Jan Gray*
8/75 **There I Said It** *Margo Smith*
53/89 **There! I've Said It Again** *Mickey Gilley*
20/79 **There Is A Miracle In You** *Tom T. Hall*
1/01 **There Is No Arizona** *Jamie O'Neal*
58/03 **There Is No War** *Donovan Chapman*

20/61 **There Must Be Another Way To Live** *Kitty Wells*
25/71 **There Must Be More To Life (Than Growing Old)** *Jack Blanchard & Misty Morgan*
1/70 **There Must Be More To Love Than This** *Jerry Lee Lewis*
5/69 **There Never Was A Time** *Jeannie C. Riley*
There She [He] Goes
3/55 *Carl Smith*
70/99 *Patsy Cline w/ John Berry*
11/77 **There She Goes Again** *Joe Stampley*
24/75 **(There She Goes) I Wish Her Well** *Don Gibson*
There Stands The Glass
1/53 *Webb Pierce*
34/73 *Johnny Bush*
36/01 **There Will Come A Day** *Faith Hill*
1/74 **There Won't Be Anymore** *Charlie Rich*
19/76 **There Won't Be No Country Music** *C.W. McCall*
12/69 **There Wouldn't Be A Lonely Heart In Town** *Del Reeves*
8/90 **There You Are** *Willie Nelson*
10/00 **There You Are** *Martina McBride*
1/57 **There You Go** *Johnny Cash*
32/91 **There You Go** *Exile*
64/67 **There You Go** *Sandy Mason*
26/01 **There You Go Again** *Kenny Rogers*
4/99 **There You Have It** *BlackHawk*
11/01 **There You'll Be** *Faith Hill*
21/61 **There'll Always Be Sadness** *Marion Worth*
There'll Be No Teardrops Tonight
86/78 *Willie Nelson*
70/80 *Vassar Clements*
5/51 **(There'll Be) Peace In The Valley (For Me)** *Red Foley*
76/84 **There'll Never Be A Better Night For Bein' Wrong** *Big Al Downing*
68/78 **There'll Never Be Another For Me** *Connie Smith*
(There'll Never Be Another) Pecos Bill
13/48 *Roy Rogers*
15/48 *Tex Ritter*
3/59 **There's A Big Wheel** *Wilma Lee & Stoney Cooper*
5/44 **There's A Blue Star Shining Bright (In A Window Tonight)** *Red Foley*
11/49 **(There's A) Bluebird On Your Windowsill** *Tex Williams*
4/44 **There's A Chill On The Hill Tonight** *Jimmie Davis*
65/81 **There's A Crazy Man** *Jody Payne*
1/85 **(There's A) Fire In The Night** *Alabama*
(There's A Fire In Your Soul) ..see: Burn Georgia Burn
16/68 **There's A Fool Born Every Minute** *Skeeter Davis*
20/96 **There's A Girl In Texas** *Trace Adkins*

There's A Honky Tonk Angel (Who'll Take Me Back In)
1/74 *Conway Twitty*
6/79 *Elvis Presley*
47/72 **There's A Kind Of Hush (All Over The World)** *Brian Collins*
96/85 **There's A Lot Of Good About Goodbye** *Judy Bailey*
There's A New Moon Over My Shoulder
1/45 *Jimmie Davis*
2/45 *Tex Ritter*
4/72 **There's A Party Goin' On** *Jody Miller*
88/87 **There's A Real Woman In Me** *Bobbi Lace*
10/75 **There's A Song On The Jukebox** *David Wills*
7/70 **There's A Story (Goin' 'Round)** *Dottie West & Don Gibson*
7/89 **There's A Tear In My Beer** *Hank Williams, Jr.*
80/88 **There's A Telephone Ringing (In An Empty House)** *Southern Reign*
13/71 **There's A Whole Lot About A Woman (A Man Don't Know)** *Jack Greene*
F/83 **There's All Kinds Of Smoke (In The Barroom)** *Loretta Lynn*
91/76 **There's Always A Goodbye** *Helen Cornelius*
There's Always Me
30/79 *Ray Price*
35/81 *Jim Reeves*
17/62 **There's Always One (Who Loves A Lot)** *Roy Drusky*
18/80 **There's Another Woman** *Joe Stampley*
1/51 **There's Been A Change In Me** *Eddy Arnold*
20/69 **There's Better Things In Life** *Jerry Reed*
21/64 **There's More Pretty Girls Than One** *George Hamilton IV*
17/03 **There's More To Me Than You** *Jessica Andrews*
1/81 **(There's) No Gettin' Over Me** *Ronnie Milsap*
14/03 **There's No Limit** *Deana Carter*
7/85 **There's No Love In Tennessee** *Barbara Mandrell*
49/81 **(There's No Me) Without You** *Sue Powell*
48/68 **There's No More Love** *Carl Smith*
63/00 **(There's No Place Like) Home For The Holidays** *Garth Brooks*
1/86 **There's No Stopping Your Heart** *Marie Osmond*
48/83 **There's No Substitute For You** *Younger Brothers*
1/85 **There's No Way** *Alabama*
6/50 **There's No Wings On My Angel** *Eddy Arnold*
88/80 **There's Nobody Like You** *Kin Vassy*
86/83 **There's Nobody Lovin' At Home** *Randy Wright*
3/49 **There's Not A Thing (I Wouldn't Do For You)** *Eddy Arnold*
21/60 **There's Not Any Like You Left** *Faron Young*

(There's Nothing Like The Love) Between A Woman And A Man
86/77 *Reba McEntire*
87/78 *Linda Cassady/Bobby Spears*
43/98 **There's Only You** *Kevin Sharp*
9/55 **There's Poison In Your Heart** *Kitty Wells*
19/71 **There's Something About A Lady** *Johnny Duncan*
84/83 **There's Still A Few Good Love Songs Left In Me** *Connie Francis*
There's Still A Lot Of Love In San Antone
48/74 *Darrell McCall*
64/83 *Connie Hanson w/ Darrell McCall*
58/87 **There's Still Enough Of Us** *Liz Boardo*
1/98 **There's Your Trouble** *Dixie Chicks*
5/69 **These Are Not My People** *Freddy Weller*
51/02 **These Are The Days** *Holly Lamar*
73/72 **These Are The Good Old Days** *Roy Rogers*
57/98 **These Arms** *Dwight Yoakam*
67/95 **These Arms** *Baker & Myers*
41/99 **These Arms Of Mine** *LeAnn Rimes*
(These Boots Are Made For Walking) ..see: Boots
87/77 **These Crazy Thoughts (Run Through My Mind)** *Warner Mack*
1/02 **These Days** *Rascal Flatts*
10/75 **These Days (I Barely Get By)** *George Jones*
64/86 **These Eyes** *Beth Williams*
5/56 **These Hands** *Hank Snow*
5/91 **These Lips Don't Know How To Say Goodbye** *Doug Stone*
9/69 **These Lonely Hands Of Mine** *Mel Tillis*
42/67 **These Memories** *Jeannie Seely*
57/86 **These Shoes** *Everly Brothers*
66/68 **(They Always Come Out) Smellin' Like A Rose** *Johnny Wright*
43/88 **They Always Look Better When They're Leavin'** *Becky Hobbs*
7/94 **They Asked About You** *Reba McEntire*
6/79 **They Call It Making Love** *Tammy Wynette*
58/72 **They Call The Wind Maria** *Jack Barlow*
12/81 **They Could Put Me In Jail** *Bellamy Brothers*
4/74 **They Don't Make 'Em Like My Daddy** *Loretta Lynn*
2/94 **They Don't Make 'Em Like That Anymore** *Boy Howdy*
32/76 **They Don't Make 'Em Like That Anymore** *Bobby Borchers*
10/69 **They Don't Make Love Like They Used To** *Eddy Arnold*
54/87 **They Don't Make Love Like We Used To** *Shenandoah*
53/86 **They Don't Make Them Like They Used To** *Kenny Rogers*
67/87 **They Killed Him** *Kris Kristofferson*
19/85 **They Never Had To Get Over You** *Johnny Lee*

19/80 **They Never Lost You** *Con Hunley*
21/87 **They Only Come Out At Night** *Shooters*
5/89 **They Rage On** *Dan Seals*
1/44 **They Took The Stars Out Of Heaven** *Floyd Tillman*
They'll Never Take Her Love From Me
5/50 *Hank Williams*
74/70 *Johnny Darrell*
57/81 **They'll Never Take Me Alive** *Dean Dillon*
3/95 **They're Playin' Our Song** *Neal McCoy*
72/71 **They're Stepping All Over My Heart** *Kitty Wells*
18/02 **Thicker Than Blood** *Garth Brooks*
14/85 **Thing About You** *Southern Pacific w/ Emmylou Harris*
Thing Called Love
21/68 *Jimmy Dean*
2/72 *Johnny Cash*
38/65 **Thing Called Sadness** *Ray Price*
49/82 **Thing Or Two On My Mind** *Gene Kennedy & Karen Jeglum*
Things
49/72 *Buddy Alan*
25/75 *Ronnie Dove*
22/76 *Anne Murray*
66/73 **Things Are Kinda Slow At The House** *Earl Richards*
75/91 **Things Are Mostly Fine** *Donna Ulisse*
23/91 **Things Are Tough All Over** *Shelby Lynne*
1/74 **Things Aren't Funny Anymore** *Merle Haggard*
17/98 **Things Change** *Dwight Yoakam*
32/01 **Things Change** *Tim McGraw*
25/69 **Things For You And I** *Bobby Lewis*
34/69 **Things Go Better With Love** *Jeannie C. Riley*
9/65 **Things Have Gone To Pieces** *George Jones*
68/88 **Things I Didn't Say** *Marcy Bros.*
31/77 **Things I Treasure** *Dorsey Burnette*
72/91 **Things I Wish I'd Said** *Rodney Crowell*
18/78 **Things I'd Do For You** *Mundo Earwood*
42/69 **Things That Matter** *Van Trevor*
24/62 **Things That Mean The Most** *Carl Smith*
95/82 **Things That Songs Are Made Of** *Ray Griff*
36/90 **Things You Left Undone** *Matraca Berg*
F/72 **Think About It Darlin'** *Jerry Lee Lewis*
1/86 **Think About Love** *Dolly Parton*
18/78 **Think About Me** *Freddy Fender*
38/71 **Think Again** *Patti Page*
74/76 **Think I Feel A Hitchhike Coming On** *Larry Jon Wilson*
84/88 **Think I'll Go Home** *Charlie Beckham*
Think I'll Go Somewhere And Cry Myself To Sleep
26/65 *Charlie Louvin*
50/78 *Billy "Crash" Craddock*
57/01 **Think It Over** *Allison Moorer*
1/66 **Think Of Me** *Buck Owens*
21/76 **Think Summer** *Roy Clark*
1/95 **Thinkin' About You** *Trisha Yearwood*
1/76 **Thinkin' Of A Rendezvous** *Johnny Duncan*
2/94 **Thinkin' Problem** *David Ball*
53/96 **Thinkin' Strait** *Rich McCready*
54/99 **Thinking About Leaving** *Dwight Yoakam*
56/84 **Thinking 'Bout Leaving** *Butch Baker*
9/70 **Thinking 'Bout You, Babe** *Billy Walker*
Third Rate Romance
11/75 *Amazing Rhythm Aces*
2/94 *Sammy Kershaw*
1/94 **Third Rock From The Sun** *Joe Diffie*
34/70 **Third World** *Johnny & Jonie Mosby*
52/73 **30 California Women** *Kenny Price*
7/55 **Thirty Days (To Come Back Home)** *Ernest Tubb*
83/76 **38 And Lonely** *Dave Dudley*
4/81 **Thirty Nine And Holding** *Jerry Lee Lewis*
39/87 **3935 West End Avenue** *Mason Dixon*
4/85 **This Ain't Dallas** *Hank Williams, Jr.*
23/75 **(This Ain't Just Another) Lust Affair** *Mel Street*
14/90 **This Ain't My First Rodeo** *Vern Gosdin*
33/01 **This Ain't No Rag, It's A Flag** *Charlie Daniels Band*
1/97 **(This Ain't) No Thinkin' Thing** *Trace Adkins*
This Ain't Tennessee And He Ain't You
93/81 *Gypsy Martin*
82/83 *Sara "Honeybear" Hickey*
66/84 *Katy Moffatt*
52/85 **This Bed's Not Big Enough** *Louise Mandrell*
F/83 **This Country Music's Driving Me Crazy** *Johnny Bailey*
This Cowboy's Hat
35/83 *Porter Wagoner*
63/91 *Chris LeDoux*
1/87 **This Crazy Love** *Oak Ridge Boys*
8/82 **This Dream's On Me** *Gene Watson*
9/01 **This Everyday Love** *Rascal Flatts*
42/03 **This Far Gone** *Jennifer Hanson*
40/69 **This Generation Shall Not Pass** *Henson Cargill*
36/77 **This Girl (Has Turned Into A Woman)** *Mary MacGregor*
46/66 **This Gun Don't Care** *Wanda Jackson*
This Heart
25/90 *Sweethearts Of The Rodeo*
74/94 *Jon Randall*
17/99 **This Heartache Never Sleeps** *Mark Chesnutt*
19/75 **This House Runs On Sunshine** *La Costa*
39/78 **This Is A Holdup** *Ronnie McDowell*
20/79 **This Is A Love Song** *Bill Anderson*
17/03 **This Is God** *Phil Vassar*
1/65 **This Is It** *Jim Reeves*
62/83 **This Is Just The First Day** *Razzy Bailey*
5/94 **This Is Me** *Randy Travis*
62/88 **This Is Me Leaving** *Lynne Tyndall*
6/95 **This Is Me Missing You** *James House*
21/75 **This Is My Year For Mexico** *Crystal Gayle*
30/63 **This Is The House** *Charlie Phillips*
52/05 **This Is The Life** *Billy Dean*
16/78 **This Is The Love** *Sonny James*
3/54 **This Is The Thanks I Get (For Loving You)** *Eddy Arnold*
67/80 **This Is True** *Steve Douglas*
25/97 **This Is Your Brain** *Joe Diffie*
93/74 **This Just Ain't My Day (For Lettin' Darlin' Down)** *Red Steagall*
68/73 **This Just Ain't No Good Day For Leavin'** *Kenny Serratt*
84/77 **This Kinda Love Ain't Meant For Sunday School** *Carl Smith*
1/98 **This Kiss** *Faith Hill*
81/78 **This Lady Loving Me** *Carl Smith*
4/58 **This Little Girl Of Mine** *Everly Brothers*
5/72 **This Little Girl Of Mine** *Faron Young*
37/04 **This Love** *LeAnn Rimes*
52/78 **This Magic Moment** *Sandra Kaye*
45/76 **This Man And Woman Thing** *Johnny Russell*
2/88 **This Missin' You Heart Of Mine** *Sawyer Brown*
93/79 **This Moment In Time** *Engelbert Humperdinck*
81/82 **This Morning I Woke Up In New York City** *John Kelley*
11/72 **This Much A Man** *Marty Robbins*
This Must Be My Ship
32/80 *Carol Chase*
62/81 *Diana Trask*
27/66 **This Must Be The Bottom** *Del Reeves*
20/70 **This Night (Ain't Fit For Nothing But Drinking)** *Dave Dudley*
This Night Won't Last Forever
49/89 *Moe Bandy*
6/97 *Sawyer Brown*
61/92 **This Nightlife** *Clint Black*
This Ol' ..see: This Old
90/89 **This Old Feeling** *Andy & The Brown Sisters*
52/88 **This Old Flame** *Robin Lee*
53/92 **This Ol' Heart** *Tim Mensy*
This Old Heart
21/60 *Skeets McDonald*
24/60 *Bobby Barnett*
This Old House
66/87 *Razorback*
24/88 *Schuyler, Knobloch & Bickhardt*
92/89 **This Old House** *Crosby, Stills, Nash & Young*
This Ole House
2/54 *Stuart Hamblen*
16/60 *Wilma Lee & Stoney Cooper*
33/87 **This Ol' Town** *Lacy J. Dalton*
22/60 **This Old Town** *Buddy Paul*

91/88 **This Old World Ain't The Same** *Jeff Golden*
3/03 **This One's For The Girls** *Martina McBride*
7/92 **This One's Gonna Hurt You (For A Long, Long Time)** *Marty Stuart & Travis Tritt*
36/68 **This One's On The House** *Jerry Wallace*
49/02 **This Pretender** *Joe Diffie*
13/93 **This Romeo Ain't Got Julie Yet** *Diamond Rio*
56/02 **This Side** *Nickel Creek*
11/90 **This Side Of Goodbye** *Highway 101*
55/98 **This Small Divide** *Jason Sellers w/ Martina McBride*
69/69 **This Song Don't Care Who Sings It** *Ray Pennington*
68/68 **This Song Is Just For You** *Bobby Austin*
14/69 **This Thing** *Webb Pierce*
11/95 **(This Thing Called) Wantin' And Havin' It All** *Sawyer Brown*
1/74 **This Time** *Waylon Jennings*
2/95 **This Time** *Sawyer Brown*
30/84 **This Time** *Tom Jones*
43/78 **This Time** *Johnny Lee*
45/99 **This Time** *Shana Petrone*
89/82 **This Time** *Skip & Linda*
43/00 **This Time Around** *Yankee Grey*
67/78 **This Time Around** *Sammy Vaughn*
12/74 **This Time I Almost Made It** *Barbara Mandrell*
20/77 **This Time I'm In It For The Love** *Tommy Overstreet*
This Time I've Hurt Her More Than She Loves Me
1/76 *Conway Twitty*
50/91 *Neal McCoy*
51/86 **This Time It's You** *Lisa Childress*
7/64 **This White Circle On My Finger** *Kitty Wells*
5/89 **This Woman** *K.T. Oslin*
1/95 **This Woman And This Man** *Clay Walker*
9/00 **This Woman Needs** *SheDaisy*
12/48 **This World Can't Stand Long** *Roy Acuff*
27/67 **This World Holds Nothing (Since You're Gone)** *Stonewall Jackson*
4/46 **Tho' I Tried (I Can't Forget You)** *Wesley Tuttle*
10/48 **Thorn In My Heart** *Bob Wills*
74/86 **Those Eyes** *Anthony Armstrong Jones*
70/74 **Those Lazy, Hazy, Crazy Days Of Summer** *Tex Williams*
Those Memories Of You
55/86 *Pam Tillis*
5/87 *Dolly Parton, Linda Ronstadt, Emmylou Harris*
52/83 **Those Nights, These Days** *David Wills*
47/83 **Those Were The Days** *Gary Stewart & Dean Dillon*
72/97 **Those Who Couldn't Wait** *David Morgan*
9/63 **Those Wonderful Years** *Webb Pierce*
59/95 **Those Words We Said** *Kim Richey*
62/84 **Those You Lose** *Ronnie Robbins*
14/54 **Thou Shalt Not Steal** *Kitty Wells*
16/61 **Thoughts Of A Fool** *Ernest Tubb*
6/59 **Thousand Miles Ago** *Webb Pierce*
2/93 **Thousand Miles From Nowhere** *Dwight Yoakam*
13/96 **Thousand Times A Day** *Patty Loveless*
52/89 **Threads Of Gold** *Marcy Bros.*
8/65 **Three A.M.** *Bill Anderson*
Three Bells
1/59 *Browns*
29/69 *Jim Ed Brown*
31/80 **3 Chord Country Song** *Red Steagall*
44/97 **Three Chords And The Truth** *Sara Evans*
Three Days
7/62 *Faron Young*
55/89 *k.d. lang*
36/02 **Three Days** *Pat Green*
90/90 **Three Flags** *Billy Joe Burnette*
2/61 **Three Hearts In A Tangle** *Roy Drusky*
66/00 **Three Little Teardrops** *Joanie Keller*
65/97 **Three Little Words** *Billy Ray Cyrus*
91/80 **Three Little Words** *Boyer Twins*
72/00 **Three Minute Positive Not Too Country Up-Tempo Love Song** *Alan Jackson*
30/03 **Three Mississippi** *Terri Clark*
81/78 **Three Nights A Week** *Ruby Falls*
53/88 **Three Piece Suit** *Russell Smith*
39/68 **Three Playing Love** *Cheryl Poole*
37/83 **3/4 Time** *Ray Charles*
20/78 **Three Sheets In The Wind** *Jacky Ward & Reba McEntire*
30/63 **Three Sheets In The Wind** *Johnny Bond*
32/68 **Three Six Packs, Two Arms And A Juke Box** *Johnny Seay*
9/61 **Three Steps To The Phone (Millions of Miles)** *George Hamilton IV*
73/69 **Three Tears (For The Sad, Hurt, And Blue)** *Ray Sanders*
1/87 **Three Time Loser** *Dan Seals*
Three Times A Lady
23/78 *Nate Harvell*
7/84 *Conway Twitty*
93/80 **Three Times In Love** *Tommy James*
4/47 **Three Times Seven** *Merle Travis*
76/80 **Three Way Love** *Shoppe*
7/52 **Three Ways Of Knowing** *Johnnie & Jack*
7/57 **Three Ways (To Love You)** *Kitty Wells*
1/03 **Three Wooden Crosses** *Randy Travis*
25/95 **Three Words, Two Hearts, One Night** *Mark Collie*
73/89 **Thrill Of Love** *Kennard & John*
14/61 **Through That Door** *Ernest Tubb*
99/76 **Through The Bottom Of The Glass** *Leon Rausch*
31/64 **Through The Eyes Of A Fool** *Roy Clark*
27/67 **Through The Eyes Of Love** *Tompall/Glaser Brothers*
5/82 **Through The Years** *Kenny Rogers*
66/72 **Throw A Rope Around The Wind** *Red Lane*
80/74 **Throw Away The Pages** *Randy Barlow*
87/77 **Throw Out Your Loveline** *Cates Sisters*
3/50 **Throw Your Love My Way** *Ernest Tubb*
51/78 **Throwin' Memories On The Fire** *Cal Smith*
68/96 **Thump Factor** *Smokin' Armadillos*
Thunder Road ..see: Ballad Of
1/91 **Thunder Rolls** *Garth Brooks*
33/76 **Thunderstorms** *Cal Smith*
54/98 **Ticket Out Of Kansas** *Jenny Simpson*
22/68 **Tie A Tiger Down** *Sheb Wooley*
Tie A Yellow Ribbon ..see: Yellow Ribbon
Tie Me Up (Hold Me Down)
75/88 *Becky Williams*
83/89 *David Speegle*
29/63 **Tie My Hunting Dog Down, Jed** *Arthur "Guitar Boogie" Smith*
17/86 **Tie Our Love (In A Double Knot)** *Dolly Parton*
24/82 **Tie Your Dream To Mine** *Marty Robbins*
96/88 **Tied To The Wheel Of A Runaway Heart** *Paul Proctor*
4/75 **Ties That Bind** *Don Williams*
15/65 **Tiger In My Tank** *Jim Nesbitt*
6/65 **Tiger Woman** *Claude King*
1/81 **Tight Fittin' Jeans** *Conway Twitty*
56/83 **Tijuana Sunrise** *Bama Band*
'Til A Tear Becomes A Rose
44/85 *Leon Everette*
13/90 *Keith Whitley & Lorrie Morgan*
'Til I Can Make It On My Own
1/76 *Tammy Wynette*
3/79 *Kenny Rogers & Dottie West*
Til I Can't Take It Anymore
46/70 *Dottie West & Don Gibson*
85/73 *Andra Willis*
31/77 *Pal Rakes*
2/90 *Billy Joe Royal*
'Til I Gain Control Again
42/79 *Bobby Bare*
1/83 *Crystal Gayle*
1/73 **'Til I Get It Right** *Tammy Wynette*
('Til) I Kissed You
8/59 *Everly Brothers*
10/76 *Connie Smith*
10/86 **Til I Loved You** *Restless Heart*
70/99 **'Til I Said It To You** *Reba McEntire*
22/92 **Til I'm Holding You Again** *Pirates Of The Mississippi*
4/89 **'Til Love Comes Again** *Reba McEntire*
19/02 **'Til Nothing Comes Between Us** *John Michael Montgomery*

Til' Santa's Gone (Milk And Cookies)
58/96 *Clint Black*
65/97 *Clint Black*
40/98 *Clint Black*
38/99 *Clint Black*
34/00 *Clint Black*
41/69 **Til Something Better Comes Along** *Bobby Lewis*
46/82 **Til Something Better Comes Along** *R C Bannon*
41/87 **'Til The Old Wears Off** *Shooters*
75/90 **Til U Love Me Again** *Tish Hinojosa*
39/83 **Til You And Your Lover Are Lovers Again** *Engelbert Humperdinck*
4/89 **'Til You Cry** *Eddy Raven*
Till ..also see: 'Til
14[S]/01 **Till Dale Earnhardt Wins Cup #8** *Kacey Jones*
12/91 **Till I Found You** *Marty Stuart*
39/90 **Till I See You Again** *Kevin Welch*
24/80 **Till I Stop Shaking** *Billy "Crash" Craddock*
7/53 **Till I Waltz Again With You** *Tommy Sosebea*
48/94 **Till I Was Loved By You** *Chely Wright*
6/87 **Till I'm Too Old To Die Young** *Moe Bandy*
32/66 **Till My Getup Has Gotup And Gone** *Ernest Tubb*
7/77 **Till The End** *Vern Gosdin*
Till The End Of The World
4/49 *Ernest Tubb*
9/49 *Jimmy Wakely*
12/49 *Johnny Bond*
10/52 *Bing Crosby & Grady Martin*
1/76 **Till The Rivers All Run Dry** *Don Williams*
8/73 **'Till The Water Stops Runnin'** *Billy "Crash" Craddock*
81/78 **Till Then** *Pal Rakes*
2/95 **Till You Love Me** *Reba McEntire*
17/91 **Till You Were Gone** *Mike Reid*
1/82 **'Till You're Gone** *Barbara Mandrell*
28/84 **Till Your Memory's Gone** *Bill Medley*
13/64 **Timber I'm Falling** *Ferlin Husky*
1/89 **Timber, I'm Falling In Love** *Patty Loveless*
55/85 **Timberline** *Emmylou Harris*
10/60 **Timbrook** *Lewis Pruitt*
2/85 **Time Don't Run Out On Me** *Anne Murray*
70/98 **Time For Letting Go** *Billy Ray Cyrus*
39/90 **Time For Me To Fly** *Dolly Parton*
14/55 **Time Goes By** *Marty Robbins*
23/92 **Time Has Come** *Martina McBride*
64/81 **Time Has Treated You Well** *Corbin/Hanner Band*
17/87 **Time In** *Oak Ridge Boys*
57/00 **Time, Love & Money** *Ronnie Milsap*
1/96 **Time Marches On** *Tracy Lawrence*
62/98 **Time On My Hands** *Deryl Dodd*
44/66 **Time Out** *Bill Anderson & Jan Howard*
7/91 **Time Passes By** *Kathy Mattea*
51/86 **Time Stood Still** *Vern Gosdin*
17/66 **Time To Bum Again** *Waylon Jennings*
72/73 **Time To Love Again** *Liz Anderson*
6/45 **Time Won't Heal My Broken Heart** *Ted Daffan*
26/90 **Time's Up** *Southern Pacific & Carlene Carter*
5/88 **Timeless And True Love** *McCarters*
30/65 **Times Are Gettin' Hard** *Bobby Bare*
Tin Man
70/94 *Kenny Chesney*
19/01 *Kenny Chesney*
25/65 **Tiny Blue Transistor Radio** *Connie Smith*
71/68 **Tiny Bubbles** *Rex Allen*
49/03 **Tiny Dancer** *Tim McGraw*
24/67 **Tiny Tears** *Liz Anderson*
Tip Of My Fingers
7/60 *Bill Anderson*
10/63 *Roy Clark*
3/66 *Eddy Arnold*
16/75 *Jean Shepard*
3/92 *Steve Wariner*
2/66 **Tippy Toeing** *Harden Trio*
50/00 **Tired Of Loving This Way** *Collin Raye w/ Bobbie Eakes*
84/85 **Tired Of The Same Old Thing** *David Walsh*
'Tis Sweet To Be Remembered
8/52 *Cowboy Copas*
9/52 *Flatt & Scruggs*
91/89 **To A San Antone Rose** *Steve Douglas*
To A Sleeping Beauty
15/62 *Jimmy Dean*
85/76 *Jimmy Dean*
1/84 **To All The Girls I've Loved Before** *Julio Iglesias & Willie Nelson*
65/68 **To Be A Child Again** *Anita Carter*
To Be Loved
85/78 *Peggy Sue*
96/88 *Jeremiah*
1/96 **To Be Loved By You** *Wynonna*
35/85 **To Be Lovers** *Chance*
34/91 **To Be With You** *Larry Boone*
51/98 **To Be With You** *Mavericks*
94/76 **To Be With You Again** *Gary Mack*
3/78 **To Daddy** *Emmylou Harris*
100/78 **To Each His Own** *Rita Remington*
12/72 **To Get To You** *Jerry Wallace*
63/00 **To Get To You** *Lorrie Morgan*
12/98 **To Have You Back Again** *Patty Loveless*
To Know Him Is To Love Him
18/72 *Jody Miller*
1/87 *Dolly Parton, Linda Ronstadt, Emmylou Harris*
25/70 **To Lonely, Too Long** *Mel Tillis*
93/78 **To Love A Rolling Stone** *Jan Howard*
To Love Somebody
22/77 *Narvel Felts*
49/79 *Hank Williams, Jr.*
87/77 **To Make A Good Love Die** *DeWayne Orender*
41/76 **To Make A Long Story Short** *Ray Price*
3/69 **To Make A Man (Feel Like A Man)** *Loretta Lynn*
1/69 **To Make Love Sweeter For You** *Jerry Lee Lewis*
1/98 **To Make You Feel My Love** *Garth Brooks*
3/84 **To Me** *Barbara Mandrell/Lee Greenwood*
To My Sorrow
2/47 *Eddy Arnold*
47/68 *Johnny Duncan*
(To My Wife With Love) ..see: Mi Esposa Con Amor
51/01 **To Quote Shakespeare** *Clark Family Experience*
1/69 **To See My Angel Cry** *Conway Twitty*
65/76 **To Show You That I Love You** *Brian Collins*
13/61 **To You And Yours (From Me And Mine)** *George Hamilton IV*
51/73 **Toast Of '45** *Sammi Smith*
56/86 **Tobacco Road** *Roy Clark*
5/81 **Today All Over Again** *Reba McEntire*
Today I Started Loving You Again
69/73 *Kenny Rogers & The First Edition*
9/75 *Sammi Smith*
74/79 *Arthur Prysock*
43/86 *Emmylou Harris*
Today My World Slipped Away
10/83 *Vern Gosdin*
3/97 *George Strait*
38/73 **Today Will Be The First Day Of The Rest Of My Life** *LaWanda Lindsey*
3/92 **Today's Lonely Fool** *Tracy Lawrence*
45/71 **Today's Teardrops** *Bobby Lewis*
21/78 **Toe To Toe** *Freddie Hart*
Together Again
1/64 *Buck Owens*
1/76 *Emmylou Harris*
19/84 *Kenny Rogers & Dottie West*
92/88 **Together Alone** *Ogden Harless*
14/72 **Together Always** *Porter Wagoner & Dolly Parton*
Togetherness
24/68 *Freddie Hart*
12/70 *Buck Owens & Susan Raye*
30/85 **Tokyo, Oklahoma** *John Anderson*
36/70 **Tom Green County Fair** *Roger Miller*
1/86 **Tomb Of The Unknown Love** *Kenny Rogers*
5/65 **Tombstone Every Mile** *Dick Curless*
9/70 **Tomorrow Is Forever** *Porter Wagoner & Dolly Parton*
Tomorrow Never Comes
3/45 *Ernest Tubb*
27/70 *Slim Whitman*
Tomorrow Night
24/59 *Carl Smith*
29/73 *Charlie Rich*
11/71 **Tomorrow Night In Baltimore** *Roger Miller*
74/90 **Tomorrow's World** *Tomorrow's World*
5/78 **Tonight** *Barbara Mandrell*
41/05 **Tonight** *Sara Evans*
1/67 **Tonight Carmen** *Marty Robbins*

4/93 **Tonight I Climbed The Wall** *Alan Jackson*
7/02 **Tonight I Wanna Be Your Man** *Andy Griggs*
26/76 **Tonight I'll Face The Man (Who Made It Happen)** *Kenny Starr*
31/66 **Tonight I'm Coming Home** *Buddy Cagle*
Tonight I'm Feeling You (All Over Again)
65/80 *"Blackjack" Jack Grayson*
38/82 *Jack Grayson*
19/84 **Tonight I'm Here With Someone Else** *Karen Brooks*
66/88 **Tonight In America** *David Lynn Jones*
30/80 **Tonight Let's Sleep On It Baby** *Mel Street*
10/72 **Tonight My Baby's Coming Home** *Barbara Mandrell*
89/88 **Tonight She Went Crazy Without Me** *Mike Lunsford*
6/79 **Tonight She's Gonna Love Me (Like There Was No Tomorrow)** *Razzy Bailey*
12/74 **Tonight Someone's Falling In Love** *Johnny Carver*
6/99 **Tonight The Heartache's On Me** *Dixie Chicks*
20/94 **(Tonight We Just Might) Fall In Love Again** *Hal Ketchum*
26/86 **Tonight We Ride** *Michael Martin Murphey*
69/69 **Tonight We're Calling It A Day** *Hugh X. Lewis*
30/77 **Tonight You Belong To Me** *Dottie West*
43/05 **Tonight's Not The Night** *Randy Rogers Band*
65/85 **Tonight's The Night** *Carlette*
28/78 **Tonight's The Night (It's Gonna Be Alright)** *Roy Head*
70/66 **Tonight's The Night My Angel's Halo Fell** *Sheb Wooley*
32/80 **Tony's Tank-Up, Drive-In Cafe** *Hank Thompson*
60/76 **Too Big A Price To Pay** *Kenny Price*
1/93 **Too Busy Being In Love** *Doug Stone*
3/90 **Too Cold At Home** *Mark Chesnutt*
58/01 **Too Country** *Brad Paisley*
Too Far Gone
72/67 *Lucille Starr*
12/73 *Joe Stampley*
73/75 *Emmylou Harris*
13/79 *Emmylou Harris*
85/76 **Too Far Gone (To Care What You Do To Me)** *Gary S. Paxton*
88/79 **Too Fast For Rapid City** *Sheila Andrews*
1/88 **Too Gone Too Long** *Randy Travis*
89/83 **Too Good To Be Through** *Dave Lemmon*
8/98 **Too Good To Be True** *Michael Peterson*
47/85 **Too Good To Say No To** *Leon Everette*
4/84 **Too Good To Stop Now** *Mickey Gilley*
50/69 **Too Hard To Say I'm Sorry** *Murv Shiner*
10/83 **Too Hot To Sleep** *Louise Mandrell*
22/63 **Too In Love** *Hank Thompson*
42/86 **Too Late** *Kendalls*
15/84 **Too Late To Go Home** *Johnny Rodriguez*
9/64 **Too Late To Try Again** *Carl Butler & Pearl*
88/74 **Too Late To Turn Back Now** *Four Guys*
Too Late To Worry Too Blue To Cry
1/44 *Al Dexter*
3/44 *Texas Jim Lewis*
6/75 *Ronnie Milsap*
11S/01 **Too Lazy To Work, Too Nervous To Steal** *BR549*
62/97 **Too Little Too Much** *Nikki Nelson*
28/81 **Too Long Gone** *Vern Gosdin*
40/82 **Too Many Hearts In The Fire** *Bobby Smith*
46/91 **Too Many Honky Tonks (On My Way Home)** *Tom Wopat*
68/82 **Too Many Irons In The Fire** *Billy Parker & Cal Smith*
1/81 **Too Many Lovers** *Crystal Gayle*
21/73 **Too Many Memories** *Bobby Lewis*
96/73 **Too Many Memories** *Billy Walker*
29/78 **Too Many Nights Alone** *Bobby Bare*
5/87 **Too Many Rivers** *Forester Sisters*
74/73 **Too Many Ties That Bind** *Jan Howard*
26/65 **Too Many Tigers** *Tex Williams*
2/86 **Too Many Times** *Earl Thomas Conley & Anita Pointer*
10/61 **Too Many Times** *Don Winters*
3/57 **Too Much** *Elvis Presley*
36/92 **Too Much** *Pirates Of The Mississippi*
58/91 **Too Much Candy For A Dime** *Eddy Raven*
4/96 **Too Much Fun** *Daryle Singletary*
62/91 **Too Much Fun** *Forester Sisters*
41/73 **Too Much Hold Back** *Little David Wilkins*
1/86 **Too Much Is Not Enough** *Bellamy Brothers/Forester Sisters*
18/77 **Too Much Is Not Enough** *Billie Jo Spears*
72/92 **Too Much Love** *Don Williams*
8/73 **Too Much Monkey Business** *Freddy Weller*
Too Much Month At The End Of The Money
25/89 *Billy Hill*
54/03 *Marty Stuart*
5/04 **Too Much Of A Good Thing** *Alan Jackson*
45/69 **Too Much Of A Man (To Be Tied Down)** *Arlene Harden*
55/68 **Too Much Of Not Enough** *Ernest Tubb*
28/67 **Too Much Of You** *Lynn Anderson*
1/85 **Too Much On My Heart** *Statler Brothers*
34/74 **Too Much Pride** *Mack White*
19/60 **Too Much To Lose** *Carl Belew*
66/00 **Too Much To Lose** *Kentucky Headhunters*
84/81 **Too Much, Too Little, Too Late** *Mary Bailey*
13/57 **Too Much Water** *George Jones*
Too Old To Cut The Mustard
5/52 *Ernest Tubb & Red Foley*
6/52 *Carlisles*
29/72 *Buck Owens & Buddy Alan*
46/87 **Too Old To Grow Up Now** *Pake McEntire*
13/80 **Too Old To Play Cowboy** *Razzy Bailey*
71/68 **Too Rough On Me** *Earl Scott*
4/53 **Too Young To Tango** *Sunshine Ruby*
Took It Like A Man, Cried Like A Baby
42/82 *Cedar Creek*
68/88 *Kevin Pearce*
2/73 **Top Of The World** *Lynn Anderson*
53/68 **Top Of The World** *Stu Phillips*
46/74 **Tore Down** *Porter Wagoner*
57/99 **Tore Up From The Floor Up** *Wade Hayes*
3/77 **Torn Between Two Lovers** *Mary MacGregor*
71/72 **Torn From The Pages Of Life** *Stonewall Jackson*
53/87 **Torn-Up** *Vicki Rae Von*
58/02 **Tortured, Tangled Hearts** *Dixie Chicks*
71/00 **Toss A Little Bone** *Confederate Railroad*
59/72 **Tossin' And Turnin'** *Ronnie Sessions*
25/59 **Total Strangers** *Hank Thompson*
70/98 **Totally Committed** *Jeff Foxworthy*
1/85 **Touch A Hand, Make A Friend** *Oak Ridge Boys*
5/88 **Touch And Go Crazy** *Lee Greenwood*
15/58 **Touch And Go Heart** *Kitty Wells*
Touch Me
7/62 *Willie Nelson*
62/77 *Howdy Glenn*
54/86 **Touch Me** *Bandana*
Touch Me (I'll Be Your Fool Once More)
18/79 *Big Al Downing*
4/83 *Tom Jones*
1/86 **Touch Me When We're Dancing** *Alabama*
15/79 **Touch Me With Magic** *Marty Robbins*
3/66 **Touch My Heart** *Ray Price*
99/77 **Touch Of Her Fingers** *Clyde Watson*
1/75 **Touch The Hand** *Conway Twitty*
6/73 **Touch The Morning** *Don Gibson*
(Touch The Wind) ..see: Eres Tu
6/72 **Touch Your Woman** *Dolly Parton*
64/98 **Touchdown Tennessee** *Kenny Chesney*
3/71 **Touching Home** *Jerry Lee Lewis*
92/74 **Touching Me, Touching You** *Vicky Fletcher*
43/85 **Touchy Situation** *Razzy Bailey*
82/80 **Tough Act To Follow** *Billy Parker*
1/03 **Tough Little Boys** *Gary Allan*
19/04 **Tougher Than Nails** *Joe Diffie*
67/95 **Tougher Than The Rest** *Chris LeDoux*
Tower Of Strength
32/75 *Sue Richards*
33/79 *Narvel Felts*

16/68 **Town That Broke My Heart** *Bobby Bare*
38/67 **Town That Never Sleeps** *Charlie Walker*
38/73 **Town Where You Live** *Mel Street*
12/49 **Toy Heart** *Bill Monroe*
99/77 **Toy Hearts** *Johnny Tillotson*
48/74 **Toy Telephone** *Johnny Bush*
75/76 **Tra-La-La-La Suzy** *Price Mitchell*
30/72 **Traces** *Sonny James*
25/71 **Traces Of A Woman** *Billy Walker*
29/74 **Traces Of Life** *Lonzo & Oscar*
11/76 **Tracks Of My Tears** *Linda Ronstadt*
2/53 **Trademark** *Carl Smith*
69/96 **Trail Of Tears** *Billy Ray Cyrus*
Train Medley
95/80 *Boxcar Willie*
61/83 *Boxcar Willie*
7/57 **Train Of Love** *Johnny Cash*
6/87 **Train Of Memories** *Kathy Mattea*
74/71 **Train Train (Carry Me Away)** *Murry Kellum*
57/88 **Trains Make Me Lonesome** *Marty Haggard*
20/89 **Trainwreck Of Emotion** *Lorrie Morgan*
14/48 **Tramp On The Street** *Bill Carlisle*
Trashy Women
63/90 *Jerry Jeff Walker*
10/93 *Confederate Railroad*
52/72 **Travelin' Light** *George Hamilton IV*
29/59 **Travelin' Man** *Red Foley*
32/82 **Travelin' Man** *Jacky Ward*
44/66 **Travelin' Man** *Dick Curless*
20/73 **Traveling Man** *Dolly Parton*
42/72 **Travelin' Minstrel Band** *Carter Family*
33/71 **Travelin' Minstrel Man** *Bill Rice*
1/03 **Travelin' Soldier** *Dixie Chicks*
51/67 **Traveling Shoes** *Guy Mitchell*
6/51 **Travellin' Blues** *Lefty Frizzell*
6/58 **Treasure Of Love** *George Jones*
3/96 **Treat Her Right** *Sawyer Brown*
12/71 **Treat Him Right** *Barbara Mandrell*
62/74 **Treat Me Like A Lady** *Sherry Bryce*
18/91 **Treat Me Like A Stranger** *Baillie And The Boys*
11/57 **Treat Me Nice** *Elvis Presley*
45/98 **Tree Of Hearts** *Bryan White*
16/64 **Triangle** *Carl Smith*
(Tribute To Luther Perkins) ..see: Cashin' In
Triflin' Gal
2/45 *Al Dexter*
3/45 *Walter Shrum*
20/04 **Trip Around The Sun** *Jimmy Buffett w/ Martina McBride*
1/73 **Trip To Heaven** *Freddie Hart*
75/93 **Tropical Depression** *Alan Jackson*
T-R-O-U-B-L-E
11/75 *Elvis Presley*
13/93 *Travis Tritt*
18/95 **Trouble** *Mark Chesnutt*
30/65 **Trouble And Me** *Stonewall Jackson*
Trouble In Mind
7/56 *Eddy Arnold*
81/77 *Hank Snow*
12/64 **Trouble In My Arms** *Johnny & Jonie Mosby*
1/74 **Trouble In Paradise** *Loretta Lynn*
24/60 **Trouble In The Amen Corner** *Archie Campbell*
57/87 **Trouble In The Fields** *Nanci Griffith*
39/99 **Trouble Is A Woman** *Julie Reeves*
61/89 **Trouble Man** *Waylon Jennings*
5/93 **Trouble On The Line** *Sawyer Brown*
53/00 **Trouble With Angels** *Kathy Mattea*
72/92 **Trouble With Diamonds** *Mac McAnally*
64/82 **Trouble With Hearts** *Roy Head*
64/95 **Trouble With Love** *Rob Crosby*
42/77 **Trouble With Lovin' Today** *Asleep At The Wheel*
66/99 **Trouble With Never** *Tim McGraw*
15/97 **Trouble With The Truth** *Patty Loveless*
4/62 **Trouble's Back In Town** *Wilburn Brothers*
Truck Driver's Heaven ..see: I Dreamed Of A Hill-Billy Heaven
71/70 **Truck Driver's Lament** *Johnny Dollar*
Truck Drivin' Cat With Nine Wives
54/68 *Charlie Walker*
63/68 *Jim Nesbitt*
3/65 **Truck Drivin' Son-Of-A-Gun** *Dave Dudley*
Truck Driving Man
11/65 *George Hamilton IV*
29/76 *Red Steagall*
53/68 **Truck Driving Woman** *Norma Jean*
44/69 **Truck Stop** *Jerry Smith*
73/74 **Trucker And The U.F.O.** *Brush Arbor*
54/73 **Trucker's Paradise** *Del Reeves*
23/67 **Trucker's Prayer** *Dave Dudley*
2/98 **True** *George Strait*
49/68 **True And Lasting Kind** *Bobby Lord*
30/93 **True Believer** *Ronnie Milsap*
45/93 **True Confessions** *Joy White*
9/69 **True Grit** *Glen Campbell*
5/88 **True Heart** *Oak Ridge Boys*
59/97 **True Lies** *Sara Evans*
F/81 **True Life Country Music** *Razzy Bailey*
4/91 **True Love** *Don Williams*
32/85 **True Love** *Vince Gill*
True Love
51/73 *Red Steagall*
88/78 *LeGardes*
22/71 **True Love Is Greater Than Friendship** *Arlene Harden*
39/86 **True Love (Never Did Run Smooth)** *Tom Wopat*
54/91 **True Love Never Dies** *Kevin Welch*
58/69 **True Love Travels On A Gravel Road** *Duane Dee*
True Love Ways
77/78 *Randy Gurley*
1/80 *Mickey Gilley*
3/66 **True Love's A Blessing** *Sonny James*
85/83 **True Love's Getting Pretty Hard To Find** *Wickline*
23/95 **True To His Word** *Boy Howdy*
True True Lovin'
46/65 *Ferlin Husky*
35/73 *Ferlin Husky*
55/69 **Truer Love You'll Never Find (Than Mine)** *Bonnie Guitar & Buddy Killen*
13/03 **Truth About Men** *Tracy Byrd*
82/89 **Truth Doesn't Always Rhyme** *Rebecca Holden*
64/78 **(Truth Is) We're Livin' A Lie** *R.C. Bannon*
2/69 **Try A Little Kindness** *Glen Campbell*
47/76 **Try A Little Tenderness** *Billy Thunderkloud*
82/79 **Try Home** *Sandy Posey*
36/80 **Try It On** *Stephanie Winslow*
61/72 **Try It, You'll Like It** *Jimmy Dickens*
32/81 **Try Me** *Randy Barlow*
68/86 **Try Me** *Billy Burnette*
2/44 **Try Me One More Time** *Ernest Tubb*
14/94 **Try Not To Look So Pretty** *Dwight Yoakam*
75/76 **Tryin' Like The Devil** *James Talley*
1/75 **Tryin' To Beat The Morning Home** *T.G. Sheppard*
Tryin' To Forget About [You] The Blues
11/56 *Porter Wagoner*
52/77 *Cristy Lane*
1/94 **Tryin' To Get Over You** *Vince Gill*
50/95 **Tryin' To Get To New Orleans** *Tractors*
6/93 **Tryin' To Hide A Fire In The Dark** *Billy Dean*
80/83 **Tryin' To Love Two** *Kin Vassy*
12/79 **Tryin' To Satisfy You** *Dottsy*
30/81 **Trying Not To Love You** *Johnny Rodriguez*
18/05 **Trying To Find Atlantis** *Jamie O'Neal*
99/76 **Trying To Live Without You Kind Of Days** *Sandy Posey*
1/80 **Trying To Love Two Women** *Oak Ridge Boys*
74/94 **Tuckered Out** *Clint Black*
94/80 **Tugboat Annie** *Lori Jacobs*
Tulsa ..also see: (Don't Let The Sun Set On You)
40/83 **Tulsa Ballroom** *Dottie West*
41/71 **Tulsa County** *Anita Carter*
1/79 **Tulsa Time** *Don Williams*
10/80 **Tumbleweed** *Sylvia*
11/48 **Tumbling Tumbleweeds** *Sons Of The Pioneers*
Tupelo County Jail
7/58 *Webb Pierce*
40/66 *Stonemans*
15/68 **Tupelo Mississippi Flash** *Jerry Reed*
87/87 **Turn Around** *Terri Gibbs*
9/56 **Turn Her Down** *Faron Young*
1/88 **Turn It Loose** *Judds*
11/91 **Turn It On, Turn It Up, Turn Me Loose** *Dwight Yoakam*
39/84 **Turn Me Loose** *Vince Gill*

76/88 **(Turn Me Loose And) Let Me Swing** *Swing Shift Band*
59/84 **Turn Me To Love** *Keith Whitley*
27/89 **Turn Of The Century** *Nitty Gritty Dirt Band*
87/78 **Turn On The Bright Lights** *Lenny Gault*
29/74 **Turn On Your Light (And Let It Shine)** *Kenny Price*
1/75 **(Turn Out The Light And) Love Me Tonight** *Don Williams*
4/92 **Turn That Radio On** *Ronnie Milsap*
61/87 **Turn The Music On** *O.B. McClinton*
53/82 **Turn The Pencil Over** *Porter Wagoner*
1/67 **Turn The World Around** *Eddy Arnold*
17/72 **Turn Your Radio On** *Ray Stevens*
80/81 **Turnin' My Love On** *Jimmy Payne*
F/72 **Turnin' Off A Memory** *Merle Haggard*
1/84 **Turning Away** *Crystal Gayle*
87/83 **Turning Back The Covers (Don't Turn Back The Time)** *Robin Lee*
(Turpentine And Dandelion Wine) ..see: My Old Kentucky Home
67/97 **'Twas The Night After Christmas** *Jeff Foxworthy*
88/77 **Tweedle-O-Twill** *Kathy Barnes*
Twelfth Of Never
17/66 *Slim Whitman*
98/77 *David Houston*
51/00 **Twentieth Century** *Alabama*
57/85 **Twentieth Century Fool** *Kenny Rogers*
F/83 **20th Century Fox** *Bill Anderson*
10/74 **Twentieth Century Drifter** *Marty Robbins*
11/56 **Twenty Feet Of Muddy Water** *Sonny James*
2/87 **Twenty Years Ago** *Kenny Rogers*
35/81 **20/20 Hindsight** *Billy Larkin*
18/77 **Twenty-Four Hours From Tulsa** *Randy Barlow*
13/61 **Twenty-Fourth Hour** *Ray Price*
3/98 **26¢** *Wilkinsons*
45/64 **Twice As Much** *Hank Thompson*
67/92 **Twilight Is Gone** *Desert Rose Band*
Twilight Time
100/76 *Carl Mann*
41/89 *Willie Nelson*
(Twin Pines Theme) ..see: Heaven Can Be Anywhere
1/88 **Twinkle, Twinkle Lucky Star** *Merle Haggard*
49/89 **Twist Of Fate** *Cee Cee Chapman & Santa Fe*
Two Brothers ..see: Ballad Of
3/84 **Two Car Garage** *B.J. Thomas*
8/49 **Two Cents, Three Eggs And A Postcard** *Red Foley*
53/72 **Two Divided By Love** *Kendalls*
68/71 **Two Dollar Toy** *Stoney Edwards*
3/77 **Two Dollars In The Jukebox** *Eddie Rabbitt*
Two Doors Down
7/78 *Zella Lehr*
F/78 *Dolly Parton*
1/89 **Two Dozen Roses** *Shenandoah*
67/87 **255 Harbor Drive** *A.J. Masters*
11/54 **Two Glasses, Joe** *Ernest Tubb*
39/74 **Two Gun Daddy** *Marty Robbins*
45/85 **Two Heart Harmony** *Kendalls*
47/05 **Two Hearts** *Zona Jones*
65/83 **Two Hearts** *Texas Vocal Company*
73/89 **Two Hearts** *Jon Washington*
73/90 **Two Hearts** *K.T. Oslin*
Two Hearts Beat (Better Than One)
75/80 *Kay Austin*
F/81 *Eddy Arnold*
Two Hearts Can't Be Wrong
94/82 *Denise Price*
63/85 *Two Hearts*
18/78 **Two Hearts Tangled In Love** *Kenny Dale*
71/72 **200 Lbs. O' Slingin' Hound** *Billy Edd Wheeler*
9/55 **Two Kinds Of Love** *Eddy Arnold*
83/87 **Two Kinds Of Woman** *Diamonds*
8/77 **Two Less Lonely People** *Rex Allen, Jr.*
73/70 **Two Little Boys** *Rusty Draper*
75/68 **Two Little Hearts** *Compton Brothers*
74/70 **Two Little Rooms** *Janet Lawson*
7/78 **Two Lonely People** *Moe Bandy*
1/78 **Two More Bottles Of Wine** *Emmylou Harris*
82/87 **Two-Name Girl** *Johnstons*
Two Of A Kind (Workin' On A Full House)
71/87 *Dennis Robbins*
1/91 *Garth Brooks*
Two Of The Usual
49/67 *Bobby Lewis*
64/67 *Don Adams*
50/71 **Two Of Us Together** *Don Gibson & Sue Thompson*
14/85 **Two Old Cats Like Us** *Ray Charles w/ Hank Williams, Jr.*
82/89 **Two Old Flames One Cheatin' Fire** *Joann Wintermute*
72/81 **Two Out Of Three Ain't Bad** *J.W. Thompson*
4/01 **Two People Fell In Love** *Brad Paisley*
75/79 **Two People In Love** *Lorrie Morgan*
1/98 **Two Piña Coladas** *Garth Brooks*
35/70 **Two Separate Bar Stools** *Wanda Jackson*
9/57 **Two Shadows On Your Window** *Jim Reeves*
64/93 **Two Ships That Passed In The Moonlight** *Cee Cee Chapman*
74/86 **Two Sides** *Jimmy Murphy*
56/68 **Two Sides Of Me** *Harold Lee*
15/65 **Two Six Packs Away** *Dave Dudley*
2/92 **Two Sparrows In A Hurricane** *Tanya Tucker*
44/82 **Two-Step Is Easy** *Michael Murphey*
71/93 **Two Steppin' Mind** *Tim McGraw*
6/79 **Two Steps Forward And Three Steps Back** *Susie Allanson*
72/86 **Two Steps From The Blues** *Carlette*
68/93 **Two Steps In The Right Direction** *Roger Ballard*
2/80 **Two Story House** *George Jones & Tammy Wynette*
2/99 **Two Teardrops** *Steve Wariner*
18/92 **Two-Timin' Me** *Remingtons*
39/86 **Two Too Many** *Holly Dunn*
85/84 **Two Will Be One** *Kenny Dale*
41/70 **Tyin' Strings** *June Stearns*
58/95 **Tyler** *Davis Daniel*

U

55/68 **U.S. Male** *Elvis Presley*
9/75 **U.S. Of A** *Donna Fargo*
8/58 **Uh-Huh—mm** *Sonny James*
F/57 **Uh, Uh, No** *George Jones*
41/03 **Ultimate Love** *Phil Vassar*
1/91 **Unanswered Prayers** *Garth Brooks*
58/88 **Unattended Fire** *Razzy Bailey*
2/99 **Unbelievable** *Diamond Rio*
29/73 **Unbelievable Love** *Jim Ed Brown*
Unbreakable Heart
51/93 *Carlene Carter*
24/00 *Jessica Andrews*
Unbreakable Hearts
79/78 *Bill White*
92/79 *Hargus "Pig" Robbins*
1/02 **Unbroken** *Tim McGraw*
50/01 **Unbroken By You** *Kortney Kayle*
Unchained Melody
41/75 *Joe Stampley*
6/78 *Elvis Presley*
26/91 *Ronnie McDowell*
3/97 *LeAnn Rimes*
49/76 **Uncle Hiram And The Homemade Beer** *Dick Feller*
Uncle Pen
14/56 *Porter Wagoner*
1/84 *Ricky Skaggs*
4/77 **Uncloudy Day** *Willie Nelson*
3/00 **Unconditional** *Clay Davidson*
27/91 **Unconditional Love** *Glen Campbell*
44/87 **Unconditional Love** *New Grass Revival*
18/62 **Under Cover Of The Night** *Dave Dudley*
66/83 **Under Loved And Over Lonely** *Katy Moffatt*
24/88 **Under The Boardwalk** *Lynn Anderson*
72/90 **Under The Gun** *Suzy Bogguss*
2/61 **Under The Influence Of Love** *Buck Owens*
54/93 **Under This Old Hat** *Chris LeDoux*
Under Your Spell Again
4/59 *Buck Owens*
5/59 *Ray Price*
39/71 *Waylon Jennings & Jessi Colter*
65/76 *Barbara Fairchild*
93/89 *Shelby Lynne*
28/78 **Undercover Lovers** *Stella Parton*
88/80 **Undercover Man** *Liz Lyndell*
26/64 **Understand Your Gal** *Margie Bowes*
1/64 **Understand Your Man** *Johnny Cash*
10/68 **Undo The Right** *Johnny Bush*
67/73 **Uneasy Rider** *Charlie Daniels*

23/72 **Unexpected Goodbye** *Glenn Barber*
79/75 **Unfaithful Fools** *Leroy Van Dyke*
8/50 **Unfaithful One** *Ernest Tubb*
32/83 **Unfinished Business** *Lloyd David Foster*
35/01 **Unforgiven** *Tracy Lawrence*
18/63 **Unkind Words** *Kathy Dee*
59/03 **Unkissed** *Holly Lamar*
14/48 **Unloved And Unclaimed** *Roy Acuff*
5/62 **Unloved Unwanted** *Kitty Wells*
7/66 **Unmitigated Gall** *Faron Young*
47/99 **Unsung Hero** *Terri Clark*
58/02 **Untangle My Heart** *Shannon Brown*
4/94 **Untanglin' My Mind** *Clint Black*
10/55 **Untied** *Tommy Collins*
54/85 **Until I Fall In Love Again** *Marie Osmond*
1/86 **Until I Met You** *Judy Rodman*
57/77 **Until I Met You** *Tom Bresh*
F/56 **Until I Met You** *Faron Young*
68/72 **Until It's Time For You To Go** *Elvis Presley*
1/69 **Until My Dreams Come True** *Jack Greene*
Until The Bitter End
39/80 *Kenny Seratt*
88/81 *Faron Young*
39/74 **Until The End Of Time** *Narvel Felts & Sharon Vaughn*
77/85 **Until The Music Is Gone** *Becky Chase*
50/78 **Until The Next Time** *Billy Parker*
92/81 **Until The Nights** *Charlie McCoy & Laney Smallwood*
20/60 **Until Today** *Elmer Snodgrass*
42/79 **Until Tonight** *Juice Newton*
46/02 **Until We Fall Back In Love Again** *Jeff Carson*
93/85 **Until We Meet Again** *Wray Brothers Band*
73/80 **Until You** *Terry Bradshaw*
4/88 **Untold Stories** *Kathy Mattea*
14/72 **Untouched** *Mel Tillis*
12/03 **Unusually Unusual** *Lonestar*
6/51 **Unwanted Sign Upon Your Heart** *Hank Snow*
Unwed Fathers
63/83 *Tammy Wynette*
56/85 *Gail Davies*
6/81 **Unwound** *George Strait*
12/03 **Up!** *Shania Twain*
9/89 **Up And Gone** *McCarters*
48/00 **Up North (Down South, Back East, Out West)** *Wade Hayes*
57/85 **Up On Your Love** *Karen Taylor-Good*
41/66 **Up This Hill And Down** *Osborne Brothers*
Up To Heaven ..see: (You Lift Me)
28/75 **Uproar** *Anne Murray*
36/04 **Upside Of Being Down** *Catherine Britt*
10/95 **Upstairs Downtown** *Toby Keith*
40/69 **Upstairs In The Bedroom** *Bobby Wright*
65/98 **Uptown Down-Home Good Ol' Boy** *Garth Brooks*
25/74 **Uptown Poker Club** *Jerry Reed*
94/81 **Urban Cowboys, Outlaws, Cavaleers** *James Marvell*
7/67 **Urge For Going** *George Hamilton IV*
55/97 **Use Mine** *Jeff Wood*
48/97 **Used To Be's** *Daryle Singletary*
3/85 **Used To Blue** *Sawyer Brown*
47/98 **Used To The Pain** *Mark Nesler*

V

9/98 **Valentine** *Martina McBride w/ Jim Brickman*
15/69 **Vance** *Roger Miller*
52/70 **Vanishing Breed** *Hank Snow*
7/76 **Vaya Con Dios** *Freddy Fender*
30/77 **Vegas** *Bobby & Jeannie Bare*
56/95 **Veil Of Tears** *Hal Ketchum*
9/83 **Velvet Chains** *Gary Morris*
5/82 **Very Best Is You** *Charly McClain*
50/91 **Very First Lasting Love** *Shelby Lynne w/ Les Taylor*
1/74 **Very Special Love Song** *Charlie Rich*
40/84 **Victim Of Life's Circumstances** *Vince Gill*
34/82 **Victim Or A Fool** *Rodney Crowell*
75/76 **Victims** *Kenny Starr*
24/84 **Victims Of Goodbye** *Sylvia*
10/96 **Vidalia** *Sammy Kershaw*
12/66 **Viet Nam Blues** *Dave Dudley*
21/67 **Vin Rosé** *Stu Phillips*
Violet And A Rose
24/58 *Mel Tillis*
10/62 *"Little" Jimmy Dickens*
36/64 *Wanda Jackson*
73/76 **Virgil And The $300 Vacation** *Cledus Maggard*
68/72 **Virginia** *Jean Shepard*
22/77 **Virginia, How Far Will You Go** *Dickey Lee*
21/00 **Visit, The** *Chad Brock*
90/79 **Visitor, The** *J.W. Thompson*
72/77 **Vitamin L** *Mary Kay Place*
3S/04 **Viva Las Vegas** *Grascals w/ Dolly Parton*
26/66 **Volkswagen** *Ray Pillow*
22/63 **Volunteer, The** *Autry Inman*
8/89 **Vows Go Unbroken (Always True To You)** *Kenny Rogers*

W

72/87 **W. Lee O'Daniel (And The Light Crust Dough Boys)** *Johnny Cash*
6/00 **www.memory** *Alan Jackson*
Wabash Cannonball
52/67 *Dick Todd*
27/70 *Dick Curless*
63/70 *Danny Davis/The Nashville Brass*
97/76 *Charlie McCoy*
91/84 *Willie Nelson & Hank Wilson*
50/66 **Waco** *Lorne Greene*
12/55 **Wait A Little Longer Please, Jesus** *Carl Smith*
98/85 **Wait Till I Get My Hands On You** *Wynn Stewart*
62/82 **Wait Till Those Bridges Are Gone** *Ray Price*
70/77 **Waitin' At The End Of Your Run** *Ava Barber*
Waitin' For A Train ..see: Waiting For A Train
39/92 **Waitin' For The Deal To Go Down** *Dixiana*
12/58 **Waitin' In School** *Ricky Nelson*
1/66 **Waitin' In Your Welfare Line** *Buck Owens*
70/89 **Waitin' On Ice** *Jason D. Williams*
28/02 **Waitin' On Joe** *Steve Azar*
50/00 **Waitin' On Sundown** *Andy Griggs*
36/05 **Waitin' On The Wonderful** *Aaron Lines*
69/87 **Waitin' Up** *George Highfill*
25/64 **Waiting A Lifetime** *Webb Pierce*
Waiting For A Train (All Around The Watertank)
F/57 *Jim Reeves*
11/71 *Jerry Lee Lewis*
72/76 **Waiting For The Tables To Turn** *Wayne Kemp*
50/89 **Waiting Here For You** *Gail Davies*
3/52 **Waiting In The Lobby Of Your Heart** *Hank Thompson*
14/74 **Wake Me Into Love** *Bud Logan & Wilma Burgess*
63/80 **Wake Me Up** *Louise Mandrell*
21/70 **Wake Me Up Early In The Morning** *Bobby Lord*
57/98 **Wake Up And Smell The Whiskey** *Dean Miller*
1/54 **Wake Up, Irene** *Hank Thompson*
37/73 **Wake Up, Jacob** *Porter Wagoner*
1/57 **Wake Up Little Susie** *Everly Brothers*
46/05 **Wake Up Older** *Julie Roberts*
2/91 **Walk, The** *Sawyer Brown*
8/03 **Walk A Little Straighter** *Billy Currington*
56/70 **Walk A Mile In My Shoes** *Joe South*
56/71 **Walk All Over Georgia** *Ray Sanders*
57/69 **Walk Among The People** *Cheryl Poole*
48/77 **Walk Away With Me** *Randy Barlow*
56/82 **Walk Me 'Cross The River** *Jerri Kelly*
28/87 **Walk Me In The Rain** *Girls Next Door*
7/63 **Walk Me To The Door** *Ray Price*
44/67 **Walk Me To The Station** *Stu Phillips*
2/90 **Walk On** *Reba McEntire*
30/83 **Walk On** *Karen Brooks*
61/95 **Walk On** *Linda Ronstadt*
74/87 **Walk On Boy** *Ogden Harless*
Walk On By
1/61 *Leroy Van Dyke*
98/79 *Robert Gordon*
43/80 *Donna Fargo*
73/87 *Perry LaPointe*
55/88 *Asleep At The Wheel*
1/91 **Walk On Faith** *Mike Reid*
5/68 **Walk On Out Of My Mind** *Waylon Jennings*
9/61 **Walk Out Backwards** *Bill Anderson*

71/93 **Walk Outside The Lines** *Marshall Tucker Band*
Walk Right Back
76/77 *LaWanda Lindsey*
4/78 *Anne Murray*
Walk Right In
23/63 *Rooftop Singers*
92/77 *Dr. Hook*
7/76 **Walk Softly** *Billy "Crash" Craddock*
Walk Softly On The Bridges
11/73 *Mel Street*
79/86 *Rodney Lay*
25/89 **Walk Softly On This Heart Of Mine** *Kentucky Headhunters*
10/65 **Walk Tall** *Faron Young*
54/89 **Walk That Way** *Mel McDaniel*
10/86 **Walk The Way The Wind Blows** *Kathy Mattea*
1/67 **Walk Through This World With Me** *George Jones*
30/70 **Walk Unashamed** *Tompall/Glaser Brothers*
2/93 **Walkaway Joe** *Trisha Yearwood w/ Don Henley*
57/67 **Walker's Woods** *Ed Bruce*
63/93 **Walkin'** *Cleve Francis*
2/85 **Walkin' A Broken Heart** *Don Williams*
Walkin' After Midnight
2/57 *Patsy Cline*
60/82 *Calamity Jane*
1/90 **Walkin' Away** *Clint Black*
2/96 **Walkin' Away** *Diamond Rio*
23/69 **Walkin' Back To Birmingham** *Leon Ashley*
29/59 **Walkin' Down The Road** *Jimmy Newman*
83/74 **Walkin' In Teardrops** *Earl Richards*
61/90 **Walkin' In The Sun** *Glen Campbell*
7/67 **Walkin' In The Sunshine** *Roger Miller*
21/59 **Walkin' My Blues Away** *Jimmie Skinner*
Walkin', Talkin', Cryin', Barely Beatin' Broken Heart
22/64 *Johnny Wright*
4/90 *Highway 101*
50/97 **Walkin' The Country** *Ranch*
3/94 **Walking Away A Winner** *Kathy Mattea*
Walking In Memphis
74/91 *Marc Cohn*
8/03 *Lonestar*
53/69 **Walking Midnight Road** *June Stearns*
7/66 **Walking On New Grass** *Kenny Price*
Walking Piece Of Heaven
6/73 *Marty Robbins*
22/79 *Freddy Fender*
64/66 **Walking Shadow, Talking Memory** *Carl Belew*
3/90 **Walking Shoes** *Tanya Tucker*
Walking The Floor Over You
18/65 *George Hamilton IV*
31/79 *Ernest Tubb w/ Merle Haggard*
28/58 **Walking The Slow Walk** *Carl Smith*
5/61 **Walking The Streets** *Webb Pierce*
58/68 **Walking Through The Memories Of My Mind** *Billy Mize*

15/95 **Walking To Jerusalem** *Tracy Byrd*
59/83 **Walking With My Memories** *Loretta Lynn*
24/59 **Wall, The** *Freddie Hart*
69/93 **Wall Around Her Heart** *Remingtons*
60/68 **Wall Of Pictures** *Darrell McCall*
40/87 **Wall Of Tears** *K.T. Oslin*
5/62 **Wall To Wall Love** *Bob Gallion*
43/66 **Wallpaper Roses** *Jerry Wallace*
Walls Of The Bottle ..see: (If I Could Climb)
97/76 **Walnut Street Wrangler** *Debi Hawkins*
58/03 **Walter** *Charlie Robison*
Waltz Across Texas
34/65 *Ernest Tubb*
81/76 *Maury Finney*
56/79 *Ernest Tubb*
10/85 **Waltz Me To Heaven** *Waylon Jennings*
Waltz Of The Angels
14/56 *Wynn Stewart*
11/62 *George Jones & Margie Singleton*
51/78 *David Houston*
8/48 **Waltz Of The Wind** *Roy Acuff*
13/62 **Waltz You Saved For Me** *Ferlin Husky*
85/81 **Waltzes And Western Swing** *Donnie Rohrs*
63/87 **Waltzin' With Daddy** *Carlette*
1/88 **Wanderer, The** *Eddie Rabbitt*
13/67 **Wanderin' Man** *Jeannie Seely*
2/81 **Wandering Eyes** *Ronnie McDowell*
52/68 **Wandering Mind** *Margie Singleton*
63/84 **Want Ads** *Robin Lee*
35/79 **Want To Thank You** *Kim Charles*
3/74 **Want-To's, The** *Freddie Hart*
3/90 **Wanted** *Alan Jackson*
41/75 **Wanted Man** *Jerry Wallace*
Wantin' And Havin' It All ..see: (This Thing Called)
63/67 **Wanting You But Never Having You** *Jack Greene*
11/60 **Wanting You With Me Tonight** *Jimmy Newman*
1/82 **War Is Hell (On The Homefront Too)** *T.G. Sheppard*
50/01 **Warm & Fuzzy** *Billy Gilman*
43/76 **Warm And Tender** *Larry Gatlin*
57/68 **Warm And Tender Love** *Archie Campbell - Lorene Mann*
53/73 **Warm Love** *Don Gibson & Sue Thompson*
8/49 **Warm Red Wine** *Ernest Tubb*
72/68 **Warm Red Wine** *Wes Buchanan*
6/75 **Warm Side Of You** *Freddie Hart*
Warm Summer Days ..see: (She Likes)
73/87 **Warmed Over Romance** *Tina Danielle*
25/70 **Warmth Of The Wine** *Johnny Bush*
4/92 **Warning Labels** *Doug Stone*
4/85 **Warning Sign** *Eddie Rabbitt*
56/97 **Warning Signs** *Bill Engvall w/ John Michael Montgomery*
61/86 **Was It Just The Wine** *Vern Gosdin*
43/76 **Was It Worth It** *Joe Stampley*
21/03 **Was That My Life** *Jo Dee Messina*

20/72 **Washday Blues** *Dolly Parton*
28/79 **Wasn't It Easy Baby** *Freddie Hart*
73/81 **Wasn't It Supposed To Be Me** *Kenny Earle*
45/81 **Wasn't That A Party** *Rovers*
62/82 **Wasn't That Love** *Susie Allanson*
1/75 **Wasted Days And Wasted Nights** *Freddy Fender*
27/60 **Wasted Love** *Red Herring*
87/82 **Wasted On The Way** *Crosby, Stills & Nash*
4/56 **Wasted Words** *Ray Price*
49/04 **Watch, The** *Scotty Emerick*
28/60 **Watch Dog** *Al Terry*
2/92 **Watch Me** *Lorrie Morgan*
Watch Out For Lucy
88/74 *Bobby Penn*
72/75 *Tony Booth*
1/04 **Watch The Wind Blow By** *Tim McGraw*
4/97 **Watch This** *Clay Walker*
10/65 **Watch Where You're Going** *Don Gibson*
4/82 **Watchin' Girls Go By** *Ronnie McDowell*
47/99 **Watching My Baby Not Coming Back** *David Ball*
7/71 **Watching Scotty Grow** *Bobby Goldsboro*
32/67 **Watchman, The** *Claude King*
57/91 **Water Under The Bridge** *Dan Seals*
16/73 **Watergate Blues** *Tom T. Hall*
Waterhole #3 ..see: Ballad Of
1/59 **Waterloo** *Stonewall Jackson*
4/94 **Watermelon Crawl** *Tracy Byrd*
49/70 **Watermelon Time In Georgia** *Lefty Frizzell*
Watermelon Wine ..see: (Old Dogs-Children And)
3/03 **Wave On Wave** *Pat Green*
Wave To Me, My Lady
3/46 *Elton Britt*
4/46 *Gene Autry*
62/70 **Wax Museum** *Dave Peel*
57/70 **Waxahachie Woman** *John Deer Company*
4/84 **Way Back** *John Conlee*
99/88 **Way Beyond The Blue** *Bonners*
1/77 **Way Down** *Elvis Presley*
5/83 **Way Down Deep** *Vern Gosdin*
39/87 **Way Down Texas Way** *Asleep At The Wheel*
46/76 **Way He's Treated You** *Nat Stuckey*
2/80 **Way I Am** *Merle Haggard*
67/75 **Way I Lose My Mind** *Carl Smith*
99/76 **Way I Loved Her** *Rick Smith*
59/89 **Way I Want To Go** *Burch Sisters*
54/74 **Way I'm Needing You** *Cliff Cochran*
17/63 **Way It Feels To Die** *Vernon Stewart*
82/78 **Way It Was In '51** *Merle Haggard*
91/85 **Way She Makes Love** *Billy Chinnock*
64/97 **Way She's Lookin'** *Raybon Bros.*
Way To Survive
7/66 *Ray Price*
82/89 *Monty Holmes*
55/02 **Way Too Deep** *Sixwire*

1/87 **Way We Make A Broken Heart** *Rosanne Cash*
98/76 **Way With Words** *Carl Smith*
F/83 **Way Without Words** *Roy Clark*
86/81 **Way You Are** *P.J. Parks*
98/88 **Way You Got Over Me** *Bill Nunley*
1/00 **Way You Love Me** *Faith Hill*
7/80 **Wayfaring Stranger** *Emmylou Harris*
99/79 **Waylon, Sing To Mama** *Darrell Thomas*
2/58 **Ways Of A Woman In Love** *Johnny Cash*
74/78 **Ways Of A Woman In Love** *Tom Bresh*
1/69 **Ways To Love A Man** *Tammy Wynette*
57/83 **Wayward Wind** *James Galway w/ Sylvia*
We Ain't Gonna Work For Peanuts ..see: Farmer's Song
45/04 **We All Fall Down** *Diamond Rio*
46/96 **We All Get Lucky Sometimes** *Lee Roy Parnell*
22/69 **We All Go Crazy** *Jack Reno*
75/87 **We Always Agree On Love** *Atlanta*
76/85 **We Are The World** *USA for Africa*
We Believe In Happy Endings
7/78 *Johnny Rodriguez*
1/88 *Earl Thomas Conley w/ Emmylou Harris*
We Belong Together
2/78 *Susie Allanson*
52/86 *Carlette*
85/84 **We Belong Together** *Tony Joe White*
3/91 **We Both Walk** *Lorrie Morgan*
71/92 **We Can Hold Our Own** *Ronna Reeves*
62/93 **We Can Love** *Larry Stewart*
6/72 **We Can Make It** *George Jones*
40/77 **We Can't Build A Fire In The Rain** *Roy Clark*
6/77 **We Can't Go On Living Like This** *Eddie Rabbitt*
6/94 **We Can't Love Like This Anymore** *Alabama*
3/74 **We Could** *Charley Pride*
96/81 **We Could Go On Forever** *E.W.B.*
86/79 **We Could Have Been The Closest Of Friends** *B.J. Thomas*
1/00 **We Danced** *Brad Paisley*
1/97 **We Danced Anyway** *Deana Carter*
2/82 **We Did But Now You Don't** *Conway Twitty*
66/89 **We Did It Once (We Can Do It Again)** *Pal Rakes*
6/84 **We Didn't See A Thing** *Ray Charles/George Jones/ Chet Atkins*
11/94 **We Don't Have To Do This** *Tanya Tucker*
16/81 **We Don't Have To Hold Out** *Anne Murray*
72/78 **We Don't Live Here, We Just Love Here** *Big Ben Atkins*
92/77 **We Fell In Love That Way** *Claude Gray*
30/73 **We Found It** *Porter Wagoner & Dolly Parton*
34/72 **We Found It In Each Other's Arms** *Roger Miller*
63/94 **We Got A Lot In Common** *Archer Park*
26/78 **We Got Love** *Lynn Anderson*
34/79 **We Got Love** *Mundo Earwood*
11/93 **We Got The Love** *Restless Heart*
20/69 **We Had All The Good Things Going** *Jan Howard*
We Had It All
28/73 *Waylon Jennings*
44/83 *Conway Twitty*
31/86 *Dolly Parton*
69/82 **We Had It All One Time** *Charlie Daniels Band*
We Have To Start Meeting Like This ..see: We've Got To Start
9/94 **We Just Disagree** *Billy Dean*
66/84 **We Just Gotta Dance** *Karen Taylor-Good*
98/77 **We Know Better** *Paul Craft*
53/85 **We Know Better Now** *Dottie West*
40/73 **We Know It's Over** *Dave Dudley & Karen O'Donnal*
89/79 **We Let Love Fade Away** *Leon Everette*
96/76 **We Live In Two Different Worlds** *Rachel Sweet*
68/98 **We Lose** *Brad Hawkins*
48/79 **We Love Each Other** *Louise Mandrell & R.C. Bannon*
8/74 **We Loved It Away** *George Jones & Tammy Wynette*
63/00 **We Made Love** *Alabama*
77/82 **We Made Memories** *Boxcar Willie & Penny DeHaven*
2/44 **We Might As Well Forget It** *Bob Wills*
7/62 **We Missed You** *Kitty Wells*
7/88 **We Must Be Doin' Somethin' Right** *Eddie Rabbitt*
We Must Believe In Magic
86/78 *Jack Clement*
84/83 *Johnny Cash*
3/63 **We Must Have Been Out Of Our Minds** *George Jones & Melba Montgomery*
68/92 **We Must Take America Back** *Steve Vaus*
43/68 **We Need A Lot More Happiness** *Wilburn Brothers*
69/70 **We Need A Lot More Of Jesus** *Skeeter Davis*
64/88 **We Need To Be Locked Away** *Jonathan Edwards*
22/88 **We Never Touch At All** *Merle Haggard*
67/83 **We Really Got A Hold On Love** *Family Brown*
4/98 **We Really Shouldn't Be Doing This** *George Strait*
12/92 **We Shall Be Free** *Garth Brooks*
47/03 **We Shook Hands (Man To Man)** *Tebey*
5/74 **We Should Be Together** *Don Williams*
2/71 **We Sure Can Love Each Other** *Tammy Wynette*
2/92 **We Tell Ourselves** *Clint Black*
60/00 **We The People** *Billy Ray Cyrus*
75/98 **We Three Kings (Star Of Wonder)** *BlackHawk*
9/75 **We Used To** *Dolly Parton*
63/80 **(We Used To Kiss Each Other On The Lips But It's) All Over Now** *Ann J. Morton*
2/97 **We Were In Love** *Toby Keith*
63/88 **We Were Meant To Be Lovers** *David Slater*
50/85 **We Work** *Hillary Kanter*
38/65 **We'd Destroy Each Other** *Carl Butler & Pearl*
2/93 **We'll Burn That Bridge** *Brooks & Dunn*
F/56 **We'll Find A Way** *Webb Pierce*
5/68 **We'll Get Ahead Someday** *Porter Wagoner & Dolly Parton*
We'll Sing In The Sunshine
43/64 *Gale Garnett*
63/70 *LaWanda Lindsey*
34/72 *Alice Creech*
54/68 **We'll Stick Together** *Kitty Wells & Johnny Wright*
63/69 **We'll Sweep Out The Ashes In The Morning** *Carl Butler & Pearl*
We're All Alone
75/77 *La Costa*
82/77 *Rita Coolidge*
We're Back In Love Again
37/74 *Johnny Bush*
59/80 *Johnny Russell*
93/81 **We're Building Our Love On A Rock** *Lou Hobbs*
47/76 **We're Getting There** *Ray Price*
13/70 **We're Gonna Get Together** *Buck Owens & Susan Raye*
14/62 **We're Gonna Go Fishin'** *Hank Locklin*
1/73 **We're Gonna Hold On** *George Jones & Tammy Wynette*
75/88 **We're Gonna Love Tonight** *Don Juan*
95/79 **We're In For Hard Times** *Breakfast Barry*
We're Livin' A Lie ..see: (Truth Is)
94/79 **We're Making Up For Lost Time** *Rex Gosdin*
15/74 **(We're Not) The Jet Set** *George Jones & Tammy Wynette*
18/80 **We're Number One** *Gatlin Bros.*
3/74 **We're Over** *Johnny Rodriguez*
20/00 **We're So Good Together** *Reba McEntire*
59/87 **We're Staying Together** *Rex Allen, Jr.*
80/77 **We're Still Hangin' In There Ain't We Jessi** *Jeannie Seely*
We're Strangers Again
42/83 *Merle Haggard & Leona Williams*
49/91 *Tammy Wynette w/ Randy Travis*
15/63 **We're The Talk Of The Town** *Buck Owens & Rose Maddox*
10/78 **We've Come A Long Way, Baby** *Loretta Lynn*
10/54 **We've Gone Too Far** *Hank Thompson*
44/66 **We've Gone Too Far, Again** *Justin Tubb & Lorene Mann*
3/86 **We've Got A Good Fire Goin'** *Don Williams*
97/83 **We've Got A Good Thing Goin'** *J.W. Thompson*

20/71 **We've Got Everything But Love** *David Houston & Barbara Mandrell*
95/75 **We've Got It All Together Now** *Guy & Ralna*
14/91 **We've Got It Made** *Lee Greenwood*
13/63 **We've Got Something In Common** *Faron Young*
73/96 **We've Got To Keep On Meeting Like This** *Paul Overstreet*
We've Got To Start Meeting Like This
84/81 *Kenny Earle*
76/82 *John Wesley Ryles*
85/84 *Memphis*
30/72 **We've Got To Work It Out Between Us** *Diana Trask*
1/83 **We've Got Tonight** *Kenny Rogers & Sheena Easton*
63/79 **We've Gotta Get Away From It All** *Tom Grant*
78/85 **We've Still Got Love** *Simon & Verity*
96/89 **Weak Men Break** *Harrell & Scott*
67/89 **Weak Nights** *Linda Davis*
57/70 **Weakest Kind Of Man** *John Wesley Ryles*
18/68 **Weakness In A Man** *Roy Drusky*
Wear My Ring Around Your Neck
3/58 *Elvis Presley*
F/83 *Elvis Presley*
26/92 *Ricky Van Shelton*
7/53 **Weary Blues From Waitin'** *Hank Williams*
Wedding Bells
2/49 *Hank Williams*
6/49 *Margaret Whiting & Jimmy Wakely*
15/49 *Jesse Rogers*
15/49 *Kenny Roberts*
78/83 *Margo Smith*
33/69 **Wedding Cake** *Connie Francis*
91/78 **Weeds Outlived The Roses** *Darrell McCall*
13/78 **Week-End Friend** *Con Hunley*
1/70 **Week In A Country Jail** *Tom T. Hall*
10/64 **Week In The Country** *Ernest Ashworth*
1/87 **Weekend, The** *Steve Wariner*
75/87 **Weekend Cowboys** *Marty Haggard*
F/75 **Weekend Daddy** *Buck Owens*
87/76 **Weep No More My Baby** *Lois Johnson*
43/80 **Weight Of My Chains** *Tompall/Glaser Brothers*
93/76 **Welcome Back** *John Sebastian*
56/74 **Welcome Back To My World** *Carl Belew*
79/74 **Welcome Home** *Peters & Lee*
24/68 **Welcome Home To Nothing** *Jeannie Seely*
Welcome To My World
2/64 *Jim Reeves*
34/71 *Eddy Arnold*
47/92 **Welcome To The Club** *Tim McGraw*
22/74 **Welcome To The Sunshine (Sweet Baby Jane)** *Jeanne Pruett*

6/70 **Welfare Cadilac** *Guy Drake*
60/80 **Well Rounded Traveling Man** *Kenny Price*
28/94 **Were You Really Livin'** *Brother Phelps*
46/86 **Weren't You Listening** *Adam Baker*
49/67 **West Canterbury Subdivision Blues** *Stonemans*
23/71 **West Texas Highway** *George Hamilton IV*
51/69 **West Virginia Woman** *Billy Edd Wheeler*
61/94 **Western Flyer** *Western Flyer*
20/90 **Western Girls** *Marty Stuart*
11/75 **Western Man** *La Costa*
4/03 **What A Beautiful Day** *Chris Cagle*
25/94 **What A Crying Shame** *Mavericks*
(What A Day For A) Day Dream ..see: Daydream
81/77 **What A Diff'rence A Day Made** *Bobby Lewis*
1/78 **What A Difference You've Made In My Life** *Ronnie Milsap*
50/71 **What A Dream** *Conway Twitty*
2/48 **What A Fool I Was** *Eddy Arnold*
43/87 **What A Girl Next Door Could Do** *Girls Next Door*
23/61 **What A Laugh!** *Freddie Hart*
16/79 **What A Lie** *Sammi Smith*
1/74 **What A Man, My Man Is** *Lynn Anderson*
53/02 **What A Memory** *Tracy Lawrence*
75/85 **What A Memory You'd Make** *Jim Collins*
What A Night
51/76 *David Houston*
71/77 *Tom Jones*
23/62 **What A Pleasure** *Connie Hall*
57/72 **What A Price** *Johnny Russell*
13/49 **What A Shame** *Merle Travis*
43/03 **What A Shame** *Rebecca Lynn Howard*
25/61 **What A Terrible Feeling** *Elmer Snodgrass*
What A Way To Go
18/77 *Bobby Borchers*
10/91 *Ray Kennedy*
70/74 **What A Way To Go** *Del Reeves*
29/68 **What A Way To Live** *Johnny Bush*
85/82 **What A Way To Spend The Night** *Zella Lehr*
45/98 **What A Woman Knows** *Kris Tyler*
44/93 **What A Woman Wants** *Lari White*
73/89 **What A Wonderful World** *Roy Clark*
71/93 **What About Love** *Desert Rose Band*
20/73 **What About Me** *Anne Murray*
22/61 **What About Me** *Don Gibson*
70/84 **What About Me?** *Kenny Rogers w/ Kim Carnes & James Ingram*
1/00 **What About Now** *Lonestar*
44/71 **What About The Hurt** *Bob Luman*
45/91 **What About The Love We Made** *Shelby Lynne*
80/82 **What About Tonight** *Gene Kennedy & Karen Jeglum*
45/99 **What About You** *Sons Of The Desert*
8/72 **What Ain't To Be, Just Might Happen** *Porter Wagoner*

13/72 **What Am I Gonna Do** *Bobby Bare*
90/80 **What Am I Gonna Do?** *Del Reeves*
What Am I Gonna Do About You
48/86 *Con Hunley*
1/87 *Reba McEntire*
37/67 **What Am I Gonna Do Now** *Ferlin Husky*
3/83 **What Am I Gonna Do (With The Rest Of My Life)** *Merle Haggard*
38/64 **What Am I Gonna Do With You** *Skeeter Davis*
77/84 **What Am I Gonna Do Without You** *Ray Price*
What Am I Living For
19/59 *Ernest Tubb*
59/71 *Conway Twitty*
7/56 **What Am I Worth** *George Jones*
19/69 **What Are Those Things (With Big Black Wings)** *Charlie Louvin*
1/81 **What Are We Doin' In Love** *Dottie West w/ Kenny Rogers*
4/81 **What Are We Doin' Lonesome** *Gatlin Bros.*
10/49 **What Are We Gonna Do About The Moonlight** *Hank Thompson*
66/91 **What Bothers Me Most** *Waylon Jennings*
97/74 **What Can I Do (To Make You Happy)** *Karen Wheeler*
92/79 **What Can I Do (To Make You Love Me)** *Hugh X. Lewis*
9/87 **What Can I Do With My Heart** *Juice Newton*
41/68 **What Can I Say** *Arlene Harden*
61/67 **What Can I Tell The Folks Back Home** *Melba Montgomery*
What Cha ..also see: What U / What You
30/78 **What Cha Doin' After Midnight, Baby** *Helen Cornelius*
82/88 **What Cha' Doin' To Me** *Day Johnston*
75/97 **What Child Is This** *Mark Chesnutt*
65/00 **What Children Believe** *Shenandoah*
What Did I Promise Her Last Night
75/77 *Billy Parker*
4/78 *Mel Tillis*
60/86 **What Did You Do With My Heart** *Chance*
7/58 **What Do I Care** *Johnny Cash*
What Do I Do With Me ..see: (Without You)
5/96 **What Do I Know** *Ricochet*
61/88 **What Do Lonely People Do** *Burch Sisters*
62/71 **What Do You Do** *Barbara Fairchild*
26/01 **What Do You Know About Love** *Dwight Yoakam*
3/00 **What Do You Say** *Reba McEntire*
4/99 **What Do You Say To That** *George Strait*
59/02 **What Do You See** *Sonya Isaacs*
53/01 **What Do You Want From Me Now** *Billy Yates*
6/88 **What Do You Want From Me This Time** *Foster & Lloyd*
48/95 **What Do You Want With His Love** *David Ball*

5/67 **What Does It Take** *Skeeter Davis*
70/69 **What Eva Doesn't Have** *Ray Pennington*
(What Ever May The Future Be) ..see: Lo Que Sea
66/72 **What Every Woman Wants To Hear** *Claude Gray*
1/76 **What Goes On When The Sun Goes Down** *Ronnie Milsap*
56/91 **What Goes With Blue** *Tammy Wynette*
28/80 **What Good Is A Heart** *Dean Dillon*
46/73 **What Got To You (Before It Got To Me)** *Ray Griff*
F/76 **What Have You Got Planned Tonight Diana** *Merle Haggard*
9/78 **What Have You Got To Lose** *Tom T. Hall*
50/89 **What He Does Best** *Lynn Anderson*
22/01 **What I Did Right** *Sons Of The Desert*
3/85 **What I Didn't Do** *Steve Wariner*
What I Feel In My Heart ..see: (How Can I Write On Paper)
50/79 **What I Feel Is You** *Billy The Kid*
What I Had With You
48/80 *Sheila Andrews w/ Joe Sun*
12/81 *John Conlee*
80/75 **What I Keep Sayin', Is A Lie** *Debi Hawkins*
18/83 **What I Learned From Loving You** *Lynn Anderson*
5/96 **What I Meant To Say** *Wade Hayes*
38/00 **What I Need** *Julie Reeves*
21/65 **What I Need Most** *Hugh X. Lewis*
8/00 **What I Need To Do** *Kenny Chesney*
1/01 **What I Really Meant To Say** *Cyndi Thomson*
1/89 **What I'd Say** *Earl Thomas Conley*
5/76 **What I've Got In Mind** *Billie Jo Spears*
23/98 **What If** *Reba McEntire*
26/97 **What If I Do** *Mindy McCready*
1/98 **What If I Said** *Anita Cochran w/ Steve Wariner*
57/83 **What If I Said I Love You** *Marty Robbins*
54/98 **What If I'm Right** *Shane Stockton*
67/00 **What If It's Me** *Jennifer Day*
80/86 **What If It's Right** *Family Brown*
15/97 **What If It's You** *Reba McEntire*
What If Jesus Comes Back Like That
57/95 *Collin Raye*
21/97 *Collin Raye*
2/02 **What If She's An Angel** *Tommy Shane Steiner*
70/92 **What If You're Wrong** *Ronna Reeves*
21/79 **What In Her World Did I Do** *Eddy Arnold*
19/72 **What In The World Has Gone Wrong With Our Love** *Jack Greene/Jeannie Seely*
What In The World's Come Over You
10/75 *Sonny James*
25/81 *Tom Jones*
1/47 **What Is Life Without Love** *Eddy Arnold*

3/70 **What Is Truth** *Johnny Cash*
31/04 **What It Ain't** *Josh Turner*
81/89 **What It Boils Down To** *Frank Burgess*
95/79 **What It Means To Be An American** *Billy Brown*
5/67 **What Kind Of A Girl (Do You Think I Am?)** *Loretta Lynn*
24/92 **What Kind Of Fool** *Lionel Cartwright*
2/92 **What Kind Of Fool Do You Think I Am** *Lee Roy Parnell*
44/78 **What Kind Of Fool (Do You Think I Am)** *Eddie Middleton*
97/77 **What Kind Of Fool (Does That Make Me)** *Brian Shaw*
79/89 **What Kind Of Girl Do You Think I Am** *Sandy Ellwanger*
11/92 **What Kind Of Love** *Rodney Crowell*
57/69 **What Kind Of Magic** *Les Seevers*
61/93 **What Kind Of Man** *Martin Delray*
75/95 **What Kind Of Man (Walks On A Woman)** *Marie Osmond*
4/66 **What Kinda Deal Is This** *Bill Carlisle*
71/74 **What Ladies Can Do (When They Want To)** *Dorsey Burnette*
2/67 **What Locks The Door** *Jack Greene*
55/93 **What Made You Say That** *Shania Twain*
8/58 **What Makes A Man Wander** *Jimmie Skinner*
25/65 **What Makes A Man Wander?** *Jan Howard*
70/69 **What Makes You So Different** *June Stearns*
61/82 **What Mama Don't Know** *Jim Stafford*
1/95 **What Mattered Most** *Ty Herndon*
2/93 **What Might Have Been** *Little Texas*
23/79 **What More Could A Man Need** *Tommy Overstreet*
6/73 **What My Woman Can't Do** *George Jones*
71/86 **What My Woman Does To Me** *Ray Griff*
1/93 **What Part Of No** *Lorrie Morgan*
21/04 **What Say You** *Travis Tritt w/ John Mellencamp*
What She Bottled Up In Me ..see: (I'm Just Pouring Out)
5/83 **What She Don't Know Won't Hurt Her** *Gene Watson*
1/88 **What She Is (Is A Woman In Love)** *Earl Thomas Conley*
8/85 **What She Wants** *Michael Martin Murphey*
1/92 **What She's Doing Now** *Garth Brooks*
2/94 **What The Cowgirls Do** *Vince Gill*
2/97 **What The Heart Wants** *Collin Raye*
14/03 **What The World Needs** *Wynonna*
What The World Needs Now Is Love
90/79 *Ron Shaw*
58/81 *Billie Jo Spears*
35/94 **What They're Talkin' About** *Rhett Akins*

47/99 **What This Country Needs** *Aaron Tippin*
56/90 **(What This World Needs Is) A Few More Rednecks** *Charlie Daniels Band*
9/78 **What Time Do You Have To Be Back To Heaven** *Razzy Bailey*
16/75 **What Time Of Day** *Billy Thunderkloud*
60/85 **What Used To Be Crazy** *Bama Band*
1/03 **What Was I Thinkin'** *Dierks Bentley*
74/74 **What Was Your Name Again?** *Kenny Vernon*
73/86 **What We Gonna Do** *Gus Hardin*
39/90 **What We Really Want** *Rosanne Cash*
4/66 **What We're Fighting For** *Dave Dudley*
43/02 **What We're Gonna Do About It** *Tommy Shane Steiner*
17/93 **What Were You Thinkin'** *Little Texas*
58/76 **What Will The New Year Bring?** *Donna Fargo*
32/96 **What Will You Do With M-E** *Western Flyer*
100/77 **What Would I Do Then?** *Carmol Taylor*
What Would You Do?
15/61 *Jim Reeves*
93/81 *John Rex Reeves*
54/86 **What Would You Do** *Shelly West*
What Would You Do? (If Jesus Came To Your House)
8/56 *Porter Wagoner*
15/56 *Red Sovine*
10/84 **What Would Your Memories Do** *Vern Gosdin*
52/05 **What You Ain't Gonna Get** *Lauren Lucas*
78/86 **What You Do To Me** *New Grass Revival*
8/86 **What You'll Do When I'm Gone** *Waylon Jennings*
27/61 **What'd I Say** *Jerry Lee Lewis*
37/76 **What'll I Do** *La Costa*
19/80 **What'll I Tell Virginia** *Johnny Rodriguez*
What'll You Do About Me?
76/84 *Steve Earle*
74/92 *Forester Sisters*
16/95 *Doug Supernaw*
79/79 **What're We Doing, Doing This Again** *Nick Nixon*
21/77 **What're You Doing Tonight** *Janie Fricke*
4/05 **What's A Guy Gotta Do** *Joe Nichols*
76/79 **What's A Little Love Between Friends** *Billy Burnette*
1/86 **What's A Memory Like You (Doing In A Love Like This)** *John Schneider*
87/80 **What's A Nice Girl Like You (Doin' In A Love Like This)** *Springer Brothers*
17/67 **What's Come Over My Baby** *Dottie West*
68/98 **What's Come Over You** *Paul Brandt*

1/82 **What's Forever For** *Michael Murphey*

1/89 **What's Going On In Your World** *George Strait*

67/82 **What's Good About Goodbye** *Cindy Hurt*

77/84 **What's Good For The Goose (Is Good For The Gander)** *Dottie West*

5/75 **What's Happened To Blue Eyes** *Jessi Colter*

1/65 **What's He Doing In My World** *Eddy Arnold*

5/94 **What's In It For Me** *John Berry*

20/63 **What's In Our Heart** *George Jones & Melba Montgomery*

1/93 **What's It To You** *Clay Walker*

2/68 **What's Made Milwaukee Famous (Has Made A Loser Out Of Me)** *Jerry Lee Lewis*

40/65 **What's Money** *George Jones*

11/81 **What's New With You** *Con Hunley*

47/79 **What's On Your Mind** *John Denver*

86/83 **What's She Doing To My Mind** *Johnny Bailey*

55/87 **What's So Different About You** *John Anderson*

81/81 **What's So Good About Goodbye** *Terry Aden*

93/89 **What's The Matter Baby** *Michael Shane*

41/99 **What's The Matter With You Baby** *Claudia Church*

30/78 **What's The Name Of That Song?** *Glenn Barber*

45/70 **What's The Use** *Jack Greene*

56/67 **What's This World A-Comin' To** *Slim Whitman*

1/73 **What's Your Mama's Name** *Tanya Tucker*

72/86 **What's Your Name** *Almost Brothers*

Whatcha ..also see: What Cha / What You / What U / What'Chu

75/89 **Whatcha Gonna Do About Her** *David Slater*

4/54 **Whatcha Gonna Do Now** *Tommy Collins*

7/92 **Whatcha Gonna Do With A Cowboy** *Chris LeDoux*

9/75 **Whatcha Gonna Do With A Dog Like That** *Susan Raye*

80/83 **Whatcha Got Cookin' In Your Oven Tonight** *Thrasher Brothers*

7/82 **Whatever** *Statler Brothers*

10/97 **Whatever Comes First** *Sons Of The Desert*

1/83 **Whatever Happened To Old Fashioned Love** *B.J. Thomas*

22/74 **Whatever Happened To Randolph Scott** *Statler Brothers*

55/80 **Whatever Happened To Those Drinking Songs** *Foxfire*

38/75 **Whatever I Say** *Donna Fargo*

44/03 **Whatever It Takes** *Kellie Coffey*

45/91 **Whatever It Takes** *J. P. Pennington*

59/94 **Whatever It Takes** *Kenny Chesney*

19/84 **Whatever Turns You On** *Keith Stegall*

81/82 **Whatever Turns You On** *Chantilly*

72/93 **Whatever Way The Wind Blows** *Kelly Willis*

2/99 **Whatever You Say** *Martina McBride*

16/72 **Wheel Of Fortune** *Susan Raye*

37/64 **Wheel Song** *Gary Buck*

1/88 **Wheels** *Restless Heart*

47/02 **Wheels** *Hometown News*

47/67 **Wheels Fell Off The Wagon Again** *Johnny Dollar*

77/84 **Wheels In Emotion** *Becky Hobbs*

71/91 **Wheels Of Love** *Emmylou Harris*

13/58 **When** *Kalin Twins*

15/80 **When** *Slim Whitman*

11/79 **When A Love Ain't Right** *Charly McClain*

When A Man Loves A Woman

72/76 *John Wesley Ryles*

18/82 *Jack Grayson & Blackjack*

60/87 *Narvel Felts*

3/70 **When A Man Loves A Woman (The Way That I Love You)** *Billy Walker*

32/73 **When A Man Loves A Woman (The Way That I Love You)** *Tony Booth*

20/87 **When A Woman Cries** *Janie Frickie*

When A Woman Cries

31/78 *David Rogers*

97/78 *Tommy O'Day*

12/96 **When A Woman Loves A Man** *Lee Roy Parnell*

24/95 **When And Where** *Confederate Railroad*

3/96 **When Boy Meets Girl** *Terri Clark*

5/78 **When Can We Do This Again** *T.G. Sheppard*

45/96 **When Cowboys Didn't Dance** *Lonestar*

93/89 **When Daddy Did The Driving** *Chris & Lenny*

87/89 **When Did You Stop** *Eddie Preston*

6/93 **When Did You Stop Loving Me** *George Strait*

67/77 **When Do We Stop Starting Over** *Don Gibson*

17/85 **When Givin' Up Was Easy** *Ed Bruce*

8/01 **When God-Fearin' Women Get The Blues** *Martina McBride*

57/89 **When He Leaves You** *Donna Meade*

48/71 **When He Touches Me (Nothing Else Matters)** *Lois Johnson*

11/71 **When He Walks On You (Like You Have Walked On Me)** *Jerry Lee Lewis*

66/95 **When He Was My Age** *Confederate Railroad*

2/90 **When I Call Your Name** *Vince Gill*

2/97 **When I Close My Eyes** *Kenny Chesney*

66/94 **When I Come Back (I Wanna Be My Dog)** *Greg Holland*

5/90 **When I Could Come Home To You** *Steve Wariner*

52/77 **When I Die, Just Let Me Go To Texas** *Ed Bruce*

When I Dream

F/78 *Jack Clement*

3/79 *Crystal Gayle*

53/85 **When I Get Home** *Bobby Bare*

16/74 **When I Get My Hands On You** *Diana Trask*

10/62 **When I Get Thru With You (You'll Love Me Too)** *Patsy Cline*

36/78 **When I Get You Alone** *Mundo Earwood*

53/98 **When I Grow Up** *Clint Daniels*

63/78 **When I Need You** *Lois Johnson*

1/99 **When I Said I Do** *Clint Black w/ Lisa Hartman Black*

65/97 **When I Say Forever** *Chris LeDoux*

When I Stop Dreaming

8/55 *Louvin Brothers*

88/75 *Debi Hawkins*

3/78 **When I Stop Leaving (I'll Be Gone)** *Charley Pride*

1/01 **When I Think About Angels** *Jamie O'Neal*

4/05 **When I Think About Cheatin'** *Gretchen Wilson*

66/77 **When I Touch Her There** *Jim Ed Brown*

54/68 **When I Turn Twenty-One** *Buddy Alan*

1/83 **When I'm Away From You** *Bellamy Brothers*

38/87 **When I'm Free Again** *Rodney Crowell*

34/79 **When I'm Gone** *Dottsy*

75/70 **When I'm Not Lookin'** *Liz Anderson*

54/87 **When I'm Over You (What You Gonna Do)** *Mickey Clark*

15/01 **When It All Goes South** *Alabama*

77/82 **When It Comes To Love** *Thom Bresh & Lane Brody*

3/92 **When It Comes To You** *John Anderson*

60/90 **When It Rains It Pours** *Merle Haggard*

17/86 **When It's Down To Me And You** *Charly McClain/Wayne Massey*

10/90 **When It's Gone** *Nitty Gritty Dirt Band*

When It's Just You And Me

19/77 *Dottie West*

31/81 *Kenny Dale*

26/65 **When It's Over** *Carl Smith*

39/67 **When It's Over** *Jeannie Seely*

1/59 **When It's Springtime In Alaska** *Johnny Horton*

49/88 **When Karen Comes Around** *Mason Dixon*

66/76 **When Lea Jane Sang** *Porter Wagoner*

When Love Comes Around The Bend

40/89 *Juice Newton*

51/92 *Dan Seals*

40/90 **When Love Comes Callin'** *Sawyer Brown*

71/94 **When Love Comes Callin'** *Robin Lee*

44/99 **When Love Fades** *Toby Keith*

3/94 **When Love Finds You** *Vince Gill*

44/73 **When Love Has Gone Away** *Jeannie C. Riley*
74/86 **When Love Is Right** *Charly McClain/Wayne Massey*
13/97 **When Love Starts Talkin'** *Wynonna*
31/99 **When Mama Ain't Happy** *Tracy Byrd*
6/53 **When Mexican Joe Met Jole Blon** *Hank Snow*
93/78 **When My Angel Turns Into A Devil** *Del Reeves*
When My Blue Moon Turns To Gold Again
5/44 *Cindy Walker*
11/48 *Cliffie Stone*
F/77 *Merle Haggard*
84/85 *Maines Brothers Band*
When My Conscience Hurts The Most
22/59 *Charlie Walker*
83/79 *Johnny Bush*
65/99 **When My Dreams Come True** *Rebecca Lynn Howard*
2/44 **When My Man Comes Home** *Buddy Johnson*
1/93 **When My Ship Comes In** *Clint Black*
2/44 **When My Sugar Walks Down The Street** *Ella Fitzgerald*
95/79 **When Our Love Began (Cowboys And Indians)** *George James*
9/92 **When She Cries** *Restless Heart*
75/80 **When She Falls** *Bobby Hood*
54/89 **When She Holds Me** *Larry Gatlin/Gatlin Brothers*
30/69 **When She Touches Me** *Johnny Duncan*
60/76 **When She's Got Me (Where She Wants Me)** *David Allan Coe*
37/04 **When Somebody Knows You That Well** *Blake Shelton*
5/01 **When Somebody Loves You** *Alan Jackson*
21/90 **When Somebody Loves You** *Restless Heart*
31/87 **When Something Is Good (Why Does It Change)** *Hank Williams, Jr.*
When Something Is Wrong With My Baby
6/76 *Sonny James*
67/85 *Joe Stampley*
37/98 **When The Bartender Cries** *Michael Peterson*
31/78 **When The Fire Gets Hot** *Zella Lehr*
2/69 **When The Grass Grows Over Me** *George Jones*
26/03 **When The Lights Go Down** *Faith Hill*
10/74 **When The Morning Comes** *Hoyt Axton w/ Linda Ronstadt*
87/83 **When The Music Stops** *Jerry "Max" Lane*
When The New Wears Off Of Our Love
25/77 *Jody Miller*
25/83 *Whites*
32/87 **When The Right One Comes Along** *John Schneider*
27/66 **When The Ship Hit The Sand** *"Little" Jimmy Dickens*
1/72 **When The Snow Is On The Roses** *Sonny James*
1/04 **When The Sun Goes Down** *Kenny Chesney & Uncle Kracker*
7/94 **When The Thought Of You Catches Up With Me** *David Ball*
2/76 **When The Tingle Becomes A Chill** *Loretta Lynn*
69/97 **When The Walls Come Tumblin' Down** *Billy Yates*
42/84 **When The Wild Life Betrays Me** *Jimmy Buffett*
37/65 **When The Wind Blows In Chicago** *Roy Clark*
30/64 **When The World's On Fire** *Tillman Franks Singers*
50/98 **When The Wrong One Loves You Right** *Wade Hayes*
When Two Worlds Collide
6/61 *Roger Miller*
6/69 *Jim Reeves*
11/80 *Jerry Lee Lewis*
66/91 **When Was The Last Time** *Donna Ulisse*
87/89 **When We Get Back To The Farm** *Bama Band*
49/84 **When We Get Back To The Farm** *David Frizzell*
1/84 **When We Make Love** *Alabama*
24/69 **When We Tried** *Jan Howard*
60/88 **When We're Together** *Gary Chapman*
When Will I Be Loved
1/75 *Linda Ronstadt*
75/00 *Rebel Hearts*
63/89 **When Will The Fires End** *Matt Benson*
7/51 **When You And I Were Young Maggie Blues** *Margaret Whiting & Jimmy Wakely*
7/68 **When You Are Gone** *Jim Reeves*
12/49 **When You Are Lonely** *Bill Monroe*
68/96 **When You Are Old** *Gretchen Peters*
46/03 **When You Come Around** *Deric Ruttan*
48/01 **When You Come Back Down** *Nickel Creek*
21/00 **When You Come Back To Me Again** *Garth Brooks*
14/82 **When You Fall In Love** *Johnny Lee*
14/81 **(When You Fall In Love) Everything's A Waltz** *Ed Bruce*
1/52 **(When You Feel Like You're In Love) Don't Just Stand There** *Carl Smith*
42/82 **When You Find Her, Keep Her** *Wright Brothers*
55/87 **When You Gave Your Love To Me** *Ray Price*
46/85 **When You Get A Little Lonely** *Nicolette Larson*
57/74 **When You Get Back From Nashville** *Susan Raye*
64/98 **When You Get To Be You** *Lisa Brokop*
20/86 **When You Get To The Heart** *Barbara Mandrell w/ Oak RidgeB oys*
62/85 **When You Held Me In Your Arms** *Rex Allen, Jr.*
37/86 **When You Hurt, I Hurt** *Ronnie McDowell*
60/02 **When You Kiss Me** *Shania Twain*
3/46 **When You Leave Don't Slam The Door** *Tex Ritter*
When You Leave That Way, You Can Never Go Back
77/83 *Sam Neely*
75/85 *Bill Anderson*
14/93 *Confederate Railroad*
8/02 **When You Lie Next To Me** *Kellie Coffey*
60/00 **When You Love Me** *Tim Rushlow*
37/99 **When You Love Someone** *Sammy Kershaw*
47/64 **When You Need A Laugh** *Patsy Cline*
15/00 **When You Need My Love** *Darryl Worley*
26/88 **When You Put Your Heart In It** *Kenny Rogers*
6/72 **When You Say Love** *Bob Luman*
When You Say Nothing At All
1/88 *Keith Whitley*
3/95 *Alison Krauss & Union Station*
28/03 **When You Think Of Me** *Mark Wills*
When You Walk In The Room
29/81 *Stephanie Winslow*
2/94 *Pam Tillis*
When You Were Blue And I Was Green
21/82 *Kin Vassy*
72/86 *Joe Stampley*
38/91 **When You Were Mine** *Shenandoah*
1/71 **When You're Hot, You're Hot** *Jerry Reed*
21/69 **When You're Hot You're Hot** *Porter Wagoner*
When You're In Love ..see: (That's What You Do)
68/79 **When You're In Love With A Beautiful Woman** *Dr. Hook*
16/83 **When You're Not A Lady** *Jim Glaser*
55/69 **When You're Seventeen** *Jimmy Dickens*
54/71 **When You're Twenty-One** *Claude King*
31/80 **When You're Ugly Like Us** *George Jones & Johnny Paycheck*
When Your Good Love Was Mine
14/74 *Narvel Felts*
92/77 *Marie Owens*
48/87 **When Your Yellow Brick Road Turns Blue** *John Anderson*
2/94 **Whenever You Come Around** *Vince Gill*
23/92 **Wher'm I Gonna Live?** *Billy Ray Cyrus*
89/80 **Where Are We Going From Here** *Cooter Daniel*
26/01 **Where Are You Christmas?** *Faith Hill*
18/77 **Where Are You Going, Billy Boy** *Bill Anderson & Mary Lou Turner*
1/91 **Where Are You Now** *Clint Black*

45/00 **Where Are You Now**
Trisha Yearwood
10/83 **Where Are You Spending Your Nights These Days**
David Frizzell
48/00 **Where Can I Surrender**
Randy Travis
92/81 **Where Cheaters Go** *Ben Marney*
Where Corn Don't Grow
67/90 *Waylon Jennings*
6/97 *Travis Tritt*
14/67 **Where Could I Go? (But To Her)**
David Houston
58/80 **Where Could You Take Me**
Sheila Andrews
79/83 **Where Did He Go Right** *Roy Head*
1/89 **Where Did I Go Wrong**
Steve Wariner
80/80 **Where Did The Money Go**
Hoyt Axton
53/89 **Where Did The Moon Go Wrong**
Daniele Alexander
55/71 **Where Did They Go, Lord**
Elvis Presley
74/84 **Where Did We Go Right**
Russell Smith
74/71 **(Where Do I Begin) Love Story**
Roy Clark
11/94 **Where Do I Fit In The Picture**
Clay Walker
87/87 **Where Do I Go From Here**
Al Garrison
42/96 **Where Do I Go To Start All Over**
Wade Hayes
1/79 **Where Do I Put Her Memory**
Charley Pride
1/88 **Where Do The Nights Go**
Ronnie Milsap
78/83 **Where Do You Go** *Streetfeet*
69/69 **Where Do You Go (When You Don't Go With Me)**
Ernie Ashworth
10/64 **Where Does A Little Tear Come From** *George Jones*
43/84 **Where Does An Angel Go When She Cries** *Osmond Brothers*
33/01 **Where Does It Hurt**
Warren Brothers
77/89 **Where Does Love Go (When It Dies)** *Jack Quist*
54/88 **Where Does Love Go (When It's Gone)** *Janie Frickie*
1/67 **Where Does The Good Times Go**
Buck Owens
40/92 **Where Forever Begins**
Neal McCoy
28/70 **Where Grass Won't Grow**
George Jones
6/70 **Where Have All Our Heroes Gone**
Bill Anderson
14/69 **Where Have All The Average People Gone** *Roger Miller*
(Where Have All The Good Times Gone) ..see: Hey Daisy
65/78 **Where Have You Been All Of My Life** *Roy Clark*
57/68 **Where He Stops Nobody Knows**
June Stearns
26/75 **Where He's Going, I've Already Been** *Hank Williams, Jr.*
37/04 **Where I Belong** *Rachel Proctor*
1/01 **Where I Come From** *Alan Jackson*

9/62 **Where I Ought To Be**
Skeeter Davis
49/95 **Where I Used To Have A Heart**
Martina McBride
11/71 **Where Is My Castle** *Connie Smith*
15/66 **Where Is The Circus**
Hank Thompson
83/77 **Where Lonely People Go**
Eddy Arnold
5/75 **Where Love Begins** *Gene Watson*
2/68 **Where Love Used To Live**
David Houston
3/01 **Where The Blacktop Ends**
Keith Urban
10/69 **Where The Blue And Lonely Go**
Roy Drusky
34/69 **Where The Blue Of The Night Meets The Gold Of The Day**
Hank Locklin
1/98 **Where The Green Grass Grows**
Tim McGraw
88/73 **Where The Lilacs Grow**
Slim Whitman
15/62 **Where The Old Red River Flows**
Jimmie Davis
72/88 **Where The Rocky Mountains Touch The Morning Sun**
Randy Vanwarmer
2/02 **Where The Stars And Stripes And The Eagle Fly** *Aaron Tippin*
63/82 **Where The Sun Don't Shine**
Ray Stevens
Where There's Smoke
71/89 *Jason D. Williams*
29/94 *Archer/Park*
35/82 **Where There's Smoke There's Fire**
Louise Mandrell & R.C. Bannon
20/94 **Where Was I** *Ricky Van Shelton*
49/88 **Where Was I** *Charley Pride*
91/89 **Where Was I** *Ray Pack*
70/88 **Where Were You When I Was Blue** *Razorback*
1/01 **Where Were You (When The World Stopped Turning)**
Alan Jackson
F/82 **Where Would I Be**
Mel Tillis & Nancy Sinatra
3/02 **Where Would You Be**
Martina McBride
95/89 **Where You Gonna Hang Your Hat**
Sylvie & Her Silver Dollar Band
18/98 **Where Your Road Leads**
Trisha Yearwood w/ Garth Brooks
41/74 **Where'd I Come From**
Bobby Bare
49/84 **Where'd That Woman Go**
Mel McDaniel
Where'd Ya Stay Last Night
14/66 *Webb Pierce*
78/83 *Tommy St. John*
8/84 **Where's The Dress**
Moe Bandy & Joe Stampley
67/87 **Where's The Fire** *Susie Allanson*
28/69 **Where's The Playground Susie**
Glen Campbell
10/90 **Where've You Been** *Kathy Mattea*
20/73 **Wherefore And Why**
Glen Campbell
49/94 **Wherever She Is**
Ricky Van Shelton

31/69 **Wherever You Are**
Johnny Paycheck
45/98 **Wherever You Are** *Mark Chesnutt*
55/99 **Wherever You Are**
Mary Chapin Carpenter
81/83 **Wherever You Are**
Thrasher Brothers
75/95 **Wherever You Are Tonight**
Keith Whitley
3/95 **Wherever You Go** *Clint Black*
4/95 **Which Bridge To Cross (Which Bridge To Burn)** *Vince Gill*
4/59 **Which One Is To Blame**
Wilburn Brothers
19/69 **Which One Will It Be** *Bobby Bare*
28/89 **Which Way Do I Go (Now That I'm Gone)** *Waylon Jennings*
31/80 **While I Was Makin' Love To You**
Susie Allanson
43/69 **While I'm Thinkin' About It**
Billy Mize
57/80 **While The Choir Sang The Hymn (I Thought Of Her)**
Johnny Russell
While The Feeling's Good
56/75 *Mike Lunsford*
46/76 *Kenny Rogers*
63/89 *Wayne Newton w/ Tammy Wynette*
26/81 **While The Feeling's Good**
Rex Allen, Jr. & Margo Smith
47/86 **While The Moon's In Town**
Shoppe
7/01 **While You Loved Me**
Rascal Flatts
46/98 **While You Sleep** *Tracy Lawrence*
21/66 **While You're Dancing**
Marty Robbins
25/69 **While Your Lover Sleeps**
Leon Ashley
69/78 **Whine, Whistle, Whine**
John Anderson
47/65 **Whirlpool (Of Your Love)**
Claude King
2/92 **Whiskey Ain't Workin'**
Travis Tritt & Marty Stuart
2/79 **Whiskey Bent And Hell Bound**
Hank Williams, Jr.
18/81 **Whiskey Chasin'** *Joe Stampley*
1/04 **Whiskey Girl** *Toby Keith*
51/81 **Whiskey Heaven** *Fats Domino*
2/87 **Whiskey, If You Were A Woman**
Highway 101
3/04 **Whiskey Lullaby**
Brad Paisley/Alison Krauss
76/82 **Whiskey Made Me Stumble (The Devil Made Me Fall)**
Bill Anderson
Whiskey River
14/72 *Johnny Bush*
12/79 *Willie Nelson*
92/81 *Johnny Bush*
84/89 **Whiskey River You Win**
Pat Minter
48/70 **Whiskey-Six Years Old**
Norma Jean
18/76 **Whiskey Talkin'** *Joe Stampley*
16/78 **Whiskey Trip** *Gary Stewart*
5/95 **Whiskey Under The Bridge**
Brooks & Dunn
Whiskey Was A River ..see: (I Remember When I Thought)

31/70 **Whiskey, Whiskey** *Nat Stuckey*
10/81 **Whisper** *Lacy J. Dalton*
57/78 **Whisper It To Me** *Bobby G. Rice*
1/94 **Whisper My Name** *Randy Travis*
84/78 **Whispering** *Maury Finney*
15/58 **Whispering Rain** *Hank Snow*
12/77 **Whispers** *Bobby Borchers*
66/76 **Whispers And Grins** *David Rogers*
86/74 **Whistle Stop** *Roger Miller*
28/65 **Whistle Walkin'** *Ned Miller*
White Christmas
7/50 *Ernest Tubb*
70/95 *Garth Brooks*
65/00 *Garth Brooks*
75/00 *Martina McBride*
62/01 *Martina McBride*
1/46 **White Cross On Okinawa** *Bob Wills*
25/68 **White Fences And Evergreen Trees** *Ferlin Husky*
72/88 **White Freight Liner Blues** *Jimmie Dale Gilmore*
49/89 **White Houses** *Charley Pride*
1/76 **White Knight** *Cledus Maggard*
21/65 **White Lightnin' Express** *Roy Drusky*
1/59 **White Lightning** *George Jones*
29/90 **White Limozeen** *Dolly Parton*
14/85 **White Line** *Emmylou Harris*
White Line Fever
68/72 *Buddy Alan*
95/80 *Flying Burrito Brothers*
67/94 **White Palace** *Clay Walker*
5/72 **White Silver Sands** *Sonny James*
1/57 **White Sport Coat (And A Pink Carnation)** *Marty Robbins*
56/02 **White Trash Wedding** *Dixie Chicks*
62/69 **Who Am I** *Red Sovine*
3/78 **Who Am I To Say** *Statler Brothers*
55/89 **Who But You** *Anne Murray*
3/59 **Who Cares** *Don Gibson*
60/84 **Who Dat** *David Frizzell*
56/92 **Who Did They Think He Was** *Conway Twitty*
64/69 **Who Do I Know In Dallas** *Kenny Price*
13/65 **Who Do I Think I Am** *Webb Pierce*
11/82 **Who Do You Know In California** *Eddy Raven*
67/91 **Who Got Our Love** *John Anderson*
96/89 **Who Have You Got To Lose** *Ernie Welch*
1/01 **Who I Am** *Jessica Andrews*
56/01 **Who I Am To You** *Coley McCabe*
10/74 **Who Left The Door To Heaven Open** *Hank Thompson*
41/66 **Who Licked The Red Off Your Candy** *"Little" Jimmy Dickens*
64/69 **Who Loves You** *Hardens*
6/48 **Who? Me?** *Tex Williams*
29/92 **Who Needs It** *Clinton Gregory*
12/99 **Who Needs Pictures** *Brad Paisley*
60/95 **Who Needs You** *Lisa Brokop*
73/89 **Who Needs You** *Sanders*
2/95 **Who Needs You Baby** *Clay Walker*
68/83 **Who Said Love Was Fair** *Billy Parker*
4/94 **(Who Says) You Can't Have It All** *Alan Jackson*
91/80 **Who Shot J.R.?** *Gary Burbank*
50/70 **Who Shot John** *Wanda Jackson*
7/59 **Who Shot Sam** *George Jones*
53/76 **Who Wants A Slightly Used Woman** *Connie Cato*
57/88 **Who Was That Stranger** *Loretta Lynn*
40/79 **(Who Was The Man Who Put) The Line In Gasoline** *Jerry Reed*
54/80 **Who Were You Thinkin' Of** *Doolittle Band*
51/92 **Who, What, Where, When, Why, How** *Martin Delray*
69/68 **Who Will Answer? (Aleluya No. 1)** *Hank Snow*
11/60 **Who Will Buy The Wine** *Charlie Walker*
91/75 **Who Will I Be Loving Now** *Carmol Taylor*
Who Will The Next Fool Be
67/70 *Charlie Rich*
20/79 *Jerry Lee Lewis*
1/03 **Who Wouldn't Wanna Be Me** *Keith Urban*
2/89 **Who You Gonna Blame It On This Time** *Vern Gosdin*
Who'll Turn Out The Lights
57/71 *Wayne Kemp*
36/80 *Mel Street*
69/89 *Ronnie McDowell*
27/63 **Who's Been Cheatin' Who** *Johnny & Jonie Mosby*
87/76 **Who's Been Here Since I've Been Gone** *Hank Snow*
43/66 **Who's Been Mowing The Lawn (While I Was Gone)** *Ray Pennington*
88/82 **Who's Been Sleeping In My Bed** *Diana*
Who's Cheatin' Who
1/81 *Charly McClain*
2/97 *Alan Jackson*
58/95 **Who's Counting** *Wesley Dennis*
82/84 **Who's Counting** *Marie Osmond*
3/85 **Who's Gonna Fill Their Shoes** *George Jones*
37/83 **Who's Gonna Keep Me Warm** *Phil Everly*
51/90 **Who's Gonna Know** *Conway Twitty*
1/69 **Who's Gonna Mow Your Grass** *Buck Owens*
14/72 **Who's Gonna Play This Old Piano** *Jerry Lee Lewis*
75/76 **Who's Gonna Run The Truck Stop In Tuba City When I'm Gone?** *Leroy Van Dyke*
41/82 **(Who's Gonna Sing) The Last Country Song** *Billy Parker*
18/69 **Who's Gonna Take The Garbage Out** *Ernest Tubb & Loretta Lynn*
61/90 **Who's Gonna Tell Her Goodbye** *Earl Thomas Conley*
97/78 **Who's Gonna Tie My Shoes** *Ray Pillow*
65/67 **Who's Gonna Walk The Dog (And Put Out The Cat)** *Ray Pennington*
10/69 **Who's Julie** *Mel Tillis*
62/86 **Who's Leaving Who** *Anne Murray*
1/90 **Who's Lonely Now** *Highway 101*
66/89 **Who's Lovin' My Baby** *John Anderson*
64/95 **Who's She To You** *Amie Comeaux*
29/75 **Who's Sorry Now** *Marie Osmond*
32/96 **Who's That Girl** *Stephanie Bentley*
1/94 **Who's That Man** *Toby Keith*
37/85 **Who's The Blonde Stranger?** *Jimmy Buffett*
1/02 **Who's Your Daddy?** *Toby Keith*
6/49 **Whoa Sailor** *Hank Thompson*
43/70 **Whoever Finds This, I Love You** *Mac Davis*
14/75 **Whoever Turned You On, Forgot To Turn You Off** *Little David Wilkins*
1/86 **Whoever's In New England** *Reba McEntire*
63/81 **Whole Lot Of Cheatin' Goin' On** *Jimmi Cannon*
1/57 **Whole Lot Of Shakin' Going On** *Jerry Lee Lewis*
18/72 **Whole Lot Of Somethin'** *Tony Booth*
65/75 **Whole Lotta Difference In Love** *George Kent*
23/96 **Whole Lotta Gone** *Joe Diffie*
18/91 **Whole Lotta Holes** *Kathy Mattea*
66/98 **Whole Lotta Hurt** *Brady Seals*
30/94 **Whole Lotta Love On The Line** *Aaron Tippin*
61/71 **Whole Lotta Lovin'** *Anita Carter*
22/73 **Whole Lotta Loving** *Hank Williams, Jr. & Lois Johnson*
2/76 **Whole Lotta Things To Sing About** *Charley Pride*
15/58 **Whole Lotta Woman** *Marvin Rainwater*
80/87 **Whole Month Of Sundays** *Jenny Yates*
14/70 **Whole World Comes To Me** *Jack Greene*
27/70 **Whole World Holding Hands** *Freddie Hart*
10/84 **Whole World's In Love When You're Lonely** *B.J. Thomas*
13/73 **Whole World's Making Love Again Tonight** *Bobby G. Rice*
59/88 **Whose Baby Are You** *Ric Steel*
11/95 **Whose Bed Have Your Boots Been Under?** *Shania Twain*
7/55 **Whose Shoulder Will You Cry On** *Kitty Wells*
24/03 **Why Ain't I Running** *Garth Brooks*
75/81 **Why Am I Doing Without** *Wayne Kemp*
Why Baby Why
4/55 *George Jones*
1/56 *Red Sovine & Webb Pierce*
9/56 *Hank Locklin*
23/61 *Warren Smith & Shirley Collie*
95/78 *Jerry Inman*
1/83 *Charley Pride*
46/93 *Palomino Road*
64/73 **Why, Because I Love You** *Buddy Alan*
7/77 **Why Can't He Be You** *Loretta Lynn*
36/04 **Why Can't We All Just Get A Long Neck?** *Hank Williams, Jr.*

46/96 **Why Can't You** *Larry Stewart*
49/66 **Why Can't You Feel Sorry For Me** *Carl Smith*
F/79 **Why Did You Have To Be So Good** *Dave & Sugar*
1/93 **Why Didn't I Think Of That** *Doug Stone*
Why Didn't I Think Of That
F/82 *Dave Rowland*
67/85 *Malchak & Rucker*
88/77 **Why Didn't I Think Of That** *Gene Simmons*
3/83 **Why Do I Have To Choose** *Willie Nelson*
45/66 **Why Do I Keep Doing This To Us** *Carl Smith*
F/70 **Why Do I Love You (Melody Of Love)** *Jim Reeves*
7/83 **Why Do We Want (What We Know We Can't Have)** *Reba McEntire*
97/78 **Why Do You Come Around** *Lyndel East*
53/68 **Why Do You Do Me Like You Do** *Sammi Smith*
1/87 **Why Does It Have To Be (Wrong Or Right)** *Restless Heart*
25/63 **Why Don't Daddy Live Here Anymore** *Bonnie Owens*
39/93 **Why Don't That Telephone Ring** *Tracy Byrd*
51/72 **Why Don't We Go Somewhere And Love** *Sandy Posey*
85/81 **Why Don't We Just Sleep On It Tonight** *Glen Campbell & Tanya Tucker*
94/79 **Why Don't We Lie Down And Talk It Over** *Jerry Inman*
92/80 **Why Don't You Believe Me** *Donna Stark*
93/80 **Why Don't You Go To Dallas** *Peggy Sue*
Why Don't You Haul Off And Love Me
1/49 *Wayne Raney*
5/49 *Mervin Shiner*
9/49 *Bob Atcher*
99/78 **Why Don't You Leave Me Alone** *Joey Davis*
Why Don't You Love Me
1/50 *Hank Williams*
15/75 *Connie Smith*
61/76 *Hank Williams*
1/80 **Why Don't You Spend The Night** *Ronnie Milsap*
12/84 **Why Goodbye** *Steve Wariner*
1/79 **Why Have You Left The One You Left Me For** *Crystal Gayle*
5/94 **Why Haven't I Heard From You** *Reba McEntire*
15/87 **Why I Don't Know** *Lyle Lovett*
Why I'm Walkin'
6/60 *Stonewall Jackson*
33/88 *Ricky Skaggs*
1/80 **Why Lady Why** *Alabama*
4/84 **Why Lady Why** *Gary Morris*
8/77 **Why Lovers Turn To Strangers** *Freddie Hart*
1/73 **Why Me** *Kris Kristofferson*
1/84 **Why Not Me** *Judds*
30/80 **Why Not Me** *Fred Knoblock*
58/85 **Why Not Tonight** *Atlanta*
69/77 **Why Not Tonight** *Jacky Ward*
3/50 **Why Should I Cry?** *Eddy Arnold*
45/66 **Why Should I Cry Over You** *Freddie Hart*
9/50 **Why Should We Try Anymore** *Hank Williams*
13/01 **Why They Call It Falling** *Lee Ann Womack*
45/95 **Why Walk When You Can Fly** *Mary Chapin Carpenter*
2/57 **Why, Why** *Carl Smith*
8/97 **Why Would I Say Goodbye** *Brooks & Dunn*
77/85 **Why Would I Want To Forget** *Joe Sun*
Why You Been Gone So Long
17/69 *Johnny Darrell*
69/83 *Jerry Lee Lewis*
50/86 *Brenda Lee*
95/79 **Why'd The Last Time Have To Be The Best** *Ronnie Robbins*
1/89 **Why'd You Come In Here Lookin' Like That** *Dolly Parton*
43/98 **Why'd You Start Lookin' So Good** *Monty Holmes*
22/76 **Wichita Jail** *Charlie Daniels Band*
Wichita Lineman
1/68 *Glen Campbell*
55/97 *Wade Hayes*
24/69 **Wicked California** *Tompall/Glaser Brothers*
9/56 **Wicked Lies** *Carl Smith*
13/48 **Wicked Path Of Sin** *Bill Monroe*
49/87 **Wicked Ways** *Patty Loveless*
1/98 **Wide Open Spaces** *Dixie Chicks*
19/64 **Widow Maker** *Jimmy Martin*
45/64 **Wife, Th'** *John D. Loudermilk*
22/67 **Wife Of The Party** *Liz Anderson*
16/77 **Wiggle Wiggle** *Ronnie Sessions*
1/82 **Wild And Blue** *John Anderson*
1/96 **Wild Angels** *Martina McBride*
8/65 **Wild As A Wildcat** *Charlie Walker*
65/98 **Wild As The Wind** *Garth Brooks w/ Trisha Yearwood*
52/96 **Wild At Heart** *Lari White*
18/68 **Wild Blood** *Del Reeves*
21/80 **Wild Bull Rider** *Hoyt Axton*
24/87 **Wild-Eyed Dream** *Ricky Van Shelton*
99/78 **Wild Honey** *Bellamy Brothers*
7/01 **Wild Horses** *Garth Brooks*
73/94 **Wild Love** *Joy Lynn White*
5/93 **Wild Man** *Ricky Van Shelton*
14/83 **Wild Montana Skies** *John Denver & Emmylou Harris*
1/94 **Wild One** *Faith Hill*
Wild River ..see: Ballad Of
Wild Side Of Life
1/52 *Hank Thompson*
6/52 *Burl Ives & Grady Martin*
13/76 *Freddy Fender*
78/76 *Maury Finney*
60/79 *Rayburn Anthony w/ Kitty Wells*
10/81 *Waylon Jennings & Jessi Colter (medley)*
Wild Side Of Me ..see: (You Bring Out)
79/88 **Wild Texas Rose** *Billy Walker*
F/82 **Wild Turkey** *Lacy J. Dalton*
2/68 **Wild Week-End** *Bill Anderson*
21/04 **Wild West Show** *Big & Rich*
15/63 **Wild Wild Wind** *Stonewall Jackson*
77/76 **Wild World** *Mike Wells*
9/88 **Wilder Days** *Baillie & The Boys*
6/88 **Wildflowers** *Dolly Parton/ Linda Ronstadt/Emmylou Harris*
Wildwood Flower
5/55 *Hank Thompson w/ Merle Travis*
100/79 *Tommy Wills*
55/83 *Roy Clark*
57/74 **Wildwood Weed** *Jim Stafford*
7/84 **Will It Be Love By Morning** *Michael Murphey*
5/49 **Will Santy Come To Shanty Town** *Eddy Arnold*
5/86 **Will The Wolf Survive** *Waylon Jennings*
37/91 **Will This Be The Day** *Desert Rose Band*
69/98 **Will You Be Here** *Anita Cochran*
97/85 **Will You Love Me In The Morning** *Clifton Jansky*
Will You Love Me Tomorrow
74/71 *Lynda K. Lance*
69/75 *Jody Miller*
56/87 *Cheryl Handy*
41/01 **Will You Marry Me** *Alabama*
67/78 **Will You Remember Mine** *Willie Nelson*
20/68 **Will You Visit Me On Sundays?** *Charlie Louvin*
8/62 **Will Your Lawyer Talk To God** *Kitty Wells*
64/94 **William And Mary** *Davis Daniel*
91/78 **Willie** *Hank Cochran w/ Merle Haggard*
43/70 **Willie And The Hand Jive** *Johnny Carver*
19/81 **Willie Jones** *Bobby Bare*
72/00 **Willie Nelson For President** *Peter Dawson Band*
5/62 **Willie The Weeper** *Billy Walker*
25/76 **Willie, Waylon And Me** *David Allan Coe*
66/81 **Willie, Won't You Sing A Song With Me** *George Burns*
72/83 **Willie, Write Me A Song** *Ray Price*
54/95 **Willin' To Walk** *Radney Foster*
10/62 **Willingly** *Willie Nelson & Shirley Collie*
46/80 **Willow Run** *Randy Barlow*
23/61 **Willow Tree** *Ferlin Husky*
10/71 **Willy Jones** *Susan Raye*
4/83 **Wind Beneath My Wings** *Gary Morris*
60/67 **Wind Changes** *Johnny Cash*
65/94 **Wind In The Wire** *Randy Travis*
20/81 **Wind Is Bound To Change** *Larry Gatlin/Gatlin Brothers*
54/83 **Windin' Down** *Lacy J. Dalton*
65/70 **Window Number Five** *Johnny Duncan*
Window Up Above
2/61 *George Jones*
1/75 *Mickey Gilley*
14/65 **Wine** *Mel Tillis*
10/86 **Wine Colored Roses** *George Jones*
44/99 **Wine Into Water** *T. Graham Brown*

Wine Me Up
2/69 *Faron Young*
19/89 *Larry Boone*
1/46 **Wine, Women And Song** *Al Dexter*
3/64 **Wine Women And Song** *Loretta Lynn*
70/94 **Wing And A Prayer** *Marc Beeson*
1/60 **Wings Of A Dove** *Ferlin Husky*
11/70 **Wings Upon Your Horns** *Loretta Lynn*
1/94 **Wink** *Neal McCoy*
13/76 **Winner, The** *Bobby Bare*
26/79 **Winners And Losers** *R.C. Bannon*
58/85 **Wino The Clown** *Bill Anderson*
Winter Wonderland
70/99 *Dolly Parton (medley)*
72/00 *Lonestar*
57/03 *Brooks & Dunn*
43/04 *Pat Green*
87/78 **Wipe You From My Eyes (Gettin' Over You)** *King Edward IV & The Knights*
8/79 **Wisdom Of A Fool** *Jacky Ward*
62/98 **Wish, The** *Blake & Brian*
2/70 **Wish I Didn't Have To Miss You** *Jack Greene & Jeannie Seely*
2/94 **Wish I Didn't Know Now** *Toby Keith*
60/72 **Wish I Was A Little Boy Again** *LaWanda Lindsey*
54/71 **Wish I Was Home Instead** *Van Trevor*
61/66 **Wish Me A Rainbow** *Hugh X. Lewis*
1/99 **Wish You Were Here** *Mark Wills*
2/81 **Wish You Were Here** *Barbara Mandrell*
83/86 **Wishful Dreamin'** *Michael Shamblin*
22/84 **Wishful Drinkin'** *Atlanta*
83/80 **Wishful Drinkin'** *Diane Pfeifer*
5/60 **Wishful Thinking** *Wynn Stewart*
32/79 **Wishing I Had Listened To Your Song** *Bobby Borchers*
F/80 **Wishing Well** *Tammy Jo*
7/65 **Wishing Well (Down In The Well)** *Hank Snow*
56/91 **With Body And Soul** *Kentucky Headhunters*
24/71 **With His Hand In Mine** *Jean Shepard*
68/77 **With His Pants In His Hand** *Jerry Reed*
5/85 **With Just One Look In Your Eyes** *Charly McClain/Wayne Massey*
10/78 **With Love** *Rex Allen, Jr.*
10/01 **With Me** *Lonestar*
1/67 **With One Exception** *David Houston*
3/68 **With Pen In Hand** *Johnny Darrell*
1/45 **With Tears In My Eyes** *Wesley Tuttle*
32/82 **With Their Kind Of Money And Our Kind Of Love** *Billy Swan*
31/91 **With This Ring** *T. Graham Brown*
7/83 **With You** *Charly McClain*
9/99 **With You** *Lila McCann*
33/86 **With You** *Vince Gill*
74/72 **Within My Loving Arms** *Kenni Huskey*
11/84 **Without A Song** *Willie Nelson*
50/88 **Without A Trace** *Marie Osmond*
78/81 **Without Love** *Johnny Cash*
1/01 **Without You** *Dixie Chicks*
Without You
79/79 *Susie Allanson*
12/83 *T.G. Sheppard*
50/76 **Without You** *Jessi Colter*
92/81 **Without You** *Buck Owens*
2/92 **(Without You) What Do I Do With Me** *Tanya Tucker*
10/56 **Without Your Love** *Bobby Lord*
22/96 **Without Your Love** *Aaron Tippin*
13/76 **Without Your Love (Mr. Jordan)** *Charlie Ross*
1/84 **Woke Up In Love** *Exile*
12/75 **Wolf Creek Pass** *C.W. McCall*
1/62 **Wolverton Mountain** *Claude King*
55/76 **Woman** *David Wills*
2/71 **Woman Always Knows** *David Houston*
4/92 **Woman Before Me** *Trisha Yearwood*
92/77 **Woman Behind The Man Behind The Wheel** *Red Sovine*
16/58 **Woman Captured Me** *Hank Snow*
38/76 **Woman Don't Try To Sing My Song** *Cal Smith*
58/73 **Woman Ease My Mind** *Claude Gray*
62/00 **Woman Gets Lonely** *Lisa Angelle*
15/66 **Woman Half My Age** *Kitty Wells*
24/68 **Woman Hungry** *Porter Wagoner*
9/57 **Woman I Need** *Johnny Horton*
1/89 **Woman In Love** *Ronnie Milsap*
4/67 **Woman In Love** *Bonnie Guitar*
3/81 **Woman In Me** *Crystal Gayle*
14/95 **Woman In Me (Needs The Man In You)** *Shania Twain*
74/81 **Woman In My Heart** *Bobby Hood*
4/75 **Woman In The Back Of My Mind** *Mel Tillis*
48/69 **Woman In Your Life** *Wilma Burgess*
Woman Left Lonely
72/71 *Charlie Rich*
F/71 *Patti Page*
54/97 **Woman Like You** *Matt King*
17/70 **Woman Lives For Love** *Wanda Jackson*
9/92 **Woman Loves** *Steve Wariner*
64/67 **Woman Needs Love** *Marion Worth*
52/66 **Woman Never Forgets** *Kitty Wells*
58/86 **Woman Of The 80's** *Donna Fargo*
1/69 **Woman Of The World (Leave My World Alone)** *Loretta Lynn*
35/75 **Woman On My Mind** *David Houston*
Woman (Sensuous Woman)
1/72 *Don Gibson*
21/94 *Mark Chesnutt*
54/76 **Woman Stealer** *Bobby G. Rice*
Woman To Woman
4/74 *Tammy Wynette*
62/98 *Wynonna*
4/78 **Woman To Woman** *Barbara Mandrell*
43/98 **Woman To Woman** *Lynns*
2/04 **Woman With You** *Kenny Chesney*
29/73 **Woman Without A Home** *Statler Brothers*
20/69 **Woman Without Love** *Johnny Darrell*
43/75 **Woman, Woman** *Jim Glaser*
12/84 **Woman Your Love** *Moe Bandy*
Woman's Hand
66/69 *Barbara Fairchild*
23/70 *Jean Shepard*
9/59 **Woman's Intuition** *Wilburn Brothers*
72/90 **Woman's Intuition** *Michelle Wright*
59/69 **Woman's Side Of Love** *Lynda K. Lance*
46/98 **Woman's Tears** *Matt King*
6/96 **Woman's Touch** *Toby Keith*
16/82 **Woman's Touch** *Tom Jones*
70/79 **Woman's Touch** *Glenn Barber*
80/89 **Woman's Way** *Mundo Earwood*
3/78 **Womanhood** *Tammy Wynette*
57/91 **Women** *Bandit Brothers*
74/81 **Women** *Wyvon Alexander*
9/66 **Women Do Funny Things To Me** *Del Reeves*
4/82 **Women Do Know How To Carry On** *Waylon Jennings*
18/80 **Women Get Lonely** *Charly McClain*
5/80 **Women I've Never Had** *Hank Williams, Jr.*
Women In Love
59/82 *Kin Vassy*
55/85 *Bill Medley*
65/81 **Won't You Be My Baby** *Keith Stegall*
Won't You Come Home (And Talk To A Stranger)
61/69 *Wayne Kemp*
70/97 *George Strait*
1/70 **Wonder Could I Live There Anymore** *Charley Pride*
37/70 **Wonder Of You** *Elvis Presley*
39/75 **Wonder When My Baby's Comin' Home** *Barbara Mandrell*
51/68 **Wonderful Day** *Ray Pillow*
Wonderful Tonight
66/89 *Butch Baker*
29/98 *David Kersh*
14/68 **Wonderful World Of Women** *Faron Young*
1/52 **Wondering** *Webb Pierce*
6/70 **Wonders Of The Wine** *David Houston*
5/71 **Wonders You Perform** *Tammy Wynette*
41/64 **Wooden Soldier** *Hank Locklin*
10/75 **Word Games** *Billy Walker*
8/79 **Words** *Susie Allanson*
12/94 **Words By Heart** *Billy Ray Cyrus*
63/73 **Words Don't Come Easy** *David Frizzell*
73/72 **Words Don't Fit The Picture** *Willie Nelson*
10/67 **Words I'm Gonna Have To Eat** *Bill Phillips*
3/02 **Work In Progress** *Alan Jackson*
55/90 **Work Song** *Corbin/Hanner*
Workin' At The Car Wash Blues
27/74 *Tony Booth*
F/80 *Jerry Reed*
40/95 **Workin' For The Weekend** *Ken Mellons*

86/83 **Workin' In A Coalmine** *Bob Jenkins*
21/64 **Workin' It Out** *Flatt & Scruggs*
50/96 **Workin' It Out** *Daryle Singletary*
Workin' Man Blues
1/69 *Merle Haggard*
48/95 *Jed Zeppelin*
4/88 **Workin' Man (Nowhere To Go)** *Nitty Gritty Dirt Band*
69/92 **Workin' Man's Dollar** *Chris LeDoux*
30/80 **Workin' My Way To Your Heart** *Dickey Lee*
37/73 **Workin' On A Feelin'** *Tommy Cash*
73/73 **Working Class Hero** *Tommy Roe*
16/86 **Working Class Man** *Lacy J. Dalton*
75/95 **Working Elf Blues** *Daron Norwood*
62/91 **Working For The Japanese** *Ray Stevens*
F/81 **Working Girl** *Dolly Parton*
33/71 **Working Like The Devil (For The Lord)** *Del Reeves*
7/85 **Working Man** *John Conlee*
16/77 **Working Man Can't Get Nowhere Today** *Merle Haggard*
7/93 **Working Man's Ph.D.** *Aaron Tippin*
59/67 **Working Man's Prayer** *Tex Ritter*
7/86 **Working Without A Net** *Waylon Jennings*
28/92 **Working Woman** *Rob Crosby*
23/70 **World Called You** *David Rogers*
90/77 **World Famous Holiday Inn** *Buck Owens*
10/66 **World Is Round** *Roy Drusky*
29/64 **World Lost A Man** *David Price*
26/05 **World Needs A Drink** *Terri Clark*
World Needs A Melody
32/71 *Red Lane*
35/72 *Carter Family w/ Johnny Cash*
1/74 **World Of Make Believe** *Bill Anderson*
1/68 **World Of Our Own** *Sonny James*
World So Full Of Love
18/60 *Ray Sanders*
28/61 *Faron Young*
66/68 **World The Way I Want It** *Tom T. Hall*
19/69 **World-Wide Travelin' Man** *Wynn Stewart*
10/85 **World Without Love** *Eddie Rabbitt*
14/72 **World Without Music** *Porter Wagoner*
52/67 **World's Biggest Whopper** *Junior Samples*
6/84 **World's Greatest Lover** *Bellamy Brothers*
18/79 **World's Most Perfect Woman** *Ronnie McDowell*
46/66 **World's Worse Loser** *George Jones*
5/96 **Worlds Apart** *Vince Gill*
47/64 **Worst Of Luck** *Bobby Barnett*
30/76 **(Worst You Ever Gave Me Was) The Best I Ever Had** *Faron Young*
30/93 **Worth Every Mile** *Travis Tritt*
73/96 **Worth The Fall** *Brett James*
25/96 **Would I** *Randy Travis*
41/87 **Would Jesus Wear A Rolex** *Ray Stevens*
36/87 **Would These Arms Be In Your Way** *Keith Whitley*
91/75 **Would You Be My Lady** *David Allan Coe*
13/58 **Would You Care** *Browns*
6/82 **Would You Catch A Falling Star** *John Anderson*
86/87 **Would You Catch Me Baby (If I Fall For You)** *Gail Veach*
5/66 **Would You Hold It Against Me** *Dottie West*
95/80 **Would You Know Love** *Marlow Tackett*
1/74 **Would You Lay With Me (In A Field of Stone)** *Tanya Tucker*
3/55 **Would You Mind?** *Hank Snow*
92/73 **Would You Still Love Me** *Ben Peters*
1/72 **Would You Take Another Chance On Me** *Jerry Lee Lewis*
21/73 **Would You Walk With Me Jimmy** *Arlene Harden*
12/72 **Would You Want The World To End** *Mel Tillis*
72/85 **Wouldn't It Be Great** *Loretta Lynn*
3/62 **Wound Time Can't Erase** *Stonewall Jackson*
18/84 **Wounded Hearts** *Mark Gray*
77/86 **Wrap Me Up In Your Love** *J.D. Martin*
12/77 **Wrap Your Love All Around Your Man** *Lynn Anderson*
38/73 **Wrap Your Love Around Me** *Melba Montgomery*
2/02 **Wrapped Around** *Brad Paisley*
46/72 **Wrapped Around Her Finger** *George Jones*
5/02 **Wrapped Up In You** *Garth Brooks*
50/76 **Wreck Of The Edmund Fitzgerald** *Gordon Lightfoot*
8/61 **Wreck On The Highway** *Wilma Lee & Stoney Cooper*
62/00 **Wreckin' Crew** *Trini Triggs*
16/03 **Wrinkles** *Diamond Rio*
61/99 **Write It In Stone** *Keith Harling*
9/75 **Write Me A Letter** *Bobby G. Rice*
16/66 **Write Me A Picture** *George Hamilton IV*
6/44 **Write Me Sweetheart** *Roy Acuff*
1/99 **Write This Down** *George Strait*
Writing On The Wall
96/88 *Kenny Carr*
31/89 *George Jones*
15/72 **Writing's On The Wall** *Jim Reeves*
35/82 **Written Down In My Heart** *Ray Stevens*
5/90 **Wrong** *Waylon Jennings*
1/99 **Wrong Again** *Martina McBride*
26/60 **Wrong Company** *Wynn Stewart & Jan Howard*
32/01 **Wrong Five O' Clock** *Eric Heatherly*
24/04 **Wrong Girl** *Lee Ann Womack*
6/74 **Wrong Ideas** *Brenda Lee*
20/74 **Wrong In Loving You** *Faron Young*
6/99 **Wrong Night** *Reba McEntire*
14/65 **Wrong Number** *George Jones*
37/96 **Wrong Place, Wrong Time** *Mark Chesnutt*
Wrong Road Again
6/75 *Crystal Gayle*
95/78 *Allen Reynolds*
5/92 **Wrong Side Of Memphis** *Trisha Yearwood*
76/78 **Wrong Side Of The Rainbow** *Jim Chesnut*
49/68 **Wrong Side Of The World** *Hugh X. Lewis*
Wrong Train
82/86 *Beth Williams*
83/89 *Judy Lindsey*
65/93 **Wrong's What I Do Best** *George Jones*
1/77 **Wurlitzer Prize (I Don't Want To Get Over You)** *Waylon Jennings*
79/87 **Wyatt Liquor** *Wyatt Brothers*
Wyoming ..see: (Oh Why, Oh Why, Did I Ever Leave)

X

1/94 **XXX's And OOO's (An American Girl)** *Trisha Yearwood*

Y

3/77 **Y'All Come Back Saloon** *Oak Ridge Boys*
4/65 **Yakety Axe** *Chet Atkins*
91/75 **Yakety Yak** *Eric Weissberg & Deliverance*
17/59 **Yankee, Go Home** *Goldie Hill*
17/92 **Yard Sale** *Sammy Kershaw*
69/95 **Yeah Buddy** *Jeff Carson*
44/03 **Year At A Time** *Kevin Denney*
1/71 **Year That Clayton Delaney Died** *Tom T. Hall*
Yearning
10/57 *George Jones & Jeanette Hicks*
22/61 *Benny Barnes*
1/80 **Years** *Barbara Mandrell*
2/85 **Years After You** *John Conlee*
12/82 **Years Ago** *Statler Brothers*
48/96 **Years From Here** *Baker & Myers*
4/63 **Yellow Bandana** *Faron Young*
59/67 **Yellow Haired Woman** *Claude King*
30/81 **Yellow Pages** *Roger Bowling*
5/73 **Yellow Ribbon** *Johnny Carver*
49/72 **Yellow River** *Compton Brothers*
1/84 **Yellow Rose** *Johnny Lee w/ Lane Brody*
7/55 **Yellow Rose Of Texas** *Ernest Tubb*
1/89 **Yellow Roses** *Dolly Parton*
3/55 **Yellow Roses** *Hank Snow*
1/00 **Yes!** *Chad Brock*
67/83 **Yes** *Billy Swan*
83/75 **Yes** *Connie Cato*
75/71 **Yes, Dear, There Is A Virginia** *Glenn Barber*
2/56 **Yes I Know Why** *Webb Pierce*
6/66 **(Yes) I'm Hurting** *Don Gibson*
12/78 **Yes Ma'am** *Tommy Overstreet*

Yes Ma'm (I [He] Found Her [Me] In A Honky Tonk)
67/73 *Glenn Barber*
98/82 *Dixie Harrison*
1/65 **Yes, Mr. Peters** *Roy Drusky & Priscilla Mitchell*
83/77 **Yes She Do, No She Don't** *Alvin Crow & The Pleasant Valley Boys*
60/79 **Yesterday** *Billie Jo Spears*
86/89 **Yesterday Is Too Far Away** *Birch Denney*
50/76 **Yesterday Just Passed My Way Again** *Don Everly*
10/80 **Yesterday Once More** *Moe Bandy*
9/69 **Yesterday, When I Was Young** *Roy Clark*
8/53 **Yesterday's Girl** *Hank Thompson*
9/77 **Yesterday's Gone** *Vern Gosdin*
40/69 **Yesterday's Letters** *Bobby Lord*
12/48 **Yesterday's Mail** *Hank Thompson*
11/63 **Yesterday's Memories** *Eddy Arnold*
57/81 **Yesterday's News (Just Hit Home Today)** *Johnny Paycheck*
99/88 **Yesterday's Rain** *Joy Ford*
4/44 **Yesterday's Tears** *Ernest Tubb*
Yesterday's Wine
62/71 *Willie Nelson*
1/82 *Merle Haggard/George Jones*
7/90 **Yet** *Exile*
25/80 **Yippy Cry Yi** *Rex Allen, Jr.*
63/98 **Yippy Ky Yay** *Lila McCann*
YoYo Man ..see: (I'm A)
93/85 **Yo Yo (The Right String, But The Wrong Yo Yo)** *Danny Shirley & "Piano Red"*
44/65 **Yodel, Sweet Molly** *Ira Louvin*
45/99 **Yodelin' Blues** *Wilkinsons*
Yonder Comes A Freight Train
56/68 *Jim & Jesse*
77/88 *Reno Brothers*
4/55 **Yonder Comes A Sucker** *Jim Reeves*
47/01 **You** *Marshall Dyllon*
1/87 **You Again** *Forester Sisters*
19/89 **You Ain't Down Home** *Jann Browne*
6/89 **You Ain't Going Nowhere** *Chris Hillman & Roger McGuinn*
13/72 **You Ain't Gonna Have Ol' Buck To Kick Around No More** *Buck Owens*
56/00 **You Ain't Hurt Nothin' Yet** *John Anderson*
5/79 **You Ain't Just Whistlin' Dixie** *Bellamy Brothers*
57/97 **You Ain't Lonely Yet** *Big House*
2/95 **You Ain't Much Fun** *Toby Keith*
46/66 **You Ain't No Better Than Me** *Webb Pierce*
2/66 **You Ain't Woman Enough** *Loretta Lynn*
You All ..also see: Y'All
7/54 **You All Come** *Arlie Duff*
You Almost Slipped My Mind
44/72 *Kenny Price*
4/80 *Charley Pride*
1/73 **You Always Come Back (To Hurting Me)** *Johnny Rodriguez*
37/76 **You Always Look Your Best (Here In My Arms)** *George Jones*
5/92 **You And Forever And Me** *Little Texas*
1/82 **You And I** *Eddie Rabbitt w/ Crystal Gayle*
You And Me
1/76 *Tammy Wynette*
92/77 *Lloyd Green*
3/56 **You And Me** *Red Foley & Kitty Wells*
15/70 **You And Me Against The World** *Bobby Lord*
24/78 **You And Me Alone** *David Rogers*
94/81 **You And Me And Tennessee** *Roger Ivie & Silvercreek*
92/79 **You And Me And The Green Grass** *Pal Rakes*
99/75 **You And Me, Me And You** *Sharon Vaughn*
4/95 **You And Only You** *John Berry*
91/89 **You And The Horse (That You Rode In On)** *Patsy Cole*
8/97 **You And You Alone** *Vince Gill*
6/69 **You And Your Sweet Love** *Connie Smith*
18/04 **You Are** *Jimmy Wayne*
You Are
48/00 *John Michael Montgomery*
48/04 *Chad Brock*
48/81 **You Are A Liar** *Whitey Shafer*
85/84 **You Are A Miracle** *Maines Brothers Band*
87/83 **You Are Love** *Bobby Vinton*
72/88 **You Are My Angel** *Billy Parker*
12/64 **You Are My Flower** *Flatt & Scruggs*
10/86 **You Are My Music, You Are My Song** *Charly McClain/Wayne Massey*
36/79 **You Are My Rainbow** *David Rogers*
You Are My Special Angel ..see: My Special Angel
69/77 **You Are My Sunshine** *Duane Eddy w/ Waylon Jennings, Willie Nelson, Kin Vassy & Deed Eddy*
1/68 **You Are My Treasure** *Jack Greene*
You Are So Beautiful
16/76 *Ray Stevens*
40/77 *Tanya Tucker*
93/78 **You Are Still The One** *Linda Hargrove*
97/83 **You Are The Music In Time With My Heart** *Joy Ford*
4/56 **You Are The One** *Carl Smith*
14/75 **You Are The One** *Mel Tillis & Sherry Bryce*
85/86 **You Are The Rock (And I'm A Rolling Stone)** *Carl Jackson*
11/76 **You Are The Song (Inside Of Me)** *Freddie Hart*
34/78 **You Are The Sunshine Of My Life** *Marty Mitchell*
86/84 **You Are What Love Means To Me** *Craig Bickhardt*
You Ask Me To
8/73 *Waylon Jennings*
80/78 *Billy Joe Shaver*
F/81 *Elvis Presley*
You, Babe
59/72 *Lefty Frizzell*
23/89 *Merle Haggard*
67/93 **You Baby You** *Highway 101*
20/67 **You Beat All I Ever Saw** *Johnny Cash*
You Belong To Me
54/75 *Jim Reeves*
93/89 *T.C. Brandon*
58/74 **You Bet Your Sweet, Sweet Love** *Kenny O'Dell*
52/67 **You Better Be Better To Me** *Carl Smith*
79/77 **(You Better Be) One Hell Of A Woman** *Glenn Barber*
49/80 **You Better Hurry Home (Somethin's Burnin')** *Connie Cato*
You Better Move On
10/71 *Billy "Crash" Craddock*
70/79 *Tommy Roe*
18/81 *George Jones & Johnny Paycheck*
2/54 **You Better Not Do That** *Tommy Collins*
28/68 **You Better Sit Down Kids** *Roy Drusky*
2/95 **You Better Think Twice** *Vince Gill*
49/66 **You Better Watch Your Friends** *Jim Nesbitt*
72/88 **You Blossom Me** *Bertie Higgins*
97/75 **You Bring Out The Best In Me** *Brenda Pepper*
66/85 **You Bring Out The Lover In Me** *Zella Lehr*
9/84 **(You Bring Out) The Wild Side Of Me** *Dan Seals*
63/84 **You Bring The Heartache (I'll Bring The Wine)** *Gary Wolf*
15/49 **You Broke My Heart (In Little Bitty Pieces)** *Hank Thompson*
95/79 **You Broke My Heart So Gently (It Almost Didn't Break)** *Sandra Kaye*
You Call Everybody Darling
71/73 *Lamar Morris*
69/91 *K.T. Oslin*
You Call That A Mountain
63/97 *Jeff Wood*
66/00 *B.J. Thomas*
78/85 **You Can Always Say Good-Bye In The Morning** *Jim Collins*
91/79 **You Can Be Replaced** *Leon Rausch*
85/78 **You Can Count On Me** *David Allan Coe*
3/92 **You Can Depend On Me** *Restless Heart*
1/86 **You Can Dream Of Me** *Steve Wariner*
1/96 **You Can Feel Bad** *Patty Loveless*
53/91 **You Can Go Home** *Desert Rose Band*
You Can Have Her
18/67 *Jim Edward Brown*
7/73 *Waylon Jennings*
49/74 *Sam Neely*
14/79 *George Jones & Johnny Paycheck*
48/85 **You Can Lead A Heart To Love (But You Can't Make It Fall)** *Tammy Wynette*

72/00 **You Can Leave Your Hat On** *Ty Herndon*
23/95 **You Can Sleep While I Drive** *Trisha Yearwood*
33/67 **You Can Steal Me** *Bonnie Guitar*
49/74 **You Can Sure See It From Here** *Susan Raye*
1/74 **You Can't Be A Beacon (If Your Light Don't Shine)** *Donna Fargo*
49/87 **You Can't Blame The Train** *Don McLean*
3/46 **You Can't Break My Heart** *Spade Cooley*
20/88 **You Can't Fall In Love When You're Cryin'** *Lee Greenwood*
66/90 **You Can't Fly Like An Eagle** *Johnny Lee*
98/75 **You Can't Follow Where He's Been** *Debra Barber*
39/97 **You Can't Get There From Here** *Lee Roy Parnell*
23/72 **You Can't Go Home** *Statler Brothers*
(You Can't Go Home Again) ..see: Flies On The Butter
You Can't Have It All ..see: (Who Says)
8/54 **You Can't Have My Love** *Wanda Jackson & Billy Gray*
10/67 **You Can't Have Your Kate And Edith, Too** *Statler Brothers*
4/03 **You Can't Hide Beautiful** *Aaron Lines*
55/69 **You Can't Housebreak A Tomcat** *Cal Smith*
60/99 **You Can't Hurry Love** *Dixie Chicks*
15/57 **You Can't Hurt Me Anymore** *Carl Smith*
96/74 **You Can't Judge A Book By The Cover** *Troy Seals*
31/86 **You Can't Keep A Good Memory Down** *John Anderson*
6/96 **You Can't Lose Me** *Faith Hill*
42/83 **You Can't Lose What You Never Had** *Lynn Anderson*
1/95 **You Can't Make A Heart Love Somebody** *George Strait*
100/79 **You Can't Make Love To A Memory** *Iris Larratt*
52/85 **You Can't Measure My Love** *Carlette*
8/60 **You Can't Pick A Rose In December** *Ernest Ashworth*
80/89 **You Can't Play The Blues (In An Air-Conditioned Room)** *Mel McDaniel*
F/79 **You Can't Remember And I Can't Forget** *Mary Lou Turner*
35/66 **You Can't Roller Skate In A Buffalo Herd** *Roger Miller*
20/85 **You Can't Run Away From Your Heart** *Lacy J. Dalton*
1/83 **You Can't Run From Love** *Eddie Rabbitt*
9/86 **You Can't Stop Love** *Schuyler, Knobloch & Overstreet*
26/97 **You Can't Stop Love** *Marty Stuart*
57/66 **You Can't Stop Me** *Billy Mize*
72/86 **You Can't Take It With You** *William Lee Golden*
58/03 **You Can't Take It With You When You Go** *Rhonda Vincent*
67/91 **You Can't Take It With You When You Go** *Gene Watson*
3/04 **You Can't Take The Honky Tonk Out Of The Girl** *Brooks & Dunn*
35/68 **You Changed Everything About Me But My Name** *Norma Jean*
You Comb Her Hair
5/63 *George Jones*
92/75 *Del Reeves*
45/85 **You Could Be The One Woman** *Chance*
10/76 **You Could Know As Much About A Stranger** *Gene Watson*
72/94 **You Could Steal Me** *Bobbie Cryner*
71/00 **You Could've Had Me** *Lace*
You Could've Heard A Heart Break
53/83 *Rodney Lay*
1/84 *Johnny Lee*
32/91 **You Couldn't Get The Picture** *George Jones*
51/02 **You Da Man** *Jameson Clark*
1/79 **You Decorated My Life** *Kenny Rogers*
55/67 **You Deserve Each Other** *Robert Mitchum*
73/88 **You Didn't Have To Jump The Fence** *Lisa Childress*
68/95 **You Didn't Miss A Thing** *Clinton Gregory*
47/92 **You Do My Heart Good** *Cleve Francis*
22/04 **You Do Your Thing** *Montgomery Gentry*
You Don't Bring Me Flowers
70/78 *Barbra Streisand & Neil Diamond*
10/79 *Jim Ed Brown/Helen Cornelius*
You Don't Care What Happens To Me
5/45 *Bob Wills*
55/70 *Wynn Stewart*
4/91 **You Don't Count The Cost** *Billy Dean*
5/95 **You Don't Even Know Who I Am** *Patty Loveless*
You Don't Have To Be A Baby To Cry
10/50 *Ernest Tubb*
63/77 *Ann J. Morton*
36/75 **You Don't Have To Go Home** *Nat Stuckey*
56/70 **You Don't Have To Say You Love Me** *Elvis Presley*
4/65 **You Don't Hear** *Kitty Wells*
4/83 **You Don't Know Love** *Janie Fricke*
You Don't Know Me
10/56 *Eddy Arnold*
61/70 *Ray Pennington*
1/81 *Mickey Gilley*
35/05 **You Don't Lie Here Anymore** *Shelly Fairchild*
1/78 **You Don't Love Me Anymore** *Eddie Rabbitt*
66/72 **You Don't Mess Around With Jim** *Bobby Bond*
36/79 **You Don't Miss A Thing** *Sylvia*
29/99 **You Don't Need Me Now** *Clint Black*
15/74 **You Don't Need To Move A Mountain** *Jeanne Pruett*
14/97 **You Don't Seem To Miss Me** *Patty Loveless & George Jones*
71/71 **You Don't Understand Him Like I Do** *Jeannie Seely*
14/61 **You Don't Want My Love** *Roger Miller*
You Done Me Wrong
7/56 *Ray Price*
37/85 *Mel Tillis*
13/59 **You Dreamer You** *Johnny Cash*
4/79 **You Feel Good All Over** *T.G. Sheppard*
41/80 **You Fill My Life** *Juice Newton*
15/66 **You Finally Said Something Good (When You Said Goodbye)** *Charlie Louvin*
76/88 **You Fit Right Into My Heart** *Sanders*
69/69 **You Fool** *Eddy Arnold*
7/69 **You Gave Me A Mountain** *Johnny Bush*
34/74 **You Get To Me** *Eddie Rabbitt*
8/73 **You Give Me You** *Bobby G. Rice*
25/99 **You Go First (Do You Wanna Kiss)** *Jessica Andrews*
55/88 **You Go, You're Gone** *David Ball*
60/75 **You Got A Lock On Me** *Jerry Reed*
77/74 **You Got Everything That You Want** *Pat Roberts*
7/89 **You Got It** *Roy Orbison*
28/83 **You Got Me Running** *Jim Glaser*
65/89 **You Got The Job** *Charly McClain*
7/56 **You Gotta Be My Baby** *George Jones*
49/67 **You Gotta Be Puttin' Me On** *Lefty Frizzell*
72/91 **You Gotta Get Serious** *J.P. Pennington*
65/83 **You Gotta Get To My Heart (Before You Lay A Hand On Me)** *Paulette Carlson*
41/70 **You Got-ta Have A License** *Porter Wagoner*
3/96 **You Gotta Love That** *Neal McCoy*
1/99 **You Had Me From Hello** *Kenny Chesney*
4/95 **You Have The Right To Remain Silent** *Perfect Stranger*
11/87 **You Haven't Heard The Last Of Me** *Moe Bandy*
59/99 **You Haven't Left Me Yet** *George Strait*
39/89 **You Just Can't Lose 'Em All** *Shooters*
54/77 **You Just Don't Know** *Mary K. Miller*
60/90 **You Just Get Better All The Time** *James House*
44/97 **You Just Get One** *Jeff Wood*
76/85 **You Just Hurt My Last Feeling** *Sammi Smith*
You Just Watch Me
43/88 *Libby Hurley*
20/94 *Tanya Tucker*
(You Know I Love You) ..see: Don't Be Stupid
You Know Just What I'd Do
48/75 *Lois Johnson*
9/80 *Conway Twitty/Loretta Lynn*

1/91 **You Know Me Better Than That** *George Strait*
20/78 **You Know What** *Jerry Reed & Seidina*
30/73 **You Know Who** *Bobby Bare*
48/87 **You Lay A Lotta Love On Me** *Wrays*
19/80 **You Lay A Whole Lot Of Love On Me** *Con Hunley*
You Lay So Easy On My Mind
3/73 *Bobby G. Rice*
70/84 *Narvel Felts*
79/87 *Bobby G. Rice*
63/87 **You Left Her Lovin' You** *Ride The River*
86/87 **You Left My Heart For Broke** *Ernie Rowell*
1/90 **You Lie** *Reba McEntire*
8/80 **(You Lift Me) Up To Heaven** *Reba McEntire*
You Light Up My Life
4/77 *Debby Boone*
48/97 *LeAnn Rimes*
94/79 **You Lit The Fire, Now Fan The Flame** *Penny Hamilton*
60/04 **You Look Good In My Shirt** *Keith Urban*
You Look Like The One I Love
33/82 *Deborah Allen*
69/86 *Osmond Bros.*
1/84 **You Look So Good In Love** *George Strait*
63/67 **You Love Me Too Little** *Lorene Mann*
76/78 **You Love The Thunder** *Hank Williams, Jr.*
24/86 **You Made A Rock Of A Rolling Stone** *Oak Ridge Boys*
3/84 **You Made A Wanted Man Of Me** *Ronnie McDowell*
47/81 **You Made It Beautiful** *Charlie Rich*
89/89 **You Made It Easy** *Sammy Sadler*
84/76 **You Made It Right** *Ozark Mountain Daredevils*
60/90 **You Made Life Good Again** *Nitty Gritty Dirt Band*
19/01 **You Made Me That Way** *Andy Griggs*
48/98 **You Make It Seem So Easy** *Kinleys*
67/79 **You Make It So Easy** *Bobby G. Rice*
61/76 **You Make Life Easy** *Joe Stampley*
7/85 **You Make Me Feel Like A Man** *Ricky Skaggs*
34/71 **You Make Me Feel Like A Man** *Warner Mack*
15/74 **You Make Me Feel More Like A Man** *Mel Street*
29/61 **You Make Me Live Again** *Carl Smith*
4/75 **(You Make Me Want To Be) A Mother** *Tammy Wynette*
1/85 **You Make Me Want To Make You Mine** *Juice Newton*
85/82 **You Make Me Want To Sing** *Joe Sun*
20/81 **You (Make Me Wonder Why)** *Deborah Allen*
69/68 **You May Be Too Much For Memphis, Baby** *Leroy Van Dyke*
9/81 **You May See Me Walkin'** *Ricky Skaggs*
You Mean The World To Me
1/67 *David Houston*
72/78 *Howdy Glenn*
44/88 **You Might Want To Use Me Again** *Johnny Rodriguez*
3/98 **You Move Me** *Garth Brooks*
45/86 **You Must Be Lookin' For Me** *Billy Swan*
26/89 **You Must Not Be Drinking Enough** *Earl Thomas Conley*
15/48 **You Nearly Lose Your Mind** *Ernest Tubb*
4/78 **You Needed Me** *Anne Murray*
6/77 **(You Never Can Tell) C'est La Vie** *Emmylou Harris*
You Never Even Called Me By My Name
8/75 *David Allan Coe*
60/94 *Doug Supernaw*
5/82 **You Never Gave Up On Me** *Crystal Gayle*
1/77 **You Never Miss A Real Good Thing (Till He Says Goodbye)** *Crystal Gayle*
31/74 **You Never Say You Love Me Anymore** *Nat Stuckey*
65/74 **You Only Live Once (In Awhile)** *Glenn Barber*
92/89 **You Only Love Me When I'm Leavin'** *Ellen Lee Miller*
7/46 **You Only Want Me When You're Lonely** *Gene Autry*
You Ought To Hear Me Cry
69/67 *Johnny Bush*
43/68 *Carl Smith*
16/77 *Willie Nelson*
100/76 **You Oughta Be Against The Law** *Rex Kramer*
90/77 **You Oughta Hear The Song** *Ruth Buzzi*
15/55 **You Oughta See Pickles Now** *Tommy Collins*
12/79 **You Pick Me Up (And Put Me Down)** *Dottie West*
58/89 **You Plant Your Fields** *New Grass Revival*
14/67 **You Pushed Me Too Far** *Ferlin Husky*
10/83 **You Put The Beat In My Heart** *Eddie Rabbitt*
10/82 **You Put The Blue In Me** *Whites*
F/77 **You Put The Bounce Back Into My Step** *Ray Griff*
59/89 **You Put The Soul In The Song** *Waylon Jennings*
62/78 **You Read Between The Lines** *Billy Parker*
37/84 **You Really Go For The Heart** *Dan Seals*
1/90 **You Really Had Me Going** *Holly Dunn*
6/73 **You Really Haven't Changed** *Johnny Carver*
You Really Know How To Break A Heart
93/84 *Jimmy Mac*
73/88 *Rhonda Manning*
16/75 **You Ring My Bell** *Ray Griff*
4/76 **You Rubbed It In All Wrong** *Billy "Crash" Craddock*
43/87 **You Saved Me** *Patty Loveless*
12/93 **You Say You Will** *Trisha Yearwood*
3/86 **You Should Have Been Gone By Now** *Eddy Raven*
56/78 **You Should Win An Oscar Every Night** *Chuck Pollard*
1/01 **You Shouldn't Kiss Me Like This** *Toby Keith*
11/79 **You Show Me Your Heart (And I'll Show You Mine)** *Tom T. Hall*
70/78 **You Snap Your Fingers (And I'm Back In Your Hands)** *David Wills*
14/89 **You Still Do** *T.G. Sheppard*
16/82 **You Still Get To Me In My Dreams** *Tammy Wynette*
62/89 **You Still Got A Way With My Heart** *Mickey Gilley*
53/96 **You Still Got Me** *Doug Supernaw*
82/90 **You Still Love Me In My Dreams** *Tim Mensy*
1/87 **You Still Move Me** *Dan Seals*
36/99 **You Still Shake Me** *Deana Carter*
47/01 **You Still Take Me There** *Collin Raye*
89/89 **You Sure Got This Ol' Redneck Feelin' Blue** *Joe Stampley*
35/82 **(You Sure Know Your Way) Around My Heart** *Louise Mandrell*
1/83 **You Take Me For Granted** *Merle Haggard*
15/62 **You Take The Future (And I'll Take The Past)** *Hank Snow*
76/87 **You Take The Leavin' Out Of Me** *Mickey Clark*
18/59 **You Take The Table And I'll Take The Chairs** *Bob Gallion*
65/82 **You To Come Home To** *Dean Dillon*
18/73 **You Took All The Ramblin' Out Of Me** *Jerry Reed*
You Took Her [Him] Off My Hands (Now Please Take Her [Him] Off My Mind)
11/63 *Ray Price*
33/64 *Marion Worth*
33/64 **You Took My Happy Away** *Willie Nelson*
37/69 **You Touched My Heart** *David Rogers*
75/98 **You Turn Me On** *Tim McGraw*
17/82 **You Turn Me On I'm A Radio** *Gail Davies*
3/85 **You Turn Me On (Like A Radio)** *Ed Bruce*
48/80 **You Turn My Love Light On** *Billy Walker*
1/45 **You Two Timed Me One Time Too Often** *Tex Ritter*
12/98 **You Walked In** *Lonestar*
6/70 **You Wanna Give Me A Lift** *Loretta Lynn*
70/00 **You Wanna What?** *Alecia Elliott*
20/84 **You Were A Good Friend** *Kenny Rogers*
You Were A Lady ..see: (Jeannie Marie)
1/73 **You Were Always There** *Donna Fargo*
1/99 **You Were Mine** *Dixie Chicks*

51/71 **You Were On My Mind** *Bobby Penn*
38/81 **You Were There** *Freddie Hart*
28/79 **You Were Worth Waiting For** *Don King*
6/94 **You Will** *Patty Loveless*
1/46 **You Will Have To Pay** *Tex Ritter*
You Win Again
10/52 *Hank Williams*
4/58 *Jerry Lee Lewis*
1/80 *Charley Pride*
75/80 *Jeris Ross*
16/91 **You Win Again** *Mary-Chapin Carpenter*
1/96 **You Win My Love** *Shania Twain*
61/00 **You With Me** *Anita Cochran*
93/89 **You Won The Battle** *Eddie Rivers*
17/00 **You Won't Be Lonely Now** *Billy Ray Cyrus*
2/99 **You Won't Ever Be Lonely** *Andy Griggs*
8/70 **You Wouldn't Know Love** *Ray Price*
66/66 **You Wouldn't Put The Shuck On Me** *Geezinslaw Brothers*
43/94 **You Wouldn't Say That To A Stranger** *Suzy Bogguss*
77/73 **You, You, You** *Lynda K. Lance*
77/83 **You'd Better Believe It** *Rod Rishard*
5/80 **You'd Make An Angel Wanna Cheat** *Kendalls*
You'd Think He'd Know Me Better
56/96 *Bobbie Cryner*
66/98 *Lorrie Morgan*
5/00 **You'll Always Be Loved By Me** *Brooks & Dunn*
64/67 **You'll Always Have My Love** *Wanda Jackson*
You'll Be Back (Every Night In My Dreams)
24/78 *Johnny Russell*
3/82 *Statler Brothers*
92/89 **You'll Be The First To Know** *Lee J. Stevens*
4/05 **You'll Be There** *George Strait*
10/58 **You'll Come Back** *Webb Pierce*
31/88 **You'll Come Back (You Always Do)** *Mel Tillis*
10/64 **You'll Drive Me Back (Into Her Arms Again)** *Faron Young*
1/76 **You'll Lose A Good Thing** *Freddy Fender*
55/68 **You'll Never Be Lonely Again** *Leon Ashley & Margie Singleton*
10/89 **You'll Never Be Sorry** *Bellamy Brothers*
97/85 **You'll Never Find A Good Man (Playing In A Country Band)** *Audie Henry*
19/98 **You'll Never Know** *Mindy McCready*
You'll Never Know
71/75 *Jim Reeves*
77/85 *Lew DeWitt*
26/86 **You'll Never Know How Much I Needed You Today** *Conway Twitty*
78/77 **You'll Never Leave Me Completely** *Johnny Bush*
73/82 **You'll Never Walk Alone** *Elvis Presley*

1/04 **You'll Think Of Me** *Keith Urban*
54/73 **You're A Believer** *Stoney Edwards*
92/86 **You're A Better Man Than I** *Perry LaPointe*
71/78 **You're A Dancer** *Eddy Raven*
18/83 **You're A Hard Dog (To Keep Under The Porch)** *Gail Davies*
96/86 **You're A Heartache To Follow** *Ken Fowler*
84/83 **You're A Keep Me Wondering Kind Of Woman** *Steve Mantelli*
You're A Part Of Me
99/78 *Gene Cotton w/ Kim Carnes*
20/79 *Charly McClain*
85/83 *Danny White & Linda Nail*
You're A Pretty Lady, Lady
93/79 *Wichita Linemen*
93/80 *Ray Sanders*
82/78 **You're A Violin That Never Has Been Played** *Billy Walker*
You're All The Woman I'll Ever Need
78/78 *Lee Dresser*
76/79 *Dusty James*
39/80 **You're Amazing** *David Rogers*
2/99 **You're Beginning To Get To Me** *Clay Walker*
5/45 **You're Breaking My Heart** *Ted Daffan*
59/72 **You're Burnin' My House Down** *Warner Mack*
31/81 **You're Crazy Man** *Freddie Hart*
41/66 **You're Driving Me Out Of My Mind** *Norma Jean*
1/98 **You're Easy On The Eyes** *Terri Clark*
49/68 **You're Easy To Love** *Arlene Harden*
47/85 **You're Every Step I Take** *Johnny Paycheck*
32/72 **You're Everything** *Tommy Cash*
10/63 **You're For Me** *Buck Owens*
You're Free To Go
6/56 *Carl Smith*
9/77 *Sonny James*
2/44 **You're From Texas** *Bob Wills*
1/84 **You're Gettin' To Me Again** *Jim Glaser*
26/59 **You're Going Back To Your Old Ways Again** *Hank Thompson*
10/85 **You're Going Out Of My Mind** *T.G. Sheppard*
4/98 **You're Gone** *Diamond Rio*
4/49 **You're Gonna Change (Or I'm Gonna Leave)** *Hank Williams*
29/74 **You're Gonna Hurt Me (One More Time)** *Patti Page*
34/83 **You're Gonna Lose Her Like That** *Moe Bandy*
44/78 **You're Gonna Love Love** *Ava Barber*
(You're Gonna Love Me Tonight) ..see: I Can Tell By The Way You Dance
You're Gonna Love Yourself In The Morning
77/73 *Wayne Carson*
35/75 *Roy Clark*
22/80 *Charlie Rich*
43/83 *Willie Nelson & Brenda Lee*

89/79 **You're Gonna Make A Cheater Out Of Me** *Bill Phillips*
45/89 **You're Gonna Make Her Mine** *Lionel Cartwright*
93/77 **You're Gonna Make Love To Me** *Lynn Niles*
97/79 **You're Gonna Miss Me** *June Neyman*
1/95 **You're Gonna Miss Me When I'm Gone** *Brooks & Dunn*
33/85 **You're Gonna Miss Me When I'm Gone** *Judy Rodman*
39/70 **You're Gonna Need A Man** *Johnny Duncan*
1/83 **You're Gonna Ruin My Bad Reputation** *Ronnie McDowell*
62/87 **You're Here To Remember (I'm Here To Forget)** *Merrill And Jessica*
61/87 **You're In Love Alone** *Jeff Stevens & The Bullets*
27/80 **You're In Love With The Wrong Man** *Mundo Earwood*
21/04 **You're In My Head** *Brian McComas*
92/74 **You're Just Gettin' Better** *Jack Scott*
38/71 **You're Just More A Woman** *Bob Yarbrough*
16↑/05 **You're Like Comin' Home** *Lonestar*
5/71 **You're Lookin' At Country** *Loretta Lynn*
62/67 **You're Lookin' For A Plaything** *Jamey Ryan*
37/99 **You're Lucky I Love You** *Susan Ashton*
7/59 **You're Makin' A Fool Out Of Me** *Jimmy Newman*
59/86 **You're Mine** *Orleans*
70/81 **You're More To Me (Than He's Ever Been)** *Peggy Forman*
1/75 **You're My Best Friend** *Don Williams*
5/82 **You're My Bestest Friend** *Mac Davis*
2/05 **You're My Better Half** *Keith Urban*
7/81 **You're My Favorite Star** *Bellamy Brothers*
2/87 **You're My First Lady** *T.G. Sheppard*
1/79 **You're My Jamaica** *Charley Pride*
14/79 **You're My Kind Of Woman** *Jacky Ward*
1/71 **You're My Man** *Lynn Anderson*
68/75 **You're My Rainy Day Woman** *Eddy Raven*
26/72 **You're My Shoulder To Lean On** *Lana Rae*
31/91 **(You're My) Soul And Inspiration** *Oak Ridge Boys*
36/74 **You're My Wife, She's My Woman** *Charlie Louvin*
3/87 **You're Never Too Old For Young Love** *Eddy Raven*
60/86 **You're Nobody Till Somebody Loves You** *Ray Price*
60/76 **You're Not Charlie Brown (And I'm Not Raggedy Ann)** *Donna Fargo*
26/82 **You're Not Easy To Forget** *Dottie West*

70/89 **You're Not Even Crying** *Marcy Bros.*
74/78 **You're Not Free And I'm Not Easy** *Arleen Harden*
16/74 **You're Not Getting Older (You're Getting Better)** *Freddy Weller*
7/96 **You're Not In Kansas Anymore** *Jo Dee Messina*
21/83 **You're Not Leavin' Here Tonight** *Ed Bruce*
4/54 **You're Not Mine Anymore** *Webb Pierce*
3/47 **You're Not My Darlin' Anymore** *Gene Autry*
13/56 **You're Not Play Love** *Wilburn Brothers*
15/75 **You're Not The Woman You Use To Be** *Gary Stewart*
60/80 **You're Only Lonely** *J.D. Souther*
2/83 **You're Out Doing What I'm Here Doing Without** *Gene Watson*
67/67 **You're Puttin' Me On** *Nat Stuckey*
7/56 **You're Running Wild** *Louvin Brothers*
38/67 **You're So Cold (I'm Turning Blue)** *Hugh X. Lewis*
75/77 **You're So Good For Me (And That's Bad)** *Bobby Wayne Loftis*
1/82 **You're So Good When You're Bad** *Charley Pride*
4/86 **You're Something Special To Me** *George Strait*
39/99 **You're Still Beautiful To Me** *Bryan White*
28/03 **You're Still Here** *Faith Hill*
3/56 **You're Still Mine** *Faron Young*
1/86 **You're Still New To Me** *Marie Osmond w/ Paul Davis*
You're Still On My Mind
28/62 *George Jones*
84/79 *Joe Douglas*
1/98 **You're Still The One** *Shania Twain*
14/81 **You're The Best** *Kieran Kane*
1/82 **You're The Best Break This Old Heart Ever Had** *Ed Bruce*
87/84 **You're The Best I Never Had** *Larry Jenkins*
1/73 **You're The Best Thing That Ever Happened To Me** *Ray Price*
1/83 **You're The First Time I've Thought About Leaving** *Reba McEntire*
57/77 **You're The Hangnail In My Life** *Hoyt Axton*
1/86 **You're The Last Thing I Needed Tonight** *John Schneider*
5/58 **You're The Nearest Thing To Heaven** *Johnny Cash*
You're The One
95/75 *Jerry Inman*
2/78 *Oak Ridge Boys*
5/91 **You're The One** *Dwight Yoakam*
75/76 **You're The One** *Billy Swan*
91/79 **You're The One Who Rewrote My Life Story** *Don Schlitz*
93/81 **You're The Only Dancer** *Pam Hobbs*
You're The Only Good Thing (That's Happened To Me)
4/60 *George Morgan*
29/78 *Jim Reeves*
1/79 **You're The Only One** *Dolly Parton*
77/84 **You're The Only Star (In My Blue Heaven)** *Mike Campbell*
1/65 **You're The Only World I Know** *Sonny James*
38/79 **You're The Part Of Me** *Jim Ed Brown*
64/80 **You're The Perfect Reason** *David Houston*
5/87 **You're The Power** *Kathy Mattea*
You're The Reason
4/61 *Bobby Edwards*
14/61 *Hank Locklin*
16/61 *Joe South*
48/68 *Johnny Tillotson*
90/81 *John Rex Reeves*
82/82 *Narvel Felts*
94/81 **You're The Reason** *Sligo Studio Band*
1/81 **You're The Reason God Made Oklahoma** *David Frizzell & Shelly West*
6/57 **You're The Reason I'm In Love** *Sonny James*
You're The Reason I'm Living
59/71 *Lamar Morris*
75/76 *Price Mitchell*
You're The Reason Our Kids Are Ugly
90/77 *L.E. White & Lola Jean Dillon*
F/78 *Loretta Lynn/Conway Twitty*
75/00 **You're The Ticket** *Billy Hoffman*
52/73 **You're Wearin' Me Down** *Kenny Price*
9/84 **You're Welcome To Tonight** *Lynn Anderson & Gary Morris*
71/00 **You're Where I Belong** *Trisha Yearwood*
98/76 **You're Wondering Why** *Hank Snow*
94/86 **You've Been My Rock For Ages** *Bobbi Lace*
75/70 **(You've Been Quite A Doll) Raggedy Ann** *Jimmy Dickens*
26/67 **You've Been So Good To Me** *Van Trevor*
9/85 **You've Got A Good Love Comin'** *Lee Greenwood*
2/83 **You've Got A Lover** *Ricky Skaggs*
54/87 **You've Got A Right** *Adam Baker*
44/84 **You've Got A Soft Place To Fall** *Kathy Mattea*
13/99 **You've Got A Way** *Shania Twain*
21/73 **You've Got Me (Right Where You Want Me)** *Connie Smith*
92/77 **You've Got Me Runnin'** *Gene Cotton*
3/76 **You've Got Me To Hold On To** *Tanya Tucker*
16/79 **You've Got Somebody, I've Got Somebody** *Vern Gosdin*
10/85 **You've Got Something On Your Mind** *Mickey Gilley*
85/79 **(You've Got That) Fire Goin' Again** *Jimmy Tucker*
77/87 **You've Got That Leaving Look In Your Eye** *Marcia Lynn*
60/83 **You've Got That Touch** *Lloyd David Foster*
89/81 **You've Got The Devil In Your Eyes** *Ann J. Morton*
1/87 **"You've Got" The Touch** *Alabama*
30/80 **You've Got Those Eyes** *Eddy Raven*
40/77 **You've Got To Mend This Heartache** *Ruby Falls*
(You've Got To) Move Two Mountains
56/71 *Dave Peel*
99/76 *Jimmy Russell*
6/91 **You've Got To Stand For Something** *Aaron Tippin*
79/76 **You've Got To Stop Hurting Me Darling** *Don Gibson*
2/98 **You've Got To Talk To Me** *Lee Ann Womack*
27/70 **You've Got Your Troubles (I've Got Mine)** *Jack Blanchard & Misty Morgan*
12/72 **You've Gotta Cry Girl** *Dave Dudley*
76/78 **You've Just Found Yourself A New Woman** *Jenny Robbins*
2/68 **You've Just Stepped In (From Stepping Out On Me)** *Loretta Lynn*
You've Lost That Lovin' Feelin'
41/75 *Barbara Fairchild*
57/87 *Carlette*
1/73 **You've Never Been This Far Before** *Conway Twitty*
2/84 **You've Really Got A Hold On Me** *Mickey Gilley*
You've Still Got A Place In My Heart
14/78 *Con Hunley*
3/84 *George Jones*
You've Still Got Me
68/80 *Jerry Wallace*
71/83 *David Rogers*
70/86 **You've Taken Over My Heart** *Bobby G. Rice*
2/02 **Young** *Kenny Chesney*
2/88 **Young Country** *Hank Williams, Jr.*
29/76 **Young Girl** *Tommy Overstreet*
12/57 **Young Hearts** *Jim Reeves*
Young Love
1/57 *Sonny James*
20/69 *Connie Smith & Nat Stuckey*
48/76 *Ray Stevens*
75/82 *Stella Parton*
70/94 *Twister Alley*
1/89 **Young Love** *Judds*
44/03 **Young Man's Town** *Vince Gill*
81/88 **Younger Man, Older Woman** *Richard And Gary Rose*
22/82 **Your Bedroom Eyes** *Vern Gosdin*
12/63 **Your Best Friend And Me** *Mac Wiseman*
3/80 **Your Body Is An Outlaw** *Mel Tillis*
1/53 **Your Cheatin' Heart** *Hank Williams*
67/81 **Your Daddy Don't Live In Heaven (He's In Houston)** *Michael Ballew*
4/00 **Your Everything** *Keith Urban*
76/84 **Your Eyes** *Bill Anderson*
91/85 **Your Eyes** *Simon & Verity*
17/67 **Your Forevers (Don't Last Very Long)** *Jean Shepard*
F/55 **Your Good For Nothing Heart** *Webb Pierce*

Your Good Girl's Gonna Go Bad
3/67 *Tammy Wynette*
13/81 *Billie Jo Spears*
65/67 **Your Hands** *Johnny Dollar*
5/64 **Your Heart Turned Left (And I Was On The Right)** *George Jones*
1/84 **Your Heart's Not In It** *Janie Fricke*
22/70 **Your Husband, My Wife** *Bobby Bare & Skeeter Davis*
56/71 **Your Kind Of Lovin'** *June Stearns*
7/79 **Your Kisses Will** *Crystal Gayle*
Your Lily White Hands
21/68 *Johnny Carver*
49/68 *Ray Griff*
12/87 **Your Love** *Tammy Wynette*
74/00 **Your Love** *Jim Brickman*
1/94 **Your Love Amazes Me** *John Berry*
3/79 **Your Love Had Taken Me That High** *Conway Twitty*
3/91 **Your Love Is A Miracle** *Mark Chesnutt*
92/77 **Your Love Is My Refuge** *Ava Barber*
71/70 **Your Love Is The Way** *Kitty Wells*
5/83 **Your Love Shines Through** *Mickey Gilley*
93/79 **Your Love Takes Me So High** *Maury Finney*
1/83 **Your Love's On The Line** *Earl Thomas Conley*
43/69 **Your Lovin' Takes The Leavin' Out Of Me** *Tommy Cash*
53/86 **Your Loving Side** *Butch Baker*
15/80 **Your Lying Blue Eyes** *John Anderson*
89/80 **Your Magic Touch** *Pat Garrett*
85/83 **Your Mama Don't Dance** *Roy Head*
64/97 **Your Mama Won't Let Me** *Little Texas*
4/77 **Your Man Loves You, Honey** *Tom T. Hall*
7/81 **Your Memory** *Steve Wariner*
5/86 **Your Memory Ain't What It Used To Be** *Mickey Gilley*
17/88 **Your Memory Wins Again** *Skip Ewing*
29/63 **Your Mother's Prayer** *Buddy Cagle*
6/58 **Your Name Is Beautiful** *Carl Smith*
5/80 **Your Old Cold Shoulder** *Crystal Gayle*
56/89 **Your Old Flame's Goin' Out Tonite** *Joe Barnhill*
73/68 **Your Old Handy Man** *Priscilla Mitchell*
10/61 **Your Old Love Letters** *Porter Wagoner*
5/60 **Your Old Used To Be** *Faron Young*
99/79 **Your Other Love** *Tommy O'Day*
27/99 **Your Own Little Corner Of My Heart** *BlackHawk*
13/76 **Your Picture In The Paper** *Statler Brothers*
56/82 **Your Picture Still Loves Me (And I Still Love You)** *Billy Swan*
11/77 **Your Place Or Mine** *Gary Stewart*
Your Pretty Roses Came Too Late
67/74 *Melba Montgomery*
20/77 *Lois Johnson*
93/73 **Your Shoeshine Girl** *Leona Williams*
36/73 **Your Side Of The Bed** *Mac Davis*
3/68 **Your Squaw Is On The Warpath** *Loretta Lynn*
90/73 **Your Sweet Love (Keeps Me Homeward Bound)** *Jimmy Dean*
Your Sweet Love Lifted Me
44/69 *Bobby Barnett*
45/70 *Ferlin Husky*
47/95 **Your Tattoo** *Sammy Kershaw*
1/67 **Your Tender Loving Care** *Buck Owens*
50/68 **Your Time Hasn't Come Yet, Baby** *Elvis Presley*
4/69 **Your Time's Comin'** *Faron Young*
13/57 **Your True Love** *Carl Perkins*
83/76 **Your Wanting Me Is Gone** *Vernon Oxford*
35/81 **Your Wife Is Cheatin' On Us Again** *Wayne Kemp*
12/59 **Your Wild Life's Gonna Get You Down** *Kitty Wells*
22/79 **Yours** *Freddy Fender*
77/75 **Yours And Mine** *O.B. McClinton*
78/79 **Yours And Mine** *Mary Lou Turner*
28/80 **Yours For The Taking** *Jack Greene*
47/69 **Yours Forever** *Wynn Stewart*
Yours Love
5/69 *Waylon Jennings*
9/69 *Dolly Parton/Porter Wagoner*
67/79 *Jerry Wallace*

Z

56/02 **'Zat You, Santa Claus?** *Garth Brooks*
56/90 **Zydeco Lady** *Eddy Raven*

TOP ARTISTS

Kings & Queens Of Country (The Top 300 Artists)

Top 50 Artists: 1944-1949 / 1950s / 1960s / 1970s / 1980s / 1990s / 2000-05

Top Artist Achievements:

- Most Chart Hits
- Most Top 40 Hits
- Most Top 10 Hits
- Most #1 Hits
- Most Weeks At The #1 Position
- Most Consecutive #1 Hits

TOP 300 ARTISTS

Point System:

Next to each artist's name is their point total. The points are totaled through the September 24, 2005, chart. Each artist's points are accumulated according to the following formula:

1. Each artist's singles are given points based on their highest charted position:

#1	=	100 points for its first week at #1, plus 10 points for each additional week at #1
#2	=	90 points for its first week at #2, plus 5 points for each additional week at #2
#3	=	80 points for its first week at #3, plus 3 points for each additional week at #3
#4-5	=	70 points
#6-10	=	60 points
#11-15	=	55 points
#16-20	=	50 points
#21-30	=	45 points
#31-40	=	40 points
#41-50	=	35 points
#51-60	=	30 points
#61-70	=	25 points
#71-80	=	20 points
#81-90	=	15 points
#91-100	=	10 points

2. Points awarded for *Top Country Singles Sales* hits:

#1	=	50 points for its first week at #1, plus 5 points for each additional week at #1
#2	=	45 points for its first week at #2, plus 3 points for each additional week at #2
#3	=	40 points for its first week at #3, plus 2 points for each additional week at #3
#4-5	=	35 points
#6-10	=	30 points
#11-15	=	25 points
#16-20	=	20 points
#21-30	=	15 points
#31-40	=	10 points

3. Total weeks charted are added in.

In the case of a tie, the artist listed first is determined by the following tie-breaker rules:

1) Most charted singles   2) Most Top 40 singles   3) Most Top 10 singles

When two artists combine for a hit single, such as Faith Hill and Tim McGraw, the full point value is given to both artists. Duos, such as Brooks & Dunn, are considered regular recording teams, and their points are not shared by either artist individually.

Headings And Special Symbols:

Old Rank: Artist ranking in *Top Country Singles 1944-2001* book

New Rank: Artist ranking in *Top Country Songs 1944-2005* book

● Deceased Solo Artist or Group Member

★ Hot Artist
- #1-10: Rank increased by at least 500 points.
- #11-40: Rank increased by at least 5 positions since previous edition
- #41-100: Rank increased by at least 10 positions since previous edition
- #101-300: Rank increased by at least 20 positions since previous edition

— Artist did not rank in the Top 300 of the previous edition.

DEBUT First time artist appears on this list.

+ Subject to change since a single is still charted as of the 9/24/2005 cut-off date.

KINGS & QUEENS OF COUNTRY (#1-96)

Old Rank	New Rank			Points
(1)	1.	Eddy Arnold		12,653
(2)	2.	George Jones		11,919+
(3)	3.	Johnny Cash	●	9,717
(5)	4.	Merle Haggard		9,101
(4)	5.	Conway Twitty	●	9,101
(6)	★6.	George Strait		9,094
(10)	7.	Willie Nelson		8,175
(7)	8.	Dolly Parton		8,109
(8)	9.	Webb Pierce	●	7,975
(9)	10.	Ray Price		7,773
(11)	11.	Buck Owens		7,492
(12)	12.	Waylon Jennings	●	7,491
(14)	13.	Reba McEntire		7,422
(13)	14.	Marty Robbins	●	7,306
(16)	15.	Hank Williams, Jr.		7,075
(15)	16.	Alabama		6,977
(17)	17.	Jim Reeves	●	6,843
(18)	18.	Ernest Tubb	●	6,474
(19)	19.	Charley Pride		6,422
(20)	20.	Loretta Lynn		6,285
(21)	21.	Sonny James		6,205
(38)	★22.	Alan Jackson		6,125
(22)	23.	Faron Young	●	6,115
(23)	24.	Hank Snow	●	6,088
(24)	25.	Ronnie Milsap		5,989
(25)	26.	Carl Smith		5,901
(27)	27.	Kenny Rogers		5,860
(26)	28.	Tammy Wynette	●	5,836
(28)	29.	Garth Brooks		5,711
(29)	30.	Bill Anderson		5,621
(30)	31.	Mel Tillis		5,385
(33)	32.	Tanya Tucker		5,359
(31)	33.	Red Foley	●	5,326
(32)	34.	Porter Wagoner		5,237
(34)	35.	Don Williams		5,211
(35)	36.	Elvis Presley	●	5,197
(36)	37.	Kitty Wells		5,134
(37)	38.	Don Gibson	●	5,090
(39)	39.	Glen Campbell		4,971
(63)	★40.	Tim McGraw		4,942+
(40)	41.	The Statler Brothers	●	4,828
(41)	42.	Hank Thompson		4,813
(62)	★43.	Brooks & Dunn		4,800+
(43)	44.	Steve Wariner		4,745
(42)	45.	Crystal Gayle		4,522
(50)	46.	Vince Gill		4,404
(44)	47.	Hank Williams	●	4,395
(45)	48.	Jerry Lee Lewis		4,365
(53)	49.	Clint Black		4,315
(52)	50.	Randy Travis		4,264
(46)	51.	David Houston	●	4,250
(48)	52.	Barbara Mandrell		4,217
(49)	53.	Oak Ridge Boys	●	4,217
(47)	54.	Bobby Bare		4,192
(51)	55.	Mickey Gilley		4,076
(110)	★56.	Toby Keith		4,071+
(54)	57.	Lynn Anderson		4,021
(55)	58.	Eddie Rabbitt	●	3,990
(56)	59.	Anne Murray		3,901
(57)	60.	Joe Stampley		3,866
(58)	61.	Dottie West	●	3,858
(61)	62.	Emmylou Harris		3,801
(59)	63.	John Anderson		3,779
(60)	64.	T.G. Sheppard		3,746
(77)	★65.	Travis Tritt		3,632
(156)	★66.	Kenny Chesney		3,606
(69)	67.	Sawyer Brown		3,545
(64)	68.	Moe Bandy		3,537
(65)	69.	Tom T. Hall		3,536
(66)	70.	Bellamy Brothers		3,532
(67)	71.	Billy Walker		3,493
(68)	72.	Earl Thomas Conley		3,482
(71)	73.	Patty Loveless		3,460
(70)	74.	Ferlin Husky		3,355
(105)	★75.	Martina McBride		3,338
(72)	76.	Johnny Paycheck	●	3,266
(73)	77.	Gene Watson		3,247
(74)	78.	Connie Smith		3,218
(75)	79.	Freddie Hart		3,209
(76)	80.	Johnny Rodriguez		3,145
(78)	81.	Jerry Reed		3,116
(89)	82.	Mark Chesnutt		3,101
(79)	83.	Charlie Rich	●	3,084
(80)	84.	Larry Gatlin & The Gatlin Brothers		3,031
(84)	85.	Ricky Skaggs		3,008
(81)	86.	Janie Fricke		2,993
(97)	★87.	John Michael Montgomery		2,983
(82)	88.	Jim Ed Brown		2,963
(94)	89.	Trisha Yearwood		2,950+
(83)	90.	Lefty Frizzell	●	2,945
(99)	91.	Joe Diffie		2,911
(115)	★92.	Diamond Rio		2,873
(103)	★93.	Faith Hill		2,827+
(85)	94.	Vern Gosdin		2,815
(86)	95.	Collin Raye		2,795
(87)	96.	Eddy Raven		2,793

KINGS & QUEENS OF COUNTRY (#97-209)

Old Rank	New Rank			Points
(88)	97.	Billy "Crash" Craddock		2,787
(90)	98.	Lee Greenwood		2,774
(146)	★99.	Lonestar		2,767 +
(91)	100.	John Conlee		2,756
(93)	101.	Kathy Mattea		2,733
(109)	102.	Tracy Lawrence		2,727
(92)	103.	Stonewall Jackson		2,721
(96)	104.	Lorrie Morgan		2,709
(95)	105.	Del Reeves		2,666
(98)	106.	Roy Drusky	●	2,658
(100)	107.	Dave Dudley	●	2,629
(101)	108.	Roger Miller	●	2,624
(102)	109.	Jean Shepard		2,612
(108)	110.	Dwight Yoakam		2,587
(120)	111.	Clay Walker		2,563
(104)	112.	Charly McClain		2,553
(139)	★113.	Shania Twain		2,539
(106)	114.	The Judds		2,529
(107)	115.	Donna Fargo		2,517
(111)	116.	Roy Clark		2,427
(112)	117.	Ronnie McDowell		2,420
(113)	118.	Bob Wills	●	2,418
(114)	119.	Ricky Van Shelton		2,405
(116)	120.	Skeeter Davis	●	2,353
(161)	★121.	Tracy Byrd		2,339
(117)	122.	George Hamilton IV		2,334
(118)	123.	Jack Greene		2,295
(119)	124.	Mel McDaniel		2,290
(121)	125.	Johnny Duncan		2,253
(122)	126.	Dan Seals		2,250
(123)	127.	The Kendalls	●	2,235
(124)	128.	Nitty Gritty Dirt Band		2,174
(125)	129.	Jimmy Wakely	●	2,171
(131)	130.	Restless Heart		2,167
(134)	131.	Sammy Kershaw		2,155
(126)	132.	Rosanne Cash		2,145
(127)	133.	Shenandoah		2,141
(128)	134.	"Tennessee" Ernie Ford	●	2,126
(129)	135.	Johnny Lee		2,107
(130)	136.	Gary Morris		2,107
(132)	137.	Gene Autry	●	2,101
(133)	138.	Pam Tillis		2,092
(158)	139.	Aaron Tippin		2,090
(135)	140.	Jimmy Newman		2,047
(136)	141.	Hank Locklin		2,044
(183)	★142.	Dixie Chicks		2,034
(137)	143.	Wilburn Brothers	●●	2,019
(138)	144.	George Morgan	●	2,015
(157)	145.	Wynonna		2,007
(140)	146.	Slim Whitman		1,996
(141)	147.	Al Dexter	●	1,996
(142)	148.	Tommy Overstreet		1,995
(143)	149.	Ed Bruce		1,993
(144)	150.	Billie Jo Spears		1,993
(145)	151.	Nat Stuckey	●	1,989
(149)	152.	Mary Chapin Carpenter		1,959
(147)	153.	Exile		1,952
(148)	154.	Narvel Felts		1,947
(155)	155.	Neal McCoy		1,938 +
(150)	156.	Michael Martin Murphey		1,911
(151)	157.	Razzy Bailey		1,908
(152)	158.	Tex Ritter	●	1,901
(153)	159.	Bob Luman	●	1,882
(219)	★160.	Jo Dee Messina		1,873 +
(154)	161.	Doug Stone		1,870
(159)	162.	Sammi Smith		1,814
(160)	163.	Rex Allen, Jr.		1,811
(162)	164.	Brenda Lee		1,799
(169)	165.	Marty Stuart		1,797
(163)	166.	Freddy Weller		1,784
(164)	167.	Jerry Wallace		1,761
(165)	168.	Claude King		1,754
(187)	169.	Billy Dean		1,717
(166)	170.	Tex Williams	●	1,715
(167)	171.	Juice Newton		1,688
(168)	172.	David Rogers	●	1,675
(179)	173.	Linda Ronstadt		1,673
(170)	174.	Wynn Stewart	●	1,670
(235)	★175.	LeAnn Rimes		1,661 +
(171)	176.	Cal Smith		1,644
(172)	177.	Jan Howard		1,644
(173)	178.	The Forester Sisters		1,636
(174)	179.	Red Sovine	●	1,621
(175)	180.	Susan Raye		1,616
(176)	181.	Lacy J. Dalton		1,614
(252)	★182.	Terri Clark		1,613
(269)	★183.	Trace Adkins		1,611 +
(177)	184.	Keith Whitley	●	1,573
(178)	185.	Ray Stevens		1,566
(180)	186.	Kenny Price	●	1,558
(181)	187.	Mac Davis		1,545
(189)	188.	Rodney Crowell		1,541
(182)	189.	Warner Mack		1,538
(190)	190.	T. Graham Brown		1,538
(259)	★191.	Lee Ann Womack		1,534 +
(184)	192.	Dickey Lee		1,527
(185)	193.	Sylvia		1,527
(194)	194.	Charlie Daniels Band		1,525
(186)	195.	Margo Smith		1,519
(188)	196.	Wanda Jackson		1,512
(191)	197.	Jimmy Dean		1,505
(389)	★198.	Brad Paisley		1,504 +
(192)	199.	David Frizzell		1,498
(193)	200.	John Denver	●	1,495
(201)	201.	Billy Ray Cyrus		1,478
—	★202.	Keith Urban	*DEBUT*	1,471
—	★203.	Rascal Flatts	*DEBUT*	1,470 +
(195)	204.	Charlie Louvin		1,465
(196)	205.	Highway 101		1,464
(312)	★206.	Gary Allan		1,460 +
(197)	207.	Melba Montgomery		1,449
(198)	208.	Louise Mandrell		1,446
(199)	209.	Holly Dunn		1,437

KINGS & QUEENS OF COUNTRY (#210-300)

Old Rank	New Rank			Points
(261)	★*210.*	**Mark Wills**		1,437
(214)	*211.*	**Lee Roy Parnell**		1,428
(200)	*212.*	**Suzy Bogguss**		1,419
(202)	*213.*	**Freddy Fender**		1,402
(203)	*214.*	**The Everly Brothers**		1,402
(204)	*215.*	**Leon Everette**		1,400
(205)	*216.*	**Gary Stewart**		1,399
(206)	*217.*	**The Browns**		1,398
(207)	*218.*	**Dave & Sugar**		1,391
(208)	*219.*	**Little Texas**		1,391
(209)	*220.*	**Mel Street**	●	1,390
(210)	*221.*	**Gail Davies**		1,388
(211)	*222.*	**Patsy Cline**	●	1,388
(212)	*223.*	**Barbara Fairchild**		1,386
(213)	*224.*	**Jeannie Seely**		1,386
(344)	★*225.*	**Sara Evans**		1,363 +
—	★*226.*	**Montgomery Gentry**	*DEBUT*	1,359 +
(215)	*227.*	**Jody Miller**		1,348
(216)	*228.*	**Ernest Ashworth**		1,342
(217)	*229.*	**Johnny Carver**		1,337
(220)	*230.*	**Bobby G. Rice**		1,321
(221)	*231.*	**Shelly West**		1,307
(218)	*232.*	**Bryan White**		1,303
(222)	*233.*	**David Allan Coe**		1,302
(223)	*234.*	**Merle Travis**	●	1,300
(224)	*235.*	**John Schneider**		1,298
(244)	*236.*	**BlackHawk**	●	1,284
(225)	*237.*	**Jacky Ward**		1,283
(226)	*238.*	**Claude Gray**		1,269
(227)	*239.*	**Cowboy Copas**	●	1,267
(246)	*240.*	**Ty Herndon**		1,265
(228)	*241.*	**Jeannie C. Riley**		1,263
(229)	*242.*	**Johnny Russell**	●	1,262
(230)	*243.*	**Tompall & The Glaser Brothers**		1,252
(231)	*244.*	**John Berry**		1,252
(232)	*245.*	**Marie Osmond**		1,246
(233)	*246.*	**Con Hunley**		1,242
(234)	*247.*	**Charlie Walker**		1,241
(236)	*248.*	**John Wesley Ryles**		1,235
(237)	*249.*	**Paul Overstreet**		1,216
(238)	*250.*	**Johnny Horton**	●	1,216
(239)	*251.*	**K.T. Oslin**		1,214
(240)	*252.*	**Flatt & Scruggs**	●	1,212
(241)	*253.*	**The Desert Rose Band**		1,205
(242)	*254.*	**Cristy Lane**		1,202
(243)	*255.*	**Jeanne Pruett**		1,199
(245)	*256.*	**Helen Cornelius**		1,183
(247)	*257.*	**Bobby Goldsboro**		1,165
(251)	*258.*	**Hal Ketchum**		1,162
(248)	*259.*	**Norma Jean**		1,160
(249)	*260.*	**Bobby Lewis**		1,156
(250)	*261.*	**Billy Joe Royal**		1,145
(253)	*262.*	**Jim Glaser**		1,089
(254)	*263.*	**"Little" Jimmy Dickens**		1,085
(255)	*264.*	**Randy Barlow**		1,072
(257)	*265.*	**Johnnie & Jack**	●	1,067
(258)	*266.*	**B.J. Thomas**		1,060
(260)	*267.*	**Leroy Van Dyke**		1,042
(256)	*268.*	**Olivia Newton-John**		1,038
(268)	*269.*	**Confederate Railroad**		1,003
(262)	*270.*	**Pee Wee King**	●	999
(370)	★*271.*	**SheDaisy**		995
(263)	*272.*	**Johnny Bush**		994
—	★*273.*	**Phil Vassar**	*DEBUT*	988 +
(264)	*274.*	**Wade Hayes**		986
(265)	*275.*	**Dick Curless**	●	981
(266)	*276.*	**Southern Pacific**		978
(267)	*277.*	**Buddy Alan**		972
(328)	★*278.*	**Chely Wright**		968
—	★*279.*	**Darryl Worley**	*DEBUT*	965
(270)	*280.*	**Ricochet**		959
(271)	*281.*	**Margaret Whiting**		953
(272)	*282.*	**Tommy Cash**		946
(273)	*283.*	**Ray Griff**		940
(274)	*284.*	**Elton Britt**	●	939
(388)	★*285.*	**Andy Griggs**		937
(288)	*286.*	**Rick Trevino**		933
(378)	★*287.*	**Jimmy Buffett**		931
(316)	★*288.*	**David Lee Murphy**		930
(275)	*289.*	**Red Steagall**		927
(276)	*290.*	**Mundo Earwood**		926
(277)	*291.*	**Patti Page**		918
(278)	*292.*	**Roy Acuff**	●	918
(323)	*293.*	**Deborah Allen**		909
(279)	*294.*	**The Whites**		908
(280)	*295.*	**Susie Allanson**		903
(281)	*296.*	**Carl Butler and Pearl**	● ●	898
(282)	*297.*	**Roy Head**		887
(283)	*298.*	**Bill Phillips**		887
(284)	*299.*	**Mark Collie**		885
(285)	*300.*	**Bobby Helms**	●	884

A-Z — TOP 300 ARTISTS

Acuff, Roy ... 292
Adkins, Trace ... 183
Alabama ... 16
Alan, Buddy ... 277
Allan, Gary ... 206
Allanson, Susie ... 295
Allen, Deborah ... 293
Allen, Rex Jr. ... 163
Anderson, Bill ... 30
Anderson, John ... 63
Anderson, Lynn ... 57
Arnold, Eddy ... 1
Ashworth, Ernest ... 228
Autry, Gene ... 137
Bailey, Razzy ... 157
Bandy, Moe ... 68
Bare, Bobby ... 54
Barlow, Randy ... 264
Bellamy Brothers ... 70
Berry, John ... 244
Black, Clint ... 49
BlackHawk ... 236
Bogguss, Suzy ... 212
Britt, Elton ... 284
Brooks, Garth ... 29
Brooks & Dunn ... 43
Brown, Jim Ed ... 88
Brown, T. Graham ... 190
Browns, The ... 217
Bruce, Ed ... 149
Buffett, Jimmy ... 287
Bush, Johnny ... 272
Butler, Carl, & Pearl ... 296
Byrd, Tracy ... 121
Campbell, Glen ... 39
Carpenter, Mary Chapin ... 152
Carver, Johnny ... 229
Cash, Johnny ... 3
Cash, Rosanne ... 132
Cash, Tommy ... 282
Chesney, Kenny ... 66
Chesnutt, Mark ... 82
Clark, Roy ... 116
Clark, Terri ... 182
Cline, Patsy ... 222
Coe, David Allan ... 233
Collie, Mark ... 299
Confederate Railroad ... 269
Conlee, John ... 100
Conley, Earl Thomas ... 72
Copas, Cowboy ... 239
Cornelius, Helen ... 256
Craddock, Billy "Crash" ... 97
Crowell, Rodney ... 188
Curless, Dick ... 275
Cyrus, Billy Ray ... 201
Dalton, Lacy J. ... 181
Daniels, Charlie, Band ... 194
Dave & Sugar ... 218
Davies, Gail ... 221
Davis, Mac ... 187
Davis, Skeeter ... 120
Dean, Billy ... 169
Dean, Jimmy ... 197
Denver, John ... 200
Desert Rose Band, The ... 253
Dexter, Al ... 147
Diamond Rio ... 92
Dickens, "Little" Jimmy ... 263
Diffie, Joe ... 91
Dixie Chicks ... 142
Drusky, Roy ... 106
Dudley, Dave ... 107
Duncan, Johnny ... 125
Dunn, Holly ... 209
Earwood, Mundo ... 290
Evans, Sara ... 225
Everette, Leon ... 215
Everly Brothers, The ... 214
Exile ... 153
Fairchild, Barbara ... 223
Fargo, Donna ... 115
Felts, Narvel ... 154
Fender, Freddy ... 213
Flatt & Scruggs ... 252
Foley, Red ... 33
Ford, "Tennessee" Ernie ... 134
Forester Sisters, The ... 178
Fricke, Janie ... 86
Frizzell, David ... 199
Frizzell, Lefty ... 90
Gatlin, Larry, & The Gatlin Brothers ... 84
Gayle, Crystal ... 45
Gibson, Don ... 38
Gill, Vince ... 46
Gilley, Mickey ... 55
Glaser, Jim ... 262
Glaser Brothers, Tompall & The ... 243
Goldsboro, Bobby ... 257
Gosdin, Vern ... 94
Gray, Claude ... 238
Greene, Jack ... 123
Greenwood, Lee ... 98
Griff, Ray ... 283
Griggs, Andy ... 285
Haggard, Merle ... 4
Hall, Tom T. ... 69
Hamilton, George IV ... 122
Harris, Emmylou ... 62
Hart, Freddie ... 79
Hayes, Wade ... 274
Head, Roy ... 297
Helms, Bobby ... 300
Herndon, Ty ... 240
Highway 101 ... 205
Hill, Faith ... 93
Horton, Johnny ... 250
Houston, David ... 51
Howard, Jan ... 177
Hunley, Con ... 246
Husky, Ferlin ... 74
Jackson, Alan ... 22
Jackson, Stonewall ... 103
Jackson, Wanda ... 196
James, Sonny ... 21
Jennings, Waylon ... 12
Johnnie & Jack ... 265
Jones, George ... 2
Judds, The ... 114
Keith, Toby ... 56
Kendalls, The ... 127
Kershaw, Sammy ... 131
Ketchum, Hal ... 258
King, Claude ... 168
King, Pee Wee ... 270
Lane, Cristy ... 254
Lawrence, Tracy ... 102
Lee, Brenda ... 164
Lee, Dickey ... 192
Lee, Johnny ... 135
Lewis, Bobby ... 260
Lewis, Jerry Lee ... 48
Little Texas ... 219
Locklin, Hank ... 141
Lonestar ... 99
Louvin, Charlie ... 204
Loveless, Patty ... 73
Luman, Bob ... 159
Lynn, Loretta ... 20
Mack, Warner ... 189
Mandrell, Barbara ... 52
Mandrell, Louise ... 208
Mattea, Kathy ... 101
McBride, Martina ... 75
McClain, Charly ... 112
McCoy, Neal ... 155
McDaniel, Mel ... 124
McDowell, Ronnie ... 117
McEntire, Reba ... 13
McGraw, Tim ... 40
Messina, Jo Dee ... 160
Miller, Jody ... 227
Miller, Roger ... 108
Milsap, Ronnie ... 25
Montgomery, John Michael ... 87
Montgomery, Melba ... 207
Montgomery Gentry ... 226
Morgan, George ... 144
Morgan, Lorrie ... 104
Morris, Gary ... 136
Murphey, Michael Martin ... 156
Murphy, David Lee ... 288
Murray, Anne ... 59
Nelson, Willie ... 7
Newman, Jimmy ... 140
Newton, Juice ... 171
Newton-John, Olivia ... 268
Nitty Gritty Dirt Band ... 128
Norma Jean ... 259
Oak Ridge Boys ... 53
Oslin, K.T. ... 251
Osmond, Marie ... 245
Overstreet, Paul ... 249
Overstreet, Tommy ... 148
Owens, Buck ... 11
Page, Patti ... 291
Paisley, Brad ... 198
Parnell, Lee Roy ... 211
Parton, Dolly ... 8
Paycheck, Johnny ... 76
Phillips, Bill ... 298
Pierce, Webb ... 9
Presley, Elvis ... 36
Price, Kenny ... 186
Price, Ray ... 10
Pride, Charley ... 19
Pruett, Jeanne ... 255
Rabbitt, Eddie ... 58
Rascal Flatts ... 203
Raven, Eddy ... 96
Raye, Collin ... 95
Raye, Susan ... 180
Reed, Jerry ... 81
Reeves, Del ... 105

TOP 50 ARTISTS

1944-49

1. **Eddy Arnold** 3,587
2. **Ernest Tubb** 2,455
3. **Bob Wills** 2,148
4. **Al Dexter** 1,996
5. **Red Foley** 1,756
6. **Gene Autry** 1,573
7. **Jimmy Wakely** 1,420
8. **Tex Ritter** 1,349
9. **Tex Williams** 1,218
10. **Merle Travis** 1,182
11. **Hank Williams** 1,047
12. **Sons Of The Pioneers** 795
13. **Elton Britt** 703
14. **Ted Daffan** 687
15. **Floyd Tillman** 656
16. **Hank Thompson** 617
17. **Cowboy Copas** 609
18. **Spade Cooley** 606
19. **Roy Acuff** 590
20. **George Morgan** 584
21. **Margaret Whiting** 469
22. **Bill Monroe** 445
23. **"T" Texas Tyler** 431
24. **Tennessee Ernie Ford** 418
25. **Jimmie Davis** 415

26. **Johnny Bond** 408
27. **Wesley Tuttle** 375
28. **Louis Jordan** 343
29. **Dick Thomas** 336
30. **Foy Willing** 330
31. **Jack Guthrie** 324
32. **Andrews Sisters** 322
33. **Hoosier Hot Shots** 287
34. **Moon Mullican** 282
35. **Roy Rogers** 265
36. **Nat "King" Cole** 260
37. **Pee Wee King** 258
38. **Wayne Raney** 255
39. **"Little" Jimmy Dickens** 254
40. **Bob Atcher** 250
41. **Jo Stafford** 230
42. **Zeke Manners** 221
43. **Cliffie Stone** 207
44. **Texas Jim Robertson** 203
45. **Lawrence Welk** 196
46. **Hawkshaw Hawkins** 195
47. **Arthur "Guitar Boogie" Smith** 193
48. **Kenny Roberts** 193
49. **Frankie Yankovic** 184
50. **Carson Robison** 182

1950s

1. **Webb Pierce** 5,056
2. **Eddy Arnold** 4,447
3. **Hank Snow** 3,933
4. **Carl Smith** 3,554
5. **Red Foley** 3,438
6. **Hank Williams** 3,203
7. **Ernest Tubb** 2,690
8. **Elvis Presley** 2,658
9. **Johnny Cash** 2,632
10. **Kitty Wells** 2,568
11. **Hank Thompson** 2,302
12. **Ray Price** 2,300
13. **Faron Young** 2,212
14. **Jim Reeves** 2,185
15. **Marty Robbins** 2,055
16. **Lefty Frizzell** 1,911
17. **"Tennessee" Ernie Ford** 1,375
18. **Ferlin Husky** 1,230
19. **The Everly Brothers** 1,075
20. **Johnnie & Jack** 1,013
21. **George Jones** 993
22. **Don Gibson** 937
23. **Jimmy Newman** 816
24. **Johnny Horton** 794
25. **The Browns** 789

26. **Sonny James** 771
27. **Wilburn Brothers** 769
28. **Jimmy Wakely** 751
29. **Pee Wee King** 741
30. **Slim Whitman** 735
31. **The Louvin Brothers** 674
32. **Jean Shepard** 648
33. **Porter Wagoner** 628
34. **The Carlisles** 605
35. **Bobby Helms** 593
36. **Hank Locklin** 546
37. **Jerry Lee Lewis** 546
38. **Margaret Whiting** 484
39. **Tommy Collins** 480
40. **George Morgan** 466
41. **Gene Autry** 463
42. **Red Sovine** 430
43. **Stuart Hamblen** 428
44. **Carl Perkins** 396
45. **Jimmie Rodgers** 389
46. **Goldie Hill** 388
47. **Moon Mullican** 386
48. **Ricky Nelson** 369
49. **Stonewall Jackson** 368
50. **Wilma Lee & Stoney Cooper** 358

TOP 50 ARTISTS

1960s

1. **Buck Owens** 4,819
2. **George Jones** 4,142
3. **Jim Reeves** 3,384
4. **Johnny Cash** 3,090
5. **Eddy Arnold** 2,803
6. **Marty Robbins** 2,631
7. **Webb Pierce** 2,594
8. **Bill Anderson** 2,577
9. **Ray Price** 2,450
10. **Faron Young** 2,428
11. **Kitty Wells** 2,378
12. **Sonny James** 2,341
13. **Porter Wagoner** 2,245
14. **Stonewall Jackson** 2,071
15. **Loretta Lynn** 1,958
16. **Roy Drusky** 1,907
17. **David Houston** 1,895
18. **Don Gibson** 1,855
19. **Merle Haggard** 1,760
20. **Roger Miller** 1,735
21. **Carl Smith** 1,696
22. **Billy Walker** 1,693
23. **Bobby Bare** 1,630
24. **George Hamilton IV** 1,609
25. **Skeeter Davis** 1,567

26. **Hank Snow** 1,509
27. **Dave Dudley** 1,504
28. **Connie Smith** 1,483
29. **Claude King** 1,454
30. **Del Reeves** 1,339
31. **Ferlin Husky** 1,333
32. **Ernest Ashworth** 1,319
33. **Hank Locklin** 1,311
34. **Glen Campbell** 1,253
35. **Jimmy Newman** 1,200
36. **Ernest Tubb** 1,168
37. **Waylon Jennings** 1,166
38. **Wilburn Brothers** 1,158
39. **Dottie West** 1,148
40. **Jimmy Dean** 1,137
41. **Tammy Wynette** 1,130
42. **Jack Greene** 1,112
43. **Warner Mack** 1,073
44. **Flatt & Scruggs** 1,061
45. **Norma Jean** 1,041
46. **Jan Howard** 1,031
47. **Wynn Stewart** 1,014
48. **Wanda Jackson** 1,010
49. **Hank Williams, Jr.** 977
50. **Hank Thompson** 969

1970s

1. **Conway Twitty** 4,274
2. **Merle Haggard** 3,656
3. **Charley Pride** 3,377
4. **Dolly Parton** 3,330
5. **Loretta Lynn** 3,246
6. **Mel Tillis** 3,217
7. **Tammy Wynette** 3,213
8. **George Jones** 3,095
9. **Waylon Jennings** 3,043
10. **Sonny James** 2,866
11. **Johnny Cash** 2,812
12. **Charlie Rich** 2,670
13. **Lynn Anderson** 2,658
14. **Willie Nelson** 2,638
15. **Tom T. Hall** 2,606
16. **Freddie Hart** 2,419
17. **Jerry Lee Lewis** 2,366
18. **Bill Anderson** 2,289
19. **Hank Williams, Jr.** 2,275
20. **Joe Stampley** 2,273
21. **Billy "Crash" Craddock** 2,259
22. **David Houston** 2,251
23. **Don Gibson** 2,230
24. **Glen Campbell** 2,170
25. **Ronnie Milsap** 2,101

26. **Buck Owens** 2,078
27. **Donna Fargo** 2,055
28. **Marty Robbins** 2,047
29. **Johnny Rodriguez** 2,044
30. **Porter Wagoner** 2,040
31. **Barbara Mandrell** 1,975
32. **Jim Ed Brown** 1,963
33. **The Statler Brothers** 1,946
34. **Elvis Presley** 1,941
35. **Johnny Paycheck** 1,928
36. **Don Williams** 1,885
37. **Ray Price** 1,883
38. **Jerry Reed** 1,845
39. **Dottie West** 1,783
40. **Bobby Bare** 1,740
41. **Tanya Tucker** 1,733
42. **Tommy Overstreet** 1,718
43. **Connie Smith** 1,709
44. **Crystal Gayle** 1,690
45. **Anne Murray** 1,643
46. **Johnny Duncan** 1,628
47. **Mickey Gilley** 1,615
48. **Susan Raye** 1,561
49. **Roy Clark** 1,492
50. **Billy Walker** 1,488

TOP 50 ARTISTS

1980s

1. **Willie Nelson** 4,009
2. **Conway Twitty** 3,517
3. **Merle Haggard** 3,509
4. **Kenny Rogers** 3,407
5. **Alabama** 3,368
6. **Ronnie Milsap** 3,278
7. **Oak Ridge Boys** 3,041
8. **Hank Williams, Jr.** 2,997
9. **Waylon Jennings** 2,974
10. **Reba McEntire** 2,912
11. **Dolly Parton** 2,871
12. **Earl Thomas Conley** 2,862
13. **George Strait** 2,854
14. **Don Williams** 2,834
15. **Crystal Gayle** 2,810
16. **Bellamy Brothers** 2,730
17. **George Jones** 2,672
18. **Steve Wariner** 2,600
19. **T.G. Sheppard** 2,513
20. **Emmylou Harris** 2,433
21. **Ricky Skaggs** 2,432
22. **Janie Fricke** 2,431
23. **Mickey Gilley** 2,430
24. **The Statler Brothers** 2,370
25. **Lee Greenwood** 2,301

26. **John Conlee** 2,291
27. **Eddie Rabbitt** 2,282
28. **Barbara Mandrell** 2,205
29. **Eddy Raven** 2,182
30. **John Anderson** 2,113
31. **Charley Pride** 2,100
32. **Anne Murray** 2,068
33. **Moe Bandy** 2,061
34. **Charly McClain** 2,057
35. **Gary Morris** 2,053
36. **Gene Watson** 1,989
37. **Rosanne Cash** 1,975
38. **The Judds** 1,961
39. **Larry Gatlin/Gatlin Brothers** . 1,832
40. **Ronnie McDowell** 1,825
41. **Johnny Lee** 1,784
42. **Nitty Gritty Dirt Band** 1,780
43. **Dan Seals** 1,739
44. **Mel McDaniel** 1,731
45. **Tanya Tucker** 1,712
46. **Michael Murphey** 1,707
47. **Vern Gosdin** 1,679
48. **Razzy Bailey** 1,600
49. **Joe Stampley** 1,593
50. **Exile** 1,556

1990s

1. **Garth Brooks** 4,646
2. **George Strait** 4,567
3. **Alan Jackson** 4,172
4. **Clint Black** 3,506
5. **Reba McEntire** 3,287
6. **Vince Gill** 3,176
7. **Alabama** 3,134
8. **Brooks & Dunn** 3,125
9. **Tim McGraw** 2,644
10. **Travis Tritt** 2,643
11. **Mark Chesnutt** 2,634
12. **Collin Raye** 2,499
13. **Joe Diffie** 2,480
14. **Trisha Yearwood** 2,463
15. **Randy Travis** 2,347
16. **Patty Loveless** 2,345
17. **John Michael Montgomery** 2,344
18. **Tracy Lawrence** 2,184
19. **Lorrie Morgan** 2,172
20. **Diamond Rio** 2,060
21. **Sawyer Brown** 2,056
22. **Sammy Kershaw** 1,948
23. **Martina McBride** 1,923
24. **Pam Tillis** 1,876
25. **Faith Hill** 1,860

26. **Clay Walker** 1,857
27. **Tanya Tucker** 1,808
28. **Doug Stone** 1,796
29. **Mary Chapin Carpenter** 1,765
30. **Shania Twain** 1,759
31. **Toby Keith** 1,714
32. **Wynonna** 1,711
33. **Steve Wariner** 1,680
34. **Neal McCoy** 1,582
35. **Aaron Tippin** 1,521
36. **Tracy Byrd** 1,495
37. **Shenandoah** 1,459
38. **Ricky Van Shelton** 1,419
39. **Dwight Yoakam** 1,415
40. **Little Texas** 1,391
41. **John Anderson** 1,383
42. **Lee Roy Parnell** 1,377
43. **Marty Stuart** 1,343
44. **Kenny Chesney** 1,339
45. **Billy Dean** 1,310
46. **John Berry** 1,252
47. **Kathy Mattea** 1,250
48. **Bryan White** 1,205
49. **Lonestar** 1,156
50. **Billy Ray Cyrus** 1,148

TOP 50 ARTISTS
2000-05

1. **Toby Keith** .... 2,357+
2. **Tim McGraw** .... 2,298+
3. **Kenny Chesney** 2,267
4. **Alan Jackson** 1,906
5. **Brooks & Dunn** .... 1,675+
6. **George Strait** 1,673
7. **Lonestar** .... 1,611+
8. **Keith Urban** 1,471
9. **Rascal Flatts** .... 1,470+
10. **Martina McBride** 1,415
11. **Brad Paisley** .... 1,288+
12. **Dixie Chicks** 1,248
13. **Montgomery Gentry** .... 1,188+
14. **Gary Allan** .... 1,027+
15. **Jo Dee Messina** .... 1,014+
16. **Sara Evans** .... 1,008+
17. **Phil Vassar** .... 988+
18. **Faith Hill** .... 967+
19. **Darryl Worley** 965
20. **Trace Adkins** .... 945+
21. **Travis Tritt** 903
22. **SheDaisy** 883
23. **Blake Shelton** 880
24. **Reba McEntire** 867
25. **Garth Brooks** 853

26. **Tracy Byrd** 844
27. **Lee Ann Womack** .... 818+
28. **Diamond Rio** 813
29. **Shania Twain** 780
30. **Mark Wills** 757
31. **LeAnn Rimes** .... 732+
32. **Joe Nichols** 731
33. **Andy Griggs** 724
34. **Clay Walker** 706
35. **Craig Morgan** .... 701+
36. **Chris Cagle** .... 679+
37. **Terri Clark** 676
38. **Jamie O'Neal** .... 650+
39. **John Michael Montgomery** 639
40. **Steve Holy** 616
41. **Pat Green** 587
42. **Aaron Tippin** 569
43. **Clint Black** 564
44. **Tracy Lawrence** 543
45. **Kenny Rogers** 543
46. **Jessica Andrews** 523
47. **Trick Pony** 522
48. **Gretchen Wilson** 503
49. **Trisha Yearwood** .... 487+
50. **Mark Chesnutt** 467

TOP ARTIST ACHIEVEMENTS

MOST CHART HITS

#	Artist	Hits
1.	George Jones	167
2.	Eddy Arnold	146
3.	Johnny Cash	139
4.	Willie Nelson	122
5.	Ray Price	109
6.	Dolly Parton	108
7.	Merle Haggard	107
8.	Hank Williams, Jr.	104
9.	Waylon Jennings	100
10.	Conway Twitty	98
11.	George Strait	98
12.	Webb Pierce	96
13.	Marty Robbins	94
14.	Carl Smith	93
15.	Ernest Tubb	92
16.	Buck Owens	90
17.	Faron Young	89
18.	Reba McEntire	88
19.	Hank Snow	85
20.	Elvis Presley	85
21.	Don Gibson	82
22.	Porter Wagoner	81
23.	Kitty Wells	81
24.	Jim Reeves	80
25.	Bill Anderson	80
26.	Hank Thompson	79

MOST TOP 40 HITS

#	Artist	Hits
1.	George Jones	143
2.	Eddy Arnold	126
3.	Johnny Cash	101
4.	Dolly Parton	86
5.	Conway Twitty	85
6.	Waylon Jennings	84
7.	Merle Haggard	83
8.	Ernest Tubb	82
9.	Willie Nelson	81
10.	Marty Robbins	81
11.	Webb Pierce	80
12.	Ray Price	80
13.	Hank Williams, Jr.	79
14.	George Strait	77
15.	Reba McEntire	75
16.	Buck Owens	74
17.	Faron Young	74
18.	Jim Reeves	69
19.	Carl Smith	69
20.	Mel Tillis	67
21.	Loretta Lynn	66
22.	Alabama	65
23.	Hank Snow	65
24.	Don Gibson	65
25.	Porter Wagoner	64
26.	Sonny James	63

MOST TOP 10 HITS

#	Artist	Hits
1.	Eddy Arnold	92
2.	George Jones	78
3.	Conway Twitty	75
4.	Merle Haggard	71
5.	George Strait	70
6.	Ernest Tubb	58
7.	Dolly Parton	56
8.	Red Foley	56
9.	Webb Pierce	54
10.	Reba McEntire	54
11.	Waylon Jennings	53
12.	Johnny Cash	52
13.	Charley Pride	52
14.	Alabama	51
15.	Jim Reeves	51
16.	Loretta Lynn	51
17.	Ronnie Milsap	49
18.	Buck Owens	47
19.	Marty Robbins	47
20.	Ray Price	46
21.	Don Williams	45
★22.	Alan Jackson	44
23.	Sonny James	43
24.	Hank Snow	43
25.	Willie Nelson	42
26.	Hank Williams, Jr.	42

MOST #1 HITS

#	Artist	Hits
1.	Conway Twitty	40
2.	George Strait	39
3.	Merle Haggard	38
4.	Ronnie Milsap	35
5.	Alabama	32
6.	Charley Pride	29
7.	Eddy Arnold	28
8.	Dolly Parton	24
9.	Sonny James	23
10.	Reba McEntire	22
11.	Alan Jackson	22
12.	Willie Nelson	21
13.	Buck Owens	21
14.	Kenny Rogers	21
★15.	Tim McGraw	21
16.	Tammy Wynette	20
17.	Brooks & Dunn	20
18.	Garth Brooks	18
19.	Crystal Gayle	18
20.	Earl Thomas Conley	18
21.	Don Williams	17
22.	Oak Ridge Boys	17
23.	Mickey Gilley	17
24.	Eddie Rabbitt	17

MOST WEEKS AT THE #1 POSITION

#	Artist	Weeks
1.	Eddy Arnold	145
2.	Webb Pierce	111
3.	Buck Owens	82
4.	Hank Williams	82
5.	George Strait	76
6.	Johnny Cash	69
7.	Sonny James	66
8.	Tim McGraw	64
9.	Marty Robbins	63
10.	Jim Reeves	58
11.	Merle Haggard	57
12.	Hank Snow	56
13.	Alan Jackson	53
14.	Conway Twitty	52
15.	Elvis Presley	50
16.	Charley Pride	49
17.	Ray Price	47
18.	Ronnie Milsap	47
★19.	Toby Keith	47
20.	Al Dexter	47
21.	Alabama	40
22.	Red Foley	40
★23.	Brooks & Dunn	38
24.	Tammy Wynette	37

MOST CONSECUTIVE #1 HITS

#	Hits	Artist
1.	21	Alabama (1980-87)
2.	16	Earl Thomas Conley (1983-89)
3.	16	Sonny James (1967-71)
4.	15	Buck Owens (1963-67)
5.	11	George Strait (1986-89)
6.	11	Conway Twitty (1974-77)
7.	10	Ronnie Milsap (1980-83)
8.	9	Merle Haggard (1973-76)
9.	9	Webb Pierce (1953-56)
10.	9	Dan Seals (1985-89)
11.	8	Eddy Arnold (1948-49)
12.	8	The Judds (1984-87)
13.	8	T.G. Sheppard (1980-83)

Excludes Christmas hits, re-issues, B-sides, and duos (unless they add to the streak).

Ties are broken according to rank in the *Top 300 Artists* section.
★ First time artist appears on this list.

CHART FACTS & FEATS

Top Hits: All-Time / 1944-49 / 1950s / 1960s / 1970s / 1980s / 1990s / 2000-05

Singles Of Longevity: 1944-49 / 1950s / 1960s / 1970s / 1980s / 1990s / 2000-05

Top Country Songwriters

Country Music Association Awards: Single of the Year / Song of the Year

Country Music Hall Of Fame

Top Country Labels

Label Abbreviations

DEBUT First time title appears on this list.

TOP 100 #1 HITS

ALL-TIME

Peak Year	Wks Chr	Wks T40	Wks T10	Wks @ #1	Rank	Title	Artist
50	44	44	44	**21**	1.	**I'm Moving On**	*Hank Snow*
47	46	46	41	**21**	2.	**I'll Hold You In My Heart (Till I Can Hold You In My Arms)**	*Eddy Arnold*
55	37	37	34	**21**	3.	**In The Jailhouse Now**	*Webb Pierce*
56	45	45	41	**20**	4.	**Crazy Arms**	*Ray Price*
54	41	41	40	**20**	5.	**I Don't Hurt Anymore**	*Hank Snow*
48	54	54	53	**19**	6.	**Bouquet Of Roses**	*Eddy Arnold*
61	37	37	29	**19**	7.	**Walk On By**	*Leroy Van Dyke*
54	36	36	32	**17**	8.	**Slowly**	*Webb Pierce*
49	28	28	27	**17**	9.	**Slipping Around**	*Margaret Whiting & Jimmy Wakely*
56	27	27	26	**17**	10.	**Heartbreak Hotel**	*Elvis Presley*
49	42	42	40	**16**	11.	**Lovesick Blues**	*Hank Williams*
46	29	29	29	**16**	12.	**Guitar Polka**	*Al Dexter*
63	30	30	24	**16**	13.	**Love's Gonna Live Here**	*Buck Owens*
46	23	23	23	**16**	14.	**New Spanish Two Step**	*Bob Wills*
47	23	23	23	**16**	15.	**Smoke! Smoke! Smoke! (That Cigarette)**	*Tex Williams*
51	31	31	31	**15**	16.	**Slow Poke**	*Pee Wee King*
52	30	30	30	**15**	17.	**The Wild Side Of Life**	*Hank Thompson*
60	36	36	30	**14**	18.	**Please Help Me, I'm Falling**	*Hank Locklin*
60	34	34	29	**14**	19.	**He'll Have To Go**	*Jim Reeves*
52	29	29	29	**14**	20.	**Jambalaya (On The Bayou)**	*Hank Williams*
51	25	25	25	**14**	21.	**The Shot Gun Boogie**	*Tennessee Ernie*
46	23	23	23	**14**	22.	**Divorce Me C.O.D.**	*Merle Travis*
47	22	22	22	**14**	23.	**So Round, So Firm, So Fully Packed**	*Merle Travis*
44	30	30	30	**13**	24.	**So Long Pal**	*Al Dexter*
55	32	32	28	**13**	25.	**Love, Love, Love**	*Webb Pierce*
56	30	30	28	**13**	26.	**Singing The Blues**	*Marty Robbins*
44	27	27	27	**13**	27.	**Smoke On The Water**	*Red Foley*
58	34	34	25	**13**	28.	**City Lights**	*Ray Price*
58	29	29	20	**13**	29.	**Alone With You**	*Faron Young*
50	20	20	20	**13**	30.	**Chattanoogie Shoe Shine Boy**	*Red Foley*
53	19	19	19	**13**	31.	**Kaw-Liga**	*Hank Williams*
55	32	32	28	**12**	32.	**I Don't Care**	*Webb Pierce*
51	28	28	28	**12**	33.	**Always Late (With Your Kisses)**	*Lefty Frizzell*
53	27	27	27	**12**	34.	**There Stands The Glass**	*Webb Pierce*
60	34	34	26	**12**	35.	**Alabam**	*Cowboy Copas*
49	31	31	26	**12**	36.	**Don't Rob Another Man's Castle**	*Eddy Arnold*
48	32	32	31	**11**	37.	**One Has My Name (The Other Has My Heart)**	*Jimmy Wakely*
51	27	27	27	**11**	38.	**I Want To Be With You Always**	*Lefty Frizzell*
51	24	24	24	**11**	39.	**I Wanna Play House With You**	*Eddy Arnold*
51	23	23	23	**11**	40.	**There's Been A Change In Me**	*Eddy Arnold*
62	24	24	22	**11**	41.	**Don't Let Me Cross Over**	*Carl Butler*
45	20	20	20	**11**	42.	**You Two Timed Me One Time Too Often**	*Tex Ritter*
60	36	36	30	**10**	43.	**Wings Of A Dove**	*Ferlin Husky*
54	29	29	27	**10**	44.	**More And More**	*Webb Pierce*
56	28	28	25	**10**	45.	**Don't Be Cruel / Hound Dog**	*Elvis Presley*
50	25	25	25	**10**	46.	**Why Don't You Love Me**	*Hank Williams*
57	27	27	21	**10**	47.	**Gone**	*Ferlin Husky*
58	23	23	19	**10**	48.	**Ballad Of A Teenage Queen**	*Johnny Cash*
55	21	21	18	**10**	49.	**Sixteen Tons**	*"Tennessee" Ernie Ford*
59	21	21	18	**10**	50.	**The Battle Of New Orleans**	*Johnny Horton*

TOP 100 #1 HITS (Cont'd)

ALL-TIME

Peak Year	Wks Chr	Wks T40	Wks T10	Wks @ #1	Rank	Title	Artist
61	19	19	18	10	51.	Don't Worry	Marty Robbins
59	19	19	17	10	52.	The Three Bells	The Browns
48	39	39	37	9	53.	Anytime	Eddy Arnold
45	31	31	31	9	54.	Shame On You	Spade Cooley
53	26	26	26	9	55.	Mexican Joe	Jim Reeves
62	26	26	21	9	56.	Wolverton Mountain	Claude King
57	24	24	20	9	57.	Young Love	Sonny James
61	23	23	18	9	58.	Hello Walls	Faron Young
66	25	24	13	9	59.	Almost Persuaded	David Houston
51	33	33	33	8	60.	Let Old Mother Nature Have Her Way	Carl Smith
48	32	32	27	8	61.	Just A Little Lovin' (Will Go A Long, Long Way)	Eddy Arnold
51	27	27	27	8	62.	The Rhumba Boogie	Hank Snow
58	34	34	26	8	63.	Oh Lonesome Me	Don Gibson
53	26	26	26	8	64.	Hey Joe!	Carl Smith
53	26	26	26	8	65.	I Forgot More Than You'll Ever Know	The Davis Sisters
57	26	26	25	8	66.	Four Walls	Jim Reeves
51	25	25	25	8	67.	Hey, Good Lookin'	Hank Williams
52	24	24	24	8	68.	(When You Feel Like You're In Love) Don't Just Stand There	Carl Smith
45	22	22	22	8	69.	At Mail Call Today	Gene Autry
53	22	22	22	8	70.	It's Been So Long	Webb Pierce
99	41	37	21	8	71.	Amazed	Lonestar
50	21	21	21	8	72.	Long Gone Lonesome Bues	Hank Williams
58	24	24	20	8	73.	Guess Things Happen That Way	Johnny Cash
57	22	22	20	8	74.	Wake Up Little Susie	The Everly Brothers
64	28	27	19	8	75.	Once A Day	Connie Smith
03	27	27	17	8	76.	It's Five O'Clock Somewhere ... *DEBUT*	Alan Jackson & Jimmy Buffett
62	21	21	14	8	77.	Devil Woman	Marty Robbins
55	32	32	29	7	78.	Loose Talk	Carl Smith
61	32	32	24	7	79.	Tender Years	George Jones
64	26	26	22	7	80.	My Heart Skips A Beat	Buck Owens
59	26	26	22	7	81.	El Paso	Marty Robbins
62	27	27	21	7	82.	Mama Sang A Song	Bill Anderson
57	26	26	21	7	83.	Bye Bye Love	The Everly Brothers
45	21	21	21	7	84.	I'm Losing My Mind Over You	Al Dexter
63	27	27	20	7	85.	Still	Bill Anderson
63	26	26	19	7	86.	Ring Of Fire	Johnny Cash
64	26	24	18	7	87.	I Guess I'm Crazy	Jim Reeves
04	21	21	18	7	88.	Live Like You Were Dying .... *DEBUT*	Tim McGraw
02	31	29	17	7	89.	The Good Stuff .... *DEBUT*	Kenny Chesney
66	23	21	15	7	90.	There Goes My Everything	Jack Greene
03	20	19	14	7	91.	There Goes My Life .... *DEBUT*	Kenny Chesney
66	19	18	13	7	92.	Waitin' In Your Welfare Line	Buck Owens
03	20	19	12	7	93.	Have You Forgotten? *DEBUT*	Darryl Worley
56	43	43	39	6	94.	I Walk The Line	Johnny Cash
53	23	23	23	6	95.	A Dear John Letter	Jean Shepard with Ferlin Husky
53	23	23	23	6	96.	Your Cheatin' Heart	Hank Williams
02	41	40	20	6	97.	Somebody Like You .... *DEBUT*	Keith Urban
44	20	20	20	6	98.	I'm Wastin' My Tears On You	Tex Ritter
03	34	33	19	6	99.	19 Somethin' .... *DEBUT*	Mark Wills
62	23	23	19	6	100.	She Thinks I Still Care	George Jones

TOP 25 #1 HITS — 1944-1949

Peak Year	Wks Chr	Wks T40	Wks T10	Wks @ #1	Rank	Title	Artist
47	46	46	41	21	1.	I'll Hold You In My Heart (Till I Can Hold You In My Arms)	Eddy Arnold
48	54	54	53	19	2.	Bouquet Of Roses	Eddy Arnold
49	28	28	27	17	3.	Slipping Around	Margaret Whiting & Jimmy Wakely
49	42	42	40	16	4.	Lovesick Blues	Hank Williams
46	29	29	29	16	5.	Guitar Polka	Al Dexter
46	23	23	23	16	6.	New Spanish Two Step	Bob Wills
47	23	23	23	16	7.	Smoke! Smoke! Smoke! (That Cigarette)	Tex Williams
46	23	23	23	14	8.	Divorce Me C.O.D.	Merle Travis
47	22	22	22	14	9.	So Round, So Firm, So Fully Packed	Merle Travis
44	30	30	30	13	10.	So Long Pal	Al Dexter
44	27	27	27	13	11.	Smoke On The Water	Red Foley
49	31	31	26	12	12.	Don't Rob Another Man's Castle	Eddy Arnold
48	32	32	31	11	13.	One Has My Name (The Other Has My Heart)	Jimmy Wakely
45	20	20	20	11	14.	You Two Timed Me One Time Too Often	Tex Ritter
48	39	39	37	9	15.	Anytime	Eddy Arnold
45	31	31	31	9	16.	Shame On You	Spade Cooley
48	32	32	27	8	17.	Just A Little Lovin' (Will Go A Long, Long Way)	Eddy Arnold
45	22	22	22	8	18.	At Mail Call Today	Gene Autry
45	21	21	21	7	19.	I'm Losing My Mind Over You	Al Dexter
44	20	20	20	6	20.	I'm Wastin' My Tears On You	Tex Ritter
45	19	19	19	6	21.	Oklahoma Hills	Jack Guthrie
44	15	15	15	6	22.	Straighten Up And Fly Right	The King Cole Trio
47	38	38	38	5	23.	It's A Sin	Eddy Arnold
49	28	28	26	5	24.	I Love You So Much It Hurts	Jimmy Wakely
46	13	13	13	5	25.	Wine, Women And Song	Al Dexter

TOP 25 #1 HITS — 1950s

Peak Year	Wks Chr	Wks T40	Wks T10	Wks @ #1	Rank	Title	Artist
50	44	44	44	21	1.	I'm Moving On	Hank Snow
55	37	37	34	21	2.	In The Jailhouse Now	Webb Pierce
56	45	45	41	20	3.	Crazy Arms	Ray Price
54	41	41	40	20	4.	I Don't Hurt Anymore	Hank Snow
54	36	36	32	17	5.	Slowly	Webb Pierce
56	27	27	26	17	6.	Heartbreak Hotel	Elvis Presley
51	31	31	31	15	7.	Slow Poke	Pee Wee King
52	30	30	30	15	8.	The Wild Side Of Life	Hank Thompson
52	29	29	29	14	9.	Jambalaya (On The Bayou)	Hank Williams
51	25	25	25	14	10.	The Shot Gun Boogie	Tennessee Ernie
55	32	32	28	13	11.	Love, Love, Love	Webb Pierce
56	30	30	28	13	12.	Singing The Blues	Marty Robbins
58	34	34	25	13	13.	City Lights	Ray Price
58	29	29	20	13	14.	Alone With You	Faron Young
50	20	20	20	13	15.	Chattanoogie Shoe Shine Boy	Red Foley
53	19	19	19	13	16.	Kaw-Liga	Hank Williams
55	32	32	28	12	17.	I Don't Care	Webb Pierce
51	28	28	28	12	18.	Always Late (With Your Kisses)	Lefty Frizzell
53	27	27	27	12	19.	There Stands The Glass	Webb Pierce
51	27	27	27	11	20.	I Want To Be With You Always	Lefty Frizzell
51	24	24	24	11	21.	I Wanna Play House With You	Eddy Arnold
51	23	23	23	11	22.	There's Been A Change In Me	Eddy Arnold
54	29	29	27	10	23.	More And More	Webb Pierce
56	28	28	25	10	24.	Don't Be Cruel / Hound Dog	Elvis Presley
50	25	25	25	10	25.	Why Don't You Love Me	Hank Williams

TOP 25 #1 HITS — 1960s

Peak Year	Wks Chr	Wks T40	Wks T10	Wks @ #1	Rank	Title	Artist
61	37	37	29	19	1.	Walk On By	Leroy Van Dyke
63	30	30	24	16	2.	Love's Gonna Live Here	Buck Owens
60	36	36	30	14	3.	Please Help Me, I'm Falling	Hank Locklin
60	34	34	29	14	4.	He'll Have To Go	Jim Reeves
60	34	34	26	12	5.	Alabam	Cowboy Copas
62	24	24	22	11	6.	Don't Let Me Cross Over	Carl Butler
60	36	36	30	10	7.	Wings Of A Dove	Ferlin Husky
61	19	19	18	10	8.	Don't Worry	Marty Robbins
62	26	26	21	9	9.	Wolverton Mountain	Claude King
61	23	23	18	9	10.	Hello Walls	Faron Young
66	25	24	13	9	11.	Almost Persuaded	David Houston
64	28	27	19	8	12.	Once A Day	Connie Smith
62	21	21	14	8	13.	Devil Woman	Marty Robbins
61	32	32	24	7	14.	Tender Years	George Jones
64	26	26	22	7	15.	My Heart Skips A Beat	Buck Owens
62	27	27	21	7	16.	Mama Sang A Song	Bill Anderson
63	27	27	20	7	17.	Still	Bill Anderson
63	26	26	19	7	18.	Ring Of Fire	Johnny Cash
64	26	24	18	7	19.	I Guess I'm Crazy	Jim Reeves
66	23	21	15	7	20.	There Goes My Everything	Jack Greene
66	19	18	13	7	21.	Waitin' In Your Welfare Line	Buck Owens
62	23	23	19	6	22.	She Thinks I Still Care	George Jones
64	27	27	18	6	23.	I Don't Care (Just As Long As You Love Me)	Buck Owens
64	22	22	17	6	24.	Understand Your Man	Johnny Cash
64	25	22	15	6	25.	Dang Me	Roger Miller

TOP 25 #1 HITS — 1970s

Peak Year	Wks Chr	Wks T40	Wks T10	Wks @ #1	Rank	Title	Artist
72	19	18	12	6	1.	My Hang-Up Is You	Freddie Hart
77	18	14	10	6	2.	Luckenbach, Texas (Back To The Basics Of Love)	Waylon Jennings
75	15	13	8	6	3.	Convoy	C.W. McCall
71	19	18	13	5	4.	Kiss An Angel Good Mornin'	Charley Pride
70	20	19	12	5	5.	Rose Garden	Lynn Anderson
77	19	14	10	5	6.	Here You Come Again	Dolly Parton
71	15	13	10	5	7.	When You're Hot, You're Hot	Jerry Reed
70	20	18	10	4	8.	Hello Darlin'	Conway Twitty
70	17	16	10	4	9.	Baby, Baby (I Know You're A Lady)	David Houston
71	16	15	10	4	10.	Empty Arms	Sonny James
71	16	14	9	4	11.	I'm Just Me	Charley Pride
70	15	14	9	4	12.	Don't Keep Me Hangin' On	Sonny James
77	18	15	8	4	13.	Don't It Make My Brown Eyes Blue	Crystal Gayle
78	16	12	8	4	14.	Mammas Don't Let Your Babies Grow Up To Be Cowboys	Waylon & Willie
73	17	14	7	4	15.	If We Make It Through December	Merle Haggard
77	20	13	7	4	16.	Heaven's Just A Sin Away	The Kendalls
70	14	13	7	4	17.	It's Just A Matter Of Time	Sonny James
71	24	22	13	3	18.	Easy Loving	Freddie Hart
71	20	18	12	3	19.	Help Me Make It Through The Night	Sammi Smith
71	19	17	12	3	20.	I Won't Mention It Again	Ray Price
72	23	17	10	3	21.	The Happiest Girl In The Whole U.S.A.	Donna Fargo
73	19	16	10	3	22.	You've Never Been This Far Before	Conway Twitty
72	16	15	10	3	23.	Carolyn	Merle Haggard
70	16	14	9	3	24.	Endlessly	Sonny James
70	16	14	9	3	25.	He Loves Me All The Way	Tammy Wynette

TOP 25 #1 HITS — 1980s

Peak Year	Wks Chr	Wks T40	Wks T10	Wks @ #1	Rank	Title	Artist
80	15	9	8	3	1.	Coward Of The County	Kenny Rogers
80	15	13	7	3	2.	My Heart	Ronnie Milsap
80	14	10	7	3	3.	Lookin' For Love	Johnny Lee
87	22	13	6	3	4.	Forever And Ever, Amen	Randy Travis
85	22	14	8	2	5.	Have Mercy	The Judds
83	23	15	7	2	6.	Islands In The Stream	Kenny Rogers With Dolly Parton
83	22	15	7	2	7.	Houston (Means I'm One Day Closer To You)	Larry Gatlin/Gatlin Brothers
84	22	15	7	2	8.	Why Not Me	The Judds
85	23	14	7	2	9.	Lost In The Fifties Tonight (In The Still Of The Night)	Ronnie Milsap
88	22	14	7	2	10.	When You Say Nothing At All	Keith Whitley
86	19	14	7	2	11.	Mind Your Own Business	Hank Williams, Jr.
84	20	13	7	2	12.	To All The Girls I've Loved Before	Julio Iglesias & Willie Nelson
80	16	12	7	2	13.	I Believe In You	Don Williams
80	14	10	7	2	14.	My Heroes Have Always Been Cowboys	Willie Nelson
89	26	24	6	2	15.	A Woman In Love	Ronnie Milsap
88	21	15	6	2	16.	I'll Leave This World Loving You	Ricky Van Shelton
82	21	15	6	2	17.	Always On My Mind	Willie Nelson
87	23	14	6	2	18.	Somewhere Tonight	Highway 101
89	22	14	6	2	19.	I'm No Stranger To The Rain	Keith Whitley
88	20	14	6	2	20.	Eighteen Wheels And A Dozen Roses	Kathy Mattea
80	16	13	6	2	21.	One In A Million	Johnny Lee
81	16	11	6	2	22.	Love In The First Degree	Alabama
81	15	11	6	2	23.	(There's) No Gettin' Over Me	Ronnie Milsap
81	15	11	6	2	24.	Never Been So Loved (In All My Life)	Charley Pride
81	15	10	6	2	25.	I Don't Need You	Kenny Rogers

TOP 25 #1 HITS — 1990s

Peak Year	Wks Chr	Wks T40	Wks T10	Wks @ #1	Rank	Title	Artist
99	41	37	21	8	1.	Amazed	Lonestar
99	28	27	16	6	2.	Breathe	Faith Hill
99	37	34	13	6	3.	How Forever Feels	Kenny Chesney
98	42	25	13	6	4.	Just To See You Smile	Tim McGraw
97	20	20	13	6	5.	It's Your Love	Tim McGraw with Faith Hill
99	39	34	16	5	6.	Something Like That	Tim McGraw
99	33	32	15	5	7.	I Love You	Martina McBride
99	24	23	15	5	8.	Please Remember Me	Tim McGraw
90	21	20	11	5	9.	Love Without End, Amen	George Strait
97	20	20	10	5	10.	One Night At A Time	George Strait
90	20	19	10	5	11.	I've Come To Expect It From You	George Strait
97	20	20	9	5	12.	Love Gets Me Every Time	Shania Twain
95	20	19	9	5	13.	I Like It, I Love It	Tim McGraw
92	20	16	9	5	14.	Achy Breaky Heart	Billy Ray Cyrus
99	37	32	14	4	15.	Write This Down	George Strait
95	20	18	11	4	16.	Check Yes Or No	George Strait
98	32	27	10	4	17.	Where The Green Grass Grows	Tim McGraw
98	27	24	10	4	18.	Wide Open Spaces	Dixie Chicks
90	20	19	10	4	19.	Jukebox In My Mind	Alabama
97	21	16	10	4	20.	Carrying Your Love With Me	George Strait
90	26	22	9	4	21.	Hard Rock Bottom Of Your Heart	Randy Travis
90	20	19	9	4	22.	Friends In Low Places	Garth Brooks
97	22	16	9	4	23.	Nobody Knows	Kevin Sharp
93	20	16	9	4	24.	Chattahoochee	Alan Jackson
92	20	19	8	4	25.	What She's Doing Now	Garth Brooks

TOP 25 #1 HITS — 2000-05

Peak Year	Wks Chr	Wks T40	Wks T10	Wks @ #1	Rank	Title	Artist
03	27	27	17	8	1.	It's Five O'Clock Somewhere	Alan Jackson & Jimmy Buffett
04	21	21	18	7	2.	Live Like You Were Dying	Tim McGraw
02	31	29	17	7	3.	The Good Stuff	Kenny Chesney
03	20	19	14	7	4.	There Goes My Life	Kenny Chesney
03	20	19	12	7	5.	Have You Forgotten?	Darryl Worley
02	41	40	20	6	6.	Somebody Like You	Keith Urban
03	34	33	19	6	7.	19 Somethin'	Mark Wills
01	29	28	17	6	8.	Ain't Nothing 'Bout You	Brooks & Dunn
03	39	27	15	6	9.	Beer For My Horses	Toby Keith with Willie Nelson
01	26	25	15	6	10.	I'm Already There	Lonestar
05	19+	19+	15+	6	11.	As Good As I Once Was	Toby Keith
00	42	41	17	5	12.	How Do You Like Me Now?!	Toby Keith
02	41	36	15	5	13.	Good Morning Beautiful	Steve Holy
00	46	28	15	5	14.	My Next Thirty Years	Tim McGraw
03	24	24	15	5	15.	I Love This Bar	Toby Keith
00	32	29	14	5	16.	I Hope You Dance	Lee Ann Womack
02	31	26	14	5	17.	My List	Toby Keith
01	28	26	14	5	18.	I Wanna Talk About Me	Toby Keith
01	27	25	14	5	19.	Austin	Blake Shelton
05	26	25	14	5	20.	Bless The Broken Road	Rascal Flatts
05	23	22	14	5	21.	Making Memories Of Us	Keith Urban
04	22	20	14	5	22.	Redneck Woman	Gretchen Wilson
04	22	22	13	5	23.	When The Sun Goes Down	Kenny Chesney & Uncle Kracker
01	20	20	12	5	24.	Where Were You (When The World Stopped Turning)	Alan Jackson
05	36	34	17	4	25.	That's What I Love About Sunday	Craig Morgan

+ = still charted as of the 9/24/2005 cut-off date

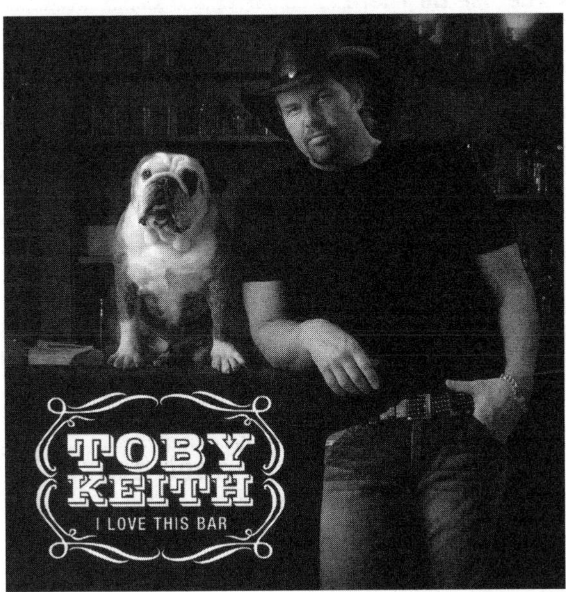

2000-05: Toby Keith has 6 of the Top 25 #1 Hits!

SINGLES OF LONGEVITY

Peak Year	Peak Pos	Peak Wks	Wks Chr	Rank	Title	Artist
					1944-49	
48	1	19	54	1.	**Bouquet Of Roses**	*Eddy Arnold*
47	1	21	46	2.	**I'll Hold You In My Heart (Till I Can Hold You In My Arms)**	*Eddy Arnold*
49	1	16	42	3.	**Lovesick Blues**	*Hank Williams*
49	1	1	40	4.	**Tennessee Saturday Night**	*Red Foley*
48	1	9	39	5.	**Anytime**	*Eddy Arnold*
47	1	5	38	6.	**It's A Sin**	*Eddy Arnold*
					1950s	
57	1	4	52	1.	**Fraulein**	*Bobby Helms*
51	1	1	46	2.	**Cold, Cold Heart**	*Hank Williams*
56	1	20	45	3.	**Crazy Arms**	*Ray Price*
50	1	21	44	4.	**I'm Moving On**	*Hank Snow*
56	1	6	43	5.	**I Walk The Line**	*Johnny Cash*
54	1	20	41	6.	**I Don't Hurt Anymore**	*Hank Snow*
					1960s	
61	1	2	39	1.	**I Fall To Pieces**	*Patsy Cline*
61	1	19	37	2.	**Walk On By**	*Leroy Van Dyke*
60	1	14	36	3.	**Please Help Me, I'm Falling**	*Hank Locklin*
60	1	10	36	4.	**Wings Of A Dove**	*Ferlin Husky*
63	1	1	36	5.	**Talk Back Trembling Lips**	*Ernest Ashworth*
60	1	14	34	6.	**He'll Have To Go**	*Jim Reeves*
					1970s	
70	1	1	26	1.	**For The Good Times**	*Ray Price*
71	1	3	24	2.	**Easy Loving**	*Freddie Hart*
72	1	3	23	3.	**The Happiest Girl In The Whole U.S.A.**	*Donna Fargo*
73	7	2	22	4.	**Let Me Be There**	*Olivia Newton-John*
72	12	1	22	5.	**To Get To You**	*Jerry Wallace*
75	1	3	21	6.	**Rhinestone Cowboy**	*Glen Campbell*
					1980s	
86	1	1	35	1.	**On The Other Hand**	*Randy Travis*
86	9	2	29	2.	**You Can't Stop Love**	*Schuyler, Knobloch & Overstreet*
85	1	1	28	3.	**Baby's Got Her Blue Jeans On**	*Mel McDaniel*
84	1	1	28	4.	**I've Been Around Enough To Know**	*John Schneider*
87	6	1	28	5.	**The Hand That Rocks The Cradle**	*Glen Campbell With Steve Wariner*
85	1	1	27	6.	**Seven Spanish Angels**	*Ray Charles (with Willie Nelson)*
					1990s	
98	1	6	42	1.	**Just To See You Smile**	*Tim McGraw*
99	1	8	41	2.	**Amazed**	*Lonestar*
99	1	5	39	3.	**Something Like That**	*Tim McGraw*
99	1	6	37	4.	**How Forever Feels**	*Kenny Chesney*
99	1	4	37	5.	**Write This Down**	*George Strait*
99	2	2	36	6.	**You Won't Ever Be Lonely**	*Andy Griggs*
					2000-2005	
01	5	1	48	1.	**Right Where I Need To Be**	*Gary Allan*
00	1	5	46	2.	**My Next Thirty Years**	*Tim McGraw*
05	2	2	46	3.	**Baby Girl**	*Sugarland*
02	1	2	45	4.	**Beautiful Mess**	*Diamond Rio*
00	6	2	45	5.	**Let's Make Love**	*Faith Hill with Tim McGraw*
00	2	3	44	6.	**I Will...But**	*SheDaisy*

TOP COUNTRY SONGWRITERS

	Points	# of Hits	
1.	**10,749**	147	**Harlan Howard**
2.	**10,396**	152	**Bob McDill**
3.	**9,921**	131	**Bill Anderson**
4.	**9,584**	124	**Billy Sherrill**
5.	**8,129**	144	**Bill Rice**
6.	**7,381**	118	**Dallas Frazier**
7.	**7,179**	99	**Merle Haggard**
8.	**7,128**	131	**Jerry Foster**
9.	**7,106**	92	**Buck Owens**
10.	**7,034**	92	**Tom T. Hall**
11.	**6,843**	105	**Hank Cochran**
12.	**6,842**	86	**Don Schlitz**
13.	**6,822**	92	**Tom Shapiro**
14.	**6,610**	107	**Rory Bourke**
15.	**6,452**	85	**Norro Wilson**
16.	**6,399**	81	**Mel Tillis**
17.	**6,281**	104	**Troy Seals**
18.	**6,243**	104	**Curly Putman**
19.	**5,987**	85	**Glenn Sutton**
20.	**5,772**	76	**Don Gibson**
21.	**5,722**	78	**Wayne Walker**
22.	**5,549**	73	**Boudleaux Bryant**
23.	**5,334**	72	**Dolly Parton**
24.	**5,193**	78	**Ben Peters**
25.	**5,032**	75	**Charlie Black**
26.	**4,837**	68	**Johnny Cash**
27.	**4,836**	60	**Marty Robbins**
28.	**4,814**	74	**Roger Murrah**
29.	**4,772**	68	**Wayland Holyfield**
30.	**4,743**	70	**Willie Nelson**
31.	**4,707**	70	**Bob DiPiero**
32.	**4,635**	76	**Dean Dillon**
33.	**4,506**	63	**Roger Miller**
34.	**4,491**	77	**Sonny Throckmorton**
35.	**4,440**	67	**Chris Waters**
36.	**4,440**	59	**Paul Overstreet**
37.	**4,428**	62	**Webb Pierce**
38.	**4,398**	64	**Craig Wiseman**
39.	**4,368**	64	**Bobby Braddock**
40.	**4,358**	60	**Don Cook**
41.	**4,279**	59	**Eddie Rabbitt**
42.	**4,198**	52	**Cindy Walker**
43.	**4,173**	74	**A.L "Doodle" Owens**
44.	**4,134**	75	**Bob Morrison**
45.	**4,123**	58	**Dennis W. Morgan**
46.	**4,105**	54	**Fred Rose**
47.	**4,104**	50	**Vince Gill**
48.	**4,037**	50	**Clint Black**
49.	**4,000**	50	**Mike Reid**
50.	**3,996**	59	**Even Stevens**

	Points	# of Hits	
51.	**3,917**	58	**Rafe Van Hoy**
52.	**3,861**	50	**Larry Gatlin**
53.	**3,827**	49	**Hank Thompson**
54.	**3,810**	50	**Mark D. Sanders**
55.	**3,773**	54	**Walt Aldridge**
56.	**3,763**	58	**Carmol Taylor**
57.	**3,737**	50	**George Jones**
58.	**3,711**	67	**Bucky Jones**
59.	**3,698**	62	**Max D. Barnes**
60.	**3,692**	69	**Red Lane**
61.	**3,647**	44	**Don Reid**
62.	**3,607**	55	**Rick Giles**
63.	**3,572**	52	**Rodney Crowell**
64.	**3,544**	55	**Don Pfrimmer**
65.	**3,512**	57	**Whitey Shafer**
66.	**3,506**	39	**Alan Jackson**
67.	**3,488**	47	**Jerry Chesnut**
68.	**3,471**	45	**Gary Burr**
69.	**3,446**	50	**George Richey**
70.	**3,385**	45	**Paul Nelson**
71.	**3,355**	53	**Keith Stegall**
72.	**3,213**	50	**Dennis Linde**
73.	**3,132**	44	**Skip Ewing**
74.	**3,094**	42	**John D. Loudermilk**
75.	**3,091**	47	**Shel Silverstein**
76.	**3,006**	42	**Tony Martin**
77.	**2,965**	39	**Jeffrey Steele**
78.	**2,965**	37	**David Bellamy**
79.	**2,916**	34	**Mutt Lange**
80.	**2,905**	38	**Garth Brooks**
81.	**2,896**	41	**Felice Bryant**
82.	**2,883**	59	**Don Goodman**
83.	**2,879**	32	**Toby Keith**
84.	**2,864**	38	**Dave Loggins**
85.	**2,825**	41	**Kent Robbins**
86.	**2,810**	45	**Gary Nicholson**
87.	**2,806**	36	**Kye Fleming**
88.	**2,770**	38	**Jack Clement**
89.	**2,766**	30	**Ronnie Dunn**
90.	**2,747**	53	**Ray Griff**
91.	**2,739**	40	**Kris Kristofferson**
92.	**2,731**	47	**Steve Bogard**
93.	**2,680**	45	**Eddy Raven**
94.	**2,672**	38	**Steve Davis**
95.	**2,666**	39	**John Jarrard**
96.	**2,656**	34	**Hayden Nicholas**
97.	**2,650**	33	**Lefty Frizzell**
98.	**2,637**	45	**Michael Garvin**
99.	**2,617**	33	**Paul Kennerley**
100.	**2,597**	36	**Kim Williams**

	Points	# of Hits	
101.	**2,563**	34	**Steve Dorff**
102.	**2,556**	37	**Larry Boone**
103.	**2,543**	40	**Jerry Reed**
104.	**2,538**	36	**Johnny MacRae**
105.	**2,536**	33	**Conway Twitty**
106.	**2,524**	33	**Kostas**
107.	**2,506**	34	**Don Robertson**
108.	**2,501**	43	**Tommy Rocco**
109.	**2,495**	35	**Tim Nichols**
110.	**2,491**	34	**Jan Crutchfield**
111.	**2,490**	41	**Waylon Jennings**
112.	**2,484**	43	**Terry Skinner**
113.	**2,456**	30	**Sonny Lemaire**
114.	**2,427**	37	**Wayne Carson**
115.	**2,417**	34	**Liz Anderson**
116.	**2,416**	35	**Earl Thomas Conley**
117.	**2,389**	28	**Shania Twain**
118.	**2,370**	31	**Freddie Hart**
119.	**2,368**	34	**Radney Foster**
120.	**2,367**	40	**Larry Kingston**
121.	**2,367**	35	**Johnny Slate**
122.	**2,366**	32	**Steve Wariner**
123.	**2,356**	26	**Ernest Tubb**
124.	**2,351**	41	**Mac Davis**
125.	**2,344**	34	**Thom Schuyler**
126.	**2,338**	32	**Robert Byrne**
127.	**2,334**	31	**Leon Payne**
128.	**2,288**	50	**Dave Kirby**
129.	**2,287**	29	**Faron Young**
130.	**2,282**	33	**Frank J. Myers**
131.	**2,279**	31	**Vic McAlpin**
132.	**2,265**	27	**Bob Wills**
133.	**2,261**	31	**Merle Kilgore**
134.	**2,252**	42	**Gene Dobbins**
135.	**2,251**	31	**Richard Leigh**
136.	**2,199**	30	**Matraca Berg**
137.	**2,196**	29	**J.P. Pennington**
138.	**2,191**	35	**Ronnie Rogers**
139.	**2,186**	31	**Kix Brooks**
140.	**2,151**	34	**Al Anderson**
141.	**2,129**	30	**Rick Bowles**
142.	**2,129**	24	**Jenny Lou Carson**
143.	**2,118**	37	**J.L. Wallace**
144.	**2,117**	34	**Larry Butler**
145.	**2,117**	25	**Cy Coben**
146.	**2,114**	25	**Marijohn Wilkin**
147.	**2,110**	32	**Tim DuBois**
148.	**2,110**	31	**Jim Weatherly**
149.	**2,093**	26	**Loretta Lynn**
150.	**2,074**	26	**Mark Wright**

COUNTRY MUSIC ASSOCIATION AWARDS

SINGLE OF THE YEAR Title...*Artist(s)*	YEAR	SONG OF THE YEAR Title...*Songwriter(s)*
There Goes My Everything...*Jack Greene*	1967	**There Goes My Everything**...*Dallas Frazier*
Harper Valley P.T.A. ...*Jeannie C. Riley*	1968	**Honey**...*Bobby Russell*
A Boy Named Sue...*Johnny Cash*	1969	**The Carroll County Accident**...*Bob Ferguson*
Okie From Muskogee...*Merle Haggard*	1970	**Sunday Morning Coming Down**...*Kris Kristofferson*
Help Me Make It Through The Night...*Sammi Smith*	1971	**Easy Loving**...*Freddie Hart*
The Happiest Girl In The Whole U.S.A. ...*Donna Fargo*	1972	**Easy Loving**...*Freddie Hart*
Behind Closed Doors...*Charlie Rich*	1973	**Behind Closed Doors**...*Kenny O'Dell*
Country Bumpkin...*Cal Smith*	1974	**Country Bumpkin**...*Don Wayne*
Before The Next Teardrop Falls...*Freddy Fender*	1975	**Back Home Again**...*John Denver*
Good Hearted Woman... *Waylon Jennings & Willie Nelson*	1976	**Rhinestone Cowboy**...*Larry Weiss*
Lucille...*Kenny Rogers*	1977	**Lucille**...*Roger Bowling & Hal Bynum*
Heaven's Just A Sin Away...*The Kendalls*	1978	**Don't It Make My Brown Eyes Blue**...*Richard Leigh*
The Devil Went Down To Georgia... *Charlie Daniels Band*	1979	**The Gambler**...*Don Schlitz*
He Stopped Loving Her Today...*George Jones*	1980	**He Stopped Loving Her Today**... *Bobby Braddock & Curly Putman*
Elvira...*Oak Ridge Boys*	1981	**He Stopped Loving Her Today**... *Bobby Braddock & Curly Putman*
Always On My Mind...*Willie Nelson*	1982	**Always On My Mind**... *Johnny Christopher, Wayne Carson & Mark James*
Swingin'...*John Anderson*	1983	**Always On My Mind**... *Johnny Christopher, Wayne Carson & Mark James*
A Little Good News...*Anne Murray*	1984	**The Wind Beneath My Wings**... *Larry Henley & Jeff Silbar*
Why Not Me...*The Judds*	1985	**God Bless The USA**...*Lee Greenwood*
Bop...*Dan Seals*	1986	**On The Other Hand**...*Paul Overstreet & Don Schlitz*
Forever And Ever, Amen...*Randy Travis*	1987	**Forever And Ever, Amen**... *Paul Overstreet & Don Schlitz*
Eighteen Wheels And A Dozen Roses...*Kathy Mattea*	1988	**80's Ladies**...*K.T. Oslin*
I'm No Stranger To The Rain...*Keith Whitley*	1989	**Chiseled In Stone**...*Max D. Barnes & Vern Gosdin*
When I Call Your Name...*Vince Gill*	1990	**Where've You Been**...*Jon Vezner & Don Henry*
Friends In Low Places...*Garth Brooks*	1991	**When I Call Your Name**...*Vince Gill & Tim DuBois*
Achy Breaky Heart...*Billy Ray Cyrus*	1992	**Look At Us**...*Vince Gill & Max D. Barnes*
Chattahoochee...*Alan Jackson*	1993	**I Still Believe In You**... *Vince Gill & John Barlow Jarvis*
I Swear...*John Michael Montgomery*	1994	**Chattahoochee**...*Alan Jackson & Jim McBride*
When You Say Nothing At All... *Alison Krauss & Union Station*	1995	**Independence Day**...*Gretchen Peters*
Check Yes Or No...*George Strait*	1996	**Go Rest High On That Mountain**...*Vince Gill*
Strawberry Wine...*Deana Carter*	1997	**Strawberry Wine**...*Matraca Berg & Gary Harrison*
Holes In The Floor Of Heaven...*Steve Wariner*	1998	**Holes In The Floor Of Heaven**... *Billy Kirsch & Steve Wariner*
Wide Open Spaces...*Dixie Chicks*	1999	**This Kiss**... *Beth Nielsen Chapman, Robin Lerner & Annie Roboff*
I Hope You Dance...*Lee Ann Womack*	2000	**I Hope You Dance**...*Mark D. Sanders & Tia Sillers*
I Am A Man Of Constant Sorrow...*Soggy Bottom Boys*	2001	**Murder On Music Row**...*Larry Cordle & Larry Shell*
Where Were You (When The World Stopped Turning)...*Alan Jackson*	2002	**Where Were You (When The World Stopped Turning)**...*Alan Jackson*
Hurt...*Johnny Cash*	2003	**Three Wooden Crosses**... *Doug Johnson & Kim Williams*
Live Like You Were Dying...*Tim McGraw*	2004	**Live Like You Were Dying**... *Tim Nichols & Craig Wiseman*

At the time of this book's publication, CMA Awards for 2005 had not yet taken place.

COUNTRY MUSIC HALL OF FAME

YEAR	INDUCTEE(S)	YEAR	INDUCTEE(S)
1961	Jimmie Rodgers Fred Rose Hank Williams	1984	Ralph Peer Floyd Tillman
1962	Roy Acuff	1985	Lester Flatt & Earl Scruggs
1963	(elections were held but no candidate received enough votes)	1986	Whitey Ford (The Duke Of Paducah) Wesley H. Rose
1964	Tex Ritter	1987	Rod Brasfield
1965	Ernest Tubb	1988	Loretta Lynn Roy Rogers
1966	Eddy Arnold James R. Denny George D. Hay Uncle Dave Macon	1989	Jack Stapp Cliffie Stone Hank Thompson
1967	Red Foley J.L. (Joe) Frank Jim Reeves Stephen H. Sholes	1990	"Tennessee" Ernie Ford
1968	Bob Wills	1991	Boudleaux & Felice Bryant
1969	Gene Autry	1992	George Jones Frances Preston
1970	Original Carter Family (A.P., Maybelle, Sara) Bill Monroe	1993	Willie Nelson
1971	Arthur Edward Satherley	1994	Merle Haggard
1972	Jimmie Davis	1995	Roger Miller Jo Walker-Meador
1973	Chet Atkins Patsy Cline	1996	Patsy Montana Buck Owens Ray Price
1974	Owen Bradley Frank "Pee Wee" King	1997	Harlan Howard Brenda Lee Cindy Walker
1975	Minnie Pearl	1998	George Morgan Elvis Presley E.W. "Bud" Wendell Tammy Wynette
1976	Paul Cohen Kitty Wells	1999	Johnny Bond Dolly Parton Conway Twitty
1977	Merle Travis	2000	Charley Pride Faron Young
1978	Grandpa Jones	2001	Bill Anderson The Delmore Brothers The Everly Brothers Don Gibson Homer & Jethro Waylon Jennings The Jordanaires Don Law The Louvin Brothers Ken Nelson Webb Pierce Sam Phillips
1979	Hubert Long Hank Snow	2002	Bill Carlisle Porter Wagoner
1980	Johnny Cash Connie B. Gay Original Sons of the Pioneers	2003	Floyd Cramer Carl Smith
1981	Vernon Dalhart Grant Turner	2004	Jim Foglesong Kris Kristofferson
1982	Lefty Frizzell Roy Horton Marty Robbins	2005	Alabama DeFord Bailey Glen Campbell
1983	"Little" Jimmy Dickens		

TOP COUNTRY LABELS

		Total Hits
1.	**RCA**	2,310
2.	**Columbia**	1,629
3.	**Capitol**	1,543
4.	**MCA**	1,329
5.	**Epic**	969
6.	**Mercury**	865
7.	**Warner**	863
8.	**Decca**	820
9.	**Curb**	670
10.	**Arista**	320
11.	**Dot**	320
12.	**United Artists**	319
13.	**ABC**	315
14.	**MGM**	305
15.	**Elektra**	236
16.	**Liberty**	207
17.	**Atlantic**	200
18.	**BNA**	193
19.	**Monument**	176
20.	**Hickory**	140
21.	**Reprise**	118
22.	**Asylum**	102
23.	**Door Knob**	100
24.	**Giant**	91
25.	**Soundwaves**	89
26.	**DreamWorks**	85
27.	**Starday**	76
28.	**Sun**	71
29.	**Lyric Street** *DEBUT*	70
30.	**Polydor**	67
31.	**Chart**	64
32.	**Republic**	57
33.	**King**	55
34.	**Imperial**	53
35.	**Step One**	52
36.	**MTM**	51
37.	**GRT**	49
38.	**Ovation**	48
39.	**Kapp**	47
40.	**Playboy**	46

DEBUT First time label appears on this list.

LABEL ABBREVIATIONS

America/Sm.	America Smash
Atlantic Amer.	Atlantic America
Capitol Amer.	Capitol Americana
Country Show.	Country Showcase America
Curb/EMI Amer.	Curb/EMI America
Full Moon/Asy.	Full Moon/Asylum
Pacific Chall.	Pacific Challenger

#1 HITS

This section lists, in chronological order, all 1,495 songs that hit #1 on *Billboard's* Country Singles charts from January 8, 1944 through October 15, 2005.

From May 15, 1948 through October 13, 1958, when *Billboard* published more than one weekly Country singles chart, the chart designation and #1 weeks on each chart are listed beneath the record title. The chart designations are:

BS: Best Sellers
JY: Jockeys
JB: Juke Box

The date shown is the earliest date that a record hit #1 on any of the Country singles charts. The weeks column lists the total weeks at #1, from whichever chart it achieved its highest total. This total is not a combined total from the various Country singles charts.

Because of the multiple charts used for this research, some dates are duplicated, as certain #1 hits may have peaked on the same week on different charts. *Billboard* also showed ties at #1 on some of these charts; therefore, the total weeks for each year may calculate out to more than 52.

Billboard has not published an issue for the last week of the year since 1976. For the years 1976 through 1991, *Billboard* considered the charts listed in the last published issue of the year to be "frozen" and all chart positions remained the same for the unpublished week. This frozen chart data is included in our tabulations. Since 1992, *Billboard* has compiled a Country singles chart for the last week of the year, even though an issue is not published. This chart is only available through Member Services of Billboard.com or by mail. Our tabulations include this unpublished chart data.

See the introduction pages of this book for more details on researching the Country singles charts.

DATE: Date single first peaked at the #1 position
WKS: Total weeks single held the #1 position
↕: Indicates single hit #1, dropped down, and then returned to the #1 spot

The top hit of each year is boxed out for quick reference. The top hit is determined by most weeks at the #1 position, followed by total weeks in the Top 10, Top 40, and total weeks charted.

#1 HITS

1/8/44 through 5/8/48: Billboard's only Country chart is the "Juke Box" chart.

1944

DATE WKS

1. 1/8 **5↕ Pistol Packin' Mama** *Bing Crosby & the Andrews Sisters*
2. 2/5 **3 Pistol Packin' Mama** *Al Dexter*
3. 2/26 **3↕ Ration Blues** *Louis Jordan*
4. 3/11 **1 Rosalita** *Al Dexter*
5. 3/18 **1 They Took The Stars Out Of Heaven** *Floyd Tillman*
6. 3/25 **13↕ So Long Pal** *Al Dexter*
7. 4/1 **2↕ Too Late To Worry** *Al Dexter*
8. 6/10 **6↕ Straighten Up And Fly Right** *King Cole Trio*
9. 7/29 **5 Is You Is Or Is You Ain't (Ma' Baby)** *Louis Jordan*
10. 9/2 **4 Soldier's Last Letter** *Ernest Tubb*
11. 9/23 **13 Smoke On The Water** *Red Foley*
12. 12/23 **6 I'm Wastin' My Tears On You** *Tex Ritter*

1945

DATE WKS

1. 2/3 **7↕ I'm Losing My Mind Over You** *Al Dexter*
2. 3/17 **1 There's A New Moon Over My Shoulder** *Jimmie Davis*
3. 3/31 **9↕ Shame On You** *Spade Cooley*
4. 4/14 **2↕ Smoke On The Water** *Bob Wills*
5. 5/19 **8↕ At Mail Call Today** *Gene Autry*
6. 7/7 **1 Stars And Stripes On Iwo Jima** *Bob Wills*
7. 7/28 **6↕ Oklahoma Hills** *Jack Guthrie*
8. 8/25 **11↕ You Two Timed Me One Time Too Often** *Tex Ritter*
9. 10/27 **4↕ With Tears In My Eyes** *Wesley Tuttle*
10. 11/24 **4↕ Sioux City Sue** *Dick Thomas*
11. 11/24 **1 Shame On You** *Lawrence Welk with Red Foley*
12. 12/8 **4↕ It's Been So Long Darling** *Ernest Tubb*
13. 12/15 **3↕ Silver Dew On The Blue Grass Tonight** *Bob Wills*

1946

DATE WKS

1. 1/5 **3↕ You Will Have To Pay** *Tex Ritter*
2. 1/5 **1 White Cross On Okinawa** *Bob Wills*
3. 2/2 **16↕ Guitar Polka** *Al Dexter*
4. 5/18 **16↕ New Spanish Two Step** *Bob Wills*
5. 9/14 **5↕ Wine, Women And Song** *Al Dexter*
6. 10/12 **14↕ Divorce Me C.O.D.** *Merle Travis*

1947

DATE WKS

1. 1/18 **2↕ Rainbow At Midnight** *Ernest Tubb*
2. 2/8 **14 So Round, So Firm, So Fully Packed** *Merle Travis*
3. 5/17 **2↕ New Jolie Blonde (New Pretty Blonde)** *Red Foley*
4. 5/24 **1 What Is Life Without Love** *Eddy Arnold*
5. 6/7 **1 Sugar Moon** *Bob Wills*

1947 (cont'd)

6. 6/14 **5 It's A Sin** *Eddy Arnold*
7. 7/19 **16↕ Smoke! Smoke! Smoke! (That Cigarette)** *Tex Williams*
8. 11/1 **21↕ I'll Hold You In My Heart (Till I Can Hold You In My Arms)** *Eddy Arnold*

1948

DATE WKS

1. 4/3 **9 Anytime** *Eddy Arnold*
   JB: 9 / BS: 3

5/15/48: Billboard's "Best Sellers" chart debuts.

2. 6/5 **19↕ Bouquet Of Roses** *Eddy Arnold*
   BS: 19↕ / JB: 18↕
3. 6/5 **3↕ Texarkana Baby** *Eddy Arnold*
   JB: 3↕ / BS: 1
4. 9/18 **8↕ Just A Little Lovin' (Will Go A Long, Long Way)** *Eddy Arnold*
   JB: 8↕ / BS: 4↕
5. 11/13 **11↕ One Has My Name (The Other Has My Heart)** *Jimmy Wakely*
   BS: 11↕ / JB: 7↕
6. 12/25 **1 A Heart Full Of Love (For A Handful of Kisses)** *Eddy Arnold*
   BS: 1

1949

DATE WKS

1. 1/22 **5↕ I Love You So Much It Hurts** *Jimmy Wakely*
   JB: 5↕ / BS: 4↕
2. 3/5 **12↕ Don't Rob Another Man's Castle** *Eddy Arnold*
   JB: 12↕ / BS: 6↕
3. 3/19 **1 Tennessee Saturday Night** *Red Foley*
   JB: 1
4. 4/2 **3↕ Candy Kisses** *George Morgan*
   BS: 3↕
5. 5/7 **16↕ Lovesick Blues** *Hank Williams*
   BS: 16↕ / JB: 10↕
6. 6/18 **3↕ One Kiss Too Many** *Eddy Arnold*
   JB: 3↕

6/25/49: First time "Country & Western" is shown as chart title.

7. 7/30 **4 I'm Throwing Rice (At The Girl That I Love)** *Eddy Arnold*
   BS: 4 / JB: 3↕
8. 9/10 **3↕ Why Don't You Haul Off And Love Me** *Wayne Raney*
   JB: 3↕ / BS: 2↕
9. 9/24 **1 Slipping Around** *Ernest Tubb*
   JB: 1
10. 10/8 **17 Slipping Around** *Margaret Whiting & Jimmy Wakely*
   BS: 17 / JB: 12↕

12/10/49: Billboard's "Jockeys" chart debuts.

11. 12/10 **4 Mule Train** *Tennessee Ernie Ford*
   JY: 4

#1 HITS

DATE WKS 1950

1. 1/7 1 **Rudolph, The Red-Nosed Reindeer** *Gene Autry*
JY: 1
2. 1/7 1 **Blue Christmas** *Ernest Tubb*
JB: 1
3. 1/14 2↕ **I Love You Because** *Leon Payne*
JY: 2↕
4. 1/14 1 **Blues Stay Away From Me** *Delmore Brothers*
JB: 1
5. 1/21 13 **Chattanoogie Shoe Shine Boy** *Red Foley*
JB: 13 / JY: 13↕ / BS: 12
6. 1/28 1 **Take Me In Your Arms And Hold Me** *Eddy Arnold*
JB: 1
7. 4/22 8↕ **Long Gone Lonesome Blues** *Hank Williams*
JY: 8↕ / BS: 5↕ / JB: 4
8. 5/27 4↕ **Birmingham Bounce** *Red Foley*
BS: 4↕ / JB: 3↕
9. 6/17 10 **Why Don't You Love Me** *Hank Williams*
JY: 10 / BS: 6↕ / JB: 5
10. 6/17 4 **I'll Sail My Ship Alone** *Moon Mullican*
JB: 4 / BS: 1
11. 7/15 1 **Mississippi** *Red Foley*
JB: 1
12. 8/19 21↕ **I'm Moving On** *Hank Snow*
BS: 21↕ / JY: 18↕ / JB: 14
13. 8/26 3 **Goodnight Irene** *Red Foley & Ernest Tubb*
JB: 3 / BS: 2
14. 12/23 3 **If You've Got The Money I've Got The Time** *Lefty Frizzell*
JB: 3
15. 12/30 1 **Moanin' The Blues** *Hank Williams*
JY: 1

DATE WKS 1951

1. 1/6 3↕ **I Love You A Thousand Ways** *Lefty Frizzell*
JY: 3↕
2. 1/6 2 **The Golden Rocket** *Hank Snow*
BS: 2 / JY: 1
3. 1/13 14 **The Shot Gun Boogie** *Tennessee Ernie Ford*
JB: 14 / BS: 3↕ / JY: 1
4. 2/10 11↕ **There's Been A Change In Me** *Eddy Arnold*
JY: 11↕ / BS: 4↕
5. 3/31 8↕ **The Rhumba Boogie** *Hank Snow*
BS: 8↕ / JB: 5 / JY: 2↕
6. 5/12 1 **Cold, Cold Heart** *Hank Williams*
JY: 1
7. 5/19 3 **Kentucky Waltz** *Eddy Arnold*
JB: 3 / BS: 3↕
8. 5/26 11 **I Want To Be With You Always** *Lefty Frizzell*
JY: 11 / BS: 6↕ / JB: 5
9. 7/14 11 **I Wanna Play House With You** *Eddy Arnold*
JB: 11 / BS: 6↕
10. 8/11 8↕ **Hey, Good Lookin'** *Hank Williams*
JY: 8↕
11. 9/1 12↕ **Always Late (With Your Kisses)** *Lefty Frizzell*
BS: 12↕ / JY: 6↕ / JB: 6
12. 11/3 15↕ **Slow Poke** *Pee Wee King*
JB: 15↕ / BS: 14 / JY: 9↕

1951 (cont'd)

13. 12/22 8↕ **Let Old Mother Nature Have Her Way** *Carl Smith*
JB: 8↕ / BS: 6 / JY: 3↕

DATE WKS 1952

1. 2/2 3↕ **Give Me More, More, More (Of Your Kisses)** *Lefty Frizzell*
JY: 3↕ / JB: 3↕
2. 3/1 4 **Wondering** *Webb Pierce*
JY: 4
3. 3/29 8↕ **(When You Feel Like You're In Love) Don't Just Stand There** *Carl Smith*
JY: 8↕ / BS: 5↕ / JB: 3↕
4. 5/3 1 **Easy On The Eyes** *Eddy Arnold*
BS: 1
5. 5/10 15 **The Wild Side Of Life** *Hank Thompson*
BS: 15 / JB: 15 / JY: 8↕
6. 7/12 3↕ **That Heart Belongs To Me** Webb Pierce
JY: 3↕
7. 7/19 1 **Are You Teasing Me** *Carl Smith*
JY: 1
8. 8/16 4↕ **A Full Time Job** *Eddy Arnold*
JY: 4↕
9. 8/23 6 **It Wasn't God Who Made Honky Tonk Angels** *Kitty Wells*
BS: 6 / JB: 5
10. 9/6 14↕ **Jambalaya (On The Bayou)** *Hank Williams*
BS: 14↕ / JY: 14↕ / JB: 12↕
11. 12/6 4↕ **Back Street Affair** *Webb Pierce*
JY: 4↕ / JB: 3 / BS: 2↕
12. 12/6 1 **Don't Let The Stars (Get In Your Eyes)** *Slim Willet*
JY: 1
13. 12/27 3 **Don't Let The Stars Get In Your Eyes** *Skeets McDonald*
JB: 3

DATE WKS 1953

1. 1/10 1 **Midnight** *Red Foley*
BS: 1
2. 1/24 2↕ **I'll Go On Alone** *Marty Robbins*
JY: 2↕
3. 1/24 1 **I'll Never Get Out Of This World Alive** *Hank Williams*
BS: 1
4. 1/31 4 **No Help Wanted** *The Carlisles*
JB: 4 / JY: 4↕
5. 1/31 3 **Eddy's Song** *Eddy Arnold*
BS: 3
6. 2/7 3 **I Let The Stars Get In My Eyes** *Goldie Hill*
JB: 3
7. 2/21 13 **Kaw-Liga** *Hank Williams*
BS: 13 / JY: 8 / JB: 8↕
8. 4/11 6↕ **Your Cheatin' Heart** *Hank Williams*
JY: 6↕ / JB: 2↕
9. 5/9 9↕ **Mexican Joe** *Jim Reeves*
JB: 9↕ / JY: 7↕ / BS: 6↕
10. 6/6 4↕ **Take These Chains From My Heart** *Hank Williams*
BS: 4↕

#1 HITS

1953 (cont'd)

11. 7/11 **8↕ It's Been So Long** *Webb Pierce*
JY: 8↕ / BS: 6 / JB: 1
12. 8/1 **3↕ Rub-A-Dub-Dub** *Hank Thompson*
JB: 3↕
13. 8/22 **8↕ Hey Joe!** *Carl Smith*
JB: 8↕ / JY: 4↕ / BS: 2↕
14. 8/29 **6↕ A Dear John Letter**
Jean Shepard & Ferlin Huskey
BS: 6↕ / JB: 4↕
15. 10/17 **8↕ I Forgot More Than You'll Ever Know**
The Davis Sisters
JY: 8↕ / BS: 6↕ / JB: 2↕
16. 11/21 **12↕ There Stands The Glass** *Webb Pierce*
BS: 12↕ / JB: 9↕ / JY: 6↕
17. 12/12 **2 Caribbean** *Mitchell Torok*
JB: 2
18. 12/19 **3↕ Let Me Be The One** *Hank Locklin*
JY: 3↕ / JB: 2↕

DATE WKS 1954

1. 1/9 **3↕ Bimbo** *Jim Reeves*
JY: 3↕
2. 2/20 **17 Slowly** *Webb Pierce*
BS: 17 / JB: 17↕ / JY: 15
3. 2/20 **2 Wake Up, Irene** *Hank Thompson*
JB: 2
4. 5/15 **1 I Really Don't Want To Know** *Eddy Arnold*
JB: 1
5. 6/12 **2 (Oh Baby Mine) I Get So Lonely**
Johnnie & Jack
JY: 2
6. 6/19 **20 I Don't Hurt Anymore** *Hank Snow*
BS: 20 / JB: 20↕ / JY: 18↕
7. 7/3 **2 Even Tho** *Webb Pierce*
JY: 2
8. 7/31 **1 One By One** *Kitty Wells & Red Foley*
JB: 1
9. 11/6 **10↕ More And More** *Webb Pierce*
JB: 10↕ / BS: 9 / JY: 8↕

DATE WKS 1955

1. 1/8 **7 Loose Talk** *Carl Smith*
BS: 7 / JY: 6↕ / JB: 4
2. 1/29 **2 Let Me Go, Lover!** *Hank Snow*
JY: 2
3. 2/26 **21 In The Jailhouse Now** *Webb Pierce*
JB: 21 / BS: 20 / JY: 15
4. 6/18 **3 Live Fast, Love Hard, Die Young**
Faron Young
JY: 3
5. 7/9 **4 A Satisfied Mind** *Porter Wagoner*
JY: 4
6. 7/16 **12 I Don't Care** *Webb Pierce*
BS: 12 / JY: 12 / JB: 12
7. 10/8 **2 The Cattle Call** *Eddy Arnold*
BS: 2
8. 10/22 **13↕ Love, Love, Love** *Webb Pierce*
JY: 13↕ / JB: 9↕ / BS: 8
9. 10/22 **2 That Do Make It Nice** *Eddy Arnold*
JB: 2
10. 12/17 **10 Sixteen Tons** *Tennessee Ernie Ford*
BS: 10 / JB: 7↕ / JY: 3↕

DATE WKS 1956

1. 2/11 **4↕ Why Baby Why** *Red Sovine & Webb Pierce*
JY: 4↕ / BS: 1 / JB: 1
2. 2/25 **5 I Forgot To Remember To Forget**
Elvis Presley
JB: 5 / BS: 2
3. 3/17 **17 Heartbreak Hotel** *Elvis Presley*
BS: 17 / JB: 13↕ / JY: 12
4. 3/17 **2 I Don't Believe You've Met My Baby**
The Louvin Brothers
JY: 2
5. 4/7 **3 Blue Suede Shoes** *Carl Perkins*
JB: 3
6. 6/23 **20↕ Crazy Arms** *Ray Price*
JY: 20↕ / BS: 11↕ / JB: 1
7. 7/14 **2 I Want You, I Need You, I Love You**
Elvis Presley
BS: 2 / JB: 1
8. 7/21 **6↕ I Walk The Line** *Johnny Cash*
JB: 6↕ / JY: 1
9. 9/15 **10 Don't Be Cruel/**
JB: 10 / BS: 5 / JY: 2
10. **10 Hound Dog** *Elvis Presley*
JB: 10 / BS: 5
11. 11/10 **13 Singing The Blues** *Marty Robbins*
BS: 13 / JB: 13 / JY: 11↕

DATE WKS 1957

1. 2/2 **9 Young Love** *Sonny James*
JY: 9 / BS: 7 / JB: 3↕
2. 3/2 **5↕ There You Go** *Johnny Cash*
JB: 5↕
3. 4/6 **10 Gone** *Ferlin Husky*
BS: 10 / JY: 9 / JB: 5↕
4. 5/13 **1 All Shook Up** *Elvis Presley*
JB: 1
5. 5/20 **5 A White Sport Coat (And A Pink Carnation)**
Marty Robbins
BS: 5 / JB: 5 / JY: 1
6. 5/20 **1 Honky Tonk Song** *Webb Pierce*
JY: 1
7. 5/27 **8↕ Four Walls** *Jim Reeves*
JY: 8↕

6/17/57: Billboard's last "Juke Box" chart.

8. 7/15 **7 Bye Bye Love** *The Everly Brothers*
JY: 7 / BS: 7↕
9. 8/5 **1 Let Me Be Your Teddy Bear** *Elvis Presley*
BS: 1
10. 9/9 **2 Whole Lot Of Shakin' Going On**
Jerry Lee Lewis
BS: 2
11. 9/16 **4↕ Fraulein** *Bobby Helms*
JY: 4↕ / BS: 3
12. 9/16 **4↕ My Shoes Keep Walking Back To You**
Ray Price
JY: 4↕
13. 10/14 **8↕ Wake Up Little Susie** *The Everly Brothers*
JY: 8↕ / BS: 7
14. 12/2 **1 Jailhouse Rock** *Elvis Presley*
BS: 1
15. 12/9 **4 My Special Angel** *Bobby Helms*
BS: 4 / JY: 1

#1 HITS

1958

	DATE	WKS	
1.	1/6	4	**The Story Of My Life** *Marty Robbins* BS: 4 / JY: 4
2.	1/6	2	**Great Balls Of Fire** *Jerry Lee Lewis* BS: 2
3.	2/3	10	**Ballad Of A Teenage Queen** *Johnny Cash* JY: 10 / BS: 8
4.	4/14	8↕	**Oh Lonesome Me** *Don Gibson* BS: 8↕ / JY: 8↕
5.	5/26	2↕	**Just Married** *Marty Robbins* JY: 2↕
6.	6/2	3	**All I Have To Do Is Dream** *The Everly Brothers* BS: 3 / JY: 1
7.	6/23	8	**Guess Things Happen That Way** *Johnny Cash* BS: 8 / JY: 3↕
8.	7/21	13	**Alone With You** *Faron Young* JY: 13
9.	8/25	2	**Blue Blue Day** *Don Gibson* BS: 2
10.	9/8	6	**Bird Dog** *The Everly Brothers* BS: 6

10/13/58: Billboard's last "Best Sellers" and "Jockeys" charts (replaced with one all-encompassing "Hot C&W Sides" chart).

	DATE	WKS	
11.	10/20	13	**City Lights** *Ray Price*

1959

	DATE	WKS	
1.	1/19	5	**Billy Bayou** *Jim Reeves*
2.	2/23	6	**Don't Take Your Guns To Town** *Johnny Cash*
3.	4/6	1	**When It's Springtime In Alaska (It's Forty Below)** *Johnny Horton*
4.	4/13	5	**White Lightning** *George Jones*
5.	5/18	10	**The Battle Of New Orleans** *Johnny Horton*
6.	7/27	5	**Waterloo** *Stonewall Jackson*
7.	8/31	10	**The Three Bells** *The Browns*
8.	11/9	4	**Country Girl** *Faron Young*
9.	12/7	2	**The Same Old Me** *Ray Price*
10.	12/21	7	**El Paso** *Marty Robbins*

1960

	DATE	WKS	
1.	2/8	14	**He'll Have To Go** *Jim Reeves*
2.	5/16	14	**Please Help Me, I'm Falling** *Hank Locklin*
3.	8/22	12	**Alabam** *Cowboy Copas*
4.	11/14	10↕	**Wings Of A Dove** *Ferlin Husky*

1961

	DATE	WKS	
1.	1/9	5	**North To Alaska** *Johnny Horton*
2.	2/27	10	**Don't Worry** *Marty Robbins*
3.	5/8	9	**Hello Walls** *Faron Young*
4.	7/10	4	**Heartbreak U.S.A.** *Kitty Wells*
5.	8/7	2	**I Fall To Pieces** *Patsy Cline*
6.	8/21	7↕	**Tender Years** *George Jones*
7.	9/25	19↕	**Walk On By** *Leroy Van Dyke*
8.	11/20	2	**Big Bad John** *Jimmy Dean*

1962

	DATE	WKS	
1.	3/10	2↕	**Misery Loves Company** *Porter Wagoner*
2.	3/17	1	**That's My Pa** *Sheb Wooley*
3.	3/31	5↕	**She's Got You** *Patsy Cline*
4.	4/28	2↕	**Charlie's Shoes** *Billy Walker*
5.	5/19	6	**She Thinks I Still Care** *George Jones*
6.	6/30	9	**Wolverton Mountain** *Claude King*
7.	9/1	8	**Devil Woman** *Marty Robbins*
8.	10/27	7↕	**Mama Sang A Song** *Bill Anderson*

11/3/62: The 'W' signifying "Western" is dropped from chart title. Chart now designated only as "Hot Country Singles."

	DATE	WKS	
9.	11/10	2↕	**I've Been Everywhere** *Hank Snow*
10.	12/29	11↕	**Don't Let Me Cross Over** *Carl Butler & Pearl*

1963

	DATE	WKS	
1.	1/5	1	**Ruby Ann** *Marty Robbins*
2.	1/19	3↕	**The Ballad Of Jed Clampett** *Flatt & Scruggs*
3.	4/13	7↕	**Still** *Bill Anderson*
4.	5/4	4↕	**Lonesome 7-7203** *Hawkshaw Hawkins*
5.	6/15	4↕	**Act Naturally** *Buck Owens*
6.	7/27	7	**Ring Of Fire** *Johnny Cash*
7.	9/14	4	**Abilene** *George Hamilton IV*
8.	10/12	1	**Talk Back Trembling Lips** *Ernest Ashworth*
9.	10/19	16	**Love's Gonna Live Here** *Buck Owens*

1964

	DATE	WKS	
1.	2/8	3↕	**Begging To You** *Marty Robbins*
2.	2/15	1	**B.J. The D.J.** *Stonewall Jackson*
3.	3/7	4	**Saginaw, Michigan** *Lefty Frizzell*
4.	4/4	6	**Understand Your Man** *Johnny Cash*
5.	5/16	7↕	**My Heart Skips A Beat** *Buck Owens*
6.	6/6	2	**Together Again** *Buck Owens*
7.	7/18	6	**Dang Me** *Roger Miller*
8.	8/29	7	**I Guess I'm Crazy** *Jim Reeves*
9.	10/17	6	**I Don't Care (Just As Long As You Love Me)** *Buck Owens*
10.	11/28	8	**Once A Day** *Connie Smith*

1965

	DATE	WKS	
1.	1/23	4	**You're The Only World I Know** *Sonny James*
2.	2/20	5	**I've Got A Tiger By The Tail** *Buck Owens*
3.	3/27	5	**King Of The Road** *Roger Miller*
4.	5/1	3↕	**This Is It** *Jim Reeves*
5.	5/15	2	**Girl On The Billboard** *Del Reeves*
6.	6/5	2	**What's He Doing In My World** *Eddy Arnold*
7.	6/19	1	**Ribbon Of Darkness** *Marty Robbins*
8.	6/26	6	**Before You Go** *Buck Owens*
9.	8/7	2	**The First Thing Ev'ry Morning (And The Last Thing Ev'ry Night)** *Jimmy Dean*
10.	8/21	2	**Yes, Mr. Peters** *Roy Drusky & Priscilla Mitchell*
11.	9/4	1	**The Bridge Washed Out** *Warner Mack*
12.	9/11	3	**Is It Really Over?** *Jim Reeves*
13.	10/2	1	**Only You (Can Break My Heart)** *Buck Owens*

1965 (cont'd)

	DATE	WKS	
14.	10/9	3↕	**Behind The Tear** *Sonny James*
15.	10/23	3	**Hello Vietnam** *Johnny Wright*
16.	11/20	2	**May The Bird Of Paradise Fly Up Your Nose** *"Little" Jimmy Dickens*
17.	12/4	3	**Make The World Go Away** *Eddy Arnold*
18.	12/25	2	**Buckaroo** *Buck Owens*

1966

	DATE	WKS	
1.	1/8	6	**Giddyup Go** *Red Sovine*
2.	2/19	7	**Waitin' In Your Welfare Line** *Buck Owens*
3.	4/9	6	**I Want To Go With You** *Eddy Arnold*
4.	5/21	4	**Distant Drums** *Jim Reeves*
5.	6/18	2	**Take Good Care Of Her** *Sonny James*
6.	7/2	6	**Think Of Me** *Buck Owens*
7.	8/13	9	**Almost Persuaded** *David Houston*
8.	10/15	1	**Blue Side Of Lonesome** *Jim Reeves*
9.	10/22	4	**Open Up Your Heart** *Buck Owens*
10.	11/19	1	**I Get The Fever** *Bill Anderson*
11.	11/26	4	**Somebody Like Me** *Eddy Arnold*
12.	12/24	7	**There Goes My Everything** *Jack Greene*

1967

	DATE	WKS	
1.	2/11	1	**Don't Come Home A'Drinkin' (With Lovin' On Your Mind)** *Loretta Lynn*
2.	2/18	4↕	**Where Does The Good Times Go** *Buck Owens*
3.	3/4	1	**The Fugitive** *Merle Haggard*
4.	3/25	1	**I Won't Come In While He's There** *Jim Reeves*
5.	4/1	2	**Walk Through This World With Me** *George Jones*
6.	4/15	2	**Lonely Again** *Eddy Arnold*
7.	4/29	2	**Need You** *Sonny James*
8.	5/13	3	**Sam's Place** *Buck Owens*
9.	6/3	2	**It's Such A Pretty World Today** *Wynn Stewart*
10.	6/17	5	**All The Time** *Jack Greene*
11.	7/22	1	**With One Exception** *David Houston*
12.	7/29	1	**Tonight Carmen** *Marty Robbins*
13.	8/5	4	**I'll Never Find Another You** *Sonny James*
14.	9/2	1	**Branded Man** *Merle Haggard*
15.	9/9	1	**Your Tender Loving Care** *Buck Owens*
16.	9/16	2	**My Elusive Dreams** *David Houston & Tammy Wynette*
17.	9/30	1	**Laura What's He Got That I Ain't Got** *Leon Ashley*
18.	10/7	1	**Turn The World Around** *Eddy Arnold*
19.	10/14	3	**I Don't Wanna Play House** *Tammy Wynette*
20.	11/4	2	**You Mean The World To Me** *David Houston*
21.	11/18	5	**It's The Little Things** *Sonny James*
22.	12/23	4	**For Loving You** *Bill Anderson & Jan Howard*

1968

	DATE	WKS	
1.	1/20	2	**Sing Me Back Home** *Merle Haggard*
2.	2/3	5	**Skip A Rope** *Henson Cargill*
3.	3/9	1	**Take Me To Your World** *Tammy Wynette*
4.	3/16	3	**A World Of Our Own** *Sonny James*
5.	4/6	1	**How Long Will My Baby Be Gone** *Buck Owens*
6.	4/13	1	**You Are My Treasure** *Jack Greene*
7.	4/20	1	**Fist City** *Loretta Lynn*
8.	4/27	2	**The Legend Of Bonnie And Clyde** *Merle Haggard*
9.	5/11	1	**Have A Little Faith** *David Houston*
10.	5/18	3↕	**I Wanna Live** *Glen Campbell*
11.	5/25	3	**Honey** *Bobby Goldsboro*
12.	6/29	3	**D-I-V-O-R-C-E** *Tammy Wynette*
13.	7/20	4	**Folsom Prison Blues** *Johnny Cash*
14.	8/17	1	**Heaven Says Hello** *Sonny James*
15.	8/24	1	**Already It's Heaven** *David Houston*
16.	8/31	4	**Mama Tried** *Merle Haggard*
17.	9/28	3	**Harper Valley P.T.A.** *Jeannie C. Riley*
18.	10/19	2	**Then You Can Tell Me Goodbye** *Eddy Arnold*
19.	11/2	1	**Next In Line** *Conway Twitty*
20.	11/9	2	**I Walk Alone** *Marty Robbins*
21.	11/23	3	**Stand By Your Man** *Tammy Wynette*
22.	12/14	1	**Born To Be With You** *Sonny James*
23.	12/21	2	**Wichita Lineman** *Glen Campbell*

1969

	DATE	WKS	
1.	1/4	6	**Daddy Sang Bass** *Johnny Cash*
2.	2/15	2	**Until My Dreams Come True** *Jack Greene*
3.	3/1	1	**To Make Love Sweeter For You** *Jerry Lee Lewis*
4.	3/8	3	**Only The Lonely** *Sonny James*
5.	3/29	2	**Who's Gonna Mow Your Grass** *Buck Owens*
6.	4/12	1	**Woman Of The World (Leave My World Alone)** *Loretta Lynn*
7.	4/19	3	**Galveston** *Glen Campbell*
8.	5/10	1	**Hungry Eyes** *Merle Haggard*
9.	5/17	2	**My Life (Throw It Away If I Want To)** *Bill Anderson*
10.	5/31	2	**Singing My Song** *Tammy Wynette*
11.	6/14	3	**Running Bear** *Sonny James*
12.	7/5	2	**Statue Of A Fool** *Jack Greene*
13.	7/19	1	**I Love You More Today** *Conway Twitty*
14.	7/26	2	**Johnny B. Goode** *Buck Owens*
15.	8/9	1	**All I Have To Offer You (Is Me)** *Charley Pride*
16.	8/16	1	**Workin' Man Blues** *Merle Haggard*
17.	8/23	5	**A Boy Named Sue** *Johnny Cash*
18.	9/27	1	**Tall Dark Stranger** *Buck Owens*
19.	10/4	3	**Since I Met You, Baby** *Sonny James*
20.	10/25	2	**The Ways To Love A Man** *Tammy Wynette*
21.	11/8	1	**To See My Angel Cry** *Conway Twitty*
22.	11/15	4	**Okie From Muskogee** *Merle Haggard*
23.	12/13	3	**(I'm So) Afraid Of Losing You Again** *Charley Pride*

#1 HITS

1970

	DATE	WKS	
1.	1/3	4	**Baby, Baby (I Know You're A Lady)** *David Houston*
2.	1/31	2	**A Week In A Country Jail** *Tom T. Hall*
3.	2/14	4	**It's Just A Matter Of Time** *Sonny James*
4.	3/14	3	**The Fightin' Side Of Me** *Merle Haggard*
5.	4/4	2	**Tennessee Bird Walk** *Jack Blanchard & Misty Morgan*
6.	4/18	2	**Is Anybody Goin' To San Antone** *Charley Pride*
7.	5/2	1	**My Woman My Woman, My Wife** *Marty Robbins*
8.	5/9	1	**The Pool Shark** *Dave Dudley*
9.	5/16	3	**My Love** *Sonny James*
10.	6/6	4	**Hello Darlin'** *Conway Twitty*
11.	7/4	3	**He Loves Me All The Way** *Tammy Wynette*
12.	7/25	2	**Wonder Could I Live There Anymore** *Charley Pride*
13.	8/8	4	**Don't Keep Me Hangin' On** *Sonny James*
14.	9/5	2	**All For The Love Of Sunshine** *Hank Williams, Jr. With The Mike Curb Congregation*
15.	9/19	1	**For The Good Times** *Ray Price*
16.	9/26	2	**There Must Be More To Love Than This** *Jerry Lee Lewis*
17.	10/10	2	**Sunday Morning Coming Down** *Johnny Cash*
18.	10/24	2	**Run, Woman, Run** *Tammy Wynette*
19.	11/7	2	**I Can't Believe That You've Stopped Loving Me** *Charley Pride*
20.	11/21	1	**Fifteen Years Ago** *Conway Twitty*
21.	11/28	3	**Endlessly** *Sonny James*
22.	12/19	1	**Coal Miner's Daughter** *Loretta Lynn*
23.	12/26	5	**Rose Garden** *Lynn Anderson*

1971

	DATE	WKS	
1.	1/30	1	**Flesh And Blood** *Johnny Cash*
2.	2/6	1	**Joshua** *Dolly Parton*
3.	2/13	3	**Help Me Make It Through The Night** *Sammi Smith*
4.	3/6	3	**I'd Rather Love You** *Charley Pride*
5.	3/27	2	**After The Fire Is Gone** *Conway Twitty & Loretta Lynn*
6.	4/10	4	**Empty Arms** *Sonny James*
7.	5/8	1	**How Much More Can She Stand** *Conway Twitty*
8.	5/15	3	**I Won't Mention It Again** *Ray Price*
9.	6/5	2	**You're My Man** *Lynn Anderson*
10.	6/19	5	**When You're Hot, You're Hot** *Jerry Reed*
11.	7/24	1	**Bright Lights, Big City** *Sonny James*
12.	7/31	4	**I'm Just Me** *Charley Pride*
13.	8/28	2	**Good Lovin' (Makes It Right)** *Tammy Wynette*
14.	9/11	3↕	**Easy Loving** *Freddie Hart*
15.	9/18	2	**The Year That Clayton Delaney Died** *Tom T. Hall*
16.	10/16	3	**How Can I Unlove You** *Lynn Anderson*
17.	11/6	1	**Here Comes Honey Again** *Sonny James*
18.	11/13	1	**Lead Me On** *Conway Twitty & Loretta Lynn*

1971 (cont'd)

	DATE	WKS	
19.	11/20	2	**Daddy Frank (The Guitar Man)** *Merle Haggard*
20.	12/4	5	**Kiss An Angel Good Mornin'** *Charley Pride*

1972

	DATE	WKS	
1.	1/8	1	**Would You Take Another Chance On Me** *Jerry Lee Lewis*
2.	1/15	3	**Carolyn** *Merle Haggard*
3.	2/5	2	**One's On The Way** *Loretta Lynn*
4.	2/19	2	**It's Four In The Morning** *Faron Young*
5.	3/4	1	**Bedtime Story** *Tammy Wynette*
6.	3/11	6	**My Hang-Up Is You** *Freddie Hart*
7.	4/22	3	**Chantilly Lace** *Jerry Lee Lewis*
8.	5/13	2	**Grandma Harp** *Merle Haggard*
9.	5/27	1	**(Lost Her Love) On Our Last Date** *Conway Twitty*
10.	6/3	3	**The Happiest Girl In The Whole U.S.A.** *Donna Fargo*
11.	6/24	1	**That's Why I Love You Like I Do** *Sonny James*
12.	7/1	2	**Eleven Roses** *Hank Williams, Jr.*
13.	7/15	1	**Made In Japan** *Buck Owens*
14.	7/22	3	**It's Gonna Take A Little Bit Longer** *Charley Pride*
15.	8/12	2	**Bless Your Heart** *Freddie Hart*
16.	8/26	2↕	**If You Leave Me Tonight I'll Cry** *Jerry Wallace*
17.	9/2	1	**Woman (Sensuous Woman)** *Don Gibson*
18.	9/16	1	**When The Snow Is On The Roses** *Sonny James*
19.	9/23	1	**I Can't Stop Loving You** *Conway Twitty*
20.	9/30	2	**I Ain't Never** *Mel Tillis*
21.	10/14	3	**Funny Face** *Donna Fargo*
22.	11/4	1	**It's Not Love (But It's Not Bad)** *Merle Haggard*
23.	11/11	1	**My Man** *Tammy Wynette*
24.	11/18	3	**She's Too Good To Be True** *Charley Pride*
25.	12/9	3	**Got The All Overs For You (All Over Me)** *Freddie Hart*
26.	12/30	3	**She's Got To Be A Saint** *Ray Price*

1973

	DATE	WKS	
1.	1/20	1	**Soul Song** *Joe Stampley*
2.	1/27	1	**(Old Dogs-Children And) Watermelon Wine** *Tom T. Hall*
3.	2/3	2	**She Needs Someone To Hold Her (When She Cries)** *Conway Twitty*
4.	2/17	1	**I Wonder If They Ever Think Of Me** *Merle Haggard*
5.	2/24	1	**Rated "X"** *Loretta Lynn*
6.	3/3	1	**The Lord Knows I'm Drinking** *Cal Smith*
7.	3/10	1	**'Til I Get It Right** *Tammy Wynette*
8.	3/17	2	**Teddy Bear Song** *Barbara Fairchild*
9.	3/31	1	**Keep Me In Mind** *Lynn Anderson*
10.	4/7	1	**Super Kind Of Woman** *Freddie Hart*
11.	4/14	1	**A Shoulder To Cry On** *Charley Pride*

#1 HITS

1973 (cont'd)

	DATE	WKS	
12.	4/21	1	**Superman** *Donna Fargo*
13.	4/28	2	**Behind Closed Doors** *Charlie Rich*
14.	5/12	1	**Come Live With Me** *Roy Clark*
15.	5/19	1	**What's Your Mama's Name** *Tanya Tucker*
16.	5/26	3↕	**Satin Sheets** *Jeanne Pruett*
17.	6/9	1	**You Always Come Back (To Hurting Me)** *Johnny Rodriguez*
18.	6/16	1	**Kids Say The Darndest Things** *Tammy Wynette*
19.	6/30	1	**Don't Fight The Feelings Of Love** *Charley Pride*
20.	7/7	1	**Why Me** *Kris Kristofferson*
21.	7/14	2	**Love Is The Foundation** *Loretta Lynn*
22.	7/28	1	**You Were Always There** *Donna Fargo*
23.	8/4	1	**Lord, Mr. Ford** *Jerry Reed*
24.	8/11	1	**Trip To Heaven** *Freddie Hart*
25.	8/18	1	**Louisiana Woman, Mississippi Man** *Loretta Lynn & Conway Twitty*
26.	8/25	2	**Everybody's Had The Blues** *Merle Haggard*
27.	9/8	3	**You've Never Been This Far Before** *Conway Twitty*
28.	9/29	1	**Blood Red And Goin' Down** *Tanya Tucker*
29.	10/6	1	**You're The Best Thing That Ever Happened To Me** *Ray Price*
30.	10/13	2	**Ridin' My Thumb To Mexico** *Johnny Rodriguez*
31.	10/27	2	**We're Gonna Hold On** *George Jones & Tammy Wynette*
32.	11/10	2	**Paper Roses** *Marie Osmond*
33.	11/24	3	**The Most Beautiful Girl** *Charlie Rich*
34.	12/15	1	**Amazing Love** *Charley Pride*
35.	12/22	4	**If We Make It Through December** *Merle Haggard*

1974

	DATE	WKS	
1.	1/19	2	**I Love** *Tom T. Hall*
2.	2/2	1	**Jolene** *Dolly Parton*
3.	2/9	1	**World Of Make Believe** *Bill Anderson*
4.	2/16	1	**That's The Way Love Goes** *Johnny Rodriguez*
5.	2/23	2	**Another Lonely Song** *Tammy Wynette*
6.	3/9	2	**There Won't Be Anymore** *Charlie Rich*
7.	3/23	1	**There's A Honky Tonk Angel (Who'll Take Me Back In)** *Conway Twitty*
8.	3/30	1	**Would You Lay With Me (In A Field Of Stone)** *Tanya Tucker*
9.	4/6	3	**A Very Special Love Song** *Charlie Rich*
10.	4/27	1	**Hello Love** *Hank Snow*
11.	5/4	1	**Things Aren't Funny Anymore** *Merle Haggard*
12.	5/11	1	**Is It Wrong (For Loving You)** *Sonny James*
13.	5/18	1	**Country Bumpkin** *Cal Smith*
14.	5/25	1	**No Charge** *Melba Montgomery*
15.	6/1	1	**Pure Love** *Ronnie Milsap*
16.	6/8	1	**I Will Always Love You** *Dolly Parton*
17.	6/15	1	**I Don't See Me In Your Eyes Anymore** *Charlie Rich*
18.	6/22	1	**This Time** *Waylon Jennings*

1974 (cont'd)

	DATE	WKS	
19.	6/29	1	**Room Full Of Roses** *Mickey Gilley*
20.	7/6	2	**He Thinks I Still Care** *Anne Murray*
21.	7/20	1	**Marie Laveau** *Bobby Bare*
22.	7/27	1	**You Can't Be A Beacon (If Your Light Don't Shine)** *Donna Fargo*
23.	8/3	2	**Rub It In** *Billy "Crash" Craddock*
24.	8/17	1	**As Soon As I Hang Up The Phone** *Loretta Lynn & Conway Twitty*
25.	8/24	1	**Old Man From The Mountain** *Merle Haggard*
26.	8/31	1	**The Grand Tour** *George Jones*
27.	9/7	2	**Please Don't Tell Me How The Story Ends** *Ronnie Milsap*
28.	9/21	1	**I Wouldn't Want To Live If You Didn't Love Me** *Don Williams*
29.	9/28	1	**I'm A Ramblin' Man** *Waylon Jennings*
30.	10/5	1	**I Love My Friend** *Charlie Rich*
31.	10/12	1	**Please Don't Stop Loving Me** *Porter Wagoner & Dolly Parton*
32.	10/19	2	**I See The Want To In Your Eyes** *Conway Twitty*
33.	11/2	1	**I Overlooked An Orchid** *Mickey Gilley*
34.	11/9	1	**Love Is Like A Butterfly** *Dolly Parton*
35.	11/16	1	**Country Is** *Tom T. Hall*
36.	11/23	1	**Trouble In Paradise** *Loretta Lynn*
37.	11/30	1	**Back Home Again** *John Denver*
38.	12/7	1	**She Called Me Baby** *Charlie Rich*
39.	12/14	2	**I Can Help** *Billy Swan*
40.	12/28	1	**What A Man, My Man Is** *Lynn Anderson*

1975

	DATE	WKS	
1.	1/4	1	**The Door** *George Jones*
2.	1/11	1	**Ruby, Baby** *Billy "Crash" Craddock*
3.	1/18	1	**Kentucky Gambler** *Merle Haggard*
4.	1/25	1	**(I'd Be) A Legend In My Time** *Ronnie Milsap*
5.	2/1	1	**City Lights** *Mickey Gilley*
6.	2/8	1	**Then Who Am I** *Charley Pride*
7.	2/15	1	**Devil In The Bottle** *T.G. Sheppard*
8.	2/22	1	**I Care** *Tom T. Hall*
9.	3/1	1	**It's Time To Pay The Fiddler** *Cal Smith*
10.	3/8	1	**Linda On My Mind** *Conway Twitty*
11.	3/15	2	**Before The Next Teardrop Falls** *Freddy Fender*
12.	3/29	1	**The Bargain Store** *Dolly Parton*
13.	4/5	1	**I Just Can't Get Her Out Of My Mind** *Johnny Rodriguez*
14.	4/12	2	**Always Wanting You** *Merle Haggard*
15.	4/26	1	**Blanket On The Ground** *Billie Jo Spears*
16.	5/3	1	**Roll On Big Mama** *Joe Stampley*
17.	5/10	1	**She's Actin' Single (I'm Drinkin' Doubles)** *Gary Stewart*
18.	5/17	1	**(Hey Won't You Play) Another Somebody Done Somebody Wrong Song** *B.J. Thomas*
19.	5/24	1	**I'm Not Lisa** *Jessi Colter*
20.	5/31	1	**Thank God I'm A Country Boy** *John Denver*
21.	6/7	1	**Window Up Above** *Mickey Gilley*

#1 HITS

1975 (cont'd)

22. 6/14 1 **When Will I Be Loved** *Linda Ronstadt*
23. 6/21 1 **You're My Best Friend** *Don Williams*
24. 6/28 1 **Tryin' To Beat The Morning Home** *T.G. Sheppard*
25. 7/5 1 **Lizzie And The Rainman** *Tanya Tucker*
26. 7/12 1 **Movin' On** *Merle Haggard*
27. 7/19 2 **Touch The Hand** *Conway Twitty*
28. 8/2 1 **Just Get Up And Close The Door** *Johnny Rodriguez*
29. 8/9 2 **Wasted Days And Wasted Nights** *Freddy Fender*
30. 8/23 3↕ **Rhinestone Cowboy** *Glen Campbell*
31. 9/6 1 **Feelins'** *Loretta Lynn & Conway Twitty*
32. 9/20 2 **Daydreams About Night Things** *Ronnie Milsap*
33. 10/4 2 **Blue Eyes Crying In The Rain** *Willie Nelson*
34. 10/18 1 **Hope You're Feelin' Me (Like I'm Feelin' You)** *Charley Pride*
35. 10/25 1 **San Antonio Stroll** *Tanya Tucker*
36. 11/1 1 **(Turn Out The Light And) Love Me Tonight** *Don Williams*
37. 11/8 1 **I'm Sorry** *John Denver*
38. 11/15 1 **Are You Sure Hank Done It This Way** *Waylon Jennings*
39. 11/22 1 **Rocky** *Dickey Lee*
40. 11/29 1 **It's All In The Movies** *Merle Haggard*
41. 12/6 1 **Secret Love** *Freddy Fender*
42. 12/13 1 **Love Put A Song In My Heart** *Johnny Rodriguez*
43. 12/20 6 **Convoy** *C.W. McCall*

DATE WKS 1976

1. 1/31 1 **This Time I've Hurt Her More Than She Loves Me** *Conway Twitty*
2. 2/7 1 **Sometimes** *Bill Anderson & Mary Lou Turner*
3. 2/14 1 **The White Knight** *Cledus Maggard*
4. 2/21 3 **Good Hearted Woman** *Waylon Jennings & Willie Nelson*
5. 3/13 1 **The Roots Of My Raising** *Merle Haggard*
6. 3/20 1 **Faster Horses (The Cowboy And The Poet)** *Tom T. Hall*
7. 3/27 1 **Til The Rivers All Run Dry** *Don Williams*
8. 4/3 1 **You'll Lose A Good Thing** *Freddy Fender*
9. 4/10 1 **'Til I Can Make It On My Own** *Tammy Wynette*
10. 4/17 1 **Drinkin' My Baby (Off My Mind)** *Eddie Rabbitt*
11. 4/24 1 **Together Again** *Emmylou Harris*
12. 5/1 1 **Don't The Girls All Get Prettier At Closing Time** *Mickey Gilley*
13. 5/8 1 **My Eyes Can Only See As Far As You** *Charley Pride*
14. 5/15 1 **What Goes On When The Sun Goes Down** *Ronnie Milsap*
15. 5/22 1 **After All The Good Is Gone** *Conway Twitty*
16. 5/29 2 **One Piece At A Time** *Johnny Cash*
17. 6/12 1 **I'll Get Over You** *Crystal Gayle*
18. 6/19 2 **El Paso City** *Marty Robbins*

1976 (cont'd)

19. 7/4 1 **All These Things** *Joe Stampley*
20. 7/10 1 **The Door Is Always Open** *Dave & Sugar*
21. 7/17 3 **Teddy Bear** *Red Sovine*
22. 8/7 1 **Golden Ring** *George Jones & Tammy Wynette*
23. 8/14 1 **Say It Again** *Don Williams*
24. 8/21 1 **Bring It On Home To Me** *Mickey Gilley*
25. 8/28 2 **(I'm A) Stand By My Woman Man** *Ronnie Milsap*
26. 9/11 2 **I Don't Want To Have To Marry You** *Jim Ed Brown &Helen Cornelius*
27. 9/25 1 **If You've Got The Money I've Got The Time** *Willie Nelson*
28. 10/2 1 **Here's Some Love** *Tanya Tucker*
29. 10/9 1 **The Games That Daddies Play** *Conway Twitty*
30. 10/16 2 **You And Me** *Tammy Wynette*
31. 10/30 1 **Among My Souvenirs** *Marty Robbins*
32. 11/6 1 **Cherokee Maiden** *Merle Haggard*
33. 11/13 2 **Somebody Somewhere (Don't Know What He's Missin' Tonight)** *Loretta Lynn*
34. 11/27 2 **Good Woman Blues** *Mel Tillis*
35. 12/11 2 **Thinkin' Of A Rendezvous** *Johnny Duncan*
36. 12/25 2 **Sweet Dreams** *Emmylou Harris*

DATE WKS 1977

1. 1/8 1 **Broken Down In Tiny Pieces** *Billy "Crash" Craddock*
2. 1/15 1 **You Never Miss A Real Good Thing (Till He Says Goodbye)** *Crystal Gayle*
3. 1/22 1 **I Can't Believe She Gives It All To Me** *Conway Twitty*
4. 1/29 1 **Let My Love Be Your Pillow** *Ronnie Milsap*
5. 2/5 2 **Near You** *George Jones & Tammy Wynette*
6. 2/19 1 **Moody Blue** *Elvis Presley*
7. 2/26 1 **Say You'll Stay Until Tomorrow** *Tom Jones*
8. 3/5 1 **Heart Healer** *Mel Tillis*
9. 3/12 1 **She's Just An Old Love Turned Memory** *Charley Pride*
10. 3/19 2 **Southern Nights** *Glen Campbell*
11. 4/2 2 **Lucille** *Kenny Rogers*
12. 4/16 1 **It Couldn't Have Been Any Better** *Johnny Duncan*
13. 4/23 1 **She's Got You** *Loretta Lynn*
14. 4/30 1 **She's Pulling Me Back Again** *Mickey Gilley*
15. 5/7 1 **Play, Guitar Play** *Conway Twitty*
16. 5/14 1 **Some Broken Hearts Never Mend** *Don Williams*
17. 5/21 6 **Luckenbach, Texas (Back to the Basics of Love)** *Waylon Jennings*
18. 7/2 1 **That Was Yesterday** *Donna Fargo*
19. 7/9 1 **I'll Be Leaving Alone** *Charley Pride*
20. 7/16 3 **It Was Almost Like A Song** *Ronnie Milsap*
21. 8/6 2 **Rollin' With The Flow** *Charlie Rich*
22. 8/20 1 **Way Down** *Elvis Presley*
23. 8/27 4 **Don't It Make My Brown Eyes Blue** *Crystal Gayle*

#1 HITS

1977 (cont'd)

24. 9/24 1 **I've Already Loved You In My Mind** *Conway Twitty*
25. 10/1 1 **Daytime Friends** *Kenny Rogers*
26. 10/8 4 **Heaven's Just A Sin Away** *The Kendalls*
27. 11/5 1 **I'm Just A Country Boy** *Don Williams*
28. 11/12 1 **More To Me** *Charley Pride*
29. 11/19 2 **The Wurlitzer Prize (I Don't Want To Get Over You)** *Waylon Jennings*
30. 12/3 5 **Here You Come Again** *Dolly Parton*

DATE WKS 1978

1. 1/7 2 **Take This Job And Shove It** *Johnny Paycheck*
2. 1/21 1 **What A Difference You've Made In My Life** *Ronnie Milsap*
3. 1/28 2 **Out Of My Head And Back In My Bed** *Loretta Lynn*
4. 2/11 1 **I Just Wish You Were Someone I Love** *Larry Gatlin & The Gatlin Brothers*
5. 2/18 2 **Don't Break The Heart That Loves You** *Margo Smith*
6. 3/4 4 **Mammas Don't Let Your Babies Grow Up To Be Cowboys** *Waylon Jennings & Willie Nelson*
7. 4/1 1 **Ready For The Times To Get Better** *Crystal Gayle*
8. 4/8 2 **Someone Loves You Honey** *Charley Pride*
9. 4/22 2 **Every Time Two Fools Collide** *Kenny Rogers & Dottie West*
10. 5/6 2 **It's All Wrong, But It's All Right** *Dolly Parton*
11. 5/20 1 **She Can Put Her Shoes Under My Bed (Anytime)** *Johnny Duncan*
12. 5/27 2 **Do You Know You Are My Sunshine** *The Statler Brothers*
13. 6/10 1 **Georgia On My Mind** *Willie Nelson*
14. 6/17 1 **Two More Bottles Of Wine** *Emmylou Harris*
15. 6/24 1 **I'll Be True To You** *The Oak Ridge Boys*
16. 7/1 1 **It Only Hurts For A Little While** *Margo Smith*
17. 7/8 1 **I Believe In You** *Mel Tillis*
18. 7/15 3 **Only One Love In My Life** *Ronnie Milsap*
19. 8/5 1 **Love Or Something Like It** *Kenny Rogers*
20. 8/12 1 **You Don't Love Me Anymore** *Eddie Rabbitt*
21. 8/19 2 **Talking In Your Sleep** *Crystal Gayle*
22. 9/2 1 **Blue Skies** *Willie Nelson*
23. 9/9 3 **I've Always Been Crazy** *Waylon Jennings*
24. 9/30 3 **Heartbreaker** *Dolly Parton*
25. 10/21 1 **Tear Time** *Dave & Sugar*
26. 10/28 1 **Let's Take The Long Way Around The World** *Ronnie Milsap*
27. 11/4 3 **Sleeping Single In A Double Bed** *Barbara Mandrell*
28. 11/25 1 **Sweet Desire** *The Kendalls*
29. 12/2 1 **I Just Want To Love You** *Eddie Rabbitt*
30. 12/9 1 **On My Knees** *Charlie Rich with Janie Fricke*
31. 12/16 3 **The Gambler** *Kenny Rogers*

DATE WKS 1979

1. 1/6 1 **Tulsa Time** *Don Williams*
2. 1/13 1 **Lady Lay Down** *John Conlee*
3. 1/20 1 **I Really Got The Feeling** *Dolly Parton*
4. 1/27 2 **Why Have You Left The One You Left Me For** *Crystal Gayle*
5. 2/10 3 **Every Which Way But Loose** *Eddie Rabbitt*
6. 3/3 3 **Golden Tears** *Dave & Sugar*
7. 3/24 3 **I Just Fall In Love Again** *Anne Murray*
8. 4/14 1 **(If Loving You Is Wrong) I Don't Want To Be Right** *Barbara Mandrell*
9. 4/21 1 **All I Ever Need Is You** *Kenny Rogers & Dottie West*
10. 4/28 1 **Where Do I Put Her Memory** *Charley Pride*
11. 5/5 1 **Backside Of Thirty** *John Conlee*
12. 5/12 1 **Don't Take It Away** *Conway Twitty*
13. 5/19 3 **If I Said You Have A Beautiful Body Would You Hold It Against Me** *Bellamy Brothers*
14. 6/9 2 **She Believes In Me** *Kenny Rogers*
15. 6/23 1 **Nobody Likes Sad Songs** *Ronnie Milsap*
16. 6/30 3 **Amanda** *Waylon Jennings*
17. 7/21 1 **Shadows In The Moonlight** *Anne Murray*
18. 7/28 2 **You're The Only One** *Dolly Parton*
19. 8/11 1 **Suspicions** *Eddie Rabbitt*
20. 8/18 1 **Coca Cola Cowboy** *Mel Tillis*
21. 8/25 1 **The Devil Went Down To Georgia** *Charlie Daniels Band*
22. 9/1 1 **Heartbreak Hotel** *Willie Nelson & Leon Russell*
23. 9/8 1 **I May Never Get To Heaven** *Conway Twitty*
24. 9/15 1 **You're My Jamaica** *Charley Pride*
25. 9/22 1 **Just Good Ol' Boys** *Moe Bandy & Joe Stampley*
26. 9/29 1 **It Must Be Love** *Don Williams*
27. 10/6 2 **Last Cheater's Waltz** *T.G. Sheppard*
28. 10/20 2 **All The Gold In California** *Larry Gatlin & The Gatlin Brothers*
29. 11/3 2 **You Decorated My Life** *Kenny Rogers*
30. 11/17 2 **Come With Me** *Waylon Jennings*
31. 12/1 1 **Broken Hearted Me** *Anne Murray*
32. 12/8 1 **I Cheated Me Right Out Of You** *Moe Bandy*
33. 12/15 3 **Happy Birthday Darlin'** *Conway Twitty*

DATE WKS 1980

1. 1/5 3 **Coward Of The County** *Kenny Rogers*
2. 1/26 2 **I'll Be Coming Back For More** *T.G. Sheppard*
3. 2/9 1 **Leaving Louisiana In The Broad Daylight** *The Oak Ridge Boys*
4. 2/16 1 **Love Me Over Again** *Don Williams*
5. 2/23 1 **Years** *Barbara Mandrell*
6. 3/1 1 **I Ain't Living Long Like This** *Waylon Jennings*
7. 3/8 2 **My Heroes Have Always Been Cowboys** *Willie Nelson*
8. 3/22 1 **Why Don't You Spend The Night** *Ronnie Milsap*

#1 HITS

1980 (cont'd)

	DATE	WKS	Title / Artist
9.	3/29	1	**I'd Love To Lay You Down** *Conway Twitty*
10.	4/5	1	**Sugar Daddy** *Bellamy Brothers*
11.	4/12	1	**Honky Tonk Blues** *Charley Pride*
12.	4/19	1	**It's Like We Never Said Goodbye** *Crystal Gayle*
13.	4/26	1	**A Lesson In Leavin'** *Dottie West*
14.	5/3	1	**Are You On The Road To Lovin' Me Again** *Debby Boone*
15.	5/10	1	**Beneath Still Waters** *Emmylou Harris*
16.	5/17	1	**Gone Too Far** *Eddie Rabbitt*
17.	5/24	1	**Starting Over Again** *Dolly Parton*
18.	5/31	3	**My Heart** *Ronnie Milsap*
19.	6/21	1	**One Day At A Time** *Cristy Lane*
20.	6/28	1	**Trying To Love Two Women** *The Oak Ridge Boys*
21.	7/5	1	**He Stopped Loving Her Today** *George Jones*
22.	7/12	1	**You Win Again** *Charley Pride*
23.	7/19	1	**True Love Ways** *Mickey Gilley*
24.	7/26	1	**Bar Room Buddies** *Merle Haggard & Clint Eastwood*
25.	8/2	1	**Dancin' Cowboys** *Bellamy Brothers*
26.	8/9	1	**Stand By Me** *Mickey Gilley*
27.	8/16	1	**Tennessee River** *Alabama*
28.	8/23	1	**Drivin' My Life Away** *Eddie Rabbitt*
29.	8/30	1	**Cowboys And Clowns** *Ronnie Milsap*
30.	9/6	3	**Lookin' For Love** *Johnny Lee*
31.	9/27	1	**Old Flames Can't Hold A Candle To You** *Dolly Parton*
32.	10/4	1	**Do You Wanna Go To Heaven** *T.G. Sheppard*
33.	10/11	1	**Loving Up A Storm** *Razzy Bailey*
34.	10/18	2	**I Believe In You** *Don Williams*
35.	11/1	1	**Theme From The Dukes Of Hazzard (Good Ol' Boys)** *Waylon Jennings*
36.	11/8	1	**On The Road Again** *Willie Nelson*
37.	11/15	1	**Could I Have This Dance** *Anne Murray*
38.	11/22	1	**Lady** *Kenny Rogers*
39.	11/29	1	**If You Ever Change Your Mind** *Crystal Gayle*
40.	12/6	1	**Smoky Mountain Rain** *Ronnie Milsap*
41.	12/13	1	**Why Lady Why** *Alabama*
42.	12/20	1	**That's All That Matters** *Mickey Gilley*
43.	12/27	2	**One In A Million** *Johnny Lee*

1981

	DATE	WKS	Title / Artist
1.	1/10	1	**I Think I'll Just Stay Here And Drink** *Merle Haggard*
2.	1/17	1	**I Love A Rainy Night** *Eddie Rabbitt*
3.	1/24	1	**9 To 5** *Dolly Parton*
4.	1/31	1	**I Feel Like Loving You Again** *T.G. Sheppard*
5.	2/7	1	**I Keep Coming Back** *Razzy Bailey*
6.	2/14	1	**Who's Cheatin' Who** *Charly McClain*
7.	2/21	1	**Southern Rains** *Mel Tillis*
8.	2/28	1	**Are You Happy Baby?** *Dottie West*
9.	3/7	1	**Do You Love As Good As You Look** *The Bellamy Brothers*

1981 (cont'd)

	DATE	WKS	Title / Artist
10.	3/14	1	**Guitar Man** *Elvis Presley*
11.	3/21	1	**Angel Flying Too Close To The Ground** *Willie Nelson*
12.	3/28	1	**Texas Women** *Hank Williams, Jr.*
13.	4/4	1	**Drifter** *Sylvia*
14.	4/11	1	**You're The Reason God Made Oklahoma** *David Frizzell & Shelly West*
15.	4/18	1	**Old Flame** *Alabama*
16.	4/25	1	**A Headache Tomorrow (Or A Heartache Tonight)** *Mickey Gilley*
17.	5/2	1	**Rest Your Love On Me** *Conway Twitty*
18.	5/9	1	**Am I Losing You** *Ronnie Milsap*
19.	5/16	1	**I Loved 'Em Every One** *T.G. Sheppard*
20.	5/23	1	**Seven Year Ache** *Rosanne Cash*
21.	5/30	1	**Elvira** *The Oak Ridge Boys*
22.	6/6	1	**Friends** *Razzy Bailey*
23.	6/13	1	**What Are We Doin' In Love** *Dottie West (with Kenny Rogers)*
24.	6/20	1	**But You Know I Love You** *Dolly Parton*
25.	6/27	1	**Blessed Are The Believers** *Anne Murray*
26.	7/4	1	**I Was Country When Country Wasn't Cool** *Barbara Mandrell*
27.	7/11	1	**Fire & Smoke** *Earl Thomas Conley*
28.	7/18	2	**Feels So Right** *Alabama*
29.	8/1	1	**Dixie On My Mind** *Hank Williams, Jr.*
30.	8/8	1	**Too Many Lovers** *Crystal Gayle*
31.	8/15	2	**I Don't Need You** *Kenny Rogers*
32.	8/29	2	**(There's) No Gettin' Over Me** *Ronnie Milsap*
33.	9/12	1	**Older Women** *Ronnie McDowell*
34.	9/19	1	**You Don't Know Me** *Mickey Gilley*
35.	9/26	1	**Tight Fittin' Jeans** *Conway Twitty*
36.	10/3	1	**Midnight Hauler** *Razzy Bailey*
37.	10/10	1	**Party Time** *T.G. Sheppard*
38.	10/17	1	**Step By Step** *Eddie Rabbitt*
39.	10/24	2	**Never Been So Loved (In All My Life)** *Charley Pride*
40.	11/7	1	**Fancy Free** *The Oak Ridge Boys*
41.	11/14	1	**My Baby Thinks He's A Train** *Rosanne Cash*
42.	11/21	1	**All My Rowdy Friends (Have Settled Down)** *Hank Williams, Jr.*
43.	11/28	1	**My Favorite Memory** *Merle Haggard*
44.	12/5	1	**Bet Your Heart On Me** *Johnny Lee*
45.	12/12	1	**Still Doin' Time** *George Jones*
46.	12/19	1	**All Roads Lead To You** *Steve Wariner*
47.	12/26	2	**Love In The First Degree** *Alabama*

1982

	DATE	WKS	Title / Artist
1.	1/9	1	**Fourteen Carat Mind** *Gene Watson*
2.	1/16	1	**I Wouldn't Have Missed It For The World** *Ronnie Milsap*
3.	1/23	1	**Red Neckin' Love Makin' Night** *Conway Twitty*
4.	1/30	1	**The Sweetest Thing (I've Ever Known)** *Juice Newton*
5.	2/6	1	**Lonely Nights** *Mickey Gilley*

#1 HITS

1982 (cont'd)

6. 2/13 1 **Someone Could Lose A Heart Tonight** *Eddie Rabbitt*
7. 2/20 1 **Only One You** *T.G. Sheppard*
8. 2/27 1 **Lord, I Hope This Day Is Good** *Don Williams*
9. 3/6 1 **You're The Best Break This Old Heart Ever Had** *Ed Bruce*
10. 3/13 1 **Blue Moon With Heartache** *Rosanne Cash*
11. 3/20 1 **Mountain Of Love** *Charley Pride*
12. 3/27 1 **She Left Love All Over Me** *Razzy Bailey*
13. 4/3 1 **Bobbie Sue** *The Oak Ridge Boys*
14. 4/10 1 **Big City** *Merle Haggard*
15. 4/17 1 **The Clown** *Conway Twitty*
16. 4/24 1 **Crying My Heart Out Over You** *Ricky Skaggs*
17. 5/1 1 **Mountain Music** *Alabama*
18. 5/8 2 **Always On My Mind** *Willie Nelson*
19. 5/22 2 **Just To Satisfy You** *Waylon Jennings & Willie Nelson*
20. 6/5 1 **Finally** *T.G. Sheppard*
21. 6/12 1 **For All The Wrong Reasons** *The Bellamy Brothers*
22. 6/19 2 **Slow Hand** *Conway Twitty*
23. 7/3 1 **Any Day Now** *Ronnie Milsap*
24. 7/10 1 **Don't Worry 'Bout Me Baby** *Janie Fricke*
25. 7/17 1 **'Till You're Gone** *Barbara Mandrell*
26. 7/24 1 **Take Me Down** *Alabama*
27. 7/31 1 **I Don't Care** *Ricky Skaggs*
28. 8/7 1 **Honky Tonkin'** *Hank Williams, Jr.*
29. 8/14 1 **I'm Gonna Hire A Wino To Decorate Our Home** *David Frizzell*
30. 8/21 1 **Nobody** *Sylvia*
31. 8/28 1 **Fool Hearted Memory** *George Strait*
32. 9/4 1 **Love Will Turn You Around** *Kenny Rogers*
33. 9/11 2 **She Got The Goldmine (I Got The Shaft)** *Jerry Reed*
34. 9/25 1 **What's Forever For** *Michael Murphey*
35. 10/2 1 **Put Your Dreams Away** *Mickey Gilley*
36. 10/9 1 **Yesterday's Wine** *Merle Haggard & George Jones*
37. 10/16 1 **I Will Always Love You** *Dolly Parton*
38. 10/23 1 **He Got You** *Ronnie Milsap*
39. 10/30 1 **Close Enough To Perfect** *Alabama*
40. 11/6 1 **You're So Good When You're Bad** *Charley Pride*
41. 11/13 1 **Heartbroke** *Ricky Skaggs*
42. 11/20 1 **War Is Hell (On The Homefront Too)** *T.G. Sheppard*
43. 11/27 1 **It Ain't Easy Bein' Easy** *Janie Fricke*
44. 12/4 1 **You And I** *Eddie Rabbitt with Crystal Gayle*
45. 12/11 1 **Redneck Girl** *The Bellamy Brothers*
46. 12/18 1 **Somewhere Between Right And Wrong** *Earl Thomas Conley*
47. 12/25 2 **Wild And Blue** *John Anderson*

DATE WKS 1983

1. 1/8 1 **Can't Even Get The Blues** *Reba McEntire*
2. 1/15 1 **Going Where The Lonely Go** *Merle Haggard*
3. 1/22 1 **(Lost His Love) On Our Last Date** *Emmylou Harris*
4. 1/29 1 **Talk To Me** *Mickey Gilley*
5. 2/5 1 **Inside** *Ronnie Milsap*
6. 2/12 1 **'Til I Gain Control Again** *Crystal Gayle*
7. 2/19 1 **Faking Love** *T.G. Sheppard & Karen Brooks*
8. 2/26 1 **Why Baby Why** *Charley Pride*
9. 3/5 1 **If Hollywood Don't Need You** *Don Williams*
10. 3/12 1 **The Rose** *Conway Twitty*
11. 3/19 1 **I Wouldn't Change You If I Could** *Ricky Skaggs*
12. 3/26 1 **Swingin'** *John Anderson*
13. 4/2 1 **When I'm Away From You** *Bellamy Brothers*
14. 4/9 1 **We've Got Tonight** *Kenny Rogers & Sheena Easton*
15. 4/16 1 **Dixieland Delight** *Alabama*
16. 4/23 1 **American Made** *The Oak Ridge Boys*
17. 4/30 1 **You're The First Time I've Thought About Leaving** *Reba McEntire*
18. 5/7 1 **Jose Cuervo** *Shelly West*
19. 5/14 1 **Whatever Happened To Old Fashioned Love** *B.J. Thomas*
20. 5/21 1 **Common Man** *John Conlee*
21. 5/28 1 **You Take Me For Granted** *Merle Haggard*
22. 6/4 1 **Lucille (You Won't Do Your Daddy's Will)** *Waylon Jennings*
23. 6/11 1 **Our Love Is On The Faultline** *Crystal Gayle*
24. 6/18 1 **You Can't Run From Love** *Eddie Rabbitt*
25. 6/25 1 **Fool For Your Love** *Mickey Gilley*
26. 7/2 1 **Love Is On A Roll** *Don Williams*
27. 7/9 1 **Highway 40 Blues** *Ricky Skaggs*
28. 7/16 1 **The Closer You Get** *Alabama*
29. 7/23 1 **Pancho And Lefty** *Willie Nelson & Merle Haggard*
30. 7/30 1 **I Always Get Lucky With You** *George Jones*
31. 8/6 1 **Your Love's On The Line** *Earl Thomas Conley*
32. 8/13 1 **He's A Heartache (Looking For A Place To Happen)** *Janie Fricke*
33. 8/20 1 **Love Song** *The Oak Ridge Boys*
34. 8/27 1 **You're Gonna Ruin My Bad Reputation** *Ronnie McDowell*
35. 9/3 1 **A Fire I Can't Put Out** *George Strait*
36. 9/10 1 **I'm Only In It For The Love** *John Conlee*
37. 9/17 1 **Night Games** *Charley Pride*
38. 9/24 1 **Baby, What About You** *Crystal Gayle*
39. 10/1 1 **New Looks From An Old Lover** *B.J. Thomas*
40. 10/8 1 **Don't You Know How Much I Love You** *Ronnie Milsap*
41. 10/15 1 **Paradise Tonight** *Charly McClain & Mickey Gilley*
42. 10/22 1 **Lady Down On Love** *Alabama*
43. 10/29 2 **Islands In The Stream** *Kenny Rogers with Dolly Parton*

#1 HITS

1983 (cont'd)

#	DATE	WKS	Title / Artist
44.	11/12	1	**Somebody's Gonna Love You** *Lee Greenwood*
45.	11/19	1	**One Of A Kind Pair Of Fools** *Barbara Mandrell*
46.	11/26	1	**Holding Her And Loving You** *Earl Thomas Conley*
47.	12/3	1	**A Little Good News** *Anne Murray*
48.	12/10	1	**Tell Me A Lie** *Janie Fricke*
49.	12/17	1	**Black Sheep** *John Anderson*
50.	12/24	2	**Houston (Means I'm One Day Closer To You)** *Larry Gatlin & The Gatlin Brothers*

1984

#	DATE	WKS	Title / Artist
1.	1/7	1	**You Look So Good In Love** *George Strait*
2.	1/14	1	**Slow Burn** *T.G. Sheppard*
3.	1/21	1	**In My Eyes** *John Conlee*
4.	1/28	1	**The Sound Of Goodbye** *Crystal Gayle*
5.	2/4	1	**Show Her** *Ronnie Milsap*
6.	2/11	1	**That's The Way Love Goes** *Merle Haggard*
7.	2/18	1	**Don't Cheat In Our Hometown** *Ricky Skaggs*
8.	2/25	1	**Stay Young** *Don Williams*
9.	3/3	1	**Woke Up In Love** *Exile*
10.	3/10	1	**Going, Going, Gone** *Lee Greenwood*
11.	3/17	1	**Elizabeth** *The Statler Brothers*
12.	3/24	1	**Roll On (Eighteen Wheeler)** *Alabama*
13.	3/31	1	**Let's Stop Talkin' About It** *Janie Fricke*
14.	4/7	1	**Don't Make It Easy For Me** *Earl Thomas Conley*
15.	4/14	1	**Thank God For The Radio** *The Kendalls*
16.	4/21	1	**The Yellow Rose** *Johnny Lee with Lane Brody*
17.	4/28	1	**Right Or Wrong** *George Strait*
18.	5/5	1	**I Guess It Never Hurts To Hurt Sometimes** *The Oak Ridge Boys*
19.	5/12	2	**To All The Girls I've Loved Before** *Julio Iglesias & Willie Nelson*
20.	5/26	1	**As Long As I'm Rockin' With You** *John Conlee*
21.	6/2	1	**Honey (Open That Door)** *Ricky Skaggs*
22.	6/9	1	**Someday When Things Are Good** *Merle Haggard*
23.	6/16	1	**I Got Mexico** *Eddy Raven*
24.	6/23	1	**When We Make Love** *Alabama*
25.	6/30	1	**I Can Tell By The Way You Dance (You're Gonna Love Me Tonight)** *Vern Gosdin*
26.	7/7	1	**Somebody's Needin' Somebody** *Conway Twitty*
27.	7/14	1	**I Don't Want To Be A Memory** *Exile*
28.	7/21	1	**Just Another Woman In Love** *Anne Murray*
29.	7/28	1	**Angel In Disguise** *Earl Thomas Conley*
30.	8/4	1	**Mama He's Crazy** *The Judds*
31.	8/11	1	**That's The Thing About Love** *Don Williams*
32.	8/18	1	**Still Losing You** *Ronnie Milsap*
33.	8/25	1	**Long Hard Road (The Sharecropper's Dream)** *Nitty Gritty Dirt Band*
34.	9/1	1	**Let's Fall To Pieces Together** *George Strait*
35.	9/8	1	**Tennessee Homesick Blues** *Dolly Parton*
36.	9/15	1	**You're Gettin' To Me Again** *Jim Glaser*

1984 (cont'd)

#	DATE	WKS	Title / Artist
37.	9/22	1	**Let's Chase Each Other Around The Room** *Merle Haggard*
38.	9/29	1	**Turning Away** *Crystal Gayle*
39.	10/6	1	**Everyday** *The Oak Ridge Boys*
40.	10/13	1	**Uncle Pen** *Ricky Skaggs*
41.	10/20	1	**I Don't Know A Thing About Love (The Moon Song)** *Conway Twitty*
42.	10/27	1	**If You're Gonna Play In Texas (You Gotta Have A Fiddle In The Band)** *Alabama*
43.	11/3	1	**City Of New Orleans** *Willie Nelson*
44.	11/10	1	**I've Been Around Enough To Know** *John Schneider*
45.	11/17	1	**Give Me One More Chance** *Exile*
46.	11/24	1	**You Could've Heard A Heart Break** *Johnny Lee*
47.	12/1	1	**Your Heart's Not In It** *Janie Fricke*
48.	12/8	1	**Chance Of Lovin' You** *Earl Thomas Conley*
49.	12/15	1	**Nobody Loves Me Like You Do** *Anne Murray (with Dave Loggins)*
50.	12/22	2	**Why Not Me** *The Judds*

1985

#	DATE	WKS	Title / Artist
1.	1/5	1	**Does Fort Worth Ever Cross Your Mind** *George Strait*
2.	1/12	1	**The Best Year Of My Life** *Eddie Rabbitt*
3.	1/19	1	**How Blue** *Reba McEntire*
4.	1/26	1	**(There's A) Fire In The Night** *Alabama*
5.	2/2	1	**A Place To Fall Apart** *Merle Haggard (with Janie Fricke)*
6.	2/9	1	**Ain't She Somethin' Else** *Conway Twitty*
7.	2/16	1	**Make My Life With You** *Oak Ridge Boys*
8.	2/23	1	**Baby's Got Her Blue Jeans On** *Mel McDaniel*
9.	3/2	1	**Baby Bye Bye** *Gary Morris*
10.	3/9	1	**My Only Love** *The Statler Brothers*
11.	3/16	1	**Crazy For Your Love** *Exile*
12.	3/23	1	**Seven Spanish Angels** *Ray Charles with Willie Nelson*
13.	3/30	1	**Crazy** *Kenny Rogers*
14.	4/6	1	**Country Girls** *John Schneider*
15.	4/13	1	**Honor Bound** *Earl Thomas Conley*
16.	4/20	1	**I Need More Of You** *Bellamy Brothers*
17.	4/27	1	**Girls Night Out** *The Judds*
18.	5/4	1	**There's No Way** *Alabama*
19.	5/11	1	**Somebody Should Leave** *Reba McEntire*
20.	5/18	1	**Step That Step** *Sawyer Brown*
21.	5/25	1	**Radio Heart** *Charly McClain*
22.	6/1	1	**Don't Call Him A Cowboy** *Conway Twitty*
23.	6/8	1	**Natural High** *Merle Haggard*
24.	6/15	1	**Country Boy** *Ricky Skaggs*
25.	6/22	1	**Little Things** *The Oak Ridge Boys*
26.	6/29	1	**She Keeps The Home Fires Burning** *Ronnie Milsap*
27.	7/6	1	**She's A Miracle** *Exile*
28.	7/13	1	**Forgiving You Was Easy** *Willie Nelson*
29.	7/20	1	**Dixie Road** *Lee Greenwood*

#1 HITS

1985 (cont'd)

30. 7/27 1 **Love Don't Care (Whose Heart It Breaks)** *Earl Thomas Conley*
31. 8/3 1 **Forty Hour Week (For A Livin')** *Alabama*
32. 8/10 1 **I'm For Love** *Hank Williams, Jr.*
33. 8/17 1 **Highwayman** *Waylon Jennings/Willie Nelson/ Johnny Cash/Kris Kristofferson*
34. 8/24 1 **Real Love** *Dolly Parton (with Kenny Rogers)*
35. 8/31 1 **Love Is Alive** *The Judds*
36. 9/7 1 **I Don't Know Why You Don't Want Me** *Rosanne Cash*
37. 9/14 1 **Modern Day Romance** *Nitty Gritty Dirt Band*
38. 9/21 1 **I Fell In Love Again Last Night** *The Forester Sisters*
39. 9/28 2 **Lost In The Fifties Tonight (In The Still Of The Night)** *Ronnie Milsap*
40. 10/12 1 **Meet Me In Montana** *Marie Osmond with Dan Seals*
41. 10/19 1 **You Make Me Want To Make You Mine** *Juice Newton*
42. 10/26 1 **Touch A Hand, Make A Friend** *The Oak Ridge Boys*
43. 11/2 1 **Some Fools Never Learn** *Steve Wariner*
44. 11/9 1 **Can't Keep A Good Man Down** *Alabama*
45. 11/16 1 **Hang On To Your Heart** *Exile*
46. 11/23 1 **I'll Never Stop Loving You** *Gary Morris*
47. 11/30 1 **Too Much On My Heart** *The Statler Brothers*
48. 12/7 1 **I Don't Mind The Thorns (If You're The Rose)** *Lee Greenwood*
49. 12/14 1 **Nobody Falls Like A Fool** *Earl Thomas Conley*
50. 12/21 1 **The Chair** *George Strait*
51. 12/28 2 **Have Mercy** *The Judds*

DATE WKS 1986

1. 1/11 1 **Morning Desire** *Kenny Rogers*
2. 1/18 1 **Bop** *Dan Seals*
3. 1/25 1 **Never Be You** *Rosanne Cash*
4. 2/1 1 **Just In Case** *The Forester Sisters*
5. 2/8 1 **Hurt** *Juice Newton*
6. 2/15 1 **Makin' Up For Lost Time (The Dallas Lovers' Song)** *Crystal Gayle & Gary Morris*
7. 2/22 1 **There's No Stopping Your Heart** *Marie Osmond*
8. 3/1 1 **You Can Dream Of Me** *Steve Wariner*
9. 3/8 1 **Think About Love** *Dolly Parton*
10. 3/15 1 **I Could Get Used To You** *Exile*
11. 3/22 1 **What's A Memory Like You (Doing In A Love Like This)** *John Schneider*
12. 3/29 1 **Don't Underestimate My Love For You** *Lee Greenwood*
13. 4/5 1 **100% Chance Of Rain** *Gary Morris*
14. 4/12 1 **She And I** *Alabama*
15. 4/19 1 **Cajun Moon** *Ricky Skaggs*
16. 4/26 1 **Now And Forever (You And Me)** *Anne Murray*
17. 5/3 1 **Once In A Blue Moon** *Earl Thomas Conley*

1986 (cont'd)

18. 5/10 1 **Grandpa (Tell Me 'Bout The Good Old Days)** *The Judds*
19. 5/17 1 **Ain't Misbehavin'** *Hank Williams, Jr.*
20. 5/24 1 **Tomb Of The Unknown Love** *Kenny Rogers*
21. 5/31 1 **Whoever's In New England** *Reba McEntire*
22. 6/7 1 **Happy, Happy Birthday Baby** *Ronnie Milsap*
23. 6/14 1 **Life's Highway** *Steve Wariner*
24. 6/21 1 **Mama's Never Seen Those Eyes** *The Forester Sisters*
25. 6/28 1 **Living In The Promiseland** *Willie Nelson*
26. 7/5 1 **Everything That Glitters (Is Not Gold)** *Dan Seals*
27. 7/12 1 **Hearts Aren't Made To Break (They're Made To Love)** *Lee Greenwood*
28. 7/19 1 **Until I Met You** *Judy Rodman*
29. 7/26 1 **On The Other Hand** *Randy Travis*
30. 8/2 1 **Nobody In His Right Mind Would've Left Her** *George Strait*
31. 8/9 1 **Rockin' With The Rhythm Of The Rain** *The Judds*
32. 8/16 1 **You're The Last Thing I Needed Tonight** *John Schneider*
33. 8/23 1 **Strong Heart** *T.G. Sheppard*
34. 8/30 1 **Heartbeat In The Darkness** *Don Williams*
35. 9/6 1 **Desperado Love** *Conway Twitty*
36. 9/13 1 **Little Rock** *Reba McEntire*
37. 9/20 1 **Got My Heart Set On You** *John Conlee*
38. 9/27 1 **In Love** *Ronnie Milsap*
39. 10/4 1 **Always Have Always Will** *Janie Fricke*
40. 10/11 1 **Both To Each Other (Friends & Lovers)** *Eddie Rabbitt & Juice Newton*
41. 10/18 1 **Just Another Love** *Tanya Tucker*
42. 10/25 1 **Cry** *Crystal Gayle*
43. 11/1 1 **It'll Be Me** *Exile*
44. 11/8 1 **Diggin' Up Bones** *Randy Travis*
45. 11/15 1 **That Rock Won't Roll** *Restless Heart*
46. 11/22 1 **You're Still New To Me** *Marie Osmond with Paul Davis*
47. 11/29 1 **Touch Me When We're Dancing** *Alabama*
48. 12/6 1 **It Ain't Cool To Be Crazy About You** *George Strait*
49. 12/13 1 **Hell And High Water** *T. Graham Brown*
50. 12/20 1 **Too Much Is Not Enough** *Bellamy Brothers*
51. 12/27 2 **Mind Your Own Business** *Hank Williams, Jr.*

DATE WKS 1987

1. 1/10 1 **Give Me Wings** *Michael Johnson*
2. 1/17 1 **What Am I Gonna Do About You** *Reba McEntire*
3. 1/24 1 **Cry Myself To Sleep** *The Judds*
4. 1/31 1 **You Still Move Me** *Dan Seals*
5. 2/7 1 **Leave Me Lonely** *Gary Morris*
6. 2/14 1 **How Do I Turn You On** *Ronnie Milsap*
7. 2/21 1 **Straight To The Heart** *Crystal Gayle*

#1 HITS

1987 (cont'd)

	DATE	WKS	
8.	2/28	1	**I Can't Win For Losin' You** *Earl Thomas Conley*
9.	3/7	1	**Mornin' Ride** *Lee Greenwood*
10.	3/14	1	**Baby's Got A New Baby** *S-K-O*
11.	3/21	1	**I'll Still Be Loving You** *Restless Heart*
12.	3/28	1	**Small Town Girl** *Steve Wariner*
13.	4/4	1	**Ocean Front Property** *George Strait*
14.	4/11	1	**"You've Got" The Touch** *Alabama*
15.	4/18	1	**Kids Of The Baby Boom** *Bellamy Brothers*
16.	4/25	1	**Rose In Paradise** *Waylon Jennings*
17.	5/2	1	**Don't Go To Strangers** *T. Graham Brown*
18.	5/9	1	**The Moon Is Still Over Her Shoulder** *Michael Johnson*
19.	5/16	1	**To Know Him Is To Love Him** *Dolly Parton, Linda Ronstadt, Emmylou Harris*
20.	5/23	1	**Can't Stop My Heart From Loving You** *The O'Kanes*
21.	5/30	1	**It Takes A Little Rain (To Make Love Grow)** *The Oak Ridge Boys*
22.	6/6	1	**I Will Be There** *Dan Seals*
23.	6/13	3	**Forever And Ever, Amen** *Randy Travis*
24.	7/4	1	**That Was A Close One** *Earl Thomas Conley*
25.	7/11	1	**All My Ex's Live In Texas** *George Strait*
26.	7/18	1	**I Know Where I'm Going** *The Judds*
27.	7/25	1	**The Weekend** *Steve Wariner*
28.	8/1	1	**Snap Your Fingers** *Ronnie Milsap*
29.	8/8	1	**One Promise Too Late** *Reba McEntire*
30.	8/15	1	**A Long Line Of Love** *Michael Martin Murphey*
31.	8/22	1	**Why Does It Have To Be (Wrong Or Right)** *Restless Heart*
32.	8/29	1	**Born To Boogie** *Hank Williams, Jr.*
33.	9/5	1	**She's Too Good To Be True** *Exile*
34.	9/12	1	**Make No Mistake, She's Mine** *Ronnie Milsap & Kenny Rogers*
35.	9/19	1	**This Crazy Love** *The Oak Ridge Boys*
36.	9/26	1	**Three Time Loser** *Dan Seals*
37.	10/3	1	**You Again** *The Forester Sisters*
38.	10/10	1	**The Way We Make A Broken Heart** *Rosanne Cash*
39.	10/17	1	**Fishin' In The Dark** *Nitty Gritty Dirt Band*
40.	10/24	1	**Shine, Shine, Shine** *Eddy Raven*
41.	10/31	1	**Right From The Start** *Earl Thomas Conley*
42.	11/7	1	**Am I Blue** *George Strait*
43.	11/14	1	**Maybe Your Baby's Got The Blues** *The Judds*
44.	11/21	1	**I Won't Need You Anymore (Always And Forever)** *Randy Travis*
45.	11/28	1	**Lynda** *Steve Wariner*
46.	12/5	1	**Somebody Lied** *Ricky Van Shelton*
47.	12/12	1	**The Last One To Know** *Reba McEntire*
48.	12/19	1	**Do Ya'** *K.T. Oslin*
49.	12/26	2	**Somewhere Tonight** *Highway 101*

1988

	DATE	WKS	
1.	1/9	1	**I Can't Get Close Enough** *Exile*
2.	1/16	1	**One Friend** *Dan Seals*
3.	1/23	1	**Where Do The Nights Go** *Ronnie Milsap*
4.	1/30	1	**Goin' Gone** *Kathy Mattea*
5.	2/6	1	**Wheels** *Restless Heart*
6.	2/13	1	**Tennessee Flat Top Box** *Rosanne Cash*
7.	2/20	1	**Twinkle, Twinkle Lucky Star** *Merle Haggard*
8.	2/27	1	**I Won't Take Less Than Your Love** *Tanya Tucker*
9.	3/5	1	**Face To Face** *Alabama*
10.	3/12	1	**Too Gone Too Long** *Randy Travis*
11.	3/19	1	**Life Turned Her That Way** *Ricky Van Shelton*
12.	3/26	1	**Turn It Loose** *The Judds*
13.	4/2	1	**Love Will Find Its Way To You** *Reba McEntire*
14.	4/9	1	**Famous Last Words Of A Fool** *George Strait*
15.	4/16	1	**I Wanna Dance With You** *Eddie Rabbitt*
16.	4/23	1	**I'll Always Come Back** *K.T. Oslin*
17.	4/30	1	**It's Such A Small World** *Rodney Crowell & Rosanne Cash*
18.	5/7	1	**Cry, Cry, Cry** *Highway 101*
19.	5/14	1	**I'm Gonna Get You** *Eddy Raven*
20.	5/21	2	**Eighteen Wheels And A Dozen Roses** *Kathy Mattea*
21.	6/4	1	**What She Is (Is A Woman In Love)** *Earl Thomas Conley*
22.	6/11	2	**I Told You So** *Randy Travis*
23.	6/25	1	**He's Back And I'm Blue** *The Desert Rose Band*
24.	7/2	1	**If It Don't Come Easy** *Tanya Tucker*
25.	7/9	1	**Fallin' Again** *Alabama*
26.	7/16	1	**If You Change Your Mind** *Rosanne Cash*
27.	7/23	1	**Set 'Em Up Joe** *Vern Gosdin*
28.	7/30	1	**Don't We All Have The Right** *Ricky Van Shelton*
29.	8/6	1	**Baby Blue** *George Strait*
30.	8/13	1	**Don't Close Your Eyes** *Keith Whitley*
31.	8/20	1	**Bluest Eyes In Texas** *Restless Heart*
32.	8/27	1	**The Wanderer** *Eddie Rabbitt*
33.	9/3	1	**I Couldn't Leave You If I Tried** *Rodney Crowell*
34.	9/10	1	**(Do You Love Me) Just Say Yes** *Highway 101*
35.	9/17	1	**Joe Knows How To Live** *Eddy Raven*
36.	9/24	1	**Addicted** *Dan Seals*
37.	10/1	1	**We Believe In Happy Endings** *Earl Thomas Conley with Emmylou Harris*
38.	10/8	1	**Honky Tonk Moon** *Randy Travis*
39.	10/15	1	**Streets Of Bakersfield** *Dwight Yoakam & Buck Owens*
40.	10/22	1	**Strong Enough To Bend** *Tanya Tucker*
41.	10/29	1	**Gonna Take A Lot Of River** *The Oak Ridge Boys*
42.	11/5	1	**Darlene** *T. Graham Brown*
43.	11/12	1	**Runaway Train** *Rosanne Cash*
44.	11/19	2	**I'll Leave This World Loving You** *Ricky Van Shelton*

#1 HITS

1988 (cont'd)

45. 12/3 1 **I Know How He Feels** *Reba McEntire*
46. 12/10 1 **If You Ain't Lovin' (You Ain't Livin')** *George Strait*
47. 12/17 1 **A Tender Lie** *Restless Heart*
48. 12/24 2 **When You Say Nothing At All** *Keith Whitley*

DATE WKS 1989

1. 1/7 1 **Hold Me** *K.T. Oslin*
2. 1/14 1 **Change Of Heart** *The Judds*
3. 1/21 1 **She's Crazy For Leavin'** *Rodney Crowell*
4. 1/28 1 **Deeper Than The Holler** *Randy Travis*
5. 2/4 1 **What I'd Say** *Earl Thomas Conley*
6. 2/11 1 **Song Of The South** *Alabama*
7. 2/18 1 **Big Wheels In The Moonlight** *Dan Seals*
8. 2/25 1 **I Sang Dixie** *Dwight Yoakam*
9. 3/4 1 **I Still Believe In You** *The Desert Rose Band*
10. 3/11 1 **Don't You Ever Get Tired (Of Hurting Me)** *Ronnie Milsap*
11. 3/18 1 **From A Jack To A King** *Ricky Van Shelton*
12. 3/25 1 **New Fool At An Old Game** *Reba McEntire*
13. 4/1 1 **Baby's Gotten Good At Goodbye** *George Strait*
14. 4/8 2 **I'm No Stranger To The Rain** *Keith Whitley*
15. 4/22 2 **The Church On Cumberland Road** *Shenandoah*
16. 5/6 1 **Young Love** *The Judds*
17. 5/13 1 **Is It Still Over?** *Randy Travis*
18. 5/20 1 **If I Had You** *Alabama*
19. 5/27 1 **After All This Time** *Rodney Crowell*
20. 6/3 1 **Where Did I Go Wrong** *Steve Wariner*
21. 6/10 1 **A Better Man** *Clint Black*
22. 6/17 1 **Love Out Loud** *Earl Thomas Conley*
23. 6/24 1 **I Don't Want To Spoil The Party** *Rosanne Cash*
24. 7/1 1 **Come From The Heart** *Kathy Mattea*
25. 7/8 1 **Lovin' Only Me** *Ricky Skaggs*
26. 7/15 1 **In A Letter To You** *Eddy Raven*
27. 7/22 1 **What's Going On In Your World** *George Strait*
28. 7/29 1 **Cathy's Clown** *Reba McEntire*
29. 8/5 1 **Why'd You Come In Here Lookin' Like That** *Dolly Parton*
30. 8/12 1 **Timber, I'm Falling In Love** *Patty Loveless*
31. 8/19 1 **Sunday In The South** *Shenandoah*
32. 8/26 1 **Are You Ever Gonna Love Me** *Holly Dunn*
33. 9/2 1 **I'm Still Crazy** *Vern Gosdin*
34. 9/9 1 **I Wonder Do You Think Of Me** *Keith Whitley*
35. 9/16 1 **Nothing I Can Do About It Now** *Willie Nelson*
36. 9/23 1 **Above And Beyond** *Rodney Crowell*
37. 9/30 1 **Let Me Tell You About Love** *The Judds*
38. 10/7 1 **I Got Dreams** *Steve Wariner*
39. 10/14 1 **Killin' Time** *Clint Black*
40. 10/21 1 **Living Proof** *Ricky Van Shelton*
41. 10/28 1 **High Cotton** *Alabama*
42. 11/4 1 **Ace In The Hole** *George Strait*

1989 (cont'd)

43. 11/11 1 **Burnin' Old Memories** *Kathy Mattea*
44. 11/18 1 **Bayou Boys** *Eddy Raven*
45. 11/25 1 **Yellow Roses** *Dolly Parton*
46. 12/2 1 **It's Just A Matter Of Time** *Randy Travis*
47. 12/9 1 **If Tomorrow Never Comes** *Garth Brooks*
48. 12/16 1 **Two Dozen Roses** *Shenandoah*
49. 12/23 2 **A Woman In Love** *Ronnie Milsap*

DATE WKS 1990

1. 1/6 1 **Who's Lonely Now** *Highway 101*
2. 1/13 1 **It Ain't Nothin'** *Keith Whitley*

1/20/90: Billboard begins compiling Country chart through their BDS system (a computerized airplay monitoring system).

3. 1/20 3 **Nobody's Home** *Clint Black*
4. 2/10 1 **Southern Star** *Alabama*

2/17/90: Chart renamed "Hot Country Singles & Tracks"

5. 2/17 2 **On Second Thought** *Eddie Rabbitt*
6. 3/3 1 **No Matter How High** *Oak Ridge Boys*
7. 3/10 1 **Chains** *Patty Loveless*
8. 3/17 4 **Hard Rock Bottom Of Your Heart** *Randy Travis*
9. 4/14 1 **Five Minutes** *Lorrie Morgan*
10. 4/21 3 **Love On Arrival** *Dan Seals*
11. 5/12 1 **Help Me Hold On** *Travis Tritt*
12. 5/19 2 **Walkin' Away** *Clint Black*
13. 6/2 1 **I've Cried My Last Tear For You** *Ricky Van Shelton*
14. 6/9 5 **Love Without End, Amen** *George Strait*
15. 7/14 3 **The Dance** *Garth Brooks*
16. 8/4 2 **Good Times** *Dan Seals*
17. 8/18 3 **Next To You, Next To Me** *Shenandoah*
18. 9/8 4 **Jukebox In My Mind** *Alabama*
19. 10/6 4 **Friends In Low Places** *Garth Brooks*
20. 11/3 1 **You Lie** *Reba McEntire*
21. 11/10 1 **Home** *Joe Diffie*
22. 11/17 1 **You Really Had Me Going** *Holly Dunn*
23. 11/24 2 **Come Next Monday** *K.T. Oslin*
24. 12/8 5 **I've Come To Expect It From You** *George Strait*

DATE WKS 1991

1. 1/12 2 **Unanswered Prayers** *Garth Brooks*
2. 1/26 1 **Forever's As Far As I'll Go** *Alabama*
3. 2/2 1 **Daddy's Come Around** *Paul Overstreet*
4. 2/9 2 **Brother Jukebox** *Mark Chesnutt*
5. 2/23 2 **Walk On Faith** *Mike Reid*
6. 3/9 2 **I'd Love You All Over Again** *Alan Jackson*
7. 3/23 2 **Loving Blind** *Clint Black*
8. 4/6 1 **Two Of A Kind, Workin' On A Full House** *Garth Brooks*
9. 4/13 3 **Down Home** *Alabama*
10. 5/4 1 **Rockin' Years** *Dolly Parton with Ricky Van Shelton*
11. 5/11 2 **If I Know Me** *George Strait*

1991 (cont'd)

12.	5/25	1	**In A Different Light** *Doug Stone*
13.	6/1	2	**Meet In The Middle** *Diamond Rio*
14.	6/15	1	**If The Devil Danced (In Empty Pockets)** *Joe Diffie*
15.	6/22	2	**The Thunder Rolls** *Garth Brooks*
16.	7/6	3	**Don't Rock The Jukebox** *Alan Jackson*
17.	7/27	1	**I Am A Simple Man** *Ricky Van Shelton*
18.	8/3	2	**She's In Love With The Boy** *Trisha Yearwood*
19.	8/17	3	**You Know Me Better Than That** *George Strait*
20.	9/7	2	**Brand New Man** *Brooks & Dunn*
21.	9/21	1	**Leap Of Faith** *Lionel Cartwright*
22.	9/28	2	**Where Are You Now** *Clint Black*
23.	10/12	2	**Keep It Between The Lines** *Ricky Van Shelton*
24.	10/26	2	**Anymore** *Travis Tritt*
25.	11/9	1	**Someday** *Alan Jackson*
26.	11/16	2	**Shameless** *Garth Brooks*
27.	11/30	1	**Forever Together** *Randy Travis*
28.	12/7	2	**For My Broken Heart** *Reba McEntire*
29.	12/21	2	**My Next Broken Heart** *Brooks & Dunn*

1992

	DATE	WKS	
1.	1/4	3	**Love, Me** *Collin Raye*
2.	1/25	1	**Sticks And Stones** *Tracy Lawrence*
3.	2/1	2	**A Jukebox With A Country Song** *Doug Stone*
4.	2/15	4	**What She's Doing Now** *Garth Brooks*
5.	3/14	1	**Straight Tequila Night** *John Anderson*
6.	3/21	1	**Dallas** *Alan Jackson*
7.	3/28	2	**Is There Life Out There** *Reba McEntire*
8.	4/11	1	**She Is His Only Need** *Wynonna*
9.	4/18	3	**There Ain't Nothin' Wrong With The Radio** *Aaron Tippin*
10.	5/9	2	**Neon Moon** *Brooks & Dunn*
11.	5/23	1	**Some Girls Do** *Sawyer Brown*
12.	5/30	5	**Achy Breaky Heart** *Billy Ray Cyrus*
13.	7/4	3	**I Saw The Light** *Wynonna*
14.	7/25	1	**The River** *Garth Brooks*
15.	8/1	4	**Boot Scootin' Boogie** *Brooks & Dunn*
16.	8/29	1	**I'll Think Of Something** *Mark Chesnutt*
17.	9/5	2	**I Still Believe In You** *Vince Gill*
18.	9/19	2	**Love's Got A Hold On You** *Alan Jackson*
19.	10/3	2	**In This Life** *Collin Raye*
20.	10/17	1	**If I Didn't Have You** *Randy Travis*
21.	10/24	4	**No One Else On Earth** *Wynonna*
22.	11/21	2	**I'm In A Hurry (And Don't Know Why)** *Alabama*
23.	12/5	2	**I Cross My Heart** *George Strait*
24.	12/19	1	**She's Got The Rhythm (And I Got The Blues)** *Alan Jackson*
25.	12/26	3	**Don't Let Our Love Start Slippin' Away** *Vince Gill*

1993

	DATE	WKS	
1.	1/16	1	**Somewhere Other Than The Night** *Garth Brooks*
2.	1/23	2	**Look Heart, No Hands** *Randy Travis*
3.	2/6	1	**Too Busy Being In Love** *Doug Stone*
4.	2/13	2	**Can I Trust You With My Heart** *Travis Tritt*
5.	2/27	3	**What Part Of No** *Lorrie Morgan*
6.	3/20	1	**Heartland** *George Strait*
7.	3/27	2	**When My Ship Comes In** *Clint Black*
8.	4/10	2	**The Heart Won't Lie** *Reba McEntire & Vince Gill*
9.	4/24	1	**She Don't Know She's Beautiful** *Sammy Kershaw*
10.	5/1	2	**Alibis** *Tracy Lawrence*
11.	5/15	3	**I Love The Way You Love Me** *John Michael Montgomery*
12.	6/5	2	**Should've Been A Cowboy** *Toby Keith*
13.	6/19	2	**Blame It On Your Heart** *Patty Loveless*
14.	7/3	1	**That Summer** *Garth Brooks*
15.	7/10	1	**Money In The Bank** *John Anderson*
16.	7/17	4	**Chattahoochee** *Alan Jackson*
17.	8/14	1	**It Sure Is Monday** *Mark Chesnutt*
18.	8/21	1	**Why Didn't I Think Of That** *Doug Stone*
19.	8/28	1	**Can't Break It To My Heart** *Tracy Lawrence*
20.	9/4	2	**Thank God For You** *Sawyer Brown*
21.	9/18	2↕	**Ain't Going Down (Til The Sun Comes Up)** *Garth Brooks*
22.	9/25	1	**Holdin' Heaven** *Tracy Byrd*
23.	10/9	1	**One More Last Chance** *Vince Gill*
24.	10/16	1	**What's It To You** *Clay Walker*
25.	10/23	2	**Easy Come, Easy Go** *George Strait*
26.	11/6	1	**Does He Love You** *Reba McEntire*
27.	11/13	1	**She Used To Be Mine** *Brooks & Dunn*
28.	11/20	1	**Almost Goodbye** *Mark Chesnutt*
29.	11/27	1	**Reckless** *Alabama*
30.	12/4	1	**American Honky-Tonk Bar Association** *Garth Brooks*
31.	12/11	1	**My Second Home** *Tracy Lawrence*
32.	12/18	2	**I Don't Call Him Daddy** *Doug Supernaw*

1994

	DATE	WKS	
1.	1/1	4	**Wild One** *Faith Hill*
2.	1/29	1	**Live Until I Die** *Clay Walker*
3.	2/5	4	**I Swear** *John Michael Montgomery*
4.	3/5	1	**I Just Wanted You To Know** *Mark Chesnutt*
5.	3/12	1	**Tryin' To Get Over You** *Vince Gill*
6.	3/19	2	**No Doubt About It** *Neal McCoy*
7.	4/2	2	**My Love** *Little Texas*
8.	4/16	2	**If The Good Die Young** *Tracy Lawrence*
9.	4/30	1	**Piece Of My Heart** *Faith Hill*
10.	5/7	1	**A Good Run Of Bad Luck** *Clint Black*
11.	5/14	1	**If Bubba Can Dance (I Can Too)** *Shenandoah*
12.	5/21	1	**Your Love Amazes Me** *John Berry*
13.	5/28	2	**Don't Take The Girl** *Tim McGraw*
14.	6/11	1	**That Ain't No Way To Go** *Brooks & Dunn*
15.	6/18	4	**Wink** *Neal McCoy*
16.	7/16	1	**Foolish Pride** *Travis Tritt*

#1 HITS

1994 (cont'd)

	DATE	WKS	
17.	7/23	3	**Summertime Blues** *Alan Jackson*
18.	8/13	2	**Be My Baby Tonight** *John Michael Montgomery*
19.	8/27	1	**Dreaming With My Eyes Open** *Clay Walker*
20.	9/3	1	**Whisper My Name** *Randy Travis*
21.	9/10	2	**XXX's And OOO's (An American Girl)** *Trisha Yearwood*
22.	9/24	2	**Third Rock From The Sun** *Joe Diffie*
23.	10/8	1	**Who's That Man** *Toby Keith*
24.	10/15	2	**She's Not The Cheatin' Kind** *Brooks & Dunn*
25.	10/29	3	**Livin' On Love** *Alan Jackson*
26.	11/19	1	**Shut Up And Kiss Me** *Mary Chapin Carpenter*
27.	11/26	1	**If I Could Make A Living** *Clay Walker*
28.	12/3	1	**The Big One** *George Strait*
29.	12/10	1	**If You've Got Love** *John Michael Montgomery*
30.	12/17	4	**Pickup Man** *Joe Diffie*

1995

	DATE	WKS	
1.	1/14	2	**Not A Moment Too Soon** *Tim McGraw*
2.	1/28	1	**Gone Country** *Alan Jackson*
3.	2/4	2	**Mi Vida Loca (My Crazy Life)** *Pam Tillis*
4.	2/18	1	**My Kind Of Girl** *Collin Raye*
5.	2/25	2	**Old Enough To Know Better** *Wade Hayes*
6.	3/11	1	**You Can't Make A Heart Love Somebody** *George Strait*
7.	3/18	2	**This Woman And This Man** *Clay Walker*
8.	4/1	2	**Thinkin' About You** *Trisha Yearwood*
9.	4/15	1	**The Heart Is A Lonely Hunter** *Reba McEntire*
10.	4/22	3×	**I Can Love You Like That** *John Michael Montgomery*
11.	4/29	1	**Little Miss Honky Tonk** *Brooks & Dunn*
12.	5/20	1	**Gonna Get A Life** *Mark Chesnutt*
13.	5/27	1	**What Mattered Most** *Ty Herndon*
14.	6/3	3	**Summer's Comin'** *Clint Black*
15.	6/24	1	**Texas Tornado** *Tracy Lawrence*
16.	7/1	3	**Sold (The Grundy County Auction Incident)** *John Michael Montgomery*
17.	7/22	2	**Any Man Of Mine** *Shania Twain*
18.	8/5	1	**I Don't Even Know Your Name** *Alan Jackson*
19.	8/12	1	**I Didn't Know My Own Strength** *Lorrie Morgan*
20.	8/19	2	**You're Gonna Miss Me When I'm Gone** *Brooks & Dunn*
21.	9/2	1	**Not On Your Love** *Jeff Carson*
22.	9/9	1	**Someone Else's Star** *Bryan White*
23.	9/16	5	**I Like It, I Love It** *Tim McGraw*
24.	10/21	1	**She's Every Woman** *Garth Brooks*
25.	10/28	2	**Dust On The Bottle** *David Lee Murphy*
26.	11/11	4	**Check Yes Or No** *George Strait*
27.	12/9	2	**Tall, Tall Trees** *Alan Jackson*
28.	12/23	2	**That's As Close As I'll Get To Loving You** *Aaron Tippin*

1996

	DATE	WKS	
1.	1/6	1	**Rebecca Lynn** *Bryan White*
2.	1/13	3	**It Matters To Me** *Faith Hill*
3.	2/3	2	**(If You're Not In It For Love) I'm Outta Here!** *Shania Twain*
4.	2/17	2	**Bigger Than The Beatles** *Joe Diffie*
5.	3/2	1	**Wild Angels** *Martina McBride*
6.	3/9	1	**I'll Try** *Alan Jackson*
7.	3/16	1	**The Beaches Of Cheyenne** *Garth Brooks*
8.	3/23	2	**You Can Feel Bad** *Patty Loveless*
9.	4/6	1	**To Be Loved By You** *Wynonna*
10.	4/13	3	**No News** *Lonestar*
11.	5/4	2	**You Win My Love** *Shania Twain*
12.	5/18	3	**My Maria** *Brooks & Dunn*
13.	6/8	2	**Blue Clear Sky** *George Strait*
14.	6/22	3	**Time Marches On** *Tracy Lawrence*
15.	7/13	1	**No One Needs To Know** *Shania Twain*
16.	7/20	2	**Daddy's Money** *Ricochet*
17.	8/3	1	**Don't Get Me Started** *Rhett Akins*
18.	8/10	3	**Carried Away** *George Strait*
19.	8/31	2	**She Never Lets It Go To Her Heart** *Tim McGraw*
20.	9/14	1	**Guys Do It All The Time** *Mindy McCready*
21.	9/21	2	**So Much For Pretending** *Bryan White*
22.	10/5	1	**Living In A Moment** *Ty Herndon*
23.	10/12	2	**Believe Me Baby (I Lied)** *Trisha Yearwood*
24.	10/26	3	**Like The Rain** *Clint Black*
25.	11/16	1	**Lonely Too Long** *Patty Loveless*
26.	11/23	2	**Strawberry Wine** *Deana Carter*
27.	12/7	3	**Little Bitty** *Alan Jackson*
28.	12/28	2	**One Way Ticket (Because I Can)** *LeAnn Rimes*

1997

	DATE	WKS	
1.	1/11	4	**Nobody Knows** *Kevin Sharp*
2.	2/8	2	**It's A Little Too Late** *Mark Chesnutt*
3.	2/22	1	**A Man This Lonely** *Brooks & Dunn*
4.	3/1	1	**Running Out Of Reasons To Run** *Rick Trevino*
5.	3/8	1	**Me Too** *Toby Keith*
6.	3/15	2	**We Danced Anyway** *Deana Carter*
7.	3/29	1	**How Was I To Know** *Reba McEntire*
8.	4/5	1	**(This Ain't) No Thinkin' Thing** *Trace Adkins*
9.	4/12	2	**Rumor Has It** *Clay Walker*
10.	4/26	5	**One Night At A Time** *George Strait*
11.	5/31	1	**Sittin' On Go** *Bryan White*
12.	6/7	6	**It's Your Love** *Tim McGraw & Faith Hill*
13.	7/19	4	**Carrying Your Love With Me** *George Strait*
14.	8/16	2	**Come Cryin' To Me** *Lonestar*
15.	8/30	3	**She's Got It All** *Kenny Chesney*
16.	9/20	1	**There Goes** *Alan Jackson*
17.	9/27	3	**How Your Love Makes Me Feel** *Diamond Rio*
18.	10/18	1	**How Do I Get There** *Deana Carter*
19.	10/25	2	**Everywhere** *Tim McGraw*
20.	11/8	5	**Love Gets Me Every Time** *Shania Twain*
21.	12/13	1	**From Here To Eternity** *Michael Peterson*
22.	12/20	3	**Longneck Bottle** *Garth Brooks*

#1 HITS

1998

	DATE	WKS	Title	Artist
1.	1/10	1	**A Broken Wing**	*Martina McBride*
2.	1/17	6	**Just To See You Smile**	*Tim McGraw*
3.	2/28	1	**What If I Said**	*Anita Cochran with Steve Wariner*
4.	3/7	2	**Round About Way**	*George Strait*
5.	3/21	2	**Nothin' But The Taillights**	*Clint Black*
6.	4/4	2	**A Perfect Love**	*Trisha Yearwood*
7.	4/18	2	**Bye-Bye**	*Jo Dee Messina*
8.	5/2	1	**You're Still The One**	*Shania Twain*
9.	5/9	1	**Two Piña Coladas**	*Garth Brooks*
10.	5/16	3	**This Kiss**	*Faith Hill*
11.	6/6	3	**I Just Want To Dance With You**	*George Strait*
12.	6/27	2	**If You See Him/If You See Her**	*Reba/Brooks & Dunn*
13.	7/11	1	**The Shoes You're Wearing**	*Clint Black*
14.	7/18	2	**I Can Still Feel You**	*Collin Raye*
15.	8/1	1	**To Make You Feel My Love**	*Garth Brooks*
16.	8/8	2	**There's Your Trouble**	*Dixie Chicks*
17.	8/22	3	**I'm Alright**	*Jo Dee Messina*
18.	9/12	3	**How Long Gone**	*Brooks & Dunn*
19.	10/3	4	**Where The Green Grass Grows**	*Tim McGraw*
20.	10/31	1	**Honey, I'm Home**	*Shania Twain*
21.	11/7	4	**Wide Open Spaces**	*Dixie Chicks*
22.	12/5	1	**It Must Be Love**	*Ty Herndon*
23.	12/12	1	**Let Me Let Go**	*Faith Hill*
24.	12/19	1	**Husbands And Wives**	*Brooks & Dunn*
25.	12/26	3	**You're Easy On The Eyes**	*Terri Clark*

1999

	DATE	WKS	Title	Artist
1.	1/16	1	**Right On The Money**	*Alan Jackson*
2.	1/23	1	**Wrong Again**	*Martina McBride*
3.	1/30	3	**Stand Beside Me**	*Jo Dee Messina*
4.	2/20	2	**I Don't Want To Miss A Thing**	*Mark Chesnutt*
5.	3/6	1	**No Place That Far**	*Sara Evans*
6.	3/13	2	**You Were Mine**	*Dixie Chicks*
7.	3/27	6	**How Forever Feels**	*Kenny Chesney*
8.	5/8	1	**Wish You Were Here**	*Mark Wills*
9.	5/15	5	**Please Remember Me**	*Tim McGraw*
10.	6/19	4	**Write This Down**	*George Strait*
11.	7/17	8	**Amazed**	*Lonestar*
12.	9/11	1	**Single White Female**	*Chely Wright*
13.	9/18	1	**You Had Me From Hello**	*Kenny Chesney*
14.	9/25	5	**Something Like That**	*Tim McGraw*
15.	10/30	5	**I Love You**	*Martina McBride*
16.	12/4	2↕	**When I Said I Do**	*Clint Black (with Lisa Hartman Black)*
17.	12/11	1	**He Didn't Have To Be**	*Brad Paisley*
18.	12/25	6	**Breathe**	*Faith Hill*

2000

	DATE	WKS	Title	Artist
1.	2/5	3	**Cowboy Take Me Away**	*Dixie Chicks*
2.	2/26	2	**My Best Friend**	*Tim McGraw*
3.	3/11	1	**Smile**	*Lonestar*
4.	3/18	5	**How Do You Like Me Now?!**	*Toby Keith*
5.	4/22	3	**The Best Day**	*George Strait*
6.	5/13	1	**Buy Me A Rose**	*Kenny Rogers With Alison Krauss & Billy Dean*
7.	5/20	4	**The Way You Love Me**	*Faith Hill*
8.	6/17	3	**Yes!**	*Chad Brock*
9.	7/8	5	**I Hope You Dance**	*Lee Ann Womack*
10.	8/12	4	**What About Now**	*Lonestar*
11.	9/9	1	**It Must Be Love**	*Alan Jackson*
12.	9/16	4	**That's The Way**	*Jo Dee Messina*
13.	10/14	2	**Kiss This**	*Aaron Tippin*
14.	10/28	3	**The Little Girl**	*John Michael Montgomery*
15.	11/18	1	**Best Of Intentions**	*Travis Tritt*
16.	11/25	1	**Just Another Day In Paradise**	*Phil Vassar*
17.	12/2	2	**We Danced**	*Brad Paisley*
18.	12/16	5	**My Next Thirty Years**	*Tim McGraw*

2001

	DATE	WKS	Title	Artist
1.	1/20	1	**Born To Fly**	*Sara Evans*
2.	1/27	1	**Without You**	*Dixie Chicks*
3.	2/3	2	**Tell Her**	*Lonestar*
4.	2/17	1	**There Is No Arizona**	*Jamie O'Neal*
5.	2/24	1	**But For The Grace Of God**	*Keith Urban*
6.	3/3	3↕	**You Shouldn't Kiss Me Like This**	*Toby Keith*
7.	3/10	2↕	**One More Day**	*Diamond Rio*
8.	4/7	3	**Who I Am**	*Jessica Andrews*
9.	4/28	6	**Ain't Nothing 'Bout You**	*Brooks & Dunn*
10.	6/9	1	**Don't Happen Twice**	*Kenny Chesney*
11.	6/16	1	**Grown Men Don't Cry**	*Tim McGraw*
12.	6/23	6	**I'm Already There**	*Lonestar*
13.	8/4	1	**When I Think About Angels**	*Jamie O'Neal*
14.	8/11	5	**Austin**	*Blake Shelton*
15.	9/15	1	**I'm Just Talkin' About Tonight**	*Toby Keith*
16.	9/22	3	**What I Really Meant To Say**	*Cyndi Thomson*
17.	10/13	3↕	**Where I Come From**	*Alan Jackson*
18.	10/27	1	**Only In America**	*Brooks & Dunn*
19.	11/10	2	**Angry All The Time**	*Tim McGraw*
20.	11/24	5	**I Wanna Talk About Me**	*Toby Keith*
21.	12/29	5	**Where Were You (When The World Stopped Turning)**	*Alan Jackson*

2002

	DATE	WKS	Title	Artist
1.	2/2	5	**Good Morning Beautiful**	*Steve Holy*
2.	3/9	1	**Bring On The Rain**	*Jo Dee Messina with Tim McGraw*
3.	3/16	1	**The Cowboy In Me**	*Tim McGraw*
4.	3/23	1	**The Long Goodbye**	*Brooks & Dunn*
5.	3/30	2	**Blessed**	*Martina McBride*
6.	4/13	1	**I Breathe In, I Breathe Out**	*Chris Cagle*
7.	4/20	5	**My List**	*Toby Keith*

#1 HITS

2002 (cont'd)

8. 5/25 **4** **Drive (For Daddy Gene)** *Alan Jackson*
9. 6/22 **2** **Living And Living Well** *George Strait*
10. 7/13 **2** **I'm Gonna Miss Her (The Fishin' Song)** *Brad Paisley*
11. 7/20 **1** **Courtesy Of The Red, White And Blue (The Angry American)** *Toby Keith*
12. 7/27 **7** **The Good Stuff** *Kenny Chesney*
13. 9/14 **1** **Unbroken** *Tim McGraw*
14. 9/21 **1** **I Miss My Friend** *Darryl Worley*
15. 9/28 **2↕** **Beautiful Mess** *Diamond Rio*
16. 10/5 **1** **Ten Rounds With José Cuervo** *Tracy Byrd*
17. 10/19 **6** **Somebody Like You** *Keith Urban*
18. 11/30 **3** **These Days** *Rascal Flatts*
19. 12/21 **1** **Who's Your Daddy?** *Toby Keith*
20. 12/28 **2** **She'll Leave You With A Smile** *George Strait*

2003

DATE WKS

1. 1/11 **6** **19 Somethin'** *Mark Wills*
2. 2/22 **3** **The Baby** *Blake Shelton*
3. 3/15 **1** **Man To Man** *Gary Allan*
4. 3/22 **1** **Travelin' Soldier** *Dixie Chicks*
5. 3/29 **1** **Brokenheartsville** *Joe Nichols*
6. 4/5 **7** **Have You Forgotten?** *Darryl Worley*
7. 5/24 **1** **Three Wooden Crosses** *Randy Travis*
8. 5/31 **2** **I Believe** *Diamond Rio*
9. 6/14 **6** **Beer For My Horses** *Toby Keith with Willie Nelson*
10. 7/26 **1** **My Front Porch Looking In** *Lonestar*
11. 8/2 **1** **Red Dirt Road** *Brooks & Dunn*
12. 8/9 **8↕** **It's Five O'Clock Somewhere** *Alan Jackson & Jimmy Buffett*
13. 9/27 **1** **What Was I Thinkin'** *Dierks Bentley*
14. 10/11 **2** **Real Good Man** *Tim McGraw*
15. 10/25 **2** **Tough Little Boys** *Gary Allan*
16. 11/8 **1** **Who Wouldn't Wanna Be Me** *Keith Urban*
17. 11/15 **5** **I Love This Bar** *Toby Keith*
18. 12/20 **7** **There Goes My Life** *Kenny Chesney*

2004

DATE WKS

1. 2/7 **2** **Remember When** *Alan Jackson*
2. 2/21 **4** **American Soldier** *Toby Keith*
3. 3/20 **2** **Watch The Wind Blow By** *Tim McGraw*
4. 4/3 **5** **When The Sun Goes Down** *Kenny Chesney & Uncle Kracker*

2004 (cont'd)

5. 5/8 **2** **You'll Think Of Me** *Keith Urban*
6. 5/22 **1** **Mayberry** *Rascal Flatts*
7. 5/29 **5** **Redneck Woman** *Gretchen Wilson*
8. 7/3 **1** **If You Ever Stop Loving Me** *Montgomery Gentry*
9. 7/10 **1** **Whiskey Girl** *Toby Keith*
10. 7/17 **7↕** **Live Like You Were Dying** *Tim McGraw*
11. 8/7 **1** **Somebody** *Reba McEntire*
12. 9/11 **1** **Girls Lie Too** *Terri Clark*
13. 9/18 **4** **Days Go By** *Keith Urban*
14. 10/16 **1** **Suds In The Bucket** *Sara Evans*
15. 10/23 **2** **I Hate Everything** *George Strait*
16. 11/6 **2** **In A Real Love** *Phil Vassar*
17. 11/20 **2** **Mr. Mom** *Lonestar*
18. 12/4 **2** **Nothing On But The Radio** *Gary Allan*
19. 12/18 **1** **Back When** *Tim McGraw*
20. 12/25 **4** **Some Beach** *Blake Shelton*

2005

DATE WKS

1. 1/22 **2** **Awful, Beautiful Life** *Darryl Worley*
2. 2/5 **1** **Mud On The Tires** *Brad Paisley*
3. 2/12 **5** **Bless The Broken Road** *Rascal Flatts*
4. 3/19 **1** **Nothin' To Lose** *Josh Gracin*
5. 3/26 **4** **That's What I Love About Sunday** *Craig Morgan*
6. 4/23 **2** **Anything But Mine** *Kenny Chesney*

4/30/05: Chart renamed "Hot Country Songs"

7. 5/7 **1** **It's Getting Better All The Time** *Brooks & Dunn*
8. 5/14 **2** **My Give A Damn's Busted** *Jo Dee Messina*
9. 5/28 **5** **Making Memories Of Us** *Keith Urban*
10. 7/2 **3** **Fast Cars And Freedom** *Rascal Flatts*
11. 7/23 **6** **As Good As I Once Was** *Toby Keith*
12. 9/3 **2** **Mississippi Girl** *Faith Hill*
13. 9/17 **1** **Play Something Country** *Brooks & Dunn*
14. 9/24 **2** **A Real Fine Place To Start** *Sara Evans*
15. 10/8 **2** **Something To Be Proud Of** *Montgomery Gentry*

THE CHARTS FROM

That's because these are the **only** books that get right to the bottom of *Billboard's* major charts, with **complete, fully accurate chart data on every record ever charted**. So they're quoted with confidence by DJ's, music show hosts, program directors, collectors and other music enthusiasts worldwide.

Each book lists every record's significant chart data, such as peak position, debut date, peak date, weeks charted, label, record number and much more, all conveniently arranged for fast, easy reference. Most books also feature artist biographies, record notes, RIAA Platinum/Gold Record certifications, top artist and record achievements, all-time artist and record rankings, a chronological listing of all #1 hits, and additional in-depth chart information.

TOP POP SINGLES 1955-2002

Over 25,000 pop singles — every "Hot 100" hit — arranged by artist. Features thousands of artist biographies and countless titles notes. Also includes the B-side title of every "Hot 100" hit. 1,024 pages. Hardcover. $64.95.

POP ANNUAL 1955-1999

A year-by-year ranking, based on chart performance, of over 23,000 pop hits. Also includes, for the first time, the songwriters for every "Hot 100" hit. 912 pages. $59.95 Hardcover / $49.95 Softcover.

POP HITS SINGLES & ALBUMS 1940-1954

Four big books in one: an artist-by-artist anthology of early pop classics, a year-by year ranking of Pop's early hits, the complete story of the early pop albums and the top 10 singles charts of every *Billboard* "Best Selling Singles" chart. Filled with artist bios, title notes, and many special sections. 576 pages. Hardcover. $49.95.

POP MEMORIES 1890-1954

Unprecedented in depth and dimension. An artist-by-artist, title-by-title chronicle of the 65 formative years of recorded popular music. Fascinating facts and statistics on over 1,600 artists and 12,000 recordings, compiled directly from America's popular music charts, surveys and record listings. 660 pages. Hardcover. $44.95.

A CENTURY OF POP MUSIC

This unique book chronicles the biggest Pop hits of the past 100 years, in yearly rankings of the Top 40 songs of every year from 1900 through 1999. Includes complete artist and title sections, pictures of the top artists, top hits and top artists by decade, and more. 256 pages. Softcover. $19.95.

TOP POP ALBUMS 1955-2001

An artist-by-artist history of the over 22,000 albums that ever appeared on *Billboard's* pop albums charts, with a complete A-Z listing below each artist of tracks from every charted album by that artist. 1,208 pages. Hardcover. $79.95.

ALBUM CUTS 1955-2001

A companion guide to our Top Pop Albums 1955-2001 book — an A-Z list of cut titles along with the artist name and chart debut year of the album on which the cut is first found. 720 pages. Hardcover. $34.95.

CHRISTMAS IN THE CHARTS 1920-2004

Every charted Christmas single and album of the past 85 years, arranged by artist. Complete title sections for both singles and albums. Bonus section – 24-page full-color Christmas Photo Album. And much more! 272 pages. Softcover. $29.95.

BILLBOARD HOT 100/POP SINGLES CHARTS:

THE NINETIES 1990-1999
THE EIGHTIES 1980-1989
THE SEVENTIES 1970-1979
THE SIXTIES 1960-1969

Four complete collections of the actual weekly "Hot 100" charts from each decade; black-and-white reproductions at 70% of original size. Over 550 pages each. Deluxe Hardcover. $79.95 each.

POP CHARTS 1955-1959

Reproductions of every weekly pop singles chart *Billboard* published from 1955 through 1959 ("Best Sellers," "Jockeys," "Juke Box," "Top 100" and "Hot 100"). 496 pages. Deluxe Hardcover. $59.95.

BILLBOARD POP ALBUM CHARTS 1965-1969

The greatest of all album eras...straight off the pages of *Billboard*! Every weekly *Billboard* pop albums chart, shown in its entirety, from 1965 through 1969. Black-and-white reproductions at 70% of original size. 496 pages. Deluxe Hardcover. $49.95.

TOP TO BOTTOM

HOT DANCE/DISCO 1974-2003
First edition! Lists every one of the over 3,800 artists and over 8,000 hits that appeared on *Billboard's* national "Dance/Disco Club Play" chart from its inception. 368 pages. Hardcover. $39.95.

ROCK TRACKS 2002 Edition
Two separate artist-by-artist listings of of every title and artist that appeared on *Billboard's* "Mainstream (Album) Rock Tracks" chart from March, 1981 through October, 2002 and every title and artist that appeared on *Billboard's* "Modern Rock Tracks" chart from September, 1988 through October, 2002. 336 pages. Hardcover. $39.95.

TOP ADULT CONTEMPORARY 1961-2001
Artist-by-artist listing of the nearly 8,000 singles and over 1,900 artists that appeared on *Billboard's* "Easy Listening" and "Hot Adult Contemporary" singles charts from July 17, 1961 through December 29, 2001. 352 pages. Hardcover. $39.95.

#1 POP PIX 1953-2003
A Record Research first! Full-color pictures of nearly 1,000 *Billboard* Pop/Hot 100 #1 hits of the past 51 years in chronological sequence. 112 pages. Softcover. $17.95.

#1 ALBUM PIX 1945-2004
A Record Research first! Full-color pictures of every #1 Pop, Country and R&B album, in chronological sequence. 176 pages. Softcover. $19.95.

TOP COUNTRY SONGS 1944-2005
The complete history of the most genuine of American musical genres, with an artist-by-artist listing of every "Country" single ever charted. 624 pages. Hardcover. $59.95.

COUNTRY ANNUAL 1944-1997
A year-by-year ranking, based on chart performance, of over 16,000 Country hits. 704 pages. Hardcover. $44.95.

TOP COUNTRY ALBUMS 1964-1997
An artist-by-artist listing of every album to appear on *Billboard's* Top Country Albums chart from its first appearance in 1964 through September, 1997. Includes complete listings of all tracks from every Top 10 Country album. 304 pages. Hardcover. $34.95.

TOP R&B/HIP-HOP SINGLES 1942-2004
Revised edition of our R&B bestseller! Every "Soul," "Black," "Urban Contemporary," "Rhythm & Blues" and "R&B/Hip-Hop" charted single, listed by artist. 816 pages. Hardcover. $59.95.

TOP R&B ALBUMS 1965-1998
An artist-by-artist listing of every album to appear on *Billboard's* "Top R&B Albums" chart from its first appearance in 1965 through 1998. Includes complete listings of all tracks from every Top 10 R&B album. 360 pages. Hardcover. $34.95.

BUBBLING UNDER THE BILLBOARD HOT 100 1959-2004
All "Bubbling Under The Hot 100" charts covered in full and organized artist by artist. 352 pages. Hardcover. $39.95.

BILLBOARD TOP 10 SINGLES CHARTS 1955-2000
A complete listing of each weekly Top 10 singles chart from *Billboard's* "Best Sellers" chart (1955-July 28, 1958) and "Hot 100" chart from its inception (August 4, 1958) through 2000. Each chart shows each single's current and previous week's positions, total weeks charted on the entire chart, original label & number, and more. 712 pages. Hardcover. $39.95.

BILLBOARD TOP 10 ALBUM CHARTS 1963-1998
This books contains more than 1,800 individual Top 10 charts from over 35 years of *Billboard's* weekly Top Albums chart (currently titled The Billboard 200). Each chart shows each album's current and previous week's positions, total weeks charted on the entire Top Albums chart, original label & number, and more. 536 pages. Hardcover. $34.95.

MUSIC YEARBOOKS 2004/2003/2002/2001/2000/1999/1998/1997/1996/1995/1994/1993/1992/1991/1990
A complete review of each year's charted music — Top Pop Singles and Albums, Country Singles and Albums, R&B Singles and Albums, Adult Contemporary Singles, Rock Tracks, and Bubbling Under Singles books. Various page lengths. Softcover. 2000-2004 $29.95 each / 1990-1999 $24.95 each / 1983-1989 $19.95 each.

Order Information

Shipping/Handling Extra — If you do not order through our online Web site (see below), please contact us for shipping rates.

Order By:

U.S. Toll-Free: 1-800-827-9810
(orders only please – Mon-Fri 8 AM-12 PM, 1 PM-5 PM CST)

Foreign Orders: 1-262-251-5408

Questions?: 1-262-251-5408 or **Email**: books@recordresearch.com

Online at our Web site: www.recordresearch.com

Fax (24 hours): 1-262-251-9452

Mail: Record Research Inc.
P.O. Box 200
Menomonee Falls, WI 53052-0200
U.S.A.

U.S. orders are shipped **via UPS**; please allow **7-10 business days** for delivery. (If only a post office box number is given, it will be shipped 4th class media mail which can lengthen the delivery time.)

Canadian and **Foreign** orders are shipped **via surface mail (book rate)**; please allow **6-12 weeks** for delivery. Orders must be paid in U.S. dollars and drawn on a U.S. bank.

For faster delivery, contact us for other shipping options/rates. We now offer **UPS Worldwide Express** service for Canadian and Foreign orders as well as **airmail** service through the postal system.

Payment methods accepted: MasterCard, VISA, American Express, Money Order, or Check (personal checks may be held up to 10 days for bank clearance).

*****Prices subject to change without notice.*****